Sports Law

Sports Law

Cases and Materials

Second Edition
REVISED PRINTING

Michael J. Cozzillio
WIDENER UNIVERSITY
SCHOOL OF LAW

Mark S. Levinstein
WILLIAMS & CONNOLLY, LLP

Michael R. Dimino, Sr.
WIDENER UNIVERSITY
SCHOOL OF LAW

Gabriel A. Feldman
TULANE UNIVERSITY SCHOOL OF LAW

CAROLINA ACADEMIC PRESS
Durham, North Carolina

ISBN-10: 1-59460-291-3
ISBN-13: 978-1-59460-291-7
LCCN: 2006938149

Carolina AcademicPress
700 Kent Street
Durham, North Carolina 27701
Telephone (919) 489-7486
Fax (919) 493-5668
www.cap-press.com

REVISED PRINTING

Printed in the United States of America

To Krista
MJC

To Terri
MSL

To Mom and Dad, who have given me a love of sports,
an appreciation of their importance,
and the ability to read and write about them
MRD

To Mom and Dad
GAF

Contents

Preface

This second edition is the product of nine years of thought, conversation, and experimentation. We have sought in this edition to expand on the features that have most contributed to the first edition's success, and to supplement those features with additional material that should make the study of sports law both practically and theoretically rewarding.

Specifically, we have updated and, in some cases, expanded our primer chapters, which offer a compact, convenient reference for the student or teacher who needs a refresher or an introduction to the principles of contracts, antitrust, and labor law. The labor chapter also contains textual and graphic synopses of work stoppages and the most recent major developments in collective bargaining. We have added a new primer chapter on torts.

Though this book is a teaching tool, we have made efforts to make the text as comprehensive as reasonably possible without making the volume unmanageable, so as to assist the student, teacher, or researcher who is interested in pursuing issues beyond the depth usually taught in the basic sports law course. Thus, we have continued our practice of using expansive notes to discuss cases that add nuance to the issues presented in principal cases.

Users of the first edition will notice other major changes. We have added two substantive chapters on torts, in addition to the primer chapter, devoted to liability affecting participants, spectators, equipment manufacturers, and others, and we have added a chapter on criminal liability arising out of sporting events. The discrimination chapter has been dramatically expanded to address a wide panoply of subject areas including discrimination based on race, gender, disability, and sexual orientation in all aspects of both professional and amateur sports. Each chapter has been thoroughly updated to take account of legislative and judicial developments, and the cases that have remained from the first edition have been re-edited to save space and eliminate unnecessary material.

We welcome your comments and suggestions.

MJC
MSL
MRD
GAF

Acknowledgments

In the first edition of this work, I expressed appreciation to scores of administrators, staff members, colleagues, friends, and family members who, in varying degrees, provided the inspiration and support leading to the book's completion. I echo those thanks adding only that the list of persons deserving acknowledgement and praise in a more private setting has grown and will not be ignored. Most of them are too unassuming and unpretentious even to think that they have made a significant contribution. I know better.

A few exceptions warrant special mention. Michael Dimino, my colleague and friend at Widener—your expertise and dedication. Your insights and fresh perspective have ensured that this work will reflect the invigoration and enthusiasm commonly associated with a first edition. The guys at 4103, the ultimate crack team—thanks for the companionship and understanding, particularly our incredible sojourn to South Bend, away from your friends as well as your "great and good friends." Krista, continued gratitude and appreciation for consenting to my desire to marry "up." 25 down, here's to another 25. What's love got to do with it? Everything!

MJC

Many matters in this casebook are matters in which I was involved. Other matters - involving Olympic sports—will be the subject of a subsequent supplement or 3rd edition. Behind-the-scenes contributions of a few are particularly memorable. All Arena Football League players owe a tremendous debt to Mike Pawlawski, perhaps the best and smartest AFL QB, and James Guidry, who almost gave his life on an AFL field. Their efforts led to AFL player rights and the AFLPA. It has also been an honor to represent the USOC for the past five years, to support our Olympic and Paralympic athletes and to work with Frank Marshall, Bill Stapleton, Gordon Gund, Chris Duplanty, and the others responsible for the 2003 reform of USOC governance. Working with USOC Athlete Ombudsman John Ruger and athletes Chris Duplanty, Rachel Godino, Mary McCagg, Cameron Myler, and others, lawyers like Jeff Benz, Bill Bock, Sean Breen, Craig Fenech, Tim Herman, Howard Jacobs, and Gary Johansen, and sports experts like Dr. Jim Stray-Gunderson has been particularly rewarding. The successful defense of Paul Hamm's right to retain his Olympic Gold Medal shows the limits of dispute resolution. Paul Hamm's comeback victory in the 2004 Olympic Men's Gymnastics All-Around Competition was one of the greatest comebacks in the history of sports, yet may be remembered for the baseless challenge by the Korean Olympic Committee.

Beyond work for teams, leagues, sponsors, licensees, and sports organizations, I have worked with some of the best athletes in the world. It has been a privilege to be involved with Andre Agassi and Lance Armstrong, whose unbelievable achievements on the court and on the bike have been equaled or exceeded by their "off-the-field" achievements. The power and potential of the positive connection that exists between athletes and their fans, particularly children, has never been harnessed. It is a spectacular experience to be a part of the efforts by Andre Lance, Warrick Dunn, Julie Foudy, Mia Hamm, Andrea Jaeger, Jackie Joyner-Kersee, Alonzo Mourning, and other great athlete philanthropists, with the help of sports industry experts and leaders like Ivan Blumberg, Mike Burg, George Cohen, Don Fehr, Allen Furst, Rachel Godino, Gordon Gund, Ross Greenburg, John Langel, Dan Levy, Mike Lynch, Frank Marshall, Peter Roby, Perry Rogers, Bill Stapleton, and Doug Ulman to form Athletes for Hope, to maximize the value of the connection between athletes and sports fans.

My contributions to this edition of the book are dedicated to my family, in particular my father's memory. It is a true pleasure to have the contributions of Gabriel A. Feldman, formerly a law firm colleague and now a Professor at Tulane University's law school, who has worked with me on so many issues, matters, negotiations, arbitrations, and lawsuits since the first edition. However, without the hard work, patience, dedication, and commitment of Michael Cozzillio, the best sports law professor in the country, neither edition of this book would exist, and without Professor Michael Dimino's tireless efforts a second edition would never have been forthcoming. I am indebted to all three of my co-authors for offering their insights and leading by example, and waiting patiently for me to do my share of the work.

MSL

I owe thanks, as all casebook authors do, to several people who have contributed their energy, talents, and patience to helping me with this text. Michael Cozzillio, who has warmly welcomed me to the project and with whom I have had the pleasure of working and discussing the most minute details of English usage, is the primary reason I can look with satisfaction on this completed book. It was a delight to work with you, and I look forward to working on the third edition.

My wife, Laura, tolerated my unending conversations with Cozzillio, even though she does not share our appreciation of the necessity for spending half the night discussing comma placement, and the time she spent managing our family allowed me to put my efforts into the book. Many thanks to you, and to our sons, Michael and Steven, who provide endless inspiration and amusement, as well as a sense of the joy that sports can bring to "children of all ages."

I am also indebted to Widener's faulty and administration for the support they have provided, and to Ben Barros, Michael Hussey, and especially Chris Robinette for the specific suggestions they made. Each of the four authors benefited tremendously from the research assistance of Niki Carter and Becky Cantor. Lastly, I wish to thank Linda Lacy and Reuben Ayres at Carolina Academic Press, who have been more than accommodating of our delays and revisions.

MRD

I owe thanks to too many people to mention them by name, but I would be remiss if I did not single a few people out for their help and inspiration over the past several years. First, I must thank John Weistart, who first introduced me to the study of sports law at Duke Law School, and who in many ways inspired me to pursue a career in sports law and in teaching. Second, I have to thank Mark Levinstein and many others at Williams & Connolly for providing me with an unbelievable opportunity to work on a variety of matters in the sports law industry. I continue to be inspired by Mark's passion and commitment to his clients, family, and friends. I also need to thank Mark for introducing me to Donald Dell, who provided me with my first opportunity to teach sports law and who taught me a tremendous amount about the practical side of sports law and sports business. I also must thank Gary Roberts and everyone at Tulane Law School for providing me with the opportunity to teach and research in the sports law field and for allowing me (I hope) to pass on to the great students here some of the many things I have learned over the years.

Finally, and most importantly, I have to thank my family for all of their help and support. To my father, for taking me to all of those Jets games in the freezing cold and for the countless ways you have helped and supported me over the years. To my mother, for the baked spaghetti and all of your guidance, encouragement, and love. And, to my brother, for all of the "Wonder Years" moments we have shared together. All three of you have inspired me, challenged me, and made me the person I am today. Thank you.

GAF

Sports Law

Chapter 1

Introduction

<hr>

Who's on First?

Excerpted from THE BASEBALL READER, p. 317 (Charles Einstein, ed., 1980)

COSTELLO: Hey, Abbott, tell me the names of the players on our baseball team so I can say hello to them.

ABBOTT: Sure, Now, Who's on first, What's on second, I-Don't-Know on third ...

COSTELLO: Wait a minute.

ABBOTT: What's the matter?

COSTELLO: I want to know the names of the players.

ABBOTT: I'm telling you. Who's on first, What's on second, I-Don't-Know on third ...

COSTELLO: Now, wait. What's the name of the first baseman?

ABBOTT: No, What's the name of the second baseman.

COSTELLO: I don't know.

ABBOTT: He's the third baseman.

COSTELLO: Let's start over.

ABBOTT: Okay. Who's on first ...

COSTELLO: I am asking YOU what's the name of the first baseman.

ABBOTT: What's the name of the second baseman.

COSTELLO: I don't know.

ABBOTT: He's on third.

COSTELLO: All I'm trying to find out is the name of the first baseman.

ABBOTT: I keep telling you. Who's on first.

COSTELLO: I'm asking YOU what's the name of the first baseman.

ABBOTT: *(Rapidly)* What's the name of the second baseman.

COSTELLO: *(More rapidly)* I don't know.

BOTH: *(Most rapidly)* Third Base!!

COSTELLO: All right. Okay. You won't tell [me] what's the name of the first baseman.

ABBOTT: I've *been* telling you. What's the name of the second baseman.

COSTELLO: I'm asking *you* who's on second.

ABBOTT: *Who's* on *first*.

COSTELLO: I don't know.

ABBOTT: He's on third.

COSTELLO: Let's do it this way. You pay the players on this team?

ABBOTT: Absolutely.

COSTELLO: All right. Now, when you give the first baseman his paycheck, who gets the money?

ABBOTT: Every penny of it.

COSTELLO: *Who?*

ABBOTT: Naturally.

COSTELLO: *Naturally?*

ABBOTT: Of course.

COSTELLO: All right. Then Naturally's on first …

ABBOTT: No. Who's on first.

COSTELLO: *I'm asking you!* What's the name of the first baseman?

ABBOTT: And I'm telling you! What's the name of the second baseman.

COSTELLO: You say third base, I'll … (*Pause*) Wait a minute. You got a pitcher on this team?

ABBOTT: Did you ever hear of a team without a pitcher?

COSTELLO: All right. Tell me the pitcher's name.

ABBOTT: Tomorrow.

COSTELLO: You don't want to tell me now?

ABBOTT: I said I'd tell you. Tomorrow.

COSTELLO: What's wrong with today?

ABBOTT: Nothing. He's a pretty good catcher.

COSTELLO: Who's the catcher?

ABBOTT: No, Who's the first baseman.

COSTELLO: All right, tell me that. What's the first baseman's name?

ABBOTT: No. What's the second baseman's name.

COSTELLO: I-don't-know-third-base.

ABBOTT: Look, it's very simple.

COSTELLO: I know it's simple. You got a pitcher. Tomorrow. He throws the ball to Today. Today throws the ball to Who, he throws the ball to What, What throws the ball to I-Don't-Know; he's on third … and what's more, I-Don't-Give-A-Darn!

ABBOTT: What's that?

COSTELLO: I said, I-Don't-Give-A-Darn!

ABBOTT: Oh, he's our shortstop!

The foregoing exchange between Bud Abbott and Lou Costello, which seems to transcend changes in styles and trendy developments in the world of comedy, has entertained generations for years and probably will continue to do so. Unfortunately, the absolute confusion that is so vexing to the hapless Costello is likely experienced by every sports fan who is trying to grasp the subtle technical aspects of professional sports jurisprudence. What was once an enjoyable hobby has become a maze of complex legal issues. Indeed, it seems as though controversy erupts as often off the field as on. The problems are even more profound for the lawyer or law student who seeks to gain a comprehensive understanding of the subtle nuances of sports law.

Yet, the term "sports law" is somewhat misleading. In reality, sports law is nothing more or less than law as applied to the sports industry. A basic appreciation of contracts, labor relations, and antitrust is a necessary prerequisite to the development of any meaningful expertise in this area. Moreover, a passing familiarity with torts, criminal law, civil procedure, administrative law, constitutional law, corporations, securities, tax, workers' compensation, estate planning, copyright, trademark, common law misappropriation, and related subdisciplines will enhance one's ability to represent athletes, leagues, teams, owners, sponsors, television companies, and other sports clients and to grasp some of the more esoteric issues that arise in the sports law arena.

This text endeavors to introduce the student to various aspects of professional sports, including, but certainly not limited to: league and association structure; the role of league commissioners; contracting between players and clubs and clubs' enforcement mechanisms to ensure compliance with those contracts; exercise of league prerogatives as a voluntary association; collective bargaining between teams/league and player representatives; protections afforded and limitations upon athletes who seek to organize and engage in collective bargaining through elected agents; application of antitrust laws as they relate to player mobility, franchise relocation, and league disciplinary power; owners' autonomy in the league framework; potential statutory and non-statutory exemptions from antitrust scrutiny; tort liability for conduct involving participants, spectators, and manufacturers; player/club property rights to performances, logos, images, etc.; and agent responsibilities and ethical considerations for any practitioner in this field.

After a few introductory chapters designed to familiarize the reader with the various components of the sports industry, with a particular focus on league commissioners, the bulk of the text is divided into four principal subject areas—contracts, antitrust, torts, and labor. Due to the significance and cosmic reach of these subjects in terms of evolving sports jurisprudence, primer chapters have been provided to introduce each of these areas. Other important subject areas have been covered but in less detail. Included among these selected additional topics are intellectual property, torts, agent representation, and discrimination. Issues affecting amateur sports have been addressed tangentially but have been left for full explication in a future supplement or another volume.

The student of sports law cannot be deluded. Before one begins to tackle the exciting and complex issues attending contract jumping, reserve clauses, player trades, and the like, he or she must have a working knowledge of offer and acceptance, consideration, conditions, remedies, etc. Likewise, one cannot undertake to explore the myriad questions surrounding the legality of league restrictions on franchise relocation, the college draft, free agency, salary caps, strikes, and lockouts without some comprehension of the rudiments of antitrust and labor law. The cases and materials have been selected with an eye toward exploring the more lofty issues without sacrificing the necessary explanation of the most basic principles.

Some of the cases may seem mundane to the contracts, antitrust, labor, or torts scholar, and correspondingly may seem baffling to the neophyte in each of these areas. Such is the potential problem of attempting to accommodate a large universe of readers and students. Hopefully, this problem will never eventuate and the "veteran" will be challenged while the rookie is edified. In any event, the material contained in this text should equip you to handle most game situations that arise in the ambit of professional sports law. Of course, there is no suggestion or guarantee that this text provides all the answers; it should merely establish the groundwork upon which you will be able to develop your expertise in this area. At the very least, you will feel comfortable discussing the prevailing issues and should emerge with a confidence that you are conversant in the rudiments of sports law. At best, it may whet your appetite to the point where you choose to pursue sports law as a career choice. In either event, let's hope that this knowledge does not compromise your appreciation for the Xs and Os, the strategy, the sights, the smells, the tastes, and the sounds of sports that may well have attracted you to sports law in the first place.

Chapter 2

The Business of Sports

I. Introduction

The study of "sports law" does not involve an entirely unique or discrete body of special principles divorced from traditional legal concepts. Rather, sports law involves the application of basic legal precepts to a specific industry. Attempting to understand sports law without becoming conversant in the subtle nuances of the sports business will likely be an unsatisfying experience. One must appreciate fully the inner workings of this industry to understand relevant sports law precedent and eventually to represent adequately a client's interests. The sports lawyer may serve a transactional function, a litigation function, a counseling function, or some hybrid combination of the three. In all capacities, an intimate knowledge of the idiosyncrasies of this relatively new enterprise is essential.

As will be discussed below, the sports lawyer may be called upon to assist in the planning and development of a new league, to negotiate individual contracts or collective bargaining agreements, to litigate complex issues in various arenas including antitrust, labor, intellectual property, and corporate law, and to provide general advice designed to avoid litigation, labor strife, or other potential disruptions to the orderly conduct of business. Simply studying and comprehending the relevant legal principles applicable to the particular subdiscipline involved (*e.g.*, antitrust, labor, contracts), while important, is but a part of the overall responsibilities that a sports lawyer assumes. The business of sports is relatively new to its participants, adjudicating bodies, and the public at large. Consequently, there is often a dearth of information available to inform the judgment of advisors regarding the more esoteric aspects of the nature of the operation. For example, contracts with television broadcast companies, league constitutions and by-laws, and similar data are often closely guarded secrets. This factor only makes it more imperative that students of sports law make every effort to assimilate as much information as possible to draw the best connection between sports jurisprudence and the business of sports.

The sports litigator who is well-versed in the details of a client's operation will be able to draw effectively on that experience to highlight similarities or distinctions between the case at bar and other precedent. The probability of success in a particular case will be substantially enhanced if the litigator is able to share with the court special knowledge of the factual settings in which a dispute arose or unique facets of the controversy that justify the relief sought or defenses offered. In a related sense, settlement negotiations to avoid litigation will enjoy a greater probability of success if the negotiator is educated in established industry custom, trade usage, and historic interpretation of ambiguous language.

In a transactional sense, sports counsel are often called upon not only to advise clients regarding the legal advisability of a particular contract, plan of action, or other non-litigation strategy, but also to provide insights and guidance regarding the business ramifications of a particular course of action. Most legal advisors are capable of explaining the legal issues and pertinent authority governing a contemplated transaction. However, the most effective counsel is one who understands the client's industry, business, and operation and is able to make recommendations that are legally tenable and, at the same time, commercially rewarding. The ability to anticipate potential legal problems and to identify and cultivate a business strategy responsive to the legal concerns necessitates an intimate familiarity with all phases of the sports business. Recognizing the differences between a league consisting of numerous teams and a circuit or tour comprised of independent contractors/participants, understanding the roles of collective bargaining versus individual contract negotiation, appreciating the necessary skills, prerequisites, and career longevity for each sport's participants, comprehending the financial underpinnings and utilization of capital in a typical league, and myriad other manifestations of one's "connection" with the sports business are as critical as a thorough knowledge of relevant case law and statutory authority.

Throughout this book, information about the business of sports is entwined with analyses of legal principles. Every case that provides some information about the particular sport also supplies valuable commercial background. Cases and other materials have been selected and edited with an eye toward providing instruction in both the legal and business aspects of sports.

As suggested above, there is often a yawning gap between information that is needed and information that is available in various aspects of sports law representation. Counsel who advise sports leagues about how to structure their operations to improve their likelihood of success in potential future antitrust or labor law litigation seldom publish articles making that same information available to other attorneys. Even information that is at hand may be difficult to locate or to comprehend out of context. For example, a list of the current year's player salaries in a league is very useful data. However, that information may be of limited utility unless it is read in conjunction with the relevant collective bargaining agreement, the terms of the contracts beyond the published salary figures, other revenue-generating opportunities for those athletes, the expected duration of the players' careers in that sport, etc. For this reason, the factual backgrounds contained in many of the cases are critical parts of the reported decisions and often the only source of reliable information in that subject area. In this regard, the full opinions at times have received only a light editing touch, so as not to disturb the reporting and discussion of important facts simply for the sake of making the case an easier read. A failure to absorb this seemingly trivial background information may compromise one's ability to apply and analogize the cases to hypothetical and real-world fact patterns.

With further regard to information flow, the business of sports is a venture of producing entertainment products, and, as a result, the public's perception and interest is one of the touchstones of the enterprise. Therefore, those involved in the sports industry work very hard to shape the public's perception of the product, the participants who produce the product, and the reasons for the participants' conduct. As a result, sports insiders may have considerable incentive to try to manipulate the media through selective disclosure of information, misinformation, and concealment of information. At the same time, the media who report on sports are dependent on those "in the sports business" as the source of information and access. The sports media are also dependent on fan interest in sports to sell the media's product; therefore, certain members of the media and those individuals or entities producing the sporting events are often willing co-conspirators in presenting an image that conceals some of the more seamy aspects of the sports business.

The earnings of athletic participants are not tied just to their performance "on the field" or "between the lines." Beyond the potential revenue streams for endorsements, licensing, appearances, autographs, and other income associated with involvement in sports, the value of many professional athletes is linked directly to their ability to attract the interest of fans or to increase the attendance or the television ratings at events in which they participate. Even non-athletes, such as boxing promoters, coaches, and others associated with the sporting event, may generate fan interest and thereby have a greater value to the teams or events with which they are associated.

In addition, it is important to remember that the business of sports is not a unitary phenomenon. Beyond the dramatic differences between professional and amateur sports and the special issues attending college athletics and the world of the National Collegiate Athletic Association ("NCAA"), specific sports present very different concerns and situations. Boxing matches, track meets, figure skating competitions and exhibitions, beach volleyball events, bowling tournaments, cycling tours, equestrian events (such as the Triple Crown horse races), marathons, triathlons, NASCAR, "extreme" sports, jai-alai, tennis tournaments, the Olympic Games, the World Cup soccer tournament, golf tournaments, and league games, all can come under the umbrella of professional sports. That list does not even begin to cover all of the sports conducted in the United States and it does not identify many of the sports generally played outside of this country. While those sports have several things in common, there are obviously dramatic differences as well.

The following sections of this chapter address a few overarching issues concerning the business of sports that have not generally been addressed in the available literature and that should be consulted from time to time as the reader proceeds through the subsequent chapters. This review will expand your perspective on many different levels. In addition, as you read the cases and other materials, you should be able to think about sports from additional angles, such as from the vantage point of: the people who have invested in the business of sports; the executives who are employed in and whose career paths, successes, and failures may be shaped by sports; the investors and executives in the television industry, who evaluate, produce and broadcast sporting events; and the investors and executives in associated industries, such as the manufacture of equipment used in professional sports and sale of licensed products (*e.g.*, apparel, memorabilia, trading cards, games, fantasy sports, etc.).

The first section discusses the collective and competitive nature of sports associations, circuits, tours, and, in particular, leagues. Given the number and significance of professional team sports, the amount of litigation those leagues have spawned, and the significant similarities and parallels between and among the leagues, the league structure is a critical aspect of certain sports. Understanding the legal and business relationships of the league and participants is critical to understanding the legal analysis related to those entities.

The second section discusses two primary league structures. The most familiar structure is the "traditional model league," with each investor or investor group owning a constituent team. The second structure, a "pure single entity league," is a relatively new phenomenon, created as a result of legal issues that have plagued traditional model leagues. The section considers some of the advantages and disadvantages of the two structures and certain "hybrid" configurations which incorporate many attributes of the two primary structures.

The third section examines the similarities and differences between "team" or "league" sports and "individual" sports. In most treatments of sports jurisprudence, individual sports are the forgotten stepchildren. Yet a sports lawyer must compare and contrast the underlying nature of both team and individual sports to understand the rationale underlying the regulations and judicial precedents affecting these enterprises. Specifically, one should be able to address how these sports operate, how one would produce a sporting event—either by producing an individual event, a circuit of events or launching an entire league and producing games as part of the league schedule—and how their profitability is determined (*i.e.,* what are their expenses and what are their likely revenue streams?). It is likely that you will find this section the most illuminating due to the paucity of literature about non-team sports.

There are many other general questions about sports that need to be considered to formulate a complete understanding of the industry. Certainly, a few general observations about sports can be made. All sports were invented—that is, none of them existed throughout all time. They all involve some sort of physical activity. They all generate winners and those who do not win. They are all supposed to have limitless possibilities so that each time the sport is played the outcome is not known when the game or event starts.

Yet, beyond those generalizations lie a plethora of observations and questions that expose the many strata of issues affecting sports law and the sports industry. These questions range from the mundane (How many different sports can you list? What makes them a sport and not a game? Which are professional sports and why?) To the esoteric (How significant are sports in the United States? What indications are there of the significance of sports? What facts would you point to in support of the significance of sports? Why are sports important? Why do people care about some sports and not about others? Why do you care about certain sports and not others?). Some of the questions probe the mercantile aspects of sport (Why are some sports very popular on television or as events to attend (*i.e.,* live gate attendance) while others are not? Why are some sports very popular as participation sports in the United States, but not as spectator sports, either with respect to live gate attendance or television? Why does the popularity of specific sports vary widely from country to country?). Other questions probe the psychology or unconscious patterns and behavior of the participants and fans (Why must an eighteen year old freshman shoot a critical free throw facing a screaming, towel-waving throng, while a veteran golfer or tennis player is unable to putt or serve without total silence? Are athletes more disposed to domestic violence than non-athletes?).

As you read the following sections that seek to answer a few of those questions, please recognize that, in addressing the issues, new and more puzzling questions may be spawned. As you ponder the questions posed above, contemplate possible variations on the theme, and try to identify other questions that you have about the business of sports.

II. Some General Observations on the Nature of Leagues, Circuits, Tours, and Collective Behavior

Generally sports leagues, circuits, and tours are viewed and structured as private associations, entitled to certain latitude in self-governance and regulation. Oftentimes the legal principles that are applied to various sports leagues and associations have a precedential root in organizations such as bar associations, medical associations, private clubs, or fraternal societies. *See* John C. Weistart & Cym H. Lowell, *The Law Of Sports* (hereinafter "WEISTART & LOWELL")§ 3.15 (1979). Some commentators have characterized these sports governing bodies as corporations, complete with management hierarchy, by-laws, and all the trappings of a modern, commercial enterprise. Others perceive sports leagues and sports associations as types of joint ventures in which the parties operate as a collective but retain considerable individual entrepreneurial control. In some respects these leagues and associations are not unlike large cartels (such as OPEC), having a common goal and objective that is best obtained through collective efforts, yet resulting in individual gains not necessarily shared with other members of the cartel. *See* Robert C. Berry, William B. Gould IV, & Paul D. Staudohar, *Labor Relations In Professional Sports* 21 n.10 (1986). *See also NCAA v. Board of Regents of Univ. of Okla.*, 468 U.S. 85, 95–96 (1984); *but see Chicago Professional Sports Ltd. Partnership v. National Basketball Ass'n*, 95 F.3d 593 (7th Cir. 1996). Of course, it is impossible to give a broad designation to all sports leagues because each entity has its own peculiarities in terms of governance, commissioner's authority, eligibility requirements, individual corporate structure, etc. Yet, common characteristics suggest that leagues such as Major League Baseball ("MLB"), the National Football League ("NFL"), the National Basketball Association ("NBA"), and the National Hockey League ("NHL"), are not corporations in the traditional sense due to the significant degree of autonomy that each league's constituents possess.

Most leagues are coalesced by some type of multi-team agreement in which each member agrees to observe a common set of by-laws and/or constitutional provisions. In essence, the wax that binds the members is a form of contract in which all teams agree to defer to the rules of the league as a whole. WEISTART & LOWELL §3.15. Unlike individual sports events, which may survive on their own, teams in most league sports, excepting, of course, barnstorming operations such as the Harlem Globetrotters, need a league or some sort of contractual relationship with other teams to exist, and they may need a league or similar structure to promote themselves on a national or international basis. Thus, the interesting paradox distinguishing sports leagues from many of their analogs is the fact that their very lifeblood is both total competition and the absence of competition. They compete on the athletic field, achieving optimum success through maximum victories. While some owners have demonstrated a greater zeal for saving money than producing the most proficient team, many owners, motivated by both the economic rewards and ego gratification of developing successful programs, do whatever is necessary to "win it all." Yet, leagues constantly insist that the key to their economic success is cooperation, not competition. One aspect of this business cooperation is an effort to control the economic competition among the teams to ensure that there will be some degree of parity. The product that they produce—athletic competitions between teams—is enhanced if the consumer perception or the fan perception is that "on any given day" one team can defeat any other team. At the opposite extreme, a perception of virtual invulnerability of one or very few teams, especially year-in and year-out dominance, may threaten the long term prosperity of a league.

This need for balance has traditionally been the leagues' claimed justification for their insistence upon communal control over the talent pool, with the alleged motivation being that no single league entrepreneur becomes dominant. All leagues have cultivated some form of reserve system, whereby players are precluded from indiscriminately switching teams upon expiration of the individual contracts with their clubs. These reserve systems in their most restrictive sense amounted to a perpetual lock on player services from the initial signing through the end of the player's career. Devices such as the college draft, in which the poorest performing teams from the previous season are given the first opportunity to select available amateur players, together with other divisions of the talent pool, discussed below, which the leagues contend have been employed to further the league's goal of stocking each club with a roughly equivalent reservoir of talent, also depress player salaries below the level that would prevail if there were free competition between and among teams. These same restrictions place severe limits on the freedom of professional athletes to select their locale of employment and choice of employer. The latest mechanism that restricts player compensation and the transmigration of players is the salary cap, which places limits on the amounts that any club can expend on player salaries, and its variation, a luxury tax penalizing any club that spends more than the amount allotted for salaries. Forms of a salary cap have been agreed to and incorporated in collective bargaining agreements in the NBA, NFL, MLS, and NHL. The most recent collective bargaining agreement in Major League Baseball contains a tax on "excess" salaries paid by a member club.

Over the years, players have resisted league attempts to circumscribe their marketability and to limit the universe of available employers. Clubs grudgingly have attempted to mollify players by, for example, permitting a player, after a certain number of years in the league, to become a free agent and sign with another club when the signing club compensates the former club with a player of commensurate value or provides some other form of compensation. They also have offered a diluted free agency, sometimes called "restricted free agency," whereby the "incumbent" club is given a right of first refusal or an opportunity to match the offer of a "rival" club. The players' attempts to secure "unrestricted free agency," a system with no institutional restrictions on a player's ability to negotiate with the team of his choice, have resulted in acrimonious collective bargaining, lockouts, strikes, and substantial litigation. *See, e.g., McNeil v. National Football League,* 790 F. Supp. 871, 878–81 (D. Minn. 1992). In most instances, the owners have argued that absolute free agency would have disastrous effects in terms of interclub competition and would signal the eventual demise of the league. Yet, courts have almost uniformly rejected the leagues' arguments in this regard and have found that the restrictions on player mobility have been unreasonable restraints of trade in violation of Section 1 of the Sherman Antitrust Act. *See, e.g., Smith v. Pro Football, Inc.,* 593 F.2d 1173 (D.C. Cir. 1978); *Mackey v. National Football League,* 543 F.2d 606 (8th Cir. 1976), These cases will be considered in Chapter Ten. The only salvation for the leagues has been their ability, at times, to argue that the particular restraint on the labor market is insulated from antitrust scrutiny by virtue of various exemptions to the antitrust laws. *See Flood v. Kuhn,* 407 U.S. 258 (1972) (baseball exemption); *Brown v. Pro-Football, Inc.,* 518 U.S. 231 (1996) (nonstatutory labor exemption). These exemptions will be explored comprehensively in Chapters 8 and 9, respectively.

There are numerous other ways in which leagues have joined to limit competition among their members, to lower their overall league costs, increase overall league revenues, and create and promote a more attractive product that will compete more effectively with other entertainment products. Included among the cooperative efforts are sharing of revenues, joint marketing of league marks, logos, and products, lucrative league-wide television packages, restrictions on marketing and television rights by individual teams or events, etc. Critical financial underpinnings of a typical sports league are gate receipts, income from concessions and parking, and similar revenue sources. For this reason, a team's prosperity, and, derivatively, league growth, turn on the development of a "user friendly," productive arena or stadium. The financial success and, for a short time, even the on-field success of the Baltimore Orioles and Cleveland Indians following construction of Orioles Park at Camden Yards and Jacobs Field, illustrate the importance of the physical plant in the scheme of league master plans. *See, e.g.,* PETER

RICHMOND, BALLPARK: CAMDEN YARDS AND THE BUILDING OF AN AMERICAN DREAM (1993). However, far and away the most important emerging long-term revenue source rests with television and radio packages, including superstation deals and cable television, along with efforts to tap potentially lucrative international markets.

The extent to which each league relies upon broadcast revenue versus ticket sales and other revenue from live attendance will vary from sport to sport. One important factor is the number of games that each team plays. For example, a Major League Baseball team produces at least eighty-one events—its eighty-one regular season home games. That number does not include spring training, exhibition, or post-season games. The NFL teams, at the other extreme, only produce eight events (regular season home games) plus an average of two home preseason games and the possibility of post-season play. Therefore, while a Major League Baseball team potentially has fans turn their turnstiles three million or more times during the regular season, a top NFL team may only fill a half a million regular season seats even if all of its games are sold out. Some sports leagues, such as Major League Baseball, have permitted more local control over television contracts whereby individual teams may negotiate local television packages. Baseball derives only 25% of its revenues from national television deals and shares only 36% of its total revenues. On the other hand, professional football operates predominantly on a national broadcasting arrangement, deriving more than 60% of its income from league-wide television arrangements and sharing equally perhaps 70% of total revenues. *See* Michael K. Ozanian, *Foul Ball*, FINANCIAL WORLD, May 25, 1993, Volume 162, No. 11, at 18. Those percentages may increase as television and national sponsorship revenue grows faster than local and stadium-related revenue. As discussed in Chapter Seven, Congress, through the Sports Broadcasting Act of 1961 and 1966, acceded to the NFL's request and granted certain sports leagues a limited antitrust exemption for purposes of negotiating league-wide, across-the-board sponsored television broadcasting packages; specifically because a prior court order would have prevented such agreements. *See generally* Stephen F. Ross, *An Antitrust Analysis of Sports League Contracts with Cable Networks*, 39 EMORY L.J. 463 (1990); Robert Alan Garrett and Phillip R. Hochberg, *Sports Broadcasting and the Law*, 59 IND. L.J. 155 (1983).

Of course, professional sports are far from a totally cooperative venture. As indicated above, while the NFL teams share regular season gate receipts on a 34% visiting team, 66% home team basis, income from certain sources such as luxury sky boxes and other stadium resources is generally not shared. In the National Hockey league, all gate receipts are retained by the home team and "only national broadcasting and licensing revenues * * * are shared equally." Ozanian, at 30–31. Likewise, while gate receipts are included in total revenues calculated in computing the NBA salary cap, they have not been shared in the NBA. *Id.* Finally, Major League Baseball only shares a small portion of gate receipts, and this failure has led to allegedly "small market" franchises claiming that they are simply unable to compete with larger market teams, especially with regard to their ability to generate sufficient revenues/profits to bid on available players under the current modified free agency system. The purported plight of these small market franchises has fueled proposals that have led to the adoption of a "luxury tax." Players have argued that, if small market franchises are flagging, then perhaps a more elaborate system of revenue sharing, rather than further restrictions on free agency, would be the alternative of choice to rectify the problem. In truth, many franchises have no desire to share revenues and could live comfortably with a free market, open bidding approach to free agency. Some owners, most notably former Oakland A's owner Charles O. Finley, have even argued that an unrestricted market for player services would be a more economically viable option for the league because the glut of free agents would increase supply and thus lower the amounts paid. In any event, while baseball owners have attempted to maintain a united front on the salary cap or luxury tax issue in negotiations with the players' union, the consensus has always been fragile (if it could ever be called a consensus), and it has always been susceptible to schism at the hands of impatient owners who have the financial wherewithal to survive and flourish under the current system or even in a free-for-all environment.

The notion that "off the field" cooperation begets "on the field" competition, which in turn will create a better product, is not without its additional tensions. At times, individual clubs may be torn between their own self-interest and the interests of the league. Issues may arise that will motivate a club owner to pursue a course of action that promotes the best interests of the club, but at the same time disserves, at least in the immediate sense, league's well being. However, given each team's long-term dependence on the league's fortunes, actions that promote the league's prosperity benefit every team to some extent. Therefore, an action that appears to serve the league at the expense of an individual team often derivatively benefits that "sacrificial" team.

It is commonly understood that in some situations, the league's members owe a fiduciary duty to each other and must act accordingly when making league decisions. As one court has noted in the context of a league formally structured as a corporation:

> [W]hen the representatives of the various teams sit as the Board of Trustees of the WHA, it is not their club, their by-laws, their personal concept of duty which control their obligations and duties as trustees. The law requires, irrespective of the competitive personal feelings of the various owners of teams may [*sic*] have towards each other, when they or their representatives sit on the Board of Directors of WHA to the extent they have common corporate goals, they have a duty to make decisions for the benefit of the cooperation, the hockey league as a whole.

Stressing the need for a unique form of *esprit d'corps*, the court added:

> The by-laws provide for Board approval of a new team owner. This requirement rests upon the unspoken premise the league as a whole will suffer if one team is financially weak, unable to meet its obligations. The league's good will, credibility and financial strength are involved. Thus, each representative on the Board owes the league as a whole the traditional fiduciary duties in this commonly shared corporate purpose. * * * To be specific, there is a duty of loyalty which requires directors-trustees not to act in their own self-interest when the interests of the corporation will be damaged thereby. This duty of undivided loyalty applies even though the members of the Board may also serve on subsidiary bodies or groups which make up the constituent element of the corporation. * * *

Professional Hockey Corp. v. World Hockey Association, 191 Cal. Rptr. 773, 777 (Cal. Ct. App. 1983).

Despite this court's grandiose view of the all-for-one, one-for-all mentality that ideally will prevail in a league structure, owners do not always toe the league line, particularly where large sums of revenue are concerned. For example, one concern among league members is the fear that franchises will relocate in an indiscriminate fashion or could be sold to owners who will eventually embarrass the league. The leagues obviously are concerned that wholesale alteration in league structure or ownership could be perceived as a demonstration of instability. This perception might have an adverse impact on fan support as well as support that derives from municipalities, business entities, the media, etc.

As a result, virtually all league constitutions and by-laws or other organizing documents contain restrictions on team owners' ability to relocate franchises, and generally prohibit such action without prior approval, in most cases approval by a majority or supermajority of team owners. Yet, owners have relocated and sold their operations without league approval on various occasions and under some extremely bizarre circumstances. These relocations have occurred without warning literally under cover of darkness (Robert Irsay's decision to transfer the Colts from Baltimore to Indianapolis), in direct contravention of a league mandate (Oakland Raiders owner Al Davis' decision to relocate to Los Angeles), and in the face of total and unequivocal support from the people of the abandoned city (Cleveland Browns owner Art Modell's migration to Baltimore). In some instances, these relocations and similar activities have triggered intense litigation challenging the league's ability to control the individual entrepreneurial urges of the "maverick" owner. *See, e.g., Los Angeles Memorial Coliseum Comm'n v. National Football League*, 726 F.2d 1381 (9th Cir. 1984) (considered in Chapter Twelve). In other circumstances, the league has simply looked the other way, unwilling to challenge a particular owner or perhaps fearing that the league's restrictions will not, as formulated or as applied to the facts presented, survive antitrust scrutiny.

In addition to disputes about the advisability of particular franchise relocations, owners have taken other independent action that concerns league management and other owners who favor collective decisionmaking and control over unilateral behavior by individual teams. Jerry Jones, flamboyant and controversial owner of the Dallas Cowboys, negotiated endorsement deals between Texas Stadium and corporate sponsors, such as American Express and Pepsi, that compete with exclusive league sponsors (*e.g.,* VISA and Coca-Cola). Jones flaunted his stadium's relationships in ways that conflicted with the league's "team concept," drawing attention to the stadium sponsors during half-time of a nationally televised Monday Night Football game. Many of Jones' fellow owners and the NFL commissioner responded by directing the league to file suit against Jones. Jones responded by challenging the NFL Trust and the NFL's pooling of all league and team marks and logos as violative of the federal antitrust laws. Closer examination by the NFL revealed that Jones' conduct, while perhaps not in the best interest of the league, was not contrary to any league rule because Jones did not permit any sponsor to utilize any of his team (as opposed to stadium) marks and logos. In December, 1996, both sides agreed to dismiss all claims without prejudice.

Beyond Jones' lawful "ambush marketing" by selling sponsors an affiliation with the stadium, which consumers associate with the Cowboys, all leagues must resolve the issue of national (league-wide) versus local (team-by-team) marketing of marks and logos to sponsors and licensees. That issue was raised in Jones' counterclaims against the NFL, and in a 1997 lawsuit filed by George Steinbrenner's New York Yankees and Adidas against Major League Baseball. *See* complaint, *New York Yankees Partnership v. Major League Baseball Enterprises, Inc.* Case No. 97-1153-CW-T-25B (M.D.Fla. May 6, 1997). Certain team owners may believe that they can generate more revenue from local sponsors of their team and licensees for their team marks and logos than their *pro rata* share of the revenue generated by an exclusive central league marketing organization.

A similar issue arises when a league seeks to negotiate exclusive national television broadcast contracts for the entire league, while certain individual teams may prefer to negotiate local broadcast contracts, including, perhaps, local contracts with television superstations. Superstation broadcasts may be picked up by cable television companies throughout the country, thereby effectively creating national dissemination of games that are only broadcast locally. This type of national versus local (superstation) controversy locked the NBA, the Chicago Bulls, and Chicago superstation WGN in more than five years of federal court litigation, including two trips to the United States Court of Appeals for the Seventh Circuit. The case was finally settled in the Fall of 1996. *Chicago Professional Sports Ltd. Partnership v. National Basketball Ass'n*, 95 F.3d 593 (7th Cir. 1996) (considered in Chapter Twelve).

A somewhat related problem has arisen in the context of owners who seek to own and operate franchises in two different sports. The NFL has attempted to limit a member's ability to own any interest in a franchise in another league, even if it involves a different sport. These restrictions have been successfully challenged as violative of the Sherman Act. *North American Soccer League v. National Football League*, 670 F.2d 1249 (2d Cir. 1981), *cert. denied*, 459 U.S. 1074 (1982) (examined in Chapter Eleven). The NFL continues to take the official position that the judicial decision holding the cross-ownership ban unlawful only applies to professional soccer (therefore, the NFL did not challenge the Major League Soccer investments by Lamar Hunt (owner of the NFL's Kansas City Chiefs) or Robert Kraft (owner of NFL's New England Patriots). In addition, there are instances in which the NFL has permitted dual ownership, notwithstanding league rules that, according to NFL Commissioner Paul Tagliabue, proscribe such activity. Blockbuster Video magnate Wayne Huizenga's ownership of the Miami Dolphins, the Florida Marlins (MLB), and the Florida Panthers (NHL), pursuant to an agreement giving Huizenga a limited exemption from the rule for a specified period of time and a subsequent modification of the rule to permit Huizenga's ownership (and all other cross-ownership of teams in the owner's NFL territory), presented a compelling example. *See* discussion in Chapter Eleven.

Interestingly, much like the franchise relocation cases, litigation in this area is often instigated by an owner who was presumably a willing participant in the formulation of the rules that are being contested. The courts consistently have held that such participation does not preclude the owner from vindicating his rights under the antitrust laws and it does not even preclude the owner from seeking treble damages for the loss that the restriction imposed upon him, unless he was basically responsible for imposing or maintaining the restraint. *See Los Angeles Memorial Coliseum Comm'n v. NFL,* 726 F.2d 1381 (9th Cir. 1984) and 791 F.2d 1356 (9th Cir. 1986); *Sullivan v. NFL,* 34 F.3d 1091, 1107-09 (1st Cir. 1994); *see also Perma Life Mufflers, Inc. v. International Parts Corp.,* 392 U.S. 134 (1968) (no common law defense of *in pari delicto* under the antitrust laws); *Kiefer-Stewart Co. v. Joseph E. Seagram & Sons,* 340 U.S. 211 (1951) (no unclean hands defense); *but see Perma Life Mufflers, Inc.,* 392 U.S. at 146 (White, J., concurring), 147 (Fortas, J., concurring in result), 149 (Marshall, J., concurring in the result), 154 (Harlan, J., with Stewart, J., concurring in part and dissenting in part) (five justices indicate that equal and voluntary participation by the plaintiff in the challenged misconduct could constitute a defense). Issues relating to franchise relocation, cross-ownership provisions and related restrictions upon entrepreneurial and operational control are addressed in Chapters Eleven and Twelve.

In numerous contexts, including the player restraint and franchise relocation cases addressed above, the various sports leagues have argued strenuously that each league is a single entity consisting of non-autonomous members. In most instances, this argument has been generated by league attempts to defend claims that its members have conspired to restrain trade in violation of the antitrust laws, particularly the Sherman Act. The rationale simply is that a single entity cannot conspire with itself. In most instances, league attempts to establish the single entity defense have proved unsuccessful. *See Sullivan v. NFL,* 34 F.3d 1091, above; *Los Angeles Memorial Coliseum Commission v. NFL,* 726 F.2d

1381 (9th Cir. 1984); *but see San Francisco Seals, Ltd. v. NHL,* 379 F. Supp. 966 (C.D. Cal. 1974) (expressly overruled in the *Los Angeles Memorial Coliseum Comm'n* case, above). *See also Chicago Professional Sports Limited Partnership v. NBA,* 95 F.3d 593 (7th Cir. 1996). As discussed below, one advantage of adopting a pure corporate model to a league would be that the resulting entity would have the singularity necessary to insulate the league from antitrust ramifications grounded in a conspiracy claim. On one hand, it is unlikely that most team owners would be willing to trade their individual operating autonomy and the historical, well-nurtured inter-franchise rivalries for absolute insulation from antitrust liability. Yet, given the plethora of litigation involving allegations that sports league owners have conspired to restrain trade, both in the labor market and in other input (*e.g.,* stadium services) and output markets, it is not surprising that leagues have considered the notion of establishing a structure modeled after a single corporation.

There could be no greater manifestation of total cooperation than a league operating as a self-contained, single entity with subsidiaries and divisions that formerly consisted of semi-autonomous teams. Carried to its extreme of a league created with a single owner or group with totally centralized control over all operations, costs, revenues, and profits, there could be no viable allegations that the "teams" had conspired among themselves to violate the antitrust laws. The myriad questions surrounding the identity of the league as an entity and the legal ramifications of such identification would be eliminated. At the same time, the lifeblood of professional sports would also be sacrificed. It is difficult to imagine the passions provoked by traditional sports rivalries, such as the New York Yankees versus the Boston Red Sox or the Boston Celtics versus the Los Angeles Lakers, where the sole basis for competition is one corporate division versus another. Another problem that obviously arises is the extent to which the corporation would transfer players, managers, and others in order to promote the corporation as a whole to the disadvantage of an individual franchise. How loyal would the local fans be to a team that trades away its top players if the team has won too many years in a row?

The notion of a league/corporation conjures several additional questions. Among the issues that would be confronted by individuals seeking to establish a new league are the following:

(1) What are the advantages and disadvantages of a league patterned after the traditional model?

(2) What are the advantages and disadvantages of a league established along the lines of a single entity/corporate model?

(3) What is the feasibility of a hybrid structure that borrows on aspects of both the traditional and single entity models?

(4) What are the advantages and disadvantages of forming a league in an already established sport, such as the Galactic Football League, as opposed to a league in a new sport with no established league?

(5) Can a league established without traditional owners survive?

(6) Is a league totally owned and operated by players a viable option?

Undeniably, the problems presented by the very thought of forming a league to compete with an existing organization are varied and most intimidating. The difficulties attending an attempt to start a league with no precedent and no current fan following whatsoever for that professional sport may be even more daunting. The following discussion addresses the questions raised above and offers a game plan for the creation and development of an innovative league structure.

III. The League: An Excursus on the "Traditional" and "Single Entity" Models[1]

Over the past forty years, many new sports leagues have been formed. During the 1960s and 1970s, the primary focus seemed to be on new leagues seeking to challenge the existing monopoly leagues in the major sports. Only Major League Baseball was left unchallenged in the United States. The WHA challenged the NHL's hockey monopoly, the AFL threatened the NFL's football monopoly, and the ABA attacked the NBA's monopoly over professional basketball in the United States. Those challenges were eliminated through the new leagues collapsing or merging, and the direct challenges to the NHL and the NBA ceased. Challenges to the NFL continued—the World Football League disbanded in 1975, *see Mid-South Grizzlies v. National Football League*, 720 F.2d 772, 776 (3d Cir. 1983); the USFL was shut down in 1986, *see United States Football League v. National Football League*, 842 F.2d 1335 (2d Cir. 1988) in Chapter Eleven; and the XFL, a WWE-NBC joint venture that ceased operations after just one season; a series of other challengers never left the ground (the International League of American Football, the Professional Spring Football League, the "A" League, and others). While there was some speculation about the possibility of the Canadian Football League increasing its United States presence and changing its name to the Continental Football League or the North American Football League to enhance its ability to compete directly with the NFL, that threat never materialized. In fact, an agreement entered into between the NFL and the Canadian Football League in April, 1997, made such an outcome extremely unlikely. A new All-American Football League to start play in the spring of 2007 was announced in mid-2006.

While the dominant leagues in the four principal sports survived, leagues in other sports were less successful. In professional soccer, the North American Soccer League and the Major Indoor Soccer League initially prospered, seemed destined to survive, then failed. The outdoor American Professional Soccer League ("APSL"), and two indoor leagues, the Continental Indoor Soccer League ("CISL") and the National Professional Soccer League ("NPSL") were launched and struggled. United States Interregional Soccer League was a very large (72 teams), lower budget minor professional soccer league that combined with the APSL and other semi-pro teams, while downsizing, to form the United States Soccer Leagues ("USL"). Major League Soccer ("MLS") launched its inaugural season in 1996 and is growing slowly but surely, and after more than ten years appears fairly well-established as its teams struggle to build soccer-specific stadiums. World Team Tennis was born in the 1970s and has only survived on a much-reduced scale.

New "minor" leagues were formed in major sports. The Continental Basketball Association ("CBA") had been formed back in 1946 and expanded during the 1970s, but then it struggled and almost died as financial problems led it to enter a series of "working agreements" with the NBA, pursuant to which it became the NBA's minor league affiliate for a few years. The United States Basketball League was formed in 1985. The indoor Arena Football League was also established in the mid-1980's, spawned its own minor league, AFL2, and has survived over 20 years. The NFL formed its "World League of American Football" ("WLAF") in the late 1980s to play in the Spring in Eu-

---

1. This section has been adapted from Mark S. Levinstein, *Legal and Business Considerations in Structuring a Professional Sports League: The "Traditional" and "Single Entity" Models*, presented to the American Bar Association Forum on Entertainment and Sports Industries (October, 1994).

rope and in U.S. cities without NFL teams, thereby foreclosing competition from any more competing Spring football leagues. Despite measured success in Europe, the project was mismanaged and poorly promoted, and the league shut down briefly before being reconstituted as a struggling, entirely non-United States enterprise, NFL Europe. Baseball's minor leagues were already in existence, and, overall they have prospered. The Major Indoor Lacrosse League existed in the East for more than ten years, and Roller Hockey International, an in-line roller skating indoor hockey league, was also introduced in the 1990s. Two women's professional leagues, the American Basketball League and the Women's National Basketball Association, were established in 1996 and 1997, respectively, and the WNBA has survived with substantial financial support from the NBA.

There has been substantial reporting that several of these leagues, including the WLAF, ABL, WNBA, and the MLS, claimed to have been organized as single entities, with the investors in those leagues owning an undivided interest in the league, rather than owning individual teams. In fact, significant questions remain about whether those leagues truly are "single entities" that cannot conspire under Section 1 of the Sherman Act. In early 1997, the Major League Soccer Players filed a class action directly challenging the MLS' claim that it is a single entity. *See* Complaint, *Fraser v. Major League Soccer*, Civil Action No. 10242 (D. Mass. 1997). A district judge dismissed the players' Section 1 claims on the basis that the MLS was a single entity that could not conspire with itself or its teams, and that dismissal was affirmed on other grounds. *Fraser v. MLS*, 97 F.Supp.2d 130, 135–39 (D.Mass. 2000), aff'd on other grounds, 284 F.3d 47 (1st Cir. 2002). While a great deal has been written in internal league memoranda about the legal and business consequences of these new "single entity" structures, few publications have attempted to identify and ventilate the issues presented. The following discussion will address these points.

(A) Revisiting the Traditional Model

When a group is convened to discuss the formation of a new professional sports league, that group is likely to begin by assuming that the league will be organized along the lines of the "traditional model" for sports leagues—the basis for the organization of Major League Baseball, the National Football League, the National Basketball Association, and the National Hockey League. There are many characteristics that are common to leagues structured according to this model.

(1) Characteristics of the Traditional Model—Structure of the League

The primary features of the traditional model involve the structure of the league and the ownership of the teams that compete in the league. The league is generally a nonprofit incorporated or unincorporated association of the member clubs, with each member club owned separately. Rules governing the ownership of teams in the league vary from league to league. *See, e.g., Sullivan v. National Football League* (discussed in Chapter Twelve). Certain common league operations are conducted by the league office, but a substantial portion of the league's operations are conducted by the individual teams.

Oversight for the league can be provided by representatives of all the member clubs (who basically constitute a "Board of Directors") or by a subset or committee of some of those representatives (*e.g.*, a Management Council or Executive Committee). Committees composed primarily of representatives of the member clubs often provide oversight and address such policy issues as the league's rules of play, finances, media policy and negotiations, franchise relocation, expansion or sale, collective bargaining, arena or stadium issues, and numerous other matters of league-wide concern.

The day-to-day common operations or "league operations" are generally run by employees of the association who answer to the owners or their Board of Directors either directly or through a "commissioner." The extent to which owners monitor day-to-day league operations in a traditional model league can vary widely. For example, league employees may report to a designated owner or committee of owners on a daily or weekly basis or may only report at periodic league meetings.

The central league operations may involve a wide variety of functions, including but not limited to: (1) scheduling games; (2) hiring and training league referees, umpires or other officials; (3) producing, managing, and marketing league (as opposed to team) events, such as an All-Star Game or Weekend, and, in some cases (or to some extent), the league playoffs or championship game(s); (4) disciplining players or team employees whose conduct is detrimental to the overall operation of the league; (5) marketing the league's marks and logos for use in association with other products (licensing); (6) maintaining and marketing the broadcast programming library created by the operation of the league, such as production and marketing of highlight films and videos; (7) marketing league and team products through other media (*e.g.*, the internet); (8) negotiating and servicing league-wide broadcasting arrangements, labor contracts, and sponsorship agreements; (9) developing press relations for and marketing of the overall league; (10) recording and compiling league statistics; (11) dealing with college and university officials and/or any associated "minor league" or other league that serves as a source of player development and player replacement; (12) conducting certain centralized lobbying (contact with federal and state governments concerning legislation related to their professional sport); (13) coordinating legal, accounting, and business services; and (14) conducting negotiations and dealings with other outside organizations (*e.g.*, the National and International Governing Bodies for the Sport, the United States and International Olympic Committees, etc.). Those functions may all be performed by the league itself, a subsidiary organization, or some affiliated entity.

The individual teams' responsibilities center around operations in their own geographic areas and activities that primarily impact their own operations. *See, e.g.*, Michael S. Jacobs, *Professional Sports Leagues, Antitrust, and the Single-Entity Theory: A Defense of the Status Quo*, 67 IND. L.J. 25, 41–42 & n.68 (1991) (discussing the responsibilities of individual teams in the National Football League). For example, each team is likely to be responsible for: (1) negotiating its own stadium, arena, or facility leases (or the team owner may own the team's stadium, arena, or facility); (2) securing training, off-season, practice, and/or preseason facilities; (3) marketing and selling season tickets and individual game tickets to their regular season and preseason home games; (4) marketing any "luxury boxes" or "sky boxes" or game-day hospitality associated with the purchase of specific tickets or ticket packages; (5) conducting press relations for, and marketing of, its individual team (including contractual relations with local team sponsors); (6) "producing" the home games (including broadcasting, half-time activities, game day promotions, team cheerleaders, bands or other music during the game, etc.); (7) negotiating local television and radio contracts (if any); and (8) hiring team employees. Team employees may include players, coaches, general managers, talent scouts, marketing and ticket sales personnel, trainers and other medical personnel, financial and legal personnel, and others. The stadium or arena owner may be responsible for certain aspects of the operation of the facilities (*e.g.*, stadium maintenance, food service, medical facilities, security, etc.), or the owner may negotiate with independent contractors to provide some or all of those services. The individual teams may also have substantial responsibilities for providing products and services to the players, such as uniforms, equipment, training facilities, food services, transportation to away games, travel and hotel accommodations, medical care, and counseling.

One common feature of the traditional model historically has been that the leagues, as opposed to the member clubs, have been operated as nonprofit entities. In fact, special federal tax legislation, part of the Sports Broadcasting Act of 1966, specifies that professional football leagues retain their not-for-profit tax status even though they administer pension plans for players and other employees. *See* 26 U.S.C. §501(c)(6). The leagues do not generally accumulate capital, but, rather, distribute all excess league income to the member clubs. In non-league sports, entities like the PGA Tour (golf) and the ATP Tour (tennis) are nonprofit organizations that generate surpluses and accumulate capital, which is used to promote the sport and for a variety of other purposes. The PGA Tour's profits are not distributed to the owners of the events that comprise the PGA Tour. In contrast, when NFL revenues exceed the NFL's expenses, the surplus is distributed to the member clubs.

Whether the member clubs are required to make annual contributions to pay for league operations or make no contributions and receive distributions from the league is a function of the custody of the league's revenue stream. If a substantial portion of the league's revenues are "common revenues," which are paid, in the first instance, to the league, it is likely that the league's revenues will exceed its expenses, and member clubs will receive periodic distributions. If, on the other hand, most of the revenues come directly to the teams and not through the league (*e.g.*, through ticket sales, local television broadcast contracts, local sponsors, concessions, and parking), the league may need to call upon the member clubs to make periodic payments to cover the costs of league operations. From a business standpoint, it is preferable to design the league revenue streams in a manner that does not force the league to collect periodic contributions or assessments from the teams. By routing sufficient revenues through the league for eventual distribution to the teams, the league can deduct all of its expenses and amounts owed by the teams from its periodic distributions to the teams.

As stated above, all leagues share revenues to some extent, but the traditional model does not presuppose the extent to which a league will make this distribution. Revenues derived from national television packages and league products (*e.g.*, jackets, hats, and other souvenirs bearing league and team logos) are often shared equally among the teams. Gate receipts may belong entirely to the home team or may be shared with the visitors. Theoretically, all revenues related to the production of the league's games could be pooled and shared equally. *See generally* Roger G. Noll, *The Economics of Sports Leagues*, 2 *Law of Professional and Amateur Sports* §17.02[1] (Gary A. Uberstine ed., 1994); WEISTART & LOWELL, §5.11, at 700–01 and materials cited therein. *See also Chicago Professional Sports Limited Partnership v. National Basketball Association*, 754 F. Supp. 1336, 1340–41 (N.D. Ill. 1991), *aff'd*, 961 F.2d 667 (7th Cir.), *cert. denied*, 506 U.S. 954 (1992); *North American Soccer League v. National Football League*, 505 F. Supp. 659, 679–80 (S.D.N.Y. 1980), *rev'd*, 670 F.2d 1249, 1256–58 (2d Cir. 1981), *cert. denied*, 459 U.S. 1074 (1982).

(2) Advantages of the Traditional Model

The primary benefit of the traditional model is a commercial, not a legal, benefit—the autonomy and economic independence of the member clubs. By permitting individual owners to run the local business operations of their teams, the major sports leagues have been able to attract wealthy entrepreneurs who are capable of operating their individual teams, while, at the same time, providing experience, oversight, and expertise to the overall league operations. *See, e.g.*, John C. Weistart, *League Control of Market Opportunities: A Perspective on Competition and Cooperation in the Sports Industry*, 1984 Duke L. J. 1013, 1049 (1984) ("[E]ach club has management responsibilities and * * * the excitement generated by the [NFL] is frequently a product of the diverse management styles adopted by the franchises."). As one court has explained, "the potential investor [in a sports league] must be reasonably compatible with the other members of the league, with a sufficient understanding of the nature of the business and the interdependence of ownership to support not only his newly-acquired team but the sports league of which it is a member." *North American Soccer League v. National Football League*, 670 F.2d at 1253.

The traditional model gives the owner of each club substantial financial incentive to further his or her interests by producing and marketing a high quality local team product. Each owner will share the fruits of the league's overall success, and will also own a separate financial asset—his or her team. That financial asset can be sold, transferred to heirs, and, with limitations, relocated to increase its value. The traditional model provides the owner with the independence and stature of owning and operating an independent business, while joining him or her with the other owners in furthering the common purposes of the league. Each owner's direct accountability and financial responsibility for the separate local operations of his or her team generally provide sufficient incentive for the owner to concentrate on producing a successful local product. Non-shared team revenues and benefits (*e.g.*, cost savings) from a well-run team are sufficient to motivate team owners to expend substantial time, effort, and resources to further their individual team's fortunes. At the same time, individual owners' fortunes are sufficiently linked with the fortunes of the overall league that the owners optimally will participate actively and aggressively in league affairs and operations, or at least to serve as active league board members, overseeing the league staff, setting league policies, and long-term league goals and strategy.

Under the traditional model, the league need not exercise substantial supervision over the individual team operations. League commissioners have no responsibility for hiring and supervising coaches, general managers, or team marketing directors. Likewise, the commissioner has no obligation to negotiate a team's stadium contract, arena lease, or concession deal. For an established league, providing and training league personnel to run all the operations of close to thirty teams would be very difficult and would involve a dramatic increase in the number of league employees. For a start-up league, requiring a fledgling league office already saddled with the responsibility for all "league operations" to assume the burden of trying simultaneously to direct a start-up business in each of at least eight cities might be overwhelming.

A related benefit of the traditional model flows indirectly from the public perception of the individual owners' economic independence. The military example serves as a suitable metaphor. The loyal fan often views the visiting team as an enemy invader and views the home team, including its players, coaches, general manager, employees, and owner, as the fan's allies or the army representing the fan and doing battle on his or her behalf. The fan considers it the owner's responsibility to further the interests of the team—to try to win the league championship each year. Again, competitive parity in the league is acknowledged to be a league goal, but not a goal of each individual owner, who is supposed to seek total league domination by his or her team. These are the rivalries that became synonymous with the sport; the coals are stoked and there is no detente. Interest in the games presented by the league depends, to some extent, on the public's perception that the participants are all striving to win—that the outcomes of the games are not predetermined, and that no one associated with the teams has any incentive to allow the opposing team to win. The traditional model and the owners' independence associated with that model fuel that public perception and, with it, the fans' interest in the league.

(3) Disadvantages of the Traditional Model

The traditional model of sports league structure was developed at a time when the centralized operations of the leagues were a much smaller, less important aspect of the overall operation of the leagues. The league commissioner had no concerns about multi-billion dollar television contracts, billions of dollars of licensed products, international marketing of the league, Olympic "dream teams," pay-per-view television opportunities, or strategic alliances designed to maximize the long-term value of the league's programming on the information super-highway. In fact, the origins of Major League Baseball date back to a time when there was no television, no radio, no telephones. There was no *national* business—there were just local businesses in each city, bound together by a schedule, league rules, and a league constitution and bylaws. Each team was, to a much greater extent, an independent local business. The parochial interests and responsibilities of the teams have increased, but not nearly as dramatically as the centralized league operations.

The centralized aspects of league operations have become more lucrative, and the conduct of individual teams has a more substantial effect on the financial success of other teams and the success of those centralized operations. Historically, ticket revenue was by far the largest revenue source for the leagues. Therefore, as long as a team owner fielded a team that put fans in the seats at away games and home games (if home revenues were shared with the visitors), the other activities of an individual owner had little impact on the profits of his or her fellow owners. As the league's common ventures have become more important and more lucrative, business decisions by individual owners have had a greater impact on league operations and, in turn, on the income and profits of other team owners. On the cost side, a team's decision to pursue free agents with lucrative offers may, in the absence of a "hard" salary cap, increase other teams' overall costs for player salaries. On the revenue side, any conduct by an individual team that affects any of the shared revenue streams-*e.g.*, national television, national sponsors, licensing—will affect all the other teams in the league. For example, the NBA has contended that the Chicago Bulls' television agreements with superstation WGN were likely to affect adversely the NBA's national television contracts. *See Chicago Professional Sports Limited Partnership v. National Basketball Ass'n*, 754 F. Supp. 1336 (N.D. Ill. 1991), *aff'd*, 961 F.2d 667 (7th Cir. 1992). Again, the central league motivation to control maverick owners who develop a penchant for cutting their own deals is self-evident.

As a result of this increased economic interdependence, the leagues have tightened controls and restrictions on their members. A greater emphasis has been placed on league office control of individual owners, rather than owner supervision of the central league office. Along with the increased importance of the central league office has come the employment and retention of experienced, sophisticated office personnel. It is not surprising that the number of league employees has increased dramatically. To keep pace with the times, the major sports leagues have hired employees with substantial backgrounds in television and other media relations, sports marketing and licensing, computers, and, needless to say, law.

One consequence of all these developments has been a general de-emphasis of the need for, and value of, the autonomy of the individual member clubs. As explained above, the primary benefit of the traditional model was precisely the independence of the member clubs. League commissioners and others associated with central league operations now assign a lesser value to an owner's rugged individualism, and even have tried to limit entrepreneurial independence to further the collective goals of the league.

While the primary advantage of the traditional model has been the business advantages that flow from autonomy of the individual teams, the primary disadvantage of the traditional model has been the substantial risk of antitrust liability under Section 1 of the Sherman Act for rules restricting economic competition between or among member clubs. As explained above, for leagues structured in accordance with the traditional model, the "league" is simply an administrative and business office created and controlled by the member clubs. Thus, as a legal matter, the league only acts as a collective decisionmaker of its members—the individual teams. Therefore, whenever the league restrains or restricts the independent behavior of its members, or the members agree to impose any restriction on individual members' dealings with third parties, adversely affected members or third parties can file antitrust claims contending that the owners have conspired to restrain trade in violation of Section 1. *See e.g., Los Angeles Memorial Coliseum Comm'n v. NFL*; *Sullivan v. NFL*; *North American Soccer League v. NFL*; *Chicago Pro Sports Limited Partnership*, discussed in Chapters Eleven and Twelve.

In addition to the potential legal issues spawned by the economic independence of member clubs, two business concerns are created. First, every member club may be adversely affected by commercial and public relations errors committed by a single member club. The team that overpays for player services is likely to increase player expectations and the amounts that must be paid by the other member clubs. This result may obtain either through salary arbitration, where applicable, or through the free agency market. The team that negotiates and signs a disadvantageous stadium lease may reduce the amount of shared revenues generated by that team. The team that is unable or unwilling to field a competitive team may devalue the product offered by the league, thereby decreasing the gate receipts for that team's home games (some of which are probably revenues that would be shared with other teams) as well as away games, the value of the league's overall broadcasting rights, and other league revenue streams. The same autonomy that helps the league attract high quality owners may create antitrust liability for league conduct in ways that will limit the league's ability to supervise and remedy individual teams' poor business practices or inadequate competitive performance.

A collateral business concern faced by traditional model leagues concerns the situation of a member club whose owner is in severe financial distress, whether that distress is caused by the club's performance or unrelated financial problems. The business of the team may be severely disrupted as the owner seeks a solution to his or her financial problems. Again, the importance of the development of a lucrative stadium arrangement with a municipality cannot be overstated. The involvement of a bankruptcy court may also limit the league's ability to control the eventual disposition and new ownership of the team. A distress sale of a team may depress the perceived value of other teams. Therefore, while some team owners may believe that their entrepreneurial zeal and expertise justify their independent actions, the fear of the consequences flowing from a weak link causes leagues to discourage individual team dealings.

(B) The Single Entity Model

(1) Legal Background—The Traditional Model and The Single Entity Defense

As explained above, courts have generally concluded that rules, regulations, and restrictions of traditional sports leagues are properly viewed as joint conduct by the constituent teams of the leagues, which satisfies the agreement requirement ("contract, combination * * *, or conspiracy") of Section 1 of the Sherman Act. Again, traditional leagues have responded that the interdependence of the member clubs and the revenue sharing by the teams are so significant that the traditional leagues are more properly viewed as a single business entity, the conduct of which cannot be held violative of Section 1, because the agreement requirement is not satisfied. This issue is considered in reported decisions, text and the *Notes and Questions* in Chapter Twelve.

The leagues' "single entity" response to challenges under Section 1 has received a positive reception from a few judges and from several law professors, but the precedential decisions have uniformly rejected the defense. *See, e.g.,* Gary R. Roberts, *The Single Entity Status of Sports Leagues under Section 1 of the Sherman Act: An Alternative View,* 60 Tulane L. Rev. 562 (1986); Myron C. Grauer, *Recognition of the National Football League as a Single Entity under Section One of the Sherman Act: Implications of the Consumer Welfare Model,* 82 Mich. L. Rev. 1 (1983). *Compare San Francisco Seals, Ltd. v. National Hockey League,* 379 F. Supp. 966, 969–70 (C.D. Cal. 1974); *Los Angeles Memorial Coliseum Comm'n v. National Football League,* 726 F.2d at 1403–10 (9th Cir. 1984) (Williams, J., concurring in part and dissenting in part) *with McNeil v. National Football League,* 790 F. Supp. 871, 878–81 (D. Minn. 1992). Many commentators considered the issue to be resolved, but the leagues contended that the Supreme Court's decision in *Copperweld Corp. v. Independence Tube Corp.,* 467 U.S. 752 (1984), required a re-examination of the issue. In *Copperweld,* the Supreme Court held only that a parent corporation and its wholly (100%) owned subsidiary have a sufficient "unity of interest" whereby they constitute a single actor for antitrust purposes. Therefore, "agreements" between the parent and wholly-owned subsidiary do not satisfy the Section 1 requirement of a "contract, combination * * *, or conspiracy." *See* Stephen F. Ross, *An Antitrust Analysis of Sports League Contracts with Cable Networks,* 39 Emory L.J. 463, 466, n.17 (1990) ("The courts have consistently and correctly held, however, that where leagues are composed of teams that are independently owned and operated and that do not share all profits and losses, they fail to qualify as 'single entities' for purposes of the antitrust laws"); Michael S. Jacobs, *Professional Sports Leagues, Antitrust, and the Single-Entity Theory: A Defense of the Status Quo,* 67 Ind. L.J. 25 (1991) (arguing that no aspect of the *Copperweld* decision militates in favor of re-examining the possibility of a "single entity defense" for sports leagues); *see also McNeil v. National Football League,* 790 F. Supp. 871, 878–81 (D. Minn. 1992). The "single entity" issue was a primary focus of the litigation between MLS players and the MLS League and owners. *See Fraser v. MLS*, 97 F.Supp.2d 130 (D.Mass. 2000). *See further* Chapter Twelve.

(2) Considering the Alternative—A Single Entity League

When new leagues are formed, their organizers hope to learn and benefit from the mistakes and experiences of existing and defunct leagues. Having watched existing leagues raise the "single entity" defense to antitrust claims under Section 1 without success, leagues formed in the last 15–20 years have often considered abandoning the traditional model in favor of a league structure in which a single entity defense might succeed. They have designed leagues based, in the first instance, on the theory that the league and all of its teams *will* be part of a single entity-*not* separate, independent businesses. All of the investors, or owners, will be owners of undivided interests in the league as a whole—sharing all expenses, revenues, profits and losses solely on the basis of their percentage ownership of the league. By creating the "complete unity of interest" addressed in the *Copperweld* case, the organizers hope they can limit player salaries, restrict or prevent franchise relocation, control output in various markets, and engage in other conduct that affects competition in a variety of ways, all without substantial concern about antitrust challenges or liability.

(3) The Single Entity League and Analogous Precedent

The argument that a single entity cannot conspire with itself is not new. Neither is the idea of a sports league or circuit organized as a single entity. World Championship Tennis, Inc. ("WCT"), formed in 1968 by Lamar Hunt and David Dixon to compete against the grand slam tennis events and the other amateur tennis events produced by the members of the International Tennis Federation, was the first world class international professional tennis circuit. As a single entity, WCT was free unilaterally to set a prize money scale for its tournaments, sell the television rights for all WCT events as a package, coordinate the scheduling of WCT tournaments, and require players to agree to play in a minimum number of WCT events as a precondition to playing in any WCT events. That same conduct by the Men's International Professional Tennis Council, an association of independent tennis event producers, arguably constituted a number of independent *per se* violations of Section 1. *See Volvo North America Corp. v. Men's International Professional Tennis Council*, 857 F.2d 55 (2d Cir. 1988), considered in Chapter Ten.

(4) Sole Purpose of the Single Entity Model

Because the federal courts are not likely to reverse a long history of holdings that agreements among teams in traditional model leagues have violated Section 1 (despite Justice Rehnquist's dissent from the denial of certiorari in the *NASL* case and Judge Easterbrook's decision in *Chicago Professional Sports Ltd. Partnership*—see Chapter Twelve), organizers of new leagues have been seeking a new league model that might reduce the leagues' antitrust exposure. The primary (if not sole) purpose is relatively simple—design a league that could engage in the conduct that was unlawful when pursued by the traditional model leagues. The organizers want their leagues to be free to limit player, coach, and general manager salaries, restrict franchise relocation and sales, and regulate all other forms of competition between or among teams in the league. The answer lies in the *Copperweld* decision—design a true single entity league and the league's concerns about Section 1 will be largely alleviated.

(5) Design of the Paradigm Single Entity League

The design of the single entity model league flows from *Copperweld*. At the outset, the new league, which we will call League, Inc., would be a for-profit corporation. The investors in the league, the "owners," would own stock in League, Inc. It would be responsible for all of the centralized league operations performed by the traditional model league, but would also be responsible for the individual team operations that traditional model team owners perform. In addition to hiring the central league employees, League, Inc. would contract directly with the players, coaches, general managers, team marketing directors and ticket managers, and all other employees who would be hired by a team in a traditional model league.

(6) Relative Advantages and Disadvantages of the Paradigm Single Entity League

(a) Advantages

Beyond the advantages of substantially reduced antitrust exposure and liability, the single entity league should yield cost savings associated with reduced competition. Without teams competing for players, general managers and coaches, League, Inc. should be able to maintain lower salaries for those team personnel, subject to possible competition from other leagues, colleges, and universities for some general managers or coaches. Similarly, League, Inc. may be able to force prospective stadium lessors to compete on a national scale to have one of the teams as a tenant, and, with the increased power to speak on behalf of the entire enterprise, it may very well be able to negotiate better lease terms. For example, if League, Inc. plans to launch a ten-team league, it can approach arenas in twenty cities, ask each arena for the best terms possible, and include those terms as a factor in the site plan decisionmaking. There may also be efficiencies and associated cost savings as a result of League, Inc. being responsible for the business operations of all the teams in the league. With one league employee negotiating the national and local television contracts, League, Inc. should be able to negotiate a better overall set of television contracts than the traditional model league and its individual teams.

Another substantial advantage flows from the complete unity of interest among the owners of the league—increased league profits benefit all the owners. Therefore, League, Inc. has a substantial financial incentive to improve and expand league operations in ways that a traditional model league will not. One glowing illustration is league expansion. In traditional model leagues, a major obstacle to expansion has always been the fact that adding a team increases the number of owners sharing league revenues. If the expansion team will pay a sufficient league expansion fee and the addition of the expansion team will increase national television revenue and other league income sources, the benefits to existing teams may offset the negative consequences. The additional sharing of league revenue and the need to compete with one more team for players, coaches, general managers, and media interest and coverage, coupled with the requirement that any expansion must be approved by a majority or a super-majority of league owners, has served as a major deterrent to expansion of the successful traditional model leagues. *See, e.g.,* Andrew Zimbalist, *Baseball And Billions* 173–74 (1992). Only the threat of adverse congressional action has been sufficient to instigate some of the traditional league expansion that has occurred. *Id.* at 140–46.

In a single entity league, market demand should dictate expansion decisions. Adding a new team does not require an additional owner of the league; thus, as long as the anticipated additional revenue from a new team exceeds the anticipated additional costs, the single entity league is likely to expand. Even though the single entity league may not receive an expansion fee from a new owner, the existing league owners receive additional revenues from the expansion team. They will be shared beneficiaries of all the local team revenues—local ticket sales, skybox revenue, local television, local sponsorship, concessions, and parking, along with the increases in league revenue streams, including national television contracts and enhanced sales of licensed products that are associated with expansion. Given that expansion teams in a traditional model league are willing to pay the expansion fee as an up-front cost before they commence operations, and then receive revenues under the terms of the league's constitution and bylaws, it is reasonable to assume that the value of those revenues will exceed the amount of the expansion fee.

Similarly, team relocation will be less controversial in a single entity league. If one of the league's teams is not prospering, the league could relocate that team to a more profitable venue. In a traditional model league, the owners in profitable cities may not care about the team that is not prospering, and they may not want the struggling team to relocate to a new venue that might otherwise yield a substantial expansion fee in which they will share. In contrast, because the owners of a single entity league all share in the team's losses, they will exert efforts to remedy the disadvantageous situation. Because the team owners in a traditional model league do not have that same unity of interest, they do not respond to problem situations in as cooperative a manner.

Another advantage of single entity leagues is flexibility to improve the league product. The single entity league can enter into innovative agreements with sponsors, television companies, and others that may not treat all the teams in the league equally. For example, if a corporate sponsor with East Coast operations wants to make a sponsorship agreement with all of the teams in the league that are located in East Coast cities, the single entity league can sign that agreement, without concern that the agreement would not benefit the remaining teams in the league. All the owners of the single entity league would profit from the agreement, no matter how many or how few teams were benefited. The traditional model league might need to obtain assent from the East Coast team owners, and might need to devise a formula for compensating the non-East Coast teams.

The dispute litigated in the *Chicago Professional Sports Limited Partnership* case would never have arisen in a paradigm single entity league. There, the Chicago Bulls sought to contract with superstation WGN for the broadcast of a large number of Bulls games. The Bulls' revenue from WGN was not shared with the other NBA teams. At the same time, the NBA league office wanted to limit individual teams' contracts with superstations, in favor of league contracts with national television networks and superstations. The revenue from the league's contracts would be divided equally by the twenty-seven NBA teams. If the NBA were a single entity league, the only concerns would be making the best deal to advance the interests of the league, regardless of whether the television broadcast revenue came to the league or to a single team.

In summary, the primary advantages of the single entity model vis-à-vis the traditional model are the freedom to engage in conduct that might otherwise subject the league to antitrust liability and the collateral benefits to be derived from an unfettered right to impose restrictions on competition. However, perhaps as significant are the benefits that flow from the fact that the owners of the teams in a traditional model league simply do not have anything approaching the complete unity of interest prompting them to act together with only the best interests of the league at heart. The single entity owners should possess such singularity of purpose.

(b) Disadvantages

The primary disadvantages of the single entity model are not legal issues, but business issues. Most of the business difficulties flow from the fact that the owners of/investors in the single entity league do not have the autonomy of traditional model owners. They do not have independent authority to run an individual team. All team responsibilities of an owner in a traditional model league are assumed by the single entity league; thus, an investor in a pure single entity league will not own a team and will not perform the traditional model owner functions—selecting, hiring, and firing the players, coaches, and general managers, negotiating contracts with such personnel, running the business of the individual team, sitting in the owner's box, and dealing with the media as the representative of the team.

While the pure single entity league investor will probably be permitted to sell his or her ownership interest in the league or to pass it on to his heirs, he or she will not be able to sell a team or relocate an individual team. The value of the single entity investor's ownership interest will be much more directly a function of the overall league value. The amount that an investor in a traditional model team is willing to pay includes a premium for the notoriety and stature associated with owning a city's or a geographic area's representative in a popular sports league, the single entity owner is not as likely to capture that type of premium when he sells his ownership interest. As a result, it may be more difficult to attract investors in a single entity league in the first place.

An issue related to the lack of individual team autonomy is the effect that it may have on public and fan perception. To the extent that a fan's interest is a function of the team battling other teams in the league, it may be disheartening to learn that the financial fortunes of the people running his or her team are not very closely correlated to the team's on-the-field success. In fact, if the team is winning every game and threatening to establish a dynasty, then it may be in management's best interest to weaken the team to achieve competitive parity in the league. It remains to be seen whether those issues would deter fans from buying tickets and watching league broadcasts.

(7) Recent Leagues Utilizing the Single Entity Model and Questions About the Efficacy of the Single Entity Model

The concept of a sports league organized pursuant to a "single entity" model is at least twenty years old. One of the first "pure" single entity leagues, the Major Indoor Lacrosse League, was founded by two individuals, and for a number of years was owned by the founders and a third investor. The NFL's developmental league, the World League of American Football, now NFL Europe is a corporate entity owned by the member clubs of the NFL. Two sports leagues that never got off the ground, the Professional Spring Football League and the "A League," were designed to be, to some extent, single entity leagues. Most recently, Major League Soccer was at its inception conceived to be a single entity league, but it was launched as a hybrid league that has substantial similarities to the traditional model. *See* Complaint, *Fraser v. Major League Soccer*, Civil Action No. 10242 (D. Mass. 1997). The American Basketball League, the women's professional basketball league that went out of business after a few seasons, claimed to be a pure single entity league. The NBC-WWE joint venture, the XFL, claimed to be a single-entity league.

The mere fact that a league claims to have been organized as a single entity may not insulate it from antitrust challenges under Section 1. First, if the league enters into agreements with third parties that restrain competition, those agreements remain subject to challenge. Second, if the owners of the league are former, present, or potential competitors, the agreements pursuant to which those owners coalesced to form and operate the league may themselves be violations of Section 1. For example, in an extreme case, if the owners of the new "single entity" league were previously owners of teams in a professional traditional model league in the same sport, and they shut down the traditional model league or terminated their involvement with that league in order to form a single entity league, the *Copperweld* concern about a "sudden joining of economic resources that had previously served different interests," 467 U.S. at 771–72, would arguably be present. Third, if any of the officers or directors of the "single entity" league have an independent personal stake in achieving the league's goals, the participation of that officer or director may satisfy the requirement of a "contract, combination * * *, or conspiracy." Fourth, if the nominal single entity league is a hybrid between a traditional model and a true single entity league, it may stray too far from the single entity model to contend that the agreements among its owners are not combinations that unreasonably restrain trade.

As a result, when forming a new league, the organizers need to consider carefully the business and legal ramifications of the structure of their league, as well as legal implications raised by the "participants" in the league—the owners, the officers and directors, and the third parties with whom the league contracts. Antitrust courts will look beyond the structure of the league to the economic realities in order to determine if the league is truly a newly created, independent economic entity, or is more properly evaluated as a combination of former, present, or potential competitors.

(C) Planning and Establishing a New League— A Suggested Analysis Drawing Upon the Traditional and Single Entity Models

(1) Introduction

When trying to plan a course of action for the creation of a new professional sports league, it is natural to start with either the traditional model or, more recently, with the single entity model, and to organize the league's business plan exclusively on one model or the other. However, such an approach channels the business plan into a mode of operation that may not adequately further the goals and objectives of the new league. It also may tend to limit creativity and innovation, which may be essential for a new league to succeed in the very competitive professional sports industry. Therefore, it may not be advisable for the organizers of a new league to feel constrained to limit their planning to a pure application of only one model.

(2) The Significance of Innovation in a New League

Historically, some very substantial improvements and innovations in professional sports have been introduced by new leagues or circuits challenging the existing leagues or events in that sport. For example, World Championship Tennis ("WCT") receives credit for introducing: (1) yellow tennis balls (much easier to see on television); (2) tiebreakers (making it easier to control and predict the duration of a match); (3) colored shirts (again, a much better selection for television); (4) no doubles lines on the court during singles matches; and (5) other significant innovations. The American Basketball Association ("ABA") introduced red, white, and blue basketballs (which disappeared along with the ABA) and three-point shots (which became an NBA mainstay after the ABA's demise).

Creating and sustaining a new league in a sport that does not already have an established league is a formidable challenge. In these circumstances, the new league will not have a fan base or an established player pool (complete with fan awareness) for which to compete. It will not have the opportunity to draw upon and satisfy the unfulfilled demand that the rival league may have created. An established professional league that has been acting as a monopoly is likely to have artificially restricted the number of franchises and otherwise limited output in the face of substantial excess demand. *See, e.g.,* Andrew Zimbalist, *Baseball and Billions* 173–75 (1992). Cities and stadia or local and state governments may be competing to secure a team for their geographic area. New sports leagues that face an established league can often place teams in cities actively seeking an expansion or relocating team in the established league. New leagues in unestablished sports do not have the same opportunities. Soccer leagues that did not survive include the North American Soccer League and the Major Indoor Soccer League. For a partial list of other sports leagues that have died an untimely death, see Berry, Gould & Staudohar at 6. World Team Tennis, the MLS, and the Arena Football League are three more examples of currently operating sports leagues that were launched without a pre-existing league in their sport (because Arena Football is a much different product than professional football in the NFL).

Despite new leagues' freedom to innovate and improve on the product offered by established leagues, an established league has tremendous advantages over a start-up league in any sport. The established league has a fan and revenue base, on-going business operations, long-term relationships with television broadcast companies and sponsors, and general public awareness of its product and its way of conducting business. At the same time, an established league may experience difficulty making changes to respond to new competition. It is very difficult for such league to alter its product significantly or to change the primary rules about how it conducts its business. Besides problems with the effects of changes on long-term contractual arrangements, and the possible challenges from individual member clubs that oppose a change, there may be tremendous fan and media resistance to changes in the league's product. *See, e.g., Chicago Professional Sports Limited Partnership (Discussed in Chapter Twelve).* For example, Major League Baseball could face tremendous opposition if it considers changing the number of games each team plays (in the absence of a strike or lockout), use of aluminum bats, or similar "innovations." Modification of schedules to include regular season inter-league play was delayed for several years as a result of concern about such opposition.

(3) Structuring a League to Achieve Various Disparate Goals

Given the tremendous hurdles faced by a new league, it is important to structure the league in ways that will maximize league revenues, minimize league costs, and draw upon as many sources of support as possible. The league needs to create a high-quality product demanded by a variety of direct or indirect league consumers, to produce the product on a low-cost basis, and to divide the revenues generated in ways that adequately reward the various participants in, and contributors to, the league. The organizers of the new league start with tremendous flexibility to plan what product or products the league will offer (rules governing the game, the format of the game, the size and character of the arenas, the atmosphere associated with the games, etc.), when it will offer the product (how many games in a season, during what months will the season take place, etc.), where it will offer the product, how it will organize its business (league structure, involvement of sponsors and television broadcast companies, etc.), how it will market its product, and so on. Therefore, to the extent possible, a new league should not make business decisions based on how other leagues operate without at least identifying and considering alternatives.

(4) Identifying the Persons and Entities Affected by or Interested in the New League

One way to organize a league planning discussion is to identify the possible "participants," those categories of people that may have an interest in, or may be affected by, the league. In large part, a league is simply formed by contracts between and among these various participants. Therefore, if each of these participants is viewed as a contracting party, the organizers can consider what each category of participants can offer or contribute to a new league, what benefits they are seeking in return, and how the league can best serve their interests.

Of course, the planning analysis is likely to be affected dramatically by the identity of the participants who are organizing the league—players, television companies, wealthy individuals with an interest in the sport, stadium or facility owners seeking a new product to offer that may make use of their facilities, national governing bodies, etc.

A preliminary, broadly-defined list of "participants" in a league organized pursuant to the "traditional model" might include the following:

- Majority or minority owners of teams or investors in the league
    a. Publicly traded corporation as owner
    b. Closely-held corporation (or partnership) as owner
    c. Individual as owner
- Non-player employees of teams
    a. General Manager
    b. Coaches
        (1) Head Coach
        (2) Assistant Coaches
    c. Marketing and sales personnel
    d. Other team employees
- Commissioner or president (and employees)
    a. Commissioner
    b. Employees of league
    c. Employee of league organizations (*e.g.,* president of league marketing organization)
    d. League outside counsel

     e. Referees/umpires/officials
- Players
       a. Superstar players

       b. Solid, non-superstar players

       c. Marginal players
- Players Agents
- Players Associations
       a. Executive Director of Players Association

       b. President (current player) of Players Association and team representatives

       c. Players Association inside and outside counsel
- Television or radio broadcast companies
       a. National network

       b. Local station

       c. Superstation

       d. Cable station

          (1) Pay-per-view television company

          (2) Sports cable station
- Owner of stadium/arena/facility
- Corporate sponsor of player, coach, league, team, radio or television broadcast, etc.
- Companies that produce and sell team and league licensed products (*e.g.*, apparel, trading cards, collectibles, etc.)
- Companies that manufacture equipment and other products purchased and/or used by the league (*e.g.*, "tools of the trade," astroturf or another court or field surface, goal posts or goals, etc.)
- Local communities/municipalities, state governments, federal government
- Fans who are the consumers of
       a. Skyboxes

       b. Regular stadium seating

       c. Concessions

       d. Television and radio broadcasts

       e. Team and league licensed products
- The "Media"—broadcast, print, etc.—that does not broadcast the games, but photographs and reports about the players, the games, and the business of the sport.

(5) Identifying and Projecting the Likely Revenues and Expenses to be Generated by the New League and its Teams

The next step in developing a strategic plan for the new league is to identify and quantify the likely expenses and revenues associated with the league. Under the traditional model, a preliminary list of revenues and expenses might be as follows:

- League Expenses
    a. Referees' and other officials' salaries and benefits
    b. League office employees' salaries, benefits, etc.
    c. Costs associated with coaching staff and trainers
    d. League marketing and advertising activities
- Team Expenses
    a. Player salaries, benefits, etc.
    b. Costs of operating the league office and the Properties division—travel expenses, office equipment, league office space, possibly ATP Tour or PGA Tour-type facilities, the costs associated with the draft, the all-star games and related activities, the playoffs, the championship game or series, etc.
    c. Salaries and benefits for team front-office personnel (president, general manager, ticket office manager and employees, public relations personnel, etc.)
    d. Cost of the stadium
    e. Expenses for office space, office furniture and equipment, and activities associated with operation of the front office
    f. Expenses associated with the players, trainers and coaches—transportation and travel expenses, training and practice facilities, weight rooms, locker rooms, medical facilities, costs associated with feeding the players, etc.
    g. Expenses associated with the production of home games—stadium costs, costs of the surface and the court, security, ticket takers and ushers, parking lot attendants and parking lot security, etc.
    h. Expenses associated with away games—transportation and travel expenses for team personnel, etc.
- League revenues
    a. National television contracts
    b. League sponsor agreements
    c. Properties-type licensing revenues
    d. Revenues associated with the draft, all-star games and related activities, non-team playoff revenues, and championship game or series revenues
- Team revenues
    a. Ticket sales, luxury box seat sales for home games
    b. Local television revenue
    c. Local sponsor revenue
    d. Concession revenue
    e. Parking revenue.

The next step is to attempt to quantify the likely amounts for each of these revenues and expenses, to the extent that such calculation is possible. It will require substantial planning concerning the product to be offered by the league. The length of the league season, the number of teams in the league, the number of games to be played by each team, the ticket prices to be charged, an estimated per game attendance figure, and other revenue figures must be considered. The organizers also must estimate player and other employee salaries, as well as the other major costs of operating the league.

Agreements with the various participants should allocate the league's revenues and expenses in ways that attract their interest, investments, and support to the league, while providing sufficient incentives to invest substantial time and effort into making the league a success. For example, in return for some form of profit sharing, revenue sharing, or another mechanism for giving them "upside potential" if the league prospers, suppliers to the league, including players, league and team employees, and owners of stadia, may agree to receive lower initial salaries or payments.

(6) Drawing on Aspects of Both the Single Entity and Traditional Models

As explained above, the primary benefits of the single entity model relate to freedom to control player and other team employee costs and freedom to control team behavior (*e.g.,* relocation, transfer of ownership, etc.) without antitrust liability. The primary problem with the single entity model, when compared with the traditional model, concerns the second "benefit"—a lack of autonomy of the teams, which may deter investment and adversely affect fan interest in the league.

Therefore, one alternative would be to create a single entity league that employs all the players, coaches, and general managers, and then contracts with city franchise owners to provide facilities for teams and to market the teams on a local basis. Each city franchise owner would provide specified minimum training and playing facilities for the team in that city, including an arena that satisfies specific league standards. The city franchise owner would be an independent contractor with rights and obligations delineated in an agreement with the league. That agreement would specify what traditional model "league" and "team" expenses would be the responsibility of the city franchise owner and would specify how the league and the city franchise owner would divide any interest that the city franchise owner may have in each of the various traditional model "league" and "team" sources of revenue. The agreement would also specify what rights, if any, the city franchise owner would have with respect to renewal of the agreement, relocation of the franchise, and sale, assignment, or transfer of the franchise owner's rights and obligations. The goal would be to create a sufficient "unity of interest" between the city franchise owner and the league such that the owner would be autonomous, but nevertheless would share the league's aspirations. Thus, the ultimate aim would be to design a league that would have the freedom to control player costs without antitrust liability by following the single entity model, while drawing on the traditional model to secure a somewhat autonomous entrepreneur to operate the local businesses of the league in a way tailored to minimize the conflicts between the local businesses and the overall league interests.

(7) Considering Other Structures

This discussion of the organization of a league and the application of the traditional and single entity models has proceeded on the assumption that the organizers do not have an independent interest in the sport. However, the organizers of a new sports league could be: (1) the players, seeking to own and control their sport; (2) the manufacturer of the tools of the trade for the sport seeking to gain an exclusive position with the new league to promote its products (*e.g.,* a company that produces volleyball equipment and apparel funding the creation of a professional volleyball league); (3) a television broadcast company, seeking additional programming (*e.g.*, the NBC co-ownership of the failed XFL); or (4) the national governing body for the sport, seeking to form a top quality professional league to further the sport. If the organizer were a player, manufacturer, television company, or national governing body, the goals may be very different, and modification of the league structure may be appropriate.

For example, if the players are organizing a league, minimizing player salaries may not be a goal of the league. The players might decide to contract with individuals who would operate the teams and limit the amount that those team operators could earn. The television broadcast company that helps to organize a league may be very concerned about placing teams in the most important television markets (or the markets that are most important to that company or where its most powerful affiliates are located) and maintaining its exclusive right to broadcast league games. The national governing body's primary concern may be furthering the sport generally.

The structure and organization of a new sports league has important implications for the future prospects of any new league. While organizers of new leagues must address all the issues discussed above, there is precious little literature to provide guidance in this area. A fuller ventilation and understanding of these issues will benefit league organizers, as well as those who deal with the leagues, and those who must litigate disputes involving the league.

Notes and Questions

1. If you were retained to counsel a group of prospective owners on the formation of a new league, what model would you recommend? Are there hybrid variations that would accomplish the dual objectives of control and competition?

2. Is there any possibility that a league owned and operated by the players themselves could survive? What would the position of the players associations be with regard to the possibility of the players exercising entrepreneurial control? Would such a league obviate the need for union representation of any type? Would players' ownership create labor law concerns because the employees are, in fact, also the employers?

3. If the players organized a league that had no traditional owners, would the participants simply be independent contractors functioning similar to professional tennis players and golfers?

4. To this point, we have explored in considerable detail the traditional league structure in the typical team sport. To date, the legal literature addressing non-league sports is remarkably sparse. Some of these questions that are seldom raised or adequately discussed are:

   a) What are the legal and competitive aspects common to team and individual sports?

   b) What are the significant points of comparison and distinction between team sports and individual sports?

   c) What aspects of team sports are inapplicable to individual sports?

   d) Are there elements of team sports that can be employed in an advantageous manner by individual sports?

   e) Who is responsible for creating, maintaining, and developing individual sports such as tennis and golf?

f) What is the significance of appearance fees, ranking systems, and related devices in terms of the success and fan acceptance of a particular individual sport or sports tour?

To understand fully the myriad legal questions that arise in sports law, a comprehension of the systems that operate in the individual sport context is necessary. The following discussion focuses on the similarities and differences between team sports and individual sports and the various legal and business approaches that must be employed in each area.

IV. Team and Individual Sports: A Comparison[2]

Many articles and books about the law and business of sports assume that sports are a unitary phenomenon. This assumption is misplaced. Some authors have demonstrated an appreciation of the fact that individual and team sports are different and they have consciously limited the scope of their writing to "league sports." Yet, there has been very little written about individual sports or the differences between individual and team sports.

Such a comparison is not an idle or academic pursuit; the fundamental differences are dramatic and the potential legal consequences are profound. For example, because participants in individual sports are generally not deemed to be "employees," labor laws are not implicated and the relationships between "participants" and "producers" follow accordingly. Similarly, many of the issues that have arisen in team sports regarding the contractual underpinnings of the employer-employee relationship have not surfaced in the individual sport arena. Moreover, in antitrust litigation involving challenges to rules and regulations of sports associations and agreements among producers of individual sport events, the purposes and competitive effects of these rules, regulations, and agreements, which often differ markedly in a team sport context, may dictate the outcome.

Understanding the similarities and differences between team and individual sports is also crucial to the success of those persons or entities involved in the production and marketing of sports events. Producers of individual sport competitions can profit from the study and imitation of other individual sports. Insights gained from the study of league sports can be applied to improve individual sporting events, and correspondingly, aspects of individual sports production can be used to benefit league sports.

(A) Competitive Differences Between Individual and Team Sports

Anyone who has played or observed both team and individual sports is aware that there are basic competitive differences. For example, as a result of the obvious differences between sports that require teamwork and those pursuits that, by definition, do not, the best individual performer will prevail in an individual competition, but the best player in a league may not be able to lead his or her team to victory. There are also

---

2. This section has been adapted from Mark S. Levinstein, *An Analysis of Legal and Business Differences Between Individual and Team Sports—Appearance Fees, Ranking Systems, and Marketing Implications*, X THE SPORTS LAWYER 1 (1990–91).

competitive differences that affect the organization of team sports. Coaches often help individual athletes prepare for competition, but, because of the need to make substitutions and to coordinate multiple players, coaches of teams usually play a more important role during the games or the team competitions themselves. There are no general managers involved in individual sports, but a team's general manager, who knows which players to draft, recruit, sign as free agents, cut or trade, and how they will mesh, may regularly direct his team to victory, even if he is not able to secure the best individual athletes.

Those *competitive* differences are occasionally discussed in articles about the mental aspects of golf, tennis, and other individual sports where top competitors do not rely on the support of teammates. The literature comparing team and individual sports is scanty, but the issues are sometimes touched upon in the daily newspapers or magazines, as sportswriters discuss and debate the importance of coaches, managers, and general managers, and the ability or inability of a single great player to lead his or her team to the league championship. The differences are also apparent when a player's great individual performance is overshadowed by the team's loss of a game.

(B) Legal and Business Differences Between Individual and Team Sports

(1) Organization of Individual Sports v. League Sports

(a) League Sports

Most sports fans are intimately familiar with team sports. Typically, a collection of team owners, each with a single team and a home facility or stadium, schedules games between teams and thereby forms a league. As discussed earlier in this chapter, the league usually has a chief executive officer who holds the title of "commissioner," the teams have coaches, managers, and/or general managers, and the players are represented individually by agents and collectively by a labor union or "players association" (*see* Chapters Three, Fourteen and Twenty).

Each team incurs its own expenses for player salaries, stadium or facility leasing, uniforms, and equipment. The league office usually absorbs the expense of training and employing umpires and/or referees and pays those expenses out of league revenues or passes them through to the individual teams to share the cost. Each team by nature is entitled to keep its own revenues from such sources as ticket sales, sales of sponsorship rights, sales or rental of sky boxes, facility agreements, parking fees, concessions, sales of team memorabilia and clothing, and sales of television broadcast rights. However, most leagues have some sort of revenue sharing that commonly involves such items as sales of team or league products (clothing, memorabilia, etc.), sales of television broadcast rights, and revenues or profits from post-season playoffs and/or championship games. Some leagues also divide regular season ticket revenues.

(b) Individual Sports

It is more difficult to generalize about individual sports, whether professional or amateur, because the great number of different individual sports lead to varied business structures. The primary organizational unit is usually the "event," which may be a "tournament," a race, or a series of races, but is generally a single competition in one geographic area or site that lasts a few hours to a few weeks. The person or entity in charge of the event is usually referred to as the "owner," "producer," or "promoter" of the event, referred to throughout this section as the "event producer."

The event producer first creates the event by selecting a location and negotiating an agreement with the owner of the site or facility where the event will be held. The event producer then attracts the athletes to play in the event, by offering prize money, appearance fees, trophies or medals, and/or the stature, satisfaction and pride associated with competing in, and perhaps winning, the event. The event producer assumes responsibility for securing necessary equipment, as well as for printing tickets, arranging for parking facilities, employing referees, umpires, timekeepers, or other neutral officials, providing security, crowd control, and/or ushers, and otherwise insuring the orderly administration of the event. The event producer is then entitled to any revenue that the event generates, including ticket sales for attending the event, sponsorship revenues from those who are willing to pay to be associated publicly with the event, parking fees, concession proceeds, revenues from the sale of broadcasting rights, programs, memorabilia, licensed products, and souvenirs, and miscellaneous other sources of income.

The event producer can absorb ultimate responsibility for all expenses and revenues, or he can sell or contract away the various rights and obligations. For example, the agreement with the facility may mandate that the parking and concessions revenues remain with the owner of the facility. Similarly, a primary sponsor of the event may make a major, long-term financial commitment to the event and demand a percentage of the profits or a percentage of the gross revenues as part of the sponsorship agreement. Many different sponsorship rights may be sold. Event producers often sell the right to be part of the title or name of the event to a "title sponsor" and the right to be identified as the entity presenting the event to a "presenting sponsor" (*e.g.*, the Colgate Classic presented by Ford). The event producer may also seek other sponsorship support, in return for a variety of benefits, such as identification as an "official" product or sponsor of the event (*e.g.*, the official golf ball or hotel), on-site identification (*e.g.*, banners, t-shirts, pages in the program), tickets to the event, the right to conduct on-site entertainment (*e.g.*, a reception area), inclusion in event advertising materials, participation in a pro-am event associated with the main event, or even a specified share of the event revenues or profits. The sponsorship support may also take different forms, from sponsorship fees to various "trade deals" or "in-kind" payments, such as free hotel rooms at the "official" hotel of the event.

In addition, a person, organization or sponsor may decide to subcontract operation of an event to a company in the business of producing and managing such events in exchange for a percentage of the profits or a guaranteed amount. It is also common for the event producer to contract with a management company or sales agent to sell the domestic and/or foreign television broadcast rights or to secure sponsorship revenue in return for a percentage of the television or sponsorship revenue generated. For all these reasons, once the original event producer has entered into short-term or long-term agreements that reallocate rights and responsibilities, the identity of the "owner" or the "producer" may become increasingly unclear.

Further complications arise when a players association is formed, or when a sports association "sanctions" events and/or a "circuit," "tour" or "series" of individual events is established. In some cases, all three of these occurrences may be implicated. In general, if any of these situations arise, the individual event producer agrees to rules and regulations about how he or she will operate the event, such as: (1) to make specified payments (*e.g.*, the promoter may have to pay fees to the organizations that sanction a boxing match); (2) to surrender certain rights (*e.g.*, television revenues may become the property of the tour and the tour may sell certain on-site sponsorship identification rights at all tour, events, thereby restricting the individual event producer's ability to generate event-specific sponsorship revenue); (3) to impose certain restrictions upon participation (*e.g.*, the rules may only allow members of the players association to compete, may give preference to athletes based on their circuit ranking or may require the producer to schedule the event where and when the circuit decides it should be scheduled); and/or (4) to yield some control over the operation of the event (*e.g.*, the players association, the sports association, or the tour may insist on supplying, selecting, or approving the officials or referees at the event). When these types of rules exist, who "owns" or "produces" the event becomes even more ambiguous.

(c) Similarities and Differences

Even after such a short analysis of the organization of league and individual sports, similarities become obvious. The teams sell on-site identification to sponsors in much the same way as individual events do. A team's stadium contract may have terms similar to the terms of a facility contract for an individual event. Although athletes in individual sports are not generally unionized and may even be more properly considered independent contractors rather than employees, players associations in both league and individual sports are supposed to fulfill the same player advocacy or player representation functions. Further, as discussed below, circuits, tours, or sports associations may perform functions paralleling those exerted by the commissioner and league offices in league sports.

In addition, there are games that are organized as if they were individual events, in which the event producer contracts with the teams to play and runs the event accordingly. College football bowl games and some college basketball tournaments are operated as if they were individual events. They even sell title sponsorships, in which a corporate identification becomes part of the event's title (*e.g.*, the Fidelity Bank Holiday Shoot-out, the FedEx Orange Bowl, etc.).

Despite the similarities, the differences remain significant. As discussed below, the need for coordination between or among separate events is not the same as the need for coordination among teams in league sports. The absence of collective bargaining and the resulting inapplicability of the antitrust labor exemption is illustrative. In addition, competing leagues seldom survive in the long run, while competing individual events often survive, even in sports with tours or circuits of events. Similarly, while exclusive contracts are the rule in major league sports, tours and circuits are generally unable to extract exclusivity commitments, assuming that such commitments would survive legal scrutiny.

Another major difference is that the league format means every game includes a range of participants, from superstars to marginal players. Fans who have an avid interest in their local teams are familiar with the entire roster. The non-superstar who fills an assigned role or a specialist who is not a great overall athlete can achieve success and cultivate substantial fan interest and support.

Individual sports tend to revolve around a much smaller number of top players. Specialization is not as rewarded in many individual sports. The tennis player with the best serve, the golfer with the best drive, or the heavyweight boxer with the best uppercut will not achieve any significant recognition or success if he or she does not become one of the best overall performers. The result is that the degree of success or failure of individual sports events tends to depend on the level of participation of the best-known, most popular athletes. Of course, some sports, such as track and field, are based on specialization and, except for events like the pentathlon and the decathlon that require diversification, *only* specialists are successful (with the possible exception being an athlete who "specializes" in several separate events—*e.g.*, sprints, long jump, hurdles.

The nature of certain other individual sports presents unique challenges and opportunities. For example, it is often not feasible to charge spectators a fee to watch a marathon or an outdoor bicycle race. It may not even be possible to sell the exclusive broadcast rights if the event is conducted in public. *See WCVB-TV v. Boston Athletic Ass'n*, 926 F.2d 42 (1st Cir. 1991) (considered in Chapter Nineteen). At the same time, fans are often less insistent on maintaining a traditional format; so there are opportunities for creativity and innovation to improve their events and increase their profitability. Producers of individual events must study the economics of their sports carefully, to assess their market, create and present their event, and maximize the long-term viability and profitability of their event and the sport as a whole.

(2) Owners of Teams Have a Much Greater Need to Coordinate Their Activities Than Do Producers of Individual Sport Competitions

Perhaps the most fundamental economic or business distinction, which has never been discussed in a reported judicial decision, is that individual sports events generally can stand on their own, and owners or producers of these events need not cooperate or coordinate their rules, schedules, or business operations with the owners or producers of any other competitions. To the contrary, teams *need* to agree on rules, schedules, and business issues about their games (or matches or meets) in order to produce a game. Two teams cannot independently decide on different rules, locations, dates, and ticket prices, or separate exclusive television contracts for the same game.

There are many examples of individual events that stand alone. The Kentucky Derby, championship boxing matches, the Boston Marathon, the Ironman Triathlon, the Figure Skating World championships, and the Indianapolis 500 are just a few examples. Even in sports that are dominated by tours or circuits, there are events in which individuals compete and succeed. For example, the British Open, produced by the Royal and Ancient Golf Club of St. Andrews, is an event for professional golfers that is not part of any tour. The United States Golf Association's U.S. Open also stands on its own, even though most professional golf events are part of a professional tour, such as the PGA Tour, the LPGA Tour, or the European PGA Tour.

In tennis, the four Grand Slam events were originally separate and independent. In the early 1970s, they became part of the Grand Prix of Tennis, which was organized and administered by the Men's International Professional Tennis Council ("MIPTC"), and, since 1988, referred to as the Men's Tennis Council ("MTC"). At the end of 1989, the MIPTC was dissolved and the Grand Slam events did not become part of the ATP Tour, the successor circuit to the Grand Prix. There now is a Grand Slam Committee that coordinates the four Grand Slam events, but the Grand Slams are again primarily independent. There is no real doubt that they could survive without any need for horizontal cooperation among them—unlike team sports. *See further* Chapter Ten.

(3) There Are Business Reasons for Individual Events to Cooperate

(a) Competition-Enhancing Reasons

Even though individual events do not need to cooperate, there may be compelling business reasons that dictate such cooperation. The "packaging" of events to be advertised and marketed together may be an effective competitive strategy. Advertisers and sponsors may want to associate with a circuit of events that lasts for several months or all year round, rather than with several unrelated events. There may be economies of scale and other efficiencies in linking events. One sports marketer can contact potential national sponsors and television companies on behalf of fifteen events, eliminating the need for fifteen individual tournament directors to make the same calls. Similarly, television companies may have greater interest in a series of events that can be broadcast during the same time slot each week, much like professional football and the baseball "game of the week" have been telecast. There may be greater fan and viewer interest if there is a circuit of events, with circuit standings or rankings of the competitors, rules that are the same from week to week, and/or a competition that leads to an end-of-season championship game, tournament, match, or series.

There are many examples of producers of individual events linking or packaging their product in an effort to increase fan and viewer interest. For example, the heavyweight unification series of boxing that took place in the 1980's benefited from the packaging of the individual fights. By linking several bouts in a tournament-style playoff, not only did the promoters attempt to "unify" the WBC, WBA and IBF titles in a single heavyweight champion, but they also sought to increase the public's familiarity with the various champions and challengers.

Television's interest in a package or series of events is also evidenced by its efforts to combine events that have not been joined by the producers of the events. Television networks and cable companies sometimes advertise and broadcast a "fight of the week" or a series of individual sporting events on that network (e.g., "Tennis on USA Network"), even if those fights, tennis tournaments, or other events are not otherwise part of a single circuit, tour, or series of events. The series format on television may increase viewer interest, as well as provide viewers with information. This approach communicates to the viewer that the network with the series will be broadcasting a number of that sport's events on a regular basis, encouraging a viewer interested in that sport to develop an allegiance to that network. Each broadcast will tell viewers about upcoming events in the series. The network is also able to market advertising time on the entire series of broadcasts to sponsors who believe that the demographics of the likely purchasers of their products are closely correlated with the demographics of the viewers likely to watch that series of sports broadcasts.

(b) Competition-Reducing Reasons

In other contexts, the greatest incentive for cooperation among individual events may be the prospect of elimination of competition between those events that would otherwise exist. For example, by coordinating scheduling, two tournaments that might be played during the same week can agree to hold their events on different dates. As a result, they need not compete directly for athletes to participate in, for television companies to broadcast, or for the media to attend and publicize their events. Of course,

THE BUSINESS OF SPORTS

because the top athletes do not participate in all events, the events still need to remain competitive and attractive to the best performers. The average number of events in which professional athletes compete varies from sport to sport, based on such factors as the nature of the competition, the number of available events, geographical considerations and compensation. For example, marathon runners generally compete in fewer events. Professional boxers seldom fight more than once a month. Tennis players and golfers tend to play more often.

In a similar vein, a television network may only be willing to broadcast fifteen golf tournaments each year, creating competition among the various tournaments to be televised by that network. However, the direct competition will be reduced substantially, achieving the competition-reducing goals underlying the formation of tours and circuits as well as the consolidation of competing circuits.

(C) Business Issues Common To Individual Sports

(1) Appearance Fees or "Guarantees"

(a) The Concept

After a league is organized and the players contract with the various league teams, players simply play wherever their teams are scheduled. Individual sports face a different competitive situation. While some individual events may not be affected significantly by the identity of the competitors, generally the opposite is true. The identity of the competitors can dramatically affect an event's revenues from television, sponsors, ticket sales, concessions, parking, and other sources. Accordingly, it is in the event producers' business interest to attract the best (or most popular) field of competitors.

There are many different ways to attract competitors. When selecting competitions, athletes may consider the significance, locations, and dates of the events, competing tournaments, their own training regimen, the likelihood of winning, the prize money or other compensation offered, and many other factors. Golfers prefer certain courses. Some track stars prefer outdoor meets to indoor meets. Tennis players prefer certain court surfaces. An athlete's endorsement contract may obligate him to compete in specific events or may pay substantial bonuses for successful participation in certain events. A specific event may be at the right time and under the right conditions to serve as a "warm-up" for a subsequent, more important, event. The above-listed factors are often beyond the control of the event producer. However, a producer does have the ability to make an event more appealing. For example, he can offer athletes top-quality facilities, superb hospitality, and luxurious accommodations. In some sports, the event manager (or similar official responsible for administering the event) may be able to adjust the schedule to accommodate a popular competitor (e.g., delay his first match or heat (in racing events) so he or she can arrive late for the competition, slot him or her to compete at night when the temperature at the facility is cooler, etc.).

The event producer also may be able to attract the most desirable athletes by offering some sort of pre-arranged recompense—paying them a flat sum of money or reimbursing them for their cost of travel, meals, or other expenses. The money may be called an "appearance fee," training expenses, or "share of the purse." The event may simply guarantee that the athlete will win a certain amount in prize money. Thus, the term "guarantee" has become synonymous with "appearance fee." In general, however, the payment, whether called a "guarantee" or an "appearance fee," is additional to any prize money that the athlete may win for his performance. In some professional individual events, there is no "prize money." In amateur events, the only tangible "prize" awarded may be a trophy or a medal. Therefore, the only compensation paid by the event producer is an appearance fee, training expense, purse, or similar payment, generally arranged in advance. However, some "amateur" events pay specified amounts of "training money" to athletes based on their performance in the event (*e.g.*, $5,000 of training money for the runner who finishes first). In these circumstances, the line between amateur and professional events may no longer be meaningful.

In an amateur competition or a professional event governed by the rules of a league or circuit, there may be restrictions upon the event's freedom to pay the participants. For those or other reasons, the payments may be camouflaged. Professional athletes have been paid hundreds of thousands of dollars for participating in pro-am events, for attending press conferences or cocktail parties, or for performing other services, where it was clear that the payments were nothing more or less than appearance fees. Likewise, the producers have dressed appearance fees in the disguise of expenses or similar ostensibly legitimate reimbursements.

(b) Payment of Appearance Fees—Competitive Reasons

As discussed above, whenever the "owner" or promoter of a competition wants to ensure that a particular athlete will participate in that competition, and the prize money or other reward for the competitors is insufficient to guarantee such participation, there is an incentive for the owner to offer the athlete an appearance fee. The benefit to the event can be very substantial. In some circumstances, payment of appearance fees to a few players could be worth a million dollars or more in increased tournament revenues. As long as the appearance fees are less than the overall benefit to the event, there will be strong economic incentive to make the payments. For example, a golf or tennis tournament that can advertise the anticipated attendance of several top names is likely to increase its sponsorship revenue, "season" ticket (tickets for every day of a multi-day event) and individual ticket sales, parking and concession revenue, and media interest. If television contracts for that year have not been finalized, the better field may even lead to increased television revenue.

Addition of the top names will also improve the assessment of the event by those who attend or are associated with the event. Increased media interest means free advertising and satisfied event sponsors. Increased viewer interest means higher television ratings. Higher ratings mean that the television broadcast company will demand and receive more advertising dollars. When television advertisers are pleased, the stations are also pleased, and the next television contract may be more lucrative as a result. The larger television audience and the larger on-site crowds will ensure greater publicity for sponsors who, in turn, will be more inclined to renew their sponsorship. The people who attend and enjoy the event and those who cannot obtain tickets for sold-out events are more likely to purchase tickets for next year's event, and the overall stature, reputation, and goodwill of the event will be enhanced.

For these reasons, it is not surprising that appearance fees have become an accepted part of the tournament culture. It is only in the past few decades that athletes in individual sports have had a substantial number of opportunities to compete in professional events. As recently as 1967, all major tennis events were only for amateur competitors. If a player at that time accepted any money, or even if he played in a tournament against a professional and *did not* receive *any* money, he could be forever banned from amateur competition by the International Tennis Federation.

In light of the fact that amateur athletes could not receive prize money, even if they were to win the events, it was sometimes difficult for producers of top amateur events to convince amateur athletes to incur the costs of travel and accommodations to compete. At the same time, these events received substantial income from sponsorships, ticket sales, concessions, and eventually television. Because they were not permitted to pay the players, the event producers' expenses were minimal. When the presence of top amateur athletes was likely to increase an event's stature (and profitability), amateur events often paid secret travel or expense reimbursement to persuade amateur athletes to compete. Not surprisingly, the reimbursements often exceeded the athletes' expenses, and events often competed to attract the top athletes by offering increased payments. This type of payment often led to charges of "shamateurism." Eventually and inevitably, professional events, accessible to both professionals and amateurs, came into existence.

(c) Prohibition of Appearance Fees—Competitive Reasons

Several arguments have been advanced in opposition to appearance fees. The most important argument may be that it is unseemly or unfair for an athlete to be compensated merely for participating, without regard to his performance. In some cases, a star athlete who loses may still receive a larger appearance fee than the prize money paid to the athlete who wins. Many observers argue that such an outcome is inappropriate and that it will decrease the public's interest in the sport if it is exposed.

The other principal business argument against appearance fees is that the top player who receives the appearance fee is thereby encouraged to lose intentionally, or, at least, is not encouraged to win, because he has already received a payment for attending and competing. Early-round losses by top-ranked tennis players and poor performances by professional golfers or track and field stars are sometimes attributed to appearance fees.

A third argument sometimes offered by sports purists is that an athlete's income should be a function of his or her performance on that date, not his ranking or past achievements, and certainly not personality or popularity. They consider appearance fees to be inconsistent with this ideal. Appearance fees, like an athlete's endorsement income, are also tied to past performances, the athlete's personality, age, cosmetic appeal, and other factors that affect media or public interest. These purists believe that the athlete's revenue from the event should be based solely on performance in that event, and that everyone should have an equal opportunity to earn the same prize money. The purists and those who believe appearance fees encourage poor performances sometimes argue that the payment of undisclosed appearance fees constitutes some sort of fraud or misrepresentation.

The responses to the criticisms of appearance fees are persuasive. First, in all sports that do not revolve around prize money, athletes' primary compensation is based on past performance. In some sports, performance incentives, such as most home runs or runs batted in, are actually prohibited. It would be naive to believe that a player's personality, popularity, and appeal to fans and the media does not affect how much compensation a team will offer. The player's charisma translates into fan interest, increased game attendance, sponsorship revenue and other economic benefits to his team.

In addition, players in team sports can often negotiate long-term contracts that guarantee their salary and/or spot on the roster, regardless of performance. Such "guarantees" may be embraced in the collective bargaining agreement between team owners and the players' bargaining representative. Even the top competitors in individual sports are generally unable to negotiate similar contractual assurances. If they cannot play, they will not be paid. If they want the same type of protection, they have to purchase insurance, provided that they are able to find someone willing to insure them not only against injury, but also against poor performance.

The argument that the appearance fee will lead to half-hearted performances or early round tournament losses is not as logical as it appears at first blush. An athlete competing in a tournament is playing for the prize money even if he or she is independently wealthy or has received an appearance fee to attend the event. Why should a multi-millionaire who has received no advance payment to compete in an event play more poorly for the $100,000 prize money than if he had already been paid $50,000 to attend and compete?

There is no reason to believe that a player competing in fifteen events offering the same prize money will perform worse at the events that paid him or her to appear. In fact, he or she may have added incentive to compete more strenuously so as to increase the likelihood of being offered an appearance fee to return the following year. Professional boxers are often paid a pre-negotiated fee for a fight, a fee that is not affected by the outcome of the bout. With certain unfortunate exceptions, they still fight hard in most cases, knowing that the outcome will affect future paydays. It is also not unheard of for a player to feel a sense of obligation to perform well at an event that paid him or her an appearance fee.

Of course, it is true that the prospect of an appearance fee may cause a player who is injured, tired or disinterested nevertheless to attend an event and conceivably perform in a subpar fashion. In general, however, fans want to see the athlete compete no matter how he or she fares, and the event producer wants him or her to compete because most financial rewards to the event are not lost if he or she plays badly (tickets are primarily sold in advance, sponsors are under contract, etc.). If the athlete performs poorly on a regular basis, appearance fees or fan interest are likely to decline. In addition, if the sport's ranking systems are designed properly and fairly, his or her ranking, stature, and income are likely to fall with a poor showing. Therefore, there remain substantial incentives for the athlete to give the best possible performance, and the market itself should police the player who consciously takes his or her money, fails to perform, and runs.

(d) Prohibition of Appearance Fees—Anticompetitive Reasons

There are additional bases for the continuation of appearance fees. Prize money and appearance fees are two of the most important means by which individual sport events compete for players' services. Because it is important for these events to ensure the participation of the top-ranked or most popular athletes, appearance fees are the most effective and most efficient means of insuring competition. If prize money is increased, all competitors in the event benefit, while appearance fees can be limited to the players who are most sought after by the event producer. In addition, prize money can only be increased through public announcements. An event producer knows that his or her competition may match increases in prize money. Appearance fees, on the other hand, can be kept secret and are likely to improve the event field.

The competitive analysis here is similar to teams' competition for players' services in league sports. While some team owners aggressively pursue free agents, others do not, partially due to their recognition that open competition for available players will increase salaries generally and thereby increase all teams' costs. Similarly, some event producers favor prohibitions on appearance fees, reducing event costs for player services but surrendering the option of improving the field at their event. Prohibiting appearance fees decreases the amounts paid for players' services overall. A more searching analysis of the legal challenges to appearance fees is contained in Chapter Ten. *See Volvo North America Corp. v. MIPTC, 857 F.2d 55 (2d Cir. 1988).*

(2) Ranking Systems in Individual Sports

Sports pages are filled with discussions of league standings, battles to qualify for playoffs, championship games, etc. Articles about high school, college, and professional sports constantly report team rankings, conference standings, and tournament possibilities. Various individual statistics also receive a great deal of attention, as do the myriad awards created to acknowledge individual achievements.

Some of these rankings, standings, awards and statistics pre-date the creation of league or NCAA marketing directors, but today they nevertheless serve many league and university objectives very effectively. They increase fan, viewer and media interest, provide additional focal points for discussions and disputes, add significance to some games that might otherwise appear to be trivial, and promote fan loyalty and commitment to individual players, teams, leagues, and entire sports. Every team or league marketing director, at one time or another, considers possible changes in individual and/or team ranking systems, post-season play format, or the statistics that are reported during broadcasts or in post-game releases to the media. The creation of new awards and statistics, alteration of award criteria and selection processes, and similar decisionmaking are seldom considered without reference to anticipated public perception or possible financial impact on the sport. Awards, rankings, and championship formats are sometimes very important aspects of the competitive viability of various leagues, conferences, and sports. These vehicles, if utilized properly, can sometimes help keep a fledgling sport, like a professional indoor soccer or arena football league, afloat.

It is not surprising that similar rankings, awards, and end-of-season championships have been utilized by producers of individual sports events, tours, and circuits. As with team sports, ranking of individual athletes gives the spectator or fan more information about the sport—who has been playing well and who has not; who is the underdog and who is the favorite, etc. In fact, the ranking system may even be more important in individual sports. In team sports, there are probably fans who will root for the local team and will be interested in the outcome of each game, even if they do not know the names of the players on their team. In individual sports, the fan may have no interest in the outcome of the events without some knowledge of the participants. A ranking system ties together performance in what may be unrelated events, and the outcome of each event affects the overall ranking. The rankings serve to reassure fans or viewers that they are watching the top competitors in the sport and to provide some objective benchmarks about how the recent performance of the athletes compares to others throughout the sport.

As a result of the ranking system, a fan who cares about a favorite golfer's ranking may also begin to care about events in which that golfer does not even compete. This response parallels team sports, where a fan who roots for the local team may be interested in the outcome of games involving the local team's competition for a conference championship or a place in the playoffs. The ranking system may also decide who will play in an individual sport's season-ending championship, thus generating fan interest in how a favorite player or his competitors are performing in otherwise unimportant events.

A savvy circuit or tour promotion office considers all of the available tools—ranking systems, year-end championship events, awards, publishing of carefully selected statistics, and similar strategies to foster interest in that circuit or tour and the overall sport. Used to provide additional information and increase fan interest, they are legitimate competitive methods that should be encouraged.

Once ranking systems, bonus pools, and official statistics are established, they assume significance in the marketplace. Athlete endorsement contracts often provide healthy bonuses if an athlete wins specific awards or achieves certain rankings. There are also often bonuses for winning specific events or for "making the cover" of various publications. In addition to affecting the endorsement bonuses to which an athlete is entitled, the awards and rankings dramatically affect the endorsement opportunities offered to athletes. The financial impact of such bonuses can be substantial. An official ranking or award is often the best available assessment of an athlete's stature and the concomitant value to the company for which he or she endorses products.

By controlling the ranking and the basis on which it is determined, a sports association, tour, or circuit can alter the system to coerce athletes to do what it wants. A distorted ranking system can sometimes provide a plausible explanation for poor performance by star or marquee players. The primary incentive in most sports that discourages lackluster performances is some sort of ranking or evaluation system that penalizes athletes who compete and lose. Players who receive appearance fees and play badly will be penalized with lower rankings, leading to reduced public and media interest and diminished endorsement income. By distorting the ranking system, a tour or circuit can encourage players to play additional events, without penalizing them for poor performances.

For example, in professional tennis prior to 1989, the computer ranking system was designed to improve the rankings of players who played more Grand Prix events. This distortion was brought about by the producers of Grand Prix events, who gained a competitive advantage vis-à-vis producers of non-Grand Prix events. In many situations, by playing in an additional Grand Prix event, a player could improve his or her ranking by playing well. At the same time, he or she would not risk any decline in his or her ranking by losing. A higher ranking could lead to more endorsement revenue and more success in gaining admission to the events with the most prestige and the highest prize money. Performance in non-Grand Prix events did not affect a player's ranking, so they could not offer those potential derivative benefits.

In 1989, the ATP Tour further distorted the system by basing rankings solely on their best fourteen results in ATP Tour-approved events in the preceding year. *See* ATP Tour Computer Ranking Rules, 1990 *Official Rulebook of the ATP Tour*, at RK-3 (2d ed. 1989). This rule obviously penalizes players who play in less than fourteen events. In addition, every tournament that a player plays beyond the minimum fourteen can only improve his or her ranking. Winning matches in an additional tournament will enhance one's ranking, and losing has no adverse consequences.

The distortion of the ranking system had its intended effect. The increase in number of events played by the top players was dramatic. During 1988–89, only twenty-three of the top one hundred players had played twenty tournaments and only one player had played in twenty-five or more. During 1989–90, sixty-eight of the top one hundred players had played twenty or more tournaments in the preceding twelve months and nineteen of them had played twenty-five or more events. The ATP Tour's elimination of competing events, ranking system, and other rules have created a situation over the past fifteen years that all but the very best players generally compete in over twenty-five events a year. For players who rarely advance past the first round of each event, the number of matches played is perhaps not as onerous as the number of weeks and the travel involved may suggest, but for players who routinely advance to the semi-finals and finals playing Tuesday (1st round), Thursday(round of 16), Friday (quarterfinals), Saturday (semi-finals), and Sunday (finals) every week is very demanding.

(D) Marketing Implications for Individual and League Sports

Understanding the advantages and disadvantages of various types of league sports and individual sports can be extremely useful to a sports marketer seeking to develop new events and to improve existing events. For example, a sports marketer can modify a team sport or take star athletes who play a team sport, separate them from their teams, and create a single event. That event, if successful, will benefit from the fans' interest in "their" teams and the players on "their" teams, and will channel that interest to make the next event a success. All-star games are an example of this phenomenon.

An advertiser or a fan who is interested in the individual sport is likely to remain interested when the individual sport is presented in a team format. In fact, the owner or promoter of the event hopes that the interest will be increased because he has taken the competition between or among individuals and added the dimensions of team rivalry and/or national pride. World Team Tennis is an example of an individual sport converted into a team competition.

The Olympics are, of course, the ultimate example of this phenomenon. Many people who have little or no interest in track and field, gymnastics, skiing, or boxing have tremendous interest in those events during the Olympic games, to a large extent because the Olympic competition may be the most important or the ultimate competition in those sports. But, perhaps more important, interest is heightened because fans are not simply watching individual athletes, but because they have a team or a nation that they can support—their ultimate "home" team.

(E) Conclusion

As a result of the collective bargaining process in league sports, media scrutiny of those sports, and numerous other factors, there has been public disclosure of substantial information about such things as player salaries, team profits, and league television contracts. Nevertheless, there are aspects of league sports operations about which very little has been written. In the case of individual sports, the problem is more acute. There simply is no public awareness about the business or economics of individual sports. To develop an understanding of individual sports, it is essential to focus on the legal and commercial issues that explain the conduct of the various participants in each sport. Such an understanding is, at a minimum, necessary to assess financial opportunities for the participants and to discern the legality of various rules, regulations, and agreements. Appreciating the similarities and differences between individual and league sports can lead to other advantages, including the development of ways to improve the events or games presented, to stimulate viewer or fan interest without altering the events or games themselves, and to enhance the financial viability of individual events or the sport as a whole.

Notes and Questions

1. The foregoing overview of leagues and associations by no means exhausts all the components of the sports industry. In fact, the old and overused adage, "you can't tell the players without a program," is nowhere more relevant than in the world of professional sports. Recognizing the players by position in the early days of sports was a formidable enough objective. Today the emergence of microscopic media coverage, high profile owners, celebrity agents, and players associations that are true trade unions have turned professional sports into its own theater. Without a playbill, one cannot identify the actors or understand their background, credentials, attitudes, and predispositions. Absent a sophisticated appreciation of this information, one will encounter considerable difficulty sorting out the various legal issues spawned by the relationships that have evolved between and among the participants. In the succeeding chapters, we will explore various additional elements of the sports industry, such as players, player agents, collective bargaining representatives (players associations), media (print and broadcast), umpires, referees and other game officials, and commissioners (including league presidents and other executives). For a thorough and well-organized treatment of the many "actors" in the sports theater, see BERRY, GOULD & STAUDOHAR at 4, 5–17.

2. As you consider these various components, exercise care in assuming who possesses the ultimate power. Over the years, the nucleus of power has shifted. The following list of the *100 Most Powerful* figures in sports according to the *Sporting News* (January 2006), may contain more than a few surprises. This list illustrates that, though owners through their leagues produce and administer the sporting event, other actors in the sports theater play substantial and, at times, starring roles. As you review this list, note any peculiarities that you find evident. Ask yourself the following questions:

   a) How do you anticipate the distribution of power in professional sports changing over the next decade? As you contemplate this question, consider whether certain collective bargaining developments could seriously alter the spheres of influence. For example, are salary caps and similar intrusions on players' ability to operate in a free market system here to stay? *See generally* Jeffrey E. Levine, *The Legality and Efficacy of The National Basketball Association Salary Cap*, 11 CARDOZO ARTS & ENT. L.J. 71 (1992). If a salary cap were ever negotiated in Major League Baseball and is maintained in the NBA, NFL, and NHL would you anticipate the usurping of power from team owners and individual agents and giving greater latitude to collective bargaining representatives? Tensions often develop between agents and players associations, particularly in the face of a cap that designates a finite amount of money to be spent on players' salaries, combined with agent regulations limiting the percentages of player salaries that can be paid to the agents. The relationship of agents and player unions, and the individual versus collective bargaining processes, will be discussed in greater detail in Chapters Fourteen through Sixteen and Chapter Twenty-One.

   b) In Chapter Nine, we will visit the applicability of antitrust law's non-statutory labor exemption as it applies in a sports industry context. It suffices to say that recent authority has exponentially expanded the scope of the exemption and has virtually foreclosed antitrust availability to any plaintiff represented by a labor organization in matters involving labor market restraints (*e.g.,* a restraint upon a player's ability to market his or her services, such as the annual draft). *See Brown v. Pro Football*, 518 U.S. 231 (1996). What is the impact of this decision in terms of the role that collective bargaining representatives will now serve as power brokers? What is its impact on the need for leagues to consider organizing themselves as single entities? Will leagues go from battling union formation to demanding that athletes unionize?

c) Half of the top ten and about a third of the top thirty are television executives. Do you find this number surprising? Why? Why would the industry consider television executives to be powerful in the industry?

d) Three of the major league commissioners—David Stern (NBA), Paul Tagliabue (NFL) since retired and replaced by Roger Goodell, Gary Bettman (NHL)—are all former partners at major law firms where they handled matters for sports clients. Bill Daly (NHL legal), Jeff Pash (NFL legal), and other high-ranking league executives also came to their leagues from major law firms at which their legal work included work for the league that now employs them. Gregg Levy, the runner-up behind Roger Goodell to replace Paul Tagliabue as NFL Commissioner, is a partner at the same firm where Paul Tagliabue worked, one of the primary firms working for the NFL—Covington & Burling in Washington, D.C. What explains this phenomenon? What might be its implications?

e) No professional sports team owner is in the top thirty. At the same time, the top thirty includes the commissioners of the four major leagues and golf, five league executives, nine television executives, and five executive of companies that sponsor sports and endorse athletes. More athletes or former athletes are on the list than team owners and executives. Do you find the small number of team owners and team executives on the list surprising? Why?

100 Most Powerful

- David Stern, commissioner, NBA
- George Bodenheimer, president, ESPN and ABC Sports; co-chair Disney Media Networks
- Paul Tagliabue, commissioner, NFL
- Bud Selig, commissioner, Major League Baseball
- Brian France, chairman and CEO, NASCAR
- Gary Bettman, commissioner, NHL
- Dick Ebersol, chairman, NBC Universal Sports and Olympics
- Sean McManus, president, CBS News and CBS Sports
- David Hill, chairman, FOX Sports; president and COO, DirecTV
- Brian Roberts, chairman and CEO, Comcast
- Ted Forstmann, chairman, IMG
- Gene Upshaw, executive director, NFLPA
- August Busch IV, president, and Tony Ponturo, V.P. of global media and sports marketing, Anheuser-Busch, Inc.
- Phil Knight, chairman, Nike, Inc.
- John Skipper, executive V.P. of content, ESPN
- Adam Silver, presumed-to-be deputy commissioner, NBA; currently president and COO, NBA Entertainment

- Bill Daly, executive V.P. and chief legal officer, NHL
- Roger Goodell, executive V.P. and COO, NFL
- William Perez, president and CEO, Nike, Inc.
- Ed Goren, president and executive producer, FOX Sports
- Steve Bornstein, president and CEO, NFL Network; executive V.P. media, NFL
- David Levy, president, Turner Sports; president, Turner Entertainment ad sales and marketing
- Erich Stamminger, executive board member responsible for North America and global marketing, Adidas; CEO, Adidas America
- Sens. John McCain and Jim Bunning and U.S. Rep. Tom Davis, congressional steroids enforcers
- Jeff Shell, president, Comcast Programming
- Jack Roush, owner and CEO, Roush Racing, NASCAR
- Tiger Woods, golfer
- Bob DuPuy, president and COO, Major League Baseball
- Tim Finchem, commissioner, PGA
- Mark Schweitzer, chief marketing officer, Sprint Nextel
- Pat Bowlen, owner, Denver Broncos; chair of the NFL Broadcast Committee and member of other NFL committees
- Colin Campbell, executive V.P. and director of hockey operations, NHL
- Tony Petitti, executive V.P. and executive producer, CBS Sports
- George Pyne, COO, NASCAR
- Tim Brosnan, executive V.P. for business, MLB
- Brendan Shanahan, forward, Detroit Red Wings; competition committee leader and rules summit organizer, NHL
- Russ Granik, outgoing deputy commissioner and COO, NBA
- Omar Minaya, general manager, New York Mets
- George Steinbrenner, unhappy owner, New York Yankees
- Jose Canseco, author
- Arn Tellem, agent
- Ken Schanzer, president, NBC Sports
- Tony Vinciquerra, president and CEO, FOX Networks Group
- Robert Kraft, owner, New England Patriots
- Yao Ming, center, Houston Rockets
- Jerry Jones, owner, Dallas Cowboys
- Pat Riley, coach, president, Miami Heat
- Brian Cashman, general manager, New York Yankees
- Larry Lucchino, president, Boston Red Sox
- Trevor Linden, president, NHLPA

- Rob Manfred, executive V.P. and labor negotiator, MLB
- Sean Bratches, executive V.P. sales and marketing, ESPN
- Charlie Weis, football coach, Notre Dame
- Lance Armstrong, seven-time Tour de France winner and big-time inspiration
- John Galloway, V.P. of sports and media, Pepsi-Cola North America
- Scott Boras, agent
- Tom Fox, senior V.P. of sports marketing, Gatorade
- Jim Delany, commissioner, Big Ten
- Micky Arison, owner, Miami Heat; chairman of the board of governors, NBA
- Ed Horne, president, NHL Enterprises
- Ozzie Guillen, manager, Chicago White Sox
- Bob Thompson, president, and Randy Freer, COO, FOX Sports Networks
- Myles Brand, president, NCAA
- Tom Brady, quarterback, New England Patriots
- Lesa France Kennedy, president, International Speedway Corp.
- Jeff Pash, executive V.P. and chief administrative officer-counsel, NFL
- Norby Williamson, executive V.P., remote and studio production, ESPN
- Jack Williams, president and CEO, Comcast SportsNet
- Shaquille O'Neal, center, Miami Heat
- Doug Perlman, senior V.P. of television and media ventures, NHL
- Billy Hunter, executive director, NBPA
- Tony Hawk, action sports entrepreneur
- Jeff Gordon, NASCAR Nextel Cup driver
- Tim Duncan, forward, San Antonio Spurs
- Jerry Richardson, owner and founder, Carolina Panthers
- Arte Moreno, owner, Los Angeles Angels of Anaheim
- Bruton Smith, chairman and CEO, Speedway Motorsports Inc.
- LeBron James, forward, Cleveland Cavaliers
- Tracy Dolgin, president and CEO, YES Network
- Sonny Vaccaro, director of grassroots basketball, Reebok
- Matt Leinart, quarterback, University of Southern California
- Archie Manning, sire extraordinaire
- Stu Jackson, senior V.P., basketball operations, NBA
- Joe Paterno, football coach, Penn State
- Joel Litvin, executive V.P., legal and business affairs, NBA
- Tom Condon, president, IMG Football
- Rich McKay, president and G.M., Atlanta Falcons; co-chair, NFL competition committee

- Larry Brown, coach, New York Knicks
- Bob Bowman, president and CEO, MLB Advanced Media
- Chuck Pagano, executive V.P., technology, ESPN
- Jerry Colangelo, men's senior national team managing director, USA Basketball; chairman, Phoenix Suns
- Al Michaels and John Madden, much-courted NFL announcers
- Michelle Wie, golfer
- Ted Saskin, executive director, NHLPA
- Mike Krzyzewski, basketball coach, Duke University; head coach, USA Basketball
- Stephen A. Smith, outspoken star, ESPN
- Roger Clemens, erstwhile hometown hero
- Dave and Dana Pump, college hoops power brokers, Double Pump
- Donna Orender, president, WNBA
- Brian Bedol, CEO and co-founder, CSTV

3. Beyond the Commissioners, there are a substantial number of NFL, NBA, MLB, and NHL employees on the list, about as many as the team owners and team employees combined. What does that suggest about the changing nature of sports leagues, from local businesses to national or international operations?

4. The list includes athletes, coaches, NCAA officials, United States senators and a congressman, and a few sports broadcasters. If you were responsible for deciding who should be on the "Power 100," would you have included those individuals on the list? How would you attempt to assess their "power" relative to sponsors, television executives, team executives, and team owners? Is it meaningful to compare Yao Ming's "power" or Notre Dame football coach Charlie Weis's "power" with that wielded by Tom Fox, the Senior VP of Sports Marketing at Gatorade? Why do you think these individuals are on the list?

5. Some commentators have challenged the traditional league wisdom regarding the correlation between a successful sports enterprise and common control, cooperation, and restrictions on player mobility. They have suggested that the following steps would create a more effective formula for league prosperity:

a) Remove all restrictions to free agency. Borrowing on former Oakland A's owner Charlie Finley's theory, they posit that an increase in the universe of available players would increase supply and reduce the price of the commodity;

b) Allow for corporate ownership in the NFL and all sports leagues that do not permit it. They reason that corporations are subsidizing many of the sports teams under the current arrangement;

c) Eradicate Major League Baseball's exemption from the antitrust laws;

d) Eliminate salary caps and permit players the same latitude as owners, making as much money as the free market permits;

e) Circumscribe revenue sharing to national television packages.

See Michael K. Ozanian, *Foul Ball*, 162 FINANCIAL WORLD, May 25, 1993, No. 11, at 31. As you proceed through this text, particularly Chapters Seven through Thirteen, ponder whether these suggestions, which will appear to be anathema to most owners, are viable. It might prove interesting to compare your gut reactions to a more searching analysis following your comprehensive understanding of the legal issues that have arisen in these contexts.

6. Finally, you should read this text both as a student and eventual practitioner seeking to gain insights into the nuances of sports law. But, inevitably and uncontrollably, you will probably also be, at some level, a fan or interested observer of sports. The importance of the fan, the ultimate purchaser of the sports product, is often lost or temporarily misplaced. Traversing all socio-economic strata, educational levels, age, race, gender, and national origins, "fans" both purchase the right to participate in a sport through attending the sports event, and serve as ultimate consumers in the purchase of the various ancillary products that the sport produces. No shopping mall, today, is complete without a store that specializes in jerseys, hats, and related products of the teams in the professional sports leagues. Sports memorabilia shows, featuring plaques, cards, autographs, and other souvenirs have become a lucrative industry. As a result, elaborate licensing arrangements have been developed in which the right to a player's likeness is an invaluable commodity.

It is true that some sports attract a certain type of fan while others attract a distinctly different type; yet, you will find that there is a certain eclecticism that pervades all sports events in terms of the range of interest and background of the people who participate. Admittedly, the composition and deportment of a crowd at the All England Club watching Wimbledon and the fans gathering to watch a NASCAR race, or a Stanley Cup playoff game at Madison Square Garden are quite different. Yet, to suggest that any of these crowds is a monolithic group or a totally homogeneous one formed along class lines is a mistake. You may find the most dignified CEO of a Fortune 500 corporation screaming and banging the glass at a Stanley Cup playoff game, and you may likewise find someone at the other end of that corporate ladder totally absorbed in the finals of the U.S. Open Tennis Tournament in New York.

Fans are incredibly demanding at some times and unbelievably resilient at others. They expect their athletes to produce on a daily basis, to be available for autographs, to subject themselves and their families to constant fishbowl observation whether it be at restaurants, theaters, or a neighborhood park. At the same time, fans have been jaded by delays of seasons, cancellations of playoff games, lockouts and strikes by game officials, and other disruptions in the regular play by their favorite and/or hometown franchises. They have watched owners and players negotiate to impasse at the expense of the season in an industry where the fans already see ticket prices rising, owners' profits soaring, and players' salaries spiraling. Depending upon their political or philosophical persuasion, they lay the blame on capitalistic owners who treat their players as cattle, or greedy players, who are fortunate to be playing professional sports and who incredibly are demanding higher salaries and better conditions. Yet, after brief periods of disenchantment and temporary boycotts or other shows of displeasure, fans return. At times, when it seems as though players and owners have embarked upon a path of self-destruction through their intransigence at the bargaining table, it isn't long before heated pennant races, electrifying playoffs, and dramatic championship games draw their fans back to the stadiums.

For the most part, fans have been passive observers of the sports scene, accepting their plight, ticket prices, inflated souvenir costs, extraordinarily expensive concessions, and the like without protest or vigorous response. Yet, they have by no means totally avoided demonstrations of dissatisfaction. *See generally* MIKE LUPICA, MAD AS

Hell: How Sports Got Away from the Fans and How We Get It Back (1996). There are times in which fans have galvanized their disenchantment with a particular sports development and have pursued a more graphic demonstration of their dissatisfaction. Fans have sued franchises attempting to move; they have sued leagues and teams—claiming the league and team extracted a stadium lease on terms too disadvantageous to the local community; they have attempted nationwide boycotts of a sport due to their displeasure with the disconcerting developments in that sport's labor relations and collective bargaining; they have staged protests to challenge sports' deliberate progress in the area of minority hiring; and they have engaged in similar shows of dismay in various other contexts. Increased media exposure that brings the most microscopic aspects of sports into the fans' living room will only serve to enhance their involvement.

7. As you review the precedent that follows in succeeding chapters, consider it from as many perspectives as possible. Consider the attorney, studying the application of law to a specialized industry. Consider the entrepreneurs investing in teams, producing events, and seeking a return on their investments. Consider the league or circuit employees— the commissioners, the league executives, and others who work for the owners, yet have their own stake, their own agendas. Consider the players, with fleeting careers, who possess unique physical talents and mental toughness that set them apart. Consider the collective bargaining representatives and player agents who have rapidly emerging and increasing roles as the athlete becomes a more dominant figure in sports. Consider the television companies, seeking sporting events as potential programming, an integral part of their overall television production lineup. Consider sponsors, who are involved in the business of sports to sell services and sports-related products, and who are linked by demographics and advertising to the fans who follow a particular sport. Consider, finally, the fans, who are forced to swallow more than a modicum of law with their normal diet of sports news. As admonished at the end of Chapter One, the only sin is if you forget to consider it from your own perspective. Be mindful of the reasons underlying your interest in sports at the outset. It is supposed to be fun; so have some!

Chapter 3

The Commissioner

I. Introduction

Given the large-scale business enterprise that professional sports has become, teams often relinquish individual power to administer league affairs to designated representatives. In fact, all sports leagues have grown to recognize the folly of attempting self-governance without some type of central voice to manage their daily affairs, regulate the activities of league members and their players, impose discipline at appropriate times, etc. For this reason, most sports leagues will appoint a commissioner to assume day-today operational control of the league's affairs.

While all sports leagues and league commissioners have their own idiosyncrasies and peculiarities, it is safe to say that the basic premises underlying the creation of the commissioner's office and the functions that it fulfills are consistent across league lines. Thus, while the specific job description of each commissioner in the area of, for example, labor relations will differ, all commissioners assume some responsibility for the development of a collective bargaining agreement that will ensure the economic viability of the league, satisfaction of the players, and labor harmony throughout the term of the agreement. This same general responsibility with regard to overseeing media relations, maintaining the integrity of the game, providing a fair and impartial forum to resolve interclub controversies, promoting the sport's public image and thereby enhancing its fan appeal, and numerous other duties rests within the purview of all league commissioners. As a general rule, most league commissioners have seen their authority vis-à-vis players limited with the evolution of collective bargaining representatives. The commissioner's role as neutral arbitrator over all matters has been circumscribed virtually to the point where the commissioner is the final word only on matters involving the integrity of the sport. In situations involving interpretations of the collective bargaining agreement above and beyond issues implicating the "best interests of the game," an arbitration panel, rather than the commissioner, often will be the appropriate dispute-resolution forum.

The prototype for today's commissioner's office was established by Major League Baseball in 1921, following the infamous Black Sox scandal. At that time, troubled by the significant negative publicity created by the affair, in which several members of the Chicago White Sox were found to have accepted money from gamblers for the purpose of "throwing" World Series games, baseball decided that it needed a facelift. There was a perceived need for a strong governing arm and a centralized source of power to demonstrate that the league was capable of governing itself and to prevent such incidents as the Black Sox scandal from recurring. Public confidence in the game and its leadership was at its nadir. A *New York Times* editorial eloquently synopsized the state of the game:

Professional baseball is in a bad way, not so much because of the Chicago scandal, as because that scandal has provoked it to bring up all the rumors and suspicions of years past. * * * [T]he general effect is to wrinkle the noses of fans who will quit going to ball games if they get the impression that this sort of thing has been going on underground for years.

GEOFFREY C. WARD & KEN BURNS, BASEBALL: AN ILLUSTRATED HISTORY 144 (1995).

Judge Kenesaw Mountain Landis was selected as the first commissioner, and he accepted such role under the strict condition that he be given plenary authority to govern the league. Given the league's concern that a dramatic statement be made regarding baseball's professionalism and ability to self-govern, the league agreed to Landis' demands, and the first commissioner became, in many respects, omnipotent.

While Judge Landis was not without his flaws, the most heinous of which was his staunch resistance to the integration of baseball, the creation of the commissioner's office and the selection of a strong individual to occupy this position provided the national pastime with a much-needed rudder. The considerable deference shown to baseball's attempts at self-governance, including the maintenance of the unique, infamous, and much criticized exemption from the antitrust laws, has been due in large part to the perceived strength of the commissioner's office.

Prior to the formation of the commissioner's office, baseball had been run by a national commission that consisted of two league presidents and a chairman selected by the two presidents. Originally, the commissioner's term was designated as seven years; however, beginning with Commissioner Peter Ueberroth, the term was shortened to five years. Under current rules, the election of a new commissioner must be effected by a three-fourths vote of the owners. However, the reappointment of a commissioner may be effected by a simple majority with a minimum of five votes coming from each league's teams. *See* ANDREW ZIMBALIST, BASEBALL AND BILLIONS 45 (1993).

Following the early dismissal of Fay Vincent in 1992, league owners had considerable difficulty settling on the selection of a new commissioner. Eventually the owners agreed to install Milwaukee Brewers' owner Allan "Bud" Selig as acting commissioner. Selig transferred control of the Brewers to his daughter, which hardly ameliorated the concerns some had about potential conflicts of interest. A telling illustration of the potential problems with making an owner commissioner is the 1994–95 baseball strike, in which the owners vehemently opposed free agency and promoted the adoption of the salary cap as the *sine qua non* of a strike settlement. Given the fact that the salary cap mechanism would benefit the small market owners, of whom Selig is a prominent member, the sport hardly has been in the hands of a disinterested party.

It was possible that Selig's status as both an owner and as commissioner made it less likely that outside agencies would continue to trust baseball to regulate itself. For example, a court may be more inclined to intervene in a commissioner's decision to suspend a player when that player is a member of a club that competes in the same division as the commissioner's club. Today's sports leagues are major industries unto themselves, and they need effective, neutral leaders with vision and fortitude. Having an owner occupy the commissioner's chair partially compromises that goal and carries implications of self-interest and other appearances of impropriety. Despite these problems, the baseball owners unanimously elevated Selig in 1998 from acting commissioner to commissioner. In 2004, the owners extended Selig's term to 2007.

Admittedly, the selection of a new commissioner has never been an easy matter, and the difficulties have not been unique to baseball. For example, Pete Rozelle, who served as NFL commissioner for almost thirty years, was appointed after a seven day, twenty-two ballot marathon session. His successor, Paul Tagliabue, was selected after over fifty hours of committee debate. *See* WILL MCDONOUGH ET AL., 75 SEASONS 180–81, 278–79 (1994). The selection of Roger Goodell to succeed in Tagliabue in 2006 was much less contentious. Baseball's Bowie Kuhn was a compromise candidate selected after nineteen acrimonious ballots. *See* JOHN HELYAR, LORDS OF THE REALM 93 (1993). Notwithstanding the obvious difficulties inherent in marshaling enough support to achieve a consensus, attempting to operate a modern sports league without a commissioner or with what becomes a "lifetime interim" commissioner is unwise. Of course, first ballot selections have always been perceived as the optimum situation from the standpoint of stability and purpose. Nonetheless, leagues must be wary of the fact that the fear of a protracted process or the unwillingness to make tough choices could operate to subvert the best interests of the sport. Indecision leading to no decision in the selection of a commissioner could have adverse consequences on two fronts. First, the league will suffer economically due to a diminution in public confidence and the absence of a centralized voice to deal with media, municipalities and others seeking to transact business with the league. Second, the league will suffer on the legal front because the historic deference shown to the sport by courts and legislators will undoubtedly be compromised if the absence of leadership and the inability even to reach agreement in the selection of a leader evinces a bankruptcy of internal government.

It is generally understood that a professional sports league commissioner's power is paramount and supreme, deriving largely from the control and governance suggested by Judge Landis's regime. Rarely have clubs or players challenged the commissioner's authority and, when they have, courts have been extremely deferential to the commissioner's decisions. *See Finley v. Kuhn*, 569 F.2d 527 (7th Cir. 1978), below; *Milwaukee American Ass'n v. Landis*, 49 F.2d 298 (N.D. Ill. 1931). Of course, the commissioner's power is not plenary, and some courts have made it clear that, though considerable deference will be shown the private association and its controlling voice, there are limits. *See, e.g., Riko Enterprises, Inc. v. Seattle Supersonics Corp.*, 357 F. Supp. 521 (S.D.N.Y. 1973). Commissioners who abuse the considerable power that they have been given could, in the extreme case, find an inhospitable judiciary. Yet, these instances have been rare in sports jurisprudence. After you have reviewed the following cases, contemplate whether recent questionable exercises of authority by commissioners, together with the insecurity and instability afflicting some league commissioners, will result in a diminished judicial and congressional respect for the commissioner's office and its decisions. You will note that most of the cases included below and most of the reported decisions involve Major League Baseball. This fact is not surprising given that much of the controversy that has surrounded league commissioners and the greatest amount of pointed *ad hominem* criticism has been reserved for baseball's czars.

Those Who Have Served
MAJOR LEAGUE BASEBALL

Judge Kenesaw Mountain Landis (1920–1944)

A.B. "Happy" Chandler (1945–1951)

Ford C. Frick (1951–1965)

General William D. Eckert (1965–1968)

Bowie K. Kuhn (1969–1984)

Peter V. Ueberroth (1984–1989)

A. Bartlett Giamatti (1989)

Francis T. "Fay" Vincent, Jr. (1989–1992)

Allan H. "Bud" Selig (Acting Commissioner 1992–1998, Commissioner 1998–Present)

NATIONAL BASKETBALL ASSOCIATION

Maurice Podoloff (1946–1963)

J. Walter Kennedy (1963–1975)

Laurence O'Brien (1975–1984)

David Stern (1984–Present)

NATIONAL FOOTBALL LEAGUE

Elmer Layden (1941–1946)

Bert Bell (1946–1959)

Alvin "Pete" Rozelle (1960–1989)

Paul Tagliabue (1989–2006)

Roger Goodell (2006–Present)

NATIONAL HOCKEY LEAGUE

Clarence Campbell (President) (1946–1977)

John M. Ziegler (President) (1977–1992)

Gil Stein (President) (1992)

Gary Bettman (Commissioner) (1992–Present)

II. Parameters of the Commissioner's Authority

Charles O. Finley & Co. v. Kuhn
569 F.2d 527 (7th Cir. 1978)

SPRECHER, Circuit Judge. The two important questions raised by this appeal are whether the Commissioner of baseball is contractually authorized to disapprove player assignments which he finds to be "not in the best interests of baseball" where neither moral turpitude nor violation of a Major League Rule is involved, and whether the provision in the Major League Agreement whereby the parties agree to waive recourse to the courts is valid and enforceable.

I

The plaintiff, Charles O. Finley & Co., Inc., an Illinois corporation, is the owner of the Oakland Athletics baseball club, a member of the American League of Professional Baseball Clubs (Oakland). Joe Rudi, Rollie Fingers and Vida Blue were members of the active playing roster of the Oakland baseball club and were contractually bound to play for Oakland through the end of the 1976 baseball season. On or about June 15, 1976,

Oakland and Blue entered a contract whereby Blue would play for Oakland through the 1979 season, but Rudi and Fingers had not at that time signed contracts for the period beyond the 1976 season.

If Rudi and Fingers had not signed contracts to play with Oakland by the conclusion of the 1976 season, they would at that time have become free agents eligible thereafter to negotiate with any major league club, subject to certain limitations on their right to do so that were then being negotiated by the major league clubs with the Players Association.

On June 14 and 15, 1976, Oakland negotiated tentative agreements to sell the club's contract rights for the services of Rudi and Fingers to the Boston Red Sox for $2 million and for the services of Blue to the New York Yankees for $1.5 million. The agreements were negotiated shortly before the expiration of baseball's trading deadline at midnight on June 15, after which time Oakland could not have sold the contracts of these players to other clubs without first offering the players to all other American League teams, in inverse order of their standing, at the stipulated waiver price of $20,000.

The defendant Bowie K. Kuhn is the Commissioner of baseball (Commissioner), having held that position since 1969. On June 18, 1976, the Commissioner disapproved the assignments of the contracts of Rudi, Fingers and Blue to the Red Sox and Yankees "as inconsistent with the best interests of baseball, the integrity of the game and the maintenance of public confidence in it." The Commissioner expressed his concern for (1) the debilitation of the Oakland club, (2) the lessening of the competitive balance of professional baseball through the buying of success by the more affluent clubs, and (3) "the present unsettled circumstances of baseball's reserve system."

Thereafter on June 25, 1976, Oakland instituted this suit principally challenging, as beyond the scope of the Commissioner's authority and, in any event, as arbitrary and capricious, the Commissioner's disapproval of the Rudi, Fingers and Blue assignments. The complaint set forth seven causes of action: (I) that the Commissioner breached his employment contract with Oakland by acting arbitrarily, discriminatorily and unreasonably; * * * (VI) that the Commissioner did not have the authority to disapprove Oakland's assignments "in the best interests of baseball"; and (VII) that Oakland have specific performance of its contracts of assignment with Boston and New York. * * *

A bench trial took place as a result of which judgment * * * was entered in favor of the Commissioner on March 17, 1977.

On August 29, 1977, the district court granted the Commissioner's counterclaim for a declaratory judgment that the covenant not to sue in the Major League Agreement is valid and enforceable. * * *

II

Basic to the underlying suit brought by Oakland and to this appeal is whether the Commissioner of baseball is vested by contract with the authority to disapprove player assignments which he finds to be "not in the best interests of baseball." In assessing the measure and extent of the Commissioner's power and authority, consideration must be given to the circumstances attending the creation of the office of Commissioner, the language employed by the parties in drafting their contractual understanding, changes and amendments adopted from time to time, and the interpretation given by the parties to their contractual language throughout the period of its existence.

Prior to 1921, professional baseball was governed by a three-man National Commission formed in 1903 which consisted of the presidents of the National and American Leagues and a third member, usually one of the club owners, selected by the presidents of the two leagues. Between 1915 and 1921, a series of events and controversies contributed to a growing dissatisfaction with the National Commission on the part of players, owners and the public, and a demand developed for the establishment of a single, independent Commissioner of baseball.

On September 28, 1920, an indictment issued charging that an effort had been made to "fix" the 1919 World Series by several Chicago White Sox players. Popularly known as the "Black Sox Scandal," this event rocked the game of professional baseball and proved the catalyst that brought about the establishment of a single, neutral Commissioner of baseball.

In November, 1920, the major league club owners unanimously elected federal Judge Kenesaw Mountain Landis as the sole Commissioner of baseball and appointed a committee of owners to draft a charter setting forth the Commissioner's authority. In one of the drafting sessions an attempt was made to place limitations on the Commissioner's authority. Judge Landis responded by refusing to accept the office of Commissioner.

On January 12, 1921, Landis told a meeting of club owners that he had agreed to accept the position upon the clear understanding that the owners had sought "an authority * * * outside of your own business, and that a part of that authority would be a control over whatever and whoever had to do with baseball." Thereupon, the owners voted unanimously to reject the proposed limitation upon the Commissioner's authority, they all signed what they called the Major League Agreement, and Judge Landis assumed the position of Commissioner. Oakland has been a signatory to the Major League Agreement continuously since 1960. The agreement, a contract between the constituent clubs of the National and American Leagues, is the basic charter under which major league baseball operates.

The Major League Agreement provides that "[t]he functions of the Commissioner shall be * * * to investigate * * * any act, transaction or practice * * * not in the best interests of the national game of Baseball" and "to determine * * * what preventive, remedial or punitive action is appropriate in the premises, and to take such action * * *." Art. I, Sec. 2(a) and (b).[11]

The Major League Rules, which govern many aspects of the game of baseball, are promulgated by vote of major league club owners. Major League Rule 12(a) provides that "no * * * [assignment of players] shall be recognized as valid unless * * * approved by the Commissioner."[13]

---

11. * * *

This language is identical to Art. I, Sec. 2(a) and (b) as originally executed on January 12, 1921, with the exception that the words in present paragraph (a) "not in the best interests of the national game of Baseball" were originally "detrimental to the best interests of the national game of baseball." The change was made in 1964. The district court implied that the change broadened the Commissioner's powers when it found that "previously the Commissioner had to find conduct 'detrimental' to the best interests of baseball in order to take remedial or preventive action * * *"

13. * * *

A federal district judge in another case has expressed his opinion that the present case was correctly decided by the district court on the sole ground that the Commissioner was given specific authority under Major League Rule 12(a) to disapprove contracts and therefore render players free agents. *Atlanta National League Baseball Club, Inc. v. Kuhn*, 432 F. Supp. 1213, 1224 n.8, 1225 (N.D. Ga. 1977).

The Major Leagues and their constituent clubs severally agreed to be bound by the decisions of the Commissioner and by the discipline imposed by him. They further agreed to "waive such right of recourse to the courts as would otherwise have existed in their favor." Major League Agreement, Art. VII, Sec. 2.

Upon Judge Landis' death in 1944, the Major League Agreement was amended in two respects to limit the Commissioner's authority. First, the parties deleted the provision by which they had agreed to waive their right of recourse to the courts to challenge actions of the Commissioner. Second, the parties added the following language to Article I, Section 3:

> No Major League Rule or other joint action of the two Major Leagues, and no action or procedure taken in compliance with any such Major League Rule or joint action of the two Major Leagues shall be considered or construed to be detrimental to Baseball.

The district court found that this addition had the effect of precluding the Commissioner from finding an act that complied with the Major League Rules to be detrimental to the best interests of baseball.

The two 1944 amendments to the Major League Agreement remained in effect during the terms of the next two Commissioners, A.B. "Happy" Chandler and Ford Frick. Upon Frick's retirement in 1964 and in accordance with his recommendation, the parties adopted three amendments to the Major League Agreement: (1) the language added in 1944 preventing the Commissioner from finding any act or practice "taken in compliance" with a Major League Rule to be "detrimental to baseball" was removed; (2) the provision deleted in 1944 waiving any rights of recourse to the courts to challenge a Commissioner's decision was restored; and (3) in places where the language "detrimental to the best interests of the national game of baseball" or "detrimental to baseball" appeared those words were changed to "not in the best interests of the national game of Baseball" or "not in the best interests of Baseball."

The nature of the power lodged in the Commissioner by the Major League Agreement is further exemplified "[i]n the case of conduct by organizations not parties to this Agreement, or by individuals not connected with any of the parties hereto, which is deemed by the Commissioner not to be in the best interests of Baseball" whereupon "the Commissioner may pursue appropriate legal remedies, advocate remedial legislation and take such other steps as he may deem necessary and proper in the interests of the morale of the players and the honor of the game." Art. I, Sec. 4.

The Commissioner has been given broad power in unambiguous language to investigate any act, transaction or practice not in the best interests of baseball, to determine what preventive, remedial or punitive action is appropriate in the premises, and to take that action. He has also been given the express power to approve or disapprove the assignments of players. In regard to nonparties to the agreement, he may take such other steps as he deems necessary and proper in the interests of the morale of the players and the honor of the game. Further, indicative of the nature of the Commissioner's authority is the provision whereby the parties agree to be bound by his decisions and discipline imposed and to waive recourse to the courts.

The Major League Agreement also provides that "[i]n the case of conduct by Major Leagues, Major League Clubs, officers, employees or players which is deemed by the Commissioner not to be in the best interests of Baseball, action by the Commissioner for each offense may include" a reprimand, deprivation of a club of representation at joint meetings, suspension or removal of nonplayers, temporary or permanent ineligibility of players, and a fine not to exceed $5,000 in the case of a league or club and not to exceed $500 in the case of an individual. Art. I, Sec. 3.[22]

The district court considered the plaintiff's argument that the enumeration in Article I, Section 3 of the sanctions which the Commissioner may impose places a limit on his authority inasmuch as the power to disapprove assignments of players is not included. The court concluded that the enumeration does not purport to be exclusive and provides that the Commissioner may act in one of the listed ways without expressly limiting him to those ways.

The court further concluded that the principles of construction that the specific controls the general, or that the expression of some kinds of authority operates to exclude unexpressed kinds, do not apply since the Commissioner is empowered to determine what preventive, remedial or punitive action is appropriate in a particular case and the listed sanctions are punitive only. In fact, from 1921 until 1964, Article I, Section 3, expressly described the enumerated sanctions as "punitive action."

In view of the broad authority expressly given by the Major League Agreement to the Commissioner, particularly in Section 2 of Article I, we agree with the district court that Section 3 does not purport to limit that authority.

III

Despite the Commissioner's broad authority to prevent any act, transaction or practice not in the best interests of baseball, Oakland has attacked the Commissioner's disapproval of the Rudi-Fingers-Blue transactions on a variety of theories which seem to express a similar thrust in differing language.

The complaint alleged that the "action of Kuhn was arbitrary, capricious, unreasonable, discriminatory, directly contrary to historical precedent, baseball tradition, and prior rulings and actions of the Commissioner." In pre-trial answers to interrogatories, Oakland * * * contend[ed] that the Commissioner could set aside assignments only if the assignments involved a Rules violation or moral turpitude.

In its briefs on appeal, Oakland summarized this branch of its argument by stating that the Commissioner's "disapproval of the assignments * * * exceeded [his] authority under the Major League Agreement and Rules; was irrational and unreasonable; and was procedurally unfair." The nub of this diffuse attack seems best expressed in a subsequent heading in the brief that the Commissioner's "abrupt departure from well-established assignment practice and his retroactive application of this change of policy to disapprove [Oakland's] assignments was made without reasonable notice and was therefore procedurally unfair."

The plaintiff has argued that it is a fundamental rule of law that the decisions of the head of a private association must be procedurally fair. Plaintiff then argued that it was "procedurally unfair" for the Commissioner to fail to warn the plaintiff that he would "disapprove large cash assignments of star players even if they complied with the Major League Rules."

In the first place it must be recalled that prior to the assignments involved here drastic changes had commenced to occur in the reserve system and in the creation of free agents. In his opinion disapproving the Rudi, Fingers and Blue assignments, the Com-

---

22. [T]he possibility of assessing a fine against an individual of up to $500 did not appear in the agreement until 1964.

missioner said that "while I am of course aware that there have been cash sales of player contracts in the past, there has been no instance in my judgment which had the potential for harm to our game as do these assignments, particularly in the present unsettled circumstances of baseball's reserve system and in the highly competitive circumstances we find in today's sports and entertainment world."

Absent the radical changes in the reserve system, the Commissioner's action would have postponed Oakland's realization of value for these players.[27] Given those changes, the relative fortunes of all major league clubs became subject to a host of intangible speculations. No one could predict then or now with certainty that Oakland would fare better or worse relative to other clubs through the vagaries of the revised reserve system occurring entirely apart from any action by the Commissioner.

In the second place, baseball cannot be analogized to any other business or even to any other sport or entertainment. Baseball's relation to the federal antitrust laws has been characterized by the Supreme Court as an "exception," an "anomaly" and an "aberration." Baseball's management through a commissioner is equally an exception, anomaly and aberration, as outlined in Part II hereof. In no other sport or business is there quite the same system, created for quite the same reasons and with quite the same underlying policies. Standards such as the best interests of baseball, the interests of the morale of the players and the honor of the game, or "sportsmanship which accepts the umpire's decision without complaint," are not necessarily familiar to courts and obviously require some expertise in their application. While it is true that professional baseball selected as its first Commissioner a federal judge, it intended only him and not the judiciary as a whole to be its umpire and governor.

As we have seen in Part II, the Commissioner was vested with broad authority and that authority was not to be limited in its exercise to situations where Major League Rules or moral turpitude was involved. When professional baseball intended to place limitations upon the Commissioner's powers, it knew how to do so. In fact, it did so during the 20-year period from 1944 to 1964.

The district court found and concluded that the Rudi-Fingers-Blue transactions were not, as Oakland had alleged in its complaint, "directly contrary to historical precedent, baseball tradition, and prior rulings." During his almost 25 years as Commissioner, Judge Landis found many acts, transactions and practices to be detrimental to the best interests of baseball in situations where neither moral turpitude nor a Major League Rule violation was involved, and he disapproved several player assignments.

On numerous occasions since he became Commissioner of baseball in February 1969, Kuhn has exercised broad authority under the best interests clause of the Major League Agreement. Many of the actions taken by him have been in response to acts, transactions or practices that involved neither the violation of a Major League Rule nor any gambling, game-throwing or other conduct associated with moral turpitude. Moreover, on several occasions Commissioner Kuhn has taken broad preventive or remedial action with respect to assignments of player contracts.

On several occasions Charles O. Finley, the principal owner of the plaintiff corporation and the general manager of the Oakland baseball club, has himself espoused that the Commissioner has the authority to exercise broad powers pursuant to the best inter-

---

27. This realization of value could come in the form of subsequent player transactions involving less cash but some returning-player value, or in box office profits attributable to these players, or possibly in the aggregate value of the club if and when eventually sold as a franchise and team.

ests clause, even where there is no violation of the Major League Rules and no moral turpitude is involved.

Twenty-one of the 25 parties to the current Major League Agreement who appeared as witnesses in the district court testified that they intended and they presently understand that the Commissioner of baseball can review and disapprove an assignment of a player contract which he finds to be not in the best interests of baseball, even if the assignment does not violate the Major League Rules and does not involve moral turpitude. Oakland contended that the district court erred in admitting this testimony since parties are bound "only by their objective manifestations and their subjective intent is immaterial." In this bench trial where Oakland was contending that it was not put on notice that transactions alleged to otherwise conform to the Major League Rules might be invalidated, the court could certainly consider what most of the current parties to the agreement believed they were put on notice of when they became signatories.

Oakland relied upon Major League Rule 21, which deals, in Oakland's characterization of it, with "(a) throwing or soliciting the throwing of ball games, (b) bribery by or of players or persons connected with clubs or (c) umpires, (d) betting on ball games, and (e) physical violence and other unsportsmanlike conduct" as indicating the limits of what is "not in the best interests of baseball." However, Rule 21(f) expressly states:

> Nothing herein contained shall be construed as exclusively defining or otherwise limiting acts, transactions, practices or conduct not to be in the best interests of Baseball; and any and all other acts, transactions, practices or conduct not to be in the best interests of Baseball are prohibited, and shall be subject to such penalties including permanent ineligibility, as the facts in the particular case may warrant.

Oakland also took issue with language in the district court's judgment order of March 17, 1977, which relied upon *Milwaukee American Ass'n v. Landis*, 49 F.2d 298 (N.D. Ill. 1931). Oakland contended that the *Landis* case was distinguishable inasmuch as it involved the violation of a certain rule. In that case Judge Lindley held that the Commissioner "acted clearly within his authority" when he disapproved a player assignment after several assignments of the same player to and from different clubs owned by a single individual. The court said in 49 F.2d at 302:

> Though there is nothing in the rules to prohibit an individual owning control of a Major League club from likewise owning control of Minor League clubs, the intent of the code is such that common ownership is not to be made use of as to give one individual, controlling all of the clubs mentioned, the absolute right, independent of other clubs, to control indefinitely a player acquired and switched about by apparent outright purchases.

We conclude that the evidence fully supports, and we agree with, the district court's finding that "[t]he history of the adoption of the Major League Agreement in 1921 and the operation of baseball for more than 50 years under it, including: the circumstances preceding and precipitating the adoption of the Agreement; the numerous exercises of broad authority under the best interests clause by Judge Landis and * * * Commissioner Kuhn; the amendments to the Agreement in 1964 restoring and broadening the authority of the Commissioner; * * * and most important the express language of the Agreement itself—are all to the effect that the Commissioner has the authority to determine whether any act, transaction or practice is 'not in the best interests of baseball,' and upon such determination, to take whatever preventive or remedial action he deems appropriate, whether or not the act, transaction or practice complies with the Major

League Rules or involves moral turpitude." Any other conclusion would involve the courts in not only interpreting often complex rules of baseball to determine if they were violated but also, as noted in the Landis case, the "intent of the [baseball] code," an even more complicated and subjective task.

The Rudi-Fingers-Blue transactions had been negotiated on June 14 and 15, 1976. On June 16, the Commissioner sent a teletype to the Oakland, Boston and New York clubs and to the Players Association expressing his "concern for possible consequences to the integrity of baseball and public confidence in the game" and setting a hearing for June 17. Present at the hearing were 17 persons representing those notified. At the outset of the hearing the Commissioner stated that he was concerned that the assignments would be harmful to the competitive capacity of Oakland; that they reflected an effort by Boston and New York to purchase star players and "bypass the usual methods of player development and acquisition which have been traditionally used in professional baseball"; and that the question to be resolved was whether the transactions "are consistent with the best interests of baseball's integrity and maintenance of public confidence in the game." He warned that it was possible that he might determine that the assignments not be approved. Mr. Finley and representatives of the Red Sox and Yankees made statements on the record.

No one at the hearing, including Mr. Finley, claimed that the Commissioner lacked the authority to disapprove the assignments, or objected to the holding of the hearing, or to any of the procedures followed at the hearing.

On June 18, the Commissioner concluded that the attempted assignments should be disapproved as not in the best interests of baseball. In his written decision, the Commissioner stated his reasons which we have summarized in Part I. The decision was sent to all parties by teletype.

The Commissioner recognized "that there have been cash sales of player contracts in the past," but concluded that "these transactions were unparalleled in the history of the game" because there was "never anything on this scale or falling at this time of the year, or which threatened so seriously to unbalance the competitive balance of baseball." The district court concluded that the attempted assignments of Rudi, Fingers and Blue "were at a time and under circumstances making them unique in the history of baseball."

We conclude that the evidence fully supports, and we agree with, the district court's finding and conclusion that the Commissioner "acted in good faith, after investigation, consultation and deliberation, in a manner which he determined to be in the best interests of baseball" and that "[w]hether he was right or wrong is beyond the competence and the jurisdiction of this court to decide."

We must then conclude that anyone becoming a signatory to the Major League Agreement was put on ample notice that the action ultimately taken by the Commissioner was not only possible but probable. The action was neither an "abrupt departure" nor a "change of policy" in view of the contemporaneous developments taking place in the reserve system, over which the Commissioner had little or no control, and in any event the broad authority given to the Commissioner by the Major League Agreement placed any party to it on notice that such authority could be used.

* * *

Finally, Oakland has also argued that the court excluded evidence which tended to show the Commissioner's malice toward Mr. Finley. Finley's own testimony on this subject, as well as the Commissioner's deposition covering the subject, were admitted as part of the record. When counsel for the Commissioner attempted to cross-examine Finley in regard to the same subject, Oakland's counsel objected on the ground of relevancy and the court sustained the objection on the ground that the Commissioner's motivation was not a serious issue in the case. When the Commissioner was being cross-examined the same objection was sustained. However, since the subject had not been covered in direct examination, the court in its discretion could restrict the cross-examination to the scope of the direct; and since the subject of malice and motivation had been covered in Finley's testimony and in the Commissioner's deposition, the court could exclude it as cumulative regardless of its relevancy. The court made an express finding that the Commissioner had not been motivated by malice.

* * *

[Part IV of this opinion deals with baseball's exemption from the antitrust laws. *See* Chapter 8.]

* * *

In this part we consider the district court's judgment of August 29, 1977, granting the Commissioner's counterclaim for a declaratory judgment that the waiver of recourse clause is valid and enforceable.

* * *

Oakland has urged us to apply the substantive law dealing with the "policies and rules of a private association" to the Major League Agreement and actions thereunder. Illinois has developed a considerable body of law dealing with the activities of private voluntary organizations and we agree that the validity and effect of the waiver of recourse clause should initially be tested under these decisions.

Even in the absence of a waiver of recourse provision in an association charter, "[i]t is generally held that courts * * * will not intervene in questions involving the enforcement of bylaws and matters of discipline in voluntary associations * * *."

Viewed in light of these decisions, the waiver of recourse clause contested here seems to add little if anything to the common law nonreviewability of private association actions. This clause can be upheld as coinciding with the common law standard disallowing court interference. We view its inclusion in the Major League Agreement merely as a manifestation of the intent of the contracting parties to insulate from review decisions made by the Commissioner concerning the subject matter of actions taken in accordance with his grant of powers.

A second situation in which the waiver of recourse clause must be tested is in conjunction with the provision immediately preceding it which provides that "[a]ll disputes and controversies related in any way to professional baseball between clubs * * * shall be submitted to the Commissioner, as Arbitrator who, after hearing, shall have the sole and exclusive right to decide such disputes and controversies." Art. VII, Sec. 1. These clauses combine to place the Commissioner in the role of binding arbitrator between disputing parties as compared to his power to act upon his own initiative in the best interests of baseball as in the present case.

Considering the waiver of recourse clause in its function of requiring arbitration by the Commissioner, its validity cannot be seriously questioned. Illinois has adopted the Uniform Arbitration Act allowing contracting parties to require that all existing and future disputes be determined by arbitration * * *. [Illinois, numerous other states, and] [t]he federal courts have * * * upheld provisions in private agreements to waive all review of an arbitrator's decision. * * * We conclude that the waiver of recourse clause is valid when viewed as requiring binding arbitration by the Commissioner for disputes between clubs.

Even if the waiver of recourse clause is divorced from its setting in the charter of a private, voluntary association and even if its relationship with the arbitration clause in the agreement is ignored, we think that it is valid under the circumstances here involved. Oakland claims that such clauses are invalid as against public policy. This is true, however, only under circumstances where the waiver of rights is not voluntary, knowing or intelligent, or was not freely negotiated by parties occupying equal bargaining positions. The trend of cases in many states and in the federal courts supports the conclusion of the district court under the circumstances presented here that "informed parties, freely contracting, may waive their recourse to the court."

Although the waiver of recourse clause is generally valid for the reasons discussed above, we do not believe that it forecloses access to the courts under all circumstances. Thus, the general rule of nonreviewability which governs the actions of private associations is subject to exceptions (1) where the rules, regulations or judgments of the association are in contravention to the laws of the land or in disregard of the charter or bylaws of the association and (2) where the association has failed to follow the basic rudiments of due process of law. Similar exceptions exist for avoiding the requirements of arbitration under the United States Arbitration Act. We therefore hold that, absent the applicability of one of these narrow exceptions, the waiver of recourse clause contained in the Major League Agreement is valid and binding on the parties and the courts.

* * *

[The concurring opinions of Chief Judge Fairchild and Judge Tone are omitted.]

Notes and Questions

1. What is the significance of the "waiver of recourse" language in the Major League Agreement? Even absent such a manifestation of the league's members' willingness to abide by the decisions of the commissioner, would courts not generally opt for a policy of deference? On the other hand, would the "waiver of recourse" be given any legal efficacy in the face of a commissioner's decision that was totally arbitrary or capricious? *See Atlanta National League Baseball Club, Inc. v. Kuhn*, 432 F. Supp. 1213 (N.D. Ga. 1977).

2. Clubs generally want to develop the most proficient team and win the most games, prompted by both a profit and an ego motive. Some owners will spend tremendous sums of money to field a winning team, even if it may not be the most prudent capital venture. The ability to provide this outlay to win a championship stems, in part, from the fact that many owners already have accumulated large amounts of capital in another business venture or through the profits gleaned from the league's development at a time when less of the pot was shared with the players. On occasion, however, club owners have jettisoned star players and compromised the success of their teams in an effort to reduce salaries and purportedly to preserve the economic viability of their enterprise. Owners Calvin Griffith, Charles Finley, and Ray Kroc, for example, have generated headlines by selling off star players without replacing them in the lineup with players of commensurate ability. With the development of the free agency system, this practice, particularly with regard to financially strapped clubs fearful of their inability to re-sign highly paid players, has become more prevalent.

Commissioners have traditionally permitted major trades of key players without intervening. In professional football, outstanding Los Angeles Rams running back Ollie Matson was once incredibly traded for eight players and a draft choice. The commissioner's office did not disturb this transaction notwithstanding its unprecedented character. Ironically, or perhaps predictably, this trade was engineered by Los Angeles Rams general manager Pete Rozelle, who later became league commissioner. It was not the only time that Rozelle involved himself in player dealings that had a certain degree of intrigue and ingenuity, to put it kindly. *See Los Angeles Rams Football Club v. Cannon*, 185 F. Supp. 717 (S.D. Cal. 1960). In baseball, superstars have been traded and sold without so much as a whimper of protest from the commissioner's office. After the 1959 season, home run champion Rocky Colavito of the Cleveland Indians was traded for batting champion Harvey Kuenn of the Detroit Tigers, igniting a storm of protest from the fans of both cities. Other deals, the outright sale of Lyman Bostock from the Minnesota Twins to the California Angels, Wayne Gretzky's departure from the Edmonton Oilers, and legions of others establish that controversial and often inexplicable player transfers have become part of sport ever since the Boston Red Sox sold Babe Ruth to the New York Yankees for a song.

In light of the foregoing, what aspects of the trades in the *Finley* case provoked Commissioner Kuhn's strong reaction? Perhaps Kuhn had a somewhat elevated assessment of his own importance.

> Kuhn was only two months on the job before he invoked his "best interests" power. The Astros had traded Rusty Staub and some throw-ins to the Montreal Expos for Donn Clendenon and some throw-ins. When Clendenon announced he'd retire rather than go to Houston, Kuhn ordered the trade restructured and consummated. The fledgling Expos, he decreed, would benefit from a young star like Staub. It was extraordinary for a commissioner—to say nothing of a pro-tem—to inject himself into a trade. But, that was Kuhn.

HELYAR at 105.

3. Would the *Finley* decision (or the commissioner's initial veto) have been different if the infamous Charlie Finley had not been involved in both transactions? At the time, Finley was regarded as a league maverick, suggesting such novel approaches to the game as orange baseballs. It is well settled that he was not a part of the "good old boy network" that characterized Major League Baseball at the time. *See* Tom Verducci, *Charley O-So-Outspoken*, NEWSDAY, Aug. 17, 1988, Sports, Inside Baseball, at 130. Given this information, one must muse whether Commissioner Kuhn would have taken the same action had these trades been instigated by Los Angeles Dodgers owner Walter O'Malley or some other well-established owner who had not, in the past, affronted the delicate sensibilities of the league's select fraternity. Certainly, the district court appeared to believe that Commissioner Kuhn's feelings of antipathy for Finley were irrelevant to the issue of whether Kuhn had abused his authority.

Yet many commentators have hinted that a commissioner's "successful" imposition of sanctions against an allegedly recalcitrant owner is limited to those circumstances where the particular owner has been deemed expendable by the remainder of the establishment. Thus, commissioners' treatment of owners may be assessed not by the validity of the sanction, but, rather, by the reputation or standing of the owner. For example, though Cincinnati Reds owner Marge Schott's numerous racist and anti-semitic remarks were plainly sufficient justification for the suspension she received, her unpopularity among fellow owners surely did not help her. By contrast, Calvin Griffith, charter member of the league's good old boy network, once explained that he decided to relocate the Washington Senators to Minnesota "[w]hen I found you only had 15,000 blacks here," but was never sanctioned. Bob Fowler, *Twins Players Raging Over Cal's Remarks*, THE SPORTING NEWS, Oct. 14, 1978. Similar examples of questionably disparate handling of recalcitrant owners such as the New York Yankees' George Steinbrenner, the Atlanta Braves' Ted Turner, and others have occurred with regularity.

4. Suggestions that Bowie Kuhn was a shill for certain owners are by no means isolated. "Kuhn was a czar with a master: Walter O'Malley. When Lou Hoynes was tapped to handle the Curt Flood case * * * he first had to make a pilgrimage to Dodger Stadium where he was received, queried and found worthy. 'It sounds like a good idea, and I'm in favor of it,' O'Malley told Hoynes. 'But don't embarrass me.'" HELYAR at 105. Other commentators have denigrated Kuhn's contribution to the game and have even questioned his integrity during and after his reign as commissioner. *See id.*; WARD & BURNS at 411, 421. Yet, the most graphic invective directed at Commissioner Kuhn was issued by former Major League Baseball Players Association Executive Director Marvin Miller:

> [Kuhn's] moves constantly backfired. * * * His inability to distinguish between reality and his prejudices, his lack of concern for the rights of players, sections of the press, and even of the stray, unpopular owner—all combined to make Kuhn a vital ingredient in the growth and strength of the union. To paraphrase Voltaire on God, if Bowie Kuhn had never existed, we would have had to invent him.

MARVIN MILLER, A WHOLE DIFFERENT BALL GAME: THE SPORT AND BUSINESS OF BASEBALL 91 (1990). For a decidedly different perspective, see BOWIE KUHN, HARDBALL: THE EDUCATION OF A BASEBALL COMMISSIONER (1987).

5. The broad powers bequeathed to the commissioner in 1921, as modified by various contractions and re-expansions, and relied upon by Bowie Kuhn in 1976, were a direct result of first commissioner Judge Landis's insistence that the Major League Agreement be rewritten. The plenary authority was the *sine qua non* of Landis's acceptance of the $50,000 position. The commissioner's exercise of authority was challenged in 1931 when Judge Landis disallowed an owner's attempt to manipulate league rules by surreptitiously assigning a player to several minor league clubs (operated by the same owner) without securing waivers from other league members. The court denied the owner's request for injunctive relief and sustained the commissioner's extensive exercise of authority, including his declaration that the player had become a free agent. *See Milwaukee American Ass'n v. Landis*, 49 F.2d 298, 302–04 (N.D. Ill. 1931). The court's reasoning and ultimate conclusion served as a harbinger of the deference that courts would show baseball and the commissioner's office:

> The facts negative any assertion that this decision was made arbitrarily or fraudulently. It was made in pursuance of jurisdiction granted to the commissioner with the expressed desire to achieve certain ends, that is, to keep the game of baseball clean, to promote clean competition, to prevent collusive or fraudulent contracts, to protect players' rights, to furnish them full opportunity to advance in accord with their abilities and to prevent their deprival of such opportunities by subterfuge, covering or other unfair conduct.

Id. at 303. Compare *American League Baseball Club of New York (Yankees) v. Johnson*, 109 Misc. 138, 179 N.Y.S. 498 (N.Y. 1919). Certainly, Judge Landis's view of his charge was no less grandiose than the court's interpretation:

> "Baseball is something more than a game to an American boy," he said. "It is his training field for life work. Destroy his faith in its squareness and honesty and you have destroyed something more;you have planted suspicion of all things in his heart."

WARD & BURNS at 143–44. Few people realize that Landis, who was only 38 years old at the time of his appointment to the bench by President Theodore Roosevelt, had the hubris to continue to serve as a federal judge for 15 months while occupying the commissioner's throne. *See Finley v. Kuhn*, 569 F.2d 527, 537 n.37 (7th Cir. 1978).

Yet, not everyone was prepared to lionize Judge Landis and mark him as the game's savior. Political commentator and baseball aficionado George Will characterized the first commissioner in the following fashion:

> Landis was a grandstanding judge — in baseball lingo, a hot dog * * *. He tried to extradite the Kaiser because a Chicagoan died when a German submarine sank the Lusitania. Landis enjoyed stiff drinks of whiskey but handed out stiff sentences to people who violated Prohibition.

ZIMBALIST at 211 n.64. Baseball historian Harold Seymour characterizes Landis as an "egocentric, eccentric goofball." *Id.* Regrettably, this strident criticism of Judge Landis was also directed at his successors in the commissioner's chair. While the commissioners of other professional sports have not been immune to some negative commentary, they have in varying degrees been credited with the development of the sports under their stewardship. Few, if any, have been subject to the vitriol reserved for the likes of Landis, Happy Chandler, Ford Frick, William Eckert, and Fay Vincent. *See* HAROLD SEYMOUR, BASEBALL: THE PEOPLE'S GAME 532 (1972); Michael J. Cozzillio, *From the Land of Bondage: The Greening of Major League Baseball Players and the Major League Baseball Players Association*, 41 CATH. U.L. REV. 117, 127–34 (1991); HELYAR at 78; ZIMBALIST at 44. Commissioners Ueberroth and Giamatti have avoided the most poisonous pens, but that is suprising given Uederroth's role in collusion against free agent players and Giamatti's conduct in the Pete Rose controversy, but this phenomenon could be attributable to Ueberroth's success as Staff Director of the Los Angeles Olympic Organizing Committee (he was Time Magazine's Man of the Year) and, in Giamatti's case, the tragic circumstances surrounding his untimely death. Nonetheless, to suggest that these two commissioners' terms will be glorified by baseball's chroniclers is far too sanguine. *See* ZIMBALIST at 41–44; MILLER at 389–401; HELYAR at 310–29. In 2004, Ueberroth became the Chair of the Board of the United States Olympic Committee.

6. *Finley v. Kuhn* and its precursors might suggest that the commissioner's power is, however, well nigh absolute. Is it? The answer is simply that the commissioner does wield considerable power but that this power is circumscribed to some degree. The *Finley* court makes it plain that baseball forfeits some of the judicial deference that it has "earned" over the years if the commissioner violates principles of due process or clearly acts in violation of law. *See, e.g., Riko Enterprises, Inc. v. Seattle Supersonics Corp.*, 357 F. Supp. 521 (S.D.N.Y. 1973).

7. Once again, Marvin Miller has suggested that the commissioner's unfettered, or apparently unfettered, authority is exclusively a function of the owners' whim. "If Fay Vincent or any other commissioner ever attempted to act 'in the best interest of baseball' *but* against the best interests of a significant group of owners, the press' illusions about the commissioner's power would be quickly shattered." MILLER at 406. Miller's prescience is evidenced by the fact that Vincent's honeymoon with baseball's establishment ended when he crossed swords with many owners over league realignment and

the 1990 lockout. *See, e.g.*, Mike Dorning, *Hockey Touted as Growth Sport of the 90s*, CALGARY HERALD, Oct. 11, 1992; Murray Chase, *On the Way Out Vincent Finally Gets a Consensus*, N.Y. TIMES, Sept. 8, 1992, § B, at 17. This sentiment has been echoed by other commentators:

> Judge Landis' dramatic Black Sox entry and his autocratic bearing had created the myth of the all-powerful commissioner; and the commissioner did, indeed, have sweeping authority to take actions in the "best interests of the game"; but in practice, that authority applied mainly to disciplinary matters. In business matters, the commissioner existed only as a tie-breaker between the two leagues.

HELYAR at 77. This issue will be addressed in the discussion of *Chicago National League Ball Club v. Vincent*, appearing in the latter part of this chapter.

8. Any delusions that baseball may have had regarding the sacrosanct nature of any and all decrees by the commissioner's office were dispelled in the landmark dispute involving Pete Rose and the late Bart Giamatti. The investigation into Rose's gambling began at the end of Ueberroth's term as commissioner, when Ueberroth appointed attorney John M. Dowd to investigate the allegations. According to a letter Ueberroth sent to Rose's counsel, the commissioner acted "[P]ursuant to the best interest of baseball authority contained in Art. 1, Sec. 2(b) of the Major League Agreement and in conformity with the Rules of Procedure contained on page one of our rules book."

Rules of Procedure

Formulated by the Commissioner and Announced Pursuant to the Major League Agreement, and the Professional Baseball Agreement

(1) NOTICE. Written notice of the time and place of hearings shall be given under the direction of the Commissioner.

(2) APPEARANCE. In all claims and disputes submitted to the Commissioner the persons or organizations concerned shall be entitled to appear and be heard in person, to present witnesses, to cross examine witnesses and to be represented by an attorney. In the case of dispute between a Major League Club and a National Association Club, or other matter involving or concerning a National Association League or National Association Club, a representative designed by the National Association shall be entitled to appear.

(3) PROCEEDINGS. Proceedings before the Commissioner shall be conducted in general like judicial proceedings and with due regard for all the principles of natural justice and fair play, but the Commissioner may proceed informally whenever he deems it desirable.

(4) PROOFS. The Commissioner will in general follow the established rules of evidence but may depart from them in cases in which the ends of justice will in his judgment best be subserved by so doing. He may receive and consider affidavits if, in his judgment, there is good reason for the non-appearance of the affiants.

(5) SUMMONS. In the case of all persons or organizations who have accorded recognition to the office and authority of the Commissioner, a summons by him, by letter or telegram to appear either as a party or as a witness before him, the Secretary-Treasurer or before any person he may designate, shall be binding upon the person or official to whom directed. Failure to respond to the summons, or to produce the documents or other evidence which it may specify, or to testify and give evidence fully and accurately to the best of his knowledge, and any offering, or attempt to offer, of any false testi-

mony or evidence, or any attempt to induce another to offer or attempt to offer any false testimony or evidence, will be treated by the Commissioner as conduct deemed not to be in the best interests of Baseball and penalties will be imposed by him pursuant to the terms of the Major League Agreement, and/or the Professional Baseball Agreement, as the case may be.

(6) DEPOSITIONS. The Commissioner, when he deems proper, may direct testimony to be taken and evidence to be produced at convenient places before a notary public or other officer, or before the Secretary-Treasurer, and in such cases will proceed substantially as if the testimony had been taken on an open commission in a judicial proceeding.

(7) DEFAULT. If any person, club or league party to any dispute, claim, complaint or charge shall fail to answer fully thereto within fifteen (15) days after notice thereof, or such further time, if any, as the Commissioner may have allowed in writing, the Commissioner shall render judgment or take action, as the case may be, against the party in default.

(8) RECORD. The Secretary-Treasurer will assist the Commissioner in matters pending before him and will preserve all documents entrusted to him. Stenographic reports of hearings may be made at the discretion of the Commissioner. Notification of all action will be given under direction of the Commissioner to all parties in interest, and public statements will be made by him in all cases where, in his judgment, publicity is either necessary or proper.

PETER V. UEBERROTH, Commissioner

Letter from New Commissioner Bart Giamatti to Judge Carl Rubin

April 18, 1989

CONFIDENTIAL
The Honorable Carl B. Rubin
Chief Judge
United States District Court
Southern District of Ohio
United States Post Office and Courthouse
5th and Main Street
Cincinnati, Ohio 45202

Re: United States v. Peters, Criminal No. 1-89-034
(USDC SD Ohio)

Dear Judge Rubin:

I am advised that Ron Peters will appear before you shortly in the above-entitled case to enter a plea of guilty to two felonies and to receive his sentence.

It is my purpose to bring to your attention the significant and truthful cooperation Mr. Peters has provided to my special counsel who is conducting the investigation into allegations concerning the conduct and activities of Pete Rose, the manager of the Cincinnati Reds Baseball Club.

Mr. Peters has been readily available at all times to my special counsel and has provided critical sworn testimony about Mr. Rose and his associates. In addition, Mr. Peters has provided probative documentary evidence to support his testimony and the testimony of others. Based upon other information in our possession, I am satisfied Mr. Peters has been candid, forthright and truthful with my special counsel.

In view of the confidential nature of my inquiry, I would respectfully request this letter to remain under the Court's seal until the completion of my inquiry.

Thank you for your consideration of this letter on behalf of Mr. Peters.

Sincerely yours
/s/
A. Bartlett Giamatti

Rose v. Giamatti
1989 Ohio App. LEXIS 2542 (Ct. App. Ham. Cty. 1989)

PLAINTIFF PETER E. ROSE'S REPLY MEMORANDUM IN SUPPORT OF MOTION FOR TEMPORARY RESTRAINING ORDER AND PRELIMINARY INJUNCTION

I. PETE ROSE'S REQUEST FOR INJUNCTIVE RELIEF IS NOT PREMATURE.

It is hornbook law that,

> Where a court's general equity jurisdiction has been invoked, it may stay an arbitration proceeding on the ground that an arbitrator was not qualified because of bias or prejudice; to permit the arbitration to proceed to a conclusion under such circumstances would be futile, since the award would certainly be vacated.

5 American Jurisprudence 2d, Arbitration & Award §100 at 596.

Defendants Giamatti and Major League Baseball make the statement that they are not aware of any case where a private association was required to disqualify its decision-maker before he had rendered a decision. Such authority exists. In *Rabinowitz v. Olewski*, 473 N.Y.S.2d 232 (N.Y. App. Div. 1984) * * * the New York Court held that:

> The law is well settled that 'in an appropriate case, the courts have inherent power to disqualify an arbitrator before an award has been rendered.' * * * The proper standard of review for the disqualification of arbitrators is whether the arbitration process is free of the appearance of bias * * *. Plaintiffs should not be required to arbitrate their claims in such a charged atmosphere. Trial Term, therefore, did not err by removing the arbitration from the DOC due to the "appearance of impropriety and specter of bias among the DDC." We accordingly affirm.

473 N.Y.S.2d at 234 (emphasis added).

The commissioners of professional sports leagues do not enjoy any particular immunity in this regard. In *Erving v. Virginia Squires Basketball Club,* 349 F. Supp. 716, 719 (E.D.N.Y.), *aff'd,* 468 F.2d 1064 (2d Cir. 1972), the Court ordered professional basketball player Julius Erving to arbitrate his claims concerning the validity of his contract with an American Basketball Association franchise as required by the terms of Erving's contract. However, Erving's contract called for arbitration before the ABA Commissioner who was a partner in a law firm that represented Erving's employers. The Court ordered arbitration but disqualified the Commissioner of the ABA holding that "[u]nder the circumstances, arbitration should proceed before a neutral arbitrator and the order so provides."

* * *

Defendants erroneously state the law to be that Courts will not intervene in the actions of private associations. Defendants' own authority shows that this is not the case.

> The decisions of any kind of voluntary society or association in disciplining or suspending, or expelling members are of a quasi judicial character. In such cases, the Courts never interfere except to ascertain whether or not the proceeding was pursuant to the rules and laws of the society, whether or not the proceeding was in good faith, and whether or not there was anything in the proceeding in violation of the laws of the land.

State ex rel. Ohio High School Athletic Ass'n v. Judges, 181 N.E.2d 261, 266 (Ohio 1962) * * *. The law of the land in Ohio included the principle "that a member who an association seeks to expel is entitled to due process and natural justice." *Bay v. Anderson Hills, Inc.,* 483 N.E.2d 491, 493 (Ohio Ct. App. 1984).

The present case falls clearly within the exception recognized by the cases which Defendants have cited to this Court. This * * * case involves the right of Pete Rose to pursue his livelihood in the only profession which he has ever known. The evidence before the Court shows that Defendants have not complied with their own rules and have not accorded Pete Rose the due process and natural justice required by the law of Ohio.

Pete Rose is not required to "exhaust" his remedies within Major League Baseball. Defendants' own authorities recognize that exhaustion is not required when internal appeal is futile or illusory. [T]here is no person or entity within Major League Baseball that has the power to review or correct the actions of Giamatti.

Exhaustion is not required as a prerequisite to judicial relief when the person or body before whom such remedies lie is biased or has prejudged the issue. The "remedy" which Defendants want Pete Rose to exhaust is submission to Giamatti's "hearing". Pete Rose is not required to exhaust that remedy because, as is shown by unequivocal evidence before the Court, Giamatti is biased and has prejudged Pete Rose's case.

* * *

II. THE COMMISSIONER IS NOT BEYOND JUDICIAL SCRUTINY IN CARRYING OUT HIS RESPONSIBILITIES.

Defendants Giamatti and Major League Baseball are, like other private organizations, entitled to some deference to exercise their own discretion in governing their internal affairs. However, * * * even the action of Major League Baseball is reviewable "1) where the rules, regulations or judgments of the association are in contravention to the laws of the land or in disregard of the charter or bylaws of the association and 2) where the association has failed to follow the basic rudiments of due process of law." [*Finley v. Kuhn,*] 569 F.2d at 544. *See also Atlanta National Baseball Club, Inc. v. Kuhn,* 432 F. Supp. 1213, 1218 (N.D. Ga. 1977) ("The extent of defendant Kuhn's contractual power is a question for the court.").

This case does not implicate the Commissioner of Baseball's discretion to determine what is or is not in the best interests of baseball. This case presents the Court with a situation where Defendant Giamatti and his agents are actually biased and have actually prejudged Pete Rose's guilt, all contrary to Baseball's own Rules of Procedure. It is not Pete Rose who seeks to have Giamatti disqualified in this case. Giamatti has disqualified himself by his words and actions taken during his proceedings against Pete Rose.

III. PETE ROSE HAS ESTABLISHED HIS ENTITLEMENT TO THE REQUESTED RELIEF.

Defendants are correct in stating that fairness includes notice of the charges and an opportunity to be heard. However, a hearing requires substance as well as form.

* * *

Giamatti and Major League Baseball would have the Court believe that this aspect of fairness does not apply to a private decision-maker like Giamatti who is not subject to any internal review procedure * * *. While a private association is not subject to all of the requirements of Fourteenth Amendment due process, Ohio law does require private entities to grant "due process and natural justice" to their members and to "comport with fundamental fairness."

Giamatti argues that his conduct has not disqualified him from deciding Pete Rose's professional fate * * *. "Bias is always difficult, and indeed often impossible to 'prove'. Unless an arbitrator publicly announces his partiality, or is overheard in a moment of private admission, it is difficult to imagine how 'proof' would be obtained." *Morelite Construction Corp. v. New York City District Council,* 748 F.2d 79, 84 (2d Cir. 1984). Pete Rose has put exactly that kind of proof before the Court.

Giamatti has stated that Ron Peters was "candid, forthright and truthful" in telling John Dowd that Pete Rose has bet on baseball and on the Cincinnati Reds. It does not matter whether Giamatti formed this conclusion from first-hand observation or simply accepted Dowd's evaluation; Giamatti has still manifested prejudgment on an issue central to the accusations against Pete Rose and has tied his own reputation to the veracity of Peters. This is not like an adverse preliminary ruling or an adverse ruling in a prior case. Giamatti's statements are manifestations of prejudgment on the merits.

* * *

Rose v. Giamatti

1989 Ohio Misc. LEXIS 1 (Ct. Comm. Pleas Ham. Cty. 1989)

TEMPORARY RESTRAINING ORDER
NORBERT A. NADEL

This cause came on to be heard on the Motion of Plaintiff Peter E. Rose ("Pete Rose") for a Temporary Restraining Order and Memorandum in Support thereof * * *.

The Court finds based on the information that is presently before the Court, that there is a substantial likelihood of success by the Plaintiff on the merits and that Defendants and persons acting on their behalf, in association with them, or in concert with them have and are about to commit the acts set forth in the Complaint as verified by the Affidavit of Robert A. Pitcairn, Jr. and will, unless enjoined by Order of this Court, continue to do so. Further, the Court finds that Pete Rose will suffer irreparable harm absent the relief granted herein in that he will be subjected to disciplinary proceedings before a biased, unfair tribunal, on charges that he bet on Baseball, and that permanent and irreparable damage will be done to his career and reputation. The Court further finds that there is a substantial likelihood that any disciplinary proceedings undertaken against plaintiff Pete Rose in which defendant A. Bartlett Giamatti is involved or participates will be conducted with improper prejudice against Pete Rose and will be inherently unfair and in violation of the rules and contracts governing Pete Rose's participation in Major League Baseball and the laws of the State of Ohio. The Court concludes that Plaintiff Pete Rose has no adequate remedy at law and that he has shown immediate and irreparable injury, loss, or damage and that as to each item of relief granted hereinafter, the injury inflicted upon Plaintiff Pete Rose by the denial of such relief would be greater than any injury that would be inflicted upon Defendants by the granting of such relief and that the granting of such relief is in the public interest. The Court therefore finds that Plaintiff Pete Rose's Motion for a Temporary Restraining Order is well taken and should be granted.

IT IS THEREFORE ORDERED, ADJUDGED AND DECREED that Defendants A. Bartlett Giamatti, Major League Baseball, the Cincinnati Reds, and their respective members, officers, agents, servants, employees, attorneys, and all persons in active concert or participation with Defendants are hereby restrained and enjoined for the term of this Order and any extension thereof, directly or indirectly, from:

1. Further involvement in deciding whether plaintiff Pete Rose should be disciplined, banned, suspended, expelled, or declared ineligible from participation in baseball pending resolution of this action;

2. Terminating Plaintiff Pete Rose's employment as Field Manager of the Cincinnati Reds or taking any action to interfere with Pete Rose's employment in that capacity in response to any order, declaration, pronouncement, decree, edict, or decision from Defendants A. Bartlett Giamatti or Major League Baseball, or in response to Plaintiff Pete Rose having filed this action.

* * *

Rose v. Giamatti
1989 Ohio App. LEXIS 2448 (Ohio Ct. App. 1989)

MOTION FOR SUSPENSION OF TEMPORARY RESTRAINING ORDER PENDING APPEAL AND FOR EXPEDITED TREATMENT

Defendants, A. Bartlett Giamatti, as Commissioner of Baseball, and Major League Baseball, hereby apply to the Court * * * for a suspension of the temporary restraining order issued by the trial court on June 25, 1989 pending the appeal of this order and for expedited treatment. It would not be practicable to request the instant relief from the trial court especially given the serious press of time in this matter.

* * *

The record herein establishes that the trial court's grant of the temporary restraining order was unjustified and without legal support. Most importantly, the pendency of the temporary restraining order presents clear irreparable injury to the Commissioner's Office.

For the last several weeks, the charges against Pete Rose have focused enormous public attention on gambling and the possible corruption of the game. Now that Pete Rose has aired these charges by bringing suit, it has become critical for the Commissioner's Office to act promptly to maintain public confidence in the integrity of the game. If every action by the Commissioner to investigate and determine matters affecting the integrity of the game were to be subject to court intervention and delay, the Commissioner's ability to safeguard the integrity of the game would be destroyed. The action of the court below threatens the very reputation of Major League Baseball, and deprives the Commissioner of the power to protect the integrity of the game. Accordingly, these defendants respectfully request the court to stay the order below pending appeal.

MEMORANDUM IN SUPPORT

A. Statement Of The Case

Plaintiff, field manager of the Cincinnati Reds baseball club, has been under investigation for allegations of gambling on baseball. The Commissioner of Baseball is empowered to investigate and act on such allegations under the Major League Agreement and plaintiff's contract with the Cincinnati Reds.

In this instance the Commissioner enlisted special counsel, John Dowd, to investigate the allegations against plaintiff. Mr. Dowd conducted an extensive investigation and submitted a comprehensive report to the Commissioner consisting of 225 pages and eight volumes of exhibits.

On May 11, 1989, the Commissioner provided a copy of the Report to plaintiff and scheduled a hearing on the matter for May 25, 1989. Plaintiff requested from the Commissioner an extension of thirty days in which to prepare for the hearing. This request was granted and the hearing was rescheduled for June 26, 1989.

Rather than prepare for the hearing before the Commissioner, plaintiff filed suit on June 19, 1989, seeking a temporary restraining order, preliminary injunction, and permanent injunction, as well as other relief. After two days of testimony, the trial court granted the temporary restraining order on June 25, 1989, concluding that there is substantial evidence the Commissioner has prejudged plaintiff's case and cannot serve as a fair and impartial decisionmaker. * * * The trial judge enjoined the Commissioner and the Cincinnati Reds baseball club from taking any disciplinary action whatsoever against plaintiff during the 14-day life of the order.

The trial judge has scheduled a hearing for a preliminary injunction beginning July 6, 1989. Accordingly, a determination by this Court is required, at the very latest, on or before that date.

B. Argument

The order of the court below violates one of the most fundamental rules governing private associations—courts may not interfere in the proceedings of such associations before such proceedings have been concluded. * * *

Where a voluntary association has yet to conduct a disciplinary hearing or to render a decision, judicial intervention to enjoin the association's proceeding or to disqualify the decisionmaker is unprecedented * * *. In these cases, injunctive relief is inappropriate both because private associations are given great deference in the initial conduct of their specialized affairs and because there can be no showing of imminent irreparable injury prior to the conclusion of an association's internal proceedings. The court below has erred on a fundamental matter of law by restraining the Commissioner of Baseball from even holding a hearing with respect to the serious allegations that Pete Rose was gambling on Major League Baseball games.

The sole basis for the court's action was Judge Nadel's finding that Commissioner Giamatti had prejudged the matter of Pete Rose's guilt. This finding, too, is incorrect. The single item of evidence relied upon by Judge Nadel was a letter, dated April 18, 1989, drafted by the Commissioner's Special Counsel John M. Dowd, signed by Commissioner Giamatti and sent to the Honorable Carl Rubin, who was about to sentence one of Pete Rose's accusers, Ron Peters * * *. The letter recites that "[b]ased upon other information in our possession, I am satisfied Mr. Peters has been candid, forthright and truthful with my special counsel." As discussed in Defendants' Brief, the claim of prejudgment based on this letter is not sustainable as a matter of law or fact.

* * *

The unrefuted evidence was that the letter was drafted by Mr. Dowd, reflected only his preliminary assessment of the quality of the testimonial and documentary evidence provided to him by Mr. Peters, represented no independent assessment of evidence by the Commissioner, and did not in any manner constitute a ruling on the ultimate issue which would be before the Commissioner.

* * *

Moreover, the type of "prejudgment" about which plaintiff complains forms an insufficient basis as a matter of law for disqualifying decisionmakers. If the rule were otherwise, judges who made preliminary findings of credibility in preliminary injunction matters, or in connection with warrants in criminal cases would be forever disqualified from subsequent proceedings over the same or related matters. This is plainly not the case.

In supervising the investigation of Pete Rose, the Commissioner was acting pursuant to specific powers given him under the Major League Agreement to investigate conduct not in the best interests of Baseball * * *. The Commissioner will inevitably make certain judgments in the course of his investigations, but there is no reason that his investigatory function should preclude the exercise of his adjudicatory function. The combination of such functions is routine in government agencies, and is certainly not inconsistent with natural justice and fundamental fairness.

In *Withrow v. Larkin*, the Supreme Court rejected the argument made by plaintiff here with the observation that any attack upon the supposed impropriety of combining investigatory and adjudicatory powers in one agency "must overcome a presumption of honesty and integrity in those serving as adjudicators." The Court noted that,

> Judges repeatedly issue arrest warrants on the basis that there is probable cause to believe that a crime has been committed and that the person named in the warrant has committed it. Judges also preside at preliminary hearings where they must decide whether the evidence is sufficient to hold a defendant for trial. Neither of these pretrial involvements has been thought to raise any constitutional barrier against the judge's presiding over the criminal trial and, if the trial is without a jury, against making the necessary determination of guilt or innocence.

* * *

Judge Nadel's suggestion that the hearing of this matter would be futile, given the supposed prejudgment of the Commissioner, is contradicted by the facts before him, and is also inconsistent with the appropriate legal standard. This rule against judicial interference in the decision-making process of a private association cannot be avoided by "[a] mere averment that a remedy is futile or illusory." * * * Even in the administrative context, where stricter standards of due process apply than here, "[a] vain act is defined in the context of lack of authority to grant administrative relief and not in the sense of lack of probability that the application for administrative relief will be granted." Here, the court below erred by holding that the pursuit of a hearing would be a futile act.

The need for the immediate and extraordinary relief here sought is critical. The subject of Pete Rose's gambling activities and the extent of gambling on Major League Baseball has been the focus of widespread speculation and intense public concern, putting a cloud over Major League Baseball and its administration. The trial court's issuance of the temporary restraining order has now raised substantial doubt as to baseball's ability to police itself and the Commissioner's power to enforce its rules. The integrity of the game has been damaged by the lower court's ruling and it will continue to suffer as long as the temporary restraining order remains in effect.

It is vital that the Commissioner be allowed to hear the evidence on the allegations against plaintiff and reach a determination as quickly as possible. Indeed, the sport of baseball will be severely damaged if the Commissioner is barred from completing his investigation and taking the actions he sees as appropriate—steps consistent with his mandate to uphold the integrity of the game. The image of a sport no longer capable of policing itself in a matter as serious as a manager betting on his own team's games could only erode public confidence in and respect for the national pastime. The ability of the Commissioner to protect the integrity of baseball, the purpose for which his office was created, is at stake.

For these reasons, it is respectfully requested that the Court of Appeals suspend the temporary restraining order pending appeal, and consider this entire matter on an expedited basis.

Rose v. Giamatti

1989 Ohio App. LEXIS 2542 (Ct. App. Ham. Cty. 1989)

PLAINTIFF-APPELLEE PETER E. ROSE'S BRIEF IN OPPOSITION TO DEFENDANTS-APPELLANTS' MOTION FOR SUSPENSION OF TEMPORARY RESTRAINING ORDER PENDING APPEAL AND FOR EXPEDITED TREATMENT

* * *

Defendants' contention that Giamatti has not prejudged the accusations against Pete Rose is patently absurd. Giamatti stated in writing to a United States District Judge that Ron Peters' accusations that Pete Rose has bet on baseball games and on Cincinnati Reds' games were "candid, forthright and truthful." This is not the kind of preliminary finding made by Judge Nadel that probable cause exists for further investigation. It is an unadorned, unqualified statement that Ron Peters' accusations are truthful. Such statements about the credibility of witnesses or parties routinely require disqualification when made by a judge. *See, e.g., Nicodemus v. Chrysler Corp.,* 596 F.2d 152, 155 (6th Cir. 1979) (statements by district judge that defendants were not "worthy of credence by anybody" and were "a bunch of villains" required disqualification of the judge.).

Defendants' assertion that Giamatti must act immediately to protect baseball from the evils of gambling simply proves the substance of Pete Rose's claims in this action. Defendants' repeated statements that baseball will be harmed by maintaining the status quo for this short period clearly show that Giamatti and Major League Baseball have determined that Pete Rose bet on baseball, without even hearing Pete Rose's evidence and witnesses.

CONCLUSION

For all of the reasons set forth above, Plaintiff Peter E. Rose respectfully requests that the Court deny the Motion of Defendants A. Bartlett Giamatti and Major League Baseball for a Suspension of Temporary Restraining Order Pending Appeal and for Expedited Treatment.

Notes and Questions

1. Has the commissioner's office been strengthened or weakened as a result of the *Rose* case? Be mindful of the fact that, subsequent to the issuance of Judge Nadel's injunction, Rose's case was removed by Commissioner Giamatti to federal court, and, past often being prologue, it was assumed that baseball eventually would have prevailed on the merits of that litigation. In any event, Rose eventually agreed to a settlement in which he was "permanently" banned from the game, with an opportunity to seek dissolution of the ban at a subsequent time. It could be argued that this settlement, which virtually sounded the death knell for Pete Rose's reentry into baseball and eventual admission into baseball's Hall of Fame, constituted a major victory for the late Bart Giamatti. Yet, it cannot be denied that this case marked one of the rare instances in which courts did not slavishly defer to a decision of an exalted league commissioner. As a side comment, there are those who consider Giamatti's actions after the settlement agreement somewhat less than honorable. The settlement agreement between Rose and Giamatti provided that there would be no conclusions drawn about Rose's guilt (regarding betting on baseball games) nor would the settlement constitute an admission of same. Yet, during the press conference announcing the settlement, Giamatti made it clear that baseball's allegations against Rose had been profoundly vindicated. *See* Miller at 397.

2. Rose has since admitted that he gambled on Reds games, both when he was a player and a manager, though he maintains that he never bet *against* the Reds. *See* Pete Rose with Rick Hill, My Prison Without Bars (2004). Should that make a difference? *See Molinas v. National Basketball Ass'n*, 190 F. Supp. 241 (1961) ("[E]ach time he either placed a bet or refused to place a bet, this operated inevitably to inform bookmakers of an insider's opinion as to the adequacy or inadequacy of the point-spread or his team's ability to win."). Perhaps more importantly, a manager may sacrifice his team's chances in certain games (by, for example, not using the team's best pitcher) if a bet placed on *another* game makes that contest more important to him. Rose has applied for reinstatement on several occasions since 1997, but Commissioner Selig has not acted favorably on the applications.

3. It is a fundamental principle of administrative law that one must exhaust adminis¬trative remedies prior to invoking the aid of the court. It is an equally recognized tenet that such exhaustion of remedies need not be exercised when it would be futile. *See Gibson v. Berryhill*, 411 U.S. 564 (1973). In Pete Rose's case, the actions of Commissioner Giamatti made it clear that certain credibility determinations had already been made before the hearing. For these reasons, Judge Nadel concluded that it was unnecessary for Rose to exhaust his remedies and that the question of Giamatti's bias and the procedural due process implications were justiciable issues. Major League Rules 2 and 3 specifically provide that all parties concerned in claims submitted to the commissioner for resolution shall be entitled to a hearing, including the right to present testimony, to cross-examine witnesses, and to be represented by an attorney. Specifically, Rule 3 declares that proceedings "shall be conducted in general like judicial proceedings and with due regard for all the principles of natural justice and fair play." Rule 3 does permit the commissioner to proceed informally if he deems it desirable, but such a qualification might not justify the total elimination of the most basic due process guarantees, especially adjudication by an unbiased tribunal. See Jeffrey A. Durney, Comment, *Fair or*

Foul? The Commissioner and Major League Baseball's Disciplinary Process, 41 EMORY L.J. 581 (1992); Matthew B. Pachman, Note, *Limits on the Discretionary Powers of Professional Sports Commissioners: A Historical and Legal Analysis of Issues Raised by the Pete Rose Controversy*, 76 VA. L. REV. 1409 (1990).

4. Should the Commissioner of Baseball be subject to *any* limitations sounding in due process? Commissioners are private individuals, not government actors, and Major League Baseball is a private association. Accordingly, it is unlikely that either the commissioner or MLB would satisfy the "state-action" requirement necessary to make the Fifth or Fourteenth Amendment's Due Process Clause binding. Nevertheless, as discussed in Chapter 17, there has been some attempt to treat some persons associated with baseball as state actors. *See Ludtke v. Kuhn*, 461 F. Supp. 86 (S.D.N.Y. 1978).

Judge Nadel's decision applying the strictures of due process to the commissioner, however, rests not on the United States Constitution, but on Ohio's law of private associations. May a state constitutionally restrict the way a private association decides to dismiss one of its members? *Cf. Boy Scouts of America v. Dale*, 530 U.S. 640 (2000); *Board of Directors v. Rotary Club*, 481 U.S. 537 (1987); *Roberts v. United States Jaycees*, 468 U.S. 609 (1984). *See* Christopher J. McKinny, *Professional Sports Leagues and the First Amendment: A Closed Marketplace*, 13 MARQ. SPORTS L. REV. 223 (2003); Pachman, *supra* at 1430–35.

5. Interestingly, Judge Landis was the subject of a disqualification proceeding before he became Commissioner of Baseball. *See Berger v. United States*, 255 U.S. 22 (1921). It may not surprise you, after reading of Judge Landis's personality earlier in this Chapter, to hear that he made rather indelicate comments about German-Americans in a case involving a German-American criminal defendant. Among other remarks, Landis said that German-Americans' "hearts are reeking with disloyalty," that "this defendant" was not loyal to the United States, and, "If anybody has said anything worse about the Germans than I have I would like to know it so I can use it." *Id.* at 28–29. *See also In re IBM*, 45 F.3d 641 (2d Cir. 1995) (requiring recusal of a judge biased against IBM); *State* ex rel. *La Russa v. Himes*, 197 So. 762 (Fla. 1940) (requiring the recusal of the judge in La Russa's criminal trial when the judge had issued a campaign statement saying that "what the people want is a judge who will put people like Philip La Russa and his associates away.").

6. Would Giamatti be impermissibly biased if he had made public statements not about Rose's *guilt*, but about the *issue* of gambling in baseball? Suppose he announced that he viewed gambling on baseball as detrimental to the game and worthy of a lifetime exclusion from baseball. Would an accused gambler prevail on a motion to disqualify in that scenario? Agency decision-makers are often predisposed to policy results: "[I]t is in the nature of persons charged with making policy to have ideas and value judgments and want to advocate those conclusions." WILLIAM F. FOX, JR., UNDERSTANDING ADMINISTRATIVE LAW 196 (4th ed. 2000). *Cf. United States v. Cooley*, 1 F.3d 985, 993 n.4 (10th Cir. 1993) ("Judges take an oath to uphold the law; they are expected to disfavor its violation."); Michael R. Dimino, *Pay No Attention to That Man Behind the Robe: Judicial Elections, the First Amendment, and Judges as Politicians*, 21 YALE L. & POL'Y REV. 301 (2003).

7. While a neutral decision-maker is at the cornerstone of administrative due process, this requirement may be qualified where there is no alternative adjudicator. Under the "rule of necessity," it is conceivable that a biased decision-maker may be preferred to no arbiter at all.

8. Another principle of administrative law that was implicated in the *Rose* case involves the commingling of the prosecutorial and administrative functions. *See Withrow*

v. Larkin, 421 U.S. 35 (1975). The Administrative Procedure Act ("APA") has specifically declared that agency personnel cannot engage in both the prosecutorial and administrative functions where a formal administrative proceeding is appropriate. 5 U.S.C. §554(d) (1994). However, the APA carves out an exception that exempts "the agency or a member or members of the body comprising the agency" from this prohibition against commingling. 5 U.S.C. §554(d)(2)(C). Can the commissioner be analogized to an agency head and thereby engage in both prosecutorial and adjudicatory functions without compromising the parties' due process? Regardless of the constitutional/administrative law analogy, it is well settled that commissioners in many sports contexts, particularly those situations involving the integrity of the game, do engage in both an investigative or quasi-prosecutorial role as well as the ultimate adjudicatory role. It is likely that they can continue to engage in such activity without implicating the Constitution both because there is probably insufficient state action and because the Supreme Court has suggested that commingling functions does not necessarily intrude upon the procedural due process to which one would be entitled. *See Withrow v. Larkin, supra.*

9. What is the significance of Judge Nadel's decision in terms of other sports, including non-traditional non-team sports? National governing bodies in Olympic contexts such as track and field, figure skating, swimming, and gymnastics must show sensitivity to the due process concerns of their participants. These sports organizations, which govern Olympic sports and international competitions, are covered by federal legislation that regulates their conduct and provides for arbitration of certain disputes. *See* Ted Stevens Olympic Amateur Sports Act, 36 U.S.C. §220501 *et seq.* Likewise, the conduct of many of the governing bodies is controlled by internal rules and regulations, the Bylaws of the United States Olympic Committee, the rules and regulations of the international federation with jurisdiction over their sport and, in some contexts, the rules and regulations of the International Olympic Committee, including the Olympic Charter.

10. The investigation into Rose's conduct is not the only time a commissioner has sought outside assistance in investigating a problem in a sport. In 2006, Commissioner Selig appointed former Senator George Mitchell to head a committee investigating the use of performance-enhancing drugs. The choice of Mitchell drew criticism, however, (by no less than John Dowd, among others) because Mitchell is currently a director of the Boston Red Sox. *See Dowd Criticizes Selig's Selection of Mitchell*, Apr.1, 2006, *at* http://sports.espn.go.com/mlb/news/story?id=2390344 (last visited August 16, 2006).

11. As discussed at several points in this text, the barrier between sports and real life is increasingly pregnable. Players, fans, owners, unions, and commissioners must be aware of the legal consequences of on-the-field activities, whether those consequences stem from the courts, legislatures, or executives. The Mitchell appointment followed congressional committee hearings in 2005, in which Commissioner Selig testified that "the eradication of performance enhancing substances from all of professional baseball is my top priority." Statement of Allan H. Selig, Commissioner of Baseball, Before the Committee on Energy and Commerce of the United States House of Representatives, May 18, 2005, available at http://energycommerce.house.gov/108/Hearings/05192005hearing1507/Selig.pdf#search=%22 commissioner%20baseball%20testify%20congress%22. We discuss MLB's history of responding to the problem of performance-enhancing substances in Chapter 14. Should Congress concern itself with the drug policies adopted by baseball and other sports? Several commentators found it ironic that Congress would take action because the public was losing trust in another institution's credibility.

The Executive Branch likewise has not been silent on this issue. FBI investigations into the use and sale of Human Growth Hormone have resulted in the outing of pitcher Jason Grimsley and Grimsley's implication of other Major League players whose identities have yet to be made public. Additionally, recently published books, including JOSE CANSECO, JUICED (2005) and MARK FAINARU-WADA & LANCE WILLIAMS, GAME OF SHADOWS (2006), continue to pressure the commissioner to take action. The commissioner's principal action so far, other than the appointment of Mitchell, was to increase the penalties for the use of performance-enhancing drugs, with the agreement of the MLBPA, to a 50-game suspension for the first positive test, a 100-game suspension for the second, and a lifetime ban for the third. Would the commissioner have authority to impose such a policy unilaterally if he deemed it "in the best interests of baseball"?

12. Should Pete Rose be permanently denied entry into the Hall of Fame? What factors should be considered in determining eligibility for the Hall? Should Rose's guilty plea and five-month sentence for tax fraud be relevant? If on-the-field performance alone qualifies one for entry, how do we justify Rose's denial? The same question persists with regard to Chicago White Sox (also "Black Sox") superstar "Shoeless" Joe Jackson. However, if sound character and other personal factors are to be considered, how do we explain the membership of Detroit Tiger and avowed racist Ty Cobb? The most notorious off-the-field stain on an athlete's reputation is O.J. Simpson's alleged double murder, but Simpson remains in football's Hall. Should Simpson's acquittal preclude a commissioner from banning the former running back from the game, or should the commissioner be able to make his own determination? The commissioner's office, unsurprisingly, has apparently determined that not-guilty verdicts do not constrain commissioner discretion — the Black Sox were acquitted after less than three hours' deliberation.

Indeed, Rose is not the only professional athlete to have engaged in gambling activities. National Football League superstars Paul Hornung and Alex Karras received one-year suspensions for betting on NFL games. They were not permanently denied access to the sport nor were they declared ineligible for the Football Hall of Fame. At the same time, Billy Cannon's election was rescinded when, years after his career was over, he was convicted of counterfeiting and other offenses having nothing to do with his NFL career. There have even been rumors to the effect that Michael Jordan's brief hiatus from the NBA to play professional baseball was a silent suspension prompted by his extensive gambling activities (unrelated to basketball). Is baseball's preoccupation with gambling dating back to the Black Sox scandal the reason for Rose's severe punishment, or was Rose's sanction predicated on something else?

13. Commissioners have also seen fit to regulate the appearance of participants, sometimes provoking the irritation of those who must abide by such rules. The Kentucky Horse Racing Authority suspended three jockeys for wearing an advertisement on their pants during the 2005 Kentucky Derby, over Hall of Fame jockey Kent Desormeaux's protests that the ban infringed his free speech rights. More well known is NBA Commissioner David Stern's decision to impose a "business-casual" dress code on NBA players for all team events, including travel to and from games. The dress code has not been challenged by the NBPA. Is it a mandatory subject of bargaining? Consider the question again when you read Chapters 14 & 15.

14. How far can a commissioner go to circumscribe an athlete's freedom of speech or expression? Incidents such as Atlanta Braves pitcher John Rocker's infamous interview in which he leveled a broadside attach on minorities, foreigners, and the City of New York in general bring the issue to the fore. There Rocker was suspended for 73 days for con-

duct deemed not in the best interests of baseball. This suspension was reduced by an arbitrator who sustained the commissioner's right to "intervene" but found the penalty to be excessive. *See* Lewis Kurlantzick, *Symposium: John Rocker: John Rocker and Employee Discipline for Speech*, 11 MARQ. SPORTS L. REV. 185 (2001). *See also* Christopher J. McKinny, *Professional Sports Leagues and the First Amendment: A Closed Market*, 13 MARQ. SPORTS L. REV. 223 (2003). An interesting freedom of expression case that never reached the formal litigation stage involved NBA star Mahmoud Abdul-Rauf, who, due to his Muslim faith, refused to stand at attention for the National Anthem. After the imposition of a suspension by Commissioner David Stern and the filing of a grievance by the NBPA, the parties reached a compromise in which Abdul-Rauf agreed to stand with his hands in a position of prayer to Allah. *See* McKinny, *supra,* at 243. What about a commissioner's power to regulate the artistic expression of players who write a song with controversial lyrics, such as Philadelphia 76ers flamboyant superstar Allen Iverson's explicit rap song, left on the cutting room floor after serious castigation by Commissioner Stern? *See* McKinny, *supra,* at 223–24. For further discussion of the commissioner's authority to sanction players for off-the-field misbehavior, see Anna L. Jefferson, *The NFL and Domestic Violence: The Commissioner's Power to Punish Domestic Abusers*, 7 SETON HALL J. SPORTS L. 353 (1997). *See* Ellen E. Dabbs, *Intentional Fouls: Athletes and Violence Against Women*, 31 COLUM. J. L. & SOC. PROBS. 167 (1998); Carrie A. Moser, *Penalties, Fouls, and Errors: Professional Athletes and Violence Against Women*, 11 SPORTS LAW J. 69 (2004).

15. *Rose v. Giamatti* sends a message that commissioners must be mindful of limits to their authority. Indeed, the power wielded by commissioners may be extremely illusory, resting on the precarious footing of the owners' caprice. The following case again illustrates that the commissioner is not sacrosanct, particularly when he has the temerity to challenge baseball's established order. Tampering with league alignment, potentially disrupting established rivalries, constitutes daring conduct by any commissioner, not to mention one whose position is somewhat tenuous. At the time of the following decision, Commissioner Fay Vincent's regime was already tottering as a result of his directive that the owners abandon the 1990 lockout and his earlier decision to assign American League clubs only a 22% share of National League expansion revenues (despite requiring those American League teams to provide their share of players for the expansion draft). One American League owner had already declared, "That's it. Fay Vincent is history." ZIMBALIST at 44–45.

Chicago National League Ball Club, Inc. v. Vincent
1992 U.S. Dist. LEXIS 14948 (N.D. Ill. 1992)

CONLON, District Judge. Plaintiff Chicago National League Ball Club, Inc. ("the Chicago Cubs") challenges the authority of defendant Francis T. Vincent, Jr., Commissioner of Major League Baseball ("the Commissioner") to transfer the Chicago Cubs to the Western Division of the National League of Professional Baseball Clubs ("the National League"). The Chicago Cubs also claim that the Commissioner's action is arbitrary and capricious. The Chicago Cubs seek declaratory and injunctive relief against the Commissioner, and now move to preliminarily enjoin him from enforcing his order. Issuance of a preliminary injunction would maintain the *status quo* and enable the Chicago Cubs to remain in the Eastern Division pending a final decision on the merits of this case.

***

FINDINGS OF FACT

* * *

3. The Chicago Cubs have continuously played baseball in Chicago since 1876, and are a charter member of the National League.

4. The Chicago Cubs have been in the Eastern Division since 1969, when the National League was divided into two divisions.

5. The position of Commissioner was created by the Major League Agreement of January 12, 1921, following the infamous Black Sox scandal. Federal Judge Kenesaw Mountain Landis served as the first Commissioner. Judge Landis insisted that proposed limitations on his authority be eliminated or he would not accept the position. The club owners agreed to Judge Landis' demands.

6. The Major League Agreement was amended in 1944 after Judge Landis' death. The club owners removed a provision that waived their right to recourse to the courts to challenge the Commissioner's actions. The amended agreement added a provision declaring that no action taken in compliance with a major league rule shall be deemed detrimental to baseball. These two amendments were in effect through the terms of the next two Commissioners, Albert B. Chandler and Ford C. Frick.

7. After Commissioner Frick's retirement in 1964, three relevant amendments were made to the Major League Agreement. First, the owners deleted the 1944 provision declaring that actions taken in compliance with major league rules shall not be deemed detrimental to baseball. Second, the provision waiving the club owners' right to challenge the Commissioner's decisions in court was restored. Third, the language pertaining to the Commissioner's broad authority was modified. Whereas the Commissioner previously had to find conduct "detrimental" to baseball, the Commissioner's modified authority extends to conduct "not in the best interest of Baseball."

8. The Commissioner derives his authority solely from the Major League Agreement.

9. The National League is governed by a constitution. The National League Constitution addresses membership, finances, officers, appeals, committees, club owner meetings, the league's championship series, player contracts, misconduct, umpires, gate receipts and divisional alignments.

10. In 1968, the National League Constitution was amended to divide the league into two divisions. Member clubs were assigned to each division. Divisional realignment required the unanimous consent of all clubs.

11. In 1982, the National League Constitution was amended to require approval by three-fourths of the clubs for league expansion and divisional realignment, provided that no club could be transferred to a different division without its consent. These provisions are still in effect.

12. On March 4, 1992, the realignment at issue was submitted to a vote by the National League clubs. Ten clubs voted in favor of the proposed realignment; the Chicago Cubs and the New York Mets object to the proposal. The proposal was defeated because the Chicago Cubs, one of the clubs to be transferred, did not consent.

13. Despite defeat of the proposal, several National League clubs continued to press for realignment of the divisions. A telephonic conference was held on April 6, 1992 to determine whether to seek the Commissioner's assistance in the dispute. Five clubs (Atlanta, Montreal, Pittsburgh, San Diego and San Francisco) agreed that the Commissioner's intervention was appropriate. Five other clubs (Cincinnati, Los Angeles, New

York, Philadelphia and St. Louis) opposed intervention by the Commissioner. The Houston and Chicago clubs did not participate in the conference. However, it was noted that Houston supported the Commissioner's intervention, while the Chicago Cubs clearly did not.

14. On May 29, 1992, the Commissioner solicited opinions from National League clubs on whether he should intervene. William D. White, President of the National League, responded:

> Changes in areas covered by the League constitution should only be achieved by members of the League and not through unprecedented individual action. The current issues simply do not justify the Commissioner invoking the extraordinary power to substitute his business judgment for that of the League.
>
> * * *
>
> To my knowledge, no commissioner has attempted * * * a wholesale intrusion into the business affairs of the Leagues such as you are apparently considering. Surely at this critical juncture in our game an abrupt reversal of these long established expectations and understandings will inflame the current divisions to such an extent that any temporary benefits obtained from your decision could become almost an afterthought in the acrimony and litigation that may result.

15. The Chicago Cubs and New York Mets voiced opinions that the Commissioner lacked authority to overturn a realignment decision governed by the National League Constitution.

16. On July 6, 1992, the Commissioner issued his "Decision on National League Realignment and Sharing of Gate Receipts" ("the decision" or "the order"). The order transfers the Chicago Cubs and the St. Louis Cardinals to the Western Division and transfers the Atlanta Braves and the Cincinnati Reds to the Eastern Division, effective in the 1993 championship season.

17. In issuing his decision, the Commissioner relied on his broad authority under the Major League agreement:

> to investigate * * * any act, transaction or practice * * * not in the best interests of the national game of Baseball * * * [and] to determine * * * what preventive, remedial or punitive action is appropriate * * * and to take such action. * * *

18. In his order, the Commissioner stated that his powers under the Major League Agreement were broad enough to overturn a decision made in conformity with the National League Constitution, notwithstanding a specific provision in Article VII of the agreement that limits his authority to resolve disputes between clubs. The Commissioner concluded that the National League constitutional provisions—requiring the transferred club's consent—did not serve the best interests of baseball because the Chicago Cubs' veto "thwarts the preferences of the great majority of National League Clubs."

19. The Major League Agreement, signed by all National and American League clubs, confers upon the Commissioner the sole and exclusive right to decide:

> All disputes and controversies related in any way to professional baseball between clubs * * * other than those whose resolution is expressly provided for by another means * * * in the constitution of either Major League. * * *

20. In challenging the Commissioner's decision, the Chicago Cubs contend that Sections 9.4 and 16.1 of the National League Constitution expressly provide for resolution

of realignment disputes. Both of these provisions flatly bar a divisional transfer if the affected club does not consent.

21. Section 9.4 of the National League Constitution provides that the composition of the Eastern and Western Divisions

> * * * shall not be changed except by a three-fourths vote of all the clubs of the League: provided, however, that no member club may be transferred to a different division without its consent.

22. Section 9.4 placed the Chicago Cubs in the Eastern Division.

23. Section 16.1 of the National League Constitution governs amendment procedures. A provision of the National League Constitution may be amended by a three-fourths vote of all member clubs. One of only two exceptions provides that:

> [N]o club may be transferred to a division different from that provided in Section 9.4 of Article 9 without its consent * * *

24. The parties' dispute centers on whether the broad "best interests of baseball" authority in the Major League Agreement empowers the Commissioner to abrogate the Chicago Cubs' right to [veto] their transfer to the Western Division. Implicit in this dispute is the question whether the Commissioner is empowered to unilaterally amend the National League Constitution simply because he finds that a constitutional provision or procedure is "not in the best interests of baseball."

25. The Commissioner's realignment order transferring the Chicago Cubs to the Western Division is without precedent.

26. The Chicago Cubs have requested expedited consideration of the emergency motion for a preliminary injunction. Under an agreement between the major league clubs and the players association, the President of the National League was to submit the schedule for the 1993 season to the players association by July 1, 1992. This deadline was extended to July 31, 1992, at the Commissioner's request.

27. If the schedule for the 1993 season is based on the Commissioner's realignment order, the Chicago Cubs would not be competing with their traditional Eastern Division rivals for the divisional championship. It is also likely that under a new divisional format, the Chicago Cubs will play fewer games against their traditional Eastern Division rivals and will play more games on the West Coast.

28. Games on the West Coast begin three hours later than those in the Eastern Time Zone, thus affecting prime time radio and television coverage for Chicago fans.

29. The Chicago Cubs have not advanced their claim that the Commissioner's decision was arbitrary and capricious as a basis for requesting a preliminary injunction. Thus, the wisdom of the Commissioner's decision is not before the court. For this reason, the court has denied several motions by fans and others for leave to file *amicus* briefs. This court is not acting as an umpire regarding the disputed merits of the realignment order. Rather, the court must preliminarily determine whether the Commissioner has exceeded his authority and impaired the Chicago Cubs' contractual rights.

CONCLUSIONS OF LAW

* * *

4. To evaluate the likelihood of success on the merits, the court must preliminarily determine whether the Major League Agreement authorized the Commissioner's trans-

fer order, in derogation of the Chicago Cubs' right to veto a divisional transfer under the National League Constitution.

* * *

13. Under Illinois rules for construing contracts, it is clear that the broad authority granted the Commissioner by Article I of the Major League Agreement is not as boundless as he suggests. Giving the language of Article I its common sense and ordinary meaning, the Commissioner's authority to investigate "acts," "transactions" and "practices" and to determine and take "preventive, remedial or punitive action" does not encompass restructuring the divisions of the National League. There has been no conduct [or misconduct] for the Commissioner to investigate, punish or remedy under Article I. The veto exercised by the Chicago Cubs as a matter of contractual right merely resulted in the maintenance of long-standing divisional assignments reflected in the National League Constitution.

14. The Commissioner relies on the Seventh Circuit's decision in *Finley v. Kuhn,* 569 F.2d 527 (7th Cir. 1978) to support his expansive view of Article I. In *Finley,* the owner of the Oakland Athletics attempted to sell contract rights for the services of three Oakland players. The Commissioner disapproved the assignments as inconsistent with the best interests of baseball. The owner sued, challenging the Commissioner's authority, and lost the case. *Finley* is distinguishable because there the Commissioner was responding to affirmative conduct. The underlying purpose for Oakland's maneuvering was to avoid an upcoming deadline after which it could not sell the players' contracts without first offering them to all other teams at a stipulated waiver price of $20,000. Unlike the Chicago Cubs, Oakland was not acting pursuant to any contractual right authorized by the American League Constitution.

15. More on point is *Atlanta National League Baseball Club, Inc. v. Kuhn,* 432 F. Supp. 1213 (N.D.Ga. 1977). There, the Atlanta Braves and their owner Ted Turner sued the Commissioner. Turner and the Braves challenged the Commissioner's authority to sanction Turner for violating major league rules against tampering with potential free agents. The Commissioner had investigated Turner's conduct in attempting to sign free agent Gary Matthews. The Commissioner found that Turner's conduct subverted a collective bargaining agreement and was not in the best interests of baseball. The Commissioner declined to interfere with the contract between Matthews and the Braves, but instead chose to suspend Turner from baseball for one year and eliminate the Braves' upcoming first round draft choice. The court upheld Turner's suspension, but found that the Commissioner exceeded his authority in eliminating the Braves' upcoming first round draft choice. Because the latter sanction is not enumerated in the Major League Agreement, the court stated:

> If the Commissioner is to have the unlimited punitive authority as he says is needed to deal with new and changing situation, the [Major League] agreement should be changed to expressly grant the Commissioner that power.

16. The Commissioner also cites two prior actions to support his position: Commissioner Kuhn's 1976 reversal of the National League's rejection of an expansion plan and Commissioner Ueberroth's 1985 approval of a new minority owner of the Texas Rangers. In both of these actions, the Commissioner overrode voting requirements of a league constitution. The Commissioner contends that these actions constitute "strong precedent" for his realignment decision. * * * These incidents did not arise under comparable factual circumstances and implicated different constitutional provisions. More importantly, the fact that these actions did not result in a court challenge is neither pro-

bative nor persuasive evidence that the Commissioner in fact acted within his authority on those occasions.

17. Even if the terms "act," "transaction" or "practice" were construed to apply to the Chicago Cubs' exercise of its veto right against divisional transfer, the Commissioner's Article I authority must be considered in light of Article VII. Article VII expressly limits the Commissioner's jurisdiction to resolution of disputes "other than those whose resolution is expressly provided for by another means in * * * the [Major League] constitution." * * *

18. Sections 9.4 and 16.1 explicitly provide the means for resolving disputes among clubs concerning divisional realignment; any decision is conditioned on the consent of a transferred club. These provisions manifest a clear intention to protect the substantial interest of an individual club in its divisional assignment from adverse action by the majority.

19. Reading Article I in light of Article VII, the Commissioner lacked authority to unilaterally abrogate the Chicago Cubs' rights under Sections 9.4 and 16.1 of the National League Constitution. Accordingly, there is a strong likelihood that the Chicago Cubs shall prevail on the merits.

20. The Chicago Cubs' contractual right to remain in the Eastern Division is unique. Money damages could not adequately compensate for the loss of the intangible benefits of this unique right. * * * The prospective loss of decades-old rivalries against Eastern Division teams constitutes sufficient evidence of irreparable harm for which there is not adequate remedy at law.

24. Harm to the Chicago Cubs absent a preliminary injunction is great. If the Chicago Cubs ultimately prevail, reversing their transfer to the Western Division would be problematic, particularly once the 1993 championship season schedule is finalized.

25. There is no discernable harm to the Commissioner in maintaining the *status quo*. If the Commissioner ultimately prevails on the merits, transfer of the Chicago Cubs to the Western Division would be delayed one year while the traditional division of the National League are maintained.

26. There is no evidence that issuance of a preliminary injunction will harm the public interest.

CONCLUSION AND ORDER

The undisputed facts reasonably support a preliminary finding that the Commissioner exceeded his authority in ordering the transfer of the Chicago Cubs to the Western Division. The Commissioner's unprecedented action violated Article VII of the Major League Agreement. By reason of Sections 9.4 and 16.1 of the National League Constitution, the Chicago Cubs may not be transferred to the Western Division without their consent.

The Chicago Cubs have satisfied the requirements for issuance of a preliminary injunction. Accordingly, defendant Francis T. Vincent, Jr., Commissioner of Major League Baseball, is enjoined from ordering the transfer of the Chicago Cubs from the Eastern Division to the Western Division of the National League, pending final resolution of the merits of this case.

On September 24, 1992 Judge Conlon issued the following Order:

Upon consideration of the parties' Joint Motion to Withdraw and Vacate Findings of Fact, Conclusions of Law and Order, Dissolve Preliminary Injunction and Dismiss, it is ORDERED:

1. that this Court's Findings of Fact, Conclusions of Law and Order of July 23, 1992 be, and are hereby, withdrawn and vacated;

2. that the preliminary injunction entered in this matter on July 23, 1992 be, and is hereby, dissolved; and

3. that this action be, and is hereby, dismissed without prejudice, each side to bear its own reimbursable court costs.

Notes and Questions

1. Eventually, Major League Baseball re-aligned itself dramatically and now even engages in inter-league play. Yet, the foregoing case, along with Commissioner Vincent's aforementioned no-lockout order and unpopular expansion revenue distribution decision, were pivotal features of the owners' eventual decision to look elsewhere for a "leader." *See* Thomas Boswell, *Down and Dirty in Scapegoat Game*, Wash. Post, Sept. 4, 1992. Close observers of Major League Baseball should not have been surprised that Vincent's belief in his own untouchability was either woefully misguided or simply constituted whistling past the graveyard. As one commentator had stated prophetically:

> [O]ver the course of a five-year term, too many controversial decisions by a commissioner are likely to create too many enemies for reappointment. Given the structural fragility of the job, it is difficult to envisage even the most enlightened of commissioners successfully leading MLB through its maze of economic and political challenges in the 1990s.

ZIMBALIST at 45. Marvin Miller formed the opinion that Vincent had become a charter member of the "Illusion of The Commissioner Having Real Power Club" as evidenced by Vincent's statement that "'I'm not going to resign * * * [T]he decision whether I stay or go is mine * * * [T]hat's the way it is.'" MILLER at 406–07. The "way it was," however, was that Vincent received a compelling 18-9 vote of "no confidence" and he resigned shortly thereafter. Vincent was not the first baseball commissioner to delude himself into thinking that his ouster was an impossibility.

Happy Chandler, successor to Judge Landis, also demanded a vote of confidence and an early extension of his then seven-year term. The owners rejected him 9-7 and he later resigned. Chandler, like Vincent, had sealed his own fate by misjudging the power and retaliatory motives of the owners: "I always regarded baseball as our National Game that belongs to 150 million men, women and children, * * * not to sixteen special people who happen to own big league teams." WARD & BURNS at 320. Again, like Vincent, Chandler was misperceived by the owners as a person who could be counted upon to follow marching orders and to do so in a congenial, obsequious fashion. A final parallel between Chandler and Vincent rests in the mixed reviews they receive as players' commissioners. For example, historian John Helyar states that Chandler was "suspiciously sympathetic to the interests of the players." HELYAR at 76. Yet, Marvin Miller disputes Chandler's sensitivity to the players and echoes venerable columnist Red Smith's characterization of Chandler as a pawn for the owners. The normally reserved Smith was particularly critical, commenting at one point, "[i]f I can get paid for thinking Happy Chandler has performed like a clown and a mountebank, then I want all that kind of money I can get. Ordinarily, I have to work for mine." MILLER at 57.

Fay Vincent, likewise, receives no consensus as a players' commissioner. On the one hand, he was scorned for ending the 1990 lockout, perceived by some observers as a betrayal of the owners. On the other hand, he has been criticized for his allegiance to the ownership component on such matters as the collusion case in which the owners were found guilty of conspiring to deny free agency opportunities to the players in violation of the collective bargaining agreement. Vincent had commented that punishing guilty owners for their collusive activity would constitute double jeopardy because the owners had already absorbed 280 million dollars in a back pay settlement. This comment prompted Marvin Miller's wry observation: "Imagine that a bank robber was caught red-handed, convicted and forced to return the loot—and then claimed that going to jail constituted double jeopardy!" *Id.* at 400. One telling comment linking the unceremonious terminations of Commissioners Vincent and Chandler is offered by baseball historian Daniel Okrent: "Fay Vincent has been cashiered by the owners, and however much we may feel for the man, we feel even worse about his job." WARD & BURNS at 467, quoting DANIEL OKRENT, ALWAYS RIGHT ON TIME (1994).

2. In any event, many commentators believe that Vincent's short tenure was characterized by an overriding concern for the best interests of the game as a whole rather than any of its constituent and often bickering factions. *See* Mike Penner, *Too Good For Game He Loves*, L.A. Times, Sept. 9, 1992, Sports, Part C, at 1. Should the commissioner be a chief executive officer or chiefoperating officer merely reporting to the owners and under their absolute control or should he be an independent force, advancing the best interests of the sport, even when those interests run counter to the individual concerns of one or all of the owners?

3. In the wake of Commissioner Vincent's departure, the owners amended the Major League Agreement to designate the commissioner as head of the Player Relations Committee. Article I, Section 2. The Player Relations Committee is the negotiating arm of baseball's owners and assumes full responsibility for collective bargaining with the Players Association. As will be discussed in detail later, the creation of this type of committee is designed to isolate labor relations responsibility to a small group of owners and to limit potential legal liability under pertinent labor laws. By "elevating" the commissioner to the chairmanship of the Player Relations Committee, the owners removed him as an independent overseer of player-club labor relations. Thus, the owners believe that commissioner intervention into the bargaining process as a non-participant (which has occurred on more than one occasion in the past) would be preempted. Of course, any questionable commissioner conduct would likely be imputed to the other owners, carrying possible attendant liability under the labor laws. Further, Major League Baseball welcomed the twenty-first century by formally expanding the commissioner's authority to block trades if they are deemed detrimental to the sport and to increase monetary fines against teams from $250,000 to $2 million. In a more undefined sense, baseball also bequeathed the commissioner with the power to ensure the long term competitive balance among the teams.

4. In the past, the Commissioner of Baseball served as "neutral" arbitrator in numerous contexts. With the coming of age of the Players Association and the development of a meaningful collective bargaining agreement, the commissioner's authority to resolve disputes without question has been circumscribed to issues pertaining to the best interests of baseball. In these areas, the commissioner may act unilaterally without regard to the grievance and arbitration mechanism of the collective bargaining agreement. In fact, such agreement expressly excludes such matters from the arbitration procedure. *See* Basic Agreement between the American League of Professional Baseball Clubs and the National League of Professional Baseball Clubs and Major League Baseball Players Association (2003–2006), Art. XI(A)(1)(b). Yet, in cases dealing with player discipline that arguably affect the best interests of baseball (such as suspensions for drug use), it

bears mention that the commissioner generally grants the player's request for an independent arbitrator. Must he do so? *See id.* at Art. XII.

5. While other sports also give the commissioner power to impose discipline in certain contexts without intervention of the collective bargaining agreement's grievance mechanism, traditional arbitration procedures typically will be employed to resolve most of these disputes. *See, e.g.,* Collective Bargaining Agreement Between National Football League and National Football League Players Association (1993–2000), Arts. IX and XI; Collective Bargaining Agreement Between National Basketball Association and the National Basketball Players Association, Art. XXI, Section B.

Section 35(d) of the NBA Constitution gives the commissioner authority to impose discipline for player misbehavior. Appeals from impositions of discipline generally proceed to arbitration for review under an arbitrary-and-capricious standard. NBA Collective Bargaining Agreement, article XXXI. Suspensions or fines "for conduct on the playing court," however, may be appealed only to the commissioner himself. NBA CBA, article XXXI, §8. In what may be the worst episode of violence at a game in the history of the NBA, a brawl between the Detroit Pistons and the Indiana Pacers resulted in players entering the stands and fighting with fans. Commissioner David Stern suspended several of the players who were involved in the incident. When the players appealed the suspensions to an arbitrator, Stern argued that the appeals were "for conduct on the playing court" and under the CBA could be appealed only to him. The arbitrator and a federal district judge rejected that argument, holding that entering the stands was not conduct "on the court." *National Basketball Ass'n v. National Basketball Players Ass'n*, 2004 U.S. Dist. LEXIS 26244 (S.D.N.Y. 2004). Indeed, the very fact that the fight was *not* on the court is what caused the incident to be so noteworthy.

6. Baseball does grant the commissioner the authority to issue a unilateral determination on matters affecting the integrity of the game, but, as stated above, baseball commissioners have not availed themselves of this prerogative in many discipline cases, choosing rather to allow review by a neutral arbitrator. At times, commissioners have rued the day that they permitted arbitral review over major disciplinary decisions. Perhaps the most significant and controversial example in this regard involved New York Yankee pitcher Steve Howe who, after six prior suspensions for drug use and an off-season incident in which Howe was arrested on a cocaine possession charge, was banned from baseball for life by Commissioner Fay Vincent. The "lifetime" ban was short-lived, however, as arbitrator George Nicolau upheld Howe's grievance and reversed Commissioner Vincent's decision. Crucial to Nicolau's decision was his opinion that Vincent had not adequately heeded the warnings of his medical advisor, who recommended that Howe be tested year-round, "every other day for the rest of his professional career." Vincent did place conditions on Howe's return, but the required testing was not as rigorous as had been suggested and was irregularly administered.

> While Howe can certainly be faulted for seeking to delay testing at a time of his admittedly increasing sense of vulnerability, the Office of the Commissioner cannot escape its measure of responsibility for what took place. * * * Based on medical advice the Commissioner had solicited, the need for continuous testing was obvious. To give Howe 'yet another chance' of returning to the game without implementing those conditions was not, in my judgment, a fair shot at success.

Major League Baseball Players Association and the Commissioner of Major League Baseball (Howe) (Nicolau, Arbitrator, 1992). Panel Decision No. 94 at 48. Did Vincent bear "responsibility" for not overseeing Howe more closely? Should the Commissioner have any duty to give offenders a "fair shot at success"? How different would the criminal justice system appear if offenders were entitled to Nicolau's version of a "fair shot at success" upon release?

To add insult to injury, Nicolau admonished Vincent and, in the process, reminded all that the awesome power of the commissioner's office should not be abused:

> What bears repeating here is that the Commissioner does not stand in the isolated position of an individual employer. He can bar the employment of a player at any level of the game regardless of the opinion or wishes of any one of a great number of potential employers. That is an awesome power. With it comes a heavy responsibility, especially when that power is exercised unilaterally and not as the result of a collectively bargained agreement as to the level of sanctions to *be imposed for particular actions.*

Id. at 49–50.

Was Arbitrator Nicolau needlessly harsh in his implications that the commissioner had abused his authority? Does the power to "bar the employment of a player at any level of the game regardless of the opinion or wishes of any one of a great number of potential employers" raise antitrust concerns? *See Molinas v. National Basketball Ass'n,* 190 F. Supp. 241 (S.D.N.Y. 1961). What is the significance of the emotional baggage that gambling and drug use carry in terms of their impact on professional sports? Of what relevance should it have been that Howe was afflicted with Attention Deficit Hyperactivity Disorder, which contributed to his drug abuse? Shortly after Howe's career ended, he was arrested for attempting to board a plane with a loaded .357 Magnum in his luggage. He died in 2006 after losing control of his car and being ejected from the vehicle.

7. The problems of drug abuse and other matters dramatically affecting the integrity of the game, and the difficulties inherent in developing a collective response to such problems will be addressed in subsequent chapters (*see* Chapters 14–16). Suffice it to say that these issues represent a significant challenge to the commissioner's office, particularly in terms of the "judgment calls" that must be made where the integrity of the game is at stake. *See further In re NFL Management Council and NFL Players Ass'n (Reese/Crowder)* (Scearce, Arbitrator, 1979).

As NHL commissioner or as a general counsel advising the commissioner, what recommendations would you make if you were confronted with the following situation? A goaltender on a contending team is arrested during the first round of the Stanley Cup playoffs for possession of mind-altering substances. The commissioner's office conducts an investigation and has no independent basis to suspect the player of drug use, but the local district attorney has decided to indict the player on a number of drug-related charges. If, on the one hand, you choose to suspend the player, and he is later exonerated, you have compromised the possible success of his club and likewise may have caused irreparable damage to his career. No amount of backpay or other monetary recompense will be adequate to remedy the effects of his suspension. On the other hand, it is arguable that as commissioner you possess your own prosecutorial authority and, in order to protect the integrity of the game, not to mention the player who could be injured as a result of his potential drug abuse, are entitled to take interim action. The potential intrusions upon one's "private" due process rights, guaranteed by the standard player contract, collective bargaining agreement, and league rules, cannot be overstated. At the same time, the potential harm to the game and its participants is likewise of paramount importance to the commissioner. To complicate matters further, what if the player with diminished capacity were a pitcher or other player whose lack of total "control" could visit serious injury upon another player or fans? *See generally* Jan Stiglitz, *Player Discipline in Team Sports*, 5 Marq. Sports. L.J. 167 (1995).

8. The quandary created in the suspension/due process context is more than an academic curiosity. In late September, 1996, Roberto Alomar, second baseman for the Baltimore Orioles, engaged in an altercation with home plate umpire John Hirschbeck over a called third strike. During the argument, Alomar spit in Hirschbeck's face. The American League President, Gene Budig, suspended Alomar for five games commencing with the start of the 1997 regular season. This decision, which was appealed by the Players Association, enabled Alomar to participate in post-season play (the Orioles had already earned the right to play the Cleveland Indians in the American League Division Series). The delayed suspension triggered protests from the umpires and others who claimed that the suspension should have taken effect immediately. This dispute presented an interesting dilemma. On the one hand, the gravity of the offense suggests that allowing Alomar to play in the post-season was too lenient. On the other hand, an immediate suspension would have subverted the player's right to a meaningful hearing, assuming that there were issues resolvable through an evidentiary proceeding (*e.g.*, material issues of fact). This dilemma could have been reconciled by conducting an expedited hearing, with an opportunity for argument, at the end of the season. A decision could have been rendered that allowed for appropriate and timely discipline without compromise to the player's due process rights. For further discussion of this incident, see Chapter 14, Part V(B), where this incident is treated in conjunction with a discussion of the current relationship between game officials and players.

9. For those who believe that everything evens out in the long run, the Alomar incident has an interesting postscript. His twelfth inning home run provided the margin of victory that catapulted the Orioles into the American League Championship Series against the New York Yankees. His crucial error in the fifth game of that series led to the Orioles' four-games-to-one demise.

10. As a result of the league's decision to postpone Alomar's suspension until the start of the 1997 season, the Association of Major League Umpires threatened to strike, notwithstanding a provision in their collective bargaining agreement with Major League Baseball prohibiting strikes. The league secured an injunction and the umpires refrained from engaging in any work stoppage. The validity of the injunction, however, is questionable given the fact that under prevailing Supreme Court precedent, a peaceful strike cannot be enjoined even in the face of a no-strike clause unless the underlying dispute is arbitrable. *See Boys Markets, Inc. v. Retail Clerks Union*, Local 770, 398 U.S. 235 (1970). Is an umpire's protest over league treatment of a player and member of a sister labor organization a grievable issue subject to the umpires' union contract's arbitration mechanism? In resolving questions of this nature, the collective bargaining agreement must be examined in detail to ascertain whether the matter in dispute is covered. *See* Chapter 14, Part IX(A).

III. Status of Commissioner

In the morass that surrounds the parameters of commissioner authority, the preeminent question is often overlooked: Who and what is a league commissioner? Is he an employer or sufficiently allied with employers so as to be their agent in terms of some type of corporate liability? If he is aligned with employers, does he owe the owners a fiduciary duty to act in their best interests? Is he a third party who answers neither to the employer nor to the employees and their collective bargaining representative? The types of problems presented by the fact that this issue has never been resolved definitively are illustrated in the following cases.

National Football League Players Ass'n v. NLRB
503 F.2d 12 (8th Cir. 1974)

HEANEY, Circuit Judge. The National Football League Player's Association [Union] petitions this Court to review an order of the National Labor Relations Board dismissing a complaint against the Employers, consisting of the National Football League [Owners] and the National Football League Management Council [Council].[1] The complaint alleged that Employers violated §8(a)(5) and (1) of the National Labor Relations Act, 29 U.S.C.§151, et seq., by unilaterally establishing a rule that "any player leaving the bench area while a fight is in progress on the field will be fined $200." The Board's decision and order is reported at 203 N.L.R.B. No. 165 (1973).

We emphasize at the outset that the wisdom of the rule is not at issue here. The sole question before us is whether the Board erred in dismissing the complaint on the ground that the rule was adopted and promulgated by the Commissioner of the NFL rather than by the Employers. A brief discussion of the facts is necessary to an understanding of the issue.

On January 22, 1971, the Union was certified by the NLRB as the exclusive bargaining representative for the professional football players employed by the NFL and its member clubs. A collective bargaining agreement was signed by the Union, Council's predecessor (*see*, n. 1, *supra*) and each of the member clubs on June 17, 1971, effective February 1, 1970. The Agreement expired on January 31, 1974.

In early 1971, the NFL Commissioner, Pete Rozelle, discussed with his staff the problem of injuries to players through violence on the football field. He directed a member of the NFL staff to discuss this problem with the competition committee (consisting of four Owners or their representatives) to deal with the effect of proposed changes in policy on the competitive aspects of football. The committee recommended that a rule be established to fine players who left the bench during a fight on the field. At the March 25th meeting of the Owners, the Commissioner explained the proposal to the clubs. The Owners then adopted a rule which read:

> Any player leaving the bench area while a fight is in progress on the field will be fined $200.

Rozelle subsequently fined thirty-four players for leaving the bench while a fight was in progress during the Minnesota-San Diego exhibition game on August 4, 1971, fifty-eight players for doing the same thing during the Atlanta-San Francisco game on August 15th, and fourteen players for identical conduct during the Chicago-New Orleans game on October 10th.

---

1. The League consists of twenty-six member clubs. The Council is an unincorporated organization designated by the clubs as their collective bargaining representative, and was formerly known as the National Football League Players Relations Association [NFLPRA]. Hereinafter, the NFLPRA is referred to as the Council.

On September 30th, the Union's Executive Director, Edward Garvey, wrote to the Commissioner requesting information with respect to the fines imposed as a result of the Minnesota-San Diego incident. On October 18th, Garvey again wrote to the Commissioner. He appealed the imposition of the fines on players who had left the bench during the Minnesota-San Diego and Atlanta-San Francisco games. He did so on the grounds that the players had not been notified of the new rule and that the rule imposing the fines was violative of the Collective Bargaining Agreement, which provided that:

> * * * any change in current practices affecting employment conditions of the players shall be negotiated in good faith.

Commissioner Rozelle replied to the two letters on October 21st. He wrote:

> While still considering your letter of September 30 regarding player fines I am now in receipt of your October 18 letter on the same subject. *The action taken as the result of the player fights was done so under a resolution passed by the member clubs* last March. It reads:
>
> "Any player leaving the bench area while a fight is in progress on the field will be fined $200."
>
> * * *
>
> It has been the long-standing policy of this office to most certainly accord any disciplined players the right of appeal to the Commissioner, either through writing or hearing, but I have serious doubts whether the [Union] has jurisdiction in the area of player fines for misconduct during the course of a game. Therefore, I believe I must request written argument from the [Union] and the [Council] on this issue before I can entertain any grievance initiated by the [Union]. (Emphasis added.)

The Union responded as follows:

> * * * [T]he Collective Bargaining Agreement makes it clear that the [Union] may appeal any grievance that it so desires. Article XII, Section (d) states:
>
> "Any such fine and amount thereof, however, may be made the subject of a grievance in accordance with the provisions of Article X hereof."
>
> Article X relates to the non-injury grievance procedure, and Step 1 states:
>
> "Any NFL player or the [Union] may present a written grievance to any member club or to the League itself within sixty days * * *"
>
> I completely reject any suggestion that we could not have jurisdiction in this matter, given the clear language of the Collective Bargaining Agreement. * * *

It also raised a series of questions going to the merits of the issue.[2]

On December 29, 1971, Garvey wrote to Commissioner Rozelle stating that he was withdrawing the entire matter from the Commissioner's hands and that he was asking the Council to begin negotiations on the matter. He stated that he understood Rozelle's

---

2. Some of the questions posed by Garvey were:
* * * [D]id the League determine the players who had left the bench while a fight was in progress on the field? If so, how did the League make this determination? Since the ball changed hands in both instances, is a player on the offensive or defensive team who would normally take the field under these circumstances, subject to a fine? Did the League study the films or did the League simply impose the fine on the clubs and ask the clubs to make the determination of who was to be fined and who was not to be fined?

position to be that he was simply implementing a decision of the Owners and that, therefore, the matter was not properly before him.

On February 1, 1972, the Council's Executive Director wrote to Garvey as follows:

> We take the position that [the Commissioner] was acting under the powers vested in him as Commissioner under the Collective Bargaining Agreement which incorporates by reference both the NFL Constitution and By-Laws and the Standard Player Contract.
>
> In the absence of language to the contrary, we contend that he has the authority to fine a player and it is reviewable as provided for in the Constitution and By-Laws and the Standard Player Contract. They provide for the right of hearing before the Commissioner.

The Union filed an unfair labor practice charge with the Board on December 10, 1971, alleging that the Employers' unilateral adoption of the rule was a refusal to bargain. Amended charges were filed on February 11 and May 10, 1972. The General Counsel of the N.L.R.B. issued a complaint on May 12, 1972. It alleged that the Employers violated §8(a)(5) of the Act by unilaterally promulgating and implementing a new rule providing for an automatic $200.00 fine against any player leaving the bench area during a fight or altercation on the football field during the game.

The Employers denied the Union's allegations, taking the position that the fines were Commissioner fines rather than Owner fines and that the Employers had not violated §8(a)(5) because they had not instituted the rule change. They contended, alternatively, that the action was taken more than six months prior to the filing of the charges by the Union and hence was barred by §10(b) of the Act, and that the Collective Bargaining Agreement contained grievance and arbitration mechanisms for resolution of the issue and that the Board should stay its hand in deference to those mechanisms.

The administrative law judge found: (1) that the rule was an Owners' fine rather than a Commissioner's fine; (2) that the statute of limitations did not start to run until late August of 1971 when the Executive Director of the Union first learned of the fines and that, therefore, the charges were not barred by §10(b) of the Act; and (3) that deferral to arbitration was not appropriate because there was no merit to the Employers' position and because the policy considerations underlying the deferral rule would not be satisfied by a procedure where "the arbitrator [Commissioner Rozelle] was determining the merits of his own conduct."

The Employers filed exceptions to the administrative law judge's decision.

The Board agreed that deferral would be inappropriate for the reason that the Commissioner was not a disinterested party and thus the purpose of the Act would not be served by having him resolve the dispute. It went on to state:

> As to the merits of the bench-fine issue, the General Counsel and the Union concede that *the Commissioner* has, and always has had, *the authority to impose fines for conduct detrimental to football with or without the approval of the owners.* This fact leads us to conclude that nothing of substance was changed by the owners' action at their March 25 meeting. *Since it is conceded that the Commissioner had the authority to impose the rule in issue,* and indeed was the moving force in securing an adoption of the rule by the owners, we do not perceive any meaningful or substantial unilateral conduct arising out of the meeting of the owners. Thus, if the owners had not met on March 25 and the Commissioner had levied the fines without prior consultation, there would be no dispute as to

the propriety of his conduct. What the General Counsel and Charging Party are asking us to find is that by approving the resolution, the Respondent unilaterally altered the terms and conditions of employment. We believe any such holding would exalt form over substance, in that mere approval of a rule initiated by the Commissioner adds nothing of substance when the facts show that such approval was neither required nor that it partook of any substantive difference over what the Commissioner could have done without such approval. We therefore find that Respondent's conduct on March 25 did not constitute a violation of Section 8(a)(5) and (1) and we shall accordingly dismiss that portion of the complaint. (Emphasis added.)

We understand the Board to have made the following findings: (1) that the Union conceded that the Commissioner had a right to adopt the bench-fine rule; (2) that the bench-fine rule had in fact been promulgated by the Commissioner rather than the Owners and that the Owners engaged in no meaningful or substantial conduct with respect to its adoption or promulgation; and (3) that, as a matter of law, there is no substantive difference between the Commissioner's imposing individual fines for conduct detrimental to the game after notice and hearing and promulgating the bench-fine rule—thus, promulgation of the rule was within the authority of the Commissioner.

(1) The record does not support the Board's finding that the Union conceded that the Commissioner had the right under the Collective Bargaining Agreement to adopt and promulgate the bench-fine rule; to the contrary, the Union denied that he had such a right. The Union agreed only that the Commissioner had a right pursuant to the Agreement to fine a player for conduct detrimental to the League or professional football after notice and hearing. The distinction is a meaningful one to the Union and also to us.[3] If

---

3. It is not necessary for us to decide this issue in this proceeding; suffice it to say that the Union's position is not without merit. Section 8.13(A) of the By-Laws of the League provide:

> Whenever the Commissioner, after notice and hearing, decides that * * * any player * * * has been or is guilty of conduct detrimental to * * * professional football, then the Commissioner shall have complete authority to:
>
>> (1) Suspend and/or fine such person in an amount not in excess of five thousand dollars ($5,000) * * *

Section II of the Standard Player Contract for the National Football League provides:

> Player acknowledges the right and power of the Commissioner * * * to fine and suspend * * * any player * * * who is guilty of any conduct detrimental to the welfare of the League or of professional football * * *

Article II, Section 2, of the Collective Bargaining Agreement provides:

> The provisions of this Agreement * * * supersede any conflicting provisions now existing or which shall exist during the life of this Agreement in the NFL Constitution and Bylaws, the Standard Player Contract, * * * and any other document affecting the wages, hours, or working conditions of NFL players.

Article III, Section 1, of the Agreement provides:

> * * * The Standard Player Contract shall govern the relationship between the clubs and the players, except that this Agreement shall govern if any terms of the Standard Player Contract conflict with the terms of this Agreement * * *

Article II, Section 3, of the Agreement provides that "disputes over the meaning, interpretation or proper application of the terms of this Agreement" will be determined by unanimous decisions of a joint committee on contract interpretation, and Article X provides that non-injury grievances will be resolved by a two-step grievance procedure culminating in submission to the Commissioner.

An addendum to the Agreement states that any changes in current practices affecting employment conditions of the players shall be negotiated in good faith.

It seems clear from the above that whether the Commissioner is an agent of the Employers, the joint agent of the Union and the Employers, or an independent third party, he has no authority to make changes in practices which affect employment conditions of the players. It also seems clear

the Commissioner's power is limited in the manner the Union suggests, each player who has been notified that he is being charged with conduct detrimental to the game can at the hearing attempt to prove that the conduct in question is not, in fact, detrimental and to prove that he did not engage in the proscribed conduct. The questions raised in footnote 2, for example, would have to be answered by the Commissioner.

(2) Nor does the record support the Board's finding that the bench rule was adopted by the Commissioner without meaningful or substantial conduct on the part of the Owners.

(a) The Commissioner stated in his letter of October 21, 1971, that the action was taken pursuant to a resolution passed by the member clubs. He was not called by the Employers to qualify that statement. Thus, it is fair to say that the Commissioner viewed the rule as one adopted and promulgated by the Owners and the individual fines as being levied pursuant to that rule.

(b) The Commissioner did discuss with his staff "his feeling that from now on if a player left the bench area during a fight, he felt he would have to fine him." But, he was obviously concerned about the reaction of the Owners to such a course of action and instead of announcing that such would be his policy or simply imposing a fine when an occasion occurred, he asked a member of the staff of the NFL to discuss the matter with the competition committee of the League—a committee in which only management is represented. When that committee indicated its approval, the Commissioner still wasn't satisfied. He had the committee bring a recommended resolution to the Owners for their approval. It was only when Owners voted twenty-four to two that the rule should be put into effect that the Commissioner had a press release sent out indicating that the bench-fine rule was now in effect.

(c) At no time prior to the press release did the Commissioner discuss the problem of players leaving the bench during fights with the Union. If, as the Employers contend, the Commissioner is the agent of both the Employers and the Union, and promulgated the rule as their agent, one must assume a serious breach of ethics by the Commissioner if he talked to only one of his principals. And, no one suggests that the Commissioner is an unethical man.

To summarize, every fact and inference supports the administrative law judge's conclusion that the rule was adopted and promulgated by the Owners.

(3) Finally, the Board held that because the Commissioner had the power to promulgate the bench-fine rule, he exercised that power. The premise is doubtful, *see*, n.3, *supra*, and the conclusion a *non sequitur*. While the Board is permitted to draw inferences from the facts in the record and while we are required to accept such inferences when supported by facts, we are not required to adopt inferences or conclusions that are totally lacking in factual support. We hold that the Employers, by unilaterally promulgating and implementing a rule providing for an automatic fine to be levied against any player who leaves the bench area while a fight or an altercation is in progress on the football field, have engaged in unfair labor practices within the meaning of Section 8(a) (5) and (1) of the Act.

We remand to the Board with instructions to it to adopt a remedy consistent with this opinion.

---

that when he acts in the capacity of an arbiter, he must act in an impartial manner within the authority given to him by the Collective Bargaining Agreement, and that he must decide matters presented to him on the basis of the evidence submitted by the parties.

MATTHES, Senior Circuit Judge (concurs). [Opinion omitted]

Oakland Raiders v. National Football League
32 Cal. Rptr. 3d 266 (Cal. Ct. App. 2005)

PREMO, J. The Oakland Raiders (Raiders), a member club of an unincorporated association known as the National Football League (NFL or League), sued the NFL and its commissioner, Paul Tagliabue. The Raiders alleged that the NFL and Tagliabue (collectively, defendants) took various actions that were discriminatory towards the Raiders and placed it at a competitive disadvantage vis-à-vis other member clubs. One legal theory that the Raiders advanced was breach of fiduciary duty. Defendants argued that this claim was without merit for a variety of reasons, including the absence of legal duty, and the requirement that courts abstain from involving themselves in disputes involving private voluntary associations. The court below, citing both reasons, agreed with defendants and granted summary adjudication. The Raiders appealed.

We are therefore called upon here to examine the parties' relationship to determine whether the NFL and its commissioner owe fiduciary duties to the Raiders. After reviewing the unique nature of the NFL business organization and the extent of the powers and duties of its commissioner, we conclude that neither defendant stands in a fiduciary relationship with the Raiders. We hold further that the nature of this conflict is one from which the courts properly abstain. Accordingly, after our de novo review, we conclude that summary adjudication was proper and we affirm the judgment.

PROCEDURAL HISTORY

The Raiders filed a [complaint] asserting that the NFL and/or Tagliabue breached their fiduciary duties to the Raiders.

Broadly speaking, the complaint alleged that the Raiders was discriminated against and treated unfavorably as compared with the other member clubs. The alleged breaches of fiduciary duty included: "singling the Raiders out" from other clubs and "treating the Raiders disparately and adversely"; permitting other member clubs to violate NFL rules, thereby giving them a competitive advantage over the Raiders; requiring that the Raiders (over its objection) participate with other member clubs in the European football league known as the "World League of American Football"; concealing information from the Raiders and excluding its participation in a lawsuit involving the former owner of the New England Patriots, William H. Sullivan, Jr.; and denying Al Davis (former Raiders' managing general partner) and his family permission to buy the Oakland Athletics baseball team, notwithstanding that defendants permitted violations of the League's "Cross-ownership Rule" by other club owners. In addition, the Raiders alleged that Tagliabue committed further breaches of fiduciary duty: by removing Davis from the Management Council Executive Committee in September 1995; by removing Raiders' representatives from NFL committees, and by excluding the Raiders from participating in significant NFL committees, thereby placing the Raiders at a competitive disadvantage; and by concealing from the Raiders certain rules violations by other member clubs.

[The trial court granted summary judgment to the NFL and Tagliabue.]

* * *

A. *Claims Arising out of Fiduciary Relationships, Generally*

We start with a recitation of some of the basic principles of the law of fiduciary duty. * * * A fiduciary must give "priority to the best interest of the beneficiary." In addition to this duty of preference toward the beneficiary, the fiduciary also is required to manage the subject matter of the relationship (or res) with due care, must account to the beneficiary, and must keep the beneficiary fully informed as to all matters pertinent to the beneficiary's interest in the res.

Our Supreme Court has acknowledged that it is difficult to enunciate the precise elements required to show the existence of a fiduciary relationship. But the high court has noted that "before a person can be charged with a fiduciary obligation, he must either knowingly undertake to act on behalf and for the benefit of another, or must enter into a relationship which imposes that undertaking as a matter of law."

Fiduciary duties arise as a matter of law "in certain technical, legal relationships." While this list of special relationships is one that "is not graven in stone" (CHODOS, THE LAW OF FIDUCIARY DUTIES 1 (2000)), it is useful to identify many of the relationships that give rise to fiduciary duties. They include relationships between: (1) principal and agent including real estate broker/agent and client and stockbroker and customer; (2) attorney and client; (3) partners; (4) joint venturers; (5) corporate officers and directors, on the one hand, and the corporation and its shareholders, on the other hand; (6) husband and wife, with respect to the couple's community property; (7) controlling shareholders and minority shareholders; (8) trustee and trust beneficiary; (9) guardian and ward; (10) pension fund trustee and pensioner beneficiary; (11) executor and decedent's estate; and (12) trustee and trust beneficiaries.

In numerous cases, however, California courts have rejected attempts to extend fiduciary obligations to relationships where the imposition of such an affirmative duty is unwarranted. For instance, no fiduciary relationship was found to exist as between the following: (1) an attorney and his cocounsel under the theory that the former's malpractice in handling of a mutual client's case caused damage to cocounsel in the loss of fees; (2) one shareholder and another by virtue of the fact that they were former partners in an entity that was later incorporated; (3) an unmarried cohabitant and his cohabitant concerning the operation of the former's business; (4) a movie distributor and movie producers under a distribution contract; (5) a homeowner's association and the buyer of an individual unit (with respect to disclosure of known construction defects); (6) a trade union and a union member (apart from the union's duty of fair representation); (7) a bank and its borrowers; (8) a corporation and its bondholders; (9) a clearing broker and an investment broker's customer; (10) an insurer and its insured; and (11) a manufacturer and an authorized dealer.

Many of the cases rejecting breach of fiduciary duty claims have been based (at least in part) upon the principle * * * that "[a] mere contract or a debt does not constitute a trust or create a fiduciary relationship." As a general rule, courts finding no fiduciary duty have done so "where other legal relationships clearly existed between the parties which 'covered' the transaction in suit and which were inconsistent with the existence of fiduciary duty." (Chodos, The Law of Fiduciary Duties, *supra,* p. 61.)

B. *Whether Fiduciary Relationship Existed as a Matter of Law*

We first examine whether * * * there was a triable issue of fact as to the existence of a fiduciary relationship, by virtue of the nature of the business relationship between the Raiders and defendants.

As the Ninth Circuit Court of Appeals has previously recognized, "[t]he NFL is [a] unique business organization." (*Los Angeles Memorial Coliseum Com'n v. N.F.L.* (9th Cir.1984) 726 F.2d 1381, 1401.) It is perhaps for this reason that there is no authority cited by the parties—or known by this court to exist—that is definitive on the question of whether the NFL or its commissioner owes fiduciary duties to one of the NFL's member clubs (in this case, the Raiders).

* * *

In *Jones* [*v. H.F. Ahmanson & Co.*, 460 P.2d 464 (1969)], the Supreme Court held definitively that majority shareholders owe fiduciary duties to the corporation and its minority shareholders "to use their ability to control the corporation in a fair, just, and equitable manner." Thus, under the circumstances presented in that case, the court concluded that "when, as here, no market [for the corporation's stock] exists, the controlling shareholders may not use their power to control the corporation for the purpose of promoting a marketing scheme that benefits themselves alone to the detriment of the minority."

Most notably, the discussion of fiduciary duties in *Jones* was premised on the existence of a *corporation, controlling shareholders, and minority shareholders.* No such organizational structure is presented in the instant appeal. To the contrary, it is without dispute that the NFL is *an unincorporated not-for-profit association* of 31 (now 32) member clubs. * * * As such, neither the NFL nor its member clubs fit the *Jones* model of fiduciary duties owed by majority shareholders to their corporation and to minority shareholders.

Even were we to ignore this glaring distinction, the claim here is that the *organization* (the NFL), not its majority members (or purported "majority shareholders"), owes the Raiders fiduciary duties. *Jones* is thus inapposite on this basis as well.

Moreover, we find the entire rationale of *Jones* to have no application to the facts of this case. In *Jones,* the Supreme Court addressed the inherent unfairness of majority shareholders of a for-profit corporation using their dominant position to further their own interests at the expense of minority shareholders. Here, the Raiders' claim is that the nonprofit organization itself (and its commissioner) acted in a manner that was prejudicial to the Raiders. This contention is a far cry from the corporate abuse that the Supreme Court addressed in *Jones,* namely, controlling shareholders misusing their position of dominance for their personal benefit and to the detriment of minority shareholders.

* * *

There are at least two significant reasons that prevent us from concluding that *Cohen* [*v. Kite Hill Community Ass'n*, 191 Cal. Rptr. 209 (1983) (holding that a homeowners' association owes a fiduciary duty to its members)] supports the Raiders' position. In the first instance, the *nature of the entity* in *Cohen* was entirely different. The homeowners' association that the court found to owe fiduciary duties to its members was a nonprofit *corporation,* not an unincorporated association as is the case with the NFL. The Raiders' attempts to trivialize this issue notwithstanding, this distinction is a significant one. As a nonprofit corporation, there were fiduciary obligations *imposed by statute* upon the officers and directors of the homeowners' association * * * [citing a case interpreting California corporations law].

Second, homeowners' associations, as the *Cohen* court noted, perform "public-service functions" and "have increasingly 'quasi-governmental' * * * responsibilities." In contrast, the NFL neither performs "public-service functions," nor acts in a manner similar to homeowners' associations. Furthermore, homeowners' associations are organized to regulate and govern various aspects of unit owners' day-to day occupancy and maintenance of their homes; the NFL is organized for a far different purpose.[11]

* * *

The Raiders has cited no cases—and we are aware of none—in which it has been held as a blanket proposition that a voluntary unincorporated association and/or its leadership owes fiduciary duties to its members. * * * We decline to reach that conclusion here.

Finally, we reject the Raiders' intimation that a fiduciary relationship exists between it and the defendants because of an alleged joint venture. A joint venture, of necessity, "requires an agreement under which the parties have (1) a joint interest in a common business, (2) an understanding that profits and losses will be shared, and (3) a right to joint control." Here, there is no sharing of profits and losses by member clubs indicative of a joint venture. As one federal district court concluded, specifically with respect to the NFL: "Strictly speaking, the NFL teams are not engaged in a joint venture. 'A joint venture is a joint business undertaking of two or more parties who share the risks as well as the profits of the business.' Though the NFL teams share revenues, they do not share profits or losses." (*Los Angeles Memorial Coliseum v. N.F.L.*, 468 F. Supp. 154, 162 n. 9 (S.D. Cal. 1979).) There is thus no merit to the Raiders' claim for breach of fiduciary duty arising out of a joint venture.[13]

We conclude therefore that the relationship between the Raiders, on the one hand, and the NFL and Tagliabue, on the other hand, is not one under which a fiduciary relationship exists as a matter of law. * * *

C. Whether Defendants Undertook Fiduciary Responsibilities

We now review whether, irrespective of the absence of fiduciary duty imposed by law, the NFL and Tagliabue undertook fiduciary responsibilities to the Raiders by agreement. After such review, we find quite the opposite to be true.

* * * "The NFL is governed by a constitution that generally requires a three-quarters vote for action. The chief executive officer is the commissioner, who is appointed by a two-thirds vote of the clubs. * * *" The Raiders admits that the NFL's constitution and bylaws (NFL constitution) govern the NFL and constitute a contract to which all member clubs agreed.

---

11. The Raiders' claim notwithstanding, *Dietz v. American Dental Ass'n.* 479 F. Supp. 554 (E.D. Mich. 1979)—a case in which a federal trial court applied Michigan substantive law—is not controlling. There, the court concluded that "[w]here a professional association has monopoly power and membership in the association significantly affects the member's practice of his profession, courts will hold the association has a fiduciary duty to be substantively rational and procedurally fair." There is no claim here that the NFL is a professional association or that it excluded the Raiders from membership status.

13. Although not controlling to our reasoning here, we note with interest that in *Los Angeles Memorial Coliseum Comm'n v. N.F.L.*, the parties there asserted positions that are essentially opposite from those made in this appeal: "The NFL contends the league structure is in essence a single entity, akin to a partnership or joint venture, precluding application of Sherman Act section 1 which prevents only contracts, combinations or conspiracies in restraint of trade. The Los Angeles Coliseum and Raiders reject this position and assert the League is composed of 28 separate legal entities which act independently."

* * * In light of the fact that the NFL and its member clubs are governed by the NFL constitution, we must examine that document carefully in our evaluation of the Raiders' breach of fiduciary duty claim.

Even the most cursory review of the NFL constitution discloses the enormous power vested in the commissioner with respect to the business operations of the League and its member clubs. As a blanket proposition, the member clubs agreed that "[t]hey, and each of them, shall be bound by and will observe all decisions of the [c]ommissioner of the League in all matters within his jurisdiction." Further, each member club agreed to a broad release of, among others, the NFL and the commissioner in connection with any official acts taken on behalf of the NFL.[14]

The commissioner's authority under the NFL constitution ranges from very broad issues to * * * minutiae. The commissioner has the power to appoint operating committees as the NFL "deems necessary and appropriate," with the commissioner directing and chairing such committees. The section of the NFL constitution that concerns the commissioner's qualifications and duties (Article VIII) consists of eight pages of text. The commissioner is empowered under that article (among other things) to: (1) arbitrate a broad array of disputes involving NFL employees, NFL members, coaches, employees of members, players, and NFL officials; (2) incur expenses on the NFL's behalf; (3) interpret and establish policy and procedure with respect to the NFL constitution and its enforcement; (4) arrange for and negotiate contracts on behalf of the NFL; (5) take disciplinary action against any owner, player, coach, officer, director, or employee of any member club, or against any NFL officer, employee or official;[17] and (6) disapprove contracts between players and member clubs.

The more mundane (but nonetheless significant) powers of the commissioner specified in the NFL constitution include: (1) deciding appropriate penalties in the event of player tampering; (2) approval of a member club's hiring of any coach, or administrative/supervisory employee; (3) approval of a member club's contract for the telecast or broadcast of its games (including the sponsorship for such games); (4) the sale of all radio and television and film rights for conference championship games and the Super Bowl; (5) control over conference championship and Super Bowl games; (6) preparing and modifying game schedules; (7) presiding over player drafts and resolving disputes arising out of the drafts; (8) approval of player trades; (9) suspension of players for violations of the NFL constitution, player contract, NFL rule, or club rule; and (10) inves-

---

14. The release reads in relevant part: "[The member clubs, as well as each club's owners, officers, directors, shareholders and partners], and each of them, to the fullest extent permitted by law, release and indemnify the [c]ommissioner, the League and every employee thereof * * * from and against any and all claims, demands, suits or other proceedings, whether for damages or otherwise, which they * * * may at any time have or assert in connection with or by reason of any action taken or not taken by the released/indemnified parties in their official capacities on behalf of the League or any committee thereof."

17. The commissioner's disciplinary powers under the NFL constitution are extremely significant. The commissioner may suspend and/or impose a fine of *up to one-half million dollars,* and/or may cancel the person's contract with the NFL or club member. The commissioner is empowered to take such action, after notice and hearing, where the commissioner decides that the person "has either violated the [NFL constitution] * * *, or has been or is guilty of conduct detrimental to the welfare of the League or professional football." The commissioner is also empowered to refer disciplinary matters to the NFL Executive Committee in instances where the commissioner believes that greater punishment is warranted. In those cases, the commissioner may recommend the most Draconian of punishments, cancellation of a member club's NFL franchise. Further, the commissioner may impose severe sanctions—including expulsion from the League—for gambling on the outcome or score of any NFL game.

tigation of a member club's placement of players on "Reserve/Injured," "Reserve," or "Reserve/Suspended" status, and (where such placement was improper) taking disciplinary action against the member club.

It is clear from a comprehensive review of the NFL constitution that neither the NFL nor Tagliabue undertook the role of a fiduciary towards any particular member club, including the Raiders. To the contrary, the expansive powers of the commissioner delineated in the NFL constitution strongly demonstrate the absence of such a fiduciary relationship. As noted, a fiduciary must give "priority to the best interest of the beneficiary." The breadth of the commissioner's powers plainly shows that there are numerous and varied potential circumstances in which the commissioner may be required to act *against* the best interests of the Raiders as a member club.

There is a vast array of potential circumstances under which the commissioner may take action that is adverse to a particular member club (such as the Raiders). Under the NFL constitution, the commissioner could act in a manner potentially adverse to the Raiders, inter alia, by: (1) arbitrating a dispute between the Raiders and a coach, player, other employee, or other member club; (2) interpreting or enforcing the NFL constitution in a manner incongruent with the Raiders' position; (3) disapproving a Raiders player contract or the proposed hiring of a Raiders coach, administrative, or supervisory employee; (4) disapproving a player trade proposed by the Raiders; or (5) resolving a player draft dispute adverse to the Raiders. Further, as we have noted, the commissioner's disciplinary powers under the NFL constitution are very extensive; those powers include the commissioner being able to discipline any Raiders' owner, player, coach, or employee, to discipline the Raiders where the club improperly assigned a player to a particular status, and to assess penalties against the Raiders for player tampering. We can readily imagine numerous scenarios where the NFL and its commissioner might take action involving a member club such as the Raiders — either through disciplinary action or other action authorized under the NFL constitution — that would leave the club without the services of a talented coach, player, or other employee.

There are thus numerous circumstances where the NFL and its commissioner would be contractually obligated to take action adverse to the Raiders. In such cases, the NFL and the commissioner would be acting in the best interests of the League but certainly *not* in the Raiders' best interests. Moreover, such official actions — at least based upon the literal wording of the constitution — might be governed by the prior release given by the Raiders under the constitution; obviously such blanket absolution for official action runs counter to the notion that the NFL or Tagliabue owes a fiduciary duty "to act with the utmost good faith for the benefit of the other party." There is simply no factual basis for concluding that either the NFL or the commissioner undertook by agreement fiduciary responsibilities to member clubs such as the Raiders.

Likewise, we find no merit to the argument that Tagliabue was the Raiders' fiduciary because he signed a 1996 settlement agreement as commissioner of the NFL on the League's behalf and on behalf of the NFL's member clubs. This lone matter does not, of itself, constitute an agreement on Tagliabue's part to act as agent for the Raiders. There is no evidence here "'of the essential characteristic of the right of control'" required for a finding of agency. Indeed, it is readily apparent—both from the text of the NFL constitution and the claims asserted by the Raiders—that the Raiders do *not* control the commissioner's actions. We therefore reject any claim by the Raiders that Tagliabue owed fiduciary duties to the Raiders under an unfounded principal-agent theory.

For all of the above reasons, we conclude that there was no fiduciary relationship between defendants and the Raiders arising either as a result of agreement or by operation of law. Accordingly, the court below properly granted summary adjudication of the second cause of action.

* * *

RUSHING, P.J., concurring. The Raiders *are* a diverse group of athletes. But despite such pluralism, the Raiders *is* a singular football team, and because of this, I must concur in the technical propriety of such phrases as "the Raiders asserts," "the Raiders does not contend," and "the Raiders was discriminated against," which appear in the main opinion. However, although these phrases may be sound, their sound, to me, is personally foul and deserves dissent, if not a 15-yard penalty and loss of down. This is especially so when the phrases are read out loud.

* * *

I believe we could have reached our goal of meaning and avoided fumbling dissonance with a judicial substitution: pulling "the Raiders" and going with a second-stringer like "the plaintiff."

Notes and Questions

1. If the court was correct to view "Raiders" as a singular noun, was the court incorrect to use the possessive form "Raiders'," as in "[t]he Raiders' claim notwithstanding * * *"? *See* WILLIAM STRUNK JR. & E.B. WHITE, THE ELEMENTS OF STYLE 1 (4th ed. 2000). This is not the first controversy involving the intersection of sports and grammar. (And by the way, is "sports" singular or plural?) Consider former broadcaster Keith Jackson's fondness for the grammatically correct plural form "times out" over "time-outs." Was *Hockey Night in Canada* broadcaster Bob Cole correct to announce that "[t]he Colorado Avalanche has won the Stanley Cup"? Would anybody say, "The Buffalo Sabres has won the Stanley Cup," even if they (it) did manage miraculously to accomplish the feat?

2. The court in *Oakland Raiders* places considerable importance on the facts that the NFL is (a) unincorporated and (b) does not exercise quasi-governmental functions. Should either of these factors matter? Do you think the NFL is distinguishable from a homeowners' association in terms of fiduciary duty? Do you think Al Davis is more concerned with his homeowners' association's regulation of his daily life or the NFL's? What rationale(s) does the court give for distinguishing the precedents on fiduciary duty?

3. The essential difficulty of this case rests in the traditional league structure, as discussed in Chapter 2. Owners of NFL franchises are both partners and competitors with each other, as their teams battle each other for championships but pursue the League's interests collectively. In light of this collaboration between competitors, how significant should it have been that the commissioner has the power to take actions that have the effect of improving some teams to the detriment of others? Would it be possible to split the commissioner's functions into internal and external responsibilities, with fiduciary duties to the member clubs only as to the latter category?

4. After reading these cases, are we any closer to resolving whether the commissioner is, in fact, an employer? In contemplating this issue, consider whether Major League Baseball and other sports have placed themselves in the following "Catch-22" situation. If the commissioner, in truth, is an employer or an agent of the employer, should his

actions not be imputed to the remainder of the club owners in terms of employer liability under pertinent labor laws or related legislation? If he is not an employer, but rather is a neutral who has serious involvement in the labor relations aspects of Major League players, then should his selection not be a mandatory subject of collective bargaining under § 8(d) of the National Labor Relations Act? Has this question been obviated by baseball's decision to make the commissioner head of the Player Relations Committee? Is there now any doubt that the commissioner stands in the shoes of the owners and will be deemed an employer for purposes of the NLRA and similar legislation? Freeze-frame this question for revisitation in subsequent chapters dealing with labor-management relations in professional sports.

5. At times, the commissioner is called upon to act as arbiter in matters far more mundane, but no less emotional, than league realignment, player discipline, and complex trades. The classic example involves on-the-field, -court, or -ice protests wherein the decisions of game officials are questioned. In these situations the commissioner, or if appropriate jurisdictionally, the league president, will generally defer to the official, especially where judgment calls are implicated. Just as the courts are extremely deferential to professional sports' internal adjudication machinery, so too commissioners are very solicitous of game officials. This deference is undoubtedly fueled by the belief that the original decision-maker has the experience and expertise to render an independent judgment as well as the belief that any officious intermeddling will prompt a flood of silly protests and protracted litigation. In many respects, part of the rationale that justifies deference to, and preference for, a voluntary dispute adjustment mechanism, assurance of some degree of finality, applies to referees and umpires.

Further, game officiating in most sports is not, as it once was, a part-time job and repository for the uncontrolled invective of players and fans alike. Today, there are 68 umpires in Major League Baseball, 34 linesmen and 37 referees in the National Hockey League, 61 referees in the National Basketball Association, and over 120 officials in the National Football League. The base salary for umpires is $84,000 per year and ranges as high as $300,000 for veterans (plus expenses, a per diem, and playoff bonuses). Umpires are paid on a year-round basis, and are represented now by the World Umpires Association after having decertified the Major League Umpires Association and its flamboyant leader, Richie Phillips (see Chapter 14, *infra*). On more than one occasion, the umpires have engaged in work stoppages in an effort to secure greater benefits. While there may be some sympathy between the umpires and players in terms of their basic labor organization goals, the players have never ceased work in sympathy with an umpires' strike, nor have they offered support on those occasions where the league has attempted to lockout the umpires.

The minimum salary for NBA referees is set forth in the recently negotiated five-year collective bargaining agreement between the National Basketball Association Referees Association and the NBA. Under the terms of this agreement, in year one, the rookie minimum will be $85,000 and maximum salary for veterans $261,000. In year five of this same collective bargaining agreement, the rookie minimum rises to $90,000 and the most highly paid veteran referee will receive $328,000. National Football League officials, who are paid on a part-time basis, receive between $2200 and $8000 per game. Finally, National Hockey League linesmen receive between $72,000 and $162,000, while referees make between $110,000 and $255,000. Thus, the heightened recognition of officials and the greater respect that they repeatedly demand may lead to even greater league deference to, and support for, officials' decisionmaking authority.

At times, however, commissioners have reversed game officials, and have ordered that the game be replayed from the point where the incorrect call had been made. The determining factors may be the timing and severity of the mistake (*i.e.*, a mistake involving the game clock may not necessitate a replay if it occurs early in the game (thus "correctable") as opposed to a mistake occurring late in the game where the victimized team does not have the opportunity to compensate for the official's error). In either event, there is considerable reluctance to overrule an official's decision both in the professional as well as amateur ranks, witness the Big Eight Conference's refusal to reverse a victory by the University of Colorado (which led to an eventual NCAA championship) even when it was unequivocally established that the winning touchdown had been scored compliments of an extra down. *Big Eight to Review Colorado's Fifth Down*, NEWSWIRE, Oct. 8, 1990, Los Angeles Sports, Part C, at 2; Michael Vega, *Loss Would've Left BC Extra Down*, BOSTON GLOBE, Sept. 9, 1995, Sports, at 26.

Perhaps the most celebrated reversal of an umpire's decision involved the infamous "Pine Tar" incident, where Kansas City Royal George Brett's game winning homer against the New York Yankees had been disallowed because his bat was covered with too much pine tar (a sticky substance that prevents the bat from slipping out of a player's hand). American League President Lee MacPhail changed the umpire's ruling and reinstated the Royals' victory, triggering a vehement protest from the Yankees. This incident spawned myriad commentary from journalists and legal scholars alike. While many of the responses simply staked out the authors' strong views on the prudence of league officials overruling umpires, some commentary reflected thoughtful and provocative scholarship. *See, e.g.,* Christopher H. Clancy & Jonathan A. Weiss, *A Pine Tar Gloss on Quasi-Legal Images*, 5 CARDOZO L. REV. 409 (1984); Jared Tobin Finkelstein, Commentary, *In re Brett: The Sticky Problem of Statutory Construction*, 52 FORDHAM L. REV. 430 (1983).

6. After further review ... if reversals by commissioners and other league officials are rare, reversals of game officials by courts are almost non-existent. Almost. In *Georgia High School Ass'n v. Waddell*, 285 S.E.2d 7 (Ga. 1981), a football referee had incorrectly applied the "roughing the kicker" rule, denying the punting team an automatic first down. The team that was the victim of the misapplication then punted again, and ultimately lost the game. They then appealed for relief to Georgia High School Association and then to the courts. The trial court ordered that the teams

> resume play at the Lithia Springs thirty[-]eight yard line with the ball being in possession of R.L. Osborne High School and it be first down and ten yards to go for a first down and that the clock be set at seven minutes one second to play [in] the fourth quarter.

The Georgia Supreme Court indefinitely stayed the order, holding "that courts of equity in this state are without authority to review decisions of football referees because those decisions do not present judicial controversies." *Id.* at 9. *See also Bain v. Gillispie*, 357 N.W.2d 47 (Iowa Ct. App. 1984) (holding that merchandisers have no cause of action against a referee whose blown call harmed their business interests).

Chapter 4

Contract Law and Sports: A Primer*

I. Introduction

In understanding the complex contract issues that have arisen in the sports industry, one must have a basic grasp of rudimentary contract law principles typically covered in the first year of law school. While any attempt to summarize an entire contracts course in a brief chapter is tantamount to Don Quixote's tilting at windmills, an effort has been made, below, to address the more pertinent concepts with a "broad-brush" review. This synopsis should provide the necessary framework to facilitate a meaningful exploration of the cases that follow in the succeeding chapters.

II. Contract Formation

The determination of mutual assent and the parties' intent to be bound legally are the threshold questions associated with contract formation. Most commentators emphasize the intent *not* to be bound and declare that, generally, "a party's intention to be legally bound is irrelevant." E. ALLAN FARNSWORTH, CONTRACTS § 3.7 (3d ed. 2003) (*hereinafter* "FARNSWORTH"). However, this characterization is misleading. A more intellectually satisfying approach is that the parties must intend to be bound, and such intent is presumed from an offer and acceptance or similar manifestation, except when the parties' words, actions, or the surrounding circumstances dictate otherwise. *See, e.g., Blackmon v. Iverson*, 324 F. Supp. 2d 602 (E.D. Pa. 2003); *Balfour v. Balfour*, 2 K.B. 571 (C.A. 1919). Of course, offer and acceptance are typical manifestations of assent, but they are not always evident or identifiable as discrete components of a transaction.

* Portions of the following synopsis have been adopted, with permission, from Michael J. Cozzillio, *The Athletic Scholarship and the College National Letter of Intent: A Contract By Any Other Name,* 35 WAYNE L. REV. 1275 (1989) and Michael J. Cozzillio, *The Option Contract: Irrevocable Not Irrejectable,* 39 CATH. U. L. REV. 491 (1990). At various points, full annotations contained in the original manuscripts have been abridged and/or placed into the text. At other points, these two articles have been referenced with "pin-point" citations to direct the reader to a more expansive discussion of the issue being addressed. The articles will hereinafter be cited as Cozzillio, *Scholarship* and Cozzillio, *Option Contract*, respectively.

Manifestation of mutual assent is the *sine qua non* of any enforceable contract and is evaluated through employment of an objective test. *See Huyett v. Idaho State Univ.*, 104 P.3d 946, 951 (Idaho 2004); *compare Hendricks v. Clemson Univ.*, 578 S.E.2d 711 (S.C. 2003) *with Ross v. Creighton Univ.*, 957 F. 2d 410 (7th Cir. 1992). A party's subjective intent is irrelevant if his words or conduct, from the perspective of a reasonable person in that position, manifest the requisite assent. The parties need not express an intent to be bound or explicitly evince their contemplation of legal consequences. . *See* JOHN CALAMARI & JOSEPH PERILLO, CALAMARI & PERILLO ON CONTRACTS (5th ed. 2003) (*hereinafter* CALAMARI & PERILLO). The entire transaction may be aborted if a party manifests an intent not to be bound, either by explicitly agreeing that the arrangement is nonbinding or by implicitly conveying such intent through his conduct. The circumstances surrounding the "agreement" may also compel the conclusion that the parties have no desire to elevate their relationship to a legally enforceable contract. *See* Otto Kahn-Freund, *Pacta Sunt Servanda, A Principle and Its Limits: Some Thoughts Prompted by Comparative Labour Law*, 48 TUL. L. REV. 894 (1974). Contracts may be implied-in-law, *i.e.*, constructed by the court, or implied-in-fact. Contracts implied-in-law are not contracts in the truest sense, characterized in some quarters as quasi-contracts. Contracts implied-in-fact are agreements that "impose contractual terms by reason of the parties expressions, inferred from the facts, circumstances and expressions of the parties' intent to be bound." *Detroit Tigers, Inc. v. Ignite Sports Media, LLC*, 203 F. Supp. 2d 789, 798 (E.D. Mich. 2002). "The only difference between an express contract and a contract implied in fact, is that in the former the parties arrive at their agreement by words, either oral or written, while in the latter, their agreement is arrived at by consideration of their acts and conduct." *Id.* The prime motivation for the latter is the court's desire to avoid unjust enrichment. *See Blackmon v. Iverson*, 324 F. Supp. 2d 602 (E.D. Pa. 2003).

"Intent to be bound" questions often arise when there is doubt about the parties' seriousness. Although the basic rudiments of offer and acceptance may be present, some outward manifestation may indicate that the parties never intended legal consequences. The parties can consummate an agreement, replete with all the trappings of a contract, but express an intention not to be legally bound. In these instances, the majority of courts will, under the prevailing objective theory, presume that there was no intention to be bound and refuse to enforce the contract. Courts will indulge the parties' express manifestations of intent that the arrangement is nothing more than a sham or gentlemen's agreement. *See Hirschkorn v. Severson*, 319 N.W.2d 475, 478 (N.D. 1982). *But see Greene v. Howard Univ.*, 412 F.2d 1128 (D.C. Cir. 1969).

A more difficult question arises when the parties' intent is not obvious, but must be derived from surrounding circumstances. For example, a husband who promises his spouse that he will take out the garbage in exchange for her agreement to attend a social event is unlikely to prevail in court on a claim that failure to perform constitutes a breach of contract. Likewise, an invitation to dinner in exchange for a return invitation will generally not rise to the level of a binding contract. It is a safe assumption that, in either event, the parties do not contemplate judicial enforcement of their agreements.

Again, the nature of a transaction, the words of the parties, and the surrounding circumstances will dictate judicial evaluation of intent. Claims that a deal was made in jest or that an agreement was signed without a clear understanding that any legal obligation would be attached are assessed in accordance with the objective standard. *Lucy v. Zehmer*, 84 S.E.2d 516 (Va. 1954). *See further Chiles v. Good*, 41 S.W.2d 738, 739 (Tex.

App. 1931), *rev'd*, 57 S.W.2d 1100 (Tex. 1933). Promises may be enforced despite the promisor's remonstrations that he or she subjectively never contemplated entering a binding contract. Indeed, while parties often enter agreements without the slightest worry about the possibility of a breach and without the remotest idea of judicial enforcement mechanisms, this mindset does not necessarily signify that mutual assent is lacking or that the parties are not absolutely serious in their commitments.

Oftentimes, commitments made in which an athlete pledges services are rendered without a full appreciation of the legal consequences or, at least, with a subjective sense that the transaction is something less than a binding contract. This absence of "subjective" intent is frequently a product of the nature of the transaction (*e.g.*, a high school student signing a letter of intent to attend a university under scholarship) or the lack of sophistication of the athlete. *See, e.g.,* Timothy Davis, *The Myth of the Superspade: The Persistence of Racism in College Athletics*, 22 FORDHAM URBAN L.J. 615 (1995); Cozzillio, *Scholarship*. In either event, the objective manifestations of the parties, rather than their subjective intent, will generally control the outcome notwithstanding the naivete of the party who would prefer to escape from the deal. Yet, it is not uncommon for a court either expressly or impliedly to consider a party's youth or innocence in assessing liability in an action to enforce a particular agreement. *See New York Football Giants, Inc. v. Los Angeles Chargers Football Club, Inc.,* 291 F.2d 471 (5th Cir. 1961); *Los Angeles Rams Football Club v. Cannon*, 185 F. Supp. 717 (S.D.Cal. 1960). Likewise, the extent to which one party has taken advantage of the other party's youth, inexperience, or ignorance may evoke a court's indulgence of the putative victim's desire to avoid a contract that has been fully formed. *See* Part IV, below.

(A) The Process of Offer and Acceptance: An Overview

The "formation" stage of a commercial agreement involves the elements of offer and acceptance that comprise the circle of assent, although these elements are not always necessary or readily identifiable as discrete entities. The offer is a demonstration of a desire to enter an agreement and represents the first volley in the formation process. RESTATEMENT (SECOND) OF CONTRACTS § 24. It renders its maker vulnerable to an acceptance that creates a binding contract. An acceptance is described as "the manifestation of assent to the terms [of an offer] made by the offeree in a manner invited or required by the offer." *Id.* § 50(1), at 128. Ascertaining whether an offer is susceptible to an acceptance or invites an act that will conclude the transaction presents many problems. For years, courts have attempted to distinguish true offers from preliminary negotiations, physicians' opinions, and offers to accept offers. Case law often reflects *post hoc*, outcome-determinative decisionmaking. Thus, the distinctions presented are quite artificial, providing little predictive value. Nonetheless, several factors are repeatedly considered in the offer/non-offer calculus, including the language of commitment, the identity of the offeror and offeree, and the specificity of quality, quantity, and overall description of the goods or services involved. Yet, there is no litmus test that can measure the weight to be accorded each factor. As Professor Murray has noted:

> The scores of cases that have sought to determine whether, in a given set of facts, an offer has been made, are notoriously deficient in suggesting clear guidelines to determine whether an offer exists. A glance at modern cases often reveals an admission that "[i]t is impossible to formulate a general principle or criterion for its determination."

JOHN MURRAY, MURRAY ON CONTRACTS § 34 (4th ed. 2001) (citations omitted) (*hereinafter* MURRAY).

The difficulty of ascertaining the offeror and offeree in a particular case is dramatically illustrated in early cases involving the attempts of rival professional sports leagues to bid for the services of college athletes. There, soon-to-be college graduates, besieged by numerous suitors, often found themselves signing agreements with more than one team. Because the league agreements frequently contained specific language requiring commissioner approval or similar third party approbation, identification of offeror and offeree became exceedingly complex. *See Los Angeles Rams Football Club v. Cannon*, 185 F. Supp. 717 (S.D. Cal. 1960); *Detroit Football Co. v. Robinson*, 186 F. Supp. 933 (E.D. La. 1960); *see also International Filter Co. v. Conroe Gin, Ice & Light Co.*, 277 S.W. 631 (Tex. Comm'n App. 1925). In the wake of decisions holding that a commissioner's approval was a condition precedent to the contract's very formation, league responses included altering the standard player contract such that the agreement was completely formed when signed by both the team and the players. *See Los Angeles Rams v. Cannon, supra; infra,* Chapter 5. *See also Bowen v. Workers Comp. Appeals Board*, 86 Cal. Rptr. 2d 95 (Cal. Ct. App. 1999) (Commissioner's approval construed as a condition subsequent—not a prerequisite to formation).

Often, even where a writing is not required by the Statute of Frauds or other legislative device, parties will claim that the absence of a memorial will evince the parties' intent not yet to be bound. The determination will turn on whether the writing was intended to be the *sine qua non* of the parties' manifestations of a desire to consummate the agreement or simply a convenient memorial of an oral agreement establishing a binding contract in its own right. Among the factors to be considered are: 1) whether the agreement is the kind typically embraced in a writing; 2) whether the agreement's complete expression can only be reflected in a writing; 3) whether the arrangement contains many details; 4) whether the magnitude of the transaction is large; 5) whether the contract is atypical; 6) whether there exist unresolved details; 7) whether the negotiations demonstrate that a writing was within the contemplation of the parties. *See Continental Laboratories v. Scott Paper Co.*, 759 F. Supp. 538, *aff'd* 938 F. 2d 184 (8th Cir. 1991); RESTATEMENT (SECOND) OF CONTRACTS § 27; *Media Sports & Arts v. Kinney Shoe Corp.*, 1997 U.S. Dist. LEXIS 12394 (S.D.N.Y. 1997), (delineating several factors to be considered in ascertaining the significance of a contemplated written memorial as the *sine qua non* of the parties' agreement); *In re The Score Board, Inc.*, 238 B.R. 585 (D.N.J. 1999) (signatures on a contract were not required as a condition precedent to formation of a valid contract when subsequent performance of executory obligations signified acceptance).

Once it has been determined that an offer has been made, it is essential to identify the character of the offer to ascertain whether a particular response constitutes a valid acceptance. This determination will depend upon the method of acceptance that the offer invites. When an offer explicitly seeks performance as the mode of acceptance, a promise to perform generally will not suffice. *See* RESTATEMENT (SECOND) OF CONTRACTS § 53; *see also* Note, *Acceptance by Performance When the Offeror Demands a Promise*, 52 S. CAL. L. REV. 1917 (1979). Likewise, when an offer seeks a promise and an offeree begins to accept by performing, this acceptance may fall short of the response necessary to form a contract. Of course, the beginning of performance may be deemed an implied promise to complete, particularly when the partial performance occurs in the offeror's presence. Full performance prior to expiration of an offer that invites a promise as acceptance may be deemed to constitute a valid acceptance if accompanied by appropriate notification. *See generally* RESTATEMENT (SECOND) OF CONTRACTS §63

(1932). Notification of an intent to accept by promise is typically required. Therefore, when the offer seeks only a promise but the offeree chooses to accept by performance, such performance should logically be an effective acceptance only if the proper notification has been tendered. *See* RESTATEMENT (SECOND) OF CONTRACTS §§ 54, 56, 63; U.C.C. § 2-206 (1977); Robert Braucher, *Offer and Acceptance in the Second Restatement,* 74 YALE L.J. 302 (1964). In other circumstances, the notice may be a condition precedent to the promisor's duty to perform, but it is not a necessary component of acceptance. *See* John Murray, *Contracts: A New Design for the Agreement Process,* 53 CORNELL L. REV. 785 (1968). When an offer is silent as to the mode of acceptance or invites *either* type of acceptance, the modern view gives the offeree an opportunity to choose the appropriate method of acceptance. *See* RESTATEMENT (SECOND) OF CONTRACTS § 32. Again, as discussed above, although a formal contract was prepared and one party did not sign, the contract may be upheld if that party performed as if it agreed to enter the contract. *See Detroit Tigers, Inc. v. Ignite Sports Media,* 203 F. Supp. 2d 789 (E.D. Mich. 2002)(defendant did not sign the formal contract but did forward the contract for necessary commissioner approval and did start to perform under the contract; therefore, a contract was formed).

An offer that seeks acceptance either by a performance or a return promise is typically revocable by the offeror any time prior to an effective acceptance. Generally, where the parties are negotiating face to face or telephonically, the offer will lapse when the conversation ends. An actual revocation is unnecessary absent evidence that the offer is still viable. Where the offer has been extended by mail, the acceptance of that offer is normally effective upon dispatch (commonly referred to as the "mailbox rule"). *See Morrison v. Thoelke,* 155 So. 2d 889 (Fla. App. 1963). The offeree may seek to forestall a spontaneous revocation by securing an option or a promise not to revoke. In most option contracts, the offeree, generally in exchange for some consideration, is provided an agreed upon or reasonable time period within which to accept an offer. *See* RESTATEMENT (SECOND) OF CONTRACTS § 25; *see also* U.C.C. § 2-205 (1977) (firm offers). The option contract has been characterized as a separate agreement, or a contract "preliminary to another one, that is, a contract entered in contemplation of another contract that may come into existence later if the grantee so elects." Saul Litvinoff, *Consent Revisited,* 47 LA. L. REV. 699, 746 (1987). In fact, there is an infinite variety of option contracts. Their bilateral or unilateral character, as well as their independence from the underlying transaction, will turn on the particular option agreement. *See, e.g.,* ARTHUR CORBIN, CORBIN ON CONTRACTS § 62 (1963). Although each option has its own nuances, its principal purpose is to freeze the offeror's prerogative to revoke for the designated period. Normally, the optionee has no duty to accept and is free to abort the transaction at any time. Some commentators have taken pains to distinguish an option contract from an "irrevocable offer." *See* D.O. McGovney, *Irrevocable Offers,* 27 HARV. L. REV. 644 (1914); Litvinoff at 747–48, 751, 753. However, these terms are generally fungible and will be used interchangeably here. *See* CALAMARI & PERILLO § 2-22.

An interesting question has arisen as to whether an option contract secured by consideration is terminated by a rejection or counter-offer made during the option period. The Second Restatement suggests that an option survives the rejection and that the optionee may still accept the offer so long as the option remains open. RESTATEMENT (SECOND) OF CONTRACTS § 37. Some courts add that an optionee may be estopped from accepting an option if the optionor has detrimentally relied upon an intervening rejection. *See Ryder v. Wescoat,* 535 S.W.2d 269 (Mo. Ct. App. 1976). A minority view argues that traditional rules governing offer and acceptance should prevail, compelling a conclusion that a rejection will terminate the power of acceptance. The most persuasive support for this position is that the optionee does not have the ability to accept and then reject during the option period; thus, he or she should have no opportunity to perform the obverse. *See* Cozzillio, *Option Contract*, at 529–33.

This issue could assume more than mere academic curiosity where the payment of bonus monies could create an option, thus inviting the possibility of a vacillating optionee. Once again, the *Cannon* case, referenced above and highlighted in Chapter 5, provides a useful illustration. There, the team seeking to enforce its alleged contract with college star Billy Cannon argued, albeit unsuccessfully, that a bonus check paid to Cannon constituted consideration to secure an option, thereby suspending Cannon's ability to revoke his "offer." The court rejected the argument, finding that the money was paid conditionally and did not cement the option.

Uniform player contracts have contained option clauses through which the clubs retain the rights to a player for a year at a salary to be agreed upon or at a salary designated by the contract and the pertinent collective bargaining agreement. Often, the standard contracts do not contain option clauses, but such clauses can be individually negotiated. *See* NFL Collective Bargaining Agreement, 1998–2005—subject to reopener, Art. XV. These contracts may also contain rights of first refusal in which a club is entitled to match the offer of another team for the services of one of its players. These rights of first refusal or "matching offers" will be visited in subsequent chapters, particularly with reference to whether they constitute unlawful, anticompetitive restrictions on player mobility. In any event, it is important to note that options and rights of first refusal, though similar in form and potential consequences, are different. *See* Cozzillio, *Option Contract*, at 522 n.155. Numerous issues have arisen in the option context, including the length of the option, the consideration necessary to secure the option, the applicable deadlines for exercising the option, and the terms governing the parties during the option year. As referenced above, standard player contracts traditionally contained option clauses that gave clubs the prerogative to renew an expressed contract on designated terms. For years, clubs argued that these option clauses renewed themselves with the contract, thus creating a system of perpetual reserve on player services. At times, the players themselves have advanced this harsh interpretation, hoping that courts would find the contract unconscionably long, fatally indefinite or wholly lacking mutuality of consideration. *See* Parts II(B) and (C), below. Further, cases arising in other sports-related contexts have generally reinforced the notion that time is "of the essence" in an option contract and have construed the time constraints as conditions precedent to the parties' duties to perform. Failure to comply strictly with the applicable deadlines could result in forfeiture of the option. *See, e.g., In re Arbitration Between Major League Baseball Players Ass'n (Carlton Fisk) and Major League Baseball Player Relations Comm., Inc. (Boston Red Sox),* Panel Decision No. 45, Grievance No. 80-35 (February 12, 1981) (Goetz, Chairman). For an illustration of judicial consideration of an option included in the contract for the benefit of the player, rather than the club, see *Community Sports, Inc. v. Denver Ringsby Rockets,* 240 A.2d 832 (Pa. 1968).

In many traditional unilateral and bilateral contracts, courts have imposed a constructive option contract in an effort to place the parties in the most equitable position. For example, when an offer invites performance, a partial performance may operate much like independent consideration to freeze the offer for a reasonable period of time, thereby precluding the offeror from revoking. *See Marchiondo v. Scheck,* 432 P.2d 405, 407 (N.M. 1967); *see also* RESTATEMENT (SECOND) OF CONTRACTS §45. This approach represents a refreshing alternative to the often inequitable and restrictive choices of either making full performance a necessary element of the acceptance, or making the beginning of performance the functional equivalent of a promise to complete. Each choice is problematic. In the former, the offeror would retain the right to revoke after an offeree has expended considerable effort to complete; in the latter, the partial performance would be deemed a promise when the offer did not indicate any indulgence of a promissory acceptance. In the constructive option contract, the offeror is not free to revoke, yet the offeree is free to reject. However, the offeror evokes little sympathy because he is the master of the offer and, with limited exceptions, could avoid the problem by demanding a promissory acceptance. *See* Henry Ballantine, *Acceptance of Offers for Unilateral Contracts by Partial Performance of Service Requested*, 5 MINN. L. REV. 94, 97 (1921). Even when a party has invited a promissory acceptance, courts may construct an irrevocable offer to achieve equity. *See Drennan v. Star Paving Co.*, 333 P.2d 757 (Cal. 1958); *see also* RESTATEMENT (SECOND) OF CONTRACTS §87. *But see James Baird Co. v. Gimbel Bros. Inc.*, 64 F.2d 344 (2d Cir. 1933).

(B) Indefiniteness and Agreements to Agree

If the terms of an agreement (particularly the essential terms) are not sufficiently definite or reasonably certain, the entire contract could fail. *See* MURRAY, *supra* §38 (4th ed. 2001); RESTATEMENT (SECOND) OF CONTRACTS §33(2). In the name of salvaging such a contract, which evinces the parties' intent to be bound in all other respects, courts will often attempt to cure the indefiniteness by supplying the missing term or terms. Simply stated, "the law leans against the destruction of contracts because of uncertainty." *Bettancourt v. Gilroy Theatre Co.*, 261 P.2d 351, 353 (Cal. Ct. App. 1953). Courts also may choose to sever the indefinite portion of the agreement and enforce the remainder, provided that the requisite elements of a binding contract are still present. *See generally Eckles v. Sharman*, 548 F.2d 905 (10th Cir. 1977), Chapter 5, Part III(C).

Where the indefiniteness exists because the parties have only reached an agreement to agree, as opposed to an inadvertent omission, courts are more reluctant to save the contract. The rationale simply is that the parties' manifestation of an intention to agree *later* suggests that they have not already reached agreement. *Compare Bornstein v. Somerson*, 341 So. 2d 1043 (Fla. Dist. Ct. App. 1977), *with Reprosystem, B.V. v. SCM Corp.*, 727 F.2d 257 (2d Cir. 1983). The question centers upon where to draw the line between reasonable gap-filling and judicial intermeddling to the point of subverting the parties' bargaining prerogative.

Of course, an approach may be too rigid if it either summarily invalidates all agreements to agree or paternalistically writes the contract for the parties where no real basis exists to provide the absent term. Recent authority has established a middle category, in which the parties may be held to their "agreement to agree" and required, at the least, to pursue good faith negotiations with an eye toward eventual settlement. *See, e.g., Thompson v. Liquichimica of Am., Inc.*, 481 F. Supp. 365 (S.D.N.Y. 1979); *see also Opdyke Inv. Co. v. Norris Grain Co.*, 320 N.W.2d 836, 838 (Mich. 1982) ("A contract to make a subsequent contract is not *per se* unenforceable; in fact, it may be just as valid as any other contract."). In a related vein, some courts have drawn a distinction between Type I and Type II Preliminary Agreements. Type I arrangements involve agreement on all essential terms, where no disputed issues remain, and a further contract is contemplated only as a formality. In a Type II agreement the parties acknowledge the existence of unresolved terms but agree to negotiate in good faith to resolve any open terms, including important ones. *Media Sports & Arts v. Kinney Shoe Corp.,* 1997 U.S. Dist. LEXIS 12394 (S.D.N.Y. 1997). The key lies in ascertaining the parties' intent, rather than simply relying in the titling of the document allegedly establishing the existence or non-existence of a contract.

The varying judicial approaches to contracts lacking precision and certitude are reflected in numerous sports contexts. In *Eckles v. Sharman,* 548 F.2d 905 (10th Cir. 1977), a club claimed the right to the services of its head coach, who had accepted a coaching position elsewhere. The Tenth Circuit reversed a lower court decision that had found the contract, which contained an agreement to agree on material terms, to be enforceable due to the presence of a severability clause. The lower court reasoned that the severability clause operated to excuse the flawed parts of the agreement, leaving a complete agreement in place. The court of appeals denied the enforcement of the contract, holding that the severability clause could not be used to excise essential contract terms without disturbing the contract's validity.

As to "material terms," compensation may not always be deemed an "essential" element. In *Echols v. Pelullo,* 377 F.3d 272 (3d Cir. 2004), a professional boxing promotional agreement left open the purse for future bouts. The court did not find such agreement fatally indefinite. Rather, the court found that while the purse amount was certainly "relevant" to the agreement, it was not "material and essential to the understanding regarding the relationship." *Id.* at 276. Additionally, the court upheld the contract because the terms of the agreement were certain enough to provide a basis for determining breach and giving an appropriate remedy. *Id.* at 277, *citing* RESTATEMENT (SECOND) OF CONTRACTS §33(2). *See also, Blackmon v. Iverson,* 324 F. Supp. 2d 602 (E.D. Pa. 2003); *Media Sport & Arts v. Kinney Shoe Corp., supra.* Often overlooked is the fact that many relationships characterized as employment "at-will" would be deemed enforceable contracts but for the indefiniteness surrounding the duration of the agreement. *See Rooney v. Tyson,* 697 N.E.2d 571, 577–79 (N.Y. 1998) (Smith, J. dissenting); Justice Smith, dissenting; CALAMARI & PERILLO §2.9(3).

In a related sports context, contracts may fail where the duration is so undefined as to render the agreement fatally indefinite. For years, Major League Baseball argued that the standard option clause renewing the contract at the will of the club also renewed the option clause itself, thus creating a "perpetual" agreement. To the extent that such an agreement is deemed to exist perpetually or indefinitely, the contract could be construed to lack precise parameters and fail on that basis. *See Kansas City Royals Baseball Corp. v. Major League Baseball Players Ass'n,* 532 F.2d 615 (8th Cir. 1976); *Central New York Baseball, Inc. v. Barnett,* 181 N.E.2d 506 (Ohio C.P. 1961). Likewise, the indefinite nature of the contracts may suggest illusoriness, jeopardizing the contract's validity on consideration grounds. *Metropolitan Exhibition Co. v. Ward,* 9 N.Y.S. 779 (Sup. Ct. 1890); *Metropolitan Exhibition Co. v. Ewing,* 42 F. Supp. 198 (S.D.N.Y. 1890). Modern approaches to consideration make it improbable that this latter argument would prevail. *See* Part IV(A), below.

Finally, in certain contexts, a "Memorandum of Intent" or similar arrangement suggesting something short of a binding contract *may* be deemed an enforceable contract based on the surrounding circumstances and the nature of the transaction. Such inferences have been drawn in cases involving professional athletes. *See Arnold Palmer Golf Co. v. Fuqua Indus., Inc.,* 541 F.2d 584 (6th Cir. 1979). For example, it has been suggested that the College National Letter of Intent signed by prospective college athletes in response to a scholarship offer, manifests a binding bilateral contract. Cozzillio, *Scholarship, supra*; *Williams v. Univ. of Cincinnati,* 752 N.E.2d 367 (Ohio Cl. Ct. 2001); *Mercer v. Duke Univ.,* 32 F. Supp. 2d 836 (M.D.N.C. 1998).

III. Terminating the Offer and Aborting the Power of Acceptance: Revocation and Rejection

Several acts can terminate an offer, including revocation by the offeror, counter-offer or outright rejection by the offeree, the death of one of the parties, the destruction of the subject matter contained in the offer, and lapse of time. *See generally* RESTATEMENT (SECOND) OF CONTRACTS §§ 37–49. For purposes of this text, revocation by the offeror and the outright rejection or counter-offer/rejection by an offeree are the critical "terminators" of an offer.

(A) Revocation

Most offers are presumed to be revocable at the will of the offeror, provided that the offeree has not already manifested his acceptance by some effective means. *See* CORBIN § 38. Thus, even though the offeror has represented that a particular offer will remain open for a designated period of time, the offeror still reserves the right to revoke the offer within that time period, barring an effective acceptance. However, as discussed in Part II(B), if the offeree has secured the offeror's pledge of irrevocability by some exchange of consideration, or through some rough equivalent, such as seal, detrimental reliance, or a statutory dispensation of the need for consideration, then that offer will remain open for the period of time agreed to, or for a reasonable timeframe. *See* Note, *The Requirement of a Definite Time Period in Option Contracts*, 34 LA. L. REV. 668 (1974).

Normally, an offeror must communicate notice of a revocation to protect the offeree from detrimentally relying upon an offer that no longer exists. Thus, while an offeree's acceptance of an offer can be effective from the moment it leaves his or her possession (as in a situation where the parties invite mailing as an appropriate mode of acceptance), revocation of an offer will not be effective until the offeree receives it. The realization that the offeror is technically the instigator of the transaction and invites the offeree's acceptance should quickly dispel any misgivings about this approach's apparent bias in favor of the offeree. Because the offer invites acceptance, the offeror should assume that the offeree expects that acceptance to form a binding contract. Moreover, the offeror should realize that an offeree will act in reliance upon that logical assumption. By contrast, the offeree does not invite the offeror to revoke and therefore has no reasonable belief that a revocation is forthcoming until it actually arrives. As master of the offer, the offeror may seek to restrict the method and time of acceptance and, theoretically, may expressly reserve the right to revoke at will and without notice. However, absent some outward manifestation of the offeror's intent to revoke, some question exists as to whether this broad reservation of rights should permit an uncommunicated revocation to bar an otherwise effective acceptance.

Under appropriate circumstances, indirect or constructive communication of a revocation to an offeree may terminate the offer. If an offeree possesses knowledge from a reliable source that an offeror has contracted with a third party concerning the same subject matter contained in the original offer, and if the information is true, then such "indirect" revocation may operate to terminate the offer. *See, e.g., Dickinson v. Dodds*, 2 Ch. Div. 463 (Ct. App. Ch. Div. 1876); RESTATEMENT (SECOND) OF CONTRACTS § 43.

This approach seems to place substance over form and to give credence to an offeree's constructive knowledge that an offer no longer exists. Absent some agreement to forestall or circumscribe the offeror's power to revoke, the offeree is at the mercy of the offeror who chooses to terminate the offer prior to an effective acceptance.

(B) Rejection

A rejection is essentially a "manifestation of intention not to accept an offer," assuming that the offeree has demonstrated no intent to consider the offer further. RESTATEMENT (SECOND) OF CONTRACTS § 38(2). A counter-offer is an "offer made by an offeree to his offeror relating to the same matter as the original offer and proposing a substituted bargain differing from that proposed by the original offer." *Id.* § 39(1). A counteroffer generally acts as a rejection and, absent qualifying language demonstrating the offeror's or offeree's intent to reserve the acceptance prerogative, will terminate the offer. *Id.* § 39(2). As suggested above, an offeree's response that deviates in any way from the offer will operate as a rejection at common law and will vitiate the offeree's power of acceptance. Further, the offeree may manifest an unconditional assent to the offer but simultaneously propose additional or varied terms. Under the common law mirror image rule, these additional terms may compel the conclusion that the offeree finds the original offer unacceptable unless the offeree has provided indications to the contrary. *Id.* Finally, a conditional acceptance, which makes a purported acceptance of the offer dependent upon the offeror's acquiescence to other terms, will also generally terminate the offer even under the more progressive approaches denigrating the mirror image rule.

Thus, an offeree may reject an offer in several ways, including: outright rejection; implied rejection drawn from the offeree's counteroffer; a qualified acceptance that purports to embrace the terms of an offer but conditions such acceptance upon the incorporation of varied or additional terms; and, in some jurisdictions, an apparently unconditional acceptance that includes varied or additional terms. With respect to acceptances that incorporate varied or additional terms, U.C.C. § 2-207 has altered the playing field in the context of the sale of goods, permitting the formation of a contract notwithstanding the existence of additional or varied terms in an acceptance—provided the "dickered" or "material" terms (for example, price or quantity) are not in dispute. *See* U.C.C. § 2-207 (1977). Section 2-207 also provides a mechanism to ascertain whether these additional terms should be embraced by the final agreement. *See generally* Paul Barron & Thomas W. Dunfee, *Two Decades of 2-207: Review, Reflection and Revision.* 24 CLEV. ST. L. REV. 171 (1975); Richard Duesenberg, *Contract Creation: The Continuing Struggle With Additional and Different Terms Under Uniform Commercial Code Section 2-207*, 34 BUS. LAW. 1477 (1979); John Murray, *The Article 2 Prism: The Underlying Philosophy of Article 2 of the Uniform Commercial Code*, 21 WASHBURN L.J. 1 (1981). While the development of § 2-207 was a positive step toward reconciliation of the mirror image rule with well-recognized commercial exigencies, it has hardly been hailed as a paragon of legislative draftsmanship. *See, e.g.,* John Murray, *The Chaos of the "Battle of the Forms": Solutions,* 39 VAND. L. REV. 1307 (1986); Charles M. Thatcher, *Battle of the Forms: Solution by Revision of Section 2-207,* 16 U.C.C.L.J. 237 (1984); Gregory M. Travalio, *Clearing the Air After the Battle: Reconciling Fairness and Efficiency in a Formal Approach to UCC Section 2-207*, 33 CASE W. RES. L. REV. 327 (1983).

Not all apparent counteroffers will act as rejections terminating the offeree's power of acceptance. *See* RESTATEMENT (SECOND) OF CONTRACTS § 39. Under prevailing objective theory, an offeror's clear manifestation of intent to indulge counteroffers, and to maintain the vitality of the offer in the face of such counteroffers, will preserve the offeree's power of acceptance notwithstanding any intervening posturing. Moreover, if the offeree apprises the offeror of an intent to continue negotiations and a desire to keep the original offer under consideration, then the counteroffer accompanying the "reservation of rights" may properly be viewed as mere intermediate negotiations and not a rejection of the original offer.

Further, acceptances that raise further inquiries, comment negatively on the offer, or request a better offer do not necessarily constitute conditional acceptances or counteroffers containing varied terms. Rather, these responses simply represent types of grumbling acceptances that do not presume to present a substitute bargain in any way, but merely place the world on notice that the acceptor would be happier with a somewhat different deal. Clearly, the key in this latter context is to assess whether the additional term proposes a new contract, demonstrating dissatisfaction with the terms (some would say "material terms") of the original offer, or constitutes an acceptance conditional upon the offeror's assent to the new terms—both of which would negate the offeree's power to accept.

In any event, the outright rejection or the counteroffer/rejection does not become effective until communicated to the offeror. Thus, while acceptance generally becomes effective upon dispatch, a rejection will terminate an offer only upon receipt. Therefore, under a scenario in which the offeree mails an acceptance and subsequently recants, the acceptance will close the circle of assent even though the offeror's receipt of the rejection antedates the receipt of the acceptance. These generalizations are qualified by significant exceptions. For example, estoppel may bar the enforcement of the subsequent contract if the offeror has detrimentally relied on the rejection. Further, and of greater significance, the "mailbox rule" should not operate in the option contract setting where time typically is "of the essence" and acceptance is only effective upon receipt, absent contrary manifestations of intent by the offeror. *See generally* Murray § 47. *See also* RESTATEMENT (SECOND) OF CONTRACTS §§ 40, 63.

IV. Validation of the Contract and Enforcement of the Promise

(A) Consideration

The proposition that the law does not enforce all promises is unassailable. The traditional method of identifying those promises entitled to legal enforcement as part of a binding contract requires a determination of whether the promise is supported by consideration. Promises unsupported by consideration will not be enforced, barring activation of some equitable enforcement machinery.

Consideration has been defined as involving some benefit to the promisor or detriment to the promisee. Many courts, however, have given little credence to the importance of demonstrating actual benefit to the promisor or detriment in fact, as opposed to legal detriment, to the promisee. For example, in the classic case of *Hamer v. Sidway*, 27 N.E. 256 (N.Y. 1891), an uncle promised his nephew a small fortune to abstain from smoking, drinking, and other vices. The court declared:

Courts "will not ask whether the thing which forms the consideration does in fact benefit the promisee or a third party, or is of any substantial value to any one. It is enough that something is promised, done, forborne or suffered by the party to whom the promise is made as consideration for the promise made to him."

Id. at 257 (quoting Anson's Prin. of Con. 63). *See also Blackmon v. Iverson,* 342 F. Supp. 2d 602, 611 (E.D. Pa. 2003).

In a similar vein, Professors Calamari and Perillo place little emphasis upon the "benefit" variable or upon the existence of any "real" detriment. Their formula, adopted from Justice Cardozo's landmark opinion in *Allegheny College v. National Chatauqua County Bank,* 159 N.E. 173 (N.Y. 1927), determines consideration by applying a three-part test:

(a) The promisee must suffer legal detriment; that is, do or promise to do what he is not legally obligated to do; or refrain from doing or promise to refrain from doing what he is legally privileged to do.

(b) The detriment must induce the promise. In other words the promisor must have made the promise because he wishes to exchange it at least in part for the detriment to be suffered by the promisee.

(c) The promise must induce the detriment. This means in effect * * * that the promisee must know of the offer and intend to accept it.

CALAMARI & PERILLO § 4.2. Applying this neatly packaged formula, certain types of promises, however unequivocal, may be unenforceable. For example, a promise to do something that the promisee is already obligated to do, will not support a counterpromise under what is called the pre-existing duty rule. The promised detriment did not induce the promise; the obligation existed independent of the ostensible bargain. *Id.* This concept exists in theory in the context of modifications of a contract by the original parties or also to negate the enforceability of promises made by a third party. Thus, under the traditional view, a promise to pay $50 in exchange for a promise to perform some service is not enforceable if the service was owed by virtue of an earlier legally binding transaction. *Id.* § 4.9. The Calamari and Perillo formula also will not dignify a promise made in exchange for some detriment that has already occurred. Past consideration is not good consideration because the promise in that instance obviously has not induced the detriment. *Id.* §§ 4.2, 4.3, 5.2.

Because courts traditionally have avoided examining the adequacy of consideration or the amount of detriment suffered by the promisee, some commentators have suggested that any terminology embracing detriment or benefit is superfluous. RESTATEMENT (SECOND) OF CONTRACTS §§ 71, 79. They would instead emphasize the importance of a bargained-for exchange, the transaction motivator. The Second Restatement defines consideration as "a performance or a return promise [that] must be bargained for. * * * A performance or return promise is bargained for if it is sought by the promisor in exchange for his promise and is given by the promisee in exchange for that promise." *Id.* § 71. The Second Restatement also disdains any emphasis upon the traditional consideration vernacular, explaining: "If the requirement of consideration is met, there is no additional requirement of a gain, advantage, or benefit to the promisor or a loss, disadvantage, or detriment to the promisee." *Id.* § 79.

Calamari and Perillo state that both Restatements "may" have embraced an approach that finds legal benefit and legal detriment irrelevant to consideration. CALAMARI &

PERILLO §4.2. Their use of the term "may" is entirely appropriate because the Restatement is not clear. As Professor Murray suggests, "[t]here is a significant difficulty in discovering definitional terminology sufficient to encompass all that is meant by 'consideration.'" Murray concedes that there is consensus on two elements that comprise consideration: (1) a "bargained-for" exchange; and (2) benefit or detriment. MURRAY §§ 55–56. The definition of consideration has expanded and contracted considerably as part of judicial attempts to fashion a means to validate contractual agreements without making the process so rigid as to frustrate the clear attempts of the parties to reach an accord. Today, the three-prong test fostered by Calamari and Perillo, even though it speaks in terms of "detriment," seems to be an appropriate articulation of the exchange principle advanced by the Second Restatement. *See generally* Michael B. Metzger & Michael J. Phillips, *The Emergence of Promissory Estoppel as an Independent Theory of Recovery*, 35 RUTGERS L. REV. 472 (1983). It certainly is a useful mechanical formula to evaluate most consideration issues. The test also appears to do no violence to Professor Murray's consensus. Cozzillio, *Scholarship*, at 1337 n.238.

Recent authority illustrates the judicial gymnastics employed to stretch the definition of consideration to fit a particular transaction. When faced with promises that by their own terms plainly manifest no commitment whatsoever, courts have often engrafted implied promises of "good faith" or "best efforts." *See Wood v. Lucy, Lady-Duff Gordon*, 118 N.E. 214 (N.Y. 1917). For example, Party A's promise to grant Party B a percentage of any sales of B's product, in exchange for Party B's promise to give Party A the exclusive right to market the product, is facially illusory and theoretically is not consideration for Party B's counter-promise. Yet, the consideration problem is erased by judicially imposing an implied promise to exercise best efforts on Party A's apparently empty representations. Similarly, an absolute "cancellation at will" clause in an agreement may not negate the commitment to perform because there is either an express or implied notice requirement that, standing alone, may constitute sufficient detriment to justify enforcement of the contract as a whole. *See Sylvan Crest Sand & Gravel Co. v. United States*, 150 F.2d 642 (2d Cir. 1945). *But see Miami Coca-Cola Bottling Co. v. Orange Crush Co.*, 296 F. 693 (5th Cir. 1924). Such judicial constructions reflect attempts to exalt substance over form, and to preserve the legitimate notion that parties would not enter into an agreement unless they truly expected to be bound in some fashion. Drawing inferences of valid promissory intent from an agreement that appears to be devoid of meaningful commitment is not a radical concept. To do less would nullify a contract freely entered and possibly permit a *post hoc* escape for a party who envisions a better deal with another contractor.

Likewise, the rules governing pre-existing duty and past consideration have been relaxed in various contexts in the name of preserving rather than destroying contracts and encouraging parties to honor their agreements. Regarding the pre-existing duty rule, the Second Restatement has adopted a view that a promise by a third party is nonetheless enforceable even though it is "supported" by a promise to perform an extant duty. RESTATEMENT (SECOND) OF CONTRACTS § 73(c), comment d. Also, Article 2 of the Uniform Commercial Code and various state laws have reduced the need for new consideration in a contract modification. U.C.C. § 2-209. With respect to past consideration, various exceptions have emerged, including support for the proposition that some promises should be enforced simply because there is a moral obligation to perform. *See Webb v. McGowan*, 168 So. 196 (1935); RESTATEMENT (SECOND) OF CONTRACTS § 86.

Consideration questions have arisen in various sports contexts. In early cases, courts would disdain the enforcement of player contracts based upon traditional notions that each agreement must have mutuality of obligation. Thus, a player's commitment to play for a one-year period in exchange for a club's promise to pay his salary, terminable by the club at will or after a brief notice period, was deemed to lack consideration. The rationale simply was that the broad cancellation prerogative held by the club rendered its promise illusory and, because both sets of promises in a bilateral contract must be supported by consideration, the entire contract became void. *See, e.g., American League Baseball Club of Chicago v. Chase*, 149 N.Y.S. 6 (Sup.Ct. 1914). Moreover, the possible interpretation of option clauses as serving as perpetual renewals of existing agreements likewise contributed to the one-sided nature of the agreements and the overall illusoriness of the transaction. *See Metropolitan Exhibition Co. v. Ward*, 9 N.Y.S. 779 (Sup. Ct. 1890); *Metropolitan Exhibition Co. v. Ewing*, 42 F. Supp. 198 (S.D.N.Y. 1890).

In *Philadelphia Ball Club v. Lajoie*, 51 A. 973 (Pa. 1902), the court rejected the player's claim that he was free to abandon his contract because it lacked consideration. The court emphasized that mutuality of obligation does not mean that each party's duties must be identical. Rather, the only requirement in this regard is that there be mutuality of consideration, some type of bargained for exchange in which each party has suffered some legal detriment. Modern cases have reinforced this practical interpretation of consideration, preserving contracts that appear to manifest an intent by both parties to bind themselves to enforceable obligations. *See Nassau Sports v. Peters*, 352 F. Supp. 870, 876 n.18 (E.D.N.Y. 1972); *Erving v. Virginia Squires Basketball Club*, 468 F.2d 1064 (2d Cir. 1972). *But see Connecticut Professional Sports Corp. v. Heyman*, 276 F. Supp. 618 (S.D.N.Y. 1967). Courts, however, are unwilling to uphold contracts that are supported solely on past consideration. *See, e.g., Blackmon, supra; R.J. Hendricks v. Clemson Univ.*, 578 S.E. 2d 711 (S.C. 2003) (student athlete could not make out a breach-of-contract claim for an implied contract for academic eligibility because, *inter alia,* he did not discuss academic concerns until after he was enrolled and was attending the university; *Passante v. McWilliams*, 53 Cal. App. 4th 1240 (Cal. Ct. App. (1997)) (because the promise in question induced a detriment that had already been suffered it was deemed gratuitous and consideration was found lacking even though there may have been some moral obligation to honor it).

Consideration can also imperil the enforceability of contracts at the amateur sports level. For example, while there seems to be little doubt that the relationship between a scholarship athlete and a university has contractual underpinnings, the typical "agreements" establishing this relationship may suffer infirmities that render the contract void for want of consideration. For example, paragraph nine of the College National Letter of Intent ("NLOI" or "Letter") provides: "This Letter must be filed with the appropriate conference by the institution with which I sign within 21 days after the date of final signature or it will be invalid. In that event, this Letter may be reissued." National Letter of Intent Regulations and Procedures, Paragraph 9. This language arguably permits the university to nullify the Letter by letting the filing period pass without action. This possibility raises several issues: (1) does the language of paragraph nine, *on its face*, give the university the option to withdraw its scholarship offer and abort the entire agreement; (2) if the university can withdraw its offer, does an implied promise by the university to file the Letter within the appropriate time frame exist; and (3) what is the meaning of the tag sentence, "In that event, this Letter may be reissued?" The sentence gives no clue as to when or to whom the NLOI will be reissued.

The university's broad license to sit on its obligations and allow the twenty-one days to expire under paragraph nine poses a serious problem. Taken at face value, the clauses, "it [the Letter] will be invalid" and "this Letter may be reissued," could allow the university to let the time lapse and refuse to "reissue" the Letter, thus removing the acceptance arc from the circle of assent. *Id.* The wording is peculiar, as the offeror could arguably be deemed master of both the offer and the acceptance. Further, the promises of a promisor who possesses such absolute power to perform or refuse to perform could be illusory, voiding the apparent agreement.

Paragraph two of the NLOI declares:

> I MUST RECEIVE IN WRITING AN AWARD OR RECOMMENDATION FOR ATHLETIC FINANCIAL AID FROM THE INSTITUTION AT THE TIME OF MY SIGNING FOR THIS LETTER TO BE VALID. The offer or recommendation shall list the terms and conditions of the award, including the amount and duration of the financial aid. If such recommended financial aid is not approved within the institution's normal time period for awarding financial aid, the letter shall be invalid.

National Letter of Intent Regulations and Procedures, Paragraph 2. The final sentence of paragraph two could be construed as giving the university total control over the purse strings and the contract's validation. Even though most recommendations are eventually approved, the paragraph does not suggest that the university must adhere to the financial aid recommendations. Certainly, the wording of the Letter implies that the continued vitality of the agreement is a function of the university's continuing satisfaction with the bargain. *See generally* RESTATEMENT (SECOND) OF CONTRACTS § 77.

Many of the responses to paragraph nine of the Letter have equal utility in the resolution of potential consideration problems raised by paragraph two. The language seems to give the university *carte blanche* to disapprove any recommended financial aid package and thereby nullify the entire Letter of Intent arrangement. The absence of any meaningful commitment again raises the specter of illusoriness that could render the agreement void for want of consideration.

These illustrations only scratch the surface of the potential problems that could arise in assessing whether a contract between an athlete and his "employer" is supported by consideration. Their inclusion here serves to itemize the typical and not so typical arguments that could be used to challenge an agreement's apparent validity. Where a contract has been deemed invalid due to a lack of consideration or similar infirmity, the athlete or the club (or university) may seek enforcement of the contract on equitable grounds. The next section explores the notion of promissory estoppel and its geometric, if not exponential, expansion over the years.

(B) Promissory Estoppel

The Second Restatement of Contracts states: "A promise which the promisor should reasonably expect to induce action or forbearance on the part of the promisee or a third person and which does induce such action or forbearance is binding if injustice can be avoided only by enforcement of the promise. * * *" RESTATEMENT (SECOND) OF CONTRACTS § 90. This doctrine, commonly referred to as promissory estoppel, was developed to remedy the harsh effects of a promisee's justifiable reliance upon a promise otherwise unenforceable in contract for want of consideration or other infirmity. Classic applications involved family gifts, gratuitous bailments, bequests of land, and other promises in which the exchange necessary to establish a valid contract was plainly lacking. *See generally* Murray §66(A). In most cases, there was not even the pretense of a bargain.

The doctrine has evolved to the point where it can alternately serve as a consideration substitute, a loophole to circumvent the Statute of Frauds, and even an independent cause of action. *See, e.g.*, Restatement (Second) of Contracts §139. Some commentators have characterized promissory estoppel as a "contort" and have intimated that the geometric expansion of the doctrine illustrates that contract law has been absorbed piecemeal by tort law. Daniel A. Farber & John H. Matheson, *Beyond Promissory Estoppel: Contract Law and the "Invisible Handshake,"* 52 U. Chi. L. Rev. 903, 905 nn.8–12 (1985). Promissory estoppel can be catalogued under the tort aegis, on the premise that the predicate for remedying the injury is the victim's reliance upon a promise carelessly made. *Id.* The traditional view that promissory estoppel should only be invoked in the context of detrimental reliance, not the product of a bargain, fuels that notion. *See* Charles J. Goetz & Robert E. Scott, *Enforcing Promises: An Examination of the Basis of Contract*, 89 Yale L.J. 1261, 1274–75 (1980). *See also Detroit Tigers, supra* (court would not recognize a promissory estoppel claim where the alleged detrimental reliance was in the form of a performance that the plaintiff had already contractually agreed to do). However, the doctrine is regularly employed in situations where some semblance of a bargain has been struck or sought, and even where reliance was not the actual predicate for relief. *See Debron Corp. v. National Homes Constr. Corp.*, 493 F.2d 352 (8th Cir. 1974); *see also Loranger Constr. Corp. v. E.F. Hauserman Co.*, 384 N.E.2d 176 (Mass. 1978). These expansive applications call into question the traditional descriptive nomenclature, "unbargained-for reliance," and demonstrate the substantial growth of a concept that was at one time narrowly circumscribed.

Promissory estoppel has been applied to bargain configurations when a binding agreement was contemplated but either remained inchoate or failed to become a binding contract due to some infirmity such as indefiniteness. *See Kearns v. Andree*, 139 A. 695 (Conn. 1928). One frequent fact pattern involves subcontractor bidding in the construction industry. In *Drennan v. Star Paving Co.*, 333 P.2d 757 (Cal. 1958), the California Supreme Court, using promissory estoppel as its predicate, construed a bid arrangement between a subcontractor and a general contractor to be an option contract irrevocable by the subcontractor for a reasonable period of time. The court concluded that the subcontractor's bid, which was relied upon by the general contractor in submitting his bid to the "owner," was a promise carrying an attendant implied promise of at least temporary irrevocability. The general contractor's reliance upon the bid in preparation of his own bid acted to freeze the subcontractor's offer, much the same as consideration will cement the irrevocability of an offer in the typical option contract. The peculiar aspect of *Drennan* is that the offer plainly invited a promissory acceptance that was not forthcoming before the offer had been revoked. Thus, the court's reasoning reflected a road historically not taken—invoking promissory estoppel when an offer seeking a bilateral contract had been made and the bargaining process was well under way. *See, e.g., Northwestern Eng'g Co. v. Ellerman*, 10 N.W.2d 879 (S.D. 1943); *see also* Restatement (Second) of Contracts §87.

Situations involving subcontractors' bids are somewhat unique, and *Drennan* should not be read as freezing *all* offers to bilateral contracts when the offeree has detrimentally relied. Rather, when an offer seeks a promissory acceptance, courts will not, in the absence of the unique circumstances presented in the subcontractor bid scenario, take away the offeror's revocation prerogative prior to receipt of a return promise. However, *Drennan* does reflect an increasing judicial predisposition to invoke promissory estoppel in other bargain contexts. *See* Stanley D. Henderson, *Promissory Estoppel and Traditional Contract Doctrine*, 78 YALE L.J. 343, 368–71 (1969). For example, courts have applied promissory estoppel when a party has relied on a bilateral contract that is later found to be fatally indefinite or otherwise deformed. *See Wheeler v. White*, 398 S.W.2d 93 (Tex. 1965). The doctrine has also been used to permit recovery based upon one party's reliance on a questionable promise made as part of preliminary negotiations undertaken with an eye toward reaching a binding agreement. *See Associated Tabulating Services, Inc. v. Olympic Life Ins. Co.*, 414 F.2d 1306 (5th Cir. 1969); *Hoffman v. Red Owl Stores, Inc.*, 133 N.W.2d 267 (Wis. 1965). These lines of authority suggest that contractual foreplay may establish a basis for recovery when the putative promisee has detrimentally relied, even though an intent to be bound and demonstration of commitment are completely lacking.

Again, plaintiffs in various sports contexts have raised promissory estoppel arguments as alternative theories of recovery. *See, e.g., Rose v. Giamatti*, 721 F. Supp. 906 (S.D. Ohio 1989); *Soar v. NFLPA*, 438 F. Supp. 337 (D.R.I. 1975). In the scholarship-athlete situation, where the contractual arguments are more tenuous, the availability of promissory estoppel as a form of equitable relief could be significant. *See Cozzillio, Scholarship*, at 1356–59. Yet, courts have been reluctant to provide relief simply on the basis of plaintiff's vacuous claim that an unjust result has occurred. *See Hall v. NCAA*, 985 F. Supp. 782 (N.D. Ill. 1997). Likewise, promissory estoppel claims have been unavailing when asserted as substitutes for sufficient consideration where the deficiency in the consideration afflicts the promissory estoppel claim in the same way, *i.e.*, the promise did not induce any detriment. *See Media Sports & Arts v. Kinney Shoe Corp.*, 1997 U.S. Dist. LEXIS 12394 (S.D.N.Y. 1997).

V. Avoidance

Several circumstances arising in a particular relationship or commercial transaction may void a putative contract. A contract that is infirm for lack of consideration or a similar defect will be deemed void with no prerogative of ratification or affirmance by either party. Other types of contracts may have been the products of negotiations that, while not voiding the entire agreement, may render the contract voidable. Such an agreement would enjoy continued viability only through ratification, acquiescence, or a failure to disavow by the "victimized" party. *See generally* FARNSWORTH §§ 4.4, 4.19–.20. (Farnsworth catalogs these types of avoidance situations as problems of "status" and "behavior." *Id.* §§ 4.1, 4.9.) Among the types of circumstances that would render a contract voidable are incapacity, duress or undue influence, fraud or misrepresentation, mutual and occasionally unilateral mistake, and unconscionability. These concepts are addressed briefly below.

(A) Incapacity

If a party attempting to enter an agreement has failed to achieve the age of majority (generally, eighteen years) or is mentally infirm, then the contract will be voidable or, in certain circumstances, void. Generally, a minor may disaffirm a contract between himself and a non-minor party by expressing his intention to disaffirm on the grounds that the executed agreement was inappropriate due to the minor's lack of capacity to contract. The prerogative to disaffirm exists during minority or within a reasonable period of time after the infant has reached majority. *See McNaughton v. Granite City Auto Sales*, 183 A. 340 (Vt. 1936); *Ryan v. Hofstra Univ.*, 324 N.Y.S.2d 964 (1971). *But see Watson v. Ruderman*, 66 A. 515 (Conn. 1907). Of course, the minor, as the potential "victim," has the exclusive power to disaffirm the agreement. *See Quality Motors v. Hays*, 225 S.W.2d 326 (Ark. 1949). A court will not, however, invalidate a contract where, upon reaching the age of majority, the "victim" ratified the agreement. *See, e.g., In re The Score Board, Inc.*, 238 B.R. 585 (D.N.J. 1999) (holding that notification occurred when, after turning 18, Kobe Bryant deposited a check from the other party and performed executory obligations).

There are situations in which the minor may forfeit his disaffirmance prerogative or may find a jurisdiction inhospitable to the general rules governing a minor's ability to escape from an agreement "freely" entered. Included among these exceptions is the doctrine of "necessaries," in which a minor, who contracts for goods or services that will provide him with food, clothing, shelter, and similar items needed to maintain his existence, may be subject to the non-minor party's action for restitution. *See* FARNSWORTH § 4.5, n.4. A second exception to the general rule exculpating a minor from restitutionary liability is when the minor is a plaintiff in the contract enforcement action. The rationale for this exception is that "[t]he privilege of infancy is to be used as a shield, and not as a sword." *Rice v. Butler*, 55 N.E. 275, 276 (N.Y. 1899). A third exception may arise when the minor has misrepresented his age to the non-minor party. Some courts and commentators have reasoned that, because a fraudulent misrepresentation of age is actionable in tort if it induces reliance, and because minors are liable for their tortious acts, full restitution should lie for the adult party who has conferred benefits on the minor in reliance upon this misrepresentation. *See, e.g.,* 2 SAMUEL WILLISTON, WILLISTON ON CONTRACTS § 245 (Walter H.E. Jaeger (3d ed. 1970)).

Finally, even in the absence of these exceptions, some jurisdictions have departed from the general rule that a minor who has lost or destroyed the product of his agreement need not make restitution of the product in its original form. New Hampshire, for example, adopts the position that the minor cannot be permitted to disaffirm his contractual obligations unless and until he is able to make full restitution. *See Porter v. Wilson*, 209 A.2d 730 (N.H. 1965); *see also Valencia v. White*, 654 P.2d 287 (Ariz. 1982).

One author of this casebook's earliest and fondest recollections of sports was accompanying his father to watch the Philadelphia Phillies play the Cincinnati Reds (at the time commonly called the Redlegs) at Connie Mack Stadium in Philadelphia. The Reds' pitcher, Joe Nuxhall, had signed his first Major League contract at the tender age of fifteen. The author found it remarkable that such a young teenager could play professional baseball with grown men. What never crept into mind was whether Nuxhall had the capacity to sign a contract or whether such an agreement was voidable. It was a simpler time. Be that as it may, capacity issues frequently arise in the sports context, due to the presence of prodigies who are physically prepared for the highest level of competition long before their age would suggest such progress. *See, e.g., Gandler v. Nazarov*, 1995 U.S. Dist. Lexis 8325 (S.D.N.Y. 1995). Oftentimes the non-minor party allows for the underage signing by requiring a co-signing adult. For example, a high school student-athlete's signature on the National Letter of Intent must be accompanied by the signature of a parent or guardian. In some jurisdictions, statutes have been enacted to circumscribe a minor's ability to disaffirm a contract. Cal. Civ. Code §§ 3(a)(2)–(3) (West 1982); Cal.Lab. Code § 1700.37 (West 1989); N.Y. GEN. OBLIG.§ 3-101(2) (Consol. 1977). As might be expected, such statutes appear in jurisdictions, such as New York and California, where there are numerous child entertainers. *See Shields v. Gross,* 448 N.E.2d 108, (N.Y. 1983). Three states (California, Florida, and New York) have passed Coogan's Laws, legislation that allows employers to enter contractual agreements with minor athletes without fear that the minor will rescind on capacity grounds. These contracts generally must be approved by the court and contain provisions for the establishment of a trust. *See* Mark Rosenthal & Brian Yates, *Sign Up the Next Lebron James Before He Leaves High School? NOT So Fast,* 74 ENT. & SPORTS LAWYER 9 (Spring 2006).

(B) Duress and Undue Influence

The Second Restatement of Contracts declares: "If a party's manifestation of assent is induced by an improper threat by the other party that leaves the victim no reasonable alternative, the contract is voidable by the victim." *See* RESTATEMENT (SECOND) OF CONTRACTS § 175(1). In certain circumstances, especially those involving physical compulsion, the duress may render the entire agreement void as opposed to merely voidable. *See Fairbanks v. Snow,* 13 N.E. 596 (Mass. 1887). The improper threat can assume many forms, including physical abuse, threats of criminal prosecution, and various types of economic duress characterized as "business compulsion." *See* FARNSWORTH §§ 4.17, 4.18. The Second Restatement of Contracts defines undue influence as "unfair persuasion of a party who is under the domination of the person exercising the persuasion or who by virtue of the relation between them is justified in assuming that that person will not act in a manner inconsistent with his welfare." RESTATEMENT (SECOND) OF CONTRACTS § 177.

Of course, once the threat has been removed, the failure to disaffirm could result in the victim's ratification of the agreement. *See Gallon v. Lloyd Thomas Co.,* 264 F.2d 821 (8th Cir. 1959). Generally, in cases involving undue influence, the court places predominant emphasis upon two factors: (1) the relationship between the parties (*i.e.,* one of "confidence" or "dominance"), *see Kase v. French,* 325 N.W.2d 678 (S.D. 1982); *Methodist Mission Home v. NAB,* 451 S.W.2d 539 (Tex. Ct. Civ. App. 1970); and (2) the degree of excessive persuasion exercised. *See McCullough v. Rogers,* 431 So. 2d 1246 (Ala. 1963). For a comprehensive list of the factors to be considered in ascertaining whether or not an agreement was voidable a product of undue influence, see *Odorizzi v. Bloomfield Sch. Dist.,* 54 Cal. Rptr. 533 (1966).

Seldom does duress form the basis for avoidance of a party's contractual obligations in a sports context. Yet, it is conceivable that a rookie being besieged with offers from rival leagues or, more likely, a high school student-athlete being rushed by a large-scale university could argue that his commitment to play was a product of duress or undue influence. In fact, several college bound athletes have sought release from their Letters of Intent on this basis. *See* Cozzillio, *Scholarship,* at 1279, 1330–35. Given the special relationships that often develop between a coach and recruit and the tremendous pressure often exerted upon the student athlete to sign, it is conceivable that many scholarship arrangements could be the products of undue influence, both in the colloquial as well as legal sense of that term. This result could obtain whether we are discussing a professional team's pressure in the context of rival leagues or the typical college coach "rushing" his top recruit. *See, e.g., Los Angeles Rams Football Club v. Cannon,* 185 F. Supp. 717 (S.D. Cal. 1960). Other motivations may prompt an athlete to sign a contract that is not the product of free choice. *See Professional Hockey Club Central Sports Club of Army v. Detroit Red Wings, Inc.,* 787 F. Supp. 706 (E.D. Mich. 1992). Further, should new leagues be established, the battle for talent could result in arm-twisting that could rise to the level of undue influence. Finally an athlete who chooses to "hold-up" his team by threatening to withhold services at a critical time in exchange for a modification in his contract may find his new deal voidable due to the economic duress or business compulsion. *See Austin Instrument Inc. v. Loral Corp.*, 272 N.E.2d 533 (N.Y. 1971) (1971). *See also VKKCorp. v. NFL*, 94 Civ. 8335 (JES) (S.D.N.Y. 1994). In a wholly different vein, an interesting question that has been raised centers upon whether conference rules governing a high school athlete's participation are enforceable when the affiliation with such conference is theoretically voluntary but practically without a meaningful choice. *See, e.g., Robinson v. Kansas State High School Ass'n,* 917 P.2d 836 (Kan. 1996).

(C) Misrepresentation/Fraud

The Second Restatement of Contracts defines misrepresentation as "an assertion that is not in accord with the facts." *See* Restatement (Second) Of Contracts § 159; *see generally* Farnsworth §§ 4.10–.14; Murray § 95. Essentially, misrepresentation will render an agreement voidable if it was either fraudulent (knowingly false) or material and induced the victim' s justifiable and reasonable reliance in entering the particular agreement. *See Boston Mutual Ins. Co. v. New York Islanders Hockey Club,* 165 F. 3d 93 (1st Cir. 1999); *see also* Restatement (Second) of Contracts §§ 162–164. At times, a passive misrepresentation may occur in the form of a concealment or nondisclosure, which, by its nature, is equivalent to an assertion of a fact. *Id.* § 161. With regard to fraudulent nondisclosure, the operating premise is that the alleged misrepresenter has no duty to disclose. However, as the common law has evolved and a greater emphasis has been placed upon consumer protection, numerous circumstances will justify the finding of a misrepresentation when relevant facts have been deliberately concealed or simply not disclosed. For example, a party may be obligated to disclose given a relationship of trust and confidence that exists between himself and the other party. Likewise, a party who knows that revealing additional facts is necessary to correct a previous erroneous assertion has a duty to disclose. *See* Calamari & Perillo §§ 9–20. Of course, as with other avoidance issues, a party who becomes aware of the misrepresentation and, in effect, waives its objection by ratifying the arrangement may be precluded from avoiding its contractual obligation. *See Time Warner Sports Management Merchandising v. Chicago Land Processing Corp.,* 974 F. Supp. 1163 (N.D. Ill. 1997).

In the early days of fledgling sports leagues, there is frequently intense competition between leagues to sign superstar amateur players. Often this competition provokes bidding wars with the established leagues. In such a situation, the player who has signed a contract with one club, only to regret his decision, may seek to avoid his contractual obligations by claiming misrepresentation, duress, or a similar avoidance predicate. As discussed earlier, the player frequently will argue that the agreement never occurred and that there was no mutual assent. However, misrepresentation may also provide the escape hatch that the athlete seeks. Again, the high school student-athlete is particularly vulnerable to the inflated egos and expansive representations of recruiters and other athletic department officials. *See, e.g., Los Angeles Rams Football Club v. Cannon,* 185 F. Supp. 717 (S.D. Cal. 1960). *See also Reedy v. Cincinnati Bengals, Inc.,* 758 N.E.2d 678 (2001); *Boston Mut. Ins. Co. v. N.Y. Islanders Hockey Club,* 165 F.3d 93 (1st Cir. 1999). Bear Bryant, renowned University of Alabama football coach, once said:

If I wanted a kid bad enough, I used every trick I could think of. Frank Leahy used to tell everybody that when I was at Kentucky, I dressed our manager Jim Murphy, in a priest's outfit to recruit Gene Donaldson away from Notre Dame. Maybe Jim Murphy did tell Donaldson he was a priest. Shucks, I'd have told him Murphy was Pope Pius the XII if I'd thought we would get Donaldson that way.

W. MORRIS, THE COURTING OF MARCUS DUPREE 51 (1986).

A rather unique application of misrepresentation to sports contracting arose in the context of the Pittsburgh Pirates refusal to pay superstar Dave Parker a portion of his promised compensation as a result of Parker's alleged drug use. The club claimed, *inter alia*, that Parker's conduct constituted a misrepresentation in terms of his commitment to perform in a satisfactory manner and to the best of his abilities. The club, therefore, argued that their contractual duties were voidable. *Pittsburgh Assocs. v. Parker*, Slip Op. (W.D. Pa. 1986). This case settled prior to litigation; yet, it presents an interesting approach for clubs who seek not only to release subpar players but also to relieve themselves of any guaranteed salary or benefit commitments. In another unique application, season ticket holders have frequently attempted to attack football teams' failure to honor holders' rights of first refusal on misrepresentation/fraud grounds. *See Charpentier v. Los Angeles Rams Football Club*, 75 Cal. App. 4th 301 (Cal. Ct. App. 2000); *Beder v. Cleveland Browns, Inc.*, 129 Ohio 3d 188 (Ohio App. 1998).

(D) Mistake

A mistake is a belief that is not in accord with the facts. *See* RESTATEMENT (SECOND) OF CONTRACTS §151. A mistake will render a contract voidable when, at the time the contract is formed, a basic erroneous assumption on which such agreement was based materially affects the exchange of performances. Mutual mistakes can assume many forms, including mistakes of identity, subject matter, transmission, etc. If the assumption made represents a conscious uncertainty on the part of both parties, particularly with regard to mistakes as to subject matter, then the risk of such mistake will have been assumed by both parties and the contract generally will not be voidable. *See Sherwood v. Walker*, 33 N.W. 919 (Mich. 1887); *Wood v. Boynton*, 25 N.W. 42 (Wis. 1885); *see also Gartner v. Eikill*, 319 N.W.2d 397 (Minn. 1982). Care should be taken to differentiate basic misunderstandings, in which there has been no mutual assent and thus no agreement, from mistakes. *See, e.g., Raffles v. Wichelhaus*, H. & C. 906, 159 Eng. Rep. 375 (1864). *Compare* RESTATEMENT (SECOND) OF CONTRACTS §20 *with* §§151–154.

Traditionally, courts have been unwilling to permit a party to escape contractual obligations based on unilateral mistake. *See Mutual of Enumclaw Ins. Co. v. Wood By-Products Inc.*, 695 P.2d 409 (Idaho 1984). Even under this strict view, a unilateral mistake may have justified avoidance by the mistaken party where the erroneous assumption was palpable and recognized by the other party. *See, e.g., Hanby v. Claymont Fire Co. No. 1*, 528 A.2d 1196 (Del. 1987). Modern jurisprudence has blurred traditional distinctions between mutual and unilateral mistakes, particularly in the context of errors in mathematical calculation. *See Boise Junior College Dist. v. Mattefs Constr. Co.*, 450 P.2d 604 (Idaho 1969); *see also* Ernest M. Jones, *The Law of Mistaken Bids*, 48 U. CIN. L. REV. 43 (1979). The factors to be considered in determining whether or not a contract can be avoided based upon unilateral mistake in this context include: (1) the materiality of the mistake; (2) the unconscionability of enforcement; (3) the mistaken party's "reasonableness" or culpability; (4) the prejudice to the non-mistaken party; and (5) the timing of notification that a mistake has been made. *See* Murray §91. The Second Restatement has embraced an approach that would expand the universe of cases voidable due to unilateral mistake beyond computational errors and similar situations. In addressing such situations, the Second Restatement considers many of the factors listed immediately above. *See* Restatement (Second) of Contracts §153.

A sports-related case that attracted considerable attention in this area involved an eleven-year-old baseball card collector who purchased a Nolan Ryan rookie card at an incredibly low price. The deal was made because a part-time clerk did not realize that the card had been mislabeled and sold it as advertised. When the shopowner attempted to rescind the sale based on a theory of mistake or misunderstanding, the purchaser (and his family) refused. The matter was resolved amicably, but presents an interesting question as to whether the law of mistake would provide the seller with an avenue of escape. Would the seller's theory rest upon the grounds that there never was a deal due to a misunderstanding or that the contract was voidable under the doctrine of mistake? *See* Restatement (Second) of Contracts §§20, 151–154. The answer to this question once again turns on the courts' general refusal to indulge errors made unilaterally and beyond the limited circumstances outlined above. *See Myskina v. Conde Nast Publications, Inc.,* 386 F. Supp. 2d 409 (S.D.N.Y. 2005).

(E) Unconscionability

An agreement may be deemed unconscionable if it involves unfair surprise (often called "procedural unconscionability") or oppressive terms (often called "substantive unconscionability"). *See* Murray §96. *See also* U.C.C. §2-302. In essence, defects in the bargaining process, such as phrasing terms in language that the average consumer cannot understand, constitute a category distinct from situations involving a lopsided transaction in which one party has received the dramatically short end of the stick. *See Resource Mgt. Co. v. Weston Ranch,* 706 P.2d 1028, 1042 (Utah 1985). *See also Williams v. Walker-Thomas Furn. Co.,* 350 F.2d 445 (D.C. Cir. 1965); *Jones v. Star Credit Corp.,* 298 N.Y.S.2d 264 (1969). In assessing whether a particular arrangement is unconscionable, courts will consider many factors, including the choices available to the contracting parties, fundamental assumptions regarding each party's duty to read and understand the agreement, the sophistication of the parties, and the time, place, and circumstances surrounding the arrangement.

Normally, unconscionability cases arise in the context of unwary consumers or other unsophisticated contracting parties. Frequently, it has become a catch-all for every bad bargain that cannot be avoided through any other device. At the same time, it represents a positive expansion of contract jurisprudence by protecting parties who have been victimized by flim-flam sales approaches, outrageously incomprehensible contract language, or adhesive bargains so one-sided and oppressive as to offend the sensibilities of any reasonable person.

In the sports context, it is conceivable that excessively long or broad negative covenants may subject an agreement to avoidance on unconscionability grounds. Thus, a player seeking to avoid an injunction on equitable grounds based on the unreasonable length or breadth of the negative covenant may also find a viable defense in the unconscionability of the agreement. *See generally Connecticut Professional Sports Corp. v. Heyman,* 276 F. Supp. 618 (S.D.N.Y. 1967); *Long Island Am. Ass'n Football Club, Inc. v.*

Manrodt, 23 N.Y.S.2d 858 (Sup. Ct. 1940). Players have also occasionally claimed, in large part unsuccessfully, that grievance mechanisms and arbitration clauses in collective bargaining agreements were unconscionable and that the agreements negotiated are contracts of adhesion. *See Morris v. New York Giants*, 575 N.Y.S. 2d 1013 (Sup. Ct. 1991); *Alexander v. Minnesota Vikings Football Club*, 649 N.W.2d 464 (Minn. Ct. App. 2002). Interestingly enough, in earlier cases, prior to the notion of unconscionability coming into legal vogue, the unbalanced nature of the transaction caused the contract to fail on consideration grounds under the rubric of "mutuality of obligation." *See* Part III(A), *supra. See also American Base Ball & Athletic Exhibition Co. v. Harper*, 54 Cent. L.J. 449 (Mo. 1902).

(F) Impossibility

At times, a party may be rendered unable to fulfill contractual obligations because the promised performance has become impossible. In that eventuality, the court will assess whether the inability to perform will serve as an excuse for the other party's refusal to honor its obligations (where the performance rendered impossible is an express condition) or as a defense to a breach (where the performance is part of a promise). Of course, an express condition ordinarily mandates strict compliance and a party's failure to meet that condition would signify that the duty of the other party has not been triggered. If the performance were part of a promise then the failure to satisfy it would constitute a breach, which if material, would likewise forgive the other party's duty to perform in addition to creating damage liability.

The Second Restatement of Contracts declares in relevant part:

> Where, at the time a contract is made, a party's performance under it is impracticable without his fault because of a fact of which he has no reason to know and the non-existence of which is a basic assumption on which the contract is made, no duty to render that performance arises, unless the language or circumstances indicate the contrary.

RESTATEMENT (SECOND) OF CONTRACTS § 266 (1). Thus, the critical features of an impossibility defense are an unforeseen event rendering performance impossible or highly impracticable that was beyond the control or outside of the assumed risk of the party claiming inability to perform. *See Sunflower Electric Cooperative, Inc. v. Tomlinson*, 638 P.2d 963 (Kan.Ct.App. 1981). If these factors have been met, then the party unable to perform would be insulated from liability, with the obvious byproduct being the release of the other party's counter-obligations — assuming that the failed performance was substantial. *See Shaw v. Mobil Oil Corp.*, 535 P.2d 756 (Ore. 1975)("'[I]f one of these promises becomes impossible of performance, the party who made it may be excused from legal duty. His failure to perform is not a breach of contract. But the fact that the law excuses him from performance does not justify him in demanding performance by the other party.' 6 CORBIN, CONTRACTS, 510–511, § 1365 (1962).").

Where the performance involves an express condition, the added wrinkle is that the party unable to perform may still insist on the other party's performance if the performance rendered impossible was material. The early English cases prove most illustrative. *Compare Poussard v. Spiers and Pond*, 1 QBD 410 (1876) *with Bettini v. Gye*, 1 QBD 183 (1876). For example, if a tennis player's appearance fee were part of a contract that contained an express condition requiring the player to meet with fans to sign autographs on the Saturday before a major tournament, and he was unable to meet that obligation due to serious illness, but was still able to play in the tournament, then the condition would probably be excused and the player would still be entitled to the appearance fee. If the condition involved a performance that was a material part of his ultimate obligation (*e.g.*, a requirement to participate in doubles *and* singles with such condition unsatisfied because the serious illness precluded the playing of doubles), then the "impossibility" would not excuse the condition and the duty to pay the appearance fee would not be triggered.

This issue could arise in other sports contexts where, for example, a team is unable to meet payroll obligations due to insolvency or where other unforeseen factors compromise a player or team's inability to satisfy its promise to play or pay. *See e.g., Stabler, supra.* Boxers, injured in preparation for a bout, frequently seek postponements due to their inability to pass the physical or to perform up to par. Of course, most personal services contracts anticipate those occurrences and address the consequences in the contract by virtue of a *force majeure* clause or similar vehicle.

An interesting collateral question surrounds situations where the performance is not impossible but its preclusion would frustrate the underlying foundation of the contract. A contract can be avoided even if the direct subject of the contract is still capable of performance. If a team advertises a contest as "Superstar X's last game" and he is unable to play due to injury, may the ticket holder obtain a refund even though the game is still played without Superstar X? *See Krell v. Henry,* 2 KB 740 (C.A.K.B. 1903).

(G) Illegality

At first blush, it would appear that the term illegality harbors serious criminal consequences. In contract law, however the term does not necessarily involve criminality. Rather, it refers to a wide range of circumstances that may render a contract unenforceable. Often it is ascribed to situations where the agreement is void on grounds of public policy. This broad iteration can mean the agreement in question is violative of a local ordinance (*see Bennett v. Hayes,* 125 Cal. Rptr. 825 (Cal. Ct. App. 1975)), a restraint of trade implicating federal or state antitrust laws (*e.g.*, overly broad covenants not to compete (see *BDO Seidman v. Hirshberg,* 690 N.Y.S. 2d 854 (N.Y. 1999)), failure to meet state licensing requirements (see RESTATEMENT (SECOND) OF CONTRACTS §181), and a variety of other arrangements involving untoward conduct (*see* RESTATEMENT (SECOND) OF CONTRACTS §§178–196).

Courts approach such illegal contracts in a variety of ways, including voiding the entire agreement, severing the illegal portion, otherwise sometimes known as blue penciling, or permitting the innocent party (if there be one) to enforce the contract or at least recover in restitution. To be sure, at times the concept of illegality is honored in the breach rather than in the enforcement. *See* CALAMARI & PERILLO §22.2(a)–(f).

In the sports context, illegal bargains could be struck in a variety of ways. Most prominently, contracts containing overly broad or unconscionable negative covenants may be deemed illegal and unenforceable on public policy grounds or because they run afoul of the antitrust laws. *Id.* §16.19; *Vanderbilt v. Dinardo,* 174 F.3d 751 (6th Cir. 1999). Agent-athlete agreements, which involve the agent's performance of functions beyond his authority (*e.g.*, providing certain types of investment advice without securing proper authorization from the Securities and Exchange Commission, could also fail due to illegality. *See generally, Zinn v. Parrish*, 644 F.2d 360 (7th Cir. 1981); *Walters v. Fullwood*, 675 F. Supp. 155 (S.D.N.Y. 1987); *Detroit Lions, Inc. v. Argovitz*, 580 F. Supp. 542 (E.D. Mich. 1984). Finally, contracts between boxers and promoters have been challenged on illegality grounds where the agreement violates state laws and pertinent agency regulations. *See De LaHoya v. Top Rank, Inc.*, 2001 U.S. Dist. LEXIS 25816 (C.D. Cal. 2001).

VI. Performance

In ascertaining the performance obligations of parties to a contract, it is first necessary to identify each party's promises and any conditions that will qualify or trigger the performance of such duties. There is a substantial difference between a condition and a promise, and the failure to fulfill either of these contractual elements has distinct and significant consequences. "A promise is generally defined as a 'manifestation of intention to act or refrain from acting in a specified way so made as to justify a promisee in understanding that a commitment has been made.'" RESTATEMENT (SECOND) OF CONTRACTS §2(1). A condition is an event, not certain to occur, which must occur, unless its non-occurrence is excused, before performance under a contract becomes due." *Id.* §224.

Express conditions generally require strict compliance. Any duty dependent upon satisfaction of an express condition will be suspended or discharged if such a condition is not completely and literally followed. *See Inman v. Clyde Hall Drilling Co.*, 369 P.2d 498 (Alaska 1962). A promise, on the other hand, creates a duty that must be fulfilled in order to avoid a breach. *See* CORBIN §633. In a typical bilateral contract, a constructive condition born of a promise must be substantially performed before a corresponding duty arises. *See generally* RESTATEMENT (SECOND) OF CONTRACTS §231. There are two key points in assessing the finding of a promise versus the finding of a condition. First, the breach of a promise renders the promisor subject to an action for damages or specific performance, whereas the failure of a condition creates no such liability. Second, the constructive condition spawned by the promise need only be substantially performed. *See Howard v. Federal Crop Ins. Corp.*, 540 F.2d 695 (4th Cir. 1976).

The concepts of substantial performance and material breach go hand in glove. If a promise giving rise to a constructive condition is materially breached, then the underlying condition has not been substantially performed. Correspondingly, an immaterial breach generally involves substantial performance of the constructive condition created by the promise. One party's failure to perform substantially in this regard justifies the other party's termination of the contract (or, at least, suspension of performance awaiting a possible "cure") as well as an action for breach. *See* MURRAY §107(B). Substantial performance of the condition may still subject the performer to suit based on the immaterial breach, but the other party's duty to perform will have been triggered. *See generally* CALAMARI & PERILLO §§11–18. The assessment of substantial performance considers the entire performance rather than the performance of each promise. *See* RESTATEMENT (SECOND) OF CONTRACTS §232 cmt. b. *See also O'Brien v. Ohio State Univ.*, 2005 Ohio 3335 (Ct. Cl. 2005). For a summary of the factors considered in determining the materiality of a breach and substantiality of performance, see RESTATEMENT (SECOND) OF CONTRACTS §§241–243. For a discussion of the "victim's" option to continue performing after a material breach, see FARNSWORTH §8.15. The underlying assumption in the above summary is that the promises in a bilateral contract are dependent. This conclusion is eminently plausible; true independent promises are rare and the notion has developed that the performance obligations in a bilateral contract setting are dependent "except in special cases," *See Corn Exch. Nat'l. Bank & Trust Co. v. Taubel*, 175 A. 55, 61 (N.J. 1934); Murray § 155.

Ponder the classic lawn-mowing hypothetical: A promises to pay B $50 (times have changed) in exchange for B's promise to mow A's lawn. The agreement also contains the following term, "lawn to be mowed with a 'Super Shred' lawn mower." This term could be deemed a promise or a condition. If the former, B's use of a substantially equivalent mower may trigger A's duty to pay, but would also leave B vulnerable to a suit for breach, albeit immaterial. If the term were interpreted as a condition, then the use of the other mower would theoretically discharge A's duty to pay because B had not strictly complied with the condition. If the clause contained additional language tailoring it as both an express condition and a promise, then A could argue that his duty was discharged *and* that he had a cause of action against B for breach of promise. To evade the harsh consequences of the strict compliance requirement, courts will often construe an obvious condition as a promise (activating a more flexible substantial performance analysis), *Jacob & Youngs v. Kent*, 129 N.E. 889 (N.Y. 1921); excuse the condition to avoid a forfeiture, *Ledford v. Adkins*, 413 S.W.2d 68 (Ky. 1967); or divide the contract to save those portions that were satisfied by compliance, *Yeargin v. Bramblett*, 156 S.E.2d 97 (Ga. App. 1967).

This hypothetical also points out the importance of the order of performance because most promises in a bilateral contract create conditions of exchange. *Corn Exch. Nat'l. Bank & Trust Co.*, 175 A. at 61 ("The order in which the things are to be done, it would seem, is now a significant, if not the controlling, factor.") For purposes of this discussion, a few general rules will suffice. First, when the parties manifest an intent to exchange all performances simultaneously, the performances are generally due simultaneously. Restatement (Second) of Contracts §234(1). When true simultaneity is impossible, it is commonly understood that tender of the requisite performance (*i.e.*, a showing of willingness and ability to perform) is sufficient. Second, when one party's performance in the exchange of promises requires time to complete, his or her performance is generally due prior to the performance of the other party. *Id.* §234(2). In a typical contract for services, the work normally must be performed before payment becomes due. *Id.* §234 cmt. e.

In addition to the aforementioned presumption favoring promises over conditions, courts consider various factors in attempting to draw the often subtle distinctions between these two concepts. The factors include the peculiarities of the transaction, any pertinent idiosyncrasies of the trade or the parties' relationship, and, most important, the nomenclature used and the objectives sought by the provision. *See* Restatement (Second) Of Contracts §§ 226–227. The oft-indulged prescription that advises courts to resolve doubts in favor of a "promissory" construction serves as a backdrop to this exercise in interpretation. Professor Williston has aptly articulated the rationale for this presumption:

> Because the enforcement of conditions frequently leads to forfeitures and penalties, courts have always been indisposed to interpret contracts as containing conditional promises, unless the language is too clear to be mistaken. * * *

> The courts have frequently disregarded plainly expressed conditions, because of their unwillingness to deprive a promisee of all rights on account of some trivial breach of condition.

6 Samuel Williston, Williston on Contracts §827 (footnotes omitted) (Walter H.E. Jaeger 3d ed., 1970).

The differentiation between a promise and a condition, and the consequences of such determination, present unique difficulties in the sports and entertainment fields. For example, in attempting to define a professional sports team's prerogative to terminate a player's contract, courts and commentators have intimated that the promise to play carries a condition of satisfaction that allows a club to terminate the agreement if it is not satisfied with the player's performance. It is unclear whether this condition is implied in fact, thereby "express," invoking a strict compliance requirement, or whether it is a constructive condition derived from a promise to perform satisfactorily. In any event, most contracts delineate the reasons justifying a team's decision to terminate a player's contract. *See, e.g.,* Article II of the National Football League Uniform Player Contract, §7(b) of Major League Baseball's Uniform Contract, and §20 (b)(2) of the National Basketball Association Uniform Player Contract. Essentially, these contracts specify that the player may be terminated if he fails to exhibit sufficient skill or ability to compete with other players on the club. Where the agreement does not explicitly outline the parameters of competency or performance, the standard is deemed to be "ordinary and reasonable skill, care and diligence." Annotation, *Employer's Termination of Professional Athlete's Services as Constituting Breach of Employment Contract*, 57 A.L.R.3d 257 (1974). *See also* Richard J. Ensor, *Comparison of Arbitration Decisions Involving Termination in Major League Baseball, the National Basketball Association and the National Football League*, 32 St. Louis L.J. 135 (1987). However, while the term "reasonable" is employed, the standard is subjective, rather than objective, and courts will generally assess the club's good faith in assessing the propriety of the termination.

The rationale for the subjective approach is that the nature of professional sports justifies considerable deference to decisions of coaching staffs and management hierarchy. *Cincinnati Bengals, Inc. v. Bergey*, 453 F. Supp. 129 (S.D. Ohio 1974). The assessment of skill is not limited to concrete examples of achievement, such as batting averages or shooting percentages; it also embraces considerations of the intangible variables of leadership, teamwork, and motivation. Courts and arbitrators will often indulge the team's determination of whether a player has demonstrated sufficient skill, based on both tangible and intangible factors. There is some authority for the proposition that the club's decision should be based on objective criteria under the reasonable person standard. *See, e.g.,* Tim Freudenberger, *Eliminating Drug Use in Sports Utilizing Contractual Remedies*, Ent. & Sports Law 20 (Summer 1987). However, application of an objective test seems to be limited to terminations based on disciplinary action rather than the player's insufficient skills. *See In re Major League Baseball Players Assoc. and the San Diego Padres and Peter Ueberroth*, Panel Decision No. 74 (June 16, 1987) (Nicolau, Arb.). Thus, to the extent the club's satisfaction is qualified by any standard, it is most often limited to this subjective, good faith requirement.

Moreover, the line between full performance and substantial performance is quite thin in any personal services contract in the sports and entertainment fields. Substantial performance could equal full performance, when the ultimate performance of the promise has no upper limit. Thus, if a Major League pitcher hurls a "perfect game" he has undeniably "performed"; but, if he pitches a two-hit shutout in the following game, he most certainly has not breached the contract, materially or otherwise. Of course, there are some examples of traditional substantial performance notions in professional sports, such as when a player (in exchange for payment and in addition to his promise to play) has pledged to engage in a limited number of club promotions. Adherence to all promises save these "minor" obligations may constitute substantial performance of the contract as a whole, but may leave the athlete vulnerable to an action for immaterial breach. *See* JOHN C. WEISTART & CYM H. LOWELL, THE LAW OF SPORTS § 3.07 (1979).

When a coach fails to produce a successful team, defined as significantly more wins than losses, there is authority supporting his/her discharge and the termination of the employer's contractual obligations. While the terminology may vary, the upshot of such a decision is that the coach's substandard performance in terms of win-loss record constitutes a material breach warranting the employer's cessation of its own performance obligations. *See Cole v. Valley Ice Garden,* 113 P.3d 275 (Mont. 2005). In various contexts, courts have suggested that coaches are employed at will. *See Kish v. Iowa Cent. County College,* 142 F. Supp. 2d 1084 (N.D. Div. 2001). In the professional sphere, the predominance of win-loss record as a factor in determining the substantiality of performance is understandable. Yet, in a college setting, it seems readily apparent that overemphasis upon winning has contributed to recruiting violations, unstable relationships and an intrusion on the academic, as opposed to professional, model for college athletics. *See* Brian Porto, *Completing the Revolution: Title IX as Catalyst for an Alternative Model of College Sports,* 8 SETON HALL J. SPORT L. 351 (1998).

VII. Need for a Writing

The Statute of Frauds, developed in England during the 16th century to eliminate problems of perjury in contract dispute resolution, has been adopted in almost every American jurisdiction by statute and by other jurisdictions in some form through judge-made law. While there are numerous peculiar statutory provisions governing the need for a writing to evince the existence of a contract, five principal provisions of the original statute of frauds have survived in most jurisdictions. Essentially, a writing is required in the following circumstances: (1) suretyship contracts; (2) contracts of executors and administrators to be personally liable for the debts of the estate; (3) agreements made in consideration of marriage; (4) contracts for the sale of land; (5) contracts that cannot be performed within one year. In addition, the Uniform Commercial Code specifically requires that certain types of transactions necessitate a writing. *See* U.C.C. § 2-201.

Interpretation of each of the above categories has spawned no small amount of litigation and critical commentary. For example, in the area of suretyship contracts, a seemingly cut and dried area, courts have developed approaches such as the "primary purpose" or "leading object" doctrine, which takes an agreement out of the Statute of Frauds if the purpose of the arrangement is to protect or further the interests of the guarantor. *See Contractor's Crane Service, Inc. v. Vermont Whey Abatement Auth.,* 519 A.2d 1166 (Vt. 1986). *See generally Power Entertainment, Inc. v. NFL Properties, Inc.,* 151 F. 3d 247 (5th Cir. 1998). The one-year rule and its nuances have been a bane to the existence of most law students searching to find consensus among the rule's numerous permutations and combinations. RESTATEMENT (SECOND) OF CONTRACTS § 130, ILL. 1–11. Similarly, with regard to the "one-year" rule, where a series of alternative performances will satisfy a party's obligations, the contract will rest outside the statute if either one is capable of performance within one year. Some courts have even found the contract to rest outside of the statute where one of the alternatives was an anticipated inability to perform fully. In such situations, the oral contract was found to be enforceable notwithstanding the fact that actual full performance could not have been effected within one year. *Compare*

Hopper v. Lennen & Mitchell, 146 F.2d 364 (9th Cir. 1944) *with Coan v. Orsinger*, 265 F.2d 575 (D.C. Cir. 1959). In terms of satisfying the statute, the requirements for a "writing" are broad and expansive. The Second Restatement declares:

§131. General Requisites of a Memorandum

Unless additional requirements are prescribed by the particular statute, a contract within the Statute of Frauds is enforceable if it is evidenced by any writing, signed by or on behalf of the party to be charged, which

(a) reasonably identifies the subject matter of the contract,

(b) is sufficient to indicate that a contract with respect thereto has been made between the parties or offered by the signer to the other party, and

(c) states with reasonable certainty the essential terms of the unperformed promises in the contract.

RESTATEMENT (SECOND) OF CONTRACTS §131. Courts have sewn together separate writings connected by express reference or inference to satisfy the requirement of a memorandum. Even where some of these separate writings had not been signed, courts still found that the "pieced-together" document satisfied the statute's writing requirement. *See Crabtree v. Elizabeth Arden Sales Corp.*, 110 N.E.2d 551 (N.Y. 1953). *See Detroit Tigers, Inc. v. Ignite Sports Media, LLC*, 203 F. Supp. 2d 789, 798 (E.D. Mich. 2002).

Clearly, it is impossible in this summary to discuss the nuances of each category and the divergent judicial opinions addressing the myriad sub-issues. It suffices to say that, given the Statute of Frauds' preoccupation with form over substance, courts will often take extreme measures and engage in the most creative sophistry to avoid application of the statute. *See, e.g.,* RESTATEMENT (SECOND) OF CONTRACTS §139, which calls for the enforcement of a promise to avoid injustice notwithstanding the presence of the Statute of Frauds. Many commentators believe that the statute has outlived its usefulness. Their opinion is entitled to considerable respect given the fact that England, the primogenitor of the Statute of Frauds, has significantly pared the original statute, limiting those types of contractual relationships necessitating proof of a writing to be enforceable. For an excellent synopsis of the Statute of Frauds, *see* MURRAY §§ 68–80.

In the world of sports, the Statute of Frauds has been implicated particularly with regard to the "one-year" rule. *See, e.g., Jim Bouton Corp. v. William Wrigley, Jr. Co.*, 1989 U.S. Dist. Lexis 7656 (S.D.N.Y. 1989); *Hennessey v. NCAA*, 564 F.2d 1136 (5th Cir. 1977); *Houston Oilers, Inc. v. Neely*, 361 F.2d 36 (10th Cir. 1966). *See Detroit Tigers, supra; Athletes & Artists, Inc. v. Millen*, 1999 U.S. Dist. LEXIS 11991 (S.D.N.Y. 1999) (former NFL linebacker and current president of the Detroit Lions Matt Millen successfully argued that he was under no obligation to pay agents for services under an oral contract because the obligations arising thereunder could not be performed in less than one year). Yet, remarkably enough, the statute has reared its head in other contexts in which professional athletes have been parties, such as suretyship contracts. *See, e.g., NFL Insurance Ltd. v. B & B Holdings, Inc.*, 1993 U.S. Dist. 3312 (S.D.N.Y. 1993). Given the types of informal exchanges that occur between coaches and players, athletic directors and student athletes, promoters and boxers, it is likely that the oral nature of many transactions will continue to be an issue in contract enforcement. *See, e.g., Madison Square Garden Boxing, Inc. v. Shavers*, 434 F. Supp. 449 (S.D.N.Y. 1977); *see also, Rooney v. Tyson*, 697 N.E.2d 571 (N.Y. 1998) (Smith, J., dissenting) (1998). Further, notwithstanding considerable judicial dissatisfaction with the Statute of Frauds, courts will continue to refuse to enforce oral agreements. For example, in *Holloway v. King*, 361 F. Supp. 2d 351 (S.D.N.Y. 2005), plaintiff/boxing managers alleged that promoter Don King had breached an oral agreement to provide plaintiffs 10% of the promoter's earnings derived from exploiting boxer Mike Tyson's fights. Because the agreement could not be performed within a year, the court, applying the Statute of Frauds, sustained King's motion to dismiss. It is noteworthy that the court differentiated contracts that contemplate the possibility of termination within one year from contracts that are terminated within one year by virtue of a failure to perform. *See also Coan v. Orsinger*, 265 F.2d 575 (D.C. Cir. 1959). *Compare Hopper v. Lennen & Mitchell*, 146 F.2d 364 (9th Cir. 1944).

VIII. The Parol Evidence Rule

Frequently parties to a written contract will attempt to show that the written agreement is not the entire embodiment of their understanding. They will ask a court to consider whether earlier verbal or written agreements, or other extraneous evidence, should be admitted for the purpose of supplementing or contradicting the formal contract. Whether such information should be admitted is governed by the parol evidence rule.

Reduced to its essentials, the parol evidence rule has been defined as follows.

> If the parties to a transaction have embodied that transaction in whole or in part in a single memorial such as a writing or writings, and if they regard that memorial as the final expression of their intention as a whole, or of a part thereof, then all other prior or contemporaneous utterances by the parties in connection with that transaction, whether oral or written, are inoperative for the purpose of ascertaining the terms of their contract, or at least so much of it as is embodied in the memorial.

JOHN MURRAY, MURRAY ON CONTRACTS §82(B).

The key inquiries that will guide application of the rule are whether the written agreement is integrated and, if integrated, whether it is completely integrated. An integrated document is one that constitutes the "final expression of one or more terms of an agreement"; a completely integrated document is "adopted by the parties as a complete and exclusive statement of the terms of the agreement." RESTATEMENT (SECOND) OF CONTRACTS §§209–210. The existence of a "merger" clause, one reflecting the parties' expressed intent that the written agreement be the sole and exclusive repository of their understanding is strong evidence that the agreement is fully integrated and not susceptible to additions or contradictions. Of course, a court may find a document to be completely integrated even in the absence of such a provision. *See Adler v. Shaykin & Wachner*, 721 F. Supp. 472, 476–77 (S.D.N.Y. 1988).

If an agreement is only partially integrated, consistent additional terms may be admissible to supplement the written agreement, but not to contradict. RESTATEMENT (SECOND) OF CONTRACTS §§213–216. If the document is completely integrated, additional terms may not be admitted to supplement or contradict. *Id.* In some formulations, the sanctity of the written contract may be disturbed if the prior oral agreement: 1) is collateral in form; 2) does not contain the expressed or implied language of the final memorial; 3) reflects an arrangement that one would not expect to find in the writing—i.e., would not naturally be included in the written agreement. *See Mitchell v. Lath*, 160 N.E. 646 (N.Y. 1928). *See also Myskina v. Conde Nast Publications, Inc.*, 386 F. Supp. 2d 409 (S.D.N.Y. 2005); *Lee v. Joseph E. Seagram & Sons*, 552 F.2d 447 (2d Cir.

1977); RESTATEMENT (SECOND) OF CONTRACTS § 216. Thus, if a player and club embody their agreement in the standard player contract, and there is evidence of a prior oral understanding that the club would provide air transportation and hotel accommodations for the players' parents to attend all away games, evidence of such an understanding may be admissible to supplement the written contract. *See Lee v. Joseph E. Seagram & Sons, supra.* This arguable exception to the parol evidence rule, which some argue only assumes importance when needed to contradict an apparently fully integrated document containing a merger clause, is commonly known as the collateral admission test. *See* FARNSWORTH, *supra,* at § 2.3.

Overall, how the parol evidence rule is applied to determine whether a document is non-integrated, integrated, or completely integrated has generated enough debate, critical commentary, and statutory language to fill this entire volume. Suffice it to say that the major contract treatises, most notably Corbin's and Williston's prolific works, the Second Restatement, and Article 2 of the Uniform Commercial Code (§ 2-302), have all advanced their own interpretations of the rule and its implications. For a comprehensive synopsis of the various approaches, *see* CALAMARI & PERILLO, *supra* §§ 3.4(c) & (d); MURRAY, *supra* § 82. While all of the formulations have their idiosyncracies, the most dramatic differences lie in Professors Corbin's and Williston's approaches. The former has expressed considerable disdain for the rule, arguing, for example, that all pertinent evidence of intent should be examined to ascertain the integrated or non-integrated nature of an agreement — thus, particularly in a non-jury trial, eviscerating the rule. Williston, on the other hand, would give significantly more credence to the document itself and apply the rule in a more expansive fashion. *See* CALAMARI & PERILLO, *supra,* §§ 3.4 (c) & (d). The debate that has raged on between these two prominent scholars continues in the even thornier questions governing the role that parol evidence should play in resolving difficult questions of contract interpretation. *Id.* §§ 3.11, 3.12. *See O'Brien v. Ohio State Univ.,* 2005 Ohio 3335 (Ohio 2005); *Fox Sports Net v. Minnesota Twins Partnership,* 2002 U.S. Dist. LEXIS 8896 (D. Minn. 2002), aff'd 319 F.3d 329 (8th Cir. 2003); *Dombrowski v. New Orleans Saints,* 764 So. 2d 980 (La. Ct. App. 2000).

Finally, in considering the possible application of the rule, bear in mind that several exceptions exist wherein parol evidence will be admitted notwithstanding its apparent inadmissibility. For example, where the parties to a written contract have verbally agreed that the obligations under an agreement are subject to the occurrence of a condition, evidence of that condition is admissible. RESTATEMENT (SECOND) OF CONTRACTS §217. Likewise, evidence of a fraud or a lack of consideration to support the promises in an agreement is admissible notwithstanding the apparent integration of the writing that purports to embody the agreement. Id. § 218. Finally, the parol evidence rule is a rule of substantive law, not a rule of evidence. Thus, most commentators agree that failure to object to the admission of evidence at trial would not preclude raising the issue on appeal. *See e.g.* MURRAY, *supra,* § 82(B); FARNSWORTH, *supra,* § 7.2. *But see Parker v. Parker,* 681 N.W.2d 735, 744 (Neb. 2004); *Chantey Music Pub. Inc. v. Malaco, Inc.,* 915 So.2d 1052, 1060 (Miss 2005).

Recent sports-related cases have turned on some of the subtle distinctions addressed above. In *Yocca v. Pittsburgh Steeler Sports, Inc.,* 854 A.2d 425 (Pa. 2004), plaintiffs had claimed that a brochure inviting applications for season tickets, was an offer whose terms were part of a contract. Plaintiffs signed a contract that, in part, contained terms that differed from the brochure. Plaintiffs' attempts to introduce the brochure as evidence were rejected. The court found that the presence of a merger clause rendered the final contract as exclusive and barred all other evidence under the parol evidence rule.

Similarly, in a slightly more provocative context, tennis professional Anastasia Myskina sued a magazine publisher contending, *inter alia*, that the defendant disseminated nude photographs of her without authorization. The crux of Myskina's argument was that there had been a prior agreement between her and the publisher to the effect that the photographs would have a limited distribution. However, subsequent thereto, Myskina signed a release authorizing a broader dissemination. The court refused to admit as evidence the alleged conversation in which the publisher agreed to circumscribe distribution holding "although the release does not contain an explicit merger or integration clause, its language * * * indicates an intention * * * to be bound only by the terms of the release." For obvious reasons, the court likewise rejected Myskina's collateral agreement argument, finding that the evidence was central not collateral, contradictory not supplementary, and a matter that one would expect to be embodied in the writing. *See also Holloway v. King*, 361 F. Supp. 2d 351 (S.D.N.Y. 2005); *White v. NFL*, 972 F. Supp. 1230 (D. Minn. 1997).

IX. Third Party Beneficiary

At times, rights may accrue to a person who derives a benefit from the performance of a contract, even when that individual is not a party to the contract; *i.e.*, neither a promisor nor a promisee. This beneficiary may become vested with such rights even though there is no privity in the traditional sense. *See* Murray, *supra* § 129. There has not been consensus as to when the rights actually vest, but the predominant commentary suggests that vesting accrues when the putative beneficiary "would be reasonable in relying on the contract." *Id.* § 130. At the very least, the third party will be deemed protected when he or she has manifested assent to the promise in question at the request of the promisor or promisee or has materially and justifiably relied on the promise. Restatement (Second) of Contracts § 361 (3).

> Two distinct types of beneficiaries exist in contract jurisprudence, intended and incidental. The Second Restatement defines each as follows:
>
> § 302. Intended and Incidental Beneficiaries
>
> (1) Unless otherwise agreed between promisor and promisee, a beneficiary of a promise is an intended beneficiary if recognition of a right to performance in the beneficiary is appropriate to effectuate the intention of the parties and either
>
>> (a) the performance of the promise will satisfy an obligation of the promisee to pay money to the beneficiary; or
>>
>> (b) the circumstances indicate that the promisee intends to give the beneficiary the benefit of the promised performance.
>
> (2) An incidental beneficiary is a beneficiary who is not an intended beneficiary.

Incidental beneficiaries have no contract rights as third party beneficiaries. Thus, if A owes B money from a pre-existing debt or perhaps seek to enrich B in some way, and C promises A that she will compensate B in exchange for a performance by A, B is an intended beneficiary. On the other hand, if B owned a haberdashery, he would only be an incidental beneficiary if C promised A that she would buy him a tie from B's establishment.

Beyond these basic rudiments, numerous questions abound as to the rights and defenses of third party beneficiaries. A comprehensive analysis obviously is beyond the scope of this chapter and this volume. Yet, as a starting point, the following general principles emerge. In terms of the parties' rights and obligations *vis a vis* each other, the third party beneficiary may enforce the contract against the promisor. But the promisor may assert any defenses available to him against the promisee. The parameters of the promisor's defense will turn on whether the promise is absolute. If C promises A that she "will pay B whatever A owes him" rather than "will pay B $500," then C will be able to assert any defenses that she could have raised against A (*e.g.*, lack of consideration). C would also be able to raise any defenses that A would have had available against B. If the obverse were true, C's ability to assert any defenses that A would have had available against B would be compromised. In a related vein, if B is a creditor beneficiary (owed a debt), B can sue either the promisor (C) or promisee (A). Finally, A can sue B and recover on the original debt. *See generally* CALAMARI & PERILLO §§ 17.12–.14.

While the third party beneficiary issue has not arisen in the sports context very often it has been raised in conjunction with arguments that the relationship between an athletic conference and a constituent member creates third party beneficiary rights of student athletes. The contention has been that a conference mission to pursue goals that will advantage student athletes, reflects the conference's intention "to assume a direct contractual relationship" with the constituent member's student athletes. *See Hairston v. Pacific 10 Conference*, 101 F.3d 1315, 1320 (9th Cir. 1996). Courts are wary of accepting this argument. *Id.* "To succeed on a third-party beneficiary claim, [plaintiffs] must show that they were intended and not merely incidental beneficiaries to the contract between the NCAA and [the university]." *Hall v. NCAA*, 985 F. Supp. 782, 796 (N.D. Ill. 1997). *See also M Sports Prod. v. Pay-Per-View Network, Inc.*, 1998 U.S. Dist. LEXIS 401 (S.D.N.Y. 1998) ("[T]he parties (sic) intent to benefit a third party must be shown on the face of the agreement, although the obligation to the third party beneficiary need not be explicitly stated"). *See also Lewis v. Rahman*, 147 F. Supp. 2d 225 (S.D.N.Y. 2001), where the plain language of a boxing/promotion contract clearly identified heavyweight champion Lennox Lewis as a third party beneficiary with rights to enforce the terms of the agreement conferring benefits upon him.

X. Assignment

The Second Restatement provides in relevant part:

> An assignment of a right is a manifestation of the assignor's intention to transfer it by virtue of which the assignor's right to performance by the obligor is extinguished in whole or in part and the assignee acquires a right to such performance.

RESTATEMENT (SECOND) OF CONTRACTS § 317. To create an effective assignment, the proprietor of the rights under the contract must demonstrate (to the assignee or a third person) an intent to convey such rights. If X and Y are parties to a contract, one of the parties, X, may transfer rights or duties to a third party, Z. X is the assignor, Y is the obligor, and Z is the assignee. The manifestation of such an intent will be assessed under an objective standard. *See generally* FARNSWORTH § 11.3.

There are no talismanic words that evince an assignment, provided that there is the requisite manifestation of intent (*e.g.*, "I hereby assign," "I authorize the transfer," etc.).

Where the assignment is exchanged for consideration or where some reliance can be shown, the assignment is is irrevocable. Where revocability is possible, such triggers may include bankruptcy or death of the assignor. If X dies, the assignment of the rights under prior arrangement with Y, is revoked. Z's rights against Y are subject to the same defenses that Y had against X * * * if they are inherent in the contract (*e.g.,* a lack of consideration). Related defenses are only available if they predated Y's knowledge of the assignment. Obviously, Y cannot raise any defenses that X may have had against Z, and Z cannot assert any claims against X when Y is unable to perform (*i.e.,* if X assigns rights to a contract to Z, Z cannot sue X for the assigned performance if Y becomes unable to perform.

The ability of an assignor to transfer the obligor's performance obligation to a third party (the assignee) is somewhat limited. Instances in which an assignment may be precluded include: (1) the assignment would materially alter the duty of the obligor or otherwise substantially change the risks assumed or the performance expected by the obligor under the contract; (2) a statute or public policy forbids the assignment; or (3) the contract itself legitimately prohibits the assignment. *Id.* For a thorough discussion of each of these three qualifiers, *see* CALAMARI & PERILLO §§ 18-12 to 18-16. Further, personal services contracts generally are not assignable. If an obligor would be bound under an assignment to perform services for someone other than the original obligee, the putative assignment would be precluded (*e.g.,* where the services are unique).

In the world of sports, the classic example of an assignment is the trading of players. When one club trades a player in exchange for another player or a future draft choice, the club has effected an assignment. Typically, in a personal services contract, this type of assignment would be prohibited. However, the Uniform Player Contract generally contains a provision in which the player explicitly consents to an assignment, thus conceivably waiving, where permissible, the aforementioned exceptions to the general rules allowing assignments. For example, Section 17 of the National Football League Uniform Player Contract provides:

> Unless this contract specifically provides otherwise, Club may assign this contract and Player's services under this contract to any successor to Club's franchise or to any other Club in the League. Player will report to the assignee Club promptly upon being informed of the assignment of his contract and will faithfully perform his services under this contract. The assignee club will pay Player's necessary traveling expenses in reporting to it and will faithfully perform this contract with Player.

See also National Basketball Association Player Contract, Section 10; National League Uniform Player Contract, Section 7. Of course, the pertinent collective bargaining agreements may proscribe the assignment of certain players. *See* Basic Agreement between the American League of Professional Baseball Clubs and the National League of Professional Baseball Clubs and Major League Baseball Players Association, Art. XIX.

A contract may contain a special covenant in which the club surrenders its prerogative to assign the contract to another club. These provisions are commonly referred to as "no-trade" clauses. Numerous issues have arisen in this area regarding the nature and scope of the no-trade language. Consider, for example, whether a change in ownership would justify a player's refusal to perform, under the rationale that the transfer of ownership functionally constitutes a change in teams. *See, e.g., Munchak Corp. v. Cunningham,* 457 F.2d 721 (4th Cir. 1972); *Washington Capitals Basketball Club, Inc. v. Barry,* 419 F.2d 472 (9th Cir. 1969). Similar questions surrounding the efficacy and breadth of no-trade provisions abound in the sports law context. *See generally* WEISTART & LOWELL §§ 3.13, 3.14. In effect, the player trade would be precluded at common law, but the UPC waiver resurrects the right to assign and the no-trade special covenant returns the process to square one.

XI. Remedies

There are three fundamental recovery interests in the typical breach of contract or contract rescission scenario: expectation; reliance; and restitution. Generally, punitive damages are unavailable in the context of a contract action except in the most unusual circumstances. *See White v. Benkowski*, 155 N.W.2d 74 (Wis. 1967). *But see Hibschman Pontiac, Inc. v. Batchelor*, 362 N.E.2d 845 (Ind. 1977). The expectation interest is intended to place the injured party in the position he would have been in had the contract been fulfilled. Thus, this interest is designed to insure that the injured party receives the benefit of his bargain. *See, e.g., United Indus. Syndicate v. Western Auto Supply Co.*, 686 F.2d 1312 (8th Cir. 1982). Oftentimes, the court will be confronted with a difficult damage calculation, based on the fact that a literal application of the expectation approach will result in considerable unjust enrichment to the plaintiff and a hardship to the defendant. For example, where a defendant has failed to complete a particular project or has done so in a defective manner, the cost of completing the performance or correcting the defects may be grossly disproportionate to the likely loss in value to the plaintiff. *See Eastlake Constr. Co. v. Hess*, 686 P.2d 465 (Wash. 1984); *Peevyhouse v. Garland Coal & Mining Co.*, 382 P.2d 109 (Okla. 1962). Where there is such a gap between the cost to remedy the defect and the actual loss in value, courts may base recovery on the reduction in market price to avoid unnecessary economic waste. *See Peevyhouse, supra.* Professor Farnsworth has criticized this approach, suggesting that, "rather than accept the Draconian choice between overcompensation through cost to remedy and undercompensation through diminution in market price, the trier of facts ought to be allowed at least to fix an intermediate amount as its best estimate * * * of the loss in value to the injured party." FARNSWORTH § 12.13; *see also* RESTATEMENT (SECOND) OF CONTRACTS §§ 347, 348.

The reliance measure of damages attempts to recompense the injured party for any change in position made in reliance on the contract (such as costs expended for performance or preparation for performance offset by any loss that the breaching party can demonstrate "with reasonable certainty the injured party would have suffered had the contract been performed"). *See* RESTATEMENT (SECOND) OF CONTRACTS § 349. The purpose of the reliance remedy is to place the injured party in the same position as he would have been had the contract not been made. Though reliance may take on many forms, including direct reliance upon the subject contract as well as other types of incidental reliance, it does not include lost profits. As a rule, reliance damages will be a subset of expectation relief and often are employed by courts to provide some relief to an injured party who is unable to establish expectation damages with the requisite certainty. Further, reliance damages presume a contract in which the injured party would, at a minimum, have broken even; thus, to the extent that a particular contract would have resulted in a loss, such loss will be employed to offset the reliance damages to which the injured party may be entitled. *See* CALAMARI & PERILLO § 14.9.

The restitution interest attempts to prevent any unjust enrichment to the breaching party and returns to the injured party benefits conferred to the one in breach. It is normally an amount less than the expectation and reliance interests, but it will be a part of the calculus in ascertaining expectation and reliance damages. *See* Restatement (Second) of Contracts § 371; *United States v. Algernon Blair, Inc.*, 479 F.2d 638 (4th Cir. 1973); *compare Johnson v. Bovee*, 574 P.2d 513 (Colo. Ct. App. 1978); *see also* Robert Childress & Jack Garamella, *The Law of Restitution and the Reliance Interest in Contract*, 64 Nw. U. L. Rev. 433 (1969). Restitution also may be available to a breaching party who has not strictly complied with the requirements of a particular contract but has conferred benefit on the non-breaching party that would result in unjust enrichment to that party. *See* Restatement (Second) of Contracts § 374; *Lancellotti v. Thomas*, 341, 491 A.2d 117 (Pa. Super. Ct. 1985). For a comprehensive analysis of the various types of recovery interests, see L.L. Fuller & William R. Perdue, Jr., *The Reliance Interest in Contract Damages*, 46 Yale L.J. 52 (1936–37). This article is universally accepted as the starting point for any analysis of monetary relief in the context of a breach of contract.

A party's entitlement to relief under any of the foregoing interests is qualified by requirements that the damages sought be foreseeable and reasonably certain. With respect to foreseeability, the injured party must be able to show either that the breaching party should have anticipated the loss as a likely result of a breach: because it follows in the "ordinary course of events"; or because it follows due to special circumstances beyond the ordinary course of events, but through a course of events within the reasonable contemplation of the breaching party. *See* Restatement (Second) of Contracts § 351; *see also Hadley v. Baxendale*, 9 Ex. 341, 156 Eng. Rep. 145 (1854). Bear in mind that the foreseeability component involves what should have been anticipated at the time of contracting, not at the time of breach, and that foreseeability focuses not on the contemplation of the breach but the contemplation of damages that would flow from such breach. Finally, be mindful of the modern view that foreseeability should be viewed from the perspective of the breaching party. *See* Farnsworth § 12.14; Murray § 120.

The certainty requirement places a responsibility upon the injured party to demonstrate that there is some reasonable basis upon which to calculate the damages sought. At times, the uncertainty feature may result in the injured party receiving no recompense. In other situations, the uncertainty feature may result in a finding that there is no adequate remedy at law, thus justifying an award of specific performance or other equitable remedy. *See Wilson v. Sandstrom*, 317 So. 2d 732 (Fla. 1975). While courts may differ in terms of the availability of specific performance in this context, it is undeniable that precluding any relief whatsoever serves a hardship on the injured party to the advantage of the party who breached the contract. Many courts will stretch their imaginations to establish some type of certainty given the fact that the alternative would be to benefit the very party whose breach has caused the uncertainty. *See* Farnsworth §12.15; *Milton v. Hudson Sales Corp.*, 313 P.2d 936 (Cal. Ct. App. 1957).

At times, where contracting parties recognize that it may be difficult if not impossible to determine damages with reasonable certainty in the event of a breach, they may establish a basis for damages on the face of the contract itself. *See Vanderbilt v. Dinardo*, 174 F.3d 751 (6th Cir. 1999). These "liquidated" damages clauses are generally enforceable, provided that they are not disproportionate to what a reasonable amount of damages would be. Some courts will also place emphasis upon the difficulty of proving actual damages and the intent of the parties at the time of contracting. *See Banta v. Stamford Motor Co.*, 92 A. 665 (Conn. 1914). Finally, the purpose of the liquidated damages clause must be to make the "victim" of a breach whole. Otherwise the liquidated damages provision will be viewed as nothing more than a subterfuge to permit a penalty, which is antithetical to the notion that contract remedies should be compensatory, not punitive. *See Lake River Corp. v. Carborundum Co.*, 769 F.2d 1284 (7th Cir. 1985). An interesting question arises in the context of liquidated damages clauses where the injured party fails or refuses to mitigate damages (*see* below). This problem is particularly acute in the area of employment contracts, where an employee, discharged in breach of such an agreement, relies on the liquidated damages clause and makes no effort to obtain other employment. *See Koenings v. Joseph Schlitz Brewing Co.*, 377 N.W.2d 593 (Wis. 1985).

The final qualifier in the damage equation obliges the injured party to avoid the accrual of unnecessary and additional damages—commonly characterized as "mitigation." The injured party's duty to mitigate damages generally only involves such mitigation that can be effected without "undue risk, burden or humiliation" and mitigation that can be effected with "reasonable" efforts. *See* RESTATEMENT (SECOND) OF CONTRACTS §350; *see also Parker v. Twentieth Century-Fox Film Corp.*, 474 P.2d 689 (Cal. 1970). Further, to the extent that the contract in question involves a non-exclusive arrangement, the mitigation requirement is diluted because it is assumed that the injured party would have been attempting to secure additional contracts independent of the other party's breach. *See Payne v. Pathe Studios, Inc.*, 44 P.2d 598 (Cal. Ct. App. 1935); *see also* CALAMARI & PERILLO §§14–16.

Specific performance is the fundamental equitable remedy awarded by a court to enforce a contract. It is the classic example of the ultimate expectation relief, in the sense that it places the injured party in exactly the position he would have occupied had the contract been fulfilled. There are numerous exceptions and limitations upon securing specific performance, including problems with a lack of precision or definiteness in a particular contract, failure to satisfy basic equitable prerequisites such as an inadequate remedy at law, irreparable injury, undue hardship, etc. *See, e.g.*, RESTATEMENT (SECOND) OF CONTRACTS §357. Further, courts will not award specific performance to remedy a breach of a personal services contract. The difficulty in administering such a remedy, together with the obvious problems of involuntary servitude, compels the conclusion that specific performance in this context is simply inappropriate. Of course, those considerations do not preclude a court from enjoining a breaching party in a personal services contract to *refrain* from specific actions, such as performing similar functions for another party in direct violation of a covenant to refrain from such activity.

Breach of the typical sports contract could visit a range of remedies upon the breaching party. A club's failure to meet its payment obligations to players could result in back pay liability and/or, if the breach is material, a declaration that the victim/player is a free agent (i.e., the player may repudiate his contractual obligations due to the club's failure to perform substantially). *See, e.g., Alabama Football, Inc. v. Greenwood*, 452 F. Supp. 1191 (W.D. Pa. 1978); *Alabama Football, Inc. v. Stabler*, 319 So. 2d 678 (Ala. 1975); *American and National Leagues of Professional Baseball Clubs v. Major League Baseball Players Ass'n*, 130 Cal. Rptr. 626 (Ct. App. 1976). This issue is addressed comprehensively in Chapter 6.

When a player "jumps" his or her contract and signs with another club, the available remedies are limited. Damage awards are infrequent because the amount due is often speculative and uncertain. *See generally* Gary A. Uberstine, *The Enforceability of Sports Industry Employment Agreements*, in LAW OF PROFESSIONAL AND AMATEUR SPORTS Ch. 9 (Gary A. Uberstine ed., 2002). Moreover, as stated above, courts will not require the player to return to his original club because such an order would constitute involuntary servitude and would be extremely difficult to administer. *See generally Lumley v. Wagner*, 482 Eng. Rep. 687 (1852). *See also* James T. Brennan, *Injunction Against Professional Athletes Breaching Their Contracts*, 34 BROOKLYN L. REV. 61 (1967). Thus, in most cases of this sort, the only avenue remaining for the club is the negative injunction, an order barring the breaching player from performing for the new club. *See, e.g., Philadelphia Ball Club v. Lajoie,* 51 A. 973 (Pa. 1902) (court cannot compel defendant to play for plaintiff, but court can restrain defendant from playing for another club); *Northeastern Univ. v. Brown,* 17 Mass. L. Rep. 443 (Mass. Super. Ct. 2004) (court would not allow university football coach to coach for competing university); *Marchio v. Letterlough,* 237 F. Supp. 2d 580 (E.D. Pa. 2002). In order to secure an injunction, the moving party must generally establish a probability of success on the merits and the potential to suffer irreparable harm. At the threshold of the analysis the plaintiff must demonstrate that there is a valid, enforceable contract and that there is no adequate remedy at law to make the victim whole.

A contract action for a negative injunction essentially involves the enforcement of a negative covenant that is expressed in the Uniform Player Contract or other arrangement between the athlete and his employer/contractor. It is essential that such a covenant be reasonable, not excessively broad in terms of geography, duration or subject matter scope. For example, a covenant that prohibits a player from participating in "any competitive event, any place in the world" for a period well in excess of the actual contractual term, may not be enforced notwithstanding the ostensible consent of the parties. Courts, generally wary of covenants not to compete, are extremely circumspect about covenants that impose oppressive conditions, particularly where there is evidence of unequal bargaining power. *See* CALAMARI & PERILLO §§ 16–19 (A)–(C). Even absent such a covenant, courts will often construct one from the surrounding circumstances. *See Lewis v. Rahman,* 147 F. Supp. 2d 225 (S.D.N.Y. 2001); *Madison Square Garden Boxing Inc. v. Shavers,* 434 F. Supp. 449 (S.D.N.Y. 1977). At times, they will help to salvage an overly onerous covenant by "blue penciling" it—excising the unreasonable parts and keeping the rest. CALAMARI & PERILLO *supra,* at § 16.21. Further, the plaintiff must also show that the defendant/player was unique. While the definition of unique has no real consensus (varying from indispensable to simply being a professional athlete—a rarity in itself), a plausible working standard is one suggesting difficulty of replacement. *See Philadelphia Ball Club v. Lajoie,* 51 A. 973 (Pa. 1902). The uniqueness issue has been largely obviated by language in Uniform Player Contracts containing a stipulation that the player is unique. *See Minnesota Muskies, Inc. v. Hudson,* 294 F. Supp. 979 (M.D.N.C. 1969); *Barnett v. Hayes,* 53 Cal. App. 3d 900 (1975). Going hand in glove with the uniqueness variable is the requirement that there be no adequate remedy at law. *Boston Professional Hockey Ass'n v. Cheevers,* 348 F. Supp. 261 (D. Mass. 1972). If one is unique, the injury caused by his repudiation of the contract is likely irreparable—damages cannot rectify the harm. *See Shavers, supra.*

Questions surrounding the issuance of a negative injunction, including the prerequisites for relief and the availability of equitable defenses are discussed at length in Chapter 6. Because the injunction is equitable, any party seeking such relief must approach the court in somewhat pristine condition. "He who comes into equity must come with clean hands." 2 JOHN N. POMEROY, *A Treatise on Equity Jurisprudence* §§ 397, 398 (1941). Therefore, a club that has pirated a player from another club, only to have the player return to the former club, may encounter considerable difficulty enjoining the player under a negative covenant. *See Weegham v. Killefer,* 215 F. 168 (W.D. Mich.), *aff'd,* 215 F. 289 (6th Cir. 1914). Of course, because the nature of equitable relief is somewhat amorphous, one court may find a plaintiff's actions tolerable while another court may deny injunctive relief based on the same conduct. *Compare Munchak Corp. v. Cunningham,* 457 F.2d 721 (4th Cir. 1972) with *Minnesota Muskies, Inc. v. Hudson, supra.*

Another oft-repeated scenario begetting claims of unclean hands has involved battles between established and upstart professional leagues seeking to enroll marquis college players prior to the exhaustion of their eligibility. The clubs have engaged in questionable behavior, courted athletes about to graduate from their undergraduate institutions, secured their signatures on standard player contracts, and lost those athletes to other teams after the players have had time to pause and reflect or has been "rushed" in a similar manner by clubs from the rival league. The jilted club seeking relief must confront their own untoward "recruiting" tactics whenever it asks a court to enforce the initial contract and provide the equitable relief of a negative injunction. *Compare New York Giants Football, Inc. v. Los Angeles Chargers Football Club, Inc.,* 291 F.2d 471 (5th Cir. 1961) *with Houston Oilers, Inc. v. Neely,* 361 F.2d 36 (11th Cir. 1966).

Chapter 5

Contracts and Sports: Negotiation, Formation and Interpretation

I. Introduction

Contracts negotiated in the sports world do not differ dramatically from contracts negotiated in other areas of enterprise. The tactics and strategies employed in the negotiating process and the potential pitfalls that beset the contracting parties traverse a wide variety of other industries. There may be shades of difference, but the basic ground rules for successful negotiation apply across the board. While there really is no adequate substitute for experience in developing a negotiating technique, the rules of thumb that are discussed below should provide a useful overview of the key elements of successful contract negotiation. After you have reviewed this section, peruse the National Football League Uniform Player Contract. It represents a typical standard agreement between player and club. Although all league contracts have their own idiosyncrasies, this agreement will provide a useful exemplar that will be referred to at various points throughout the chapter. As you review the NFL contract and other standard agreements, bear in mind that they are incorporated in, and subordinate to, the pertinent collective bargaining agreements between the clubs and the players' collective bargaining representatives.

II. Negotiating Strategy

(A) Knowledge and Understanding of All Pertinent Materials, Relevant Bargaining History, and the Particular Idiosyncrasies of Your Client's Case, as well as Knowledge of Your Adversary's Case and Proposal

Those charged with negotiating the typical sports contract for players or teams today should have a detailed knowledge and comprehension of the following: (1) all uniform player contracts in each league with which they are involved; (2) the league's constitution and by-laws, and any other relevant documents reflecting the agreements between and among various league members; (3) the nature of the league's relationship with league commissioners or any other parties acting as representatives of the league in an official or unofficial capacity; (4) all pertinent collective bargaining agreements, including "memoranda of understanding," relevant negotiation minutes, prior collective bargaining agreements, and any other documents expanding upon, clarifying, or narrowing the collective bargaining agreement; (5) pertinent performance statistics of any other players that may be relevant to the particular dispute or negotiation; and (6) all pertinent court, agency, or arbitration precedent, whether it be in the context of litigation or negotiation.

Lawyers sometime make the mistake of assuming that research is only a necessary pursuit in the context of actual litigation. In fact, understanding how a court or arbitrator may interpret a particular contractual provision may very well dictate the language that you seek to have included in the contract and may also, in appropriate circumstances, persuade you to accept vague or amorphous language in the name of resolving the dispute (*e.g.*, where interpretation of such vague language has traditionally been effected in a way favorable to your client). This point is explored in more detail in Part II(E), below.

The importance of scrutinizing every detail of your adversary's proposal cannot be overstated. On numerous occasions, negotiators have gained valuable ground by knowing and understanding parts of the other side's proposal better than the adversary himself or herself did. At times, a party will propose terms that he or she does not even realize are part of the offer (*i.e.*, it may be boilerplate language or stray remnants from an old proposal or form contract).

Once you have become totally conversant with the other party's proposal, you should attempt to ascertain the motivation underlying the language. At times, it can be difficult to divine why a particular term has been proposed, especially one that almost looks too good to be true. At this point, it becomes necessary to accommodate two potentially conflicting aphorisms: there are no free lunches; and don't look a gift horse in the mouth. In attempting to decide whether to be grateful or suspicious about certain arcane provisions, you should discuss the matter in detail with your client and explore other contracts and related situations involving similar language, especially the occurrence of litigation surrounding the questionable terms. Although there are no litmus tests in this regard, it seems a safe assumption that all language has been inserted for a reason and that those reasons relate to advancing the other side's cause.

As suggested above, negotiations are often erroneously perceived solely as a battle of wills and endurance. As discussed in Part II(C), below, one's strength and durability will undoubtedly play a part in a successful negotiation. However, emerging "on top" in a difficult negotiation requires much more and, in many respects, parallels the type of preparatory effort that is involved in your typical litigation.

(B) Negotiating From Your Own List of Demands

While it may appear insignificant, negotiating from one's own set of demands serves as a useful strategy in the bargaining process. In an ideal situation, you will want to receive the other party's proposal first so as to insure that your tentatively prepared offer has not underestimated the largesse of your adversary. Upon receipt of the other side's offer, you typically will then submit your "counteroffer," which, in large part, has already been drafted based on your client's needs and inputs.

Negotiating from your own document has its own advantages. First, it insures that the incidental oversight will not occur. There may be aspects of another side's proposal that contain little if any offensive language necessitating your intervention. However, less important items that you would prefer to include may become lost in the "counteroffer shuffle." However, if you are negotiating from your own document, where each item has been scrupulously prepared and discussed with your client, then the possibility of omission is reduced.

Second, negotiating from your document insures that the incidental or noncritical language, *i.e.*, language that you prefer but do not insist upon, will be retained as the parties negotiate and dicker over more significant provisions. In essence, if a party is going to overlook the "small stuff" in the name of bigger ticket items, let it be the other side. In this way, you will have insured that the "nonactive ingredients" as well as the more important parts of the contract are written on your terms. It is possible that such provisions will be of negligible future importance; but this language may well serve to support your position in subsequent arbitrations or as a predicate upon which to build in future contract negotiations.

Third, as negotiations wear on, particularly in hard-fought, protracted discussions, weary parties will sometimes agree more readily on well-crafted language that seems to have assumed a role subordinate to the more compelling provisions. If you have taken care to draft language for those less important provisions and make them cosmetically more acceptable to the other side, there is a likelihood that those provisions will be adopted without argument. Once again, this language may constitute simple boilerplate provisions that are subject to little controversy and no litigation; yet, there exists the possibility that such language may in a collateral sense support other language in the contract or, independently, could be useful in litigation to resolve some unanticipated dispute.

(C) Endurance, Cosmetics, Public Opinion, and Psychological Advantage

As stated above, negotiations are often perceived as simple endurance contests where only the strong survive and the weak are culled from the herd. This perception is misleading and misapprehends the true nature of the negotiating process. At the same time, negotiation can be a grueling, no-holds-barred affair in many respects. While fist pounding, cursing, shouting, and glowering are not the virtues that they are cracked up to be, physical conditioning and mental toughness can become critical factors, particularly as negotiations approach the dog days of some designated or self-imposed deadline. Diet, exercise, and rest may play pivotal roles in a given negotiation, and negotiators should be aware that total disregard for their own recreation and leisure could compromise their ability to represent their clients effectively.

In a related sense, even cosmetics can become a relevant factor in an intense negotiation, especially one that is subject to heightened media coverage or public scrutiny. While some experts place great emphasis upon the way one looks in negotiations, it is probably not a significant feature. Nonetheless, conveyance of the impression that you are fatigued, at odds with your client, less than attentive to detail in your dress and other comportment, may all create the impression that you can be beaten at the table. For this reason, while cosmetics is not to be rated over preparation and form not to be exalted over substance, it is highly recommended that parties avoid a disheveled appearance. While the rolled-up sleeve, loosened tie, removed earring, and tousled hair may suggest to the outside world that you are pressing the edge of the envelope to reach an agreement, they may likewise convey the impression to the other side that you are ready for a fall. Where the print and broadcast media have injected themselves into the process this factor assumes added importance. Negotiations are stereotypically closed door, backroom affairs, replete with the intrigue of political conventions of a bygone era. Sports negotiations, both in one-on-one situations as well as in collective bargaining, have carried that connotation in many respects. However, the media blitz that accompanies high profile negotiations, the personalities of many of the participants, and the rampaging public curiosity, assure the parties that they likely will be bargaining in a fishbowl. The public, informed by an aggressive media, is aware of every step and ploy almost before the participants. The perceived correctness of the parties' positions and the resulting pressure brought to bear by an angry public and a critical media, may be fueled by the appearance of the negotiator. Surly, unkempt, and uncooperative negotiators may be viewed as messengers of evil, and their corresponding proposals may likewise be viewed as unreasonable notwithstanding the legitimacy and prudence of the positions being advanced. While representatives should not pander, they should be aware of the degree to which their public personae could dictate the success of the negotiation in the context of an entertainment industry.

(D) Availability to Client

Client availability, particularly with regard to the emotions attached to an acrimonious negotiation, is critical. Frequently, the negotiations will have either arbitrary or set deadlines necessitating that the proceedings be conducted in an expeditious manner. Further, representing athletes or professional sports clubs, you may be dealing with individuals who virtually have their "choice of the litter" when it comes to selecting counsel. Given the substantial amount of money that could be involved, oftentimes for a minimal amount of time expended, your client may be extremely concerned about your prompt response to phone calls and questions. Moreover, your availability and need to return calls extends to your adversary as well. Controversial negotiations are often "litigated" in the court of public opinion, and the degree to which your client may lose capital and negotiating leverage because of the alienation of the public could very well dictate the success of your negotiating strategy. If the public is given the impression that negotiations have stalled due to your own dilatory tactics, the benefit derived from having a sympathetic audience could be compromised.

This availability could also extend to the press, third party mediators, or expert consultants who could play critical roles in moving the negotiating process along in a favorable way. Frequently, lawyers will relegate certain matters to the back burner, particularly in the face of pressing litigation or matters that have more formal deadlines such as court dates. Under those circumstances, lawyers may fall into the trap of postponing negotiating sessions or delaying them to the point of frustration for their client and the other side because the deadlines for the most part rest on a consensual basis. This trap should be avoided at all costs because it could be as damaging to the eventual outcome of negotiations as failure to meet a more conventional deadline could be in the context of formal litigation.

(E) Resolution of Ambiguous or Vague Terms

Generally, all vague or indefinite matters should be resolved either in the contract it-self or in some type of memorandum of understanding. Failure to resolve such terms could result in a contract that is found to be fatally indefinite or could result in outside adjudication of a term's meaning or significance that is adverse to your client. If you are in a position of strength, you should push to resolve any ambiguous terms in a more concrete fashion and in a fashion consistent with your client's desires. If, however, you are in a weak bargaining position, it may prove imprudent to force the issue in terms of quantifying a vague term such as "reasonable," "fair," etc. For example, considerable liti-gation has arisen regarding salary guarantee clauses that are stated in broad and ab-solute terms but fail to state specifically how salary would be distributed in the event of a strike or work stoppage. If you are in a position of strength, you may want to delin-eate specifically whether or not a strike or work stoppage would be included in the gen-eral designation of a salary guarantee. However, if you are in a weak bargaining position and anticipate that the other side will insist upon a clarification that is not in your client's best interests, you may wish to leave the vague term undisturbed, provided that such vagueness does not invalidate the contract due to indefiniteness. Again, consider-able research should be undertaken to gain an understanding of how the vague or am-biguous term would be interpreted in the appropriate forum. To the extent that the broad term has been interpreted in a way that is favorable to your client and, in fact, would provide you the same protection that a more concrete or quantifiable term would provide, conceivably no point would be served in pressing for more precise language.

(F) Costing Out the Contract

Prior to entering into negotiations, each party should "cost out" the contract in such a way that the "price tag" attached to each item is readily identifiable. While this exercise is much more critical in the context of collective bargaining and some types of commer-cial negotiations, where each provision should be computed on a "dollars-and-cents-per-hour" basis, it is also important in individual contract bargaining. By developing a formula that identifies the costs of each item on a line-by-line basis, each party will be able to respond to the various proposals and counter-proposals expeditiously. As part of this calculus, the parties should differentiate immediate and deferred compensation with due consideration to the tax implications and other collateral matters that could affect the ultimate costs and benefits to each party.

Numerous sources exist to assist parties in devising practical cost-out formulations, including several "loose-leaf" publications. It is highly recommended that these sources be reviewed and that appropriate consultants such as economists or accountants be re-tained when their services will enhance the process.

(G) "Know When To Hold 'Em, Know When To Fold 'Em"

Perhaps the most difficult aspect of negotiation is knowing when to attack and when to retreat. This decision requires judgment that turns on many factors, including your client's interests, the desire to push forward for potentially minimal advantages, the bargaining strength of your adversary, the amount of negotiation your adversary is conducting with other parties, the economic condition and availability of other income for your client and your adversary, etc. In any event, it is critical that your client's interests be paramount and that any strategy pursued for the purpose of derivatively benefiting other clients be scrupulously avoided. In essence, successful representation of one client could beget personal satisfaction and professional advancement of the representative. But, you must resist the urge to close a deal that enhances your own reputation at the expense of the client. If there is tension between the interests of your client and the interests of other people that you represent, then perhaps such conflict may necessitate that you cease representation of one or more of these parties.

Further, with regard to the ultimate decision as to whether to reject or accept an opponent's offer, avoid at all costs any type of machismo compulsion to beat the other side. In the event that your client's interests have been served and a satisfactory resolution has been reached, your belief that you personally have emerged victorious should be irrelevant. Negotiations have failed on numerous occasions because the party conducting the representation has become absorbed in a vendetta with another party's representative, subordinating the interests of their clients and subverting an otherwise easily resolvable matter.

Finally, it is important to remember that recognizing when to concede is more than just a question of negotiating strategy. This judgment also involves ethical considerations and the extent to which your pattern of negotiation reflects upon your professionalism and sense of responsibility. Under no circumstances should you permit the informality of the negotiation process to relax your standards of ethical behavior. Failure to observe this caveat is a formula for disaster, both in terms of your reputation among peers and potential clients, as well as the obvious danger of disqualification from practice.

Conclusion

The foregoing suggestions only scratch the surface of the approaches that we should consider in developing a workable negotiating strategy. The nuances of each negotiation will dictate the various means of securing the best deal for your client. Beyond the thumbnail sketches that are presented above, the following sources provide a comprehensive view of the matter one should consider in preparation for a successful negotiation. *See* Charles Loughran, Negotiating a Labor Contract: A Management Handbook (3d Ed. 2003); Patrick J. Cleary, The Negotiation Handbook (2001); Paul T. Steel & Tom Beasor, Business Negotiation: A Practical Workbook (1999).

NFL PLAYER CONTRACT

THIS   CONTRACT   is   between   _____,   hereinafter   "Player,"   and _____, a _____ corporation (limited partnership)(partnership), hereinafter "Club," operating under the name of the _____ as a member of the National Football League, hereinafter "League." In consideration of the promises made by each to the other, Player and Club agree as follows:

1. TERM. This contract covers _____ football season(s), and will begin on the date of execution or March 1, _____, whichever is later, and end on Febru-

ary 28 or 29, _____, unless extended, terminated, or renewed as specified elsewhere in this contract.

2. EMPLOYMENT AND SERVICES. Club employs Player as a skilled football player. Player accepts such employment. He agrees to give his best efforts and loyalty to the Club, and to conduct himself on and off the field with appropriate recognition of the fact that the success of professional football depends largely on public respect for and approval of those associated with the game. Player will report promptly for and participate fully in Club's official mandatory mini-camp(s), official pre-season training camp, all Club meetings and practice sessions, and all pre-season, regular season and post-season football games scheduled for or by Club. If invited, Player will practice for and play in any all-star football game sponsored by the League. Player will not participate in any football game not sponsored by the League unless the game is first approved by the League.

3. OTHER ACTIVITIES. Without prior written consent of the Club, Player will not play football or engage in activities related to football otherwise than for Club or engage in any activity other than football which may involve a significant risk of personal injury. Player represents that he has special, exceptional and unique knowledge, skill, ability, and experience as a football player, the loss of which cannot be estimated with any certainty and cannot be fairly or adequately compensated by damages. Player therefore agrees that Club will have the right, in addition to any other right which Club may possess, to enjoin Player by appropriate proceedings from playing football or engaging in football-related activities other than for Club or from engaging in any activity other than football which may involve a significant risk of personal injury.

4. PUBLICITY AND NFLPA GROUP LICENSING PROGRAM. (a) Player grants to Club and the League, separately and together, the authority to use his name and picture for publicity and the promotion of NFL Football, the League or any of its member clubs in newspapers, magazines, motion pictures, game programs and roster manual, broadcasts and telecasts, and all other publicity and advertising media, provided such publicity and promotion does not constitute an endorsement by Player of a commercial product. Player will cooperate with the news media, and will participate upon request in reasonable activities to promote the Club and the League. Player and National Football League Players Association, hereinafter "NFLPA," will not contest the rights of the League and its member clubs to telecast, broadcast, or otherwise transmit NFL Football or the right of NFL Films to produce, sell, market, or distribute football game film footage, except insofar as such broadcast, telecast, or transmission of footage is used in any commercially marketable game or interactive use. The League and its member clubs, and Player and the NFLPA, reserve their respective rights as to the use of such broadcasts, telecasts or transmissions of footage in such games or interactive uses, which shall be unaffected by this subparagraph.

(b) Player hereby assigns to the NFLPA and its licensing affiliates, if any, the **exclusive** right to use and to grant to persons, firms, or corporations (collectively "licensees") the right to use his name, signature facsimile, voice, picture, photograph, likeness, and/or biographical information (collectively "image") in group licensing programs. Group licensing programs are defined as those licensing programs in which a licensee utilizes a total of six (6) or more NFL player images on products that are sold at retail or used as promotional or premium items. Player retains the right to grant permission to a licensee to utilize his image if that licensee is not concurrently utilizing the images of five (5) or more other NFL players on products that are sold at retail or are used as promotional or premium items. If Player's inclusion in a particular NFLPA program is precluded by an individual exclusive endorsement agreement, and Player provides the NFLPA with timely written notice of that preclusion, the NFLPA will exclude Player from that particular program. In consideration for this assignment of rights, the NFLPA will use the revenues it receives from group licensing programs to support the objectives as set forth in the By-laws of the NFLPA. The NFLPA will use its best efforts to promote the use of NFL player images in group licensing programs, to provide group licensing opportunities to all NFL players, and to ensure that no entity utilizes the group licensing rights granted to the NFLPA without first obtaining a license from the NFLPA. This paragraph shall be construed under New York law without reference to conflicts of law principles. The assignment in this paragraph shall expire on December 31 of the later of (a) the third year following the execution of this contract, or (b) the year in which this contract expires. Neither Club nor the League is a party to the terms of this paragraph, which is included herein solely for the administrative convenience and benefit of Player and the NFLPA. The terms of this subparagraph apply unless, at the time of execution of this contract, Player indicates by striking out this subparagraph (b) and marking his initials adjacent to the stricken language his intention to not partic-ipate in the NFLPA Group Licensing Program. Nothing in this subparagraph shall be construed to supersede or any way broaden, expand, detract from, or otherwise alter in any way whatsoever, the rights of NFL Properties, Inc. as permitted under Article V (Union Security), Section 4 of the 1993 Collective Bargaining Agreement ("CBA").

5. COMPENSATION. For performance of Player's services and all other promises of Player, Club will pay Player a yearly salary as follows:

$ _____ for the 19____ season;
$ _____ for the 19____ season;
$ _____ for the 19____ season;
$ _____ for the 19____ season;
$ _____ for the 19____ season;

In addition, Club will pay Player such earned performance bonuses as may be called for in this contract; Player's necessary traveling expenses from his residence to training camp; Player's reasonable board and lodging expenses during pre-season training and in connection with playing pre-season, regular season, and post-season football games outside Club's home city; Player's necessary traveling expenses to and from pre-season, regular season, and post-season football games outside Club's home city; Player's neces-sary traveling expenses to his residence if this contract is terminated by Club; and such additional compensation, benefits and reimbursement of expenses as may be called for in any collective bargaining agreement in existence during the term of this contract. (For purposes of this contract, a collective bargaining agreement will be deemed to be "in existence" during its stated term or during any period for which the parties to that agreement agree to extend it.)

6. PAYMENT. Unless this contract or any collective bargaining agreement in exis-tence during the term of this contract specifically provides otherwise, Player will be paid 100% of his yearly salary under this contract in equal weekly or bi-weekly installments over the course of the applicable regular season period, commencing with the first reg-ular season game played by Club in each season. Unless this contract specifically pro-vides otherwise, if this contract is executed or Player is activated after the beginning of the regular season, the yearly salary payable to Player will be reduced proportionately and Player will be paid the weekly or bi-weekly portions of his yearly salary becoming due and payable after he is activated. Unless this contract specifically provides other-wise, if this contract is terminated after the beginning of the regular season, the yearly

salary payable to Player will be reduced proportionately and Player will be paid the weekly or bi-weekly portions of his yearly salary having become due and payable up to the time of termination.

7. DEDUCTIONS. Any advance made to Player will be repaid to Club, and any properly levied Club fine or Commissioner fine against Player will be paid, in cash on demand or by means of deductions from payments coming due to the Player under this contract, the amount of such deductions to be determined by Club unless this contract or any collective bargaining agreement in existence during the term of this contract specifically provides otherwise.

8. PHYSICAL CONDITION. Player represents to Club that he is and will maintain himself in excellent physical condition. Player will undergo a complete physical examination by the Club physician upon Club request, during which physical examination Player agrees to make full and complete disclosure of any physical or mental condition known to him which might impair his performance under this contract and to respond fully and in good faith when questioned by the Club physician about such condition. If Player fails to establish or maintain his excellent physical condition to the satisfaction of the Club physician, or make the required full and complete disclosure and good faith responses to the Club physician, then Club may terminate this contract.

9. INJURY. Unless this contract specifically provides otherwise, if Player is injured in the performance of his services under this contract and promptly reports such injury to the Club physician or trainer, then Player will receive such medical and hospital care during the term of this contract as the Club physician may deem necessary, and will continue to receive his yearly salary for so long, during the season of injury only and for no subsequent period covered by this contract, as Player is physically unable to perform the services required of him by this contract because of such injury. If Player's injury in the performance of his services under this contract results in his death, the unpaid balance of his yearly salary for the season of injury will be paid to his stated beneficiary, or in the absence of a stated beneficiary, to his estate.

10. WORKERS' COMPENSATION. Any compensation paid to Player under this contract or under any collective bargaining agreement in existence during the term of this contract for a period during which he is entitled to workers' compensation benefits by reason of temporary total, permanent total, temporary partial, or permanent partial disability will be deemed an advance payment of workers' compensation benefits due Player, and Club will be entitled to be reimbursed the amount of such payment out of any award of workers' compensation.

11. SKILL, PERFORMANCE AND CONDUCT. Player understands that he is competing with other players for a position on Club's roster within the applicable player limits. If at any time, in the sole judgment of Club, Player's skill or performance has been unsatisfactory as compared with that of other players competing for positions on Club's roster, or if Player has engaged in personal conduct reasonably judged by Club to adversely affect or reflect on Club, then Club may terminate this contract. In addition, during the period any salary cap is legally in effect, this contract may be terminated if, in Club's opinion, Player is anticipated to make less of a contribution to Club's ability to compete on the playing field than another player or players whom Club intends to sign or attempts to sign, or another player or players who is or are already on Club's roster, and for whom Club needs room.

12. TERMINATION. The rights of termination set forth in this contract will be in addition to any other rights of termination allowed either party by law. Termination

will be effective upon the giving of written notice, except that Player's death, other than as a result of injury incurred in the performance of his services under this contract, will automatically terminate this contract. If this contract is terminated by Club and either Player or Club so requests, Player will promptly undergo a complete physical examination by the Club physician.

13. INJURY GRIEVANCE. Unless a collective bargaining agreement in existence at the time of termination of this contract by Club provides otherwise, the following injury grievance procedure will apply: If Player believes that at the time of termination of this contract by Club he was physically unable to perform the services required of him by this contract because of an injury incurred in the performance of his services under this contract, Player may, within 60 days after examination by the Club physician, submit at his own expense to examination by a physician of his choice. If the opinion of Player's physician with respect to his physical ability to perform the services required of him by this contract is contrary to that of the Club's physician, the dispute will be submitted within a reasonable time to final and binding arbitration by an arbitrator selected by Club and Player or, if they are unable to agree, one selected in accordance with the procedures of the American Arbitration Association on application by either party.

14. RULES. Player will comply with and be bound by all reasonable Club rules and regulations in effect during the term of this contract which are not inconsistent with the provisions of this contract or of any collective bargaining agreement in existence during the term of this contract. Player's attention is also called to the fact that the League functions with certain rules and procedures expressive of its operation as a joint venture among its member clubs and that these rules and practices may affect Player's relationship to the League and its member clubs independently of the provisions of this contract.

15. INTEGRITY OF GAME. Player recognizes the detriment to the League and professional football that would result from impairment of public confidence in the honest and orderly conduct of NFL games or the integrity and good character of NFL players. Player therefore acknowledges his awareness that if he accepts a bribe or agrees to throw or fix an NFL game; fails to promptly report a bribe offer or an attempt to throw or fix an NFL game; bets on an NFL game; knowingly associates with gamblers or gambling activity; uses or provides other players with stimulants or other drugs for the purpose of attempting to enhance on-field performance; or is guilty of any other form of conduct reasonably judged by the League Commissioner to be detrimental to the League or professional football, the Commissioner will have the right, but only after giving Player the opportunity for a hearing at which he may be represented by counsel of his choice, to fine Player in a reasonable amount; to suspend Player for a period certain or indefinitely; and/or to terminate this contract.

16. EXTENSION. Unless this contract specifically provides otherwise, if Player becomes a member of the Armed Forces of the United States or any other country, or retires from professional football as an active player, or otherwise fails or refuses to perform his services under this contract, then this contract will be tolled between the date of Player's induction into the Armed Forces, or his retirement, or his failure or refusal to perform, and the later date of his return to professional football. During the period this contract is tolled, Player will not be entitled to any compensation or benefits. On Player's return to professional football, the term of this contract will be extended for a period of time equal to the number of seasons (to the nearest multiple of one) remaining at the time the contract was tolled. The right of renewal, if any, contained in this contract will remain in effect until the end of any such extended term.

17. ASSIGNMENT. Unless this contract specifically provides otherwise, Club may assign this contract and Player's services under this contract to any successor to Club's franchise or to any other Club in the League. Player will report to the assignee Club promptly upon being informed of the assignment of his contract and will faithfully perform his services under this contract. The assignee club will pay Player's necessary traveling expenses in reporting to it and will faithfully perform this contract with Player.

18. FILING. This contract will be valid and binding upon Player and Club immediately upon execution. A copy of this contract, including any attachment to it, will be filed by Club with the League Commissioner within 10 days after execution. The Commissioner will have the right to disapprove this contract on reasonable grounds, including but not limited to an attempt by the parties to abridge or impair the rights of any other club, uncertainty or incompleteness in expression of the parties' respective rights and obligations, or conflict between the terms of this contract and any collective bargaining agreement then in existence. Approval will be automatic unless, within 10 days after receipt of this contract in his office, the Commissioner notifies the parties either of disapproval or of extension of this 10-day period for purposes of investigation or clarification pending his decision. On the receipt of notice of disapproval and termination, both parties will be relieved of their respective rights and obligations under this contract.

19. DISPUTES. During the term of any collective bargaining agreement, any dispute between Player and Club involving the interpretation or application of any provision of this contract will be submitted to final and binding arbitration in accordance with the procedure called for in any collective bargaining agreement in existence at the time the event giving rise to any such dispute occurs.

20. NOTICE. Any notice, request, approval or consent under this contract will be sufficiently given if in writing and delivered in person or mailed (certified or first class) by one party to the other at the address set forth in this contract or to such other address as the recipient may subsequently have furnished in writing to the sender.

21. OTHER AGREEMENTS. This contract, including any attachment to it, sets forth the entire agreement between Player and Club and cannot be modified or supplemented orally. Player and Club represent that no other agreement, oral or written, except as attached to or specifically incorporated in this contract, exists between them. The provisions of this contract will govern the relationship between Player and Club unless there are conflicting provisions in any collective bargaining agreement in existence during the term of this contract, in which case the provisions of the collective bargaining agreement will take precedence over conflicting provisions of this contract relating to the rights or obligations of either party.

22. LAW. This contract is made under and shall be governed by the laws of the State of _____.

23. WAIVER AND RELEASE. Player waives and releases any claims that he may have arising out of, related to, or asserted in the lawsuit entitled *White v. National Football League,* including, but not limited to, any such claim regarding past NFL Rules, the College Draft, Plan B, the first refusal/compensation system, the NFL Player Contract, preseason compensation, or any other term or condition of employment, except any claims asserted in *Brown v. Pro Football, Inc.* This waiver and release also extends to any conduct engaged in pursuant to the Stipulation and Settlement Agreement in *White* ("Settlement Agreement") during the express term of that Settlement Agreement or any portion thereof. This waiver and release shall not limit any rights Player may have to performance by the Club under this Contract or Player's rights as a member of the

White class to object to the Settlement Agreement during its review by the court in Minnesota. This waiver and release is subject to Article XIV (NFL Player Contract), Section 3(c) of the CBA.

24. OTHER PROVISIONS. (a) Each of the undersigned hereby confirms that (i) this contract, renegotiation, extension or amendment sets forth all components of the player's remuneration for playing professional football whether such compensation is being furnished directly by the Club or by a related or affiliated entity); and (ii) there are not undisclosed agreements of any kind, whether express or implied, oral or written, and there are no promises, undertakings, representations, commitments, inducements, assurances of intent, or understanding of any kind that have not been disclosed to the NFL involving consideration of any kind to be paid, furnished or made available to Player or any entity or person owned or controlled by, affiliated with, or related to Player, either during the term of this contract or thereafter.

(b) Each of the undersigned further confirms that, except insofar as any of the undersigned may describe in an addendum to this contract, to the best of their knowledge, no conduct in violation of the Anti-Collusion rules of the Settlement Agreement took place with respect to this contract. Each of the undersigned further confirms that nothing in this contract is designed or intended to defeat or circumvent any provisions of the settlement agreement, including but not limited to the Rookie Pool and Salary Cap provisions; however, any conduct permitted by the CBA and/or the Settlement Agreement shall not be considered a violation of this confirmation.

(c) The Club further confirms that any information regarding the negotiation of this contract that it provided to the Neutral Verifier was, at the time the information was provided, true and correct in all material respects.

25. SPECIAL PROVISIONS.

THIS CONTRACT is executed in six (6) copies. Player acknowledges that before signing this contract he was given the opportunity to seek advice from or be represented by persons of his own selection.

_____	_____
PLAYER	CLUB
_____	_____
Home Address	By
_____	
Club Address	
_____	_____
Telephone Number	
_____	_____
Date	Date

_____
PLAYER'S CERTIFIED AGENT

_____
Address

_____

_____
Telephone Number

Date

Copy Distribution: White-League Office   Yellow-Player
                                Green-Member Office   Blue-Management Council
                                Gold-NFLPA   Pink-Player Agent

III. Specific Problems in Contract Formation

(A) Offer and Acceptance: Identifying the Offeror

Los Angeles Rams Football Club v. Cannon
185 F. Supp. 717 (S.D. Cal. 1960)

LINDBERG, District Judge. * * * Specifically, plaintiff prays for an injunction to restrain defendant from playing football or engaging in related activities for anyone other than plaintiff without the plaintiff's consent during the term of a contract or contracts allegedly entered into by the parties on November 30, 1959, and an order declaring the existence of a valid written contract or contracts.

Defendant denies he ever entered into a contract or contracts as alleged and further claims, as defenses to plaintiff's claims, fourteen affirmative defenses.

The first six, in substance, deny that the defendant ever entered a binding contract or contracts but that defendant merely made an offer which was not accepted prior to revocation. The others, in brief, consist of:

Fraud and deceit on the part of plaintiff, acting through Pete Rozelle, then the General Manager of the Rams;

The doctrine of unclean hands on the part of plaintiff barring the granting of equitable relief;

Lack of mutuality;

Breach of contract, if any, on the part of plaintiff;

That the contracts, if any, are unfair, inequitable and contrary to public policy;

That if the defendant entered into any contract he did so under a material mistake of fact; and

That the plaintiff has an adequate remedy at law.

The defendant, Billy Cannon, is a remarkable football player who has just finished his collegiate career with Louisiana State University. The last intercollegiate game he participated in was the Sugar Bowl game on January 1, 1960. Prior to that time, however, on November 28, 1959, or early in the morning of the 29th, he was contacted by telephone by Pete Rozelle, now Commissioner of the National Football League, but who was then and at all times material to the dispute here involved General Manager for the Los Angeles Rams. Mr. Rozelle was in Baltimore, Maryland and Billy Cannon was then in New York.

There is no question about the call being made but there is serious dispute as to the conversation had. However, we can safely assume that it had to do with football. (At this time I do not attempt to resolve the factual disputes but leave that for later consideration as I reach the issues.)

The telephone call mentioned occurred less than thirty-six hours before the annual selection meeting of the National Football League which was held in Philadelphia, Pennsylvania.

The Rams, after sifting an astonishing amount of information through a complex scouting system, concluded that Billy Cannon was the player of the current graduating crop they would most like to see on their team. The Rams, by virtue of ten losses and only two wins last season were tied for last place in the League, but as every cloud has its silver lining this fact also tied them for first draft choice at the above-mentioned selection meeting. The tie was to be broken by the flip of a coin. Thus it was that the Rams stood a fifty-fifty chance of having the first draft choice.

It has been the Rams' contention throughout that this position on the draft is so valuable that careful steps are undertaken to assure the team having the choice that it is not wasted on a player not willing to play for that team. The telephone call referred to was for the purpose of exploring that question.

On the 29th there was another telephone conversation between Mr. Rozelle and the defendant and on this occasion Mr. Rozelle was in Philadelphia. That night Billy Cannon took a train from New York to Philadelphia and registered at the Sheraton Hotel under the name of Billy Gunn at the suggestion and arrangement of Mr. Rozelle.

On the following day the selection meeting was held. The Rams won the toss of the coin and selected Billy Cannon as its first draft choice.

Immediately following the meeting defendant and Mr. Rozelle got together, met with members of the press, and discussed for the benefit of the press the fact that the Rams had received the first draft choice and had selected Billy Cannon.

Following the press interview Cannon and Rozelle went to Rozelle's hotel room where Cannon signed three sets of National Football Player Contract forms covering the years 1960, 1961 and 1962, and took possession of two checks, one for $10,000 and the other for $500.

Mr. Rozelle, on or about December 1st, left one set of said forms as filled out—that set embracing the 1960 season—with the then acting Commissioner, Mr. Gunsel.

Some two weeks later Billy Cannon was contacted on behalf of a Mr. K. S. Adams, Jr., who is the owner or part owner of the Houston Oilers, a football club in the recently-formed American Football League. On or about December 22nd Cannon met with Mr. Adams and others in Baton Rouge and negotiations were had with respect to a so-called personal service contract including the playing of football.

On December 30, 1959 Billy Cannon sent to the Rams a letter wherein he announced that he no longer desired to play for the Rams, purportedly revoked any offer he may have made to play for the Rams, and returned therewith the two checks above mentioned uncashed and unendorsed.

Prior thereto, however, it is contended that Mr. Gunsel approved the contract for the 1960 season, and the exhibit as admitted, Exhibit A, bears the signature of Mr. Gunsel alongside of which the date December 1, 1959 was written in.

At this point I propose to treat the question of whether or not a contract or contracts ever came into existence, dealing first with the instruments themselves before getting into the difficult matter of what transpired prior to and at the time of signing. The question, then, is, What is the nature of the several documents signed by Billy Cannon November 30, 1959? Disregarding for the moment the interpretations of the parties, the court must look to the instruments themselves.

We have three sets of instruments, in triplicate, each denominated National Football League Standard Players Contract, admitted in evidence as plaintiff's Exhibits A, B, C and H; H being a photo copy of the League copy of the first set. The printed form is identical in each case with the exception that there are three riders attached to each copy of the first set. The first set has the year 1960 typed in the appropriate blank; the second, 1961; and the third, 1962.

Each form states that it is a contract between Los Angeles Rams Football Club, thereinafter called the Club, and Billy Cannon, thereafter called the player. It states that in consideration of the respective promises contained therein the parties agree to the following terms:

Paragraph 1 thereunder reads as follows:

"1. The term of this contract shall be from the date of execution hereof until the first day of May following the close of the football season commencing in (blank for the insertion of a given year) subject, however, to rights of prior termination as specified herein."

* * *

Paragraph 13 reads, in full:

"13. This agreement contains the entire agreement between the parties and there are no oral or written inducements, promises or agreements except as contained herein. This agreement shall become valid and binding upon each party hereto only when, as and if it shall be approved by the Commissioner."

* * *

As heretofore indicated three sets of these forms were used. In the appropriate blank in Paragraph 1 the years 1960, 1961 and 1962, respectively, were inserted in the three sets. Each set contains the signature of Pete Rozelle for the Rams, Billy Cannon and the two witnesses. (I might state at this point, parenthetically, that no law this court is aware of requires this type of contract to be witnessed, nor does the contract itself set up such a requirement.)

Only one of the sets bears the signature of the Commissioner with respect to approval, and the evidence is to the effect that until late in December, 1959 the Commissioner was unaware of the other two sets.

The question germane at this point is just how important to these contracts is the Commissioner's approval. On this point, of course, the parties to the action are at opposite poles, plaintiff taking the position that it is an unimportant ministerial act concerning only the League and the Club, while the defendant takes the position that it is an act absolutely essential to the formation of a contract.

It is the opinion of this court that on this issue the defendant must prevail. Approval by the Commissioner is essential to the formation of a contract here and this is so because the terms of the document make it so.

Keeping in mind that these forms were furnished by the Rams and not Billy Cannon, the court calls particular attention to the words regarding approval:

"This agreement shall become valid and binding upon each party hereto only when, as and if it shall be approved by the Commissioner."

Paraphrasing: "Shall become valid * * * only when * * * and if * * * it shall be approved * * *."

The words "shall become valid" clearly compels the conclusion that—in the absence of approval—it is not yet a valid agreement.

The use of the word "if" clearly suggests that approval might not happen at all.

This clause is too definite to be ignored. It jumps out at you. The words employed are too strong to permit of ambiguity. Their selection was obviously made with great care so that there would be no dispute about their meaning, and this court attaches to them the only meaning it can—that is, that the agreement shall only become valid and binding if, as and when approved by the Commissioner.

If there were not reason enough for so holding there are further reasons inherent in the instruments themselves which makes this conclusion inescapable.

We have earlier noted that paragraph 1 describes the term of the agreement "from the date of execution hereof until the first day of May following the close of the football season commencing in _____" (whatever year is placed in the blank provided). This paragraph defines the term and it clearly allows for more than one year. If such a contract were executed today and the year 1970 were placed in the blank it would be, to my way of thinking, a contract for a term in excess of ten years.

Paragraph 3 obligates the Club "to pay the player *each football season* during the term of this contract" a stated sum. This again is persuasive that this form permits a term in excess of one year unless there is more than one football season in one year.

Paragraph 1 tells us when a term ends but it does not tell us when it begins. If, as contended by plaintiff, the date of execution is the date it is signed by the Club and player, we would have in the case at bar three contracts, all commencing on November 30, 1959, one running to May of 1961, the second to May of 1962, and the third to May of 1963. And as each contract calls for payment for each season within the term Billy Cannon might have a contract calling for a grand total of $95,000, including the bonus.

This, of course, is so absurd that no one would suggest that is what either side intended to do here.

This absurdity does not exist if it is determined that approval is essential to execution, as I find it is. When approval is essential to execution and that act fixes the beginning of the term, the Club, so long as it sits on the instrument, controls the beginning of the term thereunder and at the same time the number of seasons it shall cover. This, perhaps, may well be one of the reasons these instruments are not submitted for approval until just before the year typed in the blank.

Section 7 of Article XII of the Constitution and By-Laws of the National Football League, which, of course, is a part of the forms by reference, provides that the only instrument which will bind a player to any club is the form used here when executed and filed in the office of the Commissioner. It provides that the club first filing such a contract shall be awarded the player and that the time of filing shall be the time of filing it in the Commissioner's office. If two teams within the League signed the same player and the last team to sign the player were the first to file the contract with the Commissioner there can be no question under this provision who would be awarded the player.

For League purposes it may be very essential to provide this sort of arrangement in order to avoid disputes between teams within the League. But the only way this can be accomplished within the framework of law is to make the Commissioner's approval an essential part of execution, otherwise the Commissioner would be destroying the legal efficacy of binding contracts, a thing the courts would be powerless to do. This provision, which is within the four corners of the contract, is one more persuasive indication that approval is essential to execution.

Counsel for plaintiff in oral argument cited certain cases for the proposition that the signature of the Commissioner was no more than a condition precedent to performance. I do not find these cases apposite.

* * *

Here Paragraph 13 requires approval before the contract becomes valid or binding. Also in the case at bar the approval of the Commissioner was not a matter resting entirely with the Commissioner. They had to be first submitted by the Rams, and there is no showing nor am I able to find that the Rams were under any obligation to so submit them.

It is my conclusion, therefore, that until approved, these instruments are, at most, only offers.

In this respect these instruments are not like the numerous contracts we see containing conditions precedent to the creation of obligations thereunder. These instruments do contain the condition precedent of making the team before the obligation to pay the salary arises, but the requirement for approval in these instruments is much more than a condition precedent to a mere obligation; it could be characterized a condition precedent to execution but it is more properly to be denominated a part of execution, so made by the people who drew up the form.

If we are to adhere to the doctrine of freedom of contract we must allow parties to specify any degree of formality to the act of execution they wish so long as it doesn't violate public policy or some rule of law.

We may conclude, therefore, that what we have been loosely referring to as the 1961 and 1962 contracts were, at most, only offers and are now unquestionably revoked. That leaves the question of whether the 1960 instrument became a contract.

Having concluded as a matter of law that the alleged contracts—Exhibits A, B and C—under the provisions contained therein when signed by the defendant on November 30, 1959, constituted no more than an offer by Cannon to play football for the Rams until accepted by them and approved by the Commissioner. I next consider what the terms of the offer were.

It has been plaintiff's contention that they made the offer to Cannon and that he accepted that offer. That, as I have already stated, was not the result as a matter of law under paragraph 13 of the alleged contracts. Further, it must be borne in mind that plaintiff was not in a position to make a firm offer to Cannon under the Constitution and By-laws of the League until after the "flip of the coin" which occurred on Monday, November 30, 1959, some two hours or thereabouts before Cannon signed the documents.

The terms of the offer cannot be ascertained from the several documents alone, presenting as they do, if the interpretation urged by plaintiff is followed, an ambiguity as to the term of service covered under paragraph one of the documents and the compensation to be paid under paragraph three, as I have earlier pointed out.

It becomes necessary, therefore, for the purpose of determining whether there was a manifestation of mutual assent, to consider the conversations and circumstances preceding and occurring at the time of the signing of the contract forms.

The testimony of Cannon and Rozelle as to many of the facts is directly contradictory and I shall attempt to resolve their disagreement only as to the more pertinent facts and statements such as appear essential in deciding what the understanding between them was. In so doing I have weighed the conflicting testimony with particular care, trying alternately to sustain the testimony of each within the framework of the surrounding circumstances and admitted facts as developed by the evidence.

First, with respect to the proposal submitted by Rozelle to Cannon in the course of the telephone conversations of November 28th and 29th, it should be kept in mind that Rozelle had talked with Coach Dietzel on several occasions prior to his initial conversation with Cannon. On one such occasion Rozelle agrees that he told Dietzel, in substance, that, "We will give Billy Cannon a three-year contract starting in 1960 for fifteen thousand a year, and a $5,000 bonus for signing the contract, but again we would like to have assurance that he would be willing to sign such a contract."

Rozelle also testified that when he talked with Cannon first on Saturday evening, November 28th, he repeated the identical terms to Cannon * * *. While Rozelle also testified that his subsequent proposal was "a $10,000 bonus for signing, rather than five and for 1960 a $10,000 contract, rather than a $15,000 contract. And a $15,000 for '61 and a $15,000 for '62" it is clear that he was talking at all times about a three-year proposal. Furthermore, following the first telephone conversation with Rozelle, Dietzel called Cannon and told him that the offer Rozelle had made to him was the best he (Dietzel) had heard of a rookie getting. Whether or not Rozelle referred to his proposal as a "package" or not it is my conclusion that Rozelle conveyed and Cannon obtained the impression that the proposal to be submitted by the Rams in the event they won the toss of the coin was to cover a three-year period with total compensation, including a bonus, of $50,000. On the other hand, it likewise seems clear that Rozelle had in mind at the time he presented the Standard Players Contract forms to Cannon for signing, judging from the fact that he submitted the bonus, injury and armed services riders as to one and left but one form, namely, Exhibit A, with Acting Commissioner Gunsel and never submitted Exhibits B and C, that—the transaction would result in three separate and distinct contracts—one for each season to be submitted to the Commissioner for approval if the Rams so desired, as each succeeding year approached. It thus appears that there was never a meeting of the minds as between the parties with respect to the offer. Construing the Contract forms as I do, i.e. requiring not only the signing by the parties but also the approval of the Commissioner, the forms as signed by Cannon— even though signed by the Rams—must be construed as an offer by him to play for the Rams for a period of three years. This offer was never accepted by the Rams inasmuch as they requested and received the approval of the Commissioner as to the first year, 1960, only.

It is true, however, that even though the signing of the Contract forms by Cannon, because of lack of approval by the Commissioner, constituted no more than an offer, Cannon did at least take possession of the $10,000 bonus check, which, under the understanding of both parties, was payable in advance of the 1960 football season and conditioned upon the player reporting to the Rams for the 1960 training camp period. Can this be construed as an acceptance of an assumed counter-offer of the Rams for the 1960 season subject to a later approval of the Commissioner as to the proposed contract, Exhibit A? This would depend, in part at least, upon the understanding between the parties as to whether

Cannon accepted the check as payment. It is undisputed that he did not endorse the check, that he left it with his banker for safekeeping, and that he returned it before the player's copy of the proposed contract, Exhibit A, approved by the Commissioner was sent to him.

Bearing on this issue Rozelle testified:

> "I told Billy Cannon this would be kept in confidence, the signing would not be announced until after the Sugar Bowl and told him to take good care of the money." * * *

Of course, the great difficulty in resolving the factual issues involved in this case results from the fact that the signing of the alleged contracts—Exhibits A, B and C—was shrouded in secrecy due to the manner in which Rozelle handled the transaction. He knew from Cannon's coach, Dietzel, that he, Dietzel, was opposed to the signing of any contract. Rozelle nevertheless intended to get Cannon's signature to a contract when, as he testified, he carefully phrased his answer to Dietzel that "The Rams will do nothing to impair Cannon's eligibility for the Sugar Bowl." * * * Cannon, on the other hand, unwittingly, I am convinced, expressed his desire to apportion his anticipated 1960 income so as to make some of it taxable for the year 1959. This, of course, might well be construed as a compelling motive for accepting the check as payment. At this juncture, however, it should be noted, that Cannon, granting his outstanding ability and prowess on the gridiron, is anything but an astute business man. His whole life and interest has been directed toward athletics and particularly football; and while he impressed me as being somewhat naive for a college senior I feel certain that he knew he couldn't accept as payment the $10,000 check that was tendered him and remain eligible to play for his school in the Sugar Bowl, nor do I believe he would intentionally disqualify himself. He didn't need to With respect to Cannon this wasn't a chance in a lifetime to turn professional which he might lose forever if he didn't grab it immediately. By this time he must have appreciated the fact that his services were in great demand by professional football. I, therefore, am led to make the finding that Cannon did not accept the check in payment. Rather, he accepted it, believing it was not his and that he had no claim upon it until after the Sugar Bowl game.

While some, particularly those schooled—to use the vernacular—in the "game for dough" may view my interpretation of the transaction as a "Pollyanna" approach and entirely unrealistic it should be borne in mind that Cannon, while having been a highly publicized college ball player, was, in fact, and still is, it would appear, a provincial lad of 21 or 22, untutored and unwise, I am convinced, in the way of the business world. While he had entertained ambitions for years to get into professional football the proposition submitted to him by the Rams came by telephone apparently without prior notice while he was away from home and in New York for the purpose of receiving one of many rapidly accumulating honors that were being bestowed upon him. He was without counsel or advice and the whole transaction, including the signing of the alleged contracts, was completed in less than 48 hours. When Cannon arrived at the Warwick Hotel on Monday morning he did not know whether the Rams had acquired the right to draft him. He was immediately brought before the press and, as Rozelle testified, he Rozelle, heard Cannon make the statement to the effect that he would sign a contract with the Rams following the L.S.U. and Mississippi game in the Sugar Bowl on New Year's Day * * *.

At that time it is reasonable to assume that Cannon had no idea that Rozelle would expect him to sign a written contract. Thereafter, Rozelle took Cannon and no one else with him to Rozelle's room where Rozelle had waiting for signature the partially-completed forms which he presented to Cannon for signature. Just what language Rozelle used in persuading Cannon to sign the documents I do not know and I doubt if either

Cannon or Rozelle have a completely accurate recollection of what was said. I am persuaded, however, that during the 30 to 45 minutes spent in the room Rozelle conveyed the impression to Cannon that the documents would not become effective or binding upon him until after the Sugar Bowl game on New Year's Day. The admitted fact that Rozelle sought to keep their existence confidential and secret as well as the fact that Rozelle did not become concerned as to the Acting Commissioner's approval of Exhibit A until after he had learned on December 22, 1959 of the possibility that Cannon might go with the Houston Oilers lends support to the belief that Rozelle had so assured Cannon.

In view of the foregoing it is my conclusion that the accepting of possession of the check for $10,000 by Cannon was not an acceptance of payment under the alleged contract, Exhibit A.

Addressing myself, now, to the contention made by the plaintiff that the $10,000 bonus check is in the nature of consideration for a binding option; that is, consideration for holding open the offer of Billy Cannon for a reasonable length of time.

As I have indicated, Cannon took possession of the $10,000 check thinking that it would be his only if the contract he contemplated for three years' services became effective following the Sugar Bowl game and he further understood, as he testified, that even then he had to report to the club for the 1960 training camp period or he would have to return the bonus.

There can be no question but that the $10,000 check represented what is generally referred to in professional athletics as a bonus payment, customarily offered as an inducement to outstanding rookies. But under the facts as I have found them it was received conditionally.

Furthermore, if, as contended by plaintiff, the bonus constitutes consideration for holding the offer open for a reasonable time and assuming further that the offer were held open in consideration thereof but the player failed for some reason other than military service to show up for the training camp period, it is my understanding of the plain language of the bonus rider attached to Exhibit A that he would be required to return it. If that be so, the bonus so far as consideration for an option is illusory. I conclude, therefore, that in this case there was no binding or irrevocable agreement on the part of Cannon to hold his offer open.

Reaching as I have the conclusion that there did not come into existence a valid written contract or contracts binding upon plaintiff and defendant there is no basis upon which to consider plaintiff's claims for equitable relief or defendant's affirmative defenses in opposition thereto. Specifically, therefore, I make no findings as to the issues of fraud and deceit, or any other of the equitable issues raised by defendant's affirmative defenses.

It probably should be observed, however, that while I have already indicated that Cannon did not intentionally or knowingly make himself ineligible to play in the Sugar Bowl game because of his dealings with the Rams on November 30th, I did not reach the issue of what in fact would have made him ineligible to play under the rules of the N.C.A.A. I do not reach it because the matter is relevant to this litigation, if at all, only as related to defendant's affirmative defense of fraud and deceit and as I have just indicated if no valid contract came into existence that issue becomes academic as far as this litigation is concerned * * *.

Judgment will be for defendant, with costs * * *.

Notes and Questions

1. To appreciate the nuances of the *Cannon* case, one must realize that a vigorous bidding war was ongoing between the established National Football League and the up-start American Football League. As a result, numerous ploys and stratagems were devised to lure players to one league or the other. Oftentimes, these stratagems did not manifest the best elements of fair play and frequently demonstrated unscrupulous conduct on the part of the bidders. It is noteworthy that part of the intrigue of the *Cannon* case was promoted by Pete Rozelle, who eventually became NFL commissioner. For a review of the circumstances surrounding the acrimony between these two leagues and the eventual merger in the late 1960s, see DAVID HARRIS, THE LEAGUE: THE RISE AND DECLINE OF THE NFL (1986).

2. What was the relevance of Cannon's subjective understanding that the contracts would not become effective or binding until after New Year's Day? What factors led the court to take his subjective understanding into account? What was the relevance of the court's discussion of Cannon's age and lack of counsel? Clearly the *Cannon* court perceived the defendant as an unsophisticated actor in the leagues' battle for preeminence in professional football and undoubtedly tailored this decision accordingly. If Cannon were found to be the offeree in this case, the signing of the contract would have closed the circle of assent and precluded his unilateral rescission of the agreement. Accordingly, the court, confronted with a "toss-up" question as to who was the offeror or offeree, opted to find that Cannon was the offeror and that the "commissioner approval" language was a condition precedent to contract formation, rather than a condition precedent to performance. *See Detroit Football Co. v. Robinson*, 186 F. Supp. 933 (E.D. La. 1960); *see also International Filter Co. v. Conroe Gin, Ice & Light Co.*, 277 S.W. 631 (Tex. Comm'n App. 1925). If the court had concluded that the commissioner's approval was a condition precedent to performance, a contract would have been formed, but the duties of the parties would not have been triggered until the commissioner had ultimately approved the contract. During the interim, Cannon would have been ousted of any opportunity to revoke, because the contract already would have been formed.

3. Was the commissioner a party to the agreement? Was the league a party to the contract? Should the league be required to pay Cannon's salary if the Rams become bankrupt? *See United States Football League Players Ass'n v. United States Football League*, 650 F. Supp. 12, 14–16 (D. Or. 1986).

4. The court rejected the NFL's argument that an option contract had been formed as a result of the $10,000 bonus check which had been tendered to Billy Cannon. What would have been the significance of a finding that an option had been formed, and why did the court reject this argument?

5. As a result of this decision, the National Football League has changed its standard player contract language to reflect its intent that the commissioner approval language not be part of the acceptance, but rather be a condition precedent to performance. *See* NFL Uniform Player Contract, ¶18, which reads: "This contract will be valid and binding upon Player and Club immediately upon execution * * *.The Commissioner will have the right to disapprove this contract on reasonable grounds including but not limited to an attempt by the parties to abridge or impair the rights of any other club * * *." How would this language alter the disposition of the *Cannon* case, if at all?

6. Assuming that Cannon had been found to be the offeree and that a contract had been formed, what grounds would be available for him to "avoid" his contractual oblig-

ations? Consider the potential avoidance issues addressed in Chapter 4, Part V. Is there evidence of duress, undue influence, or misrepresentation, among others?

7. Is there any plausible argument that the commissioner approval language rendered the club's promise illusory, thus depriving the agreement of the requisite consideration? That is, because the commissioner had the unbridled authority to withhold approval, was Cannon's promise to play unsupported by any consideration? *See* Chapter 4, Part IV(A).

8. For an analogous "condition precedent to formation" situation, see *Huyett v. Idaho State Univ.*, 104 P.3d 946 (Idaho 2004). Huyett, a women's basketball coach, had entered a one-year contract but desired a multi-year deal. Huyett negotiated with the school and its president for a multi-year contract, but the school reneged on the deal before either party signed the draft agreement. Huyett unsuccessfully argued that a contract was formed. Idaho State Board of Education rules required the Board's approval of any contract exceeding a one-year duration. The court held that there was never any meeting of the minds without Board approval, and therefore a contract could not be formed. *Id.* at 951 ("Proof of a meeting of the minds requires evidence of mutual understanding as to all terms before a contract is formed.") Of course, "meeting of the minds" in today's contract lexicon means a meeting of the minds in the objective, not subjective, sense: "We must look to the outward expression of a person as manifesting his intention rather than his secret and unexpressed intention." *First Nat'l Exchange Bank of Roanoke v. Roanoke Oil Co.*, 192 S.E. 764, 770 (1937). Despite the fact that the school's president had the authority to negotiate a multi-year employment contract, "the material terms of the contract were always subject to Board approval." 104 P. 3d at 951. Although not titled as such by the *Huyett* court, Board approval was a condition precedent to contract formation, and therefore no contract existed. Consequently, the offeror would have the ability to revoke at any point up to the Board's approval.

9. Contract formation questions also arise in the context of student athletes and their relationships with colleges and universities. In *Ross v. Creighton Univ.*, 957 F. 2d 410 (7th Cir. 1992), an all-too familiar recruitment scenario occurred. Creighton University recruited Ross to play basketball. Ross, who did not possess outstanding academic credentials, accepted the scholarship. After his eligibility to play ceased, Ross had not received enough credits to graduate and had the academic sophistication of an elementary school student. Ross sued the school, claiming, *inter alia,* breach of contract in that Creighton promised to give him an education and the assistance he needed to succeed (such as tutoring) in exchange for his playing basketball. On appeal from the grant of a motion to dismiss, the Seventh Circuit reversed, finding that Ross alleged facts sufficient to warrant further breach of contract proceedings. *Id.* at 417.

The court noted that the basic legal relation between a student and a private university or college is contractual in nature, but all aspects of the student-university relationship are not subject to contract action remedy. *Id.* at 416. The academic abstention doctrine often prompts courts to limit their involvement in purely academic affairs, such as grading. *See* Michael J. Cozzillio, *The Athletic Scholarship and the College National Letter of Intent: A Contract By Any Other Name*, 35 Wayne L. Rev. 1275 (1989). However, where a student can point to an identifiable contractual promise that the school failed to honor, an action could be claimed. *Id.* at 416–17 (such ruling would required an objective assessment of whether school made good faith effort to perform; it would not require an inquiry into the nuances of education processes and theories). Here, Ross alleged that Creighton knew he was not academically qualified but yet made a specific promise that he would be able to participate meaningfully in the school's program thanks to the school's academic support program. *Id.* Because he was able to produce facts that would support an implied contract, Ross was able to proceed with his claim.

In *Hendricks v. Clemson University,* 578 S.E.2d 711 (S.C. 2003), a student athlete alleged a breach of contract based on inadequate academic services that rendered him ineligible to play baseball. The court found that Hendricks was unable to establish that a contract was even formed between him and the school. Hendricks failed to produce any written promise from Clemson, and unlike Ross, did not produce any real evidence that such a promise was implied. *Id.* at 717. The court emphasized that Hendricks "did not discuss NCAA academic eligibility until he was already enrolled at Clemson," *id.,* intimating that such an implied academic contract as asserted by Hendricks would lack consideration. The court abstained, reasoning that allowing this action to proceed "would invite courts to engage in * * * subjective analysis," inappropriate under today's objective theory.

10. As discussed in Chapter 4, a contract is formed when the circle of assent closes, *i.e.,* once there is offer and acceptance, supported by adequate consideration. For an interesting treatment of what constitutes acceptance, consider season ticket packages, particularly in the context of newly built stadiums. Typically in those situations, fans are sent a brochure inviting them to complete an application for a season seat in the new stadium. Often a sketch of the tentative stadium seating is included, and the fans that submit an application and down payment are later notified of their actual seats. Does the completion of the application and submission with the down payment constitute "acceptance" invited by an offer and a closing of the circle of assent? *Compare Yocca v. Pittsburgh Steelers Sports, Inc.,* 854 A.2d 425 (Pa. 2004) *with Reedy v. Cincinnati Bengals, Inc.,* 758 N.E.2d 678 (Ohio 2001).

Once a contract is found to exist, does a season ticket holder have a justified right to expect an opportunity to renew that package under a right of first refusal? Would your answer change if the team relocates to an area that is not local? Does the season ticket holder still retain a right of first refusal to renew his or her package or should it be a matter of common sense that the fan will not want season tickets in a distant area? *See Charpentier v. L.A. Rams Football Co.,* 89 Cal. Rptr. 2d 115 (Cal. Ct. App. 2000) (finding that it was unreasonable for a season ticket holder to assume a right to renew when a team relocated out of the local area); *Beder v. Cleveland Browns, Inc.,* 129 Ohio App. 3d 188 (1998) (holding that the team breached its contract with season ticket holder when it failed to offer a right of first refusal of season tickets in new stadium, even though stadium moved from Cleveland to Baltimore).

11. More than thirty years after the *Cannon* case, questions still abound regarding Billy Cannon's naïveté and Judge Lindberg's decision to err on the side of the vulnerable college student. *See generally* Michael J. Goodman, *An Utter Disaster,* THE SPORTING NEWS, May 29, 1995, at 10. Billy Cannon won the Heisman Trophy in 1959 and is a legendary figure at Louisiana State University, where he is best known for his 89-yard punt return for a game-winning touchdown against the University of Mississippi on Halloween night in 1959. His contract with the Oilers was signed on New Years Day in 1960, between the goal posts and in front of 83,000 fans at the Sugar Bowl. The contract with the Oilers included $100,000 over three years, a $10,000 "gift" for his wife, a slightly used Cadillac, and a promised chain of Cannon gas stations selling Cannonball gasoline. Cannon led the AFL in rushing in 1961, but injured his back in 1962. In 1964 he was traded to the Oakland Raiders and he ended

his career in 1970 as a tight end. During the off-seasons, while he played in the AFL, he attended dental school and subsequently developed a successful practice as an orthodontist.

Billy Cannon's jurisprudential history did not end with his NFL career. In 1980, Cannon's son, Billy, Jr., an 18 year-old high school senior, was projected to be a probable first round pick in Major League Baseball's amateur draft as a shortstop/outfielder. Billy Cannon, Sr. sent telegrams to all 26 major league teams, telling them not to waste a first-round pick on his son, because Billy, Jr., was going to college first. No one selected Cannon until the third round, when George Steinbrenner and the New York Yankees drafted him and subsequently signed him to a contract that included a $350,000 signing bonus. Three American League teams—the Toronto Blue Jays, California Angels, and Boston Red Sox—filed grievances with Commissioner Bowie Kuhn, claiming that there had been prior negotiations between Cannon and Steinbrenner and a plan to mislead the other American League teams to forego drafting Cannon, paving the way for the Yankees to draft him. After a two-day hearing, Kuhn announced that the Yankees had violated draft rules prohibiting negotiations with free agents in advance of the draft, stripped the Yankees of their draft rights, reprimanded Steinbrenner, and scheduled a supplemental lottery and draft for Cannon in which the Yankees were not permitted to participate. The Cleveland Indians drafted Cannon, but he instead opted to go to Texas A&M and was drafted by the NFL's Dallas Cowboys in the first round of the 1984 draft as a linebacker. Billy, Jr., signed a contract for $1.9 million over six years, but his career ended after just eight games when he suffered a spinal injury. Billy, Jr., filed a multi-million dollar negligence lawsuit against the Cowboys, and the case was eventually settled in 1992.

During the intervening period, Billy Cannon, Sr., again graced the courtroom, this time on the criminal side of the docket. In 1983, beset by severe financial difficulty, reportedly because of unsuccessful investments and gambling losses, Cannon Sr. was arrested and pleaded guilty to conspiracy to possess and deal in counterfeit money. He served about two and one-half years in prison. His 1983 selection for induction into the National Football Hall of Fame was revoked as a result of the counterfeiting conviction. After he left prison, he went back to practicing dentistry, but, in July of 1995, he was forced to file for bankruptcy, citing debts of $1.8 million and less than $200,000 in assets.

12. The *Cannon* decision turned on the pivotal question of who was the offeror or offeree in the scenario presented. The following case focuses not on the identities of the parties but the duration of the agreement. Frequently, in sports litigation, the length of the agreement (*e.g.*, a long-term contract with a series of one-year performances versus several one-year contracts) can profoundly impact the rights of the parties.

(B) Contract Duration

Sample v. Gotham Football Club, Inc.
59 F.R.D. 160 (S.D.N.Y. 1973)

EDELSTEIN, **Chief Judge.** * * * Defendant is the owner and operator of a professional football team popularly known as the "New York Jets." On September 1, 1968, it entered into three separately executed written agreements with plaintiff under which plaintiff was required to render services as a professional football player for the 1968, 1969 and

1970 football seasons. Each document represents the agreement between plaintiff and defendant for a different year. The current dispute only pertains to the contracts covering the 1969 and 1970 football seasons.

* * *

Turning to an examination of the second cause of action the court is confronted with the allegation that plaintiff's dismissal in 1969 entitles him to recovery of his 1970 salary under the injury-benefits clause of his contract. This allegation is grounded on plaintiff's contention that both parties intended to enter into one three-year contract covering the 1968, 1969 and 1970 football seasons, notwithstanding the existence of three separately executed documents. Accordingly, plaintiff argues that since his alleged injury was sustained during the performance of a three-year contract he is entitled to his salary for the remaining term of the contract * * *.

To the contrary, defendant contends that the three separately executed documents were intended to represent three one-year contracts. Thus, if obligated to pay at all, it would be liable only for the salary provided under the contract pertaining to the season in which the injury was sustained. After a careful and thorough independent review of the record the court finds that the parties entered into three one-year contracts, rather than a single three-year contract. Accordingly, defendant is granted summary judgment with respect to plaintiff's second cause of action.

Plaintiff argues that he subjectively believed that he was entering into one three-year contract when he affixed his signature to the documents in question. He further alleges that he was duped into the separate-contract-arrangement due to: (1) his lack of sophistication in contract negotiations; (2) his lack of representation by counsel; and (3) the unequal bargaining positions of the parties. All these arguments are unavailing.

In determining whether the simultaneous execution of several instruments results in one contract or in several separate agreements, the intention of the parties must be ascertained from a reading of the several instruments, and from an examination of the facts and circumstances at the time of execution. The New York Court of Appeals has stated that when the terms of a written contract are clear and unambiguous the intent of the parties must be ascertained from the language used to express such intent * * *. Here the contracts were plain and unambiguous. The intent of the parties is clearly manifested by the three separate executions, and because each contract pertains to a single football season. Moreover, the relevant contractual intent is that expressed in the contract (or contracts) even though it may not accord with the subjective intent of the parties * * *. It should be noted that although all three contracts were executed contemporaneously by the same parties, this does not necessarily require that they be read together as one instrument. Plaintiff's reliance on *Ripley v. International Railways of Central America*, 171 N.E.2d 443 (1960), and *Nau v. Vulcan Rail & Construction Co.*, 36 N.E.2d 106 (1941), for the contrary proposition, is misplaced. In those cases various instruments were required to be read together as one contract. But in each instance the writings were either related to the same subject matter and intended to effectuate the same purpose, *Nau* * * *, or were otherwise integrated by specific reference to the other agreements, *Ripley* * * *. Moreover, in *Ripley* the New York Court of Appeals stated:

> The circumstance that they are different documents does not necessarily mean that they do not form a single contract * * *, *but it does indicate that they are separate unless the history and subject matter shows them to be unified* * * *. (emphasis added).

Significantly, the three documents in the case at bar did not relate to the same subject matter even though they concerned the same parties. This conclusion is reached because each contract called for performance at different times, *i.e.*, each pertained to a different football season * * *.

Having determined that the parties entered into three separate contracts, it is necessary to evaluate plaintiff's second claim in light of this conclusion.

Paragraph 14 of the 1970 contract makes it unequivocally clear that the injury-benefits provision[9] is operative only during the relevant contract period. In this instance only during the 1970 football season. In pertinent part, paragraph 14 provides that if a

> Player is injured in the performance of his services *under this contract* * * * the Club will * * * continue, *during the term of this contract*, to pay Player his salary * * * if and so long as it is the opinion of the Club Physician that Player, because of such injury, is unable to perform the services required of him *by this contract* (emphasis added).

Since the injury alleged by plaintiff occurred during the term of his 1969 contract, and since the 1970 contract is a separate agreement, plaintiff can not prevail on his second cause of action. Only if plaintiff had sustained a disabling injury during the term of the 1970 contract would he be entitled to invoke the injury-benefits clause of that contract. Hence, defendant is entitled to summary judgment as a matter of law with respect to plaintiff's second claim.

The decision of the Court of Appeals for the Fifth Circuit in *Hennigan v. Chargers Football Co.*, 431 F.2d 308 (5th Cir. 1970), lends support to the conclusion reached above. In *Hennigan* the plaintiff-player brought suit against the defendant-football team under the injury-benefits provision of the AFL Standard Players Contract for salary during the option-year[10] of his contract.[11] Plaintiff was injured during the second and third years of his three-year contract and was paid his salary for those years under the injury-benefits provision of the contract. Defendant exercised the option-clause of plaintiff's contract. This had the effect of obligating plaintiff to perform as a player for a period of one year after the termination of his original three-year contract.

---

9. The injury-benefits provision, which is contained in paragraph 14, * * * allows a player to collect his entire salary under the contract if he is injured and unable to play during the term of the contract.

10. All professional football players who play for teams in the National Football League have a standard option clause in their contracts. This clause permits a team to renew the player's contract for a term of one year at not less than ninety percent of his previous salary. The option clause permits a player to leave a team by playing out his option year. The standard option clause reads as follows:

> The Club may, by sending notice in writing to the Player, on or before the first day of May following the football season referred to in ¶1 hereof, renew this contract for a further term of one (1) year on the same terms as are provided by this contract, except that (1) the Club may fix the rate of compensation to be paid by the Club to the Player during said further term, which rate of compensation shall not be less than ninety-percent (90%) of the sum set forth in ¶3 hereof and shall be payable in installments during the football season in such further term as provided in ¶3; and (2) after such renewal this contract shall not include a further option to the Club to renew the contract. The phrase "rate of compensation" as above used shall not include bonus payments or payments of any nature whatsoever and shall be limited to the precise sum set forth in ¶3 hereof.

11. Hennigan signed his three-year contract with the Houston Oilers, Inc. in 1964. He completed his three years (1964, 1965 and 1966) with the Oilers and was traded to the defendant, Chargers Football Company, pursuant to paragraph 9 of the standard players contract. The Chargers then exercised the option-clause of Hennigan's original contract with the Oilers.

Plaintiff reported to preseason training for the option-year and was examined by defendant's team physician as required by the Standard Players Contract. The team physician found plaintiff physically unfit to play and recommended that he be rejected by the team. The defendant terminated its contract with plaintiff on the basis of the physician's recommendation.

Subsequently, Hennigan brought suit against the Chargers for the salary he would have earned during the option-year of his contract. He predicated his claim on two separate grounds. First, that since he was injured during the term of the contract, which defendant extended by its exercise of the option clause, he was entitled to recovery under the injury-benefits provision of the original contract. His second argument, which is not relevant to the instant motion, concerned the applicability of the "no-cut" clause in the original contract to the option year.

After determining that the exercise of the option clause had the effect of creating a new contract with the plaintiff, the Fifth Circuit concluded:

> [I]t follows that Hennigan was not entitled to compensation for the 1967 football season from the Chargers. He suffered no injury while in the performance of any services required of him after the option was exercised. Consequently, he is not entitled to payment under paragraph 15 (the injury provision). 431 F.2d at 317–318.

The result reached above concerning Sample's second claim is thus on all fours with *Hennigan*.

* * *

Reviewing the dispositions, the court denies plaintiff's cross-motion for summary judgment on both its first and second causes of action * * *.

So ordered.

Notes and Questions

1. What was the relevance of Sample's subjective understanding that he was entering into a three-year contract? What was the relevance of Sample's lack of sophistication, absence of counsel, and inferior bargaining position? Do you agree with the court's conclusion that the contract in question constituted a series of one-year agreements rather than a long-term contract? *See* Michael J. Cozzillio, *The Athletic Scholarship and the College National Letter of Intent: A Contract By Any Other Name*, 35 WAYNE L. REV. 1275, 1320–24 (1989).

2. High school athletes signing the National Letter of Intent often speak of their scholarship as a "four year rule" or a "full ride" when, in fact, NCAA regulations prohibit scholarships in excess of one year. Refusal to renew a scholarship, thus, could spawn interesting questions of contract interpretation, parol evidence, misrepresentation, and a host of other issues, depending of course upon the correspondence exchanged. Why would either party agree to a contract that contained terms for succeeding years if the contract itself were only one year in duration? Would either party have had the right to rescind unilaterally in the second year of the agreement in question? From the club's standpoint, because of the system of perpetual reserve existing in the National Football League, arguably there was no downside risk of Sample not being bound by the second and third years of his contract. Had he chosen not to accept the second year of the agreement, he would have been bound to play for the Gotham Foot-

ball Club or not to play football at all. Perhaps the rationale of the National Football League was that the terms of the second and third year had been established with no opportunity for renegotiation by Sample while Sample really had no opportunity to negotiate a better deal elsewhere. Clearly the merger of two rival leagues compromises player mobility and tends to suppress salaries because the absence of a competing league places the player at the mercy of the existing league, barring some type of free agency or opportunity to move from club to club within that league.

3. Article XV of the 1993 NFL-NFLPA Collective Bargaining Agreement eliminated the option year from the standard NFL contract.

4. The court placed considerable reliance upon the *Hennigan* decision. As the court indicated, the exercise of the option clause in that case created a new contract, thereby precluding any type of continuous benefit under the original agreement. A perusal of the full text of that opinion demonstrates the extent to which a court will go to avoid enforcing a salary guarantee. There, the court devised a tortured definition of the term "renewal" in such a way as to conclude that a renewal option, in essence, created a new contract upon its exercise. One dissenting judge persuasively argued that the majority's interpretation of the term "renew and extend" did not support the league's position, but, rather, contradicted it. The dissent posited that the option established an extension of the existing contract, thereby justifying the conclusion that the salary guarantees and the no-cut clause contained in the original agreement should be enforced. Certainly, it created enough of an ambiguity to warrant the dissenter's determination that the contract should be construed against the "maker," the Chargers Football Company.

5. When Sample became disabled, what benefits and other amounts did the Jets owe him? Does the law give Sample any legal approach other than a breach of contract claim against the Jets to receive compensation for his pain and suffering, inability to earn a living, loss of physical function, and other damages? Generally, workers' compensation is the exclusive remedy for injuries sustained in the scope of one's employment. However, in the context of certain intentional torts or fraudulent concealment situations, additional remedies may be available. *See* Chapter 18 Part IV, *infra*.

6. The courts have been inconsistent in their interpretation of the duration of the agreement language in professional sports contracts. For example, in *Chuy v. Philadelphia Eagles*, 407 F. Supp. 717 (E.D. Pa. 1976), the court concluded that the contract's ambiguity and the resultant presumption against the drafter compelled the conclusion that the club intended a long-term contract with an attendant salary guarantee rather than a series of one-year agreements. The upshot of this legal conclusion was that plaintiff Chuy was able to insist upon a guaranty for the duration of his long-term contract as opposed to just the initial year

7. Questions of duration can affect not only the length of time that a contract is in effect but the very existence of the contract itself. In *Rooney v. Tyson*, 697 N.E.2d 571 (N.Y. 1998), the issue was whether an oral contract to train a boxer "for as long as the boxer fights professionally" was enforceable. Because contracts lacking definite duration are potentially infirm both on grounds of indefiniteness and a lack of consideration, resolution of this issue in favor of the defendant would suggest that the relationship was "at-will" rather than contractual.

The issue created an intense bout within the New York Court of Appeals, which had questions certified to it by the United States Court of Appeals for the Second Circuit as follows:

Does an oral contract between a fight trainer and a professional boxer to train the boxer 'for as long as the boxer fights professionally' establish a definite duration, or does it constitute employment for indefinite duration within the scope of the at-will rule?

The majority acknowledged that employment relationships are presumed to be at-will if there be no agreement creating a fixed duration and that an at-will presumption is activated when that putative agreement does not declare a definite employment period. Following from that precept, the court applied a two-step process that asked 1) whether the duration is definite, in which case the at-will doctrine is inapplicable, and 2) whether the employment period is indefinite or undefined, in which case then exists a rebuttable presumption that the arrangement is at-will—leaving the door open for the introduction of other factors. Interpreting the term definite in a relatively expansive fashion, the court found that the contract was enforceable and that a rebuttable presumption did not exist:

> When an agreement is silent as to duration, however, it is presumptively at-will, absent an express or implied limitation on an employer's otherwise unfettered ability to discharge an employee. Only when we discern no term of some definiteness or no express limitation does the analysis switch over to the rebuttable presumption line of cases. They embody the principle that an employment relationship is terminable upon even the whim of either either the employer or the employee. The agreement in this case is not silent and manifestly provides a sufficiently limiting framework * * * Accordingly, the certified question of the Second Circuit Court of Appeals should be answered that an oral contract between a fight trainer and a professional boxer to train the boxer "for as long as the boxer fights professionally" is a contract for a definite duration.

Rooney v. Tyson, supra at 574, 576. The dissent vigorously objected, opining that "definite" presupposes a length of employment fixed with some precision. Wryly, the dissent castigated the majority for concluding that "the ending of a boxing career is somehow more definite than death." Characterizing employment at-will as a "judicial bedrock" of employment law, the dissent declared that the majority incorrectly focused on the "definiteness of how employment might be limited rather than the definiteness of the term of employment." 697 N.E.2d at 579. The dissent concluded, "a promise of employment which might last anywhere from a day to a decade is insufficient standing alone, to indicate an actual intention to be potentially and absolutely bound * * *" *Id.* at 581.

8. Would the majority's opinion in the *Rooney* case affect the possible applicability of the Statute of Frauds? Contracts of indefinite duration are presumably not within the Statute of Frauds' one-year rule because they are potentially performable within a year. *See* CALAMARI & PERILLO §§ 19.17–.18. The dissent echoes this concern "an employment contract of definite duration beyond a year may avoid application of the at-will presumption but must be in writing to be enforceable at all. 697 N.E.2d at 583.

9. The positions staked out by the majority and dissent reflect a common debate among contracts scholars and jurists regarding contract preservation versus contract destruction. As discussed at various points in Chapter 4, courts and legislatures have become increasingly indulgent of contracts with questionable underpinnings in terms of definition, consideration, etc. Consider, for example, ways in which Article 2 of the Uniform Commercial Code has relaxed traditional rules in the name of preserving

contracts. *See e.g.* U.C.C. §§ 2-204, 2-305; *Wood v. Loyola Marymount Univ.*, 267 Cal. Rptr. 230 (Cal. Ct. App. 1990); *Sylvan Crest Sand & Gravel Co. v. United States*, 150 F. 2d 642 (2d Cir. 1945); CALAMARI & PERILLO, CONTRACTS §. Likewise, countless jurisdictions have diluted the notion of employment at will by finding implied contracts, abusive discharges actionable in tort, etc. *See, e.g., Martin Marietta v. Lorenz*, 823 P.2d 100 (Colo. 1992); *Siles v. Travenal Labs*, 433 N.E.2d 103 (Mass. Ct. App. 1982).

10. Is a contract that a party will provide training services so long as the other party boxes professionally beset with consideration problems as well as potential indefiniteness? Cannot Mike Tyson quit whenever he pleases? What is Tyson's obligation under the agreement? Professor Corbin would respond that sufficient consideration is present because Tyson's promise states a limitation upon his future liberty of action. So long as Tyson boxes professionally, Rooney is obligated to train him and vice versa. *See* ARTHUR CORBIN, CORBIN ON CONTRACTS § 160; RESTATEMENT (SECOND) OF CONTRACTS §§ 77, 78.

11. Injury grievances are much more prevalent in professional football than in any other sport. In fact, the collective bargaining agreement between the National Football League and the National Football League Players Association has specific provisions governing the grievance and arbitration procedure to be employed in the case of disputes over injuries. *See* Article X of NFL-NFLPA Collective Bargaining Agreement. Among the questions that frequently arise in this context, are the types of injuries for which the team will assume responsibility or liability, including expenses for medical care and/or salary recompense. The *Sample* case illustrates that the parameters of a team's duty to "cover" a player for injuries sustained on the field are not always subject to a facile resolution. The same difficulties have obtained in attempting to ascertain the categories of injuries that may rest within the scope of his performance for the club. *See, e.g., Matuszak v. Houston Oilers, Inc.*, 515 S.W.2d 725 (Tex. Civ. App. 1974). In any event, all parties should be aware that courts and arbitrators are extremely strict in applying and interpreting procedural prerequisites to claims for benefits arising from injuries. *See, e.g., Tillman v. New Orleans Saints Football Club*, 265 So.2d 284 (La. Ct. App. 1972). *See also Spain v. Houston Oilers, Inc.*, 593 S.W.2d 746 (Tex. Civ. App. 1979). For a comprehensive treatment of injuries, both in terms of the players' rights to compensation as well as the clubs' ability to terminate, see JOHN C. WEISTART & CYM H. LOWELL, THE LAW OF SPORTS §§ 3.05, 3.06, at 215–30 (1979).

12. As the *Sample* case makes abundantly clear, careful draftsmanship is critical to ensure that the parties' intent in a particular agreement will be honored. Yet, all too frequently, contract terms remain vague or, worse, omitted either because the parties inadvertently neglected to include such provisions or consciously left them to be resolved at a later time. As the following case illustrates, judicial resolution of these "oversights," while moving toward greater indulgence, is varied and unpredictable.

(C) Indefiniteness

Eckles v. Sharman
548 F.2d 905 (10th Cir. 1977)

BREITENSTEIN, Circuit Judge. This is an action by the owner of a professional basketball team for breach of contract by a former coach and for the inducement of that breach by the owner of another professional basketball team. Judgment was entered on a jury verdict for $250,000 against the coach and for $175,000 against the inducing owner. We reverse and remand with directions.

After these appeals were filed, the plaintiff-appellee Mountain States Sports, Inc., became bankrupt and R. T. Eckles, trustee in bankruptcy, was substituted as the appellee in each case. References herein will be to Mountain States rather than to the trustee.

Defendant-appellant Sharman was the coach of the San Francisco Warriors, a professional basketball team of the National Basketball Association, NBA. In 1968 he was persuaded to leave the San Francisco team and to coach the Los Angeles Stars of the newly formed American Basketball Association, ABA. The contract between Sharman and the Los Angeles team was for seven years and called for a starting salary of $55,000 with yearly increases of 5%. Provisions of the contract pertinent to these cases are:

(1) — Sharman was given an "option to purchase 5% ownership of the Club" at a price to be agreed upon between him and the owner.

(2) — Sharman was to participate in a "pension plan" of an undefined nature.

(3) — The parties agreed that: "In the event any one paragraph of this Agreement is invalid, this Agreement will not fail by reason thereof but will be interpreted as if the invalid portion were omitted."

(4) — California law governs the agreement.

In 1970 the Los Angeles Stars were sold for $345,000 to plaintiff Mountain States Sports, Inc., a Colorado corporation, of which Bill Daniels was the president and principal stockholder. An addendum to the sale agreement provided:

"Buyer shall not be obligated to assume the Sharman contract unless he shall have confirmed his willingness to transfer to the city selected by Buyer for operation of the team. Seller states that Sharman has orally expressed his willingness to do so."

The team was moved to Salt Lake City, Utah, and became the Utah Stars. Without anything in writing pertaining to his participation in the move, Sharman went to Salt Lake City with the team. Sharman coached the Utah Stars during the 1970–1971 season and the team won the ABA championship.

During the two years that the team was in Los Angeles with Sharman as coach nothing was done with regard to the option and pension provisions of the contract. Boryla, the general manager of the Utah Stars, told Sharman that the pension provision would be worked out. Later Sharman and Daniels, the president of Mountain States, had numerous communications, both oral and written, concerning Sharman's pension rights. No final agreement was reached. In June, 1971, Sharman resigned as coach of the Utah Stars and, in July, signed a contract to coach the Los Angeles Lakers of the NBA.

Mountain States brought suit in Utah state court charging Sharman with breach of contract. The complaint was amended to assert a claim against defendant-appellant California Sports, Inc., the owner of the Los Angeles Lakers, and two individuals for the tortious inducement of Sharman's breach of contract * * *. The case was removed to the United States District Court for the District of Utah and fell before Judge Anderson * * *.

Judge Anderson conducted extensive pre-trial proceedings and entered a comprehensive pre-trial order. Among other things, Judge Anderson ruled "that the question of what was intended by the parties with respect to the severability clause and by the paragraph 11 [pension plan] clause in particular, is a question of fact that the jury should decide." After five days of a jury trial Judge Anderson declared a mistrial because of "communications between witness and a member of the court staff." The case was then assigned to Judge Ritter.

A jury trial before Judge Ritter began about a month later. Early in that trial Judge Ritter stated: "I'm not going to pay any attention to anything that happened over on the other side of this court." At the conclusion of the plaintiff's case, Judge Ritter denied a defense motion to dismiss saying that the claim of contract invalidity because of the option and pension clauses presented nothing but a "red herring" and that Sharman and the owners of the Utah Stars had made a "good faith" effort to "clear up those terms." At the conclusion of all of the evidence, Judge Ritter directed a verdict against Sharman on the question of liability.

The case went to the jury on the questions of damages recoverable from Sharman, liability of the other defendants charged with inducement of contract breach and, if there was inducement, the damages resulting therefrom. The jury returned verdicts (1) in favor of the individuals sued for inducement, (2) against Sharman in the amount of $250,000, and (3) against California Sports in the amount of $175,000.

Implicit in the direction of a verdict against Sharman on the question of liability is a ruling that as a matter of law (1) the contract between Sharman and the Los Angeles Stars was valid and enforceable, (2) the contract was validly assigned to Mountain States Sports, and (3) the option and pension provisions of the contract were severable from the remainder thereof.

The option clause was unenforceable because it was nothing more than an agreement to agree. The pension clause did not state (1) the amount of pension, (2) the manner in which it would be funded, and (3) the age at which the pension would begin. The plaintiff does not seriously contest the defense claim that the pension clause is ambiguous.

Plaintiff relies on the severance clause which says that "[i]n the event any one paragraph of this Agreement is invalid," the agreement will not fail but will be interpreted as if the invalid portion was omitted. We have a failure of two paragraphs. Sharman and representatives of the plaintiff negotiated for about 15 months over the two mentioned clauses, principally that pertaining to the pension.

Good faith negotiations over various terms of an agreement do not make a fatally ambiguous contract valid and enforceable. The controlling California law is that for there to be an enforceable contract the parties must agree on the essential and material terms * * *. If a contract has been agreed upon and all that remains is good faith negotiations or elaboration of non-essential terms, the contract will be held legally cognizable despite the uncertainties * * *. The question is not whether good faith negotiations had taken place but whether the option and pension were so essential to the contract that failure to agree on the pertinent terms made the contract unenforceable.

Moffat Tunnel Improvement Dist. v. Denver & S.L. Ry. Co., 10 Cir., 45 F.2d 715, 731, says that a severability clause "is but an aid to construction, and will not justify a court in declaring a clause as divisible when, considering the entire contract, it obviously is not." The crucial question is whether the clauses to be severed are essential to the contract. Essentiality depends on the intent of the parties* * *.

The intent evidence is not all one way. Sharman testified that without the option and pension provisions he would not have left the well-established NBA for the newly-established ABA. His testimony was corroborated by other witnesses. On the other hand, the record reveals that Sharman never made any serious efforts to clarify or enforce the option clause. Nothing was done about the pension clause during the two years that Sharman and the team were in Los Angeles. During the fifteen months that Sharman was with the Utah Stars many communications, both written and verbal, passed between Sharman and representatives of the team owners. Nothing was accomplished. From the evidence in the record a reasonable man could have drawn an inference one way or the other on the question of intent.

We have repeatedly held that a verdict may not be directed unless the evidence all points one way and is susceptible of no reasonable inferences which sustain the position of the party against whom the motion is made * * *. On the record presented it may not be said, as a matter of law, that the option and pension clauses were unessential and hence severable. Neither can it be said, as a matter of law, that without the resolution of the controversy over those clauses Sharman agreed to the assignment of the contract to the owners of the Utah Stars. The pertinent intent questions required factual determination by the jury under proper instructions. The court erred in directing a verdict against Sharman and in favor of Mountain States on the liability issue.

The liability of California Sports depends on whether the contract between Sharman and the owner of the Los Angeles Stars was valid and whether the contract was enforceable by the owner of the Utah Stars against Sharman. If the contract was not valid, and if the contract was not enforceable by the Utah Stars, California Sports is not liable under the claim of tortious inducement of breach. The error of the court in directing a verdict on the question of Sharman's liability requires the reversal of the judgment against California Sports.

* * *

[Reversed and remanded.]

Notes and Questions

1. Why did the Tenth Circuit decide that the option to purchase and the pension plan provisions were too ambiguous to enforce? Was the severance clause intended to address this type of situation?

2. Article 2 of the Uniform Commercial Code articulates the modern view that not all contract indefiniteness should be fatal. To that end, the UCC provides numerous gap-filler provisions designed to facilitate a court's ability to supply missing or vague terms. As Professor John Murray notes, the UCC's general mandate directing courts to enforce contracts if they find demonstrable intent to be bound and a plausible predicate to fashion a remedy "served as a catalyst to chart the new, anti-technical course away from fatal indefiniteness * * *." JOHN MURRAY, MURRAY ON CONTRACTS § 38.

3. Issues surrounding contract indefiniteness, particularly in the context of "agreements to agree," have presented extremely complicated issues with no definitive judicial resolution. At times, courts have concluded that an agreement to agree, by definition, suggests no meaningful agreement and thereby will find the putative contract fatally indefinite. *See Hill v. McGregor Mfg. Corp.*, 178 N.W.2d 553 (Mich. Ct. App. 1970); *Dunhill Securities Corp. v. Microthermal Applications, Inc.*, 308 F. Supp. 195 (S.D.N.Y. 1969); ARTHUR CORBIN, CORBIN ON CONTRACTS § 29 (1952). Other courts have attempted to salvage the agreement and find the agreement to agree not fatally indefinite by applying custom and usage in the industry or other gap-filling devices to attempt to divine the

intent of the parties. *See, e.g., Itek Corp. v. Chicago Aerial Indus.*, 274 A.2d 141 (Del. 1971). Perhaps the best approach is for courts to take a middle course and attempt to enforce the agreement to agree but not to substitute their own version of the contract. In this sense, the courts will require as part of their enforcement that the parties make a reasonable effort to agree but will not impose substantive terms upon those parties. Thus, the resolution is not unlike the National Labor Relations Board's enforcement of an employer's duty to bargain in good faith with a collective bargaining representative. *See* 29 U.S.C. §§ 158(a)(5), 158(d); *see also NLRB v. Food Store Employees Union, Local 347*, 417 U.S. 1 (1974).

4. For a detailed exploration of agreements to agree and the various devices courts have employed to address the myriad problems created therein, see Harvey L. Temkin, *When Does the "Fat Lady" Sing: An Analysis of "Agreements in Principle" in Corporate Acquisitions*, 55 Fordham L. Rev. 125 (1986); Charles L. Knapp, *Enforcing the Contract To Bargain*, 44 N.Y.U. L. Rev. 673 (1969). The upshot of the reams of critical commentary is that the key feature of ascertaining the enforceability of agreements to agree will be the parties' intent. Any presumption created by the titling of the arrangement is rebuttable by establishing objective manifestations of a contrary intent. *See Dunhill*, 308 F. Supp. at 198. Is the compensation a professional is to receive for his services a "material" term of the contract?

5. If you represented the Utah Stars in the *Eckles* case, what evidence would you try to present in support of a damage claim against Sharman? What relevance would the extent of league revenue sharing have with respect to a damage claim by the Stars against Sharman?

6. Did the Utah Stars seek injunctive relief against Sharman or the Lakers? Could the club meet the burden of establishing its right to injunctive relief?

7. In some respects, we would expect that purse, or in the employment contract context, compensation, goes to the cost of the contract and would constitute fatal indefiniteness if omitted. Yet, as stated above, many lawmakers and judges have become more willing to fill gaps for unwary or careless parties and will often travel the extra mile to enforce a contract based on what the parties may have intended rather than on what the contract actually prescribed. Consider the following case with advance apologies for the confusion that *Eckles/Echols* will inevitably produce.

Echols v. Pelullo
377 F.3d 272 (3d Cir. 2004)

RENDELL, Circuit Judge. A boxing promoter seeks to recover from the District Court's knockout punch aimed, and delivered, at the enforceability of its promotional agreement. Banner Promotions, Inc. entered into a promotional agreement with boxer Antwun Echols, the terms of which left Echols's compensation for participating in bouts secured by Banner subject to negotiation between the two parties, and to renegotiation under certain circumstances. The District Court determined that the agreement's failure to specify minimum compensation for Echols's participation in these bouts rendered it so indefinite as to be unenforceable. For the reasons set forth below, we will reverse.

I.

Arthur Pelullo is the president and owner of Banner Promotions, Inc. ("Banner"), a company engaged in the promotion of professional boxers and professional boxing matches. Antwun Echols is a professional boxer with a current record of twenty nine wins, five losses and one draw.

In November 1999, Echols signed a Promotional Agreement ("the Agreement") with Banner, receiving a $30,000 signing bonus. The Agreement granted Banner "the sole and exclusive right to secure all professional boxing bouts requiring [Echols's] services as a professional boxer and to promote all such bouts" for a term of at least four years, and possibly longer, if certain conditions were met. In essence, the Agreement gave Banner the right to be Echols's sole representative in negotiations with any third parties that were interested in having Echols box on their television networks, in their arenas, or against boxers they represented.

Banner's major obligation under the Agreement was to "secure, arrange and promote" not less than three bouts for Echols during each year of the contract. Banner had sole discretion to determine the time and place of each bout. While Echols had to approve each opponent, his approval could not be "unreasonably withheld." Under Section Five of the Agreement, Banner could satisfy its obligation to secure a bout "if it shall have made a bona fide offer in writing irrespective of whether such bout actually takes place for any reason other than Banner's nonperformance."

Section Six of the Agreement delineated Echols's compensation for his appearance in the bouts secured by Banner:

> Your purse for all bouts covered by this agreement shall be structured as follows (a) non television, not less than $7,500.00 (b) Univision, not less than $10,000.00 (c) Telemundo, not less that $10,000.00 (d) ESPN 2, Fox Sports or small pay-per-view, not less than $20,000.00 plus $10,000.00 training expenses. (e) HBO AFTER DARK as a challenger or in a non title bout, not less than $45,000.00 plus $10,000.00 training expenses. (f) HBO AFTER DARK as a World Champion not less than $80,000.00 plus $10,000.00 training expenses. (g) HBO as a challenger or in a non-title bout, not less than $50,000.00 plus $10,000 training expenses. (h) HBO as a World Champion, not less than $125,000.00 plus $15,000.00 training expenses.

Thus, Banner was to pay Echols not less than a stated minimum amount for each bout in which he appeared, with the amount of the minimum depending on where the bout was televised and whether Echols appeared as a champion or not. However, these "minimum purses" could be subject to renegotiation, or the entire Agreement cancelled, at Banner's option, by operation of Section Eight, which provided that "if during the course of this Agreement Boxer should lose any bout, Banner shall [sic] the right but not the obligation to rescind this Agreement or the purses set forth in paragraph (6) shall be subject to renegotiation."

One month after entering the Agreement, Echols lost a world championship bout to Bernard Hopkins, triggering Section Eight. Banner chose not to exercise its right to rescind the Agreement, but took the position that Echols's compensation would thereafter be negotiated on a bout-by-bout basis. Indeed, the parties proceeded to negotiate several individual bout purse agreements in the years after the loss to Hopkins.

Echols, however, became dissatisfied with the situation. According to him, Banner had made him "take it or leave it" offers—offering him bouts for what he believes is below-market compensation, and then rescinding the offers if he attempted to negotiate for a larger purse. Because the operation of Section Eight eliminated the minimum purses specified in Section Six, Echols felt that he was forced to accept Banner's unsatisfactory offers in order to receive any compensation at all.

Tension also arose between the two parties over a "step-aside" fee that Banner negotiated on Echols's behalf in connection with a fight in Germany. [1] Echols believed that Banner misrepresented the amount of the "step-aside" fee, telling him that it was less than it actually was, so that Banner could pocket the difference.

Finally, in February 2003, Echols requested information about the purse for a fight on March 15 of that year. Banner offered $30,000. When Echols made a counter-offer, Banner responded by rescinding the offer and stating it would offer the March 15 fight to another boxer. Echols filed this suit shortly thereafter.

* * *

In this case, Section Nineteen of the Agreement provides that it "shall be governed and construed under the laws of the state of Delaware." Thus, our task is to predict how the courts of Delaware would resolve this issue if presented with these facts. The District Court, applying principles of Delaware contract law, held that the Agreement was unenforceable. However, we predict that the Delaware Supreme Court would conclude otherwise, and will accordingly reverse.

In Delaware, as in most jurisdictions, a court will not enforce a contract that is indefinite in any of its material and essential provisions. *Hindes v. Wilmington Poetry Society, 37 Del. Ch. 80, 138 A.2d 501, 503 (Del. Ch. 1958)*. However, a court will enforce a contract with an indefinite provision if the provision is not a material or essential term. Id. The Delaware courts have not spoken on this issue recently, nor have they ever really focused on what types of contract provisions are material and what types are not, although they noted decades ago that "the general rule is that price is an essential ingredient of every contract." *Raisler Sprinkler Co. v. Automatic Sprinkler Co., 36 Del. 57, 6 W.W. Harr. 57, 171 A. 214 (Del. Super. Ct. 1934)*.

Here, the District Court held that the operation of Section Eight of the Agreement, which required the parties to negotiate Echols's compensation for appearing in bouts secured by Banner on a bout-by-basis after the December 1999 loss, "removed any mention of price from the agreement." In its view, "the essence of the parties' agreement after [Echols's] loss became a contract to enter into a future contract." Relying on the Raisler Sprinkler court's pronouncement that "an agreement that [parties] will in the future make such contract as they may agree upon amounts to nothing," the District Court deemed the Agreement unenforceable.

We think this conclusion of the District Court is overly simplistic. It would no doubt be correct if the Agreement between Echols and Banner were nothing more than a contract for Echols to appear in a particular bout or series of bouts. If that were the case, Echols's price for appearing in a bout would be a material and essential term, and, consequently, the failure to specify the amount of that compensation or some method of determining that compensation would certainly make the contract indefinite. However,

---

1. Under certain circumstances, boxing association rules force a champion to offer to fight the next-ranking contender. If the champion wishes to fight a boxer other than the next-ranking contender, or if a boxer other than the next-ranking contender wishes to fight the champion, they may pay the next-ranking contender to decline the champion's offer and "step aside" for another boxer. Such a payment is known as a "step-aside" fee.

the Agreement does not merely deal with a bout or a series of bouts. Rather, it establishes the relationship between the two parties, a relationship in which Echols promised to fight exclusively for Banner, and Echols desired Banner's services on an ongoing basis. The consideration that Banner paid Echols to secure this promise included a $30,000 signing bonus and a guarantee that Banner would arrange at least three bouts per year for him. While the purses for these bouts were relevant, we do not view them as so material and essential to the understanding regarding the relationship such that providing that certain events could alter the price would render the contract so indefinite as to be invalid.

This is supported by the way in which the Agreement was intended to function. Under Section Four, Banner was obligated to secure three bouts for Echols per year. Under Section Five, Banner discharged its duty to secure a bout "if it shall have made a bona fide offer in writing irrespective of whether such bout actually takes place for any reason other than Banner's nonperformance." Notably absent is any requirement that Echols agree to such an offer or that Echols must agree to such an offer before Banner will be deemed to have fulfilled its obligation to him. As a result, the parties could satisfy the terms of the Agreement without any bouts occurring, as long as Echols continued to deal exclusively with Banner and Banner continued to make the required number of bona fide offers. While neither party would likely be pleased with that result, the Agreement—with or without the minimum purse structure in place—clearly contemplates such an outcome. The Agreement does not require the parties to enter into contracts for individual bouts, so it is not, as the District Court posited, "a contract to enter into a future contract." Thus, it need not specify the terms of those future contracts to be enforceable.

* * *

While the Delaware courts have not had the opportunity to construe an agreement of this type, there is one case from another jurisdiction that is clearly on point. In *Don King Prods., Inc. v. Douglas, 742 F. Supp. 741 (S.D.N.Y. 1990)*, the court was confronted with a nearly identical issue. A boxer argued that his agreements with a promoter were unenforceable for indefiniteness. The promotional agreement between the two parties provided $ 25,000 to the boxer in return for the exclusive right to promote his fights for a period of time. Compensation for individual fights was made subject to further negotiation and agreement, with the terms to be set forth in individual bout agreements. The promotional agreement specified floor levels of compensation for all bouts except title bouts, where the purse was to be "negotiated and mutually agreed upon between [the parties]." *Id. at 761.*

* * *

The court found that while the agreement left certain terms open to future negotiation, it was more than an agreement to agree, at least with respect to the exclusivity terms, as it was "explicit and definite about [the boxer's] commitment to fight only for [the promoter] during the life of those contracts and about the minimum consideration he could receive for making that commitment." *Id. at 762.* The fact that the agreement left open the compensation that would be payable under certain circumstances (i.e., title bouts) did not affect the essential subject matter of the agreement, as "the writing manifests in definite language * * * the agreement to deal exclusively with one another with respect to title defenses and to negotiate in an effort to reach a mutual understanding as to the open price term for such a defense." Id.

Similarly, the failure to specify Echols's purses does not affect the essential subject matter of the contract in the instant case, which is the exclusive nature of Echols's relationship with Banner and the services that Banner has agreed to perform for Echols in exchange for this exclusivity. The Agreement clearly indicates Echols's obligation to deal only with Banner and Banner's obligation to secure a certain number of bouts for Echols. However, nowhere does it obligate Echols to participate in those bouts, and, in the absence of such an obligation, it is unnecessary for the parties to have agreed in advance upon purses for Echols's participation. The purses were not material and essential terms, and the fact that they were left open to future negotiation does not render the contract unenforceable.

* * *

We reject not only the somewhat simplistic view of the District Court but also the impassioned view of our dissenting colleague. The issue squarely presented involved indefiniteness in specific terms, not bargaining power, oppression or other factors. The unequal bargaining power of a boxer in the boxing marketplace was not briefed, nor do we think that it should impact our analysis of certainty in contractual terms.

V.

In light of the foregoing discussion, we conclude that the District Court erred when it determined that the Promotional Agreement's failure to specify minimum compensation for Echols's participation in bouts secured by Banner rendered it so indefinite as to be unenforceable. Accordingly, we will REVERSE the District Court's order granting summary judgment in favor of Echols.

ROSENN, Circuit Judge, dissenting. Boxing is a perennial sport, stretching from the golden days of ancient Greece to present times. The professional life of a boxer, however, is ephemeral and because of the violence of the sport, is limited to a few fleeting years. The possibility of a defeat is always imminent. Thus, a purported contract between a promoter and boxer, which permits the promoter in the event the boxer "should lose any bout" to rescind its obligation to provide any minimum purses, lays all the odds in favor of the promoter.

Boxer Antwun Echols ("Echols") and his promoter, Banner Promotions, Inc. ("Banner") dispute the enforceability of the exclusive promotional agreement that they executed in 1999. The purported contract, drafted by Banner and governed by Delaware law, allowed Banner to retain the exclusive promotional rights to secure all professional boxing bouts for at least four years, but failed to maintain any price term following a defeat. As drafted, Echols must rely on Banner's good will for future compensation, hoping that the promoter will renegotiate acceptable new terms on either a bout-by-bout or collective-bout basis. If the new financial terms are unacceptable to the boxer, the purported contract does not allow him to look elsewhere. In my mind, this one-sided instrument is not a legal contract. The instrument is not worthy of judicial enforcement, and I believe that the Delaware Supreme Court would hold it unenforceable. I therefore respectfully dissent.

I.

The majority acknowledges the that Delaware Courts "will not enforce a contract that is indefinite in any of its material and essential provisions." But, the majority rationalizes that the disputed agreement "does not merely deal with a bout or a series of bouts" but with "the relationship between the two parties, a relationship in which

Echols promised to fight exclusively for Banner. * * *" Every contract between two parties deals with a relationship, but from the boxer's corner, the essential ingredients of that relationship are the bout or series of bouts and the obligation of the promoter to provide a purse for the boxer.

A professional fight is no mere exhibition. It is a contest for victory and money. The relationship between a promoter and a boxer is meaningless unless the boxer engages in his craft and receives appropriate compensation. Therefore, the bouts and their purses are not only relevant, but material and essential to the relationship. The details spelled out in Section Six of the disputed agreement with respect to the purses for all bouts reflects how important and material the related parties regarded the purses. The majority's *ipse dixit* statement that the purses are not essential completely ignores the language painstakingly set forth in Section Six.

Boxing can be a brutal business, and fighters have precious little time to capitalize on their talents and age. In this case, the price limits set forth in Section Six guaranteed the minimum compensation that Echols could expect each time he stepped into the ring. Therefore, the essentiality of the minimum price term to the bargain reached between the parties to this contract cannot be denied.

Neither party disputes that from the time the instrument was executed until Echols' first boxing loss, the contract guaranteed Echols minimum purses for each fight. However, following Echols' loss to Bernard Hopkins in 1999, Section Eight of the instrument authorized Banner to either "rescind this Agreement or the purses set forth in paragraph (6) shall be subject to renegotiation." Banner did not rescind, but elected to renegotiate. The majority interprets this clause as requiring that the price terms thereafter must be renegotiated on a "bout-by-bout" basis. However, the District Court interpreted the contract differently, and found the clause in Section Eight to be "undoubtedly ambiguous." According to the District Court, the renegotiation clause may also be interpreted to require that following a loss, the entire minimum price structure must be renegotiated all at once, establishing new price minimums to govern the agreement. Under this interpretation, the parties would be able to revitalize the instrument following the defeat by renegotiating a schedule of minimum prices that reflect Echols' market value as a fighter with one loss.

I recognize that both interpretations of the renegotiation clause present risks to the parties. If price minimums are to be renegotiated all at once, both parties risk that a new agreement will not be reached and the contract, which they otherwise would choose to maintain, would be voided. On the other hand, if prices are left to be renegotiated on a bout-by-bout basis, the boxer risks that he will be forced to accept whatever minimal price the promoter offers, or not fight at all. For the reasons described below, I believe that under the relevant contract law, the former interpretation is the only enforceable and fair option.

Echols essentially argues that he did not bargain for an agreement where following a loss, he is left to either fight for whatever price Banner offers, or not fight at all. I believe that the general rule of contract law, recognized in Delaware and other jurisdictions, that "price is an essential ingredient of every contract * * * for the rendering of services" is intended to protect against exactly the situation that Echols now faces. *Raisler Sprinkler Co. v. Automatic Sprinkler Co., 36 Del. 57, 6 W.W. Harr. 57, 171 A. 214, 219 (Del. Super. Ct. 1935)* (citation omitted). The majority holds that while the purses for the fights are "relevant," they are not material and essential because the parties could satisfy the terms of the agreement without any bouts occurring. I acknowledge that under the strict terms of the contract, Banner could make three offers per year for boxing matches with *de minimus* purses, Echols could reject all of Banner's offers, and both parties would be technically compliant with the contract terms. Under this interpretation, a court could determine when a party breaches these terms, thereby providing some level of reasonable certainty in the contract. However, I do not believe that this theoretical certainty changes the essential character and terms of this boxing promotion contract, nor does it make the contract enforceable under Delaware law. Even the most basic service contract would be deemed unenforceable if it failed to state a price term, regardless of whether the contract requires the parties to ever actually exercise their ability to purchase or sell the services. The Delaware Superior Court reinforced this idea in Raisler Sprinkler, explaining that

> one of the commonest kind of promises too indefinite for legal enforcement is where the promisor retains an unlimited right to decide later the nature or extent of his performance. This unlimited choice in effect destroys the promise and makes it merely illusory. *** But a promise to give anything whatever which the promisor may choose * * * is illusory, for such promises would be satisfied by giving something so infinitely near nothing or by performance so indefinitely postponed as to have no calculable value.

171 A. at 219 (quoting Williston on Contracts, vol. 1 § 43).

The majority portrays Section Eight of the purported agreement to allow for certain events to merely "alter" the price structure in the contract. In my view, Section Eight does more than alter the price. It removes the price structure completely, and this renders the contract fatally defective. Under the majority's holding, Echols' loss authorizes Banner to make offers for fights at any price, even below market rates, and still remain technically compliant with the contract terms. [7] I believe this holding "destroys the promise and makes it merely illusory." Id. In reality, all boxers eventually lose, and some live to fight another day. Although a loss may decrease a boxer's market value, and some mechanism to adjust price may be required to account for this lack of certainty in the boxing market, I believe that the Delaware Supreme Court would interpret the prior case law in the state to require the maintenance of some minimum price in order to deem the contract enforceable.

II.

In my view, the sparse case law on this topic also supports the premise that boxing promotions contracts must have at least some minimum price term to be enforceable. Both Banner and the majority cite to *Don King Prods., Inc. v. Douglas*, 742 F. Supp. 741 (S.D.N.Y. 1990), to support their position in this case. Yet, Don King supports the opposite conclusion. The original contract in Don King set forth minimum prices for all bouts except title bouts, and the parties later reached a second agreement establishing a $ 1.3 million purse for a title bout and a $ 1 minimum purse guarantee for the next

---

7. The majority, at note 2, opines that because the agreement requires Banner to make "*bona fide*" offers, a *de minimus* price offer would not be valid under the agreement and may trigger a breach. First, interpreting "*bona fide*" to mean that a court should imply a reasonableness standard to the price term is inconsistent with the majority's holding that the price term is non-essential. Second, I find no case law, in Delaware or elsewhere, establishing that a "*bona fide* offer" implies a reasonable price term. Rather, when used to describe an offer, the term "*bona fide*" refers to an offer intended to produce a legal contract, regardless of whether the price is reasonable. * * * Under this definition of "*bona fide*," Banner could make *bona fide* offers for fights at any price, as long as the offer is intended to bind the parties if accepted.

three fights, subject to renegotiation upwards in price if the fighter, Douglas, should win the heavyweight title. *742 F. Supp. at 748, n5.* Therefore, when the court decided the case, there were minimum price guarantees in place, and Douglas was forced to take the position that because his market value as a fighter had risen significantly, the $ 1,000,000 price minimum was "insufficient to render the contract sufficiently definite for enforcement." *Id. at 761.* The court found that the $ 1,000,000 minimum price was sufficient to bind the parties, and clearly stated that "the *minimum price terms,* together with DKP's upfront payment of $ 25,000 and its commitments to hold a set number of bouts, clearly did provide an expectancy of compensation for Douglas that was sufficiently definite to induce his promise to fight exclusively for DKP." *Id. at 763* (emphasis added). Thus, Don King stands only for the proposition that an exclusive boxing promotion contract with an indefinite price structure, supported at least by *minimum price terms,* is enforceable.

Furthermore, Don King establishes that minimum price terms are considered part of the bargain that a promoter offers a boxer to induce a promise of exclusivity. By failing to consider the minimum price term as an essential component of the bargain in the present case, the majority deviates from the rule established in Don King. Under the majority's holding, a boxer loses the certainty of minimum compensation; the promoter, however, maintains exclusive control. Echols maintains a price guarantee as long as he wins, but receives no minimum price guarantee after a loss, when he is most vulnerable. The effect of the majority's decision is to leave a boxer subject to the whim and mercy of the promoter, once the boxer loses a bout.

* * *

Even though individual boxers may be untested, the sport and spectacle of boxing is hardly a new industry with unknown production and distribution costs. If a promoter and a boxer can reasonably agree to minimum purses when the boxer is undefeated, they should be able to agree fairly on them when the boxer has one loss and both retain some bargaining power. The disputed instrument leaves the boxer with no guaranteed purses, no bargaining power, and the promoter in total control of his boxing career for the next several years.

The District Court found the contract unenforceable because the contract is an agreement to negotiate future agreements without specifying its material and essential price terms. I agree with the District Court.

III.

Therefore, I would hold the contract in this case unenforceable and affirm the judgment of the District Court.

Notes and Questions

1. Has the court exceeded all reasonable bounds in finding a binding contract, notwithstanding the vagary of the monetary recompense? Or given the clear desire of the parties to reach an agreement, has the court appropriately precluded one party from using a loophole to reinforce his remorse at entering the deal *ab initio?*

2. To what degree does boxing's unsavory reputation contribute to the possibility that the court is sending a message of caution for parties to respect their promises and adhere to agreements freely entered?

3. Would you characterize the indefiniteness surrounding Echols' compensation as an omission or as an agreement to agree? Would your conclusion affect the outcome? *See* Chapter 4, Part II (B), *supra*.

4. Does this decision downplay the materiality factor and, in effect, give courts *carte blanche* to ignore gaps in an agreement even where the missing piece seems to be an essential part of an agreement?

5. The court dismissed the argument that the boxer's unequal bargaining power *vis-à-vis* powerful promoters is a relevant inquiry stating that the issue was not briefed and that it nonetheless would "not impact our analysis of certainty in contract terms." Do you agree? If the issue had been raised originally, would it be relevant to support the boxer's claims that the contract was fatally indefinite? Would the boxer's lack of sophistication provide a basis for a contention that the contract was voidable on the basis of unconscionability? Generally, unconscionability involves unfair surprise (procedural) and/or oppressive terms (substantive). Are either of those factors present here? Would Echols have been obligated to show that *both* elements were present? *See Maxwell v. Fidelity Financial Services*, 907 P.2d 51 (Ariz. 1995). Are the promises in this case illusory, presenting problems of consideration?

(D) Salary Guarantees and the Duty to Mitigate Damages

Another problem that has arisen in professional sports contracting involves the vagaries attending salary guarantee clauses. These problems range well beyond the "duration" issues considered in the *Sample* case, above. The parties occasionally fail to clarify the extent of the guarantee and leave for judicial or arbitral determination the scope of the guarantee, the availability of "offset" protection, the relevance of damage mitigation, etc. The following case presents a telling example and demonstrates that careless manifestation of intent by both an individual club and the league can be a costly proposition.

National Football League Players Ass'n v. National Football League Management Council
233 Cal. Rptr. 147 (Cal. Ct. App. 1986)

BARRY-DEAL, Associate Justice. The National Football League Management Council (Management Council) and the Los Angeles Raiders, formerly doing business as the Oakland Raiders (Raiders), appeal from the judgment confirming an arbitration award in favor of the National Football League Players Association (Players Association) and Dante Pastorini, Jr. (Pastorini). The Raiders and Management Council contend that the arbitrator exceeded his powers (Code Civ. Proc., §1286.2, subd. (d)) in that he made an error in law by failing to apply the doctrine of mitigation of damages. They further contend that the award violates public policy and that the award was incorrectly calculated. We affirm the judgment.

I. *Background*

In 1978 Pastorini negotiated a series of six 1-year "NFL Player Contracts" to play football for the Houston Oilers (Oilers). For each of the years in question, 1981, 1982, and 1983, the contracts called for current compensation of $150,000 per year, for a total of $450,000 for the period in question, as well as for deferred compensation. Each contract contained the following provisions:

"[24.B.] 2. Despite any contrary language in Paragraph 11, Club shall pay Player the salary specified in Paragraph 5 even if at any subsequent time Player's skill or performance is judged by Club to be unsatisfactory as compared with that of other players competing for positions on Club's roster.

C. The guarantee provided in B above shall in no way affect the operation of the League's waiver system."

Pastorini was traded to the Raiders in March 1980, and the contracts in question were assumed by that team. On September 1, 1981, the Raiders placed Pastorini on waivers and released him in accordance with the provision in his contract because his skill and performance were unsatisfactory. Thereafter, Pastorini demanded that the Raiders pay him the current compensation under his contracts pursuant to paragraph 24.B.2.

Pastorini signed with the Los Angeles Rams (Rams) on September 25, 1981, and was paid $190,000 for the year. The Raiders then informed Pastorini's attorney that the Raiders were no longer obligated to pay Pastorini's salary, because they were entitled to an offset of Pastorini's earnings as a member of the Rams. Pastorini was paid by the Philadelphia Eagles $140,000 for the 1982 season and $175,000 for the 1983 season.

On November 18, 1981, pursuant to the collective bargaining agreement between the Players Association and the Management Council, the Players Association and Pastorini filed a noninjury grievance against the Raiders, seeking payment on the 1981 through 1983 contracts. The Raiders responded, contending that the doctrines of mitigation of damages and offset were applicable.

The matter proceeded to arbitration on April 9, 1983. Arbitrator Sam Kagel determined that mitigation and offset were not applicable and directed the Raiders to pay Pastorini as provided in the contracts.

The Raiders failed to comply with the arbitrator's decision, and the Players Association and Pastorini petitioned the superior court to confirm the arbitration award. The Raiders then petitioned to vacate the award. After a hearing, the arbitration award was confirmed.

II. *Discussion*

Pastorini's dispute with the Raiders clearly falls within the ambit of section 301(a) of the Labor Management Relations Act (29 U.S.C. §185(a)), which pertains to "'[s]uits for violation of contracts between an employer and a labor organization representing employees in an industry affecting commerce[.]' * * * Therefore, we must apply federal substantive law * * *. However, we may also rely on state law if it is compatible with the purposes of the federal law * * *.

A. *Evidence*

In reaching his award, Arbitrator Kagel considered testimony regarding the NFL's salary offset policy. Joel Bussert, director of personnel for the NFL, testified that the NFL's policy "'* * * was that when a player was released from a guaranteed contract and signed with a second club, that any amounts earned from that second club would be offset against the guaranteed amounts he was entitled to receive from the first club.'" Bussert conceded that the policy did not exist in writing, had never been communicated to the Players Association, and did not form part of the collective bargaining agreement.

Arbitrator Kagel also considered two Player-Club Relations Committee (PCRC) decisions, *Charles Smith v. Oakland Raiders and San Diego Chargers* and *Anthony Davis v.*

Houston Oilers. The arbitrator's decision stated that in the former, Smith had a contract with the Raiders which provided for a guaranteed $45,000 salary for the 1975 season. In mid-September 1975, Smith was released by the Raiders and subsequently signed with the San Diego Chargers (Chargers), with whom he played for five weeks. The Chargers also gave Smith a $15,000 signing bonus. Smith conceded that the Raiders were entitled to offset the $45,000 guaranteed salary by the amount he was paid by the Chargers during his five weeks with that team, but contended that the Raiders could not offset their obligation by the $15,000 signing bonus. The PCRC agreed with Smith, noting that the bonus rider specifically provided that the bonus was not to be deemed part of Smith's salary. Arbitrator Kagel emphasized that following the Smith decision, the NFL distributed to clubs an offset provision which could be negotiated into player contracts.

Arbitrator Kagel also discussed the applicability of *Anthony Davis v. Houston Oilers, supra.* Davis signed a 1979 contract which provided that the Oilers "'absolutely and unconditionally'" guaranteed payment of half his $80,000 salary if Davis was removed from the club's roster before or during the 1979 season. Davis was waived by the Oilers in November 1978 and signed as a free agent with the Rams, where he played the remainder of the 1978 season. He returned to the Rams in 1979, but was released on September 20, 1979. Davis then requested $40,000 from the Oilers. The Oilers sought to offset the obligation with the salary Davis received from the Rams in 1979. The PCRC held that the contract language guaranteeing payment was "'clear and unmistakable,'" and that the Oilers were not entitled to an offset.

Here, Arbitrator Kagel concluded that when an offset was intended, specific provisions for offset were inserted into player contracts. Because Pastorini's contract had no such provisions, Arbitrator Kagel determined that mitigation and offset did not apply to Pastorini's case.

B. *Mitigation of Damages and Offset*

The Raiders argue that the obligation to reimburse for the amount of salary wrongfully withheld may be mitigated by deducting earnings from other employment * * *. They compare the present controversy to an action for wrongful termination of employment and contend that the measure of recovery therefore is the guaranteed salary, less the amount earned from other employment * * *.

The arbitrator found that mitigation did not apply to Pastorini's contracts, stating:

> That rule is not applicable in the Pastorini case. There is no claim that Pastorini was 'wrongfully discharged.' In fact, Pastorini was not discharged—he was waived, an action *authorized* by the contract. The Raiders had a right to waive Pastorini but it also had an obligation to pay the salaries provided for in the contracts which they assumed from Houston.
>
> This case does not concern itself with an alleged breach of the contracts between the Raiders and Pastorini at the time of waiver; it is not a case seeking damages; but it is an action on the contracts themselves for the agreed-upon compensation which is set forth in the contracts between the Raiders and Pastorini. What Pastorini is seeking is the payment of a debt owed to him by the Raiders as a result of the contracts and the concept of offset by way of mitigation is not applicable in this instance.[3] (Original emphasis.)

---

3. The Raiders argue that the arbitrator exceeded his powers in making the award because he determined that the issue was not breach of contract and damages, but rather whether the Raiders were entitled to offset Pastorini's salary. The Raiders' defense, however, alleged failure to mitigate

The arbitrator concluded that when an offset was intended, specific language would be included in the contract.

* * *

The Raiders rely on *de la Falaise v. Gaumont-British P. Corp.* (1940) 39 Cal.App.2d 461, 103 P.2d 447, for the proposition that offset should have been applied to the instant facts. In that case, actress Constance Bennett de la Falaise agreed to appear in two motion pictures to be produced by the respondent, a motion picture company * * *. The agreement provided, inter alia, for a $30,000 guaranteed advance for each picture * * *. The first picture was completed, and de la Falaise was paid pursuant to the contract terms. De la Falaise was never notified of the second picture's starting date, as required by the contract, and the second picture was never made * * *. De la Falaise unsuccessfully sought employment as an actress; she did receive, however, $4,000 for two radio engagements during the period in which the second picture was to have been filmed * * *. De la Falaise sought to recover the amount guaranteed under the contract * * *, alleging that the respondent breached the contract by failing to notify her of the second picture's starting date * * *. This court found that she was entitled to the guaranteed minimum, less the $4,000 she received from the radio engagements * * *. The court noted that where an employee has been wrongfully discharged, the measure of damages is the amount of salary agreed upon, less the amount which the employee has earned or with a reasonable effort might have earned * * *.

The instant case does not involve wrongful discharge of employment; Pastorini was waived, an action authorized by his contract. Therefore, the offset provisions of *de la Falaise* are inapplicable.

Pastorini relies on *Payne v. Pathe Studios, Inc.* (1935) 6 Cal. App.2d 136, 44 P.2d 598, for the proposition that offset is inapplicable in the instant action. In that case, the plaintiff's assignor, Zazu Pitts, contracted with the defendant motion picture company to act in a motion picture * * *. The company was to employ Pitts for at least four weeks * * *. A clause in the contract provided that "'It is understood and agreed that in the event your services are not started on or before December 31, 1930, we hereby agree to pay you the sum of Five Thousand Dollars ($5000), which represents the four weeks guarantee on this agreement.'" * * * Zazu Pitts's services were never requested, and her assignee sued to recover the guaranteed $5,000 * * *. The movie studio argued that Pitts had a duty to mitigate damages by securing other employment * * *. This court, after determining that plaintiff's assignor had not been discharged * * *, stated:

> [T]he rule as to mitigation of damages in cases of contracts of hire does not apply to contracts not requiring all or the greater portion of the time of the party employed, or which do not preclude the party from undertaking and being engaged in the performance contemporaneously of other contracts * * *. Here again we must bear in mind that this is not an action for damages for breach of the contract of employment, but an action on the contract itself for the agreed compensation. The doctrine of mitigation of damages has no place in such an action * * *.

Unlike Pitts, Pastorini was under an exclusive services contract to the Raiders. Consequently, he cannot rely on the doctrine stated in the above cited case.

---

damages and right of offset. Thus, the issue before the arbitrator was the right of the Raiders to offset Pastorini's guaranteed contract.

Nevertheless, we conclude that offset is inapplicable in the instant case and that the arbitrator did not make an error in law. Paragraph 24.B. provided that Pastorini would be paid if his performance was unsatisfactory, *i.e.*, even if he did not play. Paragraph 24.C. referred to this provision as a "guarantee" and stated that it did not affect the waiver system. The evidence clearly reveals that when offset was intended, a special provision was inserted into the contract. Bussert testified that the NFL's alleged custom and practice regarding offset was not communicated to the Players Association and did not constitute part of the collective bargaining agreement. This court may reverse the arbitrator's award only if there is a manifest disregard of the agreement, totally unsupported by principles of contract construction * * *. No such manifest disregard appears in the instant case.

C. *Public Policy*

We cannot agree with the Raiders' contention that Pastorini was unjustly enriched and that the award therefore violates public policy. The contracts guaranteed Pastorini's salary even if his skill or performance was unsatisfactory. They contained no provision for offset in the event that Pastorini was waived. There was no unjust enrichment at the Raiders' expense, because Pastorini fully performed under the contracts with that team.

* * *

The judgment is affirmed.

SCOTT, Acting P.J., and MERRILL, J., concur.

Notes and Questions

1. What was the critical infirmity in the NFL's case? There simply was no evidence to support the NFL's contention that, when a player is released from a guaranteed contract and signs with a second club, the amounts earned from the second club should serve as an offset against the guaranteed amount. The NFL attempted through smoke and mirrors to persuade the court that this was the league policy, and that such policy was embraced by pertinent agreements, even though its director of personnel conceded that the policy did not exist in writing, had never been communicated to the players' collective bargaining representative, and had never been included in any collective bargaining agreement.

2. Are the *Charles Smith* and *Anthony Davis* cases cited in Justice Barry-Deal's opinion distinguishable from Pastorini's case? In *Smith*, the grievant had conceded that the original club was entitled to offset the guaranteed salary by amounts paid by the second club. In all likelihood, barring such a concession, the arbitrator would have been compelled to find that the salary offset was not due and owing the first club. In fact, subsequent to that decision, the NFL distributed to its clubs sample offset language that could be negotiated into the uniform player contracts. With regard to the *Davis* case, Arbitrator Kagel concluded that the original club was not entitled to an offset given the fact that the contract language guaranteeing payment was clear and unmistakable. Thus, because the league had provided specific offset language to the club and because the guarantee language of Pastorini's contract contained no such offset language, the court had no recourse but to affirm the arbitrator's award and to bar application of any offset.

3. In its zeal to explain the application of the "mitigation of damages" doctrine, the court perhaps sent a confusing and misleading message. The court concluded, "[t]he instant case does not involve wrongful discharge of employment: Pastorini was waived, an action authorized by his contract. Therefore, the offset provisions * * * are inapplicable." This passage suggests a rather curious and bizarre scenario: If the plaintiff had thus been terminated unlawfully, the doctrine of mitigation of damages would apply; and the club, by terminating Pastorini unlawfully, could have lessened its amount of monetary liability. John Murray, Murray on Contracts § 122 (4th ed. 2001). Plainly, the doctrine of mitigation does not apply in a salary guarantee context, but it also would not have applied in a salary guarantee context had the club materially breached the agreement by unlawfully discharging Pastorini. In either case, because the salary was guaranteed without qualification, the doctrine of mitigation or offset would not have been applicable. *See Wassenaar v. Panos*, 331 N.W.2d 357 (Wis. 1983).

4. In the *de la Falaise* case, was the plaintiff wrongfully discharged or was she simply seeking recovery pursuant to the terms of the contract? Ms. de la Falaise was suing the motion picture company for breach of contract—seeking the guaranteed amount, even though the motion picture company did not want her services. How is that distinguishable from Pastorini's claim?

5. The court's renunciation of the applicability of *Payne v. Pathe Studios, Inc.* is important in view of the fact that there the plaintiff had not entered an exclusive contract and would, as a matter of course, zealously pursue other acting opportunities. For that reason, the doctrine of mitigation would not apply because the plaintiff would seek other contracts whether or not the contract in question had been breached. Here, because Pastorini had an exclusive agreement, the termination of the contract would necessitate his attempt to secure other employment under the basic doctrine of mitigation. Again, however, mitigation had no applicability in this case due to the fact that the salary guarantee was absolute. *See also* John Calamari & Joseph Perillo, Contracts §§ 14–16 (5th ed. 2003).

6. Perhaps some of the confusion surrounding this case centers upon an inadequate understanding of what waiver means in the context of professional sports. The NFL-NFLPA collective bargaining agreement contains the following language:

ARTICLE XXII

WAIVER SYSTEM

Section 1. Release:

(a) Whenever a player who has finished the season in which his fourth year of credited service has been earned under the Bert Bell/Pete Rozelle Plan is placed on waivers between February 1 and the trading deadline, his contract will be considered terminated and the player will be completely free at any time thereafter to negotiate and sign a Player Contract with any Club, and any Club shall be completely free to negotiate and sign a Player Contract with such player, without penalty or restriction, including, but not limited to, Draft Choice Compensation between Clubs or First Refusal Rights of any kind, or any signing period. If the waivers occur after that time, the player's Player Contract will be subject to the waiver system and may be awarded to a claiming Club. However, if such player is claimed and awarded, he shall have the option to declare himself an Unrestricted Free Agent at the end of the League Year in question if he has a no-trade clause in his Player Contract. If such player does not have a no-trade clause and the Player Contract being awarded through waivers covers more than one additional season, the player shall have the right to declare himself an Unrestricted Free Agent as set forth above at the end of the League Year following the League Year in which he is waived and awarded.

(b) Whenever a player who has finished less than the season in which his fourth year of credited service has been earned under the Bert Bell/Pete Rozelle Plan is placed on waivers, the player's Player Contract will be subject to the waiver system and may be awarded to a claiming Club.

Section 2. Contact:

Coaches or any other persons connected with another NFL Club are prohibited from contacting any player placed on waivers until such time as the player is released by the waiving Club.

Section 3. Ineligibility:

Any NFL player who is declared ineligible to compete in a pre-season, regular season or post-season game because of a breach by any NFL Club by whom he is employed of waiver procedures and regulations, or any other provision of the NFL Constitution and By-laws, will be paid the salary or other compensation which he would have received if he had not been declared ineligible, which, in any event, will be a minimum of one week's salary and, when applicable, expense payments.

Section 4. Notice of Termination:

The Notice of Termination form attached hereto as Appendix G will be used by all Clubs. If possible, the Notice of Termination will be personally delivered to the player prior to his departure from the team. If the Notice of Termination has not been personally delivered to the player prior to his departure from the team, the Notice of Termination will be sent to him by certified mail at his last address on file with the Club.

NFL-NFLPA Collective Bargaining Agreement, Article XXII, §§ 1–4. There are strategic implications attending the notion of waiver. If a club is interested in claiming a player "on waivers" it may do so, but in so doing may assume the contractual obligations of the original team. If the club desiring the player chooses to roll the dice, hoping that the player "clears waivers" (is bypassed by the other teams), leaving it the freedom to renegotiate the contract, it may lose its opportunity to sign the player.

7. As discussed in the *Sample* case earlier in this chapter, the scope of a salary guarantee is often vague or ill-defined. For example, does a clause that insures one's salary for a year likewise guarantee a roster spot? If a player is released from the club, but is paid a regular salary under a guarantee, does this time constitute service as an active player for purposes of pension eligibility or other benefits? *See, e.g., In re Arbitration Between Nat'l Basketball Ass'n (Houston Rockets) and NBPA(Vallely)* (Seitz, Arbitrator, 1974). NBA player John Vallely signed a contract with a "no-cut" clause. After a trade, Vallely was removed from the roster but continued to receive a salary. When Vallely was denied pension payments because he was not eligible due to lack of sufficient roster time, Arbitrator Seitz, while refraining from interpreting no-cut clauses across the board, sustained Vallely's grievance. He ruled in favor of the grievant primarily because he did not believe that the club had offered persuasive reasons why the no-cut clause should be limited only to salary. In essence, the underpinnings of a salary assurance is that the player is constructively on the team. If he is constructively on the team, he should, absent clear contractual evidence to the contrary, likewise be able to accumulate

pension benefits. Further, Arbitrator Seitz believed that the club had ample opportunity to limit the application of the no-cut clause in the contract itself but had failed to do so.

8. In the tumultuous days of Billy Martin's on again-off again managerial stint with the New York Yankees, Martin once banished star pitcher Ken Holtzman to the bullpen, announcing that he had no intention of using Holtzman's services. Holtzman had a no-cut contract and, technically, the Yankees were honoring their obligations thereunder. Could Holtzman have filed a grievance or breach of contract action claiming that his treatment violated the spirit if not the letter of his no-cut clause? Under what theory would you proceed if you were Holtzman's attorney or counsel for the players association?

(E) Salary, Bonuses, and Incentive Awards—The Club's Failure to Pay as a Material Breach

Alabama Football, Inc. v. Stabler

319 So. 2d 678 (Ala. 1975)

SHORES, Justice. Stabler filed a complaint on December 4, 1974, seeking a declaratory judgment and other relief, contending that the defendant had breached its contract with Stabler by failing to pay the balance due in 1974 under the contract between the parties; that the terms of the contract prohibited him from negotiating a contract with any other professional football club; and that irreparable damage would result to him if the contract was not held to be null and void.

After a hearing, the trial court entered its judgment on January 6, 1975, holding that the contract between Stabler and Alabama Football, Inc. had been breached by Alabama Football, Inc. and that Stabler was free from any obligation under any of the terms of the contract.

This appeal is from that judgment.

Stabler is a professional football player. In April, 1974, he signed an agreement with Alabama Football, Inc., which was effective immediately, and which in part provided that Alabama Football, Inc. would pay him $50,000 upon signing and an additional $50,000 in the year 1974. The agreement provided that Stabler would play football for Alabama Football, Inc. for seven years after the expiration of his existing contract with the Oakland Raiders for a total consideration of $875,000, $100,000 of which was the bonus for signing and payable in 1974, $100,000 payable in 1975, and $135,000 per year thereafter through 1980.

The contract also prohibited Stabler from executing any other contract with any other football franchise or team in any football league.

The $50,000 was paid upon execution of the contract. The record indicates that at the time the contract was negotiated, some discussion was had regarding looking into the possibility of some deferred compensation plan, whereby Stabler might avoid taxes on monies due in 1974. It was subsequently determined that no effective means could be worked out to avoid taxes on the monies to be received in 1974. When this was discovered, Stabler asked for the balance due him. He received $10,000 of the balance on May 20. In June, he was told that there was no money available to pay the balance; but on June 28, an agreement was entered into which set up a schedule of payments for the $40,000 remaining unpaid. $10,000 was paid under this arrangement, but the remaining payments were not made as they became due. $30,000 remained due at that time. On October 29, Alabama Football, Inc. delivered a note to Stabler for the $30,000 payable on November 29, 1974. When this note was not paid, Stabler filed this suit seeking cancellation of the contract, and also asked the court to issue a temporary restraining order prohibiting the use of his name by Alabama Football, Inc. This was granted and was finally made permanent.

Appellant argues, on appeal, that the trial court erred in refusing to dismiss the complaint on the ground that no justiciable controversy existed between the parties. We disagree. Stabler contended that he was entitled to rescind the contract between him and Alabama Football, Inc. on the ground that it had breached the contract between them; that it prohibited him from negotiating with any other professional football team; that repeated demands had been made on Alabama Football, Inc. for the payment of the amounts promised him in 1974; that Alabama Football, Inc. had used the fact of Stabler's signing with it to promote ticket sales and to recruit other professional football players; and that it was having financial problems which prevented its ability to live up to the contract between them. At the time of the hearing, the team had no money on deposit in a bank; the chairman of the board of Alabama Football, Inc. testified that the team was unable to pay the $30,000 due Stabler at the time of the hearing; and it had been unable to pay either the September or October installments worked out by the June 28 agreement. The contention of Alabama Football, Inc. was that although it had not paid the $30,000 when due, it was trying to work out its financial problems, which the record indicates were formidable. Mr. Putnam, chairman of the board of Alabama Football, Inc., testified at the hearing in this cause that, at that time the team had indebtedness in excess of $1,600,000, and that it was overdrawn some $67,000 at the bank.

Under these circumstances, we cannot say that a justiciable controversy did not exist between the parties, which was subject to resolution by the trial court.

Appellant argues that Stabler was not entitled to a judgment rescinding the contract, because he made no offer to restore the money which had already been paid to him under the contract. While the general rule supports this argument, it is not absolute. Stabler argues, and the trial court was of the opinion that, under the facts of this case, Stabler was under no obligation to restore the money paid to him. We agree. Obviously, contracts involving professional athletes are somewhat unique. The evidence indicates that Alabama, Inc. benefited from the fact that Stabler had signed a contract to play football with it beginning in 1976. It exploited his notoriety as a successful quarterback with the Oakland Raiders to sell tickets to ball games played in 1974; he appeared at press conferences to publicize Alabama Football, Inc. and the World Football League. While it is true that the general rule is "* * *a party may not disaffirm a voidable contract and at the same time enjoy the benefits received thereunder," * * * such rule must be applied to comport with general equitable principles * * *.

The record is replete with indications that Alabama Football, Inc. was not able to fulfill its contract with Stabler. He was not paid the amount promised him in 1974, and the team was unable to pay him. Yet, under the contract, he was prohibited from negotiating a contract with any other team so long as he was under contract with Alabama Football, Inc. We agree with the trial court that the balancing of the equities would not require Stabler to return the money received during the year 1974, since there was evidence to support a conclusion that Alabama Football, Inc. had received benefits under the contract which Stabler was entitled to be paid for. We note also that the trial court, in holding the contract between the parties null and void, also cancelled the $30,000 note payable to Stabler, finding that balancing the equities between the parties could best be achieved in this manner.

It is next argued by appellant that notice of rescission is a condition to such action, and that it received no notice from Stabler of his intention to rescind. This court has held that "* * * where there is a contract involving mutual continuing duties on the part of both parties, and one party has breached, but has not repudiated, the contract, it is the duty of the other before rescission to give notice and opportunity to live up to the contract[.] * * * The purpose of such notice is to give the breaching party a chance to perform. This does not mean, however, that such notice is always a prerequisite to rescission. The conduct of the parties themselves may vitiate the necessity of this requirement * * *. Indeed in the instant case, Stabler made repeated demands upon the appellant for the amount of the bonus due him. In fact, the appellant was given an opportunity to perform through the supplemental agreement and schedule of payments agreed upon on June 28, 1974. When it did not meet the payments agreed upon in that agreement, Stabler accepted a note due November 29, 1974. This note was not paid either. It is difficult to determine what more Stabler could have done to give appellant an opportunity to perform its part of the agreement. A formal notice of intention to rescind, under the facts of the instant case, was hardly necessary to give appellant an opportunity to perform; and the trial court correctly held that Stabler was relieved of this requirement before he could maintain his suit.

It is next submitted by appellant that the breach in the instant case was not substantial and that a slight or casual breach will not justify rescission * * *. While this is a good statement of the general rule, the appellant overlooks a universal rule more applicable to the facts of this case. The evidence adduced below relating to the financial condition of appellant is uncontradicted. It overwhelmingly supports a conclusion that it was unable to perform the contract with Stabler. While it is true that financial inability to perform "* * * whether due to * * * poverty, [or] financial panic * * *." 17 Am.Jur.2d, Contracts §415, does not excuse nonperformance of a contract, it is equally true that:

> "The inability of a party to perform a contract after it is made is, as a rule, a ground for rescinding it. The fact that substantial performance by one party is impossible or that a party is unable to perform a material part of the contract is a ground for rescission * * *." 17 Am.Jur.2d, Contracts §506.

Since there was substantial evidence from which the trial court could have concluded that appellant was unable to perform its contract with Stabler, we find no basis for reversal on this point. * * *

Finding no error to reverse, the decree appealed from is, therefore, affirmed.

Affirmed.

HEFLIN, C.J., and MERRILL, MADDOX and JONES, JJ., concur.

Notes and Questions

1. What was the nature of Stabler's bonus arrangement with the Alabama club—was it remuneration for his signature and its publicity value in terms of boosting advance ticket sales and luring other players to jump leagues? Or was it simply a salary advance?

2. This decision is intellectually unsatisfying in terms of the remedy that was assessed and its abject failure to reconcile Stabler's failure in any way to return to the *status quo* as part and parcel of the rescission. For example, what was the basis for Stabler being permitted to keep $70,000? Why did the Court not require the payment of the remaining $30,000 of the $100,000 bonus to Stabler? What is the relationship between the amount paid to Stabler ($70,000) and the amount by which Stabler was damaged or the reasonable value to Alabama Football of Stabler's partial performance? Why was defendant Stabler discharged of any duties arising under this agreement? If he had promised to perform and failed to do so, does this not constitute a material breach of his obligations under the agreement? If, on the other hand, the club had materially breached *its* duties under the agreement, then the constructive condition precedent to Stabler's obligation to perform would not have been met and Stabler's duty would not have been triggered. *See* Chapter 4, Part VI. Thus, Stabler would have been justified in rescinding the contract and refusing to perform any obligations that would have arisen thereunder. The curious aspect of this opinion is the court's failure to require any type of return to the *status quo*. Where did the court arrive at a damage amount that coincidentally and remarkably equalled the amount of money that Stabler had received during the 1974 season? Should there not have been some type of proceeding before a special master to ascertain the amount of damages and to apply that amount to the money that Stabler had received during the 1974 football season? *See also* John C. Weistart & Cym H. Lowell, The Law of Sports § 3.11 (1979). Finally, did the court adequately address the issue of anticipatory breach and the timing of Stabler's lawsuit?

3. The answer to the foregoing question may turn on the characterization of the bonus as a signing bonus rather than a salary advance. If it be the former, then the player's legitimate repudiation of his contract may create no concomitant obligation to return any monies advanced.

> Where a specific portion of a defendant's performance, such as the execution of the contract, has been apportioned as the equivalent of plaintiff's performance, such as the payment of a bonus, plaintiff is not entitled to restitution if the defendant has rendered the apportioned consideration in full.

Alabama Football Club, Inc. v. Greenwood, 452 F. Supp. 1191, 1200 (W.D. Pa. 1978). *See further*, NFL-NFLPA Collective Bargaining Agreement (2006–2011), Art. XIV, § 9.

4. Because of the club's material breach, Stabler was declared a free agent. The term "free agency" has assumed monumental proportions and is today common parlance reflecting the players' qualified freedom from the restrictions of the reserve system imposed by all major sports. Yet, in the context of a breach of contract suit, it simply means that one party is liberated from any duties that it would have assumed had the other party satisfied the conditions necessary to trigger such duties. In the typical sports contract a player assumes a duty to play in exchange for the club's duty to pay. Failure to perform as promised could constitute a material breach or, phrased otherwise, a failure to satisfy the constructive condition(s) created by the promise(s). In the following case, Oakland Athletics pitcher Jim "Catfish" Hunter was declared a free agent because owner Charles Finley had neglected to provide insurance coverage to Hunter as promised in his Standard Player Contract. Hunter had made repeated requests prior to initiating legal action. As you review this case, consider whether the club's failure to pay constituted a material breach warranting rescission of the contract and declaration of Hunter as a free agent. Further, note that at the time of this decision there was no free agency in Major League Baseball; thus, Finley's failure to pay not only allowed Hunter to escape from the terms of the contract but also provided an escape hatch from the strictures of the reserve system.

American and National Leagues of Professional Baseball Clubs v. Major League Baseball Players Ass'n

130 Cal. Rptr. 626 (Ct. App. 1976)

DRAPER, P.J., with Emerson, J., concurring. This is an appeal by Oakland Athletics, Division of Charles O. Finley & Co., Inc., from a judgment denying its petition to vacate an arbitration award in favor of James A. Hunter.

Hunter, a pitcher, contracted to play baseball for the appellant for the 1974 and 1975 seasons. The contract, dated February 11, 1974, required payment to the player of $100,000 for each of the two seasons. A "special covenant" included in the agreement provided: "* * * the said Club will pay to any person, firm or corporation designated by said Player, the sum of Fifty Thousand ($50,000.00) Dollars, per year, for the duration of this contract to be deferred compensation, same to be paid during the seasons as earned." As proposed by Hunter's attorney, the last line had required the deferred compensation to be paid "at any time requested by said Player," but at the request of appellant's president, Charles O. Finley, these words had been stricken, and "during the seasons as earned" had been substituted. Four days after the contract date, Finley wrote to Hunter's attorney that the club "will be very happy to cooperate in any manner possible to defer any amount of Mr. Hunter's compensation" and "after you have decided as to how these payments should be made and who they should be made to, kindly advise us and we will cooperate accordingly."

Hunter's attorney corresponded with the Internal Revenue Service and ultimately submitted to it an agreement for deferred compensation investment account (DCIA), proposed to be executed by player and club. It provided that the value of that account be "deemed equal to the amount of the account if the deferred compensation had been invested" in annuity contracts with a named life insurance company, half in a fixed annuity contract and half in a variable annuity. This proposed agreement specifically provided "[t]he Employer has the discretion * * * to invest or not invest" and "nothing contained in this agreement shall be construed as requiring such investment." On July 15, the Internal Revenue Service wrote Hunter, in care of his attorney, that "if payments are made according to its terms * * * the amounts payable under the Agreement will not be includible in gross income until such time as those amounts are paid or otherwise made available * * * to you or your beneficiary." On August 1, Hunter delivered to Finley an agreement in the above form, together with form of application to the named life insurance company for annuity contracts. The agreement and the application for annuity contracts provided that ownership of the annuities was to be vested in the club, and not Hunter.

On August 8, Hunter's attorney wrote Finley that the papers delivered by Hunter to Finley had not been signed and returned. He demanded prompt action. Some time before August 22, Finley telephoned Hunter's attorney to say that due to domestic difficulties Finley might be unable to secure the signature of Mrs. Finley, the secretary of the club. The attorney wrote Finley, August 22, again seeking signature and return of the papers. On September 4, Finley phoned to inform the attorney that he feared other players might seek what Hunter wanted, that other club owners had urged him not to sign, and that if he did sign he [Finley] would have to pay additional taxes. Following another letter, Finley phoned the attorney on September 15 and, for the first time, stated that he would not sign as requested, nor would he pay the insurer. The attorney asked for a letter to that effect, but Finley refused, saying that he had thrown the papers away. The next day, Hunter's attorney informed Finley that "we contend* * *you have breached your contract." and formally demanded signature of the DCIA agreement and payment of $50,000 to the life insurance company. On October 4, general counsel for the Major League Baseball Players Association telegraphed Finley on behalf of Hunter, asserting termination of the contract for breach and for failure to cure the breach within 10 days. On October 17 and 18, the association filed grievances with the club owners' Player Relations Committee, one seeking to have Hunter declared a "free agent" and the other seeking payment of the $50,000 deferred compensation for the 1974 season.

The arbitration panel sustained the player's position as to both grievances and made awards accordingly. Appellant club petitioned the superior court for vacation of the award. The petition was denied and the awards affirmed. The club appeals.

It is undisputed that the club agreed to pay Hunter $100,000 per season. Of this amount, $50,000 per year was to be "deferred compensation" but was specifically to be paid to player's designee, "during the seasons as earned." It is equally undisputed that no part of the deferred compensation was in fact paid, despite demands therefor beginning August 1. As a result, the club enjoyed Hunter's not insubstantial services for the full 1974 season at a cost of but half the agreed total compensation.

It is quite true that the club's purchase of annuity contracts in August was not required by the DCIA agreement proposed by Hunter's attorney, and that this inconsistency might result in loss to Hunter of the tax benefit he sought by attempting to defer taxation of his income to years of lesser earnings. But, as the arbitration panel properly found from the documents and the testimony as to negotiations for the basic contract, the plan was designed to benefit Hunter, and not the club. Hence its success or failure was a matter for consideration by Hunter only.

Appellant club, however, asserts that its signature of the DCIA agreement and simultaneous payment to the life insurer would be illegal, and would subject the club and Finley to prosecution for aiding or assisting in a false statement in a matter arising under the internal revenue laws (26 U.S.C.A. §7206). But the club had made no representation that it would comply only with the DCIA agreement, and it would have been a minimal inconvenience, if it executed the documents delivered to it August 1, to disclose to the Internal Revenue Service both the DCIA agreement and the payments to the life insurer.

Aside from the effect upon appellant, however, it is argued that the award is illegal or against public policy. It must be remembered that we deal here with an arbitration award. Grounds for vacation of an arbitration are strictly limited by statute (Code Civ. Proc., §1286.2). Moreover, "erroneous reasoning will not invalidate an otherwise proper award." Every intendment of validity must be given the award and doubts must be resolved in its favor.

Nonetheless, arbitration awards have been vacated when they are illegal or against public policy. Hence we examine briefly the several types of decisions so holding. Of course, if the underlying contract which provides for arbitration is itself illegal, no arbitration award may be made under it * * * Similarly, if the award commands an act which is unlawful or against public policy, it will be vacated. Such authorities have no application here, since the award commands only payment of the unpaid compensation of $50,000.

Appellant, however, seems to argue that the claimed breach consisted only in its refusal to perform acts which would have violated public policy by encouraging tax evasion. He contends that thus, while neither the basic agreement nor the award itself is illegal, the award nonetheless is against public policy. As we have pointed out, both statutory and judicial policy favor finality of arbitration awards.

Moreover, courts are reluctant to declare a contract void as against public policy, and will refuse to do so if by any reasonable construction it may be upheld.

Most importantly, appellant's contention is rejected under a recent Supreme Court holding. (*Redke v. Silvertrust*, 6 Cal. 3d 94 [98 Cal.Rptr. 293, 490 P.2d 805], *cert. den.*, 405 U.S. 1041.) There, an inter vivos trust and agreement between husband and wife for testamentary disposition were attacked as working a fraud upon tax authorities and thus unenforceable. There, as here, there was "nothing illegal per se" in the agreement, for it "could have been carried out in an entirely legal manner had [the husband] disclosed its existence to the tax authorities, or chosen not to claim the* * *deduction." (P. 102.) "As a general rule, if a contract can be performed legally, a court will presume that the parties intended a lawful mode of performance" (*id.*). Absent proof that the parties entered the agreement "with the intent of fraudulently concealing its existence from the tax authorities," the agreement was valid and enforceable.

* * *

Appellant also attacks that portion of the award which declared Hunter a "free agent." He asserts that application of the "reserve clause" is not subject to arbitration. The argument involves construction of the major league rules, the basic agreement between owners and players groups, and the uniform players contract. The issue is discussed at length in a recent decision (*Kansas City Royals Baseball Corp. v. Major League Baseball Players Ass'n* (8th Cir. 1976) 532 F.2d 615). We accept the reasoning and conclusion of that decision, which affirmed an arbitration award comparable to that before us.

Judgment affirmed.

"HAROLD C. BROWN, Associate Justice" [The disenting opinion of Justice Brown is omitted."

Notes and Questions

1. Did the arbitrator and the court give Finley sufficient opportunity to pay Hunter the insurance monies owed? Did Finley's recalcitrance justify forfeiture of the entire contract and declaration of free agency—the most severe "sanction" an owner could receive, especially where the liberated player was one of Hunter's caliber? *See also In re Arbitration Between Major League Baseball Clubs (Cleveland Indians) and Major League Baseball Players Ass'n (Bibby)*, Decision No. 36, Grievance No. 78-3 (Porter, Chairman, 1978) (Pitcher Jim Bibby declared a free agent when club refused to award him incentive bonus for appearing in an agreed upon number of games); FARNSWORTH, § 8.15; MURRAY § 107.

2. With regard to bonuses, another interesting question centers upon the characterization of the bonus money. Is it pay above and beyond regular salary, or is it simply a part of the player's compensation? This issue holds more than academic curiosity given the fact that players unable to come to agreement on a new contract have been forced to play out an option year at a percentage of the prior year's salary (*e.g.*, 80%). In *In re Arbitration Between Major League Baseball Player Relations Committee (Atlanta National League Baseball Club, Inc.) and Major League Baseball Players Ass'n (Horner)*, Atlanta Braves third baseman Bob Horners claimed that certain money earmarked as "bonus" by the club was actually part of his regular compensation and thereby should be included in the formula employed to determine his compensation during his option

year. While the arbitrator acknowledged that the Major League Rules distinguish a bonus from regular salary, he likewise noted that the rule was only enforceable to the extent consistent with the player's contract or applicable collective bargaining agreement. Because arbitration panel chairman Goetz found it unreasonable to conclude that the maximum salary cut during Horner's option year could reduce a $150,000 annual income (including incentives) to a mere $21,000 (straight salary), he ruled that the incentives were to be included in the figure subject to the maximum 20% reduction. While Horner escaped unscathed in this case, the result underscores the importance of clarity in contract language, specifically the unambiguous designation of bonus, salary guarantee, no-cut clauses and similar provisions. The inclusion of salary caps in some collective bargaining agreements has elevated the importance of definitions of salary and characterizations of bonus money. Owners and players have made new sport of circumventing the salary cap and devising stratagems to avoid designating certain recompense as "salary" in order to fall within the cap. *See, e.g.,* Chapter 14, Part IX(D).

3. A similar issue was presented in Patrick Ewing's 1991 arbitration case against the New York Knicks of the NBA. Ewing's 1985 contract gave Ewing the right to terminate his contract on or before June 30, 1991, if it placed him outside the NBA's top four highest paid players in terms of salary compensation. "Salary compensation" was defined in the contract to exclude "'signing,' 'performance,' or other bonuses." The purpose of the provision in Ewing's contract was to make him a free agent in 1991 if league salaries had increased to such an extent that his 1985 contract—then by far the best contract ever given a basketball player—no longer called for payment of a salary comparable to the salaries being paid to the top few players in the league. The parties agreed that at least three other NBA players would receive more "salary compensation" than Ewing in 1991–92 (Hakeem Olajuwon, Michael Jordan, and John "Hot Rod" Williams). The question was whether Larry Bird of the Boston Celtics, who was to be paid $2.2 million in salary and a $4.87 million "signing bonus," was to be considered an NBA player earning more than Ewing. Resolution of the issue turned on the characterization of Bird's "signing bonus."

Ewing established that Bird and the Celtics had agreed on a one-year salary of $7.07 million and had only renamed $4.87 million a "signing bonus" in order to comply with an erroneous league interpretation of the NBA's salary cap. Ewing also proved that the Bird payment, while titled a "signing bonus," was unlike virtually all other payments in sports that had been called signing bonuses—it had none of the four identifying characteristics of such income: (1) it was not earned by or in consideration for signing the contract; (2) it was not in consideration for the signing of a multi-year contract; (3) it exceeded the total amount of salary under the contract; and (4) it was subject to all of the restrictions traditionally imposed on players' rights to receive salary payments. Nevertheless, the NBA arbitrator held that Ewing and the Knicks had made no attempt to define or restrict the term "signing bonus" in Ewing's contract, and they were thereby bound by the fact that Bird and the Celtics had chosen to call about 70% of Bird's salary a "signing bonus." In addition, because the contract did not provide otherwise, the arbitrator concluded "that the term 'signing bonus' was intended to have whatever meaning industry practice gave to it in 1991," not in 1985, when the contract was written. The arbitrator held that Bird did not earn more "salary compensation" than Ewing's $3.1 million, and Ewing was therefore not entitled to terminate his contract and become a free agent. *In re Arbitration Between Patrick Ewing and the New York Knickerbockers* (Collins, 1991).

4. Incentive clauses vary from sport to sport, with Major League Baseball taking a dim view of performance-related bonuses. In baseball, bonuses for such achieve-

ments as most home runs, highest batting average, etc. are strictly prohibited. The rationale presumably is that players, in their zeal to gain the economic benefit of the incentive clause, may pursue individual accomplishments to the disservice of the team. Bonuses based upon numbers of games played or certain types of awards (*e.g.,* Most Valuable Player) are permitted, again presumably because they do no violence to the notion of team play. While it would appear that these types of incentives are fairly straight-forward and non-controversial, myriad problems can result if the conditions governing their award are not clear and unequivocal. Even where the contract seems clear, application of the incentive clause may present complex questions of contract interpretation.

5. Consider the following hypotheticals:

A) Johnny Spahn, star pitcher for the New York Bombers, has a clause in his Standard Player Contract that provides for a $100,000 bonus if he appears in 75 games during the regular season. During the season, between April 6 and August 30, Spahn appears in 74 games. At this point in time, his team is mired in last place, 25 games out of first place, with no chance of winning the division title. Between August 30 and October 2, the last day of the regular season, Spahn is not called upon to pitch. He completes the season with 74 appearances and is denied his $100,000 appearance bonus. Does he have a cause of action against the club, and if so, what legal arguments should he advance? What defenses would the club offer?

B) The same Johnny Spahn has a clause in his contract calling for a $50,000 bonus if he is selected to pitch in the annual all-star game. When the time arrives to name the all-star game's pitching staff, Len Roberts, manager of the all-star team and also manager of the Bombers (last year's league champions), ignores Spahn and the fact that he leads the league in earned run average and winning percentage with an incredible 17-0 record. Does he have a legitimate claim for the $50,000 incentive bonus? What legal arguments would be advanced? As Spahn's attorney, how could you have prevented the problem?

6. Washington Redskins kicker Mark Moseley's contract gave him an incentive bonus of $5,000 whenever he broke an NFL record. Five times that season Moseley broke and extended the NFL record, because his consecutive field goal streak was five field goals longer than any previous NFL place kicker. Is he entitled to $25,000 or $5,000 or some other amount? What evidence would you gather to support your position? How would you present this issue to an arbitrator to further Moseley's or the Washington Redskins' positions?

7. Difficult questions surrounding promises versus conditions and the determination of what constitutes a material breach warranting contract termination or, in the employment context, discharges have not been limited to players and clubs. Consider the following case.

Cole v. Valley Ice Garden, LLC
113 P.3d 275 (Mont. 2005)

Justice Patricia O. Cotter delivered the opinion of the court.

Valley Ice Garden, L.L.C. and Valley Ice Garden Management, L.L.C. (hereinafter collectively referred to as VIG) and William Martel appeal the judgment of the [lower court] that the termination of Plaintiff David G. Cole as the hockey coach for the Bozeman Ice Dogs was without cause. We reverse and remand.

* * *

In June of 1997, Martel purchased the Ice Dogs, a Junior A, American West Hockey League team. Because of the time in the season that Martel purchased the Ice Dogs, he needed to find a coach immediately. Hence, Martel met with and ultimately hired Cole as the Head Coach and General Manager of the Ice Dogs.

Martel asked Cole to draw up an employment agreement, which Cole did after consulting an attorney. The applicable portion of this employment agreement stated:

> TERM: That the term of this Agreement shall be five (5) years, commencing on the 1st day of June 1997, and continuing thereafter, uninterrupted, unless employee is terminated for cause. In the event of the termination of employee for other than cause, employee shall receive one (1) full calendar year salary and a bonus equal to that paid to him for the preceding year.

The above-quoted provision of the agreement was subsequently amended in March 1998 to add the following:

> Further, the term of this Agreement shall automatically renew, so as to have five (5) years remaining, each year on the 1st day of June, unless employer notifies employee in writing prior to the 1st day of May of that Year of the non-renewal.

Cole's annual base salary was fixed at $50,000.00.

The 1997–1998 hockey season was fairly successful, but the following 1998–1999 season was not. The Ice Dogs ended that season with a record of 18 wins, 35 losses, and 7 ties. The Ice Dogs did not qualify for the playoffs, Cole did not receive any performance bonuses, and the game attendance declined to approximately 1,000 fans per game.

Thereafter, during the off-season and at Cole's suggestion, Martel expended substantial sums of money in an effort to improve the team. In particular, Martel increased his recruitment efforts; entered the Ice Dogs in pre-season tournaments and in games in Canada; and hired a goalie coach and a new trainer. Despite these efforts, the 1999–2000 season again started out poorly, with the Ice Dogs winning one game and losing six.

On October 3, 1999, Martel terminated Cole due to the Ice Dogs' poor performance. Martel then told Cole that because he had cause to fire him, he felt he was not obligated to provide him severance pay. However, Martel did offer Cole $15,000 in severance pay, which Cole accepted. When Cole arrived to pick up his check, Martel asked him to sign a release from liability form, which Cole declined to sign. Cole then sought the advice of an attorney, and thereafter requested that Martel provide him with a written statement regarding his reasons for terminating him. Martel complied with Cole's request.

After receiving Martel's explanation, Cole brought an action for breach of the employment contract and for breach of the implied covenant of good faith and fair dealing. Cole filed a motion for partial summary judgment. VIG also filed a motion for summary judgment. The District Court denied VIG's motion, and it granted Cole's motion as to liability, holding, in part, that Cole was terminated without cause.

* * *

* * * The facts relevant to the question of whether Cole was fired for cause are undisputed. VIG fired Cole from his job for unsatisfactory job performance. The contract Cole drafted allowed for certain payments to be made to him in the event he was terminated for "other than cause." "Cause" was not defined in the contract. The District

Court was therefore required to determine whether discharge for an unsatisfactory job performance constituted sufficient "cause" for discharge, so as to relieve VIG of the obligation to pay Cole upon termination of his contract.

VIG contends it had good cause to terminate Cole, and that the District Court erred in concluding that Cole was discharged without cause. In this connection, it presents several arguments. First, VIG argues that under Montana law, if any uncertainty in a contract exists, that uncertainty must be construed against the drafter. As such, VIG contends that any uncertainty as to the meaning of "cause," as contained in the contract, must be construed against Cole, as he drafted the employment agreement. In addition, VIG maintains that the ordinary meaning of "cause" should apply, and that VIG had several "good or adequate" reasons for terminating Cole's employment.

VIG likens the present case to one brought under Montana's Wrongful Discharge from Employment Act (the WDEA). While acknowledging that the WDEA does not apply here, VIG argues that since "good cause" is defined in the WDEA, that definition provides this Court with a guideline for "cause" in the present case. Namely, the WDEA defines "good cause" as "reasonable job-related grounds for dismissal based on a failure to satisfactorily perform job duties, disruption of the employer's operation, or other legitimate business reasons." *Section 39-2-903(5), MCA.* VIG maintains that based on this definition, we have before upheld termination for "good cause" on the basis of poor job performance and we should do so here as well.

As VIG notes, Cole admits he was not terminated for a capricious or false reason; in fact, he concedes his termination was the result of his losing record. Thus, there is no allegation of a pre-textual or otherwise improper motive for the discharge. VIG further maintains that firing a coach for a poor win/loss record is hardly unusual in the sports industry. Indeed, VIG contends that the expectation for Cole to win was evident by the built-in bonuses for winning listed in the employment agreement. VIG argues that it is hypocritical for Cole—who drafted the employment agreement—to claim he should be financially rewarded for winning, yet not penalized for a poor win/loss record.

Cole contends that because the plain language of the employment agreement does not list as one of Cole's duties the need to maintain a specific win/loss ratio, this Court need not analyze the contract any further, as it cannot insert terms into the contract that are not there. Hence, because the win/loss ratio was not delineated in the employment agreement, the fact that Cole was terminated because of it proves that he was not terminated "for cause." He then maintains that "the fundamental issue in this case is not whether VIG had a right to discharge Coach Cole." Rather, he argues that because coaches are commonly terminated for failing to maintain a winning record, it follows that VIG is obligated to pay off the remainder of a coach's contract, as is the case here. Cole further maintains that the WDEA's definitions do not apply to the present case. Finally, he asserts that the employment agreement should not be construed against him because VIG, as the employer, was in the superior bargaining position and took unfair advantage of him.

* * *

The District Court concluded that because "the condition to have a winning percentage or an adequate win/loss record ratio was not in the contract * * * the Plaintiff's termination was without 'cause.'" The District Court noted that the contract included "coaching" as a duty, but, stating there were no Montana cases addressing the termination of a coach's employment for a poor win/loss record, reasoned therefrom that permitting the termination of Cole's employment for this reason would require the insertion of "language into the contract which was not agreed upon by the parties." Thus, according to the District Court, because (1) there are no previous cases on point, and (2) "cause" is not defined by the contract, then (3) poor team performance cannot be "cause" for termination of employment, despite Cole's contractual duty of "coaching."

Although the District Court may have believed it was avoiding the insertion of language into the contract, what it actually did was substantially eliminate an agreed-to provision of the contract: that Cole was subject to termination for "cause." Cole's failure to define "cause" when drafting the agreement does not mean that the term has no meaning, or that the parties intended the term to have a narrow, specific meaning. Indeed, Cole concedes that coaches are routinely terminated for failing to maintain a winning record, and argues that the question is not whether VIG could fire him, but rather, whether it ought to be required to pay out the term of his contract. He acknowledged in the District Court that the "measuring stick" of a team's performance is its record, and that the win/loss record is a "big factor" in assessing a coach's performance. In essence, Cole is not disputing management's right to fire him for poor performance; he simply wants to be paid upon the occurrence of that discharge. He asks that we uphold his compensation not because the discharge was wrongful, but rather because the contract he drafted does not specify it as so.

The lack of any definition of "cause" in the contract Cole drafted meant that it was incumbent on the District Court to decide what the term means. In doing so, the court must be guided by *§ 28-3-501, MCA,* which provides: "The words of a contract are to be understood in their ordinary and popular sense * * *." Where the parties' contract fails to define a term, we look to this rule of construction, as well as to the general rule that unclear language in a contract should be construed against the drafter.

VIG offers a number of cases we have decided pursuant to the WDEA, which defines "good cause" as "reasonable job-related grounds for dismissal based on a failure to satisfactorily perform job duties * * * or other legitimate business reason." *Section 39-2-903(5), MCA.* Acknowledging that this is not a WDEA case, we nonetheless find that these cases offer persuasive guidance in this matter.

It is well settled in our pre-[wrongful discharge] Act cases that courts should not intrude in the day-to-day employment decisions of business owners * * * An employer's legitimate right to exercise discretion over whom it will employ must be balanced, however, against the employee's equally legitimate right to secure employment * * * The balance should favor an employee who presents evidence, and not mere speculation or denial, upon which a jury could determine *that the reasons given for his termination were false, arbitrary or capricious, and unrelated to the needs of the business. Morton v. M-W-M, Inc. (1994),* 263 Mont. 245, 250 (emphasis added) (alteration in original) (citing *Kestell v. Heritage Health Care Corp. (1993), 259 Mont. 518, 525).* We further explained in *Kestell* that we had defined "legitimate business reason" as "a reason that is neither false, whimsical, arbitrary or capricious, and it must have some logical relationship to the needs of the business." *Kestell,* 259 Mont. at 525 (quoting *Buck v. Billings Montana Chevrolet, Inc. (1991),* 248 Mont. 276, 281–82).

Similar standards have been applied in other jurisdictions for similar situations, including the discharge of a coach employed pursuant to a contract which allowed discharge only for good cause.

The term "good cause" is "largely relative in [its] connotation, depending upon the particular circumstances of each case." "Essentially, [it] connotes 'a fair and honest cause or reason, regulated by good faith on the part of the party exercising the power.'" The employer does not have a right to make an arbitrary or unreasonable decision about terminating an employee when there is an agreement to terminate only for good cause.

* * *

Cole did not establish, nor even assert, that the reasons for terminating his employment "were false, arbitrary or capricious, [or] unrelated to the needs of the business." *Morton*, 263 Mont. at 250. Neither did he establish, nor even assert, that VIG's reasons were "false, whimsical * * * [or did not] have some logical relationship to the needs of the business." *Kestell*, 259 Mont. at 525. As we have defined the term in both WDEA and non-WDEA cases, VIG had a "legitimate business reason" to terminate Cole, a reason "logically related to the needs of the business." Discharging the coach of a professional sports team which is performing poorly, despite management's good faith efforts, is a discretionary decision related to the legitimate needs of the business and constitutes "cause."

Had the District Court concluded on the basis of disputed facts, and after a trial on the merits, that Cole was not discharged for "cause," we would rightly be reluctant to disturb such a finding and conclusion on appeal. * * *

Reversed and remanded.

Notes and Questions

1. The court relied in part upon state law (the Wrongful Discharge From Employment Act) to determine the meaning of "just cause." Is this an appropriate reference point for purposes of interpreting the parties' intent? *See Wood v. Loyola Marymount Univ.*, 218 Cal. App. 3d 661 (Cal. Ct. App. 1980).

2. The coach asserted that the plain language of the contract did not delineate a satisfactory won-loss record as one of his duties. Accordingly, he contended that that criterion was not a valid predicate for his discharge. In essence, he posited a rule of interpretation embracing the canon "*expressio (or inclusio) unius est exclusio alterius.*" Is this an appropriate tool for interpreting the just cause provision in an employment contract? *See generally Hanson v. Mahoney*, 433 F.3d 1107 (9th Cir. 2006); *Dusen v. North Carolina Dep't of Human Resources*, 476 S.E.2d 383 (N.C. Ct. App. 1996).

3. If we were to assume that a coaching agreement rises to the level of a binding bilateral contract, and that a poor win-loss record warrants discharge or termination of the contract, is the natural yet bizarre conclusion that a coach's poor performance could result in a breach with the possibility of damages? Such a result seems unlikely. A more plausible scenario may be that a won-loss record, satisfactory to the team, is a condition precedent to the team's duty to fulfill its end of the agreement. Failure to comply strictly with the condition, *i.e.* have a "satisfactory" win-loss record, signifies that the team's duty has not been triggered. If the condition is characterized as a condition of satisfaction, it is likely that an objective, reasonable-person standard would be applied to ascertain whether the condition had been met. *See* Chapter 4, Part VI, *supra; Hutton v. Monogram Plus, Inc.*, 604 N.E.2d 200 (Ohio Ct. App. 1992).

4. In the collegiate context, coaches are routinely dismissed, or, at least, not renewed, on the basis of their win-loss records or even their failure to beat arch-rivals. In the arena of intercollegiate athletics, does using won-loss records to determine whether coaches will be retained send the wrong message? Does it reinforce the idea that college sports truly is a big business and that the academic model is a vestige of another era?

Should college coaches be awarded tenure like other members of the university community? *See* Notes and Questions following the *Northeastern* case, Chapter 6, *infra*.

5. Was Cole functionally employed at-will? Even if so, does that give universities *carte blanche* to discharge coaches with impunity? Is there no protection from abusive discharges or terminations that violate public policy?

6. In *Wood v. Loyola Marymount University, supra*, the university fired its baseball coach and claimed that it had a right to do so because the coach was employed "at will" and that there was no need to establish a just-cause basis for the termination. In the alternative, the university offered evidence demonstrating that the baseball team had a losing record and that team morale was very low. The coach argued that an implied-infact contract existed by virtue of his fifteen-year employment with the university, correspondence indicating that his employment would be continuous, and the list of "privileges and conditions" contained in the employee handbook.

The court reversed the district court grant of summary judgment to the defendant/university and found that an implied-in-fact contract existed. (*See* Chapter 4, Part II, *supra*). The court rejected the university's argument that its at-will prerogative was established by a memorandum explaining that "the appointment was * * * subject * * * to the university's continuing mutual satisfaction from the part of the university and [Wood] with regard to performance, salary, professional opportunities and working conditions." 218 Cal. App. 3d at 666. In effect, the university claimed paradoxically that there was an express contract providing that the coach was employed at-will. Forgiving the apparent contradiction and the consideration problems presented by such right to cancel (see Chapter 4, Part IV, *supra*), the court found that any at-will presumption that may have existed was rebutted by the existence of an implied-in-fact contract. This conclusion was buttressed by the coach's longevity, repeated oral assurances of job security and, of greatest significance, the university's published policies that employees like the coach would be dismissed only as a "last resort" and not as the product of an arbitrary process. *Id.* at 667–68. The court inferred the existence of a just cause termination provision as part of the implied contract.

The court also was not enamored with the university's *post-hoc* arguments regarding the coach's poor win-loss record and morale.

> "Most young people go to college not to receive training with which to further a career in professional sports, but rather to receive an education. Sports participation is considered, by the majority of students, to be but a small part of the overall academic experience. Team morale is not the sole responsibility of a coach. The players must assume their share of responsibility.
>
> A coach, like any other educator, is to be judged by his overall contribution to the success of the learning institution for which he works. Wood presented evidence to show that he was not just a baseball coach, but a counselor who influenced students in important ways."

Id. at 669.

7. Would a coach's failure to abide by NCAA regulations be deemed "good cause" for termination and material breach of the coach's contractual obligation? *See O'Brien v. The Ohio State Univ.*, 2005 Ohio 3335 (Ohio Ct. Cl. 2005). *See* Chapter 4, Part VI, *supra*.

Chapter 6

Contracts and Sports: Enforcement

I. Introduction

It is a settled principle that an affirmative injunction or "specific performance" is an inappropriate remedy for breach of a personal services contract by a party who is obligated to perform such services. The judicial rationale for declining to impose relief that requires the breaching party to perform specifically is two-fold: (1) such a remedy would constitute a violation of the Thirteenth Amendment's prohibition against involuntary servitude; and (2) the court would have considerable difficulty ascertaining whether a subsequent failure to perform was the product of an innocent shortcoming or contempt of the court's order. For example, in *Ford v. Jermon*, 6 Phil. L. Rep. 6 (1865), the court refused to grant specific performance against an actress who had breached an agreement requiring her to perform in a play. The court commented: "In order to render such a decree effectual, it would be necessary to appoint a master, whose duty should be to frequent the theater and decide whether the mistakes or incongruities by which the part might be disfigured, were in contempt of the court, or unintentional." *Id.* at 7; *see also Lumley v. Wagner*, 482 Eng. Rep. 687 (1852); Stewart E. Sterk, *Restraints on Alienation of Human Capital,* 79 Va. L. Rev. 383 (1993); Christopher T. Wonnel, *The Contractual Disempowerment of Employers,* 46 Stan. L. Rev. 87 (1993); Robert S. Stevens, *Involuntary Servitude By Injunction,* 6 Cornell L.Q. 235 (1921).

In the context of professional sports, courts have clearly recognized the repugnance of requiring someone to work against his or her will and, likewise, have acknowledged the practical problems in ascertaining compliance with any specific performance mandate. *See, e.g.,* James T. Brennan, *Injunction Against Professional Athletes Breaching Their Contracts,* 34 Brooklyn L. Rev. 61 (1967). Moreover, ascertaining damages when a professional athlete has "jumped a contract" or otherwise refused to fulfill his or her contractual obligations is likewise extremely difficult. Courts will not award money damages where the amount is too speculative or uncertain. *See, e.g., Freund v. Washington Square Press,* 314 N.E.2d 419 (N.Y. 1974); *Locke v. United States,* 283 F.2d 521 (Ct. Cl. 1960). But see *Boston Professional Hockey Ass'n v. Cheevers,* 348 F. Supp. 261 (D. Mass. 1972).

Thus, because the typical contract between player and club involves the payment of money in exchange for personal services, the remedy for a "jilted" team is often limited to a negative injunction—an order precluding the player from playing for any club other than the club to which he has pledged his services. Ordinarily, the contract contains an explicit "negative covenant" binding the player to the club and opening the door to the negative injunction in the event of a breach. Even in the absence of this type of covenant, courts will infer its existence from any number of factors. *See Madison Square Garden Boxing, Inc. v. Shavers*, 434 F. Supp. 449 (S.D.N.Y. 1977). Yet, because such an action is equitable in nature, numerous issues often come into play, including the uniqueness of the athlete, *see Central New York Basketball, Inc. v. Barnett*, 181 N.E.2d 506 (Ct. C.P. Cuyahoga Cty. Ohio 1961), below, the adequacy of a monetary penalty, the possibility of irreparable harm, the breadth of the negative covenant, etc. Also, given the equitable nature of the injunction request, it is necessary that the plaintiff approach the court with "clean hands." *See Weegham v. Killefer*, 215 F. 168 (W.D. Mich. 1914). Finally, pertinent collective bargaining agreements may contain provisions that result in judicial deferral to the voluntarily devised arbitration machinery. *See Boston Celtics v. Shaw*, 908 F.2d 1041 (1st Cir. 1990), below. Other labor contracts will exclude a club's judicial enforcement of a negative covenant from the scope of an arbitrator's jurisdiction. Each of these issues will be addressed in the cases that follow.

II. The Negative Injunction

Central New York Basketball, Inc. v. Barnett

181 N.E.2d 506 (Ct. C.P. Cuyahoga Cty. Ohio 1961)

DANACEAU, J. This is an action for injunctive relief brought by the plaintiff, Central New York Basketball, Inc., a New York corporation, against Richard Barnett and Cleveland Basketball Club, Inc., a corporation. Plaintiff owns and operates a professional basketball team under the name of Syracuse Nationals, having a franchise of the National Basketball Association, now in its 16th season.

The defendant, Richard Barnett, a professional basketball player, the No. 1 draft choice in 1959 of the plaintiff and who played for the plaintiff during the ensuing 1959 basketball season, played for the Syracuse club throughout the 1960 basketball season under a signed and executed Uniform Player Contract of the National Basketball Association under date of March 16, 1960 by and between the plaintiff and said defendant * * *.

The defendant, Cleveland Basketball Club, Inc., is a member of the American Basketball League, recently organized, and owns and operates a professional basketball team.

In July of 1961, the defendants, Barnett and Cleveland Basketball Club, Inc., made and entered into an American Basketball League Player Contract in which the club engaged the player to render his services as a basketball player for a term beginning on September 15, 1961 and ending on September 14, 1962, a copy of said contract having been received in evidence as plaintiff's Exhibit A.

* * *

Plaintiff claims that the defendant, Barnett, is a professional player of great skill and whose talents and abilities as a basketball player are of special, unique, unusual and extraordinary character; that the defendant, Cleveland Basketball Club, Inc., knew that he was under contract with the plaintiff; that in accordance with the terms and conditions of said contract the plaintiff exercised a right to renew said contract for an additional year as provided therein and so notified the defendant Barnett, that the defendant Barnett breached the said contract by failing and refusing to play with and for the said plaintiff during the 1961–1962 playing season, and that said breach of contract was committed with the knowledge and participation of the defendant, Cleveland Basketball Club, Inc.

Plaintiff claims that it cannot reasonably or adequately be compensated for damages in an action at law for the loss of defendant Barnett's services as required by said contract and an oral agreement between plaintiff and Barnett made in May of 1961, and that plaintiff will suffer immediate and irreparable damages.

* * *

The defendant, Cleveland Basketball Club, Inc., admits that the defendant Barnett is a professional basketball player but denies that he is of great skill and denies that his talents and abilities as a basketball player are of special, unique, unusual and extraordinary character; and further admits that the defendant Barnett has played professional basketball in the National Basketball Association as an employee of the plaintiff.

* * *

The separate answer of the defendant, Richard Barnett, conforms to the answer of the Cleveland Basketball Club, Inc. and further admits that on or about March 16, 1960, he and the plaintiff signed a written document and that a copy of the said document, annexed to the petition as Exhibit A, is a true copy thereof, but denies that said instrument is a contract. Said defendant further admits that he played professional basketball for plaintiff during the 1960–1961 season and that plaintiff paid him the sum of $8,500, but denies that as partial consideration therefor he promised to give the plaintiff the right to renew said contract as provided in paragraph 22 (a) thereof and promised not to play otherwise than with plaintiff. The said defendant further denies that plaintiff exercised its option to renew the alleged contract with him for the next playing season and denies that plaintiff, through its general manager, negotiated with him as to the amount to be paid for the 1961–1962 basketball season and denies that the parties agreed that he would be paid $11,500 for the next season.

* * *

The written agreement under date of March 16, 1960 and signed by the plaintiff and the defendant Barnett provides in part as follows:

"5. The Player promises and agrees (a) to report at the time and place fixed by the club in good physical condition; and (b) to keep himself throughout the entire season in good physical condition; and (c) to give his best services, as well as his loyalty, to the Club, and to play basketball only for the Club unless released, sold or exchanged by the Club; and (d) to be neatly and fully attired in public and always to conduct himself on and off the court according to the highest standards of honesty, morality, fair play and sportsmanship, and (e) not to do anything which is detrimental to the best interests of the Club or of the National Basketball Association or of professional sports.

"9. The Player represents and agrees that he has exceptional and unique skill and ability as a basketball player; that his services to be rendered hereunder are of a special, unusual and extraordinary character which gives them peculiar value which cannot be reasonably or adequately compensated for in damages at law, and that the Player's breach of this contract will cause the Club great and irreparable injury and damage. The Player agrees that, in addition to other remedies, the Club shall be entitled to injunctive and other equitable relief to prevent a breach of this contract by the Player, including, among others, the right to enjoin the Player from playing basketball for any other person or organization during the term of this contract.

"22. (a) On or before September 1st (or if a Sunday, then the next preceding business day) next following the last playing season covered by this contract, the Club may tender to the Player a contract for the term of that season by mailing the same to the Player at his address following his signature hereto, or if none be given, then at his last address of record with the Club. If prior to the November 1 next succeeding said September 1, the Player and the Club have not agreed upon the terms of such contract, then on or before 10 days after said November 1, the Club shall have the right by written notice to the Player at said address to renew this contract for the period of one year on the same terms, except that the amount payable to the Player shall be such as the Club shall fix in said notice; provided, however, that said amount shall be an amount payable at a rate not less than 75% of the rate stipulated for the preceding year.

(b) The Club's right to renew this contract, as provided in subparagraph (a) of this paragraph 22, and the promise of the Player not to play otherwise than with the Club have been taken into consideration in determining the amount payable under paragraph 2 hereof."

Plaintiff contends that the foregoing provisions provide for two alternatives: (1) that the parties may agree upon a signed new contract for the next succeeding playing season and (2) in the event a signed agreement is not made, the club has the right to renew the contract for a period of one year on the same terms, except that the salary shall be fixed by the club and shall be payable at a rate not less than the stipulated minimum.

The plaintiff contends that under the second alternative, the terms are the same as in the preceding year except for the amount of salary and that at the close of the renewal year, the contract has been completed and is at an end.

The defendants, on the other hand, interpret the contract to provide for perpetual service and, consequently, is void. It is said in 11 O. Jur.2d at page 398:

"Generally, a liberal construction should be put upon written instruments so as to uphold them, if possible, and carry into effect the intention of the parties. Courts are required, by applying known rules of law, to enforce valid and reasonable contracts of parties, with the view of carrying out their clear intent, rather than, by resorting to technical construction, to render such contracts void. A contract should be given that construction that will uphold it and preserve to the parties thereto their rights, if the same can be done without doing violence to the language of the contract. Wherever the language of a contract will permit, it should be so construed as to support rather than to destroy legal obligation * * *.

"* * *If the language of a contract is susceptible of two constructions, one of which will render it valid and give effect to the obligation of the parties, and the other will render it invalid and ineffectual, the former construction must be adopted."

Then continuing on page 399, it is said:

"In construing a written instrument, effect should be given to all of the words if this can be done by any reasonable interpretation; and it is the duty of a court to give effect to all parts of a written contract, if this can be done consistently with the expressed intent of the parties. If possible, every provision in a contract should be held to have been inserted for some purpose and to perform some office, and an attempt must be made to harmonize, if possible, all the provisions of a contract."

The construction of the contract urged by plaintiff, to which it is committed in open court, is reasonable, rational, practical, just and in accordance with the foregoing principles, and is adopted by this Court.

The defendant Barnett had previously played for the Syracuse team during the greater part of the 1959–1960 season under a signed contract.

Daniel Biasone, the President and General Manager of the Syracuse club, testified that near the close of the 1960–1961 season in March of 1961, he told the defendant Barnett that Barnett was one of seven players he would keep exempt from the forthcoming draft of players from all National Basketball Association clubs to stock the new Chicago club and that Barnett was one of the seven players he was "protecting."

In the latter part of May, 1961, Mr. Biasone reached the defendant Barnett by telephone, and they discussed salary for the next season and agreed upon an increase of $3,000 which would bring the salary of Barnett to $11,500. He further testified that Barnett said, "You mail them (contracts) down and I will sign them and return them." * * * On cross-examination Biasone said that he was not sure and did not know whether Barnett said "I will sign."

* * *

New contracts with the signature of plaintiff thereon were mailed to the defendant Barnett on May 26, 1961; and they remained with Barnett unsigned ever since.

In June of 1961, there was a telephone conversation between Jerry Walser, the Business Manager of the Syracuse club, and the defendant Barnett in which Barnett asked for an advance.

* * *

On July 10, 1961, the plaintiff, through Jerry Walser, mailed to Barnett a letter enclosing a check for $3,000.

* * *

The letter and check were received by Barnett and remained in the sealed envelope until produced in court during a hearing on an application for a preliminary injunction on October 9, 1961.

Finding that the contracts mailed to Barnett were not returned and not hearing from Barnett, Mr. Biasone made repeated attempts to contact or reach the defendant Barnett in July and August of 1961 by telephone, telegram and letter, to all of which there was no response. On November 6, 1961, a letter from the plaintiff to the defendant was written and mailed and received by Barnett which reads as follows:

> "It is our position that your 1960–61 contract with us was renewed when we came to terms and we sent you an advance. However, to abide by the letter of the contract and to make the position of the Syracuse Nationals absolutely clear, we hereby notify you that pursuant to Paragraph 22 (a) of said contract, we hereby renew the same for the period of one year ending October 1, 1962. The amount payable to you under such renewed contract is hereby fixed at $11,500."

Meanwhile, during the months of June and July of 1961, Barnett met and talked to his former coach and advisor, John B. McLendon, who was the coach of the Cleveland Pipers Basketball team of the defendant Cleveland Basketball Club, Inc. Both Barnett and McLendon stated that Barnett did not want to play for Syracuse but did want to play for the Cleveland Pipers. However, they were both concerned about the "Kenny Sears" case, then pending in the California Court. It appears that Sears was trying to "jump leagues" * * * to play for San Francisco and both wanted to see the outcome of the case. Undoubtedly, this explains the lack of communication from Barnett to the Syracuse club during June and July of 1961, his failure to return the contracts and his failure to open the envelope containing the letter and check enclosed therein.

Relying upon a newspaper story and their interpretation thereof to the effect that Sears "would not be penalized for going to this new League," Barnett and McLendon proceeded to take the necessary steps culminating in a signed contract between Barnett and the Cleveland Pipers with McLendon signing the contract on behalf of the Cleveland club.

The request of Barnett for an advance, whether it was $300 or $3,000, renders strong support to the claim of plaintiff that an oral agreement on a salary had been reached and that Barnett would play for Syracuse during the 1961–1962 season. Manifestly, unless there was such an understanding, there could be no salary upon which such an advance could be made. The evidence is overwhelming, and this Court finds that the plaintiff and the defendant Barnett reached an understanding that Barnett would play for Syracuse during the 1961–1962 season at a salary of $11,500. It is also quite clear that Barnett and McLendon of the Cleveland Pipers were acting in concert in awaiting the ruling in the Sears case; and after reading the newspaper report, decided that Barnett could "jump" without penalty and sign up with the Cleveland Pipers. Barnett and McLendon decided that they had the green light and the "jump" was made.

The defendants challenge the validity and enforceability of the renewal provisions of the contract on the ground that they lack mutuality. The renewal clauses are an integral part of the contract, and there is sufficient consideration for the obligations and duties arising thereunder.

* * *

In the celebrated case of *Philadelphia Ball Club v. Lajoie*, 51 A. 973, 975 [Pa. 1902], the opinion of the court reads:

> "We are not persuaded that the terms of this contract manifest any lack of mutuality in remedy. Each party has the possibility of enforcing all the rights stipulated for in the agreement. It is true that the terms make it possible for the plaintiff to put an end to the contract in a space of time much less than the period during which the defendant has agreed to supply his personal services; but mere difference in the rights stipulated for does not destroy mutuality of remedy. Freedom of contract covers a wide range of obligation and duty as between the parties, and it may not be impaired, so long as the bounds of reasonableness and fairness are not transgressed."

[A]nd at page 230:

> "The case now before us comes easily within the rule as above stated. The defendant sold to the plaintiff, for a valuable consideration, the exclusive right to his professional services for a stipulated period, unless sooner surrendered by the plaintiff, which could only be after due and reasonable notice and payment

of salary and expenses until the expiration. Why should not a court of equity protect such an agreement until it is terminated? The court cannot compel the defendant to play for the plaintiff, but it can restrain him from playing for another club in violation of his agreement. No reason is given why this should not be done, except that presented by the argument, that the right given to the plaintiff to terminate the contract upon ten days' notice destroys the mutuality of the remedy. But to this it may be answered that, as already stated, the defendant has the possibility of enforcing all the rights for which he stipulated in the agreement, which is all that he can reasonably ask. Furthermore, owing to the peculiar nature and circumstances of the business, the reservation upon the part of the plaintiff to terminate upon short notice does not make the whole contract inequitable."

This court holds that the renewal provisions of the contract involved herein are valid and enforceable.

Plaintiff claims that defendant Barnett is a professional basketball player of great skill and whose talents and abilities as a basketball player are of special, unique, unusual and extraordinary character.

There is some disagreement in the testimony as to the ability and standing of Barnett as a basketball player. Daniel Biasone, the general manager of the Syracuse club for the past 16 years, testified that * * *: "As of now I think Richard Barnett is one of the greatest basketball players playing the game." "[H]e is an exceptionally good shooter." * * * "He is above average * * * with other foul shooters in the National Basketball Association and that he ranked 19th in the whole league (approximately 100 players) scoring, playing as a guard." * * * He further testified * * *:

"Q. What is your opinion as to his ability, that is, as a guard, now, at driving?

"A. Terrific.

"Q. What is your opinion as to his ability as play making as a guard?

"A. Good. He has all the abilities a good basketball player should have. He has all the talent of a great basketball player. He is terrific all the way around."

Mr. Biasone also testified on cross-examination that he would place Barnett in the group of some specifically-named nine or ten unusual and extraordinary players in the National Basketball Association * * *.

Mr. Biasone also testified that Barnett was a box office attraction and was asked on cross examination: "on what basis do you say he was a great box office attraction?" He answered * * *:

"A. Because he, in my opinion, he is such a tremendous ball handler and he does things that have crowd appeal, he is noticeable. He appeals to the crowd because he does things extraordinary."

Coach McLendon of the Cleveland Pipers is not so generous in his appraisal. Barnett, in his opinion, is not in the class of the specifically named outstanding basketball players. McLendon concedes that both Barnett and Neuman, now playing for Syracuse in his first year as a professional, are both "pretty good." * * *

The defendant Barnett was asked by his counsel * * *:

"Q. Do you represent to this court that you have exceptional and unique skill and ability as a basketball player?

"A. No.

"Q. Do you represent to this court that your services are of a special, unusual and extraordinary character?

"A. No.

"Q. You do represent to the court that you are a professional basketball player; is that correct?

"A. Yes.

"Q. Do your think you are as good as Oscar Robertson?

"A. No."

The defendants also presented one James Palmer, a professional basketball player, who testified that he did not think Barnett was playing the right position as a guard; that he is very weak on defense as far as driving goes; that he "goes straight for the boards * * * rather than pass it to somebody or set up a play."* * *Palmer concedes that Barnett "is a very good shooter"* * *; Mr. Palmer does not put Barnett in the class with the specifically-named basketball players who he said, "are just about in a class by themselves."

That the defendant Barnett was 19th among the top 25 scorers in the National Basketball Association in the 1960–61 season is confirmed in the statistics published on page 113 of the official Guide. On page 190 of the Guide is the record of Richard Barnett which indicates that he played in 78 games (out of 79) in the 60–61 season for a total of 1,970 minutes; that his F.G.M. Percentage was .452; That his F. T. M. Percentage was .712 and that he scored 1,320 points for an average of 16.9. The Guide also indicates that Barnett was not among the players in the East-West All Star Game on January 17, 1961, nor was he among the players named in the U.S. Basketball Writers' All-NBA Team for 1961.

The defendant Barnett may not be in the same class with the top ten basketball players. The Syracuse manager is not a disinterested witness, and he may have given an immoderate appraisal of the playing abilities of Barnett. On the other hand, neither are McLendon nor Barnett disinterested witnesses. McLendon's eagerness to secure the services of Barnett at a high salary ($13,000) indicates a higher opinion of Barnett's playing abilities than he was willing to concede at the trial of this case. Barnett was understandably under embarrassment when asked to give his opinion of his own abilities and to make comparisons with another named player.

The increase of salary from $8,500 to $11,500 agreed to by plaintiff, the Cleveland Basketball Club's willingness to pay $13,000, and the latter's eagerness to secure his services, all point to a high regard for his playing abilities. Whether Barnett ranks with the top basketball players or not, the evidence shows that he is an outstanding professional basketball player of unusual attainments and exceptional skill and ability, and that he is of peculiar and particular value to plaintiff.

His signed contract with Syracuse provides:

"9. The Player represents and agrees that he has exceptional and unique skill and ability as a basketball player; that his services to be rendered hereunder are of a special, unusual and extraordinary character which gives them peculiar value which cannot be reasonably or adequately compensated for in damages at law, and that the Player's breach of this contract will cause the Club great and irreparable injury and damage. The Player agrees that, in addition to other remedies, the Club shall be entitled to injunctive and other equitable relief to prevent a breach of this contract by the Player, including, among others, the right to enjoin the Player from playing basketball for any other person or organization during the term of this contract."

The Cleveland contract contains a similar provision, which reads:

"12. The Player represents and agrees that he has exceptional and unique skill and ability as a basketball player; that his services to be rendered hereunder are of a special, unusual and extraordinary character, which gives them peculiar value which cannot be reasonably or adequately compensated for in damages at law, and that the Player's breach of this contract will cause the Club great and irreparable injury and damage. The Player agrees that, in addition to other remedies, the Club shall be entitled to injunctive and other equitable relief to prevent a breach of this Contract by the Player, including, among others, the right to enjoin the Player from playing basketball for any other person or organization during the term of this Contract, or any renewal thereof."

The aforesaid provisions are contained in uniform players' contracts and it would seem that mere engagement as a basketball player in the N.B.A., or A.B.L., carries with it recognition of his excellence and extraordinary abilities.

An important growth in the field of equity has been the use of injunctions against the breach of negative agreements, both express and implied. Pomeroy's Specific Performance of Contracts, Third Ed. at page 75 reads:

"Another class of contracts stipulating for personal acts are now enforced in England by means of an injunction. Where one person agrees to render personal services to another, which require and presuppose a special knowledge, skill, and ability in the employee, so that, in case of a default, the same services could not easily be obtained from others, although the affirmative specific performance of the contract is beyond the power of the court, its performance will be negatively enforced by enjoining its breach. This doctrine applies especially to contracts made by actors, public singers, artists and others possessing a special skill and ability. It is plain that the principle on which it rests is the same with that which applies to agreements for the purchase of land or of chattels having a unique character and value. The damages for the breach of such contracts cannot be estimated with any certainty, and the employer cannot, by means of any damages, purchase the same services in the labor market."

Pomeroy continues:

"The more recent American cases are in accord with the English rule stated in the text, and where one person agrees to render personal service to another which require and presuppose a special knowledge, skill and ability in the employee, so that in case of default, the same services could not be easily obtained from others, equity will negatively enforce the contract by enjoining its breach."

* * *

Professional players in the major baseball, football, and basketball leagues have unusual talents and skills or they would not be so employed. Such players, the defendant Barnett included, are not easily replaced.

The right of the plaintiff is plain and the wrong done by the defendants is equally plain, and there is no reason why the Court should be sparing in the application of its remedies.

Damages at law would be speculative and uncertain and are practically impossible of ascertainment in terms of money. There is no plain, adequate and complete remedy at law and the injury to the plaintiff is irreparable.

Professional baseball, football, and basketball require regulations for the protection of the business, the public and the players, and so long as they are fair and reasonable there is no violation of the laws on restraint of trade. The evidence before this Court does not show any unfair or unreasonable act on the part of the plaintiff and the Court concludes that the claim of the defendant that the contract is in restraint of trade is without merit* * *.

The court finds in favor of the plaintiff on all issues joined and permanent injunctions as requested for the 1961–1962 basketball playing season are decreed. Thereafter the said injunctions shall be dissolved.

Notes and Questions

1. How must the court define uniqueness for purposes of granting the plaintiff's injunction? At one point, it appears as though the court was hospitable to a definition requiring "mere engagement as a basketball player in the NBA" as *a priori* proof of the defendant's uniqueness. The court rejected any definition requiring the plaintiff to demonstrate that it was impossible to replace the defendant. This response parallels what the court articulated more than a half-century earlier in the landmark case involving National League batting champion Napolean Lajoie. *Philadelphia Baseball Club v. Lajoie,* 51 A. 973 (Pa. 1902). It would seem that the most viable approach, and one suggested by the *Barnett* court, is that the standard to determine whether a player is truly unique would be based upon how difficult it is to replace him or her, rather than a knee-jerk assumption based on the athlete's professional status on the one hand or the need to show indispensability on the other hand. In determining a player's "uniqueness," how important is the player's reputation and popularity? *See Philadephia Baseball Club,* 51 A. at 973 (defendant was a highly talented baseball player who had a "great reputation"); *Marchio v. Letterlough,* 237 F. Supp. 2d 580, 589 (E.D. Pa. 2002) (boxer was "irreplaceable" as a nationally-ranked and reputable professional fighter).

2. The court was unsympathetic to the defendant's claim that the standard player contract lacked mutuality and thus was unenforceable for lack of consideration. The court's summary repudiation of this argument reflects the modern view that identical duties and remedies are not necessary to establish the requisite mutuality. *See* Chapter 4, Part IV(A). In line with this thinking, the term "mutuality of consideration," suggesting a bargained for exchange, supplants "mutuality of obligation," which connotes an evenly balanced transaction.

3. Consider the testimony of the respective parties in this case which, were it not so disingenuous, might seem hilarious. The club willing to pay the premium rate to secure Dick Barnett's services essentially testified that he was a mediocre basketball player unworthy of any special attention. But the club unwilling to pay the higher salary, and seeking an injunction to preclude his performance for any other clubs, extols his virtues as a veritable superstar. This case reflects an analysis not unlike most injunction cases in this context, including as basic requirements a demonstration by the plaintiff that: (1)

there was a probability of success on the merits evidenced most prominently by the existence of a valid contract; and (2) irreparable injury will result if an injunction is not granted. With regard to the former, several components exist, including proof that the basic elements of a contract have been established (offer and acceptance, consideration, etc.), that a negative covenant exists (often implied by the court), and that the negative covenant is reasonable. With regard to the latter category, the uniqueness component often satisfies the irreparable injury feature and likewise will establish that there can be no adequate remedy at law. However, courts often look to other features as part of the irreparable injury calculus, including whether and to what degree the parties have been competitively disadvantaged as a result of the action that has precipitated the injunction suit. *See Harrisburg Baseball Club v. Athletic Ass'n*, 8 Pa. County Ct. 337 (1890); *see also* JOHN C. WEISTART & CYM H. LOWELL, THE LAW OF SPORTS §4.10, at 369–73 (1979). Some courts will also consider the extent to which the nonmoving party will suffer irreparable harm if the injunction is issued, and will also consider whether the issuance of an injunction is in the public interest. *Marchio, supra*, at 585.

4. What is the relevance of the contract recitations in the Uniform Player Contracts of the NBA and the ABL concerning Barnett's uniqueness and the team's ability to obtain injunctive relief? Is the entire uniqueness question and, derivatively, the need to show irreparable injury in most professional sports cases obviated in light of the language in the standard contract that acknowledges the player's unique skills and talents? *See, e.g.*, NBA Uniform Player Contract, ¶9.

5. Did Barnett and the Nationals agree to a new contract for the 1961–62 season, or did the Nationals renew the contract pursuant to the option provision in paragraph 22 of the 1960–61 contract? Does it make a difference given the court's interpretation of the option clause? Could the Nationals have renewed Barnett's contract on November 6, 1991, pursuant to paragraph 22(a) for $6,375 (75% of $8,500)?

6. Dick Barnett was a starting player on the Syracuse Nationals but he was not selected to the NBA All Star team in 1960–61. Would the outcome have been different if Barnett were the twelfth man on a team with twelve players? What if Barnett were playing for a semi-professional club or an inferior professional league and abandoned his contractual obligation to sign with an established NBA club? *See Connecticut Professional Sports Corp. v. Heyman*, 276 F. Supp. 618 (S.D.N.Y. 1967); *Dallas Cowboys Football Club, Inc. v. Harris*, 348 S.W.2d 37 (Tex. App. 1961); *see also Winnipeg Rugby Football Club v. Freeman*, 140 F. Supp. 365 (N.D. Ohio 1955).

7. Is Central New York Basketball Club, Inc. entitled to additional relief against Cleveland Basketball Club, Inc.? What cause of action might be pursued? Several years ago All-American basketball player Danny Ainge of Brigham Young University was wooed by both Major League Baseball and the National Basketball Association. After signing with the Toronto Blue Jays and playing during the spring and summer, he decided to abandon his contract and sign with the NBA's Boston Celtics. In 1981, Ainge played in 86 major league games for the Blue Jays, primarily at third base, and had a batting average of .187, the third worst average in the American League. The Blue Jays sued Ainge for breach of contract and the Celtics for tortious interference with contractual obligations. To succeed in an action for tortious interference, the jilted club must prove:

(1) there was an existing relationship between it and the athlete who was hired away;

(2) the defendant club or league interfered with that relationship in a manner which denied to the original employer benefits to which it was otherwise entitled;

(3) the new employer acted in knowing and intentional disregard of the existing relationship; and

(4) the original employer was damaged by the interference.

WEISTART & LOWELL § 4.14, at 398. What advantages are to be gained by suing the Celtics in tort as opposed to suing Ainge for breach of contract? The Restatement of Contracts declares unequivocally that punitive damages are unavailable as part of recovery for breach of contract: "Punitive damages are not recoverable for a breach of contract unless the conduct constituting the breach *is also a tort* for which punitive damages are recoverable." RESTATEMENT (SECOND) OF CONTRACTS § 355 (emphasis added). Bear in mind further that the statutes of limitations for contract and tort actions may be different. *See also American Present, Ltd. v. Hopkins,* 330 F. Supp. 2d 1217 (D. Colo. 2004); *Bauer v. Interpublic Group of Cos.,* 255 F. Supp. 2d 1086 (N.D. Cal. 2003).

8. In 1993, when Michael Jordan retired from the NBA to play baseball, with years remaining on his NBA contract, could the Chicago Bulls have prevented him from jumping sports? Would the Chicago Bulls have been obligated to show that they would suffer competitive harm from Jordan playing minor league baseball? If not, could the Bulls secure an injunction against Jordan working as an announcer, a coach, a team official, or in some other sports-related capacity? *See Matuszak v. Houston Oilers, Inc.,* 515 S.W.2d 725, 727, 729–30 (Tex. App. 1974) (appellate court affirmed the injunction against Matuszak jumping from the Oilers (NFL) to the Houston Texans (USFL) but modified the scope of the injunction; Matuszak was enjoined from playing football for anyone other than the Oilers, but the injunction against "engaging in activities related to football" was vacated).

9. On a similar note, when Magic Johnson left the NBA because of concerns about his HIV-positive status, he led a barnstorming basketball exhibition team on a tour around the world. If the Lakers could show that Johnson left voluntarily, could they enforce a restriction in his contract precluding him from playing in non-NBA basketball exhibitions? If Johnson began playing in exhibitions that were being televised in the United States, would your answer change? Why? *See Independent Entertainment Group v. NBA,* 853 F. Supp. 333 (C.D. Cal. 1994).

10. If the Bulls in the case of Michael Jordan or the Lakers in the case of Magic Johnson must prove competitive injury, what evidence would support such a claim? Many courts have held that an injunction may issue even when the new employer does not compete with the employer seeking the injunctive relief. *See New England Patriots Football Club, Inc. v. University of Colorado,* 592 F.2d 1196, 1200 (1st Cir. 1979). *See also, Northeastern Univ. v. Brown,* 17 Mass. L. Rptr. 443 (Mass. Super. Ct. 2004), below.

11. If you were the judge and the Cleveland Basketball Club, Inc. presented evidence that the ABL was a new, struggling league and it needed to attract quality NBA players to survive, would it affect your analysis? In fact, the ABL only survived a single season (the American Basketball Association ("ABA") came along several years later). *See Boston Professional Hockey Ass'n, Inc. v. Cheevers,* 348 F. Supp. 261, 268–70 (D. Mass. 1972); *see also Connecticut Professional Sports Corp. v. Heyman,* 276 F. Supp. 618 (S.D.N.Y. 1967).

12. The *Barnett* court follows the general view that proving damages to the requisite certainty in the context of an athlete's "contract jumping" is extremely difficult. However, in certain circumstances, courts may find that such damages are not speculative and that an adequate remedy at law exists. *See, e.g., Cheevers, supra.* Can you devise a formula or formulas to eliminate the uncertainty problem and recompense monetarily

the club whose contract the player breached? What if the court were to order the player to pay his former club the difference between his salary under his existing contract and the salary offered by the new club? Certainly an argument can be made that such an award is punitive in nature and beyond the remedial powers of the court in a breach of contract action. The club, however, would claim that the award is compensatory, giving it precisely what the player whose services had been pledged was worth. It has also been suggested that the jilted club would be entitled to the cost of replacing the breaching player. Criticism of this approach rests on the fact that this award in effect gives the former club a blank check and invites profligate spending at the expense of the breaching party. In this sense, this approach would also raise questions regarding the extent to which the "old" club would be required to mitigate damages in searching for a replacement. *See* Gary A. Uberstine, *The Enforceability of Sports Industry Employment Contracts, in* Law of Professional And Amateur Sports Ch. 9 (Gary A. Uberstine ed., 2002); Weistart & Lowell §4.09, at 366–69.

13. Players are not the only actors in the sports theater with a wanderlust. Coaches frequently find the grass greener on the other side of the court or campus. New York Knicks, Detroit Pistons, Philadelphia 76ers, and Kansas Jayhawks coach Larry Brown comes immediately to mind. Rules governing the enforcement of negative covenants precluding players from "jumping" contracts apply with equal force. Consider the following case.

Northeastern University v. Brown

17 Mass. L. Rptr. 443 (Mass. Super. Ct. 2004)

CONNOLLY, JUDGE. This civil action arises from an alleged case of "contract jumping" by Donald A. Brown, Jr., at the alleged instigation of and "tampering" by the University of Massachusetts at Amherst ("U. Mass.") and its athletic department.

* * *

Brown has been the head football coach at Northeastern University since 2000. On or about July 8, 2003, Northeastern entered into a written Employment Agreement ("Contract") with Brown pursuant to which Northeastern agreed to employ Brown as its head football coach through the end of the 2007–2008 football season. At the time that he signed the Contract in 2003, Brown and his assistant coaches received substantial salary increases from Northeastern.

Article VIII of the Contract, captioned "outside employment," provided as follows:

Coach [Brown] agrees to devote full time and effort to the University and agrees not to seek, discuss, negotiate for, or accept other employment during the term of this Agreement without first obtaining the written consent of the President of the University. Such consent shall not be unreasonably withheld.

Article IX of the Contract, captioned "Liquidated Damages," provides that, "except as otherwise noted herein," if Brown leaves Northeastern prior to the end of the contract period, then Brown "shall pay to the University as liquidated damages $25,000" and that in the event of an acceptance of such amount by Northeastern, it would be deemed to be "adequate and reasonable compensation to the University[.]"

In January 2004, six months after signing his contract with Northeastern, at the conclusion of the 2003–2004 football season, Brown told Northeastern's Athletic Director David O'Brien (O'Brien) that Brown wished to speak to another college (not U. Mass.)

from whom Brown claimed to have received an inquiry. O'Brien asked Brown "what it would take" to keep Brown from interviewing with that other college. Brown and O'Brien proceeded to discuss a one-year extension to Brown's contract, a raise in his and his staff's salaries, and other football program enhancements, and Brown agreed to those terms. Thereupon, Northeastern agreed to grant him a one-year extension to his contract and to enter into a new contract with him through June 2009 with concomitant salary increases.

However, before a contract could be drafted and signed, the Acting Athletic Director of U. Mass., Thorr Bjorn ("Bjorn"), called O'Brien to seek permission to speak to Brown about coaching football at U. Mass. O'Brien notified Bjorn that Northeastern would not grant permission and that Northeastern had a contractual right to prevent such discussions. The next day, O'Brien called Bjorn again and confirmed that O'Brien and Northeastern would not give permission to U. Mass. to speak with Brown.

On Friday evening, February 6, 2004, Brown called O'Brien and told O'Brien that U. Mass. Athletic Director John McCutcheon had offered him the U. Mass. football coaching job, that he, Brown, had accepted it, and that he then turned it down. Over the weekend of February 7–8, 2004, and although he had told several student football players that the rumors that he was leaving were not true, Brown cleared out his office. On Monday, February 9, 2004, Brown handed his letter of resignation to O'Brien, and O'Brien said that Northeastern would do what it needed to do to protect its legal rights.

Thereupon, U. Mass. issued a press release around 5:30 p.m. on Monday, February 9, 2004, to notify the newspapers and media outlets that it hired and signed Brown to be the new football coach at U. Mass. U. Mass. is a member of the same football conference as Northeastern, and the teams play each other every year. Northeastern's entire football program and its playbook will be available to U. Mass. Their recruitment practices and methods will be known to U. Mass. These two universities compete with each other in the same league, compete for fans to attend their games, compete for media coverage, compete for many of the same football recruits, and compete with each other for television to cover their games on a regional basis. There should be no doubt that college sports and the revenue that they draw are a major business for a university. At times, at some universities, football and basketball programs appear to be more important than the universities' duty to educate and their duty to instill in college students basic concepts of ethical conduct and adherence to legal and moral obligations.

DISCUSSION

There appears to the Court that there is no question that Brown willfully and intentionally breached his contract with Northeastern. He signed his contract and straight-out violated it. He gave his word to Northeastern and the student athletes that he was not leaving Northeastern when in fact, within a day, he was cleaning out his room to move to U. Mass. Unfortunately for Northeastern, its student athletes, and its football program, Brown's word was no good and his promises were lies. There also appears to be no question that U. Mass. actively induced the breach when it had been told of the restrictions on Brown's talking to other potential football employers and of his existing long-term contract with Northeastern.

At the hearing on these motions, counsel for Brown attempted to justify his client's actions by asserting that "everyone in collegiate football does this" and "what is the big deal?"

Well, a contract is a contract for major universities, just as it is for the rest of the world. This issue was discussed in detail in *New England Patriots v. University of Col-*

orado, 592 F.2d 1196 (1st Cir. 1979). That case involved the then Patriots head coach, Charles "Chuck" Fairbanks who decided unilaterally to breach his contract with the Patriots and to become the football coach for the University of Colorado. Id. at 1198. After an extensive discussion of Mr. Fairbanks' "explanations" for his breach of the contract and his word, the Court stated:

> Whatever may be thought rules elsewhere, the legal rules are clear. A contract is not avoided by crossed fingers behind one's back on signing, nor by unsupported and at once inconsistently self-deprecating and self-serving protests that the breach was to the other party's benefit.

Id. at 1199; see also *Boston Prof'l Hockey v. Cheevers,* 348 F. Supp. 261, 265 (1972).

Both defendants raise the issue that Article IX of the Contract contains a liquidated damage clause in the event that Brown leaves before the Contract is completed. The defendants claim that the $25,000 contained in the liquidated damage clause is all to which Northeastern is entitled. However, such a position runs counter to well-established Massachusetts case law. In *Rigs v. Sokol,* 318 Mass. 337, 342–43 (1945), the Court held that specific performance or an injunction may be granted to enforce a duty even though there is a provision for liquidated damages for breach of that duty.

> This result is reached on the assumption that the parties ordinarily contemplate that the contract be performed and that the provision for a penalty or liquidated damages in the event of a breach is intended as security for performance and not as a price for the privilege of nonperformance. A contract, of course, may provide for the payment of a fixed sum as an alternative to performance. Whether such a provision is merely security for the performance of the contract or an alternative to its performance depends upon the intention of the parties to be deduced from the whole instrument and the circumstances.

Id. at 343.

In this case, there is absolutely nothing to indicate that the liquidated damage clause in Article IX was intended as an alternate to performance. While Article IX does state that in the event of an acceptance of such amount by Northeastern, it would be deemed to be "adequate and reasonable compensation to the University[,]" Article IX deals with the money losses to Northeastern in the event Brown would leave as football coach. It appears to the Court that Article IX does not in any way prohibit injunctive relief, and merely deals with financial payments for money losses incurred by Brown for leaving the University and breaching the contract. Or, as stated in *Restatement (Second) of Contracts,* § 361: "Specific performance or an injunction may be granted to enforce a duty even though there is a provision for liquidated damages for breach of that duty."

Therefore, assuming that Brown breached his contract the Court must consider whether the circumstances warrant the issuance of injunctive relief * * *

The judge initially evaluates in combination the moving party's claim of injury and chance of success on the merits. If the judge is convinced that failure to issue the injunction would subject the moving party to a substantial risk of irreparable harm, the judge must then balance this risk against any similar risk of irreparable harm which granting the injunction would create for the opposing party. What matters as to each party is not the raw amount of irreparable harm the party might conceivably suffer, but rather the risk of such harm in light of the party's chance of success on the merits.

Here, there is strong evidence of irreparable harm to be sustained by Northeastern and its football program. Brown knows the program, the plays, and the set procedures used at Northeastern, and he will be able to use his knowledge of same against Northeastern. Northeastern and U. Mass. compete to recruit the same student athletes and compete with each other on a regional basis for television coverage for their games. As noted, U. Mass. and Northeastern are members of the same football conference, and they play each other each year. There is a strong showing of irreparable harm by Northeastern just as there was to the Patriots in *New England Patriots, 592 F.2d at 1199.*

Further, Northeastern has shown indisputably that it is likely to prevail on the merits. The breach of contract is as clear as it was by Mr. Fairbanks in *New England Patriots.* See *id. at 1198.*

On the other hand, the harm to Brown would be that he would not be able to be the football coach at U. Mass. The harm to U. Mass. would be that it would not be able to employ Brown as its football coach. The breach of contract by Brown was and is obvious, brazen, and defiant. U. Mass., as the Commonwealth's premier higher educational institution was and is likewise callous in its duty to provide ethical and moral values for its students. The persons from U. Mass. involved in this episode have clearly violated the law but above all else have brought great shame on themselves and the university. This Court finds that the irreparable harm suffered by Northeastern and its probable chance of success on the merits far outweigh the irreparable harm, if any, to Brown or U. Mass. and their negligible chance, if any, to prevail in this case.

After consideration, it appears to the Court that at this time, an injunction directed to the defendant, Donald A. Brown, Jr., will suffice to achieve the result needed in this case. A preliminary injunction will not at this time issue directed to U. Mass., and said request is denied without prejudice. A preliminary injunction will issue to the defendant, Donald A. Brown, Jr.

ORDER

The defendant, Donald A. Brown, Jr., is *ORDERED* to cease, desist, and refrain from working as an employee, consultant, aide, assistant or in any other capacity for the defendant, University of Massachusetts until further order of this Court.

The request for a preliminary injunction directed to the University of Massachusetts is *DENIED* without prejudice.

Notes and Questions

1. It is noteworthy that the court granted the injunction even though the contract contained a liquidated damages clause. Is this conclusion counter-intuitive? Does the liquidated damages clause provide an adequate remedy at law?

2. In balancing the equities, the court found that the denial of the injunction would cause far greater harm to the plaintiff than the issuance would cause for the defendant. In evaluating the harm, the court took note of the fact that the "tampering" school and the plaintiff were members of the same conference and played each other annually. Would this case have been decided differently if the defendant had accepted a coaching position in the Southwest or PAC-10 conference? Probably not. *See New England Patriots v. Univ. of Colorado, 592 F.2d 1196 (1st Cir. 1979).*

3. There is little doubt that coaching is not a job for those individuals seeking stability and job security. Even coaches who boast outstanding win-loss records have found themselves holding the proverbial pink slip. Does recognition of this fact prompt many

coaches to adopt a lifestyle in which mobility for self and family becomes part of their *raison d'etre*? Correspondingly, does it contribute to their omnipresent desire to seek better opportunities even when their job seems secure—reasoning "if I am going to move, I am going to move upward and on my terms." Would guaranteed long-term contracts or even tenure at the college level curtail some of the insecurity and resultant wanderlust? It certainly would place coaches in the university mainstream and perhaps shrink the distance between the gym and the library. Another positive by-product of granting coaches tenure is the possibility that job security will eliminate untoward recruiting practices and enhance reform to some degree in college athletics. *See* MICHAEL J. COZZILLIO AND ROBERT L. HAYMAN, JR., SPORTS AND INEQUALITY 551 (2005).

4. Was the University of Massachusetts guilty of tortious interference in this case? Could the court have awarded punitive damages? *See* RESTATEMENT (SECOND) OF CONTRACTS § 355.

5. The nether world of professional boxing is replete with incidents of participants attempting to escape contractual obligations to fight one opponent often due to the appeal of a belated but better deal elsewhere. Doubtless, these incidents arise due to the mysteries that surround boxing promotions, checkered pasts of the promoters themselves, and the alphabet soup of sanctioning organizations that govern the countless weight classes and divisions. The following case gives a flavor of the types of controversies that have surfaced.

Madison Square Garden Boxing, Inc. v. Shavers
434 F. Supp. 449 (S.D.N.Y. 1977)

OWEN, District Judge. Before me is a motion by plaintiff Madison Square Garden Boxing, Inc. (the Garden) for a preliminary injunction enjoining defendant Earnie Shavers, heavyweight championship contender, from participating in any boxing match until he fulfills his contractual obligations to plaintiff.

On June 23, 1977, I held a hearing at which Teddy Brenner of the Garden, Earnie Shavers, and Frank Luca, Shavers' business manager, testified. Also before me were various documents and affidavits. Because of time pressure, I notified the parties on Friday, June 24th, that the preliminary injunction was granted. In conformity with Rule 52(a), I now state my findings of fact and conclusions of law.

The Garden has an option contract with Muhammed Ali for a heavyweight championship bout to take place between September 1 and October 10, 1977. This option will expire on July 1, 1977 unless the Garden exercises the option by June 30, 1977.

The Garden, through Teddy Brenner, its matchmaker, entered into negotiations with Frank Luca, Shavers' business manager, for this championship fight. By about May 16, the parties were in essential agreement. In a telephone conversation between Brenner and Luca, Brenner asked Luca to send him a telegram accepting the Garden's offer. A telegram, set out in the margin,[1] signed by Shavers, Luca and Joseph Gennaro, Shavers' manager, "accepted" the Garden's "offer."

---

1. EARNIE SHAVERS WILL BOX MUHAMMED ALI FOR THE HEAVYWEIGHT CHAMPIONSHIP OF THE WORLD IN MADISON SQUARE GARDEN ON OR BEFORE OCTOBER 10 1977. SHAVERS IS TO RECEIVE A MINIMUM GUARANTEE OF $200,000.00 IF BOUT IS NOT SIGNED FOR BY JUNE 15 1977 $10,000.00 WILL BE FORFEITED TO SHAVERS. SHAVERS WILL GRANT MADISON SQUARE GARDEN BOXING OPTION OF FIRST REFUSAL ON FIRST AND SECOND TITLE DEFENSES AT TERMS MUTUALLY AGREEABLE. THANK YOU

Upon receipt of and in reliance upon this telegram, the Garden reached a multi-million dollar agreement with the National Broadcasting Company to televise the fight.

The next day Brenner prepared a "letter agreement" to "document the substance of an understanding between us." This letter agreement differed from the telegram in certain particulars:

(a) The date for the exercise of the option was extended from June 15 to July 1, 1977;

(b) The purse was set as a "total amount of $200,000" instead of "a minimum guarantee of $200,000;"

(c) There was an express non-competition clause.

On or about May 23, 1977, Brenner telephoned Luca to check that everything was in order and ask if the letter agreement had been signed. The parties worked out certain discrepancies during this conversation:

(a) The option date was extended to July 1, 1977 to coordinate with the Ali option;

(b) Shavers' compensation beyond the $200,000 was to include both closed-circuit television rights in Ohio if the bout was telecast on closed-circuit, and Shavers' training expenses at Grossingers which would normally be paid by Luca and Gennaro, as well as some other minor extras such as tickets and fare, about which I did not take testimony;

(c) There was no discussion of the non-competition clause. I find that, given the eight week training period necessary to prepare for a title bout and the practice in the industry, this term would have been implied, if it had not been expressly stated.

At this point in their conversation, I find that the contract in its final form was agreed upon. The parties "had a deal," even though the letter agreement was never signed by Shavers, Luca and Gennaro.

Luca *then* asked to "borrow" $30,000 (get an advance on the purse of $30,000). Brenner said he could guarantee him $20,000 but would have to discuss the remaining $10,000 with Michael Burke, president of Madison Square Garden, and would get back to him. There was a delay of one and one-half days in this since Brenner's attentions were directed elsewhere, and by the time Brenner was able to reach Luca, Luca told him that he had an offer from Robert Arum, president of Top Rank, Inc., for $300,000 for an Ali-Shavers fight during the same time period. The Top Rank contract, which was signed on May 26, stated that if Top Rank could not get the Ali fight, it promised to get one of several other fighters for the same $300,000 purse to Shavers. Shavers has received a $30,000 advance on this contract.

Both Luca and Shavers testified before me that they did not consider that they had a deal until they *had* the $30,000 advance. I do not credit their testimony. The advance was not mentioned in the telegram. Luca also testified that he specifically told Brenner that not only was there no deal until they received the advance, but also that until that time they would continue to negotiate with Top Rank. Brenner denies being told this and I credit him. I observed both men on the witness stand. It is inconceivable that Brenner—knowledgeable, energetic and vocal—having an option agreement with Ali which would expire on July 1 and a multi-million dollar contract in hand for television rights to the fight with NBC, would not have pinned down this alleged last item of the deal if Luca had told him what he says he told him. I reject Luca's version of this conversation.

While I have not *heard* the testimony of Robert Arum, from the affidavit of Commissioner Floyd Patterson of the New York State Athletic Commission, sworn to on June 20, 1977 and which I credit, I find it is more likely so than not so that Luca was misled into believing that Arum had the Garden's "blessings" in negotiating the subsequent contract. Besides the conversation when Commissioner Patterson was on the line, Luca also stated to Brenner on other occasions that Arum had told him that Top Rank and the Garden were partners.

It is also significant that Luca, after speaking with his lawyer, DiBlasio, told Brenner, in the presence of both Brenner's lawyer and his own, that he "had been told by Mr. DiBlasio that if you had to be sued by either one, he would prefer that it were the Garden rather than Top Rank"* * *.

On June 13, 1977, the parties, as well as Top Rank, appeared before the New York State Athletic Commission, at which time testimony was taken. On June 15, the Commission issued its opinion finding a binding contract between the Garden and Shavers, which it approved. While I would in no event be bound by the Commission's decision, it obviously is in accord with my findings, and I note that the Commission has expertise in practices in the trade, which enables it to authoritatively view the acts of the parties in context.[9]

The relationship between the parties is clearly governed by New York law. Under the law of New York and as viewed by others in this Court, the granting of negative injunctive relief in personal services contracts involving athletes is discretionary and first requires a finding by the trial court that the contract terms, including the restrictive negative covenant,[11] are not "unduly harsh or one-sided," *Connecticut Professional Sports Corp. v. Heyman*, 276 F. Supp. 618, 620 (S.D.N.Y.1967), and that the enforcement of the negative restrictive covenant would not unreasonably burden the party to be enjoined * * *.

I make such findings here. No one argues to the contrary, and I conclude that the terms of the agreement between the parties are fair and reasonable and that Shavers' purse is consistent with his being a contender for the heavyweight title. There is no question here of overreaching or unequal bargaining power between the parties. Furthermore, it would not unreasonably burden Shavers to enjoin him from fighting until October 11 or such earlier time as the agreement with the Garden is satisfied, since Shavers is protected by the required $100,000 bond plaintiff has already posted and therefore is assured of his due if he performs under the agreement with the Garden, even if ultimately he prevails in his position that there was no contract between himself and plaintiff.

Next, I conclude that plaintiff has satisfied its burden under *Sonesta International Hotels Corp. v. Wellington Associates*, 483 F.2d 247 (2d Cir. 1973), having shown the probability of ultimate success on the contractual issue before me. Also, not only is Shavers not injured by the granting of the preliminary injunction in view of the $100,000 bond * * *, but the Garden is, to a measurable extent, irreparably injured as a viable promoter of major boxing matches were Shavers with impunity able to simply

---

9. I also note that I find it more likely so than not so that Luca had agreed with Brenner when they met at the Cleveland Airport with their lawyers on June 4 to submit the dispute to the Commission to decide.

11. It is beyond question that Earnie Shavers' talents are "unusual, unique [and] extraordinary" and, accordingly, a negative covenant not to fight except as provided in the agreement with plaintiff will be implied in the event it is not explicitly so provided * * *.

disavow a prior agreement with the Garden to take advantage of a later-made more attractive offer. The Garden's credibility could be destroyed in the eyes of boxing managers, as well as various media representatives, such as television producers, or others, who, in reliance, enter into further contracts that in fact may well represent the major source of income from the event being promoted, possibly being the difference between profit and loss for the promoter. In any event, it is beyond question that the balance of hardships is in the Garden's favor.

Given the foregoing, the preliminary injunction is granted.

So Ordered.

Notes and Questions

1. Why did the court find "preliminarily" that Madison Square Garden did not have a right of first refusal with respect to Shavers' first two title defenses if he defeated Ali?

2. Is the negative covenant contained in this case overly broad? *See Machen v. Johansson*, 174 F. Supp. 522 (S.D.N.Y. 1959); *Madison Square Garden Corp. v. Braddock*, 19 F. Supp. 392 (D.N.J. 1937), *aff'd on other grounds*, 90 F.2d 924 (3d Cir. 1937). It is noteworthy that the court described the negative covenant and the relief requested as "enjoining defendant Earnie Shavers, heavyweight championship contender, from participating in any boxing match until he fulfills his contractual obligations to the plaintiff." Were the negative covenant to be construed this broadly, it may fail because the duration is indefinite and the timeframe is unconscionably long. The court itself acknowledged that the negative covenant will not be enforced if it is "unduly harsh or one-sided" or if it would unreasonably burden the party to be enjoined. Here, the court granted the injunction but precluded Shavers from fighting until October 11 or such earlier time as the agreement with the Garden was satisfied. Is this the injunction that the plaintiff sought, and is it what the negative covenant precludes Shavers from doing? It appears as though the court has employed the device of blue-penciling, or narrowing the contract by construction, so as to validate the negative covenant, which, if construed literally, would have been overly broad.

3. Why is blue-penciling frowned upon by many courts? The device is frequently employed in interpreting covenants not to compete where such covenants are outrageous and unconscionable on their face and thus are unworthy of enforcement as written. Courts may modify the harsh language to minimize the hardship of the covenant's enforcement. For example, Massachusetts courts prefer to redact the offensively broad covenant. Rather than rejecting it outright, they enforce it in a fashion that they deem reasonable. *See Nassau Sports v. Peters*, 352 F. Supp. 870 (E.D.N.Y. 1972); *Wrentham Co. v. Cann*, 189 N.E.2d 559 (Mass. 1963). Many jurisdictions, however, disdain this "blue penciling" approach, reasoning that it could have the unfortunate *in terrorem* impact of promoting the drafting of unconscionable covenants because the drafter would be assured that the covenant in some form will be enforced. It becomes a no-lose proposition for the party who has insisted upon the overly broad covenant. If, on the other hand, a court were to reject unconscionable negative covenants outright, it would encourage the parties to draft reasonable restrictions on the ability of each side to compete. *See, e.g., White v. Fletcher/Mayo/Associates*, 303 S.E.2d 746 (Ga. 1983). *Compare BDO Seidman v. Hirshberg*, 712 N.E.2d 1220 (N.Y. 1999).

4. Early in the opinion, the court concluded, "I find that the contract in its final form was agreed upon. The parties had a deal, even though the letter agreement was never

signed by Shavers, Luca and Gennaro." Why did the Statute of Frauds not apply in this case? Was the agreement of indefinite duration? If so, should it have been enforced? If not, what was the duration? *See* Note 7, *supra*, 178-79.

5. In footnote 11, the court reasoned that Earnie Shavers' talents are "'unusual, unique [and] extraordinary,' and accordingly, a negative covenant not to fight except as provided in the agreement with plaintiff will be implied in the event it is not explicitly so provided." Thus, the court suggested that, simply because Earnie Shavers satisfied the uniqueness component, he had *a fortiori* satisfied the negative covenant component by implication. Thus, if some courts will assume that one's very status as a professional athlete is indicative of his uniqueness, and if this uniqueness were to create the assumption that an implied negative covenant exists, then it is a short road to develop a theory that says a club has an automatic right to an injunction whenever a professional athlete jumps a contract. Could this be what the court intended in footnote 11? Perhaps so, because many courts, recognizing that the breach of a personal services contract is not conducive to any type of affirmative injunction and that damages are very difficult to ascertain, may want to clear the path for the jilted party to secure some type of meaningful relief. Yet, it should not be assumed that every breach of a personal service contract will result in some type of negative injunctive relief. *See Star Boxing, Inc. v. Tarver*, 2002 U.S. Dist. LEXIS 24506 (S.D.N.Y. 2002).

Several years after *Shavers*, a federal court reinforced the notion that a negative covenant could be inferred where the services of the athlete in question were unique. In *Lewis v. Rahman,*dethroned heavyweight champion Lennox Lewis sued his victor Hasim Rahman to enjoin him from engaging in any heavyweight fights for 18 months unless and until Rahman complied with his contractual obligations to fight a rematch. *Lewis v. Rahman*, 147 F. Supp. 2d 225 (S.D.N.Y. 2001). As heavyweight champion, Rahman could not escape the conclusion that he was unique and extraordinary. *Id.* at 234. The court declared further that "a negative covenant will be implied where the party from whom performance is sought is a unique and extraordinary talent." *Id.* No mystery thus surrounds the court's finding of irreparable injury and the granting of Lewis' injunction request. There, however, the injunction request did not appear to be as broad and open-ended as the one in *Shavers*. Further, because the covenant was implied, there was no need to blue pencil; *i.e.*, there would be no point served in judicially deriving or constructing an overly expansive covenant. The facts of this case illustrate the complexities of arranging boxing matches in the modern eras. One truly cannot identify the players without a scorecard. Of particular note in this regard is that Lewis secured his contract rights as a third party beneficiary.

6. In the *Shavers* case, who acted as Shavers's promoter for the fight? Who was Shavers's manager? Historically, owners of facilities promoted boxing matches and contracted directly with each fighter, through the fighter's manager. During the 1970s and 1980s, "independent" boxing promoters like Bob Arum and Don King began to promote fights. The independent promoters contracted with the fighters and the facility owners (arenas, stadia, casinos, etc.) Recently, facility owners such as Steve Wynn (owner the Mirage Hotel (and casino), among others in Las Vegas) have tried to eliminate the role of the independent promoters by having the facility again contract directly with the fighter's manager. For a discussion of the roles occupied by fight managers and promoters, *see George Foreman Associates, Ltd. v. Foreman*, 389 F. Supp. 1308 (N.D. Cal. 1974).

7. Professional boxers, however, still contract with fight promoters, and negative injunctions have been granted in those contexts as well. In *Marchio, supra*, boxing promoter Alfredo Marchio, sued boxer Julian Letterlough and his manager. *Marchio v. Let-*

terlough 237 F.Supp.2d 580 (E.D.Pa 2002). Letterlough and Marchio had previously entered into an exclusive promotional agreement, but Letterlough sought to employ the services of another promoter. Marchio sought to enjoin Letterlough from engaging in professional bouts promoted by someone else. 237 F. Supp. 2d at 581. Although noting its reluctance to grant any kind of injunction because personal services were involved, the court found that Marchio had a legal interest in promoting this particular, unique boxer. *Id.* at 590. The court fashioned a limited remedy, circumscribing the injunctive relief to a certain date and requiring Letterlough merely to indicate that fights were either promoted or co-promoted by Marchio. *Id.*

9. The Letterlough story unfortunately has a tragic ending. He was shot and killed in Reading, Pennsylvania, on July 8, 2005.

Boston Celtics Limited Partnership v. Shaw

908 F.2d 1041 (1st Cir. 1990)

BREYER, Chief Judge. On January 23, 1990, Brian Shaw signed a contract with the owners of the Boston Celtics (the "Celtics") in which he promised that he would cancel his commitment to play for an Italian basketball team next year so that he could play for the Celtics instead. When Shaw threatened to break his agreement with the Celtics, they immediately sought arbitration. The arbitrator found that Shaw must keep his promise. The Players Association that represents Shaw agreed with the arbitrator. The Celtics then asked the federal district court to enforce the arbitrator's decision. The court ordered it enforced.

Shaw now appeals the district court's order. We have examined the arbitration award, the district court's determination, the briefs, and the record. We conclude that the district court's decision is lawful, and we affirm it * * *.

The basic facts, which are not in dispute, include the following:

(a) In 1988, soon after Shaw graduated from college, he signed a one-year contract to play for the Celtics.

(b) In 1989, Shaw signed a two-year contract to play with the Italian team Il Messaggero Roma ("Il Messaggero"). The team agreed to pay him $ 800,000 for the first year and $ 900,000 for the second year. The contract contains a clause permitting Shaw to cancel the second year (1990–91). It says that Shaw has the right to rescind the second year of this Agreement * * * [if he] returns to the United States to play with the NBA * * * by delivering a registered letter to [Il Messaggero] * * * between June 20, 1990 and July 20, 1990.

(c) At the end of January 1990 Shaw signed a five-year "Uniform Player Contract" with the Celtics. The contract contains standard clauses negotiated by the National Basketball Association ("NBA") franchise owners and the National Basketball Players Association (the "Players Association"). It adopts by cross-reference arbitration provisions contained in the NBA-Players Association Collective Bargaining Agreement. In the contract, the Celtics promise Shaw a $ 450,000 signing bonus and more than $ 1 million per year in compensation. In return, Shaw promises the Celtics, among other things, that he will cancel his second year with Il Messaggero. The contract says that the Player [i.e., Shaw] and Club [i.e., the Celtics] acknowledge that Player is currently under contract with Il Messaggero Roma (the "Messaggero Contract") for the 1989–90 & 1990–91 playing seasons. The Player represents that in accordance with the terms of the Messaggero Contract, the Player has the right to rescind that contract prior to the 1990–91 season and the player hereby agrees to exercise such right of rescission in the manner and at the time called for by the Messaggero Contract.

(Emphasis added.)

(d) On June 6, 1990, Shaw told the Celtics that he had decided to play for Il Messaggero during the 1990–91 season and that he would not exercise his right of rescission * * *.

On June 11, 1990, the Celtics invoked their right under the Collective Bargaining Agreement (cross-referenced in the Contract) to an "expedited" arbitration proceeding. The arbitrator held a two-day hearing on June 13 and 14. He found that Shaw's refusal to rescind the Il Messaggero contract violated Shaw's contract with the Celtics. He ordered Shaw to rescind the Il Messaggero contract (on June 20) and not to play for any team other than the Celtics during the term of his Celtics contract. On June 15, Shaw said he still did not intend to rescind the Il Messaggero contract.

The Celtics responded immediately by asking the federal district court to use its authority under §301 of the Labor Management Relations Act, 29 U.S.C. §185, to enforce the award, * * * and the parties no longer dispute that §301 applies. The Celtics asked the court for "expedited enforcement" of the award and for a preliminary injunction. After receiving Shaw's response (in the form of an opposition, a motion to dismiss, a brief, and supporting affidavits), and after holding an oral hearing, on June 26, the court granted the Celtics' motion to expedite, ordered Shaw to cancel the Il Messaggero agreement "forthwith," and "enforced" the award. Shaw now appeals this district court decision, attacking both the preliminary injunction and the order enforcing the arbitration award.

* * *

Shaw says that the district court should not have enforced the arbitrator's award because that award was itself unlawful, for any of five separate reasons * * *.

Shaw argues that the arbitrator could not reasonably find that he broke a contractual promise to the Celtics because, he says, the Celtics had previously agreed with the Players Association that contracts with individual players such as Shaw would not contain promises of the sort here at issue, namely, a promise to cancel a contract to play with a different team. Shaw says that this previous agreement between the Celtics and the Players Association renders his promise to terminate Il Messaggero "null and void." To support this argument, he points to Article I, section 2 of the Collective Bargaining Agreement, which Shaw and the Celtics, through cross-reference, made part of their individual agreement. Section 2 says, "Any amendment to a Uniform Player Contract [of the type Shaw and the Celtics used], other than those permitted by this [Collective Bargaining] Agreement, shall be null and void." The Agreement permits amendments (a) "in * * * respect to the compensation * * * to be paid the player," (b) "in respect to specialized compensation arrangements," (c) in respect to a "compensation payment schedule," and (d) in respect to "protect[ion]" of compensation in the event of contract termination. Shaw says that his promise to cancel the Il Messaggero agreement was an amendment to the Uniform Players Contract that does not concern compensation, specialized compensation, compensation schedules, or compensation protection; therefore, it is "null and void" * * *.

Shaw's argument, while logical, fails to show that the arbitrator's contrary finding is unlawful. The reasons it fails are fairly straightforward. First, the argument concerns the proper interpretation of a contract negotiated pursuant to a collective bargaining agreement. Second, federal labor law gives arbitrators, not judges, the power to interpret such contracts. The Supreme Court, noting the strong federal policy favoring the voluntary settlement of labor disputes, has written that a labor arbitration award is valid so long as it "draws its essence" from the labor contract. *See United Steelworkers v. Enterprise Wheel & Car Corp.*, 363 U.S. 593, 597 (1960). An award "draws its essence" from the contract so long as the "arbitrator is even arguably construing or applying the contract and acting within the scope of his authority." *United Paperworkers Int'l v. Misco*, 484 U.S. 29, 38 (1987). We have held that "this language makes clear that any 'exception' to the normal rule (that forbids the court to find an arbitrator's interpretation outside the authority delegated to him by the contract) is extremely narrow." *Crafts Precision Indus., Inc. v. Lodge No. 1836, Int'l Assoc. of Machinists*, 889 F.2d 1184, 1185 (1st Cir. 1989). Consequently, "we shall uphold an arbitrator's interpretation of a contract as long as we can find some 'plausible argument that favors his interpretation.'" *Id.*

Third, one can find "plausible arguments" favoring the arbitrator's construction. Shaw's "rescission" promise defines the beginning of the compensation relationship. It also plausibly determines, at the very least, whether Shaw's compensation will begin at $ 1.1 million (and continue for three years) or whether it will begin at $ 1.2 million (and continue for only two years). *See* Appendix, *infra* (describing compensation schedule). More importantly, and also quite plausibly, Shaw's overall compensation might have been much different had he declined to promise to play for the Celtics in 1990–91, thereby forcing the Celtics, perhaps, to obtain the services of a replacement for that year. The NBA Commissioner, who reviews all player contracts, found that the term was related to "compensation," as did the arbitrator. We cannot say that their findings lack any "plausible" basis.

* * *

The district court, as we have pointed out, issued a preliminary injunction requiring Shaw to rescind "forthwith" his contract with Il Messaggero and forbidding him to play basketball for any team other than the Celtics during the term of his Celtics contract. The court also "enforced" an arbitration award containing essentially the same terms. Shaw argues that both the preliminary injunction and the enforcement order are unlawful. Since the district court correctly upheld the award's validity, Shaw's only remaining arguments are that the district court lacked discretion to award preliminary injunctive relief and that it mismanaged the proceedings below. We discuss both points briefly * * *.

The disputed award in this case resulted from arbitration procedures contained in a collective bargaining agreement between a labor organization (the Players Association) and an employers' association (the NBA). Shaw bound himself to that collective bargaining agreement in his contract with the Celtics, the terms of which are themselves a product of collective bargaining between employees and employers. Well-established public policy embodied in statute, see 29 U.S.C. §172(d), in Supreme Court decisions, see *United Steelworkers v. American Mfg. Co.*, 363 U.S. 564 (1960); *United Steelworkers v. Warrior & Gulf Navigation Co.*, 363 U.S. 574 (1960); *United Steelworkers v. Enterprise Wheel & Car Corp., supra*, and in numerous lower court opinions, strongly favors judicial action to "effectuate[]* * *the means chosen by the parties for settlement of their differences under a collective bargaining agreement* * *." *American Mfg. Co.*, 363 U.S. at 566. That judicial action clearly may include a preliminary injunction enforcing an arbitration award, * * * even if such a preliminary injunction gives the plaintiff all the relief it seeks.

The only legal question before us, therefore, is whether the district court acted outside its broad equitable powers when it issued the preliminary injunction. That is to say, did the court improperly answer the four questions judges in this Circuit must ask when deciding whether to issue a preliminary injunction. They are: (1) have the Celtics shown a likelihood of success on the merits? (2) have they shown that failure to issue the injunction would cause the Celtics "irreparable harm?" (3) does the "balance of harms" favor Shaw or the Celtics? and (4) will granting the injunction harm the "public interest?" Our examination of the record has convinced us that the court acted well within the scope of its lawful powers.

To begin with, the Celtics have shown a clear likelihood of success on the merits. As we pointed out in section "A," the arbitration award is lawful, and courts have authority to enforce lawful arbitration awards. The Celtics also have demonstrated irreparable harm. Without speedy relief, they will likely lose the services of a star athlete next year* * *and, unless they know fairly soon whether Shaw will, or will not play for them, they will find it difficult to plan intelligently for next season. Indeed, in his contract Shaw expressly represents and agrees that he has extraordinary and unique skill and ability as a basketball player, * * * and that any breach by the Player of this contract will cause irreparable injury to the Club.

Further, the court could reasonably find that the "balance of harms" favors the Celtics. Of course, a preliminary injunction, if ultimately shown wrong on the merits, could cause Shaw harm. He might lose the chance to play in the country, and for the team, that he prefers. On the other hand, this harm is somewhat offset by the fact that ultimate success on the merits—*i.e.*, a finding that Shaw was not obligated to terminate Il Messaggero after all—would likely result in the following scenario: Shaw might still be able to sign with Il Messaggero and, if not, he would always have the Celtics contract of over $ 5 million to fall back upon. At the same time, the court's failure to issue the injunction, if the merits ultimately favored the Celtics, could cause them serious harm of the sort just mentioned (*i.e.*, significantly increased difficulty in planning their team for next season). Given the very small likelihood that Shaw would ultimately prevail on the merits, and the "comparative" harms at stake, the district court could properly decide that the overall "balance" favored the Celtics, not Shaw.

Finally, the court could properly find that issuing a preliminary injunction would not harm the public interest. Indeed, as we have pointed out, the public interest favors court action that "effectuates" the parties' intent to resolve their disputes informally through arbitration * * *.Where the dispute involves a professional basketball player's obligation to play for a particular team, one could reasonably consider expeditious, informal and effective dispute-resolution methods to be essential, and, if so, the public interest favoring court action to "effectuate" those methods of dispute-resolution would seem at least as strong as it is in respect to work-related disputes typically arising under collective bargaining agreements. Shaw, while conceding that the public also has an interest in seeing that contracts between consenting adults are honored, points to a general policy disfavoring enforcement of personal service contracts. That latter policy, however, typically prevents a court from ordering an individual to perform a personal service, it does not prevent a court from ordering an individual to rescind a contract for services and to refrain from performing a service for others.

* * *

At the same time the court issued the preliminary injunction, it also ordered the arbitration award enforced. The enforcement award was the equivalent of a permanent injunction and amounted to a final judgment on the merits. This action made consider-able practical sense, for the preliminary injunction and the enforcement order, as we understand them, amounted to the same thing. Once the preliminary injunction issued, the case was virtually over for Shaw and he had lost. Nevertheless, Shaw argues that even if the preliminary injunction was lawful, the order enforcing the award was not proper, for, in Shaw's view, the entry of that final order so soon after the complaint was filed, deprived him of certain important procedural rights. In particular, he says that granting enforcement of the award was like granting the Celtics summary judgment. The Federal Rules of Civil Procedure normally require the plaintiff to wait 20 days be-fore moving for summary judgment, see Fed.R.Civ.P. 56, and only 11 days elapsed be-tween the filing of the complaint and the court's decision.

In our view, Shaw's argument is unduly formal. The important question, in respect to time limits such as those Shaw cites, is whether failure to observe them somehow in-jured Shaw. Was he prevented from making a defense he might otherwise have made? Was he unable to prove a critical fact that he might otherwise have been able to show? Shaw indicated his awareness that the district court might award relief on an expedited basis. He presented affidavits, statements, and arguments. We have not found anywhere in the record any offer by counsel to produce additional specific, significant factual evi-dence or information. We asked counsel at oral argument whether Shaw had additional evidence that might have affected the district court's decision, and he could not point to anything not already in the record.

* * *

We add that the case before us, while arising in the world of professional sports, in-volves a collective bargaining agreement between employees and employers, an agree-ment that provides for expedited arbitration. The Supreme Court has frequently em-phasized the importance of permitting unions and employers to create informal dispute-resolution mechanisms that satisfy both, and it has given courts broad author-ity to ensure that those agreed-upon mechanisms are effective.

* * *

In our view, the legal principles that grant courts broad powers to enforce arbitration agreements and to use their contempt powers or equitable powers, even enjoining strikes, all in support of arbitration, permit the district court's expedited enforcement of the arbitration award. The court used procedures that preserved basic fairness while permitting the resolution of a dispute in the expeditious manner called for by the cir-cumstances and the parties' own agreement. * * *

Notes and Questions

1. In this case, the plaintiff, Boston Celtics, invoked their prerogative under the col-lective bargaining agreement and sought an expedited arbitration. In some collective bargaining agreements the clubs reserve the right to bypass the contractual grievance mechanism and seek an injunction precluding the breaching player from honoring his contract to the new club. The "reservation" eliminates the possibility of the defendant player claiming that the injunction request is wanting because the club has failed to ex-haust its remedies under the collective bargaining agreement.

2. After the club was successful in its arbitration, it sought enforcement of the arbi-trator's award in U.S. district court. In addition to claiming that the court exceeded its equitable powers in granting the injunction, Shaw argued that the enforcement of the

arbitration award was inappropriate because it deprived him of procedural due process. Specifically, Shaw argued that the enforcement of the award within 11 days of the complaint gave the plaintiff the constructive equivalent of a summary judgment to which it would not have been entitled for at least 20 days under the Federal Rules of Civil Procedure. Is Shaw correct or does his argument, as the court suggests, elevate form over substance? To what degree was the court's off-handed dismissal of Shaw's argument fueled by a desire to reinforce the contractual grievance machinery as a legitimate and, in fact, preferred *modus operandi* to resolve disputes of this type?

3. As a final thrust in his defense, Shaw argued that the Boston Celtics had "unclean hands" and, because "he who seeks equity must do equity," they should be denied injunctive relief. Shaw contended that the Celtics took advantage of him at a weak moment when he was "homesick," disturbed by purportedly undeserved criticism from the Italian press, and unrepresented by an agent. He was also supposedly unaware at the time of his signing that, if he had honored the final year of his contract in Italy, he would become a free agent, eligible to sign with any club in the NBA. The court took a dim view of Shaw's protests and dismissed his claims of vulnerability:

> [E]vidence in the record * * * which Shaw does not deny, shows that he is a college graduate; that he has played under contract with the Celtics before; that the contract is a standard form contract except for a few * * * rather clear, additions * * *; that he had bargained with the Celtics for an offer that increased from $3.4 million to $5.4 million (less than one month later); that he looked over the contract before signing it; that he told the American consul in Rome (as he signed it) that he had read and understood it; and that he did not complain about the contract until he told the Celtics in June that he would not honor it. Given this state of the record, the district court could easily and properly conclude that the Celtics' hands were not unclean.

908 F.2d *at* 1049.

4. If the Celtics had sued Shaw for damages, could he have sought to avoid the contract based on the same facts that were offered in support of his unclean hands defense? What legal theory would you advance in support of his claim?

5. Although the court rejected Shaw's unclean hands defense, this argument has occasionally been raised successfully in cases involving professional athletes who seek to avoid an injunction. Because this defense necessitates a balancing of equities and imprecise "fair-play" determinations, there are few absolute rules governing when the defense will prevail. In the following section, we see some approaches taken by the courts in this context.

6. At about the time that the *Shaw* dispute arose, the NBA and basketball's international governing body, Federation Internationale de Basketball ("FIBA"), entered into an agreement committing the NBA and its member teams to honor "validly binding player contracts" of "teams in leagues that are affiliated with members of Federations that are members of FIBA" and vice versa. *See Agreement Between NBA and FIBA* (May 9, 1990). The Agreement provides for all disputes to be resolved in arbitration proceedings, either in accordance with the arbitration provisions in the NBA's collective bargaining agreement with the NBPA or before an international arbitrator agreed to by the parties or appointed by the International Chamber of Commerce in Paris, France. The Agreement includes expedited procedures—a hearing within ten days and an award issued no later than seventy-two (72) hours after the conclusion of the hearing. The NBPA and the players are not parties to this agreement. Can it be enforced against

them? For a further discussion of the need to exhaust contractual remedies provided by a grievance/arbitration procedure, see *Sharpe v. NFLPA*, 941 F. Supp. 8 (D.D.C. 1996).

III. Unclean Hands Doctrine—A Defense to Plaintiff's Request for Injunctive Relief

It is a settled principle that "he who seeks equity must do equity." Frequently in the professional sports context, parties seek injunctive relief when they are *in pari delicto* or at least have failed to show that they are not partially at fault in terms of the ensuing litigation. In the succeeding cases, some courts take an almost puritanical approach to the unclean hands question, finding that plaintiffs are not entitled to invoke equity if they have failed to conduct themselves in both a morally and legally unobjectionable manner. *See, e.g., Weegham v. Killefer*, below. Other courts will enforce the injunction notwithstanding some untoward conduct on the part of the plaintiff, provided that the plaintiff has not engaged in any illegal activity. *See, e.g., Munchak Corp. v. Cunningham*, below. As you consider the following cases, contemplate the extent to which the courts, much like in the *Cannon* case addressed earlier, found the sophistication and vulnerabilities of the defendants to be determinative.

Weegham v. Killefer
215 F. 168 (W.D. Mich. 1914)

SESSIONS, District Judge. This record shows that the defendant, Killefer, is a baseball player of unique, exceptional, and extraordinary skill and expertness. Unfortunately, the record also shows that he is a person upon whose pledged word little or no reliance can be placed, and who, for gain to himself, neither scruples nor hesitates to disregard and violate his express engagements and agreements. His repudiation of one contract, for the making of which he had been paid several hundred dollars, and his breach of another contract, entered into after at least a week's consideration and deliberation, give rise to the present controversy. Viewed from the standpoint of common honesty and integrity, his position in this litigation is not an enviable one.

In April, 1913, defendant Killefer entered into a written contract with the Philadelphia Ball Company (now Philadelphia National League Club) by the terms of which he bound himself to perform for the Ball Company the services of a professional baseball player during the season of 1913. Three clauses of that contract are of a special importance here:

> 1. The compensation of the party of the second part stipulated in this contract shall be apportioned as follows: 75% thereof for services rendered and 25% thereof for and in consideration of the player's covenant to sanction and abide by his reservation by the party of the first part for the season of 1914, unless released before its termination in accordance with the provisions of this contract. The party of the second part shall be entitled to and shall be paid the full consideration named herein in regular semimonthly installments, unless released prior to the termination of this contract in accordance with section 8 hereof, regardless of whether or not the contracting club exercises the privilege of reserving the party of the second part for the season of 1914.

8. It is further understood and agreed that the party of the first part may, at any time after the beginning and prior to the completion of the period of this contract, give the party of the second part ten days' written notice to end and determine all its liabilities and obligations under this contract, in which event all liabilities and obligations undertaken by said party of the first part, in this contract, shall at once cease and determine at the expiration of said ten days; the said party of the second part shall thereupon be also freed and discharged from obligation to render service to said party of the first part. If such notice be given to the party of the second part while "abroad" with the club, he shall be entitled to his necessary traveling expenses to the city of Philadelphia.

10. In consideration of the compensation paid to the party of the second part by the party of the first part as recited in clause 1 hereof, the party of the second part agrees and obligates himself to contract with and continue in the service of said party of the first part for the succeeding season at a salary to be determined by the parties to such contract.

After the close of the season of 1913, and before the first of the next year, the Philadelphia Club notified Killefer that it desired his services for another year, and would pay him an increased salary, and thereupon he again promised and agreed to play with that club during the season of 1914. Notwithstanding these agreements with the Philadelphia Club, he, upon the solicitation and at the request of the plaintiffs, entered into negotiations with the latter which, on the 8th day of January, 1914, resulted in the execution of a written contract, by the terms of which he agreed to play baseball for and with the Chicago Federal League Club, during the three seasons of 1914, 1915, and 1916, at a salary of $5,833.33 per season. At the time of the execution of this contract, plaintiffs and their manager had knowledge of Killefer's previous contract with the Philadelphia Club, and were acquainted with its provisions. Twelve days later and on January 20, 1914, Killefer executed another contract with the defendant Philadelphia National League Club, by the terms of which he agreed to play baseball for and with that club during the three seasons of 1914, 1915, and 1916, at a salary of $6,500 per annum. Since the execution of the last-mentioned contract, Killefer has entered upon its performance and intends to continue to play with the Philadelphia Club unless he is restrained from so doing. In this proceeding, plaintiffs seek an injunction restraining him from playing with any baseball team or club other than their own.

The parties concede and the authorities sustain the jurisdiction of a court of equity in a suit of this character. That the contracts of January 8th and January 20th are, in form, valid and binding upon the parties thereto must also be conceded. Therefore the questions here presented and requiring consideration are these:

First, are the provisions of the 1913 contract between the defendants, relative to the reservation of the player for the succeeding season, valid and enforceable? and, second, are the plaintiffs by their own conduct barred from seeking relief in a court of equity?

The leading authorities, with possibly one exception, are agreed that executory contracts of this nature can neither be enforced in equity nor form the basis of an action at law to recover damages for their breach. The reasons for the decisions are that such contracts are lacking in the necessary qualities of definiteness, certainty, and mutuality. The 1913 contract between these defendants, relative to the reservation of the defendant Killefer for the season of 1914, is lacking in all of these essential elements. It is wholly uncertain and indefinite with respect to salary and also with respect to terms and conditions of the proposed employment. It is nothing more than a contract to enter into a contract, in the future, if the parties can then agree to contract. Although it is founded upon sufficient consideration, it lacks mutuality, because the Philadelphia Club may terminate it at any time upon 10 days' notice while the other party has no such option and is bound during the entire contract period. A contract exists, but, if broken by either party, the other is remediless, because the courts are helpless either to enforce its performance or to award damages for its breach.

The principle embodied in the maxim, "He who comes into equity must come with clean hands," is a cardinal one, lying at the foundation of equity jurisprudence. Equity imperatively demands of suitors in its courts fair dealing and righteous conduct with reference to the matters concerning which they seek relief. He who has acted in bad faith, resorted to trickery and deception, or been guilty of fraud, injustice, or unfairness will appeal in vain to a court of conscience, even though in his wrongdoing he may have kept himself strictly "within the law." Misconduct which will bar relief in a court of equity need not necessarily be of such nature as to be punishable as a crime or to constitute the basis of legal action. Under this maxim, any willful act in regard to the matter in litigation, which would be condemned and pronounced wrongful by honest and fair-minded men, will be sufficient to make the hands of the applicant unclean. Both courts and text-writers have repeatedly spoken upon this subject in no uncertain language.

* * *

Authorities to the same effect might be multiplied indefinitely. The foregoing will suffice to state and to define the universally accepted and adopted rule upon this subject. The principle thus broadly enunciated is not confined in its application to controversies of any particular nature or class, but extends generally to all cases cognizable by courts of equity. It is, however, peculiarly appropriate and applicable to cases like the present one, where relief will not be granted as a matter of strict right, but must result from the exercise of a sound judicial discretion. Measuring and testing their conduct by this rule, are the plaintiffs in court with clean hands? Knowing that the defendant, Killefer, was under a moral, if not a legal, obligation to furnish his services to the Philadelphia Club for the season of 1914, they sent for him, and by offering him a longer term of employment and a much larger compensation induced him to repudiate his obligation to his employer. In so doing a willful wrong was done to the Philadelphia Club, which was none the less grievous and harmful because the injured party could not obtain legal redress in and through the courts of the land. Can it be doubted that, if the plaintiffs had not interfered, Mr. Killefer would have carried out his agreements with the Philadelphia Club in honesty and good faith? The plaintiffs and Killefer both expected to derive a benefit and a profit from their contract, and both knew that such contract, if performed, would work a serious injury to the Philadelphia Club. The conduct of both is not only open to criticism and censure, but is tainted with unfairness and injustice, if not with actionable fraud. To drive a shrewd bargain is one thing and to resort to unfair and unjust practices and methods in order to obtain an advantage over a business rival or competitor is another. Courts of equity may protect and enforce the former, but will not sanction nor lend their aid to the latter. While it is true that the plaintiffs and Mr. Killefer have entered into a legal and binding contract, for the breach of which the one may be compelled to respond in damages to the other, it is also true that, because both have acted wrongfully and in bad faith, a court of equity will neither adjust their differences nor balance their equities. The motion for an injunction must be denied, not because the executory part of the 1913 contract between the defendants was of superior or any legal force and effect, not because the contract between plaintiffs and defendant, Killefer, is not in itself such a one as the courts will enforce, not because there are any equities in Killefer's favor which excuse or exempt him from the performance of his engagements, and not because the merits of the controversy are with the Philadelphia Club, but solely because the actions and conduct of the plaintiffs in procuring the contract, upon which their right to relief is and must be founded, do not square with one of the vital and fundamental principles of equity which touches to the quick the dignity of a court of conscience and controls its decision regardless of all other considerations.

Notes and Questions

1. Judge Sessions clearly was not pleased with either party in the *Weegham* case, but nonetheless punished Chicago because it was the party seeking the injunctive relief. His attack upon both parties is testimony to Judge Sessions's considerable righteousness.

2. Yet, despite Judge Sessions's noble desire to have all parties toe the moral line, is this decision fair? There is little doubt that the original agreement between Philadelphia and Killefer was vague, possibly fatally indefinite and, perhaps, lacking in consideration. If such be the case, could Chicago be faulted for attempting to woo Killefer away, given the fact that the contractual obligation ostensibly binding him may have been infirm? If you were an attorney, and Killefer came to you with the Chicago offer, what would you advise him? In some sense, there is a "Catch-22" because suggesting that he cannot jump the club ignores the obvious infirmities in the Philadelphia contract; yet, recommending that he jump the club visits possible injunction action upon him if the Philadelphia club should decide to sue. The problems only become compounded when Killefer opts to return to the original Philadelphia club, prompting Chicago to seek injunctive relief notwithstanding its own unclean hands.

3. In *Northeastern University. v. Brown, supra*, although not explicitly titling it as an "unclean hands" issue, the court was unsympathetic to Brown, a football coach seeking to "jump" his contract with Northeastern University. Brown was approached by University of Massachusetts and agreed to coach for them. Northeastern sought and was granted a preliminary injunction prohibiting Brown from coaching at U. Mass. The court was particularly unconcerned about any potential harm to both Brown and U. Mass., finding that Brown "willfully and intentionally breached his contract with Northeastern," and that U. Mass. actively induced that breach. *Id.* at 6–7.

4. Compare and contrast the *Weegham* decision with Judge Stanley's opinion in the *Minnesota Muskies, Inc. v. Hudson* case that follows.

Minnesota Muskies, Inc. v. Hudson
294 F. Supp. 979 (M.D.N.C. 1969)

STANLEY, Chief Judge. The plaintiffs seek by this action to enjoin the defendant, Louis C. Hudson, from playing professional basketball for any professional basketball team other than the plaintiff, Florida Professional Sports, Inc., for the term of an alleged contract he signed with the plaintiff, Minnesota Muskies, Inc., on May 3, 1967, and assigned to the plaintiff, Florida Professional Sports, Inc., on July 31, 1968. Jurisdiction is based on diversity of citizenship and the amount in controversy. * * *

After giving due consideration to the stipulated record, briefs, and arguments, the following facts are found:

Facts

1. The plaintiff Minnesota Muskies, Inc., hereinafter referred to as "Muskies," is a corporation organized and existing under the laws of the State of Minnesota, and has its principal place of business in Minneapolis, Minnesota. For the reasons later stated, the corporation is not actively operating any business at the present time.

2. During the 1967–68 professional basketball season, the Muskies operated a professional basketball team in Minneapolis, Minnesota, under a franchise issued by the American Basketball Association, and on July 31, 1968, the franchise, nineteen player contracts, and certain other equipment belonging to the Muskies, were transferred and assigned by the Muskies to the plaintiff Florida Professional Sports, Inc.

3. The plaintiff Florida Professional Sports, Inc., hereinafter referred to as "Miami," is a corporation organized and existing under the laws of the State of Florida, and has its principal place of business in Miami, Florida. The corporation was incorporated on or about July 11, 1968, and during the 1968–69 professional basketball season is engaged in the business of operating a professional basketball team known as the Miami Floridians under the franchise originally issued by the American Basketball Association to the Muskies.

4. The defendant Louis C. Hudson is a citizen and resident of Greensboro, North Carolina. Hudson attended Dudley High School in Greensboro, North Carolina, where he participated in basketball and other sports. After graduating from Dudley High School in 1962, he enrolled in the University of Minnesota and attended that institution from the fall of 1962 until the spring of 1966. While attending the University of Minnesota, he played on the freshman and varsity basketball terms of that institution and was named to several all-tournament and all-star basketball teams. He was also named on the Helms Foundation All-American team following his junior year.

5. The defendant Atlanta Hawks Basketball, Inc., hereinafter referred to as "Atlanta," is a corporation organized and existing under the laws of the State of Georgia, and has its principal place of business in Atlanta, Georgia. Atlanta was incorporated on or about July 3, 1968, and during the current basketball season is engaged in the business of operating a professional basketball team in the City of Atlanta under a franchise issued by the National Basketball Association.

6. St Louis Hawks Basketball Club, Inc., hereinafter referred to as "St. Louis," is a corporation organized and existing under the laws of the State of Missouri, and has its principal place of business in St. Louis, Missouri. St. Louis formerly owned the National Basketball Association franchise under which Atlanta is now operating its professional basketball team.

7. The American Basketball Association, hereinafter referred to as "ABA," is an association of professional basketball teams that operate basketball teams in several cities in various sections of the United States under franchises issued by the ABA. The ABA was established in 1967, and its teams played their first regular season games during the 1967–68 professional basketball season. During the 1967–68 season, each ABA team played a number of regular season games, followed by a series of play-off games between certain ABA teams with the best regular season records. During the 1968–69 season, each ABA team will play regular season games and a series of play-off games will follow the regular season games.

8. The National Basketball Association, hereinafter referred to as "NBA," is an association of professional basketball teams that operate basketball teams in several cities in var-

ious sections of the United States under franchises issued by the NBA. During the 1967–68 season, each NBA team played a number of regular season games, followed by a series of play-off games between certain NBA teams with the best regular season records. During the 1968–69 professional basketball season, each NBA team will play regular season games and a series of play-off games will follow the regular season games.

9. NBA and ABA teams commence regular season play during the month of October of each year.

10. In the spring of 1966, Hudson was drafted by St. Louis in a player-draft held by the NBA, and on May 17, 1966, he signed an NBA Uniform Player Contract with St. Louis. The contract provided for the employment of Hudson as a basketball player for one year from October 1, 1966, with the following provision, known as a "reserve clause":

> "24. On or before September 1 next following the last playing season covered by this contract and renewals and extensions thereof, the Club may tender to the Player a contract for the next succeeding season by mailing the same to the Player at his address shown below, or if none is shown, then at his address last known to the Club. If the Player fails, neglects, or omits to sign and return such contract to the Club so that the Club receives it on or before October 1st next succeeding, then this contract shall be deemed renewed and extended for the period of one year, upon the same terms and conditions in all respects as are provided herein, except that the compensation payable to the Player shall be the sum provided in the contract tendered to the Player pursuant to the provisions hereof, which compensation shall in no event be less than 75% of the compensation payable to the Player for the last playing season covered by this contract and renewals and extensions thereof.

> "The Club's right to renew this contract, as herein provided, and the promise of the Player not to play otherwise than for the Club and its assignees, have been taken into consideration in determining the amount of compensation payable under paragraph 2 hereof."

11. The contract between Hudson and St. Louis also provided that St. Louis would pay Hudson a salary of $15,000.00 for the 1966–67 season, and contained the following provisions:

> "27. This contract is a guaranteed no-cut contract for the 1966–67 season and the compensation referred to above shall be payable to the Player in any event.

> "In addition to the annual compensation referred to in this contract, the Club agrees to and herewith does pay the Player the sum of $4,000.00 as and for a bonus."

12. Hudson played for St. Louis during the 1966–67 regular season, and during the NBA play-off games until St. Louis was eliminated from the play-off games on April 12, 1967. Hudson had an 18.4 points per game scoring average with St. Louis during the 1966–67 season, and was named NBA Rookie of the Year by the New York Sportswriters Association. His scoring average was the highest average of any player on the St. Louis team during the 1966–67 season.

13. On or about March 4, 1967, Hudson borrowed $4,000.00 from St. Louis, for which he executed a promissory note. The note has typed on its face: "To be deducted from my 1967–68 contract with the St. Louis Hawks Basketball Club." Both Ben Kerner, owner of St. Louis, and Hudson testified that the loan was repaid by Hudson

out of his salary from his 1967–68 contract. However, the original promissory note was still in Kerner's possession on October 16, 1968, and contained no notation that it had been paid.

14. The ABA began organizing in 1966, but its teams did not commence playing until the 1967–68 professional basketball season. The Muskies joined the ABA and received a franchise for the Minneapolis, Minnesota, area in January of 1967. Laurence P. Shields was and is the president and principal stockholder of the Muskies. A. E. Holman was the Muskies' vice-president and general manager from the time the Muskies were organized until March of 1968. Holman is no longer an employee or officer of the Muskies or Miami, although he is a minority stockholder in the Muskies. At the time of his deposition in September of 1968, and at the present time, he is a plaintiff in a law suit against the Muskies for two years' salary for an alleged breach of an employment contract. Robert Casey was publicity director of the Muskies. In 1967, the Muskies were interested in securing the services of basketball players who would have an appeal in Minnesota, including certain former players of the University of Minnesota. As general manager, it was Holman's responsibility to secure the services of players and negotiate contracts with them.

15. On May 3, 1967, Hudson signed an ABA Uniform Player Contract with the Muskies. The contract provided for the employment of Hudson as a professional basketball player for a period of three years from October 2, 1967. In an addendum to the contract, the Muskies agreed to pay Hudson for his services as follows:

> October 2, 1967 to October 2, 1968 — $37,500.00
>
> October 2, 1968 to October 2, 1969 — $42,500.00
>
> October 2, 1969 to October 2, 1970 — $47,500.00

16. The addendum to the contract also provided that Hudson was to be paid a bonus of $7,500.00 upon execution of the contract, which sum was paid to Hudson by the Muskies as provided.

17. The addendum to the contract between the Muskies and Hudson further provided as follows:

> "6. In the event legal proceedings be instituted to prevent and enjoin the Player from playing for the first year of this contract, and if the said legal proceeding be successful in that said Player be enjoined from playing for one year, then and in that event the Club will pay the Player the sum of $25,000.00 for the said year. The Player agrees to then play for the Club the next ensuing three years under the terms and conditions as set forth in Clause 1 of this addenum. The Club shall choose, provide and pay for legal counsel for the defense of any such legal proceedings, save and except that Player reserves the right to choose his own counsel.

> * * *

> "8. If at the end of three years (or four years if the Player is enjoined by law as referred to above) from and after October 2, 1967 the Club is nonoperative, is in receivership or bankruptcy, then the injunction proceedings as provided for in paragraph 5 of the main contract shall not apply to the Player.

> "Under all other circumstances paragraphs 5 and 17 of the main contract remain in full force and effect."

18. The contract between Hudson and the Muskies also contains the following provision:

"5. *Injunctive Relief.* The PLAYER hereby represents that he has special, exceptional and unique knowledge, skill and ability as a basketball player, the loss of which cannot be estimated with any certainty and cannot be fairly or adequately compensated by damages and therefore agrees that the CLUB shall have the right, in addition to any other rights that the CLUB may possess, to enjoin him by appropriate injunction proceedings against playing basketball, or engaging in activities related to basketball for any person, firm, corporation or institution, or injunction against any other breach of this contract."

19. As disclosed by the deposition testimony of the various individuals involved, the parties are in disagreement with respect to the details of the negotiations that led to the signing of the Hudson-Muskies contract. From the conflicting testimony, it is found that sometime in March of 1967, at a time Hudson was still playing for St. Louis in playoff games, and while his contract with St. Louis was in full force and effect, Hudson was contacted by a representative of the Muskies for the purpose of determining whether he was interested in signing a professional basketball contract with the Muskies. After a series of telephone calls between Hudson and representatives of the Muskies organization, Hudson contacted his agent, Edward M. Cohen, an attorney in Minneapolis, and advised Cohen of his conversations with representatives of the Muskies and asked him to see what the Muskies had to offer. Hudson also advised Cohen that he would be a free agent when the NBA play-offs were over. On March 29, 1967, Cohen wrote Holman that Hudson would be a free agent, effective with the termination of the NBA play-offs, and that he was Hudson's representative for the purpose of negotiating contracts for future performances by Hudson as a basketball player. Thereafter, Cohen and Holman had a series of conferences. On April 7 or 8, 1967, Hudson went to Minneapolis, and took with him a copy of his contract with St. Louis and showed it to Cohen. Cohen immediately called to Hudson's attention the "reserve clause" in the contract, and questioned whether he would be a free agent at the end of the current basketball season. Nevertheless, it was decided that Cohen would continue his negotiations with the Muskies and keep Hudson advised as to the progress of the negotiations. Pursuant to instructions, Cohen continued his negotiations with the Muskies, during which time various offers and counter-offers were made. During the latter part of April of 1967, at Holman's request, Cohen called Hudson and asked him to come back to Minneapolis for further discussion, and advised him that the Muskies would pay his travel expense. As a consequence, Hudson was in Minneapolis on May 1, 2 and 3, 1967, during which time a series of meetings were held in Cohen's office with respect to a contract between Hudson and the Muskies. Cohen, Hudson, Barnett, Holman and Shields each attended some of the meetings, but all were not present at every meeting. The meetings culminated in Hudson and the Muskies signing the aforementioned contract on May 3, 1967.

20. All responsible officials of the Muskies, including Holman and Shields, were fully aware of the contract Hudson had with St. Louis before the contract between Hudson and the Muskies was prepared and signed, and had every reason to believe St. Louis would either exercise its option under the "reserve clause" of its existing contract or negotiate a new contract with Hudson. While some doubt was expressed as to the validity of the "reserve clause" in the St. Louis contract, officials of the Muskies recognized that Hudson might very well have additional contractual responsibilities to St. Louis for the 1967–68, and possibly subsequent, basketball seasons. Holman did not recognize any

responsibility for conferring with St. Louis before executing the contract with Hudson, feeling that it was Hudson's duty to advise St. Louis as to the negotiations and the execution of the new contract.

21. Both parties to the Hudson-Muskies contract, as well as their attorneys, were uncertain as to the legal effect of the "reserve clause" in the St. Louis contract, and this uncertainty prompted Hudson to request that Paragraph 6 of the addendum be inserted in his contract with the Muskies. Further, it was Cohen's feeling that in the event St. Louis was successful in restraining Hudson from playing under his contract with the Muskies, Hudson was entitled to some financial protection.

22. On May 18, 1967, a press conference was held at the Leamington Hotel in Minneapolis, at which time the Muskies and Hudson announced that they had signed a contract. Hudson went to Minneapolis to attend the press conference. Following the press conference, a telegram, signed by Hudson, was sent to and received by Ben Kerner, the then owner of St. Louis, in which Kerner was advised that Hudson had signed with the Muskies and was not going to play with St. Louis. The telegram also stated that Hudson had been offered an extremely lucrative contract with the Muskies, and that it was his intention to make his future career in Minneapolis. The announcement of the Hudson-Muskies contract was publicized in the news media, including newspapers in St. Louis. The announcement referred to the Muskies as having gone fishing "for a Muskie," and having come up with "one of the biggest catches in sports."

23. On May 25, 1967, one week after the Hudson-Muskies contract was publicly announced, St. Louis filed suit against the Muskies, all the other members of the ABA, and George Mikan, Commissioner of the ABA, in the United States District Court for the District of Minnesota, charging a conspiracy among the defendants, with respect to the Hudson-Muskies contract, to deliberately, maliciously, wrongfully and unjustifiably interfere with the contractual relationship which existed between St. Louis and Hudson, and seeking actual damages in the sum of $2,000,000.00 and punitive damages in the sum of $1,000,000.00.

24. On May 25, 1967, St. Louis also filed suit against Hudson in the United States District Court for the District of Minnesota, seeking an injunction against Hudson from playing basketball for any other person, firm or corporation, during the 1967–68 and the 1968–69 professional basketball seasons.

25. After Kerner received the telegram from Hudson on May 18, 1967, he immediately tried to get in touch with Hudson by calling various places where he thought he might be, and by leaving messages in Minneapolis and Greensboro for Hudson to contact him.

26. At the time Kerner received said telegram from Hudson, Ritchie Guerin, the St. Louis Coach, Bill Bridges, a member of the St. Louis team and a roommate and close friend of Hudson, and some other St. Louis players, were in South America on a basketball tour. When Guerin and Bridges returned to the United States, Kerner advised them that Hudson had signed with the Muskies. Shortly thereafter, Hudson received a message at his home in Greensboro that Bridges was attempting to contact him by telephone from St. Louis. Before returning the call, Hudson called Cohen in Minneapolis and advised that certain St. Louis players, Bill Bridges for one, were desirous of seeing and talking with him. Cohen responded by telling Hudson that it was his personal business as to whether he talked with any of the St. Louis players, but reminded him of his contract with the Muskies. When Hudson returned Bridges' telephone call, Bridges mentioned that he had read in the paper about Hudson signing a contract with the Muskies, and questioned the wisdom of Hudson signing the contract.

27. It is apparent that sometime during the early part of June of 1967 Hudson had become dissatisfied with the contract he had signed with the Muskies, and had decided to see if he could reach another agreement with St. Louis. The record is unclear as to whether Hudson first approached Kerner concerning his dissatisfaction with the Muskies contract, or whether the dissatisfaction was brought about by action initiated by Kerner. In any event, Hudson was in Atlanta on June 4, 1967, playing golf with Bridges and some other people. Either before or after his golf game, he wrote Kerner in St. Louis expressing regrets for the trouble he had caused St. Louis, and stating that he would like to continue with the St. Louis Club. On the same day, apparently after the letter was written, Hudson called Kerner in St. Louis and made inquiry concerning the possibility of a meeting. Kerner readily agreed, and it was arranged that the meeting would be held in Atlanta.

28. On June 5, 1967, Hudson and St. Louis executed an NBA Uniform Player Contract covering a period of five years from October 1, 1967. The contract provided that Hudson would be paid the sum of $34,000.00 per year during the five-year period, in addition to a bonus of $15,000.00 for executing the contract.

29. There is evidence that the contract was actually signed by Hudson and Kerner on June 4, 1967, in Atlanta, and that the blanks in the contract were filled in by typewriter in St. Louis the following day. In any event, the contract was signed and is being honored by both parties, and it would appear to be irrelevant and immaterial as to where, or on what day, the signatures were actually affixed. Neither is it deemed relevant nor material as to whether Hudson first approached Kerner, or whether Kerner or some other representative of St. Louis first approached Hudson, with respect to the new contract. For the record, the Court will find that the contact was initiated by St. Louis, and that the meeting in Atlanta was prearranged in order to induce Hudson to enter into another contract with St. Louis.

30. Shortly after the signing of the Hudson-St. Louis contract on June 5, 1967, St. Louis submitted to a voluntary dismissal of the two actions it had brought in the United States District Court for the District of Minnesota against the Muskies, and others, and against Hudson. Answers had not been filed when the actions were dismissed.

31. Sometime in June or July of 1967, Hudson advised Cohen of the signing of the new St. Louis contract and instructed Cohen to return to the Muskies the $7,500.00 bonus the Muskies had paid him at the time he signed the Muskies contract. After receiving the ininstructions, Cohen called Holman and offered to return $5,000.00 of the $7,500.00 bonus, stating that this was all the money Hudson had at that time and that the balance would be paid "very shortly." Holman refused to accept the tender of $5,000.00, and also stated that he would refuse to take the full $7,500.00 should it be tendered.

32. In August of 1967, Hudson entered the Army for approximately six months. While in the Army he played for St. Louis occasionally on weekends and holidays. He was released from active military status the latter part of January of 1968, and resumed playing for St. Louis on a full-time basis.

33. On October 13, 1967, Holman wrote a letter to Hudson, in care of his attorney, Cohen, in which he stated that the Muskies were agreeable to Hudson playing out a one-year option with St. Louis, but that he was expected to perform his contract with the Muskies at the end of the one-year option period, which was understood to be October 2, 1968. Hudson was requested to respond to the letter and acknowledge that he intended to honor his contract with the Muskies. The letter was received by Hudson,

but he has never responded to same. Hudson was of the opinion that he had advised St. Louis of the receipt of the letter, but Kerner has no recollection of the matter. On May 3, 1968, in response to an inquiry, Cohen advised the Muskies that Hudson's position was that he did not have any contractual obligation to perform for the Muskies.

34. Before May 6, 1968, the Muskies had retained attorneys in Minnesota and St. Louis in an effort to commence an action against Hudson, seeking an injunction. Pleadings were actually drafted, but when Hudson could not be located in Missouri or Minnesota, the Muskies secured the services of attorneys in Greensboro in an effort to locate Hudson. When eventually advised of Hudson's presence in Greensboro, the Muskies authorized the immediate institution of this action. The complaint was filed on May 22, 1968, and Hudson was served with copy of summons and complaint on May 23, 1968.

35. On May 3, 1968, Thomas G. Cousins and Carl E. Sanders, residents of Atlanta, Georgia, entered into a contract to purchase the NBA franchise owned by St. Louis, ten player contracts, including the Hudson contract dated June 5, 1967, and miscellaneous equipment for $3,200,000.00. Of the total purchase price, $2,990,000.00 was allocated to player contracts. Immediately after the purchase contract was executed, a public announcement of the pending sale was made. The announcement appeared in newspapers in New York, Philadelphia, Atlanta, and St. Louis, among others.

36. The purchase of the St. Louis franchise, player contracts, and other property, by Cousins and Sanders was consummated on May 10, 1968. There is no evidence that either Cousins or Sanders, or anyone else connected with the Atlanta purchase, had any knowledge of the Muskies having asserted a claim against Hudson until after the transaction with St. Louis had been closed. There is substantial evidence, however, that the transaction would not have been consummated, certainly not at the purchase price involved, if there had been any question about the Hudson contract.

37. On July 3, 1968, Sanders and Cousins transferred and assigned the NBA franchise, player contracts, and other assets they had purchased from St. Louis, to defendant Atlanta Hawks Basketball, Inc., a corporation in which Cousins and Sanders were the sole stockholders. Atlanta now owns the Hudson contract signed with St. Louis on June 5, 1967.

38. On July 31, 1968, as earlier noted, the Muskies sold and transferred to Miami the Muskies' ABA franchise, 19 player contracts, and other assets, including the contract Hudson signed with the Muskies on May 3, 1967. In consideration for the franchise, player contracts, and other assets, Miami paid the Muskies $75,000.00 in cash, executed a promissory note for $125,000.00, and delivered to the Muskies 75,000 shares of stock of Miami with a par value of $1.00 per share, making the total consideration $275,000.00. The 75,000 shares of stock transferred to the Muskies represent 50% of the outstanding stock of the Miami corporation.

39. Miami knew that this action was pending at the time it purchased the franchise and player contracts from the Muskies. Inquiry was made on behalf of Miami as to Hudson's intention, and Miami was advised by the Muskies that Hudson had stated that he would play for whichever team the Court decided he should play for. Miami will not owe the Muskies any additional consideration, and the Muskies will not be indebted to Miami for any amount, regardless of whether or not the injunction sought in this action is issued.

40. On October 3, 1968, counsel for Hudson tendered to counsel for plaintiffs a certified check in the amount of $7,500.00, as reimbursement for the bonus paid Hudson

by the Muskies. The tender was refused by counsel for the plaintiffs. Counsel for Hudson have informed counsel for the plaintiffs by letter that the tender remains open for acceptance by the plaintiffs.

41. Hudson is presently playing with Atlanta, and has testified that he wants to continue to play for Atlanta. He has been Atlanta's high scorer in several games this season.

42. As of March 31, 1968, the Muskies had sustained an operating loss of $493,374.75 from their professional basketball operations during the 1967–68 season. As of April 30, 1968, the operating loss was $554,902.32.

43. The officers and stockholders of Miami have furnished Hudson personal guaranties of Miami's performance of its obligations as assignee of the Muskies-Hudson contract.

44. Hudson is highly skilled and talented, and possesses special, exceptional, and unique knowledge, skill and ability as a basketball player.

Discussion

The sole question presented for decision is whether the plaintiffs are entitled to an injunction restraining Hudson from playing professional basketball with any team or club other than Miami for the term of the contract he signed with the Muskies on May 3, 1967, and assigned by the Muskies to Miami on July 31, 1968. Jurisdiction is not questioned, and the fact that Hudson possesses special, exceptional, and unique knowledge, skill and ability as a basketball player has been conceded.

It is generally held that where a person agrees to render personal services to another, which require special and unique knowledge, skill and ability, so that in default the same services cannot easily be obtained from others, a court of equity is empowered to negatively enforce performance of the agreement by enjoining its breach. While acknowledging this principle of law, the defendants correctly assert that equitable relief should be denied to a suitor who comes into court with unclean hands.

> One of the most fundamental principles of equity jurisprudence is the maxim that "he who comes into equity must come with clean hands." Equity demands of suitors fair dealings with reference to matters concerning which they seek relief.

* * *

In *Precision Instrument Mfg. Co. v. Automotive Maintenance Machinery Co.*, 324 U.S. 806 (1945), it is stated:

> "The guiding doctrine in this case is the equitable maxim that [HN5] 'he who comes into equity must come with clean hands.' This maxim is far more than a mere banality. It is a self-imposed ordinance that closes the doors of a court of equity to one tainted with inequitableness or bad faith relative to the matter in which he seeks relief, however, improper may have been the behavior of the defendant. That doctrine is rooted in the historical concept of court of equity as a vehicle for affirmatively enforcing the requirements of conscience and good faith. This presupposes a refusal on its part to be 'the abetter of iniquity.' Thus while 'equity does not demand that its suitors shall have led blameless lives,' *Loughran v. Loughran, 292 U.S. 216, 229* as to other matters, it does require that they shall have acted fairly and without fraud or deceit as to the controversy in issue.

"This maxim necessarily gives wide range to the equity court's use of discretion in refusing to aid the unclean litigant. It is 'not bound by formula or restrained by any limitation that tends to trammel the free and just exercise of discretion.' Accordingly one's misconduct need not necessarily have been of such a nature as to be punishable as a crime or as to justify legal proceedings of any character. Any willful act concerning the cause of action which rightfully can be said to transgress equitable standards of conduct is sufficient cause for the invocation of the maxim by the chancellor." (citations omitted)

* * *

Measured by these fundamental principles of equity jurisprudence, the conclusion is inescapable that the Muskies, in its dealings with Hudson, soiled its hands to such an extent that the negative injunctive relief sought should be denied. This is not to say that Hudson was an innocent bystander, or that he was an unwilling participant in his dealings with the Muskies. On the contrary, viewed strictly from the standpoint of business morality, his position in this litigation, like that of the Muskies, is not an enviable one.

On May 17, 1966, Hudson, an adult with four years of university education, freely and voluntarily executed a contract to play professional basketball with St. Louis for one year, with the provision that St. Louis might renew the contract for successive basketball seasons under certain prescribed conditions. A sizeable bonus for executing the contract was paid by St. Louis and received by Hudson.

Beyond question, both Hudson and St. Louis anticipated that the contract would be renewed for subsequent years. A short time before his initial contact with the Muskies, Hudson had borrowed $4,000.00 from St. Louis with the specific provision that it was to be repaid by deductions from his 1967–68 contract with St. Louis. Additionally, by his leading his team in scoring, and his being named Rookie of the Year in the NBA, Hudson's skill and ability as a professional basketball player had been well established during his first year with St. Louis.

While not a controlling factor, the Court is convinced that the Muskies, admittedly desirous of acquiring a winning basketball team as quickly as possible, either contacted Hudson, or caused him to be contacted by someone on its behalf, while he was still actively engaged in play-off games with St. Louis. Without this unwarranted interference on the part of the Muskies, there is every likelihood that Hudson would have fulfilled his contractual and moral obligations with St. Louis. The fact that Hudson advised Cohen, who in turn advised Holman, that Hudson would be a free agent, effective with the termination of the NBA play-offs, is of no consequence. Even if this information had been conveyed in good faith, everyone involved in the negotiations had seen a copy of Hudson's contract with St. Louis, and had full knowledge of its contents, long before the Hudson-Muskies contract was drafted and signed.

Basically, the plaintiffs argue that Hudson's original contract with St. Louis, because it provides for perpetual service, and is lacking in the necessary qualities of definiteness, certainty, and mutuality, is void. The contract being void and unenforceable beyond the 1966–67 season, the plaintiffs contend that their contract with Hudson is in all respects valid, and that the Hudson-St. Louis contract executed on June 5, 1967, with knowledge of the existence of the Hudson-Muskies contract executed on May 3, 1967, is likewise void. Under these circumstances, plaintiffs assert that they are entitled to have their contract enforced in a court of equity. There is no merit to this argument. Even if the "reserve clause" in the St. Louis contract is of doubtful validity, the fact remains that the Muskies, knowing that Hudson was under a moral, if not a legal, obligation to furnish his services to St. Louis for the 1967–68 and subsequent seasons, if St. Louis chose to exercise its option, sent for Hudson and induced him to repudiate his obligation to St. Louis. Such conduct, even if strictly within the law because of the St. Louis contract being unenforceable, was so tainted with unfairness and injustice as to justify a court of equity in withholding relief.

St. Louis furnished a forum for Hudson and the Muskies to test the legality of the "reserve clause" in its contract by the commencement of actions against the Muskies and other members of the ABA, and Hudson, in the United States District Court for the District of Minnesota one week after the Hudson-Muskies contract was publicly announced. Hudson chose not to defend the action, but instead signed another contract with St. Louis. The Muskies chose to let Hudson return to St. Louis for the 1967–68 season rather than litigate the matter. The Muskies explained its inaction by stating that it recognized that Hudson was perhaps obligated to play for St. Louis for one more year. Notwithstanding its recognition of this obligation, the Muskies agreed to pay Hudson to sit out the 1967–68 season even if the Court should decree that the St. Louis contract was enforceable. This alone is sufficient for a court of equity to refuse relief.

Finally, plaintiffs insist that they are entitled to relief, notwithstanding their unfair and unjust conduct, because St. Louis was also guilty of inequitable and unlawful conduct in signing Hudson to a second contract on June 5, 1967, when it knew that Hudson had signed a valid contract with the Muskies on May 3, 1967. This argument is also lacking in merit. The doors of a court of equity are closed to one tainted with unfairness or injustice relative to the matter in which he seeks relief "however improper may have been the behavior of the defendant." *Precision Instrument Mfg. Co. v. Automotive Maintenance Machinery Co.*, 324 U.S. 806, 814 (1945). It is irrelevant that the conduct of St. Louis may have been more reprehensible than that of the Muskies, since it is the devious conduct of the Muskies that created the problems presented in this litigation. Consequently, a determination of the validity of the "reserve clause" in the St. Louis contract is immaterial to a resolution of this controversy. No effort was made to avoid the contract in an honest way, but instead the Muskies consciously attempted to nullify and ignore it to the manifest injury of St. Louis. In so doing, it foreclosed its right to seek the aid of a court of equity.

The injunctive relief sought by the plaintiffs must be denied, not because the Hudson-St. Louis contract was of "any legal force and effect" or is one that "the courts will enforce," and not because the merits of the controversy are necessarily with St. Louis, "but solely because the actions and conduct of the [Muskies] in procuring the contract, upon which [its] right to relief is and must be founded, do not square with one of the vital and fundamental principles of equity which touches to the quick the dignity of a court of conscience and controls its decision regardless of all other considerations." *Weegham v. Killefer*, 215 F. 168, 173 (W.D.Mich.), aff'd 6 Cir., 215 F. 289 (1914).

There can be no question but that Miami acquired no greater rights to the services of Hudson than those acquired by the Muskies in its contract of May 3, 1967, and that Atlanta's rights to his services are not superior to those of St. Louis.

Conclusions of Law

1. The Court has jurisdiction over the parties and the subject matter.

2. The plaintiffs are not entitled to the negative injunctive relief sought.

Accordingly, a judgment will be entered dismissing the complaint with prejudice.

Notes and Questions

1. As in the *Barnett* case considered earlier, the standard player contract ordained that the player was unique. Again, given the custom in the NBA of "suiting up" 11 or 12 players, but playing less than that number, can we assume that a court would find every NBA player to be unique simply by virtue of a boiler-plate contract clause that says so? Is it, as said in Lewis Carroll's THROUGH THE LOOKING GLASS, "so because I say it is so?" If uniqueness presupposes the existence of a negative covenant, are we reaching the point where the demonstration of irreparable injury in the case of an athlete's abdication of contractual obligations, is a mere "formal" exercise, and the issuance of the injunction a foregone conclusion?

2. This court adopts an approach to unclean hands that, like Judge Sessions in *Weegham v. Killefer,* is somewhat puritanical:

> Basically, the plaintiffs argue that Hudson's original contract with St. Louis, because it provides for perpetual service, and is lacking in the necessary qualities of definiteness, certainty, and mutuality, is void * * * Under these circumstances, plaintiffs assert that they are entitled to have their contract enforced in a court of equity. There is no merit to this argument. Even if the "reserve clause" in the St. Louis contract is of doubtful validity, the fact remains that the Muskies, knowing that Hudson was under a moral, if not a legal, obligation to furnish his services to St. Louis for the 1967–68 and subsequent seasons, if St. Louis chose to exercise its option, sent for Hudson and induced him to repudiate his obligation to St. Louis. Such conduct, even if strictly within the law because of the St. Louis contract being unenforceable, was so tainted with unfairness and injustice as to justify a court of equity in withholding relief.

Is this conclusion realistic? Should the facial invalidity of a contract never be a factor in the defense of a party who has sought escape by contracting with another? In effect, should the court penalize the party who, albeit for its own self interest, has rescued a party from an agreement that palpably fails to satisfy the basic rudiments of contract formation and consideration?

3. In *Munchak v. Cunningham,* 457 F.2d 721 (4th Cir. 1972), the Fourth Circuit took a decidedly different tack in considering whether the ABA's Carolina Cougars had unclean hands when they sought to enjoin star player Billy Cunningham from playing with his original club, the Philadelphia 76ers, after he had jilted the Sixers, only to resign with them after signing with the Cougars. There, the Cougars, aware that Cunningham was under contract with the 76ers, including an option for the succeeding season, began negotiations culminating in a three-year contract. Cunningham was to receive a $125,000 signing bonus, $80,000 of which was reflected in a promissory note from the Cougars. The note, however, would be cancelled if Cunningham decided to continue to play for the 76ers during the option year at a salary of less than $80,000 (or, by some testimony, $100,000). If he declined to play for Philadelphia during the option year, the Cougars would be bound to honor it in full. When Cunningham reneged on the Cougars deal and signed a new agreement with Philadelphia, Carolina sued and asked the court to enjoin him from playing for anyone but the Cougars. The District Court denied the injunction based on unclean

hands, adopting a position not unlike the courts in *Weegham* and *Muskies*. However, the 4th Circuit reversed, finding that the Cougars did not have unclean hands and adding that equity does not require the performance of a futile act—in this instance, not paying the note.

Among the more bizarre and inexplicable reasons for the Fourth Circuit's reversal of the lower court and refusal to find unclean hands was the court's tortured reasoning that the cancellability of the promissory note provided an incentive for Cunningham to play for the 76ers if they paid him less than $80,000. The court stated, "the giving of the note was an incentive to Cunningham to perform his contract with the 76ers, not a tortious interference with the performance of his contract." Does this suggestion survive meaningful scrutiny? How does the note/guarantee provide Cunningham with an incentive to satisfy his contractual obligations to the 76ers?

Is it appropriate that Team B should be able to commence negotiating with a player during the term of a contract between that player and Team A? What is the rationale for permitting contact negotiations between Team B and the player prior to the time that his or her contract with Team A expires? In other walks of life and fields of employment, isn't it advisable to have a new job before you quit your old job? Should the determination of whether or not a party has unclean hands turn on the party's immorality and inappropriate behavior rather than a stricter standard of illegality?

2. Billy Cunningham contended that his contract could not be assigned and that, therefore, the change in ownership excused his continued performance. The court concluded that a change in ownership is not nearly as onerous as an assignment to a new club. Given today's mercurial and flamboyant owners, is this a realistic assessment of the impact of new ownership upon a player?

3. The *Munchak* case has been cited for the proposition that, absent special facts, rights arising under personal services contracts cannot be assigned, or are not assignable generally. *See* WEISTART & LOWELL § 3.13, at 293–94. The presumption arises because the various exceptions to the general premise that contract rights may be assigned occur frequently in the context of personal services contracts, particularly contracts between a team and a player. As discussed in Chapter 4, the restrictive effects of these exceptions can be ameliorated if the team secures the player's consent to be assigned through the Uniform Player Contract (provided that such consent is not prohibited by the pertinent collective bargaining agreement). The individual player, however, may negotiate a special "no-trade" clause that, in effect, has the opposite impact, precluding any and all assignments without the player's consent. In *Munchak*, the player argued that his no-trade clause applied to any change in the identity of the shareholders. The court reasoned that the identity of the owners should have no impact on the player's obligations to perform and that the no-trade clause was inapplicable in this context. Do you agree?

The ability of a club to transfer contract rights of a player to another club has generated considerable litigation in the sports arena. Included among the issues addressed are the scope of the assignment clause, the applicability and effectiveness of no-trade clauses, the liability of the assigning team when the assignee team is unable to meet its contract demands (in particular, the player's compensation), etc. *See generally* WEISTART & LOWELL §§ 3.13–.14.

5. The following case adopts the more indulgent view of unclean hands than *Minnesota Muskies v. Hudson* and *Weegham v. Killefer* did. Is the rationale more tenable or, at least, satisfying than the bizarre justification advanced in *Munchak*?

Washington Capitols Basketball Club, Inc. v. Barry
304 F. Supp. 1193 (N.D. Cal.), *aff'd*, 419 F.2d 472 (9th Cir. 1969)

LEVIN, District Judge. This action was commenced by Washington Capitols Basketball Club, Inc., (hereafter "Washington") for declaratory and equitable relief and for damages. The relevant facts which are undisputed are as follows:

On June 19, 1967, Richard F. Barry III (hereafter "Barry") granted to Charles E. "Pat" Boone (hereafter "Boone") and S. D. Davidson (hereafter "Davidson") an option to acquire his services as a professional basketball player for the 1967–68 season, and received an assignment for the transfer of a certain undivided interest in the Oakland franchise of the American Basketball Association (hereafter "ABA"), a Delaware corporation, organized and existing for the purposes, among others, of forming, managing, operating and advising a professional basketball league with member clubs in various cities of the United States.

On the same date Boone executed a guaranty and agreement guaranteeing, among other things, certain earnings to Barry for his services and also agreeing to cause Oakland Basketball, Inc., (hereafter "Oaks") to indemnify and hold Barry harmless from any and all liability Barry may incur by reason of his execution of the option. Such an indemnity agreement was executed on September 29, 1967, by Barry, Boone, Davidson and Oaks.

Pursuant to the option Barry signed an ABA Uniform Player Contract with Oaks, the owner and operator of the ABA franchise for Oakland, California, of a professional basketball team under the name of Oaks. Barry also signed an amendment to the aforesaid ABA contract, dated October 31, 1967, which provides that the term of the employment of Barry by Oaks is for three years commencing on October 2, 1968,

> "or such earlier date as Player's services as a basketball player are not enjoined by order or decree of any court of competent jurisdiction and there is no adjudication by such a court denying Player the right and freedom to contract for his services without restraint or damages by others."

This agreement, as amended, provides "for a salary of $75,000.00 per year plus an amount equal to the lesser of (a) Five (5%) per cent of all gross gate receipts received by the Club per year in excess of the sum of $60,000.00 plus Player's compensation, or (b) $15,000.00." The agreement also provides in paragraph 6 thereof:

> "The Club shall have the right to sell, exchange, assign and transfer this contract to any other professional basketball club in the Association and the Player Agrees to accept such assignment and to faithfully perform and carry out this contract with the same force and effect as if it had been entered into by the Player with the assignee Club instead of with this Club."

On August 28, 1969, Washington and Oaks entered into an agreement of purchase which provides, among other things, for the sale by Oaks and the purchase by Washington of all of Oaks:

> "property and assets of every kind and nature whatsoever related to operation of the SELLER'S professional basketball team * * * all of the SELLER'S right and interest in and to contracts with all professional basketball players * * * as well as all other right and interest the SELLER has in and to any and all basketball players whether or not such players are under written contract with the SELLER."

After recitation of the purchase price the agreement contains the statement:

> "The above described purchase price is allocated as follows:

* * *

"2. $750,000.00 For Rick Barry Contract."

A bill of sale dated September 8, 1969, from Oaks to Washington was executed by the president and secretary of Oaks and an assignment from Oaks to Washington as of the same date was similarly executed. On August 29, 1969, Barry entered into a contract to play professional basketball with defendant San Francisco Warriors (hereafter "Warriors"), a limited partnership, organized and existing under the laws of the State of California, the owner of a professional basketball team franchise of the National Basketball Association (hereafter "NBA") for a term of five years commencing October 2, 1969, and terminating October 1, 1974. Defendant Lemat Corporation (hereafter "Lemat"), a Delaware corporation qualified to do business in the State of California, is the sole general partner of the aforesaid limited partnership.

At this stage of the proceedings plaintiff seeks a preliminary injunction to enjoin Barry from playing professional basketball with any team other than plaintiff "for so long as Barry remains in default under his contract with plaintiff."

The grant or refusal of injunctive relief is a matter of equitable jurisdiction. 43 C.J.S. Injunctions §12, p. 419. A Court of Equity will grant the relief when it determines it essential to restrain an act contrary to equity and good conscience. 43 C.J.S. Injunctions §1, p. 405.

I.

The purpose of the preliminary injunction is to maintain the status quo between the litigants pending final determination of the case. *Hamilton Watch Co. v. Benrus Watch Co.*, 206 F.2d 738, 742 (2d Cir. 1953). In order for plaintiff to succeed in its motion for a preliminary injunction, it is fundamental that it show at least first, a reasonable probability of success in the main action and second, that irreparable damage would result from a denial of the motion.

A. The Status Quo

The status quo is the last, peaceable, uncontested status between the parties which preceded the present controversy * * *.

The parties have differed in their interpretation of the meaning of the status quo in this case. It seems exceedingly clear that the status quo of the parties to the action was that peaceable state of affairs existing when Barry was under contract to Oaks and, prior to his injury, playing professional basketball for that team during the 1968–69 season. Although it is manifest that Barry cannot now play basketball for Oaks, their assets having been sold to Washington, the assignment of Barry's contract to Washington makes his obligations to them the closest to the status quo that can be attained. Most assuredly, permitting Barry to play with Warriors, which Barry indicated he would do if the preliminary injunction were not granted, would not be preserving any semblance of the situation as it existed just prior to the commencement of the present litigation.

B. Probability of Success at Trial

* * *

Defendants have not shown that the contract between Oaks and Barry, which was assigned by Oaks to Washington, is itself unconscionable, unenforceable or otherwise void. It is under this contract that Washington seeks to assert its rights to Barry's services and the protection of this Court from violation of those rights. The precedents for granting injunctive relief against "star" athletes "jumping" their contracts—and certainly defendants do not deny that Barry is a unique, a "star" athlete—are numerous * * *.

C. Showing of Irreparable Injury

* * *

Irreparable injury is that which cannot be compensated by the award of money damages; it is injury which is certain and great. Such injury exists when an athletic team is denied the services of an irreplaceable athlete. Barry is just such an irreplaceable athlete. He was the leading collegiate basketball scorer in the United States during the 1964–65 season and was voted Rookie of the Year during his first season of professional basketball in 1965–66 while playing with the Warriors. He was the leading scorer in the NBA during the 1966–67 season and was voted Most Valuable Player in the 1967 National Association All Star Basketball Game. Finally, while playing for Oaks during the 1968–69 season, he was the team's and ABA's leading scorer until an injury forced him to cease play. It is apparent today that with such a surfeit of fine basketball players in the United States graduating annually from collegiate ranks, the mere signing of a player to a professional basketball contract is substantial evidence of his outstanding qualities. When, like Barry, a player has proven his superior ability under the rigorous conditions of professional basketball, it is clear that money alone cannot replace his loss.

II.

* * *

A. The Contract between the Oaks and Barry Was Not Breached by Oaks

1. The Contract was Assignable

Although defendants dispute the validity of the assignment of Oaks' franchise and the contract with Barry to Washington, Barry's contract with Oaks clearly provided for such assignment, and it is not otherwise contrary to public policy or the law of this State. The language of the contract is clear and unambiguous * * *.

In the opinion of the Court, Barry's contract with Oaks was an integrated agreement which included the ABA Uniform Player Contract as amended, the Option, the Assignment, the Guaranty and Agreement, and the Indemnity Agreement. Even if the contract between Barry and Oaks is determined to be the sole document governing the contractual relationship of the parties, the same result ensues, for there is no doubt about the assignability of the agreement of the parties embodied therein.

2. Barry Remains Obligated to Perform under the Contract

Defendants next contend that Barry does not remain obligated to perform for Washington under the assignment because Oaks' actions constituted a breach of its contract with Barry. That contract provides that Barry shall receive compensation in the following form for a three year period: (1) a salary of $75,000.00 per year, plus (2) the lesser of 5% of all gross gate receipts received by the Oaks in excess of the sum of $60,000.00 or $15,000.00 plus (3) an ownership interest in the Oakland franchise to consist of 15% of the shares to be issued thereon (upon payment of $5,000.00 by Barry), plus 4) a guaranty of indemnity by the Oaks for any expenses incurred by Barry in making a legal defense of his agreement with the Oaks.

Defendants claim that the assignment of Barry's contract from Oaks to Washington diluted the value of Barry's 5% "gate interest", because the only available arenas in which Washington would play basketball have capacities of 6500–7000 persons, while the arena in which the Oaks had played had a capacity of approximately 12,000. In answer to this, it need only be pointed out that despite the capacity of its playing arena the Oaks drew an average attendance of only 1800 persons per game during the 1968–69 season, a number that may be accommodated easily in the available Washington arenas.

Defendants also claim that Barry's 15% ownership interest has been rendered null by the assignment of his contract with Oaks. If Barry's interest has been rendered nugatory, it is because of Oaks' disastrous financial condition and not because of its assignment to Washington. After all, as a shareholder Barry still was entitled to realize his proportionate share of any amount Oaks realized upon the sale of its assets to Washington. In any event, what would Barry's ownership interest be worth even if the prayed-for preliminary injunction were not granted? Oaks' financial condition raises serious doubts about Barry's ability to sell his ownership interest for any profit, even were a buyer available. No matter what the outcome of this case at trial, Oaks cease to exist. Therefore, it is illogical for Barry to argue that the denial of an injunction against him will in any way increase the value of his ownership interest in Oaks. In fact, Earl Foreman, the owner of Washington, has offered to purchase Barry's ownership interest in the defunct Oaks in order that Barry play with Washington.

B. Plaintiff Is Entitled to Equitable Relief Because It Comes to a Court of Equity with Clean Hands

It is a settled and ancient maxim that, "He who comes into equity must come with clean hands"* * *. In determining this point the Court examined the principle enunciated by courts that if plaintiff's hands are not clean equity must deny him relief no matter how improper defendant's conduct may have been * * *. Consequently, Barry's conduct in breaching his original contract with Warriors and executing the contract with Oaks has not been given weight in considering the question of injunctive relief. Certainly it is not every instance or allegation of misconduct that will leave plaintiff's hands soiled, and it is wholly within the discretion of the Court to find plaintiff's claim for relief barred by his own alleged misconduct* * *.

Defendants seek to invoke the doctrine of clean hands to bar injunctive relief in favor of Washington on the basis that since Washington's predecessor in interest, Oaks, was guilty of misconduct at an earlier time, Washington must be tainted similarly by imputation. The inducement by Oaks of Barry to contract with Oaks in 1967 while he still had a year to play under his contract "option" year with Warriors was the particular misconduct ascribed to Oaks. In *Lemat Corp. v. Barry*, 275 Cal. App.2d 671, 275 A.C.A. 732, 80 Cal.Rptr. 240 (1969), an injunction was granted Warriors to prevent Barry from playing under his subsequently signed contract with Oaks. The Court of Appeal affirmed the finding of the trial court that Oaks had induced Barry to breach his contract with Warriors.

Even if such conduct by Oaks would be sufficient to invoke the defense of unclean hands were Oaks a party to this suit, it is inapplicable to defeat the claim of Washington, for the two reasons discussed hereafter.

1. Oak's Unclean Hands, If Any, Do Not Taint Plaintiff

In order for defendants to invoke successfully the doctrine of clean hands, they must show that it is the plaintiff in this action, Washington, who is tainted. This defendants have failed to do and they have not cited any persuasive authorities to support their view that Washington, the successor, is tainted in equity by the malfeasance of Oaks, its predecessor.

* * *

No reason is presented to this Court why the instant case poses a situation where justice requires that equitable relief be denied to plaintiff. On the contrary, the very exercise of the conscience and discretion of the Court demands that plaintiff be able to make its arrangements free of any alleged taint of its predecessor.

2. The Misconduct Alleged, If Any, Is Not Referable to the Transaction Which Is The Subject of This Suit

The maxim of clean hands will not be invoked unless the inequitable conduct sought to be attributed to plaintiff is referable to the very transaction which is the source of the instant controversy * * *.

* * *

In the instant case the "transaction" which is the subject matter of the suit is the offer by Warriors to Barry of a contract which provides that Barry play basketball for Warriors while Barry still was under contract to play basketball for Oaks. Any misconduct for which Oaks is responsible by reason of its entering into a contract with Barry while he still was under his original contract with Warriors is, at most, a case of misconduct which is remote or misconduct which affects the instant case only indirectly.

Furthermore, it must be noted that Oaks' contract, under which Barry played for a season and received sizable compensation, did not go into effect by its own terms until after Barry's original contract with Warriors ended. In any event, Warriors were able to obtain redress for Oaks' alleged earlier misconduct through the issuance of an injunction enjoining Barry from playing for any other team until September 30, 1968, which in effect prevented Barry from playing with Oaks in 1967–68. (See Lemat Corp. v. Barry, supra.) Thus Warriors incur no continuing harm as a result of Oaks' earlier actions, and the Court believes that it would be inequitable and untenable to impute to Washington the prior, redressed wrongful action of Oaks in inducing the breach of contract between Warriors and Barry.

Minnesota Muskies, Inc. v. Hudson, 294 F. Supp. 979 (M.D.N.C. 1969), relied upon by defendants is distinguishable. In that case, Lou Hudson, a professional basketball player, negotiated and signed a contract to play with the Minnesota Muskies of the ABA while still subject to an "option" year under his then-existing contract with the St. Louis Hawks of the NBA. Hudson signed a three-year contract with Minnesota but before playing a game for that team he became discontented and he was able to procure a new five-year contract from the Hawks. In an action by Minnesota and its assignee, Florida Professional Sports, Inc., to enjoin Hudson from playing for anyone except Minnesota, defendants raised the defense of plaintiffs' unclean hands. The Court agreed, finding plaintiffs' hands too soiled to award them relief, and so denied injunctive relief.

Unlike the instant case, Minnesota, the original party which induced Hudson's breach of contract, was a plaintiff in the action for an injunction, and thus sought to benefit by its own wrongdoing. Furthermore, Minnesota's assignee intended that Hudson begin to play for it while he was still under contract to the Hawks by reason of an option agreement. In addition, there seemed little doubt that the Hawks would exercise the option. The Hawks had received no other redress for the wrong done to it when Minnesota encouraged Hudson to breach his contract with the Hawks. Finally, Hudson had not received any benefits under the Minnesota contract, a factor which distinguishes it from the instant case. Barry realized substantial benefits even during the year 1967–68 when he did not play for Oaks as well as in the year 1968–69 when he did play for Oaks.

III.

The other arguments of the defendants are illusory. Barry claims that an undesirable situation would be created if he were forced to play for a party with whom he is now in litigation and with whose arrangements he is dissatisfied. The simple answer is that in granting a preliminary injunction this Court is not forcing Barry to play for Washington. He is free to "sit it out" if he so desires, the course of action which Barry took in 1967–68.

Barry alludes to his goodly personal and financial interests in the San Francisco Bay Area, all of which he claims would be jeopardized by a move to the Washington, D.C. area. Again, the answer is that Barry need do nothing, if he so desires, while this preliminary injunction is in effect. Every famous athlete may suffer some damage to his local business and personal interests or other inconvenience when the assignment of his contract requires him to relocate in another city; but nothing is more commonplace in the history of organized professional sports in America than such moves, through trades and otherwise. Even were Barry to go to Washington, we see nothing preventing him from developing similar business interests and opportunities flowing from his unique basketball skills, if he desires to utilize them * * *.

IV.

Although the consequences of this determination may result in the departure of Barry from the San Francisco Bay Area to his claimed detriment, equitable considerations constrain this Court to sign this day the proposed findings of fact, conclusions of law, and order granting to plaintiff a preliminary injunction.

Any relief granted herein is without prejudice to defendant Barry's right to seek damages for any loss he may suffer and prove legally during the existence of this preliminary injunction.

* * *

Notes and Questions

1. The court granted the plaintiff's request for preliminary injunction and denied the applicability of the unclean hands defense for two principal reasons. First, the transaction that was the subject matter of the suit (the Warriors' offer to Barry while he was still under contract to play basketball for the Oakland Oaks) is unrelated to the Oaks' tampering with Barry's Warrior contract originally, misconduct which is "remote or misconduct which affects the instant case only indirectly." Second, the court concluded that it would be inequitable and untenable to impute to Washington, a successor employer, the wrongful action of the Oakland Oaks in inducing Barry's breach. The court distinguished cases such as *Minnesota Muskies Inc. v. Hudson*, 294 F. Supp. 979 (M.D.N.C. 1969), on the grounds that the original party inducing Barry's breach of

contract was not the plaintiff in the action seeking injunctive relief. Thus, in this case, the Washington Capitols, not trying to gain benefit from its own wrongdoing, but, rather, simply trying to enforce a valid contract right, sought equity with "clean hands."

2. If it were proven that the successor or assignee club knew of the untoward activities of the predecessor or assignor club, would that alter the result in the *Barry* case?

> The basic issue is whether the defense is one which attaches to the contract or operates only against the particular plaintiff. A review of the historical origins of the defense suggests that it was thought to be personal in nature and no bar to enforcement by other suitors. The basis of the doctrine is that equity will not use its special powers to aid a wrongdoer. While the equity order is highly discretionary, this concern would seemingly not apply where the party before the court had not in any way participated in the improper activities.

WEISTART & LOWELL §4.12, at 390–91. The question remaining is whether a successor club, knowing that part of its assets were obtained in an illegal or, at least, immoral fashion, should be permitted to enjoy the fruits of this transaction. In some respect, is the accessorizing after the fact, so to speak, conduct that should be considered as part of the balancing process that is characteristic of any equitable determination?

3. How significant is the fact that the Warriors at an earlier time had secured an injunction to preclude Barry from playing for the Oaks?

4. Is the court's conclusion that the transaction was "remote" realistic? That is, would this conclusion have been the same if the Oakland Oaks, rather than the Washington Capitols, had been the plaintiff? Language from the opinion suggests that the court considered these factors to be separate and distinct bases for repudiating the unclean hands defense. Thus, the court left the impression that, even if the Oakland Oaks had been the plaintiff, the remoteness of the earlier improper transaction would have precluded applicability of the unclean hands defense. Would such a conclusion eliminate this defense in almost every case involving an athlete who has jumped from one club to another?

5. Frequently, unclean hands cases arise not in the context of one club that has "pirated" a player from another club, but, rather, due to improprieties in the initial contract negotiations. This phenomenon was particularly prevalent during the pre-merger days of the National Football League and the American Football League, where vying for college talent was almost more sport than the playing of the games on the field. As you consider the following cases, reflect upon whether the court's conclusions were based upon meaningful factual distinctions or whether the sophistication of the parties involved and the particular judges' predilections provide a more intellectually honest rationale for the divergent opinions.

New York Football Giants, Inc.
v. Los Angeles Chargers Football Club, Inc.
291 F.2d 471 (5th Cir. 1961)

TUTTLE, **Chief Judge.** In the case of *Detroit Football Company v. Robinson*, 186 F.Supp. 933, 934, Judge Wright, of the District Court for the Eastern District of Louisiana, said:

> "This case is but another round in the sordid fight for football players, a fight which begins before these athletes enter college and follows them through their professional careers. It is a fight characterized by deception, double

dealing, campus jumping, secret alumni subsidization, semi-professionalism and professionalism. It is a fight which has produced as part of its harvest this current rash of contract jumping suits. It is a fight which so conditions the minds and hearts of these athletes that one day they can agree to play football for a stated amount for one group, only to repudiate that agreement the following day or whenever a better offer comes along. So it was with Johnny Robinson."

We have read cases cited in Judge Wright's opinion and we share his disgust at the sordid picture too often presented in this kind of litigation. So much so, in fact, that we conclude that in an appropriate case the federal equity court, which is the tribunal usually appealed to for a decree of specific performance or injunction, must decline to lend its aid to either party to a transaction that in its inception offends concepts of decency and honest dealing, such as the case before us.

In the fall of 1959 Flowers was an outstanding football player on the University of Mississippi team. His team was to play a post-season game on January 1, 1960, at the Sugar Bowl in New Orleans against a traditional rival, Louisiana State University.

He well understood rules of the Southeastern Conference (SEC) and the National Collegiate Athletic Association (NCAA)[1] made ineligible from further participation in intercollegiate games any player who had signed a contract to play with a professional team. Flowers wanted above all else to play in the Sugar Bowl game. On a trip to New York City for other purposes he was invited by the Giants' official Mara to come to his office where he was urged to sign a contract to play two seasons, beginning in 1960, with the Giants. He told Mara he wanted to retain his eligibility to play in the Sugar Bowl game. The manner in which this was made clear to Mara and the device by which Mara persuaded Flowers to sign the contract and deceive his coach, the University and the opposing team, as well as the college football public, can most satisfactorily be expressed by quoting Mara's own testimony on cross-examination:

"Q. Prior to the signing of any instrument in your office between you and Charles Flowers, Flowers made it clear to you, didn't he, that the University of Mississippi Football Team had been invited to play in the Sugar Bowl Game on January 1st in New Orleans. You knew that? A. Yes, sir.

"Q. Didn't he make it clear to you prior to the signing of the contract, or paper, in your office on December 1st, he did not want to do anything that would destroy his eligibility as a player in that game? A. We discussed that earlier.

"Q. Did he make that crystal clear he did not want to do anything, or sign any paper in your office on December 1st, that would destroy his eligibility as a player in that game? A. I certainly understood that. Yes, sir.

"Q. He made it crystal clear to you that was his attitude about it, wasn't it? A. I knew that was his attitude.

---

1. SEC Constitution and By-Laws, 1959, Rule VIII:
"Professionalism.
Any student who signs a contract or enters into any agreement, explicit or implicit, with a professional team * * * shall not be eligible for intercollegiate athletics."
NCAA Constitution, 1958–1959, Article III:
"Principle of Amateurism * * *. One who takes or has taken pay, or has accepted the promise of pay, in any form, for participation in athletics * * * does not meet [the] definition of an amateur."

"Q. In order for you to have a binding contract with Mr. Flowers in the paper that was signed and exhibited here as #3 to your testimony, and allow him to play in the Sugar Bowl Game, what proposal did you make to Mr. Flowers as to how he could sign the paper and play in the game?* * *A. That the signing of the contract would be kept confidential.

"Q. Kept confidential. So your proposal was that he could sign the paper and play in the game and you would keep it a secret. Is that correct? A. That is correct.

"Q. Why did you want to keep it a secret? A. I knew if it were revealed, that Flowers would not be permitted to play in the Sugar Bowl Game.

"Q. You knew Coach Vaught, the Head Coach at Ole Miss? A. Yes, sir.

"Q. You had known him a number of years? A. I first met him in '58, I believe.

"Q. You knew that if Coach Vaught knew this young man, Flowers, had signed a contract in your office on December 1st, obligating his service to your team, Coach Vaught would not have allowed him to play in that Sugar Bowl Game, didn't you?* * *A. That was my feeling.

"Q. That was your feeling. That was one reason you wanted to keep the matter a secret, wasn't it? A. That's correct."

Following such proposal by Mara, Flowers signed the standard form of contract of the National Football league, and received checks totalling $3500 as a sign-on bonus, and then returned to Mississippi. One of the terms of the contract was that: "This agreement shall become valid and binding upon each party hereto only when, as and if it shall be approved by the Commissioner." Part of the deceit agreed to between the parties was an agreement that Mara would not submit the contract to the Commissioner until after January 1st. Flowers later made some effort by telephone on or about December 5th to withdraw from the contract. Thereafter, the Giants promptly filed the contract with the Commissioner, and he "approved" it on December 15th. However, at Mara's request, he withheld announcement of his approval until after January 1st. On December 29th Flowers had negotiations with the Los Angeles Chargers, as a result of which he was offered a better contract, but which was not formally executed until after the Sugar Bowl game on January 1st. He wrote a letter to the Giants on December 29th stating that he was withdrawing from his agreement with them. He returned the uncashed checks for the bonus money. Flowers played in the game, all of his fans presumably thinking that he was still an eligible player, thanks to the deception proposed by the Giants and entered into by him.

The trial court held that until the "contract" was approved by the Commissioner it was not binding. It held, therefore, that when Mara, contrary to his agreement not to submit the contract to the Commissioner until after January 1st, did so, the approval by the Commissioner was not effective to make it binding and that Flowers still had the legal right to cancel until January 1st. The trial court, therefore, entered judgment for both defendants.

> Without considering the legal issues on the merits, we affirm the judgment of the trial court. We do so by application of the age-old, but sometimes overlooked, doctrine that "he who comes into equity must come with clean hands."

* * *

Here the plaintiff's whole difficulty arises because it admittedly took from Flowers what it claims to be a binding contract, but which it agreed with Flowers it would, in effect, represent was not in existence in order to deceive others who had a very material and important interest in the subject matter. If there had been a straightforward execution of the document, followed by its filing with the Commissioner, none of the legal problems now presented to this court to untangle would exist. We think no party has the right thus to create problems by its devious and deceitful conduct and then approach a court of equity with a plea that the pretended status which it has foisted on the public be ignored and its rights be declared as if it had acted in good faith throughout.

When it became apparent from uncontradicted testimony of Mara that this deceit was practiced in order to bring into being the "contract" sued upon, the trial court should have dismissed the suit without more on the basis of the "clean hands" doctrine.

To the extent that the final judgment of the trial court dismissed the complaint as amended, with costs adjudged against the plaintiff, the said judgment is affirmed. To the extent that the judgment proceeded to a legal determination as to the validity of the contracts between the parties, we conclude that, in the view we take of the equitable principles applicable, these judgments should not have been reached. The judgment of the trial court is, therefore, modified by striking therefrom paragraphs B and C of section 5 of the said judgment.

Houston Oilers, Inc. v. Neely
361 F.2d 36 (10th Cir. 1966)

PICKETT, Circuit Judge. This appeal concerns the validity of a professional football contract signed by Ralph Neely, a University of Oklahoma football player, and Houston Oilers, Inc., a Texas corporation which owns and operates a professional football team in the American Football League. Neely, a high school athlete of great promise, graduated from the Farmington, New Mexico high school in 1961, and found his way to the University of Oklahoma at Norman, Oklahoma. There his proficiency in football continued to develop, and in his senior year he became one of the nation's outstanding collegiate football players. He intended to play professional football and desired to take full advantage of the financial benefits arising from the rapidly growing popularity of professional football and the rivalry existing between the two major professional football leagues. Upon completion of the regular football schedule at the University of Oklahoma on November 28, 1964, the right to contract for Neely's services was awarded under a draft process to the Houston Oilers in the American Football League and to the Baltimore Colts in the National Football League. On December 1, 1964, Neely signed American Football League Standard Players Contracts with Houston, each containing a "no-cut" clause, for the seasons 1965 through 1968, and received therefor a $25,000 bonus check. Thereafter Neely signed contracts with the Dallas Cowboys of the National Football League, which had acquired Baltimore's draft rights to Neely, and returned the Houston contracts and the $25,000 bonus check.

Houston thereupon brought this action for a judgment, declaring its contract with Neely to be valid and enforceable, and for an injunction restraining him from playing professional football with any team other than Houston. The trial court, in denying the relief sought, found that the contract was tainted with fraud and violative of the Texas Statute of Frauds. We hold that the undisputed facts in the record disclose a valid and enforceable contract.

Immediately after the draft on November 28, 1964, both Baltimore and Houston had set in motion their contract machinery to acquire the services of Neely. On that date Neely, while enroute to New York City to accept honors awarded him as an All-American choice and to participate in the Ed Sullivan television show, discussed his plans with representatives of the Baltimore team and was given a firm offer to sign a contract. On the same day, Breen, the personnel director of the Houston team, went to New York for the sole purpose of obtaining a commitment from Neely. Neely was accompanied by his father-in-law, Robert Forte, an Oklahoma City businessman, who participated in all the negotiations as advisor to Neely. In New York City, Neely advised Breen of the Baltimore offer, but indicated that he preferred to play in the southwest. Neely told Breen that in any contract negotiations he wanted to discuss an arrangement for off-season work. Breen assured Neely and Forte that such an arrangement could be worked out, but only K. S. Adams, Jr., President of the Houston Club, could discuss such proposals. For the purpose of continuing contract discussions, the three traveled to Houston, arriving there on November 30th. At a meeting attended by Neely, Forte, Adams and Martin, the club's General Manager, a four-year contract with a "no-cut" clause was offered to Neely. The offer provided for a $25,000 bonus and a salary of $16,000 per year. In addition, Adams agreed to secure employment for Neely with a local real estate firm at a guaranteed annual income of not less than $5,000. Adams also agreed that an oil company which he owned and controlled would construct a "conventional Phillips '66 Service Station" on a suitable location in Harris County, Texas, at an approximate cost of $30,000 to $60,000, and convey the same to Neely by special warranty deed, subject to the Phillips '66 lease and a deed of trust.

Neely was impressed with the offer but desired further time to consider it. On December 1, 1964, Adams was advised that the offer was accepted. In the meantime, Neely had conferred with his wife and the owner of the Baltimore Club. The Standard Players Contracts were then prepared and executed by the parties, but were left undated. The letter agreement for additional employment, the filling station agreement, and the bonus check were dated December 1, 1964 and executed and delivered on that date. It is stipulated that these instruments constitute a single transaction. From the beginning of the discussions, Neely, for tax reasons, had insisted that the bonus money must be paid in 1964, and further, that the signing of the contract and the acceptance of the bonus money be kept secret to prevent him being declared ineligible to participate in the post-season Gator Bowl game on January 2, 1965, to which the University of Oklahoma had accepted an invitation. Any rational consideration of the evidence leads to the conclusion that all the parties knew that if Neely signed a professional football contract and received money therefor, under the rules of the N.C.A.A. and the Big Eight Conference, of which the University of Oklahoma was a member, he would consequently become ineligible to compete in the post-season game. Neely and Forte were advised that such a large sum of money could not be paid without a signed contract. It was then agreed that when the contract was signed, the $25,000 bonus check would be made payable to Forte as Trustee and that all the contract transactions would remain confidential, with no public announcement until after the Gator Bowl game.

After the contracts were executed, copies were delivered to Neely, he and Forte returned to Oklahoma. Later that day Houston's General Manager inserted the date "December 1, 1964" on the Standard Players Contracts and thereafter copies were filed with the A.F.L. Commissioner. Neely testified that he understood the arrangement to mean that the contracts would not be effective or filed until after the post-season game. However the contracts provide in plain language that they shall be valid and binding immediately upon execution and that a copy shall be filed with the League Commissioner within ten days thereafter.[4] The A.F.L. rules also require the filing of all player contracts within 10 days after execution.

---

4. Each of the Players Contracts contain this provision:
    18 Upon its execution, this contract shall be valid and binding immediately upon the par-

Immediately upon his return to Oklahoma, Neely was advised that the Dallas Cowboys, another team in the N.F.L., had obtained Baltimore's draft rights and desired contract discussions with him. Forte made several trips on behalf of Neely, and, unknown to Houston, Neely's contracts were forwarded to Dallas' attorneys for examination. Neely signed letters dated December 29, 1964, prepared by attorneys for Dallas, addressed to Houston and Adams, advising that he did not consider himself bound by the contracts and was withdrawing therefrom. The $25,000 bonus check was returned. These letters were received by Houston and Adams on December 31st. On that date the Dallas Club deposited $25,000 to the account of Neely in a Dallas bank. Prior to any publicity of the matter, Neely, apparently sensing trouble after the return of the Houston contracts, advised his coach in Jacksonville, Florida, where the Oklahoma team was preparing for the Gator Bowl game, of his activities in regard to the Houston contract. At about midnight on December 31st, Neely was notified that there had been some publicity concerning his signing with Houston. On January 1, 1965, Neely was advised that he had been declared ineligible to participate in the Gator Bowl game. There is no evidence from which it can be inferred that any publicity by Houston brought about this action. That evening Neely signed a contract to play with Dallas for the 1965 through 1968 seasons. He played for Dallas during the 1965 season and will continue to do so unless enjoined therefrom.

Neely was over the age of 21 years, and it is stipulated that he had "special, exceptional, unique knowledge, skill and ability as a football player." He was competent to enter into a valid contract to perform these services exclusively for a designated person or organization, and upon agreeing to so limit his services, he was subject under Texas law, which the parties agree is controlling, to be enjoined from performing them for anyone else.[5] *Dallas Cowboys Football Club, Inc. v. Harris*, Tex.Civ.App., 348 S.W.2d 37 * * *.

Disagreement over the validity of these contracts does not arise out of the provisions contained therein, but from an extrinsic oral understanding that their existence was to be kept secret until after the post-season game. The essence of Neely's contentions before the trial court and here is that the contracts are unenforceable because Houston falsely represented that the effective date of the agreement would be January 2, 1965, and that Houston's filing of the contract copies with the Commissioner was a violation of its promise to keep the matter secret. The trial court was of the opinion that these alleged misrepresentations constituted fraud in the inducement of the contract which would subject it to rescission. As has been heretofore stated, each contract specifically provides otherwise. Neely does not say he was so naive that he did not know his eligibility for further inter-collegiate football competition would be destroyed when he signed a professional football contract and received the bonus money. The record is too clear for any misunderstanding that the purpose of secrecy surrounding the execution of the

---

ties hereto. A copy of this contract shall be filed by the club with the Commissioner within ten (10) days after execution. Within ten (10) days after its filing in the League office, the Commissioner shall have the right to terminate this contract by his disapproval in accordance with and pursuant to the powers vested in him by the Constitution and the By-Laws of the League. If so terminated, the Commissioner shall promptly give both parties written notice of such termination and thereupon both parties shall be relieved of their respective rights and obligations hereunder.

5. The players contracts signed by Neely provide:

The Player promises and agrees that during the term of this contract he will not play football or engage in activities related to football for any other person, firm, corporation or institution except with prior written consent of the Club and the Commissioner* * *.

contracts was not to preserve Neely's eligibility, but rather to prevent his ineligibility from becoming known; otherwise there was no need for secrecy. This is illustrated by his later dealings with Dallas which similarly were not publicized, although a $25,000 deposit was made to his credit on the 31st day of December, 1964, thereby permitting him to report that amount as income for the year 1964 in his income tax return. The acceptance of this money ended his eligibility.

The trial court's conclusion that Houston represented to Neely that he would remain eligible if the contracts were kept secret is not supported by the record. As has been stated, it is apparent that Neely knew his eligibility was lost the instant he completed the Houston transaction and took the bonus money. Furthermore, the only claimed violation of the secrecy agreement was that Houston filed the contract with the League Commissioner. Nothing issued from the Commissioner's office occasioned the declaration of ineligibility. The scheme to mislead Neely's school, his coaches, his team, and the Gator Bowl opponents, no doubt would have succeeded but for Neely's own double dealing with Dallas, resulting in his attempt to avoid the Houston contracts. While we do not for a moment condone the ruthless methods employed by professional football teams in their contest for the services of college football players, including the lavish expenditure of money, it must be conceded that there is no legal impediment to contracting for the services of athletes at any time, and the above-mentioned conduct, while regrettable, does not furnish athletes with a legal excuse to avoid their contracts for reasons other than the temptations of a more attractive offer. Although there are many dismal indications to the contrary, athletes, amateur or professional, and those connected with athletics, are bound by their contracts to the same extent as anyone else, and should not be allowed to repudiate them at their pleasure.

Fraud has been defined in Texas as "the successful employment of cunning, deception or artifice to circumvent, cheat or defraud another to his injury" * * *. This court has said that fraud "is never imputed or presumed and the court should not sustain findings of fraud upon circumstances which at the most create only suspicion" * * *. The draft system in professional football limited Neely's negotiations initially to Baltimore and Houston. His collegiate football record was such that he and his father-in-law could anticipate that his services would be in demand and would command a premium contract. The opportunity presented to Neely would come but once in his lifetime, and it is understandable that the situation would be exploited to the maximum. It was with this background that Neely negotiated with Houston and Baltimore. Neely, a bright young man,[8] ably advised by his father-in-law, knew exactly what he wanted. With commendable foresight, he sought not only a favorable contract, but also a business arrangement extending beyond his football days. Houston, through its president, undertook to meet this requirement. Neely, after consulting his wife and father-in-law, and after further discussion with Baltimore, accepted Houston's final proposal, which he characterized as a "fine offer." Unexpectedly Dallas arrived on the scene, and Neely found another bidder for his services. He welcomed this new opportunity and apparently plans were set in motion designed to convince him that he could ignore the existing agreements with Houston. The first indication that Houston had of Neely's dissatisfaction with his arrangement was when the contracts were received in the mail on December 31, 1964. Up to that time there had been no publicity, and Neely was in Jacksonville prepared to play in the January 2nd game. Representatives of Houston were

---

8. Neely graduated from the College of Business Administration at the University of Oklahoma with a double major in accounting and finance.

there to arrange for the photographing of a simulated contract-signing ceremony immediately after the game. It was Neely, not Houston, who disclosed to his coach the facts which brought about a declaration of his ineligibility. Even then Neely had lost his eligibility through his transactions with Dallas. There is insufficient evidence to sustain a finding of material misrepresentation on the part of Houston amounting to fraud which would affect the validity of the contracts. It is true that Neely testified that it was his understanding that the contracts were not to become effective until after the game on January 2nd. The contracts, however, provided otherwise, and we are not at liberty to rewrite then. Furthermore, the letter of employment, the filling station arrangement, and the $25,000 bonus check which was delivered upon the execution of the contracts, were all dated December 1, 1964.

The trial court, in denying the relief sought, apparently applied the equitable maxim that "he who comes into equity must come with clean hands." This doctrine, fundamental in equity jurisprudence, means that equity will not in any manner aid a party whose conduct in relation to the litigation matter has been unlawful, unconscionable, or inequitable * * *. But the doctrine does not exclude all wrongdoers from a court of equity nor should it be applied in every case where the conduct of a party may be considered unconscionable or inequitable * * *. The maxim admits of the free exercise of judicial discretion in the furtherance of justice * * *. While it is not contended here that Houston did not have a legal right to sign Neely to a professional player's contract, it is urged that when Houston participated in a scheme to conceal that fact for the purpose of permitting an ineligible player to participate in a post-season game, it was such deceit upon others that a court of equity should not intervene to assist in the enforcement of the contract. With this argument we cannot agree. It is neither unlawful nor inequitable for college football players to surrender their amateur status and turn professional at any time. Neely was free to bind himself to such a contract on December 1, 1964 as he would have been after January 2, 1965. Nor was Houston under any legal duty to publicize the contract or to keep it secret. Its agreement to keep secret that which it had a legal right to keep secret cannot be considered inequitable or unconscionable as those terms are ordinarily used in contract negotiations. Neely relies on the case of *New York Football Giants v. Los Angeles Chargers F. Club, Inc.*, 291 F.2d 471 [(5th Cir.)], where, in a somewhat similar situation, the court applied the clean hands doctrine. It is quite apparent that the player contract in that case was acquired under circumstances much different from those in this case, but if the rule announced in that case was intended to apply to every instance in which a contract is entered into with a college football player before a post-season game with an understanding that it be kept secret to permit that player to compete in the game, then we must respectfully disagree with the conclusion.

The trial court held that the service station agreement violated the Texas Statute of Frauds, * * * in that it is vague, indefinite, uncertain and unenforceable. The letter agreement specifically provides that the service station will be for the sale and distribution of Phillips '66 products and that Ada Oil Company will arrange for the construction of a "conventional Phillips '66 Service Station of either Series ER 2000, ARS 201 or DRS 201", and be financed according to the plan selected. It is clear from the unqualified language of the instrument that the station site, the type of station, and the financing thereof is to be determined by Ada Oil Company within the limits specified, without the necessity of further agreement. Such writing satisfies the Texas Statute of Frauds.

Reversed and remanded with instructions to grant the injunction.

Notes and Questions

1. Why was an injunction granted in *Neely* but not in *Flowers*? To what degree did the sophistication or gullibility of the athletes involved motivate the courts' conclusions? Are the factual distinctions made by the *Neely* court significant or are we simply dealing with a jurisdiction that is more cavalier about unclean hands and the need to "do equity?"

2. As discussed earlier in this chapter, the pre-merger days of the NFL-AFL were characterized by no small amount of bitterness and acrimony. *AFL v. NFL*, 323 F.2d 124 (4th Cir. 1963). The often unscrupulous interleague battles for players' services represented some of the more colorful and regrettable tactics employed during this period by the leagues and their member clubs. The merger of the two leagues brought peace and prosperity and even evoked congressional approval and limited exemptions from antitrust scrutiny. *See, e.g.,* 15 U.S.C. §§ 1291–1295. As will be discussed later, these types of mergers certainly eliminate the issues arising in the *Flowers* and *Neely* cases, but they likewise seriously compromise an athlete's ability to demand top dollar, particularly in the absence of free agency. The free agency question obviously assumed greater importance when the merger was completed, because there was only one league with a comprehensive reserve system within which a player could attempt to market his services.

3. What is the possible impact of the Statute of Frauds upon the oral agreements that supposedly had occurred regarding the secrecy of the contracts?

4. What arguments would you make and what theories would you advance to support the players' attempts to "avoid" any contractual obligations that may have arisen in these cases? In particular, discuss whether the club's activities constituted misrepresentation, duress, undue influence, or unconscionability. What responses would you offer as counterarguments for the club? If the players were able to demonstrate that one or more of the avoidance arguments referenced above were valid, is there any evidence that the players nonetheless ratified the agreements, thereby precluding their disaffirmance or renunciation of the deals?

5. A) Hub Carlson, star pitcher for the New York Debts, had won 67 games and lost only 15 during the 1983, '84, and '85 Major League Baseball seasons. During those years, the Debts were drawing over 35,000 people per home game when Hub pitched. In all other games, average home game attendance was about 9,000 fans. In truth, Hub had become a cult figure in New York and was nicknamed the Mealticket II. (Who was the original "Mealticket"? No points, just curious.) Despite Hub's outstanding record, each year (1983, '84, and '85) the Debts finished last in their division with the worst record in baseball. Midway through the 1986 season, with the Debts again occupying the division cellar (last place), Hub became "fed up" with the game and announced his retirement. Hub was in the second year of a lucrative four year-four million dollar contract package. This contract provided in pertinent part:

> The player promises and agrees that during the term of this contract he will not play baseball or engage in activities related to baseball for any other person, firm, corporation or institution, or on his own behalf, except with the prior written consent of the Club.

Also, Hub was the beneficiary of a $100,000 signing bonus, which he received upon signing his current four-year contract. The purpose of the bonus was to dissuade Hub from signing with a team in the newly formed, but now defunct, Galactic Baseball Association.

Hub announced that he was leaving to pursue a broadcasting career and that, in fact, he had signed a three-year contract at $1.5 million per year to host "Hubcap," a television program that would be aired every weeknight, Monday through Friday, from 8:00 p.m. to 10:00 p.m. The show, which aired immediately after Hub signed his TV contract, consists of film footage, in-depth interviews, pitching hints, scouting reports on the various clubs and some variety spots featuring Hub's many diverse talents, including singing, dancing, and impersonations.

During the week following Hub's defection, the Debts were still floundering in the cellar, drawing an average of 9,000 fans for each home game. Meanwhile, the local network's ratings were soaring. The Debts initiated suit and the case was assigned to the judge for whom you are clerking. The Debts have sued Hub for breach of contract and have sought: an affirmative injunction requiring him to report back to the Debts immediately; an injunction precluding Hub from "performing" for the TV network; and damages. The judge asks you to prepare a detailed memorandum examining the merits of the Debts' lawsuit and the availability of the relief requested. Prepare this memorandum, addressing the advantages *and* disadvantages of each potential argument.

B) Assume the foregoing facts, but consider the additional evidence that, subsequent to Hub's defection, he returned to the Debts in breach of his agreement and negative covenant with the network. Assume further that prior to Hub's latest change of heart, the network's ownership had changed hands. Would it matter if Hub's contract with the network had contained a prohibition against assignments?

Chapter 7

Antitrust Law and Sports:
A Primer

I. Introduction

Antitrust issues related to professional sports cannot be considered separately from the overall body of antitrust law. There are at least two antitrust issues—the "baseball exemption" and the Sports Broadcasting Act of 1961 and 1966 exemptions—that only arise in the context of professional sports, and there are several issues that arise more frequently in sports cases. However, sports cases involving the antitrust laws are just one type of antitrust case, and lawyers and judges addressing such cases analyze them within the overall framework of the law of antitrust.

It is, of course, not possible for a casebook that focuses on many different legal issues related to professional sports to explain all antitrust law, in much the same way as it is not possible for a sports law course to provide you with the antitrust law background that is provided by a full introductory course dedicated solely to antitrust. Nevertheless, a basic understanding of the antitrust laws is necessary to appreciate the subtleties of the antitrust decisions involving professional sports. To that end, this chapter is intended to provide a basic overview of some of the relevant antitrust statutes, terms, and concepts, as well as a basic understanding of the economics behind the operation of sports leagues and the production of other professional sporting events.

The normal context in which antitrust law is applied involves traditional businesses that buy a variety of inputs, create a product or service, and sell that product or service to others. Many businesses that sell products operate in a traditional framework, in which a manufacturer buys raw materials and employs workers to manufacture a product, which is then sold to wholesalers or distributors. The wholesalers or distributors then sell the product to retailers, who stock the product and sell it to the ultimate consumers, who are the end users. There are, of course, modifications to this traditional framework even in normal business contexts, as there may be various levels in the chain of distribution. However, over the past one hundred years most judicial opinions concerning antitrust have involved businesses that resemble the traditional manufacturer-wholesaler-retailer economic structure.

When sports leagues and producers of circuits or tours of individual events have been sued by plaintiffs challenging their rules, regulations and other conduct, the leagues, circuits, and tours have contended that the differences between the business of sports and more traditional enterprises are so significant that the antitrust precedent developed in the context of traditional business should not be applied to their operations. Even when courts have held the antitrust laws applicable to the sports industry, leagues and circuits have argued that the differences in the business of professional sports mandate different rules or modification of the traditional antitrust rules.

In general, efforts to persuade courts not to apply the antitrust laws to the business of professional sports have been unsuccessful (with the business of baseball as the single, glaring exception). However, "sports defendants" have had some success convincing judges that the special nature of professional sports requires greater scrutiny and greater factual development before traditional antitrust rules (*e.g.,* the Sherman Act §1 *per se* rule, see below) are applied. In addition, some judges, while holding basic antitrust rules applicable to sports, have either been sympathetic to the idea that sports are different or have had difficulty understanding how to adapt traditional antitrust principles to the unique structure within which professional sports operate.

Nevertheless, for the past forty years antitrust law has played a major role in reshaping professional sports. Even in situations in which judicial decisions have not mandated changes, many modifications have been made at least in part because the decisionmakers were operating with an antitrust Sword of Damocles hovering above. Many decisions made by those who control professional sports events are a result of antitrust advice and interpretations of the potential impact of the antitrust laws upon contemplated plans of action.

While antitrust has had a major impact on the business of sports, antitrust cases arising out of sports business disputes also have had a major role in overall antitrust jurisprudence. Antitrust decisions related to professional sports often have been landmark decisions, significantly affecting the transactional advice of practitioners counseling clients engaged in traditional businesses. For example, a substantial percentage of the leading judicial opinions concerning the scope of the antitrust labor exemption, including the landmark decision of the Supreme Court in *Brown v. Pro-Football, Inc.*, 518 U.S. 231 (1996), have arisen in the context of disputes between professional athletes and the teams that employ them.

To apply the antitrust laws to any business, it is important to understand how the business works, what are the inputs used to create the final product, who purchases the inputs, who sells the inputs, what products are created, to whom are the products sold, who are the competitors in the sale of those products, who are buyers of those products, and other basic questions. Answers to those questions are necessary to appreciate fully the framework in which the business is conducted. Once the professional sport is understood as a business, it is then possible to apply the laws and precedents developed in the context of other businesses to reach determinations about the likely anticompetitive effects of various agreements and conduct of those entities involved in professional sports.

II. Statutes: What Antitrust Laws Apply to Professional Sports?

Over the past one hundred fifteen years, the United States Congress and the fifty states have passed legislation designed to promote competition and prevent unfair practices that may lead to monopolies or suppression of competition. The primary antitrust statute is the Sherman Antitrust Act, which was enacted in 1890 and has maintained its original basic form. The following is a summary of the major antitrust provisions, all of which could, in certain circumstances, be applied to conduct involving professional sports. Again, the most significant antitrust provisions for the business of professional sports are Section 1 and Section 2 of the Sherman Act, 15 U.S.C. §§1 and 2.

(A) Section 1 of the Sherman Act, 15 U.S.C. §1, provides that "[e]very contract, combination in the form of trust or otherwise, or conspiracy, in restraint of trade or commerce among the several States, or with foreign nations, is hereby declared to be illegal." This provision is the primary antitrust provision applied to agreements or joint action by the teams in a league, the owners of events in a sports tour or circuit, or other groups involved in the business of professional sports. This simple declaration against "contract[s], combination[s] * * * [and] conspirac[ies]" is applied to a very broad range of conduct, including bid rigging; price fixing; horizontal market division; group boycotts; territory, customer, and location restrictions; tying; exclusive dealing; and other restrictive agreements. Section 1 requires an agreement between two or more separate economic actors. It does not apply to unilateral conduct by a single firm, agreements between a parent corporation and a wholly-owned subsidiary, or "conspiracies" between two employees who work for a single corporation and are acting on behalf of that corporation. While by its terms it purports to prohibit *all* contracts, combinations, or conspiracies that are "in restraint of trade or commerce," it was interpreted early on only to prohibit agreements that *unreasonably* restrain trade. *See, e.g., Texaco v. Dagher*, 126 S.Ct. 1276, 1279 (2006); *State Oil Co. v. Khan*, 522 U.S. 3, 10 (1997).

(B) Section 2 of the Sherman Act, 15 U.S.C. §2, prohibits monopolization, attempts to monopolize, and conspiracies to monopolize. This section is the back-up provision of the Sherman Act and does not require proof of an agreement. It restricts even unilateral conduct by a single firm. However, Section 2 is only implicated by single firm conduct when a defendant has achieved "monopoly power" (a term to be explained later) or is attempting to achieve a "monopoly position" in a "relevant market" and has a dangerous probability of succeeding. The Section 1 prohibitions against agreements in restraint of trade already prohibit virtually all (if not all) conduct that could be a conspiracy to monopolize.

(C) Section 3 of the Clayton Act, 15 U.S.C. §14, prohibits leases or sales of "goods * * * or other commodities * * * on the condition, agreement or understanding that the lessee or purchaser thereof shall not use or deal in the goods * * * or other commodities of a competitor * * * where the effect * * * may be to substantially lessen competition or tend to create a monopoly in any line of commerce." This prohibition on sales or leases on condition is applied to tying arrangements and exclusive dealing agreements that involve "goods * * * or other commodities." Because professional sports antitrust cases do not generally involve goods (except for cases about equipment, they usually involve player services, broadcast rights, sponsorship rights, franchise ownership, etc.) and Section 1 of the Sherman Act has been interpreted to prohibit everything prohibited by Section 3 of the Clayton Act, whether it involves goods or services or intangible rights, this section seldom adds to antitrust analysis involving professional sports.

(D) Section 7 of the Clayton Act, 15 U.S.C. §18, prohibits mergers and acquisitions where the effect may be substantially to lessen competition or to create a monopoly in any line of commerce. Its scope and its relevance to professional sports are generally limited to mergers or acquisitions, such as the merger of two previously independent sports leagues (*e.g.*, AFL-NFL, ABA-NBA). *But see* 15 U.S.C. §1291, *et seq.* (the Sports Broadcasting Act, discussed below).

(E) Section 5 of the Federal Trade Commission Act, 15 U.S.C. §45, prohibits "unfair methods of competition in or affecting commerce. * * *" There is no implied right of action under Section 5 of the Federal Trade Commission Act. *See, e.g., Summey v. Ford Motor Credit Co.*, 449 F. Supp. 132, 135 (D.S.C. 1976), *aff'd mem.*, 573 F.2d 1306 (4th Cir. 1978); *Naylor v. Case & McGrath, Inc.*, 585 F.2d 557, 561 (2d Cir. 1978); *Fulton v. Hecht Co.*, 580 F.2d 1243, 1249 n.2 (5th Cir. 1978), *cert. denied*, 440 U.S. 981 (1979). Only the FTC is empowered to proceed after notice and hearing against persons who violate Section 5. Section 5(b) empowers the FTC to issue "cease and desist" orders against respondents found to have engaged in unfair methods of competition or unfair or deceptive acts or practices. *See* 15 U.S.C. §45(b). At the conclusion of all appeals or, if there are no appeals, sixty days after service of the cease and desist order on the respondent, the order becomes final. If a final cease and desist order is violated, the FTC can apply to a federal district court for the imposition of civil penalties, injunctions, and other equitable relief.

Section 5 is broader than the other federal antitrust provisions. It gives the FTC the authority to "define and proscribe an unfair competitive practice, even though the practice does not infringe either the letter or the spirit of the antitrust laws" and "to proscribe practices as unfair or deceptive in their effect upon consumers regardless of their nature or quality as competitive practices or their effect on competition." *FTC v. Sperry & Hutchinson Co.*, 405 U.S. 233, 244 (1972).

While the scope of Section 5 is potentially much greater than the other federal antitrust laws, its significance in the area of professional sports is limited by the fact that it can only be invoked in litigation by the FTC. That qualifier provides the main limitation on the volume of litigation under this provision. *But see* State "Baby FTC" Acts, discussed below.

(F) Section 2 of the Clayton Act, as amended by the Robinson-Patman Act, 15 U.S.C. §13, among other things, makes it unlawful in certain circumstances for a seller engaged in commerce to discriminate in price between different buyers. That prohibition appears in Section 2(a), the most frequently invoked provision in the Robinson-Patman Act. 15 U.S.C. §13(a). Section 2(f) makes it unlawful for a buyer "knowingly to induce or receive" a discriminatory price. 15 U.S.C. §13(f). Section 2(c) prohibits sellers from paying to or receiving from a buyer certain commissions, brokerage fees, or other types of compensation. 15 U.S.C. §13(c). Sections 2(d) and 2(e) prohibit discriminatory payments by a seller for a product's handling, promotion, or advertising. 15 U.S.C. §13(d)–(e). The Robinson-Patman Act rarely applies to professional sports disputes.

(G) State Antitrust Laws generally mirror the Sherman Act. They prohibit the same practices as those addressed by Sections 1 and 2 of the Sherman Act, and are usually interpreted in accordance with federal case law, but remove the ne-

cessity that the plaintiff demonstrate an effect on interstate or foreign commerce. These provisions generally add little to the federal prohibitions. Further, in many instances, they may be held inapplicable to conduct by national or international sports leagues and associations in light of the interstate nature of professional sports, the federal court precedents in the past forty years broadening the scope of "interstate commerce" and limiting the plaintiff's burden in that respect, and the federal constitutional limitations such as preemption (under the Supremacy Clause) and prohibition of undue interference with interstate commerce under the Commerce Clause. *See, e.g., Flood v. Kuhn*, 407 U.S. 258 (1972), in Chapter 8.

(H) State "Baby FTC" Acts, as the name suggests, are similar in nature to the federal FTC Act, but there are significant differences from state to state. Some statutes prohibit "unfair methods of competition." Some others prohibit "unfair or deceptive trade practices." Some of the state statutes limit enforcement of these provisions to the state Attorney General's office or a similar governmental authority, while others explicitly provide a private cause of action to any person injured by reason of a violation of the statute. Still other states limit the private cause of action to consumers who are purchasing for personal, as opposed to business, use. Some of the statutes explicitly mandate that they be interpreted consistently with federal precedents, opinions, and rules of the Federal Trade Commission. These statutes have had little applicability in antitrust cases involving professional sports for the reasons explained above that state antitrust laws are seldom of significance.

III. An Overview of Sections 1 and 2 of the Sherman Act

As explained above, the antitrust provisions most relevant to professional sports cases are Sections 1 and 2 of the Sherman Act. The primary difference between the two provisions is that Section 1 is aimed at *agreements*, which the Sherman Act calls "contracts, combinations or conspiracies." To prevail, a plaintiff who can establish an agreement under Section 1 only has to show that the agreement unreasonably restrained competition. If the plaintiff cannot establish an agreement but can only prove that the challenged conduct was by a single firm or a single business entity, the plaintiff cannot bring an action under Section 1, and instead must rely on Section 2. Even under Section 2, the plaintiff cannot challenge the conduct as a "conspiracy to monopolize" without proving the existence of an agreement.

When challenging single firm conduct, the plaintiff must prove either that: (1) the defendant is a monopolist and has used, acquired, or maintained its monopoly position in some improper way; or (2) the defendant is guilty of an attempt to monopolize, in that the defendant had the specific intent to achieve monopoly power in a relevant market and that the defendant has a dangerous probability of succeeding in that effort by improper means if not restrained by the court. As a result, various sports leagues have attempted to convince courts that their teams should be considered parts of a single entity, judged only under the analysis of Section 2, and that the league should be considered a single actor, not a participant in joint activity. As explained above, if viewed as joint activity by the teams, rather than unilateral conduct by a league, league rules, regulations and other conduct will be proscribed by Section 1 if they unreasonably restrain trade.

Over the years, as federal courts have seen hundreds and thousands of antitrust cases, they have developed a mode of economic analysis and have grouped agreements into categories or types of agreements that may violate Section 1. For each type of conduct, such as bid rigging, price fixing, horizontal market division, group boycotts, tying, and exclusive dealing, basic rules of analysis have been developed. Accordingly, when a plaintiff brings a case under Section 1, the plaintiff often has separate causes of actions, challenging various agreements as price fixing, group boycotts, horizontal market division, and so on. For each one of these legal theories and types of conduct, there are leading United States Supreme Court and United States court of appeals precedents that guide the lower court judges when they are evaluating the claims.

Similarly, in cases brought under Section 2, there are certain types of wrongful conduct in which defendants are repeatedly alleged to have engaged. Plaintiffs contend that these practices, such as predatory pricing, abuse of administrative or judicial processes to prevent entry, and denial of access to essential facilities, constitute anticompetitive conduct intended to achieve or maintain a monopoly position. Over the years, a fairly discrete set of judicial precedents has developed rules for assessing the legality of these types of conduct.

IV. Analysis of Section 1 of the Sherman Act

(A) Introduction

Section 1 of the Sherman Act states, in pertinent part, that:

> Every contract, combination in the form of trust or otherwise, or conspiracy, in restraint of trade * * * is declared to be illegal. * * *

15 U.S.C. §1 (1980). Since 1911, the courts have interpreted Section 1 to only prohibit "contract[s], combination[s] * * *, or conspirac[ies]" that *unreasonably* restrain trade. *See Standard Oil of N. J. v. United States*, 221 U.S. 1 (1911). *See also Texaco, Inc. v. Dagher*, 126 S.Ct. 1276, 1279 (2006); *State Oil Co. v. Khan*, 522 U.S. 3, 10 (1997). Some agreements, including price fixing, horizontal market division, and certain group boycotts and tying arrangements, are said by courts to be *per se* (automatically) unlawful. *See, e.g., Arizona v. Maricopa Cty. Medical Soc'y*, 457 U.S. 332 (1982) (price fixing); *United States v. Topco Associates, Inc.*, 405 U.S. 596 (1972) (horizontal market division); *Northwest Wholesale Stationers v. Pacific Stationery Printing Co.*, 472 U.S. 85 (1985) (group boycotts); *Illinois Tool Works, Inc. v. Independent Ink, Inc.*, 126 S.Ct. 1281 (2006) and *Jefferson Parish Hosp. Dist. No. 2 v. Hyde*, 466 U.S. 2 (1984) (tying arrangements). *See* Section D, below.

Most restraints, however, are analyzed by applying the "Rule of Reason," under which the fact finder must determine whether the challenged agreement imposes an *unreasonable* restraint on competition. *See, e.g., Arizona v. Maricopa Cty. Medical Soc'y*, 457 U.S. at 343. As the Supreme Court stated in *National Society of Professional Engineers v. United States*:

> There are, thus, two complementary categories of antitrust analysis. In the first category are agreements whose nature and necessary effect are so plainly

anticompetitive that no elaborate study of the industry is needed to establish their illegality—they are "illegal *per se*." In the second category are agreements whose competitive effect can only be evaluated by analyzing the facts peculiar to the business, the history of the restraint, and the reason why it was imposed.

435 U.S. 679, 692 (1978).

The basic analytical process for evaluating claims under Section 1 involves asking and answering a series of questions. Some of these questions relate to a specific element of a Section 1 claim, but others are merely guides that help antitrust lawyers and courts distinguish agreements that are lawful from anticompetitive agreements that violate Section 1. Some of the most important questions are as follows:

(1) Did the challenged conduct involve an agreement—was the "contract, combination * * * or conspiracy" requirement met?

(2) If so, was it a horizontal or a vertical agreement?

(3) Was it an agreement that can fairly be said to fit into one of the categories of *per se* violations (*e.g.*, price fixing (horizontal or vertical), bid rigging, horizontal market division, group boycotts, or tying arrangements)?

(4) Even if it could fairly be said to fit into one of the *per se* categories, does it merit *per se* treatment?

(5) If it does not merit *per se* treatment, under the Rule of Reason (a) what are its anticompetitive effects, (b) what are its procompetitive benefits, and (c) if the procompetitive benefits exceed the anticompetitive effects, is there a less restrictive means by which the procompetitive benefits could be achieved without causing the anticompetitive effects?

(B) Concerted Action—An Agreement Between Two or More Persons

The first element of both the *per se* and the Rule of Reason analyses under Section 1 is to assess whether the challenged conduct involved a "contract, combination * * * or conspiracy." 15 U.S.C. §1. *See, e.g., Copperweld Corp. v. Independence Tube Corp.*, 467 U.S. 752, 768 (1984) ("Section 1 of the Sherman Act * * * reaches unreasonable restraints of trade effected by a 'contract, combination * * * or conspiracy' between *separate* entities. It does not reach conduct that is 'wholly unilateral.' Concerted activity subject to §1 is judged more sternly than unilateral activity under §2."). As defined by the Supreme Court, the requirement of a combination or conspiracy is satisfied when two or more persons have a "unity of purpose or a common design and understanding or a meeting of minds in an unlawful arrangement." *See, e.g., Monsanto Co. v. Spray-Rite Serv. Corp.*, 465 U.S. 752, 764 (1984); *American Tobacco Co. v. United States*, 328 U.S. 781 (1946).

Courts have consistently held that the three terms "contract, combination, and conspiracy" are all simply ways of saying that the challenged conduct had to be pursuant to some sort of agreement between two separate economic entities. The agreement can be written, oral, or tacit, express or implied, and enforceable or unenforceable. All these arrangements constitute agreements for purposes of Section 1. In applying the requirement of two separate entities, courts have held that "agreements" between parent companies and wholly-owned subsidiaries, between employees and the company that employs them, or among employees of a single firm do not constitute agreements between or among separate entities as required to state a claim under Section 1. In the context of professional sports, as explained above, a related issue is whether the teams in a league should be considered a single entity for antitrust purposes, such that actions of its member clubs would not constitute an agreement under Section 1.

(C) Horizontal Versus Vertical Agreements

(1) Vertical Agreements

Vertical agreements are agreements such as those between: (1) a manufacturer and sellers of inputs (such as labor, materials, utilities, and facilities); (2) a manufacturer and distributors, wholesalers, or retailers; (3) a distributor or wholesaler and its supplier(s) of inputs (besides the product from the manufacturer that they buy to resell- *e.g.,* labor to operate the distributorship, facilities, etc.); (4) a distributor or wholesaler and its retailers; and (5) a retailer and consumers. Virtually every sale of products or services constitutes a vertical agreement. These arrangements are referred to as "vertical" agreements because they follow the "vertical" chain of distribution from basic inputs to an end product sold to consumers. Vertical agreements are an essential aspect of every business. No industry or business operates without vertical agreements. In the sports world, agreements between athletes and teams or events, agreements between teams and facilities, agreements between teams or leagues and television companies, and agreements between coaches or umpires and leagues or teams are all examples of vertical agreements.

(2) Horizontal Agreements

Horizontal agreements are agreements between or among firms or persons at the same level of the market. For example, agreements between two or more manufacturers, agreements between employees, and agreements between retailers all constitute horizontal agreements. Therefore, horizontal agreements are agreements between current or potential competitors. Two manufacturers agree to create a joint research facility to develop new products; two distributors agree to establish a joint buying unit to increase their total purchases and take advantage of volume discounts; or all the competing television networks agree to limit the violence and language used on their broadcasts from 7 to 10 p.m. Each of the preceding arrangements is a horizontal agreement. In the sports world, teams in a league may agree to honor each other's exclusive territories; competing circuits may agree on the location and time of their particular events; leagues may agree to work together to lobby Congress for favorable legislation; and players may agree (through their union) not to play unless a more favorable set of terms and conditions of employment is established. Again, these examples illustrate classic horizontal arrangements.

(3) Different Analysis of Horizontal Versus Vertical Agreements

Vertical agreements are essential. Horizontal agreements are rarely essential. Vertical agreements usually improve the functioning of markets and facilitate the development, manufacture, distribution and sale of products and services. Many horizontal agreements reduce the amount of competition between competitors. If extended to all or almost all competitors in a relevant market, horizontal agreements to substitute cooperation for competition could lead to joint exercise of monopoly power, lower payments to the sellers of inputs by the collaborators, and higher prices paid by the purchasers of products or services from those horizontal collaborators.

Vertical agreements can also adversely affect competition. For example, an exclusive agreement between a manufacturer and the owner of a quarry could deny all the manufacturer's competitors access to raw material only available from that quarry. However, the effect of vertical agreements on competition is more indirect and usually requires agreements that foreclose a major percentage of the supply or the customers for a particular product. The idea is that one competitor can improve its market position by entering into agreements that limit other competitors' access to the inputs or the customers that they need. If the firm entering into the vertical agreement cannot completely cut-off its competitors' access to inputs or consumers, it may at least be able to increase its competitors' costs of doing business and thereby improve its own competitive position. However, it is difficult in most cases to achieve these results with vertical agreements. The effect on competition of horizontal agreements between competitors limiting the scope or intensity of competition between them is more direct. Accordingly, horizontal agreements are viewed much more skeptically and more harshly by antitrust commentators and tribunals. Therefore, in assessing the legality of agreements that are alleged to restrain trade unreasonably, the antitrust laws distinguish horizontal and vertical agreements.

(4) Distinguishing Procompetitive and Anticompetitive Agreements

The primary concern of antitrust law is with horizontal agreements by which competitors agree to limit or eliminate the competition between or among themselves. For example, sellers of oil could gather together and agree to limit production or raise prices, to increase their sales and profitability, rather than independently expanding production and lowering prices. Such an arrangement would cause all consumers of oil to face higher prices. The competitive system is thereby subverted. By bid rigging, price fixing, dividing up markets, and other anticompetitive practices, horizontal competitors can undermine the competitive system on which our economy is based and increase their profits at the expense of all who purchase their products or services. In addition, those "consumers" who purchase other products or services for which the noncompetitive products or services are an input may also face higher prices.

However, not all agreements between or among horizontal competitors are anticompetitive. For example, two small firms, unable to afford the equipment necessary for a research and development facility, might agree to pool their resources to finance the facility. A group of independent retailers might agree to create a cooperative to buy their products and office supplies in bulk, thereby reducing their costs and making it possible for them to lower the prices that they charge. Such lower prices may help those retailers improve the quality of their competition against a large retail chain, thereby increasing competition and benefiting consumers.

Having recognized that not all horizontal agreements are anticompetitive, courts interpreting the antitrust laws must distinguish those arrangements that serve to eliminate competition from agreements that foster competition. Similarly, while most vertical agreements do not adversely affect competition, the courts must recognize that some vertical agreements lock up supply or distribution channels for a product and may act to stifle or prevent competition.

(D) Per Se Violations of Section 1 of the Sherman Act

The traditional form of Section 1 analysis has been the Rule of Reason, under which the competitive effects of a challenged agreement are assessed by examining a wide range of issues, including the history behind and reasons for the agreement, its purpose, its scope and duration, and its likely competitive effects. *See, e.g., Texaco, Inc. v. Dagher*, 126 S.Ct. 1276, 1279 (2006). In the early cases, this broad analysis led to the introduction of a broad range of evidence and creation of extensive trial records for submission to juries that were called upon to assess the "reasonableness" of agreements. Over time, however, the federal courts came to the conclusion that they were seeing certain types of agreements repeatedly, and those agreements were consistently held to violate Section 1 under the Rule of Reason. *See, e.g., Nynex Corp. v. Discon, Inc.*, 525 U.S. 128, 133–34 (1998). As a result, from the 1920s through the early 1970s, courts pronounced certain categories of agreements *per se* or "automatic" violations of Section 1, without the need for applying the Rule of Reason. Plaintiffs challenging *per se* violations did not have to prove any actual adverse effects on competition—those effects were presumed, and courts generally held that there were no affirmative defenses to *per se* claims. As explained above, the primary categories of agreements characterized as *per se* violations were price fixing, horizontal market division, group boycotts, and tying arrangements.

In the early cases in which these *per se* categories were developed, the conduct at issue was obviously anticompetitive. However, having announced broad categories of *per se* violations, the courts were then called upon to assess exactly what conduct constituted "price fixing," "horizontal market division," "group boycotts," and "tying arrangements." The problem was complicated by imaginative and creative plaintiffs who sought to expand each of these *per se* categories to include the conduct that they were challenging in particular cases. Plaintiffs tried to describe all challenged agreements as within one or more of the *per se* categories.

The courts have responded in a variety of ways, both defining and limiting the scope of these *per se* categories. As a result, a significant portion of litigation under Section 1 involves a determination of whether specified agreements are within one or more of the *per se* violations or whether, alternatively, the plaintiff must prove that the agreements violate the Rule of Reason.

(1) Price Fixing*

The Supreme Court has stated that "protection of price competition from conspiratorial restraint is an object of special solicitude under the antitrust laws," *United States v. General Motors Corp.*, 384 U.S. 127, 148 (1966), because restrictions on free and open price competition pose an "actual or potential threat to the central nervous system of the economy." *United States v. Socony-Vacuum Oil Co.*, 310 U.S. 150, 224–26 n.59 (1940). As a result, the Supreme Court has declared a variety of agreements among competitors that raise, lower, or stabilize prices to be unlawful as *per se* violations of Section 1. At the same time, the Court has recognized that "[n]ot all arrangements among actual or potential competitors that have an impact on price are *per se* violations

---

* This overview only addresses horizontal price fixing; bid rigging and vertical price fixing have not generally been at issue in antitrust cases involving professional or amateur sports.

of the Sherman Act or even unreasonable restraints." *Broadcast Music, Inc. v. Columbia Broadcasting Sys., Inc.,* 441 U.S. 1, 23 (1979).

There are cases in which agreements that have had an impact on price have been found not to be *per se* unlawful when the effect on price was incidental to an agreement designed to improve the competitive working of the marketplace. The Supreme Court has stated that "'price fixing' is a shorthand way of describing certain categories of business behavior" that are *per se* unlawful, but in that same case declared that classifying conduct as price fixing "is not a question simply of determining whether two or more potential competitors have literally 'fixed' a price.'" *Broadcast Music, Inc. v. CBS, Inc.,* 441 U.S. at 9. *See also Texaco, Inc. v. Dagher,* 126 S.Ct. at 1280.

Moreover, price-fixing violations are not limited to agreements that directly concern price. For example, in *Socony-Vacuum,* 310 U.S. 150, the Court was called upon to evaluate an agreement among the major oil companies that they would purchase excess gasoline supplied by independent oil companies to prevent prices in the gasoline market from falling sharply. The defendants' conduct served to stabilize the gasoline price level even though there was no explicit agreement among the oil companies about the prices that they would charge. The Court held that concerted action to tamper with price structures is unlawful, advancing the broad proposition that "[u]nder the Sherman Act a combination formed for the purpose and with the effect of raising, depressing, fixing, pegging, or stabilizing the price of a commodity in interstate or foreign commerce is illegal *per se*." 310 U.S. at 224–26 n.59.

(2) *Horizontal Market Division*

Horizontal agreements among competitors that restrict their competition at the same level of the market have traditionally been held to constitute *per se* violations of Section 1. In a series of cases dating back to the early years of the Sherman Act, the Supreme Court repeatedly applied a standard of *per se* illegality to horizontal conspiracies allocating territories, dividing up customers, or otherwise imposing non-price restraints upon actual or potential competitors. *See, e.g., United States v. Topco Associates, Inc.,* 405 U.S. 596 (1972); *Timken Roller Bearing Co. v. United States,* 341 U.S. 593 (1951); *United States v. National Lead Co.,* 332 U.S. 319 (1947); *Hartford Empire Co. v. United States,* 323 U.S. 386 (1945). Rather than limiting the competition between them by agreeing to raise prices or limit output, the defendants in those cases had simply agreed to avoid each others' territories or customers.

If a dominant firm in the eastern United States agreed not to sell products in the west in return for the dominant west coast firm agreeing not to move east, that conduct would traditionally have been held to be a clear *per se* violation. In some recent cases, however, courts have expressed dissatisfaction with a rigid *per se* analysis. For example, the United States Court of Appeals for the Fourth Circuit has carved out a narrow "affirmative defense" if the defendants acted with the purpose and effect of achieving a legitimate public policy objective. *See, e.g., Hospital Building Co. v. Trustees of the Rex Hospital,* 691 F.2d 678 (4th Cir. 1982), *cert. denied,* 464 U.S. 890 (1983); *see also NCAA v. Board of Regents of Univ. of Okla.,* 468 U.S. 85 (1984). Thus, recent precedent has been moving toward a broader Rule of Reason inquiry for many horizontal restraints that were formerly governed by a more rigid *per se* analysis. *See, e.g., Chicago Professional Sports Ltd. Partnership v. NBA,* 754 F. Supp. 1336 (N.D. Ill. 1991) *aff'd,* 961 F.2d 667 (7th Cir.), *cert. denied,* 506 U.S. 954 (1992); *Rothery Storage & Van Co. v. Atlas Van Lines, Inc.,* 792 F.2d 210, 224–29 (D.C. Cir. 1986), *cert. denied,* 479 U.S. 1033 (1987);

General Leaseways v. National Truck Leasing, 744 F.2d 588 (7th Cir. 1984). *But see Palmer v. BRG of Ga., Inc.*, 498 U.S. 46 (1990) (per curiam) (*per se* horizontal market division).

(3) Group Boycotts

(a) Introduction

An antitrust "boycott" is a concerted refusal, usually by horizontal competitors, to deal with others. This type of agreement is generally referred to as a "group boycott" or a "concerted refusal to deal." The practice generally is regarded as unreasonable *per se* under the federal antitrust laws because it denies parties to the agreement the freedom to decide independently whether to deal with the boycotted party, and it prevents the boycotted party from dealing in an open market. As discussed below, the extent to which group boycotts are *per se* illegal, rather than subject to Rule of Reason scrutiny, is unsettled after the Supreme Court's decision in *Northwest Wholesale Stationers v. Pacific Stationery & Printing Co.*, 472 U.S. 85 (1985). Yet, even prior to the *Northwest Wholesale Stationers* decision, the type of conduct that constituted an unlawful group boycott had not been clearly defined. The Supreme Court had stated that "boycotts are not a unitary phenomenon'" and numerous Supreme Court decisions had "reflect[ed] a marked lack of uniformity in defining the term." *St. Paul Fire & Marine Ins. Co. v. Barry*, 438 U.S. 531, 543 (1978), (quoting Phillip Areeda, *Antitrust Analysis* at 381 (2d ed. 1974)); *see also Cha-Car, Inc. v. Calder Race Course, Inc.*, 752 F.2d 609, 613 (11th Cir. 1985) (although a "concerted refusal to deal is generally subject to a rule of *per se* illegality * * * a confusing array of exceptions and qualifications to this rule have developed, and case law in this area is unsettled"); *Organization of Minority Vendors, Inc. v. Illinois Cent. Gulf R.R.*, 579 F. Supp. 574, 602 (N.D. Ill. 1983) ("there remains a great deal of confusion over the scope and operation of the *per se* rule against group boycotts").

An agreement among several traders which precludes trade relations with a third party will generally be considered a boycott—and *per se* illegal—even though only one member of the combination will in effect be refusing to deal with that party. On the other hand, an agreement not specifically aimed at a third party—although having the effect of a refusal to deal with that third party—may be upheld. For example, requirements contracts and other vertical exclusive dealing agreements may be lawful, and are generally judged under a Rule of Reason analysis, even though they have the effect of a refusal to deal with all others during the term of the agreement.

(b) Judicial Analysis of the Legal Standard for Group Boycotts—Pre- and Post-Northwest Wholesale Stationers

In general, courts have held group boycotts and concerted refusals to deal to be *per se* unlawful. *See, e.g., Radiant Burners, Inc. v. People's Gas, Light & Coke Co.*, 364 U.S. 656, 659–680 (1961); *Klor's v. Broadway-Hale Stores, Inc.*, 359 U.S. 207, 212 (1959). *But see Tropic Film Corp. v. Paramount Pictures Corp.*, 319 F. Supp. 1247, 1253 n.7 (S.D.N.Y. 1970) (the Supreme Court "has not ruled that group boycotts are *per se* violations of the Act.") *See also United States Trotting Ass'n v. Chicago Downs Ass'n, Inc.*, 665 F.2d 781, 788 (7th Cir. 1981) ("[t]he Supreme Court has found *certain* group boycotts *per se* illegal") (emphasis added).

The Supreme Court, in *Northwest Wholesale Stationers*, stated, "[t]his Court has long held that certain concerted refusals to deal or group boycotts are so likely to restrict competition without any offsetting efficiency gains that they should be condemned as per se violations of section 1 of the Sherman Act." 472 U.S. at 290 (citations omitted). However, the problem in that case, as well as in many cases, was that "[e]xactly what types of activity fall within the forbidden category is, however, far from certain." *Id.* at 294. The Supreme Court proceeded in that case to describe the forbidden category:

> Cases to which this Court has applied the per se approach have generally involved joint efforts by a firm or firms to disadvantage competitors by "either directly denying or persuading or coercing suppliers or customers to deny relationships the competitors need in the competitive struggle." L. SULLIVAN, *Law of Antitrust* 261–62 (1977). *See, e.g., Silver* (denial of necessary access to exchange members); *Radiant Burners* (denial of necessary certification of product); *Associated Press* (denial of important sources of news); *Klor's* (denial of wholesale supplies). In these cases, the boycott often cut off access to a supply, facility, or market necessary to enable the boycotted firms to compete, *Silver, Radiant Burners*, and frequently the boycotting firms possessed a dominant position in the relevant market. *E.g., Silver, Associated Press, Fashion Originators Guild. See generally* Brodley, *Joint Ventures and Antitrust Policy*, 95 HARV. L. REV. 1523, 1533, 1563–65 (1982). In addition, the practices were generally not justified by plausible arguments that they were intended to enhance overall efficiency and make markets more competitive. Under such circumstances the likelihood of anticompetitive effects is clear and the possibility of countervailing procompetitive effects is remote.
>
> Although a concerted refusal to deal need not necessarily possess all of these traits to merit per se treatment, not every cooperative activity involving a restraint or exclusion will share with the per se forbidden boycotts the likelihood of predominantly anticompetitive consequences.

Id. at 294–95. *See Nynex Corp. v. Discon, Inc.*, 525 U.S. 128, 135–36 (1998) ("precedent limits the *per se* rule in the boycott context to cases involving horizontal agreements among direct competitors").

The pre-*Northwest Wholesale Stationers* case that set the legal standards for evaluating group boycotts by industry self-regulatory groups was the Supreme Court's decision in *Silver v. New York Stock Exchange*, 373 U.S. 341 (1963). In *Silver*, the Court held the New York Stock Exchange ("NYSE") liable to a nonmember broker-dealer under Section 1 of the Sherman Act for denying the broker-dealer the right to connect to a member firm's teletype and the right to connect to a stock ticker service which transmitted information directly from the floor of the exchange. The basis for the Court's decision in *Silver* was its view that the NYSE and its members had exercised their power over the market to deny the plaintiffs access to "a valuable business service which they needed in order to compete effectively as broker-dealers" without providing the broker-dealer "notice, assigning him any reason for the action, or affording him an opportunity to be heard." *Id.* at 343, 347. The Court went on to state the general rule that "absent any justification derived from the policy of another statute *or otherwise*, the Exchange acted in violation of the Sherman Act." *Id.* at 348–49 (emphasis added).

In *Silver*, however, the policy of another statute was implicated. Defendant NYSE was a major participant in the self-regulatory scheme of the federal securities laws; thus, the Court was called upon to reconcile the *per se* rule of the antitrust laws with the statutory mandate of self-regulation by the NYSE. The Court acknowledged the clear public policy in favor of some regulation by the NYSE; therefore, it focused on whether or not the NYSE had adopted adequate procedural safeguards that would prevent the regulation from being utilized for anticompetitive purposes. Because no procedural safeguards had been employed by the NYSE, the policy of the federal securities laws did not shield the NYSE from civil liability. Nevertheless, the analysis in *Silver* was interpreted by some courts as creating an exception to the *per se* rule. *See, e.g., Brenner v. World Boxing Council*, 675 F.2d 445, 454 (2d Cir.), *cert. denied*, 459 U.S. 835 (1982).

The cases interpreting *Silver* prior to the *Northwest Wholesale Stationers* decision utilized different tests to ascertain *per se* vulnerability, but a four-step analysis was applied by several courts. First, the courts determined whether the challenged industry self-regulatory scheme brought about a group boycott or other anticompetitive injury. If the court so found, there remained three criteria to apply for determining whether an association that engages in a concerted refusal to deal qualified for an exception to the *per se* rule.

The most commonly applied test was first outlined in *Denver Rockets v. All-Pro Management, Inc.*, 325 F. Supp. 1049, 1064–65 (D.C. Cal. 1971). Under the *Denver Rockets* test, for conduct to fall within the *Silver* exception to *per se* invalidation of concerted refusals to deal, there had to be proof that:

(i) There is a group boycott or similar concerted action injurious to the plaintiff, and

then it must be established that:

(ii) There is a legislative mandate for self-regulation "or otherwise." * * *

(iii) The collective action [(a)] is intended to * * * accomplish an end consistent with the policy justifying self-regulation, (b) is reasonably related to that goal, and (c) is no more extensive than necessary [and]

(iv) The association provides procedural safeguards which assure that the restraint is not arbitrary and which [furnish] a basis for judicial review.

Denver Rockets, 325 F. Supp. at 1064–65. *See also Brenner v. WBC*, 675 F.2d at 454–56 (citing the *Denver Rockets* test approvingly); *Linesman v. World Hockey Ass'n*, 439 F. Supp. 1315 (D. Conn. 1977) (same).

Further, some pre-*Northwest Wholesale Stationers* cases had held that the *per se* proscription was limited to "concerted attempt[s] by a group of competitors at one level to protect themselves from competition from non-group members who seek to compete at that level." *See, e.g., United States Trotting Association v. Chicago Downs Ass'n, Inc.*, 665 F.2d at 788; *M&H Tire Co., Inc. v. Hoosier Racing Tire Corp.*, 560 F. Supp. 591, 601 (D. Mass. 1983), *rev'd on other grounds*, 733 F.2d 973 (1st Cir. 1984); *Smith v. Pro-Football, Inc.*, 593 F.2d 1173 (D.C. Cir. 1978). Those cases then applied general Rule of Reason analysis to fact situations which did not fit the paradigm. The Rule of Reason analysis is similar to the analysis conducted under the four-part test, but in the cases applying this analysis less rigorous scrutiny was applied to individual rules when it appeared clear that the rules were nondiscriminatory and were instituted for a positive purpose unrelated to the suppression of competition. *See, e.g., Brenner v. WBC*, 675 F.2d at 454–55 (discussing various tests and varied approaches utilized by lower courts).

The continued vitality of the *Silver* decision and the above-referenced four-part analysis is in doubt in the aftermath of *Northwest Wholesale Stationers*. To the extent that portions of the *Silver* analysis are still viable, prong two will almost always be satisfied in a legitimate league context, and prong four has been virtually eliminated as a factor. *See, e.g., Northwest Wholesale Stationers,* 472 U.S. at 291–93 ("If the challenged action would not amount to a violation of §1, no lack of procedural protections would convert it into a *per se* violation because the antitrust laws do not themselves impose on joint ventures a requirement of process."); *see also Weight Rite Golf Corp. v. USGA,* 766 F. Supp. 1104 (M.D. Fla. 1991), *aff'd.,* 953 F.2d 651 (11th Cir. 1992). More recently, courts have looked to the above-quoted language from *Northwest Wholesale Stationers* to determine whether a *per se* analysis is appropriate. Interestingly, there is also language in the *Northwest Wholesale Stationers* decision that may allow plaintiffs to attack, as an unlawful group boycott, conduct that gives defendants an unfair competitive advantage, even if the defendants did not completely refuse to deal with the plaintiffs but only agreed to deal with them on unreasonable terms:

> Because Pacific has not been wholly excluded from access to Northwest's wholesale operations, there is perhaps some question whether the challenged activity is properly characterized as a concerted refusal to deal. To be precise, Northwest's activity is a concerted refusal to deal with Pacific on substantially equal terms. Such activity might justify *per se* invalidation if it placed a competing firm at a severe competitive disadvantage.

Northwest Wholesale Stationers, 472 U.S. at 295 n.6 (citations omitted). This language, of course, is somewhat anomalous, or at least confusing, as it introduces the concept of likely anticompetitive effects and, therefore, a Rule of Reason-type calculus (the assessment of anticompetitive effects versus procompetitive effects) into the preliminary analysis of whether a *per se* rule should be applied.

(4) Tying

A "tying arrangement" or "tie-in" is "an agreement by a party to sell one product but only on the condition that the buyer also purchases a different (or tied) product." *Northern Pacific Ry. v. United States,* 356 U.S. 1, 5 (1958). The seller requires the buyer who wants or needs to purchase the "tying product" to purchase a specified quantity (or all of the buyer's needs) of a second, "tied product." Section 1 of the Sherman Act and Section 3 of the Clayton Act are the provisions most commonly applied to tying arrangements. Section 5 of the Federal Trade Commission Act could be applied as well.

The rationale underlying prohibitions on tying arrangements is readily apparent. If a seller has economic power or control over the first, or tying product, he will be able to use or "leverage" that power to achieve control over a second product. By limiting sales of the tying product to buyers who agree to buy the tied product from him or her, the seller might attempt to drive competing tied product sellers out of the tied product market. Through such a restriction, it is feared, a seller who dominates one market might be able to wield that control to dominate another market. The harm to competition was explained by the Supreme Court in the *Northern Pacific* case:

> [Tying arrangements] deny competitors free access to the market for the tied product, not because the party imposing the tying requirement has a better product or lower price but because of his power or leverage in another market. At the same time buyers are forced to forego their free choice between competing products.

Northern Pacific Ry., 356 U.S. at 6. More recent Supreme Court decisions concerning tying arrangements are *Jefferson Parish Hosp. Dist. No. 2 v. Hyde,* 466 U.S. 2 (1984), and

Eastman Kodak Co. v. Image Technical Services, Inc., 504 U.S. 451 (1992), and *Illinois Tool Works Inc. v. Independent Ink, Inc.*, 126 S.Ct. 1281 (2006).

The primary tying lawsuits in the context of professional sports were generally unsuccessful and concerned whether requiring professional football season ticket holders to purchase preseason game tickets illegally ties the regular season and preseason tickets. *See, e.g., Driskill v. Dallas Cowboys Football Club, Inc.*, 498 F.2d 321 (5th Cir. 1974); *Coniglio v. Highland Services*, 495 F.2d 1286 (2d Cir.), *cert. denied*, 419 U.S. 1022 (1974); *Laing v. Minnesota Vikings Football Club*, 372 F. Supp. 59 (D. Minn. 1973), *aff'd per curiam*, 492 F.2d 1381 (8th Cir.), *cert. denied*, 419 U.S. 832 (1974); *Grossman Development Co. v. Detroit Lions*, 1973 Trade Cas. ¶74,790 (E.D. Mich.), *aff'd*, 530 F.2d 1404 (6th Cir. 1974). In the 1980s, the Minnesota Twins and Minnesota North Stars faced antitrust litigation by a television company alleging, among other things, that the Twins and North Stars had unlawfully tied their broadcast rights. *See Midwest Communications, Inc. v. Minnesota Twins, Inc.*, 779 F.2d 444 (8th Cir. 1985). More recently, issues have arisen concerning owners of NHL and NBA teams requiring season ticket applicants to purchase season tickets for both the NHL and NBA teams that play in a single arena. However, to date there are no reports of any litigation concerning those requirements.

(E) Rule of Reason Analysis

(1) Introduction and General Analysis

All conduct challenged under Section 1 of the Sherman Act that is not analyzed under a *per se* rule will be analyzed under the Rule of Reason. To prove a claim under the Rule of Reason, a plaintiff must establish that: (1) there was an agreement between or among two or more persons or distinct business entities, as explained above; (2) the agreement or the conduct pursuant to the agreement adversely affected competition in a relevant market; and (3) the anticompetitive effects of the agreement exceeded the procompetitive benefits, or there were less restrictive (i.e., less anticompetitive) alternatives by which the same procompetitive benefits could have been achieved.

The courts have stated different formulations of the elements, but the formulations do not generally lead to different analyses and results. *See, e.g., Los Angeles Memorial Coliseum Comm'n v. National Football League*, 726 F.2d 1381 (9th Cir.), *cert. denied*, 469 U.S. 990 (1984):

> To establish a cause of action, plaintiff must prove these elements: "(1) An agreement among two or more persons or distinct business entities; (2) which is intended to harm or unreasonably restrain competition; (3) and which actually causes injury to competition."

Id. at 1391 (quoting *Kaplan v. Burroughs Corp.*, 611 F.2d 286, 290 (9th Cir. 1979), *cert. denied*, 447 U.S. 924 (1980)). Under the Ninth Circuit test, once the plaintiff has shown that the challenged conduct restrains competition, the court applies a balancing test that requires a "thorough investigation of the industry at issue and a balancing of the arrangement's positive and negative effects on competition." *Id.* at 1391 (quoting *Northrop Corp. v. McDonnell Douglas Corp.*, 705 F.2d 1030, 1050 (9th Cir.), *cert. denied*, 464 U.S. 849 (1983)). If "an observer with even a rudimentary understanding of economics could conclude that the arrangements in question would have an anticompetitive effect on customers and markets," "quick look" rule of reason analysis can be applied to hold an arrangement unlawful under Section 1. *See, e.g., California Dental Ass'n v. Federal Trade Comm'n*, 526 U.S. 756, 769–770 (1999) and cases cited therein.

The purpose of the Rule of Reason inquiry is to determine if the challenged conduct and agreements constitute *unreasonable* restraints. If the plaintiff can identify and establish potential or actual anticompetitive effects, the court will examine whether the restraint will *benefit* competition in any way—whether it will have any *procompetitive* benefits. If procompetitive benefits that exceed the anticompetitive effects can be identified, the court should then ask whether the restraint is reasonably necessary to achieve the legitimate, or procompetitive, purposes and whether there is a way of achieving the procompetitive benefits while causing substantially fewer anticompetitive effects.

As mentioned above, competitive effects, both anticompetitive and procompetitive, must be assessed in the context of a relevant market. Competitive effects cannot be assessed without first determining who are the buyers and sellers in the market and what is the scope and significance of the challenged agreements in that market. The theory is that plaintiffs who establish a *per se* violation do not need to establish a relevant market, because in a *per se* case the inherently anticompetitive nature of the agreement yields a presumption of anticompetitive effects. In practice, as the law has evolved, there have been significant departures from the theory. In any event, Rule of Reason plaintiffs must plead and prove the relevant market as a preliminary step toward establishing anticompetitive effects in that relevant market. Because most of the cases developing the concept of a relevant market have been decided under Section 2 of the Sherman Act, this issue is discussed in the monopolization portion of this chapter. *See* Section V.

(2) What Purposes or Effects Constitute Procompetitive Benefits Recognized by Antitrust Tribunals?

In *National Society of Professional Engineers v. United States*, 435 U.S. 679 (1978) ("*NSPE* case"), the Supreme Court held that not all purposes deemed "reasonable" by a jury are considered procompetitive benefits for the purposes of applying the Rule of Reason. A general assertion that a restraint serves the public interest was held to be insufficient in that case. There, the defendant society of engineers promulgated rules and standards designed to discourage competitive bidding. 435 U.S. at 683–84. The society conceded that its actions would tend to discourage price competition and were likely to lead to higher prices paid by buyers of engineers' services. It argued, however, that engineers who bid low would be forced to reduce quality and, if their low bids were accepted, would build defective structures injurious to the public. *Id.* at 684–85. The Supreme Court rejected this argument, stating that the Rule of Reason inquiry into procompetitive benefits "is confined to a consideration of the impact on competitive conditions," *id.* at 690 (footnote omitted), and "[i]n sum, the Rule of Reason does not support a defense based on the assumption that competition itself is unreasonable." *Id.* at 696.

Thus, in the eyes of the *NSPE* Court, a rule limiting competition is not legitimized simply because the competition that the plaintiff seeks to preserve would allegedly not be in the public interest. The Supreme Court declared that the cases interpreting the Sherman Act "foreclose the argument that because of the special characteristics of a particular industry, monopolistic arrangements will better promote trade and commerce than competition." *Id.* at 689.

However, there is also language in the *NSPE* case to the effect that "[t]he true test of legality is whether the restraint imposed is such *as merely regulates and perhaps thereby promotes competition* or whether it is such as may suppress or even destroy competition." *Id.* at 691 (quoting *Chicago Bd. of Trade v. United States*, 246 U.S. 231, 238 (1918); *Continental T.V., Inc. v. GTE Sylvania Inc.*, 433 U.S. 36, 49 n.15 (1977)) (footnote omitted) (emphasis added). Recent authority may be construed as reinforcing a more cosmic definition of reasonable and greater latitude for defendants to justify certain anticompetitive conduct by pointing to the overall public benefit. Some counsel for sports antitrust defendants have contended that the Supreme Court's decision in *NCAA v. Board of Regents of the Univ. of Okla.*, 485 U.S. 85 (1984), effectively broadened the scope of procompetitive benefits that will be recognized under the Rule of Reason. Under the language of *NSPE* and under a possible broadening of procompetitive benefits recognized in the *NCAA* case, defendants argue that their rules, regulations, and other conduct merely involve regulation of their sport in ways that promote competition.

V. Analysis of Section 2 of the Sherman Act

(A) Introduction to Section 2

While Section 1 of the Sherman Act is directed at concerted action, *i.e.*, action by two or more persons or entities, which can be considered a contract, combination, or a conspiracy in restraint of trade, Section 2 prohibits *unilateral* monopolization and attempted monopolization, as well as monopolization by combination or through some sort of conspiracy. The relevant language of Section 2 is as follows:

> Every person who shall monopolize, or attempt to monopolize, or combine or conspire with any other person or persons, to monopolize any part of the trade or commerce among the several states, or with foreign nations, shall be deemed guilty of a felony. * * *

15 U.S.C. §2.

(B) Overall Legal Theory of Monopolization

Unlawful monopolization has been defined by the courts as the possession of monopoly power plus some element of wrongful conduct that constitutes an improper use of the monopolist's power, preserves the monopolist's power, or increases the monopolist's power. A plaintiff seeking to prove unlawful monopolization must therefore define a relevant market in which the plaintiff contends the defendant has achieved monopoly power. The burden is on the plaintiff to prove the relevant market.

Monopoly power has generally been defined as the power to control prices or exclude competition. The plaintiff must establish the relevant market, prove that the defendant has monopoly power in the market, and show that: (1) the monopoly power was acquired through some sort of wrongful, exclusionary, or predatory conduct; (2) the wrongful conduct helped the monopolist maintain its monopoly power when otherwise new competitors or existing competitors would have eroded that power; or (3) the conduct of the monopolist constituted an improper use or abuse of its monopoly power.

As explained above, monopoly power is not defined as a specific market share, but, rather, is characterized in terms of ability to raise market prices or exclude competition. However, market share is considered as a starting point and some courts have treated market share as the end of the analysis. Therefore, as a practical matter, to establish the monopoly power element of a monopolization claim, the plaintiff should generally be able to establish that the defendant has a market share of about 70% or greater in the relevant market. The plaintiff will then attempt to prove that the defendant's market position was achieved or enhanced through wrongful, predatory, or exclusionary conduct or that, having achieved a monopoly position lawfully, the monopolist then engaged in some sort of wrongful, predatory, or exclusionary conduct which injured its rivals and preserved its monopoly position.

Conversely, the defendant will seek to show that it does not have monopoly power, either by expanding the size of the relevant market so as to minimize the defendant's market share, or by showing that the defendant does not have the power to control price or exclude competition. If the defendant fails in that effort, it will seek to show that its monopoly position was achieved through exercise of superior skill, foresight, or industry, rather than through any predatory or exclusionary conduct.

(C) Attempt to Monopolize Distinguished from Monopolization

The differences between a monopolization claim and an attempt to monopolize claim are slight. As stated above, a monopolization claim requires that the plaintiff establish the defendant's monopoly power, usually by showing that the defendant had a market share of 70% or greater and dominated the market. To sustain a claim for an attempt to monopolize, the plaintiff's burden in this area is less onerous. The plaintiff must establish that the defendant has the specific intent to achieve a monopoly and that the wrongful conduct in which the defendant is engaging has a "dangerous probability of success" in moving the defendant into a monopoly position. Accordingly, to prove an attempt to monopolize claim, the plaintiff must generally show that the defendant's market share is at least 30% of a relevant market and that the challenged conduct is moving the defendant at a steady rate toward higher market shares. Because there is often a long lag time between the filing of an antitrust complaint and the eventual trial, it is important for the plaintiff to establish a substantial increase in the defendant's market share during the pendency of the monopolization litigation.

(D) Conspiracy to Monopolize

Section 2 of the Sherman Act also prohibits combinations or conspiracies "to monopolize any part of * * * trade or commerce." The elements of a conspiracy to monopolize claim are: (1) the existence of an agreement—the contract, combination, or conspiracy requirement; (2) an overt act by one of the parties to the agreement in furtherance of the conspiracy; (3) the fact that a substantial amount of commerce was affected or would be affected by the planned conduct of the conspiring parties; and (4) specific intent on the part of the agreeing parties to monopolize.

There is not a considerable amount of case law about conspiracies to monopolize. The reason is that Section 2 is primarily aimed at unilateral conduct and imposes a much more significant burden on a plaintiff than does proving an agreement in restraint of trade under Section 1. Accordingly, a party who has a legitimate conspiracy to monopolize claim will most certainly have the ability to establish a Section 1 violation—a contract, combination or conspiracy to restrain trade—and there is often not much for a plaintiff to gain by proving both a Section 1 violation and a conspiracy to monopolize claim.

(E) Analysis of Certain Elements of Section 2 Claims

(1) Monopoly Power

As stated above, monopoly power has been defined as "the power to control market prices or exclude competition." *United States v. E.I. du Pont de Nemours & Co.*, 351 U.S. 377, 391 (1956). The issue is not whether prices have been raised or whether competition has actually been excluded, but whether the defendant has the power to raise prices or exclude competition whenever it desires. *See, e.g., American Tobacco Co. v. United States*, 328 U.S. 781, 811 (1946). In order to determine whether the defendant has monopoly power, it is first necessary to define a relevant market in which the power over price or the power to exclude competition is to be measured, for "[w]ithout a definition of that market there is no way to measure [the defendant's] ability to lessen or destroy competition." *Walker Process Equipment, Inc. v. Food Mach. & Chem. Corp.*, 382 U.S. 172, 177 (1965).

In other words, if the defendant becomes the only seller of broadcast rights for professional tennis tournaments held around the world, the court at first blush may not be concerned. If the broadcast rights for all sporting events were completely fungible, then it might be that the purchasers of the broadcast rights, the networks and cable companies, would be willing to substitute other sports broadcasts. If viewers did not have specific preferences regarding the sporting events that they watched, the courts might not fear a dominance over tennis broadcast rights, because the mere monopoly over those rights might not give the defendant the power to raise prices or exclude competition. If the defendant attempted to raise the price for tennis broadcast rights, the purchasers would simply purchase broadcast rights to golf tournaments, baseball games, football games, and other sporting events.

Therefore, to determine whether the defendant charged with monopolization has monopoly power, the analysis must first focus on the market being analyzed before an effort can be made to measure the defendant's power over that market.

(a) Defining the Relevant Market

Every relevant market has two dimensions: a geographic dimension and a product dimension. The relevant market is the "area of effective competition" within which the defendant operates. *Brown Shoe Co. v. United States*, 370 U.S. 294, 324–26 (1962); *Standard Oil Co. v. United States*, 337 U.S. 293, 299 n.5 (1949). The definition of a relevant market is to some extent circular with the definition of monopoly power. As set forth above, monopoly power is defined as the power to control market prices or exclude competition. Many inquiries define a relevant market by asking whether, if the defendant controlled the entire market as described, the defendant could raise its prices to a level well above its costs plus a reasonable return without losing substantial sales volume to sellers outside the market. If the defendant's increases in price would be limited significantly by the prices charged for products outside the market as defined, the market has been defined too narrowly. In other words, if the court were examining the sale of Honda cars in Washington, D.C. and plaintiff contends that that is the relevant market, the court would ask whether a distributor of Honda automobiles in Washington, D.C. would be able to raise prices significantly without losing a sufficient number of customers to sellers of other automobiles (indicating a broader relevant product market) or sellers of Honda automobiles (same product market) who are located outside of Washington, D.C. (indicating a broader relevant geographic market).

As that example makes clear, definition of a relevant market is far from an exact science and is always a question of degree. Almost all products compete with one another for a consumer's dollar. As a particular product has its price escalate, customers will substitute other products. Nevertheless, the antitrust laws were passed in response to concern about monopolies, and the definition of a relevant market is focused on identifying an area of trade or commerce, which, if controlled by a single seller or buyer, would lead to prices that would be too high and a corresponding reduction in output. As a result, definition and proof of a relevant market generally involve expert testimony focusing on various indicia. In addition, courts generally state that definition of the relevant market is a question for the trier of fact, whose findings on this issue, like other issues of fact, will be set aside only if "clearly erroneous." *International Boxing Club, Inc. v. United States*, 358 U.S. 242, 245 (1959); *see also Borough of Landsdale v. Philadelphia Electric Co.*, 692 F.2d 307 (3d Cir. 1982) (stating that the jury, not the court, should decide geographic market question).

As explained above, to define a relevant market the plaintiff must establish both the product scope and the geographic scope of the market.

(b) Relevant Product Market

The leading Supreme Court case on definition of the relevant product market is the so-called "cellophane" case—*United States v. E.I. du Pont de Nemours & Co.*, 351 U.S. 377 (1956). In that case the issue was whether the relevant product market was cellophane (du Pont's market share in cellophane was 75%) or all flexible packaging material, including wax paper, aluminum foil, and other materials (du Pont had a share of less than 20% of the larger market). The court in that case stated that:

> The "market" which one must study to determine when a producer has monopoly power will vary with the part of commerce under consideration. The tests are constant. That market is composed of products that have reasonable interchangeability for the purposes for which they are produced—price, use and qualities considered.

Id. at 404. In determining whether cellophane was reasonably interchangeable with other flexible packaging materials, the Supreme Court considered the cross-elasticity of demand for the two products, which is "the responsiveness of the sales of one product to price changes of the other." *Id.* at 400. As explained by the Court, "[i]f a slight decrease in the price of cellophane causes a considerable number of customers of other flexible wrappings to switch to cellophane, it would be an indication that a high cross-elasticity of demand exists between them; that the products compete in the same market." *Id.* Similarly, if a slight increase in the price of cellophane causes a considerable number of customers to stop purchasing cellophane and to switch their purchases to other flexible wrappings, it would be an indication that a high cross-elasticity of demand exists between them and that the products compete in the same market.

In defining the relevant product market, most courts have emphasized reasonable interchangeability and cross-elasticity of *demand*, thereby focusing on the consumer of the product rather than the producer. Nevertheless, some courts have also considered the cross-elasticity of *supply*. This analysis focuses on the ease with which a seller of a similar or related product could switch its production facilities to make the same product as the defendant, in response to defendant's attempts to raise the price of his product significantly. For example, in *Twin City Sportservice, Inc. v. Charles O. Finley & Co.*, 512 F.2d 1264 (9th Cir. 1975), the Ninth Circuit observed that two products with a high degree of substitutability in use (*demand* substitutability) "should be considered in the same market," and also that:

> [a] like analysis applies when the market is viewed from the production rather than the consumption standpoint; the degrees of substitutability in production is measured by cross-elasticity of supply. Substitutability in production refers to the ability of firms in a given line of commerce to turn their productive facilities toward the production of commodities in another line because of similarities in technology between them. Where the degree of substitutability in production is high, cross-elasticity of supply will also be high, and again the two commodities in question should be treated as part of the same market.

Id. at 1271.

(c) Relevant Geographic Market

The geographic scope or dimension of a relevant market is often defined as the area of effective competition in which the product or its reasonably interchangeable substitutes are traded. *See, e.g., L.A. Draper & Son v. Wheelabrator-Frye, Inc.*, 735 F.2d 414, 423 (11th Cir. 1984); *Hornsby Oil Co. v. Champion Spark Plug Co.*, 714 F.2d 1384, 1393 (5th Cir. 1983); *Hecht v. Pro-Football, Inc.*, 570 F.2d 982, 988 (D.C. Cir. 1977), *cert. denied*, 436 U.S. 956 (1978). The relevant geographic market "is not ordinarily susceptible to a 'metes and bounds definition,' [but] it is the area in which 'producers effectively compete.'" *White & White, Inc. v. American Hospital Supply Corp.*, 723 F.2d 495, 503 (6th Cir. 1983) (quoting *Tampa Electric Co. v. Nashville Coal Co.*, 365 U.S. 320, 327 (1961)).

In determining the relevant geographic market, many diverse factors must be considered. For example, "such economic and physical barriers to expansion as transportation costs, delivery limitation and customer convenience and preference must be considered." *L.A. Draper & Son*, 735 F.2d at 423 (quoting *Hornsby Oil Co. v. Champion Spark Plug Co.*, 714 F.2d at 1394). The location and facilities of other sellers of the relevant product are also critical factors to be considered in determining the relevant market. *See, e.g., L.A. Draper & Son*, 735 F.2d at 423; *Tampa Electric Co. v. Nashville Coal Co.*, 365 U.S. at 327. In addition, several discrete submarkets may be integrated within a larger geographic market. *See, e.g., Brown Shoe Co.*, 370 U.S. at 326; *Hornsby Oil Co.*, 714 F.2d at 1393.

As explained by the commentators, each factual situation must be examined individually to ascertain the relevant geographic market:

> The geographic market should be defined in a realistic way. If a particular region or local area such as a municipality is asserted to constitute a separate geographic market in which the power of a firm is to be evaluated, several questions must be asked. One should begin with practical, commercial reali-

ties. Do those in the industry perceive the region as a separate market and customarily treat it as one, in the sense that those outside of it make little or no attempt to sell or promote within it? Are sales actually made within the region responsive to changes in conditions of demand and supply elsewhere? Are traders beyond the bounds of the region disadvantaged by transportation costs, or the lack of available storage or distribution facilities? Freight rates, and like factors, may be relevant to those inquiries, but the ultimate question is one of seller and buyer conduct—who are the actual traders who are competitive forces?

Again, the question is one of degree. Seldom will there be blatant divisions between geographic market areas.

LAWRENCE ANTHONY SULLIVAN, LAW OF ANTITRUST 68 (1977).

The above cases indicate that geographic market definition in section 2 cases depends on the characteristics of the product or service at issue, methods of distribution, areas within which purchasers can reasonably choose from alternative sources, and other considerations which can be analyzed only case by case. If any generalization is appropriate, it is that geographic markets should be analyzed so as to distinguish market power where it exists, even in a small area, so long as that area is economically significant.

2 EARL W. KINTER, FEDERAL ANTITRUST LAW 349–50 (1980) (footnote omitted).

Determination of the relevant geographic market is generally a question of fact to be decided by the jury. *See, e.g., United States v. Connecticut Nat'l Bank,* 418 U.S. 656 (1974); *L.A. Draper,* 735 F.2d at 425; *Aspen Highlands Skiing Corp. v. Aspen Skiing Co.,* 738 F.2d 1509, 1514 n.4 (10th Cir. 1984), *aff'd on other grounds,* 472 U.S. 585 (1985), and cases cited therein. Plaintiff is required to show the relevant geographic market by "competent economic evidence." *Joseph Ciccone & Sons, Inc. v. Eastern Indust., Inc.,* 559 F. Supp. 671, 674 (E.D. Pa. 1983). "[A] 'pragmatic, factual approach' is required, * * * not a 'scientifically precise definition.'" *Id.* (quoting *Brown Shoe Co.,* 370 U.S. at 336, and *United States v. M.P.M., Inc.,* 397 F. Supp. 78, 88 (D. Colo. 1975)).

(d) Proof of Monopoly Power

One way of proving monopoly power is through direct evidence that the defendant exercised control over prices or excluded competitors. If that proof is not available, analysis must focus on the defendant's market share. When there is no proof that the defendant has exercised the power to control price or exclude competition, the traditional cases first stress market share. If market share figures are inconclusive, they consider other structural and behavioral factors that might demonstrate a firm's economic power. In this regard, note that market power, economic power, and monopoly power are all related terms. Economic power and market power are the same thing, and monopoly power simply indicates a high degree of market or economic power.

(i) Market Share as an Indicator of Market Power

In most antitrust cases, once the relevant market is determined, it is a relatively easy task to compute the market shares for the defendant and the other firms in the market:

Once the product and geographic markets are determined, the actual computation of market shares is often a simple or at least straight-forward task. It is accomplished by setting the defendant's production or sales as the numerator and then dividing that by the larger denominator constituting total production or sales in the defined area.

See, e.g., American Tobacco Co. v. United States, 328 U.S. 781, 794–96 (1946); Ernest Gellhorn, *Antitrust Law and Economics* 106 (1981); *see also In re IBM Peripheral EDP Devices Antitrust Litigation,* 481 F. Supp. 965, 975 (N.D. Cal. 1979), *aff'd sub nom. Transamerica Computer Co. v. International Business Machines Corp.,* 698 F.2d 1377 (9th Cir.), *cert. denied,* 464 U.S. 955 (1983) ("With the relevant market defined, the defendant's share of that market can be measured. * * * The larger defendant's market share, the stronger is the inference that competitors would be unable to effectively check exercises of monopoly power.")

The court then assesses market or monopoly power based on market share. In *United States v. Aluminum Co. of America* ("*Alcoa*"), 148 F.2d 416, 424 (2d Cir. 1945), Judge Learned Hand, writing for the Second Circuit after the case was certified to a special three judge panel of the Second Circuit from the Supreme Court, stated that a defendant who supplies 90% of a relevant market has "enough to constitute a monopoly; it is doubtful whether sixty or sixty-four percent would be enough; and certainly thirty-three percent is not." In a subsequent case, analyzing a merger, the Supreme Court stated:

> We do not undertake to prescribe any set of percentage figures by which to measure the reasonableness of a corporation's enlargement of its activities by the purchase of the assets of a competitor. The relative effect of percentage command of a market varies with the setting in which that factor is placed.

United States v. Columbia Steel Co., 334 U.S. 495, 527–28 (1948).

(ii)   Other Indicators of Market Power

As stated above, market share is not the only factor considered by courts in determining whether a defendant has market power or has monopoly power. *See, e.g., Berkey Photo, Inc. v. Eastman Kodak Co.,* 603 F.2d 263, 273 n.11 (2d Cir. 1979), *cert. denied,* 444 U.S. 1093 (1980). Monopoly power may also be demonstrated by a firm's ability to maintain its market share even when it produces an inferior product or service. *See, e.g., Byars v. Bluff City News Co.,* 609 F.2d 843, 853 n.26 (6th Cir. 1979). The relative size of a dominant firm's competitors, the performance of those competitors, the degree of barriers to entry or barriers to expansion, the stability of market share over time, and many other factors may be considered in measuring a firm's monopoly power when market share alone is inconclusive. Consistent extraction of above normal profits may also be evidence of monopoly power. *See, e.g., Borden Inc. v. FTC,* 674 F.2d 498, 512 (6th Cir. 1981), *vacated and remanded,* 461 U.S. 940 (1983) (above-normal profits supported finding of monopoly power). Other indicia of monopoly power are discussed in the 1984 Department of Justice Merger Guidelines.

(2) *The Additional Element—Purpose, Intent, and/or Conduct— Required to Make Monopoly Unlawful "Monopolization"*

As set forth above, the mere possession of monopoly power does not by itself violate Section 2. Nevertheless, it is not clear what purpose, intent, or conduct distinguishes a lawful monopoly from illegal monopolization. The early Sherman Act cases stated that the element of intentional monopolization could be found if the monopoly was a probable result of the monopolist's conduct, "for no monopolist monopolizes unconscious of what he is doing." *American Tobacco Co.,* 328 U.S. at 814 (quoting *Alcoa,* 148 F.2d at 432). Similarly, in *dictum* in the *Cellophane* case, the Court observed that "when an alleged monopolist has power over price and competition, an intention to monopolize in a proper case may be assumed." *E.I. du Pont de Nemours & Co.,* 351 U.S. at 392.

In *Alcoa,* the Second Circuit found that Alcoa illegally monopolized the aluminum ingot market. The court held that, because Alcoa was not "the passive beneficiary of a monopoly, following upon an involuntary elimination of competitors by automatically operative economic forces," it was guilty of unlawful monopolization. 148 F.2d at 430. However, the court observed that "the successful competitor, having been urged to compete, must not be turned upon when he wins." *Id.* The *Alcoa* court also contrasted the facts of that case with situations in which one company has achieved a monopoly position through "superior skill, foresight, and industry." *Id.*

The most recent decisions have held that a defendant's monopoly position may be lawful even if the defendant did not *involuntarily* acquire and maintain its monopoly position. Rather, these decisions have sought to distinguish conduct that is "honestly industrial," *Alcoa,* 148 F.2d at 431, "legal and ordinary," *Telex Corp. v. IBM,* 510 F.2d 894, 926 (10th Cir.), *cert. denied,* 423 U.S. 802 (1975), from activity that is "predatory," "unnecessarily" exclusionary, *Greyhound Computer Corp. v. IBM,* 559 F.2d 488, 498 (9th Cir. 1977), *cert. denied,* 434 U.S. 1040 (1978), *see also Byars v. Bluff City News,* 609 F.2d at 853 ("unreasonably exclusionary"), "unreasonably restrictive," *California Computer Prods., Inc. v. IBM,* 613 F.2d 727, 735–36 (9th Cir. 1979), "unreasonably anticompetitive," *Byars v. Bluff City News,* 609 F.2d at 860, or otherwise improper.

Evolving precedent has generally evaluated the exclusionary effects of the conduct at issue and balanced the "evils" against the "virtues." In making this assessment, courts have analyzed whether the defendant's conduct was aimed at furthering its own competitive position through provision of a better product and creating increased efficiencies in its own operations or was directed at deterring competition and thereby preserving or acquiring monopoly power. In this area, as in the analysis under Section 1, the emphasis is on whether the challenged conduct has procompetitive purposes and whether the anticompetitive effects exceed the procompetitive benefits in light of less restrictive means by which the defendant could have achieved the procompetitive purposes without causing as great an anticompetitive effect. The cases have not generally been explicit in utilizing this analysis, but this summary illustrates the overall analysis employed. While the standard for assessing less restrictive alternatives is not settled, the growing consensus is that the means selected by the defendant need not be the least restrictive means for achieving the procompetitive benefits, but, as with analysis under the Rule of Reason under Section 1, the means employed by the defendant that have anticompetitive effects must be reasonably necessary to achieve the procompetitive benefits.

VI. Antitrust Exemptions

As set forth above, the federal antitrust laws were enacted to prohibit certain agreements and conduct that adversely affect competition. In some circumstances, those laws must be reconciled with Constitutional limitations, other statutory provisions that may conflict with the antitrust laws, explicit antitrust exemptions enacted by Congress, or exemptions implied by the courts. For example, Congress has enacted several statutes that grant agricultural producers, associations, and cooperatives an exemption; the Communications Act of 1934 as amended renders the antitrust laws inapplicable to interstate and foreign radio and television communications and leaves regulation to the Federal Communications Commission; the McCarran-Ferguson Act created an antitrust exemption for the "business of insurance," and federal regulation of railroads and other form of transportation, natural gas and other natural resources, and securities have all led to the creation of limited antitrust exemptions. *See generally* ABA Antitrust Section, *Antitrust Law Developments* (4th ed. 1997).

Other important exemptions, which extend beyond the scope of any particular industry, are the state action and *Noerr-Pennington* exemptions. The former shields from antitrust scrutiny certain conduct by state or local government bodies that limits competition. The latter, which takes its name from two Supreme Court cases, *Eastern Railroad Presidents Conference v. Noerr Motor Freight, Inc.*, 365 U.S. 127 (1961) and *United Mine Workers v. Pennington*, 381 U.S. 657 (1965), provides antitrust immunity for efforts, whether conducted by a single firm or a group of competitors, to solicit administrative, executive, judicial, or legislative action that restricts competition. Recent Supreme Court cases concerning the *Noerr-Pennington* doctrine include *City of Columbia v. Omni Outdoor Advertising, Inc.*, 499 U.S. 365 (1991) and *Professional Real Estate Investors, Inc. v. Columbia Pictures, Indus.*, 508 U.S. 49 (1993).

In addition to the occasional relevance of the state action and *Noerr-Pennington* doctrines in sports antitrust cases, there are three categories of antitrust exemption issues specific to the business of sports: the baseball exemption, the statutory and non-statutory labor exemptions, and the exemptions created by the Sports Broadcasting Act of 1961 and 1965. With respect to sports antitrust cases involving the *Noerr-Pennington* doctrine, see, for example, *United States Football League v. National Football League*, 634 F. Supp. at 1170–71; *Mid-South Grizzlies v. National Football League*, 720 F.2d at 784–85 and n.7. Courts have permitted plaintiffs to offer evidence about sports antitrust exemption legislation, and have expressly held that abuse of monopoly power acquired as a result of the legislation is not exempt. However, they have generally held that evidence about the reasons or motives that led the NFL to seek the legislation is not admissible, and the NFL's lobbying efforts related to the passage of that legislation are immune from antitrust challenge under the *Noerr-Pennington* doctrine. The state action exemption was recently invoked in response to antitrust claims brought by the Florida Panthers against the owner of the arena where the Panthers play their home games. *See Florida Panthers Hockey Club, Ltd. v. Miami Sports and Exhibition Authority*, 939 F. Supp. 855, 856 n.1 (S.D. Fla. 1996).

(A) The Baseball and Labor Exemptions

In the area of professional sports, the baseball exemption and the labor-related exemptions have been the most important. As a result, Chapter 8 provides a comprehensive review of the history of the baseball exemption. An in-depth analysis of the statutory and non-statutory labor exemptions is presented in Chapter 9.

(B) The Sports Broadcasting Act of 1961 and 1966

The Sports Broadcasting Act, 15 U.S.C. §1291, *et seq.*, essentially consists of two separate provisions, the first enacted in 1961 and the second in 1966. The first provision, which exempts certain joint agreements among professional football, baseball, basketball, or hockey teams to pool their sponsored television broadcasts rights for sale as a package, was passed in response to a judicial decision involving the National Football League (see below). *United States v. National Football League*, 196 F. Supp. 445 (E.D. Pa. 1961). *See generally* S. Rep. No. 1087, 87th Cong., 1st Sess. (1961) *reprinted in* 1961 U.S.C.C.A.N. 3042–44. *See also WTWV, Inc. v. National Football League*, 678 F.2d 142, 144–45 (11th Cir. 1982) (discussing background and history of the legislation). The second provision was passed to permit the merger of the American Football League ("AFL") and the National Football League ("NFL") into a single league to operate under the latter name. The remaining provisions of this legislation are primarily specifications of limitations on the scope of the exemptions created by the first provision.

(1) Exemption for Pooling of Television Broadcast Rights

In 1951, the Justice Department filed a civil antitrust action against the National Football League and its member clubs, challenging NFL by-laws that restricted televising and radio broadcasting of NFL games. After trial, the district court held that certain of the restrictions violated the Sherman Act. *See United States v. National Football League*, 116 F. Supp. 319 (E.D. Pa. 1953). Following the issuance of the court's opinion, a judgment containing permanent injunctive provisions was entered. About eight years later, the NFL and its member clubs filed a petition, seeking a declaration that an exclusive contract between the NFL and the Columbia Broadcasting System ("CBS") did not violate the previous judgment. *See United States v. National Football League*, 196 F. Supp. 445, 446 (E.D. Pa. 1961). The district court held that this "pooling" of broadcast rights by the member clubs eliminated competition between and among those clubs and thereby violated the prior judgment. At that time, teams in the AFL and other professional sports leagues, including the National Basketball Association ("NBA") and the National Hockey League ("NHL"), had been pooling their broadcast rights for sale to television networks. At the request of the NFL, which claimed unequal treatment, Congress passed the Sports Broadcasting Act of 1961 and "overrule[d] the effect of" the court's decision.

The Sports Broadcasting Act exempts agreements by the members of professional baseball, basketball, football, or hockey leagues to pool their sponsored television broadcast rights for sale in a package to purchasers, such as television networks, for airing as sponsored television. However, the exemption comes with several specific limitations.

First, the exemption does not apply to agreements with territorial limits on the purchaser's broadcast area, except restrictions that protect a home team from competing games broadcast into its home territory on a day when it is playing a game at home. These restrictions are known as "blackout rules." The courts adjudicating challenges to the NFL's blackout rules have held that the Sports Broadcasting Act shields them from antitrust scrutiny. *See WTWV, Inc. v. National Football League*, 678 F.2d at 145–46; *Blaich v. National Football League*, 212 F. Supp. 319, 321–22 (S.D.N.Y. 1962).

Second, the exemption does not apply to a pooled agreement that permits telecasting of football games where and when college and high school football teams traditionally play their games. *See Ass'n of Independent Television Stations, Inc. v. College Football Ass'n*, 637 F. Supp. 1289, 1300 n.11 (W.D. Okla. 1986). This provision was "designed to provide greater protection for in person attendance at college football contests and carrie[d] out the recommendations of the NCAA." S. Rep. No. 108, 87th Cong., 1st Sess.

(1961), *reprinted in* 1961 U.S.C.C.A.N. 3042, 3043–44. The 1966 Act extended the prohibition from college games to both high school and college games.

Third, the exemption is limited to its express terms and is specifically not intended "to change, determine, or otherwise affect the applicability or nonapplicability of the antitrust laws" to any other aspect of the professional sports identified in the statute.

Litigation has focused on the scope of the antitrust exemption created by the Sports Broadcasting Act. One question that has arisen is whether the exemption is limited to a single contract with one network. *See, e.g., United States Football League v. National Football League*, 842 F.2d 1335, 1353–55, 1358–61 (2d Cir. 1988) (exemption is not limited to contact with a single network, but if the intent and effect of agreements is to exclude a competing league or its members from selling their television rights, they may be unlawful). The Chicago Bulls' litigation with the National Basketball Association, addressed in Chapter 12, focused on whether the Act exempts league efforts to force an unwilling member club to pool its broadcast rights and what limits are imposed by the exemption's specification of "sponsored telecasting"—for example, closed circuit, cable, subscription, or pay-per-view television?

(2) Exemption for Football League Mergers

The second provision of the Sports Broadcasting Act was passed in 1966, five years after the initial statute; it is more narrow in scope. It was passed to allow the NFL and AFL to merge without fear of antitrust challenge. The exemption is limited to professional football, and it insulates agreements by "the member clubs of two or more professional football leagues * * * [to] combine their operations in [an] expanded single league * * * if such agreement increases rather than decreases the number of professional football clubs so operating. * * *"

As explained above, this second provision of the Sports Broadcasting Act is limited to football leagues. As a result, it did not protect the National Basketball Association ("NBA") and the American Basketball Association ("ABA") from antitrust challenge when they discussed a possible merger in the early 1970s. The issue soon became academic as eventually the ABA became defunct, and four former ABA teams were awarded expansion franchises by the NBA.

VII. Impact of the Federal Antitrust Laws on Professional Sports

It is difficult to overemphasize the impact of the federal antitrust laws on the business of professional sports in the United States. Even baseball, which has long operated with the protection of the baseball exemption considered in Chapter 8, has had to remain vigilant, continually lobbying Congress to maintain the exemption, attempting to keep cases involving the most egregious conduct out of the courts, anticipating the consequences of a judicial recanting or legislative repeal of the exemption, and speculating upon what conduct might be outside the scope of the exemption.

The following is just a partial description of the many business aspects of professional basketball, football, and hockey that have been the subject of litigation under the antitrust laws. A review of the following partial histories is useful to derive some indication of the many ways that antitrust has insinuated itself into the inner workings of professional sports. However, it is important to be aware that the significance of antitrust law to these sports ranges well beyond the reported decisions of state and federal courts. For example, there are lawsuits that are filed and resolved without ever leaving a reported decision, lawsuits that are threatened and settled without any action having been commenced, and lawsuits that are feared and avoided without even the need for the issuance of a formal threat of litigation.

Many of the cases described below were not exclusively antitrust cases. In fact, the antitrust claims may not have been the strongest claims asserted in certain lawsuits that are referenced. However, in these cases, the antitrust laws were the basis for some or all of the allegations. As you peruse this section, please note that it is intended neither to analyze every case mentioned nor to explicate the facts and holdings of such decisions. Rather, it is offered to show you a partial laundry list of the lawsuits that have been brought over the past few decades and to expose the nature of the conduct that provoked such litigation. Many of the cases referenced below are covered in detail in Chapters 8 through 13.

(A) Antitrust and Professional Basketball

In the early twentieth century, college rather than professional basketball was the dominant attraction in the large municipalities. In 1937, after more than thirty years of professional barnstorming and the appearance of small professional basketball leagues, ten independent professional teams and three teams previously representing the Goodyear and Firestone Rubber Companies in Akron Ohio and General Electric Company in Fort Wayne, Indiana in the Midwest Industrial League came together to form the National Basketball League ("NBL"). Over the next several years the league alternately expanded and contracted, but continued to operate without interruption.

Meanwhile, eleven owners of hockey teams and several operators of large arenas met in 1946 in New York City to establish the Basketball Association of America ("BAA"). This league consisted of the Boston Celtics, New York Knickerbockers, Philadelphia Warriors, Providence Steamrollers, Toronto Huskies, Washington Capitols, Chicago Stags, Cleveland Rebels, Detroit Falcons, Pittsburgh Ironmen, and the St. Louis Bombers. Four of the original teams folded after a single season (Detroit, Cleveland, Toronto, and Pittsburgh) and the Baltimore Bullets were added in 1947 to make the BAA an eight-team league. In 1948, four of the best teams from the NBL—the Minneapolis Lakers, the Rochester Royals, the Fort Wayne Zollner Pistons, and the Indianapolis Kautskys—left to join the BAA, and in 1949 the remaining six NBL franchises joined with the remaining BAA franchises to form a unified seventeen-team league, the National Basketball Association ("NBA").

The NBA faced early antitrust challenges in the 1950s and 1960s, when it disapproved the sale of a member club, see *Washington Professional Basketball Corp. v. NBA*, 131 F. Supp. 596 (S.D.N.Y. 1955) and 1956 Trade Cas. ¶68,560 (S.D.N.Y. 1956), and when it exiled players who were alleged to have been involved in gambling on games or associating with known gamblers. *See, e.g., Hawkins v. NBA*, 288 F. Supp. 614 (W.D.Pa. 1968); *Molinas v. NBA*, 190 F. Supp. 241 (S.D.N.Y. 1961). In the 1970s, the NBA was sued by players challenging restrictions on player compensation and mobility. These early "player mobility/player restraint" cases were a harbinger of a rash of antitrust lawsuits in basketball and other professional sports. One of the more celebrated cases involved Spencer Haywood, a young superstar who was precluded from joining the NBA under league rules that barred his "admission" until his high school class would have graduated from college. Haywood successfully challenged the rule as an unreasonable restraint of trade in violation of the Sherman Act. *See Denver Rockets v. All-Pro Management*, 325 F. Supp. 1049 (C.D.Cal. 1971).

During this period, the NBA was also involved in antitrust litigation with a group that sought unsuccessfully to purchase the Boston Celtics, *Levin v. NBA*, 385 F. Supp. 149 (S.D.N.Y. 1974), and was sued by the ABA and by the players of both leagues when the ABA and the NBA discussed a merger. *See, e.g., Robertson v. NBA*, 389 F. Supp. 867 (S.D.N.Y. 1975). The ABA had been established in 1967 and had attempted to introduce innovations designed to offer an alternative to the NBA (red, white and blue basketballs, three-point field goals, etc.). Given its success in signing prominent superstars such as Julius Erving and Dan Issel, the ABA's threat to the NBA was becoming obvious and merger talk became inevitable. In 1976, the lawsuits by the players and the ABA were settled—the ABA folded, and four ABA teams (Denver Nuggets, Indiana Pacers, New Jersey Nets, and San Antonio Spurs) became NBA expansion teams in 1976. Since that time, the NBA and its players have entered into a series of collective bargaining agreements with the National Basketball Players Association ("NBPA").

The 1980s brought additional antitrust litigation to the NBA, including lawsuits by two groups that sought to purchase the Chicago Bulls. *See Fishman v. Estate of Wirtz*, 807 F.2d 520 (7th Cir. 1987). Attempts by competing league franchises to relocate also visited antitrust controversy on the league when the New Orleans Jazz moved to Utah in 1979 (the stadium in the city that lost the team sued the league), *HMC Management Corp. v. New Orleans Basketball Club*, 375 So. 2d 300 (La. Ct. App. 1979), and when the Clippers relocated from San Diego to Los Angeles (in 1984). *NBA v. SDC Basketball Club, Inc.*, 815 F.2d 562 (9th Cir. 1987).

At the time of the 1983 collective bargaining agreement, the NBA contended that a majority of its teams were losing money and convinced the NBPA to agree to a salary cap. The NBA then faced antitrust litigation from a rookie who challenged the salary cap and other terms of the collective bargaining agreement. *Wood v. NBA*, 602 F. Supp. 525 (S.D.N.Y. 1984), *aff'd*, 809 F.2d 954 (2d Cir. 1987). The dismissal of that lawsuit was affirmed by the Second Circuit based on the non-statutory labor exemption. When the 1983 bargaining agreement expired in 1987, the NBA players again filed an antitrust lawsuit alleging that the restrictions on player mobility violated the Sherman Act. *See Bridgeman v. NBA*, 675 F. Supp. 960 (D.N.J. 1987). After a year of litigation, culminating in a settlement, the players and the league entered into a new collective bargaining agreement that embraced the *Bridgeman* settlement and modified, but did not totally eliminate, the player restraints. This agreement expired in 1994. When collective bargaining negotiations broke down in 1994, the league sued its players and the players filed counterclaims before the NBA received favorable labor exemption decisions from the courts. *See NBA v. Williams*, 45 F.3d 684 (2d Cir. 1995). As a sideline feature of this litigation and negotiation, many players, disenchanted with the fact that union representation blocked the door to full litigation of the antitrust claims, briefly and unsuccessfully sought to decertify the NBPA as collective bargaining representative. After a stormy negotiation period, a new agreement was reached in 1996 (see Chapter _____, Section IX(D)).

In the early 1990s, the NBA faced antitrust litigation from the businesses that tried to produce an off-season Magic Johnson versus Michael Jordan one-on-one game for pay-per-view television, see *Independent Entertainment Group v. NBA*, 853 F. Supp. 333

(C.D.Cal. 1994), and from the owners of the Chicago Bulls who challenged the league's restrictions on the sale of television broadcast rights by individual teams. *See Chicago Professional Sports Ltd. Partnership v. NBA*, discussed in Chapter 12. There was also antitrust litigation, however short-lived, between the NBA and a group that attempted to purchase the Minnesota Timberwolves to relocate the team to New Orleans. *See NBA v. Minnesota Professional Basketball*, 56 F.3d 866 (8th Cir. 1995). In 2002, the NBA successfully moved to dismiss a consumer antitrust action challenging the league's agreement with Direct TV. *See Kingray, Inc. v. NBA, Inc.*, 188 F.Supp.2d 1177 (S.D.Cal. 2002). For a general history of the National Basketball Association, see *The Official NBA Basketball Encyclopedia* (Zander Hollander and Alex Sachare eds., 1989).

(B) Antitrust and Professional Football

In the early twentieth century, professional football, like basketball, began to emerge and develop in small towns and cities that did not have major colleges. In 1920, the American Professional Football Association ("APFA") was formed at a meeting in Canton, Ohio, with each team owner paying a $100 franchise fee. One of the initial owners was George Halas, who operated the Decatur Staleys, soon to become the Chicago Bears. The league was initially composed of fourteen teams in five states and its first president was Jim Thorpe. In 1922 the APFA changed its name and became the National Football League ("NFL"). The names of the early founders still resonate through the "halls" of professional football. Tim Mara's New York Giants (1925), Charles Bidwill's Chicago Cardinals (1933), Arthur Rooney's Pittsburgh Pirates (1933) (soon to be Steelers), and Bert Bell's Frankford Yellow Jackets (soon to be Philadelphia Eagles) were early entrants.

In 1944, the All-American Football Conference ("AAFC") was formed to compete with the NFL. The AAFC started as an eight-team league and folded by 1950, when three AAFC teams, the Baltimore Colts, the Cleveland Browns, and the San Francisco 49ers, were merged into the NFL. The Colts were defunct by the end of the 1950 season, but were revived when the league sold Carroll Rosenbloom the franchise to operate an expansion team in Baltimore in 1953.

The history of the NFL since the early 1950s contains a litany of antitrust litigation. William Radovich had played for the Detroit Lions in the NFL before and just after World War II. In 1947, after a two year stint in the rival AAFC, Radovich tried to return to the NFL. However, as a result of his show of "disloyalty" by jumping leagues, Radovich was suspended by the NFL for five years. *See Radovich v. NFL*, 231 F.2d 620, 621 (9th Cir. 1956). He filed an antitrust suit against the NFL, but the trial judge dismissed Radovich's claims based on the Supreme Court's earlier rulings that Major League Baseball was exempt from the antitrust laws. *See Toolson v. New York Yankees*, 346 U.S. 356 (1953), discussed in Chapter 8. The Court of Appeals affirmed, holding that football was more like baseball than like boxing, an individual sport recently deemed to be non-exempt by the Supreme Court. *See United States v. International Boxing Club of New York*, 348 U.S. 236 (1955). *Radovich v. NFL*, 231 F.2d at 622–23. The United States Department of Justice intervened in support of Radovich, and in 1957 the Supreme Court reversed, holding that football was not entitled to an antitrust exemption, and that Radovich had stated a viable antitrust claim. *Radovich v. NFL*, 352 U.S. 445 (1957). The decision came too late to aid Radovich's career, but it signaled the dawning of a new day for NFL player relations and antitrust litigation.

As discussed in Chapter Fourteen, at about the same time that the Supreme Court issued its decision in *Radovich*, the players formed the NFL Players Association ("NFLPA"), modeled after the union formed by Major League Baseball players ten years earlier. After a somewhat anemic beginning, the union strengthened in the early 1970s and fueled and funded much of the antitrust litigation that followed during that decade and succeeding years. In fact, many commentators have speculated that the selection of John Mackey (all-pro tight end of the Baltimore Colts) for entry into the Football Hall of Fame was delayed several years as retribution for his service as president of the NFLPA.

By the late 1950s, there was an excess demand for ownership of professional football teams. Many people contacted the NFL expressing interest in owning an NFL team, but the existing owners manifested little interest in expansion. As a result, a number of groups began to explore the possibility of starting a competing league. In 1958, Lamar Hunt, who had vainly sought an NFL expansion team in Dallas and who had attempted to purchase the Chicago Cardinals to relocate them to Dallas, decided to found his own league. The American Football League ("AFL") started with Hunt in Dallas (Texans), Bud Adams in Houston (Oilers), Bob Howsam in Denver (Broncos), and Max Winter in Minneapolis (Vikings).

Hunt believed that the new league needed a team in Los Angeles and a team in New York. Barron Hilton placed a team in Los Angeles (Chargers), and Harry Wismer, a former broadcaster, owned the first team in New York (Titans). Ralph Wilson wanted to place a team in Miami, but when the City of Miami refused to let Wilson use the Orange Bowl, Wilson settled for Buffalo (Bills). Billy Sullivan, whom we will revisit later, was awarded a team in Boston (Patriots). Before the AFL had played its first game, Winter announced that he would abandon the AFL and place his franchise in the established NFL. Winter's Vikings were replaced by the Oakland Raiders, owned by Wayne Valley. After the 1960 season, the Chargers relocated from Los Angeles to San Diego; the Miami Dolphins and the Cincinnati Bengals joined the league in the years that followed. At the outset, revenue sharing was a part of the AFL's plan; the leaguewide pooling of television rights and revenues, starting with its first television contract with ABC in 1960, was a critical component of the program. In fact, the AFL later contended that its television revenue sharing plan had been copied by the NFL.

In the early 1960s, the AFL claimed that the NFL had established a monopoly in violation of Section 2 of the Sherman Act. After a full trial on liability, the district court held that the NFL did not have monopoly power and that there was insufficient evidence of the NFL's specific intent to monopolize. *See American Football League v. National Football League*, 205 F. Supp. 60 (D.Md. 1962), *aff'd*, 323 F.2d 124 (4th Cir. 1963). In 1966, the NFL and AFL agreed to merge. Shortly thereafter, the first Super Bowl was played and, since that time, it has grown into the most spectacular media event in professional sports.

The World Football League ("WFL") was formed in 1973 and operated a full season in 1974 and a partial season in 1975 before going out of business. One WFL team, the Mid-South Grizzlies, applied for NFL membership as an expansion team. When that request was denied, it instituted antitrust litigation against the NFL under Sections 1 and 2 of the Sherman Act. *See Mid-South Grizzlies v. National Football League*, 720 F.2d 772 (3d Cir. 1983), *cert. denied*, 467 U.S. 1215 (1984). The court rejected the Grizzlies' claim, holding that they were not seeking to remedy an alleged restriction on competition. Rather, because the Grizzlies had sought to join the alleged illegal monopoly, the court concluded that they therefore had not suffered the requisite injury.

The control by the NFL or individual NFL owners of football stadia, and their agreements that prevent potential owners or operators of football teams in competing leagues from using those stadia, have also been subject to antitrust litigation. In *Hecht v. Pro-Football, Inc.*, 570 F.2d 982 (D.C. Cir. 1977), *cert. denied*, 436 U.S. 956 (1978), the court held that RFK Stadium in Washington, D.C., then home of the Washington Redskins, was an "essential facility" and that the denial of access to a competing football team violated the antitrust laws. Other antitrust plaintiffs have not been as successful for a variety of reasons. *See, e.g., Scallen v. Minnesota Vikings Football Club, Inc.*, 574 F. Supp. 278 (D. Minn. 1983). *See also United States Football League v. National Football League*, 634 F. Supp. 1155 (S.D.N.Y. 1986).

The most significant antitrust litigation brought against the NFL by a competing league was filed in 1984 by the United States Football League ("USFL"). The USFL had started play in March 1983, with twelve teams and contracts with the American Broadcasting Company ("ABC") and the Entertainment and Sports Programming Network ("ESPN"). Six additional franchises were added to the USFL between the 1983 and 1984 seasons. Over its three seasons of Spring football, USFL teams were owned by thirty-nine different principal owners and played in twenty-two different cities. After the three seasons yielded close to $200 million in losses, the USFL played its last game in July, 1985. The USFL unsuccessfully sought a network television contract for games to be played in the Fall of 1986, and one of the principal allegations of the USFL's antitrust case was that the NFL had pressured the major television networks not to enter into such an agreement. After forty-eight days of trial and five days of deliberations, the jury held that the NFL had unlawfully monopolized major league professional football in the United States and had injured the USFL. Yet, the jury only awarded the USFL one dollar of damages (three dollars after trebling), and it totally rejected the USFL's other claims. The district judge then refused the USFL's requests for injunctive relief, but ordered the NFL to pay the USFL $5.52 million of attorneys' fees. The jury's verdict was sustained, in its entirety, on appeal. *United States Football League v. National Football League*, 842 F.2d 1335 (2d Cir. 1988). The award of attorneys fees was also affirmed on appeal. *United States Football League v. National Football League*, 887 F.2d 408 (2d Cir. 1989).

The NFL and its member clubs also have faced antitrust challenges to their policy of "blacking-out" the television broadcast of a club's unsold-out home games in its home territory, *see WTWV, Inc. v. National Football League*, 678 F.2d 142 (11th Cir. 1982), and their "blacking-out" of the Super Bowl broadcast in the city where the Super Bowl was played. *See Campo v. National Football League*, 334 F. Supp. 1181 (E.D. La. 1971). The NFL has even faced an antitrust challenge because it *did not* black out NFL broadcasts within seventy-miles of a state football championship game. *Colorado High School Activities Ass'n v. National Football League*, 711 F.2d 943 (10th Cir. 1983).

More recently, the NFL has faced antitrust litigation challenging its pooling of teams' television broadcast rights for sale to satellite broadcasters at artificially high and non-competitive prices. The Court rejected the NFL's claim that its conduct was exempt from antitrust scrutiny, holding that the Sports Broadcasting Act of 1961 and 1966 exempts only the pooling of broadcast rights for commercially sponsored free broadcasts. *See Shaw v. Dallas Cowboys Football Club*, 172 F.3d 299 (3d Cir. 1999).

Yet, over the past forty years, the greatest volume of antitrust litigation involving the NFL has concerned "player restraints." In particular, players have challenged the draft system and various limitations upon a player's ability to sign with the team of choice after his or her existing contract has expired. *See* Chapter 10. A threshold issue in most of that litigation has been the applicability of the nonstatutory labor exemption to the challenged conduct. *See* Chapter 9. Most of the decisions that have found the exemption inapplicable have, on the merits, found the underlying conduct to be an unreasonable and unlawful restraint of trade.

For example, in *Mackey v. National Football League*, 543 F.2d 606 (8th Cir. 1976), *cert. dismissed*, 434 U.S. 801 (1977), considered in detail in Chapters 9 and 10, the court determined that the "Rozelle Rule" (allowing the league commissioner to determine and award "compensation" to a team losing a free agent) violated the antitrust laws. Following the Eighth Circuit's decision in *Mackey*, the NFLPA sponsored a class action lawsuit against the NFL, seeking damages and other relief on behalf of 5706 former and then present pro football players. *See Alexander v. National Football League*, 1977-2 Trade Cas. ¶61,730 (D.Minn. 1977); *Reynolds v. National Football League*, 584 F.2d 280 (8th Cir. 1978). That litigation was settled simultaneous to the negotiation of a collective bargaining agreement between the NFL and the NFLPA. 584 F.2d at 281-83.

In *Smith v. National Football League*, 593 F.2d 1173, 1184–85 (D.C. Cir. 1979), the court held that the NFL's player draft as it existed in 1968 also violated the antitrust laws. The lower court had found a *per se* violation; however, while affirming the result, the United States Court of Appeals for the D.C. Circuit rejected the *per se* approach and applied a Rule of Reason analysis. *See also Chuy v. Philadelphia Eagles*, 407 F. Supp. 717 (E.D. Pa. 1976) (player whose career was cut short by injury filed a complaint asserting a wide variety of claims, including unsuccessful antitrust challenges to the NFL standard player contract, the NFL's player draft, and other conduct by the NFL and its member teams), *aff'd*, 595 F.2d 1265 (3d Cir. 1979). The NFL's 1984 "supplemental draft" of players under contract to USFL teams was also the subject to an antitrust challenge, which the NFL successfully defended. *See Zimmerman v. National Football League*, 632 F. Supp. 398 (D.D.C. 1986).

Several lawsuits, filed by the NFL players against the league, including the *Powell*, *McNeil*, *Jackson*, and *White* cases, resulted in judgments against the league and led in 1993 to the most recent collective bargaining agreement. These decisions, together with the subsequent landmark decision of the Supreme Court in the *Brown* case, which gave the labor exemption its most expansive reading, are discussed in considerable detail in Chapter 9. All these cases involved player mobility or player compensation issues ("labor market restraints"). One of the NFL's responses to the battery of antitrust lawsuits filed by the players was to file their own, ill-conceived antitrust lawsuit against the NFLPA and agents representing NFL players; that lawsuit was summarily dismissed. *See Five Smiths, Inc. v. NFL Players Association*, 788 F. Supp. 1042 (D.Minn. 1992).

While these lawsuits were being litigated, the NFL's affiliated properties organization also faced antitrust litigation from the NFL Players Association concerning alleged unreasonable restraints and attempted monopolization of markets related to licensed products. *See NFL Players Association v. NFL Properties, Inc.*, 1991 U.S. Dist. LEXIS 19590 (S.D.N.Y. 1991).

The NFL's draft rules were subject to antitrust scrutiny in 2004 when Maurice Clarett, a freshman running back who led Ohio State University to a national championship, brought a Section 1 claim against the NFL after being denied entry into the 2004 draft. As discussed in Chapters 9 and 10, the district court granted summary judgment in favor of Clarett and ordered that he be permitted to enter the NFL draft. *Clarett v. NFL*, 306 F.Supp.2d 379 (S.D.N.Y.), rev'd, 369 F.3d 124 (2d Cir. 2004). The district court opinion was reversed by the Second Circuit on the grounds that the draft eligibility rule was part of the NFL CBA and was thus protected by the non-statutory labor exemption. *Clarett v. NFL*, 369 F.3d 124 (2d Cir. 2004).

In unrelated litigation, various NFL teams faced antitrust challenges when they began requiring fans to purchase tickets to all of their home preseason games as a condition to purchasing season tickets for the regular season. *See, e.g., Coniglio v. Highwood Services*, 495 F.2d 1286 (2d Cir.), *cert. denied*, 419 U.S. 1022 (1974); *Driskill v. Dallas Cowboys Football Club, Inc.*, 498 F.2d 321 (5th Cir. 1974); *Laing v. Minnesota Vikings Football Club*, 372 F. Supp. 59 (D. Minn. 1973), *aff'd per curiam*, 492 F.2d 1381 (8th Cir.), *cert. denied*, 419 U.S. 832 (1974); *Grossman Development Co. v. Detroit Lions*, 1973 Trade Cas. ¶74,790 (E.D. Mich.), *aff'd*, 530 F.2d 1404 (6th Cir. 1974). For the most part, fan efforts to claim that such ticket arrangements constituted illegal tying have failed. *See supra*, this chapter at Section IV(D)(4).

Another area of seemingly continuous antitrust litigation for the NFL has concerned its efforts to prevent any relocation by NFL teams outside their home territories. During his tenure as league commissioner, Pete Rozelle was committed to keeping all NFL teams in their "75-mile radius home territories," while satisfying new demand for NFL teams. To enforce this policy, the owners implemented Article 4.3 of the NFL Constitution & Bylaws, which required unanimous consent by the owners of all of the teams to permit any team to relocate. This policy was first challenged by the Los Angeles Memorial Coliseum Commission (the "Coliseum") in 1979.

The Los Angeles Rams, in 1978, had decided to relocate within their home territory, from the Coliseum to Anaheim's "Big A", commencing with the 1980–81 football season. Aware that no team could relocate to the Coliseum unless it secured approval by all other NFL teams, the Coliseum sued, seeking an injunction against the enforcement of Article 4.3. As the litigation progressed, the Coliseum convinced the Oakland Raiders to enter into a lease to play their home games at the Coliseum, and the Raiders were dropped as a defendant and added as a plaintiff. In response to the Coliseum/Raider lawsuit, the NFL had amended Article 4.3, to require only three-fourths of the owners to approve a relocation, but the Raiders' relocation was nevertheless rejected by an overwhelming 22 "No", 0 "Yes" and 5 "Abstention" vote. After an initial hung jury and mistrial, the jury in the second trial found for the Coliseum and the Raiders, awarding them approximately $50 million in damages (after trebling). The jury's verdict on liability was affirmed on appeal. *Los Angeles Memorial Coliseum Comm'n v. NFL*, 726 F.2d 1381 (9th Cir. 1984) (discussed in Chapter 12).

Shortly after the Ninth Circuit's affirmance was issued, Robert Irsay, the owner of the Baltimore Colts, loaded up the Colts' uniforms, equipment, and other assets in Mayflower moving vans under cover of darkness and literally relocated to Indianapolis in the middle of the night without any NFL opposition (*i.e.*, without NFL approval or disapproval). *See* discussion in *Mayor and City Council of Baltimore v. Baltimore Football Club, Inc.*, 624 F. Supp. 278, 279–80 (D.Md. 1985). Under less intriguing circumstances, the New York Jets encountered no opposition when they relocated from Shea Stadium to Giants Stadium in East Rutherford, New Jersey. There has been some suggestion that, absent the Coliseum and Raiders' lawsuit, the NFL might not have permitted the Jets' relocation, even though the move was within the Jets' home territory, because the effect of the move was to leave New York City without an NFL team. *See, e.g., United States Football League v. National Football League*, 84 Civ. 7484 (PKL), LEXIS Slip Op. at 2–5 (S.D.N.Y. May 15, 1986).

In December, 1984, when financially beleaguered Philadelphia Eagles owner Leonard Tose and his daughter were contemplating a move and meeting with stadium officials in Phoenix, Arizona, Commissioner Rozelle filed a preemptive strike, sued Tose and the Eagles in Philadelphia, sought a declaratory judgment that Article 4.3 was lawful, and requested an injunction to keep Tose from relocating the Eagles out of Philadelphia. *See* Complaint in *National Football League v. Philadelphia Eagles Football Club*, Civil Action No. 84-6131 (E.D. Pa. 1984). One week later, Commissioner Rozelle issued procedures for proposed franchise relocations under Article 4.3. *See* Chapter 12. The litigation with the Eagles was resolved when Norman Braman purchased the Eagles from Tose and agreed to keep the team in Philadelphia.

In 1986, the Ninth Circuit finally issued its decision on the damages award in the *Coliseum* case, reversing and remanding that portion of the jury's verdict and instructing the district court to conduct a damages re-trial that was likely to lead to a reduction in the jury's prior award. *See Los Angeles Memorial Coliseum Comm'n v. National Football League*, 791 F.2d 1356 (9th Cir. 1986). A few months before the Ninth Circuit's second decision, Bill Bidwill sought to relocate his Cardinals out of St. Louis, and he sued for the right to do so because he believed that the NFL would reject his relocation application. Bidwill was concerned because of Rozelle's commitment to prevent relocation and the perceived unlikelihood of ever getting approval by three-fourths of the owners. His pessimism was exacerbated by an alleged agreement between Rozelle and the United States Football League ("USFL") to the effect that the NFL would not permit relocation to cities that were already home to USFL teams. *See* Complaint in *St. Louis Football Cardinals, Inc. v. Rozelle*, Civil Action No. 86 Civ. 1262 (JES) (S.D.N.Y. 1986). The dispute with the Cardinals was resolved when the club agreed to pay the other owners $7.5 million in return for permission to relocate.

For the next eight years, the NFL was successful in preventing all relocation. The NFL prevented Victor Kiam II from relocating the New England Patriots from Foxboro Massachusetts when Kiam owned the team from 1988–1992. The Patriots' financial woes, combined with other financial problems during the recession of the early 1990's forced Kiam to sell the Patriots to avoid bankruptcy. The League then refused to approve Kiam's sale of the Patriots to James Orthwein unless and until Kiam signed a general release. The release was upheld over Kiam's claims that it was an unenforceable part of the NFL's antitrust conspiracy and that it was the result of economic duress, but the NFL's challenges to Kiam's claims against the entities in Jacksonville that agreed not to deal with Kiam were rejected. *VKK Corp. v. NFL*, 244 F.3d 114 (2d Cir. 2001). In 1995, the Los Angeles Rams announced that they were relocating to St. Louis. After the Rams and the Attorney General of Missouri threatened the NFL with antitrust litigation, the NFL owners recanted their initial rejection of the proposed move and approved the relocation subject to the payment of several million dollars in penalties to other owners.

After the Rams' move, a number of other relocations were announced and approved—Al Davis's Raiders back to Oakland, Art Modell's Browns (now Ravens) from Cleveland to Baltimore, and Bud Adams' Oilers from Houston to Nashville. This series of attempted and approved relocations led to the institution of antitrust litigation: by the Maryland Stadium Authority against the NFL, challenging the league's interference with the Browns' move to Baltimore; by Seattle to try to prevent a move by the Seahawks; by the NFL against the Raiders, *see* Complaint in *National Football League v. Los Angeles Raiders*, Civil Action No. 95-5885 (C.D. Cal. 1995); by the Raiders against the NFL, *see* Complaint in *Oakland Raiders v. National Football League*, Civil Action No. 95-05547 (SBA) (N.D. Cal. 1995); and by the St. Louis stadium operator against the league, *see St. Louis Convention and Visitors Commission v. National Football League*, 154 F.3d 851 (8th Cir. 1998). During this period, the NFL also stifled an attempt by Seattle Seahawks' owner David Behring to relocate his club to Los Angeles.

Throughout the past twenty-five years, the NFL repeatedly and unsuccessfully has asked Congress for an exemption that would permit relocation restrictions without fear of antitrust reprisals. A substantial number of bills have been introduced and a significant number of Congressional hearings have been held, but no bill has ever proceeded out of committee.

In addition to the challenges to the league's restrictions on relocation, the NFL's limitations on the ownership of the teams have come under antitrust attack. In the late 1970s and early 1980s, certain NFL owners and the North American Soccer League successfully challenged the NFL's cross-ownership ban, which prohibited owners of majority interests in NFL teams and members of their families from acquiring any interest in any other major team sport. *North American Soccer League v. National Football League*, 670 F.2d 1249 (2d Cir. 1981), *cert. denied*, 459 U.S. 1074 (1982). In the early 1990s, former New England Patriots owner Billy Sullivan successfully challenged the NFL's restrictions on public ownership of NFL teams, securing a jury verdict for $38 million ($114 million after trebling), which was reduced by the district judge to $17 million ($51 million after trebling). However, Sullivan's victory was short-lived, as the district court decision was reversed and remanded for a new trial, based on questions concerning the jury instructions, as well as a potential cloud on Sullivan's claim due to his initial involvement in, support of, and prior use of the NFL rule. *Sullivan v. National Football League*, 34 F.3d 1091 (1st Cir. 1994). After a second jury agreed on the illegality of the rule, but could not agree on the question of the significance of Sullivan's involvement with the rule, the NFL settled the case by paying Sullivan $11.1 million. The NFL succeeded in litigation regarding the same ownership restriction from another former owner of the Patriots. *See Murray v. National Football League*, 1998-1 Trade Cas (CCH) ¶72,147 (E.D. Pa. 1998).

In the last few years, antitrust suits have also been brought against the NFL and its member clubs regarding terms of stadium lease deals extracted from communities desperate to keep their local teams from relocating. The first suit was dismissed because the plaintiff, a local taxpayer, lacked standing. *Warnock v. NFL*, 154 Fed.Appx. 291 (3d Cir. 2005) (Pittsburgh Steelers). The second suit was dismissed because the relevant statute of limitations had expired before the suit was filed. *Hamilton County, Ohio v. NFL*, 2006-1 Trade Cas. (CCH) ¶75,243 (S.D. Ohio 2006) (Cincinnati Bengals).

Another recent subject of antitrust litigation has been the NFL teams' exclusive pooling of their marks and logos to be marketed by NFL Properties, Inc. pursuant to the terms of the NFL Trust agreement. When the NFL sued the Dallas Cowboys and their owner, Jerry Jones, in 1995, seeking damages under the Lanham Act and various state common law theories (Verified Complaint in *National Football League Properties, Inc. v. Dallas Cowboys Football Club, Ltd.*, 95 Civ. 7951 (SAS) (S.D.N.Y. 1995)), the Cowboys responded with antitrust claims challenging the NFL's conduct as violations of Sections 1 and 2 of the Sherman Act in the professional football sponsorship and merchandise markets. *See* Amended Complaint in *Dallas Cowboys Football Club, Ltd. v. National Football League Trust*, 95 Civ. 9426 (SAS) (S.D.N.Y. 1996). The cases were settled in December of 1996, with both sides simply agreeing to dismiss their claims without prejudice.

The NFL and its member clubs have even faced antitrust litigation relating to their operation of the World League of American Football ("WLAF") and their decision to terminate the WLAF's operation of teams in the United States. *See, e.g., Orlando Thunder, L.P. v. National Football League*, 1995-1 Trade Cas. ¶70,857 (9th Cir. 1994) (per curiam). Yet, the NFL is not the only professional football league that has faced antitrust litigation. For example, in 1984 a court sustained a challenge to the USFL's "Eligibility Rule," which provided that potential players were not eligible to play for any USFL team "unless (1) all college football eligibility of such player has expired, or (2) at least five (5) years shall have elapsed since the player first entered or attended a recognized junior college, college or university or (3) such player received a diploma from a recognized college or university." *See Boris v. United States Football League*, 1984-1 Trade Cas. ¶66,012 (C.D. Cal. 1984). Even fledgling operations such as the Arena Football League and the World Football League have found themselves in the position of defendants in antitrust litigation. *See Tampa Bay Storm, Inc. v. Arena Football League, Inc.*, 932 F. Supp. 281 (M.D. Fla. 1996); *New England Colonials Football Club, Inc. v. World Football League*, 1980–81 Trade Cas. ¶63,710 (D. Mass. 1980). For an exhaustive history of the National Football League, see DAVID HARRIS, *The League: The Rise and Decline of the NFL* (1986). For additional background on the emergence of professional football, see WILL MCDONOUGH ET AL., *75 Seasons* (1995); MYRON COPE, *The Game That Was* (1974); MIKE RATHET ET AL., *Pro Football* (1970).

(C) Antitrust and Professional Hockey

In the early 1900s, amateur and professional hockey leagues appeared throughout the United States and Canada. North America's first significant professional league may have been the International Hockey League, created in 1904 with several teams in Michigan, a team in Pittsburgh, and a team in Ontario. In 1908, the Eastern Canada Amateur Hockey Association launched a professional league, followed in 1909 by the National Hockey Association and the Canadian Hockey Association, with all three leagues operating exclusively in Canada. The Pacific Coast Hockey Association organized another Canadian league in 1911. In 1917, the members of the National Hockey Association disbanded their league and created a new association, the National Hockey League ("NHL").

When the NHL first came into existence in 1917, it had four teams, all located in Canada—two in Montreal (the Wanderers and the Canadiens) and one each in Toronto and Ottawa. The Montreal Wanderers ceased to operate midway through the first year, as a fire claimed their "home ice," the Montreal Arena. In 1919, the Quebec Bulldogs were briefly a part of the NHL; they were then sold, becoming the Hamilton Tigers for the 1920 season. In 1924, after seven years of operating as a four (or three team) league, the NHL added its first United States team, the Boston Bruins, and another team in Montreal—the Maroons. The NHL further increased its size and its United States presence in 1925, when the Hamilton Tigers were purchased and relocated to Madison Square Garden as the New York Americans; they joined the Pittsburgh Pirates as new league members. Further expansion occurred in 1926, when the New York Rangers, the Chicago Black Hawks, and Detroit Cougars were added to the league.

Over the next forty years, certain teams changed their names, relocated, shut-down operations for a season or two, and/or disbanded, yielding a league with six teams. In 1967 the league doubled in size, as six more United States teams were added—in Los

Angeles, Minneapolis, Oakland, Philadelphia, Pittsburgh, and St. Louis. In 1970, owners of expansion teams in Vancouver and Buffalo each paid more than eight million dollars as expansion fees to acquire the local minor league hockey team in each of those cities and to join the NHL. In 1971, the NHL selected Nassau County, New York (Long Island) and Atlanta as the expansion cities for two more NHL teams, raising the total number of teams for the 1972–73 season to sixteen.

Success breeds new entry and competition, and in 1971 the World Hockey Association ("WHA") began to challenge the NHL's position as the only producer of major league professional hockey games in North America. By the time that its founders had formed the WHA, there were already three minor league professional hockey associations in North America (the American, Central, and Western Hockey Leagues), with a total of about twenty-four teams. There were also two "amateur" or semi-professional leagues (the Eastern and International Leagues). The WHA sought to establish a fully operational, twelve-team major league in a single year, with a salary structure competitive with the salaries being paid to NHL players.

The competition between the NHL and WHA was intense, as the WHA's strategy included signing well-known NHL players, such as Bobby Hull, Derek Sanderson, Gerry Cheevers, Andre Lacroix, and J.C. Tremblay. *See, e.g., Boston Professional Hockey Ass'n, Inc. v. Cheevers*, 348 F. Supp. 261 (D. Mass.), *remanded*, 472 F.2d 127 (1st Cir. 1972). Another key element of the WHA's competitive strategy was the initiation of antitrust litigation against the NHL, to challenge the perpetual control over NHL players that the NHL "reserve clause" purported to give NHL teams. *See, e.g., Philadelphia World Hockey Club, Inc. v. Philadelphia Hockey Club, Inc.*, 351 F. Supp. 462 (E.D. Pa. 1972). During 1972, fifteen separate lawsuits were filed against the NHL, and those actions were all transferred to the United States District Court for the Eastern District of Pennsylvania for consolidated pretrial proceedings. In 1974, after a series of major rulings adverse to the NHL and its member clubs, all parties except one WHA team reached an antitrust settlement agreement. *See generally In re Professional Hockey Antitrust Litigation*, 531 F.2d 1188 (3d Cir. 1976). Two years later, the United States Supreme Court summarily reinstated a district court order dismissing the remaining claims as a sanction for discovery abuse by the remaining WHA litigants. *NHL v. Metropolitan Hockey Club, Inc.*, 427 U.S. 639 (1976).

In a separate litigation, a plaintiff who was seeking to establish a WHA franchise at the Nassau Memorial Coliseum ("Coliseum") in Long Island sued the NHL. The gravamen of his case, which was filed in 1971 and did not end until 1981, was that the NHL created the New York Islanders to foreclose the plaintiff's access to the Coliseum and thereby block the entry of the WHA into the New York metropolitan area. *See Shayne v. NHL*, 504 F. Supp. 1023 (E.D.N.Y. 1980).

As if that tumultuous history in such a short period of time were not enough antitrust litigation for one sport to endure, both the NHL and WHA faced substantial additional antitrust lawsuits in the 1970s. For example, when the NHL and thirteen of its member clubs sued to enjoin a manufacturing firm from producing and selling embroidered emblems with the NHL team marks and logos, the defendants raised the antitrust laws as a *defense*. They claimed that the NHL's exclusive license agreement constituted tying, price fixing, and a series of other violations of the antitrust laws, thereby defeating the NHL's rights under the Lanham Act and the common law of unfair competition. The district court rejected those defenses and that portion of the decision was affirmed. *See Boston Professional Hockey Ass'n, Inc. v. Dallas Cup & Emblem Manufacturing, Inc.*, 510 F. 2d 1004, 1013–14 (5th Cir. 1975), *rev'g and remanding*, 360 F. Supp. 459 (N.D.

Tex. 1973). The NHL also faced antitrust litigation: (1) by one of its own member clubs after the NHL denied the team's request to relocate from San Francisco to Vancouver, see *San Francisco Seals, Ltd. v. NHL*, 379 F. Supp. 966 (C.D. Cal. 1974); (2) in courts on both coasts of the United States by a one-eyed hockey player who was not allowed to play in the NHL, see *Neeld v. NHL*, 594 F.2d 1297 (9th Cir. 1979) and *Neeld v. NHL*, 439 F. Supp. 446 (W.D.N.Y. 1977); and (3) again by players challenging the NHL reserve system in effect at the end of the 1970s. See *McCourt v. California Sports, Inc.*, 600 F.2d 1193 (6th Cir. 1979).

The fledgling WHA soon learned that even less established sports leagues can be antitrust defendants, as it faced antitrust litigation from a nineteen year-old player who challenged the WHA rule prohibiting players under 20 from playing. See *Linsemen v. WHA*, 439 F. Supp. 1315 (D. Conn. 1977). It was a co-defendant with the NHL in a lawsuit filed by a referee who alleged that, after an aborted NHL-WHA merger, some sort of NHL-WHA agreement led to both leagues refusing to hire him. See *Dowling v. United States*, 476 F. Supp. 1018 (D. Minn. 1979).

In the 1980s, both the NHL and WHA faced antitrust litigation brought by a number of active and former professional hockey players. *See, e.g., Adduono v. WHA*, 824 F.2d 617 (8th Cir. 1987). In addition, owners of a minor league hockey team in the Western Hockey League ("WHL") asserted antitrust claims against the NHL, alleging that the NHL wrongfully denied the plaintiffs an NHL franchise, denied the plaintiffs the opportunity to join the WHA, and eventually damaged the WHA and destroyed the Western Hockey League. See *Seattle Totems Hockey Club, Inc. v. NHL*, 1986-1 Trade Cas. [CCH] ¶66,968 (9th Cir. 1986). In 1983, the Ralston Purina Co., owner of the NHL's St. Louis Blues, agreed to sell the team for $11.5 million to Canadian investors who planned to move the team to Saskatoon, Saskatchewan. The NHL refused to approve the sale and relocation, and Ralston Purina filed an antitrust suit seeking $60 million. When Ralston Purina threatened to dissolve the team, the NHL assumed operation of, and eventually sold, the team, and countersued Ralston Purina for $78 million in damages. Two weeks into the jury trial in 1985, the case settled on undisclosed terms. Tim Bryant, *Blues, NHL Lawsuit Settled*, UPI, June 27, 1985.

In 1990 and 1991, the NHL and its member clubs became embroiled in antitrust litigation concerning the league's requirement that suppliers of equipment to NHL teams pay a fee to the NHL as compensation for the NHL permitting the brand names and logos of the equipment to be displayed during NHL games. See *NHL v. Karhu Canada, Inc.*, 1991 U.S. Dist. LEXIS 1693 (E.D. Pa. 1991). Later in 1991, when negotiations between the NHL and the NHL Players Association ("NHLPA") failed to yield a new collective bargaining agreement, the NHL filed a preemptive antitrust action, unsuccessfully seeking a declaratory judgment that their continued adherence to specific provisions of the expired 1988 agreement were lawful. See *NHL v. NHLPA*, 789 F. Supp. 288 (D. Minn. 1992).

More recently, the NHLPA brought a suit alleging that the Ontario Hockey League (the "OHL") violated Section 1 of the Sherman Act by adopting a rule that prohibited 20-year olds from playing in the OHL, if they had previously played at a NCAA school. The Sixth Circuit rejected the NHLPA's claim holding that the players had failed to prove that the rule actually caused t he harm alleged in the complaint. *National Hockey League Players Association v. Plymouth Whalers*, 419 F.3d 462 (6th Cir. 2005), For a comprehensive treatment of professional hockey's history, see STAN & SHIRLEY FIS-CHBEIN ET AL., *Twentieth Century Hockey Chronicles* (1994).

(D) Antitrust and Other Professional Sports Leagues

As discussed in Chapter Two, the number of professional team sports has increased dramatically in recent years. Professional leagues produce games of soccer, lacrosse, arena football, roller hockey, team tennis, women's basketball, and other sports. There are also minor leagues and semi-professional leagues for basketball, hockey, baseball, and other team sports. Antitrust is not as important an influence in some of those leagues, primarily because they are less likely to have "market power." Thus, while their conduct may restrain trade, a plaintiff may be unable to prove that conduct by one of these leagues adversely affects overall market competition in a relevant market. For example, if Arena Football is determined to compete with NFL football in the relevant market at issue, it is unlikely that Arena Football would be able to restrain trade in that overall market. If, however, the case concerns the market for Arena player services or if Arena Football is deemed to be a separate product, so that the teams in the Arena Football League collectively define and control the market, an antitrust challenge may be viable. The other major obstacle to antitrust litigation involving those sports that generate less revenue is the sheer cost of antitrust litigation. Proving relevant markets through testimony of expert witnesses and addressing all the issues necessary to establish an antitrust violation may be prohibitively expensive. If the plaintiff can afford the litigation cost, he may succeed in the lawsuit and, in the process, put the league (and the entire sport, in some circumstances) out of business. Therefore, while threatened antitrust litigation is not uncommon even in these sports, it is likely that the matter would be resolved in some fashion outside the courtroom.

Nevertheless, antitrust concerns still motivate much of the decisionmaking in certain "non-major" professional sports leagues. As discussed in Chapter 2, when preliminary decisions are being made about the composition of a new league, competent counsel should structure the league to avoid potential future litigation. The mere fact that a league has not yet reached "the big time" does not guarantee insulation from antitrust scrutiny. *See, e.g., Tampa Bay Storm, Inc. v. Arena Football League, Inc.*, 932 F. Supp. 281 (M.D. Fla. 1996)(complaint includes count alleging violation of Florida Antitrust Act). For example, while a professional roller hockey league may not have market power in any television market or with respect to stadia or arena where their games are played, the league's restrictions on competition among the teams for the services of roller hockey players may be attacked under the antitrust laws by disgruntled players. Therefore, antitrust concerns must be considered carefully in much of the decisionmaking concerning even these "lesser" professional sports leagues.

These antitrust concerns were in the forefront of the minds of Major League Soccer ("MLS") and its players before a single game had even been played. As discussed in chapters 2, 10, and 12, the MLS players decided not to form a union in order to preserve their ability to pursue an antitrust lawsuit against the MLS. The MLS, however, had structured itself as a "single entity" league, or at least a hybrid thereof, and claimed it was thus immune from scrutiny under Section 1 of the Sherman Act. The players brought an antitrust suit against the MLS in 1997, alleging that the MLS and its teams, along with the United States Soccer Federation, had violated the Sherman Act by agreeing to restrict player salaries and preventing any other organization in the United States from competing with the MLS. The district court granted summary judgment for the MLS on the plaintiffs' Section 1 claims, holding that the MLS was a true "single entity." On appeal, the United States Court of Appeals for the First Circuit affirmed on other grounds, the players' Section 1 claims because the MLS did not have market power in the worldwide market for player services, based on the jury's finding that there was a worldwide relevant geographic market for player services when the jury found for the defendants at the trial of the players' monopolization claims. *See Fraser v. MLS*, 294 F.3d 47 (1st Cir. 2002).

(E) Antitrust and Individual Sports

While most professional sports antitrust litigation has focused on the major team sports leagues, professional boxing, golf, tennis, horse racing, auto racing, beach volleyball, and other "individual" sports have not been immune from antitrust litigation. For a comprehensive discussion of individual sports, see Chapter 2. *See also Volvo North America Corp. v. Men's International Professional Tennis Council*, discussed in Chapter 10; *International Boxing Club v. United States*, 358 U.S. 242 (1959). In addition, investigations by government antitrust enforcement agencies have been major subjects of concern for certain individual professional sports. For example, rules governing PGA Tour players' participation in non-PGA Tour events as well as other collateral issues were focal points of the United States Federal Trade Commission's investigation of the PGA Tour in the early 1990s.

It is more difficult to discuss antitrust issues concerning individual sports as a group than with league sports as a group. The different structures of the individual sports (*e.g.*, sanctioning bodies, ranking systems, circuits or tours), the nature and idiosyncrasies of each sport, the various entities and persons that may be important, the extent to which the sport is domestic or international in character, and similar issues make it questionable whether conclusions reached in the context of one sport would be directly applicable to another. For example, in *Blalock v. LPGA*, 359 F. Supp. 1260 (N.D. Ga. 1973), the court found that a suspension of a player for cheating constituted a *per se* violation of Section 1 of the Sherman Act because the governing body ruling on the suspension consisted exclusively of plaintiff's competitors. Other lawsuits by professional golfers alleging denial of eligibility or imposition of disciplinary sanctions have been dismissed because the restraint impacted only the competitor rather than competition and/or because the alleged restraint was deemed reasonable. *See Deesen v. PGA*, 358 F.2d 163 (9th Cir. 1966); *O'Grady v. PGA Tour, Inc.*, 1989 U.S. Dist. LEXIS 4301 (S.D. Cal. 1989); *Manok v. Southeast District Bowling Ass'n*, 306 F. Supp. 1215 (C.D. Ca. 1969). Antitrust analysis of particular agreements or conduct in an individual sport can only be undertaken after the attorney, expert economist, government agency, or court believes that it has a relatively full understanding of the sport and how it operates. This point is especially compelling in the context of equipment restriction cases where the nature of the players' expectations, fan response, and similar factors may have a pivotal effect on validity of the restraint. *See, e.g., Gunter Harz Sports, Inc. v. USTA, Inc.*, 511 F. Supp. 1103 (D. Neb.), *aff'd*, 665 F.2d 222 (8th Cir. 1981); *Weight-Rite Golf Corp. v. USGA*, 766 F. Supp. 1104 (N.D. Fla. 1991), *aff'd without op.*, 953 F.2d 651 (11th Cir. 1992); *Gilder v. PGA Tour, Inc.*, 936 F. 2d 417 (9th Cir. 1991). In Chapters 2, 10, and 13, we explore these cases and refer to numerous other decisions that illustrate the unique nuances of the antitrust inquiries arising in individual sports. By examining the other sports antitrust cases, the student of antitrust law can develop an understanding of the theory of antitrust and ways in which the antitrust concepts can be applied to the particular facts of the individual sport at issue.

As the National Association of Stock Car Racing ("NASCAR") has gained popularity and evolved into a financial success over the last several years, it has also attracted more threats of litigation from those looking to gain a share of the success. In 2005, Kentucky Speedway filed a complaint alleging that NASCAR and the International Speedway Association monopolized and attempted to monopolize the market for hosting national stock car racing and wrongfully denied it a "NEXTEL Cup Series Race." The district court denied NASCAR's motion to dismiss. *Kentucky Speedway, LLC v. NASCAR*, 410 F.Supp.2d (E.D.K.Y. 2006). Even the horse racing industry has not been immune from antitrust lawsuits, as Churchill Downs, Inc., brought a Section 1 claim against the Jockey Guild in 2005 in response to the jockeys' boycott of various races.

VIII. Conclusion

Antitrust claims asserted against defendants involved in professional sports are, first and foremost, claims that must be analyzed under the federal antitrust laws. In particular, they are primarily examined under Sections 1 and 2 of the Sherman Act. To understand the judicial opinions, to advise clients involved in the business of professional sports, and to predict the likely outcome (or at least the likely analysis) of future disputes, you must read the opinions carefully in the context of the antitrust framework set out above. As you progress through the subsequent antitrust chapters, Chapters 8 through 13, please consider the impact that antitrust considerations have had on the ways that the business of professional sports is conducted and refer back to this overview chapter to facilitate your understanding of the governing legal precedents.

Chapter 8

Antitrust and Sports:
The Baseball Exemption

I. Introduction

Casey Stengel, from *The Congressional Record*

Excerpted from THE BASEBALL READER 278 (Charles Einstein ed., 1980)

SENATOR KEFAUVER: Mr. Stengel, you are the manager of the New York Yankees. Will you give us very briefly your background and your views about this legislation?

MR. STENGEL: Well, I started in professional ball in 1910. I have been in professional ball, I would say, for forty-eight years. I have been employed by numerous ball clubs in the majors and in the minor leagues.

I started in the minor leagues with Kansas City. I played as low as Class D ball, which was at Shelbyville, Kentucky, and also Class C ball and Class A ball, and I have advanced in baseball as a ballplayer.

I had many years that I was not so successful as a ballplayer, as it is a game of skill. And then I was no doubt discharged by baseball in which I had to go back to the minor leagues as a manager, and after being in the minor leagues as a manager, I became a major-league manager in several cities and was discharged, we call it discharged because there was no question I had to leave.

And I returned to the minor leagues at Milwaukee, Kansas City and Oakland, California, and then returned to the major leagues.

In the last ten years, naturally, in major-league baseball with the New York Yankees; the New York Yankees have had tremendous success, and while I am not a ballplayer who does the work, I have no doubt worked for a ball club that is very capable in the office.

I have been up and down the ladder. I know there are some things in baseball thirty-five to fifty years ago that are better now than they were in those days. In those days, my goodness, you could not transfer a ball club in the minor leagues, Class D, Class C ball, Class A ball.

How could you transfer a ball club when you did not have a highway? How could you transfer a ball club when the railroad then would take you to a

317

town, you got off and then you had to wait and sit up five hours to go to another ball club?

How could you run baseball then without night ball?

You had to have night ball to improve the proceeds, to pay larger salaries, and I went to work, the first year I received $135 a month.

I thought that was amazing. I had to put away enough money to go to dental college. I found out it was not better in dentistry. I stayed in baseball. Any other question you would like to ask me?

SENATOR KEFAUVER: Mr. Stengel, are you prepared to answer particularly why baseball wants this bill passed?

MR. STENGEL: Well, I would have to say at the present time, I think that baseball has advanced in this respect for the player help. That is an amazing statement for me to make, because you can retire with an annuity at fifty and what organization in America allows you to retire at fifty and receive money?

I want to further state that I am not a ballplayer, that is, put into that pension fund committee. At my age, and I have been in baseball, well, I will say I am possibly the oldest man who is working in baseball. I would say that when they start an annuity for the ballplayers to better their conditions, it should have been done, and I think it has been done.

I think it should be the way they have done it, which is a very good thing.

The reason they possibly did not take the managers in at that time was because radio and television or the income to ball clubs was not large enough that you could have put in a pension plan.

Now I am not a member of the pension plan. You have young men here who are, who represent the ball clubs.

They represent the players and since I am not a member and don't receive pension from a fund which you think, my goodness, he ought to be declared in that, too, but I would say that is a great thing for the ballplayers.

That is one thing I will say for the ballplayers, they have an advanced pension fund. I should think it was gained by radio and television or you could not have enough money to pay anything of that type.

Now the second thing about baseball that I think is very interesting to the public or to all of us that it is the owner's own fault if he does not improve his club, along with the officials in the ball club and the players.

Now what causes that?

If I am going to go on the road and we are a traveling ball club and you know the cost of transportation now—we travel sometimes with three Pullman coaches, the New York Yankees and remember I am just a salaried man, and do not own stock in the New York Yankees. I found out that in traveling with the New York Yankees on the road and all, that it is the best, and we have broken records in Washington this year, we have broken them in every city but New York and we have lost two clubs that have gone out of the city of New York.

Of course, we have had some bad weather, I would say that they are mad at us in Chicago, we fill the parks.

They have come out to see good material. I will say they are mad at us in Kansas City, but we broke their attendance record.

Now on the road we only get possibly 27 cents. I am not positive of these figures, as I am not an official.

If you go back fifteen years or so if I owned stock in the club, I would give them to you.

SENATOR KEFAUVER: Mr. Stengel, I am not sure that I made my question clear.

MR. STENGEL: Yes, sir. Well, that is all right. I am not sure I am going to answer yours perfectly, either.

SENATOR O'MAHONEY: How many minor leagues were there in baseball when you began?

MR. STENGEL: Well, there were not so many at that time because of this fact: Anybody to go into baseball at that time with the educational schools that we had were small, while you were probably thoroughly educated at school, you had to be—we only had small cities that you could put a team in and they would go defunct.

Why, I remember the first year I was at Kankakee, Illinois, and a bank offered me $550 if I would let them have a little notice. I left there and took a uniform because they owed me two weeks' pay. But I either had to quit but I did not have enough money to go to dental college so I had to go with the manager down to Kentucky.

What happened there was if you got by July, that was the big date. You did not play night ball and you did not play Sundays in half of the cities on account of a Sunday observance, so in those days when things were tough, and all of it was, I mean to say, why they just closed up July 4 and there you were sitting there in the depot.

You could go to work someplace else, but that was it.

So I got out of Kankakee, Illinois, and I just go there for the visit now.

SENATOR CARROLL: The question Senator Kefauver asked you was what, in your honest opinion, with your forty-eight years of experience, is the need for this legislation in view of the fact that baseball has not been subject to antitrust laws?

MR. STENGEL: No.

SENATOR LANGER: Mr. Chairman, my final question. This is the Antimonopoly Committee that is sitting here.

MR. STENGEL: Yes, sir.

SENATOR LANGER: I want to know whether you intend to keep on monopolizing the world's championship in New York City.

MR. STENGEL: Well, I will tell you. I got a little concern yesterday in the first three innings when I saw the three players I had gotten rid of, and I said when I lost nine what am I going to do and when I had a couple of my players I thought so great of that did not do so good up to the sixth inning I was more confused but I finally had to go and call on a young man in Baltimore that we don't own and the Yankees don't own him, and he is doing pretty good, and I would actually have to tell you that I think we are more the Greta Garbo type now from success.

We are being hated, I mean, from the ownership and all, we are being hated. Every sport that gets too great or one individual—but if we made 27 cents and it pays to have a winner at home, why would not you have a good winner in your own park if you were an owner?

That is the result of baseball. An owner gets most of the money at home and it is up to him and his staff to do better or they ought to be discharged.

SENATOR KEFAUVER: Thank you very much, Mr. Stengel. We appreciate your presence here. Mr. Mickey Mantle, will you come around? * * * Mr. Mantle, do you have any observations with reference to the applicability of the antitrust laws to baseball?

MR. MANTLE: My views are just about the same as Casey's.

The foregoing exchange occurred in 1958 at hearings conducted by the Senate's Antitrust and Monopoly Subcommittee (part of the Judiciary Committee). In considering H.R. 10378 and S. 4070, bills introduced to exempt baseball and other professional sports from antitrust coverage, the Subcommittee called several witnesses including New York Yankee manager Casey Stengel and Yankee superstar Mickey Mantle. Stengel's rambling and hilarious monologue, totally undeterred and unaffected by Senator Estes Kefauver's questions, was characteristic of his famous *non sequiturs* that entertained sportswriters and readers for decades.

Yet, Casey's "insights" into the exemption question are no more bizarre or indecipherable than a half-century of arcane Supreme Court precedent addressing the same basic issue. Congress has never chosen to exempt any professional sport from antitrust coverage, with limited exceptions pertaining to the merger of the American and National Football Leagues and the negotiation of league-wide television contracts. The Court, however, through a trilogy of bizarre decisions, has bestowed upon Major League Baseball a blanket exemption from the coverage of the antitrust laws. During roughly the same time frame, the Court incredibly concluded that no other professional sport is to be similarly blessed. A reading of the cases following immediately below provides all the "explanation" that is necessary.

II. The Baseball Exemption—From Federal Base Ball to Flood

Federal Base Ball Club of Baltimore, Inc. v. National League of Professional Base Ball Clubs
259 U.S. 200 (1922)

MR. JUSTICE HOLMES delivered the opinion of the Court. This is a suit for threefold damages brought by the plaintiff in error under the [Sherman Act and the Clayton Act]. The defendants are the National League of Professional Base Ball Clubs and the American League of Professional Base Ball Clubs, unincorporated associations, composed respectively of groups of eight incorporated base ball clubs, joined as defendants; the presidents of the two Leagues and a third person, constituting what is known as the National Commission, having considerable powers in carrying out an agreement between the two Leagues; and three other persons having powers in the Federal League of Professional Base Ball Clubs, the relation of which to this case will be explained. It is alleged that these defendants conspired to monopolize the base ball business, the means adopted being set forth with a detail which, in the view that we take, it is unnecessary to repeat.

The plaintiff is a base ball club incorporated in Maryland, and with seven other corporations was a member of the Federal League of Professional Base Ball Clubs, a corporation under the laws of Indiana, that attempted to compete with the combined defendants. It alleges that the defendants destroyed the Federal League by buying up some of the constituent clubs and in one way or another inducing all those clubs except the plaintiff to leave their League, and that the three persons connected with the Federal League and named as defendants, one of them being the President of the League, took part in the conspiracy. Great damage to the plaintiff is alleged. The plaintiff obtained a verdict for $80,000 in the Supreme Court and a judgment for treble the amount was entered, but the Court of Appeals, after an elaborate discussion, held that the defendants were not within the Sherman Act. The appellee, the plaintiff, elected to stand on the record in order to bring the case to this Court at once, and thereupon judgment was ordered for the defendants. *National League of Professional Baseball Clubs v. Federal Baseball Club of Baltimore*, 269 Fed. 681, 688, 50 App. D.C. 165. It is not argued that the plaintiff waived any rights by its course. *Thomsen v. Cayser*, 243 U.S. 66.

The decision of the Court of Appeals went to the root of the case and if correct makes it unnecessary to consider other serious difficulties in the way of the plaintiff's recovery. A summary statement of the nature of the business involved will be enough to present the point. The clubs composing the Leagues are in different cities and for the most part in different States. The end of the elaborate organizations and sub-organizations that are described in the pleadings and evidence is that these clubs shall play against one another in public exhibitions for money, one or the other club crossing a state line in order to make the meeting possible. When as the result of these contests one club has won the pennant of its League and another club has won the pennant of the other League, there is a final competition for the world's championship between these two. Of course the scheme requires constantly repeated travelling on the part of the clubs, which is provided for, controlled and disciplined by the organizations, and this it is said means commerce among the States. But we are of opinion that the Court of Appeals was right.

The business is giving exhibitions of base ball, which are purely state affairs. It is true that, in order to attain for these exhibitions the great popularity that they have achieved, competitions must be arranged between clubs from different cities and States. But the fact that in order to give the exhibitions the Leagues must induce free persons to cross state lines and must arrange and pay for their doing so is not enough to change the character of the business. According to the distinction insisted upon in *Hooper v. California*, 155 U.S. 648, 655, the transport is a mere incident, not the essential thing. That to which it is incident, the exhibition, although made for money would not be called trade or commerce in the commonly accepted use of those words. As it is put by defendants, personal effort, not related to production, is not a subject of commerce. That which in its consummation is not commerce does not become commerce among the States because the transportation that we have mentioned takes place. To repeat the illustrations given by the Court below, a firm of lawyers sending out a member to argue a case, or the Chautauqua lecture bureau sending out lecturers, does not engage in such commerce because the lawyer or lecturer goes to another State.

If we are right the plaintiff's business is to be described in the same way and the restrictions by contract that prevented the plaintiff from getting players to break their bargains and the other conduct charged against the defendants were not an interference with commerce among the States.

Judgment affirmed.

Notes and Questions

1. What was the basis for the antitrust allegations in the foregoing case? Why did the Supreme Court refuse to reach the merits of plaintiff's antitrust claims?

2. What changes have occurred since 1922 that might justify a reevaluation of *Federal Base Ball*? Were these altered circumstances in place at the time that the *Toolson* and *Flood* cases were decided in 1953 and 1972, respectively?

3. The plaintiff's brief in the *Federal Base Ball* case included the following statements:

> Millions of people follow the daily reports of the results of the games in the press, and in the large cities gather in the afternoons around the newspaper offices to see the bulletin reports of the scores. Not only so, but vast numbers of people travel from one city to another for the purpose of witnessing the games. Telegraph facilities are installed at all the ball parks in the Major Leagues, and in those of the more important Minor Leagues, where reports of the games are sent out and are received throughout the country. * * *

> These incidents, while in themselves not determinative of the question of whether or not the business is interstate in character, yet, when considered in connection with its main features, emphasize the truth of what has before been said, that there is scarcely any business which can be named in which the element of interstate commerce is as predominant as that in which defendants are engaged.

Federal Base Ball Club of Baltimore, Inc. v. National League of Professional Base Ball Clubs, 259 U.S. 200, 205 (1922). Do you agree with the plaintiff? What was the response of the Supreme Court to these factual assertions?

4. The Court of Appeals in *Federal Base Ball* had said: "The fact that the appellants produce baseball games as a source of profit, large or small, cannot change the character of the games. They are still sport, not trade." 269 F. at 685. Did the Supreme Court hold that baseball was a sport and a recreational activity, and not a business or commercial enterprise?

5. It appears that the Court said both that baseball exhibitions were not commerce *and* that the exhibitions were not interstate. Do you see a significance in these different statements?

6. Applying the decision in *Federal Base Ball*, is there any basis for reaching a different result in cases brought against football, basketball, or any other sports league?

Toolson v. New York Yankees, Inc.

346 U.S. 356 (1953)

PER CURIAM. * * * In *Federal Baseball Club of Baltimore v. National League of Professional Baseball Clubs,* 259 U.S. 200 (1922), this Court held that the business of providing public baseball games for profit between clubs of professional baseball players was not within the scope of the federal antitrust laws. Congress has had the ruling under consideration but has not seen fit to bring such business under these laws by legislation having prospective effect. The business has thus been left for thirty years to develop, on the understanding that it was not subject to existing antitrust legislation. The present cases ask us to overrule the prior decision and, with retrospective effect, hold the legislation applicable. We think that if there are evils in this field which now warrant application to it of the antitrust laws it should be by legislation. Without re-examination of the underlying issues, the judgments below are affirmed on the authority of *Federal Baseball Club of Baltimore v. National League of Professional Baseball Clubs, supra*, so far as that decision determines that Congress had no intention of including the business of baseball within the scope of the federal antitrust laws.

Affirmed.

MR. JUSTICE BURTON, with whom MR. JUSTICE REED concurs, dissenting.

* * * Whatever may have been the situation when the *Federal Baseball Club* case was decided in 1922, I am not able to join today's decision which, in effect, announces that organized baseball, in 1953, still is not engaged in interstate trade or commerce. In the light of organized baseball's well-known and widely distributed capital investments used in conducting competitions between teams constantly traveling between states, its receipts and expenditures of large sums transmitted between states, its numerous purchases of materials in interstate commerce, the attendance at its local exhibitions of large audiences often traveling across state lines, its radio and television activities which expand its audiences beyond state lines, its sponsorship of interstate advertising, and its highly organized "farm system" of minor league baseball clubs, coupled with restrictive contracts and understandings between individuals and among clubs or leagues playing for profit throughout the United States, and even in Canada, Mexico and Cuba, it is a contradiction in terms to say that the defendants in the cases before us are not now engaged in interstate trade or commerce as those terms are used in the Constitution of the United States and in the Sherman Act.

In 1952 the Subcommittee on Study of Monopoly Power, of the House of Representatives Committee on the Judiciary, after extended hearings, issued a report dealing with organized baseball in relation to the Sherman Act. In that report it said:

"'Organized baseball' is a combination of approximately 380 separate baseball clubs, operating in 42 different States, the District of Columbia, Canada, Cuba, and Mexico * * * .

"Inherently, professional baseball is intercity, intersectional, and interstate. At the beginning of the 1951 season, the clubs within organized baseball were divided among 52 different leagues. Each league is an unincorporated association of from 6 to 10 clubs which play championship baseball games among themselves according to a prearranged schedule. Such a league organization is essential for the successful operation of baseball as a business.

"Of the 52 leagues associated within organized baseball in 1951, 39 were interstate in nature."

In the *Federal Baseball Club* case the Court did not state that even if the activities of organized baseball amounted to interstate trade or commerce those activities were exempt from the Sherman Act. The Court acted on its determination that the activities before it did not amount to interstate commerce. The Court of Appeals for the District of Columbia, in that case, in 1920, described a major league baseball game as "local in its beginning and in its end." This Court stated that "The business is giving exhibitions of base ball, which are purely state affairs," and the transportation of players and equipment between states "is a mere incident. * * *" The main thrust of the argument of counsel for organized baseball, both in the Court of Appeals and in this Court, was in support of that proposition. Although counsel did argue that the activities of organized baseball, even if amounting to interstate commerce, did not violate the Sherman Act, the Court significantly refrained from expressing its opinion on that issue.

That the Court realized that the then incidental interstate features of organized baseball might rise to a magnitude that would compel recognition of them independently is indicated by the statement made in 1923 by Mr. Justice Holmes, the writer of the Court's opinion in the *Federal Baseball Club* case. In 1923, in considering a bill in equity alleging a violation of the Sherman Act by parties presenting local exhibitions on an interstate vaudeville circuit, the Court held that the bill should be considered on its merits and, in writing for the Court, Mr. Justice Holmes said "The bill was brought before the decision of the *Base Ball Club* Case, and it may be that what in general is incidental, in some instances may rise to a magnitude that requires it to be considered independently."

The 1952 report of the Congressional Subcommittee previously mentioned also said:

"Under judicial interpretations of this constitutional provision [the commerce clause], the Congress has power to investigate, and pass legislation dealing with professional baseball, or more particularly 'organized baseball,' if that business is, or affects, interstate commerce. * * *

"After full review of all of the foregoing facts and with due consideration of modern judicial interpretation of the scope of the commerce clause, it is the studied judgment of the Subcommittee on the Study of Monopoly Power that the Congress has jurisdiction to investigate and legislate on the subject of professional baseball." H.R.Rep. No. 2002, 82d Cong., 2d Sess. 4, 7, and see 111-139.

In cases Nos. 18 and 23 the plaintiffs here allege that they are professional baseball players who have been damaged by enforcement of the standard "reserve clause" in their contracts pursuant to nationwide agreements among the defendants.[10] In effect they charge that in violation of the Sherman Act, organized baseball, through its illegal monopoly and unreasonable restraints of trade, exploits the players who attract the profits for the benefit of the clubs and leagues. Similarly, in No. 25, the plaintiffs allege that because of illegal and inequitable agreements of interstate scope between organized baseball and the Mexican League binding each to respect the other's "reserve clauses" they have lost the services of and contract rights to certain baseball players. The plaintiffs also allege that the defendants have entered into a combination, conspiracy and monopoly or an attempt to monopolize professional baseball in the United States to the substantial damage of the plaintiffs.

Conceding the major asset which baseball is to our Nation, the high place it enjoys in the hearts of our people and the possible justification of special treatment for organized

---

10. "The reserve clause is popularly believed to be some provision in the player contract which gives to the club in organized baseball which first signs a player a continuing and exclusive right to his services. Commissioner Frick testified that this popular understanding was essentially correct. He pointed out, however, that the reserve clause is not merely a provision in the contract, but also incorporates a reticulated system of rules and regulations which enable, indeed require, the entire baseball organization to respect and enforce each club's exclusive and continuous right to the services of its players." * * *

sports which are engaged in interstate trade or commerce, the authorization of such treatment is a matter within the discretion of Congress. Congress, however, has enacted no express exemption of organized baseball from the Sherman Act, and no court has demonstrated the existence of an implied exemption from that Act of any sport that is so highly organized as to amount to an interstate monopoly or which restrains interstate trade or commerce. In the absence of such an exemption, the present popularity of organized baseball increases, rather than diminishes, the importance of its compliance with standards of reasonableness comparable with those now required by law of interstate trade or commerce. It is interstate trade or commerce and, as such, it is subject to the Sherman Act until exempted. Accordingly, I would reverse the judgments in the instant cases and remand the causes to the respective District Courts for a consideration of the merits of the alleged violations of the Sherman Act.

Notes and Questions

1. The *per curiam* majority opinion affirmed based on *Federal Base Ball* "so far as that decision determines that Congress had no intention of including the business of baseball within the scope of the federal antitrust laws." Is this interpretation of *Federal Base Ball* appropriate?

2. Justice Burton, in dissent, explained that, given the developments in the thirty-one years since the Supreme Court's decision in *Federal Base Ball*, he was not able to join a decision that "in effect, announces that organized baseball, in 1953, still is not engaged in interstate trade or commerce." Did Justice Burton correctly state the majority's position in *Toolson*?

3. How do you reconcile the Supreme Court's decisions in *Federal Base Ball* and *Toolson* with the Second Circuit's decision in the case that follows?

Salerno v. American League of Professional Baseball Clubs
429 F.2d 1003 (2d Cir. 1970)

FRIENDLY, Circuit Judge. * * * [The plaintiffs were umpires in the American League who were fired by the league President. The league claimed the discharge was due to the umpires' incompetence, but the umpires claimed they were fired because they were trying to unionize American League umpires. The umpires filed a complaint asserting antitrust claims under Sections 1 and 2 of the Sherman Act and a claim for defamation. In addition, they pursued their claims before the National Labor Relations Board ("NLRB"). The NLRB issued a complaint against the American League, accusing it of unfair labor practices in violation of §§8(a)(1) and 8(a)(3) of the National Labor Relations Act and the labor case was set for a hearing. The only defendant who was served was baseball commissioner Bowie Kuhn. He moved to dismiss the case for lack of jurisdiction and the district court granted his motion. On appeal, the Second Circuit expressed doubt about whether the challenged conduct, even if proved, violated the antitrust laws, and doubt about whether a federal court could proceed after the NLRB proceedings had commenced.] * * *

Apart from these exceedingly serious obstacles, plaintiffs recognize that they can prevail only if we should be willing to predict the likely overruling of the holdings in *Federal Baseball* * * * and *Toolson* * * *, that professional baseball is not subject to the antitrust laws. Cf. *Green v. Board of Elections of City of New York*, 380 F.2d 445, 448 (2d Cir. 1967), and cases there cited. They say that changes in the economics of the sport even since *Toolson*, especially the increasing importance of revenues from interstate television broadcasts, make baseball's immunity from the antitrust laws more anomalous than ever. But the ground upon which *Toolson* rested was that Congress had no intention to bring baseball within the antitrust laws, not that baseball's activities did not sufficiently affect interstate commerce. *Cf. Gardella v. Chandler*, 172 F.2d 402, 407–08 (2d Cir. 1949). We freely acknowledge our belief that *Federal Baseball* was not one of Mr. Justice Holmes' happiest days, that the rationale of *Toolson* is extremely dubious and that, to use the Supreme Court's own adjectives, the distinction between baseball and other professional sports is "unrealistic," "inconsistent" and "illogical." *Radovich v. National Football League*, 352 U.S. 445, 452 (1957). We add that *Boys Markets, Inc. v. Retail Clerks Local 770*, 398 U.S. 235, decided June 1, 1970, overruling *Sinclair Refining Co. v. Atkinson*, 370 U.S. 195 (1962), despite Congress' failure to act on invitations to do so, may presage a change from the attitude with respect to such inaction that was expressed in *Toolson*, 346 U.S. at 357, which Mr. Justice Black in dissent invoked to no avail, 398 U.S. at 255. However, putting aside instances where factual premises have all but vanished and a different principle might thus obtain, we continue to believe that the Supreme Court should retain the exclusive privilege of overruling its own decisions, save perhaps when opinions already delivered have created a near certainty that only the occasion is needed for pronouncement of the doom. While we should not fall out of our chairs with surprise at the news that *Federal Baseball* and *Toolson* had been overruled, we are not at all certain the Court is ready to give them a happy d[i]spatch.

Affirmed.

Notes and Questions

1. What is the significance of the National Labor Relations Board's assertion of jurisdiction over disputes involving Major League umpires? Do the NLRB's jurisdictional standards differ from the standards typically applied by a federal court in a matter arising under the Sherman Act? *See American League of Professional Baseball Clubs*, 180 NLRB 190 (1969).

2. The NLRB has refused to exercise jurisdiction over the horse racing industry. *See* 29 C.F.R. § 103.3. Given the apparent impact of this industry upon commerce, is the NLRB's refusal to assert jurisdiction as inexplicable as the Supreme Court's original and continuing refusal to apply the Sherman Act to Major League Baseball activities? *See also* 29 U.S.C. § 164(c). What differences are there between the horse racing industry and professional baseball with respect to state involvement, the centrality of interstate commerce, alternative sources of regulation, and other issues that might lead the NLRB to decline to assert its own jurisdiction and thereby to defer to state regulation? If such differences exist, are they significant enough to justify the NLRB's declination of jurisdiction?

3. As you peruse the final side of the Supreme Court exemption triangle, below, question whether Justice Blackmun wore the hat of a fan or a jurist in assessing the continuing viability of the baseball exemption.

Flood v. Kuhn

407 U.S. 258 (1972)

Mr. Justice Blackmun delivered the opinion of the Court. * * * For the third time in 50 years the Court is asked specifically to rule that professional baseball's reserve system is within the reach of the federal antitrust laws.[1] Collateral issues of state law and of federal labor policy are also advanced.

I

The Game

It is a century and a quarter since the New York Nine defeated the Knickerbockers 23 to 1 on Hoboken's Elysian Fields June 19, 1846, with Alexander Jay Cartwright as the instigator and the umpire. The teams were amateur, but the contest marked a significant date in baseball's beginnings. That early game led ultimately to the development of professional baseball and its tightly organized structure.

The Cincinnati Red Stockings came into existence in 1869 upon an outpouring of local pride. With only one Cincinnatian on the payroll, this professional team traveled over 11,000 miles that summer, winning 56 games and tying one. Shortly thereafter, on St. Patrick's Day in 1871, the National Association of Professional Baseball Players was founded and the professional league was born.

The ensuing colorful days are well known. The ardent follower and the student of baseball know of General Abner Doubleday; the formation of the National League in 1876; Chicago's supremacy in the first year's competition under the leadership of Al Spalding and with Cap Anson at third base; the formation of the American Association and then of the Union Association in the 1880's; the introduction of Sunday baseball; interleague warfare with cut-rate admission prices and player raiding; the development of the reserve "clause"; the emergence in 1885 of the Brotherhood of Professional Ball Players, and in 1890 of the Players League; the appearance of the American League, or "junior circuit," in 1901, rising from the minor Western Association; the first World Series in 1903, disruption in 1904, and the Series' resumption in 1905; the short-lived Federal League on the majors' scene during World War I years; the troublesome and discouraging episode of the 1919 Series; the home run ball; the shifting of franchises; the expansion of the leagues; the installation in 1965 of the major league draft of potential new players; and the formation of the Major League Baseball Players Association in 1966.

Then there are the many names, celebrated for one reason or another, that have sparked the diamond and its environs and that have provided tinder for recaptured thrills, for reminiscence and comparisons, and for conversation and anticipation in-season and off-season: Ty Cobb, Babe Ruth, Tris Speaker, Walter Johnson, Henry Chadwick, Eddie Collins, Lou Gehrig, Grover Cleveland Alexander, Rogers Hornsby, Harry Hooper, Goose Goslin, Jackie Robinson, Honus Wagner, Joe McCarthy, John McGraw, Deacon Phillippe, Rube Marquard, Christy Mathewson, Tommy Leach, Big Ed Delahanty, Davy Jones, Germany Schaefer, King Kelly, Big Dan Brouthers, Wahoo Sam Crawford, Wee Willie Keeler, Big Ed Walsh, Jimmy Austin, Fred Snodgrass, Satchel Paige, Hugh Jennings, Fred Merkle, Iron Man McGinnity, Three-Finger Brown, Harry and Stan Coveleski, Connie Mack, Al Bridwell, Red Ruffing, Amos Rusie, Cy Young, Smokey Joe Wood, Chief Meyers, Chief Bender, Bill Klem, Hans Lobert, Johnny Evers, Joe Tinker, Roy Campanella, Miller Huggins, Rube Bressler, Dazzy Vance, Edd Roush, Bill Wambsganss, Clark Griffith, Branch Rickey, Frank Chance, Cap Anson, Nap Lajoie,

---

1. The reserve system, publicly introduced into baseball contracts in 1887, *see Metropolitan Exhibition Co. v. Ewing*, 42 F. 198, 202–04 (C.C.S.D.N.Y. 1890), centers in the uniformity of player contracts; the confinement of the player to the club that has him under the contract; the assignability of the player's contract; and the ability of the club annually to renew the contract unilaterally, subject to a stated salary minimum. * * *

Sad Sam Jones, Bob O'Farrell, Lefty O'Doul, Bobby Veach, Willie Kamm, Heinie Groh, Lloyd and Paul Waner, Stuffy McInnis, Charles Comiskey, Roger Bresnahan, Bill Dickey, Zack Wheat, George Sisler, Charlie Gehringer, Eppa Rixey, Harry Heilmann, Fred Clarke, Dizzy Dean, Hank Greenberg, Pie Traynor, Rube Waddell, Bill Terry, Carl Hubbell, Old Hoss Radbourne, Moe Berg, Rabbit Maranville, Jimmie Foxx, Lefty Grove. The list seems endless.

And one recalls the appropriate reference to the "World Serious," attributed to Ring Lardner, Sr.; Ernest L. Thayer's "Casey at the Bat"; the ring of "Tinker to Evers to Chance"; and all the other happenings, habits, and superstitions about and around baseball that made it the "national pastime" or, depending upon the point of view, "the great American tragedy."

II
The Petitioner

The petitioner, Curtis Charles Flood, born in 1938, began his major league career in 1956 when he signed a contract with the Cincinnati Reds for a salary of $4,000 for the season. He had no attorney or agent to advise him on that occasion. He was traded to the St. Louis Cardinals before the 1958 season. Flood rose to fame as a center fielder with the Cardinals during the years 1958–1969. In those 12 seasons he compiled a batting average of .293. His best offensive season was 1967 when he achieved .335. He was .301 or better in six of the 12 St. Louis years. He participated in the 1964, 1967, and 1968 World Series. He played errorless ball in the field in 1966, and once enjoyed 223 consecutive errorless games. Flood has received seven Golden Glove Awards. He was co-captain of his team from 1965–1969. He ranks among the 10 major league outfielders possessing the highest lifetime fielding averages.

Flood's St. Louis compensation for the years shown was:

1961	$13,500 (including a bonus for signing)
1962	$16,000
1963	$17,500
1964	$23,000
1965	$35,000
1966	$45,000
1967	$50,000
1968	$72,500
1969	$90,000

These figures do not include any so-called fringe benefits or World Series shares.

But at the age of 31, in October 1969, Flood was traded to the Philadelphia Phillies of the National League in a multi-player transaction. He was not consulted about the trade. He was informed by telephone and received formal notice only after the deal had been consummated. In December he complained to the Commissioner of Baseball and asked that he be made a free agent and be placed at liberty to strike his own bargain with any other major league team. His request was denied.

Flood then instituted this antitrust suit in January 1970 in federal court for the Southern District of New York. The defendants (although not all were named in each cause of action) were the Commissioner of Baseball, the presidents of the two major leagues, and the 24 major league clubs. In general, the complaint charged violations of the federal antitrust laws and civil rights statutes, violation of state statutes and the common law, and the imposition of a form of peonage and involuntary servitude contrary to the Thirteenth Amendment and 42 U.S.C. §1994, 18 U.S.C. §1581, and 29 U.S.C. §§102 and 103. Petitioner sought declaratory and injunctive relief and treble damages.

Flood declined to play for Philadelphia in 1970, despite a $100,000 salary offer, and he sat out the year. After the season was concluded, Philadelphia sold its rights to Flood to the Washington Senators. Washington and the petitioner were able to come to terms for 1971 at a salary of $110,000. Flood started the season but, apparently because he was dissatisfied with his performance, he left the Washington club on April 27, early in the campaign. He has not played baseball since then.

III
The Present Litigation

Judge Cooper, in a detailed opinion, first denied a preliminary injunction, 309 F.Supp. 793 (S.D.N.Y. 1970), observing on the way:

> "Baseball has been the national pastime for over one hundred years and enjoys a unique place in our American heritage. Major league professional baseball is avidly followed by millions of fans, looked upon with fervor and pride and provides a special source of inspiration and competitive team spirit especially for the young.

> "Baseball's status in the life of the nation is so pervasive that it would not strain credulity to say the Court can take judicial notice that baseball is everybody's business. To put it mildly and with restraint, it would be unfortunate indeed if a fine sport and profession, which brings surcease from daily travail and an escape from the ordinary to most inhabitants of this land, were to suffer in the least because of undue concentration by any one or any group on commercial and profit considerations. The game is on higher ground; it behooves every one to keep it there." 309 F.Supp., at 797.

Flood's application for an early trial was granted. The court next deferred until trial its decision on the defendants' motions to dismiss the primary causes of action, but granted a defense motion for summary judgment on an additional cause of action.

Trial to the court took place in May and June 1970. An extensive record was developed. In an ensuing opinion, 316 F.Supp. 271 (S.D.N.Y.1970), Judge Cooper first noted that:

> "Plaintiff's witnesses in the main concede that some form of reserve on players is a necessary element of the organization of baseball as a league sport, but contend that the present all-embracing system is needlessly restrictive and offer various alternatives which in their view might loosen the bonds without sacrifice to the game. * * *

> "Clearly the preponderance of credible proof does not favor elimination of the reserve clause. With the sole exception of plaintiff himself, it shows that even plaintiff's witnesses do not contend that it is wholly undesirable; in fact they regard substantial portions meritorious. * * *" 316 F.Supp., at 275–276.

He then held that *Federal Baseball Club v. National League*, 259 U.S. 200 (1922), and *Toolson v. New York Yankees, Inc.*, 346 U.S. 356 (1953), were controlling; that it was not necessary to reach the issue whether exemption from the antitrust laws would result because aspects of baseball now are a subject of collective bargaining; that the plaintiff's state-law claims, those based on common law as well as on statute, were to be denied because baseball was not "a matter which admits of diversity of treatment," 316 F.Supp., at 280; that the involuntary servitude claim failed because of the absence of "the essential element of this cause of action, a showing of compulsory service," 316 F.Supp., at 281—282; and that judgment was to be entered for the defendants. Judge Cooper included a statement of personal conviction to the effect that "negotiations could produce an accommodation on the reserve system which would be eminently fair and equitable to all concerned" and that "the reserve clause can be fashioned so as to find acceptance by player and club." 316 F.Supp., at 282 and 284.

On appeal, the Second Circuit felt "compelled to affirm." 443 F.2d 264, 265 (1971). It regarded the issue of state law as one of first impression, but concluded that the Commerce Clause precluded its application. Judge Moore added a concurring opinion in which he predicted, with respect to the suggested overruling of *Federal Baseball* and *Toolson*, that "there is no likelihood that such an event will occur." 443 F.2d, at 268, 272.

We granted certiorari in order to look once again at this troublesome and unusual situation.

IV

The Legal Background

* * *

[The Court recounted the precedential history of the baseball exemption focusing on *Federal Base Ball Club of Baltimore, Inc. v. Nat'l League of Professional Base Ball Clubs*, 259 U.S. 200 (1922) and *Toolson v. New York Yankees*, 346 U.S. 356 (1953).]

United States v. Shubert, 348 U.S. 222 (1955), was a civil antitrust action against defendants engaged in the production of legitimate theatrical attractions throughout the United States and in operating theaters for the presentation of such attractions. The District Court had dismissed the complaint on the authority of *Federal Baseball* and *Toolson*, 120 F.Supp. 15 (S.D.N.Y. 1953). This Court reversed. Mr. Chief Justice Warren noted the Court's broad conception of "trade or commerce" in the antitrust statutes and the types of enterprises already held to be within the reach of that phrase. He stated that *Federal Baseball* and *Toolson* afforded no basis for a conclusion that businesses built around the performance of local exhibitions are exempt from the antitrust laws. He then went on to elucidate the holding in *Toolson* by meticulously spelling out the factors mentioned above:

> "In *Federal Baseball*, the Court, speaking through Mr. Justice Holmes, was dealing with the business of baseball and nothing else. * * * The travel, the Court concluded, was 'a mere incident, not the essential thing.'* * *

> "In *Toolson*, where the issue was the same as in *Federal Baseball*, the Court was confronted with a unique combination of circumstances. For over 30 years there had stood a decision of this Court specifically fixing the status of the baseball business under the antitrust laws and more particularly the validity of the so-called 'reserve clause.' During this period, in reliance on the *Federal Baseball* precedent, the baseball business had grown and developed. * * * And Congress, although it had actively considered the ruling, had not seen fit to reject it by amendatory legislation. Against this background, the Court in *Toolson* was asked to overrule *Federal Baseball* on the ground that it was out of step

with subsequent decisions reflecting present-day concepts of interstate commerce. The Court, in view of the circumstances of the case, declined to do so. But neither did the Court necessarily reaffirm all that was said in *Federal Baseball*. Instead, '[w]ithout re-examination of the underlying issues,' the Court adhered to *Federal Baseball* 'so far as that decision determines that Congress had no intention of including the business of baseball within the scope of the federal antitrust laws.' In short, *Toolson* was a narrow application of the rule of *stare decisis*.

" * * * If the Toolson holding is to be expanded—or contracted—the appropriate remedy lies with Congress."

E. *United States v. International Boxing Club*, 348 U.S. 236 (1955), was a companion to *Shubert* and was decided the same day. This was a civil antitrust action against defendants engaged in the business of promoting professional championship boxing contests. Here again the District Court had dismissed the complaint in reliance upon *Federal Baseball* and *Toolson*. The Chief Justice observed that "if it were not for *Federal Baseball* and *Toolson*, we think that it would be too clear for dispute that the Government's allegations bring the defendants within the scope of the Act." 348 U.S., at 240–241. He pointed out that the defendants relied on the two baseball cases but also would have been content with a more restrictive interpretation of them than the *Shubert* defendants, for the boxing defendants argued that the cases immunized only businesses that involve exhibitions of an athletic nature. The Court accepted neither argument. It again noted that "*Toolson* neither overruled *Federal Baseball* nor necessarily reaffirmed all that was said in *Federal Baseball*." It stated:

> "The controlling consideration in *Federal Baseball* and *Hart* was, instead, a very practical one—the degree of interstate activity involved in the particular business under review. It follows that *stare decisis* cannot help the defendants here; for, contrary to their argument, *Federal Baseball* did not hold that all businesses based on professional sports were outside the scope of the antitrust laws. The issue confronting us is, therefore, not whether a previously granted exemption should continue, but whether an exemption should be granted in the first instance. And that issue is for Congress to resolve, not this Court." 348 U.S., at 243.

The Court noted the presence then in Congress of various bills forbidding the application of the antitrust laws to "organized professional sports enterprises"; the holding of extensive hearings on some of these; subcommittee opposition; a postponement recommendation as to baseball; and the fact that "Congress thus left intact the then-existing coverage of the antitrust laws." 348 U.S., at 243–244.

MR. JUSTICE FRANKFURTER, joined by MR. JUSTICE MINTON, dissented. "It would baffle the subtlest ingenuity," he said, "to find a single differentiating factor between other sporting exhibitions * * * and baseball insofar as the conduct of the sport is relevant to the criteria or considerations by which the Sherman Law becomes applicable to a 'trade or commerce.'" 348 U.S., at 248. He went on:

> "The Court decided as it did in the *Toolson* case as an application of the doctrine of *stare decisis*. That doctrine is not, to be sure, an imprisonment of reason. But neither is it a whimsy. It can hardly be that this Court gave a preferred position to baseball because it is the great American sport. * * * If *stare decisis* be one aspect of law, as it is, to disregard it in identic situations is mere caprice.

"Congress, on the other hand, may yield to sentiment and be capricious, subject only to due process. * * *

"Between them, this case and *Shubert* illustrate that nice but rational distinctions are inevitable in adjudication. I agree with the Court's opinion in *Shubert* for precisely the reason that constrains me to dissent in this case." 348 U.S., at 249–250.

Mr. Justice Minton also separately dissented on the ground that boxing is not trade or commerce. He added the comment that "Congress has not attempted" to control baseball, and boxing. The two dissenting Justices, thus, did not call for the overruling of *Federal Baseball* and *Toolson*; they merely felt that boxing should be under the same umbrella of freedom as was baseball and, as Mr. Justice Frankfurter said, they could not exempt baseball "to the exclusion of every other sport different not one legal jot or title from it."

F. The parade marched on. *Radovich v. National Football League*, 352 U.S. 445 (1957), was a civil Clayton Act case testing the application of the antitrust laws to professional football. The District Court dismissed. The Ninth Circuit affirmed in part on the basis of *Federal Baseball* and *Toolson*. The court did not hesitate to "confess that the strength of the pull" of the baseball cases and of *International Boxing* "is about equal," but then observed that "[f]ootball is a team sport" and boxing an individual one. 231 F.2d 620, 622.

This Court reversed with an opinion by Mr. Justice Clark. He said that the Court made its ruling in *Toolson* "because it was concluded that more harm would be done in overruling *Federal Baseball* than in upholding a ruling which at best was of dubious validity." 352 U.S., at 450. He noted that Congress had not acted. He then said:

"All this, combined with the flood of litigation that would follow its repudiation, the harassment that would ensue, and the retroactive effect of such a decision, led the Court to the practical result that it should sustain the unequivocal line of authority reaching over many years.

"[S]ince *Toolson* and *Federal Baseball* are still cited as controlling authority in antitrust actions involving other fields of business, we now specifically limit the rule there established to the facts there involved, *i.e.*, the business of organized professional baseball. As long as the Congress continues to acquiesce we should adhere to—but not extend—the interpretation of the Act made in those cases.
* * *

"If this ruling is unrealistic, inconsistent, or illogical, it is sufficient to answer, aside from the distinctions between the businesses, that were we considering the question of baseball for the first time upon a clean slate we would have no doubts. But *Federal Baseball* held the business of baseball outside the scope of the Act. No other business claiming the coverage of those cases has such an adjudication. We, therefore, conclude that the orderly way to eliminate error or discrimination, if any there be, is by legislation and not by court decision. Congressional processes are more accommodative, affording the whole industry hearings and an opportunity to assist in the formulation of new legislation. The resulting product is therefore more likely to protect the industry and the public alike. The whole scope of congressional action would be known long in advance and effective dates for the legislation could be set in the future without the injustices of retroactivity and surprise which might follow court action."

Mr. Justice Frankfurter dissented essentially for the reasons stated in his dissent in *International Boxing*. Mr. Justice Harlan, joined by Mr. Justice Brennan, also dissented because he, too, was "unable to distinguish football from baseball." Here again the dissenting Justices did not call for the overruling of the baseball decisions. They merely could not distinguish the two sports and, out of respect for *stare decisis*, voted to affirm.

G. Finally, in *Haywood v. National Basketball Assn.*, 401 U.S. 1204 (1971), Mr. Justice Douglas, in his capacity as Circuit Justice, reinstated a District Court's injunction pendente lite in favor of a professional basketball player and said, "Basketball * * * does not enjoy exemption from the antitrust laws." 401 U.S., at 1205.

H. This series of decisions understandably spawned extensive commentary, some of it mildly critical and much of it not; nearly all of it looked to Congress for any remedy that might be deemed essential.

I. Legislative proposals have been numerous and persistent. Since Toolson more than 50 bills have been introduced in Congress relative to the applicability or nonapplicability of the antitrust laws to baseball. A few of these passed one house or the other. Those that did would have expanded, not restricted, the reserve system's exemption to other professional league sports. And the [Sports Broadcasting] Act of Sept. 30, 1961 and the merger addition thereto effected by the Act of Nov. 8, 1966, 15 U.S.C. §§1291–1295, were also expansive rather than restrictive as to antitrust exemption.

V

In view of all this, it seems appropriate now to say that:

1. Professional baseball is a business and it is engaged in interstate commerce.

2. With its reserve system enjoying exemption from the federal antitrust laws, baseball is, in a very distinct sense, an exception and an anomaly. *Federal Baseball* and *Toolson* have become an aberration confined to baseball.

3. Even though others might regard this as "unrealistic, inconsistent, or illogical," see *Radovich*, the aberration is an established one, and one that has been recognized not only in *Federal Baseball* and *Toolson*, but in *Shubert, International Boxing*, and *Radovich*, as well, a total of five consecutive cases in this Court. It is an aberration that has been with us now for half a century, one heretofore deemed fully entitled to the benefit of *stare decisis*, and one that has survived the Court's expanding concept of interstate commerce. It rests on a recognition and an acceptance of baseball's unique characteristics and needs.

4. Other professional sports operating interstate—football, boxing, basketball, and, presumably, hockey[11] and golf[12]—are not so exempt.

5. The advent of radio and television, with their consequent increased coverage and additional revenues, has not occasioned an overruling of *Federal Baseball* and *Toolson*.

6. The Court has emphasized that since 1922 baseball, with full and continuing congressional awareness, has been allowed to develop and to expand unhindered by federal legislative action. Remedial legislation has been introduced repeatedly in Congress but none has ever been enacted. The Court, accordingly, has concluded that Congress as yet has had no intention to subject baseball's reserve system to the reach of the antitrust statutes. This, obviously, has been deemed to be something other than mere congres-

---

11. *Peto v. Madison Square Garden Corp.*, 1958 Trade Cases ¶69,106 (S.D.N.Y. 1958).
12. *Deesen v. Professional Golfers' Assn.*, 358 F.2d 165 (CA 9), *cert. denied*, 385 U.S. 846 (1966).

sional silence and passivity. *Cf. Boys Markets, Inc. v. Retail Clerks Union*, 398 U.S. 235, 241–242 (1970).

7. The Court has expressed concern about the confusion and the retroactivity problems that inevitably would result with a judicial overturning of *Federal Baseball*. It has voiced a preference that if any change is to be made, it come by legislative action that, by its nature, is only prospective in operation.

8. The Court noted in *Radovich*, 352 U.S., at 452, that the slate with respect to baseball is not clean. Indeed, it has not been clean for half a century.

This emphasis and this concern are still with us. We continue to be loath, 50 years after *Federal Baseball* and almost two decades after *Toolson*, to overturn those cases judicially when Congress, by its positive inaction, has allowed those decisions to stand for so long and, far beyond mere inference and implication, has clearly evinced a desire not to disapprove them legislatively.

Accordingly, we adhere once again to *Federal Baseball* and *Toolson* and to their application to professional baseball. We adhere also to *International Boxing* and *Radovich* and to their respective applications to professional boxing and professional football. If there is any inconsistency or illogic in all this, it is an inconsistency and illogic of long standing that is to be remedied by the Congress and not by this Court. If we were to act otherwise, we would be withdrawing from the conclusion as to congressional intent made in *Toolson* and from the concerns as to retrospectivity therein expressed. Under these circumstances, there is merit in consistency even though some might claim that beneath that consistency is a layer of inconsistency.

The petitioner's argument as to the application of state antitrust laws deserves a word. Judge Cooper rejected the state law claims because state antitrust regulation would conflict with federal policy and because national "uniformity [is required] in any regulation of baseball and its reserve system." 316 F.Supp., at 280. The Court of Appeals, in affirming, stated, "[A]s the burden on interstate commerce outweighs the states' interests in regulating baseball's reserve system, the Commerce Clause precludes the application here of state antitrust law." 443 F.2d, at 268. As applied to organized baseball, and in the light of this Court's observations and holding in *Federal Baseball*, in *Toolson*, in *Shubert*, in *International Boxing*, and in *Radovich*, and despite baseball's allegedly inconsistent position taken in the past with respect to the application of state law, these statements adequately dispose of the state law claims.

The conclusion we have reached makes it unnecessary for us to consider the respondents' additional argument that the reserve system is a mandatory subject of collective bargaining and that federal labor policy therefore exempts the reserve system from the operation of federal antitrust laws.

We repeat for this case what was said in *Toolson*:

> "Without re-examination of the underlying issues, the [judgment] below [is] affirmed on the authority of *Federal Baseball Club of Baltimore v. National League of Professional Baseball Clubs, supra*, so far as that decision determines that Congress had no intention of including the business of baseball within the scope of the federal antitrust laws." 346 U.S., at 357.

And what the Court said in *Federal Baseball* in 1922 and what it said in *Toolson* in 1953, we say again here in 1972: the remedy, if any is indicated, is for congressional, and not judicial, action.

The judgment of the Court of Appeals is

Affirmed.

Mr. Justice white joins in the judgment of the Court, and in all but Part I of the Court's opinion.

Mr. Justice Powell took no part in the consideration or decision of this case.

Mr. Chief Justice Burger, concurring. I concur in all but Part I of the Court's opinion but, like Mr. Justice DOUGLAS, I have grave reservations as to the correctness of *Toolson v. New York Yankees, Inc.,* 346 U.S. 356 (1953); as he notes in his dissent, he joined that holding but has "lived to regret it." The error, if such it be, is one on which the affairs of a great many people have rested for a long time. Courts are not the forum in which this tangled web ought to be unsnarled. I agree with Mr. Justice DOUGLAS that congressional inaction is not a solid base, but the least undesirable course now is to let the matter rest with Congress; it is time the Congress acted to solve this problem.

Mr. Justice Douglas, with whom Mr. Justice Brennan concurs, dissenting. This Court's decision in *Federal Baseball,* made in 1922, is a derelict in the stream of the law that we, its creator, should remove. Only a romantic view[13] of a rather dismal business account over the last 50 years would keep that derelict in midstream.

In 1922 the Court had a narrow, parochial view of commerce. With the demise of the old landmarks of that era, particularly *United States v. E. C. Knight Co.,* 156 U.S. 1, *Hammer v. Dagenhart,* 247 U.S. 251, and *Paul v. Virginia,* 8 Wall. 168, the whole concept of commerce has changed.

Under the modern decisions such as *Mandeville Island Farms v. American Crystal Sugar Co.,* 334 U.S. 219; *United States v. Darby,* 312 U.S. 100; *Wickard v. Filburn,* 317 U.S. 111; *United States v. South-Eastern Underwriters Assn.,* 322 U.S. 533, the power of Congress was recognized as broad enough to reach all phases of the vast operations of our national industrial system. An industry so dependent on radio and television as is baseball and gleaning vast interstate revenues (see H.R.Rep.No.2002, 82d Cong., 2d Sess., 4, 5 (1952)) would be hard put today to say with the Court in the *Federal Baseball Club* case that baseball was only a local exhibition, not trade or commerce.

Baseball is today big business that is packaged with beer, with broadcasting, and with other industries. The beneficiaries of the *Federal Baseball Club* decision are not the Babe Ruths, Ty Cobbs, and Lou Gehrigs.

The owners, whose records many say reveal a proclivity for predatory practices, do not come to us with equities. The equities are with the victims of the reserve clause. I use the word "victims" in the Sherman Act sense, since a contract which forbids anyone to practice his calling is commonly called an unreasonable restraint of trade.[14] *Gardella v. Chandler,* 172 F.2d 402 (CA 2). And *see Haywood v. National Basketball Assn.,* 401 U.S. 1204 (Douglas, J., in chambers).

If congressional inaction is our guide, we should rely upon the fact that Congress has refused to enact bills broadly exempting professional sports from antitrust regulation.[15]

---

13. While I joined the Court's opinion in *Toolson v. New York Yankees, Inc.,* I have lived to regret it; and I would now correct what I believe to be its fundamental error.

14. Had this same group boycott occurred in another industry, *Klor's, Inc. v. Broadway-Hale Stores, Inc.,* 359 U.S. 207; *United States v. Shubert,* 348 U.S. 222; or even in another sport, *Haywood v. National Basketball Assn.,* 401 U.S. 1204 (Douglas, J., in chambers); *Radovich v. National Football League,* 352 U.S. 445; *United States v. International Boxing Club,* 348 U.S. 236; we would have no difficulty in sustaining petitioner's claim.

15. The Court's reliance upon congressional inaction disregards the wisdom of *Helvering v. Hallock,* 309 U.S. 106, 119–121, where we said: "Nor does want of specific Congressional repudia-

H.R.Rep. No. 2002, 82nd Cong., 2d Sess. (1952). The only statutory exemption granted by Congress to professional sports concerns broadcasting rights. 15 U.S.C. §§1291–1295. I would not ascribe a broader exemption through inaction than Congress has seen fit to grant explicitly.

There can be no doubt "that were we considering the question of baseball for the first time upon a clean slate" we would hold it to be subject to federal antitrust regulation. *Radovich v. National Football League*, 352 U.S. 445, 452. The unbroken silence of Congress should not prevent us from correcting our own mistakes.

Mr. Justice Marshall, with whom Mr. Justice Brennan joins, dissenting. * * *

Petitioner brought this action in the United States District Court for the Southern District of New York. He alleged, among other things, that the reserve system was an unreasonable restraint of trade in violation of federal antitrust laws.[19] The District Court thought itself bound by prior decisions of this Court and found for the respondents after a full trial. 309 F. Supp. 793 (1970). The United States Court of Appeals for the Second Circuit affirmed. 443 F.2d 264 (2d Cir. 1971). We granted certiorari on October 19, 1971 in order to take a further look at the precedents relied upon by the lower courts.

This is a difficult case because we are torn between the principle of *stare decisis* and the knowledge that the decisions in *Federal Baseball Club v. National League*, 259 U.S. 200 (1922), and *Toolson v. New York Yankees, Inc.*, 346 U.S. 356 (1953), are totally at odds with more recent and better reasoned cases.

In *Federal Baseball Club*, a team in the Federal League brought an antitrust action against the National and American Leagues and others. In his opinion for a unanimous Court, Mr. Justice Holmes wrote that the business being considered was "giving exhibitions of base ball, which are purely state affairs." 259 U.S., at 208. Hence, the Court held that baseball was not within the purview of the antitrust laws. Thirty-one years later, the Court reaffirmed this decision, without re-examining it, in *Toolson*, a one-paragraph *per curiam* opinion. Like this case, *Toolson* involved an attack on the reserve system. The Court said:

"The business has * * * been left for thirty years to develop, on the understanding that it was not subject to existing antitrust legislation. The present cases ask us to overrule the prior decision and, with retrospective effect, hold the legislation applicable. We think that if there are evils in this field which now warrant application to it of the antitrust laws it should be by legislation." *Id.*, at 357.

Much more time has passed since *Toolson* and Congress has not acted. We must now decide whether to adhere to the reasoning of *Toolson*—*i.e.*, to refuse to re-examine the

---

tions * * * serve as an implied instruction by Congress to us not to reconsider, in the light of new experience * * * those decisions. * * * It would require very persuasive circumstances enveloping Congressional silence to debar this Court from re-examining its own doctrines. * * * Various considerations of parliamentary tactics and strategy might be suggested as reasons for the inaction of * * * Congress, but they would only be sufficient to indicate that we walk on quicksand when we try to find in the absence of corrective legislation a controlling legal principle." And *see United States v. South-Eastern Underwriters Assn.*, 322 U.S. 533, 556–561.

19. Petitioner also alleged a violation of state antitrust laws, state civil rights laws, and of the common law, and claimed that he was forced into peonage and involuntary servitude in violation of the Thirteenth Amendment to the United States Constitution. Because I believe that federal antitrust laws govern baseball, I find that state law has been pre-empted in this area. Like the lower courts, I do not believe that there has been a violation of the Thirteenth Amendment.

underlying basis of *Federal Baseball Club*—or to proceed with a re-examination and let the chips fall where they may.

In his answer to petitioner's complaint, the Commissioner of Baseball "admits that under present concepts of interstate commerce defendants are engaged therein." * * * There can be no doubt that the admission is warranted by today's reality. Since baseball is interstate commerce, if we re-examine baseball's antitrust exemption, the Court's decisions in *United States v. Shubert*, 348 U.S. 222 (1955), *United States v. International Boxing Club*, 348 U.S. 236 (1955), and *Radovich v. National Football League*, 352 U.S. 445 (1957), require that we bring baseball within the coverage of the antitrust laws. *See also Haywood v. National Basketball Assn.*, 401 U.S. 1204 (Douglas, J., in chambers).

We have only recently had occasion to comment that:

> "Antitrust laws in general, and the Sherman Act in particular, are the Magna Carta of free enterprise. They are as important to the preservation of economic freedom and our free-enterprise system as the Bill of Rights is to the protection of our fundamental personal freedoms. * * * Implicit in such freedom is the notion that it cannot be foreclosed with respect to one sector of the economy because certain private citizens or groups believe that such foreclosure might promote greater competition in a more important sector of the economy." *United States v. Topco Associates, Inc.*, 405 U.S. 596, 610 (1972).

The importance of the antitrust laws to every citizen must not be minimized. They are as important to baseball players as they are to football players, lawyers, doctors, or members of any other class of workers. Baseball players cannot be denied the benefits of competition merely because club owners view other economic interests as being more important, unless Congress says so.

Has Congress acquiesced in our decisions in *Federal Baseball Club* and *Toolson*? I think not. Had the Court been consistent and treated all sports in the same way baseball was treated, Congress might have become concerned enough to take action. But, the Court was inconsistent, and baseball was isolated and distinguished from all other sports. In *Toolson* the Court refused to act because Congress had been silent. But the Court may have read too much into this legislative inaction.

Americans love baseball as they love all sports. Perhaps we become so enamored of athletics that we assume that they are foremost in the minds of legislators as well as fans. We must not forget, however, that there are only some 600 major league baseball players. Whatever muscle they might have been able to muster by combining forces with other athletes has been greatly impaired by the manner in which this Court has isolated them. It is this Court that has made them impotent, and this Court should correct its error.

We do not lightly overrule our prior constructions of federal statutes, but when our errors deny substantial federal rights, like the right to compete freely and effectively to the best of one's ability as guaranteed by the antitrust laws, we must admit our error and correct it. We have done so before and we should do so again here. *See, e.g., Blonder-Tongue Laboratories, Inc. v. University of Illinois Foundation*, 402 U.S. 313 (1971); *Boys Markets, Inc. v. Retail Clerks Union*, 398 U.S. 235, 241 (1970).[20]

---

20. In the past this Court has not hesitated to change its view as to what constitutes interstate commerce. Compare *United States v. Knight Co.*, 156 U.S. 1 (1895), with *Mandeville Island Farms v. American Crystal Sugar Co.*, 334 U.S. 219 (1948), and *United States v. Darby*, 312 U.S. 100 (1941).

"The jurist concerned with 'public confidence in, and acceptance of the judicial system' might well consider that, however admirable its resolute adherence to the law as it was, a

To the extent that there is concern over any reliance interests that club owners may assert, they can be satisfied by making our decision prospective only. Baseball should be covered by the antitrust laws beginning with this case and henceforth, unless Congress decides otherwise.

Accordingly, I would overrule *Federal Baseball Club* and *Toolson* and reverse the decision of the Court of Appeals.

This does not mean that petitioner would necessarily prevail, however. Lurking in the background is a hurdle of recent vintage that petitioner still must overcome. In 1966, the Major League Players Association was formed. It is the collective-bargaining representative for all major league baseball players. Respondents argue that the reserve system is now part and parcel of the collective-bargaining agreement and that because it is a mandatory subject of bargaining, the federal labor statutes are applicable, not the federal antitrust laws. The lower courts did not rule on this argument, having decided the case solely on the basis of the antitrust exemption. * * *

While there was evidence at trial concerning the collective-bargaining relationship of the parties, the issues surrounding that relationship have not been fully explored. As one commentary has suggested, this case "has been litigated with the implications for the institution of collective bargaining only dimly perceived. The labor law issues have been in the corners of the case—the courts below, for example, did not reach them—moving in and out of the shadows like an uninvited guest at a party whom one can't decide either to embrace or expel."[24]. * * *

In light of these considerations, I would remand this case to the District Court for consideration of whether petitioner can state a claim under the antitrust laws despite the collective-bargaining agreement, and, if so, for a determination of whether there has been an antitrust violation in this case.

Notes and Questions

1. In *Flood*, the Court again raised the specter of "congressional inaction" to justify its refusal to correct the long-standing aberration of baseball's solitary exemption from the antitrust laws. Is the Court to be praised for prudent restraint or condemned for abdication of its "judicial responsibility?" In answering this question, consider the myriad factors that are involved in the introduction of a bill and its enactment into law. For example, ponder the small constituency that would benefit in any way from the exposure of baseball to antitrust review. Is it realistic to expect that Congress would initiate legislation to remove the baseball exemption—especially when the byproduct of such action could be legal prohibitions against owners' attempts to restrict player mobility. Arguably, most fans would oppose any legislation that would expand players' ability to enhance their income growth given the common perception that the upshot of higher salaries would be higher ticket prices. Is Justice Marshall correct that only Major League Baseball players would benefit from elimination of baseball's antitrust exemption?

2. If there were an error in the initial creation of the baseball exemption, it was an error of judicial making. Under these circumstances, is any notion of *stare decisis* ap-

---

decision contrary to the public sense of justice as it is, operates, so far as it is known, to diminish respect for the courts and for law itself." Szanton, Stare Decisis; A Dissenting View, 10 HASTINGS L.J. 394, 397 (1959).

24. Jacobs & Winter, *Antitrust Principles and Collective Bargaining by Athletes: Of Superstars in Peonage*, 81 YALE L.J. 1, 22 (1971).

propriate? Consider further *Boys Markets, Inc. v. Retail Clerks Union, Local 770*, 398 U.S. 235 (1970), where the Supreme Court abruptly overruled *Sinclair Refining Co. v. Atkinson*, 370 U.S. 195 (1962), a case decided only eight years earlier. *Boys Markets* profoundly altered the legal landscape in the area of labor management relations by carving out an exception to the Norris-LaGuardia Act's anti-injunction provisions. The Court held that lower courts could enjoin a peaceful strike in breach of a collective bargaining agreement's no-strike clause where the dispute was subject to the collective bargaining agreement's grievance and arbitration mechanism. The Court suggested that its reversal of field was prompted by a need to reconcile conflicting decisions handed down subsequent to *Sinclair Refining*. It is more probable that the Court simply reconsidered *Sinclair Refining* and concluded that harmonious labor relations would be better served by the approach adopted by *Boys Markets*. In any event, this type of precedent establishes that the notion of *stare decisis* is by no means a wooden absolute. Indeed, given the dramatic changes occurring in baseball since 1922, *stare decisis* seems an anemic excuse for the continuation of the baseball exemption. This point was addressed directly by Justices Marshall and Brennan in dissent:

> The jurist concerned with 'public confidence in, and acceptance of the judicial system' might well consider that, however admirable its resolute adherence to the law as it was, a decision contrary to the public sense of justice as it is, operates, so far as it is known, to diminish respect for the courts and for law itself.

See *Flood v. Kuhn*, 407 U.S. at n.20 (1972). *See also Garcia v. San Antonio Metro. Transit Auth.*, 469 U.S. 528 (1985), in which Justice Blackmun, writing for a 5-4 majority, overruled a decision issued just nine years earlier, *National League of Cities v. Usery*, 426 U.S. 833 (1976). In *Garcia*, Justice Blackmun did not even mention *stare decisis*, stating only that "We do not lightly overrule recent precedent." 426 U.S. at 557. In dissent, Justice Powell observed that *National League of Cities* was not only a recent precedent, but (a) it had been cited and quoted approvingly in opinions joined by all nine Members of the Court that decided the *Garcia* case, (b) its reasoning and the principle it applied had "been reiterated consistently over the past eight years," and (c) less than three years earlier, a unanimous Court, deciding *Transportation Union v. Long Island R. Co.*, 455 U.S. 678 (1982), had reaffirmed its principles. *Garcia* at 557–58.

3. In *Wisconsin v. Milwaukee Braves, Inc.*, 144 N.W.2d 1 (Wis. 1966), the Milwaukee Braves had argued that *state* antitrust laws were preempted by the Commerce Clause, thus insulating it from liability even absent the baseball exemption. The Wisconsin Supreme Court sustained this argument and dismissed plaintiff's claim. See *Flood v. Kuhn*, 407 U.S. at 283 n.19 (MARSHALL, J., dissenting), where Justice Marshall, joined by Justice Brennan, declared: "Because I believe that federal antitrust laws govern baseball I find that state law has been pre-empted in this area." *See also HMC Management Corp. v. New Orleans Basketball Club*, 375 So. 2d 700 (La. Ct. App. 1979). However, in *Morsani v. Major League Baseball*, 663 So. 2d 653 (Fla. Dist. Ct. App. 1995), the court rejected Major League Baseball's contention that the Commerce Clause barred application of the antitrust laws to sports activities. "State antitrust laws not in direct conflict with federal antitrust laws are neither preempted nor precluded by any federal considerations." *Id.* at 657.

4. The decisionmaking process by which the Supreme Court issued the *Flood* opinion is chronicled in Bob Woodward & Scott Armstrong's classic discussion of the Supreme Court, THE BRETHREN. THE BRETHREN's analysis sheds substantial light on the development of the various opinions in the case:

Earlier at the March 24 conference, [Justice Potter] Stewart had found himself the senior member of a majority for the first time in his career. The case (*Flood v. Kuhn*) concerned Curt Flood, a former star outfielder for the St. Louis Cardinals, who had refused to be traded to the Philadelphia Phillies. He had filed an antitrust suit against professional baseball. Flood wanted to break the reserve clause that allowed teams to trade baseball players without their consent.

Oral argument had failed to clarify the issues. Former Justice Arthur Goldberg, in his first appearance before the Court since resigning in 1965 to become Ambassador to the United Nations, had offered such a poor presentation of Flood's case that his former colleagues were embarrassed.

Powell withdrew from the case, because he held stock in Anheuser-Busch, Inc., whose principal owner, August Busch, Jr., also owned the St. Louis Cardinals. The Chief, Douglas and Brennan voted for Flood, leaving Stewart to assign the opinion for a five-member majority.

Stewart thought that the opinion would be easy to write. The Court had twice before decided that baseball was exempt from the antitrust laws. It was, Stewart said, "a case of '*stare decisis*' double dipped." There seemed little chance of losing the majority as long as the two earlier precedents were followed. He assigned the opinion to Blackmun.

Blackmun was delighted. Apart from the abortion assignment, he felt that he had suffered under the Chief, receiving poor opinions to write, including more than his share of tax and Indian cases. He thought that if the antitrust laws were applied to baseball, its unique position as the national pastime would be undermined. A devoted fan first of the Chicago Cubs and later the Minnesota Twins, he welcomed this chance to be one of the boys.

With his usual devotion to detail, Blackmun turned to the *Baseball Encyclopedia*, which he kept on the shelf behind his desk. He set down minimum lifetime performance standards—numbers of games played, lifetime batting averages or earned-run averages. He picked out representative stars from each of the teams, positions, and decades of organized baseball. Then, closeted away in the Justices' library, Blackmun wrote an opening section that was an ode to baseball. In three extended paragraphs, he traced the history of professional baseball. He continued with a list of "the many names, celebrated for one reason or another, that have sparked the diamond and its environs and that have provided timber for recaptured thrills, for reminiscence and comparisons, and for conversation and anticipation in season and off season: Ty Cobb, Babe Ruth. * * *" There were more than seventy names. "The list seems endless," Blackmun wrote. He paid homage to the verse "Casey at the Bat," and other baseball literature. When he had finished, Blackmun circulated his draft.

Brennan was surprised. He thought Blackmun had been in the library researching the abortion cases, not playing with baseball cards.

One of Rehnquist's clerks called Blackmun's chambers and joked that Camilo Pascual, a former Washington Senators pitcher, should have been included in the list of greats.

Blackmun's clerk phoned back the next day. "The Justice recalls seeing Pascual pitch and remembers his fantastic curve ball. But he pulled out his Encyclopedia and looked up his record. He decided Pascual's 174 wins were not enough.

It is difficult to make these judgments on who to include but Justice Blackmun felt that Pascual is just not in the same category with Christy Matthewson's 373 wins. I hope you will understand."

Calling Blackmun's chambers to request that some favorite player be included became a new game for the clerks.

Stewart was embarrassed that he had assigned the opinion to Blackmun. He tried to nudge him into recognizing the inappropriateness of the opening section, jokingly telling him that he would go along with the opinion if Blackmun would add a member of Stewart's home-town team, the Cincinnati Reds.

Blackmun added a Red.

Marshall registered his protest. The list included no black baseball players. Blackmun explained that most of the players on his list antedated World War II. Blacks had been excluded from the major leagues until 1947.

That was the point exactly, Marshall replied.

Three black players were added—Jackie Robinson, Roy Campanella, and Satchel Paige.

Marshall decided to switch anyhow and write his own opinion in Flood's favor. The Court was now split 4 to 4, and word circulated that White was considering following Marshall. That would give him a majority.

White owed a great deal to professional sports. His career in football had paid for a first-rate law school education. He remembered the years he had spent touring the country playing football. In those days, teams were real teams, brotherhoods of young men. It was different now. There were too many prima donnas, concerned only with their own statistics. White had difficulty feeling sorry for Curt Flood, who had turned down a $100,000 annual salary.

The antitrust issues were not easy in the case. White thought that if the federal laws did not apply, state antitrust laws might. His clerks used his hesitation to negotiate small changes in the Marshall opinion. White would probably join if the changes were made, one clerk offered.

When Marshall balked at a change that seemed trivial, his clerk protested that it was necessary to get White's vote.

"Says who?" Marshall asked.

A White clerk, he was told.

"He'll never join," Marshall responded.

Finally, White indicated he would stay with Blackmun's opinion against Flood, but he flatly refused to join the section listing the baseball greats.

Blackmun ignored the insult. He still had only four votes. If the tie stood, no opinion would be published.

At the end of May, Powell's clerks made a last-ditch effort to get him back in the case. They knew that he favored Flood's position. Since he would be voting against the major leagues, he could not be accused of a conflict of interest, his clerks argued. He would only be hurting his own interests. It was in fact possible that he could be accused of conflict if he did not vote.

No, Powell told them. He was out and he would stay out.

The Court was still deadlocked in the last half of May. After all his work, it seemed that Blackmun was to be deprived of his opinion.

The Chief's Saturday visit to Blackmun, and Blackmun's subsequent withdrawal of the abortion opinion, had spawned vicious rumors among the clerks of vote trading. Then, as the term drew to a close, Burger announced that he would switch to the Blackmun opinion in the Flood case, giving him the fifth vote. He too, however, initially declined to join the first section.

After the opinion had come down, a clerk asked Blackmun why he hadn't included Mel Ott, the famous New York Giants right fielder on his list of baseball greats.

Blackmun insisted that he had included Ott.

The clerk said that the name was not in the printed opinion.

Blackmun said he would never forgive himself.

Bob Woodward & Scott Armstrong, THE BRETHREN: INSIDE THE SUPREME COURT 189–92 (1979).

5. At this point, the dubious "logic" of the baseball exemption and the "anchor leg" run by Justice Blackmun in *Flood* should be obvious. It is no surprise that the arcane insulation of baseball from antitrust scrutiny has been scorned by legions of commentators. *See* Latour Rey Lafferty, *The Tampa Bay Giants and the Continuing Vitality Of Major League Baseball's Antitrust Exemption: A Review of* Piazza v. Major League Baseball, 21 FLA. ST. U.L.REV. 1271 (1994); John J. Scura, Comment, *The Time Has Come: Ending the Antitrust Non-Enforcement Policy in Professional Sports*, 2 SETON HALL J. SPORT L. 151 (1992); H. Ward Classen, *Three Strikes And You're Out: An Investigation of Professional Baseball's Antitrust Exemption*, 21 AKRON L. REV. 369 (Spring, 1988); Robert G. Berger, Essay, *After The Strikes: A Reexamination of Professional Baseball's Exemption from the Antitrust Laws*, 45 U. PITT. L. REV. 209 (Fall, 1983).

6. Justice Marshall's dissent declared in relevant part:

This does not mean that petitioner would necessarily prevail, however. Lurking in the background is a hurdle of recent vintage that petitioner still must overcome. In 1966, the Major League Players Association was formed. It is the collective-bargaining representative for all major league baseball players. Respondents argue that the reserve system is now part and parcel of the collective-bargaining agreement and that because it is a mandatory subject of bargaining, the federal labor statutes are applicable, not the federal antitrust laws. The lower courts did not rule on this argument, having decided the case solely on the basis of the antitrust exemption. * * * Petitioners suggest that the reserve system was thrust upon the players by the owners and that the recently formed players' union has not had time to modify or eradicate it. If this is true, the question arises as to whether there would then be any exemption from the antitrust laws in this case. (Footnotes omitted)

The labor exemption and its substantial impact upon antitrust litigation in the sports industry will be addressed comprehensively in Chapter 9. Justice Marshall's dissent also foreshadowed the Congressional passage of the Curt Flood Act and the issue of the baseball exemption as applied to player-team relations as opposed to issues such as agreements among major league and minor league teams, league restrictions on team relocation, league consideration of contracting the number of major league teams, and other issues beyond restraints on player compensation and mobility.

7. The lower courts visiting the baseball exemption question have engaged in heroic gymnastics to avoid following *Flood v. Kuhn* and have pressed the end of the analytical envelope to circumscribe the scope of the exemption to the fullest extent possible. Is that behavior consistent with the spirit of Justice Blackmun's opinion and the obligations of state and lower federal courts in terms of traditional notions of *stare decisis*? Consider the efforts of Judge McDonald, Judge Padova and Justice Harding in the *Henderson*, *Piazza*, and *Butterworth* cases that follow.

III. The Baseball Exemption after *Flood* and before the Curt Flood Act

Henderson Broadcasting Corp. v. Houston Sports Ass'n, Inc.
541 F. Supp. 263 (S.D. Texas 1982)

McDONALD, District Judge. * * * Henderson Broadcasting Corporation, radio station KYST-AM (KYST), has sued Houston Sports Association (HSA), the owner of the Houston Astros baseball team, and Lake Huron Broadcasting Corporation, owner of KENR-AM radio (KENR), charging: violations of the Sherman Act, 15 U.S.C. §§1 and 2 and of the Texas Antitrust laws; breach of contract; inducing the repudiation of a contract, and interference with business relationships. Plaintiff seeks injunctive relief and over two and a half million dollars in damages. Federal jurisdiction is premised solely on the Clayton Act violations under 15 U.S.C. §§15 [damages] and 26 [injunctive relief]. Defendants have moved to dismiss for lack of subject matter jurisdiction and failure to state a claim on the grounds that defendants' actions fall within the baseball exemption from the antitrust laws.

The gist of the complaint is that HSA cancelled KYST's contract to broadcast Astro baseball games. Plaintiff alleges that HSA as "the network" entered into station contracts with both plaintiff and defendant KENR; that plaintiff KYST and defendant KENR have overlapping broadcast signals and compete for listeners and advertising revenue; and that defendant HSA breached its contract with plaintiff in a conspiracy with KENR to divide and allocate advertising and audience territories in the greater Houston-Galveston radio broadcasting market, to eliminate competition for advertising revenue and listening audiences, and thus to impose horizontal restraints on that radio market area. * * *

The Court holds that defendants' alleged actions are not exempt from the antitrust laws. This decision rests on three considerations. First, the United States Supreme Court has implied that broadcasting is not central enough to baseball to be encompassed in the baseball exemption. Second, Congressional action does [sic] not support an extension of the exemption to radio broadcasting. Third, lower federal courts have declined to apply the baseball exemption in suits involving business enterprises which, like broadcasting, are related to but separate and distinct from baseball.

I. The Supreme Court's Baseball Exemption

The United States Supreme Court has held in three decisions that baseball is exempt from the antitrust laws. It has not considered the precise question of whether radio broadcasting of baseball games is also exempt, but its opinions imply that the exemption covers only those aspects of baseball, such as leagues, clubs and players which are integral to the sport and not related activities which merely enhance its commercial success.

* * *

The *stare decisis* basis for both the *Toolson* and *Kuhn* decisions and thus the narrow scope of the baseball exemption is reflected in the court's failure to make reference to an important decision by the Court of Appeals for the Second Circuit, several years before *Toolson*, which confronted the impact of the media on the baseball exemption. In *Gardella v. Chandler*, 172 F.2d 402 (2d Cir. 1949), plaintiff was barred from playing with the organized baseball clubs after he violated the terms of the reserve clause of his contract and sued the commissioner of baseball and the National and American Leagues' presidents for anti-trust violations. Judges Frank and Hand, forming the majority of a three judge panel, reversed and remanded the district court's dismissal for lack of jurisdiction on the basis of the baseball exemption. Although broadcasting itself was not at issue, Judge Frank wrote that defendants' lucrative contracts for interstate communication distinguished the case from *Federal Base Ball* since, "the interstate communication by radio and television is in no way a means, incidental or otherwise, of performing the intra-state activities (the local playings of the games) * * * [H]ere the games themselves because of radio and television, are so to speak, played interstate as well as intrastate. * * *" *Id.*, at 411–412, and thus the court should view a monopoly in baseball as it would one "related to the production of stage-plays in radio and television studios." *Id.* at 414.

Judge Hand took the analysis a step further. To him "the only debatable question [wa]s whether the defendants' connection with these activities [radio and television broadcasting] makes them a part of their business and enough a part of it to color the whole." He found that "[t]he contracts with the [radio and television broadcasting] companies are mutual arrangements in which each contributes a share to a common venture," and that these arrangements are not

> merely incidents of the business, as were the interstate features in *Federal Base Ball Club v. National League* * * * On the contrary, they are part of the business itself, for that consists in giving public entertainment. The players are the actors, the radio listeners and the television spectators are the audiences; together they form as indivisible a unit as do actors and spectators in the theatre.

Id. at 407–408. Concluding, that defendants were "*pro tanto* engaged in interstate commerce," he posed the question to the district court whether "these features of the business no matter now insignificant they may prove, necessarily subjected it as a whole to the antitrust laws," and stated that for the plaintiff to prevail

> he must show that the defendant's conduct, by which he was injured, was itself subject to the law that he invokes * * * not * * * that he was injured by the broadcasting and television; but that * * * those activities together with any other interstate activities marked the business as a whole. Certainly that was implied in *Federal Baseball* * * * itself * * * [where] nobody questioned that many interstate activities were in fact involved in professional baseball; the court merely thought them not important enough to fix the business-at-large with an interstate character.

Id. at 408. The question of the effect of broadcasting on the baseball exemption was left unresolved because *Gardella* was settled without further proceedings.

Additional evidence of the narrow scope of the Supreme Court's judicially-created baseball exemption is the court's consistent refusal to extend the exemption to other professional sports, in part because of the interstate broadcasting of the sports. In *United States v. International Boxing*, 348 U.S. 236, 243 (1955), the Court found that the "controlling consideration [in *Federal Base Ball*] was a very practical one—the degree of interstate activity involved in the particular business under review," and held that such activity in boxing subjected it to the antitrust laws. * * *

Similarly, in *Radovich v. National Football League*, 352 U.S. 445, 451–452 (1957), the court wrote that it had "not extend[ed] the baseball exemption from the antitrust laws to boxing or the theatre because we believe that the volume of interstate business in each, the rationale of *Federal Base Ball*, was such that both activities were in the Act." The court repeated plaintiff's argument that

> "part of the business of professional football itself" and "directly tied in and con-
> nected" with its football exhibitions is the transmission of games over radio and
> television into nearly every State of the Union. This is accomplished by contracts
> which produce a "significant portion of the gross receipts" and without which
> "the business of operating a professional football club would not be profitable."
> The playing of the exhibitions themselves "is essential to the interstate transmis-
> sion by broadcasting and television" and that the actions of respondents against
> [plaintiff] were necessarily related to these interstate activities.

Id. at 449.[6] It held the volume of interstate business in football placed it within the pro-visions of the Sherman Act. Thus, the Supreme Court has refused to extend the baseball exemption to boxing and football because it recognized that extensive broadcasting of those sports thrust them into interstate commerce.

The question posed by defendants HSA and KENR is the obverse of that posed by Judge Hand in *Gardella*: is radio broadcasting so much a part of baseball that it, as well as baseball, is exempt from the antitrust laws. The fact that interstate broadcasting has on the one hand subjected other professional sports to the antitrust laws, but has not on the other hand affected the baseball exemption, is perplexing. One implication of the Supreme Court's upholding of the baseball exemption despite interstate broadcasting would seem to be that the broadcasting is not central enough to the "unique character-istics and needs" of baseball which the exemption was created to protect, to affect that exemption. Thus, although the exhibition of baseball is now a big business "packaged with beer, broadcasting, and other industries," *Kuhn*, Douglas dissent, 407 U.S. at 287, radio broadcasting is not a part of the sport in the way in which players, umpires, the league structure and the reserve system are. However, the most reasonable interpreta-tion of the baseball exemption that has emerged from player challenges to the reserve

---

6. A year later a federal judge in Texas applied this reasoning to baseball. Finding not that broad-casting is essential to baseball, but that baseball is essential to the broadcasting of baseball, he held that broadcasting of baseball was therefore covered by the baseball exemption. Judge Dooley com-mented from the bench:

> The telecasting simply lifts the horizon, so to speak, and brings in another set of viewers
> of the same identical game that those present in the grandstand are seeing at the same
> time, ordinarily, and I believe it's straining reality to suggest that this television business
> has become a new facet of activity that you can look at apart from the ordinary business
> of baseball; and I can't follow that because there couldn't be such broadcasting except for
> the old-fashioned baseball game being played somewhere—the very gist and essence of
> the baseball business.

Hale v. Brooklyn Baseball Club, Inc., Civil Action No. 1294 (N.D.Tex.1958).

clause system is simply that it is an aberration. This Court's reading of the Supreme Court's opinions is that it should leave the aberration as it finds it, on the narrow ground of *stare decisis*.

II. Congressional Action

The Supreme Court in *Toolson* and *Flood v. Kuhn*, found that Congress had by its inaction implicitly ratified the *Federal Baseball* exemption. Congress, however, clearly has not extended the exemption to cover other businesses related to baseball. In fact, it has recognized that professional organized sports are involved in extraneous business activities and expressed its judgment that an extension of the baseball exemption to other activities as well as to other sports would contravene the federal antitrust laws. The 1952 House Subcommittee Report No. 2002, entitled "Organized Baseball," 82d Cong., 2d Sess., 230, submitted to the full House by the House Subcommittee on the Study of Monopoly Power pursuant to House Resolution 95, 82d Cong., 1st Sess., which the court relied on in declining to extend the baseball exemption to boxing in *International Boxing Club of New York*, concluded that extension of the baseball exemption "to all professional sports enterprises and to all acts in the conduct of such enterprises" would

> no longer require competition in any facet of business activity of any sport enterprise. Thus the sale of radio and television rights, the management of stadia, the purchase and sale of advertising, the concession industry and many other business activities as well as the aspects of baseball which are solely related to the promotion of competition on the playing field would be immune and untouchable. Such a broad exemption could not be granted without substantially repealing the antitrust laws.

The Subcommittee recommended against enactment of legislation on baseball, pending judicial interpretation of *Federal Baseball*, and Congress declined to extend the exemption to other sports and activities.

Congress has, contrary to the court's observations in *Flood v. Kuhn*, focused on the question of exemption of the television broadcast of sports from the antitrust laws and has legislated with regard to baseball no differently than it has with regard to football, basketball and hockey. Section 1291 of 15 U.S.C., (1966) (amending 15 U.S.C. §1291 (1961)) provides in part:

> The antitrust laws as defined in §12 of this title or in the Federal Trade Commission Act, as amended, shall not apply to any joint agreement by or among persons engaged in or conducting the organized professional team sports of football, baseball, basketball, or hockey, by which any league of clubs participating in professional football, baseball, basketball, or hockey contests sells or otherwise transfers all or any part of the rights of such league's member clubs in the sponsored telecasting of the games of football, baseball, basketball, or hockey, as the case may be, engaged in or conducted by such clubs.

The purpose of this exemption, as stated in Senate Report No. 1087, accompanying H.R. 9096, September 20, 1961, was precisely Justice Holmes' purpose in creating the baseball exemption in *Federal Baseball*, to protect the league structure, to give a league

> the power to make 'package' sales of the television rights of its member clubs to assure the weaker clubs of the league continuing television income and television coverage on a basis of substantial equality with the stronger clubs.

* * * [Since] should these weaker teams be allowed to flounder, there is danger that the structure of the league would become impaired and its continued operation imperiled.

The league structure is obviously not implicated in the instant case. Congress has not exempted radio broadcasting from the antitrust laws, and there is no reason to believe Congress intended to exempt radio broadcasting of baseball from those laws. In sum, Congressional action with regard to antitrust exemptions for professional sports do not support defendants' position.

III. Judicial Application of the Exemption

The baseball exemption arose and has been applied by the courts solely in disputes between players and team owners or a league. By contrast, in antitrust actions involving contracts between baseball teams or players on the one hand, and non-exempt business enterprises on the other, no court has granted a dismissal on the ground that baseball is somehow implicated. In fact, in such cases, the baseball exemption has not been raised in a jurisdictional challenge either by the parties or by the courts which are bound by the law to raise jurisdictional issues.

The Court of Appeals for the Seventh Circuit in *Charles O. Finley & Co., Inc. v. Kuhn*, 569 F.2d 527, 540–541 (7th Cir. 1978), *cert. denied*, 439 U.S. 876 (1978), rejected the argument that the baseball exemption applies only to the reserve system and not to a baseball club owner's claim that the Commissioner of Baseball, by disapproving the club's agreement to sell its contract rights for players services conspired to eliminate the club from baseball in violation of federal antitrust laws. The court concluded from its reading of *Federal Base Ball, Toolson, Flood v. Kuhn*, and *Radovich* that "the Supreme Court intended to exempt the business of baseball, not any particular facet of that business, from the federal antitrust laws." However, it "recognize[d] that this exemption does not apply wholesale to all cases which may have some attenuated relation with the business of baseball," *id.*, at 541, n.5, and cited as an example *Twin City Sportservice, Inc. v. Charles O. Finley & Co.*, 365 F.Supp. 235 (N.D.Cal.1972) *rev'd on other grounds* 512 F.2d 1264 (9th Cir. 1975).

In *Twin City* defendant, owner of a baseball team, counterclaimed for antitrust violations challenging a twenty-year-term exclusivity "follow the franchise" provision in his contract with a concessionaire. Under the parties' contract plaintiff concessionaire exchanged $150,000 and twenty-nine percent of the receipts from concession items sold to spectators for concession equipment and a $100,000 loan. The concession services included advertising and program printing as well as food. Nevertheless, neither the concessionaire nor the court raised the baseball exemption as a jurisdictional defense to this antitrust claim. The radio broadcasting contract at issue in the instant case, like a concession contract, brings revenue to the baseball team. If the contract of a concessionaire, whose programs, advertising and food are part of the spectators' experience of the baseball game, is not covered by the baseball exemption, then neither should the broadcasting contract which provides transmission of merely an aural version of the game across the airwaves.

In the recent case of *Fleer Corporation v. Topps Chewing Gum, Inc.*, 658 F.2d 139 (3rd Cir. 1981), plaintiff sued Topps and the major league baseball players association (MLBPA), which negotiates and enforces collective bargaining agreements between players and team owners and is the exclusive marketing agent for the publicity rights of the players as a group, on the grounds that defendants excluded competition in the sale of baseball cards by individual licensing agreements with each player and an agreement between Topps and the MLBPA which renegotiated the players' earlier contracts. Defendants did not urge, and the court did not raise, the baseball exemption. Clearly, the exemption is no more applicable to an antitrust suit on a broadcasting contract than it is to a suit on baseball players' licensing agreements for baseball cards.

IV. Conclusion

The focus of the court in an antitrust action is the particular activity and the particular market in question. * * *

In the instant case the Court must reconcile the Supreme Court's rulings exempting baseball from antitrust proscriptions with the antitrust laws favoring competition. The issue in the case is not baseball but a distinct and separate industry, broadcasting. Defendant, HSA, is sued in its capacity as a "network." The reserve clause and other "unique characteristics and needs" of the game have no bearing at all on the questions presented. To hold that a radio station contract to broadcast baseball games should be treated differently for antitrust law purposes than a station's contract to broadcast any other performance or event would be to extend and distort the specific baseball exemption, transform it into an umbrella to cover other activities and markets outside baseball and empower defendants radio station and "network" to use that umbrella as a shield against the statutes validly enacted by Congress.[8]

With all due respect, this Court concurs with Judge Friendly in his "belief that *Federal Baseball* was not one of Mr. Justice Holmes' happiest days, that the rationale of *Toolson* is extremely dubious and that, to use the Supreme Court's own adjectives, the distinction between baseball and other professional sports is 'unrealistic,' 'inconsistent' and 'illogical.' *Radovich v. National Football League*, 352 U.S. 445, 452 (1957)." It shares his view that "changes in the economics of the sport even since *Toolson*, especially the increasing importance of revenues from interstate television broadcasts, make baseball's immunity from the antitrust laws more anomalous than ever." *Salerno v. American League*, 429 F.2d 1003, 1005 (2d Cir. 1970), *cert. denied, sub nom. Salerno v. Kuhn*, 400 U.S. 1001 (1971). The baseball exemption today is an anachronism. Defendants have not presented a reason to extend it. Accordingly, defendants' Motions to Dismiss are DENIED.

Notes and Questions

1. In Part III of her opinion, Judge McDonald stated that "[t]he baseball exemption arose and has been applied by the courts solely in disputes between players and team owners or a league." Was that an accurate statement?

2. What do you consider to be the significance of the fact that the MLBPA and the Third Circuit in the *Fleer* case, and the concessionaire and court in the *Twin City* case did not raise the baseball exemption defense?

3. Given Judge McDonald's discussion of the questionable applicability of the baseball exemption in the context of agreements between baseball teams and the broadcast

---

8. The Court is also persuaded by plaintiff's argument that an exempt baseball team, like a labor union or agricultural cooperative which is exempted from the Sherman Act by statute, loses its exemption when it combines with a non-exempt radio station. *Ramsey v. United Mine Workers*, 401 U.S. 302 (1971). This is another expression of the principle that antitrust laws are applied or not applied to specific conduct in a specific market.

media, should the baseball exemption apply to: (1) an agreement among all major league baseball owners pooling all radio and television broadcasting revenue; (2) an agreement among all baseball owners that they would not own teams in other sports; (3) an agreement setting a wage scale for all players; (4) an agreement between and among the owners of Major League teams and owners of Minor League teams; (5) an agreement among the teams in Major League Baseball restructuring the relocation of teams; (6) an agreement among Baseball owners and NFL football team owners not to award new franchises or hold All-Star, Pro Bowl, or Super Bowl games in states that permit gambling on sporting events? Can you conceive of any situations in which an agreement between Major League Baseball and another professional sports league would be insulated by the baseball exemption?

4. Judge McDonald declared "radio broadcasting is not a part of the sport in the way in which players, umpires, the league structure and the reserve clause are." Should the baseball exemption as construed by *Flood* apply to antitrust claims about baseball's employment relations with its umpires? *See Postema v. National League of Professional Baseball Clubs*, 799 F. Supp. 1475, 1489 (S.D.N.Y. 1992). What about antitrust claims concerning the business of amateur softball? *See Amateur Softball Ass'n of Am. v. United States*, 467 F.2d 312, 314 (10th Cir. 1972).

5. Does Judge McDonald's opinion persuasively distinguish the case at bar from the infamous exemption trilogy (*Federal Base Ball*, *Toolson*, and *Flood*) or is it merely a thinly veiled effort to ignore Supreme Court precedent that Judge McDonald perceives to be unworthy of any "*stare decisis*" homage? Consider her approach and compare it to Judge Padova's analysis in *Piazza*.

Piazza v. Major League Baseball
831 F. Supp. 420 (E.D. Pa. 1993)

PADOVA, J. Plaintiffs allege that the organizations of professional major league baseball and an affiliated individual frustrated their efforts to purchase the San Francisco Giants baseball club (the "Giants") and relocate it to Tampa Bay, Florida. Plaintiffs charge these defendants with infringing upon their rights under the United States Constitution and violating federal antitrust laws and several state laws in the process. * * *

I. BACKGROUND

A. The Allegations

Plaintiffs are Vincent M. Piazza and Vincent N. Tirendi, both Pennsylvania residents, and PT Baseball, Inc. ("PTB"), a Pennsylvania corporation wholly owned by Piazza and Tirendi. Pursuant to a written Memorandum of Understanding ("Memorandum") dated August 18, 1992, Piazza and Tirendi agreed with four other individuals, all Florida residents, to organize a limited partnership for the purpose of acquiring the Giants. (The parties to the Memorandum will be referred to collectively as the "Investors".) * * *

On August 6, 1992, the Investors had executed a Letter of Intent with Robert Lurie, the owner of the Giants, to purchase the Giants for $115 million. Pursuant to this Letter of Intent, Lurie agreed not to negotiate with other potential buyers of the Giants and to use his best efforts to secure from defendant Major League Baseball approval of the sale." As required by the rules of Major League Baseball, the Partnership submitted an application to that organization on September 4, 1992 to purchase the Giants and move the team to St. Petersburg. In connection with this application, Major League Baseball and its "Ownership Committee" undertook or purported to undertake a personal background check on the Investors. On September 10, 1992, defendant Ed Kuhlmann, Chairman of the Ownership Committee, stated at a press conference that, among other things, the personal background check on the Investors had raised a "serious question in terms of some of the people who were part of that group" and that "a couple of investors will not be in the group." Kuhlmann elaborated that there was a "background" question about two of the investors rather than a question of financial capability and that something had shown up on a "security check." Kuhlmann also stated that the "money" of the two investors "would not have been accepted." Immediately following Kuhlmann at the news conference, Jerry Reinsdorf, a member of the Ownership Committee, added that the Ownership Committee's concern related to the "out-of-state" money and that the "Pennsylvania People" had "dropped out."

As the only principals of the Partnership who reside in Pennsylvania, Piazza and Tirendi aver that the clear implication of Kuhlmann's and Reinsdorf's comments, combined with the fact that Piazza and Tirendi are of Italian descent, was that the personal background check had associated them with the Mafia and/or other criminal or organized criminal activity. Piazza and Tirendi further allege that they have never been involved in such activity; nor had they "dropped out" of the Partnership. They also allege that they were never apprised by Baseball or anyone else of the charges against them nor given an opportunity to be heard.

On September 11, 1992, plaintiffs' counsel sent letters to Major League Baseball, Kuhlmann, and Reinsdorf requesting immediate correction of these statements and their implications. Plaintiffs' counsel never received a response to these letters, but on September 12, 1992, defendant Kuhlmann admitted to some members of the media that "there was no problem with the security check."

On the same day that the Partnership submitted its application to purchase and relocate the franchise, Kuhlmann directed Lurie to consider other offers to purchase the Giants, in knowing violation of Lurie's exclusive agreement with the Partnership. On September 9, 1992, Bill White, President of the National League, invited George Shinn, a North Carolina resident, to make an alternative bid to purchase the Giants in order to keep the team in San Francisco. An alternative offer was ultimately made by other investors to keep the Giants in San Francisco. Even though this offer was $ 15 million less than the $115 million offer made by the Partnership, Major League Baseball formally rejected the proposal to relocate the Giants to the Tampa Bay area on November 10, 1992.

Plaintiffs allege that Baseball never intended to permit the Giants to relocate to Florida and failed to evaluate fairly and in good faith their application to do so. They claim that to avoid relocation of the Giants, Baseball set out to "destroy the financial capability of the Partnership by vilifying plaintiffs." And in addition to preventing plaintiffs' purchase and relocation of the Giants, plaintiffs allege that Baseball's allegedly defamatory statements cost them the loss of a significant contract in connection with one of their other businesses, which depends upon "impeccable personal reputations." * * *

D. Antitrust * * *

1. Relevant Market

Absent a per se violation, which neither party argues has been alleged here, a cause of action under the Sherman Act requires, inter alia, an allegation of injury to competition in relevant product and geographic markets. Baseball argues that plaintiffs have not alleged an injury to competition in a relevant product market because plaintiffs were seeking to join Baseball, rather than compete with it. * * *

Plaintiffs aver that they were competing in the team franchise market with other potential investors located primarily outside of Major League Baseball for ownership of the Giants, and that Baseball interfered directly and substantially with competition in that market. I therefore reject Baseball's contention that plaintiffs have failed to allege a restraint on competition in a relevant product market. * * *

3. Exemption from Antitrust Liability

I now turn to the heart of Baseball's motion to dismiss plaintiffs' Sherman Act claim—that in *Federal Baseball Club of Baltimore, Inc.* v. *National League of Professional Baseball Clubs, Inc.*, 259 U.S. 200 (1922); *Toolson* v. *New York Yankees*, 346 U.S. 356 (1953); and *Flood* v. *Kuhn*, 407 U.S. 258 (1972), the United States Supreme Court exempted Baseball from liability under the federal antitrust laws. Plaintiffs do not deny that these cases recognize some form of exemption from antitrust liability related to the game of baseball, but argue alternatively that the exemption either does not apply in this case, cannot be applied as a matter of law to the facts of this case, or should no longer be recognized at all.

a. Evolution of the exemption. * * *

The next and most recent time the Supreme Court directly considered the exemption was in *Flood* v. *Kuhn*, 407 U.S. 258 (1972). Like Toolson, the plaintiff in Flood was a professional baseball player dissatisfied with the reserve clause in his contract and the "reserve system" generally. After an extensive analysis of the history of the exemption, Justice Blackmun, who delivered the opinion of the Court, produced a list of statements that can be made regarding the exemption and its circumstances:

1. Professional baseball is a business and it is engaged in interstate commerce.

2. With its reserve system enjoying exemption from the federal antitrust laws, baseball is, in a very distinct sense, an exception and an anomaly. *Federal Baseball* and *Toolson* have become an aberration confined to baseball.

3. Even though others might regard this as "unrealistic, inconsistent, or illogical," the aberration is an established one* * *, heretofore deemed fully entitled to the benefit of stare decisis, and one that has survived the Court's expanding concept of interstate commerce. * * *

4. Other professional sports operating interstate—football, boxing, basketball, and, presumably, hockey and golf—are not so exempt.

5. The Court has emphasized that since 1922 baseball, with full and continuing congressional awareness, has been allowed to develop and to expand unhindered by federal legislative action. * * * The Court accordingly has concluded that Congress as yet has had no intention to subject baseball's reserve system to the reach of the antitrust statutes. * * *

b. Discussion

(i) Scope of the exemption

In each of the three cases in which the Supreme Court directly addressed the exemption, the factual context involved the reserve clause. Plaintiffs argue that the exemption is confined to that circumstance, which is not presented here. Baseball, on the other hand, argues that the exemption applies to the "business of baseball" generally, not to one particular facet of the game.

Between 1922 and 1972, Baseball's expansive view may have been correct. Although *Federal Baseball* involved the reserve clause, that decision was based upon the proposition that the business of exhibiting baseball games, as opposed to the business of moving players and their equipment, was not interstate commerce and thus not subject to the Sherman Act. *Toolson*, also a reserve clause case, spoke in terms of the "business of baseball" enjoying the exemption. Likewise, *Radovich*, a 1957 decision concerning football, recognized the exemption as extending to the "business of organized professional baseball."

In 1972, however, the Court in *Flood* v. *Kuhn* stripped from *Federal Baseball* and *Toolson* any precedential value those cases may have had beyond the particular facts there involved, *i.e.*, the reserve clause. The *Flood* Court employed a two-prong approach in doing so. First, the Court examined the analytical underpinnings of *Federal Baseball*—that the business of exhibiting baseball games is not interstate commerce. In the clearest possible terms, the Court rejected this reasoning, removing any doubt that "[p]rofessional baseball is a business * * * engaged in interstate commerce." *Flood*, 407 U.S. at 282.

Having entirely undercut the precedential value of the reasoning of *Federal Baseball*, the Court next set out to justify the continued precedential value of the result of that decision. To do this, the Court first looked back to Toolson and uncovered the following four reasons why the Court there had followed *Federal Baseball*:

> (a) Congressional awareness for three decades of the Court's ruling in *Federal Baseball*, coupled with congressional inaction. (b) The fact that baseball was left alone to develop for that period upon the understanding that the reserve system was not subject to existing antitrust laws. (c) A reluctance to overrule *Federal Baseball* with consequent retroactive effect. (d) A professed desire that any needed remedy be provided by legislation rather than court decree.

* * * [T]he *Flood* Court viewed the disposition in *Federal Baseball* and *Toolson* as being limited to the reserve system, for baseball developed between 1922 and 1953 with the understanding that its reserve system, not the game generally, was exempt from the antitrust laws. This reading of *Flood* is buttressed by (1) the reaffirmation in *Flood* of a prior statement of the Court that "'*Toolson* was a narrow application of the doctrine of stare decisis,'" and (2) the *Flood* Court's own characterization, in the first sentence of its opinion, of the *Federal Baseball*, *Toolson*, and *Flood* decisions: "For the third time in 50 years the Court is asked specifically to rule that professional baseball's reserve system is within the reach of the antitrust laws."

Viewing the dispositions in *Federal Baseball* and *Toolson* as limited to the reserve clause, the *Flood* Court then turned to the reasons why, even though analytically vitiated, the precise results in *Federal Baseball* and *Toolson* were to be accorded the continuing benefit of stare decisis. Like *Toolson*, the *Flood* Court laid its emphasis on continued positive congressional inaction and concerns over retroactivity. In particular, the *Flood* Court "concluded that Congress as yet has had no intention to subject baseball's reserve system to the reach of the antitrust statutes." Finally, the Court acknowledged that "[w]ith its reserve system enjoying exemption from the federal antitrust laws, baseball is, in a very distinct sense, an exception and an anomaly. *Federal Baseball* and *Toolson* have become an aberration confined to baseball." Thus in 1972, the Supreme Court made clear that the Federal Baseball exemption is limited to the reserve clause.

Relying primarily upon *Charles O. Finley & Co.* v. *Kuhn*, 569 F.2d 527 (7th Cir. 1978), *cert. denied*, 439 U.S. 876 (1978), defendant Baseball offers a different reading of *Flood*. * * * Finding the Commissioner exempt from the antitrust laws under *Federal Baseball*, the district court granted summary judgment in favor of the Commissioner, and Finley appealed.

Like plaintiffs here, Finley argued on appeal that the exemption applies only to the reserve system. The Seventh Circuit disagreed, finding that "[d]espite the two references in the Flood case to the reserve system, it appears clear from the entire opinions in the three baseball cases, as well as from *Radovich*, that the Supreme Court intended to exempt the business of baseball, not any particular facet of that business, from the federal antitrust laws."

In reaching this conclusion, the Seventh Circuit looked back to *Federal Baseball*, *Toolson*, and *Radovich*, as I have done here, and concluded that the Court had focused in those cases upon the business of baseball, not just the reserve clause. Then the court discussed *Flood*:

> In *Flood* v. *Kuhn*, the Court said that "Professional baseball is engaged in interstate commerce" and "we adhere once again to *Federal Baseball* and *Toolson* and to their application to professional baseball."

This single paragraph represents the Seventh Circuit's entire substantive discussion of *Flood*—the Supreme Court's most recent and most thorough explanation of the *Federal Baseball* exemption. The court discounted two references in *Flood* to the reserve clause and made no mention of the fact that *Flood* refers to the reserve clause at least four times, the two not discussed by the court indicating that (1) the Supreme Court reads *Federal Baseball* and *Toolson* as reserve clause cases, and (2) the Court continues to follow the precise disposition of those decisions because Congress continues to express no intention of subjecting the reserve clause to the antitrust laws* * *.

But there is an even more significant flaw in the Seventh Circuit's analysis of *Flood* than in failing to note the extent to which that decision turned upon the reserve clause: Application of the doctrine of stare decisis simply permits no other way to read *Flood* than as confining the precedential value of *Federal Baseball* and *Toolson* to the precise facts there involved. To understand why this is so, one must fully understand the doctrine of stare decisis and its application by lower courts to Supreme Court decisions. The Third Circuit recently offered the following explanation:

> [Supreme Court] * * * opinions usually include two major aspects. First, the Court provides the legal standard or test that is applicable to laws implicating a particular * * * provision. This is part of the reasoning of the decision, the ratio decidendi. Second, the Court applies that standard or test to the particular facts of the case that the Court is confronting—in other words, it reaches a specific result using the standard or test.

As a lower court, we are bound by both the Supreme Court's choice of legal standard or test and by the result it reaches under the standard or test. As Justice Kennedy has stated, courts are bound to adhere not only to results of cases, but also "to their explications of the governing rules of law." Our system of precedent or stare decisis is thus based on adherence to both the reasoning and result of a case, and not simply to the result alone. This distinguishes the American system of precedent, sometimes called "rule stare decisis," from the English system, which historically has been limited to following the results or disposition based on the facts of a case and thus referred to as "result stare decisis."

Like lower courts, the Supreme Court applies principles of stare decisis and recognizes an obligation to respect both the standard announced and the result reached in its prior cases. Unlike lower courts, the Supreme Court is free to change the standard or result from one of its earlier cases when it finds it to be "unsound in principle [or] unworkable in practice."

Applying these principles of stare decisis here, it becomes clear that, before *Flood*, lower courts were bound by both the rule of *Federal Baseball* and *Toolson* (that the business of baseball is not interstate commerce and thus not within the Sherman Act) and the result of those decisions (that baseball's reserve system is exempt from the antitrust laws). The Court's decision in *Flood*, however, effectively created the circumstance referred to by the Third Circuit as "result stare decisis," from the English system. In *Flood*, the Supreme Court exercised its discretion to invalidate the rule of *Federal Baseball* and *Toolson*. Thus no rule from those cases binds the lower courts as a matter of stare decisis. The only aspect of *Federal Baseball* and *Toolson* that remains to be followed is the result or disposition based upon the facts there involved, which the Court in *Flood* determined to be the exemption of the reserve system from the antitrust laws.

Neither *Finley* nor any other case cited by Baseball in support of its view of the exemption has undertaken such an analysis of the Supreme Court's baseball trilogy. And as none of these decisions is binding upon this Court, I will not follow them. It is well settled that exemptions from the antitrust laws are to be narrowly construed. Application of this principle is particularly appropriate, if not absolutely critical, in this case because the exemption at issue has been characterized by its own creator as an "anomaly" and an "aberration." For these reasons, I conclude that the antitrust exemption created by *Federal Baseball* is limited to baseball's reserve system, and because the parties agree that the reserve system is not at issue in this case, I reject Baseball's argument that it is exempt from antitrust liability in this case.

(ii) Nature of the exemption

Although it would be appropriate to end here my discussion of the *Federal Baseball* exemption, for the purpose of providing a complete record of decision in the event of certification for immediate appeal under 28 U.S.C.A. §1292(b), I will press on to consider the implications of applying "rule stare decisis" to *Federal Baseball* and plaintiffs' complaint.

Assuming, as Baseball would have it, that *Finley* is correct and the exemption extends beyond the reserve system, I must determine exactly how far the exemption reaches. I find that stating, as did the *Finley* court, that the exemption covers the "business of baseball" does little to delineate the contours of the exemption.

As mentioned above, to state a claim under the Sherman Act, plaintiffs must allege injury to competition in a relevant product market. Although the Supreme Court has not couched its explanation of the exemption in these terms, I believe that the only arguably surviving rule to be gleaned from the Court's baseball trilogy is that if the relevant product market involved is the market defined as the "business of baseball," injury to competition in that market may not be redressed under the Sherman Act. * * * Cf. *Henderson Broadcasting Corp.* v. *Houston Sports Ass'n*, 541 F. Supp. 263 (S.D. Tx. 1982)(exemption does not apply to market for broadcast of baseball games). *Federal Baseball* itself made this clear. The focus in that case was upon competition in two different businesses or markets. The first was defined as the business of "giving exhibitions of base ball [sic]." *Federal Baseball*, 259 U.S. at 208. The second was defined as the business of "moving players and their paraphernalia from place to place." *D.C. Opinion*, 269 F. at 686. The Sherman Act was held not to apply to restraints in the first market because that market did not implicate interstate commerce. *Federal Baseball*, 259 U.S. at 208–09. Restraints in the second market, however, were redressable under the Sherman Act because that market did implicate interstate commerce. *D.C. Opinion*, 269 F. at 687–88. Thus, assuming the validity of *Finley*, the *Federal Baseball* exemption is one related to a particular market—the market comprised of the exhibition of baseball games—not a particular type of restraint (such as the reserve clause) or a particular entity (such as Major League Baseball).

It follows from having expressed the exemption as relating to a particular market that the next question is whether the plaintiffs in this case seek relief for restraints in that market or some other market. If Baseball's allegedly unlawful conduct merely restrained competition in the market comprised of baseball exhibitions, Baseball is immune from liability under the Act. If some other market was involved, however, even the expansive version of the *Federal Baseball* exemption would not apply.

A "market" may be defined as "any grouping of sales whose sellers, if unified by a hypothetical cartel or merger, could raise prices significantly above the competitive level." Phillip E. Areeda & Herbert Hovenkamp, ANTITRUST LAW ¶518.1b (Supp. 1991)(footnote omitted). As stated above, plaintiffs allege that the relevant product market in this case is the market for ownership of existing major league professional baseball teams. Reduced to its essentials, one can infer at this stage of the proceedings that this market has the following components: (1) the product being sold is an ownership interest in professional baseball teams; (2) the sellers are team owners; and (3) the buyers are those who would like to become team owners. Viewing the complaint in the light most favorable to plaintiffs, it would not be unreasonable also to infer that if the team owners combined, they could increase the price of teams considerably and control the conditions of sale.[25]

The market to which the expansive version of the *Federal Baseball* exemption applies, on the other hand, has the following components: (1) the product is the exhibition of baseball games; (2) the sellers, as with the market defined by plaintiffs, are team owners; and (3) the buyers are fans and, perhaps, the broadcast industry. Thus the two markets have different products—baseball teams versus baseball games—and different consumers.

Although not expressed in market terms, the Court of Appeals in *Federal Baseball* attributed great weight to such differences. The court distinguished for Sherman Act purposes between the business that encompassed the exhibition of baseball games (the "game exhibition market") and the business that involved the movement of players and their paraphernalia (the "player transportation market"). *D.C. Opinion*, 269 F. at 686. The focus of the exemption was on the exhibition of games only, which Justice Holmes characterized in affirming the Court of Appeals as "purely state affairs." *Federal Baseball*, 259 U.S. at 208. Other aspects of a baseball team's business—interstate aspects distinguishable from but nonetheless related to the games such as the movement of players and equipment—were not part of the exemption. Thus the anticompetitive nature of

---

25. One might also view the relevant market more narrowly as the market for the purchase and transfer of the Giants only, where there was but one seller, Robert Lurie, constituting a monopoly, with the buyer group including only those interested in the Giants, as opposed to other professional baseball teams. On a motion to dismiss, I must view the relevant market in the manner most favorable to plaintiffs.

the reserve clause in the game exhibition market was found not to violate the Sherman Act, but could have given rise to a claim under the Act had it directly affected other markets. A similar distinction may be made here. The plaintiffs in this case target not anticompetitive activity in the market for the exhibition of baseball games; but anticompetitive activity in the market for the sale of ownership interests in baseball teams—a market seemingly as distinguishable from the game exhibition market as the player transportation market.

Recent courts construing the expansive version of the exemption, although not focusing upon the distinction made by the Court of Appeals in *Federal Baseball*, have defined the exempted market (characterized as the "business of baseball") as that which is central to the "'unique characteristics and needs'" of baseball. * * * There seems to be agreement among these courts and others that, defined in this way, the exempted market includes (1) the reserve system and (2) matters of league structure. * * *

I do not view these decisions as conflicting with the analysis of the Court of Appeals in *Federal Baseball*. Applying their logic, the Court of Appeals can be understood as essentially viewing the movement of players and their equipment from game to game as a market activity not central to the unique characteristics and needs of exhibiting baseball games. Thus, when these decisions are considered together, the following list of activities or markets that are not within the exempted market can be generated: (1) the movement of players and their equipment from game to game; (2) the broadcast of baseball games; and, perhaps, (3) employment relations between organized professional baseball and non-players.

No court, however, has analyzed or applied the expansive view of the Federal Baseball exemption to the market for ownership interests in existing baseball teams. Thus I must determine whether this market is central to the unique characteristics and needs of baseball exhibitions. I conclude that such a determination is not possible without a factual record, and that, viewing plaintiffs' complaint in their favor, plaintiffs may be able to demonstrate that team ownership is not central to baseball's unique characteristics.

Plaintiffs plead that they were attempting to acquire an interest in a business owned by Robert Lurie engaged in the exhibition of baseball games—the San Francisco Giants. As stated above, the products being sold in this market (teams) are different from those being sold in the exempted market (games). And acquiring an ownership interest in a team may very well be no more unique to the exhibition of baseball games than is moving players and their equipment from game to game. Although players and their equipment are, beyond doubt, uniquely necessary to a baseball game, the Court of Appeals in *Federal Baseball* found, on a trial record, that their movement—which essentially involves the transportation of men and equipment—was not. Likewise, although teams, as business entities engaged in exhibiting baseball games, are undoubtedly a unique necessity to the game, the transfer of ownership interests in such entities may not be so unique. Moreover, anticompetitive conduct toward those who seek to purchase existing teams has never been considered by any court to be an essential part of the exhibition of baseball games.

On the other hand, it is conceivable that, although the precise products in plaintiffs' market and the exempted market are different, these markets nonetheless overlap to such an extent that they should be treated identically for purposes of the expansive view of *Federal Baseball*. In other words, the acquisition of a business that is engaged in baseball exhibitions may be central in some way not apparent on the face of the complaint to the unique characteristics of baseball exhibitions. Without a factual record, I would be engaged in mere speculation in deciding now whether it is or is not.

Accordingly, I conclude that if "rule stare decisis" and the *Finley* expansive view were applied, this case would not be ripe for determination of whether the *Federal Baseball* exemption applies. Thus, even under this analysis, Baseball's motion would be denied. One additional observation bears mentioning. I have considered plaintiffs' complaint in the light most favorable to plaintiffs and have accepted their definition of the relevant market as the market for team ownership. But the gravamen of plaintiffs' case may be Baseball's interference with plaintiffs' efforts to acquire and relocate the Giants to Florida. As stated earlier, matters of league structure have been viewed by other courts as being unique to baseball. The physical relocation of a team and Baseball's decisions regarding such a relocation could implicate matters of league structure, and thus be covered by the exemption. If, therefore, the expansive view of *Federal Baseball* were applied and a factual record were developed showing that this case concerns only restraints on the market for ownership and relocation of the Giants as inseparable activities, "rule stare decisis" could require application of the exemption.

III. CONCLUSION

Baseball's motion to dismiss is granted in part and denied in part. Plaintiffs' direct claims under the U.S. Constitution are dismissed. In all other respects the motion is denied. Because I have not dismissed all of plaintiffs' claims over which this Court has original jurisdiction, I will continue to exercise supplemental jurisdiction over plaintiffs' state law claims.

Notes and Questions

1. This opinion reflects the substantial effort courts will exert to avoid applying the baseball exemption. As was evident in *Henderson Broadcasting*, lower courts, though constrained somewhat by the message of *Flood v. Kuhn*, will often make every attempt to circumscribe the scope of that opinion so as not to extend the aberrational baseball exemption beyond its most narrow confines.

2. Is Judge Padova's decision correct in terms of its interpretation of the scope of the exemption? Specifically, Judge Padova suggested that all baseball exemption cases have involved baseball's reserve clause, and he circumscribed the exemption accordingly. Although *Flood* and *Toolson* indeed involved the reserve system, *Federal Base Ball* addressed broad questions surrounding a league's ability to absorb all or part of a competing league. Judge Padova's tortured analysis, including his painstaking differentiation between result *stare decisis* and rule *stare decisis,* was largely predicated upon his desire to limit the exemption. Following upon a basic assumption that the business of baseball as applied to baseball's antitrust exemption is limited to reserve system cases, Judge Padova left himself free to conclude that neither rule *stare decisis* nor result *stare decisis* was implicated. Yet, as indicated above, it is a mischaracterization to suggest that *Federal Base Ball* was a reserve system case or to suggest that Blackmun in *Flood* would have limited the exemption simply to the reserve clause. While Judge Padova's aspirations and any concomitant attempt to reduce the baseball exemption to its absolute minimum are commendable, the implication that the business of baseball in pertinent litigation has been limited to the reserve system may be intellectually infirm and a somewhat too convenient escape hatch from the captivity of the baseball exemption. If the exemption were limited to the reserve clause or player restraints, would you expect an explicit statement to that effect in at least one of the Supreme Court decisions?

3. In addition to his potentially overly restrictive view of existing baseball exemption precedent, Judge Padova complicated matters unnecessarily by pursuing an analysis of the impact of the exemption upon the market involved. Arguably, Judge Padova erred by resorting to an analysis of the relevant market and, in effect, assessing the merits of the underlying antitrust claim to assess the breadth of the exemption. Is it not singularly inappropriate to evaluate the possible applicability of an exemption by ascertaining the extent to which the non-exempt conduct would substantively affect the product market? All questions regarding the impact on the market and the reasonableness of the restraint should await the threshold determination of whether an exemption in fact exists. Consider, for example, an employee who allegedly is exempt from the wage-hour laws based on a particular statutory exemption. It defies logical explanation to evaluate the applicability of the exemption by ascertaining how much money this employee would lose as a result of his exemption from minimum wage and overtime protection. A market analysis prior to determination of whether or not the conduct is even subject to antitrust scrutiny is likewise counterintuitive.

4. Even assuming that a market analysis is an appropriate inquiry at the exemption stage, Judge Padova immersed himself in more hot water by attempting to characterize certain parts of baseball as interstate in nature and therefore not within the limitations that Justice Holmes placed upon the exemption in *Federal Base Ball*. Judge Padova thus concluded that the "anticompetitive nature" of the reserve clause was found not to violate the Sherman Act, but he added that it could have given rise to a claim under the Act had it directly affected other markets. Again, Judge Padova arguably missed the point because the reserve clause has a profound effect on the market for player services. It is somewhat anomalous to suggest that the exemption is limited to the reserve clause when, in fact, the reserve clause is a glowing example of an interstate aspect, distinguishable from the movement of players and equipment, for example. The upshot is that in his zeal to establish a distinction in the instant case (as he suggests, the plaintiffs here target not anticompetitive activity in the market for the exhibition of baseball games but anticompetitive activity in the market for the sale of ownership interests in baseball teams), he attempted to create distance between the infamous exemption trilogy and the case at bar. However, this distinction fails to pass muster because the reserve system's impact on the market for player services is conceptually similar to the anticompetitive affect on the market for the sale of ownership interests in baseball franchises. Therefore, although Judge Padova's motives were pure in attempting to prove that the baseball exemption should not apply to the case at hand, his suggestions that the three earlier cases were reserve clause cases and that the reserve clause situation is distinguishable are tenuous at best.

5. Following the issuance of the *Piazza* opinion, Major League Baseball sought appellate review, but Judge Padova denied the defendants' request that he certify his decision about the baseball exemption for immediate appeal. *See Piazza v. Major League Baseball*, 836 F. Supp. 269, 271–73 (E.D.Pa. 1993). One year later, on the eve of jury selection in the case, the parties settled in *Piazza*, with the plaintiff receiving a substantial monetary "award," reported to be $6 million. *See, e.g.*, Hank Grezlak, *Early Settlement Rains Out Baseball Antitrust Trial*, Pennsylvania Law Weekly, Oct. 10, 1994; Thomas Tobin, *State Court Deals Blow to Baseball*, St. Petersburg Times, Oct. 7, 1994.

6. Did Major League Baseball take the *Piazza* suit seriously at the time of its filing? Given the baseball exemption, baseball may have assumed blithely that the court

would never reach the merits. In fact, baseball did not notify its insurance carriers of the existence of the *Piazza* litigation until 19 months after the suit had been filed. As a result of baseball's cavalier attitude, the carriers were absolved of any obligation to defend and indemnify baseball for claims that otherwise might have been covered. *See Hartford Fire Ins. Co. v. Baseball Office of the Commissioner*, 654 N.Y.S.2d 21 (1997).

7. During the 1990's, as baseball endured multiple labor-management disputes, some members of Congress made attempts to reduce the impact of the exemption or to eliminate it altogether. In 1994, Senator Howard Metzenbaum's attempt to eliminate the exemption through S. 500 was killed in the Judiciary Committee by a vote of 10-7. Throughout the discussion of S.500 and its companion, H.R. 1459, serious concerns focused upon two factors: the independence of the commissioner, and the possibility of expansion. Is this inquiry at all pertinent? How does the possibility of the establishment of additional franchises in other American cities or the functional independence of a commissioner implicate the scope of antitrust coverage? Certainly, we cannot trust the commissioner of baseball to serve as the substitute for a United States District Court in terms of governing the collusive activities and the anticompetitive conduct of the various team owners. More importantly, the question of expansion into numerous cities seems almost to suggest a venal preoccupation with each legislator protecting the interests of his or her constituents rather than a consideration of the overall negative impact of the exemption upon competition. Is a congressional motive that seeks to protect Major League Baseball's unfettered control over the minor leagues and minor league players any more noble in terms of the baseball exemption?

Butterworth v. National League of Professional Baseball Clubs
644 So. 2d 1021 (Fla. 1994)

HARDING, Justice. We have for review *Butterworth v. National League of Professional Baseball Clubs*, 622 So. 2d 177 (Fla. 5th DCA 1993), in which the Fifth District Court of Appeal certified the following question to be one of great public importance:

> Does the antitrust exemption for baseball recognized by the United States Supreme Court in *Federal Base Ball* * * * and its progeny exempt all decisions involving the sale and location of baseball franchises from federal and Florida antitrust law? * * *

We answer the certified question in the negative and quash the decision below because we find that baseball's antitrust exemption extends only to the reserve system.

This case arose from the unsuccessful attempt of a group of investors to purchase the San Francisco Giants Major League Baseball franchise and relocate it to Tampa Bay, Florida. After the baseball owners voted against approval of the sale to the Tampa investors and the Giants owner signed a contract to sell the franchise to a group of San Francisco investors, Florida Attorney General Robert Butterworth (Attorney General) issued antitrust civil investigative demands (CIDs) to the National League of Professional Baseball Clubs and its president William D. White. * * * According to the CIDs, the specific focus of the investigation was "[a] combination or conspiracy in restraint of trade in connection with the sale and purchase of the San Francisco Giants baseball franchise."

The National League petitioned the Circuit Court of the Ninth Judicial Circuit to set aside the CIDs, based upon an assertion that the matters under investigation involved a transaction exempt from the application of both federal and state antitrust laws * * * [T]he circuit court issued an order quashing the CIDs. The circuit court determined that "[d]ecisions concerning ownership and location of baseball franchises clearly fall within the ambit of baseball's antitrust exemption." On appeal, the district court affirmed that order and certified the question to this Court. * * *

Based upon the Supreme Court's trilogy of baseball cases, baseball clearly enjoys some form of exemption from antitrust laws. However, there is some disagreement as to the scope of that exemption. * * *

Several federal courts have interpreted the scope of the exemption broadly. For example, the United States Court of Appeals for the Seventh Circuit concluded that the "Supreme Court intended to exempt the business of baseball, not any particular facet of that business, from the federal antitrust laws." *Finley,* 569 F.2d at 541; *accord Professional Baseball Schs. & Clubs, Inc. v. Kuhn,* 693 F.2d 1085, 1086 (11th Cir. 1982) (concluding that business of baseball, including franchise location system, is exempt from antitrust laws); *Salerno v. American League of Professional Baseball Clubs,* 429 F.2d 1003 (2d Cir. 1970), *cert. denied,* 400 U.S. 1001 (1971) (finding exemption applicable to former umpires' claim of antitrust violation following umpires' discharge).

However, in a recent decision involving two Pennsylvania citizens who were part of the same investment group as the Tampa Bay investors in the instant case the United States District Court for the Eastern District of Pennsylvania stated that the "antitrust exemption created by *Federal Baseball* is limited to baseball's reserve system." * * * After an extensive analysis of the Supreme Court's baseball trilogy, the *Piazza* court concluded that *Flood* invalidated the rule *stare decisis* of *Federal Baseball* and *Toolson* and left only the result *stare decisis* under the facts of the case, namely the exemption of baseball's reserve system from federal antitrust law.

Even though the *Piazza* court is the only federal court to have interpreted baseball's antitrust exemption so narrowly, the language of the *Flood* opinion supports such an interpretation. * * *

Based upon the language and the findings in *Flood*, we come to the same conclusion as the *Piazza* court: baseball's antitrust exemption extends only to the reserve system.

Accordingly, we answer the certified question in the negative, quash the decision below, and remand this case for proceedings consistent with this opinion.

It is so ordered. * * *

OVERTON, Justice, specially concurring.

At the outset I believed that baseball franchises were exempt from any type of federal or state antitrust laws. I concur in the majority opinion, however, because I am now convinced that *Piazza v. Major League Baseball,* 831 F. Supp. 420 (E.D. Pa. 1993), which holds otherwise, properly analyzes the trilogy of decisions of the United States Supreme Court addressing this issue. * * *

Times have changed significantly since the exemption was initially created. Several other professional sports now operate in a manner similar to professional baseball but do not enjoy a similar antitrust exemption. All of these major professional sports teams are important business entities in the broad communities of interest in which they operate. In my personal view, why one professional sport would have a judicially created antitrust exemption, but others do not, is a question that defies legal logic and common sense. * * *

Now is the time for this question to be finally resolved and the United States Supreme Court should take jurisdiction of this case to do so. * * *

McDONALD, Senior Justice, dissenting.

I would approve the decision under review and answer the certified question in the affirmative. In doing so, I adopt portions of the trial judge's order as follows: * * *

It is not the individuals involved with professional baseball that are exempt, nor the entity calling itself baseball, it is the business of baseball which is exempt. The exemption protects business activities which are directly related to the unique needs and characteristics of professional baseball. One area of business activity which has clearly and consistently been considered exempt is the matter of the structure of the league. The composition of the leagues, that is, where professional baseball is played and with whom, is a fundamental consideration of professional baseball and at the heart of its business activity. Decisions concerning ownership and location of baseball franchises clearly fall within the ambit of baseball's antitrust exemption. * * *

The application of baseball's exemption to antitrust laws in this area is clear and the Attorney General is without authority to investigate activity which is clearly exempt.

Notes and Questions

1. The dissent adopted the trial judge's conclusions that decisions concerning ownership and location of baseball franchises are covered by the baseball exemption. As profoundly unsatisfying as such a conclusion might be, is the dissent correct?

2. Prior to *Piazza*, it was generally understood that the minor league system was protected by the baseball exemption. For example, in *Professional Baseball Schools and Clubs, Inc. v. Kuhn*, 693 F.2d 1085, 1086 (11th Cir. 1982) (*per curiam*), the Eleventh Circuit, affirming the district court's dismissal of an antitrust challenge to the minor league player assignment and franchise location systems and other minor league rules, reasoned that "the exclusion of the business of baseball from the antitrust laws is well established." Similarly, in *Portland Baseball Club, Inc. v. Kuhn*, 368 F. Supp. 1004, 1007 (D. Or. 1971), *aff'd per curiam*, 491 F.2d 1101, 1103 (9th Cir. 1974), the district court and the Ninth Circuit found Major League Baseball's agreement with the minor leagues and rules governing territorial allocation and compensation for territorial infringement to be insulated from federal antitrust challenge by the baseball exemption. Subsequent to *Piazza*, but prior to *Butterworth*, the United States District Court for the Eastern District of Louisiana granted summary judgment dismissing antitrust challenges to territorial allocation rules of the minor leagues. *New Orleans Pelicans Baseball, Inc. v. National Association of Professional Baseball Leagues, Inc.*, Civil Action No. 93-253, 1994 WL 631144 at 20–21 (E.D.La. 1994). The court adopted the Seventh Circuit's reasoning in *Finley v. Kuhn*, *supra*, and expressly rejected the "cramped view" of *Piazza*; but the court acknowledged that Judge Padova's reasoning was "impressive."

3. In assessing the wisdom of Judge Padova's decision, compare Latour Ray Lafferty, *The Tampa Bay Giants and The Continuing Vitality of Major League Baseball's Antitrust Exemption: A Review of Piazza v. Major League Baseball*, 21 FLA. ST. U. L. REV. 1271 (1994) *with* Neal R. Stoll & Shepard Goldfein, *The Narrowing of Baseball's Exemption*, N.Y.L.J., December 21, 1993. *See also McCoy v. Major League Baseball*, 911 F. Supp. 454

(W.D. Wash. 1995); *Morsani v. Major League Baseball,* 663 So. 2d 653 (Fla. Dist. Ct. App. 2 1995).

4. It is interesting that Major League Baseball's owners, after fighting for seventy years to preserve baseball's exemption, have inadvertently surrendered many of the "benefits" through myopic collective bargaining. Several years ago, during negotiations over free agency, both sides agreed, at the owners' instigation, not to "act in concert with other clubs [or players]" regarding the "utilization or non-utilization of rights" with respect to free agency. *See* Major League Baseball, Basic Agreement, Art. XVIII. The players subsequently relied on this CBA provision and filed a grievance, alleging that during the years 1985, 1986, and 1987, the owners conspired in a collusive effort to restrict or eliminate free agency. Two arbitration decisions sustained the grievances, holding that the owners had breached Article XVIII. The Players Association and the owners agreed to a settlement calling for payment of 280 million dollars in back pay to the affected players. In retrospect, when the owners insisted upon the non-collusion provision, the players must have mused, "please don't throw us into that briar patch." *See In Re Arbitration Between Major League Baseball Players Ass'n and The Twenty-Six Major League Baseball Clubs,* Grievance No. 86-2, Chapter 16.

5. In the latter part of 1996, Major League Baseball and the MLBPA settled their lengthy dispute and agreed on a five-year collective bargaining agreement. Nonetheless, the protracted strike, the failure to name a new commissioner, and other evidence of baseball's penchant for self-destruction resulted in the thinning of congressional patience. In 1996, the Senate Judiciary Committee reported out a bill (S. 415) calling for a partial removal of the exemption. Ironically, as players and owners grappled over a new union contract, they reached agreement on jointly petitioning Congress to repeal the baseball exemption insofar as Major League labor relations matters and Major League labor market restraints were implicated. Read the Curt Flood Act carefully and consider what it does to the continued viability or existence of the baseball exemption.

6. Proposed legislation introduced in the 1990s without the support of Major League Baseball called for dramatic changes in baseball's exempt status. *See, e.g.,* S. 15, 104th Cong., 1st Session (1995) (would eliminate the exemption, but leave baseball protected by the Sports Broadcasting Act); H.R. 106, 104th Cong., 1st Session (1995) (would simply eliminate the exemption in its entirety); H.R. 735, 104th Cong., 1st Session (1995) (would establish a national commission to oversee and regulate baseball); H.R. 105, 104th Cong., 1st Session (1995) (would eliminate baseball's right to pool television broadcast rights by withdrawing from baseball the protection of the Sports Broadcasting Act). What should have been the primary areas of concern for Congress as it crafted a legislative solution: player-club relations; Major League-Minor League agreements; franchise relocation; or other issues? What should be the scope, if any, of the baseball exemption?

7. In Chapter 2, we discussed league disenchantment with maverick owners, such as the Dallas Cowboys' Jerry Jones, who circumvent either the spirit or the letter of league policy and attempt to negotiate individual endorsement deals. In 1997, New York Yankees' owner George Steinbrenner had ruffled his colleagues' feathers by making overtures to individual corporate "sponsors" about the possibility of entering private agreements independent of any arrangements that may have been made by the league. Major League Baseball attempted to block Steinbrenner's efforts and he responded by initiating litigation in federal court in Florida, claiming that the league's action violated federal and state antitrust law and constituted various common law torts. See Complaint,

New York Yankees Partnership v. MLB Enterprises, Inc., Case No. 97-1153-CW-T-25B (M.D. Fla. May 6, 1997). Does the baseball exemption foreclose his lawsuit?

IV. The Curt Flood Act

In 1997, Major League Baseball, involved in labor disputes with the Major League Baseball Players Association ("MLBPA"), came under attack in Congress. Many pundits and sportswriters opined that the reason Major League Baseball has been plagued by strikes and lockouts to an extent greater than other professional sports leagues (e.g., NBA and NFL) may be baseball's exemption from antitrust scrutiny. The MLBPA, perceiving an opportunity to gain public and congressional support for elimination of the exemption, fanned the flames, publicly asserting a causal connection between the exemption and MLB's labor relations problems. Major League Baseball may have been concerned about the possible success of congresssional efforts to repeal the baseball exemption. In addition, MLB certainly received legal advice that the existence and broadened scope of the labor exemption (as clarified by the 1996 US Supreme Court decision in *Brown v. Pro-Football, Inc.*, 518 U.S. 231 (1996), and addressed in detail in Chapter 9) and the strength and success of the MLBPA (with the corresponding low likelihood that the MLBPA would cease to be the MLB players' collective bargaining representative in order to pursue antitrust claims) generally rendered the baseball exemption redundant in the context of MLB's dealings with the MLBPA concerning major league players.

The collective bargaining agreement signed by the MLB and MLBPA in March of 1997 provided that the parties agreed to:

> jointly request and cooperate in lobbying Congress to pass a law that will clarify that Major League Baseball players are covered under the antitrust laws (i.e. that Major League Players have the same rights under the antitrust laws as do other professional athletes, *e.g.*, football and basketball players), along with a provision that makes it clear that passage of that bill does not change the application of the antitrust laws in any other context or with respect to any other person or entity.

1997 MLB-MLBPA Collective Bargaining Agreement, Article XXVIII. Pursuant to that agreement, MLB and the MLBPA jointly submitted the Curt Flood Act to Congress and it was enacted.

Curt Flood Act of 1998

SECTION 1. SHORT TITLE.

This Act may be cited as the "Curt Flood Act of 1998."

SEC. 2. PURPOSE.

It is the purpose of this legislation to state that major league baseball players are covered under the antitrust laws (i.e., that major league baseball players will have the same rights under the antitrust laws as do other professional athletes, e.g., football and basketball players), along with a provision that makes it clear that the passage of this Act does not change the application of the antitrust laws in any other context or with respect to any other person or entity.

SEC. 3. APPLICATION OF THE ANTITRUST LAWS TO PROFESSIONAL MAJOR LEAGUE BASEBALL.

The Clayton Act (15 U.S.C. Sec. 12 et seq.) is amended by adding at the end the following new section:

SEC. 27. (a) Subject to subsections (b) through (d), the conduct, acts, practices, or agreements of persons in the business of organized professional major league baseball directly relating to or affecting employment of major league baseball players to play baseball at the major league level are subject to the antitrust laws to the same extent such conduct, acts, practices, or agreements would be subject to the antitrust laws if engaged in by persons in any other professional sports business affecting interstate commerce.

(b) No court shall rely on the enactment of this section as a basis for changing the application of the antitrust laws to any conduct, acts, practices, or agreements other than those set forth in subsection (a). This section does not create, permit or imply a cause of action by which to challenge under the antitrust laws, or otherwise apply the antitrust laws to, any conduct, acts, practices, or agreements that do not directly relate to or affect employment of major league baseball players to play baseball at the major league level, including but not limited to—

(1) any conduct, acts, practices, or agreements of persons engaging in, conducting or participating in the business of organized professional baseball relating to or affecting employment to play baseball at the minor league level, any organized professional baseball amateur or first-year player draft, or any reserve clause as applied to minor league players;

(2) the agreement between organized professional major league baseball teams and the teams of the National Association of Professional Baseball Leagues, commonly known as the 'Professional Baseball Agreement', the relationship between organized professional major league baseball and organized professional minor league baseball, or any other matter relating to organized professional baseball's minor leagues;

(3) any conduct, acts, practices, or agreements of persons engaging in, conducting or participating in the business of organized professional baseball relating to or affecting franchise expansion, location or relocation, franchise ownership issues, including ownership transfers, the relationship between the Office of the Commissioner and franchise owners, the marketing or sales of the entertainment product of organized professional baseball and the licensing of intellectual property rights owned or held by organized professional baseball teams individually or collectively;

(4) any conduct, acts, practices, or agreements protected by Public Law 87-331 (15 U.S.C. Sec. 1291 et seq.) (commonly known as the 'Sports Broadcasting Act of 1961');

(5) the relationship between persons in the business of organized professional baseball and umpires or other individuals who are employed in the business of organized professional baseball by such persons; or

(6) any conduct, acts, practices, or agreements of persons not in the business of organized professional major league baseball.

(c) Only a major league baseball player has standing to sue under this section. For the purposes of this section, a major league baseball player is—

(1) a person who is a party to a major league player's contract, or is playing baseball at the major league level; or

(2) a person who was a party to a major league player's contract or playing baseball at the major league level at the time of the injury that is the subject of the complaint; or

(3) a person who has been a party to a major league player's contract or who has played baseball at the major league level, and who claims he has been injured in his efforts to secure a subsequent major league player's contract by an alleged violation of the antitrust laws: Provided however, That for the purposes of this paragraph, the alleged antitrust violation shall not include any conduct, acts, practices, or agreements of persons in the business of organized professional baseball relating to or affecting employment to play baseball at the minor league level, including any organized professional baseball amateur or first-year player draft, or any reserve clause as applied to minor league players; or

(4) a person who was a party to a major league player's contract or who was playing baseball at the major league level at the conclusion of the last full championship season immediately preceding the expiration of the last collective bargaining agreement between persons in the business of organized professional major league baseball and the exclusive collective bargaining representative of major league baseball players.

(d)(1) As used in this section, 'person' means any entity, including an individual, partnership, corporation, trust or unincorporated association or any combination or association thereof. As used in this section, the National Association of Professional Baseball Leagues, its member leagues and the clubs of those leagues, are not 'in the business of organized professional major league baseball'.

(2) In cases involving conduct, acts, practices, or agreements that directly relate to or affect both employment of major league baseball players to play baseball at the major league level and also relate to or affect any other aspect of organized professional baseball, including but not limited to employment to play baseball at the minor league level and the other areas set forth in subsection (b), only those components, portions or aspects of such conduct, acts, practices, or agreements that directly relate to or affect employment of major league players to play baseball at the major league level may be challenged under subsection (a) and then only to the extent that they directly relate to or affect employment of major league baseball players to play baseball at the major league level.

(3) As used in subsection (a), interpretation of the term 'directly' shall not be governed by any interpretation of section 151 et seq. of title 29, United States Code (as amended).

(4) Nothing in this section shall be construed to affect the application to organized professional baseball of the nonstatutory labor exemption from the antitrust laws.

(5) The scope of the conduct, acts, practices, or agreements covered by subsection (b) shall not be strictly or narrowly construed.

Notes and Questions

1. If *Piazza* and *Butterworth* were correct, what is left of the baseball exemption after the Curt Flood Act of 1998?

2. The Curt Flood Act says it does not create a private cause of action relating to, among other things, "any conduct, acts, practices, or agreements of persons engaging in, conducting or participating in the business of organized professional baseball relating to or affecting franchise expansion, location or relocation, franchise ownership issues, including ownership transfers, the relationship between the Office of the Com-

missioner and franchise owners, the marketing or sales of the entertainment product of organized professional baseball and the licensing of intellectual property rights owned or held by organized professional baseball teams individually or collectively." Does this mean that Congress is saying that the baseball exemption includes all issues related to expansion, location and relocation of MLB teams, issues related to team ownership and sales of teams, MLB and MLB team marketing and sales, and MLB licensing?

3. When a Court is called upon to interpret the Curt Flood Act in a case involving *minor* league baseball, how should it proceed?

V. Cases and Commentary After the Curt Flood Act

Major League Baseball v. Butterworth
181 F. Supp. 2d 1316 (N.D. Fla. 2001)

Hinkle, J. * * * Major League Baseball has announced its intention to contract from 30 clubs to 28 for the 2002 season. The issue in this action is whether the federal and state antitrust laws apply to the proposed contraction. The defendant Attorney General of the State of Florida asserts that the antitrust laws do apply. Pursuant to his statutory authority to investigate possible violations of the federal and state antitrust laws, the Attorney General has issued civil investigative demands to plaintiffs Major League Baseball, its Commissioner, and the two Florida major league baseball clubs. Plaintiffs seek declaratory and injunctive relief against the Attorney General on the grounds that the "business of baseball," including the decision whether to contract, is exempt from the federal and state antitrust laws. Plaintiffs are correct * * *

Major League Baseball is an unincorporated association of the 30 major league baseball clubs. It is governed by a Constitution adopted in January 2000. The Constitution authorizes contraction on the affirmative vote of three-fourths of the clubs.

On November 6, 2001, the clubs voted 28 to 2 in favor of contracting from 30 clubs to 28 for the 2002 season. The two Florida clubs voted in favor of contraction. On December 13, 2001, Major League Baseball announced that negotiations with the Players Association, an organization representing major league baseball players, had failed and that Major League Baseball was proceeding with the planned contraction. As this opinion is written, it appears that contraction is imminent. * * *

On December 10, 2001, plaintiffs filed this action, contending that, as a matter of federal law, the "business of baseball," a concept that plaintiffs assert includes the proposed contraction from 30 teams to 28, is exempt from the federal and state antitrust laws. Plaintiffs' complaint demanded declaratory and injunctive relief.

IV
The Merits

Under an unbroken line of United States Supreme Court decisions,[4] as well as under numerous decisions of lower courts,[5] including the United States Court of Appeals for

---

4. *See Flood v. Kuhn,* 407 U.S. 258 (1972); *Toolson v. New York Yankees, Inc.,* 346 U.S. 356 (1953); *Federal Baseball Club v. National League,* 259 U.S. 200 (1922).

5. *See, e.g., Triple-A Baseball Club Assocs. v. Northeastern Baseball, Inc.,* 832 F.2d 214 (1st Cir.1987); *Erving v. Virginia Squires Basketball Club,* 468 F.2d 1064 (2d Cir.1972); *Kowalski v. Chan-*

the Eleventh Circuit,[6] the federal antitrust laws do not apply to the "business of baseball"; the business of baseball is, as it is sometimes phrased, exempt from the antitrust laws. The exemption applies as well to state antitrust laws, which are, to the extent otherwise applicable to baseball, invalid.[7]

The Attorney General asserts the exemption applies only to the "reserve clause," part of the contract between clubs and players reserving each club's right to its players, subject to various terms. The Attorney General's assertion cannot be squared with the plain language and clear import of the many reported cases in this area. Nor can the Attorney General's assertion be squared with the United States Supreme Court's oft repeated rationale for continuing to recognize the exemption of the business of baseball: that any change in this long standing interpretation of the antitrust laws should come from Congress (which has left the decisions intact in relevant respects for now 79 years), not from the courts.

Although one might think it sufficient to dispose of this issue simply by citing the Supreme Court (and Eleventh Circuit) decisions on point, the Attorney General asserts their inapplicability so adamantly that a more detailed discussion seems appropriate. Moreover, two courts, a United States District Court in Pennsylvania[8] and the Florida Supreme Court,[9] have adopted a contrary reading of the cases, further confirming the need for close examination.

In Part A ... I address in excruciating detail the Supreme Court's decisions regarding the exemption of baseball from the federal antitrust laws. In Part B, I address the Eleventh Circuit's decision on this subject, which is squarely controlling and would be dispositive of the issue, standing alone. In Part C, I address the Attorney General's contention that ... the proposed contraction of Major League Baseball from 30 clubs to 28 nonetheless is not, or may not be, part of the exempt "business of baseball." In Part D, I address the impact of the federal antitrust exemption on the Florida Antitrust Act. Finally, in Part E, I address the Attorney General's contention that his CIDs can be sustained under other provisions of Florida law, even if the federal and state antitrust laws are indeed inapplicable to the proposed contraction.

A. *The Baseball Exemption in the Supreme Court*

The United States Supreme Court has issued three opinions in baseball antitrust cases, each time holding the antitrust laws inapplicable to the business of baseball, and never suggesting in the slightest that the result turned on whether the antitrust claim at issue did or did not involve the reserve clause. Other decisions of the Supreme Court confirm this result.

The first baseball case was *Federal Baseball Club v. National League*, 259 U.S. 200 (1922). The case arose from the attempt of a new league-known as the "Federal League" — to compete with the National and American Leagues, which then, as now, constituted the major leagues. The new venture failed, and one of its clubs sued the Na-

---

dler, 202 F.2d 413 (6th Cir.1953); *Charles O. Finley & Co. v. Kuhn,* 569 F.2d 527 (7th Cir.1978); *Portland Baseball Club, Inc. v. Baltimore Baseball Club, Inc.,* 282 F.2d 680 (9th Cir.1960); *Smith v. Pro Football, Inc.,* 593 F.2d 1173 (D.C.Cir.1978); *Morsani v. Major League Baseball,* 79 F.Supp.2d 1331 (M.D.Fl.1999); *McCoy v. Major League Baseball,* 911 F.Supp. 454 (W.D.Wash.1995); *New Orleans Pelicans Baseball, Inc. v. National Association of Professional Baseball Leagues, Inc.,* 1994 WL 631144 (E.D.La.1994); *Minnesota Twins Partnership v. State,* 592 N.W.2d 847 (Minn.1999); *State v. Milwaukee Braves,* 31 Wis.2d 699 (Wis.1966).

6. *Professional Baseball Schools and Clubs, Inc. v. Kuhn,* 693 F.2d 1085 (11th Cir.1982).
7. *See Flood v. Kuhn,* 407 U.S. at 284–85.
8. *Piazza v. Major League Baseball,* 831 F.Supp. 420 (E.D.Pa.1993).
9. *Butterworth v. National League,* 644 So. 2d 1021 (Fla.1994)

tional and American Leagues and their member clubs, asserting that they "destroyed the Federal League by buying up some of the constituent clubs and in one way or another inducing all those clubs except the plaintiff to leave their League. * * *" *Federal Baseball,* 259 U.S. at 207.

The Supreme Court upheld a judgment for the defendants, concluding that the Sherman Act, which was then just 32 years old, did not apply to major league baseball. The Court said that baseball games "would not be called trade or commerce in the commonly accepted use of those words," and that major league baseball thus was not interstate commerce, despite the incidental travel of players and fans in connection with the games. *Federal Baseball,* 259 U.S. at 209.

The Court gave no indication this result had anything to do with the reserve clause. Indeed, the Court mentioned the reserve clause only once, *after* concluding its analysis of the inapplicability of the antitrust laws to baseball. The Court said:

> If we are right [that baseball games are purely state affairs] the plaintiff's business is to be described in the same way and the restrictions by contract that prevented the plaintiff from getting players to break their bargains *and the other conduct charged against the defendants* were not an interference with commerce among the States.

Federal Baseball, 259 U.S. at 209 (emphasis added). The "other conduct" to which the Court referred presumably was that described at the outset of the opinion: "destroy[ing] the Federal League by buying up some of the constituent clubs and in one way or another inducing all those clubs except the plaintiff to leave their League. * * *" *Federal Baseball,* 259 U.S. at 207. The assertion that this was solely a reserve clause case is simply not true.[10] *Federal Baseball* held that professional baseball, not just the reserve clause, was outside the scope of the antitrust laws.

The Supreme Court next addressed the applicability of the antitrust laws to baseball in *Toolson v. New York Yankees, Inc.,* 346 U.S. 356 (1953). That consolidated decision dealt with three different antitrust cases against major league baseball clubs. The cases were dismissed by the district courts, and the dismissals were affirmed by the courts of appeals, on the authority of *Federal Baseball.*

Although the three cases addressed in Toolson *had been brought by baseball players and dealt overwhelmingly with reserve clause issues, the Supreme Court did not even mention that in its opinion, and its language gave not a hint that the applicability of the antitrust laws turned on that circumstance. Instead, the Court said that in* Federal Baseball *it had held that "the business of providing public baseball games for profit between clubs of professional baseball players was not within the scope of the federal antitrust laws." The Court explicitly adhered to that decision so far as it held the "business of baseball" exempt from the antitrust laws. The Court said that any change in that approach would have to come from Congress, not from the Court.*

It is impossible to glean from *Toolson* any inkling that the applicability of the antitrust laws to baseball turned on whether the issue was the reserve clause, on the one

---

10. In *Piazza v. Major League Baseball,* 831 F.Supp. 420 (E.D.Pa.1993), the court concluded that *Federal Baseball* was really just a reserve clause case, citing the opinion of the lower court. *See National League v. Federal Baseball Club,* 269 F. 681 (C.C.D.C.1920). Whatever the lower court might have thought, the Supreme Court thought *Federal Baseball* dealt with other issues, over and above the reserve clause. It is an odd approach to interpreting Supreme Court cases to disregard that Court's own description of a case in favor of a lower court's description.

hand, or something else, on the other. Quite to the contrary, it was the "business of baseball" that was exempt, and that, according to the Court, was to remain exempt, unless and until Congress said otherwise.

Before the Supreme Court would decide its third baseball antitrust case, it dealt with attempts to expand the baseball exemption into other areas. In *United States v. Shubert*, 348 U.S. 222 (1955), the Court held local theater exhibitions not exempt, rejecting the assertion that *Federal Baseball* and *Toolson* required a contrary result. The Court said that in *Federal Baseball* it "was dealing with the *business of baseball* and nothing else." *Shubert*, 348 U.S. at 228 (emphasis added). The Court said that in *Toolson* it was faced with a long standing decision that Congress had considered but had elected not to change and that, as a result, the Court had simply adhered to *Federal Baseball*, "so far as that decision determines that Congress had no intention of including the *business of baseball* within the scope of the federal antitrust laws." *Shubert*, 348 U.S. at 230 (emphasis added), *quoting Toolson*, 346 U.S. at 356. Had the baseball exemption been limited to the reserve clause, the Court surely would have said so; that would, after all, have provided a succinct and irrefutable basis for rejecting the claim that the same exemption should apply to the theater, which has no reserve clause. But the Court did not say this, for one reason: the exemption was (and is) for the business of baseball, not just the reserve clause.

In *United States v. International Boxing Club*, 348 U.S. 236 (1955), decided the same day as *Shubert*, the Court held the antitrust laws applicable to boxing, saying that *Federal Baseball* did not hold all professional sports beyond the scope of the antitrust laws. The Court said:

> The issue before us is, therefore, not whether a previously granted exemption should continue, but whether an exemption should be granted in the first instance. And that issue is for Congress to resolve, not this Court.

International Boxing, 348 U.S. at 243. The Court referred to baseball's reserve clause not at all, an odd approach if, as the Attorney General now asserts, the baseball exemption really only applied to the reserve clause, which has no counterpart in boxing. If the exemption were only for the reserve clause, one would have expected the Court to say so in rejecting the claimed exemption for boxing.[11]

Next came *Radovich v. National Football League*, 352 U.S. 445 (1957), an antitrust case brought by a football player challenging practices very similar to those taken under baseball's reserve clause. The Ninth Circuit held for the NFL, concluding that football, like baseball but unlike boxing, was a team sport. If the baseball antitrust exemption had turned on the reserve clause, one might have expected the Supreme Court to affirm, but it reversed. The Court made clear that the antitrust exemption of the business of baseball was just that: an exemption of the business of baseball, created long ago and never changed by Congress, that would remain in existence but would be limited to the business of baseball. After discussing *Federal Baseball* and *Toolson* and the Court's earlier statements "limiting them to baseball," the Court said:

---

11. Indeed, in dissent Justice Frankfurter, a jurist of no small intellect, said it would "baffle the subtlest ingenuity to find a single differentiating factor between other sporting exhibitions, whether boxing or football or tennis, and baseball insofar as the conduct of the sport is relevant to the criteria or considerations by which the Sherman Law becomes applicable to a 'trade or commerce.'" 348 U.S. at 248. Justice Frankfurter underestimated the Florida Attorney General's subtle ingenuity: baseball has a reserve clause, but boxing does not. Had the baseball exemption been limited to the reserve clause, this distinction between baseball and boxing would not have been so baffling to the justices of the Supreme Court, who missed it clean.

> [W]e now specifically limit the rule there established to the facts there involved, *i.e., the business of organized professional baseball.* As long as Congress continues to acquiesce we should adhere to—but not extend— the interpretation of the Act made in those cases.

Radovich, 352 U.S. at 451 (emphasis added). The Court suggested not at all that the rule of *Federal Baseball* or *Toolson* was limited to the reserve clause; instead, the Court very explicitly defined the antitrust exemption as applicable to "the business of organized professional baseball." And the Court continued,

> [W]ere we considering the question of baseball for the first time upon a clean slate we would have no doubts. But Federal Base Ball held the business of baseball outside the scope of the Act. No other business claiming the coverage of those cases has such an adjudication. We, therefore, conclude that the orderly way to eliminate error or discrimination, if any there be, is by legislation and not by court decision.

Radovich, 352 U.S. at 452 (emphasis added). The Attorney General's assertion now that the rationale of *Federal Baseball* (that big league baseball is not interstate commerce) has been undermined, and that the case thus should be limited narrowly to its facts (purportedly only the reserve clause) simply ignores the undeniable truth that, long after it was clear that big league baseball was interstate commerce, the Court still adhered to the explicit exemption for the "business of baseball," not based on any outdated view of interstate commerce, but because of the rationale (still just as applicable today) that any change in this long standing interpretation of the antitrust laws should come from Congress, not the courts. *That* rationale has not been questioned by the Court nor undermined by the passage of time.

It was against this backdrop that the Court addressed its third and most recent baseball antitrust case, *Flood v. Kuhn,* 407 U.S. 258 (1972). Curt Flood, one of the game's great center fielders, brought an antitrust action challenging the reserve clause. The district court and court of appeals rejected the claim, as did the Supreme Court. The Court recounted in detail its earlier decisions in this area, including all those discussed above. The Court acknowledged again, as it had done earlier, that if the slate were clean, the business of baseball would not garner an exemption from the antitrust laws. But the Court also said again, as it had said earlier, that the long history of decisions holding the business of baseball exempt ought not be changed by the judiciary. The Court explicitly adhered to the exemption, saying any change would have to come from Congress.

The Court's statements to this effect were numerous, and they were by no means limited to the reserve clause. While the fact that the case involved the reserve clause was mentioned, there was not the slightest suggestion that that was significant to the result. Not once did the Court intimate in any way that it was only the reserve clause that was exempt. To the contrary, the Court's articulation of the exemption was always phrased as the business of baseball, never as simply the reserve clause.

Thus, for example, after starting its discussion with a description of *Federal Baseball,* the Court noted that that decision had been "generally and necessarily accepted as controlling authority" by lower courts. *Flood,* 407 http://www.westlaw.com/Find/Default .wl?rs=FIPI1.0&vr=2.0&DB=708&FindType=Y&SerialNum=1972127159U.S. at 272. The examples the Court cited included cases having nothing to do with the reserve clause. *See, e.g., State v. Milwaukee Braves, Inc.,* 31 Wis.2d 699 (1966) (holding proposed transfer of Braves from Milwaukee to Atlanta exempt from antitrust challenge). Had the Court believed its earlier decisions recognizing an antitrust exemption could properly be limited to the reserve clause, it surely would not have said the lower courts "necessarily" found those cases controlling in other contexts, but it did. The Court's point was that *Federal Baseball* had long been followed, and properly so, thus supporting the conclusion that any change should come only from Congress.

The *Flood* Court next discussed *Toolson*, which, the Court said, cited *Federal Baseball* "as holding 'that the *business of providing public baseball games* for profit between clubs of professional baseball players was not within the scope of the federal antitrust laws.'" *Flood*, 407 U.S. at 273 (emphasis added), *quoting Toolson*, 346 U.S. at 357. The Court said *Toolson* adhered to *Federal Baseball* "so far as that decision determines that Congress had no intention of including the *business of baseball* within the scope of the federal antitrust laws." *Flood*, 407 U.S. at 273 (emphasis added), *quoting Toolson*, 346 U.S. at 357. The Court said, "The emphasis in *Toolson* was on the determination, attributed even to *Federal Baseball*, that Congress had no intention to include *baseball* within the reach of the federal antitrust laws." *Flood*, 407 U.S. at 274 (emphasis added). There was not a hint that *Toolson's* holding or rationale could be limited to the reserve clause or that the Court intended now so to confine it. * * *

In sum, although in *Flood* the Court was asked to overrule *Federal Baseball* and *Toolson*, the Court explicitly declined to do so, holding instead that the business of baseball was exempt from the antitrust laws, just as *Federal Baseball* and *Toolson* had said. The Court reached this result not based on any original antitrust analysis but instead because of its explicit determination that any change should come from Congress. *Flood* was, therefore, not so much a decision about antitrust law as about the appropriate role of the judiciary within our constitutional system. The Sherman Act had been in effect for 82 years. For 50 of those years, the Sherman Act had been interpreted as inapplicable to the business of baseball. Congress had considered the issue many times but had never changed the result: the business of baseball remained exempt. The Court held that, unless and until changed by the Congress, that would remain the law.

Phrased differently, *Flood* was a ruling not about whether the antitrust exemption should be terminated but about *who* should make that decision. The Court determined that the decision whether to terminate baseball's antitrust exemption should be made by Congress, not by the Court. That was explicitly the basis for *Flood's* holding. The Court's rationale remains every bit as valid today as it was when *Flood* was decided.

Nothing of substance has changed since *Flood*. The arguments for and against application of the antitrust laws to baseball are about the same. More significantly, the arguments for and against having the courts, rather than Congress, make any change in this area also are the same today as they were when *Flood* was decided, except that now nearly 30 more years have passed without congressional action.[16]

---

16. Plaintiffs assert that the Curt Flood Act, 15 U.S.C. § 27a, adopted in 1998, constitutes an endorsement by Congress of the exemption of the business of baseball. I disagree. In that Act, Congress expressly subjected matters directly affecting employment of baseball players (including the reserve clause) to the antitrust laws, to the same extent those laws are applicable to other professional sports. But Congress also made clear that this did not render the antitrust laws applicable to baseball in any other respect. *See* 15 U.S.C. § 27a(b). Properly construed, this does not affect the issues in the case at bar one way or the other, because Congress explicitly indicated its intention not to affect issues other than direct employment matters. Thus Congress said, "No court shall rely on the enactment of this section as a basis for changing the application of the antitrust laws to any conduct, acts, practices, or agreements other than" player issues. *Id.* I take Congress at its word and resolve this case without reliance on the Curt Flood Act as affecting the outcome one way or the other. I conclude that the business of baseball *is* exempt; the exemption was well established long prior to adoption of the Curt Flood Act and certainly was not *repealed* by that Act.

Flood constitutes an unequivocal, binding decision of the United States Supreme Court, establishing that the business of baseball is exempt from the antitrust laws, as it has been since 1922, and as it will remain unless and until Congress decides otherwise. Period.

C. *Applying the Baseball Exemption to Contraction*

The Attorney General asserts that, even if the "business of baseball" is exempt from the antitrust laws, that does not necessarily dispose of this case, because, the Attorney General says, the proposed contraction may not be part of the "business of baseball."

It is difficult to conceive of a decision more integral to the business of major league baseball than the number of clubs that will be allowed to compete. It might be possible to have an open and unrestricted assortment of teams, with new teams being formed and entering the fray at will, and with each team playing whatever other teams it chooses, whenever it chooses. But that would not be major league baseball as it developed before 1922 and as it has continued to exist. To the contrary, since before *Federal Baseball,* there has always been a defined National League and a defined American League, each with a set number of specific clubs, and there has always been a schedule of games involving major league clubs only. That league structure—and the ability to keep out the competing Federal League—were part of the business of baseball that *Federal Baseball* held exempt from antitrust scrutiny.

The basic league structure, including the number of teams, remains an essential feature of the business of baseball, exempt from the antitrust laws. *Professional Baseball Schools* [and *Clubs, Inc. v. Kuhn,* 693 F.2d 1085 (11th Cir. 1982)], a binding decision of the Eleventh Circuit, so held, and it did so not based on any factual record, but on a motion to dismiss.

D. *Applicability of the Florida Antitrust Act*

The Florida Antitrust Act explicitly exempts the same subjects as are exempt under federal law:

> Any activity of conduct exempt under Florida statutory or common law or exempt from the provisions of the antitrust laws of the United States is exempt from the provisions of this chapter

§ 542.20, Fla. Stat. (2001). The Florida legislature adopted this provision in 1980, just eight years after *Flood v. Kuhn* was decided, presumably with full knowledge of the baseball exemption. Any contention that the Florida Antitrust Act applies to the business of baseball thus fails for the same reasons the contention fails with respect to federal law.

Moreover, any effort to apply the Florida Antitrust Act to the business of baseball would remain invalid even if the Act by its terms did not incorporate the federal exemption. The United States Supreme Court held in *Flood v. Kuhn* that state antitrust laws could not be applied to the business of baseball because state antitrust regulation would conflict with federal policy, would prevent needed national uniformity in the regulation of baseball, and thus would run afoul of the Commerce Clause.

The need for national uniformity is no less in the case at bar than it was in *Flood.* Major League Baseball cannot have 30 teams in Florida but 28 in another state. The Devil Rays and Marlins cannot be required to compete against a 29th or 30th team if the Yankees and Braves do not. And Major League Baseball cannot properly be required to eliminate only teams in other states, not Florida, just because the Florida courts, unlike those of any other state, view this as an matter for resolution in an antitrust court.

In short, the various states properly cannot, in the name of state antitrust laws, impose different standards in this area. The business of baseball, including the decision to contract, is exempt from the antitrust laws, federal and state.

E. *Applying the Baseball Exemption to the CIDs at Issue*

As set forth above, the proposed contraction of Major League Baseball is exempt from the federal or state antitrust laws, and the Attorney General thus has no authority to enforce the antitrust laws against the proposed contraction or to issue CIDs as part of an investigation of whether to file an enforcement action.

VII
Remaining Issues

For purposes of plaintiffs' motion for a preliminary injunction, the record is closed, and what has been said establishes that plaintiffs are likely (indeed, virtually certain) to prevail on the merits. Plaintiffs also meet the other criteria for issuance of a preliminary injunction. A preliminary injunction therefore has been separately entered and will remain in effect in accordance with its terms. * * *

Notes and Questions

1. The district court's decision was affirmed by the United States Court of Appeals for the Eleventh Circuit as *Major League Baseball v. Crist*, 331 F.3d 1177 (11th Cir. 2003), which stated that the district court "persuasively established" that the "business of baseball" is exempt from federal antitrust laws, and concluded that the possibility of contracting the number of major league teams "implicates the heart of the 'business of baseball.'" 331 F.3d at 1183. The Eleventh Circuit went so far as to state that "the district court forcefully destroyed the notion that the antitrust exemption should be narrowly cabined to the reserve system." *Id.* at 1181 n.10. Do you agree? Who is right? Judge Padova and the Florida Supreme Court or Judge Hinkle and the Eleventh Circuit?

2. The district judge declined MLB's invitation that he rely on the Curt Flood Act as evidence that the baseball exemption is broader than player restraints:

> Thus Congress said, 'No court shall rely on the enactment of this section as a basis for changing the application of the antitrust laws to any conduct, acts, practices, or agreements other than' player issues. I take Congress at its word and resolve this case without reliance on the Curt Flood Act as affecting the outcome one way or the other.

Was it honest for MLB to attempt to rely on the Curt Flood Act when the explicit agreement between the MLB and MLBPA was that no court should rely on the Curt Flood Act for that purpose? Despite the Court's claim that it was not relying on the Curt Flood Act (which might have rendered its decision reversible on appeal), do you believe the Curt Flood Act may be considered as supporting a broad scope for the exemption?

3. If the limitation on the exemption advocated by Judge Padova is not accepted, where do the limitations proposed by Judge McDonald in the *Henderson Broadcasting* case stand?

4. There have been other baseball exemption decisions since the Curt Flood Act. In *Minnesota Twins Partnership v. Minnesota*, the Minnesota Supreme Court held that the proposed sale and relocation of the Minnesota Twins was an integral part of the business of baseball, and was therefore within the baseball exemption, and for that reason the Minnesota Attorney General could not compel compliance with subpoenas that had been issued in connection with an antitrust investigation of the transaction. *Minnesota Twins Partnership v. Minnesota*, 592 N.W.2d 847 854–56, (Minn.1999).

In another 1999 case, a Florida federal district court judge expressed doubt (to put it charitably) about the line of cases consistent with *Piazza*:

> Notwithstanding abundant and controlling federal precedent to the contrary, *Butterworth v. National League of Prof'l Baseball Clubs*, 644 So. 2d 1021 (Fla. 1994), purports to determine that professional baseball's antitrust exemption applies only to the player reserve system. Utterly foreign to the unquestionable weight of governing federal authority, this view, most charitably construed, amounts to a prediction that the Supreme Court of the United States (which, after all, determines such matters without reference to the inclinations of Florida's Supreme Court,) will recede from *Flood v. Kuhn* in due course. Perhaps so. However, the boundaries of the federal antitrust laws in general and the baseball exemption in particular are not subject to accretion or reliction in response to a change of tide at the Florida Supreme Court. * * *

Morsani v. Major League Baseball, 79 F. Supp. 2d 1331, 1335 (M.D. Fla. 1999).

In light of this case law, how would you advise MLB or an owner if they were concerned about facing an antitrust suit involving (a) restrictions on minor league players, (b) agreements restricting competition between minor league and major league teams, (c) a league decision to deny an owner's request to approve relocation of his team, (d) a league decision to reduce the number of MLB teams by two (contraction), (e) a league agreement with one national television network, giving that network exclusivity with respect to all MLB national and local games, or (f) an exclusive league sponsorship agreement with a single bat manufacturer or apparel manufacturer, only permitting players to use product from that manufacturer?

5. The Curt Flood Act also spawned an entire symposium on the Act and other law review articles. *See, e.g.,* Roger Abrams, *Before the Flood: The History of Baseball's Antitrust Exemption,* 9 MARQ. SPORTS L.J. 307 (1999); Ted Curtis, *The Flood Act's Place in Baseball Legal History,* 9 MARQ. SPORTS L.J. 403 (1999); Jennifer Dyer, *The Curt Flood Act of 1998: After 76 Years, Congress Lifts Baseball's Antitrust Exemotion on Labor Relations But Leaves Franchise Relocation Up to the Courts,* 3 T.M. Cooley J. Prac. & Clinical L. 247 (2000); Edmund Edmonds, *The Curt Flood Act of 1998: A Hollow Gesture After All These Years?* 9 MARQ. L.J. 315 (1999); J. Gordon Hylton, *Why Baseball's Antitrust Exemption Still Survives,* 9 MARQ. SPORTS L.J. 391 (1999); Joshua P. Jones, *A Congressional Swing and Miss: The Curt Flood Act, Player Control, and the National Pastime,* 33 Ga. L. Rev. 639 (1999); Lacie L. Kaiser, *Revisiting the Impact of the Curt Flood Act of 1998 on the Bargaining Relationship Between Players and Management in Major League Baseball,* DEPAUL SPORTS L.J. 230 (2004); Marianne McGettigan, *The Curt Flood Act of 1998: The Players' Perspective,* 9 MARQ. SPORTS L.J. 379 (1999); Thomas J. Ostertag, *Baseball's Antitrust Exemption: Its History and Continuing Importance,* VA. SPORTS & ENT. L.J. 54 (2004); Gary Roberts, *A Brief Appraisal of the Curt Flood Act of 1998 from the Minor League Perspective,* 9 MARQ. SPORTS L.J. 413 (1999). As you read Chapter 9 and gain an understanding of the labor exemption, ask yourself, did the MLBPA really gain any-

thing? On the other hand, does the Curt Flood Act increase the likelihood that (a) Congress will never "repeal" or eliminate the baseball exemption, (b) courts will hold that the exemption includes the "business of baseball" as broadly defined, and (c) the Supreme Court, with the congressional mandate in the Curt Flood Act that the exemption beyond the Major League reserve clause and other player restraints shall not be disturbed, will now have a basis to say that Congress has effectively considered the issue and decided that the exemption should remain in effect? Was MLB's agreement to the Curt Flood Act a major victory for the owners?

Chapter 9

Antitrust and Sports: The Labor Exemption

I. Introduction

Probably the most complex and elusive concept encountered in sports law, which extends beyond sports jurisprudence, is the labor exemption to the antitrust laws. This exemption, which insulates certain types of employer and union conduct from antitrust scrutiny, is divided into two parts: a precise, narrowly drawn statutory immunity; and a judicially constructed, amorphous non-statutory component.

The statutory exemption is embraced in Sections 6 and 20 of the Clayton Antitrust Act. CLAYTON ANTITRUST ACT, 38 STAT. 730 (1914), as amended, 15 U.S.C. § 17 (1988), 29 U.S.C. § 52 (1988). It is addressed in Part II of this chapter. The non-statutory exemption has evolved through decades of judicial precedent in which the case authority often has done more to confuse than to clarify. It will be addressed at length in Parts III to VI of this chapter.

Suffice it to say at this point that the innate tension between labor and antitrust law creates a conundrum that may make the labor exemption beyond an explication that is wholly satisfying or even mildly reassuring. The purpose of much labor legislation is to provide protection for certain collective action that in part is designed to suppress competition. Antitrust law, on the other hand, is intended to punish activity that unreasonably restrains trade and stifles competition. Therein lies the problem in attempting to devise a calculus that is sensitive to the goals of meaningful collective bargaining and healthy marketplace competition.

Notwithstanding the formidable challenge, the remainder of this chapter will attempt to outline the parameters of the labor exemption, its current application in the sports industry, and its likely impact on future antitrust litigation. In particular, the succeeding sections will trace the exemption from its statutory origins to its general non-statutory beginnings and finally to its unique implications for sports-related cases, most notably restraints in the labor market area—the market for player services. You will observe that the exemption has evolved from a concept that was applied to immunize a narrow set of labor management agreements to situations where no agreement exists and, in fact, had been resisted by one of the parties.

II.Statutory Exemption

The Clayton Act provides, in pertinent part:

> Sec. 6. The labor of a human being is not a commodity or article of commerce. Nothing contained in the antitrust laws shall be construed to forbid the existence and operation of labor, agricultural, or horticultural organizations, instituted for the purposes of mutual help, and not having capital stock or conducted for profit, or to forbid or restrain individual members of such organizations from lawfully carrying out the legitimate objects thereof; nor shall such organizations, or the members thereof, be held or construed to be illegal combinations or conspiracies in restraint of trade, under the antitrust laws.

> Sec. 20. No restraining order or injunction shall be granted by any court of the United States, or a judge or the judges thereof, in any case between an employer and employees, or between employers and employees, or between employees, or between persons employed and persons seeking employment, involving, or growing out of, a dispute concerning terms or conditions of employment, unless necessary to prevent irreparable injury to property, or to a property right, of the party making the application, for which injury there is no adequate remedy at law, and such property or property right must be described with particularity in the application, which must be in writing and sworn to by the applicant or by his agent or attorney.

> And no such restraining order or injunction shall prohibit any person or persons, whether singly or in concert, from terminating any relation of employment, or from ceasing to perform any work or labor, or from recommending, advising, or persuading others by peaceful means so to do; or from attending at any place where any such person or persons may lawfully be, for the purpose of peacefully obtaining or communicating information, or from peacefully persuading any person to work or to abstain from working; or from ceasing to patronize or to employ any party to such dispute, or from recommending, advising, or persuading others by peaceful and lawful means so to do; or from paying or giving to, or withholding from, any person engaged in such dispute, any strike benefits or other moneys or things of value; or from peaceably assembling in a lawful manner, and for lawful purposes; or from doing any act or thing which might lawfully be done in the absence of such dispute by any party thereto; nor shall any of the acts specified in this paragraph be considered or held to be violations of any law of the United States.

Clearly, this exemption, on its face, does not address combinations between labor and non-labor groups. Yet, to foster meaningful collective bargaining, some accommodation was necessary to insulate certain types of employer/employee agreements that might restrain trade in a relevant market from the reach of the antitrust laws. Enter the non-statutory exemption.

III. Non-Statutory Exemption

Clarett v. National Football League
369 F.3d 124 (2d Cir. 2004)

SOTOMAYOR, Circuit Judge:

* * *

I.

Although "the interaction of the [antitrust laws] and federal labor legislation is an area of law marked more by controversy than by clarity," *Wood v. Nat'l Basketball Ass'n, 809 F.2d 954, 959 (2d Cir. 1987)* (citing R. Gorman, *Labor Law, Unionization and Collective Bargaining* 631–35 (1976)), it has long been recognized that in order to accommodate the collective bargaining process, certain concerted activity among and between labor and employers must be held to be beyond the reach of the antitrust laws. *See United States v. Hutcheson, 312 U.S. 219; Apex Hosiery Co. v. Leader, 310 U.S. 469 (1940).* Courts, therefore, have carved out two categories of labor exemptions to the antitrust laws: the so-called statutory and non-statutory exemptions.[11] We deal here only with the non-statutory exemption.

The non-statutory exemption has been inferred "from federal labor statutes, which set forth a national labor policy favoring free and private collective bargaining; which require good-faith bargaining over wages, hours, and working conditions; and which delegate related rulemaking and interpretive authority to the National Labor Relations Board." *Brown v. Pro Football, Inc., 518 U.S. 231, 236 (1996).* The exemption exists not only to prevent the courts from usurping the NLRB's function of "determin[ing], in the area of industrial conflict, what is or is not a 'reasonable' practice," but also "to allow meaningful collective bargaining to take place" by protecting "some restraints on competition imposed through the bargaining process" from antitrust scrutiny. *Id. at 237.*

The Supreme Court has never delineated the precise boundaries of the exemption, and what guidance it has given as to its application has come mostly in cases in which agreements between an employer and a labor union were alleged to have injured or eliminated a competitor in the employer's business or product market. In the face of such allegations, the Court has largely permitted antitrust scrutiny in spite of any resulting detriment to the labor policies favoring collective bargaining.

In the first case to deal squarely with the non-statutory exemption, *Allen Bradley Co. v. Local No. 3, International Brotherhood of Electrical Workers, 325 U.S. 797 (1945)*, the New York City electrical workers union negotiated a series of agreements in which local manufacturers and contractors agreed to deal only with other manufacturers and contractors that employed the union's members. *Id. at 799–800.* A non-local manufacturer

---

11. The statutory exemption, so named because it is derived from the texts of the Clayton Act, *15 U.S.C. § 17, 29 U.S.C. § 52,* and the Norris-LaGuardia Act, *29 U.S.C. § 101 et seq.*, shields from the antitrust laws certain unilateral conduct of labor groups such as boycotts and picketing. *See H.A. Artists & Assocs., Inc. v. Actors' Equity Ass'n, 451 U.S. 704, 714–15 (1981).* Because the statutory exemption does not provide any protection for "concerted action or agreements between unions and nonlabor parties," *Connell Constr. Co. v. Plumbers & Steamfitters Local No. 100, 421 U.S. 616, 622 (1975),* the NFL does not rely on the statutory exemption in arguing that its eligibility rules are immune from the antitrust laws.

that was excluded from the market as a result successfully sued under the antitrust laws, establishing that these agreements were "but one element in a far larger program in which contractors and manufacturers united with one another to monopolize all the business in New York City, to bar all other business men from that area, and to charge the public prices above a competitive level." *Id. at 809.* Although the Court recognized that the union sought the agreements out of "a desire to get and hold jobs for themselves at good wages and under high working standards," it held that the non-statutory exemption did not apply where unions "combine with employers and with manufacturers of goods to restrain competition in, and to monopolize the marketing of, such goods." *Id. at 798.*

Twenty years later, the Court considered two cases dealing with the non-statutory exemption. Although the Court again refused to apply the non-statutory exemption in the first, *United Mine Workers v. Pennington, 381 U.S. 657 (1965)*, it did apply the exemption in *Local No. 189, Amalgamated Meat Cutters & Butcher Workmen v. Jewel Tea Co., 381 U.S. 676 (1965)*. In *Pennington*, a small coal mine operator claimed that a miners union violated the antitrust laws by agreeing with large coal mine companies that the union would demand a higher wage scale from small coal mine operators in an effort to drive the small mine operators from the market. Echoing its decision in *Allen Bradley*, the Court held that while "a union may make wage agreements with a multi-employer bargaining unit and may in pursuance of its own union interests seek to obtain the same terms from other employers" without incurring antitrust liability, "a union forfeits its exemption from the antitrust laws when it is clearly shown that it has agreed with one set of employers to impose a certain wage scale on other bargaining units." *Pennington, 381 U.S. at 665.*

The Court, however, reached a different result in *Jewel Tea*, which involved a challenge to a collective bargaining agreement between the butchers union and meat sellers in Chicago, whereby the meat sellers agreed to limit the operation of meat counters to certain hours. *See Jewel Tea, 381 U.S. at 679–80.* The union sought the restriction not only to cabin the hours in the workday but also to diminish the threat posed to members' job security by evening sales of prepackaged meat and the nighttime use of unskilled labor. *Id. at 682.* Jewel Tea was one of the meat sellers that signed the agreement. It did so, however, only under pressure from the union and then challenged the hours restriction on antitrust grounds. Jewel Tea notably did not allege that the hours restriction eliminated competition among the meat sellers that made up the bargaining unit or that the union sought the hours restriction from Jewel Tea at the behest of other meat sellers. *Id. at 688.*

A majority of the Court agreed that the hours restriction fell within the non-statutory exemption, but the Justices disagreed as to the reason for applying the exemption. Justice White, writing for himself and two other Justices, advocated that the application of the non-statutory exemption should be determined by balancing the "interests of union members" served by the restraint against "its relative impact on the product market." *Id. at 690 n.5.* Applying that test, Justice White held that the hours restriction was

> so intimately related to wages, hours and working conditions that the unions' successful attempt to obtain that provision through bona fide, arm's-length bargaining in pursuit of their own labor union policies, and not at the behest of or in combination with nonlabor groups, falls within the protection of the national labor policy and is therefore exempt from the Sherman Act.

Id. at 689–90.[12]

Concurring in *Jewel Tea* but dissenting in *Pennington*, Justice Goldberg, writing for himself and two Justices, found that no such balancing was necessary. Because federal labor law obligates the union and employer to bargain in good faith and permits unions to strike over those issues that relate to workers' wages, hours, or terms and conditions of employment, Justice Goldberg found that it would "stultify the congressional scheme" to expose collective bargaining agreements on these so-called mandatory bargaining subjects to antitrust liability. *Id. at 712.* Therefore, according to Justice Goldberg, all "collective bargaining activity concerning mandatory subjects of bargaining under the [labor laws] is not subject to the antitrust laws." *Id. at 710.*

Another ten years later, in *Connell Construction Co. v. Plumbers & Steamfitters Local Union No. 100, 421 U.S. 616 (1975),* the Court held the non-statutory exemption did not protect a union's agreement with a contractor that bound the contractor to deal only with subcontractors that employed the union's members. The challenged agreement was not a collective bargaining agreement, and the union did not represent the contractor's employees; rather, the contractor acceded to the agreement only after the union picketed one of its facilities. *Id. at 619.* The Court refused to apply the exemption to this "kind of direct restraint on the business market[, which] has substantial anticompetitive effects, both actual and potential, that would not follow naturally from the elimination of competition over wages and working conditions." *Id. at 625.*

* * *

Notes and Questions

1. The foregoing synopsis by the Second Circuit provides a workable overview of the development of the labor exemption outside of the sports industry. It, by no means, addresses every permutation and combination of the nebulous calculus that has evolved. Moreover, most of the non-sports precedent that informed the early construction of the labor exemption involved alleged restraints in a product, as opposed to a labor, market. Parenthetically, and as will be discussed later in this chapter, this fact could call into question the utility of relying upon the early cases in ascertaining the availability of the exemption in the unique labor market context. *See Brown v. Pro-Football, Inc.,* 50 F. 3d 1041 (D.C. Cir. 1955), *aff'd,* 518 U.S. 231 (1996), and the notes that follow in Part VI. Pay particular attention to the context in which Justice Goldberg offered his straightforward concurrence in *Jewel Tea* and draw your own conclusions as to whether he would approve of its application in the *Brown*-type scenario. Justice Stevens's dissent may be illuminating in that respect.

2. Consider this evolution of the non-statutory exemption as you read the following cases that apply the foregoing principles to the unique circumstances prevailing in the sports industry. Proceeding through the various scenarios presented in the remainder of this chapter, assess whether the idiosyncrasies of sport and the prevalence of labor market restraints affecting professional athletes warrant a retooling of the exemption as it has emerged.

---

12. When confronted with allegations that agreements between labor and employers damaged competition in the business or product market, we have previously regarded Justice White's decision in *Jewel Tea* as setting forth the "classic formulation" of the non–statutory exemption. See *Local 210 v. Associated Gen. Contractors of Am.,* 844 F.2d 69, 79 (2d Cir. 1988); *Berman Enterprises, Inc. v. Local 333, United Marine Div.,* 644 F.2d 930, 935 n.8 (2d Cir. 1981).

IV. Application of the Labor Exemption to Professional Sports

Mackey v. National Football League

543 F.2d 606 (8th Cir. 1976)

LAY, Circuit Judge. This is an appeal by the National Football League (NFL), twenty-six of its member clubs, and its Commissioner, Alvin Ray "Pete" Rozelle, from a district court judgment holding the "Rozelle Rule" to be violative of §1 of the Sherman Act, and enjoining its enforcement.

This action was initiated by a group of present and former NFL players, appellees herein, pursuant to §§4 and 16 of the Clayton Act, 15 U.S.C. §§15 and 26, and §1 of the Sherman Act, 15 U.S.C. §1. Their complaint alleged that the defendants' enforcement of the Rozelle Rule constituted an illegal combination and conspiracy in restraint of trade denying professional football players the right to freely contract for their services. Plaintiffs sought injunctive relief and treble damages.

The district court, the Honorable Earl R. Larson presiding, conducted a plenary trial which consumed 55 days and produced a transcript in excess of 11,000 pages. At the conclusion of trial, the court entered extensive findings of fact and conclusions of law. The court granted the injunctive relief sought by the players and entered judgment in their favor on the issue of liability. This appeal followed.

The district court held that the defendants' enforcement of the Rozelle Rule constituted a concerted refusal to deal and a group boycott, and was therefore a per se violation of the Sherman Act. Alternatively, finding that the evidence offered in support of the clubs' contention that the Rozelle Rule is necessary to the successful operation of the NFL insufficient to justify the restrictive effects of the Rule, the court concluded that the Rozelle Rule was invalid under the Rule of Reason standard. Finally, the court rejected the clubs' argument that the Rozelle Rule was immune from attack under the Sherman Act because it had been the subject of a collective bargaining agreement between the club owners and the National Football League Players Association (NFLPA).

The defendants raise two basic issues on this appeal: (1) whether the so-called labor exemption to the antitrust laws immunizes the NFL's enforcement of the Rozelle Rule from antitrust liability; and (2) if not, whether the Rozelle Rule and the manner in which it has been enforced violate the antitrust laws. Ancillary to these contentions, appellants attack a number of the district court's findings of fact and raise several subsidiary issues.

HISTORY

* * *

Throughout most of its history, the NFL's operations have been unilaterally controlled by the club owners. In 1968, however, the NLRB recognized the NFLPA as a labor organization, within the meaning of 29 U.S.C. §152(5), and as the exclusive bargaining representative of all NFL players, within the meaning of 29 U.S.C. §159(a). Since that time, the NFLPA and the clubs have engaged in collective bargaining over various terms and conditions of employment. Two formal agreements have resulted. The first, concluded in 1968, was in effect from July 15, 1968 to February 1, 1970. The second, entered into on June 17, 1971, was made retroactive to February 1, 1970, and expired on January 30, 1974. Since 1974, the parties have been negotiating; however, they have not concluded a new agreement.

For a number of years, the NFL has operated under a reserve system whereby every player who signs a contract with an NFL club is bound to play for that club, and no other, for the term of the contract plus one additional year at the option of the club. The cornerstones of this system are §15.1 of the NFL Constitution and Bylaws, which requires that all club-player contracts be as prescribed in the Standard Player Contract adopted by the League, and the option clause embodied in the Standard Player Contract. Once a player signs a Standard Player Contract, he is bound to his team for at least two years. He may, however, become a free agent at the end of the option year by playing that season under a renewed contract rather than signing a new one. A player "playing out his option" is subject to a 10% salary cut during the option year.

Prior to 1963, a team which signed a free agent who had previously been under contract to another club was not obligated to compensate the player's former club. In 1963, after R. C. Owens played out his option with the San Francisco 49ers and signed a contract with the Baltimore Colts, the member clubs of the NFL unilaterally adopted the following provision, now known as the Rozelle Rule, as an amendment to the League's Constitution and Bylaws:

> Any player, whose contract with a League club has expired, shall thereupon become a free agent and shall no longer be considered a member of the team of that club following the expiration date of such contract. Whenever a player, becoming a free agent in such manner, thereafter signed a contract with a different club in the League, then, unless mutually satisfactory arrangements have been concluded between the two League clubs, the Commissioner may name and then award to the former club one or more players, from the Active, Reserve, or Selection List (including future selection choices) of the acquiring club as the Commissioner in his sole discretion deems fair and equitable; any such decision by the Commissioner shall be final and conclusive.

This provision, unchanged in form, is currently embodied in §12.1(H) of the NFL Constitution. The ostensible purposes of the rule are to maintain competitive balance among the NFL teams and protect the clubs' investment in scouting, selecting and developing players.

During the period from 1963 through 1974, 176 players played out their options. Of that number, 34 signed with other teams. In three of those cases, the former club waived compensation. In 27 cases, the clubs involved mutually agreed upon compensation. Commissioner Rozelle awarded compensation in the four remaining cases.

We turn now to the contentions of the parties.

THE LABOR EXEMPTION ISSUE

We review first the claim that the labor exemption immunizes the Commissioner and the clubs from liability under the antitrust laws. Analysis of this contention requires a basic understanding of the legal principles surrounding the labor exemption and consideration of the factual record developed at trial.

History.

The concept of a labor exemption from the antitrust laws finds its basic source in §§6 and 20 of the Clayton Act, 15 U.S.C. §17 and 29 U.S.C. §52, and the Norris-LaGuardia

Act, 29 U.S.C. §§104, 105 and 113. Those provisions declare that labor unions are not combinations or conspiracies in restraint of trade, and specifically exempt certain union activities such as secondary picketing and group boycotts from the coverage of the antitrust laws. The statutory exemption was created to insulate legitimate collective activity by employees, which is inherently anticompetitive but is favored by federal labor policy, from the proscriptions of the antitrust laws.

The statutory exemption extends to legitimate labor activities unilaterally undertaken by a union in furtherance of its own interests. It does not extend to concerted action or agreements between unions and non-labor groups. The Supreme Court has held, however, that in order to properly accommodate the congressional policy favoring free competition in business markets with the congressional policy favoring collective bargaining under the National Labor Relations Act, certain union-employer agreements must be accorded a limited nonstatutory exemption from antitrust sanctions.

The players assert that only employee groups are entitled to the labor exemption and that it cannot be asserted by the defendants, an employer group. We must disagree. Since the basis of the nonstatutory exemption is the national policy favoring collective bargaining, and since the exemption extends to agreements, the benefits of the exemption logically extend to both parties to the agreement. Accordingly, under appropriate circumstances, we find that a non-labor group may avail itself of the labor exemption. * * *

The clubs and the Commissioner claim the benefit of the nonstatutory labor exemption here, arguing that the Rozelle Rule was the subject of an agreement with the players union and that the proper accommodation of federal labor and antitrust policies requires that the agreement be deemed immune from antitrust liability. The plaintiffs assert that the Rozelle Rule was the product of unilateral action by the clubs and that the defendants cannot assert a colorable claim of exemption.

To determine the applicability of the nonstatutory exemption we must first decide whether there has been any agreement between the parties concerning the Rozelle Rule.

The Collective Bargaining Agreements.

The district court found that neither the 1968 nor the 1970 collective bargaining agreement embodied an agreement on the Rozelle Rule, and that the union has never otherwise agreed to the Rule. Ordinarily, we review findings of fact under the clearly erroneous standard. F.R.C.P. 52(a). We note, however, that to the extent that these findings turn upon a construction of the parties' collective bargaining agreements, which are before this court, we are not required to defer to the interpretation given them by the district court. We look, then, to the parties' collective bargaining history.

The 1968 Agreement.

At the outset of the negotiations preceding the 1968 agreement, the players did not seek elimination of the Rozelle Rule but felt that it should be modified. During the course of the negotiations, however, the players apparently presented no concrete proposals in that regard and there was little discussion concerning the Rozelle Rule. At trial, Daniel Shulman, a bargaining representative of the players, attributed their failure to pursue any modifications to the fact that the negotiations had bogged down on other issues and the union was not strong enough to persist.

The 1968 agreement incorporated by reference the NFL Constitution and Bylaws, of which the Rozelle Rule is a part. Furthermore, it expressly provided that free agent rules shall not be amended during the life of the agreement.

The 1970 Agreement.

At the start of the negotiations leading up to the 1970 agreement, it appears that the players again decided not to make an issue of the Rozelle Rule. The only reference to the Rule in the union's formal proposals presented at the outset of the negotiations was the following:

> The NFLPA is disturbed over reports from players who, after playing out their options, are unable to deal with other clubs because of the Rozelle Rule. A method should be found whereby a free agent is assured the opportunity to discuss contract with all NFL teams.

There was little discussion of the Rozelle Rule during the 1970 negotiations. Although the 1970 agreement failed to make any express reference to the Rozelle Rule, it did contain a "zipper clause":

> (T)his Agreement represents a complete and final understanding on all bargainable subjects of negotiation among the parties during the term of this Agreement* * *

While the agreement did not expressly incorporate by reference the terms of the NFL Constitution and Bylaws, it did require all players to sign the Standard Player Contract, and provided that the Standard Contract shall govern the relationship between the clubs and the players. The Standard Player Contract, in turn, provided that the player agreed at all times to comply with and be bound by the NFL Constitution and Bylaws. At trial, Tex Schramm, a bargaining representative of the club owners, and Alan Miller, a bargaining representative of the players, testified that it was their understanding that the Rozelle Rule would remain in effect during the term of the 1970 agreement.

Since the beginning of the 1974 negotiations, the players have consistently sought the elimination of the Rozelle Rule. The NFLPA and the clubs have engaged in substantial bargaining over that issue but have not reached an accord. Nor have they concluded a collective bargaining agreement to replace the 1970 agreement which expired in 1974.

Based on the fact that the 1968 agreement incorporated by reference the Rozelle Rule and provided that free agent rules would not be changed, we conclude that the 1968 agreement required that the Rozelle Rule govern when a player played out his option and signed with another team. Assuming, without deciding, that the 1970 agreement embodied a similar understanding, we proceed to a consideration of whether the agreements fall within the scope of the nonstatutory labor exemption.

Governing Principles.

Under the general principles surrounding the labor exemption, the availability of the nonstatutory exemption for a particular agreement turns upon whether the relevant federal labor policy is deserving of pre-eminence over federal antitrust policy under the circumstances of the particular case. * * *

Although the cases giving rise to the nonstatutory exemption are factually dissimilar from the present case, certain principles can be deduced from those decisions governing the proper accommodation of the competing labor and antitrust interests involved here.

We find the proper accommodation to be: First, the labor policy favoring collective bargaining may potentially be given pre-eminence over the antitrust laws where the restraint on trade primarily affects only the parties to the collective bargaining relationship. * * * Second, federal labor policy is implicated sufficiently to prevail only where the agreement sought to be exempted concerns a mandatory subject of collective bargaining. * * * Finally, the policy favoring collective bargaining is furthered to the degree necessary to override the antitrust laws only where the agreement sought to be exempted is the product of bona fide arm's-length bargaining. * * *

Application.

Applying these principles to the facts presented here, we think it clear that the alleged restraint on trade effected by the Rozelle Rule affects only the parties to the agreements sought to be exempted. Accordingly, we must inquire as to the other two principles: whether the Rozelle Rule is a mandatory subject of collective bargaining, and whether the agreements thereon were the product of bona fide arm's-length negotiation.

Mandatory Subject of Bargaining.

Under §8(d) of the National Labor Relations Act, 29 U.S.C. §158(d), mandatory subjects of bargaining pertain to "wages, hours, and other terms and conditions of employment* * *." See NLRB v. Borg-Warner Corp., 356 U.S. 342 (1958). Whether an agreement concerns a mandatory subject depends not on its form but on its practical effect* * *. Thus, in Meat Cutters v. Jewel Tea, the Court held that an agreement limiting retail marketing hours concerned a mandatory subject because it affected the particular hours of the day which the employees would be required to work. In Teamsters Union v. Oliver, 358 U.S. 283 (1959), an agreement fixing minimum equipment rental rates paid to truck owner-drivers was held to concern a mandatory bargaining subject because it directly affected the driver wage scale.

In this case the district court held that, in view of the illegality of the Rozelle Rule under the Sherman Act, it was "a nonmandatory, illegal subject of bargaining." We disagree. The labor exemption presupposes a violation of the antitrust laws. To hold that a subject relating to wages, hours and working conditions becomes nonmandatory by virtue of its illegality under the antitrust laws obviates the labor exemption. We conclude that whether the agreements here in question relate to a mandatory subject of collective bargaining should be determined solely under federal labor law.* * *

On its face, the Rozelle Rule does not deal with "wages, hours and other terms or conditions of employment" but with inter-team compensation when a player's contractual obligation to one team expires and he is signed by another. Viewed as such, it would not constitute a mandatory subject of collective bargaining. The district court found, however, that the Rule operates to restrict a player's ability to move from one team to another and depresses player salaries. There is substantial evidence in the record to support these findings. Accordingly, we hold that the Rozelle Rule constitutes a mandatory bargaining subject within the meaning of the National Labor Relations Act.

Bona Fide Bargaining.

The district court found that the parties' collective bargaining history reflected nothing which could be legitimately characterized as bargaining over the Rozelle Rule; that, in part due to its recent formation and inadequate finances, the NFLPA, at least prior to 1974, stood in a relatively weak bargaining position vis-à-vis the clubs; and that "the Rozelle Rule was unilaterally imposed by the NFL and member club defendants upon the players in 1963 and has been imposed on the players from 1963 through the present date."

On the basis of our independent review of the record, including the parties' bargaining history as set forth above, we find substantial evidence to support the finding that there was no bona fide arm's-length bargaining over the Rozelle Rule preceding the execution of the 1968 and 1970 agreements. The Rule imposes significant restrictions on players, and its form has remained unchanged since it was unilaterally promulgated by the clubs in 1963. The provisions of the collective bargaining agreements which operated to continue the Rozelle Rule do not in and of themselves inure to the benefit of the players or their union. Defendants contend that the players derive indirect benefit from the Rozelle Rule, claiming that the union's agreement to the Rozelle Rule was a *quid pro quo* for increased pension benefits and the right of players to individually negotiate their salaries. The district court found, however, that there was no such *quid pro quo*, and we cannot say, on the basis of our review of the record, that this finding is clearly erroneous.

In view of the foregoing, we hold that the agreements between the clubs and the players embodying the Rozelle Rule do not qualify for the labor exemption. The union's acceptance of the status quo by the continuance of the Rozelle Rule in the initial collective bargaining agreements under the circumstances of this case cannot serve to immunize the Rozelle Rule from the scrutiny of the Sherman Act.[18]

CONCLUSION

In conclusion, although we find that non-labor parties may potentially avail themselves of the nonstatutory labor exemption where they are parties to collective bargaining agreements pertaining to mandatory subjects of bargaining, the exemption cannot be invoked where, as here, the agreement was not the product of bona fide arm's-length negotiations. Thus, the defendants' enforcement of the Rozelle Rule is not exempt from the coverage of the antitrust laws. Although we disagree with the district court's determination that the Rozelle Rule is a *per se* violation of the antitrust laws, we do find that the Rule, as implemented, contravenes the Rule of Reason and thus constitutes an unreasonable restraint of trade in violation of §1 of the Sherman Act.

We note that our disposition of the antitrust issue does not mean that every restraint on competition for players' services would necessarily violate the antitrust laws. Also, since the Rozelle Rule, as implemented, concerns a mandatory subject of collective bargaining, any agreement as to interteam compensation for free agents moving to other teams, reached through good faith collective bargaining, might very well be immune from antitrust liability under the nonstatutory labor exemption.

It may be that some reasonable restrictions relating to player transfers are necessary for the successful operation of the NFL. The protection of mutual interests of both the players and the clubs may indeed require this. We encourage the parties to resolve this question through collective bargaining. The parties are far better situated to agreeably resolve what rules governing player transfers are best suited for their mutual interests than are the courts. However, no mutual resolution of this issue appears within the present record. Therefore, the Rozelle Rule, as it is presently implemented, must be set aside as an unreasonable restraint of trade.

With the exception of the district court's finding that implementation of the Rozelle Rule constitutes a *per se* violation of §1 of the Sherman Act and except as it is otherwise modified herein, the judgment of the district court is AFFIRMED. The cause is remanded to the district court for further proceedings consistent with this opinion.

---

18. 8 In view of our holding, we need not decide whether the effect of an agreement extends beyond its formal expiration date for purposes of the labor exemption.

Notes and Questions

1. Those already familiar with the most recent developments in the labor exemption saga (see Part VI of this chapter) may question the continued viability of *Mackey*. The response is two-fold. A consideration of *Mackey* has historical value and, along with the next case, provides the background necessary to comprehend fully the extent of the exemption's evolution thereby representing more than a mere academic curiosity. Of greater importance, there is language in the Supreme Court's most recent iteration of the exemption, *Brown v. Pro-Football, Inc.*, 518 U.S. 231 (1996), suggesting strongly that the heart of *Mackey* has not been disturbed. *See* Notes and Questions following *Clarett v. NFL, infra*, at the conclusion of this chapter. Moreover, given the arcane and mercurial nature of the exemption and the questions that it continues to provoke a revisitation of the exemption and the assessment of the Supreme Court's pronouncement is not beyond the realm of possibility. For these reasons, *Mackey* and *Powell* (following below) and the questions that they spawn are worthy of attention.

2. Is *Mackey* limited to restraints involving the labor market? Does the significance of the test lie in the fact that it is uniquely suited to restrictions upon player mobility, particularly where the players' collective bargaining representative is an unwilling partner?

3. In *McCourt v. California Sports, Inc.*, 600 F.2d 1193, 1198 (6th Cir. 1979), the Sixth Circuit expressly acknowledged that the proper labor exemption standards are set out in *Mackey*, but concluded:

> We believe that in holding that the reserve system had not been the subject of good faith, arm's length bargaining, the trial court failed to recognize the well-established principle that nothing in the labor law compels either party negotiating over mandatory subjects of collective bargaining to yield on its initial bargaining position. Good faith bargaining is all that is required. That the position of one party on an issue prevails unchanged does not mandate the conclusion that there was no collective bargaining over the issue.* * *
>
> From the express findings of the trial court, fully supported by the record, it is apparent that the inclusion of the reserve system in the collective bargaining agreement was the product of good faith, arm's-length bargaining, and that what the trial court saw as a failure to negotiate was in fact simply the failure to succeed, after the most intensive negotiations, in keeping an unwanted provision out of the contract. This failure was a part of and not apart from the collective bargaining process, a process which achieved its ultimate objective of an agreement accepted by the parties.

600 F.2d at 1200, 1203. What is the relevance of the *Mackey* test's third prong (*bona fide* bargaining)? Does it unnecessarily and inappropriately merge the antitrust exemption inquiry with an assessment of the conduct's legitimacy under the labor laws? Should the collective bargaining strength of the labor organization be deemed pertinent in any equation employed to ascertain the applicability of the labor exemption? Is it safe to say that, given the state of the labor organizations and collective bargaining in most professional sports, conduct that satisfies the first two prongs of *Mackey* (conduct primarily affects only the parties to the collective bargaining relationship and the agreement concerns a mandatory bargaining subject) will be exempt from antitrust scrutiny? Does *McCourt* suggest that a sophisticated labor negotiator, who discusses all issues and refuses to yield on any significant issue, will nevertheless satisfy the third prong? Does an affirmative answer signify that the third

prong is merely a trap for the unwary, naïve, or inexperienced league and players association representatives?

4. As a practical matter, has the emergence of professional sports unions rendered the third prong nugatory? *See generally* Richard E. Bartok, *NFL Free Agency Restrictions Under Antitrust Attack*, 2 DUKE L.J. 503 (1991).

5. In *McCourt*, Judge Edwards dissented, declaring in relevant part: "I do reject one feature of the *Mackey* and *Reynolds* decisions upon which the majority relies. The fact that a particular provision restricting competition is a mandatory subject of collective bargaining and has been agreed upon by management and labor in a collective bargaining contract does not necessarily exempt the restriction from the Sherman Act." Is he suggesting that the majority opinion has *de facto* accepted the rationale articulated by Justice Goldberg in the *Jewel Tea* case? Is he right?

6. Judge Edwards, in his *McCourt* dissent, reasoned that "[t]he antitrust laws were adopted to protect the free enterprise system and the general public. It is easy to postulate situations where the profit interests of capital and the wage-hour interests of labor could be mutually served by introducing into collective bargaining agreements restrictions upon competition which are greatly contrary to the public interest and have nothing to do with the labor interests protected by the Clayton and Norris-LaGuardia Acts * * *." Does this comment in one fell swoop expose the frailties of Justice Goldberg's approach?

7. One question raised by the first prong of *Mackey* (restraint primarily affects only the parties to the collective bargaining relationship) was whether future members of the union are deemed to be parties. In *Wood v. National Basketball Association*, 809 F.2d 954 (2d Cir. 1987), Cal. State Fullerton's Leon Wood was subject to the NBA draft and other restraints starting in 1984. He brought an antitrust challenge against those restraints, which were part of the collective bargaining agreement (through a "Memorandum of Understanding") that had been reached between the NBA and the National Basketball Players Association ("NBPA") in 1983. Wood was a member of the gold medal-winning United States Olympic basketball team and a first round draft pick of the Philadelphia 76ers. The NBA-NBPA collective bargaining agreement provided for a cap on team salaries, such that "a team that has reached its maximum allowable team salary may sign a first round draft choice like Wood only to a one-year contract for $75,000." 809 F.2d at 957. Wood, among other things, sought damages to compensate him for the difference between his salary and the salary that he would have received in a market of free competition among the NBA teams. Wood claimed that he could challenge the salary cap, draft, and other restraints because he was not a party to those restraints—he was still in college and was therefore not a member of the NBPA in 1983. Both the district court and the court of appeals held that the NBA-NBPA agreements were labor exempt because of their view that to hold otherwise would subvert federal labor policy and long-term collective bargaining agreements. *Wood v. National Basketball Association*, 602 F.Supp. 525 (S.D.N.Y. 1984), *aff'd*, 809 F.2d 954 (2d Cir. 1987). *Wood* involved salary caps applicable to all players. What would be the effect of rookie salary caps (in more recent NBA and NFL collective bargaining agreements) that benefit all members of the union and only restrict future members? Historically, league management has been successful in making small concessions that benefit current players in return for restrictions on future players who have no voting franchises when the agreement is approved. For example, the 1982 NFL-NFLPA collective bargaining agreement expired in 1987, with one exception—the 1982 agreement authorized the NFL draft for ten years. Therefore, in 1982, NFL players received certain concessions in return for agreeing that the NFL

could impose restrictions on future NFL players who were in the sixth grade at the time that the agreement was signed. Should those restrictions be exempt? This issue is joined in the Notes and Questions following *Clarett v. NFL,* 369 F. 3d 124 (2d Cir. 2004), *infra,* Part VI.

8. The courts in *Mackey* and *McCourt* were not presented with the thorny issue of whether to apply the non-statutory labor exemption to conduct, the subject of which at one time had been included in collective bargaining agreements now expired. The following case and the cases discussed in the *Notes and Questions* that follow, addressed that issue directly. While the decisions achieved no real consensus, their conclusions harbored profound consequences for the affected professional sports and set the stage for the Supreme Court's subsequent consideration of the *Brown* case.

V. Availability and Scope of the Exemption When the Collective Bargaining Agreement Expires

Powell v. National Football League
930 F.2d 1293 (8th Cir. 1989)

GIBSON, Circuit Judge. The National Football League appeals from a district court order which denied the League's motion for partial summary judgment, ruling that the nonstatutory labor exemption to the antitrust laws expires when, as here, the parties have reached "impasse" in negotiations following the conclusion of a collective bargaining agreement. This antitrust action was brought by Marvin Powell, eight other professional football players, and the players' collective bargaining representative, the National Football League Players Association (hereinafter the "Players"). Although this action also includes claims that both the League's college draft and its continued adherence to its uniform Player Contract constitute unlawful player restraints, the only League practice at issue in this interlocutory appeal is that provision of the Players' collective bargaining agreement establishing a "Right of First Refusal/Compensation" system. These employment terms restrict the ability of players to sign with other teams, a right commonly termed "free agency." On appeal, the League contends that the challenged practices are the product of bona fide, arm's-length collective bargaining and therefore are governed by federal labor law to the exclusion of challenge under the Sherman Act, 15 U.S.C. §§1–7 (1982). The Players, on the other hand, argue that the labor exemption to the antitrust laws expires when parties reach "impasse" in negotiations, and that the First Refusal/Compensation system therefore may be challenged as an unlawful restraint of trade. As we conclude that this action is at present governed by federal labor law, and not antitrust law, we reverse.

* * *

Now that the 1982 Agreement is terminated, however, we must decide whether the nonstatutory labor exemption has also expired or, alternatively, whether under the circumstances of this case the exemption continues to protect the League from potential antitrust liability.

The district court adopted "impasse" as the point at which the nonstatutory labor exemption expires, holding that "once the parties reach impasse concerning player restraint provisions, those provisions will lose their immunity and further imposition of those conditions may result in antitrust liability." The court reasoned that its impasse standard "respects the labor law obligation to bargain in good faith over mandatory bargaining subjects following expiration of a collective bargaining agreement," and that it "promotes the collective bargaining relationship and enhances prospects that the parties will reach compromise on the issue." *Powell I*, 678 F.Supp. at 789. The League attacks the district court's standard as providing a union, such as the Players, with undue motivation to generate impasse in order to pursue an antitrust suit for treble damages. * * *

The Players contend that we should accept the district court's impasse test as "inherently balanced." For support, the Players cite the language of *Bridgeman v. National Basketball Association*, 675 F.Supp. 960 (D.N.J.1987), which involved a challenge by professional basketball players to the National Basketball Association's college player draft, salary cap, and right of first refusal:

> Impasse is certainly a plausible point at which to end the labor exemption, for by its very definition it implies a deadlock in negotiations, which could in some cases imply that the employees' consent to the restraints of the prior agreement has ended. The moment of impasse in negotiations is significant, for an employer may, after bargaining with the union to impasse, make "unilateral changes that are reasonably comprehended within his pre-impasse proposals."

* * * *Bridgeman* held that the labor exemption survives "only as long as the employer continues to impose that restriction unchanged, and reasonably believes that the practice or a close variant of it will be incorporated in the next collective bargaining agreement." * * * The Players argue that *Bridgeman* rejected the impasse test, at least in part, on a belief that the labor exemption could expire prior to impasse:

> Because an impasse occurs only when the entire negotiating process has come to a standstill, the prospects for incorporating a particular practice into a collective bargaining agreement may also disappear before a full impasse in the negotiations is actually reached.

* * * The *Bridgeman* standard was rejected by the district court as not giving proper regard to the labor law policy promoting the collective bargaining process, in that this standard would encourage employees to exhibit steadfast, uncompromising adherence to stated terms. * * * Instead, the district court suggested that its impasse standard strikes an appropriate balance between labor policy and antitrust policy:

> By allowing a labor exemption to survive only until impasse, the law will not insulate a practice from antitrust scrutiny, but will only delay enforcement of the substantive law until continued negotiations over the challenged provision become pointless. * * *

Our evaluation of the district court's impasse standard cannot proceed without a firm appreciation of the remedies available under the federal labor laws to the parties involved in labor negotiations or disputes. After the expiration of a collective bargaining agreement, a comprehensive array of labor law principles govern union and employer conduct. For both sides, there is a continuing obligation to bargain. * * * Before the parties reach impasse in negotiations, employers are obligated to "maintain the status quo as to wages and working conditions." * * * Such conduct is often conducive to further collective bargaining and to stable, peaceful labor relations. * * * After impasse, an employer's continued adherence to the status quo is authorized. At the same time, once an impasse in bargaining is established, employers become entitled to implement new or different employment terms that are reasonably contemplated within the scope of their pre-impasse proposals. * * * If employers exceed their labor law rights in implementing employment terms at impasse, the full range of labor law rights and remedies is available to unions.

The Supreme Court has recognized that disputes over employment terms and conditions are not the central focus of the Sherman Act. For example, in holding that a union did not have standing to assert antitrust claims against a multi-employer bargaining association with which it had a collective bargaining relationship, the Court stated that Congress has developed "a separate body of labor law specifically designed to protect and encourage the organizational and representational activities of labor unions." * * * Under these laws, a union "will frequently not be part of the class the Sherman Act was designed to protect, especially in disputes with employers with whom it bargains." * * * In this context, we must decide the extent to which a labor union may employ the antitrust laws to attack restraints imposed by management which are derived from an expired collective bargaining agreement. * * *

Other courts have concluded that in certain circumstances labor market restraints imposed in a collective bargaining context do not raise Sherman Act issues * * *

While the League invites us to read these cases as establishing a rule to the effect that the Sherman Act is concerned only with product markets and not those for player services, we need not read them so broadly. We do, however, interpret them as precedent supporting the proposition that, in certain circumstances, such as in this case, the nonstatutory labor exemption may be invoked even after a collective bargaining agreement has expired.

Our reading of the authorities leads us to conclude that the League and the Players have not yet reached the point in negotiations where it would be appropriate to permit an action under the Sherman Act. The district court's impasse standard treats a lawful stage of the collective bargaining process as misconduct by defendants, and in this way conflicts with federal labor laws that establish the collective bargaining process, under the supervision of the National Labor Relations Board, as the method for resolution of labor disputes.

In particular, the federal labor laws provide the opposing parties to a labor dispute with offsetting tools, both economic and legal, through which they may seek resolution of their dispute. A union may choose to strike the employer, * * * and the employer may in turn opt to lock out its employees. * * * Further, either side may petition the National Labor Relations Board and seek, for example, a cease-and-desist order prohibiting conduct constituting an unfair labor practice. * * * To now allow the Players to pursue an action for treble damages under the Sherman Act would, we conclude, improperly upset the careful balance established by Congress through the labor law. * * *

The labor arena is one with well established rules which are intended to foster negotiated settlements rather than intervention by the courts. The League and the Players have accepted this "level playing field" as the basis for their often tempestuous relationship, and we believe that there is substantial justification for requiring the parties to continue to fight on it, so that bargaining and the exertion of economic force may be used to bring about legitimate compromise.

The First Refusal/Compensation system, a mandatory subject of collective bargaining, was twice set forth in collective bargaining agreements negotiated in good faith and at arm's-length. Following the expiration of the 1982 Agreement, the challenged restraints were imposed by the League only after they had been forwarded in negotiations and subsequently rejected by the Players. The Players do not contend that these proposals were put forward by the League in bad faith. We therefore hold that the present lawsuit cannot be maintained under the Sherman Act. Importantly, this does not entail that once a union and management enter into collective bargaining, management is forever exempt from the antitrust laws, and we do not hold that restraints on player services can never offend the Sherman Act. We believe, however, that the nonstatutory labor exemption protects agreements conceived in an ongoing collective bargaining relationship from challenges under the antitrust laws. "[N]ational labor policy should sometimes override antitrust policy," * * * and we believe that this case presents just such an occasion.

Upon the facts currently presented by this case, we are not compelled to look into the future and pick a termination point for the labor exemption. The parties are now faced with several choices. They may bargain further, which we would strongly urge that they do. They may resort to economic force. And finally, if appropriate issues arise, they may present claims to the National Labor Relations Board. We are satisfied that as long as there is a possibility that proceedings may be commenced before the Board, or until final resolution of Board proceedings and appeals therefrom, the labor relationship continues and the labor exemption applies. Since the matter before us concerns an interlocutory appeal, we need not decide issues left unresolved by this opinion.

III.

In sum, we hold that the antitrust laws are inapplicable under the circumstances of this case as the nonstatutory labor exemption extends beyond impasse. We reverse the order of the district court and remand the case with instructions to enter judgment in defendants' favor on Counts I, II, and VIII of plaintiffs' amended complaint.

HEANEY, Senior Circuit Judge, dissenting.

Today, the majority permits the owners to violate the antitrust laws indefinitely. Because such a result is not justified by the labor laws, I dissent. * * *

The majority purports to reject the owners' argument that the labor exemption in this case continues indefinitely. The practical effect of the majority's opinion, however, is just that—because the labor exemption will continue until the bargaining relationship is terminated either by a NLRB decertification proceeding or by abandonment of bargaining rights by the union. The majority asserts that the players can seek a cease and desist order from the NLRB to prohibit conduct constituting an unfair labor practice. Implicit in this assertion is the idea that it may be an unfair labor practice for employers to insist on a package of player restraints which violate the antitrust laws. The problem is that the NLRB will not decide that question. The NLRB will say that it is for the courts to decide whether the antitrust laws are being violated. We should accept our responsibility and direct the district court to make that determination.

The majority also suggests that the union can strike to eliminate or modify the player restraints. This is, of course, an alternative, but should players be forced to strike to alter owner conduct which violates the antitrust laws? I think not.[8]

---

8. *See* Lock, *The Scope of the Labor Exemption in Professional Sports*, 1989 DUKE L.J. 339. Lock notes that there are several features that distinguish the professional athletes' unions from the great majority of industrial unions. First, professional athletes do not possess homogeneous skills; a wide range of ability and expertise exists among players. Thus, different players have dramatically different needs from a union. Second, the nature of professional sports presumes that the owners retain nearly complete discretion to make necessary personnel changes to produce a winning team. Typically, a professional athlete has virtually no job security. For example, the NFL standard player con-

Neither scenario, decertification nor economic strife, harmonizes the antitrust laws with the labor laws. * * * The majority opinion will, moreover, discourage collective bargaining. Players will be considerably less likely to enter into any agreement with respect to player restraints because of the certainty that the terms of the agreement will become the terms of employment ad infinitum, unless they strike and win. *See* National Labor Relations Act §1, 29 U.S.C. §151 ("experience has proved that protection by law of the right of employees to organize and bargain collectively * * * promotes the flow of commerce * * * by encouraging practices fundamentally to the friendly adjustment of industrial disputes"). In practical terms the majority has eliminated the owners' fear of the antitrust lever; therefore, little incentive exists for the owners to ameliorate anticompetitive behavior damaging to the players. * * *

To argue that continuing the exemption beyond impasse is conducive to a stable bargaining environment and judicial nonintervention, as the majority has done, is untenable. * * * Rather, the majority's view undercuts the labor law principles of freedom to contract and the promotion of bona fide, arm's length negotiations. Under the majority's rule, an agreement to a particular restraint for a finite period of time operates to waive, indefinitely or permanently, a union's right to challenge that restraint after the expiration of the agreement under the antitrust laws. The ultimate result is that the majority has intervened to remove the players' rights under the antitrust laws from the bargaining table and has unjustifiably given the owners a continuing right to circumvent the antitrust laws.

It may be argued that both successful and unsuccessful strikes and lockouts are normal parts of the collective bargaining process and that this Court should not give the players through court action what they are unable to win at the bargaining table or through economic action. I subscribe to that view, but this view cannot be controlling where the employers are engaging in practices which may well be illegal. There must be a point at which the validity of the package of player restraints can be tested without the union resorting to a strike or terminating its collective bargaining rights. In my view, impasse is the appropriate point at which to do this.

LAY, Chief Judge, with whom McMILLIAN, Circuit Judge, joins, dissenting [from subsequent denial of rehearing en banc].

I dissent from this court's denial of rehearing en banc. This case is undoubtedly one of the more significant cases this court has confronted in several years. A 2-1 panel opinion now serves as an important precedent of newly-declared law in the accommodation of congressional policies favoring both free competition and collective bargaining. In all due respect, two judges of this court have impliedly overruled this court's long-standing, well-recognized precedent in *Mackey.* * * * In doing so, the panel majority concedes its own uncertainty as to when the antitrust exemption ends, and, in addition, needlessly treats the issue as ripe for resolution. * * *

---

tract contains no injury protection beyond the season in which the injury occurs and grants the team sole discretion to terminate a player's contract at any time for lack of skill. Only five percent of all NFL players have been able individually to limit this discretion. In addition, the professional life of an athlete is short, resulting in high turnover of union members. The NFL Players Association experiences an average yearly turnover of twenty-five percent. Thus, a strike jeopardizes a significant portion of the career and earning potential of many athletes. Moreover, most professional athletes possess highly specialized skills that are rarely marketable in any other industry. As a result, players are extremely vulnerable to explicit and implicit management pressure.

The panel majority purports to apply *Mackey*, yet ignores these principles. The undeniable reality is that the panel opinion does not apply *Mackey*, it rejects it by destroying its carefully constructed limitations.

The panel majority notes that *Mackey* left open the question whether the exemption continues after a bona fide agreement formally terminates. However, the panel then proceeds to extend the law based on a premise which completely ignores the rationale of *Mackey*. In the present case the collective bargaining agreement containing the exempted restraint has not only come to an end, but, under the panel majority's erroneous assumption, the parties have unsuccessfully bargained over its continuance to the point of impasse. Clearly, at this point the restraint can no longer be considered "the product of bona fide arm's-length negotiation." Once impasse has been reached, after termination of an agreement, it is a complete nonsequitur to hold that continued restraints are protected as an accommodation of the good faith bargaining of the parties.

The panel decision destroys the very foundation of the limits we carefully constructed in *Mackey*. The panel majority reasons that, notwithstanding impasse, as long as the restraint was at onetime contained within a terminated agreement it retains immunity as the "product" of collective bargaining. Surely this cannot be the law. If the exemption does not end at impasse, when does it end? The majority's view does not accommodate labor policy, it instead offers an employer's Shangri-la of everlasting immunity from the antitrust laws.

The rationale underlying the panel decision appears to be that a union should not be entitled to invoke the antitrust laws to gain something it could not win at the bargaining table. This overlooks the fact that the restraint involved is clearly beneficial to management, and is illegal unless otherwise exempt. The panel majority fails to comprehend that it was not the union that failed to win a concession, but *the employer* who gained victory in the first instance by obtaining the antitrust exemption *through union consent*.

The only labor policy of which I am aware that is accommodated by exempting the laws protective of free competition is bona fide collective bargaining. Yet, this court's unprecedented decision leads to the ineluctable result of union decertification in order to invoke rights to which the players are clearly entitled under the antitrust laws. * * * The plain and simple truth of the matter is that the union should not be compelled, short of self-destruction, to accept illegal restraints it deems undesirable. Union decertification is hardly a worthy goal to pursue in balancing labor policy with the antitrust laws.

The panel decision, left undisturbed by the failure of the en banc court to rehear the case today, not only fails to adhere to our precedent in *Mackey*, but substantially amends the antitrust laws. In doing so, it ignores the Supreme Court's admonition that "exemptions from antitrust laws are to be narrowly construed." * * * For these reasons, I would grant petitioner's suggestion for rehearing en banc, and would vote to overturn the panel opinion.

Notes and Questions

1. In the court below, Judge Doty had ruled that the labor exemption should expire upon impasse. *See Powell*, 678 F. Supp. 777, 788 (D. Minn.1988). Doty's reasoning followed the recommendations of a student note appearing in the New York University law review. *See* Michael Hobel, Note, *Application of the Labor Exemption After the Expiration of Collective Bargaining Agreements in Professional Sports*, 57 N.Y.U. L. Rev. 164 (1982). In this note, the author suggests that impasse is the ideal departure point for the

applicability of the labor exemption. Any suspension of the exemption prior to impasse could frustrate the collective bargaining process and encourage parties to forego the negotiating table in favor of costly and acrimonious antitrust litigation. On the other hand, to apply the exemption in perpetuity does not foster meaningful bargaining and does not remain faithful to the rationale underlying the development of non-statutory exemptions. Judge Doty was persuaded by the author's "compromise" approach, which bridged a gap between the positions of the two parties: the owners' contention that the exemption survived the expiration of the collective bargaining agreement indefinitely; and the players' view that the exemption ended at the expiration date of the collective bargaining agreement. This latter view, commonly labelled the "union consent" theory, had been embraced and persuasively argued by several commentators. *See* Note, *Releasing Superstars From Peonage: Union Consent and the Nonstatutory Labor Exemption*, 104 HARV. L. REV. 874 (1991); Ethan Lock, *The Scope of the Labor Exemption in Professional Sports*, 1989 DUKE L.J. 339. The question joined and the solution offered by proponents of the "union consent" approach has been articulated as follows:

> Union consent is thus essential to any nonstatutory labor exemption justified as accommodating national labor policy. If courts do not define the temporal boundaries of the union consent requirement, however, the requirement loses its labor policy foundation.

> A rule giving unions unlimited control over their employers' ability to raise the labor exemption as a defense might appear pro-union and thus justified by labor policy. In practice, however, allowing unions to grant and withdraw consent to labor market restraints at will would inhibit collective bargaining and minimize the relevance of the labor exemption. If the union's apparent consent to a restraint were not legally binding, employers would neither trade benefits for that consent nor enter agreements containing potentially illegal restraints. Even restraints that the union itself proposed—such as a uniform wage scale— would often be rejected by employers worried that "concessions won at the bargaining table could be quickly lost in court" and that agreement with the union today might mean treble damages tomorrow. Collective bargaining, the heart of national labor policy, would be suppressed, and the labor exemption would become nugatory, as employers would adopt only legal restraints, leaving the labor exemption nothing to exempt.

> Thus, courts must clearly define the points at which union consent attaches and expires. The next two sections conclude that to accommodate labor policy, union consent to an employment restraint should be deemed coterminous with the union-employer agreement that incorporates that restraint. The labor exemption should attach when the agreement is executed and should expire as soon as the agreement expires. (*citations omitted*)

104 HARV. L. REV. at 885–86.

2. In a case involving the National Basketball Association, the district court declared that the labor exemption should survive "only as long as the employer continues to impose that restriction unchanged, and reasonably believes that the practice or a close variant of it will be incorporated in the next collective bargaining agreement." The court reasoned that when the employer ceases to have such a reasonable belief, the restraint in question is no longer the product of arm's length negotiation between the employer and the union:

> This formulation is meant to determine the point at which agreement ends on the practices at issue, instead of tying the fate of the exemption to progress in

the negotiation as a whole. In any particular case, the exemption may expire before, during or after impasse, and the facts bearing on the impasse question may also bear on the determination of the expiration of the labor exemption.

Bridgeman v. National Basketball Association, 675 F. Supp. 960, 967 (D.N.J. 1987). Is this test useful? How does a court discern when an employer "reasonably believes that the practice* * *will be incorporated into the next collective bargaining agreement"? If you were counsel for the players association, would you not simply advise the owners that you will *never* agree to the practice in question, thereby attempting to create a reasonable belief that the new agreement will not include the practice and thus precluding applicability of the labor exemption? Is there anything in the federal labor laws to prevent this tactic? How does the culture of labor negotiations, in which yesterday's vehement denials become tomorrow's labor contract, affect your response?

3. While the court's formulation in *Bridgeman* leaves something to be desired in terms of precision and predictability, it is noteworthy in the sense that it reaffirmed the third prong of *Mackey* long after *McCourt* suggested its demise. The emphasis upon the arm's length negotiation variable indicates that inquiries into this factor may still be appropriate and that *Mackey*'s three-part calculus survives, at least in some form. *See Brown v. Pro Football, Inc.*, 518 U.S. 231 (1996), *infra*, Part VI.

4. Does the Eighth Circuit's opinion in *Powell* provide any end to the labor exemption, short of terminating the collective bargaining relationship? In the wake of the court's decision in *Powell*, the NFLPA asked NFL players to sign a petition formally revoking the authority of the NFLPA or any other person or entity to engage in collective bargaining on their behalf. When a majority of NFL players had signed the petition, "the NFLPA filed a labor organization termination notice with the United States Department of Labor." *See Powell v. National Football League* (*Powell* IV), 764 F. Supp. 1351, 1356 (D. Minn. 1991). After the NFLPA formally terminated its right to represent players in labor negotiations, NFL players initiated an antitrust action against the NFL and its member teams, challenging the league's restrictions on free agency under Section 1 of the Sherman Act. *See McNeil v. National Football League*, 790 F. Supp. 871 (D. Minn. 1992).

Although the NFLPA continued to coordinate conduct by NFL players and made no significant alterations in its operations, it publicly took the position that, as a matter of law, the signing of the petition by a majority of NFL players, together with the NFLPA's disclaimer of interest, terminated the nonstatutory labor exemption under the court's holding in *Powell*. The *McNeil* plaintiffs filed a motion for summary judgment striking the NFL's nonstatutory labor exemption defense. The defendants presented affidavits that the disclaimer of interest was pretextual and a sham, and that the NFLPA's phony disclaimer of interest violated its duty to negotiate in good faith. Moreover, defendants argued that the plaintiffs' contentions were inconsistent with the Court's decision in *Powell*. Nevertheless, the district court granted summary judgment, reasoning that, even if the NFLPA's disclaimer of interest were not made in good faith, the fact that the NFLPA had caused a majority of the players to petition to terminate the NFLPA's collective bargaining status aborted the nonstatutory labor exemption as a matter of law. *Powell IV*, 764 F. Supp. at 1357 n.6.

The court's conclusion paved the way for the *McNeil* case to proceed to trial. In September of 1992, a jury found that the NFL's Plan B rules, which placed restrictions upon the players' desired free agency prerogatives, violated Section 1 of the Sherman Act, awarded no money damages to four plaintiff players, and awarded the remaining four plaintiffs damages ranging from $50,000 to $240,000. *See Jackson v. National Football League*, 802 F. Supp. 226, 228–29 & nn. 1–2 (D. Minn. 1992); *McNeil v. National Football League*, 1992-2 Trade Cas. ¶69,982 (D. Minn. 1992). On September 17, 1992, the district court entered judgment in *McNeil* based on the jury's verdict.

Just four days after the jury returned its verdict in *McNeil*, ten NFL players filed suit, challenging the same NFL rules and conduct at issue in *McNeil* and seeking injunctive relief and monetary damages. *Jackson v. National Football League*, 802 F. Supp. 226, 228 (D. Minn. 1992). Four of the *Jackson* plaintiffs, including the named plaintiff, Keith Jackson, sought a temporary restraining order and a preliminary injunction enjoining all NFL teams from enforcing Plan B or any other rules or agreements that would restrict those four players from contracting with any NFL team for the remainder of the 1992 season. On September 24, 1992, the district court granted the plaintiffs' motion for a temporary restraining order in *Jackson*, after concluding that the issues presented therein were identical to the issues raised in *McNeil*, and that it was likely that the plaintiffs in *Jackson* would prevail through application of collateral estoppel. *Id.* at 229–30.

After the filing of the *Jackson* complaint based on the jury verdict in *McNeil*, the NFL players filed a class action seeking damages and injunctive relief for *all* NFL players, in particular the players whose contracts were about to expire early in 1993. *White v. National Football League*, 822 F. Supp. 1389, 1395 (D. Minn. 1993). In the months immediately following the *McNeil* verdict, while the NFL players were pursuing their TROs (*Jackson*), preliminary injunctions (*Jackson* and *White*), and a permanent injunction (*White*) against Plan B and all NFL restrictions on free agency (including the college draft), the NFL, the NFLPA and the NFLPA's counsel engaged in negotiations designed to settle all pending litigation and to consummate a collective bargaining agreement.

The NFLPA, which was funding *McNeil*, *Jackson*, and *White*, and whose attorneys were representing the plaintiff players, including the class in *White*, was unwilling to settle the players' antitrust claims without an agreement with the NFL concerning the terms of a new collective bargaining agreement. Similarly, the NFL needed to capture the terms of any antitrust settlement agreement that restricted player mobility in a collective bargaining agreement in order to re-qualify for the nonstatutory labor exemption. While both the NFL and NFLPA desired to settle the pending antitrust claims by way of a collective bargaining agreement, federal labor law prohibited the "decertified" NFLPA from negotiating with the NFL on behalf of NFL players. However, the NFLPA representatives were unwilling to re-achieve majority representational status prior to knowing the terms of the "deal" because re-recognition might risk the resurrection of the antitrust labor exemption.

Eventually, either disregarding the labor law concerns or willing to risk incurring unfair labor practice liability, the parties agreed on the substantive terms of a "global settlement" that purportedly achieved labor peace. The settlement was embraced in a new collective bargaining agreement between the NFL and the "re-certified" NFLPA. This agreement and the bargaining that created it was challenged by the Philadelphia Eagles, who filed unfair labor practice charges with Region Five of the National Labor Relations Board. These charges alleged that the NFL and NFLPA had engaged in unlawful bargaining because the NFLPA had negotiated the terms of the agreement at a time when it was specifically not authorized to act on behalf of the NFL players and did not represent a majority of those players. The charges were eventually withdrawn when the Eagles were sold; and the 1993 agreement between the NFL and the NFLPA has been extended several times and its basic terms are still in effect. Under the terms of that agreement, the parties acknowledged the continued existence of the labor exemption for the remainder of the contract, and they agreed that the league will not assert a labor exemption defense if the Players Association should decertify subsequent to a post-expiration impasse (*i.e.*, the NFL will not attack the decertification as a sham should the NFLPA utilize this ploy again to avail itself of antitrust coverage). The fairly transparent stratagem of the NFL and NFLPA to have their cake and eat it too, and the apparent violence done to the labor laws, have not gone unnoticed. *See* Robert A. McCormick, *Interference on Both Sides: The Case Against the NFL-NFLPA Contract*, 53 WASH. & LEE L. REV. 397 (1996); *See* Michael C. Harper, *Essay: Multi-Employer Bargaining, Antitrust Law and Team Sports, The Contingent Choice Of A Broad Exemption*, 38 WM. & MARY L. REV. 1663 (1997). This issue, particularly the legitimacy of the NFL and NFLPA's conduct under Sections 8(a)(2) and 8(b)(1)(A), is addressed in Chapters Fourteen and Fifteen.

5. A collateral issue arising in the wake of the NFL-NFLPA's settlement was player refusals to pay union dues notwithstanding a union shop clause in the collective bargaining agreement. An interesting question lying at the root of the controversy was the applicability of right to work legislation in jurisdictions where teams like the Washington Redskins practiced, albeit having their home field in a non-right to work state. This issue is addressed in Chapters 14 and 16, *infra. See NFLPA v. Pro-Football, Inc.*, 857 F. Supp. 71 (D.D.C. 1994); *Orr v. NFLPA*, 35 Va. Cir. 156 (Va. Cir. Ct. 1994).

6. Having read *Powell* and the synopsis of the events that followed, what is your position regarding the availability of the labor exemption upon expiration of a collective bargaining agreement? The underlying purpose of the Eighth Circuit's indefinite extension of the labor exemption undeniably was to force the parties back to the bargaining table. Did the Eighth Circuit in its wildest dreams contemplate that the path to the eventual labor settlement would be so circuitous and intriguing?

7. The question that remained after the Eighth Circuit's sweeping decision in *Powell* was whether the labor exemption would apply to all bargainable issues arising pursuant to a collective bargaining relationship, even where such matters had not been incorporated into a collective bargaining agreement. In *Brown v. Pro Football, Inc.*, 782 F. Supp. 125 (D.D.C. 1991), the district court held that there could be no exemption absent an agreement between the labor and non-labor group. Adopting part of the rationale for the union consent theory, the court held:

> Under the nonstatutory labor exemption, employers are exempt from certain applications of the antitrust law. Such exemption is consistent with the policies behind labor laws and the exemption which together seek to encourage employers and unions to agree on terms relating to conditions of employment. Terms included within a collective bargaining agreement are protected. Extension of the exemption beyond expiration of that agreement frustrates the relevant policies because it treats the parties as if there is a collective bargaining agreement when in fact there is none. If the parties have not expressly agreed to terms relating to conditions of employment, this court can find no discernible justification for granting the employer any exemption from the antitrust laws. To do so would reward employers simply for being part of a collective bargaining relationship where employers and labor had at one time agreed on terms relating to conditions of employment.

782 F. Supp. at 133. On appeal, however, the Court of Appeals for the D.C. Circuit reversed, holding that the labor exemption could apply even where no agreement was in evidence. The Supreme Court affirmed, reasoning that a failure to apply the labor exemption in this situation would threaten labor peace and subvert multi-employer bargaining. Relevant portions of those two decisions follow immediately below.

VI. The Non-Statutory Labor Exemption and Its Outer Limits

Brown v. Pro-Football, Inc.
50 F.3d 1041 (D.C. Cir. 1995)

EDWARDS, Chief Judge.

* * *

I. BACKGROUND

This case arises from a labor dispute over salaries for a limited number of professional football players whose jobs required them to practice with regular NFL players, and to replace regular players who became injured, but not otherwise to play in NFL football contests. In 1987, a collective bargaining agreement governing the terms and conditions of employment for all professional football players expired, and the NFL and NFLPA began negotiations for a new agreement. In early 1989, with the two sides making little progress toward such an agreement, the owners adopted an amendment to the NFL Constitution that altered the rules governing players on the clubs' injured-reserve lists and established new Developmental Squads of practice and replacement players. The amendment, known as Resolution G-2, allowed each club to maintain a Developmental Squad of as many as six rookie or "first-year"[1] practice and replacement players in addition to its usual 47-player roster. Resolution G-2 departed from the customary NFL practice of setting player salaries through individual negotiation. It anticipated a fixed salary for the Developmental Squad players, though it did not establish the amount of that salary.

The NFL and NFLPA engaged in fruitless negotiations over Resolution G-2. On April 7, NFL Management Committee ("NFLMC") Executive Director Jack Donlan solicited a meeting with NFLPA Executive Director Gene Upshaw to negotiate the terms and conditions of employment for Developmental Squad players. On May 17, 1989, a league management committee proposed that the salary for Developmental Squad players be set at $1,000 per week. On May 18, Donlan again sought a meeting with Upshaw. Subsequently, on May 30, 1989, Upshaw responded with a letter stating that the NFLPA agreed only "that players can be listed on a developmental squad of an NFL club if they have all of the benefits and protections which players on the Active List have," including "the right to negotiate their own salaries." * * * Donlan and Upshaw met on June 16, 1989, to discuss the Developmental Squad portion of Resolution G-2. In a letter to Donlan memorializing the discussions at that meeting, Upshaw rejected the fixed salary component of the Developmental Squad proposal, holding to the position that "all players, including developmental, should have the right to negotiate salary terms, and that no fixed wage for any group of players is acceptable to the NFLPA." * * * As a result, Donlan concluded that the issue was "clearly at impasse" for "implementation purposes." * * *

The NFL then unilaterally implemented the Developmental Squad program by distributing uniform contracts for Developmental Squad players to all teams. Club officials

---

1. A first-year player is a player who, in a previous year, attended an NFL training camp but played in fewer than three regular season games.

were advised that paying any such player more or less than $1,000 per week would result in disciplinary action, including loss of future draft choices.* * * Resolution G-2 allowed the clubs to form their Developmental Squads from players remaining available after each club reduced its regular roster to 47 players on September 4. Under the resolution, the clubs could sign Developmental Squad players to contracts after 4 p.m. on September 5, 1989. During the 1989 season, 236 players signed Developmental Squad contracts.

On May 9, 1990, appellee Antony Brown and eight other Developmental Squad players ("the Players") brought a class action lawsuit against all 28 NFL clubs and the NFL itself on behalf of 235 of the 1989 Developmental Squad players, alleging that the defendants engaged in price-fixing in violation of the Sherman Act by setting a $1,000 fixed salary for such players. On June 4, 1991, the District Court granted the Players' motion for partial summary judgment, and denied the NFL's cross-motion, on the issue of whether the Players' suit was precluded by the nonstatutory labor exemption to the antitrust laws. *Brown v. Pro Football, Inc.*, 782 F. Supp. 125 (D.D.C. 1991). The District Court relied on three alternative rationales to support its judgment. First, it held that the exemption ended when the parties' collective bargaining agreement expired in 1987. *Id.* at 130–34. Second, the court held that, even if the exemption survived the expiration of the collective bargaining agreement, it ended when the parties reached impasse regarding the issue of Developmental Squad player salaries. *Id.* at 134–37. Finally, the District Court held that, in any event, the exemption was inapplicable because it protects only restraints on competition contained in collective bargaining agreements, and the fixed salary had not previously been encompassed in any agreement between the NFL and NFLPA. *Id.* at 137–39.

On March 10, 1992, the District Court granted the Players' motion for summary judgment on the issue of antitrust liability. With liability established, the District Court on September 21, 1992, began a ten-day jury trial on the issues of antitrust injury and damages. The jury awarded damages to the players in the class that, when trebled in accordance with section 4 of the Clayton Act, 15 U.S.C. §15 (1988), totaled $30,349,642. *Brown v. Pro Football, Inc.*, Civ. Action No. 90-1071 (D.D.C. Oct. 5, 1992) (judgment on the verdict). In the wake of this verdict, the District Court denied the clubs' motion for judgment as a matter of law, or a new trial, and granted the Players' request for a permanent injunction barring the clubs from ever again setting a uniform regular season salary for any category of players.* * *Finally, on March 1, 1994, the District Court awarded the Players' counsel $1,744,578.41 in attorney's fees. *Brown v. Pro-Football, Inc.*, 846 F. Supp. 108 (D.D.C. 1994).[3]

II. ANALYSIS

* * *

Appellants contend that the nonstatutory labor exemption applies to all restraints on competition imposed through the collective bargaining process, even those imposed unilaterally by an employer. In their view, any other rule would disrupt the balance of power between unions and employers that exists under federal labor law. The Players, meanwhile, argue that the exemption applies only where a union has consented to a restraint on competition. They contend that the exemption must be narrowly construed to apply only where unions act in tandem with employers, as, for example, by entering into collective bargaining agreements.

---

3. Meanwhile, the NFLMC and the NFLPA finally agreed to a new seven-year collective bargaining agreement on January 6, 1993.

After reviewing relevant Supreme Court precedent and the policies underlying both the NLRA and the Sherman Act, we conclude that the nonstatutory labor exemption shields from antitrust challenge alleged restraints on competition imposed through the collective bargaining process, so long as the challenged actions are lawful under the labor laws and primarily affect only a labor market organized around a collective bargaining relationship. Because the fixed salary for Developmental Squad players is such an action, we hold that the exemption shields the clubs and the NFL from liability in this case.

* * *

B. The NLRA

The NLRA makes clear that federal labor policy focuses on collective bargaining as a process, rather than collective bargaining agreements alone. In the NLRA, Congress established "the mutual obligation of the employer and the representative of the employees to meet at reasonable times and confer in good faith with respect to wages, hours, and other terms and conditions of employment." 29 U.S.C. §158(d). This obligation "is premised on the belief that collective discussions backed by the parties' economic weapons will result in decisions that are better for both management and labor and for society as a whole." *First Nat'l Maintenance Corp. v. NLRB*, 452 U.S. 666, 678 (1981). Thus, two factors define the collective bargaining process under federal law: the "necessity for good-faith bargaining between parties, and the availability of economic pressure devices to each to make the other party incline to agree on one's terms." *Insurance Agents' Int'l Union*, 361 U.S. at 489.

As the foregoing suggests, collective bargaining under the NLRA is a carefully defined bilateral process. Unions and employers alike enjoy protections under the collective bargaining process. Unions are not the sole beneficiaries of the NLRA. For example, unions may strike; but employers may lock out their workers. Further, unions are protected against unilateral action by employers with respect to subjects of mandatory bargaining while negotiations over such subjects are ongoing, *see NLRB v. Katz*, 369 U.S. 736, 743 (1962), and continue to enjoy this protection until negotiations end in impasse. At that point, however, "an employer does not violate the Act by making unilateral changes that are reasonably comprehended within his pre-impasse proposals." *NLRB v. McClatchy Newspapers, Inc.*, 964 F.2d 1153, 1165 (D.C. Cir. 1992) (Edwards, J., concurring in denial of petition for enforcement). Employers may not fire workers engaged in economic strikes, and must rehire such workers at the conclusion of such a strike absent "legitimate and substantial business justifications" for doing otherwise. *NLRB v. Fleetwood Trailer Co., Inc.*, 389 U.S. 375, 378 (1967) (quoting *NLRB v. Great Dane Trailers*, 388 U.S. 26, 34 (1967)). Under an exception to this rule, however, employers may hire permanent replacements for strikers. Finally, while the NLRA requires both employers and unions to bargain collectively, it does not require either side to agree. *See* 29 U.S.C. §158(d) (providing that duty to bargain "does not compel either party to agree to a proposal or require the making of a concession"). Rather, the statute generally leaves the outcome of negotiations to the parties, with government intervention largely proscribed.

Thus, a careful reading of the federal labor laws militates strongly against the Players' argument that the nonstatutory labor exemption shields restraints on competition only when unions have consented to them by signing collective bargaining agreements, for that argument necessarily incorporates the premise that federal labor policy somehow favors unions in the collective bargaining process. As the terms of the NLRA amply demonstrate, federal labor policy favors neither party to the collective bargaining process, but instead stocks the arsenals of both unions and employers with economic weapons of roughly equal power and leaves each side to its own devices.

Some commentators have suggested that union agreement ought to be a precondition to any invocation of the nonstatutory labor exemption, because, in their view, the federal labor laws are primarily designed to foster employee rights to engage in collective bargaining. At one level, this argument is a nonsequitur, for the right to engage in collective bargaining does not encompass the right of agreement. At another level, the argument expresses more an aspiration than a reality. It is true that the NLRA strongly protects the right to join and form unions, but at least since Congress passed the Labor Management Relations Act of 1947, 29 U.S.C. §141 et seq. (1988) ("LMRA"), federal labor law has expressed a "policy of voluntary unionism." *Pattern Makers' League v. NLRB*, 473 U.S. 95, 105 (1985). The LMRA expressly gave employees the right to refrain from collective bargaining activity, *see* 29 U.S.C. §157, and, while it maintained the obligation of employees to pay union dues under union security agreements, it established that an employer would commit an unfair labor practice by discharging an employee "for failing to abide by union rules or policies with which he disagrees." *Pattern Makers' League*, 473 U.S. at 106; *see* 29 U.S.C. §158(a)(3). Thus, under the NLRA, employees have an equal right to join or refrain from joining unions and engaging in collective bargaining.

Accordingly, to accommodate federal labor policy, we must preserve the delicate balance of countervailing power that characterizes the process. Injecting the Sherman Act into the collective bargaining process would disrupt this balance by giving unions a powerful new weapon, one not contemplated by the federal labor laws. With such a weapon at their disposal, union workers could do what the plaintiff class has done here: invoke the antitrust laws and their threat of treble damages to gain an advantage in bargaining over a salary provision about which union members do not care deeply enough to strike. In sum, a proper respect for the national labor policy expressed in the NLRA and the LMRA requires us to recognize the nonstatutory labor exemption as a potential shield for all lawful actions taken by either unions or employers pursuant to the collective bargaining process. Indeed, only the most crude accommodation of the federal labor and antitrust policies would shield union-employer agreements from Sherman Act liability, but leave exposed the lawful means employed in the process to reach those agreements.

* * *

C. The Sherman Act

As the policy underlying the NLRA supports the principle that the nonstatutory labor exemption shields the entire collective bargaining process, so too the policy underlying the Sherman Act supports the principle that the case for applying the exemption is strongest where a restraint on competition operates primarily in the labor market. The Sherman Act states simply that "[e]very contract, combination in the form of trust or otherwise, or conspiracy, in restraint of trade or commerce among the several States, or with foreign nations, is declared to be illegal." 15 U.S.C. §1.

* * *

We recognize, of course, that, as a general matter, the antitrust laws may apply to restraints on competition in non-unionized labor markets. *See, e.g., Radovich v. NFL*, 352 U.S. 445, 449–52 (1957). However, we think the inception of a collective bargaining relationship between employees and employers irrevocably alters the governing legal regime. Once employees organize a union, federal labor law necessarily limits the rights of individual employees to enter into negotiations with their employer. Indeed, employers are positively prohibited from seeking to bargain with individual employees, absent consent from the union. *See J.I. Case Co. v. NLRB*, 321 U.S. 332, 338–39 (1944). Moreover, employers may lawfully reduce competition in the labor market by forming multi-employer bargaining units, allowing for standardization of wage rates and working conditions within an industry. Thus, once collective bargaining begins, the Sherman Act paradigm of a perfectly competitive market necessarily is replaced by the NLRA paradigm of organized negotiation—a paradigm that itself contemplates collusive activity on the parts of both employees and employers. Stubborn adherence to antitrust principles in such a market can only result in "a wholesale subversion" of federal labor policy.

When this case is put in proper perspective, it is very difficult to take seriously the Players' claim that the action of the NFL violated the Sherman Act. If the Players had been negotiating with a single football team (instead of the multi-employer group), there is no doubt whatsoever that that single employer lawfully could have taken unilateral action to impose a fixed salary for practice team players after bargaining in good faith to a point of impasse. Indeed, the players do not assert otherwise, for they recognize that this is standard fare in labor law. And nothing in the antitrust law is intended to proscribe such unilateral action by a single employer. So the heart of the Players' position appears to be that the presence of a multi-employer bargaining unit should make a difference under the antitrust law. This is a wholly untenable position.

* * *

D. Application of the Exemption

Based on our review of relevant Supreme Court precedent and the policies underlying both the NLRA and the Sherman Act, we conclude that injecting antitrust liability into the system for resolving disputes between unions and employers would both subvert national labor policy and exaggerate federal antitrust concerns. Accordingly, we hold that the nonstatutory labor exemption waives antitrust liability for restraints on competition imposed through the collective bargaining process, so long as such restraints operate primarily in a labor market characterized by collective bargaining. Our conclusion dictates that the exemption bars the plaintiff class in this case from challenging the fixed salary for Developmental Squad players under the antitrust laws. The clubs and the NFL imposed the fixed salary only after negotiations over the issue reached impasse, and the fixed salary was encompassed within their pre-impasse proposals. Thus, their action was a lawful part of the collective bargaining process established by the NLRA. Further, the fixed salary operates as a restraint on competition in the labor market, specifically, the market for Developmental Squad player services, which is organized around the collective bargaining relationship between the NFL and the NFLPA.

* * *

In our view, the nonstatutory labor exemption requires employees involved in a labor dispute to choose whether to invoke the protections of the NLRA or the Sherman Act. If employees wish to seek the protections of the Sherman Act, they may forego unionization or even decertify their unions. We note that the NFL players took exactly this latter step after the Eighth Circuit's Powell decision. Decertification also occurs when newly organized unions are unable to negotiate their first contract. We do not mean to encourage this practice, but we believe that employees, like all other economic actors, must make choices. If they choose to avail themselves of the advantages of the collective bargaining process, their protections are as defined by the federal labor laws. The system established by those statutes offers employees many benefits: recognition of organized workers as a bargaining unit, thereby giving them bargaining strength; establishment of mandatory subjects of bargaining; protection of the right to strike; allowance for the possibility of negotiated grievance procedures and pooled benefit plans; and judicial enforcement of collective bargaining agreements. Further, it establishes a significant list of employer actions that, if taken, constitute unfair labor practices for which employees and unions may seek redress before the NLRB. However, under the system established by the federal labor laws, employees win concessions not by filing antitrust lawsuits, but with shrewd bargaining, favorable grievance settlements, victories in arbitration, and, when necessary, by striking.

We recognize that the history of bargaining between the NFL and the NFLPA, which includes a failed strike by the players during the 1987 season, has prompted some commentators to conclude that "[t]he union cannot effectively strike." Ed Garvey, *Foreword* to *The Scope of the Labor Exemption in Professional Sports: A Perspective on Collective Bargaining in the NFL*, 1989 DUKE L.J. 328, 337 (1989). While we express no opinion on the NFLPA's ability to win the concessions it desires through organized activity, we reject the notion that an inequality of bargaining power in any industry justifies judicial intervention under the auspices of the Sherman Act. Federal labor law guarantees a process, not any particular result. Thus, it does not "contain a charter for the National Labor Relations Board"—or, we believe, for the courts— "to act at large in equalizing disparities of bargaining power between employer and union." *Insurance Agents' Int'l Union*, 361 U.S. at 490.

* * *

III. CONCLUSION

In sum, the clubs and the NFL are exempt from Sherman Act liability in this case. Our holding does not mean that, freed of the threat of treble damages, employers will henceforth seek to force every set of negotiations with employees to impasse so that they may unilaterally implement the employment terms they desire. Employers always face the threat of a strike for such actions. Perhaps more importantly, they face the pressures toward settlement that inhere in an ongoing employer-employee relationship in which each side needs the other to accomplish its goals.

Initially it may be only fear of the economic consequences of disagreement that turns the parties to facts, reason, a sense of responsibility, a responsiveness to government and public opinion, and moral principle; but in time these forces generate their own compulsions, and negotiating a contract approaches the ideal of informed persuasion. Nor does our holding mean that the antitrust laws are completely without force where labor agreements are at issue. Employers and unions certainly face liability when they conspire to use a collective bargaining agreement as an economic weapon against their competitors in the product market. However, where, as here, an alleged restraint on competition imposed through the collective bargaining process affects only the bargaining parties, and has no impact on the product market, the nonstatutory labor exemption shields those parties from antitrust liability. Accordingly, the judgment of the District Court is reversed and the case is remanded for further proceedings consistent with this opinion.

So ordered.

WALD, Circuit Judge, dissenting. Today the majority holds that the so-called "nonstatutory labor exemption" totally immunizes employers from antitrust liability when they unilaterally impose industry-wide terms of employment, in restraint of competition in the labor market, so long as the employers have previously engaged in unsuccessful collective bargaining with their employees over those issues. In so holding, the majority decides that employees who exercise their statutory rights to bargain collectively automatically forfeit antitrust rights to which they otherwise would be entitled. Thus, employees must now choose between foregoing collective bargaining altogether, thereby retaining antitrust protection against employer restraints on the labor market; or engaging in collective bargaining at the risk of forfeiting all antitrust remedies if bargaining fails and the employers unilaterally foist unagreed-to industry-wide terms upon them.

The majority insists its ruling does no more than maintain a level playing field in employer-employee relations and carry out the congressional mandate favoring collective bargaining as the primary means of resolving labor disputes. I do not think so. The reality is that today's decision sharply tilts the playing field in employers' favor, and because of that, will erode the vitality of collective bargaining itself. The rule announced today gives multiemployer groups both renewed incentives and unprecedented power to impose industry-wide terms of employment regardless of union consent and without fear of antitrust liability. Multiemployer groups will enjoy new freedom to harden bargaining positions, secure that if the employees do not submit at the bargaining table, the employers may impose their negotiating proposals after bargaining has irretrievably stalled. Employees in a weak bargaining position will likely opt in favor of clinging to antitrust protection as the less risky course of action; these employees will henceforth have powerful incentives not to engage in collective bargaining at all, since any collective bargaining opens the door to employer imposition of labor market restraints if bargaining fails. It could in extreme cases drive employees to decertify their unions, as the only guarantee against threats by multiemployer groups to unilaterally impose industry-wide wage caps and unacceptable working conditions.

All this suggests less, not more, collective bargaining and fewer, not more, successfully negotiated collective bargaining agreements. The majority decision thus poses a threat to the central purpose of our labor laws of promoting collective bargaining as the primary vehicle for ensuring labor peace. This result neither harmonizes labor law with antitrust law, nor comports with the congressional design of our statutory labor law regime.

I. APPLICABILITY OF ANTITRUST LAWS TO RESTRAINTS ON THE LABOR MARKET

Absent special statutory or judge-made exemption, a multiemployer agreement unilaterally imposing uniform industry-wide terms of employment, and thereby restraining competition in the labor market, runs afoul of the antitrust laws.[1] Concededly, employer-imposed restraints on the labor market are most prominent in professional sports. Employers in other fields generally favor open competition in the labor market,

---

1. The majority characterizes the players' position as an ill-begotten effort to "import" and "inject" antitrust principles into collective bargaining * * * This of course turns the question inside-out. Historically and logically, antitrust comes first; the antitrust statutes antedate our labor laws and are of general applicability, applying to labor markets unless some statutory or judge-made exemption creates an exception. The question before us then, is whether we should now extend a judicially-created exemption from antitrust coverage for collective bargaining agreements into the previously uncharted territory of post-collective bargaining imposition of the employers' terms. Thus we might better ask to what extent we must "import" and "inject" labor law practices beyond the collective bargaining context into antitrust laws that would otherwise apply.

believing that, in the absence of chronic labor shortages, competition for jobs will generally hold down wages and produce higher quality and better motivated workers. Historically, restraints on competition in the labor market have originated in employees' attempts to counter this downward pressure on wages through collective bargaining agreements fixing uniform wages and terms of employment. In professional sports, however, the situation is reversed. Because top-level athletic talent is scarce, competition tends to drive salaries up, at least for the top performers. Thus professional athletes have sought to maximize competition among employers for their unique athletic skills.[2] Predictably, the owners have reacted with multiemployer efforts to restrain competition for professional athletes' services.

* * *

Admittedly, a few commentators have suggested that antitrust laws should not apply to restraints on labor markets. They argue that, despite the broad language of the antitrust statutes prohibiting every restraint on trade, the central purpose of the antitrust laws is not to promote competition per se, but to protect consumers from anticompetitive practices. Thus if an anticompetitive restraint affects only input markets, e.g., labor, and not output markets, e.g., products, it should not be subject to antitrust scrutiny. It is, however, not possible to square this minority view with the development of our antitrust jurisprudence. The Supreme Court has clearly held that antitrust laws apply not only to restraints on output markets, but to input markets as well, including both labor and input commodities.

* * *

Economists, too, have long recognized that market inefficiencies created by anticompetitive restraints on input markets can be as destructive of a free market economy (and therefore ultimately damaging to consumers) as restraints on output markets. While antitrust prosecutions for restraints on input markets are relatively rare, this is explained by the fact that restraints on input markets arise only in the unusual circumstance of an effective monopsony—a single purchaser, or a group of purchasers acting in concert. And monopsony in turn arises only when the resource is uniquely valuable in its current use, so that even if the price is depressed by monopsony, sellers are unable to find alternative buyers.

* * *

Athletic prowess is, of course, a unique and highly specialized resource, of precisely the genre vulnerable to monopsony manipulation. With a few notable exceptions, athletes typically excel in a single sport, and their labor has greater market value in that sport than in any other profession. If team owners join together to suppress the price of athletic services through monopsony practices, most athletes will not be able to switch profitably to other lines of work. Thus, the labor market for professional athletes' services is one of a very few areas where there is real potential for anticompetitive monopsonistic practices. Economic theory tells us, however, that monopsony will diminish output over time. Because some talented athletes will switch to other sports or other

---

2. Ironically, athletes have sought to achieve employer competition through the same collective bargaining processes that other employees use to restrain labor market competition. Players' unions typically bargain for such mobility-enhancing and competition-maximizing measures as "free agency" and the elimination of reserve clauses, salary caps and player drafts. Simultaneously, however, players' unions have embraced more traditional union demands such as league-wide minimum salaries and standardized pension plans. *See* Ethan Lock, *The Scope of the Labor Exemption in Professional Sports*, 1989 DUKE L.J. 339, 341 n.12.

professions, or decide not to enter the field, the overall quality of athletic performance in the sport will then decline, to the detriment of consumers. Thus, both legal precedent and economic theory instruct that—absent some special exemption—antitrust principles do and should apply to such monopsonistic practices. As the majority acknowledges * * * professional athletes presumptively have antitrust protection against monopsonistic restraints on the market for their services, as long as they forego collective bargaining with their employers.

In sum, antitrust law has a significant role to play as an antidote to anticompetitive restraints on labor markets. That role should be ousted only as necessary to implement clear congressional directives.

* * *

The majority presses a deceptively simple solution: whenever antitrust coverage potentially overlaps with activities authorized by labor law, and only the labor market is affected by the challenged restraint, antitrust law must give way. The majority's is a bright-line rule, no mistake. Additionally, it keeps federal courts out of messy labor-management disputes. There is much to be said for the twin virtues of economy and elegance, but they may be purchased at too high a price—in this case the substantial interests of players and fans in guarding against uncontrolled labor market restraints. Over the long haul, the majority's approach will not serve the interests of labor law by promoting collective bargaining. And it certainly will not comport with our judicial duty to carve out only the narrowest antitrust exemption compatible with the effective implementation of the labor laws.

III. MAINTAINING THE EMPLOYER-EMPLOYEE BALANCE

The majority insists its rule granting employers an antitrust exemption for terms unilaterally imposed after a bargaining impasse is required so that employers can engage in hard bargaining as permitted by the labor laws, and thereby "preserve the delicate balance of countervailing power," * * * that is necessary to keep unions from gaining the upper hand. The majority rightly points out that the labor laws contemplate a system of countervailing economic pressure between employers and employees, under which both sides have incentives to bargain. But we must also be mindful that "a primary purpose of the National Labor Relations Act was to redress the perceived imbalance of economic power between labor and management * * * by conferring certain affirmative rights on employees and by placing certain enumerated restrictions on the activities of employers." *American Ship Bldg. Co. v. NLRB*, 380 U.S. 300, 316 (1965). Once Congress established this scheme, it contemplated that neither the courts nor the National Labor Relations Board would intervene on a case-by-case basis to adjust the parties' relative bargaining power, but rather leave them to fight it out at the bargaining table. Of course, Congress itself from time to time adjusts the balance, as it did in enacting the Taft-Hartley Act of 1947 and the Landrum-Griffin Act of 1957, further limiting union conduct.

In my view, the majority's rule does much more than "preserve the delicate balance" in labor-management relations already established by labor law. It decisively tips the balance by giving employers important new rights, together with new incentives to harden their bargaining positions. Because employers can now unilaterally impose labor market restraints that heretofore might have exposed them to antitrust liability, the majority's rule provides new incentives to raise the stakes in bargaining in hope of winning industry-wide labor market restraints that might never before have been attempted. It also encourages employer groups to hang tough on their demands, since at impasse they may be able to impose any bargaining proposals the employees have rejected without fear of antitrust liability. The majority's rule does not just protect hard bargaining; it positively encourages it. It makes impasse more likely and successful collective bargaining less likely.

On the employees' side, the majority's rule also creates new incentives, none of them helpful to the bargaining process. First, some employees—especially those in a weak bargaining position—are under pressure not to enter into collective bargaining at all, lest the existence of a bargaining relationship license unilateral employer imposition of anticompetitive terms. Second, as the majority recognizes, some employees will be encouraged to decertify their unions rather than risk unilateral multiemployer imposition of terms at impasse. * * * Such a consequence is not mere speculation, but represents the actual upshot of the Eighth Circuit's decision in Powell upholding a broad nonstatutory labor exemption like that of the majority here. Faced with anticompetitive industry-wide terms forced upon them without their consent, the players in Powell promptly responded by terminating union representation. New incentives for employees not to engage in collective bargaining—and the bizarre prospect of employers attempting to force employees to remain in a union so as to preserve the employers' valuable antitrust exemption—run directly contrary to the overarching purpose of the labor laws to encourage bona fide collective bargaining.

The majority seems to suggest that because the labor laws mandate a process and not an agreement we should not be concerned if the rule ends up encouraging more nonagreements than agreements. I do not see how they can be right. "The basic theme of* * *[the National Labor Relations] Act was that through collective bargaining the passions, arguments, and struggles of prior years would be channeled into constructive, open discussions leading, it was hoped, to mutual agreement." *H.K. Porter Co. v. NLRB*, 397 U.S. 99, 103 (1970). A rule that ousts antitrust law only to encourage fewer collective bargaining agreements seems contrary to the purposes of both the labor laws and the antitrust laws.

The majority's rule also creates new asymmetries in bargaining relationships still in effect. Employers, now shielded from antitrust liability, can unilaterally impose terms restraining the labor market, while employees have no such capability because unions do not hold sufficient economic power to unilaterally force terms on unwilling employers. Prior to today's ruling, employers and employees could jointly agree to restraints on the labor market through collective bargaining agreements, and those restraints would be free from antitrust scrutiny. In that limited sense, employees had the right to bargain away (or waive) their antitrust protection, but always with the prospect of getting something in return. Employers could also acquire antitrust immunity for labor market restraints through the quid pro quo of collective bargaining. But today's ruling "effectively gives the party benefitting from a potentially anticompetitive restraint [i.e., employers] * * * the benefit of the antitrust exemption without having to pay for it" through concessions at the bargaining table.

* * *

In the end, the wide open field given employers by so broad an exemption from antitrust laws cannot be justified by any rationale based on the requirements of collective bargaining.

IV. "TERMS" VERSUS "TACTICS"

The majority's analysis goes astray, I believe, by relying on a too-facile equation of terms of employment that restrain the labor market and are unilaterally imposed by employers at impasse, with "bargaining tactics," "hard bargaining," and the "economic weapons" used by each side in jockeying for position at the bargaining table. Unilaterally-imposed terms are not mere bargaining tactics. It is true, of course, that "the use of economic pressure by the parties to a labor dispute is * * * part and parcel of the process of collective bargaining," *Insurance Agents'*, 361 U.S. at 495, and the Supreme Court itself has suggested that post-impasse unilateral imposition of terms may qualify as an economic pressure tactic. Still, the statutory structure of the National Labor Relations Act and the logic of collective bargaining suggest that an employer's right to unilaterally impose terms after impasse is best understood not as a "bargaining tactic" but as part of the employer's residual right to continue operating as dictated by business necessity once her statutory duty to bargain has been exhausted.

Prior to enactment of the NLRA (and even today outside the collective bargaining context), employers remained free to unilaterally impose new terms of employment at any time; but those unilaterally-imposed terms were subject to antitrust scrutiny. The NLRA, however, restricts an employer's freedom to unilaterally impose terms. The employer's central duty under §8(a)(5) of the NLRA is to bargain in good faith over mandatory subjects of bargaining. To give substance to that obligation, §8(a)(5) has been interpreted to prohibit an employer from unilaterally imposing at impasse new terms not previously submitted to collective bargaining and rejected by the union, for to do so "is necessarily inconsistent with a sincere desire to conclude a [ ] [collective bargaining] agreement," *NLRB v. Katz*, 369 U.S. 736, 745 (1962). Moreover, because unilateral imposition of new terms during bargaining "tends to subvert the union's position as the representative of the employees," *Insurance Agents'*, 361 U.S. at 485, the employer must observe the status quo while bargaining continues. But after impasse, the employer is free to unilaterally impose terms reasonably encompassed in bargaining proposals already rejected by the union, because at that point the employer has exhausted its statutory duty to bargain.

Why then is it necessary, or even helpful in advancing the collective bargaining process, to grant additional antitrust immunity to terms unilaterally imposed by the employer as part of his residual right to conduct his business, after he has been relieved of his statutory duty to bargain? I should think that the antitrust interest in unilaterally-imposed industry-wide terms remains as great after impasse, when the employer's duty to bargain over those terms has ceased under the labor laws, as at any other time. Congress could, of course, assign some new, significant labor law role to an employer's right to unilaterally impose terms at impasse, such that the terms must be immune from antitrust scrutiny. But the majority can point to nothing in the statute or in its legislative history to support any such intention. * * * In short, there is simply no fundamental conflict between the well-established interest of the antitrust laws in preventing employers from unilaterally imposing restraints on the labor market through anticompetitive terms, and the interest of the labor laws in promoting collective bargaining.

* * *

The present case offers a striking illustration of how employers may now execute an end run around the antitrust laws. Here, there is no indication that the employers' unilateral imposition of a fixed salary of $1,000 per week on rookie and first-year developmental squad players was a "tactic" or "economic weapon" aimed at bringing an intransigent union back to the bargaining table. The employers frankly admitted they wanted a $1,000 fixed salary for developmental squad players to save money, and because they could not enforce existing prohibitions against "stashing" players on the injured reserve list. Thus their primary purpose for unilaterally imposing the fixed salary had nothing to do with tactical advantages in the bargaining process or pressuring the union to re-sume bargaining. They basically thought the new terms were a better way to run their business. The purpose, effect, and content of their unilaterally-imposed terms would have been the same had there been no union in the picture at all.

V. STRIKING THE BALANCE BETWEEN ANTITRUST AND LABOR LAW

The majority suggests that without the rule adopted today, employees will rely on antitrust litigation to secure gains they could not win at the bargaining table but were unwilling to strike over. That argument is a nonstarter.

First, the majority's rule applies whether or not the employees strike. Second, deny-ing employers antitrust exemption for unilaterally-imposed terms does not place any new offensive plays in the employees' playbook. Rather, it affords them a defense against unilateral employer actions that offend antitrust principles. Preserving antitrust protec-tion does not guarantee unions a win at impasse because multiemployer bargaining units still have many other options. They can maintain the status quo, and employ eco-nomic pressure tactics such as joint lockouts, or hiring temporary replacements for strikers. A multiemployer group can be disbanded (by mutual consent with the union) upon the failure of bargaining, and each employer can resume bargaining separately. Although generally not free to unilaterally withdraw from the multiemployer bargain-ing unit absent "unusual circumstances," individual employers are still free to negotiate interim agreements with the union. Finally, even if the multiemployer group does pro-ceed to unilaterally impose anticompetitive terms, thereby courting an antitrust lawsuit, the outcome of that litigation is far from a foregone conclusion under a rule-of-reason balancing. Under any of these scenarios, employees will be hard-pressed to gain any easy victory. Indeed, the range of choices left to employers without post-impasse an-titrust immunity more closely tracks the "delicate balance" of the collective bargaining process as we now know it, than any wholesale exemption such as that announced by the majority today.

For all these reasons, I would hold ultimately, in accord with the district court, that terms of employment unilaterally imposed by employers after impasse are not exempt from antitrust scrutiny under the nonstatutory labor exemption. Under our rule, the symmetry and mutuality of the bargaining process are preserved. Either side may pro-pose and bargain for terms restraining the labor market, but can win those restraints only at the bargaining table by making concessions and securing agreement from the opposing side. Incentives to bargain remain. But at the point of impasse—when an agreement is no longer in sight or even being sought—immunity from antitrust liabil-ity for terms employers unilaterally impose should terminate. Extending antitrust im-munity undercuts the substantial interests of antitrust law in protecting the freedom of the labor market, and serves no ascertainable purpose within the collective bargaining framework.

This outcome, I believe, accomplishes a superior balancing of the competing interests of antitrust and labor policy. Rather than casting out antitrust principles whenever any as-pect of labor law enters the scene, it preserves antitrust protection alongside the collective bargaining process in situations where they do not fundamentally conflict. And it better comports with our duty to construe implied antitrust exemptions narrowly; the majority's global interpretation of the nonstatutory exemption goes far beyond what is necessary to make the collective bargaining process work. *Cf. id.* Finally, because it preserves the sym-metry, mutuality, and balance of the collective bargaining process as crafted by Congress over the past 60 years, it more faithfully follows the design of our labor laws as well.

With time running out in a bitterly fought scoreless tie, this court would allow the owners an unearned critical fifth down.

I respectfully dissent.

Notes and Questions

1. The non-statutory exemption ideally represents an accommodation of the competing concerns of the antitrust laws and the labor laws. Does Judge Edwards start from that premise or does he, at the threshold, appear to concede the preeminence of labor law and the labor law regulatory scheme for addressing controversies implicating arguable restraints in the labor market? His "body language" is evident in the initial sentence addressing the "applicability of the exemption": "[W]e conclude that *injecting* antitrust liability into the system for resolving disputes between unions and employers would both subvert national labor policy and exaggerate federal antitrust concerns." 50 F.3d at 1056 (emphasis added). Is this approach consistent with the non-statutory exemption's underlying purpose, derived as it is from the statutory exemption, which was designed to insulate union collective action from antitrust scrutiny, not to eviscerate claims arising in a non-product market? As you contemplate the path that the non-statutory labor exemption has taken in the sports industry, reflect upon the origins of the non-statutory exemption. Given its underpinnings in the statutory exemption, which insulated union conduct exclusively, is application of the non-statutory exemption to conduct that does not involve voluntary union participation a corruption?

2. Judge Edwards cavalierly declared that employees who seek the benefits of the Sherman Act must, in certain circumstances, "forego unionization." Is there anything in the statutory or non-statutory exemptions that visits this type of "Hobson's choice" upon employees? Judge Edwards seemed satisfied that the availability of decertification as an option allays fears that unionization will permanently foreclose redress through antitrust. Is his comfort level in this regard somewhat exaggerated, given the nature of decertification and the extreme infrequency with which it occurs? The difficulties involved in gathering enough employee support for a decertification, including employee apathy, fear of reprisal, and the procedural hoops through which employees must jump to complete the decertification process, might suggest that this option is not as redeeming as Judge Edwards would have us believe. *See* Michael C. Harper, *Essay: Multiemployer Bargaining, Antitrust Law and Team Sports: The Contingent Choice of a Broad Exemption*, 38 Wm. & Mary L. Rev. 1663 (1997).

3. Judge Wald's dissent favored a less mechanical, and certainly less predictable, application of the non-statutory exemption to labor market restraints in the sports industry. Yet, she did not confront employees with the NLRA/Sherman Act mutually exclusive choice presented by Judge Edwards. Does Judge Edwards' approach reflect a desire to eliminate the mystery of the exemption even at the cost of a proper balancing of the labor and antitrust concerns? Conversely, did Judge Wald's attempt to devise a delicate balance between the labor and antitrust agendas subvert the exemption and, in fact, delve into an analysis of market restraints when the inquiry should have been limited to an examination of whether the allegedly unlawful conduct was exempt from such analysis?

4. Judge Wald suggested that the majority opinion creates needless hysteria by equating multi-employer bargaining tactics with unilaterally imposed terms by the multi-employer group. Wald differentiated the two concepts, making clear that the renunciation

of the labor exemption on the facts of *Brown* does not signal antitrust vulnerability each and every time that a multi-employer bargaining group meets to confer on the strategy to be pursued in negotiations. She emphasized the unilateral implementation of terms which should present the same antitrust concerns "after impasse, when employer's duty to bargain * * * has ceased under the labor laws, as at any other time." Judge Wald concluded: "There is simply no fundamental conflict between the well-established interest of the antitrust laws in preventing employers from unilaterally imposing restraints on the labor market through anticompetitive terms and the interest of the labor laws in promoting collective bargaining." 50 F.3d at 1067 (Wald, dissent).

5. Judge Winter, as jurist and legal commentator, has been a notorious opponent of the utilization of the antitrust laws to redress complaints regarding limitations on player mobility. *See Wood v. National Basketball Ass'n*, 809 F.2d 954 (2d Cir. 1987). Is his view, which functionally makes union representation and the availability of the antitrust laws mutually exclusive options, appropriate? In one sense, Judge Winter's decision seems to be the propagation of legal theories that he had advanced decades before. *See* Michael S. Jacobs & Ralph Winter, *Antitrust Principles and Collective Bargaining by Athletes: Of Superstars in Peonage*, 81 YALE L.J. 1 (1971). As recently as 1995, Judge Winter authored the Second Circuit's opinion in *National Basketball Ass'n v. Williams*, 45 F.3d 684 (2d Cir. 1995), where the court held that the antitrust laws did not apply to collective bargaining negotiations between the NBA and the NBA Players Association. The plaintiff had claimed that the NBA's college draft, right of first refusal and salary cap provisions were in violation of Section 1 of the Sherman Act. Judge Winter extolled the history, virtue, and numerous benefits of multi-employer bargaining and reasoned that terminating the exemption at the end of the collective bargaining agreement would subvert this long-standing collective bargaining technique.

> The claim before us, if adopted, would prevent employers in all industries from jointly bargaining hard with a common union. Although the Players' claim as presently formulated would allow employees jointly to make proposals, they could not maintain the status quo after expiration of the agreement and before bargaining to an impasse, nor could they implement new terms after impasse without fear of antitrust sanctions.

45 F.3d at 693. Is his fear legitimate?

6. In essence, Judge Winter's approach served as a harbinger of the view embraced by Judge Edwards in *Brown*. As a result of the *Williams* decision, and the NBA players' disenchantment with the NBA Players Association, a number of players accepted Judge Winter's tacit invitation and filed a decertification petition, seeking to remove the Players Association as collective bargaining representative. The union and the NBA had agreed in principle on a new collective bargaining agreement. The decertification effort threatened the agreement and an uneasy labor peace that it would have achieved. In an election conducted by the National Labor Relations Board, the players rejected the decertification and voted to retain the union as collective bargaining representative. One NBA player, Mitch Richmond, filed unfair labor practices and objections to the election, claiming that the vote was tainted by NBA threats to lock out the players if the agreement between the league and the union were disturbed by the successful decertification. The matter was settled, and the NBA and the NBPA agreed on a new multi-year collective bargaining agreement. In a sense, the expansive interpretation of the labor exemption indirectly brought about a labor settlement. Was the circuitous path to the bargaining table what the Eighth Circuit in *Powell* and the Second Circuit in *Williams* contemplated? As seen at the conclusion of this chapter, the Second Circuit continues to

adopt a view that categorically favors resolution of labor market restraints such as those addressed herein through the labor laws. *Clarett v. National Football League*, 369 F. 3d 124 (2d Cir. 2004).

7. Acting Major League Baseball Commissioner Bud Selig claimed that the *Williams* decision had constructively pre-empted the need for, or relevance of, a revisitation of the baseball exemption as applied to labor market restraints. He reasoned that the breadth of Judge Winter's opinion takes all collective bargaining matters out of the antitrust arena—whether or not they had at some point been incorporated into a collective bargaining agreement. If there were any doubt that Selig correctly read the tea leaves, the D.C. Circuit's adoption of the *Williams* approach certainly helped to resolve them. The Supreme Court's decision in *Brown* put the matter to rest. The breadth of the labor exemption probably hastened and precipitated Major League Baseball's and the MLBPA's concurrence on the content of what was to become the Curt Flood Act for passage by Congress. *See* Chapter 8, *supra*.

Brown v. Pro-Football, Inc.
518 U.S. 231 (1996)

JUSTICE BREYER delivered the opinion of the court. The question in this case arises at the intersection of the Nation's labor and antitrust laws. A group of professional football players brought this antitrust suit against football club owners. The club owners had bargained with the players' union over a wage issue until they reached impasse. The owners then had agreed among themselves (but not with the union) to implement the terms of their own last best bargaining offer. The question before us is whether federal labor laws shield such an agreement from antitrust attack. We believe that they do. This Court has previously found in the labor laws an implicit antitrust exemption that applies where needed to make the collective bargaining process work. Like the Court of Appeals, we conclude that this need makes the exemption applicable in this case.

* * *

II

The immunity before us rests upon what this Court has called the "nonstatutory" labor exemption from the antitrust laws. The Court has implied this exemption from federal labor statutes, which set forth a national labor policy favoring free and private collective bargaining. * * *

* * *

The petitioners and their supporters concede, as they must, the legal existence of the exemption we have described. They also concede that, where its application is necessary to make the statutorily authorized collective-bargaining process work as Congress intended, the exemption must apply both to employers and to employees. * * * Nor does the dissent take issue with these basic principles. Consequently, the question before us is one of determining the exemption's scope: Does it apply to an agreement among several employers bargaining together to implement after impasse the terms of their last best good-faith wage offer? We assume that such conduct, as practiced in this case, is unobjectionable as a matter of labor law and policy. On that assumption, we conclude that the exemption applies.

Labor law itself regulates directly, and considerably, the kind of behavior here at issue—the postimpasse imposition of a proposed employment term concerning a mandatory subject of bargaining. Both the Board and the courts have held that, after impasse, labor law permits employers unilaterally to implement changes in preexisting conditions, but only insofar as the new terms meet carefully circumscribed conditions. For example, the new terms must be "reasonably comprehended" within the employer's preimpasse proposals (typically the last rejected proposals), lest by imposing more or less favorable terms, the employer unfairly undermined the union's status. The collective-bargaining proceeding itself must be free of any unfair labor practice, such as an employer's failure to have bargained in good faith. These regulations reflect the fact that impasse and an accompanying implementation of proposals constitute an integral part of the bargaining process.

Although the caselaw we have cited focuses upon bargaining by a single employer, no one here has argued that labor law does, or should, treat multiemployer bargaining differently in this respect. Indeed, Board and court decisions suggest that the joint implementation of proposed terms after impasse is a familiar practice in the context of multiemployer bargaining. * * * We proceed on that assumption.

Multiemployer bargaining itself is a well-established, important, pervasive method of collective bargaining, offering advantages to both management and labor. * * * The upshot is that the practice at issue here plays a significant role in a collective-bargaining process that itself comprises an important part of the Nation's industrial relations system.

In these circumstances, to subject the practice to antitrust law is to require antitrust courts to answer a host of important practical questions about how collective bargaining over wages, hours and working conditions is to proceed—the very result that the implicit labor exemption seeks to avoid. And it is to place in jeopardy some of the potentially beneficial labor-related effects that multiemployer bargaining can achieve. That is because unlike labor law, which sometimes welcomes anticompetitive agreements conducive to industrial harmony, antitrust law forbids all agreements among competitors (such as competing employers) that unreasonably lessen competition among or between them in virtually any respect whatsoever. Antitrust law also sometimes permits judges or juries to premise antitrust liability upon little more than uniform behavior among competitors, preceded by conversations implying that later uniformity might prove desirable (* * * or accompanied by other conduct that in context suggests that each competitor failed to make an independent decision).

If the antitrust laws apply, what are employers to do once impasse is reached? If all impose terms similar to their last joint offer, they invite an antitrust action premised upon identical behavior (along with prior or accompanying conversations) as tending to show a common understanding or agreement. If any, or all, of them individually impose terms that differ significantly from that offer, they invite an unfair labor practice charge. Indeed, how can employers safely discuss their offers together even before a bargaining impasse occurs? A preimpasse discussion about, say, the practical advantages or disadvantages of a particular proposal, invites a later antitrust claim that they agreed to limit the kinds of action each would later take should an impasse occur. The same is true of postimpasse discussions aimed at renewed negotiations with the union. Nor would adherence to the terms of an expired collective-bargaining agreement eliminate a potentially plausible antitrust claim charging that they had "conspired" or tacitly "agreed" to do so, particularly if maintaining the status quo were not in the immediate economic self-interest of some. All this is to say that to permit antitrust liability here threatens to introduce instability and uncertainty into the collective-bargaining process, for antitrust law often forbids or discourages the kinds of joint discussions and behavior that the collective-bargaining process invites or requires.

We do not see any obvious answer to this problem. We recognize, as the Government suggests, that, in principle, antitrust courts might themselves try to evaluate particular kinds of employer understandings, finding them "reasonable" (hence lawful) where justified by collective-bargaining necessity. But any such evaluation means a web of detailed rules spun by many different nonexpert antitrust judges and juries, not a set of labor rules enforced by a single expert administrative body, namely the Labor Board. The labor laws give the Board, not antitrust courts, primary responsibility for policing the collective-bargaining process. And one of their objectives was to take from antitrust courts the authority to determine, through application of the antitrust laws, what is socially or economically desirable collective-bargaining policy.

III

Both petitioners and their supporters advance several suggestions for drawing the exemption boundary line short of this case. We shall explain why we find them unsatisfactory.

A

Petitioners claim that the implicit exemption applies only to labor-management agreements—a limitation that they deduce from caselaw language, see, e.g., Connell, 421 U.S. at 622 (exemption for "some union-employer agreements") (emphasis added), and from a proposed principle—that the exemption must rest upon labor-management consent. The language, however, reflects only the fact that the cases previously before the Court involved collective-bargaining agreements.

Nor do we see how an exemption limited by petitioners' principle of labor-management consent could work. One cannot mean the principle literally—that the exemption applies only to understandings embodied in a collective-bargaining agreement—for the collective-bargaining process may take place before the making of any agreement or after an agreement has expired. Yet a multiemployer bargaining process itself necessarily involves many procedural and substantive understandings among participating employers as well as with the union. Petitioners cannot rescue their principle by claiming that the exemption applies only insofar as both labor and management consent to those understandings. Often labor will not (and should not) consent to certain common bargaining positions that employers intend to maintain. Similarly, labor need not consent to certain tactics that this Court has approved as part of the multiemployer bargaining process, such as unit-wide lockouts and the use of temporary replacements.

Petitioners cannot save their consent principle by weakening it, as by requiring union consent only to the multiemployer bargaining process itself. This general consent is automatically present whenever multiemployer bargaining takes place. As so weakened, the principle cannot help decide which related practices are, or are not, subject to antitrust immunity.

B

The Solicitor General argues that the exemption should terminate at the point of impasse. After impasse, he says, "employers no longer have a duty under the labor laws to maintain the status quo," and "are free as a matter of labor law to negotiate individual arrangements on an interim basis with the union."

Employers, however, are not completely free at impasse to act independently. The multiemployer bargaining unit ordinarily remains intact; individual employers cannot withdraw. The duty to bargain survives; employers must stand ready to resume collective bargaining. And individual employers can negotiate individual interim agreements with the union only insofar as those agreements are consistent with "the duty to abide by the results of group bargaining." Regardless, the absence of a legal "duty" to act jointly is not determinative. This Court has implied antitrust immunities that extend beyond statutorily required joint action to joint action that a statute "expressly or impliedly allows or assumes must also be immune." 1 P. AREEDA & D. TURNER, ANTITRUST LAW ¶¶ 224, 145 (1978).

More importantly, the simple "impasse" line would not solve the basic problem we have described above. Labor law permits employers, after impasse, to engage in considerable joint behavior, including joint lockouts and replacement hiring. * * * Indeed, as a general matter, labor law often limits employers to four options at impasse: (1) maintain the status quo, (2) implement their last offer, (3) lock out their workers (and either shut down or hire temporary replacements), or (4) negotiate separate interim agreements with the union. What is to happen if the parties cannot reach an interim agreement? The other alternatives are limited. Uniform employer conduct is likely. Uniformity—at least when accompanied by discussion of the matter—invites antitrust attack. And such attack would ask antitrust courts to decide the lawfulness of activities intimately related to the bargaining process.

The problem is aggravated by the fact that "impasse" is often temporary * * *; it may differ from bargaining only in degree; it may be manipulated by the parties for bargaining purposes; and it may occur several times during the course of a single labor dispute, since the bargaining process is not over when the first impasse is reached. How are employers to discuss future bargaining positions during a temporary impasse? Consider, too, the adverse consequences that flow from failing to guess how an antitrust court would later draw the impasse line. Employers who erroneously concluded that impasse had not been reached would risk antitrust liability were they collectively to maintain the status quo, while employers who erroneously concluded that impasse had occurred would risk unfair labor practice charges for prematurely suspending multiemployer negotiations.

The Solicitor General responds with suggestions for softening an "impasse" rule by extending the exemption after impasse "for such time as would be reasonable in the circumstances" for employers to consult with counsel, confirm that impasse has occurred, and adjust their business operations; by reestablishing the exemption once there is a "resumption of good-faith bargaining"; and by looking to antitrust law's "rule of reason" to shield * * * such joint actions as the unit-wide lockout or the concerted maintenance of previously-established joint benefit or retirement plans. But even as so modified, the impasse-related rule creates an exemption that can evaporate in the middle of the bargaining process, leaving later antitrust courts free to second-guess the parties' bargaining decisions and consequently forcing them to choose their collective-bargaining responses in light of what they predict or fear that antitrust courts, not labor law administrators, will eventually decide. * * *

C

Petitioners and their supporters argue in the alternative for a rule that would exempt postimpasse agreement about bargaining "tactics," but not postimpasse agreement about substantive "terms," from the reach of antitrust. They recognize, however, that both the Board and the courts have said that employers can, and often do, employ the imposition of "terms" as a bargaining "tactic." This concession as to joint "tactical" implementation would turn the presence of an antitrust exemption upon a determination of the employers' primary purpose or motive. *See, e.g.,* 50 F.3d, at 1069 (Wald, J., dissenting). But to ask antitrust courts, insulated from the bargaining process, to investigate an employer group's subjective motive is to ask them to conduct an inquiry often more amorphous than those we have previously discussed. And, in our view, a labor/antitrust line drawn on such a basis would too often raise the same related (previously discussed) problems.

D

The petitioners make several other arguments. They point, for example, to cases holding applicable, in collective-bargaining contexts, general "backdrop" statutes, such as a state statute requiring a plant-closing employer to make employee severance payments, and a state statute mandating certain minimum health benefits. Those statutes, however, "'neither encourage[d] nor discourage[d] the collective-bargaining processes that are the subject of the [federal labor laws].'" *Fort Halifax [Packing Co. v. Coyne,* 482 U.S. 1 (1987)] at 21. Neither did those statutes come accompanied with antitrust's labor-related history.

Petitioners also say that irrespective of how the labor exemption applies elsewhere to multiemployer collective bargaining, professional sports is "special." We can understand how professional sports may be special in terms of, say, interest, excitement, or concern. But we do not understand how they are special in respect to labor law's antitrust exemption. We concede that the clubs that make up a professional sports league are not completely independent economic competitors, as they depend upon a degree of cooperation for economic survival. In the present context, however, that circumstance makes the league more like a single bargaining employer, which analogy seems irrelevant to the legal issue before us.

We also concede that football players often have special individual talents, and, unlike many unionized workers, they often negotiate their pay individually with their employers. But this characteristic seems simply a feature, like so many others, that might give employees (or employers) more (or less) bargaining power, that might lead some (or all) of them to favor a particular kind of bargaining, or that might lead to certain demands at the bargaining table. We do not see how it could make a critical legal difference in determining the underlying framework in which bargaining is to take place. Indeed, it would be odd to fashion an antitrust exemption that gave additional advantages to professional football players (by virtue of their superior bargaining power) that transport workers, coal miners, or meat packers would not enjoy.

The dissent points to other "unique features" of the parties' collective bargaining relationship, which, in the dissent's view, make the case "atypical." It says, for example, that the employers imposed the restraint simply to enforce compliance with league-wide rules, and that the bargaining consisted of nothing more than the sending of a "notice," and therefore amounted only to "so-called" bargaining. Insofar as these features underlie an argument for looking to the employers' true purpose, we have already discussed them. Insofar as they suggest that there was not a genuine impasse, they fight the basic assumption upon which the District Court, the Court of Appeals, the petitioners, and this Court, rest the case. Ultimately, we cannot find a satisfactory basis for distinguishing football players from other organized workers. We therefore conclude that all must abide by the same legal rules.

* * *

For these reasons, we hold that the implicit ("nonstatutory") antitrust exemption applies to the employer conduct at issue here. That conduct took place during and immediately after a collective-bargaining negotiation. It grew out of, and was directly related to, the lawful operation of the bargaining process. It involved a matter that the parties were required to negotiate collectively. And it concerned only the parties to the collective-bargaining relationship.

Our holding is not intended to insulate from antitrust review every joint imposition of terms by employers, for an agreement among employers could be sufficiently distant in time and in circumstances from the collective-bargaining process that a rule permitting antitrust intervention would not significantly interfere with that process. We need not decide in this case whether, or where, within these extreme outer boundaries to draw that line. Nor would it be appropriate for us to do so without the detailed views of the Board, to whose "specialized judgment" Congress "intended to leave" many of the "inevitable questions concerning multiemployer bargaining bound to arise in the future."

The judgment of the Court of Appeals is affirmed.

JUSTICE STEVENS, dissenting.

* * *

I

The basic premise underlying the Sherman Act is the assumption that free competition among business entities will produce the best price levels. Collusion among competitors, it is believed, may produce prices that harm consumers. Similarly, the Court has held, a market-wide agreement among employers setting wages at levels that would not prevail in a free market may violate the Sherman Act.

The jury's verdict in this case has determined that the market-wide agreement among these employers fixed the salaries of the replacement players at a dramatically lower level than would obtain in a free market. While the special characteristics of this industry may provide a justification for the agreement under the rule of reason, at this stage of the proceeding our analysis of the exemption issue must accept the premise that the agreement is unlawful unless it is exempt.

The basic premise underlying our national labor policy is that unregulated competition among employees and applicants for employment produces wage levels that are lower than they should be. Whether or not the premise is true in fact, it is surely the basis for the statutes that encourage and protect the collective-bargaining process, including the express statutory exemptions from the antitrust laws that Congress enacted in order to protect union activities. Those statutes were enacted to enable collective action by union members to achieve wage levels that are higher than would be available in a free market.

The statutory labor exemption protects the right of workers to act collectively to seek better wages, but does not "exempt concerted action or agreements between unions and nonlabor parties." It is the judicially crafted, nonstatutory labor exemption that serves to accommodate the conflicting policies of the antitrust and labor statutes in the context of action between employers and unions. *Connell Constr. Co. v. Plumbers*, 421 U.S. 616, 621–22 (1975).

The limited judicial exemption complements its statutory counterpart by ensuring that unions which engage in collective bargaining to enhance employees' wages may enjoy the benefits of the resulting agreements. The purpose of the labor laws would be frustrated if it were illegal for employers to enter into industry-wide agreements providing supracompetitive wages for employees. For that reason, we have explained that "a proper accommodation between the congressional policy favoring collective bargaining under the NLRA and the congressional policy favoring free competition in business markets requires that some union-employer agreements be accorded a limited non-statutory exemption from antitrust sanctions."

Consistent with basic labor law policies, I agree with the Court that the judicially crafted labor exemption must also cover some collective action that employers take in response to a collective bargaining agent's demands for higher wages. Immunizing such action from antitrust scrutiny may facilitate collective bargaining over labor demands. So, too, may immunizing concerted employer action designed to maintain the integrity of the multi-employer bargaining unit, such as lockouts that are imposed in response to "a union strike tactic which threatens the destruction of the employers' interest in bargaining on a group basis."

In my view, however, neither the policies underlying the two separate statutory schemes, nor the narrower focus on the purpose of the nonstatutory exemption, provides a justification for exempting from antitrust scrutiny collective action initiated by employers to depress wages below the level that would be produced in a free market. Nor do those policies support a rule that would allow employers to suppress wages by implementing noncompetitive agreements among themselves on matters that have not previously been the subject of either an agreement with labor or even a demand by labor for inclusion in the bargaining process. That, however, is what is at stake in this litigation.

II

In light of the accommodation that has been struck between antitrust and labor law policy, it would be most ironic to extend an exemption crafted to protect collective action by employees to protect employers acting jointly to deny employees the opportunity to negotiate their salaries individually in a competitive market. Perhaps aware of the irony, the Court chooses to analyze this case as though it represented a typical impasse in an unexceptional multiemployer bargaining process. In so doing, it glosses over three unique features of the case that are critical to the inquiry into whether the policies of the labor laws require extension of the nonstatutory labor exemption to this atypical case.

First, in this market, unlike any other area of labor law implicated in the cases cited by the Court, player salaries are individually negotiated. The practice of individually negotiating player salaries prevailed even prior to collective bargaining. The players did not challenge the prevailing practice because, unlike employees in most industries, they want their compensation to be determined by the forces of the free market rather than by the process of collective bargaining. Thus, although the majority professes an inability to understand anything special about professional sports that should affect the framework of labor negotiations in this business it is the employers, not the employees, who seek to impose a noncompetitive uniform wage on a segment of the market and to put an end to competitive wage negotiations.

Second, respondents concede that the employers imposed the wage restraint to force owners to comply with league-wide rules that limit the number of players that may serve on a team, not to facilitate a stalled bargaining process, or to revisit any issue previously subjected to bargaining. The employers could have confronted the culprits directly by stepping up enforcement of roster limits. They instead chose to address the problem by unilaterally forbidding players from individually competing in the labor market.

Third, although the majority asserts that the "club owners had bargained with the players' union over a wage issue until they reached impasse," that hardly constitutes a complete description of what transpired. When the employers' representative advised the union that they proposed to pay the players a uniform wage determined by the owners, the union promptly and unequivocally responded that their proposal was inconsistent with the "principle" of individual salary negotiation that had been accepted in the past and that predated collective bargaining. The so-called "bargaining" that followed amounted to nothing more than the employers' notice to the union that they had decided to implement a decision to replace individual salary negotiations with a uniform wage level for a specific group of players.

Given these features of the case, I do not see why the employers should be entitled to a judicially crafted exemption from antitrust liability. We have explained that the "[t]he nonstatutory exemption has its source in the strong labor policy favoring the association of employees to eliminate competition over wages and working conditions." I know of no similarly strong labor policy that favors the association of employers to eliminate a competitive method of negotiating wages that predates collective bargaining and that labor would prefer to preserve.

Even if some collective action by employers may justify an exemption because it is necessary to maintain the "integrity of the multiemployer bargaining unit," no such justification exists here. The employers imposed a fixed wage even though there was no dispute over the pre-existing principle that player salaries should be individually negotiated. They sought only to prevent certain owners from evading roster limits and thereby gaining an unfair advantage. Because "the employer's interest is a competitive interest rather than an interest in regulating its own labor relations," there would seem to be no more reason to exempt this concerted, anticompetitive employer action from the antitrust laws than the action held unlawful in *Radovich v. National Football League,* 352 U.S. 445 (1957).

The point of identifying the unique features of this case is not, as the Court suggests, to make the case that professional football players, alone among workers, should be entitled to enforce the antitrust laws against anti-competitive collective employer action. Other employees, no less than well-paid athletes, are entitled to the protections of the antitrust laws when their employers unite to undertake anticompetitive action that causes them direct harm and alters the state of employer-employee relations that existed prior to unionization. Here that alteration occurred because the wage terms that the employers unilaterally imposed directly conflict with a pre-existing principle of agreement between the bargaining parties. In other contexts, the alteration may take other similarly anticompetitive and unjustifiable forms.

III

Although exemptions should be construed narrowly, and judicially crafted exemptions more narrowly still, the Court provides a sweeping justification for the exemption that it creates today. The consequence is a newly-minted exemption that, as I shall explain, the Court crafts only by ignoring the reasoning of one of our prior decisions in favor of the views of the dissenting Justice in that case. Of course, the Court actually holds only that this new exemption applies in cases such as the present in which the parties to the bargaining process are affected by the challenged anticompetitive conduct.

But that welcome limitation on its opinion fails to make the Court's explanation of its result in this case any more persuasive.

The Court explains that the nonstatutory labor exemption serves to ensure that "antitrust courts" will not end up substituting their views of labor policy for those of either the Labor Board or the bargaining parties. The Court concludes, therefore, that almost any concerted action by employers that touches on a mandatory subject of collective bargaining, no matter how obviously offensive to the policies underlying the Nation's antitrust statutes, should be immune from scrutiny so long as a collective-bargaining process is in place. It notes that a contrary conclusion would require "antitrust courts, insulated from the bargaining process, to investigate an employer group's subjective motive," a task that it believes too "amorphous" to be permissible.

The argument that "antitrust courts" should be kept out of the collective-bargaining process has a venerable lineage. Our prior precedents subscribing to its basic point, however, do not justify the conclusion that employees have no recourse other than the Labor Board when employers collectively undertake anticompetitive action. In fact, they contradict it.

We have previously considered the scope of the nonstatutory labor exemption only in cases involving challenges to anticompetitive agreements between unions and employers brought by other employers not parties to those agreements. Even then, we have concluded that the exemption does not always apply.

* * * [T]he mere fact that an antitrust challenge touches on an issue, such as wages, that is subject to mandatory bargaining does not suffice to trigger the judicially fashioned exemption.

* * *

Here, however, the Court does not undertake a review of labor law policy to determine whether it would support an exemption for the unilateral imposition of anticompetitive wage terms by employers on a union. The Court appears to conclude instead that the exemption should apply merely because the employers' action was implemented during a lawful negotiating process concerning a mandatory subject of bargaining. Thus, the Court's analysis would seem to constitute both an unprecedented expansion of a heretofore limited exemption, and an unexplained repudiation of the reasoning in a prior, nonconstitutional decision that Congress itself has not seen fit to override.

The Court nevertheless contends that the "rationale" of our prior cases supports its approach. As support for that contention, it relies heavily on the views espoused in Justice Goldberg's separate opinion in *Meat Cutters v. Jewel Tea Co.*, 381 U.S. 676 (1965). At five critical junctures in its opinion, the Court invokes that separate concurrence to explain why, for purposes of applying the nonstatutory labor exemption, labor law policy admits of no distinction between collective employer action taken in response to labor demands, and collective employer action of the kind we consider here.

It should be remembered that *Jewel Tea* concerned only the question whether an agreement between employers and a union may be exempt, and that even then the Court did not accept the broad antitrust exemption that Justice Goldberg advocated. Instead, Justice White, the author of *Pennington*, writing for Chief Justice Warren and Justice Brennan, explained that even in disputes over the lawfulness of agreements about terms that are subject to mandatory bargaining, courts must examine the bargaining process to determine whether antitrust scrutiny should obtain. *Jewel Tea*, 381 U.S., at 688–697. "The crucial determinant is not the form of the agreement—*e.g.*, prices or wages—but its relative impact on the product market and the interests of union members." *Id.*, at 690, n.5 (emphasis added). Moreover, the three dissenters, Justices Douglas, Clark, and Black, concluded that the union was entitled to no immunity at all. *Id.*, at 735–738.

It should also be remembered that Justice Goldberg used his separate opinion in *Jewel Tea* to explain his reasons for dissenting from the Court's opinion in *Pennington*. He explained that the Court's approach in *Pennington* was unjustifiable precisely because it permitted "antitrust courts" to reexamine the bargaining process. The Court fails to explain its apparent substitution in this case of Justice Goldberg's understanding of the exemption, an understanding previously endorsed by only two other Justices, for the one adopted by the Court in *Pennington*.

The Court's silence is all the more remarkable in light of the patent factual distinctions between *Jewel Tea* and the present case. It is not at all clear that Justice Goldberg himself understood his expansive rationale to require application of the exemption in circumstances such as those before us here. Indeed, the main theme of his opinion was that the antitrust laws should not be used to circumscribe bargaining over union demands. * * * Moreover, Justice Goldberg proved himself to be a most unreliable advocate for the sweeping position that the Court attributes to him.

Not long after leaving the Court, Justice Goldberg served as counsel for Curt Flood, a professional baseball player who contended that major league baseball's reserve clause violated the antitrust laws. *Flood v. Kuhn*, 407 U.S. 258 (1972). Although the *Flood* case primarily concerned whether professional baseball should be exempt from antitrust law altogether, *see Federal Baseball Club of Baltimore v. National League of Professional Baseball Clubs*, 259 U.S. 200 (1922); *Toolson v. New York Yankees, Inc.*, 346 U.S. 356 (1953), the labor law dimensions of the case did not go unnoticed.

The article that first advanced the expansive view of the nonstatutory labor exemption that the Court appears now to endorse was written shortly after this Court granted certiorari in *Flood*, *see* Jacobs & Winter, *Antitrust Principles and Collective Bargaining by Athletes: Of Superstars in Peonage*, 81 YALE L. J. 1 (1971), and the parties to the case addressed the very questions now before us. Aware of both this commentary, and, of course, his own prior opinion in *Jewel Tea*, Justice Goldberg explained in his brief to this Court why baseball's reserve clause should not be protected from antitrust review by the nonstatutory labor exemption.

> "This Court has held that even a labor organization, the principal intended beneficiary of the so-called labor exemption, may not escape antitrust liability when it acts, not unilaterally and in the sole interests of its own members, but in concert with employers 'to prescribe labor standards outside the bargaining unit,' And this is so even when the issue is so central to bargaining as wages." *Mine Workers v. Pennington*, 381 U.S., at 668. * * *

> "The separate opinion on which respondents focus did express the view that 'collective bargaining activity on mandatory subjects of bargaining' is exempt from antitrust regulation, without regard to whether the union conduct involved is 'unilateral.' *Meat Cutters v. Jewel Tea Co.*, 381 U.S., at 732 (concurring opinion). But the author of that opinion agreed with the majority that agreements between unions and nonlabor groups on hard-core restraints like 'price-fixing and market allocation' were not exempt. 381 U.S., at 733. And there is no support in any of the opinions filed in *Meat Cutters* for Baseball's essential, if tacit, contention that unilateral, hard-core anticompetitive activity by em-

ployers acting alone—the present case—is somehow exempt from antitrust regulation."

Moreover, Justice Goldberg explained that the extension of antitrust immunity to unilateral, anticompetitive employer action would be particularly inappropriate because baseball's reserve clause predated collective bargaining.

> "This case is in fact much clearer than *Pennington*, *Meat Cutters*, or *Ramsey*, for petitioner does not challenge the fruits of collective bargaining activity. He seeks relief from a scheme—the reserve system—which Baseball admits has been in existence for nearly a century, and which the trial court expressly found was 'created and imposed by the club owners long before the arrival of collective bargaining.'" *Id.*, at 14.

I would add only that this case is in fact much clearer than *Flood*, for there the owners sought only to preserve a restraint on competition to which the union had not agreed, while here they seek to create one.

Adoption of Justice Goldberg's views would mean, of course, that in some instances "antitrust courts" would have to displace the authority of the Labor Board. The labor laws do not exist, however, to ensure the perpetuation of the Board's authority. That is why we have not previously adopted the Court's position. That is also why in other contexts we have not thought the mere existence of a collective-bargaining agreement sufficient to immunize employers from background laws that are similar to the Sherman Act.

IV

Congress is free to act to exempt the anticompetitive employer conduct that we review today. In the absence of such action, I do not believe it is for us to stretch the limited exemption that we have fashioned to facilitate the express statutory exemption created for labor's benefit so that unions must strike in order to restore a prior practice of individually negotiating salaries. I therefore agree with the position that the District Court adopted below.

> "Because the developmental squad salary provisions were a new concept and not a change in terms of the expired collective bargaining agreement, the policy behind continuing the nonstatutory labor exemption for the terms of a collective bargaining agreement after expiration (to foster an atmosphere conducive to the negotiation of a new collective bargaining agreement) does not apply. To hold that the nonstatutory labor exemption extends to shield the NFL from antitrust liability for imposing restraints never before agreed to by the union would not only infringe on the union's freedom to contract, but would also contradict the very purpose of the antitrust exemption by not promoting execution of a collective bargaining agreement with terms mutually acceptable to employer and labor union alike. Labor unions would be unlikely to sign collective bargaining agreements with employers if they believed that they would be forced to accept terms to which they never agreed." 782 F. Supp. 125, 139 (D.C. 1991) (footnote omitted).

Accordingly, I respectfully dissent.

Notes and Questions

1. Justice Breyer suggested that terminating the labor exemption at the point of impasse or upon expiration of the collective bargaining agreement (where one has been in

effect) would jeopardize multi-employer bargaining. Why? Is there any viable argument that, because the Sherman Act prohibits conspiracies to restrain trade in the labor as well as product markets, employers opting to bargain as a group may risk antitrust repercussions whenever they unilaterally implement terms upon the occurrence of an impasse? They may, in terms of Section 8(a)(5) of the National Labor Relations Act, retain the prerogative to implement these terms without bargaining, much the same as an individual employer in a post-impasse posture. However, the collective nature of their action, absent the insulation provided by an agreement with a labor organization, could subject their conduct to the scrutiny of the Sherman Act.

2. Is there a legitimate cause for concern that such a limitation upon a multi-employer bargaining group's post-impasse unilateral implementation option will sound the death knell for multi-employer bargaining and the labor peace that it has engendered in several industries? Even if there is no labor exemption, would not the employees or other potential plaintiffs still have the onerous burden of establishing that the alleged restraint is unreasonable (under the Rule of Reason) or a *per se* violation? How many unilaterally imposed restraints would truly rise to the level of a Sherman Act violation? Did the NFL create a slippery slope hysteria that persuaded the court to extend the labor exemption to situations in which the particular restraint was never part of an agreement, and, in neither party's wildest dreams, would ever be included in such an agreement? If the court is correct that the labor exemption should apply to conduct that never was agreed to by the union, what is the statutory predicate for this construction? Certainly, no support can be found in the Sherman Act itself, nor do Sections 6 and 20 of the Clayton Act offer any reinforcement unless one were to embrace the attenuated and decidedly minority view of those commentators who argue that the antitrust laws do not reach labor market restraints. *See Brown v. Pro-Football, Inc.*, 50 F.3d 1041, 1060–62 (D.C. Cir. 1995)(Wald, J., dissenting).

3. The Court's emphasis upon whether the conduct involves a mandatory subject of bargaining on the surface parallels Justice Arthur Goldberg's concurring opinion in the *Jewel Tea* case decided almost 30 years earlier. Yet, Justice Stevens' dissent pointed out that Justice Goldberg's *Jewel Tea* concurrence was never intended to apply to a restraint implicating a labor market where the employees' collective bargaining representative unilaterally opposed its implementation. Do you agree?

4. It is now inevitable that unionized professional athletes who seek to challenge restraints upon player mobility (or similar restraints) through antitrust will have virtually no alternative but to decertify their bargaining representative and terminate the collective bargaining relationship. Is this the goal that the Court hopes to achieve? Will this decision insure labor peace or create a new host of problems in which professional athletes choose to deal *mano-a-mano* with owners as virtual independent contractors. The Curt Flood Act of 1998 (see Chapter 8, *supra*) may render Major League Baseball subject to the same dynamic, and other professional sports may find that stable collective bargaining relationships are threatened by the omnipresent possibility of decertification as the gateway to antitrust relief. *See* Note 6, *below*. In a related vein, an expansive view of the labor exemption may negate the significance of the Flood Act's exclusion of player restraints from the baseball exemption. That is, if baseball's exemption is only circumscribed to the extent that it implicates matters having to do with labor market restraints, then it is a toothless consensus because many of those matters would be exempted by the now proliferated non-statutory exemption. *But see, Piazza v. Major League Baseball*, 831 F. Supp. 420 (E.D. Pa. 1993) (where the court found that the exemption only applied to reserve clause-type issues *ab initio*). *Compare Minnesota Twins*

Partnership v. State of Minnesota, 592 N.W. 2d 847 (Minn. 1999), *cert. denied sub. nom., Hatch v. Minnesota Twins,* 528 U.S. 1013 (2000).

5. Are today's sports unions willing to assume the risk of a decertification and possibly forecast their own obsolescence in the name of opening the doors of the courts for antitrust litigation in the labor market area? This question is particularly compelling in the context of an antitrust claim that affects a substantially small portion of the bargaining unit. For example, would a union disclaim interest in a bargaining unit or would a majority of players marshall a decertification effort to remove the labor exemption and provide an antitrust forum for those players affected by a rookie salary cap or the "developmental squad" issue in *Brown*? By the same token, what manner of self-destruction would prompt a union to strike or otherwise exert economic pressure in support of bargaining demands affecting such a small number of unit members? Given the unalterable fact that all members of the bargaining unit are represented by the union, and, in many states, may be required to pay dues pursuant to a lawfully executed union security clause, is this remotely fair to the disaffected unit members whose claims would otherwise be justiciable under the Sherman Act? Once again, this point resurrects the question posed throughout this section as to whether it is appropriate to present organized employees with the Hobson's choice of antitrust with no union versus labor organization with no antitrust fallback.

6. At least one union apparently plans to continue using the "recognition, de-certification, antitrust litigation, settlement, and re-recognition" approach. The collective bargaining agreement that the NFLPA negotiated with the NFL includes the following provision:

> The Parties agree that, after the expiration of the express term of this Agreement, in the event that at that time or at any time thereafter a majority of players indicate that they wish to end the collective bargaining status of the NFLPA on or after expiration of this Agreement, the NFL and its Clubs and their respective heirs, executors, administrators, representatives, agents, successors and assigns waive any rights they may have to assert any antitrust labor exemption defense based upon any claim that the termination by the NFLPA of its status as a collective bargaining representative is or would be a sham, pretext, ineffective, requires additional steps, or has not in fact occurred.

Collective Bargaining Agreement Between the NFL Management Council and the NFL Players Association, Article LVII, Section 3(b)(Feb 25, 1998). Is this provision enforceable? In 2006, talks surrounding the extension of the CBA temporarily broke down. The gravamen of the dispute centered on the salary cap, particularly the percentage of revenues to be allocated to the players under the cap provisions. NFLPA Executive Director Gene Upshaw had postured that their contract extension would be imperiled if the players' demands on the salary cap issue were not resolved. As leverage, Upshaw threatened to decertify and seek redress through the antitrust laws, signaling a possible end to the salary cap in any form. The threat bore fruit as the parties settled with an increase in the salary cap without litigation. *See* Chapter 14, Part IX (Recent Developments), *infra*.

7. Consider the following hypotheticals:

A) If a collective bargaining representative agreed to a provision in a collective bargaining agreement that, a small group of employees maintains, violates Title VII of the Civil Rights Act, would those employees be precluded from initiating an action under this law, Section 1981 or other anti-discrimination legislation? In fact, have not the National Labor Relations Board and the courts categorically denied such employees the right to bypass their authorized representative and to engage in collective action to protest such discrimination, advising the allegedly disenfranchised employees to seek redress through Title VII or similar avenue? *See Emporium Capwell Co. v. Western Addition Community Org.,* 420 U.S. 50 (1975).

B) What if the NFL pressured the NFL Players Association into an agreement whereby all quarterbacks were declared ineligible to become free agents? What if such agreement had expired and the clause was "on the bargaining table"? What if the matter had never been incorporated into the CBA and was being proposed for the first time? Would the labor exemption apply to any or all of these situations?

C) If a group of owners and the Players Association agreed that only college graduates who have graduated in the top 15% of their class are eligible for the NFL draft, would a student ranked 20 out of 100 have a cause of action against the owners, the union, or both? Would *Brown* dictate that this matter be found to be labor exempt?

In addressing these hypotheticals, ask whether *Brown* has sounded the death knell for the three-pronged test of *Mackey*. While it appears as though the third prong has been dealt a severe blow (again), it is unlikely that *Brown,* read literally or constructively, has done violence to the *first* two prongs of the *Mackey* test. *See* Notes and Questions following *Clarett, infra.*

8. The *Brown* majority cited numerous cases establishing that post-impasse unilateral changes are permissible in both a single employer and multi-employer setting. Clearly, the individual employer that avails itself of this prerogative does so without fear of Sherman 1 reprisal because it is incapable of conspiring with itself. When a group of employers even under a legitimate multi-employer bargaining configuration likewise engages in post-impasse unilateral action, it does so without fear of labor law sanction. But does it follow necessarily that it takes such action without fear of ramifications under the Sherman Act when, by its very nature, it is a form of combination or conspiracy? Stated otherwise, what if a single employer's collective bargaining devices, including post-impasse implementation of terms, result in monopolization or an attempt to monopolize a particular market? Is the conduct insulated from antitrust scrutiny simply because the unilateral implementation does not constitute a refusal to bargain under Section 8(a)(5) of the National Labor Relations Act? *See generally* Thomas J. Campbell, *Labor Law and Economics,* 38 STAN. L. REV. 991 (1986).

9. If the NLRB or a court subsequently determines that there was no impasse when the multi-employer group unilaterally implemented its final proposal or determines that the implementation was not consistent with terms contained in management's final proposal, are the employees free to pursue antitrust as well as labor law remedies? If the exemption is not available under those circumstances, does *Brown* leave employers with the same dilemma that the court sought to avoid—antitrust liability or eligibility for the exemption turning on the difficult determination of whether an impasse occurred?

Clarett v. National Football League
369 F.3d 124 (2d Cir. 2004)

SOTOMAYOR, Circuit Judge: Defendant-appellant National Football League ("NFL" or "the League") appeals from a judgment of the United States District Court for the

Southern District of New York (Scheindlin, J.) ordering plaintiff-appellee Maurice Clarett ("Clarett") eligible to enter this year's NFL draft on the ground that the NFL's eligibility rules requiring Clarett to wait at least three full football seasons after his high school graduation before entering the draft violate antitrust laws. In reaching its conclusion, the district court held, *inter alia*, that the eligibility rules are not immune from antitrust scrutiny under the non-statutory labor exemption. We disagree and reverse.

BACKGROUND

Clarett, former running back for Ohio State University ("OSU") and Big Ten Freshman of the Year, is an accomplished and talented amateur football player. After gaining national attention as a high school player, Clarett became the first college freshman since 1943 to open as a starter at the position of running back for OSU. He led that team through an undefeated season, even scoring the winning touchdown in a double-overtime victory in the 2003 Fiesta Bowl to claim the national championship. Prior to the start of his second college season, however, Clarett was suspended from college play by OSU for reasons widely reported but not relevant here. Forced to sit out his entire sophomore season, Clarett is now interested in turning professional by entering the NFL draft. Clarett is precluded from so doing, however, under the NFL's current rules governing draft eligibility.

Founded in 1920, the NFL today is comprised of 32 member clubs and is by far the most successful professional football league in North America. Because of the League's fiscal success and tremendous public following, a career as an NFL player "represents an unparalleled opportunity for an aspiring football player in terms of salary, publicity, endorsement opportunities, and level of competition." *Clarett, 306 F. Supp. 2d at 384.* But since 1925, when Harold "Red" Grange provoked controversy by leaving college to join the Chicago Bears, the NFL has required aspiring professional football players to wait a sufficient period of time after graduating high school to accommodate and encourage college attendance before entering the NFL draft. For much of the League's history, therefore, a player, irrespective of whether he actually attended college or not, was barred from entering the draft until he was at least four football seasons removed from high school. The eligibility rules were relaxed in 1990, however, to permit a player to enter the draft three full seasons after that player's high school graduation.

Clarett "graduated high school on December 11, 2001, two-thirds of the way through the 2001 NFL season" and is a season shy of the three necessary to qualify under the draft's eligibility rules. Clarett Decl. at P 6. Unwilling to forego the prospect of a year of lucrative professional play or run the risk of a career-compromising injury were his entry into the draft delayed until next year, Clarett filed this suit alleging that the NFL's draft eligibility rules are an unreasonable restraint of trade in violation of Section 1 of the Sherman Act, *15 U.S.C. §1,* and Section 4 of the Clayton Act, *15 U.S.C. §15.*

Because the major source of the parties' factual disputes is the relationship between the challenged eligibility rules and the current collective bargaining agreement governing the terms and conditions of employment for NFL players, some elaboration on both the collective bargaining agreement and the eligibility rules is warranted. The current collective bargaining agreement between the NFL and its players union was negotiated between the NFL Management Council ("NFLMC"), which is the NFL member clubs' multi-employer bargaining unit, and the NFL Players Association ("NFLPA"), the NFL players' exclusive bargaining representative. This agreement became effective in 1993 and governs through 2007. Despite the collective bargaining agreement's comprehensiveness with respect to, *inter alia*, the manner in which the NFL clubs select rookies through the draft and the scheme by which rookie compensation is determined, the eligibility rules for the draft do not appear in the agreement.

At the time the collective bargaining agreement became effective, the eligibility rules appeared in the NFL Constitution and Bylaws, which had last been amended in 1992. Specifically, Article XII of the Bylaws ("Article XII"), entitled "Eligibility of Players," prohibited member clubs from selecting any college football player through the draft process who had not first exhausted all college football eligibility, graduated from college, or been out of high school for five football seasons. Clubs were further barred from drafting any person who either did not attend college, or attended college but did not play football, unless that person had been out of high school for four football seasons. Article XII, however, also included an exception that permitted clubs to draft players who had received "Special Eligibility" from the NFL Commissioner. In order to qualify for such special eligibility, a player was required to submit an application before January 6 of the year that he wished to enter the draft and "at least three NFL seasons must have elapsed since the player was graduated from high school." The Commissioner's practice apparently was, and still is, to grant such an application so long as three full football seasons have passed since a player's high school graduation.

Although the eligibility rules do not appear in the text of the collective bargaining agreement, the NFL Constitution and Bylaws that at the time of the agreement's adoption contained the eligibility rules are mentioned in three separate provisions relevant to our discussion. First, in Article III, Section 1 (Scope of Agreement), the collective bargaining agreement states:

> This Agreement represents the complete understanding of the parties as to all subjects covered herein, and there will be no change in the terms and conditions of this Agreement without mutual consent. * * * The NFLPA and the Management Council waive any rights to bargain with one another concerning any subject covered or not covered in this Agreement for the duration of this Agreement, *including the provisions of the NFL Constitution and Bylaws*; provided, however, that if any proposed change in the NFL Constitution and Bylaws during the term of this Agreement could significantly affect the terms and conditions of employment of NFL players, then the [NFLMC] will give the NFLPA notice of and negotiate the proposed change in good faith.

(emphasis added). Second, Article IV, Section 2 (No Suit) provides generally that "neither [the NFLPA] nor any of its members" will sue or support a suit "relating to the presently existing provisions of the Constitution and Bylaws of the NFL as they are currently operative and administered." Third, Article IX, Section 1 (Non-Injury Grievance) makes "any dispute * * * involving the interpretation of, application of, or compliance with, * * * any applicable provision of the NFL Constitution and Bylaws pertaining to terms and conditions of employment of NFL players" subject to the grievance procedures afforded under the collective bargaining agreement.

Before the collective bargaining agreement became effective, a copy of the Constitution and Bylaws, as amended in 1992, was provided by the NFL to the NFLPA along with a letter, dated May 6, 1993, that "confirm[ed] that the attached documents are the presently existing provisions of the Constitution and Bylaws of the NFL referenced in Article IV, Section 2, of the Collective Bargaining Agreement." The May 6 letter was signed by representatives of the NFL and the NFLPA. The only other evidence presented to the district court by the NFL concerning the negotiation of the collective bargaining agreement were the two declarations of Peter Ruocco, Senior Vice President of Labor

Relations at the NFLMC. In the second declaration, Ruocco attests that "during the course of collective bargaining that led to the [collective bargaining agreement], the [challenged] eligibility rule itself was the subject of collective bargaining."

In 2003, ten years into the life of the collective bargaining agreement, Article XII was amended. Although the substance of most of the eligibility rules was retained, the "Special Eligibility" provision was removed and substituted with the following:

> If four seasons have not elapsed since the player discontinued high school, he is ineligible for selection, but may apply to the Commissioner for special eligibility.

The Bylaws then refer to a separate memorandum issued by the Commissioner on February 16, 1990 — three years before the current collective bargaining agreement became effective — pursuant to his authority under the Bylaws to establish necessary policies and procedures. That memorandum states that "applications for special eligibility for the 1990 draft will be accepted only from college players as to whom three full *college* seasons have elapsed since their high school graduation." (emphasis added). It is this version of the eligibility rules that the NFL relies upon in refusing Clarett special eligibility for this year's draft, and it is this version of the eligibility rules that Clarett seeks to invalidate.

* * *

The NFL asserted that Clarett lacked "antitrust standing" and that, as a matter of law, the eligibility rules were immune from antitrust attack by virtue of the non-statutory labor exemption. On February 5, 2004, the district court granted summary judgment in favor of Clarett and ordered him eligible to enter this year's draft. *Clarett, 306 F. Supp. 2d at 410–11*. First, relying on the test articulated by the Eighth Circuit in *Mackey v. National Football League, 543 F.2d 606 (8th Cir. 1976)*, the district court rejected the NFL's argument that the antitrust laws are inapplicable to the eligibility rules because they fall within the non-statutory labor exemption to the antitrust laws. *Clarett, 306 F. Supp. 2d at 397*. Specifically, the district court held that the exemption does not apply because the eligibility rules: 1) are not mandatory subjects of collective bargaining, 2) affect only "complete strangers to the bargaining relationship, "and 3) were not shown to be the product of arm's-length negotiations between the NFL and its players union. *Id. at 393–97*.

Second, the district court ruled against the NFL on its contention that Clarett lacked standing because he had not demonstrated a sufficient "antitrust injury" to maintain this suit, holding that the "inability to compete in the market" for NFL players' services is sufficient injury for antitrust purposes. *Id. at 403*.

Third, on the merits of Clarett's antitrust claim, the district court found that the eligibility rules were so "blatantly anticompetitive" that only a "quick look" at the NFL's procompetitive justifications was necessary to reach the conclusion that the eligibility rules were unlawful under the antitrust laws. *Id. at 408*. The NFL had argued that because the eligibility rules prevent less physically and emotionally mature players from entering the league, they justify any incidental anticompetitive effect on the market for NFL players. *Id.* In so doing, according to the NFL, the eligibility rules guard against less-prepared and younger players entering the League and risking injury to themselves, prevent the sport from being devalued by the higher number of injuries to those young players, protect its member clubs from having to bear the costs of such injuries, and discourage aspiring amateur football players from enhancing their physical condition through unhealthy methods. *Id. at 408–09*. The district court held that all of these justifications were inadequate as a matter of law, concluding that the NFL's purported concerns could be addressed through less restrictive but equally effective means. *Id. at 410.* Finding that the eligibility rules violated the antitrust laws, the district court entered judgment in favor of Clarett, and, recognizing that this year's draft was then just over two months away, issued an order deeming Clarett eligible to participate in the draft.

The NFL subsequently moved for a stay pending appeal, which the district court denied. *Clarett v. Nat'l Football League,* 306 F. Supp. 2d 411 (S.D.N.Y. 2004). After filing a notice of appeal, the NFL petitioned to have the appeal heard on an expedited basis and again moved to stay the district court's order pending appeal. On March 30, 2004, we agreed to hear the appeal on an expedited basis and set a substantially compressed briefing schedule. Following oral argument on April 19, we granted the NFL's motion to stay the district court's order, citing the NFL's "likelihood of success on the merits" and noting that the resulting harm to Clarett was mitigated by the NFL's promise to "hold a supplemental draft for [Clarett] and all others similarly situated" were the district court's judgment affirmed. Order of April 19, 2004. Clarett thereafter made successive applications to two Justices of the Supreme Court to lift this Court's stay order. Both applications were denied. Clarett did not participate in the NFL draft held on April 24 and 25, 2004.

DISCUSSION

Clarett argues that the NFL clubs are horizontal competitors for the labor of professional football players and thus may not agree that a player will be hired only after three full football seasons have elapsed following that player's high school graduation. That characterization, however, neglects that the labor market for NFL players is organized around a collective bargaining relationship that is provided for and promoted by federal labor law, and that the NFL clubs, as a multi-employer bargaining unit, can act jointly in setting the terms and conditions of players' employment and the rules of the sport without risking antitrust liability. For those reasons, the NFL argues that federal labor law favoring and governing the collective bargaining process precludes the application of the antitrust laws to its eligibility rules. We agree.

* * *

Relying on *Mackey,* the district court below held that the non-statutory exemption provides no protection to the NFL's draft eligibility rules, because the eligibility rules fail to satisfy any of the three *Mackey* factors. Specifically, the district court found that the rules exclude strangers to the bargaining relationship from entering the draft, do not concern wages, hours or working conditions of current NFL players, and were not the product of bona fide arm's-length negotiations during the process that culminated in the current collective bargaining agreement.

We, however, have never regarded the Eighth Circuit's test in *Mackey* as defining the appropriate limits of the non-statutory exemption. Moreover, we disagree with the Eighth Circuit's assumption in *Mackey* that the Supreme Court's decisions * * * dictate the appropriate boundaries of the non-statutory exemption for cases in which the only alleged anticompetitive effect of the challenged restraint is on a labor market organized around a collective bargaining relationship. Indeed, we have previously recognized that these decisions are of limited assistance in determining whether an athlete can challenge restraints on the market for professional sports players imposed through a collective bargaining process, because all "involved injuries to *employers* who asserted that they were being excluded from competition in the product market." *Wood v. Nat'l Basketball Ass'n,* 809 F.2d 954, 963 (2d Cir. 1987) (emphasis in original).

Clarett does not contend that the NFL's draft eligibility rules work to the disadvantage of the NFL's competitors in the market for professional football or in some manner protect the NFL's dominance in that market. He challenges the eligibility rules only on the ground that they are an unreasonable restraint upon the market for players' services. Thus, we need not decide here whether the *Mackey* factors aptly characterize the limits of the exemption in cases in which employers use agreements with their unions to disadvantage their competitors in the product or business market, because our cases have counseled a decidedly different approach where, as here, the plaintiff complains of a restraint upon a unionized labor market characterized by a collective bargaining relationship with a multi-employer bargaining unit. *See Caldwell v. Am. Basketball Ass'n,* 66 F.3d 523 (2d Cir. 1995); *Nat'l Basketball Ass'n v. Williams,* 45 F.3d 684 (2d Cir. 1995); *Wood v. Nat'l Basketball Ass'n,* 809 F.2d 954 (2d Cir. 1987). Moreover, as the discussion below makes clear, the suggestion that the *Mackey* factors provide the proper guideposts in this case simply does not comport with the Supreme Court's most recent treatment of the non-statutory labor exemption in *Brown v. Pro Football, Inc., 518 U.S. 231 (1996).*

II.

Our decisions in *Caldwell, Williams,* and *Wood* all involved players' claims that the concerted action of a professional sports league imposed a restraint upon the labor market for players' services and thus violated the antitrust laws. In each case, however, we held that the non-statutory labor exemption defeated the players' claims. Our analysis in each case was rooted in the observation that the relationships among the defendant sports leagues and their players were governed by collective bargaining agreements and thus were subject to the carefully structured regime established by federal labor laws. We reasoned that to permit antitrust suits against sports leagues on the ground that their concerted action imposed a restraint upon the labor market would seriously undermine many of the policies embodied by these labor laws, including the congressional policy favoring collective bargaining, the bargaining parties' freedom of contract, and the widespread use of multi-employer bargaining units. Subsequent to our decisions in this area, similar reasoning led the Supreme Court in *Brown* to hold that the non-statutory exemption protected the NFL's unilateral implementation of new salary caps for developmental squad players after its collective bargaining agreement with the NFL players union had expired and negotiations with the union over that proposal reached an impasse.

* * *

That same year, in *Caldwell,* we heard the appeal of Joe L. Caldwell, a former professional basketball player who after four successful seasons of play was suspended from his team in 1974 and never returned to the game. *Caldwell,* 66 F.3d at 525–26. While a basketball player, Caldwell represented the players in labor negotiations with the league and claimed to have incurred the scorn of his league, the American Basketball Association ("ABA"), as a result. *Id.* at 526. He alleged that the teams consequently agreed among themselves, in violation of the antitrust laws, that he should be fired and then blacklisted from professional play. *Id.* Despite the district court's finding that the case could "be entirely resolved without any reference whatsoever to the" collective bargaining agreement between the ABA and its players union, *id. at* 529 n. 1, we held that the non-statutory exemption defeated Caldwell's claims, *id.* at 527.

In *Caldwell,* our analysis began with the observation that "the inception of a collective bargaining relationship between employees and employers irrevocably alters the governing legal regime." *Id.* at 527–28. We found that as a consequence of the collective bargaining relationship between the ABA and its players union, Caldwell's claims, insofar as they concerned the "circumstances under which an employer may discharge or refuse to hire an employee," involved a mandatory bargaining subject. *Id.* at 529. Thus, federal labor law afforded Caldwell a host of administrative and judicial remedies to contest the parties' agreements on the subject, as well as his firing and any team's refusal to rehire him. *Id.* Drawing upon our discussion of multi-employer bargaining units in *Williams*, we then observed that the legality *vel non* of his treatment did not become a question of antitrust law simply because the "employers acted jointly in refusing employment." *Id.* Because such issues are remediable under labor law, we concluded that the non-statutory exemption applied.

The following year, in *Brown*, the Supreme Court was presented with facts similar to *Williams*, and eight Justices agreed that the non-statutory exemption precludes antitrust claims against a professional sports league for unilaterally setting policy with respect to mandatory bargaining subjects after negotiations with the players union over those subjects reach impasse. There, a class of professional football players challenged the NFL's unilateral institution of a policy that permitted each team to establish a new squad of developmental players and capped those players' weekly salaries after negotiations with the players union over that proposal became deadlocked. Approaching the issue largely as a "matter of logic," the Court found that to permit antitrust liability in such a case would call into question a great deal of conduct, such as multi-employer bargaining, that federal labor policy promotes and for which labor law provides an array of rules and remedies. The Court held that the non-statutory labor exemption necessarily applied not only to protect such labor policies but also to prevent "antitrust courts" from usurping the NLRB's responsibility for policing the collective bargaining process.

The Court also rejected a number of potential limits on the exemption that were raised by the players and their supporters. First, the Court held that the exemption was not so narrow as to protect only agreements between the parties that are embodied in an existing collective bargaining agreement. Second, in finding that the League's post-impasse action was protected by the exemption, the Court dismissed the suggestion that the exemption should insulate the concerted action of employers only up to the point at which negotiations reach impasse or a "reasonable time" thereafter. Third, the Court rejected the notion that courts in applying the exemption could distinguish between bargaining "tactics," which the players argued should be exempt, and unilaterally imposed "terms." Finally, the Court refused the players' contention that the labor of professional sports players was unique and that the market for players' services therefore should be treated differently than other organized labor markets for purposes of the non-statutory exemption.

Although the Court in *Brown* held that the non-statutory exemption applied, it left the precise contours of the exemption undefined. In so doing, the Court found it unnecessary to embrace, and indeed expressed some reservations about, the broader holding of the court of appeals that the non-statutory exemption "waiv[es] antitrust liability for restraints on competition imposed through the collective-bargaining process, so long as such restraints operate primarily in a labor market characterized by collective bargaining."

Clarett argues that his case differs in material respects from *Brown*, but he does not argue, nor do we find, that the Supreme Court's treatment of the non-statutory exemption in that case gives reason to doubt the authority of our prior decisions in *Caldwell*, *Williams*, and *Wood*. Because we find that our prior decisions in this area fully comport—in approach and result—with the Supreme Court's decision in *Brown*, we regard them as controlling authority. In light of the foregoing jurisprudence, we therefore proceed to the merits of this appeal.

B.

Clarett argues that he is physically qualified to play professional football and that the antitrust laws preclude the NFL teams from agreeing amongst themselves that they will refuse to deal with him simply because he is less than three full football seasons out of high school. Such an arbitrary condition, he argues, imposes an unreasonable restraint upon the competitive market for professional football players' services, and, because it excludes him from entering that market altogether, constitutes a *per se* antitrust violation. The issue we must decide is whether subjecting the NFL's eligibility rules to antitrust scrutiny would "subvert fundamental principles of our federal labor policy." *Wood,* 809 F.2d at 959. For the reasons that follow, we hold that it would and that the non-statutory exemption therefore applies.

Although the NFL has maintained draft eligibility rules in one form or another for much of its history, the "inception of a collective bargaining relationship" between the NFL and its players union some thirty years ago "irrevocably alter[ed] the governing legal regime." *Caldwell,* 66 F.3d at 527. Our prior cases highlight a number of consequences resulting from the advent of this collective bargaining relationship that are relevant to Clarett's litigation. For one, prospective players no longer have the right to negotiate directly with the NFL teams over the terms and conditions of their employment. That responsibility is instead committed to the NFL and the players union to accomplish through the collective bargaining process, and throughout that process the NFL and the players union are to have the freedom to craft creative solutions to their differences in light of the economic imperatives of their industry. Furthermore, the NFL teams are permitted to engage in joint conduct with respect to the terms and conditions of players' employment as a multi-employer bargaining unit without risking antitrust liability. The arguments Clarett advances in support of his antitrust claim, however, run counter to each of these basic principles of federal labor law.

Because the NFL players have unionized and have selected the NFLPA as its exclusive bargaining representative, labor law prohibits Clarett from negotiating directly the terms and conditions of his employment with any NFL club, and an NFL club would commit an unfair labor practice were it to bargain with Clarett individually without the union's consent. The terms and conditions of Clarett's employment are instead committed to the collective bargaining table and are reserved to the NFL and the players union's selected representative to negotiate.

The players union's representative possesses "powers comparable to those possessed by a legislative body both to create and restrict the rights of those whom it represents." *Trans World Airlines, Inc. v. Indep. Fed'n of Flight Attendants,* 489 U.S. 426, 458–59 (1989). In seeking the best deal for NFL players overall, the representative has the ability to advantage certain categories of players over others, subject of course to the representative's duty of fair representation. *See Vaca v. Sipes,* 386 U.S. 171, 177 (1967). The union representative may, for example, favor veteran players over rookies, and can seek to preserve jobs for current players to the detriment of new employees and the exclusion of outsiders. This authority and exclusive responsibility is vested in the players' representative "once a mandatory collective bargaining relationship is established and continues throughout the relationship." *Caldwell,* 66 F.3d at 528. For the duration of that relationship, federal labor law then establishes a "'soup-to-nuts array' of rules, tribunals and remedies to govern [the collective bargaining] process." *Id.* at 529.

Clarett's argument that antitrust law should permit him to circumvent this scheme established by federal labor law starts with the contention that the eligibility rules do not constitute a mandatory subject of collective bargaining and thus cannot fall within the protection of the non-statutory exemption. Contrary to the district court, however, we find that the eligibility rules are mandatory bargaining subjects. Though tailored to the unique circumstance of a professional sports league, the eligibility rules for the draft represent a quite literal condition for initial employment and for that reason alone might constitute a mandatory bargaining subject. But moreover, the eligibility rules constitute a mandatory bargaining subject because they have tangible effects on the wages and working conditions of current NFL players. Because the unusual economic imperatives of professional sports raise "numerous problems with little or no precedent in standard industrial relations," *Wood, 809 F.2d at 961,* we have recognized that many of the arrangements in professional sports that, at first glance, might not appear to deal with wages or working conditions are indeed mandatory bargaining subjects, *see Silverman v. Major League Baseball Player Relations Comm., Inc.,* 67 F.3d 1054, 1061 (2d Cir. 1995).

* * *

Furthermore, by reducing competition in the market for entering players, the eligibility rules also affect the job security of veteran players. *See Fibreboard, 379 U.S. at 210–15.* Because the size of NFL teams is capped, the eligibility rules diminish a veteran player's risk of being replaced by either a drafted rookie or a player who enters the draft and, though not drafted, is then hired as a rookie free agent. Consequently, as was true in *Silverman,* we find that to regard the NFL's eligibility rules as merely permissive bargaining subjects "would ignore the reality of collective bargaining in sports." *Silverman,* 67 F.3d at 1061–62.

Clarett, however, argues that the eligibility rules are an impermissible bargaining subject because they affect players outside of the union. But simply because the eligibility rules work a hardship on prospective rather than current employees does not render them impermissible. The eligibility rules in this respect are not dissimilar to union demands for hiring hall arrangements that have long been recognized as mandatory subjects of bargaining. In such hiring hall arrangements, the criteria for employment are set by the rules of the hiring hall rather than the employer alone. Nevertheless, such an arrangement constitutes a permissible, mandatory subject of bargaining despite the fact that it concerns prospective rather than current employees.

As a permissible, mandatory subject of bargaining, the conditions under which a prospective player, like Clarett, will be considered for employment as an NFL player are for the union representative and the NFL to determine. Clarett, however, stresses that the eligibility rules are arbitrary and that requiring him to wait another football season has nothing to do with whether he is in fact qualified for professional play. But Clarett is in this respect no different from the typical worker who is confident that he or she has the skills to fill a job vacancy but does not possess the qualifications or meet the requisite criteria that have been set. In the context of this collective bargaining relationship, the NFL and its players union can agree that an employee will not be hired or considered for employment for nearly any reason whatsoever so long as they do not violate federal laws such as those prohibiting unfair labor practices, or discrimination. Any challenge to those criteria must "be founded on labor rather than antitrust law." *Caldwell,* 66 F.3d at 530.

Even accepting that an individual club could refuse to consider him for employment because he is less than three full seasons out of high school, Clarett contends that the

NFL clubs invited antitrust liability when they agreed amongst themselves to impose that same criteria on every prospective player. As a consequence of the NFL's unique position in the professional football market, of course, such joint action deprives Clarett of the opportunity to pursue, at least for the time being, the kind of high-paying, high-profile career he desires. In the context of collective bargaining, however, federal labor policy permits the NFL teams to act collectively as a multi-employer bargaining unit in structuring the rules of play and setting the criteria for player employment. Such concerted action is encouraged as a matter of labor policy and tolerated as a matter of antitrust law, despite the fact that it "plainly involve[s] horizontal competitors for labor acting in concert to set and to implement terms of employment," *Caldwell*, 66 F.3d at 529. Multi-employer bargaining in professional sports, moreover, offers the added advantage of allowing the teams to agree with one another and, as required, bargain with the union over the host of uniform rules needed for the successful operation of the league, such as the "number of games, length of season, playoff structures, and roster size and composition." *Williams*, 45 F.3d at 689. The fact that the challenged rules govern eligibility for the NFL draft, thereby excluding some potential employees from consideration, does not render the NFL's adherence to its eligibility rules as a multi-employer bargaining unit suspect.

The threat to the operation of federal labor law posed by Clarett's antitrust claims is in no way diminished by Clarett's contention that the rules were not bargained over during the negotiations that preceded the current collective bargaining agreement. The eligibility rules, along with the host of other NFL rules and policies affecting the terms and conditions of NFL players included in the NFL's Constitution and Bylaws, were well known to the union, and a copy of the Constitution and Bylaws was presented to the union during negotiations. Given that the eligibility rules are a mandatory bargaining subject for the reasons set out above, the union or the NFL could have forced the other to the bargaining table if either felt that a change was warranted. Indeed, according to the declaration from the NFLMC's Vice President for Labor Relations, Peter Ruocco, this is exactly what the NFL did.

Although this declaration was the only evidence on this point and went uncontradicted by Clarett below, the district court found that this evidence was insufficient to entitle the NFL to a non-statutory exemption defense as a matter of law. But even disregarding this evidence entirely, the collective bargaining agreement itself makes clear that the union and the NFL reached an agreement with respect to how the eligibility rules would be handled. In the collective bargaining agreement, the union agreed to waive any challenge to the Constitution and Bylaws and thereby acquiesced in the continuing operation of the eligibility rules contained therein—at least for the duration of the agreement. The terms of that waiver not only keep the eligibility rules in effect for the length of the agreement but also leave the NFL in control of any changes to the eligibility rules on the condition that any significant change potentially affecting the terms and conditions of players' employment would be preceded by notice to the union and an opportunity to bargain. The value of such a clause to the NFL is obvious, as control over any changes to the eligibility rules is left in the hands of management at least until the expiration of the collective bargaining agreement. Although it is entirely possible that the players union might not have agreed entirely with the eligibility rules, the union representative might not have regarded any difference of opinion with respect to the eligibility rules as sufficient to warrant the expenditure of precious time at the bargaining table in light of other important issues.

Clarett would have us hold that by reaching this arrangement rather than fixing the eligibility rules in the text of the collective bargaining agreement or in failing to wrangle over the eligibility rules at the bargaining table, the NFL left itself open to antitrust liability. Such a holding, however, would completely contradict prior decisions recognizing that the labor law policies that warrant withholding antitrust scrutiny are not limited to protecting only terms contained in collective bargaining agreements. The reach of those policies, rather, extends as far as is necessary to ensure the successful operation of the collective bargaining *process* and to safeguard the "unique bundle of compromises" reached by the NFL and the players union as a means of settling their differences. It would disregard those policies completely to hold that some "particular *quid pro quo* must be proven to avoid antitrust liability," *id.* at 962 n.5, or to allow Clarett to undo what we assume the NFL and its players union regarded as the most appropriate or expedient means of settling their differences, *id.* at 961. We have cautioned before that "to the extent that courts prohibit particular solutions for particular problems, they reduce the number and quality of compromises available to unions and employers for resolving their differences." *Id.* Clarett would have us disregard our own good advice.

The disruptions to federal labor policy that would be occasioned by Clarett's antitrust suit, moreover, would not vindicate any of the antitrust policies that the Supreme Court has said may warrant the withholding of the non-statutory exemption. This is simply not a case in which the NFL is alleged to have conspired with its players union to drive its competitors out of the market for professional football. Nor does Clarett contend that the NFL uses the eligibility rules as an unlawful means of maintaining its dominant position in that market. This lawsuit reflects simply a prospective employee's disagreement with the criteria, established by the employer and the labor union, that he must meet in order to be considered for employment. Any remedies for such a claim are the province of labor law. Allowing Clarett to proceed with his antitrust suit would subvert "principles that have been familiar to, and accepted by, the nation's workers for all of the NLRA's [sixty years] in every industry except professional sports." *Caldwell*, 66 F.3d at 530. We, however, follow the Supreme Court's lead in declining to "fashion an antitrust exemption [so as to give] additional advantages to professional football players * * * that transport workers, coal miners, or meat packers would not enjoy." *Brown*, 518 U.S. at 249.

CONCLUSION

For the foregoing reasons, the judgment of the district court is REVERSED and the case REMANDED with instructions to enter judgment in favor of the NFL. The order of the district court designating Clarett eligible to enter this year's NFL draft is VACATED.

Notes and Questions

1. The Second Circuit's cynicism about the continuing vitality of *Mackey* is clear: "We, however, have never regarded the Eighth Circuit's test as defining the appropriate limits of the non-statutory exemption." Is the court's denigration of the *Mackey* test valid? Is it even justified by the controlling precedent? Compare the following:

> We find the proper accommodation to be: First, the labor policy favoring collective bargaining may potentially be given pre-eminence over the antitrust laws where the restrain on trade primarily affects only the parties to the collective bargaining relationship. * * * Second, federal labor policy is implicated sufficiently to prevail only where the agreement sought to be exempted concerns a mandatory subject of collective bargaining. * * * Finally, the policy favoring collective bargaining is furthered to the degree necessary to override the

antitrust laws only where the agreement sought to be exempted is the product of bona fide arm's-length bargaining. * * *

Mackey v. National Football League, 543 F. 2d 606, 614 (8th Cir. 1976).

For these reasons, we hold that the implicit ("nonstatutory") antitrust exemption applies to the employer conduct at issue here. That conduct took place during and immediately after a collective-bargaining negotiation. It grew out of, and was directly related to, the lawful operation of the bargaining process. It involved a matter that the parties were required to negotiate collectively. And it concerned only the parties to the collective-bargaining relationship.

Brown v. Pro-Football, Inc., 518 U.S. 231, 250 (1996). Do the *Mackey* criteria and the factors apparently deemed critical in *Brown* bear any resemblance? Perhaps a striking resemblance?

2. On the other hand, is the Second Circuit's reversal of the District Court's rejection of the labor exemption decision at all surprising given *Brown's* application of the labor exemption to the facts of that case? Has the court's decision set the stage for a possible conflict among the circuits leading to more Supreme Court treatment? Or has *Brown* sent a definitive message to the lower courts that the labor exemption is to weigh heavily toward the labor process as the preferred method to resolve such disputes? In one respect, *Brown's* message to the lower courts could not have been too explicit, witness the District Court's decision in *Clarett* embracing *Mackey* and finding the league's arguments in support of the exemption unavailing. *See Clarett v. NFL,* 306 F. Supp. at 393–97.

3. The NBA collective bargaining agreement provides that commencing in 2006, the age for entering the NBA draft increased from 18 to 19. U.S. players must be at least one year removed from high school and reach the age of 19 by the end of that calendar year. Would *Brown/Clarett* preclude antitrust challenge by a high school senior who seeks entry into the NBA? Is a rule that purports to govern hiring and the eligibility of individuals not yet employed by the NBA a proper subject of the labor exemption? While there seems to be little doubt as to the direction that the Second Circuit would take, are other courts of appeals likely to follow lockstep? Or is there enough flex in *Brown* to prompt a lower court to entertain a challenge to the NBA's rule on the merits? Further, does this rule have a disproportionate impact on minority student-athletes? If so, can it survive scrutiny under Title VII, 42 U.S.C. § 2000e. *See* Chapter 17, *infra*.

4. In order to become eligible to represent players in the major professional sports, agents typically must be certified by the players' collective bargaining representatives. The players associations wield considerable power in the certification of agents and have broad authority to govern the conduct of agents within their "jurisdiction." For example, the NHLPA's agent certification regulations provide in relevant part:

No person (other than a player representing himself) shall conduct individual contract negotiations on behalf of a player, and/or assist in or advise with respect to such negotiations with NHL Clubs unless he:

(1) is currently certified as an agent pursuant to these Regulations.

* * *

These Regulations govern the activities and conduct of agents in the provision of advice, counsel, information or assistance to players with respect to negotiating their individual contracts with Clubs and/or thereafter in enforcing those contracts; the conduct of negotiations regarding compensation with the Clubs on behalf of individual players; and any other activity or conduct which directly or indirectly bears upon an agent's integrity, competence or ability to properly represent individual NHL players and the NHLPA in individual contract negotiations, the management of funds, tax preparation and counseling, and financial advice and investment services.

NHLPA Regulations of Agent Certification, §§ 1 (A)(1) & (B). If questions arise surrounding the revocation of an agent's certification, or any other matter involving the interpretation of the Regulations, they are resolved as follows:

> In establishing a system for regulating agents, it is the intention of the NHLPA that the arbitration process set forth herein be the sole and exclusive method for resolving any and all disputes that may arise from the interpretation, application or enforcement of these Regulations and the resulting agreements between agents and individual players. This will ensure that those disputes—which involve essentially internal matters concerning the relationship between individual players, the NHLPA in its capacity as their exclusive bargaining representative, and agents performing certain delegated representative functions relating particularly to individual Player compensation negotiations—will be handled and resolved expeditiously by the decision-maker established herein, without need to resort to costly and time-consuming formal adjudication.

* * *

> The NHLPA shall appoint a panel of at least three (3) skilled, experienced and impartial persons to serve as single Arbitrators for all disputes arising hereunder. Each panel member shall be appointed for a one (1) year term which shall be automatically renewed from year to year unless the member resigns or is discharged by the NHLPA. The NHLPA may discharge a panel member at the conclusion of a one (1) year term by serving written notice upon him on or before the expiry of the term. The panel member so discharged shall render decisions in all cases he previously heard but will hear no further cases. The NHLPA shall thereupon select a successor panel member. If there is an interim period between the discharge of the panel member and the selection of a successor panel member, an Arbitrator shall be selected on a case by case basis under the Voluntary Labor Tribunal Rules of the American Arbitration Association then in effect. The panel members shall hear disputes on a rotating basis.

> The NHLPA shall assign the dispute to the next panel member in the rotation at the time the Grievance is received by the NHLPA.

NHLPA Regulations of Agent Certification, §§ 5(A) & (D).

Without commenting on the viability of an antitrust challenge to the agent certification regulations as unreasonable restraints of trade, or any resemblance that these procedures bear to traditional due process, would such an action be barred by the non-statutory labor exemption? Again, assuming that the Sherman 1 claim could survive the "laugh" test, is there anything in the history of the labor exemption that would or should preclude the controversy from being heard? Is agent certification a mandatory or permissive subject of bargaining? Could a union demand that the employer bargain over this issue and file a successful 8(a)(5) bad faith bargaining charge in the event of an employer's refusal to discuss it? Would a union's strike over such an issue constitute protected concerted activity? If not, even under the expansive view of *Brown,* could the exemption apply in this scenario? A similar certification scheme was challenged in

Collins v. Grantham, 850 F. Supp. 1468 (D. Colo. 1991), *aff'd per curiam,* 976 F. 2d 740 (10th Cir. 1992), where the court found the exemption applicable:

> [T]he nonstatutory exemption * * * immunizes the Regulations from Sherman Act scrutiny. The Regulations were unilaterally developed in response to player complaints and to further NBPA labor policies. The NBPA-NBA Agreement, including Article XXXI, was agreed to in arms-length collective bargaining. The provision was not sought 'at the behest of or in combination with' any employer or other non-labor group as forbidden by *Jewel Tea.* There is no economic benefit to the NBPA or the NBA member teams as a result of this provision and there is no effect on the employer's product or service market as a result of the provision.

850 F. Supp. at 1480. Again, if *Mackey* still has life, would the exemption be imperiled by its application? If a court were to conclude either that the agreement was not limited to the parties to the CBA *or* that the agent certification agreement was not a mandatory bargaining subject, then the *Mackey* (and probably *Brown*) criteria, phrased in the conjunctive as they were, would not be satisfied. *See* Lori J. Lefferts, *The NFL Players Association's Agent Certification Plan: Is It Exempt from Antitrust Review?*, 26 Ariz. L. Rev. 699 (1984).

5. The hypothetical concerns became a reality in 1999 in a dispute involving the Arena Football League. Conjuring memories of the NFL-NFLPA situation following the *Powell* decision, the labor exemption played a prominent part in the development of that case.

THE ARENA FOOTBALL SAGA AND THE LABOR EXEMPTION

Arena Football is an indoor football game invented by an NFL Properties executive in the early 1980's as a way to take the tremendous public interest in professional football and create a product that could be played inside basketball and hockey facilities. By the end of the second millennium, despite substantial franchise turnover and relocations, Arena Football had survived seventeen seasons and had spawned a minor league, Arena II, to bring its game to smaller cities. Fueled in part by the success of Arena Football veteran, Kurt Warner, as the Super Bowl MVP for the Los Angeles Rams, national public awareness of the AFL had increased substantially.

Despite the increased awareness and the stability of the league, AFL wages and working conditions were sources for some consternation among AFL players. As a threshold matter, the game was played on a relatively thin carpet placed over very hard surfaces, including in some cases, concrete or ice. Walls surround the field with only a few inches between the sidelines and the walls. The walls are in play, and teams advertised the fact that players may get tackled over the walls and into the laps of the spectators—hockey-like—without the glass to separate the players from the stands. Tackle football that involves contact with walls and hard floors yields injuries, but many AFL players did not have health insurance. The AFL rules required certain players to play on both offense and defense and AFL awards recognized the endurance of these "Iron Men." Some players played for only $200 per game (or less). Moreover, a significant part of AFL team budgets was for workers compensation and AFL teams were involved in various plans and manipulations to limit the extent to which they had to pay, witness the Albany Firebirds busing their players to practice in Vermont every day, contending that the players were entitled to the lower workers compensation benefits provided by Vermont, as opposed to New York.

In the summer of 1999, with the help of the United Food and Commercial Workers Union (UFCW), over ninety percent of the players in the Arena Football League

("AFL") signed a petition for recognition as a labor organization. Representatives of the players and the UFCW met with AFL officials and presented the petition, asking the AFL to recognize the UFCW as a labor organization representing all the players.

During the next several weeks, while the AFL contemplated its response, UFCW officials met with Gene Upshaw and other NFL Players Association representatives and were advised about the Supreme Court's 1996 decision in *Brown v. Pro Football, Inc.*, and the possibility that AFL players might be better served by pursuing relief under the antitrust laws, an avenue that would be precluded if the players unionized. As a result, the UFCW sent a letter to the AFL in the late fall of 1999, withdrawing the request for recognition and specifically disclaiming any intention to unionize the players or to represent AFL players in collective bargaining. At the same time, players from all 17 AFL teams gathered together and formed the AFL Players Association, an organization with a Constitution that expressly forbade the AFLPA from acting as a labor organization or engaging in any conduct that might cause the players to lose their right to pursue antitrust claims against the AFL and its owners.

After a brief moment of relief that the players had abandoned their organizational efforts, the AFL leadership realized that they faced the potential of major antitrust litigation. At the time, the AFL was courting various NFL owners to own and operate AFL teams, and the AFL turned to the NFL's outside antitrust counsel for advice. The AFL and its owners decided that they would be much better off negotiating with a players union, rather than facing antitrust litigation seeking three times the difference between the wages a competitive market would have yielded and the amounts the AFL had paid players under the AFL's comprehensive system of player restraints. The dilemma that the AFL faced was how to force the players to form a union—a situation not dramatically unlike the NFL's post-*Powell*, post-decertification situation in 1992.

The AFL's first gambit involved selecting leading players on the various teams and flying them to the Chicago O'Hare Hilton for a meeting with AFL representatives. The AFL flew players to Chicago for the purpose of organizing and engaging in collective bargaining with those players. In response, the AFLPA booked its own conference room in the same hotel and, as the players selected by the AFL (whose flights were paid for by the AFL) arrived at the hotel, the AFLPA leaders ushered those players into the AFLPA conference room for meetings with the AFLPA's antitrust counsel and for player-only meetings. Only a few players who were missed by the AFLPA upon arrival in Chicago ever attended the meeting with the AFL owners. Eventually, the AFLPA and the players who had joined their meeting offered to attend a negotiating session with the AFL representatives, but only if every AFL representative and every AFL owner in attendance would agree in writing that the meeting was not a collective bargaining session—but rather would be characterized merely as a settlement conference to discuss the possible resolution of antitrust claims that the players were considering filing against the AFL and its owners. When the AFL representatives refused to sign the proffered agreement, the AFLPA conducted its own meeting and the players headed home without ever having met with the AFL or the owners who had financed their trip.

The AFL's next step was to film a December fireside chat (complete with an artificial fireplace in the background) in which AFL Commissioner David Baker told the players that the AFL was a family and the outside interference from the UFCW and the NFLPA was threatening to destroy the AFL family. Commissioner Baker said the AFL owners were willing to sit down with a group of players to discuss improvements in compensation and working conditions for all AFL players. The video of Commissioner Baker's fireside chat was sent to players throughout the AFL, and it was accompanied by public statements by the AFL that the 2000 AFL season (which ran from April to August 2000) would be canceled if the players did not form a union and meet with the owners to engage in collective bargaining.

Despite an organized AFL campaign, the players stood together and refused to organize. Shortly thereafter, the AFL Players Union ("AFLPU"), allegedly backed by the Teamsters, surfaced and initiated efforts to unionize the players. The AFLPU tried to get a majority of the players to sign union cards, calling for player representation by the AFLPU, but the AFLPA persuaded the players to resist the organizing efforts. The league continued to threaten to cancel the 2000 season if the players did not capitulate and support the AFLPU.

In response to the AFL's threat to cancel the season and the other efforts to coerce the AFL players to form a union, several AFL players filed unfair labor practice charges with the NLRB, alleging violations of §8(a)(1) and (2) and 8(b)(1)(A) of the NLRA and claiming, *inter alia*, that the AFL and AFLPW had interfered with their right to choose whether or not to form a labor organization as part of an effort to assert federal antitrust claims.

To break the deadlock before the league-imposed deadline, the AFL Buffalo Destroyers paid three of their players who worked for the team in the off-season, to lead an effort to enlist player support for the AFLPU (without disclosing that the effort was being financed by the Destroyers). When those efforts were also unsuccessful, the players began forging AFL players' names on union cards supporting the AFLPU and faxing them to the AFLPU's office. In the final hours before the league's deadline, the AFLPU claimed to have secured enough signatures, the AFL (aware of the questionable nature of the AFLPU's claim to majority status and not wanting to have possession of evidence that the AFLPU did not have majority support) made it clear that it did not want to see the signatures but nevertheless accepted the AFLPU's claim of majority status and recognized the AFLPU as a union representing all AFL players. The season was not canceled and within a couple of weeks the AFL and AFLPU reached agreement on a collective bargaining agreement that yielded de minimis benefits for AFL players while yielding dues to the AFLPU and locking the AFLPU in as the representative of all AFL players.

With ULPs already pending before the NLRB, the AFLPA alleged further that the AFLPU was a "company union" without majority support and that authorization cards had been falsified. The NLRB accepted the players' charges, issued a complaint against the AFL and its member teams, and scheduled an evidentiary hearing for January of 2001 in Tampa, Florida. The NLRB claimed not just that player signatures had been forged, but also that many of the players whose signatures had been submitted were not part of the bargaining unit, and even if the signatures of players in the possession of the AFLPU were all proper, they did not constitute a majority of the players in any properly defined bargaining unit.

Throughout this time period, the players' class action antitrust lawsuit was proceeding in the United States District Court for the District of New Jersey, in Newark, New Jersey. The players added the AFLPU as a defendant. The AFL and its member teams sought dismissal based on the labor exemption, given the league's claim that the players had chosen, by forming a union and negotiating a long-term collective bargaining agreement, to exercise their rights under federal labor laws and to relinquish their rights under the antitrust laws. The players demanded the right to move ahead, based on their claims that (a) the players had not chosen to be represented by a union—the vast majority of the signatures had been forged, and (b) any "choice" to form a union in response to a threat to shutdown the league and all employment opportunities if the players did not form a union was not within the broadest parameters of the non-statutory example. The players relied upon the NLRB's complaint against the AFL leadership as further support for their opposition to the application of the labor exemption.

The district court denied the motion to dismiss and allowed the antitrust case to continue while the NLRB moved toward its unfair labor practice hearing. A major open question was whether the decision by the NLRB on the unfair labor practice claims would have to be resolved in favor of the players for the labor exemption to be inapplicable, or whether the court needed to make an independent decision of whether the players had chosen the labor laws over the antitrust laws.

Facing the inevitable and imminent disclosures at the NLRB hearing that the AFL recognition of the AFLPU was improper, the AFL and AFLPU agreed to a class action antitrust settlement agreement modeled after prior settlement agreements between the NFL and its players. Under the terms of the settlement, the AFL agreed to: 1) pay damages to AFL players plus attorneys' fees; 2) rescind its recognition of the AFLPU; and, 3) increase dramatically the wages and working conditions of AFL players. Further, players agreed to recognize and to incorporate the terms of the settlement into any collective bargaining agreement with the new collective bargaining representative. The AFLPA and AFLPU campaigned for the right to represent the players. An election was conducted and supervised by the NLRB, and the AFLPA was certified as exclusive bargaining representative for all AFL players.

6. Is the intrigue that surrounded the foregoing account a product of a non-statutory exemption that now runs amuck? Does it provoke employers to engage in tactics of domination and forced unionization to the disservice of employee choice, clear violations of 8(a)(1) and (2) of the NLRA, to avoid antitrust liability whenever they have acted in concert to impose unreasonable restraints in a labor market?

Chapter 10

Antitrust and Sports: Player Restraints

I. Introduction

The cases that follow address several issues dealing with restraints on player participation in sports, including player mobility, eligibility, and discipline. These issues will be addressed from the standpoint of both team or "league" sports and individual sports such as golf and tennis.

In the area of restrictions on player mobility and player compensation, antitrust challenges have focused on such league sport restraints as the amateur drafts, age restrictions, reserve clauses, no-tampering rules, salary caps, caps on certain players—e.g., rookies or "developmental" players—and "compensation" systems (that require a club obtaining the services of a "free agent" to provide some remuneration through a draft choice, a player, or money to the team that has lost the services of the "free agent"). Each of these limitations has restricted players' compensation, or their capability to enter the league or association or move between and among the various teams within a league. In the preceding chapter, courts considered league arguments that many of the allegedly violative provisions were embraced in collective bargaining agreements and thus were "labor-exempt" from antitrust scrutiny. In many instances, however, the labor exemption has been found to be inapplicable, necessitating a review of the allegations on the merits. Several of the opinions contained in this chapter include a portion, not reprinted herein or printed in the previous chapter, that considered the alleged applicability of the labor exemption.

In addition to the player mobility issues, other issues have arisen dealing with player eligibility, such as participation in professional golf and tennis tours (as well as in traditional team sports) and discipline for failing to observe the rules of a league or association. Due to the absence of any collective bargaining relationships in "individual sports" and the possibility that individual athletes may be independent contractors who would not be able to unionize under the protection of federal labor laws, such conduct may not fall within the labor exemption; it is thus vulnerable to judicial scrutiny under the antitrust laws. The *Molinas, Blalock* and *Volvo* cases considered in this chapter illustrate some of the foregoing points.

Restrictions in agreements between players and teams, or athletes and the producers of events in which the athletes compete, have been the subject of considerable controversy and a tremendous amount of antitrust litigation for two primary reasons. First,

445

because top quality players are the most essential element of professional sports and are definitely the central focus of sports fans, ensuring their availability is a primary concern of every league, team owner, circuit of events, or individual event producer. From the vantage point of employers or management, it is very important that contracts with the best athletes guarantee the availability and loyalty of those athletes. Therefore, agreements with players in established leagues and circuits are always major barriers to a new league or circuit that wants to employ top quality players. Restrictions in agreements with elite athletes that restrain new leagues or competing events have historically been the subjects of intense antitrust battles, where the success or failure of a new league or a competing event or series of events hangs in the balance. Antitrust is the sword that competing leagues use to force themselves into a marketplace when player restraints block their access.

Second, because the services of the most proficient athletes are so essential to success or failure of a sporting event and the businesses that produce the event, the single most expensive input for many sports is the compensation paid to the athletes. Competition between teams or events seeking those players increases the level of compensation. Agreements among teams or events and between teams or events and the athletes often limit that competition and restrict the level of player compensation. Antitrust litigation is one of the weapons that athletes use to remove restraints that limit their ability to negotiate for higher salaries or for changes in other aspects of their working conditions. One central aspect of the player's working conditions in team sports is the freedom to change teams, enabling him to seek a winning team, a style of play more suited to the athlete's talents, or a different domicile. The tenuous nature and relatively short length of a professional athlete's career increase the incentive for an athlete to bring an antitrust claim to ensure earlier access into the league or higher salaries and better working conditions once he or she is in the league.

Courts hearing antitrust challenges to player restraints must examine a series of issues. The initial questions concern the applicability of any antitrust exemptions—primarily the baseball exemption (Chapter 8) and the labor exemption (Chapter 9). Then, as explained in Chapter 7, for the restraint to be violative of Section 1 of the Sherman Act, it must be the result of an agreement—the requirement of a "contract, combination * * *, or conspiracy." In professional sports, as explained in Chapter 2 and Chapter 12, that issue is generally presented as a dispute about whether the teams in a league or events in a circuit constitute a single entity, incapable of "conspiring" with itself. While the argument that an agreement among the teams in a traditional model league is the action of a single competitor has not yet been pronounced dead in cases involving inter-league competition or ancillary markets (*e.g.*, television broadcasting of sporting events), such a contention in the context of player restraints may have taken its last breath. Hybrid single entity leagues have had some success in arguing that an agreement among its teams is the action of a single competitor, *see, e.g., Fraser v.* MLS, 97 F. Supp. 2d 130, 135–39 (D. Mass. 2000), but even these claims of single entity status face severe judicial scrutiny. *See, e.g., Fraser v. MLS*, 294 F.3d 47 (1st Cir. 2002).

If the agreement requirement is satisfied, the court must consider what mode of Sherman Act §1 analysis should be applied—*per se*, Rule of Reason, or the "quick look" Rule of Reason. Restraints like the amateur draft, reserve clause, and anti-tampering rules have been challenged as agreements among teams not to compete with each other for the players' services. Players challenge those agreements as *per se* unlawful horizontal market divisions (agreements to divide potential employees), group boycotts (agreements by all the teams without rights to the player to refuse to deal with that player), and price fixing (agreements that reduce competition and thereby decrease the amount for which the player can negotiate). Teams counter that they are joint venturers who must cooperate to produce the games—their product—and for that reason should not be subject to *per se* rules applied to horizontal agreements where cooperation is unnecessary. Ford and General Motors have no need to cooperate—they can each produce cars independently, while the Dallas Cowboys and New York Giants must agree on the rules, the schedule, the officials, and other issues, for their product—the game—to be created.

As you read the cases that follow, ask yourself the following questions. (1) Did the court apply a *per se* rule, the Rule of Reason, or the "quick look" Rule of Reason? Why? (2) If the Rule of Reason (or "quick look" Rule of Reason) was applied, what did the court identify as the relevant market? (3) What were the anticompetitive effects in that market? (4) What were the procompetitive benefits, if any, of the challenged agreements? (5) Were there reasonably less restrictive means by which the procompetitive benefits could be achieved without causing the anticompetitive effects? (6) Are the rules at issue in the case similar to rules now in effect in that sport? If not, how have the rules changed? Are they now exempt from antitrust scrutiny due to some exempt status? If not, are the new rules unlawful?

II. Restraints of Trade in the Market for Player Services

(A) Player Restraints and Application of the Per Se Rule

Kapp v. National Football League
390 F. Supp. 73 (N.D. Cal. 1974)

SWEIGERT, District Judge. Plaintiff Joe Kapp, once an All-American (1958) for the University of California Bears, later a Professional quarterback of considerable renown in the Canadian League (1959–1966) and with the Minnesota Vikings (1967–1969) and finally a quarterback for the New England Patriots (1970), brings this suit against the defendants National Football League (NFL), its Commissioner Pete Rozelle and its 26 member professional football clubs and other related defendants, alleging antitrust conspiracy and monopoly among defendants, whereunder defendants in July, 1971, caused his discharge by the New England Patriots with which he claims to have had an October 6, 1970 contract to play for the 1970, 1971 and 1972 seasons for a stated compensation of $600,000, alleging, further, that defendants, in effect, drove plaintiff out of professional football in the United States. * * *

While Kapp was with the University of California and a prospective professional player, the Washington Redskins "drafted" him pursuant to a so-called "selection" or "draft" rule, embodied in the NFL Constitution and By-Laws, Section 14.3(A) and 14.5, providing that at a Selection Meeting of the NFL Clubs, held annually in January or February, each club participating therein can select prospective players of its own choice; the selecting club will have the exclusive right to negotiate for the services of each player selected by it and placed on its Reserve List—even if the selecting club's offer to the prospective player might be unacceptable and even if the selecting club makes no offer at all, no other league club may negotiate with him without the consent of the selecting club.

The NFL Constitution and By-Laws, Section 9.2 also contains a so-called "tampering" rule which provides that if a member club shall tamper, negotiate with or make an offer to a player on the active, reserve or selection list of another club, then the offending club, in addition to being subject to all other penalties provided in the NFL Constitution and By-Laws, shall lose its selection choice in the next succeeding selection meeting in the same round in which the affected player was originally chosen and, if such offense was intentional the Commissioner shall have power to fine the offending club and may award the offended club 50% of the amount of the fine imposed by the Commissioner.

When the Washington Redskins made no satisfactory offer to Kapp, he went to the Canadian Football League and played there for seven years (1959–1966) during which period the Redskins kept him on their reserve list until April, 1966 and thus barred other NFL Clubs from negotiating with him.

Kapp's last Canadian contract expired after the 1966 season, subject to an option of his Canadian team to renew his contract for 1967—an option which was exercised. The Canadian Club, however, then suspended Kapp because of his covert negotiations, during December, 1966, with the Houston Oilers of the then American Football League.

Those negotiations had resulted in a contract between Kapp and the Oilers, dated February 10, 1967, whereunder Kapp was to be paid a $10,000 bonus to report to Houston in 1967 if his Canadian team did not exercise its option and, if it did, then he was to report to Houston in 1968 and play for two years at a salary of $100,000 a year.

On April 12, 1967, the Kapp-Oilers contract was declared invalid by NFL Commissioner Rozelle and by the then President of the AFL, acting together, according to plaintiff, pursuant to an understanding between the NFL and the Canadian League that players would not be permitted to contract during their contract periods for moving from one league to another.

Although Kapp still preferred to play for the Oilers, he eventually obtained clearance to play for the Minnesota Vikings when the latter paid Kapp's Canadian team $50,000 for his release and (apparently) made satisfactory arrangements with the Washington Redskins for any claim they might have. Kapp's contract with the Vikings, dated September 3, 1967, was for the 1967–1968 seasons with an option to have him also in 1969 for a total compensation of $300,000.

Kapp played with the Vikings during 1967 and 1968; the Vikings then exercised their option for a third year, 1969, during which Kapp contributed considerably to the Vikings NFL championship and participation at the Super Bowl.

The Vikings offered Kapp a contract for another two years upon the same compensation terms but Kapp declined to sign. Other clubs, needing a quarterback of Kapp's ability, expressed interest—the Philadelphia Eagles and the Houston Oilers—but neither club followed up with an offer.

According to plaintiff, this was because those teams were restrained by the so-called "Ransom" or "Rozelle" rule which, as embodied in the NFL Constitution and By-Laws

(Sec. 12.1(H)), provides that no league club will employ a player even if he has become a free agent by playing out his contract (as did Kapp) unless the new employing club either makes satisfactory arrangements with the former employing club, or, absent such satisfactory arrangements, employs the player subject to the power of the NFL Commissioner to name and award one or more players to the former club from the active reserve or selection list of the acquiring club as the Commissioner in his sole discretion deems fair and reasonable.

Eventually, the New England Patriots, needing a quarterback of Kapp's abilities, sought assurances from the Minnesota Vikings concerning what they would require as a ransom in the event the Patriots employed Kapp. This resulted in a transfer agreement between the Vikings and the Patriots under which the Patriots surrendered to the Vikings the Patriots' first round of draft choice for 1972 and, in addition, their number-one draft selection of 1967.

Under these conditions the Patriots contracted with Kapp under date of October 6, 1970, for his services as a Patriot for the remainder of the 1970 season and for 1971 and 1972 at a total compensation of $600,000. (Defendants contend that there is some evidence in the record that this claimed contract was merely a memorandum intended by the parties to be effective only when Kapp signed a Standard Player Contract).

Nevertheless, Kapp played for the Patriots under that agreement for the remaining eleven games of the 1970 season and was paid $154,000 of the contracted amount.

In January, 1971, the Patriots, acting pursuant to the NFL Constitution and By-Laws and at the direction of the Commissioner, sent Kapp a form of Standard Player Contract but Kapp refused to sign it. This Standard Player Contract is required by the NFL Constitution and By-Laws, Sections 15.1 and 15.4, to the effect that all contracts between the clubs and players shall be in the form adopted by the member clubs of the league, each club to have the right to modify such standard contract but subject to the right of the Commissioner to disapprove any such modification which is in violation of the Constitution and By-Laws or if either contracting party is guilty of conduct detrimental to the league or to professional football.

The Standard Player Contract (Pars. 4, 6 and 11), so required, provides that the player becomes bound by the Constitution, By-Laws, Rules and Regulations of the league and of his club, including future amendments thereto and to the discipline of the club—subject only to the right to a hearing by the Commissioner whose decisions shall be final and unappealable.

The Standard Player Contract, Par. 10 also contains the so-called "option" rule which gives the employing club an unilateral option to renew the contract for a further term of one year at a reduced rate of compensation, i.e., 90% of the amount paid by the player in the previous year—the purpose of this rule being, according to plaintiff, to coerce the player to sign a new contract on the owner's terms under peril of having to serve another year at the reduced compensation.

On May 28, 1971, Commissioner Rozelle wrote to the Patriots reminding the club that Articles 17.5(B) and 15.6 of the NFL Constitution and By-Laws provide that no player may play in a game or practice with a member club unless an executed Standard Player Contract is on file with the Commissioner.

Kapp was permitted to report to the Patriots (1971) training camp and to take the physical examination and participate in team meetings and light workouts but, when he persisted in his refusal to sign the Standard Player Contract he was, in effect, told by the Patriots to leave.

In July, 1971, the defendant clubs instituted a grievance procedure against Kapp, pursuant to the NFL Constitution and By-Laws §§8.3, 8.5 and 8.13(F), complaining that he had refused to sign a Standard Player Contract and, upon reference of the grievance to Commissioner Rozelle for decision, the Commissioner, (Kapp failing to appear) reaffirmed his previous decision by ordering Kapp to sign a Standard Player Contract as a condition of eligibility to continue his participation in football activity on behalf of the Patriots or any other NFL Club. * * *

Even after Kapp's departure from the Patriots' training camp the Patriots retained him on their reserve list in the expectation that, under the so-called "Ransom" or "Rozelle" Rule, already above mentioned, the Patriots could claim a ransom if Kapp should sign with any other NFL Club. * * *

PLAINTIFF'S CONTENTIONS

Plaintiff contends that the foregoing rules contained in the NFL Constitution and By-Laws * * * constitute a combination among defendants to refuse to deal with players except under the above stated conditions—in effect a boycott or blacklist—and as such a *per se* violation of the Sherman Act.

Plaintiffs further contend that, apart from the *per se* rule, the combination is illegal even under the "rule of reason" because the restraint obviously goes far beyond what would be reasonably necessary to achieve the business goals involved. * * *

DEFENDANTS' CONTENTIONS

Defendants contend (1) that the rules contained in the NFL Constitution and By-Laws and in the Standard Player Contract, do not amount to a violation of the antitrust laws—certainly not to such a refusal to deal as would amount to a per se violation of Section 1 of the Sherman Act as contended by plaintiff, and (2) that, even if these rules might otherwise amount to an antitrust violation, all of these rules are now immunized from antitrust laws by having become since at least from February 1, 1970, the subject of, and the result of, collective bargaining between the NFL, as an employer, and the NFL Football Players Association as the certified collective bargaining labor union representative of all NFL players.

Deferring consideration of defendants' asserted collective bargaining defense, we take up first the question whether the rules contained in the NFL Constitution, By-Laws and Standard Player Contract, amount to a violation of the Sherman Act *per se* or otherwise.

THE ANTITRUST ISSUE—CONTENTIONS OF THE PARTIES

* * *

[D]efendants argue that professional league sport activities, such as football, must be distinguished from other kinds of business activities which have been held to be per se antitrust violations; that league sports activities are so unique that the per se rule is inapplicable; that, although club teams compete on the playing field, the clubs are not, and indeed cannot be, competitors with one another in a business way because the very purpose of a professional sports league is to provide reasonably matched teams for field competition to attract and sustain the interest and patronage of the fans; that the success of the league as a joint venture of its clubs depends upon the ability of each club to do this; that, if each member club were allowed by the league to engage in free-for-all competition for the best or better players, then the most strongly financed or otherwise better advantaged clubs would be able to sign up and monopolize the best or better players, leaving only average or mediocre players for the other clubs with the effect of destroying the evenly matched field competition that brings fans to the games.

For this reason, defendants say, there must be league agreements and rules which, restricting the freedom of the clubs to compete for players, impinge to some extent upon the freedom of players to choose their own clubs. * * *

THE ANTITRUST ISSUE—CONCLUSIONS

* * *

[S]ince plaintiff contends that the challenged rules are illegal *per se*, while defendant argues for the test of *reasonableness*, we must now determine which test to apply in this case.

There is authority to the effect that combinations of the kind shown by the record here, constitute *per se* antitrust violations. * * *

Under the holdings of those cases the combination here shown would be a per se violation of the antitrust laws. In *Washington State Bowling Assn. v. Pacific Lanes* [356 F.2d 371 (9th Cir. 1966)], the Court applied the principle that in league sports activities all jointly enforced regulations, limiting the right of each club to deal with anyone it chooses and consequently limiting to some extent the players' free choice of employment, are *per se* illegal—regardless of whether the regulation is designed to promote the league sport rather than to constitute a boycott.

However, we are of the opinion that for reasons to be hereinafter set forth it is not necessary to rest our decision in this pending case on an application of the *per se* rule.

In the first place, there are cases which, recognizing the unique nature and purpose of sports league activities, hold * * * that the *per se* rule is inappropriate and inapplicable to sports league activities. * * *

In our pending case and in similar cases the only alleged anti-competitive practice is joint club enforcement, through the league, of player-employee contracts whereunder the player agrees to accept and the clubs agree among themselves to enforce certain restrictions on the players' right to freely pursue his trade with other club-employers and the clubs yield to that extent their free choice to employ.

There is a well-settled rule of contract law that employer-employee contracts, restricting an employee's right to freely pursue his trade, may be illegal as against public policy *if, but only if,* the restraint is *unreasonable,* taking into consideration the nature of the business, the duration of the restraint, the area in which it operates, the situation of the parties and all circumstances bearing on whether the restriction is such only as to afford fair protection to the interests of the employer without imposing such an undue hardship on the employee as to interfere with the public interest. * * *

We have in mind, of course, that when two or more club employers agree through league rules that individual player-employees, who violate such individual club-employee contracts will be in effect boycotted by all member club-employers, the situation goes beyond mere employer-employee contracting and falls within the antitrust law *per se* prohibition of *combinations* not to deal—even though the reasonableness test would have been applicable to the individual player contract.

It is arguable, however, that in this unique field of sports league activities (wherein to achieve fairly evenly matched teams on the field, there must be some degree and kind of restriction on the right of clubs to hire and players to sign as they please) the test of legality of league rules for that purpose should be the same test, *i.e.*, reasonableness test, as would be applicable to the individual player-club contract.

A further argument for preferring the reasonableness test is the existence of the player-employee/club-employer relationship—a relationship which lends itself to collective bargaining. Application of the absolute antitrust *per se* rule to *all* league rules enforcing restrictions upon the players' free choice of employment tends to preclude collective bargaining negotiations for league enforcement of some rules in this category which, considering the unique nature and purpose of league sports, may be regarded by both players and clubs as reasonably necessary in furtherance of their long-range *mutual* interests. For the foregoing reasons we conclude that in this particular field of sports league activities the purposes of the antitrust laws can be just as well served (if not better served) by the basic antitrust reasonableness test as by the absolute *per se* test sometimes applied by the courts in other fields.

In applying the reasonableness test we have in mind that the issue of reasonableness is ordinarily in such genuine dispute that a case cannot be resolved on a motion for summary judgment and must go to full trial of that issue.

However, in the present case, league enforcement of most of the challenged rules is so patently unreasonable that there is no genuine issue for trial.

The "Ransom" or "Rozelle" rule, provides in effect that a player, even after he has played out his contract under the option rule and has thereby become a free agent, is still restrained from pursuing his business to the extent that all league members with whom he might otherwise negotiate for new employment are prohibited from employing him unless upon consent of his former employer or, absent such consent, subject to the power of the NFL Commissioner to name and award one or more players to the former employer from the active reserve or selection list of the acquiring club—as the NFL Commissioner in his sole discretion deems fair and reasonable.

A conceivable effect of this rule would be to *perpetually* restrain a player from pursuing his occupation among the clubs of a league that holds a virtual monopoly of professional football employment in the United States.

We conclude that such a rule imposing restraint virtually unlimited in time and extent, goes far beyond any possible need for fair protection of the interests of the club-employers or the purposes of the NFL and that it imposes upon the player-employees such undue hardship as to be an unreasonable restraint and such a rule is not susceptible of different inferences concerning its reasonableness; it is unreasonable under any legal test and there is no genuine issue about it to require or justify trial.

Similarly, the draft rule * * * is also patently unreasonable insofar as it permits virtually perpetual boycott of a draft prospect even when the drafting club refuses or fails within a reasonable time to reach a contract with the player.

Similarly, the so-called "one-man rule" * * *, vesting final decision in the NFL Commissioner, is also patently unreasonable (particularly where considered in the light of principles of impartial arbitration embodied in the Federal Arbitration Act, 9 U.S.C. §1-14, and underlying the decision of the Supreme Court in *Commonwealth Corp. v. Casualty Co.*, 393 U.S. 145 (1968)), insofar as that unilateral kind of arbitration is used to interpret or enforce other NFL rules involving restrictions on the rights of players or clubs to free employment choice.

Similarly, the tampering rule * * * and the Standard Player Contract rule * * * are also patently unreasonable insofar as they are used to enforce other NFL rules in that area.

The Option Rule, which appears only in the Standard Contract (Par. 10), gives the club an option for one additional year of service at 90% of the contract salary unless otherwise agreed. Since NFL rules leave the matters of duration and salary to free negotiation between players and clubs, this lone prescribed option provision cannot be said to so extend the original term and salary as to render it patently unreasonable; its legality cannot, therefore, be determined on summary judgment.

However, it is not necessary to hold that NFL league enforcement is illegal as to all restrictive employment or tenure rules; it is sufficient if we can determine on summary judgment the illegality of league enforcement of one or more such rules to the detriment of plaintiff.

It remains, therefore, only to determine whether NFL enforcement of the rules which we have held to be patently unreasonable and illegal can be deemed to have been the cause or at least one of the causes of injury to plaintiff.

We have in mind that the record here shows that the immediate cause of plaintiff's discharge by the New England Patriots was his refusal to comply with demands that he sign the Standard Player Contract.

However, as already explained, signing of the Standard Player Contract (including its paragraphs 4, 5 and 6) would bind a player to the whole NFL Constitution and By-Laws which, in turn, include the rules herein held to be illegal.

As already indicated, we are mindful that it may be held on review that application of the per se test renders NFL enforcement illegal as to all restrictive employment or tenure rules regardless of reasonableness for sports league purposes. If so, such holding could be made on the present record without trial or further proceedings. * * *

[The Court then explains that the defendants' conduct was not labor exempt because the Collective Bargaining Agreement had not been executed at the time of the conduct challenged by Kapp.]

Further, even if the NFL Standard Player Contract requirement had been accepted through collective bargaining, there would still remain the question, well put by Marshall, J. in *Flood* * * * as to what are "the limits to the antitrust violations to which labor and management can agree." We are of the opinion that, however broad may be the exemption from antitrust laws of collective bargaining agreements dealing with wages, hours and other conditions of employment, that exemption does not and should not go so far as to permit immunized combinations to enforce employer-employee agreements which, being unreasonable restrictions on an employee's right to freely seek and choose his employment, have been held illegal on grounds of public policy long before and entirely apart from the antitrust laws.

We conclude, therefore, that upon the record before us it appears with no genuine dispute as to any material fact that the NFL Standard Contract Rule under which plaintiff was discharged from his employment, had not been contractually accepted by plaintiff or the Players Association as the result of collective bargaining.

It is unnecessary to decide the further question whether collective bargaining contracts, insofar as they bind members of a union to employer enforcement of individual contract restrictions upon the employee's right to pursue his trade with other employers, really fall within the NLRA requirement for collective bargaining concerning "wages, hours and other terms and conditions of employment." * * *

For the above reasons, the plaintiff's motion for summary judgment should be and hereby is granted in part in accordance with the views set forth herein. * * *

Notes and Questions

1. The Court concluded that the NFL's rules—the draft, the "Rozelle rule," the "one-man rule," and the "tampering rule"—violated the antitrust laws, but the court refused to find a *per se* violation. Why?

2. One reason given for the court's refusal to apply the *per se* rule was that such a rule might tend "to preclude collective bargaining negotiations for league enforcement of some rules * * * which, considering the unique nature and purpose of League sports, may be regarded by both players and clubs in furtherance of their long-range *mutual* interests." What did the court mean? If the rules further both the players' and teams' long-range mutual interests, does that mean the rules are procompetitive or, in some sense of the word, "reasonable"? After he decided to apply the Rule of Reason, how and why did Judge Sweigert take the fact-specific application of the Rule of Reason away from the jury? Consider Judge Sweigert's approach and compare it to the "quick look" Rule of Reason announced and applied by the Supreme Court ten years later in *NCAA v. Board of Regents*, 468 U.S. 85 (1984).

3. In *Smith v. Pro-Football*, 593 F.2d 1173 (D.C. Cir. 1978), the court of appeals affirmed a lower court finding that the NFL draft was an unreasonable restraint of trade in violation of Section 1 of the Sherman Act. However, the court refused to affirm the lower court's finding of a *per se* violation, opting instead to apply a Rule of Reason analysis. Employing the Rule of Reason approach, the D.C. Circuit dismissed out of hand the NFL's contentions that the competitive balance and the league's operational integrity would suffer if the draft were eliminated. The court reasoned first that comparing the on-the-field competitive benefits to off-the-field, economically anticompetitive disadvantages was tantamount to comparing apples to oranges. *See also National Society of Professional Engineers v. United States*, 435 U.S. 679 (1978). Further, the court questioned the legitimacy of the league's claims that the draft and similar player restraints were necessary to insure the continuation of competitive balance and the avoidance of dynasties. Is the court's assessment of the procompetitive vs. anticompetitive balancing test fair? Could a league argue persuasively that the relevant product market is entertainment and that on-the-field competitiveness, if it can be demonstrably related to the restraint in question, creates a better, more competitive product *vis-à-vis* other entertainment fare? Should treatment of a professional sports league be different than other types of industries for purposes of a typical antitrust inquiry? In this regard, is the application of a *per se* rule to professional sports ever appropriate given the fact that some type of economically anticompetitive behavior lies at the heart of most league structures? *See* Joseph P. Bauer, *Antitrust and Sports: Must Competition On the Field Displace Competition in the Marketplace?*, 60 Tenn. L. Rev. 263 (1993); Gary R. Roberts, *The Evolving Confusion of Professional Sports, Antitrust, The Rule of Reason and The Doctrine of Ancillary Restraints*, 61 S. Cal. L. Rev. 943 (1988).

4. In 2004, Maurice Clarett, a star running back for Ohio State University, brought a similar claim against the NFL's draft eligibility rule. According to the NFL's rules, a

player could not enter the NFL draft until he was at least three full football seasons removed from high school, or after that player's high school graduation. Clarett, who graduated high school on December 11, 2001, was denied entry into the 2004 NFL draft and therefore brought a Section 1 claim against the NFL.

Although both parties agreed that the Rule of Reason applied, U.S. District Judge Scheindlin held that the draft eligibility rule should be analyzed under the "quick look" Rule of Reason "because its anticompetitive effects are so obvious." *Clarett v. NFL*, 306 F. Supp. 2d 379, 408 (S.D.N.Y.), *rev'd*, 369 F.3d 124 (2d Cir. 2004).

Given Judge Scheindlin's conclusion that the NFL's draft eligibility rule was "blatantly" anticompetitive, the burden shifted to the NFL to identify the procompetitive benefits of the rule. The NFL, much like it did in *Kapp* and in subsequent antitrust suits, argued that there were four primary procompetitive benefits that justified the imposition of the age restriction. First, the NFL argued that the rule protected players who were physically and emotionally unprepared for the risk of injury in the NFL. Second, the NFL claimed that injuries to these young players would devalue the sport in the public eye. Third, the NFL argued that the rule protected the NFL and its teams from the costs and liability associated with injuries to these players. Fourth, the NFL claimed that the rule protected the young players from the risk and temptation of self-abuse and steroid use. *Id.* at 408–10.

Judge Scheindlin held that each of these justifications was inadequate as a matter of law and that all of the NFL's alleged goals could be achieved through less restrictive means, and therefore ruled in favor of Clarett. According to Judge Scheindlin, the NFL's concern regarding the "health of younger players is laudable, but it has nothing to do with promoting competition." *Id.* at 408. Is there an argument that the protection of young players and potential future NFL stars is procompetitive?

Moreover, as in *Smith*, 593 F.2d 1173 (see note 3 above) Judge Scheindlin rejected the NFL's contention that any potential anticompetitive effects in the player's market may be justified by procompetitive effects in the overall entertainment market. "Even if it could be said with certainty that the (eligibility rule) is procompetitive in this sense—and the League has certainly submitted no evidence to that effect—the League may not enact a policy that, effectively, 'determine[s] the respective values of competition in various sectors of the economy.'" *Clarett*, 306 F. Supp. 2d at 408–09 (quoting *United States v. Topco Assocs., Inc.*, 405 U.S. 596, 610. *Topco*, cited for support by Judge Scheindlin, has come under intense criticism from judges and commentators. *See, e.g., Rothery Storage & Van Co. v. Atlas Van Lines, Inc.*, 792 F.2d 210, 226 (D.C. Cir. 1986) (citing *Broadcast Music, Inc. v. Columbia Broadcasting System*, 441 U.S. 1 (1979); *National Collegiate Athletic Association v. Board of Regents*, 468 U.S. 85 (1984), and *Northern Wholesale Stationers, Inc. v. Pacific Stationery & Printing Co.*, 472 U.S. 284 (1985)); Robert H. Bork, The Antitrust Paradox: A Policy at War with Itself, 276–277 (1978). Additionally, other courts have held that it can be appropriate to balance the anticompetitive effects of one market with the procompetitive benefits in the overall sports or entertainment market. *See, e.g., MLS v. Fraser*, 7 F.Supp.2d 73, 77 (D. Mass. 1998) (noting that "a restraint on competition in the market for player services might have corresponding, and necessary, procompetitive effects in the market for soccer matches or for sports entertainment generally"); *Sullivan v. NFL*, 34 F.3d 1091, 1112 (1st Cir. 1994) (stating that it is appropriate "in some cases to balance the anticompetitive effects on competition in one market with certain procompetitive benefits in other markets").

In dismissing the NFL's argument, Judge Scheindlin stated that "[t]he NFL's reference to 'protecting the NFL's entertainment product' is somewhat obscure. The NFL never explains how protecting its entertainment product enhances competition." *Clarett*, 306 F. Supp. 2d at 409, n.184. If you were counsel for the NFL, what arguments would you make to explain how protecting the NFL's product enhances competition?

As discussed more fully in Chapter 9, Judge Scheindlin's opinion was reversed by the Second Circuit on the grounds that the draft eligibility rule was protected by the non-statutory labor exemption. *Clarett*, 369 F.3d 124 (2d Cir. 2004).

5. In *National Hockey League Players Association v. Plymouth Whalers*, 419 F.3d 462 (6th Cir. 2005), the NHL Players Association brought a suit alleging that the Ontario Hockey League (the "OHL") violated Section 1 of the Sherman Act by adopting a rule that prohibited 20-year olds from playing in the OHL[23] if they had previously played at an NCAA school. The NHLPA argued that the rule, known as the "Van Ryn Rule," was established to prevent NCAA players from achieving free agency without having signed a contract with the NHL team that drafted them. *Id.* at 467.

The Sixth Circuit held that the *per se* rule was inappropriate, stating that "courts consistently have analyzed challenged conduct under the Rule of Reason when dealing with an industry in which some horizontal restraints are necessary for the availability of a product such as sports leagues." *Id.* at 469 (internal quotation and citation omitted). After applying the Rule of Reason, however, the court rejected the NHLPA's claim, holding that the NHLPA had failed to prove that the Van Ryn Rule actually caused the harm alleged by the plaintiffs. *Id.* at 475–76. Instead, the court found that any restrictions on free agency were caused by agreements in the NHL's collective bargaining agreement, and such agreements were protected by the non-statutory labor exemption. *Id.* at 474.

Should the OHL players, who are not members of the NHLPA and therefore have no part in the negotiation of the NHL collective bargaining agreement, be bound by the terms of an agreement negotiated without them? And, should the OHL players be prevented from bringing an antitrust claim against an agreement that was created to exclude them? *See Clarett v. NFL*, 369 F.3d 124 (2d Cir. 2004). For a complete discussion of the non-statutory labor exemption, *see* Chapter 9.

6. Should players be permitted to negotiate with another club while under contract? If so, what was the justification in *Kapp* for the "understanding between the NFL and the Canadian League that players would not be permitted to contract during their contract periods for moving from one league to another?"

7. What did the *Kapp* court decide about the contract requirement that player-team disputes be decided in final, binding arbitration before the commissioner? Article 3.11(D) of the present NFL Constitution & Bylaws requires every NFL team to "include in every contract between any member club and its employees, including coaches and players, a clause wherein the parties * * * agree to be bound by the Constitution and Bylaws" and Article 8.3(B) gives the commissioner "full, complete, and final jurisdiction and authority to arbitrate" any dispute between any NFL team and any player, coach, or team employee. Is that requirement enforceable to the extent that it is compatible with relevant provisions of the collective bargaining agreement between the NFL and the NFLPA?

---

23. The OHL was made up of twenty teams, each of which was permitted to carry players aged sixteen through nineteen and three players who were twenty years old.

8. As we saw in Chapter 9, restrictions legally agreed to as part of collective bargaining or even restrictions unilaterally implemented by a league after impasse between the league and its players association are insulated from antitrust attack. Players thus sacrifice the ability to bring certain antitrust claims when they unionize and collectively bargain with their respective leagues. One group of players, the professional soccer players playing in Major League Soccer ("MLS")—decided not to form a union in order to preserve the ability bring an antitrust lawsuit against the MLS.

The MLS began its first season in 1996, and the non-unionized soccer players filed an antitrust claim against the MLS in February 1997, claiming that the MLS and its teams (and the United States Soccer Federation) violated Section 1 of the Sherman Act by agreeing not to compete for player services and violated Section 2 of the Sherman Act by preventing any other organization from competing against the MLS. *Fraser v. MLS*, 284 F.3d 47 (1st Cir. 2002).

The first response by the MLS was that it was a "single entity" and therefore, by definition, could not form an agreement or conspiracy in violation of Section 1 of the Sherman Act. The "single entity" concept and defense as well as the structure of the MLS will be discussed at length in Chapter 12, but the crux of the MLS's argument was that, unlike the NBA, NFL, NHL, and MLB, the MLS "retains significant centralized control over both league and individual team operations." *Id.* at 53. Most significantly, according to the MLS, the league—and not the individual owners of the MLS teams—"recruits the players, negotiates their salaries, pays them from league funds, and, to a large extent, determines where each of them will play." *Id.* The district court agreed, granting summary judgment for the MLS and concluding that they comprised a single entity incapable of conspiring in violation of Section 1 of the Sherman Act. *Fraser v. MLS*, 97 F. Supp. 2d 130, 135–39 (D.Mass. 2000).

On appeal, the First Circuit concluded that it need not decide whether the MLS was a single entity because the players had failed to prove a relevant United States market and thus could not sustain a claim under Section 1 or Section 2. In rejecting the players' case, however, the First Circuit made clear that in cases involving "interdependent multi-party enterprises," the Rule of Reason—and not the *per se* analysis—is the appropriate framework for analyzing antitrust claims. *Fraser*, 284 F.3d at 58. According to the First Circuit:

> Sports leagues are a primary example [of interdependent multi-party enterprises,] but so are common franchising arrangements and joint ventures that perform specific services for competitors. Certainly the trend of section 1 law has been to soften *per se* rules and to recognize the need for accommodation among interdependent enterprises. * * *

> [E]ven if we assume that section 1 applies, it is clear to us that the [MLS] cannot be condemned by *per se* rules and presents at best a debatable case under the rule of reason. * * *

> The rejection of the *per se* rule is straightforward. Although players portray MLS as a sham for horizontal price fixing, the extent of real economic integration is obvious. * * *

> [T]he effects of the MLS arrangement are simply too uncertain to warrant application of the *per se* rule.

Id. at 58, 59 (internal quotations and citations omitted). Does the Second Circuit's holding signal the end of the debate regarding the application of the *per se* versus Rule of Reason tests? Are sports leagues such as the MLS, NBA, MLB, NBA, and NHL truly "interdependent multi-party enterprises"?

9. What was the court's antitrust analysis of the NFL requirement that compensation be given by a team that signs a player (like Kapp) who has become a free agent by playing out his option? Is it arguable that the requirement is procompetitive because it gives the team an opportunity to recover the investment made in coaching and training young players?

The MLS made a similar argument in its suit against the MLS players, in which MLS claimed that it had to restrict salaries in order to survive as a league. In briefly discussing the actual restraints at issue in the case, the Second Circuit noted that the "best arguments for upholding MLS's restrictions [are] that it is a new and risky venture" and that "[w]ithout the restrictions, MLS might not exist or, if it did, might have larger initial losses and a shorter life. This would hardly enhance competition." *Id.* at 59. Is this consistent with the Supreme Court's statement in *National Society of Professional Engineers v. United States*, 435 U.S. 679, 696 (1978) that "the Rule of Reason does not support a defense based on the assumption that competition itself is unreasonable?" Should the financial status and stability of a league be a factor in the actual Rule of Reason analysis or should it be relevant only in terms of deciding whether to apply the *per se* rule or the Rule of Reason in the first instance? If you were a representative of a new league, what factors would you focus on to show that your league was at risk of failure?

10.   Another issue involving the MLS and its players was a challenge to soccer's international transfer fee system, enforced by FIFA, soccer's international governing body. *Fraser v. MLS*, 7 F. Supp. 2d 73 (D. Mass. 1998). According to the players' complaint in *Fraser*, "once a player has signed with the MLS to play for an MLS Member Team, he cannot sign a contract with a team in another soccer league in another country without the payment of a significant transfer fee, even if the player's contract with the MLS has expired." FIFA does not require a team signing the free agent player to pay compensation in the form of replacement players; the transfer fee is monetary compensation. The district court held that the Rule of Reason should be applied to this transfer fee system, because "there is no accumulated judicial experience analyzing the rules of international sports federations in light of antitrust principles." *Id.* at 77. How would you defend this rule under the Rule of Reason? Should United States courts apply United States antitrust law to an internationally mandated, worldwide set of rules?

11. If the draft rule at issue in this case is held unlawful, why do players associations agree to draft rules in collective bargaining agreements? What is the significance of the number of rounds of a draft to substantive antitrust analysis under the Rule of Reason? Why did the NFL and the NBA, but not Major League Baseball, reduce significantly the number of rounds of their respective amateur drafts?

12. What did Judge Sweigert mean when he referred to the question of "what are 'the limits to the antitrust violations to which labor and management can agree'"? Knowing what you do about the labor exemption, are there still limits other than a requirement that the matter involve a mandatory subject of bargaining? What about the agreements Sweigert refers to—"unreasonable restrictions on an employee's right to freely seek and choose his employment * * * [which] have been held illegal on grounds of public policy long before and entirely apart from the antitrust laws"—are they exempt if included in a collective bargaining agreement? What if they are imposed unilaterally by management after impasse?

13. Following Judge Sweigert's opinion, the matter was heard before a jury. The judge had reserved for trial the issue of whether NFL enforcement of the challenged

rules precipitated Kapp's damages. After a lengthy trial, the jury found that the rules did not cause any injury and returned a verdict against Kapp on all issues. *See Kapp v. NFL*, 586 F.2d 644 (9th Cir. 1978). On appeal, the Ninth Circuit held that Kapp's failure to prove actual damage "eliminate[d] any harm that the NFL may have suffered by virtue of the summary judgment" and rendered the NFL's appeal moot. 586 F.2d at 650. All plaintiffs seeking remedy under the antitrust laws must establish, at a minimum, the existence of injury to themselves, often referred to as "the fact of damage." *See, e.g., Story Parchment Co. v. Paterson Parchment Paper Co.*, 282 U.S. 555 (1931). *See also Midwest Communications v. Minnesota Twins, Inc.*, 779 F.2d 444 (8th Cir. 1985).

Mackey v. National Football League
543 F.2d 606 (8th Cir. 1976)

LAY, Circuit Judge. Prior to 1963, a team which signed a free agent who had previously been under contract to another club was not obligated to compensate the player's former club. In 1963, after R. C. Owens played out his option with the San Francisco 49ers and signed a contract with the Baltimore Colts, the member clubs of the NFL unilaterally adopted the following provision, now known as the Rozelle Rule, as an amendment to the League's Constitution and Bylaws:

> Any player, whose contract with a League club has expired, shall thereupon become a free agent and shall no longer be considered a member of the team of that club following the expiration date of such contract. Whenever a player, becoming a free agent in such manner, thereafter signed a contract with a different club in the League, then, unless mutually satisfactory arrangements have been concluded between the two League clubs, the Commissioner may name and then award to the former club one or more players, from the Active, Reserve, or Selection List (including future selection choices) of the acquiring club as the Commissioner in his sole discretion deems fair and equitable; any such decision by the Commissioner shall be final and conclusive.

This provision, unchanged in form, is currently embodied in §12.1(H) of the NFL Constitution. The ostensible purposes of the rule are to maintain competitive balance among the NFL teams and protect the clubs' investment in scouting, selecting and developing players.

During the period from 1963 through 1974, 176 players played out their options. Of that number, 34 signed with other teams. In three of those cases, the former club waived compensation. In 27 cases, the clubs involved mutually agreed upon compensation. Commissioner Rozelle awarded compensation in the four remaining cases.

* * *

ANTITRUST ISSUES.

We turn, then, to the question of whether the Rozelle Rule, as implemented, violates §1 of the Sherman Act, which declares illegal "every contract, combination * * * or conspiracy, in restraint of trade or commerce among the several States." 15 U.S.C. §1. The district court found the Rozelle Rule to be a *per se* violation of the Act. Alternatively, the court held the Rule to be violative of the Rule of Reason standard.

Players' Services as a Product Market.

The clubs and the Commissioner first urge that the only product market arguably affected by the Rozelle Rule is the market for players' services, and that the restriction of competition for players' services is not a type of restraint proscribed by the Sherman Act. In support of this contention, defendants rely on §6 of the Clayton Act, 15 U.S.C. §17, and on language construing that statute in *Apex Hosiery Co. v. Leader*, Section 6 of the Clayton Act provides:

> The labor of a human being is not a commodity or article of commerce. Nothing contained in the antitrust laws shall be construed to forbid the existence and operation of labor, agricultural, or horticultural organizations, instituted for the purposes of mutual help, and not having capital stock or conducted for profit, or to forbid or restrain individual members of such organizations from lawfully carrying out the legitimate objects thereof; nor shall such organizations, or the members thereof, be held or construed to be illegal combinations or conspiracies in restraint of trade, under the antitrust laws.

Based on this section, the Supreme Court, in *Apex*, observed:

> [I]t would seem plain that restraints on the sale of the employee's services to the employer, however much they curtail the competition among employees, are not in themselves combinations or conspiracies in restraint of trade or commerce under the Sherman Act.

310 U.S. at 503.

On the surface, the language relied on by defendants lends merit to the defense. However, we cannot overlook the context in which the language arose. Section 6 of the Clayton Act was enacted for the benefit of unions to exempt certain of their activities from the antitrust laws after courts had applied the Sherman Act to legitimate labor activities. In *Apex*, the Court condoned restrictions on competition for employee services imposed by the employees themselves, not by employers.

In other cases concerning professional sports, courts have not hesitated to apply the Sherman Act to club owner imposed restraints on competition for players' services. *See Kapp v. National Football League*, 390 F.Supp. 73 (N.D.Cal.1974); *Robertson v. National Basketball Ass'n*, 389 F.Supp. 867 (S.D.N.Y.1975). *See also Radovich v. National Football League, supra; Smith v. Pro-Football, supra; Boston Professional Hockey Ass'n, Inc. v. Cheevers, supra; Denver Rockets v. All-Pro Management, Inc.*, 325 F.Supp. 1049 (C.D.Cal.1971), *stay vacated*, 401 U.S. 1204 (1971) (Justice Douglas, Opinion in Chambers). In other contexts, courts have subjected similar employer imposed restraints to the scrutiny of the antitrust laws. *See also Mandeville Farms v. Sugar Co.*, 334 U.S. 219 (1948), in which the Court held that businessman may not act in concert to eliminate competition in the procurement of commodities essential to the operation of their businesses.[24]

We hold that restraints on competition within the market for players' services fall within the ambit of the Sherman Act.

Per Se Violation.

We review next the district court's holding that the Rozelle Rule is *per se* violative of the Sherman Act. * * *

---

24. In *Mandeville Farms v. Sugar Co.*, 334 U.S. 219 (1948), Mr. Justice Rutledge observed at 236: The statute does not confine its protection to consumers, or to purchasers, or to competitors, or to sellers. Nor does it immunize the outlawed acts because they are done by any of these. *Cf. United States v. Socony-Vacuum Oil Co.*, 310 U.S. 150; *American Tobacco Co. v. United States*, 328 U.S. 781. The Act is comprehensive in its terms and coverage, protecting all who are made victims of the forbidden practices by whomever they may be perpetrated.

The district court found that the Rozelle Rule operates to significantly deter clubs from negotiating with and signing free agents. By virtue of the Rozelle Rule, a club will sign a free agent only where it is able to reach an agreement with the player's former team as to compensation, or where it is willing to risk the awarding of unknown compensation by the Commissioner. The court concluded that the Rozelle Rule, as enforced, thus constituted a group boycott and a concerted refusal to deal, and was a *per se* violation of the Sherman Act.

There is substantial evidence in the record to support the district court's findings as to the effects of the Rozelle Rule. We think, however, that this case presents unusual circumstances rendering it inappropriate to declare the Rozelle Rule illegal *per se* without undertaking an inquiry into the purported justifications for the Rule.

First, the line of cases which has given rise to *per se* illegality for the type of agreements involved here generally concerned agreements between business competitors in the traditional sense. * * * Here, however, as the owners and Commissioner urge, the NFL assumes some of the characteristics of a joint venture in that each member club has a stake in the success of the other teams. No one club is interested in driving another team out of business, since if the League fails, no one team can survive. *See United States v. National Football League*, 116 F.Supp. 319, 323 (E.D.Pa. 1953). Although Businessmen cannot wholly evade the antitrust laws by characterizing their operation as a joint venture, we conclude that the unique nature of the business of professional football renders it inappropriate to mechanically apply *per se* illegality rules here, fashioned in a different context. This is particularly true where, as here, the alleged restraint does not completely eliminate competition for players' services. * * * In similar circumstances, when faced with a unique or novel business situation, courts have eschewed a *per se* analysis in favor of an inquiry into the reasonableness of the restraint under the circumstances. * * *

Second, one of the underpinnings of the *per se* analysis is the avoidance of lengthy and burdensome inquiries into the operation of the particular industry in question. Here, the district court has already undertaken an exhaustive inquiry into the operation of the NFL and the effects of and justifications for the Rozelle Rule. Accordingly, the instant case lacks much of the basis for application of the *per se* doctrine.

In view of the foregoing, we think it more appropriate to test the validity of the Rozelle Rule under the Rule of Reason.

Rule of Reason.

The focus of an inquiry under the Rule of Reason is whether the restraint imposed is justified by legitimate business purposes, and is no more restrictive than necessary * * *

In defining the restraint on competition for players' services, the district court found that the Rozelle Rule significantly deters clubs from negotiating with and signing free agents; that it acts as a substantial deterrent to players playing out their options and becoming free agents; that it significantly decreases players' bargaining power in contract negotiations; that players are thus denied the right to sell their services in a free and open market; that as a result, the salaries paid by each club are lower than if competitive bidding were allowed to prevail; and that absent the Rozelle Rule, there would be increased movement in interstate commerce of players from one club to another.

We find substantial evidence in the record to support these findings. Witnesses for both sides testified that there would be increased player movement absent the Rozelle Rule. Two economists testified that elimination of the Rozelle Rule would lead to a substantial increase in player salaries. Carroll Rosenbloom, owner of the Los Angeles Rams, indicated that the Rams would have signed quite a few of the star players from other teams who had played out their options, absent the Rozelle Rule. Charles De Keado, an agent who represented Dick Gordon after he played out his option with the Chicago Bears, testified that the New Orleans Saints were interested in signing Gordon but did not do so because the Bears were demanding unreasonable compensation and the Saints were unwilling to risk an unknown award of compensation by the Commissioner.[27] Jim McFarland, an end who played out his option with the St. Louis Cardinals, testified that he had endeavored to join the Kansas City Chiefs but was unable to do so because of the compensation asked by the Cardinals. Hank Stram, then coach and general manager of the Chiefs, stated that he probably would have given McFarland an opportunity to make his squad had he not been required to give St. Louis anything in return.[28]

In support of their contention that the restraints effected by the Rozelle Rule are not unreasonable, the defendants asserted a number of justifications. First, they argued that without the Rozelle Rule, star players would flock to cities having natural advantages such as larger economic bases, winning teams, warmer climates, and greater media opportunities; that competitive balance throughout the League would thus be destroyed; and that the destruction of competitive balance would ultimately lead to diminished spectator interest, franchise failures, and perhaps the demise of the NFL, at least as it operates today. Second, the defendants contended that the Rozelle Rule is necessary to protect the clubs' investment in scouting expenses and player developments costs. Third, they asserted that players must work together for a substantial period of time in order to function effectively as a team; that elimination of the Rozelle Rule would lead to increased player movement and a concomitant reduction in player continuity; and that the quality of play in the NFL would thus suffer, leading to reduced spectator interest, and financial detriment both to the clubs and the players. Conflicting evidence was adduced at trial by both sides with respect to the validity of these asserted justifications.

The district court held the defendants' asserted justifications unavailing. As to the clubs' investment in player development costs, Judge Larson found that these expenses are similar to those incurred by other businesses, and that there is no right to compen-

---

27. Gordon himself testified that he was fined by the Chicago Bears for missing training camp and exhibition games even though he had played out his option with that club and was no longer under contract to them. His testimony reflected that Los Angeles called Chicago to get the Bears' consent to have Gordon work out with the Rams so that Los Angeles management could observe his performance. He further stated that he received indications from Cincinnati that Chicago's compensation requests were unreasonable; that "they (Chicago) were asking almost for their (Cincinnati's) entire defensive line." Gordon missed pre-season camp and the first few games of the 1972 season because of Chicago's unreasonable requests under the player compensation rule. He testified that this affected his physical condition and contributed to an injury that year.

28. Among other examples which support Judge Larson's findings are:
Marlin Briscoe indicated that he had to sign a three-year contract with Miami even though he would have preferred a single-year contract. He stated that "they would not accept anything less than a three-year contract because of what they would have to give up. * * *"
Alan Page testified that the Rozelle Rule was a hindrance to free player movement, but that the principal effect is on players' salaries. Steven Falk, an attorney for Bob Hayes, testified that Dallas told the Redskins that "they (Dallas) were not trading Hayes to anybody within their own division. * * *"
William Sullivan, president of the Patriots, said he didn't want to sign Joe Kapp, Minnesota's quarterback, and then take a chance on what Minnesota would demand.

sation for this type of investment. With respect to player continuity, the court found that elimination of the Rozelle Rule would affect all teams equally in that regard; that it would not lead to a reduction in the quality of play; and that even assuming that it would, that fact would not justify the Rozelle Rule's anticompetitive effects. As to competitive balance and the consequences which would flow from abolition of the Rozelle Rule, Judge Larson found that the existence of the Rozelle Rule has had no material effect on competitive balance in the NFL. Even assuming that the Rule did foster competitive balance, the court found that there were other legal means available to achieve that end, *e.g.*, the competition committee, multiple year contracts, and special incentives. The court further concluded that elimination of the Rozelle Rule would have no significant disruptive effects, either immediate or long term, on professional football. In conclusion the court held that the Rozelle Rule was unreasonable in that it was overly broad, unlimited in duration, unaccompanied by procedural safeguards, and employed in conjunction with other anticompetitive practices such as the draft, Standard Player Contract, option clause, and the no-tampering rules. We agree that the asserted need to recoup player development costs cannot justify the restraints of the Rozelle Rule. That expense is an ordinary cost of doing business and is not peculiar to professional football. Moreover, because of its unlimited duration, the Rozelle Rule is far more restrictive than necessary to fulfill that need.

We agree, in view of the evidence adduced at trial with respect to existing players turnover by way of trades, retirements and new players entering the League, that the club owners' arguments respecting player continuity cannot justify the Rozelle Rule. We concur in the district court's conclusion that the possibility of resulting decline in the quality of play would not justify the Rozelle Rule. We do recognize, as did the district court, that the NFL has a strong and unique interest in maintaining competitive balance among its teams. The key issue is thus whether the Rozelle Rule is essential to the maintenance of competitive balance, and is no more restrictive than necessary. The district court answered both of these questions in the negative.

We need not decide whether a system of inter-team compensation for free agents moving to other teams is essential to the maintenance of competitive balance in the NFL. Even if it is, we agree with the district court's conclusion that the Rozelle Rule is significantly more restrictive than necessary to serve any legitimate purposes it might have in this regard. First, little concern was manifested at trial over the free movement of average or below average players. Only the movement of the better players was urged as being detrimental to football. Yet the Rozelle Rule applies to every NFL player regardless of his status or ability. Second, the Rozelle Rule is unlimited in duration. It operates as a perpetual restriction on a player's ability to sell his services in an open market throughout his career. Third, the enforcement of the Rozelle Rule is unaccompanied by procedural safeguards. A player has no input into the process by which fair compensation is determined. Moreover, the player may be unaware of the precise compensation demanded by his former team, and that other teams might be interested in him but for the degree of compensation sought * * *

In sum, we hold that the Rozelle Rule, as enforced, unreasonably restrains trade in violation of §1 of the Sherman Act.

Notes and Questions

1. The court concluded that the National Football League's restrictions upon free agency as manifested by the Rozelle Rule violated the antitrust laws; but, as in *Kapp*, the court refused to find a *per se* violation. Why?

2. Given the nature of the sports industry and the fact that some type of anticompetitive behavior may be endemic to league survival (leaving aside the question of whether behavior that is endemic to league survival is, on balance, anticompetitive), the question again arises: can there ever be a *per se* violation in the context of a player restraint in professional football or other professional sports? For a relatively recent analysis of this question, see the district court opinions in *Brown v. Pro-Football, Inc.*, 1992-1 Trade Cas. (CCH) ¶69,747 and 812 F. Supp. 237 (D.D.C. 1992), which were subsequently reversed by the D.C. Circuit on other grounds (the conduct was deemed beyond the reach of the antitrust laws due to the labor exemption). As fully explored in Chapter 9, the D.C. Circuit decision was affirmed by the United States Supreme Court.

Even more recently, in Maurice Clarett's antitrust suit over the NFL's draft eligibility rule, both parties agreed that the Rule of Reason, and not the *per se* rule, applied because the challenged restraint was instituted by a sports league. *Clarett v. NFL*, 306 F.Supp.2d 379, 405 (S.D.N.Y. 2004), rev'd, 369 F.3d 124 (2d Cir. 2004). Why would Clarett agree to application of the Rule of Reason? Does this concession signal the end of the debate over the application of the *per se* rule versus the Rule of Reason?

3. Some commentators believe that there can be no Sherman §1 violation for restraints in the market for player services. This view suggests that the labor of a human being, as a non-commodity or article of commerce, cannot be subject to the prohibitions of Sherman §1. *See* Gary R. Roberts, *Sports League Restraints on the Labor Market: The Failure of Stare Decisis*, 47 U. Pitt. L. Rev. 337 (Winter, 1986). Yet, Professor Roberts is one of the few commentators clinging to the view that a player mobility restraint is not one properly subject to Sherman §1 scrutiny. For a better and more persuasive view of player mobility restraints as Sherman §1 violations, see Robert A. McCormick, *Baseball's Third Strike: The Triumph of Collective Bargaining in Professional Baseball*, 35 Vand. L. Rev. 1131 (October, 1982); *see also* Matthew C. McKinnon, *Professional Football's Draft Eligibility Rule: The Labor Exemption and the Antitrust Laws*, 33 Emory L. J. 375 (Spring, 1984); Myron C. Grauer, *Recognition of the National Football League as a Single Entity Under Section 1 of the Sherman Act: Implications of the Consumer Welfare Model*, 82 Mich. L. Rev. 1 (October, 1983). *See also* the lower court opinions in *Brown v. Pro-Football*, cited in Note 2, above.

In the *Clarett* case, the NFL argued that the relevant market must be drawn broadly, to include football players in the Arena Football League and the Canadian Football League. The district court rejected the NFL's contention, holding that the relevant market consisted exclusively of NFL players. According to Judge Scheindlin, the NFL's

> suggestion that one of the other professional football leagues in North America is a fair substitute for the NFL cannot be taken seriously. "[M]arket definition is guided by an analysis of the interchangeability of use or the cross-elasticity of demand for potential substitute products." Todd v. Exxon Corp., 275 F.3d 191, 201 (2d Cir.2001) (quotation marks and citations omitted). In the case of a labor market or buyer-side conspiracy, these factors are reversed. "In such a case, the market is not the market of competing sellers but of competing buyers. This market is comprised of buyers who are seen by sellers as being reasonably good substitutes." Id. at 202 (quotation marks and citations omitted). No elaborate factual record need be developed to recognize that no football player would see the Arena League or the Canadian League as a reasonably good substitute for the NFL.

Clarett v. NFL, 306 F. Supp. 2d 379, 408 (S.D.N.Y. 2004), rev'd, 369 F.3d 124 (2d Cir. 2004). Is this an appropriate analysis of the relevant market? Is Judge Scheindlin's summary conclusion justified? The Second Circuit later reversed Scheindlin's opinion on other grounds, holding that the draft eligibility rule was protected by the non-statutory labor exemption.

4. Another issue troubling some commentators is the fact that, unlike price fixing by sellers, which raises the prices to consumers, agreements among teams to restrict player salaries reduces team costs and may lead to lower prices charged to fans and others who "consume" the teams' products. They suggest that perhaps the antitrust laws need not be concerned about this type of conflict between teams and owners which may benefit football consumers. *See, e.g.,* Paul C. Weiler and Gary R. Roberts, *Sports and The Law: Cases, Materials and Problems* 130 (1993). Do you agree? *See also, e.g., MLS v. Fraser,* 97 F.Supp.2d 130, 135–39 (D.Mass. 2000) (stating that "[w]hile it is not immediately clear * * * it is not obviously out of the question that one of the effects of lower player salaries is lower prices for the consumer. Under a rule of reason, depending on all the circumstances that may or may not justify the restraint."); *Kartell v. Blue Shield of Mass., Inc.,* 749 F.2d 922, 931 (1st Cir.1984) (noting that "the Congress that enacted the Sherman Act saw it as a way of protecting consumers against prices that were too high, not too low. * * * These facts suggest that courts at least should be cautious—reluctant to condemn too speedily—an arrangement that, on its face, appears to bring low price benefits to the consumer.") The district court opinion in *Brown v. Pro-Football, Inc.,* 1992-1 Trade Cas. (CCH) ¶69,747 at 67,402 (D.D.C. 1992), dismissed that argument out-of-hand, relying on a long-line of cases that hold wage-fixing or price fixing by purchasers unlawful and stating that "[t]he court finds no discernible reason, given that the Sherman Act applies to services as well as goods, * * * why wage-fixing by purchasers of services should be treated differently then price-fixing by sellers of goods." *See also, e.g, Clarett,* 306 F. Supp. at 409, *rev'd,* 369 F.3d 124 (2d Cir. 2004) (stating that "[t]he NFL's desire to keep its costs down is not a legitimate procompetitive justification. The fact that the League and its teams will save money by excluding players does not justify that exclusion."); *Law v. NCAA,* 134 F.3d 1010 (10th Cir. 1998) (holding that "cost-cutting by itself is not a valid procompetitive justification"); *Mandeville Island Farms, Inc. v. American Crystal Sugar Co.,* 334 U.S. 219, 235 (1948). Should employers be permitted to enter into agreements to restrict the amount that they pay for inputs in order to lower their costs, potentially leading to lower prices for consumers? Why not?

5. Although *per se* violations in the context of player mobility restraints are virtually non-existent and certainly do not seem to be in the offing in future litigation, there have been instances where trial courts have given such anticompetitive restraints *per se* treatment. *See, e.g., Denver Rockets v. All-Pro Management, Inc.,* 325 F. Supp. 1049 (C.D. Cal. 1971); *Smith v. Pro Football, Inc.,* 420 F. Supp. 738 (D.D.C. 1976), *aff'd in part, rev'd in part,* 593 F. 2d 1173 (D.C.Cir. 1978); *Mackey v. National Football League,* 407 F. Supp. 1000 (D. Minn. 1975), *aff'd in part, rev'd in part,* 543 F. 2d 606 (8th Cir. Minn. 1976). The following decision finds a *per se* violation in a league conspiring to restrain trade in the player services market. Is this type of group boycott contemplated by the Supreme Court in its attempts to delineate specific types of *per se* violations? *See Northwest Wholesale Stationers v. Pacific Stationery & Printing Co.,* 472 U.S. 85 (1985).

Boris v. United States Football League
1984-1 Trade Cas. (CCH) ¶66,012 (C.D. Cal. 1984)

Order Specifying Facts Which Appear to Be Without Substantial Controversy

WATERS, D.J. This matter is before the Court on the motion of plaintiff Robert F. Boris ("Boris") for an order adjudicating and declaring the defendants United States Football

League ("USFL") and the Arizona Wranglers ("Wranglers") liable to Boris under Count One of the complaint for damages and Count Two of the complaint for an injunction.

Count One of the complaint alleges that defendant USFL and Wranglers violated section one of the Sherman Act (15 U.S.C. §1) and seeks damages for that breach under section four of the Clayton Act (15 U.S.C. §15).

Count Two of the complaint alleges that defendants USFL and Wranglers violated section one of the Sherman Act (15 U.S.C. §1), and seeks a preliminary and permanent injunction under section 16 of the Clayton Act (15 U.S.C. §26).

Statement of Uncontroverted Facts

Having considered the pleadings and other papers on file and the parties' briefs, and evidence submitted in connection with this motion for summary judgment, and having ruled on the motion, the Court hereby finds that there is no genuine issue as to the following material facts:

1. Plaintiff Boris was a varsity football player at the University of Arizona during the 1980–81 and 1981–82 seasons and for the first three games of the 1982 season.

2. After the third game of the 1982 season, Boris voluntarily withdrew from the University of Arizona.

3. Boris is not currently eligible to nor is he playing college football.

4. Boris will not be eligible to play college football in the fall of 1984 or any time thereafter under the rules and regulations of the NCAA.

5. Defendant USFL is an unincorporated association.

6. During the 1983 playing season, the USFL consisted of 12 member teams; and during the 1984 playing season, the USFL will consist of 18 member teams. These 18 teams are referred to herein as the "USFL member teams." Six additional franchises have been added to the USFL between the 1983 and 1984 seasons.

7. Defendant Wranglers is an Arizona corporation with its principal place of business in Phoenix, Arizona. Its principal business is the operation of a professional football team.

8. The USFL conducts its business in such a manner as to constitute interstate commerce.

9. The USFL and its member teams have agreed with each other to abide by an "Eligibility Rule" which provides:

> No person shall be eligible to play or be selected as a player unless (1) all college football eligibility of such player has expired, or (2) at least five (5) years shall have elapsed since the player first entered or attended a recognized junior college, college or university or (3) such player received a diploma from a recognized college or university.

10. The USFL and all of the USFL member teams, including defendant Wranglers, have agreed among themselves to adhere to and to enforce the Eligibility Rule quoted in the paragraph above.

11. The reasons advanced by the defendants in support of the Eligibility Rule, as it existed relative to the USFL's 1983 football season, are (in summary): The Eligibility Rule promotes on-field competitive balance among USFL teams; very few college-age athletes are physically, mentally, or emotionally mature enough for professional foot-

ball; abolition of the Eligibility Rule will not benefit the college athlete; the Eligibility Rule promotes the concept of the importance of a college education; the Eligibility Rule promotes the efficient operation of the USFL by strengthening the sport at the college level so that the USFL does not have to develop players at that level; the Eligibility Rule is not inflexible; since 1983 was the USFL's first season of play, competitive conditions required it to adopt and enforce the same Eligibility Rule previously adopted and enforced by the two powerful and established existent major professional football leagues (the National Football League and the Canadian Football League), if it cannot enforce the Eligibility Rule, its very existence will be threatened, and the best chance that college football players have for increased remuneration (viz, inter-league economic competition) will be gone.

12. The Court finds that although the above listed reasons may have varying degrees of merit, the principal reason for the adoption by the USFL and its member teams of the Eligibility Rule was to respond to apparent demands made by college football programs and thereby to gain better access to these programs towards the end of selecting the best college players available.

13. The Eligibility Rule of the USFL, as it existed relative to the USFL's 1983 football season, involved combining for the primary purpose of coercing or excluding third parties, and did in fact have the effect of coercing or excluding those third party individuals deemed ineligible by the Rule. * * *

14. While in certain areas cooperation and not competition among professional sports teams is required and thus the USFL might in some respects be considered to be an economic entity, as measured against issues presented in this case the Court finds that the USFL teams are economic competitors. *Los Angeles Memorial Coliseum, Inc. v. National Football League*, 468 F.Supp. 154 (C.D. Cal. 1979).

15. The USFL and its member teams have agreed upon a Territorial Schools Rule. During 1983, this Rule provided, in essence, that each member team of the USFL shall be assigned five "territorial schools." Each year, each USFL member team may select five players from each of its "territorial schools" and identify those players to other teams in the league. After those players have been so identified, all the other teams in the league, pursuant to the USFL member teams' agreement, will not deal with any of those players, unless the team selecting those players sells or waives its rights to such a player.

16. The USFL and its member teams have applied the Eligibility Rule and the Territorial Schools Rule so as to render plaintiff Boris ineligible to play professional football with any USFL member team.

17. The USFL does not provide procedural safeguards whereby an individual may contest his exclusion under the Eligibility Rule.

18. As written, the Eligibility Rule imposes an absolute exclusion on all persons who still have theoretical collegiate athletic eligibility remaining.

19. During 1982 and 1983, the University of Arizona, which Boris attended, was a "territorial school" of the Wranglers. Thus, under the Territorial Schools Rule, the Wranglers had the option to select Boris in the January, 1985 USFL draft, after his theoretical college eligibility had expired.

20. Under the terms of the USFL Territorial Schools Rule, the Wranglers were not required to exercise their option to select Boris as a territorial draft choice until December, 1984.

21. Until November, 1983, the Wranglers refused to consider waiving or selling their rights to Boris as a player from one of the Wrangler's territorial schools.

22. In October, 1982, after he had voluntarily become ineligible to participate in collegiate athletics, Boris entered into a contract with Professional Sports Management, Inc. ("PSMI"), a management firm for professional athletes. As a result of entering into this contract, Boris became ineligible to ever again participate in amateur collegiate football.

23. At that time, Boris desired, and he still desires, to play professional football for a team in the USFL.

24. After signing a contract with Boris, PSMI attempted to obtain employment for Boris with a team in the USFL. These attempts took place between February, 1983, and May, 1983. PSMI was unsuccessful in obtaining any position for Boris or even a tryout with a USFL team.

25. Boris' application for a tryout or employment with teams in the USFL between February and May, 1983, was rejected because of the USFL Eligibility Rule and the Territorial Schools Rule.

Order Re Plaintiff's Motion for Partial Summary Judgment

* * *

It Is Hereby Ordered:

1. Plaintiff's motion for partial summary judgment is granted in part in that the Court finds that the "Eligibility Rule" of the United States Football League ("USFL"), as it existed in 1983, and which provided as follows:

> No person shall be eligible to play or be selected as a player unless (1) all college football eligibility of such player has expired, or (2) at least five (5) years shall have elapsed since the player first entered or attended a recognized junior college, college or university or (3) such player received a diploma from a recognized college or university.

as it was applied to plaintiff Robert F. Boris, constituted a "group boycott," and was, therefore, a per se violation of section one of the Sherman Act (15 U.S.C. §1). Pursuant to 28 U.S.C. §1292(b), the Court is of the opinion that the foregoing order involves a controlling question of law as to which there is substantial ground for difference of opinion and that an immediate appeal from this order may materially advance the ultimate termination of the litigation.

2. Plaintiff's motion for partial summary judgment is denied in part in that the court finds that the issue of whether the "Territorial Schools Rule" of the USFL, as it existed in 1983, constituted a violation of section one of the Sherman Act (15 U.S.C. §1) is an issue that must be resolved under the "rule of reason" at the trial of this action.

Notes and Questions

1. The *Boris* court concluded that the refusal to permit certain college players to join the United States Football League prior to the graduation of their class constituted a group boycott and justified the finding of a *per se* violation. How does this case square with the notion that some type of anticompetitive behavior is necessary for the league to survive? Should the USFL have been given an opportunity to explain the reasons un-

derlying its refusal to consider freshmen, sophomores and juniors for its annual draft? Many perceive the draft rules in this regard as evincing a cozy relationship wherein: (1) the NCAA is assured that those players who have been given lucrative scholarships will play their entire college career rather than opting to join a professional league prior to graduation; and, at the same time, (2) professional sports league are bequeathed with a free and extremely productive farm system where their future players can cultivate the necessary skill and development. *See Clarett v. NFL*, 306 F.Supp.2d 379, 408, n.181 (S.D.N.Y. 2004), *rev'd*, 369 F.3d 124 (2d Cir. 2004) (Clarett argued that the NFL draft eligibility rule "perpetuates and maintains the NCAA as its free minor league system."); Note, *Sherman Act Invalidation of the NCAA Amateurism Rules*, 105 HARV. L. REV. 1299 (April 1992); Deborah E. Klein, *Proposition 48 and the Business of Intercollegiate Athletics: Potential Antitrust Ramifications Under the Sherman Act*, 67 DENV. U. L. REV. 301 (1990); Marianne Jennings, *Student-Athletes, Athlete Agents and Five Year Eligibility: An Environment of Contractual Interference, Trade Restraint and High-Stake Payments*, 66 U. DET. L. REV. 179 (Winter, 1989). To what extent may this perception color the court's determination as to whether or not *per se* treatment is appropriate?

2. If the "draft" rule were a part of a collective bargaining agreement, would it have been immune from antitrust scrutiny under the non-statutory labor exemption? *See* Kieran M. Corcoran, Note, *When Does the Buzzer Sound?: The Nonstatutory Labor Exemption in Professional Sports*, 94 COLUM. L. REV. 1045 (April, 1994); Daniel C. Nester, Comment, *Labor Exemption to Antitrust Scrutiny in Professional Sports*, 15 S. ILL. U. L. J. 123 (Fall, 1990); Robert A. McCormick and Matthew C. McKinnon, *Professional Football's Draft Eligibility Rule: The Labor Exemption and The Antitrust Laws*, 33 EMORY L. J. 375 (Spring, 1984).

3. Difficult questions often arise in the context of league or association decisions to limit or preclude a player's participation in a particular sport. In many instances, there is little doubt that these actions compromise the player's earning capacity. The persistent issue, however, is whether the antitrust laws are the proper vehicle through which to seek redress. In this regard, courts will frequently place emphasis upon the impact of the league's or association's action upon competition rather than just the competitor. If the *Boris* court had applied the Rule of Reason rather than a *per se* rule, could Boris have proven an anticompetitive effect on the overall market, rather than just an adverse effect on Boris?

4. In *Clarett v. NFL*, 306 F.Supp.2d 379, 405 (S.D.N.Y. 2004), *rev'd*, 369 F.3d 124 (2d Cir. 2004), Judge Scheindlin found that the NFL's draft eligibility rule did in fact have an anticompetitive effect on the overall market, not merely an adverse effect on a single player—"Indeed, one can scarcely think of a more blatantly anticompetitive policy than one that excludes certain competitors from a market altogether. Because the [eligibility rule] has the actual anticompetitive effect of excluding players—including Clarett—from the NFL, it is a naked restriction." Judge Scheindlin's conclusion was rejected by many commentators, and her opinion was subsequently reversed by the Second Circuit because the NFL's eligibility rule was protected by the non-statutory labor exemption. *See, e.g.,* Symposium, *Panel II: Maurice Clarett's Challenge*, 15 FORDHAM INTELL. PROP. MEDIA & ENT. L.J. 391, 405 (Winter 2005).

5. Questions surrounding the legitimacy of league or association decisions to impose disciplinary suspensions or otherwise to circumscribe competition are often complicated by the nature of the alleged conduct prompting the discipline as well as the composition of the body vested with the authority to make the ultimate decision. Consider these factors as you read the *Molinas* and *Blalock* cases that follow.

(B) Player Restraints: Limitations on Participation

Molinas v. National Basketball Ass'n

190 F. Supp. 241 (S.D.N.Y. 1961)

KAUFMAN, District Judge. Plaintiff, Jack Molinas, is a well-known basketball player. In 1953, upon his graduation from Columbia University, he was "drafted" by the Fort Wayne Pistons, then a member of the defendant National Basketball Association (now the Detroit Pistons). Subsequently, in the fall of 1953, he signed a contract to play with the Pistons. In January of 1954, however, he admitted, in writing, that he placed several bets on his team, the Pistons, to win. The procedure he followed was that he contacted a person in New York by telephone, who informed him of the "point spread" on the particular game in question. The plaintiff would then decide whether or not to place a bet on the game. The plaintiff admitted that he received some $400 as a result of these wagers, including reimbursement of his telephone calls to New York. After the plaintiff admitted this wagering, Mr. Podoloff, the president of the league, acting pursuant to a clause (Section 15) in plaintiff's contract and a league rule (Section 79 of the League Constitution) prohibiting gambling, indefinitely suspended the plaintiff from the league. This suspension has continued until the present date. Since the suspension, plaintiff has made several applications, both oral and written for reinstatement. All of these have been refused, and Mr. Podoloff has testified that he will never allow the plaintiff to re-enter the league. He has characterized the plaintiff as a "cancer on the league" which must be excised.

In the meantime, plaintiff attended and graduated from the Brooklyn Law School, and was then admitted to the New York State Bar. He has also been playing basketball for Williamsport and Hazelton of the Eastern Basketball League.

In 1954, shortly after the suspension, plaintiff brought an action in the New York State Supreme Court, alleging that he had been denied notice and hearing prior to the suspension, and that there was no authority for the indefinite suspension imposed by Mr. Podoloff. The court, after a trial, found against the plaintiff, holding that since he had engaged in reprehensible and morally dishonest conduct, he was not entitled to seek the aid of an equity court. The court also found that even if a hearing was required by league rules, it would have been a futile formality in this case, since the plaintiff had admitted violations of his contract and the league rules. An appeal was taken to the Appellate Division but was subsequently dismissed.

In the action presently before the court, the plaintiff alleges that the defendant National Basketball Association has entered into a conspiracy with its member teams and others in restraint of trade, and thus has violated the anti-trust laws. It is alleged that the operation of the so-called reserve clause, by which players are allocated among the league teams, and through which a team holding a player's contract is given an option to renew it each year, is an unreasonable restraint of trade in violation of the anti-trust laws. It is further alleged that the suspension of the plaintiff by the league, and its subsequent refusal to reinstate him, is the result of a conspiracy in violation of these laws. Finally, plaintiff charges that the league has, through this conspiracy, imposed certain collateral restraints upon him, affecting his opportunities to play in "exhibition games" against league personnel.

Plaintiff seeks treble damages in the sum of three million dollars, an injunction against the conspiracies alleged, and reinstatement to the league.

* * *

The law is clear that, in order for a private plaintiff in a civil anti-trust suit to recover, he must establish a clear causal connection between the violation alleged and the injuries allegedly suffered. * * * With respect to the plaintiff's contention based on the so-called reserve clause, no causal connection whatsoever has been established between the reserve clause and any damage which he may have sustained. Plaintiff has not shown that he suffered any damage at the time he signed his contract with the Fort Wayne Pistons, in the fall of 1953, following the so-called college draft. It does not appear that Molinas was in any way displeased over playing for the Pistons, and were it not for his suspension in January of 1954, it is likely that he would have continued to play for them without complaint. Following the suspension, the refusal of the league or its member clubs to deal with the plaintiff was clearly due to the suspension, rather than the reserve clause. These teams would obviously have refused to deal with the plaintiff even if the reserve clause had never existed. Thus, the plaintiff has not sustained his burden of proof on this claim.

* * *

With respect to plaintiff's suspension from the league in January of 1954, and the subsequent refusal by the league to reinstate him, plaintiff has patently failed to establish an unreasonable restraint of trade within the meaning of the anti-trust laws. A rule, and a corresponding contract clause, providing for the suspension of those who place wagers on games in which they are participating seems not only reasonable, but necessary for the survival of the league. Every league or association must have some reasonable governing rules, and these rules must necessarily include disciplinary provisions. Surely, every disciplinary rule which a league may invoke, although by its nature it may involve some sort of a restraint, does not run afoul of the anti-trust laws. And, a disciplinary rule invoked against gambling seems about as reasonable a rule as could be imagined. Furthermore, the application of the rule to the plaintiff's conduct is also eminently reasonable. Plaintiff was wagering on games in which he was to play, and some of these bets were made on the basis of a "point spread" system. Plaintiff insists that since he bet only on his own team to win, his conduct, while admittedly improper, was not immoral. But I do not find this distinction to be a meaningful one in the context of the present case. The vice inherent in the plaintiff's conduct is that each time he either placed a bet or refused to place a bet, this operated inevitably to inform bookmakers of an insider's opinion as to the adequacy or inadequacy of the point-spread or his team's ability to win. Thus, for example, when he chose to place a bet, this would indicate to the bookmakers that a member of the Fort Wayne team believed that his team would exceed its expected performance. Similarly, when he chose not to bet, bookmakers thus would be informed of his opinion that the Pistons would not perform according to expectations. It is certainly reasonable for the league and Mr. Podoloff to conclude that this conduct could not be tolerated and must, therefore, be eliminated. The reasonableness of the league's action is apparent in view of the fact that, at that time, the confidence of the public in basketball had been shattered, due to a series of gambling incidents. Thus, it was absolutely necessary for the sport to exhume gambling from its midst for all times in order to survive.

The same factors justifying the suspension also serve to justify the subsequent refusal to reinstate. The league could reasonably conclude that in order to effectuate its important and legitimate policies against gambling, and to restore and maintain the confidence of the public vital to its existence, it was necessary to enforce its rules strictly, and to apply the most stringent sanctions. One can certainly understand the reluctance to permit an admitted gambler to return to the league, and again to participate in championship games, especially in light of the aura and stigma of gambling which has clouded the sports world in the past few years. Viewed in this context, it can be seen that the league was justified in determining that it was absolutely necessary to avoid even the slightest connection with gambling, gamblers, and those who had done business with gamblers, in the future. In addition, conduct reasonable in its inception certainly does not become unreasonable through the mere passage of time, especially when the same factors making the conduct reasonable in the first instance, are still present. At any rate, plaintiff must show much more than he has here in order to compel a conclusion that the defendant's conduct was in fact unreasonable. Thus, it is clear, that the refusal to reinstate the plaintiff does not rise to the stature of a violation of the anti-trust laws.

With respect to the alleged "collateral restraints"—those involving various exhibition games in which league teams or players allegedly refused to play because of the plaintiff's presence—the plaintiff has completely failed to establish that any of these alleged incidents was the result of any conspiracy involving the league or its president, Mr. Podoloff. Once again, it must be remembered that the plaintiff has the burden of proof, and it is clear that there is a complete failure of proof on this issue. It was not established that the league or Mr. Podoloff, gave any instructions whatsoever concerning these matters, or that any agreement or conspiracy was ever entered into. The proof established at most that several league owners, coaches or players may have felt that it was unwise, possibly because of the likelihood of adverse publicity, to participate in a game, in which the plaintiff, an admitted gambler, was also involved. This falls far short of the conspiracy required to establish a violation of the anti-trust laws.

* * * Plaintiff's complaint, therefore, must be dismissed.

Notes and Questions

1. *Molinas* illustrates that even though the player's suspension, in a sense, restrained trade by precluding him from pursuing his profession as a National Basketball Association player, this action does not necessarily rise to the level of a restraint of trade under the Sherman Act. Moreover, the court refused even to entertain a balancing test to determine whether or not the procompetitive effects outweighed the anticompetitive effects, perhaps because Molinas' suspension and expulsion had no meaningful anticompetitive impact. Was the court saying that suspending athletes for something as important as gambling is *per se* reasonable? In effect, while failing to state so explicitly, the court may have tacitly accepted the notion that the antitrust laws were designed to protect competition but not necessarily competitors. *See Weight-Rite Golf Corporation v. United States Golf Association*, 766 F. Supp. 1104 (M.D.Fla. 1991) *aff'd without opinion*; 953 F.2d 651 (11th Cir. 1992); *Volvo North America Corp. v. Men's International Professional Tennis Council*, 857 F.2d 55 (2d Cir. 1988); *Fishman v. Wirtz*, 807 F.2d 520 (7th Cir. 1986); *Midwest Communications, Inc. v. Minnesota Twins, Inc.*, 779 F.2d 444 (8th Cir. 1985); *Banks v. NCAA*, 746 F. Supp. 850 (N.D.Ind. 1990); *Les Shockley Racing, Inc. v. National Hot Rod Ass'n*, 884 F.2d 504 (9th Cir. 1989); *Deesen v. Professional Golfers Association of America*, 358 F. 2d 165 (9th Cir. 1966). While most competitors are, in fact, protected by a rigid promotion of competition in the marketplace, *Molinas* indicated that there are times when an individual competitor may be harmed by a particular group action but competition as a whole will be unaffected. In the *Shockley* case, the plaintiffs alleged that they had been banned from drag racing events as a result of an unlawful conspiracy. The Ninth Circuit affirmed the district court's dismissal of the case, stating:

Plaintiffs correctly argue that removal of one or more competing sellers from any market necessarily has an effect on competitive conditions within that market. But removal of one or a few competitors need not equate with injury to competition. * * * [S]ection one claimants must plead and prove a reduction of competition in the market in general and not mere injury to their own positions as competitors in the market.

884 F.2d at 508. In many of these instances, no *prima facie* case under the antitrust laws is established because the Rule of Reason requires the plaintiff to prove overall anticompetitive effects in a relevant market. If the plaintiff can prove the injury to market competition, he must still prove that his injury is "antitrust injury"—harm of the type that the antitrust laws are concerned about. For a general discussion of the "antitrust injury" concept, see *Cargill, Inc. v. Monfort of Colorado, Inc.,* 479 U.S. 104 (1986); *Brunswick Corp. v. Pueblo Bowl-O-Mat, Inc.,* 429 U.S. 477 (1977). *See also, Deesen v. PGA,* 358 F.2d 163 (9th Cir. 1966); *O'Grady v. PGA Tour, Inc.,* 1989 U.S. Dist. LEXIS 4301 (C.D. Cal. 1989).

2. What is the significance of the fact that Molinas was guilty of, or at least seemingly admitted, some participation in gambling? For a subsequent case about a player who was held ineligible for the 1964 NBA draft because of his alleged involvement in a college point shaving scandal in 1961, see *Hawkins v. NBA,* 288 F. Supp. 614 (W.D.Pa. 1968). Connie Hawkins was eventually vindicated and later starred for several years in both the ABA and the NBA. *See* David Wolf, *Foul!* (1972). Following the Black Sox scandal, all professional sports have been extremely sensitive to any participation in gambling activities even if it did not involve gambling in the participant's sport. Pete Rose's well-chronicled fall from grace, allegations about the Philadelphia Phillies' Lenny Dykstra playing "high stakes poker," and the considerable flap surrounding revelations of basketball star Michael Jordan's and baseball slugger Albert Belle's gambling propensities, are glaring recent examples. Some other historical examples include suspensions of NFL quarterback Art Schlicter (suspended by the NFL in 1983 after admitting to associations with gamblers and losing more than $700,000 in bets on NFL games and other sporting events), Alex Karras and Paul Hornung (suspended from the NFL for one year in 1963—allegedly betting on their own teams to win), and Leo Durocher (suspended in 1947 for allegations that he was associated with gamblers). There was also the famous showdown between Broadway Joe Namath and NFL Commissioner Pete Rozelle, in which Rozelle ordered Namath to sell his interest in the Bachelors III restaurant because alleged gamblers frequented the establishment, and gambling information had supposedly been collected by law enforcement officials through wiretaps on the restaurant's telephones. For a controversial discussion of relationships between NFL personnel and gambling, see DAN E. MOLDEA, INTERFERENCE: HOW ORGANIZED CRIME INFLUENCES PROFESSIONAL FOOTBALL (1989).

3. Compare and contrast the treatment that Molinas received in his case with the *Rose* case discussed earlier. Would Pete Rose have had a colorable claim under the antitrust laws for his suspension from baseball and all baseball related activities if the baseball exemption had not been in place? Further, could Pete Rose have sued under the antitrust laws for any type of collusive activity that virtually precluded Rose from membership in baseball's Hall of Fame? For many years it was reported that Rose had never sought reinstatement by Major League Baseball. How would that affect a legal challenge by Rose?

4. Having witnessed the concern of professional sports for gambling or similar untoward activity, consider the following case in which plaintiff, Jane Blalock, successfully argued that her suspension for cheating during a golf tournament was a *per se* violation of the antitrust laws.

Blalock v. Ladies Professional Golf Ass'n

359 F. Supp. 1260 (N.D. Ga. 1973)

MOYE, District Judge. Plaintiff and defendants Cynthia Sullivan, Judy Rankin, Linda Craft, Penny Zavichas and Sharon Miller are professional women golfers who regularly compete against one another in tournament play sponsored by defendant LPGA for profit. Plaintiff and these defendants are all active members of defendant LPGA which is organized under the laws of the State of Ohio and is the sole owner of the defendant LPGA Tournament Players Corporation, a Texas corporation which was organized for carrying on the business matters of defendant LPGA. The officers of defendant LPGA and defendant LPGA Tournament Players Corporation are the same. The policies, business and affairs of defendant LPGA are directed by the Executive Board, which is comprised of defendants Sullivan, Rankin, Craft, Zavichas and Miller, who are officers of defendant LPGA as well as player-competitors of plaintiff.

During the week of May 15, 1972, defendant Gene McCauliff III, Tournament Director of defendant LPGA, appointed four observers at the second round of the LPGA Tournament in Louisville, Kentucky, to observe the play of the plaintiff. The observers claimed that plaintiff had illegally moved her ball. A meeting of the Executive Board of defendant LPGA was convened on May 20, 1972, which resulted in a decision to disqualify plaintiff as to the Louisville tournament, to place her on probation for the remainder of the 1972 season and to impose a fine of $500 for cheating. Plaintiff was informed of the Executive Board's decision on May 26, 1972, when she was summoned before the Executive Board in Southern Pines, North Carolina.

On May 28, 1972, the Executive Board again convened to discuss plaintiff's case. The meeting was attended by two non-Board members—Marlene Hagge and Kathy Farrer—both player-competitors of plaintiff. Defendants Sullivan and Rankin related that plaintiff had made certain statements on May 26, 1972, when informed of her probation and fine which were considered by them to be admissions of her improper conduct. Marlene Hagge, speaking on behalf of the tournament committee, recommended that plaintiff be suspended. The members of the Executive Board who were present (defendants Sullivan, Rankin and Miller) discussed the suspension of plaintiff and voted to suspend plaintiff for one year. Defendant Craft in Baltimore, Maryland, was called, and, after the case was explained to her, she, too, cast her vote for suspension. Defendant Zavichas, who was in Colorado, was unable to be reached.

On May 30, 1972, plaintiff was again called before the Executive Board which had convened in Baltimore, Maryland. All members of the Executive Board were present. After extended discussion with plaintiff, the Executive Board informed plaintiff that she was suspended from June 1, 1972, until May 31, 1973. That suspension was agreed to by all members of the Executive Board.

Plaintiff contends that suspension from defendant LPGA for a period of one year constitutes a group boycott and a *per se* restraint of trade.

Initially, it must be pointed out that professional golf is subject to the antitrust laws. Although not expressly deciding that professional golf is so governed, Justice Blackmun, in *Flood v. Kuhn*, 407 U.S. 258 (1972), having determined that baseball is exempt from the antitrust laws, stated that:

> " * * * Other professional sports operating interstate—football, boxing, basketball, and, presumably, hockey and golf—are not so exempt * * *"

That professional golf is governed by the antitrust laws is further substantiated by *Deesen v. Professional Golfers Assn. of America*, 358 F.2d 165 (9th Cir. 1966), *cert. denied*, 385 U.S. 846 (1966). * * *

Before a concerted refusal to deal can be illegal under this section, two threshold elements must be present: (1) there must be some effect on "trade or commerce among the several States", and (2) there must be sufficient agreement to constitute a "contract, combination * * * or conspiracy." * * *

It is undisputed that both of these elements are present in the instant case. As to the first element, it is clear that defendant LPGA conducts its business in such a manner as to constitute interstate commerce. The golf tournaments, co-sponsored by defendant LPGA Tournament Players Corporation, are conducted in and among the several states and the rights to televise and broadcast certain tournaments for interstate transmission have been sold. As to the second element, defendants Sullivan, Rankin, Craft, Zavichas, Miller and the members of the LPGA, by the imposition of a one-year suspension, have agreed, through the LPGA's constitution and by-laws, not to deal with plaintiff.

The fundamental principle for determining the legality of conduct under the Sherman Antitrust Act is the "rule of reason" announced in *Standard Oil Co. of New Jersey v. United States*, 221 U.S. 1 (1911). * * *

* * * From this general principle has been carved a well-defined exception within which fall group boycotts:

"* * * Certain arrangements are conclusively presumed to be unreasonable restraints of trade, simply by virtue of their obvious and necessary effect on competition. Once the existence of such an arrangement has been established, no evidence of actual public injury is required * * * and no evidence of the reasonableness of defendant's conduct will be considered in justification. This rule of *per se* illegality has been applied thus far to horizontal and vertical price fixing agreements, divisions of markets between competitors, tying arrangements, *and certain collective refusals to deal, or "group boycotts."* * * *

* * * [T]he Court finds that the purpose and effect of the arrangement in this case (the agreement by defendants Sullivan, Rankin, Craft, Zavichas and Miller to suspend plaintiff from defendant LPGA for one year) was to exclude plaintiff from the market and is therefore a "naked restraint of trade." Plaintiff is a member in good standing of defendant LPGA. Suspension therefrom is tantamount to total exclusion from the market of professional golf. Not only would plaintiff be excluded from LPGA sponsored tournaments, but, as defendant LPGA's Constitution and By-Laws provide in Article VIII:

"A member of the Ladies Professional Golf Association may not compete for prize money in tournament, professional-amateur, or qualifying event that is not co-sponsored by the LPGA Tournament Players Corporation, or approved in writing by the LPGA Executive Director * * *"

The suspension was imposed upon plaintiff by defendants Sullivan, Rankin, Craft, Zavichas and Miller in the exercise of their completely unfettered, subjective discretion as is evident from the fact that they had initially imposed upon plaintiff only probation and a fine, but then, without hearing from plaintiff, determined to impose the suspension at issue here. Furthermore, the suspension was imposed by competitors of plaintiff who stand to gain financially from plaintiff's exclusion from the market.

The Court therefore determines that the arrangement in this case is illegal *per se*. Consequently, it is not necessary that it inquire as to the reasonableness of the suspension. * * *

Defendants have argued throughout their briefs that the instant case is governed by the "rule of reason" on the ground that the suspension of plaintiff was a valid exercise of self-regulation. Defendants principally rely on the case of *Silver v. New York Stock Exchange*, 373 U.S. 341 (1963). * * *

The Court believes that defendants' reliance upon *Silver* in this case is misplaced. There is no statute here involved which might be construed *in pari materia* with the antitrust laws which justifies defendant LPGA's "self-regulation." The Supreme Court in *Silver* created an exception to the *per se* rule when there is present another statute which justifies concerted action which would otherwise be a *per se* violation of Section 1 of the Sherman Act. *Silver* did not sanction concerted actions not justified by some other federal statute. Some courts have focused on the phrase "or otherwise" in the Supreme Court's opinion in *Silver* and have concluded that the Court intended to include within its exception cases wherein self-regulatory activities providing for notice and an opportunity for hearings exist without legislative mandate. * * * However, this Court does not construe the exception to the *per se* rule announced in *Silver*, notwithstanding the "or otherwise" language, to sweep that broadly. * * *

Defendants have also cited the cases of *Molinas v. National Basketball Association*, 190 F. Supp. 241 (S.D.N.Y. 1961), and *Deesen v. Professional Golfers' Association of America*, 358 F.2d 165 (9th Cir. 1966). The Court finds these cases to be inapposite. The facts in Molinas demonstrate that Molinas, a professional basketball player, was suspended by the president of the National Basketball Association who was acting pursuant to a clause in Molinas's contract and a league rule prohibiting gambling. The suspension was not imposed by Molinas's competitors.

In the *Deesen* case, Deesen, a professional golfer and a member of the Professional Golfer's Association, had his approved tournament player status terminated by the PGA's national tournament committee. The national tournament committee was largely composed of non-competitors of Deesen (the only exception being Bob Rosburg). Furthermore, the Court of Appeals relied heavily on the fact that notwithstanding that Deesen's tournament status had been terminated, Deesen was not completely excluded from the market (tournaments) as he could still participate therein, if he chose to become a golf teacher employed by a golf club. The termination in *Deesen* was based upon virtually a mathematical application of pre-determined standards. It did not involve a completely unfettered, subjective and discretionary determination of an exclusionary sanction by a tribunal wholly composed of competitors, as here. Consequently, we are not persuaded that the holding in *Deesen* is contrary to *McQuade* or *Fashion Originators' Guild* in regard to the *per se* illegality of group boycotts.

Pursuant to the requirements of Fed. R. Civ. P. 56(d), the Court finds that the following facts are not in dispute:

(1) Defendant LPGA conducts its business in such a manner as to constitute interstate commerce;

(2) Defendants Sullivan, Rankin, Craft, Zavichas, and Miller, members of defendants LPGA's Executive Committee and competitors of plaintiff, combined to impose upon plaintiff a one-year suspension from defendant LPGA.

By reason of these undisputed facts and for the reasons stated above, the Court orders that partial summary judgment in favor of plaintiff be GRANTED to the limited extent of ruling that plaintiff's suspension by her competitors, defendants Sullivan, Rankin, Craft, Zavichas and Miller through the mechanism of defendant LPGA, was in violation of §1 of the Sherman Act. This ruling does not reach the self-policing activities of defendant LPGA which are less than exclusionary in their effect. The Defendants Erickson and McCauliff have moved for summary judgments contending that they were not voting members of the Executive Committee and did not vote to suspend plaintiff. Notwithstanding the fact that these two defendants did not vote to suspend plaintiff, there is inter alia, a genuine issue of material fact as to whether these defendants acquiesced in and implemented the suspension of plaintiff by her competitors. Therefore, the motions for summary judgment filed by defendants Erickson and Mc-Cauliff are denied.

In conjunction with the trial of the other issues raised in the complaint, a determination of whether permanent injunctive relief, money damages or both are appropriate will be made.

Since plaintiff's suspension has expired by its own terms, no further injunctive relief seems required, and the preliminary injunction heretofore granted is dissolved. Likewise, defendants' request for an increase in bond is denied as the import of this order is that the prior suspension, which was enjoined, violated the antitrust laws and plaintiff is entitled to her winnings during the period of the purported suspension.

Notes and Questions

1. Would the *Blalock* case have been decided differently if her competitors had comprised less than a majority of the panel that determined her guilt and imposed her suspension? What is the significance of the fact that the panel's initial decision was a $500 fine and a year of probation?

2. If this case were subject to a Rule of Reason analysis, what would be the relevant market, and what factors would the court consider in balancing the procompetitive versus the anticompetitive effects? *See Deesen v. Professional Golfers Association*, 358 F.2d 165 (9th Cir. 1966).

3. This case presents an interesting irony. Arguably, if the court had not found a *per se* violation, predicated upon the fact that Blalock's *competitors* reached the ultimate determination of guilt and penalty, it is unlikely that she would have been able to establish that, on balance, the anticompetitive effects of the discipline outweighed the procompetitive effects. Indeed, while Blalock was suspended, another golfer would simply have taken her place, and the likely anticompetitive impact would have been negligible. If Blalock were the top player on the tour, and there were evidence that the suspension was motivated, in part, by personal animus and a desire by the other players to have a better shot at the available prize money, would that satisfy the requirement of anticompetitive market effects or injury to competition? If Blalock's antitrust claim failed, would she have any other potential legal recourse?

4. What is the significance of the fact that there were no other tours in which Blalock could have participated during the term of her suspension? If there had been other tours for which Blalock would have been eligible during her suspension, would that have changed in any way the court's finding of a *per se* violation? Would these facts have compromised further Blalock's claim under a Rule of Reason analysis that the anticompetitive effects of her suspension outweighed the procompetitive effects? What if each of those tours unilaterally decided to honor the LPGA's suspension by another tour?

5. The next case, *Volvo North American Corp. v. Men's International Professional Tennis Council*, 857 F.2d 55 (2d Cir. 1988), presents several interesting antitrust issues unique to "individual" sports, particularly tennis. In order to appreciate fully the cul-

ture of professional tennis and the nuances of the *Volvo* decision, the following background is offered as orientation.

(C) Player Restraints: Sponsors, Tours and Special Events

(1) Background of Men's Professional Tennis

Prior to 1968, participation in the most important and prestigious men's tennis events was limited to amateur tennis players and was governed by the International Tennis Federation ("ITF") (previously the International *Lawn* Tennis Federation). The ITF is a membership organization composed of the national tennis associations of the countries around the world. For example, the United States Lawn Tennis Association (which became the United States Tennis Association "USTA"), the French Tennis Federation, the Japanese Tennis Federation, and over 100 other national federations are the members of the ITF. Prior to 1968, the ITF and its members exercised total control over all amateur events. *See further Gunter Harz Sports, Inc. v. USTA*, 511 F. Supp. 1103 (Neb. 1981).

Events run by the ITF and its members included all the Grand Slam events (Wimbledon and the championships of the United States, France, and Australia), the Davis Cup (an international team competition), and many other tournaments around the world (*e.g.*, the national championships of Canada, Italy, Germany, and all the other member countries of the ITF). The ITF had the power to determine which events would be "sanctioned," and sanctioning required that events remain "amateur." Therefore, until 1968, the Wimbledon champion received a silver plate.

If a tournament violated the rules of the ITF, it would lose its "sanction." If a player competed in an unsanctioned event, he or she would surrender his or her eligibility. For example, if a player participated in a "professional tournament," he or she would lose eligibility, even if he or she did not accept any payment from the tournament. If a sanctioned tournament permitted a player who had lost eligibility to compete in the event, the tournament would lose its sanction. Therefore, any player who played in a professional event was banished from competition in the Grand Slam events, the Davis Cup, and all other ITF-sanctioned events. If a tennis center presented a non-sanctioned event, the tennis center sacrificed its sanction, and could not produce sanctioned events. In this manner, the ITF could keep everyone in line—violation of any ITF mandate could mean banishment from the sport.

There were a few players who nevertheless "turned professional," but they were relegated to barnstorming exhibitions against other travelling professionals and were excluded from the prestigious events, often playing in high school gymnasiums, converted ice rinks, and parking lots.

By the mid-1960s, the demand for tennis events had heightened, and a few top players, including 1962 Grand Slam winner Rod Laver, Ken Rosewall, Lew Hoad, and Pancho Gonzales, had instigated efforts to develop a professional tour and abandon the ITF. The absence of these top players began to take a toll on the image of the ITF and its events. In addition, the great demand for tennis events, coupled with the high cost to an amateur player associated with playing amateur events around the world, was causing many producers of ITF-sanctioned "amateur" events to compete for amateur players by offering them secret "expense money." This led to public allegations that the ITF's claims of amateurism were a sham—hence the term "shamateurism."

In late 1967, Lamar Hunt, the founder of the American Football League and owner of the Kansas City Chiefs, launched World Championship Tennis, Inc. ("WCT"), a worldwide tour of professional tennis events. The first players to leave the amateur ranks to join the WCT were 1967 Wimbledon Champion John Newcombe, Tony Roche, Dennis Ralston, Roger Taylor, Nikki Pilic, and Cliff Drysdale. With Laver, Rosewall, and Gonzales who were already professionals, the Grand Slam events were facing the prospect that WCT events might have more of the top players in the world than Wimbledon and the other Grand Slam events.

In December, 1967, the British Lawn Tennis Association and the All England Club responded by declaring the 1968 Wimbledon Championship open to all categories of players—amateur and professional—and by appropriating prize money for the event. The United States Lawn Tennis Championships at Forest Hills responded in kind and announced that in 1968 the event would become the U.S. Open Tennis Championships—open to all players, amateur and professional—and would pay a total of $50,000 in prize money. The French and Australian Opens soon followed, and the "open era" of tennis—professional tennis as we know it—was born.

The WCT was a for-profit business, and it operated a series of events, which it called a "tour." The ITF and its members responded in 1970, at Jack Kramer's suggestion, by creating the "Grand Prix" tour, which was a series of events produced by or sanctioned by ITF members, including the Grand Slam events, the other major ITF national championships (*e.g.*, the Italian Open and the Canadian Open), and other leading independently owned and operated (but ITF-sanctioned) tournaments. Over the next twelve years, competition between WCT and the ITF alternated between periods when the competition between the ITF's Grand Prix and the WCT was intense, and periods when the ITF and WCT, declaring a "truce," would divide up the calendar. In 1972, the two sides reached a "cease-fire," which provided that WCT would limit its events to the first five months of each year—January through the WCT Finals in mid-May. The Grand Prix would limit its events to May through December, starting with the French Open and ending with the Australian Open. This calendar-dividing arrangement existed from 1973 through 1976. Then, as the demand for tennis events grew dramatically in the 1970s, the number of Grand Prix events increased correspondingly. When the truce expired, the Grand Prix sought to increase its portion of the calendar. After "peace talks" failed, a period of year-roundhead-to-head competition resulted, with the players becoming the biggest beneficiaries of the tournaments' efforts to attract the best fields to their events. Both the WCT and the Grand Prix sought ways to induce, entice, or force the top players to play in as many of their events as possible. For the Grand Prix, their primary devices to serve these purposes were their commitment agreement, bonus pool, and ranking system rules, which are discussed in the case that follows this historical excursus.

In 1973, the ITF suspended Yugoslavian Nikki Pilic from playing at Wimbledon because he allegedly failed to pay in a Davis Cup competition to which he had committed. The Yugoslavian national federation added to this insult by declaring him not in good standing. Many of the top players, led by Arthur Ashe, Stan Smith, agent/attorney Donald Dell, and their recently-formed Association of Tennis Professionals ("ATP"), boycotted Wimbledon. The boycott forced the ITF to acknowledge the players' organization and their right to representation, and led to the formation of the Men's International Professional Tennis Council ("MIPTC") in 1974. The MIPTC included player representatives and was given the power to sanction and schedule events and to control the qualifications and requirements for players desiring to participate in the Grand Prix tour. The Grand Prix, operated under the control of the MIPTC, continued to compete against the WCT. Late in the 1970s, as part of the most recent truce between the WCT and the MIPTC, WCT events became part of the Grand Prix.

In 1981, the MIPTC's power exceeded the punch of the WCT, and the MIPTC refused to accept the WCT's demands for preferential treatment within the Grand Prix. WCT responded by withdrawing its events from the Grand Prix, attempting to reestablish its own independent tennis event schedule for 1982, and filing suit on January 21, 1983 in federal court in New York. The history of competition between WCT and the Grand Prix and the expansion of the number of professional tennis events is summarized in the following chart.

Year	Circuit	No. of Tournaments	Time Period	Total Tournaments
1970	Grand Prix	21 (1 in WCT, too)	May-December	63
	WCT	13 (1 in GP, too)	February-October	
	Other	31	January-October	
1971	Grand Prix	32 (2 in WCT, too)	April-December	67
	WCT	21 (2 in GP, too)	February-November	
	Other	16	January-August	
1972	Grand Prix	34	February-December	86
	WCT	24	February-November	
	Other	28	January-December	
1973	Grand Prix	52	May-December	99
	WCT	24	January-May	
	Other	23	January-June	
1974	Grand Prix	48	May-December	96
	WCT	27	January-May	
	Other	21	January-June/December	
1975	Grand Prix	43	January-December	98
	WCT	29	January-May	
	Other	26	January-May, July September-October	
1976	Grand Prix	49	May-December	100
	WCT	28	January-May	
	Other	23	January-May, September-October, December	
1977	Grand Prix	77	January-December	102
	WCT	16	January-May, September-December	
	Other	9	January-May/September	
1978	Grand Prix	86	January-December	122
	WCT	(merged in GP + 4 additional events)	December-May	
	Other	32	January-December	
1982	Grand Prix	81	January-December	144
	WCT	21	January-December	
	Other	42	January-November	
1983	Grand Prix	71	January-December	118
	WCT	9	January-May	
	Other	38	January-November	

The *WCT* lawsuit was settled in October, 1983 under terms that limited the number of WCT events to five, but gave them favored status within the Grand Prix. By 1984, having absorbed the WCT and ending that competitive threat, the MIPTC began to focus on other competing non-Grand Prix events. The MIPTC referred to these events as "special events" or exhibitions. Many of the "special events" that concerned the MIPTC were small tournaments or round robin events. Producers of special events invited the players generating the greatest fan interest, negotiated directly with their agents to guarantee them a substantial fee for participation, and operated without constraints to select the players with the highest ATP rankings at the time of the event. Thus, in 1985 the producers of special events were able to create an eight-man event for Jimmy Connors, John McEnroe, Ivan Lendl, Yannick Noah, Boris Becker, Mats Wilander, Stefan Edberg, and Bjorn Borg. The producer of a special event could thereby provide television coverage for an entire series of very attractive match-ups for viewers. At the same time, a Grand Prix tournament could not guarantee its television network those types of match-ups even if all those players started in the draw of the event. With single elimination tournaments, even if the initial draw of 32, 64 or 128 players originated with all those stars, it is unlikely that they would all reach the later rounds of the event.

The producers of Grand Prix events considered the special events a major threat and sought to eliminate them. The way to eliminate those events was clear—keep the top players from participating. The devices that they employed were both "carrots" and "sticks". One "stick" was that the Grand Prix forced players to sign Commitment Agreements that directly imposed certain restrictions on the players. The Commitment Agreements required the players to play minimum numbers of Grand Prix events and specified weeks when the players were not permitted to participate in special events, even if they were not playing Grand Prix events during those time periods. A player who refused to sign a Commitment Agreement would be excluded from all Grand Prix events, including the WCT events and the Grand Slam events. The "carrots" were the ranking system and the bonus pool. These devices rewarded players who played more Grand Prix events with extra money (bonus pool) and higher rankings, which led in turn to greater potential for endorsements and other ancillary income. The Grand Prix Bonus Pool and the ranking system forced individual special events to compete for top player participation not just against Grand Prix events scheduled at the same time but against the entire Grand Prix.

The Grand Prix also decided to pass rules targeted at the companies that produced special events and helped those events secure players—the tennis agents/sports management companies, Donald Dell's ProServ, Inc. and Mark McCormack's International Merchandising Corporation (doing business as "IMG"). The management companies responded, along with jilted Grand Prix tour sponsor Volvo North America Corporation, by filing the following antitrust challenge in 1985.

(2) The Volvo Affair

Volvo North America Corp. v. Men's International Professional Tennis Council

857 F.2d 55 (2d Cir. 1988)

PIERCE, Circuit Judge. This is an appeal from so much of an order entered in the United States District Court for the Southern District of New York, Kevin Thomas Duffy, Judge, as dismissed Counts One through Seven of an amended complaint filed by appellants Volvo North America Corporation ("Volvo"), International Merchandising Corporation ("IMC"), and ProServ, Inc. ("ProServ"), for failure to state a claim upon which relief can be granted. *See Volvo N. Am. Corp. v. Men's Int'l Professional Tennis Council*, 678 F. Supp. 1035 (S.D.N.Y. 1987), *appeal dismissed in part*, 839 F.2d 69 (2d Cir. 1988). Counts One through Five allege that appellees, the Men's International Professional Tennis Council ("MIPTC"), its chairman, Philippe Chatrier, and its administrator, M. Marshall Happer, III, have conspired in violation of §§1 and 2 of the Sherman Act, 15 U.S.C. §§1,2 (1982), to monopolize and restrain trade in the markets for the production of men's professional tennis events, the tennis-playing services of men's professional tennis players, and the rights to broadcast men's professional tennis events. * * * For the reasons stated below, we vacate the dismissal of certain of appellants' antitrust and common law claims and remand with instructions to dismiss these claims with leave to replead; and we reverse as to the remaining claims on appeal.

I

A. The Business of Men's Professional Tennis

According to the amended complaint, the production of a men's professional tennis event requires: (1) selecting a site and arranging for a suitable facility for the event; (2) marketing the event; and (3) raising revenue to cover the costs of the event through the sale of sponsorship rights, the sale of tickets to attend the event, the sale of concessions, programs, or other products at the event, and the sale of rights associated with the event, including the rights to broadcast the event on television. The production of a men's professional tennis event often involves several different participants. The "owner" of the event is the person or entity that is obligated to pay the expenses of the event, including compensation to the players and the costs for the facility or site where the event is played, and that is entitled to receive the revenues generated by the event. Frequently, the owner of an event will contract with a third person, such as a player-agent, to advertise or market the event or certain rights associated with the event, or to manage the day-to-day operation of the event. An event also may have several different "sponsors," including: (a) a title sponsor, which purchases the right to have its name included in the title of the event; (b) a presenting sponsor, which purchases the right to have the event identified and advertised as an event that is "presented by" this sponsor; and (c) secondary sponsors, which pay for specific subsidiary sponsorship rights, such as the right to have the sponsor's product identified as the official product of the event. Volvo is an owner, producer, and sponsor of certain men's professional tennis events. IMC and ProServ own and produce certain tennis events, and also provide representational and management services to men's professional tennis players. At the present time, men's professional tennis events fall into one of two categories. The first category consists of events that are sanctioned by either MIPTC or the International Tennis Federation ("ITF"). These events include the Davis Cup events and the "Grand Prix" events; the latter consist of (1) the four "Grand Slam" tournaments, that is, Wimbledon, the U.S. Open, the French Open, and the Australian Open; (2) the Masters Tournament; (3) the World Championship Tennis Finals; (4) "Super Series" events; (5) "Regular Series" events; and (6) "Open Week Series" events. The second category consists of tournaments known as "Special Events," which include all events other than MIPTC- or ITF-sanctioned events and the Davis Cup events. Until recently, Volvo owned, produced, and sponsored only sanctioned events; IMC and ProServ, on the other hand, have owned and produced both sanctioned events and Special Events.[1]

---

1. On appeal, Volvo claims that, since this litigation was commenced, it has become the owner of one Special Event.

B. The Recent History of Men's Professional Tennis

1. ITF, WCT, and MIPTC

The amended complaint alleges that, up until the late 1960s, only amateur tennis players were allowed to compete in the prestigious men's tennis tournaments sanctioned by ITF, a governing body that consists of various national tennis associations, including the United States Tennis Association. In the late 1960s, however, a rival organization, World Championship Tennis, Inc. ("WCT"), began sponsoring a series of men's professional tennis tournaments to compete with the events sanctioned by ITF. A substantial number of top men's tennis players thereafter turned professional and began to participate in WCT-sponsored events. In response, ITF eventually changed its rules to permit professional players to compete in ITF-sanctioned tournaments. In 1974 ITF joined in establishing MIPTC, which currently consists of nine members: three members representing ITF; three members representing men's professional tennis players; and three members representing men's professional tennis tournament directors. As noted above, MIPTC sanctions and schedules the tournaments that comprise the Grand Prix.

From 1974 to 1981, MIPTC increased the number of its Grand Prix events from fifty to ninety. At the same time, MIPTC began to require men's professional tennis players, as a condition of their participation in any Grand Prix event, to execute "Commitment Agreements" which required the players to participate in a minimum number of Grand Prix events, and to limit their participation in events not sanctioned by MIPTC. As a result, WCT agreed to obtain MIPTC sanctions for its entire circuit of events. By 1981, WCT owned eight Grand Prix events sanctioned by MIPTC.

2. The MIPTC-WCT Agreement

In 1981, a dispute arose between MIPTC and WCT over the terms and conditions of WCT's continued participation in the Grand Prix. WCT withdrew from the Grand Prix in April, 1981, and unsuccessfully attempted to establish its own independent tennis circuit for 1982. WCT thereafter commenced an action in the United States District Court for the Southern District of New York, alleging that MIPTC, ITF, and the Association of Tennis Professionals had violated the antitrust laws by engaging in a combination to monopolize the production and presentation of championship caliber men's professional tennis throughout the world. The lawsuit was settled in the fall of 1983, and WCT events were integrated into the Grand Prix. The resulting agreement (the "MIPTC-WCT Agreement") provided, inter alia, that: (1) MIPTC would sanction a specified minimum number of WCT tournaments; (2) MIPTC would give the WCT tournaments scheduling and sanctioning protection and priority; (3) WCT would not sponsor, own, or promote any Special Event or Grand Prix event that might adversely affect another Grand Prix event without prior MIPTC approval; (4) if certain conditions were satisfied, WCT would terminate its involvement in the business of acting as an agent or representative of men's professional tennis players; (5) if WCT decided to operate its WCT Tournament of Champions or its WCT World Doubles Championship as Special Events, MIPTC would (a) exempt these events from all Special Event restrictions, (b) continue to grant these events scheduling priority, and (c) exempt all players from any rules that would restrict their participation in these events; (6) MIPTC would limit the number of events it would sanction; (7) MIPTC would alter the players' Commitment Agreements to require all players who qualified to participate in the WCT Finals; (8) MIPTC would increase the minimum number of MIPTC-sanctioned events in which players would be required to participate; (9) MIPTC would use its power over the services of men's professional tennis players to encourage players to participate in both WCT and other MIPTC events; (10) MIPTC and WCT would fix minimum and maximum levels of compensation to be offered to players at WCT events; and (11) MIPTC rules would be altered to provide that no Super Series event would be held in the same week as a WCT event.

3. Volvo's Involvement with Men's Professional Tennis

Volvo began its involvement in professional tennis in 1973 with a small tournament in New Hampshire known as the Volvo International Tennis Tournament. Volvo began producing and sponsoring the Washington, D.C. Volvo Classic tennis tournament in 1975 and the Volvo Tennis Games in Palm Springs, California in 1979. Late in 1979 Volvo agreed to become the overall sponsor of the entire series of Grand Prix tournaments for the years 1980, 1981, and 1982, with the option to sponsor the Grand Prix for 1983 and 1984. Volvo exercised its option to continue sponsoring the Grand Prix in 1983 and 1984, and offered to continue its overall sponsorship of the Grand Prix into the future. However, in February, 1984, MIPTC announced that it was awarding the Grand Prix sponsorship for 1985 to Nabisco Brands, Inc.

Relations between Volvo and MIPTC began to sour shortly after MIPTC chose to award the Grand Prix sponsorship to Nabisco. For several years the Masters Tournament, the final event of the annual Grand Prix series, had been held in Madison Square Garden in the week following professional football's Super Bowl. Although Volvo's right to sponsor the Grand Prix was to end in 1984, Volvo had acquired contractual rights to the use of Madison Square Garden for the Masters Tournament week in January, 1985. Volvo also entered into contractual commitments with the National Broadcasting Company ("NBC") for the televising of a men's professional tennis event during that week in future years. In response, appellee Philippe Chatrier, chairman of MIPTC, sent a letter to Volvo claiming that Volvo's negotiation of these contracts was legally improper and unethical. In January, 1985, Volvo agreed to assign its rights under the contracts with Madison Square Garden and NBC to MIPTC. In return, MIPTC agreed to approve Volvo's application for a sanction for the production of a tennis event at a site to be selected by Volvo, on the condition that Volvo sponsor no Special Events in North America during weeks in which Grand Prix tournaments were being conducted or in any city in which a Grand Prix event was held. In addition, the contract provided that MIPTC and Volvo would cooperate with each other's reasonable promotional activities.

Volvo claims, however, that despite the foregoing agreement to cooperate, appellee M. Marshall Happer, III, the administrator of MIPTC, embarked on a campaign to "dissuade and intimidate" tournament owners and producers from associating with Volvo or permitting Volvo to participate in the ownership, production, and sponsorship of Grand Prix events. * * *

C. The Litigation

In April, 1985, Volvo filed a complaint in the United States District Court for the Southern District of New York, alleging federal antitrust and common law claims against MIPTC, Chatrier, and Happer. In September, 1985, IMC and ProServ, two sports management companies that provide representational and management services to tennis players and produce and own certain men's professional tennis events, joined Volvo as plaintiffs when an amended complaint was filed.

The amended complaint alleges, inter alia, that appellees have violated §§1 and 2 of the Sherman Act, 15 U.S.C. §§1, 2 (1982), by conspiring to monopolize and restrain trade in the market for men's professional tennis. Appellants claim that this market includes: (1) the submarket for the production of men's professional tennis events; (2) the submarket for the tennis-playing services of men's professional players; and (3) the submarket for the rights to broadcast men's professional tennis events on television in the United States. Appellants identify several ways in which MIPTC allegedly has violated the Sherman Act.

First, appellants allege that MIPTC's administration of the Grand Prix has violated the Sherman Act in at least three ways. The amended complaint states that appellants, in their capacity as owners and producers of sanctioned events, "have been denied the opportunity to produce tennis events in the manner they seek, with respect to matters such as site location, player compensation and scheduling." With respect to player compensation in particular, the amended complaint states that MIPTC will not sanction a tournament unless the owner agrees to a ceiling on player compensation.

Next, appellants claim that MIPTC has "further inhibited the development of events that could compete effectively with them by coercing WCT to agree, in the MIPTC-WCT Agreement, not to own or become involved in promoting any Special Event that adversely affects any MIPTC-sanctioned event, without prior approval from the MIPTC." Appellants also assert that "the MIPTC-WCT Agreement gave the WCT competitive advantages, and used the MIPTC's monopoly power to benefit the WCT," insofar as the Agreement "included covenants not to compete and agreements horizontal competitors to divide markets, fix prices, limit output, and limit outside competition."

Further, appellants contend that MIPTC has decreased the number of non-sanctioned tournaments in which players may compete by requiring all players who wish to participate in Grand Slam events to sign Commitment Agreements which include certain restrictive provisions. A player signing a Commitment Agreement agrees to participate in a minimum of fourteen Grand Prix events, and in the Masters Tournament or the WCT Finals, if he so qualifies. According to appellants, this restriction prevents players from competing in non-sanctioned tournaments for up to twenty-one weeks out of the year. The player also agrees not to participate in any Special Event that is held in the same week as, inter alia, a Grand Slam event, the Masters Tournament, or the WCT Finals. According to appellants, this requirement prevents players from participating in Special Events during sixteen weeks out of the year. In addition, the player agrees not to participate in any Special Event that is held within thirty days of a Grand Slam event, the Masters Tournament, the WCT Finals, or any Super Series event if the Special Event is held within one hundred miles of that event. And still further, no player may participate in more than four Special Events that are held during the same week and on the same continent as one of the MIPTC Super Series events.

Appellants also allege that MIPTC requires the owners and producers of sanctioned events to agree to contribute to a "bonus pool," which provides additional compensation to players who perform well at sanctioned events throughout the course of the year. This latter requirement provides players with an additional incentive to maximize their participation in sanctioned events.

Finally, appellants claim that certain proposed restrictions would further limit their ability to compete in the market for men's professional tennis events. Among these proposed rules is a "Special Event" Rule, which would require all owners, agents, consultants, and associates of a sanctioned event to agree not to "promote" any Special Event during the week of any Grand Prix tournament. Since Grand Prix tournaments occupy forty-eight weeks of the year, this rule allegedly would preclude any person associated with an existing sanctioned event from producing any Special Events at all. There is also a proposed rule, known as the "Best Interest" Rule, which would give MIPTC the right to refuse to sanction any event whenever "in the sole judgment of the MIPTC" sanctioning that event would not serve "the best interest of the sport." Another proposal, the "Conflicts of Interest" Rule, would allow MIPTC to prohibit owners and producers from inviting certain players to participate in their tournaments as "wild cards." And last, there is a proposed rule that would permit MIPTC to serve as the exclusive representative and agent for the pooled sale of television broadcasting rights to sanctioned events.

Appellants claim that, as a result of the foregoing restrictions, they have been injured in their capacities as owners and producers, or potential owners and producers, of Special Events, as well as in their capacities as owners and producers of sanctioned events. IMC and ProServ claim that MIPTC's rules have injured them in their capacities as owners and producers of Special Events in three ways: by restricting the ability of IMC and ProServ to obtain a sufficient supply of players' services for Special Events; by causing them to own and produce fewer Special Events than they otherwise would have owned and produced; and by causing the Special Events which they do own or produce to have been less profitable than they otherwise would have been. Volvo claims that it has been injured in similar fashion, but only in its capacity as a potential owner and producer of Special Events. All three appellants claim that they have been injured in their capacities as owners and producers of MIPTC-sanctioned events, primarily because compliance with the foregoing rules has limited their ability "to compete freely and vigorously with the events owned and produced by the defendants and their co-conspirators."

* * *

In an opinion dated August 10, 1987, Judge Duffy granted the motion to dismiss Counts One through Seven and Thirteen. * * * In dismissing the amended complaint, however, Judge Duffy did not rely primarily on the arguments raised by appellees in support of the motion to dismiss. Instead, he dismissed every count of the complaint, except the counts claiming breach of contract and fraud, on the ground that appellants had failed to state a claim upon which relief could be granted.

* * *

III. Sua Sponte Dismissal

* * * We agree with appellants that the court erred by dismissing the complaint on grounds that were not briefed by either party. * * *

Conceivably, we could remand with instructions that the district court consider appellees' arguments relating to antitrust injury and extend to appellants an opportunity to brief the issues which the court did address. In their submissions to the court, however, all the parties have addressed the issue of antitrust injury, and we think the better course is to resolve this issue ourselves. In addition, since appellants have devoted substantial portions of their appellate briefs to the issues discussed in the district court's opinion, and for the sake of judicial economy, we think it is appropriate for us to decide whether appellants have stated claims for relief under §§1 and 2 of the Sherman Act and under the common law of tortious interference with prospective business relationships and unfair competition. We therefore address these issues seriatim.

IV. Antitrust Injury

* * *

* * * MIPTC argues that none of the practices challenged by appellants-MIPTC's administration of the Grand Prix circuit, the MIPTC-WCT Agreement, the Commitment Agreements, the bonus pool system, and so on—have caused appellants to suffer "injury of the type the antitrust laws were intended to prevent." In connection with each of these challenged practices, MIPTC raises the following argument in one form or another: if appellants' theory is correct, and MIPTC is the vehicle through which tournament owners and producers have organized a cartel in the market for men's professional tennis, then appellants lack standing to challenge the cartel because, as owners and producers of sanctioned tournaments, appellants themselves are members of the cartel who stand to benefit from the cartel's unlawful activity. * * * Taken to its logical conclusion, appellees' argument suggests that we adopt a per se rule prohibiting putative [cartel] members from asserting antitrust claims against other members of the cartel.

We decline to adopt a rule precluding cartel members from raising antitrust challenges against the cartel. As one commentator has noted, "even absent legal restraint the cartel is inherently more fragile than the single-firm monopolist. The interests of the cartel as a whole often diverge substantially from the interests of individual members. * * *" Individual members of the cartel may face different costs; some may be more efficient than others, and "some may produce slightly different products, which cost either a little less or a little more than the product sold by other cartel members. * * *" Thus, even though a particular trade restraint adopted by a cartel presumably operates to the cartel's aggregate benefit, the restraint may operate to the detriment of an individual member. Of course, the mere fact that a particular restraint may cause a cartel member to suffer injury is not a sufficient condition to establish antitrust standing; as noted above, the harm must be "injury of the type the antitrust laws were intended to prevent." Thus, a restraint that merely prevents a cartel member from acquiring a greater share of the fruits of the cartel would not cause the member to suffer antitrust injury, because "the antitrust laws * * * were enacted for 'the protection of *competition*, not *competitors*.'" * * * But to the extent a cartel member credibly asserts that it would be better off if it were free to compete—such that the member's interest coincides with the public interest in vigorous competition—we believe that the individual cartel member satisfies the antitrust injury requirement. * * *

2. Applying Antitrust Injury Analysis

a. MIPTC's Administration of the Grand Prix Circuit

As noted above, appellants claim that, in administering the Grand Prix, MIPTC has denied appellants "the opportunity to produce tennis events in the manner they seek with respect to matters such as site location, player compensation and scheduling." In response, appellees argue that, to the extent appellants themselves are owners and producers of events sanctioned by MIPTC, they "are only helped by rules minimizing scheduling conflicts," and that "the MIPTC rule limiting the amount of prize money which can be awarded by an event * * * cannot possibly hurt appellants in their association with MIPTC sanctioned events" because appellants stand to "benefit from a ceiling on one of the key costs of running an event."

For the following reasons, we conclude that appellants have standing to challenge the administration of the Grand Prix circuit. Because the individual cartel member's interests may diverge from the interests of the cartel as a whole, MIPTC's decisions relating to site location and scheduling might not work to appellants' advantage, even though appellants are owners and producers of sanctioned events. Appellants claim that MIPTC uses its power "to shield tournaments favored by MIPTC from the rigors of competition," and, in our view, this allegation satisfies the antitrust injury requirement. Moreover, as Volvo argues on appeal, the rule limiting the amount of prize money that may be awarded by sanctioned events may injure appellants, as owners and producers of such events, by preventing them from "compet[ing] against other Grand Prix events for the services of highly ranked players by offering more prize money." Once again, although a particular rule may work to the aggregate benefit of the owners and producers of sanctioned events, it may not benefit an individual owner or producer such as Volvo, ProServ, or IMC. Thus, because appellants' individual interests may coincide with the public interest in promoting competition, we believe that appellants have satisfied the first element of the standing analysis. Finally, we see no reason why, on the facts of this case, the "other reasons" set forth in *Associated General Contractors*—relating to the directness or speculativeness of the injury, the difficulty of apportioning damages, and so on-should foreclose appellants from proceeding with their challenge to the MIPTC's administration of the Grand Prix.

b. The MIPTC-WCT Agreement

* * *

We believe * * * that appellants have standing to challenge the MIPTC-WCT Agreement for essentially the same reasons that appellants have standing to challenge MIPTC's decisions relating to scheduling and location. A conspiracy on the part of MIPTC and WCT to restrain trade would not necessarily work to the equal benefit of every member of the alleged tennis cartel; therefore, to the extent that MIPTC and WCT may have agreed unlawfully to divide the market and to fix prices in such a way as to favor WCT events over events owned and produced by appellants, appellants have standing to challenge the agreement. * * *

c. Commitment Agreements

The amended complaint alleges that the Commitment Agreements inhibit men's professional tennis players from competing in Special Events. Appellees counter the attack on the Commitment Agreements by arguing, first, that "appellants stand only to gain from each of the alleged restrictions on the market for men's tennis playing services," because "any incentives for players to sell their services to the Grand Prix * * * can only benefit appellants" in their capacity as owners and producers of MIPTC-sanctioned events. Appellees also urge that "appellants' allegations respecting the Commitment Agreement[s] * * * at most state a claim that is purely derivative of an antitrust claim which players might have," and that this court "has steadfastly refused to recognize antitrust standing for parties harmed only derivatively. * * *" Finally, appellees contend that IMC and ProServ, in their capacities as owners and producers of Special Events, lack standing to challenge the Commitment Agreements because (1) "they do not plead any events which have failed or even suffered because of the Commitment Agreements," and (2) the amended complaint does not allege that the Commitment Agreements prohibit players from participating in Special Events, but only that appellants will have to pay more to induce players who participate in Grand Prix events to participate in non-sanctioned events.

Notwithstanding the foregoing arguments, we conclude that appellants have standing to challenge the Commitment Agreements. As alleged, the Commitment Agreements discourage players from participating in non-sanctioned events and, therefore, increase the cost of producing these events. * * *

Appellees' argument that appellants' claim is "purely derivative" of whatever claim the players may have is unpersuasive in light of our analysis above; appellants' alleged injury is not so "indirect" as to deny them the right to challenge the Commitment Agreements. And, despite the fact, as noted by appellees, that IMC and ProServ have not alleged any particular tournaments that "failed or suffered" as a result of the Commitment Agreements, we do not believe that the alleged injury is so inherently speculative as to merit dismissal at this stage of the litigation.

d. Bonus Pool

* * *

In our view, * * * IMC and ProServ, as owners and producers of Special Events, have standing to attack the bonus pool system to the extent that this system, like the Commitment Agreements, may discourage players from competing in Special Events. Moreover, as owners and producers of sanctioned events, IMC, ProServ, and Volvo have standing for two reasons. First, like the Commitment Agreements, the bonus pool system may discourage appellants from attempting to compete against MIPTC. Second, because the interest of an individual cartel member may diverge from the aggregate interest of the cartel, Volvo, ProServ, and IMC may be better off choosing for themselves how much to invest to encourage players to participate in sanctioned tournaments rather than being compelled to invest however much the alleged cartel dictates. We thus conclude that appellants also have standing to contest the bonus pool system.

e. Special Events Rule

Finally, we believe that appellants have standing to attack the proposed Special Events Rule because the rule, if adopted, might discourage appellants, as owners and producers of sanctioned events, from becoming involved with non-sanctioned tournaments that could compete with MIPTC events. Moreover, ProServ and IMC have standing to challenge the rule, in their capacity as owners and producers of non-sanctioned events, to the extent that the rule might coerce them into abandoning their involvement with Special Events.

* * *

V. Section 1 Claim

1. "Contract, Combination * * * or Conspiracy"

* * *

* * * [T]he district court held that appellants failed to state a claim for relief under §1, because they failed to allege an agreement between two or more persons. According to the district court:

> The only co-conspirator named in the complaint is the ITF. The ITF formed MIPTC originally, participates in MIPTC's operation, and ITF members make up one-third of MIPTC. Because ITF makes up part of MIPTC, and because it is legally impossible to conspire with oneself, * * * plaintiffs can make out no claim of conspiracy to restrain trade or to monopolize against ITF and MIPTC.

Plaintiffs also allege that other co-conspirators exist, "some of whom may not be known to the plaintiffs at this time."

* * * However, no conspiracy claim can stand against unidentified and unknown third parties.

* * * Although we agree with the principle that it is impossible to conspire with oneself, we do not believe that the district court was correct to apply this principle in the present case. As we have noted, MIPTC is an association consisting of representatives of national tennis associations, tournament owners and directors, and professional tennis players. Courts have consistently held that, since joint ventures—including sports leagues and other such associations—consist of multiple entities, they can violate §1 of the Sherman Act. * * * We therefore hold that appellants have adequately alleged the element of contract, combination, or conspiracy.

2. "In Restraint of Trade"

On appeal Volvo, IMC, and ProServ contend that their complaint alleges three "classic forms of per se illegal conduct": price fixing, horizontal market division, and group boycott. We address each of these theories in turn.

a. Price Fixing

The amended complaint clearly alleges that MIPTC has engaged in price fixing * * * [T]he amended complaint states that MIPTC has "fixed the compensation that can be paid to players at other men's professional tennis events. * * *" [T]he amended complaint states that "all owners and producers seeking sanction for their events must agree * * * to ceilings on player compensation. * * *" Finally, in relevant part, * * * of the amended complaint states that appellants, "as owners and producers of men's professional tennis events sanctioned by MIPTC, have been harmed in that, among other things, * * * they have been denied the opportunity to produce tennis events in the manner they seek, with respect to such matters as * * * player compensation." Accordingly, we reverse so much of the district court's order as dismissed appellants' claim for relief from the alleged price-fixing conspiracy.

Assuming that appellants succeed in proving the foregoing allegations, however, we express no opinion at this time as to whether appellees' conduct should be condemned as per se unlawful or, instead, should be analyzed under the Rule of Reason. Normally, "agreements among competitors to fix prices on their individual goods and services are among those concerted activities" that are considered per se illegal under §1 of the Sherman Act. * * * The relevant inquiry, however, involves more than "a question simply of determining whether two or more potential competitors have literally 'fixed' a 'price. * * *'" Instead, "'price fixing' is a shorthand way of describing certain categories of business behavior to which the per se rule has been held applicable." *Id. See also* Hovenkamp §4.4, at 128 ("Once a court has properly characterized a practice as price fixing, it is per se illegal. However, determining when a practice should be so characterized can be very difficult, and may involve a fair amount of sophisticated economic inquiry.") Moreover, we recognize that professional sporting events cannot exist unless the producers of such events agree to cooperate with one another to a certain extent, and that the antitrust laws do not condemn such agreements when coordination is essential if the activity is to be carried out at all. *See, e.g., NCAA v. Board of Regents*, 468 U.S. 85 at 101 (1984). * * * Thus, on remand, the district court should carefully consider whatever arguments appellees may offer in support of their practices relating to player compensation before deciding whether the per se rule or the Rule of Reason should apply.

b. Horizontal Market Division

Appellants also claim that appellees have unlawfully agreed to a horizontal market division. * * * According to appellants, "one of the prime continuing objectives of defendants' cartel is minimizing any direct competition among Grand Prix tournaments or with the ITF's events by agreeing to schedule their events during different weeks and in different cities." The district court did not expressly consider appellants' horizontal market division theory.

In our view, the complaint adequately alleges an unlawful horizontal market division. * * * [A]s we noted above, appellants have alleged that the 1983 MIPTC-WCT Agreement resulted in the division of the market between the two competing tennis circuits. * * * Accordingly, we reverse so much of the lower court's order as dismissed appellants' claims relating to horizontal market division. We express no opinion as to whether the horizontal restraints alleged in the amended complaint should be subject to a per se rule or to the Rule of Reason. * * *

c. Group Boycott or Concerted Refusal to Deal

Finally, appellants claim that appellees have unlawfully agreed to engage in a group boycott or concerted refusal to deal. According to appellant ProServ, "the Grand Prix tournaments have collectively agreed not to permit the participation by any player who fails to accept the conditions the group imposes upon the player's activities for an entire year." Thus, men's professional tennis players "confront through the Commitment Agreements a horizontal agreement among competing producers of tennis tournaments setting forth the terms under which they will collectively decline to deal with the players."

Judge Duffy considered the Commitment Agreements to be "essentially employment contracts that require employee players to play only for MIPTC for thirty-six weeks a year. * * *" The court then stated that "employers may impose reasonable employment conditions for a reasonable period of time," and that "even accepting plaintiffs' assertion that creating an independent tennis event series is not feasible during the remaining weeks of the year, I cannot find that an exclusive employment contract for thirty-six weeks a year is imposed for an unreasonable length of time. * * *"

In our view, the amended complaint adequately alleges that appellees have threatened to engage in a group boycott or concerted refusal to deal. Generally, a group boycott is "an agreement by two or more persons not to do business with other individuals, or to do business with them only on specified terms. * * *" To prevail on a group boycott or refusal to deal claim, a plaintiff must demonstrate that the defendant intends to restrain competition, or to enhance or expand his monopoly, and has acted coercively. * * *

As with the allegations relating to price fixing and horizontal market division, we see no need at this stage of the litigation to express an opinion whether, on remand, the district court should apply a per se rule or the Rule of Reason to the restrictions that allegedly constitute a concerted refusal to deal. We note only that "certain concerted refusals to deal or group boycotts are so likely to restrict competition without any offsetting efficiency gains that they should be condemned as per se violations of §1," Northwest Wholesale Stationers, Inc. v. Pacific Stationery & Printing Co., 472 U.S. 284, 290 (1985), * * * while others do not "share with the per se forbidden boycotts the likelihood of predominantly anticompetitive consequences * * *" Whether the threatened boycott alleged in the amended complaint falls into the former or the latter category is a matter for the district court to consider in due course.

B. Section 2 Claim

* * * Appellants argue that MIPTC has violated §2 by engaging in monopolization, attempted monopolization, and conspiracy to monopolize. We address each of these theories *seriatim.*

1. Monopolization

The offense of monopolization under §2 of the Sherman Act consists of two elements: (1) the possession of monopoly power in the relevant market; and (2) the willful acquisition or maintenance of that power, as distinguished from growth or development as a consequence of a superior product, business acumen, or historic accident. * * * Appellants clearly have alleged that MIPTC possesses monopoly power over the production of first-rate men's professional tennis events. Paragraph 50 of the amended complaint, for example, alleges that in 1985 the top one hundred men's professional tennis players all signed Commitment Agreements. Moreover, the amended complaint alleges that appellees have willfully maintained their monopoly power (1) by merging with WCT in 1983; (2) by requiring players to sign Commitment Agreements; and (3) by requiring owners of sanctioned events to contribute to the bonus pool. Although the facts may eventually bear out the district court's conclusion that MIPTC has not willfully maintained its monopoly power, and that MIPTC instead has benefited from "the recent historical development of men's professional tennis," we do not believe that the district court was correct to draw this conclusion on a motion to dismiss.

2. Attempted Monopolization

The offense of attempted monopolization under §2 of the Sherman Act requires proof of three elements: (1) anti-competitive or exclusionary conduct; (2) specific intent to monopolize; and (3) a dangerous probability that the attempt will succeed. * * *

In the present case, the district court did not address appellants' attempted monopolization claim. For the reasons stated above, however, we believe that the complaint clearly alleges the first two elements of an attempted monopolization claim, exclusionary conduct and specific intent to monopolize. In addition, since the complaint alleges both exclusionary conduct and the existence of monopoly power, the third element, a dangerous probability of success, may be inferred.

3. Conspiracy to Monopolize

Under §2 of the Sherman Act, the offense of conspiracy to monopolize requires proof of (1) concerted action, (2) overt acts in furtherance of the conspiracy, and (3) specific intent to monopolize. * * * For reasons already stated, we believe that the complaint alleges concerted action and specific intent to monopolize. Moreover, the various practices to which appellants object could qualify as overt acts. Accordingly, appellants have stated a claim of conspiracy to monopolize.

* * *

CONCLUSION

For the reasons stated above, we vacate so much of the district court's order as dismissed with prejudice appellants' antitrust challenges to the Best Interest Rule, the Conflicts of Interest Rule, and the rule relating to pooled television broadcasting rights, and we remand with instructions that the district court dismiss the challenges to these rules with leave to replead in the event that the rules are actually adopted. * * *

With respect to the remaining issues on appeal, we reverse. In our view, appellants have standing to attack MIPTC's administration of the Grand Prix circuit, the MIPTC-WCT Agreement, the Commitment Agreements, the bonus pool system, and the Special Event Rule. The complaint adequately alleges that appellees have engaged in price fixing, horizontal market division, and that they have threatened a concerted refusal to deal. The complaint further alleges, properly, that appellees have engaged in monopolization, attempted monopolization, and conspiracy to monopolize. * * * Accordingly, we remand for further proceedings consistent with this opinion.

Notes and Questions

1. The saga of the *Volvo* case illustrates one of the major risks of sports-related antitrust litigation: jurists who have difficulty applying antitrust laws, which were developed primarily in the context of traditional industries, to the world of professional sports. As the Second Circuit explained, the conduct challenged by the plaintiffs was either *per se* unlawful or conduct similar to *per se* offenses that might have to be assessed under the Rule of Reason. Yet, the district court judge concluded that no antitrust claim had even been stated:

> The decision on this motion for summary judgment submitted in January of 1986 has been a long time in coming. The reason for this is that I had difficulty (as often happens) in articulating the obvious. Sometimes it is necessary to explain the obvious, something that district court judges are competent to do. * * * It is necessary in this case.

678 F. Supp. at 1036.

In large part because he ruled on the merits of the case without the benefit of any briefs on those issues from the parties, the judge did not fully comprehend the significance of issues such as how an effort by the MIPTC to enact an "internal rule" forcing all the tournaments to pool their television broadcast rights could violate the antitrust laws. Just three years earlier, the Supreme Court had held that mandatory pooling of college football television broadcast rights was unlawful. See *NCAA v. Board of Regents*, 468 U.S. 85 (1984). As part of his sweeping housecleaning of the antitrust claims, the judge likewise dismissed various antitrust counterclaims against plaintiff ProServ.

Six years after the Second Circuit's decision in *Volvo*, the same district judge held both that the NBA's salary cap and other restrictions were protected by the labor exemption *and that even without an exemption those restrictions were permissible because they were reasonable! See NBA v. Williams*, 857 F. Supp. 1069, 1079 (S.D.N.Y. 1994). While the court's decision on the labor exemption was affirmed, 45 F.3d 684 (2d Cir. 1995), and the correctness of its holding concerning the labor exemption was subsequently confirmed by the Supreme Court in *Brown v. Pro-Football, Inc.*, 518 U.S. 231 (1996), the Second Circuit made it clear that the district court's application of the Rule of Reason, rendered without an appropriate exposition of the relevant facts, was not endorsed. 45 F.3d at 688 ("We need not * * * address the various arguments pro and con regarding the Rule of Reason").

2. As an attorney advising a potential plaintiff in a sports antitrust case, or when novel issues are presented in the context of a fledgling industry, how do you assess for your client the risk that the decisionmaker will not appreciate the magnitude of the alleged offenses and the subtle factual bases for the allegations? How should that risk affect a potential plaintiff's strategy? What are the likely consequences of judicial delay?

The *Volvo* plaintiffs filed their lawsuit in 1985; it was dismissed in 1987 and reinstated and remanded by the Second Circuit in 1988. No trial date had been set, depositions had not commenced, and a full evidentiary proceeding in the case remained unlikely for at least another eighteen months. In the Second Circuit, cases are generally remanded to the same judge; thus, despite the judge's initial conclusions that all the challenged conduct was reasonable, he was directed to determine whether the MIPTC's conduct should be assessed under a *per se* rule or under the Rule of Reason. Does this seem appropriate? The question was resolved when the district judge recused himself, and the parties settled the case before a new judge was assigned.

3. On remand, with respect, for example, to the plaintiffs' group boycott, price fixing, and horizontal market division claims, should a lower court judge or a jury decide whether a *per se* rule or a Rule of Reason should be applied? Did the *Volvo* court suggest that the reasonableness of the rules in the context of the tennis industry must be considered and, if the rules are "unreasonable" or "anticompetitive," they should be held *per se* unlawful? How does this differ (if it does) from the analysis of Judge Sweigert in the *Kapp* case? Is this approach not somewhat counter-intuitive given that the "reasonableness" balancing test should not be part of the equation in a *per se* situation? Once again, the imprecise "guidance" of *Northwest Wholesale Stationers* rears its head. *Northwest Wholesale Stationers v. Pacific Stationery & Printing Co.*, 472 U.S. 85 (1985). If additional factual analysis is necessary to decide whether to apply a *per se* rule, does this issue have to be submitted to the jury, with appropriately explicit instructions?

4. When the *Volvo* case settled, the MIPTC told the tennis community that it had agreed to eliminate or modify significantly many of the restrictions challenged by the plaintiffs and not to enact most of the proposed rules. The settlement was part of an effort by the ITF and the MIPTC to maintain their almost total control over professional tennis. However, the effort was unsuccessful, and the Association of Tennis Professionals ("ATP") announced that it was forming a new tour—the ATP Tour, modeled in large part after the golf counterpart, the PGA Tour. While nominally "owned" or "controlled" by the players, the ATP Tour is a not-for-profit entity that has continued to employ most of the same restrictions found by the *Volvo* court to be *per se* unlawful. In fact, some of the ATP Tour's rules are even more restrictive. *See, e.g.,* the changes in ATP ranking system causing players to play in more ATP Tour events, discussed in Chapter 2. Over time, those restrictions virtually eliminated the significance of competition from "special events." The producers of "special events" generally turned their events into more traditional tournaments and applied for membership in the ATP Tour, or they simply shut their events down. Any MIPTC promises not to enact such rules obviously do not bind the ATP Tour.

5. In 2002, two ATP Tour-sanctioned tournaments brought an antitrust suit against the ATP Tour, challenging these new restrictions and the ATP Tour's agreements with the International Tennis Federation and the Grand Slam tennis events, and arguing that the ATP Tour was trying to eliminate all events that might compete with it. The parties eventually settled the case before it reached trial, and the ATP Tour continues to employ many of the restrictions the *Volvo* court held might be *per se* violations. How can a circuit continue to engage in conduct that may be *per se* unlawful?

6. The ATP Tour would likely assert that a major difference between its restrictions and those imposed by the MIPTC is the ITF's non-involvement in the ATP Tour. While certain events produced by national federations are part of the ATP Tour, the Grand Slams and Davis Cup are not. In fact, the ITF sanctioned a year-end event, the Grand Slam Cup, which, together with the Grand Slams, constituted a type of circuit. There-

fore, to the extent that the MIPTC's authority was derived from their direct control over the Grand Slams, the ATP Tour lacks that power. However, the ITF and ATP Tour coordinate the scheduling of their events (either explicitly or implicitly) to avoid conflicts and since 1998 there have been agreements between the ITF and the ATP Tour on scheduling, producing competing events, and other issues, which included an agreement that the ITF would shut down the Grand Slam Cup. If the restrictions imposed by the MIPTC are *per se* violations of Section 1, would it matter (or should it matter) that the ATP Tour does not have as much power as MIPTC had or that the ATP Tour does not control the Grand Slam events?

7. Traditional horizontal market division cases have involved two competitors agreeing not to infringe upon each other's exclusive geographic territories. *See, e.g., Palmer v. BRG of Ga., Inc.,* 498 U.S. 46 (1990) (per curiam); *United States v. Topco Associates, Inc.,* 405 U.S. 596 (1972); *Timken Roller Bearing Co. v. United States,* 341 U.S. 593 (1951); *United States v. Sealy, Inc.,* 388 U.S. 350 (1967). Was the agreement by WCT and MIPTC to divide the year a comparable restraint? In what respects would that division eliminate competition between the events in the two tours? In what ways would they continue to compete? Taking the analysis one step further, does the ATP Tour's exclusive scheduling of one or two events per week constitute horizontal market division? Does a circuit of events have to schedule all the events to ensure that they are spread over the calendar and do not conflict with each other? What procompetitive benefits can that type of "tournament of the week" scheduling yield and are they sufficient to outweigh the anticompetitive impact of the restraint?

8. Six of the nine members of the MIPTC—the three ITF representatives and the three tournament representatives—ran tournaments or represented producers of MIPTC tournaments. As members of the Council, those tournament producers sat in judgment about issues relating to sanctioning, scheduling, and other business issues that directly impacted their own tournaments and other tournaments. They enacted or proposed all the rules that ProServ, IMC and Volvo challenged. What is the relevance of the *Blalock* analysis to the facts in *Volvo*? *See Blalock v. LPGA,* 359 F. Supp. 1260 (N.D. Ga. 1973). Are the decisions by the Council that adversely affect competing tournaments or favor tournaments produced by the Council members *per se* unlawful? *See further Gilder v. PGA Tour, Inc.* 936 F.2d 417 (9th Cir. 1991), discussed in Chapter 13.

9. The district court judge believed that the restrictions imposed by the MIPTC would not prevent a new circuit of events from competing—the new circuit would simply have to convince players to forego all participation in MIPTC events (Grand Slams plus approximately 100 other tournaments) in order to compete in the new circuit. The district court was correct; the restrictions imposed by the MIPTC were designed to yield precisely that result—only an entire alternative circuit could compete. Why would it be virtually impossible to create such a competing tour? The district court apparently did not understand that the restrictions rendered it impossible for individual, unaffiliated events to compete with the Grand Prix and survive, thus signalling an elimination of competition. *See, e.g.,* the discussion in Chapter 2 questioning whether agreements between individual sport events (like tennis tournaments) are essential, as compared with agreements between and among teams in league sports.

10. The *Volvo* court discussed at length whether the plaintiffs suffered "antitrust injury" as a result of the various restraints. The complications arose from the variety of conduct challenged and the plaintiffs' dual roles—they produced both Grand Prix events and non-Grand Prix or "special" events. With respect to rules that substituted regulation for competition between events *within* the Grand Prix and limited, among

other things, the amounts plaintiffs could pay for players and when and where they could hold their tournaments, the plaintiffs were similarly situated to the colleges in *NCAA v. Board of Regents*, 468 U.S. 85 (1984). On the other hand, rules that limited players' ability to participate in non-Grand Prix events were specifically intended to put special event producers, like the plaintiffs, out of that business. The restraints on the players were the means, but hamstringing the plaintiff and injuring the competition was the motivation. The MIPTC used its market power to force the players, sellers of an essential input, to agree not to play in special events, except under limited circumstances. It is clear that the disadvantaged, boycotted competitors are proper antitrust plaintiffs. The closer question is whether the party through whom the restraint operates, the players, may also bring a damage action. *See, e.g., Blue Shield v. McCready*, 457 U.S. 465 (1982); *Associated General Contractors v. California State Council of Carpenters*, 459 U.S. 519, 541 (1983); *see further North American Soccer League v. NFL*, 670 F.2d 1249 (2d Cir.), *cert. denied*, 459 U.S. 1074 (1982); *International Entertainment Group v. NBA*, 853 F. Supp. 333 (C.D. Cal. 1994); *Philadelphia World Hockey Club, Inc. v. Philadelphia Hockey Club, Inc.*, 351 F. Supp. 462 (E.D.Pa. 1972).

11. Which rules challenged in *Volvo* injured non-Grand Prix competing events? Do those rules benefit the plaintiffs when they are producing Grand Prix events? Which restraints restrict producers of Grand Prix events? Do those restrictions help special events compete? If a rule hurts the plaintiffs in one capacity, but helps them in another, how does that affect the plaintiffs' antitrust claims, including the amount of damages? *See, e.g., Los Angeles Mem. Coliseum Comm'n v. NFL*, 791 F.2d 1356 (9th Cir. 1986), discussed in Chapter 12.

12. The primary attack on the "player restraints" in *Volvo*—the commitment agreement, bonus pool, and ranking system—was not based on those restraints reducing player compensation or mobility. Rather, the restraints on the top world class players, an essential input to produce professional tennis events, were the means by which a circuit of events battled its rivals. As we move to the next chapter, we consider other restraints alleged to prevent the production or sale of sports events that have been challenged by competitors.

13. Undoubtedly, the tour arrangements under fire in *Volvo* had some advantageous aspects and promoted competition in some fashion. Had the *Volvo* case or the 2002 case against the ATP Tour proceeded to a more searching inquiry under Rule of Reason analysis, what procompetitive reasons would the defendants offer to justify their conduct? Would these procompetitive benefits be sufficient to outweigh the anticompetitive impact of the restraints?

Chapter 11

Antitrust and Sports: Monopolization and Restraints on Inter-League Competition

I. Introduction

Two unusual features that distinguish professional sports from the vast majority of industries are: (1) it is rare for two competing entities in the same sport—two major leagues in one country or two top international professional circuits—to survive; and (2) many consumers and other market participants who would benefit from competition nevertheless are not troubled by, and frequently favor, the absence of competition—control of the sport by a single league, circuit or sports association. In other industries, consumers seek and often demand that there be competing producers or suppliers because of the recognition that competition generally leads to higher quality products and greater innovation, all at lower prices. Similarly, proposals to merge the only two competitors in a non-sports market are generally viewed with skepticism and protest because of a recognition that the elimination of competition is likely to injure all who have business dealings with the to-be-merged firms. The public reaction to such circumstances in the professional sports industry is often very different.

The antitrust laws approach professional sports in the same way that they approach all other industries—with enthusiasm for competition and hostility toward monopoly or other anticompetitive conduct. However, consumers and fans in the United States often voice the opinion that each sport should be (or must be) represented or controlled at the highest professional level by a single league or circuit. Announcements of the launch of new, competing leagues are typically greeted with criticism or derision, and any adverse consequences of monopoly control are often accepted as inevitable. In addition, the success of new leagues or circuits frequently leads to calls for the competitors to merge or, at least, to schedule season-ending competitions between the best competitors or teams from the rival leagues, with the ultimate goal of identifying a "national" or "world" champion. In many cases, the mergers or joint activity sought by the fans would constitute clear violations of the federal antitrust laws that were enacted by Congress to protect those very consumers. Nevertheless, the fans still seek consolidation. That sentiment even motivated Congress to pass unprecedented legislation to override the antitrust laws to permit one such merger. As explained in Chapter 7, the 1966 amendments to the Sports Broadcasting Act of 1961 were enacted to permit the merger of the American Football League and the National Football League into a single league.

The history of successful major professional sports leagues in the United States is generally continuous and repetitive: (1) a single major league gains control of the highest level of a sport and becomes its dominant professional league; (2) the league achieves stability and a period of perceived prosperity; (3) the demand for ownership of the existing teams in the league substantially exceeds the supply of teams, and/or the demand by cities without teams for the creation of additional teams substantially exceeds the existing owners' interest in expansion; (4) a new, competing league is created; and either (5a) the new league simply fails and its teams or personnel are, to some extent, absorbed by the existing league, or (5b) the new league survives and shows some signs of stability, and competition between the two leagues ends when the new league is absorbed in some manner by the existing league. In this manner, the existing league further enhances its control over the highest level of the sport. As a result, the next putative challenger league will face an even tougher, more established and generally more dominant league. Individuals in the new group, seeking to form the next challenger league, can learn from the preceding failure, but may have an even tougher road to convince investors that the new venture is likely to succeed. Subsequently, the historical cycle begins again. Eventually, a new group, hoping to build on the strategies and profit from the mistakes of the predecessor challengers forms another competing league.

More recently, entrepreneurs have often opted to forego challenging the entrenched, dominant, major leagues, each of which have about thirty teams located throughout the United States (or North America). The alternative strategy has been to focus instead on the creation, expansion, or enhancement of a "minor league" with lower player costs, smaller arenas and attendance, cheaper ticket prices, and an entertainment product that delivers more than just admission to a sporting event—pregame and halftime entertainment, activities for young fans, and a more interactive, audience-participatory environment.

At the same time, individual sports (tennis, golf, etc.) have also seen the development of circuits of events for women, "minor league" circuits, and the organization of "senior tours." Senior tours generally seek to promote the continued fan interest in former top professionals and satisfy the excess market demand for professional events in that sport, which is not satisfied by the major league, minor league, and women's tours.

The cases that follow concern the manner in which major professional sports leagues and their teams have responded to competition, potential competition, or a perception of competition from teams in rival leagues. The *Volvo* case was included at the end of the previous chapter because its primary focus was on player restraints. However, those player restraints were also the central part of one circuit's war against competing events. The commitment agreement, bonus pool, and ranking system in *Volvo* were all part of an effort by the producers of the events in the most established circuit of professional tennis, the Grand Prix, to prevent present or future competition from any other circuit. The cases in this chapter concern other competitive struggles between competing producers of events as well as skirmishes between competing leagues and between the teams in those leagues.

The first two cases in this chapter, *American Football League v. National Football League* and *Hecht v. Pro-Football, Inc.*, concern the battles between the AFL and the NFL in the 1960s. The AFL was created by a number of wealthy individuals who had previously sought in vain to own NFL franchises. Shortly after the organization of the AFL was announced, the NFL awarded expansion franchises to owners who would otherwise have owned AFL teams. The AFL sued, contending that this conduct and other conduct by the NFL restrained trade and was part of an attempt by the NFL to maintain its monopoly position. The *Hecht* case involved a group of investors who had unsuccessfully sought an AFL franchise to play in Washington, D.C. Norman Hecht claimed that their effort failed because an NFL team, the Washington Redskins, had enforced an exclusive provision in its lease with RFK Stadium to prevent anyone from leasing that facility for a competing football franchise and had thereby maintained the Redskins' monopoly position over professional football in Washington, D.C.

The third case, *United States Football League v. National Football League*, was brought by another challenger to the NFL's position as the sole major professional football league, the USFL. The USFL had commenced operation as a spring football league, but eventually adopted a fall schedule and sought to engage the NFL in direct competition. The USFL failed and sought vindication through the antitrust laws alleging that it was the victim of the NFL's monopolization. The *USFL* case is extremely important from both a sports law and sports business perspective because it: (1) manifested the only significant challenge to sport's dominant major league from the late 1970s until the World Wrestling Entertainment's and NBC's XFL in 2001; (2) provided an opportunity for the federal courts to adjudicate allegations that the dominant league had engaged in a wide variety of conduct directed at the new entrant; and (3) represented a concept that had potential to succeed and would serve as a model to be used by others planning competing leagues and by the NFL in launching its World League of American Football, which became the NFL Europe.

The first three cases in this chapter concerned classic battles between, on one side, existing teams in the dominant league and the league itself, and, on the other side, their fledgling competitors. The fourth and final featured case in this chapter also implicated the NFL, but the competition at issue was from a league in another sport—called football in Europe and elsewhere in the world, and known as soccer in the United States. Certain owners of NFL teams were involved in the ownership of teams in the North American Soccer League ("NASL"). The controversy centered upon the NFL's attempt to force them to choose—own an NFL team or a team in another league (NASL, National Basketball Association, Major League Baseball, National Hockey League, etc.), but not both. Is such a restriction merely the right of teams in a league to demand that every owner's full attention and loyalty not be diverted by ownership of teams in another sport? Or, does such a rule—a "cross-ownership ban"—constitute an impermissible attempt to deprive a competing league of the involvement and capital investment from experienced owners of professional sports teams in another league? Does such a prohibition possibly compromise the economic viability of the "other" league? Given the amount of money necessary to fund a professional sports franchise, are there a limited number of potential owners who would be willing and able to provide the necessary capital investment? If so, how significant is this factor in any assessment of the reasonableness of a league "cross-ownership" limitation? *See North American Soccer League v. National Football League*, below.

As you read these cases, consider the following additional questions:

(1) Was the defendants' conduct challenged as a violation of Sherman Act Section 1 ("contract, combination * * *, or conspiracy" that restrains trade) or Section 2 (monopolization, attempt to monopolize, conspiracy to monopolize) or both?

(2) What was the particular conduct engaged in by the defendants and how did it adversely impact the plaintiff(s)?

(3) What was the market(s) that the plaintiff(s) contended was monopolized by the defendants or in which competition was restrained?

(4) How does the analysis of the legality of the challenged conduct differ under Section 1 as opposed to Section 2 of the Sherman Act? Is there evidence that is relevant under Section 2 that is irrelevant under Section 1?

II. AFL-NFL Pre-Merger Competition

American Football League v. National Football League
323 F.2d 124 (4th Cir. 1963)

HAYNSWORTH, Circuit Judge. The American Football League and owners of its franchises are contending against the National Football League and the owners of its franchises for victory in the courts. The American Football League and the owners of its franchises lost in the Court below, when the District Court held that there had been no violation of Sections 1, 2 or 3 of the Sherman Act by the National Football League and the owners of its franchises. We affirm. * * *

In 1959, the National Football League operated with twelve teams located in eleven cities. There were two teams in Chicago and one each in Cleveland, New York, Philadelphia, Pittsburgh, Washington, Baltimore, Detroit, Los Angeles, San Francisco, and Green Bay, Wisconsin. In 1960, two additional franchises were placed, one in Dallas and one in Minneapolis-St. Paul, the Dallas team beginning play in 1960 and the Minneapolis-St. Paul team in 1961. In 1961, one of the Chicago teams, the Cardinals, was transferred to St. Louis.

The American Football League was organized in 1959, and began with a full schedule of games in 1960. Affiliated with it were eight teams located in eight cities, Boston, Buffalo, Houston, New York, Dallas, Denver, Los Angeles and Oakland. After the 1960 season, the Los Angeles team was moved to San Diego. * * *

Many of the National League owners were interested in expanding the league. * * * [T]he interest of the owners centered on Houston, Dallas, and two or three other cities. * * * [I]t was thought that Houston and Dallas, with their natural rivalry, could each support a team. Those two cities were considered by National's owners as the most likely prospects for expansion, with Minneapolis-St. Paul, Buffalo and Miami close behind.

Meanwhile, there were people actively interested in acquiring franchises to operate National League teams in Houston and Dallas. Clint Murchison, Jr. and his father, of Dallas, had sought to purchase the San Francisco 49'ers, the Washington Redskins and the Chicago Cardinals, intending, if successful in acquiring one of those teams, to move it to Dallas. In 1957 and 1958, Lamar Hunt, of Dallas, and the Houston Sports Association applied to National for franchises to operate teams in those two cities. Hunt also sought to acquire the Chicago Cardinals and move that team to Dallas. Early in 1959, Murchison and Hunt (Dallas) and Cullinan, Kirksey and Adams (Houston Sports Association) were all actively seeking National League franchises. * * *

* * * [I]n the spring of 1959, Hunt, of Dallas, decided that a new league was feasible and could be successfully organized. He had been told by [Bert] Bell [the NFL Commissioner] that he might submit a formal application for the Dallas franchise at the January 1960 annual meeting. However, he was either unsure of National's expansion into Dallas, of when it would occur, or of his chances of obtaining the franchise in competition with Murchison.

The remainder of 1959 was very eventful. Hunt proceeded actively with his plan to organize a new league. In July he disclosed his intention to Commissioner Bell. On July 28, Bell, with Hunt's permission, told a congressional committee of Hunt's plans, and stated that the National League owners favored organization of the new league. Early in August, Hunt and Adams publicly announced the formation of the new league, with teams owned by them to be located, respectively, in Dallas and Houston. Hunt and his associates were actively in touch with interested persons in a number of other cities. On August 22, representatives from Los Angeles, Dallas, Houston, New York, Minneapolis and Denver signed articles of association. Representatives from many other cities had been in touch with Hunt. Wilson, of Detroit, sought an American franchise for Miami, and later for Buffalo, and the Buffalo franchise was formally granted in October. In November, an application for a franchise to be placed in Boston was approved. Thus, in late November, American had tentative arrangements for teams in Houston, Dallas, Minneapolis, New York, Boston, Denver, Buffalo and Los Angeles.

In the meanwhile, Murchison, of Dallas, and Cullinan and Kirksey, who had been associated with Adams in efforts to obtain a National franchise for Houston, continued their efforts to obtain National franchises for those two cities. In late August, at their insistence, Halas, with the approval of a number of National owners, publicly announced that National's expansion committee would recommend to the 1960 meeting franchises for Dallas and Houston to begin play in 1961, the Houston franchise to be conditioned upon the availability of an adequate stadium. Construction of a new stadium in Houston was in contemplation, and there was hope that a National League team might obtain use of the Rice University Stadium until a new municipal stadium was constructed and available. * * *

In October, however, it became known that the Rice University Stadium would not be made available for use by a National League team, and all further consideration of a National League franchise in Houston was then abandoned.

A number of people in Minnesota had been seeking a National League football team, but after Hunt's plans for a new league had been disclosed to them, Winter, Boyer and Skoglund, of Minneapolis, entered into American's Articles of Association, which were executed in August 1959. * * * When it became known that an appropriate stadium in Houston was not available, Johnson and Winter sought definite commitments from the National League. They obtained telegraphic commitments in November. * * *

In January 1960, Winter, of Minneapolis, and Haugsrud, of Duluth, formally applied to the National League for a franchise. Boyer joined in its presentation, stating that he had withdrawn from the American League and had obtained a complete release and a return of the $ 25,000 deposit, which he, Winter and Skoglund had made. At National's annual meeting on January 28, 1960, franchises were granted to Dallas and Minneapolis-St. Paul, the grant to Minneapolis-St. Paul being conditioned upon the enlargement of the Minneapolis stadium and the sale of 25,000 season tickets for the 1961 season when play was to commence. The Dallas franchise, however, permitted it to operate in 1960, for Murchison was very anxious that his National League team commence play in Dallas the same year. Hunt's American League team commenced play there.

On the next day, the American League had its annual meeting, during which it granted a franchise to Oakland, which took the place of Minneapolis-St. Paul. The American League owners preferred Oakland to other applicants, because they wanted a second team on the West Coast and because they regarded the Oakland area as promising.

It thus came to pass that in the 1960 season, teams of the two leagues were in direct competition in New York, Dallas, Los Angeles, and in the San Francisco-Oakland area.

Each league had teams in other cities in which there was no direct competition between the leagues. The two leagues were competing on a national basis for television coverage, outstanding players and coaches, and the games of each league competed for spectators with the televised broadcast of a game of the other.

The first and most important question on appeal, therefore, is a review of the District Court's determination of the relevant market. The District Court recognized that the two leagues and their member teams competed with each other in several ways, and that the relevant market with respect to one aspect of their competition would not necessarily be the relevant market with respect to another. Since each league recruited players and coaches throughout the nation, he concluded that the relevant market with respect to their competition in recruiting was nationwide. He necessarily found that their competition for nationwide television coverage, with a blackout only of the area in which the televised game was played, was nationwide. As for the competition for spectators, he found the relevant market to be those thirty-one metropolitan areas in the United States having a population of more than 700,000 people according to the 1960 census. This determination was based upon testimony that a metropolitan area of that size might be expected to support a major league professional football team. Indeed, Hunt, of the American League, had testified that a metropolitan area of 500,000 might support such a team. The District Court's determination was influenced by American's contention that the bare existence of the National League and its member teams foreclosed certain markets to it and limited its capacity to operate successfully. It is reinforced by the evidence of many applications from other cities which were actively pressed upon American, some of which, at least, were thought worthy of real consideration.

In addition to those cities in which American actually placed franchises, Hunt testified that there was substantial interest in a franchise in Vancouver, Seattle, Kansas City, Louisville, Cincinnati, Philadelphia, Jacksonville, Miami, Atlanta, St. Louis and Milwaukee. The eighth franchise was placed in Oakland only after consideration of the "strong case" made by Atlanta. In short, it abundantly appears that cities throughout the United States and one Canadian city were actively competing for league franchises, there being many more applicants than available franchises.

In this Court, the plaintiffs contend that the relevant market is composed of those seventeen cities in which National now either has operating franchises, or which it seriously considered in connection with its expansion plans in 1959. They would thus include in the relevant market, New York, Chicago, Philadelphia, Cleveland, Pittsburgh, Washington, Los Angeles, San Francisco, Baltimore, Detroit and Green Bay, in which National teams were operating in 1959, plus Dallas and Minneapolis-St. Paul, in which franchises were authorized in 1960, plus Houston, Buffalo and Miami, which were considered by National for expansion, and St. Louis, to which the Chicago Cardinals were transferred in 1961 after American's first operating season. They include in the relevant market all of the closed cities in which there is a National League team, but no American League team, but exclude from the relevant market all of those closed cities in which there is an American League team but no National League team, and all of those other cities in which there is now no major league professional football team, but which would be hospitable to a franchise and which have a potential for adequate support of a professional football team. They advance the unquestioned principle that the relevant market should be geographically limited to the area in which the defendants operate, or the area in which there is effective competition between the parties.

In very different contexts, the relevant market has been found to be a single city, a group of cities, a state, or several states. In considering an attempt to monopolize, it, of course, is appropriate to limit the relevant geographic market to the area which the defendant sought to appropriate to itself, and, if monopoly power has been acquired in a separably identifiable and normally competitive market, it is irrelevant that the defendant did not possess the same monopoly power in an unrelated market elsewhere.

Plaintiff's contention here, however, is a simple fractionalization of a truly national market. Each league has teams franchised to cities on the Atlantic, on the Pacific and in the midlands. Each team in each league travels back and forth across the country to play before many different audiences in many different cities. Most of the official season games are played in a city in which there is a franchised team, but that is not invariable,[11] and most of the preseason exhibition games are played in cities in which there is no franchised team. In locating franchises, neither league has restricted itself to any geographic section of the country or limited itself to any particular group of cities. In American's brief history, it has moved one team from Los Angeles to San Diego, and the many changes which have occurred in National's franchises belie any notion of geographic limitation.

Though we may concentrate our attention upon competition between the leagues for franchise locations and lay aside for the moment clearly national aspects of their competition for players, coaches and television coverage, location of the franchise is only a selection of a desirable site in a much broader, geographically unlimited market. It is not unlike the choice a chain store company makes when it selects a particular corner lot as the location of a new store. It preempts that lot when it acquires it for that purpose, but, as long as there are other desirable locations for similar stores in a much broader area, it cannot be said to have monopolized the area, or, in a legal sense, the lot or its immediate vicinity.

The National League was first upon the scene. In 1959, it had franchises in eleven cities, the two Chicago teams being in direct competition with each other. It now has franchises in fourteen cities, some of which the District Court found capable of supporting more than one professional football team. Obviously, the American League was of that opinion, for it placed teams in New York, Los Angeles, and the San Francisco-Oakland area, where National, at the time, had well established teams. Most of the other cities in which each league operates, however, are incapable of supporting more than one professional football team. In such a city, a professional football team, once located there, enjoys a natural monopoly, whether it be affiliated with the National or American League, but the fact that National had teams located in such cities before American's advent does not mean that National had the power to prevent or impede the formation of a new league, or that National's closed cities should be included in the relevant market if American's closed cities are to be excluded. The fact is that the two leagues are in direct competition for regular season spectators only in New York, Dallas, and the San Francisco-Oakland area, and, during the 1960 season, in Los Angeles. If the relevant market is not to be limited to those cities, it must be, geographically, at least as broad as the United States, including Hawaii and portions of Canada.[12]

Though there may be in the nation no more than some thirty desirable sites for the location of professional football teams, those sites, scattered throughout the United

---

11. Green Bay, for instance, regularly plays a number of its games in Milwaukee, approximately 120 miles from Green Bay.

12. There was interest in a franchise for Honolulu. Vancouver's interest in obtaining an American franchise has been previously mentioned.

States, do not constitute the relevant market. The relevant market is nationwide, though the fact that there are a limited number of desirable sites for team locations bears upon the question of National's power to monopolize the national market.

The District Court's finding that National did not have the power to monopolize the relevant market appears plainly correct. In 1959, it occupied eleven of the thirty-one apparently desirable sites for team locations, but its occupancy of some of them as New York and San Francisco-Oakland was not exclusive, for those metropolitan areas were capable of supporting more than one team. Twenty of the thirty-one potentially desirable sites were entirely open to American. Indeed, the fact that the American League was successfully launched, could stage a full schedule of games in 1960, has competed very successfully for outstanding players, and has obtained advantageous contracts for national television coverage strongly supports the District Court's finding that National did not have the power to prevent, or impede, the formation of the new league. Indeed, at the close of the 1960 season, representatives of the American League declared that the League's success was unprecedented.

American advances a theory, however, that, since the National League won Minneapolis-St. Paul in competition with American, National could have taken several other cities away from American had it undertaken to do so. This is only a theory, however, unsupported by evidence. It ignores the fact that American won Houston over National's competition, and that each league has won one and lost one in their direct competition for franchise locations. It ignores the fact that National was committed to expansion from twelve to sixteen teams in two separate steps, two teams at a time, so that it had but two franchises to place at the time American was being organized. American questions the finding that sixteen teams is a maximum that one league can efficiently accommodate, but the finding is based upon evidence and was not clearly erroneous. In short, there is no basis for a contention that the evidence required a finding that National, had it wished, could have placed a team in every location sought by American, or in a sufficient number of them to have destroyed the league.

American complains that National, the first upon the scene, had occupied the more desirable of the thirty-one potential sites for team locations. Its occupancy of New York and San Francisco-Oakland was not exclusive, however, and the fact that its teams in other locations, such as Baltimore and Washington, enjoyed a natural monopoly does not occasion a violation of the antitrust laws unless the natural monopoly power of those teams was misused to gain a competitive advantage for teams located in other cities, or for the league as a whole. It frequently happens that a first competitor in the field will acquire sites which a latecomer may think more desirable than the remaining available sites, but the firstcomer is not required to surrender any, or all, of its desirable sites to the latecomer simply to enable the latecomer to compete more effectively with it. There is no basis in antitrust laws for a contention that American, whose Boston, Buffalo, Houston, Denver and San Diego teams enjoy natural monopolies, has a right to complain that National does not surrender to it other natural monopoly locations so that they too may be enjoyed by American rather than by National. When one has acquired a natural monopoly by means which are neither exclusionary, unfair, nor predatory, he is not disempowered to defend his position fairly.

American also charges the defendants with an attempt to monopolize. They say that National offered franchises to be located in Dallas and Houston, and later to Minneapolis-St. Paul in substitution for Houston, for the sole purpose of preventing organization of the American League. It relies upon certain statements made by Marshall, of the National League Washington Redskins, and it discounts all of National's earlier discussion of its expansion plans as froth designed to influence congressional action upon a pending bill granting certain exemptions from the antitrust laws to professional football. * * *

[T]he District Court found that there was substantial business and economic reasons for advocacy by National League owners of the planned expansion.[18] The statement attributed to Marshall, of the Washington Redskins, that he had heard of no reason for expansion except to prevent formation of the American League, the District Judge found to be untrue, for Marshall had been present when business and economic reasons for the expansion had been discussed. Marshall, himself, consistently opposed expansion, though at the 1960 meeting, after some personal differences with Murchison and some of Murchison's associates had been adjusted, he acquiesced in the granting of franchises to Dallas and Minneapolis-St. Paul. Marshall may have made the statement attributed to him, but, in light of his opposition to expansion and the evidence of business considerations which induced other National League owners to advocate expansion, the District Court was not required to find that Marshall's statement was true. * * *

We conclude, therefore, that the District Court properly held that the plaintiffs have shown no monopolization by the National League, or its owners, of the relevant market, and no attempt or conspiracy by them, or any of them, to monopolize it or any part of it. No violation of the Sherman Act having been established, the judgment of the District Court is affirmed.

Affirmed.

Notes and Questions

1. Monopoly power is generally defined as the power to control price or to exclude competition. Did the court find that the NFL lacked the power to exclude the AFL? What was the basis for the court's conclusion?

2. Two factual conclusions upon which the district court's decision was based were that there were thirty-one suitable locations where a professional football franchise could locate and "sixteen teams is a maximum that one league can efficiently accommodate." Are those factual conclusions still supportable today, given the facts that: (1) there are now thirty-two NFL teams; (2) there are only four or perhaps six NFL teams sharing a metropolitan area; and (3) there are no NFL teams presently in Birmingham, Hartford, Hawaii, the entire Los Angeles/Anaheim area (which may be able to support two teams), Memphis, Nassau County, New York, Orlando, Portland, Raleigh-Durham, Sacramento, San Antonio, the Tidewater area of Virginia, or in any city in Canada or anywhere else outside the United States? *See, e.g., Mid-South Grizzlies v. National Football League*, 720 F.2d 772, 786 n.8 (3rd Cir. 1983) (discussing study prepared for NFL Expansion Committee of potential locations for new NFL franchises).

3. In more recent years, NFL owners have generally been opposed to expansion because one of its primary consequences is that the revenues from the league's lucrative television contracts would have to be divided among more team owners. Nevertheless, various pressures, combined with the attraction of large expansion fees, have seen the NFL grow to thirty-two teams. Would a decision by NFL owners to expand in order to avoid giving a new league a foothold in cities with no NFL team constitute illegal mo-

---

18. It is elementary that in order to find the offense of conspiracy or attempt to monopolize, there must be a specific, subjective intent to gain an illegal degree of market control. *Times-Picayune Publishing Co. v. United States*, 345 U.S. 594, 626 [(1953)].

nopolization? What about the World League of American Football, which became NFL Europe and was created to foreclose competition in the spring? Does the NFL have market power? Consider the analysis of the Supreme Court in *Aspen Skiing Co. v. Aspen Highlands Skiing Corp.*, 472 U.S. 585, 608–610 (1985) (sacrificing short-run economic benefits and consumer goodwill in exchange for a perceived long-run impact on smaller rival constituted unlawful monopolization). What antitrust ramification could result from the five year "alliance" between the NFL and the Canadian Football League? See Jim Taylor, *Goodwill Has Little to do with CFL Deal*, THE FINANCIAL POST, APR. 10, 1997, at 59. What about NFL owners owning Arena Football League teams and an NFL-Arena Football League agreement? What about the NBA's long-standing agreement (since terminated) with the Continental Basketball League?

4. When identifying the relevant geographic market, it is very important to ascertain for what purpose the market is being defined. Who are the buyers and sellers in the market, what is the product or service being sold, and what are the reasonable substitutes for that product or service? In the *American Football League* case, the court concluded that the issue involved competition between the AFL and the NFL, on a league-wide basis, for owners and cities. The district court concluded that this competition took place on a national basis. How would you characterize competition between AFL and NFL teams for local television and radio contracts? How would you characterize competition between AFL and NFL teams located in the same cities for local sponsors, sales of luxury boxes and club seats, all-purpose fans (purchasers of season tickets and individual game tickets—home game attendance), and media coverage? What is the relevant market when the competition allegedly restrained is between two teams in the same geographic area? *See Los Angeles Memorial Coliseum Comm'n v. National Football League*, 726 F.2d 1381 (9th Cir. 1984), in Chapter 12. The next case concerns allegations that the local team used its contractual control over the best stadium in town to block entry by a competing team. What should be the relevant market for purposes of analyzing the competition at issue in that controversy?

Hecht v. Pro-Football, Inc.

570 F.2d 982 (D.C. Cir. 1977)

WILKEY, Circuit Judge. This is a private antitrust action. Plaintiffs Hecht, Kagan, and Miller (hereafter collectively "Hecht") are a group of promoters who in 1965 sought unsuccessfully to obtain an American Football League (AFL) franchise for Washington, D.C. Defendants are Pro-Football, Inc., operator of the Washington Redskins (the Redskins), and the District of Columbia Armory Board, an unincorporated instrumentality of the District of Columbia which operates and maintains Robert F. Kennedy (RFK) Stadium under contract with the Interior Department.[1] The Armory Board leases RFK Stadium to the Redskins. Hecht attacks a restrictive covenant in that lease.[2]

Hecht contends that RFK Stadium is the only stadium in the Washington metropolitan area suitable for the exhibition of professional football games; that the restrictive covenant prevented him from obtaining the use of the stadium; and that his inability to obtain the use of the stadium prevented him from submitting an acceptable franchise

---

1. The land on which the stadium is located is owned by the United States.
2. The lease runs from 1961 to 1990. Paragraph II(e) thereof provides that "at no time during the term of this Lease Agreement shall the Stadium be let or rented to any professional football team other than the Washington Redskins." * * *

application to the AFL owners, and thus from competing with the Redskins in the Washington professional football market. Hecht's complaint alleges that the restrictive covenant constitutes a contract in restraint of trade, in violation of Sherman Act §§1 and 3 [Section 3 of the Sherman Act is the same as Sherman Act §1, but it expressly applies to United States territories and the District of Columbia]; and that the Redskins, in obtaining the covenant and refusing to waive it, have monopolized professional football in Washington, D.C., in violation of Sherman Act §2. The case was tried to a jury,[5] which rendered a verdict for defendants. Hecht appeals numerous instructions and evidentiary rulings. We reverse and remand for a new trial.

I. FACTS

Formed in 1959–60 with eight franchised teams, the AFL by 1965 was seriously considering expansion. It planned to grant two new franchises, one to a city with an NFL franchise and one to a city with no professional football team. The granting of any new franchise required the affirmative votes of six clubs. In June 1965 Hecht and his associates organized an original group of investors. This group had no football experience and limited financial strength, but possessed a general familiarity with business affairs. * * *

In July 1965 Hecht submitted a written offer to purchase an AFL franchise, couching the application in a form suggested by [AFL] Commissioner Foss. * * * Hecht presented evidence which tended to show that his promotional activities were serious and that at least some members of the AFL expansion committee favored his application; he presented one piece of evidence which suggested that if he got the stadium he would get the franchise. The Redskins presented evidence which tended to show that the AFL owners never seriously considered expansion to Washington and that Hecht's application never had a chance of being approved.

On 7 September 1965 Hecht submitted a written proposal to the Armory Board for shared use of RFK Stadium. The Board told Hecht that it could not negotiate a lease with him owing to the restrictive covenant in the Redskins' lease. The Board also said, however, that it would gladly consider any arrangement acceptable to the Redskins under which Hecht could use the stadium (*i.e.*, a waiver of the restrictive covenant) and by which the Board's financial condition would be improved. There was conflicting evidence about the practicality of any plan for sharing the stadium between two professional football teams.

On 4 October 1965 Hecht received a memorandum from the Interior Department expressing its opinion that the restrictive covenant in the Redskins' lease violated the antitrust laws. Hecht distributed copies of this memorandum to the AFL owners and to the Armory Board. Months of intermittent and frustrating meetings followed. The Redskins presented evidence which tended to show that they had reason to doubt the sufficiency of Hecht's financial resources and the integrity with which he pursued the negotiations. During this period, Hecht was whipsawed between the positions of the Redskins and the AFL. The Redskins would not seriously negotiate for Hecht's use of the stadium unless Hecht had an AFL franchise; the AFL would not seriously consider Hecht's application for a franchise unless he had the use of RFK Stadium. In his

---

5. The trial was held on remand from this Court. *Hecht v. Pro-Football, Inc. (Hecht I)*, 444 F.2d 931, 947 (1971), *cert. denied*, 404 U.S. 1047 (1972). In *Hecht I*, the district court granted summary judgment for the defendants on the ground that the Board's leasing of RFK Stadium was governmental action immune from the antitrust laws. We reversed and remanded for trial on the merits, concluding that Congress had evinced no intention to confer such immunity.

quandary, Hecht made representations to both sides which were optimistic at best. In August 1966 the Redskins broke off negotiations. In October 1966 Hecht filed his original complaint in this action.

II. OVERALL ANALYSIS

At the outset, the Redskins contend that we need not reach Hecht's various assignments of error because the trial conclusively demonstrated that Hecht lacks standing to sue. * * * Section 4 of the Clayton Act confers the right to sue for treble damages on "any person who shall be injured in his business or property by reason of anything forbidden in the antitrust laws. * * *" This section establishes a two-fold standing requirement: the plaintiff must show both an injury-in-fact to his "business or property" and a causal connection between that injury and the defendant's allegedly illegal acts. The Redskins contend that Hecht has shown neither.

* * * [T]he courts have generally not insisted that a plaintiff actually be engaged in a going business in order to have antitrust standing; it is sufficient if he has manifested an intention to enter the business and has demonstrated his preparedness to do so. Our review of the record indicates that the evidence presented a question of fact for the jury on these issues. We cannot hold that Hecht lacked "business or property" as a matter of law.

Second, the Redskins argue that Hecht's inability to submit an acceptable franchise application was due entirely to his own bad faith in negotiating with them for use of RFK Stadium, and that Hecht consequently failed to show a causal connection between his injury and the restrictive covenant in the Redskins' lease. We find this argument sanctimonious and somewhat sophistical. The negotiations, plainly, were frustrating for all concerned. The question, in any event, was peculiarly one for the jury. We cannot hold, in defiance of plain evidence and common sense, that the restrictive covenant was causally unrelated to the injury of which Hecht complains; the degree of causality may be another matter. * * *

III. INSTRUCTIONS
A. Relevant Geographic Market.

In suits brought under the Sherman Act the threatened foreclosure of competition must be assessed "in relation to the market affected." The relevant product market in this case is indisputably the business of professional football. The parties disagree, however, as to the relevant geographic market. Hecht contends that it is the metropolitan area of Washington, D.C.; the Redskins contend that it is the entire United States. The trial judge effectively instructed the jury that the relevant geographic market was the nation as a whole.[13] We hold that his instruction was clearly erroneous as a matter of law.

The relevant geographic market is "the area of effective competition," the area "in which the seller operates, and to which the purchaser can practically turn for supplies." It is well settled that the relevant market "need not be nationwide," and that "where the relevant competitive market covers only a small area the Sherman Act may be invoked

---

13. the trial judge purported to leave the question of relevant geographical area to the jury, * * *, he defined that area as the area of competition for football franchises. * * * Since the trial established beyond peradventure that numerous cities were competing for franchises, the judge's instruction virtually directed the jury to find a national market. Not surprisingly, the jury seems to have been confused by the "relevant market" instructions. * * *

to prevent unreasonable restraints within that area." Indeed, courts have regularly identified relevant geographic markets as single cities or towns, and even portions thereof.

In this case Hecht sought to enter the market for professional football in Washington, D.C. He argues that the Redskins frustrated his entry by denying him use of RFK stadium, access to which was a condition precedent to his submitting a successful franchise application. Given this posture of the case, it seems evident that the relevant geographical market is the D.C. metropolitan area: it is here that "the seller operates." It is here alone that the Redskins' customers (primarily, their ticket purchasers) can "practicably turn" for the supply of professional football. Hecht sought to compete for these customers by obtaining a franchise of his own, and it can scarcely be doubted that "the area of effective competition" between him and the Redskins would be the nation's capital. * * *

The trial court, however, defined the relevant geographical market as "the area of effective competition for the acquisition, location and operation of a professional football franchise in the years 1965 and 1966." It is true, of course, that Hecht had to "compete" with other cities before he could assure himself of a franchise for Washington; yet this is hardly the competition that is at issue here. Hecht is not complaining that the Redskins' restrictive covenant prevented him from entering "the national market for football franchises;" obviously, Hecht could have entered that market, notwithstanding the Redskins' lease, from any other city. Hecht is complaining, rather, that the restrictive covenant on RFK Stadium in Washington, D.C., prevented him from entering the market for professional football in Washington; this is "the area which the alleged restraints affect."[20] The "national competition" was but a preliminary, if necessary, step to a distinctly local end. We hold, therefore, that the trial judge erred in failing to instruct the jury that the relevant geographic market is the area of metropolitan Washington, D.C., in which Hecht and the Redskins would have effectively competed for customers.[21]

B. Monopolistic Intent and "Natural Monopoly."

The offense of "monopolization" under Sherman Act §2 implicates both the possession of monopoly power—"monopoly in the concrete"—and an element of willfulness or intent. To demonstrate intent to monopolize, however, a plaintiff need not always prove that the defendant acquired or maintained his monopoly power by means of exclusionary, unfair, or predatory acts. At least since *Alcoa*, it has been clear that the requisite intent can be inferred if a defendant maintains his power by conscious and willful business policies, however legal, that inevitably result in the exclusion or limitation of actual or potential competition. In accordance with *Alcoa*, Hecht requested an instruction that the jury could find monopolistic intent if it found that the Redskins had consciously engaged in acts or contracts, whether lawful or unlawful, that "maintained and

---

20. *United States v. Columbia Steel Co.*, 334 U.S. 495, 520 (1948). Defendants' citation of *American Football League v. National Football League*, 323 F.2d 124 (4th Cir. 1963), is inapposite. That case concerned the "competition between the leagues for franchise locations;" since each league was considering expansion to a host of desirable sites, the court properly held that the market, geographically, was "at least as broad as the United States, including Hawaii and portions of Canada." * * * This case, by contrast, concerns the potential competition between two teams for customers in one location. Unlike the NFL, the Redskins as "sellers" do not operate nationally; unlike the AFL, Hecht is not trying to expand nationally. He sought merely to compete with the Redskins on their home turf.

21. These customers would include potential season ticket holders and occasional ticket buyers, and, to a lesser extent, purchasers of local radio and pre-season television broadcasting rights. * * *

protected" their monopoly over professional football in Washington. The trial judge refused to give this instruction. Instead, he ruled that the *Alcoa* theory of intent (viz., an inference of monopolistic intent without a showing of specific unfair practices) was not available to Hecht unless he proved that the Washington metropolitan area could support two professional football teams. We hold that this instruction was error.

In order to explain the trial judge's chain of reasoning, it is necessary to elaborate somewhat the teaching of *Alcoa*. In that opinion, Judge Hand recognized, as noted above, that monopolistic intent may be inferred from conscious business practices that inevitably produce or maintain monopoly power. Judge Hand also recognized, of course, that there are situations in which an inference of monopolistic intent absent a showing of specific unfair practices would be improper. One such situation is where defendant has a "natural monopoly"—where, in Judge Hand's words, "[a] market [is] so limited that it is impossible to produce at all and meet the cost of production except by a plant large enough to supply the whole demand." In the wake of *Alcoa*, accordingly, a substantial body of case law has developed, holding that the "characteristics of a natural monopoly make it inappropriate to apply the usual rule that success in driving competitors from the market is evidence of illegal monopolization." These cases hold, in short, that a natural monopolist does not violate §2 unless he "acquired or maintained [his] power through the use of means which are 'exclusionary, unfair or predatory.'" In this case, therefore, the trial judge properly told the jury that if it found the Redskins to have a natural monopoly, "such a monopoly does not violate the antitrust laws unless it was acquired or maintained by exclusionary, unfair, or predatory means."

The trial judge further instructed the jury, however, that Hecht bore the burden of proving that the Redskins did not have a natural monopoly:

> In this connection, you are instructed that an established operating professional football team may be said to have a natural monopoly in a particular city, if that city cannot support two professional teams under existing circumstances. Accordingly, the plaintiffs must prove by a preponderance of the evidence that [the D.C. metropolitan area,] in 1965 and 1966, could have reasonably supported both the defendant Redskins and an [AFL] team.

This part of the instruction, we think, was incorrect. It is the clear thrust of *Alcoa* that, once a plaintiff has proven the defendant's maintenance of its monopoly power through conscious business practices, a rebuttable presumption is established that defendant has the requisite intent to monopolize. The defendant can defeat this presumption by showing that it had monopoly, as some have greatness, "thrust upon it"—that its power derives from "superior skill, foresight and industry" or (as is particularly relevant here) from the advantages of natural monopoly conditions. Both the Supreme Court, and the lower courts, have echoed this position. We are not called upon in this case to elaborate the various circumstances under which the burden of proof in §2 cases might shift to defendant; we hold merely that when, as here, a defendant seeks to avoid a charge of monopolization by asserting that it has a natural monopoly owing to the market's inability to support two competitors, the defendant, and not the plaintiff, bears the burden of proof on that score.

This holding finds firm grounding in antitrust policy. To hold otherwise could effectively mean that a defendant is entitled to remain free of competition unless the plaintiff can prove, not only that he would be a viable competitor, but also that he and defendant both would survive. This result would be ironic indeed: we cannot say that it is in the public interest to have the incumbent as its sole theatre, or its sole newspaper, or its sole football team, merely because the incumbent got there first. Assuming that there is no identity of performance, the public has an obvious interest in competition, "even though that competition be an elimination bout." "It has been the law for centuries," Justice Holmes once wrote, "that a man may set up a business in a small country town, too small to support more than one, although thereby he expects and intends to ruin some one already there, and succeeds in his attempt." The newcomer and the incumbent may both succeed, or either or both may fail; this is what competition is all about.

C. Essential Facility.

Hecht contends that the District Court erred in failing to give his requested instruction concerning the "essential facility" doctrine. We agree. The essential facility doctrine, also called the "bottleneck principle," states that "where facilities cannot practicably be duplicated by would-be competitors, those in possession of them must allow them to be shared on fair terms. It is illegal restraint of trade to foreclose the scarce facility." This principle of antitrust law derives from the Supreme Court's 1912 decision in *United States v. Terminal R.R. Ass'n*,[37] and was recently reaffirmed in *Otter Tail Power Co. v. United States*;[38] the principle has regularly been invoked by the lower courts. To be "essential" a facility need not be indispensable; it is sufficient if duplication of the facility would be economically infeasible and if denial of its use inflicts a severe handicap on potential market entrants. Necessarily, this principle must be carefully delimited: the antitrust laws do not require that an essential facility be shared if such sharing would be impractical or would inhibit the defendant's ability to serve its customers adequately.

In this case Hecht presented evidence that RFK stadium is the only stadium in the D.C. metropolitan area that is suitable for the exhibition of professional football games. He also presented evidence that proper agreements regarding locker facilities, practice sessions, choice of playing dates, and so forth would have made sharing of the stadium practical and convenient. Accordingly, Hecht requested an instruction that if the jury found (1) that use of RFK stadium was essential to the operation of a professional football team in Washington; (2) that such stadium facilities could not practicably be duplicated by potential competitors; (3) that another team could use RFK stadium in the Redskins' absence without interfering with the Redskins' use; and (4) that the restrictive covenant in the lease prevented equitable sharing of the stadium by potential competi-

---

37. 224 U.S. 383 (1912). In *Terminal R.R.*, a group of railroads had won control of all railroad switching facilities in St. Louis; topographical factors prevented potential competitors from gaining access to the city via other routes. The Court held:

> [W]hen, as here, the inherent conditions are such as to prohibit any other reasonable means of entering the city, the combination of every such facility under the exclusive ownership and control of less than all of the companies under compulsion to use them violates both the first and second sections of the [Sherman Act].

Id. at 409. The Court ordered the railroads to amend their agreement to provide "for admission of any existing or future railroad to joint ownership and control of the combined terminal properties" on equal terms. *Id.* at 411.

38. 410 U.S. 366, 377–78 (1973), *affirming in relevant part* 331 F. Supp. 54, 59–61 (D. Minn. 1971). In *Otter Tail*, municipalities sought to compete with defendant power company by building their own electric facilities. The municipalities could not afford to construct their own subtransmission lines, however, and defendant refused to "wheel" power for them over its own lines. The court found that Otter Tail's subtransmission lines were a scarce facility and that its refusal to share them violated §2. 331 F. Supp. at 61.

tors, then the jury must find the restrictive covenant to constitute a contract in unreasonable restraint of trade, in violation of Sherman Act §§1 and 3.[44] His instruction was substantially correct and failure to give it was prejudicial error.[45]. * * *

E. Unreasonable Restraint of Trade.

Hecht contends, however, that the instruction was incomplete: although the court told the jury what *factors* to consider, it failed to tell them what those factors *must prove*—it failed, in other words, to explain what an unreasonable restraint *was*. Hecht argues that the jury should have been instructed that a restraint is unreasonable if it "has a substantially adverse effect upon competition* * *, that is, [if] it suppresses or prevents competition." This is the standard definition of an "unreasonable" restraint, sanctioned both by *Chicago Board of Trade*[64] and later cases, and the trial judge should have included it in his instruction.

Elaborating the *Chicago Board of Trade* factors, the judge told the jury that in considering whether the restrictive covenant was reasonable they should "consider whether the provision [was] fairly related to business considerations that the Redskins or the Armory Board had to deal with at the time they entered into the lease." The court thus implied that if there existed good business reasons for the restrictive covenant the jury should not find the restraint unreasonable. As Hecht points out, however, it is settled that the "antitrust outcome does not turn merely on the presence of sound business reason or motive" and that the "promotion of self-interest alone does not invoke the rule of reason to immunize otherwise illegal conduct." The latter part of the judge's instruction was thus misleading and should have been deleted. * * *

IV. EVIDENTIARY RULINGS

* * *

C. Expert Testimony.

The trial judge admitted into evidence testimony of plaintiffs' experts that it was customary and usual business practice for tenants and landlords in the D.C. area to bargain for restrictive covenants in leases. Hecht argues that this testimony was irrelevant and should have been excluded. We agree. The witnesses concededly possessed no expertise about football stadiums, and testified only about garden-variety com-

---

44. It seems clear that the essential facility doctrine would also support an allegation that the Redskins' refusal to waive the restrictive covenant constituted illegal monopolization under §2. * * * Cf. *Otter Tail*, supra note 38 and *Terminal R.R.*, supra note 37. Hecht, however, did not request an instruction to this effect.

45. Defendants offer two objections to this conclusion. First, they argue that the requested instruction presupposes the area of competition to be restricted to Washington, D.C. In view of our disposition of the relevant market issue,* * *, this argument need not detain us further. Second, defendants argue that, notwithstanding the essential facility doctrine, the jury could still have found the restrictive covenant reasonable. * * * This argument robs the essential facility doctrine of any significance, and we reject it. The garden-variety restrictive covenant does not violate §1 unless it unreasonably restrains trade; when the restrictive covenant covers an essential facility, however, all possible competition is by definition excluded and the restraint is thus unreasonable *per se* —provided, of course, that the facility can be shared practically. The requested instruction adequately accommodated this proviso.

64. 246 U.S. 231, 238 (1918) ("The true test of legality is whether the restraint imposed is such as merely regulates and perhaps thereby promotes competition or whether it is such as may suppress or even destroy competition."

mercial leases. There is, however, no analogy between a shopping center lease which, *e.g.*, stipulates that only one drug store can rent space in the center, and the restrictive covenant in the Redskins' lease: another drug store can be built down the road, whereas RFK Stadium is an essential facility that cannot be duplicated. It is settled, moreover, that evidence of customs and practices in an industry is irrelevant in determining whether the defendant has violated the antitrust laws. Although we would not reverse on this point alone, we conclude that the trial judge erred in admitting the experts' testimony.

CONCLUSION

Because the trial judge erred in giving, or failing to give, at least four important instructions to the jury, and in admitting, or failing to admit, at least two important pieces of evidence, the judgment must be reversed and the case remanded for another trial. On remand, we strongly suggest that the trial judge use his discretion to submit the case to the jury on special interrogatories, rather than elicit a mere general verdict. Antitrust cases present difficult problems for jurors; written interrogatories would help them to focus on the salient issues, and would help to pinpoint what went wrong should this case, *horribile dictu*, come to this Court a third time.

So ordered.

Notes and Questions

1. The court's discussion of the plaintiffs' standing raises an interesting issue—if a monopolist is able to prevent a potential competitor from ever entering the market, he can defend on the basis that: (1) the plaintiff never launched a business and therefore lacks standing; (2) the plaintiff has made an insufficient showing that he ever would have survived, and his claim to any damage is too speculative—thus, because there is no proof of damage, his case must be dismissed (*see, e.g.*, the discussion following the *Kapp* case in Chapter 10); and (3) even if the plaintiff has standing and can prove the fact of damage, he cannot possibly quantify how successful he would have been with the specificity necessary to sustain a damage award. Compare *Peller v. International Boxing Club*, 227 F.2d 593 (7th Cir. 1955) (plaintiff who sought to promote boxing matches had never progressed beyond preliminary negotiations for promotion of match and had not suffered antitrust injury; summary judgment against plaintiff affirmed) with *Washington Professional Basketball Corp. v. National Basketball Association*, 147 F. Supp. 154, 155 (S.D.N.Y. 1956) (plaintiff's allegations that defendants interfered with his efforts to acquire "the remnants of the defunct Baltimore Bullets" were sufficient to state an antitrust claim). The plaintiff must prove that he would have been part of a new league destined to have prospered if it were not for the defendants' obstruction. This showing will be difficult if the new league does not survive and prosper because start-up leagues generally lose money and fail. Does this analysis suggest that the best strategy for a dominant league or team might be to take decisive steps to insure that a fledgling competitor never gets started?

2. Both the *AFL v. NFL* and *Hecht* decisions discuss the concept of "natural monopoly" markets, meaning markets that, as a practical matter, might not be able to support two teams. If there is going to be only one team in a market that survives, why is the competition over who will be the monopolist a concern of the antitrust laws? If the identity of the eventual monopolist will not affect consumers, can the plaintiff establish

an adverse affect on competition as opposed to an adverse affect on one competitor? *See Fishman v. Wirtz*, 807 F.2d 520, 532–538 (7th Cir. 1987) and 807 F.2d at 563–585 (Easterbrook, J., dissenting in part). The introduction to this chapter discussed many sports fans' general opposition to the existence of competing leagues at the highest level of the sport. Would such opposition, when combined with proof that many cities could only support a single team, establish a viable defense? Could a sole surviving league defend its anticompetitive conduct on the ground that it is a natural monopolist? *See, e.g., Philadelphia World Hockey Club, Inc. v. Philadelphia Hockey Club*, Inc., 351 F. Supp. 462, 511–513 (E.D. PA. 1972).

3. The "essential facility" doctrine, applied in *Hecht*, involved a particular kind of refusal to deal where the following factors are present: (1) one or more competitors control access to a "facility" that cannot practically or reasonably be duplicated; (2) access to the facility is essential; and (3) it is feasible to provide access to the facility to another competitor, but access is refused. *See, e.g., MCI Communications Corp v. American Telephone & Telegraph Co.*, 708 F.2d 1081, 1132 (7th Cir.), *cert. denied*, 464 U.S. 891 (1983). Is the doctrine limited to tangible items? Does the term "facility" suggest that the doctrine should be limited to tangible items? If only one major professional league can survive, as a practical matter, does that mean membership in the league could be an essential "facility"? *See, e.g., North American Soccer League v. National Football League*, 465 F. Supp. 665, 676 n.20 (S.D.N.Y. 1979) (all of the essential facility cases "deal with tangible physical objects as essential facilities"), *rev'd on other grounds*, 670 F.2d 1249 (2d Cir. 1981); *Mid-South Grizzlies v. National Football League*, 550 F. Supp. 558, 570 n.32 (E.D. Pa. 1982) ("The cases applying the doctrine involved the denial of access to physical structures per discreet services. * * * In contrast, plaintiffs seek to participate in an entire business organization. Thus, the principles enunciated in these cases seem inapposite."), *aff'd on other grounds*, 720 F.2d 772, 787 (3d Cir. 1983), *cert. denied*, 467 U.S. 1215 (1984). More recent cases have questioned or rejected the idea that the doctrine is limited to tangible items. *See, e.g., Bellsouth Advertising & Publishing Corp. v. Donnelley Information Publishing*, 719 F. Supp. 1551, 1556 (S.D. Fla. 1988) ("Although the doctrine of essential facilities has been applied predominantly to tangible assets, there is no reason why it could not apply, as in this case, to information wrongfully withheld. The effect in both situations is the same: a party is prevented from sharing in something essential to compete."), *aff'd*, 933 F.2d 952 (11th Cir. 1991). *See also American Health Systems v. Visiting Nurse Ass'n*, 1994-1 Trade Cas. (CCH) ¶70,633 (E.D. Pa. 1994) (holding that a hospital's provision of patient referrals could be an essential facility); *Advanced Health Care Sys. v. Radford Community Hosp.*, 910 F.2d 139, 150–51 (4th Cir. 1990) (same). For a general discussion of issues related to the essential facility doctrine, see James R. Ratner, *Should There Be an Essential Facility Doctrine?* 21 U. CAL. DAVIS L. REV. 327 (1988); Gregory J. Werden, *The Law and Economics of the Essential Facility Doctrine*, 32 ST. LOUIS U. L. J. 433 (1987); Daniel E. Troy, Note, *Unclogging the Bottleneck: A New Essential Facility Doctrine*, 83 COLUM. L. REV. 441 (1983); Note, *Refusals to Deal by Vertically Integrated Monopolists*, 87 HARV. L. REV. 1720 (1974).

4. The *Hecht* case involved allegations that one team in the dominant league blocked one group of investors from establishing an expansion team in the competing league; the court defined the market and conducted its analysis accordingly. How does the analysis change if all the teams in the competing league sue, claiming that the dominant league and all of its members have been involved in anticompetitive conduct? The following case addresses those issues, among others.

III. Monopolization and Rival Leagues

United States Football League v. National Football League
842 F.2d 1335 (2d Cir. 1988)

WINTER, Circuit Judge. This appeal follows a highly publicized trial and jury verdict of $1.00. The plaintiff is a now-defunct professional football league that began play in this decade; the defendant is a football league founded nearly seventy years ago. The older of the two leagues, the National Football League, is a highly successful entertainment product. So many Americans watched NFL games between 1982 and 1986 that its twenty-eight teams shared $ 2.1 billion in rights fees from the three major television networks, and perhaps as much as $ 1 billion in gate receipts. The newer league, the United States Football League, began play in March 1983 with twelve teams and network and cable television contracts with the American Broadcasting Company ("ABC") and the Entertainment and Sports Programming Network ("ESPN"). After three seasons and losses in the neighborhood of $ 200 million, the USFL played its last game in July 1985. Meanwhile, in October, 1984, blaming its older competitor for its difficulties, the USFL instituted this litigation. Plans to play in the fall of 1986 were abandoned after the jury's verdict that is the principal subject of this appeal.

The USFL and certain of its member clubs brought this suit in the Southern District of New York against the NFL, its commissioner, Alvin R. "Pete" Rozelle, and twenty-seven of its twenty-eight member clubs. Seeking damages of $ 1.701 billion and appropriate injunctive relief, the USFL alleged that the NFL violated Sections 1 and 2 of the Sherman Anti-Trust Act, 15 U.S.C. §§1 and 2 (1982), and the common law. Forty-eight days of trial before Judge Leisure produced a trial transcript of nearly 7100 pages and thousands of additional pages in exhibits.

After five days of deliberations, the jury found that the NFL had willfully acquired or maintained monopoly power in a market consisting of major-league professional football in the United States. The jury also found that the NFL's unlawful monopolization of professional football had injured the USFL. The jury awarded the USFL only $ 1.00 in damages, however, an amount that, even when trebled, was no consolation for the USFL.

The jury rejected the remainder of the USFL's claims. It found that the NFL had neither monopolized a relevant television submarket nor attempted to do so; that the NFL did not commit any overt act in furtherance of a conspiracy to monopolize; that the NFL did not engage in a conspiracy in restraint of trade; that the NFL's television contracts were not unreasonable restraints of trade; that the NFL did not control access to the three major television networks; and that the NFL did not interfere either with the USFL's ability to obtain a fall television contract or with its spring television contracts. The USFL's common law claims were also rejected.

Judge Leisure denied the USFL's motions for judgment notwithstanding the verdict on its claims of monopolization of the television submarket, attempted monopolization, unreasonable restraint of trade by means of the network television contracts and essential facilities, and for a new trial on damages on the monopolization of professional football claim, or in the alternative for a new trial. * * * The district court also denied the USFL's request for injunctive relief.

On this appeal, the USFL claims that a "litany of erroneous opinions, rulings and instructions" by Judge Leisure resulted in a "verdict of confusion" that "sent one of the most egregious violators in the history of the federal antitrust laws on its way with a pat on the back." * * * Specifically, the USFL contends that the NFL could not legally enter into a pooled-rights agreement with all three networks; that Judge Leisure's jury instructions "destroyed" the effectiveness of the USFL's proof of its television claims and set improperly high standards of liability; that he improperly allowed the NFL to introduce evidence that the USFL was mismanaged; that he excluded other evidence critical to establishing the USFL's claims; and that his incorrect rulings and instructions on damages prevented the USFL from receiving appropriate relief. We affirm.

SUMMARY

We briefly summarize our principal rulings. The jury's finding of illegal monopolization of a market of major-league professional football was based upon evidence of NFL attempts to co-opt USFL owners, an NFL Supplemental Draft of USFL players, an NFL roster increase, and NFL conduct directed at particular USFL franchises. These activities, however, were hardly of sufficient impact to support a large damages verdict or to justify sweeping injunctive relief. For that reason, the USFL candidly admits that "at the heart of this case" are its claims that the NFL, by contracting with the three major networks and by acting coercively toward them, prevented the USFL from acquiring a network television contract indispensable to its survival. The jury expressly rejected the television claims.

The jury was clearly entitled by the evidence to find that the NFL's fall contracts with the three networks were not an anticompetitive barrier to the USFL's bidding against the NFL to acquire a network contract. Moreover, there was ample evidence that the USFL failed because it did not make the painstaking investment and patient efforts that bring credibility, stability and public recognition to a sports league. In particular, there was evidence that the USFL abandoned its original strategy of patiently building up fan loyalty and public recognition by playing in the spring. The original plan to contain costs by adherence to team salary guidelines was discarded from the start. Faced with rising costs and some new team owners impatient for immediate parity with the NFL, the idea of spring play itself was abandoned even though network and cable contracts were available. Plans for a fall season were therefore announced, thereby making 1985 spring play a "lame-duck" season. These actions were taken in the hope of forcing a merger with the NFL through the threat of competition and this litigation. The merger strategy, however, required that USFL franchises move out of large television markets and into likely NFL expansion cities. Because these moves further eroded fan loyalty and reduced the value of USFL games to television, the USFL thereby ended by its own hand any chance of a network contract.

Notwithstanding the jury's evident conclusions that the USFL's product was not appealing largely for reasons of the USFL's own doing and that the networks chose freely not to purchase it, the USFL asks us to grant sweeping injunctive relief that will reward its impatience and self-destructive conduct with a fall network contract. It thus seeks through court decree the success it failed to achieve among football fans. Absent a showing of some unlawful harm to competition, we cannot prevent a network from showing NFL games, in the hope that the network and fans will turn to the USFL. The Sherman Act does not outlaw an industry structure simply because it prevents competitors from achieving immediate parity. This is particularly so in the case of major-league professional football because Congress authorized a merger of the two leagues existing in 1966 and thus created the industry structure in question.

THE TRIAL

1. The Parties' Contentions

The USFL contended at trial that the NFL maintained a monopoly in the market for major league professional football and in a submarket for the network broadcasting rights to such football by the following allegedly predatory tactics:

a. Signing multiyear contracts with the three major television networks;

b. Pressuring the major networks to abstain from televising USFL games in the spring or fall, and successfully preventing any network telecasts of the USFL in the fall, by threatening not to renew NFL contracts or by assigning unattractive NFL games under existing contracts;

c. Establishing contracts with the networks for artificially high rights fees that, because of the so-called "dilution effect" on demand for advertising during NFL games, precluded network broadcasts of the USFL;

d. Seeking to prevent any of the three major networks from signing a contract for the USFL's initial 1983 spring playing season;

e. Rotating the Super Bowl among the three networks and not submitting the Super Bowl, playoff and even regular-season television rights to competitive bidding;

f. Pursuing a strategy outlined in the so-called "Porter Presentation" to "conquer" and bankrupt the USFL, including: co-opting powerful USFL owners, such as Donald Trump and Alfred Taubman, by offering them NFL franchises; encouraging ABC not to continue USFL broadcasts; pressuring ABC by giving it an unattractive schedule for its Monday Night Football program in 1984; targeting important USFL players for signing with the NFL through means such as the NFL's Supplemental Draft and expanded roster; and attempting to bankrupt the weakest USFL teams by driving up USFL player salaries in order to diminish the USFL's size and credibility;

g. Collaborating with the City of Oakland to destroy the Oakland Invaders of the USFL in order to hurt the credibility and image of the Invaders and the entire USFL;

h. Threatening to move an existing NFL franchise or to create a new NFL franchise solely to injure the USFL franchise in Oakland; and

i. Attempting to preclude the USFL's New Jersey Generals from moving to New York City.

The NFL contended that the relevant television submarket included entertainment broadcasting generally and that it had not monopolized either the market for major league professional football or the television submarket because:

a. Its contracts with the three major networks were not exclusionary;

b. The USFL's failure to secure a fall network contract was the result of the independent judgment of each network that the USFL was an inferior product, and of the USFL's self-destructive strategy of forcing a merger with the NFL;

c. It never pressured a network by threatening non-renewal or by assigning a schedule of unattractive games;

d. It never undertook the strategy outlined in the Porter Presentation;

e. It never sought to injure the USFL's Oakland franchise or to preclude the New Jersey Generals from playing in New York City; and

f. The losses suffered by the USFL were due to its own mismanagement.

2. The History of Major-League Professional Football

* * *

In 1974, the World Football League ("WFL") was founded. The WFL lasted for one-and-one-half seasons before disbanding. Its teams were underfinanced and played in mostly smaller markets. The WFL never obtained a television contract with a major network, although its games were televised by a syndicated network. At least one of the league's teams tried unsuccessfully to enter the NFL through litigation. *See Mid-South Grizzlies v. National Football League*, 720 F.2d 772 (3d Cir. 1983) (rejecting antitrust claim by WFL team denied admission to NFL).

The USFL was founded in May 1982 by David Dixon as a league that would play spring football. The league began play in March 1983 with teams in Birmingham, Boston, Chicago, Denver, Los Angeles, Michigan, New Jersey, Oakland, Philadelphia, Phoenix, Tampa and Washington. In part because of the location of its teams in major television markets, the USFL was able to obtain multimillion dollar network and cable television contracts with ABC and ESPN. Nevertheless, for reasons explored in detail infra, the USFL demonstrated little stability. Over its three seasons of spring football (one of which was a "lame-duck" season commenced after an announced decision to shift to fall play), the USFL clubs played in twenty-two cities, and had thirty-nine principal owners. None of the majority owners of an original USFL team was a majority owner by 1986 when a planned fall schedule was aborted by the $ 1.00 verdict.

3. The NFL's Television Contracts

* * *

In 1970, the NFL entered into a contract with ABC to televise a game nationally on Monday nights. Since then, all three major television networks have broadcast NFL games,[8] and the NFL's annual revenues from television have increased by more than 800 percent. The NFL teams received approximately $ 186 million for the 1970–73 seasons; $ 268 million for the 1974–77 seasons; $ 646 million for the 1978–81 seasons; and $ 2.1 billion over the five-year period 1982–86.

The ABC, CBS and NBC contracts from 1970 onward have given each network rights of first negotiation and first refusal to decide whether to continue its NFL contract for subsequent years. The NFL's 1982–86 contracts were nonexclusive and did not forbid a network from televising another football league's games at any time when it was not

---

8. ABC now televises Monday night games and certain prime-time games. CBS televises National Football Conference ("NFC") games throughout the season, on Thanksgiving Day, and on Saturdays in December. NBC televises American Football Conference ("AFC") games throughout the season, Thanksgiving Day, and on Saturdays in December. Interconference games are televised by the network with the rights to the conference of the visiting team. CBS televises NFC playoff games, and NBC televises AFC playoff games. The first Super Bowl, held in 1967, was broadcast by both CBS and NBC. Since 1967, CBS and NBC have alternated telecasts of the Super Bowl, except that pursuant to its 1982–86 contract with the NFL, ABC televised the Super Bowl played in January 1985. Broadcasting rights to Super Bowl games are not bid for separately but are rotated among the networks.

broadcasting NFL games. NBC was thus legally free to televise to a particular city another league's games on Sunday afternoons directly opposite NFL games on CBS when there was no NFL game scheduled for NBC to be televised to that city. CBS had a similar option. ABC was legally free to televise another league's games all afternoon each Sunday. All three networks were legally free to telecast another league's games in prime time. Because the NFL was forbidden by its network contracts to televise games on cable, cable television contracts were open to a competing league, although such contracts are less lucrative than network contracts. When the NFL's network contracts expired in 1981 and 1986, the networks were free to contract with a competing league's games for all time slots.

The NFL's three-network "tie-up" was a central issue at trial. The USFL claimed that the NFL intentionally set out to tie up the three networks as a means of excluding competitors. In support of its theory, the USFL introduced a memorandum from NFL general counsel Jay Moyer written during the NFL's 1973 network contract negotiations stating that "an open network may well be an open invitation to formation of a new league." Commissioner Rozelle testified, however, that in 1970, before contacting ABC and signing the Monday night football contract with it, he unsuccessfully approached CBS and NBC, both of which already televised NFL games, about their interest in prime-time football. The USFL also emphasized at trial a June 1984 CBS business study suggesting that the fall broadcast of USFL games on Sundays would reduce the network's advertising revenues from NFL games by $ 49 million to $ 53 million over three years. This "dilution effect," the USFL argued, created a $ 50 million barrier to entry by a new league.

The USFL also sought to show that the NFL had placed unlawful pressure on the networks to prevent the broadcast of USFL games. Much of this evidence consisted of statements by USFL representatives and hearsay and speculation by third parties.[9] Officials from the three networks and one cable network testified that the NFL had not exerted any pressure on them regarding the broadcast of USFL games. Several network officials did testify, however, that they feared that televising the USFL in the fall might jeopardize their NFL relationships[10]—a fear somewhat at odds with the USFL claim that the NFL needed three network contracts to produce the "dilution effect." Executives from all three major networks also testified that by 1986, after the USFL had left several large television markets and was encountering financial and other difficulties, the USFL was not an attractive entertainment product.[11]

---

9. USFL Commissioner Harry Usher testified that he was told by Roone Arledge, the president of ABC Sports, that Arledge "had had negative reaction from the NFL for putting the USFL on initially." ABC sportscaster Howard Cosell testified that he was told by Arledge that Commissioner Rozelle was "all over" Arledge because ABC was televising the USFL in the spring. (Arledge testified unequivocally that he had never made such a statement to Cosell.) Jim Spence, a senior vice-president at ABC, testified that he believed that the NFL was "less than enamored" of the network's dealings with the USFL, although he did not recall that any NFL official had directly expressed any displeasure to him.

10. For example, CBS Sports President Neil Pilson testified that he would consider televising the USFL in the fall only if another network was involved. This double exposure would increase the USFL's value and also not leave CBS in a position that would induce the NFL to give the other networks better treatment, including a better schedule of games.

11. NBC Sports President Watson testified that his network did not conduct a business study concerning the feasibility of broadcasting USFL games on Saturday in the fall because of the network's commitments to other sporting events, including baseball, college basketball, golf, and thoroughbred racing.

4. "Conquering the USFL": Predatory Tactics

The USFL also sought to prove monopolization by the NFL through predatory tactics unrelated to television. It thus introduced a memorandum prepared by NFL labor negotiator Jack Donlan entitled "Spending the USFL dollar," which urged NFL owners to bid for USFL players to drive up USFL costs. The USFL's proof of predatory behavior, however, consisted primarily of allegations concerning the recommendations of the so-called "Porter Presentation," and of the so-called Oakland and New York "conspiracies."

The Porter Presentation was a two-and-one-half hour presentation, entitled *USFL v. NFL*, by Harvard Business School Professor Michael Porter to sixty-five NFL executives attending a multiday seminar on labor negotiations. Porter's presentation, which was not previewed by anyone in the NFL, set out a strategy for the NFL to "conquer the USFL."

The USFL claimed that the NFL implemented a recommendation of the Porter Presentation by attempting to "co-opt" USFL owners with promises of an NFL franchise. Donald Trump, owner of the USFL's New Jersey Generals, testified that he was offered an NFL franchise by Commissioner Rozelle in exchange for his blocking the USFL's proposed move to the fall and his preventing the league from filing the instant action. Rozelle denied that he made such an offer to Trump. In addition, hearsay testimony by Al Davis, owner of the NFL's Los Angeles Raiders, a team not sued by the USFL, indicated an attempt to co-opt Alfred Taubman of the Michigan Panthers. Taubman, however, denied that he was offered an NFL team.

The USFL also claimed that the NFL followed Professor Porter's recommendation to "dissuade" ABC from continuing its USFL contract. Supporting evidence consisted largely of hearsay introduced to show the state of mind of the networks. The declarants denied making any such statements. Jim Spence of ABC did testify, however, that the NFL informed him that the NFL owners were "not enamored" with the network's USFL contract. Nevertheless, ABC subsequently offered the USFL a four-year, $ 175 million contract for spring football beginning in 1986. The USFL also claimed that the NFL used a method recommended by Porter to pressure ABC by offering it unattractive Monday night games that would and did earn low ratings in 1984. In response, NFL officials testified that the 1984 *Monday Night Football* schedule was settled before the Porter Presentation, that "weak" teams such as Buffalo and Cincinnati appeared on that schedule fewer times than in prior years, and that any change in ABC's ratings was due to economic conditions that affected the entire sports television marketplace.

Finally, the USFL claimed that the NFL followed Porter's recommendations for competing for players. This evidence consisted of the NFL's decision to conduct a supplemental draft of players still under USFL contract in March 1984, an increase in NFL roster size from forty-five to forty-nine, conversations between the Dallas Cowboys and USFL star Herschel Walker, and NFL salary offers to relatively unknown USFL players such as Todd Fowler. * * *

5. Damages

The USFL's evidence of damages consisted of the testimony of economist Nina Cornell, who sought to estimate the league's losses by two methods. Method A was based on the assumption that the gate and television revenues of an unhindered USFL could be estimated by using the gate receipts and television revenues of the old AFL. Dr. Cornell estimated the USFL's damages under this method at $565 million. Method B was based on the June 1984 CBS business study examining the fall broadcast of USFL games. She estimated the USFL's damages under this method at $301 million.

Dr. Cornell's damage calculations rested on several other assumptions. First, of course, she assumed that illegal NFL conduct was the cause of the USFL's failure to obtain a network contract. Second, Dr. Cornell assumed that the NFL could lawfully contract with only one network. Third, her calculations attributed the USFL's damages entirely to illegal NFL conduct and not at all to the USFL's own mismanagement.

Finally, she assumed that there would be no increased player costs to the USFL resulting from the shift to fall play and that salaries would remain stable from 1986 to 1992. Tension existed between her assumption of stable salaries and her projections of large increases in USFL revenues as a result of playing in the fall during the 1986 to 1992 seasons. Player salaries had already increased dramatically because of the two leagues' competition for players, even when they were playing in different seasons. No reason was given to expect a stabilization of wages when the leagues would play in the same season and the USFL would have substantially greater revenues to compete for players. Moreover, a cornerstone of the USFL's television claim was that a network contract was essential so that it could compete for quality players, a position that is hardly consistent with stability in player salaries.

6. Management of the USFL

The USFL was conceived and organized in 1981 to play in the spring rather than the fall. Its founders believed that public demand for football was not satisfied by the NFL's and the colleges' fall seasons; that cable television, which could not televise NFL games under the existing NFL-network contracts, would offer unique opportunities for television revenues and exposure; that a spring football league would face limited competition; that there was a sufficient supply of football players for two leagues; and that a spring league could draft college players and put them on the field even before the NFL draft.

The USFL's founders placed a high priority on the fans' perception of the quality of play. They intended to use major stadiums and to hire well-known coaches. At the same time, they wanted the league to control costs. For its first season, therefore, the USFL established budget guidelines for player salaries of between $ 1.3 and $ 1.5 million per team.

The USFL's founders did not seek to obtain a television contract for fall play. Before fielding a team, however, the USFL received bids for a spring television contract from ABC and NBC and from two cable networks, ESPN and the Turner Broadcasting System. The league entered a four-year contract with ABC, and a two-year contract with ESPN. The ABC agreement provided for ABC to pay the USFL $ 18 million for the 1983 and 1984 seasons, with options exercisable by ABC at $ 14 million for 1985 and at $ 18 million for 1986. ESPN contracted to televise USFL games for two years at rights fees of $ 4 million for 1983 and $ 7 million for 1984. The USFL began with eight of its twelve teams in the nation's top ten television markets. The ABC contract required the USFL to field teams in the three largest television markets (New York, Los Angeles and Chicago) and in at least four of the five other top-ten television markets in which teams were originally located (Philadelphia, Boston, Detroit, San Francisco/Oakland and Washington).

The USFL's first year of play, 1983, was a mixed success. The league received extensive media exposure when it signed Heisman Trophy winner Herschel Walker to a three-year, $ 3,250,000 contract. The Nielsen television rating for the first week of games was 14.2, a figure comparable to NFL ratings. As the season went on, however, the USFL's television ratings declined; average television ratings for the year were 6.23 on ABC and

3.28 on ESPN. Average attendance for the year was approximately 25,000. Nevertheless, these figures were consistent with the league's and networks' preseason projections.

On the financial side, the picture was not as bright. The USFL lost a total of almost $ 40 million, or an average of $ 3.3 million per team. The league had projected losses of only about $ 2 million per year for each team over the first three years. The unanticipated financial losses were chiefly the result of the failure to stay within the original salary guidelines. Indeed, in a November 1983 letter to other owners, Tad Taube of the Oakland team warned that: "If we are not successful in establishing player [salary] caps I can guarantee you that there will not be a USFL within three years, irrespective of improved revenue [from] television. * * * We have sighted the enemy and they are us!"

The USFL's second year was marked by change. Four teams shifted locations. For example, the owner of the Chicago franchise exchanged that franchise for the Phoenix franchise, taking his winning Chicago coach and players while the original Phoenix team moved to Chicago under a new owner. The league, over the objection of some owners, expanded from twelve teams to eighteen. Five of the original owners left the league. Some of the new owners, notably Donald Trump of the New Jersey Generals, believed that the USFL ought to play in the fall. Thereafter, the issue of when to play became divisive, and several owners came to believe that Trump was trying to bring about a merger with the NFL that would include only some USFL teams.[16]

The NFL introduced extensive evidence designed to prove that the USFL followed Trump's merger strategy, and that this strategy ultimately caused the USFL's downfall. The merger strategy, the NFL argued, involved escalating financial competition for players as a means of putting pressure on NFL expenses, playing in the fall to impair NFL television revenues, shifting USFL franchises out of cities where NFL teams played into cities thought to be logical expansion (through merger) cities for the NFL, and, finally, bringing the antitrust litigation now before us.

Throughout the second half of 1983 and early 1984, several USFL owners escalated spending on player salaries. USFL teams, for example, signed established NFL players such as running back Joe Cribbs and defensive back Gary Barbaro. Trump, in particular, signed a number of players who were still under contract with the NFL to future contracts, including superstar Lawrence Taylor of the New York Giants. USFL owners also signed many top players coming out of college, for example, wide receiver Anthony Carter and quarterback Jim Kelly. The USFL's spending on players greatly outpaced its revenues. The owner of the Los Angeles team, for example, committed the team to $ 13.1 million in salaries and bonuses for just one season. He even entered into a multiyear, $ 40 million contract with just one player, Steve Young of Brigham Young University.

By the end of the 1984 season, USFL franchises in two of the top three television markets, Chicago and Los Angeles, had failed, and only four of the original owners remained in the league. The league was not a failure as entertainment, however. Despite a decline in the USFL's television ratings to 5.7 on ABC and 2.8 on ESPN, ABC exercised its option to carry the USFL in the spring of 1985 at $ 14 million and offered a new contract worth $ 175 million for four years in the spring beginning in 1986. ESPN offered a contract worth $ 70 million over three years.

---

16. After a January 1984 USFL owners' meeting, Myles Tanenbaum of the Philadelphia franchise complained that the "'Original' franchise owners" had become outnumbered, and expressed his outrage that "one of the group believes it would be fair or appropriate to simply 'pay off' others in the event there is a potential big hit by way of merger or whatever."

Nevertheless, during an August 1984 owners' meeting, the USFL decided to move to the fall in 1986. This decision was made despite: (i) ABC's warning that such a move would breach its contract for the spring of 1985 and 1986; (ii) the contrary recommendations of a management consulting firm, McKinsey & Company, which the USFL had retained for $ 600,000 to consider the advisability of a fall season; and (iii) the contrary recommendations of the USFL's directors of operations and marketing.

Moreover, Eddie Einhorn, a USFL owner who was to represent the USFL in negotiations to secure a network contract for the fall, warned that moving from large television markets to "merger" cities too quickly might preclude the securing of a network contract. Nevertheless, in the ensuing months, the USFL withdrew from Chicago, Detroit, Philadelphia, Pittsburgh and Washington, D.C.—each a large television market with an NFL team—and moved into Baltimore (which had lost its NFL team in 1984) and Orlando (which had no NFL team). Through mergers, the USFL bolstered franchises in Oakland (which had lost the NFL Raiders to Los Angeles) and Phoenix (which had been discussed as a possible NFL expansion city). The decision to move to the fall damaged the USFL's relations with ABC and ESPN. The former withheld a significant portion of the USFL's rights fees for the 1985 season, while the latter demanded a renegotiation of its proposed 1985–87 USFL contract. * * *

In October 1984, the instant litigation was begun. The USFL's 1985 "lame-duck" spring season appears to have been affected adversely by the now publicly announced move to the fall. The league's television ratings declined to 4.1 on ABC and 2.0 on ESPN. By the end of the season, several owners had withdrawn financial support for their teams, and a number of clubs were no longer meeting their payrolls and other bills. The USFL scheduled eight teams for its fall 1986 season, which was ultimately cancelled after the verdict in this case. Only one team (New Jersey), was in a top-ten television market. One other team (Tampa Bay), was in a top-twenty market. Three teams were located in Florida (Jacksonville, Orlando and Tampa Bay) but only one was west of the Mississippi River (Phoenix). In three years, USFL teams had left fourteen of the twenty-two cities in which they had played.

7. The Verdict

The jury found the NFL liable on the USFL's claim of actual monopolization, concluding that the older league had willfully acquired or maintained monopoly power in a market consisting of major league professional football in the United States (Question No. 4). The jury also found that the NFL's unlawful monopolization had caused injury to the USFL (Question No. 5). In ruling on the NFL's motion for judgment notwithstanding the verdict with respect to these findings, the district court held that sufficient evidence existed that the NFL had engaged in predatory conduct. This evidence related to: (1) NFL efforts to co-opt USFL owners and potential owners; (2) the NFL Supplemental Draft of USFL players; (3) the NFL's move to a forty-nine-man roster; and (4) the NFL's activity directed at specific USFL franchises such as the Oakland Invaders. * * *

The USFL was unsuccessful on its remaining claims. * * * The fatal blow * * * was the complete rejection of the USFL's television claims. The jury found that the NFL had not willfully acquired or maintained a monopoly in a relevant television submarket (Question No. 4). It further found that the NFL's contracts with all three television networks for the right to broadcast the league's regular season and championship games through the 1986–87 season were not an unreasonable restraint of trade violative of Section 1 (Question No. 24). Finally, the jury rejected the USFL's "essential facilities" claim, specifically finding that "defendants [did not] have the ability to deny actual or potential competitors access to a national broadcast television contract" (Question No. 33), although it also found that such a contract was "essential to the ability of a major league professional football league to compete successfully in the United States" (Question No. 31) and "that potential competitors of the NFL, cannot as a practical matter, duplicate the benefits of a network contract" (Question No. 32).

DISCUSSION

* * *

1. Liability

a. The Sports Broadcasting Act

The USFL contends that the Sports Broadcasting Act of 1961 limits the antitrust exemption for pooled-rights contracts to a single contract with one network. Therefore, it argues, the NFL's multiple contractual arrangements with three networks violates the injunction in *United States v. National Football League*, 116 F. Supp. 319 (E.D. Pa. 1953), a decision claimed by the USFL collaterally to estop the NFL from denying that its arrangements with the networks violate Section 1 of the Sherman Act. * * *

* * * [T]he passage of the 1966 NFL-AFL merger statute provides conclusive evidence that Congress did not intend the 1961 Act to prohibit NFL contracts with more than one network. When considering this legislation, Congress was explicitly informed that the merged league would continue to broadcast its games on "at least 2 networks," and no concern whatsoever was expressed in Congress that such conduct was either undesirable or would go beyond the scope of the 1961 Act's exemption. * * * The lack of a "one network" limitation in the 1966 merger bill thus dooms the USFL's claims. Accordingly, we hold that the mere existence of the NFL contracts with the three networks does not violate the antitrust laws. Having made this determination, we need not consider whether the decree in *United States v. National Football League* has any collateral-estoppel effect.

b. The "Dilution Effect"

* * *

The term "dilution effect" comes from a CBS business study ordered by Neil Pilson, CBS Sports' President, and completed in June 1984. CBS conducted the study because it was apprehensive over ABC's signing a USFL fall contract and desired the leverage a second league would afford it in its negotiations with the NFL. The study estimated the economic impact on CBS of the televising of USFL games in the fall under various scenarios. * * *

As explained by Pilson, the value of a USFL fall contract to CBS was determined (in simplified fashion) as follows. From the estimated gross advertising revenues would be subtracted estimates of: (i) expenses related to production; (ii) losses in revenues that would otherwise have been earned by programs preempted by USFL games, or "preemptive impact"; (iii) decreases in advertising revenues from NFL games resulting from the addition of USFL games, or "dilution effect"; and (iv) rights fees to the USFL. Pilson testified that when these estimates were made in June 1984, the resultant calculation, CBS's profit, was negative. The USFL argues that, but for the "dilution effect" of $ 50 million, the sum would have been sufficiently positive to make a USFL contract attractive. The USFL assumes that the "dilution effect" was experienced equally by all three networks and thus concludes that the effect of NFL's network contracts was to exclude all competition.

* * * The jury rejected the USFL's claims as to the "dilution effect" in finding that the NFL had not monopolized a television submarket, that the NFL television contracts were not an unreasonable restraint, and that the NFL did not have the power to exclude a competing league from obtaining a network contract. There was ample evidence to support these conclusions.

First, the USFL concedes, as it must, that the "dilution effect" is nonexistent when the NFL network contracts expire and negotiations over new contracts are under way. Whatever exclusionary effect exists is only for the term of the three NFL network contracts, and all leagues are free to compete on the basis of the quality of their product upon the expiration of these contracts. The district court's instructions directed the jury to consider the length of these contracts, then five years, in determining whether they were reasonable. Its verdict, therefore, is dispositive because the duration of the contracts was hardly unreasonable as a matter of law.

Second, there was no evidence that the result of the calculations described above would be the same for ABC as for CBS. ABC's contract was largely confined to televising a single NFL game in prime time on a weekday night. Its Sundays were free of football, and it would not encounter the scheduling problems faced by CBS in televising both NFL and USFL games on Sunday afternoons. ABC was thus free to schedule games so as to maximize revenue. Moreover, whatever "dilution effect" ABC's prime-time games might suffer was not necessarily identical to that faced by CBS. * * *

Third, the conduct of the NFL and the networks indicates that neither believed their contracts to be exclusionary. Notwithstanding the early opinion of the NFL's Moyer about a network without a contract being "open invitation to a new league," the NFL's actual conduct displayed no marked desire to lock up all three networks. Prime-time weekday telecasts were offered to NBC and CBS, both of whom already had NFL contracts, before ABC was approached. It was the testimony of both the ABC executives and CBS's Pilson, elicited by counsel for the USFL, that Rozelle routinely used the threat of leaving them without an NFL contract in order to extract from them the largest possible rights fees. If the "dilution effect" theory of exclusion were correct, the NFL could not credibly threaten to leave one network without a contract. If the theory were correct, moreover, the last network to sign with the NFL would have a bargaining advantage because its agreement would be essential to the NFL's monopoly, much as the owner of the last lot in a tract of land needed for a construction project can demand the highest price. In the NFL-network negotiations, the opposite was the case, and the last network to sign was at a bargaining disadvantage. * * *

Fourth, even if the "dilution effect" theory were alive and well in 1986, the jury could have found that that "effect" was not a cause of the USFL's failure to get a network contract in that year* * *. [T]here were the problems of the USFL itself. The league had failed to establish fan loyalty in most places because of repeated franchise moves. Most importantly, the USFL had abandoned most major television markets, thereby rendering telecasts of its games much less valuable than had been estimated by the earlier CBS study. Finally, the disagreements among the USFL owners, the financial condition of some of the franchises, and the "lame-duck" spring season of 1985 further lessened the value of USFL telecasts in 1986. In fact, Pilson himself testified that by 1986 the events described above had rendered the "dilution effect" irrelevant to CBS's decision not to televise the USFL. In light of this evidence, the jury was free to conclude that the revenues to be expected from USFL telecasts were so low that no network would purchase them even if there were no "dilution effect."

c. "Intent and Effect" Charge

* * *

The Supreme Court has repeatedly defined monopolization as the "willful acquisition or maintenance" of monopoly power. *E.g., Aspen Skiing Co. v. Aspen Highlands Skiing Corp.*, 472 U.S. 585, 596 n.19 (1985) * * * The willfulness element certainly requires proof of intent. * * * Proof of effect is required by definition alone to satisfy the "acquisition or maintenance" requirement.

A requirement that both intent *and* effect be proven is necessary to enable a trier of fact to make the critical distinction between conduct that defeats a competitor because of efficiency and consumer satisfaction, and conduct that "not only (1) tends to impair the opportunities of rivals, but also (2) either does not further competition on the merits or does so in an unnecessarily restrictive way." * * * Hopes and dreams alone cannot support a Section 2 claim of monopolization. * * * If they did, the nationwide advertisement "Ford wants to be your car company" would constitute an open-and-shut Section 2 case. Success alone is not enough or the antitrust laws would have their greatest impact on the most efficient entrepreneurs and would injure rather than protect consumers.

Proof of intent and effect is also of evidentiary value. Distinguishing between efficient and predatory conduct is extremely difficult because it is frequently the case that "competitive and exclusionary conduct look alike." * * * Evidence of intent *and* effect helps the trier of fact to evaluate the actual effect of challenged business practices in light of the intent of those who resort to such practices. * * *

The present case is in fact a useful example of the intent-*and*-effect approach to determining whether certain practices are predatory. As the preceding discussion of the "dilution effect" indicates, the jury's conclusion that the NFL's three network contracts were not exclusionary was supported by evidence that a quality league could either have overcome the "dilution effect" or have acquired a contract when the NFL's contracts expired. The conduct of the NFL itself and the networks showed their disbelief in any exclusionary effect by the NFL's threatening to leave a network without NFL games and the networks' taking the threat seriously. The evidence also supported the conclusion that when the NFL locked up the third network, CBS, in the 1982 negotiations, it did so to obtain $ 736 million in rights fees, not to exclude competitors.

* * * We disagree with the USFL that proof of either anticompetitive intent *or* effect is sufficient in a Rule-of-Reason case under Section 1. Unlike a *per se* price-fixing case, a Rule-of-Reason case requires the fact finder to balance the procompetitive and anticompetitive *effects* of any restraint. *See, e.g., National Soc'y of Professional Eng'rs v. United States*, 435 U.S. 679, 691 & n.17 (1978). * * * We have previously stated * * * that "it is difficult to conceive of a viable private action for damages under section 1 if some unreasonable restraint of trade has not been effected" * * * and we now hold, for reasons stated in our discussion of the Section 2 claim, that an anticompetitive effect must be shown to make out a Section 1 Rule-of-Reason violation. * * *

2. The District Court's Evidentiary Rulings

a. The USFL's Merger Strategy

The USFL vigorously contends that the NFL's introduction of evidence of its merger strategy enabled the NFL to present an impermissible *in pari delicto* or unclean-hands defense under the guise of damage causation. This claim is frivolous.

It is true that a plaintiff's own anticompetitive conduct generally cannot be raised as a defense to liability in an antitrust action. *See Perma Life Mufflers, Inc. v. International Parts Corp.*, 392 U.S. 134, 139 (1968) (rejecting *in pari delicto* defense that plaintiff's participation in challenged scheme barred recovery); *Kiefer-Stewart Co. v. Joseph E. Seagram & Sons, Inc.*, 340 U.S. 211, 214 (1951) (rejecting unclean hands defense based on plaintiff's involvement in unrelated conduct). The defense may be available, however, when the plaintiff was present at the creation and had a complete and continuing involvement in the monopolization scheme. * * *

Whatever its force or content, the *in pari delicto* defense was never interposed by the NFL, and the evidence in question was quite properly admitted as relevant to causation and damages. Stretching dictum in *Perma Life* beyond recognition, the USFL misreads that decision to proscribe the introduction of evidence that might "prejudice the jury improperly into evaluating 'the relative moral worth of the parties.'" * * * Neither *Perma Life* nor *Kiefer-Stewart* suggests that otherwise readily admissible evidence must be excluded because it might also be relevant to an *in pari delicto* or unclean-hands defense. In fact, *Perma Life* explicitly states that such evidence "can of course be taken into consideration in computing damages." 392 U.S. at 140 * * *

As with any evidence, therefore, the district judge had broad discretion to determine whether the probative value of the evidence of a merger strategy was "substantially outweighed by the danger of unfair prejudice, confusion of the issues, or misleading the jury." Fed. R. Evid. 403. His decision that evidence of business decisions made by the USFL pursuant to the merger strategy was highly relevant to the issues of causation and damages and not outweighed by any prejudicial effect was clearly correct. This evidence was highly probative on the central issue of whether the USFL's alleged injury and damages, particularly with regard to its failure to obtain a fall network contract, were caused by the NFL's anticompetitive conduct or by the USFL's own deliberate business judgments. * * *

b. Prior NFL Antitrust Judgments

In his Opinion No. 3, Judge Leisure excluded from evidence prior court decisions that found the NFL to have violated Section 1 of the Sherman Act. 634 F. Supp. at 1171–75. The USFL contends on appeal that this ruling was error, and that the NFL used this ruling as a "shield" to present a "good monopolist" defense.

Prior antitrust violations and the history of competition in a market may, in appropriate cases, be admissible to establish market power and intent to monopolize. * * * Such evidence also may be admissible to establish the intent, motive and method of a conspiracy under Section 1. * * * In order for the NFL's prior antitrust judgments to be admissible, however, the USFL bore the burden of demonstrating that the conduct underlying those prior judgments had a direct, logical relationship to the conduct at issue in this case. * * *

Judge Leisure found that the USFL never made such a showing, and, although we do not fully embrace his reasoning, we agree that the prior judgments should not have been admitted as evidence of a longstanding conspiracy somehow casting light on current alleged illegalities. Two of the decisions in question, *Smith v. Pro Football, Inc.*, 593 F.2d 1173 (D.C. Cir. 1978) (invalidating rules for NFL player draft); *Mackey v. National Football League*, 543 F.2d 606 (8th Cir. 1976) (invalidating "Rozelle Rule" for compensation of free agents), are not consistent with our decision in *Wood v. National Basketball Ass'n*, 809 F.2d 954 (2d Cir. 1987). The three others, *Los Angeles Memorial Coliseum*

Comm'n v. National Football League, 726 F.2d 1381 (9th Cir.) (invalidating NFL Rule 4.3 limiting franchise relocation), *cert. denied*, 469 U.S. 990 (1984), later opinion, 791 F.2d 1356 (9th Cir. 1986), *cert. denied*, 484 U.S. 826 (1987); *North Am. Soccer League v. National Football League*, 670 F.2d 1249 (2d Cir.) (invalidating rule forbidding franchise owners from owning other professional sports teams), *cert. denied*, 459 U.S. 1074 (1982), and *United States v. National Football League*, 116 F. Supp. 319 (E.D. Pa. 1953) (invalidating rules limiting broadcast of games into home territories of other teams), involve difficult antitrust questions that were (and, in circuits other than the place of decision, may still be) fair game for litigation. Accordingly, these cases are at best marginally probative of an ongoing intent to exclude competitors.

Judge Leisure excluded the latter three judgments on the ground that they involved intraleague restraints, whereas the instant litigation involves interleague competition. Although we hesitate to adopt a rule that anticompetitive restraints among competitors can never reveal monopolistic intent toward would-be entrants, we do note that sports leagues raise numerous difficult antitrust questions involving horizontal restraints and group boycotts. The very concept of a league involving separate business entities (teams) requires concerted behavior among them and the exclusion of outsiders. Even the drawing up of a schedule requires that horizontal competitors (teams) conform to jointly made decisions and necessarily excludes others. * * * Moreover, the antitrust law governing horizontal arrangements among competitors and group boycotts has been fluid. * * *

Accordingly, we are wary of allowing a trier of fact to draw inferences of intent from the outcome of prior lawsuits in an area so fraught with uncertainty and doubt. Our wariness in this regard is enhanced by the fact that the lawsuits most pertinent to the instant action—involving claims by another league or a team in another league—were in fact won by the NFL. *American Football League v. National Football League*, 323 F.2d 124 (4th Cir. 1963); *Mid-South Grizzlies v. National Football League*, 720 F.2d 772 (3d Cir. 1983). The district court thus acted within its discretion in excluding evidence of prior antitrust judgments against the NFL on the grounds that their prejudicial value outweighed their probative value under Fed. R. Evid. 403. * * *

c. Legislative Process Evidence

The USFL claims that the district court erroneously excluded evidence relating to the activities of the NFL in Congress. This evidence included (1) the NFL's lobbying activities in connection with the 1961 Sports Broadcasting Act and the 1966 NFL-AFL merger legislation, (2) Congress's motives in enacting this legislation, and (3) Senator Alphonse D'Amato's knowledge of the NFL's use of "pressure" tactics in its congressional lobbying.

Legislative lobbying efforts cannot of course be the basis of antitrust liability. *See Eastern R.R. Presidents Conference v. Noerr Motor Freight, Inc.*, 365 U.S. 127, 135–36 (1961); *United Mine Workers of Am. v. Pennington*, 381 U.S. 657, 669–72 (1965). Evidence of such lobbying may be admitted, however, "if it tends reasonably to show the purpose and character of the particular transactions under scrutiny," *Pennington*, 381 U.S. at 670 n.3 (quoting *FTC v. Cement Inst.*, 333 U.S. at 705), and that evidence is more probative than prejudicial. *Id.*

We address first the exclusion of evidence about the Sports Broadcasting Act and the 1966 merger legislation. The USFL objects to the exclusion of a House Committee Report on the Sports Broadcasting Act, which stated that Congress expected professional sports leagues to institute competitive bidding for their television rights as soon as existing contracts expired. * * * The USFL sought to demonstrate by this report that the NFL had misled Congress by promising to put NFL telecasts (especially of the championship game) up for competitive bidding. Judge Leisure properly ruled that the interpretation of legislative history was not an issue of fact for the jury, * * * and that such evidence was otherwise excludable under Fed. R. Evid. 403 as overly prejudicial and confusing.

As to the NFL-AFL merger legislation, the USFL sought to introduce evidence that it was approved in part because the NFL had promised two powerful Louisiana lawmakers that a franchise would be awarded to New Orleans. The district court's refusal to admit such evidence was not an abuse of discretion * * *

Finally, we address the district court's exclusion of Senator D'Amato's testimony about the NFL's use of "pressure" tactics in Congress. These tactics allegedly included threats to certain members of the House and Senate to remove franchises from their states and promises to others to move franchises to their states. The USFL argued that these lobbying activities fell within the "sham" exception to *Noerr-Pennington*. We agree, however, with Judge Leisure that efforts to persuade government officials simply by appealing to their political interests have *Noerr-Pennington* protection. * * *

Finally, with regard to all of the excluded evidence relating to the legislative process, we tend to share the view of the Third Circuit that, "if these allegations are true, * * * they are, perhaps, instructive on the nature of the federal legislative process. For purposes of [the Sherman Act], however, they are irrelevant." *Mid-South Grizzlies*, 720 F.2d at 784. * * *

3. The District Court's Damages Instructions

The USFL contends that it received an award of only $ 1.00 because of incorrect jury instructions regarding damages. Again, we disagree. Specifically, the USFL challenges the instructions with respect to an antitrust plaintiff's burden of proving the amount of damages and with respect to nominal damages.

a. The $ 1.00 Award

The jury was given the following nominal damages instruction:

> Just because you have found the fact of some damage resulting from a given unlawful act, that does not mean that you are required to award a dollar amount of damages resulting from that act. You may find, for example, that you are unable to compute the monetary damages resulting from the wrongful act, except by engaging in speculation or guessing, or you find that you cannot separate out the amount of the losses caused by the wrongful act from the amount caused by other factors, including perfectly lawful competitive acts and including business decisions made by the plaintiffs or the plaintiffs' own mismanagement. Or you may find that plaintiffs failed to prove an amount of damages.

> You may decline to award damages under such circumstances, or you may award a nominal amount, say $ 1.

The jury's $ 1.00 award was consistent with this instruction. The NFL offered much evidence of self-destructive USFL decisions, and the jury's nominal award suggests that it credited this proof, as it was free to do. Moreover, it is now clear that Dr. Cornell's testimony was based on a number of assumptions entailing legal premises that were incorrect or factual conclusions that were rejected by the jury. In awarding only nominal damages, the jury might reasonably have concluded that the USFL had failed to prove any damages. * * *

4. The District Court's Denial of Injunctive Relief

Finally, the USFL claims that the district court should have granted sweeping injunctive relief under Section 16 of the Clayton Act, 15 U.S.C. §26 (1982). In particular, the USFL requested membership in the NFL, separation of the NFL into two leagues, each league being limited to one network, or a prohibition on the NFL from broadcasting its games in more than one afternoon time slot on Sunday. Judge Leisure held that the requested relief was unrelated to the monopolization of the market for major-league professional football verdict and not justified by the record as a whole.

The USFL contends that the jury's monopolization verdict compelled the district court to "pry open to competition [the] market that has been closed by defendants' illegal restraints." * * * However, this argument simply glosses over the critical fact that the jury did not find the NFL liable on any of the USFL's television-related claims. With regard to the findings implied by the monopolization verdict that the NFL engaged in predatory conduct through attempts to co-opt USFL owners, creation of a Supplemental Draft, or expansion in roster size, Judge Leisure denied relief on the ground that the USFL provided no evidence that such conduct was likely to continue or recur. The USFL has not asked us to overturn that denial of relief.

Instead, the USFL seeks sweeping injunctive relief on the ground that the NFL's single league structure, in conjunction with television contracts with the three networks, creates an impenetrable barrier to entry by a competing league into the market of professional football. No matter what the jury found, however, such relief would not have been appropriate. First, Congress has authorized the NFL's single-league structure and its joint economic operations. Second, at the time the district court denied the relief, the NFL's contracts with the networks had expired. There was thus no "tie-up" of the three networks and no barrier to entry created by the "dilution effect." There was only free competition between the NFL's product and the USFL's product. Of course, the district court also properly rejected this claim in view of the jury's outright rejection of all of the USFL's television-related claims.

What the USFL seeks is essentially a judicial restructuring of major-league professional football to allow it to enter. Because of the explicit congressional authorization in 1966 for the NFL-AFL merger and single-league operation, the USFL does not attack the league structure directly. Instead, the USFL asks us to prevent networks from broadcasting, and fans from watching, NFL games in the hope that they will turn to the USFL. Absent a showing of an unlawful barrier to entry, however, new sports leagues must be prepared to make the investment of time, effort and money that develops interest and fan loyalty and results in an attractive product for the media. The jury in the present case obviously found that patient development of a loyal following among fans and an adherence to an original plan that offered long-run gains were lacking in the USFL. Instead, the USFL quickly changed to a strategy of competition with the NFL in the fall, hoping thereby to force a merger of a few USFL teams into the NFL. That led to a movement of USFL teams out of large television markets and a resultant reduction in value of USFL games to television. As USFL owner and negotiator Einhorn predicted, abandoning major television markets precluded the possibility of obtaining a network contract. The USFL hoped, however, that if a merger did not occur, a jury verdict in the instant litigation followed by a decree effectively forcing a network to televise its product would save the day. Instead, the jury found that the failure of the USFL was not the result of the NFL's television contracts but of its own decision to seek entry into the NFL on the cheap.

CONCLUSION

For the foregoing reasons, we affirm the jury's verdict and the judgments entered thereon. We thus need not consider the NFL's conditional cross-appeal.

Affirmed.

Notes and Questions

1. Following the jury's announcement of its verdict, one of the six jurors, Mrs. Miriam Sanchez, a high school English teacher, told reporters that she had favored awarding the USFL substantial damages (perhaps between $200 and $300 million—which would have been trebled), but that she had agreed on the award of nominal damages—one dollar—based on the understanding that the district judge could and would increase the amount. *See, e.g.,* Lionel S. Sobel, *The USFL v. NFL Case: A Review of the Issues Before, During and After the Trial, Including Speculation on the Reason for the $1 Jury Verdict and on Possible Grounds for Appeal,* 8 ENTERTAINMENT L. REP., Sept., 1986; Dave Goldberg, *Sports News,* ASSOCIATED PRESS, July 31, 1986; Richard Hoffer, *USFL Awarded Only $3 in Antitrust Decision; Jury Finds NFL Guilty on One of Nine Counts,* LOS ANGELES TIMES, July 30, 1986. Do you understand how a juror may have come to that conclusion based on the jury instruction quoted by the Second Circuit? The district court rendered the post-trial statements by the jurors inadmissible and refused to consider them. *See United States Football League v. National Football League,* 644 F. Supp. 1040, 1043–45 (S.D.N.Y. 1986).

2. As explained in Judge Winter's opinion, the USFL's damages expert only gave the jury two damage figures to consider—$301 million and $565 million. After trebling, those damage figures, if awarded by the jury and sustained on appeal, would have yielded a verdict of $903 million or $1.695 billion. How would those figures compare to the value, in 1986, of the twenty-eight teams in the NFL? In 1984, Clint Murchison sold the Dallas Cowboys along with Texas Stadium for a total of $80 million and Edgar Kaiser sold the Denver Broncos for $70 million. When Gene Klein sold his 56% interest in the San Diego Chargers shortly thereafter to Alex Spanos, it was based on a team valuation of $80 million. *See, e.g.,* Gene Klein and David Fisher, Excerpts from *First Down and a Billion: The Funny Business of Pro Football,* THE SAN DIEGO UNION-TRIBUNE, Dec. 23, 1986, at C-1. If you take into account that those teams were among the most valuable in the NFL, that the Cowboys' deal included the stadium itself, and that Spanos bought total control over the team without having to purchase 100% of the stock, it is safe to conclude that the average NFL team was worth $60 million or less. That assumption would yield a value for the twenty-eight teams of $1.680 billion. Thus, the stake in the *USFL* case and the importance of the jury's decision to both leagues is readily apparent. If the USFL had been awarded $1.695 billion and the verdict had been sustained on appeal, the USFL owners would have been the primary (perhaps sole?) beneficial owners of the NFL! Suppose that, in the face of such a major antitrust threat, the NFL owners had agreed to award NFL expansion franchises to some or most of the USFL teams and that the USFL became defunct. Would such a combination of the teams in the two leagues have violated the antitrust laws? Could the USFL and NFL have defended against an antitrust challenge by arguing that the demise of the USFL was inevitable, and that the survival of a few USFL teams at least preserved the availability of major league professional

football for the fans in the areas where those USFL teams played? Could the NFL owners have defended on the grounds that a pro-USFL damage award in the litigation would have meant that the two leagues were under common ownership (by the USFL owners) and that their settlement was less anticompetitive than that result?

3. Under Section 4 of the Clayton Act:

> [A]ny person who shall be injured in his business or property by reason of anything forbidden in the antitrust laws may sue therefor * * * and shall recover threefold the damages by him sustained, and the cost of suit, including a reasonable attorney's fee.

15 U.S.C. §15(a). Given the outcome of the USFL's case against the NFL, should it have been awarded attorneys' fees? *See United States Football League v. National Football League*, 887 F.2d 408 (2d Cir. 1989) (affirming district court judgment awarding the USFL $5,529,247.25 in attorneys' fees and also taxing costs of $62,220.92 against the NFL). Was the USFL the "prevailing party"? *Id.* at 412.

4. The Porter Presentation discussed by the court was a two and one-half hour analysis of the USFL's strengths, weaknesses, and potential strategies by Professor Michael Porter of the Harvard Business School, guest columnist for the Wall Street Journal, and author of, *inter alia, Competitive Strategy: Techniques for Analyzing Industries and Competitors* (1980). The audience consisted of over fifty NFL executives who were attending the NFL's annual multi-day labor relations seminar in Cambridge, Massachusetts. The seminars were established to educate the various NFL team executives concerning strategy to be employed when negotiating NFL player contracts. The NFL Players Association had been critical of the seminars as presenting opportunities for NFL teams to collude to suppress player salaries.

In 1984, with the NFL facing the adverse consequences of competition by the USFL—both for players and in other markets—Michael McCaskey, the President of the Chicago Bears, asked that the focus of the seminar be changed and that Professor Porter be invited to discuss competitive strategies for responding to the USFL threat. Not an attorney, Porter proposed a wide range of improper conduct, including interfering with contracts and prospective business relations, offering NFL franchises to the most substantial USFL owners, and targeting the weakest USFL teams for elimination. NFL Commissioner Pete Rozelle testified that he was not at the presentation and that he became physically ill when he heard what Porter had proposed. He immediately sent a letter to Porter disavowing Porter's recommendations. When the USFL sought to establish that the NFL had implemented Porter's plan, the NFL produced evidence purporting to prove that they had done nothing of the kind. In retrospect, Commissioner Rozelle's immediate, decisive response to the Porter Presentation may have saved NFL owners over $1 billion in damages.

Given the dominant professional leagues' monopoly position in their sports, should it be a major responsibility of the league commissioner to keep the conduct of the league and its owners within the constraints of the antitrust laws? Could that phenomenon explain why these leagues, in recent years, have generally called upon antitrust counsel at major law firms to serve as general counsel and commissioners?

5. Judge Winter seemed to think that the USFL's moving its games to the Fall would significantly raise the USFL's player costs, apparently assuming that there would be more direct competition for players. Do you agree? In light of the fact that players already had to choose between the USFL and NFL and could not play in both leagues, how would simultaneous seasons change the competition for players?

6. One remedy sought by the USFL was an injunction ordering the NFL to merge USFL teams into the NFL. Would that relief have remedied the NFL's unlawful monopolization or would it have merely allowed the USFL teams to share the monopoly? *See, e.g., Mid-South Grizzlies v. National Football League*, 720 F.2d 772, 787 (3rd Cir. 1983). If the NFL's unlawful monopolization had included limiting expansion, so that cities with tremendous demand for major league professional football (the potential expansion cities) were deprived of a team, such "mandated" expansion conceivably would provide a solution to that aspect of the monopoly's adverse consequences. Does that result justify a court's ordering such injunctive relief?

7. When two professional sports leagues or circuits are in direct competition, any resulting antitrust litigation inevitably focuses on allegations that the dominant league or circuit in some way used its controlling position to block competition from the new entrant. Analytically, the two primary ways in which a dominant league or circuit can attack its competition are interfering with the new entrant's ability to secure the necessary inputs to produce its product at a reasonable cost and interfering with the entrant's ability to sell its product and to generate the revenue necessary to stay in business.

The first category of interference can include: (1) limiting the new entrant's ability to contract with the players or athletes necessary to produce a major league product, *see, e.g.,* the *Volvo* case in Chapter 10; *Philadelphia World Hockey Club, Inc. v. Philadelphia Hockey Club, Inc.*, 351 F. Supp. 462 (E.D. Pa. 1972)), or raising the price that the new entrant has to pay players (*e.g.,* allegations in the *USFL* case about NFL raising the price of players to the USFL—"spending the USFL dollar"); (2) impeding the new entrant's ability to contract with the necessary facilities for exhibiting the games, *see, e.g.,* the *Hecht* case, above; *United States Football League v. National Football League*, 634 F. Supp. 1155, 1176–77 (S.D.N.Y. 1986); (3) preventing top quality referees, umpires, etc. from officiating the new league's games, *see United States Football League*, 634 F. Supp. at 1184–89; or (4) compromising the new entrant's efforts to attract investors with sports background, experience, and expertise to finance and operate its teams or events. *See, e.g., Volvo; AFL v. NFL*, above; *NASL v. NFL*, below).

The second category of interference—regarding the competitor's effort to sell its product—requires blocking one or more of the revenue streams available to a sports league or circuit. As discussed in Chapter 2, these income sources potentially include revenue from ticket sales (including personal seat licenses, luxury boxes, and club seats), television, sponsors, licensees, and, in some cases, fees for the purchase of the rights to operate expansion teams. In general, the dominant league can only interfere with a competitor's revenue source if the dominant league has business dealings with that source. Therefore, it would be very difficult for one league to deprive another of ticket sales (unless it blocked the new league's access to a stadium or some other essential input). Nevertheless, the USFL alleged that the NFL had sought that very result through a "deliberate and widespread campaign" designed to defame and disparage the USFL. *See, e.g., United States Football League*, 634 F. Supp. at 1182–84. Similarly, while a league could pressure its sponsors not to endorse a new league, there should still be other sponsors for the new league unless the universe of potential sponsors is very limited. The same principle applies to licensees interested in selling league-approved products. Therefore, television is the most likely way to interfere with revenues and the most likely source of allegations of a new league or circuit seeking to apply antitrust pressure to the existing league.

Many of these strategies had been discussed by Professor Michael Porter in his infamous presentation, and they provided the reinforcement for many of the arguments advanced by the USFL. *See, e.g.,* Thomas Moore, *It's 4th & 10—The NFL Needs the Long*

Bomb, TIME, Aug. 4, 1986, at 160. While the jurors heard all about the Porter presentation and its strategies, for a variety of legal and factual reasons the jury never heard about the other conduct alleged by the USFL. *See, e.g., United States Football League v. National Football League*, 634 F. Supp. at 1175–90. A careful reading of the district court and court of appeals opinions leaves the impression that the judges may have been motivated by a concern that the jury might become angered at the NFL, and award the USFL a verdict not reasonably related to the USFL damages that were actually caused by the NFL as opposed to those losses that were self-inflicted.

8. Some of the conduct engaged in by the NFL and challenged by the USFL was arguably unilateral, and thereby not subject to scrutiny under Section 1 of the Sherman Act, particularly if the NFL were determined to be a single entity with respect to inter-league disputes. *See* Chapters 2 and 12. However, the NFL's agreement with the three television networks were not so insulated, and, if those contracts unreasonably restrained competition in a relevant market, they would violate Section 1. The USFL did not have to prove that a market was *monopolized*—only that competition in the market was restrained. If, however, the USFL had limited its challenge to Section 1 to avoid a need to prove that the NFL had monopoly power, what would the adverse consequences be for the USFL's litigation strategy? The USFL might not have been permitted to introduce evidence of prior conduct by the NFL because such history might be deemed irrelevant to whether competition was being restrained in the mid-1980s. The USFL could have responded that the history of the restraint was relevant under the Rule of Reason as set forth by the Supreme Court in *Chicago Board of Trade*, 246 U.S. 231, 238 (1918); but that rejoinder would certainly not have been applicable to judicial decisions holding the NFL guilty of antitrust violations in other cases addressing different restraints. In addition, the USFL sought far-ranging injunctive relief (*e.g.*, USFL membership in the NFL or "separation of the NFL into two leagues") to remedy what it contended was the NFL's long-standing illegal monopoly. If the USFL had only contended and proved that the NFL's contracts with the networks unreasonably restrained trade, what injunctive relief could it have reasonably sought, especially after those agreements had expired? Was the emphasis on illegal monopolization necessary to render certain evidence relevant and to support claims for sweeping injunctive relief? What other differences are there between claims under Section 1 and Section 2?

9. Many who watched the USFL compete with the NFL and listened to the witnesses at trial were convinced that the USFL design—a lower cost professional league playing in the Spring—might have succeeded if the initial strategy had not been abandoned. Ever since the USFL's fate was sealed by the jury's one dollar verdict, there have been efforts to form a new league that would build upon and improve upon the USFL model. One NFL response was the establishment of the World League of American Football ("WLAF"), a low cost spring league that would not compete with the NFL and would make it less likely that a competing league not dominated by the NFL would be launched. Initially, the WLAF had eight teams, four in the United States in cities that do not have an NFL franchise, and four overseas. The NFL subsidized the WLAF (to the tune of about $500,000 annually per team) before shutting it down. The NFL defended the losses as necessary to introduce "American football" outside the United States. The NFL re-launched the WLAF as NFL Eurpoe—a league with all its teams outside the United States.

The cost of dealing with a competing league would obviously be more than $500,000 per team, per year. Therefore, as a business decision it was unassailable. However, if it could be proved that the NFL owners launched a league, knowing it would lose money, as part of a plan to foreclose competition, should such a stratagem violate the antitrust laws as illegal maintenance of the NFL's monopoly position? *See Philadelphia World Hockey Club, Inc. v. Philadelphia Hockey Club, Inc.*, 351 F. Supp. 462, 511–513 (E.D. Pa. 1972).

10. Despite the *USFL* court and jury rejecting the USFL's television claims, people attempting to organize competing professional football leagues frequently consider a network television contract a key to success. As league counsel Jay Moyer cautioned, a network without an NFL contract may be "an open invitation to formation of a new league." Therefore, when Fox outbid CBS for the right to broadcast the NFL's National Football Conference contests, there was tremendous speculation that CBS might agree to broadcast a competing league's games. As the negotiations for the next NFL television contracts commenced, the NFL faced a dilemma. Should they leave one network without a contract to force them to compete and thereby to increase their payments to the NFL, an approach carrying the risk that the jilted network would support a competing league? When in fact, NBC was left without an NFL contract it co-founded the XFL with World Wrestling Entertainment, Inc. and its founder, Vince McMahon, and then NBC tried broadcasting Arena Football League games. Should the NFL enable all four networks (and ESPN) to broadcast NFL games? When the NFL contracts with all four networks, as well as with cable sports channels, does it substantially increase its antitrust exposure?

11. As explained by Judge Winter, the district judge excluded evidence about a number of prior antitrust cases involving the NFL, including the case that follows, *North American Soccer League v. National Football League*. The district court's reasoning was that this case involved an intra-league, rather than an inter-league dispute. While the court was obviously correct—the NASL challenged a rule that only directly applied to NFL owners—do you agree that the characterization rendered the decision not relevant to the USFL's case against the NFL? Did the court in the following case find that the NFL was concerned about its *intra*-league competition (internal operations) or *inter*-league competition when it enforced its cross-ownership ban? Do you agree with Judge Winter's alternative theory as to why the evidence should be excluded—that the *NASL* case and the other "intra-league" cases all "involve[d] difficult antitrust questions" concerning an "area so fraught with uncertainty and doubt" and "were (and in circuits other than the place of decision, may still be) fair game for litigation"? As you read the *NASL* case, attempt to identify what is "fraught with uncertainty and doubt." Is it whether the NFL's conduct is subject to analysis under Section 1 in light of defendants' contention that the NFL is a single entity incapable of conspiring with itself or is it the court's market definition or whether the court's application of the Rule of Reason analysis was appropriate? *See North American Soccer League v. National Football League*, 459 U.S. 1074 (1982) (Rehnquist, J., dissenting from denial of certiorari). As you read the following opinion, ask yourself whether you would have allowed the USFL to tell the jury about the *NASL v. NFL* case.

IV. Inter-Sport Competition and Cross-Ownership Bans

North American Soccer League v. National Football League
670 F.2d 1249 (2d Cir. 1981)

MANSFIELD, Circuit Judge. The central question in this case is whether an agreement between members of one league of professional sports teams (NFL) to prohibit its members from making or retaining any capital investment in any member of another league of professional sports teams (in this case NASL) violates the antitrust laws. The answer requires an analysis of the facts and application of governing antitrust principles. Most of the facts are not in dispute. The NFL is an unincorporated joint venture consisting of 28 individually owned separate professional football teams, each operated through a distinct corporation or partnership, which is engaged in the business of providing public entertainment in the form of competitive football games between its member teams. It is the only major league professional football association in the United States. Upon becoming a member of the NFL a team owner receives a non-assignable franchise giving him the exclusive right to operate an NFL professional football team in a designated home city and "home territory," and to play football games in that territory against other NFL members according to a schedule and terms arranged by the NFL.

The success of professional football as a business depends on several factors. The ultimate goal is to attract as many people as possible to pay money to attend games between members and to induce advertisers to sponsor TV broadcasts of such games, which results in box-office receipts from sale of tickets and revenues derived from network advertising, all based on public interest in viewing games. If adequate revenues are received, a team will operate at a profit after payment of expenses, including players' salaries, stadium costs, referees, travel, maintenance and the like. Toward this goal there must be a number of separate football teams, each dispersed in a location having local public fans willing to buy tickets to games or view them on TV; a group of highly skilled players on each team who are reasonably well-matched in playing ability with those of other teams; adequate capital to support the teams' operations; uniform rules of competition governing game play; home territory stadia available for the conduct of the games; referees; and an apparatus for the negotiation and sale of network TV and radio broadcast rights and distribution of broadcast revenues among members.

To perform these functions some sort of an economic joint venture is essential. No single owner could engage in professional football for profit without at least one other competing team. Separate owners for each team are desirable in order to convince the public of the honesty of the competition. Moreover, to succeed in the marketplace by attracting fans the teams must be close in the caliber of their playing ability. * * *

Earlier in this century various professional football leagues existed, outstanding of which were the NFL and AFL (American Football League). In 1970 the AFL merged into the NFL, after receiving Congressional approval to avoid violation of antitrust laws that would otherwise occur. Since then the NFL has assumed full responsibility for national promotion of professional football, granting of team franchises, negotiation of network TV contracts for broadcast rights with respect to its members' games, employment of referees, adoption of game rules, scheduling of season games between members leading up to the league championship game known as the Super Bowl, and many other matters pertaining to the national sport. Although specific team profit figures were not introduced at trial, the record is clear that the NFL and most of its members now generally enjoy financial success. The NFL divides pooled TV receipts equally among members. Pre-season gate receipts from each game are shared on a 50/50 basis between opposing teams, and regular season gate receipts are divided on the basis of 60% for the home team and 40% for the visiting team.

Although NFL members thus participate jointly in many of the operations conducted by it on their behalf, each member is a separately owned, discrete legal entity which does not share its expenses, capital expenditures or profits with other members. Each also derives separate revenues from certain lesser sources, which are not shared with other members, including revenues from local TV and radio, parking and concessions. A member's gate receipts from its home games varies from those of other members, depending on the size of the home city, the popularity of professional football in the area and competition for spectators offered by other entertainment, including professional soccer. As a result, profits vary from team to team. Indeed as recently as 1978, the last year for which we have records, 2 of the 28 NFL teams suffered losses. In 1977 12 teams experienced losses. Thus, in spite of sharing of some revenues, the financial performance of each team, while related to that of the others, does not, because of the variables in revenues and costs as between member teams, necessarily rise or fall with that of the others. The NFL teams are separate economic entities engaged in a joint venture.

The North American Soccer League ("NASL") was founded in 1968 upon the merger of two pre-existing soccer leagues. Like the NFL, the NASL is an unincorporated association of professional soccer teams whose members are separately owned and operated, and are financially independent. Its *raison d'etre* and the needs of its member teams are essentially the same as those of members of other major professional sports leagues, including the NFL. However, professional soccer is not as mature or lucrative as professional football. Just as was the case with NFL member teams a quarter of a century ago, NASL is struggling to achieve wider popularity and with it greater revenues. Consequently, the risk of investing in an NASL team is considerably greater than that of investing in the NFL.

Soccer was not a widely followed or popular sport when the NASL was founded, and several earlier attempts to put together a professional soccer league failed due to lack of fan interest. The NASL has been the most successful soccer league to date. The district court found that since the NASL was organized "professional soccer has experienced substantial and accelerated growth in fan interest, media following, paid attendance, number of franchises and geographic scope. * * *" With this success NASL teams have become increasingly more effective competitors of the NFL teams. The two sports are somewhat similar. Their seasons substantially overlap. The teams have franchises from their respective leagues in the same locations and frequently use the same stadia. An increasing, although small, percentage of the public are switching their interest as fans and TV viewers from professional football to professional soccer, threatening to reduce revenue which NFL teams derive from gate receipts and TV broadcast rights. Competition between NFL and NASL teams has not only increased on an inter-league basis but also between individual NFL and NASL teams. On the league front both organizations compete for a greater share of finite national and regional TV broadcast and advertising revenues. At the local level NFL teams compete against NASL teams for greater fan support, gate attendance, and local broadcast revenues.

In spite of its success relative to other leagues that have attempted to make soccer a viable competitor, the NASL and its member teams have been, to this point, financially unsuccessful. Last year the teams collectively lost approximately $ 30 million. Individual NASL franchises have been very unstable; for example, since the trial of this case 8 of the 24 NASL teams have folded. Thus the NASL is the weakest of the major professional sports leagues (the NFL, the NASL, the National Basketball Association, the National Hockey League, and Major League Baseball).

Because of the interdependence of professional sports league members and the unique nature of their business, the market for and availability of capital investment is limited. As the district court found, the economic success of each franchise is dependent on the quality of sports competition throughout the league and the economic strength and stability of other league members. Damage to or losses by any league member can adversely affect the stability, success and operations of other members. Aside from willingness to take the risk of investing in a member of a league in which members have for the most part not demonstrated a record of profits, the potential investor must be reasonably compatible with other members of the league, with a sufficient understanding of the nature of the business and the interdependence of ownership to support not only his newly-acquired team but the sports league of which it is a member. As the district court further noted, these conditions have tended to attract individuals or businesses with distinct characteristics as distinguished from the much larger number of financiers of the type prevailing in most business markets. Although, as the district court observed, the boundaries of this "sports ownership capital and skill" market are not as confined as NASL contends and not limited strictly to present major league sports owners, the sources of sports capital are limited by the foregoing conditions and existing sports league owners constitute a significant source. In short, while capital may be fungible in other businesses, it is not fungible in the business of producing major league professional sports. Regardless of the risk involved in the venture, which may vary greatly from league to league, league members look not merely for money but for a compatible fellow owner, preferably having entrepreneurial sports skill, with whom the other members can operate their joint business enterprise. League members recognize, for example, that if the owner of one team allowed it to deteriorate to the point where it usually lost every game, attendance at games in which that team was playing would fall precipitously, hurting not just that team, but every other team that played it during the season. In view of this business interdependence team owners, through their leagues, are careful about whom they allow to purchase a team in their league and leagues invariably require that the sale of a franchise be approved by a majority of team owners rather than by the selling owner alone.

For these reasons individuals with experience in owning and operating sports teams tend to be the most sought-after potential owners. Indeed, the NFL made clear that it values proven experience in a potential owner. When in 1974 it expanded by 2 teams, 5 of the 8 prospective owners it considered seriously had professional sports team ownership experience; a sixth had experience in non-team sports. The two ownership groups to whom it awarded franchises included individuals with prior professional sports team ownership experience, and the NFL did not award the franchises to the highest bidder, a procedure that would have provided the most immediate financial reward to its owners.

The attractiveness of existing owners of major sports teams as sources of potential capital is further evidenced by the large number of members of major sports leagues who control or own substantial interests in members of other leagues. The record reveals some 110 instances of cross-ownership and some 238 individuals or corporations having a 10% or greater interest in other teams. Over the last 13 years there have been 16 cross-ownerships between NFL and NASL teams. Indeed, since the NASL was organized Lamar Hunt, the owner of the NFL's Kansas City Chiefs, has been involved as an NASL team owner, first of the Dallas Tornado team, then of the Tampa Bay team, and as a promoter of NASL. Since 1975 Elizabeth Robbie, the wife of the NFL's Miami Dolphins owner Joseph Robbie, has been the majority owner of the NASL's Fort Lauderdale franchise. Mr. Robbie has apparently been the actual operator of the soccer team as well as the football team. In the words of the district court, these cross-owners have provided the NASL with an "important element of stability," 465 F. Supp. at 669, which led to professional soccer's becoming a major league sport, and withdrawal of their interests "would have a significantly adverse effect on the *NASL*," 505 F. Supp. at 668.

Beginning in the 1950s NFL commissioners had a policy against a team owner maintaining a controlling interest in a team of a competing league, which was first put in writing by the owners themselves in January 1967, at a time when 12 owners of old NFL or AFL teams (the leagues had by then agreed to merge to form the present NFL) were involved in the formation of the predecessors of the NASL. The resolution, which was approved at an owners' meeting, called for the drafting of amendments to the NFL constitution and by-laws prohibiting cross-ownership, but nothing was ever done to comply with it. In 1972 the NFL owners passed another resolution providing that NFL owners were not to acquire operating control of a team in a competing league. The participants agreed that any member holding such a controlling interest would make a "best effort" to dispose of it.

For the next five years the NFL members repeatedly passed the same resolution at meetings, except through inadvertence in 1975. During this period the NASL, which had come close to disbanding in 1968, grew more successful, due in no small part to the efforts of Hunt, who worked tirelessly to promote professional soccer and raise capital for it. NFL owners began to feel competition from the NASL. Leonard Tose, the owner of the Philadelphia Eagles, became one of the most vocal opponents of Hunt's soccer holdings. At approximately the same time the NASL Philadelphia Atoms were leading that league in attendance, and Tose's NFL football team, the Philadelphia Eagles, was losing money. (The Eagles lost money from at least 1969 to 1974, and in 1976 and 1977.) Tose became particularly incensed when Hunt began doing promotional work for the NASL. For example, at one NFL owners' meeting Tose denounced Hunt for allegedly stating in an interview that soccer is the sport of the future. Tose later explained one of the reasons for his concern, stating, "in my view when our truck drivers [fans] have X number of dollars to spend for entertainment in sport, and [sic] any dollar that they spend in another sport could affect what they spend for football." In short, Mr. Tose's business, the NFL Philadelphia Eagles, was suffering from the competition from the NASL Philadelphia Atoms.

Tose was not the only NFL owner upset by competition from a soccer league team. Max Winter, the owner of the NFL's Minnesota Vikings, became concerned about competition from the Minnesota Kicks, an NASL member. As Tose had done, Winter complained about Hunt's NASL soccer team interest at NFL owners' meetings. At his deposition he stated, "I think I said it to the league, in the room, that I object very much that an American Football Conference President [i.e., Hunt] is going to Minneapolis to advance soccer, introduce soccer in my city." Winter discussed Hunt's activities with Tose, stating that he felt that the Kicks "are hurting us, the sports dollar, that they are drawing very well, that we are losing ground as far as media exposure, fan participation. [It g]enerally hurts us."

Finally in 1978 the NFL owners moved to take strong action against Hunt and Robbie. An amendment to the NFL by-laws was proposed that would require both to divest their soccer holdings if they wished to continue to own an NFL team. The proposed amendment, which was to have been voted on at an October 1978 NFL owners' meeting, would also have prevented all majority owners, certain minority owners, officers and directors of NFL teams, and certain relatives of such persons from owning any interest in a team in a "major team sport." * * *

On September 28, 1978, the NASL and various of its members commenced this action by serving the NFL with a complaint and an order to show cause why it should not be preliminarily enjoined from adopting the proposed amendment. On February 21, 1979, after hearing oral argument, Judge Haight issued a preliminary injunction prohibiting the enactment of the amendment. The judge found that the NASL would be irreparably injured if the NFL were allowed to adopt the amendment, that there were serious questions going to the merits, and that the balance of the hardships tipped in favor of the NASL. * * * The NFL did not appeal the injunction.

A lengthy trial followed, and on November 17, 1980, Judge Haight issued his decision. * * * Although he found that the purpose and impact of the NFL cross-ownership ban was to suppress competition in interstate commerce on the part of NASL and its members, he denied relief on the ground that in competing against NASL and its members the NFL and its members must be regarded as a "single economic entity," rendering §1 of the Sherman Act inapplicable for the reason that it is limited to a plurality of actors. Recognizing that individual NFL teams compete with individual NASL teams for the consumer's dollar in their respective localities, the district court nevertheless concluded that this NFL team-member versus NASL team-member competition is subsumed in league versus league competition in the general entertainment market, which he described as "the primary economic competition in professional sports," stating that in all relevant markets the competition is "between two single economic entities uncomplicated by any relevant competition between the member clubs of a league." * * * Decisions rejecting sports leagues' contentions that they should be treated as "single economic entities" were distinguished on the ground that they involved different types of markets in which the members of a sport league were competing individually against each other (e.g., for players' services, hiring availability and terms, reserve clauses, college drafts, etc.), whereas here the court considered them to act monolithically as one joint enterprise. Supreme Court decisions in non-sports antitrust cases rejecting arguments that business trade restraints were justified on the ground that two or more participants had acted as a joint venture or "single business entity," e.g., *Timken Roller Bearing Co. v. United States*, 341 U.S. 593 (1951), and *Perma Life Mufflers, Inc. v. International Parts Corp.*, 392 U.S. 134 (1968), were distinguished on the ground those combinations, unlike sports leagues, were unnecessary to the successful production and marketing of the product involved, the district judge here stating, "No interdependence or joint action is necessary to make a bearing or a muffler." 505 F. Supp. at 686. Because individual teams acting alone could not produce "Pro Football," Judge Haight reasoned, the combination of those teams through the NFL was justified by its "dominant purpose," the production of the league sport, and was legal under *Timken* and *Perma Life*. For the same reason the judge refused to apply the rule of reason as articulated in *National Society of Professional Engineers v. United States*, 435 U.S. 679 (1978).

Judge Haight further concluded that, while a sports ownership capital market may exist as a submarket of the broad capital funds market, the NASL and its members had failed to prove that the submarket was, as claimed by them, limited to present owners of major sports league teams. He declined to make any finding as to the scope of the submarket and whether the NFL cross-ownership ban foreclosed NASL teams from access to any significant share of it or restrained them from competing against NFL teams in the entertainment market. Instead he chose to rest his decision on the "single economic entity" theory. * * *

DISCUSSION

The first issue is whether §1 of the Sherman Act, which prohibits "[e]very contract, combination in the form of trust or otherwise, or conspiracy, in restraint of trade or commerce among the several States, with foreign nations * * *" applies to the cross-ownership ban adopted by NFL and its members. The NFL contends, and the district court held, that §1 does not apply for the reason that the NFL acted as a "single economic entity" and not as a combination or conspiracy within the meaning of that law. We disagree. As the Supreme Court long ago recognized, the Sherman Act by its terms applies to "every" combination or agreement concerning trade, not just certain types. *Chicago Board of Trade v. United States*, 246 U.S. 231, 238 (1918). The theory that a combination of actors can gain exemption from §1 of the Sherman Act by acting as a "joint venture" has repeatedly been rejected by the Supreme Court and the Sherman Act has been held applicable to professional sports teams by numerous lesser federal courts. * * * We are unpersuaded by the efforts of the district judge to distinguish these cases from the present one. Although many involved player relations or playing sites, which affect competition between member teams, at least one raised issues between leagues. In *Radovich v. National Football League*, * * * the issue was whether an NFL boycott of a player who had previously accepted employment with a competing pro football league, the All America Conference, violated §1 of the Sherman Act. The Court held in *Radovich* that it did, even though that boycott might not, in the words of the district court, "implicate [or] impinge[ ] upon competition between member clubs." * * *

The characterization of NFL as a single economic entity does not exempt from the Sherman Act an agreement between its members to restrain competition. To tolerate such a loophole would permit league members to escape antitrust responsibility for any restraint entered into by them that would benefit their league or enhance their ability to compete even though the benefit would be outweighed by its anticompetitive effects. Moreover, the restraint might be one adopted more for the protection of individual league members from competition than to help the league. For instance, the cross-ownership ban in the present case is not aimed merely at protecting the NFL as a league or "single economic entity" from competition from the NASL as a league. Its objective also is to shield certain individual NFL member teams as discrete economic entities from competition in their respective home territories on the part of individual NASL teams that are gaining economic strength in those localities, threatening the revenues of such individual teams as the NFL Philadelphia Eagles, owned by Leonard Tose, because of competition by the NASL's Philadelphia team, and the revenues of the NFL Minnesota Vikings because of competition by the successful NASL Minnesota Kicks. The NFL members have combined to protect and restrain not only leagues but individual teams. The sound and more just procedure is to judge the legality of such restraints according to well-recognized standards of our antitrust laws rather than permit their exemption on the ground that since they in some measure strengthen the league competitively as a "single economic entity," the combination's anticompetitive effects must be disregarded.

Having concluded that §1 of the Sherman Act is applicable, we next must decide whether the NFL teams' cross-ownership ban violates that statute. The plaintiffs, characterizing the ban as a "group boycott" and "concerted refusal to deal," contend that the conduct is a species of the patently pernicious anticompetitive kind that must be condemned as per se unlawful without further proof. * * * We disagree.

Combinations or agreements are per se violations of the Sherman Act only if they are so "plainly anticompetitive," *National Society of Professional Engineers v. United States*, 435 U.S. 679, 692 (1978), and so lacking in any "redeeming virtue," *Northern Pac. R. Co. v. United States*, 356 U.S. 1, 5 (1958), that "because of [their] unquestionably anticompetitive effects," *United States v. United States Gypsum Co.*, 438 U.S. 422, 440 (1978), "they are conclusively presumed illegal without further examination under the rule of reason generally applied in Sherman Act cases," *Broadcast Music, Inc. v. CBS*, 441 U.S. 1, 8 (1979). Examples are agreements between competitors fixing prices at which they will sell their competing products, limiting their respective marketing areas, or restricting customers to whom their products will be sold or from whom they will be purchased. The cross-ownership ban, though anticompetitive, does not meet these stringent conditions. * * *

Because agreements between members of a joint venture can under some circumstances have legitimate purposes as well as anticompetitive effects, they are subject to scrutiny under the rule of reason. * * *

I

In this case, the procompetitive effect claimed by the defendants for the cross-ownership ban is that the ban is necessary for the NFL owners to compete efficiently in the professional sports league market. On the other hand, the voluminous trial record discloses that the NFL's cross-ownership ban would foreclose NASL's teams from continued enjoyment of and access to a significant segment of the market supply of sports capital and skill, thereby restraining at least some NASL teams from competing effectively against NFL teams for fan support and TV revenues. Any resulting restraint would benefit not merely the NFL as a league but those NFL teams that would be otherwise weakened individually and disproportionally (as compared with other NFL teams) by competing NASL teams. This evidence of the defendants' anticompetitive purpose is relevant in judging its potential anticompetitive effect. * * *

NFL argues that there is no such thing as a limited market or submarket for sports capital and skill, only a general market in which "capital is fungible." It further urges that in this much larger market the effect of the cross-ownership ban would be de minimis, working no appreciable anticompetitive restraint on NASL teams, and that their difficulty in attracting capital is attributable to the poor financial outlook of their franchises rather than to the ban.[6] * * *

Since we have rejected the "single economic theory" in the context of this case, it is necessary to determine whether the record discloses a separate market for sports capital and skill. We are satisfied that it does. * * *

Because of the economic interdependence of major league team owners and the requirement that any sale be approved by a majority of the league members, an owner may in practice sell his franchise only to a relatively narrow group of eligible purchasers, not to any financier.[7] The potential investor must measure up to a profile having certain characteristics. Moreover, on the supply side of the sports capital market the number of investors willing to purchase an interest in a franchise is sharply limited by the high risk, the need for active involvement in management, the significant exposure to publicity that may turn out to be negative, and the dependence on the drawing power and financial success of the other members of the league. The record thus reveals a market which,

---

6. The NFL claims that no special skills are required to run a major league sports team.

7. For example, Steve Rosenbloom, the son of the former owner of the NFL's Baltimore Colts, said of the family's experience in attempting to sell the Colts:

> "As I say from experience, it is a small market, because it was no secret we might have sold the thing and that we were talking to people. A few people came around, and those that came around never came up with a concrete proposal. I would take that experience and say, theoretically or practically, or realistically, there didn't seem to be a large market for it."

while not limited to existing or potential major sports team owners, is relatively limited in scope and is only a small fraction of the total capital funds market. The evidence further reveals that in this sports capital and skill market owners of major professional sports teams constitute a significant portion. Indeed the existence of such a submarket and the importance of the function of existing team owners as sources of capital in that market are implicitly recognized by the defendants' proven intent in adopting the cross-ownership ban. If they believed, as NFL now argues, that all sources of capital were fungible substitutes for investment in NASL sports teams and that the ban would not significantly foreclose the supply of sports capital, they would hardly have gone to the trouble of adopting it. Unless the ban has procompetitive effects outweighing its clear restraint on competition, therefore, it is prohibited by §1 of the Sherman Act. That law does not require proof of the precise boundaries of the sports capital market or the exact percentage foreclosed; it is sufficient to establish, as was done here, the general outlines of a separate submarket of the capital market and that the foreclosed portion of it was likely to be significant.

NFL argues that the anticompetitive effects of the ban would be outweighed by various procompetitive effects. First it contends that the ban assures it of the undivided loyalty of its team owners in competing effectively against the NASL in the sale of tickets and broadcasting rights, and that cross-ownership might lead NFL cross-owners to soften their demands in favor of their NASL team interests. We do not question the importance of obtaining the loyalty of partners in promoting a common business venture, even if this may have some anticompetitive effect. But in the undisputed circumstances here the enormous financial success of the NFL league despite long-existing cross-ownership by some members of NASL teams demonstrates that there is no market necessity or threat of disloyalty by cross-owners which would justify the ban. Moreover, the NFL was required to come forward with proof that any legitimate purposes could not be achieved through less restrictive means. This it has failed to do. The NFL, for instance, has shown no reason why it could not remedy any conflict of interest arising out of NFL-NASL competition for broadcast rights by removing cross-owners from its broadcast rights negotiating committee.

For the same reasons we reject NFL's argument that the ban is necessary to prevent disclosure by NFL cross-owners of confidential information to NASL competitors. No evidence of the type of information characterized as "confidential" is supplied. Nor is there any showing that the NFL could not be protected against unauthorized disclosure by less restrictive means. Indeed, despite the existence of NFL cross-owners for some years there is no evidence that they have abused confidentiality or that the NFL has found it necessary to adopt confidentiality rules or sanctions. Similarly, there is no evidence that cross-ownership has subjected the personnel and resources of NFL cross-owners to conflicting or excessive demands. On the contrary, successful NFL team owners have been involved in ownership and operation of other outside businesses despite their equal potential for demands on the owners' time and resources. Moreover, a ban on cross-ownership would not insure that NFL team owners would devote any greater level of their resources to team operations than they otherwise would.

Although there may be some merit in NFL's contentions that the ban would prevent dilution of the good will it has developed, that it would avoid any disruption of NFL operations because of disputes between its owners or cross-owners, or that it would prevent possible inter-league collusion in violation of the antitrust laws, these procompetitive effects are not substantial and are clearly outweighed by its anticompetitive purpose and effect. Its net effect is substantially to restrain competition, not merely competitors. It therefore violates the rule of reason. * * *

We reverse the order granting judgment of the NFL and remand with directions to enter a permanent injunction prohibiting the ban. Because the district court's decision made it unnecessary for it to consider the issue of damages, we remand for consideration of that issue. We affirm the dismissal of NFL's counterclaim requesting an injunction against cross-ownership.

Notes and Questions

1. The Second Circuit directed the district court to "enter a permanent injunction prohibiting the [NFL's cross-ownership] ban." Nevertheless, the position of the NFL remains that the decision only held the ban unlawful when applied to prevent investment in the NASL. The NFL advises owners that the cross-ownership ban "was held invalid as to the North American Soccer League, but the policy continues to apply to the major league sports." Despite that aggressive interpretation of the court's opinion, the NFL decided not to apply the cross-ownership ban to prevent NFL owners from investing in the next major United States professional soccer league—Major League Soccer ("MLS"). Once again, Lamar Hunt—the moving force behind World Championship Tennis (*see* the *Volvo* case in Chapter 10), the American Football League (*see AFL v. NFL*, in this chapter), and the North American Soccer League—has played a central role in the development of MLS and owned and operated the Kansas City Wizards and the Columbus Crew. Another NFL owner, Bob Kraft (owner of the New England Patriots and Foxboro Stadium), is an owner of the MLS and the operator of the New England Revolution in that league. If the NFL sought to enforce the cross-ownership ban against Hunt and Kraft with respect to their investments and involvement in MLS, would they be forced to relitigate the *NASL v. NFL* case issues, or would that case establish, by collateral estoppel and/or principles of *res judicata*, the illegality of the cross-ownership ban as applied to the MLS, the leading professional soccer league in the United States?

2. Outside the context of professional soccer, should an owner of an NFL team and a team in another major sport have to relitigate the *NASL v. NFL* issues? If so, would an NFL owner who sought to become the owner of a Major League Baseball, National Basketball Association, or National Hockey League team have to prove that the cross-ownership ban is likely to compromise the economic viability of the "other" league? Owners of professional football teams (especially those individuals who own their stadiums) are likely to be interested in soccer teams because they can usually utilize the same facilities (*e.g.*, Bob Kraft's MLS New England Revolution share Kraft's Foxboro Stadium with the New England Patriots). Owners of football stadia are less likely to be important to leagues that play in smaller arenas (explaining the common ownership of a number of NHL and NBA teams, which often share a single arena). Therefore, NFL owners have not historically played a major role in the NHL or NBA. Given the recent prosperity of the NBA and the self-inflicted problems facing the NHL, would it be possible for a potential cross-owner to show any adverse effect of the NFL ban on the NBA or NHL? Would an antitrust challenge survive? How could the NHL prove that damage was caused by a ban when it survived and prospered without NFL owners and was almost crippled by labor problems and its misguided strategy of massive expansion into U.S. sunbelt cities?

3. While the NFL never attempted to apply the cross-ownership ban to Hunt's and Kraft's MLS ownership, the league has never given a general waiver of the ban with respect to ownership of teams in the NBA, NHL, or Major League Baseball. At the same time, the ban has not been enforced consistently. For example, Edward Debartolo, Jr.

purchased the San Francisco 49ers in 1977, at a time when his father, Edward Debartolo, Sr., owned the NHL Pittsburgh Penguins. *See* DAVID HARRIS, *The League—The Rise and Decline of the NFL* 278–80 (1986). This situation presented a family conflict similar to one posed by the Robbie family interests in the Miami Dolphins and the NASL Fort Lauderdale Strikers. Of more concern to the league, however, was Ed Sr.'s subsequent purchase of the USFL Pittsburgh Maulers. During numerous meetings, NFL owners agreed that the family ownership of both the 49ers and the Maulers was a conflict of interest in violation of the league rule; however, the uncertainty regarding the legality of such a rule after the *NASL* case and the *Los Angeles Memorial Coliseum Comm'n* litigation prevented the league from taking action. *Id.* at 554–55. The fact that the two teams were owned by separate members of the same family technically meant that there was no violation of the specific terms of the cross-ownership rule. However, given the close father-son relationship between Ed Sr. and Ed Jr. and the fact that Ed Sr.'s company guaranteed the loan which allowed Ed Jr. to purchase the 49ers, the league did not hesitate to assert that the situation amounted to a conflict of interest which violated at least the spirit of the cross-ownership rule. Ultimately, this conflict was resolved when Ed Jr. agreed to do the following: (1) withdraw the 49ers from the scouting combine shared with several other teams; (2) refrain from signing any Pittsburgh Mauler players; (3) absent himself from NFL discussions of the USFL; and (4) decline to participate on any NFL committees. *Id.* at 612. Does cross-ownership of a team in the same sport raise more substantial concerns than cross-ownership of a team in a different league? Could owning two teams, one in each football league, give that owner a competitive advantage? For example, a player drafted by both the Maulers and the 49ers would have had difficulty playing one team against the other during contract negotiations. If the Maulers and 49ers had drafted the same players, they could have kept their team salaries down through collusion between the Maulers' and 49ers' personnel who negotiated the players' contracts. In addition, while the NFL scouting combine information would have been valueless to an NHL or NASL team, it would have been of great benefit to a USFL team.

4. A more recent example of the NFL's failure to enforce the ban occurred in March, 1994, when the NFL permitted Wayne Huizenga, Blockbuster Video magnate and owner of the Florida Marlins baseball team and the Florida Panthers hockey franchise, to purchase a controlling share of the Miami Dolphins. At that time, the NFL approved Huizenga's purchase conditionally. Huizenga and the NFL agreed that Huizenga could own the Dolphins until June 1, 1996 (extended to June 1, 1997 to allow the NFL time to "study" the issue). Huizenga agreed to place his Dolphins stock in the hands of a trustee during that "interim study period" and gave the NFL the power to order the trustee to sell the stock if the NFL concluded, at the end of that interim period, that the ban should be enforced. *See* Eric Conrad, *NFL Puts Trust in Huizenga*, FORT LAUDERDALE SUN-SENTINEL, Mar. 24, 1994, at 1C. Huizenga was required to sign a release, waiving his right to sue to challenge the cross-ownership ban in the event that the NFL decided to enforce it against him at the end of the interim period. The enforceability of that release was never tested, because in March, 1997, by a vote of 24-5, with one abstention, the NFL passed a resolution permitting cross-ownership, as long as the NFL owner only owns sports franchises in the same home territory as his NFL team or in territories not occupied by an NFL franchise and not otherwise reserved as "home territories owned by the NFL" (presently territories recently vacated by relocating teams are owned by the NFL. The NFL's change in the cross-ownership rules was designed to permit Huizenga to maintain his NFL ownership and to pave the way for the acquisition of the Seattle

Seahawks by Paul Allen, the owner of the NBA's Portland Trail Blazers. *See generally* Tony Grossi, *NFL Changes Policy; New Rule Allows Cross-Ownership*, THE PLAIN DEALER, Mar. 12, 1997, at 1D. Allen, the co-founder with Bill Gates of computer software maker Microsoft, purchased an exclusive option to purchase the Seahawks, but he conditioned his exercise of the option upon public funding for a new football stadium. The NFL had been concerned that Allen's failure to purchase the Seahawks might result in their relocation out of the Seattle area. Huizenga's other teams (Major League Baseball's Florida Marlins and the NHL's Florida Panthers) are located within the Dolphins' home territory, and there is no NFL team in Portland. Does the NFL's "relaxed" approach to Huizenga's multiple ownership and eventual approval of certain cross-ownership signal a surrender to the *NASL v. NFL* conclusions regarding the potential illegality of cross-ownership bans? How do the "Huizenga/Allen modifications" to the cross-ownership ban affect the likelihood that it would withstand future antitrust scrutiny if applied to block an NFL owner from owning an interest in a team in Major League Baseball, the NHL, or the NBA?

5. Assume hypothetically that the owner of the Seattle Seahawks informs you that he has put his team up for sale and has been contacted by the following potential purchasers: (a) Peter Angelos, the principal owner of Major League Baseball's Baltimore Orioles; (b) George Steinbrenner, the controversial owner of Major League Baseball's New York Yankees; and (c) the CEO of a corporation that owns the NHL's Ducks of Anaheim, California. Assume that the Seahawks' owner advises you that Angelos, Steinbrenner, and the CEO of the NHL corporate owner have each offered over $250 million for the Seahawks. Assume further that the next best offer the Seahawks' owner has received, less than $200 million, was made by Paul Allen, a potential purchaser who does not implicate the NFL's cross-ownership ban (because there is no NFL team in Portland, the cross-ownership ban does not apply). How would you analyze the situation and what advice would you give the Seahawks' owner? Is the ban enforceable at all, or as applied to these three potential owners? Does the analysis vary among the three potential cross-owners?

6. The court's recitation of the history of the NFL's cross-ownership policies noted that the NFL was about to expand the ban to "prevent[] all majority owners, certain minority owners, officers and directors of NFL teams," and certain relatives of such persons from owning any interest in a team in a "major team sport." This event triggered the NASL's lawsuit. Similarly, in the *Volvo* case included in Chapter 10, the MIPTC was about to enact its "Special Event Rule," which would have forced the thousands of people associated with Grand Prix events (all "owners, agents, consultants, and associates") to agree not to "promote" any competing events. That rule would have forced ProServ, IMC, Volvo, and others to choose between any association with the events in the dominant circuit and an association with any competing event. The breadth of both the proposed NFL rule and the proposed MIPTC rule strongly suggests that their purpose was not to protect legitimate interests of the league or circuit, but rather was to leverage the dominant league or circuit's large sphere of influence to foreclose as many people as possible from "owning any interest in," or "promoting," the rival. Once the league or circuit has manifested an intent to harm the rival, is it extremely difficult to argue that the market is so broad that the dominant league or circuit's efforts could not have a deleterious effect? If the NFL owners were simply vengeful, and wanted to hurt the NASL, but a careful analysis revealed that they simply did not have power over any relevant market and that Lamar Hunt and Joe Robbie could easily be replaced as owners, should the NFL's conduct be held lawful? If the conduct does not violate the antitrust laws under those circumstances, are there other legal theories that might be used to challenge the same conduct?

7. If the NFL owners asked you to draft cross-ownership rules and procedures that would both prevent cross-ownership and withstand antitrust scrutiny, what would you recommend?

Chapter 12

Antitrust and Sports: Intra-League Restraints Limitations on Ownership, League Membership, Sale of Broadcast and Sponsorship Rights and Franchise Relocation

I. Introduction

Earlier in this text we addressed the potential conflicts that develop between a team's desire to promote itself in the best way possible and its obligation to the rest of the league. The last case in the previous chapter, *North American Soccer League v. National Football League*, while primarily involving an inter-league dispute, arose when the NFL was preparing to enforce an internal league rule prohibiting NFL owners from investing in teams in other major sports leagues. The NFL contended that Joe Robbie and Lamar Hunt were neglecting and even undermining their collective obligations to the NFL by expending their energies to promote the North American Soccer League at the expense of their fellow NFL owners. Similarly, the *Volvo* case in Chapter 10, which primarily focused on player restraints imposed by the dominant circuit of tennis events, involved an intra-circuit dispute, an effort by the Grand Prix to regulate and restrict the businesses and competitive efforts of virtually everyone associated with the circuit.

Two other areas in which the potential conflict between an owner's self-interest and the needs of the league become most evident are a team decision to relocate its franchise or an owner's decision to sell his or her operations. These issues have generated a considerable amount of controversy and major antitrust litigation, particularly with respect to a league's ability to circumscribe a team's franchise relocation decision. *See, e.g., Los Angeles Memorial Coliseum Comm'n v. National Football League* and *National Basketball Association v. SDC Basketball Club, Inc.*, below. Derivative questions have also surfaced, including whether a league can prevent a club owner from selling his franchise to a foreign-based person or corporation, whether a club leaving a city is vulnerable to lawsuits by the abandoned city or stadium owner, and whether the league can prohibit the sale of ownership interests in its teams to publicly-held corporations or to the public through offerings of publicly traded stock. *See, e.g., Sullivan v. National Football League*, below.

This chapter will also address other questions relating to a league's ability to restrict its membership, for example, limiting sales of local television rights or licensing of team name and logos to sponsors. *See Chicago Pro Sports Limited Partnership v. National Basketball Association*, below. In effect, while certain business decisions are generally left to the judgment of the individual team owners, those decisions are generally reviewed or at least reviewable by the overall league. What standards can or should the league apply in reviewing its team owners' business decisions? What recourse is available to team owners when the league seeks to overrule their decisions or when the league enacts new rules that increase revenue sharing or circumscribe independent team decisionmaking? *See generally* Matthew J. Mitten and Bruce W. Burton, *Professional Sports Franchise Relocations from Private Law and Public Law Perspectives: Balancing Marketplace Competition, League Autonomy, and the Need for a Level Playing Field*, 56 MD. L. REV. 57 (1997); John K Harris, Jr., *Fiduciary Duties of Professional Team Sports Franchise Owners*, 2 SETON HALL J. SPORT L. 255 (1992); Daniel B. Rubanowitz, Note, *Who Said 'There Is No Place Like Home?': Franchise Relocation in Professional Sports*, 10 LOY. L.A. ENT. L. J. 163 (1990); Kenneth L. Shropshire, *Opportunistic Sports Franchise Relocations: Can Punitive Damages in Actions Based on Contract Strike a Balance?*, 22 LOY. L.A. L. REV. 569 (1989); Daniel S. York, *The Professional Sports Community Protection Act: Congress' Best Response to Raiders?*, 38 HASTINGS L. J. 345 (1987); John Beisner, *Sports Franchise Relocation: Competitive Markets and Taxpayer Protection*, 6 YALE L. & POL'Y REV. 429 (1988); Richard Amoroso, Note, *Controlling Professional Sports Team Relocations: The Oakland Raiders' Antitrust Case and Beyond*, 17 RUTGERS L. J. 283 (1986); Thane N. Rosenbaum, *The Antitrust Implications of Professional Sports Leagues Revisited: Emerging Trends in the Modern Era*, 41 U. MIAMI L. REV. 729 (1987); Charles Gray, *Keeping The Home Team At Home*, 74 CALIF. L. REV. 1329 (1986); James L. Brock, Jr., *A Substantive Test for Sherman Act Plurality: Applications for Professional Sports Leagues*, 52 U. CHI. L. REV. 999 (1985); Christian M. McBurney, Note, *The Legality of Sports Leagues' Restrictive Admissions Practices*, 60 N.Y.U. L. REV. 925 (1985); Gary R. Roberts, *Sports Leagues and The Sherman Act: The Use and Abuse of Section 1 to Regulate Restraints on Intra-League Rivalry*, 32 U.C.L.A. L. REV. 219 (1984); Daniel E. Lazaroff, *The Antitrust Implications of Franchise Relocation Restrictions In Professional Sports*, 53 FORDHAM L. REV. 157 (1984).

II. Franchise Relocation: The Relevant Legal Precedent

Los Angeles Memorial Coliseum Comm'n v. National Football League

726 F.2d 1381 (9th Cir. 1984)

J. BLAINE ANDERSON, Circuit Judge. These appeals involve the hotly contested move by the Oakland Raiders, Ltd. professional football team from Oakland, California, to Los Angeles, California. We review only the liability portion of the bifurcated trial; the damage phase was concluded in May 1983 and is on a separate appeal. After a thorough review of the record and the law, we affirm.

I. FACTS

In 1978, the owner of the Los Angeles Rams, the late Carroll Rosenbloom, decided to locate his team in a new stadium, the "Big A," in Anaheim, California. That left the Los Angeles Coliseum without a major tenant. Officials of the Coliseum then began the search for a new National Football League occupant. They inquired of the League Commissioner, Pete Rozelle, whether an expansion franchise might be located there but were told that at the time it was not possible. They also negotiated with existing teams in the hope that one might leave its home and move to Los Angeles.

The L.A. Coliseum ran into a major obstacle in its attempts to convince a team to move. That obstacle was Rule 4.3 of Article IV of the NFL Constitution. In 1978, Rule 4.3 required unanimous approval of all the 28 teams of the League whenever a team (or in the parlance of the League, a "franchise") seeks to relocate in the home territory of another team. Home territory is defined in Rule 4.1 as

> the city in which [a] club is located and for which it holds a franchise and plays its home games, and includes the surrounding territory to the extent of 75 miles in every direction from the exterior corporate limits of such city.
> * * *

In this case, the L.A. Coliseum was still in the home territory of the Rams.

The Coliseum viewed Rule 4.3 as an unlawful restraint of trade in violation of 1 of the Sherman Act, 15 U.S.C. 1, and brought this action in September of 1978. The district court concluded, however, that no present justiciable controversy existed because no NFL team had committed to moving to Los Angeles. 468 F. Supp. 154 (C.D. Cal. 1979).

The NFL nevertheless saw the Coliseum's suit as a sufficient threat to warrant amending Rule 4.3. In late 1978, the Executive Committee of the NFL, which is comprised of a voting member of each of the 28 teams, met and changed the rule to require only three-quarters approval by the members of the League for a move into another team's home territory.

Soon thereafter, Al Davis, managing general partner of the Oakland Raiders franchise, stepped into view. His lease with the Oakland Coliseum had expired in 1978. He believed the facility needed substantial improvement and he was unable to persuade the Oakland officials to agree to his terms. He instead turned to the Los Angeles Coliseum.

Davis and the L.A. Coliseum officials began to discuss the possibility of relocating the Raiders to Los Angeles in 1979. In January, 1980, the L.A. Coliseum believed an agreement with Davis was imminent and reactivated its lawsuit against the NFL, seeking a preliminary injunction to enjoin the League from preventing the Raiders' move. The district court granted the injunction, 484 F. Supp. 1274 (C.D. Cal. 1980), but this court reversed, finding that an adequate probability of irreparable injury had not been shown. 634 F.2d 1197 (9th Cir. 1980).

On March 1, 1980, Al Davis and the Coliseum signed a "memorandum of agreement" outlining the terms of the Raiders' relocation in Los Angeles. At an NFL meeting on March 3, 1980, Davis announced his intentions. In response, the League brought a contract action in state court, obtaining an injunction preventing the move. In the meantime, the City of Oakland brought its much-publicized eminent domain action against the Raiders in its effort to keep the team in its original home. The NFL contract action was stayed pending the outcome of this litigation, but the eminent domain action is still being prosecuted in the California courts.

Over Davis' objection that Rule 4.3 is illegal under the antitrust laws, the NFL teams voted on March 10, 1980, 22 0 against the move, with five teams abstaining. That vote did not meet the new Rule 4.3's requirement of three-quarters approval.

The Los Angeles Memorial Coliseum Commission then renewed its action against the NFL and each member club. The Oakland-Alameda County Coliseum, Inc., was permitted to intervene. The Oakland Raiders cross-claimed against the NFL and is currently aligned as a party plaintiff.

The action was first tried in 1981, but resulted in a hung jury and mistrial. A second trial was conducted, with strict constraints on trial time. The court was asked to determine if the NFL was a "single business entity" and as such incapable of combining or conspiring in restraint of trade. Referring to the reasoning in its opinion written for the trial, 519 F. Supp. 581, 585 (C.D. Cal. 1981), the court concluded the League was not a "single entity. * * *"

* * * On May 7, 1982, the jury returned a verdict in favor of the Los Angeles Memorial Coliseum Commission and the Oakland Raiders on the antitrust claim and for the Raiders on their claim of breach of the implied promise of good faith and fair dealing. The court then continued the case to September 20, 1982, to begin the damages trial.

On June 14, 1982, the court issued its judgment on the liability issues, permanently enjoining the NFL and its member clubs from interfering with the transfer of the Oakland Raiders' NFL franchise from the Oakland Coliseum to the Los Angeles Memorial Coliseum. * * *

The damages trial was completed in May 1983 with the jury returning a verdict awarding the Raiders $11.55 million and the Los Angeles Coliseum $4.86 million. These awards were trebled by the district court pursuant to 15 U.S.C. 15. The NFL and the other defendants have appealed. * * * This panel will hear and decide the damage appeals. But, because these appeals were expedited, the damage appeals will be decided in a later opinion after briefing, possible argument, and submission.

II. SHERMAN ACT 1

The jury found that Rule 4.3 violates 1 of the Sherman Act. * * *

In the present case, the district judge found that the unique nature of the business of professional football made application of a *per se* rule inappropriate. * * * The court therefore instructed the jury that it was to decide whether Rule 4.3 was an unreasonable restraint of trade. The parties do not contest the appropriateness of this basic reasonableness inquiry. The NFL, however, raises two arguments against the lower court's judgment finding section 1 liability. First, the NFL contends that it is a single entity incapable of conspiring to restrain trade under section 1. Second, it insists that Rule 4.3 is not an unreasonable restraint of trade under section 1.

A. Single Entity

The NFL contends the league structure is in essence a single entity, akin to a partnership or joint venture, precluding application of Sherman Act section 1 which prevents only contracts, combinations or conspiracies in restraint of trade. The Los Angeles Coliseum and Raiders reject this position and assert the League is composed of 28 separate legal entities which act independently.

The district court directed a verdict for plaintiffs on this issue and as a preliminary matter the NFL states the jury should have been allowed to decide the question. * * *

It is true, as the NFL contends, that the nature of an entity and its ability to combine or conspire in violation of 1 is a fact question. * * * It would be reversible error, then, to take the issue from the jury if reasonable minds could differ as to its resolution. * * * Here, however, the material facts are undisputed. How the NFL is organized and the nature and extent of cooperation among the member clubs is a matter of record; the NFL Constitution and Bylaws contain the agreement. Based on the undisputed facts and the law on this subject, the district court correctly decided this issue.

The district court cited three reasons for rejecting the NFL's theory. Initially, the court recognized the logical extension of this argument was to make the League incapable of violating Sherman Act 1 in every other subject restriction yet courts have held the League violated 1 in other areas. * * * Secondly, other organizations have been found to violate 1 though their product was "just as unitary * * * and requires the same kind of cooperation from the organization's members. * * *" Finally, the district court considered the argument to be based upon the false premise that the individual NFL "clubs are not separate business entities whose products have an independent value. * * *" We agree with this reasoning.

NFL rules have been found to violate 1 in other contexts. Most recently, the Second Circuit analyzed the NFL's rule preventing its member-owners from having ownership interests in other professional sports clubs. * * * It recognized the cooperation necessary among league members, even characterizing the NFL as a joint venture, but nonetheless applied rule of reason analysis and found the cross-ownership rule violated 1. Other courts have held the League rules governing player contracts violate 1 of the Sherman Act. * * * As noted by the Second Circuit in *Soccer League*, a finding of single entity status would immunize the NFL from 1 scrutiny. * * *

* * * [T]his circuit has found the threshold requirement of concerted activity missing among "multiple corporations operated as a single entity" when "corporate policies are set by one individual or by a parent corporation. * * *" The facts make it clear the NFL does not fit within this exception. While the NFL clubs have certain common purposes, they do not operate as a single entity. NFL policies are not set by one individual or parent corporation, but by the separate teams acting jointly.

It is true the NFL clubs must cooperate to a large extent in their endeavor in producing a "product" the NFL season culminating in the Super Bowl. The necessity that otherwise independent businesses cooperate has not, however, sufficed to preclude scrutiny under 1 of the Sherman Act. * * *

* * * The League itself is only in very limited respect an identity separate from the individual teams. It is an unincorporated, not-for-profit, "association." It has a New York office run by the Commissioner, Pete Rozelle, who makes day-to-day decisions regarding League operations. Its primary functions are in the areas of scheduling, resolving disputes among players and franchises, supervising officials, discipline and public relations. The decision involved here on territorial divisions is made by the NFL Executive Committee which is comprised of a representative of each club. Even though the individual clubs often act for the common good of the NFL, we must not lose sight of the purpose of the NFL as stated in Article I of its constitution, which is to "promote and foster the primary business of League members." Although the business interests of League members will often coincide with those of the NFL as an entity in itself, that commonality of interest exists in every cartel. * * * [W]e must look behind the label proffered by the defendants to determine the substance of the entity in question. * * *

Our inquiry discloses an association of teams sufficiently independent and competitive with one another to warrant rule of reason scrutiny under 1 of the Sherman Act.

The NFL clubs are, in the words of the district court, "separate business entities whose products have an independent value. * * *" Although a large portion of League revenue, approximately 90%, is divided equally among the teams, profits and losses are not shared, a feature common to partnerships or other "single entities." In fact, profits vary widely despite the sharing of revenue. The disparity in profits can be attributed to independent management policies regarding coaches, players, management personnel, ticket prices, concessions, luxury box seats, as well as franchise location, all of which contribute to fan support and other income sources.

In addition to being independent business entities, the NFL clubs do compete with one another off the field as well as on to acquire players, coaches, and management personnel. In certain areas of the country where two teams operate in close proximity, there is also competition for fan support, local television and local radio revenues, and media space.

These attributes operate to make each team an entity in large part distinct from the NFL. It is true that cooperation is necessary to produce a football game. However, as the district court concluded, this does not mean, "that each club can produce football games only as an NFL member. * * *" This is especially evident in light of the emergence of the United States Football League.

For the foregoing reasons, we affirm the district court's rejection of the NFL's single entity defense. Of course, the singular nature of the NFL will need to be accounted for in discussing the reasonableness of the restriction on team movement, but it is not enough to preclude 1 scrutiny. The NFL's related argument that Rule 4.3 is valid as a restraint ancillary to a joint venture agreement will be discussed in the rule of reason analysis that follows. Contrary to the NFL's apparent belief, the ancillary restraint doctrine is not independent of the rule of reason. * * *

B. Rule of Reason

* * * As elaborated upon by this circuit: "Rule of reason analysis calls for a 'thorough investigation of the industry at issue and a balancing of the arrangement's positive and negative effects on competition.'" * * * This balancing process is not applied, however, until after the plaintiff has shown the challenged conduct restrains competition. * * * To establish a cause of action, plaintiff must prove these elements: "(1) An agreement among two or more persons or distinct business entities; (2) Which is intended to harm or unreasonably restrain competition; (3) And which actually causes injury to competition. * * *"

Our rejection of the NFL's single entity defense implicitly recognized the existence of the first element the 28 member clubs have entered an agreement in the form of the NFL Constitution and Bylaws. As will be developed in more detail, we have no doubt the plaintiffs also met their burden of proving the existence of the second element. Rule 4.3 is on its face an agreement to control, if not prevent, competition among the NFL teams through territorial divisions. The third element is more troublesome. It is in this context that we discuss the NFL's ancillary restraint argument. Also, a showing of injury to competition requires "[p]roof that the defendant's activities had an impact upon competition in a relevant market, * * *" proof that "is an absolutely essential element of a rule of reason case. * * *"

Other courts have applied rule of reason analysis to determine the legality of concerted action undertaken by the NFL and for the most part have found such action illegal. * * *

* * * [T]his lawsuit requires us to engage in the difficult task of analyzing the negative and positive effects of a business practice in an industry which does not readily fit into the antitrust context. Section 1 of the Sherman Act was designed to prevent agreements among competitors which eliminate or reduce competition and thereby harm consumers. Yet, as we discussed in the context of the single entity issue, the NFL teams are not true competitors, nor can they be.

The NFL's structure has both horizontal and vertical attributes. * * * On the one hand, it can be viewed simply as an organization of 28 competitors, an example of a simple horizontal arrangement. On the other, and to the extent the NFL can be considered an entity separate from the team owners, a vertical relationship is disclosed. In this sense the owners are distributors of the NFL product, each with its own territorial division. In this context it is clear that the owners have a legitimate interest in protecting the integrity of the League itself. Collective action in areas such as League divisions, scheduling and rules must be allowed, as should other activity that aids in producing the most marketable product attainable. Nevertheless, legitimate collective action should not be construed to allow the owners to extract excess profits. In such a situation the owners would be acting as a classic cartel. Agreement among competitors, *i.e.,* cartels, to fix prices or divide market territories are presumed illegal under 1 because they give competitors the ability to charge unreasonable and arbitrary prices instead of setting prices by virtue of free market forces. * * *

On its face, Rule 4.3 divides markets among the 28 teams, a practice presumed illegal, but, as we have noted, the unique structure of the NFL precludes application of the per se rule. * * * Instead, we must examine Rule 4.3 to determine whether it reasonably serves the legitimate collective concerns of the owners or instead permits them to reap excess profits at the expense of the consuming public.

1. Relevant Market

* * * The claims of the Raiders and the L.A. Coliseum, respectively, present somewhat different market considerations. The Raiders attempted to prove the relevant market consists of NFL football (the product market) in the Southern California area (the geographical market). The NFL argues it competes with all forms of entertainment within the United States, not just Southern California. The L.A. Coliseum claims the relevant market is stadia offering their facilities to NFL teams (the product market) in the United States (the geographic market). The NFL agrees with this geographic market, but argues the product market involves cities competing for all forms of stadium entertainment, including NFL football teams. * * *

To some extent, the NFL itself narrowly defined the relevant market by emphasizing that NFL football is a unique product which can be produced only through the joint efforts of the 28 teams. Don Shula, coach of the Miami Dolphins, underscored this point when he stated that NFL football has a different set of fans than college football.

The evidence from which the jury could have found a narrow pro football product market was balanced, however, with other evidence which tended to show the NFL competes in the first instance with other professional sports, especially those with seasons that overlap with the NFL's. On a broader level, witnesses such as Pete Rozelle and Georgia Frontierre (owner of the L.A. Rams) testified that NFL football competes with other television offerings for network business, as well as other local entertainment for attendance at the games.

In terms of the relevant geographic market, witnesses testified, in particular Al Davis, that NFL teams compete with one another off the field for fan support in those areas where teams operate in close proximity such as New York City-New Jersey, Washington, D.C.-Baltimore and formerly San Francisco-Oakland. * * * Al Davis also testified at length regarding the potential for competition for fan support between the Raiders and the Los Angeles Rams once his team relocated in Los Angeles.

Testimony also adequately described the parameters of the stadia market. On one level, stadia do compete with one another for the tenancy of NFL teams. Such competition is shown by the Rams' move to Anaheim. Carroll Rosenbloom was offered what he considered to be a more lucrative situation at the Big A Stadium, so he left the L.A. Coliseum. In turn, the L.A. Coliseum sought to lure existing NFL teams to Los Angeles. Competition between the L.A. Coliseum and the Oakland Coliseum for the tenancy of the Raiders resulted.

It is true, as the NFL argues, that competition among stadia for the tenancy of professional football teams is presently limited. It is limited, however, because of the operation of Rule 4.3. Prior to this lawsuit, most teams were allowed to relocate only within their home territory. That is why Carroll Rosenbloom could move his team to Anaheim. This is not to say the potential for competition did not previously exist. There was evidence to the effect that the NFL in the past remained expressly noncommitted on the question of team movement. This was done to give owners a bargaining edge when they were renegotiating leases with their respective stadia. The owner could threaten a move if the lease terms were not made more favorable.

The NFL claims that it is places, not particular stadia, that compete for NFL teams. This is true to a point because the NFL grants franchises to locales (generally a city and a 75 mile radius extending from its boundary). It is the individual stadia, however, which are most directly impacted by the restrictions on team movement. A stadium is a distinct economic entity and a territory is not.

It is also undoubtedly true, as the NFL contends, that stadia attempt to contract with a variety of forms of entertainment for exhibition in their facilities. In the case of the L.A. Coliseum, this includes college football, concerts, motorcycle races and the like. An NFL football team, however, is an especially desirable tenant. The L.A. Coliseum, for example, had received the highest rent from the Rams when they played there. We find that this evidence taken as a whole provided the jury with an adequate basis on which to judge the reasonableness of Rule 4.3 both as it affected competition among NFL teams and among stadia.

We conclude with one additional observation. In the context of this case in particular, we believe that market evidence, while important, should not become an end in itself. Here the exceptional nature of the industry makes precise market definition especially difficult. * * * [T]he critical question is whether the jury could have determined that Rule 4.3 reasonably served the NFL's interest in producing and promoting its product, *i.e.*, competing in the entertainment market, or whether Rule 4.3 harmed competition among the 28 teams to such an extent that any benefits to the League as a whole were outweighed. As we find below, there was ample evidence for the jury to reach the latter conclusion.

2. The History and Purpose of Rule 4.3

The NFL has awarded franchises exclusive territories since the 1930s. In the early days of professional football, numerous franchises failed and many changed location in the hope of achieving economic success. League members saw exclusive territories as a means to aid stability, ensuring the owner who was attempting to establish an NFL team in a particular city that another would not move into the same area, potentially ruining them both.

Rule 4.3 is the result of that concern. Prior to its amendment in 1978, it required unanimous League approval for a move into another team's home territory. That, of course, gave each owner an exclusive territory and he could vote against a move into his territory solely because he was afraid the competition might reduce his revenue. Notably, however, the League constitution required only three-quarters approval for all other moves. The 1978 amendment removed the double-standard, and currently three-quarters approval is required for all moves.

That the purpose of Rule 4.3 was to restrain competition among the 28 teams may seem obvious and it is not surprising the NFL admitted as much at trial. It instead argues that Rule 4.3 serves a variety of legitimate League needs, including ensuring franchise stability. We must keep in mind, however, that the Supreme Court has long rejected the notion that "ruinous competition" can be a defense to a restraint of trade. * * * Conversely, anticompetitive purpose alone is not enough to condemn Rule 4.3. * * * The rule must actually harm competition, and that harm must be evaluated in light of the procompetitive benefits the rule might foster. * * *

3. Ancillary Restraints and the Reasonableness of Rule 4.3

The NFL's primary argument is that it is entitled to judgment notwithstanding the verdict because under the facts and the law, Rule 4.3 is reasonable under the doctrine of ancillary restraints. The NFL's argument is inventive and perhaps it will breathe new life into this little used area of antitrust law, but we reject it for the following reasons.

The common-law ancillary restraint doctrine was, in effect, incorporated into Sherman Act section 1 analysis by Justice Taft in *United States v. Addyston Pipe & Steel Co.*, 85 F. 271 (6th Cir. 1898), *aff'd as modified*, 175 U.S. 211 (1899). * * * Most often discussed in the area of covenants not to compete, the doctrine teaches that some agreements which restrain competition may be valid if they are "subordinate and collateral to another legitimate transaction and necessary to make that transaction effective. * * *"

Generally, the effect of a finding of ancillarity is to "remove the *per se* label from restraints otherwise falling within that category. * * *" We assume, with no reason to doubt, that the agreement creating the NFL is valid and the territorial divisions therein are ancillary to its main purpose of producing NFL football. The ancillary restraint must then be tested under the rule of reason, * * * the relevance of ancillarity being it "increases the probability that the restraint will be found reasonable. * * *"

The competitive harms of Rule 4.3 are plain. * * * The harm from Rule 4.3 is especially acute in this case because it prevents a move by a team into another existing team's market. If the transfer is upheld, direct competition between the Rams and Raiders would presumably ensue to the benefit of all who consume the NFL product in the Los Angeles area.

The NFL argues, however, that territorial allocations are inherent in an agreement among joint venturers to produce a product. * * * We agree that the nature of NFL football requires some territorial restrictions in order both to encourage participation in the venture and to secure each venturer the legitimate fruits of that participation.

Rule 4.3 aids the League, the NFL claims, in determining its overall geographical scope, regional balance and coverage of major and minor markets. Exclusive territories aid new franchises in achieving financial stability, which protects the large initial investment an owner must make to start up a football team. Stability arguably helps ensure no one team has an undue advantage on the field. Territories foster fan loyalty which in turn promotes traditional rivalries between teams, each contributing to attendance at games and television viewing.

Joint marketing decisions are surely legitimate because of the importance of television. Title 15, U.S.C. 1291 grants the NFL an exemption from antitrust liability, if any, that might arise out of its collective negotiation of television rights with the networks. To effectuate this right, the League must be allowed to have some control over the placement of teams to ensure NFL football is popular in a diverse group of markets.

Last, there is some legitimacy to the NFL's argument that it has an interest in preventing transfers from areas before local governments, which have made a substantial investment in stadia and other facilities, can recover their expenditures. In such a situation, local confidence in the NFL is eroded, possibly resulting in a decline in interest. All these factors considered, we nevertheless are not persuaded the jury should have concluded that Rule 4.3 is a reasonable restraint of trade. The same goals can be achieved in a variety of ways which are less harmful to competition.

* * * Here, the district court correctly instructed the jury to take into account the existence of less restrictive alternatives when determining the reasonableness of Rule 4.3's territorial restraint. * * *

The NFL argues that the requirement of Rule 4.3 that three-quarters of the owners approve a franchise move is reasonable because it deters unwise team transfers. While the rule does indeed protect an owner's investment in a football franchise, no standards or durational limits are incorporated into the voting requirement to make sure that concern is satisfied. Nor are factors such as fan loyalty and team rivalries necessarily considered.

The NFL claims that its marketing and other objectives are indirectly accounted for in the voting process because the team owners vote to maximize their profits. * * * Under the present Rule 4.3, however, an owner need muster only seven friendly votes to prevent three-quarters approval for the sole reason of preventing another team from entering its market, regardless of whether the market could sustain two franchises. A basic premise of the Sherman Act is that regulation of private profit is best left to the marketplace rather than private agreement. * * *

The NFL's professed interest in ensuring that cities and other local governments secure a return on their investments in stadia is undercut in two ways. First, the local governments ought to be able to protect their investment through the leases they negotiate with the teams for the use of their stadia. Second, the NFL's interest on this point may not be as important as it would have us believe because the League has in the past allowed teams to threaten a transfer to another location in order to give the team leverage in lease negotiations.

Finally, the NFL made no showing that the transfer of the Raiders to Los Angeles would have any harmful effect on the League. Los Angeles is a market large enough for the successful operation of two teams, there would be no scheduling difficulties, facilities at the L.A. Coliseum are more than adequate, and no loss of future television revenue was foreseen. Also, the NFL offered no evidence that its interest in maintaining regional balance would be adversely affected by a move of a northern California team to southern California.

It is true, as the NFL claims, that the antitrust laws are primarily concerned with the promotion of interbrand competition. * * * Here, the jury could have found that the rules restricting team movement do not sufficiently promote interbrand competition to justify the negative impact on intraband competition.

To withstand antitrust scrutiny, restrictions on team movement should be more closely tailored to serve the needs inherent in producing the NFL "product" and competing with other forms of entertainment. An express recognition and consideration of those objective factors espoused by the NFL as important, such as population, economic projections, facilities, regional balance, etc., would be well advised. * * * Fan loyalty and location continuity could also be considered. * * * Al Davis in fact testified that in 1978 he proposed that the League adopt a set of objective guidelines to govern team relocation rather than continuing to utilize a subjective voting procedure.

Some sort of procedural mechanism to ensure consideration of all the above factors may also be necessary, including an opportunity for the team proposing the move to present its case. * * * In the present case, for example, testimony indicated that some owners, as well as Commissioner Rozelle, dislike Al Davis and consider him a maverick. Their vote against the Raiders' move could have been motivated by animosity rather than business judgment.

Substantial evidence existed for the jury to find the restraint imposed by Rule 4.3 was not reasonably necessary to the production and sale of the NFL product. Therefore, the NFL is not entitled to judgment notwithstanding the verdict.

III. JURY INSTRUCTIONS

The NFL also claims it is entitled to a new trial because of error in the jury instructions. In particular, the NFL argues that the instructions lacked the specificity required in a complex lawsuit such as this, that certain of its legal theories should have been presented to the jury, and that the instructions failed to articulate all the requirements of the law for finding an unlawful restraint of trade. * * *

The NFL also argues it was unduly prejudiced by the instructions because they focused on issues of competition among the NFL teams (intraband competition) rather than competition between the NFL "product" and other forms of entertainment (interbrand competition). * * * The trial court instructed the jury on the NFL's relevant market claim that it competes with all forms of entertainment. * * * In light of this instruction, the jury was not constrained to ascertain the reasonableness of Rule 4.3 solely in view of the internal NFL market.

There also was no error in the failure of the district court to charge the jury that it could balance the loss of competition in the San Francisco Bay Area against that to be gained in the Los Angeles area. The extent of the loss and gain to competition in these locations was a fact question that could be argued to the jury. * * *

V. CONCLUSION

The NFL is an unique business organization to which it is difficult to apply antitrust rules which were developed in the context of arrangements between actual competitors. This does not mean that the trial court and jury were incapable of meeting the task, however. The lower court correctly applied and described the law. The reasonableness of a restraint is a "paradigm fact question, * * *" and our review of the record convinces us the jury had adequate evidence to answer that question.

We believe antitrust principles are sufficiently flexible to account for the NFL's structure. To the extent the NFL finds the law inadequate, it must look to Congress for relief.

The judgment finding the NFL liable to the Los Angeles Coliseum and the Raiders, and enjoining the NFL from preventing the Raiders from relocating in Los Angeles is AFFIRMED.

* * *

Notes and Questions

1. One important aspect of the *Raiders* case was the finding by the district court, affirmed by the Ninth Circuit, that the National Football League is not a single entity. The court, though acknowledging the various indicia of commonality among the NFL teams, noted that the teams did not share profits and losses, a significant feature tending to establish that the league was not a single entity. The court directly linked the disparity in profits and losses to independent management policies with regard to coaches, players, supervisory personnel, ticket prices, concessions, etc. The single entity issue has been a primary focus in almost all litigation about intra-league restraints. *See, e.g., Sullivan v. National Football League,* below, and *Chicago Professional Sports Limited Partnership v. National Basketball Association,* below. In the wake of the *Raiders* and *NASL* cases in the Ninth and Second Circuits, respectively, it was generally understood that any future decision by a non-exempt, traditional model professional sports league to circumscribe the rights of its member clubs to relocate a franchise would be subject to review under Sherman § 1. *See generally* Charles Gray, *Keeping the Home Team At Home,* 74 CALIF. L. REV. 1329 (1986); Daniel E. Lazaroff, *The Antitrust Implications of Franchise Relocation Restrictions,* 53 FORDHAM L. REV. 157 (1984). Prior to the *Raiders* decision, there had been suggestions by some courts that, under the appropriate circumstances, a sports league that is an association of separately-owned teams may still constitute a single entity. *See, e.g., San Francisco Seals, Ltd. v. National Hockey League,* 379 F. Supp. 966, 969 (C.D. Cal. 1974); *Levin v. National Basketball Ass'n,* 385 F. Supp. 149, 152 (S.D.N.Y. 1974). Further, Justice Rehnquist's dissent from the Supreme Court's denial of the NFL's request for certiorari in the *NASL* case, *NASL v. NFL,* 459 U.S. 1074 (1982), and the opinions of Judge Easterbrook in the *Chicago Professional Sports Limited Partnership* case, below, have kept the leagues' hopes alive. As discussed in detail later in this chapter, leagues have been unwilling to abandon the so-called "single entity defense" because its judicial or legislative adoption would harbor dramatic ramifications for traditional model leagues. *See* Section IV for a retrospective and analysis of the "single entity" question as it applies to traditional sports leagues.

2. Within days of Al Davis' announcement that the Raiders were leaving Oakland for Los Angeles, the City of Oakland brought an eminent domain action to acquire the team. Summary judgment was granted for the Raiders but the California Supreme Court reversed, holding that the California eminent domain statute permitted the condemnation of intangible property and that the city could attempt to establish at trial the Raiders' acquisition as a valid public use. *See City of Oakland v. Oakland Raiders,* (Cal. 1982). The case subsequently went to trial in May 1983, and the court again entered judgment for the Raiders. *See City of Oakland v. Oakland Raiders,* 220 Cal. Rptr. 153, 154–55 (1985). On appeal, that judgment was remanded to the trial court, with directions to consider certain remaining objections to plaintiff's suit which had not been previously addressed by the court. *Id.* On remand, the trial court once again entered judgment for the Raiders on the grounds that: (1) the city's stated purpose in acquiring the team was not a public use; (2) the city's action was invalid under the antitrust laws; and (3) the city's conduct constituted undue interference with interstate

commerce and therefore violated the commerce clause of the United States Constitution. *Id.*

The court of appeals affirmed the trial court's decision on the grounds that the city's proposed acquisition would impermissibly burden interstate commerce. *Id.* at 157–58. In reaching this decision, the court first found that the league's success was dependent upon its ability to conduct business nationwide. *Id.* Based on this finding, the court next found that uniform national regulation was appropriate in this area because local laws, such as eminent domain statutes, only take into consideration parochial interests, sometimes at the expense of larger national concerns. *Id.* Thus, the court concluded that the city's attempted condemnation of the Raiders franchise represented "the precise brand of parochial meddling with the national economy that the commerce clause was designed to prohibit." *Id.* at 157. There is substantial doubt that a state's exercise of the power of eminent domain would violate the dormant commerce clause, especially in light of more recent Supreme Court precedents. Therefore, the use of eminent domain legislation as a response to a relocation threat is still likely in the future. For a discussion of some of the eminent domain issues, see further Charles Gray, *Keeping the Home Team at Home,* 74 Calif. L. Rev. 1329 (1986); Lisa J. Tobin-Rubio, *Eminent Domain and the Commerce Clause Defense: City of Oakland v. Oakland Raiders,* 41 U. Miami L. Rev. 1185 (1985); Thomas Merrill, *The Economics of Public Use,* 72 Cornell L. Rev. 61 (1986).

3. After the jury verdict in *Raiders,* but before the Ninth Circuit decision affirming the liability decision, Robert Irsay, the owner of the Baltimore Colts, considered moving his team to Indianapolis. *See generally Mayor and City Council of Baltimore v. Baltimore Football Club, Inc.,* 624 F. Supp. 278, 279 (D. Md. 1985). During this same period, Irsay was engaged in negotiations with Maryland and Baltimore officials about keeping the Colts in Baltimore. When ongoing negotiations between the Colts and Indianapolis became public, the Maryland legislature responded with a statute that would have authorized the City of Baltimore to condemn professional sports franchises under the doctrine of eminent domain. The bill was introduced in the Maryland Senate on February 24, 1984. On February 28, 1984, the Ninth Circuit's decision affirming liability was issued. Three days later, the NFL held a special meeting in Chicago to review the decision and its implications. In an NFL executive session, from which Colts' personnel were excluded, the league decided that it would take no action with respect to any move by the Colts. Later in the day, Irsay officially announced that he was considering moving the Colts to Indianapolis. The league did not approve or disapprove this possible move.

During the remainder of March 1984, Irsay continued negotiations with Baltimore and Indianapolis. On the morning of March 28, 1984, Irsay learned from a Chicago newspaper that, on March 27, 1984, the Maryland Senate had passed the eminent domain legislation mentioned above. That day, Irsay directed his general counsel to execute the deal offered by Indianapolis and to move all of the Colts' property from Owing Mills, Maryland to Indianapolis. During the night of March 28–29, the Colts' property was loaded into Mayflower moving vans; the caravan left for Indianapolis on the morning of March 29, 1984. On March 30, 1984, the Maryland legislature enacted the eminent domain statutes, and the City of Baltimore immediately initiated state court condemnation proceedings to acquire the Colts' franchise. The Colts subsequently filed an interpleader action in federal court in Indianapolis to enjoin the eminent domain action in Baltimore. The suit was dismissed. *See Indianapolis Colts v. Mayor and City Council of Baltimore,* 733 F.2d 484 and 741 F.2d 954 (7th Cir. 1984). The City of Baltimore's eminent domain action was also subsequently dismissed, based on the fact that the Colts' property was outside the state when the action was filed. *See Mayor and City Council of Baltimore v. Baltimore Football Club, Inc.,* 624 F. Supp. 278, 289 (D. Md. 1985).

Why did the NFL owners decide to ignore the proposed relocation of the Colts from Maryland to Indiana? Did the decision in the *Raiders* case mean that any action to block the Colts' move would be unlawful? Did the *Raiders* decision hold NFL Rule 4.3 illegal on its face, or only as applied to the Raiders' relocation from Oakland to Los Angeles?

4. The majority opinion in *Raiders* advised the NFL that "[t]o withstand antitrust scrutiny, restrictions on team movement should be more closely tailored to serve the needs inherent in producing the NFL 'product' and competing with other forms of entertainment." The opinion identified some of the factors that the NFL should consider as part of a more appropriate analysis of proposed relocations. What rules would you propose? Could you draft objective standards? Who should be the ultimate decisionmaker? If the owners are the decisionmakers, what vote should be necessary to disapprove a proposed relocation? Are there rules that would be responsive to the majority's concern about owners voting against a move out of animosity toward the relocating owner?

5. Nine months after the Colts went to Baltimore, another NFL team, the Philadelphia Eagles, contemplated relocation as a means of improving its financial situation. Reportedly because of dissatisfaction with his stadium lease and because of personal financial problems, Eagles owner Leonard Tose began negotiating a deal to sell a minority interest in the Eagles to Phoenix real estate developer James Monaghan. *See* Joe Juliano, UNITED PRESS INTERNATIONAL, Dec. 17, 1984. As part of this deal, the Eagles would have relocated to Phoenix. Tose initially denied reports that he was considering selling or moving the team. However, rumors of the deal were fueled when Tose and his daughter, the Eagles' vice president, traveled to Phoenix in late November, 1984. *See* David Harris, THE LEAGUE: THE RISE AND DECLINE OF THE NFL 622 (1986).

Notwithstanding the continued legal uncertainty following the *Raiders* decision, Commissioner Rozelle filed suit against Tose and the Eagles in federal court in Philadelphia, seeking a declaration that an NFL evaluation of a proposed Eagles move, under "orderly league procedures," would not violate the antitrust laws. The lawsuit became moot a few days after it was filed when Tose signed a new deal with Philadelphia officials that kept the Eagles in Philadelphia. *See* Joe Juliano, UNITED PRESS INTERNATIONAL, Dec. 17, 1984.

6. The jury in the *Raiders* case found that the team's move from Oakland to Los Angeles would promote competition, and, concomitantly, that the league's efforts to block that move were anticompetitive and unlawful. Considering the same move, no NFL owner voted to allow the Raiders to relocate (22 voted "no," and 5 owners abstained). What does that tally say about the standards being applied by the owners or their motivations? Does it support the NFL's claim that they lost the jury trial because Los Angeles area jurors wanted to bring the Raiders to their Coliseum? *See Los Angeles Memorial Coliseum Comm'n v. NFL,* 89 F.R.D. 497 (C.D. Cal. 1981).

7. Judge Anderson stated that the anticompetive effect of Rule 4.3 was "especially acute in this case because it prevents a move by a team into another existing team's market." Does that mean that a relocating team only has a viable antitrust claim if it is moving into another team's home territory? When the St. Louis Cardinals sued the NFL seeking the right to relocate, *St. Louis Football Cardinals, Inc. v. Rozelle,* Civil Action No. 86 Civ. 1262 (JES) (S.D.N.Y. February 11, 1986), the NFL took the position that blocking a move to Phoenix, where there was no NFL team, would not even raise a claim under the antitrust laws. *See* Motion to Dismiss and Memorandum of Points and Au-

thorities in Support, *St. Louis Football Cardinals, Inc. v. Rozelle*, No. 86 Civ. 1262 (JES) (S.D.N.Y. October 9, 1986). The dispute was eventually resolved when the Cardinals agreed to pay the other owners $7.5 million and the league voted 26-0 to allow the move, with Raiders' owner Al Davis and Miami Dolphins' owner Joe Robbie abstaining. *See* Gerald Eskenazi, *NFL Approves Team Shift*, NEW YORK TIMES, Mar. 16, 1988, at B9.

8. Could the Cardinals have argued that the NFL's interference with their move to a "non-NFL" city unlawfully restrained trade in the market for stadium services, the market alleged by the Los Angeles Memorial Coliseum Commission in *Raiders*? As buyers in the market that was restrained, would the Cardinals have standing to challenge a restraint on that market? In the alternative, could the Cardinals have argued that precluding all entry into the Phoenix market, to leave that market unsatisfied, and to ensure that a possible future NFL expansion team will have a monopoly, violates the antitrust laws? Is it possible that blocking market entry that will give consumers an alternative supplier of the product violates the antitrust laws, but preventing consumers from having any access to the product at all is legitimate?

9. When considering the single entity question, the court was laboring under the erroneous assumption that 90% of NFL revenues are shared equally among the teams. In 1979, about 45% of NFL revenues—$336 million or $12 million per team—were shared equally. By 1997 those numbers had grown, to 55% of team revenue and about $70 million per year, per team. The 90% of all revenues cited by the judge probably came from the fact that 90% of all NFL revenue was shared to some extent, but that figure includes revenues that are not shared equally. If all NFL revenues were shared equally, and the Raiders received only their 1/28th share of the revenue increases that their relocation to Los Angeles yielded, would their interest in relocating have diminished? If the other twenty-seven team owners were each going to receive an equal share of all revenue increases related to the Raiders' move, do you believe that more NFL owners might have voted in favor of the relocation?

10. More than two years after the Ninth Circuit's opinion affirming the jury's liability finding, and almost two years after oral argument, a different Ninth Circuit panel issued a long and very complicated opinion addressing the NFL's appeal of the damages portion of the jury verdict. *See Los Angeles Memorial Coliseum Comm'n v. National Football League ("Raiders II")*, 791 F.2d 1356 (9th Cir. 1986). After the court affirmed the damage award in favor of the Coliseum Commission, it responded to the NFL's argument that the district court erred in refusing to instruct the jurors that they could consider, as a damages offset, the *benefits* that the Raiders realized as a result of receiving the right to play in Los Angeles instead of Oakland. The court found that the permanent injunctive relief, giving the NFL the right to play in Los Angeles in the future, provided the Raiders the value accumulated as a result of the NFL's lawful cultivation of the Los Angeles market a "commodity" that the NFL could have sold to an expansion team in Los Angeles.

The court in *Raiders II* remanded the case and instructed the district court to offset "the value of the NFL's Los Angeles expansion opportunity in 1980, prior to the NFL's illegal conduct, less the value of the Oakland opportunity returned to the league." 791 F.2d at 1372. The dissent criticized the majority opinion because there was no evidence that the NFL had a right to charge the Raiders a so-called "expansion opportunity" fee, or that it would have done so. *See* 791 F.2d at 1376 (Nelson, J., dissenting in part). In analyzing this issue, the majority preliminarily found it necessary to interpret whether the jury's verdict meant that Rule 4.3 was illegal as applied to the Raiders' attempted move, or whether the rule was illegal on its face. Examining the evidence presented at trial and the court's instructions to the jury, the Ninth Circuit concluded that the jury found only that Rule 4.3 was illegal as applied by the NFL to the Raiders' proposed relocation to Los Angeles. 791 F.2d at 1369. If the NFL had known that the initial *Raiders* decision only held Rule 4.3 unlawful as applied to the Raiders' move to Los Angeles, is it likely that the league would have responded in a different manner to the Colts' 1984 departure for Indianapolis?

On remand, the district court, in June, 1988, addressed the issue of whether the NFL's potential offset would be limited to the $11.55 million in damages awarded to the Raiders (thus resulting in no damage award to either side), or whether the NFL could argue that the expansion opportunity value was more than $11.55 million and that therefore the Raiders owed the league money. *See Two Rulings Go against the Raiders,* ASSOCIATED PRESS, June 14, 1988. The NFL argued that the Raiders' move increased the franchise value by $25 million and convinced the district court judge that the NFL was entitled to seek to recapture that entire amount from the jury. The case was eventually settled, with the NFL agreeing to pay the Raiders approximately $18 million.

11. When the Ninth Circuit issued its initial *Raiders* decision, the NFL was not the only league affected. The San Diego Clippers in the NBA, like the Baltimore Colts, saw that decision as an opportunity to relocate. The Los Angeles Memorial Coliseum Commission entered into an agreement to relocate the Clippers to Los Angeles, and both the Clippers and the Coliseum threatened the National Basketball Association with antitrust litigation if the NBA took any steps to interfere with the Clippers' move. The NBA permitted the relocation but sought a declaration of its rights under these circumstances. The relocation and the proceedings in the district court were completed before the Ninth Circuit issued its decision in *Raiders II.* Consider carefully the analysis and holdings of the Ninth Circuit in the *SDC* case that follows.

National Basketball Ass'n v. SDC Basketball Club, Inc.

815 F.2d 562 (9th Cir. 1987)

WARREN J. FERGUSON, Circuit Judge. Once again this court must consider the application of federal antitrust law to a sports league's effort to restrain the movement of a member franchise. In this case, the league, the National Basketball Association (NBA), seeks declaratory judgment that it may restrain the movement of its franchise, the Los Angeles Clippers (nee San Diego Clippers), and that it may impose a charge upon them for the Clippers' unilateral usurpation of the "franchise opportunity" available in the Los Angeles market. The NBA also seeks declaratory judgment on similar grounds against the Los Angeles Memorial Coliseum Commission (the Coliseum). The district court, believing the result controlled by the decision in the first *Los Angeles Raiders* case, dismissed the case upon the Clippers' motion for summary judgment. Finding genuine issues of material fact, we reverse and remand to the district court for further proceedings.

I.

The Clippers currently operate a professional basketball franchise in the Los Angeles Sports Arena. The franchise is a member of the NBA, an organization of professional basketball teams that operates as a joint venture under New York law. In the early 1980s, the then San Diego Clippers desired to move their franchise to Los Angeles. The Clippers abandoned their effort after the NBA filed suit in the Southern District of California. The suit was resolved via a stipulation that any subsequent suits regarding a move must be brought in the Southern District.

In 1984, this court rendered the decision in *Raiders I*. The *Raiders I* panel found that the National Football League (NFL) was not immune from the antitrust laws as a single business entity. * * * Possible antitrust violations within the league thus properly are tested by "rule of reason" antitrust analysis. The *Raiders I* panel found that a reasonable jury applying the rule of reason standard could have found that the NFL violated antitrust laws in restraining Al Davis's Oakland Raiders from moving to the Los Angeles Coliseum. * * *

The then extant clause directly governing the movement of franchises within the NBA, Article 9 of the NBA constitution, was similar to a clause abandoned by the NFL prior to the Raiders litigation as potentially violative of federal antitrust laws. Seeing the *Raiders I* decision as a window of opportunity, the Clippers, through their president Alan Rothenberg, on May 14, 1984, announced to the NBA their move to Los Angeles. They asserted that the move was to take place on the following day and that any action taken by the NBA to restrain that move would violate the antitrust laws. The NBA attempted to appoint an investigatory committee to examine the move, but abandoned the effort in the face of the Clippers' continued assertions that the investigation violated antitrust law. To avoid potential liability, the NBA scheduled the Clippers games in Los Angeles and made no effort to sanction the club.

The NBA asserts that Article 9 was not the only limitation upon franchise movement. Article 9 provided that no team could move into a territory operated by another franchise without that franchise's approval. The Clippers complied with this requirement, as the Los Angeles Lakers agreed in writing to waive their rights under Article 9. The NBA argues, however, that the league as a body must be permitted to consider moves in order to give effect to a number of constitutional provisions for the exclusiveness of franchise territories. Article 9, it contends, limits the actions of the NBA as a league and does not prescribe the only strictures on franchise movement.

The NBA also began proceedings to adopt a new rule governing the consideration of franchise moves, later adopted as Article 9A. The NBA argues that Article 9A is a new constitutional provision codifying previous practice. The Clippers argue that Article 9A is rather an amendment to Article 9 that, by virtue of the NBA constitution, must be unanimously approved by the member teams. The Clippers thus argue that Article 9A was not properly adopted at the time of the Clippers' move, when the Clippers voted against it.

The NBA brought suit in the Southern District for declaratory judgment that it could as a league consider the Clippers' move to Los Angeles and sanction the Clippers for failing to seek league approval without violating the antitrust laws. It also sought damages from the Clippers on a variety of state-law claims, including breach of fiduciary duty and breach of contract. The NBA sought damages from the Coliseum for tortious interference with the contractual relations between the Clippers and the NBA. The Clippers and the Coliseum responded and counterclaimed against the NBA and individually against its member teams for declaratory judgment that consideration by the NBA of the Clippers' move would violate the antitrust laws.

After voluminous pleading and the denial of five summary judgment motions, the district judge suggested on the eve of trial that the NBA could not possibly win its case under the guidelines established in *Raiders I*. The judge further expressed doubt that the league had any valid provision for the consideration of franchise movement. At the hearing on the final summary judgment motions, he repeated his continuing frustration with the case by noting that he couldn't "see spending my time * * * on this case without some instruction from the circuit." The district judge also refused NBA counsel's request for a written opinion.

The district judge entered an order granting summary judgment for the Clippers on April 28, 1986. The order awarded the Clippers and the Coliseum declaratory relief but not damages on their antitrust claims. The order dismissed all of the NBA's claims. Although it is not entirely clear, the district court appears to have dismissed the antitrust claims as nonmeritorious, and the pendent state claims due to the dismissal of the primary federal claim. The Clippers' and Coliseum's other counterclaims were dismissed by stipulation, and thus the judgment is final for appeal.

After the district court granted summary judgment, the *Raiders* panel rendered its opinion regarding damages and state-law claims. Resting on that decision's award in offset for the "expansion opportunity" lost to the league by the Raiders' move, * * * the NBA requests that this court enter judgment in its favor for the expansion opportunity taken by the Clippers in their move to Los Angeles. The NBA also requests summary judgment on its pendent claims for declaratory relief regarding the effect of the NBA constitution. The NBA further requests that summary judgment on all other counts be reversed and the case remanded for trial. * * *

IV.

* * *

The antitrust issues are directly controlled by the two *Raiders* opinions, although the district judge had the benefit only of *Raiders I* when he rendered judgment. Collectively, the *Raiders* opinions held that rule of reason analysis governed a professional sports league's efforts to restrict franchise movement. More narrowly, however, *Raiders I* merely held that a reasonable jury could have found that the NFL's application of its franchise movement rule was an unreasonable restraint of trade. * * * *Raiders II* confirmed that the jury's liability verdict affirmed in *Raiders I* "held Rule 4.3 [the franchise movement rule] invalid only as it was applied to the Raiders' proposed move to Los Angeles." *Raiders II*, 791 F.2d [1356,] 1369 [(9th Cir. 1986)]. The Clippers' and the Coliseum's efforts to characterize *Raiders I* as presenting guidelines for franchise movement rules are thus unavailing. Neither the jury's verdict in *Raiders*, nor the court's affirmance of that verdict, held that a franchise movement rule, in and of itself, was invalid under the antitrust laws.

Raiders I did establish the law of this circuit in applying the rule of reason to a sports league's franchise relocation rule, "a business practice in an industry which does not readily fit into the antitrust context." * * * Any antitrust plaintiff "must prove these elements: '(1) An agreement among two or more persons or distinct business entities; (2) Which is intended to harm or unreasonably restrain competition; (3) And which actually causes injury to competition." * * * The *Raiders I* panel carefully examined the structure of professional football * * *, a structure in which the "teams are not true competitors, nor can they be." * * * The *Raiders I* panel concluded that the relevant market for professional football, the history and purpose of the franchise-movement rule, and the lack of justification of the rule under [the] ancillary-restraint doctrine all supported the jury's verdict. In so doing, of course, the panel set down no absolute rule for sports leagues. Instead, it examined the facts before it and concluded that the jury's conclusion that the NFL violated the antitrust laws was supported by the record.

Yet the Clippers argue, as they must to support summary judgment, that the "NBA three-quarters rule * * * is illegal under *Raiders I*" *i.e.*, either that the NBA rule is void as a matter of law under *Raiders I*, or that the NBA has not adduced genuine issues of fact to allow the rule to stand. The Clippers assert that the rule "is illegal as applied * * * [but that under *Raiders I*], a professional sports league's club relocation rule must at least be 'closely tailored' and incorporate objective standards and criteria such as population, economic projections, playing facilities, regional balance, and television revenues." Putting to the side, for the moment, NBA's adamant and repeated assertions that such standards have been incorporated in the evaluation of franchise movements, the Clippers misperceive the effect of the *Raiders* cases. The Clippers' confusion, and that of a number of commentators, may derive from the *Raiders I* panel's painstaking efforts to guide sports leagues toward procedures that might, in all cases, withstand antitrust analysis. *See Raiders I*, 726 F.2d at 1397. The objective factors and procedures recounted by the Clippers are "well advised," *id.*, and might be sufficient to demonstrate procompetitive purposes that would save the restriction from the rule of reason. They are not, however, necessary conditions to the legality of franchise relocation rules.

Since a careful analysis of *Raiders I* makes it clear that franchise movement restrictions are not invalid as a matter of law, for the district judge to grant summary judgment against the NBA, he must have found that the NBA had adduced no facts upon which a reasonable jury could have found that NBA consideration of the Clippers' move was a reasonable restraint of trade. As we have demonstrated, antitrust analysis under *Raiders I* indicates that the question of what restraints are reasonable is one of fact. We believe that numerous issues of fact remain.

The NBA asserts a number of genuine issues of fact: (1) the purpose of the restraint as demonstrated by the NBA's use of a variety of criteria in evaluating franchise movement, (2) the market created by professional basketball, which the NBA alleges is substantially different from that of professional football, and (3) the actual effect the NBA's limitations on movements might have on trade. The NBA's assertions, if further documented at trial, create an entirely different factual setting than that of the Raiders and the NFL. Further, as the NBA correctly notes, the antitrust issue here is vastly different than that in the Raiders cases: the issue here is "whether the mere requirement that a team seek [NBA] Board of Governor approval before it seizes a new franchise location violates the Sherman Act." The NBA here did not attempt to forbid the move. It scheduled the Clippers in the Sports Arena, and when faced with continued assertions of potential antitrust liability, brought this suit for declaratory relief. Given the *Raiders I* rejection of *per se* analysis for franchise movement rules of sports leagues, and the existence of genuine issues of fact regarding the reasonableness of the restraint, the judgment against the NBA must be reversed.

* * * *Raiders II* * * * reemphasized that only the particular application of the franchise movement rules in that case violated antitrust law. The mere existence of Article 9, Article 9A, and various provisions for franchise movement evaluation, cannot violate antitrust law. Further, the NBA has adduced sufficient facts to create a genuine issue of the reasonability of the restraint. * * *

The NBA requests that this court enter judgment for it under the "expansion opportunity" theory of damages discussed in *Raiders II*. * * * The majority in *Raiders II*, however, found only that the expansion opportunity taken by the Raiders in their move to Los Angeles limited the Raiders' recovery of antitrust damages. The majority revealed nothing about the origin of that offset. Therefore, the existence of a recovery for expansion opportunity must find its source somewhere other than antitrust law: *i.e.*, the express or implied provisions of the NBA constitution. This theory, however, presents issues of fact and is properly left to the district court.

CONCLUSION

The pervasive issues of material fact that remain warrant the return of this case, in its entirety, to the district court for trial. We therefore reverse the district court's grant of summary judgment and remand the case to the district court for trial.

REVERSED and REMANDED.

Notes and Questions

1. In the aftermath of the *Clippers* decision, an oft-debated issue is whether a professional sports league can properly approve a proposed relocation, conditioned upon the relocating team's agreement to pay some financial consideration to the other owners in return for their votes of approval ("expansion opportunity" or "relocation fees"). The NBA, like the NFL in the *Raiders II* case, publicly took the position that the Clippers' move enhanced the value of that franchise by $25 million, see The American Lawyer, June, 1987, at 24, and the dispute eventually settled when the Clippers agreed to pay the NBA $5.6 million. *See* Robert L. Caporale, *Wandering Team Owners Change Rules of the Game*, Boston Business Journal, Apr. 9, 1993. The NFL extracted a $29 million fee, $17 million of personal seat license revenue, waiver by the Rams of their right to share in expansion fees paid by other teams for a period of years, and a number of other financial assessments from the Rams as the basis on which the NFL owners permitted the relocation from Los Angeles to St. Louis. The League claimed that the fact that the $29 million fee worked out to $1 million per other NFL team was a "coincidence." The NFL also "taxed" the Browns for moving to Baltimore (to become the Ravens) and the Oilers for the right to relocate from Houston to Nashville. If a league approves a move, but assesses a relocation fee, can the relocating owner challenge that charge as violative of federal antitrust law? Can the assessment be challenged as a matter of private association or contract law? Can the owners all vote, on the eve of a relocation vote, to change their league's Constitution & Bylaws to authorize them to assess the relocating team? If the team passes that fee on to the owner of the new stadium to which the team is relocating, can the owner claim that as antitrust damages? *See, e.g., St. Louis Convention & Visitors Commission v. NFL*, 154 F.3d 851 (8th Cir. 1998).

2. Is it appropriate for team owners to condition their approval of a relocation application on non-financial conditions imposed on the relocating team? For example, would it be permissible for the owners considering a relocation application to insist that an unpopular relocating owner sell his or her team within a specified period after the relocation? Would it be permissible for the owners to insist that the relocating owner agree not to transfer the team to his or her heirs upon the death of the owner? Does your answer to these questions depend on whether the owner has met the league's criteria for relocation? If the owner has not met the league's criteria, can the other owners take the position that, because the criteria were not satisfied, they can disapprove the request to relocate, and thus impose any conditions, however unreasonable, upon the relocating team? These questions are not purely hypothetical. When the Rams applied for approval to move to St. Louis, Commissioner Tagliabue and other NFL owners initially sought to force owner Georgia Frontiere to sell the Rams to minority owner Stan Kroenke, and subsequently sought her agreement not to leave the Rams to her heirs. When those efforts were unsuccessful, Commissioner Tagliabue took the position that

the league could impose any conditions that it desired, because the Rams had not satisfied the NFL's Guidelines. Could the Rams challenge that conduct as a violation of the antitrust laws, as a breach of contract, as a breach of fiduciary duty, or as tortious interference with contract or with business relations?

3. As a result of the *Raiders* and *Clippers* decisions, the National Basketball Association enacted the following Constitution & Bylaws provisions concerning franchise location and relocation. Do the NBA's rules appear to be consistent with the antitrust laws? With the Ninth Circuit's opinions?

NBA PROVISIONS CONCERNING FRANCHISE RELOCATION
National Basketball Association Constitution & Bylaws
(RELEVANT EXCERPTS)

9A.   A Member may transfer its franchise, city of operation, or playing site of any or all of its home games, to a different location, within or outside its existing Territory, as defined in Article 10, only in accordance with and subject to the following provisions:

* * *

(b)   No application to relocate may be made after the first day of March preceding the season in which the proposed relocation is to take effect. Within ten (10) days of the receipt of an application to relocate, the Commissioner shall refer the application to a Committee to investigate the application. The Committee shall be appointed by the Commissioner and shall consist of no fewer than five Governors or Alternate Governors. * * * The recommendation of the Committee shall be based solely and exclusively upon the following factors:

(i)   Whether the proposed new location can support a franchise in the Association or, if the proposed new location is within the existing Territory of a Member, whether the proposed new location can support another franchise. In evaluating this factor, the Committee shall consider: existing and projected population, income levels and age distribution; existing and projected markets for radio, broadcast television, cable television, and other forms of audio-visual transmission of Association games; the size, quality and location of the arena in which the Member proposes to play its home games; and the presence, history and popularity in the proposed new location of other professional sports teams and major college basketball teams.

(ii)   Whether the applicant has demonstrated that it will be able successfully to operate an Association team in the proposed new location. In evaluating this factor, the committee shall consider the applicant's present and projected financial condition and resources and its past performance in operating a team in the Association.

(iii)   Whether the proposed relocation is likely to have an adverse effect upon the Association's ability to market and promote Association basketball on a nationwide basis in a diverse group of geographic markets.

(iv)   Whether the proposed new location presents particular disadvantages for the operation of the Association, such as by creating significant traveling or scheduling difficulties or because of adverse state or local laws or regulations.

(v)   Whether other Association Members, in addition to the applicant, are interested in transferring their franchises to the proposed new location, or whether there are persons or entities interested in obtaining an expansion franchise in the proposed new location. * * *

(d)   The report and recommendation of the Committee shall be delivered to each Member of the Board of Governors. * * * The question whether to approve the proposed relocation shall be decided by a majority vote of all of the members, and no vote by proxy shall be permitted. The vote of each Governor on the proposed relocation shall be based solely and exclusively upon the factors listed in subparagraph (b)(i through v) of this Article * * *

TRANSFER OF PLAYING SITE

9B. Article 9A shall not apply to a request by a Member, in accordance with this Article 9B, to transfer the home playing site of one or more of its Regular Season or Playoff Games to a different facility under the following circumstances: * * *

(a) the Member seeks to schedule up to four (4) of its Regular Season home games at another playing site within its Territory.

In order for a Member to transfer the home playing site of any of its Regular Season or Playoff Games under the circumstances set forth in subparts (1), (b), or (c) above, the Member must make an application in writing to the Commissioner, who is empowered to grant or deny such application, either unconditionally or upon specific conditions, as in his judgment shall be in the best interests of the Association. * * *

TERRITORY

10. (a) Except as provided in Paragraphs (b) and (c) of this Article 10, the Territory of a Member shall be the territory incorporated within an area of seventy-five (75) air miles of the corporate limits of the city of operation, except that when the line circumscribing the Territory of a Member intersects with the line circumscribing the Territory of another Member, the respective Territories shall be evenly divided by a line between the two (2) points of intersection.

(b) Notwithstanding the provisions of Paragraph (a) of this Article 10, the Territory of the respective holders of the New York and Philadelphia franchises shall be the territory incorporated within an area of seventy-five air miles of the corporate limits of those two (2) cities, except as the limits of these Territories have been modified by the provisions of a certain written agreement heretofore made by the holders of the New York and Philadelphia franchises.

(c) A Team operated by a Member shall have no right to play in the Territory of another Member without the consent of the resident Member.

(d) In addition to the territorial rights above provided, a Member shall have priority within the corporate limits of any city in which its Team has played not less than three (3) home Regular Season Games during the preceding Season. Such priority shall continue so long as such Member's Team continues to play not less than three (3) home Regular Season Games in such city in each succeeding consecutive Season; * * * . "Priority," as used in this Paragraph (d), means a preference granted to schedule and play home Regular Season Games and home preseason Exhibition Games within the corporate limits of such city.

4. What has been the result of the *Raiders* and *Clippers* decisions? Have they caused a dramatic increase in the number of team relocations in the four major sports leagues? Is relocation a relatively new phenomenon? As the major sports leagues have grown to a point that there are about thirty teams in each league, does that render expansion less attractive to the leagues, and thereby increase the demand for relocation? Consider

those issues as you review the following histories of league location, expansion, and relocation in the four major professional sports leagues.

NATIONAL BASKETBALL ASSOCIATION FRANCHISE RELOCATION

ATLANTA HAWKS — National Basketball League's Buffalo Bisons in 1945–46, moved to become Tri-Cities Blackhawks (Moline and Rock Island, Illinois and Davenport, Iowa), merged into Basketball Association of America and League renamed the NBA for 1949–50 season, moved to Milwaukee and renamed the Hawks in 1951, moved to St. Louis in 1955, moved to Atlanta in 1968.

BOSTON CELTICS — Original Team in Basketball Association of America formed in 1946, League renamed the NBA in 1949.

CHARLOTTE BOBCATS — 2004 Expansion Team.

CHICAGO BULLS — 1966 Expansion Team.

CLEVELAND CAVALIERS — 1970 Expansion Team, in 1974 moved 25 miles to Richfield, Ohio, in 1994 returned to downtown Cleveland and Gund Arena.

DALLAS MAVERICKS — 1980 Expansion Team.

DENVER NUGGETS — Denver Rockets Original Team in American Basketball Association, founded in 1967, became the Denver Nuggets in 1974, became an NBA Expansion Team in 1976.

DETROIT PISTONS — Fort Wayne Zollner Pistons joined the National Basketball League in 1941, became the Fort Wayne Pistons, withdrew from the NBL in 1948 to join the rival Basketball Association of America, in 1949 BAA renamed the NBA, in 1957 moved to Detroit, in 1988 moved to Auburn Hills, Michigan.

GOLDEN STATE WARRIORS — Philadelphia Warriors Original Team in Basketball Association of America formed in 1946, League renamed the NBA in 1949, team moved to San Francisco in 1962, moved to Oakland in 1971 and became the Golden State Warriors.

HOUSTON ROCKETS — 1967 Expansion Team San Diego Rockets, moved to Houston in 1971.

INDIANA PACERS — Original team in American Basketball Association, founded in 1967, became an NBA Expansion Team in 1976, play in Indianapolis.

LOS ANGELES CLIPPERS — 1970 Expansion Team Buffalo Braves, moved in 1978 and became the San Diego Clippers, moved to Los Angeles in 1984.

LOS ANGELES LAKERS — 1948 Minneapolis Lakers join the Basketball Association of America, League renamed the NBA in 1949, moved to the Inglewood Forum in 1961 and became the Los Angeles Lakers.

MEMPHIS GRIZZLIES — 1995 Expansion Team Vancouver Grizzlies moved to Memphis, Tennessee in 2001.

MIAMI HEAT — 1988 Expansion Team play in Overtown.

MILWAUKEE BUCKS — 1968 Expansion Team

MINNESOTA TIMBERWOLVES — 1989 Expansion Team in Minneapolis.

NEW JERSEY NETS — 1967 Original Team in the American Basketball Association the New Jersey Americans, moved to Commack, New York (on Long Island) and became the New York Nets, became an NBA Expansion Team in 1976, played at other suburban sites in Long Island and then in New Jersey, becoming the New Jersey Nets in 1977, moved to East Rutherford, New Jersey in 1981.

NEW ORLEANS/OKLAHOMA CITY HORNETS—1988 Expansion Team Charlotte Hornets, moved to New Orleans in 2002, temporarily moved team's base of operations to Oklahoma city for 2005–06 and 2006-07 seasons.

NEW YORK KNICKERBOCKERS—1946 Original Team in Basketball Association of America, which was renamed the NBA in 1949.

ORLANDO MAGIC—1989 Expansion Team.

PHILADELPHIA 76ERS—1946 Syracuse Nationals in National Basketball League, merged into Basketball Association of America and League renamed the NBA for 1949–50 season, moved in 1963 to become Philadelphia 76ers (also known as the "sixers" for short).

PHOENIX SUNS—1968 Expansion Team.

PORTLAND TRAIL BLAZERS—1970 Expansion Team.

SACRAMENTO KINGS—1945 Rochester Royals joined National Basketball League, 1948 withdrew from NBL to join the Basketball Association of America, which was renamed the NBA for 1949–50 season, 1957 moved to Cincinnati, 1972 moved to become the Kansas City Omaha Kings (playing home games in both cities), became the Kansas City Kings in 1975, moved to Sacramento in 1985.

SAN ANTONIO SPURS—1967 Original Dallas Chaparrals of the American Basketball Association, in 1970 became the Texas Chaparrals ("regional franchise" playing home games at several locations), 1971 again became the Dallas Chaparrals, 1973 moved to become San Antonio Spurs, became an NBA Expansion Team in 1976.

SEATTLE SUPERSONICS—1967 Expansion Team, played 1994–95 season in Tacoma, returned to Seattle.

TORONTO RAPTORS—1995 Expansion Team.

UTAH JAZZ—1974 Expansion Team New Orleans Jazz, moved to Salt Lake City to become the Utah Jazz in 1979.

WASHINGTON WIZARDS—1961 Expansion Team Chicago Packers, 1962 became the Chicago Zephyrs, 1963 moved to become the Baltimore Bullets, 1973 moved to Landover, Maryland and became the Capital Bullets, renamed the Washington Bullets in 1974, 1997 moved to downtown Washington, D.C. and renamed the Washington Wizards.

NATIONAL FOOTBALL LEAGUE FRANCHISE RELOCATION
NATIONAL FOOTBALL CONFERENCE

ARIZONA CARDINALS—1920 Racine Cardinals in Chicago were one of the 11 charter members of the American Professional Football League, name changed to Chicago Cardinals in 1922, in 1944 during World War II combined with the Pittsburgh Steelers to play as one team, with home games at Comiskey Park (Chicago) and Forbes Field (Pittsburgh), moved to St. Louis in 1960, moved to Phoenix (Tempe) in 1988, renamed Arizona Cardinals in 1994. moved to Glendale (in greater Phoenix) in 2006.

ATLANTA FALCONS—1966 Expansion Team.

CAROLINA PANTHERS—1995 Expansion Team.

CHICAGO BEARS—1920 Decatur Staleys of the American Professional Football League, moved and became Chicago Staleys in 1921, became Chicago Bears in 1922.

DALLAS COWBOYS—1960 Expansion Team, moved to Irving, Texas in 1971.

DETROIT LIONS—1930 Expansion Franchise Portsmouth Spartans, moved in 1934 to become the Detroit Lions, moved to Pontiac, Michigan Silverdome in 1975.

GREEN BAY PACKERS—1921 Green Bay Packers, starting in 1950s for forty years played games in Green Bay and Milwaukee, now play all home games in Green Bay.

MINNESOTA VIKINGS—1961 Expansion Team.

NEW ORLEANS SAINTS—1967 Expansion Team.

NEW YORK GIANTS—1925 New York Giants, in the 1970s played in four different home stadiums in three states (N.Y., N.J., CT), moved to East Rutherford, New Jersey (Meadowlands) in 1976.

PHILADELPHIA EAGLES—Founded in 1933

SAN FRANCISCO 49ERS—Founded in AAFC in 1946, joined NFL in 1950.

SEATTLE SEAHAWKS—1976 NFL Expansion Team

ST. LOUIS RAMS 1937 Cleveland Rams, moved to Los Angeles Memorial Coliseum in 1946, moved to Anaheim in 1980, moved to St. Louis in 1995.

TAMPA BAY BUCCANEERS—1976 Expansion Team.

WASHINGTON REDSKINS—1932 Boston Braves, became Boston Redskins in 1933, moved to become Washington Redskins in 1937, moved to Raljon, Maryland in 1997.

AMERICAN FOOTBALL CONFERENCE

BALTIMORE RAVENS—1946 Founded in AAFC as the Cleveland Browns, joined NFL in 1950, shifted to American Football Conference at start of interleague play in 1970 after merger, moved to Baltimore in 1996 and renamed the Ravens.

BUFFALO BILLS—Original AFL Team founded in 1960.

CINCINNATI BENGALS—1968 AFL Expansion Team.

CLEVELAND BROWNS—1999 NFL Expansion Team

DENVER BRONCOS—Original AFL Team founded in 1960.

HOUSTON TEXANS—2002 NFL Expansion Team.

INDIANAPOLIS COLTS—originally New York Yanks moved to Dallas, Texas in 1952, moved to Baltimore in 1953, (replaced Baltimore Colts, who had been the Miami Seahawks of the All-America Football Conference, became NFL Baltimore Colts in 1950, withdrew from NFL in 1951) moved to Indianapolis in 1984.

JACKSONVILLE JAGUARS—1995 Expansion Team.

KANSAS CITY CHIEFS—Original AFL Team founded in 1960 as Dallas Texans, moved to Kansas City in 1963.

MIAMI DOLPHINS—1966 AFL Expansion Team moved to suburban Dade County in 1987.

NEW ENGLAND PATRIOTS—Original AFL Team founded in 1960 as Boston Patriots, moved to Foxboro, Massachusetts in 1971.

NEW YORK JETS—Purchased assets of New York Titans out of bankruptcy, became New York Jets original AFL Team founded in 1960, moved to East Rutherford, New Jersey (Meadowlands) in 1984.

OAKLAND RAIDERS—Original AFL Team Founded in 1960 as Oakland Raiders, moved to Los Angeles Memorial Coliseum in 1982 (see Raiders case), moved back to Oakland in 1995.

PITTSBURGH STEELERS—1933 Pittsburgh Pirates, became Pittsburgh Steelers in 1940, shifted to American Football Conference at start of interleague play in 1970.

SAN DIEGO CHARGERS—1960 AFL Los Angeles Chargers, moved to San Diego in 1961.

TENNESSEE TITANS—Original AFL Team Founded in 1960 as the Houston Oilers, played 1997 season in Memphis, moved to Nashville in 1998 and became Tennessee Titans.

NATIONAL HOCKEY LEAGUE

FRANCHISE RELOCATION

ANAHEIM DUCKS—1993 Expansion Team (originally Mighty Ducks of Anaheim, named after Disney movie, name changed to Anaheim Ducks).

ATLANTA THRASHERS—1999 Expansion Team.

BOSTON BRUINS—Founded in 1924.

BUFFALO SABRES—1970 Expansion Team.

CALGARY FLAMES—1972 Expansion Team the Atlanta Flames, moved to Calgary in 1980.

CAROLINA HURRICANES—World Hockey Association Team New England Whalers, merged into NHL in 1979 (NHL called it an expansion), and became the Hartford Whalers. Moved to Greensboro, North Carolina, in 1997 then to Raleigh, North Carolina, upon completion of new arena in Raleigh.

CHICAGO BLACKHAWKS—Founded in 1926.

COLORADO AVALANCHE—World Hockey Association Team Quebec Nordiques, merged into NHL in 1979 (NHL called it an expansion), moved to Denver, Colorado, in 1995 and became the Colorado Avalanche.

COLUMBUS BLUE JACKETS—2000 Expansion Team.

DALLAS STARS—1967 Expansion Team Minnesota North Stars, merged with the Cleveland Browns (formerly California Seals, and then Oakland Seals) in 1978, moved to Dallas in 1993.

DETROIT RED WINGS—Detroit Cougars Founded in 1926, became Detroit Falcons in 1930, became Detroit Red Wings in 1932.

EDMONTON OILERS—World Hockey Association Alberta Oilers, moved to be WHA's Edmonton Oilers in 1973, merged into NHL in 1979 (NHL called it an expansion).

FLORIDA PANTHERS—1993 Expansion team.

LOS ANGELES KINGS—1967 Expansion Team plays in Inglewood.

MINNESOTA WILD—2000 Expansion Team.

MONTREAL CANADIENS—Founded in 1917.

NASHVILLE PREDATORS—1998 Expansion Team.

NEW JERSEY DEVILS—1974 Expansion Team Kansas City Scouts, moved to Denver and became the Colorado Rockies in 1976, moved to East Rutherford, New Jersey (Meadowlands), in 1981 and became the New Jersey Devils.

NEW YORK ISLANDERS—1972 Expansion Team, plays in Uniondale.

NEW YORK RANGERS—Founded in 1926.

OTTAWA SENATORS—1992 Expansion Team.

PHILADELPHIA FLYERS—1967 Expansion Team.

PHOENIX COYOTES—1972 World Hockey Association Team Winnipeg Jets, merged into NHL in 1979 (NHL called it an expansion), moved to Phoenix, Arizona, in 1996 and became the Phoenix Coyotes.

PITTSBURGH PENGUINS—1967 Expansion Team.

ST. LOUIS BLUES—1967 Expansion Team.

SAN JOSE SHARKS—1991 Expansion Team.

TAMPA BAY LIGHTNING—1992 Expansion Team.

TORONTO MAPLE LEAFS—Toronto Arenas founded in 1917, became Toronto St. Patricks in 1919, became Toronto Maple Leafs in 1927.

VANCOUVER CANUCKS—1970 Expansion Team.

WASHINGTON CAPITALS—1974 Expansion Team played in Landover, Maryland, moved to downtown Washington, D.C., in 1997.

MAJOR LEAGUE BASEBALL FRANCHISE RELOCATION

NATIONAL LEAGUE

ATLANTA BRAVES—The Boston Red Stockings of the National Association were founded in 1872, the National Association dissolved in 1875 and the Boston Red Stockings moved to the National League in 1876; by 1883 the team was called the Boston Beaneaters, by 1901 were called the Boston Nationals, became the Boston Doves in 1907, the Boston Rustlers in 1911, and in 1912 became the Boston Braves, Braves moved to Milwaukee in 1953, moved to Atlanta in 1966.

ARIZONA DIAMONDBACKS—1998 Expansion Team plays in Phoenix.

CHICAGO CUBS—Chicago White Stockings were founded as part of the National League in 1876, became Chicago Cubs in 1905.

CINCINNATI REDS—1882 American Association Team, Cincinnati Reds, 1889 merged with Washington Senators, National League Cincinnati Reds 1890–1943, Cincinnati Redlegs 1944–45, 1946 Cincinnati Reds.

COLORADO ROCKIES—1993 Expansion Team plays in Denver.

FLORIDA MARLINS—1993 Expansion Team plays in Suburban Dade county, part of Miami.

HOUSTON ASTROS—Houston Colts were a 1962 Expansion Team, became the Houston Colt 45's, then became the Houston Astros in 1965.

LOS ANGELES DODGERS—1884 Brooklyns, 1889 Brooklyn Bridegrooms, 1899, Brooklyn Superbas, 1911 Brooklyn Infants, 1914 Brooklyn Robins, 1932 Brooklyn Dodgers, moved to Los Angeles in 1958.

MILWAUKEE BREWERS—1969 Expansion Team Seattle Pilots, moved to Milwaukee in 1970.

NEW YORK METS—1962 Expansion Team.

PHILADELPHIA PHILLIES—1880 Worcester Brown Stockings move to become Philadelphia Phillies in 1883.

PITTSBURGH PIRATES—Founded in 1887.

ST. LOUIS CARDINALS—Founded in 1892.

SAN DIEGO PADRES—1969 Expansion Team.

SAN FRANCISCO GIANTS—1879 Troy Trojans, 1883 New York Gothams, 1885 New York Giants, moved to San Francisco in 1958.

WASHINGTON NATIONALS—1969 Expansion Team Montreal Expos, purchased by MLB in 2001, moved to Washington, D.C. in 2005.

AMERICAN LEAGUE

BALTIMORE ORIOLES—1901 Milwaukee Brewers, moved in 1902 to become St. Louis Browns, moved to Baltimore in 1954.

BOSTON RED SOX—Boston Americans of Boston Pilgrims in 1901, became Boston Red Sox in 1907.

LOS ANGELES ANGELS OF ANAHEIM—Los Angeles Angels were a 1961 Expansion Team, moved to Anaheim for 1966 season, became Los Angeles Angels of Anaheim in 2005.

CHICAGO WHITE SOX—Founded in 1901.

CLEVELAND INDIANS—1901 Cleveland Broncos, 1902 Cleveland Blues, 1905 Cleveland Naps, 1912 Cleveland Molly McGuires, 1915 Cleveland Indians.

DETROIT TIGERS—Founded in 1901.

KANSAS CITY ROYALS—1969 Expansion Team.

MILWAUKEE BREWERS—Seattle Pilots were a 1969 Expansion Team, moved to become Milwaukee Brewers in 1970.

MINNESOTA TWINS—1901 Washington Senators, moved to Minneapolis in 1961 and became the Minnesota Twins.

NEW YORK YANKEES—Defunct 1901–02 Baltimore Orioles franchise purchased in 1903 and began play as the New York Highlanders, moved to Polo Grounds and became New York Yankees in 1913 (it has been reported that sportswriters used the name "Yankees" unofficially prior to 1913 because "Highlanders" was too long to put in headlines).

OAKLAND ATHLETICS (OR A's)—1901 Philadelphia Athletics, moved to Kansas City in 1955, moved to Oakland in 1968.

SEATTLE MARINERS—1977 Expansion Team.

TAMPA BAY RAYS—1998 Expansion Team Tampa Bay Devil Rays, name changed from "Devil Rays" to Rays in 2007, plays in St. Petersburg, Florida.

TEXAS RANGERS—1961 Expansion Team, originally the "second" Washington Senators, moved to Arlington, Texas, in 1972.

TORONTO BLUE JAYS—1977 Expansion Team.

Notes and Questions

1. Since the decision of the Ninth Circuit in *Raiders I*, the major sports leagues have tried to avoid any denial of a relocation request that could lead to judicial scrutiny. Several NFL relocations have been approved under threat of antitrust challenge. In addition, when the NBA, in 1994, confronted a request by an owner to sell to a purchasing group that intended to relocate the team, the league denied the request to sell, thereby obviating the need to rule on a request to relocate. *See generally National Basketball Association v. Minnesota Professional Basketball, L.P.*, 56 F.3d 866 (8th Cir. 1995). On June 5, 1994, the owner of the Minnesota Timberwolves signed an agreement to sell the team to Top Rank of Louisiana, Inc. ("Top Rank"), a corporation led by boxing promoter Bob Arum. Top Rank intended to relocate the team to New Orleans for the 1994–95

season, and the team and Top Rank submitted applications to the NBA Board of Governors for approval of the sale and relocation. On June 15, 1994, an NBA committee voted to recommend that the sale not be approved because Top Rank had refused to disclose the source of funds that would be used to purchase the team. 56 F.3d at 869. That same day, the NBA filed a lawsuit in federal district court in Minneapolis, seeking an injunction to prohibit the team and Top Rank from relocating the team unless and until the transactions were approved by the league. When asked about the speed with which the NBA prepared and filed the complaint, NBA Commissioner David Stern replied, "Sometimes, we have lawsuits in a drawer for special occasions—birthdays, weddings and franchise transfers." Greg Boeck, *NBA Committee Says T-Wolves Should Stay*, USA TODAY, June 16, 1994, at 1C . On June 23, 1994 the federal district court issued a temporary injunction sought by the NBA; Top Rank responded the next day by filing a lawsuit in state court in Louisiana. Four days later, the state court enjoined the NBA and the team from finalizing their 1994–95 schedule. On July 1, 1994 the federal district court enjoined the sale to Top Rank, enjoined the defendants from moving the team, enjoined the defendants from participating in the case in Louisiana, and enjoined the Louisiana court from conducting any further proceedings in its case. *See NBA v. Minnesota Professional Basketball, L.P.*, 56 F.3d at 869–70. About one year after the district court's rulings, the Eighth Circuit affirmed those rulings, except for the lower court's injunction precluding the Louisiana court from conducting further proceedings in its pending case. *Id.* at 871–73.

2. Could the owner of the Timberwolves and Top Rank have challenged the NBA's conduct under the antitrust laws as a subterfuge to prevent relocation? Would your assessment change if there were documents showing that the NBA committee's discussion had focused on ways to block a relocation without relying on the NBA's franchise transfer provisions, specifically to avoid *Raiders*-type litigation?

3. Why did the NBA believe that it was so important to file first? Is that a strategy that you would advise a sports league to follow? If the relocating owner could prove that the league was preparing its complaint long before the NBA committee had ever deliberated about the proposed sale and relocation, could he or she challenge the league's conduct on the theory that the league's pre-judgment denied him the fair hearing that the NBA Constitution & Bylaws guarantees? Think back to the arguments made by Pete Rose in Chapter 3 and by figure skater Tonya Harding in her disputes with the United States Olympic Committee and the United States Figure Skating Association. Would proof of prejudgment or other manifestation of bias help a plaintiff asserting a *Raiders*-type antitrust claim?

III. Franchise Relocation and the Business of Professional Sports Leagues

(A) Introduction

Media coverage of franchise relocation is often dominated by emotional descriptions of the "perpetrators" and the "victims": "Greedy teams are abusing city officials." "The ungrateful, heartless relocating team is abandoning loyal fans." "Cities without teams are behaving like hostile raiders, seeking to steal a team from a poor, unsuspecting city and its fans." "Team owners are extorting both the stadium authority where they now play as well as potential relocation cities, demanding free stadia with luxury boxes and club seats, state-of-the-art training and practice facilities, special tax treatment, and a variety of other unreasonable financial concessions that are likely to burden taxpayers for years to come." "The financial concessions demanded by the avaricious owner are improperly diverting public funds away from public education and the construction of schools and other facilities needed by the children in the community."

The business analysis is much less emotional. The franchise relocation phenomenon flows inevitably from the economics of the major professional sports leagues and their teams. An examination of the recent history and economics of major sports league franchise relocation, and the incentives of the league office and the owners reviewing a team's relocation proposal speaks to the inevitability of franchise relocation and league efforts to restrict it.

(B) Recent History of Major Sports League Franchise Relocation

The Raiders' relocation from Oakland to Los Angeles and the associated litigation in the early 1980s created tremendous national interest in franchise shifts. The Raiders left sell-out crowds and "loyal fans" in Oakland, in search of a better business situation in Los Angeles. The Los Angeles Memorial Coliseum Commission, having lost the Rams to the "Big A" in Anaheim, was desperately in search of a replacement major league professional football team tenant. Prior to the departure of the Raiders, and despite the long history of franchise relocation revealed by the charts above, only the near-simultaneous coastal migration of baseball's Dodgers from Brooklyn's Ebbets Field to Los Angeles and the Giants from New York's Polo Grounds to San Francisco had been the subject of such intense national attention.

In response to the Raiders' lawsuit and jury verdict, the NFL sought sanctuary from Congress, threatening that, without an antitrust exemption, the major sports leagues would be defenseless against the inevitability of massive franchise relocation. Despite a number of hearings and the introduction of a series of legislative measures, Congress as a whole expressed very little interest in the issue. At the same time, despite their predictions of imminent doom, the NFL and NBA managed to prevent almost all team relocation for over ten years. Except for the Clippers and the Colts, who moved within three months of the Ninth Circuit's issuance of the *Raiders I* decision, only the NBA's Kansas City Kings to Sacramento (1985) and the NFL's St. Louis Cardinals to Phoenix (1987) moved in the succeeding ten years.

The issue of franchise relocation resurfaced in a major way in 1995, as unprecedented NFL player free agency placed competitive and financial pressure on NFL teams. At the same time, the NFL expansion process, promised since the early 1980s and ongoing through the early 1990s, concluded at the end of 1993. The NFL had expanded by two teams in 1977 (Seattle Seahawks and Tampa Bay Buccaneers) and had delayed the next expansion for eighteen years (the Charlotte Panthers and Jacksonville Jaguars began play in 1995).

States and cities that had been unsuccessful participants in the NFL expansion process had planned first class football-only stadia and associated facilities, moved favorable enabling legislation through state legislatures, and developed ways to finance their projects, including the sale of season tickets in conjunction with personal seat licenses or the use of other modern financing techniques. These cities and states were offering extremely generous financial packages to the owner of any NFL team that located in, or relocated to, their stadia. The expansion process had whetted the appetite of these cities and states for an NFL football team, and they were unwilling to wait for the next NFL expansion, which might never come to fruition. NFL owners' and league officials' expressions of hostility toward the notion of dividing national television revenues among any more teams and other factors led to predictions that the next NFL expansion might not occur for another eighteen (or more) years.

Three of the unsuccessful expansion candidates, St. Louis, Baltimore, and Oakland, were ex-NFL towns, and they believed that they had earned NFL franchises. During the expansion process, they were very deferential to the NFL; several candidates even agreed, at the behest of the NFL league office, not to discuss relocation with league owners while this process was ongoing. Now that they had been rejected, they saw relocation as their only viable means for securing an NFL franchise in the next ten to twenty years. In fact, relocation led to expansion as the NFL continues to issue expansion teams to replace teams that leave cities. The Cleveland Browns replaced the Browns who departed to become the Baltimore Ravens. The Houston Texans replaced the Houston Oilers who had become the Tennessee Titans. The NFL continues to explore options for replacing the Rams and/or the Raiders in the Los Angeles area.

(C) Restriction of the Number of Teams Creates Competitive Pressure

A potential team purchaser or city or state wanting to attract a major professional football team has only one league to approach. The same is true for baseball, hockey, and basketball. As mentioned in the introduction to this chapter, public pressure from fans and legislators has permitted, and perhaps even driven, each of the major sports to combine into a single surviving league. Putting aside the question of the extent of competition between leagues in different sports, each league, together with its member teams, has a monopoly position with respect to the location of teams within that league. If the relevant market is broader than a single sport, the league and its member clubs will not have a monopoly in the antitrust sense; but, to a city, a stadium authority, a state, or a politician seeking to open the door to professional football in their local region, the NFL teams hold the keys. At the same time, the leagues have expanded much more slowly than the number of locations that can support teams have increased, both domestically and internationally. The demand for teams has continued to rise while the supply has lagged, thereby creating what would generally be described as a deficit.

(D) The Only Long-Term Solution Increasing the Supply of Teams to Satisfy the Excess Demand Is Not Likely in the Near Future

Many of the leading commentators, including even commentators who consistently voice only positions advocated by the leagues, have written and testified before Congress that the only long-term solutions are government regulation, mandated expansion, or forced division into at least two competing leagues. *See, e.g.,* Testimony of Stephen R.

Ross, "Antitrust Issues in Relocation of Professional Sports Franchises," Hearing before the Subcommittee on Antitrust, Business Rights, and Competition of the Senate Committee on the Judiciary, 104th Cong., 1st Sess. (November 29, 1995); Testimony of Andrew Zimbalist, "Professional Sports: The Challenges Facing the Future of the Industry," Hearing before the Senate Committee on the Judiciary on Challenges Facing the Future of the Professional Sports Industry, 104th Cong., 2d Sess. (January 23, 1996); Testimony of Andrew Zimbalist, "The Economics of Stadiums, Teams and Cities," Hearing before the Subcommittee on Commerce, Trade and Hazardous Materials of the House Committee on Commerce on H.R. 2740: The Fan Freedom and Community Protection Act of 1995, 104th Cong., 2d Sess. (May 16, 1996); Testimony of Gary R. Roberts, "Professional Sports Franchise Relocation: Antitrust Implications," Hearing before the House Committee on the Judiciary, 104th Cong., 2d Sess. (February 6, 1996). However, it is apparent that Congress is not going to act to bring about any of those results. Therefore, it is economically inevitable that there will be more cities and stadium authorities seeking to attract or retain teams than the number of available franchises.

(E) Many Factors Combine to Limit the Number of Teams Both Willing and Able to Relocate

Another inevitability is that the number of cities and stadium authorities seeking to attract teams at any point in time will be much greater than the number of teams willing and able to relocate. Teams in major professional sports leagues generally have very long-term leases at least ten year terms and often thirty year terms or longer. Some teams have negotiated for the right to terminate their leases before their expiration, which gives them additional flexibility if a better situation is offered. However, there typically will be few teams that are free to walk away from their existing lease in a given year.

For a variety of reasons, many team owners are reluctant to relocate, even when their lease or its expiration permits them to do so. An owner may own the stadium, the owner and/or the owner's family may be committed to stay in that geographic area, or the owner may own other businesses in that area (including other sports teams or sports businesses). The owner is likely to have achieved a prominent place in the community, with strong civic, business, and social ties, much of which may be lost if the owner relocates one of the community's prize "possessions" out of the area. In addition, the relocating owner may bear a great number of other costs that are associated with a relocation out of the team's home territory.

From the perspective of an owner, the prospect of relocating a major professional sports franchise is a daunting and risky endeavor. Therefore, a rational owner will generally not want to move his or her team unless there are problems in the current location and a much better situation somewhere else. The costs of moving may include one or more "lame duck" seasons in the original location and/or one or more seasons playing in an inferior stadium or arena in the new city while a new facility is being constructed. The ultimate disaster would be for the team to be forced to remain in its original location. Owners who seek to relocate their teams are often subject to intense local hostility from media, fans, and the business community.

There are also potential problems awaiting the owner in the new location. If the move is based on government funding of a new facility, withdrawal of approval for any number of reasons could leave the new team without an arena. It is not uncommon for legal issues to arise concerning the permissibility of using certain tax revenues and other sources of government funding to construct a sports facility that will benefit private parties. Construction delays can also create tremendous problems for the relocating owner. In effect, the owner is leaving the known problems of the existing facility and home territory for the unknown problems in the new territory.

The litigation and disapproval risks of a proposed relocation are perhaps the most substantial. As discussed above, the response to any major sports team's announcement of a proposed relocation is likely to include litigation by fans, taxpayers, the stadium authority, and governmental bodies in the abandoned locale. Even litigation that is completely without merit can be costly. League approval may not be forthcoming, and the league may even file preemptive litigation to restrain the relocation. In the alternative, the league may approve the relocation but condition approval upon payment of a relocation fee and other financial and non-financial concessions that will render the decision to relocate unprofitable. During the league relocation process, the league and other team owners may take positions adverse to the relocation, criticizing the team, the owner, and its management, and blaming them for the financial circumstances that led to the decision to move. The league may "punish" a relocating owner in many different ways, all in an effort to deter relocation in general and to deflect criticism away from the league. Congressional hearings are often convened, and there is even a risk that Congress will add additional costs and consequences to relocations, forcing relocating owners to leave their team marks and logos behind. As a result, among the very small number of owners able to move at any point in time, an even smaller number will even seriously consider relocation.

(F) Reasons Why Owners May Seek to Relocate

The business and personal considerations that may motivate an owner to relocate are too numerous to catalog. However, as competition intensifies among teams for players and coaches, the pressure to identify additional revenue sources increases dramatically. It is generally safe to assume that the relocation will yield very significant financial benefits to the relocating owner. Those benefits may include revenue streams that will not be shared with the other owners in the league, as well as many other forms of compensation. Relocating owners have been promised lucrative real estate propositions, ownership of stadia and practice facilities, and other financial inducements.

The importance of the team's improved financial condition may vary from owner to owner. An owner who acquired a team many years ago may have no debt to service and may be content with the financial performance of the team. On the other hand, a newer owner, who recently paid market value for a team, may need to service a large debt and may have a greater drive to increase the team's profitability. Moreover, an owner who does not own other businesses and who depends on the team to generate sufficient positive cash flow for financial support may not be content with the fact that the team is increasing in value.

(G) League Office and Owner Consideration of Proposed Team Relocation

Once an owner has made the decision to relocate a team and has commenced negotiations to bring about that result, an important consideration is the likelihood that the relocation will receive league approval. An analysis of the effects of relocation on the other owners in the league suggests that, under most circumstances, there is likely to be an inherent bias among owners against permitting relocations by other teams in the league.

(1) The Commissioner and the League Office Are Likely to Oppose Relocation Strenuously

Whenever a team in a major professional league announces that it is considering relocating, everyone desiring to retain the team is likely to contact their league office, legislators, and other interested parties. The typical result is that the criticism of the relocation that is not directed at the relocating owner is leveled at the league itself. The league office has to attend congressional hearings to explain and defend the league policy, conduct the league's review of the proposed relocation and issue a recommendation, schedule and run potentially contentious league meetings, consult with league counsel about the legal ramifications if the league approves or disapproves the relocation, meet with representatives of the city and stadium from which the team seeks to depart, spend several months answering the media's questions about the relocation and the league's intentions, confer with the owners to elicit their views about the move, and participate in any litigation that results. In addition, if the relocation is approved by the league, the league office is likely to receive a cool reception from public officials who opposed the relocation, especially when the league is seeking legislative assistance in other contexts. The attention that has to be focused on relocation issues is also likely to detract from the league commissioner's efforts to advance other aspects of his or her agenda.

If the relocation eventually occurs, there is likely to be substantial animosity from some fans of the abandoned city directed toward the league. The commissioner may be vilified as an ineffective leader unable to control the teams. At the same time, it is unlikely that the fans in the new city will have warm feelings toward the league office, which may be perceived as a thorn in the side of the relocating owner and potential impediment to the municipality's securing of a franchise. The league may feel compelled to award an expansion team to an owner in the "abandoned" city as happened when the NFL created the Cleveland Browns and the Houston Texans after the original Browns became the Baltimore Ravens and the Houston Oilers moved to Nashville to be the Tennessee Titans. That will require additional division of league profit.

If, however, the league is successful in blocking the relocation and resolving the situation in a way that keeps the team in its home territory, such conduct is generally viewed by the national media as evidence of the strength and power of the commissioner and his control over the operations of the league and its teams. For example, NBA Commissioner David Stern generally received very positive reviews for his handling of the attempt by the owner of the Timberwolves to sell the team for eventual relocation to New Orleans.

For all these reasons, there is a great incentive for the league office to use its power and influence to block relocations. When a relocation is announced, if the league can develop a plan by which the home territory matches or approaches matching the offer from the team's new destination, the league office emerges a winner, while achieving what the league wants—a general improvement in the facilities and financial condition of a member team in its home territory. Therefore, it is not surprising that the commissioners and league counsel of the major professional sports leagues have testified in congressional hearings that they oppose team relocation and that they need legislative assistance to permit the league to block relocations without fear of liability.

(2) Reasons Owners May Support a Proposed Relocation

There are several reasons underlying a fellow owner's vote in favor of an owner's decision to relocate. He or she may believe that the move is good for the league. Most relocations improve the quality of the team's game facilities, thereby enhancing the overall quality of the league product. A relocation may also lead to increased home game attendance for the relocating team, which may be shared with visiting teams under the league rules. The relocation of the team to a new geographic area is likely to generate substantial local, and sometimes national, interest in licensed merchandise of the relocating team, and the profits from those sales are generally shared on some basis among all owners in the league. If the relocation leads to a higher market valuation of the relocating team, that valuation may raise the asking price when a non-relocating owner seeks to sell his own team.

In addition, a non-relocating owner may simply believe that the league's Constitution & Bylaws were intended to give owners the prerogative to relocate unless there are overwhelming reasons to block the exercise of that right. The non-relocating owner may want to help the relocating owner and may vote for approval out of friendship. Other owners, from a selfish standpoint, may vote to approve a relocation as a precedent because: (1) they may want to relocate in the near future and may consider a vote of disapproval to be a negative league precedent; (2) they may need a credible threat that the league will permit relocation to convince their current landlord to improve their situation; and/or (3) they may be considering a sale of their team, and they will recognize that a team permitted to relocate without interference will be worth more to potential buyers.

Finally, owners may believe that stopping the relocation would be illegal, and would subject the league and its member teams to costs and other problems associated with major antitrust and business tort litigation. The more lucrative the relocating owner's deal, the greater the damage a league disapproval decision would inflict, and the greater the potential sustainable damage award from a jury. Except for owners who support relocation and vote to approve based on principle, and those individuals who want the potential indirect benefits from a pro-relocation precedent, the primary motivation for voting to approve relocation is likely to be this threat of litigation.

(3) Reasons Owners May Oppose a Proposed Relocation

While a non-relocating owner may perceive a proposed relocation as advantageous, the basic economics of professional sports leagues makes that an unlikely possibility for a number of reasons. First, teams in the major professional sports leagues generally do not have anything approaching a unity of interest with respect to the categories of revenue that are likely to increase as a result of the relocation. For example, consider stadium-related revenues of NFL teams. Certain categories, such as parking, concessions, and luxury box rental fees, are not shared at all. In addition, contrary to popular understanding, even those stadium revenues that are shared to some extent are certainly not shared equally among the teams in the league. One such category is gate receipts, which are shared on the basis of 66% to the home team and 34% to the visiting team. Assume that an NFL team moves to a new stadium and, as a result, sells an extra 20,000 tickets per regular season game at $50 per ticket. For eight home regular season games, those seats will generate an extra one million dollars of revenue per game, with $660,000 per game and $5.28 million per season going to the home team. Eight visiting teams will each receive $340,000. The remaining twenty-one teams in the league will not receive any of the eight million dollars of increased revenue that season. Over an eight-year period, the four teams in the same division of the NFL will each receive 4.255% of the extra revenue, the ten other teams in the same conference will each receive about one percent, and the fifteen teams in the other conference will each play only one game in eight years at the new stadium, and will therefore each receive about one-half of one percent (.55%) of the extra revenue. The home team (the relocating team) will receive 66% of the revenue. It is clear that the thirty teams hardly have anything approaching a complete unity of interest with respect to those additional ticket sales, even though they are among the revenue streams that are "shared."

Second, while the league office will bear the brunt of the media attacks and the congressional inquiries, the other owners in the league will not be immune from the negative fallout of a proposed relocation. To the extent that relocations cause any fan disillusionment with the league or any reduction in television ratings of national television broadcasts, all the owners will suffer their *pro rata* share of the harm.

Third, as explained above, many owners have no intention of ever moving outside their home territory, and their primary concern about relocation is the prospect that another team might relocate into their home territory. Therefore, any league policy or precedent that permits relocation or makes it easier to relocate increases the risk that an exclusive territory might be invaded in the future. For example, if the league permits relocations into unoccupied territories, it will be very difficult for the league to block relocations that would hurt another team (such as the Raiders' relocations, first to Los Angeles to compete with the Rams, and then to Oakland to compete with the San Francisco 49ers). In Major League Baseball, the Baltimore Orioles strenuously resisted the League's relocation of the Montreal Expos to become the Washington Nationals. The Orioles received substantial concessions from the League as compensation for the Nationals moving into the Orioles' "territory."

Fourth, and perhaps most important, it must be remembered that the teams in a traditional model league all compete with each other. They compete for players and for coaches, and a relocation that improves the financial condition of a competitor will increase the costs of every other team in the league. Teams with greater financial strength can offer more money, better facilities, and greater amenities to attract the best players and coaches. These factors are all interrelated, creating a positive synergy wherein one advantage begets another (excellent coaches attract excellent players, excellent facilities attract excellent coaches, etc.).

Fifth, in the world of salary caps, the effect of the relocation depends on the collective bargaining agreement and whether it places a cap on team expenditures for players. However, even in a league that presently has negotiated a salary cap, the owners must anticipate that a future collective bargaining agreement may not include any limitation on the amounts paid to players. In addition, even when a salary cap is in place, computation of the overall league cap and the individual team minimum and maximum salaries may take into account stadium revenue streams that will be increased as a result of the relocation. If so, a relocation by a single team will increase the salary cap. Given that a number of teams in the league will "spend to the cap," any increase in the cap is likely to cause at least an equal increase in the spending by a number of teams and an overall increase in league-wide team costs. Therefore, while the non-relocating teams will not receive anything approaching a *pro rata* share of the increased revenues, they will suffer a proportional increase in costs caused by the relocation's effect on the league salary cap.

Sixth, as counter-intuitive as it may seem, a number of owners do not want to increase the market value of teams in their league because of estate tax and estate planning concerns. For owners who have no intention of selling their teams, an increase in value is not generally a benefit. While an increased valuation might make it possible to borrow more money, with the team as collateral, league rules often cap the amount that a team can borrow well below the amount of a loan that the team value would support. Therefore, the primary effect of an increased valuation would be to increase the amount of estate tax due when an owner dies. When the Internal Revenue Service attempts to support a high valuation for a team upon the death of its owner, the primary evidence will be recent sale prices for other teams in the league. While there are other complex, negative estate planning consequences, the general conclusion is that anything increasing the value of other teams is likely to lead to higher valuations and higher estate tax obligations for the other owners' estates, unless and until estate taxes are repealed.

Seventh, as explained above, relocation may lead to pressure to award an expansion team to an owner in the abandoned city, yielding one more owner to share the league's profits and one more team to compete annually for the league championship.

As the Ninth Circuit observed in *Raiders I*, when a league has a requirement that a proposed relocation receive approval from a super-majority of the other owners, like the NFL's ¾ (24 out of 32) requirement, it will not be difficult for a league office that opposes a relocation to convince the necessary number of owners to block the relocation. While there will always be, for each relocation, at least one owner who is adamantly in favor of approval (the relocating owner), there will probably be a substantial number of owners who believe that approving the relocation is directly contrary to their economic interests.

(H) Conclusions

This analysis of the incentives and tendencies of the participants in league decisionmaking concerning relocation suggests a number of possible conclusions. First, except for relocations threatened as a negotiation tactic to improve a team's situation in its home territory, a major professional sports league team is likely to attempt to relocate out of its home territory only when the relocation will cause a major improvement in its financial condition. Second, if fans and politicians in the current territory of the team are willing to protest and fight the relocation, most owners and the league office are likely to disapprove. Third, if there is not a credible threat of litigation against the league and/or its owners, they are likely to disapprove the relocation. Fourth, if Congress eliminates all threats of litigation against sports leagues arising out of such disapproval, almost all relocation requests will be denied, unless the relocating owner can offer the other owners sufficient financial incentives to gain their approval. While not everyone will agree with these conclusions, the legislators who have introduced many of the recent bills in Congress share the expectation that leagues with antitrust immunity will prevent almost all relocations.

Notes and Questions

1. In the *Raiders I* opinion, the Ninth Circuit opined that "[t]o the extent the NFL finds the law inadequate, it must look to Congress for relief." The NFL has heeded that advice and encouraged congressional intervention. Whenever a team seeks to relocate out of a state, even if the relocation is within the team's "home territory," the members of Congress from that state often call for congressional hearings to block the relocation. At the same time, legislators representing other states with teams considering relocation often ally themselves with the anti-relocation forces.

Congressional hearings concerning these issues were held shortly after the *Raiders* jury verdict, at the time the St. Louis Cardinals were considering relocating to Phoenix, and most recently when a number of relocations were announced by owners in the NFL and other major sports leagues. *See, e.g.,* "Professional Sports Antitrust Immunity," Hearings before the Senate Committee on the Judiciary on S. 2784 and S. 2821, 97th Cong., 2d Sess. (August 16, September 16, 20 and 29, 1982); "Professional Sports Antitrust Immunity," Hearings before the Senate Committee on the Judiciary on S. 172, S. 259, and S. 298, 99th Cong., 1st Sess. (February 6, March 6, and June 12, 1985); "Antitrust Issues in Relocation of Professional Sports Franchises," Hearing before the Subcommittee on Antitrust, Business Rights, and Competition of the Senate Committee on the Judiciary, 104th Cong., 1st Sess. (November 29, 1995); "Professional Sports: The Challenges Facing the Future of the Industry," Hearing before the Senate Committee on the Judiciary, 104th Cong., 2d Sess. (January 23, 1996); "Professional Sports Franchise Relocation: Antitrust Implications," Hearing before the House Committee on the Judiciary, 104th Cong., 2d Sess. (February 6, 1996); Hearing before the Subcommittee on Commerce, Trade and Hazardous Materials of the House Committee on Commerce concerning H.R. 2740: The Fan Freedom and Community Protection Act of 1995, 104th Cong., 2d Sess. (May 16, 1996). Many of the bills that have been introduced by members of Congress and debated in these congressional hearings would incorporate some or all of the NFL's 1984 Guidelines. Those bills generally provide that if a major professional sports league evaluates proposed team relocations under some or all of the criteria in the Guidelines, any decision by the sports leagues to approve the relocation, to disapprove the relocation, or to approve the relocation subject to conditions (such as substantial financial transfers from the relocating team to the other teams in the league) would be exempt from antitrust scrutiny. Should Congress give the NFL this type of an antitrust exemption?

2. Federal legislation concerning relocation could assume many different forms. What legislative and public policy goals should Congress seek to achieve as it considers alternative legislation to address relocation issues? Various bills considered by the Senate and/or the House of Representatives have included some of the following objectives: (1) prevent all relocation of teams; (2) create a "seniority" system, in which cities with major league teams keep their teams and cities still seeking teams await league expansion; (3) force owners who want to relocate to sell their teams to new owners who will not relocate; (4) leave all decisions about relocation in the hands of the sports leagues; (5) place the final decisions about the relocation of sports teams in the hands of the courts or independent arbitration panels; (6) punish teams that relocate or leagues that permit relocation by requiring the league to replace relocating teams with expansion teams or requiring the relocating team to leave its logos and marks, team name, team colors, and team history behind for use by the next expansion or relocating team in that city; (7) encourage cities and stadium authorities to spend a reasonable amount of money on an ongoing basis to maintain the quality of the stadia and arenas where fans watch sporting events and other entertainment products; (8) permit the relocation of teams when relocation will increase fan interest and improve the quality of the stadium or arena where the team will play; (9) restrict relocation that does not involve movement to larger television markets or to markets where tickets to attend the team's games will be in greater demand; (10) ensure that relocation only occurs after fans, politicians, and other "interested parties" have an opportunity to express their views about the relocation; (11) outlaw leagues' conditioning of relocation on payments by the relocating team to eliminate one incentive for the other owners to approve relocation; and (12) encourage leagues to increase the transfer payments from high revenue to low revenue

teams (revenue sharing). In the alternative, should Congress mandate that professional sports leagues expand the number of teams in their leagues to accommodate cities that could support, but do not presently have, teams? If Congress decides to regulate relocation, should the legislators enact laws that insulate the cities in their states from competition from cities in other states that do not now have teams?

3. Could vigorous legislative action create a sort of seniority system, in which the cities would retain their teams forever, notwithstanding changes in demographics, population migration, or other exigencies? Would the legislation encourage or discourage improvements in the quality of the leagues' stadia, arenas, and other facilities? Is expansion more or less likely as a result of the legislation? Most important, will the system that you envision replace market competition with market regulation by team owners, and, if so, is that result in the public's best interest?

4. Certain bills that have been introduced would require leagues to consider whether the relocating owner had received a fair market value offer to purchase the team from a local owner or a prospective owner who would not move the team. Is it appropriate for either Congress or a sports league to try to coerce a team owner to sell his or her team? Is such conduct consistent with the obligations owed by the league to its owners or by owners to each other? How would you evaluate whether a relocating owner had received a fair market value offer for his team? Should you assess the team's value under the best terms offered by the stadium authority in the new city or under the best terms offered in the team's current location or within the team's home territory? How important would be the amounts most recently paid to purchase other teams in the league? Should you reduce the fair market value to account for any local hostility prompted by the team's announced desire to relocate? Once it is generally known that offers to buy the team will be considered, is the fact that potential owners might bid low, hoping to purchase the team under "fire sale" circumstances, relevant?

5. Despite the absence of legislation, the NFL conspiracy to prevent relocation appears to have continued unabated. Only coercing departing owners to release all claims, see *VKK Corp. v. NFL*, 154 F.3d 851 (8th Cir. 1998), saved the league and its member teams from treble damages of hundreds of millions of dollars.

6. The disputes between the NFL and the Raiders continued for another decade, including not just antitrust claims, but a wide variety of state statutory and common law claims. *See, e.g., NFL Properties, Inc. v. Superior Court*, 75 Cal Rptr.2d 893, 65 Cal.App.4th 100 (Cal.App. 6 Dist. 1998); *Oakland Raiders v. NFL*, 81 Cal.Rptr.2d 773, 69 Call.App.4th 680 (Cal.App. 6 Dist. 2001) and 25 Cal.Rptr.3d 141, 126 Cal.App.4th 1564 (Cal.App. 2 Dist. 2005) and 32 Cal.Rptr.3d 266 (Cal.App. 6 Dist. 2005). At what point could a league (or its Commissioner) take severe disciplinary action (including perhaps exclusion from the league) against a team that pursues a series of unsuccessful legal actions against the league, its member clubs, and individual league employees, including the Commissioner?

7. The *NASL* case and, more importantly, the *Raiders* decision, drew attention to the fact that league restrictions on individual teams might violate federal antitrust law. The NFL's cross-ownership ban had been held unlawful in *NASL*, and its rules that restricted relocation had been held unlawful as applied to the Raiders' efforts to move to Los Angeles. The NFL's blanket prohibition on public ownership of NFL teams or public ownership of any entity that owns an interest in an NFL team came under attack in a lawsuit by Billy Sullivan, the former owner of the New England Patriots. The decision in that case follows, below.

Sullivan v. National Football League

34 F.3d 1091 (1st Cir. 1994)

TORRUELLA, Chief Judge. * * * Under Article 3.5 of the NFL's constitution and by-laws, three-quarters of the NFL club owners must approve all transfers of ownership interests in an NFL team, other than transfers within a family. In conjunction with this rule is an uncodified policy against the sale of ownership interests in an NFL club to the public through offerings of publicly traded stock. The members, however, retain full authority to approve any given transfer by a three-quarters vote according to Article 3.5.

[William H. Sullivan II owned the New England Patriots from the team's inception in 1959 until October of 1988. When Sullivan formed the Patriots, the team was part of the old American Football League ("AFL"), which was separate from the NFL, and which had no policy against public ownership of teams. Sullivan and his partner sold non-voting shares of the team to the public beginning in 1960.] In 1966, the AFL and the old NFL merged into a single league. Under the terms of the merger, the new NFL adopted the old NFL's policy against public ownership. The Patriots, however, were allowed to retain their level of public ownership as a special exception to the rule under a grandfather clause.

[In 1976, Sullivan sought to "take the Patriots private." He did this by acquiring all of the publicly held shares of the Patriots through a merger of the club into a new Sullivan-owned company. Stockholders approved the transfer and the transaction was subsequently consummated, but some shareholders subsequently brought suit, challenging the sufficiency of the purchase price Sullivan had paid for the public shares.] After protracted litigation, the shareholders obtained a judgment requiring Sullivan to pay them a higher price for their shares. The Patriots then became a fully privately owned club.

Sullivan and his son, Chuck Sullivan, who owned the stadium where the Patriots played [Sullivan Stadium], began to experience financial difficulties and increasing debt burdens in the mid-1980s. The Sullivans decided that they needed to raise capital to alleviate their financial problems. After the Boston Celtics professional basketball franchise made a public offering of 40% of the team in December of 1986, the Sullivans decided to pursue a similar deal with the Patriots to raise cash to cover some of their debts.

On October 19, 1987, the Sullivans met with Stephens, Inc., a small investment banking firm in Little Rock, Arkansas. They discussed a debt financing deal whereby Stephens would loan the Sullivans $80 million dollars, with half going to the Patriots and the other half to Chuck Sullivan's company which owned the Patriots' stadium. The Patriots' portion of the loan would be repaid out of the proceeds of the sale of 49% of the Patriots through the offering of public stock. Stephens agreed to look into the possibility of arranging the deal, but informed the Sullivans that they would first have to get NFL approval. Sullivan ultimately never obtained NFL approval and the deal with Stephens never progressed beyond some preliminary discussions.

At a meeting of the NFL owners on October 27, 1987, Sullivan raised his stock sale idea with the other owners and asked for a modification of the NFL's policy against public ownership to allow for certain controlled sales of minority interests in NFL clubs. Alternatively, Sullivan requested a waiver from the public ownership policy for his contemplated public offering of the Patriots. Sullivan's request was eventually tabled at this meeting. Discussions continued among the owners and, at one point, Sullivan counted 17 of the 21 owners needed for approval as being in favor of allowing him to make his public offering (seven owners were still undecided). Pete Rozelle, NFL Commissioner at the time, told Sullivan that he was not in favor of Sullivan's proposals and that league approval was "very dubious." Sullivan ultimately never asked for a vote on amending the ownership policy or on waiving the policy for the Patriots, and the NFL never held such a vote. Sullivan claims that he did not ask for a vote because it would have been futile.

In October of 1988, Sullivan sold the Patriots for approximately $83.7 million to KMS Patriots L.P. ("KMS"), a limited partnership owned by Victor Kiam and Francis Murray. * * *

On May 16, 1991, Sullivan sued the NFL claiming that, among other things, the NFL had violated the Sherman Antitrust Act, 15 U.S.C. 1 2, by preventing him from selling 49% of the Patriots to the public in an equity offering. [Sullivan alleged that, absent the NFL's public ownership policy, he would have been able to retain a majority share of a rapidly appreciating asset with a high potential for future profits. Instead, Sullivan asserted, he was forced to sell the Patriots at a depressed price to private buyers.] Sullivan alleged that, as a result, he was forced to sell the entire team to a private buyer at a fire sale price in order to pay off existing debts. Prior to trial, the district court dismissed Sullivan's claim under 2 of the Sherman Act along with various state law claims. After a trial on Sullivan's claim under 1 of the Sherman Act, the jury rendered a verdict for Sullivan in the amount of $ 38 million, which the judge later reduced through remittitur to $17 million. Pursuant to 15 U.S.C. 15, which provides for treble damages for antitrust violations, the court entered a final judgment for Sullivan of $51 million.

II. ANALYSIS

The NFL has raised a number of issues on appeal concerning the application of 1 of the Sherman Act to the facts of this case, which, according to the NFL, entitle it to judgment as a matter of law. We address these issues first to see if the present case should be dismissed, and we ultimately conclude that it should not. We next address the NFL's allegations of trial error and we find that several of them require that we overturn the verdict in this case and order a new trial. * * *

III. ISSUES ALLEGEDLY REQUIRING JUDGMENT FOR THE NFL

A. Lack of Antitrust Injury

* * *

The jury determined in this case, via a special verdict form, that the relevant market is the "nationwide market for the sale and purchase of ownership interests in the National Football League member clubs, in general, and in the New England Patriots, in particular." The jury went on to find that the NFL's policy had an "actual harmful effect" on competition in this market.

The NFL argues on appeal that Sullivan has not established the existence of any injury to competition, and thus has not established a restraint of trade that can be attributed to the NFL's ownership policy. The league's attack is two-fold, asserting (1) that NFL clubs do not compete with each other for the sale of ownership interests in their teams so there exists no competition to be injured in the first place; and (2) Sullivan did not present sufficient evidence of injury to competition from which a reasonable jury could conclude that the NFL's policy restrains trade. Although we agree with the NFL that conceptualizing the harm to competition in this case is rather difficult, precedent and deference to the jury verdict ultimately require us to reject the NFL's challenge to the finding of injury to competition.

Critically, the NFL does not challenge on appeal the jury's initial finding of the relevant market and no corresponding challenge was raised at trial. As a result, the NFL faces an uphill battle in its attack on the presence of an injury to competition. Given the existence of a relevant market for ownership interests in NFL teams, it is reasonable to presume that a policy restricting the buying and selling of such ownership interests injures competition in that market. The NFL nevertheless maintains that NFL teams do not compete against each other for the sale of their ownership interests, even if we accept that a market exists for such ownership interests.

1. No Competition Subject to Injury as Matter of Law

The NFL correctly points out that member clubs must cooperate in a variety of ways, and may do so lawfully, in order to make the football league a success. * * * On the other hand, it is well established that NFL clubs also compete with each other, both on and off the field, for things like fan support, players, coaches, ticket sales, local broadcast revenues, and the sale of team paraphernalia. * * * The question of whether competition exists between NFL teams for sale of their ownership interests, such that the NFL's ownership policy injures this competition, is ultimately a question of fact. The NFL would have us find, however, that, as a matter of law, NFL teams do not compete against each other for the sale of their ownership interests. We decline to make such a finding.

The NFL relies on a series of cases which allegedly stand for the "well established" rule that a professional sports league's restrictions on who may join the league or acquire an interest in a member club do not give rise to a claim under the antitrust laws. * * * These cases, all involving a professional sport's league's refusal to approve individual transfers of team ownership or the creation of new teams, do not stand for the broad proposition that no NFL ownership policy can injure competition. * * *

None of the cases cited by the NFL considered the particular relevant market that was found by the jury in this case or a league policy against public ownership. *Seattle Totems* and *Mid-South Grizzlies* considered potential inter-league competition when a sports league rejected plaintiffs' applications for new league franchises. *Seattle Totems*, 783 F.2d [1347,] 1349 50 [(9th Cir.), *cert. denied*, 479 U.S. 932 (1986)]; Mid-South Grizzlies, 720 F.2d [772,] 785 86 [(3d Cir. 1983), *cert. denied*, 467 U.S. 1215 (1984)]. Those decisions found no injury to competition because the plaintiffs were not competing with the defendant sports leagues, but rather, were seeking to join those leagues. * * * *Mid-South Grizzlies* left open the possibility that potential intra-league competition between NFL football clubs could be harmed by the NFL's action, but found that the plaintiff in that case had not presented sufficient evidence of harm to such competition. * * *

The *Fishman* and *Levin* cases concerned the National Basketball Association's ("N.B.A.") rejection of plaintiffs' attempts to buy an existing team. * * * Those cases also based their finding that there was no injury to competition on the fact that the plaintiffs were seeking to join with, rather than compete against, the N.B.A. * * * Neither case considered whether competition between teams for investment capital was injured. As pointed out in *Piazza v. Major League Baseball*, 831 F. Supp. 420 (E.D. Pa. 1993), Fishman explicitly recognized the potential for competition in the market for ownership of teams, although the plaintiff had failed to raise the issue, and *Levin* simply presumed, incorrectly, that there could never be any competition among league members. * * *

The important distinction to make between the cases cited by the NFL and the present case is that here Sullivan alleges that the NFL's policy against public ownership generally restricts competition between clubs for the sale of their ownership interests, whereas in the aforementioned cases, a league's refusal to approve a given sale transaction or a new team merely prevented particular outsiders from joining the league, but did not limit competition between the teams themselves. To put it another way, the NFL's public ownership policy allegedly does not merely prevent the replacement of one club owner with another an action having little evident effect on competition it compromises the entire process by which competition for club ownership occurs.

We take a moment to briefly address a related argument raised by the NFL to the effect that NFL clubs are unable to conspire with each other under 1 of the Sherman Act because they function as a single enterprise in relation to the league's public ownership policy. The NFL asserts that the Supreme Court's holding in *Copperweld Corp. v. Independence Tube Corp.*, 467 U.S. 752 (1984), controls the facts of this case and overturns prior caselaw holding that NFL clubs do not constitute a single enterprise but rather, are separate entities which were capable of conspiring with each other under 1. * * *

We do not agree that *Copperweld*, which found a corporation and its wholly owned subsidiary to be a single enterprise for purposes of 1 * * * applies to the facts of this case or affects the prior precedent concerning the NFL. *See McNeil v. National Football League*, 790 F. Supp. 871, 879 80 (D. Minn. 1992) (holding that *Copperweld* did not apply to the NFL and its member clubs and finding the clubs to be separate entities capable of conspiring together under 1). *Copperweld's* holding turned on the fact that the subsidiary of a corporation, although legally distinct from the corporation itself, "pursued the common interests of the whole rather than interests separate from those of the corporation itself." * * * [T]he critical inquiry is whether the alleged antitrust conspirators have a "unity of interests" or whether, instead, "any of the defendants has pursued interests diverse from those of the cooperative itself." * * * As we have already noted, NFL member clubs compete in several ways off the field, which itself tends to show that the teams pursue diverse interests and thus are not a single enterprise under 1.

Ultimately, the NFL's *Copperweld* challenge is subsumed under the question of whether or not the evidence can support a finding that NFL teams compete against each other for the sale of their ownership interests. Proof of such competition defeats both the NFL's challenge to the existence of an injury to competition and the NFL's *Copperweld* argument as well. Insufficient proof of such competition would require a judgment in favor of the NFL anyway, regardless of the implications under *Copperweld*. As we discuss below, the jury's finding that there exists competition between teams for the sale of ownership interests was based on sufficient evidence.

2. Insufficient Evidence of Harm to Competition

The NFL contends that Sullivan did not present sufficient evidence concerning: (1) the existence of competition between NFL clubs for the sale of ownership interests, or (2) a decrease in output, an increase in prices, a detrimental effect on efficiency or other incidents of harm to competition in the relevant market, from which a reasonable jury could conclude that the NFL's policy injured competition. Although we agree that the evidence of all these factors is rather thin, we disagree that the evidence is too thin to support a jury verdict in Sullivan's favor.

With respect to evidence of the existence of competition for the sale of ownership interests, one of Sullivan's experts, Professor Roger Noll, testified that "one of the ways in which the NFL exercises monopoly power in the market for the franchises and ownership is by excluding certain people from owning all or part any type part of an NFL franchise." Dr. Noll explained that this "enables a group of owners, in this case, you only need eight owners, to exclude from the League and from competing with them, people who might be more effective competitors than they are." The record also contains statements from several NFL owners which could reasonably be interpreted as expressions of concern about their ability to compete with other teams in the market for investment capital in general, and for the sale of ownership interests in particular. For example, Arthur Rooney II of the Pittsburgh Steelers stated in a letter that he did not "believe that the individually or family owned teams will be able to compete with the consolidated groups." Ralph Wilson of the Buffalo Bills stated that big corporations should not own teams because it gives them an "unfair competitive advantage" over other teams since corporations will funnel money into the team and make it "more competitive" than the other franchises. Former NFL Commissioner Pete Rozelle admitted that similar sentiments had been expressed by NFL members.

Although it is not precisely clear that the "competition" about which Noll, Rooney, and Wilson were discussing is the same competition at issue here that is competition for the sale of ownership interests a jury could reasonably interpret these statements as expressing a belief that the competition exists between teams for the sale of ownership interests. The statements of the two NFL owners imply that greater access to capital for all teams will put increased pressure on some teams to compete with others for that capital, and all the statements reveal that the ownership rules, particularly the rule against public ownership, is the main obstacle preventing such access. The fact that ownership by "consolidated groups" is not necessarily the same as public ownership does not affect the conclusion that teams face competitive pressure in selling their ownership interests generally to whoever might buy them. We also note that evidence of actual, present competition is not necessary as long as the evidence shows that the potential for competition exists. It would be difficult indeed to provide direct evidence of competition when the NFL effectively prohibits it.

The NFL focuses on the fact that Professor Noll testified that many of the purchasers of Patriots' stock would be New England sports fans and others in the New England area. The NFL points out that other NFL teams would not compete with the Patriots for the sale of stock to their own fans. This argument slightly distorts Professor Noll's testimony. Professor Noll stated that local souvenir buyers would be one portion of the market for Patriots stock. Professor Noll also testified several times that other investors would buy Patriots stock as well, for investment purposes. Noll's point was that the souvenir buyers would serve to bid up the price of the stock above what the price would normally be if the Patriots were a regular company. His testimony did not preclude a finding that NFL teams compete against each other for investment capital via the sale of ownership interests.

The record also contains sufficient evidence of the normal incidents of injury to competition from the NFL's policy reduced output, increased prices, and reduced efficiency to support the jury's verdict. As Dr. Noll pointed out in his testimony, the NFL's policy "excludes individuals * * * who might want to own a share of stock in a professional football team." Several NFL officials themselves admitted that the policy restricts the market for investment capital among NFL teams. There is thus little dispute that the NFL's ownership policy reduces the available output of ownership interests.

The NFL is correct that, in one sense, the overall pool of potential output is fixed because there are only 28 NFL teams and, although their value may fluctuate, the quantity of their ownership interests cannot. However, the NFL's public ownership policy completely wipes out a certain type of ownership interest public ownership of stock. By restricting output in one form of ownership, the NFL is thereby reducing the output of ownership interests overall. In other words, the NFL is literally restricting the output of a product a share in an NFL team.

There was considerable testimony concerning the price effects of the NFL policy. Both of Sullivan's experts testified that the policy depressed the price of ownership interests in NFL teams because NFL franchises would normally command a premium on the public market relative to their value in the private market, which is all that the league currently permits. Professor Noll testified that fan loyalty would push up the price of ownership interests if sales to the public were allowed. Even former Commissioner Pete Rozelle acknowledged that "it was pointed out, with justification, it has been over the years, that [the ownership policy] does restrict your market and, very likely, the price you could get for one of our franchises if you wanted to sell it, because you are eliminating a very broad market. * * * And they have said that there is a depression on the price they could get for their franchise."

The NFL points out that the alleged effect of its ownership policy is to reduce prices of NFL team ownership interests, rather than to raise prices which is normally the measure of an injury to competition. * * * We acknowledge that it is not clear whether, absent some sort of dumping or predatory pricing* * *, a decrease in prices can indicate injury to competition in a relevant market. The Supreme Court has emphasized, however, that overall consumer preferences in setting output and prices is more important than higher prices and lower output, per se, in determining whether there has been an injury to competition. *NCAA*, 468 U.S. at 107. In this case, regardless of the exact price effects of the NFL's policy, the overall market effects of the policy are plainly unresponsive to consumer demand for ownership interests in NFL teams. Dr. Noll testified that fans are interested in buying shares in NFL teams and that the NFL's policy deprives fans of this product. Moreover, evidence was presented concerning the public offering of the Boston Celtics professional basketball team which demonstrated, according to some of the testimony, fan interest in buying ownership of professional sports teams. Thus, a jury could conclude that the NFL's policy injured competition by making the relevant market "unresponsive to consumer preference." * * * *3

As for overall efficiency of production in the relevant market,4 Sullivan's experts testified that the NFL's policy hindered efficiency gains, and that allowing public ownership would make for better football teams. Professor Noll stated that the NFL's public ownership policy prevented individuals who might be "more efficient and much better at running a professional football team" from owning teams. Dr. Noll also stated that

---

3. The NFL maintains that price and output are not affected because its ownership policy does not limit the number of games or teams, does not raise ticket prices or the prices of game telecasts and does not affect the normal consumer of the NFL's product in any other way. Such facts might be relevant to an inquiry of whether the NFL's policy harms overall efficiency, *see infra* note 4, but it is not relevant to whether the policy affects output and prices in the relevant market for ownership interests. Just because consumers of "NFL football" are not affected by output controls and price increases does not mean that consumers of a product in the relevant market are not so affected. In this case, two types of consumers are denied products by the NFL policy: consumers who want to buy stock of the Patriots or other teams, and consumers like Sullivan who want to "purchase" investment capital in the market for public financing.

4. Although the product at issue in the relevant market is "ownership interests," efficiency in production of that product can be measured by the value of the ownership interest. That is, an improved product produced more efficiently will be reflected in the value of the output in question (regardless of the price). In this case, the value of the product depends on the success of the Patriots' football team, the overall efficiency of its operations, and the success of the NFL in general.

publicly owned NFL teams would be better managed, and produce higher quality entertainment for the fans. Noll testified that the ownership rule excluded certain types of management structures which would likely be more efficient in running the teams, resulting in higher franchise values. One NFL owner, Lamar Hunt, acknowledged that increased access to capital can improve a team's operations and performance. A memorandum prepared by an NFL staff member stated that changes to the NFL's public ownership policy could contribute to each NFL team's own financial strength and viability, which in turn would benefit the entire NFL because the league has a strong interest in having strong, viable teams.

The NFL presented a large amount of evidence to the contrary and now claims on appeal that Sullivan's position was based on nothing more than sheer speculation. We have reviewed the record, however, and we cannot say that the evidence was so overwhelming that no reasonable jury could find against the NFL and in favor of Sullivan. We therefore refuse to enter judgment in favor of the NFL as a matter of law.

B. Ancillary Benefits

The NFL next argues that even if its public ownership policy injures competition in a relevant market, it should be upheld as ancillary to the legitimate joint activity that is "NFL football" and thus not violative of the Sherman Act. We take no issue with the proposition that certain joint ventures enable separate business entities to combine their skills and resources in pursuit of a common goal that cannot be effectively pursued by the venturers acting alone. * * * We also do not dispute that a "restraint" that is ancillary to the functioning of such a joint activity *i.e.* one that is required to make the joint activity more efficient does not necessarily violate the antitrust laws. * * * We further accept, for purposes of this appeal, that rules controlling who may join a joint venture can be ancillary to a legitimate joint activity and that the NFL's own policy against public ownership constitutes one example of such an ancillary rule. Finally, we accept the NFL's claim that its public ownership policy contributes to the ability of the NFL to function as an effective sports league, and that the NFL's functioning would be impaired if publicly owned teams were permitted, because the short-term dividend interests of a club's shareholder would often conflict with the long-term interests of the league as a whole. That is, the policy avoids a detrimental conflict of interests between team shareholders and the league.

We disagree, however, that these factors are sufficient to establish as a matter of law that the NFL's ownership policy does not unreasonably restrain trade in violation of 1 of the Sherman Act. The holdings * * *, do not throw the "rule of reason" out the window merely because one establishes that a given practice among joint venture participants is ancillary to legitimate and efficient activity the injury to competition must still be weighed against the purported benefits under the rule of reason * * *

One basic tenet of the rule of reason is that a given restriction is not reasonable, that is, its benefits cannot outweigh its harm to competition, if a reasonable, less restrictive alternative to the policy exists that would provide the same benefits as the current restraint. * * * The record contains evidence of a clearly less restrictive alternative to the NFL's ownership policy that may yield the same benefits as the current policy. Sullivan points to one proposal to amend the current ownership policy by allowing for the sale of minority, nonvoting shares of team stock to the public with restrictions on the size of the holdings by any one individual. Dividend payments, if any, would be within the firm control of the NFL majority owner. Under such a policy, it would be reasonable for a jury to conclude that private control of member clubs is maintained, conflicts of interest are avoided, and all the other "benefits" of the NFL's joint venture arrangement are preserved while at the same time teams would have access to the market for public investment capital through the sale of ownership interests. * * *

C. Causation of Injury in Fact

The NFL next argues that Sullivan did not present sufficient evidence to support a finding by the jury that the NFL's public ownership policy caused injury in fact to Sullivan. An antitrust plaintiff must prove that he or she suffered damages from an antitrust violation and that there is a causal connection between the illegal practice and the injury. * * *"Plaintiffs need not prove that the antitrust violation was the sole cause of their injury, but only that it was a material cause." * * *

Sullivan asserted at trial that the NFL's ownership policy forced him to sell the Patriots at a depressed price, far below what the team would have been worth in a market that included public ownership of the team. "But for" the NFL's policy, Sullivan claims, he would have been able to offer 49% of the Patriots to the public for $ 70 million, pay off his debts, and retained ownership of a much more valuable and profitable team.

The NFL contends that Sullivan failed to establish a causal connection between his "forced" sale of the Patriots and the NFL's ownership policy because (1) Sullivan never officially requested a vote on his proposals to amend or waive the policy so there is no way of knowing whether the policy would have prevented a public offering in the first place; and (2) Sullivan never established that the public stock sale was feasible or potentially successful and thus an alternative to what ultimately happened (*i.e.*, even if the NFL did not have a policy against public ownership, Sullivan would still have had to sell his team because the Patriots stock sale would not have happened or would not have raised enough money to pay off Sullivan's debts and prevent a fire sale of the team). Although the evidence of causation is not overwhelming, it is nevertheless sufficient to support the verdict.

Regarding the NFL's first claim that Sullivan never called for a vote from the owners to change or waive the ownership policy, Sullivan presented sufficient evidence to show that the NFL essentially rejected Sullivan's request, even though no official vote was taken. Under certain circumstances, an antitrust plaintiff must make a demand on the defendant to allow the plaintiff to take some action or obtain some benefit, which the defendant's challenged practice is allegedly preventing the plaintiff from taking or obtaining, in order to prove that the practice caused injury in fact to the plaintiff. * * * Such a requirement only applies, however, where the plaintiff cannot otherwise prove that the illegal practice exists or that the practice is preventing the plaintiff from competing in the relevant market; in such cases, a refused demand is the only reliable evidence of causation. * * * In cases like the present one, an official request and official refusal is not necessary to establish causality because there is other evidence showing that defendant's practice caused injury in fact to the plaintiff. * * * There is certainly no blanket requirement, as the NFL maintains * * * that Sullivan must call for a vote and obtain an official refusal from the NFL, even if such a request would be futile. * * * Certainly, if Sullivan can prove futility independent of any official request, he need not show that he actually called for a vote and received a denial from the other NFL owners.

The jury in this case heard evidence that would allow it to conclude that the NFL effectively denied Sullivan's request for a waiver or amendment of the public ownership policy, and that an official vote would indeed have been futile. * * *

Sullivan also presented sufficient evidence to support a finding that the Patriots stock sale was both feasible and potentially successful. Sullivan met with Stephens, Inc., an investment banking firm, to discuss a deal whereby Stephens would arrange for a loan of $80 million to Sullivan and his son, half of which would be paid back out of the proceeds of the Patriots stock offering, which Stephens would also arrange. In a subsequent letter, Stephens stated that it had been retained to assist in the "private placement of $80 million of debt" and set out some preliminary terms and conditions. Although specifics of the public offering were not discussed, and Stephens did not determine whether the stock offering was ultimately feasible, Stephens repeatedly made it clear to Sullivan that NFL approval was required indeed Stephens specifically singled out NFL approval as the prerequisite before Stephens could proceed any further with efforts to prepare for the placement of Patriots stock.

As discussed above, NFL approval was never obtained. Therefore, the jury could conclude that lack of approval was the reason Stephens was unwilling to proceed with the deal, even though Stephens also expressed some concern about Sullivan's financial and legal troubles. The jury also heard testimony that Charles Allen, a prominent investment banker in New York, thought the Patriots public offering was feasible and that he was potentially interested in arranging the deal. Sullivan himself testified that the stock sale was feasible based on his experience with the previous public offering of Patriots stock in 1960, and based on the public offering of the Boston Celtics. Finally, one of Sullivan's experts, Patrick Brake, testified that the public offering would have been feasible had the NFL not blocked it.

In addition, despite significant financial and legal problems with the Patriots, the evidence is sufficient to support a finding that Sullivan could have solved these problems in the course of the public offering and, further, that he could have brought off a successful stock sale that would have raised at least $70 million. * * *

Although we share the NFL's skepticism that Sullivan would have succeeded in his public offering if the NFL had allowed him to try it, we cannot say that, as a matter of law, the evidence was so overwhelming that no reasonable jury could find that the NFL's policy harmed Sullivan by preventing him from doing something he would otherwise have been able to do. We therefore reject the NFL's claim that it is entitled to a judgment in its favor on the basis that Sullivan failed to prove his injury was caused by the alleged antitrust violation. * * *

The NFL's arguments concerning the application of 1 of the Sherman Act to the facts of this case raise a substantial challenge to the jury verdict and are certainly weighty enough to give us pause. Upon careful consideration of the issues, however, we find Sullivan's theory of the case to be a plausible one and ultimately find the evidence sufficient to support it. For the foregoing reasons, therefore, we see no justification, as a matter of law, for ringing the death knell on this litigation.

IV. TRIAL ERRORS

Having reviewed those issues which would have warranted a judgment in favor of the NFL, had we decided any of those issues in the NFL's favor, we now turn to the NFL's claim that it is entitled to a new trial because of allegedly erroneous jury instructions and other trial errors. In particular, the NFL asserts that the district court failed to provide the jury with several crucial jury instructions that were required in order to present to the jury certain legal theories that were potentially dispositive of the verdict. The NFL argues that the court's failure to give the instructions was prejudicial error requiring a new trial. * * *

In this case, we find that the failure to give certain instructions was prejudicial error and we therefore vacate the judgment and order a new trial.

A. Equal Involvement Defense

* * * A plaintiff's "complete, voluntary, and substantially equal participation" in an illegal practice under the antitrust laws precludes recovery for that antitrust violation. In order to establish an "equal involvement" defense, an antitrust defendant must prove, by a preponderance of the evidence, that the plaintiff bears at least substantially equal responsibility for an anticompetitive restriction by creating, approving, maintaining, continually and actively supporting, relying upon, or otherwise utilizing and implementing, that restriction to his or her benefit. * * * It is not essential to the defense that the plaintiff actually helped author or create the policy, although such facts would be highly probative, as long as the plaintiff was substantially responsible for maintaining and otherwise effectuating the policy. * * * On the other hand, proof that the plaintiff benefitted from the challenged policy or failed to object to the policy, without more, is not sufficient to show "substantially equal participation." * * * Moreover, proof that the plaintiff was coerced ("economically" or otherwise) into supporting the policy, that the plaintiff attempted to oppose the illegal conduct, or that the plaintiff's participation was otherwise not voluntary, is highly probative of the absence of complete and equal involvement by the plaintiff in an antitrust violation. * * *

In this case, the evidence in the record was sufficient to support a jury instruction on the equal involvement defense. Sullivan was one of the three AFL members on the Joint Committee that established the policies, including the ownership policies, that were to govern the new expanded NFL. That Committee agreed, in a merger agreement signed by Sullivan, to adopt the NFL's policy against public ownership for the new NFL. Sullivan's son, Chuck, stated that Sullivan was the central figure in the merger negotiations. Sullivan subsequently relied on the NFL's public ownership policy to justify his purchase, through the merger of his team into a wholly owned company, of the outstanding stock of the Patriots in 1976. In the proxy statement for that transaction, Sullivan listed the NFL's policy against public ownership as one of the "Reasons for the Merger", and he attached a letter from the NFL justifying the public ownership policy and explaining that the continued presence of public stockholders conflicted with the interests of the league. Sullivan also affirmatively supported the policy in sworn testimony during the litigation with his former shareholders following the Patriots merger. Sullivan stated that the NFL's public ownership policy, and the justifications underlying the policy, were the reasons for his desire to purchase all outstanding shares of the team. There is no evidence that Sullivan ever opposed or objected to the ownership policy prior to the circumstances surrounding this case.

Taken together, this evidence is sufficient for a reasonable jury to conclude that Sullivan bears substantially equal responsibility for the NFL's public ownership policy because Sullivan helped adopt the policy, he relied upon it, and he actively supported it. The jury, however, was never given an opportunity to consider this evidence in light of the equal involvement defense.

Sullivan claims that he was not at the meetings in which Lamar Hunt, the chairman of the AFL committee, agreed to the NFL's public ownership policy, and that he did not know in advance that the old NFL's public ownership rule would be adopted by the new NFL. Mr. Hunt himself testified, however, that he always spoke for the entire AFL committee at his various meetings with NFL owners, and that he discussed various negotiating points with the other AFL owners, including Sullivan, before any decisions were made. Moreover, Sullivan's own team obtained a specific waiver from the ownership policy, which, a reasonably jury could infer, indicates that Sullivan was involved in the decision to adopt the policy. In any event, it is the jury's responsibility to weigh the evidence and make a choice in circumstances like this where the same evidence supports two different yet reasonable conclusions.

The district court erred by failing to give the jury the opportunity to choose between these versions of the facts. The court's "finding" that Sullivan's involvement in the public ownership policy was minimal ignores evidence in the record. The court's view that the NFL imposed the ownership policy on the AFL owners, rendering their participation involuntary, is largely unsupported by the record. Ultimately, however, these are factual questions for the jury and none of the instructions provided by the district court served to adequately instruct the jury on this issue or send the issue to the jury. Therefore, the district court erred in refusing to give the NFL's proffered instruction on the "equal involvement" defense. * * *

B. Failure to Request an Official Vote of the Owners

As discussed in Section II.C. above, in order to establish that the policy actually caused injury to himself, Sullivan must prove that the NFL effectively denied his request to waive or amend its policy against public ownership. While there is evidence that supports a finding that the NFL's policy effectively blocked Sullivan from pursuing his public offering, there is also sufficient evidence to support a contrary finding. Sullivan's failure to request a vote from the owners after he discovered that he was four votes shy of obtaining a waiver with seven owners still undecided, combined with former Commissioner Rozelle's testimony that he told Sullivan that Rozelle would put to the owners any plan that Sullivan wished, could support a finding that Sullivan was a "dormant plaintiff" who did not "spring into action" until it was "time to file suit." * * * As such, a jury could conclude that the NFL did not prevent Sullivan from pursuing his stock sale, but instead, Sullivan simply dropped the idea for reasons unrelated to the NFL's policy. If the jury had reached such a conclusion, Sullivan would have failed to prove that his injury was caused by the antitrust policy, and judgment for the NFL would be required.

* * * The failure of Sullivan to request a vote is a critical and potentially dispositive issue in this case. If the alleged restraint of trade does not even exist in practice, the whole case essentially disappears. Therefore, the jury should have been directed to make a specific finding as to whether the public ownership policy was enforced against Sullivan. * * * The failure to give some instruction concerning the failure of Sullivan to request a vote was error. * * *

* * *

D. Balancing Procompetitive and Anticompetitive Effects in the Relevant Market

As we noted above, the rule of reason analysis requires a weighing of the injury and the benefits to competition attributable to a practice that allegedly violates the antitrust laws. * * * The district court instructed the jury on its verdict form to balance the injury to competition in the relevant market with the benefits to competition in that same relevant market. The NFL protested, claiming that all procompetitive effects of its policy, even those in a market different from that in which the alleged restraint operated, should be considered. The NFL's case was premised on the claim that its policy against public ownership was an important part of the effective functioning of the league as a joint venture. Although it was not readily apparent that this beneficial effect applied to the market for ownership interests in NFL teams, the relevant market found by the jury, the NFL argued that its justification should necessarily be weighed by the jury under the rule of reason analysis. Sullivan responded, and the district court agreed, that a jury cannot be asked to compare what are essentially apples and oranges, and that it is impossible to conduct a balancing of alleged anticompetitive and procompetitive effects of a challenged practice in every definable market.

The issue of defining the proper scope of a rule of reason analysis is a deceptive body of water, containing unforeseen currents and turbulence lying just below the surface of an otherwise calm and peaceful ocean. The waters are muddied by the Supreme Court's decision in *NCAA* one of the more extensive examples of the Court performing a rule of reason analysis where the Court considered the value of certain procompetitive effects that existed outside of the relevant market in which the restraint operated. *NCAA*, 468 U.S. at 115 20 (considering the NCAA's interest in protecting live attendance at televised games and the NCAA's "legitimate and important" interest in maintaining competitive balance between amateur athletic teams as a justification for a restraint that operated in a completely different market, the market for the telecasting of collegiate football games). Other courts have demonstrated similar confusion. *See, e.g., L.A. Coliseum*, 726 F.2d at 1381,1392, 1397, 1399 (stating that the "relevant market provides the basis on which to balance competitive harms and benefits of the restraint at issue" but then considering a wide variety of alleged benefits, and then directing the finder of fact to "balance the gain to interbrand competition against the loss of intrabrand competition", where the two types of competition operated in different markets).

To our knowledge, no authority has squarely addressed this issue. On the one hand, several courts have expressed concern over the use of wide ranging interests to justify an otherwise anticompetitive practice, and others have found particular justifications to be incomparable and not in correlation with the alleged restraint of trade. * * * We agree that the ultimate question under the rule of reason is whether a challenged practice promotes or suppresses competition. Thus, it seems improper to validate a practice that is decidedly in restraint of trade simply because the practice produces some unrelated benefits to competition in another market.

On the other hand, several courts, including this Circuit, have found it appropriate in some cases to balance the anticompetitive effects on competition in one market with certain procompetitive benefits in other markets. * * *

In any event, we need not enter these dangerous waters to resolve the instant dispute. The NFL wanted the jury to consider its proffered justifications for the public ownership policy namely that the policy enhanced the NFL's ability to effectively produce and present a popular entertainment product unimpaired by the conflicting interests that public ownership would cause. These procompetitive justifications should have been considered by the jury, even under Sullivan's theory of the proper scope of the rule of reason analysis. * * * [T]o the extent the NFL's policy strengthens and improves the league, resulting in increased competition in the market for ownership interests in NFL clubs through, for example, more valuable teams, the jury may consider the NFL's justifications as relevant factors in its rule of reason analysis. The danger of the proffered instructions on the verdict form is that they may have mislead the jury into thinking that it was precluded from considering the NFL's justifications for its ownership policy. Therefore, the relevant market language on the verdict form should be removed, or else the jury should be informed that evidence of benefits to competition in the relevant market can include evidence of benefits flowing indirectly from the public ownership policy that ultimately have a beneficial impact on competition in the relevant market itself.

E. References to Prior Antitrust Cases Against the NFL

Despite a pretrial motion in limine and repeated objections by the NFL, the district court allowed the jury to hear numerous references to prior antitrust cases against the NFL. Evidence about prior antitrust violations by the defendant may, in appropriate cases, be admissible to show things like market power, intent to monopolize, motive, or method of conspiracy. * * * Because of the inherently prejudicial nature of such evidence, however, evidence of prior antitrust cases involving the NFL are only admissible if Sullivan can demonstrate that the conduct underlying those prior judgments had a direct, logical relationship to the conduct at issue in the present case. * * *

In many of the instances where Sullivan or his counsel made references to prior antitrust cases at trial, Sullivan failed to satisfy this burden.

Sullivan argues that the prior cases were relevant either to certain testimony regarding the reasonableness of the NFL's ownership policy and voting requirements or to the issue of defining the relevant market. Because none of the cases mentioned at trial concerned the NFL's ownership policy at issue here, evidence of those prior cases is not relevant to the reasonableness of the NFL's policy against public ownership. The general voting requirements are not in dispute, so cases touching solely upon them are also not relevant. Certain limited portions of some prior antitrust decisions are relevant to the issue of defining the relevant market. The testimony and commentary at trial concerning these prior cases, however, was not limited to the relevant market portions of these cases and, on the contrary, focused primarily on the issue of whether the NFL's public ownership policy was unreasonable. As such, that evidence was prejudicial, without any balancing relevance to justify its admission into evidence. * * *

* * * [R]eferences to prior NFL cases are not relevant to the issue of the reasonableness of the NFL's public ownership policy and such references should be excluded if they contain information about the unreasonableness of other policies of the NFL which were at issue in the other cases.

Reversed and remanded.

Notes and Questions

1. Why is an owner's "corporate character" important to the league as a whole?

2. In terms of control, what legitimate concerns might a league have if the team were publicly owned and its stock were traded publicly? Do those concerns apply if only a minority interest is sold to the public or if the public can only purchase non-voting shares?

3. Do the actions of the Raiders, the Clippers, and the Sullivan family reflect a growing independence of sports league owners and less of a "one for all, all for one" ethic among league members? This question becomes more poignant when one is reminded that, within the past few years, many owners have openly challenged or ignored league orders: (a) Philadelphia Eagles owner Norman Braman objected to the NFL's settlement with the NFL Players Association and filed unfair labor practice charges against the league; (b) Baltimore Orioles owner Peter Angelos threatened to defy his fellow owners' mandate to use replacement players during the baseball strike; (c) Dallas Cowboys owner Jerry Jones and, to a lesser extent, New England Patriots owner Robert Kraft ignored the NFL's pooling of team marks and logos for sponsorship and licensing; (d) New York Yankees owner George Steinbrenner repudiated Major League Baseball's sponsorship program; and, (e) the NBA's Mark Cuban has been openly critical of NBA Commissioner

David Stern, (f) as described below, the Chicago Bulls challenged the NBA's national television program. How do such demonstrations of defiance affect the sport as a whole?

4. The *Sullivan* opinion addressed at length whether Rule of Reason analysis permits the balancing of procompetitive benefits in one market against anticompetitive effects in another, perhaps primary, market. Resolution of that issue may be extremely important in a case concerning franchise relocation, but it was only addressed in passing in the *Raiders I* opinion. For example, in 1995, the Rams were leaving a metropolitan area (Los Angeles/Anaheim) where they were in direct competition with the Raiders (until Al Davis announced, one month later, that the Raiders were leaving Los Angeles as well). The Rams moved to a city where they are not in significant direct competition with any other NFL team for live attendance (it is 240 or more miles from St. Louis to Kansas City, Indianapolis, or Chicago). If the Rams' request to relocate had been denied, should an antitrust jury have been instructed to consider the preservation of competition between the Rams and the Raiders as a procompetitive justification for the disapproval? If a judge were to instruct a jury in that fashion, how would a jury conduct that sort of a balancing test?

5. Think back to the *Hecht* case in Chapter 11 and the Redskins' argument that Hecht could not state a claim because he had not proceeded far enough with his business plans to secure an AFL franchise. Is that similar to the NFL's argument that Sullivan's failure to request a vote should bar his claim? Consider the NFL's conduct in light of Note 1 following *Hecht*. By making sure that Sullivan's request for permission to make a public offering was never subject to a vote, while at the same time taking steps to guarantee that Sullivan was never able to implement his plans, did the NFL achieve its business objectives and simultaneously strengthen its future antitrust defense? *See* Will McDonough, *Sullivan Suited for Litigation*, THE BOSTON GLOBE Aug. 17, 1996, at E1 ("later jurors said they couldn't find in favor of Sullivan because he had never even asked for a vote to change the rule on public stock").

6. After the First Circuit's opinion in *Sullivan*, the case was remanded and tried again, ending in a hung jury. Although the jury had reached agreement that the NFL was not a single entity and that its prohibition on public ownership was unlawful, they could not reach unanimous agreement on issues relating to Billy Sullivan's injury or his alleged "equal involvement." *See* David M. Halbfinger, *Mistrial in Sullivan-NFL Suit: Ex-Pats Owner Seeks 3d Trial Against League*, THE BOSTON GLOBE, February 8, 1996, at 57. After the district court declared a mistrial, the case settled six months later, with the NFL paying Sullivan a reported $11.5 million. *See* Will McDonough, *Sullivan Suited for Litigation*, THE BOSTON GLOBE, Aug. 17, 1996, at E1; Patti Myers, *Legal Battles Over for Sullivan*, THE PATRIOT LEDGER, Aug. 13, 1996, at 27.

7. With the settlement of the *Sullivan* case, the NFL did not end the challenges to its ownership policies. In June, 1996, a district court denied the NFL's motion to dismiss a challenge similar to Sullivan's in a case brought by Francis W. Murray. Murray was a minority owner of the New England Patriots toward the end of Billy Sullivan's ownership of the team and he remained a minority owner when Sullivan sold his majority interest to Victor K. Kiam, II in 1988. *See Murray v. National Football League*, 1996 U.S. Dist. LEXIS 9108 (E.D. Pa. 1996). The *Murray* case was eventually dismissed when the district judge granted the NFL's motion for summary judgment April 24, 1988.

8. While the NFL struggled with intra-league challenges to its franchise relocation and ownership policies, the NBA spent the first half of the 1990s litigating about its restrictions on the sale of television broadcast rights by its member teams. The following case marked the second time that the Seventh Circuit was called upon to review district court

rulings enjoining certain NBA television restrictions upon five-time NBA Champion Chicago Bulls and its local television station, WGN. As discussed in more detail below, this decision has fueled new sports league hope that the so-called single entity defense, presumed dead after the First Circuit's decision in *Sullivan*, might be resuscitated.

Chicago Professional Sports Limited Partnership v. National Basketball Ass'n
95 F.3d 593 (7th Cir. 1996)

EASTERBROOK, Circuit Judge. In the six years since they filed this antitrust suit, the Chicago Bulls have won four National Basketball Association titles and an equal number of legal victories. Suit and titles are connected. The Bulls want to broadcast more of their games over WGN television, a "superstation" carried on cable systems nationwide. The Bulls' popularity makes WGN attractive to these cable systems; the large audience makes WGN attractive to the Bulls. Since 1991 the Bulls and WGN have been authorized by injunction to broadcast 25 or 30 games per year. 754 F. Supp. 1336 (1991). We affirmed that injunction in 1992, see 961 F.2d 667, and the district court proceeded to determine whether WGN could carry even more games and whether the NBA could impose a "tax" on the games broadcast to a national audience, for which other superstations have paid a pretty penny to the league. After holding a nine-week trial and receiving 512 stipulations of fact, the district court made a 30-game allowance permanent, 874 F. Supp. 844 (1995), and held the NBA's fee excessive, 1995-2 Trade Cas. [CCH] 71,253. Both sides appeal. The Bulls want to broadcast 41 games per year over WGN; the NBA contends that the antitrust laws allow it to fix a lower number (15 or 20) and to collect the tax it proposed. With apologies to both sides, we conclude that they must suffer through still more litigation.

Our 1992 opinion rejected the league's defense based on the Sports Broadcasting Act, 15 U.S.C. 1291 95, but our rationale implied that the NBA could restructure its contracts to take advantage of that statute. 961 F.2d at 670 72. In 1993 the league tried to do so, signing a contract that transfers all broadcast rights to the National Broadcasting Company. NBC shows only 26 games during the regular season, however, and the network contract allows the league and its teams to permit telecasts at other times. Every team received the right to broadcast all 82 of its regular-season games (41 over the air, 41 on cable), unless NBC telecasts a given contest. The NBA-NBC contract permits the league to exhibit 85 games per year on superstations. Seventy were licensed to the Turner stations (TBS and TNT), leaving 15 potentially available for WGN to license from the league. It disdained the opportunity. The Bulls sold 30 games directly to WGN, treating these as over-the-air broadcasts authorized by the NBC contract not to mention the district court's injunction. The Bulls' only concession (perhaps more to the market than to the league) is that WGN does not broadcast a Bulls game at the same time as a basketball telecast on a Turner superstation.

Back in 1991 and 1992, the parties were debating whether the NBA's television arrangements satisfied 1 of the Sports Broadcasting Act, 15 U.S.C. 1291. We held not, because the Act addresses the effects of "transfers" by a "league of clubs," and the NBA had prescribed rather than "transferred" broadcast rights. The 1993 contract was written with that distinction in mind. The league asserted title to the copyright interests arising from the games and transferred all broadcast rights to NBC; it received some back, subject to contractual restrictions. Section 1 has been satisfied. But the league did not pay enough attention to 2, 15 U.S.C. 1292, which reads:

Section 1291 of this title shall not apply to any joint agreement described in the first sentence in such section which prohibits any person to whom such rights are sold or transferred from televising any games within any area, except within the home territory of a member club of the league on a day when such club is playing at home.

The NBA-NBC contract permits each club to license the broadcast of its games, and then, through the restriction on superstation broadcasts, attempts to limit telecasts to the teams' home markets. Section 2 provides that this makes 1 inapplicable, so the Sports Broadcasting Act leaves the antitrust laws in force.

Our prior opinion observed that the Sports Broadcasting Act, as a special-interest exception to the antitrust laws, receives a beady-eyed reading. A league has to jump through every hoop; partial compliance doesn't do the trick. The NBA could have availed itself of the Sports Broadcasting Act by taking over licensing and by selling broadcast rights in the Bulls' games to one of the many local stations in Chicago, rather than to WGN. The statute offered other options as well. Apparently the league did not want to use them, in part for tax reasons and in part because it sought to avoid responsibilities that come from being a licensor, rather than a regulator, of telecasts. Such business decisions are understandable and proper, but they have consequences under the Sports Broadcasting Act. By signing a contract with NBC that left the Bulls, rather than the league, with the authority to select the TV station that would broadcast the games, the NBA made its position under the Sports Broadcasting Act untenable. For as soon as the Bulls picked WGN, any effort to control cable system retransmission of the WGN signal tripped over 2. The antitrust laws therefore apply, and we must decide what they have to say about the league's effort to curtail superstation transmissions.

Three issues were left unresolved in 1992. One was whether the Bulls and WGN, as producers, suffer antitrust injury. 961 F.2d at 669–70. The NBA has not pursued this possibility, and as it is not jurisdictional (plaintiffs suffer injury in fact), we let the question pass. The other two issues are related. We concluded in 1992 that the district court properly condemned the NBA's superstation rule under the quick-look version of the Rule of Reason, see *National Collegiate Athletic Association v. Board of Regents of the University of Oklahoma*, 468 U.S. 85 (1984), because (a) the league did not argue that it should be treated as a single entity, and (b) the anti-free riding justification for the superstation rule failed because a fee collected on nationally telecast games would compensate other teams (and the league as a whole) for the value of their contributions to the athletic contests being broadcast. 961 F.2d at 672–76. Back in the district court, the NBA argued that it is entitled to be treated as a single firm and therefore should possess the same options as other licensors of entertainment products; outside of court, the league's Board of Governors adopted a rule requiring any club that licenses broadcast rights to superstations to pay a fee based on the amount the two Turner stations pay for games they license directly from the league.

Plaintiffs say that the single-entity argument was forfeited by its omission from the first appeal, but we think not. As our 1992 opinion observed, the case went to initial trial and decision within seven weeks, 961 F.2d at 676, a salutary development made possible in part by judicial willingness to entertain in subsequent rounds of the case arguments that could not be fully developed in such short compass. If defendants in complex cases feared that any arguments omitted from the first phase of the case would be lost forever, they would drag their heels in order to ensure that nothing was overlooked, a step that would benefit no one. * * * That is why we noted that the argument would be available in the ensuing stages of the case, 961 F.2d at 672–73, and why the district court properly entertained and resolved it on the merits.

The district court was unimpressed by the NBA's latest arguments. It held that a sports league should not be treated as a single firm unless the teams have a "complete unity of interest" which they don't. The court also held the fee to be invalid. Our opinion compelled the judge to concede that a fee is proper in principle. 961 F.2d at 675–76. But the judge thought the NBA's fee excessive. Instead of starting with the price per game it had negotiated with Turner (some $ 450,000), and reducing to account for WGN's smaller number of cable outlets, as it did, the judge concluded that the league should have started with the advertising revenues WGN generated from retransmission on cable (the "outer market revenues"). Then it should have cut this figure in half, the judge held, so that the Bulls could retain "their share" of these revenues. The upshot: the judge cut the per game fee from roughly $ 138,000 to $ 39,400.

The district court's opinion concerning the fee reads like the ruling of an agency exercising a power to regulate rates. Yet the antitrust laws do not deputize district judges as one-man regulatory agencies. The core question in antitrust is output. Unless a contract reduces output in some market, to the detriment of consumers, there is no antitrust problem. A high price is not itself a violation of the Sherman Act. * * * WGN and the Bulls argue that the league's fee is excessive, unfair, and the like. But they do not say that it will reduce output. They plan to go on broadcasting 30 games, more if the court will let them, even if they must pay $ 138,000 per telecast. Although the fee exceeds WGN's outer-market revenues, the station evidently obtains other benefits for example, (i) the presence of Bulls games may increase the number of cable systems that carry the station, augmenting its revenues 'round the clock; (ii) WGN slots into Bulls games ads for its other programming; and (iii) many viewers will keep WGN on after the game and watch whatever comes next. Lack of an effect on output means that the fee does not have antitrust significance. Once antitrust issues are put aside, how much the NBA charges for national telecasts is for the league to resolve under its internal governance procedures. It is no different in principle from the question how much (if any) of the live gate goes to the visiting team, who profits from the sale of cotton candy at the stadium, and how the clubs divide revenues from merchandise bearing their logos and trademarks. Courts must respect a league's disposition of these issues, just as they respect contracts and decisions by a corporation's board of directors. *Charles O. Finley & Co. v. Kuhn*, 569 F.2d 527 (7th Cir. 1978); *cf. Baltimore Orioles, Inc. v. Major League Baseball Players Association*, 805 F.2d 663 (7th Cir. 1986).

According to the league, the analogy to a corporate board is apt in more ways than this. The NBA concedes that it comprises 30 juridical entities 29 teams plus the national organization, each a separate corporation or partnership. The teams are not the league's subsidiaries; they have separate ownership. Nonetheless, the NBA submits, it functions as a single entity, creating a single product ("NBA Basketball") that competes with other basketball leagues (both college and professional), other sports ("Major League Baseball", "college football"), and other entertainments such as plays, movies, opera, TV shows, Disneyland, and Las Vegas. Separate ownership of the clubs promotes local boosterism, which increases interest; each ownership group also has a powerful incentive to field a better team, which makes the contests more exciting and thus more attractive. These functions of independent team ownership do not imply that the league is a cartel, however, any more than separate ownership of hamburger joints (again useful as an incentive device, see Benjamin Klein & Lester F. Saft, *The Law and Economics of Franchise Tying Contracts*, 28 J.L. & Econ. 345 (1985)) implies that McDonald's is a cartel. Whether the best analogy is to a system of franchises (no one expects a McDonald's outlet to compete with other members of the system by offering pizza) or to a corporate holding company structure (on which see *Copperweld Corp. v. Independence Tube Corp.*, 467 U.S. 752 (1984)) does not matter from this perspective. The point is that antitrust law permits, indeed encourages, cooperation inside a business organization the better to facilitate competition between that organization and other producers. To say that participants in an organization may cooperate is to say that they may control what they make and how they sell it: the producers of Star Trek may decide to release two episodes a week and grant exclusive licenses to show them, even though this reduces the number of times episodes appear on TV in a given market, just as the NBA's superstation rule does.

The district court conceded this possibility but concluded that all cooperation among separately incorporated firms is forbidden by 1 of the Sherman Act, except to the extent *Copperweld* permits. *Copperweld*, according to the district court, "is quite narrow, and rests solely upon the fact that a parent corporation and its wholly-owned subsidiary have a 'complete unity of interest'" (quoting from 467 U.S. at 771). Although that phrase appears in *Copperweld*, the Court offered it as a statement of fact about the parent-subsidiary relation, not as a proposition of law about the limits of permissible cooperation. As a proposition of law, it would be silly. Even a single firm contains many competing interests. One division may make inputs for another's finished goods. The first division might want to sell its products directly to the market, to maximize income (and thus the salary and bonus of the division's managers); the second division might want to get its inputs from the first at a low transfer price, which would maximize the second division's paper profits. Conflicts are endemic in any multi-stage firm, such as General Motors or IBM, see Robert G. Eccles, *Transfer Pricing as a Problem of Agency,* in *Principals and Agents: The Structure of Business* 151 (Pratt & Zeckhauser eds. 1985), but they do not imply that these large firms must justify all of their acts under the Rule of Reason. Or consider a partnership for the practice of law (or accounting): some lawyers would be better off with a lockstep compensation agreement under which all partners with the same seniority have the same income, but others would prosper under an "eat what you kill" system that rewards bringing new business to the firm. Partnerships have dissolved as a result of these conflicts. Yet these wrangles every bit as violent as the dispute among the NBA's teams about how to generate and divide broadcast revenues do not demonstrate that law firms are cartels, or subject to scrutiny under the Rule of Reason their decisions about where to open offices or which clients to serve.

Copperweld does not hold that only conflict-free enterprises may be treated as single entities. Instead it asks why the antitrust laws distinguish between unilateral and concerted action, and then assigns a parent-subsidiary group to the "unilateral" side in light of those functions. Like a single firm, the parent-subsidiary combination cooperates internally to increase efficiency. Conduct that "deprives the marketplace of the independent centers of decisionmaking that competition assumes," 467 U.S. at 769, without the efficiencies that come with integration inside a firm, go on the "concerted" side of the line. And there are entities in the middle: "mergers, joint ventures, and various vertical agreements" (*id.* at 768) that reduce the number of independent decisionmakers yet may improve efficiency. These are assessed under the Rule of Reason. We see no reason why a sports league cannot be treated as a single firm in this typology. It produces a single product; cooperation is essential (a league with one team would be like one hand clapping); and a league need not deprive the market of independent centers of decisionmaking. The district court's legal standard was therefore incorrect, and a judgment resting on the application of that standard is flawed.

Whether the NBA itself is more like a single firm, which would be analyzed only under 2 of the Sherman Act, or like a joint venture, which would be subject to the Rule of Reason under 1, is a tough question under *Copperweld*. It has characteristics of both. Unlike the colleges and universities that belong to the National Collegiate Athletic Association, which the Supreme Court treated as a joint venture in NCAA, the NBA has no existence independent of sports. It makes professional basketball; only it can make "NBA Basketball" games; and unlike the NCAA the NBA also "makes" teams. After this case was last here the NBA created new teams in Toronto and Vancouver, stocked with players from the 27 existing teams plus an extra helping of draft choices. All of this makes the league look like a single firm. Yet the 29 clubs, unlike GM's plants, have the right to secede (wouldn't a plant manager relish that!), and rearrange into two or three leagues. Professional sports leagues have been assembled from clubs that formerly belonged to other leagues; the National Football League and the NBA fit that description, and the teams have not surrendered their power to rearrange things yet again. Moreover, the league looks more or less like a firm depending on which facet of the business one examines. *See* Phillip E. Areeda, 7*Antitrust Law* 1478d (1986). From the perspective of fans and advertisers (who use sports telecasts to reach fans), "NBA Basketball" is one product from a single source even though the Chicago Bulls and Seattle Supersonics are highly distinguishable, just as General Motors is a single firm even though a Corvette differs from a Chevrolet. But from the perspective of college basketball players who seek to sell their skills, the teams are distinct, and because the human capital of players is not readily transferable to other sports (as even Michael Jordan learned) the league looks more like a group of firms acting as a monopsony. That is why the Supreme Court found it hard to characterize the National Football League in *Brown v. Pro Football, Inc.*, 116 S. Ct. 2116, 2126 (1996): "the clubs that make up a professional sports league are not completely independent economic competitors, as they depend upon a degree of cooperation for economic survival. * * * In the present context, however, that circumstance makes the league more like a single bargaining employer, which analogy seems irrelevant to the legal issue before us." To say that the league is "more like a single bargaining employer" than a multi-employer unit is not to say that it necessarily is one, for every purpose. * * *

Most courts that have asked whether professional sports leagues should be treated like single firms or like joint ventures have preferred the joint venture characterization. *E.g.*, *Sullivan v. NFL*, 34 F.3d 1091 (1st Cir. 1994); *North American Soccer League v. NFL*, 670 F.2d 1249 (2d Cir. 1982); *Smith v. Pro Football, Inc.*, 593 F.2d 1173, 1179 (D.C. Cir. 1978). But Justice Rehnquist filed a strong dissent from the denial of certiorari in the soccer case, arguing that "the league competes as a unit against other forms of entertainment," *NFL v. North American Soccer League*, 459 U.S. 1074, 1077 (1982), and the fourth circuit concluded that the Professional Golf Association should be treated as one firm for antitrust purposes, even though that sport is less economically integrated than the NBA. *Seabury Management, Inc. v. PGA of America, Inc.*, 878 F. Supp. 771 (D. Md. 1994), affirmed in relevant part, 52 F.3d 322 (4th Cir. 1995). Another court of appeals has treated an electric cooperative as a single firm, *Mt. Pleasant v. Associated Electric Cooperative*, 838 F.2d 268 (8th Cir. 1988), though the co-op is less integrated than a sports league. These cases do not yield a clear principle about the proper characterization of sports leagues and we do not think that *Copperweld* imposes one "right" characterization. Sports are sufficiently diverse that it is essential to investigate their organization and ask *Copperweld*'s functional question one league at a time and perhaps one facet of a league at a time, for we do not rule out the possibility that an organization such as the NBA is best understood as one firm when selling broadcast rights to a network in competition with a thousand other producers of entertainment, but is best understood as a joint venture when curtailing competition for players who have few other market opportunities. Just as the ability of McDonald's franchises to coordinate the release of a new hamburger does not imply their ability to agree on wages for counter workers, so the ability of sports teams to agree on a TV contract need not imply an ability to set wages for players. *See* JESSE W. MARKHAM & PAUL V. TEPLITZ, *Baseball Economics and Public Policy* (1981); ARTHUR A. FLEISHER III, BRIAN L. GOFF & ROBERT D. TOLLISON, *The National Collegiate Athletic Association: A Study in Cartel Behavior* (1992).

However this inquiry may come out on remand, we are satisfied that the NBA is sufficiently integrated that its superstation rules may not be condemned without analysis under the full Rule of Reason. We affirmed the district court's original injunction after applying the "quick look" version because the district court had characterized the NBA as something close to a cartel, and the league had not then made a *Copperweld* argument. After considering this argument, we conclude that when acting in the broadcast market the NBA is closer to a single firm than to a group of independent firms. This means that plaintiffs cannot prevail without establishing that the NBA possesses power in a relevant market, and that its exercise of this power has injured consumers. Even in the *NCAA* case, the first to use a bobtailed Rule of Reason, see Diane P. Wood, *Antitrust 1984: Five Decisions in Search of a Theory*, 1984 SUP. CT. REV. 69, 110 12, the Court satisfied itself that the NCAA possesses market power. The district court had held that there is a market in college football telecasts on Saturday afternoon in the fall, a time when other entertainments do not flourish but college football dominates. Only after holding that this was not clearly erroneous did the Court cast any burden of justification on the NCAA. 468 U.S. at 111 13; *see also International Boxing Club v. United States*, 358 U.S. 242 (1959).

Substantial market power is an indispensable ingredient of every claim under the full Rule of Reason * * * During the lengthy trial of this case, the NBA argued that it lacks market power, whether the buyers are understood as the viewers of games (the way the district court characterized things in NCAA) or as advertisers, who use games to attract viewers (the way the Supreme Court characterized a related market in *Times-Picayune Publishing Co. v. United States*, 345 U.S. 594 (1953)). College football may predominate on Saturday afternoons in the fall, but there is no time slot when NBA basketball predominates. The NBA's season lasts from November through June; games are played seven days a week. This season overlaps all of the other professional and college sports, so even sports fanatics have many other options. From advertisers' perspective likely the right one, because advertisers are the ones who actually pay for telecasts the market is even more competitive. Advertisers seek viewers of certain demographic characteristics, and homogeneity is highly valued. A homogeneous audience facilitates targeted ads: breakfast cereals and toys for cartoon shows, household appliances and detergents for daytime soap operas, automobiles and beer for sports. If the NBA assembled for advertisers an audience that was uniquely homogeneous, or had especially high willingness-to-buy, then it might have market power even if it represented a small portion of airtime. The parties directed considerable attention to this question at trial, but the district judge declined to make any findings of fact on the subject, deeming market power irrelevant. As we see things, market power is irrelevant only if the NBA is treated as a single firm under *Copperweld*; and given the difficulty of that issue, it may be superior to approach this as a straight Rule of Reason case, which means starting with an inquiry into market power and, if there is power, proceeding to an evaluation of competitive effects.

Perhaps this can be accomplished using the materials in the current record. Although the judge who presided at the trial died earlier this year, the parties may be willing to agree that an assessment of credibility is unnecessary, so that a new judge could resolve the dispute after reviewing the transcript, exhibits, and stipulations, and entertaining argument. *See* Fed. R. Civ. P. 63. At all events, the judgment of the district court is vacated, and the case is remanded for proceedings consistent with this opinion. Pending further proceedings in the district court or agreement among the parties, the Bulls and WGN must respect the league's (and the NBC contract's) limitations on the maximum number of superstation telecasts.

CUDAHY, Circuit Judge, concurring. Although I agree with the majority's firm conclusion that the "quick look" doctrine does not apply to these complex facts, I must indicate some differences in significant matters that are reached in the course of the majority opinion. Thus, in arriving at its conclusion that a full Rule of Reason analysis is required, the majority seems to be extrapolating from its discussion of whether the NBA may be a "single entity." Classification as a "single entity" means immunity from Sherman Act 1 considerations, a distinction much more drastic than the conclusion that the conduct in question here deserves a "quizzical look" rather than a mere "quick look." So, although it is not entirely clear, the majority seems to be saying that, since the NBA may be a single entity, its conduct certainly merits more than a quick look. Perhaps so, but, since the single entity question is unresolved, I would prefer to address the problem from a slightly different direction.

For the "quick look" approach should have a narrow application, reflecting its recent and sharply delimited origin in the *NCAA* case. *Nat'l Collegiate Athletic Ass'n v. Bd. of Regents of the Univ. of Oklahoma*, 468 U.S. 85 (1984). That case, involving a loose alliance of colleges which had agreed on price and output restrictions on broadcast of their football games, held that under some circumstances a full analysis of market power is not required to determine that an agreement is anticompetitive. This framework should not be extended to the more highly integrated and economically unitary NBA. * * *

* * * I turn to the single entity issue, where the discussion of the majority is deserving of comment both as to substance and to procedure. My first reservation is procedural and concerns whether this issue may be reached at all. The majority announces an exception without precedent to my knowledge from the usual rules of waiver of issues on appeal. The exception applies, according to the majority, to "defendants in complex cases" without elaboration. Why we should have more forgiving policies for highly skilled and highly compensated counsel in big corporate cases than for *pro se* litigants or appointed counsel of perhaps lesser qualification is certainly unclear to me. Our earlier opinion in this case states that "the NBA did not contend in the district court that the NBA is a single entity, let alone that it is a single entity as a matter of law." *Chicago Professional Sports Ltd. Partnership v. National Basketball Ass'n*, 961 F.2d 667, 673 (7th Cir. 1992), *cert. denied*, 506 U.S. 954 (1992). We also stated that: Characterization is a creative rather than exact endeavor. Appellate review is accordingly deferential. The district court held a trial, heard the evidence, and concluded that the best characterization of the NBA is the third we have mentioned: a joint venture in the production of games but more like a cartel in the sale of its output. Whether this is the best characterization of professional sports is a subject that has divided courts and scholars for some years, making it hard to characterize the district judge's choice as clear error. *Id.* at 672. No one seems to have argued that the basic structure of the NBA has changed since that opinion. I think, therefore, that, despite dicta in our earlier opinion speculating that "perhaps the parties will join issue more fully [regarding the single entity status of the NBA] in the proceedings still to come in the district court," *id.* at 673, there is a real question whether we can reach the single entity issue fascinating though it may be.

However, on the assumption that the "single entity" question may be reached (and presumably will be reached on remand) a number of considerations will be relevant. Assuming as I must that the sole goal of antitrust is efficiency or, put another way, the maximization of total societal wealth, the question whether a sports league is a "single entity" turns on whether the actions of the league have any potential to lessen economic competition among the separately owned teams. The fact that teams compete on the floor is more or less irrelevant to whether they compete economically it is only their economic competition which is germane to antitrust analysis. In principle, of course, a sports league could actually be a single firm and the individual teams could be under unified ownership and management. Such a firm would, of course, be subject to scrutiny only under 2 of the Sherman Act and not under 1. From the point of view of wealth maximization, a league of independently-owned teams, if it is no more likely than a single firm to make inefficient management decisions, should be treated as a single entity. The single entity question thus would boil down to "whether member clubs of a sports league have legitimate economic interests of their own, independent of the league and each other." Sports Leagues Revisited at 127. It follows that a sports league, no matter what its ownership structure, can make inefficient decisions only if the individual teams have some chance of economic gain at the expense of the league. Another form of the same question is whether a sports league is more like a single firm or like a joint venture. With efficiency the sole criterion, a joint venture warrants scrutiny for at least two reasons (1) the venture could possess market power with respect to the jointly produced product (essentially act like a single firm with monopoly power) or (2) the fact that the venturers remain competitors in other arenas might either distort the way the joint product is managed or allow the venturers to use the joint product as a smoke-screen behind which to cut deals to reduce competition in the other arenas. The most convincing "single entity" argument involving the NBA is that the teams produce only the joint product of "league basketball" and that there is thus no significant economic competition between them. * * * If this is the case, the argument goes, type (2) concerns drop out and only type (1) concerns remain. Type (1) concerns, of course, are exactly those appropriate for 2 analysis of a single firm.

There are, however, flaws in this single entity argument. The assumption underlying it is that league sports are a different and more desirable product than a disorganized collection of independently arranged games between teams. For this reason, it is contended that joining sports teams into a league is efficiency-enhancing and desirable. I will accept this premise.[8] It is perhaps true, as argued by the NBA and many commentators, that sports are different from many joint ventures because the individual teams cannot, even in principle, produce the product league sports. However, the fact that cooperation is necessary to produce league basketball does not imply that the league will necessarily produce its product in the most efficient fashion. There is potential for inefficient decisionmaking regarding the joint product of "league basketball" even when the individual teams engage in no economic activity outside of the league. This potential arises because the structure of the league is such that all "owners" of the league must be "owners" of individual teams and decisions are made by a vote of the teams. This means that the league will not necessarily make efficient decisions about the number of teams fielded or, more generally, the competitive balance among teams. Thus, the fact that several teams are required to make a league does not necessarily imply that the current makeup of the league is the most desirable or "efficient" one.

---

8. But the Green Bay Packers and the Chicago Bears played, presumably before enthusiastic crowds, before there was a National Football League.

The NBA's justification for its restriction of Bulls broadcasts centers on the need to maintain a competitive balance among teams. Such a balance is needed to ensure that the league provides high quality entertainment throughout the season so as to optimize competition with other forms of entertainment. Competitive balance is not the only contributor to the entertainment value of NBA basketball, however. Fan enjoyment of league sports depends on both the opportunity to identify with a local or favorite team and the thrill of watching the best quality of play. A single firm owning all of the teams would presumably arrange for the number of teams and their locations efficiently to maximize fan enjoyment of the league season. There is, however, no reason to expect that the current team owners will necessarily make such decisions efficiently, given their individual economic interests in the financial health of their own teams.

It's not surprising that farflung fans want to watch the Bulls' superstars on a superstation. The NBA argues that the broadcasting of more Bulls games to these fans will disturb the competitive balance among teams. However, one can also speculate that, since sports viewing has become more of a television activity than an "in the flesh" activity, these fans might prefer to have a league composed of fewer, better teams (like the Bulls). If this were the case, league policies designed to shore up all of the current teams would be inefficient. The point, of course, is not that this speculation is necessarily correct, but that the efficient number of teams (or, more generally, the efficient competitive balance) may not be obtained as a matter of course given the current league ownership framework. * * *

In any event, sports leagues argue that they must maintain independent ownership of the teams because separate ownership enhances the appearance of competitiveness demanded by fans. But the leagues cannot really expect the courts to aid them in convincing consumers that competition exists if it really does not. If consumers want economic competition between sports teams, then independent ownership and preservation of independent economic interests is likely an efficient choice for a sports league. But that choice, as with other joint ventures, brings with it the attendant antitrust risks. The NBA cannot have it both ways.

Relating all of this to the majority's treatment of the single entity issue, I see two problems with the majority analysis. First, as already noted, divorcing the question of single entity from the question of ownership is likely to lead to messy and inconsistent application of antitrust law. The bottom line may be that the inquiry into whether separate economic interests are maintained by the participants in a joint enterprise is likely to be no easier than a full Rule of Reason analysis.

Second, some of the majority's discussion of independent interests is puzzling. The majority contends that the district court "concluded that all cooperation among separately incorporated firms is forbidden by 1 of the Sherman Act, except to the extent *Copperweld* permits." * * * *Copperweld* concluded that a parent corporation and its wholly-owned subsidiary have a "complete unity of interest" and hence should be treated as a single entity. Here the district court simply concluded that the NBA, because it involved cooperation between separately-owned teams, was subject to antitrust analysis. * * * This conclusion is a far cry from deciding that all cooperation among separately incorporated firms is forbidden.

I also cannot agree with the majority's analysis of the type of "unity of interest" required for single entity status. The majority states * * * that "even a single firm contains many competing interests." The opinion goes on to cite the competition for salary and bonuses between division managers as an example. However, when *Copperweld* talks about unity of interests in the single entity context, I think it must be taken to mean unity of economic interests of the decisionmakers. *See Copperweld*, 467 U.S. at 769. A single firm does not evidence diverse economic interests to the outside world because final decisions are made by the owners or stockholders, who care only about the overall performance of the firm. Only because this is the case can single firms be assumed to behave in the canonical profit-maximizing fashion. The diverse interests mentioned in the majority opinion seem as irrelevant to the antitrust analysis as is the on-court rivalry between teams in the NBA. Thus, when Copperweld refers to conduct that "deprives the marketplace of the independent centers of decisionmaking that competition assumes," it does not refer to "decisionmakers" whose economic independence is only potential. The antitrust issue is really whether, as a result of some cooperative venture, economic interests which remain independent coordinate their decisions. As *Copperweld* notes, "the officers of a single firm are not separate economic actors pursuing separate economic interests. * * *" *Id.* Therefore, their joint decisionmaking is of no antitrust concern. Employees or divisions within a firm, on the other hand, may remain separate economic actors pursuing separate economic interests but they do not make the final decisions governing the firm's operations. They may compete for shares of the firm's revenues, but they do not decree how that revenue will be shared. Thus their conflict or cooperation does not pose antitrust issues either. Joint ventures, on the other hand, are subject to antitrust scrutiny precisely because separate economic interests are joined in decisionmaking, with the potential for distorted results.

As long as teams are individually owned and revenue is not shared in fixed proportion, the teams both retain independent economic interests and make decisions in concert. Where this is the case, there is a strong argument that sports leagues should be treated as joint ventures rather than single entities because there remains a potential that league policy will be made to satisfy the independent economic interests of some group of teams, rather than to maximize the overall performance of the league. Thus, it is possible, if more Bulls games were broadcast, league profits might increase. But, if the revenue from the broadcast of Bulls games goes disproportionately to the Bulls, the other league members may not vote for this more efficient result.

Notes and Questions

1. The *Sullivan* and *Bulls* cases illustrate just how long sports antitrust cases can percolate in the federal courts. The *Sullivan* case settled after two trials and one trip to the court of appeals, thereby avoiding the need for a third trial. The *Bulls* case, which originally proceeded on an expedited basis, involved two trials and two excursions to the court of appeals in six years. When the plaintiffs' request for a rehearing *en banc* by the Seventh Circuit was denied, the case settled. The precise terms of the settlement agreement are not clear, but it was reported that the NBA, the Bulls, and WGN-TV agreed to a five-year deal that allows the Bulls and WGN to broadcast all of the Bulls' games locally, permits fifteen superstation broadcasts of Bulls games each year, exempts the Bulls from paying any fee to the NBA for the future superstation broadcasts, reduces the amount of the superstation tax to be paid by the Bulls to the NBA for the games played before the settlement, and splits the advertising spots on national cable among the parties. *See generally NBA and Chicago Bulls Settle Antitrust Lawsuit Over WGN Telecasts of Bulls Games*, 18 ENT. L. REP. (December, 1996); *Chicago Bulls and NBA Settle Antitrust Suit; Bulls Increase Games on 'Free TV' and Reinstate Nationwide Cable Coverage*, BUS. WIRE, Dec. 12, 1996.

2. As you recall from Chapter 2, while the NBA was in the middle of its dispute with Jerry Reinsdorf's Bulls over team versus league sale of television broadcast rights, the NFL became embroiled in a dispute with Jerry Jones' Cowboys. In September, 1995, NFL Properties, Inc. sued Jones, the Cowboys, and the corporation that owns Texas Stadium, the Cowboys' home venue. Verified Complaint, *National Football League Properties, Inc. v. Dallas Cowboys Football Club, Ltd.*, 95 Civ. 7951 (SAS) (S.D.N.Y. 1995). NFL Properties claimed that the Cowboys had violated the October 1, 1982 trust agreement, pursuant to which the NFL owners transferred the right to use all team and league marks and logos for commercial purposes to the NFL Trust and then to NFL Properties. NFL Properties contended that the agreements between Texas Stadium and sponsors such as Pepsi, American Express, and Nike were prohibited, and pressed claims for breach of contract, breach of fiduciary duty, misappropriation of property, tortious interference with contract, and violations of the Lanham Act. Less than two months later, the Cowboys responded with a lawsuit alleging that the NFL Trust and the NFL's mandatory pooling of team marks and logos violated the antitrust laws, and asserting a number of other statutory and common law claims against the NFL, NFL Properties, the NFL Trust, individual league office personnel, and the member clubs of the NFL. Verified Complaint, *Dallas Cowboys Football Club, Ltd. v. National Football League Trust* (S.D.N.Y. 1995). The Cowboys produced substantial evidence discounting NFL Properties' claims that the Cowboys had violated NFL rules, but the district court refused to dismiss the case before full discovery. *See National Football League Properties, Inc. v. Dallas Cowboys Football Club, Ltd.*, 922 F. Supp. 849 (S.D.N.Y. 1996). Nevertheless, in November, 1996, the parties agreed simply to dismiss their respective cases without prejudice, to bring Jones and the Cowboys "back into the fold," and to avoid any further airing of their "dirty laundry" in public. Whenever intra-league disputes go to court, the parties may find themselves disclosing (purportedly) important proprietary information about the league and its members, team finances, and any prior misconduct. Can the league enact rules or amendments to the league Constitution & Bylaws to anticipate that problem and to prevent it from occurring? Would a mandatory arbitration provision or a waiver of recourse clause be enforceable?

3. In lawsuits that involve *current* team owners, such as the *Raiders*, *Bulls*, and *Cowboys* cases, are the parties sufficiently adverse to join the issue on the single entity status of the league? If the league prevails, and a court determines that the league is a single entity, would that outcome both harm the team in its prosecution of its antitrust claim against the league, and still benefit the league (and, derivatively, the team) in future antitrust litigation? Therefore, in some circumstances, should the courts be wary that they could have nominally opposing litigants seeking the same outcome on certain issues before the court?

4. How can sports teams, owned by different owners who compete in so many ways (recounted earlier), contend that they constitute a single entity? On the other hand, because the teams are units of a league that create a single product — NFL football games or NHL hockey games — how can opposing parties characterize them as completely independent competitors? Are NFL teams really similar to the divisions of General Motors, and are the owners of the teams really similar to the general managers of those divisions? These questions are difficult, but the additional information set forth below about the history of the "single entity defense," the operation of professional sports leagues, and the legal evolution in this area may further illuminate the issue.

IV. The "Single Entity Defense" by Traditional Model Sports Leagues: A Historical and Functional Analysis

The major, traditional model sports leagues have enjoyed little success with the argument that their need for cooperation to operate a league renders them a single entity. Almost uniformly, courts refused to hold that Section 1 of the Sherman Act, which requires a "contract, combination * * *, or conspiracy," should not apply to agreements among teams in a league. As discussed earlier, this virtual consensus has not been joined by every judge or legal commentator. *See* Chapter 2.

In any event, after the Second Circuit's decision in the *NASL* case and the Ninth Circuit's decision in *Raiders I*, it seemed as though the single entity argument had taken its last breath. However, the Supreme Court's decision in *Copperweld Corp. v. Independence Tube Corp.*, 467 U.S. 752 (1984), resurrected league contentions that the single entity defense was viable.

Prior to 1984, lower federal courts had already recognized that the Sherman Act's "contract, combination * * *, or conspiracy" requirement was not satisfied by allegations that a corporation "conspired" with its officers, directors, or employees, or that a single entity's officers, directors, and/or employees had "conspired" among themselves. *See, e.g., Walker v. Providence Journal Co.*, 493 F.2d 82, 87 (1st Cir. 1974); *Tose v. First Pennsylvania Bank*, 648 F.2d 879, 893–94 (3d Cir.), *cert. denied*, 454 U.S. 893 (1981); *Greenville Publishing Co. v. Daily Reflector, Inc.*, 496 F.2d 391, 399 (4th Cir. 1974); *H&B Equipment Co. v. International Harvester*, 577 F.2d 239, 244 (5th Cir. 1978); *Smith v. North Michigan Hospitals, Inc.*, 703 F.2d 942, 950 (6th Cir. 1983); *Chapman v. Rudd Paint & Varnish Co.*, 409 F.2d 635, 643 n.9 (9th Cir. 1969); *Card v. National Life Insurance Co.*, 603 F.2d 828, 834 (10th Cir. 1979). However, the Supreme Court had not yet specifically addressed those issues, and there was prior Supreme Court precedent suggesting that two corporations under common ownership could conspire in violation of Sherman Section 1. *See Kiefer-Stewart Co. v. Joseph E. Seagram & Sons*, 340 U.S. 211 (1951). It was unclear under what circumstances joint conduct by a corporation and its wholly-owned subsidiary would constitute a violation. *See, e.g., Ogilvie v. Fotomat Corp.*, 641 F.2d 581, 587–89 (8th Cir. 1981); *Columbia Metal Culvert Co. v. Kaiser Aluminum & Chemical Corp.*, 579 F.2d 20, 22–25 (3d Cir.), *cert. denied*, 439 U.S. 876 (1978).

In *Copperweld*, the Supreme Court considered these questions and confirmed that officers, directors, and employees of a single firm engage in unitary, not joint, conduct for the purposes of the Sherman Act, and that the same is true of a corporation and its unincorporated divisions. The court concluded that Section 1 of the Sherman Act requires a "contract, combination * * *, or conspiracy" among separate economic entities or persons, not unitary action by persons or entities that always share "complete unity of interest." *See* 467 U.S. at 769–71. The Court proceeded to hold that because a parent corporation and its wholly owned subsidiary "have a complete unity of interest," and their joint conduct does not involve a "sudden joining of economic resources that had previously served different interests," they constitute a single economic actor for purposes of the Sherman Act. *Id.* at 771–72.

The *Copperweld* court was only considering parent corporations and their wholly-owned subsidiaries, and expressly limited its holding to "the narrow issue squarely presented." *Id.* at 767. Lower courts have applied the theory upon which *Copperweld* was based to hold that multiple wholly-owned subsidiaries of a single parent corporation (sometimes called "brother and sister corporations") cannot conspire with each other for purposes of the Sherman Act. *See, e.g., Advanced Health Care Services v. Radford Community Hospital,* 910 F.2d 139, 146 (4th Cir. 1990); *Garshmen v. Universal Resources Holding Inc.,* 824 F.2d 223, 230 (3d Cir. 1984). *But see In re Ray Dobbins Lincoln Mercury, Inc.,* 604 F. Supp. 203, 205 (W. D. Va. 1984) (*Copperweld* does not apply to conspiracies between two wholly-owned subsidiaries). Similarly, lower courts have concluded that corporations with completely common ownership are incapable of conspiring for Sherman Act purposes. *See, e.g., Century Oil Tool, Inc. v. Production Specialties, Inc.,* 737 F.2d 1316 (5th Cir. 1984); *Gucci v. Gucci Shops, Inc.,* 651 F. Supp 194, 197 (S.D.N.Y. 1986); *Guzowski v. Hartman,* 969 F.2d 211 (6th Cir. 1992). However, beyond those situations that are very similar to *Copperweld,* separate economic entities have generally been treated as potential conspirators.

The cases extending *Copperweld* are limited, generally requiring complete common ownership, majority ownership, a *complete* unity of interest, or an absolute right to control. *See generally* Stephen Calkins, *Copperweld in the Courts: The Road to Caribe,* 63 ANTI. L.J. 345 (1995). Thus, post-*Copperweld* precedents outside the sports realm do not bode well for a judicial recognition of the sports leagues' proposed single entity defense. First, common ownership and majority ownership do not apply to traditional model sports leagues. Second, while league constitutions and bylaws place certain restrictions on the individual member clubs, that is not the type of control referenced in *Copperweld.* The leagues do not have a right to operate the individual clubs, except perhaps under very extreme circumstances. The league does not have *any* ownership interest in the teams, much less the majority ownership interest that the post-*Copperweld* cases have required. The individual teams are separate businesses, linked by their constitution and by-laws but not under common ownership. For example, the NFL's Constitution & Bylaws even includes provisions governing member clubs' withdrawal from the NFL, presumably to join or form another league. NFL Constitution & Bylaws Article 3.6. *See further Mid-South Grizzlies v. National Football League,* 720 F.2d 772, 786 (3d Cir. 1983), *cert. denied,* 467 U.S. 1215 (1984).

Third, while the leagues emphasize the extent of league *revenue* sharing to support a claim that the teams have a unity of interest, there is no significant sharing of costs, and the teams' profits and losses vary widely. In addition, the fact that a revenue source is shared does not alone create a sufficient commonality of interest. To say, for example, that all ticket revenues are shared is relatively meaningless and does not beget the conclusion that the firms sharing those revenues are incapable of conspiracy. *See, e.g.,* Team Relocation and the Business of Professional Sports Leagues, above. Therefore, the observation that a traditional model league shares a high percentage of its revenues proves very little, and certainly does not establish a complete unity of interest. *See, e.g., Chicago Professional Sports Ltd. Partnership v. National Basketball Ass'n,* 754 F. Supp. 1336, 1341 (N.D. Ill. 1991), *aff'd,* 961 F.2d 667 (7th Cir.) (1992); *but see Chicago Professional Sports Ltd. Partnership v. National Basketball Ass'n,* above.

Fourth, even if a league's efforts to promote revenue could serve to increase the teams' commonality of interests to the point of complete unity of interests, it would involve the "joining of economic resources that had previously served different interests," thus, on its face, not satisfying the requirements of the *Copperweld* opinion. *See* 467 U.S. at 771–72. Finally, all cases evaluating joint ventures and independent businesses formed and operating as a joint business have concluded that the agreements between or among the joint venturers, or between or among the independent, but aligned, businesses, constitute the common conduct necessary to trigger application of Section 1. See, e.g., *Rothery Storage & Van Co. v. Atlas Van Lines*, 792 F.2d 210 (D.C. Cir. 1986); *Northwest Wholesale Stationers v. Pacific Stationery & Printing Co.*, 472 U.S. 284 (1985); *NCAA v. Board of Regents of the Univ. of Okla.*, 468 U.S. 85 (1984). As a result of this analysis, the leagues' argument that the *NASL* and *Raiders* decisions were somehow inconsistent with *Copperweld* has not been very persuasive. *See, e.g.*, Stephen F. Ross, *An Antitrust Analysis of Sports League Contracts with Cable Networks*, 39 EMORY L.J. 463, 466 and n.17 (1990) ("The courts have consistently and correctly held, however that where leagues are composed of teams that are independently owned and operated and that do not share all profits and losses, they fail to qualify as 'single entities' for purposes of the antitrust laws"); Michael S. Jacobs, *Professional Sports Leagues, Antitrust, and the Single-Entity Theory*, 67 IND. L.J. 25 (1991) (arguing that no aspect of the *Copperweld* decision militates in favor of re-examining the possibility of a "single entity defense" for sports leagues); *see also McNeil v. National Football League*, 790 F. Supp. 871, 878–81 (D. Minn. 1992).

By 1991, the courts seemed to have rejected the "single entity" defense so conclusively that the National Basketball Association did not even raise the issue in response to a Section 1 challenge by one of its member teams. *See Chicago Professional Sports Ltd. Partnership v. National Basketball Ass'n*, 754 F. Supp. 1336, 1349 (N.D. Ill. 1991) ("The NBA has not argued that it is a single entity and therefore altogether immune from Section 1 attacks"), *aff'd*, 961 F.2d 667, 673 (7th Cir), *cert. denied*, 506 U.S. 954 (1992). However, Judge Easterbrook's first opinion in the *Chicago Professional Sports* case invited further examination. *Chicago Professional Sports Ltd. Partnership v. NBA*, 961 F.2d at 673 ("whether a sports league is a single entity for antitrust purposes has significance far beyond this case, and it would be imprudent to decide the question after such cursory dialogue"). This judicial invitation further fueled the leagues' academic antitrust defenders' calls for a judicial reconsideration of the "single entity" defense. *See, e.g.*, Gary Roberts, *Antitrust Issues in Professional Sports*, 2 Law of Professional and Amateur Sports 19-21 to 19-22 (Gary A. Uberstine ed., 1994).

A sports league's status after *Copperweld* was squarely at issue in the *Sullivan* case. The NFL had argued that the Supreme Court's decision in *Copperweld* "overturns prior case law holding that NFL clubs do not constitute a single enterprise but rather, are separate entities which were capable of conspiring with each other under 1." *Sullivan v. National Football League*, 34 F.3d 1091, 1099 (1st Cir. 1994) (citations omitted). The district court and the First Circuit both rejected the NFL's argument, holding that "the critical inquiry is whether the alleged antitrust conspirators have a 'unity of interests' or whether, instead, 'any of the defendants has pursued interests diverse from those of the cooperative itself.'" 34 F.3d at 1099, quoting *City of Mt. Pleasant, Iowa v. Associated Elec. Co-op., Inc.*, 838 F.2d 268 (8th Cir. 1988). The First Circuit held that the NFL teams competing against each other in the relevant antitrust market proved that they did not have the "unity of interest" required in *Copperweld*. *Id*. The same basic analysis led a district court to deny the NFL's motion to dismiss based on the "single entity defense" in a lawsuit brought by another former owner of the New England Patriots, Fran Murray. *See Murray v. National Football League*, 1996 U.S. Dist. LEXIS 9108 (E.D. Pa. 1996).

It was generally assumed that the First Circuit's post-*Copperweld* decision in *Sullivan*, when combined with the Second and Ninth Circuit's prior decisions in *NASL* and *Raiders*, respectively, would put to rest the leagues' continued assertion that they constitute single entities. However, the questions raised by Judge Easterbrook in his first

Chicago Professional Sports Ltd. Partnership decision remained unresolved. Before he assumed his place on the bench, Judge Easterbrook had been counsel for the NCAA and had been unsuccessful in defending the NCAA's restrictions on competition in the television market before the Supreme Court *NCAA v. Board of Regents of the Univ. of Okla.*, 468 U.S. 85 (1984); therefore, he was seen as a judge who would be particularly inclined toward the positions advanced by sports leagues such as the NBA.

The NBA was not disappointed. In his second opinion, Judge Easterbrook went beyond any reported decision and held that *Copperweld* does not require members to have a "unity of interest." *Chicago Professional Sports Ltd. Partnership v. NBA*, 95 F.3d 593, 598 (7th Cir. 1996). Without specifying any legal standard, and despite significant questions concerning the issue's justiciability, see 95 F.3d at 601, 602 (Cudahy, J., concurring), Judge Easterbrook held that the district court should conduct some sort of a comprehensive "functional" investigation of the organization of the NBA to determine whether it should be treated as a single entity. *Id.* at 598–99.

At various points, Judge Easterbrook's opinion seemed to confuse the issue of whether conduct should be judged under the Rule of Reason or under a *per se* standard with the question of whether the defendants are a single entity and therefore not subject to scrutiny under Section 1. *Id.* at 598. He purported to rely on the treatise of antitrust authority, Professor Phillip Areeda, as support for the proposition that, in certain respects, a sports league may be a single entity. *Id.* at 599, citing Phillip E. Areeda, 7 *Antitrust Law* 1478d (1986). However, the decision failed to identify Professor Areeda's primary conclusion, that, in antitrust markets where individual member teams or their owners remain significant economic actors, the fact that they have come together to form a joint venture does not shield them from scrutiny under Section 1. Phillip E. Areeda, 7 *Antitrust Law* 1478d (1986). The same is true of the market for television broadcast rights, where the NBA teams have been independent economic actors.

Of course, if the antitrust issue concerned hiring of league officials or referees, or similar function in which the member clubs do not compete with each other, and in which league control is essential to the creation and/or success of the joint venture, the NBA may very well be deemed a single entity. The teams have a complete unity of interest with respect to the hiring of referees, they cannot reasonably compete with one another in that market, and they have never been actual or potential competitors for referees' services. For those reasons, a league decision about referee wages should not be subject to scrutiny under Section 1.

Judge Easterbrook's opinion also apparently reflected a fundamental misunderstanding of the decision in *Seabury Management, Inc. v. Professional Golfers' Ass'n of America, Inc.*, 878 F. Supp. 771 (D.Md. 1994), *aff'd in part and rev'd and remanded in part*, 52 F.3d 322 (4th Cir. 1995). The *Seabury* case was brought against a trade association of professional golfers, the PGA of America, *not* against the producer of professional golf events in the United States, PGA Tour, Inc. 878 F. Supp. at 777–78. Judge Easterbrook relied on the *Seabury* case as support for his holding, stating that:

> [T]he fourth circuit concluded that the Professional Golf Association should be treated as one firm for antitrust purposes, even though that sport is less economically integrated than the NBA.

95 F.3d at 599–600. While Judge Easterbrook was correct in declaring that the sport of golf, and the PGA Tour and its constituent tournaments, are less economically integrated than the NBA, those facts had nothing to do with the *Seabury* decision. The Professional Golf Association is not the PGA Tour or the sport of golf—it is an unrelated

trade association. In *Seabury*, the court simply held that a trade association and a separately incorporated division of the association should be treated as a single entity for antitrust purposes because the two entities had a "complete unity of interest" and functioned as a "single economic unit." 878 F. Supp. at 777. Contrary to Judge Easterbrook's suggestion, the evidence in the *Seabury* case established that the defendants in the *Seabury* case were much more economically integrated than the teams of the NBA.

Similarly, in *City of Mt. Pleasant, Iowa v. Associated Elec. Co-op., Inc.*, 838 F.2d 268, 276 (8th Cir. 1988), another case upon which Judge Easterbrook relied, the court expressly found no evidence that "any two of the defendants are, or have been, actual or potential competitors." The defendants' interests were not "sufficiently divergent so that a reasonable juror could conclude that the entities have not always worked together for a common cause." *Id.* In the case of the NBA teams, no reasonable juror could conclude that they had not been actual and potential competitors or that they had always worked together, as opposed to having competed.

Professor Areeda was prescient comparing traditional model leagues to a league organized as a true single entity:

> It may be helpful to compare a different structure. Imagine that investors create a new Hypothetical Football League (HFL); that the league is the only business entity involved; that it hires and fires and designates certain divisions to which it assigns and reassigns players and managers; that it decides how many teams to have; where to locate them, and when to move them; that it contracts with cities, stadiums, broadcasters, etc.; and that it receives all the revenues, decides what to retain, and distributes the remainder to shareholders. The HFL would not be immune from Sherman Act 2. But apart from agreements limiting the opportunities of its investors, broadcasters (etc.) to deal with a rival league, the HFL would escape Sherman Act 1 in deciding to "boycott" teenagers [referring to *Linsemen v. World Hockey Ass'n*, 439 F. Supp. 1315 (D. Conn. 1977)], one-eyed players [referring to *Neeld v. National Hockey League*, 594 F.2d 1297 (9th Cir. 1979) and 439 F. Supp. 446 (W.D.N.Y. 1977)], or students still in college [referring to Spencer Haywood's suit *Denver Rockets v. All-Pro Management*, 325 F. Supp. 1049 (C.D.Cal. 1971)]; to set salaries and assign or re-assign players among its divisions; or to add, subtract, or re-locate playing divisions.

> The HFL saga naturally suggests this question: why should antitrust courts largely ignore the HFL while involving themselves so deeply in the affairs of the actual sports leagues? Are the HFL and NFL so different? Perhaps it is enough to be grateful that professional sports have not been organized in the HFL way, which creates so much uncorrected power. Here, as elsewhere, we take industrial organization as we find it, and here we find entities with separate market significance, albeit entities which need more collaboration than we tolerate for ordinary business firms.

PHILLIP E. AREEDA, 7 *Antitrust Law* 1478d at 358–59 (1986).

In answer to Professor Areeda's question, the true single entity league and the traditional model league *are* so different. As explained in detail in Chapter 2, a single, integrated sports league is a very different business, with significant advantages and disadvantages that exist precisely because the teams all have a complete unity of interest. Many investors in traditional model leagues who control their own individual teams would never consider investing to own less than a controlling interest in a business that was as economically integrated as the hypothetical single entity league. They should not be permitted to adopt a league structure of independent teams and, at the same time, claim antitrust immunity as a single entity.

In addition, the antitrust laws presume that, if the league were created by investors simply pooling their money to create a league, and with no outside business interests in the sport, another league could be formed by the same means to challenge the first, in the absence of the exclusionary conduct referenced by Professor Areeda. However, when the traditional model league is formed by people located in the leading cities around the country, who each control the local stadium or arena, have left another league to join the dominant league, or have built a local business to operate a team in their city, it is much more difficult for another league to establish itself in the same fashion to challenge the first. Therefore, having invested in a league structured as a traditional model league and having benefitted over the years from all the business and competitive advantages that such a configuration afforded, the traditional model leagues have no viable argument that they should be treated as single entities.

As Professor Areeda suggested, the comparison between a traditional model league and a pure single entity league is very instructive. As more true single entity leagues are launched, the striking differences between these two different forms of doing business will become readily apparent. As a result, it should become even clearer that, excepting functions that the leagues must perform as a single entity (*e.g.*, hiring umpires and referees and other league officials, negotiating national television contracts under the protection of the Sports Broadcasting Act, and producing "league events" such as the All-Star Game), the rules and regulations of the leagues and the agreements among the member teams to eliminate competition should be subject to antitrust scrutiny under Section 1.

Even leagues nominally organized as single entity leagues may not actually be single entities for antitrust purposes. The World League of American Football ("WLAF") presents a glowing illustration. In a number of litigated cases, discussed in detail in Chapter 10, federal courts have determined that the NFL member clubs are competitors conspiring to restrain trade in, and to monopolize, the market for professional football player services. Those competitors joined together to form, own, and operate the WLAF. An antitrust plaintiff may be able to prove that a primary purpose of the NFL member clubs in forming and subsidizing the WLAF was to foreclose the creation of a league that would compete directly with the NFL. Further, the NFL ostensibly sought to establish a league that could supply the NFL with talent (like a minor league) while minimizing player compensation to avoid putting inflationary pressure on NFL team salaries. Therefore, an antitrust plaintiff could argue that the WLAF salary scale, the other WLAF restrictions on its player compensation, and the WLAF itself constitute agreements among competitors designed to restrain competition in the market for professional football player services. The plaintiff would contend that the owners were even willing to incur years of substantial losses (in excess of half a million dollars per team, per year in the early years) to reap the benefits to each of the NFL member clubs' businesses. The plaintiff might also challenge the agreements between the NFL and the WLAF as agreements that restrain competition. The NFL eventually converted the WLAF to a league operating solely outside the United States (NFL Europe). The Purpose to restrain competition from a new league in the United States remains a motivation for NFL Europe, but issues concerning extraterritorial application of U.S. antitrust laws complicates the analysis.

Another useful illustration is Major League Soccer. Although nominally structured as a single entity (a limited liability company), individual league investors have operational control over individual teams and have autonomy in decisionmaking and profit generation similar to the autonomy of owners of teams in traditional model leagues.

The flexibility of this structure under most state laws would be sufficient for each traditional model league to reconstitute the entire league and all its teams as a single limited liability company without any significant changes in its economic relationships. Therefore, the fact that player contracts are nominally with the league and that the league, and to some extent all the teams are owned by a single entity (the limited liability company) may not shield the MLS from challenge under Section 1 if a review of the economic realities reveals the direct competition and lack of unity between owners (or operators) of teams symptomatic of traditional model leagues. Those precise issues were the subject of a class action lawsuit filed by the MLS players against their league. *See* Complaint, *Fraser v. Major League Soccer*, Civ. No. 10242 (D.Mass. 1997). The MLS convinced the district court that it was a single entity, requiring dismissal of the players' Section 1 claims. *See Fraser v. Major League Soccer, L.L.C.*, 97 F.Supp.2d 130 (D.Mass. 2000); The case proceeded to trial on the Section 2 claims and the MLS prevailed there, based primarily on the jury's finding of a worldwide market for players. On appeal, the US Court of Appeals for the First Circuit refused to affirm the single entity decision, instead affirming dismissal of all claims based on the defendants not having market power or monopoly power in the worldwide market for professional soccer player services. *See Fraser v. Major League Soccer, L.L.C.*, 284 F.3d 47 (1st Cir. 2002)

The consequences of a broad judicial recognition of the "single entity" defense for traditional model leagues would be dramatic. *See Chicago Professional Sports Ltd. Partnership v. NBA*, 95 F.3d at 601 (Cudahy, J., concurring); *Los Angeles Memorial Coliseum Comm'n v. National Football League*, 726 F.2d 1381, 1387–90 (9th Cir.), *cert. denied*, 469 U.S. 990 (1984). Advocates of the defense consistently argue that Section 2 of the Sherman Act, which proscribes monopolization and does not entail demonstration of a conspiracy or other combination, would remain a constraint on league behavior. Yet, as a single entity, the member teams of the league could still set a wage scale or agree in other ways on all of the contract terms to be offered to each and every player in the league. *See, e.g.,* John Weistart, *League Control of Market Opportunities: A Perspective on Competition and Cooperation in the Sports Industry*, 1984 DUKE L.J. 1013, 1035–37 (1984). The antitrust laws would be unable to distinguish that situation from a corporate decision to pay all the corporation's employees at plants across the United States the same wage, or to issue a wage scale that applied to all of the corporation's divisions. In addition, league decisions restricting sale or transfer of franchises or limiting output to raise prices would likely be immune from antitrust sanctions. Most, if not all, of the cases holding league drafts and other player restraints unlawful would no longer be meaningful precedents. *See, e.g., Smith v. Pro-Football, Inc.*, 593 F.2d 1173 (D.C.Cir. 1978); *Mackey v. National Football League*, 543 F.2d 606 (8th Cir. 1976). Similarly, while a court might decide to expand Section 2 liability to avoid the consequences that recognition of a "single entity" defense might engender, without such expansion it is likely that the conduct in the *NASL* and *Raiders* cases would no longer be unlawful. The need for the league to convince Congress to grant antitrust immunity or exemptions for specific conduct currently deemed to be unlawful, efforts that have generally been unsuccessful for the past thirty years, would be obviated.

Thus, it is not surprising that the traditional leagues and their academic supporters persist in their efforts to convince lower courts to endorse a defense that is contrary to so many lower court decisions and, arguably, is contrary to the Supreme Court's decision in *NCAA v. Board of Regents of the Univ. of Oklahoma*, 468 U.S. 85 (1984), as well. Reinvigorated by Judge Easterbrook's opinion in the *Chicago Professional Sports Limited Partnership* case, the leagues will be litigating this issue at every opportunity, in search of a federal judge who might be convinced that such entities should be able to exercise unitary control over all issues relating to competition between and among their member teams. However, in the period following Judge Easterbrook's opinion, the leagues have had little success. *See, e.g., St. Louis Convention and Visitors Comm'n v. NFL,* Case No. 4:95, CV 2443 JCH, Slip op. at 7–17 (E.D. Mo. May 2, 1997) (denying motion to strike NFL's "single economic enterprise" defense, but stating that the *Bulls* case did not change the law and that single entity decisions against the NFL in *McNeil* and *Sullivan* collaterally estop the NFL from defending on the basis that teams are incapable of conspiring). *See also NFL v. Los Angeles Raiders,* CV 95-5808 KN (SHX), slip op at 7 n.3 (C.D. Cal. May 22, 1997).

Chapter 13

Antitrust and Sports: Equipment Restrictions

I. Introduction

One aspect of sports that seems to reflect a consensus is the need to devise a uniform set of rules governing all participants. As the Supreme Court recognized in *NCAA v. Board of Regents*, 468 U.S. 85 (1984), agreements regarding applicable "ground rules" are necessary in league sports for the product to be available at all.

A key component of the rules of the game concerns what equipment or accessories can be used by participants. In ancient times, there were sports that simply did not involve equipment. Races (running or swimming, for example) and wrestling or fighting competitions did not even necessitate the wearing of clothes! However, it is difficult to imagine a modern sport in which the competitors do not use some form of equipment, from clothing and footwear to bats, clubs, helmets, sticks, rackets, gloves, paddles, guns and ammunition, bows and arrows, skis (water or snow), poles (for skiing or vaulting), skates, snowboards, bobsleds, hurdles, shotputs, javelins, balls, pucks, pads and other protective equipment, nets, baskets, goals, goal posts, wickets, tees, automobiles, trucks, boats, weights, mats, zambonis, gymnastics equipment-balance beams, rings, pommel horses, parallel and uneven parallel bars, floor exercise mats, powders and resins, swords, epees, bowling balls, pins, fishing rods, and many other categories of equipment. A stroll around any sporting goods store will reveal a great variety of equipment associated to some extent with one or more sports. A race track, swimming pool, ping-pong ("table tennis" to purists) table, basketball or tennis court, artificial playing surface, or stadium enclosure may also, in some circumstances, be considered "equipment."

Part and parcel of a league's or association's self-governance involves its ability to control on-the-field or on-the-court competition and to place reasonable restrictions upon the style of play and equipment used in the playing of the games. For example, Major League Baseball may outlaw aluminum bats or other paraphernalia that, it believes, may compromise the league's notions of tradition, fair play, competitiveness, or safety. Likewise, professional golf or tennis tours may decide to limit the extent to which a player may use an innovative piece of equipment that, the tour organizers believe, threatens the delicate balance of competition existing in the sport. Oftentimes, these restrictions on equipment use and limitations upon the development of new ideas have prompted the filing of antitrust suits by manufacturers and/or players alleging that the actions constitute a conspiracy to restrain trade and suppress, rather than foster, meaningful competition.

621

The cases that follow explore the factors to be considered in determining whether a particular equipment restriction runs afoul of the antitrust laws. In reviewing these decisions, you should attempt to discern the parameters of permissible self-regulation, differentiating a restriction that is part of legitimate self-governance from a restriction that restrains trade in an unreasonable fashion. This line of demarcation is often difficult to draw.

Consider the following list of possible reasons why a league or tour may select one type or brand of equipment to the exclusion of other types or brands. What is the relevance of the offered rationale to a typical antitrust inquiry?

1) The new equipment would actually change competition in a detrimental way. For example, an engine on a bicycle would not be permitted in cycling. Likewise, the NFL may not permit NFL quarterbacks to have walkie-talkies in their helmets that they might use to communicate with their receivers during a particular play.

2) The new equipment is "non-traditional," and, although it would not change the competition (*e.g.*, the outcome would not be different a player's performance would not be affected), it is contrary to the traditional concept of "the game." For example, despite the popularity of the movies *Tin Cup* and *Happy Gilmore*, the PGA Tour or the United States Golf Association may decide to continue its prohibition on "clubs" that do not conform to Rules of Golf. Thus, players would be precluded from using hockey sticks, shovels, or hoes as clubs, or pool cues as putters, even though officials may be certain that the use of such alternative "clubs" would hurt, not improve, the players' performance.

3) The league or tour wants to use a standardized product developed by a single manufacturer to equalize the competition and to ensure that differences in equipment are eliminated. For example, all competitors in an auto race will use a single brand of tire, all cyclists will use the same bicycle model, or all MLB, NBA, or NFL games will be played with the same brand of ball.

4) The manufacturer enters into a sponsorship agreement with the league or circuit, and the agreement requires the league or circuit to use that manufacturer's product exclusively — *e.g.*, tennis balls, football helmets, etc.

5) The same as No. 4, but the exclusive manufacturer is selected through competitive bidding.

II. Equipment Restrictions and Professional Tennis

Gunter Harz Sports, Inc. v. United States Tennis Ass'n, Inc.
511 F. Supp. 1103 (D. Neb. 1981)

SCHATZ, District Judge. * * * The present controversy grew out of the decision of the United States Tennis Association (USTA) to honor a temporary ban imposed by the International Tennis Federation (ITF) on the use of "double-strung" tennis rackets, and the USTA's subsequent adoption of a new rule of tennis defining a tennis racket, which was promulgated by the ITF and replaced the temporary ban. The plaintiff alleges that the USTA's actions constitute a conspiracy with various others, not made defendants to this action, to restrain competition in the sale of tennis rackets and tennis racket stringing systems in the United States and abroad, in violation of Section 1 of the Sherman Act.

I. FACTS

The plaintiff, Gunter Harz Sports, Inc. (Harz Sports) * * * is engaged in commerce in the business of manufacturing and distributing tennis rackets and tennis racket strings and stringing systems in the United States, as well as internationally. The president and incorporator of Harz Sports is Gunter Harz.

The defendant USTA is a Type A not-for-profit corporation, organized under the laws of the State of New York, with its headquarters located in New York, New York. The USTA is a voluntary membership organization made up of Sectional Associations, Member Clubs, Individual Members and Honorary Members from all over the United States. * * *

The USTA is the recognized sanctioning organization governing tournament tennis, both amateur and professional, in the United States. Sanctioning indicates that a particular tournament is an official USTA approved tournament and insures that the international Rules of Tennis, promulgated by the ITF, and the Tournament Regulations of the USTA will be followed. The results of sanctioned events are the input for a multi-level ranking system administered by the USTA which ranks every person who participates in sanctioned events in the United States, whether amateur or professional.

The USTA is a member of the ITF, an international body made up of 104 national tennis associations from all over the world. The ITF is a democratic body and is managed by representatives of the member national associations who assemble in an Annual General Meeting and are referred to as "The Council." Every two years, the Council appoints a Committee of Management (COM), consisting of eleven persons, which has administrative powers to carry on the work of the ITF between Annual General Meetings, and to administer the finances of the Federation.

The primary purpose of the ITF is to foster and promote the integrity of tennis competition internationally. One of the ITF's objects in pursuing that purpose is to uphold the uniform, international Rules of Tennis promulgated by the ITF and to make such alterations and additions to such Rules as may appear necessary or desirable.

As a condition of membership in the ITF, all member national associations agree that the ITF Rules of Tennis will be obeyed in all tournaments sanctioned by the national associations. Accordingly, official USTA Tournament Regulation No. 1 provides in relevant part:

> The Tournament Regulations herein contained and the international Rules of Lawn Tennis shall be observed throughout all tournaments held by clubs, associations or organizations belonging directly or indirectly to the USTA.

During the early 1970's, a novel method of stringing a tennis racket, dubbed "double-stringing," was developed in West Germany by a Bavarian horticulturist, Werner Fischer. The main and cross strings of a conventional tennis racket are interlaced or interwoven, and are all on the same plane. In contrast, Fischer's double-strung racket has two layers of main strings, one layer on each side of the cross strings, and the main strings are independent, and not interlaced or interwoven with the cross strings. Short lengths of protective nylon tubing are placed on the main strings at each intersection with the five double cross strings, and each layer of main strings is tied together with five tie cords, one knotted directly below each of the five rows of protective tubing. Epoxy (adhesive coating) is used to keep the short nylon tubes and the tie cords in place.

The double-strung racket was first brought to the attention of the ITF by a May 2, 1977, telex from the Swiss Tennis Association asking whether the ITF accepted a new tennis racket with double strings which was being marketed. Other inquiries and comments from member associations, players and the press followed. At its meeting at Wimbledon in June, 1977, the ITF COM examined and discussed a sample of the double-strung racket, provided by Dr. Grimm, the General Secretary of the European Tennis Association. Deciding the matter deserved attention, the COM took the matter a week later to the Annual General Meeting of the Council of the ITF in Hamburg, where the President of the ITF reported that a new type of tennis racket was on the market which was strung to give far more spin to the ball and told the delegates of member associations that the COM was interested in receiving reports from associations and players on the racket.

Between the July, 1977, Annual General Meeting in Hamburg, and October, 1977, the ITF office in London received a number of reports of player reaction to the double-strung racket, including written reports from the Swiss, German and Austrian federations where the racket had become widely used.

On October 1–3, 1977, the COM met in Barcelona, Spain, to consider, among other items on its agenda, the double-strung racket. At the Barcelona meeting, the COM witnessed a demonstration game using both the double-strung rackets and conventional rackets, and considered written reports regarding double-strung rackets from the German, Austrian and Swiss tennis federations, and oral reports concerning the racket from representatives from France and Spain. The COM also considered press reports concerning the threatened boycott of the 1977 French Championships by players to protest the use of the double-strung rackets, and "strange" results at the Coupe Poree Grand Prix tournament on September 19–26, 1977, in Paris, the Gold Racquet Grand Prix tournament in Aix-en-Provence, France, on September 26–October 2, 1977, and the U.S. Open in Forest Hills, New York, in September, 1977, where several top-ranked world class professionals were upset by lower ranked players using double-strung rackets.

After consideration of the evidence before them, and acting under their emergency power under ITF Rule 57 to settle all urgent questions subject to confirmation at the next Annual General Meeting, the COM issued a temporary ban on the use of rackets with double strings or protuberances. * * * The stated purpose of the temporary "freeze" was to enable the ITF to collate research on the effects of the racket on match play. The release noted that the "Committee of Management does not want to stand in the way of technological progress, but it must be sure that new developments benefit the game." The COM appointed a Technical Sub-Committee to investigate and forward suggestions to the COM on the standardization of rackets.

On October 18, 1977, the USTA distributed USTA Press Release No. 120-77, announcing that the USTA would honor the ITF's temporary prohibition on the use of tennis rackets with double strings or protuberances, in order to permit an in-depth study by the ITF, technical groups, and the USTA. The USTA's stated reasons for honoring the ban were that "the USTA, as a member of the ITF, believes uniformity of rules is especially important in tennis because of the worldwide tournament schedule" and that "in addition * * * it has been suggested that the use of double stringing may result in a double hit.'" The press release stated that the ban would be in effect until further notice and would apply to international team matches such as the Davis Cup and all ITF sanctioned tournaments, as well as to all USTA sanctioned events, whether amateur or professional.

At the COM meeting held in Monte Carlo on April 13–16, 1978, the COM heard reports from the Technical Sub-Committee on its studies to date on double-strung rackets and considered all comments and information that had been collected by the ITF office in London. The COM adopted a formulation of a proposed rule for tennis rackets, and a procedure whereby tennis rackets could be submitted to the ITF for a ruling on whether or not they complied with the proposed rule. Included in this procedure was the right to appeal an adverse ruling.

In a statement dated May 12, 1978, the ITF gave notice that it was proposing to introduce a rule on the definition of a tennis racket, which would become effective from July 13, 1978, in a final form if approved at the Annual General Meeting in Stockholm on that day. The notice contained the text of the proposed rule and approval procedures and solicited comments on the proposed definition from players, administrators and manufacturers of tennis equipment. It was announced that such comments would be taken into account by the COM when it made its final recommendation to the annual meeting. All national associations were asked to circulate this request as widely as possible. * * *

Designers and manufacturers were encouraged to seek advance ruling or approval on any questionable racket designs or prototypes.

After the May 12, 1978, statement and agenda were released, the Technical Sub-Committee recommended that a revised draft of the proposed rule be put before the Annual General Meeting on July 13, based on further study done by the sub-committee and suggestions and comments made by a number of manufacturers and stringers. A statement dated June 29, 1978, was prepared by the ITF office in London, containing the revised draft[3] of the proposed rule. The statement was immediately distributed to a number of people, including Werner Fischer and other equipment manufacturers, who had contributed to discussion of the proposed rule or who had particularly asked to be kept informed. The ITF office asked to receive comments on the revised draft prior to July 10, 1978, when the ITF staff would leave for the Stockholm meeting.

At its meeting in Wimbledon on July 6 and 7, 1978, the COM approved the revised draft and voted to submit it to the Council of national associations at the Stockholm Annual General Meeting, with the COM's recommendation that the rule be approved.

At the Annual Meeting in Stockholm on July 13 and 14, 1978, the revised draft of the rule was presented to the Council and approved by the requisite two-thirds majority of the votes cast. All of the votes of the USTA were cast in favor of the proposed rule. On approval at the Annual Meeting, the revised draft of the proposed rule became Rule 4 of the Rules of Tennis. Therefore, as a condition of membership, all na-

---

3. The following is the text of the revised rule:

The Racket

The racket shall consist of a frame and a stringing.

The Frame

The frame may be of any material, weight, size or shape.

The Stringing

The strings must be alternately interlaced or bonded where they cross and each string must be connected to the frame.

If there are attachments, they must be used only to prevent wear and tear and must not alter the flight of the ball.

The density in the center must be at least equal to the average density of the stringing.

Note to the Rule

The spirit of this rule is to prevent undue spin on the ball that would result in a change in the character of the game.

The stringing must be made so that the moves between the strings will not exceed what is possible for instance with 18 mains and 18 crosses uniformly spaced and interlaced in a stringing area of 75 square inches.

tional associations belonging to the ITF, including the USTA, agreed from that date on that the new Rule 4 would be obeyed in all tournaments sanctioned by the national associations. * * *

The president of plaintiff corporation, Gunter Harz, became a business associate of Werner Fischer in the summer of 1977. Prior to the temporary ban of the double-strung racket in October of 1977, Harz was employed by Fischer's German company, Fischer Besaitungstechnik GMBH (Fischer GMBH), as its international sales manager, to find licensees to market the double-strung racket * * *

During the period Harz was employed by Fischer GMBH he began working on improving the Fischer double-strung racket to decrease the topspin imparted to the ball and to give the ball more speed, in response to comments from tennis players at the club level in Southern Germany where the Fischer racket had the widest exposure. By the time Harz left Fischer GMBH to come to the United States, he had developed a modification of Fischer's double stringing. In place of nylon tubing and knotted tie cords used in Fischer's stringing system, Harz's modification uses four rows of pre-molded plastic pieces per layer of main strings to both encase the main strings in tubes and bind the main strings of a layer together. Harz's variation also uses six single cross strings between the layers of the main strings, in contrast to the five double cross strings of Fischer's racket, and uses a different gauge of string for the mains and crosses. Fischer-America began to market both rackets and stringing kits using Harz's modification of Fischer's double stringing under the name "Play Spaghetti" prior to the July, 1978, approval of Rule 4.

* * *

No written request to appear before the USTA concerning the double-strung racket was made by either Fischer or Harz until Harz, through his attorney, requested in an August 8, 1979, letter to the General Counsel of the USTA that Harz be given a hearing at the Annual Meeting of the USTA to be held later that month in Flushing Meadows, and that, in addition, he be permitted to provide a demonstration on the use of the "Play Spaghetti" racket. In a letter of August 20, 1979, the USTA, through its General Counsel, responded that Harz might wish to apply to the ITF for further testing and demonstration, commenting that because of the international character of the game, it is important that the USTA and the other national bodies follow a uniform set of rules. The letter stated that the rules Harz complained of are reasonable and well within the discretion of the governing sports body. The letter also stated that while the Executive Committee of the USTA was to meet in New York City, the Annual Meeting was not scheduled until February, 1980. On December 28, 1979, plaintiff filed the present suit.

APPLICABLE LAW

Plaintiff characterizes the actions of the defendant USTA, and those of the ITF and its member nations who were not made parties to this suit, as a group boycott of double-strung tennis rackets, having the express purpose as well as the effect of restraining competition in the manufacture and distribution of tennis rackets and tennis racket stringing systems in violation of Section 1 of the Sherman Act. * * *

Where the purpose of a "group boycott" has been to protect fair competition in sports and games, courts have eschewed a per se analysis in favor of an inquiry into the reasonableness of the restraint under the circumstances. The Court agrees that * * * the rule of reasonableness should govern the analysis of the present controversy. * * *

Since the need for collective action is inherent in organized sports, in analyzing the rules and regulations of sanctioning organizations under the rule of reason, courts have relied on the Supreme Court's analysis in *Silver v. New York Stock Exchange*, 373 U.S. 341 (1963). In *Silver*, the defendant Stock Exchange ordered the termination of direct wire connections to certain non-member security dealers. Because the Securities Exchange Act of 1934 established a statutorily imposed duty of self-regulation on the exchange, which involved the obligation to formulate rules governing the conduct of exchange members, the Court found the defendant's "group boycott" should be judged under the rule of reason so that the policy in favor of self-regulation could be accommodated. However, the Court found the defendant's actions to be unreasonable under Section 1 of the Sherman Act because the Exchange could offer no justification stemming from its statutorily imposed duty of self-regulation for its collective action in denying the non-members the private wire connections without notice and an opportunity for a hearing.

Courts have extended the reasoning of *Silver* beyond situations involving statutorily created duties of self-regulation to areas where a need for self-regulation is inherent in an industry. * * *

Professional and amateur sports have been included in this extension. Under the reasoning of *Silver* the inquiry under the rule of reason focuses on (1) whether the collective action is intended to accomplish an end consistent with the policy justifying self-regulation; (2) whether the action is reasonably related to that goal; (3) whether such action is no more extensive than necessary; and (4) whether the association provides procedural safeguards which assure that the restraint is not arbitrary and which furnish a basis for judicial review. * * *

Defendants contend that the actions of the USTA are exempt from this type of analysis under the circumstances of this case because the ITF actually initiated and promulgated the temporary ban and Rule 4, while the USTA was forced to adopt the rule as a condition of its membership. The Court finds that contention without merit. In rejecting a similar defense, the court in *Linseman v. World Hockey Ass'n*, 439 F. Supp. 1315, 1321–22 (D. Conn. 1977)] noted that "courts have uniformly rejected any defense that an antitrust violation was 'forced' onto the defendant," and that the "Supreme Court has held that 'acquiescence in an illegal scheme is as much a violation of the Sherman Act as the creation and promotion of one,'" * * *

While it is true that the plaintiff challenges the reasonableness of the actions of the ITF as well as those of the USTA, the USTA made a voluntary decision to delegate its rule-making authority to the ITF and to adopt the ITF's temporary ban of double-strung rackets and Rule 4. Thus, it is the USTA's decision that requires the Court to inquire into the actions of the ITF, as well as those of the USTA. The Court concludes that while the USTA's relationship to the ITF cannot absolve the USTA from all liability under Section 1 of the Sherman Act, it is an important factor to be taken into consideration by the Court under a rule of reason analysis.

Turning to an analysis of the actions of the USTA under the rule of reason, the Court specifically finds that the collective action of the USTA, ITF, and other member national associations of the ITF was intended to accomplish the legitimate goals of preserving the essential character and integrity of the game of tennis as it had always been played, and preserving competition by attempting to conduct the game in an orderly fashion. The record is totally devoid of any evidence from which an intent to injure the plaintiff or any other manufacturer or distributor of tennis equipment can be inferred. As noted previously, the Court finds no agreement between the USTA or ITF and any manufacturer or distributor of tennis equipment to exclude plaintiff from competing in the market for rackets or stringing systems.

The evidence shows that the ITF solicited, received, and acted upon comments and suggestions from equipment manufacturers, including Fischer and Harz. The original draft of the proposed rule was revised partly in response to comments of manufacturers suggesting that many conventional rackets on the market would be banned by the original draft of the proposed rule, although such rackets did nothing to alter the character of the game. However, the Court finds nothing impermissible in such communication or response. Both the USTA and the ITF had the right to solicit such information and act upon it in attempting to make reasonable informed decisions concerning racket specifications and in attempting to draft the rule so that it would be the least restrictive of technological improvements and developments, but still address the legitimate concern that such development not adversely alter the character of the game of tennis as it had been played historically or artificially enhance the skill and ability of players, thereby harming the integrity of competitive tennis.

Secondly, the Court concludes that the actions of the USTA and the ITF were reasonably related to the goals discussed above. In reaching that conclusion, the Court is not to substitute its own judgment for that of the ITF or the USTA. It is irrelevant whether the Court might or might not independently reach the same decision based on the same evidence. * * *

Plaintiff contends that the actions of the ITF in enacting the temporary ban on double-strung rackets were arbitrary because the basis for the ban was a false and misleading assessment by the German Federation of a study made by the Braunschweig Technical University on the effect of double-strung rackets, and a playing demonstration using poor copies of the Fischer double-strung racket, not strung according to Fischer's specifications on stringing tension.

The Court finds that despite the actual conclusion of the Braunschweig study that double stringing did not revolutionize the character of the game and should not be banned, the study's findings did lend support to the concerns which prompted the temporary ban. The study found that strokes at high speed, as well as stroke types which primarily utilized cross strings, could be played under certain conditions only; that double stringing resulted in strokes with a very strong spin being played almost exclusively since those strokes were most effective; and that on red gravel and coarse fiber courts, when high topspin strokes were played in the baseline area, balls could bounce over the back fence and such balls could only be returned when hit right after they bounced.

The Germans represented that the study established:

a) that the range of strokes is limited or curtailed, that is to say certain strokes can only be partially played, thus the game itself is restricted.

b) that there is a handicap in that very fast balls can only be returned under certain conditions.

Based on the study's findings summarized above, the Court is unconvinced that these conclusions are not supported by the study.

Additionally, the Court finds that several manufacturers were marketing double-strung rackets at the time of the temporary ban and that some players were using homemade versions of the double-strung racket which they strung themselves. In view of this finding, the Court concludes that it was immaterial that Fischer's rackets were not used at the Barcelona demonstration since the temporary ban was aimed at the use of all double-strung rackets and not just Fischer's products.

Contrary to plaintiff's assertions, the Court finds that the ITF's temporary ban bore a rational relationship to its goal of attempting to conduct organized tennis competitions in an orderly fashion. The COM at Barcelona acted not only on the basis of the demonstration, and the German Federation's assessment of the Braunschweig study, but also on the basis of actual and threatened players' strikes against use of the double-strung racket, publicity concerning upsets of high-ranking players by virtual unknowns using double-strung rackets, and adverse reports of several national federations based on their experience with the racket in match play and in training situations. This evidence provided an objective basis from which the COM could have concluded that a temporary freeze on the use of the rackets was necessary pending further investigation and subsequent action by the ITF Council. * * *

Because of the international character of the game of tennis and its worldwide tournament schedules, the USTA considered uniformity of rules in tennis tournaments an important factor in preserving the integrity of tennis competition. Based on this view, it was reasonable for the USTA to honor the ITF's temporary ban after deciding it was not enacted arbitrarily.

The Court also rejects plaintiff's argument that the USTA at no time had any evidence before them upon which they could base a conclusion that the proposed rule on racket specifications had a rational ground or justification. The USTA conducted no independent tests concerning double-strung rackets based on the management committee's decision that it was proper for the ITF, as the recognized rule-making authority, to conduct the tests and formulate a rule. This decision was also based on their feelings that the majority of the manufacturers of double-strung systems were then in Europe and that the ITF was closer to the technical side of tennis than the USTA. * * *

The Court concludes that the information garnered by the ITF Technical Sub-Committee and relayed to the ITF COM and USTA management committee provided an objective basis from which the ITF and the USTA could reasonably conclude that Rule 4 was necessary to the preservation of the character of the game of tennis. Plaintiff spent a great deal of time at trial attempting to establish that no written definition of the "character of the game" exists and concludes from that fact that the ITF and the USTA relied on an arbitrary standard in respectively promulgating and adopting Rule 4. The Court finds it immaterial that no written definition of the "character of the game" exists, since the evidence in the case clearly establishes that it is widely understood merely as referring to the way the game has been traditionally played over scores of years. The ITF and the USTA talked about changes in the character of the game only in relation to the excessive amount of topspin, *i.e.*, ball rotation, imparted to the ball by a double-strung racket.

The evidence that a double-strung racket, as compared to a conventional racket, imparts more ball rotation to a ball hit with a topspin stroke, *i.e.*, an upswing stroke, is uncontroverted. Harz conceded at trial that a double-strung racket was actually designed to impart more topspin to the ball. The independent main strings of both sides of the racket face slide from side to side on impact, causing the ball to be held on the racket face longer. This in turn causes the ball to come off the racket with a greater number of ball revolutions per minute, *i.e.*, exaggerated topspin.

The Technical Sub-Committee and COM of the ITF viewed film studies made by Sportalma, an independent Italian testing laboratory, which showed the effect of double-strung rackets on ball rotation. A subsequent study by Sportalma concluded that double-strung rackets imparted an average of seventeen per cent more ball rotation to the ball on an upswing stroke than a conventional racket. In addition, a study prepared for the USTA in anticipation of this litigation by the Coto Sports Research Center, using computerized bio-mechanical analysis, concluded that a "Play Spaghetti" racket demonstrates a twenty per cent to sixty per cent greater ability to maintain and impart spin on the ball than does the standard racket, depending on where the ball impacts with the pre-molded plastic pieces.

The Court finds that a rule on racket specifications designed to prohibit rackets which impart exaggerated topspin to the ball on impact is rationally related to the goal of preserving the character of the game of tennis.

* * *

The Court also concludes that the actions of the USTA in honoring the temporary ban and adopting Rule 4 were not more extensive than necessary to serve the legitimate goals of the USTA and ITF. Based on the players' strikes and walkouts occasioned by use of the double-strung racket, the Court concludes that the temporary freeze on the use of double-strung rackets in sanctioned play was no more extensive than necessary to further the legitimate goal of conducting the game in an orderly fashion, especially in view of the provision that member nations could apply for permission to experiment with the racket at club level. The Court finds it reasonable for the ITF and USTA to have concluded that the alternative of taking no action and letting the racket have a twenty-four month trial period would not have furthered that goal.

Rule 4 itself was narrowly drawn to proscribe only rackets and stringing systems that imparted exaggerated topspin to the ball, since the ITF concluded that it was that feature which changed the character of the game. The breadth of the rule was additionally narrowed by provision of appeal procedures whereby a racket that failed to conform to the face of the rule could be approved under the standard that it did not impart exaggerated topspin to the ball or change the character of the game. * * *

Finally, the Court rejects the contention that a lack of procedural safeguards afforded the plaintiff must necessarily result in a finding of unreasonableness under Section 1 of the Sherman Act. While it may be that neither the actions of the ITF nor the USTA would serve as a model of procedural due process, the Court finds the procedural safeguards provided adequate to meet the requirements of *Silver* and its progeny and thus avoid liability under Section 1 of the Sherman Act.

* * *

In sum, the Court ultimately finds under the rule of reason analysis, that the concerted action engaged in by the defendant, USTA, was intended to further the legitimate goals of preserving the essential integrity of the game of competitive tennis and conducting that game in an orderly fashion; that the temporary freeze of double-strung rackets and the subsequent adoption of Rule 4 were rationally related to those goals and no more extensive than necessary; and that adequate procedural safeguards were provided. Any effect the USTA's actions had on plaintiff's ability to compete in the market for tennis rackets and tennis racket stringing systems was incidental to the USTA's primary purpose in promoting tennis competition.

The Court, therefore, concludes that the defendant's actions do not constitute a violation of Section 1 of the Sherman Act. A separate order dismissing the action on the merits shall be entered in accordance with this memorandum opinion.

Gunter Harz Sports, Inc. v. United States Tennis Ass'n, Inc.

665 F.2d 222 (8th Cir. 1981)

PER CURIAM. This matter involves a rule of the United States Tennis Association (USTA) which effectively prohibits the use of a certain tennis racket in sanctioned tournaments. The manufacturer of the racket, Harz Sports, brought an antitrust action against the USTA. The district court * * * ruled that the USTA is subject to the Sherman Act but, following a trial on the merits, found no antitrust violation. We affirm.

The district court applied a thorough rule of reason analysis. Briefly, the court found that the USTA legitimately functions as a private, nonprofit regulating body to ensure that competitive tennis is conducted in an orderly fashion and to preserve the essential character of the game as played in organized competition. USTA regulation of racket characteristics is rationally related to these goals. Moreover, the court found that the particular rule at issue here does not extend beyond what is necessary to further such goals and provides adequate procedural safeguards to protect against arbitrary enforcement of the rule. These findings have substantial support in the record and we find no merit in the contrary assertions by Harz Sports.

The USTA does not dispute the district court's findings, but contends that it should not be subject to the antitrust laws in the first instance. The International Tennis Federation, as *amicus curiae*, similarly argues against judicial involvement absent evidence of "extraordinary anticompetitive animus." We cannot agree. Antitrust regulation is proper when, as here, an association wields enormous economic clout by virtue of its exclusive control over the conduct of a major sport.[3] Nonprofit amateur sports associations also have been subject to antitrust regulation. *See, e.g., Hennessey v. National Collegiate Athletic Ass'n*, 564 F.2d 1136 (5th Cir. 1977). When an athletic association's action serves to protect fair competition in the game and does not involve improper collusion with commercial interests or "an agreement with business competitors in the traditional sense," courts have followed a rule of reason approach. *Id*. The district court here properly focused on the factors outlined in *Silver v. New York Stock Exchange*, 373 U.S. 341 (1963).

In affirming the district court, we emphasize that the challenged USTA rule provides a procedure by which an interested party may obtain approval of a racket upon showing that its use will not "significantly change the character of the game." Whether this rule may be arbitrarily enforced in the future is a question not presently before us. We note simply that on its face, the rule provides adequate procedural safeguards.

Notes and Questions

1. Would this case have changed if the USTA or ITF also produced its own tennis rackets for profit? Conceivably, this fact could position *Gunter Harz* closer to *Blalock v. LPGA*, 359 F. Supp. 1260 (N.D.Ga. 1973), given that the persons responsible for the potential elimination of a competitor would be other competitors. What relationships between the USTA or ITF, on the one hand, and one or more tennis racket manufacturers, on the other hand, would change the analysis or outcome? For example, if several man-

---

3. Although the USTA does not manufacture or sell commercial goods, its actions may substantially influence the marketplace for products used in the sport.

ufacturers of "traditional" tennis rackets pay the USTA to be sponsors of USTA events, or if one traditional racket manufacturer pays for the right to label its product as the "official racket of the US Open," the USTA's most important event, is that enough to infer a USTA-bias or an unlawful agreement not to approve the double-strung racket? What if the "official racket" manufacturer were the primary manufacturer submitting information in opposition to the "double-strung" racket? What if a letter in opposition from that manufacturer to the USTA declared: "As you know, for the past ten years we have been major supporters of the USTA and all of its programs that benefit tennis in the United States * * *"? Can you infer that the USTA might have considered itself bound to reward a long-time supporter? Varying the theme, what if members of the ITF or USTA board, as tennis event producers or current or former players, had sponsorship relationships with traditional racket manufacturers? *See Gilder v. PGA Tour, Inc.*, later in this chapter.

2. Would this case have been decided differently if the plaintiffs were actually professional tennis players? Should there be any significance attached to the fact that the complainants in a particular equipment restriction context are participants, rather than simply manufacturers, seeking to enter the product market in a particular sport?

3. Today, it seems unlikely that anything other than an outrageous restriction by a league or association upon its participants' use of various types of equipment would be found violative of the Sherman Act. For example, Major League Baseball outlaws aluminum bats and likewise restricts the size of its gloves, and has done so without reprisal from any manufacturer or player. Before 2002, MLB's only requirement for bats was that they had to be made from a single piece of wood. In 2002, MLB announced that bat manufacturers must pay a $10,000 administrative fee to defray MLB's costs of inspecting, testing, and approving bats, and must purchase $10 million of insurance. In direct response, the number of accredited MLB bat makers dropped from 48 to 14. In certain respects, a league's prerogative to govern itself is viewed as almost sacrosanct by reviewing courts. In *Gunter Harz*, the fear that the "spaghetti" tennis racket would virtually change the entire complexion of professional tennis was partial motivation for the USTA's elimination of the innovative racket. The question that persists centers around where the line is to be drawn? There are those experts who insist that composition rackets, larger head faces, and more sophisticated racket design have changed the course of the tennis game and, on certain surfaces such as grass, have turned the game into a serve and volley power play, rather than the pure ground-stroking game that tennis was designed to be. In this vein, others have suggested that, while amateurs should be permitted to use any type of racket that will facilitate their game, professional tennis players should be required to use the standard wood racket that was used by Jack Kramer and other players of his vintage.

4. In *Gunter Harz*, Judge Schatz opined, "the Court is not to substitute its own judgment for that of the ITF or the USTA." What does that mean? If that is an accurate statement of the law, why does the opinion devote so much time explaining how the evidence submitted to the ITF and the USTA demonstrates that their conclusions were reasonable? Is the court saying that it will not substitute its judgment if the sports organization is resolving a close question or that it will not substitute its judgment even if there is overwhelming evidence of the imprudence of the sports organization's decision? What would have happened if Gunter Harz had been able to convince the court that the new racket was much less revolutionary than aluminum rackets had been when they began to replace wood rackets?

5. What market did the district court deem relevant to its inquiry? What were the anticompetitive effects of the USTA's conduct on the market for tennis rackets and tennis racket stringing systems? What were the procompetitive effects in that market?

6. The district court seemed to say that some of the USTA's conduct was justified by the fact that certain players (presumably players who did not use the new rackets) were boycotting or threatening to boycott tour events. Would it be lawful for an association of traditional racket-using players to threaten a boycott of all USTA events to force the USTA to ban the rackets used by players with whom the members of the Association compete? Compare the conduct in *Federal Trade Commission v. Superior Court Trial Lawyers Ass'n*, 493 U.S. 411 (1990) and *Federal Trade Commission v. Indiana Federation of Dentists*, 476 U.S. 447 (1986). Does it matter if they are employees whose concerted activities may be protected by federal labor laws? *See further* Chapters 14 and 15. Would the analysis of claims against the USTA change if it were later discovered that the striking players were all under long-term contracts with traditional racket manufacturers requiring those players to use their products? If the player strikes were organized and supported by traditional racket manufacturers because of concern about the introduction of new, patented technology that might put them out of business, would that change the analysis of the lawsuit against the USTA?

7. As the district court noted, the Braunschweig study said that on red gravel and coarse fiber tennis courts high topspin strokes played in the baseline area could cause the balls to bounce over the fence. Hypothetically, if a regulation tennis court called for the fence to be thirty feet behind each baseline to eliminate this problem, but many recreational courts around the world did not comply with that standard, how would that affect the analysis?

8. Tennis is an international sport, and the district court acknowledged the USTA's view that "uniformity of rules in tennis tournaments [is] an important factor in preserving the integrity of tennis competition." The court proceeded to say that the USTA acted reasonably in honoring the ITF's temporary ban in the interest of uniformity "after deciding it was not enacted arbitrarily." However, what if the USTA had opposed the ITF's decision, had voted against it as an ITF member, and had believed that the decision was arbitrary. Could the USTA have nevertheless honored the ban, applied throughout the rest of the world, based on a view that the need for uniformity was of paramount importance?

9. Frequently, international events are the pinnacle of a particular sport. For example, in many sports the Olympic Games and/or world championships are the most important competitions. If the international federation warned a United States national governing body that failure to observe the international federation's equipment restrictions would disqualify United States athletes from international competition, would that give the United States governing body *carte blanche* to impose the restriction without fear of antitrust reprisal? For a discussion of somewhat related issues see *Behagen v. Amateur Basketball Ass'n of the United States*, 884 F.2d 524 (10th Cir. 1989); *Reynolds v. International Amateur Athletic Federation*, 841 F. Supp. 1444 (S.D. Ohio 1992).

10. The district court stated that the USTA did not have to conduct its own tests. Could it have simply honored a ban based solely on a view "that the ITF was closer to the technical side of tennis than the USTA"? Would the court then reconsider substituting its judgment for the views expressed by the associations?

11. As stated earlier, the problems with any attempt to differentiate equipment limitations that promote legitimate association interest from those restraints that are in-

valid, anticompetitive and contrary to the antitrust laws, are not conducive to a ready solution. In endeavoring to draw these difficult distinctions, consider the *Weight-Rite Golf Corporation* and *Gilder* cases, below. As you read these opinions, ponder what antitrust market is at issue in the case and whether an equipment restriction that only applies to professional participants has a sufficient derivative impact upon the relevant market to implicate the Sherman Act.

III. Equipment Restrictions and Professional Golf

Weight-Rite Golf Corp. v. United States Golf Ass'n
766 F. Supp. 1104 (M.D. Fla. 1991)

NEWCOMER, District Judge. The action arises out of the USGA's determination that a shoe manufactured and distributed by the Plaintiffs does not conform to Rule 14-3 of the Rules of Golf published by the USGA. * * *

II. MOTION FOR SUMMARY JUDGMENT

* * *

A. Factual Background

The USGA is a non-profit association of golf courses and golf clubs. The USGA publishes the Rules of Golf and applies the Rules in the thirteen national championships it conducts each year. The Rules of Golf limit the kinds of equipment that a golfer may use in an event that is played pursuant to the Rules. The purpose of the Rules is "to preserve the traditions of the game, and to insure that a player's score is the product of his skill, rather than his equipment."

Other entities that conduct golf competitions, such as the PGA Tour, Inc., are separate from and independent of the USGA. However, the Rules, as interpreted by the USGA, are typically followed in major amateur and professional golf tournaments.

Plaintiffs manufacture and distribute a golf shoe with a patented sole design which incorporates an angled wedge on the outside of the sole. The shoes apparently assist golfers in distributing their weight so as to better resist the tendency to push away from the ball during the swing. On March 1, 1990, Frank Thomas, the Technical Director of the USGA, and his staff determined that use of the Weight-Rite shoes would violate Rule 14-3 of the Rules of Golf. Rule 14-3 provides that a "player shall not use any artificial device or unusual equipment * * * which might assist him in gripping the club, in making a stroke or in his play."

The USGA notified Plaintiffs and other professional golf associations of its determination on March 7, 1990. Following the USGA's determination, a number of retailers stopped ordering Plaintiffs' shoes and returned the stock they had previously ordered. Plaintiffs have since commenced marketing their product directly to consumers.

Weight-Rite appealed the USGA staff determination to the Equipment Standards Committee and to the USGA Executive Committee. Both committees determined that the Weight-Rite shoe did not conform to Rule 14-3 of the Rules of Golf.

* * *

A. Sherman Act Section 1 (Count I). * * *

1. Conspiracy

Plaintiffs do not contend that the USGA and its members conspired to adopt the interpretation of Rule 14-3 challenged by Plaintiffs. Rather, Plaintiffs contend that the USGA enforces its interpretation of the Rules of Golf on its members who must, therefore, disqualify any golfer using equipment which the USGA Executive Committee has determined does not conform to the Rules of Golf.

Plaintiffs have identified no direct evidence in the record which shows that USGA members must disqualify golfers from play on their courses if the golfer uses non-conforming equipment. Plaintiffs also have identified no record evidence to show that the USGA has taken adverse action against a member for allowing a golfer to use non-conforming equipment on the member's course.

Plaintiffs have presented evidence that the scorecards at most USGA courses state that "USGA rules govern all play." Plaintiffs contend that USGA enforcement may be inferred based on the statement on the scorecards and based on a provision in the USGA by-laws which provides, in part, that all USGA members are required to "accept and enforce all rules and decisions of the [USGA] Executive Committee" as a condition of membership.

The USGA has submitted a complete copy of the USGA by-laws and the affidavit of David Fay, USGA Executive Director. * * * The Fay affidavit states that when the by-laws refer to the Rules of Golf, the full capitalized title "Rules of Golf" is used. A review of the by-laws discloses that the full capitalized title is used in Articles IV and VII. The affidavit also states that although the USGA applies its interpretation of the Rules of Golf in the thirteen national championships it conducts each year, the USGA has never required its members to enforce the USGA's interpretation of the Rules of Golf in competitions conducted by its members.

The Court concludes that a fact finder could not reasonably find, based on the evidence in the record, that the USGA requires member courses to enforce the USGA's interpretation of the Rules of Golf in tournaments conducted by its members. Accordingly, the USGA is entitled to summary judgment on Count I.

2. Unreasonable Restraint of Trade

* * *

As a threshold matter, the Court observes that Plaintiffs have not presented evidence to clearly define the relevant product market. The Plaintiffs' memorandum refers to the golf equipment industry and the golf shoe industry, as does the affidavit of Samuel Kursh. Moreover, it is unclear precisely what the relevant geographical boundary is, although Plaintiffs' memorandum suggests that it is the United States. This lack of clarity is a reflection of the lack of evidence presented in support of Plaintiffs' claims. The Court will assume that Plaintiffs define the relevant product market as the market for golf shoes in the United States. Accordingly, Plaintiffs must show injury to competition in that market.

Plaintiffs contend that the USGA has the power to bar entry into the golf shoe industry in the United States because the USGA's interpretation of the Rules of Golf is followed in virtually all major professional and amateur golf tournaments. They contend further that the USGA has exercised its power in such a way as to restrain competition in the industry.

Plaintiffs have presented evidence that the USGA's interpretation of the Rules of Golf are followed in virtually all major professional and amateur golf tournaments in the

United States. Plaintiffs also have presented evidence that, after the USGA determined that the shoe did not conform to Rule 14-3, some retailers returned their stock of Weight-Rite shoes, and many retailers discontinued ordering more stock.

However, showing merely injury to oneself as a competitor is insufficient.

> Injury to a competitor need not result in injury to competition. The use of un-
> fair means in substituting one competitor for another without more does not
> violate the antitrust laws. * * * [The plaintiff] must show harm to competition
> in general, as well as its own injury as a competitor.

As evidence of injury to competition, Plaintiffs have submitted the affidavit of Samuel J. Kursh. Mr. Kursh states his conclusion that the USGA has restrained competition in the golf equipment industry generally, and the golf shoe industry in particular, by its interpretations of the Rules of Golf. However, a party may not avoid summary judgment solely on the basis of an expert's opinion affidavit which does not provide specific facts from the record to support its conclusions. * * *

Plaintiffs have presented evidence that the USGA currently has 5,296 member clubs and 1,966 member courses in the United States. Plaintiffs contend that USGA members are required by the USGA to disqualify any golfer using equipment which the USGA Executive Committee has determined does not conform to the Rules of Golf.[7] Plaintiffs contend further that "it requires no great exercise of imagination to conclude that pro and specialty shops will not allocate shelf space to products that subject their users to disqualification in any round of golf played on a member course or under the auspices of a member club." Mr. Kursh thus opines that the USGA's interpretation of the Rules of Golf has barred the entry of competitors into the market and thereby reinforced the concentrated market structure.

However, Mr. Kursh identifies only one instance of USGA Rule interpretation other than that associated with the Weight-Rite shoe: the USGA's determination that Ping EYE 2 golf clubs were non-conforming. Mr. Kursh states that Ping's market share in the golf club market declined following the USGA's determination.

The affidavit contains no specific facts to support the conclusion that the USGA's determination that the Weight-Rite shoe does not conform to the Rules of Golf substantially restrained competition in the golf shoe market in the United States. There also is no other evidence in the record to support this conclusion. At most, Plaintiffs have presented evidence from which a fact finder could find that the USGA has the power to substantially decrease the marketability of certain types of golf shoes and that the marketability of Plaintiffs' shoe (as currently designed and manufactured) has been substantially diminished. Evidence that a single competitor has been removed from a relevant product market, in and of itself, is insufficient to establish a violation of the rule of reason. * * *

Plaintiffs have not presented evidence from which a fact finder could find that the USGA's determination has significantly restrained the operation of the free market with respect to the golf shoe industry. Plaintiffs also have not submitted evidence to controvert the USGA's showing that the purpose of Rule 14-3 of the Rules of Golf is to "preserve the traditions of the game, and to insure that a player's score is the product of his

---

7. The Court already has determined that Plaintiffs have failed to raise a genuine issue of fact with respect to the concerted action element of a section 1 claim. The Court accepts this contention as true, however, for purposes of determining whether Plaintiffs have created a genuine issue of fact with respect to the injury to competition element.

skill, rather than his equipment." The USGA is, therefore, entitled to summary judgment on Plaintiffs' claim under section 1 of the Sherman Act.

B. Sherman Act Section 2 (Count II)

In their response to the USGA's motion for summary judgment, Plaintiffs state that they do not oppose the motion with respect to their monopolization claim under section 2 of the Sherman Act. Accordingly, the USGA is entitled to summary judgment with respect to Count II of the complaint. * * *

Upon due consideration, therefore, there is no genuine issue of material fact for trial and the USGA is entitled to summary judgment as a matter of law. The Clerk is directed to enter judgment for the USGA and against the Plaintiffs, costs to be assessed according to law.

IT IS SO ORDERED.

Notes and Questions

1. This court emphasized that the goal of the antitrust laws is to protect competition, not competitors. Is there a meaningful difference? Does it adversely affect competition to exclude a new and innovative product that would give consumers an alternative? Does it hurt competition if an aggressive, innovative competitor with a very small market share is excluded from a market dominated by a few large competitors? *See, e.g., United States v. Aluminum Co. of America (Rome Cable)*, 377 U.S. 271 (1964).

2. In a portion of this opinion that was abridged, the court resurrected the following language of *Northwest Wholesale Stationers*:

> The absence of procedural safeguards can in no sense determine the antitrust analysis. If the challenged concerted activity * * * would amount to a *per se* violation of section 1 of the Sherman Act, no amount of procedural protection would save it. If the challenged action would not amount to a violation of section 1, no lack of procedural protections would convert it into a *per se* violation because the antitrust laws do not themselves impose on joint ventures a requirement of process.

472 U.S. at 293, n.10. Do you agree that the due process inquiry, which had been part of Supreme Court analysis in the past (*e.g., Silver v. New York Stock Exchange*), should be irrelevant? *See* Chapter 7.IV.(D).(3), above.

3. Should the decisions of a not-for-profit sports governing body or an "independent sanctioning organization with no financial stake" be subject to less rigorous scrutiny under the antitrust laws? *See M&H Tire Co., Inc. v. Hoosier Racing Tire Corp.*, 733 F.2d 973, 982–83 (1st Cir. 1984). In the *M&H Tire* case, the district court held that the defendant's "single tire rule," which specified a sole tire supplier for certain auto races, was a *per se* violation and, alternatively, would not withstand scrutiny under the Rule of Reason. *M&H Tire Co., Inc. v. Hoosier Racing Tire Corp.*, 560 F. Supp. 591 (D. Mass. 1983). The court of appeals reversed, holding, among other things, that a *per se* standard should not be applied to sports organizations. Further, this court, applying a "business judgment" standard, supported the sanctioning organization's view that a short-term exclusivity to a single supplier was "a reasonable way to regulate and improve modified class auto racing." 733 F.2d at 989. *See Amer. Soc'y of Mech. Engs., Inc. v. Hydrolevel Corp.*, 456 U.S. 556 (1982), for a discussion of anticompetitive conduct by a not-for-profit entity.

Gilder v. PGA Tour, Inc.

936 F.2d 417 (9th Cir. 1991)

TANG, Circuit Judge. Karsten Manufacturing Corporation and eight professional golf players challenge the implementation of a new rule by the PGA Tour (PGA) banning clubs with U-shaped grooves. Karsten and the professional player plaintiffs challenge the actions of the PGA on antitrust and state law grounds. After a three day hearing, the district court granted a preliminary injunction enjoining the PGA from implementing the rule. 727 F. Supp. 1333. The PGA appeals. We affirm.

FACTUAL AND PROCEDURAL BACKGROUND

This action concerns a rule change implemented by the PGA that bans all clubs on which the cross-section of the grooves on the face of the club is in the shape of a square or "U" as opposed to a "V" * * *

Karsten Manufacturing Corporation (Karsten) designs, manufactures, and sells a variety of golf equipment including: putters, woods, golf bags and "Ping Eye 2" golf clubs. All of Karsten's Ping Eye 2 golf clubs have U-shaped grooves. Karsten's Ping Eye 2 golf clubs are top selling clubs in the United States for both professional and amateur players. Karsten's marketing strategy is that it supplies the same equipment to the amateur as to the professional. Karsten maintains that the U-groove rule will harm its reputation if it is forced to make what the company feels is an inferior product with V-grooves.

Bob Gilder and the seven other plaintiffs in this action are eight professional golfers who are members of the PGA. Each of the eight professionals players uses Karsten's Ping Eye 2 clubs on the Tour. Karsten is paying the attorney's fees for these players.

The defendants in this action are the PGA; Deane A. Beman, the Commissioner and Chief Executive Officer of the PGA; and E. Mandell deWindt, Roger E. Birk, and Hugh E. Culverhouse, members of the PGA Tour Tournament Policy Board. The PGA is the organization which administers professional golf tournaments for the regular Tour and the Senior Tour.

The PGA Policy Board is composed of ten directors. Four of the directors are players elected from the membership of the PGA. The board also includes three officers of the PGA of America and three independent directors with no ties to golf. The independent directors volunteer their time.

In 1984, the United States Golf Association (USGA) changed the rules of golf to allow grooves in the shape of a U. Karsten developed its U-groove club. In 1985, players on the Tour began to complain that the U-groove golf clubs were detracting from the skill level of the game. These players complained that the U-grooves imparted more spin on the golf ball and thus provided greater control for shots from grassy lies of the rough. This characteristic offsets the advantage of players with the skill necessary to keep the golf shot in the fairways.[1]

---

1. The grass on the fairways is kept short enough to provide a good lie for the golf ball. The areas of the "rough" have taller grass which provides for a bad lie for the golf ball. A golfer in the fairway has an advantage over a golfer whose ball lands in the grassy area of the "rough."

In January 1987, the USGA conducted tests and concluded that the U-grooves impart more spin on the ball than V-grooves. However, in June 1987, the USGA concluded that there was not enough information to bar clubs with the U-grooves.[2]

On August 10, 1987, the PGA released the results of an equipment survey. One hundred seventy-one of the two hundred golfers on the tour had responded. Of those, seventy-three percent responded that they used U-groove clubs. When asked the advantages of the club, seventy-four percent indicated that the grooves provide for greater control from the wet grass and rough. When asked if the PGA should ban the U-groove, sixty percent responded in the affirmative.

In September 1987, Commissioner Beman wrote to all the golf club manufacturers advising them that the PGA had engaged two technical experts to study the issue of the U-groove. The letter asked the manufacturers to provide pertinent information and relevant data. Karsten did not respond to this request.

In November of 1987, the independent testing expert conducted elaborate field tests trying to localize the effect of the groove. The PGA gave the resulting data to two separate consulting groups, one at the University of Texas and one at the University of Delaware. Each of the Universities devised its own methodology to interpret the data. Both studies concluded that the U-grooves impart more spin to the golf ball than the V-grooves. Commissioner Beman testified that in the lesser lofted clubs,[3] the spin of the golf ball was affected to a much lesser extent, if at all.

On May 12, 1988, Commissioner Beman recommended to the board that a proposed rule change banning U-grooves be circulated for public comment. On May 24, 1988, the board accepted Beman's recommendation. The PGA received comments from some manufacturers and the PGA made some changes in the rule.

On August 16, 1988, the PGA deferred action on the proposed rule until the USGA conducted further player study. The USGA tests confirmed that balls hit from the rough with U-grooves have a different spin rate than those hit with V-grooves. The USGA determined, however, that the tests did not show a significant enough difference to ban the clubs with U-grooves.

Beman recommended that the PGA Policy Board adopt the U-groove ban. The PGA's bylaws at that time required a majority of the directors present and three of the player directors to vote on any rule change. At its February 28, 1989 meeting, the four player directors and the PGA officer directors abstained from voting because of conflicts of interest. Each of the abstaining directors had ties to golf club manufacturers. The three independent directors unanimously voted for the rule. The effective date of the rule was January 1, 1990.

Karsten contacted the PGA on June 23, 1989. Karsten met with the PGA to express its concerns on August 14, 1989. At that meeting, Karsten argued, based on its own testing, that the U-grooves do not affect the spin of the ball.

On August 11, 1989, Karsten sued the USGA challenging its June 1987 decision relating to the groove-to-land ratio which had effectively banned Karsten's U-groove clubs.

---

2. The USGA did however adopt a new method for measuring the groove-to-land (space between the grooves) ratio which had the effect of banning the Ping Eye 2 clubs. Karsten and the USGA have settled their differences and Ping Eye 2 clubs are considered a conforming club for purposes of the USGA.

3. The five iron through the one iron.

The USGA rule applied to USGA tournaments effective in 1990 and in all amateur tournaments in 1996. Karsten and the USGA have settled this lawsuit. Karsten filed the instant lawsuit against the PGA on December 1, 1989. The complaint sought injunctive relief and alleged that the actions of the PGA and its directors (1) violated sections 1 and 2 of the Sherman Antitrust Act, 15 U.S.C. §§1, 2; (2) violated the Arizona antitrust laws, Ariz. Rev. Stat. 44-1401 *et seq.*; and (3) interfered with the Karsten's and the professionals' business relationships. The complaint also charged the PGA directors with breaching their fiduciary duties and sought to hold them liable for their allegedly tortious conduct.

On December 5, 1989, all ten members of the PGA board met in a special session. At that meeting, all ten directors voted to change the by laws of the PGA so that the disinterested members could take binding action on behalf of the PGA policy board when the majority of the directors could not vote because of a conflict. The three disinterested directors then unanimously voted to readopt the groove rule.

Karsten's suit came on for an evidentiary hearing on December 15, 19, and 20, 1989. At the hearing, John Solheim, Karsten's Vice-President, testified that he believes that the U-grooves do not improve player performance.

At the hearing, Karsten presented an economist from Arizona State University, Dr. Richard Smith, who testified that the grooves have not had a negative effect on the PGA. Smith testified that the percentage of prize money that Ping Eye 2 players won is less than the percentage of players who used the Ping Eye 2 clubs. Thus, the Ping Eye 2 clubs do not give the players who use them an advantage. Smith also concluded that the Ping golf clubs do not help the players get their ball to the greens in less than regulation.[4] The expert testified that there is a correlation between a consumer's choice of golf clubs and the professional's choice of clubs.[5] Smith testified that Karsten had experienced a drop in its market share in its sales of golf clubs and other products because of the PGA ban of U-groove clubs. The PGA's expert challenged these last two assertions in his declaration. Smith testified that Karsten would experience harm to its reputation if forced to manufacture a club conforming to the PGA rule. Smith testified that the professional players would lose endorsements to the extent that the change in clubs adversely affects their performance on the Tour.

Two of the plaintiff players testified at the hearing. Bob Gilder testified that switching clubs would hurt his game, which in turn would affect his endorsement income. Gilder has been using Ping clubs since 1970. He likes the design and dynamics of the club. He cannot identify a difference in the club based on the shape of the grooves. He had switched to the Ping Eye 2 clubs in October of 1989. Gilder testified that he would probably use the Ping Eye 2 clubs with V-grooves if Karsten manufactured them.

---

4. "Regulation" is a term used to indicate the number of strokes it takes a golfer to reach the green on a particular hole. Regulation for each hole in golf is based on "par" for that hole. Par is the score expected of an expert golfer on a given hole and allows for two strokes on the putting green. Regulation is the number of strokes left after subtracting the two strokes on the putting green from par. For example, regulation on a par three hole is one. On a par five hole, regulation is three.

5. On cross-examination, the PGA brought out the fact that the professionals use a different ball than the average consumer. When asked why this does not affect the golf ball market, John Solheim responded that the professional's ball has a much shorter life span and thus is not economical for the average golfer. Additionally, John Solheim responded, the golf ball manufacturers do not advertise this distinction but concentrate on the name of the ball, not the actual type. By contrast, the U-groove has been extensively identified with Karsten and its Ping Eye 2 clubs.

George Lanning testified that he is a left-handed golfer. Lanning testified to his belief that Karsten makes the only quality left-handed clubs on the market. He further testified that he might lose his exemption card, which allows him to play on the Tour, if he is forced to change clubs.

Tom Kite, the all-time leading money winner on the Tour, testified that U-grooves diminished the skill factor of the game because the clubs offset the traditional advantage of being able to hit the ball in the fairway of the golf course.

Commissioner Beman testified that the issuance of the preliminary injunction would have dire consequences for the PGA. He testified that the PGA would not be able to propagate any rules for the professional tournaments that it oversees.

After this lengthy evidentiary hearing, the district court held that Karsten and the professional player plaintiffs had demonstrated that (1) they had a reasonable chance of success on the merits, (2) they would suffer irreparable injury if the injunction were not imposed, (3) the balance of hardships tips sharply in favor of the plaintiffs, and (4) there are serious questions for litigation. The PGA appeals.

JURISDICTION

* * *

In this case, the antitrust claims allege that the actions of the PGA in banning the U-groove clubs amount to a boycott of Karsten's product and a restraint of competition with the individual players. We have jurisdiction over these anti-trust claims pursuant to 28 U.S.C. §1337. We conclude that these antitrust claims are not insubstantial. *See, e.g., Gunter Harz*

Sports, Inc. v. United States Tennis Ass'n, 511 F.Supp. 1103, 1114–24 (D. Neb. 1981, *aff'd*, 665 F.2d 222 (8th Cir. 1981); *M & H Tire Co. v. Hoosier Racing Tire Corp.*, 733 F.2d 973, 980–87 (1st Cir. 1984); *Blalock v. Ladies Professional Golf Ass'n*, 359 F.Supp. 1260, 1263–68 (N.D. Ga. 1973).[6] Thus, we conclude that the district court had pendent jurisdiction over Karsten's and the professional plaintiffs' state claims.

When pendent jurisdiction is present, an injunction may issue on the basis of the pendent claims alone. * * * We review Karsten and the professional plaintiffs' pendent claims to determine if the district court abused its discretion in granting the injunction.

STANDARD OF REVIEW

We will reverse a grant of a preliminary injunction "only where the district court abused its discretion or based its decision on an erroneous legal standard or clearly erroneous factual findings." * * *

DISCUSSION

In seeking a preliminary injunction, Karsten and the professional player plaintiffs must show either (1) a likelihood of success on the merits and the possibility of irreparable injury, or (2) the existence of serious questions going to the merits and the balance of hardships tipping in their favor. "The critical element in determining the test to be applied is the relative hardship to the parties. If the balance of harm tips decidedly

---

6. We note that the parties have extensively briefed the antitrust issues raised in this case. We emphasize that we express no opinion on the antitrust issues other than they are not insubstantial.

toward the plaintiff, then the plaintiff need not show as robust a likelihood of success on the merits as when the balance tips less decidedly."

The PGA challenges the district court's analysis of (1) the balance of hardships, and (2) whether there are serious questions to be resolved on the merits. In applying the principles outlined above, we conclude that the district court did not abuse its discretion in granting the preliminary injunction.

I. Balance of Hardships

The district court determined that the balance of hardships tips sharply in favor of Karsten and the professional player plaintiffs. The PGA disputes this finding, contending both that the possible harm to the PGA is substantial and the possible harm to Karsten and the professional player plaintiffs is minimal. The district court did not abuse its discretion on this issue.

A. Harm to Karsten and the Professional Player Plaintiffs

The district court concluded that the professional player plaintiffs would be irreparably harmed if they were forced to abandon their Ping Eye 2 clubs and use different clubs. Testimony supported this conclusion. The players' testimony showed that the ban would affect the ability of the professional player plaintiffs to qualify in future tournaments and their ability to secure endorsements.

The PGA argues that the harm that the individual player plaintiffs suffered was purely speculative and thus could not be considered irreparable injury * * *

Here, the district court found that the professional player plaintiffs have demonstrated they will suffer an immediate threatened injury. The professionals will be irreparably harmed if they are forced to change clubs because they would be at a competitive disadvantage. They testified that the ban on clubs will force them to change their club selection and will have a detrimental effect on their golf game. They further testified that this forced club change would have an immediately discernible but unquantifiable adverse impact on their earnings, their ability to maintain their eligibility for the tour, and for endorsement contracts. This testimony was supported by cross-examination of Commissioner Beman and Tom Kite. The difficulty in quantifying the injury done to the professionals does not make their injuries speculative * * * Additionally, where the threat of injury is imminent and the measure of that injury defies calculation, damages will not provide a remedy at law * * * Thus, the immeasurable injuries likely to be suffered by the individual plaintiffs supports the district court's conclusion that they will be irreparably harmed. Therefore, the district court's conclusion that the professionals have established that they will suffer irreparable harm if the ban is enforced is not clearly erroneous.

With regard to Karsten Manufacturing, the district court found that Karsten would be required to redesign its clubs, retool its manufacturing process, and abandon its well-established U-groove market. Additionally, Karsten has produced evidence tending to show that the U-groove ban appears to have harmed Karsten's reputation as a golf club manufacturer.

PGA argues that Karsten has not demonstrated harm because the president of the company testified that customers do not rely on the grooves when they buy his clubs. This argument ignores testimony by John Solheim that Ping Eye 2 clubs have been identified with the U-groove. Secondly, Dr. Smith, Karsten's expert, testified that Karsten would suffer injury to its reputation if forced to switch to V-grooves.

PGA argues that Karsten's irreparable harm is due solely to Karsten's delay in complying with the rule change. Moreover, Karsten unjustifiably delayed bringing this action * * *

This case does not present a delay of several years. Here, the district court specifically found that Karsten and the professional player plaintiffs had pursued this action with reasonable diligence. Karsten sought a meeting with the PGA in June of 1989, four months after the PGA approved the rule change. Karsten met with the PGA one month later. John Solheim testified that he requested and received the test data PGA relied upon. He further testified that it took a couple of months to review the data. The district court's conclusion that Karsten brought this suit with reasonable diligence is not clearly erroneous.

B. Harm to the PGA

Contrasted with these harms, the district court found that the PGA's potential damage is based on its claim that the injunction will damage its reputation as a sports governing body. The district court concluded that the balance of harms tips sharply towards Karsten and the professional player plaintiffs.

The PGA asserts that it will be damaged due to its inability to promulgate rules which bind its members. PGA cites *Heldman v. United States Lawn Tennis Ass'n*, 354 F. Supp. 1241, 1252 (S.D.N.Y. 1973) for the proposition that the failure of the district court fully to evaluate the ban of the U-groove under the rule of reason before granting an injunction will unduly damage the prestige and operation of the PGA. The harm to PGA's prestige and operation may be substantial. *See STP Corp. v. United States Auto Club, Inc.*, 286 F. Supp. 146, 150 (S.D. Ind. 1968). Nonetheless, Karsten and the professional player plaintiffs have demonstrated severe financial and reputational injury; by contrast the PGA has demonstrated injury only to its reputation. On this record, we cannot say that the district court abused its discretion in determining that the balance of hardships tips sharply in favor of the Karsten and the professional player plaintiffs. The next consideration is whether the district court abused its discretion in determining that serious questions exist which should be resolved in a hearing on the merits.

II. Serious Questions

We need not decide whether the rule of reason or *per se* analysis will govern the plaintiff's antitrust claims. We hold instead that the district court did not abuse its discretion in determining that there are serious questions indicating a fair chance of success on the merits with regard to the circumstances surrounding the PGA Board's vote to approve the U-groove ban.

A. Fiduciary Duty and By-Law Analysis

The district court held that there were substantial questions raised about the propriety of the manner in which the board passed the U-groove ban. The individual professional player plaintiffs have alleged that the PGA directors breached their fiduciary duties by breaching the by-laws, directly and indirectly, and by voting on an issue in which they had conflicting financial interests.

To the extent that the individual plaintiffs are members of the PGA organization, the individual plaintiffs argue that the members of the board of directors owe them a fiduciary duty * * * The professional player plaintiffs argue that the player directors and the officer directors have a duty to act "in the best interests of the corporation and [they are] prohibited from using [their] position * * * for [their] private gain." * * * The PGA argues that Maryland law allows interested directors to act after full disclosure to the board and approval by the non-interested directors. *See* Md. Corps. & Ass'ns Ann. Code §2-419. However, that statute only states that a contract or transaction is not void or voidable solely on the basis that an interested director voted on it. That section does not address whether there is a violation of the director's fiduciary duties when the interested director votes. The district court did not misapprehend Maryland law in the present case * * *

The district court held that the first vote of the PGA Policy Board violated the by-laws of the PGA. The by-laws required the player directors to vote on rule changes. However, the district court found that none of the player directors voted to adopt the U-groove ban in violation of those by-laws because each of the player directors had a financial conflict. This conflict was due to ties to competing manufacturers of golf clubs. Subsequently, each of the directors voted to change the by-laws to allow the noninterested directors to vote, in the very same meeting and possibly with the intention of allowing the other directors to pass the regulation. Voting on a matter on which a director has a conflict of interest may violate that director's fiduciary duty. A court "may intervene to prevent (or annul) conduct on the part of directors that is fraudulent or represents a breach of their fiduciary obligations." * * *

We are not prepared to rule on the merits of these questions at this stage of the litigation and on this undeveloped record. We hold only that the district court did not abuse its discretion in determining that this case raises serious questions that must be resolved at trial.

CONCLUSION

The preliminary injunction is necessary to preserve the status quo ante litem pending a hearing and a decision on the merits. * * * The district court did not err in determining that there are serious questions that should be resolved at trial and that the balance of hardships tips sharply in favor of the plaintiffs. Therefore, the district court did not abuse its discretion in granting the preliminary injunction. The judgment of the district court is

Affirmed.

Notes and Questions

1. In *Gilder*, what was the possible relevance of the fact that both players and manufacturers had sued the PGA over the restrictions on the U-groove golf club? What is the difference, if any, between a PGA rule circumscribing one's ability to wear a shoe that facilitates his or her swing with a rule prohibiting a golf club that enables one to put greater spin and action on the ball? Seemingly, in both cases, the overall impact on play and the compromise of the purity of the sport are very similar.

2. In attempting to divine the rationale of the court in each case, how relevant is it that other competitors remain in the market after the competitor affected by the rule has functionally been removed from such market, and a particular producer is engaged only in the business of manufacturing the product that has been declared invalid by the particular association's regulation?

3. What is the significance of the PGA's breach of fiduciary duty in the decision to prohibit the use of U-groove clubs? Should it be a factor in the overall determination of reasonableness?

4. Should a professional sports league or association be permitted to enter into an exclusive deal with one manufacturer of equipment? In *Schutt Athletic Sales Co. v. Riddell, Inc.*, 727 F. Supp. 1220 (N.D. Ill. 1989), defendant Riddell and National Football

League Properties, Inc., the NFL's licensing arm, entered into an agreement that gave Riddell the exclusive right to display its logo on its own helmets during NFL games, in exchange for certain "perks" available to players and teams. Players wearing helmets of manufacturers other than Riddell could not display the logos of those competing brands. The court rejected Schutt's argument that the agreement was a *per se* violation, held that Schutt had not demonstrated an adverse affect upon competition in the relevant market. Schutt advanced a theory that high school and college consumers would make their purchasing decisions based on what they saw NFL players wear. The court responded that there was not enough evidence to prove that competition in that broad market would be affected. If there were evidence that a high percentage of consumers would behave in the manner that Schutt suggested, would that render the NFL-Riddell agreement unlawful? Should it matter if Schutt and Riddell had actively competed to be the NFL's supplier?

5. If *Gilder* had not been resolved by the district court pursuant to a *per se* theory, could plaintiffs have proven that the PGA Tour rule had an adverse effect on competition in an overall (not just professionals) golf club market? Could conduct that constitutes a *per se* violation in some bizarre fashion survive scrutiny under the Rule of Reason? *See Notes and Questions* following the *Blalock* case in Chapter 10.

6. Before Karsten Manufacturing sued the PGA Tour, it had already sued the USGA and the Royal & Ancient Golf Club of St. Andrews ("the R&A") in a separate, somewhat unrelated, lawsuit, also in the United States District Court for the District of Arizona. That lawsuit also concerned Ping Eye 2 Irons and arose out of the dispute referenced in footnote 2 of the Ninth Circuit's opinion in *Gilder*. The R&A is, among other things, the organization responsible for promulgating the Rules of Golf outside the United States, and Mexico. The latter two jurisdictions are the areas where the USGA is responsible for the Rules of Golf. Karsten alleged that the nominally independent decisions by the R&A and the USGA declaring that the grooves on the face of Karsten's Ping Eye 2 irons were too close together furthered a conspiracy—an agreement violative of Section 1. Karsten's case against the R&A was dismissed due to lack of personal jurisdiction, *see Karsten Manufacturing Corp. v. USGA*, 728 F. Supp. 1429 (D. Az. 1990), and the court ordered Karsten to reimburse the R&A for its fees and costs incurred in defending the lawsuit. However, the case proceeded against the USGA, with the allegation remaining that the USGA's actions were pursuant to a conspiracy with the R&A. Is that the kind of conspiracy Sherman Act §1 was designed to proscribe? An agreement between two rule-making organizations for different parts of the world is certainly not an agreement between competitors. If a single organization set the rules worldwide, the plaintiff would have to prove monopolization or an attempt to monopolize. Should the law be different if two rule-making bodies cooperate to achieve global uniformity?

7. Equipment issues proliferate in the world of golf. Consumers can purchase devices to help the golfer measure the distance to the pin, calculate the direction and force of the wind, and clean the ball. Equipment manufacturers have marketed balls that will not curve (hook or slice), balls that allegedly "fly too far" to conform to the rules, gloves that lock the golfer's wrist in one position, clubs that can be adjusted to serve as the various irons (*e.g.*, a two-iron through nine-iron), and many other products designed to improve the golfer's score. Another development is the "long putter," a club with an extended shaft that supposedly helps "cure the yips," a condition that interferes with the golfer putting with a smooth stroke and an efficient follow-through. The USGA considered whether the long putter was in compliance with the Rules of Golf while Karsten's suit against the USGA was pending; eventually, the USGA approved the club. Is there

any cognizable difference between the marginal benefits provided by the U-groove clubs and the advantages offered by the long putter? Might the USGA's approval of the latter have been prompted by the pendency of the Karsten lawsuit and fear of more unwanted litigation?

8. One aspect of golf that some believe distinguishes it from all other sports is the concept that one can compare a round of golf played on a particular course by a top professional in 1960 with a round played on that same court by anyone else. Professionals and amateurs and even recreational golfers play by the same rules with equipment governed by the same rules. Therefore, if you are fortunate enough to play at Pebble Beach or the Old Course at St. Andrews in Scotland, you can compare your score to the best rounds recorded at those courses by Tiger Woods, Jack Nicklaus, Arnold Palmer, Gary Player, Sam Snead, or Greg Norman. In fact, there are many variables that might render the comparison questionable—such as changes in equipment (clubs and balls), weather, pin placement, fairway condition, and so on—but the sport and its participants cling to the idea that nothing significant has changed and inter-decade comparisons remain meaningful. New technology threatens the illusion of comparability. New technology also pushes golf course designers and managers to increase the length and difficulty of their holes to preserve 72 as a meaningful par for 18 holes played by the top professionals. To preserve the comparability in the face of titanium clubs, "Big Bertha" drivers, and new technology balls, many argue that the Royal and Ancient Golf Club of St. Andrews ("R&A") and the US Golf Association (USGA") should set limits on how far balls can travel and limits on what clubs can be used. Others argue that the PGA Tour and other major professional golf events should make the professional equipment rules different than the rules for non-professionals. The PGA tour's prohibition of "U-groove" irons was the PGA Tour's only foray in that direction, departing from the USGA rules. Golf club and golf ball manufacturers respond to any proposals about limitations on their new products by threatening antitrust lawsuits. Would such claims have merit if the PGA Tour changed its rules or the USGA and R&A changed the rules for everyone to freeze certain technological advances at the 2006 level?

9. In this area, the age-old debate of whether art imitates life or life imitates art irresistibly comes to mind. Decades ago, in the movie *It Happens Every Spring*, Ray Milland played the part of a college chemistry professor/baseball fanatic who inadvertently stumbled upon a compound that repelled wood. The compound, when applied to a baseball, precluded any forceful contact with a Louisville slugger or other wood bat. Armed with, but not divulging, his innovation, Milland secured a tryout with his favorite Major League team and led them to the World Series. Romance and humor aside, this type of invention clearly would change the face of the game and would provoke an immediate and understandable response from league officials. Is this not the type of intrusion upon the tradition of the game and the integrity of play that rules committees were designed to police? Admittedly, there are equipment advances less dramatic than Milland's chemical compound that warrant league or association review and perhaps sanction. Yet, does a "wedged" golf shoe or a U-groove golf club rise to that level? Is there a meaningful differentiation between an aluminum vs. wood racket, U-groove vs. V-groove club, regular vs. "wedged" golf shoes, a twelve and one-half inch baseball glove and a twelve inch glove, and an aluminum vs. wood bat? Associations and leagues, with judicial approval in some instances, have drawn such distinctions. In this regard, if you have trouble comprehending how a rule allowing for an extra-long, cosmetically unappealing putter has less impact upon the traditions and play of the game of golf than a wedged golf shoe, you are certainly not alone.

10. Often, the predicate for an equipment regulation is a concern for the safety of participants or fans. Such concerns have also prompted regulations beyond mere limi-

tations on the use of certain equipment. The NHL has foreclosed league participation to players with certain handicaps such as vision in only one eye. In *Neeld v. National Hockey League*, 594 F. Supp. 1297 (9th Cir. 1979), a player challenged such rules as *per se* violations of the Sherman Act. The court dismissed the *per se* contentions out of hand and, applying the Rule of Reason, concluded that the purpose and effect of the rule was the promotion of safety. The court stressed that the plaintiff's condition posed a danger to his own physical well-being as well as to the health of his fellow competitors. Finding that these factors outweighed any incidental anti-competitive effects, the court dismissed the plaintiff's claims. While there can be no doubt that insuring the safety of the game's participants is a noble aspiration and indeed "reasonable" in the dictionary definition of that term, is it pro-competitive in the sense of the typical antitrust inquiry? Does the promotion of safety vs. restraint in the market for player services constitute a type of "apples and oranges" analysis repudiated in other sports litigation. *See Smith v. Pro-Football, Inc.*, 593 F.2d 1173 (D.C. Cir. 1978). *See further National Society of Professional Engineers v. United States*, 435 U.S. 679 (1978). What if Major League Baseball had adopted a rule banning all players with one arm or hand? All-star, one-handed pitcher Jim Abbott, regarded as an inspiration to millions, would have never played a Major League game. The same unfortunate result would have occurred in the case of the St. Louis Cardinals' one-armed outfielder Pete Gray.

In the context of equipment restrictions, how relevant is the promotion of safety to the defense of a manufacturer's or player's claim that the restriction unreasonably restrains trade? Can a league or association refusing to permit participation by players who neglect to wear safety helmets or other protective devices be liable under the antitrust laws? What about a league that does not allow a quarterback with broken ribs to wear a "flak jacket" or similar protection under his jersey? What about a soccer league that does not allow a player who has suffered concussions to wear protective headgear? This issue could present an interesting quandary for the club, as well as other employers in the industrial sector. Imposition of strict rules governing safety could invite legal reprisals in terms of antitrust or right to privacy; however, the failure to insist upon proper protective devices could visit liability under tort law, occupational safety and health regulations, etc.

Hypothetical Problem

During a hotly contested National Football League game in the third week of the regular NFL season, the Maine Icebergs' star rookie quarterback Lee Crosby was injured when he attempted to tackle a defensive back who had intercepted one of his forward passes. Crosby suffered serious damage to the wrist of his throwing arm. The team physician declared that there was severe trauma to the tendons of the wrist and also that there was "some arterial trauma". Prior to the injury, Crosby was leading the league in passing with a 65% completion percentage, including eight touchdown passes and no interceptions. Notwithstanding this injury, Crosby declared that he was ready to return and he was pronounced fit by team physician Hugh Betterplay. In fact, at private workouts in the Hula Bowl Stadium, Crosby seemed to be throwing without any hint of pain or problem.

Accordingly, Crosby was activated for the Icebergs' eleventh game, a sellout at the Icebergs' home park, "Frostbite Stadium." Crosby's return, unfortunately, was less than auspicious. He completed two of 17 passes for 12 yards, with four interceptions. The next two games ended the same way for Crosby as the home fans were treated to consecutive losses "highlighted" by his seven interceptions. Throughout these games, Crosby complained to head coach Ulysses Zola that his throwing hand felt numb and that he "could not seem to get a good feel for the ball". He repeated these complaints during practice before each game and on post-game television interviews. The average temperature during each game was 22 degrees.

Remarkably, Crosby's lament found the ears of a local amateur inventor and engineer Jack Flacket. Within three days, Flacket had devised a special jersey with battery-powered heated pockets. Crosby wore the jersey in the next game (average temperature of 27 degrees) and was rejuvenated. He led the Icebergs to victory with a 25 for 35 completion rate, three touchdown passes and no interceptions. Flacket was so elated that he began to draw up plans to mass produce the jerseys.

Unfortunately, the story does not end here. The NFL Rules Committee (consisting of representatives of all NFL clubs) convened an "emergency meeting" to discuss the "Handwarmer Jersey." As a result of its deliberation, the League wrote the following letter to each NFL club: "No players may wear any version of the new 'Handwarmer Jersey' during the NFL regular season or postseason play. In the opinion of the Rules Committee, this jersey compromises the integrity of the game and detracts from the rugged individualism concept that has made the NFL great."

As a result of the NFL's rule, several teams canceled new orders for the jerseys, and Flacket ceased production. Also, during the next game, played in Minnesota in subfreezing temperatures, Crosby, without the Handwarmer Jersey, fumbled two snaps from center and tossed four more interceptions.

Both Flacket and Crosby have filed suit in United States district court alleging that the League's actions constitute a violation of the Sherman Antitrust Act. Discuss the issues raised by this suit and provide arguments for both plaintiffs and the defendant(s).

Chapter 14

Labor Law and Sports: A Primer

I. Introduction*

Law school courses of three, four, and even five credits have attempted to synopsize all that there is to know about labor management relations in both the private and the public sectors. Most of these courses and this casebook will not even attempt to address the myriad issues arising in the context of equal employment law, occupational safety and health administration, and fair labor standards (*e.g.*, minimum wage, overtime, etc.). Even with these omissions, it is virtually impossible to address all the remaining subtle and sophisticated issues arising in the context of labor law.

With that disclaimer in mind, the following outline should at least provide some background for those readers who have never taken a labor law course and should provide a useful review for those readers with labor law experience. It has been included here to facilitate a working understanding of labor law principles as they apply to the world of professional sports. Again, it is by no means intended to be a substitute for a labor law course or even to be a poor person's hornbook. Rather, it is simply a road map that should be enhanced and amplified through specific cases as they apply uniquely to the sports industry.

II. The Relevant Statutes

The statute that governs labor-management relations in the private sector is the National Labor Relations Act, which embraces the Wagner Act of 1935, the Taft-Hartley Act of 1947, and the Landrum-Griffin Act of 1959. They will be collectively referred to as the National Labor Relations Act or the NLRA. 29 U.S.C. §151 *et seq.* (1973). This federal statute gives all employees the right: (1) to organize and bargain collectively with

---

* While this chapter is derived from numerous sources, the authors wish to acknowledge specially the outstanding encyclopedic treatise, THE DEVELOPING LABOR LAW, originally compiled by Charles Morris, and now edited by Patrick Hardin and John E. Higgins, Jr. It has been an invaluable resource for all members of the labor law community. *See* THE DEVELOPING LAW (4th ed. 2001) ("HARDIN"). With regard to labor law jurisprudence and professional sports, the following excellent works are deserving of special mention: PAUL D. STAUDOHAR, PLAYING FOR DOLLARS (1996) ("STAU-DOHAR"); ROBERT C. BERRY, WILLIAM B. GOULD IV & PAUL D. STAUDOHAR, LABOR RELATIONS IN PROFESSIONAL SPORTS (1986) ("BERRY"); JAMES B. DWORKIN, OWNERS V. PLAYERS: BASEBALL AND COLLECTIVE BARGAINING (1981) ("DWORKIN").

a representative of their own choosing; and (2) to engage or refuse to engage in protected, concerted activity with respect to their wages, hours, and conditions of employment. 29 U.S.C. §157, referred to commonly as "Section 7 rights." The National Labor Relations Board ("NLRB" or the "Board") has defined concerted activity broadly, focusing on the nature of the conduct and the extent to which it affects, reflects, or relates to group concerns in the workplace.

In certain circumstances, representation of the interests of other employees by a single employee in matters concerning wages, hours, or working conditions may be deemed to be "concerted." For example, an individual's attempt to enforce provisions of a collective bargaining agreement is not "isolated" but, rather, is part of the "concerted" activity that reached its culmination in the union contract. *See Interboro Contractors, Inc.*, 157 NLRB 1295 (1966), *enforced*, 388 F.2d 495 (2d Cir. 1967); *NLRB v. City Disposal Systems, Inc.*, 465 U.S. 822 (1984); *Mike Yurosek & Sons*, 310 NLRB 831 (1993), aff'd, 53 F.3d 261 (9th Cir. 1995); *NLRB v. P.I.E. Nationwide, Inc.*, 923 F.2d 506 (7th Cir. 1991). Even in a non-union setting, where no collective bargaining agreement exists, the NLRB and the courts recognize that action by a single employee may be deemed "concerted" when that employee acts on behalf of fellow employees or seeks to promote group action by consolidating the complaints of other employees. *See, e.g., Medeco Security Locks v. NLRB*, 142 F.3d 733 (4th Cir. 1998). *See also* Leonard Page and Daniel W. Sherrick, *The NLRB's Deferral Policy and Union Reform: A Union Perspective*, 24 U. Mich. J. L. Rev. 647 (1991). Indeed, the Board has also adopted the view that in a non-union setting an employer rule prohibiting employees from discussing wages and salaries violated the NLRA because such action by employees was protected, concerted activity. *NLRB v. Main Street Terrace Care Center*, 218 F.3d 531 (6th Cir. 2000).

Yet, there are limits upon this expansive view of "concerted" activity. The Board and the courts have manifested a reluctance to characterize employee complaints to governmental agencies or employee attempts to assert rights under federal or state legislation as "concerted." For example, the NLRB has rejected arguments that individual employee action taken pursuant to other statutory mandates is automatically concerted given the broad constituency that such legislation covers. *See Hollings Press, Inc.*, 343 NLRB No. 45 (2004). Where the employee activity has involved safety concerns, the circuit courts have failed to establish any clear line of demarcation. *See Williams v. Watkins Motor Lines, Inc.*, 310 F.3d 1070 (8th Cir. 2002); *NLRB v. Caval Tool Div., Chromalloy Gas Turbine Corp.*, 362 F.3d 184 (2d Cir. 2001). The NLRB differentiates the invocation of contract rights, which are part of a continuous pattern of concerted activity, from statutory rights, which lack such continuity. *Meyers Industries*, 281 NLRB 882 (1988), *aff'd sub nom. Prill v. NLRB*, 835 F.2d 1481 (D.C. Cir. 1987), *cert. denied*, 487 U.S. 1205 (1988). *See also Ewing v. NLRB*, 861 F.2d 353 (2d Cir. 1988); Jean C. Love, *Retaliatory Discharge for Filing a Workers' Compensation Claim: The Development of a Modern Tort Action*, 37 Hastings L. J. 551 (1986). Moreover, in order to be "protected" by the NLRA, concerted activities must have lawful objectives and must be executed in a lawful manner. For example, certain types of trespass, destruction of property, sit-down strikes, and other untoward activities, including the use of crude and derogatory language directed at supervisors, are not protected, though they may be concerted. *See, e.g., Media General Operations, Inc. v. NLRB* 394 F.3d 207 (4th Cir. 2005); *NLRB v. Fansteel Metallurgical Corp.*, 306 U.S. 240 (1939); *compare Overhead Door Corp.*, 220 NLRB 431 (1975), *enforcement denied in part*, 540 F.2d 878 (7th Cir. 1976). *See also* Melinda Branscomb, *Labor, Loyalty, and the Corporate Campaign*, 73 B. U. L. Rev. 293 (1993).

At times, employers' property rights and the freedom from trespass collides with employees' rights to organize and seek a bargaining representative. The need to maintain workplace order with regard to employee organizing efforts and to insulate themselves from trespassory activity by non-employee union organizers has prompted employers to promulgate broad no-solicitation/no-distribution clauses. These provisions are governed by strict rules (through evolving NLRB and judicial precedents) insuring that there is the proper accommodation between the employers' property interests and the employees' Section 7 rights. The attempts to reconcile these competing concerns, especially adapting the rules to specific industries and unique logistical situations (*i.e.*, hospitals, retail stores), have generated reams of cases and critical commentary. *See, e.g., Lechmere, Inc. v. NLRB*, 502 U.S. 527 (1992); *NLRB v. Babcock & Wilcox Co.*, 351 U.S. 105 (1956); *Nabors Alaska Drilling, Inc. v. NLRB*, 190 F. 3d 1008 (9th Cir. 1999); *Tri-County Medical Center, Inc.*, 222 NLRB 1089 (1976). *See also* Stephanie Goss John, *Oakland Mall, Ltd.: A Further Limitation on Union Access to Private Property*, 57 La. L. Rev. 361 (1996); Harry G. Hutchison, *Through the Pruneyard Coherently: Resolving the Collision of Private Property Rights and Nonemployee Union Access Claims*, 78 Marq. L. Rev. 1 (1994); Cynthia L. Estlund, *Labor, Property, and Sovereignty After Lechmere*, 46 Stan. L. Rev. 305 (1994); John H. Fanning, *Union Solicitation and Distribution of Literature on the Job—Balancing the Rights of Employees and Employers*, 9 Ga. L. Rev. 367 (1975).

Finally, it bears emphasis that concerted activity need not involve union activity, although it most often does. *See Lewittes Furn. Enterprises*, 244 NLRB 810 (1979). Further, the NLRA protects both those employees who seek to join a union or to engage in concerted activities, as well as those employees who wish to refrain from affiliating with a labor organization or engaging in any type of collective activity. Hardin at 72. This point is addressed more fully in the discussion of "right to work" legislation and "union security" clauses, Part VII, below.

III. Responsible Government Agency

The agency responsible for administering and enforcing the National Labor Relations Act is the National Labor Relations Board. The NLRB is divided into several regions and sub-regions throughout the United States and has two operating components: (1) the Board; and (2) the General Counsel. The Board "side" acts as a labor court and consists of several Administrative Law Judges as well as a five-member review panel. The General Counsel serves as an attorney general of labor, prosecuting unfair labor practice charges filed by various charging parties. If the General Counsel concludes that a particular charge has merit, a complaint will be issued, and the General Counsel will assume responsibility for the prosecution of that complaint on behalf of the charging party. The charging party, however, retains the right, in most cases, to participate with the General Counsel in the development of the litigation.

IV. Coverage of the NLRA

Statutorily, several persons are exempt from the coverage of the Act, including the following employees: agricultural workers; domestic servants; persons employed by a parent or spouse; employees under the protection of the Railway Labor Act; and government employees. HARDIN at 2092. In addition, independent contractors and supervisors are not afforded the same protection of the NLRA as are employees. *See, e.g. NLRB v. Kentucky River Community Care, Inc.,* 532 U.S. 706 (2001) for the latest discussion by the Supreme Court on "supervisory status" under the NLRA. As to the Board's recent "independent contractor" status standards *see Roadway Package System, Inc.* 326 NLRB 842 (1998). *Employers* exempt from the NLRA include: the United States government; Federal Reserve Banks; wholly-owned government corporations; and employers under the Railway Labor Act. HARDIN at 1601–05. *See generally* 29 U.S.C. §§152(2)-(14). Section 2 of the NLRA explicitly defines several "players" in the labor law game, including "employer," "employee," "supervisor," and "labor organization." *See* 29 U.S.C. §§ 152 (1)–(14).

The NLRB has been given broad statutory jurisdiction over all businesses affecting interstate commerce. As part of this broad discretion, the Board may decline to assert jurisdiction in a variety of cases, provided that it does not refuse to exercise jurisdiction over any labor dispute within its jurisdiction under the standards prevailing in August, 1949 (the date of the most recent statutory amendments regarding NLRB assertion of jurisdiction). *See generally* 29 U.S.C. §164. The Board has assumed jurisdiction over most aspects of the professional sports industry. Yet, oddly enough, the NLRB has chosen not to assert jurisdiction over the horse and dog racing industries despite their apparent impact on interstate commerce. *See Eatz v. DME Unit of Local Union Number 3 of the International Brotherhood of Electrical Workers,* 973 F.2d 64 (2d Cir. 1992); *NLRB v. California Horse Racing Board,* 940 F.2d 536 (9th Cir. 1991). Recently, however, the Board did decide to exercise jurisdiction over an Indian gaming casino on tribal lands. *San Manuel Indian Bingo and Casino,* 341 NLRB No. 138 (2004).

The Board has developed a complete set of jurisdictional standards governing retail and non-retail businesses, public utilities, newspapers, etc. These standards essentially involve a fixed-dollar amount reflecting particular entities' total volume of business. With incidental exceptions, all major sports and the employees within those major sports have been deemed to rest within the jurisdiction of the National Labor Relations Act. *See, e.g., Salerno v. American League of Professional Baseball Clubs,* 429 F.2d 1003 (2d Cir. 1970).

For purposes of this text, the employers in the sports industry will consist of owners, leagues, and properly designated management groups (*e.g.,* The NFL Management Council, The Major League Baseball Player Relations Committee, etc). Employees will be defined as players, batboys and batgirls, ballboys and ballgirls, umpires, groundskeepers, concession employees, etc. Managers and coaches are presumed to be supervisors, as are general managers and other upper echelon club executives. The relevant labor organizations will be the Major League Baseball Players Association ("MLBPA"), the National Basketball Players Association ("NBPA"), the National Hockey League Players Association ("NHLPA"), and the "on-again, off-again" National Football League Players Association ("NFLPA"). Of course, there are other labor organizations that we will touch upon throughout this text, such as the World Umpires Association ("WUA") and similar trade unions.

One of the more difficult questions governing the identity and definition of the various entities that we will encounter in sports law is the role occupied by the league commissioners. The question as to whether the commissioner is truly management, *i.e.,* "an employer", as defined in the Act, has never been definitively resolved. There is ample basis upon which to conclude that the commissioner is, in fact, an employer, or at least a representative of the owners and, thus, an employer's agent. However, owners have attempted to distance themselves from words or conduct of league commissioners to avoid unfair labor practice liability. *See, e.g., NFLPA v. NLRB*, 503 F.2d 12 (8th Cir. 1974); *Silverman v. Major League Baseball Player Relations Comm., Inc.*, 516 F. Supp. 588 (S.D.N.Y. 1981). Many commentators believe that the commissioner does not enjoy true independence from league ownership. For an interesting commentary strongly criticizing the characterization of a league commissioner as independent, see MARVIN MILLER, A WHOLE DIFFERENT BALLGAME: THE SPORT AND BUSINESS OF BASEBALL 389, 406 (1990). For comments on a new proposal that would restructure the baseball commissioner's authority whereby the commissioner would act in a role similar to a chief executive officer of a corporation, see Depak Sathy, *Reconstruction: Baseball's New Future*, 4 SETON HALL J. SPORT L. 27 (1994); Michael J. Willisch, *Protecting the "Owners" of Baseball: A Governance Structure to Maintain the Integrity of the Game and Guard the Principals' Money Investment*, 88 NW. U.L. REV. 1619 (1994). The relatively recent decision to make the baseball commissioner part of the management "team" in collective bargaining matters creates some interesting scenarios as discussed in Chapter 3, *supra*. Certainly, the commissioner will not occupy the same role and pose the same "threat" to the owners as Fay Vincent occupied in ordering the end of the lockout in the 1990s. However, today's commissioner also will not be able to insulate himself from unfair labor practice liability that would attach to league owners as employers.

In earlier chapters, we addressed in considerable detail owners, league commissioners, and other individuals responsible for league governance. In labor law parlance, these individuals, to different degrees, comprise the employing entities. An excursus on the nature of the employees in the sports world (the players) and their collective bargaining representatives follows below. Some discussion of umpires and their representatives will also be entertained. In this section, brief mention will be made of players' individual agents. They will be considered at length in Chapter 23.

V. The Covered Employees and their Collective Bargaining Representatives

(A) The Players

It is difficult to imagine an industry more labor intensive than professional sports. Discount the uniforms and equipment, and the inventory becomes largely an irrelevancy. The game must be played with players, and no amount of automation or substitution will permit its operation without them. Professional sports leagues are peopled by the most exquisitely gifted athletes in the world, whose skills and talents have been honed through the training grounds of the minor leagues and intercollegiate athletics. They generally range in age from 18 to 45, but most team-sport athletes are in their prime between the ages of 22 and 35. The "average life expectancy" of a professional athlete will vary from sport to sport. In football, for example, it is commonly understood that a player can count on a career of approximately four years. In ice hockey the average career is approximately five years, and most players begin their professional careers at an early age due to the minor league programs and NHL rules which permit them to be drafted as early as 17 years of age. *See* STAUDOHAR at 148. The professional careers in other sports may be slightly longer, but in no event is the average expectancy in excess of ten years. Doubtless, the average career length will be influenced in the future by several factors, including high annual salaries, injuries resulting from the increased size and speed of the participants, artificial playing surfaces, and expanded schedules.

Today, aside from the fan resentment that has grown proportionately to the labor unrest in each sport, athletes are lionized as folk heroes and role models. Playgrounds are densely populated with young athletes who aspire to professional careers. Popular advertisements such as "I wanna be like Mike", referring to the idolatry reserved for Chicago Bulls' superstar Michael Jordan, capitalize on, and accurately reflect, the hero worship accorded the professional athlete.

Ball players were not always held in such high esteem. In the early part of the twentieth century athletes were often viewed as ruffians and hooligans who were unwilling or unable to secure more respectable employment. The image of the professional athlete was in no way enhanced by the infamous Black Sox scandal of 1919 in which several Major League Baseball players were accused of gambling on, or "throwing", World Series games. The injection of criminal elements into professional sports only served to reinforce the public perception that this industry was morally bankrupt and culturally unredeeming.

Several factors probably led to the emergence of the athlete from a status as virtual ne'er do well into a respected member of society. First, in professional football and basketball, most of the participants received their "training" at the college level. The number of college graduates in the professional ranks in these sports may have suggested to the public that these individuals possessed some type of pedigree or, at least, that they had achieved a level of professionalism worthy of some respect. While a college degree by no means is an absolute indicator of one's intelligence, culture, or even decency, it has carried a connotation that the recipient is entitled to some credit for his or her efforts. Further, the universal appeal of athletics, attracting fans from all socio-economic strata, may suggest further that putting on exhibitions and showcasing one's talents in professional sports was much like legitimate theater or other fine arts, presumably professions of some nobility. Finally, the more fans became fascinated with the playing of the game, the more familiar they became with the players themselves. Increased press coverage, the development of more sophisticated communications, and the advent of television shrank the distance between player and fan. Thus, the public quickly saw the professional athlete in a more positive light—a typical worker with a family much like themselves, but a worker with special and enviable skills.

As athletes evolved, both in terms of the refinement of skills and overall sophistication, they came to recognize their own self-worth and the importance of securing meaningful wages and benefits during their brief careers. This recognition led athletes to seek the advantages of collective strength and solidarity. While the 1950s are commonly recognized as the era when labor organizing in professional sports began, the notion of players banding together in some type of concerted effort had germinated many years earlier. *See* James R. Devine, *Baseball's Labor Wars In Historical Context: The 1919 Chicago White Sox As a Case-Study in Owner-Player Relations*, 15 MARQ. SPORTS L. J. 1 (1994). In 1885, the players established the National Brotherhood of Baseball Players. Even then, over 100 years ago, the principal impetus for the organizing effort was the reserve system and a $3,000 cap on salaries. Five years later, the players, upset over their inability to move freely from club to club (history continues to repeat itself), went so far as to form their own league. This "Players League" disassembled after only one year largely through the orchestration of the magnates who had been challenged by this novel concept. LEE LOWENFISH & TONY LUPIEN, THE IMPERFECT DIAMOND (1980). *See also* James O. Castagnera and

Michael R. Ostrowski, *Players Without Picket Signs: A Plan For Employee Ownership In Professional Athletics*, 42 WAYNE L. REV. 73 (1995). The Brotherhood also faded into oblivion as did numerous other player groups organized to deal with baseball's establishment in labor relations matters. *See* DWORKIN at 12–20; BERRY at 51–52. Thus, as the sports industry burgeoned, the idea that athletes could bond together in an effort to gain economic advantage and to share in the profits of the enterprise did not seem to be subversive. Yet, these early attempts to have leagues recognize the players' collective representatives and pay heed to their needs and demands hardly constituted collective bargaining. The players did not view themselves as typical trade unionists, and the teams certainly did not consider themselves "unionized" in the traditional sense.

The Major League Baseball Players Association was formed in 1954. It selected former Cleveland Indians pitcher and Hall of Famer Bob Feller as its representative. Feller epitomized the notion that his organization was much more of a social club or fraternal association than any type of trade union. *See* DWORKIN at 27–29. In fact, the players seemed almost insulted at the notion that they could be compared to teamsters or electricians or others who sought the benefits of strength through an adversarial collective bargaining process. It is almost as if this organization assumed that a friendly roundtable discussion with management would redound to the collective benefit and assure contentment across the board. Perhaps, the prosperity that the sport enjoyed created a false sense of security in players that "there was plenty to go around."

> The earliest formal stirrings of labor organizing in professional football occurred in the mid-Fifties. Dante Lavelli, Cleveland Browns Hall of Famer, takes credit for being at the forefront of the organizing efforts, claiming that he postponed his retirement after the 1955 season in order to promote the players' union. *See* WILL McDONOUGH ET AL., 75 SEASONS 111 (1995). By some accounts, the NFLPA was established in November, 1956, when a majority of NFL players designated the NFLPA and private attorney Creighton Miller to represent them in collective bargaining. Ironically, Miller had previously served as general manager and general counsel of the Cleveland Browns. One again, this union was a mere shadow of a typical trade union. Even the modest initial statement issued by the NFLPA spoke to its rather unambitious designs: The football man, when dissatisfied, thinks not of a revolt, but of recognition. It is hoped that the modern club executive faced with player grievances will think not of the divine right of management, but of making feasible adjustments.

Id.

Paralleling the formation of the labor organizations in baseball and football, the National Basketball Players Association ("NBPA") was established in 1954 under the leadership of eventual Boston Celtics Hall of Famer Bob Cousy. The NBA recognized the NBPA in 1957 after two years of ignoring the union's complaints and requests for action. Part of the impetus for the voluntary recognition was Commissioner Maurice Podoloff's fear that the Players Association would execute its threat to affiliate with a larger labor organization such as the American Guild of Variety Artists ("AGVA"). Again, mirroring the early frustration of the players associations in other sports, the NBPA was largely ineffectual in its embryonic stage. *See* STAUDOHAR at 105. Finally, the National Hockey League players, receiving the cue from the other professional sports, established themselves as a union in 1957. In a recurring theme, the NHLPA did little to further the interests of the players during their initial decade.

The real emergence of players as union members and of players associations as true labor organizations occurred in the mid-1960s. At that point, Marvin Miller, former Steelworkers' Union pension expert, became Executive Director of the Major League Baseball Players Association. Ed Garvey, an attorney and player advocate, became Executive Director of the National Football League Players Association. Larry Fleischer and Alan Eagleson assumed leadership of the National Basketball Players Association and the National Hockey League Players Association, respectively. They represented a change in direction for players and their unions. Under the guidance of these advocates, the social club concept that had become identified with existing players associations soon was vitiated; players associations matured into "trade unions," and the labor relations landscape changed dramatically and irreversibly.

Miller has been hailed as the prototype and, in some quarters, the paragon of sports union leadership. While few league officials would share this viewpoint, many observers believe that Miller's influence on the game rivals Babe Ruth, Branch Rickey, and others who, on the field and in the front office, have left indelible marks. It has even been suggested that Miller should be enshrined in baseball's Hall of Fame in Cooperstown, New York. During Miller's tenure, baseball players secured salary arbitration, liberal (if not unqualified) free agency, exponential increases in salaries, and a change in status that virtually made them equal partners with owners as purveyors of the product of Major League Baseball. Given the tumultuous history of labor relations in Major League Baseball and the continuing militancy of the MLBPA in the wake of Miller's retirement in 1983, it is unlikely that there will ever be a consensus on his contributions to, or effect upon, the game. There, however, can be little doubt of the large shadow that he has cast in terms of the development of the Players Association as a trade union and the benefits enjoyed by its members, and, derivatively, the members of other labor unions representing professional athletes. *See* DWORKIN at 29; *see also* Michael J. Cozzillio, *From the Land of Bondage: The Greening of Major League Baseball Players And The Major League Baseball Players Association*, 41 CATH. U. L. REV. 117 (1991) (reviewing MARVIN MILLER, A WHOLE DIFFERENT BALL GAME: THE SPORT AND BUSINESS OF BASEBALL (1991)).

The appearance of Garvey in 1971, Fleisher in 1962, and Eagleson in 1967, affected football, basketball and ice hockey in ways similar to, if not so momentous as, the impact that Miller had on baseball. Garvey's influence was felt in both the litigation and negotiation spheres. During Garvey's reign, the draft and the Rozelle rule were challenged and defeated, *Smith v. Pro-Football, Inc.*, 593 F.2d 1173 (D.C. Cir. 1979); *Mackey v. NFL*, 543 F.2d 606 (8th Cir. 1976) subjects about which the league was required to bargain in good faith were expanded and clarified, commissioner's authority was circumscribed in favor of neutral arbitrators, and the NFLPA progressed from a loose amalgam of athletes to a group unified in their efforts to secure better wages, hours, and working conditions. *See* STAUDOHAR at 65–68. During this period, as might be expected, battle lines were frequently drawn, and relationships between Garvey and Commissioner Rozelle and the Management Council's Jack Donlin were far from cordial.

Fleisher's role in the NBPA was not as pronounced as Miller's and Garvey's but was significant nonetheless. In particular, through his leadership, the NBPA began to function as a viable labor organization that advanced players' interests in terms of free agency, salary guarantees, and limitations upon the amateur draft. Fleisher parlayed the union's apparent solidarity with the threat of litigation and collective action (strikes) to accomplish the union's goals. Yet, during Fleisher's term of office, there was little litigation and no work stoppage. Even when it appeared as though litigation was the answer or a strike would produce more immediate or dramatic results, Fleisher often adopted a policy of restraint. *See* BERRY at 57–59; STAUDOHAR at 104–06.

Alan Eagleson, like Garvey and Fleisher, a prominent attorney, coalesced NHL players and gained the league's voluntary recognition in 1967. Interestingly, Eagleson is both praised and criticized for his early leadership in the areas of player salaries and benefits. While there is little doubt that hockey players secured numerous gains under Eagleson's guidance, his record is shadowed by the fact that he, like Larry Fleisher, represented individual players while serving as Executive Director. The apparent and potential conflict of interest has prompted some critics to question his commitment to the union and his ability to serve both masters. *See* BERRY at 206–08; STAUDOHAR at 147–50. Intervening events have done little to remove the doubts, as Eagleson was indicted in 1994 for, among other alleged offenses, misappropriating union funds. STAUDOHAR at 149. *See* Chapter 23.

The efforts of these second stage Players Association leaders have been significant in several respects. Groups that were once fraternal societies or social clubs are now trade unions negotiating with the same solidarity, vigor, threat of strike, and legal arsenals as any member of the AFL-CIO. The role of executive director is no longer a symbolic position, but, rather, one that occupies the status of a staunch adversary of the ownership and, at times, the league commissioner. Finally, labor-management relations in sports have been altered such that the successors, Donald Fehr in baseball, Gene Upshaw in football, James Hunter in basketball, and Bob Goodenow in hockey, no longer need to blaze a trail to be recognized, legally or psychologically. In most instances and from most perspectives, the demands that they make and the tactics that they employ are no longer viewed as radically militant stratagems; instead, they are simply part of the labor relations game played on both sides by professionals who know the rules and operate within their unique framework.

Reflective of the surprise with which management has received these developments is the fact that each of these unions had been *voluntarily* recognized by the league and its owners. It is unusual in the private industrial sector for a union to become a representative of a unit of employees absent some type of vigorous electioneering and campaigning on the part of both parties. Yet, the leagues in every major sport, with the exception of the NASL in soccer, honored the players associations' requests for recognition. While the leagues have not been quite so hospitable to demands for recognition from umpires and referees (see Part IX(A), below), they probably never anticipated that the players associations would function as trade unions or that the players would develop to the point where the demands regarding free agency, pension benefits and the like would reach their current level. If they had contemplated such developments, it is likely that the leagues would have offered stiff opposition to the players' organizing efforts. Of course, the silver lining for management has been that the unionization of the athlete may provide some type of derivative benefit by way of the labor exemption from the antitrust laws. As discussed in Chapter 9, the existence of a collective bargaining relationship will insulate most labor market restraints (free agency, college draft, etc.) from antitrust scrutiny. *See Brown v. Pro-Football, Inc.,* 518 U.S. 231(1996).

When the average fan or league owner thinks of players associations today, he or she identifies them with work stoppages, lockouts, and other types of industrial relations unrest. All major sports now have been confronted with strikes or threats of strikes, with the most traumatic occurrences arising in the fields of Major League Baseball and the National Football League. Nothing brought the reality of labor travail home quite as resoundingly as the 1994–95 baseball strike that deprived baseball fans of the World Series. These incidents will be addressed in Part IX, below, and throughout Chapters 15 and 16.

Among the additional stereotypes that fans and outsiders develop regarding representatives of professional athletes is a presumed camaraderie between unions and players' individual agents. In some respects, these two groups proceed on parallel lines in an effort to secure the greatest advancement for their constituencies. However, there are points at which the interests, goals and *modus operandi* of these entities come into direct conflict. *See generally* Keith N. Hylton, *The Changing Workplace: A Theory of Minimum Contract Terms, With Implications for Labor Law*, 74 Tex. L. Rev. 174 (1996); Katherine Van Wezel Stone, *The Legacy of Industrial Pluralism: The Tension Between Individual Employment Rights and the New Deal Collective Bargaining System*, 59 U. Chi. L. Rev. 575 (1992). For example, under relevant labor law precedent, once a union is certified as collective bargaining representative, it becomes the exclusive representative regarding all matters involving wages, hours, or other conditions of employment. Accordingly, players represented by a union are, with certain exceptions, precluded from negotiating individual deals with their employers.

The union's status as exclusive bargaining representative creates an interesting question in terms of the extent to which an individual's benefit could be detrimental to the interests of the whole. Pertinent labor law authority prescribes narrow qualifications to the notion of exclusivity, permitting a union to waive its right to bargain over mandatory subjects so long as the individual arrangement provides advantages over and above the benefits guaranteed by the collective bargaining agreement. *See* Part VIII(B), below. In Chapter 15, we will consider cases that help define the parameters of collective bargaining and the limited extent to which players may divorce themselves from the collective body to bargain their own terms. Also, the certification and regulation of agents by the Players Associations in the major team sports will be considered. As you will see, the lines are by no means clearly drawn and likely will be subject to more conflict and definition over the next several years.

At times, individual players (such as superstars) have suffered financially through agreements that benefit the entire unit. Frustrations spawned by the impediments presented by collective representation have sparked efforts by some players to decertify their union and open the door for unfettered individual bargaining, antitrust litigation, etc. On occasion, players' agents have engaged in direct confrontation, including litigation, over issues stemming from union-management accords that disserve the individual player. In the days following the historic settlement in *Bridgeman v. National Basketball Association*, 675 F. Supp. 960 (D.N.J. 1987) (*see* Chapter 9) several players challenged the agreement and threatened litigation to insure that their individual rights were not compromised by a resolution ostensibly benefiting the bargaining unit as a whole. *See Bridgeman v. National Basketball Association*, Civ. Action No. 87-4001 (D.N.J.).

An interesting illustration of the types of conflicts that may develop between one's collective bargaining responsibilities and the obligations owed individual players was presented by a controversy between two competing labor organizations, the Major Indoor Soccer League Players Association ("MISLPA") and the Professional Soccer Players Association ("PROSPA"). The MISLPA claimed that PROSPA's petition to represent the soccer league's players should be denied because PROSPA was controlled by persons who also represented players in their individual contract negotiations with the clubs. The NLRB honored PROSPA's petition and permitted PROSPA to seek representation of the soccer players, with the qualification that PROSPA would not be certified as collective bargaining representative if a player agent served in any labor relations capacity with PROSPA. *See Major Indoor Soccer League and Professional Soccer Players Association (PROSPA)*, Decision of NLRB Regional Director, November 15, 1983, 5-RC-11987, 5-RC-12001. *See also* Darryl Hale, *Step Up the Scale: Wages and Unions In the Sports Industry*, 5 MARQ. SPORTS L. J. 123 (1994). Decertification of agents and similar imposition of discipline has also prompted litigation. See *Black v. NFLPA*, 87 F. Supp. 2d 1 (D.D.C. 2000).

Another example of the tension between an individual player agent and a collective bargaining representative arises in the context of a salary cap. *See* Part IX (e)(ii), *infra*. Although there is no precedent discussing the potential conflict, there is some concern that a particular agent could represent two players on the same team in a sport where a salary cap exists. With a salary cap there is no "deep pocket", and owners are precluded from spending above a certain amount of money. Therefore, any advances that are secured for one client will deplete the available resources for another client. While this situation may not present direct conflicts or compromise one's standing as a member of the bar, it certainly has the appearance of impropriety and may even suggest such a radical notion as limiting an agent in a salary cap context to the representation of one player per team. These issues and the nature of the relationship between player and agent will be explored comprehensively in succeeding chapters. See Chapter 23, *infra*, Notes and Questions following *Sims v. Argovitz*, 580 F. Supp 542 (E.D. Mich. 1984) Chapter 23 will also entertain a discussion of agents' ethical responsibilities and the various types of legislation and internal governance mechanisms that have been employed to regulate agents' activity. Derivately, it will address potential abuses by collective bargaining representative in the regulation of agents and administration of the rules governing agent conduct.

(B) Umpires and Other Game Officials

It is often said that the best officials are those individuals who are unnoticed. Whenever a game is played entirely without controversial calls, it is generally presumed to have been a proficient performance by the umpiring or refereeing crew. Yet, officials have played critical roles in sports, and their importance cannot be overstated. While, in the early days of sports, umpiring or refereeing was more or less an *ad hoc*, part-time position, today's modern officials are, for the most part, full-time employees represented by labor unions. The program for today's officials and their union affiliate is as follows: Major League Baseball, World Umpires Association ("WUA"); National Football League, National Football League Referees Association ("NFLRA"); National Basketball Association, National Basketball Referees Association ("NBRA"); and, National Hockey League, National Hockey League Officials Association ("NHLOA").

As discussed in Chapter 3, professional sports officials have emerged from the dark ages of labor management relations. Union representation, at times viewed as quite militant, has altered the playing field and has contributed to the increased wages and benefits that officials now enjoy. With that modest prosperity has come a more aggressive umpire and referee, more willing to do battle with players, exchange verbal taunts, and possibly engage in physical contact. This emerging dynamic between umpires and players began to take hold several years ago in an incident involving the Baltimore Orioles' Roberto Alomar, who spat on umpire John Hirschbeck during an altercation over a called third strike. The event exacerbated tensions existing between umpires and players, and the league's response, a five game suspension to be served at the outset of the 1997 season, permitting Alomar to play in the League Championship Series, did little to relieve the tension. *See* Part IX, *infra*; Chapter 3, *supra* (where the Alomar incident has been revisited). The umpires' feelings were hardly mollified when Orioles owner Peter Angelos announced that Alomar would be paid during his suspension. In an effort to calm the waters and relax tensions between the players and umpires, an unprecedented summit meeting was convened in February, 1997. While the summit, attended by representatives of the league, players, and umpires, identified the problem areas and reflected the parties' sensitivity to the issues, it is unlikely that umpires will revert to a culture of responding to player overaggressiveness with passivity and indulgence.

Further, today's arbiters are not afraid to adopt a more aggressive posture in terms of their collective bargaining relationship with the lords of the sports industry realm. *See* Part IX, *infra*. As discussed below, the omnipresent sports work stoppage has attended the relationships between umpires and leagues as well as the oft-repeated strikes and lockouts involving players. Some of the labor-management disputes and the strategies devised by the leadership of the officials' unions have provoked serious internal discord and have resulted in the decertification of a major bargaining representative, the Major League Umpires' Association ("MLUA").

In 1999, MLUA leader Richie Phillips exhorted umpires to resign in an effort to put pressure on the league to meet demands for better wages and benefits. Phillips' belief was that the league would capitulate and refuse to accept the resignation of so many umpires. The ploy proved to be disastrous as the league called the union's bluff, resulting in a loss of jobs for a substantial number of the league's arbiters. Later, Arbitrator Alan Symonette ruled that 9 of the 22 umpires were entitled to reinstatement based largely on the infirmities in the initial termination process. Later, four more umpires were returned to their former positions, albeit without back pay. The U.S. District Court for the Eastern District of Pennsylvania and later the United States Court of Appeals for the Third Circuit affirmed the arbitrator's decision. *See MLUA v. American League of Professional Baseball Clubs*, 357 F. 3d 272 (3d Cir. 2005). As a result of this ill-fated strategy, among other areas of discontent, the umpires decertified the MLUA. As indicated in earlier chapters, the umpires are now represented by the World Umpires Association, led by former umpire John Hirshbeck.

It is clear that the salary scale and the conditions of employment for umpires and referees have changed considerably over the years. *See* Chapter 3, Notes and Questions following *NFLPA v. NLRB*, 503 F.2d 12 (8th Cir. 1974). Cynics who question the appropriateness of paying the staggering salaries that today's players currently receive, might likewise question a system wherein some basketball referees earn in excess of $300,000. Yet, the impact of the free agency era and increased salaries for players have dramatically affected the pay scale for game officials. In essence, umpires and referees are enjoying somewhat improved wages and conditions, both because professional sports has taken on tremendous proportions in terms of the role it plays in American life and because the "men in blue" and "zebras" are derivatively enjoying the fruits of the players' litigation and collective bargaining advances.

Even before umpires and referees began to secure some of their financial "due" through collective bargaining, competition for these positions was fierce. A perusal, for example, of the vast numbers of people who register for the various types of umpiring schools compared with the few who make it to the Major Leagues illustrates the highly competitive nature of this vocational pursuit. The difficulty in ascending to the level of an NBA referee, an NFL umpire, or an NHL linesman is similar. It should come as no surprise that women and minorities encounter even greater obstacles in attempting to become officials in professional sports leagues. For example, in professional baseball, Amanda Clement was the first woman umpire, serving from 1905–1911 in various semi-professional leagues. Astoundingly, no other women became umpires until 1992, when Bernice Gera umpired her first minor league game. *See* Gai Ingham Berlage, Women in Baseball 63–65 (1994). In the entire history of professional baseball, only four women have reached the minor leagues. In professional basketball, the all-male referee situation underwent a dramatic change. Two female officials, Dee Kantner and Violet Palmer, were hired by the NBA for the 1997–98 season. Ms. Kantner was terminated following the 2002 season. Richard O'Brien and Hank Hersch, eds., *Scorecard*, Sports Illustrated, May 5, 1997, Vol. 86, No. 18, at 23. (In Chapter 17, we will address this issue in considerable detail, including the lawsuit instigated by Pam Postema, a female umpire who was denied a Major League position. *See Postema v. National League of Professional Baseball Clubs* 799 F. Supp. 1475 (S.D. N.Y. 1992), *rev'd and remanded*, 998 F.2d 60 (2d Cir 1993).

VI. Labor Disputes Covered by the NLRA

The types of labor disputes that the NLRA has been created to address are representation (commonly called "R") and unfair labor practice (commonly called "C") cases. Representation questions involve the myriad issues surrounding attempts by employees to seek and obtain a representative for purposes of collective bargaining, and the NLRB's role in governing and monitoring the organizing process. 29 U.S.C. §159. Unfair labor practice cases involve a variety of proscribed activities engaged in by employers and labor organizations, particularly with regard to the exercise of rights to organize and bargain collectively guaranteed by §7 of the NLRA. 29 U.S.C. §§157, 158. In succeeding sections, you will find outlines of the procedures governing the typical representation and unfair labor practice cases as well as synopses of employer and union unfair labor practices.

VII. The Representation Case and the Organizing Process

(A) Request for Recognition

A union often will ask an employer directly to recognize it as the employees' representative for purposes of collective bargaining. Typically, the union will attempt to prove its representative status by presenting signed "authorization cards" to an employer. It has been held generally that authorization cards are inherently unreliable determinants of a union's majority status. *Linden Lumber v. NLRB*, 419 U.S. 301 (1974). Therefore, an employer is typically free to refuse to recognize a union based simply on a presentation of authorization cards. *See generally Jefferson Smurfit Corp.*, 331 NLRB 809 (2000); Charles J. Morris, *A Blueprint for Reform of the National Labor Relations Act*, 8 Admin. L. J. Am. U. 517 (1994); Sheila Murphy, *A Comparison of the Selection of Bar-*

gaining Representatives In the United States and Canada: Linden Lumber, Gissel, and the Right to Challenge Majority Status, 10 Corp. Lab. L. 65 (1988). However, if the employer should acknowledge that review of those cards is an appropriate method for determining majority status and conducts a poll using such cards as the method for ascertaining majority, then a majority of signed cards in favor of the union may be sufficient to establish a bargaining relationship and the employer loses its right to insist on a secret ballot election. *NLRB v. English Bros. Pattern & Foundry*, 679 F.2d 787 (9th Cir. 1982). Because an employer is required to negotiate in good faith with the employees' collective bargaining representative, a refusal to bargain with the union that has established majority status will constitute an unfair labor practice. *See NLRB v. Gissel Packing Co.*, 395 U.S. 575 (1969); *see generally* Hardin at 693–705. *See also* James J. Brudney, *A Famous Victory: Collective Bargaining Protections and the Statutory Aging Process*, 74 N. C. L. Rev. 939 (1996); Note, *The Propriety of Section 10(j) Bargaining Orders in Gissel Situations*, 82 Mich. L. Rev. 112 (1983).

As indicated above, employers normally will refuse to acknowledge the union's request for recognition or to consider the union's authorization cards as a basis for establishing majority status. When such a recognition request is denied, the union typically will file a Petition for Representation asking that the Board schedule an election. If the union can demonstrate a showing of interest (*i.e.*, a demonstration by cards, signatures on a petition, or similar device that at least 30% of subject employees seek an election), the NLRB will entertain the petition, and the representation process will be activated.

In professional sports, most labor organizations have been voluntarily recognized by the leagues. Thus, there have been few acrimonious election campaigns and very little litigation regarding the scope of the bargaining unit and the individuals eligible to vote in an election. *See Morio v. North American Soccer League*, 501 F. Supp. 633 (1980). While there have been some skirmishes involving players' decertification efforts (a process whereby a group of employees seeks to "de-unionize"), these events, for the most part, have been prompted, not by player dissatisfaction, but by a desire to open the doors to an antitrust suit unencumbered by the labor exemption.

Given the fact that an overwhelming preponderance of employers will not voluntarily recognize a union, the leagues' willingness to dispense with their election prerogative to embrace collective bargaining with open arms may seem perplexing. Yet, considering the aforementioned modest demands and casual nature of these players associations in their embryonic stages, the owners never contemplated that true trade unionism would blossom in their respective sports. Ironically, as mentioned above, the evolution of unionization among professional athletes has taken a tortuous path through which unions that at one point presented owners with a formidable force in all matters concerning players' conditions of employment now serve as precious insulation from the reach of the antitrust laws, at least in matters involving labor market restraints. *See Brown v. Pro-Football, Inc.*, 518 U.S. 231 (1996). A recent fiasco involving the Arena Football League and the machinations that the league ownership employed to stimulate unionization provides a glowing illustration. A vivid account of this series of events is contained in the Notes and Questions following the *Clarett* case in Chapter 9, Part VI, *supra*.

(B) The Appropriate Bargaining Unit

Prior to the holding of an election, the NLRB must determine the appropriateness of the bargaining unit sought. That is, the petitioning labor organization must designate the unit of employees that it purports to represent. For example, at a typical manufacturing facility, the union: (1) may seek to represent all production and maintenance employees within the plant facility; (2) may attempt to narrow that unit to a segment of the production and maintenance employees; or (3) may endeavor to broaden that unit to encompass other employer facilities within the area. The designation of the unit and the employer's response (and the litigation that often ensues) may have a profound impact on the eventual determination of whether the union represents a majority. Some schools of thought suggest that employers should attempt to convince the NLRB to certify the broadest possible unit because it would render the union's efforts to organize and achieve majority status more difficult. The obvious fly in the ointment is that, if the employer should then lose the election, the union will represent an even greater number of employees than it might have otherwise.

Frequently, the employer and petitioning union will stipulate to a particular bargaining unit. Often, the employer's stipulation is exchanged for concessions by the union in terms of the length of time between the petition and the election, the place and hours of the election, etc. When the parties are unable to agree on a unit designation, the NLRB will make the ultimate decision. In ascertaining the appropriateness of a particular bargaining unit, the NLRB will consider several factors to determine whether the employees involved have a sufficient "community of interest" (*i.e.*, commonality of supervision, similarity of wage scale and benefits structure, vacations programs, wearing of uniforms, common cafeteria privileges, similarity of skills, employee preferences, the extent of union organization, etc.). *See* HARDIN at 592–93.

With the exception of the North American Soccer League, professional sports has seen no unit determinations made by the NLRB. The collective bargaining has been conducted on a league-wide basis (*i.e.*, the entire sport, as in Major League Baseball, the National Football League, etc.). The players comprise one bargaining unit; this unit does not include umpires or other employees. It is difficult to assess who has benefitted most from the league unit configuration. On the one hand, it could be argued that the larger unit benefits the players because it stabilizes the bargaining and minimizes the possibility of fragmentation and piecemeal depletion of the unit by decertification or general disinterest. On the other hand, it is possible that gains secured on a team-by-team or other smaller unit basis could exceed those advances secured as a larger unit because each settlement would raise the floor for future negotiations. If the bargaining were staggered, the various units could exert economic pressure upon the employer/owners in a whipsaw fashion.

In terms of labor management harmony and long-term peace, it appears as though the larger unit is the most advantageous. Yet, interesting questions have arisen regarding possible variations in the existing bargaining unit structure. While not a mandatory subject of bargaining, the unit size and composition could be renegotiated by the parties as a "permissive subject of bargaining." A permissive subject is a matter that is within the ambit of allowable bargaining but is not a subject that the parties are required by law to discuss. *See NLRB v. American Nat'l. Ins. Co.,* 343 U.S. 395 (1952); Section 8(d) of the NLRA, 29 U.S.C. §158(d). *See also* Part VIII(B), below. Further, the NLRB could alter the existing unit through a unit clarification or other procedural device that provides the agency with an opportunity to revisit an earlier unit determination or stipulation.

Among the possible unit configurations that a new determination could bring would be "all players on a team," "all pitchers," "all offensive players," and various other permutations and combinations reflecting the pockets of common interest. This possibility is not so bizarre when one considers that, in other contexts, players have banded together to promote their self interests. The development of NFL Quarterback Club, Inc. in which several NFL quarterbacks joined together with NFL Properties to market themselves and their licensed products as a group, is but one illustration. The rationale supporting the smaller units obviously would be that the players would still derive a measure of strength from being part of a collective, but would not be saddled with the idiosyncratic concerns of other players with whom they share only peripheral interests.

The foregoing possibilities presuppose that the employing entity is continuing to negotiate on a multi-employer basis. Even in the team-by-team unit, the players could continue to bargain with a multi-team employer. The same holds true for the more specialized, boutique-type units discussed above. Yet, as we saw in Chapter 9, particularly the *Brown* court's extensive treatment of, and homage to, league-wide negotiations, multi-employer bargaining generally is consensual unless the nature of the employing entity is such that a joint-employer bargaining arrangement is the only appropriate device. *See North American Soccer League v. NLRB*, 613 F.2d 1379 (5th Cir. 1980). *See also, WJA Realty Ltd. Partnership*, 310 NLRB 862 (1993); *Major League Rodeo, Inc.*, 246 NLRB 743 (1979).

Assuming the existence of a voluntarily established multi-employer bargaining group, members of that group may withdraw at certain points in time. Absent unusual circumstances, such withdrawal generally will not be permitted during negotiations. The employer seeking to escape sustains a substantial burden in terms of proving unusual circumstances. For example, a sharply divided Supreme Court has held that such unusual circumstances do not include an impasse in negotiation, a fairly significant event in other respects. *See Charles D. Bonanno Linen Service v. NLRB*, 454 U.S. 404 (1982). *See further Sheet Metal Workers Local 104 v. Simpson Sheet Metal*, 954 F.2d 554 (9th Cir. 1992); *Action Electric Inc. v. IBEW Local 292*, 856 F.2d 1062 (8th Cir. 1988). *See also Luterbach Constr.*, 315 NLRB 976 (1994).

At any rate, the existence of this withdrawal possibility multiplies the number of potential unit structures that could be formed. For example, if the NLRB did not conclude as a matter of labor law that the teams constituted an inseparable single or joint employer, then each team could conceivably withdraw from the larger unit and bargain with players on its own. Likewise, the union could partially withdraw from group bargaining and negotiate with one employer on behalf of certain employees, but continue to bargain on a multi-employer basis on behalf of the remainder. The problems expand exponentially where a group of players want team-by-team bargaining but neither the union nor the employer is willing to withdraw from the larger bargaining configuration. In this situation, the players may have a host of options, including decertification, that would trigger the NLRB's representation procedures and resurrect the initial unit determination. *See further* JOHN C. WEISTART & CYM W. LOWELL, THE LAW OF SPORTS at §6.04, 792–800 (1979), where the authors provide a comprehensive and thought-provoking analysis of the appropriate bargaining units in professional sports. *See further* Douglas Leslie, *Multi-Employer Bargaining Rules*, 75 VA. L. REV. 241 (1989).

(C) The Election

If the NLRB honors the petition and reaches a unit determination, it will direct that an election be held, normally within a three to four week period following the determination of the unit questions. During the period between filing of the petition and the election, often called the "critical period", both the union and management have opportunities to persuade employees to vote in a certain way. During this period, there are strict rules governing the conduct of election campaigning. *See Dal-Tex Optical Co.*, 137 NLRB 1782 (1962); *General Shoe Corp.*, 77 NLRB 124 (1948). Violations of such rules could constitute unfair labor practices or be the basis for objections that result in an order for a new election or, in extreme cases, an order for the employer to bargain. *See NLRB v. Gissel Packing Co.*, 395 U.S. 575 (1969); *see also* Part VIII(C), below.

(D) Conducting the Election

Typically, the election is conducted by agents of the NLRB by secret ballot. The petitioning union must secure votes from 50% plus one of the employees voting to be certified as collective bargaining representative ("tie goes to the employer", so to speak). Those employees deemed eligible have the opportunity to vote for or against the labor organization (including any intervening labor organizations that may appear on the ballot). Any employee who is not on the eligible voters list but still seeks to vote may be challenged by management, the union, or the NLRB representatives. For more information on voter eligibility and voting procedures, see HARDIN at 549–60.

(E) Certification of Election Results

Once the election results are tallied, the NLRB will certify such results and declare a winner. Within seven days of the election, either side may file objections to the conduct of the election and contest the election results. If neither side files objections, then the tally will be deemed final. If objections to the election are filed, the NLRB's Regional Director for the affected Regional Office will conduct an investigation of the allegedly objectionable conduct. This investigation may also be accompanied by unfair labor practice proceedings (discussed below) when the objectionable conduct rises to the level of activity prohibited by Section 8 of the NLRA. As a result of these objections and/or unfair labor practice charges, the election results will either be sustained or they will be overturned. If the election results are overturned, the NLRB will direct that a new election be held. If an employer's conduct is deemed to be so outrageous and pervasive as to preclude a meaningful employee choice in a second election, the employer may be ordered to bargain with the union notwithstanding the fact that the employer was successful in the election. *See further NLRB v. Gissel Packing Co.*, 395 U.S. 575 (1969). Either party may appeal the Regional Director's or Administrative Law Judge's decision, as the case may be, by filing exceptions with the Board in Washington, D.C. After all appeals have been exhausted, the election results will be certified. There is little recourse to the courts in a representation case. *See Leedom v. Kyne*, 358 U.S. 184 (1958). However, the results in an unfair labor practice case may be appealed to the NLRB in Washington, D.C., the appropriate United States Court of Appeals, and the United States Supreme Court. For a thorough update on the NLRB's approach to pre-election misconduct, see THEODORE ST. ANTOINE, CHARLES B. CRAVER AND MARION G. CRAIN, LABOR RELATIONS LAW, CASES AND MATERIALS (11TH ED. 2005).

(F) The One-Year Waiting Period

No election may be held within one year after a valid unsuccessful election has been held among employees in the same or broader bargaining unit. The rationale for this rule is to protect employers from constant organizing attempts by the same union or several different unions with respect to the same group or groups of employees. *See Brooks v. NLRB*, 348 U.S. 96 (1954).

(G) Impact of Unionization Once a Union Has Been Certified as Collective Bargaining Representative

If a union becomes the exclusive collective bargaining representative, management loses all prerogative to make decisions regarding wages, hours, or working conditions in a unilateral fashion. All matters dealing with such "mandatory subjects" must be discussed with the union prior to implementation. *See generally NLRB v. Katz*, 369 U.S. 736 (1962).

If the union and employer bargain in good faith to an impasse, the employer may unilaterally implement terms or conditions that have been discussed and are consistent with proposals exchanged between the parties. *See generally* Hardin at 840–47; *see infra*, Part VIII(B). Further, there are circumstances that may justify an employer's by-passing the exclusive representative and bargaining directly with individual employees. *See J.I.Case Co. v. NLRB*, 321 U.S. 332 (1944); *Midland Broadcasting Co.*, 93 NLRB 455 (1951); *see further* George Schatzki, *Majority Rule, Exclusive Representation, and the Interests of Individual Workers: Should Exclusivity be Abolished?*, 123 U. Pa. L. Rev. 897 (1975). For example, drug testing programs for professional athletes are mandatory subjects of bargaining because they constitute "condition(s) of employment." *Johnson-Bateman Co.*, 295 NLRB No. 26 (1986). Yet, under certain circumstances, individual athletes, even though represented by a players association, may be able to negotiate individual covenants with management regarding substance use and testing. *See* Part VIII(B), below. *See further* Edward Rippey, *Contractual Freedom Over Substance-Related Issues in Major League Baseball*, 1 Sports Law. J. 143 (1994). Other issues worthy of discussion include whether league owners must bargain over decisions to relocate a franchise, decrease the number of teams in a league, etc. *See, e.g., First National Maintenance Corp. v. NLRB*, 452 U.S. 661 (1981); *Dubuque Packing Co.*, 303 NLRB 386 (1991), *enf. sub. nom. Food & Commercial Workers Local 150-A v. NLRB*, 1 F.3d 24 (D.C.Cir. 1993). *See also* Bryan Day, *Labor Pains: Why Contraction Is Not The Solution to Major League Baseball's Competitive Balance Problems*, 12 Fordham Intell. Prop. Media & Ent. L.J. 521 (2001); *Metropolitan Sports Facilities Commission v. Minnesota Twins Partnership*, 638 N.W. 2d 214 (Minn. 2002).

(H) Union Security and Right To Work

The "closed shop", which required union membership as a condition of employment, is now illegal. However, the union and agency shops, through which an employer and union agree that an employee must join the union within a designated period of time, or tender periodic dues, is permissible. Still, Section 14(b) of the Act allows states to prohibit "union" and "agency" shops even when the parties would be willing to enter agreement on some type of "union security." *See* 29 U.S.C. §164(b). *See Retail Clerks Local 1625 v. Schermerhorn*, 373 U.S. 746 (1963). At present, 22 states have adopted right to work legislation outlawing "union" or "agency" shops. Further, while employers can be required to enforce union security clauses by disciplining recalcitrant employees, Section 8(a)(3) declares that no employee may be terminated for reasons other than the failure to pay periodic dues. 29 U.S.C. §158(a)(3). Thus, in terms of the employees' job security, there is no functional difference between a union and agency shop arrangement. Of course, distinctions may still exist in other areas, such as where membership is a prerequisite to eligibility for certain union benefits or where internal union discipline is concerned. Union security provisions are mandatory subjects of bargaining requiring management's good faith negotiation. *See NLRB v. General Motors Corp.*, 373 U.S. 734 (1963).

The "right to work" issue has interesting ramifications in the area of professional sports. For example, if a team practices exclusively in a right to work state but palys its home games in a non-right to work jurisdiction, which state's laws will determine whether union security is permitted? A recent decision, arising in the aftermath of the controversial NFL-NFLPA settlement that resulted in the 1993 collective bargaining agreement, assessed the applicability of Virginia's right to work laws to the Washington Redskins football club and its players. *NFLPA v. Pro-Football, Inc.*, 857 F. Supp. 71 (D.D.C. 1994). The court reasoned that the number of hours expended at the Virginia practice facility outweighed the city of "affiliation," and therefore applied Virginia law:

> The NFLPA may have some legitimate equitable arguments about the financial significance of the games that are played in the District of Columbia, as opposed to the practices that occur in Virginia. Nevertheless, when the Redskins players get up in the morning to go to work, they usually go to Redskins Park [in Virginia] not RFK Stadium [in Washington, D.C.].

Id. at 78. Thus, the court found that an earlier arbitration decision was incorrect and that, under Virginia's right to work law, Redskins players had no obligation to join the NFLPA or pay dues pursuant to the collective bargaining agreement's union security clause. This decision, which is discussed in greater detail in Chapter 16, adopts an approach that could, in certain circumstances, permit players to fragment the union and threaten its stability as bargaining representative. It is noteworthy that this potential inter-jurisdictional tension has surfaced in other contexts, such as application of workers' compensation or taxation of income earned by athletes while playing games "on the road." *See, e.g., Pro-Football, Inc. v. District of Columbia Dep't. of Employment Servs.*, 588 A.2d 275 (D.C. 1991).

VIII. Unfair Labor Practices ("ULPs")

(A) Unfair Labor Practice Procedures

(1) Charge Filed

Any person may file an unfair labor practice charge with the NLRB, provided that the charge is filed within six (6) months of the conduct giving rise to the allegations. This charge is normally filed in one of the NLRB's Regional Offices.

(2) Determination of Merit

Once a charge has been filed, the NLRB Regional Director conducts an investigation to determine whether or not the charge has merit. During this investigation, agents of the NLRB may visit the employer (or union) to ask questions, take affidavits, and gather relevant information. If the investigation shows the charge to be meritorious, the Regional Director will issue a complaint. If not, the charge will be dismissed. The dismissal of an unfair labor practice charge may be appealed to the NLRB's Office of Appeals in Washington, D.C.

(3) Hearing

If a complaint is issued, the General Counsel's office of the NLRB would represent the charging party in an evidentiary hearing before an Administrative Law Judge. As stated above, the charging party may participate in the prosecution of the complaint. The hearing will approach a formal trial without a jury. Although there is limited discovery, the Federal Rules of Evidence are applicable, and subpoenas *ad testificandum* and subpoenas *duces tecum* may be obtained.

(4) Administrative Law Judge's Decision

After the hearing, the Administrative Law Judge will issue findings of fact and conclusions of law. Either party may appeal the Administrative Law Judge's decision to the NLRB in Washington, D.C. If either party is dissatisfied with the NLRB's disposition of the appeal, that party may seek review in the appropriate United States court of appeals and, in rare instances, may find its way to the United States Supreme Court.

(5) Appeal

If the Board petitions a court of appeals for enforcement or if a person aggrieved by a Board order seeks review by such court, the Board's findings of fact, if supported by substantial evidence on the record, will be conclusive. 29 U.S.C. §160(e) and (f). The initiation of a petition for enforcement or other appeal does not operate as a stay of the Board order, unless such stay has been ordered by the court. 29 U.S.C. §160(g).

(B) Unfair Labor Practices—Prohibited Employer Conduct

The following outline will, in a very broad sense, list the various types of employer and union activity prohibited by the NLRA. *See generally* 29 U.S.C. §§157, 158(a)(1)-(a)(5), 158(b)(1)-(b)(7). The prohibited conduct delineated below is, in common labor law parlance, often characterized by shorthand reference to section numbers of the Act. For example, more often than not, "interference with protected rights" is referred to simply as an 8(a)(1) violation. Thus, familiarity with this vernacular will facilitate one's ability to converse with members of the labor law community, most importantly the NLRB.

(1) Section 8(a)(1)—Interference with employees' right to organize and bargain collectively

The following employer conduct violates Section 8(a)(1) of the Act.

(a) Threatening to close a facility, discharge employees, discontinue benefits, or take similar reprisals against employees because of their union activities or affiliation. *See NLRB v. Gissel Packing Co.*, 395 U.S. 575 (1969); *see also AP Automotive Systems*, 333 NLRB 581 (2001).

(b) Interrogating employees about their union activities, affiliation, etc. Often, the most benign interrogations can constitute unfair labor practices. In theory, an interrogation is not *per se* unlawful; yet, the Board and the courts tend to view such activity in an extremely circumspect fashion. The rationale for such strict scrutiny over employee interrogations is that they frequently are the forerunners of retaliation by employers who suspect employees of union organizing activities. *See Struksnes Construction Co.*, 165 NLRB 1062 (1967); *Blue Flash Express, Inc.*, 109 NLRB 591 (1954). Employers may formally poll employees to ascertain whether a collective bargaining representative is still favored by a majority of employees provided that employer demonstrates it has a reasonable doubt, based on objective considerations, that the continued majority support exists. *See Allentown Mack Sales and Service v. NLRB*, 522 U.S 359 (1998).

(c) Promising to grant benefits or otherwise reward employees to discourage their participation in union activity or other protected concerted activities. This tack is often metaphorically referenced as the "fist inside of a velvet glove." *See NLRB v. Exchange Parts Co.*, 375 U.S. 405, 409 (1964); *NLRB v. Erie Resistor Corp.*, 373 U.S. 221 (1963); *NLRB v. Curwood, Inc.*, 397 F.3d 548 (7th Cir. 2005) (employer violated NLRB when it announced possible pension plan improvements but blamed union organizing activity for inability to implement the improvements).

(d) Surveilling or giving the impression of spying upon employees' union activities, such as meetings, informal discussions, etc. Again, this type of activity was often employed to identify union sympathizers and mark them for future recriminations. *See Consolidated Edison Co. v. NLRB*, 305 U.S. 197 (1938); *Timken Co. v. NLRB*, 171 LRRM 3215 (6th Cir. 2002); *Crown Cork and Seal Co., Inc.*, 254 NLRB 1340 (1981); *Idaho Egg Producers, Inc.*, 111 NLRB 93 (1955), *enforced*, 229 F.2d 821 (9th Cir. 1956).

Any activity constituting a violation of Sections 8(a)(2)-8(a)(5) is automatically and derivatively a violation of Section 8(a)(1). The rationale simply is that such unlawful activity cannot help but interfere with employees' fundamental right to organize and seek a collective bargaining representative (or refrain from same). *See generally* Samuel Estreicher, *Labor Reform in a World of Competitive Product Markets*, 69 CHI. KENT L. REV. 3 (1993); Robert J. Lalonde and Bernard D. Meltzer, *Hard Times for Unions: Another Look at the Significance of Employer Illegalities*, 58 U. CHI. L. REV. 953 (1991).

A classic example of these types of offenses in the professional sports arena would be an owner's threat to trade or release union activists or otherwise to alter their working conditions as a result of their concerted activity or desire to refrain from such activity. *See, e.g., Seattle Seahawks*, 292 NLRB 899 (1989), *aff'd sub nom, Nordstrom v. NLRB*, 984 F. 2d 479 (D.C.Cir.1993), covered in Chapter 15. The victims of this type of misconduct would typically be player representatives. Another example would be a promise to award a pay increase or some other arrangement that would reward a professional athlete for repudiating his or her collective bargaining representative.

(2) Section 8(a)(2)—Domination and assistance

Employers can violate Section 8(a)(2) of the NLRB in numerous ways, including creating or controlling a particular labor organization, playing favorites or supporting one union over another, or destroying or endangering the independence of a labor organization. Differentiating a legitimate expression of preference from unlawful support, domination, or control is extremely difficult. The purpose of the section is to insure that employees' selection of a bargaining representative of their own choosing is unfettered. Obviously, an employer's "sweetheart" arrangement with a union in derogation of the employees' choice violates the letter and spirit of this provision. Concerns about employer support for, or domination of, a union stem from the evils that arise with "company unions" or other groups that purport to represent employees but in reality are instruments of management. *See NLRB v. Pennsylvania Greyhound Lines, Inc.*, 303 U.S. 261 (1938). At the same time, the NLRA in no way should be interpreted to discourage cooperative programs between management and labor that are implemented to promote greater productivity for the employer and better wages, hours, and working conditions for the workforce. *See* Joseph B. Ryan, *The Encouragement of Labor-Management Cooperation: Improving American Productivity Through Revision of the National Labor Relations Act,* 40 U.C.L.A. L. Rev. 571 (1992); Charles C. Jackson, *An Alternative To Unionization And The Wholly Unorganized Shop: A Legal Basis For Sanctioning Joint Employer-Employee Committees And Increasing Employee Free Choice,* 28 Syracuse L. Rev. 809 (1977). *But see Electromation, Inc.,* 309 NLRB 990 (1992), *enforced,* 35 F.3d 1148 (7th Cir. 1994) and *Crown Cork & Seal,* 334 NLRB 699 (2001). *See also* Madelyn C. Squire, *Electromation: A Metaphor for the Ills of the NLRA—Is A Representation Standard A Cure,* 73 U. Det. Mercy L. Rev. 209 (1996).

There are various ways through which an employing entity can violate Section 8(a)(2) in a sports context. A classic illustration, although one which did not result in unfair labor practice charges, was the manner in which the Major League Baseball Players Association was treated in its infancy. There, baseball ownership played a pivotal role in the selection of the union's executive director, contributed funds to the association, and otherwise blatantly interfered in the conduct of that labor organization's activities to a point at which it was little more than a "company union." *See* Marvin Miller, A Whole Different Ballgame: The Sport and Business of Baseball 68 (1991). Ironically, Section 8(a)(2) was specifically designed to eliminate the company union—a labor organization that, in effect, was owned lock, stock, and barrel by the employer. This type of arrangement was evident in the early days of labor-management relations in Major League Baseball. *See* Dworkin at 28.

An example of possible 8(a)(2) conduct in the professional football arena is found in the unfair labor practice charges filed by the Philadelphia Eagles against the NFL and the NFLPA following a spate of successful player antitrust lawsuits against the NFL. The players had "decertified" the union as their exclusive bargaining representative in order to remove the labor exemption and to pave the way for antitrust litigation over various league restrictions on player mobility. As a result of these lawsuits and potential future litigation, the NFL recognized the significant risk of substantial monetary liability. Consequently, the NFL sought to insulate itself by negotiating a new collective bargaining agreement and restoring the labor exemption that had been rendered inoperative as a result of the NFLPA's "decertification."

The Eagles alleged that the NFL and NFLPA had bargained and reached agreement in derogation of the employees' Section 7 rights. That is, the NFL had achieved its objective by bargaining with the NFLPA while it was still decertified and not a representative of a majority of the players, thus violating Sections 8(a)(2) and 8(b)(1)(A). In this situation, the fact that a majority of the players eventually re-selected the NFLPA as bargaining representative is irrelevant. The status at the point that negotiating begins determines the legitimacy of the bargaining. *See ILGWU v. NLRB*, 366 U.S. 731 (1961); *Majestic Weaving Co.*, 147 NLRB 859 (1964), *enforcement denied*, 355 F.2d 854 (2d Cir. 1966). Likewise, the owners' good faith, but erroneous, belief that the union enjoyed majority status would not insulate them from liability under Section 8(a)(2). *Id. See* Shant H. Challan, *Fourth and Goal: Player Restraint in Professional Sports, A Look Back and A Look Ahead*, 67 St. John's L. Rev. 593, 613–20 (1993). When Eagles owner Norman Braman sold the club to entertainment mogul Jeffrey Lurie, the unfair labor practice charges were withdrawn. Yet, there persists serious doubt as to whether the seven year NFL-NFLPA agreement negotiated in 1993, which has been extended several times and is still in effect, rests on a proper foundation. *See* Robert A. McCormick, *Interference on Both Sides: The Case Against the NFL-NFLPA Contract*, 53 Wash. & Lee L. Rev. 397 (1996). *See further* Chapter 15, where the Notes and Questions following the *Seattle Seahawks* case revisits this incident in more detail. This issue was also treated in Chapter 9 relative to the decertification efforts to remove the labor exemption as a bar to the prosecution of the players' antitrust claims. Any doubts surrounding an employer's willingness to absorb the burdens of a collective obligation to forestall possible antitrust violations were removed recently in a bizarre series of events involving the Arena Football League. As related in Chapters 9 and 15, the owners there exhausted every effort imaginable to develop a collective bargaining relationship with a hand-picked labor organization to insure insulation from potential antitrust litigation. The veritable control that the owners attempted to establish over the representation process spawned unfair labor practices alleging violations of Sections 8(a)(1) and (2).

(3) Section 8(a)(3)—Discrimination

Employers engaging in discrimination (including demotion, discharge, reduction in pay, transfer, etc.) against employees to encourage or discourage their membership in any labor organization violate Section 8(a)(3). Likewise, employers who refuse to hire qualified applicants based upon their union activity or affiliation contravene the NLRA. Oftentimes, employers will engage in proscribed conduct by denying economic strikers the opportunity to return to work when available positions exist. *See Laidlaw Corp.*, 171 NLRB 1366 (1966), *enforced*, 414 F.2d 99 (7th Cir. 1969), *cert. denied*, 397 U.S. 920 (1970). *See also NLRB v. Great Dane Trailers*, 388 U.S. 26 (1967). Another illustration of an employer's across-the-board disparate treatment of employees involves the "runaway shop" or other operational change in which the employer discontinues or modifies part of its business to avoid continuation of a bargaining relationship with the union and the satisfaction of duties attending such relationship. *See generally Darlington Textile Workers v. Darlington Manufacturing Co.*, 380 U.S. 263 (1965); *Garwin Corp.*, 153 NLRB 664 (1965), *enforced in part*, 374 F.2d 295 (D.C. Cir. 1967).

In order to establish a case of discriminatory treatment under 8(a)(3), the General Counsel must prove that the employer had knowledge of union activity and manifested some type of anti-union motive. *See Yellow Ambulance Serv.,* 342 NLRB No. 77 (2004). Difficulties often arise when the employer offers ostensibly legitimate reasons for its conduct other than, or in addition to, anti-union motives. In such pretextual or mixed motive contexts, the NLRB attempts to determine whether or not an employer's motives were based on anti-union animus and, if so, whether the allegedly unlawful conduct would have occurred notwithstanding such anti-union sentiment. *See Wright Line,* 251 NLRB 1980, *enforced,* 662 F.2d 899 (1st Cir. 1981), *cert. denied,* 455 U.S. 989 (1982). For a discussion of *Wright Line* and its application in a sports context see Jeffrey Goore, *Discriminatory Discharge in a Sports Context: A Reassessment of the Burden of Proof and Remedies Under the National Labor Relations Act,* 51 FORDHAM L. REV. 615 (1984). Although there is no doubt that a demonstration of anti-union animus is a critical component of a Section 8(a)(3) violation, such a showing is not theoretically necessary to establish a violation of Section 8(a)(1). These assumptions create an interesting question as to whether the General Counsel who alleges that certain discriminatory conduct independently violates Section 8(a)(1) needs to show an anti-union motive. *See* Note 3 following the *NFL Management Council* case, 309 NLRB 78 (1992), Chapter 15. *See also NLRB v. Burnup & Sims, Inc.,* 379 U.S. 21 (1964); Walter Oberer, *The Scienter Factor in Sections 8(a)(1) and (3) of the Labor Act: Of Balancing, Hostile Motive, Dogs and Tails,* 52 CORNELL L. Q. 491 (1967).

A typical example of an 8(a)(3) violation in professional sports is a decision to trade, reassign, or release a professional athlete as a result of his preference for a labor organization or service as player representative. This type of retaliation has occurred after player representatives voiced pro-union sentiments regarding negotiations, schedules, striking activities, etc. *See Seattle Seahawks,* 292 NLRB 899 (1989), *aff'd, Nordstrom v. NLRB,* 984 F. 2d 479 (D.C.Cir.1993). With regard to the aforementioned discriminatory treatment of strikers, the NLRB recently affirmed an Administrative Law Judge's decision finding that the league's refusal to honor in a timely fashion the players' unconditional offer to return to work was motivated by anti-union animus and was in violation of Section 8(a)(3). A substantial backpay order resulted. *See National Football League and The National Football League Players Ass'n,* 309 NLRB 78 (1992). These cases are fully explored in Chapter 15.

(4) Section 8(a)(4)—Retaliation

As a corollary to Section 8(a)(3), Section 8(a)(4) proscribes employer reprisals against employees who have availed themselves of the NLRB's processes. Essentially, Section 8(a)(4) prohibits any employer discriminatory treatment against employees who file charges, give testimony before the NLRB, or otherwise cooperate with NLRB investigative efforts. *See Pickle Bill's, Inc.,* 224 NLRB 413 (1976). Again, a classic 8(a)(4) violation would involve trading, reassigning, or otherwise discriminatorily treating a player representative or other employee who has attempted to cooperate with the NLRB's investigative or litigation efforts. To date, there has been little litigation involving sports ownership's reprisals against players for utilizing the offices of the NLRB or asserting rights arising under the NLRA.

(5) Section 8(a)(5)—Refusal to bargain in good faith

Again, when a union is certified as the exclusive collective bargaining representative of employees within a particular bargaining unit, the employer must bargain with that representative about all matters involving wages, hours, or working conditions—mandatory subjects of bargaining. *See* 29 U.S.C. §158(d). While it is not necessary that employers actually make concessions or accede to specific demands, a persistent unwillingness to accept any union proposal is evidence of bad faith. *See generally NLRB v. Reed & Prince Manufacturing Co.*, 96 NLRB 850 (1951), *enforced*, 205 F.2d 131 (1st Cir. 1953), *cert. denied*, 346 U.S. 887 (1953). The problem of determining what is a mandatory bargaining subject is particularly vexing, especially because the term "conditions of employment" is extremely broad and quite vague. *See* 29 U.S.C. §158(d); *Ford Motor Co. v. NLRB*, 441 U.S. 488 (1979). In a sports context, numerous questions have arisen regarding management decisions that ostensibly implicate mandatory subjects (*e.g.*, artificial turf, television timeouts, salary arbitration, etc.). As discussed below, these issues have surfaced both in terms of management's unilateral action and its failure to furnish relevant information about these topics to the players associations during negotiations.

In addition to mandatory subjects, there are permissive and illegal subjects of bargaining. Permissive subjects are matters over which the parties may agree to bargain but have no statutory obligation. *See NLRB v. Borg Warner Corp., Wooster Div.*, 356 U.S. 342 (1958) (*e.g.*, internal union matters, interest arbitration, etc.) Thus, parties may not insist to impasse on the inclusion of a permissive subject. The agreement upon a permissive subject and its inclusion in a collective bargaining agreement does not alter its character; it remains a permissive subject. *See Allied Chemical & Alkali Workers Local No. 1 v. Pittsburgh Plate Glass Co.*, 404 U.S. 157 (1971). Illegal subjects are matters about which the parties may not bargain at all (*e.g.*, "closed shop" clause). *See* HARDIN at 949–54.

As will be addressed in Chapter 15, employers may run afoul of their bargaining obligations in several respects, including: (1) engaging in surface or sham bargaining with the employees' certified collective bargaining representative, or pursuing dilatory tactics to protract negotiations unnecessarily, *see Crane Company*, 244 NLRB 103 (1979); *Irvington Motors Inc.*, 147 NLRB 565 (1964), *enforced*, 343 F.2d 759 (3rd Cir. 1965); (2) bypassing the collective bargaining representative by taking unilateral action regarding wages, hours or working conditions without consultation with the union, *see NLRB v. Katz*, 369 U.S. 736 (1962); *NLRB v. Insurance Agents' Union*, 361 U.S. 477 (1960); (3) dealing with individual employees directly without regard to the collective bargaining agreement or the collective bargaining representative, *see J.I. Case v. NLRB*, 321 U.S. 332 (1944); *but see, Americare Pine Lodge Nursing and Rehab. Center v. NLRB*, 164 F. 3d 867(4th Cir. 1999); and (4) refusing to furnish relevant information necessary for the collective bargaining representative to process grievances, conduct arbitrations, or engage in collective bargaining. *See NLRB v. Truitt Manufacturing Co.*, 351 U.S. 149 (1956); *Liquor Indus. Bargaining Group*, 333 NLRB 1219 (2001). Generally, an employer may engage in "hard bargaining" so long as it is not merely "going through the motions" and subverting the bargaining process by *de facto* insisting on proposals that guarantee virtual control over wages, hours, and working conditions. *See NLRB v. American National Insurance Co.*, 343 U.S. 395 (1952); *Public Serv. Co. of Oklahoma v. NLRB*, 318 F. 3d 1173 (10th Cir. 2003).

With regard to unilateral changes, post-impasse implementation is permissible, provided that the matter has been bargained about in good faith and the change is no more favorable than proposals offered to the union during negotiations. *See Litton Business Systems, Inc. v. NLRB*, 501 U.S. 190 (1991); *Colorado Ute Elec. Ass'n v. NLRB*, 939 F.2d 1392 (10th Cir. 1991); *Atlas Tack Corp.*, 226 NLRB 222 (1976), *enforced* 559 F.2d 1201 (1st Cir. 1977). The difficulty with this approach rests with determining a precise point at which impasse occurs. *See Taft Broadcasting*, 163 NLRB 475 (1967). It is noteworthy that any unilateral change made under the mistaken, albeit good faith, notion that an impasse occurred will violate Section 8(a)(5). *See Columbia Portland Cement*, 294 NLRB 410 (1989). In ascertaining whether the parties have reached impasse on an issue or set of issues, several factors will be considered, including statements of the parties, nature of the issues in dispute, number, duration and timing of negotiating sessions, evidence of anti-union animus, etc. *See* HARDIN at 918–25; Peter Guyon Earle, *The Impasse Doctrine*, 64 CHI. KENT L. REV. 407 (1988). Even where impasse has not occurred, unusually compelling circumstances may justify an employer's unilateral implementation of changes in employment conditions, but such an occurrence is rare. *See Raleigh Water Heater Mfg. Co.*, 136 NLRB 76 (1962); *see also NLRB v. Pinkston-Hollar Construction Services*, 954 F.2d 306 (5th Cir. 1992).

At times, an employer may be compelled to assume the collective bargaining obligations of a predecessor employer. Whether a purchasing employer is a "successor" who is required to bargain with the incumbent union will turn on several factors, including the extent to which the new workforce is comprised of the predecessor's employees. *See Fall River Dyeing and Finishing Corp. v. NLRB*, 482 U.S. 27 (1987); *NLRB v. Burns International Security Services, Inc.*, 406 U.S. 272 (1972). In rare circumstances, the successor may even be bound by the predecessor's collective bargaining agreement. *See, e.g., John Wiley & Sons, Inc. v. Livingston*, 376 U.S. 543 (1964). For recent treatments of the successorship doctrine, see David M. Lester, *Reopening a Warn Issue: A Two-Step Approach to Determining an Employer's Obligation to Recognize a Union When It Reopens a Plant*, 22 PEPP. L. REV. 467 (1995); Wilson McLeod, *Rekindling Labor Law Successorship in an Area of Decline*, 11 HOFSTRA LAB. L. J. 271 (1996); Norman J. Fry, *The Decontextualization of Labor Relations in Successorship Cases: Williams Enterprises v. NLRB and Sullivan Industries v. NLRB*, 61 GEO. WASH. L. REV. 1616 (1994). Of importance is the NLRB's on- and off-again approach to the question of whether a union enjoys a honeymoon period after a succession in which the new employer must bargain. The NLRB's most recent pronouncement is that an incumbent union commands only a rebuttable presumption of majority status *vis-à-vis* the successor employer. *M.V. Transp.*, 337 NLRB 770 (2002). Thus, the NLRB will entertain an election petition filed by the employees of the successor.

Further, in certain circumstances, a union may waive its status as exclusive bargaining agent and thereby permit limited individual bargaining (*e.g.*, where there are substantial variations in skill levels). *See generally J.I.Case Co. v. NLRB*, 321 U.S. 332 (1944); *Midland Broadcasting Co.*, 93 NLRB 455 (1951). There also may be situations in which certain employees, by mutual agreement, are "red-circled" or designated for special treatment apart from the remainder of the bargaining unit. In such cases, the union's consent permits the employer to bypass the employees' exclusive collective bargaining representative. Also, in individual contract, in certain circumstances, may be enforceable in state court notwithstanding the subsequent negotiation of a collective bargaining agreement that covers the affected employee. *Caterpillar Inc. v. Williams*, 482 U.S. 386 (1987).

A union may also surrender its right to demand good faith bargaining by its expressed or implied agreement. The expressed waiver often assumes the form of a zipper clause, which identifies the contract as the complete and only agreement covering unit employees' wages, hours, and working conditions, or a broad management rights clause, which vests the prerogative to make decisions affecting such matters in the employer. *See generally* HARDIN at 934–51; *GTE Automatic Elec., Inc.*, 261 NLRB 1491 (1982); *LeRoy Machine Co.*, 147 NLRB 1431 (1964). *See also Martinsville Nylon Employ-*

ees' Council v. NLRB, 969 F.2d 1263 (D.C. Cir. 1992); *Milwaukee Spring Div. of Illinois Coil Spring Co.*, 268 NLRB 601 (1984), *aff'd sub. nom. UAW v. NLRB*, 765 F.2d 175 (D.C. Cir. 1985). These waivers must be clear and unmistakable. HARDIN, *id.*; *Tide Water Associated Oil Co.*, 85 NLRB 1096 (1949). The union's willingness to cede its right to bargain over certain mandatory subjects may also occur through the parties' negotiation history. *See Daniel I. Burk Enterprises*, 313 NLRB 1263 (1994); *Proctor Mfg. Corp.*, 131 NLRB 1166 (1961). *See also* Keith Hylton, *An Economic Theory of the Duty to Bargain*, 83 GEO. L. J. 19 (1994). An interesting collateral issue centers on whether an employer can insist to impasse on a clause conferring broad management prerogatives. *See NLRB v. American National Insurance*, 343 U.S. 395 (1952); *compare Stuart Radiator Core Mfg. Co.*, 173 NLRB 125 (1968).

There are numerous illustrations of the above-referenced types of refusals to bargain in the context of professional sports, and in several instances, the leagues have been found in violation of the NLRA. In particular, the NFLPA and the MLBPA have sued management (or grieved under the collective bargaining agreement) for failing to furnish relevant information during collective bargaining, *Silverman v. Major League Baseball Player Relations Comm., Inc.*, 516 F. Supp. 588 (S.D.N.Y. 1981)); *NFL Management Council and NFLPA*, NLRB Case No. 2-CA-13379 (June 30, 1976)); for bypassing the collective bargaining agent in the area of commissioner/owner fines for on-the-field fighting, *see NFLPA v. NLRB*, 503 F.2d 12 (1974)); and for unilaterally implementing changes in wages, hours, or working conditions. *Silverman v. Major League Baseball Player Relations Comm., Inc.*, 67 F.3d 1054 (2d Cir. 1995).

In most professional sports, the players associations have agreed to allow players and owners to negotiate individually over salary and for certain other special benefits where such "special covenants" do not result in any reduction in the gains secured by the collective bargaining agreement. For example, Article II of Major League Baseball's Collective Bargaining Agreement provides in pertinent part:

> The Clubs recognize the Association as the sole and exclusive collective bargaining agent for all Major League Players, and individuals who may become Major League Players during the term of this Agreement, with regard to all terms and conditions of employment, provided that an individual Player shall be entitled to negotiate in accordance with the provisions set forth in this Agreement, (1) an individual salary over and above the minimum requirements established by this Agreement and (2) Special Covenants to be included in an individual Uniform Player's Contract, which actually or potentially provide additional benefits to the Player.

With regard to such clauses, controversy may be generated by clubs and players negotiating special covenants that arguably cede benefits secured by the collective. *See In the Matter of Arbitration Between MLBPA and The Player Relations Comm., Inc.*, Grievance No. 80-18 (Goetz, Impartial Arbitrator, 1981). A persistent question has centered upon the validity of a special covenant that amounts to a club paying a player additional moneys or other significant compensation in exchange for that player's surrender of some benefit guaranteed by the collective bargaining agreement. The fear is that permitting this type of conduct will result in the employer's gradual "buy-out" of the labor contract and subversion of the collective bargaining relationship. This issue is addressed in Chapter 15.

In a recent development, the NLRB's General Counsel found reasonable cause to believe that Major League Baseball owners had violated Section 8(a)(5) of the NLRA by unilaterally implementing new terms governing player mobility and related issues. Although the owners had the right to take such action upon impasse, the General Counsel concluded that no impasse had been reached, thus invalidating the implementation. Specifically, the owners unilaterally implemented provisions regarding a salary cap, limitations on free agency, and elimination of salary arbitration. After the General Counsel had issued a complaint, the owners agreed to remove the salary cap. However, following the General Counsel's suspension of unfair labor practice proceedings, the owners unilaterally declared that salary arbitration would be eliminated and that certain free agency restrictions (including a revocation of a prohibition against collusive activity) would be resurrected. The General Counsel rejected the owners' position that such matters were not mandatory bargaining subjects and issued a complaint alleging that pre-impasse implementation without bargaining violated §8(a)(5) of the National Labor Relations Act.

The NLRB obtained an injunction requiring the owners to return to the *status quo ante* and negating the changes that the owners had established. The issuance of the injunction was affirmed by the Court of Appeals for the Second Circuit. *See Silverman v. Major League Baseball Player Relations Comm., Inc.*, 67 F.3d 1054 (2d Cir. 1995). As a result, the players, who had struck for over 200 days, made an unconditional offer to return to work, ending the strike. After approximately another eight months of bargaining, the NLBPA and Major League Baseball reached agreement on a five year collective bargaining agreement. This agreement contains no salary cap, but it does provide for a luxury tax penalizing teams that exceed a designated salary ceiling. It also provides for inter-league play, revenue sharing and a continuation of salary arbitration. *See* Chapter 16; *see also* Part IX(D), below. Several potential issues exist, but have never been fully litigated before the NLRB. The duty to bargain in good faith over drug testing, especially at a time when steroid abuse is a cutting edge controversy warrants attention. Finally, as touched upon earlier, a league's ability to contract and eliminate franchises and a team's ability to relocate profoundly impact employee working conditions but these concerns may be outweighed by the owner's need to conduct its business free from the constraints of the bargaining process. *See First National Maintenance Corp. v. NLRB*, 452 U.S. 661 (1981); *Dubuque Packing Co.*, 303 NLRB 386 (1991), *enf. sub. nom. Food & Commercial Workers Local 150-A v. NLRB*, 1 F.3d 24 (D.C. Cir. 1993); *Metropolitan Sports Facilities Commission v. Minnesota Twins Partnership*, 638 N.W. 2d 214 (2002).

(C) Employer Liability for Unfair Labor Practices

An employer who is found guilty of an unfair labor practice may be "punished" in a variety of ways, including the remedies discussed below.

(1) Backpay

In the case of an unlawful discharge or refusal to hire or reinstate (or, in the sports context, a trade, release, or reassignment), the employer may be liable for the amount of backpay (plus interest) that the employee would have received if he or she had not been discriminatorily and unlawfully treated. *See, e.g., Freeman Decorating Co.*, 288 NLRB 1235 (1988); *New Horizons for the Retarded, Inc.*, 283 NLRB 1173 (1987). Of course, any income earned in the interim may be set off against the total backpay that is due. *See Tubari, Ltd. v. NLRB*, 959 F.2d 451 (3d Cir. 1992); *see also F.W. Woolworth Co.*, 90 NLRB 289 (1950). However, unemployment benefits generally will not be part of the mitigation calculation. *See NLRB v. Gullet Gin Co.*, 340 U.S. 361 (1951). The Board generally will not award backpay or front pay to remedy a refusal to bargain. The rationale for the Board's restraint rests upon the premise that such a remedy would constitute setting the terms of an agreement, an exercise that is beyond the Board's province. *See Tiidee Products, Inc.*, 194 NLRB 1234 (1972), *enforced*, 502 F.2d 349 (D.C. Cir. 1974), *cert. denied*, 421 U.S. 991 (1995). But see HARDIN at 2531–47. *See further Virginia Concrete Co. v. NLRB*, 75 F.3d 974 (4th Cir. 1996).

(2) Reinstatement

An employer might be required by the NLRB to reinstate an employee who was found to have been illegally discharged, denied employment, or, in the sports context, traded or released, because of some union preference or for engaging in protected, concerted activities. *See* 29 U.S.C. §160(c). Often this requirement is much more onerous than economic liability because the employer is compelled to retain an employee that it, rightly or wrongly, deems to be unsatisfactory. *See Phelps Dodge Corp. v. NLRB*, 313 U.S. 177 (1941); *see also Sure-Tan, Inc.*, 277 NLRB 302 (1985); *Haberman Constr. Co.*, 236 NLRB 79, *enf'd*, 618 F.2d 288 (5th Cir. 1980).

(3) Bargaining Order

If an employer's pre-election conduct is so flagrant as to deprive employees of a free choice in an NLRB election, the employer might be ordered to bargain with the petitioning union—despite the election results. A "bargaining order" also will result if an employer has refused to bargain with a union that it ostensibly recognized or has by-passed a union certified as bargaining representative. *See NLRB v. Gissel Packing, Co.*, 395 U.S. 575 (1969).

(4) Rerun Election

Unlawful, pre-election conduct by an employer could result in the invalidation of election results and the direction of a new election. *See Caron Int'l.*, 246 NLRB 1120 (1979); *Lufkin Rule Co.*, 147 NLRB 341 (1964). Generally, such conduct must occur during the critical period between the filing of the petition and the holding of the election. *See Goodyear Tire & Rubber Co.*, 138 NLRB 453 (1962); *Ideal Electric & Mfg. Co.*, 134 NLRB 1275 (1961).

(5) Cease and Desist Order

An order may be issued requiring an employer to cease engaging in the illegal conduct that is the subject of the unfair labor practice allegations. This remedy is simply a version of a negative injunction that precludes the employer from engaging in the prohibited activity for which he or she has been found guilty. *See Steelworkers v. NLRB*, 646 F.2d 616 (D.C. Cir. 1981); *Hickmott Foods*, 242 NLRB 1357 (1979). For additional information regarding remedies provided for employer's misconduct, see HARDIN chapter 32.

(6) *Injunctive Relief*

Section 10(j) of the Act states in pertinent part:

> The Board shall have power, upon issuance of a complaint as provided in sub-section (b) charging that any person has engaged * * * in an unfair labor prac-tice, to petition any district court of the United States * * * for appropriate temporary relief or restraining order. Upon the filing of any such petition the court shall cause notice thereof to be served upon such person, and thereupon shall have jurisdiction to grant to the Board such temporary relief or restrain-ing order as it deems just and proper.

29 U.S.C. §160(j) (1947). Considerable debate has been generated by the words "just and proper." Among the more salient questions is whether the party seeking the injunc-tion must satisfy traditional equitable prerequisites, including a demonstration of ir-reparable harm. The United States courts of appeals have wrestled with this question with no definitive resolution. *See* HARDIN at 2497–2509. The majority of courts sub-scribe to an approach that asks whether the Act has been, and will continue to be, frus-trated by the conduct giving rise to the charge. *See Colatrello v. "Automatic" Sprinkler Corp.*, 55 F.3d 208 (6th Cir. 1995); *Arlook v. S. Lichtenberg & Co.*, 952 F.2d 367 (11th Cir. 1992); *Pascarell v. Vibra Screw Inc.*, 904 F.2d 874 (3d Cir. 1990); *Fleishert v. Nixon Detroit Diesel, Inc.*, 859 F.2d 26 (6th Cir. 1988); *Boise v. Pilot Freight, Inc.*, 515 F.2d 1185 (5th Cir. 1975); *Minnesota Mining & Mfg. Co. v. Meter*, 385 F.2d 265 (8th Cir. 1967). The "frustration of the Act" standard calls for the injunction "when the nature of the al-leged unfair labor practices are likely to jeopardize the integrity of the collective bar-gaining process. *Vibra Screw*, 904 F.2d at 878. The remaining circuits focus upon tradi-tional equitable principles in ascertaining the appropriateness of injunctive relief. *See Miller v. California Pac. Medical Ctr.*, 19 F.3d 449 (9th Cir. 1994); *Kinney v. Pioneer Press*, 881 F.2d 485 (7th Cir. 1989); *Macau v. Universidad Interamericana De Puerto Rico, Inc.*, 722 F.2d 1026 1953 (1st Cir. 1983); *Kaynard v. Mego Corp.*, 633 F.2d 1026 (2d Cir. 1980). Essentially, the equitable principles test considers: (1) the probability of success on the merits; (2) the possibility of irreparable harm to the moving party; (3) the bal-ance of hardships; and (4) the benefit to the public interest by the granting of relief. Clearly, the "frustration of the Act" standard favors the Board and defers considerably to the General Counsel's judgment regarding the finding of reasonable cause and the even-tual issuance of a complaint.

(D) Unfair Labor Practices—Prohibited Union Conduct

(1) *Section 8(b)(1)(A) and Section 8(b)(1)(B)—Interfering with employees' rights*

A union's restraint of employees' attempts to exercise Section 7 rights violates the NLRA much the same as similarly coercive employer conduct. Specifically, a union vio-lates 8(b)(1)(A) by: (1) engaging in threats, coercion, violence, or other activities where the object is to force employees to join or assist in the creation of a particular labor or-ganization, to partake or cease partaking in concerted activities, etc., *see Harborside Health Care*, 343 NLRB No. 100 (2004) (pro-union supervisor asking employees to sign union authorization cards during an election campaign violated 8(b)(1)(A) and tainted union election victory results; *Operating Engineers' Local 450(Houston AGC)*, 267 NLRB

775 (1983); (2) fining or otherwise disciplining member/employees for refusing to engage in unlawful or unprotected activity, (*see Pattern Makers' League v. NLRB*, 473 U.S. 95 (1985); *UAW Local 594 v. NLRB*, 776 F.2d 1310 (6th Cir. 1985); *UFCW Local 1439 (Rosauer's Supermarkets, Inc.)*, 275 NLRB 30 (1985); *compare NLRB v. Allis-Chalmers Mfg. Co.*, 388 U.S. 175 (1967); (3) retaliating against member/employee for filing unfair labor practices or otherwise legitimately protesting activities of the union. *See Operating Engineers' Local 450, supra*; *ILA Local 333 (ITO Corp.)*, 267 NLRB 1320 (1983). Similarly, a union violates Section 8(b)(1)(B) by: (1) restraining or coercing an employee in the selection of representatives for purposes of collective bargaining or handling grievances; (2) fining or otherwise disciplining supervisor/members who perform certain collective bargaining functions for an employer. *See generally IBEW Local 340 v. NLRB*, 481 U.S. 1 (1987). *See generally* Kevin Marcoux, *Section 8(b)(1)(A) from Allis-Chalmers to Pattern Makers' League: A Case Study in Judicial Legislation*, 74 CALIF. L. REV. 1409 (1986).

From a slightly different perspective, an attempt to provide union officials, such as shop stewards, with added benefits violates both the letter and spirit of Section 8(b)(1)(A). While acknowledging the importance of according limited superseniority for layoff and recall purposes (given the need to provide stability in the collective bargaining scheme), the NLRB has cautioned that such "largesse" is to be narrowly circumscribed. *See Dairylea Coop.*, 219 NLRB 656, *enforced sub. nom, NLRB v. Teamsters Local 338*, 531 F.2d 1162 (2d Cir. 1976); *Gulton Electric Voice*, 266 NLRB 406 (1983), *enforced sub. nom, Electrical Workers' Local 900 v. NLRB*, 727 F.2d 1184 (D.C. Cir. 1984). *See also* Sharon Lee Davies, *New Limits on Superseniority: Ignoring The Importance of Union Operation*, 86 COLUM. L. REV. 631 (1986). The scenario described earlier regarding the Philadelphia Eagles' Section 8(a)(2) challenge to the negotiation and resulting collective bargaining agreement between the NFL and the NFLPA presented a possible finding of an 8(b)(1)(A) violation against the NFLPA. The Eagles argued that the NFLPA's attempt to secure a labor contract on behalf of "employees" that it ceased to represent subverted the players' rights to organize and bargain collectively with a representative of their own choosing. The Arena Football League story, mentioned above and recounted in Chapters 9 and 15. likewise involved union conduct that arguably violated Section 8(b)(1)(A).

Moreover, if a players association or other group of players in any way threatened or coerced an employee who sought to avoid participation in particular players association activities, an action under Section 8(b)(1)(A) would lie. With regard to Section 8(b)(1)(B), if a player-coach/member or player-manager/member were fined by the labor organization for performing his or her routine management functions (*e.g.*, during a strike), the union could be guilty of an unfair labor practice. Finally, an agreement to provide extra seniority to "player representatives," the sports equivalent to plant "shop stewards," could violate Section 8(b)(1)(A).

(2) Section 8(b)(2)—Discriminating Against Employees

As stated above, an employer violates Section 8(a)(3) by discriminating against employees due to their union activities or affiliation (or similar concerted activity). Section 8(b)(2) renders unlawful any union conduct that coerces an employer to engage in such discriminatory conduct, such as: (1) causing or attempting to cause an employer to discriminate against an employee in hiring or other condition of employment, *see Wolf Trap Foundation for the Performing Arts*, 287 NLRB 1040 (1988); (2) causing or attempting to cause an employer to have an employee fired because of a legitimate refusal to participate in union activities or refraining from same, *see Teamsters Local 439(Tracy American Ready Mix)*, 281 NLRB 1232 (1986); or (3) refusing to refer an employee for employment or otherwise maintaining an exclusive hiring hall without objective criteria. *See NLRB v. Teamsters*, 778 F.2d 207 (5th Cir. 1985). *See also* Roger Hartley, *Constitutional Values and the Adjudication of Taft-Hartley Dues Objection Cases*, 41 HASTINGS L. J. 1 (1989); Heidi Marie Werntz, *Waiver of Beck Rights and Resignation Rights: Infusing the Union Member Relationship with Individualized Commitment*, 43 CATH. U. L. REV. 159 (1993); *see also* Mark D. Meredith, *From Dancing Halls to Hiring Halls: Actors Equity and the Closed Shop Dilemma*, 96 COLUM. L. REV. 178 (1996). Further, a union's failure to represent its members appropriately could constitute violations of Section 8(b)(2) and 8(b)(1)(A), in addition to implicating other sections of the NLRA. *See Miranda Fuel Co.*, 140 NLRB 181 (1962), *enforcement denied*, 326 F.2d 172 (2d Cir. 1963); *Graphics Arts Local 96B (Williams Printing Co.)*, 235 NLRB 1153 (1978). *See also* Madelyn C. Squire, *The National Labor Relations Act and Unions' Invidious Discrimination—A Case Review of a Would Be Constitutional Issue*, 30 How. L. J. 491 (1987).

Although rarely seen in the professional sports area, an 8(b)(2) violation could be found if, for example, the players association exerted pressure upon the Management Council, Player Relations Committee, or other ownership arm to take reprisals against a particular employee who is not sensitive to the union's concerns, does not attend union meetings, etc. If a players association neglects to represent its members fairly or adequately, such as by failing to process a grievance, a violation of Section 8(b)(1)(A) or 8(b)(2) could lie. Yet, establishing this type of transgression is difficult. See *Peterson v. NFLPA*, 771 F.2d 1244 (9th Cir. 1985). Likewise, a violation of this section could be found if the players association forced a player to tender periodic dues or forced an employer to discipline an employee for failing to pay such dues under an unlawful union security clause. Again, the situation in the *Eagles* case could have prompted a colorable claim under Section 8(b)(1)(B) if it were found that the collective bargaining agreement had been entered improvidently, and if dues had been deducted pursuant to union security language in such agreement. *See R. Waldo, Inc.*, 280 NLRB 1237 (1986); *see further UFCW Local 425 (Hudson Foods, Inc.)*, 282 NLRB 1413 (1987).

(3) Section 8(b)(3)—Refusing to Bargain In Good Faith

Unions as well as employers must bargain in good faith. Although the number of employer unfair labor practices in this regard dwarfs the incidents of union refusals to bargain, a labor organization can violate Section 8(b)(3), for example, by: insisting to impasse on issues that are illegal subjects of bargaining, *see Nassau Insurance Co.*, 280 NLRB 878 (1986); or refusing to furnish relevant information to the employer. *See UFCW Local 1439 (Layman's Market)*, 268 NLRB 780 (1984)). Activity by a players association, including work stoppages to achieve bargaining demands that are unlawful, could violate Section 8(b)(3). To date, the players generally have only engaged in work stoppages or similar economic pressure in support of bargaining demands over mandatory bargaining subjects.

(4) Section 8(b)(4)—Secondary Boycotts

Section 8(b)(4) of the NLRA has spawned the most complex litigation since the promulgation of the Wagner Act in 1935 and the Taft-Hartley Act in 1947. It is folly to attempt to summarize the myriad issues arising under this section or to provide a simple explanation of its complicated terms. Suffice it to say, the purpose of this provision is generally to prohibit a labor organization from engaging in activity that has the effect of immersing a neutral party in a dispute between that labor organization and the employer whose employees it represents. This secondary activity may assume several forms, including: a union's attempt to induce an employee to engage in a strike or to threaten any person with an object of forcing that person or other persons to cease doing business with the "primary employer;" forcing an employer to recognize Labor Organization "A" where Labor Organization "B" is already certified as the collective bargaining representative, or forcing an employer to assign work to employees in a certain labor organization not certified as collective bargaining representative. *See, e.g., NLRB v. Servette, Inc.*, 377 U.S. 46 (1964); *NLRB v. Denver Bldg. and Constr. Trades Council*, 341 U.S. 675 (1951).

Several factors may complicate already complex secondary boycott issues. For example, picketing a construction site "housing" several different employers or picketing ambulatory sites such as a ship docked in a shipyard harbors serious ramifications in terms of the potential effect upon neutral employers. Union attempts to isolate the picketing to the primary employer without compromising its ability to reach its intended audience can be a difficult accommodation. *See, e.g., IUE Local 761 v. NLRB*, 366 U.S. 667 (1961); *Sailor's Union (Moore Dry Dock)*, 92 NLRB 547 (1950). Ascertaining the object of picketing or related activity is often a difficult task, and the lines drawn between activity that has an unlawful objective and activity that, for example, is simply designed to advise the public of certain facts can be extremely thin. Even distinguishing picketing from certain types of handbilling or similar non-prohibited conduct can be problematic.

Numerous issues arise in terms of union activity that may have a secondary effect or appear to enmesh neutral parties but, for a variety of reasons, may rest outside the ambit of Section 8(b)(4)'s proscriptions. A classic illustration is presented by the "ally" doctrine, in which an ostensibly neutral or secondary party may be subject to a union's picketing without recourse because it is, or has become, in some fashion allied with the primary employer. In a typical situation, the formerly neutral employer surrenders its insulated status because it begins to perform work that, but for the dispute, would have been performed by the primary employer. Thus, the performance of "struck work" places the secondary employer in the shoes of the "primary." *See NLRB v. Business Mach. & Office Appliance Mechanics Conference Bd., Local 459*, 228 F.2d 553 (2d Cir. 1955), *cert. denied*, 351 U.S. 962 (1956) (commonly referred to as the *Royal Typewriter* case). There are also other situations in which the facts peculiar to a dispute may create an ally situation enabling the picketing union to expand the reach of its protest (*e.g.*, two employers that, for all intents and purposes are the same entity, straight line operations in which the continuity of the process lends singularity to the operation, etc.). *See, e.g., Teamsters Local 560 (Curtin Matheson Scientific, Inc.)*, 248 NLRB 1212 (1980).

Another illustration of the difficulties inherent in identifying the true neutrals in a labor dispute arises in the context of consumer handbilling and picketing. Oftentimes, a labor organization will seek to reach a primary employer through another entity that stocks its products (*e.g.*, a union on strike against a ketchup manufacturer may seek to picket in front of a grocery store). The courts and the NLRB have articulated rules that permit qualified picketing of the struck product and, derivatively, the neutral party. To comply with these rules, the union must tailor the location, timing, and description of the protest in such a way as to minimize the impact upon the neutral employer. *See NLRB v. Fruit and Vegetable Packers Local 760*, 377 U.S. 58 (1964). *See also* Lee Modjeska, *The Tree Fruits Consumer Picketing Case—A Retrospective Analysis*, 53 U. OF CIN.

L. Rev. 1005 (1984). The already difficult task of ascertaining the secondary nature and violability of picketing to discourage the purchase of struck goods is exacerbated considerably in a situation where the struck goods comprise a substantial portion of the secondary entity's inventory or revenue source. In addressing this problem, the Supreme Court has condemned picketing that would, *de facto*, cause ruination or substantial loss to the neutral employer, notwithstanding the fact that the union may have exhausted efforts to direct its appeal to the struck goods and the primary disputant. *See NLRB v. Retail Clerks Local 1001*, 447 U.S. 607 (1980).

Where the union's appeal is made via handbilling rather than picketing, the conduct may rest within a proviso to Section 8(b)(4) permitting truthfully advising to the public, including customers of a neutral employer, that such secondary employer is selling or otherwise distributing a struck product. Thus, even though the handbilling exhorts customers not to do business with the neutral employer, it will be valid, so long as it does not have the impact of inducing an employee, not employed by the primary employer, to withhold the performance of services or assigned duties. *See, e.g., Edward J. DeBartolo Corp. v. Fla. Gulf Coast Bldg. & Constr. Trades Council*, 485 U.S. 568 (1988); James Gray Pope, *Labor-Community Coalitions and Boycotts: The Old Labor Law, the New Unionism, and the Living Constitution*, 69 Tex. L. Rev. 889 (1991); Thomas C. Kohler, *Setting the Conditions for Self-Rule: Unions Associations, Our First Amendment Discourse and the Problem of DeBartolo*, 1990 Wis. L. Rev. 149 (1990).

Finally, certain types of labor-management agreements that have "secondary" features are prohibited by the NLRA. For example, hot cargo clauses, in which an employer agrees to cease using the product of another employer, *may* violate Section 8(e) of the NLRA. Union efforts to coerce an employer to enter such an agreement likewise may contravene the NLRA's secondary boycott proscriptions. *See* Section 8(b)(4)(a). *See also National Woodwork Mfrs. Ass'n v. NLRB*, 386 U.S. 612 (1967); *NLRB v. ILA*, 473 U.S. 61 (1985); *Maui Trucking, Inc., v. Operating Engineers Local 3*, 37 F.3d 436 (9th Cir. 1994). These "hot cargo" clauses also have invited challenges predicated on the Sherman Antitrust Act, triggering extensive inquiry into the applicability of the labor exemption. *See* Chapter 9; *Woelke & Romero v. NLRB*, 456 U.S. 645 (1982); *Connell Construction Co. v. Plumbers Local 100*, 421 U.S. 616 (1975).

While there are few examples of secondary activity arising in a sports context, several possibilities exist. In the appropriate circumstance, a players association may exert pressure on a league by appealing to equipment manufacturers and suppliers, businesses that distribute the league's authorized products, minor league affiliates, ticket sellers, etc. In another vein, the players association may picket an arena or stadium that houses games and attempt to dissuade the public from patronizing the event. Given the critical impact of the media upon sports and the success of sporting events, a union representing players may picket, or threaten to exact reprisals against, television stations or crews assigned to cover a particular game or event. Although highly unlikely, the Major League Baseball Players Association, for example, and the league could agree that the owners will not use certain equipment because its manufacturer does not have a contract with a particular union, thus triggering an inquiry under Section 8(e) of the Act. In each of these situations, the principles touched on briefly above could be implicated. Of course, the extremely complex nature of most secondary boycott situations compels the disclaimer that the foregoing treatment is cursory at best and should only be a starting point for a more searching review of the statute and relevant precedent. Advancing this disclaimer further, we caution that this section only touches upon the nature of prohibited secondary activity and the difficulties inherent in differentiating legitimate

conduct to protest a primary dispute from those activities that unlawfully absorb innocent bystanders into the fray. Many issues resting in the highly involved subtext of the
NLRA's secondary boycott jurisprudence have been bypassed due to the *extreme* unlikelihood that they would ever arise in a sports context.

(5) Section 8(b)(5)—Paying Excessive Dues

Section 8(b)(5), a rarely activated section of the NLRA, simply proscribes union
conduct wherein the labor organization requires the payment of excessive dues to satisfy
union security clauses authorized under Section 8(a)(3). Expanding dues geometrically
or otherwise attempting to secure an excessive amount of money from All-Star game
revenues or other special projects for the purpose of payment of union dues would rest
within this section. To date, there have been no allegations of excessive dues infractions
in professional sports.

(6) Section 8(b)(6)—Featherbedding

Section 8(b)(6) of the NLRA prohibits featherbedding or union efforts to "make
work" for its members where no legitimate work exists. Few cases arise under this section in the wake of two Supreme Court cases limiting its applicability. *American Newspaper Publisher's Ass'n v. NLRB*, 345 U.S. 100 (1953); *NLRB v. Gamble Enterprises*, 345
U.S. 117 (1953). These decisions, read in tandem, hold essentially that a union may
persist in its demands for work and compensation for its members—even if the employer neither needs nor wants the work to be performed—provided that the members
actually do the work. *See* HARDIN at 1848–54. This conduct seldom would occur in the
sports context, but may arise much more often in the entertainment industry where, for
example, an employer seeking live music may be forced to hire several musicians (some
of whom are not necessary) in order to obtain the necessary personnel from a union
representing musicians. *See, e.g., NLRB v. Gamble Enterprises, Inc., supra; New Orleans
Opera Guild, Inc. v. Local 174, Musicians Mutual Protective Union*, 134 So.2d 901 (La.
1961).

(7) Section 8(b)(7)—Picketing

Picketing with an attempt to force the employer to recognize or bargain with a labor
organization is prohibited conduct. *See International Hod Carriers Local 840 (Blinne
Construction Co.)*, 135 NLRB 1153 (1962). Specifically, such activity is unlawful where:
(1) the employer has lawfully recognized another labor organization with respect to the
employees involved and cannot legally recognize another labor organization; (2) in the
preceding twelve (12) months, a valid election was conducted; or (3) picketing was conducted for a period of 30 days without any attempt by the union to go through the procedures of Section 9 in seeking an election petition. Of course, if the purpose of the
pickets is simply to publicize an employer's failure to satisfy prevalent area standards for
wages, hours, and working conditions, or advising the public of the non-existence of a
collective bargaining relationship, then the conduct is not proscribed. Area standards
picketing is not deemed to be recognitional and thus rests outside Section 8(b)(7)'s
ambit. *See Houston Bldg. & Constr. Trades Council (Claude Everett Construction Co.)*,
136 NLRB 321 (1962). Further, picketing "for the purpose of truthfully advising the
public" that the employer does not have a collective bargaining agreement with the subject union may be permissible. Informational picketing is presumed to be recognitional

in part, but it is insulated by a proviso to Section 8(b)(7). *See, e.g., Smitley v. NLRB*, 327 F.2d 351 (9th Cir. 1964). Yet, as in the case of secondary activity described above, it is often difficult to ascertain the union's true objectives. The differentiation between legitimate area standards activity and potentially unlawful recognitional picketing is by no means a simple task. *See generally* HARDIN at 1569–76. *See also NLRB v. Operating Eng'rs, Local 571*, 624 F.2d 846 (8th Cir. 1980).

In the context of a new league, a union (*e.g.*, the NFL Players Association, the Teamsters, the Steelworkers, etc.) may seek to represent the players. If it engages in picketing to achieve representative status, it could be in violation of Section 8(b)(7). For the reasons discussed earlier, the various unions representing professional athletes have had no need to resort to recognitional or organizational picketing. Nonetheless, the advent of a new league or even a new professional sport could resurrect the possibility of demands for recognition that could be accompanied by economic pressure from the labor organization seeking recognition.

(E) Union Liability For Unfair Labor Practices

(1) Injunctions

As part of its remedy, the NLRB/General Counsel may seek to have particular labor organization activity enjoined. While injunctive relief pending resolution of unfair labor practice charges is by no means commonplace, Congress has earmarked certain types of unlawful conduct that warrant immediate relief. *See* 29 U.S.C. §10(j). For example, Section 10(l) of the Act instructs the General Counsel's office to seek injunctive relief whenever there is reasonable cause to believe that the charged labor organization has violated Sections 8(b)(4), 8(b)(7) or 8(e) of the Act.

(2) Bargaining Order

Again, as with employer violations of the duty to bargain requirement, unions may be ordered to bargain in good faith as part of the NLRB's remedy for similar unlawful activity.

(3) Cease and Desist Order

Any union engaging in activity in violation of Section 8(b) may be required to cease and desist from engaging in such activity, particularly in the context of restraining or coercing employees in the exercise of their Section 7 rights. *See National Maritime Union of Am.*, 78 NLRB 971 (1948), *enforced*, 175 F.2d 686 (2d Cir. 1949), *cert. denied*, 338 U.S. 954 (1950).

(4) Damages

Section 303 of the NLRA specifically permits an affected party to seek damages in an appropriate U.S. district court for violations of Section 8(b)(4). *See* 29 U.S.C. §187. Thus, if a union engages in activity whereby the object is to force a neutral employer to cease doing business with a primary disputant in a labor controversy, and the neutral employer suffers monetary losses, damages may be recoverable. A damage award may be appropriate in a variety of other contexts to remedy the effects of unlawful union activity, such as damage to property or person as part of unlawful coercion. *See generally UFCW Local 1439 (Allied Employers, Inc.),* 275 NLRB 995 (1985); *ILA Local 333 (Morania Oil Tankers, Inc.),* 233 NLRB 387 (1977). In professional sports, if the NBA Players Association sought to enmesh a neutral, for example, broadcasters or others doing business with the NBA, by picketing their facilities or otherwise engaging in activity designed to force this neutral party to cease doing business with the NBA or other league structure, then the union could be guilty of a secondary boycott violation and liable for damages accordingly.

(5) Disestablishment of the Union or Withdrawal of Recognition

When a union is found in violation of Section 8(b)(1)(A), stemming from an unlawful recognition under Section 8(a)(2), the remedy could include withdrawal of the employer's recognition, or disestablishment of the union. *See Carpenter Steel Co.,* 76 NLRB 670 (1948). If the Board had found the NFLPA guilty of Section 8(a)(2) or 8(b)(1)(A) violations in the Eagles case referenced above, the NFL's recognition of the union and the current seven-year labor contract would have been jeopardized.

IX. Miscellaneous Issues

(A) Work Stoppages

In general, the NLRA specifically gives employees the right to strike as part of their overall prerogative to engage in protected, concerted activities. *See* 29 U.S.C. §§157, 163. This right to strike is enhanced by the Norris-LaGuardia Act, which precludes the issuance of an injunction to require the cessation of any peaceful work stoppage. *See* 47 Stat. 70 (1932), 29 U.S.C. §§101–15 (1988). However, the employees' strike prerogative and the anti-injunction provisions are by no means absolute. They are qualified in the following ways.

(1) If an employer and a union have negotiated a collective bargaining provision in which the employer agrees to engage in binding arbitration in exchange for the union's agreement not to strike, then the anti-injunction provisions of the Norris-LaGuardia Act will cede, and the employer can obtain an injunction for the union's breach of the no-strike clause (action brought under Section 301 of the NLRA). *See Textile Workers v. Lincoln Mills,* 353 U.S. 448 (1957); *Boys Markets, Inc. v. Retail Clerks Union, Local 770,* 398 U.S. 235 (1970). *But see Mastro Plastics Corp. v. NLRB,* 350 U.S. 270 (1956). This exception will not obtain in the context of a sympathy strike, which, by its nature, is presumed to be non-arbitrable and, therefore, outside of the *quid pro quo* (arbitration for waiver of the right to strike) that warrants the exception. *See Buffalo Forge Co. v. Steelworkers,* 428 U.S. 397 (1976); *Indianapolis Power & Light Co.,* 291 NLRB 1039 (1988); *see further NLRB v. Rockaway News Supply Co.,* 345 U.S. 71 (1953) (addressing "protected" status of sympathy strikes in violation of collective bargaining agreement's no-strike clause).

Courts will often infer the existence of a no-strike pledge from a grievance/arbitration clause. Some courts will also assume that where both no-strike and arbitration clauses are contained in an agreement, they are to be read coterminously-*i.e.,* the no-strike agreement has no efficacy independent of the arbitration clause, thus negating the no-strike clause's enforceability in the context of a non-arbitrable matter. *See Delaware Coca-Cola Bottling Co. v. Teamsters Local 326*, 624 F.2d 1182 (3d Cir. 1980). Other courts find that the coterminous reading is appropriate for purposes of the injunction question (there can be no injunction without underlying arbitrability) but reject such an interpretation in the context of a damage action brought under §301 of the NLRA. *Ryder Truck Lines, Inc. v. Teamsters Local 480*, 727 F.2d 594 (6th Cir.), *cert. denied*, 469 U.S. 825 (1984).

(2) Employees engaging in an economic strike (*i.e.*, a strike to obtain better wages, hours, and working conditions) versus an unfair labor practice strike (a strike over an employer's unfair labor practices) may be permanently replaced. *See NLRB v. MacKay Radio & Tel. Co.*, 304 U.S. 333 (1938). Thus, while an economic striker cannot be fired, *see NLRB v. International Van Lines*, 409 U.S. 48 (1972), he or she can be replaced as long as the replacement is desirous of retaining the position. The difference between discharge and permanent replacement is that in a discharge situation the employee is permanently deprived of any reinstatement prerogative. If a striking employee makes an unconditional offer to return to work, he or she is entitled to reinstatement if a vacancy exists in his or her former job or a substantially equivalent job that he or she is capable of performing. *See NLRB v. Fleetwood Trailers Co.*, 389 U.S. 375 (1967). It has been argued by various labor organizations that management's prerogative to "permanently replace" has a chilling effect on strikers and effectively subverts the NLRA's right to strike. *See generally* William R. Corbett, *A Proposal For Procedural Limitations on Hiring Permanent Striker Replacements: "A Far, Far Better Thing" Than the Workplace Fairness Act*, 72 N. C. L. Rev. 813 (1994); Michael H. LeRoy, *The MacKay Radio Doctrine of Permanent Striker Replacements and the Minnesota Picket Line Peace Act: Questions of Preemption*, 77 Minn. L. Rev. 843 (1993). As part of general labor reform debate, Congress has considered the elimination of the *MacKay Radio*/permanent replacement rule on several occasions but to no avail. Unfair labor practice strikers cannot be permanently replaced. *Collins & Aikman Corp.*, 165 NLRB 678 (1967), *enf'd*, 395 F.2d 277 (4th Cir. 1968).

An interesting question was posed by Major League Baseball's threat to use replacement players during the 1994–95 strike. Labor laws in certain Canadian provinces prohibit the use of replacements during a labor dispute. Thus, one or more Canadian teams could be precluded from employing a tactic arguably available to other teams in the league. The expansion of the NBA into Canada and increased militancy of the NHL Players Association make it clear that this issue is certainly not limited to baseball. *See* J. Jordan Lippner, *Replacement Players For the Toronto Blue Jays? Striking The Appropriate Balance Between Replacement Worker Law in Ontario, Canada and the United States*, 18 Fordham Int'l L. J. 2026 (1995). The impact of this legislation upon Canadian teams' ability to employ replacement players in games played in the United States has not been fully explicated. A related issue is whether a state can prohibit the use of replacements notwithstanding governing federal labor law that permits employers to do so. Relevant precedent stands for the proposition that such action by a state or local authority is preempted. *See, e.g., Golden State Transit Corp. v. City of Los Angeles*, 475 U.S. 608 (1986); *Michigan State Chamber of Commerce v. Michigan*, 115 LRRM 2887 (Mich. Cir. Ct. 1984); Peter F. Giamporcaro, *No Runs, No Hits, Two Errors: How Maryland Erred in Prohibiting Replacement Players From Camden Yards During the 1994–95 Major League Baseball Strike*, 17 Loy. L. A. Ent. L. J. 123 (1996). *See also* Chapter 15, Notes and Questions following *Silverman v. Major League Baseball Player Relations Comm., Inc.*, 67 F.3d 1054 (2d Cir. 1995).

(3) Employees are not paid during a strike, and, in many instances, may be ineligible for unemployment compensation. *See Baker v. General Motors Corp.*, 478 U.S. 621

(1986); *New York Telephone Co. v. New York State Dept. of Labor*, 440 U.S. 519 (1979). To ascertain eligibility for unemployment benefits during a strike, reference should be made to pertinent state law.

(4) Various types of employee conduct may corrupt the strike and render the activity unprotected. For example, partial strikes, in which employees slow down production or engage in similar "counter-productive" activity, may result in discipline without recourse to Section 7. *See Elk Lumber Co.*, 91 NLRB 333 (1950). Likewise, strikes in derogation of the employees' authorized collective bargaining representative may be unprotected. *See Emporium Capwell Co. v. Western Addition Community Organization*, 420 U.S. 50 (1975). Employees who engage in violence or other picket line misconduct will also surrender the protections afforded by Section 7. *See, e.g., NLRB v. Fansteel Metallurgical Corp.*, 306 U.S. 240 (1939); *Clear Pine Mouldings, Inc.*, 268 NLRB 1044 (1984). Finally, employees who breach a collective bargaining agreement's no-strike clause engage in unprotected activity and may be subject to discharge or other discipline. *See NLRB v. Sands Mfg. Co.*, 306 U.S. 332 (1939). *See further Mastro Plastics Corp. v. NLRB*, 350 U.S. 270 (1956); *Arlan's Department Store*, 133 NLRB 802 (1961).

A lockout is a tactical measure taken by employers whereby employees are precluded from working and earning income. The lockout may involve an entire shutdown of the employer's operation or it may simply entail a foreclosure of work opportunity for the affected employees. This strategy may be employed to avoid the consequences of a union work stoppage called at an inopportune time (*e.g.,* in the context of perishable goods), to counteract the effects of a whipsaw strike wherein one member of a multi-employer group is victimized by a work stoppage, or to gain an advantage in the negotiating process. In the past, the NLRB and the courts differentiated offensive and defensive lockouts, and the legal consequences arising therefrom. However, the Supreme Court has eroded the offensive/defensive distinction and generally has validated the utilization of a lockout as a viable negotiating ploy. *See American Ship Building Co. v. NLRB*, 380 U.S. 300 (1965); *NLRB v. Brown*, 380 U.S. 278 (1965); *NLRB v. Truck Drivers Union, Local No. 449*, 353 U.S. 87 (1957); *International Brotherhood of Boilermakers, Local 88 v. NLRB*, 858 F.2d 756 (D.C. Cir. 1988). Yet, there is still some dispute regarding the implementation of an offensive lockout while employing replacement workers. *Compare Inter-Collegiate Press, Graphic Arts Division v. NLRB*, 486 F.2d 837 (8th Cir. 1973) *with Inland Trucking Co. v. NLRB*, 440 F.2d 562 (7th Cir. 1971). *See* HARDIN at 1535–37. *See also* DOUGLAS E. RAY AND EMERY W. BARTLE, MANAGEMENT RELATIONS: STRIKES, LOCKOUTS AND BOYCOTTS (1992).

From the owners' perspective, the lockout is an important weapon because it enables them to dictate the timing of a work stoppage or other economic pressure. If baseball owners anticipate a strike being called over Memorial Day or Labor Day weekend, historically high attendance periods, they may seek to seize the initiative and lockout the players in order to force an agreement. At times, owners expecting a strike have locked out players only to characterize the cessation of play as a strike. *See* MILLER at 271.

During the past thirty years, strikes, lockouts, and other economic pressure have become prominent parts of the sports collective bargaining landscape. Baseball has experienced strikes or owner lockouts in 1972, 1976, 1980–81, 1985, 1990, and 1994–95. The controversies have centered upon several issues, the most prominent of which have been pension contributions, salary arbitration, the salary cap, and restrictions upon free agency. Owners' attempts to circumscribe a player's ability to move from one club to another upon expiration of his or her standard player contract have generated the most acrimonious disputes, both at the bargaining table and in litigation. *See Flood v.*

Kuhn, 407 U.S. 258 (1972); *Kansas City Royals Baseball Corp. v. Major League Baseball Players Ass'n*, 532 F.2d 615 (8th Cir. 1976).

Prior to the watershed *McNally-Messersmith* decision (*National & American League Professional Baseball Clubs v. Major League Baseball Players Ass'n*, 66 LA 101 (1996)), in which Arbitrator Peter Seitz declared all players free agents after the option year of their standard player contract expired, the players had attempted to secure free agency at the bargaining table. Subsequent to Seitz's decision, every negotiation and work stoppage has focused on free agency. The issue has assumed several forms and has manifested itself in various proposals, but the upshot has been the same—the owners' attempts to limit player mobility and the free market for player services. Owners have attempted to qualify the unequivocal free agency declared by Arbitrator Seitz in several ways: imposing qualifications on eligibility based on years of league service; player compensation systems where the signing club compensates the former club with a player or draft choice of comparable worth; and the infamous salary cap (including its stepchild, "luxury tax"). These issues and some of the work stoppages and litigation that they have generated are addressed in Chapters 15 and 16.

Professional football likewise has been beset with its share of labor woes since 1968, encountering strikes or lockouts in 1968, 1970, 1974, 1975, 1982, and 1987. The early strikes (1968–1975) were notable primarily because they evinced early stirrings of player militancy; but they were largely ineffectual due to the strength of the league and the lack of solidarity among the players. The issues provoking the players discontent during this period involved pension contributions and restrictions upon free agency.

During the 1974–1977 time frame, players successfully initiated litigation to contest the draft, the Rozelle Rule, and other limitations upon player mobility. *Smith v. Pro-Football, Inc.*, 593 F.2d 1173 (D.C. Cir. 1978); *Mackey v. National Football League*, 543 F.2d 606 (8th Cir. 1976). As in baseball, a significant part of collective bargaining since these pro-player decisions has been devoted to owners' efforts to dilute their effect and players' resistance to these efforts. Yet, during the 1977 bargaining, the players ceded back some of their litigation gains on the free agency front in exchange for other benefits. Among the reasons offered for this conciliatory posture was the prevailing view that, even with free agency, football owners were less interested in signing "available" players because "of their uncertain impact on winning games" and because income supply was "secure regardless of team personnel." BERRY at 134. During negotiations in 1982, free agency remained a prominent issue, but the players' principal demand was for 55% of gross revenues to be allocated for pension and salary benefits. The parties reached impasse on these issues and a strike ensued. The players alleged that the strike was provoked by the owners' bad faith bargaining and their discriminatory treatment of player representatives. Accordingly, the NFLPA filed unfair labor practice charges alleging violations of Section 8(a)(1), (3), and (5) of the NLRA. While the union hoped that these charges would give them additional bargaining leverage, it also recognized that the finding of an unfair labor practice strike would paralyze any owner plan to replace permanently the striking players. The strike was settled after 57 days at a substantial cost to owners and players. *See* STAUDOHAR at 71–73.

The most recent strike called by the NFLPA occurred in 1987 and was notable for the NFL's use of replacement players. After several weeks, the players' resolve waned, and the poorly conceived work stoppage ended. During this time frame and thereafter, the players, acknowledging their limitations at the bargaining table and on the strike front, moved the battle to the courts where successes in the *McNeil* case and related litigation eventually led to a global settlement and the current, seven year collective bargaining agreement. Issues surrounding these strikes and the companion litigation were addressed in Chapter 9, and will be considered further in Chapters 15 and 16.

For several years the NBA and the NHL shared a common achievement—neither organization had been involved in a major work stoppage. Basketball has remained untouched in this regard with the exception of a brief lockout in 1995. This lockout stemmed from disputes over several issues including the perennial salary cap/free agency debate. A tentative agreement was reached in late September, and the NBA regular season was undisturbed. Yet, this lockout exposed the tenuous labor relations situation in the NBA as well as the lack of consensus among the players themselves, as evidenced by the move for decertification of the union by some star players. The possibility of a decertification probably was prompted as much by a desire to open the gates to individual or class action antitrust lawsuits (free of the labor exemption) as by players' disenchantment with the union itself.

Hockey's recent labor past has not been so benign, and indeed has suffered what may be ·he single worst work stoppage in American sports history, forcing the cancellation of the entire 2004–05 season. Trade-unionist Robert Goodenow's 1992 selection as executive director of the National Hockey League Players Association (after the previous executive director, Alan "the Eagle" Eagleson, resigned amid charges of fraud, racketeering, and embezzlement stemming from Eagleson's theft of money from the NHLPA pension fund, charges which eventually landed him in prison) foreshadowed future conflicts between the Association and NHL owners. In April of that year, after working without a CBA since the previous September, the players called a strike over the NHL's limitations on free agency. While the strike was settled in a relatively expeditious fashion, the Stanley Cup playoffs were delayed and both parties suffered economic consequences.

This strike served as a precursor to other labor travail in hockey. In 1994, NHL owners locked the players out of training camp after unsuccessful negotiations for a new collective bargaining agreement. Again, with baseball providing a grim parallel, the dispute centered primarily on the owners' desire to assist small market franchises and to place a rein on some of the league's more profligate spenders by imposing a salary cap or luxury tax. The work stoppage resulted in the cancellation of almost half of the entire season. *See* STAUDOHAR at 151–52.

The 1994 work stoppage seems mild, however, compared to the lockout that cancelled the 2004–05 season. A new agreement was reached in time to begin the 2005 season, with the players largely caving to the owners' demands to a salary cap tied to league revenues (and initially set at $39 million). Goodenow resigned that summer and was replaced by the NHLPA's Senior Director of Business Affairs and Licensing, Ted Saskin.

Finally, even game officials have been involved in work stoppages to secure better wages and working conditions. NBA and NHL referees have struck and have been locked out for brief periods of time. In 1977, virtually on the eve of the playoffs, NBA referees unanimously voted to strike in support of their demand that the league recognize and bargain with them and their union, the National Association of Basketball Referees ("NABR") (now the National Basketball Referees Association ("NBRA")). Following a 16-day strike, the NBA recognized the NABR as the referees' exclusive bargaining representative and reached agreement on an interim contract. It is interesting that, despite a practice wherein professional sports leagues consistently extended voluntary recognition to players' unions, in this instance the NBA had insisted that it would not bargain until the NABR had demonstrated majority representation in an NLRB election. Almost a decade earlier, Major League Baseball had forced league umpires to prove their desire to be recognized through the Board's election processes. This posture undoubtedly was prompted by the leagues' increasing awareness that labor relations in professional sports had become a type of economic warfare. *See* DWORKIN at 275–77.

Major League Baseball umpires, represented by the Association of Major League Umpires ("AMLU"), struck in 1970, 1979, and 1991, and they threatened to withhold their labor for the League Championship Series in 1996. During these strikes, replacement umpires have been used amid controversy and vocal protests by players and fans. Yet, the players have never struck in sympathy. This failure to honor the umpires' picket lines could be a product of the players' fear of reprisal in terms of their contractual no-strike clause, or it simply could represent an unwillingness to utilize tactics employed by the more traditional trade unions. It raises an interesting question as to whether the current uneasiness between players and officials may stem, in part, from a belief that players have failed to show the proper *esprit de corps* to a sister labor organization.

The issues provoking the umpires' work stoppages generally involved higher pay, primarily for post-season work (umpiring games in the League Championship Series and the World Series). In addition to these strike incidents, major league umpires were locked out in 1995 to preempt a strike during the season. During spring training and the early part of the regular season, the league hired replacement umpires. The lockout ended in April with the negotiation of a five year agreement.

In October, 1996, when Baltimore Orioles'second baseman Roberto Alomar spat upon umpire John Hershbeck in a dispute over a called third strike (a pitch, not a work stoppage), the umpires threatened to strike if Alomar were permitted to play in the succeeding League Championship Series. Alomar was advised that he would be suspended, but the suspension was scheduled to begin at the start of the regular season in 1997. When the umpires rattled their strike sabres to force the league to suspend Alomar immediately, the league sought and secured an injunction in federal court.

The legal predicate for the injunction was that the threatened action was a direct violation of the no-strike clause contained in the collective bargaining agreement between Major League Baseball and the umpires' union. Yet, it is settled law that, even if the no strike clause has been violated, no injunction should issue unless the strike is over an arbitrable dispute. *See Boys' Markets*, above.In particular, the Supreme Court has declared unequivocally that peaceful sympathy strikes not subject to a collective bargaining agreement's grievance machinery (because the underlying dispute involves parties beyond such agreement) are not enjoinable. *Buffalo Forge Co. v. Steelworkers*, 428 U.S. 397 (1976). Thus, the injunction granted in the Alomar matter must give pause. If the umpires' contract contained language that would have made the umpires' protest against the league's handling of the Alomar incident an arbitrable matter, the injunction may have been proper. If, however, there was no contractual basis upon which the umpires could have sought redress, the injunction was probably improvident and in direct contravention of the Norris-LaGuardia Act's anti-injunction provisions. *See* 29 U.S.C. § 101 (1932).

A further review of incidents involving collective economic pressure and owner lockouts will be provided in succeeding chapters, together with cases that explore the ramifications of, and the owners' response to, such action. Samples of some of the many work stoppages that have dotted the sports landscape appear in the pages that follow.

NHL Strikes

Strikes	Main Issue	Date	No. of Days	Type	Number of Games Cancelled	Result	Replacement Players Used	Source
1992	(1) Salary arbitration and (2) free agency	April 1, 1992– April 11, 1992	10	Player strike	30 but rescheduled	(1) Union won right to choose arbitrators in salary disputes; (2) reduction in age for unrestricted free agency, from 31 to 30; (3) increase in players' post season revenue share; (4) two year contract for players; (5) players received marketing rights they wanted; (6) playoff money fund rose from $3.2 mil to $7.5 mil; (7) compromise on disability benefits; and (8) four games were added to regular schedule to pay for increased league costs	No	Paul D. Staudohar
1994-95	Salary cap	October 1, 1994– January 11, 1995	104	Owner lockout	468	(1) Owners dropped payroll tax; (2) rookie salary cap was raised; and (3) free agency was severely limited	No	Paul D. Staudohar
2004-2005	(1) Fines for misbehavior; (2) reducing the number of games; (3) minimum salaries: (4) playoff bonuses; (5) free agency; (6) salary arbitration; (7) revenue sharing; and (8) maximum team salary cap linked to league revenues	September 16, 2004 - July 22, 2005	310	Owner lockout	1230	(1) Payroll cap of $39 million for 2005-06; (2) player compensation limited to 54% of league revenues; (3) minimum payroll of $21 million; (4) rookie salaries capped at $850,000 w/top signing bonus of 10% annually; (5) NHL players will also deposit an adjustable percentage of their salary into an escrow account out of which teams receive funds if the league wide payroll exceeds 54% of revenues. If less than 54% it is paid back to players; (6) players under contract had salaries cut by 24%; (7) teams had the one-time opportunity to buy out player contracts for two-thirds of their remaining value, minus the 24% cut; no one player can account for more than 20% of team's total player; (9) minimum salaries raised to $450,000 in 2005j-06 and after two years the minimum rises again to $475,00 in 2005j-06 and finally $500,000; (10) in 2005-06, players still become free agents at 32 with age decreasing to 29 then 27.	No	Paul D. Staudohar

MLB Strikes

Strikes	Main Issue	Date	Number of Days	Type	No. of Games Cancelled	Result	Replacement Players Used	Source
1972	(1) Pensions; and (2) binding arbitration	April 1, 1972	14 (per cbs news.com) 13 (per Staudohar article)	Strike called by the MLBPA	86	$500k increase in pension fund payments	No	http://www.cbsnews.com/elements/2002/07/10/archive/timeline514679.shtml
1973	Salary arbitration	February 1973	12	Owner lockout	No games cancelled but spring training is delayed	Players win (1) higher minimum salaries; and (2) a bigger owner contribution to the pension fund	No	http://www.cbsnews.com/elements/2002/07/10/archive/timeline514679.shtml
1976	Free agency	March 1976	17	Owner lockout	None	Judge upholds the decision of an arbitrator making two pitchers free agents	No	http://www.cbsnews.com/elements/2002/07/10/archive/timeline514679.shtml
1980	Free agency	April 1980	8	Player Strike	No games were missed but the player did not participate in the last eight days of spring training	The parties agree on a contract which pushes the decision on free agency back a year	No	http://www.cbsnews.com/elements/2002/07/10/archive/timeline514679.shtml
1981	Free Agency	June 12, 1981–August 9, 1981 (City of Cincinnati v. Cincinnati Reds, 19 Ohio App. 3d, 483 N.E.2d 1181 (App. Ct. 1st App. Dist. 1984).	50	Player Strike	712	Teams that lost a "premium" player could be compensated by drawing from a pool of players left unprotected from all clubs rather than just the signing club	No	http://www.cbsnews.com/elements/2002/07/10/archive/timeline514679.shtml

MLB Strikes, continued

Strikes	Main Issue	Date	Number of Days	Type	No. of Games Cancelled	Result	Replacement Players Used	Source
1985	(1) Salaries; and (2) Pension fund	August 1985	2	Player Strike	25 (games made up at end of season, Staudohar)	Owners agree to increase both the salaries and the pension fund	No	http://www.cb-snews.com/ele-ments/2002/07/10/a rchive/time-line514679.shtml
1990	(1) Salary Cap; (2) ar-bitration	February 15, 1990–March 18, 1990	32	Owner lockout	None, although training camps opened late but the season started on time	(1) top 17% of 2nd year players eligible for arbitration; (2) 23 man roster returned; (3) $100K minimum salary; (4) increase in World Series shares to both teams; (5) $55 mil increase in pension fund; (6) joint commit-tee created to study salary cap and revenue sharing	No	http://www.cb-snews.com/ele-ments/2002/07/10/a rchive/time-line514679.shtml
1994–9 5	(1) revenue sharing; (2) salary cap; (3) free agency; (4) salary arbi-tration; and (5) mini-mum salary	August 12, 1994–March 31, 1995	232 days (World Series cancelled) 920 games missed	Player Strike	920; and post season cancelled, including World Series	Judge Sonia Sontomayor granted an injunction against the owners and ordered them to resume under the conditions of the 1990 CBA	Spring train-ing opened with replace-ments (17 Loy. L.A. Ent. L.J. 123)	60 Alb. L. Rev. 205, 223-229; 17 Loy. L.A. Ent. L.J. 123
2002	Labor disagreements	August 30, 2002	None	No Strike as players and own-ers signed an 11th hour contract	None	(1) Each team contributes 34% of net local revenue (after de-ductions for expenses) and it is redistributed equally to all 30 teams; (2) luxury tax was im-posed on a graduated scale and expired on final day of 2006 season; (3) all players will be randomly drug tested for steroids: (4) an agreement was reached on arbitration but de-tails were not released	No	http://www.cb-snews.com/ele-ments/2002/07/10/a rchive/time-line514679.shtml

Collective Bargaining Agreements, MLB

League	Governing Body/ Committee	Testing Practices	Drugs that are Positives	Penalties	Appeal Procedures
MLB Attachment 18 of the Basic Agreement. "Major League Baseball's Joint Drug Prevention and Treatment Program"	-Joint Drug Prevention and Treatment Program -Health Policy Advisory Committee oversees the Program -The HPAC is comprised of one medical professional/representative (licensed physicians expert in the diagnosis and treatment of chemical use and abuse problems) from the Commissioner's Office and the MLBPA and one representative (licensed attorneys) each from the same two entities -The representatives can be appointed and removed by the Commissioner's Office or the MLBPA	-Steroid testing - all players will be randomly selected for testing once at an unannounced time during each championship season -Additionally, the Office of the Commissioner has the right during each of the calendar years to conduct additional testing of randomly-selected players at unannounced times for the presence of Steroids. The number, schedule and timing of these tests is to be determined by the HPAC. Each player shall remain subject to additional tests throughout the calendar year regardless. -A player must be tested for dugs of abuse if any HPAC member has information that gives him/her reasonable	-Drugs that are on Schedule II of the Code of Federal Regulations Schedule of Controlled Substances and all drugs that are included on Schedule I that is attached to the Agreement -The following drugs are always considered drugs of abuse, their schedule classification notwithstanding -Cocaine, LSD, Marijuana, Opiates, MDMA (ecstasy), GHB, Phencyclidine (PCP), Ephedra -The Program also covers all anabolic androgenic steroids covered by Schedule III of the Code of Federal Regulations' Schedule of Controlled Substances. Additionally, steroids that are not on the schedule but may not	-If a player tests positive, they are admitted to the Program and placed either on the Clinical track or the administrative Track to participate in treatment. -If the HPAC determines by a majority vote that the player has failed to comply with his treatment program, the following penalties will result: (1) first failure to comply, at least a 15-day but no more than 25-day suspension or $10k fine; (2) second failure to comply, at least a 25-day failure but no more than 50-day suspension or up to a $25k fine; (3) third failure, at least a 50-day but not more than a 75-day suspension, or up to a $50k fine; (4) fourth failure to comply, at least a one-year suspension or	-All disputes regarding failure to comply with treatment program are subject to the Basic Agreement's Article XI.B grievance procedures. -Within 24 hours of receiving notice of a player's positive result, the Association attorney representing HPAC shall notify the player of the result. The player has two business days to inform the HPAC rep if he intends to challenge the result.

Collective Bargaining Agreements, MLB, continued

League	Governing Body/ Committee	Testing Practices	Drugs that are Positives	Penalties	Appeal Procedures
(MLB)		cause to believe that a player has, in the previous 12-month period, engaged in the use, possession, sale or distribution of a prohibited substance. There will be a meeting called to conduct a vote between HPAC members as to the reasonable cause. If the majority vote concludes there is reasonable cause, the player will be subject to immediate testing.	be lawfully obtained are also covered by the program.	up to a $100k fine; (5) any subsequent failure to comply shall result in further discipline imposed by the Commissioner. All suspensions are without pay. -Steroid positives: (1) first positive result - 10 day suspension or a $10k fine; (2) second positive result - a 30 day suspension or a $25K fine; (3) third positive result - 60-day suspension or a $50k fine; (4) fourth positive result - a one year suspension or up to a $100k fine; (5) any subsequent failure to comply shall result in further discipline imposed by the Commissioner. All suspensions are without pay.	

Collective Bargaining Agreements, NBA

League	Governing Body/ Committee	Testing Practices	Drugs that are Positives	Penalties	Appeal Proc.
NBA Article XXXIII of the Collective Bargaining Agreement	-The NBA and Players' Association jointly select a Medical Director how is in charge of selecting and supervising the Counselors and other personnel necessary for the effective implementation of the Program. NBA Counselors shall, when practicable, be retired NBA players. -The NBA and Players' Association shall also jointly select an Independent Expert who is responsible for issuing authorizations for testing. -The NBA and players' Association shall also form a Prohibited Substances Committee comprised of one NBA rep, one Players' Association rep, and three individuals jointly selected who	-If the NBA or Players' Association has information that gives it reasonable cause to believe that a players is engaged in the use, possession, or distribution of a prohibited substance, the parties shall convene for a conference with the Independent Expert and the IE shall immediately decide whether there is reasonable cause and if there is reasonable cause an authorization for testing will be issued for such player. -first year players may be, in addition to the reasonable cause testing, be required to undergo testing for prohibited substances at any time in the sole discretion of the NBA and without prior notice to the player during the following periods: (1) Not more than once during training camp or within 15 days of joining a team if the player does not	-Amphetamine and its analogs (including but not limited to methamphetamine and MDMA) Cocaine LSD Opiates (Heroine, Codeine, Morphine(Phencyclidine ("PCP") -Marijuana and its by-products -Steroids, Performance Enhancing Drugs, and Masking Agents (SPEDs) -Diuretics	-Any player who (i) tests positive for marijuana pursuant to Section 5 ... shall suffering the following penalties: (A) For the first such violation, the player shall be required to enter the Marijuana Program; (B) For the second such violation, the player shall be fined $25,000 and, if the player is not then subject to in-patient or aftercare treatment in the Marijuana Program, be required to enter the Marijuana Program; (C) For the third such violation, the player shall be suspended for five (5) games and, if the player is not then subject to in-patient or aftercare treatment in the Marijuana Program, be required to enter the Marijuana Program; and (D) For any subsequent violation, the player shall be suspended for five (5) games longer than his immediately preceding suspension for violating the Marijuana Program and, if the player is not then subject to in-patient or aftercare treatment in the Marijuana Program, be required to enter the Marijuana Program.	

Collective Bargaining Agreements, NBA, continued

League	Governing Body/ Committee	Testing Practices	Drugs that are Positives	Penalties	Appeal Proc.
(NBA)	shall be experts in the field of testing and treatment for drugs of abuse and performance-enhancing substances.	participate in training camp; (2) no more than three times during the then-current regular season or for a player who does not sign until after March 1, no more than three times during the regular season following the signing. -veteran players may be required to undergo testing for prohibited substances by the NBA no more than one time during each season during regular training camp or in the case of a veteran player who did not participate in training camp, during the first 15 days after such player reports to his team.		-Any player who (i) tests positive for a SPED ... shall suffer the following penalties: (A) For the first such violation, the player shall be suspended for (10) games and required to enter the SPED program; (B) For the second such violation, the player shall be suspended for twenty-five (25) games and, if the player is not then subject to in-patient or aftercare treatment in the SPED Program, be required to enter the SPED program; (C) For the third such violation, the player shall be suspended for one (1) year from the date of such violation and, if the player is not then subject to in-patient or aftercare treatment in the SPED Program, be required to enter the SPED Program; and (D) For the fourth such violation, the player shall be immediately dismissed and disqualified from any association with the NBA or any of its Teams in accordance with the provisions of Section 11(a)	

Collective Bargaining Agreements, NFL

League	Governing Body/ Committee	Testing Practices	Drugs that are Positives	Penalties	Appeal Procedures
NFL	-Parties will select a medical director and regional teams of evaluation clinicians, a medical advisor for substances of abuse, a team clinician, a team substance abuse physician, a chief forensic toxicologist, drug program agents, and a club physician.	-Rookies and eligible veterans will be subjected to a pre-employment test -All players will be tested preseason by team or position group -All players in intervention stage will be tested -By agreement Steroids -All players at least once per year, usually in preseason -Weekly preseason regular season and postseason tests, and periodic off-season tests with players selected by computer on a coded or "blind" basis -Reasonable cause testing for players with prior steroid involvement or when medical or behavioral evidence warrants	-Anabolic Steroids -Peptide Hormones (hGH, hCG, etc.) -Beta-2 Agonists (Clenbuterol, etc.) -Diuretics and Other Masking Agents -Ephedrine, Amphetamines and Certain Other Stimulants -Dietary "Supplements" Containing Prohibited Substances -Other Substances Related to the Above	-Based on the Intervention Stage that the player is in, different penalties apply. -A player will normally be subject to discipline up to and including suspension without pay for four regular and/or postseason games for a first violation of the law related to substances of abuse other than alcohol and for six regular and/or postseason games for a second violation of the law related to substances of abuse other than alcohol. -The Commissioner will review and may impose a fine, suspension, or other appropriate discipline if a player is convicted of or admits to a violation of the law (including within the context of a diversionary program, degreed adjudication, disposition of supervision, or similar arrangement including but no limited to nolo con-	-A player can appeal a fine or suspension in writing within five (5) days of receiving notice from the NFL.

Collective Bargaining Agreements, NFL continued

League	Governing Body/ Committee	Testing Practices	Drugs that are Positives	Penalties	Appeal Procedures
(NFL)				tendre) relating to the use of alcohol. Steroids -First Positive Test: Medical evaluation (if Advisor directs) and suspension for a minimum of four regular and/or postseason games. -Second Positive Test: Medical evaluation (if advisor directs) and suspension for a minimum of eight regular and/or postseason games. -Third Positive Test: Minimum one-year suspension -Players will not be paid during suspensions. -Players are subject to discipline for positive tests at any time during the year.	

Collective Bargaining Agreements, NHL

League	Governing Body/ Committee	Testing Practices	Drugs that are Positives	Penalties	Appeal Procedures
NHL http://www.nhlpa.com/ PerformanceEnhancing /index.asp	-Performance-Enhancing Substances Program Committee -comprised of an equal number of NHL and NHLPA representatives	-Following orientation session, every player will be subject to up to two "no-notice" tests from the start through the end of the regular season	-Performance-enhancing substances list maintained by the World Anti-Doping Agency (WADA) for out-of-competition testing -Changes to the items included on the Prohibited List can only be negotiated by the NHL and NHLPA -Players can request information on specific supplements	-First positive test results in a mandatory 20-game suspension without pay and mandatory referral to the NHLPA.NHL Substance Abuse & Behavioral Health Program for evaluation, education and possible treatment -Second positive test results in a mandatory 60-game suspension without pay -Third positive test results in a mandatory permanent suspension. A player is eligible to apply for reinstatement after a two-year period The application will be considered by the Performance-Enhancing Substances Program Committee	-The NHLPA may appeal on a player's behalf to an impartial arbitrator -Test results are kept confidential and there will be no public announcement until the appeal process has been completed and a final disciplinary determination has been imposed

(B) Arbitration

Over the past thirty years, arbitration and related voluntary dispute adjustment mechanisms have replaced traditional litigation devices. In various commercial contexts, domestic relations and, of course, labor law, arbitration has become a viable method for adjudicating disputes. The National Labor Relations Board and the courts have shown considerable deference to the arbitration process and voluntary dispute adjustment machinery. *See Boys' Markets v. Retail Clerks*, 398 U.S. 235 (1970); *Steelworkers v. Enterprise Wheel & Car Corp.*, 363 U.S. 593 (1961); *Steelworkers v. American Mfg. Co.*, 363 U.S. 564 (1960); *Steelworkers v. Warrior & Gulf Navigation Co.*, 363 U.S. 574 (1960); *Olin Corp.*, 268 NLRB 573 (1984); *Collyer Insulated Wire*, 192 NLRB 837 (1971); *Spielberg Mfg. Co.*, 112 NLRB 1080 (1955). *See also* Dennis O. Lynch, *Deferral, Waiver, and Arbitration Under the NLRA: From Status to Contract and Back Again*, 44 U. MIAMI L. REV. 237 (1989).

Because most professional sports are governed by collective bargaining agreements containing broad grievance-arbitration clauses, a significant amount of litigation in this arena involves extra-judicial forums. For example, free agency in Major League Baseball was achieved through the filing of a grievance after almost a century of futility in which the players sought this result through the courts. Further, major advances in players' salaries have been achieved through salary arbitration (employed in baseball and ice hockey). For a more detailed discussion of arbitration in professional sports, *see* Frederick N. Donegan, *Examining the Role of Arbitration in Professional Baseball*, 1 SPORTS LAW. J. 183 (1994) (Chapter 16); James Gilbert Rappis, *The Use of Contract Interpretation by Professional Sports Arbitrators*, 3 MARQ. SPORTS L.J. 215 (1993). For an outstanding overview of salary arbitration and a critical review of its utility, see DWORKIN at 144–72.

Chapter 16 is devoted exclusively to labor arbitration and developments in sports law that have emerged from arbitral decisions. A review of the decisions in that chapter reflects the significant impact of the arbitration process upon sports/labor jurisprudence. Given the long-term labor contracts that currently prevail in professional sports, the breadth of the grievance/arbitration machinery in those agreements, and the parties' willingness to avail themselves of, and defer to, the arbitration process, it is likely that this method of dispute resolution will continue to have a profound effect upon labor relations in professional sports. The Supreme Court's expansive reading of the antitrust-labor exemption, and homage to the process and results of collective bargaining will only heighten the role and importance of the neutral arbitrator.

The pre-eminence of arbitration as a vehicle for dispute resolution in professional sports is not limited to traditional labor-management controversies. The elaborate regulations governing the various players unions' regulation of player agents mandate arbitration as the exclusive forum for resolving questions of agent certification and discipline. As will be discussed in Chapter 16, these arbitration procedures weigh heavily in favor of the players' associations as custodians of the agent certification process and, in some respects, lack the character of a true voluntary arbitration machinery.

(C) Recent Developments in Collective Bargaining

The collective bargaining process has continued unabated in recent years. While it is beyond the scope of this book to detail all of the changes in professional sports that have occurred as a result of collective bargaining, four areas of development: salary arbitration, free agency, salary caps, and drug testing, all worthy of separate attention. Salary arbitration is addressed in Chapter 16, *infra*, but the rest will be introduced in the succeeding paragraphs. Also, a recent development in which the NBA and NBPA have agreed upon a rule prohibiting players younger than 19 from entering the league is discussed in Chapter 9, *supra*.

(i) Free Agency

Baseball

Most free agents that make national headlines achieve that status by playing six years in the major leagues. Nevertheless, there are other ways of becoming a free agent. Obviously, a club's material breach of its contractual obligations will provoke a court or arbitrator to honor a player's repudiation of the contract—thus a rebuke. *See Amer. & Nat'l Etc. Baseball Clubs v. Major League Baseball Players Ass'n.*, 59 Cal. App. 3d 493 (1976). The club may release the player voluntarily. Once released, a player may sign with any team. Major League Rule 8. A player with three years of service who is sent to the minor leagues may refuse the assignment and become a free agent. MLB CBA art. XX, §§ D(1), (2). A final category of free agents is the "non-tenders," players who have not been offered a contract by December 20. *See id.* § A. Often these players have not performed sufficiently well to earn a position on the team's forty-player roster, but others are not offered contracts because the club will not be able to pay the salary that could be expected to be awarded after arbitration. (Recall that players with three years of service are eligible for arbitration.) *See generally* Moorad & Parker, *supra*, § 5:31.

A player eligible for free agency has a fifteen-day window within which to declare his free agency. That window begins on the day after the last game of the World Series or on October 15, if the World Series has finished by that date. Even after making such a declaration, however, the player may not immediately sign with another club. Instead, his prior club retains the exclusive right to re-sign him until the end of the fifteen-day window, though the player may negotiate with other clubs during that period. After the window has closed, then a player may sign with any team. *See* MLB CBA art. XX, § B(2).

The player may ultimately elect to re-sign with his incumbent team, but the team faces obstacles to re-signing free agents if it fails to do so quickly enough. The old team can negotiate with a free agent until December 7 just as other teams can. The old team can extend this deadline if it offers salary arbitration to the player, in which case the player has until December 19 to accept the offer. *See* MLB CBA art. XX, § B(3). If the player accepts the offer, he is signed for the next season, and an arbitration proceeding will occur as described above. If the player rejects the offer or does not respond, the current team may not negotiate with or sign the player from January 8 until May 1. *Id.*

Teams that lose free agents to other clubs are entitled to compensation in the form of additional draft choices. No compensation is required, however, if the former club has lost the right to negotiate with the player because the December 7 deadline has passed and the club has not offered the player salary arbitration. Thus, the former club is entitled to compensation if one of its free agents is signed by another club by December 7, or if the club does offer arbitration and the offer is rejected. *See* MLB CBA art. XX, §B(4)(c).

The precise type of compensation is determined by the quality of free agent lost, again as evaluated by the Elias statistical rankings. The loss of a "Type A" player, *i.e.*, a player in the top 30% of players at his position, entitles the former club to a "regular" draft choice of the club signing the free agent, as well as an additional "special" choice between the first and second rounds of the amateur draft. The "regular" draft choice surrendered by the signing team is determined by the following formula:

> If the signing Club is among the first half of selecting Clubs [in the draft], then the choice to be assigned for the highest ranking free agent Player signed by such Club shall be its second choice, with choices in the next following rounds to be assigned as compensation for the signing of the other Players in descending order of ranking. If the signing Club is among the second half of selecting Clubs, then such compensation shall begin with the Club's first choice.

MLB CBA art. XX, §B(4)(d).

The loss of a "Type B" player, *i.e.*, a player in the top 50% but not in the top 30%, entitles the former team to the signing team's draft choice, as determined by the preceding formula. *See id.*, §§B(4)(c), (d). The loss of a "Type C" player, *i.e.*, a player in the top 60% but not in the top 50%, entitles the former team to an additional "special" draft choice between the second and third rounds. *See id.* No compensation is due for the loss of a free agent in the bottom 40%.

Obviously, the compensation system renders "free" agency a misnomer. To the extent that signing a player will cost the signing team a draft choice, that team will be unwilling to offer the player the full value of his services. Instead, the signing team's offer will be discounted by the loss of value triggered by the compensation system. For the same reason, the player's former club will not offer the player his full value to stay with the club, even if the club is financially able to pay. Instead, the club will discount its offer by the amount it expects to receive in draft compensation. As Moorad and Parker note, however, because former teams typically receive this compensation only if they are willing to offer arbitration to the surrendered players, financially poor teams that cannot afford arbitration may not be able to benefit from the compensation scheme. *See* Moorad & Parker, *supra*, at §5:29.

Another restriction on baseball's "free" agency is the limit on the number of free agents each club may sign, which is calculated based on the number of free agents available in a given off-season. If fourteen or fewer Type A or B players elect to become free agents, each club may sign no more than one of them. If there are fifteen to thirty-eight Type A or B free agents, each club may sign up to two. If there are thirty-nine to sixty-two Type A or B free agents, each club may sign up to three. MLB CBA art. XX, §B(5)(a). A club that loses free agents, however, may sign at least the number of free agents that it has lost. *Id.* at §B(5)(b).

A cautionary note: the 2002 Collective Bargaining Agreement is in effect only until December 2006. Expect the information in the preceding paragraphs to change somewhat when the next CBA goes into effect.

Football

Players in the National Football League have radically different rights depending on their seniority. Until players have been in the NFL for three years, they may negotiate and sign with only the teams that drafted them. Of course, with such a restricted market, there often is little "negotiation." If, however, the team fails to make an offer to a player by March 1 for at least the league minimum salary, the player may sign with any team, without restriction, and no compensation need be paid to the first club. NFL CBA art. XVIII, § 2.

Players who have three years of experience (or, in the last year of a CBA, which is not subject to a salary cap, four years of experience) and whose contracts have expired have the oxymoronic title of restricted free agent (RFA). A RFA may negotiate with other teams, but his ability to sign with another club depends on actions that his old club takes. If the RFA has been offered a contract with a sufficiently high salary, the old club will have a right of first refusal when the player receives a contract offer from another team, and will receive draft-pick compensation if the player is lost to another team. The amount of salary that must be offered depends on the player's salary in the previous year (at least 110% of the previous year's salary must be offered for the team to receive draft-pick compensation). If, however, the player's salary is below a threshold, then the amount that must be offered depends on a schedule that is adjusted annually in accordance with projections of revenue. The 2004 figures are as follows:

$628,000 for a right of first refusal.

The greater of $628,000 or 110% of the prior year's salary for a right of first refusal and a draft pick in the round in which the RFA was drafted.

The greater of $1,368,000 or 110% of the prior year's salary for a right of first refusal and a first-round draft pick.

The greater of $1,824,000 or 110% of the prior year's salary for a right of first refusal, a first-round draft pick, and a third-round draft pick.

See Leigh Steinberg & Scott G. Parker, *Representing the Professional Football Player, in* LAW OF PROFESSIONAL AND AMATEUR SPORTS § 6:32 (Gary A. Uberstine ed., 2004). If no such offer is made or if one is withdrawn, the player becomes an unrestricted free agent.

Unrestricted free agents are those players who have four seasons of experience in the NFL (or five seasons in the last, uncapped year of the CBA (the meaning of "uncapped" will be explained *below* in Part IX(c)(ii))). Unrestricted free agents may negotiate with any team during the signing period, and if they sign a contract with a new team no compensation is due the former team. The signing period runs from late-February or early-March until the later of July 22 or the first day of training camp. If the player has not signed a contract by June 1, the old club can offer him a contract for 110% of his last year's salary, thereby ensuring that the club will have exclusive negotiating rights for the player if he remains unsigned at the end of the signing period. *See* NFL CBA art. XIX, § 1; Steinberg & Parker, *supra*, § 6:33.

The NFL's free-agency system is moderated by the teams' ability to designate one player a "franchise player" or "transition player." A transition player, though he may otherwise be eligible for unrestricted free agency, is subject to his old club's right of first refusal. To maintain that right, however, the club must tender a contract offering a one-year salary of 120% of the player's previous year's salary or the average of the ten largest salaries at the transition player's position in the prior year. *See* NFL CBA art. XX, § 16; Steinberg & Parker, *supra*, § 6:34.

The designation of franchise players is similar, but clubs may choose between two types of restrictions on the mobility of franchise players. The first restriction is a right of first refusal, plus compensation of two first-round draft picks. To gain this benefit, the team must tender a contract at the greater of 120% of the player's previous year's salary or the average of the five largest salaries for that player's position in the prior year. The second restriction prohibits the franchise player from negotiating with other clubs at all, but requires that the club tender an offer of a contract at the greater of 120% of the player's previous year's salary or the average of the top five salaries for players at the franchise player's position for the *current* year. *See* NFL CBA art. XX, § 2(c); Steinberg & Parker, *supra*, § 6:35. *See also* Bernard Pellegrino, *Assessing the Impact of the NFL Free Agency Compromise in McNeil v. National Football League*, 1993 ENT. AND SPORTS LAW. 1, 4 (Summer, 1993).

Basketball

In general terms, the NBA's free agency system is simpler than that of the other three major sports. There are no unrestricted free agents in the NBA; rather, each player's team has a right of first refusal as against offers a player has obtained from competing clubs. Once a player has come to an agreement with a new team, he and the team execute an "offer sheet" containing the terms of the contract to which they have agreed. The offer sheet is then presented to the prior team, which has seven days to decide whether to agree to those terms or to allow the player to sign with the new team on those terms. A player may sign only one offer sheet, so the player may not take advantage if a better deal materializes after the offer sheet is signed.

Though NBA players have this free agency right on paper, in actuality the right presents little practical opportunity to increase one's salary and even less to change teams. Ironically, one reason for this ineffectiveness of the NBA free agency system is that clubs losing free agents to other clubs receive no compensation for the losses. Ordinarily compensation is thought to depress the free agent market because the new team will be forfeiting something to obtain the "free" agent. But when the lack of compensation is coupled with a right of first refusal, there is great pressure on the prior team to retain the rights of the player, meaning that the player's ability to change teams will be severely compromised. And if the player is not going to change teams at the end of the day, then competitor clubs are unlikely to make offers that would trigger the right of first refusal in the first place. *See* Ted Steinberg, *Negotiating National Basketball Association Contracts*, in LAW OF PROFESSIONAL AND AMATEUR SPORTS §§ 7:34–7:35 (Gary A. Uberstine ed., 2002).

This system is likely to be in place for a substantial time, as the latest NBA/NBPA agreement was executed in 2005 and will be in effect at least through the 2010–11 season. The NBA holds an option to extend the agreement one season longer. Though basketball's free agency rules appear to favor management, bear in mind that the soft salary cap in the NBA (discussed *infra*) allows for salary increases that would not be possible in the NFL.

Hockey

The NHL has both unrestricted and restricted free agents. There are several types of unrestricted free agents, each with its own set of qualifications based on such factors as age, years played, games played, and salary earned. *See* NHL CBA art. 10, § 10.1. Unrestricted free agents may sign with any club, "without penalty or restriction, or being subject to any Right of First Refusal, Draft Choice Compensation or any other compensation or equalization obligation of any kind." *Id.*

Restricted free agents (who qualify for such status through a combination of age and professional experience) may negotiate and sign with another club, but the former clubs have a right of first refusal and draft pick compensation if the clubs have tendered adequate contractual offers to the restricted free agents. The minimum salaries in such offers depend on the players' salaries in the previous year. Players who made less than $660,000 must be offered 110% of that salary. Players who made between $660,000 and $1,000,000 must be offered 105% of that salary. Players who made more than $1,000,000 must be offered at least that salary. Such offers are subject to salary arbitration if the player is otherwise eligible for arbitration.

(ii) Salary Cap

The notion of a salary cap, and the machinations surrounding its development (or variation of same), is far too involved to be explained comprehensively here. However, the following synopsis should provide a workable understanding of how caps operate and their impact on player mobility and league financial stability.

Baseball

Major League Baseball has no salary cap *per se*, but imposes a "Competitive Balance Tax" (called a "luxury tax" by fans and perhaps Milton Bradley "Monopoly" afficianados) on clubs whose "Actual Club Payrolls" exceed a set figure. In 2006 (the last year of the current Collective Bargaining Agreement), the "tax threshold" was $136.5 million. MLB CBA art. XXIII § B(2). For purposes of the Competitive Balance Tax, the Actual Club Payroll is determined by adding players' salaries, the pro-rata share of players' signing bonuses, and the amount paid as performance bonuses in year under consideration to the team's 1/30 share of the Player Benefit Costs. *See id.*, §§ C(1), E. Deferred compensation is allocated to the year in which it is earned, not the one in which it was paid. *See id.* § E(6).

The tax rate paid by clubs exceeding that figure varies depending on the clubs' recidivism. No club will pay a tax if it exceeds the 2006 limit but its 2005 payroll was below the 2005 threshold of $128 million. *Id.* § B(3). Teams exceeding the threshold in 2005 and 2006 (but not in 2004) are assessed a tax of 30% of the amount by which the club's payroll exceeds the threshold. Teams that violate the threshold for the third or fourth consecutive year pay 40% of the amount by which they exceed the threshold. Taxes are assessed in December for violations occurring in the previous season. The only two teams to be assessed a tax in December 2005 were the New York Yankees and the Boston Red Sox, who paid $34 million and $4 million, respectively. The Yankees' tax was 40% of its excess because New York had exceeded the threshold three times, while the Red Sox' tax was 30% of its excess because Boston had violated the limit twice. In 2004, the Yankees, the Red Sox, and the Angels were required to pay taxes under this provision. *See* Barry M. Bloom, *Yanks, Red Sox Hit with Luxury Tax Bills*, Dec. 21, 2005, at <http://mlb.mlb.com/NASApp/mlb/news/article.jsp?ymd=20051221&content_id=1286225&vkey=news_mlb&fext=.jsp&c_id=mlb>.

It is unclear whether there will be a Competitive Balance Tax in the next CBA, after the current one expires at the end of 2006. The current CBA provides that there will be no tax after the 2006 season, and the provisions of the CBA dealing with the tax "shall not survive the expiration of this Agreement." MLB CBA art. XXIII, § I.

In addition to the Competitive Balance Tax, Major League Baseball uses revenue sharing as a way of protecting small-market teams from the harsh reality of free enterprise. The details of the revenue-sharing plan, which was decades in the making and, at times, resisted by parties on both sides of the table, are contained in article XXIV of the CBA, the most important of which provides that clubs pool 34% of their local revenue, which is then distributed to each team equally. Teams are obligated to use the money received under the plan "to improve [their] performance on the field." MLB CBA art. XXIV, § B(5)(a).

Football

The NFL's salary cap, which places both a floor and a ceiling on the amount of money that each team can spend on player salaries, was instituted in the 1993 collective bargaining agreement. The purpose of the cap is to provide some limitations on free-agent spending and to address the owners' concern over spiraling salaries. The cap, characterized as a "hard cap" because it allows for few exceptions or variances, goes into effect in when salaries equal 67% of league revenue, but does not apply to the last year of the CBA.

To compute the figure that will serve as the salary cap, the league's costs for player benefits are subtracted from the gate receipts and broadcast revenues. Each team is then given a percentage of the total, and may not exceed that figure in distributing funds to players. As of 2006 the cap is set at approximately $102 million, with a minimum of approximately $75 million. In the case of deferred compensation, funds are credited against the cap for the year in which they are earned, rather than the one in which they will be paid. Signing bonuses are pro-rated across the term of the contract. The current cap ceiling was the product of a negotiation conducted pursuant to a re-opener provision in the existing collective bargaining agreement that was due to expire in 2007. The acrimonious negotiation culminated in agreement only after considerable positioning imperiled the continuation of the cap through the 2007 season and provoked the union to threaten decertification and a challenge to the entire salary cap scheme via the antitrust laws. *See* Chapter 9.

While this agreement has been hailed as a welcome assurance of long-range labor peace, some players and other observers believe that the NFLPA negotiated a deal that was more advantageous to the union than to the players themselves. Given the outright victory in the *McNeil* litigation and virtual assurance of similar results in other lawsuits alleging that free agency restrictions violated the antitrust laws, concessions on the salary cap and certain aspects of free agency could be viewed as excessive. *See generally* Brian E. Dickerson, *The Evolution of Free Agency in the National Football League: Unilateral and Collective Bargaining Restrictions*, 3 SPORTS LAW. J. 165 (Spring 1996). This suspicion is fueled by reports that the union also was given a monstrous monetary settlement and the rights to group licensing of players formerly held by NFL Properties. This exchange, which was part of the global settlement that addressed pending antitrust litigation as well as existing labor unrest, infuriated some owners and many players who correctly envisioned the termination of their lucrative licensing arrangements with the league. *See* Chapter 9, Chapter 15.

Further, specifics about the salary cap are extremely intricate, and are contained in article XXIV of the NFL's collective bargaining agreement. For additional information, see Steinberg & Parker, *supra*, §§ 6:22–6:24.

Basketball

As with football and hockey, basketball's salary cap is tied to league revenue. In 2006 the salary cap is $53,135,000 per team. The NBA's salary ceiling—in contrast to the

NFL's—has been characterized as a "soft" cap because it allows latitude to maneuver and circumvent the outer limits of spending. The most notable stratagem has been the "Larry Bird" rule, which permits a team to exceed the cap for the purpose of re-signing its own free agents who have been with the same team for three years.

For a general discussion of developments relating to the NBA salary cap, see Jonathan C. Latimer, *The NBA Salary Cap: Controlling Labor Costs Through Collective Bargaining*, 44 Cath. U. L. Rev. 205 (1994). *See also* David Rothstein, *The Salary Cap: A Legal Analysis of and Practical Suggestions for Collective Bargaining in Professional Basketball*, 11 U. Miami Ent. & Sports L. Rev. 251 (1994).

Hockey

As discussed in the preceding section, the NHL instituted a salary cap in 2005 after a lockout that lasted nearly a full year and required the league to cancel the entire 2004–05 season. The cap is tied to league revenues and provides for both a minimum and a maximum amount teams may spend on players' salaries. Players receive at least 54% of the league's hockey-related revenue. Beginning in 2006 the minimum amount teams may spend on player salaries will be set at $16 million below the maximum. In 2005–06 the figures were $21.5 million and $39 million; in 2006–07 they are $28 million and $44 million.

(iii) Drug Testing
Baseball

The MLB's program is overseen by a Health Policy Advisory Committee ("HPAC"), comprised of two physicians and two attorneys, one of each profession representing management and one representing the players. There are provisions for both random and reasonable cause tests. There are random tests throughout the calendar year, though 90% of the 600 random tests will take place during spring training or the season. Reasonable cause tests take place if the HPAC agrees that there is reasonable cause to believe a player is using a banned substance. If the HPAC is evenly divided on the question, the HPAC itself appoints a fifth member to break the tie. Interestingly, when that tie-breaking procedure is employed, the fifth member is not told the identity of the player under suspicion. MLB CBA Exhibit 18, § 3(A).

The 2003–06 CBA originally provided mild penalties for players testing positive for steroids. For the first offense a player was required to undergo treatment, while the second offense visited a fifteen-day suspension or a fine, and further offenses resulted in more severe punishment. On the fifth offense, a player would receive a one-year suspension. As a result of the pressure put on baseball by Congress and the public owing to recent scandals over the use of steroids and other performance-enhancing substances by players, baseball has greatly increased the penalties applicable for positive tests. Now the first offense results in a fifty-game suspension; the second results in a one-hundred-game suspension; and the third offense results in a lifetime ban. A player subject to the lifetime ban can petition the commissioner for restatement after one year. *See* Lisa Pike Masteralexis, *Drug Testing Provisions: An Examination of Disparities in Rules and Collective Bargaining Agreement Provisions*, 40 New Eng. L. Rev. 775, 785 (2006).

The next CBA may well re-address the applicable rules and suspensions relating to drug use. Though the steroid penalties have been increased, the result has stood uncomfortably next to the CBA's declarations that criminal convictions for possession of controlled substances shall result in only a fifteen-to-thirty-day suspension or a fine, and even a conviction for *sale* of a controlled substance shall result in a sixty-to-ninety-day suspension and a fine. MLB CBA Exhibit 18, § 9 (C), (D). Marijuana use or possession will not result in any suspension at all. *See id.* § 9(E). The MLB agreement does, however, reach many drugs, including amphetamines, opiates, PCP, and marijuana, among many others, beyond just the steroids that are subject to regulation under Schedule III of the Federal Controlled Substances Act. (The CSA places addictive drugs with no approved medical use on Schedule I. Schedule II regulates drugs that are legal if prescribed, but that have significant dangers of addiction. Schedule III drugs, such as most steroids, are legal if prescribed, but carry a danger of addiction somewhat less severe than those drugs on Schedules I and II.)

Football

The NFL was the first of the four major professional sports leagues to test its athletes for banned substances, commencing with a formal program in 1987. The league subjects its players to an unlimited number of random drug tests throughout the season and the playoffs, plus one test during the pre-season physical and up to two random off-season tests. Each player is tested at least once annually, and a total of 10,000 tests are conducted each year, according to the NFL. Mike Cranston, *NFL Assailed on Drug Testing*, CHI. TRIBUNE, Aug. 29, 2006, at 3. Players testing positive are suspended for a minimum of four games for the first offense, a minimum of six games for the second offense, and a year for the third. Appeals are heard by the commissioner.

Though the NFL steroid policy prohibits steroids, hormones, amphetamines, and masking agents, human growth hormone is not the subject of any test, and as a result there is speculation that the use of that hormone is more widespread than one would hope. *See id.*

Basketball

Uniquely, the NBA provides a voluntary program allowing players who have used a prohibited substance to enter treatment without subjecting themselves to penalties, providing that they follow the treatment regimen. The NBA also provides for involuntary testing, with random testing possible once per season in training camp for veterans (four times throughout the season for rookies), and reasonable cause testing possible throughout the season. The reasonable cause provision is triggered whenever the union or management believes that a player is using a banned substance. At that point a hearing is held with the other party before an independent expert, who determines whether in fact there is reasonable cause to believe the player has violated the policy. If so, the expert authorizes testing. NBA CBA art. XXXIII, § 5.

If a player is found to have violated the policy, he is suspended for ten games for the first violation, twenty-five games for the second, and one year for the third. In addition, for each of those violations, the player must enroll in the league's drug treatment program. For the fourth violation, the player is banned from the league. Players are entitled to an appeal before an arbitrator and thirty days to prepare such an appeal, and the test results are confidential throughout the appeal process. *Id.* art. XXXI, §§ 2–3.

Prohibited substances include amphetamines, steroids, performance-enhancing drugs, masking agents, and such Schedule I drugs as cocaine, LSD, opiates, and marijuana.

Hockey

The NHL instituted its steroid testing policy with the 2005 collective bargaining agreement, though "[t]he policy still has some issues that the players association and management are working out." Masteralexis, *supra*, at 783. In particular, though it is clear that a joint committee of officials from the NHL and the NHLPA will play a role in the formation of the policy, there is no doubt exactly what they will do. *See id.* at 783–84.

It is clear, however, that players will be subject to "up to two" tests, and that the penalty structure will be as follows: players will receive a twenty-game suspension and mandatory drug treatment for the first offense, a sixty-game suspension and mandatory drug treatment for the second offense, and a permanent ban (requiring Commissioner approval for reinstatement after two years) for the third offense. *See NHL, NHLPA Team Up Against Performance-Enhancing Substances*, July 22, 2005, at <http://www.nhl .com/nhlhq/cba/drug_testing072205.html>. The only drugs prohibited, however, are performance-enhancing substances, in accordance with the list maintained by the World Anti-Doping Agency ("WADA").

For more detail about the different sports' provisions regarding drug testing, see Masteralexis, *supra*.

Chapter 15

Labor-Management Relations and Sports: Representation and Unfair Labor Practices

I. Introduction

In this chapter we will consider representation and unfair labor practice issues as they have arisen in the world of sports. As you consider the cases that follow in this chapter, ask yourself the following questions:

(1) What is the likelihood of any variation in the current bargaining unit structure in the major professional sports? What factors would be considered in ascertaining the validity of an employer designation different from the existing joint employer arrangement? Is any employee bargaining unit smaller than the present unit feasible?

(2) Why is it extremely difficult to establish that an owner has unlawfully discriminated against a particular employee by trade, demotion or outright release?

(3) If a union that is certified as collective bargaining representative constitutes the exclusive agent for purposes of collective bargaining, how do professional athletes obtain the right to bargain regarding salary on an individual, one-to-one, basis with team owners? What are the limitations upon such individual bargaining?

(4) What are the limitations upon a bargaining representative's right to obtain proprietary information in furtherance of its negotiation and grievance adjustment functions?

(5) In the 1994–95 baseball strike, the NLRB's General Counsel determined, *inter alia*, that the owners had failed to reach impasse prior to implementing unilaterally their salary cap proposal. The General Counsel issued a complaint alleging violations of Section 8(a)(5) and Judge Sonia Sotomayor issued an injunction requiring the owners to return to the *status quo* pending the full adjudication of the unfair labor practices before the NLRB. As a result, the players unconditionally offered to return to work. What would have been the result if the owners had decided to lockout the players after they voted to end the strike?

II. The Representation Process

The foregoing chapter explained in detail the procedures involved in the selection of a collective bargaining representative by employees. As indicated, unionization in most professional sports has been the result of the ownership's voluntary recognition of the collective bargaining representative, and many of the procedures considered in the preceding chapters have never been invoked. Therefore, questions concerning vigorous unionization campaigns and the complex appropriate unit questions that often result from a union's petition for an election have received little play in the professional sports industry. Thus, with the exception of a few North American Soccer League cases, appropriate unit issues have rarely arisen in the professional sports context, and the "stipulated" units have included all players on a "sport-wide" or "league-wide" basis (*i.e.*, all players in the Major Leagues, all NFL players, etc.). *See, e.g., Morio v. NASL*, 501 F. Supp. 633 (S.D.N.Y. 1980); *NASL v. NLRB*, 613 F.2d 1379 (5th Cir. 1980). *See also Major League Rodeo, Inc. and Major League Rodeo Players Association*, 246 NLRB 743 (1979).

The question as to whether or not there is room for changes in the basic unit configurations in professional sports remains open. For example, if a new league were formed and a request for recognition were made by a labor organization, it is conceivable that appropriate unit questions could surface. While it is unlikely that such issues will ever become commonplace in professional sports, the advent of new leagues and increasing labor unrest could result in a new unit determination or a revisitation of old unit questions formerly resolved through the parties' stipulations. The *Morio* case, following immediately below, provides a rare illustration of the appropriate unit case in a sports context, and gives some instruction as to the approach that the NLRB and the courts may adopt.

North American Soccer League v. NLRB
613 F.2d 1379 (5th Cir. 1980)

RONEY, Circuit Judge. The correct collective bargaining unit for the players in the North American Soccer League is at issue in this case. Contrary to our first impression, which was fostered by the knowledge that teams in the League compete against each other on the playing fields and for the hire of the best players, our review of the record reveals sufficient evidence to support the National Labor Relations Board's determination that the League and its member clubs are joint employers, and that a collective bargaining unit comprised of all NASL players on clubs based in the United States is appropriate. Finding petitioners' due process challenge to be without merit, we deny the petition for review and enforce the collective bargaining order on the cross-application of the Board.

The North American Soccer League is a non-profit association comprised of twenty-four member clubs. The North American Soccer League Players Association, a labor organization, petitioned the NLRB for a representation election among all NASL players. The Board found the League and its clubs to be joint employers and directed an election within a unit comprised of all the soccer players of United States clubs in the League. Excluded from the unit were players for the clubs based in Canada, because the Board concluded its jurisdiction did not extend to those clubs as employers.

Players in the unit voted in favor of representation by the Association. After the League and its clubs refused to bargain, the Board found them in violation of Sections 8(a)(1) and (5) of the National Labor Relations Act, 29 U.S.C.A. §§158(a)(1) and (5), and ordered collective bargaining. The League and its member clubs petitioned this Court for review. The Board's cross-application seeks enforcement of that order.

* * *

The settled law is not challenged on this petition for review. Where an employer has assumed sufficient control over the working conditions of the employees of its franchisees or member-employers, the Board may require the employers to bargain jointly. The Board is also empowered to decide in each case whether the employee unit requested is an appropriate unit for bargaining. The Board's decision will not be set aside unless the unit is clearly inappropriate. Thus the issues in this case are whether there is a joint employer relationship among the League and its member clubs, and if so, whether the designated bargaining unit of players is appropriate.

JOINT EMPLOYERS

Whether there is a joint employer relationship is "essentially a factual issue," and the Board's finding must be affirmed if supported by substantial evidence on the record as a whole.

The existence of a joint employer relationship depends on the control which one employer exercises, or potentially exercises, over the labor relations policy of the other. In this case, the record supports the Board's finding that the League exercises a significant degree of control over essential aspects of the clubs' labor relations, including but not limited to the selection, retention, and termination of the players, the terms of individual player contracts, dispute resolution and player discipline. Furthermore, each club granted the NASL authority over not only its own labor relations but also, on its behalf, authority over the labor relations of the other member clubs. The evidence is set forth in detail in the Board's decision and need be only briefly recounted here. *North American Soccer League*, 236 NLRB (No. 181).

The League's purpose is to promote the game of soccer through its supervision of competition among member clubs. Club activities are governed by the League constitution, and the regulations promulgated thereunder by a majority vote of the clubs. The commissioner, selected and compensated by the clubs, is the League's chief executive officer. A board of directors composed of one representative of each club assists him in managing the League.

The League's control over the clubs' labor relations begins with restrictions on the means by which players are acquired. An annual college draft is conducted by the commissioner pursuant to the regulations, and each club obtains exclusive negotiating rights to the players it selects. On the other hand, as the Board recognized, the League exercises less control over the acquisition of "free agent" players and players "on loan" from soccer clubs abroad.

The regulations govern interclub player trades and empower the commissioner to void trades not deemed to be in the best interest of the League. Termination of player contracts is conducted through a waiver system in accordance with procedures specified in the regulations.

The League also exercises considerable control over the contractual relationships between the clubs and their players. Before being permitted to participate in a North

American Soccer League game, each player must sign a standard player contract adopted by the League. The contract governs the player's relationship with his club, requiring his compliance with club rules and the League constitution and regulations. Compensation is negotiated between the player and his club, and special provisions may be added to the contract. Significantly, however, the club must seek the permission of the commissioner before signing a contract which alters any terms of the standard contract.

Every player contract must be submitted to the commissioner, who is empowered to disapprove a contract deemed not in the best interest of the League. The commissioner's disapproval invalidates the contract. Disputes between a club and a player must be submitted to the commissioner for final and binding arbitration.

Control over player discipline is divided between the League and the clubs. The clubs enforce compliance with club rules relating to practices and also determine when a player will participate in a game. The League, through the commissioner, has broad power to discipline players for misconduct either on or off the playing field. Sanctions range from fines to suspension to termination of the player's contract.

Although we recognize that minor differences in the underlying facts might justify different findings on the joint employer issue, the record in this case supports the Board's factual finding of a joint employer relationship among the League and its constituent clubs.

Having argued against inclusion of the Canadian clubs in the NLRB proceeding, petitioners contend on appeal that their exclusion renders the Board's joint employer finding, encompassing 21 clubs, inconsistent with the existence of a 24-club League. The jurisdictional determination is not before us on appeal, however, and the Board's decision not to exercise jurisdiction over the Canadian clubs does not undermine the evidentiary base of its joint employer finding.

Even assuming the League and the clubs are joint employers, they contend that *Greenhoot, Inc.*, 205 NLRB 250 (1973), requires a finding of a separate joint employer relationship between the League and each of its clubs, and does not permit all the clubs to be lumped together with the League as joint employers. In *Greenhoot*, a building management company was found to be a joint employer separately with each building owner as to maintenance employees in the buildings covered by its contracts. The present case is clearly distinguishable, because here each soccer club exercises through its proportionate role in League management some control over the labor relations of other clubs. In *Greenhoot*, building owners did not exercise any control through the management company over the activities of other owners.

APPROPRIATE UNIT

The joint employer relationship among the League and its member clubs having been established, the next issue is whether the leaguewide unit of players designated by the Board is appropriate. Here the Board's responsibility and the standard of review in this Court are important.

The Board is not required to choose the most appropriate bargaining unit, only to select a unit appropriate under the circumstances. The determination will not be set aside "unless the Board's discretion has been exercised 'in an arbitrary or capricious manner.'"

Notwithstanding the substantial financial autonomy of the clubs, the Board found they form, through the League, an integrated group with common labor problems and a high degree of centralized control over labor relations. In these circumstances the Board's designation of a leaguewide bargaining unit as appropriate is reasonable, not arbitrary or capricious.

In making its decision, the Board expressly incorporated the reasons underlying its finding of a joint employer relationship. The Board emphasized in particular both the individual clubs' decision to form a League for the purpose of jointly controlling many of their activities, and the commissioner's power to disapprove contracts and exercise control over disciplinary matters. Under our "exceedingly narrow" standard of review, no arguments presented by petitioners require denial of enforcement of the bargaining order.

Thus the facts successfully refute any notion that because the teams compete on the field and in hiring, only team units are appropriate for collective bargaining purposes. Once a player is hired, his working conditions are significantly controlled by the League. Collective bargaining at that source of control would be the only way to effectively change by agreement many critical conditions of employment.

* * *

PETITION FOR REVIEW DENIED, ORDER ENFORCED.

Notes and Questions

1. What is the significance of the court's finding that the league and its member clubs constituted "joint employers" for purposes of collective bargaining? Is there a distinction between joint employers and a "single employer" in terms of the status of the employing entity? *See Greenhoot, Inc.,* 205 NLRB 250 (1973).

2. As indicated above, professional sports leagues have seldom been beset with difficult unit determinations. Yet, it is not beyond the realm of belief that incumbent unions could be challenged by other labor organizations seeking to represent players. Such challenges could prompt new representation proceedings implicating current bargaining configurations. Imagine smaller bargaining units consisting of "all players occupying skill positions," "all pitchers and catchers," or any number of permutations and combinations of the existing unit structure. *See further* JOHN C. WEISTART & CYM W. LOWELL, THE LAW OF SPORTS §6.04, at 792–802 (1985). Moreover, the possibility exists that new leagues will be formed without voluntarily recognizing any labor organization. In that event, competing labor organizations or a single labor organization could vie for the right to represent the players in collective bargaining. Thus, issues involving appropriate units may be worthy of more than mere academic curiosity.

3. Another interesting question that could arise is whether the league commissioner would or should be included as an "employer" and thus a part of the employing entity. Such status would visit additional responsibilities—and potential liabilities—upon an already taxed commissioner's office. *See also, Silverman v. Major League Baseball Player Relations Comm., Inc.,* 516 F. Supp. 588 (S.D.N.Y. 1981). The "assignment" of the commissioner to the Major League Baseball Player Relations Committee certainly places him in the position of an employer at least insofar as the duty to bargain in good faith is concerned.

4. Assume that tomorrow the Galactic Baseball League is formed and each team is stocked with a roster of forty players. What steps would you take as a union business agent to organize their players for purposes of collective bargaining? In answering this

question, several issues must be addressed, including the possibility of voluntary recognition, the size of the requested unit, the identification of the employing entity, the description of the positions (or jobs) covered in the requested unit, the ideal length of time for an election campaign, and the campaign strategy to be employed.

5. Soccer has been one sport in the United States in which players seeking to unionize have faced considerable resistance. As chronicled in *NASL v. NLRB*, the NASL fought unionization of its players for several years, despite clear and consistent majority support by the players for a union. The NASL folded in 1984. In 1997, the top soccer players in the United States decided not to unionize in order to preserve their antitrust claims against Major League Soccer, in light of the Supreme Court's decision in *Brown v. Pro Football, Inc.* (discussed in Chapter 9). *See* Complaint, *Fraser v. MLS*, Civil Action No. 10242 (D. Mass. 1997). In 1995, the members of the United States Men's National Soccer Team, the team that represents the United States in the World Cup and other international competitions, opted to unionize. After initial recognition by their employer, the United States Soccer Federation ("USSF"), the players faced a refusal to bargain. The players filed unfair labor practice charges with the NLRB alleging violations of Section 8(a)(5) of the NLRA. After rejecting the USSF's contention that the Amateur Sports Act of 1978, 36 U.S.C. §371, *et seq.*, preempts the NLRA, the NLRB's General Counsel issued a complaint against the USSF to force them to recognize and bargain with the players' representative. *See* Complaint, *USSF, Inc. and the United States Men's National Soccer Team Players*, Case 5-CA-26593 (May 30, 1997).

6. If you were an owner in the new league, what measures would you adopt to insulate yourself from a union's organizing attempts? If unionization were inevitable, what problems would you confront by voluntarily recognizing the labor organization that, in your mind, would be the least onerous? If you were engaged in a lengthy union campaign, what rules would govern your conduct?

Major League Rodeo, Inc. and Its Constituent Members and Major League Rodeo Players Association
246 NLRB 743 (1979)

Upon a petition duly filed under Section 9(c) of the National Labor Relations Act, as amended, a hearing was held before Hearing Officer Richard R. Paradise. After the hearing and pursuant to Section 102.67 of the National Labor Relations Board Rules and Regulations, Series 8, as amended, this proceeding was transferred to the Board for decision. Thereafter, Major League Rodeo, Inc., and Major League Rodeo Players Association filed briefs.

Pursuant to the provisions of Section 3(b) of the National Labor Relations Act, as amended, the National Labor Relations Board has delegated its authority in this proceeding to a three-member panel.

The Board has reviewed the Hearing Officer's rulings made at the hearing and finds that they are free from prejudicial error. They are hereby affirmed.

Upon the entire record in this proceeding, the Board finds:

1. Major League Rodeo, Inc. (hereinafter MLR or the League), is an association of professional rodeo teams which was formed in 1977 as a nonstock, nonprofit corporation under the laws of Nevada. Its purpose is to administer and coordinate professional team rodeo. During its first season, 1978, the League consisted of teams in Denver, Col-

orado; Kansas City, Missouri; Los Angeles, California; Salt Lake City, Utah; San Antonio, Texas; and Tulsa, Oklahoma.

League policy is made by a board of representatives consisting of the principal owners of the teams. The chief executive officer of the League is the commissioner, a position currently held by Michael Shapiro. All teams are subject to the provisions of the MLR constitution, bylaws, fiscal rules, operating rules, playing rules, and decisions of the board of representatives. Each team pays uniform dues, assessed from time to time by the board of representatives, to finance the operations of the League.

The League, through its staff and/or the board of representatives, *inter alia*, establishes team size, schedules the games, conducts the annual player draft, and enforces the various rules. The commissioner has the power to act as a final and binding arbitrator over disputes which arise within the League. He also "speaks for the teams on most matters."[2]

The League is also involved in the contractual relationship between the team and the player. The commissioner has the power to discipline, including the power to fine, suspend, or expel a player for a breach of specific provisions of the contract, or for conduct injurious to the League. The commisioner's arbitration powers extend to disputes between a team and a player. Finally, the League can declare a contract null and void if the team fails to meet its obligations under the contract.

In 1978, each team played approximately 14 home games, and traveled to other States for approximately 14 away games.[3] In addition to the regular season, the League sponsored an All-Star game, playoff games, and a championship game.

The petition herein was filed on August 30, 1978. On October 24, 1978, the Regional Director for Region 31 ordered that a hearing be held on November 13, 1978.

* * *

At the hearing, the parties stipulated that Major League Rodeo, Inc.'s constituent members during the fiscal year ending September 30, 1978, purchased goods and services valued in excess of $ 50,000 directly from sellers or suppliers outside the State of California, and outside the home States of the respective constituent members. They further stipulated that each constituent member of the League, during the fiscal year ending September 30, 1978, directly purchased from sellers or suppliers located outside their respective home States in excess of $ 15,000 each for goods and services.

The Employer asserts that the Board lacks statutory jurisdiction because professional team rodeo is essentially local in character, and has no substantial impact on interstate commerce. It also contends that the Board should decline to assert its discretionary jurisdiction, because professional team rodeo is similar to horseracing, an industry over which the Board has declined to assert jurisdiction. In the alternative, the Employer argues that the Board should apply its $ 500,000 retail standard to the Employer, and, since the gross revenues of MLR and its teams total far less than this amount, the Board should decline to assert jurisdiction.

---

2. The parties agreed at the hearing, and we find, that Major League Rodeo, Inc., and its Constituent Members properly constitute a joint-employer bargaining unit. Hereinafter, Major League Rodeo, Inc., and its Constituent Members will be referred to as the Employer.

3. A professional team rodeo game consists of two teams competing in the traditional rodeo events of bareback (horse) riding, barrel racing, team roping (of a steer), saddle bronc riding, calf roping, steer wrestling, and bull riding. Unlike a traditional rodeo, however, a member of one team competes in an event simultaneously against a member of the other team.

Petitioner contends that the Board has statutory jurisdiction over the Employer, and that the Board should assert its discretionary jurisdiction because professional team rodeo is an interstate enterprise by nature, similar to other professional sports over which the Board has asserted jurisdiction without establishing a specific monetary jurisdictional standard. It further argues that even accepting, *arguendo*, the Employer's asserted 1978 gross income as valid, its revenues are not insubstantial. * * *

The stipulation of the parties with respect to the out-of-state expenditures of the League and its constituent members establishes that the Employer is engaged in commerce within the meaning of Section 2(6) of the Act, and that, therefore, the Board has statutory jurisdiction over the Employer. In addition, we conclude that assertion of our discretionary jurisdiction over professional team rodeo is warranted. Professional team rodeo is an interstate enterprise. The games are held in six States in the western portion of the country, and involve travel across state lines by the teams. Thus, any labor disputes which may arise in the industry will be at least regional in scope, and will radiate their impact far beyond individual state boundaries.

The gross income information in the record varies considerably and, as discussed *infra*, is largely unreliable. The Employer, however, in the document it submitted summarizing its revenues, conceded that it received in excess of $ 281,000 during its first season. Furthermore, as set forth above, the parties stipulated that, during the past fiscal year, each constituent member of the League, respectively, made out-of-state purchases in excess of $ 50,000. Based on the foregoing, we find that the Employer has a substantial impact on interstate commerce. [7]

Accordingly, in view of the interstate nature of the industry, and its impact on commerce, we find that a labor dispute involving professional team rodeo will have a substantial effect on commerce. We therefore conclude that the Employer is engaged in commerce within the meaning of the Act, and that it will effectuate the purposes of the Act to assert jurisdiction herein.

* * *

2. Petitioner claims to represent certain employees of the Employer. Major League Rodeo Players Association (MLRPA) was organized in July and August 1978 by William Hines, who currently serves as its acting director. Among its purposes, as set forth in its constitution, is to promote and advance all rodeo players through "the negotiation, execution and administration of collective-bargaining agreements." Hines was aided in his organizing effort by Ernie Wright, western regional director of the National Football League Players Association (NFLPA), and by Professional Athletes International, an affiliation of existing sports players' unions. Hines testified without contradiction, however, that MLRPA was not affiliated with any other labor organization.

At the hearing, the Employer contended that Petitioner was not a labor organization nor, in the alternative, that it was affiliated with the NFLPA, and such affiliation should

---

7. *Volusia Jai Alai, Inc.*, 221 NLRB 1280 (1975). The Employer urges us to apply our $ 500,000 retail jurisdictional standard to professional sports employers. The Board, in its assertion of jurisdiction over professional sports employers, has not previously established a specific discretionary jurisdictional standard, and we decline to do so herein. See *The North American Soccer League and its Constituent Member Clubs*, 236 NLRB 1317 (1978); *Volusia Jai Alai, Inc., supra; American Basketball Association Players Association*, 215 NLRB 280 (1974); *National Football League Management Council*, 203 NLRB 958 (1973), reversed on other grounds 503 F.2d 12 (8th Cir. 1974); and *American League of Professional Baseball Clubs, supra*.

appear on the ballot in the event an election is directed herein. These contentions were not raised in the Employer's post-hearing brief to the Board.

We find no merit in the Employer's contentions. We conclude that Petitioner is a labor organization within the meaning of Section 2(5) of Act, and that it was not affiliated with any other labor organization at the time of the hearing.

3. A question affecting commerce exists concerning the representation of employees of the Employer within the meaning of Section 2(6) and (7) and Section 9(c)(1) of the Act.

4. Petitioner seeks to represent a unit including all rodeo players on the Employer's active and inactive lists, and all players who have played out their contracts, excluding managerial personnel, all other employees and supervisors as defined in the Act. The Employer agrees that players on the active and inactive lists are properly included in the unit, but contends that players who have played out their contracts should not be included in the unit.

The record discloses that each player signs a standard contract with his or her team which initially binds the player to the team from the time of signing until December 31 of the same year. The contract provides that during December of the first contract year the team can, by exercising a one-time option, compel the player to play for an additional 2-year period at the same compensation rate as the first year. The contract further allows the team to trade the player or to terminate the contract, if, "in the sole opinion of the team," the player's services are deemed "not sufficient." Also, as noted above, the League can declare a contract null and void if the team fails to meet its obligations under the contract.

Players can be on a team's active list or its inactive (or reserve) list. Players on the active list are those currently playing in games. The inactive list includes players held in reserve who do not actually compete in games, players temporarily disabled, or players under suspension by the commissioner.

During the Employer's first season of operation, 1978, each team had 16 players on the active list and 9 on the inactive list. For the 1979 season, the board of representatives decided to increase the active list to 18, and decrease the inactive list to 2.

The teams begin their official player selection process in December, when they must exercise their options on players with initial contracts. Players are deemed to have played out their contracts if their team fails to exercise their options, or when they have played the full 3 years under a contract. They then become free agents. Players previously employed by an expelled team, e.g., San Antonio, along with all other persons seeking a position on a team, are also free agents. Free agents can sign with any team until they are selected by a team in the League's annual draft.

The draft occurs in the first few months of the calender [sic] year. The formal procedures for the draft for the 1979 season had not been established by the board of representatives at the time of the hearing, but the teams essentially will take turns selecting players from the pool of free agents. Once a player is selected, he or she may only be employed by the selecting team.

All teams were to have completed their preliminary hiring by mid-March. Team tryouts and practice sessions then were to have been held and, based on these preliminary sessions, the teams were to make their final active and inactive list selections. The 1979 regular season was to begin in early April and continue through August.

Petitioner asserts that the appropriate unit also should include players who have played out their contracts because they are essentially between contracts, most likely seeking employment with the same or different teams for subsequent seasons and are subject to the League's draft. In addition, Petitioner contends that these players share a community of interest with players who continue under contract with regard to wages, hours, and working conditions for the upcoming season, as well as with respect to procedures for, and restrictions on, seeking employment with other teams.

The Employer contends that players who have played out their contracts are no longer employees of a team, and have no expectation of further employment with a team. It argues, therefore, that they should be excluded from the unit.

As of the time of the hearing, the Employer had completed its first season of operation, all players were under their initial contracts, and the 1979 draft had not yet been conducted. Thus, as of the time of the hearing the hiring practices of the teams with respect to players who have played out their contracts had not had sufficient time to develop. Further, there is no other basis in the record for determining the degree to which a player who has played out his or her contract has a reasonable expectation of reemployment with the Employer. We therefore shall not include in the appropriate unit players who have played out their contracts. Accordingly, we find that the following employees constitute a unit appropriate for the purposes of collective bargaining within the meaning of Section 9(c) of the Act:

> All professional rodeo players employed by Major League Rodeo, Inc., and its constituent members, including players on the active list and players on the inactive list; excluding all officials of Major League Rodeo, Inc., all managerial or executive personnel of Major League Rodeo, Inc., or its constituent members, and all other employees and supervisors, as defined in the Act.

Notes and Questions

1. The NLRB, through rulemaking and administrative order, consistently has declined to assert jurisdiction over the horse racing industry. The employer in this case plausibly argued that, if the horse racing industry fails to satisfy the NLRB's jurisdictional standards, then the rodeo industry as described in the facts should likewise rest outside of such coverage. The majority responded:

> Contrary to the Employer's contentions, Member Penello finds none of the reasons for the Board's declining to assert jurisdiction over the horseracing industry is applicable here. Professional team rodeo is not highly regulated by the States, and the industry is essentially interstate, rather than local, in nature. Further, the work force in the unit sought is sufficiently stable that it does not present the difficult administrative problems associated with the horseracing industry. Sec. 103.3 of the National Labor Relations Board Rules and Regulations, Series 8, as amended. Chairman Fanning and Member[s] Truesdale believe that, in any event, the Board should reconsider Sec. 103.3 of its Rules and Regulations. See their dissenting opinion in *American Totalisator Company, Inc.,* 243 NLRB 314 (1979).

Major League Rodeo, 246 NLRB at 745. Oddly enough, the NLRB continues, however stubbornly, to refuse to assert jurisdiction over horse racing.

2. Do you agree with the NLRB's decision regarding the exclusion of employees who had "played out their contract?"

3. In the cases that follow, we will examine typical unfair labor practices that have arisen in professional sports. By far, the most significant amount of litigation has cen-

tered on the owners' refusal to bargain in good faith with various players associations, and owners' discriminatory treatment of those players who have acted in concert to promote their collective bargaining efforts. There will be little attention devoted to unfair labor practices involving unlawful union activity because there simply is a paucity of litigation in this area. For a review of union activity that would rise to the level of an unfair labor practice, see Chapter 14, Section VIII(D).

III. Unfair Labor Practices

(A) Discriminatory Treatment for Engaging in Protected Concerted Activity

National Football League Management Council and National Football League Players Ass'n
309 NLRB 78 (1992)

This case presents significant questions arising from the 1987 strike by the National Football League's professional football players. These include: whether the Respondents lawfully adopted and enforced a rule requiring strikers to report for work by Wednesday of a given week in order to be eligible to play in and be paid for the following weekend's games; whether the Respondents lawfully refused to pay the salaries of certain injured players during the strike; whether the Respondents unlawfully bypassed the Union and dealt directly with the employees; whether Respondent Dallas Cowboys unlawfully threatened to withhold deferred compensation from certain players on account of their participation in the strike; and whether the New England Patriots unlawfully threatened reprisal against strikers* * *.

The Board has considered the exceptions in light of the record and briefs and has decided to affirm the judge's rulings, findings, and conclusions as modified and to adopt the recommended Order as modified.[2]

* * *

I. Factual Findings

A. Collective-Bargaining Agreements and Strikes During the Period 1971–1987

The Union was certified in 1971 as the representative of the active and certain inactive players on the rosters of all National Football League clubs. Since 1971, the parties have negotiated successive collective-bargaining agreements, the most recent of which was effective from 1982 to 1987. Each of these agreements was signed after strikes of varying duration.

---

2. * * * In the absence of exceptions, we adopt the judge's finding that Respondent National Football League Management Council and the 28 constituent member clubs—which are also respondents—are not a single employer. However, the Respondents conceded, the judge found, and we agree that the Respondents are jointly and severally liable for the violations found herein. For ease of reference only, we have referred in this decision to the Respondents collectively where appropriate.

In 1982, the players struck for 57 days during the NFL season before an agreement was reached with the Respondents. The Respondents did not hire replacements during this strike. According to NFL Management Committee Executive Director Jack Donlan's uncontradicted testimony, the Respondent Clubs collectively lost $ 200 million as a result of the strike. Donlan also testified that the Respondents obtained state court injunctions prohibiting strikers from engaging in "All Star" games staged independently of the NFL.[4] There was no testimony concerning efforts by the players to maintain their physical condition during the 1982 strike.

During the 1982 strike, the Respondents determined that each Club had to play nine games in order for the season to have "integrity." Because of certain scheduling requirements, this could be accomplished only if the strike were settled in time to play the games scheduled for November 22–23, 1982. The strike was settled on November 17, 1982, a Tuesday, and nearly all the strikers reported for work the following day. All NFL Clubs played a normal schedule of games the following weekend. Consistent with the Union's request, none of the returning strikers were given medical examinations or formal conditioning tests to determine their fitness to play football. Some Clubs asked players to indicate whether their physical condition had changed; however the parties stipulated that the Dallas Cowboys were the only Club which compiled or administered written conditioning tests.

B. The 1987 Contract Negotiations and Strike

The parties began negotiations for a successor to the 1982–1987 agreement early in 1987. These negotiations were unsuccessful and, on September 21, 1987, after the second week of regular season play, the players went out on strike. The Respondents immediately began hiring temporary replacements for the striking players. Because certain Clubs were unable to assemble complete teams in time for the games scheduled for September 27–28, 1987, the Respondents canceled those games.

The Respondents also substantially modified the NFL's complex personnel rules governing the hiring of players and their eligibility to play in a game. In 1987, the Respondents' (nonstrike) personnel rules permitted each Club to have no more than 60 players under contract between the start of preseason training camps and the completion of the football season (i.e., the Super Bowl). At any given time, each such player had to be classified by the Club on one of the following categories or lists: Active, Inactive, Reserve, or Exempt. The Active list and Inactive lists combined could not exceed 47 players and the Active list could not exceed 40.

A Club's Reserve list could consist of players who (1) retired while under contract, (2) did not report, (3) left the squad (quit team), (4) were injured, (5) were found physically unable to perform at the time of their training camp physical, (6) had a non-football injury or illness, (7) were in military service, (8) were drafted but never signed a contract, and (9) were suspended or declared ineligible or expelled from the NFL. Complex rules not material to this case restrict a Club's ability to move a player from

---

4. Each NFL player is required to sign a standard "NFL Player Contract" which provides, inter alia, that "[w]ithout prior consent of club, player will not play football or engage in activities related to football otherwise than for club or engage in any activity other than football which may involve a significant risk of personal injury * * * club will have the right * * * to enjoin player by appropriate proceedings from playing football or engaging in football-related activities other than for club or from engaging in any activity other than football which may involve a significant risk of personal injury."

certain of the reserve categories to active status. A player could be placed on the Exempt list only with the approval of the NFL Commissioner. Exempt players did not count against the Club's Active list limit but could practice with their Club. This list was used for players who failed to report to their Club at the prescribed time (*e.g.*, players "holding out" in connection with contract negotiations), but in such cases the player's exempt status could last for only two games. Exemptions could also be granted for players who left their Club without permission after reporting, both for the time the player was absent and, if the Commissioner deemed it reasonable that the player was not in shape, for a period of time after the player returned.

Only players on a Club's Active list were eligible to play in a game. The Respondents' rules usually provide that, for games played on a Saturday or Sunday, each Club must establish its Active list for the game by 2 p.m. New York time the day prior to that game. For Monday night games, the deadline is 2 p.m. New York time the day of the game.

In response to the strike, the Respondents substantially modified these rules. On September 29, 1987, the NFL Management Council Executive Committee (CEC) eliminated roster limits until 4 p.m. New York time on October 3, 1987.[7] Clubs were permitted an unlimited number of players on their Inactive lists with a 45-player Active list limit for participating in the games on October 4–5. The deadline for establishing the Active lists was set at 4 p.m. New York time on October 3, and a deadline of 12 p.m. noon local time on Friday (October 2) was established for signing nonroster players. The CEC also established a deadline of 12 p.m. noon local time on October 2 for strikers to report in order to be eligible to play in the Sunday or Monday games.

On October 1, the above rules were modified to establish a 3 p.m. Friday New York time deadline for strikers to report in order to be eligible for that weekend's games or for Clubs to sign nonroster players.

On October 5, the CEC further modified its eligibility rules for returning strikers. The deadline for signing nonroster players was moved back to 4 p.m. New York time Saturday for teams playing on Sunday, and to 4 p.m. New York time on Monday for teams playing that night. For strikers, however, the reporting deadline was set at 1 p.m. New York time on Wednesdays. Strikers reporting after that time were not eligible to play in the following weekend's game, could not be paid for that game, and were exempt from counting against the Club's Active or Inactive list until 4 p.m. New York time on the day following that game. This rule was in effect on Thursday October 15, when the Union advised the Respondents that the strike was over; on the basis of this rule all strikers who had not reported prior to the deadline were declared ineligible to play in the games scheduled for October 18–19 and were not paid for that game.

On October 16, the CEC modified its eligibility rules to return the eligibility deadline to prestrike status for the games on October 25–26. Clubs were allowed to retain up to 85 players on their Active and Inactive lists for those games, including all returned strikers not on the Reserve list. Clubs were permitted to activate players from their Inactive list until 5 minutes prior to kickoff if a player on the Active list refused to participate. Players on the Inactive list for the October 25–26 games were paid their contractual salary for that game.

---

7. All dates hereafter are in 1987 unless otherwise noted.

The Respondents also established special rules for injured players during the strike. The standard "NFL Players Contract" essentially provides that a player injured in the performance of services to the Club is entitled to medical treatment, at the Club's expense, and to continuation of his salary for the rest of that season only, "in accordance with the Club's practice." In general, injured players are expected to cooperate in any prescribed treatments or rehabilitation program, and to attend team meetings and practices to the extent requested and able to do so. However, with the advent of the strike, the Respondent CEC ordered Clubs not to pay injured players who did not report to team facilities or who picketed. The Clubs were also ordered to arrange for such players to continue to receive medical treatment at an offsite facility.

* * *

II. Analysis

A. Deadline Rule

The judge found, and we agree, that the Union unconditionally offered to return to work on Thursday, October 15. For the reasons that follow, we find that the Respondents unlawfully discriminated against the strikers by maintaining and enforcing the Wednesday eligibility deadline to preclude their participation in or payment for the games played on October 18–19.

The Supreme Court has recognized that "there are some practices which are inherently so prejudicial to union interests and so devoid of significant economic justification* * *that the employer's conduct carries with it an inference of unlawful intent so compelling that it is justifiable to disbelieve the employer's protestations of innocent purpose." *American Ship Building Co. v. NLRB*, 380 U.S. 300 (1965). If an employer's conduct falls within this category, "the Board can find an unfair labor practice even if the employer introduces evidence that the conduct was motivated by business considerations." *NLRB v. Great Dane Trailers*, 388 U.S. 26, 34 (1967).

On the other hand, if the impact on employee rights of the discriminatory conduct is comparatively slight, an antiunion motivation must be proved to sustain the charge if the employer has come forward with evidence of legitimate and substantial business justifications for the conduct. Thus, in either situation, once it has been proved that the employer engaged in discriminatory conduct which could have adversely affected employee rights to some extent, the burden is upon the employer to establish that it was motivated by legitimate objectives since proof of motivation is most accessible to him. *Id.* at 34. Applying these principles to this case, we find as an initial matter that the Wednesday deadline rule clearly constitutes discriminatory conduct which adversely affects employee rights. On its face, the rule discriminates against strikers by applying different, and more stringent, standards for eligibility to participate in NFL games (and to be paid for such participation). Moreover, the rule also adversely affects one of the most significant rights protected by the Act—the right to strike. The Board and the courts, applying the principles of *Great Dane*, have long recognized that the right to strike includes the right to full and complete reinstatement upon unconditional application to return. *NLRB v. Fleetwood Trailer Co.*, 389 U.S. 375, 380–381 (1967); *see also Laidlaw Corp.*, 171 NLRB 1366, 1368–1369 (1968), *enfd.* 414 F.2d 99 (7th Cir. 1969), *cert. denied*, 397 U.S. 920 (1970).

As in *Laidlaw*, the Respondents—in reliance on their Wednesday reporting deadline—offered the striking employees who reported for work on October 15 "less than the rights accorded by full reinstatement" (*i.e.*, the right to participate in the games scheduled for October 18–19 and to be paid for those games). *Laidlaw, supra,* 171 NLRB at 1368. Thus, the Wednesday deadline adversely affected the striking employees in the exercise of their right to strike or to cease participating in the strike, by prohibiting the full and complete reinstatement, for the October 18–19 games, of those employees who chose to return to work after the Respondents' deadline had passed.

We need not decide whether, as the General Counsel contends, the Respondents' conduct was inherently destructive of employee rights. Even assuming that the impact on employee rights of the Wednesday deadline rule for strikers was "comparatively slight," the burden still rests with the Respondents to establish "legitimate and substantial business justifications" for the rule. For the reasons that follow, we find that the Respondents have not made the required showing.

The Respondents assert that the Wednesday deadline was justified by the Clubs' need for sufficient time to prepare returning players for game conditions. In this regard, the Respondents presented evidence that the strikers' physical condition would be expected to deteriorate as the strike progressed. In addition, NFL Management Council official Eddie LeBaron testified that players could not maintain their "football condition" without participating in practices involving physical contact. The Respondents also assert that they particularly did not wish to risk injuries to so-called franchise players. The Respondents also assert that the rule is justified by their goal of ensuring that each Club operates from the same competitive position. Thus, the Wednesday deadline would give each Club the same amount of preparation time with returning players, prevent situations in which a replacement squad was "mismatched" against a squad composed of veterans who had reported late in the week, and ensure that Clubs could prepare for specific players during the Wednesday and Thursday practices when game plans were typically practiced.

Finally, the Respondents assert that the Wednesday deadline was justified in light of substantial administrative difficulties allegedly posed if strikers returned at a late date in the week. These alleged difficulties included the question of how to merge replacement squads and strikers, as well as the logistics of practicing and evaluating two squads of players at the same time and arranging transportation to away games for late-reporting players.

In evaluating the Respondents' justifications, we initially note the unprecedented nature of the Wednesday deadline and the absence of any evidence that the Respondents have imposed a deadline of this type on employees outside of a strike setting. In particular, the record shows that players who withheld their services in pursuit of individual goals (i.e., players holding out for a more lucrative contract) are not subject to comparable restraints on their status on their return. Rather, such players are eligible to play immediately so long as they are included in the Club's active roster. If the Club determines that the player is not in shape to play, he may be placed on an Exempt list, as noted above. However, there is no automatic disqualification from participation in NFL games, or from being paid for a game while on the Exempt list, as was the case with the striking employees in 1987. This is so whether or not the individual is considered a "franchise player." Likewise, after the 1982 strike, players were immediately restored to their prestrike status—including players who did not report or practice until the Thursday prior to the next weekend's games. In this regard, NFL Management Council Executive Director Jack Donlan testified that the safety of returning players was not considered either way in 1982 because the NFL's goal of completing the season could only be accomplished if the games were played.

It is undisputed that the Wednesday deadline was only applicable to striking players. The Respondents could and did sign nonstrikers to contracts subsequent to the date the strikers were declared ineligible; the nonstrikers were eligible to play in and were paid for the October 18–19 games. Similarly, after the 1987 strike, Clubs retained a substantial number of replacement players on their Inactive lists for up to two games. Although not eligible to play to the extent that they were not activated, these individuals were paid for those games.

Under these circumstances, we find that the Respondents have not established legitimate and substantial justifications for the deadline rule.[20] While it may be true that some striking employees' physical conditioning declined during the strike, the same considerations were present in the case of holdouts and of replacement players.[21] Likewise, safety concerns did not preclude the immediate reinstatement of the striking players in 1982, even though they had been out for 57 days, while the 1987 strike lasted only 25 days. While most of the strikers in 1982 reported a day earlier in the week than was the case with most 1987 strikers, there is no evidence in the record to suggest that the extra day would be sufficient to overcome the far greater loss of conditioning one would expect after the longer 1982 strike.[22] We also find that the Respondents' asserted competitiveness concerns are unpersuasive. Although the Respondents were entitled to ensure that all clubs operated under the same rules, adopting a deadline which discriminated against strikers was unnecessary to the achievement of this goal. The Respondents' argument that Clubs needed the practice time provided by the Wednesday deadline to prepare the strikers to play (and, for the purpose of those practices, needed to know who would be playing for its opponent) is contradicted by their willingness to allow nonstrikers with substantially less preparation time to play in those games.[23]

---

20. In this regard, we reverse the judge's finding that the Respondents never committed themselves to paying the players even if they were ineligible to play. This finding ignores the uncontradicted evidence, set forth above, that the Respondents' obligation to compensate players is based on the terms of the NFL Players Contract, not their eligibility status, that ineligible players on the Inactive, Reserve, and Exempt lists are compensated in circumstances indistinguishable from those presented here.

21. In this regard, there is substantial evidence that many players practiced as a group during the strike and also continued their physical conditioning programs on an individual basis. These activities were conducted in many cases at the direction of club officials, often using facilities and equipment which the Clubs arranged to be made available. Although there were no contract drills, such activities were prohibited by the NFL Player Contracts and the strikers had every reason to believe that the Clubs would enforce that prohibition. Under these circumstances, and considering that the Clubs did not administer any physical exams or conditioning tests after the strike, we find that the Respondents have not established that the strikers were not in sufficient physical condition to participate in an NFL game.

22. We also note that, in 1982, the Lions and Jets did not practice until the Thursday prior to the first poststrike games, but nevertheless were not subject to any automatic ineligibility rule like that imposed by the Respondents on strikers reporting on Thursday October 15, 1987. Moreover, the record shows that the Lions and Jets played teams which had practiced for an additional day, without any apparent ill effect.

23. The Respondents' competitiveness concerns are also belied by the substantial evidence that the strikers, who generally were veteran players familiar with their Clubs' offensive and defensive strategies, needed less preparation time than replacement players with little or no familiarity with these matters. In this regard, we note that the Board in Laidlaw found that "the employer's preference for strangers over tested and competent employees is sufficient basis for inferring" that its refusal to reinstate them was motivated by antiunion animus. *Laidlaw, above* at 1369 fn. 14. To the extent that the Respondents seek to justify the Wednesday deadline based on a preference for the replacement players we find that such preference is not a legitimate or substantial justification for the rule.

Moreover, the Respondents' claim that late-returning strikers would have a disproportionate impact on the game unless Clubs had an opportunity to prepare their players to face them would seem to contradict their prior claim that these same players were so out of shape that it would be unsafe to play them. Again, in the case of returning hold-outs, replacement players, and the players returning from the 1982 strike, competitiveness concerns did not dictate the imposition of an eligibility deadline like the Wednesday deadline at issue here. We find that such concerns did not justify that deadline in 1987 either.

In addition, we find that the logistical and administrative burden of reinstating the strikers does not justify the rule either. In this regard, the Respondents' arguments are premised entirely on the burden of reinstating the entire 1100 player complement, even though the rule on its face would apply to a single striker who elected to return to work. The Respondents provide no justification for the application of the rule in these circumstances.[24] We also note that the Respondents maintained a substantial complement of replacement players well after the strikers had been fully reinstated. Accordingly, we find that any administrative burden associated with maintaining two separate squads for the games on October 18–19 is not a legitimate and substantial justification for the Wednesday deadline.

The Respondents also provide no explanation for the fact that the initial deadline for returning strikers, 12 p.m. noon on Friday (later modified to 3 p.m. New York time), would have provided the Clubs with less time to accomplish the reinstatement of returning strikers than they actually had when the strikers reported on October 15. To the contrary, LeBaron admitted that he did not take logistical problems into account when he set that deadline because he did not expect the strike to end at that time, and the Friday deadline gave Clubs more opportunity to obtain players, including striking players.

We also find unpersuasive LeBaron's testimony that, early in the strike a Friday deadline was appropriate because the strikers had been out for less than 2 weeks, but that "suddenly you go past that two week cycle, and you're into the third week, and you start getting very concerned about their conditioning." Rather, we think the true explanation for the change is that, as LeBaron subsequently stated, the Respondents wanted a late reporting deadline early in the strike in order to assist them in assembling replacement teams. As LeBaron noted, "if you can get a striking player, then you are better off." Only after the Respondents had assembled the replacement teams was a separate, earlier deadline viewed as desirable. Under these circumstances, we find that the Respondents' claimed logistical and administrative problems are not a legitimate and substantial justification for the Wednesday deadline.[25]

---

24. Indeed, we note that the deadline rule was anomalous in other respects as well. Thus, as the judge noted, it was applied to preclude even specialty players such as kickers from participation in the games, notwithstanding the lack of any evidence that the Respondents' asserted justifications applied in their case. Likewise, the rule was applied to players on injured reserve throughout the strike even though those players would not have been eligible in any event and the only effect of the Wednesday deadline was to prevent them from receiving compensation to which they would otherwise have been entitled as injured players. The Wednesday deadline was also applied to players whose next scheduled game was on Monday, October 19, even though they had as much time to prepare for that game as players reporting by the Wednesday deadline had to prepare for a Sunday game. The Respondents admit that safety or logistical reasons could not justify the application of the rule to these individuals.

25. In so holding, we are mindful that logistical or administrative problems can prevent an employer from immediately reinstating economic strikers who have not been permanently replaced. However, we decline to find that such considerations were present here, in light of the Respondents'

Finally, the Respondents assert that the Wednesday deadline was privileged by the rule established in the Board's *Drug Package Co.*[26] case, granting employers 5 days to reinstate unfair labor practice strikers. As the Respondents note, the October 18–19 games fell within 5 days after the Union's October 15 offer to return to work. However, the Respondents had already reinstated the strikers on October 15, when they were welcomed back, requested to "immediately" begin practicing under their Club's direction and paid a per diem if they did. We also note that the *Drug Package* holding was limited by the Board to orders for reinstatement and backpay for unfair labor practice strikers who had not sought reinstatement prior to the hearing. In contrast, "where a Board order issues after unfair labor practice strikers have already made an offer to return which has been rejected by the employer, backpay runs from the date of the offer to return with no 5-day period allowed." *Drug Package, above* at 114. Even assuming that the *Drug Package* 5-day grace period for reinstatement applies to economic strikers, the Board has refused to give the benefit of any grace period to an employer who unduly delays or unlawfully denies reinstatement. *Aztec Bus Lines*, 289 NLRB 1021, 1030 fn. 23 (1988). For all the forgoing reasons, we find that the Respondents are not entitled to the *Drug Package* grace period for reinstating the strikers in this case.

In sum, the Respondents' Wednesday deadline prohibited employees who returned from the strike on October 15 from playing in the following weekend's games and prohibited their Club from paying them for that game on the basis of their absence from the Club during the strike. The only players subject to such restrictions were those who chose to participate in the strike, a concerted activity protected by the Act. Players absent from their Club for other reasons were not subject to any similar restriction on their eligibility to participate in games; players ineligible to play for other reasons were nevertheless still entitled to be paid. Accordingly, for the reasons stated above, we find that the Respondents' maintenance and enforcement of its Wednesday deadline rule violated Section 8(a)(1) and (3) of the Act.

* * *

Notes and Questions

1. The Board, affirming the Administrative Law Judge, found that the National Football League and its member clubs had violated Sections 8(a)(1) and (3) of the National Labor Relations Act. To find a violation of Section 8(a)(3), the General Counsel must establish that the employer had an antiunion motive and knowledge of union activity. Where was the demonstration of antiunion animus in this case?

2. As part of its analysis, the Board applied the rationale of *NLRB v. Great Dane Trailers*, a case that typically is applied in contexts where wholesale discriminatory activity, such as refusal to reinstate strikers, certain types of lockouts, and similar conduct that could be inherently destructive of employee rights, has been alleged as violative of Sections 8(a)(1) and (3). Under *Great Dane*, if there is a comparatively slight impact on employee rights, the General Counsel must demonstrate anti-union motivation to sustain the charge, provided that the employer has manifested a legitimate and substantial business justification for the discriminatory conduct. Did the employer establish some business justification in this case? If not, was the demonstration

---

demonstrated willingness and ability to reinstate nonstrikers and returning strikers in 1982 to active status under circumstances presenting the same alleged difficulties.

26. 228 NLRB 108 (1977), *enfd. in relevant part*, 570 F.2d 1340 (8th Cir. 1978).

of antiunion motive inferred, or did the Board dispense with any need for it given the clear discriminatory impact of the conduct? In Footnote 15 of the unedited opinion, the Board declared that the General Counsel had no need to establish an antiunion motive for the rule due to the absence of any legitimate business justification demonstrated by the league. Yet, it is axiomatic that the General Counsel must establish some type of antiunion animus in order to prove a violation of Section 8(a)(3). Despite the inartful wording of the opinion, the Board presumably concluded that motive can be inferred from the discriminatory conduct of the owners together with the absence of any legitimate business justification. *See further Lone Star Industries*, 309 NLRB 430 (1992); *Glover Bottled Gas Corp.*, 292 NLRB 873 (1989), *enforced*, 905 F.2d 681 (2d Cir. 1990).

3. The NFL offered numerous reasons ostensibly justifying its decision to delay the return of the economic strikers for one week, costing those players significant amounts of money. Among the justifications presented were administrative difficulties, fear of injury as a result of the short period of time for replacement players to prepare, and potential compromise of the competitive position of the various clubs. For obvious reasons, the Board found that these defenses were pretextual in nature and could not withstand close scrutiny as a legitimate basis for denying the return of the strikers. *See generally Wright Line, Wright Line Div.*, 251 NLRB 1083 (1980), *enforced*, 662 F.2d 899 (1st Cir. 1981); *see also Greco & Haines*, 306 NLRB 634 (1992); *Cine Enterprises, Inc.*, 301 NLRB 446 (1991).

A troubling question that has plagued labor lawyers for decades is the need to show anti-union motive in a Section 8(a)(3) context, but arguably no need to demonstrate animus in the context of an 8(a)(1). If the General Counsel were to allege that a discharge violated Section 8(a)(1), would there be a dispensation of the need to establish motive? Such a result is highly unlikely; motive, whether explicitly or implicitly, would probably become part of the calculus to determine the validity of the employer's action. *See* HARDIN at 82–84; Walter Oberer, *The Scienter factor in Sections 8(a)(1) and (3) of the Labor Act: Of Balancing Hostile Motive, Dogs, and Tails*, 52 CORNELL L.Q. 491 (1967).

4. During the 1987 strike, each player lost approximately $15,000.00 per game, with an overall deficit of $80 million. The owners, however, did not suffer a concomitant loss of income due to the utilization of replacement players. Approximately 70% of the players who struck were replaced. The owners' income, however, was depleted substantially as a result of a requirement that they reimburse the networks $60 million over the succeeding two years for losses occasioned by the games missed during one weekend, a lowering of ratings, and a decline in advertising revenue. *See* PAUL D. STAUDOHAR, *Playing for Dollars*, 74–76 (1996). In any event, it had become increasingly obvious that, if the players were to secure free agency, the route to be taken was not the bargaining table; they simply lacked the war chest, solidarity, and expertise necessary to wage a lengthy economic battle with the owners. Thus, the remaining avenue to eliminate the shackles of the reserve system rested on antitrust grounds. As discussed at length in Chapter 9, the labor exemption temporarily postponed litigation of these issues in federal court. However, once the NFLPA was decertified, paving the way for antitrust litigation, the players were successful in a variety of lawsuits challenging the impediments to free agency as violations of the Sherman Act. These victories resulted in the aforementioned willingness of the NFL to hammer out a new collective bargaining agreement following the reestablishment of the NFLPA as collective bargaining representative. *See* Chapter 9, *Notes and Questions* following the *Powell* decision.

5. In the next case, the Board examined a pretextual discharge in the context of a club's disparate treatment of a player who was a known union adherent. As you review this decision, consider how much the broad discretion typically given a coach or general manager in terms of personnel decisions complicates the analysis.

Seattle Seahawks
292 NLRB 899 (1989)

On November 23, 1983, Administrative Law Judge Bernard Ries issued the attached decision. The Respondent filed exceptions and a supporting brief, the General Counsel filed a brief in reply to the Respondent's exceptions, the Charging Party filed cross-exceptions and a supporting brief, and the Respondent filed a brief in answer to the Charging Party's cross-exceptions. The Respondent also filed a motion to disqualify and the Charging Party filed a response opposing the motion.

The National Labor Relations Board has delegated its authority in this proceeding to a three-member panel.

The Board has considered the decision and the record in light of the exceptions and briefs and has decided to affirm the judge's rulings, findings, and conclusions and to adopt the recommended Order as modified.

This is a factually complex case. In its exceptions to the judge's decision, the Respondent attacks not only the judge's factual findings but also the legal standards that he applied. We are satisfied that the judge applied the appropriate standards and that his factual findings are supported by the record, but we address below certain of the Respondent's specific objections and the views of our dissenting colleague.

1. The Respondent challenges the judge's formulation of the test for determining whether the decision to release Sam McCullum violated Section 8(a)(3) of the Act. Specifically, the Respondent contends that the judge failed to apply the *Wright Line* test and that this failure is demonstrated by his use of the terms "in part" and "predominant motive," in describing what the General Counsel must prove as to unlawful motive before the burden shifts to the Respondent either to rebut the General Counsel's case or to show, as an affirmative defense, that the action in question would have been taken in any event, whether or not the Respondent was motivated by the employee's protected activities. We disagree.

It is true that in *Wright Line, supra*, the Board rejected "in part" and "dominant motive" tests, but it did so because those earlier tests of the lawfulness of a particular employment decision stopped with the conclusion whether the decision was dominantly or "in part" motivated by discriminatory sentiments. 251 NLRB at 1087. The Board changed to a test under which, after the General Counsel had presented evidence "sufficient to support an inference that protected conduct was 'a motivating factor' in the employer's decision," the Respondent could avoid liability by demonstrating, as an affirmative defense, that "the same action would have taken place even in the absence of the protected conduct." *Id*. at 1089. In the Supreme Court's subsequent endorsement of the *Wright Line* test in *NLRB v. Transportation Management Corp.*, 462 U.S. 393, 400–403 (1983), the Court made clear its understanding that the significant change in the Board's test was not the characterization of the General Counsel's initial burden, but rather, the addition of a new step by which the Board was required to consider an employer's affirmative defense even when the presence of unlawful motivation had been established. Thus, the Court saw "substantial or motivating factor" as nothing more than the way the Board now "puts it" in describing the General Counsel's initial burden. *Id.* at 401.

It is incontestable that the judge, notwithstanding his occasional use of the term "in part" to describe the extent of the Respondent's unlawful motivation, found that antiunion considerations were a motivating factor in the decision that produced McCullum's release, and that he fully considered the Respondent's Wright Line defense. We therefore find that his analysis fully comports with the Wright Line standard.

2. The Respondent has also excepted to the judge's implicit finding that certain remarks that Sam McCullum made in his role as the team's player representative at a February 19, 1982 press conference and that produced negative reactions from both the team's general manager, John Thompson, and its head coach, Jack Patera, are in fact protected under Section 7 of the Act. In particular, the Respondent argues that McCullum's expression of his view that team doctors, whom he saw as identified with management, released injured players for games too soon, when the players were not fully recovered, constituted "disloyal" disparagement of the employer, which, pursuant to the theory of *NLRB v. Electrical Workers IBEW Local 1229 (Jefferson Standard)*, 346 U.S. 464 (1953), is not protected activity under Section 7. The Respondent also argues, as to the "solidarity handshake" episode, that any hostility would naturally be against the Union—as the author of this activity throughout the league—rather than against McCullum. We disagree with both contentions.

a. In *Jefferson Standard*, the Supreme Court held that a union's public attacks on the quality of the employer's product were not protected under Section 7 in which they had no connection with the employee's working conditions or any current labor controversy. It seems indisputable, however, that the relative haste with which injured players are returned to the football field is a matter that directly affects the players' working conditions. Although McCullum's views may have been exaggerated or not soundly based, that does not withdraw the protection of the Act from them. Indeed, employees and employers frequently differ greatly in their views whether the employees are properly treated.

b. We do not mean to suggest, of course, that it was unlawful for either Thompson or Patera to take issue with McCullum's statements. The fact remains, however, that McCullum established himself at this press conference as a fairly aggressive union spokesman. McCullum's role as player representative was highlighted again when he and two other players approached Patera in August to apprise him of the players' intention to support the Union's "solidarity handshake" plan by engaging in such a handshake with the opposing team in the upcoming August 13 game with St. Louis. Although it was another player who mentioned the "union solidarity" symbolism of the handshake, it was McCullum who—after Patera had expressed his opposition—said that the players might go ahead and do it anyway. We agree with the judge that Patera's prediction of the subsequent fines ("I'll fine you as much as I can") and the heavy fines that the Respondent sought to impose reveal animus toward union activity for which, at this point, McCullum was the obvious focus on the team. Thus, we see no merit in the Respondent's argument that, because the solidarity handshake was an activity planned by the Union, the Respondent's animus had nothing to do with the individual Seattle players who participated. It was those players whom the Respondent sought to fine (a fine averted only because the Management Council ordered rescission after an unfair labor practice charge was filed). It was McCullum who had vowed to go through with the handshake after Patera said he opposed it.

3. The Respondent attacks the judge's discrediting of Patera—which is essential to his findings of unlawful motive—by insisting that it rests fundamentally not on observations of witness demeanor but rather on a flawed logical analysis of the plausibility of Patera's account of an urgent search, beginning as early as January 1982, for a "deep threat" wide receiver. We do not agree that the judge's logic is fatally flawed, but in any event it is apparent that the judge's decision is based in part on his observation of Patera, who he found "not one of the most impressive witnesses at the hearing."

Thus, for example, the judge saw and heard Patera testify that he was merely "bothered" by McCullum's remarks at the February 19 press conference, but the judge found that Patera's reaction had been "considerably stronger than that." (The judge found his impression corroborated by Patera's later involvement in the fines for the solidarity handshakes.) Similarly, on the question of whether Patera and Rhome had jointly agreed prior to the trade for Carr that McCullum was to be released if the trade went through, the judge was clearly influenced by the manner in which this testimony "popped out" of Patera on cross-examination.

We, of course, recognize that the judge's evaluation of all the testimony was influenced by his view of how it fit together logically or failed to do so, but we are necessarily reluctant to disregard the demeanor component of credibility resolutions by a trier of fact. We therefore decline the Respondent's invitation to reverse the judge's assessment of the credibility of Patera's testimony.

4. Finally, we address two of the Respondent's arguments concerning alleged inconsistencies between the judge's factual findings and the record evidence. These are both matters raised also by our dissenting colleague.

a. First, the Respondent argues that a finding that it was seeking to obtain Carr in order to rid itself of McCullum is inconsistent with the evidence that the Respondent had declined to accept Baltimore's offer of Carr in late spring for a first round draft choice, that it had declined another Baltimore offer in August for a "high" draft choice, and that the Respondent had even toughened its position by insisting on September 2 that it would give up only a fourth round draft choice for Carr. We do not see that conduct as inconsistent with the judge's motivation finding for the reasons essentially given by the judge.

An employer may harbor an unlawful intent to rid itself of a troublesome employee but still wish to do so on the most advantageous terms possible. Furthermore, the testimony of the Respondent's own witnesses shows that they reasonably believed that Baltimore wanted to be rid at all costs of the injury-prone Carr, particularly in August, by which time he had missed a preseason minicamp and commented to the press about his dissatisfaction with Baltimore. The Respondent knew that Baltimore would willingly take a fourth-round draft choice if that was all that were offered. Thus, the Respondent's conduct of negotiations with Baltimore is not at all inconsistent with a desire to make a trade that would produce an apparent justification for releasing McCullum.

b. The Respondent also contends that the judge's findings concerning Patera's influence over the release of McCullum are inconsistent with evidence concerning the role of Seattle's offensive coordinator, Jerry Rhome, in the decision to release McCullum and the role of the team's owner, John Thompson, and its director of football operations, Michael McCormick, in the decision to acquire Roger Carr just prior to McCullum's release. We see no fatal inconsistency.

It is undeniable that Rhome was responsible for rating the wide receivers throughout training camp and the preseason games and that Patera would reasonably take seriously his judgment, after the Carr-trade, that McCullum should be released rather than Steve Largent, Byron Walker, or Paul Johns. But it is clear from Rhome's testimony that he was not consulted about the desirability of having Carr, as opposed to McCullum, at the point in the season that Carr was finally acquired. Thus, Rhome testified that he could not rate Carr because he had not seen him play very recently. Rhome obviously approached the evaluation process with the realization that Carr was not for cutting. As he testified, "You can't just eliminate Roger Carr because you just got through trading for him." Hence, having Carr as one of the wide receivers going into the new season was essentially imposed on Rhome by the trade. He made no considered judgment that an injury-prone player who had not participated in any training camp that summer and did not know Seattle's system of offensive plays would be more valuable than McCullum.

Although Carr's name was first mentioned by McCormick when he joined the Respondent's organization in March and the initial decision to make inquiries about Carr occurred after a conversation among McCormick, Patera, and Thompson about the matter, Patera made the initial call, while subsequent negotiations with Baltimore were carried out first by McCormick and later by Thompson. But Patera's role was crucial. As Thompson testified, Patera was the one to decide who would make the team. Given the time at which Carr was finally acquired—just before the opening of the season—it was clear that, as Rhome recognized, acquiring him meant bringing him onto the team. Nothing in the record suggests that efforts to acquire players would have been made without continuing consultation with the head coach. Thus, it had to be up to Patera whether negotiations to acquire Carr would continue just before the start of the season, when cuts were to be made. Contrary to our dissenting colleague, we do not rely simply on an absence of evidence as to Patera's role in the acquisition of Carr. We rely on admissions of the Respondents' own witnesses that Patera determined who would be on the team (testimony of Thompson) and that the trade for Carr, given its timing, was tantamount to a decision that Carr would be on the team (testimony of Rhome). We then find that there is no record evidence contradicting the clear implication of those admissions considered together, namely, that Patera's views were necessarily taken into account in the decision to make the trade just before the regular season was to begin.

Given the reports that Rhome says he made to Patera about the progress of players Walker and Johns in the training camp and preseason games, the continued pursuit of Carr is suspect. McCullum was rated a very good wide receiver in many respects—allegedly all except for the ability to go deep and catch "the bomb." But this was an area in which Johns and Walker were now rated highly, so the need to obtain Carr for that particular skill was diminishing rapidly according to the Respondent's own witnesses.

The Respondent simply has not shown that the acquisition of Roger Carr on September 3 would have occurred even in the absence of the animus of the Respondent's management—most notably, but not solely, the animus of Patera—against McCullum as an outspoken representative of union sentiment on the team. The animus against the Union's solidarity had been powerfully expressed, but thwarted in August, when the Respondent imposed fines for the "solidarity handshake" that greatly exceeded those imposed by any other NFL team and then was forced to rescind the fines. The opportunity for the Respondent to rid itself of the most visible team symbol of that solidarity was finally seized upon in September through the acquisition of Carr.

* * *

DISSENTING OPINION BY MEMBER JOHANSEN: OMITTED.

Notes and Questions

1. In 1993, ten years after the ALJ's decision and four years after the NLRB's affirmance, the United States Court of Appeals for the District of Columbia Circuit enforced the Board's order and back pay award. *See Nordstrom v. NLRB*, 984 F.2d 479 (D.C. Cir. 1993).

2. The *Wright-Line* test, alluded to in the early part of the Board's opinion, was developed in part to provide additional protection to an employer who is able to demonstrate that, even though a particular course of conduct was prompted by unlawful motivation, the conduct would have been undertaken independent of such motivation. The owners in the subject case misperceived the scope and impact of this test when they suggested that the Administrative Law Judge had erred by using such terms as "in part" and "predominant motive"—terms that had been rejected in *Wright-Line*. In reality, such terminology had been eliminated in *Wright-Line* because, in prior decisions, the determination of an employer's liability turned *solely* on whether or not unlawful motivation existed. The critical aspect of *Wright-Line*, therefore, is not the elimination of the words "in part" or "predominant motive," but, rather, the additional opportunity provided an employer to demonstrate that, notwithstanding the unlawful motive, the conduct would have occurred nonetheless. For a useful discussion of *Wright-Line* in this regard, see Jeffrey Goore, *Discriminatory Discharge In a Sports Context: A Reassessment of the Burden of Proof and Remedies Under The National Labor Relations Act*, 53 FORDHAM L. REV. 615 (1984).

3. Significantly, the Administrative Law Judge discredited head coach Jack Patera's testimony that the decision made regarding the player representative, Sam McCullum, was based solely on his abilities as a football player. The majority of the Board panel had no difficulty affirming these factual conclusions. It is extremely rare to find the Board reversing an Administrative Law Judge's credibility findings given the fact that he or she has had the opportunity to observe the demeanor of the witnesses. An interesting question involves the degree to which a reviewing court should consider the factfinder's conclusions where such conclusions have been reversed by an agency review panel (*e.g.*, an Administrative Law Judge being reversed by the NLRB). *See* 5 U.S.C. §§ 556, 557; *Universal Camera Corp. v. NLRB*, 340 U.S. 474 (1951).

4. This case is somewhat unusual in that it reflects the rare situation in which a club decision regarding a personnel move was found to violate the National Labor Relations Act. As discussed in Chapter 14, this decision is inherently subjective, given the myriad variables that are involved in staffing decisions affecting professional athletes. Even though it is difficult to establish that an employer's decision was not made in good faith under a subjective standard, it was clear to the Administrative Law Judge and the Board in this case that the Seahawks' decision was motivated by antiunion motive and could not be explained by any business justification. Under the *Wright-Line* test, the Seahawks could have emerged unscathed if they had been able to show that, notwithstanding their antiunion motive, the decision affecting the charging party still would have been made. However, even with this more relaxed standard in the context of a pretextual discharge, the respondents were unable to make the requisite showing.

5. By far the most commonplace unfair labor practice allegations regarding mistreatment of employees implicate Sections 8(a)(1) and (3) of the Act and predominantly in-

volve the discouragement of union activity or affiliation. However, it is likewise an un-fair labor practice for an employer or labor organization to coerce employees in the ex-ercise of their right *not* to engage in collective bargaining or to seek representation. When an employer dominates a labor organization or otherwise establishes a relation-ship with the union that acts in derogation of the wishes of the majority of the employ-ees, an unfair labor practice violation could arise under Section 8(a)(2) and Section 8(b)(1)(A).

At various points in this text, we have referred to allegations of such conduct arising in the wake of the ultimate resolution of the infamous 1987 NFL strike, specifically through the collective bargaining agreement and litigation settlement occurring in 1993. After decertifying the union to enable themselves to file individual and class ac-tion lawsuits under the antitrust laws (unencumbered by the labor exemption), the players eventually sought recognition anew to allow negotiation of the collective bar-gaining agreement that is currently in effect. The fly in the ointment was that Norman Braman, owner of the Philadelphia Eagles, and a party to the settlement negotiations regarding the pending antitrust litigation as well as the collective bargaining for a new labor contract, claimed that the labor agreement had been reached prior to the time that the Players Association had been recertified as bargaining representative. Such con-duct, if true, would constitute a blatant violation of the NLRA, which precludes an em-ployer and a union from reaching agreement if that union does not represent a majority of employees (except in the construction industry where prehire agreements generally are permissible. *See* 29 U.S.C. § 158(f)).

The charges filed with the NLRB alleging violations of Sections 8(a)(2) and 8(b)(1)(A) were dropped when all pending litigation was withdrawn as part of Bra-man's decision to sell the Eagles. Nonetheless, the specter of illegality hangs over the settlement, which, in many circles, has been hailed as a paragon of collective bargaining and labor peace. There have been accusations that the sense of relief experienced as a result of the settlement following a half decade of acrimony and litigation has obscured the fact that the legal footing upon which the agreement rests is somewhat tenuous. Even with the gloss placed over this agreement, several players, including many super-stars, are disgruntled about the settlement, particularly its salary cap provisions, its continued new limitations on free agency for certain players, and other less significant aspects. NFL Commissioner Paul Tagliabue, NFL owners, NFLPA Executive Director Eugene Upshaw, and many others contend that the settlement provided benefits to both sides and that the advances made in terms of free agency overall were a valid exchange for certain concessions by the NFLPA, such as the salary cap.

Critics point to the fact that, as part of this settlement and a global agreement to re-solve existing litigation, the league surrendered the rights to player licensing formerly owned by NFL Properties and paid $45 million in "damages." A large portion of these damages was applied to defray approximately $18 million in legal fees and also to estab-lish a war chest for future collective bargaining negotiations. To that end, it has been suggested that the real winners in the negotiation were the NFL and the Players Associ-ation, with the players themselves deriving only incidental benefit. For a discussion of the potential unfair labor practices stemming from the negotiation of the agreement in 1993, see Robert A. McCormick, *Interference on Both Sides: The Case Against the NFL-NFLPA Contract*, 53 WASH. & LEE L. REV. 397 (1996).

6. The strike that served as a backdrop to the *Seattle Seahawks* case began in Septem-ber, 1982 and constituted the most extensive work stoppage in NFL history. The grava-men of this controversy centered upon the players' demand for a percentage of gross

revenues, the proceeds of which were to be placed in a fund to be distributed as deferred compensation and pension. Related pension benefits issues and the players' continuing demand for liberalization of free agency also posed impediments to a quick resolution of the dispute. These issues, together with the players' alternative request that wages be tied to television revenues, reflected an increased player militancy in terms of their desire to share in the profits that the prosperous NFL was beginning to enjoy. Certainly, the 1982 strike served as an indicator that the NFLPA had emerged as a labor organization in the traditional sense and that true player solidarity was on the horizon. The fifty-seven-day strike ended on November 21, 1982, with substantial losses suffered by both players and owners. The seven regular season games that were sacrificed resulted in a $210 million deficit for the owners and lost salaries of $63 million for the players. The owners and players were not the only sports industry casualties resulting from this strike. Numerous municipalities and many of their independent businesses suffered considerably as well, with some cities losing between one and two million dollars in hotel and restaurant revenue, as well as other miscellaneous reversals. *See* Robert C. Berry, William B. Gould IV & Paul D. Staudohar, Labor Relations in Professional Sports 146–48 (1986).

7. When players' demands were not met in 1982, they filed unfair labor practice charges claiming that the strike was at least in part prompted by the owners' unlawful activity. Why would the NFLPA claim that the strike was caused by the employer's unfair labor practices rather than employed as a form of economic pressure to secure the demands made at the bargaining table?

8. In a scenario not unlike the NFL-NFLPA saga recounted above, the Arena Football League attempted to foist a union upon its players in large part to avoid antitrust repercussions. This incident and the attendant unfair labor practice charges are discussed at length in Chapter _____, Part VI. It is noteworthy that a six-year collective bargaining agreement improvidently negotiated with a union that did not represent a majority of the players was rescinded. *See* Glenn M. Wong, Essentials of Sports Law (3d Ed. 2003), § 11.3.6.2, at 511. Repudiation of a collective bargaining agreement negotiated in derogation of rights guaranteed by Section 7 and in violation of Sections 8(a)(2) and 8(b)(1)(A) is not an uncommon remedy. *See* 2 Patrick Hardin and John E. Higgins, Jr., The Developing Labor Law 436, 2520 (4th ed. 2001).

9. The following case illustrates that the NLRB places a considerable burden on the General Counsel alleging violations of Sections 8(1) and (3) to demonstrate that the charging party had engaged in activity both concerted and protected and that the employer's allegedly discriminatory treatment was motivated in part by anti-union animus.

Palace Arena Football, LLC
and Arena Football League Players Association
2003 NLRB LEXIS 190 (2003)

The General Counsel alleges that on November 28, 2001, Respondent threatened to terminate Antoine Worthman, the Detroit Fury's player representative for the Union, the Arena Football League Players Association, for engaging in union activity. He also alleges that on December 7, 2002, Respondent terminated Worthman's employment in retaliation for his protected activities.

* * *

Antoine Worthman, the alleged discriminatee, played professional football for nine years. He played three years (1992–94) in the Canadian Football League (CFL) and then six (1996–2001) in the Arena Football League (AFL). In November 2000, he signed a three-year contract with the Detroit Fury, a team about to play its initial season in the AFL. This contract did not obligate the Fury to retain Worthman as a player, it only set forth his compensation for three years if he was retained.

In 2001 and 2002, the AFL season began in April and ended in July. The Arena Football game is designed to be a high-scoring game, featuring more scoring and more passing than the National Football League (NFL). The playing field is 50 yards long and 85 yard wide; there are eight players on the field, rather than eleven. To facilitate scoring, one receiver, the "high motion man" is allowed to move forward towards the line of scrimmage. In the NFL and in American college and high school football, offensive players are prohibited from moving forward before the ball is snapped.

Three players on the field are defensive backs. Two of these are called defensive specialists (OS); the other is called a cornerback, who plays an offensive position as well. Generally six of the eight players on the field are playing offense and defense. Antoine Worthman started every game for the Fury in 2001 at a defensive specialist position (DS) and was the team's leading tackler. He was awarded three game balls during the season for being the team's outstanding player of the game. Worthman did not play any offensive position.

In July 2001, the AFL players chose to be represented by the Union. The Detroit Fury players elected Andy Chilcote to be their player representative and Antoine Worthman to be the alternate player representative. When Chilcote sustained a neck injury, ending his career with the Fury, Worthman, at least unofficially, assumed his duties.

On or about November 16, 2001, the Fury paid for Worthman to fly to Detroit to attend a season ticket promotion. On or about November 27, 2001, Worthman had a telephone conversation with Jay Gruden, who had recently announced that he was stepping down as coach of the AFL's Orlando Predators, to resume his playing career. Worthman and Gruden had been teammates in 1996 on the AFL Tampa Bay Storm.

During their conversation, Gruden mentioned that his team, the Orlando Predators, might lose some of its players who were free agents. Worthman told Gruden that the Fury was negotiating with some of its players. At some point in the conversation Worthman mentioned Kelvin Kinney, a Fury lineman, who was not eligible for free agency. Worthman concedes that he told Gruden that Kinney wanted more money than the Fury was paying him and that other players were being paid substantially more. Worthman denies suggesting to Gruden that the Predators might be able to obtain Kinney's services. I find, however, that at least implicitly, Worthman indicated to Gruden that Orlando might be able to acquire Kinney.

Within an hour of this conversation, Jay Gruden called Darrel "Mouse" Davis, then the Fury's coach.[6] Gruden mentioned that he talked to Worthman and that he understood that io Kelvin Kinney was available to other AFL teams. Davis told him that was not so. On November 28, 2001, Davis left a message on the telephone answering machine at Worthman's home. Davis' message was that he had just heard some disturbing

---

6. The Fury fired Davis and Rich Stubler, his defensive co-coordinator, another of Respondent's witnesses, in July 2002, at the conclusion of a 1-13 season.

news that made him think of cutting (terminating) Worthman from the Fury. However, Davis said he wanted to discuss what he had heard with Worthman.

The same day Davis and Worthman had a forty-minute telephone conversation. Davis made it very clear that he was angry with Worthman. He told Worthman that he had heard that Worthman spoke with Jay Gruden and was trying to sell some of the Fury's players to the Orlando Predators.[7] After a thorough venting of this subject, Worthman mentioned that he had been advising players to look at the AFLPA website and providing them information about the team's salary cap. I credit Davis' testimony that he indicated that these activities didn't bother him.

On December 6, 2001, Torey Hunter, a defensive specialist, signed a contract with Respondent. The next day, Davis called Worthman to inform him that he was being released from the team. On or about December 10, 2001, the Fury selected Carl Greenwood, a defensive specialist, in a "dispersal draft" of players who had become available by virtue of the demise of the AFL Houston franchise. Greenwood signed a contact with the Fury in February 2002.

In late April or early May of 2002, after the Fury had lost their first three games of the 2002 season, Worthman called Davis to inquire about rejoining the team. Davis told Worthman that the defensive backs he had were better than Worthman. On May 8, 2002, the Fury signed OS Kenny Wheaton. On May 13, it waived Torey Hunter. On May 14, the team suspended Wheaton. On May 21, the Fury signed OS Quincy Davis. On May 28, it activated Kenny Wheaton from suspension and on June 3, it waived Carl Greenwood. [8]

Analysis

In order to prove a violation of Section 8(a)(3) and (1), the General Counsel must show that union activity or other protected concerted activity has been a substantial factor in the employer's adverse personnel decision. To establish discriminatory motivation, the General Counsel must show union or protected concerted activity, employer knowledge of that activity, animus or hostility towards that activity and an adverse personnel action caused by such animus or hostility. Inferences of knowledge, animus and discriminatory motivation may be drawn from circumstantial evidence as well from direct evidence. Once the General Counsel has made an initial showing of discrimination, the burden of persuasion shifts to the employer to prove its affirmative defense that it

---

7. "I credit Davis over Worthman and find that the initial part of their telephone conversation concerned Worthman's telephone conversation with Gruden. Worthman's testimony, that this subject didn't come up until late in the conversation, is illogical and incredible. Worthman's testimony on direct, makes it clear that Davis called Worthman on November 28 to discuss Worthman's recent conversation with Gruden and Davis' belief that Worthman was "acting like an agent for players on the team" and "contacting other teams, trying to sell our players." I also credit Davis' testimony that he indicated that he had no problem with Worthman's other activities on behalf of the Union and the Fury players. As Davis testified, somebody was going to act as player representative and there was no reason for him to be angry with Worthman for doing so. Moreover, there is absolutely no evidence of anti-union animus on the part of Davis or any other management official—apart from Worthman's account of his November 28, 2001 telephone conversation with Davis.

8. Hunter, Greenwood and Wheaton were selected in the National Football League draft and played briefly in the NFL in the 1990s. Worthman was not drafted by an NFL team nor did he play in the NFL. Although the Fury publicized the NFL experience of its players, it does not appear that such experience played any role in the Fury's decisions as to which players to acquire, keep or terminate.

would have taken the same action even if the employee had not engaged in protected activity. *Wright Line*, 251 NLRB 1083 (1980), enfd. 662 F.2d 899 (1st Cir. 1981).

In the instant case, there is no evidence of anti-union animus, except for Antoine Worthman's testimony regarding his November 28, 2001 conversation with Darrel Davis. The lack of reliable evidence of anti-union animus is the single most important factor in my decision to dismiss the Complaint. The General Counsel essentially seeks a finding of discrimination on the basis on Worthman's account of his conversation with Davis and evidence that indicates that Respondent's stated reasons for waiving Worthman are pretextual. As evidence of pretext, the General Counsel argues that Respondent has advanced shifting reasons for releasing Worthman and that the testimony of Davis and Stubler is inconsistent with Respondent's position statement. While Respondent and its witnesses have not been consistent in their explanation for the release of Worthman, I find this insufficient, when considering the record as a whole, to infer illegal motive.

Respondent argues that it waived Worthman because it found players it thought were better and because it considered him disloyal in suggesting to Jay Gruden that he might be able to acquire Fury player Kelvin Kinney. Although Respondent may not have been completely content with Mr. Worthman's play, I find that it had no plans to release him until late November 2001. Further, I conclude that but for Davis' conversation with Jay Gruden concerning Worthman's call to Gruden, the Fury would not have released Worthman on December 7, 2001. However, I conclude that Davis' decision to release Worthman was motivated by Worthman's conversations with Gruden regarding Kelvin Kinney and not about Worthman's other activities on behalf of the Union or Fury players. In this regard, Worthman's protected activities were quite unremarkable and appear not to be the sort of endeavors that would provoke discrimination by a unionized employer.

The General Counsel relies on *Boeing Airplane* Co., 110 NLRB 147 (1954) in arguing that Worthman's efforts on behalf of Kelvin Kinney were insufficiently disloyal to be deemed unprotected. However, that case is distinguishable in that unlike the *Boeing* employees, Worthman was only acting on behalf of Kelvin Kinney; his activity was not protected concerted activity. The *Boeing* employees arranged a job fair with other employers during a collective bargaining impasse. There was no issue as to whether their conduct was concerted, only whether it was sufficiently disloyal to lose the protections of the Act. Moreover, *Boeing* is also distinguishable in that the Boeing employees were attempting to persuade their employer to meet their demands. By way of contrast, there is no evidence that Worthman was attempting to obtain any result from Respondent For these reasons I find *Boeing Airplane* irrelevant to this case.

While I credit Davis and find that Torey Hunter's availability was a factor in the timing of Worthman's release, Respondent concedes that it did not have to release Worthman to make room on its roster for Torey Hunter. Respondent could have invited Worthman to training camp in the spring of 2002 had the team desired his presence. At that time Respondent could have re-evaluated the relative merits of Worthman, Hunter and other defensive specialists. The only significance I find in Worthman's performance during the 2001 season was the it was obviously not so superior to cause Davis to overlook his anger towards Worthman's conduct regarding Kelvin Kinney.

In conclusion, I find that the General Counsel has not established that Respondent threatened Antoine Worthman with termination due to union or other protected concerted activity or that it terminated his employment due to such activity. Rather, I conclude that Davis was motivated to release Worthman due to his conversation with Jay

Gruden in which he attempted to interest Gruden in acquiring Kelvin Kinney for the Orlando Predators. This activity is unprotected by the Act.[14]

On these findings of fact and conclusions of law and on the entire record, I issue the following recommended

ORDER

The complaint is dismissed.

Notes and Questions

1. Do you agree that there was no evidence of anti-union motive? Could such motive be inferred from the facts as presented?

2. As you recall from earlier discussions and decisions, employee disloyalty may render certain types of concerted activity as "unprotected." Was the employee conduct in this case *neither* concerted *nor* protected? Was it either?

(B) The Refusal to Bargain in Good Faith

At the threshold of an employer's bargaining obligation lies a duty to negotiate in good faith with the employees' exclusive representative about mandatory subjects of bargaining (wages, hours, and working conditions). *See* 29 U.S.C. § 158 (d). In all professional sports, there is no doubt concerning the identity of the labor organizations representing the employees and the owners' duty to bargain. However, recognizing those items that constitute mandatory bargaining subjects is not always a simple endeavor. Unfortunately, there is no litmus test to be applied in ascertaining the often subtle distinctions between mandatory subjects requiring good faith bargaining and the host of other subjects that rest within management's broad prerogative to implement unilaterally. Frequently, the identification of those subjects is anecdotal—we know that they are mandatory because the NLRB or the court has told us so. But, we do not necessarily know why or how they are distinguished from permissive subjects or even certain illegal subjects.

Perhaps no section of the National Labor Relations Act has been implicated in the sports context as much as Section 8(a)(5), which prohibits an employers' refusal to bargain in good faith. This refusal to bargain can assume many forms including, but certainly not limited to: engaging in surface bargaining (going through the motions); refusing to furnish relevant information (particularly in the context of claiming financial inability to meet the union's economic demands); by-passing the collective bargaining representative (especially when collective bargaining agreements permit certain types of exceptions to the exclusivity principle); and unilaterally implementing changes in wages, hours, or working conditions, as amplified at the close of this chapter. A union's refusal to bargain is prohibited by Section 8(b)(3) of the NLRA. However, most of the allegations of bad faith bargaining in the arena of professional sports have involved conduct by league owners. The following cases are illustrative.

---

14. General Counsel emphasizes the fact that Jay Gruden was no longer a coach with the Orlando Predators at the time of this telephone conversation, It argues that Gruden was a fellow bargaining unit member with whom Worthman was free to discuss Kelvin Kinney's status. Although Gruden was no longer officially a coach, I find that Worthman understood that, at least unofficially, Gruden had input into personnel decisions made by the Orlando Predators' management.

(1) Refusal to Furnish Information
Silverman v. Major League Baseball Player Relations Comm., Inc.
516 F. Supp. 588 (S.D.N.Y. 1981)

WERKER, District Judge. This is an action brought by petitioner, the Regional Director of the Second Region of the National Labor Relations Board for and on behalf of the National Labor Relations Board (the "Board") seeking temporary injunctive relief pursuant to Section 10(j) of the National Labor Relations Act, as amended (the "Act"), 29 U.S.C. § 160 (j), pending the final disposition of matters presently before the Board. Respondents in this action are the Major League Baseball Player Relations Committee, Inc., ("PRC") and twenty-four of its constituent member clubs. A hearing on petitioner's application was held on June 3 and 4, 1981. The Major League Baseball Players Association (the "Players Association") was granted leave to participate at the hearing in support of petitioner. All parties were afforded full opportunity to be heard, to present evidence bearing on the issues and to argue on the evidence and the law. After duly considering all the evidence and arguments presented, the petition for injunctive relief is denied.

FACTS

Since 1966 the Major League baseball players have been represented by the Players Association. During this time the respondent PRC has been the exclusive collective bargaining agent of twenty-six Major League clubs. The Board of Directors of the PRC is empowered to formulate labor relations policy for the clubs and direct all negotiations with the Players Association. C. Raymond Grebey, Director of Player Relations of PRC, has been designated by the PRC Board as the official spokesman for the PRC in all collective bargaining matters. To assist the PRC Board of Directors in dealing with the Players Association, the Board has designated a bargaining team, which includes Mr. Grebey, to conduct all negotiations.

The Players Association and the PRC bargain to establish an agreement on pensions, allowances and a variety of rules governing players' employment. Except as to a base salary, under the various agreements negotiated by the parties, the Players Association has waived its right to bargain with the PRC about individual player salaries. Thus, above a minimum salary, the subject has been left to each individual player to negotiate with his club.

Prior to 1975, when a Major League baseball player's employment contract expired, he was precluded from negotiating for employment with any other team except his own. In December 1975, as the result of grievances filed by the Players Association on behalf of John Messersmith and David McNally, an arbitrator found that Major League clubs could not reserve a player for more than one year ("option year") past the expiration of his contract. A player who completes the option year without signing a renewal contract with his team becomes a "free agent" who is able to negotiate with other clubs.

In 1976 the Players Association and the PRC entered into a collective bargaining agreement, effective January 1, 1976 through December 31, 1979, which provided, inter alia, for "free agency" as established by the Messersmith-McNally decision. Pursuant to this agreement, however, a player was required to serve six years in the Major Leagues before becoming a "free agent." The agreement also provided for "compensation" in the form of an amateur player draft choice to each club which lost a "free agent" player selected by more than two clubs for negotiation rights. After four years of experimenting with this new system, the Players Association and the PRC commenced negotiations for a new collective bargaining agreement on November 11, 1979.

On January 16, 1980, the PRC presented a proposal which recognized the difference in quality, as measured by skill and ability, among the various players choosing to become "free agents." Under this proposal, as finally offered on May 12, 1980, a team losing a "free agent" selected by less than four clubs will not be afforded replacement player "compensation." If a player is selected for negotiation rights by four to seven clubs, the club signing a contract with the player must compensate the player's former club with an amateur draft choice, as before. However, if a player is selected by eight or more clubs, and meets certain minimum performance standards, the signing club must compensate the former club with not only an amateur draft choice, but also a professional player of the former club's choice from a list of unprotected players under contract with the signing club. In this third category, the player is referred to as a "ranking free agent" or "premium" player. Each club may retain 40 players under the contract. Depending upon the performance level of the "free agent" signed, the signing team may protect from 15 to 18 of its 40 players. The Players Association adamantly opposed this proposal as having a negative impact on player salaries. Since the proposal requires a club signing a "ranking free agent" to give up a professional player as well as an amateur draft choice, the Association predicts that the number of clubs willing to bid for a "premium" player and the salaries they would offer would be limited by the knowledge that they would be required to forfeit a player of perhaps comparable quality.

Correspondingly, the player's present club could then offer him less to insure his remaining with the team.

As negotiations progressed, various matters were being resolved, but it became apparent that the issue of additional replacement player "compensation" was a significant impediment to settlement. Unable to reach agreement on the PRC's proposal, a strike deadline was established for May 23, 1980. On the eve of that deadline the PRC and the Players Association entered into a collective bargaining agreement ("basic agreement"), effective January 1, 1980 through December 31, 1983, establishing the terms and conditions of employment of Major League baseball players. As part of that agreement, a joint study committee was appointed to consider the unresolved matter of replacement player "compensation" for a club which loses a "free agent." The committee was to report to the PRC and the Players Association no later than January 1, 1981.

On December 8, 1980, Bowie Kuhn, Commissioner of Baseball, delivered a speech at the Annual Convention of Professional Baseball. Commenting on the financial difficulties facing the industry, Commissioner Kuhn expressed concern about escalating player salaries brought about by "free agency." He cited the companion problem of "compensation" as a threat to competitive balance in baseball and thus expressed a concern about adequate replacement talent for the loss of a "free agent." Sounding a clarion call to owners and players alike to recognize the need to correct the system of "free agency" which has given rise to these problems, he predicted further financial loss without cooperation between the two groups. Meanwhile, the joint study committee met on several occasions between August 7, 1980 and January 22, 1981. At one of the meetings, Marvin Miller, the Executive Director of the Players Association, referring to the press reports of Commissioner Kuhn's statements at the Annual Baseball Convention on December 8, 1980, asserted that the clubs' "compensation" proposal was motivated by financial concerns and by a desire to reduce player salaries. Mr. Grebey rebutted these statements and clearly stated that reduction of player salaries was not a goal of the clubs' proposal and that no question of the clubs' ability to pay was relevant or was being raised on behalf of the clubs.

Failing to agree on a joint report, separate reports were issued by the PRC on February 17, 1981 and by the Players Association on February 19, 1981. The players' position, as reflected in its report, is that the additional compensation for a "ranking free agent" diminishes that "free agent's" bargaining position with the new team by the value of the player that the signing club expects to lose. The clubs repeated their position in the report submitted by its members, stating that its current approach is not designed to attack the subject of player salaries.

This impasse ended round one of negotiations over the PRC's proposal and set the stage for round two as provided for in Article XVIII, Section D(2) of the basic agreement:

> Negotiations. Subsequent to receiving the report of the study committee, the parties shall promptly meet to commence negotiations on the subject of the study. If the parties are unable to reach agreement on the matter of player selection rights as compensation to a Club which loses a free agent player after receiving the report of the study committee and by February 15, 1981, the Clubs may thereafter but before February 20, 1981 unilaterally adopt and put into effect as part of the Basic Agreement the proposal on this matter* * *(see attachment 9) or a variation not less favorable to the Players Association. In the event the Clubs put such proposal into effect unilaterally, the Players Association may reopen the Basic Agreement with respect to the player selection rights provision put into effect by the Clubs and strike with respect thereto. The Player Association may reopen the Basic Agreement with respect to the player selection rights provision put into effect by the Clubs and strike with respect thereto. The Player Association shall give the Clubs notice of such reopening by March 1, 1981 and in such notice shall indicate the date on which it will strike, which date shall not be later than June 1, 1981. In the event the Players Association does not so strike, there shall be no further strike on this subject during the term of the Basic Agreement; provided, however, that the Players Association may, prior to March 1, 1981, offer to waive the right to strike described above and may request the Clubs to agree to a substitute right to strike in 1982 on a date not later than June 1, with no obligation on the part of the Clubs to accept such request.

On February 19, 1981, the parties having failed to reach an agreement on the "compensation" issue, the clubs invoked their option under the basic agreement and unilaterally adopted as part of that agreement their last proposal on the issue. On February 26, 1981, the Players Association likewise exercised one of its options under the agreement, reopening the basic agreement on the unresolved issue and setting a strike deadline of May 29, 1981. As a result of this reopener, the second round of negotiations began.

By letter of February 27, 1981, the Players Association requested the PRC to provide certain financial information for all member clubs. The Players Association premised the appropriateness of its request on Commissioner Kuhn's December 1980 speech which the Association interpreted as an affirmation of its belief that the "compensation" proposal was motivated by financial concerns.

Mr. Miller explained that the requested financial data was "necessary for the Players Association to properly discharge its duties and responsibilities* * *as the exclusive collective bargaining representative of all major league players, for purposes of preparation for and conduct of the ongoing negotiations." On March 13, 1981, the PRC, through Mr. Grebey, refused to comply with the Association's request, repeating the PRC's position that its bargaining stance regarding "compensation" was not based on "economic incapacity or inability." By letters of April 7 and 20, 1981, the Players Association sought reconsideration of the PRC's decision not to comply with its request. Specifically, the Association focused on the sharp increase in player salaries since the 1976 agreement. Noting a causal relationship between the "free agency" provisions of that agreement and the escalation of player salaries, the Association challenged the PRC to deny that its proposal is "designed to negatively impact upon the salaries of free agent players."

Grebey responded by letter of April 24, 1981, and again refused to comply with the Association's request. First, he noted the Association's failure to seek disclosure of club financial data until it exercised its option to reopen the basic agreement, more than sixteen months after the commencement of negotiations on the issue of player "compensation." Grebey further stated that the PRC had "never advanced the position nor taken refuge in argumentation which either directly or indirectly claims an inability to pay as a defense for (its) position in collective bargaining." Rather, the objective of the PRC in proposing the plan for "compensation," explained Mr. Grebey, "is to enhance player balance between clubs losing a quality free agent over the long term by providing replacement personnel that will: (1) compensate for the loss of a player; (2) compensate for the general inability of clubs to overcome this added turn-over on a club roster through additions from the Minor Leagues; and (3) provide equity balance in compensation, reflecting the different levels of skill and ability of players who chose to become free agents as evidenced by our experience of the past four years."

Meanwhile, during this second round of negotiations, various statements by club owners appeared in the media. These statements all reflect an expression of concern about the financial well-being of the baseball industry and/or the level of player salaries. Specifically, in an article appearing in The Sporting News on March 21, 1981, Ruly Carpenter, President of the Philadelphia Phillies, stated that "salaries have basically gotten to ridiculous proportions." Ray A. Kroc, Chairman of the Board of the San Diego Padres, made a statement which was quoted in The Sporting News magazine dated May 21, 1981, warning the players not to strike because there is a limit to the salaries they can be paid. He is also quoted as saying that only three or four clubs out of twelve in the National League are still making money.

On March 21, 1981, Toronto Blue Jays President, Peter Bavasi, predicted in a radio interview that the rise in salaries as a result of "free agency" would force the clubs into bankruptcy if the situation were not corrected. He further commented that cooperation from the players regarding the "compensation" proposal would be helpful in restraining clubs from expending large sums on "free agents" since they would have to give up a promising player as a price for signing a "premium" player.

On April 7, 1981, during a television interview, Ted Turner, President of the Atlanta Braves, similarly voiced concern about the financial state of the baseball industry due to salaries, as did Joseph Burke, in his capacity as Executive Vice President of the Kansas City Royals. Burke linked the rise in salaries to "free agency."

Believing that the PRC's bargaining position on the issue of player "compensation" was based at least in part on the financial difficulties of certain member clubs, on May 7, 1981, the Players Association filed an unfair labor practice charge with the Board alleging respondents' failure to bargain in good faith by refusing to comply with the Players Association's request for financial disclosure in violation of Sections 8(a)(1) and (5) of the Act, 29 U.S.C. §§158(a)(1) and (5).

Following investigation and pursuant to Section 10(b) of the Act, 29 U.S.C. §160(b), the Board filed a complaint charging respondents with violating Sections 8(a)(1) and

(5) of the Act. A hearing on this complaint before an Administrative Law Judge of the Board is scheduled to commence on June 15, 1981.

The temporary injunctive relief sought by petitioner requires respondents to rescind their February 19, 1981, action by which they exercised their right under the 1980 basic agreement and unilaterally implemented their bargaining proposal regarding "compensation." This relief, if granted, would thus preclude the Players Association, under the terms of the basic agreement, from commencing a strike. Petitioner argues that if its request for relief is not granted, the Players Association and the baseball player-employees it represents will be forced to strike within forty-eight hours after this Court rules, or be bound through the end of 1983 by the PRC's proposal. Petitioner emphasizes that obvious irreparable harm to the players, owners and fans would flow from a decision by the Players Association to strike.

The Association contends that if petitioner should prevail in the proceedings presently before the Administrative Law Judge, the Board would be unable to adequately remedy the PRC's alleged unfair labor practice by ordering the clubs to disclose the financial information which the Association seeks, since the Board cannot undo the effects of a strike which would ensue as a result of the denial of petitioner's instant request for relief.

Respondents vigorously oppose petitioner's application as a tactic by the Players Association to avoid the consequences of a contract freely bargained for and entered into by it.

DISCUSSION

To obtain a Section 10(j) injunction, petitioner must satisfy a two-fold test. First, this Court must find that there is reasonable cause to believe that an unfair labor practice has been committed. Second, the Court must determine whether the requested relief is just and proper. *Kaynard v. Mego Corp.*, 633 F.2d 1026, 1030 (2d Cir. 1980). Regarding issues of fact, petitioner "should be given the benefit of the doubt," and with respect to questions of law, "the Board's view should be sustained unless the court is convinced that it is wrong." *Kaynard v. Palby Lingerie, Inc.*, 625 F.2d at 1051.

Unfair Labor Practice Claim

Section 7 of the Act provides that "(employees) shall have the right to* * *bargain collectively through representatives of their own choosing * * *." 29 U.S.C. §157. Section 8(a)(5) of the Act implements this right by making it an unfair labor practice for an employer "to refuse to bargain collectively with the representatives of his employees * * *." 29 U.S.C. §158(a)(5). Section 8(d) defines collective bargaining as, inter alia, "the mutual obligation of the employer and the representative of his employees to meet at reasonable times and confer in good faith with respect to wages, hours and other terms and conditions of employment * * *." 29 U.S.C. §158(d).

Information concerning subjects at issue in bargaining is presumed to be necessary and relevant to negotiations, and employers and unions alike must provide such information when requested in the course of bargaining. *NLRB v. General Electric Co.*, 418 F.2d 736, 753 (2d Cir. 1969).

Since the Players Association exercised its option under the 1980 basic agreement on February 26, 1981, and reopened negotiations with regard to the PRC's "compensation" proposal, collective bargaining has been limited to one issue: the level of "compensation" to be paid to a club when a former player of the club, upon the expiration of his employment contract becomes a "free agent" and contracts with another club for employment.

The Board alleges in its petition that the public statements by club owners regarding claims of financial difficulties created a reasonable belief on the part of the Players Association that respondents' bargaining position during this second round of negotiations was based, "at least in part, on the present or prospective financial difficulties of certain of Respondents' member clubs." Although Marvin Miller has expressed some doubt as to club owners' inability to pay rising player salaries, he nevertheless takes the position that the Players Association must have the financial information it requests if it is to fulfill its duty of fair representation. If deprived of that information, the Association claims that it must blindly decide whether to press its demands and risk the loss of jobs for its members if the clubs cannot survive under the "compensation" terms proposed by the Association, or to recede from it position and accept the PRC's proposal without verifying owners' claims of financial distress caused by "free agency." Thus, the Association brought an unfair labor practice charge against the PRC for its failure to disclose the requested financial data after the clubs allegedly put into issue their inability to pay.

In *NLRB v. Truitt Manufacturing Co.*, 351 U.S. 149, 76 S. Ct. 753, 100 L. Ed. 1027 (1956), the Supreme Court laid to rest the question of whether an employer, bound by the National Labor Relations Act to bargain in good faith, could claim that it was financially unable to pay higher wages and then refuse a union's request to produce financial data to substantiate the claim. Holding that such conduct supported a finding of failure to bargain in good faith, in violation of Section 8(a)(5) of the Act, 29 U.S.C. §158(a)(5), the Court explained:

Good-faith bargaining necessarily requires that claims made by either bargainer should be honest claims. This is true about an asserted inability to pay an increase in wages. If such an argument is important enough to present in the give and take of bargaining, it is important enough to require some sort of proof of its accuracy. *Id*. at 152–53, 76 S. Ct. at 755–756.

However, Truitt's progeny have held that an employer is required to disclose its financial condition only when the employer claims an inability to pay, however phrased, during the course of bargaining.

Petitioner admits that at no time during bargaining sessions have respondents made a claim of inability to pay. Nevertheless, petitioner urges the Court to find that public statements made by several club owners as well as the Commissioner of Baseball about the financial condition of the industry are sufficient to support a finding of reasonable cause to believe that respondents have injected the inability to pay into the negotiations.

The cases cited by petitioner in support of its position are simply inapposite. In each case, inability to pay was put in issue at the bargaining table. Thus, no consideration of extrinsic events was necessary or relied upon in determining under Truitt, whether an employer raised the issue of inability to pay at the bargaining table.

Thus, Petitioner concedes, as it must, that the Board and courts have never found that an employer has injected financial condition into negotiations, absent statements or conduct by the employer at the bargaining table. Nevertheless, it urges this Court to find, on the basis of statements by Commissioner Kuhn and various owners, that the financial issue has become relevant to the negotiations regarding "compensation" because of the unique nature of collective bargaining in baseball. Mindful that this Court must be "hospitable" to the views of the Regional Director, however novel, I am nevertheless convinced that the Board's position is wrong, and thus will not "defer to the statutory construction urged by (it)."

It is the PRC Board of Directors which is charged with the exclusive authority to formulate the collective bargaining position of the clubs and to negotiate agreements with the Players Association. Indeed, Grebey, the official spokesman for the PRC in collective bargaining matters, has consistently denied that the clubs' financial status is at issue in the current negotiations.

Commissioner Kuhn's remarks in December 1980 at the convention cannot be imputed to the PRC as a statement of its bargaining position. First, petitioner's attempt to establish an agency relationship between the Commissioner and the PRC is unavailing. As Commissioner of Baseball, Kuhn presides at the regular joint meetings of the Major Leagues, but does not request nor preside at special meetings called by the PRC. Moreover, while Kuhn is responsible for disciplining players who may then file grievances against him in his capacity as Commissioner, he has likewise ordered the clubs to cease certain action when the interests of baseball warranted his intercession, as when he directed the clubs to open their training camps in the spring of 1976.

There can be little doubt that there is a correlation between "free agency" and the rise in player salaries. Commissioner Kuhn addressed this problem and expressed his concern about the high salaries negotiated between individual players and clubs. During his 1980 speech at the clubs' convention, he also voiced concern for a companion problem, and called for cooperation between the players and owners in combating the threat to competitive balance. He expressed optimism that a solution would be found by the joint study committee that was then considering the "compensation" issue. Fairly read, I cannot find that the Commissioner's speech supports the proposition that the clubs' bargaining position on the replacement player "compensation" proposal is motivated by financial inability.

Indeed, viewing the companion problem of player "compensation" as a separate issue, Commissioner Kuhn made a statement appearing in The Sporting News on January 24, 1981 that he did "not believe that 'compensation' as proposed by the clubs would have any effect on salaries or certainly not more than a marginal effect at most."

In a multi-employer bargaining unit as large and publicly visible as the Major League Baseball Clubs, it is inevitable that extraneous statements will be made by individuals affiliated in some way with the group which are inconsistent with the official position of the unit. This only underscores the necessity, recognized by the PRC, for centralized bargaining responsibility and authority. Clearly, individual expressions of opinion cannot serve to bind the entire bargaining unit in the absence of authority to speak for the group.

Petitioner and the Association strain to emphasize the uniqueness of collective bargaining in the baseball industry to avoid the consequences of the established labor law regarding the inability to pay. However, this Court cannot accept "collective bargaining through the press" as a basis for a 10(j) injunction.

The Act has provided for collective bargaining between the parties through their authorized representatives. If this Court were to find that the several public statements by club officials and the Commissioner were sufficient to support a finding that the PRC and its negotiating team view the respondents' "compensation" proposal as related to the financial condition of the clubs, it would do violence to the intent and purpose of the Act which limits the jurisdiction of this Court.

To accept petitioner's argument would permit disgruntled employers in a multi-employer unit who disagreed with the negotiation policies of their representatives to force negotiation issues into the courts, thereby "conducting labor management relations by way of an injunction," *id.* at 850, a result clearly contrary to the purpose of the Act. The Players Association and the PRC entered into a valid contract on May 23, 1980. As part of that contract they agreed that if the parties were unable to reach an agreement on the "compensation" issue, the PRC could implement its proposal, thereby triggering one of the Players Association's options, that is, to reopen the agreement on that issue and set a strike deadline of no later than June 1, 1981. This Court will not alter the terms of this contract for which the parties freely bargained by delaying implementation of the proposal and a possible strike on the basis of a tortured reading of the law regarding inability to pay.

Thus, I cannot find that the comments by several club officials and the Commissioner, relied upon by petitioner, are statements of policy on behalf of the PRC which would support a claim of inability to pay.

Moreover, the issue of salary, above a minimum rate, is not a subject of collective bargaining between the Players Association and the PRC. Rather, individual players negotiate independently with the clubs as to their salary. Indeed, it is the high player salaries which have resulted from the negotiation of individual contracts by players and clubs which Commissioner Kuhn addressed in his 1980 speech. Noting that player salaries are increasing at a more rapid rate than revenues, he opined that bargaining of individual contracts has led to this problem. He called upon players and owners to cooperate in this regard to arrest the trend and avoid loss to all, including the fans who will be required to pay higher ticket prices.

The evidence adduced at the hearing is insufficient to support a finding that the replacement player "compensation" proposal implemented by the PRC presents economic issues. Rather, the proposal is addressed to the inequities which flowed from the "compensation" for "free agents" as provided for in the 1976 agreement. Specifically, the proposal implemented by the PRC in February 1981, recognized the difference in skill and ability among "free agents" by the type of compensation provided to a club losing the player. In addition, the proposal is designed to more adequately assist the clubs in replacing players lost in the "free agent" draft. Under the 1976 agreement, clubs were unable to replace lost players through the Minor League and amateur systems within a meaningful time period, if at all.

Finally, I find an insufficient basis for the Board's assertion that the Players Association has a reasonable and rational belief in the clubs' inability to pay in view of its delay in requesting financial data for more than one year after the "compensation" proposal was first introduced by respondents.

As early as 1975 there were reports about club financial losses. In response to these reports, Miller characterized the claims as "phony." In 1977, again in response to reports of financial loss, Miller stated that the clubs had been making that claim for years. In January 1979, Miller claimed that the concern about the escalation of salaries was ill-founded since Major League clubs pay players a smaller proportion of income than most other industries. Tr. 56–60. A few days following the Commissioner's speech in December 1980, Miller likewise commented on the credibility of statements regarding alleged club losses by focusing on the rise in capital gains over the preceding five years. Tr. 63. Indeed, as recently as March or April of this year, Miller predicted that the clubs would refuse to produce the requested financial data because they were not losing money. Tr. 64.

Despite the presentation of a "compensation" proposal in January 1980 and Miller's apparent knowledge for several years of the losses claimed by club owners, the Players

Association first requested financial information from the clubs on February 27, 1981. This delayed request coupled with Miller's expressed opinion that the clubs were not losing money leads to the inescapable conclusion that the proceedings brought before the Board, resulting in the instant action, was not a sincere effort to obtain access to the clubs' financial records, but rather a bargaining tactic by the Association to prevent the implementation of the PRC's proposal.

The court is mindful that a strike may result from its denial of petitioner's request for a 10(j) injunction. Indeed, the industry has suffered a strike in the past. Nevertheless, in struggling with a temptation and even compulsion to prevent a strike in the public interest, I am bound by the law. The possibility of a strike, although a fact of life in labor relations, offers no occasion for this Court to distort the principles of law and equity. The resolution of the "compensation" issue is left to the parties through the negotiation process.

CONCLUSION

In accordance with the foregoing, I find there is no reasonable cause to believe that an unfair labor practice has been committed by respondents. The petition is therefore dismissed.

PLAY BALL!!!

SO ORDERED.

Notes and Questions

1. Did Judge Werker miss the point when he stressed the Players Association's apparent knowledge of the losses claimed by club owners *prior* to the initial request for financial information? Werker concluded: "This delayed request coupled with [Marvin] Miller's expressed opinion that the clubs were not losing money leads to the inescapable conclusion that the proceedings brought before the Board* * *was not a sincere effort to obtain access the club's financial records, but rather a bargaining tactic by the Association to prevent the implementation of the PRC's proposal". Judge Werker's commentary may reflect a lack of sophistication in the area of labor relations and collective bargaining. Is Miller's preconceived, cynical assessment of the owners' claims of losses pertinent to whether or not the players have a legitimate right to inspect information that would substantiate or refute the claims of such financial distress? *See generally* Brent Robbins, *Rethinking Financial Information Disclosure Under the National Labor Relations Act,* 47 Vand. L. Rev. 1905 (1994).

2. The strike that began on June 12, 1981, lasted approximately 50 days and resulted in the cancellation of 713 games. Hailed by Marvin Miller as a paragon of solidarity, the players had voted 967 to 1 in favor of a strike. In a recurrent theme, this strike was prompted by the players' unwillingness to surrender any more restrictions on free agency and their absolute resistance to other demands for increased compensation to the team losing a free agent. Because of the unusual backdrop, in which the 1981 strike had loomed on the horizon since the middle of the 1980 season, owners had purchased a $50 million strike insurance policy and had created a $15 million strike fund to enable them to weather the strike storm. The strike ended on July 31, 1981, with the players adamantly refusing to accede to any owner demand for free agency compensation. By most accounts, the owners were the losers in this strike, suffering $72 million in losses even after insurance policy recompense had been made. The players lost $34 mil-

lion, approximately $52,000 apiece. However, in 1982, average player salary had increased by $56,000 per player, and in 1985 had risen to $371,000. In 1990, the average salary had more than tripled, averaging $597,000. MARVIN MILLER, A WHOLE DIFFERENT BALL GAME, THE SPORT AND BUSINESS OF BASEBALL 295, 318 (1991).

3. The decision rendered by Judge Werker in many respects accelerated and, in fact, guaranteed the occurrence of a strike in the 1981 season. How?

4. Among the questions presented by this case is once again the status of the commissioner either as an independent party or an agent of the league owners/employers. While this case ultimately turned on whether the employer raised the issue of an inability to pay at the bargaining table or in peripheral discussions, the unaddressed question remained whether or not the commissioner's statements could be imputed to the ownership. If the peripheral comments had been interpreted to constitute actual "bargaining table" negotiations, could the owners have been found liable for a refusal to bargain by failing to disclose the requested financial information? Likewise, could statements made by the commissioner to the effect that his employer/principals were unable to meet the union's demands have visited a requirement upon the owners that their books be divulged to the Players Association?

5. As discussed in earlier chapters, questions concerning the degree of involvement of the commissioner in labor negotiations has arisen on numerous occasions, the most recent of which prompted the termination of Commissioner Fay Vincent. While numerous reasons were offered for Vincent's ouster, it is well known that one source of consternation among the owners was Vincent's calling a halt to the lockout in 1990, which many construed as a show of disloyalty to the ownership.

6. Throughout the history of negotiations between the MLBPA and the ownership, the most prevalent ungranted request has been the players' demand to examine the owners' books. This persistent demand has been prompted by constant complaints from teams, particularly those teams located in small markets, that they are simply incapable of meeting the salary demands of the players. As a result, owners have suggested various devices to limit player mobility, such as restrictions on free agency, salary caps, compensation systems, etc. The players, however, flushed with the success of negotiating individual deals with owners for extremely high salaries, steadfastly have refused to surrender the free agency secured several years ago and have demanded that the owners expose their "books" to public scrutiny to prove the dire financial conditions allegedly afflicting the league.

Although there has been some "confidential" disclosure of those Major League teams that are "in financial trouble", the owners have failed to comply with the union's request for more telling financial data. Interestingly, by mutual agreement, those teams that have been designated as flagging franchises cannot be identified. Players Association Executive Director Don Fehr has expressed the view that many teams have "cried wolf" and have misrepresented their weak economic position. Given the considerable distrust between the players and the owners, particularly after the owners' collusive activities in the mid-1980's, it is unlikely that the players will ever feel comfortable acceding to ownership's demands for concessions in the area of free agency unless and until they can visibly identify the areas of the owners' financial distress. The players' adamant refusal to accept a salary cap notwithstanding their grudging acceptance of a luxury tax is illustrative.

7. The owners' intransigence in this area stands in marked contrast to NBA owners who, several years ago, supported the call for a salary cap by opening their books for the

Players Association's review. The players' eventual acquiescence in the original salary cap was a product of their belief in the owners' claims of financial travail as evidenced by hard economic data.

8. Clearly, Judge Werker's *denial* of the injunction in *Silverman* played a vital role in the lengthy strike of 1981. Ironically, almost fifteen years later, Judge Sotomayor's *issuance* of an injunction in April, 1995, in response to the MLBPA's filing of unfair labor practice charges, the General Counsel's finding of "merit," and the NLRB's request for injunctive relief, ended the longest strike in baseball history. Both injunction requests stemmed from player allegations that the owners had failed to bargain in good faith, the former based on a refusal to furnish information and the latter predicated on the owners' unilateral changes in working conditions.

9. The duty to furnish information is not limited to the negotiating table. Labor organiations are entitled to relevant information in the processing of grievances and related administration of the collective bargaining agreement. *See National Hockey League,* 1999 NLRB LEXIS 395 (1999); 2-CA-29510; 2-CA-3022; 2-CA-30397.

10. As discussed in Chapter 14, a union that is recognized by an employer or certified as collective bargaining representative by the NLRB is the employees' exclusive representative for purposes of negotiating wages, hours, and working conditions of employment. Accordingly, any unilateral action by management or any attempts to bargain individually with employees who are represented by a labor organization would constitute bad faith bargaining in violation of Section 8(a)(5) of the NLRA. There are circumstances, however, in which the union may waive its right to serve as exclusive bargaining representative, particularly when the differences in skill levels of the employees in the bargaining unit may dictate that some type of individual bargaining is the most prudent course. *See J.I. Case v. NLRB,* 321 U.S. 332 (1944). The sports industry presents some unique circumstances that allow for limited individual dealing, particularly with regard to player salaries. *See generally* WEISTART & LOWELL §6.07, at 806–13. The exclusivity principle and pertinent exceptions are addressed in the cases that follow.

(2) Bypassing the Collective Bargaining Representative
Morio v. North American Soccer League
501 F. Supp. 633 (S.D.N.Y. 1980)

MOTLEY, District Judge. This is an action brought by Petitioner, the Regional Director, Region 2, National Labor Relations Board, for and on behalf of the National Labor Relations Board (the Board) in which she seeks a temporary injunction pursuant to Section 10(j) of the National Labor Relations Act, as amended (the Act), pending the final disposition of matters presently pending before the Board. Respondents in this action are the North American Soccer League and its 21 constituent member clubs in the United States. The action is now before the court upon the issuance of an order to show cause why the temporary injunctive relief prayed for by Petitioner should not be granted. Petitioner filed her order to show cause for a temporary injunction, verified complaint, affidavits and brief in support of her application on July 30, 1980. Respondents' answer was served on August 5, 1980. A hearing was held on August 6 and 7, 1978. The North American Soccer League Players Association (the Union) was permitted to intervene in the action and to participate in the hearing. All parties were given an opportunity on the hearing to present evidence and to argue the legal issues. Thereafter, Petitioner and Respondents were given an opportunity to submit proposed findings of fact, conclusions of law, and briefs. The court has now considered the verified petition of Winifred D. Morio, Regional Director of Region 2 of the National Labor Relations Board, the answer of Respondents, the evidence adduced at the hearing, the arguments of the parties and intervenor and the proposed findings of fact and conclusions of law and briefs. Upon the entire record, the court finds and concludes that Petitioner has reasonable cause to believe and there is reasonable cause to believe that Respondents have engaged in unfair labor practices and that Petitioner is entitled to the temporary injunctive relief sought in this action.

On August 16, 1977, the Union filed a petition for an election under Section 9(c) of the Act alleging that the League and each of its affiliated members constituted a single employer for purposes of collective bargaining. Hearings were held from September 8 to September 30, 1977, and briefs were submitted on the unique and complex issues of the appropriate unit in the professional soccer industry. On June 30, 1978, exactly nine months later, the Board issued a decision and direction of election among the soccer player employees of those teams listed in the petition as well as other employers who had been granted franchises by the League and commenced operations of teams during the intervening period.

On or about July 27, 1978, through August 4, 1978, the employees of Respondent Clubs participated in a secret ballot election conducted under the supervision of the Board, wherein a majority of the valid votes counted were cast for the Union. On September 1, 1978, the Union was certified as the exclusive collective bargaining representative of the employees of Respondent Clubs.

Subsequent to the certification, Respondents refused to bargain with the Union and contested the Board's determination of a single "League-wide unit" as being appropriate for collective bargaining. The Union filed an unfair labor practice charge on October 30, 1978 in Case No. 2-CA-15966. The General Counsel issued a complaint on November 24, 1978, against Respondents which alleged, inter alia, that Respondents had failed and refused to recognize and bargain with the Union in violation of Section 8(a)(1) and (5) of the Act. Following a summary judgment proceeding, the Board, on April 30, 1979, issued an order directing Respondents to bargain with the Union (241 NLRB No. 199). The Respondents appealed the Board's order to the United States Court of Appeals for the Fifth Circuit.

On March 21, 1980, the United States Court of Appeals for the Fifth Circuit issued its decision enforcing the Board's Order (103 L.R.R.M. 2976) and on May 14, 1980, issued its mandate. The mandate contained language directing the Respondents to recognize and bargain with the Union as exclusive collective bargaining representative of Respondent's professional soccer players.

Respondents have filed a petition for a writ of certiorari in the United States Supreme Court. Their petition for rehearing has been denied by the Fifth Circuit and no stay of the Fifth Circuit's mandate has been secured.

On March 28, 1979, the Union, pursuant to provisions of the Act, filed with the Board a charge alleging that Respondents have engaged in and are engaging in unfair labor practices within the meaning of Section 8(a)(1) and (5) of the Act.[7] Other such unfair labor practice charges were filed by the Union on June 25, 1979, alleging violations of 8(a)(1), (3) and (5) of the Act. These charges were referred to Petitioner for

---

7. The Board has found that the Respondent League and its constituent member clubs are joint employers and that a collective bargaining unit comprised of all NASL players on clubs based in the United States is appropriate. 236 N.L.R.B. No. 181 (1978). This determination has been affirmed by the Fifth Circuit. 613 F.2d 1379 (5th Cir. 1980), *rehearing denied,* 616 F.2d 568 (5th Cir. 1980).

adjudication. Thereafter, on October 20, 1979, a complaint and notice of hearing pursuant to Section 10(b) of the Act, alleging that Respondents have engaged and are engaging in unfair labor practices within the meaning of the Act, was issued by the Regional Director. On November 30, 1979, the Union filed more charges of unfair labor practices by Respondents which were again referred to the Regional Director and again on January 18, 1980, a complaint and notice of hearing with respect to these latest charges were issued by Petitioner. All charges by the Union were ordered consolidated for hearing by Petitioner on February 14, 1980. On February 19, 1980, Petitioner amended the consolidated complaint. Subsequently, hearings were held before Administrative Law Judge Benjamin Schlesinger. These hearings were held between March 4 and May 1, 1980, in four cities around the country. On May 28, 1980, the General Counsel of the Board moved to amend the consolidated complaint. The hearing before the Administrative Law Judge has not been concluded. Petitioner seeks a temporary injunction pending the final disposition of the charges presently before the Administrative Law Judge and the final action of the Board with respect thereto.

Respondent, the North American Soccer League, is a non-profit association. It currently comprises about 24 professional soccer teams, 21 of which are located in the United States and three of which are located in Canada. The League's principal office is at 1133 Avenue of the Americas, County, City and State of New York, where it has been engaged in its operation as a non-profit association. Each of the constituent members is engaged primarily in the business of promoting and exhibiting professional soccer contests for viewing by the general public. Collectively, these clubs annually gross revenue in excess of half a million dollars and purchase and cause to be imported in interstate commerce goods and materials valued in excess of $ 50,000. The Respondent League and its constituent member clubs constitute and have constituted at all times material herein joint employers for the purpose of collective bargaining.

The Union is an unincorporated association and is an organization of employees which exists for the purpose, in whole or in part, of dealing with employees concerning grievances, labor disputes, wages, rates of pay, hours of employment or conditions of employment. The Union maintains its principal offices at 1300 Connecticut Avenue, N.W., Washington, D. C.

Philip Woosman is the Commissioner of the North American Soccer League. Ted Howard is Director of Operations of the League. Derek Carroll is Chairman of the Labor Relations Committee of the constituent member clubs and president of the New England Tea Men.

All professional soccer players, whether on loan or otherwise, employed by Respondent League and Respondent Clubs constitute a unit appropriate for the purposes of collective bargaining within the meaning of Section 9(b) of the Act. This unit includes players on the following eligibility lists: active, temporarily inactive, disabled, suspended, ineligible, and military. The unit does not include officials of Respondent League or managerial or executive personnel of Respondent League and Respondent Clubs or players employed by the Edmonton Drillers, Toronto Metros and Vancouver Whitecaps. All other employees and supervisors as defined in the Act are also included. Since September 1, 1978, the Union, by virtue of Section 9(a) of the Act has been and is now the exclusive representative of all the employees in the unit for the purpose of collective bargaining with respect to the rates of pay, wages, hours of employment and other terms and conditions of employment.[8]

---

8. 29 U.S.C. §159(a).

In this case Petitioner alleges that she has reasonable cause to believe that Respondent interfered with, restrained and coerced employees in the exercise of rights guaranteed them by Section 7 of the Act by engaging in the following acts and conduct:

1. On or about October 19, 1978, and continuing thereafter, Respondents unilaterally changed the employment conditions of the employees in the Unit by requiring them to obtain permission from their respective clubs whenever a particular brand of footwear, other than selected by each of Respondent Clubs, is desired by an employee.

2. On April 10, 1979, Respondent, acting through their agents, Phil Woosman and Ted Howard, unilaterally changed the employment conditions of the employees in the unit by initiating plans for a new winter indoor soccer season which began in November, 1979, and ended in March, 1980.

3. On or about November 24, 1979, and continuing to the present, Respondents, acting through their agents, Phil Woosman and Ted Howard, and other agents presently unknown, unilaterally changed and are continuing to change the employment conditions of the employees in the unit by requiring them to play or otherwise participate in the winter indoor soccer season.

4. On or about October 16, 1979, Respondents, acting through the same agents named above, unilaterally changed the employment conditions of employees in the unit by initiating plans to increase the 1980 regular summer outdoor soccer season schedule by two games and two weeks over the 1979 format and by subsequently implementing said plans and maintaining them in full force and effect.

5. On or about October 16, 1979, Respondents, acting through their said agents, unilaterally changed the employment conditions of employees in the unit by initiating plans to reduce the maximum roster of all the Respondent Clubs during the regular summer outdoor summer season from 30 to 26 players and by subsequently implementing said plan and maintaining them in full force and effect.

6. Commencing on or about October 19, 1978, until on or about March, 1979, and continuing thereafter, Respondents by-passed the Union and dealt directly with employees in the unit. Respondents solicited employees to enter into individual employment contracts, negotiated individual employment contracts, and actually entered into individual employment contracts with the employee members of the unit.

The evidence introduced at the hearing conducted by the court established that Petitioner has reasonable cause to believe that Respondents have entered into individual contracts with employees since September 1, 1978, and continue to do so and that these individual contracts constitute 96.8% of the existing individual contracts. The other 3.2% of the current individual player contracts were entered into prior to the Union's certification on September 1, 1978.

Respondents conceded that they have unilaterally changed the conditions of employment by requiring employees to obtain permission from their respective clubs before wearing a particular brand of footwear other than that selected by each Respondent Club; that they have changed the conditions of employment by initiating plans for a new winter indoor soccer season which began in November, 1979, and ended in March, 1980; that they unilaterally changed conditions of employment by requiring employees to play or otherwise participate in the winter indoor soccer season; that they unilaterally changed conditions of employment by initiating plans to increase the 1980 summer outdoor soccer season by two games and two weeks over the 1979 format, which is presently in operation; and that they unilaterally changed employment conditions by initiating plans to reduce the maximum roster of all the Respondent Clubs during the regular summer outdoor season from 30 players to 26 players beginning on or about October 16, 1979, and continuing to the present.

Petitioner has therefore established that she has reasonable cause to believe that the Respondents have engaged in the foregoing unfair labor practices and is, therefore, entitled to temporary injunctive relief, pending the final determination of these charges presently pending before the Administrative Law Judge and the Board, as provided by Section 10(j) of the Act.

The court therefore finds and concludes that there is reasonable cause to believe Respondents have engaged in unfair labor practices in violation of the Act and that Petitioner is entitled to temporary injunctive relief as prayed for in the petition.

Respondents' first claim that some of the constituent clubs throughout the United States did not receive notice of the petition and order to show cause and therefore the court could not proceed to hear the petition as to them. The court finds that pursuant to the order of this court Petitioner personally served the Respondent League at its New York office and served Respondents' constituent member clubs by certified mail with a copy of the petition and order to show cause before 5:00 p.m. on July 31st. The court also finds that in addition counsel for Petitioner notified the joint employers' attorneys for Petitioner's intention to seek injunctive relief should settlement efforts fail, as early as June 17, 1980. The court therefore concludes that Petitioner has satisfied Rule 4(d)(7) of the Federal Rules of Civil Procedure and that all Respondents received timely and sufficient notice of the application for a temporary injunction and the hearing.

Respondents next claim that injunctive relief should be denied since the Board, itself, is responsible for delaying its own final determination of the charges of unfair labor practices which have been filed before it by the Union. This court finds that delay was caused in part by Respondents and that there has been no such delay by the Board as to warrant a denial of the requested injunctive relief. The section pursuant to which Petitioner invokes this court's jurisdiction for temporary injunctive relief contemplates that there will be need for relief pending the final determination of matters pending before the Board, as the legislative history indicates. (S.Rep. No. 105, 80th Cong., 1st Sess. 8 (1947)). Section 10(j) of the Act provides that the Board shall have the power on the issuance of a complaint charging unfair labor practices to petition any district court of the United States, in any district wherein the unfair labor practice in question is alleged to have occurred or wherein such person resides or transacts business, for appropriate temporary relief, or a restraining order. That section confers jurisdiction upon this court to grant the relief requested after notice and hearing.

The unilateral changes which Respondents admit have occurred since September 1, 1978, in the terms and conditions of employment, may violate the employer's obligations to bargain with the exclusive bargaining representative of the players. The duty to bargain carries with it the obligation on the part of the employer not to undercut the Union by entering into individual contracts with the employees. In *NLRB v. Katz*, 369 U.S. 736 (1962), the Supreme Court noted: "A refusal to negotiate in fact as to any subject which is within §8(d) and about which the Union seeks to negotiate violates §8(a)(5)."

It is undisputed that Respondents have since September 1, 1978, refused to bargain with the Union. Respondents claim that they had a right to refuse to bargain with the Union since they were pursuing their right to appeal the Board's determination that all of the players referred to above constitute a unit for collective bargaining purposes. Respondents' duty to bargain with the Union arose from the time the Union was certified as the exclusive bargaining representative of the players—September 1, 1978. The fact that Respondents were pursuing their right to appeal did not, absent a stay of the Board's order, obviate their duty to bargain with the Union and does not constitute a defense to an application for relief under Section 10(j) of the Act where, as here, Respondents have apparently repeatedly refused to bargain with the Union and have continued to bypass the Union and deal directly with employees. As Petitioner says, Respondents could have bargained subject to later court decision adverse to Petitioner and the Union and can do so now. Negotiations between Respondents and the Union were scheduled to commence August 12, 1980, notwithstanding Respondents' petition for a writ of certiorari.

Respondents' most vigorous opposition comes in response to Petitioner's application for an order requiring Respondents to render voidable, at the option of the Union, all individual player contracts, whether entered into before or after the Union's certification on September 1, 1978. Respondents' claim that such power in the hands of the Union, a non-party to this action, would result in chaos in the industry and subject Respondents to severe economic loss and hardship since these individual contracts are the only real property of Respondents.

It should be noted, at the outset, that the relief requested by Petitioner is not a request to have all individual contracts declared null and void. It should be emphasized that Petitioner is not requesting that the "exclusive rights" provision of the individual contracts, which bind the players to their respective teams for a certain time, be rendered voidable. Moreover, the Board seeks an order requiring Respondents to maintain the present terms and conditions in effect until Respondents negotiate with the Union—except, of course, for the unilateral changes—unless and until an agreement or a good faith impasse is reached through bargaining with the Union. Petitioner does not, however, seek to rescind that unilateral provision which provided for the present summer schedule. The Board has consciously limited its request for relief to prevent any unnecessary disruption of Respondents' business. The Board is seeking to render voidable only those unilateral acts taken by the Respondents, enumerated above, which Respondents admit have in fact occurred.

These unilateral changes appear to modify all existing individual contracts entered into before September 1, 1978, in derogation of the Union's right to act as the exclusive bargaining agent of all employees in the unit.

The court finds that Petitioner is entitled to the temporary injunctive relief which it seeks with respect to all of the individual contracts. The individual contracts entered into since September 1, 1978, are apparently in violation of the duty of the Respondents to bargain with the exclusive bargaining representative of the players. The Act requires Respondents to bargain collectively with the Union. The obligation is exclusive. This duty to bargain with the exclusive representative carries with it the negative duty not to bargain with individual employees. *Medo Photo Supply Corp. v. NLRB*, 321 U.S. 678 (1944).

With respect to the individual contracts entered into prior to September 1, 1978, Petitioner is entitled to an injunction enjoining Respondents from giving effect to these individual contracts of employment or any modification, continuation, extension or renewal thereof "to forestall collective bargaining." *J. I. Case Co. v. NLRB*, 321 U.S. 332, 341 (1944). The evidence adduced at the hearing disclosed that Respondents have refused to recognize that only the Union has the right to waive, if it so desires and to the extent it so desires, its right to be the exclusive bargaining representative. Respondents had also refused to negotiate with the Union since September 1, 1978, pending resolution of their appeal.

In *National Licorice Co. v. NLRB*, 309 U.S. 350 (1940), the Supreme Court held that the Board has the authority, even in the absence of the employees as parties to the proceeding, to order an employer not to enforce individual contracts with its employees which were found to have been in violation of the NLRA. Petitioner is seeking temporary relief to this effect as to those individual contracts entered into before September 1, 1978, as well as relief with respect to those contracts entered into prior to September 1, 1978. The evidence discloses that Petitioner has reasonable cause to believe that Respondents have used, and will continue to use, the individual contracts entered into prior to September 1, 1978, to forestall collective bargaining.

With such contracts in place, Petitioner has reasonable cause to believe that Respondents' determination not to bargain with the Union has been well fortified and that there simply is no incentive for Respondents to bargain with the Union with those contracts in place. Petitioner has reasonable cause to believe that the ability of Respondents to enter into individual contracts and to continue to enforce them is to bypass and to undermine support for the Union. The court therefore finds that there is reasonable cause to believe that Respondents have used the individual contracts entered into prior to September 1, 1978, to forestall collective bargaining.

The Board is, therefore, entitled to the relief which it seeks requiring Respondents to render voidable certain provisions in the existing individual contracts which the Union requests, as set forth above. The Union has been permitted by the court to intervene in this action as a party petitioner. The court finds that it is not the intent of the Petitioner, as Respondents claim, to visit punitive actions on Respondents and that the requested relief with respect to the individual contracts has been carefully tailored to avoid chaos in Respondents' industry and to avoid any economic hardship to Respondents.

Finally, the court finds that under the circumstances of this case a temporary injunction would be just and proper. In so holding, this court does not intend to pass on the merits of any pending unfair labor charges before the Board. Those are matters for determination by the Board. The court notes, however, that these charges are still pending before the Board and that Respondents are still pursuing all available remedies in the courts. It may therefore be a long time before final resolution of these matters. The court also notes that after the instant hearing was concluded, but before this court's decision, Respondents and the Union were scheduled to commence negotiations. However, those negotiations, if commenced, may take months to complete. In the interim, the purposes of the NLRA may be defeated and the public interests harmed.

Notes and Questions

1. What was the purpose of NASL teams negotiating individual contracts with their players? Should these individual contracts have been voided completely given the fact that the union had become the exclusive bargaining representative, and the fact that any individual contracting immediately before, or subsequent to, that certification could have had a chilling effect on union organizing and negotiating efforts? Why did the court conclude that the appropriate remedy was to render the contracts voidable?

2. The *Midland Broadcasting* case, following immediately below, considered the parameters of potential exceptions to the exclusivity principle discussed earlier. As you will see, there hardly was Board unanimity on the approach to be taken in developing a workable formula. Has *Midland* misperceived the proper accommodation of individual

negotiation and the collective bargaining process? Resolution of this question will assist your response to the problem following the *Midland* case.

Midland Broadcasting Co.
93 NLRB 445 (1951)

Decision and Order

On February 8, 1950, Trial Examiner Myers D. Campbell, Jr., issued his Intermediate Report in the above-entitled case, copy of which is attached, finding that the Respondent has not engaged in any of the unfair labor practices alleged in the complaint, and recommending that the complaint be dismissed in its entirety. The General Counsel and American Federation of Radio Artists, A. F. of L., filed exceptions to the Intermediate Report together with supporting briefs. The Respondent filed a brief and reply brief in support of the Intermediate Report.

All parties participated in oral argument before the Board on September 8, 1950.

The Board has reviewed the rulings of the Trial Examiner at the hearing and finds that no prejudicial error was committed. The rulings are hereby affirmed. The Board has considered the Intermediate Report, the briefs and exceptions, the contentions advanced at oral arguments, and the entire record in the case, and hereby adopts the findings, conclusions, and recommendations of the Trial Examiner, with the following additions and modifications:

1.   The General Counsel and the Union contend that the Respondent violated Section 8(a) (5) and (1) of the Act by executing and continuing in effect individual or "talent" contracts with its staff actors and singers; notwithstanding that the union was the exclusive bargaining agent of such artists. In agreeing with the Trial Examiner's finding that the Respondent did not violate the Act in this respect, we are particularly persuaded by the following considerations:

Section 6 of the 1946 and 1948 contracts between the Union and the Respondent covering its staff artists expressly authorized direct negotiations between the Respondent and the artists.[1] The Union and our dissenting colleagues do not question the fact that, under the special circumstances present in this industry, these individual bargaining provisions were themselves consistent with the Respondent's bargaining obligations under the Act.

They are expressly limited, however, to the negotiation of better terms than those contained in the union contracts. Relying on this authorization, the Respondent negotiated individual, or "talent," contracts with its artists. Generally speaking, these talent

---

1. Section 6 of the 1946 and 1948 union contracts read as follows:

* * * The Company agrees that no staff artist will be employed or engaged at Station KMBC upon terms and conditions less favorable to the staff artist than those set forth in Schedule I * * *. The Company further agrees that nothing in this contract shall be deemed to prevent any staff artist from negotiating for or obtaining better terms than the minimum terms provided herein * * *. (1946 contract.)

The Company agrees that no full-time staff artist will be employed * * * upon terms and conditions less favorable to the full-time staff artist than those contained in this contract and Schedule I * * *and that the Company further agrees that nothing in this contract shall be deemed to prevent any full-time staff artist from negotiating for or obtaining better terms than the minimum terms provided herein. (1948 contract.)

93 NLRB No. 65.

contracts differed from the union contracts in that they afforded the artist an opportunity to earn a bonus over and above the minimum rates of pay guaranteed by the union contracts, but at the same time imposed certain restrictions on the artist, designed in general to assure that the Respondent would receive the exclusive benefit of its investment in the artist.

The General Counsel contends, however, that certain provisions of the talent contracts are less favorable than the union contracts, and that in negotiating and continuing such provisions in effect the Respondent has therefore exceeded the scope of its authority to negotiate directly with individual artists for *better* terms, thereby violating Section 8(a) (5) and (1) of the Act. We do not agree that the present record supports that contention.

Among the provisions of the talent contracts claimed to be less favorable are those relating to the artists' compensation. However, we agree that the Trial Examiner that the talent contracts, as administered by the Respondent, have not had the effect of reducing any artist's pay below the union minimum.

The General Counsel contends further that the talent contracts are less favorable in that they impose certain restrictions on the artist's freedom to sell his services on the open market, both during his employment by the Respondent and for some time thereafter. Assuming that these restrictions are in derogation of the provisions of the union contracts, we nevertheless find that the General Counsel has not established by the preponderance of the evidence that, in negotiating or maintaining the talent contracts in effect, the Respondent exceeded the scope of its authority under Section 6 of the union contracts to bargain directly with its artists with respect to better or more favorable terms that those contained in the Union contracts.

It is not sufficient, in our opinion, to show that a particular provision of the talent contracts, taken by itself, is less favorable than a particular term of the union contract. The talent contracts are self-contained, collateral agreements, conferring certain benefits upon the artists in the form of a bonus arrangement, in consideration for which the artists accept certain responsibilities and restrictions. If we were to strike down the burdensome provisions and leave only the bonus provisions of the talent contracts in effect, we would be making a new and different contract for the parties. That is not the function of this Board.

It is not without significance that while the union contract established grievance machinery, it does not appear from the record that the question whether the talent contracts are less favorable than the union contracts has been taken up by the Union, or by any artist, as a grievance. This is not the sort of controversy which Congress established this Board to consider or decide.

We find, therefore, in agreement with the Trial Examiner, that the Respondent did not violate the Act by negotiating the talent contracts or by continuing them in effect.

* * *

Order

Upon the entire record in this case, and pursuant to Section 10(c) of the National Labor Relations Act, as amended, the National Labor Relations Board orders that the complaint in this case against the Respondent, Midland Broadcasting Company, be and it hereby is, dismissed.

MEMBERS HOUSTON and STYLES, dissenting in part:

We disagree with the decision of the majority of the Board in this case insofar as it finds that the Respondent did not violate Section 8(a)(5) of the Act by negotiating, executing, and continuing in effect certain provisions of its individual contracts with its staff artists at a time when the Union was the acknowledged statutory bargaining representative of such artists. It is well settled that the statutory representative has the exclusive right to bargain for the employees it represents, and that any direct negotiations between an employer and such employees is in derogation of that right, and hence violative of Section 8(a)(5).

The Respondent contends, however, that various provisions in its 1946 and 1948 contracts with the Union authorized the Respondent to negotiate and execute all the provisions of such individual "talent" contracts.

The Respondent relies principally on the following language of Section 6 of the 1946 and 1948 union contracts.:

> * * * The Company agrees that no staff artist will be employed or engaged at Station KMBC upon terms and conditions less favorable to the staff artist than those set forth in Schedule I* * *.The Company further agrees that nothing in this contract shall be deemed to prevent any staff artist from negotiating for or obtaining better terms than the minimum terms provided herein* * *.(1946 contract.)

> * * * The Company agrees that no full-time staff artist will be employed* * *upon terms and conditions less favorable to the full-time staff artist than those contained in this contract and schedule I * * * and the Company further agrees that nothing in this contract shall be deemed to prevent any full-time staff artist from negotiating for or obtaining better terms than the minimum terms provided herein. (1948 contract.)

We construe these provisions as permitting the Respondent to negotiate and execute contracts with individual artists, but only insofar as they (1) relate to matters covered by the union contracts, and (2) provide terms more favorable than those contained in the union contracts. Under this view, negotiations by the Respondent with individual artists were not authorized by the Union contracts if (1) they did not relate to matters covered by such contracts, or (2) they did relate to such matters, but involved terms not more favorable to the artist than the terms contained in such contracts.

Such a view not only accords with our settled policy of construing strictly any waiver by a union of its rights under the Act, but also constitutes the most reasonable interpretation of the meaning of the foregoing quoted provisions. There can be no question that such provisions did not authorize the negotiation of an individual contract provision which, while relating to a matter covered by the union contract—such as wages— was not more favorable than the terms of the union contract. The union contracts are unequivocal on this point. As to matters not covered by the union contracts—*e.g.,* the artists's property right in his own compositions, his right to seek other employment after leaving Respondent's employ—there was no warrant in the union contracts for any negotiations whatsoever on these subjects. The Union had consented only to the negotiation of "more favorable" terms than those contained in the union contracts. This test necessarily implied in our opinion that the negotiations must relate to matters which were susceptible of comparison with some term of the union contracts; otherwise, the requirement that the terms negotiated with individuals be more favorable than the collectively bargained terms would be meaningless. Clearly, it would be impossible to determine whether a provision in a talent contract which had no counterpart in the union contracts was more favorable than anything in the union contracts. Consequently, it is clear that the only way to give effect to the "more favorable" test in the union contracts is to construe those contracts as permitting individual bargaining only with respect to matters covered by the union contracts, and as to those matters, as already stated, the bargaining must be limited to terms more favorable than those contained in the union contracts.

Under the circumstances of this case, we believe that the Union might, if it wishes, effectively waive its exclusive bargaining rights to the limited extent indicated in Section 6 of its contracts with the Respondent, and that the Respondent was free, *within those limits*, to bargain directly with individual artists. However, we find that the Respondent exceeded those limits by bargaining for, and incorporating in the talent contracts, provisions which were either less favorable than comparable provisions in the union contract or which related to matters outside the scope of such contracts.

The majority holds further that it is not sufficient to show that certain provisions of the talent contracts may be less favorable to the artists than corresponding provisions of the union contracts, because the contracts also confer certain benefits upon the artists. We know of no basis for this view. The union contracts forbid the negotiation of less favorable "terms and conditions" of employment, and authorize the negotiation of better "terms," than the union minimum. Under this language, the negotiation of *any*"term" of employment, which was not more favorable than the union minimum would violate the union contracts.

In the parlance of labor relations each distinct provision of an employment contract is a term of employment. Thus, when the contract embodies a number of clauses, one relating to wages, another to hours, a third to seniority, etc., each such clause is deemed to be a term of the employment relation.

We believe therefore that, in drafting Section 6 of the union contracts, the parties intended to preclude the negotiation of *any* provision which, in itself, was to more favorable to the artist than the union contracts, and did not intend to permit the negotiation of such a provision upon the condition that the Respondent simultaneously agreed with the individual artists on other provisions, the sum of which was more favorable to the artists than the union contracts. And, unlike the majority, we can attach no significance to the fact that no grievance may have been filed under the union contract on the issuance of whether the talent contracts are less favorable than the union contracts.

We would find, therefore, that the Respondent violated its statutory duty to bargain with the majority representative by negotiating provisions in the talent contracts which were less favorable than the union contracts. Contrary to the assumption of the majority, such a finding would not require that we engage in the function of rewriting the talent contracts for the parties. Our order need merely direct the Respondent to cease and desist from engaging in the conduct found to be unlawful and to bargain with the Union on the inclusion in *future* talent contracts of provisions not authorized by the existing union contract.

Notes and Questions

1. Union consent to limited individual bargaining for better terms than those provided by the applicable collective bargaining agreement presumably reflected recognition by the union of the great differences in the earning power of radio artists. In *J. I. Case*, the court said:

Of course, where there is great variation in circumstances of employment or capacity of employees, it is possible for the collective bargain to prescribe only minimum rates or maximum hours or expressly to leave certain areas open to individual bargaining.

321 U.S. at 338.

2. Is it unrealistic to apply conventional rules governing rank and file production employees to professional athletes? While there are numerous points of comparison, the differences in terms of skill levels and salary potential dictate the need for an approach that permits more latitude in individual bargaining over wages and special benefits. It is not surprising that most major sports collective bargaining agreements provide for some waiver of the union's status as exclusive bargaining agent. In Chapter 14, we cited such language from the collective bargaining agreement between Major League Baseball and the Major League Baseball Players Association. Article XXXIV of the NBA/NBPA bargaining agreement provides another illustration:

> The NBA recognizes the Players Association as the exclusive collective bargaining representative of persons who are employed by NBA Members as professional basketball players (and/or who may become so employed during the term of this Agreement or any extension thereof); and the Players Association warrants that it is duly empowered to enter into this Agreement for and on behalf of such persons. The NBA and the Players Association agree that, notwithstanding the foregoing, such persons and NBA Members may, on an individual basis, bargain with respect to and agree upon the provisions of Player Contracts, but only as and to the extent permitted by this Agreement.

Notwithstanding this language, the possible additions to, or deletions from, the standard NBA player contract are narrowly circumscribed. *See* NBA Collective Bargaining Agreement, Article II, §2(a). Baseball's special covenant exception does not contain such explicit restrictions, leaving the door ajar for further litigation to interpret the validity of standard player contract language arguably intruding upon the benefits provided by the CBA.

3. In various professional sports contexts the quandary presented by this type of "exculpatory" language may manifest itself. For example, an individual payment to a player in exchange for his or her agreement to submit to random drug testing (hypothetically prohibited by the collective bargaining agreement) may rest squarely within the Special Covenants proviso or may independently violate both Section 8(a)(5) of the NLRA and the drug testing proscription of the collective bargaining agreement. The issue will turn on the extent to which the special deal corrupts the benefits derived from such agreement. If the special covenant is perceived to detract from the collective or if it appears as though the special benefit is employed to buy out or, in a piecemeal fashion, dismantle the union contract, then a violation of 8(a)(5) and/or the agreement may arise. The interesting question is whether arbitrators or perhaps the NLRB should employ a totality of circumstances approach whereby the overall detriment to the collective is weighed against the individual benefits to be derived from the special arrangement. Most unions would oppose this approach, reasoning that any intrusion into the collective bargaining agreement goes beyond the limited waiver of exclusivity and threatens the continuing viability of the union and the agreement that it has negotiated. Again, the respective arguments in this regard are contained in the *Midland* opinions.

4. On several occasions, arbitrators have been confronted with the difficult accommodation of recognizing the peculiarities of sports and the unique range of abilities

possessed by professional athletes, while at the same time avoiding the subversion of the bargaining process that would result from subordinating the labor organization's concerns to the needs of individual players. For example, in a case involving pitcher Dick Tidrow, the arbitrator sustained the MLBPA's grievance that had contested a right of first refusal clause contained in Tidrow's standard player contract. The union urged that the clause operated to reduce the effectiveness of the collective bargaining agreement's free agency provisions. Reasoning that the right of first refusal provision certainly was less beneficial than absolute free agency, the arbitration panel concluded that this club prerogative ran afoul of the collective bargaining agreement. In a sense, the fear was that the right of first refusal could have been exchanged for monetary concessions by the club, thus creating the impression and continuing possibility of a management buyout resulting in the gradual erosion of the collective bargaining agreement. *See Major League Baseball Players Association v. Chicago Cubs (Tidrow)*, Grievance No. 80-18 (November 14, 1980).

Ironically, in other contexts, the bargaining representative has acknowledged the players' ability to negotiate their own deals notwithstanding basic principles of exclusivity. Atlanta Braves player Alvin Moore negotiated a special covenant whereby the club agreed that Moore could veto any assignment and could declare free agency at the conclusion of the 1977 season. When the National League's president negated the clause because it allegedly conflicted with the CBA, the Players Association grieved. The league argued that, by giving Moore unfettered free agency unencumbered by the prerequisites contained in the CBA, the Braves and Moore nullified the modified reserve system and qualified free agency that had become part of the union contract. The arbitration panel rejected the league's contentions, holding that nothing precluded the Braves and Moore from reaching agreement on a provision that so plainly gave Moore an added benefit beyond, albeit inconsistent with, the benefits provided in the CBA. The panel acknowledged that, while the Braves could not be barred from agreeing to allow Moore free agency status earlier than the agreement provided, the club could *not* surrender the rights of other clubs by waiving the requirement that Moore be included in the reentry draft. At the time, the reentry draft, wherein a pool of free agents were eligible for selection by a number of teams, was a part of the CBA's free agency provisions. *See Major Leagues of Professional Baseball Clubs v. Major League Baseball Players Ass'n (Moore and Atlanta Braves)*, Grievance No. 77-18 (September 7, 1977); *see further Major Leagues of Professional Baseball Clubs v. Major League Baseball Players Ass'n (Marshall and Minnesota Twins)*, Grievance No. 78-15 (October 25, 1978) (where the arbitration panel negated a special covenant in which the Minnesota Twins had agreed to waive any obligation that a club signing Marshall would owe them recompense).

Problem

Various collective bargaining agreements in professional sports contain provisions that operate as a waiver of the union's status as exclusive representative on all matters involving wages, hours and working conditions. Major League Baseball's Basic Agreement (collective bargaining agreement), excerpted earlier, contains the following language:

> The Clubs recognize the Association as the sole and exclusive collective bargaining agent for all Major League Players, and individuals who may become Major League Players during the term of this Agreement, with regard to all terms and conditions of employment, provided that an individual Player shall be entitled to negotiate in accordance with the provisions set forth in this

Agreement (1) an individual salary over and above the minimum requirements established by this Agreement and (2) Special Covenants to be included in an individual Uniform Player's Contract, which actually or potentially provide additional benefits to the Player.

The agreement also expressly prohibits "all random drug testing of any player without the express permission of the player *and* the players association". Dr. Courtney Sonn, team physician for the Chicago Cubs, has developed a legal, synthetic steroid-like drug that, for certain individuals, enhanced strength, speed and hand-eye coordination. The Cubs agreed in three players' individual contracts to give daily doses (worth approximately $200 per dose) to the Cub players (free of charge) in exchange for the players' agreement that the club could "conduct random blood tests to ascertain any elevations or reductions in blood count and to detect the presence of any foreign substances that might adversely affect the player's tolerance to the drug or his general health." The Players Association filed an unfair labor practice charge with the National Labor Relations Board and a grievance under the collective bargaining agreement.

What are the legal predicates for the Players Association contentions and what defenses would the Cubs offer? Discuss any policy considerations that you deem pertinent.

(3) Unilateral Implementation of a Mandatory Subject of Bargaining

Silverman v. Major League Baseball Player Relations Comm., Inc.
67 F.3d 1054 (2d Cir. 1995)

WINTER, Circuit Judge. This is an appeal by the Major League Baseball Player Relations Committee, Inc. ("PRC") and the constituent member clubs of Major League Baseball ("Clubs") from a temporary injunction issued by Judge Sotomayor pursuant to Section 10(j) of the National Labor Relations Act ("NLRA"), 29 U.S.C. § 160(j). The PRC is the collective bargaining representative for the twenty-eight Clubs. The Major League Baseball Players Association is a union that is the exclusive bargaining representative for the forty-man rosters of each major league club. The injunction is based on the district court's conclusion that appellants violated NLRA §§ 8(a)(1) and (5), 29 U.S.C. §§ 158(a)(1) and (5), by unilaterally implementing terms and conditions of employment that differed from those in the last collective agreement. It orders the PRC and the Clubs to: (i) abide by the terms of an expired collective agreement, (ii) rescind any actions taken that are inconsistent with that agreement and (iii) bargain in good faith with the Players Association. *See Silverman v. Major League Baseball Player Relations Comm., Inc.,* 880 F. Supp. 246, 261 (S.D.N.Y. 1995). The injunction is to remain in effect until either (i) the expired agreement is replaced by a new collective bargaining agreement, (ii) the National Labor Relations Board ("NLRB") renders a final disposition of the matters pending before it in the related administrative case, or (iii) the district court finds, upon petition of either of the parties, that an impasse has occurred. *See id.* We affirm.

BACKGROUND

On January 1, 1990, the most recent collective agreement ("Basic Agreement") between appellants and the Players Association became effective. It contained provisions implementing a combination of free agency and a reserve system—that is, a compromise between free competitive bidding for a player's services and an individual club's exclusive rights to those services.

* * *

Article XX of the Basic Agreement that became effective in 1990 contains a series of provisions that govern free agency and reserve rights. Players with six or more years of major league service are free agents and may seek competing bids in an effort to obtain the best contract, which may of course give exclusive rights to the club for a stipulated number of years. *See Silverman,* 880 F. Supp. at 250. Free agency is guaranteed by an anti-collusion provision, Article XX(F), which prohibits the Clubs from acting in concert with each other with respect to the exercise of rights under Article XX. *See id.* Article XX(F) thus prevents the Clubs from agreeing either to refuse to bid for the services of free agents or to offer only low bids to them. Article XX(F) also prohibits players from acting in concert with regard to Article XX rights. *See id.*

Players with less than six years of service remain under reserve to their individual clubs, although a club may reserve a player only once. Although a minimum annual salary is provided, players with less than three years of major league service must negotiate with their clubs to determine their salary for the coming season. Article XX allows certain reserved players—generally those with more than three but less than six years of service—to demand salary arbitration. *See id.* at 251. Salary arbitration is a mechanism for determining the individual salaries for that group of reserved players if they cannot arrive at an agreement with their clubs. The player and the club each present the arbitrator with a suggested salary figure for a new one-year contract. The arbitrator then inserts either the player's or the club's figure into a blank uniform contract that the parties have already signed. *See id.*

* * *

The Basic Agreement expired on December 31, 1993, pursuant to the PRC's notice of termination. Although negotiations for a successor agreement did not get underway until March 1994, the PRC and the Players Association continued to observe the terms of the expired Basic Agreement. Prior to the commencement of negotiations, the Clubs and the Players Association had completed individual salary arbitration hearings and had entered into individual player contracts for the 1994 baseball season, which began in April 1994. *See Silverman,* 880 F. Supp. at 251.

Negotiations for a new collective bargaining agreement continued unsuccessfully. The PRC offered its first formal economic proposal to the Players Association at a meeting on June 14, 1994. It included a "salary cap," a mechanism that establishes a ceiling on the total player salaries paid by each club. The ceiling may allow some flexibility, depending on the details. Generally, the aggregate salaries of each team are determined by an agreed upon formula and must remain above a minimum percentage of industry revenues, also determined by an agreed upon formula, but below a maximum percentage of those revenues. The PRC proposal also eliminated the salary arbitration system and substituted restricted free agency rights for those reserved players previously eligible for salary arbitration. As an alternative to the PRC's proposed salary cap, the Players Association suggested a revenue sharing and luxury "tax" plan that would impose a tax on high-paying clubs. Subsequent proposals reflected disagreement over appropriate tax rates and payroll thresholds above which clubs would be subject to the tax. *See Silverman,* 880 F. Supp. at 251–52.

The players struck on August 12, and the 1994 baseball season never resumed. On December 22, 1994, the PRC declared an impasse in negotiations and stated that it intended unilaterally to impose a salary cap and to implement other changes in the terms and conditions of employment, including the elimination of salary arbitration. *See Sil-*

verman, 880 F. Supp. at 252. The Players Association responded with a unilateral ban on players signing individual contracts with the Clubs.

Thereafter, cross-charges of unfair labor practices were filed with the National Labor Relations Board ("NLRB") by the Players Association and the Clubs. The Players Association alleged that the Clubs had engaged in unfair labor practices by unilaterally implementing the salary cap and other terms because the parties were not at an impasse.

On February 3, 1995, counsel for the PRC notified the NLRB General Counsel that the PRC would revoke the implementation of unilateral changes and restore the status quo ante. The General Counsel indicated that the Players Association charges would be dismissed as a result. Counsel for the PRC informed the General Counsel, however, that the PRC did not believe itself obligated to maintain provisions of the Basic Agreement that involved non-mandatory subjects of bargaining. He mentioned salary arbitration in that regard and also suggested that the Clubs might decide to bargain exclusively through the PRC. The NLRB General Counsel declined to offer an advisory opinion on these matters.

Three days later, by memorandum dated February 6, counsel for the PRC notified the Clubs that, until a new collective bargaining agreement was ratified or until further notice, individual clubs had no authority to negotiate contracts with individual players because the PRC was now the Clubs' exclusive bargaining representative. This amounted to an agreement among the Clubs not to hire free agents and thus was a departure from the anti-collusion provision, Article XX(F) of the Basic Agreement. It also amounted to an elimination of salary arbitration, because salary arbitration is a method of arriving at a wage for an individual player contract with a club.

The Players Association thereupon filed a new unfair labor practice charge, and the General Counsel issued a complaint alleging, *inter alia*, that the Clubs and the PRC had violated Sections 8(a)(1) and (5) of the NLRA by unilaterally eliminating, before an impasse had been reached, competitive bidding for the services of free agents, the anti-collusion provision, and salary arbitration for certain reserved players. The NLRB found that these matters were related to wages, hours, and other terms and conditions of employment and were therefore mandatory subjects for collective bargaining. It then authorized its General Counsel to seek an injunction under NLRA §10(j). On March 27, the NLRB Regional Director filed a petition seeking a temporary injunction restraining the alleged unfair labor practices.

The district court agreed that the NLRB had reasonable cause to conclude that free agency and salary arbitration were mandatory subjects of bargaining and that the Clubs' unilateral actions constituted an unfair labor practice. The district court also concluded that injunctive relief was warranted. This appeal followed. We denied a stay on April 4.

DISCUSSION

* * *

Section 8(d) of the NLRA mandates that employers and unions bargain in good faith over "wages, hours, and other terms and conditions of employment." 29 U.S.C. §158(d). These are so-called mandatory subjects of bargaining. Under caselaw, the parties may propose and bargain over, but may not insist upon, permissive subjects of bargaining. When a collective agreement expires, an employer may not alter terms and conditions of employment involving mandatory subjects until it has bargained to an impasse over new terms. *NLRB v. Katz*, 369 U.S. 736, 741–43 (1962). Thereafter, it may implement the new terms. Generally, when an agreement expires, an employer need not bargain to an impasse over terms and conditions involving permissive subjects but may alter them upon expiration.

Many of the usual issues that arise in impasse cases are not disputed in the instant matter. The parties agree that the PRC, in directing the Clubs to decline to bargain individually with free agents, unilaterally departed from much of Article XX, which provides for a limited form of free agency and forbids collusive behavior by the Clubs in negotiating with free agents. It is also undisputed that the PRC unilaterally departed from the Basic Agreement's provisions with regard to salary arbitration. The PRC does not claim that it had bargained to an impasse over the free agency, the anti-collusion, or the salary arbitration provisions. Finally, it is also agreed that, if those provisions involved mandatory subjects of bargaining, their unilateral abrogation before impasse was a refusal to bargain in good faith.

The PRC and the Clubs argue that the anti-collusion and free agency provisions of the Basic Agreement do not involve mandatory subjects of bargaining and are therefore not subject to the Katz rule that unilateral implementation of new terms is an unfair labor practice unless the employer has bargained to an impasse over these new terms. *See Silverman*, 880 F. Supp. at 254. The PRC and the Clubs contend that an injunction compelling them to maintain the free agency and anti-collusion provisions undermines their right as a multiemployer group to bargain collectively through an exclusive representative. If so, they would be permissive subjects of bargaining. *See Borg Warner*, 356 U.S. at 349. With regard to salary arbitration, the PRC and the Clubs argue that it is the equivalent of interest arbitration—arbitration of the terms of a new collective agreement—and thus not a mandatory subject of bargaining.

We are unpersuaded that an injunction compelling the PRC and the Clubs to observe the anti-collusion and free agency provisions of the Basic Agreement infringes on their right as a multiemployer group to bargain through an exclusive representative. Free agency and the ban on collusion are one part of a complex method—agreed upon in collective bargaining—by which each major league player's salary is determined under the Basic Agreement. They are analogous to the use of seniority, hours of work, merit increases, or piece work to determine salaries in an industrial context. The PRC and the Clubs describe free agency and the ban on collusion as provisions undermining their right to select a joint bargaining representative because those provisions entail individual contracts with clubs. However, the argument ignores the fact that free agency is simply a collectively bargained method of determining individual salaries for one group of players. The anti-collusion provision is not designed to prevent the PRC from representing the Clubs. Rather, that provision guarantees that free agency will be a reality when permitted by the Basic Agreement. The injunction thus does not in any way prevent the PRC from bargaining as the Clubs' exclusive representative with the Players Association over the elimination of free agency in its entirety or for a modified version of the same, and thereafter from implementing any proposals incorporated into a collective bargaining agreement.

The question, therefore, is whether the free agency, anti-collusion, and reserve issues are—or there is reasonable cause to believe they are—otherwise mandatory subjects of bargaining. Section 8(d) of the NLRA defines the duty to bargain as "the obligation * * * to meet * * * and confer in good faith with respect to wages, hours, and other terms and conditions of employment * * *." In *Wood v. Nat'l Basketball Ass'n*, 809 F.2d 954 (2d Cir. 1987), we noted that free agency and reserve issues are "at the center of collective bargaining in much of the professional sports industry," *id*. at 961, and that "it is precisely because of [free agency's] direct relationship to wages and conditions of employment that [it is] so controversial and so much the focus of bargaining in professional sports." Id. at 962.

Wood noted that collective bargaining between professional athletes and leagues raises "numerous problems with little or no precedent in standard industrial relations." Id. at 961. Such is the case with a free agency and reserve system. For the most part, unionized employees in the industrial sector may leave one employer for another without restriction. The employee may have no bargaining rights with regard to the terms of hire by the new employer, which may be set by a collective agreement, but is nevertheless generally free to go from one unionized job to another.

The professional sports industry has a very different history and very different economic imperatives. Most professional sports leagues have always had some form of what has become known as the reserve system. As noted, this is a system by which the right to a player's services becomes the property of a particular club with limited freedom for the player to seek employment with another club. The reserve system in one form or another has been used in major league baseball for over a century. Until the arbitration decision in 1976, the reserve system prevented players from offering their athletic services to competing teams. A player's services were thus the property of a single team until he was traded or released. In enforcing a complete reserve system, Major League Baseball was exercising monopsony power—a buyer's monopoly.

However, there are many reasons, apart from maximizing the transfer of revenues from players to clubs, why reserve systems exist within professional sports. Fans might not be interested in games between teams that had entirely new lineups for every contest. Moreover, high quality play may require that individuals practice and play with the same teammates for at least some period of time. Teams may also want to recoup what they regard as training costs invested in players while they gained experience. In antitrust litigation, the leagues perennially argue that some form of reserve system is necessary for competitive balance. Indeed, even in a system of complete free agency, one would expect to see many long-term agreements binding individual players to particular clubs.

There are also reasons, apart from maximizing the transfer of revenues to players, why a union of professional athletes would seek free agency. It is very difficult to set individual salaries in professional sports through collective bargaining. Although unions of professional athletes may bargain for uniform benefits and minimum salaries, they do not usually follow their industrial counterparts and seek relatively fixed salaries by job description, seniority, or other formulae. Players often play positions requiring very different skills. Moreover, the level of performance and value to a team in attracting fans differs radically among players, with star athletes or popular players being far more valuable than sub-par or nondescript players. Usually, therefore, players unions seek some form of free agency as a relatively simple method of setting individual salaries.

Most importantly, however, both the leagues and the players unions view free agency and reserve issues as questions of what share of revenues go to the clubs or to the players. The more restrictive the reserve system is, the greater the clubs' share. The greater the role of free agency, the greater the players' share.

To hold that there is no reasonable cause for the NLRB to conclude that free agency and reserve issues are mandatory subjects of bargaining would be virtually to ignore the history and economic imperatives of collective bargaining in professional sports. A mix of free agency and reserve clauses combined with other provisions is the universal method by which leagues and players unions set individual salaries in professional sports. Free agency for veteran players may thus be combined with a reserve system, as in baseball, or a rookie draft, as in basketball, *see Wood*, 809 F.2d at 957, for newer players. A salary cap may or may not be included. *See id.* To hold that any of these items, or others that make up the mix in a particular sport, is merely a permissive subject of bargaining would ignore the reality of collective bargaining in sports.

Indeed, free agency is in many ways nothing but the flip side of the reserve system. A full reserve system does not eliminate individual bargaining between teams and players. It simply limits that bargaining to one team. If free agency were a permissive subject of collective bargaining, then so would be the reserve system.

With regard to salary arbitration, we will assume, but not decide, that if it is a form of interest arbitration, it may be unilaterally eliminated. Interest arbitration is a method by which an employer and union reach new agreements by sending disputed issues to an arbitrator rather than settling them through collective bargaining and economic force. The salary arbitration provisions of the Basic Agreement are a method by which salaries for some players who are not eligible for free agency—those with three to six years of major league service—are set. The Basic Agreement sets forth criteria by which the arbitrator is to reach a decision. These criteria include the player's performance in the prior year, the length and consistency of career contribution, physical or mental defects, recent performance of the team on the field and at the gate, and salaries of certain comparable players. The Basic Agreement also forbids the arbitrator from considering certain facts that might otherwise be relevant. Finally, the Basic Agreement requires that the arbitrator pick either the club's suggested salary or the player's.

We decline to analogize Article VI(f) of the Basic Agreement to interest arbitration. Salary arbitration provides limited discretion to the arbitrator to set salaries for designated players who are not eligible for free agency. The discretion afforded the arbitrator is arguably less than the discretion afforded arbitrators in grievance arbitration involving disputes arising under an existing collective agreement, which is beyond question a mandatory subject of bargaining. In grievance arbitration, an arbitrator may permissibly imply a term even though the term has no explicit support in the text of the collective agreement. Similarly, a term may be implied from past practices even though somewhat inconsistent with the agreement. We thus decline to analogize salary arbitration to interest arbitration, and, therefore, we hold that there is reasonable cause to believe that it is a mandatory subject of bargaining.

With regard to whether the granting of relief was "just and proper," 29 U.S.C. §160(j), we review the district court's determination only for abuse of discretion* * *.We see no such abuse in the present matter. Given the short careers of professional athletes and the deterioration of physical abilities through aging, the irreparable harm requirement has been met. The unilateral elimination of free agency and salary arbitration followed by just three days a promise to restore the status quo. The PRC decided to settle the original unfair labor practice charges while embarking on a course of action based on a fallacious view of the duty to bargain. We see no reason to relieve it of the consequences of that course.

We therefore affirm.

Notes and Questions

1. In an edited portion of this case, the court explained:

The NLRB is authorized under Section 10(j) of the NLRA to petition for temporary injunctive relief from a district court to enjoin ongoing unfair labor practices. 29 U.S.C. §160(j). If the court has reasonable cause to believe that an unfair labor practice has occurred and that injunctive relief would be just and proper, it should grant appropriate relief. *Kaynard v. MMIC, Inc.*, 734 F.2d 950, 953 (2d Cir. 1984). The court need not make a final determination that the conduct in question is an unfair labor practice. *Kaynard v. Mego Corp.*, 633 F.2d 1026, 1033 (2d Cir. 1980). It need find only reasonable cause to support such a conclusion. *See id.*; *MMIC*, 734 F.2d at 953. Appropriate deference must be shown to the judgment of the NLRB, and a district court should decline to grant relief only if convinced that the NLRB's legal or factual theories are fatally flawed. *See Mego*, 633 F.2d at 1031, 1033; *Kaynard v. Palby Lingerie, Inc.*, 625 F.2d 1047, 1051 (2d Cir. 1980). In reviewing a district court's grant of injunctive relief pursuant to Section 10(j), a court of appeals must also accord deference to the district court's decision, at least with regard to those aspects that are traditionally left to the district court's discretion. *Mego*, 633 F.2d at 1030.

Would you consider this standard "relaxed"? What is involved in demonstrating that the injunctive relief would be "just and proper"? If you recall the discussion of remedies in Chapter 14, this "just and proper" standard has been subject to varying interpretations. The construction of the standard, at one level, may be critical because it will dictate the extent to which the traditional equitable criteria such as irreparable injury are prerequisites to the issuance of a 10(j) injunction. Clearly, those courts that liberally construe the just and proper language give considerable deference to the Board and, in a sense, severely limit the respondent's ability to oppose the injunction once the General Counsel has decided to issue a complaint. Was an injunction justified in the *Silverman* case? How would the differing interpretations of the term "just and proper" compel a contrary conclusion in *Silverman*? *See* Chapter 14, Section VIII(C)(6). Does the continued existence of the arcane baseball exemption have any influence upon agencies such as the NLRB in its determination of the appropriateness of injunctive relief in the context of cases such as *Silverman*?

2. Shortly after the injunction was granted in the above case, the Major League Baseball Players Association unconditionally offered to return to work and abandoned the strike. Why?

3. The 1994–95 strike erased the end of the 1994 season and left fans with no World Series for the first time in 90 years. The owners, galvanized by small market teams (including Acting Commissioner Bud Selig's Milwaukee Brewers) and a group of hard-liners, vigorously promoted the institution of a salary cap, elimination of salary arbitration and the CBA's anti-collusion provisions, and generally committed themselves to a policy of restraint in terms of the proliferation of players' wages. It is unlikely that any work stoppage in sports has attracted the media attention, public debate, fan vitriol and internecine squabbling that characterized the 1994–95 strike. The involvement of federal mediators, senators, congressmen and congresswomen, and President Clinton did nothing to break the impasse and salvage the 1994 season. The costs in terms of salaries, lost revenues, and sacrifice of good will were astronomical. The image of the game may never be fully restored.

The battles waged in the relevant legal forums eventually dictated the outcome of the strike. Congressional threats to remove baseball's exemption from the antitrust laws did little to chasten the ownership, break their resolve, or relax their absolute insistence upon a salary cap (or its hybrid, a punitive luxury tax). However, as reflected in *Silver-*

man, above, the union's filing of unfair labor practice charges and the General Counsel's issuance of complaints called into question the owners' negotiating strategy and commanded a change in course. It is conceivable that the government's "official" sanction of the owners' posture and approach had additional consequences both in terms of public perception as well as the fragmentation of the owners' fragile alliance. Ironically, the ultimate settlement in part resulted from personal pique. Chicago White Sox owner, Jerry Reinsdorf, was the prime mover in developing the owners' strategy to hold firm on the salary cap issue, ostensibly to preserve and protect the small markets and to put a lid on the owners' profligate spending. Yet, after the penultimate vote rejecting the players' offer, Reinsdorf signed Cleveland Indians resident troublemaker, Albert Belle, to a multi-year contract calling for $55 million—one of the most lucrative deals in baseball history for one of the sport's most nefarious competitors. Many owners felt that Reinsdorf had betrayed his own philosophy and had disserved his colleagues in the process. Within a matter of days, another vote was taken in which the owners overwhelmingly accepted the players' offer.

4. The length of the work stoppage and the surrounding acrimony raised several questions about management's strategic options during an economic strike. The most prevalent concern centered on the owners' ability to hire permanent replacements. As addressed in Chapter 14, Section IX(A), employers are free to replace economic strikers. However, they must reinstate strikers who make an unconditional offer to return to work provided a vacancy exists in a job that the striker is capable of performing. *NLRB v. Fleetwood Trailers Co.*, 389 U.S. 375 (1967); *NLRB v. MacKay Radio & Tel. Co.*, 304 U.S. 333 (1938). Unfair labor practice strikers may *not* be permanently replaced. *See Philip Carey Mfg. Co. v. NLRB*, 331 F.2d 720, 729 (6th Cir. 1964).

At one point during the 1994–95 strike, the owners announced that they would hire replacements to insure an uninterrupted season. This announced strategy created several possible conflicts. Baltimore Orioles owner Pete Angelos declared that he would not field a team of permanent replacements regardless of the league's decision. His refusal presents an interesting question in terms of his liability to the rest of the owners for failing to observe a league mandate and, potentially, for forfeiting scheduled games. Maryland lawmakers showed their support for Angelos' position by passing legislation, signed by Governor Parris Glendening, that effectively barred the use of replacement players in the State of Maryland. The law stated that no games could be played at Camden Yards, the Orioles home field, unless 75% of the players on the participating teams were on Major League rosters in 1994. American League President, Gene Budig, claimed that the legislation was ineffectual. Was he correct? Given governing Supreme Court precedent that permits the use of permanent replacements, would such legislation be preempted by federal labor law? *See Golden State Transit Corp. v. City of Los Angeles*, 475 U.S. 608 (1986); *Michigan State Chamber of Commerce v. Michigan*, 115 LRRM 2887 (Mich. Cir. Ct. 1984); Chapter 14, *supra*.

Further, certain Canadian jurisdictions prohibit the use of replacements, thus posing a dilemma for one or more Canadian clubs. In particular, the issue irresistibly joined is whether the Canadian law would apply across the board to teams like the Toronto Blue Jays or whether such legislation would only apply to games played in those Canadian jurisdictions. Would the prohibitions have any impact on United States' teams?

5. We saw in Chapter 9 that Judge Winter vigorously has advocated the preeminence of labor over antitrust in determining applicability of the non-statutory labor exemption. In so doing, he strenuously has urged labor organizations and employees to avail themselves of the labor laws to redress arguable restraints of trade in the labor market.

Is his opinion in *Silverman* consistent with his views articulated in labor exemption cases such as *National Basketball Ass'n v. Williams*, 45 F.3d 684 (2d Cir. 1995)? In *Clarett*, discussed at length in Chapter 9, the Second Circuit remained consistent in its predilection for favoring the labor forum over the antitrust avenue to redress labor market grievances. *See Clarett v. NFL*, 369 F. 3d 124 (2d Cir. 2004), *cert. denied*, 544 U.S. 961 (2005).

6. As we will see in the succeeding chapter, interest arbitration is a term used to describe resolution of disputes involving the setting of the terms in a collective bargaining agreement as opposed to interpreting terms of such an agreement. Interest arbitration is generally considered to be a permissive subject of bargaining. *See Columbus Printing Pressmen Union No. 252*, 219 NLRB 268 (1975), *enforced*, 543 F.2d 1161 (5th Cir. 1976). Judge Winter concluded that baseball salary arbitration, through which salaries of some players are determined by a neutral arbitrator, did not constitute interest arbitration. As a result, Winter found that salary arbitration was a mandatory, not permissive, subject of collective bargaining. Accordingly, the owners' unilateral implementation of its proposal regarding elimination of salary arbitration (prior to impasse) violated Section 8(a)(5) of the NLRA. Why does salary arbitration rest outside the definition of interest arbitration? As a threshold matter, should interest arbitration be a mandatory subject?

7. Shortly after the 2001 baseball season, Major League Baseball announced plans to contract the league by purchasing and then jettisoning the two teams that had produced the least revenue. The likely candidates were the Minnesota Twins and the Montreal Expos. If the two teams were eliminated as part of this contraction, several Major League jobs would have been sacrificed. As a result, the Players' Association filed grievances claiming that the league's action would constitute a mandatory subject of bargaining, and any unilateral action would run afoul of §8(a)(5) of the Act. As a result of this grievance, baseball agreed to defer the contraction decision.

Is contraction a mandatory subject of collective bargaining? *See* Bryan Day, *Labor Pains, Why Contraction Is Not The Solution To Major League Baseball's Competitive Balance Problems*, 12 FORDHAM INTELL. PROP., MEDIA & ENT. L. J. 521 (2001); *see also, Metropolitan Sports Facilities Commission v. Minnesota Twins Partnership*, 678 N.W. 2d 214 (2002). If the league unilaterally implemented its plan and the Players' Association filed unfair labor practices, would the NLRB defer to the collective bargaining agreement's arbitration machinery? *See Collyer Insulated Wire*, 192 NLRB 837 (1971); *see also Public Serv. Co.*, 319 NLRB 984 (1995).

8. In an unrelated vein, if a franchise decided to relocate in a different city and secured league approval, would it be obligated to bargain with the players' collective bargaining representative about the decision? About its effects on the bargaining unit? *See First National Maintenance Corp. v. NLRB*, 452 U.S. 666 (1981); *Dubuque Packing Co.*, 303 NLRB 389 (1981), *enforced sub. nom., United Food & Commercial Workers Local 150-A v. NLRB*, 1 F. 3d 2 (D.C. Cir. 1993).

9. Failure to abide by the terms of a collective bargaining agreement plainly constitutes a breach of contract actionable in federal or state court under Section 301 of the NLRA. Would such conduct likewise be deemed a violation of Section 8(a)(5)? The NLRB answers that question in the affirmative. In *WJA Limited Partnership*, 310 NLRB 862 (1993), the NLRB found that several jai alai franchises' failure to make contractually mandated monthly contributions to the World Jai Alai Players' Association retirement plan constituted an unlawful refusal to bargain, notwithstanding the teams' claim

that they were financially unable to pay and that they lacked the intent to repudiate the contract. The NLRB held:

> We find that on or about January 1992, the Respondent, without obtaining the Union's consent, failed to make contractually required retirement plan contributions. The terms and conditions of the agreement the Respondent has failed to continue in full force and effect are mandatory subjects of bargaining.
>
> Accordingly, we conclude that the Respondent has failed to bargain collectively and in good faith with the Union as the exclusive representative of its employees, and that the Respondent has thereby engaged in unfair labor practices in violation of Section 8(a)(5) and (1) of the Act.

(4) Refusal to Bargain by a Labor Organization (Section 8(b)(3))

While the typical refusal to bargain charge implicates employer misconduct in violation of Section 8(a)(5), labor organization behavior may also run afoul of the Act's prohibition of bad faith bargaining. In the following case, the NLRB found that the United Basketball Players' Association violated Section 8(b)(3) of the NLRA by insisting to impasse that the Harlem Globetrotters agree to terms expressly proscribed by other provisions of the Act.

United Basketball Players Association and Harlem Globetrotters, Inc.
294 NLRB 1191 (1989)

* * *

The Employer and the Respondent were parties to a collective-bargaining agreement that was effective from September 1, 1983, to August 31, 1986. The employees of the Employer described in article 1, section 1, and article 2, section 1 of that agreement constitute a unit appropriate for collective bargaining under Section 9(b) of the Act. Since at least 1980, and at all material times, the Respondent has been the lawfully designated collective-bargaining representative of the employees of the Employer. Such recognition has been embodied in successive collective-bargaining agreements, the most recent of which has been described above. At all relevant times, the Respondent, by virtue of Section 9(a) of the Act, has been and is the exclusive collective-bargaining representative of the employees in the unit described above.

At various times during July, August, September, and October 1986, the Employer and the Respondent met to engage in negotiations regarding wages, hours, and other terms and conditions of employment of the employees in the unit described above. During those negotiations, the Respondent demanded as a condition of consummating any collective-bargaining agreement that the Employer agree to include the following provisions:

Public Relations. The Company shall have the right to use [e]mployees to assist and take part in public relations and other promotional activities in a reasonable manner, and the Company will endeavor to give all of the players a reasonable opportunity to participate in such activities * * *. Whenever the Company receives compensation for such appearances, the Company shall pay the [Respondent] and/or player who appears, one third (⅓) of the proceeds it receives for such appearances within ten (10) days of receipt.

Network Television Shows. Whenever a network television show, such as ABC Wide World of Sports, is contracted by the Company, then the [Respondent] shall receive additional compensation over and above the individual contracts of the various employees and said compensation shall be a sum equal to one third (⅓) of the net revenue generated by such contract. The one third (⅓) net revenue shall also be applicable for any second showing of the network television show for which any additional money is received by the Company.

Bonus. Employees shall share and participate at the end of each regular season in a bonus fund which shall not be less than One Hundred Fifty Thousand ($150,000.00) Dollars. The Bonus fund shall be paid directly to * * * [the Respondent] * * * and * * * [the Respondent] shall distribute the money to the employees in such proportion as * * * [the Respondent] shall determine.

The provisions demanded by the Respondent as set forth above, insofar as they would require the Employer to make payments to the Respondent, are prohibited by Section 302 of the Act. In furtherance and support of those demands, the Respondent bargained to impasse and, about September 17, 1986, engaged in a strike. By demanding as a condition of consummating any collective-bargaining agreement that the Employer make payments to the Respondent that are prohibited by Section 302, and by bargaining to impasse and striking in support of those demands, the Respondent has violated Section 8(b)(3) of the Act.

Since about November 11, 1986, the Employer has requested the Respondent to furnish the following information, which is relevant and necessary for the purposes of collective bargaining:

Documents, records or other information indicating (a) the names and addresses of individuals who received payments from the Emergency Relief Fund and Scholarship Funds during 1983–86, (b) the amounts received by each individual in either Emergency Relief or Scholarship Fund payments, (c) whether [the Respondent] retained any of the Emergency Relief and/or Scholarship Fund monies, and if so, for what years and in what amounts, and (d) the criteria used by [the Respondent] in selecting recipients for these payments.

Since about November 21, 1986, the Respondent has failed and refused to furnish to the Employer the information described above. By failing and refusing to provide that information to the Employer, the Respondent has violated Section 8(b)(3) of the Act.

Conclusions of Law

By demanding, as a condition of consummating any collective-bargaining agreement, that the Employer make payments to the Respondent that are prohibited by Section 302 of the Act, by bargaining to impasse and striking in support of those demands, and by failing and refusing to provide information requested by the Employer that is relevant and necessary to collective bargaining, the Respondent has failed and refused, and is failing and refusing, to bargain collectively and in good faith with the Employer as required by Section 8(d) of the Act, and thereby has engaged in unfair labor practices affecting commerce within the meaning of Section 8(b)(3) and Section 2(6) and (7) of the Act.

Remedy

Having found that the Respondent has engaged in certain unfair labor practices, we shall order it to cease and desist and to take certain affirmative action designed to effectuate the policies of the Act. We shall require the Respondent, on request, to furnish the Employer with information that is relevant and necessary to collective bargaining.

* * *

Notes and Questions

1. Typically, it is in the union's best interests to bargain in good faith; what prompted the NLRB to find that the United National Basketball Players' Association had violated Section 8(b)(3)?

2. Other situations in which a union may contravene Section 8(b)(3) include a refusal to execute an agreed-upon contract, repudiation of an existing collective bargaining agreement, insistence upon permissive subjects of bargaining to impasse, etc. *See, e.g.,* HARDIN AND HIGGINS, *supra,* at 792–93.

Chapter 16

Labor-Management Relations and Sports: Arbitration

I. Introduction

In the early 1960s, arbitration began to emerge as a viable and, in fact, preferable vehicle to resolve disputes in the area of labor management relations. A trio of Supreme Court opinions enunciated the judicial inclination to favor arbitration as a dispute adjustment mechanism and served as a harbinger of continued judicial deference to voluntary grievance resolution machinery. *Steelworkers v. American Mfg. Co.*, 363 U.S. 564 (1960); *Steelworkers v. Warrior & Gulf Navigation Co.*, 363 U.S. 574 (1960); *Steelworkers v. Enterprise Wheel & Car Corp.*, 363 U.S. 593 (1960). A few years earlier, the Supreme Court had concluded that a binding arbitration clause was the *quid pro quo* for a no-strike clause, thus establishing the Court's lofty placement of arbitration in the overall scheme of labor relations litigation. *See Textile Workers Union v. Lincoln Mills*, 353 U.S. 448 (1957). This decision ultimately served as one of the cornerstones for the Court's landmark decision in *Boys Markets, Inc. v. Retail Clerks Union, Local 770*, 398 U.S. 235 (1970), where the presence of an arbitration clause in conjunction with a no-strike clause was found to warrant the issuance of an injunction in a peaceful strike notwithstanding the anti-injunction provisions of the Norris-LaGuardia Act. The critical underpinnings of the decision, which, reduced to its simplest form, judicially repealed part of Norris-LaGuardia, was the existence of arbitration as an effective way for the union to seek redress for its grievances.

During the past forty years, the evolution of arbitration as the *modus operandi* for maintaining stability and industrial peace has been readily apparent. Its acceptance has been manifested by its prevalence in most collective bargaining agreements (its inclusion is almost a foregone conclusion) and by the substantial respect that it is shown in other litigation forums. The NLRB, for example, has expressed its homage both in terms of its policy of deferring some unfair labor practice charges (that also present arbitrable claims under a union contract) to the agreed-upon arbitration process and also with respect to its reluctance to disturb arbitration awards once they have been issued.

For example, in *Collyer Insulated Wire*, 192 NLRB 837 (1971), the NLRB announced standards to be applied in determining whether to defer consideration of unfair labor practice charges to the collective bargaining agreement's grievance/arbitration machinery. The Board, confronted with allegations that the employer had refused to bargain in good faith by implementing unilateral changes in working conditions, deferred the Section 8(a)(5) charges to the CBA's arbitration procedure. The standards enumerated to assess the appropriateness of deferral include whether: (1) the matter arose in the context of a "long and productive collective bargaining relationship"; (2) the employer or union charged was demonstrably willing to submit the dispute in question to the arbitration process; (3) the collective bargaining agreement and interpretation of terms within such agreement rested at the core of the grievance. Patrick Hardin & John E. Higgins, Jr., The Developing Labor Law 1380 (4th Ed. Vol. 11 2001). Over the years, the *Collyer* doctrine has been expanded, contracted, clarified, praised and condemned through volumes of case law and scholarly commentary. *Id.* at 1386–90. After a brief period in which the doctrine was narrowly circumscribed to situations involving Sections 8(a)(5) and 8(b)(3), the Board returned to its earlier stance of invoking the deferral approach also in cases involving, *inter alia*, Sections 8(a)(1), 8(a)(3), 8(b)(1)(A), and 8(b)(2). *Compare General American Transportation Corp.*, 228 NLRB 808 (1977) *to United Technologies Corp.*, 268 NLRB 557 (1984). While the Board now adopts a liberal deferral policy consistent with the emerging significance of arbitration as a dispute resolution mechanism, there are unfair labor practice contexts in which the *Collyer* deferral doctrine will be disregarded. *See Shaw's Supermarkets, Inc.*, 339 NLRB No. 108 (2003) (§8(a)(5) refusal to bargain claim stemming from an employer's failure to provide relevant information).

Once arbitrators have ruled on a case that arguably implicates the National Labor Relations Act (as well as the collective bargaining agreement), the Board will honor the arbitrator's award where certain criteria are satisfied. First, the grievance proceedings must be fair. This criterion is important because an unfair labor practice case, for which the arbitrator serves as substitute, involves an evidentiary proceeding with the full panoply of due process protection. Second, the parties must have agreed to be bound by the arbitration decision. The voluntary nature of the arrangement and the consent to permit the arbitrator to resolve the dispute are critical components of this criterion. Third, the arbitrator's decision must be consistent with the NLRA and in no way contravene its purposes and policies. Finally, the issue presented by the alleged unfair labor practice must have been part of the case before the arbitrator. *See Spielberg Mfg. Co.*, 112 NLRB 1080 (1955). *See also Olin Corp.*, 268 NLRB 573 (1984); *Derr and Gruenewald Constr. Co.*, 315 NLRB 266 (1994).

There are two predominant types of arbitration: interest arbitration and grievance arbitration. Interest arbitration, which seldom arises in the private sector, consists of an arbitration mechanism to establish the terms of a collective bargaining agreement. It is employed more in the public sector where there is often no right to strike and where some type of resolution by a third party is the only weapon in the employees' arsenal. Grievance arbitration, on the other hand, does not involve a third party setting the terms of an agreement, but, rather, entails the interpretation of those terms.

Salary arbitration, on one level, would seem to be a classic example of interest arbitration and probably the only example of interest arbitration in professional sports. That is, it involves seeking the aid of a neutral arbitrator to set the terms rather than interpret the terms of an agreement. Recently, baseball owners urged that, because interest arbitration is *not* a mandatory subject of bargaining, salary arbitration is not a subject about which employers must bargain. The Second Circuit rejected this contention and found that salary arbitration is *not* interest arbitration. Thus, the leagues are indeed bound to bargain over salary arbitration proposals. *See Silverman v. Major League Baseball Player Relations Comm.*, 67 F.3d 1054 (2d Cir. 1995).

Grievance arbitration is traditionally an item that management will concede, particularly and typically in exchange for a pledge by the union not to engage in a strike. In this respect, it promotes, rather than impedes, industrial harmony. *See Boys Markets, Inc., above; Textile Workers Union v. Lincoln Mills,* above. Labor arbitration in the private sector almost always refers to grievance arbitration. Private parties, specifically management, rarely will surrender the prerogative to negotiate or, after impasse, set the terms of an agreement. *See generally,* Christopher Bavis, *Labor Arbitration As An Industrial Relations Dispute Settlement Procedure in World Labor Markets,* 45 LAB. L. J. 147 (1994); Karl Klare, *Workplace Democracy and Market Reconstruction: An Agenda For Legal Reform,* 38 CATH. U. L. REV. 1 (1988). In those few instances where weak unions have suggested that a festering strike or stalled negotiations be resolved through some form of interest arbitration, employers have typically demurred. Work stoppages involving the NFL and NFLPA provide a classic illustrations.

Collective bargaining agreements governing professional sports contain grievance/arbitration machinery in the areas of injury, salary, discipline, and general disputes arising under the various terms of the agreements in question. We have seen that, once parties have voluntarily agreed to settle their differences through the arbitration process, courts and agencies are extremely deferential to the arbitration process and, where possible, will make every effort to avoid intervening in that process. *See Kansas City Royals v. MLBPA,* below. A great deal of the litigation arising in professional sports has been resolved through various voluntary dispute adjustment mechanisms. The broad arbitration clause contained in the typical collective bargaining agreement has insured that most disputes will be resolved without resort to the courts or the federal agencies regulating professional sports. As discussed in Chapter 3, the role of league commissioner as "impartial" arbitrator has diminished considerably with the evolution of the players' collective bargaining representatives. His or her arbitral function has been circumscribed primarily to matters involving the integrity of the sport. Now, most sports litigation is resolved through the arbitration procedures of the collective bargaining agreements. Often, the procedures include provisions for an arbitration panel consisting of a representative of the owners and the players, and an impartial chairman. These procedures are very elaborate (several pages in length), and their filing requirements and other qualifications are strictly enforced. Sample grievance adjustment language appears below.

> Any dispute (hereinafter referred to as a "grievance") arising after the execution of this Agreement and involving the interpretation of, application of, or compliance with, any provision of this Agreement, the NFL Player Contract, or any applicable provision of the NFL Constitution and Bylaws pertaining to terms and conditions of employment of NFL players, will be resolved exclusively in accordance with the procedure set forth in this Article, except wherever another method of dispute resolution is set forth elsewhere in this Agreement, and except wherever the Settlement Agreement provides that the Special Master, Impartial Arbitrator, the Federal District Court or the Accountants shall resolve a dispute.

NFL Collective Bargaining Agreement, Article IX, Section 1.

In the discussion that follows, we will consider several arbitration decisions, including two grievance arbitrations that have dramatically altered the labor relations landscape in Major League Baseball, particularly with respect to free agency. In this regard, we will also visit a grievance challenging football's reserve system. In addition, we will explore briefly the procedures employed to resolve grievances, the need for strict compliance with procedural requirements, and the degree to which courts will defer to the arbitral process. Further, we will consider the thorny question of salary continuation during a work stoppage and steps that the parties have taken to ensure that their respective interpretations are explicitly delineated in the standard player contracts. Finally, we will address baseball's salary arbitration mechanism and invite you to decide whether it constitutes "grievance" or "interest" arbitration as you have come to understand those terms.

The case appearing immediately below gutted baseball's entrenched reserve system and made "free agency" the hot topic in every labor negotiation that has followed. In the second *Silverman* case at the latter part of Chapter 15, the Second Circuit provided a pithy summary of the free agency-reserve clause debate. It is a useful introduction to the next case.

> Free agency, in its purest form, is a status in which the rights to a player's athletic services are not owned by a club and may be shopped around by the player in a quest for the most attractive bid. However, for more than a century, Major League Baseball has had a reserve system that to one degree or another affords individual clubs exclusive property rights to the athletic services of certain players. Before the players were organized and a collective bargaining relationship was established, the standard players contract with a club reserved to the club exclusive rights to a player's services and provided for an annual right of renewal of the contract by the club in question. The Clubs interpreted the contract as allowing the club in question to renew all of an individual player's contract, including the right of renewal provision. So interpreted, this provision—known generally as the "reserve clause"—bound a player to one club in perpetuity until traded or released. After the Clubs recognized the Players Association and entered into a collective agreement with it, an arbitrator held in a grievance proceeding that the reserve clause allowed a renewal for only one year rather than a succession of years. *See National & American League Professional Baseball Clubs v. Major League Baseball Players Ass'n*, 66 Lab. Arb. (BNA) 101 (1976) (Seitz, Arb.). Since then, appellants and the Players Association have struggled to accommodate their conflicting interests in the free agency and reserve issues, and a variety of compromises have from time to time been reached. However, relations have been acrimonious, and several strikes and lockouts have occurred.

67 F.3d at 1056.

II. Grievance Arbitration

(A) Free at Last—Almost

Kansas City Royals Baseball Corp.
v. Major League Baseball Players Ass'n
532 F.2d 615 (8th Cir. 1976)

HEANEY, Circuit Judge. The owners of the twenty-four Major League Baseball Clubs seek reversal of a judgment of the District Court for the Western District of Missouri. The court refused to set aside and ordered enforced an arbitration panel's award rendered in favor of the Major League Baseball Players Association. The arbitration panel was established pursuant to a collective bargaining agreement between the Club Owners and the Players Association. The award relieved pitcher Andy Messersmith of any contractual obligation to the Los Angeles Dodgers, and pitcher Dave McNally of any similar obligation to the Montreal Expos. It directed the Dodgers and Expos to remove Messersmith and McNally, respectively, from their reserve or disqualified lists. It ordered the American and National Leagues to inform and instruct their member clubs that the provisions of Major League Rule 4-A (reserve list rule) and Rule 3(g) (no-tampering rule) do not inhibit, prohibit or prevent such clubs from negotiating or dealing with Messersmith and McNally with respect to employment.

We hold that the arbitration panel had jurisdiction to resolve the dispute, that its award drew its essence from the collective bargaining agreement, and that the relief fashioned by the District Court was appropriate. Accordingly, we affirm the judgment of the District Court.

I

On February 25, 1973, the Club Owners and the Players Association entered into a collective bargaining agreement to be in effect from January 1, 1973 to December 31, 1975.

Article X of the agreement set forth a comprehensive procedure for the resolution of certain grievances. "Grievance" was defined as "a complaint which involves the interpretation of, or compliance with, the provision of any agreement between the Association and the Clubs or any of them, or any agreement between a Player and a Club. * * *" Certain disputes not pertinent here were excepted. A player having a grievance was first required to present the matter to his club. Either the player or Players Association could then appeal the matter to the clubs' Player Relations Committee and to the appropriate League President. Grievances not satisfactorily resolved by these procedures could be submitted to a tripartite panel for binding arbitration. The panel was comprised of one member to be appointed by the Club Owners, one member to be appointed by the Players Association, and an impartial chairman to be chosen jointly by the other two members. The agreement defined the arbitrators' authority as follows:

> With regard to the arbitration of Grievances, the Arbitration Panel shall have jurisdiction and authority only to interpret, apply or determine compliance with the provisions of agreements between the Association and the Clubs or any of them, and agreements between individual Players and Clubs. The Arbitration Panel shall not have jurisdiction or authority to add to, detract from, or alter in any way the provisions of such agreements.

On October 7, 1975, the Players Association filed a grievance on behalf of Andy Messersmith. The grievance alleged that Messersmith played for the Los Angeles Dodgers in 1975 under a renewed 1974 contract, that the renewal year was completed on September 28, 1975, that Messersmith thus became a free agent on that date, and that the Club Owners had denied him his right to deal with other teams for his services in 1976. The Players Association asked that the Club Owners be ordered to treat Messersmith as a free agent and to compensate him for any financial detriment he might incur due to their delay in doing so. On October 9, 1975, the Players Association filed a companion grievance on behalf of Dave McNally, alleging similar circumstances.

The Club Owners responded to both grievances on October 24, 1975. Their primary contention was that the claims raised fell outside the scope of the agreed upon grievance procedures and were, therefore, not subject to the jurisdiction of the arbitration panel. They argued that Article XV of the 1973 agreement excluded disputes concerning the "core" or "heart" of the reserve system from the grievance procedures set forth in Article X. Article XV provided:

> Except as adjusted or modified hereby, this Agreement does not deal with the reserve system. The Parties have differing views as to the legality and as to the merits of such system as presently constituted. This Agreement shall in no way prejudice the position or legal rights of the Parties or of any Player regarding the reserve system. During the term of this Agreement neither of the Parties will resort to any form of concerted action with respect to the issue of the reserve system, and there shall be no obligation to negotiate with respect to the reserve system.

With respect to the merits of the dispute, the Club Owners argued that under the Uniform Player's Contract, the Dodgers and the Expos had the right to renew Messersmith's and McNally's contracts from year to year for a reasonable number of years. They alternatively argued that under the Major League Rules, the two clubs could obligate the pitchers to play for them and no other Major League Club, simply by placing their names on the clubs' reserve lists.

The arbitration panel set the matter for hearing. Thereafter, on October 28, 1975, the Kansas City Royals Baseball Corporation commenced an action in the United States District Court for the Western District of Missouri seeking a declaratory judgment that the aforesaid grievances were non-arbitrable and an injunction prohibiting the Players Association from proceeding with arbitration. The remaining twenty-three Major League Clubs then joined the action as plaintiffs-intervenors. Subsequently, the Players Association filed a counterclaim, pursuant to §301 of the Labor-Management Relations Act, 29 U.S.C. §185, seeking to compel the plaintiffs to arbitrate.

At a pretrial conference on November 6, 1975, the parties agreed to go forward with the scheduled arbitration. It was stipulated that the arbitration panel should initially determine its own jurisdiction, but that the question could later be presented to the District Court on the basis of the record compiled in the arbitration proceeding as well as any other relevant and material evidence which either side might wish to present.

* * * [T]he Messersmith-McNally grievances were submitted to arbitration* * *. On December 23, 1975, the panel rendered its decision, holding that the grievances were within the scope of its jurisdiction and that Messersmith and McNally were free agents. It directed that both parties be removed from the reserve or disqualified lists of their respective clubs, and that the leagues promptly notify their member clubs that they may negotiate with Messersmith and McNally with respect to future employment. The panel denied the Players Association's prayer for damages as premature, but retained jurisdiction as to that and other questions pertaining to the appropriate nature and extent of relief. Following the issuance of the arbitrators' decree, the dormant District Court action was revived in accordance with the parties' stipulation of November 6, 1975.

* * *

The District Court held that the Messersmith-McNally grievances were within the scope of the arbitration panel's jurisdiction, and that neither the arbitrators' resolution of the merits nor the relief awarded exceeded the bounds of the panel's authority. It ordered enforcement of the arbitration panel's award.

The Club Owners perfected a timely appeal. On appeal, they renew their contention that the Messersmith-McNally grievances are not within the purview of the arbitration panel's jurisdiction. They additionally argue that the arbitration panel's award exceeded the scope of its authority. They further maintain that the District Court's decree is fatally defective in that it operates against persons who were not parties to the proceedings before the arbitration panel or the court, and that it is ambiguous and indefinite.

The Supreme Court articulated the legal principles applicable to the arbitration of labor disputes in the Steelworkers trilogy,[6] and recently reaffirmed them in *Gateway Coal Co. v. United Mine Workers of America*, 414 U.S. 368 (1974).

A party may be compelled to arbitrate a grievance only if it has agreed to do so. *Gateway Coal Co. v. United Mine Workers of America, supra; United Steelworkers of America v. Warrior & Gulf Navigation Co.*, 363 U.S. 574 (1960). The question of arbitrability is thus one of contract construction and is for the courts to decide. *See, e.g., Wiley & Sons v. Livingston*, 376 U.S. 543.

In resolving questions of arbitrability, the courts are guided by Congress's declaration of policy that arbitration is the desirable method for settling labor disputes. See §203 of the Labor-Management Relations Act, 29 U.S.C. §173(d). Accordingly, a grievance arising under a collective bargaining agreement providing for arbitration must be deemed arbitrable "unless it may be said with positive assurance that the arbitration clause is not susceptible of an interpretation that covers the asserted dispute. Doubts should be resolved in favor of coverage." *United Steelworkers of America v. Warrior & Gulf Navigation Co., supra*, 363 U.S. at 582–583. Consistent with these principles, a broad arbitration provision may be deemed to exclude a particular grievance in only two instances: (1) where the collective bargaining agreement contains an express provision clearly excluding the grievance involved from arbitration; or (2) where the agreement contains an ambiguous exclusionary provision and the record evinces the most forceful evidence of a purpose to exclude the grievance from arbitration.

If it is determined that the arbitrator had jurisdiction, judicial review of his award is limited to the question of whether it "draws its essence from the collective bargaining agreement." *United Steelworkers of America v. Enterprise Wheel & Car Corp.*, 363 U.S. 593, 597. We do not sit as an appellate tribunal to review the merits of the arbitrator's decision.

We turn first to the question of the jurisdiction of the panel to arbitrate the Messersmith-McNally grievances.

III

We begin with the proposition that the language of Article X of the 1973 agreement is sufficiently broad to require arbitration of the Messersmith-McNally grievances. We think this clear because the disputes involve the interpretation of the provisions of agreements between a player or the Players Association and a club or the Club Owners. The grievances require the construction of agreements manifested in paragraphs 9(a) and 10(a) of the Uniform Player's Contract.

9. (a) The Club and the Player agree to accept, abide by and comply with all provisions of the Major League Agreement, the Major League Rules, the Rules or Regulations of the League of which the Club is a member, and the Professional Baseball Rules, in effect on the date of this Uniform Player's Contract, which are not inconsistent with the provisions of this contract or the provisions of any agreement between the Major

---

6. *United Steelworkers of America v. American Mfg. Co.*, 363 U.S. 564, 4 L. Ed. 2d 1403, 80 S. Ct. 1343 (1960); *United Steelworkers of America v. Warrior & Gulf Navigation Co.*, 363 U.S. 574 (1960); *United Steelworkers of America v. Enterprise Wheel & Car Corp.*, 363 U.S. 593 (1960).

League Clubs and the Major League Baseball Players Association, provided that the Club, together with the other Clubs of the American and National Leagues and the National Association, reserves the right to modify, supplement or repeal any provision of said Agreement, Rules and/or Regulations in a manner not inconsistent with this contract or the provisions of any then existing agreement between the Major League Clubs and the Major League Baseball Players Association [sic].

10. (a) On or before December 20 (or if a Sunday, then the next preceding business day) in the year of the last playing season covered by this contract, the Club may tender to the Player a contract for the term of that year by mailing the same to the Player at his address following his signature hereto, or if none be given, then at his last address of record with the Club. If prior to the March 1 next succeeding said December 20, the Player and the Club have not agreed upon the terms of such contract, then on or before 10 days after said March 1, the Club shall have the right by written notice to the Player at said address to renew this contract for the period of one year on the same terms, except that the amount payable to the Player shall be such as the Club shall fix in said notice; provided, however, that said amount, if fixed by a Major League Club, shall be an amount payable at a rate not less than 80% of the rate stipulated for the next preceding year and at a rate not less than 70% of the rate stipulated for the year immediately prior to the next preceding year. The interpretation of paragraph 9(a), in turn, requires the construction of Major League Rules 3(g) and 4-A(a).

* * *

The Messersmith-McNally grievances might also be viewed as involving construction of the 1973 collective bargaining agreement itself. The provisions set forth above were made a part of that agreement under Article III, which incorporated by reference the terms of the Uniform Player's Contract.

Although we find that the grievances are arbitrable under Article X standing alone, we cannot ignore the existence of Article XV, which provides, *inter alia*, that the agreement "does not deal with the reserve system."

The provisions of the Uniform Player's Contract and the Major League Rules cited above are among the many contract provisions and rules which together constitute the reserve system. In fact, the Club Owners maintain that they are the very "core" or "heart" of the reserve system. The Club Owners argue that Article XV removed grievances arising out of the cited clauses from the coverage of Article X, and that when the agreement is read as a whole, as it must be, the Messersmith-McNally grievances are not arbitrable.

The District Court rejected this argument. It recognized that the agreement must be construed as a whole, but concluded that Article XV could not be interpreted to exclude any grievances from the procedures set forth in Article X.

We find the question more difficult than did the District Court. We cannot say that Article XV, on its face, constitutes a clear exclusionary provision. First, the precise thrust of the phrase "this Agreement does not deal with the reserve system" is unclear. The agreement incorporates the provisions which comprise the reserve system. Also, the phrase is qualified by the words "except as adjusted or modified hereby." Second, the impact of the language "This Agreement shall in no way prejudice the position ... of the Parties" is uncertain. Third, the "concerted action" which the parties agree to forego does not clearly include bringing grievances. Fourth, Article XV affords no basis for the Club Owners' distinction between the "core" and the periphery of the reserve system. Finally, Article X(A)(1), which declares certain disputes non-grievable, is silent as to the reserve system. We find, however, that Article XV creates an ambiguity as to whether the grievances here involved are arbitrable. Accordingly, we must look beyond the face of the agreement and determine whether the record as a whole evinces the most forceful evidence of a purpose to exclude these grievances from arbitration.

We proceed to an examination of the evidence presented to the District Court pertaining to the parties' intent. Of particular relevance is the history of collective bargaining between the parties.

A. 1968 Basic Agreement.

* * *

The 1968 agreement established the grievance procedures which continued in effect through the 1973 agreement. The agreement excluded disputes relating to benefit plans and the dues check-off agreement from the grievance and arbitration procedures. The Commissioner of Baseball was designated as the impartial arbitrator.

During the period that the 1968 agreement was in force, the provisions of the Uniform Player's Contract and the Major League Rules set forth above were in effect in substantially similar form. The 1968 agreement incorporated by reference those provisions in the same manner as the later agreements.

The 1968 agreement contained no provision analogous to Article XV of the 1973 agreement. With respect to the reserve system, Article VIII provided:

> The parties shall review jointly the matters of (a) the length of the championship season and (b) possible alternatives to the reserve clause as now constituted.

> The joint review of the matter of the length of the championship season shall commence as early as practicable and shall be completed prior to the drawing up of the preliminary schedules for 1969.

> The joint review of the reserve clause shall be completed prior to the termination date of this Agreement.

> Subject to Article III, Section B, it is mutually agreed that the Clubs shall not be obligated to bargain or seek agreement with the Players Association on either of the above matters during the term of this Agreement.

Pursuant to Article VIII, the parties held three meetings to discuss possible modification of the reserve system. No agreement was reached. At trial, Marvin Miller, Executive Director of the Players Association and a participant in those meetings, testified that no further discussions were held because the Club Owners refused to consider significant changes in the reserve system.

B. 1970 Basic Agreement.

* * *

The 1970 agreement provided for grievance procedures similar to those established in 1968. Two significant changes were made which were carried over into the 1973 agreement. First, the tripartite panel replaced the Commissioner of Baseball as the impartial arbitrator. Second, the agreement excepted two additional categories of disputes from the grievance procedures, namely complaints involving actions against players taken by the Commissioner involving the integrity of the game, and complaints involving pictures and public appearances.

The 1970 agreement incorporated the Uniform Player's Contract and the Major League Rules in the same manner as the 1968 and 1973 agreements.

During the negotiations leading up to the 1970 agreement, the Players Association submitted a number of proposed modifications of the reserve system, including a provision which would give each player the option of becoming a free agent once every three years. The Club Owners rejected these proposals as unacceptable, stating that they went to the heart of the game and the reserve system. In February, 1970, it became apparent that the parties had reached an impasse on the reserve system. Richard Moss, General Counsel to the Players Association, recollected that Marvin Miller then suggested:

> We are not making any progress on modifications in the Reserve System. We are running out of time, in terms of the date of the negotiations, the approach of the season, and if it is mutually desirable to make an agreement we have got to do something about this issue that we are not making any progress on, and therefore we ought to set it aside.

At approximately the same time that the 1970 negotiations were reaching an impasse on the reserve system, Curt Flood, an outfielder traded by the St. Louis Cardinals to the Philadelphia Phillies, filed suit in federal court challenging the validity of the reserve system. Flood's complaint defined the reserve system as a number of provisions designed to bind a player to the club for the duration of his career. He claimed that the reserve system violated federal antitrust laws.

The Club Owners asserted, as a defense to the Flood action, that the parties had agreed to the reserve system through collective bargaining, and that the system was, therefore, exempt from federal antitrust laws. *See Amalgamated Meat Cutters v. Jewel Tea Co.*, 381 U.S. 676 (1965). As a result of the assertion of that defense, Arthur Goldberg, Chief Counsel for Flood, suggested to the Players Association's negotiators that a provision be included in the 1970 agreement which would obviate the Jewel Tea defense.

In accordance with Goldberg's suggestion, and their desire to enter into a collective bargaining agreement despite the parties' differences on the reserve system, the Players Association proposed that the following provision be included in the 1970 agreement:

> Regardless of any provision herein to the contrary, the Basic Agreement does not deal with the reserve system. The parties have differing views as to the merits of such system as presently constituted. This Agreement shall in no way prejudice the parties or any player's position or legal rights related thereto.

> During the pendency of any present litigation relating to the reserve system, it is agreed that the parties will not during the term of this Agreement resort to strike or lockout on that issue. However, upon the rendering of a final court decision in such litigation, either party may upon the giving of 30 day's written notice to the other party, reopen this Agreement and thereafter the parties may resort to any legal and appropriate action in support of their respective positions on this issue.

Richard Moss testified that the proposal was designed to insure that the agreement would not prejudice the Flood litigation; to provide for reopening the agreement on the subject of the reserve system upon the termination of the lawsuit; and to immunize the Players Association from any potential liability as a co-conspirator in an agreement claimed to be in violation of federal antitrust laws.

Louis Hoynes, Counsel to the National League, testified that he was aware of the Players Association's desire to neutralize the Jewel Tea defense, but was unsure as to what other motivations the Association had in making the proposal set forth above. He stated:

> [There] was a lot of discussion among ourselves that evening as to exactly what the Association had in mind, what its purposes, its motives were. We were well satisfied then as we have continued to be satisfied throughout the rest of our relationship with the Association that the reasons that they gave as their motive for certain proposals need not bear any relationship to the real motive that they have and that is true of people generally.

He later testified that both parties were often less than candid in disclosing the purposes behind bargaining proposals.

According to Hoynes, the Club Owners' objections to the Players Association's proposal centered primarily around the language "the Basic Agreement does not deal with the reserve system." They were concerned that the reserve system would be unenforceable if totally excluded from the agreement. They also wanted to retain the Jewel Tea defense in the Flood case. They were further apprehensive that the language would remove the reserve system from the coverage of the "zipper clause," which provided that there was no obligation to negotiate on bargainable subjects during the term of the collective bargaining agreement.

The Club Owners were also dissatisfied with the Players Association's proposal regarding the means by which the parties could seek to further their respective positions on the reserve system. Although the proposal proscribed strikes and lockouts, the Club Owners felt that it permitted other types of actions which could be equally disruptive to their operations.

In an effort to obviate these objections, the Club Owners submitted the following counterproposal:

> Regardless of any provision herein to the contrary, this Basic Agreement does not constitute an agreement between the parties as to the merits or legality of the reserve system. This Agreement shall in no way prejudice the position or legal rights of the parties or of any player regarding the reserve system.
>
> It is agreed that during the term of this Agreement neither of the parties will resort to any form of concerted action, or encourage or support, directly or indirectly, any claim or litigation (other than *Flood v. Kuhn*, et al., pending in the U.S. District Court for the Southern District of N. Y.) on the issue of the reserve system, or any part thereof, and neither of the parties shall be obligated to negotiate regarding the reserve system. [Emphasis added.]

The parties finally agreed upon the following language, which became Article XIV of the 1970 agreement:

Reserve System

> Regardless of any provision herein to the contrary, this Agreement does not deal with the reserve system. The parties have differing views as to the legality and as to the merits of such system as presently constituted. This Agreement shall in no way prejudice the position or legal rights of the Parties or of any Player regarding the reserve system.
>
> It is agreed that until the final and unappealable adjudication (or voluntary discontinuance) of *Flood v. Kuhn* et al., now pending in the federal district court of the Southern District of New York, neither of the Parties will resort to

any form of concerted action with respect to the issue of the reserve system, and there shall be no obligation to negotiate with respect to the reserve system. Upon the final and unappealable adjudication (or voluntary discontinuance) of *Flood v. Kuhn* et al., either Party shall have the right to reopen negotiations on the issue of the reserve system as follows:

a. in the event such adjudication (or discontinuance) occurs between October 15 in any year and January 15 in the following year, inclusive, either Party may thereafter reopen such negotiation, upon 10 days' prior written notice, provided that such notice is given on or before January 15;

b. in the event such adjudication (or discontinuance) occurs between January 16 and October 14, inclusive, in any year, either Party may thereafter reopen such negotiation on or after November 1, upon 10 days' prior written notice, provided that such notice is given on or before January 15 in any following year.

Hoynes testified that the Club Owners agreed to accept the language "this Agreement does not deal with the reserve system" on the basis of assurances given by Miller. Hoynes stated that during negotiations, he questioned the enforceability of the reserve system. He quoted Miller as responding: "It is going to be outside the Agreement. It will not be subject to the Agreement, but we will acquiesce in the continuance of the enforcement of the rules as house rules and we will not grieve over those house rules." Evidence that Miller made a statement that the Players Association would not grieve over house rules appears in contemporaneous notes of attorneys representing the Club Owners. Miller denies that he made the statement attributed to him.

The Club Owners also compromised on their desire to retain the Jewel Tea defense. They felt that the language finally agreed upon weakened but did not necessarily destroy the defense.

Both parties compromised on the question of reserve system negotiations, addressing that issue expressly in the second paragraph of Article XIV. Both parties also compromised on the actions they could take in furtherance of their positions on the reserve system. They agreed that "neither of the parties will resort to any form of concerted action with respect to the reserve system."

Richard Moss testified that Article XIV, as finally agreed upon, excluded the reserve system from the 1970 agreement for purposes of litigation only. It did not preclude arbitration of any grievances otherwise arbitrable.

* * *

During the term of the 1970 agreement, a few grievances which involved one or more of the provisions that comprise the reserve system were submitted to arbitration. The Club Owners raised no jurisdictional objections. They felt that the grievances did not concern the "core" or "heart" of the reserve system, and that they were, therefore, arbitrable.

C. 1973 Basic Agreement.

* * *

During the negotiations, the Players Association proposed a number of changes in the reserve system, all but two of which were rejected by the Club Owners. The parties did agree upon a provision allowing a player who had been in the Major Leagues at least ten years and had played for his present club at least the past five years to veto a trade. The parties also agreed to arbitrate salary disputes.

In the course of negotiating salary arbitration procedures, the Club Owners proposed that both the player and his club be required to execute a new contract before either would be permitted to initiate salary arbitration. The contract would leave the amount of salary undetermined, to be filled in by the arbitration panel. The Players Association agreed to such a procedure where the player initiated arbitration, but objected to the imposition of that requirement where the salary grievance was filed by the club. Marvin Miller recalled that he stated his objection as follows:

> I said to the owners' representatives, "It is clear to us what you are trying to do and it ought to be equally clear why it is not acceptable. Under the present set of restrictive rules, there is one procedure left to the player; that is, he can refuse to sign and can play under the owner's option for one year." I continued by saying, "What you have proposed is not only to not modify the reserve system, as we have proposed, but also to close the last vestige of rights, the right of the player to become a free agent after a one-year renewal."

Contemporaneous notes taken by Richard Moss largely corroborate Miller's account of his statement. According to those notes, Miller stated: "What you propose is not only to not modify Reserve System but also to close last tiny loophole." Written across the phrase "last tiny loophole" in Moss's notes are the words "Right of Player to become a free agent."

Hoynes, who also participated in the salary arbitration discussions, testified to a different recollection of Marvin Miller's statement. He did not view the statement as relating to free agency. Rather, he thought Miller was referring to a player's right to do what Ted Simmons had done: begin the season under a renewed contract, perform well, and obtain a higher salary on the basis of that performance than was originally offered.

In any event, the parties finally agreed to a provision under which a player could withdraw from club-initiated salary arbitration and thus avoid being compelled to sign a new contract. If the player initiated arbitration, however, he was required to sign a contract.

Aside from the provisions discussed above, the parties were deadlocked on the issue of further reserve system modifications. That impasse, which was delaying execution of the 1973 agreement, continued into early February, 1973. With the status of the collective bargaining agreement in doubt, the Club Owners withdrew previously-issued invitations to players to attend pre-spring training conditioning, which was scheduled to begin shortly. Marvin Miller then proposed that the parties set aside the reserve system as they had in 1970. He suggested that language similar to Article XIV of the 1970 agreement be adopted for that purpose.

Hoynes testified that the Club Owners were amenable to setting aside the reserve system from the agreement, but that they opposed adopting the language "this Agreement does not deal with the reserve system." He stated:

> We felt that we were in the process of making some rather substantial changes in the wide area of the Reserve System and we wanted some appropriate recognition of that because we knew that Mr. Miller would be going to Congress as he already had and was clearly planning to again seek some sort of relief following the invitation of the Supreme Court in the Flood case, and we did not want Mr. Miller to be armed with a banner in the form of a new article in this Agreement that said that the Agreement did not deal with the Reserve System and which would permit Mr. Miller to say here again that management has insisted on retaining its historic rights outside of the Agreement without our agreement

and would not, with that, mention to the people that he was addressing the various changes, important changes in Players' rights that we thought we had made in the broad area of the Reserve System, so we wanted some language in this very article that would suggest that something had been done—

Hoynes then proposed that the agreement provide that it doesn't deal with "free agency." The Players Association rejected that proposal, stating that it did not want to adopt new language. The Club Owners continued to press for recognition, however, that changes had been made in the reserve system. Hoynes stated:

> We discussed the possibility of listing the things we had changed, and then we got into an argument about whether the things we had changed really affected what we were talking about whether they really affected the Reserve System or not. It became obvious that we were never going to resolve that in a short matter of time, so I suggested some language that I hoped was sufficiently ambiguous that we would be able to use it to make our point later and the Association would be entitled to make their points later and that language was the preamble that you now have as to the first sentence of Article XV, except as adjusted or modified hereby.

> Now, the Association, so it seemed to me, and we discussed this, said, well, there really weren't adjustments or modifications and we don't know what they meant when they put that language in and we can say well, we think they were things that were important here, and we would want to point out, this language simply was an ambiguous, intentionally ambiguous, compromise of a point that would give both parties an opportunity to get up before a Congressional Committee and argue whether or not something had been done in the area of the Reserve System, and Mr. Miller indicated that he had a favorable reaction to that language, that he would review it and then we proceeded to other matters.

The parties finally agreed to carry over the language of Article XIV of the 1970 agreement into the 1973 agreement, with two exceptions. First, the clause "except as adjusted or modified hereby" was substituted as the prefatory language to "this Agreement does not deal with the reserve system". Second, reference to the Flood litigation was deleted. Article XIV of the 1970 agreement, as modified, was incorporated into the 1973 agreement as Article XV. Hoynes stressed that both parties recognized that the clause "except as adjusted or modified hereby" was ambiguous.

Marvin Miller testified that while Article XV was being discussed, it occurred to him that deleting reference to the Flood litigation might allow the Club Owners to assert that they could now make unilateral changes in the reserve system. The Players Association was also anxious to continue to protect itself from potential liability as a co-conspirator in the reserve system. Accordingly, the Players Association requested and obtained the following side letter from the Club Owners:

> The following will confirm our understandings with regard to Article XV of the Basic Agreement effective January 1, 1973:

> 1. Notwithstanding the above provision, it is hereby understood and agreed that the Clubs will not during the term of the Agreement, make any unilateral changes in the Reserve System which would affect player obligations or benefits.

> 2. It is hereby understood and agreed that during the term of the Agreement the Clubs will indemnify and save harmless the Players Association in any ac-

tion based on the Reserve System brought against the Association as a party defendant. Richard Moss testified that the purpose and effect of Article XV, as finally agreed upon, was to treat the reserve system in the same manner as the parties had in 1970.

Other than the *Messersmith-McNally* grievances, only one grievance was filed during the term of the 1973 agreement which the Club Owners felt concerned the "core" or "heart" of the reserve system. That grievance was filed by Bobby Tolan, an outfielder who played in 1974 under a renewed contract. Tolan's grievance was similar to those involved in this case. The Club Owners responded that the grievance was not within the scope of the grievance procedures provided for in the 1973 agreement; however, that issue was never resolved. Tolan signed a retroactive contract at the end of the season and withdrew his grievance before it was submitted to arbitration.

We cannot say, on the basis of the evidence discussed above, that the record evinces the most forceful evidence of a purpose to exclude the grievances here involved from arbitration.

(a) The 1968 agreement clearly permitted the arbitration of grievances relating to the reserve system. It, therefore, cannot be said that the Club Owners never consented to the arbitration of such grievances. The Club Owners might have argued that they agreed to arbitrate such grievances because the Commissioner of Baseball was designated as the arbitrator, and that he, recognizing the importance of the reserve system to baseball, would interpret the disputed provisions to allow perpetual control by a Club Owner over its players. That argument, however, was not advanced before either the arbitration panel, the District Court or this Court. Moreover, the argument would not be particularly flattering to any Commissioner of Baseball.

(b) Article XIV, the predecessor to Article XV, was suggested by the Players Association for rather specific purposes and the Club Owners clearly did what they could to preserve their right to argue that the reserve system remained a part of the collective bargaining agreement. Indeed, if the Club Owners' counterproposals with respect to Article XIV had been accepted, the reserve system would clearly have remained subject to arbitration.

Article XV was clearly designed to accomplish the same purposes as Article XIV. If in accomplishing these purposes the players had clearly agreed to exclude disputes arising out of the operation of the reserve system from arbitration, the Messersmith-McNally grievances would not be arbitrable. For the reasons discussed in this opinion, however, no such agreement can be found.

(c) From 1970 to 1973, a number of grievances concerning the reserve system were submitted to arbitration. The Club Owners raised no jurisdictional objections. While this fact alone is not of controlling significance, because the grievances submitted did not go to what the Club Owners regard as the "core" or "heart" of the reserve system, the submission of grievances relating to the reserve system is certainly a fact that detracts from the Club Owners' contention that the parties clearly understood Article XIV to mean that grievances relating to the reserve system would not be subject to arbitration.

(d) The fact that Marvin Miller may have given assurances, during the 1970 negotiations, that the players would not grieve over house rules cannot be viewed as the most forceful evidence of a purpose to exclude the Messersmith-McNally grievances from arbitration. First, there is some dispute in the record as to whether Miller made such a statement. Second, assuming he did, the term "house rules" is ambiguous. Third, and we think most important, the weight of the evidence, when viewed as a whole, does not support the conclusion that Article XV was intended to preclude arbitration of any grievances otherwise arbitrable.

(e) The essence of the Club Owners' arguments on the question of arbitrability was perhaps best articulated in the testimony of Larry McPhail, President of the American League, in which he stated: "Isn't it fair to say that our strong feelings on the importance of the core of the reserve system would indicate that we wouldn't permit the reserve system to be within the jurisdiction of the arbitration procedure?" The weaknesses in this argument have been previously discussed in paragraphs (a), (b) and (c) above. We add only that what a reasonable party might be expected to do cannot take precedence over what the parties actually provided for in their collective bargaining agreement.

V

The Club Owners contend that even if the arbitration panel had jurisdiction, the award must be vacated. They argue that the award exceeded the scope of the panel's authority by "fundamentally altering and destroying the Reserve System as it historically existed and had been acquiesced in by the Association."

* * *

The nub of the Club Owners' argument is that both they and the Players Association understood the reserve system to enable a club to perpetually control a player, that this understanding was reflected in the 1973 agreement, and that the arbitration panel was without authority to alter the agreed upon operation of the reserve system.

We cannot agree that the 1973 collective bargaining agreement embodied an understanding by the parties that the reserve system enabled a club to perpetually control a player. First, the agreement contained no express provision to that effect. Second, while there is evidence that the reserve system operated in such a manner in recent years, the record discloses that various Players Association representatives viewed the system as allowing a player to become a free agent by playing under a renewed contract for one year.

Moreover, it can be argued that the arbitration panel's award did not "alter" the reserve system. To the extent that the reserve system did enable a club to perpetually control a player, it was not necessarily by virtue of successive invocations of the renewal clause, or application of the reserve list and no-tampering rules in the absence of a contractual obligation. Other provisions operate to deter a player from "playing out his option," as is evidenced by the fact that few players have done so. On this basis, it may be said that the arbitration panel's decision did not change the reserve system, but merely interpreted various elements thereof under circumstances which had not previously arisen.

The 1973 agreement empowered the arbitration panel to "interpret, apply or determine compliance with the provisions of agreements" between the players and the clubs. We find that the arbitration panel did nothing more than to interpret certain provisions of the Uniform Player's Contract and the Major League Rules. We cannot say that those provisions are not susceptible of the construction given them by the panel. Accordingly, the award must be sustained.

* * *

CONCLUSION

We hold that the arbitration panel had jurisdiction to hear and decide the Messersmith-McNally grievances, that the panel's award drew its essence from the collective bargaining agreement, and that the relief fashioned by the District Court was appropriate. Accordingly, the award of the arbitration panel must be sustained, and the District Court's judgment affirmed. In so holding, we intimate no views on the merits of the reserve system. We note, however, that Club Owners and the Players Association's representatives agree that some form of a reserve system is needed if the integrity of the game is to be preserved and if public confidence in baseball is to be maintained. The disagreement lies over the degree of control necessary if these goals are to be achieved. Certainly, the parties are in a better position to negotiate their differences than to have them decided in a series of arbitrations and court decisions. We commend them to that process and suggest that the time for obfuscation has passed and that the time for plain talk and clear language has arrived. Baseball fans everywhere expect nothing less.

This Court's mandate affirming the judgment of the District Court shall issue seven days from the date this opinion is filed. Our previous order staying enforcement of the District Court's decree shall continue in effect until the issuance of the mandate.

[The concurring opinion of Cheif Judge Gibson is omitted.]

Notes and Questions

1. The arbitration panel was chaired by Peter Seitz, the only true neutral among a panel that also consisted of Marvin Miller, Executive Director of the Major League Baseball Players Association, and John Gaherin, the club owners' representative, who, as no surprise, concurred and dissented, respectively. Do you agree with Arbitrator Seitz's conclusion that the continued viability of the reserve system was arbitrable? Doesn't it appear as though there was a strong effort made by Major League Baseball to limit the substantive arbitrability of the reserve system so as to prevent the very conclusion that eventuated here: a third party's determination of whether the owners could keep the players perpetually tied to their original clubs? See further *National & American League Professional Baseball Clubs v. Major League Baseball Players Ass'n*, 66 LA 101 (1976).

2. In truth, Seitz observed what probably should have been obvious: both sides wanted to eat their cake and have it too (the authors' version of the old aphorism). The owners wanted the reserve clause cloaked in the apparent "bipartisanship" of a collectively bargained agreement while, at the same time, did not want it to be subject to scrutiny by that agreement's neutral third party—the arbitrator. The players, on the other hand, did not want to compromise possible antitrust litigation through the owners' invocation of the labor exemption defense in the event that the baseball exemption were "overruled", but, at the same time, they wanted to be able to challenge the reserve system through the process of the grievance mechanism (if and when the antitrust claim failed). It is almost as though Seitz, however reluctantly, realized that this matter was somewhat ambiguous and therefore justified the exercise of as much arbitral authority as he could muster. The bottom line is that Seitz's decision to consider the case and the court's affirmance of same is probably correct, albeit a "bang bang play." Further, notwithstanding Arbitrator Luskin's decision addressed in Note 6, below, Seitz's decision on the merits seems absolutely unassailable because a system of perpetual reserve, or an option provision that perpetually repeats itself (rendering the contract infinite and fatally indefinite in duration), would fail to survive even the most liberal contract interpretation. See, e.g., *Metropolitan Exhibition Co. Baseball Club v. Ewing*, 42 F. 198 (C.C.S.D.N.Y. 1890); *Metropolitan Exhibition Co. v. Ward*, 9 N.Y.S. 779 (Sup. Ct. 1890). See further *Central New York Basketball, Inc. v. Barnett*, 181 N.E. 2d 506 (Ct.C.P. Cuyahoga Cty. Ohio 1961).

3. This case is significant in several respects. First, it should be well-understood that the ability to reverse a decision of an arbitrator selected as part of a collective bargaining agreement is very narrowly circumscribed. In the absence of a clear abuse of discretion or a decision that is manifestly at war with all relevant authority, the arbitrator generally will be affirmed. *See, e.g., MLBPA v. Garvey*, 532 U.S. 504 (2001). This deference stems from a prevailing view emerging in the early 1960s that courts would do well to permit and, in fact, encourage parties to develop their own grievance adjustment mechanisms. *See Steelworkers v. Enterprise Wheel & Car Corp.*, 363 U.S. 593 (1960); *Steelworkers v. American Mfg. Co.*, 363 U.S. 564 (1960); *Steelworkers v. Warrior & Gulf Navigation Co.*, 363 U.S. 574 (1960).

4. Arbitrator Seitz's decision is probably the most profoundly significant case in baseball's checkered jurisprudence. It undid a reserve system that had existed for almost a hundred years. It has sparked considerable debate at the bargaining table in every collective bargaining session that has ensued since 1976. It has provoked impasses, strikes, lockouts and labor unrest due to the owners' failure to accept the decision and their continued resistance to any notion of a player being able to negotiate a contract with the employer of choice at the expiration of an existing contract. Finally, and not unexpectedly, it has generated reams of critical commentary, and has spawned other arbitration decisions occasioned by the owners' conspiratorial activity to limit the effect of free agency outside their unsuccessful attempts to do so at the bargaining table. *See infra Matter of Arbitration Between Major League Baseball Players Ass'n and The Twenty-Six Major League Baseball Clubs*, Grievance No. 86-2 (1986).

5. The selection of Arbitrator Seitz itself was significant. Earlier, he had decided an arbitration initiated by an MLBPA grievance filed on behalf of Jim "Catfish" Hunter of the Oakland Athletics. Hunter claimed that he should be declared a free agent because owner Charlie Finley had failed to satisfy a contract provision calling for payment of certain types of insurance monies and premiums. Arbitrator Seitz sustained the player's grievance and concluded that, because the failure to pay monies due and owing constituted a material breach, Hunter was free to rescind his contract and become a free agent. Commissioner Bowie Kuhn, among others, questioned the prudence of selecting Seitz as the impartial arbitrator (the third and deciding member of the arbitration panel) in a case that would ultimately resolve the free agency debate. In truth, Seitz's selection was entirely appropriate. His reputation as an arbitrator of vision and integrity had never been questioned before and, with the exception of Kuhn's "Monday morning" criticism, has rarely been questioned thereafter.

6. The perpetual nature of the option year in the NFL's standard player contract was also challenged through the NFL-NFLPA's collective bargaining agreement's grievance machinery. However, Arbitrator Bert Luskin, unlike Arbitrator Seitz, was not hospitable to the Players Association's claims. The union contended that a player who was compelled to re-sign with his old team and who signed a one-year contract pursuant to Article XV of the CBA was free the following year to seek employment with other NFL teams—without restrictions. The relevant portion of Article XV read as follows:

> Section 1. Applicability: Commencing with players who play out the options in their contracts or whose contracts otherwise expire (hereinafter referred to as "veteran free agent") in 1977, and with respect to veteran free agents through at least 1982, the following principles will apply:

Section 3. Offer Sheet: When a veteran free agent receives an offer to sign a contract or contracts from a new club, which he desires to accept, he will on or before April 15 give to his old club a completed Offer Sheet substantially in the form of Exhibit A attached hereto, signed by the player and by the chief operating officer of the new club, which will contain the "principal terms" (as defined in Section 7 below) of the new club's offer. Subject to Section 10 below, the player's old club, upon receipt of the Offer Sheet, may exercise its "right of first refusal," which will have the legal consequences set forth in Section 4 below.

Section 4. First Refusal Exercise Notice: Subject to Section 18 below, if, within seven days from the date it receives an Offer Sheet, the veteran free agent's old club gives to him a First Refusal Exercise Notice substantially in the form of Exhibit B attached hereto, such player and his old club will be deemed to have entered into a binding agreement, which they will promptly formalize in an NFL Player Contract(s), containing all the "principal terms" of the Offer Sheet and those terms of the NFL Player Contract(s) not modified by the "principal terms."

Section 17. Re-Signing: If a veteran free agent receives no offer to sign a contract or contracts with a new NFL club pursuant to this Article, and his old club advises him in writing by June 1 that it desires to re-sign him, the player may, at his option within 15 days, sign either (a) a contract or contracts with his old club at its last best written offer given on or before February 1 of that year, or (b) a one-year contract (with no option year) with his old club at 110% of the salary provided in his contract for the last preceding year (if the player has just played out the option year, the rate will be 120%). If the player's old club does not advise him in writing by June 1 that it desires to re-sign him, the player will be free on June 2 to negotiate and sign a contract or contracts with any NFL club, and any NFL club will be free to negotiate and sign a contract or contracts with such player, without any compensation between clubs or first refusal rights of any kind.

National Football League Players Ass'n and National Football League Management Council (Arbitrator Luskin, May 14, 1980). In essence, the claims paralleled the argument raised by the MLBPA in *McNally-Messersmith* that the option clause did not become part of the new contract and could not perpetually renew the team's prerogative to bind the player to the same club forever. The NFL Management Council argued that Section 17 did not allow for unrestricted free agency after the option year and that the CBA as a whole still imposed limitations (*e.g.,* offer sheets, first refusal, etc.) on a player's freedom to negotiate with the team of choice—even after he had played out his option year. According to the Players Association, the members of the Management Council had conspired to adopt a uniform interpretation of Section 17 that would create a system of perpetual reserve on players' services. The union claimed further that the Management Council fraudulently and in bad faith neglected to disclose this interpretation during contract negotiations.

Arbitrator Luskin concluded that nothing in the contract limited the number of options exercisable by the club. Finding no evidence that the Management Council had engaged in a fraudulent conspiracy, he dismissed the grievance and, in effect, gave credence to the notion that the agreement could and did bestow on the NFL clubs a perpetual option on player services, except where clearly qualified:

> In instances where the parties made provision for total free agent status, the
> contractual language explicitly provides for a team's loss of first refusal or com-

pensation rights * * *. The arbitrator cannot infer from the absence of affirmative or negative language that the parties reached an agreement or understanding that would serve to confer total free agent status to a veteran player who had completed a year of service pursuant to a Section 17(b) contract * * *. The arbitrator has further found that a team is not precluded from continuing to exercise the options available to a team after a veteran free agent resigned with his old team.

National Football League Players Ass'n and National Football League Management Council (Arbitrator Luskin, May 14, 1980) at 41, 45. Do you agree with Arbitrator Luskin's conclusion? Recognizing that the CBA limits arbitral authority and precludes the arbitrator from adding to, subtracting from, or altering in any way the provisions of the agreement, is the interpretation of the option year as "perpetually renewing" plausible or consistent with common law contract principles? *See also* Chapter 4 Part II(B).

7. The NFL-NFLPA's most recent collective bargaining agreement contains a modified approach to free agency, replete with such qualifiers as "franchise player" designations. *See* Collective Bargaining Agreement Between The NFL Management Council and NFL Players Association ("NFL CBA"), Art. XVIII, XIX, XX.

8. The next case stemmed from a conspiracy by the owners to place a lid on their expansive spending propensities. The plan allegedly was conceived and pursued in response to exhortations from the league commissioner that the owners show greater restraint in signing available free agents. After years of internecine economic warfare to win the free agent sweepstakes, the owners decided that enough was enough. Unfortunately for the league, the collective bargaining agreement expressly prohibited any collective action to suppress the free agency process.

In the Matter of the Arbitration Between Major League Baseball Players Ass'n and the Twenty-Six Major League Baseball Clubs
Grievance No. 86-2 (1986)

The Matters Put At Issue By Grievance No. 86-2

Grievance No. 86-2 was filed by the Players Association on January 31, 1986. It asserts the twenty-six Major League Clubs "have been acting in concert with each other with respect to individuals who became free agents under Article XVIII after the 1985 season." Article XVIII of the Basic Agreement (negotiated by the parties in 1976) establishes a system of free agency available to eligible members of the bargaining unit. This contractual provision recites that free agency is limited to players who have achieved a total of six years of major league service and who have additionally provided the proper notice of free agency intent or who have been released or not tendered renewal contracts. Paragraph H of Article XVIII is entitled "Individual Nature of Rights." It reads:

> "The utilization or non-utilization of rights under this Article XVIII is an individual matter to be determined solely by each Player and each Club for his or its own benefit. Players shall not act in concert with other Players and Clubs shall not act in concert with other Clubs."

Paragraph H of Article XVIII was originally proposed by the Clubs during the 1976 negotiations in response to a fear that individual players might join to "package" or sell their newly created free agency rights in a manner reminiscent of the earlier joint holdout attempt of Dodger players Sandy Koufax and Don Drysdale. The Players Association responded to the proposal by insisting the clubs be subject to the same constraint and thus in the clause as finally adopted appears a similar prohibition running against concerted club action. As presently constructed, the provision recognizes the tradition of individual salary negotiations in major league baseball but it is designed to guarantee that individual players negotiate with individual clubs.

The Hearing Before The Arbitration Panel

Grievance No. 86-2 was heard in arbitration over thirty-two days of presentation commencing on June 25, 1986 and continuing through May 20, 1987. A total of 5,674 pages of verbatim transcript was produced and 288 exhibits received. Finally, post-hearing briefs were submitted and on August 31, 1987 the arbitration panel met in executive session.

Decision Of The Arbitration Panel

Following the completion of the 1984 championship season sixteen of the twenty-six major league clubs signed free agents who had been playing for other clubs. In addition thereto, several other players eligible for free agency generated considerable interest from clubs other than their employer during the 1984 season. The experience during the winter of 1985–1986 was entirely different, however. Twenty-nine of the 1985–1986 re-entry free agents (plus three players who had not been tendered renewal contracts) signed with their former clubs. Only one of those twenty-nine players (Carlton Fisk) received a bona fide offer from a club other than his employer during the 1985 season (i.e., his "former" club) until such time as his former club announced it did not desire to re-sign the player. The clubs showed no interest in the available free agents at any price until such time as their former club declared the player no longer fit into their plans.

The Players Association characterizes what occurred in the free agency market during the 1985–1986 off season as a "boycott" in which all twenty-six major league clubs participated with an intent to destroy free agency. It is argued no club would turn its back on free agency unless confident all of the other clubs would do likewise. The Players Association states the clubs thus carried out an understanding designed to once and for all do away with free agency, a goal entertained since the December 23, 1975 decision of Chairman Seitz in the Messersmith-McNally case.

In their turn, the clubs contend that what occurred during the 1985–1986 winter was nothing more than the culmination of a predictable evolution to a more sober and rational free agent market from that present during the 1970s. It is argued no agreement existed among the clubs concerning free agency and in fact each of the clubs individually made rational independent decisions regarding the employment of free agents, decisions based upon legitimate baseball, business management and financial factors. The clubs declare that what occurred was the result of the general economic condition of the industry, certain changes in the Basic Agreement, and the least attractive pool of free agents in recent years. The clubs add that the depressed level of activity in the 1985 free agency market was simply the culmination of a ten-year trend rather than the sudden result of a conspiracy.

The positions taken by the parties in this case put directly at issue the meaning, intent and application of Article XVIII(H). As noted, that clause was negotiated in 1976 with the stated purpose of precluding either players or clubs from entering into an agreement, plan or understanding regarding their rights under Article XVIII. The provision declares that the utilization or non-utilization of free agency shall be an individual matter determined solely by each player and club for his or its own benefit. With regard to free agency, players may not act in concert with other players and clubs may not act in concert with other clubs. Thus, in the context of the present inquiry any agreement or plan involving two or more of the clubs and governing the manner in which they will or will not deal with free agents is contractually forbidden. It is not required that such an agreement or understanding be in writing and accompanied by all of the formalities of contract. A common scheme or plan directed to a common benefit is in violation of the bargain of the parties.

Article XVIII(H) is not designed to prohibit the established practice of the clubs whereby their representatives regularly meet to exchange information, express views and seek the counsel of the Player Relations Committee. The clubs, the Player Relations Committee, the Players Association and player agents remain free to exchange information. What is prohibited is a common scheme involving two or more clubs and/or two or more players undertaken for the purpose of a common interest as opposed to their individual benefit.

It is appropriate to pause here and recall something of the history of the free agent market subsequent to its creation in 1976. In that regard the evidence discloses that the arrival of free agency on the major league scene generated considerable enthusiasm and a resultant lively bidding for the services of the relatively few players eligible for such status. In 1976, for example, eleven of the twenty-six clubs signed a total of sixteen significant free agents. Player contract prices began to rise and multi-year contracts were negotiated. This is not to say, however, that all clubs viewed the free agent market as a panacea. Indeed, some of the clubs have never become active in the competition for free agents while others have shied away after experiencing initial disappointing results. Yet, this pattern of history does not explain the sudden and abrupt termination of all efforts to secure the services of free agents from other clubs as present during the winter of 1985–1986.

The clubs argue that the experience of the free agents following the completion of the 1985 championship season was the direct result not of a conspiracy launched by management but rather the deteriorating economics of the game, the increased cost of free agents and the number of "disastrous" club experiences with free agents coupled with a trend in recent years toward the development of young players through the farm system procedure. These contentions will be considered separately.

In the course of the 1985 negotiations the clubs for the first time distributed to the Players Association and to one another a statement of their financial situation including profit and loss balances. This was followed by the urging of the Commissioner that the clubs develop policies and practices designed to solve their economic problems. It is to be noted, however, that Article XVIII(H) provides no exemption from its precepts based upon fiscal needs or constraints. Acting in concert with regard to free agency rights is prohibited whatever may be the economic situation of the individual clubs. Nothing in that provision would prevent any of the twenty-six clubs from offering a free agent a salary and contract term consistent with its budget. In 1985, however, no free agent received an offer *at any price* until and unless his former club declared a lack of interest.

The contention is advanced by the clubs that the quiescence of the 1985 free agent market was set in part by the conviction of the owners that most players who signed long-term contracts thereafter exhibited a pronounced decline in performance, frequently accompanied by long periods on the disabled list. It is argued this perception caused all of the clubs to reduce the guarantee of such contracts to a term of two years for pitchers and three years for position players. While the contracts of all free agents are not long-term, most premiere free agents make such an arrangement a condition of signing. Indeed, it may be said that multi-year contracts are a direct result of the availability of free agency. It follows from this that if free agency can be weakened or destroyed the long-term contract will disappear. This may be a happy result from the perspective of the clubs but it may only be accomplished within the constraints of the provisions of the basic agreement, including the precepts of Article XVIII(H).

A certain number of clubs have always emphasized minor league development and a strong scouting system. In more recent years a view has emerged that young players have now become as productive as many veteran players but at substantially more modest salaries and this phenomenon has been reflected in the quality of the amateur draft. A number of clubs have thus turned from free agency to the perceived advantages attendant to the utilization of young players developed in the farm system coupled with the incidental benefit of avoiding forfeiture of a first or second round draft pick. It is further argued that a rampant resort to free agency has also been dampened by the demise of the free agency re-entry draft process and its attendant publicity. Additionally, the 1985 Basic Agreement introduced a new system of deadlines imposed upon free agent negotiations so that if a club now fails to offer a free agent employee salary arbitration by December 7 (or if an offer of salary arbitration has been made and not accepted) that club must sign the player by January 8 or lose the right to negotiate with him until May 1. Once again, however, these contractual realities of contemporary baseball life do not provide assurance that a free agent will remain with his former club. Only a common understanding that no club will bid on the services of a free agent until and unless his former club no longer desires to sign the free agent will accomplish such a universal effect. In the case at hand, just such a result obtained. This, in itself, constitutes a strong indication of concerted action.

As noted above, and confirmed by history, not all clubs have been active in the free agent market. The Kansas City Royals, for example, have never signed a significant free agent from another club. The same is true of the Minnesota Twins, Oakland Athletics and Seattle Mariners. A number of other clubs have, however, tasted of free agency with the signing of at least one significant player. The Toronto Blue Jays signed free agent Dennis Lamp in 1983, the San Francisco Giants signed Joel Youngblood in 1982, the St. Louis Cardinals signed Darrell Porter in 1980, the Los Angeles Dodgers signed Dave Goltz and Don Stanhouse in 1979, the Milwaukee Brewers signed Roy Howell in 1980, the Philadelphia Phillies signed Pete Rose in 1978, and in the same year the Pittsburgh Pirates signed Lee Lacy while the Montreal Expos signed Elias Sosa. The Boston Red Sox have not signed a significant free agent since 1979 and the New York Mets have not done so since 1980. The Chicago Cubs signed Dave Kingman in 1977 and Bill Campbell in 1981. The Cleveland Indians have signed but one significant free agent, *i.e.*, Wayne Garland in 1976.

More recent free agency activity has seen the Houston Astros sign Omar Moreno in 1982, the same year the Chicago White Sox signed Floyd Bannister. In 1983 the Cincinnati Reds signed Dave Parker and the Detroit Tigers signed Darrell Evans. 1984 saw three significant free agents move to the Baltimore Orioles, *i.e.*, Don Aase, Lee Lacy and Fred Lynn.

The five clubs who have been the most active participants in free agency are the Atlanta Braves, the California Angels, the New York Yankees, the San Diego Padres and the Texas Rangers. In 1981 the Angels signed Reggie Jackson and Frank LaCorte was signed in 1983. The Braves signed Bruce Sutter in 1984 while the Yankees signed Bob Shirley and Steve Kemp in 1982, plus Ed Whitson in 1984. Also in 1984 the Padres signed Tim Stoddard and the Rangers signed Cliff Johnson, Dave Rozema and Burt Hooten.

In the winter of 1984–1985, twenty-six of the forty-six re-entry free agents changed clubs. The situation was dramatically different during the winter of 1985–1986. Prior to the commencement of spring training in 1986 twenty-nine re-entry free agents plus at least three "non-tender" free agents (Dave Kingman, Al Cowens and Joel Youngblood) signed major league contracts. All but four of that total of thirty-two free agents (*i.e.*, Juan Beniquez, Al Holland, Dane Iorg and David Palmer) signed with their former clubs. True enough, after the commencement of spring training nine other free agents signed with new clubs. It is to be noted, however, that in each such case the free agent had not been signed by his former club. Indeed, with the exception of Carlton Fisk no free agent received an offer from a new club until and unless his former club was no longer interested.

The situation of Kirk Gibson will serve as an example of the foregoing. Gibson became eligible for free agency while employed by the Detroit Tigers. The Kansas City Royals sought to initiate discussions with his agent and went so far as to entertain Gibson on a hunting trip at the conclusion of the 1985 season. The interest of the Royals in Gibson suddenly cooled, however, concurrently with a meeting of the owners at St. Louis, Missouri in October of 1985 and a gathering of the general managers in Tarpon Springs, Florida during November of 1985. These meetings were convened contemporaneously with a public announcement of the Royals that they were not going to make an effort to sign any free agents, including Kirk Gibson. The Atlanta Braves also initiated discussions with Gibson's agent but abruptly terminated the exchange. Other established performers on the field received no offers at all except from their former club. These players included Donnie Moore, Tony Bernazard, Tom Brookens, Jamie Easterly, Phil Niekro, Joe Niekro and Aurelio Lopez. Carlton Fisk received a single private overture from the owner of the New York Yankees but that contact was not even revealed to the other members of the management of the New York Yankees. The climate of the market had abruptly changed.

To return for a moment to the commencement of spring training in 1986, it is to be noted that only four free agents had by that time changed clubs. Of that number, Al Holland and Dave Iorg were never offered employment by their former clubs while David Palmer and Juan Beniquez declined such offers. None of the four were offered salary arbitration by their former club prior to the December 7 contract deadline. This removed the former club from a negotiating position until at least May 1, 1986 and Palmer as well as Beniquez ultimately signed for a salary less than the offer of their former club. The result of all of this was a preemption of free agency negotiating rights by the former club, a result that could only be obtained through common consent in violation of Article XVIII(H).

The clubs argue that those free agents signed following the completion of the 1985 championship season enjoyed the benefits of a free competitive market as witness the contracts of Donnie Moore (one million dollars per year for three years), Carlton Fisk ($875,000.00 for 1986) and Kirk Gibson (four million dollars payable over a span of three years). It is further claimed the clubs offered generous salaries to their own free agents because of a fear the players might be lured away by other clubs. The approach of the clubs to free agency negotiations during this period was, however, not consistent with the existence of a free market. Their conduct demonstrated a conviction and belief that none of the other clubs would interfere in the negotiations with their own players until and unless they announced they no longer desired to retain the services of the player. No enthusiasm remained to sign their own players before they could declare for free agency. Nor are we speaking here of only "significant" free agents. Each and every free agent had the same experience, i.e., no offers until their former clubs stated they were no longer interested. This is precisely the result forbidden by Article XVIII(H).

The individual clubs have attempted to explain their conduct during the 1985–1986 winter as a uniform disenchantment with free agency and not a form of prohibited concerted action. Thus, it is said the Atlanta Braves adopted the philosophy of their new General Manager (Bobby Cox) that a team is most effectively developed through its farm system while Vice President Mike Port of the Angels introduced a change of emphasis to scouting and internal development so as to avoid the need to surrender a high draft choice in return for signing a free agent. Port also testified that in 1985 the Angels had no need for a starting pitcher or a catcher. The clubs state that in 1985 the Rangers adopted a written commitment to scouting and minor league development while the San Diego Padres signed only re-entry free agent Dane Iorg because President Ballard Smith was seriously concerned about the financial health of the franchise. The Milwaukee Brewers lost 5.4 million dollars in 1985 and could not afford to sign a free agent while the Kansas City Royals decided to stand pat after winning the 1985 World Series. Director of Player Personnel Al Campanis of the Los Angeles Dodgers testified he was pleased with the composition of his team and saw no reason to become involved in a bidding war for available free agents. Similar testimony was presented on behalf of the New York Yankees, the Baltimore Orioles, the Chicago Cubs and the Cincinnati Reds. Indeed, each and every club representative who testified at the hearing denied a common agreement or understanding. Yet it must be noted that the 1985 class of free agents was unattractive only to clubs other than the club for whom they were employed during that season. It is further to be recalled that those players who declare for free agency are not all superstars. It is reasonable to anticipate that interest in the services of at least some of them will be expressed by a team other than the club by whom they were employed at the time they elect free agency. They surely had a value at some price and yet no offers were advanced.

At the conclusion of the 1985 championship season and early on during the off-season that followed, a series of meetings of the management of major league baseball was convened. Thus, a regularly scheduled quarterly meeting of the owners or their representatives took place at Itasca, Illinois on September 27, 1985, a meeting chaired by the Commissioner. Also in attendance were the two League Presidents, representatives of the Player Relations Committee and counsel. A report was made by a subcommittee of the Long Range Planning Committee concerning the player development systems in place and the cost of those enterprises. The next meeting of the owners took place on October 22, 1985 during the World Series at St. Louis, Missouri. On that occasion a vote was taken to terminate the Joint Drug Agreement previously entered into with the Players Association and a further report of the subcommittee of the Long Range Planning Committee was received. Additionally, the retiring Director of the Player Relations Committee, Leland S. MacPhail, distributed a memorandum (dated October 16, 1985) that had as its message the undesirability of long-term contracts because players signed to such agreements frequently do not thereafter perform to the level of their ability or suffer injuries that force them to leave baseball while still enjoying the salary benefits of the contracts. MacPhail urged the clubs to "exercise more self-discipline in making their operating decisions" and resist the temptation to "give in to the unreasonable demands of experienced marginal players." MacPhail declared, "We must stop day dreaming that one free agent signing will bring a pennant. Somehow we must get our operations back to the point where a normal year for the average team at least results in a break-even situation, so that clubs are not led to make rash moves in the vain hope that they might bring a pennant and a resulting change in their financial position. This requires resistance to fan and media pressure and is not easy." The Commissioner then asked that the comments of MacPhail be given serious consideration and following an informal poll certain club representatives stated their intent to avoid long-term contracts.

The Major League Baseball General Managers met at Tarpon Springs, Florida on November 6, 1985. At that session the Commissioner repeated his concern regarding the financial commitment made by the clubs under long-term player contracts and stated, "It is not smart to sign long-term contracts." He further described such signings as "dumb." There followed the annual Major League Baseball Meeting in San Diego, California on December 11, 1985. At that meeting Mr. MacPhail, on behalf of the Player Relations Committee, distributed a list of the players who had declared for free agency. As noted herein, the distillation of the message of these meetings resulted in every major league club abstaining from the free agency market during that winter until an available free agent was "released" by his former club upon the announcement that the former club was no longer interested in his services. That result was obtained through the conduct of the clubs uniformly established and maintained. The right of the clubs to participate in the free agency provisions of the Basic Agreement no longer remained an individual matter to be determined solely for the benefit of each club. The contemplated benefit of a common goal was substituted. This action constituted a violation of the prohibition against concerted conduct found in Article XVIII(H) and Grievance No. 86-2 is therefore sustained. Pursuant to the stipulation of the parties, argument and evidence regarding an appropriate remedy will be entertained at hearings to be scheduled at the earliest convenience of counsel and the Chairman of the Arbitration Panel.

AWARD

1) The Clubs violated Article XVIII(H) of the Basic Agreement following the completion of the 1985 championship season by acting in concert with regard to the free agency provisions of the said Article XVIII.

2) The question of the construction of an appropriate remedy shall forthwith be set for hearing before the Arbitration Panel.

Notes and Questions

1. The eventual award in this case was a product of a settlement between the Players Association and the owners in the amount of $280 million. Several players who had been bound to other clubs were released and were given the opportunity to declare free agency.

2. Ironically enough, the collusion decision was a result of the owners' own devices. During labor negotiations in 1976 and 1980, they had expressed concern that the players would join together and attempt to whipsaw the owners into signing prohibitive free agency contracts. Purportedly recalling the tandem negotiation by Sandy Koufax and Don Drysdale of the Los Angeles Dodgers decades earlier, the owners demanded that the players agree not to engage in any type of collusion to force the owners to accede to their free agency demands.

Again, the owners employed a bargaining strategy that could only be described as remarkable in its ineptitude. The Koufax/Drysdale tandem negotiation was a result of the fact that there was no free agency at the time. Consequently, the only way that these two superstars could achieve a bargaining position to enable them to demand suitable compensation was to double-team the Dodgers. There was no real likelihood that players would employ this strategy under a system of free agency in which they are free to negotiate with the club of choice. However, Marvin Miller, seizing on the moment, agreed to refrain from engaging in conspiracies if the owners would agree to do the same in terms of *restricting* free agency opportunities. The owners quickly concurred, thereby constructively surrendering, at least in terms of conspiring to curtail free agency, one of the advantages of the precious antitrust exemption. The collusion case, therefore, was a direct byproduct of the owners' insistence upon an anti-collusion provision that they promptly (within a few years) violated.

3. Other collective bargaining agreements in professional sports contain lengthy anti-collusion clauses that explicitly delineate prohibited club conduct and prescribed remedies. *See,* NFL CBA; NBPA COLLECTIVE BARGAINING AGREEMENT ("NBA CBA"), XIV.

(B) Judicial Response to the Arbitration Process: Respect for the Process but Not Categorical Deference

As emphasized above, courts are extremely deferential to arbitral decisions, particularly in the labor relations area where voluntary dispute adjustment has become a way of life. However, this policy of deferral, adopted by both the NLRB and the courts, has its limits. Certain types of unfair labor practices are not conducive to resolution in the arbitration forum and will not be deferred, or "*Collyerized*" in common labor law parlance. Certain awards will not be enforced because their issuance will frustrate the purposes of the NLRA or otherwise run afoul of those criteria that have been established as standards for NLRB review. *Spielberg Mfg. Co.,* 112 NLRB 1080 (1955); *Olin Corp.,* 268 NLRB 573 (1984). Finally, the arbitrator simply may have exceeded the collective bargaining agreement's jurisdictional boundaries, and his or her interpretation may have been so manifestly at war with the contract's intent or relevant authority as to justify reversal. In the two cases that follow immediately, we see classic illustrations of judicial deference to the arbitral process. In the first instance we are guided by no less an authority than the Supreme Court. In the succeeding case, by contrast, we consider precedent in which the court refused to sustain an arbitrator's decision, notwithstanding the predilection for deferral. The opinion is instructive for several reasons, one of which is the obvious delight that some jurists take in injecting their analyses of these types of cases with a healthy dose of football metaphors.

Major League Baseball Players Association v. Garvey
532 U.S. 504 (2001)

Per Curiam.

The Court of Appeals for the Ninth Circuit here rejected an arbitrator's factual findings and then resolved the merits of the parties' dispute instead of remanding the case for further arbitration proceedings. Because the Court's determination conflicts with our cases limiting review of an arbitrator's award entered pursuant to an agreement between an employer and a labor organization and prescribing the appropriate remedy where vacation of the award is warranted, we grant the petition for a writ of certiorari and reverse. * * *

In the late 1980's, petitioner Major League Baseball Players Association (Association) filed grievances against the Major League Baseball Clubs (Clubs), claiming the Clubs had colluded in the market for free-agent services after the 1985, 1986 and 1987 base-ball seasons, in violation of the industry's collective-bargaining agreement. A free agent is a player who may contract with any Club, rather than one whose right to contract is restricted to a particular Club. In a series of decisions, arbitrators found collusion by the Clubs and damage to the players. The Association and Clubs subsequently entered into a Global Settlement Agreement (Agreement), pursuant to which the Clubs established a $ 280 million fund to be distributed to injured players. The Association also designed a "Framework" to evaluate the individual player's claims, and, applying that Framework, recommended distribution plans for claims relating to a particular season or seasons.

The Framework provided that players could seek an arbitrator's review of the distribution plan. The arbitrator would determine "only whether the approved Framework and the criteria set forth therein have been properly applied in the proposed Distribution Plan." *Garvey* v. *Roberts*, 203 F.3d 580, 583 (CA9 2000) *(Garvey I)*. The Framework set forth factors to be considered in evaluating players' claims, as well as specific requirements for lost contract-extension claims. Such claims were cognizable "'only in those cases where evidence exists that a specific offer of an extension was made by a club prior to collusion only to thereafter be withdrawn when the collusion scheme was initiated.'" *Id.* at 584.

Respondent Steve Garvey, a retired, highly regarded first baseman, submitted a claim for damages of approximately $3 million. He alleged that his contract with the San Diego Padres was not extended to the 1988 and 1989 seasons due to collusion. The Association rejected Garvey's claim in February 1996, because he presented no evidence that the Padres actually offered to extend his contract. Garvey objected, and an arbitration hearing was held. He testified that the Padres offered to extend his contract for the 1988 and 1989 seasons and then withdrew the offer after they began colluding with other teams. He presented a June 1996 letter from Ballard Smith, Padres' President and CEO from 1979 to 1987, stating that, before the end of the 1985 season, Smith offered to extend Garvey's contract through the 1989 season, but that the Padres refused to negotiate with Garvey thereafter due to collusion.

The arbitrator denied Garvey's claim, after seeking additional documentation from the parties. In his award, he explained that "'there exists * * * substantial doubt as to the credibility of the statements in the Smith letter.'" He noted the "stark contradictions" between the 1996 letter and Smith's testimony in the earlier arbitration proceedings regarding collusion, where Smith, like other owners, denied collusion and stated that the Padres simply were not interested in extending Garvey's contract. The arbitrator determined that, due to these contradictions, he "'must reject [Smith's] more recent assertion that Garvey did not receive [a contract] extension'" due to collusion, and found that Garvey had not shown a specific offer of extension. He concluded that:

> "'the shadow cast over the credibility of the Smith testimony coupled with the absence of any other corroboration of the claim submitted by Garvey compels a finding that the Padres declined to extend his contract not because of the constraints of the collusion effort of the clubs but rather as a baseball judgment founded upon [Garvey's] age and recent injury history.'"

Garvey moved in Federal District Court to vacate the arbitrator's award, alleging that the arbitrator violated the Framework by denying his claim. The District Court denied the motion. The Court of Appeals for the Ninth Circuit reversed by a divided vote. The court acknowledged that judicial review of an arbitrator's decision in a labor dispute is extremely limited. But it held that review of the merits of the arbitrator's award was warranted in this case, because the arbitrator "'dispensed his own brand of industrial justice.'" *Id.* at 589. The court recognized that Smith's prior testimony with respect to collusion conflicted with the statements in his 1996 letter. But in the court's view, the arbitrator's refusal to credit Smith's letter was "inexplicable" and "bordered on the irrational," because a panel of arbitrators, chaired by the arbitrator involved here, had previously concluded that the owners' prior testimony was false. *Id.* at 590. The court rejected the arbitrator's reliance on the absence of other corroborating evidence, attributing that fact to Smith and Garvey's direct negotiations. The court also found that the record provided "strong support" for the truthfulness of Smith's 1996 letter. *Id.* at 591–592. The Court of Appeals reversed and remanded with directions to vacate the award.

The District Court then remanded the case to the arbitration panel for further hearings, and Garvey appealed. The Court of Appeals, again by a divided vote, explained that *Garvey I* established that "the conclusion that Smith made Garvey an offer and subsequently withdrew it because of the collusion scheme was the only conclusion that the arbitrator could draw from the record in the proceedings." No. 00-56080, 2000 WL 1801383, at *1 (Dec. 7, 2000), judgt. order to be reported at 243 F.3d 547. (*Garvey II*). Noting that its prior instructions might have been unclear, the Court clarified that *Garvey I* "left only one possible result — the result our holding contemplated — an award in Garvey's favor." *Ibid.* The Court of Appeals reversed the District Court and directed that it remand the case to the arbitration panel with instructions to enter an award for Garvey in the amount he claimed.

The parties do not dispute that this case arises under § 301 of the Labor Management Relations Act, 1947, 61 Stat. 156, 29 U.S.C. § 185(a), as the controversy involves an assertion of rights under an agreement between an employer and a labor organization. Although Garvey's specific allegation is that the arbitrator violated the Framework for resolving players' claims for damages, that Framework was designed to facilitate payments to remedy the Clubs' breach of the collective-bargaining agreement. Garvey's right to be made whole is founded on that agreement.

Judicial review of a labor-arbitration decision pursuant to such an agreement is very limited. Courts are not authorized to review the arbitrator's decision on the merits despite allegations that the decision rests on factual errors or misinterprets the parties' agreement. *Paperworkers* v. *Misco, Inc.*, 484 U.S. 29. We recently reiterated that if an "'arbitrator is even arguably construing or applying the contract and acting within the scope of his authority,' the fact that 'a court is convinced he committed serious error does not suffice to overturn his decision.'" *Eastern Associated Coal Corp.* v. *Mine Workers*, 531 U.S. 57 (2000) (quoting *Misco, supra*, at 38). It is only when the arbitrator strays from interpretation and application of the agreement and effectively "dispenses his own brand of industrial justice" that his decision may be unenforceable. *Steelworkers* v. *Enterprise Wheel & Car Corp.*, 363 U.S. 593, 597 (1960). When an arbitrator resolves disputes regarding the application of a contract, and no dishonesty is alleged, the arbitrator's "improvident, even silly, factfinding" does not provide a basis for a reviewing court to refuse to enforce the award. *Misco*, 484 U.S. at 39.

In discussing the courts' limited role in reviewing the merits of arbitration awards, we have stated that "'courts * * * have no business weighing the merits of the grievance [or] considering whether there is equity in a particular claim.'" *Id.* at 37 (quoting *Steelworkers* v. *American Mfg. Co.*, 363 U.S. 564, 568 (1960)). When the judiciary does so, "it usurps a function which * * * is entrusted to the arbitration tribunal." *Id.* at 569; see also *Enterprise Wheel & Car Corp., supra*, at 599 ("It is the arbitrator's construction [of the agreement] which was bargained for * * * "). Consistent with this limited role, we said in *Misco* that "even in the very rare instances when an arbitrator's procedural aberrations rise to the level of affirmative misconduct, as a rule the court must not foreclose further proceedings by settling the merits according to its own judgment of the appropriate result." 484 U.S. at 40–41, n. 10. That step, we explained, "would improperly substitute a judicial determination for the arbitrator's decision that the parties bargained for" in their agreement. *Ibid.* Instead, the court should "simply vacate the award, thus leaving open the possibility of further proceedings if they are permitted under the terms of the agreement." *Ibid.*

To be sure, the Court of Appeals here recited these principles, but its application of them is nothing short of baffling. The substance of the Court's discussion reveals that it overturned the arbitrator's decision because it disagreed with the arbitrator's factual findings, particularly those with respect to credibility. The Court of Appeals, it appears, would have credited Smith's 1996 letter, and found the arbitrator's refusal to do so at worst "irrational" and at best "bizarre." *Garvey I,* 203 F.3d at 590–591. But even "serious error" on the arbitrator's part does not justify overturning his decision, where, as here, he is construing a contract and acting within the scope of his authority. *Misco,* *supra,* at 38.

In *Garvey II,* the court clarified that *Garvey I* both rejected the arbitrator's findings and went further, resolving the merits of the parties' dispute based on the court's assessment of the record before the arbitrator. For that reason, the court found further arbitration proceedings inappropriate. But again, established law ordinarily precludes a court from resolving the merits of the parties' dispute on the basis of its own factual determinations, no matter how erroneous the arbitrator's decision. *Misco, supra,* at 40, n. 10; see also *American Mfg. Co.,* 363 U.S. at 568. Even when the arbitrator's award may properly be vacated, the appropriate remedy is to remand the case for further arbitration proceedings. *Misco, supra,* at 40, n. 10. The dissent suggests that the remedy described in *Misco* is limited to cases where the arbitrator's errors are procedural. *Post,* at 1 (opinion of STEVENS, J.) *Misco* did involve procedural issues, but our discussion regarding the appropriate remedy was not so limited. If a remand is appropriate *even* when the arbitrator's award has been set aside for "procedural aberrations" that constitute "affirmative misconduct," it follows that a remand ordinarily will be appropriate when the arbitrator simply made factual findings that the reviewing court perceives as "irrational." The Court of Appeals usurped the arbitrator's role by resolving the dispute and barring further proceedings, a result at odds with this governing law.

For the foregoing reasons, the Court of Appeals erred in reversing the order of the District Court denying the motion to vacate the arbitrator's award, and it erred further in directing that judgment be entered in Garvey's favor. The judgment of the Court of Appeals is reversed, and the case is remanded for further proceedings consistent with this opinion.

* * *

CONCUR: JUSTICE GINSBURG, concurring in part and concurring in the judgment. I agree with the Court that in *Garvey* v. *Roberts,* 203 F.3d 580 (CA9 2000) (*Garvey I*), the Ninth Circuit should not have disturbed the arbitrator's award. Correction of that error sets this case straight. I see no need to say more.

* * *

JUSTICE STEVENS, dissenting. It is well settled that an arbitrator "does not sit to dispense his own brand of industrial justice." *Steelworkers* v. *Enterprise Wheel & Car Corp.,* 363

U.S. 593, 597(1960). We have also said fairly definitively, albeit in dicta, that a court should remedy an arbitrator's "procedural aberrations" by vacating the award and remanding for further proceedings. *Paperworkers* v. *Misco, Inc.*, 484 U.S. 29, 40–41, n.10 (1987). Our cases, however, do not provide significant guidance as to what standards a federal court should use in assessing whether an arbitrator's behavior is so untethered to either the agreement of the parties or the factual record so as to constitute an attempt to "dispense his own brand of industrial justice." Nor, more importantly, do they tell us how, having made such a finding, courts should deal with "the extraordinary circumstance in which the arbitrator's own rulings make clear that, more than being simply erroneous, his finding is completely inexplicable and borders on the irrational." *Garvey* v. *Roberts*, 203 F.3d 580, 590 (CA9 2000) (case below). Because our caselaw is not sufficiently clear to allow me to conclude that the case below was wrongly decided — let alone to conclude that the decision was so wrong as to require the extraordinary remedy of a summary reversal — I dissent from the Court's disposition of this petition.

Without the benefit of briefing or argument, today the Court resolves two difficult questions. First, it decides that even if the Court of Appeals' appraisal of the merits is correct — that is to say, even if the arbitrator did dispense his own brand of justice untethered to the agreement of the parties, and even if the correct disposition of the matter is perfectly clear — the only course open to a reviewing court is to remand the matter for another arbitration. That conclusion is not compelled by any of our cases, nor by any analysis offered by the Court. As the issue is subject to serious arguments on both sides, the Court should have set this case for argument if it wanted to answer this remedial question.

Second, without reviewing the record or soliciting briefing, the Court concludes that, in any event, "no serious error on the arbitrator's part is apparent in this case." *Ante*, at 7, n. 3. At this stage in the proceedings, I simply cannot endorse that conclusion. After examining the record, obtaining briefing, and hearing oral argument, the Court of Appeals offered a reasoned explanation of its conclusion. See 203 F.3d at 589–592; see also *id.* at 593–594 (Hawkins, J., concurring). Whether or not I would ultimately agree with the Ninth Circuit's analysis, I find the Court's willingness to reverse a factbound determination of the Court of Appeals without engaging that court's reasoning a troubling departure from our normal practice.

Accordingly, I respectfully dissent.

* * *

Notes and Questions

1. The Court characterized the Court of Appeals' application of traditional arbitral review principles as "baffling." Is this assessment unduly harsh?

2. The arbitration mechanism in this case was not the product of a mutual selection process that characterizes typical grievance machinery in a collective bargaining agreement. Should the somewhat unusual nature of this process negate the overwhelming deference that courts traditionally give arbitrations where the entire procedure conjures images of pure voluntariness?

3. As discussed in Chapter 14, unions representing players in all of the major professional sports have developed elaborate regulations for the certification and governance of player agents. The regulations all contain grievance and arbitration procedures for the resolution of disputes between the agent and the collective bargaining representa-

tive. However, once again, the arbitrator selection process is not neutral. Consider the following case.

Black v. National Football League Players Association
87 F. Supp. 2d 1 (D.D.C. 2000)

ROBERTSON, District Judge. William Black claims that the National Football League Players Association (NFLPA) unlawfully initiated disciplinary proceedings against him, affecting his livelihood as a player agent. NFLPA moves for summary judgment. Plaintiff opposes that motion and moves for leave to amend. Plaintiff will be permitted to take discovery on his claim of discrimination under 42 U.S.C. § 1981, but defendant is entitled to judgment as a matter of law on the claims of tortious interference and violation of the Federal Arbitration Act. Leave to file new claims of defamation and trade disparagement will de denied. The reasons for those rulings are set forth below.

Background

* * *

NFLPA is the exclusive collective bargaining representative of NFL players pursuant to Section 9(a) of the National Labor Relations Act, 29 U.S.C. § 159(a). NFLPA nevertheless permits individual agents, or "contract advisors," to represent individual players in negotiations with NFL Clubs. NFLPA "certifies" contract advisors pursuant to a set of regulations. Those regulations set forth a code of conduct for contract advisors, and require that issues regarding the activities of contract advisors be resolved by arbitration.

Mr. Black was first certified as a NFLPA contract advisor in March 1995. He submitted a sworn application to continue his certification on September 9, 1998. The application contained this statement:

> In submitting this Application, I agree to comply with and be bound by these Regulations ... I agree that if I am denied certification or if subsequent to obtaining certification it is revoked or suspended pursuant to the Regulations, the exclusive method for challenging any such action is through the arbitration procedure set forth in the Regulations. In consideration for the opportunity to obtain certification and in consideration of NFLPA's time and expense incurred in the processing of this application for such certification, I further agree that this Application and the Certification, if one is issued to me, along with the NFLPA Regulations Governing Contract Advisors shall constitute a contract between NFLPA and myself.

In May 1999, Mr. Black received a disciplinary complaint from NFLPA's Disciplinary Committee.[2] He commenced this action a month later, asserting that the disciplinary

---

2. The disciplinary complaint alleged, inter alia, that, in violation of the regulations: (1) at various times in 1997 and 1998 Mr. Black provided cash payments to several college players before their eligibility had expired; (2) in late December 1998 Mr. Black arranged the purchase of a Mercedes-Benz automobile for a University of Florida player who was still competing at the college level; (3) in December 1998 Mr. Black met with an assistant coach at Louisiana State University and admitted to purchasing the Mercedes-Benz for the University of Florida football player; (4) in December 1998 an agent identifying himself as Mr. Black's representative offered a bribe to an assistant coach at LSU to encourage an LSU player to enlist Mr. Black as his agent; (5) at various times in 1996 Mr. Black sold stock in a publicly-traded company to several players; (6) over the past three years Mr. Black has provided a bill paying service for his clients whereby they deposit funds in accounts which Mr. Black's firm jointly controls; (7) on his application for certification as a contract advisor, Mr. Black untruthfully answered "NO" when asked: "Do you manage, invest, or in any other manner handle

complaint was the product of an antitrust conspiracy and a secondary boycott, in violation of the Sherman Antitrust Act and the National Labor Relations Act, and that the arbitration system established by the regulations violates the Federal Arbitration Act. Mr. Black's motion for a temporary restraining order was denied on June 22, 1999 by Judge Hogan, and Mr. Black filed an answer to the disciplinary complaint on July 6, 1999.

On July 27, 1999, the Disciplinary Committee issued a proposed ruling revoking Mr. Black's contract advisor certification for a minimum of three years. The regulations provide that Mr. Black may challenge the proposed ruling only by taking the matter to arbitration before an arbitrator selected by NFLPA—in this case, Roger P. Kaplan, Esq.

On July 29, 1999, Mr. Black filed an amended complaint. This first amended complaint jettisons the antitrust and secondary boycott claims and adds two new claims: that NFLPA's initiation of the disciplinary proceedings was based on race discrimination in violation of Section 1981; and that NFLPA tortiously interfered with Mr. Black's business relations (and those of his corporate entity Professional Management, Inc.) by invoking disciplinary action. Mr. Black continues to claim that the arbitration process established by the regulations is illegal under the FAA.

Now before the Court are NFLPA's motion to dismiss or, in the alternative, for summary judgment on all three counts in plaintiffs' first amended complaint, and plaintiffs' motion for leave to file a second amended complaint that would add claims of defamation and trade disparagement.

Analysis

A. Section 1981 Claim

Mr. Black asserts that NFLPA deprived him and his company of full enjoyment of their contractual relationship with NFLPA in violation of 42 U.S.C. § 1981. He asserts that three white agents subjected to disciplinary action by the NFLPA—Joel Segal, Jeffrey Irwin and James Ferraro—were treated more favorably than he.

To establish a prima facie case of discrimination under Section 1981, Mr. Black must demonstrate that his non African-American comparators were similarly situated to him in all material respects. This standard makes it questionable whether Mr. Black's claim can succeed. The timing and gravity of the charges against Mr. Segal appear to be quite different from those against Mr. Black. Mr. Black has not yet had an opportunity for discovery, however, and he has asked * * * for "a chance to obtain affidavits and take depositions and other discovery" pursuant to Fed. R. Civ. P. 56(f). Because Rule 56(f) requests should be "liberally construed," Mr. Black will have a "reasonable opportunity" to justify his opposition. The same ruling will apply with respect to the other alleged comparators, Messrs. Irwin and Ferraro, as to whom the NFLPA has made no factual response to Mr. Black's section 1981 claims.

B. Tortious Interference

Mr. Black and PMI allege that NFLPA, by means of its racially discriminatory actions and by making defamatory statements, tortiously interfered with their existing and prospective business and contractual relations. NFLPA's motion argues that these state law based claims are preempted by Section 301 of the Labor Management Rela-

---

funds for NFL players?"; and (8) in May 1997 Mr. Black filed suit in South Carolina state court against Brantley Evans, Jr., in contravention of exclusive arbitration procedures in the regulations.

tions Act. It is undisputed that NFLPA is a labor union and that the NFLPA contract advisor regulations were formulated in accordance with the collective bargaining agreement.

In *Allis-Chalmers Corp. v. Lueck*, 471 U.S. 202, 213 (1985), the Supreme Court applied the rule that a tort claim "inextricably intertwined with consideration of the terms of the labor contract" is preempted under Section 301. Mr. Black and PMI are not parties to the labor contract, but, as contract advisors, they have agreed to be bound by the regulations promulgated under the collective bargaining agreement. Their license to act as agents for NFL players comes by delegation from the NFLPA, which is a party to the collective bargaining agreement.

State law based claims that depend on construction and application of terms in a collective bargaining agreement are preempted. Those that have a basis wholly independent of the labor contract are not. *Compare United Steelworkers v. Rawson*, 495 U.S. 362, 371(1990) and *International Brotherhood of Electrical Workers v. Hechler*, 481 U.S. 851, 862 (1987) *with Lingle v. Norge Div. of Magic Chef, Inc.*, 486 U.S. 399, 411–12 (1988).

The gravamen of Mr. Black's tortious interference claim is that NFLPA engaged in "discriminatory treatment * * * under the pretext of a disciplinary proceeding" and thereby deliberately interfered with his contractual relationships with NFL players. He does not assert a violation of a right to contract "owed to every person in society," *Rawson*, 495 U.S. at 370, or any other generalized statutory right. Mr. Black's complaint is about the way in which NFLPA has conducted and will conduct his disciplinary. proceeding. That complaint turns upon the proper application of the regulations to Mr. Black's alleged illegal activities as a contract advisor. Thus, *Rawson*, *Hechler* and their progeny, rather than the *Lingle* line of cases, control. Mr. Black's state law claim "cannot be described as independent of the collective-bargaining agreement." *Id.* at 370.

The validity of PMI's contracts with "various football players relating to certain marketing, promotional and public relations services that PMI was to render for players," and PMI's expectancy that those contracts would continue in effect are derivative of Mr. Black's position. Thus, even though PMI's tortious interference claim is in some sense further removed from the regulations than Mr. Black's individual claim, its very existence depends upon interpretation and application of the regulations.

C. Federal Arbitration Act

Mr. Black attacks NFLPA's arbitration system as inherently biased, asserts that Arbitrator Kaplan, who is scheduled to hear the appeal of his disciplinary complaint, is not "neutral" under the terms of the regulations, and demands that Mr. Kaplan be removed. As authority for his demand, Mr. Black invokes Section 10 of the FAA, which empowers a federal court to vacate an arbitration award in limited and specified circumstances, one of which is evident partiality or corruption of the arbitrator.

Mr. Black consented to be bound by NFLPA's contract advisor regulations and agreed that, if his certification should be "suspended or revoked, the exclusive method for challenging any such action is through the arbitration procedure set forth in the Regulations." Section 5.D of the regulations provides: "NFLPA shall select a skilled and experienced person to serve as the outside impartial Arbitrator for all cases arising hereunder."

A written agreement to arbitrate a dispute is "valid, irrevocable, and enforceable" except on grounds that would exist at law or in equity for the revocation of contract. 9

U.S.C. § 2. The Supreme Court has observed that "Section 2 is a congressional declaration of a liberal federal policy favoring arbitration agreements." *Perry v. Thomas*, 482 U.S. 483, 489 (1987). Any questions or doubts as to the intentions of the parties "are generously construed as to issues of arbitrability." *Mitsubishi Motors Corp. v. Soler Chrysler-Plymouth, Inc.*, 473 U.S. 614, 626 (1985).

Mr. Black's legal proposition is that a federal court may step in to preempt agreed-upon arbitration methods and appoint a "neutral" arbitrator where "the potential bias of a named arbitrator makes arbitration proceedings a prelude to later judicial proceedings challenging the arbitration award." He relies for that proposition on a single district court decision, *Third National Bank v. Wedge Group, Inc.*, 749 F. Supp. 851 (M.D. Tenn. 1990). That case is factually distinguishable from this one, however, and it has been disavowed by the very court on whose opinions it relied. *See Aviall, Inc. v. Ryder System, Inc.*, 110 F.3d 892, 896 (2d Cir. 1997).

The *Aviall* decision is more on point. In that case, the court held that a parent company's outside auditor, KPMG Peat Marwick, could not be removed prior to arbitration with a subsidiary because "*Aviall* was fully aware of KMPG's relationship with Ryder when the [agreement] was executed." Distinguishing *Wedge*, the Ryder court noted that "the touchstone in [cases where arbitrators have been removed] was that the arbitrator's relationship to one party was undisclosed, or unanticipated and unintended, thereby invalidating the contract." *Id.* at 896; *see also NFLPA v. OPEIU*, No. 97-1517 at 5–7 (D.D.C. March 25, 1999).

Mr. Black admits that he was aware of and freely agreed to the arbitration terms contained in the regulations, and he makes no allegation about infirmities in the drafting of the regulations. As *Aviall* makes clear, it is of no moment that Mr. Black did not have a hand in the structuring of the arbitration process. *See Aviall*, 110 F.3d at 896. An NFL-selected arbitrator may have an incentive to appease his or her employer, but "the parties to an arbitration choose their method of dispute resolution, and can ask no more impartiality than inheres in the method they have chosen." *Merit Ins. Co. v. Leatherby Insurance Co.*, 714 F.2d 673, 679 (7th Cir. 1983). Mr. Black's peremptory challenge to the neutrality of the NFLPA arbitrator must accordingly be rejected. "He remains free to challenge on the ground of evident partiality any [penalty] ultimately" approved through arbitration. *Aviall*, 110 F.3d at 897.

* * *

Notes and Questions

1. Is the plaintiff correct in his attack on the neutrality of the arbitration mechanism? Should there at least be a presumption in favor of the arbitrator's ability to adjudicate the dispute in an unbiased fashion notwithstanding the selection process?

2. While the arbitration machinery should not be presumptively flawed simply because the selection process is skewed, should that factor at least militate against the escalated degree of deference accorded the typical arbitration decision arising from a purely voluntary procedure?

3. As referenced above, all of the major sports collective bargaining representatives have assumed responsibility for certification and monitoring of individual agents and their representation of players in dealings with league owners. The authority for such oversight derives from the NLRA and the players' association's status as exclusive collective bargaining representatives. Conceivably, the fact that individual bargaining can

only be conducted with the approval of the union fuels the argument that that body can set the standard and ordain eligibility for individuals seeking to represent players who are part of the bargaining unit.

The agent certification agreement and regulations typically contain an elaborate grievance and arbitration mechanism governing all disputes arising under this arrangement. For example, the NHLPA regulations provide as follows:

A. Purpose and Scope

In establishing a system for regulating agents, it is the intention of the NHLPA that the arbitration process set forth herein be the sole and exclusive method for resolving any and all disputes that may arise from the interpretation, application or enforcement of these Regulations and the resulting agreements between agents and individual players. This will ensure that those disputes—which involve essentially internal matters concerning the relationship between individual players, the NHLPA in its capacity as their exclusive bargaining representative, and agents performing certain delegated representative functions relating particularly to individual Player compensation negotiations—will be handled and resolved expeditiously by the decision-maker established herein, without need to resort to costly and time-consuming formal adjudication.

* * *

D. Arbitrator

The NLPA shall appoint a panel of at least three (3) skilled, experienced and impartial persons to serve as single Arbitrators for all disputes arising hereunder. Each panel member shall be appointed for a one (1) year term which shall be automatically renewed from year to year unless the member resigns or is discharged by the NHLPA. The NHLPA may discharge a panel member at the conclusion of a one (1) year term by serving written notice upon him on or before the expiry of the term. The panel member so discharged shall render decisions in all cases he previously heard but will hear no further cases. The NHLPA shall thereupon select a successor panel member. If there is an interim period between the discharge of the panel member and the selection of a successor panel member, an Arbitrator shall be selected on a case by case basis under the Voluntary Labor Tribunal Rules of the American Arbitration Association then in effect.

The panel members shall hear disputes on a rotating basis. The NHLPA shall assign the dispute to the next panel member in the rotation at the time the Grievance is received by the NHLPA.

In Chapter 9, *supra*, we considered whether the agent certification procedures would survive meaningful scrutiny under the antitrust laws and whether the labor exemption would insulate the current arrangements from antitrust sanction. The one-sided, non-voluntary-but-binding arbitration procedure likewise must give pause regarding the due process provided agents prior to a decision that could result in decertification of the agent and the virtual death penalty in terms of the ability to pursue his or her chosen profession. Certain unreported arbitration decisions reinforce the notion that some arbitral determinations carry the malodorous scent of a tribunal lacking at least the appearance of neutrality or diligence.

4. Given the inherent tension between individual agents and collective bargaining representatives, are the players' associations the best custodians of agent eligibility and conduct?

National Football League Players Ass'n v. Pro-Football, Inc.
857 F. Supp. 71 (D.D.C. 1994)

HOGAN, District Judge. The history of professional football is dotted with moments where last minute heroics produced stunning victories. For example, on December 28, 1958, with the score tied 17-17 in overtime, Johnny Unitas handed the ball to Alan ("the Horse") Ameche, who burst into the endzone to give the Baltimore Colts a championship victory over the New York Giants. This case presents the Court with the opportunity to address another type of last minute activity: a last minute legal battle that at one point threatened to stop the last game of the Washington Redskins' 1993 football season.

The parties in this suit seek to resolve a dispute arising out of the labor agreement governing the players and teams in the National Football League ("NFL"). The parties normally rely upon an arbitrator to act as a referee when disputes arise, but in this particular case, the Court is forced to don a black and white striped shirt and interpret the rules by which the parties have agreed to be bound. Having carefully considered the parties' cross-motions for summary judgment, the oral arguments of counsel, and the entire record in this case, the Court will grant the defendants' motions for summary judgment and dismiss this case.

BACKGROUND

The facts in this case are undisputed. The plaintiff, the National Football League Players Association ("NFLPA"), is the union representing NFL players. The defendants are Pro-Football, Inc. d/b/a the Washington Redskins ("the Redskins") and the NFL Management Council ("Management Council"). The NFLPA and the NFL Management Council signed a collective bargaining agreement ("CBA") on May 6, 1993, that governs the employment of professional football players. In executing the CBA, the NFLPA acted as the sole and exclusive representative of the individuals who play football for NFL teams and the Management Council acted as the sole and exclusive representative of the NFL teams that employ these football players. CBA, Preamble.

Article V of the agreement contains a standard agency shop provision that requires NFL players to pay union dues or an equivalent service fee within 30 days of employment. The agreement states that this provision is applicable "wherever and whenever legal." CBA, Art. V, §1. If, after written notification to the NFL Management Council that a player has not paid the proper fees, the matter is not resolved within seven days, the agreement indicates that the player should be suspended without pay. Additionally, Article V states that "any dispute over compliance with, or the interpretation, application or administration of this Article" will be resolved through arbitration. CBA, Art. V, §6. The resulting arbitration decision "will constitute full, final and complete disposition of the dispute, and will be binding on the player(s) and Club(s) involved and the parties to this agreement." *Id.*

On December 17, 1993, the NFLPA sent a written notice to the Management Council which identified the players who had not paid dues or fees to the NFLPA for 1993. The Management Council then informed the Redskins that the team should suspend any players who failed to pay their fees or dues by December 24, 1993. On December 24, 1993, the NFLPA advised the Redskins that 37 Redskins players should be suspended for failing to pay the required fees. The Redskins refused to suspend the delinquent players, asserting that Virginia's right-to-work law prohibited the club from suspending the players.

Based on the refusal of the Redskins to suspend the players, on December 24, 1993, the NFLPA then filed a grievance pursuant to the CBA and obtained an expedited hearing before an arbitrator, Herbert Fishgold. The arbitrator conducted a six-hour hearing on December 28, 1993. During the hearing, the Redskins argued that the club is a Virginia employer, subject to Virginia's right-to-work laws. Since the club's players spend the vast majority of their working hours at Redskins Park in Loudoun County, Virginia, the Redskins took the position that it would be illegal to enforce the agency shop provision against the Redskins and the team's players. The NFLPA argued that the players' predominant job situs was in the District of Columbia and that Virginia's right-to-work law did not apply to the Redskins. Specifically, the NFLPA pointed out that the Redskins play two preseason and eight regular season games at Robert F. Kennedy Stadium ("RFK Stadium") in the District of Columbia, the club's revenue is predominantly derived from playing football games, and players' salaries are related to the number of games in which they remain on the club's roster.

On December 29, 1993, the arbitrator issued his finding. The arbitrator ordered the Redskins to comply with the agreement and to suspend players who failed to pay their dues or fees. Interpreting the Supreme Court's decision in *Oil, Chemical, and Atomic Workers, International Union v. Mobil Oil Corp.*, 426 U.S. 407 (1976), the arbitrator found that the District of Columbia, not Virginia, was the players' predominant job situs because the Redskins play more games there (at RFK stadium) than anywhere else. Plaintiff's Exhibit H at 6-7. Although the players spend the majority of their time practicing in Virginia, the arbitrator found that the team's games are the "*raison d'etre*" of the players' employment and produce the team's revenues. *Id.* Therefore, the arbitrator issued an award that required the Redskins to suspend any players who failed to pay the proper fees. Plaintiff's Exhibit I.

On December 27, 1993, prior to the arbitration hearing, Terry Orr, a Redskins player who is not a party to this suit, sought a temporary restraining order ("TRO") in the Circuit Court of Loudoun County, Virginia. Orr sought to enjoin the enforcement of the agency shop provision on the grounds that the provision was illegal under Virginia's right-to-work law. On December 30, 1993, Judge Thomas D. Horne granted the temporary restraining order and enjoined the Redskins from suspending Orr. *Orr v. National Football League Players Ass'n* No. 15460, 1993 WL 604063 (Va. Cir. Ct. December 30, 1993). Judge Horne interpreted *Mobil Oil* to mean that Virginia's right-to-work law applies to Orr and his teammates because the players spend the vast majority of their time in Virginia. *Id.* at 2.[6]

Following Judge Horne's action, the NFLPA filed this suit seeking injunctive relief and a TRO ordering the defendants to comply with the arbitration award. The NFLPA sought to have the players suspended prior to the Redskins' December 31 game against the Minnesota Vikings. Judge Joyce Hens Green denied the motion on December 30, 1993. *National Football League Players Ass'n v. Pro-Football, Inc.*, 849 F. Supp. 1, 1993 WL 548828 (D.D.C. 1993). Judge Green found that the NFLPA was unable to demonstrate a substantial likelihood of success on the merits. Additionally, Judge Green expressed concern that granting the TRO could cause the Redskins to forfeit the December 31 game, the only NFL game scheduled to be broadcast on New Year's Eve. Such a result would harm ticket holders, fans planning to watch or listen to the game in the mass media, and the teams that were still competing for a berth in the NFL playoffs. *Id.* at 2.

Although the 1993 NFL season is over, the parties have pursued this matter. The Redskins have filed a counterclaim against the NFLPA seeking a declaratory judgment

---

6. In response to Judge Horne's ruling, the arbitrator amended his prior award and excluded Orr from the list of players whom the Redskins should suspend.

finding the arbitrator's award to be unlawful and unenforceable. The NFLPA filed a motion for summary judgment and the defendants have filed cross-motions for summary judgment. The Court heard oral arguments on these motions on April 21, 1994.

DISCUSSION

In this case, the Court needs to determine whether the Redskins can make an end run around the arbitrator's decision. In order to make such a determination, the Court needs to address two issues: (1) the standard of review to apply; and (2) whether the arbitrator correctly interpreted *Mobil Oil* when he found the job situs of Redskins players to be the District of Columbia. The Court finds that it is required to act much like the mysterious individual in the NFL's instant replay booth and review the prior decision de novo. After conducting a slow-motion de novo review of the arbitrator's decision, the Court finds that the arbitrator incorrectly interpreted *Mobil Oil*. Accordingly, the Court finds that the defendants are entitled to summary judgment.

I. The Appropriate Standard for Reviewing the Arbitrator's Decision

Under §301(a) of the Labor Management Relations Act, 29 U.S.C. §185, federal courts have jurisdiction to enforce collective bargaining agreements. The parties do not dispute that this Court has jurisdiction to review and enforce the arbitrator's decision. However, the parties dispute the level of deference that the Court should give to the arbitrator's decision.

The defendants start out in the position of a football team that is behind on the scoreboard and buried in its own territory with less than a minute to play. They face a difficult challenge because ordinarily, "a federal court may not overrule an arbitrator's decision simply because the court believes its own interpretation of the contract would be a better one." *W.R. Grace & Co. v. Local Union 759, Int'l Union of United Rubber, Cork, Linoleum & Plastic Workers*, 461 U.S. 757, 764 (1983). This rule makes sense because parties who choose to have a dispute resolved by an arbitrator should not then be able to go into federal court and seek to reject the interpretation for which the parties bargained. Much like a referee's pass interference call, the key is not necessarily the correctness of the decision, but its finality. Without a final resolution of the matter, play cannot proceed.

In order to keep the game of labor-management relations going, courts ordinarily defer to arbitrator's decisions. The arbitrator's award is legitimate so long as it "draws its essence from the collective bargaining agreement," but may be set aside if it does not draw its essence from the agreement. *United Steelworkers v. Enterprise Wheel & Car Corp.*, 363 U.S. 593, 597 (1960). A mere ambiguity in the arbitrator's decision is not adequate to demonstrate that the arbitrator exceeded his or her authority *Id.* at 597–98. In fact, the scope of judicial review of an arbitrator's decision is the "narrowest known in the law." *Southern Pacific Transp. Co. v. United Transp. Union*, 789 F. Supp. 9, 13 (D.D.C. 1992).

Undaunted by this field position, the defendants' first play is to argue that the arbitrator's award is not legitimate because it did not draw its essence from the collective bargaining agreement. This argument does little to advance the defendants toward the end zone. An award fails to draw its essence from a contract if it is "based on external legal sources, wholly without regard to the terms of the parties' contract." *American Postal Workers Union v. United States Postal Service*, 789 F.2d 1, 8 (D.C. Cir. 1986). Here, the arbitrator looked to external legal sources, but did so only in order to interpret the "wherever and whenever legal" provision of the collective bargaining agreement. Since the arbitrator did not look directly to external legal sources, but did so in order to interpret a provision of the agreement, the arbitrator's decision in fact draws its essence from the agreement * * *. Thus, this argument fails to gain any yardage for the defendants.

The defendants' next challenge to the arbitrator's decision also falls short—an incomplete pass. The defendants argue that the arbitrator's decision concerning the meaning of the term "wherever and whenever legal" in the CBA merits no deference because the arbitrator implausibly and incorrectly interpreted the Supreme Court's Mobil Oil decision. The District of Columbia Circuit has indicated that it would not disturb an arbitrator's plausible reading that a contract incorporated state law. The defendants argue that such deference is not appropriate here because the arbitrator's award was implausible.

Even assuming that the arbitrator's interpretation of *Mobil Oil* was incorrect, it was not implausible. The arbitrator based his decision on the fact that football games are the "*raison d'etre*" of the relationship between the Redskins and the team's players. The arbitrator drew this French phrase directly from Justice Marshall's majority opinion. Although the French may not know much about American football, the arbitrator's reliance on the phrase in making his decision was not implausible; he drew directly upon language in a Supreme Court decision. Thus, as the defendants return to the huddle, their prospects for victory look bleak.

The defendants next turn to the "Hail Mary" of challenges to an arbitrator's decision, public policy. Decisions of arbitrators are given deference even if the arbitrator makes errors of fact and law, unless the arbitrator's award "compels the violation of law or conduct contrary to accepted public policy." *Washington-Baltimore Newspaper Guild, Local 35 v. The Washington Post Company*, 442 F.2d 1234, 1239 (D.C. Cir. 1971). This is consistent with the Supreme Court's statement that "a court may not enforce a collective-bargaining agreement that is contrary to public policy." *W.R. Grace & Co.*, 461 U.S. at 766. In determining whether a clear policy exists, courts look to "the laws and legal precedents" not "general considerations of supposed public interests." *Id.* (quoting *Muschany v. United States*, 324 U.S. 49, 66 (1945)). Such public policy arguments, much like Hail Mary passes, are usually unsuccessful.

Despite the difficulty of creating a successful public policy argument, the defendants present a credible claim based upon the law of Virginia. The Virginia Code states that "it is hereby declared to be the public policy of Virginia that the right to work shall not be denied or abridged on account of membership or nonmembership in any labor union or labor organization." Va. Code Ann. §40.1-58. Section 40.1-62 of the Virginia Code prohibits employers from requiring employees to pay union dues or similar fees to labor unions. A violation of this prohibition is a misdemeanor. *Id.* §40.1-69. If these laws apply to the Redskins, enforcing the agency shop provision of the CBA would violate Virginia's law and public policy.

The difficulty presented by the defendants' argument is that it is intertwined with the merits. If the arbitrator was correct in finding that the players' job situs is the District of Columbia, the Court should defer to his award because it does not violate Virginia's public policy. However, if the arbitrator was incorrect, the Court should not defer to the award because it violates Virginia's public policy. The only reasonable way to determine the amount of deference to give to the arbitrator is to review the merits of the arbitrator's decision to determine whether he made an error of law that compels the defendants to violate Virginia law and public policy. This is the route that the District of Columbia Circuit took in *Washington Post v. Washington-Baltimore Newspaper*

Guild, Local 35, 787 F.2d 604, 606 (D.C. Cir. 1985). In that case, the plaintiff challenged a remedy ordered by an arbitrator on the grounds that it violated a provision of the Labor Management Relations Act, 29 U.S.C. §186. The *Washington Post* court recognized that arbitrator's awards are normally entitled to significant deference, but noted that deference is not appropriate where an award contemplates a violation of law. It stated that in circumstances where legal interpretation is necessary, "we are informed by the views of the arbitrator* * *, but we approach the task with an awareness that the final responsibility is solely our own." 787 F.2d at 606. The Court went on to interpret the statute and found that the arbitrator's award was lawful. *Id.* at 609. Guided by this precedent, the Court will not punt this issue to the arbitrator, but will follow the same course as Washington Post and review the merits of the arbitrator's decision de novo in order to determine whether or not it compels a violation of Virginia law. By articulating a credible public policy argument, the defendants have completed their Hail Mary pass. Nevertheless, to win the game by succeeding on the merits, the defendants must persuade the Court that the arbitrator incorrectly interpreted *Mobil Oil*.

II. Determining the Job Situs of Redskins' Players Under *Mobil Oil*

An analysis of the arbitrator's decision must start with the United States Supreme Court's decision in *Mobil Oil*. In *Mobil Oil*, an oil company filed a lawsuit seeking to invalidate an agency shop provision in its CBA with unlicensed seamen who worked on its oil tankers. 426 U.S. at 410. The company argued that the provision was invalid because it violated Texas' right-to-work laws. *Id.* The sole issue before the Supreme Court was whether the right-to-work laws of Texas could void the agency shop provision of the CBA. *Id.* This determination involved an interpretation of §§8(a)(3) and 14(b) of the National Labor Relations Act. In examining the issue, the Court considered three possible methods for evaluating the contacts between the state and the employment relationship: (1) applying the law of the employee's principal job situs; (2) evaluating the whole employment relationship to determine whether a state had sufficient contacts with the employment relationship; and (3) applying the law of the jurisdiction where the hiring process took place. *Id.* at 413–14. The Court held that:

> In light of what we understand Congress' concerns in both §8(a)(3) and §14(b) to have been, we conclude that it is the employees' predominant job situs rather than a generalized weighing of factors or the place of hiring that triggers the operation of §14(b). We hold that under §14(b), right-to-work laws cannot void agreements permitted by §8(a)(3) when the situs at which all the employees covered by the agreement perform most of their work is located outside of a state having such laws.

Id. at 414. Because most of the employment work of the seamen was performed on the high seas, the Court found that Texas' right to work laws did not apply to them. *Id.* at 420.

In the course of reaching its conclusion, the Court rejected the tests that would require courts to evaluate contacts or look to the location of the hiring process. For example, the Court rejected the latter test because §14(b) addressed concerns related to the post-hiring employment relationship, not the hiring process. *Id.* at 417. In emphasizing that §14(b) is concerned with the post-hiring relationship as opposed to the place of hiring, the Court stated that:

> It is evident, then, that §14(b)'s primary concern is with state regulation of the post-hiring employer-employee-union relationship. And the center of the

post-hiring relationship is the job situs, the place where the work that is the very *raison d'etre* of the relationship is performed.

Id.

The Court went on to explain that two practical concerns supported its decision to adopt a rule that an employee's predominant job situs should determine the applicability of state right-to-work laws: (1) the rule minimizes the possibility of "patently anomalous extra-territorial applications" of right-to-work laws and (2) the rule provides an easy and predictable method of determining whether an agency shop provision will apply. *Id.* at 419.

The parties in this case seize upon different language in *Mobil Oil* to support their positions. The NFLPA argues that the arbitrator correctly relied upon the *raison d'etre* language because of the unique employment status of professional athletes. Despite their lengthy practices, the real purpose of their work is to play in football games. Since more of the Redskins' games are played at RFK Stadium than any place else, the NFLPA reasons that the District of Columbia is the predominant job situs of the Redskins players. The defendants argue that the arbitrator fumbled his interpretation of *Mobil Oil* by taking the *raison d'etre* language out of context. According to the defendants, *Mobil Oil* creates a quantitative test. Because the Redskins players spend most of their time in Virginia, not the District of Columbia, the defendants assert that Virginia is the players' predominant job situs and that its right-to-work law should apply to the Redskins players.

A review of the *Mobil Oil* decision and the few cases interpreting it convince this Court that the arbitrator's decision was erroneous. The *raison d'etre* language appears only once in the *Mobil Oil* opinion. It arises only in the context of the Supreme Court's explanation of why, under §14(b), the post-hiring employment relationship was more significant than the location where the hiring process took place. Contrary to the arbitrator's interpretation, the Supreme Court did not use this phrase as a means of defining the term "predominant job situs." By treating the passing use of the term *raison d'etre* as the definition of "predominant job situs," the arbitrator read the term out of its appropriate context and gave it a significance that the Supreme Court had not intended. Nothing in the case suggests that the Supreme Court intended an employee's predominant job situs to be the place that is the *raison d'etre* of his or her employment, as opposed to the place where the employee spends the most time.

This can be clearly seen by examining the manner in which the Supreme Court determined the predominant job situs of the seamen in *Mobil Oil*. When the Supreme Court applied its new test in *Mobil Oil*, it made no reference to the *raison d'etre* of the seamen's employment, but only referred to the place where most of the work was performed. 426 U.S. at 420. Because the seamen spent most of their time on the high seas, the Court had little difficulty finding that Texas' right-to-work laws did not apply to the seamen. *Id.* A full reading of the *Mobil Oil* opinion can only lead to the conclusion that the Supreme Court adopted a quantitative test for determining an employee's predominant job situs.

* * *

The two judges who have already considered the matter have disagreed with the arbitrator's analysis. In granting a TRO in favor of Terry Orr, Judge Horne of the Loudoun County Circuit Court rejected the arbitrator's interpretation of *Mobil Oil* and found that because Terry Orr spends over 90 percent of the time required to perform his contract in Virginia, Virginia is his predominant job situs. *Orr*, 1993 WL 604063 at 2. The

NFLPA tries to distinguish Judge Horne's holding because Orr did not actually play any games in the District of Columbia in 1993. While this may be true, it was simply not a factor that was addressed in Judge Horne's opinion and did not affect Judge Horne's analysis. Judge Joyce Hens Green denied the plaintiff's motion for a TRO for substantially the same reasons stated by Judge Horne and stated that the facts in Orr's case were equally applicable to the other Redskins who spend most of their time practicing at Redskins Park. The Court recognizes that it need not give any weight to these preliminary determinations because they are neither law of the case nor res judicata. Without giving these decisions any substantive weight, the Court notes that these decisions suggest that today's ruling is not based on a wholesale reinterpretation of existing law.

Because the NFLPA has little relevant authority to support its position, it attempts a misdirection play by directing the Court's attention to a District of Columbia Court of Appeals decision in which some Redskins players were found to be covered by the District of Columbia's Workers' Compensation Act, *Pro-Football, Inc. v. District of Columbia Dep't of Employment Servs.*, 588 A.2d 275 (D.C. 1991). In *Pro-Football*, the Court was asked to determine whether the District of Columbia's Department of Employment Services was clearly erroneous when it applied a test that sought to determine the place "from which the employee performs the principal service(s) for which he was hired." *Id.* at 278. Applying that standard, the Court found that the Department had not been clearly erroneous in finding that players who had actually played football games at RFK Stadium were subject to District of Columbia law. *Id.* at 279.

If this Court were applying the same test in this case, it conceivably could reach the same result. However, *Mobil Oil* did not establish a "principal services" test, but a "predominant job situs" test based upon where an employee spends most of his or her time. 426 U.S. at 414. The *Pro-Football* case specifically noted that the Redskins players spend the majority of their time in Virginia, but found that the players' principal services were performed in the District of Columbia. 588 A.2d at 278–79. The factual findings in *Pro-Football* thus support a finding that the predominant job situs of the players under the quantitative *Mobil Oil* test is Virginia. Accordingly, the *Pro-Football* case provides no relevant guidance for interpreting *Mobil Oil* and does nothing to support the NFLPA's position.

It appears that the arbitrator simply misread *Mobil Oil*. The Supreme Court was concerned with developing a workable test and rejected the use of a flexible balancing test. Nevertheless, at the arbitration hearing, the parties presented evidence that attempted to establish the contacts between the Redskins and the District of Columbia. The NFLPA presented evidence showing that the Redskins' revenues come predominantly from football games and that the players' contracts were linked to game performance. Transcript of Arbitration at 110–122. The NFLPA also tried to support its position by demonstrating that the Redskins' fight song includes the phrases "sons of Washington" and "Fight on for old D.C." *Id.* at 225–26. The mere fact that such evidence was presented suggests the folly of adopting the arbitrator's *raison d'etre* test. It would present a clear risk of creating a flexible and nebulous test despite the Supreme Court's pronouncement that a bright line test is appropriate. *Mobil Oil*, 426 U.S. at 418–19.

It is true that the Redskins would not exist if the team did not play its games in the District of Columbia and elsewhere. The team's revenue comes primarily from playing games, not practicing. However, to adopt an economic-based *raison d'etre* test would potentially create difficulties in application. Professional athletes, musicians, actors, and others who may spend most of their time in one place practicing, but earn their revenue based upon a limited number of performances, would face the possibility that the application of agency shop provisions may vary from year to year depending on the location of their performances in a given year. Further, the Redskins themselves may be presented with situations where players are under contract but do not play in the District of Columbia at all because of injuries or some other concerns. If a player does not participate in a single game in the District of Columbia (*e.g.* Terry Orr), the player could possibly be subject to Virginia's right-to-work laws, because the *raison d'etre* would be different. This could create the anomalous situation in which players on the same team would be covered by the labor laws of different jurisdictions. This is not the type of situation envisioned by the Supreme Court when it adopted the job situs test.

The Court's primary concern must be with predictability. The NFLPA may have some legitimate equitable arguments about the financial significance of the games that are played in the District of Columbia, as opposed to the practices that occur in Virginia. Nevertheless, when the Redskins players get up in the morning to go to work, they usually go to Redskins Park, not RFK stadium. Practices, conditioning, and meetings are an integral part of game preparation. Since the players spend most of their time working in Virginia, *Mobil Oil* indicates that Virginia law should apply to them. Regardless of the intuitive appeal of the arbitrator's decision, it does not conform with the current state of the law. Carving out exceptions to *Mobil Oil* for the Redskins (and eventually others) would limit the predictability and usefulness of *Mobil Oil*.

Because the arbitrator in this case clearly erred in interpreting *Mobil Oil*, he placed the Redskins in the unenviable position of being ordered to violate the law and public policy of Virginia. Although the Court is ordinarily quite reluctant to act as a Monday morning quarterback and second-guess an arbitrator, public policy mandates that the Court step in and act in this particular case. The Court finds that the arbitrator's decision violated the law and public policy of Virginia and therefore cannot stand. Thus, although the team has struggled recently on the gridiron, the Redskins have won a surprising come-from-behind victory here in the judicial arena.

CONCLUSION

For the foregoing reasons, the Court finds that this case presents no genuine issue of material fact and that the defendants are entitled to a judgment as a matter of law pursuant to Fed. R. Civ. P. 56. Therefore, the Court will vacate the arbitrator's award and enter a declaratory judgment finding that the award is unenforceable because it is contrary to the laws and public policy of Virginia. Accordingly, the Court will grant the defendants' motions for summary judgment, deny the plaintiff's motion for summary judgment, and dismiss this case.

Notes and Questions

1. Was the judge's reversal of the arbitrator's decision appropriate in this case?

2. The foregoing decision was addressed earlier in Chapter 14, Part VII(H), dealing with the applicability of right to work laws where an employee "works" in both "right to work" and "union shop" states. Do you agree that the practice times should take precedence over the locale of half the regular season games? Is it insignificant that the Redskins "are inextricably and indelibly connected to the District of Columbia in the public eye" and in all league matters? While the court notes the financial importance of the actual playing of the games in the District of Columbia, it stresses the need for pre-

dictability, and the clear message of the *Mobil Oil* decision regarding the emphasis to be placed on the employees' daily work situs.

3. In drawing its reasoning and conclusions from the "essence" of a collective bargaining agreement, to what degree should an arbitrator employ outside sources and rely on extra-arbitral authority? For example, in interpreting a contract's "non-discrimination" clause, should an arbitrator consider decisions of the EEOC, the courts, or any other forum charged with investigating, prosecuting or adjudicating claims of disparate treatment or other discriminatory conduct? *See generally* FRANK ELKOURI AND EDNA ASPER ELKOURI, HOW ARBITRATION WORKS 321–64 (6th ed. 2003).

4. Not all arbitration review proceedings result in absolute affirmances or reversals. At times, courts have found certain portions of an arbitrator's report to be sustainable while questioning the prudence of other portions (such as the remedy). Likewise, arbitrators have been called upon to review decisions of league commissioners, and have modified the remedy while acknowledging the commissioner's broad authority to act.

Former Atlanta Braves relief pitcher John Rocker tested the boundaries of employee free speech when he commented in a magazine interview on the evils of New York, focusing mainly on the subway and its habituees. In particular, Rocker declared:

> I'm not a very big fan of foreigners. You can walk an entire block in Times Square and not hear anybody speaking English. Asians and Koreans and Vietnamese and Indians and Russians and Spanish people and everything up there. How the hell did they get in this country? ... Imagine having to take the [number] 7 train to the ball park looking like you're [riding through] Beirut next to some kid with purple hair next to some queer with AIDS, right next to some dude who just got out of jail right next to some 20-year-old mom with four kids.

See Roger I. Abrams, *Symposium: John Rocker: Off His Rocker: Sports Discipline and Labor Arbitration,* 11 MARQ. SPORTS L. REV. 167 (2001).

Invoking the best interests of baseball clause, Commissioner Bud Selig suspended Rocker for seventy-four days, fined him $20,000, and required him to undergo sensitivity training. Arbitration Shaym Das modified the discipline imposed by the commissioner, reducing the suspension to two weeks and the fine to $500, finding that Rocker had been penalized more severely than other players for comparable offenses. *Id.*

5. The foregoing case raises serious questions about the parameters of a player's off-the-field misconduct and the extent to which behavior away from the playing arena should be regulated by the league. Among the questions that it poses for future incidents are: whether league a league commissioner has authority under the broad umbrella of "best interests" and "integrity of the game" clauses to circumscribe a player's freedom of speech and expression; whether the commissioner can legislate or impose discipline for other off-the-field conduct such as domestic violence; whether such matters are a mandatory subjects of bargaining requiring good faith negotiations with the players' collective bargaining representative; and whether the player is entitled to be heard by a neutral arbitrator or is to be afforded other due process protections. *See* Christopher J. McKinny, *Professional Sports Leagues and the First Amendment: A Closed Marketplace,* 13 MARQ. SPORTS L. REV. 223 (2003); Matthew Pachman, *Limits On The Discretionary Powers of Professional Sports Commissioners: A Historical and Legal Analysis of Issues Raised by the Pete Rose Controversy,* 76 VA. L. REV. 1409 (1990); Carrie A. Moser, *Penalties, Fouls and Errors,* 11 SPORTS LAW J. 69 (2004).

6. One of the more celebrated incidents triggering a major arbitration decision involved former Golden State Warrior Latrell Sprewell. Sprewell, during a team practice, assaulted coach P.J. Carlisimo and attempted to choke him. After leaving the court, Sprewell returned and attempted to finish the deed, suggesting more malice than heat of passion. The response was twofold as the Warriors terminated Sprewell's contract and the league suspended him for one year. As a result of the contract repudiation and the league discipline, the NBPA filed a grievance claiming that the punishment violated the just cause language of the collective bargaining agreement. Arbitrator John D. Ferrick, former Dean of the Fordham Law School, sustained the grievance in large part, requiring the Warriors to reinstate Sprewell's contract and reducing the suspension to the remainder of the season (still costing Sprewell over six million dollars). Sprewell was unsuccessful in his appeal to the federal courts on the portion of Ferrick's opinion that he deemed unfavorable. *See Sprewell v. Golden State Warriors*, 231 F.3d 520 (9th Cir. 2000). *See also*, GLENN M. WONG, ESSENTIALS OF SPORTS LAW (3d ed. 2003) 925.

7. In the following case, another District of Columbia federal judge considered a football player's claim under the NFL-NFLPA collective bargaining agreement. Here, the player sued the Players Association for breach of its duty to represent him fairly. The lawsuit stemmed from the player's original contention that his club, the Green Bay Packers, had wrongfully terminated him after he was unable to perform due to a football related injury. When the league, through the Management Council and the NFLPA, attempted to resolve the matter amicably, including removing the dispute from the injury grievance machinery, the plaintiff claimed that his rights under the agreement had been compromised. He sought immediate redress in court, bypassing the procedures outlined in the collective bargaining agreement and short-circuiting the process already initiated.

Sharpe v. National Football League Players Ass'n
941 F. Supp. 8 (D.C. 1996)

GREEN, District Judge.

I. Introduction

This matter is before the Court on the Defendant National Football League Players Association's ("Defendant") Motion to Dismiss. The Court holds that before it may consider the Plaintiff's complaint, the Plaintiff must receive, at least, an adverse decision from an arbitrator on his contract claim against his former employer. Since the arbitrator has not decided that claim, the Plaintiff's Complaint must be dismissed.

II. Facts

The Plaintiff was a professional football player for the Green Bay Packers ("Packers") of the National Football League ("NFL"). The Plaintiff was also a member of the collective bargaining unit represented by the Defendant with the right to be represented by the Defendant in individual grievance matters against the Packers. The Defendant is the exclusive collective bargaining representative for present and future professional football players in the NFL, representing such players in injury grievance claims against the players' employer-clubs.

In May 1993, the Defendant and the NFL Management Council signed a new collective bargaining agreement that controlled employment disputes between players and teams. In particular, the agreement provides for the filing of injury grievances by players against their employer-teams.

In 1991, the Plaintiff signed a contract that obligated him to play for the Packers through the year 2000. The Plaintiff was scheduled to be paid an installment on his 1995 salary by March 15, 1995. In the final week of the 1994 NFL season, the Plaintiff participated in a game and did not receive any injury. The Plaintiff alleges that, in February 1995, the Packers coerced him into having surgery and led him to believe that the team would pay his 1995 salary. After the surgery, the Plaintiff became physically unable to perform under the contract he signed with the Packers. The Packers subsequently terminated the Plaintiff.

On March 8, 1995, the Plaintiff submitted to arbitration an injury grievance against the Packers seeking the remainder of his 1995 salary. He alleged that the Packers wrongfully terminated him when he was physically unable to perform under his contract.

The Plaintiff alleges that the Defendant urged him to withdraw his grievance and then, without Plaintiff's knowledge, secretly agreed with the NFL Management Council that the Defendant would expedite Plaintiff's claim and not treat it as an injury grievance. In addition, the Plaintiff alleges that the Defendant has left the arbitrator and the Management Council with the "impression" that the Defendant did not believe in the legitimacy of Plaintiff's claim. The Plaintiff argues that the secret agreement would deprive the Plaintiff of the following: (1) the ability "to fully pursue the injury grievance claim[;]" (2) due process rights and important guidelines and procedures; (3) the necessary time to prepare his case; (4) the right to supplement the hearing record. The Plaintiff, therefore, believes that the Defendant did not represent him in good faith.

The Plaintiff then filed this action alleging that the Defendant breached its duty of fair representation of the Plaintiff.

III. Discussion

Under the contract that the Plaintiff signed with the Packers, he agreed that any contractual dispute between the Packers and him would "be submitted to final and binding arbitration in accordance with the procedure called for in any collective bargaining agreement in existence at the time the event giving rise to any such dispute occurs." (Mot. to Dismiss Ex. B, P 20.) The extant collective bargaining agreement contains two grievance procedures, each of which results in binding arbitration: (1) an injury grievance procedure; and (2) a non-injury grievance procedure, through which all other disputes "pertaining to terms and conditions of employment of NFL players will be resolved exclusively. * * *" (Mot. to Dismiss Ex. A.)

The Plaintiff has chosen to arbitrate his dispute with the Packers while suing the Defendant before this Court. Yet, a suit against an employer alleging a breach of the collective bargaining agreement and a suit against the union for breach of the union's duty of fair representation are "inextricably interdependent." *DelCostello v. International Brotherhood Of Teamsters*, 462 U.S. 151, 164, (1983). To prevail on either claim, an employee-union member must prove a violation of the employment contract and demonstrate the union's breach of duty. "The employee may, if he chooses, sue one defendant and not the other; but the case he must prove is the same whether he sues one, the other, or both." *DelCostello v. International Brotherhood Of Teamsters*, 462 U.S. at 165.

The Plaintiff is obligated to arbitrate his contract claim against the Packers by virtue of his employment contract, the collective bargaining agreement and federal labor policy. Indeed, the Plaintiff has submitted his claim against the Packers to arbitration and it is pending. (Compl. P 26.) The focus, therefore, "is no longer on the reasons for the union's failure to act but on whether, contrary to [an] arbitrator's decision, the employer breached the contract and whether there is substantial reason to believe that a union breach of duty contributed to [an] erroneous outcome of the contractual proceedings." *Hines v. Anchor Motor Freight, Inc.*, 424 U.S. at 568. Consequently, before the Court can entertain the Plaintiff's claim against the Defendant for breach of its duty of fair representation, the Plaintiff must receive, at least, an adverse decision from an arbitrator on his claim against the Packers. Since no such decision has yet been rendered, the Plaintiff's complaint is premature and must be dismissed.

The Court shall, therefore, grant the Defendant's Motion to Dismiss.

IV. Conclusion

In order to consider the Plaintiff's claim that the Defendant breached its duty of fair representation, the Plaintiff must submit his contract claim against the Packers to arbitration and, at least, receive an adverse decision. Since the arbitrator has not resolved this dispute, the Plaintiff's complaint must be dismissed.

Notes and Questions

1. This case reinforces the idea that parties who have established procedures to resolve disputes must utilize that mechanism prior to seeking redress in a judicial forum. *McKart v. United States*, 395 U.S. 185 (1969); *Myers v. Bethlehem Shipbuilding Corp.*, 303 U.S. 41 (1938). This need to exhaust one's remedies or, alternatively, the importance of deferral to pertinent administrative forums or contractually agreed upon dispute adjustment mechanisms, is permanently etched in our litigation consciousness. *See Steelworkers v. American Mfg. Co.*, 363 U.S. 564 (1960); *Steelworkers v. Warrior & Gulf Navigation Co.*, 363 U.S. 574 (1960); *Steelworkers v. Enterprise Wheel & Car Corp.*, 363 U.S. 593 (1960). *See also Collyer Insulated Wire*, 192 NLRB 837 (1971). Of course, as reflected in the Pete Rose case, Chapter 3, the need to exhaust administrative remedies may be suspended when the ultimate outcome in that forum is a foregone conclusion. Courts will not require a party to waste its energies when such efforts would be clearly futile.

2. The court in *Sharpe* granted the defendant's motion to dismiss because the plaintiff had failed to exhaust his contractual remedies, specifically by neglecting to follow the prescribed grievance/arbitration procedure. Is this decision fair in light of Sharpe's claim that the NFLPA had breached its duty of fair representation? What purpose would be served by requiring Sharpe to avail himself of a procedure wherein the very union that, in part, allegedly aggrieved him would be serving as his representative? The Supreme Court has declared that the courts and the NLRB share concurrent jurisdiction over claims alleging a breach of the duty of fair representation. *Vaca v. Sipes*, 386 U.S. 171 (1967). Thus, a court is not precluded from asserting jurisdiction over this type of claim notwithstanding the arguable jurisdiction of the NLRB. Under these circumstances, and given the obvious "futility" factor, would it have been proper for the court to bypass the contractual grievance procedure and exercise jurisdiction over Sharpe's claim? Is it relevant that Sharpe had already activated the grievance machinery? It is conceivable that the concurrent jurisdiction argument theoretically would be inap-

propriate, even by analogy, because the plaintiff had already opted to employ the contract's grievance mechanism and use the arbitration forum for ultimate review. *See* WILLIAM J. FOX, JR., UNDERSTANDING ADMINISTRATIVE LAW 238 (1986). If so, then Sharpe's strongest argument would have been that the NFLPA's apparently cozy relationship with the NFL and, derivatively, his club, would render proceeding through the grievance procedure, with the union as his "champion," a futile exercise. If Sharpe sought to raise his injury dispute through the tort route, would a court assert jurisdiction or would such claims be preempted? *See Holmes v. NFL*, 939 F. Supp. 517 (N.D. Tex. Da. Div. 1996).

3. Once again, the importance of following procedures outlined in the collective bargaining agreement cannot be overemphasized. Failure to observe all relevant time periods and jurisdictional boundaries could lead to dismissal of the claim(s). Thus, while arbitration procedures are more informal than more traditional forums, the filing prerequisites and other requirements are often strictly applied. *See generally Davis v. Pro Basketball, Inc.*, 381 F. Supp. 1 (S.D.N.Y. 1974).

4. The *Sharpe* case involved a common dispute in professional football, the extent to which an athlete's ability to play and, concomitantly, the club's right to terminate, have been affected by an injury. The NFL's injury grievance provisions have given rise to numerous questions, often focusing upon the cause of a deterioration in player skill and the relationship between such deterioration and a prior injury. *In re McCauley* represents an arbitration decision that attempted to clarify the parameters of a club's options and responsibilities in the context of an injury allegedly contributing to a player's inability to play. There, Arbitrator Smith was confronted with a player who had diminished skills yet was still technically "cleared" to play (*i.e.*, earlier "on the field" injuries had healed). He declared that a club would assume no financial liability for the player's termination year unless: (1) the pre-season physical was wrong and the incapacity was caused by the injury in question; (2) after the pre-season physical and during the season, the player suffered a new injury leading to the decision to terminate; and (3) during the season, intervening events served to exacerbate the earlier injury to a degree that the player was incapacitated, causing the termination. *See* WEISTART & LOWELL §3.06, at 225; *In Re Williams* (Arbitrator Stark, May 15, 1977). *See further Tillman v. New Orleans Football Club*, 265 So. 2d 284 (La. Ct. App. 1972); *Schultz v. Los Angeles Dons, Inc.*, 238 P.2d 73 (Cal. Dist. Ct. App. 1951).

5. The NFL's current injury grievance language reads as follows:

ARTICLE X

INJURY GRIEVANCE

Section 1. **Definition:** An "injury grievance" is a claim or complaint that, at the time a player's NFL Player Contract was terminated by a Club, the player was physically unable to perform the services required of him by that contract because of an injury incurred in the performance of his services under that contract. All time limitations in this Article may be extended by mutual agreement of the parties.

Section 2. **Filing:** Any player and/or the NFLPA must present an injury grievance in writing to a Club, with a copy to the Management Council, within twenty-five (25) days from the date it became known or should have become known to the player that his contract had been terminated. The grievance will set forth the approximate date of the alleged injury and its general nature. If a grievance is filed by a player without the involvement of the NFLPA, the Management Council will promptly send copies of the grievance and the answer to the NFLPA.

Section 3. **Answer:** The Club to which an injury grievance has been presented will answer in writing within seven (7) days. If the answer contains a denial of the claim, the general grounds for such denial will be set forth. The answer may raise any special defense, including but not limited to the following:

(a) That the player did not pass the physical examination administered by the Club physician at the beginning of the pre-season training camp for the year in question. This defense will not be available if the player participated in any team drills following his physical examination or in any pre-season or regular season game; provided, however, that the Club physician may require the player to undergo certain exercises or activities, not team drills, to determine whether the player will pass the physical examination;

(b) That the player failed to make full and complete disclosure of his known physical or mental condition when questioned during the physical examination;

(c) That the player's injury occurred prior to the physical examination and the player knowingly executed a waiver or release prior to the physical examination or his commencement of practice for the season in question which specifically pertained to such prior injury;

(d) That the player's injury arose solely from a non-football-related cause subsequent to the physical examination;

(e) That subsequent to the physical examination the player suffered no new football-related injury;

(f) That subsequent to the physical examination the player suffered no football-related aggravation of a prior injury reducing his physical capacity below the level existing at the time of his physical examination as contemporaneously recorded by the Club physician.

Section 4. **Neutral Physician:** The player must present himself for examination by a neutral physician in the Club city or the Club city closest to the player's residence within twenty (20) days from the date of the grievance. This time period may be extended by mutual consent if the neutral physician is not available. Neither Club nor player may submit any medical records to the neutral physician, nor may the Club physician or player's physician communicate with the neutral physician. The player will notify the Club of the identity of the neutral physician by whom he is to be examined as soon as possible subsequent to a selection by the player. The neutral physician will not become the treating physician nor will the neutral physician examination involve more than one office visit without the prior approval of both the NFLPA and Management Council. The neutral physician may review any objective medical tests which all parties mutually agree to provide. The neutral physician is further authorized to perform any necessary diagnostic tests after consultation with the parties. The neutral physician is required to submit to the parties a detailed typewritten medical report of his examination. In order to facilitate settlement of grievances, the parties periodically will consult with neutral physicians by telephone conference call to obtain preliminary opinions as to the length of time, if any, after their examinations before players would be physically able to perform contract services. The NFLPA will use its best efforts to make the neutral physicians in each Club city equally available to the players who file injury grievances.

Section 5. **Neutral Physician List:** The NFLPA and the Management Council will maintain a jointly approved list of neutral physicians, including at least two orthopedic physicians in each city in which a Club is located. This list will be subject to review and modification between February 1 and April 15 of each year, at which time either party may eliminate any two neutral physicians from the list by written notice to the other party. When vacancies occur, the NFLPA and the Management Council will each submit a list of three (3) orthopedic physicians to the other party within thirty (30) days for each NFL city where a vacancy exists. If the parties are unable to agree on a replacement, within ten (10) days they will select a neutral physician for each city by alternately striking names. The party to strike a name first will be determined by a flip of a coin. If either party fails to cooperate in the striking process the other party may select one of the nominees on its list, and the other party will be bound by such selection. The next vacancy occurring will be filled in similar fashion with the party who initially struck first then striking second. The parties will alternate striking first for future vacancies occurring thereafter during the term of this Agreement.

* * *

Section 9. **Miscellaneous:** The arbitrator will consider the neutral physician's findings conclusive with regard to the physical condition of the player and the extent of an injury at the time of his examination by the neutral physician. The arbitrator will decide the dispute in light of this finding and such other issues or defenses which may have been properly submitted to him. The Club or the Management Council must advise the grievant and the NFLPA in writing no later than seven (7) days before the hearing of any special defense to be raised at the hearing. The arbitrator may award the player payments for medical expenses incurred or which will be incurred in connection with an injury.

* * *

Section 13. **Presumption of Fitness:** If the player passes the physical examination of the Club prior to the pre-season training camp for the year in question, having made full and complete disclosure of his known physical and mental condition when questioned by the Club physician during the physical examination, it will be presumed that such player was physically fit to play football on the date of such examination.

* * *

NFL Collective Bargaining Agreement (1998), Art. X. Does this provision still leave room for interpretation and further clarification?

(C) A Change of Position: The Union as Respondent in Grievance Arbitration

The typical arbitration case finds its origin as a dispute that spawns an employee or union's attempt to seek redress by activating the collective bargaining agreement's grievance machinery. A close look at many such provisions reveals that any party can initiate the arbitration process and, in fact, may be obligated to exhaust that avenue of recourse prior to filing suit in an appropriate court. Decisions considered earlier in this chapter have found players' associations in the unusual position of respondent. In the following case, the Miami Dolphins, an employer, as statutorily defined in variouis contexts, instigated a grievance claiming breach of the collective bargaining agreement by running back Ricky Williams. In addition to presenting an unusual alignment of grievant and respondent, this case reinforces the premise advanced earlier that a judicial review of an arbitrator's decision is narrowly circumscribed.

Miami Dolphins Ltd. v. Williams
356 F. Supp. 2d 1301 (S.D. Fla. 2005)

COHN, District Judge.

* * *

I. BACKGROUND

Errick L. "Ricky" Williams ("Williams") played football for the Miami Dolphins pursuant to a contract containing various compensation provisions involving a signing bonus and incentive bonuses. Before the 2002 season, Miami traded three draft picks to the New Orleans Saints to obtain Williams. The Dolphins and Williams negotiated a new contract including various incentive bonuses available to Williams based on his performance in each season for the remainder of the term of the original contract. The Dolphins Contract also specifically incorporated (and attached) the Additional Consideration Signing Bonus provisions that were part of Williams' contract with New Orleans.

In late July, 2004, Williams informed the Dolphins that he would no longer play football. The Dolphins then filed a grievance under the collective bargaining agreement in place between the football player's union, the National Football League Player's Association ("NFLPA") and the owner's association, the National Football League Management Council ("NFL"). The grievance was based upon several clauses in the Contract between the Dolphins and Williams. One relevant clause states:

Upon Player's failure to perform for the above enumerated reasons under Player's contracts for the [1999–2006] seasons, Player shall forfeit all future payments and amounts not yet received, and shall immediately return and refund to the Club any of the Additional Consideration previously paid by Club in the proportionate amount of the Additional Consideration as follows: * * * K. Voluntary Breach of Failure to Perform after January 31, 2004, and before or during the 8th game of the 2004 regular season: 37.50% ($ 3,316,343).

* * *

With regard to performance incentive bonus payments, the Contract states in PP 12–12.6 that:

In the event Player fails or refuses to report to Club, or fails or refuses to practice or play with Club at any time for any reason * * *, or leaves Club without its consent during the duration of the above league years, or if Player is otherwise in breach of this Contract, then Player shall be in default ("Default"). If Player is in Default, then upon demand by Club, Player shall * * * return and refund to the Club any and all incentive payments previously paid by Club * * * relinquish and forfeit any and all earned but unpaid incentives.

On August 19, 2004, the Dolphins notified Williams of the Default and demanded payment of $ 8,616,343.00 in forfeited bonus payments. The Dolphins then filed a grievance against Williams pursuant to the NFL Collective Bargaining Agreement ("CBA") on September 1, 2004. The grievance was heard by an arbitrator pursuant to the CBA on September 21, 2004. On September 24, 2004, the arbitrator notified the parties that his decision was to grant the Dolphins' grievance. A twelve-page written opinion was entered by the arbitrator on October 5, 2004. On October 28, 2004, the Dolphins filed this action to confirm the arbitration award pursuant to the Federal Arbitration Act. Williams subsequently filed a motion to vacate the award. The parties completed briefing these motions on January 25, 2005. The Court then granted Williams' January 28, 2005 request to hold a hearing on the motions.

II. DISCUSSION

The provisions of the Federal Arbitration Act, 9 U.S.C. §§ 1, et seq. ("FAA"), control this Court's review of an arbitration award, whether presented by a motion to confirm or a motion to vacate. It is well-settled that the Federal Arbitration Act was intended to relieve congestion in the courts and provide the parties with an alternative method for dispute resolution that would be quicker and less expensive than litigation. Judicial review of arbitration awards is "narrowly limited," and the FAA presumes that arbitration awards will be confirmed. Great deference is afforded to arbitration awards.

This deference is even greater in the context of collective bargaining agreements and labor-management disputes. The United States Supreme Court has stated that:

> Judicial review of a labor-arbitration decision pursuant to such an agreement is very limited. Courts are not authorized to review the arbitrator's decision on the merits despite allegations that the decision rests on factual errors or misinterprets the parties' agreement. *Paperworkers v. Misco, Inc.*, 484 U.S. 29, 36 (1987). We recently reiterated that if an "'arbitrator is even arguably construing or applying the contract and acting within the scope of his authority,' the fact that 'a court is convinced he committed serious error does not suffice to overturn his decision.'" *Eastern Associated Coal Corp. v. Mine Workers*, 531 U.S. 57, 62 (2000). It is only when the arbitrator strays from interpretation and application of the agreement and effectively "dispense [s] his own brand of industrial justice" that his decision may be unenforceable.

Major League Baseball Players Ass'n v. Garvey, 532 U.S. 504, 509 (2001).

The Eleventh Circuit has long followed this standard:

> Courts are not to vacate the award because of substantive mistake except in rare instances of egregious error, such as when the award is irrational, when it fails to draw its essence from the collective bargaining agreement, or when the arbitrator has exceeded a specific contractual limitation on the scope of his authority. Although such extreme deference has its costs in the particular case, those costs are far outweighed by the general benefits that accrue to the national labor scheme from giving arbitral awards a strong presumption of finality.

Wallace v. Civil Aeronautics Bd., 755 F.2d 861, 863–864 (11th Cir. 1985).

In applying this standard of review, the FAA sets forth four grounds for vacating an arbitration award:

> (1) the award was procured by corruption, fraud, or undue means;

> (2) there was evident partiality or corruption in the arbitrators; (3) the arbitrators were guilty of misconduct in refusing to postpone the hearing when there was good cause to postpone, or in refusing to hear pertinent and material evidence, or were guilty of any other misbehavior which may have prejudiced

any party; or (4) the arbitrators exceeded their powers so much so that a mutual, final, and definite award upon the subject matter submitted was not made.

See 9 U.S.C. §10(a). The burden is on the party requesting vacatur of the award to prove one of these four bases.

In addition to the four statutory grounds, none of which are applicable in the present case, the Eleventh Circuit Court of Appeals has recognized three non-statutory bases for vacatur of an arbitration award. The award may be vacated (1) if it is arbitrary and capricious, (2) if its enforcement is contrary to public policy, or (3) if it evinces a manifest disregard for the law. *Montes v. Shearson Lehman Bros., Inc.,* 128 F.3d 1456, 1458–59, 1461–62 (11th Cir. 1997). In adding the "manifest disregard for the law" basis in *Montes*, the Eleventh Circuit emphasized "that this ground is a narrow one. We apply it here because * * * the arbitrators recognized that they were told to disregard the law (which the record reflects they knew) in a case in which the evidence to support the award was marginal." *Montes,* 128 F.3d at 1462 (11th Cir. 1997).

Williams argues that the award must be vacated because it manifestly disregards state law regarding liquidated damages that are unenforceable penalty provisions with no relation to actual damages. Williams also asserts that the award must be vacated because enforcement of the liquidated damages provisions violates the public policy of Louisiana and Florida.

A. Arbitrator's Decision

In the arbitration, the Dolphins argued that the plain language of the default provisions in the player contract is clear that Williams must refund the bonuses paid to him. Williams argued that such provisions are liquidated damages bearing no relationship to the extent of the loss suffered by the Dolphins as a result of Williams' decision to retire. The arbitrator then reviewed the contract provisions at issue. The arbitrator clearly considered the state-law argument regarding liquidated damages presented by Williams. He concluded that whether or not the default provisions constituted a penalty, "what was bargained here was a comprehensive incentive and default mechanism."

B. Manifest Disregard for the Law

Williams argues that the default provisions are intended to punish him for failing to perform under the contract in violation of the state law of Florida and Louisiana. This Court concludes that if necessary, only Florida law applies, as Louisiana law does not appear to apply to the Dolphins-Williams Contract. The Contract specifically states that it is governed by Florida law, and that the Contract, including any attachments, sets for the entire agreement. Thus, the initial Saints contract specifically does not apply, except for the Additional Consideration Signing Bonus provisions, which where specifically made part of the Dolphins-Williams Contract, and which do not reference Louisiana law.

Williams further argues that the arbitrator's decision was in manifest disregard of such state law, relying upon *Montes,* 128 F.3d at 1461 (quoted above). However, in this case, the Dolphins argued in the arbitration that state law forbidding such penalty provisions did not apply as a legal matter. That is not the same as urging the arbitrator to "manifestly disregard" state law, as the Court of Appeals found to have occurred in *Montes*. Rather, such argument and decision that the anti-penalty, even if wrong, at worst is a "misinterpretation, misstatement or misapplication of the law," which cannot constitute a basis to vacate an award. *Montes,* 128 F.3d at 1461–62.

C. Public Policy Violation

In a closely related argument, Williams asserts that the arbitrator's decision violates public policy, relying heavily upon a decision involving the NFLPA and the NFL out of the District of Columbia. In National Football League Players Ass'n v. Pro-Football, Inc., 857 F. Supp. 71, 75 (D.D.C. 1994), the NFL succeeded in having the court vacate an arbitration award against the Washington Redskins. The issue in that case involved the payment of union dues or union service fee by certain players. The CBA provided that players who have failed to pay the dues by a certain time are to be suspended by their team. In this case, the team refused to suspend the players, arguing that as a Virginia-based company, Virginia law forbids employers to enforce such a "closed-shop" labor provision. The NFLPA filed a grievance. An arbitrator concluded that the job situs was in the District of Columbia, and granted the union's grievance.

The court, in deciding to vacate the arbitration award, stated that "decisions of arbitrators are given deference even if the arbitrator makes errors of fact and law, unless the arbitrator's award 'compels the violation of law or conduct contrary to accepted public policy,'" citing to authority from the Circuit Court of Appeals for the District of Columbia. The district court reasoned that: "The only reasonable way to determine the amount of deference to give to the arbitrator is to review the merits of the arbitrator's decision to determine whether he made an error of law that compels the defendants to violate Virginia law and public policy." 857 F. Supp. at 76. After reviewing the merits of the decision regarding job situs, the Court concluded that the correct legal decision was that the job situs was Virginia, and therefore vacated the arbitration award.

In attempting to distinguish this case, the Dolphins argued that confirming the arbitration award in the present case would not require Williams to violate public policy. Although not mentioned by either party at the hearing, it appears that the Redskins decision was vacated on appeal as being moot. National Football League Players Ass'n v. Pro Football, Inc., 56 F.3d 1525, 1526 (D.C. Cir. 1995) ("we decline to reach the merits of this appeal and vacate the District Court's judgment and order"). The Court therefore declines to follow this decision.

The public policy argument of Williams has some merit. It is true that under Florida law, agreements between parties to apply liquidated damages upon default can be deemed unenforceable as penalty provisions by a court. This Court recognizes that the default provisions of the Dolphins-Williams contract could be construed as valid liquidated damages or as an unenforceable penalty. However, the Court finds that the arbitrator in this case was well within the scope of his authority in interpreting the default provisions of the contract in the context of the NFL's CBA and Florida law.[3] The fact that the arbitrator construed the contract in a manner that avoided consideration of whether the actual damages were proportional to the default provisions does not render his decision in manifest disregard or against the public policy of Florida.

---

3. On the issue of whether the default provisions are valid liquidated damages or an unenforceable penalty, the Dolphins argue that under *H.D. Hutchison v. Tompkins*, 259 So.2d 129, 132 (Fla. 1972), the fact that its damages from Williams' breach were not readily ascertainable at the time the contract was signed allows the liquidated damages clause to be valid. This Court does agree that given the personal nature of the services in question, those of a starting running back in the NFL, it would be difficult if not impossible in 2002 for the parties to ascertain what the damages to the Dolphins would be if Williams breached the agreement in July, 2004.

III. CONCLUSION

The Court therefore concludes that Williams and the NFLPA have not met their burden to vacate the arbitration award. They failed to establish that the arbitrator manifestly disregarded the law, or that enforcement of the award would violate public policy, or that the award is arbitrary and capricious. The Court will therefore deny their motion to vacate and grant the Petitioners' motion to confirm the award.

* * *

Notes and Questions

1. This case illustrates that courts are reluctant to disturb an arbitration decision absent the most dramatic abuses of arbitral authority. Do you agree that the arbitrator's decision herein was entitled to deference and that this case was distinguishable from *NFLPA v. Pro-Football, Inc.*?

2. Historically, binding arbitration has been an employer's trade-off for a union's pledge not to strike during the term of a collective bargaining agreement. *See Textile Workers v. Lincoln Mills*, 353 U.S. 448 (1957). The foregoing case illustrates that management may avail itself of the arbitration machinery, and do so successfully.

(D) Salary Recompense During A Strike

An issue that has generated considerable controversy is the application of salary guaranty provisions in the context of a strike or other work stoppage. It is axiomatic that striking employees are not entitled to compensation while they are withholding services. Of course, if the employees had accrued benefits that were due and owing at the inception of the strike, then an employer's failure to provide such compensation could violate the NLRA or pertinent collective bargaining agreement provisions. *See Emerson Electric Co., E.L. Wiegand Div. v. NLRB*, 650 F.2d 463 (3d Cir. 1981), *cert. denied*, 455 U.S. 939 (1982); *Arbitration Between MLBPA and Major League Baseball PRC, Inc.*, Panel Decision No. 49 (Goetz, Impartial Arbitrator)(June 29, 1983). To sustain a claim for such benefits in an unfair labor practice context, the General Counsel typically must prove that the strike was the basis for the employer's refusal to pay the *accrued* amounts. *See Texaco, Inc.*, 285 NLRB 241, 245 (1987). The employer may justify the refusal to pay by establishing legitimate reasons for such conduct, such as explicit contractual language evincing a waiver of entitlement to the benefits. *See, e.g., Johns-Manville Sales Corp.*, 289 NLRB 358 (1988).

Of course, the employer may not suspend payment during a strike if it has contractually agreed to guarantee payment. The problem arises when the contract does not clearly explicate those circumstances under which the guarantee will be triggered. In earlier chapters, we discussed salary guarantee clauses and the extent to which those provisions would apply in the context of an injury, assignment, waiver or other change in employment conditions. *See Sample v. Gotham Football Club*, 59 F.R.D. 160 (S.D.N.Y. 1973). We also explored the applicability of doctrines such as mitigation of damages to ascertain the nature of a club's liability for the entire amount of salary allegedly owed under a salary guarantee. *NFLPA v. NFL Management Council*, 233 Cal. Rptr. 147 (Ct. App. 1986). In the following case, we address the applicability of a salary guarantee in the face of a strike or other work stoppage. Often, the contract does not precisely define the parameters of the guarantee, particularly where a strike is concerned. In such instances, the arbitrator, NLRB, or the courts will explore several factors to ascertain the employee's eligibility for compensation. The *Tommy John* arbitration, below, is illustrative.

In the Matter of the Arbitration Between
Major League Baseball Player Relations Comm., Inc.
and Major League Baseball Players Ass'n
Panel Decision No. 50D
Salary Guarantee Grievances (1983)

* * *

New York Yankees and Tommy John (50D)

Tommy John is the only player who has been signed to a long-term guaranteed contract with the New York Yankees since January 1, 1976, and the advent of free agency, that did not contain an express exclusion from the salary obligation during strike by the Players Association. He is claiming salary continuation during the 1981 strike under his contract with the Yankees for the years 1979 through 1981, which provided as follows in paragraph 5 of the Special Covenants:

> 5. Any other provision *to the contrary* notwithstanding and except as provided below in this paragraph *all compensation and benefits payable to the Player hereunder shall be paid in any event, provided the Player does not arbitrarily refuse to render his professional services.* Compensation and benefits do not have to be paid if Player becomes incapacitated or dies while on the Major League Player Roster of Club because of intentional self injury, suicide, drugs, alcoholism, or because of participation in automobile or motorcycle racing, piloting of aircraft, fencing, parachuting or sky diving, boxing, wrestling, karate, judo, softball, football, basketball, soccer, skiing, hockey, "Superstar" or "Superteam" competition, and other activities prohibited by the Uniform Player's Contract ("Contract"), paragraph 5(b).
>
> *It is the intent and understanding of the parties* hereto *that this entire Contract shall be a "no-cut", guaranteed contract, despite any inability of the Player to exhibit sufficient skill or competitive ability, and despite any mental or physical handicap or injury or death* except as provided in the previous paragraph. (Underscoring added.)

The underscored wording is identical to corresponding portions of the provision recommended in the Players Association memorandum of January 7, 1977, and followed in a number of other guaranteed contracts referred to in earlier portions of this Decision. What makes this contract unusual is not its wording, but its erratic negotiating and drafting history.

a) Background of Preliminary Draft

Prior to signing with the Yankees, John had been under contract with the Los Angeles Dodgers for the 1977 and 1978 seasons. His contract with the Dodgers—negotiated on his behalf by his lawyer, Robert Cohen—had included a special covenant that was a verbatim copy of the Players Association recommendation that actually had been suggested to Cohen by Dodgers' Vice President Campanis. After John declared free agency at the end of the 1978 season and was selected by the Yankees and 12 other Clubs in the reentry draft, Cohen contacted a number of those Clubs and then proceeded to negotiate an "agreement in principle" on basic contract terms with Yankees' President Al Rosen during the first three weeks of November, 1978. The Yankees announced John's signing the day before Thanksgiving, although no formal written contract had yet been executed.

This agreement in principle included specific terms of salary and bonuses for each of the three years of the contract, with an option for 1982, deferred compensation, life insurance, and a loan, as well as an understanding that this was to be a guaranteed contract with a no-trade clause. During the course of negotiating these basic terms, when Cohen mentioned that the contract was to be guaranteed, Rosen asked him what he had in mind. Cohen replied that it would be "a complete guarantee as to almost every contingency, except if Tommy just arbitrarily refuses to play baseball." Rosen told Cohen he would have no problem with that and asked him to prepare a draft of the language.

In a later conversation, Rosen informed Cohen that Yankees' Owner George Steinbrenner insisted on including in any contract guarantee a prohibition of the Player engaging in certain dangerous sports and other prohibited activities. Cohen indicated he would have no objection to that, and Rosen then sent him the following suggested language:

> A. The Club agrees that if this contract is terminated because the player fails in the opinion of the Club's management, to exhibit sufficient skill or competitive ability to qualify or continue as a member of the Club's team the player shall continue to receive the unpaid balance of the salary stipulated in the contract for the term of the contract: provided, however that if the contract is terminated for any of the following reasons the player shall only receive such termination pay, if any, provided for in the basic agreement applicable at the time of such termination:

> 1. Fail, refuse or neglect to conform his personal conduct to the standards of good citizenship and good sportsmanship or to keep himself in first-class physical condition or to obey the Club's training rules: or

> 2. Fail to render his services due to physical or mental incapacity or death directly or indirectly due to or attributable to "intentional self injury, suicide, drugs, alcoholism, activities or sports prohibited by the contract of a criminal or felonious act":

> 3. Fail, refuse or neglect to render his services under the contract or in any other manner materially breach the contract.

After reviewing this, Cohen advised Rosen the only portion that would be acceptable was the wording on incapacity or death due to certain of the causes specified in subparagraph 2. On December 6, 1978, Cohen sent Rosen a four-page double-spaced typewritten draft entitled "SPECIAL COVENANTS" that included the following Paragraph 5:

> 5. Regardless of any provision herein to the contrary, all compensation and benefits payable to the Player hereunder shall be paid in any event, provided the Player does not arbitrarily refuse to render his professional services. Compensation and benefits do not have to be paid if Player becomes incapacitated or dies while on the Major League Player Roster of Club because of "intentional self injury, suicide, drugs, alcoholism, activities or sports prohibited by the Contract".

> It is the intent and understanding of the parties hereto that this entire Contract shall be a "no-cut", guaranteed contract, despite any inability of the Player

to exhibit sufficient skill or competitive ability, and despite any mental or physical handicap or injury or death except as provided in the previous paragraph.
(Quotation marks in original.)

The first and third sentences were taken from the special covenants in John's contract
with the Dodgers, while the second sentence incorporated (in the quotation marks) the
portion of the Yankees' suggested language Cohen considered acceptable. This draft also
set forth the various forms of compensation that had been agreed upon, plus the no-
trade restriction, and was signed by John before transmittal, but was never signed by
the Yankees.

b) First and Second Executed Contracts

Two changes were then made in Cohen's December 6, 1978, draft of the Special
Covenants. At Rosen's request, Cohen expanded the list of prohibited sports beyond
those specified in paragraph 5(b) of the Uniform Player's Contract, to include the
comprehensive listing set forth in the second sentence of paragraph 5 of the Special
Covenants in the final John contract quoted first above. In addition, a change was
made in the $500,000 face amount of life insurance provisions in paragraph 4 to pro-
vide that John would become owner of the policy on December 31, 2002, instead of
January 2, 2008, but left unchanged the specified cash surrender value of $350,000 for
the new transfer date. This change was made at Cohen's request because he had learned
in the interim that the Yankee's limited partnership agreement terminated on the earlier date.

These changes were worked out over the telephone by Cohen with Rosen and Peter
Alkalay, a New York City attorney who was assisting the Yankees on certain technical aspects of the John contract and compensation arrangements. Cohen prepared a revised
draft of the Special Covenants incorporating these changes, had it signed by John, and
sent it to Alkalay on December 29 or 30 via KWIP (a telephonic copying machine) for
Steinbrenner's signature. On January 2, 1979, Cohen received back, via KWIP, a copy
signed by Steinbrenner, without change.

Shortly after the execution of this contract, Cohen received a telephone call from
Rosen informing him the Yankees were having difficulty obtaining the full $500,000 face
amount of life insurance called for by paragraph 4 of the Special Covenants at the premium rate Cohen had quoted during the negotiations. Rosen asked that instead of
maintaining the $500,000 face amount for the full period, the Club be permitted to pro-
vide a substantial amount in the neighborhood of $250,000 initially and increase that
amount gradually to the full $500,000. After checking with John, Cohen called Rosen
back and informed him the requested reduction in life insurance coverage would be
agreeable if the Club could "send some documentation."

Before any revised contract had been prepared, Cohen received another telephone
call from Rosen, who then was on vacation in the Virgin Islands. Rosen told Cohen that
Steinbrenner had called about a "big problem" with the contract signed on January 2.
Rosen explained the problem was that Steinbrenner had discovered the contract "did
not have any provision in it that Tommy would not be paid in the event of a Player
strike." Cohen replied:

> That's correct, I am well aware of that, that the contract did not have that lan-
> guage, it was not supposed to have that language, and that we had bargained
> for almost a complete guarantee contract with the exception of the few things
> that we agreed to, and as far as I was to assume, we had a contract.

Rosen told Cohen Steinbrenner "was coming down on him very hard" for failing to include the strike exception in the contract and wanted Cohen to talk to John about this to see if it couldn't be changed. Cohen replied that they had signed a contract and saw no reason to change it, but that he would talk to John.

Cohen did discuss the matter with John, but before he could get back to Rosen with any decision, Rosen again called Cohen—this time from New York—and asked permission to talk to John about changing the contract because he (Rosen) was "in hot water with George." (Before receiving this call, Cohen had also had a telephone conversation with Alkalay in which Alkalay had indicated that Steinbrenner was very upset with Rosen and wanted to change the contract.)

After some further discussion with John, Cohen advised Rosen that John would be willing to give the Yankees a provision that he would not be paid in the event of a strike if (1) the Yankees would return the life insurance to the original face amount of $500,000 for the entire period until 2002 and (2) the Club would include a provision that John would be paid in the event of a lockout by the Clubs.

Apparently this was agreeable to Rosen and Alkalay since Cohen prepared a revised draft of the Special Covenants incorporating these changes. Cohen sent Alkalay a signed copy on January 26, 1979, which retained the provision in paragraph 4 (d) that "At no time shall the insurance payable pursuant to the policy be less than $500,000," and added a new paragraph 8 stating:

> 8. In the event of a strike by the Major League Players Association and as a result of the strike, Player is unavailable to participate in any regular season games, the Club will not be obligated to pay that portion of Player's salary stated in paragraph one (1) of these Special Covenants as it relates to the number of openings not played compared to the total number of openings scheduled in the regular season. No other payments due Player under the terms of this contract will be so affected. In the event of a lock-out by management, Player will receive all compensation due under paragraph one (1) of these Special Covenants as well as all other payments due under this contract.

On January 29, Cohen received from the Yankees a duplicate original signed by Steinbrenner.

c) The Final Contract

About a week after receiving the second contract signed by Steinbrenner, Cohen received a telephone call from Steinbrenner. In the course of exchanging greetings, Cohen found—to his surprise—that Steinbrenner had arranged a five-way conference call, and that Rosen and Alkalay, as well as John, were all already on the line. Steinbrenner told Cohen that the American League President would not approve John's latest contract because of the clause in paragraph 8 of the Special Covenants requiring that he be paid in the event of a lockout and that it "had to come out." Steinbrenner asked if John and Cohen would be willing to take out the lockout provision, but retain the strike exception and the new provision for the full $500,000 life insurance effective immediately.

After further discussion, Cohen agreed to talk over the Club's proposal with John and call back in half and hour. Cohen then conferred privately with John by telephone, but before he could call Steinbrenner back, Steinbrenner himself called Cohen—again with Rosen and John already on the line on a conference call (perhaps with Alkalay also). Cohen told Steinbrenner they would not be agreeable to making the requested changes, and that they felt under no obligation to make such changes because they "had a signed contract." At that point Steinbrenner became very upset and commented, "Maybe we should call the whole thing off." Cohen told him that would be fine and that he would like to contact the Kansas City Royals, who would be very receptive to having John play for them.

Cohen testified that Steinbrenner responded as follows:

> At that point in time George said, "no, no, don't react so quickly." After a short conversation he said, "All right, you win, strike language is out, lock-out language is out, the insurance goes back to the way we wanted to put originally, i.e., payable in 30 years," and that's it.

Cohen and John agreed. A third contract, at issue here, was executed the day before spring training. Paragraph 5 of the Special Covenants was in the form quoted first above, with no strike or lockout exception; paragraph 4 provided $500,000 face amount of life insurance after 30 years and transfer of the policy then, with $350,000 cash value.

d) Support for the Strike

When the strike started on June 12, 1981, John had been on the Disabled List for approximately one week and was visiting relatives in Indiana with permission from the Club. A member of Players Association for many years and a former Players Representative and member of the Association's Executive Board, John has acknowledged that he supported the 1981 strike. During the strike, he never made any attempt to contact any Yankee official or report to the stadium for medical treatment, nor did any Club official contact him or request him to perform any services for the Club.

e) Opinion

As a minimum, John would be entitled to salary continuation during the strike for the entire period of his inability to perform due to disability. In this regard, his case is indistinguishable from Panel Decision 50B involving Larry Hisle and the Milwaukee Brewers. As in that case, the contractual provision that "compensation ... shall be paid in any event ... despite any ... physical handicap or injury" gave him a right to salary continuation for the duration of disability that became "accrued" or "vested" at the time of onset of his disability. That Decision recognized that because such a vested benefit has already been earned, it cannot be cut off upon commencement of a strike. Here John had upheld his side of the bargain by performing when he was physically able.

John could not be considered to be "arbitrarily refusing" to perform services within the meaning of the proviso to the salary payment provision in the first sentence of paragraph 5 of his Special Covenants, notwithstanding his admitted support for the strike. As has been noted in other portions of Decision 50, that phrase seems designed to exclude from the guarantee *willful* conduct rendering a Player unable to perform. In John's case, he was not in any position to withhold his services when the strike started, but instead was *prevented* from doing so by the fact that he already was *physically unable* to perform. (In fact, his placement on the Disabled List precluded him form performing for at least 21 days thereafter even if he wanted to, under Major League Rule 2(e) (1).)

One of the principal purposes of the salary guarantee—evidenced by the wording of the third sentence of paragraph 5 of John's Special Covenants—was to assure continuation of salary notwithstanding inability to perform due to disability. It would defeat that purpose to deny salary to John during his disability. His failure to perform when the strike started on June 12, 1981, was not due to the strike, but to circumstances beyond his control that prevented him from performing regardless of the strike.

The difficulty here is that the evidence in the record does not show how long John's disability continued. Presumably this would have been rather difficult to determine since he had no occasion to perform during the strike and apparently was not under the care of any physician, but had been ordered by the Club's doctors "just to rest" and not aggravate his injury. It therefore seems necessary to make a determination whether under paragraph 5 of his Special Covenants he was entitled to salary continuation during the strike, in the absence of inability to perform due to disability.

On this question, the Yankees make essentially the same arguments as were made by the Dodgers in Decision 50C: namely, that compensation to an employee on strike is highly unusual; that basic purpose of salary guarantees was to protect the Player against termination due to injury or loss of skill; that the "arbitrarily refuse" proviso encompasses participation in a strike by the Players Association; that there was nothing in the special covenants or discussions between the parties affirmatively stating that salary *would* be continued during a strike; that the history of providing strike exceptions in some contracts is not reliable evidence of intent to cover strike situations in others; and that any ambiguity in the guarantee provision should be resolved against the Players Association.

Based on the Panel Decisions that have already been rendered, these arguments would have considerable merit if all we had in this case was the language of paragraph 5 of John's Special Covenants, coupled with the pattern of exceptions for strike and other contingencies in all other Yankees' guaranteed contracts. Circumstances, however, alter cases, and this case is replete with special circumstances. The vital importance of such surrounding circumstances on questions of contract interpretation has been emphasized as follows in *Corbin on Contracts*, Section 536 (1952):

> In view of all this, it can hardly be insisted on too often or too vigorously that language at its best is always a defective and uncertain instrument, that words do not define themselves, that terms and sentences in a contract, a deed, or a will do not apply themselves to external objects and performances, that the meaning of such terms and sentences consists of the ideas that they induce in the mind of some individual person who uses or hears or reads them, and that seldom in a litigated case do the words of a contract convey one identical meaning to the two contracting parties or to third persons. Therefore, it is invariably necessary, before a court can give any meaning to the words of a contract and can select one meaning rather than other possible ones as the basis for the determination of rights and other legal effects, that extrinsic evidence shall be heard to make the court aware of the "surrounding circumstances," including the persons, objects, and events to which the words can be applied and which caused the words to be used.

Accordingly, even though the wording of John's salary guarantee on its face may seem much the same as other contracts that have been held not to provide salary continuation during the strike, it is entirely possible for such similar wording to take on a different meaning because of the *context* in which it was agreed upon. It must be borne in mind that, as has previously been explained, the general language of the salary payment provision is inherently vague, and the "arbitrarily refuse" proviso is capable of more than one meaning. Thus, the Club's mercurial fluctuations in position on these Special Covenants, together with the accompanying statements and surrounding circumstances, could well cast this commonly-used wording in an entirely different light than if John had simply renewed his prior contract with the Dodgers. The crucial question here is under these circumstances, what meaning would be put upon these words by a reasonable person in the position of these parties?

In this connection, the key factors are: (a) the Club's frantic efforts—after a carefully negotiated set of detailed Special Covenants had already been drafted, reviewed by counsel for both sides, and executed by the principals—*to add an express exclusion* for strike by the Players Association, followed by (b) the *grudging deletion* of this exclusion by the Club in order to gain other concessions. Upon execution of the second contract, the unavoidable impression on Cohen and John must have been that for some unstated reason, the strike exclusion was of exceptional importance to this Club. Of the possible reasons for such an exclusion previously discussed in this Decision, the one that would seem the more logical to any reasonable person in this peculiar case—after the unheard of lengths to which the Club felt obliged to go—would be to exclude a contingency the Club strongly felt might otherwise be covered by the vague general wording. (The fact that no Club representative took the witness stand to provide any other explanation as to why this was done would seem to indicate there was none.)

Then when the Club, under protest, finally evidences a willingness to withdraw this hard-won exclusion—about which such a fuss had previously been made—it would be only reasonable for Cohen and John to assume the Club was *giving up something of substance* it otherwise would have had, which left John with a salary guarantee broad enough to cover the strike situation previously eliminated. On top of this, in exchange for this revision (which was obviously a concession by the Club) John was asked to give up two valuable features in the legally binding signed contract he already had: (i) the stated right to payment in the event of a lockout, and (ii) several hundred thousand dollars of life insurance coverage with access to the cash value six years earlier. Under these circumstances, the Club could not help but realize that a sought-after premier free agent in John's bargaining position, being represented by an experienced negotiator such as Cohen (who Steinbrenner conceded was a "helluva lawyer" he wished had been on his side) would not be foregoing these benefits *for nothing*. In this setting, when Steinbrenner said in resignation, "You win," he was admitting he had been forced to give up something of genuine significance to him to gain elimination of the lockout clause, whose deletion was essential to the League President.

John testified that when all was said and done, he "took it to mean" that he had a guaranteed contract that would provide his salary in the event of a strike. Although unstated understandings of one of the parties usually are not of controlling significance, here the Club had *reason to know* of this understanding. If it did not actually know, it *should have known*, because the totality of the Club's conduct would have given any reasonable person the same impression; neither Cohen nor John had said or done anything to indicate *any other* understanding on their part. At most there may have been a mutual misunderstanding, but it was of the Club's own making. Under established principles of contract law, where the parties attach different meanings to the words used and one party has reason to know of the meaning attached by the other, who had no reason to know of the meaning attached by the first, the wording is interpreted in accordance with the meaning attached by the other. *Restatement of Contracts Second*, Section 20(2) (1981).

Applying this principle to the case at hand, John's liberal interpretation of the vague provision that his salary "be paid in any event," and his narrow interpretation of the ambiguous "arbitrarily refuse" proviso are entitled to prevail. These interpretations not only are reasonable in light of the unique sequence of events, but also give effect to the principle that a party who enters into a contract with reason to know of a probable misunderstanding by the other is sufficiently at fault to justify his being subjected to the other party's understanding. *Farnsworth on Contracts*, Sections 7.9 and 7.10 (1982). In short, the Club is bound by John's understanding because it was not unreasonable, the Club's conduct induced it, and the Club should have been aware of it. In a situation such as this, there clearly would be no equitable reason to interpret the wording of John's special covenants against him. Moreover, the whole series of revealing actions by the Club outlined above—beginning with Rosen's first suggested wording and ending with Steinbrenner's final capitulation—inevitably added specific substance to the statement of general purpose in paragraph 5.

f) Award

Paragraph 5 of the Special Covenants to the final contract executed between Tommy John and the New York Yankees for the years 1979 through 1981 provided for guaranteed payment of salary to John for the duration of his physical disability and thereafter, notwithstanding the 1981 strike by the Players Association. Accordingly, any grievance filed by John, or on his behalf by the Players Association, claiming such salary payments must be sustained, and any grievance filed by the Yankees against John claiming reimbursement of any salary payments made to him under protest must be denied. Any salary payments attributable to the period of the 1981 strike that were not paid shall promptly be paid to John by the Club. * * *

Notes and Questions

1. Why did the arbitrator sustain Tommy John's grievance in this case?

2. How would the disposition of this grievance inform your judgment in your negotiation of a uniform player contract on behalf of a player? On behalf of the club?

3. In cases involving difficult questions of contract interpretation, should the close calls go against the contract drafter, particularly where the drafter is a Major League Baseball team? *See* Restatement (Second) of Contracts § 206.

4. Would the result in this case have been different if John had declared that he would have supported the strike and refused to work even if he were not disabled? If John did not have a guarantee that covered strikes, would he have been able to recover based on the theory that he was not in a position to offer his services when the strike commenced? What is the relevance of the fact that the strike terminated play and that there were no services to be performed? Could a player, under a guarantee clause, be required to provide services other than his normal athletic participation when all games have been suspended due to a strike?

5. The brooding omnipresence of possible work stoppages in professional sports hangs over all contract negotiations and salary guarantee clauses—assuming that the collective bargaining agreement language does not definitively resolve the issue. In individual player contract negotiations that preceded the 1990 lockout in baseball, considerable controversy arose over the clubs' decision to deny the inclusion of any salary guarantee clause that didn't explicitly disclaim the team's liability for wages lost as a result of a strike or lockout. The owners already had begun to orchestrate their plan to lockout the players in 1990 and, to that end, were attempting to eliminate the possibility of funding the players and strengthening their resolve through

payments due under a broad salary guarantee provision. The Player Relations Committee, the owners' negotiating arm, supported two types of clauses: one that plainly precluded payments during a strike or lockout; and a second that ostensibly vested a neutral arbitrator with authority to determine eligibility for recompense. Murray Chass, *In 1990, Look Out for a Lockout*, Sporting News, Jan. 9, 1989, at 39. As a sad commentary on the state of distrust in Major League Baseball, even this second variation, vague enough by its own terms, was subject to attack because it allegedly induced players into thinking that the arbitrator would be deciding the legality of the lockout rather than simply the players' eligibility for payment. According to the Players Association, the owners and the PRC knew that the players assumed the former and fraudulently withheld from the union their own interpretation of the language. Steve Fainaru, *Who Gets Paid, Lockout Clauses Points of Dispute*, Boston Globe, Mar. 15, 1990, at 30.

6. Anticipation of strikes has led to various creative approaches to salary guarantees and deferred compensation. Included among the possible responses were long term contracts devised in a way to minimize the impact of the anticipated work stoppage upon the compensation paid over the life of the agreement. In some instances, contracts were "front-end loaded" such that payments scheduled to be made at a time when the work stoppage was contemplated would be for minimal amounts (relatively speaking).

(E) Salary Arbitration In Major League Baseball

Major League Baseball players are entitled to salary arbitration after three years in the big leagues, and free agency after six years. The top 17% of players who have completed two years, measured by their performance statistics in a range of categories according to the so-called Elias rankings (after the Elias Sports Bureau, which compiles the statistics), are also entitled to arbitration should they desire it. The arbitration process including factors governing player eligibility is delineated in Article VI of the MLB-MLBPA Collective Bargaining Agreement. Of course, both arbitration and free agency come into play only where the player is not under contract. A player who has a contract to play for a particular salary may not submit that salary to arbitration and may not negotiate with another team until that agreement has expired.

Players who are eligible for arbitration may begin the arbitration process by filing between January 5 and January 15 of the year in which they qualify. In fact, the teams may also submit cases to arbitration, but as two commentators and agents note, "In practice, on January 15 the MLBPA submits all eligible players' cases to arbitration * * * because contracts are being negotiated, completed, and reported throughout January, and thus the later the date, the more market information is available." Jeffrey S. Moorad & Scott G. Parker, *Negotiating for the Professional Baseball Player*, in Law of Professional and Amateur Sports, § 5:26 at 5–61 (Gary Uberstine ed., 2005).

Baseball uses "final offer" arbitration, which means that the arbitration panel — three individuals jointly chosen by the MLBPA and the Labor Relations Department (LRD) of Major League Baseball — must select one of the proposed salaries submitted by the player and the LRD, but may not choose a figure of its own. MLB CBA, art. VI, § F(5). Consequently, both the player (in consultation with the MLBPA) and the LRD must be prudent in submitting a figure that is likely to provide the most possible benefit without causing the arbitrators to select the other party's figure. Both parties submit their figures three days after the filing for arbitration.

Hearings are held between February 1 and February 20. At the hearing, each side is free to present its position, and briefs are sometimes submitted, though they are not required. *See* Moorad & Parker, *supra*, at § 5:26. The Collective Bargaining Agreement instructs the panel, in deciding the case, to consider

> the quality of the Player's contribution to his Club during the past season (including but not limited to his overall performance, special qualities of leadership and public appeal), the length and consistency of his career contribution, the record of the Player's past compensation, comparative baseball salaries * * * and the recent performance record of the Club including but not limited to its League standing and attendance as an indication of public acceptance."

Art. VI, § F(12)(a). "[P]articular attention" is to be paid to the comparative salaries of players who have no more than one additional year of seniority in Major League Baseball than the player under consideration. *Id.* Five-year veterans in arbitration may compare their salaries to any other players, regardless of those other players' years of service.

Because of the central role of comparative salaries in the arbitration process, and because the arbitrators may not consider the wealth of the player or the team, *id.* art. VI, § F(12)(b), arbitration can significantly undermine the ability of small-market teams to retain players who have been in the league at least three years. As Commissioner Selig said, as owner of the Milwaukee Brewers, "If I want to overpay my shortstop, that's my stupidity; but why should I have to pay my shortstop relative to what some idiot in New York pays his?" Jack Sands & Peter Gammons, Coming Apart at the Seams 61 (1993).

Of course, for the three years before a player is eligible for arbitration, he is susceptible to his team's underpayment, relative to his talents. Further, Commissioner Selig's polestar for what constitutes "overpay[ment]" is unclear. Generally one's worth is what he can command on the open market; if the profligate spender in New York pays a salary that is sufficiently representative of the market that the arbitrator takes it into account, then the Brewers—and not the Yankees or Mets—may well be the outliers. Such a conclusion seems particularly likely when one considers the success rates of a particular franchise. A club may simply be unwilling to pay the price that talent commands, and have rationalized that decision by characterizing the price tag as extravagant. Similarly, free-agent signings impact the arbitration market because a five-year veteran undergoing arbitration will compare his salary to recently signed free agents. Four-year veterans will compare their salaries to those of the five-year veterans, and on down the line. *See* Moorad & Parker, *supra*, at § 5:27.

The arbitration panel issues a decision within 24 hours of the hearing, simply announcing which figure—the player's or the LRD's—was chosen. The panel does not issue an opinion explaining its choice. Obviously, the ability to obtain review of such a decision is virtually non-existent. To be sure, the traditional notion of deference to the arbitral process are even more compelling in the context of salary arbitration, which by it nature is extremely discretionary. For further explanation of salary arbitration and its nuances, see Melanie Aubut, *Salary Arbitration and Salary Cap Systems*, 10 Sports Law J. 189 (2003); Frederick Donegan, *Examining the Role of Arbitration in Major League Baseball*, 1 Sports Law J. 183 (1984).

Notes and Questions

1. Salary arbitration employs a "final offer" or "last best offer" procedure. Why? Does it suppress the parties' ability to engage in a meaningful give-and-take or does it ensure a salary negotiation free of "blue sky" demands and silly posturing?

2. Major League owners for years have regretted agreeing to salary arbitration. What has been the effect of this device upon free agency and the salaries demanded by players who are free to negotiate with the team of choice upon expiration of their contracts?

3. Having familiarized yourself with the nuances of salary arbitration, would you now characterize it as "interest" or "grievance" arbitration? Should it be a subject over which management is obligated to bargain?

Chapter 17

Discrimination and Sports

I. Preface

When Jackie Robinson broke Major League Baseball's color barrier in 1947, a giant step toward the elimination of discrimination in sports presumably had been taken. Unfortunately, progress since that time has been slow; women and minorities continue to suffer indignities ranging from overt bias to more subtle, subterranean manifestations of disparate treatment. The areas in which discrimination continues to exist and, at points, flourish are too numerous to list here. Among the issues that cast a large shadow are: the scarcity of African Americans in upper-echelon, managerial positions (especially in those sports where black players dominate both in terms of numbers and impact); unequal treatment of women and women's athletic programs in intercollegiate athletics; alarmingly low proportions of African Americans in professional golf and tennis; gross discrepancies in purses between men's and women's events in professional golf and tennis and corresponding discrepancies in salaries for men and women coaches at various amateur levels; absence of women umpires and referees at all levels of athletic competition; exploitation of all young athletes (especially African Americans) by high-powered college sports programs; patronizing and demeaning treatment of people with disabilities; and abject intolerance for those individuals whose sexual orientation is at war with traditional notions.

The problems engendered by discrimination in and out of sports have been addressed by courts, legislatures, and countless commentators. The available areas of potential redress include the Fourteenth Amendment of the United States Constitution, Title VII of the Civil Rights Act of 1964 as amended by the Civil Rights Act of 1991 (42 U.S.C. § 2000e), the Civil Rights Act of 1866 (42 U.S.C. § 1981), the Civil Rights Act of 1871 (42 U.S.C. § 1983), the Equal Pay Act of 1963 (29 U.S.C. § 206(d)(1)(1988)), Title IX (20 U.S.C. § 1981(a)(1988)), state and local legislation, and numerous common law vehicles. Each of these avenues may provide a cause of action for an alleged victim of discrimination in the sports universe.

Of course, such putative discriminatees may also find their path to relief blocked by any number of legal defenses or pragmatic considerations. For example, a coach or manager who believes that his employer has discriminated against him based on race may find sanctuary in the Fourteenth Amendment, but such access may be denied if the employer is not a state actor. A woman who has been denied an opportunity to advance in a particular sport may file charges with the Equal Employment Opportunity Commission under Title VII; however, she may be confronted with a defense that gender is a *bona fide* occupational qualification for the job in question. An African American, who

845

is repeatedly refused managerial positions in the hierarchy of a sport in which he excelled and in which hundreds of African Americans participate, may also claim that he was a victim of his employer's discriminatory treatment in violation of Title VII; yet, he may have been passed over for a reason other than race. A woman coach who contends that her lower salary is a direct product of sex discrimination in contravention of the Equal Pay Act must first demonstrate that her job was substantially identical to the job of higher paid male coaches in terms of skill, effort, and responsibility. Assuming that the coach is able to meet this criterion, the employer may rebut the *prima facie* case by establishing that the pay differential was based on factors other than sex.

Discussion of many of these issues with illustrative articles and case authority will follow. Again, these exemplars barely scratch the surface of the myriad problems involving diversity in the sports arena. This chapter, however, will expose you to the malaise that afflicts the sports industry insofar as discrimination is concerned, will heighten your consciousness in this area, and ideally will provoke you to pursue these questions further. A more comprehensive treatment of the topics addressed herein can be found in MICHAEL J. COZZILLIO AND ROBERT L. HAYMAN, JR., SPORTS AND INEQUALITY (2005). Portions of the material included below have been adopted from that text.

II. Sports and Popular Culture

Team logos and mascots that adopt and parody ethnic groups, particularly Native Americans, are by no means unique in our professional and amateur sports culture. On the contrary, hundreds of professional teams and colleges have generic nicknames such as Indians, Redskins, Braves, Warriors, Chiefs, Redmen, etc. Others sport more specific appellations such as Chippewas, Seminoles, Sioux, Choctaws, etc. Many schools have responded to the public pressure by changing their nickname or, at least, replacing their mascots. For example, the Stanford Indians are now the Stanford Cardinal, and the Marquette Warriors have become the Golden Eagles. Most professional teams and many colleges have refused to change their "trademark" identities, arguing that the characterizations are not demeaning and that the logos have become so identified with the franchise that it would be inappropriate to change.

Many Native Americans believe that they bear the brunt of most of this commonly accepted ethnic slurring and that similarly demeaning characterizations of African Americans or other minorities would not be tolerated. They argue that a team sobriquet such as the New York Jews or a logo carrying versions of the infamous "N" word are simply unheard of today, and properly so. Leaders of various Native American groups posit that they should be accorded similar respect. While most of the pressure to date has been directed to colleges and professional sports teams through intense lobbying efforts and public awareness campaigns, some court action has been pursued. The following case presents an illustration.

Harjo v. Pro-Football, Inc.
50 U.S.P.Q.2d 1705 (T.T.A.B. 1999)

WALTERS, ADMINISTRATIVE TRADEMARK JUDGE: [Petitioners brought this action to cancel certain trademarks relating to the Washington Redskins, which were owned by

Pro-Football.] Petitioners allege that they are Native American persons and enrolled members of federally recognized Indian tribes. As grounds for cancellation, petitioners assert that the word "redskin(s)" or a form of that word appears in the mark in each of the registrations sought to be canceled; that the word "redskin(s)" "was and is a pejorative, derogatory, denigrating, offensive, scandalous, contemptuous, disreputable, disparaging and racist designation for a Native American person"; that the marks in Registration Nos. 986,668 and 987,127 "also include additional matter that, in the context used by registrant, is offensive, disparaging and scandalous"; and that registrant's use of the marks in the identified registrations "offends" petitioners and other Native Americans. Petitioners assert, further, that the marks in the identified registrations "consist of or comprise matter which disparages Native American persons, and brings them into contempt, ridicule, and disrepute" and "consist of or comprise scandalous matter"; and that, therefore, under Section 2(a) of the Trademark Act, 15 U.S.C. § 1052(a), the identified registrations should be canceled.

Respondent, in its answer, denies the salient allegations of the petition to cancel and asserts that "through long, substantial and widespread use, advertising and promotion in support thereof and media coverage, said marks have acquired a strong secondary meaning identifying the entertainment services provided by respondent in the form of professional games in the National Football League"; and that "the marks sought to be canceled herein cannot reasonably be understood to refer to the Petitioners or to any of the groups or organizations to which they belong [as] the marks refer to the Washington Redskins football team which is owned by Respondent and thus cannot be interpreted as disparaging any of the Petitioners or as bringing them into contempt or disrepute."

* * *

Section 2(a)

The relevant portions of Section 2 of the Trademark Act (15 U.S.C. § 1052) provide as follows:

No trademark by which the goods of the applicant may be distinguished from the goods of others shall be refused registration on the principal register on account of its nature unless it—

(a) Consists of or comprises immoral, deceptive, or scandalous matter; or matter which may disparage or falsely suggest a connection with persons, living or dead, institutions, beliefs, or national symbols, or bring them into contempt, or disrepute;

Scandalous Matter

[D]etermining whether matter is scandalous involves, essentially, a two-step process. First, the Court or Board determines the likely meaning of the matter in question and, second, whether, in view of the likely meaning, the matter is scandalous to a substantial composite of the general public.

Matter Which May Disparage

The plain language of the statute makes clear that disparagement is a separate and distinct ground for refusing or canceling the registration of a mark under Section 2(a).

[T]he "ordinary and common meaning" of "scandalous" looks at the reaction of American society as a whole to specified matter to establish whether such matter violates the mores of "American society" in such a manner and to such an extent that it is "shocking to the sense of truth, decency or propriety," or offensive to the conscience or moral feelings, of "a substantial composite of the general public." On the other hand, the "ordinary and common meaning" of the word "disparage" has an entirely different focus, as disparagement has an identifiable object which, under Section 2(a) of the Trademark Act, may be "persons, living or dead, institutions, beliefs or national symbols."

A further difference between scandalousness and disparagement is found in the language of Section 2(a). While Section 2(a) precludes registration of matter that is scandalous, it does not preclude registration of matter that is disparaging. It precludes registration of matter that may be disparaging. There is no legislative history or precedent that specifically addresses this distinction between the two statutory provisions. Respondent's linguistics experts herein have testified that, as they understand the meaning of the word "disparage," disparagement of someone or something usually requires some degree of intent by the speaker to cause offense, although, as petitioners' expert notes, this may be inferred from the circumstances and from evidence regarding the acceptability of the language or imagery used. Thus, we believe the use of the term "may" is necessary in connection with "disparage" in Section 2(a) to avoid an interpretation of this statutory provision that would require a showing of intent to disparage. Such a showing would be extremely difficult in all except the most egregious cases. Rather, this provision, as written, shifts the focus to whether the matter may be perceived as disparaging.

In determining whether or not a mark is disparaging, the perceptions of the general public are irrelevant. Rather, because the portion of Section 2(a) proscribing disparaging marks targets certain persons, institutions or beliefs, only the perceptions of those referred to, identified or implicated in some recognizable manner by the involved mark are relevant to this determination.

1. Meaning of the Matter in Question.

Considering the meaning of the term "redskin(s)" in connection with the services identified in the challenged registrations, respondent contends that the term "Redskins," considered in connection with professional football games, denotes respondent's football team and its entertainment services. Respondent contends that, over its six decades of use, respondent's marks have "acquired a strong and distinctive meaning identifying respondent's entertainment services * * * in the context of professional football"; that "Redskins" has become "denotative of the professional football team"; and that, although "deriving from the original, ethnic meaning of 'redskin,'" the word "'Redskins' was perceived in 1967, and today, to be a distinct word, entirely separate from 'redskin' and the core, ethnic meaning embodied by that term."

This is not a case where, through usage, the word "redskin(s)" has lost its meaning, in the field of professional football, as a reference to Native Americans in favor of an entirely independent meaning as the name of a professional football team. Rather, when considered in relation to the other matter comprising at least two of the subject marks and as used in connection with respondent's services, "Redskins" clearly both refers to respondent's professional football team and carries the allusion to Native Americans inherent in the original definition of that word. This conclusion is equally applicable to the time periods encompassing 1967, 1974, 1978 and 1990, as well as to the present time.

2. Whether the Matter in Question May Disparage Native Americans.

We turn, now, to the second part of our analysis, the question of whether the matter in question may disparage Native Americans. We have found that, as an element of respondent's marks and as used in connection with respondent's services, the word "redskin(s)" retains its meaning as a reference to Native Americans, as do the graphics of the spear and the Native American portrait. In view thereof, we consider the question of whether this matter may disparage Native Americans by reference to the perceptions of Native Americans. Our standard, as enunciated herein, is whether, as of the relevant times, a substantial composite of Native Americans in the United States so perceive the subject matter in question. In rendering our opinion, we consider the broad range of evidence in this record as relevant to this question either directly or by inference.

Several of petitioners' witnesses expressed their opinions that the use of Native American references or imagery by non-Native Americans is, essentially, per se disparaging to Native Americans or, at the very least, that the use of Native American references or imagery in connection with football is per se disparaging to Native Americans. We find no support in the record for either of these views. Consequently, we answer the question of disparagement based on the facts in this case by looking to the evidence regarding the views of the relevant group, the connotations of the subject matter in question, the relationship between that matter and the other elements that make up the marks, and the manner in which the marks appear and are used in the marketplace.

While petitioners' have framed their allegations broadly to include in their claim of disparagement all matter in the subject marks that refers to Native Americans, their arguments and extensive evidence pertain almost entirely to the "Redskins" portion of respondent's marks. We note that there is very little evidence or argument by either side regarding the other elements of respondent's marks that refer to Native Americans, namely, the spear design and the portrait of a Native American in profile. Both graphics are realistic in style. Respondent acknowledges that the portrait depicts a Native American individual, although it is unclear if it is a portrait of a real individual. There is no evidence that these graphics are used in a manner that may be perceived as disparaging, or that a substantial composite of the Native American population in the United States so perceives these graphics as used in the subject marks in connection with the identified services. Thus, with respect to the spear design and the portrait of a Native American in profile, as these elements appear in two of the registered marks herein, we find that petitioners have not established, under Section 2(a), that this matter may disparage Native Americans.

The remaining question in relation to disparagement is whether the word "redskin(s)" may be disparaging of and to Native Americans, as that word appears in the marks in the subject registrations, in connection with the identified services, and during the relevant time periods.

We find petitioners have clearly established, by at least a preponderance of the evidence, that, as of the dates the challenged registrations issued, the word "redskin(s)," as it appears in respondent's marks in those registrations and as used in connection with the identified services, may disparage Native Americans, as perceived by a substantial composite of Native Americans. No single item of evidence or testimony alone brings us to this conclusion; rather, we reach our conclusion based on the cumulative effect of the entire record. We discuss below some of the more significant evidence in the record. We look, first, at the evidence establishing that, in general and during the relevant time periods, the word "redskin(s)" has been a term of disparagement of and to Native Americans. Then we look at the evidence establishing that, during the relevant time periods, the disparaging connotation of "redskin(s)" as a term of reference for Native Americans extends to the word "Redskin(s)" as it appears in respondent's subject marks and as used in connection with respondent's identified services. We have considered the perceptions of both the general public and Native Americans to be probative. For example, we have found that the evidence supports the conclusion that a substantial composite of the general public finds the word "redskin(s)" to be a derogatory term of reference for Native Americans. Thus, in the absence of evidence to the contrary, it is reasonable to infer that a substantial composite of Native Americans would similarly perceive the word. This is consistent with the testimony of the petitioners.

We look, first, at the evidence often considered in the decisional law concerning Section 2(a) scandalousness and disparagement, namely, dictionary definitions. Both petitioners and respondent have submitted excerpts defining "redskin" from numerous well-established American dictionary publishers from editions covering the time period, variously, from 1966 through 1996. Across the time period, the number of publishers including in their dictionaries a usage label indicating that the word "redskin" is disparaging is approximately equal, on this record, to those who do not include any usage label. For example, Random House publishers include the label "often offensive" in dictionaries published from 1966 onward. American Heritage publishers indicate that "redskin" is "informal" in 1976 and 1981 editions and that it is "offensive slang" in 1992 and 1996 editions. The *World Book Dictionary* includes no usage label regarding "redskin" in either its 1967 or 1980 edition and more recent editions are not in evidence. From the testimony of the parties' linguistics experts, it is clear that each entry in a dictionary is intended to reflect the generally understood meaning and usage of that word. Thus, from the fact that usage labels appear in approximately half of the dictionaries of record at any point in the time period covered, we can conclude that a not insignificant number of Americans have understood "redskin(s)" to be an offensive reference to Native Americans since at least 1966.

Discussing the substantial body of historical documents he reviewed in connection with his testimony herein, Dr. Geoffrey Nunberg, petitioners' linguistics expert, concluded that the word "redskin(s)" first appeared in writing as a reference to Native Americans in 1699 and that, from 1699 to the present, the word "redskin(s)," used as a term of reference for Native Americans, evokes negative associations and is, thus, a term of disparagement. Additional evidence of record that is consistent with the opinions expressed Dr. Nunberg includes excerpts from various articles and publications about language. These writings include, often in a larger discussion about bias in language, the assumption or conclusion that the word "redskin(s)" as a term of reference for Native Americans is, and always has been, a pejorative term.

Petitioners made of record a substantial number of writings, including, *inter alia*, excerpts from newspapers and other publications, encyclopedias, and dictionaries, evidencing the use of the word "redskin(s)" from the late 1800's through the first half of this century. As agreed by both parties' linguistics experts, the vast majority of newspaper headlines, newspaper articles, and excerpts from books and periodicals from the late 1800's and early 1900's, which include the word "redskin(s)" as a reference to Native Americans, clearly portray Native Americans in a derogatory or otherwise negative manner. For example, the newspaper articles in evidence from the late 1800's reflect a view by Anglo-American society of Native Americans as the savage enemy and the events reported are armed conflicts. The entry for "North American Indian" in the *Encyclopedia Britannica* (11th edition, 1910) clearly refers to "the aboriginal people of North America" as "primitive" people, and includes a detailed table describing the degree to which individual tribes have been "civilized" or remain "wild and indolent." An excerpt from a book entitled *Making the Movies*, by Ernest Dench (MacMillan Company, 1919), includes a chapter entitled "The Dangers of Employing Redskins as Movie Actors," which states: "The Red Indians * * * are paid a salary that keeps them well provided with tobacco and their worshipped 'firewater,'" and "It might be thought that this would civilise (sic) them completely, but it has had a quite reverse effect, for the work affords them an opportunity to live their savage days over again * * * ."

Writings in evidence from the 1930's through the late 1940's, which include the word "redskin(s)" as a reference to Native Americans, reflect a slightly less disdainful, but still condescending, view of Native Americans. For example, an article entitled "Redskin Revival—High Birthrate Gives Congress a New Overproduction Headache," in *Newsweek*, February 20, 1939, while complaining about the financial and administrative burden of "caring" for Native Americans, recognizes that the inequities suffered by Native Americans are a result of actions by the U.S. government.

From the 1950's forward, the evidence shows, and neither party disputes, that there are minimal examples of uses of the word "redskin(s)" as a reference to Native Americans. Most such occurrences are in a small number of writings about the character of the word itself, or in writings where we find that "redskin(s)" is used in a metaphorical sense juxtaposed with "white man" or "paleface." Both parties agree that, during this same time period, the record reflects significant occurrences of the word "redskin(s)" as a reference to respondent's football team.

We agree with respondent's conclusion that the pejorative nature of "redskin(s)" in the early historical writings of record comes from the overall negative viewpoints of the writings. However, this does not lead us to the conclusion that, as respondent contends, "redskin(s)" is an informal term for Native Americans that is neutral in connotation. Rather, we conclude from the evidence of record that the word "redskin(s)" does not appear during the second half of this century in written or spoken language, formal or informal, as a synonym for "Indian" or "Native American" because it is, and has been since at least the 1960's, perceived by the general population, which includes Native Americans, as a pejorative term for Native Americans.

We find the context provided by Dr. Hoxie's historical account, which respondent does not dispute, of the often acrimonious Anglo-American/Native American relations from the early Colonial period to the present to provide a useful historical perspective from which to view the writings, cartoons and other references to Native Americans in evidence from the late 19th century and throughout this century.

Finally, we note petitioners' telephone survey, as described herein, purporting to measure the views, at the time of the survey in 1996, of the general population and, separately, of Native Americans towards the word "redskin" as a reference to Native Americans. When read a list of seven words referring to Native Americans, 46.2% of participants in the general population sample (139 of 301 participants) and 36.6% of participants in the Native American sample (131 of 358 participants) indicated that they found the word "redskin" offensive as a reference to Native Americans. We have discussed, supra, several of the flaws in the survey that limit its probative value. Additionally, the survey is of limited applicability to the issues in this case as it sought to measure the participants' views only as of 1996, when the survey was conducted, and its scope is limited to the connotation of the word "redskin" as a term for Native Americans, without any reference to respondent's football team. However, considering these limitations, we find that the percentage of participants in each sample who responded positively, i.e., stated they were offended by the word "redskin(s)" for Native Americans, to be significant. While the survey polls a relatively small sample and the positive results reflect less than a majority of that sample, we find these results supportive of the other evidence in the record indicating the derogatory nature of the word "redskin(s)" for the entire period from, at least, the mid-1960's to the present, to substantial composites of both the general population and the Native American population.

The evidence we have discussed so far pertains, generally, to the word "redskin(s)" as it refers to Native Americans. From this evidence we have concluded, *supra*, that the word "redskin(s)" has been considered by a substantial composite of the general population, including by inference Native Americans, a derogatory term of reference for Native Americans during the time period of relevance herein. We have also concluded, *supra*, that the word "Redskins" in respondent's marks in the challenged registrations, identifies respondent's football team and carries the allusion to Native Americans inherent in the original definition of the word. Evidence of respondent's use of the subject marks in the 1940's and 1950's shows a disparaging portrayal of Native Americans in connection with the word "Redskin(s)" that is more egregious than uses of the subject marks in the record from approximately the mid-1960's to the present. However, such a finding does not lead us to the conclusion that the subject marks, as used in connection with the identified services during the relevant time periods, are not still disparaging of and to Native Americans under Section 2(a) of the Act. The character of respondent's allusions to Native Americans in its use of the subject marks is consistent with the general views towards Native Americans held by the society from approximately the 1940's forward.

In particular, the evidence herein shows a portrayal in various media of Native Americans, unrelated to respondent's football team, as uncivilized and, often, buffoon-like characters from, at least, the beginning of this century through the middle to late 1950's. As we move through the 1960's to the present, the evidence shows an increasingly respectful portrayal of Native Americans. This is reflected, also, in the decreased use of "redskin(s)," as a term of reference for Native Americans, as society in general became aware of, and sensitive to, the disparaging nature of that word as so used.

The evidence herein shows a parallel development of respondent's portrayal of Native Americans in connection with its services. For example, various covers of respondent's game program guides and other promotional efforts, including public relations stunts presenting players in Native American headdresses, from the 1940's through the middle to late 1950's show caricature-like portrayals of Native Americans as, usually, either savage aggressors or buffoons. Similarly, for the same time period, the costumes and antics of the team, the Redskins Marching Band, and the "Redskinettes" cheerleaders reflect a less than respectful portrayal of Native Americans.

During the late 1950's and early 1960's, the evidence shows respondent's game program covers with realistic portraits of actual Native American individuals, reflecting society's increased respect for, and interest in, Native American culture and history. During the 1960's through to the present, the evidence establishes that respondent has largely substituted football imagery for Native American imagery on its game program covers; that it has modified the lyrics of its theme song, "Hail to the Redskins" and modified its cheerleaders' uniforms; and Mr. Cooke testified that respondent has, for several years, had a strict policy mandating a restrained and "tasteful" portrayal of Native American imagery by its licensees. Of course, the allusion to Native Americans in connection with respondent's team has continued unabated, for example, in respondent's name, its trademarks, and through the use of Native American imagery such as the headdresses worn for many years by the Redskins Band.

Both parties have submitted voluminous excerpts from newspapers, including cartoons, headlines, editorials and articles, from the 1940's to the present, that refer to respondent's football team in the context of stories and writings about the game of football. These excerpts show that, despite respondent's more restrained use of its Native American imagery over time, the media has used Native American imagery in connection with respondent's team, throughout this entire time period, in a manner that often portrays Native Americans as either aggressive savages or buffoons. For example, many headlines refer to the "Redskins" team, players or managers "scalping" opponents, seeking "revenge," "on the warpath," and holding "pow wows"; or use pidgin English, such as "Big Chief Choo Choo—He Ponder." Similarly, petitioners have submitted evidence, both excerpts from newspapers and video excerpts of games, showing respondent's team's fans dressed in costumes and engaging in antics that clearly poke fun at Native American culture and portray Native Americans as savages and buffoons. As we have already stated, we agree with respondent that it is not responsible for the actions of the media or fans; however, the actions of the media and fans are probative of the general public's perception of the word "redskin(s)" as it appears in respondent's marks herein. As such, this evidence reinforces our conclusion that the word "redskin(s)" retains its derogatory character as part of the subject marks and as used in connection with respondent's football team.

Regarding the views of Native Americans in particular, the record contains the testimony of petitioners themselves stating that they have been seriously offended by respondent's use of the word "redskin(s)" as part of its marks in connection with its identified services. The record includes resolutions indicating a present objection to the use of this word in respondent's marks from the NCAI, which the record adequately establishes as a broad-based organization of Native American tribes and individuals; from the Oneida tribe; and from Unity 94, an organization including Native Americans. Additionally, petitioners have submitted a substantial number of news articles, from various time periods, including from 1969–1970, 1979, 1988–1989, and 1991–1992, reporting about Native American objections, and activities in relation thereto, to the word "Redskins" in respondent's team's name. These articles establish the public's exposure to the existence of a controversy spanning a long period of time. Also with respect to Native American protests, we note, in particular, the testimony of Mr. Gross regarding his 1972 letter, in his role as director of the Indian Legal Information Development Service, to Mr. Williams, then-owner of the Washington Redskins, urging that the name of the team be changed; and regarding his 1972 meeting with Mr. Williams, along with colleagues from several other Native American organizations. Mr. Gross testified that the individuals representing the Native American organizations expressed their views to Mr. Williams that the team name, "Washington Redskins," is disparaging, insulting and degrading to Native Americans. This evidence reinforces the conclusion that a substantial composite of Native Americans have held these views for a significant period of time which encompasses the relevant time periods herein.

We are not convinced otherwise by respondent's contentions, argued in its brief, that Native Americans support respondent's use of the name "Washington Redskins"; and that Native Americans regularly employ the term "redskin" within their communities. Respondent has presented no credible evidence in support of either contention.

Thus, we conclude that the evidence of record establishes that, within the relevant time periods, the derogatory connotation of the word "redskin(s)" in connection with Native Americans extends to the term "Redskins," as used in respondent's marks in connection with the identified services, such that respondent's marks may be disparaging of Native Americans to a substantial composite of this group of people.

* * *

Decision: As to each of the registrations subject to the petition to cancel herein, the petition to cancel under Section 2(a) of the Act is granted on the grounds that the subject marks may disparage Native Americans and may bring them into contempt or disrepute. As to each of the registrations subject to the petition to cancel herein, the petition to cancel under Section 2(a) of the Act is denied on the ground that the subject marks consist of or comprise scandalous matter. The registrations will be canceled in due course.

Notes and Questions

1. The *Harjo* case seems to have a life of its own. Years after the trademark judge's decision, the United States District Court for the District of Columbia reversed a finding that the claim should have been barred by the equitable defense of laches. 191 F. Supp. 2d 77 (D.D.C. 2002). This decision, in turn, was reversed by the United States Court of Appeals for the D.C. Circuit and remanded for further consideration. 415 F. 3d 44 (D.C. Cir. 2005). While on remand, the petitioners requested leave for further discovery, but the motion was denied by the district court. 2006 U.S. App. Dist. LEXIS 51086 (D.D.C. July 26, 2006).

2. Several commentators have supported the use of trademark cancellation and other causes of action to challenge the use of offensive racial or ethnic symbols. *See, e.g.,* Aaron Goldstein, *Intentional Infliction of Emotional Distress: Another Attempt At Eliminating Native American Mascots,* 3 J. GENDER, RACE & JUST. 689 (2000) (claiming that certain images may be so offensive as to be "outrageous" and may give rise to claims of intentional infliction of emotional distress); *Note, A Public Accommodations Challenge to the Use of Indian Team Names and Mascots in Professional Sports,* 112 HARV. L. REV. 904 (1999) (suggesting that public facilities that utilize offensive symbols may be discriminating in violation of Title II of the Civil Rights Act of 1964); *but see* Michelle B. Lee, *Section 2(A) of the Lanham Act As a Restriction On Sports Team Names: Has Political Correctness Gone Too Far?,* 4 SPORTS LAW J. 65 (1997) (arguing that the Lanham Act and similar legislation that prohibits trademark protection for "disparaging" or "scandalous" marks should be deemed void for vagueness, and that employing Section 2(A) of the Lanham Act to control the "offensive" mark amounts to a proscribed taking under the Fifth Amendment).

3. Any legal action challenging offensive logos is likely to raise two difficult issues. The first involves the magnitude of the harm caused by the logo. How precisely does one quantify that harm, and just how great must the harm be? Professor Nancy Levit summarizes the obstacles that have restrained courts in their recognition of "ethereal" harms:

> Significant institutional barriers on several levels have artificially restricted the development of ethereal torts. Part of the restraint is due to factors inherent in the enterprise of doctrinal development: If emphasis is placed on predictability of outcomes, compensation of individual harms will suffer. Another part of the confinement of ethereal torts concerns the courts' unwillingness to admit an inability to assess social science evidence generally. More fundamental, though, the limitation of ethereal torts relates to the value courts place on emotional, mental, psychic, relational, and probabilistic injuries.

Nancy Levit, *Ethereal Torts,* 61 GEO. WASH. L. REV. 136, 164 (1992). For a thorough discussion of the various legal theories that could be advanced to attack the use of disparaging logos and mascots, see Cathryn L. Claussen, *Ethnic Team Names and Logos—Is There a Legal Solution?*, 6 MARQ. SPORTS L.J. 409 (1996)(addressing a laundry list of potential legal challenges to offensive logos); Justin Blankenship, *The Cancellation of Redskins as a Disparaging Trademark: Is Federal Trademark Law an Appropriate Solution for Words That Offend?*, 72 U. COLO. L. REV. 415 (2001) (positing that trademark law is an appropriate tool for the government to intervene on behalf of minorities "harmed by the actions of an uninformed majority."

The second issue raised by these claims is one of perspective: From whose vantage point is the harm to be measured? Professor Charles Lawrence describes how he felt when, as the only black student in a New York City kindergarten classroom, his teacher shared with the class the illustrated *Little Black Sambo*. Charles Lawrence, *The Id, the Ego, and Equal Protection: Reckoning with Unconscious Racism*, 39 STAN. L. REV. 317 (1987). "I am certain that my kindergarten teacher was not intentionally racist," Professor Lawrence remarks, but "[w]e were all victims of our culture's racism." *Id.* at 318. But Professor Lloyd Cohen objects to Professor Lawrence's interpretation: "The theme of *Little Black Sambo* is not racist * * *. Any racist association with the story is merely an historic and linguistic accident." Lloyd Cohen, *A Different Black Voice in Legal Scholarship*, 37 N.Y.L. SCH. L. REV. 301, 318–19 (1992). What distinction is Professor Cohen relying on? Is it a meaningful one? "It seems to me," Professor Cohen concludes, "that Professor Lawrence has failed to distinguish between what he sees in a work of literature and what it means to others." *Id.* at 320. Do you think Professor Lawrence is unaware of this distinction? Is Professor Cohen?

Consider too a 2001 incident involving Olympic gold medalist Billy Mills:

> Mills is sitting in first class [on a commercial airliner]. A flight attendant, the words steward and stewardess are frowned upon today, checks on him every so often. The man is African-American, the preferred designation for his racial background; before that, society called him black or colored or Negro. The man is friendly, doing his job. Each time he addresses Mills, he calls him Chief. Mills doesn't know if the flight attendant realizes that he is Lakota. Maybe he calls everyone Chief. Maybe he means it as a compliment. Mills motions him over.
>
> "I want to tell you something," Mills says. The man leans in. "I'm Native American, and you calling me Chief, it turns my stomach. It'd be very similar to somebody calling you Nigger."
>
> The flight attendant looks at Mills. He says, "Calling you Chief doesn't bother me, * * * Chief."

S.L. Price, *The Indian Wars*, SPORTS ILLUSTRATED, March 4, 2002. "Who is right," asks writer S.L. Price, "and who wrong? Whose feelings take precedence? Most important, who gets to decide what we call one another?" *Id.*

Price suggests that the Ute tribe's experience with the University of Utah "might serve as a model for successful resolution of conflicts over Indian nicknames."

> [In 1998] the council met with university officials, who made it clear that they would change their teams' name, the Running Utes, if the tribe found it objectionable. (The university had retired its cartoonish Indian mascot years before.) The council was perfectly happy to have the Ute name continue to circulate in the nations' sports pages, but council members said they intended to keep a close eye on its use. "We came away with an understanding that as long as the university used the Ute name in a positive manner that preserved the in-

tegrity of the Ute tribe, we would allow the use of the name and the Ute logo [two eagle feathers and a drum]," says [tribal council member Roland] Mc-Cook. Florida State, likewise, uses the name Seminoles for its teams with the express approval of the Seminole nation.

Id.

4. In late summer 2005, the NCAA announced that, effective February 2006, any institution bearing a logo that could be deemed by the NCAA to be "hostile" or "abusive" in a racial or ethnic sense would be precluded from displaying or otherwise using them in post-season events. Further, effective 2008, cheerleaders, band members, and others would not be permitted to sport Native-American symbols on their uniforms. Of greater significance, perhaps, several schools were included in a list of offenders who would be prohibited from hosting future tournament games or matches.

Not surprisingly, various groups, such as the National Coalition on Racism in Sports and Media applauded the ban, but offered that the NCAA could have taken stronger steps including banning outright the use of the nicknames and mascots in question. On the other hand, several universities opposed the new rules and threatened legal action in response. Florida State University and the University of Utah were two schools who vehemently protested their insertion among the "offenders" for use of the "Seminoles" and "Ute" mascots, respectively. Litigation did not ensue because the NCAA honored the appeals of those institutions recognizing the "unique relationship" between those schools and the Seminole and Ute tribes.

Should the FSU and Utah appeals have been granted? Is there a meaningful distinction between use of "Seminole," "Ute," or "Apache" and the term "Redskins?" What about words like "Warrior," "Brave," etc.? Do some suggest pride while the others connote disparagement?

5. Is the brouhaha surrounding the use of mascots and adoptions of caricatures of certain ethnic groups much ado about nothing? *See* John B. Rhode, *The Mascot Name Change Controversy: A Lesson in Hypersensitivity*, 5 MARQ. SPORTS L.J. 141 (1994). Or do these exaggerated depictions serve only to perpetuate stereotypes that have operated to disserve our minority populace in various contexts such as employment, education, or property? It would seem as though the latter suggestion is more persuasive. As one commentator has stated: "Native people complain that the use of names and images is dehumanizing. * * * [And] reinforcing the dehumanizing influence of these images is the fact that they are presented as ahistorical and contextless." Nell Jessup Newton, *Memory and Misrepresentation: Representing Crazy Horse*, 27 CONN. L. REV. 1003–04, 1006 (1995). Certainly, in the case of Native Americans, as well as that of many other minorities, debasing or even discounting their rich traditions, noble cultures, and colorful histories is the worst form of disparagement. See Kimberly A. Pace, *The Washington Redskin Case and the Doctrine of Disparagement: How Politically Correct Must a Trademark Be?*, 22 PEPP. L. REV. 7 (1994).

6. Some newspapers have eliminated or limited their use of Native-American logos: the *Lincoln* (Nebraska) *Journal Star*, the *Oregonian*, the *Minnesota St. Cloud Times*, the *Minneapolis Star Tribune*, and the *Kansas City Star*. But in D.C., where the Native American population is decidedly small, the *Washington Post* hailed the hiring of Joe Gibbs with the headline "New Era for the Redskins."

This newspaper that serves the "capital of the free world" still prints that insult in bold headlines. It may be true that stereotyping nonwhites is as American as apple pie and such deeply ingrained cultural habits die hard, but the lack of public outrage at these continuing racial slurs is a bit surprising. After all, there's little debate that the use of people as mascots is, at best, humiliating. As the American Jewish Committee noted in a 1998 report, "The use of mascots is a reflection of the limits of dehumanization our culture will allow."

Salim Muwakkil, *Racist Slurs Taint U.S. Sports*, IN THESE TIMES, Feb. 16, 2004, at 9.

7. In 1992, the University of North Dakota Fighting Sioux hockey team announced that it would replace its old Indian-head team logo, which resembled the logo used by the Chicago Blackhawks, with the more abstract Indian-head design used by the school's other teams. It made no plans to change its nickname. In 1998, Las Vegas multimillionaire Ralph Engelstad announced that he was donating $100 million to the University, half to be used to build a new arena for the hockey team, and half for unspecified other uses. Englestad, whose fascination with Adolph Hitler and the Third Reich approaches (or includes, according to his critics) genuine admiration, ultimately placed a number of conditions on the grant: among them, that the school retain the "Fighting Sioux" nickname, and adopt a "new" logo that looks very much like the one it abandoned in 1992. The University initially balked, a University committee heard from nine tribes in the Dakotas who urged rejection of the logo and the nickname, but ultimately acquiesced; in the interim, Englestad approved expenditures for the hockey arena that consumed the entire $100 million grant. All the seats in the new arena are leather with cherry armrests; granite tiles cover all the floors; chandeliers decorate the lobby; and the controversial Indian-head logo appears over 1,000 times throughout the arena. Hockey coach Dean Blais notes that the new arena is a big draw for recruits and fans: "More people are getting to enjoy Sioux hockey, he says. Others are less sanguine: "This arena stands for greed and racism," says University professor Lucy Ganje. "This 'gift' has torn the campus apart." George Dohrmann, *Face Off: A Bullying North Dakota Alumnus Built the School a $100 Million Rink but Tore Its Campus Asunder*, SPORTS ILLUSTRATED, October 8, 2001.

8. During the spring of 2002, a University of Northern Colorado intramural basketball team adopted as its nickname "The Fightin' Whities." The multiethnic team adopted the moniker after several of its players failed in their efforts to persuade a local high school to change its symbols; the high school uses a cartoon American Indian caricature on its logo, replete with misshapen nose, an eagle feather, and either a loincloth or bare buttocks, and its teams are named the "Fightin' Reds." The intramural team designed and wore t-shirts bearing a mascot, a 1950s style caricature of a middle-aged white man, and the phrase "Every thang's gonna be all white!"

In the fall, the team began selling T-shirts on its website. By the end of the year, the team had raised $100,000 for scholarships for Native American college students. "We could have given the money to an organization to help fight Indian mascots," explains Charlie Cuny, a team founder and Oglala Lakota student, "but most of us felt it would be better to help Native American students at this school. We just want to do the right thing." "We couldn't have asked for much more," says Jeff Van Iwarden, an Anglo teammate. "We got the message out there, and we're helping Native American students."

Cuny hopes the message is heard, and understood. "If it were any other race," he says of the Indian mascots, "people wouldn't stand for it. But because it's Indians, people look over it. That's got to change." And for those who think its all about "political correctness" or over-sensitivity, teammate Solomon Little Owl, a member of the Crow Nation and director of Native American Student Services at UNC, offers the following: "People say this is a nonissue, but what they're really saying is, 'I don't want to change my beliefs about other ethnicities.' This is an issue of identity." Coleman Cornelius, *Fightin' Whities Fund Scholarships, T-shirt Sales Reap $100,000 for Indians*, Denv. Post, December 1, 2002, at B.01.

9. The University of Hawaii recently changed the nickname of the school's football team from the "Rainbow Warriors" to the "Warriors," and simultaneously replaced the school's 77-year-old rainbow logo. The reason: the association of the rainbow with homosexuality. "That logo," said Athletic Director Hugh Yoshida, "really put a stigma on our program at times in regards to its part in the gay community, their flags and so forth. Some of the student-athletes had some feelings in regards to that." The change "ends a very bad message, responded Ken Miller, co-chair of the Gay and Lesbian Community Center in Honolulu, "not only to the students but the (gay) athletes who happen to be struggling with that." *Rainbow Logo Removal Puts Hawaii under a Cloud*, Associated Press, July 29, 2000.

III. Race And Sports

A. The Color Barrier and The Professional Athlete

During the early part of the twentieth century, as a clear color line of demarcation was drawn between white and black professional baseball players, what are commonly characterized as the Negro Leagues emerged. What precisely were the Negro Leagues? As Professor Neil Lanctot's encyclopedic work explains, there was no single league for black ballplayers in the days of segregation, and no central administration for the collected leagues. *See* Neil Lanctot, Negro League Baseball: The Rise and Ruin of a Black Institution (2004). The Negro Leagues were, on the contrary, a loose pastiche of organizations that co-existed with the variety of white professional and semi-professional leagues. As Robert Peterson, likely the dean of Negro Leagues scholarship, explains:

> Tracing the course of the organized Negro leagues is rather like trying to follow a single black strand through a ton of spaghetti. The footing is infirm, and the strand has a tendency to break off in one's hand and slither back into the amorphous mass.

> Leagues were born and died within a single season, franchises were often shifted from city to city in the middle of summer, and a number of teams had a brief fling at glory in the sun of big-time Negro baseball before returning to the scrubby obscurity of semipro lots.

Robert Peterson, Only the Ball Was White 80 (Oxford Paperback ed. 1992).

Some leagues did predominate in the twentieth century: the American Negro League, the Eastern Colored League (home to the Hilldale club), the Negro American League (eventual home of the Kansas City Monarchs), the Negro Southern League, and above all, the Negro National League, which in its first incarnation operated from 1920 to 1931, and in its second operated from to 1933 to 1948 (and which was, in its second incarnation, home to the Homestead Grays). *See generally id.* at 257–311 (summarizing league records from 1920 to 1950). Moreover, mixed among the various entrepreneurial motives, the leagues shared a coherent purpose: to allow black ballplayers an opportunity to play professional baseball, an opportunity categorically denied them by white organized baseball since the turn of the century.

Like so much of Jim Crow, racial segregation in baseball was rooted in "custom," a custom forged in the nineteenth century in the post-emancipation South (but modeled, for the most part, on the *de facto* segregation that characterized the antebellum North), frequently formalized in compulsory segregation laws, and eventually sanctioned by the United States Supreme Court in its 1896 opinion in *Plessy v. Ferguson.*

Baseball's version of Jim Crow had its own strange career. Cf. C. VANN WOODWARD, THE STRANGE CAREER OF JIM CROW (1955). The first league, the National Association of Base Ball Players, banned black ballplayers by rule in 1868, but the league expired in 1871, and neither its successor, nor any subsequent league, felt compelled to memorialize the color line by rule. After 1871, then, no official rules banned black ballplayers, and through the remainder of the nineteenth century, some black players, Moses Fleetwood Walker, Bud Fowler, and a score of others, crossed the color line to play in "organized baseball." But the customary color line hardened with the century's end, and from 1899 to 1947 (when Jackie Robinson re-integrated the game), no black ballplayer, excepting those who "passed" for white, Indian, Asian, or "Cuban," played in white baseball. *See id.* at 16–51.

Professional baseball, it should be noted, was not alone in segregating by "gentleman's agreement." Alan H. Levy describes the drawing of the color line in the National Football League:

> [T]he NFL owners met after the 1933 season and dealt with the race question. They left no written records of their meetings, but it is abundantly clear that at the end of the 1933 season they chose to ban African Americans from the league. With shameful disingenuousness, George Halas denied that any sort of ban had been established. When asked why blacks did not appear in the NFL from 1933 to 1946, Halas mused pathetically that the game "didn't have the appeal to black players at the time." * * *
>
> In regard to the drawing of the racial bar, other owners provided points of evidence. Art Rooney said, with a combination of psychological denial and legalistic honesty, that he felt there never was any "racial bias." There may or may not have been provable bias, but, while smoking guns in regard to what lies in someone's heart can seldom be found, Rooney side-stepped the question of a "ban," and the omission was revealing. Tex Schramm, who later ran both the Los Angeles Rams and the Dallas Cowboys, was more honest about the attitude about signing blacks in the '30s and early '40s: "You just didn't do it," he recalled. Schramm's point, of course, contradicts Halas's assertions that the game must not have had any appeal to blacks. The point was that the talent was there, and everyone knew it. Moreover, since owners had previously signed talented African American football players, and then reached a point where one just did not do it, logically there had to have been a point when people made the choice to stop doing what they had been doing. This is exactly what occurred after the 1933 season.

ALAN H. LEVY, TACKLING JIM CROW: RACIAL SEGREGATION IN PROFESSIONAL FOOTBALL 55 (2003).

Some players, such as Buck O'Neil, recount fond memories of the Negro League experience, while acknowledging the obvious infirmities. For example, commenting on Ken Burns's classic documentary *Baseball,* O'Neil declares: "The best thing about the film * * * was that it gave me a chance to tell folks about the Negro Leagues, about what a glorious enterprise black baseball was, and about what a wonderful thing baseball is * * *. Waste no tears for me. I didn't come along too early, I was right on time." BUCK O'NEIL, *I Was Right On Time* at 2–3. Regrettably, Mr. O'Neil passed away in October 2006 at age 94.

Others remarking about the Negro Leagues were neither as philosophical nor forgiving. Robert Peterson synopsizes the Negro Leagues as follows: "Perhaps three general statements might be advanced with some degree of temerity: (1) that the leagues (and most of the teams) were underfinanced; (2) that, except for a brief period at the beginning, they lacked leadership; and (3) that due chiefly to points (1) and (2) the Negro Leagues never approached the level of white organized baseball in stability and discipline." PETERSON, *supra* at 80.

Interestingly, although Major League Baseball, and its Hall of Fame at Cooperstown, gradually acknowledged and eventually honored the achievements of Negro Leagues' players, it has been less hospitable to the Leagues' executives. "A magnificent innovator such as John Leslie Wilkinson," writes Mark Ribowsky, "who as owner of the fabled Kansas City Monarchs rigged up light towers and fathered baseball's original night games, will likely never be bronzed at Cooperstown (even with the knowledge that Wilkinson happened to be white)." MARK RIBOWSKY, A COMPLETE HISTORY OF THE NEGRO LEAGUES, 1884 TO 1955, xvi (1995).

Ribowsky suggests that the slight is at least partly deserved: "the tragedy of the Negro leagues was that there were too few J. L. Wilkinsons around to counterbalance the cast of plug-uglies, night riders, and hoodlums who held top positions in the Negro leagues in the thirties and forties," men like Abraham Manley, who made his money in a numbers-running racket. *Id.* "In the end," Ribowsky concludes, "legitimacy in the baseball gentility could not be bought at any price by men whose social register was the police blotter." *Id.*

Not all historians of the leagues agree that this is a fair assessment of its executives: Professor Lanctot, for example, has been highly critical of Ribowsky's relatively "cynical view" of black owners. *See* Neil Lanctot, *Book Review*, J. SPORT HISTORY, Vol. 22, No. 3 (Fall 1995). But the histories seem to find common ground in recognizing that the Negro Leagues generally offered black ballplayers, and their fans, relatively "precarious fortunes"; that much of this, perhaps all of it, was due to the severe economic disadvantages under which those Leagues operated; that many of those disadvantages, perhaps the great bulk of them, were visited upon the Leagues by white organized baseball; and that much of the remaining disadvantage, perhaps all of it, can be traced to the oppression experienced by black businesses and black Americans generally. As Ribowsky concedes, the leagues may at times have been dependent upon "soiled black seed money," but "soiled" money "was preferable to no seed money," and, besides, "soiled" is a relative term, in more ways than one. Ribowsky, *supra*, at xvi; *see also id.*, (suggesting that activities of the owners was not inconsistent with "the ethos of the 'hood"); *cf.* Regina Austin, *"The Black Community," Its Lawbreakers, and a Politics of Identification*, 65 S. CAL. L. REV. 1769, 1815–17 (1992) (noting the formation among minority groups of an "informal economy" that is "really the illegitimate offspring of legal regulation" and calling for a politics of identification that requires that its legal adherents work the line between the legal and the illegal, the formal and the informal, the socially (within 'the community') acceptable and the socially despised, and the merely different and the truly deviant."); Regina Austin, *"An Honest Living": Street Vendors, Municipal Regulation, and the Black Public Sphere*, 103 YALE L.J. 2119, 2119 (1994) ("I, like many blacks, believe that an oppressed people should not be too law abiding, especially where economics is concerned. The economic system that has exploited us is not likely to be effectively exploited by us if we pay too much attention to the law.").

Notes and Questions

1. The relative stability of white Organized Baseball partly explains why black ballplayers may have wanted to cross baseball's color line. But why else was it that those players continued to wish for integration? Why might they the desires been shared by black America generally? And why were those aspirations evidently not shared by most white ballplayers, white baseball executives, white fans, or most of white America?

Occasionally, black barnstorming teams would play exhibitions against Major League clubs. Frequently, the teams from the established league were defeated. As a result, many teams were wary of further interracial competition. For white baseball—including white baseball fans—a loss to a Negro Leagues team was widely viewed as a disgrace. Through the early twentieth century, notions of white racial supremacy apparently included a belief in white athletic supremacy—at least when it came to the skills needed to play baseball. The upshot of the negative reaction from fans and clubs, was that prior to the 1916 season the American and National Leagues banned players from barnstorming absent written permission from their team. *See generally,* NEIL LANCTOT, FAIR DEALING AND CLEAN PLAYING: THE HILLDALE CLUB AND THE DEVELOPMENT OF BLACK PROFESSIONAL BASEBALL 1910–1932 (1994).

2. What was the most significant contribution of the Negro Leagues in terms of society's perceptions of African Americans? Did the opportunity to showcase talent in this forum enhance acceptance of this segment of our community or did they pigeon-hole African Americans as having limited roles to play, many of which were to provide entertainment to white Americans? One irresistibly may conjure images of other entertainment media (such as cinema) as examples of white America's somewhat patronizing acceptance of African Americans for whom other fields of endeavor would be inaccessible.

3. Did baseball help enlighten society in general or did progress in other venues allow for the breaking of the color barrier in baseball? *See* Ira Glasser, *Branch Rickey and Jackie Robinson: Precursors to the Civil Rights Movement,* WORLD AND I, March 1, 2003 Vol. 18, Issue 3.

4. The relationship between the Negro Leagues and Jackie Robinson has sparked no small amount of discussion and debate in several contexts. Perhaps the two most common themes have been: 1) the role that the Negro Leagues played in exposing the talents of players like Jackie Robinson and promoting his entry into the big leagues; and 2) the breaking of the color barrier as the harbinger of the Negro Leagues' eventual demise.

5. At this point, few readers are unfamiliar with baseball's infamous color barrier and how it was eradicated when Branch Rickey and the Brooklyn Dodgers signed Jackie Robinson to a professional baseball contract. The first step toward the desegregation of baseball had been taken. Most commentators attribute the demise of the Negro Leagues to the integration of Major League baseball. *See, e.g.,* JACOB MARGOLIES, THE NEGRO LEAGUES, THE STORY OF BLACK BASEBALL 84 (1993). ("When Robinson made it to the Dodgers, the Negro Leaguers were largely forgotten." BRUCE CHADWICK, WHEN THE GAME WAS BLACK AND WHITE: THE ILLUSTRATED HISTORY OF THE NEGRO LEAGUES 172 (1992). "Despite the deep satisfaction felt by many at the integration of the Major Leagues, it effectively killed the Negro Leagues.") Yet, others see the integration of baseball as but one event that led to the Negro Leagues' failure as an institution. *See* Alfred Dennis Mathewson, *Major League Baseball's Monopoly Power and the Negro Leagues,* 35 AM. BUS. L.J. 291 (1998). Professor Mathewson attributes this failure to numerous factors, including weak relational structures, the need for Negro Leagues to compete with

an institution that had acquired monopoly power over the market, and Negro League owners' concession that extinction was inevitable. He is not alone in his refusal to lay the demise of the Negro Leagues solely at the feet of Jackie Robinson. Other factors include the lack of capital, abandonment by the press, and emerging social disenchantment with the "separate but equal" concept. *See e.g.,* PETERSON, *supra* at 80, 201; RIBOWSKY, *supra* at 288.

6. Professor Mathewson has also acknowledged the harm that integration of the NBA did to the Harlem Globetrotters by diminishing available black talent. Yet, he has not accorded the same "accountability" to the integration of baseball *vis-à-vis* the Negro Leagues? Perhaps it is because there was no immediate influx of black players into Major League baseball after Jackie Robinson; the progress in that regard was actually very deliberate. Yet, one cannot discount the obvious change in fan interest that would occur as soon as blacks were permitted to occupy center stage in the premier league: "Inevitably, as full integration became a reality on organized baseball's rosters, prospective stars were signed by big league organizations directly out of high school and placed on their minor league affiliates, thus eliminating the middle man—the Negro clubs." PETERSON, *supra* at 20.

7. How much of an influence did Robinson's non-violent, passive aggression have on the civil rights movement as it evolved? In some respects, was Robinson too passive? Much like tennis's Arthur Ashe, Jackie Robinson developed a renaissance persona—a quiet, often conciliatory demeanor, assertive and aggressive when necessary, and dignified at all times. It was a character that appealed to blacks and whites, men and women, Democrats and Republicans. Was his universal appeal at times almost too "mainstream" to push the buttons that needed to be pushed? Robinson became an active member of the Republican Party, certainly marking him as a rarity among those individuals who would be hailed as civil rights leaders. For an excellent overview of African-American athletes and the impact that they have had on popular culture, see Alfred Dennis Mathewson, *Grooming Crossovers*, 4 J. GENDER, RACE & JUST. 225 (2001).

8. Historian and biographer Jules Tygiel observed that Robinson's "obvious intelligence, self-deprecating wit, and public willingness to forgive and understand his tormentors, made him an American hero." JULES TYGIEL, BASEBALL'S GREAT EXPERIMENT 193 (1983). Robinson's character soon won the respect of his teammates as well. Could it be that the Dodgers' collective desire to win games overshadowed any misgivings about having a black teammate? This question begets a larger issue that asks whether the timing of baseball's decision to integrate was motivated and governed by economic factors independent of some desire finally to correct the sad mistakes of the past.

9. Robinson was not the only player to suffer abuse because of his race or ethnicity. Hank Greenberg described the bench jockeying from the Yankees in the 1930s.

> They always had a couple of guys in the dugout just doing that to you. Some of the things they yelled were pretty nasty but I could always handle it pretty well. That's because everybody got it. Italians were wops, Germans were krauts, and the Polish players were dumb polacks. Me, I was a kike or a sheeny or a mockey. I was big so I made a good target. The only thing that bothered me was there were a lot of Italians, and Germans, and Poles, but I was the only Jewish player who was making a name for himself and so they reserved a little extra for me.

HANK GREENBERG, THE STORY OF MY LIFE 40 (1989).

Greenberg's teammate, Birdie Tebbets, elaborates on that "little extra":

There was nobody in the history of the game who took more abuse than Greenberg, unless it was Jackie Robinson * * *. I was there with Hank when it was happening and I heard it. However, Hank was not only equal to it, he was superior to most of the people who were yelling at him. And in the case of Jackie Robinson, Jackie had no place to go after a ball game and Greenberg could go anyplace in the world. Greenberg had to bear that terrible burden on the field, Jackie had to bear it all his life. I wasn't in the National League with Jackie, but I was with Hank and Hank consistently took more abuse than anybody I had ever known.

Id. at 98. Hank Greenberg shared Jackie Robinson's sense of purpose. "Being Jewish," he noted, "did carry with it a special responsibility. After all, I was representing a couple of million Jews among a hundred million gentiles, and I was always in the spotlight. * * * I felt responsibility. I was there every day, and if I had a bad day, every son of a bitch was calling me names so that I had to make good. I just had to show them that a Jew could play ball." *Id.* at 110–111.

Still, Greenberg concluded, "Jackie had it tough, tougher than any ballplayer who ever lived. I happened to be a Jew, one of the few in baseball, but I was white * * *." *Id.* at 183. Greenberg, interestingly, was one of the first Major Leaguers to befriend Jackie Robinson; "I identified with Jackie Robinson," he said. "I had feelings for him because they treated me the same way." "Class tells," Robinson observed during his rookie year; "It sticks out all over Mr. Greenberg." *Id.* at 181.

10. Once Jackie Robinson became a member of the Brooklyn Dodgers, was there any reasonable doubt that the future of the Negro Leagues would be in serious jeopardy? If Robinson's signing were truly a harbinger of a more complete establishment of integration of baseball, was it not inevitable that the Negro Leagues' premier attractions would soon be headed to the "big show"? Would fans continue to spend money to watch Negro League games or simply wait until they had an opportunity to see their stars play in a Major League uniform?

11. Some commentators have suggested that true integration, without the scarring manifested by the elimination of the Negro Leagues, would have been better accomplished by assimilating a few Negro League teams into the Major Leagues or by merging with the Negro Leagues. Do you agree?

12. In other contexts, premier teams from rival leagues have been absorbed by established leagues, lock, stock and barrel. The merger of the National Basketball Association and teams from the upstart American Basketball Association is illustrative. What would have been the negative consequences, or at least the perceivable adverse effects, of inviting several of the more prominent and fiscally sound Negro League franchises to join the Major Leagues?

13. Perhaps the saddest part of the Jackie Robinson saga is that during the period from 1947–1957, the Negro Leagues were in decline, ceasing to be a viable showcase for black talent, but the Major Leagues had not yet come to accept blacks as part of their game. Thus, many great players were caught in the switches—languishing in the growing anonymity of the Negro Leagues, but not yet welcome in the "bigs."

14. Baseball's color line was clear and unequivocal. The near-systematic exclusion of blacks from other sports has been almost as pervasive but not as blatant. The woefully low number of blacks in professional tennis, golf, horseracing, and auto racing suggests an in-

visible color line that may be attributable to countless reasons ranging from a disinterest in those sports among minorities to an inevitable discontent prompted by feelings of alienation and disaffection by the purveyors of those sports and the fans that support them.

15. Are tennis and golf, for example, "racist" sports? Does the emergence of the Williams sisters, Venus and Serena (winners of several Grand Slam events) and James Blake suggest that the tide is turning? Or, are they merely notable because they are simply too good to be excluded? At some point, will the presence of black tennis players be unremarkable? Or might the presence of black tennis players become, or continue to be, threatening—to white tennis or to white America? Do the norms of "civility" and "elegance" that foster the pristine image of tennis, though facially neutral, serve to maintain the racial exclusivity of tennis? For some members of tennis's upper crust, have terms like civility and elegance become code words used to describe only wealthy Caucasians? *See generally,* Peter Bodo, The Courts of Babylon: Tales of Greed and Glory From the Harsh New World of Professional Tennis (1995).

Is it significant that the Williams sisters seem to provoke much stronger criticism and controversy than has ever been stoked by black player Chanda Rubin, who is infinitely more conservative in terms of style? Does that fact rebut claims of racism or does it simply say that Rubin is more accepted because she is "more white?"

16. While there have been few legal challenges or official protests regarding the treatment of African Americans by the tennis community, occasionally attacks have been made. One player brought suit claiming that the USTA's system of tournament selection and seeding discriminated against African Americans. In particular, he alleged that he was denied a wild card entry based on his race in violation of Title VII of the Civil Rights Act of 1964. The suit was dismissed for failure to state a claim. The court concluded that there was insufficient evidence to establish that the denial of the wild card had a disproportionate impact on African Americans. In addition, the plaintiff failed to show that he was an employee of the defendant, thus precluding applicability of Title VII. Is there any basis to demonstrate an employer/employee relationship between professional tennis players and the USTA and/or tournament sponsors? *See Washington v. United States Tennis Association,* 290 F. Supp. 2d 323 (E.D.N.Y. 2003).

On another front, former umpire Cecil Hollins has argued that the USTA never appointed a woman or a minority as chair of the U.S. Open men's final. Hollins' allegations have provided impetus for an investigation by the New York Attorney General's office into various aspects of the USTA's treatment of women and minorities.

17. One commentator has asked, "Can golf impose its courtly mores without also imposing the racial and social exclusiveness on which this courtliness was once predicated?" *See* Scott Stossel, *The Golfing of America,* The New Republic (August 3, 1998). Must the eventual character of golf change if it is to absorb a more representative range of classes and cultures? How compatible, really, are golf's aristocratic culture and America's multi-cultural democratic values?

It has been suggested that golf is no longer a rich person's game. Is this true? If the youth truly dictate trends, how can inner-city or rural youth afford the equipment, greens fees, and lessons that are necessary to pursue golf in any kind of meaningful fashion? Tiger Woods has truly revolutionized golf and he has become a cult figure to all young people, especially black youths. Has it really provoked a groundswell of support for and participation in golf among young African Americans? The reviews and prognoses are decidedly mixed. *See* Jill Lieber, *Few Can Afford Membership in Private Club,* USA Today, Sports, April 10, 2003; Mike Hembree, *Growing the Next Tiger,*

GREENVILLE NEWS, Sports, C, May 9, 2003. Matt Winkeljohn, *Tiger's Impact on the Youth Movement*, THE ATLANTA JOURNAL-THE ATLANTA CONSTITUTION, Sports, November 2, 1997; Avis Thomas-Lester, *Blacks Break into the Swing of Golf*, THE WASHINGTON POST, P6, Extra, August 17, 2000.

18. Tiger Woods's father has compared him to Jackie Robinson and early in Woods's career predicted that Tiger's influence would be profoundly felt. Do you agree? Did family, friends, colleagues, and the media place an inordinate amount of pressure on a twenty year-old? To the extent that Woods might have been able to maintain some perspective, how has his astounding fifty-four PGA Tour wins, including twelve major championships affected his equanimity? While attempting nobly to be viewed simply as a professional golfer, he may be compelled to confront the reality that his race will never be irrelevant. Does he bear the onerous burden of serving as a spokesman for the entire African-American community?

Shortly after the Masters, fellow golf professional, Fuzzy Zoeller, made a few regrettable remarks that, while offered in jest, perpetuated unfortunate stereotypes of African Americans. Specifically, Zoeller asked whether Woods, as champion and host of the Masters dinner, would be serving collard greens and fried chicken. If Woods personally viewed the remarks as harmless when placed in context, did have a larger responsibility to the minority community and a duty to assess the comments from the perspective of a larger audience?

19. How would you compare the travail of Jackie Robinson with the difficulties that Tiger Woods has encountered and is likely to encounter as his professional career matures? Do you concur in the following comparisons—

WHY IT MAY BE EASIER FOR TIGER WOODS:

Today's public is more enlightened than the sports audiences in 1947. Further, Woods will encounter less resistance from fellow competitors.

There is less likelihood of fan abuse, verbal or otherwise, given the more genteel nature of golf audiences.

Travel conditions are much better because Woods will not be denied premier hotel accommodations, access to restaurants, or other amenities that can hamper or enhance one's performance.

There is no physical contact in golf; therefore Woods will not be subject to "cheap shots" and other risk of injury at the hands of opponents.

Assuming that umpires could be guilty of bias, there is little problem of mistreatment on close judgment calls or other on-the-field (course) arbitrariness.

WHY IT MAY BE MORE DIFFICULT FOR TIGER WOODS:

Tremendous pressure from family, press, and others to become golf's answer to Michael Jordan could be both intimidating as well as inspiring.

Golf has never been accessible to blacks. Many private country clubs still discriminate on the basis of race. When Jackie Robinson broke into baseball, blacks had played the game for years. Thus, Woods to a degree is blazing a trail through rougher terrain.

Woods may be unable to influence younger blacks to play golf because the sport is expensive and often unavailable to inner city youth. Likewise the lily white nature of the sport may create the impression of inaccessibility.

Early successes in tournaments, while heartening, may mean that any future failures will be magnified—otherwise stated as the "what has he done lately" phenomenon.

As is often the case, one of the authors of this casebook owes a vote of thanks to his precocious offspring for inspiration and resources on this issue. *See* Robert L. Cozzillio, *The Ordeal of Jackie Robinson*, Seventh Grade History Day Project—Triumph and Tragedy, St. Margaret Mary School, Harrisburg, Pennsylvania (February, 1997). *See also* Christopher M. Cozzillio, *Jackie Robinson and Satchel Paige*, Second Grade Book Report, St. Margaret Mary School, Harrisburg, Pennsylvania (February, 1997).

20. Have the senior Woods's predictions approached or reached fruition? While an assessment of Woods's legacy would be premature, no one would question that he already must be numbered among the greatest golfers of all time. Occupying that lofty position, has Woods emerged as an off-the-course leader reflective of his public prominence? Does he have any responsibility to fulfill that role any more so than black leaders in other industries?

21. Is there a political agenda behind the elevation of Tiger Woods-or other minority athletes-to the status of cultural icon? Professor John Hoberman thinks there may be, and it is not the egalitarian one that appears on the surface.

> The Tiger Woods mania also revealed once again how easy it is for whites to "solve" the race problem by extolling black sports stars. White conservatives love to imagine that the sports world where whites own everything and blacks exhibit their physical prowess is "color-blind" racial integration at its finest. Tiger Woods, said Rush Limbaugh, "is going to show others how to live their lives, and it isn't going to matter that he's black or white." Not Thurgood Marshall. Not Toni Morrison. Not the angry Henry Aaron. No, the guiding light for all of us is a politically immature golfer whose public persona has been created by a shoe company.

John Hoberman, *How We've Whitewashed Race in the World of Sports*, NEWSDAY Jan. 11, 1998, at B06.

22. The non-existence of a welcome mat for African Americans may not be limited to the more elitist sports. The declining number of American-born blacks in Major League Baseball may suggest a reaction to the inhospitable way in which minorities have been treated at various stages of history and in various levels of baseball's hierarchy. Columnist Ralph Wiley declares: "Baseball has a problem, a deeply rooted problem, but it is not the pace of the game or the performance or interest level of any human subgrouping; no, it's baseball's uneasy truce with the social construct called race * * * . The problem now, 100 years later, is in the lower levels of baseball." Wiley goes on to say:

> Make no mistake, baseball is a strictly inherited game; it's not something you can pick up on the street like basketball or even football. It is a game of acquired, refined, specialized skills that are hardly translatable to any other sport. It is a game of inherited knowledge. Its Byzantine set of rules, skills, dimensions and culture are so esoteric and oftentimes so bizarre that they must be explained, passed down, by rote, statistic, history, usually from father to son, most often from an early age. This is where, normally, another statistic would be spouted, like "63 percent of young black males grow up in single-parent homes where the head of household is a woman who doesn't have time, inclination or knowledge to make baseball part of the kid's daily bill of fare * * * ." This is a baseball killer in places like Maryland, Georgia, even L.A. * * *

And let's not forget, baseball was never that welcoming for black players in the first place, which is why they had to form their own leagues in the first half of the 20th Century, if they wanted to play. It wasn't until 1947 that Jackie Robinson integrated the big leagues, and, frankly, we are still waiting for the day when American-born blacks are treated with like respect in the game.

Wiley argues that blacks' legacies in the baseball history books is often denigrated:

It is usually the American-born blacks' records and place that are resented instead of celebrated. For example, it's the stolen base that is denigrated as a weapon by baseball sabermaticians like Bill James, at precisely the time when a Rickey Henderson steals 130 bases in a season. There are sour grapes when a baseball man uses stats to tell you a stolen base isn't important. Any time a baseball manager will give up an out for a base, as with a sac bunt or groundball to the right side, any time a base is so precious, then it goes without saying that the stolen base must be important. Not the CS, the caught stealing, or stats of success rates, but the stolen base itself.

So Rickey Henderson becomes, in the media and our oral history of the day, a bad guy, "this guy," who did something meaningless, and refers to himself in the third person and, oh yeah (with a decidedly sour look), maybe the best leadoff hitter ever, whatever that means. Barry Bonds becomes somebody who is excoriated for the limitations of his personality, even though we do not know him as a late-night talk-show host, but as a big-league baseball player. That skill set is all that should matter. But anything to keep from judging him on those merits. Look at the personalities of most timeless baseball stars; Ty Cobb, Ted Williams, Joe DiMaggio-none of them was a day at the beach. But not being a day at the beach becomes Bonds' full metal straitjacket.

Wiley concludes:

So there is this general underlying resentment of the black baseball player, I feel, and it's spun now so that this dogged resentment comes from blacks themselves. In a way, it's like the notion that doing well in school is "acting white." Sure, there are black kids who wind up saying baseball is "a white man's game," and even believing it, but that's not their concept. That is what they have felt, sensed as the general societal tenor, and they picked up on it.

Ralph Wiley, *Squeeze Play: Baseball's Troubling Issue,* ESPN ONLINE, http://msn.espn.go .cm/page2/s/wiley/030715.html (2003). A short time ago, Ralph Wiley passed away prematurely. His incisive commentary will be missed.

Major League baseball is attempting to respond these problems, particularly the absence of youth baseball in inner-city areas such as Los Angeles. In August 2003, Commissioner Bud Selig revealed plans for a unique $3 million baseball academy designed to stimulate a declining interest in baseball among inner-city youths. Compton College, in downtown Los Angeles, will host the academy that Selig hopes will serve as the prototype for replication in Major League cities throughout the country. Selig commented, "I have always believed that baseball is an important social institution with enormous social responsibilities * * *. It is our intention to bring baseball back to urban America, and this is a major step in that direction." Ben Bolch, *Building $3 Million Bridge: Major League Baseball Officials Pledge To Construct Academy in Compton as Part of an Effort to Invigorate Urban Interest in Sport,* LOS ANGELES TIMES, Aug. 5, 2003, Sports, 4-1.

23. Not unlike tennis and golf, horse racing, the proverbial "sport of kings," has also enjoyed an interesting and checkered history in terms of African-American participation. Black jockeys were ubiquitous on U.S. racetracks in the 19th century. 14 of the 15 riders in the inaugural Kentucky Derby, in 1875, were black, and 15 of the first 28 Derbies were won by black riders. Several factors, such as racial discrimination and an absence of opportunities to learn to ride, have led to the virtual disappearance of black jockeys today. However, in the nineteenth century, African Americans, who grew up on or around plantations and farms, were naturally drawn to horses. As a result, many became riders by profession. Jim Bolus, *Honest Isaac's Legacy: The Greatest U.S. Jockey of the 19th Century Was a Black*, SPORTS ILLUSTRATED, April 29, 1996.

24. It is noteworthy that many of the black jockeys were known only by first names, reflecting a failure to appreciate or even acknowledge their full identity. EDWARD HOTALING, THE GREAT BLACK JOCKEYS (2001). This phenomenon of referring to members of oppressed groups by their first names is not uncommon. Legal commentators have noted that the media, particularly in certain sports, will refer to women athletes by their first names with astoundingly greater frequency than male athletes. *See* Mary Jo Kane, *Gender and Sports: Setting a Course for College Athleticism, Media Coverage For The Post Title IX Athlete: "A Feminist Analysis of Sport, Gender, and Power,"* 3 DUKE J. GENDER & POL'Y 95, 111–112 (1996). Does the familiar or first-name basis suggest a lack of respect or some view of the object as almost infantile or of some lower social standing?

25. Hotaling notes three developments that compromised the future of black jockeys: 1) raw racism; 2) African-American migration from the South, shrinking the numbers of agrarian, rural blacks; 3) the infusion of larger sums of money attracted more white riders who were able to command greater shares of the purses. Also, "big money" made it difficult for small stables which had trained and retained many black jockeys. *See* HOTALING, *supra*, at 281–284.

Once again, the scenario is repeated: blacks who were welcome in one area of sports at the turn of the century mysteriously disappeared. Why? In addition to the emerging "racialism," as it was called, playing a major part, a less obvious cause was the fear-engendering success of blacks in other arenas, such as boxing. *See id.* at 325–32. In the case of the black athlete, success certainly did *not* breed success. Legislative opposition to gambling in general, and horse racing in particular, did not help. Further, as Hotaling points out in his illuminating text, when a separate racing meet for black jockeys was proposed, it was soundly rejected by the moneyed interests. When confronted with the "interracial or not" option, white America chose to do without the services of black jockeys. As a result, black jockeys became a dying breed, a phenomenon that has not changed dramatically as we entered the 21st century. Does this Hobson's choice validate the Negro Leagues as an option even in their flawed state? Unfortunately, it is not uncommon for members of a bigoted group to sacrifice financial benefit to preserve their hegemonic position *vis-à-vis* members of a disadvantaged class. *See* MARCIA CHAMBERS, THE UNPLAYABLE LIE 34–36 (1995).

26. NASCAR (the National Association of Stock Car Auto Racing) contends that it is the second most popular sport in America, behind only football. It may be the whitest.

On December 1, 1963, Wendell Scott overcame the handicaps of overt racism and inferior equipment to win a NASCAR Grand National Race in Winston-Salem, North Carolina. Scott, who is black, beat his nearest competitor, Buck Baker, by two full laps. His victory was not well-received:

> When a race official told the beauty queen, who was white, of course, that she would have to kiss a black man in Victory Lane, she literally ran from the

premises. Officials feared a riot from the rowdy crowd if they awarded Scott the victory, so they called Scott over and told him they were giving the win to Baker, even though they knew Baker had not won. It was the most deplorable moment in racing history's most shameful chapter.

JOE MENZER, THE WILDEST RIDE 161–162 (2001). Scott was eventually recognized as the victor, and was awarded a wooden trophy with no nameplate in a private ceremony. He was the first black driver to win at NASCAR's highest level-and also its last. *See* Robert F. Casey, NASCAR's Lack of Diversity 14 (May 10, 2003) (unpublished manuscript, on file with the authors).

The auto racing industry's failure to reach out is further reflected in the fact that only 8.8% of the sports fan base of 75 million are African American. Some African Americans, such as controversial director Spike Lee, have voiced cynicism about the industry and its fans, declaring an unwillingness even to attend a NASCAR event. Tim Aust, Vice-President of Toyota Motor Sports, Racing Division of Toyota Motor Sales USA, Inc., offers that Toyota supports programs and policies designed to attract more African Americans and other minorities. Yet, he is concerned about a lack of progress perpetuated by the nature of NASCAR itself—largely a "family business." This concern is shared by African American Randi Payton, President of On Wheels, Inc., publisher of *African Americans on Wheels*. Payton noted that in recent profiles of the NASCAR fan base performed by West Coast consultants Edgar, Dunn Co., NASCAR followers saw drivers as "people like me." Payton explained that the "people like me" mentality results in the exclusion of "people like us." "Sponsors don't want to take a chance on black drivers because they believe they won't be accepted." Warren Brown, *NASCAR's Diversity Dearth May Be Sponsor-Driven*, WASH. POST, July 24, 2004, at G2.

But there are signs of change. NASCAR now has its first minority team owners, and black driver Bill Lester finished 17th in points in 2002. Tubby Smith, African-American head basketball coach at the University of Kentucky, has joined with Joe Nemencheck to form a Busch Grand National Series racing team to commence operations in 2005. SPORTS ILLUSTRATED, *Scorecard*, For the Record, Nov. 1, 2004, at 26. NASCAR itself adopted a Diversity Initiative in 2002; a Minority Council is charged with finding ways to diversify the sport and its fan base. And some of the white drivers, at least, are on board. The drivers, Jeff Burton says, "do have a role to play in it * * *. You can't change anything in our society without people being involved in it and I'm in this sport and we need to be a cross-section of America and we are not. I therefore have a responsibility to try and help that * * *" Casey at 24.

27. Would Title VII be a viable avenue of recourse for an African-American driver who was a victim of discrimination either in the denial of a position on a racing team or in his/her mistreatment as a member of that team? The answer to this question will turn, in part, on the driver's characterization as an employee or independent contractor. One commentator has determined that the latter characterization controls:

> Each driver is an independent contractor. Either the driver controls the licensing of each of his/her likenesses or the team negotiates licensing matters for him/her. This allows teams to have a choice of how they want to handle the licensing of their driver's merchandise. They may either contract out to a marketing company or they may handle licensing matters internally.

Michael A. Cokley, *In the Fast Lane to Big Bucks: The Growth of NASCAR*, 8 SPORTS L.J. 67, 86–87 (2004). Of course, the ultimate determination of a driver's employee status would turn on a variety of factors including the skill required, duration of the relationship between the parties, method of compensation, the hired party's discretion in terms of when and how long to work, employee benefits, and tax treatment. *Schwieger v. Farm Bureau Insurance Co.,* 207 F.3d 480 (8th Cir. 2000).

B. Minorities and Management

Kenneth L. Shropshire,
Merit, Ol' Boy Networks, and the Black-Bottomed Pyramid
47 HASTINGS L.J. 455 (1996).

> *They've [blacks] got everything. If they take over coaching like everybody wants them to, there's not going to be anything left for white people.*
>
> —Former CBS broadcaster Jimmy "the Greek" Snyder

> *We [white people] decide when, how many and which ones.*
>
> —Sociologist Andrew Hacker regarding the hiring of African Americans in top-level positions in corporate America

Introduction

Suppose that at some moment in the future, no one questions the merit of African-Americans seeking management positions in corporate America. Imagine further that merit issues are satisfied but the statistics reveal that a disproportionate number of these positions are still filled by white males. Further, what if African-Americans possessed these qualifications for decades but the underrepresentation of African-Americans at the management level persists decades later?

The sports industry, often considered a microcosm of society, provides an opportunity to examine these issues. In terms of merit, the sports industry represents the best we could hope for in America—in one respect—large numbers of qualified African-Americans for every position at the highest levels. Without question African-Americans are qualified to be commissioners, head coaches, and other front office executives; yet the top positions are still largely filled by white males. In the harshest of terms, the sports industry resembles a black-bottomed pyramid: large numbers of African-American athlete-participants, but few African-Americans in non-playing positions at the highest levels. The sports industry's efforts at remedying this situation may provide lessons as to how the rest of American society may deal with discrimination once objective questions of merit are resolved. And, as will be illustrated, the initial efforts to address the black-bottomed pyramid in the sports industry have been inadequate.

Snyder's comments in the opening epigraph reflect today's "angry white male" in other contexts. But here the fear expressed by Snyder is not of someone presumably less qualified. The fear is of losing long possessed employment territory. If there is no question regarding the qualifications or merit of African-Americans, then why does the underrepresentation continue? And once underrepresentation is recognized, will the sports industry-and soon society-then agree that it is time to aggressively introduce (or re-introduce) race-conscious measures such as affirmative action? Seemingly, the only other alternative to affirmative action is to allow those in power to continue to employ definitions of merit in the context of their own personal affirmative action. These are the broad issues this essay examines.

I. PROBLEM: AFRICAN-AMERICAN UNDERREPRESENTATION IN THE FRONT OFFICE

The most visible non-player personnel in sports are those who reside in the front office. Although there is no rigid definition as to which jobs constitute positions in the front office, the top-level positions generally include chief executive officers, team presidents, general managers, and the head coach who straddles both the field or court and the administrative offices. The front office also includes non-sports professionals such as team doctors, lawyers, and accountants. At present, minorities account for less than five percent of these key management positions in professional sports.

On the playing field or court, it is a different story. In 1995 African-Americans constituted nearly eight out of every ten players in the National Basketball Association, sixty-eight percent of the players in the National Football League, and nineteen percent of the players in Major League Baseball.

Although it may be argued that the on-the-field percentages are an indicator of equality, equal achievement has not occurred in terms of success at the highest levels. Despite the statistics on the field, with less than five percent representation at the top levels, African-Americans remain woefully underrepresented in the front office.

For those athletes who do desire a career in management following their playing days—and not all do—the transition up the sports management business ladder occurs for some, but generally not for African-Americans. For example, it has happened for white players Pete Rose, Larry Bowa, and Lou Piniella, who became managers in baseball shortly after retiring from playing the game. The day that Kansas City Royals star George Brett announced his retirement in 1993, he also announced that the following year he would become the Royals' Vice President for baseball operations. Rarely are such promotions included in retirement ceremonies featuring African-American athletes.

The concept of African-Americans lacking merit to manage is quickly and easily disproved at all levels in sports by comparing the qualifications of those who hold or have held the power positions with those African-Americans seeking to make the move to the management side of the table. In Major League Baseball, while Rose, Piniella, and Bowa are just a few examples of whites who went straight from the playing field to managing, Don Baylor and Dusty Baker are representative of African-Americans who have arguably been even more successful in making that same transition. But the time that it takes for African-Americans to obtain such positions is far greater. Dan Duquette, Kevin Malone, Bill Bavasi, Jim Bowden, Ed Lynch, and Randy Smith are examples of the young white men, some just barely in their thirties, occupying baseball general manager positions in the early 1990s. Where are the young African-Americans, both with and without playing experience, in these positions of power?

David Shula, the youthful Cincinnati Bengals head coach, is an example of a fast-tracker in the National Football League. Shula is an excellent illustration of racial advantage. His father, Don Shula, has been a head coach in the NFL for over three decades. No African-American has benefitted from a similar connection. David Shula offers in his merit package a long-term understanding of the NFL that only someone with similar long-term family connections could possess. Therefore, when African-American candidates are compared to him, none measure up. Shula is exceptional among all coaches, but the Shula relationship to a position of power illustrates the type of relationship whites can define as merit in a former roommate, teammate, or friend.

Corporate America has been under pressure to attain equality in hiring since the civil rights movement and subsequent legislation in the 1960s and 1970s. Some companies responded after legal action; others responded voluntarily for moral reasons or as part of a public relations program. Even with years of this type of activity, however, one still will rarely find an African-American in a top position at a Fortune 500 corporation. Only 2.8 percent of top level managers in corporations are African-American. Although the percentages in sports management are similar, one should recall the higher percentages of African-Americans that have been long-term participants in the sports industry. The larger numbers of African-Americans prepared to move into management, relative to other industries, is significant.

Then why do the disparities in African-American representation still continue at the management level in sports? Racism—both institutionalized and unconscious—is certainly part of the answer. As Charles Lawrence has observed, racism persists in all of us. Lawrence writes:

> Americans share a common historical and cultural heritage in which racism has played and still plays a dominant role. Because of this shared experience, we also inevitably share many ideas, attitudes, and beliefs that attach significance to an individual's race and induce negative feelings and opinions about nonwhites. To the extent that this cultural belief system has influenced all of us, we are all racists. At the same time, most of us are unaware of our racism. We do not recognize the ways in which our cultural experience has influenced our beliefs about race or the occasions on which those beliefs affect our actions. In other words, a large part of the behavior that produces racial discrimination is influenced by unconscious racial motivation.

A product of this unconscious racial motivation, in sports as well as in the rest of America, is the informal or "ol' boy" networks that have traditionally excluded minorities. In sports, as has been noted, being part of the network is an indicator of merit. According to Hall of Fame football coach Bill Walsh, coaching positions in football are "[a] very fraternal thing. You end up calling friends, and the typical coach hasn't been exposed to many black coaches."

There is nothing unique about Walsh's view. In the non-sports industry these networks are the reality as well. Jason Wright, an African-American vice president at RJR Nabisco, Inc., said about the business world, "The reality of life in America is that if you're white, most of the people you know are white. If someone says to you, 'Do you know anyone for this job?' the people you recommend will probably be white." The tendency to create candidate pools through this networking method often leaves blacks out of the running for positions.

Informal social and managerial networks have long been an institutionalized part of both sports and other business settings. These networks combined with the absence of anti-discrimination laws have historically worked to ensure the dominance of the white majority. The continued existence of these networks, even with the existence of stronger antidiscrimination laws, provides a justification for affirmative action.

II. Affirmative Action as a Solution?

A. Breaking Down Barriers to Networks

The ol' boy networking cycle is hard to break. It will take affirmative steps to bring greater diversity into the sports hiring networks, and systems aimed at breaking down this key barrier are not easily implemented. Even top level management has difficulty building diversity, especially on the field. The qualifications used to select personnel, particularly for on-the-field jobs, can be extremely subjective. The comfort level a hiring party has with another may also include race. These powerful institutional and structural barriers to entry support the need for affirmative action. Affirmative action ensures that 'qualified' minorities are included in any given contracting situation. Justice Harry Blackmun's dissent in *Regents of the University of California v. Bakke* is often cited in support of employing this brand of race consciousness to combat racism. In Blackmun's opinion, "In order to get beyond racism, we must first take account of race. There is no other way. And in order to treat some persons equally, we must treat them differently."

Strategies that "take account of race" may hold the key where underrepresentation exists. Implementation of such strategies, however, has become difficult. The most formidable barriers to such programs are arguments that selections of this sort should be based solely on merit-and racism persists when the determination of what constitutes merit is subjective.

B. The Conundrum of Anti-Discrimination Law

Competing tensions in anti-discrimination law create a conundrum that will not easily be solved. Unquestionably this issue is not limited to the sports industry. Any form of affirmative action, even with regard to broadening networks alone, may be viewed as reverse discrimination and a violation of the law. On the other hand, racial preferences designed to remedy the effects of past discrimination, even societal discrimination, may be benign and legal. The sports industry, like most industries, faces the pressure from both sides.

The Supreme Court has cautioned that racial preferences must be employed with great caution. In *Wygant v. Jackson Board of Education*, Justice White wrote, "Any preference based on racial or ethnic criteria must necessarily receive a most searching examination to make sure that it does not conflict with constitutional guarantees." Justice John Paul Stevens observed earlier that, "[r]acial classifications are simply too pernicious to permit any but the most exact connection between justification and classification."

The law embraces two goals in any effort to bring about change in an industry troubled by discrimination. The first goal is to prohibit racial discrimination; the second is to improve the economic condition of the underrepresented group. Absent an act that approaches malicious discrimination, the law can do little to force sports leadership to change. The law allows for remedial steps when specific individual discrimination can be identified. The emphasis of anti-discrimination law is on specific events of discrimination in that particular industry, not discrimination that occurs in society at large.

C. The Appropriate Affirmative Action Approach

At least four forms of affirmative action have been identified: the concerted effort to recruit members of the underrepresented group; the utilization of programs such as diversity and sensitivity training; the modification of employment practices which tend to underutilize underrepresented individuals; and-the most controversial conception of affirmative action-the preferential hiring and promotion of members of underrepresented groups. The last, and most extreme, version is not necessary in sports, at least if racism is not, in fact, the universal barrier to African-American hiring. What is needed are strategies that open up the hiring networks, and encourage the recognition that merit can be measured in a manner that does not include long-term membership in traditional networking groups.

Absent specific identifiable acts of discrimination, very little can be done legally to force the owners to change their hiring practices. However, a commissioner or an individual team owner can assume a strong leadership role in promoting voluntary affirmative action. Increasing the numbers of minorities in management and coaching positions in sports could be the flagship item on a league commissioner's or team owner's agenda. The presentation of a meaningful plan for change, one incorporating strong affirmative action principles, could be a part of such an agenda.

Any commissioner-initiated plan would both signal that a league was serious about reform and provide a roadmap for those owners interested in bringing about change and promoting diversity in league and franchise management areas. Any such plan would have to pass legal scrutiny before race could be factored into the bundle of qualifications.

As has been noted, affirmative action in sports is unique in that no valid meritorious basis supports the presumption of the African-American being less qualified than a white candidate. The only missing element in the resume of African-Americans in the industry is long-term membership in networks with the power-wielding parties in the industry. Affirmative action in sports should be concerned with access for those who do not normally have access to these hiring networks. This is not a question of lack of merit but rather a lack of opportunity. More importantly, it is these forms of affirmative action which will increase the comfort and knowledge level of decisionmakers regarding truly meritorious African-American candidates. This type of effort presumes racism is not the sole reason for the numerical shortfall.

The implementation of any type of affirmative action program will meet resistance. Those who implement such programs will have to find ways to counter pervasive charges of reverse racism, paternalism and the presumption of necessity.

(1) Countering "Reverse Racism"

The conscientious managers of sports enterprises must be concerned with moving cautiously in establishing any affirmative action program. The nature of the law is that it is illegal to discriminate against any race. Accordingly, the argument that affirmative action programs are in fact a form of discrimination, or reverse discrimination, is not lost on either its supporters or its critics. The anti-discrimination laws are generally intended and interpreted to disallow discrimination against any race. This creates the obvious problem of devising ways to help one race without harming another. Hence, the use of terms such as 'reverse discrimination' and 'reverse racism' in response to affirmative action plans is not constructed within the guidelines of the law.

While cautiously putting guidelines in place, the management public relations focus should be on the broadening of the traditional recruitment networks. It is important from both a legal and business standpoint to convey that there is no exception being made in the quality of person being hired.

(2) Countering Paternalism

Another major criticism of affirmative action is that it is paternalistic and places a stamp of approval on the concept that African-Americans are inferior and need help to succeed. The view by some commentators is that this image is too dear a price to pay, even if a few African-Americans do benefit from affirmative action programs. A further argument is that the programs create a "presumption" that any black that succeeds does so at the expense of a more qualified white, and, were it not for the program, the African-American would not succeed. T. Alexander Aleinikoff provides an example from the University of Michigan Law School student newspaper. He cites an article where a white student calls for the abolition of a program at the school which provides academic and non-academic support to non-white students. The white student wrote that the program "[i]mplicitly brands every minority student with a scarlet 'D.' I can't believe so many bright people allow themselves to be insulted and stigmatized in such an obnoxious way * * * ." Broadening his attack to reach affirmative action programs in general, he stated, "I see stirrings of resentment everywhere. If a black student makes a silly classroom comment (and we all do), some white students—not racists, mind you—will think in their heart of hearts about affirmative admissions policies."

The truth is that whether or not formal programs are in place, the qualifications of African-Americans will continue to be questioned. It is the nature of the racism and discrimination that have been present in this country since its earliest days. It is a permanent part of our American culture. This perception of paternalism will not easily be overcome. The public relations focus here should be on the historic absence of African-Americans in upper management, and the need for corrective measures in the industry to counteract those historic deficiencies.

(3) Countering the Presumption of Necessity

Maybe the most compelling argument against the use of network broadening affirmative action programs comes from African-Americans who participate in them. "This has now become a prerequisite for brothers to get an NFL job," one African-American college coach said regarding an NFL coaching internship program. "White guys less qualified don't have to do this—but they're ready [to do the job] * * * I'm not unless I do."

It is unfortunate that society is not yet at the point that broad-based networking comes naturally. Following the infamous statements by former Los Angeles Dodgers executive Al Campanis that blacks lacked the "necessities," to manage in Major League Baseball, Hall of Famer Reggie Jackson wrote "[b]ecause of the unfortunate things Mr. Campanis said, the time has come to break down the wall between whites and blacks. The time has come to say we have a problem and to address it. Together." Jackson's point is that the sacrifice necessary to close the networking gaps must be made by African-Americans as well as whites. The best counter to the necessity presumption is the argument that effective affirmative action may be as much in the interests of whites as blacks.

III. CONCLUSION: SELLING AFFIRMATIVE ACTION TO THE SPORTS INDUSTRY AND PUBLIC

Affirmative action is still necessary because appropriate standards of merit have not yet become the sole determinant in society of who gets a particular job. The definition of merit seemingly continues to incorporate participation in key networks as a component. This is particularly the case in the business of sports where institutionalized and unconscious racism persists.

For affirmative action to be successful, there must be evidence to all that such programs are for the good of all involved. A good example of this is the "cut-out curbs" in our cities today that were put in place to improve wheelchair accessibility. Society overall has benefitted from these curbs because of easier access not only for wheelchairs, but for bicycles, strollers, and by foot. In the area of sports it is difficult to articulate what this overall societal benefit would be. Certainly the value of society's microcosm successfully tackling the diversity issue is, in an abstract sense, compelling. If increased diversity did occur, the sports industry could be pointed to as the model for equal opportunity and diversity at all employment levels. The sense of diversity as an overriding positive principle has not been enough for all people in other segments of society. The convincing argument by those in the power positions in sports must be that diversity is good for the sport; there has been much racism in the past and the strong medicine of corrective change is necessary.

Notes and Questions

1. Professor Shropshire identifies the problem as something far more than just aversive or unconscious racism. He claims that among "today's 'angry white male[s]'", there is also a fear that blacks will occupy the territory formerly "owned" by Caucasian men. Do you agree?

2. What precisely is the "ol' boys network"? Is it more than just a network of friendship and collegiality? Is it discriminatory—either in intent or effect? Are affirmative action programs needed to counter it?

3. Note that the hiring criteria for sports executive positions are not only highly subjective, they are also quite mutable. In Major League Baseball, for example, the current trend in measuring general manager candidates is to compare them to Oakland's Billy Beane, the master of cost efficiency. "I think we're in a cycle right now," says Phillies Assistant GM Mike Arbuckle, "where the prototype is a young, high-powered graduate who went to an Ivy League school." Thus the Dodgers filled their GM vacancy with Paul DePodesta, a thirty-one year old Harvard graduate and Beane disciple; the Red Sox hired twenty-eight year-old Theo Epstein, a Yale graduate with a law degree (from the University of San Diego). "I don't know if it's right, wrong, or whatever," says the fifty-three year-old Arbuckle, a baseball lifer. "But I don't fit that profile. I'm more a through-the-ranks baseball guy. But I know these things run in cycles and there will be a shift." Paul Hagen, *Jilt by Association: He's No Beane Brain*, Phila. Daily News, Feb. 20, 2004.

4. Professor Shropshire has developed a program that requires a great deal of initiative at the league level. Is his reliance upon the commissioner's office too optimistic given the earlier assumption that the commissioners are agents of the club owners and, in some instances, are former club owners themselves? Baseball Commissioner Bud Selig has announced that he wants clubs to "show him that they are serious." The NFL, NBA, and Major League Baseball all have implemented programs that are best described as voluntary affirmative action. Are there plausible explanations for baseball's disproportionately low figures in the general manager category? Is there a correlation between this figure and the percentage of African-American Major League players? Doubtless, the ascendancy of African Americans to ownership positions and top executive levels will or should result in greater sensitivity to minority hiring at upper ends of the management hierarchy.

Despite having no set policy, the NBA has become the sports leader in management diversity, with women constituting 49% of the middle- to upper-management staff of its league office and blacks and Latinos about 22%. In the absence of a specific policy, much of this success can be attributed to a determined effort on the part of Commissioner David Stern to lobby league owners on the verge of filling important front office positions.

The NFL created an equal employment department which instituted one of the most creative diversity programs in professional sports—a minority coaching fellowship.

Each summer, minority college coaches were invited to work with NFL coaching staffs during training camp. As of 1995, seventeen graduates of that program had become NFL assistant coaches. More recently, NFL minority coaches and executives have established the Fritz Pollard Alliance (named for the first black NFL coach), a group designed to ensure a greater sensitivity to the need for diversity in professional football. Former Hall of Fame tight-end Kellen Winslow will chair the group, which will be represented by attorneys Cyrus Merhi and Johnnie Cochran, Jr. *Formal Group To "Level The Playing Field,"* ESPN Online (March 12, 2003), http://espn.go.com/nfl/news/2003/0312/1522454.html. Obviously, a key to the success of this program will be the extent to which these assistants leap the heretofore high hurdle to head coaching jobs.

Major League Baseball contracted with the law firm of Alexander & Associates, Inc., after Dodger Executive Al Campanis declared on national television that blacks lacked the necessities to hold managerial positions. The law firm was retained to survey and impose sanctions on teams that do not make the requisite attempts to achieve diversity. As of 1995, no fines had been assessed and the results of its findings are kept confidential. Bill Plaschke, *Campanis Embarrassment: A Call to Sports Diversity Management,* L.A. TIMES, July 23, 1995.

5. Former Major Leaguer and general manager Bob Watson, a finalist for the California Angels' general managerial position, noted that one of the difficulties confronting minority candidates for upper echelon executive positions is that "we still don't sit in the same steam room with the owners." This comment highlights the importance of black-white social interaction in terms of influencing progress up the business ladder for African Americans and other disadvantaged groups. Ross Newhan, *Clubs Balking At Hiring Minority General Managers,* LOS ANGELES TIMES, November 19, 1999.

Former Kansas City Royals field manager Hal McRae, commenting on his candidacy for two managerial jobs, offers a rather sanguine view of opportunities for African Americans, at least at the lower echelon managerial level:

> All you can ask for is a thorough and honest process, and I feel that I got two fair shots. I'm happy. I got to home plate, and that's a lot farther than a lot of guys got. I also think the minority environment is a lot more positive than it has been and that things are moving in the right direction. It's a slow drip, but the spigot is open.

Newhan, *supra.* McRae's positive experience and outlook are by no means universally shared. Many black managerial candidates refuse to discuss the issue. Hall of Famers Joe Morgan and Ozzie Smith express their frustration in similar fashion. Says Morgan, "[E]very time I talk about it, I get frustrated * * * I don't want to go on the air mad." Smith iterates, "There's no sense talking about it, because nothing's happened * * *. There's been a lot of talk, but nobody has done anything. We haven't gotten the response that's needed. They just continue to recycle, recycle, recycle, and are getting the same results." Rubin E. Grant, *Minority Hiring: Good Ol' Boys Still Call Shots,* SCRIPPS HOWARD NEW SERVICE, Oct. 26, 1999.

6. One commentator posed the issue as one of establishment "fear":

> One has to wonder what exactly scares baseball so much about having a non-white manager in the dugout * * *. All questions about whether blacks and Latinos are talented enough, smart enough and tough enough to survive and thrive in baseball (or any other walk of life) have pretty much been answered. There's no reason to waste breath or space trying to explain why the Billy Williams and Willie Randolphs, for example, deserve the same opportunities

to succeed or fail as Joe Torre (on his fourth job), Bobby Cox (his third) or Bobby Valentine or Jimmy Williams (their second).

David Steele, *No Race to Hire Minorities,* SAN FRANCISCO CHRONICLE, Oct. 21, 1999.

7. What are the ingredients that should comprise the general manager's credentials list? Is it more important that he know baseball or the business end of baseball? If emphasis were placed on one's status as a former player, would that help or hinder African American chances for front office managerial promotion?

8. Football, both at the professional and amateur level, has been equally inhospitable to black managerial candidates. Currently there are four black head football coaches among 115 major colleges. This 3.5 percentage is higher than the percentage of black head coaches at the Division I-AA, Division II and Division III levels. Incredibly, only 14 of 547 head football coaches are black, if historically black institutions are excluded from the mix. *See* Michael Marot, *Black Coaches Association Unhappy with Lack of Progress,* ASSOCIATED PRESS, Jan. 14, 2002. How do you explain these figures?

The problem affecting college coaches is being replicated among professional coaches. This result is hardly surprising since many teams will hire coaches directly from the college ranks. In August of 2002, the Black Coaches Association unveiled its "hiring report card," in an effort to help football recruits and their families keep track of the schools that are hiring black football coaches. Jeff Shain, *Group to Target Recruits: Black Coaches Association Wants Prospects to Consider School's Minority Hiring Record,* CHAR. OBSVR., Nov. 1, 2002, 1C.

In this regard, Kellen Winslow, former All-Pro tight end for the San Diego Chargers created no small amount of controversy when he placed considerable pressure on his heavily recruited son to attend Michigan State rather than the University of Washington because M.S.U. had a black head coach, Bobby Williams. The dispute caused a rift between Winslow and his offspring, culminating in Kellen, Jr.'s decision to attend the University of Miami. Ironically, the issue gave double meaning to the term "academic" as Williams was fired after a stormy season characterized by a 6-15 record in the Big Ten combined with off-the-field incidents involving alcohol and substance abuse among the players. Steve Wieberg, USA TODAY, http://www.usatoday.com/sports/college/football/bigten/2002-11-04-cover-michigan (2002). In the 2004 NFL draft, the younger Winslow was drafted in the first round by the Cleveland Browns.

Bill Walsh, highly respected and enormously successful former coach of the San Francisco 49ers, says that the "good old boy network is not a problem any longer." Is his guarded optimism misplaced? Walsh, who has consistently championed the cause of black coaches, declares:

> There are a bunch of young black assistants coming into the league who have head coaching potential * * *. It takes time, though, for an assistant to get the experience he needs to cope with all the aspects of a head coaching job.

He adds:

> There's always going to be some general managers who want to hire somebody they know, because they played with him or coached with him — and that may eventually work to the benefit of some black candidates as there are more and more black players — but mostly, teams just want to have a good coach.

Glenn Dickey, *Progress Slow For Black Coaches,* San Francisco Chronicle, Jan. 5, 2002.

9. Problems confronting African Americans in the college coaching profession are not limited to refusals to hire. Nolan Richardson, former head basketball coach at the University of Arkansas, sued the Arkansas Razorback Foundation and the University of Arkansas alleging that he was discriminatorily terminated. Interestingly, among his collateral claims is his allegation that the Foundation assigned him to speaking engagements in which no other black people were present. With regard to his termination allegations, Richardson, who headed the Arkansas basketball program for 17 seasons, claimed that he was fired almost immediately after he had publicly declared that the university had mistreated him because he was black. The court found that the coach had failed to demonstrate that a prima facie case of retaliation existed or that his race formed the basis for his termination. The case was dismissed. *See Richardson v. Sugg,* 325 F. Supp. 2d 919 (E.D. Ark. 2004), *aff'd* 448 F.3d 1046 (8th Cir. 2006). *See also* Linda Satter, *Richardson Details UA Bias Claim,* Arkansas Democrat-Gazette (Little Rock), March 19, 2004.

10. Whether due to the initiatives described above, greater black entrepreneurial involvement, or a more enlightened view by the lords of the sports realm, positive signs are certainly evident. Robert Johnson, founder of Black Entertainment Television (BET), recently purchased the NBA's expansion franchise in Charlotte for $300 million. Michael Jordan has also manifested a serious intention to assume ownership of an NBA franchise. Phil Taylor, *Franchise Player,* Sports Illustrated, May 5, 2003, 35–37. The following partial list is reflective of the progress that African Americans have made in professional sports:

> **Labor Leaders:** Gene Upshaw, Executive Director of the NFL Players' Association; Billy Hunter, Executive Director of the NBA Players' Association, Pamela Wheeler, Director of Operations for the NBA Players' Association

> **League Officials:** Jimmy Lee Solomon, Senior Vice President of Baseball Operations for Major League Baseball; Harold Henderson, Executive Vice President for Labor Relations and Chairman of the Management Council for the NFL; Stu Jackson, Senior Vice President of Basketball Operations for the NBA; Bob Watson, Vice President of Major League Baseball; Jonathan Mariner, CFO of Major League Baseball; Leah Wilcox, Vice President of Player and Talent Relations for NBA Entertainment; Gene Washington, Director of Football Operations for the NFL

> **Team Executives:** Ulice Payne, President of the Milwaukee Brewers (and first African American president of a major league team); Terdema Ussery, President and CEO of the Dallas Mavericks; Ozzie Newsome, Senior Vice President for Football Operations of the Baltimore Ravens; Joe Dumars, President of Basketball Operations for the Detroit Pistons; Billy King, General Manager of the Philadelphia '76ers; Kim Ng, Vice President and Assistant General Manager for the Los Angeles Dodgers; Rod Graves, Vice President of Football Operations for the Arizona Cardinals; James Harris, Vice President of Player Personnel for the Jacksonville Jaguars; Wayne Cooper, Vice President of Basketball Operations for the Sacramento Kings; Hank Aaron, Senior Vice President of the Atlanta Braves; Kenny Williams, General Manager of the Chicago White Sox; Ed Tapscott, Executive Vice President and COO of a new NBA franchise in Charlotte.

Richard Deitsch, *New World Order,* Sports Illustrated, May 5, 2003, at 38–46. In addition to the foregoing, African Americans have assumed high level positions as athletic directors, media executives, and other managerial positions in sports-related contexts.

Moreover, other minorities and women have risen to prominent positions in the sports industry, including Arturo Mareno, owner of the Anaheim Angels and the first Latino owner of a Major League franchise, and Omar Minaya, General Manager of the Washington Nationals and the first Latino general manager in Major League Baseball.

11. Despite the apparent progress, executives and head coaches in the four major men's professional leagues remain overwhelmingly white. At the end of the 2002 season (or 2001–2002 season), 21 of the 28 MLB managers were white (74%); so too were 15 of the 29 NBA head coaches (52%); 30 of the 32 NFL head coaches (94%); and all 30 NHL head coaches (100%). Among General Managers or Directors of Player Personnel, 94% in Major League Baseball were white, and so too were 83% in the NBA, 94% in the NFL, and 100% in the NHL. As for Club Presidents or Board Chairs, 100% in MLB were white, and so too were 96% in the NBA, 97% in the NFL, and 100% in the NHL. Richard E. Lapchick, 2003 Racial and Gender Report Card 22–25, 33–35 (2003). By way of reference, the Census Bureau estimates that 77.7% of the American population at this time was white.

12. At times the most well-intentioned program can suffer somewhat in the execution. In the early part of 2003, the Detroit Lions were fined $200,000 by the NFL for failing to interview minority candidates for a head coaching position. Lions president Matt Millen hired former San Francisco 49ers head coach Steve Mariucci without interviewing viable black candidates. Millen had asked several black coaches to interview for the position, but each one declined. The declinations were due to the fact that the prospective applicants knew that Millen already had decided on former teammate Mariucci as his choice and, in fact, had fired the Lions existing head coach as soon as Mariucci was "available." The other black candidates were aware of the uniqueness of the situation and offered support for Millen. Black coach Sherman Lewis, who felt that Millen was being unfairly harassed, declared, "Here, Matt knew who he wanted. We have no problem with that." *See* Jon Saraceno, *Keeping Score: In Spite of NFL Fine, Color Millen Honest,* USA Today, July 28, 2003, 7C. Are Millen and the Detroit Lions paying for the sins of others or is a zero-tolerance policy necessary to insure that diversity will be respected as an important goal of professional sports leagues?

In that same off-season, the San Francisco 49ers hired Dennis Erickson (who is white) as their head coach, preferring him over Jets defensive coordinator Ted Cottrell (who is black) because Erickson had head coaching experience: he amassed a 31-33 record as coach of the Seahawks in the late 90s. It was the seventh time that Cottrell had interviewed for a head coaching job, and his seventh rejection. "[W]hat it came down to was pretty simple." reports a team official. "Dennis had won as a head coach. No knock on Ted, but you always wonder: Can he make the jump?" Peter King, *Niners Believe Erickson Will Be Better Second Time Around, available at* http://sportsillustrated .cnn.com/inside_game/peter_king/news/2003/02/11/niners_erickson/.

13. In many respects the problem of black underrepresentation in managerial positions may be linked directly to the absence of meaningful entrepreneurial involvement by minorities. Although there are some examples of African-American team ownership interests, this phenomenon is quite rare. Again Professor Shropshire's visionary scholarship provides a useful polestar. *See* Kenneth L. Shropshire, *Diversity, Racism, and Professional Sports Franchise Ownership: Change Must Come From Within,* 67 U. Colo. L. Rev. 47 (1996). Yet, as discussed earlier in this chapter, even when African Americans have occupied controlling positions, there have been instances of discrimination. As alluded to earlier, there are numerous circumstances in which African-American owners have been very reluctant to hire minorities in various front office capacities. In the formative days of the Negro Leagues, this problem was particularly acute. This practice of overlooking

or deliberately demeaning qualified African-American candidates infuriated many commentators, as illustrated by this reprinted editorial in the Philadelphia Tribune:

> It is a reflection on the ability and intelligence of colored people. *Are we still slaves?* Is it possible that colored players are so dumb that they will resent one of their own race umpiring the game? Or is it that the management of Hilldale is so *steeped in racial inferiority that it has no faith in Negroes?* Aside from the economic unfairness of such a position the employment of white umpires at Negro games brands Negroes as inferior. It tells white people in a forceful manner that colored people are unable to even play a ball game without white leadership. It is a detestable, mean attitude. There is no excuse for it.

MARK RIBOWSKY, A COMPLETE HISTORY OF THE NEGRO LEAGUES, 1884 TO 1955, at 135 (1995) (emphasis in original). *See also* Kenneth L. Shropshire, *Sports Agents, Role Models, and Race Consciousness,* 6 MARQ. SPORTS L. J. 267, 269–70 (1996). *See also* Lateef Mtima, *The Road to the Bench: Not Even Good (subliminal) Intentions,* 8 U. CHI. L. SCH. ROUNDTABLE 135, 142 (2001) ("'Since the white commercial community hardly ever used the services of black lawyers, the black lawyers never developed wealth or influence in the commercial community.' Indeed, even 'black clients often used black lawyers in almost hopeless criminal matters but turned to white lawyers in the more lucrative civil case.'" (citing J. CLAY SMITH, JR., EMANCIPATION: THE MAKING OF THE BLACK LAWYER 1844–1944 (Pennsylvania 1993) at 11 and 4).) "The bottom line is that for many blacks, not only are we concerned about discrimination by whites because of the color of our skin, sometimes we are also concerned about the discrimination we face by other blacks." Leonard Baynes, *If It's Not Just Black and White Anymore, Why Does Darkness Cast a Longer Discriminatory Shadow Than Lightness? An Investigation and Analysis of The Color Hierarchy,* 75 DENV. L. REV. 131 (1997). *See also* Clark Freshman, *Beyond Atomized Discrimination: Use of Acts of Discrimination Against "Other" Minorities to Prove Discriminatory Motivation Under Federal Employment Law,* 43 STAN. L. REV. 241 (1990); Leonard Baynes, *Book Review, Blinded By The Light; But Now I See,* 20 N. ENG. L. REV. 491 (1998); Richard Storrow, *Same-Sex Sexual Harassment Claims After* Oncale: *Defining the Boundaries of Actionable Conduct,* 47 AM. U. L. REV. 677 (1998); Deb Lussier, Oncale v. Sundowner Offshore Services Inc. *and The Future of Title VII Sexual Harassment Jurisprudence,* 39 B.C. L. REV. 937 (1998); Henry Chambers, *Discrimination, Plain And Simple,* 36 TULSA L.J. 557 (2001). This issue was frequently confronted in the early days of the Negro Leagues where black owners seemed reluctant to hire black umpires. As Robert Peterson observes in his history of the Negro Leagues:

> The league * * * had troubles with umpiring and player conduct. When the league began, it had no staff of umpires. The home club furnished the umpires—often white—and this led to charges of favoritism and lack of race pride. Even [Rube] Foster, who clearly hoped for and expected the advancement of Negroes in baseball and in the nation's life generally, hired white umpires for his games.

ROBERT PETERSON, ONLY THE BALL WAS WHITE 90 (1970).

14. Is black skepticism about black doctors or lawyers or agents a function of their own "black-bashing" prejudice, a reflection of fear that bigotry has precluded black professionals from getting the same quality training as white professionals, or presumptions that whites may have greater access to valuable resources or contacts? Has affirmative action alleviated such a problem or has it made the concerns more acute? One commentator has suggested that several reasons underscore the failure of black athletes

to retain the services of black agents, including the historical loyalty black athletes have for white agents, negative commentary of white agents, the abundant resources available to white agents, and the media's demeaning portrayal of black agents' sophistication and ability. *See* James G. Sammataro, *Business and Brotherhood: Can They Coincide? A Search Into Why Black Athletes Do Not Hire Black Agents,* 42 How. L.J. 535, 547–48 (1999); Kenneth L. Shropshire, *Sports Agents, Role Models, and Race Consciousness,* 6 MARQ. SPORTS L.J. 267 (1996). He adds, however, that other factors may play a part in the dearth of black agents representing black players, including internal dissension and hostile competition among black agents themselves, and internalized racial stereotypes about blacks by black athletes. As Charles Farrell, head of the Rainbow Coalition for Fairness in Athletics, laments: "'We still think that white doctors, white attorneys and white agents are somehow better because of the color of their skin.'" *Id.* at 551.

15. In any event, there are indications that today's minority executives do not intend to repeat the sins of the past in terms of bypassing other minorities. Robert Johnson, new owner of the NBA's Charlotte franchise, hired hundreds of minorities while serving as president of the Black Entertainment Television network. His executive vice-president is a fellow African American, Ed Tapscott. Further, Johnson has stated, "I'm going to create an experienced pool of people who work in sports—many of them black, many of them other minorities—for all those employers who say 'we'd love to hire you if you had more experience.'" He adds:

> My mission is to create a profitable franchise that the people of Charlotte can be excited about and proud of. One of the by-products of that will be that people will see something they've never seen before—a successful sports team owned by an African-American, with other African-Americans in major positions of authority. The message that sends is powerful, to both black and white people. If we can do that, everybody wins.

Taylor, *Franchise Player,* at 37.

C. Race and Athlete Exploitation

Leroy D. Clark,
New Directions for the Civil Rights Movement:
College Athletics as a Civil Rights Issue
36 How. L.J. 259 (1993).

* * *

III. College Athletics-A Form of Exploitation of Minority (And Other) Youth?

College athletics present civil rights organizations with a new frontier, and one in which healthy reform could be achieved, albeit against great odds. Because over fifty percent of the college football players and over seventy percent of the college basketball players are black, it is appropriate for a civil rights organization to seize the initiative in addressing the problems in college sports. For many years, college athletics has been replete with corruption if one uses only the standards of the Amateur Athletic Associations and has, arguably, promoted the disparagement and exploitation of minority youth.

A brief background on the structure and operation of collegiate sports is in order. The National Collegiate Athletic Association (NCAA) is a voluntary association that sets standards for and monitors the athletic programs of over 1,000 member colleges and universities. The NCAA has divided its member colleges into divisions for purposes of defining which schools will compete against one another. This article focuses primarily on Division I and Division IA (consisting of over ninety schools) that have made a major commitment in terms of facilities, resources, and personnel to basketball and football. This focus is adopted for two reasons. First, in these two sports the NCAA has a virtual monopoly, working through the colleges and universities, over the pool from which the professional teams choose their new entrants. Second, the average young athlete probably needs further physical maturation and refining of his skills in a team setting in these two sports, before attempting to enter the professional ranks.

The monopoly by the colleges of pre-professional sports talent is reinforced by the practices of the professional basketball and football leagues. The National Football League (NFL) and the National Basketball Association (NBA) bar the formal drafting of athletes, until they have exhausted their NCAA eligibility. The NCAA, in turn, ends a student's eligibility to play for his college, if he accepts any compensation from a sports agent or enters into a contract for the prospective receipt of pay. While there are minor professional leagues in basketball (e.g., the Continental league) and in football, as well as some limited opportunity for professional work abroad, none of these options have maintained the fan interest which the colleges have garnered. The student-athlete with professional potential is well-advised to take advantage of the visibility that the NCAA multi-million dollar television and cable contracts provide, because the visibility increases his chances of acceptance by the professional leagues and influences the level of salary he can demand.

The NCAA has two functions which impinge directly on the student-athlete recruited to play football or basketball. The Association is supposed to insure the integration of the student-athlete into the college's academic program and to insure that the student remains an "amateur"; that is, that the student receives no real wages for his athletic labors. The major problem that the NCAA faces in achieving these goals is that when colleges run what is, in effect, a large-scale commercial enterprise with full-time "employees" (the football and basketball players), they often find it grossly incompatible with their primary mission of providing a bona fide high-quality education for those "employees" who are also required to be full-time students.

The problem is further complicated by the fact that successful football and basketball teams directly, or indirectly, generate significant financial rewards for the NCAA and for the Division I and I-A schools. Given the potential for substantial financial gain and the enthusiasm of alumni for successful teams, there is enormous pressure on the colleges and alumni to covertly pay the star high school athletes to secure their attendance at a given university. Colleges are also pressured to admit stellar athletes who do not meet the normal academic standards, and then to devise an undemanding curriculum or, worse yet, to doctor academic records in order to maintain the student's eligibility to play.

The articles, reports, and books documenting these scandals in academe are legion and have been published over many years. One would imagine that institutions normally committed to lofty ideals and to the nurturing and protection of our youth would be very sensitive to these repeated charges, and that such institutions would, therefore, support and institute radical reform. However, only minor changes have been adopted, and the NCAA, the institution devoted to policing college athletics, has been ineffective in eradicating the practices which violate amateur athletic standards.

Naturally, one questions how repeatedly criticized college athletics programs can continue to function in the same mode without change? The answer is two-fold. First, the covert illegal arrangements with top athletes is a "crime," and our experience in every area of human activity, where all the participants are willing cooperators, confirms that it is nearly impossible to suppress such voluntary behavior. Secondly, and more importantly, even if one of the ostensibly "willing" participants is ultimately being injured or exploited, when all of the other major participants are satisfied and making huge profits, the activity will continue because the only real victim is weak and unorganized.

All of the youth, black or white, who participate in the major college athletics of football and basketball are the real victims. They are being exploited, or they are not receiving appropriate recompense for providing entertainment for the public. These young athletes have often spent endless hours honing their skills before coming to college. And while in college, they may spend the equivalent of a thirty hour week in practice sessions, traveling, and playing games. In return, the average student-athlete receives only a scholarship and room and board. First, while many student-athletes serve the school for the full period of their athletic eligibility, the majority of student-athletes in the revenue-producing sports of football and basketball never graduate; thus, their graduation rates are significantly below that of non-athletes. Secondly, even those who manage to graduate may not have a marketable degree, if they had a pablum education.

The diminished returns which accrue to the student-athlete as contrasted with the profits of other actors in the system are discouraging. The athletic program may reap millions of dollars in prize money, if a basketball championship is won or if the football team secures an invitation to a major bowl. Television networks make millions of dollars from advertisers when they televise major college sports events. Consequently, the professional football and basketball leagues receive reams of publicity for the athletes they ultimately draft.

Head coaches at public universities sometimes have been known to receive a higher salary than the governor of the state, and these salaries are sometimes fattened by endorsement contracts with manufacturers of athletic equipment. Everyone who works in conjunction with college athletics, including the NCAA officials, receives a full-time salary; that is, everyone except the student-athlete who actually provides the live performance that the spectator public is paying to view. Only the student-athlete is supposed to operate gratis-for school honor and glory.

The alumni and the fans of college teams provide an important element of the college athletic system. Alumni with extreme pride in their alma mater have often been the conduit for illegal support of the student-athlete. Alumni may also greatly increase their contributions to the college or university that has a winning sports team. Thus, the presidents of the colleges and universities might face withdrawal of alumni support if they were to institute policies which tended to hamper a sports team's success.

A college team may draw even more support than that provided by its alumni, because the populace of some towns or entire states may come to identify closely with the team. College sports may provide an important form of entertainment in an area. College officials may be well aware of the reliance of local residents on the team, and they know that they receive general public approval and support. This may be particularly important to the presidents of state universities that require political support.

The total effect is that practically everyone is reaping enormous financial benefits from college sports except the student-athlete who has no organizational backing devoted exclusively to confronting and reorganizing the system for his benefit. Elsewhere in this article, the exploited college athlete is compared to the vulnerable drug addict and the street prostitute. Note that blacks, in relation to their percentage of the population, occupy a disproportionate portion of all three groups. In my estimation, society becomes sluggish and inefficient in problem-solving when, at some subliminal level, the white American public perceives or defines a problem as primarily "black." If this speculation has any merit, then some civil rights organization may appropriately enter the fray and begin to struggle, on behalf of a group of talented black youth, for a more equitable distribution of the financial gain that flows through amateur sports. Organizational backing is necessary, for the vested interests in, and emotional commitment to, the status quo of many individuals and institutions is strong and must be challenged. Athletes should be organized to assert new and radical, yet equitable, demands to protect their collective interests.

IV. Legal Tactics for Confronting the Exploitation of Minority Youth: The Need for a Civil Rights Organization

What could civil rights organizations do on behalf of youth who have the physical gifts to engage in college athletics? They could bring some of the same strengths to this problem that were brought to bear in attacking and breaking down all forms of racial segregation and discrimination—namely, educating the public, organizing the athletes, gathering white allies, and litigating to expose the unjust arrangements. However, the process of educating the public should entail a close examination of the entire inter-collegiate sport system. Although the challenges of education may necessitate devising recommendations which collide with some of the more cherished myths about college athletics, civil rights organizations are uniquely positioned to argue to the public that the continuation of the status quo is an indirect form of racial discrimination and exploitation.

Civil rights organizations should confront those commentators who oppose the recent efforts of colleges and universities to assure that all entering students have the minimum preparation to adequately complete a normal course of study. These battles, which always receive intense media coverage, wound the images of young black males, that already suffer from public suspicion that they are violent, gangprone, irresponsible babymakers, whose prime activity is using or selling crack. These young men do not need the "dumb jock" appellation to intensify the already high public disdain and suspicion. The debate in recent years about "qualifications" and minorities may be the ploy of some with ulterior racist motivations, but it behooves the black community not to reject all standards which are reasonably related to sensible educational goals. Young athletes should not be admitted to a college where, even with remediation, they are likely to fail; it is a scandal and disgrace that illiterate athletes have been admitted to college.

Civil rights organizations should publicly demand a complete separation of sports teams and college attendance. Playing on a major college team is, in effect, a full-time semi-professional sports job. Players should be recruited and paid exclusively on the basis of their athletic ability and contribution to the team. One may quite possibly be a superb athlete, even though one lacks a formal education. The proposal would also end the charade and deception of feigning academic or attendance records at a college where there is no potential for earning a degree.

One must question whether this means that a number of black youth will opt for semi-professional status, never complete college, and never go on to become professional athletes. Only a very small fraction of the athletes leaving college will be absorbed into the ranks of the professionals. However, this proposal may allow some young athletes, who have the ability to enter professional sports, to do so without feeling the need to falsify attendance records. Additionally, these may likely be the young athletes who rely most heavily upon professional sports, because their other options are limited by poor academic capacity, poor preparation, or lack of interest. These are the young men who will likely be harmed by the current proposals to tighten academic requirements for collegiate athletes.

Moreover, these "quasi-collegiate" sports could retain much of the current structure, such as the four-year limitation on eligibility as a semi-professional. A key element in the proposal is that the semi-professional athlete would be adequately paid, so that he would have the funds saved to pay college expenses at the end of the four-year term. Naturally, the semi-professional athlete would be able to earn extra money through the endorsement of athletic equipment, and other products, a practice which is currently barred to student-athletes because they are forced into the "amateur mold." A semi-professional athlete who had completed his four years of eligibility would only be admitted to the college where he played if he met the same academic requirements of all other students who applied.

The proposal could mean that an athlete might attend a college other than the one for which he played, a college prepared to provide the kind of remediation needed to assist him toward successful completion. In practice, a number of black athletes might attend historically black colleges at the end of their athletic careers, since those colleges have experience in coping with students from disadvantaged backgrounds as well as with top scholars. Thus, black colleges may have a stake in backing the civil rights organizations that carry out such reform because they may be losing black students to the wasteful student-athlete process which now exists at predominantly white institutions.

The present arrangement has been a disaster for the black youth who are admitted to college under athletic scholarships. The vast majority of these youth do not succeed in professional sports, and their graduation rates are even lower than those of white student-athletes. They have been forced or steered into majors that accommodate their rigorous sports activity, but in fields which show declining opportunities for blacks. The proposal set forth herein would enhance the opportunity for successful completion of college, since the athlete would be studying without the distraction of a full-time sports job and without having to follow a course of study that does not enhance his opportunities for gainful employment in the future. Moreover, more attention to attendance at college will be generated because the athlete will know, definitively, that he has no prospect of playing professional sports; and, thus, he has more incentive to study vigorously, since college will be his only means of preparation for a vocation or profession other than sports. The proposal simply recognizes what many law schools already practice when they try to discourage first-year law students from holding jobs or when they close their night classes: it is extremely difficult to adequately perform two full-time jobs simultaneously.

* * *

The only thing unique about this proposal is the suggestion that civil rights organizations seek the reform. Well-meaning individuals have been suggesting reforms of college athletics for many years, but to no avail. Organizational muscle is needed to challenge the complex institutions and arrangements that sustain the current exploitative structure.

The ultimate goal of civil rights organizations would be to form a player's union to negotiate team contracts for all of the players at major colleges. For political, moral, and legal reasons, the organization would seek to represent all of the players, regardless of their race or ethnic background.

* * *

Another legal challenge that civil rights organization could mount against the current structure of college athletics would be to bring suits against colleges—alleging that the student-athletes were "employees" within the meaning of the Fair Labor Standards Act (FLSA), and that the colleges have violated the minimum wage provisions of that statute.

* * *

Civil rights organizations could also file more "educational malpractice" suits against educational institutions for failing to perform the implied contract to provide an educational opportunity for the student-athletes. Generally, these suits have been unsuccessful, because the courts have been reluctant to enter into a management role over the educational enterprise. Strong arguments exist, however, that those cases have not thoroughly analyzed the problem.

* * *

The civil rights organizations that undertake this effort would have to reeducate the public away from the current view that there is something noble and romantic in young athletes working in sports for their colleges without pay. Although an occasional commentator will attack the legitimacy of the strict rules barring any compensation for athletes, much of the writing on this topic is replete with statements concerning the so-called "corruptive" influence in paying athletes for their talents and performances. It is often not made clear that it is not the payment which is corrupting, but the fact that it is done surreptitiously. This is especially true in the many cases where the student-athletes are from poor families in dire need of financial assistance. The problem should be attacked by civil rights organizations, because the current system involves black youths who, unlike some of their peers, have not opted for criminal activity out of despair and as a means of survival. However, the college athletic environment forces these young athletes into the corrosive self-abuse of lying and functioning in a sleazy, underhanded manner. These young men are a product of an oppressive and a deprived environment, and they deserve to have their talents protected and rewarded. The answer, therefore, is to legitimize and to make adequate their payment, since they are the most important part of a multimillion dollar commercial enterprise.

* * *

Notes and Questions

1. Professor Clark's article offers an innovative solution to the problem presented by the exploitation of young African-American athletes. He suggests that civil rights organizations should actively pursue avenues to eliminate athlete exploitation much the same as those organizations fought to remove segregation and discrimination in other contexts. Specifically, he espouses making the public aware of the problem, amalgamating the athletes themselves into some form of cohesive structure, endorsing the support of whites, and sponsoring litigation to attack the conditions plaguing the victims. Among the targets would be those commentators who favor special treatment for young African-American athletes and who implicitly or explicitly oppose regulations directed toward insuring that students are students first and athletes second. He believes that

African-American youth who proceed through college on athletic scholarships, under the mistaken belief that lucrative professional sports await them with open arms, are victims of the worst type of seduction and abandonment.

The upshot of Professor Clark's approach is that students should be educated and athletes should be paid. For that reason, he favors payment to student-athletes, with the funding coming from professional sports leagues who, to date, have skimmed the profits (college talent) from a no-expense minor league (big-time intercollegiate sports). He concludes:

> Today many youths from poor families, who have worked hard to develop their talents, are being treated like indentured servants; they receive the equivalent of room and board, while working on a full-time basis to the financial benefit of everyone else but themselves. Civil rights organizations, who should be responding to new forms of exploitation of blacks, particularly of black youth, have the experience and techniques for dramatizing and ending the exploitation.

Leroy D. Clark, *New Directions for the Civil Rights Movement: College Athletics as a Civil Rights Issue*, 36 How. L.J. 259, 289 (1993). *See also* Raymond L. Yasser, *Are Scholarship Athletes at Big-Time Programs Really University Employees?—You Bet They Are*, 9 Black L.J. 65 (1984).

2. The foregoing proposal is no doubt a radical step. Professor Clark is suggesting that sports programs at the university level be divorced from the university as a whole and, in effect, have a semi-professional affiliation. If that be the case, why would the athlete have a four-year eligibility curve presupposed in Professor Clark's piece? In all likelihood, preserving the four-year eligibility will maintain the current structure as much as possible in terms of the ages and development of the athletes participating. That is, the semi-pro teams will consist of athletes who are in the same general category as current college players. The added question is whether full-time students would be precluded from participating in their college's semi-pro team. Nothing in Professor Clark's article discounts that possibility, but the clear implication is that most students would be discouraged from such involvement.

3. Professor Clark's article presents a plethora of additional problems that may give colleges and universities pause in pursuing his semi-professional team model. The notion of an employer-employee relationship between athletes and university, which may already exist at some levels, would become a reality, replete with concerns about unionization, workers and unemployment compensation, compliance with federal and state legislation, contractual responsibility, etc. *See* Michael J. Cozzillio, *The Athletic Scholarship and the College National Letter of Intent: A Contract By Any Other Name*, 35 Wayne L. Rev. 1275, 1299 n. 95 (1989).

4. In any event, Professor Clark's novel concept has become something of a reality. Last year, Brigham Young University purchased an amateur soccer league franchise-affiliated with a league operating beyond the NCAA's control. The school would participate in a league, The Premier Development League, consisting of approximately 50 teams (whose competitive status would be similar to the level of a Class A minor league baseball team). BYU officials acknowledged that the $40,000 franchise fee (funded largely by donors) was considerably less than the $500,000 that would have been needed to field a competitive varsity soccer team.

Critics have suggested that this approach is problematic in several ways. First, it compromises the academic mission because participation in such "for-profit" endeavors connotes a semi-professional venture even though the players themselves might not be paid. Second, it has been perceived as a stratagem to circumvent Title IX because theoretically no new men's team has been added. Therefore, there would be no need to add an equivalent women's team.

In terms of profitability, it is anticipated that the team will turn a profit from an operating budget that could run as high as $150,000. While this venture is not a replica of the prototype proposed by Professor Clark, it certainly represents a step in that direction. See Jere Longman, *Soccer; College Team Finds Novel Alternative to NCAA*, N.Y. Times, March 7, 2003, at A1.

5. This problem has also been addressed in detail by Professor Timothy Davis. Professor Davis argues that racism exists in college athletics but that the bias is subtle and not conducive to ready identification. Nonetheless, he posits that the "racism persisting in the modern inter-collegiate athletic enterprise, though more illusive, continues to inflict educational, social, economic and psychological damage on African-American participants." Timothy Davis, *The Myth of the Superspade: The Persistence of Racism in College Athletics*, 22 Fordham Urban L.J. 615, 622–623 (1995). Professor Davis suggests that the remedy for the victimization of African-American student-athletes lies in contract law. While skeptical about the utility of §1981 (the Civil Rights Act of 1866, 42 U.S.C. §1981) due to the difficulty of establishing the requisite intent, he urges persuasively that common law contract principles, such as the "duty to serve" and "good faith," are useful anti-discrimination norms and viable predicates for contract actions against a university. *Id.* at 686 *et seq.*

Cureton v. National Collegiate Athletic Association
37 F. Supp. 2d 687 (E.D. Pa. 1999)

Buckwalter, District Judge. This is a putative class action lawsuit brought by four African-American student-athletes (Tai Kwan Cureton, Leatrice Shaw, Andrea Gardner, and Alexander Wesby), alleging that they were unlawfully denied educational opportunities as freshmen through the operation of initial eligibility rules by the NCAA. Specifically, they claim that these rules ("Proposition 16") utilize a minimum test score requirement that has an unjustified disparate impact on African-American student-athletes.

All four named plaintiffs failed to achieve initial eligibility under these rules because they did not meet the minimum standardized test cutoff score and consequently, were denied the opportunity to compete in intercollegiate athletics during their freshman year at Division I schools, denied admission to Division I schools, denied athletic scholarships by Division I schools (or provided with less athletically related financial aid), and/or denied recruiting opportunities by Division I schools (or provided with fewer recruiting opportunities).

It would be difficult to summarize the enormous amount of factual information presented in the record, particularly since much of it is in the form of charts, tables, and graphs. However, some background on the NCAA and Proposition 16 is necessary for an understanding of this Court's opinion.

The NCAA is a voluntary, unincorporated association of approximately 1,200 members, consisting of colleges and universities, conferences and associations, and other educational institutions. Its active members are four-year colleges and universities located throughout the United States. The active members are divided, for purposes of bylaw legislation and competition in intercollegiate championship events, into Division I, II, and III, with further classification of Division I members into Division I-A Football and Division I-AA Football. The only funds received by the NCAA from its members are in the form of annual dues determined by the members. The record, however, is not clear as to whether the NCAA directly receives federal financial assistance.

While some bylaws of the NCAA are applicable to all divisions, each division may, and has, adopted bylaws applicable only to that division. This lawsuit deals with the promulgation of a bylaw affecting initial eligibility only in Division I. Prior to 1971, freshmen were not eligible to participate in varsity athletics. Various eligibility rules affecting freshman participation in athletics were put into effect thereafter. During the early 1980s, public attention focused on the perceived lack of adequate academic preparation and success of student-athletes. Evidence existed that student-athletes were being exploited for their athletics talents and were exhausting their athletics eligibility without any realistic hope of obtaining an undergraduate degree. However, at the same time, student-athletes were graduating at rates comparable to non-athletes, and African-American student-athletes were graduating at rates higher than African-American students in general.

After debating the issue for several years, the Division I membership implemented Proposition 48 during the 1986–1987 academic year, requiring high school graduates to present a 2.000 GPA in 11 academic core courses and a minimum score of 700 on the SAT (or a composite score of 15 on the ACT) before being allowed to participate in freshman athletics. If the criteria in this "double-cut" or "conjunctive" rule were met, student-athletes were declared "eligible" for competition, practice, and athletically related financial aid immediately upon enrollment. Otherwise, they were barred from such opportunities during their first year. The standards, however, neither addressed a student-athlete's admission to a particular institution, nor precluded a student-athlete from receiving institutional financial aid generally available to all students. The Proposition 48 requirements were phased in by the 1988–1989 academic year and, over time, student-athletes have improved their academic performance—particularly African-American student-athletes—as measured by an increase in their graduation rates.

The initial eligibility rules were modified in 1992 (fully implemented in the 1996–1997 academic year) with the adoption of Proposition 16 (ultimately codified at NCAA Bylaw 14.3), which increased the number of required core courses to 13 and introduced an initial eligibility index or "sliding scale." Using the index, the student-athlete could establish eligibility with a GPA as low as 2.000, provided the student also presented an SAT score of 1010 or an ACT sum (as opposed to composite) score of 86. At the other end of the index, a minimum 820 SAT or 68 ACT sum score establishes the floor for students with GPAs of 2.500 or higher. Statistically speaking, the resultant effect of Proposition 16 was to modify Proposition 48 [as follows]: while the core GPA cutoff score of 2.000 is set at two standard deviations below the national mean, the SAT/ACT test cutoff scores are set at only one standard deviation below the national mean, resulting in a heavier weighting of the standardized test. A student-athlete not qualifying under Proposition 16 may become a partial qualifier by presenting an SAT score between 720 and 810 (ACT score between 59 and 67) and a core GPA that produces a GPA-test combination score comparable to that required of qualifiers. Partial qualifiers may not compete in intercollegiate athletics, but may be eligible for athletically related financial aid.

Is the NCAA Subject to Title VI?

[T]he NCAA is subject to Title VI for claims relating to programs or activities to which those federal funds are directed. The statute proscribes discrimination "on the ground of race under any program or activity receiving Federal financial assistance." 42 U.S.C. § 2000d. Thus, because there is a nexus between the NCAA's allegedly discriminatory conduct with regards to intercollegiate athletics and the sponsorship of such programs by federal fund recipients, the NCAA is subject to Title VI for a challenge to Proposition 16.

Accordingly, the Court holds that, under either the "indirect recipient" or "controlling authority" theories, the NCAA is subject to Title VI for a challenge to Proposition 16.

Does Proposition 16 Have an Unjustified Disparate Impact?

In *Griggs v. Duke Power Co.*(1971), the Supreme Court introduced the theory of disparate impact discrimination by holding that a plaintiff need not necessarily prove intentional discrimination in order to establish that an employer has violated Title VII of the Civil Rights Act of 1964. Since then, "facially neutral employment practices that have significant adverse effects on protected groups have been held to violate the Act without proof that the employer adopted those practices with a discriminatory intent." *Watson v. Fort Worth Bank and Trust* (1988) (O'Connor, J., plurality opinion).

The disparate impact theory is premised upon the notion that "some employment practices, adopted without a deliberately discriminatory motive, may in operation be functionally equivalent to intentional discrimination." *Id.* That is, it does not purport to strive for equal results at the institution, but to ensure that individuals are not the victims of unintentional discrimination and thus, treated unequally. Moreover, "[t]he evidence in these 'disparate impact' cases usually focuses on statistical disparities, rather than specific incidents, and on competing explanations for those disparities."

Although the disparate impact theory was originally developed in cases involving employment discrimination, courts have subsequently applied the theory to claims brought pursuant to the regulations implementing Title VI.

In order to establish a *prima facie* case of disparate impact discrimination, a plaintiff must initially demonstrate that the application of a specific facially neutral selection practice has caused an adverse disproportionate effect, to wit, excluding the plaintiff and similarly situated applicants from an educational opportunity. *See Wards Cove Packing Co. v. Atonio* (1989) (superseded in part by statute). Where such a showing has been made, the burden of rebuttal shifts to the defendant, who must demonstrate that the selection practice causing the disproportionate effect is nonetheless justified by an "educational necessity," which is analogous to the "business necessity" justification applied under Title VI. *See Board of Educ. of the City Sch. Dist. of New York v. Harris* (1979). The defendant bears only a burden of producing evidence to sustain its educational necessity.

Finally, even where a defendant meets that burden, a plaintiff may ultimately prevail by discrediting the asserted educational justification, or by proffering an equally effective alternative practice that results in less racial disproportionality while still serving the articulated educational necessity. The ultimate burden of proving that the selection practice caused a discriminatory effect against a protected group always remains with the disparate-impact plaintiff.

Whether Proposition 16 Causes a Racially Disproportionate Effect

In *Wards Cove*, the Supreme Court emphasized that a racially disproportionate effect is typically shown through the presentation of competent statistical evidence comparing the racial composition of candidates who are selected by the practice in question and the racial composition of the qualified candidate pool. Without such carefully tailored statistical proof, there may be an insufficient basis to conclude that the causation requirement is satisfied. Plaintiffs have not presented their evidence of racially disproportionate effect in this fashion, and the NCAA has not drawn the Court's attention to this. Due to the interplay between enrollment and eligibility, the Court highly doubts that either party could have presented accurate statistics in this manner.

In any event, Plaintiffs are not limited to such a showing because "statistical proof can alone make out a prima facie case," and there is no rigid mathematical threshold of disproportionality that must be met to demonstrate a sufficiently adverse impact on African-Americans in a disparate impact case. Instead, the plaintiff may offer statistical evidence sufficient to show that the practice in question has caused the exclusion of candidates for a particular opportunity because of their membership in a protected group. The Supreme Court's "formulations" have only "stressed that statistical disparities must be sufficiently substantial that they raise an inference of causation."

Accordingly, Plaintiffs contend they have established their *prima facie* case by pointing to a July 27, 1998 NCAA memorandum to the Division I membership in which NCAA research data relating to Proposition 16 is summarized. In that memorandum, the NCAA makes the following observations about Proposition 16:

> African-American and low-income student-athletes have been *disproportionately impacted* by Proposition 16 standards. Of those African-American student-athletes appearing on a Division I Institution Request List submitted to the NCAA Initial Eligibility Clearinghouse, 26.6 percent did not meet Proposition 16 standards in 1996 and 21.4 percent did not qualify in 1997 (compared to 6.4 percent of white student-athletes in 1996 and 4.2 percent in 1997). This *disproportionate impact* also is seen (to a lesser degree) for other ethnic-minority groups.

> * * *

> Preliminary enrollment data for 1994–1996 show a drop in the proportion of African-Americans among first-year scholarship athletes in Division I from 23.6 percent to 20.3 percent (accompanied by a 2.0 percent increase in white student-athletes and a 1.3 percent increase in student-athletes from all other ethnic groups combined).

> For both African-American and low-income student-athletes, the single largest reason for not meeting Proposition 16 standards was a failure to meet the minimum standardized test score.

> *The impact of the minimum standardized test score in Proposition 16 is partly a result of this standard being twice as stringent as the GPA minimum in terms of national norms.* Specifically, the cut score on the ACT/SAT (68/820) is set about one standard deviation below the national mean while the core GPA cut score (2.000) is set at two standard deviations below the mean. *Among a representative national population of students, it would be expected that more than 15 percent would be affected by the test minimum while less than three percent would be affected by the GPA minimum.* Differences in the Proposition 16 impact on minority groups and low-income student-athletes are in line with current group differences in national ACT/SAT score distributions.

(emphasis Plaintiffs').

Despite these and other similar admissions from its own documents, the NCAA suggests that the issue of disproportionate effect should be framed somewhat differently.

The NCAA characterizes Plaintiffs as focusing on the alleged disparate impact of Proposition 16 on African-Americans because of the "well-known and continuing discrepancy" in the distribution of standardized test scores for black and white students. And yet, the NCAA notes that Plaintiffs are not alleging that either the SAT or the ACT is racially biased. While recognizing that this black-white gap in test scores necessarily means that a larger share of black students than white students who take the test will score below a given minimum, the NCAA instead posits that the educational opportunity at issue here is not the opportunity to participate in college athletics during the freshman year but rather, the opportunity to obtain a college degree.

The NCAA further argues that the ultimate goal of Proposition 16 is to raise the African-American student-athlete graduation rate. That is, the standards project that the black graduation rate will increase to 59.2%, which would be 94.8% of the projected white graduation rate of 62.5%. The NCAA maintains that Plaintiffs have not disputed that African-Americans are graduating at higher rates; that the gap between African-Americans and white graduation rates has declined since the adoption of stricter initial eligibility rules; or that more African-American student-athletes are graduating since the adoption of the test score requirement.

The NCAA also contends that the increased number of African-Americans receiving athletic scholarships relative to their composition in the general student body is further proof of how college athletics has, in fact, benefited this group. According to the NCAA, although the initial eligibility rules have reduced the number of incoming African-American student-athletes, they have concomitantly resulted in creating more opportunities to graduate for those athletes that meet the eligibility standards. Thus, if graduation, and not freshman-year athletics, is the opportunity at stake here, the NCAA maintains that Plaintiffs have failed to demonstrate the requisite disproportionate effect.

Notwithstanding its attempt to reframe the lawsuit, the NCAA never disputes the veracity of the statements made in their own documents. These admissions and the bare statistics themselves plainly evince that African-Americans are being selected by Proposition 16 at a rate disproportionately lower than whites sufficient to infer causation.

Because Proposition 16 relies, in part, on standardized test scores, it is undeniable that there will be some disparity between blacks and whites at some point in the eligibility determination. "The data suggest that *any* rule that is imposed will have a disproportionate effect on minority student-athletes (because of the difference in the distribution of minority [GPAs] and test scores) both in terms of false negatives and overall number declared ineligible." *NCAA Special Comm. to Review Initial Eligibility Standards Mem.*, May 29, 1994, at 1(emphasis in original). It is precisely *this* educational opportunity that Plaintiffs are challenging, and not the opportunity to graduate.

Moreover, the Court finds unpersuasive the NCAA's argument that a selection practice having a disproportionate "beneficial" impact on the protected group can compensate for any disproportionate adverse impact on that same group. That singular fact misdirects the Court's inquiry. The alleged beneficial impact (increased graduation rates) redounds at the "back-end" while the adverse impact occurs up-front.

Whether Proposition 16 Is Justified by an Educational Necessity

Under the educational necessity prong of the analysis, "the dispositive issue is whether a challenged practice serves, in a significant way, the legitimate [educational] goals of the [institution]." That is, the practice in question must bear a demonstrable "manifest relationship" to a legitimate goal. "The touchstone of this inquiry is a reasoned review of the [institution's] justification for [its] use of the challenged practice . [T]here is no requirement that the challenged practice be 'essential' or 'indispensable'" to the institution. Rather, the defendant's burden of production at this stage is met only when the institution is able to offer

> some proof that the device serves identified legitimate and substantive [educational] goals. That is, the defendant's burden [is] to identify the particular [educational] goal and to present evidence of how the [challenged practice] "serves in a significant way" the identified goal. Merely being abstractly rational, as opposed to arbitrary, would not suffice. The defendant, therefore, has some burden of presenting objective evidence * * *factually showing a nexus between the selection device and a particular [educational] goal. Without evidence of such a relationship it cannot be said that the defendant has presented any evidence that the "challenged" practice serves, in a significant way, the legitimate [educational] goals of the [institution].

The NCAA has proffered the following two goals as underlying the promulgation of Proposition 16: (1) raising student-athlete graduation rates, and (2) closing the gap between black and white student-athlete graduation rates. The Court will address the legitimacy of these goals before continuing to discuss whether a manifest relationship exists between Proposition 16 and those goals.

Are these legitimate goals of the NCAA?

Preliminarily, the Court notes that it cannot seriously be disputed that the NCAA, acting only as the members' "surrogate with respect to athletic rules,"have no legitimate interest in promulgating academic standards that affect the graduation rates of students in general. The proper scope of their authority must be circumscribed to requirements pertaining only to student-athletes. While the Court is sure that both parties are cognizant of this fact, their submissions have not always been as careful in making that distinction when discussing whether Proposition 16 is justified by an educational necessity.

With respect to the NCAA's first proffered objective of raising student-athlete graduation rates, this Court concludes that it is a legitimate educational goal. An educational institution's primary mission is to educate and graduate as many students as possible who meet the level of academic proficiency deemed sufficient by the institution. Thus, raising graduation rates is directly in line with that mission. Here, as the surrogate of the colleges and universities in Division I, the NCAA is properly setting academic standards for student-athletes in hopes of improving the rate at which they graduate.

What is more probative than this kind of facial inquiry, however, is an examination of what specifically motivated the membership to undertake the promulgation of Proposition 16, and its predecessor, Proposition 48. After reading transcripts of the multiple NCAA convention proceedings, examining the NCAA research results and summaries, and analyzing the various NCAA memoranda and other documents in the record, the Court concludes that there is overwhelming and abundant support for the proposition that the membership was concerned about raising student-athlete graduation rates.

The same conclusion cannot be reached for the NCAA's second proffered objective of closing the gap between black and white student-athlete graduation rates. Not only is there no support for an educational institution (let alone its surrogate) to engage in such a goal, but the proffered goal was unequivocally not the purpose behind the adoption of the initial eligibility rules. Absolutely nothing in the record-transcripts of convention proceedings, research results, or memoranda—even suggest that this was a goal that motivated the promulgation of Proposition 16 or 48. Indeed, the Court finds it difficult to reconcile the NCAA's current articulation of such a goal with their own documents plainly evincing that only two goals motivated the adoption of Proposition 16 and 48: "(1) raising of graduation rates, and (2) allowing more individuals access to the finite number of athletics opportunities available."

Accordingly, the Court concludes that raising student-athlete graduation rates is a legitimate goal of the NCAA, but closing the gap between black and white student-athlete graduation rates is not.

Is there a manifest relationship?

The NCAA claims that its own research demonstrates that the use of standardized test scores not only serves these goals but has, in fact, been instrumental in achieving some success. Moreover, the NCAA argues that the use of standardized test cutoffs has been accepted as a legitimate means of achieving educational goals even when a cutoff disproportionately disqualifies one racial group.

As a general matter, it is well accepted that the SAT has some predictive ability of academic success in college as measured by college grades. That is, the College Board has shown that there is a significant correlation between the combined SAT Math and Verbal scores and predicted college GPA. In fact, the College Board's statistical research shows that there is a 0.51 mean correlation between the SAT total score and college course grades. However, it bears noting that the SAT has only been validated as a predictor of first-year GPA, and not college graduation. This is why it makes sense for college and universities to rely, at least in part, on the SAT in making admissions decisions.

The anti-discrimination statutes do not require the proponents of standardized tests "to introduce formal 'validation studies' showing that particular criteria predict actual * * * performance." But by the same token, using a standardized test to achieve objectives for which it was neither intended nor validated would be improper.

As with all facially neutral practices challenged under the disparate impact theory, the use of a SAT cutoff score as a selection practice would be proper so long as it is justified. That is, an arbitrarily selected SAT cutoff score, in the sense that the particular cutoff in question was randomly chosen from the universe of possible choices (400 through 1600), would be invalid.

Nonetheless, "[m]erely being abstractly rational, as opposed to arbitrary," will not suffice. Instead, a particular cutoff score affecting (in this case) student-athlete graduation rates "should normally be set so as to be reasonable and consistent with normal expectations of the acceptable proficiency" of student-athletes towards attaining a college degree.

"Consequently, there should generally be some independent basis for choosing the cutoff." For example, the NCAA "might establish a valid cutoff score by using a professional estimate of the requisite ability levels, or, at the very least, by analyzing test results to locate a logical 'break-point' in the distribution of scores."

Under the above-articulated standards, it is plainly apparent that the NCAA has offered no such basis in this case. It chose a cutoff that seemed acceptable from its consideration of, among other things, the "essential tension between two conflicting goals: (1) raising of graduation rates, and (2) allowing more individuals access to the finite number of athletics opportunities available." *NCAA Division I Academics/Eligibility/Compli-*

ance Cabinet Subcommittee on Initial-Eligibility Issues Mem., July 27, 1998, at 4 Then it essentially engaged in a "wait and see" strategy to see if the predicted effects and outcomes would come to pass.

Initially, the Court notes that the NCAA has not validated the use of the SAT, or any particular cutoff score of the SAT, as a predictor of student-athlete graduation rates.

Aside from the validity of using the SAT as an accurate predictor of student-athlete graduation rates, the record makes abundantly clear that, prior to adopting Proposition 16, the NCAA devoted substantial discussion towards the anticipated effects (raising graduation rates) and desired outcomes (increasing access to opportunities) of requiring additional high school coursework, using core GPA and SAT cutoff scores, and allowing for the index or sliding scale. Specifically, the 820 cutoff score being challenged in this action is roughly one standard deviation below the SAT national mean, suggesting that the NCAA referred to an independent objective standard in identifying this particular cutoff score.

But these facts only demonstrate that the NCAA was being abstractly rational. "[U]nder *Wards Cove* the defendant's burden of production involves something beyond mere articulation of a rational basis for the challenged practice." It is apparent that, because the NCAA has relied exclusively on the predictive ability of the SAT on graduation rates of student-athletes in justifying the cutoff score, it has failed to analyze the issue in terms of what factors affect the graduation rate in addition to Proposition 16, thereby concomitantly failing to control for those variables. By simply pointing to the end result of graduation rates, the NCAA can all too obviously point to some relationship between choosing a particular cutoff score and increased graduation rates. However, it cannot possibly know with any degree of certainty whether the predicted increases in graduation rates are attributable to numerous factors other than the 820 cutoff score.

Significantly, the NCAA has failed to articulate in any meaningful manner the decisionmaking process behind the selection of the 820 cutoff score.

The lack of justification behind the choice of the 820 cutoff is circumstantially revealed, for example, by the student-athletes in the partial qualifier region, whom the NCAA admits "look very similar in performance to several groups of student-athletes who are full qualifiers with lower GPAs * * * . The data indicate that partial qualifiers are performing at a slightly higher level than low-GPA full qualifiers. Taken as a whole, it is difficult to distinguish the academic performance of the partial qualifier from the performance of some qualifiers."

Because the NCAA has failed to analyze the issue in terms of what constitutes an acceptable level of proficiency for a student-athlete to attain a college degree, or what constitutes the minimal ability necessary to graduate, the current choice of the 820 cutoff score results in this anomaly. "If the goal of the standard is to delineate those who would be successful in college from those who would not, then it would seem that it is not serving its intended purpose and in fact, may preclude students who would be academically successful from attending Division I schools."

Accordingly, the Court concludes that the NCAA has not produced any evidence demonstrating that the cutoff score used in Proposition 16 serves, in a significant way, the goal of raising student-athlete graduation rates.

In reaching this result, the Court stresses that this case does not preclude the use of the SAT, or any particular cutoff score of the SAT, in the NCAA's adoption of an initial eligibility rule. It may be "that no strong statistical basis exist[s] for the use of any particular single minimum test score," but that is for the NCAA to determine more definitively after undertaking an appropriate analysis justifying an independent basis for choosing a cutoff score.

* * *

Notes and Questions

1. What is the infirmity in the NCAA's preferred defense that the opportunity in question is the chance to graduate and not the chance to participate in college athletics during one's freshman year?

2. The court concluded that a legitimate goal of the NCAA was raising student-athlete graduation rates, but the court found that the NCAA offered no support for the proposition that the goal was furthered by Proposition 16. This court required that the NCAA as defendant demonstrate more than abstract rationality or more than a rational basis for its decision. The NCAA simply failed to isolate the variables leading to differences in graduation rates. Regarding the NCAA's defense that additional justification may be found in the desire to narrow the gap between black and white graduation rates, the court holds that such a goal was not legitimate. Do you agree? *See* Dennis L. Martin, Cureton v. NCAA: *Was the Federal District Court out of Bounds When It Enjoined the NCAA from Continued Operation of Proposition 16,* 22 Campbell L. Rev. 233 (1999); Tyler J. Murray, *Illegalizing The NCAA's Eligibility Rules: Did* Cureton v. NCAA *Go Too Far or Not Far Enough?*, 26 J. Legis. 101 (2000).

3. The District Court decision in *Cureton v. NCAA* was reversed by the Third Circuit Court of Appeals, which held that the NCAA was not subject to the "disparate impact" regulations implementing Title VI; the case was remanded to the district court with instructions for the entry of judgment for the NCAA. *Cureton v. NCAA*, 198 F.3d 107 (3d Cir. 1999). Just over a year later, the Supreme Court ruled that the "disparate impact" regulations implementing Title VI afford no basis for a private right of action, *Alexander v. Sandoval* 532 U.S. 275 (2001); Justices Stevens, Souter, Ginsburg, and Breyer dissented.

On remand to the district court, the plaintiffs moved to amend their complaint to add a claim of intentional discrimination. The motion was denied on the grounds that, among other reasons, the amendment would be unduly prejudicial, and the Court of Appeals affirmed. *Cureton v. NCAA*, 252 F.3d 267 (3d Cir. 2001).

In 2000, a second lawsuit was filed, contending *inter alia* that the adoption and retention of Proposition 16 constituted intentional racial discrimination under Title VI. The plaintiffs advanced two theories: first, that the NCAA's "deliberate indifference" to the foreseeable racial disparities produced by Proposition 16 constituted intentional discrimination; and second, that knowledge of these disparities, combined with additional "circumstantial evidence," suggests that Proposition 16 was "at least partially motivate[d]" by improper considerations of race. In July 2001, Judge Buckwalter—the same judge who presided over the *Cureton* litigation—granted the NCAA's motion to dismiss. The Court of Appeals reversed, finding that in their second theory, the plaintiffs had stated a plausible clam of intentional discrimination, and had alleged sufficient facts to support their claim. *Pryor v. NCAA*, 288 F.3d 548 (3d Cir. 2002). The complaint alleged, the Court of Appeals noted, that "the NCAA openly considered race in formulating Proposition 16," and also that "it had reason to know that the adoption of Proposition 16 would lead to the greater exclusion of black athletes." *Id.* at 566. Accordingly, the complaint stated a claim of intentional racial discrimination, and this was so whether the NCAA harbored the "sinister" motive of attempting to screen out more black student athletes than white, *id.* at 565–66, or harbored the more "laudable" goal of improving black graduation rates, but did so in a way that ultimately disadvantaged black athletes. *Id.* at 567. The case was remanded to the district court.

4. Subsequent events have effectively mooted a central element of the dispute. In October 2002, the NCAA Division I Board of Directors approved a series of revisions to the eligibility standards. Most of the reforms, which took effect in August 2003, were designed to ensure progress toward graduation. To remain eligible, student-athletes need to pass twenty-four semester hours in their first year, only six of which can be in remedial work, and must pass at least eighteen hours during each subsequent year, with a minimum of six hours per semester. They must have at least a 1.9 grade point average to be eligible in their third year, and a 2.0 to be eligible in their fourth. By their third year, student athletes need to have completed forty percent of the course credits necessary to a degree (up from twenty-five percent); sixty percent by their fourth year (up from fifty); and eighty percent by their fifth year (up from seventy-five).

Initial eligibility rules were also modified. The 2.0 grade point average in core high school courses was retained, but the number of core courses was increased from thirteen to fourteen. Most significantly, the NCAA eliminated the use of a cutoff score on the SAT. Eligibility will still be based on a sliding scale that considers both the core GPA and the SAT, but there is no SAT minimum. Thus a student with a 2.50 core GPA would need the 820 that served as the pervious minimum, but a student with a 3.0 core GPA would need only a 620, while a student with a 3.55 or higher would need only a 400.

"The message being sent to young men and women who want to succeed in intercollegiate athletics," said Myles Brand, now the NCAA president, "is that they need to do well academically in high school * * * That's what's going to tell us whether they graduate or not. So I think this is headed in the right direction."

William DeLauder, president of Delaware State University, a historically black institution, concurred. "The problem with the [SAT cutoff] scores was that it was eliminating a lot of kids who the data was showing could have been successful if given an opportunity. And by using that cut score, they never did have an opportunity." Mark Asher, *NCAA Adjusts Eligibility; Minimum Score on Standardized Tests Is Eliminated*, Wash. Post, Nov. 1, 2002, at D3.

What caused the NCAA to drop the SAT cutoff? Academic consultants appointed by the Division I Board of Directors were charged with recommending ways "to maximize graduation rates while minimizing the adverse impact on minority students." Their research indicated

> that a key means of minimizing adverse impact is by eliminating the overweighting of test scores used in determining initial-eligibility. The current NCAA cut-score on the test is twice as stringent as that on the high-school grade-point average. Data indicate that the grade-point average is a better predictor of college success and should be weighted at least equally, if not higher than the test score when using these variables to predict success in college.

Proposal 02-22-B: Initial-Eligibility Requirements—Core-Course Units and Index, available at http://www.ncaa.org/databases/legislation/2002/2002-022-B.htm.

An April 2002 position paper presented to the NCAA Management Council cited this research in support of the proposal. It offered two additional rationales for the proposal: that the Educational Testing Service had consistently claimed that the cutoff represented a misuse of its tests, and that it would be "prudent * * * to choose initial-eligibility standards * * * so as to best position the Association against further legal challenges."

According to NCAA President Brand, "the new progress-toward-degree benchmarks—particularly in the student-athlete's first two years—will put athletes on track to graduate at even higher rates than they already do." *Athlete Graduation Rates Continue Climb: First Class to Matriculate Under Prop 16 Shows Marked Improvement*, THE NCAA NEWS, Sept. 1, 2003.

Andre Dennis, attorney for the *Cureton* plaintiffs, believes the lawsuit ended the cutoff. "I don't know if the NCAA will ever admit it, but I think that's what happened," he says. "I think the truth is that the NCAA doesn't respond to anything but pressure and litigation." "That was the catalyst," agrees Adele Kimmel, staff attorney for the Trial Lawyers for Public Justice. "That's what got the NCAA moving in the proper direction. I'm just sorry it took as long as it did." Rich Hoffman, *Finally, Passing on Test: Lawsuit's Effect Felt with NCAA Change on SATs*, PHILA. DAILY NEWS., Nov. 6, 2002, at 98.

5. On April 29, 2004, the NCAA Board of Directors approved a new series of academic reforms, "the beginning of a sea change in college sports," according to Brand. The new measures call for the establishment of an Academic Progress Rate (APR), designed to measure the progress of student-athletes toward their degree. Starting with the 2006–2007 academic year, schools that do not meet the APR will receive warnings; for the 2007–2008 year, schools that do not meet the standard will lose athletic scholarships. Repeat offenders may be banned from postseason tournaments. Eric Prisbell, *NCAA Approves Plan for Reform; Academic Progress Formula Will Be Introduced; Some Find New Blueprint Unfair*, WASH. POST, April 30, 2004, at D01.

Robert Hemenway, University of Kansas chancellor and chairman of the NCAA board of directors, says the message to athletes is simple: "If you come to our institutions, we're going to do everything in our power to make sure you graduate." "This," Hemenway concludes, "is a very significant day in the history of the NCAA." David Wharton, *NCAA Approves Academic Reforms; Schools Faced with Threats of Postseason Bans and Scholarship Cuts If Athletes Fall Short. But Some Fear the Plan Doesn't Go Far Enough*, L.A. TIMES, April 30, 2004, at D1.

Not everyone perceived the same message. "The day a college president has the spine to stand up and say, 'I will defend the athletic scholarship with my last breath and moreover sports have intellectual content and are consistent with education even when athletes don't graduate,' is the day I will trust him or her," writes Sally Jenkins. "Until then, count me as a cynic who regards most NCAA officials and college administrators as phony pipe suckers and glad-handers who have only occasional moral spasms. Furthermore, put me down as a stone skeptic when it comes to this latest piece of cover-their-butts policy." Sally Jenkins, *NCAA Flunking Its Graduation Test*, WASH. POST, May 1, 2004, at D01. "When a university's grad rate is woeful," Jenkins asks,

> who gets blamed? Usually the coach, and the recruit from the blighted high school who is labeled a mercenary and an academic fraud because he uses college as a steppingstone to the pros. The president gets off scot-free and goes on preaching the evil of professionalism while he sells his school to ABC for a rights fee. So let me ask you something: Of the three, who is the biggest cynic?

Id. Former Georgetown basketball coach John Thompson agrees. "It's legislation predicated on thievery and dishonesty," he says. "It's, 'You steal, and I steal, and we both know it.' They act on public perception, not the best interest of the kids." *Id.*

6. Professor Davis, referenced earlier, posits that the internal inconsistencies in the regulatory process cause student-athletes to discredit the regulators thus promoting unacceptable conduct. *See* Timothy Davis, *African-American Student-Athletes Marginalizing the NCAA Regulatory Structure,* 6 MARQ. SPORTS L.J. 199 (1996). That is, the NCAA regulatory structure is marginalized because those governed give no credence to the process or the goals sought to be achieved. In particular, the hypocrisy that attends the big business aspects of college sports defies the primacy of education and amateurism principles. Is this a valid criticism? Can amateurism and revenue production co-exist at some level? If not, is it far too late to try to put the genie back into the lamp? Has the landscape of college athletics changed so dramatically that the rah-rah/boolah-boolah days are gone forever? *See* Orion Riggs, *The Façade Of Amateurism: The Inequities Of Major College Athletics,* 5 KAN. J.L. & PUB. POL'Y 137 (1996); Matthew J. Mitten, *Applying Antitrust Law to NCAA Regulation of Big Time College Athletics: The Need to Shift from Nostalgic 19th and 20th Century Ideals of Amateurism to the Economic Realities of the 21st Century,* 11 MARQ. SPORTS L. REV. 1 (2000).

7. In September 2003, the NCAA reported the following:

> Graduation rates, which college and university presidents have longed to improve, took another jump in the right direction as data from the entering class of 1996 show student-athletes obtained degrees at a record rate.

> The latest NCAA graduation-rates research indicates student-athletes matriculating in 1996 graduated at a rate of 62 percent, which not only is two percentage points higher than last year's all-time high, but three percentage points higher than the overall student body—the largest separation between the two groups in more than a decade.

> The 1996 class represents a milestone cohort, not just because of its success, but because it is the first to have gone through college under the eligibility standards known as Proposition 16. Prop 16 was landmark legislation because it established a sliding scale index that combined high-school grade-point averages and standardized-test scores to determine initial eligibility. When it was approved at the 1992 NCAA Convention, researchers predicted that graduation rates would increase to about 62 percent, which proved to be accurate.

> In addition to the overall increase, the 1996 class also graduated at higher rates by group than the 1995 cohort. Blacks in men's basketball made a significant jump—from 35 percent in 1995 to 41 percent in 1996. Division I-A black football players also rose three percentage points-from 46 to 49 percent. Other groups, including white male and white female basketball student-athletes, black female basketball student-athletes and white football student-athletes were within one percentage point, plus or minus, of their 1995 counterparts.

Athlete Graduation Rates Continue Climb: First Class to Matriculate under Prop 16 Shows Marked Improvement, NCAA NEWS, Sept. 1, 2003.

"College presidents and athletics administrators have known for a long time that the federally mandated methodology does not accurately reflect the academic success at most of our programs," NCAA President Myles Brand said. "Still, even under the flawed federal rate, our student-athletes regularly achieve higher graduation marks than their student body counterparts. And there is reason to believe that success will increase, since subsequent classes in the research will have been better prepared to meet Prop 16 standards." *Id.*

8. In a 2001 report, the Knight Foundation Commission on Intercollegiate Athletics noted that only 48% of Division I football players earned degrees; the proportion declined to 42% for black players. Among the commission's recommendations was a rule requiring teams to graduate at least half of their players to qualify for post-season play. "We're not in the entertainment business; nor are we a minor league for professional sports," insisted Father Theodore Hesburgh, co-chairman of the Commission and president emeritus of Notre Dame. "Your school is not worthy to be the champion of the country if you're not educating your kids." David Wharton, *NCAA Graduation Rates Success, To Some Degree,* Los Angeles Times Jan. 3, 2002.

Is this measure an effective response or will it simply provoke grade inflation and an artificial success ratio? Consider the enormous pressure that this places upon a teacher who knows that the issuance of a failing grade could cost the university millions of dollars from a lost bowl appearance.

9. Are student-athlete graduation rates at all relevant if they are not compared to the graduation rates of the institution generally? The late Jim Valvano, coach of the 1983 NCAA basketball champion North Carolina State Wolfpack, frequently lamented that criticism of his players' graduation rates was unfair because the absolute figures belied how well his players fared relative to the rest of the student population. Meanwhile, Richard Lapchick, director emeritus of the Center for the Study of Sport in Society at Northeastern University, suggests that football players, for example, should do even better because they receive special tutoring. "Unlike the general population," he notes, "we're bringing these students to a college campus to perform services for the school. We owe them a little bit more." Wharton, *supra.*

Should the rates be adjusted to exclude transfers? What of students who leave early to pursue professional careers? Notes Dennis Leblanc, associate athletic director for academic and student services at the University of Nebraska: "I can't graduate someone who's not here." *Id.*

10. Athletes traditionally receive special tutoring and academic support. Is this step a positive one or does it merely add to the notion that athletes on campus are pampered and privileged ... and perhaps intellectually inferior?

11. Would awarding tenure or long-term contracts to college coaches alleviate some of the recruiting pressure and derivatively reduce the urge or perceived need to skirt the rules? If schools were to treat their coaches the same as or similar to regular tenure-track faculty members, perhaps the gap between the classroom and the weight room would be bridged and the term student-athlete would become a reality once again. While the notion may seem subversive at first blush, and certainly would meet resistance from coaches as well as faculty members, it could be a reform measure with long-range benefit. Indeed, the current system of providing many coaches with gaudy salaries in exchange for job security makes the "win at any cost" *raison d'etre* a self-fulfilling prophecy of doom for the concept of true amateurism.

This suggestion is not without its problems. Traditional criteria for tenure such as teaching, scholarship, and service may not translate easily into an evaluation of a coach's eligibility for a permanent appointment to the faculty. With some tinkering, could the standards could be adapted?

The proposal might require some adjustments in traditional mind sets. Coaches would be required to acknowledge that they do not operate in a vacuum answerable only to conference chairpersons, influential alumni, and university presidents (or lower-level officials at many NCAA Division III institutions). They would be part of the academic community as a whole. Faculty members and members of the university administration, meanwhile, would need to abandon any presumptions that the hallowed halls of academia are off-limits to members of the coaching fraternity or sorority. In any event, if coaches and faculty undertook to share the responsibility for education, the entire enterprise might be more rewarding and gratifying for all concerned, particularly the student-athlete.

IV. Gender and the Amateur Athlete

A. Title IX — An Introduction

Cohen v. Brown University (Cohen I)
991 F.2d 888 (1st Cir. 1993)

SELYA, Circuit Judge.

* * *

III. TITLE IX AND COLLEGIATE ATHLETICS

* * *

A. Scope of Title IX.

At its inception, the broad proscriptive language of Title IX caused considerable consternation in the academic world. The academy's anxiety chiefly centered around identifying which individual programs, particularly in terms of athletics, might come within the scope of the discrimination provision, and, relatedly, how the government would determine compliance. The gridiron fueled these concerns: for many schools, the men's football budget far exceeded that of any other sport, and men's athletics as a whole received the lion's share of dedicated resources—a share that, typically, was vastly disproportionate to the percentage of men in the student body.

Part of the confusion about the scope of Title IX's coverage and the acceptable avenues of compliance arose from the absence of secondary legislative materials. Congress included no committee report with the final bill and there were apparently only two mentions of intercollegiate athletics during the congressional debate. *See* 118 Cong. Rec. 5,807 (1972) (statement of Sen. Bayh on privacy in athletic facilities); 117 Cong. Rec. 30,407 (1971) (statement of Sen. Bayh noting that proposed Title IX will not require gender-blended football teams). Nevertheless, under congressional direction to implement Title IX, the Secretary of Health, Education and Welfare (HEW) promulgated regulations in 1975 which included specific provisions for college athletics. Four years later, HEW's Office of Civil Rights (OCR) added another layer of regulatory exegesis when, after notice and comment, it published a "Policy Interpretation" that offered a more detailed measure of equal athletic opportunity.

In 1984, the Supreme Court radically altered the contemporary reading of Title IX. The Court held that Title IX was "program-specific," so that its tenets applied only to the program(s) which actually received federal funds and not to the rest of the university. *Grove City College v. Bell*, 465 U.S. 555, 574 (1984). Because few athletic departments are direct recipients of federal funds—most federal money for universities is channeled through financial aid offices or invested directly in research grants—*Grove City* cabined Title IX and placed virtually all collegiate athletic programs beyond its reach.

In response to *Grove City*, Congress scrapped the program-specific approach and re-instated an institution-wide application of Title IX by passing the Civil Rights Restoration Act of 1987, 20 U.S.C. §1687 (1988). The Restoration Act required that if any arm of an educational institution received federal funds, the institution as a whole must comply with Title IX's provisions. Although the Restoration Act does not specifically mention sports, the record of the floor debate leaves little doubt that the enactment was aimed, in part, at creating a more level playing field for female athletes* * *.

The appellants do not challenge the district court's finding that, under existing law, Brown's athletic department is subject to Title IX. Accordingly, we devote the remainder of Part III to determining the meaning of Title IX, looking first at the statute and then at the regulations.

B. Statutory Framework.

Title IX, like the Restoration Act, does not explicitly treat college athletics. Rather, the statute's heart is a broad prohibition of gender-based discrimination in all programmatic aspects of educational institutions:

> No person in the United States shall, on the basis of sex, be excluded from participation in, be denied the benefits of, or be subjected to discrimination under any education program or activity receiving Federal financial assistance.

20 U.S.C. §1681(a) (1988).

After listing a number of exempt organizations, section 1681 makes clear that, while Title IX prohibits discrimination, it does not mandate strict numerical equality between the gender balance of a college's athletic program and the gender balance of its student body.

* * *

Put another way, a court assessing Title IX compliance may not find a violation solely because there is a disparity between the gender composition of an educational institution's student constituency, on the one hand, and its athletic programs, on the other hand.

That is not to say, however, that evidence of such a disparity is irrelevant. Quite the contrary: under the proviso contained in section 1681(b), a Title IX plaintiff in an athletic discrimination suit must accompany statistical evidence of disparate impact with some further evidence of discrimination, such as unmet need amongst the members of the disadvantaged gender.

C. Regulatory Framework.

As we mentioned above, the Secretary of HEW, following Congress's instructions, promulgated regulations implementing Title IX in the pre-*Grove City* era. *See* 40 Fed. Reg. 24,128 (1975). Thereafter, in 1979, Congress split HEW into the Department of Health and Human Services (HHS) and the Department of Education (DED). *See* 20 U.S.C. §§3401–3510 (1988). In a wonderful example of bureaucratic muddle, the existing Title IX regulations were left within HHS's arsenal while, at the same time, DED replicated them as part of its own regulatory armamentarium. Compare 45 C.F.R. §86 (1992) (HHS regulations) with 34 C.F.R. §106 (1992) (DED regulations). Both sets of regulations were still in effect when the Restoration Act passed. They are identical, save only for changes in nomenclature reflecting the reorganization of the federal bureaucracy * * *. Therefore, like the parties, we treat DED, acting through its OCR, as the administrative agency charged with administering Title IX.

Recognizing the agency's role has important practical and legal consequences. Although DED is not a party to this appeal, we must accord its interpretation of Title IX appreciable deference. *See Chevron U.S.A. Inc. v. Natural Resources Defense Council, Inc.*, 467 U.S. 837, 844 (1984); *see also Udall v. Tallman*, 380 U.S. 1, 16 (1965) (noting that the Supreme Court "gives great deference to the interpretation given the statute by the officers or agency charged with its administration"). The degree of deference is particularly high in Title IX cases because Congress explicitly delegated to the agency the task of prescribing standards for athletic programs under Title IX.

It is against this backdrop that we scrutinize the regulations and the Policy Interpretation.

1. The Regulations. DED's regulations begin by detailing Title IX's application to college athletics. The regulations also recognize, however, that an athletic program may consist of gender-segregated teams as long as one of two conditions is met: either the sport in which the team competes is a contact sport or the institution offers comparable teams in the sport to both genders.

Finally, whether teams are segregated by sex or not, the school must provide gender-blind equality of opportunity to its student body. The regulations offer a non-exclusive compendium of ten factors which OCR will consider in assessing compliance with this mandate:

> (1) Whether the selection of sports and levels of competition effectively accommodate the interests and abilities of members of both sexes;

* * *

2. The Policy Interpretation. In the three years next following the initial issuance of the regulations, HEW received over one hundred discrimination complaints involving more than fifty schools. In order to encourage self-policing and thereby winnow complaints, HEW proposed a Policy Interpretation. *See* 43 Fed. Reg. 58,070 (1978). It then promulgated the Policy Interpretation in final form, *See* 44 Fed. Reg. 71,413 (1979), a matter of months before the effective date of the statute through which Congress, emulating King Solomon, split HEW. The parties are in agreement that, at DED's birth, it clutched the Policy Interpretation, and, as a practical matter, that appears to be the case* * *. Although we can find no record that DED formally adopted the Policy Interpretation, we see no point to splitting the hair, particularly where the parties have not asked us to do so. Because this document is a considered interpretation of the regulation, we cede it substantial deference.

In line with the Supreme Court's direction that, "if we are to give [Title IX] the scope that its origins dictate, we must accord it a sweep as broad as its language," *North Haven Bd. of Educ. v. Bell*, 456 U.S. 512, 521 (1982) (quoting *United States v. Price*, 383 U.S. 787, 801 (1966)) (collecting cases) (brackets in original), the Policy Interpretation limns three major areas of regulatory compliance: "Athletic Financial Assistance (Scholarships)," *see* 34 C.F.R. §106.37(c); "Equivalence in Other Athletic Benefits and Opportunities," *see* 34 C.F.R. §106.41(c)(2)–(10); and "Effective Accommodation of Student Interests and Abilities," *see* 34 C.F.R. §106.41(c)(1). The court below, and a number of other district courts, have adopted this formulation and ruled that a university violates Title IX if it ineffectively accommodates student interests and abilities regardless of its performance in other Title IX areas.

Equal opportunity to participate lies at the core of Title IX's purpose. Because the third compliance area delineates this heartland, we agree with the district courts that have so ruled and hold that, with regard to the effective accommodation of students' interests and abilities, an institution can violate Title IX even if it meets the "financial assistance" and "athletic equivalence" standards. In other words, an institution that offers women a smaller number of athletic opportunities than the statute requires may not rectify that violation simply by lavishing more resources on those women or achieving equivalence in other respects.

3. Measuring Effective Accommodation.

* * *

In [determining] * * * whether an athletic program effectively accommodates students' interests and abilities, the Policy Interpretation maps a trinitarian model under which the university must meet at least one of three benchmarks:

> (1) Whether intercollegiate level participation opportunities for male and female students are provided in numbers substantially proportionate to their respective enrollments; or

> (2) Where the members of one sex have been and are underrepresented among intercollegiate athletes, whether the institution can show a history and continuing practice of program expansion which is demonstrably responsive to the developing interest and abilities of the members of that sex; or

> (3) Where the members of one sex are underrepresented among intercollegiate athletes, and the institution cannot show a continuing practice of program expansion such as that cited above, whether it can be demonstrated that the interests and abilities of the members of that sex have been fully and effectively accommodated by the present program.

44 Fed. Reg. at 71,418.

* * *

It seems unlikely, even in this day and age, that the athletic establishments of many coeducational universities reflect the gender balance of their student bodies. Similarly, the recent boom in Title IX suits suggest that, in an era of fiscal austerity, few universities are prone to expand athletic opportunities. It is not surprising, then, that schools more often than not attempt to manage the rigors of Title IX by satisfying the interests and abilities of the underrepresented gender, that is, by meeting the third benchmark of the accommodation test. Yet, this benchmark sets a high standard: it demands not merely some accommodation, but full and effective accommodation. If there is sufficient interest and ability among members of the statistically underrepresented gender, not slaked by existing programs, an institution necessarily fails this prong of the test.

Although the full-and-effective-accommodation standard is high, it is not absolute. Even when male athletic opportunities outnumber female athletic opportunities, and the university has not met the first benchmark (substantial statistical proportionality) or the second benchmark (continuing program expansion) of the accommodation test, the mere fact that there are some female students interested in a sport does not ipso facto require the school to provide a varsity team in order to comply with the third benchmark. Rather, the institution can satisfy the third benchmark by ensuring participatory opportunities at the intercollegiate level when, and to the extent that, there is "sufficient interest and ability among the members of the excluded sex to sustain a viable team and a reasonable expectation of intercollegiate competition for that team. * * *" 44 Fed. Reg. at 71,418. Staying on top of the problem is not sport for the short-winded: the institution must remain vigilant, "upgrading the competitive opportunities available to the historically disadvantaged sex as warranted by developing abilities among the athletes of that sex," *id.*, until the opportunities for, and levels of, competition are equivalent by gender.

* * *

Notes and Questions

1. Few anti-discrimination mandates have generated as much controversy as Title IX of the Education Amendments of 1972. The language of the federal mandate is disarmingly simple: "[N]o person in the United States shall, on the basis of sex, be excluded from participation in, be denied benefits of, or be subjected to discrimination under any educational program or activity receiving federal financial assistance." 20 U.S.C. § 1681 (a) (2000). Although Title IX is not limited to athletics, the sports arena has been the venue in which the most significant controversy has appeared.

Part of the controversy might be traced to an amendment by Senator Jacob Javits, calling for the executive branch to implement regulations governing gender-based discrimination in intercollegiate athletics. *See* 20 U.S.C. § 1681 (1974); Kimberly A. Yuracko, *One for You and One for Me: Is Title IX's Sex-Based Proportionality Requirement for College Varsity Athletic Positions Defensible?*, 97 Nw. U. L. Rev. 731 (2003). Initially, the Department of Health, Education, and Welfare ("HEW") assumed responsibility for enforcement of Title IX and, pursuant to such authority, promulgated initial regulations in 1975. In 1979, Congress divided HEW into the Department of Health and Human Services and the Department of Education. *Id.* at §§ 3401–3510 (2000). Since that time, the Department of Education, Office for Civil Rights ("OCR"), has been responsible for the promulgation of regulations and the administration of Title IX. As a result of this history, you will find that OCR and HEW are often used fungibly in the cases and pertinent articles addressing the government entities responsible for the administrative aspects of Title IX.

The pertinent regulations require that members of both sexes receive equal athletic opportunity, which OCR evaluates based on the following non-exclusive list of ten factors:

> 1) whether the selection of sports and levels of competition effectively accommodate the interests and abilities of members of both sexes; 2) the provision of equipment and supplies; 3) scheduling of games and practice times; 4) travel and per diem allowances; 5) opportunity to receive coaching and academic tutoring; 6) assignment and compensation of coaches and tutors; 7) provision of locker rooms, practice and competitive facilities; 8) provision of medical and training facilities and services; 9) provision of housing and dining facilities and services; and 10) publicity.

34 C.F.R. 106.41 (c) (1).

2. As the *Cohen* court notes, the regulations initially left educational institutions in something of a quandary as to the methods of compliance, prompting numerous com-

plaints and calls for greater clarification in the early years of Title IX. In 1979, OCR issued interpretative guidelines for determining whether an affected educational institution complied with the statutory mandates. In particular, this "Policy Interpretation" identified three areas of regulatory compliance:

1) athletic financial assistance (scholarships), 34 C.F.R.§ 106.37 (c);

2) equivalence in other athletic benefits and opportunities, 34 C.F.R. § 106.41 (c)(2)–(10); and

3) effective accommodation of student interests and abilities, 34 C.F.R. 106.41 (c)(1).

Covered institutions must comply in all three areas. *See also* Yuracko, *supra*; Ellen J. Staurowsky, *Title IX and College Sport: The Long Painful Path to Compliance and Reform,* 14 MARQ. SPORTS L. REV. 95 (2003).

The Policy Interpretation delineated a more detailed test for the third compliance area. It provides that the third compliance area will be satisfied where:

a school provides athletic opportunities for its male and female students in numbers substantially proportional to their respective enrollments;

the members of one sex have been and are underrepresented among intercollegiate athletes, a school can show a history and continuing practice of program expansion which is demonstrably responsive to the developing interest and abilities of the members of the underrepresented sex;

the members of one sex are underrepresented among intercollegiate athletes, and the institution cannot show a continuing practice of program expansion, the school can show that the interests and abilities of the members of that sex have been fully and effectively accommodated by the present program.

44 Fed. Reg. 71,413 (December 11, 1979). Satisfaction of any one of the benchmarks insulates the institution from liability under the statute. As a practical matter, however, the proportionality standard contained in the first prong has emerged as the critical inquiry, and the area of greatest controversy. *See* Yuracko *supra* at 731. *But see* Part B, *infra.*

3. Since their original promulgation in 1975, the regulations have exempted "contact sports" from much of Title IX's reach:

(b) Separate Teams. Notwithstanding the requirements of paragraph (a) of this section, a recipient may operate or sponsor separate teams for members of each sex where election of such teams is based on competitive skill or the activity involved is a contact sport. However, where a recipient operates or sponsors a team in a particular sport for members of one sex but operates or sponsors no such team for members of the other sex, and athletic opportunities for members of that sex have previously been limited, members of the excluded sex must be allowed to try-out for the team offered unless the sport is a contact sport. For the purposes of this part, contact sports include boxing, wrestling, rugby, ice hockey, football, basketball and other sports the purpose or major activity of which involves bodily contact.

34 C.F.R. § 106.41 (2001). Should there be any exception for contact sports? Is the line between sexism and chivalry becoming blurred? *See also* Suzanne Sangree, *Title IX and the Contact Sport Exception: Gender Stereotypes In a Civil Rights Statute,* 32 CONN. L. REV. 381 (2000). *See also,* Part D, *infra.*

4. In what respects is Title IX controversial? Proponents of the statute and its attendant regulations point to the staggering exponential leap in female athletic participation as a key indicator of Title IX's success. In 1972, fewer than 32,000 women competed in intercollegiate athletics; by 2003, 150,000 women were participating in collegiate sports. In 1971, less than 300,000 girls nationwide participated in high school sports; by 2002, the number had swelled to 2.8 million. Meanwhile, the derivative impact of Title IX—reflected in the increased interest in sports among young women and the expansion of professional sports opportunities for women—is more difficult to quantify, but is clearly substantial. At the same time, budgets for female athletics still lag significantly behind the budgets for male athletics, and the "contact sports" exception still excludes girls and women from participation in many sports.

Opponents of Title IX, on the other hand, frequently deride the statute as a "reverse discrimination" law or complain that it mandates "quotas." The enhancement of female athletic opportunity, they note, has often come with a price: the elimination of some men's sports. The principal area of concern rests with the administrative and judicial approval of "compliance by contraction," i.e., satisfying the proportionality requirements of Title IX not by increasing women's programs, but by eliminating some men's programs. The hardship to male athletes caused by such contractions—inevitably visited on non-revenue-producing sports—leaves some to question whether Title IX is accomplishing its goals in the least burdensome way. For an informative overview of Title IX developments in these areas, among others, see Diane Heckman, *The Glass Sneaker: Thirty Years of Victories and Defeats Involving Title IX and Sex Discrimination in Athletics,* 13 FORDHAM INTELL. PROP. MEDIA & ENT. L. J. 551 (2003).

5. It is important to remember that Title IX applies to any educational program that receives federal funding; high schools must also comply with the statutory mandates. *See Horner v. Kentucky High School Athletic Ass'n,* 43 F.3d 265 (6th Cir. 1994); *Williams v. School District of Bethlehem,* 998 F.2d 168 (3d Cir. 1993). One very significant case involving a high school, *Franklin v. Gwinnett County Public Schools,* 503 U.S. 60 (1992), established that plaintiffs can recover monetary damages for a violation of Title IX. *See* Heckman, *supra.*

High school students have also used Title IX as a vehicle for sexual harassment claims. For an overview of peer sexual harassment cases under Title IX, see Diane Heckman, *Tracing the History of Peer Sexual Harrassment in Title IX Cases,* 183 WEST'S EDUC. LAW REP. 1, Jan. 29, 2004. *See also, e.g., Davis v. Monroe County Bd. of Educ.,* 526 U.S. 629 (1999) (case involving sexual harassment by a fifth-grade student in which the Court held that a school could be liable for deliberate indifference to peer sexual harassment); *Gebser v. Lago Vista Indep. Sch. Dist.,* 524 U.S. 274 (1998) (school district did not violate Title IX when school district had no notice of the sexual relations between a teacher and student); *Franklin v. Gwinnett County Pub. Sch.,* 503 U.S. 60 (1992) (allowing damages in a Title IX suit against school district because of coach's sexual harassment of female student).

6. In a related high school context, the Sixth Circuit recently held that the Michigan High School Athletic Association's scheduling of girls sports at times that were disadvantageous to the participants (to the benefit of male sports) and contrary to traditional scheduling of the sports in question violated Title IX. *See Communities for Equity v. Michigan High School Athletic Association,* 459 F.3d 676 (6th Cir. 2006). The court found that motive was not necessary to establish a violation for intentional discrimination under Title IX.

7. During the presidential election campaign of 2000, then-candidate George W. Bush promised to revisit Title IX and find a "reasonable approach" toward enforcing its equality mandate. A year after he took office, the National Wrestling Coaches Association attempted to cash in this pledge by challenging the proportionality rules in a lawsuit against the Department of Education. *See* June Kronhol, *College Coaches Press Bush on Title IX*, WALL ST. J., Aug. 27, 2002 at A4. In July 2002, the Bush administration responded through Secretary of Education Roderick P. Paige, who announced the formation of a commission — the Commission on Opportunities in Athletics — designed to re-examine Title IX's compliance standards and recommend to the Secretary "whether those standards should be revised and, if so, how the standards should be revised." Sally Jenkins, *See How They Run*, WASH. POST, July 15, 2002, at D01. After six months of investigation, and two days of "sometimes contentious" meetings, the fifteen-member Commission issued a report proposing a series of recommendations. The most sweeping proposal before the Commission — eliminating entirely the proportionately requirement — was defeated by a vote of 11-4; less radical measures, most focusing on the processes for calculating opportunities for Title IX purposes, were adopted, but over vigorous dissents. *See Commission Rejects Title IX Proposals*, ASSOC. PRESS, Jan. 30, 2003. Congress, meanwhile, expressed its support for the prevailing standards in a series of hearings and draft resolutions, and the District Court hearing the Wrestling Coaches' challenge dismissed the suit in June 2003. A few weeks later, Secretary Paige issued a brief "clarification" report reaffirming the existing standards of compliance for Title IX. *See* Nicole Stern, *Preserving and Protecting Title IX: An Analysis and History of Advocacy and Backlash*, 10 SPORTS LAW. J. 155 (2003).

B. Proportionality

While Title IX has produced little consensus in any area, one emerging assumption is that the proportionality benchmark of the Policy Interpretation referenced above (the third compliance area (interests and abilities) is met if the school provides athletic opportunities for its male and female students in numbers substantially proportional to their respective enrollments) is the key standard by which to judge a particular institution's compliance with Title IX. Professor Julia Lamber has observed: "While institutions have attempted to comply with all three provisions of the Policy Interpretation, most of the litigation and legal commentary has focused on the substantial proportionality standard * * *. Most commentators simply assume that compliance will, at the end of the day, be measured in terms of substantial proportionality * * *." Julia Lamber, *Intercollegiate Athletics: The Program Expansion Standard Under Title IX's Policy Interpretation*, 12 S. CAL. REV. L. & WOMEN'S STUD. 31, 33 (2002). Professor Kimberly Yuracko explained the phenomenon as follows:

> In practice, compliance with respect to participation most often comes down to the proportionality requirement for two reasons. First, in light of the thirty years since Title IX's passage, it is difficult for any college to boast a history and continuing practice of program expansion for women if the school still does not provide proportionally equal opportunities for both sexes. Second, any time female students bring a Title IX lawsuit arguing that they are entitled to have a particular athletic team funded, it is difficult for a college to defend its lack of proportional opportunities by arguing that it has fully accommodated women's interests and abilities.

Kimberly Yuracko, *One for You and One for Me: Is Title IX's Sex-Based Proportionality Requirement for College Varsity Athletic Positions Defensible?*, 97 Nw. U.L. Rev. 731, 741

(2003). *See also,* Patrick N. Findlay, *The Case for Requiring a Proportionality Test to Assess Compliance with Title IX in High School Athletics,* 23 N. ILL. U. L. REV. 29 (2002).

In *Pederson v. Louisiana State University,* 213 F.3d 858 (5th Cir. 2000), the court did little to rebut the foregoing notion, reversing a lower court finding that compliance with Title IX should, in effect, not begin and end with the proportionality prong. The district court, in *dicta,* had denigrated the significance of the proportionality standard both from the standpoint of providing a "safe harbor" to potential defendants and also from the standpoint of giving an automatic litmus test of liability for putative plaintiffs:

> Plaintiffs and defendants desire this Court to find that, so long as males and females are represented in athletics in the same proportion as found in the general student population and are given numerically proportionate opportunity to participate in advanced competition, the university should be found in compliance with Title IX and, if numerical proportionality is not found, the institution should be found to be in violation of Title IX. This Court disagrees with either [sic] proposition.

Pederson v. Louisiana State University, 912 F. Supp. 892, 913–14 (N.D. La. 1996). The Fifth Circuit, while not negating the relevance of prongs two and three, refuted this statement and reinforced the idea that most Title IX compliance roads lead to the first prong of the Policy Interpretation:

> Appellees would have us hold that, although the student population of LSU is 51% male and 49% female, the population participating in athletics is 71% male and 29% female. Given this breakdown, they argue that it is improper to consider proportionality because to do so would be to impose quotas and that the evidence shows that female students are less interested in participating in sports than male students * * *. LSU's hubris in advancing this argument is remarkable, since of course fewer women participate in sports, given the voluminous evidence that LSU has discriminated against women in refusing to offer them comparable athletic opportunities to those it offers its male students.

Pederson v. Louisiana State University, 213 F.3d 858, 878 (5th Cir. 2000). Other circuits have similarly disdained the district court's *dicta* regarding the insignificance of the first prong. *See Neal v. Board of Trustees California State University,* 198 F.3d 763, 773 (9th Cir. 2000); *see also* Diane Heckman, *The Glass Sneaker: Thirty Years of Victories and Defeats Involving Title IX and Sex Discrimination in Athletics,* 13 FORDHAM INTELL. PROP. MEDIA & ENT. L. J. 551, 572–73 (2003).

In rejecting the plaintiff's arguments that Title IX's substantial proportionality requirement imposed a quota system or otherwise constituted an affirmative action program, the Fifth Circuit joined other circuits who have soundly repudiated such remonstrations. The First Circuit's unequivocal pronouncement is illustrative:

> Title IX is not an affirmative action statute; it is an anti-discrimination statute, modeled explicitly after another anti-discrimination statute, Title VI. No aspect of the Title IX regime at issue in this case—inclusive of the statute, the relevant regulation, and the pertinent agency documents—mandates gender-based preferences or quotas, or specific timetables for implementing numerical goals.

Cohen v. Brown University, 101 F.3d 155, 170 (1st Cir. 1996).

The proportionality prong perhaps has generated the most intense debate over Title IX's enforcement and the use of the benchmark criteria to aid in the determination of compliance. The scholarship surrounding this debate has been heated and prolific. As will be addressed in Part C, below, the gravamen of the controversy has been that the courts and pertinent regulations have made it clear that institutions can comply with the proportionality benchmark by eliminating men's sports to achieve the requisite equilibrium. The persistent question is whether contracting men's sports to achieve compliance furthers the ultimate goals of Title IX.

In March 2005, the Office of Civil Rights of the U.S. Department of Education provided schools with the "Additional Clarification of Intercollegiate Athletics Policy: Three-Part Test—Part Three." The purpose of the clarification memorandum was to delineate the factor OCR deems relevant in making a compliance determination under the third benchmark ("interests and abilities"). *See* Part IV(A) Note 2, *supra.* In pertinent part, the OCR announced:

> Under the third compliance option, an educational institution is in compliance with Title IX's mandate to provide equal athletic participation opportunities if, despite the underrepresentation of one sex in the intercollegiate athletics program, the institution is fully and effectively accommodating the athletic interests and abilities of its students who are underrepresented in its current varsity athletic program offerings. An institution will be found in compliance with part three unless there exists a sports(s) for the underrepresented sex for which all three of the following conditions are met: (1) unmet interest sufficient to sustain a varsity team in the sport(s); (2) sufficient ability to sustain an intercollegiate team in the sport(s); and (3) reasonable expectation of intercollegiate competition for a team in the sport(s)within the school's normal competitive region. Thus, schools are not required to accommodate the interests and abilities of all their students or fulfill every request for the addition or elevation of particular sports, unless all three conditions are present. In this analysis, the burden of proof is on OCR (in the case of an OCR investigation or compliance review), or on student (in the case of a complaint filed with the institution under its Title IX grievance procedures), to show by a preponderance of the evidence that the institution is not in compliance with part three.

This memorandum suggests that the third benchmark criterion, which has always been viewed as somewhat amorphous, may be the ultimate safe harbor for colleges and universities. Indeed, at one point, the memorandum declares that:

> The presumption of compliance can only be overcome if OCR finds direct and very persuasive evidence of unmet interest sufficient to sustain a varsity team such as the recent elimination of a viable team for the underrepresented sex or a recent, broad-based petition from an existing club team for elevation to varsity status.

Notes and Questions

1. Does the new interpretation advanced in OCR's clarification memorandum give many institutions a free pass? Has the burden shifted dramatically from the institution to OCR and any student seeking to challenge a school's failure to satisfy the benchmark criteria?

2. Is it conceivable that, by opening the doors for compliance through the third benchmark criterion, OCR has diminished the significance of the proportionality mandate? Will schools feel less of a need to contract men's programs because the presumption of compliance under the third prong will negate the importance of satisfying the

numbers game of the first prong? Does this "clarification" represent a step backward for Title IX as an effective mechanism for assuring gender equity in amateur athletics?

3. In the *Pederson* case, referenced above, the Fifth Circuit addressed issues other than the proportionality standard. Of particular significance is the court of appeals' review of the district court's finding that the plaintiffs in *Pederson* lacked standing because they failed to allege the injury of having been denied the *opportunity to compete* on a specific varsity team. The district court's finding would have necessitated a conclusion that a putative plaintiff's inability to *make* a team, if it had existed, would deprive that individual of standing. The court of appeals found such a standard to be too stringent. Dismissing the need to show that plaintiffs possessed the requisite skills to *make* one of the "unfielded varsity team squads," the Fifth Circuit declared, "A party need only demonstrate that she is 'able and ready' to compete for a position on the unfielded team. 213 F.3d at 871. The court cautioned, however, that standing to challenge a university's failure to provide an effective accommodation of the interest and abilities of its students does not *ipso facto* mean standing exists to challenge the *treatment* of current varsity athletes. *Id.* at 872; *see also Boucher v. Syracuse University*, 164 F.3d 113 (2d Cir. 1999). Those issues may be separate and distinct, potentially requiring a different demonstration of injury. For a useful overview of recent standing decisions in the context of Title IX, *see* Heckman, *The Glass Slipper, supra*, at 573–77. Do you agree with the court of appeals' assessment of the plaintiffs' standing in *Pederson*? Is the court's conclusion regarding the type of injury called for by Article III consistent with your understanding of Title IX's statutory mandate, as amplified by pertinent regulations?

As part of its overall standing analysis, the Fifth Circuit rejected defendant's companion contention that all of the plaintiffs' claims were moot. The court acknowledged that, because all named plaintiffs had graduated, their claims for injunctive relief would be moot. Such a result would not obtain, however, with regard to members of the putative class represented by these plaintiffs. Further, the court held that the plaintiffs' claims for monetary relief likewise were not rendered moot. Of particular relevance in a Title IX compliance scenario, the court noted that a party's claim could be deemed moot if: "(1) it can be said with assurance that there is no reasonable expectation * * * that the alleged violation will recur, and (2) interim relief or events have completely *and* irrevocably eradicated the effects of the alleged violation." (emphasis supplied). 213 F.2d at 874. Do you agree with the court in *Pederson* that defendants failed to satisfy both prongs of the quoted mootness test? Either prong? How would a defendant in LSU's situation effectively demonstrate that no reasonable expectation of recurrence exists?

In *Cook v. Colgate University*, 992 F.2d 17 (2d Cir. 1993), the court addressed an exception to the mootness doctrine for cases that are "capable of repetition, yet evading review." The two elements needed to meet the exception when the case is not a class action are: (1) the challenged action is too short in duration to be fully litigated prior to its cessation or expiration, and (2) there is a reasonable expectation that the same complaining party would be subjected to the same action again. In *Cook*, the district court had ordered Colgate to raise its female club ice hockey team to varsity status and to provide equal funding to its men's and women's ice hockey programs. *See Cook v. Colgate University*, 802 F. Supp. 737 (N.D.N.Y. 1972). The women's hockey team operated with a $4,000 total annual budget, $3,000 of which came from the university and $1,000 from alumni contributions. The men's hockey team allocated $12,500 per year for sticks alone. Yet, due to the graduation of the named plaintiffs and the absence of any allegations offered on behalf of a class of similarly situated persons, the Second Circuit found the Title IX claim moot and vacated a lower court judgment in favor of the plaintiffs.

4. In *NCAA v. Smith*, 525 U.S. 459 (1999), a prospective student-athlete sued the NCAA because it had denied her the opportunity to play intercollegiate volleyball at two member institutions that were recipients of federal funds. The plaintiff had contested the NCAA's post-baccalaureate by-laws, which precluded a postgraduate student-athlete from participating in intercollegiate athletics at any school other than the institution from which she had received her undergraduate degree. She had played volleyball at St. Bonaventure University for two years. After graduating from St. Bonaventure, she pursued post-graduate studies at Hofstra University and the University of Pittsburgh, and she sought to use her remaining eligibility to play volleyball at those schools. The U.S. Supreme Court held that although the NCAA received dues from these and other federally-funded institutions, the NCAA itself was not covered by Title IX. The statutory section in question, 20 U.S.C. § 1681(a), prohibited gender discrimination by "any educational program or activity receiving Federal financial assistance." The court concluded that the NCAA does not fall within the ambit of this language, and further found no evidence, or even an assertion, that the NCAA's constituent members paid dues with any "federal funds earmarked for that purpose." *Id.* at 468. Given the nexus between the NCAA and its member institutions, is there a viable argument that Title IX should reach the NCAA? Would the same arguments be workable regarding the institution's conference affiliation? *See generally Tarkanian v. NCAA*, 488 U.S. 179 (1988).

C. Compliance By Contraction

In footnote 15 of *Cohen I*, the court acknowledged compliance by contraction, allowing a university to cut men's sports in order to achieve proportionality and meet the first benchmark test. This interpretation was consistent with 1979 DCR regulations that sanctioned as a valid form of compliance the elimination or curtailment of men's intercollegiate athletic programs. Thus, the battle lines were drawn as the potential for the wholesale elimination of men's programs was born. In a sense, universities were invited to take the back door solution by cutting non-revenue producing men's teams rather than develop creative ideas to level the playing field without leaving scars. The debate rages as to whether this approach comports with the letter and spirit of Title IX.

Consider the following hypotheticals. You are the parent of a male high school senior who is a phenomenal golfer, heavily recruited by several Division 1 universities. Some of the schools are nationally ranked football and basketball powerhouses. Your son chooses State University partly because of its location, and partly because it boasts an outstanding golf team and your son wants to bypass the professional tour to play golf at the intercollegiate level. In his sophomore year of college, after a freshman year in which he distinguished himself as an outstanding member of the golf team, excelled in the classroom, and developed several close friendships with coaches, teachers, and peers, the university terminates the golf team to achieve compliance with Title IX.

How would you react?

Consider this as well: at this same university women comprise 70% of the student body, but only 30% of the student-athletes, despite numerous requests to elevate many women's club sports to varsity status. Consider further that the university is unable to demonstrate that it is financially unable to allocate more university dollars to women's athletic programs and, even if it did, it could demonstrate no related need to impose the austerity program reflected in belt-tightening measures such as the evisceration of the men's golf team. Finally, consider that the high school all-state softball player who desperately wants to play inter-collegiate softball at State University is somebody's daughter; in the next hypothetical, she could be yours.

The following case joins the issue and perhaps explains why the diminution of men's programs is both scorned by dissenters as a non-viable option and accepted by advocates as perhaps the only port in some compliance storms.

Neal v. Board of Trustees of the California State Universities
198 F.3d 763 (9th Cir. 1999)

HALL, Circuit Judge.

* * *

The instant case requires us to consider whether Title IX prevents a university in which male students occupy a disproportionately high percentage of athletic roster spots from making gender-conscious decisions to reduce the proportion of roster spots assigned to men. We hold that Title IX does not bar such remedial actions.

The Board of Trustees of the California State Universities and other defendants appeal from the district court's order granting the motion of Neal and other plaintiffs for a preliminary injunction. Neal's suit alleged that the decision of California State University, Bakersfield ("CSUB") to reduce the number of spots on its men's wrestling team, undertaken as part of a university-wide program to achieve "substantial proportionality" between each gender's participation in varsity sports and its composition in the campus's student body, violated Title IX and the Equal Protection Clause of the United States Constitution. The district court determined that regulations promulgated pursuant to Title IX, and CSUB's program, which was modeled after those regulations, violated Title IX. The district court declined to reach the merits of the constitutional challenge, but did hold that the regulations interpreting Title IX "raised serious constitutional questions" and rejected Plaintiffs' construction of Title IX on that alternative ground. This Court has jurisdiction to review the district court's granting of a preliminary injunction under 28 U.S.C. § 1292(a)(1). We reverse, and vacate the injunction.

I.

Defendant/Appellant CSUB is a large public university where female students outnumbered male students by roughly 64% to 36% in 1996. The composition of CSUB's varsity athletic rosters, however, was quite different. In the 1992–93 academic year, male students took 61% of the university's spots on athletic rosters and received 68% of CSUB's available athletic scholarship money.

This imbalance helped prompt a lawsuit by the California chapter of the National Organization for Women, alleging that the California State University system was violating a state law that is similar to the federal government's Title IX. That lawsuit eventually settled, resulting in a consent decree mandating, inter alia, that each Cal State campus have a proportion of female athletes that was within five percentage points of the proportion of female undergraduate students at that school. This portion of the consent decree was patterned after the first part of the three-part Title IX compliance test promulgated by the Department of Education's Office for Civil Rights ("OCR").

When the university agreed to the consent decree, California was slowly emerging from a recession, and state funding for higher education was declining. As a result, CSUB administrators were seriously constrained in what they could spend on athletic programs. The university chose to adopt squad size targets, which would encourage the expansion of the women's teams while limiting the size of the men's teams. In order to comply with the consent decree, CSUB opted for smaller men's teams across the board, rejecting the alternative of eliminating some men's teams entirely. CSUB's plan was designed to bring it into compliance with the consent decree by the 1997–98 academic year, meaning that female students would fill at least 55% of the spaces on the school's athletic teams.

As part of this across-the-board reduction in the number of slots available to men's athletic teams, the size of the men's wrestling team was capped at 27. Although the reduction was protested vigorously by wrestling coach Terry Kerr, and team captain Stephen Neal expressed concerns that a smaller squad would prove less competitive, the smaller CSUB team performed exceptionally well, winning the Pac-10 Conference title and finishing third in the nation in 1996. In 1996–97, the men's wrestling roster was capped at 25, and four of these spots went unused. Nevertheless, in response to the rumored elimination of the men's wrestling team, on January 10, 1997, the team filed the instant lawsuit, alleging that the university's policy capping the size of the men's team constituted discrimination on the basis of gender in violation of Title IX and the Equal Protection Clause of the Federal Constitution.

The team sought declaratory and injunctive relief to prevent the squad size reductions. CSUB responded by filing a motion to dismiss. The district court initially granted a temporary restraining order preventing the reductions, then granted a preliminary injunction to prevent CSUB from reducing the size of the wrestling team. The district court concluded as a matter of fact that CSUB's primary motivation for capping the size of the men's teams was to meet the gender proportionality requirements in the consent decree. The district court concluded as a matter of law that capping the male teams in order to comply with the consent decree violated Title IX. Although the district court refused to rule on Plaintiffs' equal protection challenge to the CSUB policy, the court did reject a reading of Title IX that created a "safe harbor" for any school that achieved substantial proportionality between the percentage of athletes of one gender and the percentage of students of that same gender. The court concluded that such an approach would raise serious questions under the Equal Protection Clause, and that a desire to avoid reaching such questions, in and of itself, constituted "ample reason for rejecting the safe harbor idea as part of Title IX."

* * *

III.

This case has its origins in Congress's passage of Title IX in 1972. Title IX was Congress's response to significant concerns about discrimination against women in education. In the words of the legislation's primary sponsor, Senator Birch Bayh, Title IX was enacted to "provide for the women of America something that is rightfully theirs—an equal chance to attend the schools of their choice, to develop the skills they want, and to apply those skills with the knowledge that they will have a fair chance to secure the jobs of their choice with equal pay for equal work."

The regulations promulgated pursuant to Title IX require schools receiving federal funding to "provide equal athletic opportunity for members of both sexes". 34 C.F.R.

§ 106.41(c). In evaluating schools' compliance with that provision, one factor that will be considered is "whether the selection of sports and levels of competition effectively accommodate the interests and abilities of members of both sexes". At the same time, "it would require blinders to ignore that the motivation for promulgation of the regulation on athletics was the historic emphasis on boys' athletic programs to the exclusion of girls' athletic programs in * * * colleges." The drafters of these regulations recognized a situation that Congress well understood: Male athletes had been given an enormous head start in the race against their female counterparts for athletic resources, and Title IX would prompt universities to level the proverbial playing field.

Appellees recognize that, given this backdrop, it would be imprudent to argue that Title IX prohibits the use of all gender-conscious remedies. Appellees therefore suggest that gender-conscious remedies are appropriate only when necessary to ensure that schools provide opportunities to males and females in proportion to their relative levels of interest in sports participation. By contrast, Appellants contend that schools may make gender-conscious decisions about sports-funding levels to correct for an imbalance between the composition of the undergraduate student body and the composition of the undergraduate student athletic participants pool. This disagreement has real significance: Men's expressed interest in participating in varsity sports is apparently higher than women's at the present time—although the "interest gap" continues to narrow—so permitting gender-conscious remedies until the proportions of students and athletes are roughly proportional gives universities more remedial freedom than permitting remedies only until expressed interest and varsity roster spots correspond.

Appellees' argument that equal opportunity is achieved when each gender's athletic participation roughly matches its interest in participating is hardly novel. Several courts of appeals have considered and rejected Appellees' approach as fundamentally inconsistent with the purpose of Title IX.

Cohen v. Brown University, (*Cohen I*) was the first case to rule on the issues raised in the instant appeal.

* * *

The *Cohen I* court explicitly rejected Brown's argument that, because male athletes were more interested in athletics, the school could bring itself into Title IX compliance by providing females with fewer athletic roster spots "as long as the school's response is in direct proportion to the comparative levels of interest." In *Cohen II,* the rejection of Brown's argument was even more emphatic: "Brown's relative interests approach cannot withstand scrutiny on either legal or policy grounds, because it disadvantages women and undermines the remedial purposes of Title IX by limiting required program expansion for the underrepresented sex to the status quo level of relative interests."

Under *Cohen I,* if a university wanted to comply with the first part of the three-part test, it had to provide "athletics opportunities in proportion to the gender composition of the student body," not in proportion to the expressed interests of men and women. *See also Favia v. Indiana Univ. of Penn.*, 7 F.3d 332, 343 (3d Cir.1993) (observing that a university whose student body was 56% female, but whose athletic teams were 43% female, would "appear not to be in Title IX compliance"). The reason for *Cohen I*'s rejection of Brown's/Appellees' "interest" test was clear enough: "Given that the survey of interests and abilities would begin under circumstances where men's athletic teams have a considerable head start, such a rule would almost certainly blunt the exhortation that schools should 'take into account the nationally increasing levels of women's interests and abilities' and avoid 'disadvantag[ing] members of an underrepresented sex. * * *'"

In other words, Appellees' interpretation of Title IX would have allowed universities to do little or nothing to equalize men's and women's opportunities if they could point to data showing that women were less interested in sports. But a central aspect of Title IX's purpose was to *encourage* women to participate in sports: The increased number of roster spots and scholarships reserved for women would gradually increase demand among women for those roster spots and scholarships. As the First Circuit held in *Cohen II*, "[t]o assert that Title IX permits institutions to provide fewer athletics participation opportunities for women than for men, based upon the premise that women are less interested in sports than are men, is (among other things) to ignore the fact that Title IX was enacted in order to remedy discrimination that results from stereotyped notions of women's interests and abilities."

Appellees and the district court relied heavily on a lone district court opinion, *Pederson v. Louisiana State Univ.*, 912 F.Supp. 892 (M.D.La.1996), which criticized the Policy Interpretation test's first part. However, this criticism is entirely dicta: The court still found Louisiana State University ("LSU") to be in violation of Title IX and ordered it to bring itself into Title IX compliance immediately, hinting that it should do so by funding women's soccer and softball teams. *See id.* at 922. The court never addressed the issue of whether LSU could bring itself into Title IX compliance by cutting the opportunities available to male athletes because the parties there never suggested such an approach. Moreover, the *Pederson* court misunderstood the reasoning behind *Cohen* [and similar circuit court opinions]. The *Pederson* court held that these circuit court opinions relied upon an erroneous assumption that men and women were equally interested in playing sports. As is explained above, those courts emphasized that women's interest in sports appeared to be lower than men's, but that the genders' interests were slowly but surely converging, which was precisely the reason why requiring only that each gender's expressed interest in participating be accommodated equally would freeze the inequality of the status quo.

Title IX is a dynamic statute, not a static one. It envisions continuing progress toward the goal of equal opportunity for all athletes and recognizes that, where society has conditioned women to expect less than their fair share of the athletic opportunities, women's interest in participating in sports will not rise to a par with men's overnight. The percentage of college athletes who are women rose from 15% in 1972 to 37% in 1998, and Title IX is at least partially responsible for this trend of increased participation by women. Title IX has altered women's preferences, making them more interested in sports, and more likely to become student athletes. Adopting Appellees' interest-based test for Title IX compliance would hinder, and quite possibly reverse, the steady increases in women's participation and interest in sports that have followed Title IX's enactment.

A number of courts of appeals have addressed another potentially dispositive issue in this appeal—namely, whether Title IX permits a university to diminish athletic opportunities available to men so as to bring them into line with the lower athletic opportunities available to women. Every court, in construing the Policy Interpretation and the text of Title IX, has held that a university may bring itself into Title IX compliance by increasing athletic opportunities for the underrepresented gender (women in this case) *or* by decreasing athletic opportunities for the overrepresented gender (men in this case). An extensive survey of Title IX's legislative history and the regulations promulgated to apply its provisions to college athletics concluded that boosters of male sports argued vociferously before Congress that the proposed regulations would require schools to shift resources from men's programs to women's programs, but that Congress nevertheless sided "with women's advocates" by deciding not to repeal the HEW's athletics-related Title IX regulations. Congress thus appears to have believed that Title IX would result in funding reductions to male athletic programs. If a university wishes to comply with Title IX by leveling down programs instead of ratcheting them up, as Appellant has done here, Title IX is not offended.

There is a second reason why a reversal of the district court's order granting injunctive relief on the Title IX claim is warranted. The district court failed to defer properly to the interpretation of Title IX put forward by the administrative agency that is explicitly authorized to enforce its provisions. It is well-established that the federal courts are to defer substantially to an agency's interpretation of its own regulations. The Department of Education, "acting through its OCR [is] the administrative agency charged with administering Title IX." In this instance, Congress explicitly delegated to the agency the task of prescribing standards for athletic programs under Title IX. Under *Chevron,* where Congress has expressly delegated to an agency the power to "elucidate a specific provision of the statute by regulation," that agency's regulations should be accorded "controlling weight unless they are arbitrary, capricious, or manifestly contrary to the statute."

Appellees deem *Chevron* inapplicable on the ground that OCR's interpretation violates the plain meaning of the statute. Under their interpretation, Title IX bars universities from disadvantaging any student athlete on the basis of his or her gender. But the plain meaning of the nondiscrimination principle set forth in 20 U.S.C. §1681(a) does not bar remedial actions designed to achieve substantial proportionality between athletic rosters and student bodies. Indeed, Appellees' interpretation of 20 U.S.C. §681(a)'s plain meaning would render 1681(b) superfluous. After all, §1681(b) states that Title IX does not *require*

> any education institution to grant preferential or disparate treatment to the members of one sex on account of an imbalance which may exist with respect to the total number or percentage of persons of that sex participating in or receiving the benefits of any federally supported program or activity, in comparison with the total number or percentage of persons of that sex in any community* * *.

If §1681(a) already bars the type of remedial action that Appellant engaged in pursuant to the consent decree, then §1681(b)'s provision that Title IX does not require such remedial action would be mere surplusage. "Statutes must be interpreted, if possible, to give each word some operative effect."

Moreover, we deem it highly instructive that, at oral argument, Appellees conceded that their proposed interpretation of Title IX, whereby a university could permissibly discriminate on the basis of sex in order to ensure that each gender's interests in athletic participation were equally accommodated, is just as contrary to 1681(a)'s purported plain meaning as the interpretation advanced by the OCR and Appellants is.

We also note that Appellees' interpretation of Title IX's text has been rejected explicitly by the Seventh Circuit, as well as the OCR, and implicitly rejected by the other circuits that have held that a school may cut the number of male athletic slots in order to bring itself into compliance with Title IX. Under such circumstances, it is clear that OCR's interpretation of Title IX's athletics provisions merits deference under *Martin* and *Chevron.* In *Cohen II* and *Kelley* the courts held that 34 C.F.R. §106.41 deserved controlling weight under *Chevron* and that the OCR Policy Interpretation deserved substantial deference under *Martin.* Similarly, in the case before us, the 1996 OCR Clarification and the Cantu letter explaining it merit deference under *Martin*. These clarifications essentially adopted the reasoning of *Cohen I* as OCR policy. Under these clarifications' clear wording, an institution in which male athletes are overrepresented can bring itself into Title IX compliance by reducing sufficiently the number of roster spots available to men.

Finally, the district court below rejected the interpretation of Title IX advocated by the OCR and Appellants on the ground that such a reading of the statute might violate the Constitution. In the court's words, OCR's interpretation would effectively transform Title IX from an anti-discrimination statute to a statute enacted to remedy past discrimination, thus subjecting it to heightened scrutiny. Without speculating whether Title IX would survive such searching constitutional scrutiny, the court notes that it remains unsatisfied with the *Cohen* majority's treatment of these important questions. The court is satisfied that avoiding serious constitutional questions such as an equal protection challenge to a very important Congressional statute is itself ample reason for rejecting the safe harbor idea as part of Title IX.

The district court thus strained to interpret Title IX in a way that ostensibly would avoid these concerns. In doing so, it followed the interpretive methodology laid out by the Supreme Court in *NLRB v. Catholic Bishop of Chicago* (1979). Chief Justice Burger, writing for the *Catholic Bishop* majority, announced that the Court would decline to construe an act of Congress "in a manner that could in turn call upon the Court to resolve difficult and sensitive questions arising out of the guarantees of the First Amendment Religious Clauses." Under *Catholic Bishop*, the inquiry properly raised on appeal is not whether the OCR's interpretation of Title IX is unconstitutional, but whether it "raises serious constitutional questions." We answer that question in the negative.

The First and Seventh Circuits both have considered at length the constitutionality of the first prong of the OCR's test. In *Cohen I, Cohen II*, and *Kelley*, the courts emphatically rejected the claim that the Policy Interpretation was unconstitutional under the Fourteenth Amendment. The separate reasoning in the two *Cohen* opinions is particularly well-developed. It applied intermediate scrutiny, which we would also do were we addressing the constitutional merits. *Cohen II* noted that the Policy Interpretation furthered the "clearly important" objectives of "avoid[ing] the use of federal resources to support discriminatory practices, and provid[ing] individual citizens effective protection against those practices." Moreover, it found that "judicial enforcement of federal anti-discrimination statutes is at least an important governmental objective." And *Cohen II* held that the district court's relief, which was essentially identical to what the OCR Policy Interpretation calls for, was "clearly substantially related" to these objectives. Along the same lines, the Seventh Circuit has held that "the remedial scheme established by Title IX and the applicable regulation and policy interpretation are clearly substantially related to" the objective of prohibiting "educational institutions from discriminating on the basis of sex." We adopt the reasoning of *Cohen I, Cohen II*, and *Kelley*, and hold that the constitutional analysis contained therein persuasively disposes of any serious constitutional concerns that might be raised in relation to the OCR Policy Interpretation. The district court's final basis for rejecting the OCR's interpretation of Title IX was therefore erroneous.

IV.

This past summer, 90,185 enthusiastic fans crowded into Pasadena's historic Rose Bowl for the finals of the Women's World Cup soccer match. An estimated 40 million television viewers also tuned in to watch a thrilling battle between the American and

Chinese teams. The match ended when American defender Brandi Chastain fired the ball past Chinese goalkeeper Gao Hong, breaking a 4-4 shootout tie. The victory sparked a national celebration and a realization by many that women's sports could be just as exciting, competitive, and lucrative as men's sports. And the victorious athletes understood as well as anyone the connection between a 27-year-old statute and tangible progress in women's athletics. Title IX has enhanced, and will continue to enhance, women's opportunities to enjoy the thrill of victory, the agony of defeat, and the many tangible benefits that flow from just being given a chance to participate in intercollegiate athletics. Today we join our sister circuits in holding that Title IX does not bar universities from taking steps to ensure that women are approximately as well represented in sports programs as they are in student bodies. We REVERSE, and VACATE the preliminary injunction.

Notes and Questions

1. Wrestling has been an oft-cited example of the casualties created by tolerance of a compliance by contraction approach. *See, e.g., Chalenor v. Univ. of N.D.*, 291 F.3d 1042 (8th Cir. 2002); *Nat'l Wrestling Coaches Ass'n v. United States Dep't of Educ.*, 263 F. Supp. 2d 82 (D.D.C. 2003); *Gonyo v. Drake Univ.*, 879 F. Supp. 1000 (S.D. Iowa 1995). Similar fates have befallen teams in swimming, *Kelly v. Bd. of Trs.*, 35 F.3d 265 (7th Cir. 1994); lacrosse, *Barret v. West Chester Univ.*, 2003 WL 22803477 (E.D. Pa. 2003); tennis, *Miami Univ. Wrestling Club v. Miami Univ.*, 302 F.3d 608 (6th Cir. 2002); and soccer, *id.*

2. What purpose does the court's concluding paragraph serve? Does it amount to a cost-benefit analysis in which the benefits overwhelmingly carry the day?

3. Commentators sharply criticize compliance by contraction because of the harm that it causes to men's sports, and the wrestling coach and team in *Neal* expressed great concern about the reduction in their team size. However, after the wrestling team's size was capped, it won the Pac-10 Conference and finished third in the nation. The following year, with the cap still in place, the team had four more slots for team members than they actually needed. The question irresistibly becomes, were they really harmed at all?

4. California State University, Bakersfield chose to limit the size of men's teams across the board to comply with a consent decree requiring substantial proportionality. Although the wrestling team vigorously protested and filed this lawsuit, it is likely that other affected teams strongly opposed the university's action. Why do you think the administrators chose to cap numerous men's teams instead of eliminating just a few teams? Again, is this a product of some type of academic social democracy? What role is likely played by alumni pressure? Is the historic excellence and reputation of a particular sport at a particular school (*e.g.*, golf at Wake Forest University) relevant?

5. Do you think the court's decision would have been any different if the men's wrestling program had been totally eliminated? *See Miami University Wrestling Club v. Miami University*, 302 F.3d 608 (6th Cir. 2002).

D. The Contact Sports Exception

Perhaps the easiest way to understand the scope of the "contact sports" exception is to envision the regulatory scheme in four parts. The *general rule* is that athletic opportunities must be afforded on a non-discriminatory basis, which means, under the regulations, on a non-segregated basis. 34 C.F.R. § 106.41 (a). *Gender segregated teams are permitted* under two circumstances: where selection for the team is based on "competitive skill" or where the activity is a "contact sport." A *single gender exclusive team*—i.e., a team for just one sex, with no such team for the other sex—is permitted for teams based on "competitive skill," subject to this proviso: if the excluded sex is one for whom "athletic opportunities * * * have previously been limited," then members of the excluded sex must be permitted to try out for the team. *Categorical exclusion, with no opportunity for try outs*, is permitted for "contact sports"; boxing, wrestling, rugby, ice hockey, football, basketball, "and other sports the purpose or major activity of which involves bodily contact," are explicitly excepted from the try outs requirement for single, gender exclusive teams. 34 C.F.R. §106.41 (b).

Does the contact sports exception survive scrutiny under the equal protection clause? As Professor Sangree notes, one putative purpose for the rule—probably *the* putative purpose—is that it will protect athletes from injury. *See* Suzanne Sangree, *Title IX and the Contact Sports Exception: Gender Stereotypes in a Civil Rights Statute*, 32 CONN L. REV 381 (2000)Such a purpose is, in all likelihood, an "important" one. But is a categorical gender exclusion "substantially related" to that important governmental purpose? On the one hand, there is no denying that female athletes are, on average, not as big, not as strong, and not as fast as their male counterparts, and it is not illogical to suppose that, by virtue of these differences, they will be more prone to injury in coeducational athletics. On the other hand, reliance on average differences obscures the fact that many women are big enough, strong enough, and fast enough to compete in at least some coeducational athletic settings. *Cf. Virginia*, 518 U.S. at 542. The exclusion, then, clearly relies on an over-generalization; is that generalization so overbroad that it is invalid?

"[It] is far from clear," a District Court judge in Texas recently opined, "that the refusal to sanction a mixed-gender contact sport violates the Fourteenth Amendment." *Barnett v. Texas Wrestling Ass'n*, 16 F. Supp. 2d 690, 696 (N.D.Tex. 1998). Most courts that have considered the question, however, have ruled that the contact sports exception *is* impermissibly overbroad. Thus courts have rejected the categorical ban as it has been applied to football, *see, e.g., Force v. Pierce City R-VI School District*, 570 F. Supp. 1020 (W.D. Mo. 1983) (generalizations about the "typical" girl athlete cannot justify exclusion of every girl); soccer, *see, e.g., Hoover v. Meiklejohn*, 430 F. Supp. 164 (D. Colo. 1977) (exclusion rooted in "a cultural anachronism unrelated to reality"); and wrestling, *Adams v. Baker*, 919 F. Supp. 1496 (D. Kan. 1996) (safety arguments "suggest the very sort of well-meaning but overly 'paternalistic' attitude about females which the Supreme Court has viewed with such concern"); *see also Saint v. Nebraska Sch. Activities Assoc.*, 684 F. Supp. 626 (D. Neb. 1998) (impermissible to presume that girls are "innately inferior"); have rejected attempts to exclude female ballplayers from baseball on the premise that baseball is a "contact sport," *see, e.g., Carnes v. Tennessee Secondary Schools Athletic Ass'n.*, 415 F. Supp. 569 (E.D. Tenn. 1976); *see also Fortin v. Darlington Little League*, 514 F.2d 344 (1st Cir. 1975) (contention that girls will be injury prone in Little League Baseball "is unsupported"); and have held that the categorical exclusion of girls from all boys' "contact sports" violates due process, because "girls must be given the opportunity to compete with boys in interscholastic contact sports if they are physically qualified." *Yellow Springs Exempted Village School Dist. Bd. of Ed. v. Ohio*, 443 F. Supp. 753, 758 (D.C. Ohio 1978), *rev'd on other grounds*, 647 F.2d 651 (6th Cir. 1981).

In addition, the Seventh Circuit relied on the contact-sports exception to bolster its decision upholding a company "fetal protection policy" that barred women from working in high lead exposure positions in the battery manufacturing division. "The risk of injury to women from contact sports," the court insisted, "is based upon the recognized innate physical differences between men and women, matters analogous to Johnson's fetal protection policy's concern with the differences between men and women relating to childbearing capacity." *International Union, United Auto., Aerospace and Agr. Implement Workers of America, UAW v. Johnson Controls, Inc.*, 886 F.2d 871, 895 (7th Cir., 1989). But the Supreme Court reversed, holding that the policy was discriminatory under Title VII, and could not be justified on the grounds that gender was a "bona fide occupational qualification." "Our cases," Justice Blackmun wrote for the court, "have stressed that discrimination on the basis of sex because of safety concerns is allowed only in narrow circumstances." *International Union, United Auto., Aerospace and Agr. Implement Workers of America, UAW v. Johnson Controls, Inc.*, 499 U.S. 187, 202 (1991).

On the other hand, a rule prohibiting a girl from trying out for the boys' basketball team was upheld on the theory that it was substantially related to the important interest in "maximizing sports participation." The plaintiff, the court concluded, "never disputes defendants' assertion that boys [her] age are substantially better than girls at basketball * * * [and] has never attempted to prove that the generalization is sufficiently unreliable so that it should not be given conclusive weight." *O'Connor v. Board of Educ. of School Dist. 23*, 545 F. Supp. 376, 381 (D.Ill. 1982). And the exception has been upheld by one court as it applies to boxing. *See Lafler v. Athletic Board of Control*, 536 F. Supp. 104 (W.D. Mich. 1982).

A irresistible corollary question is whether boys have a right to play on "girls' teams"? Recall that Title IX permits sex segregated teams where membership is based on competitive skill, but requires open try-outs where the school offers just one gender exclusive team in a sport if the excluded sex is one for whom "athletic opportunities * * * have previously been limited." Can boys plausibly maintain that their "athletic opportunities * * * have previously been limited"? Part of the answer to that question likely depends on the specificity of the inquiry. While boys may well have had limited opportunities in specific sports—field hockey, softball, perhaps volleyball at some institutions—it is unlikely that their general opportunities have been limited. Which is the more appropriate focus? The dominant view—not quite a consensus—has been that the Title IX regulations are concerned with overall athletic opportunities, not the history of exclusion from a particular sport. *See, e.g., Williams v. School District of Bethlehem, Pa.*, 998 F.2d 168, 174 (3rd Cir. 1993) ("If Congress had intended the inquiry into 'athletic opportunities' to be limited to a 'particular sport,' it would have so stated, particularly since the phrase 'particular sport' was used earlier in the same sentence."); *Kleczek v. Rhode Island Interscholastic League, Inc.*, 768 F. Supp. 951, 955 (D.R.I. 1991) ("Under the obvious plain meaning of the regulation, [plaintiff] need not be provided the opportunity to play on the girls' field hockey team because athletic opportunities at South Kingstown High School have not previously been limited for members of his sex."); *but see Gomes v. Rhode Island Interscholastic League*, 469 F. Supp. 659, 665 (D.R.I. 1979) ("At least in terms of volleyball at Rogers High, athletic opportunities for males have been severely limited."). *See also* Adam Darowski, *For Kenny, Who Wanted To Play Women's Field Hockey,* 12 DUKE J. GENDER L. & POL'Y 153 (Spring 2005).

Partly as a consequence of this reading of Title IX, the majority of reported opinions has rejected challenges to the exclusion of boys from all-girls teams. *See, e.g., Williams, supra* (girls volleyball); *Kleckek, supra* (field hockey); *B.C. v. Board of Educ., Cumberland Regional School Dist.*, 531 A.2d 1059 (N.J. Super. Ct. App. Div. 1987) (field hockey). Some schools and school districts, however, have granted boys' requests to play field hockey, without apparent harm either to the sport or its participants. *See* Mike Wise, *In Field Hockey, a Twist on Title IX*, N.Y. TIMES, Oct. 18, 2001. It has been suggested that the crossover of girls to boys' sports and vice versa could result in the gradual takeover of girls' teams by boys. For example, if boys were permitted to compete for positions on the girls' softball team, could the softball team eventually be dominated by boys who failed to secure a spot on the boys' baseball team or who prefer softball over baseball? Is the concern that boys will seek to infiltrate girls' teams on a wholesale basis realistic?

The impulse in the cases is to treat the issue largely as a physiological one: Are the physical differences between the sexes substantial enough to justify the exclusion? Articulating the subsidiary issues reveals the difficulty with this approach: How much bigger, stronger, and faster do male athletes have to be to justify the generalization, and how many exceptions to the generalization must we tolerate before it becomes impermissibly overbroad? An alternative approach, perhaps, would focus on the harm of exclusion. To some extent, the question remains empirical—how many "otherwise qualified" athletes are excluded by the categorical ban—but to a larger extent, the question is more theoretical: Does the exclusion perpetuate a gender-based hierarchy? As the district court in Missouri noted in striking down the exclusion of girls from football, "a gender based classification which results from ascribing a particular trait or quality to one sex, when not all share that trait or quality, is not only inherently unfair but generally tends only to perpetuate 'stereotypic notions' regarding the proper roles of men and women." *Force v. Pierce City R-VI Sch. Dist.*, 570 F. Supp. 1020, 1026 (W.D. Mo. 1983).

Mercer v. Duke University
190 F.3d 643 (4th Cir. 1999).

LUTTIG, Circuit Judge. Appellant Heather Sue Mercer challenges the federal district court's holding that Title IX provides a blanket exemption for contact sports and the court's consequent dismissal of her claim that Duke University discriminated against her during her participation in Duke's intercollegiate football program. For the reasons that follow, we hold that where a university has allowed a member of the opposite sex to try out for a single-sex team in a contact sport, the university is, contrary to the holding of the district court, subject to Title IX and therefore prohibited from discriminating against that individual on the basis of his or her sex.

I.

Appellee Duke University operates a Division I college football team. During the period relevant to this appeal (1994–98), appellee Fred Goldsmith was head coach of the Duke football team and appellant Heather Sue Mercer was a student at the school.

Before attending Duke, Mercer was an all-state kicker at Yorktown Heights High School in Yorktown Heights, New York. Upon enrolling at Duke in the fall of 1994, Mercer tried out for the Duke football team as a walk-on kicker. Mercer was the first—and to date, only—woman to try out for the team. Mercer did not initially make the team, and instead served as a manager during the 1994 season; however, she regularly attended practices in the fall of 1994 and participated in conditioning drills the following spring.

In April 1995, the seniors on the team selected Mercer to participate in the Blue-White Game, an intrasquad scrimmage played each spring. In that game, Mercer kicked the winning 28-yard field goal, giving the Blue team a 24-22 victory. The kick was subsequently shown on ESPN, the cable television sports network. Soon after the game, Goldsmith told the news media that Mercer was on the Duke football team, and Fred Chatham, the Duke kicking coach, told Mercer herself that she had made the team. Also, Mike Cragg, the Duke sports information director, asked Mercer to participate in a number of interviews with newspaper, radio, and television reporters, including one with representatives from "The Tonight Show."

Although Mercer did not play in any games during the 1995 season, she again regularly attended practices in the fall and participated in conditioning drills the following spring. Mercer was also officially listed by Duke as a member of the Duke football team on the team roster filed with the NCAA and was pictured in the Duke football yearbook.

During this latter period, Mercer alleges that she was the subject of discriminatory treatment by Duke. Specifically, she claims that Goldsmith did not permit her to attend summer camp, refused to allow her to dress for games or sit on the sidelines during games, and gave her fewer opportunities to participate in practices than other walk-on kickers. In addition, Mercer claims that Goldsmith made a number of offensive comments to her, including asking her why she was interested in football, wondering why she did not prefer to participate in beauty pageants rather than football, and suggesting that she sit in the stands with her boyfriend rather than on the sidelines.

At the beginning of the 1996 season, Goldsmith informed Mercer that he was dropping her from the team. Mercer alleges that Goldsmith's decision to exclude her from the team was on the basis of her sex because Goldsmith allowed other, less qualified walk-on kickers to remain on the team. Mercer attempted to participate in conditioning drills the following spring, but Goldsmith asked her to leave because the drills were only for members of the team. Goldsmith told Mercer, however, that she could try out for the team again in the fall.

On September 16, 1997, rather than try out for the team again, Mercer filed suit against Duke and Goldsmith, alleging sex discrimination in violation of Title IX of the Education Amendments of 1972, 20 U.S.C. §§ 1681–1688, and negligent misrepresentation and breach of contract in violation of North Carolina law. Duke and Goldsmith filed a motion to dismiss for failure to state a claim under Title IX, and, after discovery was completed, Duke and Goldsmith filed additional motions for summary judgment and a motion to dismiss for lack of subject-matter jurisdiction. On November 9, 1998, the district court granted the motion to dismiss for failure to state a claim under Title IX, and dismissed the state-law claims without prejudice, refusing to exercise supplemental jurisdiction over those claims. The district court declined to rule on any of the other outstanding motions. The district court subsequently denied Mercer's motion to alter judgment.

From the district court's order dismissing her Title IX claim for failure to state a claim upon which relief can be granted and its order denying the motion to alter judgment, Mercer appeals.

II.

Title IX prohibits discrimination on the basis of sex by educational institutions receiving federal funding. *See* 20 U.S.C. § 1681(a) ("No person in the United States shall, on the basis of sex, be excluded from participation in, be denied the benefits of, or be subjected to discrimination under any education program or activity receiving Federal financial assistance * * *"). Soon after enacting Title IX, Congress charged the Department of Health, Education, and Welfare (HEW) with responsibility for developing regulations regarding the applicability of Title IX to athletic programs. *See* Pub.L. No. 93-380, §844, 88 Stat. 484 (1974). Acting upon that charge, HEW duly promulgated 34 C.F.R. §106.41, which reads in relevant part as follows:

Athletics.

(a) General. No person shall, on the basis of sex, be excluded from participation in, be denied the benefits of, be treated differently from another person or otherwise be discriminated against in any interscholastic, intercollegiate, club or intramural athletics offered by a recipient, and no recipient shall provide any such athletics separately on such basis.

(b) Separate teams. Notwithstanding the requirements of paragraph (a) of this section, a recipient may operate or sponsor separate teams for members of each sex where selection for such teams is based upon competitive skill or the activity involved is a contact sport. However, where a recipient operates or sponsors a team in a particular sport for members of one sex but operates or sponsors no such team for members of the other sex, and athletic opportunities for members of that sex have previously been limited, members of the excluded sex must be allowed to try out for the team offered unless the sport involved is a contact sport. For the purposes of this part, contact sports include boxing, wrestling, rugby, ice hockey, football, basketball and other sports the purpose or major activity of which involves bodily contact.

34 C.F.R. §106.41(a)–(b). The district court held, and appellees contend on appeal, that, under this regulation, "contact sports, such as football, are specifically excluded from Title IX coverage." We disagree.

Subsections (a) and (b) of section 106.41 stand in a symbiotic relationship to one another. Subsection (a) establishes a baseline prohibition against sex discrimination in intercollegiate athletics, tracking almost identically the language in the parallel statutory provision prohibiting discrimination by federally funded educational institutions. In addition to generally barring discrimination on the basis of sex in intercollegiate athletics, subsection (a) specifically prohibits any covered institution from "provid[ing] any such athletics separately on such basis."

Standing alone, then, subsection (a) would require covered institutions to integrate all of their sports teams. In order to avoid such a result—which would have radically altered the face of intercollegiate athletics—HEW provided an explicit exception to the rule of subsection (a) in the first sentence of subsection (b), allowing covered institutions to "operate or sponsor separate teams for members of each sex where selection for such teams is based upon competitive skill or the activity involved is a contact sport." By its terms, this sentence permits covered institutions to operate separate teams for men and women in many sports, including contact sports such as football, rather than integrating those teams.

The first sentence of subsection (b), however, leaves unanswered the question of what, if any, restrictions apply to sports in which a covered institution operates a team for one sex, but operates no corresponding team for the other sex. HEW addressed this question in the second sentence of subsection (b).

This second sentence is applicable only when two predicate criteria are met: first, that the institution in question "operates or sponsors a team in a particular sport for members of one sex but operates or sponsors no such team for members of the other sex," and second, that "athletic opportunities for members of that sex have previously been limited." In this case, appellees do not dispute that athletic opportunities for women at Duke have previously been limited, and thus we assume that the second condition has been met. Further, we assume, without deciding, that Duke operated its football team "for members of one sex"—that is, for only men—but did not operate a separate team "for members of the other sex," and therefore that the first condition has also been satisfied. Thus, insofar as the present appeal is concerned, we consider the predicate conditions to application of the sentence to have been met.

Provided that both of the conditions in the protasis of the second sentence of subsection (b) have been met, the apodosis of the sentence requires that "members of the excluded sex must be allowed to try out for the team offered unless the sport involved is a contact sport." The text of this clause, on its face, is incomplete: it affirmatively specifies that members of the excluded sex must be allowed to try out for single-sex teams where no team is provided for their sex except in the case of contact sports, but is silent regarding what requirements, if any, apply to single-sex teams in contact sports. As to contact sports, this clause is susceptible of two interpretations. First, it could be read to mean that "members of the excluded sex must be allowed to try out for the team offered unless the sport involved is a contact sport, *in which case the anti-discrimination provision of subsection (a) does not apply at all.*" Second, it could be interpreted to mean that "members of the excluded sex must be allowed to try out for the team offered unless the sport involved is a contact sport, *in which case members of the excluded sex need not be allowed to try out.*"

Appellees advocate the former reading, arguing that HEW intended through this clause to exempt contact sports entirely from the coverage of Title IX. We believe, however, that the latter reading is the more natural and intended meaning. The second sentence of subsection (b) does not purport in any way to state an exemption, whether for contact sports or for any other subcategory, from the general anti-discrimination rule stated in subsection (a). And HEW certainly knew how to provide for a complete exemption had it wished, Congress itself having provided a number of such exemptions in the very statute implemented by the regulation. Rather, the sentence says, and says only, that covered institutions must allow members of an excluded sex to try out for single-sex teams in non-contact sports. Therefore, the "unless" phrase at the end of the second clause of the sentence cannot (logically or grammatically) do anything more than except contact sports from the tryout requirement that the beginning of the second clause of the sentence imposes on all other sports.

Contrary to appellees' assertion, this reading of the regulation is perfectly consistent with the evident congressional intent not to require the sexual integration of intercollegiate contact sports. If a university chooses not to permit members of the opposite sex to tryout for a single-sex contact-sports team, this interpretation respects that choice. At the same time, however, the reading of the regulation we adopt today, unlike the one advanced by appellees, ensures that the likewise indisputable congressional intent to prohibit discrimination in all circumstances where such discrimination is unreasonable—for example, where the university itself has voluntarily opened the team in question to members of both sexes—is not frustrated.

We therefore construe the second sentence of subsection (b) as providing that in non-contact sports, but not in contact sports, covered institutions must allow members of an excluded sex to try out for single-sex teams. Once an institution has allowed a member of one sex to try out for a team operated by the institution for the other sex in a contact sport, subsection (b) is simply no longer applicable, and the institution is subject to the general anti-discrimination provision of subsection (a). To the extent that the Third Circuit intended to hold otherwise in *Williams v. School Dist. of Bethlehem, Pa.,* 998 F.2d 168, 174 (3d Cir.1993), with its lone unexplained statement that, "[i]f it is determined that [a particular sport] is a contact sport, no other inquiry is necessary because that will be dispositive of the title IX claim," we reject such a conclusion as inconsistent with the language of the regulation.

Accordingly, because appellant has alleged that Duke allowed her to try out for its football team (and actually made her a member of the team), then discriminated against her and ultimately excluded her from participation in the sport on the basis of her sex, we conclude that she has stated a claim under the applicable regulation, and therefore under Title IX. We take to heart appellees' cautionary observation that, in so holding, we thereby become "the first Court in United States history to recognize such a cause of action." Where, as here, however, the university invites women into what appellees characterize as the "traditionally all-male bastion of collegiate football," we are convinced that this reading of the regulation is the only one permissible under law.

The district court's order granting appellees' motion to dismiss for failure to state a claim is hereby reversed, and the case remanded for further proceedings.

REVERSED AND REMANDED

Notes and Questions

1. On remand, a jury concluded that head coach Fred Goldsmith had discriminated against Mercer on the basis of her gender and that Duke was liable for such discrimination under Title IX. The jury awarded Mercer $1 in compensatory damages and $2,000,000 in punitive damages. The district court denied Duke's subsequent motion for judgment as a matter of law, and its alternative motion for a new trial and/or a remittitur, relying upon the following information to support the jury verdict:

> (1) Goldsmith made gender-biased comments towards Mercer; (2) Goldsmith treated Mercer differently with respect to her membership on the football team because she was a woman, particularly in light of the fact that he would not permit her to play on the scout team, would not permit her to stand on the sidelines during the home games with her teammates, would not issue her pads or a uniform, and created an inactive status solely for her; (3) [Duke University] President [Nan] Keohane and Athletic Director [Tom] Butters had actual knowledge of Mercer's treatment while on the football team and of the fact that she was alleging discrimination based upon her gender; (4) Keohane and Butters failed to respond to or to investigate Mercer's allegation in a timely or reasonable manner aimed at uncovering and remedying any discriminatory conduct; and (5) Goldsmith's conduct towards Mercer was discriminatory and was based upon her gender in violation of Title IX.

Mercer v. Duke Univ., 181 F. Supp. 2d 525, 547–48 (M.D.N.C. 2001). The District Court also awarded attorneys' fees to Mercer.

On appeal, the Fourth Circuit vacated the award of punitive damages, *Mercer v. Duke Univ.,* 50 Fed. Appx. 643 (4th Cir. 2002) (per curiam); the court found that punitive damages are not an available remedy under Title IX following the Supreme Court's decision in *Barnes v. Gorman,* 536 U.S. 181 (2002). The court of appeals also vacated the award of attorneys' fees and costs and remanded the case to the district court for reconsideration of the issue of attorneys' fees and costs. On January 22, 2004, the district court held that Mercer was a successful plaintiff under *Farrar v. Hobby,* 506 U.S. 103 (1992), in spite of the fact that her damages were merely nominal.

> First, Mercer brought a case of first impression that led the Fourth Circuit to specifically recognize that a cause of action would exist under Title IX when an educational institution that receives federal funds discriminates on the basis of sex against women who are permitted to try out for a previously all-male contact-sports team. As the court of appeals noted in its decision remanding the question of attorney's fees to this Court, "Mercer's claim against Duke was the first of its kind, and the jury's conclusion that Duke violated Title IX may serve as guidance for other schools facing similar issues." Second, Mercer achieved a not-so-easily-obtainable victory when the jury found that Duke, as an institution, acted with deliberate indifference to Mercer's allegations of discrimination on the basis of her sex. Moreover, the Court finds that Mercer furthered a public goal by bringing much national attention to Title IX's objective of combating sex discrimination in federally funded educational institutions. The Court also finds merit to Jocelyn Samuels' declaration that "[d]enying Mercer adequate fees would undermine such efforts to enforce Title IX because individuals are unlikely to seek to vindicate their rights if they have to secure monetary damages in addition to a judgment of liability in order to be compensated for attorneys' fees." Finally, even though Duke contends that, as a result of Mercer's lawsuit, coaches will be less likely to permit female athletes to try out for traditionally male contact-sports teams, the Court finds this argument to be unpersuasive because Title IX does not require that such permission be granted, but rather Title IX does apply to female athletes who are given the opportunity to try out for men's contact-sports teams. Therefore, the lesson to be learned from Mercer's lawsuit is that female athletes who are permitted to try out for a men's contact-sports team at a federally funded institution are entitled to the same rights as their male counterparts to be free from discrimination on the basis of gender.

Mercer v. Duke Univ., 301 F. Supp. 2d 454, 465 (2004). The court ordered the payment of $349,243.96 in attorney's fees.

2. The *Mercer* decision means that schools partially waive the "contact sports" exception when they allow members of the excluded sex to try out for a contact sports team: once it permits the try out, the school is prohibited from subsequently discriminating against the player who was allowed to try out. Does that rule create a disincentive to allow, for example, women to try out for college football teams? In the abstract, it clearly does; in practice, it might not. Gene Murphy, football coach at Fullerton College, thinks that a coach's self-interest would prevent such a result: "I don't think there's a football coach in the country, at any level, who wouldn't keep a player good enough to help him win." Diane Pucin, *Verdict Is Kick in the Pants,* L.A. TIMES, Oct. 20, 2000, at D1.

3. In 2002, Katie Hnida transferred from the University of Colorado to the University of New Mexico, and became a third-string kicker on the football team as a junior walk-on. On Christmas Day, 2002, she became the first woman to play in a Division I-A football game; her extra-point attempt was blocked. The following season, on August

30, 2003, she became the first woman to score in a Division I-A football game, as she kicked two extra-points in New Mexico's 72-8 win over Texas State-San Marcos.

E. The Future

After 32 years, Title IX continues to be at the center of considerable controversy. At a time when one would expect a statute and its regulations to have matured to a point where some consensus has been achieved, the battle lines remain drawn. Each side has proposed reforms that broaden and circumscribe the statute's reach. At one end of the spectrum sit advocates of exempting revenue-producing sports from the proportionality equation. Critics of this approach argue that such a "business model" misplaces emphasis upon the commercial aspects of college sports and further denigrates the concept of amateurism and the student-athlete. In this regard, there is concern that this "business model" reinforces a paternalistic notion of "let the revenue-producing sports survive so they preserve and maintain all other sports, especially nonrevenue-producing women's sports." Such a notion perpetuates the male dominance and superiority that serves to frustrate the goal of greater female independence, particularly in the athletic arena. *See* Ellen J. Saurosky, *Title IX and College Sports: The Long Painful Path to Compliance and Reform,* 14 MARQ. SPORTS L. REV. 95 (2003). Part of the purpose of Title IX is to encourage and develop women's sports at the university and high school levels and, hopefully, to cultivate an environment whereby women's sports will eventually be self-sustaining. A second problem with the business model, as discussed earlier, is that it is predicated on an assumption that revenue producing sports are cash cows for the rest of the university, especially its athletic programs. *See generally* Rodney K. Smith and Robert D. Walker, *From Inequity to Opportunity,* 1 Nev. L.J. 160, 161 (2001) ("It is clear that 'big-time' intercollegiate athletics is often very profitable * * *. Indeed it is clear that funds generated by profitable Division 1-A men's basketball and football programs are being diverted to cover expenses generated by nonrevenue-producing programs.") Yet, some statistical analyses would indicate that such a premise is faulty. *See* Brian Porto, *Completing the Revolution: Title IX as Catalyst for an Alternative Model of College Sports,* 8 SETON HALL J. SPORT L. 351, 378 (1998). In short, there is no consensus for the notion that the revenues derived from big-time college sports are used to fund other non-athletic aspects of a university or to advance sports that, in and of themselves, do not produce income. *See* Barbara R. Bregmanns, *Do Sports Really Make Money For the University,* 77 ACADEME 28, 29 (Jan.–Feb. 1991); Arthur Padilla & David Baumer, *Big-Time College Sports: Management and Economic Issues,* 18 J. SPORT AND SOC. ISSUES 123, 139 (1994). The question that irresistibly arises is whether a situation in which the athletic departments were no longer autonomous units, but integrated fully in the university community, would produce a result in which there would be less emphasis upon the revenue-producing sport, given the fact that the revenue-producing sport would not be deriving the direct benefit of any gains that were enjoyed.

Those who oppose compliance by contraction inevitably ask what choice does a university saddled with a tight budget have to meet Title IX's mandates. While expanding programs to achieve the equality sought by Title IX is a noble aspiration, many universities claim that there simply is inadequate funding to meet that goal. As a result, equity results in the elimination of men's programs, particularly those that do not typically generate revenue. *See* Walter B. Connolly, Jr. & Jeffrey D. Adelman, *A University's Defense to a Title IX Gender Equity in Athletics Lawsuit: Congress Never Intended Gender Equity Based on Student Body Rations,* 71 U. DET. MERCY L. REV. 845 (1994).

Finally, the lack of consensus is most dramatically reflected in the fact that minorities within the class sought to be protected by Title IX find the statute to be wanting. Recent commentary has noted that the African-American female is a member of a discrete minority and a minority that is often overlooked or disserved by prevailing anti-discrimination legislation. *See* Marilyn V. Yarbrough, *If You Let Me Play Sports*, 6 MARQ. SPORTS L.J. 229, 233 (1996); Alfred Dennis Mathewson, *Black Women, Gender Equity and the Function at the Junction*, 6 MARQ. SPORTS L.J. 239, 240–41 (1996). This issue must be exzplored if Title IX is to meet is ambitious goals of expanding

V. Gender and The Professional (Athletes, Coaches, Officials, and Journalists)

A. Introduction

Female participation in professional and amateur sports dates back to the early twentieth century. Women were actively involved as owners, players, and game/match officials. For example, Helene Britton assumed ownership of the St. Louis Cardinals in 1911 and held the position for six years. Alta Weiss, Lizzie Arlington, and Lizzie Murphy, among others, were outstanding professional baseball players. *See* BARBARA GREGORICH, WOMEN AT PLAY (1993). Amanda Clement was an outstanding umpire in the minor leagues, and earned the respect of players, fellow umpires, and fans. *See* GAI INGHAM BERLAGE, WOMEN IN BASEBALL: THE FORGOTTEN HISTORY (1994). Babe Didrikson Zaharias's renown as a great athlete is recognized by even the most casual observer. She achieved unparalleled success in track and field, basketball, golf, and countless other sports. Women's baseball leagues and barnstorming teams were established and featured play both among women and, on occasion, in competition with men. At the amateur level, several colleges and universities sponsored women's teams that competed with area high school clubs and other undergraduate institutions. *Id.*

Yet, given the early stirrings of female involvement in traditional male sports, there was no dramatic progression in terms of league formation and overall female participation. A glaring illustration is that from 1911 until the mid-1970s, there were virtually no female umpires at any professional level, despite the fact that Amanda Clement was praised as an exemplary arbiter by men and women alike. Perhaps, more significantly, those women who donned the umpiring equipment, Bernice Gera and Christine Wren, were constantly subjected to harassment from fans, players, and league officials. Gera quit after a lengthy legal battle to secure her position—the taunting was simply too much to bear. *Id.* at 61.

Females were not totally absent when the sports picture was taken in the mid-twentieth century. To be sure, World War II saw the formation of the All-American Girls' Professional Baseball League, which drew almost one million fans in 1948. The Negro Leagues allowed women to play, witness the success of Indianapolis Clowns' second basewoman Toni Stone. Effa Manley made her presence felt in no small way as co-owner of the Negro Leagues' Newark Eagles. The WNBA has provided a showcase for outstanding talent and produced entertainment that is gaining gradual acceptance. In the early 1970s, Billie Jean King gave Bobby Riggs a tennis lesson in the Battle of the Sexes and, of more recent vintage, Anika Sorenstam has competed in men's PGA Tour events. Women executives, journalists, and coaches are casting a larger shadow in the sports world. Undoubtedly, Title IX and the exponential leap in female athletic participation that it has fostered will lead to more expansive professional involvement in the future.

Yet, the progress over the past one hundred years can only be characterized as agonizingly deliberate when one recalls the early success of female athletes at the turn of the century. In 1952 Eleanor Engle became only the second woman to enter "organized" baseball. After she signed a contract to play for the Harrisburg Senators, the response was vicious, culminating in a ruling by Major League Commissioner Ford Frick barring female participation in baseball at both the major league and minor league levels. The AAGPBL was dismantled in 1954 after experiencing declining interest and attendance once men returned to the teams after World War II. We have yet to see women grace a Major League baseball diamond, an NFL football field, or NBA court. As the talk of opening the men's golf tours to more active female involvement surfaces, there is no small amount of consternation, much of it having other professional golfers as its source. Despite the progress, there is a dearth of female entrepreneurship and upper echelon management in most leagues. Achieving equal status and reception through equal pay has been a difficult struggle in many respects. Unisex competition, while visible to some degree among young athletes, is not likely to gain acceptance in the near future.

The somewhat arrested evolution of female participation in traditional sports, whether through separate leagues or direct inter-gender competition, can be attributed to many factors. At one level, men may feel threatened by the intrusion of women into traditionally male enclaves. Physiological differences, real or imagined, may persuade the purveyors of sport that certain endeavors are not well suited to the proverbial fairer sex. Finally, the line between paternalism and protection is difficult to draw, especially with the conflicting views of the gender-relativeness of strength and stamina. The material that follows will expand upon the foregoing commentary and no doubt generate further dialogue on the emerging role of female athletes and the future of professional women's sports.

B. The Female Athlete: Chivalry or Sexism?

Garrett v. New York State Athletic Commission
82 Misc. 2d 524 (N.Y. Sup. Ct. 1975)

FRANK, J. Petitioner Jacqueline Garrett, also known as Jackie Tonawanda, * * * seeks a judgment requiring the respondents New York State Athletic Commission (Commission) and Edwin Dooley, commissioner, to issue a boxing license to the petitioner * * * In notifying the petitioner that her application for a boxing license had been denied, respondents wrote the petitioner as follows:

"Your application for a license to box in New York State was considered by the Commission at a meeting on January 16, 1975.

"The matter of licensing women boxers is regulated by Rule 205.15 of Part 205, the Commission Its Powers and Procedures, of the rules promulgated by the Commission which reads as follows:

"'205.15 Disqualification of women. No women may be licensed as a boxer or second or licensed to compete in any wrestling exhibition with men.'

"Please be advised that the Commission after considering your application and reviewing its rules and regulations unanimously denied your application for a license to box in this State."

Respondents now cross-move to dismiss the petition herein upon the grounds that it fails to state a cause of action. Although the court is not called upon to rule upon the ultimate merit of petitioner's application, a determination must be reached as to whether it states a cognizable cause of action. In support of their cross motion respondents note that the State Legislature has vested the Commission with broad authority to regulate professional boxing and wrestling in this State. In accordance with that authority it is mandated that no boxing or wrestling license may be issued except if the Commission determines that the "experience, character and general fitness of an applicant * * * are such that participation of such applicant will be consistent with the public interest, convenience or necessity and with the best interests of boxing or wrestling generally and in conformity with the purposes of this act".

Commissioner Dooley in an affidavit included in respondents' submission observes:

"The image that boxing presents to the public is all important to its acceptability as a professional sport. It is 'the manly art of self-defense'. The licensing of women as professional boxers would at once destroy the image that attracts serious boxing fans and bring professional boxing into disrepute among them, to the financial detriment of those whose livelihoods depend upon this activity.

"Neither is the Commission satisfied that women boxers would not be unduly endangering their reproductive organs and breasts; despite the use of whatever protective devices may be available. The avoidance of serious physical injury is a major responsibility of the Commission.

"Finally, the Commission is not satisfied that there are a sufficient number of qualified women available as professional competition for petitioner."

Petitioner's attorney states "that it is not the intention of the petitioner to box with men but that she should be permitted to box with other women".

As authority in support of their cross motion to dismiss the petition, respondents rely, *inter alia*, upon *Matter of Calzadilla v Dooley*, in which the Appellate Division, Fourth Department, reversed a decision at Special Term which denied a motion to dismiss an application to annul the Commission's refusal to issue a professional wrestling license to a woman. In so holding, the court concluded that the Commission had not exceeded its authority in denying wrestling licenses to women, especially in view of the broad discretion vested in the Commission by the Legislature to regulate the sport of wrestling. Considering whether the Commission's determination was violative of the equal protection clause of the Fourteenth Amendment of the United States Constitution and section 11 of article I of the New York State Constitution, Mr. Justice Goldman, writing for the court, stated:

The Fourteenth Amendment does not require that all persons be treated exactly alike. It recognizes that a State may classify its citizens but mandates that the classification should not be arbitrary and that all persons within a class be treated equally * * *.

Notwithstanding any personal opinion or attitude we may hold in this respect, there is legal justification and support, under the legislation which created the Commission, for the determination made by it.

Parenthetically, the Commission thereafter altered its position regarding the licensing of women as professional wrestlers.

The respondents' claims that the licensing of women as professional boxers would be detrimental to the sport and would create inordinate risk of physical injury among women participants, are highly questionable and require a denial of the respondents' cross motion. While there are many who would deplore the spectacle of women engaging in professional boxing, there are certainly many who deplore that very same activity by men. This court will not hold that women should be precluded from professionally exploiting whatever skills or aptitude they may have in the sport of boxing merely because they are women, particularly in view of the long overdue recognition of the capacity of women to undertake the most diverse activities and occupations. Respondents apparently seek to continue the attitudes espoused a century ago in *Bradwell v State,* wherein the court opined:

> Man is, or should be, woman's protector and defender. The natural and proper timidity and delicacy which belongs to the female sex evidently unfits it for many of the occupations of civil life. The constitution of the family organization, which is founded in the divine ordinance, as well as in the nature of things, indicates the domestic sphere as that which properly belongs to the domain and functions of womanhood. The harmony, not to say identity, of interests and views which belong, or should belong, to the family institution is repugnant to the idea of a woman adopting a distinct and independent career from that of her husband.

Patronizing male chauvinism of this type not only has no place in our legal system, but should not be countenanced at any level in our society and has hopefully been relegated to the historical oblivion which it deserves.

Accordingly, the court finds that the petition states a cognizable cause of action, and respondents' cross motion is denied. The petitioner is directed to serve an amended petition reflecting the respondents' denial of her application for a boxing license. Thereafter, the respondents are directed to submit an answer thereto.

Notes and Questions

1. If petitioner had sought a license to box men, would the court's disposition have changed?

2. This opinion reflects the thin line existing between paternalism and protection. Is not the court's acknowledgment that to many individuals male boxing is repugnant a telling observation? Independent of the question of denying women access to the boxing ring are issues surrounding the sport itself, including the need for regulations in the areas of safety, promotion, agent representation, etc. Calls for federal and state legislation stalk the sport continuously. Doubtless, the unsavory elements that have populated the boxing world have made it even more difficult for women to gain access. The thin line between chivalry and sexism becomes even more difficult to demarcate in this context. *See generally,* Jonathan McElroy, *Current Proposed Federal Regulation Of Professional Boxing,* 9 SETON HALL J. SPORTS L. 463 (1999); David Altschuler, *On the Ropes: New Regulations and State Cooperation Step into the Ring to Protect Boxing from Itself,* 4 VAND. ENT. L. & PRAC. 74 (2002).

3. Assuming that the legislature had banned all female pugilism, would such prohibition be able to survive scrutiny under the Fourteenth Amendment?

4. Christy Martin, the first female boxer to achieve any significant notoriety and widely viewed as the best in the sport for several years, has followed the lead of many female sports stars; she has been reluctant to assume the role of trailblazer or spokesperson for the female athlete/boxer. *See* Stephanie Storm, *Ditch the Lipstick, Selfish Christy*, Orlando Sentinel, Nov. 15, 1996, Metro. Her unwillingness to serve as a role model for aspiring female boxers and to promote the sport beyond her own ambitions has been a source of consternation for many women. *Id.*; *see also* Maggie Hall, *As Women Win Round One in the Battle to Box, We Meet the Girl Who's the Champ in the Beauty, Brains and Braun Stakes*, Sunday Mail, November 24, 1996.

Many early sports heroines were reluctant to serve as champions of the women's movement or as representatives of an evolving feminism. Current stars often share the same aversion to the spotlight in terms of promoting the cause of women's liberation in the classic sense:

> Today's young American women are more feminist in their values than any previous generation, but they are deeply reluctant to identify with the leaders or the movement itself, partly because of its perceived failure to address the issues facing many ordinary women: the problems of child care, coping as a single parent, balancing work and home.

Helen Wilkinson, *Germaine's Desperate Bid For Attention*, Independent, May 19, 1995, at 19.

Is this reluctance fueled by a fear that they will be labeled as unfeminine, lesbian, or otherwise not part of the mainstream?

> Take, for example, the problem of homophobia–the perception that female athletes are lesbians, a stereotype that many girls go well out of their way to avoid. It is one of the most damaging backlashes to the entry of women into competitive athletics: the Ladies Pro Golf Tour is mocked as the Lesbian Pro Golf Tour; basketball players at Texas are dubbed "the lesbian team;" to be labeled butch or dyke can ruin a girl's reputation. These "sex scares" undermine women's independence by stripping athletic women of their female sexuality. Now the "new athletic girl" must not only endure criticism that she is "manly" but that she is also homosexual. Whether she is or not is irrelevant* * * . [F]ew 14 year-old girls are mature enough to have a strong sense of their own sexuality; they are likely to avoid anything that threatens it. By playing sports, girls often feel that they have to trade in their femininity for their varsity jacket. They opt out of the sports game to make it in the dating game.

Cheryl Hanna, *Bad Girls and Good Sports: Some Reflections on Violent Female Juvenile Delinquents, Title IX & The Promise of Girl Power*, 27 Hastings Const. L.Q. 667, 704–05 (2000).

C. Coaches: Equal Work for Equal Pay

Stanley v. University Of Southern California (Stanley II)

178 F.3d 1069 (9th Cir. 1999)

HUG, **Chief Judge.** Appellant Marianne Stanley appeals from the district court's order granting summary judgment in favor of defendants University of Southern California and Michael Garrett on Stanley's claims of discrimination and breach of employment contract. Stanley also appeals the denial of her motion to recuse Judge Davies, and her motion to re-tax costs. Appellants move for an award of sanctions against Stanley for filing the latter two appeals.

FACTUAL AND PROCEDURAL BACKGROUND

Marianne Stanley was hired as head coach of the women's basketball team for the University of Southern California ("USC") in 1989. Her initial contract, signed in July of that year, was for a four-year term, expiring June 30, 1993. The contract provided that she would make a base salary of $60,000 per year. This base salary was increased to $62,000 per year in 1992. The women's basketball program at USC enjoyed much success during Stanley's tenure.

Defendant Michael Garrett is the Athletic Director at USC. On April 20, 1993, two months prior to the expiration of Stanley's contract, Stanley and Garrett had an initial meeting to negotiate a new contract. The parties disagree over what took place at this meeting. Stanley contends that on that date she entered into a contract for a salary equivalent to that of George Raveling, the USC men's basketball coach. It is undisputed that Garrett expressly stated that USC could not pay her that salary, but that he would make her a formal offer in writing shortly after that meeting.

On April 27, 1993, Garrett offered Stanley, in writing, a three-year contract providing $80,000 in year one, $90,000 in year two, and $100,000 in year three, with a $6,000 per year housing allowance for each of the three years. The parties met again on May 27, 1993, at which point Garrett claims that Stanley rejected the April 27 offer because she insisted that her compensation should be equivalent to Raveling's. Stanley argues that she never rejected this offer, but simply disagreed as to the amount of compensation, because the April 27 offer was inconsistent with the April 20 offer—for Raveling's salary level—that she already had accepted.

On June 7, 1993, Stanley proposed a three-year contract providing $96,000 per year for the first eighteen months, and a salary equivalent to that of Raveling for the remainder of the term. Garrett rejected this offer. Stanley then retained an attorney who, on June 18, 1993, proposed to Garrett a three-year contract with an automatic two-year renewal provision, and total compensation of $88,000 for year one, $97,000 for year two, and $112,000 for year three, plus additional incentives. Garrett rejected this offer and withdrew the April 27 offer.

On June 21, 1993, Garrett sent to Stanley's attorney a written offer for a one-year contract for $96,000. Stanley's existing contract expired on June 30, 1993, but Stanley continued to perform her duties. On July 13, while on a recruiting trip, Stanley asked Garrett if he would still offer her a multi-year contract. He indicated that his June 21 one-year contract offer was USC's final offer, and that Stanley would have to accept or reject it by the end of the day. Stanley did not respond, but sent a memo to Garrett on July 14 requesting additional time to consider the offer. On July 15 Garrett revoked the offer, informed Stanley that he was seeking a new coach for the team, and requested that Stanley perform no further services for USC.

On August 5, 1993, Stanley initiated this action in Los Angeles County Superior Court, making claims of sex discrimination and retaliatory discharge. On August 6, 1993, the Superior Court granted Stanley's request for a temporary restraining order reinstating Stanley as head coach of the women's team at $96,000 per year pending the hearing on Stanley's motion for preliminary injunction. On that same day, defendants removed the action to federal court on the ground that the complaint stated claims arising under federal law.

On August 30, 1993, the district court denied the motion for preliminary injunction, and Stanley appealed. This court affirmed the denial of the preliminary injunction in an opinion filed January 6, 1994. *Stanley v. University of Southern California*, 13 F.3d 1313 (9th Cir.1994) (*Stanley I*). Between September 1993 and February 1994, Stanley amended her complaint several times, and defendants' motions to dismiss were granted as to several claims. Stanley's Third Amended Complaint alleges the following causes of action: (1) violation of the Equal Pay Act, 29 U.S.C. §206(d)(1) and California Fair Employment and Housing Act ("FEHA"); (2) violation of Article I, §8 of the California Constitution; (3) violation of Title IX of the Civil Rights Act of 1972, 20 U.S.C. §1681; (4) retaliation; (5) wrongful discharge in violation of public policy; (6) breach of express contract; (7) breach of implied-in-fact contract; and (8) breach of implied covenant of good faith and fair dealing. Stanley sought reinstatement, declaratory relief, injunctive relief preventing USC from further discriminating against her, back pay, three million dollars in compensatory damages, and five million dollars in punitive damages.

On October 17, 1994, defendants filed a motion for summary judgment. After Stanley was allowed additional time to conduct discovery, on March 10, 1995, the district court granted summary judgment for USC and Garrett. This appeal followed.

DISCUSSION

I. Discrimination Claims

We review the district court's grant of summary judgment de novo. *Margolis v. Ryan*, 140 F.3d 850, 852 (9th Cir.1998). We address each claim in turn.

A. Equal Pay Act Claim

The Equal Pay Act provides in relevant part:

> No employer having employees subject to any provisions of this section shall discriminate, within any establishment in which such employees are employed, between employees on the basis of sex by paying wages to employees * * * at a rate less than the rate at which he pays wages to employees of the opposite sex in such establishment for equal work on jobs the performance of which requires equal skill, effort, and responsibility, and which are performed under similar working conditions. * * *

29 U.S.C. §206(d)(1). In an Equal Pay Act case, the plaintiff has the burden of establishing a prima facie case of discrimination by showing that employees of the opposite sex were paid different wages for equal work. The prima facie case is limited to a comparison of the jobs in question, and does not involve a comparison of the individuals who hold the jobs. To make out a prima facie case, the plaintiff bears the burden of showing that the jobs being compared are "substantially equal." Significantly, under the Act, the plaintiff need not demonstrate that the jobs in question are identical; she must show only that the jobs are substantially equal.

Because we are reviewing an appeal from the grant of summary judgment, the question is whether, viewing the evidence in the light most favorable to Stanley, and resolving all inferences in her favor, a genuine issue of material fact exists regarding the substantial equality of the jobs. This analysis is quite different from that conducted by our court in *Stanley I*, where we considered an appeal from the denial of a mandatory preliminary injunction.

Circuit courts employ a two-step "substantially equal" analysis in Equal Pay Act cases. In *Brobst v. Columbus Srvs. Int'l,* (1985), the Third Circuit described this approach, writing that "[t]he crucial finding on the equal work issue is whether the jobs to be compared have a 'common core' of tasks, i.e. whether a significant portion of the two jobs is identical." When a plaintiff establishes such a "common core of tasks," the court must then determine whether any additional tasks, incumbent on one job but not the other, make the two jobs "substantially different." Both the Seventh and Fourth Circuits have also adopted this approach to Equal Pay Act cases.

Here, we may assume that the men's and women's coaching jobs share a common core of tasks. Garrett—U.S.C.'s athletic director and a defendant in this case—has acknowledged that the women's and men's coaches "have the same basic responsibilities" with regard to recruiting athletes and administering the basketball programs. In his declaration, Garrett also stated:

> Both the women's and men's head basketball coaches have the following general duties and responsibilities: basketball program; coaching and discipline of team members; general supervision over the personal and academic lives of the student athletes; and supervision over assistant coaches, part-time coaches and other athletic department personnel involved in the women's and men's basketball programs.

The parties are in serious dispute, however, as to whether the additional responsibilities borne by the men's coach, but not by the women's coach, suffice to make the two jobs "substantially different." The defendants point out that the men's coach bears greater revenue generating responsibilities, that he is under greater media and spectator pressure to produce a winning program, and that he actually generates more revenue for the University.

Stanley claims that the differences between the two jobs are attributable to previous gender-based decisions on the part of the University. Essentially, Stanley claims that the differences between the two jobs result from the University's historically disparate treatment of male and female teams; namely, its decisions to invest in and promote the men's program more than the women's program. She then claims that because the differences between the jobs derive from previous gender-based decisions on the part of the University, the differences cannot be relied on to determine that the jobs are "substantially different."

The University, on the other hand, argues that the differences between the two jobs are not attributable to anything it has done or failed to do in the past. According to USC, the reason that women's basketball does not generate the same amount of revenue as men's basketball, and that the women's coach is not under the same pressure as the men's coach, is that there simply is not a sufficient spectator or media market for women's basketball games. Accordingly, it contends that the differences in responsibilities in the two jobs legitimately suffice to make them "substantially different."

We need not decide which party is correct regarding the reason for the differences that exist. Even assuming that Stanley has succeeded in raising a genuine issue of fact as to this question, the University is entitled to summary judgment on other grounds. A defendant may rebut a prima facie case by showing that the disparity in pay is a "differential based on any * * * factor other than sex." 29 U.S.C. §206(d)(1). Defendants here assert an affirmative defense (that is, a nondiscriminatory reason for the pay differential) based on Stanley and Raveling's markedly disparate levels of experience and qualifications. The record convincingly supports their claim. When Raveling began coaching at U.S.C., he had thirty-one years of coaching experience. He had been the coach of the men's Olympic basketball team. He had been *twice* named national coach of the year, and *twice* named PAC-10 coach of the year. On top of his coaching experience, Raveling also had nine years of marketing and promotional experience, and was the author of several books on basketball. When Stanley started coaching at U.S.C., three years after Raveling became head coach of the men's team, she had seventeen years of experience coaching basketball, or *fourteen years less experience* than Raveling. She never coached an Olympic team. She had no marketing or promotional experience other than that she gained as a coach. She had never published a book about basketball.

The EEOC Notice cited above, on which *the plaintiff* relies extensively, recognizes this type of affirmative defense, stating that "[s]uperior experience, education, and ability may justify pay disparities if distinctions based on these criteria are not gender based." In *Stanley I*, moreover, we wrote that "[e]mployers may reward professional experience and education without violating the EPA. *Stanley I*. Coaches with substantially more experience and significantly superior qualifications may, of course, be paid more than their less experienced and qualified counterparts, even when it is the male coach who has the greater level of experience and qualifications. By alleging that the pay differential at issue here was due to Stanley and Raveling's markedly different levels of experience and qualifications, the defendants have proffered a factor "other than sex" to explain the difference in pay.

Garrett's testimony, moreover, supports the University's explanation. In explaining the disparity between Raveling and Stanley's salaries, Garrett referred extensively to the coaches' divergent levels of experience and differences in qualifications. He stressed Raveling's thirty-one years of experience, his experience as an Olympic coach, his nine years in marketing and promotion positions, and his authorship of several books on basketball. Garrett highlighted the fact that Raveling had been twice honored as national coach of the year, twice voted PAC-10 coach of the year, and was "widely recognized as one of the top basketball recruiters in the nation." Garrett then contrasted Stanley's lesser experience and qualifications. While he mentioned some of Stanley's accomplishments, he pointed out that she had only seventeen years coaching experience, had never coached an Olympic team, and had never authored any books on basketball.

Where the defendant demonstrates that a pay differential was based on a factor other than sex, the employee may prevail by showing that the employer's proffered nondiscriminatory reason is a "pretext for discrimination." On this appeal, Stanley bears the burden of demonstrating a material fact regarding pretext in order to survive summary judgment. Stanley's pretext argument, however, fails to meet even this minimal burden. In her briefs, Stanley disputes that Raveling had greater qualifications and experience than she. For example, Stanley states that "Mr. Raveling does not have substantially different qualifications and experience than Ms. Stanley." Unsupported allegations made in briefs are not sufficient, however, to defeat a motion for summary judgment. Stanley has conspicuously failed, moreover, to present any meaningful evidence in support of her claim that she and Raveling had comparable levels of experience. Stanley points first to her deposition testimony that she was responsible for securing donors for the women's team. Such evidence, while important in assessing Stanley's revenue raising responsibilities, says nothing of her relative level of experience. She next points to her testimony that she worked briefly as a color analyst on a Philadelphia cable station. Again, this evidence does not undermine the University's claim that Raveling possessed far greater experience as a coach and marketer than Stanley. Stanley also argues that Raveling's marketing abilities are in dispute because "Raveling was not able to successfully promote nor market a summer basketball [camp] during his entire employment at USC." However, Raveling's ability to market this camp sheds no light on his previous *experience* in marketing. Stanley, moreover, does not dispute the fact that Raveling has nine years of experience in marketing, while she had no work experience outside coaching.

In the end, therefore, we are left with these *undisputed* facts: Stanley had far less relevant experience and qualifications than Raveling. She had fourteen years less experience as a basketball coach. She, unlike Raveling, never coached the Olympic team. She had no marketing experience outside coaching. She had never written any books on basketball. Accordingly, Stanley has failed to raise a genuine issue of fact as to Raveling's markedly "superior experience," and qualifications. In short, she has failed to raise a genuine issue of fact as to the University's non-discriminatory reason for paying Raveling a higher salary.

Accordingly, we affirm the district court's decision to grant the defendants' motion for summary judgment on the Equal Pay Act claim.

* * *

CONCLUSION

We affirm the district court's grant of summary judgment in favor of USC and Garrett and its denial of the motion for disqualification. However, we remand its denial of the motion to re-tax costs. We deny appellees' motions for sanctions. Each side shall bear its own costs on appeal.

PREGERSON, Circuit Judge, dissenting:

By focusing on the differences between Stanley's and Raveling's qualifications, the majority skips over the many ways in which gender discrimination insidiously affected the University's treatment of the women's basketball program and Stanley as its Head Coach. The University's half-hearted promotion of the women's basketball program, its intensive marketing of the men's basketball program, and the formidable obstacles Stanley faced as a woman athlete in a male-dominated profession contributed to this disparate treatment.

It is hard for me to square these realities with the majority's ruling denying Stanley relief without a trial.

Therefore, I dissent.

Notes and Questions

1. The two-pronged test to ascertain substantial equality of the jobs in question involves: a) whether the two jobs have a common core of tasks; b) whether, assuming that part "a" above is met, any additional tasks substantially differentiate the two jobs. With regard to the latter, how relevant is the revenue production aspect of the two jobs?

2. Note that the *prima facie* case is established by a comparison of the jobs. But, once made, the *prima facie* case can be rebutted by differentiating the *ad hominem* credentials and qualifications of the individuals holding those jobs (*i.e.,* demonstrating a compensation decision based on factors other than gender). The court characterizes this response as an affirmative defense. At this point, Ms. Stanley needed to show that the proferred reasons for the pay differentials were pretextual. The court says that she failed to do so. Do you agree?

3. Stanley filed numerous other claims of discrimination based on Title VII (retaliation), Title IX, and the Fourteenth Amendment, etc. While arguing in the alternative can be important litigation strategy, did that approach here diminish the strength of some of her claims?

4. Stanley's contract claims failed much like her discrimination allegations. If the court had found that there had been an objective meeting of the minds, would the absence of a writing have doomed the alleged agreement? Would the deal not have been for more than a year by Stanley's own admission and, in fact, assertion, thus necessitating a memorialization under the Statute of Frauds?

5. Do you agree with Judge Pregerson's suggestion that the differences in qualifications claimed by the university are of their own creation? Should it matter in this case?

6. If a court has determined that two sports, such as baseball and softball, are *not* substantially equal for purposes of equal protection or Title IX, is it still free to determine that the coaching of these two sports is substantially equal? The variables employed to ascertain whether two sports are substantially equal are markedly different from the determinants of whether two jobs require equal skill, effort, and responsibility. *See generally* John Gage, et al., *Gender Based Pay Disparities in Intercollegiate Coaching: The Legal Issues*, 28 J.C. & U.L. 519 (2002).

7. In *EEOC v. Madison Community Unit School District No. 12*, 818 F.2d 577 (7th Cir. 1987), the Seventh Circuit dismissed allegations claiming that disparate pay to coaches of different teams (such as the girls' tennis coach versus the boys' soccer coach) constituted unlawful discrimination. Should a disparate compensation scheme predicated on the sex of team members elude sanction under pertinent equal pay legislation?

Further, in *EEOC v. Madison Community*, the court noted that the sex of the team members might justify a defense based on "a factor other than sex" (presumably meaning a factor other than the sex of the coach). While the court acknowledged that discouraging females from coaching boys' teams might negate that defense, it nonetheless recognized that discriminating on the basis of the sex of those being coached was okay. Is this consistent with the spirit of the Equal Pay Act?

The Eleventh Circuit has not felt constrained to dismiss equal pay claims solely on the basis of the fact that coaches are coaching different sports. Isn't the Eleventh Circuit correct here in the sense that such differentiation should not preclude the finding of a *prima facie* case, but, rather, should only come into play in ascertaining whether the pay difference was based on a factor other than sex? *Brock v. Georgia Southwestern College*, 765 F.2d 1026, 1032 (11th Cir. 1985).

EEOC guidelines, promulgated in 1998, declare that "it is possible for jobs coaching different sports to be substantially equal for purposes of the Equal Pay Act and for coaches of different sports to be appropriate comparatives under Title VII." *See* EEOC Notice No. 915-002, Enforcement Guidance on Sex Discrimination in the Compensation of Sports Coaches in Educational Institutions, Empl. Proc. Guide (CCH) ¶ 5527 (Oct. 27, 1997); Mel Narol and Joseph A. Martin, *A New Defense to the Old Defense: The EEOC Equal Pay Act Guidelines*, 9 Marq. Sports L.J. 175 (1998).

8. There is often significant difficulty isolating and differentiating those elements of the *prima facie* EPA case from defenses that the disparity is based on factors other than age. That is, consider the male college coach whose team draws large crowds versus an equally adept female coach in the same sport whose team generates far less fan interest and support. Does the attendance factor alone (with the obvious revenue differential)

justify a higher salary for the male coach? Where does it fit in the analysis: as a reason for concluding that the jobs are so different that they are not substantially identical, or as a rebuttal to the *prima facie* case?

9. The Equal Pay Act and Title VII do not reach the related issue of coaches who are paid less money not because of their gender but because of the gender of the teams that they coach. Should there be some recourse under one of these statutes to vindicate coaches who are discriminatorily compensated based on the gender of their "charges?"

Several "factors other than sex" have been raised as affirmative defenses once a plaintiff has established a prima facie case of an Equal Pay Act violation. Included among the factors are revenue generation, value in the marketplace, prior compensation arrangements, and the gender of the athletes coached. EEOC Guidelines, however, caution that courts should be circumspect in assessing the validity of the defenses, and the extent to which they may subvert the purposes underlying equal pay legislation. *See* Barbara Osborne & Marilyn V. Yarbrough, *Pay Equity for Coaches and Athletic Administration: An Element of Title IX*, 34 U. MICH. J.L. REFORM 231 (2001).

D. Officials

Notwithstanding the presence of female umpires as early as 1910, women have had considerable difficulty securing umpiring positions in professional baseball. As discussed above, women have encountered no small amount of difficulty entering the ranks of umpire and referee. Those individuals who have been fortunate enough to penetrate the lowest levels of professional sports officiating often have found the path to be strewn with impediments to advancement and the entire experience to be somewhat unrewarding.

Postema v. National League of Professional Baseball Clubs
799 F. Supp. 1475 (S.D.N.Y. 1992)

PATTERSON, District Judge. This is an action for damages and injunctive relief alleging employment discrimination in violation of: (1) Title VII of the Civil Rights Act of 1964, as amended by the Civil Rights Act of 1991, 42 U.S.C. §2000e-2(a)(1); (2) New York's Human Rights Law, N.Y. Exec. L. §296; and (3) the common law of restraint of trade.

* * *

II. EVENTS UNDERLYING THIS LAWSUIT

After graduating from umpiring school with the rank of 17th in a class of 130 students, Plaintiff began work in 1977 as a professional baseball umpire in the Gulf Coast League, a rookie league. At that time, she was the fourth woman ever to umpire a professional baseball game. Plaintiff worked in the Gulf Coast League during 1977 and 1978. In 1979, she was promoted to the Class A Florida State League, where she umpired during the 1979 and 1980 seasons. In 1981, Plaintiff was promoted to the AA Texas League, and she umpired there in 1981 and 1982. She was the first woman to ever umpire a professional baseball game above the Class A level.

In 1983, Plaintiff was promoted to the AAA Pacific Coast League, where she umpired from 1983 to 1986. In 1987, her contract was acquired by Triple-A, and she umpired in that league from 1987 until her discharge in 1989.

Plaintiff alleges that during her employment as a Triple-A umpire, Defendants conferred on her significant duties and responsibilities, including the following:

In 1987, Plaintiff was the home plate umpire for the Hall of Fame exhibition game between the New York Yankees and the Atlanta Braves.

In 1988, Plaintiff was selected to umpire the Venezuela All Star game.

In 1988 and 1989, Plaintiff was the chief of her umpiring crew, with ultimate responsibility for its umpiring calls and performance.

In 1988 and 1989, Plaintiff was appointed to umpire major league spring training games.

In 1989, Plaintiff was the home plate umpire for the first Triple-A Minor League All Star Game.

In 1989, Plaintiff was asked by Triple-A to become a supervisor for umpires in the minor league system.

From 1987 to 1989, Plaintiff received high praise from qualified and experienced baseball people, including Chuck Tanner, Tom Trebelhorn, Hal Lanier, and Roger Craig, all current or former managers of major league teams.

Notwithstanding these responsibilities and honors, Plaintiff alleges that throughout her career as a minor league umpire she was subjected to continual, repeated, and offensive acts of sexual harassment and gender discrimination. Such acts included the following:

On numerous occasions, players and managers addressed her with a four-letter word beginning with the letter "c" that refers to female genitalia.

Players and managers repeatedly told Plaintiff that her proper role was cooking, cleaning, keeping house, or some other form of "women's work," rather than umpiring.

Bob Knepper, a pitcher with the Houston Astros, told the press that although Plaintiff was a good umpire, to have her as a major league umpire would be an affront to God and contrary to the teachings of the Bible.

During arguments with players and managers, Plaintiff was spat upon and was subjected to verbal and physical abuse to a greater degree than male umpires.

In 1987, the manager of the Nashville Hounds kissed Plaintiff on the lips when he handed her his lineup card.

At a major league spring training game in 1988, Chuck Tanner, then the manager of the Pittsburgh Pirates, asked Plaintiff if she would like a kiss when he gave her his lineup card.

Although Plaintiff was well known throughout baseball as an excellent ball and strike umpire, she was directed and required by Ed Vargo, the Supervisor of Umpiring for the National League, to change her stance and technique to resemble those used by him during his career. No such requirement was placed on male umpires.

Plaintiff continually took action against such conduct through warnings, ejections, and reports. Although the existence of such conduct was well known throughout baseball, no one in a position of authority, including Defendants, took action to correct, stop, or prevent such conduct.

Plaintiff alleges that at the time she began her service with Triple-A, she was fully qualified to be a major league umpire, and she had repeatedly made known to Defendants her desire for employment in the major leagues. While she was not promoted to or hired by the National League or American League, male umpires having inferior experience, qualifications, and abilities were repeatedly and frequently promoted and hired by the National and American Leagues.

Plaintiff alleges that in 1988 and 1989, "events came to a head" in her effort to become a major league umpire. Specifically, in July 1987, Dick Butler, then Special Assistant to the President of the American League and the former supervisor of umpires for the American League, told Newsday that for Plaintiff to become a major league umpire: "She realizes that she has to be better than the fellow next to her. She's got to be better because of the fact that she's a girl. I'm not saying it's fair, but it exists and she's not going to change it." These comments were widely reported in the media, including in the Los Angeles Times. Defendants neither issued any statements contradicting, retracting, or correcting Butler's statements, took any remedial or disciplinary action with respect to Butler, nor otherwise said or did anything to communicate that Butler had not stated the true position of professional baseball, including Defendants.

In 1988, Bob Knepper made the above referenced remarks which resulted in national press coverage and widespread public controversy. On May 14, 1989, Larry Napp, Assistant Supervisor of Umpires for the American League, told the Richmond Times-Dispatch that Plaintiff would never become a major league umpire. He stated: "She's a nice person, and she knows the rules. But the thing is, she's got to do the job twice as good as the guy, if he's a good one to get the job." Defendants neither issued any statements contradicting, retracting, or correcting Napp's statements, took any remedial or disciplinary action with respect to Napp, nor otherwise said or did anything to communicate that Napp had not stated the true position of professional baseball, including Defendants. During the 1989 season, Ed Vargo required Plaintiff to adopt the above mentioned changes in her umpiring technique.

Plaintiff alleges that during the 1989 season, Defendants either ignored or criticized her. She and her partner were the only two of the nine minor league umpires invited to 1989 spring training who were not given the opportunity to fill in for ill or vacationing major league umpires, an opportunity which was given to male umpires with inferior abilities, experience, and qualifications. At the end of the 1989 season, Plaintiff received an unfairly negative written performance evaluation which alleged that she had a "bad attitude." Prior to 1989, Plaintiff had never received a written performance evaluation.

On November 6, 1989, Triple-A discharged and unconditionally released Plaintiff from her employment as an umpire. The reason for Plaintiff's discharge was that the National League and American League were not interested in considering her for employment as a major league umpire. Plaintiff alleges that the sole reason for her discharge, for her inability to obtain a job in the major leagues, and for the Defendants' other discriminatory conduct was Defendants' malicious, wanton, willful, knowing, and intentional discrimination on the basis of gender.

* * *

DISCUSSION

I. TITLE VII CLAIMS

* * *

Plaintiff asserts essentially two separate Title VII claims against the American League: a claim for failure to hire or promote, and a claim for wrongful termination.

1. Hiring or Promotion Claim

The American League maintains that it is entitled to summary judgment with respect to Plaintiff's claim for failure to hire or promote because * * * Plaintiff cannot establish a *prima facie* case of discrimination in promotion or hiring where no one, either male or female, was hired for or promoted to the position sought.

* * *

The American League argues that because it did not hire or promote any umpires during that period, the absence of a vacancy for the position sought prevents Plaintiff from establishing her requisite *prima facie* case of employment discrimination.

In *McDonnell Douglas Corp. v. Green* (1973), the Supreme Court ruled that an individual Title VII plaintiff must carry the initial burden of proof by establishing a *prima facie* case of discrimination. On the specific facts there involved, the Court found that the burden was met by showing that a qualified applicant, who was a member of a protected group, had unsuccessfully sought a job for which there was a vacancy and for which the employer continued thereafter to seek applicants with similar qualifications. The American League argues that because there was no vacancy in the position sought by Plaintiff, she is unable to satisfy the *McDonnell Douglas* test, and she therefore cannot establish a *prima facie* case.

McDonnell Douglas does not, however, outline the only possible way a Title VII plaintiff can establish a *prima facie* case. Indeed, in *International Brotherhood of Teamsters v. United States* (1977), the Court noted:

The importance of *McDonnell Douglas* lies, not in its specification of the discrete elements of proof there required, but in its recognition that any Title VII plaintiff must carry the initial burden of offering evidence adequate to create an inference that an employment decision was based on discriminatory criterion illegal under the [Civil Rights] Act [of 1964].

Thus, Plaintiff's inability to satisfy the *McDonnell Douglas* test does not bar her Title VII complaint, so long as she may establish a *prima facie* case by some other method.

Plaintiff relies on *Trans World Airlines, Inc. v. Thurston* (1985), and argues that *McDonnell Douglas* is irrelevant because she can establish her *prima facie* case by direct evidence. Specifically, she intends to offer the statements of American League officials Larry Napp and Dick Butler which suggested that Plaintiff would have to outperform male umpires to obtain a position in the major leagues.

In *Thurston*, the plaintiffs challenged a policy whereby vacant positions were created for airline pilots under age 60 who were forced to stop flying, but not for pilots forced into retirement at age 60. The defendant raised the absence of vacancies as a defense, but the Court refused to shield the defendant from liability where the existence of vacancies was due solely to the effect of the discriminatory policy under attack. The Court noted that because there was direct evidence of discrimination, namely the facially discriminatory policy at issue, the plaintiffs need not satisfy the *McDonnell Douglas* test: "The *McDonnell Douglas* test is inapplicable where the plaintiff presents direct evidence of discrimination. The shifting burdens of proof set forth in *McDonnell Douglas* are designed to assure that the 'plaintiff [has] his day in court despite the unavailability of direct evidence.'"

Plaintiff's reliance on *Thurston* is, however, misplaced. *Thurston* does not stand for a general proposition that a plaintiff may sue for discrimination in hiring or promotion where there was no vacancy in the position sought and no person, either within or without the protected group, was hired. *Thurston* did not hold, and Plaintiff has not cited any case which holds, that a plaintiff may sue under Title VII for discriminatory hiring or promotion where there was no vacancy in the position sought. As the Supreme Court has explained, "It is a [Title VII] plaintiff's task to demonstrate that similarly situated employees were not treated equally." The essence of a Title VII plaintiff's *prima facie* case must be differential treatment of similarly situated employees. Here, where the American League did not hire or promote any umpires during the relevant time period, either male or female, Plaintiff cannot show that she was treated any differently than male applicants, and her complaint does not make out a *prima facie* case of discrimination in hiring or promotion.

Accordingly, the American League is also entitled to summary judgment on Plaintiff's hiring and promotion claim arising from events which occurred within 300 days of the filing of her EEOC charge.

2. Termination Claim

The Complaint alleges that the reason for Triple-A's November 6, 1989 termination of Plaintiff was that the American League and National League were not interested in considering her for employment as a major league umpire.

The American League argues that it is entitled to summary judgment on Plaintiff's termination claim because when it expressed a lack of interest in hiring Plaintiff in October 1989, it treated her no differently than it treated male umpires. Martin J. Springstead, the American League's Supervisor of Umpires, states that in October 1989, Edwin L. Lawrence, the Executive Director of [the Baseball Office for Umpire Development ("BOUD")], submitted to him the names of a number of umpires employed by Triple-A, including Plaintiff's, and inquired whether the American League had a current interest in hiring any of these umpires. Mr. Springstead asserts that he advised Lawrence that the American League had no interest in hiring any of the umpires because it had no vacancies in its umpiring staff.

Plaintiff's Local Rule 3(g) Statement and an affidavit submitted by Plaintiff's counsel pursuant to Rule 56(f) suggest that in the American League's communications with BOUD in October 1989, the American League did more than simply tell BOUD that it had no umpire vacancies at that time. Rather, Plaintiff raises the possibility that the submission of her name was intended to give the American League an opportunity to express whether it ever intended to hire Plaintiff. Furthermore, Plaintiff implies that the American League either understood that its expressed lack of interest in Plaintiff would cause her termination by Triple-A, or otherwise intended to encourage Triple-A to terminate Plaintiff. Plaintiff requests that she be given an opportunity to conduct discovery to explore, inter alia, the content and nature of the October 1989 communications between the American League and BOUD.

The American League was not Plaintiff's employer at the time of her termination. Nevertheless, if Plaintiff shows such involvement by the American League in her termination by Triple-A, then she will allege a violation of Title VII against the American League. "It is clear from the language of the statute that Congress intended that the rights and obligations it created under Title VII would extend beyond the immediate employer-employee relationship." Where a third-party takes discriminatory action that causes an employer to terminate an employee, that third-party may be held liable under Title VII.

Accordingly, Plaintiff will have an opportunity to conduct discovery to determine whether the American League was involved in her termination. The American League's motion for summary judgment on Plaintiff's termination claim is therefore denied without prejudice to its renewal after discovery has been completed.

* * *

CONCLUSION

With regard to the Title VII claims: the American League's motion for summary judgment is granted in part and denied in part, and Defendants' motions to strike the jury demand and prayer for compensatory and punitive damages are denied.

IT IS SO ORDERED.

Notes and Questions

1. What explanation can be offered for the differences in treatment received by Amanda Clement in 1905 and Bernice Gera and Pam Postema in the 1980s? Are we becoming less refined as our civilization evolves or is an unfortunate byproduct of the women's movement the abandonment of any notion of male-to-female gentility? That is, are men saying, "you want equal treatment, this is how we treat one another"? In terms of collegiality, must women entering the workforce do so at their own risk at the peril of alienation?

2. In several respects, baseball's failure to promote Pam Posetma in large part stemmed from its inherent bias against women and, to some degree, the failure of her colleagues to evince a team spirit that characterizes the way in which male umpiring crews cooperate with each other. *See* Phil Rogers, *Bad Calls Part of the Game, Baseball Should Not Allow Replays,* CHI. TRIB., April 25, 2003. What are an employer's responsibilities to insure that fellow workers maintain a collegial spirit *vis-à-vis* minorities and women, especially where co-operation and team-play are important aspects of the job?

3. What procedural infirmities plagued Postema's Title VII claim? Note that, on appeal, the Second Circuit reversed the lower court's findings regarding the applicability of the 1991 amendments to Postema's claim. The Second Circuit held specifically that the amendments providing plaintiffs the right to a jury trial and compensatory and punitive damages do not apply retroactively. 998 F.2d 60 (2d Cir. 1993).

4. *Postema* presented a typical problem in terms of the standards to be applied in a sports context. Subjective judgments become the norm because there are so many variables inherent in what makes good player or an effective umpire. *See* JOHN C. WEISTART & CYM H. LOWELL, THE LAW OF SPORTS § 3.07, at 230–32 (1979); *see also* BARBARA LINDEMANN & PAUL GROSSMAN, EMPLOYMENT DISCRIMINATION LAW 197–216 (3D ED. 1996). As one commentator has stated:

> Postema will have an uphill climb convincing the courts that her performance merits an opportunity to work in the major leagues. The problem is that the decision to fire her, like the past decisions that promoted her, was made subjectively by supervisors who work without score cards.

Sharlene A. McEvoy, *The Umpire Strikes Out:* Postema v. National League: *Major League Gender Discrimination,* 11 U. MIAMI ENT. & SPORTS L. REV. 1, 5 (1993). Yet, it seems as though the factors, particularly the abstract or non-concrete indicia, that are endemic to an assessment of a player (team play, attitude, etc.) would have less utility in the evaluation of one's umpiring skills.

5. In 1997, *Sports Illustrated* columnist Grant Wahl brought us up-to-date on the details of Postema's life eight years after she was fired from her job as an umpire.

> The second shift runs from 3:30 p.m. to midnight at an auto-parts factory in Mansfield, Ohio. Pam Postema likes to work those hours because they match the schedule she used to have as a professional baseball umpire. Nine years ago, when she appeared on our cover, Postema was tantalizingly close to becoming the first female umpire in the major leagues. It never happened, of course, for her or any other woman. Postema hasn't called a game at any level since 1989. Today, the lady is a welder.
>
> Postema, 43, works on the muffler line at Newman Technology Incorporated. Her job consists of inserting tailpipes into muffler housings, turning the assemblages over to a robot for welding and, if need be, repairing the welds bungled by the robot—which happens often enough to keep Postema busy. "The robots aren't perfect," she says with mock wonderment. "Imagine that."
>
> In other words, they're a lot like umpires. In 1988 Postema was one of seven candidates the National League was considering for two vacant umpiring positions. But she was passed over that spring and then again the following year. After the '89 season, her seventh in Triple A, she was released. (Rarely do umpires work longer than four years in Triple A, which looks to uncover fresh talent for the majors.) Postema moved from Phoenix to San Clemente, California, where she drove a Federal Express truck and wrote an angry memoir, *You've Got To Have Balls To Make It In This League.* In 1991 she filed a sex-discrimination suit against Major League Baseball. She settled out of court, under two conditions: that she wouldn't reveal the amount of the settlement and wouldn't apply for umpiring jobs in any league affiliated with Major League Baseball.
>
> A year ago Postema moved to Mansfield 30 miles from her hometown of Willard, Ohio, where her 77-year-old father, Phil, still lives. She found work at Newman Tech, first as a temp and then, last June, full time. She had never welded before. "It's real laid-back, and they have a good insurance plan," she says. "But I like umpiring, and I'd rather be doing that than a factory job." In fact, Postema is thinking of moving to Florida to umpire at the college and high school levels, and women's fast-pitch softball also interests her.
>
> As for big league baseball, she rarely watches it, even on television. "If I'm channel surfing and see a game, I'll stop for 10 minutes, then move on," she says. "I don't care too much about Major League Baseball. They didn't care too much about me."

Grant Wahl, *Catching Up with Baseball Umpire Pam Postema,* SPORTS ILLUSTRATED, April 28, 1997. Do you consider it ironic that Postema chose to enter what has historically been another male-dominated profession—that of a welder?

6. If the league were to establish that Postema, while technically a very proficient umpire, was not respected by her fellow umpires and players, would these be relevant reasons to deny her a Major League position? As we discussed with regard to female reporters and television personalities, what if studies were to establish that employment of female umpires would have a substantial adverse impact in terms of fan patronage?

Courts have been reluctant to indulge employer claims that Title VII compliance will compromise business relationships or offend consumers. In this regard, is the nature of the business a relevant line of inquiry? Is an employer who is engaged in an enterprise that offers numerous consumer options in a better position to assert a consumer acceptance defense than an employer who, for example, provides airline services? That is, there is only one way to get from New York to California in a day; but there are infinite choices in other areas such as public entertainment. *See, e.g., Gerdom v. Continental Airlines, Inc.*, 692 F.2d 602 (9th Cir. 1982); *Wilson v. Southwest Airlines Co.*, 517 F. Supp. 292 (N.D. Tex. 1981). *See also* Lindemann & Grossman at 408–10. In the latter situation, is an employer's argument that viewer preference justifies rejection of a woman candidate for employment a viable argument? Again, the answer is likely no. *See Diaz v. Pan American World Airways*, 442 F.2d 385 (5th Cir. 1971), (BFOQ denied where passengers had expressed a preference for environment created by female flight attendants).

7. In particularly violent sports such as hockey or football, could the NHL or NFL or assert a defense claiming that gender is a *bona fide* occupational qualification? Is this defense even relevant to a claim of disparate impact? As suggested earlier, the less stringent business necessity test would probably apply to a disparate impact claim. With regard to the probability of success of the BFOQ defense, the league enjoys little hope for success. *See Dothard v. Rawlinson*, 433 U.S. 321, 335 (1977). The courts seemingly embrace the notion that there is a marked difference between chivalry and sexism. League remonstrations that they are primarily concerned with safety will likely be dismissed as paternalism. *See* Lindemann & Grossman at 404. Interestingly, though, regulations promulgated pursuant to Title IX permit special treatment (presumably including exclusion) of women insofar as contact sports such as basketball, football, and ice hockey are concerned. *See* 34 C.F.R. § 106.41(b). *See also* Syda Kosofsky, *Toward Gender Equality in Professional Sports*, 4 Hastings Women's L.J. 209, 235 (1993).

8. Questions of discrimination aside, becoming a Major League umpire or other professional official is a rare occurrence. For every umpire who attains the Major League level, thousands have failed. A perusal of the number of applicants that enroll in (former umpire) Harry Wendelstadt's school compared with the few who are fortunate enough to secure a professional position is revealing. Out of 160 *selected* candidates in the February, 1994 graduating class, only ten were hired by Major League Baseball's Umpire Development Program. These ten candidates are assigned to the low minors with no assurances of elevation to the Major Leagues. Gordon Monson, *Brothers in Blue*, Salt Lake Tribune, Sports, Aug. 21, 1994, at C1. At present, there is only one female umpire in professional baseball, Ria Cortesio. Cortesio is in her fourth season umpiring Double A games in the Southern league.

Given the difficulty inherent in securing a position as a Major League umpire, can women expect little help from the umpires' union? Is it even more likely that male umpires will resent women as competitors for jobs and threats to their economic security? Because good umpiring requires on-the-field cooperation and a degree of teamwork, could this insecurity result in a female umpire's male counterparts giving less than the maximum cooperative effort, thus leading to a less than optimum performance by the underrepresented women arbiters? In fact, many of Postema's minor league "colleagues" expressed the following sentiment: "If you have to, work with her, but don't help her, don't make it 'easy'." McEvoy, *supra*, at 3. This type of inter-employee hostility reflects the archaic notion that women "enter a male-dominated profession at their own risk." Melissa M. Beck, *Note, Fairness on the Field: Amending Title VII to Foster Greater Female*

Participation in Professional Sports, 12 CARDOZO ARTS & ENT. L.J. 241, 261 (1994). The first female to attempt to break the "all male umpire barrier" since the retirement of Amanda Clement in the early 1900s, Bernice Gera, was awarded a minor league position after initiation of a lawsuit. *See New York State Division of Human Rights v. New York-Pennsylvania Professional Baseball League*, 320 N.Y.S.2d 788 (N.Y. App. Div. 1971). Unfortunately, Gera resigned shortly thereafter, prompted in part by the abuses to which she was subjected by fans and players. *See* Beck, *supra*, 12 CARDOZO ARTS & ENT. L. J. 241 (1994). How do you explain the sixty-three year hiatus and the astonishingly low numbers of female umpires?

10. Given the way that other umpires responded to Pam Postema (ditto players), bringing a Title VII suit based on a hostile work environment was a prudent strategy. Why did it ultimately fail? In terms of the refusal to hire, was she doomed by: a) the absence of vacancies; b) her own admission of mediocre or "less than outstanding" minor league performance; or, c) the subjectivity factor that is a constant concern in cases like hers?

11. Not all female challenges to the "good 'ol boy" network in sports umpiring and refereeing have been dismissed as summarily as Pam Postema's. In *Ortiz-Del Valle v. National Basketball Association*, 42 F. Supp. 2d 334 (S.D.N.Y. 1994), the court found that the NBA had intentionally discriminated against the plaintiff through its gender-based refusal to hire her as a referee. She was awarded punitive damages as well as monthly relief for lost wages and emotional distress. The NBA has had two female referees, Dee Kantner and Violet Palmer. Kantner was dismissed for poor performance after the 2001–2002 season. To date, she has not pursued any legal recourse.

12. Today more women than ever occupy positions in professional sports that historically were held predominately by men. Female reporters now roam NFL sidelines and anchor popular sports news shows. However, as demonstrated by the following cases, the road to gender equality in professional sports jobs, particularly sports journalism, has never been easy.

F. Off The Field: Women and The Sports Media

Ludtke v. Kuhn
461 F. Supp. 86 (S.D.N.Y. 1978)

MOTLEY, District Judge.

* * *

On April 2, 1975, defendant [Commissioner] Bowie Kuhn wrote the general managers of all major league baseball teams indicating that baseball should maintain a "unified stand" against the admission of women sportswriters to major league clubhouses. During the 1977 World Series that policy was applied to plaintiff Melissa Ludtke, a sportswriter for Sports Illustrated, a weekly sports magazine published by plaintiff Time Incorporated. After the 1977 World Series and after the commencement of this action, baseball reconfirmed its policy of excluding women reporters from the clubhouse.

Kuhn's 1975 "unified stand" letter followed discussions within the Office of the Commissioner triggered by the decision of the National Hockey League All-Star teams to allow women reporters to conduct interviews in the locker rooms following the January 1975 National Hockey League All-Star Game. In the course of those discussions, the

Commissioner's office questioned no baseball players concerning their opinions. Public relations directors of the major league teams were questioned and their opinions were varied. On July 22, 1976, Robert Wirz, Director of Information of the Office of the Commissioner of Baseball, wrote the Public Relations Directors of all Major League Baseball teams a reminder of baseball's stance in opposition to allowing women reporters access to clubhouses and asking whether any women had requested such access. On August 4, 1976, by letter, and shortly thereafter orally, the public relations director of defendant New York Yankees told Mr. Wirz that the Yankee players had concluded by an "overwhelming majority" that women could be allowed access to the clubhouse if they conducted themselves professionally. Mr. Wirz then told the Yankee public relations director that action by one team to allow women reporters in the clubhouse would be a "definite threat to breaking down the overall barrier". Thereafter, Yankee management reversed the position of the players and said "no more" to women reporters in the Yankee clubhouse.

At the 1977 Baseball World Series games between the New York Yankees and the Los Angeles Dodgers, Melissa Ludtke, an accredited reporter assigned by Sports Illustrated to cover the Series, was informed by the Commissioner's office that she was not permitted, solely on the basis of her sex, to enter either team's clubhouse after the Series games. The Commissioner's office was aware that the Dodgers had already told Ludtke that she would have access to their clubhouse after the games. The Commissioner's office was also aware that Ludtke had been given access to the manager's office in the Yankees' clubhouse during the American League playoff games.

The Commissioner's office assigned Larry Shenk, the public relations director for the Philadelphia Phillies, to try to bring players out of the clubhouse to speak with Ludtke in the tunnel where she was made to stand. Shenk subsequently stated at the 1977 annual major league public relations meeting, chaired by the Commissioner's Director of Information, that women reporters should be given postgame access to the clubhouse.

During the World Series, the Commissioner was also told by Henry Hecht, a baseball writer for the New York Post, that he and other "regular writers on the beat" thought that women reporters should be given equal access to teams' clubhouses. The Commissioner's office spoke to no players concerning their views either during or after the World Series. After the commencement of this action, in January 1978 and again in March, the Commissioner reconfirmed his policy of excluding women reporters from baseball clubhouses. Leland MacPhail, the President of the American League, has stated that he supports the Commissioner's policy regarding women reporters.

In March 1978, at the Yankees' spring training camp in Fort Lauderdale, Florida, the Yankees' manager gave one or more women journalists access to the Yankees' locker room. Shortly thereafter the Yankees were instructed that they were to comply with the Commissioner's policy, and the Yankees' manager stated that women reporters would be excluded from the clubhouse once the regular season began.

* * *

Central to the resolution of this case is the undisputed fact that all accredited female sports reporters are excluded from the Yankee clubhouse at Yankee Stadium solely because they are women, whereas, all accredited male sports reporters (to the extent that space limitations permit) are permitted access to the clubhouse after games for the purpose of interviewing ballplayers.

Defendants say women reporters are excluded in order 1) to protect the privacy of those players who are undressed or who are in various stages of undressing and getting ready to shower; 2) to protect the image of baseball as a family sport; and 3) preservation of traditional notions of decency and propriety.

Another pivotal fact which is also not disputed is that fresh-off-the-field interviews are important to the work of sports reporters and will give a competitive advantage to those who have access to the ballplayers at that juncture, particularly during the World Series games.

Another critical consideration is the admission that there are several other less sweeping alternatives to the present policy of blanket exclusion of women reporters. Counsel for defendants admitted that those players who are desirous of undressing can retreat to their cubicles in the clubhouse. There the players can be shielded from the "roving eyes" of any female reporters by having each cubicle furnished with a curtain or swinging door. It is also conceded that the player who is undressed and wishes to move about in that state can use a towel to shield himself from view.

Since the Kuhn policy determination is based solely on sex, and since that policy results in denial of equal opportunity to plaintiff Ludtke to pursue her profession as a sports reporter, and since there are several less restrictive alternatives to the total exclusion of women, and since the material facts regarding New York City's involvement in Yankee Stadium and the lease of those premises to the Yankees are not disputed, the only questions remaining for decision are questions of law.

A. State Action

The first question is whether New York City's involvement with Yankee Stadium and the lease arrangement with the Yankees is such as to make the Kuhn policy determination state action within the contemplation of the Fourteenth Amendment.

It must by now be regarded as well settled that state action may be found where the direct perpetrator of allegedly discriminatory acts is, though a private entity, "so entwined" with an agency of the state that that agency must be deemed responsible for the private entity's acts. *Burton v. Wilmington Parking Authority* (19601. There is, however, no rigid yardstick against which the relationship may be measured to determine the presence of state action. As the Supreme Court has explained: "Only by sifting facts and weighing circumstances can the nonobvious involvement of the State in private conduct be attributed its true significance."

Burton, like the instant case, involved discrimination against the plaintiff on the ground of a class-based characteristic, in that case race. The discrimination there took place on ostensibly private premises (those of the defendant Eagle Coffee Shoppe), operated under lease from a public authority (the Wilmington Parking Authority). Here the discrimination also takes place on ostensibly private premises (the Yankee Clubhouse) located on premises (Yankee Stadium) operated under lease from a public authority (The City of New York). The Court in *Burton* found that the coffee shop, located in an otherwise public building owned by the Wilmington Parking Authority, enjoyed a "symbiotic relationship" with the publicly operated portions of the premises, consisting of parking facilities. The proximity of the coffee shop was found to be essential in establishing the fiscal viability of the parking garage. The Yankee clubhouse in this case has been opened to the press immediately after games, particularly during the World Series, so that players fresh-off-the-field may be interviewed. Moreover, it is undisputed that television cameras were permitted in the clubhouse after the World Series games for the same purpose. Advertising and massive publicity about the Yankees and individual Yankee ballplayers is essential to the profitability of the Yankee Stadium.

* * *

The facts of the case at hand so nearly resemble those of *Burton* that there can be little doubt that state action exists here, making 42 U.S.C. §1983 an appropriate statute for plaintiffs to employ in seeking redress of the injuries flowing from the defendants' discriminatory conduct, and vesting this court with jurisdiction.

Here, as in *Burton*, the place where the discriminatory acts occurred is owned by the state (the City of New York) and leased pursuant to special legislative provisions to the Yankees. In this case, as in *Burton*, the facility involved is maintained and improved with the use of public funds. The Court noted in *Burton* that the relationship of the public and private entities in that case placed them in a relationship of interdependence. The same observation can be made on these facts, where the annual rentals to be paid to the City for use of the stadium depend directly on the drawing power of Yankee games, and the City has in turn invested substantial sums of public money to enhance that drawing power by modernizing and improving the stadium itself.

* * *

It is an undisputed fact that the City's profit from its lease with the Yankees escalates when attendance at Yankee games increases. Thus the City has a clear interest in the preservation and maintenance of baseball's audience, image, popularity and standing.

Furthermore, the City has not stepped in, pursuant to the lease provision requiring the Yankees to comply with all local, state, and federal laws, to stop the Yankees' discriminatory conduct. This is so despite the City's indication of its conviction "that a less restrictive alternative to the policy of total exclusion of female reporters from the clubhouses at Yankee Stadium ought to be devised", in an affidavit by its counsel.

Defendants have argued that because the City has not explicitly directed the Yankees to adopt the policy in dispute, a finding of state action cannot be made here. The state of the law is otherwise, however. State involvement sufficient to support a finding of state action may be predicated on mere failure to act. "The failure of a city and its public officials to act constitutes state action when the municipality is under a duty to act and the inaction results in the deprivation of constitutional rights."

* * *

B. Sex Discrimination

Having found that the Kuhn determination mandating total exclusion of women from the locker room of the Yankee clubhouse constitutes state action, the next question is whether that state action has infringed any right of plaintiff Ludtke which is guaranteed by the Constitution and/or laws of the United States. 42 U.S.C. §1983. This court finds that the state action complained of here infringes both equal protection and due process rights of plaintiff Ludtke.

* * *

1. Equal Protection

On the basis of the undisputed facts, plaintiff Ludtke, while in pursuit of her profession as a sports reporter, was treated differently from her male counterparts (other properly accredited sportswriters) solely because she is a woman. Defendants have "controverted", but have not adequately disputed for purposes of Fed.R.Civ.P. 56(e), plaintiffs' allegation that the result of this differentiation was to deny plaintiff Ludtke an equal opportunity to get a story or gather news on the same basis as her male counterparts, thus giving the latter a substantial competitive advantage.

Unless a sufficient justification can be advanced, on these facts and given the involvement of the state in the conduct complained of, the court must hold that plaintiff Ludtke was deprived of equal opportunity to interview ballplayers solely on account of her sex, contrary to the equal protection clause of the Fourteenth Amendment.

"To withstand constitutional challenge * * * classifications by gender must serve important governmental objectives and must be substantially related to achievement of those objectives." *Craig v. Boren* (1976). Defendants have asserted, as justification for the complete exclusion of female reporters from the clubhouse at Yankee Stadium, their interest in protecting the privacy of the ballplayers while undressing in the locker room.

The right to privacy is of constitutional dimension, *see Roe v. Wade* (1973), and its protection is thus undeniably an important objective. It cannot be said on these facts, however, that there is a sufficiently substantial relationship between that objective on one hand and the total exclusion of women from the Yankee locker room on the other to pass constitutional muster." "Inquiry into the actual purposes' of the discrimination * * * proves the contrary." *Califano v. Goldfarb* (1977).

At least during World Series games, male members of the news media with television cameras have been allowed to enter the Yankee locker room immediately after the games and broadcast live from that location. In this connection, only a backdrop behind the player standing in front of the camera is provided to shield other players from the "roving eye" of the camera. These locker room encounters are viewed by mass audiences, which include many women and children. This practice, coupled with defendants' practice of refusing to allow accredited women sports reporters to enter the locker room, shows that the latter is "substantially related" only to maintaining the locker room as an all-male preserve.

This court need look no further than to the statements of defendants' counsel at the hearing on these cross-motions for summary judgment to find a number of alternative approaches which defendants might have implemented that would adequately protect the Yankee players' interests in privacy while at the same time enabling female sportswriters to enjoy precisely the same conditions of employment as their male colleagues.

THE COURT: With respect to the assertion of privacy, at least by some of these players, isn't it possible for them to use curtains in front of this cubicle * * * to undress and hide (themselves) from these women?

MR. CLIMENKO: It's possible, your Honor.

THE COURT: Or put swinging doors if he wants to get behind the door when a woman comes in, he can do that?

MR. CLIMENKO: It's possible. It's possible to do what the plaintiff in this case says, wear towels. It's not the way people who play baseball are accustomed to (sic) have the freedom of access after their own game.

If defendants' practice of total exclusion is derived, as counsel would appear to suggest, from a mere "custom", then it surely cannot stand against constitutional attack. The Supreme Court has held that mere administrative convenience cannot justify discrimination on account of sex.

The court holds that defendants' policy of total exclusion of women sports reporters from the locker room at Yankee Stadium is not substantially related to the privacy protection objective and thus deprives plaintiff Ludtke of that equal protection of the laws which is guaranteed her by the Fourteenth Amendment.

2. Due Process

An analysis of these same facts from the perspective of substantive due process leads us to an identical result. The right to pursue one's profession is a fundamental "liberty" within the meaning of the Fourteenth Amendment's due process guarantee. *Greene v. McElroy* (1960); *Meyer v. Nebraska* (1923); *Allgeyer v. Louisiana* (1897). Further, it is settled law that:

> Even though the governmental purpose be legitimate and substantial, that purpose cannot be pursued by means that broadly stifle fundamental personal liberties when the end can be more narrowly achieved.

Shelton v. Tucker (1960).

As noted above, the Kuhn policy substantially and directly interferes with the right of plaintiff Ludtke to pursue her profession as a sports reporter. Her male counterparts are able to get to the ballplayers fresh-off–the-field when comments about plays may still be in progress, for example.

hen a statutory classification significantly interferes with the exercise of a fundamental right, it cannot be upheld unless it is supported by sufficiently important state interests and is closely tailored to effectuate only those interests.

The undisputed facts show that the Yankees' interest in protecting ballplayer privacy may be fully served by much less sweeping means than that implemented here. The court holds that the state action complained of unreasonably interferes with plaintiff Ludtke's fundamental right to pursue her profession in violation of the due process clause of the Fourteenth Amendment.

The other two interests asserted by defendants, maintaining the status of baseball as a family sport and conforming to traditional notions of decency and propriety, are clearly too insubstantial to merit serious consideration. Weighed against plaintiff's right to be free of discrimination based upon her sex, and her fundamental right to pursue her profession, such objectives cannot justify the defendants' policy under the equal protection or due process clauses of the Fourteenth Amendment.

Since plaintiff Ludtke has been deprived, under color of the authority of the state, of rights secured to her by both the due process and equal protection clauses of the Fourteenth Amendment to the Federal Constitution, 42 U.S.C. §1983, she is entitled to the injunctive relief sought and to an award of counsel fees. 42 U.S.C. §1988.

Having ruled for plaintiffs on Ludtke's §1983 claim, the court finds it unnecessary to rule on any other federal or state law claim in order to afford plaintiffs all of the relief to which they are presently entitled.

An injunction will therefore issue enjoining defendants from enforcing the policy of total exclusion of accredited women sports reporters from the locker rooms of the clubhouses at Yankee Stadium and requiring them to adopt one of the above alternative means of preserving player privacy.

Notes and Questions

1. For a similar discussion of state action at the collegiate level, see *National Collegiate Athletic Association v. Tarkanian*, 488 U.S. 179 (1988), where the NCAA was found

not to be a state actor for purposes of a claim raised under §1983. Does *Tarkanian* preclude a constitutional claim by an aggrieved athlete attending a state university or a reporter seeking to gain access to the locker room at such institution? *See Hall v. University of Minnesota*, 530 F. Supp. 104 (D. Minn. 1982).

2. How relevant to the court's decision was its recognition that the players had voted to permit women reporters to enter the locker room? Is the league's concern really privacy or is it the more delicate question of sexual tension? What would the league's position be with regard to a gay male reporter's access? Is it the league's belief that the locker room is a last bastion of maleness and that a woman should not intrude? If so, is that really a privacy issue?

3. In *Ludtke*, the defendants expressed concerns about the privacy rights of *male* professional athletes. Would the court have given greater deference to a privacy argument by a female professional athlete seeking to protect her interests in the locker room context, or is that scenario also "too insubstantial to merit serious consideration?" This issue is a product of more than mere academic curiosity given the emergence of women's professional teams in basketball and baseball.

4. How far should the courts be willing to go in terms of access? Would the *Ludtke* court permit male reporters to have equal access to the locker room of a women's field hockey or basketball team at a *state university*? What about the same scenario at a public secondary school with a high profile women's athletic program?

5. Although women have occupied the position of sports writer for several decades, they have not been welcomed as equal members of the "fraternity." Columnist Tim Crothers offers the following account of sports writer Mary Garber's experience in the field:

> Mary Garber discovered her guardian angel in the summer of 1947 when she traveled to Brooklyn's Ebbets Field to watch Jackie Robinson. At the time, Garber was a pioneering sportswriter in a male domain, observing the first African-American to play major league baseball. "Jackie became the most important influence in my life," Garber says. "When people would step on me and hurt my feelings, I would look at how he kept his mouth shut and did his job as best he could with the belief that someday he would be accepted."
>
> In the year 2000 Garber is embarking on her seventh decade as a sportswriter in Winston-Salem, N.C., having worked first at the Twin-City Sentinel and now at the Winston-Salem Journal. The job at the Sentinel was thrust upon her near the end of World War II when a teenage boy who produced the sports page after school enlisted in the Navy and there wasn't any man to take his place. After the war Garber began to feel the sting of male chauvinism. In that era the press box was off-limits to women, children and pets. "Once, I was sent to cover a football game at Duke, but they stuck me in the wives' box," Garber recalls. "All through the game the wives blabbed and the kids screamed, and I thought I would lose my mind."
>
> Garber was one of the first women to cover the college football and basketball beats, and there she was often stereotyped by her gender. One day a high school basketball player tore his shorts during a game, and the coach asked Garber to sew them up. Indiana coach Bob Knight interrupted an NCAA tournament press conference to ask Garber if his language was proper. A 1958 Sentinel article reporting Garber's acceptance of a writing award said, "Miss Garber has received nationwide publicity as one of the few full-time female sportswriters. In addition, she bakes a mighty fine cake."

Tim Crothers, *Miss Mary's History Lesson; Mary Garber's Inspiration During a 56-Year Sportswriting Career Has Been Jackie Robinson*, SPORTS ILLUSTRATED, March 20, 2000.

6. Years after her case had been decided, Melissa Ludtke observed:

> The locker-room incidents are a stark and valuable reminder that the battles that I and others waged for equality in the 1970s didn't bring an end to discrimination. They only kept the more overt forms from showing. We've learned that changing the rules doesn't necessarily alter attitudes. Stereotypical, outmoded and confining images of women, not at all suited to the reality of their actual lives, still pop up and sting us. To be sportswriters, women learn quickly that they must observe certain unwritten rules. They must tolerate an interminable onslaught of teasing tossed at them. They must bury female sensibilities at the door. If they linger in the locker room or converse in too friendly a fashion with players, they are accused of flirting and talked about in unflattering ways that in time undermine their credibility and wear them down. Even so, the women-in-the-locker-room system for the most part works when league commissioners, team executives and players want it to. In the National Basketball Association, which gave women equal access without rancor or lawsuits, these altercations have not taken place. The players use bathrobes or rely on towels to ensure their privacy. But even in baseball, the policy of equal access can and does work. Often when I was in locker rooms in the '70s, players would politely ask me to return in five minutes, after they had dressed. The point is, there are sensible ways to make this work for everybody, without making it impossible for women to report sports or humiliating those who choose to do so. Women in locker rooms should not be the issue in 1990. Rather, the finger ought to be pointed at the infantile and repugnant behavior of some ballplayers and their inability to adjust to changing times, when gender equality should be assumed.

Leslie Whitaker, *Trouble in the Locker Rooms: More Women Reporters Face Hostility That Threatens Their Access*, TIME, Oct. 15, 1990.

Are women reporters threatening to male athletes? To men generally? Why would they be? "[It] is not the mere presence of women that is so problematic," write Mary Jo Kane and Lisa J. Disch; "it is the fact that they are present as an authoritative critic that so fundamentally threatens male power and privilege." Mary Jo Kane & Lisa J. Disch, *Sexual Violence and the Reproduction of Male Power in the Locker Room: The "Lisa Olson Incident,"* 10 Sociology Sport J. 331, 338 (1993).

7. A related problem arises in the context of a woman who is denied a sports-related media position by her employer. For example, what if the *Ludtke* court had ruled in favor of baseball, thereby diminishing the value of Ludtke and other female reporters? That is, if Ludtke is denied access to the locker room, while her male counterparts are permitted to take advantage of this venue's availability, won't her employer's competitive position in the sports news marketplace be compromised? In this event, would her employer be justified in a hiring decision that bypasses her in favor of a male applicant?

8. In the case that follows, the court considered claims that a female was denied the position of staff director for television programming at NBC Sports. As you review this decision, ponder whether denial of access in general or a perception that women are not in touch with athletes in male-dominated sports was part of the unstated motivation underlying the station's ultimate choice for staff director.

Equal Employment Opportunity Comm'n
v. National Broadcasting Co.
753 F. Supp. 452 (S.D.N.Y. 1990)

SWEET, District Judge. Plaintiff Equal Employment Opportunity Commission ("EEOC") and plaintiff-intervenor Enid Roth ("Roth") brought this action against the defendant National Broadcasting Company, Inc. ("NBC") alleging a violation of Title VII of the Civil Rights Act of 1964 as amended, 42 U.S.C. 2000e et seq. ("Title VII"), arising out of NBC's refusal to employ Roth as a staff director of television programs for NBC Sports.

* * *

On May 13, 1980 following certain of the events set forth below, the Directors Guild of America ("DGA") filed a charge of discrimination with the EEOC against NBC, alleging that NBC had discriminated against Roth because of her sex by refusing to hire her to direct television sports programs. The DGA subsequently amended the charge to include NBC's failure to offer another woman an Associate Director position in Sports.

The EEOC investigated the charge, and on July 13, 1983 issued its determination that there was "reasonable cause" to believe that the NBC sports department ("Sports") had discriminated against Roth in particular and females as a class based on their sex in filling Sports Director positions.

* * *

In a Title VII case, the plaintiff bears the initial burden of establishing, by a preponderance of the evidence, a *prima facie* case of discrimination. If the plaintiff succeeds in doing so, the burden then shifts to the defendant to produce evidence which rebuts the accusation of discrimination, by showing that there was a legitimate, non-discriminatory reason for its actions. Finally, if the defendant carries this burden, the plaintiff may respond by showing that the reason asserted by the defendant is merely pretextual. *See Texas Dept. of Community Affairs v. Burdine* (1981) (citing *McDonnell Douglas Corp. v. Green* (1973)).

In order to establish a *prima facie* case of sex discrimination, the plaintiff must show that (1) she applied for the job in question; (2) she was qualified for the job; (3) she did not receive the job; and (4) the job was held open for or filled by men whose qualifications were the same as hers.

Roth has attempted to cast this case as a "mixed motives" case, asserting that she has presented direct evidence that NBC allowed her gender to influence its decision not to hire her in Sports. If that were true, then the burden of proof—rather than the burden of production—would shift to NBC to demonstrate that its hiring decision would have been the same, absent any discrimination.[1]

However, the "direct evidence" referred to by Roth is insufficient to establish that her gender played a part in the decision. The fact that Roth had been the object of several sex—stereotyped remarks during her attempts to re-enter Sports—for example, she testified that she was told by several men that she wouldn't want to hear "all that lousy language" or go into locker rooms—is inadequate, because she has not shown that any such remarks were made by those responsible for the decision not to hire her, or that such remarks influenced that decision at all.

---

1. In contrast, under the test set forth in *Burdine* and *McDonnell*, a plaintiff who succeeds in establishing a *prima facie* case of discrimination thereby shifts the burden of production to the defendant, but the burden of persuasion remains on the plaintiff.

* * *

Roth has adequately demonstrated that she applied for the position of Sports Director, but has failed to establish a *prima facie* case of discrimination because she has not shown that she was qualified for the job. Although she had experience in directing and seems to have had ample technical skills, she has not proven that she possessed the requisite sports directing ability. Assuming, without deciding, that her sports expertise was sufficient for her to direct a sports broadcast, Roth simply lacked the creativity and leadership necessary in a Sports Director. Her background in directing studio events did not prepare her for the demands of broadcasting a live sports event, where the Sports Director must both anticipate the action and guide the cameras to capture that action in order to be prepared to deliver images which will satisfy the television audience.

Following her first directing opportunity, Nathanson communicated to Roth that she was not managing the cameras enough, that she should get more involved in directing them rather than simply taking the shots they offered. When she later directed an entire game, Finkel registered a similar complaint, stating that she "tended to be a shot caller, rather than a director." In light of this uncontradicted evidence that Roth simply lacked an ability which was essential for the position of Sports Director, it cannot be said that Roth was qualified for the job.

Of course, proof of competence sufficient to make out a *prima facie* case of discrimination was never intended to encompass proof of superiority or flawless performance. If an employer is dissatisfied with the performance of an employee, he can properly raise the issue in rebuttal of the plaintiff's showing. However, where, as here, the employer's evidence relates to the plaintiff's basic competence for the position at issue, it is appropriate to consider evidence which indicates that lack of skill when determining whether a *prima facie* case of discrimination has been made out. Because this evidence shows that Roth was not qualified for the position of Sports Director, she has not established a *prima facie* case.

* * *

Alternatively, even if Roth was qualified to be Sports Director, so that a *prima facie* case was established, NBC has presented legitimate non-discriminatory reasons for hiring its Sports Directors. Although the men who were selected as Sports Directors over Roth may not have had the absolute length of experience in television that she did, each of them demonstrated superior ability in the specific skills required of a Sports Director. In particular, Gonzalez, Gunts, and Rosenberg each demonstrated the creativity and initiative necessary to succeed as Sports Directors—qualities which both Nathanson and Finkel had found lacking in Roth's directing opportunities. Roth has not proven that NBC's expressed reasons for hiring these three men were pretextual.

* * *

With respect to the position of associate director, however, Roth has established a *prima facie* case of discrimination. Assuming that she was qualified to fill this position, and she actively sought such a position in 1988 for the Olympic Games, one of the two available positions was held open for a man instead of Roth. These elements are all that is required to state a *prima facie* case under *McDonnell* and its progeny.

NBC's rebuttal is that Roth was passed over for the associate director position for the weightlifting events in Seoul in favor of a more qualified candidate. "With some objective measure for the comparison, * * * the decision that one potential employee possesses superior ability and is better qualified than another" is a legitimate business decision. *Ibrahim v. New York State Department of Health* (2d Cir. 1990). The comparison here, between an applicant with limited sports broadcasting experience and no demonstrated knowledge of weightlifting and one with broadcasting experience from the prior Winter Olympics who had been recommended for the position by the producer of the event, satisfies the *Ibrahim* requirement of being a legitimate business decision.

Roth has not demonstrated that this proffered justification is a pretext. Although she suspected that her interview with Ewert was merely a set-up because of her litigation against NBC, Ewert in fact had no knowledge that her lawsuit was still ongoing at the time of the interview. His refusal to hire her as a logger or runner for the Olympics was based on legitimate business concerns, both for NBC as a whole and for the Olympic sports broadcasting endeavor. Thus although Roth may have been qualified for an Associate Director position, NBC had valid non-pretextual reasons for not offering her the job.

* * *

CONCLUSION

Roth has not established a *prima facie* case of discrimination with respect to the position of Sports Director. Alternatively, if a *prima facie* case was established, NBC has demonstrated legitimate non-discriminatory reasons for not making Roth a Sports Director, and she has not proven that these reasons were pretextual. * * *

Although Roth may have established a *prima facie* case of discrimination regarding the Associate Director position at the 1988 Olympics, NBC has presented valid non-discriminatory reasons for selecting a man as Associate Director for the weightlifting event, and Roth has not proven that those reasons were pretextual. EEOC has not shown discrimination in the selection of Associate Directors because, aside from Roth, it has not shown that any qualified woman applied and was rejected in favor of a man, and because Roth's rejection was supported by valid, non-discriminatory reasons.

Neither Roth nor NBC has shown any discrimination in the assignment of freelance directing opportunities because there was no evidence that any women had sought such an assignment and was denied the position in favor of a man.

Notes and Questions

1. Prohibited discrimination under Title VII generally falls into one of several categories. Included among these categories are claims alleging unlawful discrimination based upon disparate treatment, mixed or dual motives, and disparate impact. Disparate treatment involves deliberate or intentional discrimination; thus, the plaintiff must establish that the defendant's conduct was the product of discriminatory motive. The proof may be direct or indirect, but some evidence of intent is the *sine qua non* of the discriminatory treatment case. *See St. Mary's Honor Center v. Hicks,* 509 U.S. 502 (1993); *Texas Dep't of Comm. Affairs v. Burdine,* 450 U.S. 248 (1981); *McDonnell Douglas Corp. v. Green,* 411 U.S. 792 (1973). The proof regimen developed through this trilogy of decisions includes the following stages: (1) plaintiff's establishment of a *prima facie* case; (2) defendant's rebuttal supported by legitimate, non-discriminatory reasons; and (3) plaintiff's proof that the defendant's purported good faith rationale for the discriminatory conduct was pretextual, obfuscating the actual, unlawful motive. In order to establish a *prima facie* case and trigger the second stage of the allocation of proof formula, a plaintiff typically must show that: (1) he or she applied for the job at issue; (2) he or she was qualified for that job; (3) he or she was not awarded the job; and (4) the

job was available to, or filled by, a person or persons whose qualifications were no better than the plaintiff's. *McDonnell Douglas,* 411 U.S. at 802.

Once the *prima facie* case has been established, the defendant assumes the burden of production—proceeding with evidence that the decision was prompted by valid, non-discriminatory reasons. If the defendant is successful, the plaintiff, saddled with the ultimate burden of persuasion, must demonstrate that this ostensibly legitimate predicate for the conduct is a subterfuge and a pretext, hiding the true nature of the unlawful conduct. Thus, the plaintiff is ultimately required to show that, more likely than not, defendant's discrimination provoked the employment decision at issue. Of course, if the plaintiff satisfies the *prima facie* case by adducing direct, uncontroverted evidence of unlawful intent, he or she will have carried the burden of persuasion, leaving the defendant little recourse but to put forth an affirmative defense (*e.g., bona fide* occupational qualification ("BFOQ"), discussed below) or demonstrate some type of immunity. *See* BARBARA LINDEMANN AND PAUL GROSSMAN, EMPLOYMENT DISCRIMINATION LAW 40 (3d ed. 1996); HAROLD S. LEWIS, JR. & ELIZABETH J. NORMAN, EMPLOYMENT DISCRIMINATION LAW AND PRACTICE § 3.10 (2D ED. 2004). Further, if plaintiff can show that discrimination was a *motivating* factor in the decision, the burden of persuasion would shift to the defendant, requiring a demonstration that it would have taken the same action independent of the unlawful motive. *Id.* at 41; *Price Waterhouse v. Hopkins,* 490 U.S. 228 (1989). *See also Thomas v. NFLPA,* 131 F.3d 198 (D.C. Cir. 1997).

In *Price Waterhouse,* the plurality opinion does not require "direct evidence" to establish discriminatory motivation; however, Justice O'Connor, through her concurring opinion, identified such evidence as a necessary ingredient of the *prima facie* case. The 1991 amendments to the Civil Rights Act of 1964 reinforced the *McDonnell Douglas-Burdine* calculus in the typical disparate treatment case. See 42 U.S.C. § 2000e-5(g)(2)(B). Further, the 1991 legislation resolved any remaining doubts about the level of causation required to make a prima facie case in a mixed motive context. Under the amendments, where the employer's action was prompted by dual motives, the plaintiff needs only to show that one's race or other protected category was a motivating factor in the decision. If the employer can show that the decision would have been made notwithstanding the unlawful motive, it will escape some liability (e.g., back pay, reinstatement order) but may also still be subject to declaratory and injunctive relief as well as attorney's fees. *See* 42 U.S.C. §§ 2000e-5(g)(2)(B)(i), 2000e-2(m). While the amendments did not resolve the apparent tension between the *Price Waterhouse* plurality and concurring opinions regarding the need to adduce direct evidence, recent Supreme Court pronouncements have held that there is no need to produce direct evidence in a mixed-motive case. *See Desert Palace, Inc. v. Costa,* 539 U.S. 90 (2003) (jury instructed that no direct evidence is needed for mixed motive case); *Reeves v. Sanderson Plumbing Prods., Inc.,* 530 U.S. 133 (2000) (holding that discrimination should be treated like any other questions of fact). See also CHARLES A. SULLIVAN, EMPLOYMENT DISCRIMINATION LAW AND PRACTICE 21–22, 24 (3d ed. 2002, 2004 SUPP.). Compare the Title VII approach to the National Labor Relations Board's treatment of mixed motive cases in the context of pre-textual discharges under the National Labor Relations Act. *Wright Line, Wright Line Div.,* 251 NLRB 1083 (1980), *enforced,* 662 F.2d 899 (1st Cir. 1981).

The disparate impact case typically involves facially neutral policies or practices that have an adverse affect upon a protected class of employees. *See, e.g., Albemarle Paper Co. v. Moody,* 422 U.S. 405 (1975); *Griggs v. Duke Power Co.,* 401 U.S. 424 (1971). Thus, a particular course of conduct may be benign on the surface, but may have a significant deleterious impact on a disproportionate number of "protected" employees. Although the allocation of proof has been subject to some modifications and debate over the past 25 years, the 1991 amendments clarified any questions regarding the burden of proof regimen applicable to a disparate impact case. Once the plaintiff establishes a *prima facie* case, burdens of production and persuasion shift to the employer, who must show that the allegedly discriminatory practice was "job related for the position in question and consistent with business necessity." 42 U.S.C. §2000e-2(K)(1)(A)(j). At this point, the plaintiff has an opportunity to refute the employer's business-necessity defense by proving that there were options available with a less onerous impact on the protected class. For a detailed review of the sub-issues that occur in the last volley of the shifting burdens game, See LINDEMANN & GROSSMAN at 89–113; SULLIVAN, at 33.

Because the plaintiff failed to offer evidence sufficient to establish a *prima facie* case, the *Roth* court applied the *McDonnell Douglas-Burdine* analysis. (*Hicks* had not yet been decided, but the foregoing allocation of proof formula was undisturbed by that decision.) Roth's failure to persuade the court of the legitimacy of her claims is partially a product of the subjectivity attached to managerial decisions, particularly in a sports context.

2. If a local station conducted a marketing profile indicating that its existing audience would switch network allegiances upon the hiring of a female sports reporter, would that be a valid defense to a claim of sex discrimination stemming from the deliberate denial of such a position to a female applicant? Would a network be permitted to establish different standards for female reporters than male reporters in terms of cosmetics, age, etc.? The employer's argument would be that retaining females as sports reporters would compromise the station's profitability and economic viability. Section 703(e)(1) (42 U.S.C. §2000-2(e)) allows an employer to discriminate on the basis of sex where one's gender is a *bona fide* occupational qualification. However, this defense is construed narrowly; it is not a statutory catch-all for employers' intentional exclusion of protected employees from designated jobs. In fact, it cannot be raised as a defense to claims of discrimination based on race. Indicative of the narrow reading to be accorded the BFOQ defense is the following caveat from the United States Supreme Court:

> The wording of the BFOQ defense contains several terms of restriction that indicate that the exception reaches only special situations. The statute thus limits the situations in which discrimination is permissible to "certain instances" where sex discrimination is "reasonably necessary" to the "normal operation" of the "particular" business. Each one of these terms—certain, normal, particular— prevents the use of general subjective standards and favors an objective, verifiable requirement. But the most telling term is "occupational"; this indicates that these objective, verifiable requirements must concern job-related skills and aptitudes.

UAW v. Johnson Controls, Inc. 499 U.S. 187, 201 (1991). The BFOQ defense applies in the context of intentional discrimination or "disparate treatment." It does not apply in the context of disparate or adverse impact, where the practice or policy, while facially neutral, operates to discriminate against a protected group. There, the employer may assert that the discrimination has been occasioned by "business necessity." This "business necessity" defense is deemed to be less stringent for the employer than the statutorily prescribed BFOQ. *Id.* at 198. Under either standard, it is unlikely that consumer desires will justify the discriminatory impact or treatment. *See, e.g., Vigars v. Valley Christian Ctr.,* 805 F. Supp. 802 (N.D. Cal. 1992); *Diaz v. Pan-American World Airways, Inc.,* 442 F.2d 385 (5th Cir. 1971) (rejecting BFOQ for hiring decision based on female flight attendant's sexual attractiveness to male passengers and comforting nature for female passengers, concluding that the essence of the job is the promotion of safe transportation). *But see Wilson v. Southwest Airlines Co.,* 517 F. Supp. 292 (N.D. Tex. 1981).

3. Congress enacted the Civil Rights Act of 1991 to provide courts with the power to award victims of employment discrimination both compensatory damages (including emotional distress, mental anguish, loss of enjoyment of life, etc.) and punitive damages, in addition to equitable remedies. A victim of discrimination may now recover compensatory damages if the employer has discriminated intentionally, but may recover punitive damages only if the employer acts with malice or reckless indifference toward the victim's rights. *See generally* 3 Barbara Lindemann & Paul Grosman, Employment Discrimination Law 1775–79, 1821–27 (3d ed. 1996).

The 1991 amendments limit the amount of non-economic compensatory and punitive damages an employee may recover depending on the size of the employer, and also provide for jury trials. *Id.* at 1469–70. Section 1981, which is not limited to disputes arising in an employer-employee relationship, and has now been expanded to include discrimination in contract administration as well as formation, provides victims of intentional racial employment discrimination a right to compensatory and punitive damages—with no cap, as exists in the Title VII cases. *Id.* at 1823–26. Section 1981 has no administrative exhaustion requirement and provides for jury trials in which plaintiffs must prove discriminatory intent, not merely discriminatory impact. *Id.* at 971–76. Attorneys' fees also may be awarded prevailing parties in Title VII or §1981 actions. *Id.* at 1859.

4. Not all discrimination is overt; not all is easy to discern. "Neutral" criteria often conceal profound biases, and "objective" assessments often depend upon highly subjective prejudices; even very real "objective" differences among applicants may reflect the advantages and disadvantages that flow from generations of systemic inequalities. Were any of these manifest in the *Roth* case? In *Roth*, the court concludes that Enid Roth failed to establish a *prima facie* case of discrimination with respect to the sports director job because she did not prove she was "qualified for the job"; specifically, the court concluded, she "lacked the creativity and leadership necessary in a Sports Director." Alternatively, the court insisted, even if Roth were qualified, NBC had non-discriminatory reasons for preferring the men it hired: They demonstrated "the creativity and initiative" that Roth lacked. Could gender biases have influenced any of these judgments, either by NBC or by the court?

As for the associate director position, Roth did establish a *prima facie* case, but according to the court, NBC had "legitimate business" reasons for its hire: The man it chose "had broadcasting experience from the prior Winter Olympics" and "had been recommended for the position by the producer." But why did the man have more experience; why did he receive the recommendation? Is it possible that Roth was significantly disadvantaged by the history of gender exclusion in American sports?

5. Do female broadcasters have to contend with age discrimination as well as sex discrimination? Consider the situation of Leslie Visser, a longtime NFL reporter for CBS and ABC. In 2000, Visser was fired as a sideline reporter for Monday Night Football and replaced with Melissa Stark, who is 20 years Visser's junior. In explaining his move, Don Ohlmeyer only stated that "he 'wanted to go in another direction.'" Sports Illustrated, Aug. 21, 2000. Would Visser have a valid age discrimination claim? Consider how many middle-aged and older female journalists there are on TV. Would we ever see a female in the same position that Walter Cronkite had for many years—that of the wise elder statesman? Is age discrimination in broadcasting limited to women? Seventy-one year-old Pat Summerall was recently let go by Fox Sports, ending his 21-year run in the NFL broadcasting booth with John Madden. Some have suggested that Summerall not being brought back was due to his age. *See* Phil Mushnick, *No Sympathy for Summerall: Fraudulent Pat Was Bad Guy in Split with Fox,* New York Post, Feb. 3, 2002.

"Women are gradually getting good commentator and reporting jobs in men's professional sports," notes Donna Lopiano, Executive Director of the Women's Sports Foundation. But, she insists, the inequities still include "too few opportunities, too slow in growing and too much of a preoccupation with good looks compared to male commentators who are allowed to be bald, old or ugly * * * [and] sometimes all three." Tim Stephens, *A Conversation with Donna Lopiano: Women's Sports Hurting, and Leader Blames TV Favoritism*, Orlando Sentinel, Oct. 7, 2003, at D2.

VI. Sports and Sexual Orientation

A. The Female Athlete

A persistent concern in terms of female participation in competitive athletics is the stereotyping of all women athletes as lesbians, the mistreatment that lesbian athletes receive, and finally, the abuse suffered by all female athletes because they are perceived as lesbians. In some respects, all three issues are inextricably entwined. Conceivably, Title IX hastened the eradication of the "woman-athlete as lesbian" stereotype. That is, when few women participated in athletics it was assumed that they occupied the same small minority of the population as gays—the percentage of female athletes (in the public's mind) was roughly the same as the percentage of gay women. But, the expansion of opportunities for and resultant participation of female athletes should convince even the most narrow-minded observers that "they can't all be gay." One commentator argues that homophobia is a political tool used by men to keep women in their place. If women athletes are labeled as lesbians, they are stigmatized to the extent that they will avoid choosing careers in sports. *See generally* Cheryl Hanna, *Bad Girls and Good Sports: Some Reflections on Violent Female Juvenile Delinquents, Title IX and The Promise of Girl Power*, 27 Hastings Const. L.Q. 667 (2000). The problem that persists is whether there is a difficulty with the stereotyping of athletes as lesbians or with the way society views homosexuality. In other words, the stereotype, as unfair as it is, would not be nearly as pernicious if homosexuality itself did not conjure such a negative image.

Professor Francisco Valdes describes "sex," "gender," and "sexual orientation" as "a triangled web with three 'legs' inter-connecting these three constructs, or endpoints." Francisco Valdes, *Queers, Sissies, Dykes, and Tomboys: Deconstructing the Conflation of "Sex," "Gender," and "Sexual Orientation" in Euro-American Law and Society*, 83 Calif. L. Rev. 1, 12 (1995). All of the terms, he insists, are conflated in this web; for present purposes, the most significant conflation is of "gender" and "sexual orientation." Professor Valdez explains:

> At first blush, the notion that gender and sexual orientation are integrally related may tend to spark some skepticism. If so, this skepticism is due to the practice within legal (and social) culture of relegating gender to the realm of "women's issues" and sexual orientation to the realm of "sexual minorities' issues"; the twain are assumed hardly ever to meet. Nevertheless, the generally recognizable linkage between "queers" and "dykes" on the one hand, and "sissies" and "tomboys" on the other, suggests that some correlation between sex-determined gender and sexual orientation is at work.
>
> Although the first set of these terms invokes images regarding sexual orientation and the second set invokes images regarding gender, the two sets of images

collapse into an undifferentiated jumble within the consciousness of children, legislators, judges, and others. This collapse, or conflation, reflects the historical and contemporary fact that sexual orientation serves as the sexual component of gender. This fact is exemplified by the delineation and exposition of earlier clinical theories such as inversion and fixation, and by the current construction(s) of "gender identity disorder(s)" as a formal type of personality disorder: all use(d) gender to explain sexual orientation. In other words, sexual orientation has been and still is part and parcel of gender because gender encompasses both social and sexual dimensions or components. This [conflation] * * * thus exists both in theory and in practice, and both in law and in society.

Id. at 14–15.

Professors Anthony E. Varona and Jeffrey M. Monks contend that discrimination based on sexual orientation is indeed discrimination "because of sex":

> The principles regarding sex stereotyping seen in *Price Waterhouse* can also be applied to gay people. This is because gay people, simply by identifying themselves as gay, are violating the ultimate gender stereotype—heterosexual attraction. Since there is a "presumption and prescription that erotic interests are exclusively directed to the opposite sex," those who are attracted to members of the same sex contradict traditional notions about appropriate behavior for men and women. Just like the plaintiff in *Price Waterhouse*, gays fail to match the stereotype associated with their group and any employment discrimination against a gay person is "because of sex" under Title VII.
>
> Exactly how anti-gay discrimination is "because of sex" becomes clear when one asks whether the employer would still have engaged in discriminatory conduct had the employee been a member of the opposite sex. Specifically, would the employer subject a woman who was sexually attracted to men to the same adverse treatment to which he/she subjected a man also sexually attracted to men? Similarly, would the employer have treated a masculine man in the same manner that he/she may have treated a man who exhibited a feminine affect? Of course, the answer would be no.

Anthony E. Varona & Jeffrey M. Monks, *En/Gendering Equality: Seeking Relief Under Title VII Against Employment Discrimination Based on Sexual Orientation*, 7 Wm. & Mary J. Women L. 67, 84 (2000). The case for a "sex stereotyping" claim, Professors Varona and Monks note, is especially strong for effeminate gay men and masculine lesbians. *Id.* at 85.

The connection between sexual orientation and sexual stereotypes may be most obvious in the cases of "effeminate" gay men (or "masculine" lesbians), but it is not limited to those cases. Commenting on his case studies of eight gay men, Professor R.W. Connell observes that

> the familiar heterosexual definition of homosexual men as effeminate is an inaccurate description of men like the ones interviewed here, who mostly do "act like a guy." But it is not wrong in sensing the outrage they do to hegemonic masculinity. A masculine object-choice subverts the masculinity of character and social presence. This subversion is a structural feature of homosexuality in a patriarchical society in which hegemonic masculinity is defined as exclusively heterosexual and its hegemony includes the formation of character in the [education] of boys.

R.W. Connell, *A Very Straight Gay: Masculinity, Homosexual Experience, and the Dynamic of Gender*, 57 Am. Soc. Rev. 735, 748 (1992).

The complex overlap of gender and sexual orientation might also be seen in a distinct economic hierarchy. A study by economist Lee Badgett of the University of Massachusetts revealed the following earnings differences; the numbers represent the average annual earnings for the group, expressed in 1991 dollars:

> Heterosexual Men $28,680
> Homosexual/Bisexual Women $21,331
> Homosexual/Bisexual Men $21,258
> Heterosexual Women $19,738

Professor Badgett subjected the data to a multiple regression analysis that controlled for confounding variables, e.g., education, race, geography, occupational category. Only group identity-and the presence or absence of discrimination against that group-could account for the differences. Other studies confirm the basic findings: a significant disadvantage to gay men; no disadvantage, possibly an advantage, to lesbian and bisexual women, relative to other women. *See* WILLIAM N. ESKRIDGE, JR. & NAN HUNTER, SEXUALITY, GENDER AND THE LAW 867 (2004). What would account for this peculiar hierarchy? Consider the following:

> Gay men often are discriminated against because our rejection of the traditional male gender role (i.e., rejection of the domination of women in opposite-sex relationships) undermines male supremacy. We are discriminated against not solely because of how and with whom we have sex, but because of what that sex represents.
>
> Because all things associated with femininity have traditionally been de-valued, gay men are likewise viewed as inferior. Gay men threaten the patriarchal stronghold because, by declining to participate in the sexual subordination of women and by adopting traditionally feminine characteristics, we blur the gender distinctions upon which male dominance is dependent.

Varona & Monks, *supra*, at 82–83.

Not all gay-rights advocates are convinced that discrimination based on sexual orientation is best treated as discrimination "because of sex." Professor Suzanne B. Goldberg notes that "this may or may not be a very good argument from a theoretical perspective, but from a litigation perspective is has not enjoyed a great success record." Suzanne B. Goldberg, *Parallel Lives: Women's Rights and Lesbian Rights Litigation*, 23 WOMEN's RTS. L. REP. 223, 225 (2002). But the claim has at times prevailed, at least in the initial stages of litigation.

Notes and Questions

1. In the context of high school or college sports, is a prospective student-athlete entitled to inquire about the sexual preference of his or her coach? Conversely, is the coach within his or her "rights" to ask about the sexual preferences of a recruit or team member? For an enlightening look at recruiting efforts directed toward female high school athletes, *see* Steve Lopez, *Full Court Dress*, SPORTS ILLUSTRATED, Jan. 19, 1998. Vol. 8, No. 2.

2. In 2005, Penn State refused to renew the athletic scholarship of basketball player Jen Harris. Harris claimed that she had been dismissed from the team because head coach Rene Portland perceived her to be gay. Over the previous several years, rumors had circulated that Portland was hostile to lesbians. At this writing, Harris had initiated a lawsuit in federal court. On its own initiative, Penn State conducted an investigation

culminating in the imposition of a $10,000 fine against Portland. The university concluded that the coach had violated school policy prohibiting discrimination on the basis of race, sexual orientation, and similar protected status. This issue takes on even added importance when considered in light of the fact that WNBA superstar Cheryl Swopes recently announced that she was gay. Several women athletes have made similar announcements in the past, including tennis stars Martina Navratilova and Amelie Mauresmo. Do you believe that these pronouncements have affected or will affect these athletes' popularity? In your judgment, would a similar announcement from a male athlete provoke the same reaction?

B. Coming Out

R.W. Connell describes the "the process of coming out" as "establishing oneself as homosexual in a homophobic world." R.W. Connell, *supra*, at 746. Thus understood, what sort of qualities must someone possess before he or she can "come out"?

Michael Muska was the Athletic Director at Oberlin College from 1998 to 2002; he was the first openly gay athletic director in the nation. "When I visit schools and colleges," he writes , "I ask people to take part in two role-playing scenarios."

> First, I say, imagine that the whole world is gay, and that you, a straight person, are the exception. How would you view the world differently? How would you feel in situations that a gay person faces repeatedly in today's society? Next, I ask people to pair off and enact the scene of a gay person coming out to a straight person. Then I ask both to share their thoughts and emotions. It's always a powerful moment when each person realizes how difficult it is for the other.

Michael Muska, *Reflections of a Gay Athletics Director*, Chronicle Higher Ed., Oct. 13, 2000, at B10.

Coming out seems particularly difficult in athletics, because sports are so notably hostile to homosexuality. Sport seems to lag, in this sense, not only behind the broader culture, but behind its own evolutionary arc, which largely describes a more inclusionary ethos.

> It is important to note that while college sports may provide a model of building community from difference in terms of race and ethnicity, socio-economic status, and even gender (in the case of men's and women's teams in track and field or swimming and diving that often travel together and share coaches), they are generally intolerant in the area of sexual orientation. This is, of course, an issue across higher education. What is unique about athletics in regard to the issue of homosexuality, according to Wolf-Wendel, Toma, and Morphew, is that the homophobic views held by athletes, coaches, and athletics administrators seem to lie in sharp contrast to their conceptualizations of other forms of difference. Second, the extent to which those in athletics openly express hostility to gays and lesbians seems above and beyond that found on other segments of campus.

J. Douglas Toma & Thomas Kecskemethy, *College Sports, the Collegiate Ideal, and the Values of the American University*, 28 J.C. & U.L. 697, 709 n.19 (reviewing James L. Shulman & William G. Bowen, The Game of Life (2001)) (citing Lisa E. Wolf-Wendel, et al., *There's No 'I' in Team* * * * *and Other Lessons from Intercollegiate Athletics in Creating Community from Difference*, 24 Rev. Higher Educ. 369 (2001).

"To date only one male athlete has revealed his homosexuality while still competing, figure skater Rudy Galindo." Bob Padecky, *Sports Closet Full, But No One Is Coming Out*, SANTA ROSA PRESS DEMOCRAT, May 23, 2001. No athlete in Major League Baseball, the National Basketball Association, the National Football League, or the National Hockey League has acknowledged being gay while still in the league.

A very small number revealed their sexual orientation after their careers ended. Dave Kopay, who played in the NFL for 10 years, revealed his sexual orientation in 1975. He was the first to come out. "Football," he says, "is even farther back into the closet in the 25 years since I came out." Joan Ryan, *His Pride Is On Display*, S.F. CHRONICLE, May 18, 2001. Glenn Burke was the first acknowledged gay ballplayer in the Major Leagues. He retired in 1980 as his "secret" was emerging, and was publicly outed in a national sports magazine in 1982. Billy Bean revealed that he was gay after his six-year baseball career ended in 1994; he thinks it would be professional suicide for most gay players today to disclose their sexual orientation. Jeff Jacobs, *Stands by His Story, and His Man*, HARTFORD COURANT, Aug. 5, 2001. "If it was a Shaquille O'Neal who was gay there would be no problem," Bean says. "If you are talking about marginal players, that is different." Vincent J. Schodolski, *Taking off the Mask*, CHICAGO TRIBUNE, June 24, 2001. "Many in the sports media echo Bean's fears," says sports columnist Jeff Jacobs.

> An NHL player, for instance, once told me he'd cut the testicles off any gay teammate. False bravado? Of course. But there can be no denying barriers exist. A locker room can be juvenile, cruel and the guys you'd figure would be the most secure in their sexuality are the most neurotic. Yet a carpet mistrust of athletes' kindness and tolerance, especially when they are removed from the group dynamic, not only is cynical, it's probably exaggerated.

Jacobs, *supra*. "Perhaps," Jacobs concludes, "we fear the unknown too much."

Roy Simmons, an offensive lineman in the NFL from 1979–1984, revealed on the Phil Donahue show in 1992 that he was gay. He disappeared from public life for 12 years, and recently re-emerged to expand on his story. Simmons, who has battled substance abuse and faced a number of emotional and economic struggles, says he wants to reach athletes who may still be in the closet and as tortured as he was. Interestingly, Butch Woolfolk, a former teammate of Simmons, recalls that "I played with four gay guys. Roy is the only one I didn't know about." Jim Buzinski *Gay Ex-NFL Player Public Again: Lineman Roy Simmons Breaks His 12-Year Silence*, available at http://www.outsports.com/nfl/2003/1201roysimmons.htm (last visited March 3, 2004).

Most recently—in October 2002—Esera Tuaolo, NFL linebacker from 1991–1999, told HBO's *Real Sports* that he was gay. Former teammate Sterling Sharpe made it clear during the program that Tualo was wise *not* to reveal his secret while he played. "He would have been eaten alive and he would have been hated for it," Sharpe said. "Had he come out on a Monday, with Wednesday, Thursday, Friday practices, he'd have never gotten to the other team." Asked why, Sharpe explained that it was to avoid the stigma of association with a gay man: "Birds of a feather flock together." Joe O'Connor, *Zero Men Out: A Gay Porn Video Tossed Baseball One of Its Biggest Curves this Week, Largely Because the Sports World Insists Athletes Play It Straight*, NAT'L POST, Jan. 29, 2004, at S3.

Tennis player Martina Navratilova, meanwhile, was the first openly gay athlete to be featured in a national advertising campaign: She was hired by Subaru to promote their cars. "We view her as an active lifestyle-woman," company spokesman Tim Bennett said, "and the other stuff as no one's business." Jim Litke, *Champion Gets Her Due*, SEATTLE TIMES, March 20, 2000. Does this fact suggest a response to the earlier question asking whether the public response to an athlete that "comes out" would be more difficult for a man than for a woman? Don Sabo suggests that it might be more difficult for male athletes, because of the somewhat more intense hostility toward gay men. "One possible explanation for the harsher treatment of male than female homosexuals," he writes, "is that gay men represent a more serious challenge to the political dominance of male elites than lesbians." Don Sabo, *The Politics of Homophobia in Sport*, in Sex, Violence & Power in Sports: Rethinking Masculinity 101, 109 (Michael A. Messner & Donald F. Sabo, eds. 1994).

At least part of the difficulty confronting gay male athletes is the sense that they are living oxymorons: male athletes—male sports—are almost definitionally heterosexual. Professor Kenji Yoshino notes that sports provided part of the camouflage for his homosexuality:

> My response, as the weeks passed, was to adopt what I now call a "counterfeiting" strategy. I went to the company's singles night and spoke vaguely about past girlfriends. I was conspicuous about my friendships with women. I told (or at least laughed at) the right jokes and didn't say too much about my interest in theater. On a friend's suggestion, I read the sports section of the *New York Times* and at least twice dragged myself to Yankee Stadium. For a time, I even hid a small notepad in my desk on which I scribbled key biographical information about "Heather," a quite imaginary young woman with brains, looks, and the good sense to have dated me in college. Heather had unfortunately moved to Maine.

Kenji Yoshino, *Covering*, 111 Yale L.J. 769, 813 (2002).

Minor league baseball had a coming out of sorts in early 2004. Cleveland Indians minor league pitcher Kazuhito Tadano held a press conference to acknowledge that he had appeared in a gay porn video when he was a college student in Japan. "I did participate in a video and I regret it very much," he said in a prepared statement. "It was a one-time incident that showed bad judgment and will never be repeated. I was young, playing baseball, and going to college and my teammates and I needed money." After he finished his statement, Tadano added through his interpreter: "I'm not gay. I'd like to clear that fact up right now." O'Connor, *supra*.

The initial reaction from Tadano's teammates was encouraging. Grady Sizemore, sometimes roommate of Tadano's, noted that the pitcher had shared his story with his teammates in a locker room meeting during the previous season. "You could tell he was nervous," Sizemore said. "But I don't think it changed anybody's opinion of him. After it was said and done, nobody thought anything more of it. He's a great guy and a great pitcher." Starting pitcher C.C. Sabathia concurred. "This is the right team and the right organization for him. Everybody has done something that they regret in their lives. He's a person just like everyone else." Shelly Anderson, *Road Ahead Could Get Bumpy for One Japanese Player in United States*, Pittsburgh Post-Gazette, Jan. 30, 2004.

Not all reactions were so sanguine. After the news broke, Florida Marlins pitcher Brad Penny was asked if the Marlins clubhouse would still be "the tightest, most fun clubhouse in baseball" if one of the players acknowledged that he was gay. "What it would be," Penny replied, "is very uncomfortable in here." Reliever Tim Spooneybarger agreed. "I wouldn't have a problem with it, but some people in here would." They would not be alone. When he was asked how he would react to a gay teammate, Atlanta Braves outfielder Andruw Jones said he would just ask "What the hell is wrong with you?" *The Ultimate Sports Taboo Hasn't Evolved with the Times*, Miami Herald, Feb. 27, 2004.

One not uncommon reaction among (presumably) straight athletes to the prospect that a teammate might "come out" is the suggestion that sexuality—or more precisely, homosexuality—is personal and private and should remain that way. Sports, Billy Bean says, "is kind of the ultimate don't ask-don't tell environment." Madeline Baro Diaz, *Bean, Nyad: Gay Athletes Face Big Hurdles*, S. Fl. Sun-Sentinel, March 13, 2001. A comparable phenomenon may be taking place on a broader cultural level. "Friends, employers, and family," Professor John Culhane writes, "may have thought they had a 'pretty good idea' of who among them had a same-sex orientation, but a tacit agreement not to discuss the matter was in evidence. Indeed, the discussion concerning same-sex marriage at times reflects ill-concealed anger at gays and lesbians for breaching this unspoken understanding." John G. Culhane, *Uprooting the Arguments Against Same-Sex Marriage*, 20 Cardozo L. Rev. 1119, 1177 (1999).

A recurring theme in the objections to an open homosexual presence in sports is the concern about "the shower." Florida Marlins reliever Tim Spooneybarger insists that baseball, for example, is different from other professions in this regard. "This is a very personal work environment. Very intimate. Not many lawyers get together after work and shower with 30 other lawyers." *The Ultimate Sports Taboo Hasn't Evolved with the Times*, Miami Herald, Feb. 27, 2004. The locker room, one commentator suggests, seems to evoke "the classic heterosexual fear of being ogled by a 'queer' in the shower—the true motivating force behind purging gays from the military—or of being propositioned by one in public, the usually imaginary justification for gay bashing." Norah Vincent, *Adults Lead the Class in Anti-Gay Bigotry*, L.A. Times, Jan. 2, 2003, at B13. "I don't know what it is," says Jim Buzinski, co-founder of Outsports.com, "but it freaks people out—this notion of somehow being attacked by another man." O'Connor, *supra*.

Joe O'Connor suggests that the "disdain for homosexuals in the dressing room is not limited to baseball and football." Former Olympic swimmer Mark Tewksbury, he notes, witnessed plenty of it in the change room at university swim meets. "The traditional old boys' club has been blown apart in the real world, but for some reason in sports, it remains fairly solid," Tewksbury recalls. "Even in competitive swimming you are a Nelly or a gay boy or a fag—whatever they will call you—the language is still there." *Id.*

Notes and Questions

1. Who benefits when an athlete comes out? Mariah Button Nelson suggests that, eventually, the athlete benefits. "There's a tremendous amount of personal freedom in telling the truth, and a lot of political power. Ever notice how no one *accuses* Martina Navratilova of being a lesbian anymore?" Mariah Burton Nelson, Embracing Victory: Life Lessons in Competition and Compassion 206 (1998). Pat Griffin suggests that others benefit as well:

> One of the most effective tools in counteracting homophobia is increased gay and lesbian visibility. Stereotypes and the fear and hatred they perpetuate will lose their power as more lesbian and gay people in sport disclose their identities. Although some people will never accept diversity of sexual identity in sport or in the general population, research indicates that, for most people, contact with "out" lesbian and gay people who embrace their sexual identities reduces prejudice.

Pat Griffin, *Changing the Game: Homophobia, Sexism, and Lesbians in Sport*, 44 QUEST 251, 262 (1992). "The athletic world," Griffin concludes, "desperately needs more lesbian and gay coaches and athletes to step out of the closet." *Id.*

And, she suggests, they will need support from the homosexual and heterosexual communities alike.

> Another aspect of visibility is the willingness of heterosexual athletes and coaches, as allies of lesbian and gay people, to speak out against homophobia and heterosexism. In the same way that it is important for white people to speak out against racism and for men to speak out against sexism, it is important for heterosexual people to object to antigay harassment, discrimination, and prejudice. It isn't enough to provide silent, private support for lesbian friends. To remain silent signals consent. Speaking out against homophobia is a challenge for heterosexual women in sport that requires them to understand how homophobia is used against them as well as against lesbians. Speaking out against homophobia also requires that heterosexual women confront their own discomfort with being associated with lesbians or being called lesbian because that is what will happen when they speak out: The lesbian label will be used to try and intimidate them back into silence.

Id. at 262–63.

2. Are things changing and has the public become more accepting of the gay athlete? Consider the following:

> The Los Angeles Sparks of the WNBA launch a marketing campaign targeting lesbian fans—and are widely applauded. Sacramento Kings guard Jason Williams and Chicago Cubs pitcher Julian Tavarez make slurs against gays—and are widely condemned.

> At the University of Virginia, gay student groups call for an end to an antigay chant after Cavalier touchdowns—and find support from varsity athletes.

> Slowly and cautiously, gays are beginning to make their presence felt in the sports world, long one of society's locked closets.

Kristie Ackert & Luke Cyphers, *Out of the Shadows Gays Finally Getting in Game after Years of Fighting for Rights*, N.Y. DAILY NEWS, May 13, 2001, at 86.

In 1999, Corey Johnson was the senior co-captain of his Massachusetts high school football team. He is gay. He decided to tell his teammates. His parents feared for his safety, but the fears proved—in this case—unfounded. The players were surprised, but they rallied around him. After one victory, they sang songs in his honor on the bus ride home: They chose "YMCA" and "It's Raining Men." Gwen Knap, *The Closet Remains Shut Tight in Majors*, S.F. CHRONICLE, May 20, 2001.

His story made the front page of the *The New York Times*, and was told in *Sports Illustrated*. Mitchell Gold furniture featured him—as Corey Johnson, a "tough football captain," nothing more or less—in print ads. The response to all of it was overwhelmingly positive. "My story shows that this can happen, this is possible," said Johnson. "There are stories of hope out there. There are stories of love and compassion. The teenagers out there need hope." Joan Ryan, *His Pride Is on Display*, S.F. CHRONICLE, May 18, 2001.

"If kids can be that sophisticated," writes columnist Gwen Knap, "surely professional athletes can match them. It's almost insulting, a dumb-jock stereotype, to assume otherwise." Knap, *supra*. Is this projection too sanguine?

VIII. The Disabled Athlete

PGA Tour, Inc. v. Casey Martin
532 U.S. 661 (2001)

JUSTICE STEVENS delivered the opinion of the court. This case raises two questions concerning the application of the Americans with Disabilities Act of 1990, 104 Stat. 328, 42 U.S.C. § 12101 *et seq.*, to a gifted athlete: first, whether the Act protects access to professional golf tournaments by a qualified entrant with a disability; and second, whether a disabled contestant may be denied the use of a golf cart because it would "fundamentally alter the nature" of the tournaments to allow him to ride when all other contestants must walk.

I

Petitioner PGA Tour, Inc., a nonprofit entity formed in 1968, sponsors and cosponsors professional golf Tournaments conducted on three annual Tours. About 200 golfers participate in the PGA Tour; about 170 in the NIKE Tour; and about 100 in the SENIOR PGA Tour. PGA Tour and NIKE Tour Tournaments typically are 4-day events, played on courses leased and operated by petitioner. The entire field usually competes in two 18-hole rounds played on Thursday and Friday; those who survive the "cut" play on Saturday and Sunday and receive prize money in amounts determined by their aggregate scores for all four rounds. The revenues generated by television, admissions, concessions, and contributions from cosponsors amount to about $300 million a year, much of which is distributed in prize money.

There are various ways of gaining entry into particular Tours. For example, a player who wins three NIKE Tour events in the same year, or is among the top-15 money winners on that Tour, earns the right to play in the PGA Tour. Additionally, a golfer may obtain a spot in an official Tournament through successfully competing in "open" qualifying rounds, which are conducted the week before each Tournament. Most participants, however, earn playing privileges in the PGA Tour or NIKE Tour by way of a three-stage qualifying Tournament known as the "Q-School."

Any member of the public may enter the Q-School by paying a $3,000 entry fee and submitting two letters of reference from, among others, PGA Tour or NIKE Tour members. The $3,000 entry fee covers the players' greens fees and the cost of golf carts, which are permitted during the first two stages, but which have been prohibited during the third stage since 1997. Each year, over a thousand contestants compete in the first stage, which consists of four 18-hole rounds at different locations. Approximately half of them make it to the second stage, which also includes 72 holes. Around 168 players survive the second stage and advance to the final one, where they compete over 108 holes. Of those finalists, about a fourth qualify for membership in the PGA Tour, and the rest gain membership in the NIKE Tour. The significance of making it into either Tour is illuminated by the fact that there are about 25 million golfers in the country.

Three sets of rules govern competition in Tour events. First, the "Rules of Golf," jointly written by the United States Golf Association (USGA) and the Royal and Ancient Golf Club of Scotland, apply to the game as it is played, not only by millions of amateurs on public courses and in private country clubs throughout the United States and worldwide, but also by the professionals in the Tournaments conducted by petitioner, the USGA, the Ladies' Professional Golf Association, and the Senior Women's Golf Association. Those rules do not prohibit the use of golf carts at any time.

Second, the "Conditions of Competition and Local Rules," often described as the "hard card," apply specifically to petitioner's professional Tours. The hard cards for the PGA Tour and NIKE Tour require players to walk the golf course during Tournaments, but not during open qualifying rounds. On the SENIOR PGA Tour, which is limited to golfers age 50 and older, the contestants may use golf carts. Most seniors, however, prefer to walk.

Third, "Notices to Competitors" are issued for particular Tournaments and cover conditions for that specific event. Such a notice may, for example, explain how the Rules of Golf should be applied to a particular water hazard or man-made obstruction. It might also authorize the use of carts to speed up play when there is an unusual distance between one green and the next tee.

The basic Rules of Golf, the hard cards, and the weekly notices apply equally to all players in Tour competitions. As one of petitioner's witnesses explained with reference to "the Masters Tournament, which is golf at its very highest level * * * the key is to have everyone tee off on the first hole under exactly the same conditions and all of them be tested over that 72-hole event under the conditions that exist during those four days of the event."

II

Casey Martin is a talented golfer. As an amateur, he won 17 Oregon Golf Association junior events before he was 15, and won the state championship as a high school senior. He played on the Stanford University golf team that won the 1994 National Collegiate Athletic Association (NCAA) championship. As a professional, Martin qualified for the NIKE Tour in 1998 and 1999, and based on his 1999 performance, qualified for the PGA Tour in 2000. In the 1999 season, he entered 24 events, made the cut 13 times, and had 6 top-10 finishes; coming in second twice and third once.

Martin is also an individual with a disability as defined in the Americans with Disabilities Act of 1990 (ADA or Act).[2] Since birth he has been afflicted with Klippel-Trenaunay-Weber Syndrome, a degenerative circulatory disorder that obstructs the flow of blood from his right leg back to his heart. The disease is progressive; it causes severe pain and has atrophied his right leg. During the latter part of his college career, because of the progress of the disease, Martin could no longer walk an 18-hole golf course. Walking not only caused him pain, fatigue, and anxiety, but also created a significant risk of hemorrhaging, developing blood clots, and fracturing his tibia so badly that an amputation might be required. For these reasons, Stanford made written requests to the Pacific 10 Conference and the NCAA to waive for Martin their rules requiring players to walk and carry their own clubs. The requests were granted.

When Martin turned pro and entered petitioner's Q-School, the hard card permitted him to use a cart during his successful progress through the first two stages. He made a request, supported by detailed medical records, for permission to use a golf cart during the third stage. Petitioner refused to review those records or to waive its walking rule for the third stage. Martin therefore filed this action. A preliminary injunction entered by the District Court made it possible for him to use a cart in the final stage of the Q-School and as a competitor in the NIKE Tour and PGA Tour. Although not bound by the injunction, and despite its support for petitioner's position in this litigation, the USGA voluntarily granted Martin a similar waiver in events that it sponsors, including the U.S. Open.

---

2. 42 U.S.C. § 12102 provides, in part:
   "The term 'disability' means, with respect to an individual—
   "(A) a physical or mental impairment that substantially limits one or more of the major life activities of such individual * * *"

* * *

IV

Congress enacted the ADA in 1990 to remedy widespread discrimination against disabled individuals. In studying the need for such legislation, Congress found that "historically, society has tended to isolate and segregate individuals with disabilities, and, despite some improvements, such forms of discrimination against individuals with disabilities continue to be a serious and pervasive social problem." Congress noted that the many forms such discrimination takes include "outright intentional exclusion" as well as the "failure to make modifications to existing facilities and practices." After thoroughly investigating the problem, Congress concluded that there was a "compelling need" for a "clear and comprehensive national mandate" to eliminate discrimination against disabled individuals, and to integrate them "into the economic and social mainstream of American life."

In the ADA, Congress provided that broad mandate. In fact, one of the Act's "most impressive strengths" has been identified as its "comprehensive character," and accordingly the Act has been described as "a milestone on the path to a more decent, tolerant, progressive society," *Board of Trustees of Univ. of Ala. v. Garrett*, 531 U.S. 356, 375 (2001) (Kennedy, J., concurring). To effectuate its sweeping purpose, the ADA forbids discrimination against disabled individuals in major areas of public life, among them employment (Title I of the Act), public services (Title II), and public accommodations (Title III). At issue now, as a threshold matter, is the applicability of Title III to petitioner's golf Tours and qualifying rounds, in particular to petitioner's treatment of a qualified disabled golfer wishing to compete in those events.

Title III of the ADA prescribes, as a "[g]eneral rule":

"No individual shall be discriminated against on the basis of disability in the full and equal enjoyment of the goods, services, facilities, privileges, advantages, or accommodations of any place of public accommodation by any person who owns, leases (or leases to), or operates a place of public accommodation."

The phrase "public accommodation" is defined in terms of 12 extensive categories, which the legislative history indicates "should be construed liberally" to afford people with disabilities "equal access" to the wide variety of establishments available to the nondisabled.

It seems apparent, from both the general rule and the comprehensive definition of "public accommodation," that petitioner's golf Tours and their qualifying rounds fit comfortably within the coverage of Title III, and Martin within its protection. The events occur on "golf course[s]," a type of place specifically identified by the Act as a public accommodation. §12181(7)(L). In addition, at all relevant times, petitioner "leases" and "operates" golf courses to conduct its Q-School and Tours. As a lessor and operator of golf courses, then, petitioner must not discriminate against any "individual" in the "full and equal enjoyment of the goods, services, facilities, privileges, advantages, or accommodations" of those courses.

* * *

[P]etitioner reframes the coverage issue by arguing that the competing golfers are not members of the class protected by Title III of the ADA.

According to petitioner, Title III is concerned with discrimination against "clients and customers" seeking to obtain "goods and services" at places of public accommodation, whereas it is Title I that protects persons who work at such places. As the argument goes, petitioner operates not a "golf course" during its Tournaments but a "place of exhibition or entertainment," and a professional golfer such as Martin, like an actor in a theater production, is a provider rather than a consumer of the entertainment that petitioner sells to the public. Martin therefore cannot bring a claim under Title III because he is not one of the "'*clients or customers* of the covered public accommodation.'" Rather, Martin's claim of discrimination is "job-related" and could only be brought under Title I—but that Title does not apply because he is an independent contractor (as the District Court found) rather than an employee.

* * *

We need not decide whether petitioner's construction of the statute is correct, because petitioner's argument falters even on its own terms. If Title III's protected class were limited to "clients or customers," it would be entirely appropriate to classify the golfers who pay petitioner $3,000 for the chance to compete in the Q-School and, if successful, in the subsequent Tour events, as petitioner's clients or customers. In our view, petitioner's Tournaments (whether situated at a "golf course" or at a "place of exhibition or entertainment") simultaneously offer at least two "privileges" to the public—that of watching the golf competition and that of competing in it. Although the latter is more difficult and more expensive to obtain than the former, it is nonetheless a privilege that petitioner makes available to members of the general public* * *. We need not decide whether petitioner's construction of the statute is correct, because petitioner's argument falters even on its own terms. If Title III's protected class were limited to "clients or customers," it would be entirely appropriate to classify the golfers who pay petitioner $3,000 for the chance to compete in the Q-School and, if successful, in the subsequent Tour events, as petitioner's clients or customers. In our view, petitioner's Tournaments (whether situated at a "golf course" or at a "place of exhibition or entertainment") simultaneously offer at least two "privileges" to the public—that of watching the golf competition and that of competing in it. Although the latter is more difficult and more expensive to obtain than the former, it is nonetheless a privilege that petitioner makes available to members of the general public* * *. It would be inconsistent with the literal text of the statute as well as its expansive purpose to read Title III's coverage, even given petitioner's suggested limitation, any less broadly.[33]

* * *

V

As we have noted, 42 U.S.C. § 12182(a) sets forth Title III's general rule prohibiting public accommodations from discriminating against individuals because of their disabilities. The question whether petitioner has violated that rule depends on a proper construction of the term "discrimination," which is defined by Title III to include:

---

33. Contrary to the dissent's suggestion, our view of the Q-School does not make "everyone who seeks a job" at a public accommodation, through "an open tryout" or otherwise, "a customer." *Post* (opinion of Scalia, J.). Unlike those who successfully apply for a job at a place of public accommodation, or those who successfully bid for a contract, the golfers who qualify for petitioner's tours play at their own pleasure (perhaps, but not necessarily, for prize money), and although they commit to playing in at least 15 tournaments, they are not bound by any obligations typically associated with employment. Furthermore, unlike athletes in "other professional sports, such as baseball," *post*, in which players are employed by their clubs, the golfers on tour are not employed by petitioner or any related organizations. The record does not support the proposition that the purpose of the Q-School "is to hire," *ibid.*, rather than to narrow the field of participants in the sporting events that petitioner sponsors at places of public accommodation.

"a failure to make reasonable modifications in policies, practices, or procedures, when such modifications are necessary to afford such goods, services,
facilities, privileges, advantages, or accommodations to individuals with disabilities, *unless the entity can demonstrate that making such modifications would
fundamentally alter the nature* of such goods, services, facilities, privileges, advantages, or accommodations." (emphasis added).

Petitioner does not contest that a golf cart is a reasonable modification that is necessary if Martin is to play in its Tournaments. Martin's claim thus differs from one
that might be asserted by players with less serious afflictions that make walking the
course uncomfortable or difficult, but not beyond their capacity. In such cases, an accommodation might be reasonable but not necessary. In this case, however, the narrow dispute is whether allowing Martin to use a golf cart, despite the walking requirement that applies to the PGA Tour, the NIKE Tour, and the third stage of the
Q-School, is a modification that would "fundamentally alter the nature" of those
events.

In theory, a modification of petitioner's golf Tournaments might constitute a fundamental alteration in two different ways. It might alter such an essential aspect of
the game of golf that it would be unacceptable even if it affected all competitors
equally; changing the diameter of the hole from three to six inches might be such a
modification. Alternatively, a less significant change that has only a peripheral impact on the game itself might nevertheless give a disabled player, in addition to access
to the competition as required by Title III, an advantage over others and, for that
reason, fundamentally alter the character of the competition. We are not persuaded
that a waiver of the walking rule for Martin would work a fundamental alteration in
either sense.

As an initial matter, we observe that the use of carts is not itself inconsistent with the
fundamental character of the game of golf. From early on, the essence of the game has
been shot-making—using clubs to cause a ball to progress from the teeing ground to a
hole some distance away with as few strokes as possible. That essential aspect of the
game is still reflected in the very first of the Rules of Golf, which declares: "The Game of
Golf consists in playing a ball from the *teeing ground* into the hole by a *stroke* or successive strokes in accordance with the rules." Rule 1-1, Rules of Golf, App. 104 (italics in
original). Over the years, there have been many changes in the players' equipment, in
golf course design, in the Rules of Golf, and in the method of transporting clubs from
hole to hole. Originally, so few clubs were used that each player could carry them without a bag. Then came golf bags, caddies, carts that were pulled by hand, and eventually
motorized carts that carried players as well as clubs. "Golf carts started appearing with
increasing regularity on American golf courses in the 1950's. Today they are everywhere.
And they are encouraged. For one thing, they often speed up play, and for another, they
are great revenue producers." There is nothing in the Rules of Golf that either forbids
the use of carts, or penalizes a player for using a cart. That set of rules, as we have observed, is widely accepted in both the amateur and professional golf world as the rules
of the game. The walking rule that is contained in petitioner's hard cards, based on an
optional condition buried in an appendix to the Rules of Golf, is not an essential attribute of the game itself.

Indeed, the walking rule is not an indispensable feature of Tournament golf either.
As already mentioned, petitioner permits golf carts to be used in the SENIOR PGA
Tour, the open qualifying events for petitioner's Tournaments, the first two stages of the
Q-School, and, until 1997, the third stage of the Q-School as well. Moreover, petitioner

allows the use of carts during certain Tournament rounds in both the PGA Tour and the NIKE Tour. In addition, although the USGA enforces a walking rule in most of the Tournaments that it sponsors, it permits carts in the Senior Amateur and the Senior Women's Amateur championships.

Petitioner, however, distinguishes the game of golf as it is generally played from the game that it sponsors in the PGA Tour, NIKE Tour, and (at least recently) the last stage of the Q-School—golf at the "highest level." According to petitioner, "[t]he goal of the highest-level competitive athletics is to assess and compare the performance of different competitors, a task that is meaningful only if the competitors are subject to identical substantive rules." The waiver of any possibly "outcome-affecting" rule for a contestant would violate this principle and therefore, in petitioner's view, fundamentally alter the nature of the highest level athletic event. The walking rule is one such rule, petitioner submits, because its purpose is "to inject the element of fatigue into the skill of shot-making," and thus its effect may be the critical loss of a stroke. As a consequence, the reasonable modification Martin seeks would fundamentally alter the nature of petitioner's highest level Tournaments even if he were the only person in the world who has both the talent to compete in those elite events and a disability sufficiently serious that he cannot do so without using a cart.

The force of petitioner's argument is, first of all, mitigated by the fact that golf is a game in which it is impossible to guarantee that all competitors will play under exactly the same conditions or that an individual's ability will be the sole determinant of the outcome. For example, changes in the weather may produce harder greens and more head winds for the Tournament leader than for his closest pursuers. A lucky bounce may save a shot or two. Whether such happenstance events are more or less probable than the likelihood that a golfer afflicted with Klippel-Trenaunay-Weber Syndrome would one day qualify for the NIKE Tour and PGA Tour, they at least demonstrate that pure chance may have a greater impact on the outcome of elite golf Tournaments than the fatigue resulting from the enforcement of the walking rule.

Further, the factual basis of petitioner's argument is undermined by the District Court's finding that the fatigue from walking during one of petitioner's 4-day Tournaments cannot be deemed significant. The District Court credited the testimony of a professor in physiology and expert on fatigue, who calculated the calories expended in walking a golf course (about five miles) to be approximately 500 calories—"nutritionally * * * less than a Big Mac." What is more, that energy is expended over a 5-hour period, during which golfers have numerous intervals for rest and refreshment. In fact, the expert concluded, because golf is a low intensity activity, fatigue from the game is primarily a psychological phenomenon in which stress and motivation are the key ingredients. And even under conditions of severe heat and humidity, the critical factor in fatigue is fluid loss rather than exercise from walking.

Moreover, when given the option of using a cart, the majority of golfers in petitioner's Tournaments have chosen to walk, often to relieve stress or for other strategic reasons. As NIKE Tour member Eric Johnson testified, walking allows him to keep in rhythm, stay warmer when it is chilly, and develop a better sense of the elements and the course than riding a cart.

Even if we accept the factual predicate for petitioner's argument—that the walking rule is "outcome affecting" because fatigue may adversely affect performance—its legal position is fatally flawed. Petitioner's refusal to consider Martin's personal circumstances in deciding whether to accommodate his disability runs counter to the clear language and purpose of the ADA. As previously stated, the ADA was enacted to eliminate discrimination against "individuals" with disabilities, and to that end Title III of the Act requires without exception that any "policies, practices, or procedures" of a public accommodation be reasonably modified for disabled "individuals" as necessary to afford access unless doing so would fundamentally alter what is offered. To comply with this command, an individualized inquiry must be made to determine whether a specific modification for a particular person's disability would be reasonable under the circumstances as well as necessary for that person, and yet at the same time not work a fundamental alteration.

To be sure, the waiver of an essential rule of competition for anyone would fundamentally alter the nature of petitioner's Tournaments. As we have demonstrated, however, the walking rule is at best peripheral to the nature of petitioner's athletic events, and thus it might be waived in individual cases without working a fundamental alteration. Therefore, petitioner's claim that all the substantive rules for its "highest-level" competitions are sacrosanct and cannot be modified under any circumstances is effectively a contention that it is exempt from Title III's reasonable modification requirement. But that provision carves out no exemption for elite athletics, and given Title III's coverage not only of places of "exhibition or entertainment" but also of "golf course[s]," its application to petitioner's Tournaments cannot be said to be unintended or unexpected. Even if it were, "the fact that a statute can be applied in situations not expressly anticipated by Congress does not demonstrate ambiguity. It demonstrates breadth." *Pennsylvania Dept. of Corrections v. Yeskey*, 524 U.S., at 212, 118 S.Ct. 1952 (internal quotation marks omitted).[51]

Under the ADA's basic requirement that the need of a disabled person be evaluated on an individual basis, we have no doubt that allowing Martin to use a golf cart would not fundamentally alter the nature of petitioner's Tournaments. As we have discussed, the purpose of the walking rule is to subject players to fatigue, which in turn may influence the outcome of Tournaments. Even if the rule does serve that purpose, it is an uncontested finding of the District Court that Martin "easily endures greater fatigue even with a cart than his able-bodied competitors do by walking." The purpose of the walking rule is therefore not compromised in the slightest by allowing Martin to use a cart. A modification that provides an exception to a peripheral Tournament rule without impairing its purpose cannot be said to "fundamentally alter" the Tournament. What it can be said to do, on the other hand, is to allow Martin the chance to qualify for and compete in the athletic events petitioner offers to those members of the public who

---

51. Hence, petitioner's questioning of the ability of courts to apply the reasonable modification requirement to athletic competition is a complaint more properly directed to Congress, which drafted the ADA's coverage broadly, than to us. Even more misguided is Justice Scalia's suggestion that Congress did not place that inquiry into the hands of the courts at all. According to the dissent, the game of golf as sponsored by petitioner is, like all sports games, the sum of its "arbitrary rules," and no one, including courts, "can pronounce one or another of them to be 'nonessential' if the rulemaker (here the PGA Tour) deems it to be essential." *Post.* Whatever the merit of Justice Scalia's postmodern view of "What Is [Sport]," *post,* it is clear that Congress did not enshrine it in Title III of the ADA. While Congress expressly exempted "private clubs or establishments" and "religious organizations or entities" from Title III's coverage, Congress made no such exception for athletic competitions, much less did it give sports organizations carte-blanche authority to exempt themselves from the fundamental alteration inquiry by deeming any rule, no matter how peripheral to the competition, to be essential. In short, Justice Scalia's reading of the statute renders the word "fundamentally" largely superfluous, because it treats the alteration of any rule governing an event at a public accommodation to be a fundamental alteration.

have the skill and desire to enter. That is exactly what the ADA requires. As a result, Martin's request for a waiver of the walking rule should have been granted.

The ADA admittedly imposes some administrative burdens on the operators of places of public accommodation that could be avoided by strictly adhering to general rules and policies that are entirely fair with respect to the able-bodied but that may indiscriminately preclude access by qualified persons with disabilities. But surely, in a case of this kind, Congress intended that an entity like the PGA not only give individualized attention to the handful of requests that it might receive from talented but disabled athletes for a modification or waiver of a rule to allow them access to the competition, but also carefully weigh the purpose, as well as the letter, of the rule before determining that no accommodation would be tolerable.

The judgment of the Court of Appeals is affirmed.

It is so ordered.

JUSTICE SCALIA, with whom JUSTICE THOMAS joins, dissenting.

In my view today's opinion exercises a benevolent compassion that the law does not place it within our power to impose. The judgment distorts the text of Title III, the structure of the ADA, and common sense. I respectfully dissent.

I

The Court holds that a professional sport is a place of public accommodation and that respondent is a "custome[r]" of "competition" when he practices his profession.

* * *

For many reasons, Title III will not bear such an interpretation. The provision of Title III at issue here is a public-accommodation law, and it is the traditional understanding of public-accommodation laws that they provide rights for *customers*. "At common law, innkeepers, smiths, and others who made profession of a public employment, were prohibited from refusing, without good reason, to serve a customer." *Hurley v. Irish-American Gay, Lesbian and Bisexual Group of Boston, Inc.,* 515 U.S. 557, 571 (1995). See also *Heart of Atlanta Motel, Inc. v. United States,* 379 U.S. 241 (1964). This understanding is clearly reflected in the text of Title III itself. Section 12181(7) lists 12 specific types of entities that qualify as "public accommodations," with a follow-on expansion that makes it clear what the "enjoyment of the goods, services, etc." of those entities consists of-and it plainly envisions that the person "enjoying" the "public accommodation" will be a *customer*.

* * *

The Court, for its part, assumes that conclusion for the sake of argument, but pronounces respondent to be a "customer" of the PGA Tour or of the golf courses on which it is played. That seems to me quite incredible. The PGA Tour is a professional sporting event, staged for the entertainment of a live and TV audience, the receipts from whom (the TV audience's admission price is paid by advertisers) pay the expenses of the Tour, including the cash prizes for the winning golfers. The professional golfers on the Tour are no more "enjoying" (the statutory term) the entertainment that the Tour provides, or the facilities of the golf courses on which it is held, than professional baseball players "enjoy" the baseball games in which they play or the facilities of Yankee Stadium. To be sure, professional ballplayers *participate* in the games, and *use* the ballfields, but no one in his right mind would think that they are *customers* of the American League or of Yankee Stadium. They are themselves the entertainment that the customers pay to watch. And professional golfers are no different.

* * *

As the Court points out, the ADA specifically identifies golf courses as one of the covered places of public accommodation. See § 12181(7)(L) ("a gymnasium, health spa, bowling alley, golf course, or other place of exercise or recreation"); and the distinctive "goo[d], servic[e], facilit[y], privileg [e], advantag[e], or accommodatio[n]" identified by that provision as distinctive to that category of place of public accommodation is "exercise or recreation." Respondent did not seek to "exercise" or "recreate" at the PGA Tour events; he sought to make money (which is why he is called a *professional* golfer). He was not a customer *buying* recreation or entertainment; he was a professional athlete *selling* it.

* * *

The Court relies heavily upon the Q-School. It says that petitioner offers the golfing public the "privilege" of "competing in the Q-School and playing in the Tours; indeed, the former is a privilege for which thousands of individuals from the general public pay, and the latter is one for which they vie." But the Q-School is no more a "privilege" offered for the general public's "enjoyment" than is the California Bar Exam. It is a competition for entry into the PGA Tour—an open tryout, no different in principle from open casting for a movie or stage production, or walk-on tryouts for other professional sports, such as baseball* * * . [T]he purpose of holding those tryouts is not to provide entertainment; it is to hire. At bottom, open tryouts for performances to be held at a place of public accommodation are no different from open bidding on contracts to cut the grass at a place of public accommodation, or open applications for any job at a place of public accommodation. Those bidding, those applying—and those trying out—are not converted into customers. By the Court's reasoning, a business exists not only to sell goods and services to the public, but to provide the "privilege" of employment to the public; wherefore it follows, like night the day, that everyone who seeks a job is a customer.

* * *

II

[T]he Court must then confront the question whether respondent's requested modification of the supposed policy, practice, or procedure of walking would "fundamentally alter the nature" of the PGA Tour game. The Court attacks this "fundamental alteration" analysis by asking two questions: first, whether the "essence" or an "essential aspect" of the sport of golf has been altered; and second, whether the change, even if not essential to the game, would give the disabled player an advantage over others and thereby "fundamentally alter the character of the competition." It answers no to both.

Before considering the Court's answer to the first question, it is worth pointing out that the assumption which underlies that question is false. Nowhere is it writ that PGA Tour golf must be classic "essential" golf. Why cannot the PGA Tour, if it wishes, promote a new game, with distinctive rules (much as the American League promotes a game of baseball in which the pitcher's turn at the plate can be taken by a "designated hitter")? If members of the public do not like the new rules—if they feel that these rules do not truly test the individual's skill at "real golf" (or the team's skill at "real baseball") they can withdraw their patronage. But the rules are the rules. They are (as in all games) entirely arbitrary, and there is no basis on which anyone—not even the Supreme Court of the United States—can pronounce one or another of them to be "nonessential" if the rulemaker (here the PGA Tour) deems it to be essential.

If one assumes, however, that the PGA Tour has some legal obligation to play classic, Platonic golf—and if one assumes the correctness of all the other wrong turns the

Court has made to get to this point—then we Justices must confront what is indeed an awesome responsibility. It has been rendered the solemn duty of the Supreme Court of the United States, laid upon it by Congress in pursuance of the Federal Government's power "[t]o regulate Commerce with foreign Nations, and among the several States," U.S. Const., Art. I, §8, cl. 3, to decide What Is Golf. I am sure that the Framers of the Constitution, aware of the 1457 edict of King James II of Scotland prohibiting golf because it interfered with the practice of archery, fully expected that sooner or later the paths of golf and government, the law and the links, would once again cross, and that the judges of this august Court would some day have to wrestle with that age-old jurisprudential question, for which their years of study in the law have so well prepared them: Is someone riding around a golf course from shot to shot *really* a golfer? The answer, we learn, is yes. The Court ultimately concludes, and it will henceforth be the Law of the Land, that walking is not a "fundamental" aspect of golf.

Either out of humility or out of self-respect (one or the other) the Court should decline to answer this incredibly difficult and incredibly silly question. To say that something is "essential" is ordinarily to say that it is necessary to the achievement of a certain object. But since it is the very nature of a game to have no object except amusement (that is what distinguishes games from productive activity), it is quite impossible to say that any of a game's arbitrary rules is "essential." Eighteen-hole golf courses, 10-foot-high basketball hoops, 90-foot baselines, 100-yard football fields-all are arbitrary and none is essential. The only support for any of them is tradition and (in more modern times) insistence by what has come to be regarded as the ruling body of the sport—both of which factors support the PGA Tour's position in the present case. (Many, indeed, consider walking to be *the central feature* of the game of golf—hence Mark Twain's classic criticism of the sport: "a good walk spoiled.") I suppose there is some point at which the rules of a well—known game are changed to such a degree that no reasonable person would call it the same game. If the PGA Tour competitors were required to dribble a large, inflated ball and put it through a round hoop, the game could no longer reasonably be called golf. But this criterion—destroying recognizability as the same generic game—is surely not the test of "essentialness" or "fundamentalness" that the Court applies, since it apparently thinks that merely changing the diameter of the *cup* might "fundamentally alter" the game of golf.

Having concluded that dispensing with the walking rule would not violate federal-Platonic "golf" (and, implicitly, that it is federal-Platonic golf, and no other, that the PGA Tour can insist upon) the Court moves on to the second part of its test: the competitive effects of waiving this nonessential rule. In this part of its analysis, the Court first finds that the effects of the change are "mitigated" by the fact that in the game of golf weather, a "lucky bounce," and "pure chance" provide different conditions for each competitor and individual ability may not "be the sole determinant of the outcome." I guess that is why those who follow professional golfing consider Jack Nicklaus the *luckiest* golfer of all time, only to be challenged of late by the phenomenal *luck* of Tiger Woods. The Court's empiricism is unpersuasive. "Pure chance" is randomly distributed among the players, but allowing respondent to use a cart gives him a "lucky" break every time he plays. Pure chance also only matters at the margin—a stroke here or there; the cart substantially improves this respondent's competitive prospects beyond a couple of strokes. But even granting that there are significant nonhuman variables affecting competition, that fact does not justify adding another variable that always favors one player.

In an apparent effort to make its opinion as narrow as possible, the Court relies upon the District Court's finding that even with a cart, respondent will be at least as fatigued as everyone else. This, the Court says, *proves* that competition will not be affected. Far from thinking that reliance on this finding cabins the effect of today's opinion, I think it will prove to be its most expansive and destructive feature. Because step one of the Court's two-part inquiry into whether a requested change in a sport will "fundamentally alter [its] nature," consists of an utterly unprincipled ontology of sports (pursuant to which the Court is not even sure whether golf's "essence" requires a 3-inch hole), there is every reason to think that in future cases involving requests for special treatment by would-be athletes the second step of the analysis will be determinative. In resolving that second step-determining whether waiver of the "nonessential" rule will have an impermissible "competitive effect"—by measuring the athletic capacity of the requesting individual, and asking whether the special dispensation would do no more than place him on a par (so to speak) with other competitors, the Court guarantees that future cases of this sort will have to be decided on the basis of individualized factual findings. Which means that future cases of this sort will be numerous, and a rich source of lucrative litigation. One can envision the parents of a Little League player with attention deficit disorder trying to convince a judge that their son's disability makes it at least 25% more difficult to hit a pitched ball. (If they are successful, the only thing that could prevent a court order giving the kid four strikes would be a judicial determination that, in baseball, three strikes are metaphysically necessary, which is quite absurd.)

The statute, of course, provides no basis for this individualized analysis that is the Court's last step on a long and misguided journey. The statute seeks to assure that a disabled person's disability will not deny him *equal access* to (among other things) competitive sporting events—not that his disability will not deny him an *equal chance to win* competitive sporting events. The latter is quite impossible, since the very *nature* of competitive sport is the measurement, by uniform rules, of unevenly distributed excellence. This unequal distribution is precisely what determines the winners and losers—and artificially to "even out" that distribution, by giving one or another player exemption from a rule that emphasizes his particular weakness, is to destroy the game. That is why the "handicaps" that are customary in social games of golf—which, by adding strokes to the scores of the good players and subtracting them from scores of the bad ones, "even out" the varying abilities—are *not* used in professional golf. In the Court's world, there is one set of rules that is "fair with respect to the able-bodied" but "individualized" rules, mandated by the ADA, for "talented but disabled athletes." The ADA mandates no such ridiculous thing. Agility, strength, speed, balance, quickness of mind, steadiness of nerves, intensity of concentration—these talents are not evenly distributed. No wild-eyed dreamer has ever suggested that the managing bodies of the competitive sports that test precisely these qualities should try to take account of the uneven distribution of God-given gifts when writing and enforcing the rules of competition. And I have no doubt Congress did not authorize misty-eyed judicial supervision of such a revolution.

* * *

My belief that today's judgment is clearly in error should not be mistaken for a belief that the PGA Tour clearly *ought not* allow respondent to use a golf cart. *That* is a close question, on which even those who compete in the PGA Tour are apparently divided; but it is a *different* question from the one before the Court. Just as it is a different question whether the Little League *ought* to give disabled youngsters a fourth strike, or some other waiver from the rules that makes up for their disabilities. In both cases, whether they *ought* to do so depends upon (1) how central to the game that they have organized (and over whose rules they are the master) they deem the waived provision to be, and

(2) how competitive—how strict a test of raw athletic ability in all aspects of the competition—they want their game to be. But whether Congress has said they *must* do so depends upon the answers to the legal questions I have discussed above—not upon what this Court sententiously decrees to be "decent, tolerant, [and] progressive."

And it should not be assumed that today's decent, tolerant, and progressive judgment will, in the long run, accrue to the benefit of sports competitors with disabilities. Now that it is clear courts will review the rules of sports for "fundamentalness," organizations that value their autonomy have every incentive to defend vigorously the necessity of every regulation. They may still be second-guessed in the end as to the Platonic requirements of the sport, but they will *assuredly* lose if they have at all wavered in their enforcement. The lesson the PGA Tour and other sports organizations should take from this case is to make sure that the same written rules are set forth for all levels of play, and never voluntarily to grant any modifications. The second lesson is to end open tryouts. I doubt that, in the long run, even disabled athletes will be well served by these incentives that the Court has created.

Complaints about this case are not "properly directed to Congress." They are properly directed to this Court's Kafkaesque determination that professional sports organizations, and the fields they rent for their exhibitions, are "places of public accommodation" to the competing athletes, and the athletes themselves "customers" of the organization that pays them; its Alice in Wonderland determination that there are such things as judicially determinable "essential" and "nonessential" rules of a made-up game; and its Animal Farm determination that fairness and the ADA mean that everyone gets to play by individualized rules which will assure that no one's lack of ability (or at least no one's lack of ability so pronounced that it amounts to a disability) will be a handicap. The year was 2001, and "everybody was finally equal." K. Vonnegut, *Harrison Bergeron*, in ANIMAL FARM AND RELATED READINGS 129 (1997).

Notes and Questions

1. As a threshold matter, the Court had to determine whether the PGA Tour was covered by the ADA. Because Casey Martin was not an employee of the PGA Tour—he was, the Court concluded, an "independent contractor"—he cannot claim protection under Title I of the Act. The question then became whether the Tour was a "public accommodation" under Title III. The Court concluded that it was. In this regard, the Court rejected the PGA's argument that Casey Martin was neither a customer nor client of the Tour, because he was not a spectator of the event; as such, he was not attempting to obtain the benefits of a "public accommodation." The Court held instead that one need not be a spectator to qualify as a customer or client, or otherwise a beneficiary of the PGA's services. Golfers like Martin, who paid fees to participate in the event, were in fact customers and clients, and certainly were availing themselves of the services that the PGA provides.

2. What is the fundamental nature of the game of golf in terms of the key elements of competition? Clearly, hitting the ball into the hole with the minimum number of strokes is the ultimate challenge. Is walking such a critical part of the endeavor that alleviating one party of the obligation to walk produces a fundamental disturbance of the game's very essence? Note that Justice Stevens concluded that a change of the rules could produce a "fundamental alteration" in one of two ways: it might "alter such an essential aspect of the game of golf that it would be unacceptable even if it affected all competitors equally," or it might be a lesser change that "nevertheless give a disabled

player, in addition to access to the competition as required by Title III, an advantage over others and, for that reason, fundamentally alter the character of the competition." Does allowing Casey Martin to ride a cart produce either of these two results?

As to the first, Justice Stevens concluded that "From early on, the essence of the game has been shot making." Regarding the second, he noted expert testimony that the calories expended walking an 18 hole golf course approximated an expense of 500 calories; nutritionally "less than a Big Mac." Moreover, even if fatigue was a part of the game and walking contributed to that fatigue, "Martin easily endures greater fatigue even with a cart than his able-bodied competitors do by walking."

The Court stressed the ADA's mandate that disabled persons be evaluated "on an individual basis" and, in evaluating the impact of Martin's requested accommodation on the game, it accordingly used an individualized analysis. Is the individualized analysis appropriate? Consider the following:

> It is unacceptable to always have an individualized analysis; however, it is just as undesirable to never have one. Clearly, a new approach is needed * * *. The proposed approach contains three steps. At the first step the plaintiff-athlete has the burden to demonstrate that the requested accommodation is reasonable in a general sense. If the plaintiff is able to meet this burden then, under step two of the proposed analysis, the burden shifts to the defendant to prove that the asked-for change would fundamentally alter the game. At this point, before the defendant has to offer proof that a modification for this particular plaintiff would fundamentally alter the sport, the defendant must be allowed to show that the rule is so important that any deviation from it would generate fundamental change. If so, the rule cannot be changed, and the analysis is over. This is an extremely difficult factual inquiry, and this article will propose a question set that goes far beyond the analysis in either the *Martin* or *Olinger* cases for reaching an answer to that inquiry. Finally, under step three of the proposed analysis, if the defendant cannot demonstrate that the rule is so important to the sport that it can never be changed, then the defendant must prove that modifying the rule for this particular plaintiff would cause fundamental change. At this point, the court must undertake an individualized analysis of this plaintiff's circumstances. If the defendant cannot demonstrate, with specificity, that making this individualized exception would cause fundamental change, then the accommodation must be made.

Michael Waterstone, *Let's Be Reasonable Here: Why The ADA Will Not Ruin Professional Sports,* 2000 B.Y.U. L. Rev. 1489, 1531–32 (2000).

3. Justice Stevens described Casey Martin as "a gifted athlete" and "a talented golfer." Is he right? Is Martin as gifted and talented as the golfers who can walk? What would Justice Scalia say? Note, in this regard, Justice Scalia's insistence that "no wild-eyed dreamer has ever suggested that the managing bodies of the competitive sports * * * should try to take account of the uneven distribution of God-given gifts when writing and enforcing the rules of competition." Does Casey Martin, by virtue of his impairment, simply have fewer "God-given gifts" than other golfers? One way to understand Justice Stevens's observations is as a suggestion that Casey Martin shares those "God-given gifts," and also has an impairment that, through its rules, the PGA—not God—has turned into a disability.

4. Referring to the "fundamental alteration" dispute, Justice Scalia suggests that the Court, "[e]ither out of humility or out of self-respect * * * should decline to answer this

incredibly difficult and incredibly silly question." What would he have the Court do? One possible answer is found in Justice Scalia's suggestion that the rules of all games are "entirely arbitrary, and there is no basis on which anyone—not even the Supreme Court of the United States—can pronounce one or another of them to be 'nonessential' if the rulemaker (here the PGA Tour) deems it to be essential." Would such an approach immunize all sports rules from ADA claims? What else could Justice Scalia mean when he says "the rules are the rules"?

5. Justice Scalia mocks the Court's search for the "essence" or "fundamental nature" of golf; he invokes Plato's other-worldly "forms of justice" in his derisive dismissals of "federal-Platonic golf." Is there any irony here? In a general philosophical sense, is this an unusual stance for a jurist generally committed to formalism in adjudication? In the instant dispute, is it easy to reconcile this critique with Justice Scalia's own exegesis on the essence of sport: "the very *nature* of competitive sport is the measurement, by uniform rules, of unevenly distributed excellence," and "artificially to 'even out' that distribution, by giving one or another player exemption from a rule that emphasizes his particular weakness, is to destroy the game"? Justice Scalia, Professor Aviam Soifer writes, "sardonically condemned the majority for its concern for 'classic, Platonic golf.' Yet the essentialist worldview of private ordering that Scalia advances could hardly be more clearly the workproduct of a Platonic Guardian at full throttle." *Disabling the ADA: Essences, Better Angels, and Unprincipled Neutrality Claims*, 44 Wm. & Mary L. Rev. 1285, 1307 (2003).

6. Commentary on the *Martin* decision was rather sharply divided. Columnist Sally Jenkins wrote:

> The problem is that while the Supreme Court ruling speaks to our compassionate instincts and equal-opportunity sensibilities on Martin's behalf, it is ruinously interventionist. Golf, and a number of other sports, stand to be fundamentally altered thanks to this decision.
>
> We all suffer from some sort of physical limitation that prevents us from doing things we would like to do, from reaching the canned goods at the supermarket to becoming Olympians. Where is it written that to play a sport at the most elite level is a constitutional right? Until yesterday, nowhere.

Sally Jenkins, *A Good Walk is Truly Spoiled*, Wash. Post D01 (May 30, 2001). For other negative reviews, see David Broder, *Decreeing the DH?*, News & Observer (Raleigh, N.C.), June 3, 2001, at 31A; Suzanne Fields, *Advantages for the Disadvantaged; Supreme Court Lowers Standards*, Wash. Times A17 (June 4, 2001); John Leo, *Duffers in the Court; The Supremes Shouldn't Bend the Rules for a Disabled Golfer*, U.S. News & World Rep., June 11, 2001, at 16; Scott Mills, *Casey Martin Case Sets Bad Precedent*, Balt. Sun, Feb. 22, 1998, at 6F (criticizing the *Martin* decision); Terrance Moore, *Ruling Allowing Martin To Use Cart Disregards the Essence of Golf*, Atlanta J. Const., Feb. 13, 1998, at E3; Joe Queenan, *Differently-Abled Athletes*, Wall St. J., Mar. 2, 1998, at A18; George Will, *Meddling in Games*, News & Observer (Raleigh, N.C.), June 3, 2001, at 31A.

Columnist Dave Anderson, meanwhile, approved of Justice Stevens's observation that from early on, "the essence of the game has been shot making." "In other words," Anderson wrote

> the cart doesn't hit the ball, the golfer does. That has been Martin's argument, and the belief here, throughout his long and winding journey through the courts. Martin may also be unique: someone who, despite a disability, can be a competitive touring pro as long as he's allowed to ride a cart between shots.

Dave Anderson, *Sports of the Times; The Cart Doesn't Hit the Ball*, N.Y. Times D1 (May 30, 2001). Anderson recalled this incident:

> During the final round of last year's Kemper Insurance Open, Casey Martin's 20-foot putt on the 12th green just slid past the cup. Most of those in his gallery groaned, "Ohhh," but one voice blurted, "Too bad, you cheater!" Before limping off the green to his cart, Martin turned and stared in the direction of that voice.

Id. "A common perception toward people with disabilities," Martin explained, "is that you're going to have an advantage, and that's just a gross distortion of the truth. I'm sure a lot of players would love to take a cart, but I guarantee you they would not like to take a cart with my leg." *Id.* For other positive reviews, see Ira Berkow, *Sports of the Times; Fairness and Riding a Golf Cart*, N.Y. Times, Feb. 1, 1998, at § 8 (arguing that because the PGA Tour has enacted several rule modifications in the past, the Tour should grant Martin a cart); Rich Brooks, *Objections to Disabled Golfer Just Aren't Up to Par*, Sarasota Herald-Tribune BV1 (June 2, 2001); Rick Reilly, *Give Casey Martin a Lift*, Sports Illustrated, Feb. 9, 1998, at 140, 140; S. Scott Rohrer, *Martin Case is Victory for Human Decency*, Deseret News (Salt Lake City, Utah) AA08 (June 10, 2001); Bill Wallace, *Overreacting to Casey Martin's Golf Cart*, Bridge News (June 12, 2001).

7. California State Supreme Court Justice Stanley Mosk wrote in response to the opinion:

> I was thrilled by the Supreme Court's decision * * * but disheartened by the reaction of Tour officials and players who fear that the Tour could be overrun by carts. The innate bigotry fueling their fears is the same bigotry that lay behind the Caucasian—only clause barring blacks from Tour events until 1961, when a fight that I had initiated forced the PGA of America to drop that offensive and illegal provision.

My Shot; The Tour's Fear of Carts Is the Same Form of Bigotry that Caused the Caucasian-Only Clause, Sports Illustrated G46 (June 11, 2001).

The Libertarian Party, meanwhile, issued a press release asking: "What's next? Federally mandated stilts so * * * midgets can play professional basketball? Should Roger Clemens be ordered by the court to throw slower fastballs to near-sighted hitters?" Quoted in Dave Kindred, *Doomsday Is Not Nigh*, Sporting News, June 11, 2001, at 62, 62. The hypotheticals might warrant a brief response. It is not clear, first, that either one involves a "disability" within the meaning of the ADA. As for "midgets," the term references no discernible impairment. Read charitably, it is an imprecise (and outmoded and derogatory) reference to someone with a form of dwarfism, and in one reported case, a United States District Court did hold that an employee with achondroplastic dwarfism was disabled for purposes of Section 504 of the Rehabilitation Act. *See Dexler v. Tisch*, 660 F. Supp. 1418 (D. Conn.1987) (holding that Act did *not* require restructuring of postal job as a reasonable accommodation). Near-sightedness, meanwhile, is certainly *not* a disability, at least not if it can be corrected with eyeglasses. The effect of an impairment, the Supreme Court has ruled, is to be measured *with* corrective or mitigating measures (e.g., eyeglasses, prescription drugs). *See, e.g., Sutton v. United Airlines, Inc.*, 527 U.S. 471 (1999) (twin sisters with severe myopia are not "disabled" under ADA, since their vision was 20/20 with corrective lenses). As for the suggestion that the hypothetical claimants are "qualified" and can meet the "necessary" or "essential" requirements of their positions, or that the accommodations they request are "reasonable" and would not "fundamentally alter" their games, the less said, the better.

8. Recently, the United States Golf Association reversed an earlier decision and permitted MacKinzie Kline to participate in the U.S. Girls Junior and the U.S. Women's Amateur using an oxygen tank and golf cart. Kline was born with one rather than two ventricles in the heart, causing shortness of breath and fatigue. *See* MacKinzie Kline, *Change of Heart,* SPORTS ILLUSTRATED, TEEING OFF (July ___, 2006). The USGA's decision is perhaps a harbinger of other incidental accommodations to rules that would otherwise disqualify disabled persons from participation. *See* Rick Woelfel, *Nobody Told the Officials,* REFEREE (August, 2006) (High school football officials prohibited player without legs from participating in interscholastic game shortly after the player entered the contest. The incident resulted in the vilification of the refereeing crew from several sources, prompting the crew's response that its actions were consistent with Ohio High School Athletic Association rules.)

9. The *Martin* decision has not opened the floodgates of litigation, at least not if reported decisions are a reliable guide. As some commentators have predicted, ADA cases in sports contexts remain quite rare.

> The decision in favor of Martin will not result in a slippery slope in which a large number of ADA claims requesting accommodations will be brought in other professional sports. Unlike the Martin and [Ford] Olinger cases, most of the nation's 15,000 annual ADA cases concern whether the plaintiff fits under the definition of disabled individual. Further, it will be an extremely rare situation in professional sports when a disabled athlete will otherwise have the skill necessary to compete at the highest level, as do Martin and Olinger. Therefore, the professional sports arena is unlikely to confront many cases where disabled individuals will require only a slight accommodation in order to compete at the professional level. Lastly, the inherent differences between the game of golf and more rigorous sports, such as football, basketball, hockey and baseball, simply make it frivolous to argue that a ruling giving golf carts to specific disabled golfers would have a serious negative impact on other sports. Golf requires far more skill than athleticism, and walking is not an integral part of the game. Contrarily, in professional sports such as baseball, hockey, football, and basketball, where the best athletes in the world dominate the game, walking, running, or skating is a vital part of the game.

Charles A. Omage, *Comment: Caught In The Rough Of The PGA Tour And USGA Rules: Casey Martin and Ford Olinger's Fight For The Use Of A Golf Cart Under The Americans With Disabilities Act,* 29 HOFSTRA L. REV. 1401 (2001). *See also* Martha Lee Walters and Suzanne Bradley Chanti, *When the Only Way to Equal Is to Acknowledge Difference: PGA Tour, Inc. v. Martin,* 40 BRANDEIS L.J. 727 (2002).

Chapter 18

Tort Law and Sports: A Primer

> Had the parties been upon the play-grounds of the school, engaged in the usual boyish sports, the defendant being free from malice, wantonness, or negligence, and intending no harm to plaintiff in what he did, we should hesitate to hold the act of the defendant unlawful, or that he could be held liable in this action. Some consideration is due to the implied license of the play-grounds.

Vosburg v. Putney, 50 N.W. 403, 403–04 (Wis. 1891).

Sport combines athleticism with drama, placing teams and individuals in competition with each other for goals, points, runs, and ultimately championships. We watch sporting events not just because they are displays of skill, but because of the competition. The cliché "the thrill of victory and the agony of defeat" captures the emotion that is central to playing a sport and essential to maintaining an audience. We want to see our team win; and even where we do not care about the outcome of any particular contest, the event attracts our attention because the players so care about the outcome that they put their all into each "game."

This competition, however, makes inevitable the injuries that occur when bodies crash into walls or each other, pucks strike players blocking shots, splintered bats fly at opposing players, and gymnasts tumble off equipment. And where there are injuries, there are lawsuits. The states have struggled to craft tort doctrine that encourages safety and discourages carelessness, provides compensation to injured parties, and corrects injustices committed by defendants, while ensuring that the potential for legal liability does not stifle the competition that is essential to everyone's enjoyment of athletics.

If NHL defenseman Scott Stevens "lines-up" an opposing player and delivers a hip-check that sends the opponent flying head-over-heels to the ice, or if former heavyweight champion Lennox Lewis lands an uppercut to the jaw of another boxer, none of us would consider the action a tort. But if either event occurred outside the playing arena, there is little question that each would constitute battery. The chief difficulty faced by courts considering tort cases arising out of sporting events is discerning the difference between conduct inherent in the sport (and thus implicitly consented to by all involved) and conduct that, while having a connection to a sporting event, is outside the normal understanding of the game and goes beyond that which the plaintiff should have anticipated.

This chapter summarizes tort doctrines that are particularly relevant in the sports context. Accordingly, some important portions of tort law are ignored or treated summarily here, where application of those doctrines to the sporting context presents few intricacies beyond those presented in other areas. Those seeking a more comprehensive treatment may consult MARSHALL S. SHAPO, PRINCIPLES OF TORT LAW (2d ed. 2003), KENNETH S. ABRAHAM, THE FORMS AND FUNCTIONS OF TORT LAW (2d ed. 2002), or DAN B. DOBBS, THE LAW OF TORTS (2000).

The predicate for a tort action resulting from an injury inflicted on one participant by another may rest on several grounds. First, the allegation could sound in intentional tort—a claim that the injury was a result of the defendant's assault and battery. Second, the victim could claim negligence on the part of the other player (or his club, under a theory of vicarious liability). Third, the injured player could claim that the conduct was "reckless," something beyond negligent but not deliberate or intentional. *See* Raymond L. Yasser, *Liability for Sports Injuries, in* 3 LAW OF PROFESSIONAL AND AMATEUR SPORTS § 15:4 (Gary A. Uberstine ed., 2002); Bradley Nielsen, *Controlling Sports Violence: Too Late for the Carrots—Bring on the Big Stick*, 74 IOWA L. REV. 681, 696–99 (1989). *See also Nabozny v. Barnhill*, 334 N.E.2d 258 (Ill. Ct. App. 1975); *Bourque v. Duplechin*, 331 So.2d 40 (La. Ct. App. 1976).

As a general matter, sports participants are liable for intentional torts just as are non-athletes. They are immune, however, from ordinary negligence actions, on the theory that sports, if played with the proper vigor and enthusiasm, preclude the exercise of "ordinary care." *See* Stanley L. Grazis, Annotation, *Liability of Participant in Team Athletic Competition for Injury to Or Death of Another Participant*, 55 A.L.R. 5th 529. In jurisdictions that adopt that theory, sports participants are usually liable for conduct that is reckless. As Professors Weistart and Lowell summarize the doctrine,

> [V]oluntary, *sui juris* participants in lawful sporting activity assume, as a matter of law, all of the ordinary and inherent risks of that sport, so long as the activity is played in good faith and the injury is not the result of an intentional or willful act.

WEISTART & LOWELL §8.02, at 936.

There are notable exceptions to this general rule, however. As you will see in the next chapter, even some intentional conduct that causes injury will not lead to liability, if the conduct is considered a part of the game. (Consider the boxing example. *See McAdams v. Windham*, 94 So. 742 (Ala. 1922).) On the flip side, some jurisdictions apply ordinary negligence to sporting events, reasoning that the standard of "ordinary care *under the circumstances*" can take account of the events accompanying the playing of sports.

I. Intentional Torts

Two intentional torts, assault and battery, have particular relevance for sports participants and spectators. The two are closely related, for a plaintiff has been assaulted when he or she has been placed intentionally in apprehension of a battery. The battery is a harmful or offensive touching of another person, made intentionally and without consent.

A. Assault

Liability for assault seeks to compensate the plaintiff for the apprehension or loss of dignity he or she felt anticipating an imminent battery. *See* RESTATEMENT (SECOND) OF TORTS §§ 21, 32. Accordingly, the plaintiff must be aware that the battery is about to occur. *See, e.g., McCraney v. Flanagan*, 267 S.E.2d 404 (N.C. Ct. App. 1980). The person struck from behind by surprise may have a cause of action for battery, but not for assault.

The tortfeasor must intend to place the plaintiff in apprehension of the battery, or know with substantial certainty that his or her conduct will create that apprehension. *See* DOBBS, *supra*, § 33. The driver who carelessly backs into a bicyclist has not committed an assault, even if the bicyclist (but not the driver) was aware of the impending collision. It is not necessary, however, that the defendant intend to commit the battery. One may assault another if the intention is merely to scare the other person. *See id.*

For an assault to occur, there must be an act, and that act must be the reason the plaintiff fears the offensive contact. Mere threats are not enough. *See Webbier v. Thoroughbred Racing Protective Bureau, Inc.*, 254 A.2d 285, 290 (R.I. 1969). The act, however, can be minimal if accompanied by threats. *See, e.g., Muslow v. A.G. Edwards & Sons, Inc.*, 509 So. 2d 1012, 1020 (La. Ct. App. 1987); *Johnson v. Bollinger*, 356 S.E.2d 378 (N.C. Ct. App. 1987). The key question, according to the Restatement, is whether the plaintiff was "in reasonable apprehension of imminent battery." RESTATEMENT (SECOND) OF TORTS § 31 (1965). Rolling up one's sleeves, for example, can be enough of an "act" to constitute an assault if accompanied by other indications that sleeves are being rolled up in preparation for a battery. *See* SHAPO, *supra*, at 15 (*discussing Read v. Coker*, 138 Eng. Rep. 1437 (1853)).

B. Battery

Battery is the intentional, unconsented, and unprivileged harmful or offensive touching of another. RESTATEMENT (SECOND) OF TORTS § 13 (1965). Unlike assault, where the chief evil remedied is the mental distress felt by the plaintiff, battery compensates the plaintiff for the harm done by the contact itself. For liability to attach, the defendant must touch the plaintiff or something closely associated with the plaintiff, such as his or her clothing or the chair into which he or she was about to sit. *See Garratt v. Dailey*, 279 P.2d 1091 (Wash. 1955).

To be actionable, contact must be both unconsented-to and unprivileged. Thus, the physician that receives her patient's consent for surgery does not commit a battery upon making the incision. Consent is often in dispute in sports-related cases, for participants will be deemed to consent to contact typically occurring in the sport. Marginal applications of this rule are difficult and will be discussed in the following chapter, but at the extreme the application is simple. When Evander Holyfield agrees to fight Mike Tyson, Holyfield consents (explicitly or implicitly) to blows to his face and torso, but not to ear-bites. Football players consent to being tackled, at least when they are the ball-carriers. When Nancy Kerrigan agrees to participate in a figure-skating competition, she does not consent to being knee-capped by a jealous opponent's boyfriend. Fraud, however, can negate consent. If Mutt promises Jeff that the football game they are about to play is "two-hand touch," intending all the while to tackle him, Jeff's agreement to play will not amount to consent when Mutt buries Jeff's face into the ground.

The battery must be done "intentionally" for the defendant to be liable, but it is not clear exactly what must be intended. In the Restatement's phrasing, a defendant is liable for an offensive touching if he intended "to cause a harmful or offensive contact with" the plaintiff or another person, "or an imminent apprehension of such a contact." RESTATEMENT (SECOND) OF TORTS § 13 (1965). But that formulation is ambiguous, as it fails to specify whether intentional contact which is unintentionally harmful or offensive satisfies the standard. Some courts hold that the contact must be intended, but a defendant could be liable for battery if he intended neither harm nor offense. *See, e.g., White v. University of Idaho*, 797 P.2d 108 (Idaho 1990). Others conclude that a defendant will not be liable unless he intends to contact the plaintiff and he intends that the contact be harmful or offensive. *See Gouger v. Hardtke*, 482 N.W.2d 84 (Wis. 1992); *Caudle v. Betts*, 512 So. 2d 389, 390 (La. 1987). Another approach is to hold a defendant liable if he intends the contact, and if a reasonable person would believe the contact would be likely to cause harm or offense. *See* DOBBS, *supra*, § 30.

These complexities should not blind us to the basic doctrinal lesson that intention is required for battery, but that an intention to commit either assault or battery qualifies. Thus, if Cozzillio tries to scare Dimino by using a prop gun to fire a blank at him, but part of the blank flies out of the gun and into Dimino's eye, blinding him, Cozzillio is liable for battery. *See Brown v. Martinez*, 361 P.2d 152 (N.M. 1961); RESTATEMENT (SECOND) OF TORTS § 20 (1965). In addition, intent may be "transferred," so that the injured party may recover if the defendant intended to strike or scare someone else. Thus, in the prior example, if Cozzillio tried to scare Dimino with the prop gun, but part of the blank ejected and blinded Levinstein, Cozzillio would be liable for his assault of Dimino and his battery of Levinstein. *See Alteiri v. Colasso*, 362 A.2d 798 (Conn. 1975). In any event, purely accidental contact is not battery. *See Janelsins v. Button*, 648 A.2d 1039 (Md. Ct. Spec. App. 1994). (It may, of course, be negligence, which is discussed below.)

Whether a particular intentional touching will be harmful or offensive, and thus actionable, depends on the circumstances. Each of us must tolerate some amount of contact daily, simply because those contacts are consistent with norms in our society. *See McCracken v. O.B. Sloan*, 252 S.E.2d 250 (N.C. Ct. App. 1979). A tap on the shoulder, for example, is not a battery if done with slight force and designed to get the attention of the person touched. *See* SHAPO, *supra*, at 25 (citing *Coward v. Baddeley*, 157 Eng. Rep. 927 (Excheq. 1859)). Actions that would be reasonable, and thus inoffensive, in certain situations can become offensive in others. A coach's slapping of a player on the rear end after a good play may be commonplace and not a battery, but a much different result is likely for the person who slaps the rear end of a co-worker in an office. *See, e.g., Johnson v. Ramsey County*, 424 N.W.2d 800 (Minn. Ct. App. 1988) (kissing); *Regina v. Burden*, 1 W.W.R. 193 (B.C. Ct. App. 1982) (hand on thigh).

Damages for intentional torts include all the harm actually suffered, even if the extent of the harm caused is not foreseeable. The defendant must take the plaintiff as he is found, even if the plaintiff is unusually susceptible to injury—the so-called "eggshell plaintiff." *See, e.g., Stockett v. Tolin*, 791 F. Supp. 1536 (S.D. Fla. 1992); *Vosburg v. Putney*, 50 N.W. 403 (Wis. 1891).

C. Defamation

The media coverage surrounding professional sports is often harsh and unrelenting in its criticism of professional athletes. However, because professional athletes are "public figures," it is quite difficult for such a plaintiff to win a defamation suit. *See generally* Andrea K. Craig, *The Rise in Press Criticism of the Athlete and the Future of Libel Litigation Involving Athletes and the Press*, 4 SETON HALL J. SPORTS L. 527 (1994). Defamation comprises two separate torts, libel and slander, which are essentially the same except that libel is written defamation, while slander is spoken defamation.

Professor Prosser describes defamation as "an invasion of the interest in reputation and good name * * * Because defamation involves a person's reputation and the opinion others have of him, communication of an alleged defamatory statement must be made to a third party." PROSSER & KEETON § 111, at 771; *see also* RESTATEMENT (SECOND) OF TORTS §§ 558, 559 (1965). A communication is defamatory "[i]f it tends to harm the reputation of another as to lower him in the estimation of the community or to deter third persons from associating or dealing with him." RESTATEMENT (SECOND) OF TORTS § 559 (1965). The elements of the typical defamation include:

(a) a false and defamatory statement concerning another;

(b) an unprivileged publication to a third party; and

(c) fault amounting at least to negligence on the part of the publisher;

RESTATEMENT (SECOND) OF TORTS § 558 (1965).

By far, the most controversial criterion in the defamation scheme as it relates to professional sports is the "*unprivileged* publication" requirement. There are numerous illustrations of "privilege," both "absolute" and "qualified," that may be asserted to defend a defamation claim. Professor Prosser states that the notion of privilege rests upon the same conceptual footing as self-defense in an assault and battery context:

> [C]onduct which otherwise would be actionable is to escape liability because the defendant is acting in furtherance of some interest of social importance, which is entitled to protection even at the expense of uncompensated harm to the plaintiff's reputation.

PROSSER & KEETON § 114, at 815.

Given the obvious high profile of many professional and amateur athletes, the constitutional privilege reserved for matters involving public officials and public figures usually compels a judgment in the defendant's favor. *See generally New York Times v. Sullivan*, 376 U.S. 254 (1964); *Curtis Publishing Co. v. Butts*, 388 U.S. 130 (1967). Once the athlete or sports personality is deemed to be a "public figure," then an action for defamation will fail unless he or she can prove that the defamatory statements were made with "actual malice" and with knowledge of the statements' falseness or "reckless disregard" for their accuracy or truth. 376 U.S. at 279–80. (Private figures can recover for negligent defamatory statements, though punitive damages are available to private figures only after satisfying the *New York Times* "actual malice" standard. *See Gertz v. Robert Welch, Inc.*, 418 U.S. 323 (1974). The First Amendment protection has been invoked in numerous cases involving defamation claims by celebrated sports personages. *See, e.g., Sellers v. Time, Inc.*, 423 F.2d 887 (3d Cir. 1970); *Cepeda v. Cowles Magazines and Broadcasting, Inc.*, 392 F.2d 417 (9th Cir. 1968); *Dempsey v. Time, Inc.*, 252 N.Y.S.2d 186 (N.Y. Sup. Ct.), *aff'd*, 254 N.Y.S.2d 80 (N.Y. App. Div. 1964).

Statements of "opinion" are protected by the First Amendment and beyond the reach of defamation law, provided that the opinions expressed do not imply falsely that the speaker has facts to back up his claim. *See Milkovich v. Lorain Journal*, 497 U.S. 1 (1989); *Parks v. Steinbrenner*, 496 N.Y.S.2d 25 (App. Div. 1985).

D. Invasion of Privacy

Professional sports figures, along with other well known entertainers and other celebrities, occasionally suffer invasions of their privacy. Those invasions of privacy may

lead to tort liability under that term or under the label "intrusion." For liability to attach, there must be intentional intrusion into the plaintiff's private sphere, performed
in a manner "highly offensive to a reasonable person." RESTATEMENT (SECOND) OF
TORTS §652B (1977). Photographers can intrude on this zone of privacy if their activities become overzealous. *See Galella v. Onassis*, 487 F.2d 986 (2d Cir. 1973).

Invasion of privacy can assume any of these forms:

(1) "Unreasonable and highly offensive intrusion upon the seclusion of another;"
    PROSSER & KEETON §117, at 854.

(2) "Public disclosure of private facts;" *Id.* at 856.

(3) "Publicity which places plaintiff in a false light in the public eye." *Id.* at 863.

All of these causes of action have been implicated to some degree in cases involving
sports figures. For a summary of these examples of invasion of privacy as they relate to
athletes and other sports persona, see Yasser, *supra*, at 15:34 to 15–40. *See also Town &
Country Properties, Inc. v. Riggins*, 457 S.E.2d 356 (Va. 1995), discussed *infra* Chapter
19, Part V.

E. Appropriation and the Right of Publicity

Individuals have a right to control the use of their identities for commercial purposes, under certain situations. Because sports figures are effective spokespersons for
products and services, merchants often pay large amounts of money to use athletes in
advertisements. Other advertisers attempt to obtain the benefit of an athlete's endorsement without paying the athlete. This right is a species of intellectual property, and tort
law has developed the Right of Publicity as a way of protecting that property, just as
other tort doctrines protect plaintiffs' persons and physical property.

Courts have held that subject to certain limitations—most notably the privilege for
use of celebrities in news programs or stories—advertisers may not obtain a commercial advantage by using the likeness or name of a celebrity, or by using that person's
identity in other ways, without permission. *See Abdul-Jabbar v. General Motors Corp.*,
85 F.3d 407 (9th Cir. 1995) (involving the use of a former name); *Hirsch v. S.C. Johnson & Sons, Inc.*, 280 N.W.2d 129 (Wis. 1979) (involving the use of "Crazylegs"
Hirsch's nickname); *Spahn v. Julian Messner, Inc.*, 250 N.Y.S.2d 529 (N.Y. Sup. Ct.
1964). Though this tort is sometimes subsumed as part of the right of privacy, the
right of publicity primarily protects against the monetary value of an individual's
identity, rather than that individual's privacy. *See* DOBBS, *supra*, §425 (noting that
right-of-publicity cases "are closer to the fields of intellectual property, unfair competition, and trademarks than to the purely dignitary torts"). Some commentators and
courts use this difference to distinguish between appropriation and the right of publicity, with the former more concerned with compensating plaintiffs for the dignitary
harm caused by public disclosure and the right of publicity being a way of compensating plaintiffs for damage to celebrities' intellectual property in their identities. *See*
MICHAEL A. EPSTEIN, EPSTEIN ON INTELLECTUAL PROPERTY §13.02(E) (5th ed. 2006).
Large portions of this doctrine are unsettled, and it is uncertain how much the First
Amendment will inform the judgment of the tort's permissible scope. We will explore
some issues about the intersection of free speech and the right of publicity in the next
chapter.

II. Negligence

In most situations, we owe others a duty to act with reasonable care, i.e., non-negligently, to prevent foreseeable harms. Negligence generally involves careless conduct and an unintentional breach of that duty, causing injury to another. *See* RESTATEMENT (SECOND) OF TORTS § 281 (1965); WILLIAM L. PROSSER AND W. PAGE KEETON, *Prosser and Keeton on Torts* § 30, at 164 (5th ed. 1984). Accordingly, to prove a claim for negligence, the plaintiff must show (1) the existence of a duty of care from the defendant to the plaintiff; (2) the defendant's breach of that duty, i.e., that the defendant behaved negligently; (3) the causal connection between the breach and the plaintiff's injuries; and (4) damages. The existence of a duty is a question of law, while the others are questions of fact.

Causation and damages are rarely at issue in sports tort cases. Plaintiffs need to demonstrate both legal and proximate cause, *see, e.g., Palsgraf v. Long Island Railroad Co.*, 162 N.E. 99 (N.Y. 1928), and one can certainly imagine a scenario where proximate cause is in doubt: A batter carelessly neglects to apply pine tar to his bat to prevent slippage; the bat flies from his hands during a swing, into the stands; trying to get out of the way, a lemonade vendor dives to the floor, throwing his wares onto a nearby spectator; the spectator, very much surprised by the lemonade that has landed in his lap, springs up and elbows a neighboring spectator, knocking out her tooth; the second spectator sues the batter for negligence. *See Bain v. Gillespie*, 357 N.W.2d 47 (Iowa Ct. App. 1984) (holding that the harm to a business selling University of Iowa merchandise was an unforeseeable result of a basketball referee's allegedly bad call, which caused Iowa to be eliminated from the Big Ten Championship). In practice, however, most cases involve direct physical contact between the defendant and the plaintiff, resulting in injuries predictable for that sort of contact. A few examples from Chapters 19 and 20 illustrate that causation in these cases is typically a simple matter: a foul ball strikes a spectator in the eye (*Friedman v. Houston Sports Association*); a football player is struck across the neck by an opponent, resulting in a neck fracture (*Hackbart v. Cincinnati Bengals*); and a golfer is struck by a club in the head, killing him (*Brahatcek v. Millard School District*).

Often disputed, however, is the question of the duties of care owed between sports participants, between coaches or other supervisors and participants, between participants and spectators, etc. Also contested is the scope of the duty, where one exists at all. Do sports participants have a duty to behave non-negligently, or simply non-recklessly? Some courts have concluded that negligence is out of place in the sports context because if sports are played with the proper vigor there will be considerable "negligent" conduct resulting in injury. Negligence liability, these courts allege, will unduly deter sports participants and related personnel from playing with the appropriate level of enthusiasm. Others have insisted that athletes and supervisors must not create excessive dangers, and a negligence standard is the appropriate tool to encourage them to abide by that rule.

"The gist of a negligence-based claim is that the conduct involves a risk of harm that is not outweighed by the benefits to be derived from engaging in the conduct." Yasser, *supra*, § 15:3, at 15-4 to 15-5. *See United States v. Carroll Towing Co.*, 159 F.2d 169 (2d Cir. 1947). *See also Lee v. Mitchell Funeral Home Ambulance Service*, 606 P.2d 259 (Utah 1980). Although courts define negligence somewhat differently, the Restatement's "well-accepted general definition," SHAPO, *supra*, at 77, is "conduct which falls below the standard established by law for the protection of others against unreasonable risk of harm." RESTATEMENT (SECOND) OF TORTS § 282 (1965).

That "standard established by law" is generally the standard of "ordinary care under the circumstances." Defendants are expected to anticipate risks of which an average person would be aware, and negate those risks when doing so would be consistent with the ordinary actions a reasonable person would take.

Certain defendants, notably professionals such as physicians, are held to a higher standard of care. For them, they must not only comply with the standard of the ordinary, reasonable person, but they must provide that care that is provided by the reasonable professional. *See, e.g., Keebler v. Winfield Carraway Hospital*, 531 So. 2d 841, 845 (Ala. 1988); *Purtill v. Hess*, 489 N.E.2d 867 (Ill. 1986); *Rogers v. Price*, 698 So. 2d 723 (La. Ct. App. 1997); Dobbs, *supra*, § 242. Thus, a doctor whose conduct is consistent with the reasonable person standard may be negligent if it falls below the standard employed by a reasonable doctor in the defendant's community.

Following the reasoning of Judge Learned Hand in *Carroll Towing Co., supra*, several courts and commentators have attempted to assess when a defendant's conduct is negligent by comparing the cost of preventing accidents with the expected cost of the accidents themselves. As delineated in *Carroll Towing*, negligence means failing to prevent an accident when the cost of preventing it (B) is less than the product of the cost of the accident (L) and the probability of that accident occurring (P): thus, negligence is when B<PL. According to the devotees of the Hand test (and the law-and-economics movement as applied to negligence law), it makes little sense to force defendants to prevent accidents when the cost of preventing them exceeds the cost of the accidents themselves. By the same token, it is inefficient—and thus negligent—to allow accidents to occur when it would be less costly to prevent them. The Restatement provides for a similar standard: an "act is negligent if the risk is of such magnitude as to outweigh what the law regards as the utility of the act or of the particular manner in which it is done." Restatement (Second) of Torts § 291 (1965).

A negligence claim is subject to two principal defenses: contributory (or comparative) negligence and assumption of risk. Contributory negligence is defined as "conduct on the part of the plaintiff which falls below the standard to which he should conform for his own protection and which is a legally contributing cause co-operating with the negligence of the defendant in bringing about the plaintiff's harm." Restatement (Second) of Torts §463 (1965). The standard to which the plaintiff must conform is one of an objective, similarly situated, reasonable person—unless the plaintiff is a child or incapacitated person. *See* Restatement (Second) of Torts §464 (1965). If the plaintiff is found to be contributorily negligent, *i.e.*, the defendant establishes that the plaintiff's conduct was a significant feature leading to the injury, then the negligence claim will fail.

The doctrine of comparative negligence has supplanted contributory negligence for the most part, permitting the plaintiff to recover when both he and the defendant are negligent, but in an amount proportionately decreased by the plaintiff's fault. *See* Christopher J. Robinette & Paul G. Sherland, *Contributory or Comparative: Which is the Optimal Negligence Rule*, 24 N. Ill. U. L. Rev 41 (2003). In one popular formulation, comparative negligence "allows partial recovery for a plaintiff who is no more than 50% at fault." *See Friedman v. Houston Sports Ass'n*, 731 S.W.2d 572, 573 (Tex. App., 1st Dist. 1987). Others allow recovery only when the plaintiff is *less* at fault than the defendant, which is significantly different from the previous formulation because of juries' propensity to apportion fault 50-50. Still others have no threshold. In these "pure comparative negligence" jurisdictions, defendants pay their share of damages resulting from their conduct, regardless of the proportion of fault attributable to the plaintiff. For an excellent overview of the various comparative negligence regimes, see Victor E. Schwartz,

Comparative Negligence 56–88 (4th ed., 2002); *see also* Thomas J. DuFour, *The Proper Application of Judicial Decisions Overruling Established Tort Doctrines*, 65 B. U. L. Rev. 315 (1985).

The doctrine of assumption of risk comes in many forms. Express assumption of the risk, as the name implies, is an express waiver of the right to sue made in advance of the occurrence of the injury. *See, e.g., Dalury v. S-K-I, Ltd.*, 670 A.2d 795 (Vt. 1995). Implied assumption of the risk itself comes in two varieties: primary and secondary. Implied primary assumption of the risk is equivalent to a conclusion that the defendant owes no duty to protect the plaintiff from the risk or, as a matter of law, has not breached any such duty. There is no need for the defendant to show that the plaintiff specifically appreciated the risk of his activity; rather, the court will consider the risk to be an inherent part of the activity, and relieve the defendant of any obligation to negate it. For this reason, some argue that "assumption of the risk" is improperly used in this context, and that courts should instead say either that there was no duty or the duty of reasonable care was not breached. *See, e.g., Meistrich v. Casino Area Attractions, Inc.*, 155 A.2d 90 (1959); *Dobbs, supra*, §§ 211–215; Thomas C. Galligan, Jr., *A Most Dangerous Ball, in* Courting the Yankees: Legal Essays on the Bronx Bombers 69, 73 (Ettie Ward ed., 2003); Stephen D. Sugarman, *Assumption of Risk*, 31 Val. U. L. Rev. 833, 835 (1997) ("[W]hen we are tempted to say 'assumption of risk' we should instead say something else."); Symposium, *Assumption of Risk*, 22 La. L. Rev. 1 (1961).

Implied secondary assumption of the risk, by contrast, is the plaintiff's conscious taking of the risk that results in injury. Implied secondary assumption of the risk is a complete bar to recovery, but usually represents a question of fact to be decided by a jury, whereas express assumption of the risk and implied primary assumption of the risk are issues of law. To summarize,

> If the phrase assumption of the risk is used in the no-breach or no-duty context it is not being used to describe a traditional affirmative defense on which defendant would bear the burden of proof. Rather, it is being used in a manner which implies that the plaintiff has failed to establish its prima facie case.

Id. You should note that some states have codified their approaches to assumption of the risk, in legislation such as the following: "A person who takes part in any sport accepts as a matter of law the dangers that inhere therein insofar as they are obvious and necessary." 12 V.S.A. § 1037.

Either contributory negligence or assumption of risk could operate to bar a negligence claim by a typical sports participant. The availability of such defenses, however, may be more limited where the plaintiff has charged the defendant with reckless behavior. As the Restatement declares, recklessness is an act or omission by someone with a duty of care to the victim, when the actor

> know[s] or has reason to know of facts which would lead a reasonable man to realize, not only that his conduct creates an unreasonable risk of physical harm to another, but also that such risk is substantially greater than that which is necessary to make his conduct negligent.

Restatement (Second) of Torts § 500 (1965); Brendon D. Miller, *Hoke v. Cullinan Recklessness as the Standard for Recreational Sports Injuries*, 23 N. Ky. L. Rev. 409 (1996). Thus, recklessness differs from negligence in two ways. First, the degree of risk is "substantially greater" in recklessness than in negligence. Second, the defendant must know of the risk, or a reasonable person in his or her position would be aware of the risk. Mindless carelessness is negligent, but not always reckless.

One recurrent issue, both in and out of the sports context, is the duty owed by possessors of land to people injured on that land. Traditionally, the duty owed depended on the injured party's relationship to the land; that is to some extent true today, though some jurisdictions have adopted different rules. *See generally* Dobbs, *supra*, § 237. *Pinnell v. Bates*, 838 So.2d 198, 199 (Miss. 2002) (noting the widespread reconsideration of the categories of relationships). If the plaintiff was an "invitee," that is, he was invited on the land either as a member of the public or to transact business on the premises, the defendant was under the greatest duty. The defendant was required to inspect the land for potential dangers, and would be liable for injuries even if he was previously unaware of the dangerous situation. *See id.* § 235.

Persons in the second category, licensees, were entitled to less protection. Licensees, often social guests, are permitted on the land by consent of the possessor but are there for their own purposes — not those of the possessor. The possessor is obliged to make the licensee aware of any dangers of which the possessor knows or should know, but is not obliged to inspect the land for dangerous conditions. *See id.* § 233.

Trespassers, who make up the third category, are entitled to the least protection. As to these persons, who are on the land despite not having permission to be there, possessors need not abide by the duty of reasonable care. Instead, the duty is only not to conceal traps on land that could cause death or serious bodily injury. *See id.* § 232. As to a child trespasser, however, the possessor often faces a heightened duty. *See id.* § 236.

In recent years there has been a movement away from evaluating landowners' duties within these three categories, and toward requiring landowners to fulfill the obligation of "reasonable care." *See, e.g., Rowand v. Christian*, 443 P.2d 561 (Cal. 1968); *Pinnell, supra*, at 199; Dobbs, *supra*, § 237.

Overwhelmingly, in states that retain the traditional formulation, sports tort cases involving the duties owed by land possessors involve injury to invitees. Whatever standard applies, however, it is necessary to assess whether the danger on the land is the result of a breach of that duty.

Because the sports context presents dangers that are the very reason the invitees are in attendance, some risks of injury that would be considered unreasonable in another context will not amount to a breach of the reasonable-care duty when the injury is sports-related. In Chapter 20 we will consider the duties owed by possessors of sports facilities to spectators, who are subjected to risks of flying balls, sticks, pucks, and portions of stock cars, to name a few potential dangers. Courts have generally concluded that operators of those facilities have an obligation to construct some barriers to protect spectators from projectiles, but have not required facilities to insure the safety of their patrons. Fans who sit in unprotected areas by and large do so at their own peril.

Further, the obviousness of a risk may itself satisfy the duty, because a danger that is obvious is one that usually can be avoided. *See, e.g., Green v. City of New York*, 693 N.Y.S.2d 43 (App. Div. 1999) (holding that there was no breach when the plaintiff slipped on a basketball court, because he was aware of the defect). As Professor Dobbs explains, "the risk created by the defendant must be judged in the light of the plaintiff's apparent capacity to deal with it." Dobbs, *supra*, § 212, at 541 n.3. Again, some courts will consider this an issue of duty; others will consider it one of breach; and others will consider the issue one of (primary) assumption of risk.

III. Products Liability

Section 402A of the Restatement sets forth the rule that sellers of defective and unreasonably dangerous products are strictly liable for injuries caused by those products. RESTATEMENT (SECOND) OF TORTS § 402A. *See also* RESTATEMENT OF PRODUCTS LIABILITY § 1. Strictly liable means that the defendant is liable even though it took reasonable care to ensure the safety of the product, *i.e.*, that it was not negligent. There are three types of cases for which strict products liability may be an available theory of recovery.

First, sellers of products with *manufacturing defects* will be liable for injuries caused by those defects. *See generally* DOBBS, *supra*, § 355. Thus, if a car is sold without brakes because the assembly-line worker fell asleep and forgot to install them, sellers of the car—including the manufacturer—will be strictly liable. *See, e.g., Lee v. Crookston Coca-Cola Bottling Co.*, 188 N.W.2d 426 (Minn. 1971).

Second, if a product is *defectively designed, i.e.*, that the product was made according to specifications, but those specifications could have called for the manufacture of a safer product, then sellers may be strictly liable. This aspect of strict products liability is more controversial than is liability for manufacturing defects, because in designing products manufacturers must account for several considerations, only one of which is safety from a particular danger. Juries must often consider the reasonableness of a design in light of the sacrifices, for example to cost and style, that would need to be made to make the product safer. *See* RESTATEMENT OF PRODUCTS LIABILITY § 2. As a result, defective-design cases can resemble negligence actions. *See* DOBBS, *supra*, §§ 357, 359.

Third, sellers may be liable for *failure to warn* consumers about dangerous aspects of products. *See, e.g., Ross Labs. v. Thies*, 725 P.2d 1076 (Alaska 1986). There is widespread disagreement, however, about when this duty to warn should be applicable, and whether it is (or should be) significantly different from a negligence duty.

IV. Workers' Compensation

In general, state legislatures have responded to injuries arising in the workplace by developing a no-fault system of compensation. At present, all 50 states have adopted workers' compensation laws. *See* 1 ARTHUR LARSON & LEX K. LARSON, LARSON'S WORKERS' COMPENSATION LAW § 2.02, at 2–15 (2004). (Florida, however, has statutorily excluded professional athletes from workers' compensation. *See* Fla. Stat. Ann. § 440.04(2); *Rudolph v. Miami Dolphins, Ltd.*, 447 So.2d 284 (Fla. Dist. Ct. App. 1983).) In most jurisdictions, workers' compensation is now the exclusive remedy against the employer for on-the-job injuries or illnesses; various actions that may have rested on tort grounds have been absorbed. In exchange for the ceiling on liability and the virtual elimination of negligence as an actionable offense, the employer is forced to surrender such defenses as contributory negligence and assumption of risk. *See* MARTIN J. GREENBERG, SPORTS LAW PRACTICE § 12.03, at 1103 (1993). The exclusiveness of the remedy provisions of the typical workers' compensation scheme have operated in the sports context to deprive a player of common law tort and contract claims when the athlete is found to be eligible for the no-fault benefits. *See, e.g., Brinkman v. Buffalo Bills*, 433 F. Supp. 699 (W.D.N.Y. 1977); *Ellis v. Rocky Mountain Empire Sports*, Inc., 602 P.2d 895

(Colo. Ct. App. 1979). For an excellent overview of the interplay of traditional tort law and various workers' compensation schemes, see Jean Macchiaroli Eggen, *Toxic Reproductive and Genetic Hazards in the Workplace—Challenging the Myths of the Tort and Workers' Compensation Systems*, 60 FORDHAM L. REV. 843 (1992).

Still, notwithstanding the basic exclusivity principle that governs work-related injuries or illnesses, there are circumstances in which remedies beyond workers' compensation will be available. Of relatively recent vintage are decisions holding that certain types of intentional torts will not be barred even though the governing legislation touts workers' compensation as the exclusive remedy. *See Johns-Manville Products Corp. v. The Superior Court Contra Costa County*, 612 P.2d 948 (Cal. 1980); *Mandolidis v. Elkins Indus. Inc.*, 246 S.E.2d 907 (W. Va. 1978). *See also* Theodore F. Haas, *On Reintegrating Workers' Compensation and Employers' Liability*, 21 GA. L. REV. 843, 844 (1987); Mark Zebrowski, *Indemnity Clauses and Workers' Compensation: A Proposal for Preserving the Employers' Limited Liability*, 70 CAL. L. REV. 1421 (1982). Thus, certain employer conduct may be so egregious as to warrant disqualification from the broad escape hatch for typical negligence claims that most workers' compensation regimes provide. There may also be numerous situations in which the conduct of third parties is implicated, thus calling into question the continued exclusivity of workers' compensation as a remedy. Depending, of course, on the particular workers' compensation statute, these events are often deemed to rest outside of the workers' compensation regime and thus actionable in tort. *See* Karen M. Moran, *Indemnity Under Workers' Compensation: Recognizing a Special Legal Relationship Between Manufacturer and Employer*, 1987 DUKE L. J. 1095, 1096–97.

In some instances, the athlete may vigorously argue that his cause of action is covered by workers' compensation so as to be assured of some guaranteed recompense without facing an employer's contributory negligence defense. In other situations, the athlete may contend that his situation is *not* covered in order to avoid the relatively insignificant recovery provided by the statute in favor of the larger payday that may be available through a tort claim. Virtually all courts, however, have held that professional athletes are covered by workers' compensation, and thus may not sue for on-the-job injuries. *See* 2 LARSON, *supra*, § 22.04(1)(b), at 22-11 ("Injuries in [professional] sports are so routinely treated as compensable in the great majority of jurisdictions that they seldom appear in reported appellate decisions."); *Pro-Football, Inc. v. Uhlenhake*, 558 S.E.2d 571 (Va. 2002); *Larramore v. Richardson Sports, Ltd., d/b/a Carolina Panthers*, 540 S.E.2d 768 (N.C. Ct. App. 2000), *aff'd* 546 S.E.2d 87 (N.C. 2001) (upholding an award to a player injured during training camp based on the weekly average of his salary, even though he might have been cut and not received any salary if he remained healthy); *Bayless v. Philadelphia National League Club*, 472 F. Supp. 625 (E.D. Pa. 1979), *aff'd*, 579 F.2d 37 (3d Cir. 1978). *But see Palmer v. Kansas City Chiefs Football Club*, 621 S.W.2d 350 (Mo. App. 1981).

There have been some controversies in determining whether injuries that result from long-term demands of the job, rather than from specific isolated events, are the sort of injuries that are compensable. The few available cases have treated those long-term injuries as falling within workers' compensation. *See Pittsburgh Steelers, Inc. v. W.C.A.B. (Williams)*, 814 A.2d 788 (Pa. Commw. Ct. 2002) (football player's knee); *Sielicki v. New York Yankees*, 388 So. 2d 25 (Fla. Dist. Ct. App. 1980) (pitcher's arm). In *Sielicki*, for example, a Yankee pitcher was released after developing problems with his elbow that made it impossible for him to pitch. He had a history of elbow trouble, and had surgery to relocate his ulnar nerve in 1974. Sielicki pitched without incident in the 1976 and 1977 seasons, but in 1978 spring training he felt elbow tightness and muscle spasms. The Yankees argued that Sielicki could not recover under the workers' compensation policy because there had not been any specific incident during a game when Sielicki was pitching in which the injury was aggravated. The court held otherwise, concluding that Sielicki had demonstrated through doctors' testimony that the elbow condition was the result of repetitive stress caused by pitching, and awarded Sielicki benefits.

One important facet of workers' compensation is that such compensation satisfies the obligations of (i.e., preempts a tort suit against) not only the employer itself, but also "coemployees," including supervisors. Recently, the Supreme Court of Minnesota applied this doctrine to preclude a tort suit by a widow of a deceased Minnesota Viking against two coemployees—members of the Vikings' training staff. *Stringer v. Minnesota Vikings Football Club, LLC.*, 705 N.W.2d 746 (Minn. 2005). (Despite the caption, Mrs. Stringer did not present any claim against the Vikings before the Minnesota Supreme Court. *See id.* at 748 n.1) The plaintiff had alleged that the trainers were grossly negligent in failing to diagnose and treat the decedent's heat stroke, which occurred while the player was practicing at the club's training camp. The court held that workers' compensation covered the acts and omissions alleged, because the trainers were acting within the scope of their employment. The court reasoned that permitting injured workers to recover in tort from fellow employees would shift the burden of compensating injured workers from employers to employees. Accordingly, "when the alleged breach of duty falls within the workers' compensation compromise between employers and employees, the coemployee should not be held liable." *Id.* at 756.

Another unresolved question is whether participation in an individual sport such as tennis or golf, renders an athlete eligible for workers' compensation. These cases will turn on whether the athlete meets the statutory definition of "employee," or whether he or she is properly classified as an independent contractor. Broadly stated, the determination of employee status will necessitate an examination of the degree to which the putative employer exercises control over the claimant or an assessment of the nature of the work performed in relation to the employer's overall business enterprise. *See* Benjamin T. Boscolo & Gerald Herz, *Professional Athletes and the Law of Workers' Compensation Rights and Remedies, in* Law of Professional and Amateur Sports § 17:3 (Gary A. Uberstine ed., 2004). *See also Thompson v. Travelers Indem. Co.*, 777 S.W.2d 722 (Tex. App. 1989); *Mundy v. Churchill Downs, Inc.*, 600 S.W.2d 487 (Ky. App. 1980).

Most courts have held that *officials* are independent contractors not entitled to workers' compensation for injuries during games, but a few courts have found them to be employees. *Compare Gale v. Greater Washington, D.C., Softball Umpires Ass'n*, 311 A.2d 817 (Md. Ct. Spec. App. 1973) (independent contractor), *with Ford v. Bonner County School Dist.*, 612 P.2d 557 (Idaho 1980) (employee).

Perhaps the most significant current dispute at the intersection of sports law and workers' compensation is whether college scholarship athletes are entitled to workers' compensation coverage. Is the relationship between a student and a university contractual in nature? If so, is the scholarship athlete a party to an employment contract and thereby vested with the benefits of other university employees? *See* Michael J. Cozzillio, *The Athletic Scholarship and the College National Letter of Intent, A Contract By Any Other Name*, 35 Wayne L. Rev. 1275, 1299 n.95 (1989); *see also* Eric D. LeBeau & Thomas H. Sawyer, *Worker's Compensation and Scholarship Athletes: Are They Protected?*, 10 J. Legal Aspects of Sports 18 (2000); Sean Alan Roberts, *College Athletes, Universities, and Workers' Compensation: Placing the Relationship in the Proper Context by Recognizing Scholarship Athletes as Employees*, 37 S. Tex. L. Rev. 1315 (1996). There is a split of authority on the question of a scholarship-athlete's eligibility for workers' compensation benefits. For cases finding that the athlete is not an employee entitled to such coverage, see *Waldrep v. Texas Employers Insurance Ass'n*, 21 S.W.3d 692 (Tex. Ct. App. 2000); *Rensing v. Indiana State University Board of Trustees*, 444 N.E.2d 1170 (Ind. 1983); *Coleman v. Western Mich. Univ.*, 336 N.W.2d 224 (Mich. Ct. App. 1983). For a countervailing view, see *Van Horn v. Industrial Accident Comm'n*, 33 Cal. Rptr. 169 (Cal. Ct. App. 1963); *University of Denver v. Nemeth*, 257 P.2d 423 (Colo. 1953).

If a player under a salary guarantee clause is eligible for workers' compensation, the player will not be doubly indemnified as a result of a work-related injury. In all likelihood, the club will be permitted to deduct workers' compensation benefits from any income substitution payments paid to the player (for time not worked) under the contract. *See generally* Boscolo & Herz § 17:16. The standard player contract often directly addresses this question. For example, Paragraph 10 of the National Football League Player Contract provides:

> Any compensation paid to Player under this contract * * * for a period during which he is entitled to workers' compensation benefits * * * will be deemed an advance payment of workers' compensation benefits due Player, and Club will be entitled to be reimbursed the amount of such payment out of any award of workers' compensation.

* * *

In the succeeding chapters, we will see the ways in which these tort doctrines have been applied in the peculiar context of sports. We will evaluate the place of intentional torts where the very rules of the sports call for violent collisions. Then we will analyze negligence law, as applied to both on-the-field injuries and spectator injuries. We will also look at liability of supervisors, injuries caused by defective equipment, and injuries to athletes' dignitary and economic rights before turning to the question when on-the-field conduct crosses the line from vigorous competition to criminal violence.

Chapter 19

Torts and the Sports Participant: Volenti Non Fit Injuria ("To a Willing Person a Wrong Is Not Done")?

I. Introduction

There are myriad examples of tortious conduct in the world of professional and amateur sports. For the most part, traditional tort approaches to problems arising in more typical settings apply with equal force to the sports scene. Of course, sports contexts may present unusual scenarios that call for somewhat unique and interesting applications. In the succeeding sections, we will address questions of liability stemming from physical injuries suffered due to (a) intentional conduct between participants, (b) negligent or reckless conduct between participants or by supervisors, and (c) equipment defects. Following this examination of injuries occurring in athletic competition mostly due to the actions of co-participants, we turn to the supervisory duties of game officials, coaches, schools and other entities. Lastly, we will consider the torts of defamation and intrusions upon athletes' or other sports figures' rights to privacy and publicity. Chapter 20 will examine issues relating to spectator injuries and Chapter 21 will consider when on-the-field actions become so violent as to subject sports participants to criminal liability.

The following material will not exhaust the possible areas of controversy that could arise under the broad heading of tort law. It will, however, provide an overview of some classic tort principles as they have been applied in the idiosyncratic universe of sports and sports celebrities.

II. On-the-Field Disputes: Aggressiveness or Assault?

One of the more troublesome questions in competitive athletics, particularly in the context of team sports, is the differentiation between legitimate, intense contact and activity that rises to the level of actionable and, perhaps, even criminal, conduct. The problem is made more difficult by the fact that the leagues or other governing bodies have devised penalties or other sanctions for conduct that goes beyond the prescribed rules of play. Thus, the line of demarcation is not simply acceptable versus unacceptable behavior. There is an entire range of activity that is punishable (assessment of a foul or penalty) by game officials but is not remotely considered to be against societal rules or actionable either in a civil or criminal sense. Thus, if an employee on an assembly line punches a co-worker as they are heading for the cafeteria, he may be viewed much more critically than a football player who strikes an opponent after the whistle has blown. Still, there are limits to the "boys will be boys" type of attitude that pervades many professional and amateur athletic events. Drawing the line is no easy matter and requires an understanding of the differentiation between, and, at times, overlap of, concepts such as intentional tort, recklessness, and negligence.

Hackbart v. Cincinnati Bengals, Inc.
601 F.2d 516 (10th Cir. 1979)

DOYLE, Circuit Judge:

The question in this case is whether in a regular season professional football game an injury which is inflicted by one professional football player on an opposing player can give rise to liability in tort where the injury was inflicted by the intentional striking of a blow during the game.

The injury occurred in the course of a game between the Denver Broncos and the Cincinnati Bengals, which game was being played in Denver in 1973. The Broncos' defensive back, Dale Hackbart, was the recipient of the injury and the Bengals' offensive back, Charles "Booby" Clark, inflicted the blow which produced it.

* * *

Clark was an offensive back and just before the injury he had run a pass pattern to the right side of the Denver Broncos' end zone. The injury flowed indirectly from this play. The pass was intercepted by Billy Thompson, a Denver free safety, who returned it to mid-field. The subject injury occurred as an aftermath of the pass play.

As a consequence of the interception, the roles of Hackbart and Clark suddenly changed. Hackbart, who had been defending, instantaneously became an offensive player. Clark, on the other hand, became a defensive player. Acting as an offensive player, Hackbart attempted to block Clark by throwing his body in front of him. He [Hackbart] thereafter remained on the ground. He turned, and with one knee on the ground, watched the play following the interception.

The trial court's finding was that Charles Clark, "acting out of anger and frustration, but without a specific intent to injure * * * stepped forward and struck a blow with his right forearm to the back of the kneeling plaintiff's head and neck with sufficient force to cause both players to fall forward to the ground." Both players, without complaining to the officials or to one another, returned to their respective sidelines since the ball had changed hands and the offensive and defensive teams of each had been substituted. Clark testified at trial that his frustration was brought about by the fact that his team was losing the game.

Due to the failure of the officials to view the incident, a foul was not called. However, the game film showed very clearly what had occurred. Plaintiff did not at the time report the happening to his coaches or to anyone else during the game. However, because of the pain which he experienced he was unable to play golf the next day. He did not seek medical attention, but the continued pain caused him to report this fact and the incident to the Bronco trainer who gave him treatment. Apparently he played on the specialty teams for two successive Sundays, but after that the Broncos released him on waivers. (He was in his thirteenth year as a player.) He sought medical help and it was then that it was discovered by the physician that he had a serious neck fracture injury.

Despite the fact that the defendant Charles Clark admitted that the blow which had been struck was not accidental, that it was intentionally administered, the trial court ruled as a matter of law that the game of professional football is basically a business which is violent in nature, and that the available sanctions are imposition of penalties and expulsion from the game. Notice was taken of the fact that many fouls are overlooked; that the game is played in an emotional and noisy environment; and that incidents such as that here complained of are not unusual.

* * *

The evidence at the trial uniformly supported the proposition that the intentional striking of a player in the head from the rear is not an accepted part of either the playing rules or the general customs of the game of professional football. * * *

[T]he district court's assumption was that Clark had inflicted an intentional blow which would ordinarily generate civil liability and which might bring about a criminal sanction as well, but that since it had occurred in the course of a football game, it should not be subject to the restraints of the law; that if it were it would place unreasonable impediments and restraints on the activity. The judge also pointed out that courts are ill-suited to decide the different social questions and to administer conflicts on what is much like a battlefield where the restraints of civilization have been left on the sidelines.

We are forced to conclude that the result reached is not supported by evidence.

* * *

Plaintiff, of course, maintains that tort law applicable to the injury in this case applies on the football field as well as in other places. On the other hand, plaintiff does not rely on the theory of negligence being applicable. This is in recognition of the fact that subjecting another to unreasonable risk of harm, the essence of negligence, is inherent in the game of football, for admittedly it is violent. Plaintiff maintains that in the area of contributory fault, a vacuum exists in relationship to intentional infliction of injury. Since negligence does not apply, contributory negligence is inapplicable. Intentional or reckless contributory fault could theoretically at least apply to infliction of injuries in reckless disregard of the rights of others. This has some similarity to contributory negligence and undoubtedly it would apply if the evidence would justify it. But it is highly questionable whether a professional football player consents or submits to injuries caused by conduct not within the rules, and there is no evidence which we have seen which shows this. However, the trial court did not consider this question and we are not deciding it.

Contrary to the position of the court then, there are no principles of law which allow a court to rule out certain tortious conduct by reason of general roughness of the game or difficulty of administering it.

Indeed, the evidence shows that there are rules of the game which prohibit the intentional striking of blows. Thus, Article 1, Item 1, Subsection C, provides that:

> All players are prohibited from striking on the head, face or neck with the heel, back or side of the hand, wrist, forearm, elbow or clasped hands.

Thus the very conduct which was present here is expressly prohibited by the rule which is quoted above.

The general customs of football do not approve the intentional punching or striking of others. That this is prohibited was supported by the testimony of all of the witnesses. They testified that the intentional striking of a player in the face or from the rear is prohibited by the playing rules as well as the general customs of the game. Punching or hitting with the arms is prohibited. Undoubtedly these restraints are intended to establish reasonable boundaries so that one football player cannot intentionally inflict a serious injury on another. Therefore, the notion is not correct that all reason has been abandoned, whereby the only possible remedy for the person who has been the victim of an unlawful blow is retaliation.

* * *

The Restatement of Torts Second, § 500, distinguishes between reckless and negligent misconduct. Reckless misconduct differs from negligence, according to the authors, in that negligence consists of mere inadvertence, lack of skillfulness or failure to take precautions; reckless misconduct, on the other hand, involves a choice or adoption of a course of action either with knowledge of the danger or with knowledge of facts which would disclose this danger to a reasonable man. Recklessness also differs in that it consists of intentionally doing an act with knowledge not only that it contains a risk of harm to others as does negligence, but that it actually involves a risk substantially greater in magnitude than is necessary in the case of negligence. The authors explain the difference, therefore, in the degree of risk by saying that the difference is so significant as to amount to a difference in kind.

Subsection (f) also distinguishes between reckless misconduct and intentional wrongdoing. To be reckless the Act must have been intended by the actor. At the same time, the actor does not intend to cause the harm which results from it. It is enough that he realized, or from the facts should have realized, that there was a strong probability that harm would result even though he may hope or expect that this conduct will prove harmless. Nevertheless, existence of probability is different from substantial certainty which is an ingredient of intent to cause the harm which results from the act.

Therefore, recklessness exists where a person knows that the act is harmful but fails to realize that it will produce the extreme harm which it did produce. It is in this respect that recklessness and intentional conduct differ in degree.

In the case at bar the defendant Clark admittedly acted impulsively and in the heat of anger, and even though it could be said from the admitted facts that he intended the act, it could also be said that he did not intend to inflict serious injury which resulted from the blow which he struck.

In ruling that recklessness is the appropriate standard and that assault and battery is not the exclusive one, we are saying that these two liability concepts are not necessarily opposed one to the other. Rather, recklessness under §500 of the Restatement might be regarded, for the purpose of analysis at least, a lesser included act. Assault and battery, having originated in a common law writ, is narrower than recklessness in its scope. In essence, two definitions enter into it. The assault is an attempt coupled with the present ability to commit a violent harm against another. Battery is the unprivileged or unlawful touching of another. Assault and battery then call for an intent, as does recklessness. But in recklessness the intent is to do the act, but without an intent to cause the particular harm. It is enough if the actor knows that there is a strong probability that harm will result. Thus, the definition fits perfectly the fact situation here.Surely, then, no reason exists to compel appellant to employ the assault and battery standard which does not comfortably apply fully in preference to the standard which meets this fact situation.

* * *

The cause is reversed and remanded for a new trial in accordance with the foregoing views.

Notes and Questions

1. Is a "late hit" in football or a "low blow" in boxing *ever* a foreseeable event? Is the fact that one sees the possibility of a heinous act a *de facto* consent to its occurrence and the injury that results? A plausible interpretation would seem to be that late hits and low blows, "within reason," are anticipated events in a football game or boxing match, even though they are punishable by a fifteen yard penalty (football) or the occasional surrender of a point or a round (boxing). Further, it is equally reasonable to assume that the more blatant the offense (*e.g.*, a hit ten seconds after the whistle blows, repeated punches below the beltline, or a debilitating bite to the facial area), the greater the likelihood of criminal sanctions. *See generally* Diane V. White, *Sports Violence as Criminal Assault: Development of the Doctrine by Canadian Courts*, 1986 DUKE L. J. 1030, 1041–44 (1986). We will return to the theme of criminal liability in Chapter 21.

2. Take particular note of the court's discussion of the recklessness standard. If this event occurred outside of the sports context, would Hackbart's conduct be considered reckless or intentional? *Cf., e.g., Garratt v. Dailey*, 279 P.2d 1091 (Wash. 1955) (discussing the intent necessary for one to be liable to another for battery when removing a chair into which the victim was about to sit); *Vosburg v. Putney*, 50 N.W. 403 (Wis. 1891) (holding that a student's kick to the leg of a classmate constituted battery).

3. Suppose an injury-causing action was prohibited by the playing rules but accepted by what *Hackbart* called "the general customs of the game." The next case presents that vexing situation.

Avila v. Citrus Community College District
131 P.3d 383 (Cal. 2006)

Werdegar, J.

* * *

Jose Luis Avila, a Rio Hondo Community College (Rio Hondo) student, played baseball for the Rio Hondo Roadrunners. On January 5, 2001, Rio Hondo was playing a preseason road game against the Citrus Community College Owls (Citrus College). During the game, a Roadrunners pitcher hit a Citrus College batter with a pitch; when Avila came to bat in the top of the next inning, the Citrus College pitcher hit him in the head with a pitch, cracking his batting helmet. Avila alleges the pitch was an intentional "beanball" thrown in retaliation for the previous hit batter or, at a minimum, was thrown negligently.

Avila staggered, felt dizzy, and was in pain. The Rio Hondo manager told him to go to first base. Avila did so, and when he complained to the Rio Hondo first base coach, he was told to stay in the game. At second base, he still felt pain, numbness, and dizziness. A Citrus College player yelled to the Rio Hondo dugout that the Roadrunners needed a pinch runner. Avila walked off the field and went to the Rio Hondo bench. No one tended to his injuries. As a result, Avila suffered unspecified serious personal injuries.

* * *

To recover for negligence, Avila must demonstrate, inter alia, that the District breached a duty of care it owed him. Generally, each person has a duty to exercise reasonable care in the circumstances and is liable to those injured by the failure to do so. * * *

The existence of " " " [d]uty" is not an immutable fact of nature " 'but only an expression of the sum total of those *considerations of policy* which lead the law to say that the particular plaintiff is entitled to protection.' " " " Thus, the existence and scope of a defendant's duty is an issue of law, to be decided by a court, not a jury. When the injury is to a sporting participant, the considerations of policy and the question of duty necessarily become intertwined with the question of assumption of risk.

The traditional version of the assumption of risk doctrine required proof that the plaintiff voluntarily accepted a specific known and appreciated risk. The doctrine depended on the actual subjective knowledge of the given plaintiff and, where the elements were met, was an absolute defense to liability for injuries arising from the known risk.

California's abandonment of the doctrine of contributory negligence in favor of comparative negligence led to a reconceptualization of the assumption of risk. * * * Applied in the sporting context, it precludes liability for injuries arising from those risks deemed inherent in a sport; as a matter of law, others have no legal duty to eliminate those risks or otherwise protect a sports participant from them. Under this duty approach, a court need not ask what risks a particular plaintiff subjectively knew of and chose to encounter, but instead must evaluate the fundamental nature of the sport and the defendant's role in or relationship to that sport in order to determine whether the defendant owes a duty to protect a plaintiff from the particular risk of harm. A majority of this court has since embraced the [recklessness standard].

Here, the host school's role is a mixed one: its players are coparticipants, its coaches and managers have supervisorial authority over the conduct of the game, and other representatives of the school are responsible for the condition of the playing facility. [C]oparticipants have a duty not to act recklessly, outside the bounds of the sport and coaches and instructors have a duty not to increase the risks inherent in sports participation. [T]hose responsible for maintaining athletic facilities have a similar duty not to increase the inherent risks * * *. In contrast, those with no relation to the sport have no such duty.

In interscholastic and intercollegiate competition, the host school is not a disinterested, uninvolved party vis-à-vis the athletes it invites to compete on its grounds. Without a visiting team, there can be no competition. Intercollegiate competition allows a school to * * * offer its students the benefits of athletic participation and * * * reap the economic and marketing benefits that derive from maintenance of a major sports program. * * * In light of those benefits, we hold that in interscholastic and intercollegiate competition, the host school and its agents owe a duty to home and visiting players alike to, at a minimum, not increase the risks inherent in the sport. Schools and universities are already vicariously liable for breaches by the coaches they employ, who owe a duty to their own athletes not to increase the risks of sports participation. No reason appears to conclude intercollegiate athletics will be harmed by making visiting players, necessary coparticipants in any game, additional beneficiaries of the limited duty not to increase the risks of participation. * * *

* * * The duty of a host school to its own and visiting players in school-supervised athletic events is an exception to the general absence of duty, an exception plainly warranted by the relationship of the host school to all the student participants in the competitions it sponsors.

* * *

We consider next whether Avila has alleged facts supporting breach of the duty not to enhance the inherent risks of his sport. * * * Being hit by a pitch is an inherent risk of baseball. The dangers of being hit by a pitch, often thrown at speeds approaching 100 miles per hour, are apparent and well known: being hit can result in serious injury or, on rare tragic occasions, death.[9]

Being *intentionally* hit is likewise an inherent risk of the sport, so accepted by custom that a pitch intentionally thrown at a batter has its own terminology: "brushback," "beanball," "chin music." In turn, those pitchers notorious for throwing at hitters are "headhunters." Pitchers intentionally throw at batters to disrupt a batter's timing or back him away from home plate, to retaliate after a teammate has been hit, or to punish a batter for having hit a home run. Some of the most respected baseball managers and pitchers have openly discussed the fundamental place throwing at batters has in their sport. * * * As Los Angeles Dodgers Hall of Fame pitcher Don Drysdale and New York Giants All Star pitcher Sal "The Barber" Maglie have explained, intentionally throwing at batters can also be an integral part of pitching tactics, a tool to help get batters out by upsetting their frame of mind. Drysdale and Maglie are not alone; past and future Hall of Famers, from Early Wynn and Bob Gibson to Pedro Martinez and Roger Clemens, have relied on the actual or threatened willingness to throw at batters to aid their pitching.

While these examples relate principally to professional baseball, "[t]here is nothing legally significant * * * about the level of play" in this case. The laws of physics that make a thrown baseball dangerous and the strategic benefits that arise from disrupting a batter's timing are only minimally dependent on the skill level of the participants, and we see no reason to distinguish between collegiate and professional baseball in applying primary assumption of the risk.

It is true that intentionally throwing at a batter is forbidden by the rules of baseball. But "even when a participant's conduct violates a rule of the game and may subject the violator to internal sanctions prescribed by the sport itself, imposition of *legal liability* for such conduct might well alter fundamentally the nature of the sport by deterring participants from vigorously engaging in activity that falls close to, but on the permissible side of, a prescribed rule." It is one thing for an umpire to punish a pitcher who hits a batter by ejecting him from the game, or for a league to suspend the pitcher; it is quite another for tort law to chill any pitcher from throwing inside, i.e., close to the batter's body—a permissible and essential part of the sport—for fear of a suit over an errant pitch. For better or worse, being intentionally thrown at is a fundamental part and inherent risk of the sport of baseball. It is not the function of tort law to police such conduct.

[A]n athlete does not assume the risk of a coparticipant's intentional or reckless conduct "totally outside the range of the ordinary activity involved in the sport." Here, even if the Citrus College pitcher intentionally threw at Avila, his conduct did not fall

---

9. Most famously, in August 1920, Cleveland Indians shortstop Roy Chapman was hit by a pitch from the New York Yankees' Carl Mays. He died the next day. At least seven other batters in organized baseball have been killed by pitches.

outside the range of ordinary activity involved in the sport. The District owed no duty to Avila to prevent the Citrus College pitcher from hitting batters, even intentionally. Consequently, the doctrine of primary assumption of the risk bars any claim predicated on the allegation that the Citrus College pitcher negligently or intentionally threw at Avila.

* * * "One who enters into a sport, game or contest may be taken to consent to physical contacts consistent with the understood rules of the game." (Prosser & Keeton, Torts (5th ed.1984) § 18, p. 114.) Thus, the boxer who steps into the ring consents to his opponent's jabs; the football player who steps onto the gridiron consents to his opponent's hard tackle; the hockey goalie who takes the ice consents to face his opponent's slapshots; and, here, the baseball player who steps to the plate consents to the possibility the opposing pitcher may throw near or at him. The complaint establishes Avila voluntarily participated in the baseball game; as such, his consent would bar any battery claim as a matter of law.

* * *

Kennard, J. [concurring in part and dissenting in part]

* * *

Central to the majority's holding is its reliance on the legal rule that there is no duty to avoid risks "inherent" in a recreational sport. * * * I have repeatedly voiced my disagreement with this court's adoption of that rule * * * because it "distort[s] the negligence concept of due care to encompass reckless and intentional conduct." Moreover, because the question of what is "inherent" in a sport is amorphous and fact-intensive, it is impossible for trial courts "to discern, at an early stage in the proceedings, which risks are inherent in a given sport." As explained below, this case illustrates that the no-duty-for-sports rule is unworkable and unfair.

* * *

Relying on the no-duty-for-sports rule, the majority, in essence, concludes that even if the District's coaches had ordered the Citrus pitcher to hit Avila in the head with a pitched ball, the District is not liable for Avila's injuries because the risk that a batter will be injured by a pitch intentionally thrown at his head is "an inherent risk of the sport." According to the majority, "[s]ome of the most respected baseball managers and pitchers have openly discussed the fundamental place [that] throwing at batters has in their sport." The majority acknowledges that those comments were made in the context of *professional* baseball. The majority then proceeds to hold that throwing at batters is a risk as inherent in college baseball as it is in professional baseball. My concerns are threefold.

First, the determination whether being hit by a pitched ball intentionally aimed at one's head is an inherent risk of baseball, whether professional or intercollegiate, is a question of fact to be determined in the trial court. * * * Here, the trial court never heard, and thus never considered, the comments from professional baseball managers and pitchers on which the majority relies; indeed, not only did the District offer no evidence on this issue, but the District did not even *argue* that Avila's complaint was barred by the no-duty-for-sports rule. Undeterred, the majority has done its own research and made its own factual findings on this issue, thus invading the province of the trial court.

I recognize that this court must take judicial notice of "[f]acts and propositions of generalized knowledge that are so universally known that they cannot reasonably be the subject of dispute." But the majority's assertion that intentionally throwing a ball at a batter's head is inherent in intercollegiate baseball is not a fact so "universally known" that it "cannot reasonably be the subject of dispute."

Had Avila been given the opportunity in the trial court, he might well have called expert witnesses who could have refuted the majority's factual determination that aiming at a batter's head is inherent in professional baseball. And he could have pointed to the official comments accompanying Major League Baseball's Rule 8.02(d), which prohibits pitchers from trying to hit the batter: "To pitch at a batter's head is unsportsmanlike and highly dangerous. It should be—and is—condemned by everybody. Umpires should act without hesitation in enforcement of this rule."

Alternatively, Avila could have called expert witnesses to refute the majority's finding, which is unsupported by any citation of authority, that the conduct in question is as inherent in intercollegiate baseball as it is in professional baseball. And he could have pointed out that, unlike the rules of professional baseball, the rules of the National Collegiate Athletic Association provide that a pitcher who intentionally throws at a batter is not only ejected from the game in which the pitch was thrown, but is also suspended for the team's next four games, and a pitcher who intentionally throws at a batter on three occasions must be suspended for the remainder of the season. (NCAA Baseball Rules (Dec.2005) rule 5, § 16(d).)

I turn to my second concern. This matter is here after an appeal from the trial court's order sustaining a demurrer. * * * [B]y relying on the no-duty-for-sports rule to hold that the District's demurrer was properly sustained, the majority imposes on trial courts the obligation to decide—in ruling on a demurrer—a question of *fact*: that is, whether a particular sports injury arises from an activity inherent in the game. Questions of fact cannot be decided on demurrer, however; they must be decided on summary judgment or at trial. * * *

My third concern is that the majority's application of the no-duty-for-sports rule to include pitches intentionally thrown at a batter's head is an ill-conceived expansion of that rule into intentional torts. * * * Even if I were to accept the majority's misguided no-duty-for-sports rule, I would apply it only to causes of action for negligence, not for intentional torts.

I would analyze Avila's claim under the traditional doctrine of assumption of risk. Under that doctrine, the pertinent inquiry is not what risk is inherent in a particular sport; rather, it is what risk the plaintiff consciously and voluntarily assumed. That issue, as I explained earlier, is not one involving a duty of care owed to another, to be resolved on demurrer; rather, it is an affirmative defense, to be resolved on summary judgment or at trial.

Under traditional assumption-of-risk analysis, "sports participants owe each other a duty to refrain from unreasonably risky conduct that may cause harm." Intentionally hitting another person in the head with a hard object thrown at a high speed is highly dangerous and is potentially tortious, no matter whether the object is a ball thrown on a baseball field or is a rock thrown on a city street. Thus, if the District here was complicit in a decision by the pitcher to hit Avila in the head with the baseball, it may be held liable for Avila's injuries if Avila did not assume the risk that the pitcher would hit him in this manner. * * *

* * * Whether Avila assumed that risk is a question of fact that has no bearing on the District's duty of care toward Avila. Therefore, it cannot be decided on demurrer, but should be decided on a motion for summary judgment or at trial.

* * *

Notes and Questions

1. The court states that "'[t]here is nothing legally significant * * * about the level of play' *in this case* * * * we see no reason to distinguish *between collegiate and professional baseball*"(emphasis added). Does the court mean to imply that the level of play could be significant if the level were not the collegiate one? Is there a reasonable basis for a distinction between this case and one involving a high school game? What about a recreational league for adults or an intramural league for college students?

2. Would it make any difference if the defendant were the pitcher, rather than the community college district?

3. What exactly is the rationale of the majority? Why does it hold that this conduct cannot give rise to liability? How significant is its concern about deterring "activity that falls close to, but on the permissible side of, a prescribed rule"?

4. Do you think some version of the "no-duty-for-sports rule" is necessary if sports are to be played competitively? How much would it change baseball if a pitcher who is merely *negligent* in hitting a batter could be sued? Does that reasoning extend to intentionally hitting batters? Why or why not?

5. What if the injury was caused by *reckless* conduct? (Was the conduct in this case reckless? What about pitching with a tired arm or on three days' rest? What about pitching with a hangover? With a wet baseball? Are any of those negligent?) Take another look at *Hackbart*'s definition of recklessness. Recklessness differs from negligence in two ways: First, while negligence is the careless creation of an unreasonable risk, recklessness is the *conscious* disregard of a known risk. Second, the risk of injury must be greater for the conduct to qualify as reckless.

In the sports context, it appears that the second difference is much more important than the first. Doesn't pitching *always* qualify as the conscious disregard of a known risk of injury? Pitching may still not be "reckless," however, if the risk of injury is not great enough. That risk, in turn, may be different for each pitcher, depending on his or her control. Do you see any substantive difference for sports torts between a standard of "gross negligence" and one of "recklessness"?

6. Was the majority willing to lessen tort liability in this case because of the centrality of baseball in the national culture? Does the majority's invocation of "past and future Hall of Famers, from Early Wynn and Bob Gibson to Pedro Martinez and Roger Clemens" remind you of the maudlin beginning to Justice Blackmun's majority opinion in *Flood, supra* Chapter 8? Would a sport viewed as carrying less romance get the benefit of a similar rule? Would a hockey player, for example, receive immunity for an illegal, injury-causing, stick-swinging incident? *See* Chapter 21, *infra.* Would a stock-car driver receive the same immunity for a potentially lethal act of "intimidation" on the race track?

7. How should courts determine which types of intimidation are "inherent" in a given sport? *Cf. PGA Tour, Inc. v. Martin*, 532 U.S. 661, 699–701 (2001) (Scalia, J., dissenting):

> To say that something is "essential" is ordinarily to say that it is necessary to the achievement of a certain object. But since it is the very nature of a game to have no object except amusement (that is what distinguishes games from productive activity), it is quite impossible to say that any of a game's arbitrary rules is "essential." Eighteen-hole golf courses, 10-foot-high basketball hoops, 90-foot baselines, 100-yard football fields —all are arbitrary and none is essential.

But cf. Aside, *The Common Law Origins of the Infield Fly Rule*, 123 U. Pa. L. Rev. 1474, 1476–77 (1975) (asserting that the infield-fly rule is a "technical" one, and contrasting that type with other "core principles," such as "the diamond itself or the concepts of 'out' and 'safe,'" which are "necessary to the game"). Is this another way in which sports familiar to judges may be favored, in that judges will be less likely to appreciate the value of any individual rule in a sport with which they are unfamiliar? (Note, however, that in *Martin*, it was Justice Stevens—an avid golfer—who wrote the Court's opinion declaring that walking was not "fundamental" to golf.)

8. The dissent argued that whether certain injury-causing conduct is "inherent" in a sport is a question of fact. In response, the majority claimed (in an omitted footnote) that it could take judicial notice that "pitchers have been throwing at batters for the better part of baseball's century-plus history," and because the pitcher accordingly owed the batter no duty, the case "may properly be disposed of on demurrer, without further waste of judicial resources." How should a trial court in a future case approach this issue if reasonable people could differ as to whether some action is inherent in a sport?

9. How would dissenting Justice Kennard respond in a case brought by a boxer who claimed facial injuries resulting from battery? Should such a suit proceed to the summary judgment stage, or should a motion to dismiss be sufficient?

10. Assuming that one is to decide the question whether intentionally throwing at batters is part of baseball, should the court have drawn a line at throwing at a batter's *head*? *Avila* quoted Sal Maglie's philosophy of throwing at batters, as reported in Roger Kahn, The Head Game: Baseball Seen from the Pitcher's Mound (2000):

> You have to make the batter afraid of the ball or, anyway, aware that he can get hurt. * * * A good time is when the count is two [balls] and two [strikes]. He's looking to swing. You knock him down then and he gets up shaking. Now [throw a] curve [to] him and you have your out.

For an historical ode to the beanball, see Greg Couch, *Like It Or Not, Hitmen Have Their Place*, Chi. Sun-Times, June 16, 2006, at 129. For a somewhat different perspective, consider Jon Saraceno, *Baseball's 'Silent Code' May Have to Become Lethal Before Sanity Returns*, USA Today, June 16, 2006, at 7C.

Both columns were written in response to the actions of Chicago White Sox manager Ozzie Guillen, who dressed-down his pitcher Sean Tracey and then sent Tracey to the minors after Tracey failed to execute Guillen's demand that he hit Texas Ranger Hank Blalock in retaliation for the Rangers' hitting White Sox catcher A.J. Pierzynski. Was Guillen within his rights to order the retaliation? Under what circumstances can/should a pitcher refuse such an order? Consider Couch, *supra*:

> [Pitcher Goose] Gossage recalled his first spring training with the New York Yankees, 1978, when he barely had spoken with his new manager, Billy Martin.
>
> "He says, 'I want you to hit that blankety-blank Billy Sample in the head,'" Gossage said. "I throw 100 miles an hour. If I hit him in the head, it'll kill him. Martin says, 'I don't care if you do kill him.'
>
> "I said I wasn't going to hit him, and Martin says, 'You're telling me you're not going to do it?' He hated me from then on."

While courts are unwilling to second-guess a team for releasing a player due to poor performance, *see* Chapter 5, Part III, how would they react to a release for insubordination because of the player's refusal to throw at an opposing player?

11. In a footnote edited from the majority opinion, the court referenced a notorious case where a pitcher threw at an opponent who was warming up in or near *the on-deck circle*, *before the game*. *See Molina v. Christensen*, 44 P.3d 1274 (Kan. 2001). Such a situation, the court said, "would present an entirely different scenario." Indeed it would. There, the pitcher struck the plaintiff on the head, apparently upon the instruction of one of his coaches. Though the claimed motivation for the conduct was the same as in *Avila*, *viz.*, "keeping the batter from getting too close to home plate," the court thought the conduct "unconscionable," "deliberate[,] and unjustifiable." As the court explained, "the game had not started, the plaintiff had every right to be where he was and Christensen had no right whatsoever to be throwing a baseball anywhere near him." *Id.* at 1276. *Molina* presents another illustration of courts' attempts to determine the bounds of conduct acceptable in particular sports.

III. Unintentional Torts: Negligence or Recklessness?

Most courts have determined that unintentional torts occurring as the result of sports participation should be judged under the recklessness standard, rather than the negligence standard of "ordinary reasonable care." *See* Stanley L. Grazis, Annotation, *Liability of Participant in Team Athletic Competition for Injury to Or Death of Another Participant*, 55 A.L.R. 5th 529. According to the Restatement, conduct is reckless if the actor "know[s] or ha[s] reason to know of facts which would lead a reasonable man to realize not only that his conduct creates an unreasonable risk of physical harm to another, but also such risk is substantially greater than that which is necessary to make his conduct negligent." Restatement (Second) of Torts § 500. The adoption of the recklessness standard for sports torts represents a partial rejection of the Restatement's position that participating in sports

> does not manifest consent to contacts which are prohibited by rules and usages of the game if such rules and usages are designed to protect the participants and not merely to secure the better playing of the game as a test of skill. This is true although the player knows that those with or against whom he is playing are habitual violators of such rules.

Restatement (Second) of Torts § 50, comment b (1965).

Because the negligence standard incorporates the standard of ordinary care under the applicable circumstances (which would naturally include the fact that an incident occurred as part of a sporting event), however, it is unclear whether this distinction in terminology translates into a practical difference. Nobody suggests, for example, that an unintentionally errant throw in a softball game that strikes a batter-runner should subject the thrower or the league to liability. *See Allen v. Dover Co-Recreational Softball League*, 807 A.2d 1274 (N.H. 2002). Consider the following cases.

Gauvin v. Clark
537 N.E.2d 94 (Mass. 1989)

ABRAMS, Justice. * * * On January 30, 1980, the varsity hockey team of Worcester State College played against the team from Nichols College. Gauvin played center position for the Worcester State College team. Clark played center for the Nichols College team. During the second period, Gauvin was involved in a face-off with Clark, in which the referee dropped the puck, and both men vied for possession. Clark won the face-off. As the puck slid down the ice toward the Nichols College team's net, Gauvin felt a stick in his abdomen. Gauvin saw Clark's hockey stick coming away from Gauvin's abdomen, with the back of the hockey stick, called the "butt-end," protruding from Clark's hands. At trial, Harry Maxfield, a teammate of Gauvin, testified that he saw Clark give Gauvin a shot to the midsection after the puck slid down toward the Nichols goal. The blow to Gauvin's abdomen came after the face-off had been completed. The blow was struck when Gauvin and Clark were no longer competing for the puck.

As a result of the blow to his abdomen, Gauvin was hospitalized and underwent surgery. His spleen was removed. He missed seven weeks of school. Gauvin still suffers from bladder and abdominal pain.

The safety rules which govern the game of hockey prohibit "butt-ending." Butt-ending is the practice of taking the end of the stick which does not come into contact with the puck and driving this part of the stick into another player's body. Butt-ending is unexpected and unsportsmanlike conduct for a hockey game. The rules also prohibit a player, during a face-off, from making any physical contact with his opponent's body by means of his stick, except in the course of playing the puck. Butt-ending is penalized as a major penalty and also results in a disqualification of the penalized player.

Both Gauvin and Clark understood that the game was played according to a recognized set of rules, which prohibited butt-ending. Clark understood that the prohibition on butt-ending was designed for the protection of the players. * * *

* * * The jury rendered a special verdict in which it answered six specific questions and found the following facts. Clark had butt-ended Gauvin. Clark had violated a safety rule, thus causing Gauvin's injuries. By playing hockey, Gauvin did not consent to the act which caused his injury. The jury concluded, however, that Clark had not acted wilfully, wantonly, or recklessly in causing Gauvin's injury. The jury assessed damages in the amount of $30,000. Based on the jury's answer to the question whether Clark acted wilfully, wantonly, or recklessly, the judge entered judgment in favor of the defendant Clark.

1. *Standard of care.* Gauvin argues that, since the jury found that Clark violated a safety rule, and Clark's action caused Gauvin's injury, judgment should have been entered in favor of Gauvin, despite the fact that the jury found that Clark had not acted recklessly. We do not agree.

The problem of imposing a duty of care on participants in a sports competition is a difficult one. Players, when they engage in sport, agree to undergo some physical contacts which could amount to assault and battery absent the players' consent. Restatement (Second) of Torts § 50 comment b (1965). The courts are wary of imposing wide tort liability on sports participants, lest the law chill the vigor of athletic competition. Nevertheless, "some of the restraints of civilization must accompany every athlete on to the playing field." * * *

The majority of jurisdictions which have considered this issue have concluded that personal injury cases arising out of an athletic event must be predicated on reckless disregard of safety.

We adopt this standard. Allowing the imposition of liability in cases of reckless disregard of safety diminishes the need for players to seek retaliation during the game or future games. Precluding the imposition of liability in cases of negligence without reckless misconduct furthers the policy that "[v]igorous and active participation in sporting events should not be chilled by the threat of litigation."

* * *

Judgment affirmed.

Lestina v. West Bend Mutual Insurance Company
501 N.W.2d 28 (Wisc. 1993)

SHIRLEY S. ABRAHAMSON, Justice.

* * * For the reasons set out below, we conclude that the rules of negligence govern liability for injuries incurred during recreational team contact sports. * * *

I.

Robert F. Lestina, the plaintiff, filed this personal injury tort action against Leopold Jerger, the defendant, and Jerger's homeowner's insurer, West Bend Mutual Insurance Company, after the plaintiff was injured in a collision with the defendant. The collision occurred during a recreational soccer match organized by the Waukesha County Old Timers League, a recreational league for players over the age of 30. The plaintiff (45 years of age) was playing an offensive position for his team and the defendant (57 years of age) was the goalkeeper for the opposing team on April 20, 1988, when the injury occurred. Shortly before the plaintiff was injured, he had scored the first goal of the game. After his goal the plaintiff regained possession of the ball and was about to attempt a second goal when the defendant apparently ran out of the goal area and collided with the plaintiff. The plaintiff asserted that the defendant "slide tackled" him in order to prevent him from scoring.[1] Although slide tackles are allowed under some soccer rules, this league's rules prohibit such maneuvers to minimize risk of injury. The defendant claimed that the collision occurred as he and the plaintiff simultaneously attempted to kick the soccer ball.

The plaintiff seriously injured his left knee and leg in the collision and commenced this action, alleging that the defendant's conduct was both negligent and reckless. * * * Thereafter the parties agreed to limit the trial to the issue of negligence and to preserve the right to appeal regarding the appropriateness of the negligence standard. * * *

After the jury returned a unanimous verdict finding the defendant 100% causally negligent, the defendant filed motions raising, among other issues, the question whether negligence was the appropriate legal standard. The circuit court denied the post-verdict motions and entered judgment in favor of the plaintiff. The defendant appealed one issue to the court of appeals—whether negligence was the appropriate legal standard in this case. The court of appeals certified the cause to this court.

II.

* * *

---

1. A player "slide tackles" by sliding on his or her knee, with one foot forward, across the front of another player. The objective is to dispossess the opponent of the ball.

Courts in other jurisdictions have applied three divergent legal theories to uphold actions for sports-related injuries: 1) intentional torts, 2) willful or reckless misconduct, and 3) negligent conduct. See generally Raymond L. Yasser, *Liability for Sports Injuries,* in Law of Professional and Amateur Sports (Gary A. Uberstine ed., 1992) at sec. 14.01.

Courts have historically been reluctant to allow participants in contact sports to recover money damages for injuries, absent a deliberate attempt to injure. The intentional tort in a recreational team contact sport is assault and battery. A battery is the intentional, unprivileged, harmful or offensive touching of a person by another. Both parties agree that a player in a recreational team contact sport should be liable for an intentional tort. Neither party urges us to hold that a player should be held liable only for intentional torts. The defendant asks the court to adopt the recklessness standard. The plaintiff urges that the negligence standard is appropriate.

* * *

A third basis for actions for sports-related injuries is negligence. Negligence consists of failing to use that degree of care which would be exercised by a reasonable person under the circumstances.

Few sports cases can be found which have allowed a complainant to recover on proof of negligence. One commentator has concluded that this scarcity results from fear that the imposition of liability in such cases would discourage participation in sports-related activities. Cameron J. Rains, *Sports Violence: A Matter of Societal Concern,* 55 Notre Dame Lawyer 796, 799 (1980). We do not agree that the application of the negligence standard would have this effect. We believe that the negligence standard, properly understood and applied, accomplishes the objectives sought by the courts adopting the recklessness standard, objectives with which we agree.

Because it requires only that a person exercise ordinary care under the circumstances, the negligence standard is adaptable to a wide range of situations. An act or omission that is negligent in some circumstances might not be negligent in others. Thus the negligence standard, properly understood and applied, is suitable for cases involving recreational team contact sports.

The very fact that an injury is sustained during the course of a game in which the participants voluntarily engaged and in which the likelihood of bodily contact and injury could reasonably be foreseen materially affects the manner in which each player's conduct is to be evaluated under the negligence standard. To determine whether a player's conduct constitutes actionable negligence (or contributory negligence), the fact finder should consider such material factors as the sport involved; the rules and regulations governing the sport; the generally accepted customs and practices of the sport (including the types of contact and the level of violence generally accepted); the risks inherent in the game and those that are outside the realm of anticipation; the presence of protective equipment or uniforms; and the facts and circumstances of the particular case, including the ages and physical attributes of the participants, the participants' respective skills at the game, and the participants' knowledge of the rules and customs.

Depending as it does on all the surrounding circumstances, the negligence standard can subsume all the factors and considerations presented by recreational team contact sports and is sufficiently flexible to permit the 'vigorous competition' that the defendant urges. We see no need for the court to adopt a recklessness standard for recreational team contact sports when the negligence standard, properly understood and applied, is sufficient.

* * *

WILCOX, Justice (*dissenting*).

* * *

I disagree with the majority's conclusion that "the negligence standard, properly understood and applied, accomplishes the objectives sought by the courts adopting the recklessness standard. * * *" In the instant case, the standard ordinary negligence instruction was read to the jury. That instruction states:

> A person is negligent when he fails to exercise ordinary care. Ordinary care is the degree of care which the great mass of mankind ordinarily exercises under the same or similar circumstances. *A person fails to exercise ordinary care when, without intending to do any wrong, he does an act or omits a precaution* under circumstances in which a person of ordinary intelligence and prudence ought reasonably to foresee that such act or omission will subject him or his property, or the person or property of another, to an unreasonable risk of injury or damage. (Emphasis added).

Wis. JI-Civil 1005. No instruction was given to the jury setting forth the factors it was to consider in properly applying the negligence standard to this case. The jurors were not instructed that, "[t]he very fact that an injury is sustained during the course of a game in which participants voluntarily engage and in which the likelihood of bodily contact and injury could reasonably be foreseen materially affects the manner in which each player's conduct is to be evaluated under the negligence standard." While the defendant's action clearly violated a rule of the game, the action occurred during the heat of the game and should not form the basis of a negligence action.

* * *

Participants in contact sports assume greater risks than do others involved in non-physical recreational activities. Because rule infractions, deliberate or unintentional, are virtually inevitable in contact games, I believe imposition of a different standard of conduct is justified where injury results from such contact. I would adopt the rationale of the majority rule and hold that a participant in a contact sport such as soccer is liable for injuries in a tort action only if his or her conduct is in reckless disregard for the safety of the other player, but is not liable for ordinary negligence. The allegation as to ordinary negligence did not state a cause of action and should have been dismissed.

I am authorized to state that Justices STEINMETZ and BABLITCH join in this dissent.

Notes and Questions

1. Should it make any difference whether the defendant violated a "safety rule"? *Gauvin* says it should not. Revisit this question after you read the next case.

2. If the recklessness standard is appropriate for some sports, how should a court determine which sports qualify? *Lestina* recognized (in deleted footnote 10) that most cases applying a negligence standard do not involve contact team sports. *See, e.g., Auckenthaler v. Grundmeyer*, 877 P.2d 1039 (Nev. 1994) (applying negligence standard to horse-riding); *LaVine v. Clear Creek Skiing Corp.*, 557 F.2d 730 (10th Cir. 1977) (applying negligence standard to injury in collision between snow skiers); *Gray v. Houlton*, 671 P.2d 443 (Colo. Ct. App. 1983) (same); *Duke's GMC, Inc. v. Erskine*, 447 N.E.2d 1118 (Ind. Ct. App. 1983) (applying negligence standard to golf injury); *Bourque v. Duplechin*, 331 So.2d 40 (La.Ct.App. 1976) (applying negligence standard

to injury in softball game); *Jenks v. McGranaghan*, 299 N.Y.S.2d 228 (N.Y. App. Div. 1969) (applying negligence standard to golf injury); *Gordon v. Deer Park School District*, 426 P.2d 824 (Wash. 1967) (applying negligence standard to softball spectator injured when struck on the head with a bat). If a bowler is negligent, but not reckless, in allowing the ball to slip during the backswing and strike (ha!) another player, should he be liable?

Most jurisdictions apply the recklessness standard to injuries occurring during sporting events, so long as physical contact is a predictable occurrence in the sport (and sometimes even when it is not). *See, e.g., Yoneda v. Tom*, 133 P.3d 796 (2006) (golf); *Schick v. Ferolito*, 767 A.2d 962 (N.J. 2001) (golf); *Kiley v. Patterson*, 763 A.2d 583 (R.I. 2000) (softball); *Hoke v. Cullinan*, 914 S.W.2d 335, 337 (Ky. 1995) (tennis); *Crawn v. Campo*, 643 A.2d 600, 601 (N.J. 1994) (softball); *Hathaway v. Tascosa Country Club, Inc.*, 846 S.W.2d 614, 616 (Tex. Ct. App. 1993) (golf); *Picou v. Hartford Ins. Co.*, 558 So. 2d 787 (La. Ct. App. 1990) (softball); *Turcotte v. Fell*, 502 N.E.2d 964 (N.Y. 1986) (horseracing); *Ross v. Clouser*, 637 S.W.2d 11, 14 (Mo. 1982) (softball).

Some cases adopting a recklessness standard have explicitly limited their analysis to contact sports, implying that negligence might be appropriate in cases involving non-contact sports. *See Zurla v. Hydel*, 681 N.E.2d 148 (Ill. Ct. App. 1997); *Jaworski v. Kiernan*, 696 A.2d 332 (Conn. 1997); *Knight v. Jewett*, 834 P.2d 696 (Cal. 1992) (applying this "contact" sports rule to a touch football game); *Dotzler v. Tuttle*, 449 N.W.2d 774 (Neb. 1990); *Kabella v. Bouschelle*, 672 P.2d 290 (N.M. Ct. App. 1983). Other cases agree with *Lestina*'s negligence standard, even when applied to contact sports. *See Babych v. McRae*, 567 A.2d 1269 (Conn. Super. Ct. 1989) (applying negligence standard to a professional hockey game).

3. If "all" sports qualify for the recklessness standard, one must decide which activities qualify as "sports." Cheerleading? Go-kart driving? Foosball? Juggling? "Ultimate Frisbee"? *Eddy v. Syracuse University*, 433 N.Y.S.2d 923 (N.Y. App. Div. 1980). Kick-the-can? *Marchetti v. Kalish*, 559 N.E.2d 699 (Ohio 1990). The inquiry is complicated further by the fact that "competitive" sports presenting the strongest cases for a recklessness standard are often *practiced* in a non-competitive or less competitive environment, as in the next principal case, which involves recreational ice skating. How broadly do you think the recklessness standard should apply?

Ritchie-Gamester v. City of Berkley

597 N.W.2d (Mich. 1999)

YOUNG, J.

* * * According to plaintiff, she was skating at the Berkley Ice Arena during an "open skating" period when defendant, then twelve years old, ran into her, knocking her down and causing serious injury to her knee. Plaintiff alleged in her complaint that defendant was skating backwards in a "careless, reckless, and negligent manner" at the time of the collision. * * *

For purposes of appeal, defendant admits that there is a question of fact regarding whether her conduct was negligent. Similarly, plaintiff has admitted that defendant's conduct did not rise to the level of recklessness. Thus, the only question before this Court is which standard governs this case: If it is ordinary negligence, we must affirm the Court of Appeals and remand for trial; if it is recklessness, we must reverse the Court of Appeals and reinstate the trial court's grant of summary disposition for defendant.

* * *

In developing the common law in this area, we must recognize the everyday reality of participation in recreational activities. A person who engages in a recreational activity is temporarily adopting a set of rules that define that particular pastime or sport. In many instances, the person is also suspending the rules that normally govern everyday life. For example, it would be a breach of etiquette, and possibly the law, to battle with other shoppers for a particularly juicy orange in the grocery store, while it is quite within the rules of basketball to battle for a rebound. Some might find certain sports, such as boxing or football, too rough for their own tastes. However, our society recognizes that there are benefits to recreational activity, and we permit individuals to agree to rules and conduct that would otherwise be prohibited.

There are myriad ways to describe the legal effect of voluntarily participating in a recreational activity. The act of stepping onto the field of play may be described as "consent to the inherent risks of the activity," or a participant's knowledge of the rules of a game may be described as "notice" sufficient to discharge the other participants' duty of care. Similarly, participants' mutual agreement to play a game may be described as an "implied contract" between all the participants, or a voluntary participant could be described as "assuming the risks" inherent in the sport. No matter what terms are used, the basic premise is the same: When people engage in a recreational activity, they have voluntarily subjected themselves to certain risks inherent in that activity. When one of those risks results in injury, the participant has no ground for complaint.

* * * One cannot ice skate without ice, and the very nature of ice—that it is both hard and slippery—builds some risk into skating. In addition, an "open skate" invites those of various ages and abilities onto the ice to learn, to practice, to exercise, or simply to enjoy skating. When one combines the nature of ice with the relative proximity of skaters of various abilities, a degree of risk is readily apparent: Some skaters will be unable to control their progress and will either bump into other skaters, or fall. All skaters thus take the chance that they will fall themselves, that they will be bumped by another skater, or that they will trip over a skater who has fallen.

* * *

With these realities in mind, we join the majority of jurisdictions and adopt reckless misconduct as the minimum standard of care for coparticipants in recreational activities. We believe that this standard most accurately reflects the actual expectations of participants in recreational activities. As will be discussed in more detail below, we believe that participants in recreational activities do not expect to sue or be sued for mere carelessness. A recklessness standard also encourages vigorous participation in recreational activities, while still providing protection from egregious conduct. Finally, this standard lends itself to common-sense application by both judges and juries.[9]

* * *

Applying a recklessness standard in this case, we conclude that summary disposition was properly granted to defendant. Although plaintiff used the word "reckless" in her complaint, a review of the pleadings, depositions, and other documentary evi-

---

9. We recognize that we have stated this standard broadly as applying to all "recreational activities." However, the precise scope of this rule is best established by allowing it to emerge on a case-bycase basis, so that we might carefully consider the application of the recklessness standard in various factual contexts.

dence reveals that plaintiff merely contends that defendant was skating backward without keeping a proper lookout behind her. These allegations amount to, at most, carelessness or ordinary negligence. Thus, the trial court properly granted summary disposition for defendant.

V
Response to the Concurrence

Whatever else we disagree upon, those in the concurrence do agree that defendant's conduct in this case is not actionable. The fundamental difference between the two opinions turns on the standard of care each believes should apply to this and cases of like kind. As stated above, we believe that a recklessness standard most nearly comports with the expectations of participants in recreational activities. While reasonable people can differ on this issue, in rejecting our standard, the concurrence purports to apply an ordinary negligence standard. In fact, it does not.

* * *

The instant case provides a prime illustration of our point: As noted in the statement of facts, defendant concedes that questions of fact exist regarding whether her conduct was negligent. Even without this admission, it seems readily apparent that questions of fact abound under a negligence standard. All agree that defendant was permitted to skate backward at an open skate, but, as the concurrence acknowledges, an ordinary negligence standard required defendant to maintain a lookout in order to avoid running into other skaters. Here, defendant says she kept a lookout, but admits that she still bumped into plaintiff and knocked her down. Under these circumstances, could not reasonable jurors conclude that defendant failed to maintain a *sufficient* lookout? Surely, the question whether defendant's conduct was sufficiently careful under an ordinary negligence standard presents a question of material fact. Yet the concurrence declares, as a matter of law, that defendant's conduct was not negligent. The concurrence can only reach that point by ignoring the appropriate standard of review * * *, which requires us to draw inferences in favor of plaintiff, and by ignoring defendant's admission that questions of fact exist regarding whether her conduct was negligent. We find it hard to reconcile the concurrence's position with the facts of this case and traditional negligence law, and we are not persuaded that the concurrence's position corners the market on common sense.

Ignoring the foregoing problem, the concurrence attempts to support its hybrid negligence standard by suggesting that participants who conduct themselves within the rules of the game are not subject to liability under its proposed standard. It is proposed that breaches of "formal or informal rules of safety" should be actionable, but apparently breaches of other rules should not. We think this endeavor to draw a distinction between "safety rules" (which apparently are inviolate) and non-safety rules (which apparently may be disregarded with legal impunity) attempts to draw a fruitless distinction that even participants themselves do not, and probably cannot, draw. The concurrence's revised formulation of the conventional negligence standard would lead to profound doctrinal confusion, and more, rather than fewer, ancillary disputes. * * *

Let us consider real-world examples to test whether the concurrence has presented a workable standard. In the case of soccer, which is officially a "non-contact" sport, where would the concurrence draw the "negligence line" if a participant is injured when she is fouled? Is a minor foul actionable? Is a foul that draws a "yellow card" actionable? Or would the concurrence find the foul actionable if it results in a "red card"? Similarly, in hockey, is a player who receives a two-minute penalty for slashing liable for any injuries caused by his rule violation, or is he even liable for the type of foul that results in a major misconduct penalty? [*sic*—Majors and misconducts are different categories of penalties.—Eds.] Presumably, the concurrence would not preclude liability where a referee missed a foul, but what about a case where the referee saw the activity and concluded that no rule violation was committed? May a jury look beyond that decision and overturn it?

Surely all who participate in recreational activities do so with the hope that they will not be injured by the clumsiness or over-exuberant play of their coparticipants. However, we suspect that reasonable participants recognize that skill levels and play styles vary, and that an occasional injury is a foreseeable and natural part of being involved in recreational activities, however the "informal and formal rules" are structured and enforced.

* * * We do not believe that a player expects an injury, even if it results from a rule violation, to give rise to liability. Instead, we think it more likely that players participate with the expectation that no liability will arise unless a participant's actions exceed the normal bounds of conduct associated with the activity.

Consequently, we believe that the line of liability for recreational activities should be drawn at recklessness. Recklessness is a term with a recognized legal meaning and, more importantly, is a term susceptible of a common-sense understanding and application by judges, attorneys, and jurors alike in the myriad recreational activities that might become the backdrop of litigation. Just as important, our standard more nearly comports with the common-sense understanding that participants in these activities bring to them. While the concurrence may disagree whether we have accurately assessed participant expectations, we think that our standard has the significant value of providing an explicit, easy to apply rule of jurisprudence. The concurrence has failed to present a sounder, clearer alternative standard.

* * *

BRICKLEY, J. (*concurring* [*in the judgment*]).

* * *

[N]one of the advantages of the recklessness standard that the majority cites actually support its conclusion. * * *

I

I begin with the majority's assertion that the recklessness standard "encourages vigorous participation in recreational activities." * * *

[T]his state has observed the more exacting "ordinary care" standard in sporting and recreational events at least since 1932, and, despite this higher standard of care, there is no sign of any wane in the "vigorousness" of recreational sports in Michigan. Perhaps the majority would like to see even greater vigorousness in these activities, and plainly believes that the recklessness standard would serve this end. But, without any empirical evidence that participation or vigorousness in the state's recreational sports and activities would reach even greater heights under the recklessness standard, this Court should not attempt any social engineering in this area by altering long-existing rules of tort law.

The majority assumes that its decisions regarding tort standards of care are relevant considerations for those deciding whether to participate in recreational activities. I have my doubts regarding this proposition. But, even if we accept it as true, the majority's conclusion does not necessarily follow. Indeed, if participants in recreational activities have the legal foresight with which the majority credits them, it is just as likely that many would choose not to participate in these activities because the recklessness standard might encourage dangerous behavior or make it too difficult for participants to recover in the event they are injured. This heightened possibility of injury and unavailability of recovery would discourage vigorous participation, or any participation at all, by those who are less bold, or who might not want to take the financial risks presented by the possibility of injury.

These questions warn us that such policy issues are difficult for courts. * * *

II

* * *

Certainly, there is a sense in which assumption of risk has been recognized as surviving the adoption of contributory negligence schemes. This has been described as "primary assumption of risk," or the "duty perspective" on assumption of risk. * * *

This doctrine does not, however, support the majority's result in this case. The plaintiff did not consent to *any* conduct of the defendant or the other participants in the free skate. The plaintiff's implied consent in entering into this recreational activity is based upon the relationship that she entered into with her coparticipants. Since most recreational activities and sporting events have formal or informal rules regarding safety,[13] we must assume that the plaintiff entered into this relationship with her coparticipants with knowledge of these rules, and the expectation that they would be obeyed. We cannot assume most participants in such activities consent to others' behavior that is either accidentally or purposefully outside those safety rules.

Indeed, it would likely be a great surprise to the millions of participants in Michigan's recreational sports and activities that, by participating, they were legally consenting to their coparticipants' breach of the safety rules of those activities. One must wonder about the effect on the "vigorousness" of these sports, if it became common knowledge that this Court sanctioned breaches of these activities' safety rules, as long as the breaches did not amount to recklessness.

The fact that such rules exist supplies a ready definition of the legal duties that participants in sporting activities must observe: Participants have a tort-enforceable duty to one another to obey the safety rules of the sport or activity. If a participant engages in conduct outside these rules, that participant has potentially breached her legal duty to her coparticipants, and the factfinder must determine whether her conduct was reasonable under the circumstances. Participants in a sporting or recreational activity consent to actions by their coparticipants that would not satisfy the strictures of "ordinary care" in everyday activity, but they do not consent to behavior unconstrained by the safety rules of the particular activity.

---

13. A formal safety rule would be a safety rule that is written into the rule books of a particular sport or activity, while an informal safety rule would be one that is widely recognized by participants in the absence of a formal rule. The parties in the instant case agree that the relevant safety rule of free skating is that a skater looks behind her when skating backward. This would presumably be an "informal" rule, as no rule book has been presented by the parties.

A "safety" rule, as opposed to a non-safety rule, is a rule that increases the safety of the sport or activity, rather than merely increasing the fairness or competitiveness of the activity. The parties to the instant case have agreed that the relevant safety rule of free skating is that a backward-skating participant should look behind her while skating backward; there is no basis for questioning whether this is a safety rule or not.

By participating in the open skate, the plaintiff in the instant case impliedly consented to the defendant's backward skating, knowing that this was likely to be more dangerous than behavior that the plaintiff would encounter, for example, on a walk in her neighborhood. The parties agree, however, that one of the safety rules of free skating is that, while skating backward, the skater should periodically look behind her to see if she is going to run into anyone. Thus, the plaintiff consented to the heightened risk of the defendant's behavior with the knowledge that the defendant would lessen that risk by periodically looking behind her as she was skating backward.

If the defendant was skating backward and obeying the safety rules by looking behind her, and then collided with the plaintiff, she cannot be held liable because she had no duty to behave more cautiously. If, however, the defendant ran into the plaintiff while she was skating backward and *not* periodically looking behind her, then she engaged in conduct that the plaintiff had not consented to, and can be held to have breached her duty toward the plaintiff if she did not act with reasonable care.

Because there is no basis in fact or law for holding that participants impliedly consent to any behavior that is more dangerous than that allowed by the activity's safety rules, primary assumption of risk is not a basis for holding that coparticipants in sporting activities have only the duty to refrain from acting recklessly. This Court should not dash participants' expectations by insisting, without reason, that their participation indicates their consent to more dangerous conduct.

III

Despite my disagreement with the majority's reasoning, I reach its result because the plaintiff in this case submitted no evidence that the defendant breached any safety rules during free skating. The plaintiff has urged that the relevant rule of free skating is that "the skater has the responsibility for looking behind her when skating backward and should not rely upon others." The only evidence in the record regarding whether the defendant did look behind her while skating backward, is the defendant's deposition testimony[.]

* * *

While it is clear that the defendant partially relied on those skating with her to warn her about other skaters, she also unambiguously stated that she "looked" or "checked" behind her. Thus, there is no basis on which to say that she violated any safety rules of the free skate, and no basis for finding that she violated any duty that she owed to the plaintiff. The trial court properly granted her motion for summary disposition, and, like the majority, I would reverse the judgment of the Court of Appeals.

MICHAEL F. CAVANAGH and MARILYN J. KELLY, JJ., concur with BRICKLEY, J.

Notes and Questions

1. The majority and dissent disagree as to whether imposition of a recklessness standard is likely to increase participation in sports. Which argument do you find more persuasive?

2. Is a recklessness or negligence standard more "susceptible of a common-sense understanding and application"?

3. The Michigan Legislature passed two statutes—the Roller Skating Safety Act and the Ski Area Safety Act—after the Michigan Supreme Court in an earlier case elimi-

nated assumption of the risk as a defense to negligence actions. The statutes reinstated assumption of the risk for injuries occurring at roller rinks and ski resorts. The majority treated the statutes as irrelevant because this case involved neither roller-skating nor skiing. The concurrence saw the statutes as significant for what they did not say: by reinstating assumption of the risk as to roller-skating and skiing, the legislature must have meant that the defense should not be available elsewhere. One might also argue that the two statutes represented a legislative attitude against negligence liability, which should be applied more broadly than the statutory terms required. What are the arguments in favor of each approach? What reason could there be for the legislature to create a different rule for only those two forms of recreation? Might it be that those two industries were particularly influential in the legislature? How should courts treat a statute like this if it appears to be the product of rent-seeking (i.e., the use of the legislative process to advantage a small group at the expense of the greater populace)?

4. In footnote 9, the court cryptically suggests that "the precise scope" of the recklessness standard for "recreational activities" "is best established by allowing it to emerge on a case-by-case basis." Do you consider this approach to be responsible? How will the court determine whether to apply the rule to a future case?

5. If the appropriate standard were negligence, do you agree with the concurrence that the defendant should be granted summary judgment? Do you agree with the majority that the defendant's conduct was, as a matter of law, not reckless?

6. Courts have taken different approaches to delineating the activities for which the recklessness standard is applicable, as you might expect. Compare the following positions on the proper standard for evaluating jet-skiing and water-skiing accidents:

> Applying a recklessness standard to any use of a jet ski in order to encourage vigorous participation is neither a legitimate nor necessary policy goal. Moreover, the nature of jet skiing does not present the same potential for a flood of litigation as do certain contact sports. Jet skiing simply does not raise the concern * * * that if "simple negligence were to be adopted as the standard of care, every punter with whom contact is made, every midfielder high sticked, every basketball player fouled, every batter struck by a pitch, and every hockey player tripped would have the ingredients for a lawsuit if injury resulted."

Davis v. LeCuyer, 849 N.E.2d 750 (Ind. Ct. App. 2006) *transfer denied*, 2006 Ind. LEXIS 959 (Ind. Oct 27, 2006). *See also Cruz v. Gloss*, 57 Pa. D&C 4th 449 (Pa. Ct. Common Pleas 2002) (applying a negligence standard to non-competitive skiing and snowboarding).

> [T]he decisions that have recognized the existence of only a limited duty of care in a sports situation generally have reasoned that vigorous participation in the sport likely would be chilled, and, as a result, the nature of the sport likely would be altered, in the event legal liability were to be imposed on a sports participant for ordinary careless conduct. This reasoning applies to water skiing. Even when a water skier is not involved in a "competitive" event, the skier has undertaken vigorous, athletic activity, and the ski boat driver operates the boat in a manner that is consistent with, and enhances, the excitement and challenge of the active conduct of the sport. Imposition of legal liability on a ski boat driver for ordinary negligence in making too sharp a turn, for example, or in pulling the skier too rapidly or too slowly, likely would have the same kind of undesirable chilling effect on the driver's conduct that the courts in other cases feared would inhibit ordinary conduct in various sports. As a re-

sult, holding ski boat drivers liable for their ordinary negligence might well have a generally deleterious effect on the nature of the sport of water skiing as a whole. Additionally, imposing such liability might well deter friends from voluntarily assisting one another in such potentially risky sports. Accordingly, the general rule limiting the duty of care of a coparticipant in active sports to the avoidance of intentional and reckless misconduct, applies to participants engaged in non-competitive but active sports activity, such as a ski boat driver towing a water skier.

Ford v. Gouin, 834 P.2d 724, 728 (Cal. 1992).

7. More fundamentally, one might question why courts are willing to conclude that society should and does accept a greater risk of injury from sports than from other activities. Granting that, for example, a recklessness standard is necessary to allow pitchers effectively to pitch on the inside corner, why should we take that risk, rather than forcing the sport to adjust? Do you find the following explanation convincing?

One might well conclude that something is terribly wrong with a society in which the most commonly-accepted aspects of play—a traditional source of a community's conviviality and cohesion—spurs litigation. The heightened recklessness standard recognizes a commonsense distinction between excessively harmful conduct and the more routine rough-and-tumble of sports that should occur freely on the playing fields and should not be second-guessed in courtrooms.

Crawn v. Campo, 643 A.2d 600 (N.J. 1994).

Consider an analogy to other areas of life: It may well be that more effective medicines would be developed if pharmaceutical companies were immune from negligence liability, but tort law forces companies to pay damages when negligent and, in some cases, when the companies are not at fault at all. Is it more important to encourage competition in sports or industry? The *Ritchie-Gamester* dissent, in a footnote omitted from the opinion, argued that it was perverse to protect "the vigorousness of sports" by adopting a recklessness standard, when "more compelling policy rationales" supported charitable tort immunity and interfamily tort immunity, both of which were jettisoned in earlier cases. What is the best argument for sports' preferred position?

IV. Liability of Sports Supervisors, Employers, and Facilities

A. Coaches and Instructors

Brahatcek v. Millard School District

273 N.W.2d 680 (Neb. 1979)

[**Spencer, J.**] This is a wrongful death action brought by Darlene Brahatcek as administratrix of the estate of her son, David Wayne Brahatcek, hereinafter called David, against Millard School District No. 17. David died as a result of being accidentally struck in the left occipital region of his skull by a golf club during a physical education class. Trial was had to the court. The District Judge entered judgment in favor of the plaintiff in the amount of $ 3,570.06 special damages, $ 50,000 general damages, and costs. Defendant appeals.

Defendant essentially alleges four assignments of error: (1) The insufficiency of the evidence; (2) the failure to find decedent contributorily negligent; (3) the failure to hold the negligence of the classmate who struck decedent was an intervening cause of death; and (4) the award of general damages was excessive. We affirm.

David, who was a ninth grade student 14 years of age, was injured on April 3, 1974, during a physical education class conducted in the gymnasium of Millard Central Junior High School. He was struck by a golf club swung by a fellow student, Mark Kreie. He was rendered unconscious and died 2 days later without regaining consciousness.

Mandatory golf instruction during physical education classes at the school began on Monday, April 1, 1974. Because decedent was absent from school on that day, his first exposure to the program was when his class next met on Wednesday, the day of the accident. Classes on both dates were conducted in the school gymnasium because of inclement weather. Instruction was coeducational. Decedent's class of 34 boys combined with a girls' physical education class having an enrollment of 23. Two teachers, one male and one female, were responsible for providing supervision and instruction. The faculty members present on Monday were Max Kurtz and Vickie Beveridge, at that time Vickie Lindgren.

On Monday, after attendance was taken, the students were gathered around in a semicircle and received instruction on the golf grip, stance, swing, etiquette, and safety. Mr. Kurtz then explained to them the procedure that would be followed in the gym.

With the bleachers folded up, the gym was nearly as wide as it was long. Approximately 12 mats were placed across the width of the gym, in two rows of six each. One row of mats was located in the south half of the gym about even with the free throw line on the basketball court. The other row was placed along the free throw line in the north half of the gym. The mats measured about 2 feet square and were spaced 10 to 12 feet apart. Each row contained approximately six mats. A golf club and three or four plastic "wiffle" balls were placed by each mat.

The students were divided into groups of four or five students and each group was assigned to the use of one of the mats. The boys used the mats on the south side of the gym and hit in a southerly direction. The girls used the mats on the north, and hit the golf balls in a northerly direction. At the start of the class all of the students were to sit along the center line of the basketball court between the two rows of mats. On the signal of one of the instructors one student from each group would go up to the assigned mat, tee up a ball, and wait for the signal to begin. After the student had hit all of the balls on the mat he was to lay the club down and return to the center of the gym. When all of the students were back at the center line, the next student in each group was directed to retrieve the balls and the procedure was repeated.

Mr. Kurtz was not present for class on Wednesday, the day of the accident, because his wife had just given birth to a baby. His place was taken by a student teacher, Tim Haley, who had been at the school for approximately 5 weeks and had assisted with four to six golf classes on Monday and Tuesday. At the beginning of the class on Wednesday, Mrs. Beveridge repeated the instructions which had been given by Mr. Kurtz on Monday. The groups were again divided. One student went up to each mat and Mrs. Beveridge testified she gave the signal for the first balls to be hit.

Plaintiff's decedent, who prior to the date of his death had never had a golf club in his hands, was either the second or third student to go up to the easternmost mat on the boys' side of the gym. He had difficulty and asked his group if anyone could help him. Mark Kreie, who had been the last to use the club, came forward and showed decedent how to grip the club and told him that he (Kreie) would take two practice swings then hit the ball. Decedent moved to the east and stood against the folded up bleachers about 10 feet to the rear of Kreie. Kreie looked over his shoulder to observe decedent before taking two practice swings. He then stepped up to the ball and took a full swing at it. Unaware that decedent had moved closer, he hit decedent with the club on the follow-through. During all of this time, Mr. Haley was helping another boy a few mats away. Mark did not know whether Mr. Haley saw decedent and him standing together at the mat. Mrs. Beveridge was positioned along the west end of the girls' line.

Mark Kreie testified Mrs. Beveridge gave instructions to the students as to the proper use of the clubs. They were also told to remain behind a certain line on the gym floor when they were not up at the mats. He also testified on Wednesday Mrs. Beveridge told them they were to help any of the students who didn't understand. Mrs. Beveridge denied making this statement. The fact that the deceased asked for help of the students might support Kreie's statement.

* * *

Ike F. Pane, principal of Millard Central Junior High School, testified golf was a mandatory course of instruction. Golf instruction was provided to ninth grade students in April of 1974, with the first class on Monday, April 1, 1974. Pane identified exhibit 9 as his school's written rules of instruction which stated the objectives to be achieved in teaching golf to the ninth grade class, and specifically setting forth in what manner or procedure the instruction was to be undertaken and achieved. The objectives were to develop the skills and appreciation for the sport of golf, with the coequal consideration that the instruction be accomplished with safety. On page 2 of exhibit 9, the following appears: "Safety should be stressed at all times, especially when you are rained out. If in the gym, one can set up stations on the floor along one side of the bleachers, divide all students into that many stations and have them sit on the outstretched bleachers on the opposite side. Have the first person hit four or five balls, (sic) to the second person across the gym. When the first is done hitting, he will go to the end of his group and the second person hits and the third retrieves the ball and so on."

On the next page of exhibit 9, the following appears under "Safety Hints:" "1. Never hit a shot until you are sure those in front of you are out of your range. If you hit another player, you may be liable for damages. 2. Never swing a club, especially on the tees, unless you are sure no one is standing close to you."

Pane testified he approved of exhibit 9 and the procedure set forth therein, and that it was his understanding the instruction was undertaken in conformity with exhibit 9. However, after David's fatal injury he discovered that the physical arrangements for instruction were quite different than that specified.

Pane acknowledged that if the instructions had been followed it would have been difficult to have two people on a mat at the same time. It was not until after the accident that he realized the arrangement was different from what was recommended. He recognized that in any of the areas where there might be danger there is a potential for harm if the students were not properly supervised. If the procedure recommended had been followed, it would have made it more difficult for another student from the group to walk across the width of the gymnasium. It was Mr. Kurtz and Mrs. Beveridge who decided to vary the placement of the mats from that recommended in exhibit 9.

Mr. Kurtz testified that on Monday when he was giving the instruction, one from each group would go up all at the same time to the respective mats. Both he and Mrs. Beveridge would see that only one individual was at each mat when the students were to commence their swings. While the students were shooting their two or three balls, he would walk up and down in the back of them, more or less patrolling to make sure everything was okay. They walked the students through the hitting of the first ball. The second ball the students would hit on their own. In the instruction, he followed the curriculum guide, which is exhibit 9.

After each person had hit his three balls, he was supposed to lay his club down on the carpet and go back to his group and sit down. After all the stations had been cleared and no one else was standing, the next golfer would be told to go out and gather the wiffle balls, bring them back, and set them on the carpet, standing there by the proper mat. Then when that group had gathered all the balls and the designated students were standing at their respective mats, they would go through the same procedure again.

It is evident the instruction procedure used Monday was not followed on Wednesday. If it had been, the instructor would have observed the dilemma of the deceased and given him the instruction he had missed. Also, the students would not have been assisting one another.

Mr. Haley testified he had received no instruction from any of the regular teachers or faculty prior to the commencement of the class, nor did he have a lesson plan because Mrs. Beveridge was going to handle that. He further stated he gave no oral instruction to any of the students as a whole. He recognized he was teaching unskilled young people in a game dealing with potentially dangerous instruments. At the time David was injured, Haley was at the fifth mat, giving some individual instruction. Haley testified that if he had seen another student approach the mat, he would have directed him to sit down. At the time in question his attention was diverted from those students who were supposed to be observing rather than using the clubs. When he was giving specialized instruction the only persons he was seeing were the individuals who were using that particular mat he was working with. Haley was asked the following question: "'Who told you after—instructed you, if anybody, that once the instructions started on the mat that you were to lead the group from center court and go down and pass in review, more or less, in front of the mats, and if the students needed help to give them help. A. Who told me personally to do that? Q. Yes. A. No one.'"

Plaintiff called a retired school gym teacher who had a B.A. degree in physical education. He had been an instructor in golf until he entered the naval service. He played golf regularly, besides teaching and supervising the instruction of the sport. He knew, understood, and appreciated the basic techniques used in pursuing the sport of golf. He would have used the procedure outlined in exhibit 9 rather than that used on the occasion of the accident. He testified the teacher should be supervising and keeping an eye on all the students using the mats; that if he noticed a boy or girl having difficulty or needing specialized instruction, the appropriate way would be to blow the whistle, call the class to a halt, and stop the children from talking or engaging in conversation, if any, on the bleachers, so as to gain their control and attention. Then he would demonstrate to the one student in need while all students, those seated and those standing by the mats, would watch and listen, and thereby, in effect, give a public lesson to all in attendance.

Mr. Kurtz and Mrs. Beveridge testified they did not use the procedure outlined in exhibit 9 because they did not want the wiffle balls hit toward other students. They also felt there was a danger of a golf club flying loose. Mrs. Beveridge also envisioned a problem with wiffle balls going underneath the bleachers if they were hit across the width of the gym.

In determining the sufficiency of the evidence to sustain a judgment, it must be considered in the light most favorable to the successful party. Every controverted fact must be resolved in his favor and he is entitled to the benefit of every inference that can reasonably be deduced from the evidence.

In an action for negligence, the burden is on the plaintiff to show that there was a negligent act or omission by the defendant and that it was a proximate cause of the plaintiff's injury or a cause which proximately contributed to it. Negligence must be measured against the particular set of facts and circumstances which are present in each case.

Negligence is defined as doing something which an ordinary, prudent person would not have done under similar circumstances or failing to do something which an ordinary, prudent person would have done under similar circumstances.

* * *

Recovery in this case is sought on the ground of lack of supervision. Where lack of supervision by an instructor is relied on to impose liability, such lack must appear as the proximate cause of the injury, with the result that the liability would not lie if the injury would have occurred notwithstanding the presence of the instructor.

In the instant case, we are dealing with a ninth grader who had never before swung a golf club. The instruction was conducted indoors, in close quarters. There was some testimony, which the trial court could have accepted, that the physical arrangement, which was contrary to defendant's suggestion, as indicated by exhibit 9, would have prevented the opportunity for injury if followed. There is a question as to whether there was adequate safety instruction regarding the use of a golf club prior to the commencement of the class at which the fatal injury occurred. There is evidence, which the court could have accepted, that on the day the accident occurred the teaching procedure outlined by the regular instructor was not followed by the student teacher. The record would also indicate the student teacher may not have been properly informed as to the procedure to be followed. There is no question the trial judge could have found that, at the very best, there was ineffective observation and attention on the part of the student teacher when ordinary care or supervision would have prevented the occurrence which resulted in the death of David. * * *

* * *

In this instance, working with ninth graders, who were not familiar with the rules of golf, and in the case of the deceased, who had never before been exposed to the game, includes a duty to anticipate danger that is reasonably foreseeable.

We have no difficulty in finding that the lack of supervision was a proximate cause of the death of David. "Proximate cause" as used in the law of negligence is that cause which in the natural and continuous sequence, unbroken by an efficient intervening cause, produces the injury and without which the injury would not have occurred.

Defendant contends that even if it were guilty of negligence its negligence was superseded by that of Mark Kreie, decedent's classmate, and Kreie's negligence was an efficient intervening cause which produced the injury. * * * "Generally, the effect of an intervening negligent act is tested by determining whether it was such as might reasonably have been foreseen as a consequence of the claimed negligence of the original actor." * * * There should be no question about foreseeability in this case. If defendant's employees had exercised proper supervision, the death would not have occurred.

Defendant further argues that the deceased is guilty of contributory negligence. One who is capable of understanding and discretion and who fails to exercise ordinary care and prudence to avoid obvious danger is negligent or contributorily negligent. * * * "A minor is held to the exercise of that degree of care which an ordinarily prudent child of the same capacity to appreciate and avoid danger would use."

Whether or not a minor 14 years of age is of sufficient knowledge, discretion, and appreciation of danger that he may be subject to the defense of contributory negligence is generally a question of fact for the jury. The trial court in this instance must have found the deceased was not contributorily negligent. The golf instruction was a required subject. David, a ninth grader, had no understanding of the game and the record is not clear that he was properly warned of the apparent danger in the sport. If the testimony of Mark Kreie is accepted, Mark was complying with the directions of Mrs. Beveridge and giving help to another student. The mere fact there is a recognized amount of danger in the activity by reason of a swinging club is not contributory negligence unless the knowledge of the danger is made known to the child. The doing of an act with appreciation of the amount of danger is necessary in order to say as a matter of law a person is negligent. It cannot be said that deceased had sufficient knowledge of the danger involved, considering the fact he was not familiar with the game of golf and had never before had a golf club in his hands. He had not attended the first class where instruction and practice were provided. He had not received any instruction on any aspect of the game by any teacher prior to his attempted use of the club. The only instruction he received was that provided by the fellow student who struck the fatal blow. On the record in this case, we cannot say that the findings of the trial court are clearly wrong.

* * *

Affirmed.

Colwell, District Judge, dissenting.

I respectfully dissent on the issue of contributory negligence.

David Wayne Brahatcek was a normal, healthy, responsible 14-year-old boy who had a part-time job * * *. On the day of the fatal accident he attended the golf class instruction, which included the subject of safety. He followed instructions given concerning his waiting to take his turn and then advancing alone to the mat where he held the club and attempted to use it. He had the opportunity to examine the golf club and become aware of its size and weight. After fellow student Kreie briefly explained the fundamentals, Brahatcek retreated to the side and rear from Kreie about 10 feet, and Kreie informed him that he would take two practice swings with the club and then hit the ball. After two practice swings, Kreie advanced further away from Brahatcek towards the ball and hit it. Thereafter, in some unexplained circumstance, Brahatcek came into the area of the golf swing arc and he was struck, causing his tragic death.

Considering these facts and circumstances, Brahatcek had an opportunity for knowledge and appreciation of possible injury to him. However, he failed to exercise ordinary and reasonable care to avoid danger and injury to himself. Brahatcek was negligent to a degree more than slight.

The golf class included group and personal instruction and student participation. This same circumstance occurs daily in all schools, whether it be sport programs or the curriculum related to science, home economics, shop, agriculture, mechanics, and other courses, many involving potential injury to students. The standard of care of the defendant and its teachers here does not require continuous and direct supervision and surveillance of each student. The test is what a person of ordinary prudence, charged with the same duties involved, would exercise under the same circumstances.

Although the record could support a finding by the trial court that defendant was negligent, such negligence was less than gross.

The negligence of Brahatcek was more than slight and the negligence of the defendant was less than gross. Plaintiff's petition should be dismissed.

The judgment of the trial court was clearly wrong and it should be reversed.

McCown, J., joins in this dissent.

Notes and Questions

1. How much specialized golf knowledge does it take to understand that a fast-moving piece of metal, designed to propel a ball in excess of one hundred yards, presents a danger when swung near one's head? Should states impose liability on supervisors even when a defect is open and obvious? *See Tiemann v. Indep. Sch. Dist. No. 740*, 331 N.W.2d 250 (Minn. 1983) (holding that the plaintiff student did not assume the risk of a defective pommel horse, despite the obviousness of the defect).

2. Precisely what does the court find to constitute negligence in this case? Were the teachers negligent in their "supervision" of the class or in their set-up of the mats? Should the teachers have paid more attention to each individual student? To Brahatcek alone?

3. Note that the plaintiffs sued the school district. Often in sports tort cases plaintiffs will attempt to collect from employers or leagues, rather than from the comparatively shallow pockets of the individual tortfeasors. Issues of vicarious liability are therefore present whether the tortfeasor is a player, coach, or some other individual. In evaluating whether an employer assumes vicarious liability for the intentional, reckless, or negligent acts of its employee, see generally PROSSER & KEETON §69, at 499; Steven I. Rubin, *The Vicarious Liability of Professional Sports Teams for On-the-Field Assaults Committed by Their Players*, 1 VA. J. SPORTS & L. 266 (1999). Generally, a court will excuse a club from liability if its player "commits an act wholly independent and foreign to the scope of his employment." *Averill v. Luttrell*, 311 S.W.2d 812, 813–14 (Tenn. App. 1957). In the following scenarios, consider whether the *team* should be vicariously liable for the actions of the players.

> a. A relief pitcher for a visiting baseball team, warming-up in the bullpen, becomes aggravated at the heckling of a fan and hurls a baseball at a screen separating the bullpen from the stands. The ball penetrates the screen and hits a spectator. *See Manning v. Grimsley*, 643 F.2d 20 (1st Cir. 1981).

> b. After dropping a pop fly and losing the game for his semi-pro team, a left-fielder throws the ball out of the park, striking a customer at a nearby gas station. *See Bonetti v. Double Play Tavern*, 274 P.2d 751 (Cal. Super. Ct. 1954).

> c. A player physically climbs into the grandstand to assault a fan who had been criticizing his play. *See Atlanta Baseball Co. v. Lawrence*, 144 S.E. 351 (Ga. Ct. App. 1928).

Again, the difficult questions center, in the first instance, upon the nature of zealous physical contact that is an accepted, and often encouraged, part of the game. Proceeding further, where along the spectrum do we place the *overly* aggressive "take-out" slide at second base, the aforementioned "late hit", or conduct that walks a tightrope between behavior warranting intra-league punishment (a game ejection, penalty or fine) and behavior actionable in tort? The reed-thin distinction is complicated by the fact that aggression or some type of controlled hostility is often precisely what is expected of a player and, in fact, may be the basis for a reward from his employer. For example, unverified rumor has it that some NFL coaches reinforce and encourage tackles where the opposing player's head hits the ground before the rest of his body. This type of exhortation makes it difficult to identify with any certainty conduct that crosses the line of demarcation into activity "beyond the scope" of employment. *See* Carlsen at 16-13 to 16-16; MARTIN J. GREENBERG & JAMES T. GRAY, *Sports Law Practice* §11.08 (1)(d)–(f) (1998).

4. With regard to vicarious liability, a related question asks what a club's liability would be if a player suffers injury as a result of inappropriate medical advice from the team physician. For example, what happens if a player suffers a serious exacerbation of a previous injury after he has been cleared to resume play by the team doctor or trainer? Football fiction, in books and movies, repeatedly portrays the injured player pumped with cortisone and pushed to "play with the little hurts." The wholesale distribution of steroids and other artificial performance-enhancing drugs, which are administered not as therapy to promote recovery but simply to create body mass and alter one's physique, raises similar concerns.

Anecdotally, the issues generally arise in a few limited contexts: (1) a player is injured during the game and is reinserted after a cursory examination by the team's medical personnel; (2) a player who complains of an injury or who is recovering from a known injury or illness and is advised that he is fit to resume competitive play; and (3) a player is issued a prescription for steroids or other "legal" drugs. One need not refer to fiction to witness horrific and sobering examples of player suffering and even death in such contexts. Loyola Marymount's basketball star Hank Gathers died of a heart attack during an NCAA game after he had been diagnosed with, and was receiving treatment for, a life threatening cardiac condition. *See* Cathy J. Jones, *College Athletes: Illness or Injury and the Decision to Play*, 40 BUFFALO L. REV. 113, 114–16 (1992). All-pro defensive end Lyle Alzado died from cancer that he is believed to have contracted, in part, because of his liberal use of anabolic steroids. *See* Stephen F. Brock et al., *Drug Testing College Athletes: NCAA Does Thy Cup Runneth Over?*, 97 W. VA. L. REV. 53, 58 n.11 (1994).

A determination of a physician's liability and the club's derivative responsibility for such injuries or illnesses will be governed by general negligence principles, especially those tests employed to determine medical malpractice. *See* WEISTART & LOWELL §8.08, at 984–96; *Searles v. Trustees of St. Joseph's College*, 695 A.2d 1206 (Me. 1997). The degree to which the club would be liable for the tortious acts of its doctors will turn on the nature of the team-physician relationship. In particular, a court will explore various factors to ascertain whether the physician is an independent contractor or an employee of the club. *See* Yasser at §15:13. There is also the possibility of a breach of contract action if the physician has elevated his or her duty by promising a certain result or making similar representations amounting to a guarantee or a warranty. *See Sullivan v. O'Connor*, 296 N.E.2d 183 (Mass. 1973); *Hawkins v. McGee*, 146 A. 641 (N.H. 1929).

Koffman v. Garnett
574 S.E.2d 258 (Va. 2003)

OPINION BY JUSTICE ELIZABETH B. LACY

* * *

In the fall of 2000, Andrew W. Koffman, a 13-year old middle school student at a public school in Botetourt County, began participating on the school's football team. It was Andy's first season playing organized football, and he was positioned as a third-string defensive player. James Garnett was employed by the Botetourt County School Board as an assistant coach for the football team and was responsible for the supervision, training, and instruction of the team's defensive players.

The team lost its first game of the season. Garnett was upset by the defensive players' inadequate tackling in that game and became further displeased by what he perceived as inadequate tackling during the first practice following the loss.

Garnett ordered Andy to hold a football and "stand upright and motionless" so that Garnett could explain the proper tackling technique to the defensive players. Then Garnett, without further warning, thrust his arms around Andy's body, lifted him "off his feet by two feet or more," and "slammed" him to the ground. Andy weighed 144 pounds, while Garnett weighed approximately 260 pounds. The force of the tackle broke the humerus bone in Andy's left arm. During prior practices, no coach had used physical force to instruct players on rules or techniques of playing football.

In his second amended motion for judgment, Andy, by his father and next friend, Richard Koffman, and Andy's parents, Richard and Rebecca Koffman, individually, (collectively "the Koffmans") alleged that Andy was injured as a result of Garnett's simple and gross negligence and intentional acts of assault and battery. * * *

I.

[T]his Court [has] defined gross negligence as "that degree of negligence which shows indifference to others as constitutes an utter disregard of prudence amounting to a complete neglect of the safety of [another]. It must be such a degree of negligence as would shock fair minded [people] although something less than willful recklessness." Whether certain actions constitute gross negligence is generally a factual matter for resolution by the jury and becomes a question of law only when reasonable people cannot differ.

* * *

As the trial court observed, receiving an injury while participating in a tackling demonstration may be part of the sport. The facts alleged in this case, however, go beyond the circumstances of simply being tackled in the course of participating in organized football. Here Garnett's knowledge of his greater size and experience, his instruction implying that Andy was not to take any action to defend himself from the force of a tackle, the force he used during the tackle, and Garnett's previous practice of not personally using force to demonstrate or teach football technique could lead a reasonable person to conclude that, in this instance, Garnett's actions were imprudent and were taken in utter disregard for the safety of the player involved. Because reasonable persons could disagree on this issue, a jury issue was presented, and the trial court erred in holding that, as a matter of law, the second amended motion for judgment was inadequate to state a claim for gross negligence.

II.

[The court held that there could be no recovery for assault because the allegations of Koffman's surprise at being tackled by his coach negated any reasonable inference that he was placed in apprehension of an impending battery.]

* * *

The [facts as alleged are sufficient] to establish a cause of action for the tort of battery. The Koffmans pled that Andy consented to physical contact with players "of like age and experience" and that neither Andy nor his parents expected or consented to his "participation in aggressive contact tackling by the adult coaches." Further, the Koffmans pled that, in the past, coaches had not tackled players as a method of instruction. Garnett asserts that, by consenting to play football, Andy consented to be tackled, by either other football players or by the coaches.

Whether Andy consented to be tackled by Garnett in the manner alleged was a matter of fact. [R]easonable persons could disagree on whether Andy gave such consent. Thus, we find that the trial court erred in holding that the Koffmans' second amended motion for judgment was insufficient as a matter of law to establish a claim for battery.

For the above reasons, we will reverse the trial court's judgment that the Koffmans' second amended motion for judgment was insufficient as a matter of law to establish the causes of actions for gross negligence and battery and remand the case for further proceedings consistent with this opinion.

Reversed and remanded.

JUSTICE KINSER, concurring in part and dissenting in part.

I agree with the majority opinion except with regard to the issue of consent as it pertains to the intentional tort of battery. In my view, the second amended motion for judgment filed by the plaintiffs * * * was insufficient as a matter of law to state a claim for battery.

Absent fraud, consent is generally a defense to an alleged battery. In the context of this case, "taking part in a game manifests a willingness to submit to such bodily contacts or restrictions of liberty as are permitted by its rules or usages." However, participating in a particular sport "does not manifest consent to contacts which are prohibited by rules or usages of the game if such rules or usages are designed to protect the participants and not merely to secure the better playing of the game as a test of skill." Restatement (Second) of Torts § 50, cmt. b (1965).

The thrust of the plaintiffs' allegations is that they did not consent to "Andy's participation in aggressive contact tackling by the adult coaches" but that they consented only to Andy's engaging "in a contact sport with other children of like age and experience." They further alleged that the coaches had not previously tackled the players when instructing them about the rules and techniques of football.

It is notable, in my opinion, that the plaintiffs admitted in their pleading that Andy's coach was "responsible * * * for the supervision, training and instruction of the defensive players." It cannot be disputed that one responsibility of a football coach is to minimize the possibility that players will sustain "something more than slight injury" while playing the sport. A football coach cannot be expected "to extract from the game the body clashes that cause bruises, jolts and hard falls." Instead, a coach should ensure that players are able to "withstand the shocks, blows and other rough treatment with which they would meet in actual play" by making certain that players are in "sound physical condition," are issued proper protective equipment, and are "taught and shown how to handle [themselves] while in play." The instruction on how to handle themselves during a game should include demonstrations of proper tackling techniques. By voluntarily participating in football, Andy and his parents necessarily consented to instruction by the coach on such techniques. The alleged battery occurred during that instruction.

The plaintiffs alleged that they were not aware that Andy's coach would use physical force to instruct on the rules and techniques of football since neither he nor the other coaches had done so in the past. Surely, the plaintiffs are not claiming that the scope of their consent changed from day to day depending on the coaches' instruction methods during prior practices. Moreover, they did not allege that they were told that the coaches would not use physical demonstrations to instruct the players.

Additionally, the plaintiffs did not allege that the tackle itself violated any rule or usage of the sport of football. Nor did they plead that Andy could not have been tackled by a larger, physically stronger, and more experienced player either during a game or practice. Tackling and instruction on proper tackling techniques are aspects of the sport of football to which a player consents when making a decision to participate in the sport.

* * *

Notes and Questions

1. Adults participating in children's athletic events (even when the conduct is not as egregious as in *Koffman*) can create increased risks of harm to the children, which may lead to increased tort liability for the adults. Courts have divided in such cases, with some concluding that the participation of adults can make injury more likely and therefore allowing cases to go to juries, and others concluding that the risk inherent in the game was not increased appreciably by the presence of the adult. *Compare Prejean v. East Baton Rouge Parish School Board*, 729 So. 2d 686 (La. Ct. App. 1999) (holding that a coach did not breach his duty of care by participating in a youth basketball game); *and Behar v. Fox*, 642 N.W.2d 426 (Mich. Ct. App. 2001) (holding that an adult's participation in a youth soccer game did not amount to recklessness), *with Mauner v. Feinstein*, 623 N.Y.S.2d 326 (N.Y. App. Div. 1995) (holding that a jury might reasonably conclude that the presence of an adult unreasonably increased the risks of a rugby match).

2. What should be the duty of a coach whose players might be suffering from heat-related health problems? Should there be an affirmative duty to inspect players to see if they appear to be in good health? Should the duty exist only when the coach is informed of a player's poor condition? What if a coach refuses a player's request for a water break? Should it make any difference if the coach is responsible for raising the risk of health problems by requiring players to undergo extraordinarily rigorous activity (e.g., by requiring players to run until one vomits)? What difference should it make if the team is at the high-school, collegiate, or professional level? *See Draughton v. Harnett County Board of Education*, 580 S.E.2d 732 (N.C. Ct. App. 2003). *Cf. Stringer v. Minnesota Vikings Football Club, LLC.*, 705 N.W.2d 746 (Minn. 2005).

3. For a more thorough discussion of the liability of coaches and administrators, see GIL FRIED, SAFE AT FIRST: A GUIDE TO HELP SPORTS ADMINISTRATORS REDUCE THEIR LIABILITY (1999) and Anthony S. McCaskey, *A Guide to the Legal Liability of Coaches for a Sports Participant's Injuries*, 6 SETON HALL J. SPORTS L. 7 (1996).

B. Liability of Sports Facilities and the Effect of Liability Waivers

Dalury v. S-K-I, Ltd.

670 A.2d 795 (Vt. 1995)

JOHNSON, Justice.

* * *

While skiing at Killington Ski Area, plaintiff Robert Dalury sustained serious injuries when he collided with a metal pole that formed part of the control maze for a ski lift line. Before the season started, Dalury had purchased a midweek season pass and signed a form releasing the ski area from liability. The relevant portion reads:

RELEASE FROM LIABILITY AND CONDITIONS OF USE

1. I accept and understand that Alpine Skiing is a hazardous sport with many dangers and risks and that injuries are a common and ordinary occurrence of the sport. As a condition of being permitted to use the ski area premises, I freely accept and voluntarily assume the risks of injury or property damage and release Killington Ltd., its employees and agents from any and all liability for personal injury or property damage resulting from negligence, conditions of the premises, operations of the ski area, actions or omissions of employees or agents of the ski area or from my participation in skiing at the area, accepting myself the full responsibility for any and all such damage or injury of any kind which may result.

Plaintiff also signed a photo identification card that contained this same language.

Dalury and his wife filed a complaint against defendants, alleging negligent design, construction, and replacement of the maze pole. Defendants moved for summary judgment, arguing that the release of liability barred the negligence action. The trial court, without specifically addressing plaintiffs' contention that the release was contrary to public policy, found that the language of the release clearly absolved defendants of liability for their own negligence.

* * *

[P]laintiffs contend that the release was ambiguous as to whose liability was waived and that it is unenforceable as a matter of law because it violates public policy. We agree with defendants that the release was quite clear in its terms. Because we hold the agreement is unenforceable, we proceed to a discussion of the public policy that supports our holding.

I.

This is a case of first impression in Vermont. While we have recognized the existence of a public policy exception to the validity of exculpatory agreements, in most of our cases, enforceability has turned on whether the language of the agreement was sufficiently clear to reflect the parties' intent.

Even well-drafted exculpatory agreements, however, may be void because they violate public policy. Restatement (Second) of Torts §496B comment e (1965). According to the Restatement, an exculpatory agreement should be upheld if it is (1) freely and fairly made, (2) between parties who are in an equal bargaining position, and (3) there is no social interest with which it interferes. §496B comment b. The critical issue here concerns the social interests that are affected.

Courts and commentators have struggled to develop a useful formula for analyzing the public policy issue. The formula has been the "subject of great debate" during "the whole course of the common law," and it had proven impossible to articulate a precise definition because the "social forces that have led to such characterization are volatile and dynamic." *Tunkl v. Regents of Univ. of Cal.*, 383 P.2d 441, 444 (Cal. 1963).

The leading judicial formula for determining whether an exculpatory agreement violates public policy was set forth [in *Tunkl*]. An agreement is invalid if it exhibits some or all of the following characteristics:

[1.] It concerns a business of a type generally thought suitable for public regulation. [2.] The party seeking exculpation is engaged in performing a service of great importance to the public, which is often a matter of practical necessity for some members of the public. [3.] The party holds [it]self out as willing to perform this service for any member of the public who seeks it, or at least for any member coming within certain established standards. [4.] As a result of the essential nature of the service, in the economic setting of the transaction, the party invoking exculpation possesses a decisive advantage of bargaining strength against any member of the public who seeks [the party's] services. [5.] In exercising a superior bargaining power the party confronts the public with a standardized adhesion contract of exculpation, and makes no provision whereby a purchaser may pay additional reasonable fees and obtain protection against negligence. [6.] Finally, as a result of the transaction, the person or property of the purchaser is placed under the control of the seller, subject to the risk of carelessness by the seller or [the seller's] agents.

Id. at 445–46 (footnotes omitted). Applying these factors, the court concluded that a release from liability for future negligence imposed as a condition for admission to a charitable research hospital was invalid.

* * *

[W]e recognize that no single formula will reach the relevant public policy issues in every factual context. [U]ltimately the "determination of what constitutes the public interest must be made considering the totality of the circumstances of any given case against the backdrop of current societal expectations."

II.

Defendants urge us to uphold the exculpatory agreement on the ground that ski resorts do not provide an essential public service. They argue that they owe no duty to plaintiff to permit him to use their private lands for skiing, and that the terms and conditions of entry ought to be left entirely within their control. Because skiing, like other recreational sports, is not a necessity of life, defendants contend that the sale of a lift ticket is a purely private matter, implicating no public interest. We disagree.

Whether or not defendants provide an essential public service does not resolve the public policy question in the recreational sports context. The defendants' area is a facility open to the public. They advertise and invite skiers and nonskiers of every level of skiing ability to their premises for the price of a ticket. At oral argument, defendants conceded that thousands of people buy lift tickets every day throughout the season. Thousands of people ride lifts, buy services, and ski the trails. Each ticket sale may be, for some purposes, a purely private transaction. But when a substantial number of such sales take place as a result of the seller's general invitation to the public to utilize the facilities and services in question, a legitimate public interest arises.

The major public policy implications are those underlying the law of premises liability. In Vermont, a business owner has a duty "of active care to make sure that its premises are in safe and suitable condition for its customers." * * * We have already held that a ski area owes its customers the same duty as any other business—to keep its premises reasonably safe.

The policy rationale is to place responsibility for maintenance of the land on those who own or control it, with the ultimate goal of keeping accidents to the minimum level possible. Defendants, not recreational skiers, have the expertise and opportunity to foresee and control hazards, and to guard against the negligence of their agents and employees. They alone can properly maintain and inspect their premises, and train their employees in risk management. They alone can insure against risks and effectively spread the cost of insurance among their thousands of customers. Skiers, on the other hand, are not in a position to discover and correct risks of harm, and they cannot insure against the ski area's negligence.

If defendants were permitted to obtain broad waivers of their liability, an important incentive for ski areas to manage risk would be removed with the public bearing the cost of the resulting injuries. It is illogical, in these circumstances, to undermine the public policy underlying business invitee law and allow skiers to bear risks they have no ability or right to control.

* * * A recognition of the principles underlying the duty to business invitees makes clear the inadequacy of relying upon the essential public service factor in the analysis of public recreation cases. While interference with an essential public service surely affects the public interest, those services do not represent the universe of activities that implicate public concerns.

* * *

Defendants argue that the public policy of the state, as expressed in the "Acceptance of inherent risks" statute, 12 V.S.A. 1037,[2] indicates a willingness on the part of the Legislature to limit ski area liability. Therefore, they contend that public policy favors the use of express releases such as the one signed by plaintiff. On the contrary, defendants' allocation of responsibility for skiers' injuries is at odds with the statute. The statute places responsibility for the "inherent risks" of any sport on the participant, insofar as such risks are obvious and necessary. A ski area's own negligence, however, is neither an inherent risk nor an obvious and necessary one in the sport of skiing. Thus, a skier's assumption of the inherent risks of skiing does not abrogate the ski area's duty "'to warn of or correct dangers which in the exercise of reasonable prudence in the circumstances could have been foreseen and corrected.'"

Reversed and remanded.

Notes and Questions

1. What form of assumption of the risk was the defendant arguing—express, implied primary, or implied secondary? What form of assumption of the risk was governed by the statute? See Chapter 18, Part II, supra.

2. Waivers such as those at issue here are often upheld by courts, but even those courts typically construe them narrowly, resolving ambiguities against the drafters. *See, e.g., Kissick v. Schmierer*, 816 P.2d 188 (Alaska 1991) (construing a waiver of negligence claims for "any loss, damage or injury to my person or my property" not to reach a negligence claim for death); *Covert v. South Florida Stadium Corp.*, 762 So. 2d 938 (Fla. Ct. App. 2000); *Hertzog v. Harrison Island Shores, Inc.*, 251 N.Y.S.2d 164 (N.Y. App. Div. 1964).

3. Though courts divide on whether negligence liability may be waived, there is more agreement that claims of gross negligence or recklessness may not. Do you agree with this distinction?

---

2. "[A] person who takes part in any sport accepts as a matter of law the dangers that inhere therein insofar as they are obvious and necessary." 12 V.S.A. § 1037.

4. Should parents be able to waive the negligence claims of their children? *Compare Hojnowski v. Vans State Park*, 901 A.2d 381, (N.J. 2006) (refusing to enforce the waiver); *Hawkins v. Peart*, 37 P.3d 1062 (Utah 2001) (same); and *Scott v. Pacific West Mountain Resort*, 834 P.2d 6 (Wash. 1992) (same), *with Sharon v. City of Newton*, 769 N.E.2d 738 (Mass. 2002) (upholding the waiver); and *Zivich v. Mentor Soccer Club, Inc.*, 696 N.E.2d 201 (Ohio 1998) (same). Should adults be able to waive the liability of adult family members? *See Huber v. Hovey*, 501 N.W.2d 53 (Iowa 1993). Should children themselves be able to waive their right to sue? *See Dilallo v. Riding Safely, Inc.*, 687 So. 2d 353 (Fla. App. 1997) (invalidating a 14-year-old's waiver).

5. In *Hojnowski*, the New Jersey Supreme Court refused to enforce the waiver of liability signed by the parent, but it did enforce the provision of the agreement providing for mandatory arbitration. Is there a meaningful distinction between those two types of waivers? What if the waiver included a choice-of-law provision?

C. Liability of Game Officials

Santopietro v. City of New Haven
682 A.2d 106 (Conn. 1996)

BORDEN, J.

* * *

* * * On October 16, 1988, the plaintiffs attended a softball game played at East Shore Park in New Haven by teams belonging to an organized league. The defendants David Brennan and Bruce Shepard served as the umpires for that game. The defendant Mark Piombino was a participant in the game.

The plaintiff Raymond Santopietro, Jr., observed the softball game from a position behind the backstop and was not on the field of play. The plaintiff Raymond Santopietro, Sr., was approximately ten to fifteen feet from his son watching another game being played on an adjacent field.

In the sixth inning, Piombino came to bat in the game that Santopietro, Jr., was watching and hit a fly ball. In frustration, he intentionally flung his bat toward the backstop. Somehow the bat passed through the backstop and struck Santopietro, Jr., in the head. As a result, Santopietro, Jr., suffered a fractured skull and other serious injuries.

Both Santopietro, Jr., and Santopietro, Sr., appeal from the judgment of the trial court * * * following a directed verdict in favor of Brennan and Shepard on Santopietro, Jr.'s claim of negligence. * * *[4]

* * *

A review of the evidence in the light most favorable to the plaintiffs indicates that the jury might reasonably have found the following facts. During the course of the game that Santopietro, Jr., was watching when he was injured, there occurred several incidents of unruly behavior by players who were on the same team as Piombino. Some players used vulgar language in a loud and angry manner. Players taunted members of the other team in an attempt to intimidate them. Players threw their gloves and kicked

---

4. The judgment against Piombino [entered after a jury verdict in favor of Santopietro, Jr.] is not involved in this appeal.

the dirt, and one player kicked a garbage can, upsetting its contents and creating a loud noise. After his turn at bat resulted in an out, another player angrily threw a bat along the ground in the direction of the bats not in use. Another player threw his glove from the pitcher's mound into the dugout. A player inside the dugout repeatedly banged a bat against the dugout, producing a loud noise. Furthermore, the jury could have inferred from the evidence presented that Brennan and Shepard were aware or reasonably should have been aware of these incidents.

After passing a written examination, Brennan and Shepard were both trained and approved to be softball umpires by the Amateur Softball Association (association), a national organization that regulates the conduct of organized amateur softball in the United States. Both Brennan and Shepard possessed years of experience and had umpired hundreds of games. Shepard had received an award honoring him for being the best umpire in New Haven. Brennan testified that, as an umpire, he possesses specialized knowledge about softball and softball rules that is greater than the average person's knowledge. Both Brennan and Shepard were familiar with the association's rules governing the conduct of umpires.

Brennan and Shepard testified that when they observed unsportsmanlike conduct, they would issue a warning and, if the warning was disregarded, they would eject the player from the game. Specifically, they testified that they would have taken such action if they had observed the disruptive behavior described by several witnesses, including taunting, loud swearing, kicking a garbage can, hitting the inside of the dugout with a bat, or throwing a glove from the pitcher's mound into the dugout.

Brennan and Shepard further testified that when they give a warning, it usually has the effect of stopping the disruptive behavior and preventing future improper acts. They testified that any player who tosses a bat should be ejected immediately, and Brennan testified that if he had seen a player toss a bat as described by the witnesses, he would have ejected that player without warning. They testified that such disciplinary action is an effective means by which to control the actions of players.

Shepard testified that, as an umpire, he had the duty to maintain control of the game to prevent harm to spectators, and that warnings constitute the primary means by which to maintain that control. Moreover, Brennan testified that umpires have the authority to suspend the game if necessary to keep order or to prevent harm to spectators.

Brennan and Shepard also testified that the decision of whether to impose discipline in any given instance of unruly behavior is a discretionary matter for the umpire. Brennan testified that the rule against unsportsmanlike conduct gives the umpire authority "at his discretion, to disqualify any player who exhibits unsportsmanlike conduct in the judgment of the umpire." He further testified that decisions whether to take disciplinary action in response to loud swearing, throwing a glove or kicking dirt "are umpire judgment or umpire discretion calls." Shepard testified that the question of whether unruly behavior, such as using loud and abusive language, throwing a glove or kicking a garbage can, constitutes unsportsmanlike conduct will depend on the particular situation. * * *

We note that this testimony confirms what is the common understanding of the umpire's task. In the absence of exceptional circumstances, a softball umpire, when confronted with unruly behavior by a player that arguably constitutes unsportsmanlike conduct, faces a spectrum of discretionary options. At one end of the spectrum is taking no action; at the other end is ejection of the player or suspension of the game. In between are warnings and other appropriate disciplinary action. The umpire has discretion, within the spectrum, to respond to the offensive behavior in the manner that the umpire finds to be most appropriate in the given circumstances.

* * * We conclude that the plaintiffs were required to establish by expert testimony that the failure of Brennan and Shepard to act in the present case constituted a breach of duty, and that the plaintiffs' evidence did not satisfy that burden.

* * *

If the determination of the standard of care requires knowledge that is beyond the experience of an ordinary fact finder, expert testimony will be required.

We note that the plaintiffs' claims in the present case are akin to allegations of professional negligence or malpractice, which we have previously defined as "the failure of one rendering professional services to exercise that degree of skill and learning commonly applied under all the circumstances in the community by the average prudent reputable member of the profession with the result of injury, loss, or damage to the recipient of those services." As Brennan testified, he possesses specialized knowledge as an umpire that is greater than the average person's knowledge. An umpire obtains, through formal training and experience, a familiarity with the rules of the sport, a technical expertise in their application, and an understanding of the likely consequences of officiating decisions. As a result, the umpire possesses knowledge of the standard of care to which an umpire reasonably may be held, and of what constitutes a violation of that standard, that is beyond the experience and ken of the ordinary fact finder. Moreover, the fact finder's lack of expertise is exacerbated by the highly discretionary nature of the umpire's task. Thus, the fact finder must determine, not just whether in hindsight the umpire erred, but also whether the umpire's error constituted an abuse of his broad discretion. In such cases in which the fact finder's decision requires specialized knowledge, expert testimony is necessary "to assist lay people, such as members of the jury and the presiding judge, to understand the applicable standard of care and to evaluate the defendant's actions in light of that standard."

In the present case, the plaintiffs do not articulate clearly the umpire's duty upon which they base their claim. The plaintiffs principally rely upon the testimony of Shepard that an umpire's duty is "to maintain control on the field so it does not spill over to spectators." Thus, the plaintiffs appear to postulate a duty owed by the umpires to maintain control of the game in such a way as to prevent harm to others. On appeal, Brennan and Shepard do not concede that such a duty exists, but argue that even if we were to assume its existence, the plaintiffs failed to define the duty. Our research indicates that no other jurisdiction has explicitly considered whether to impose or how to define such a legal duty.

Therefore, for the purposes of this appeal, we assume, without deciding, that umpires such as Brennan and Shepard[17] have a duty, essentially as postulated by the plaintiffs, to exercise reasonable judgment as umpires in order to maintain control of a game so as to prevent an unreasonable risk of injury to others. The breach of this duty, however, must be proved, in the absence of exceptional circumstances, by expert testimony establishing that the allegedly negligent action or failure to act by the umpire constituted an abuse of the umpire's discretion to evaluate the particular circumstances and to take only such disciplinary action as the umpire deems appropriate. Moreover, the ex-

---

17. We note that Brennan and Shepard had been formally trained and were paid to officiate the game at which Santopietro, Jr., was injured. Although this information does not affect the resolution of the present case, we acknowledge that it may be relevant if, in the future, we are required to decide whether such a duty exists. The existence or extent of a duty might be affected by whether the umpire is a paid professional or an unpaid volunteer without formal training.

pert testimony must establish an abuse of that discretion sufficient to permit a jury to infer that the umpire's action or failure to act constituted such a loss of control of the game as to give rise to an unreasonable risk of injury to the plaintiff.

In fact, in the present case, the plaintiffs concede that expert testimony was required to establish whether the applicable standard of care was breached by Brennan and Shepard. The plaintiffs argue that, through the testimony of Brennan and Shepard, they presented sufficient positive evidence of an expert nature from which the jury could have reasonably concluded that Brennan and Shepard were negligent.

* * *

We conclude, in the present case, that the plaintiffs failed to produce sufficient evidence that Brennan and Shepard had breached the applicable standard of care. * * *

The plaintiffs did present evidence that, arguably, would support the conclusion that Brennan and Shepard improperly failed to act in response to two incidents. First, witnesses testified that a player tossed a bat toward other bats after an unsuccessful plate appearance. Brennan and Shepard testified that the local rule required them to eject immediately any player who throws a bat. Brennan further testified that the incident described by the witnesses would "merit an ejection." If we were to interpret this testimony to constitute an expert opinion that a reasonable umpire must have ejected the player in those circumstances, then this evidence would support the conclusion that Brennan and Shepard improperly failed to act with respect to that particular incident. Second, a witness testified that some players taunted members of the other team. Shepard testified that an umpire should take immediate action in response to taunting. Brennan and Shepard do not dispute the plaintiffs' evidence that they did not take any disciplinary action during the game.

The testimony of Brennan and Shepard concerning these two incidents supports a possible conclusion that they failed to exercise their discretion in a reasonable manner on two occasions during the game. The plaintiffs do not contend, however, that these two incidents suffice to establish that Brennan and Shepard breached a duty, which we assume exists, to maintain control of the game in order to prevent unreasonable risk of harm to others. The plaintiffs do not argue, and we do not assume, that Brennan and Shepard possess a duty to make every discretionary call that arises during the course of the game error free. Umpire liability, if it were to exist, must be predicated on facts sufficient to support the conclusion that their unreasonable actions or failure to act led to such a loss of control of the game as to imperil unreasonably the safety of others. We conclude, as a matter of law, that these two incidents of arguably negligent behavior are not sufficient to support such a conclusion.

We conclude, therefore, that the plaintiffs have failed to prove by expert testimony that Brennan and Shepard breached a duty of care to prevent an unreasonable risk of the injuries suffered by Santopietro, Jr. Because the jury could not have reasonably and legally concluded that the plaintiffs had established the elements of a negligence cause of action, a directed verdict was properly granted.

* * *

The judgment is affirmed.

Notes and Questions

1. The court holds that even if officials owe a duty to protect spectators (and, one would assume, contestants), the plaintiffs here failed to produce expert testimony

showing that the umpires exceeded their discretion. Accordingly, the court places considerable weight on the discretion entrusted to umpires to deal with unsportsmanlike conduct. Are all decisions of sports officials similarly discretionary? What if there were a rule in the league forbidding metal spikes? If an umpire ignored the rule and a participant were injured as a result, should the umpire be liable?

2. Many sports rules are drafted in absolute terms but are applied with discretion. Officials must use judgment in evaluating situations as disparate as when to eject a pitcher for throwing at a batter, when to assess a penalty for an "avoidable" body check in hockey, and what consequences result from a boxing punch that might be a low blow. What problems do you foresee with allowing expert testimony on the question how strictly a rule is applied? Do you think other officials will admit to failing to enforce a seemingly categorical rule? Or will the expert witnesses be too willing to proclaim the judgment that goes into their job, creating a different kind of "'blue' wall of silence" behind an official whose enforcement standards are too lax?

3. The *Santopietro* court opted not to decide the question whether officials owe a duty to protect spectators or participants, but there is little doubt that courts will soon need to decide whether game officials owe a duty of care to those who may be harmed as a result of their actions or omissions. Should there be such a duty? If so, what should it be? *See Rolison v. City of Meridian*, 691 So. 2d 440 (Miss. 1997) (finding no duty to protect a baserunner from a bat negligently thrown by the batter); Michael Mayer, *Stepping In to Step Out of Liability: The Proper Standard of Liability for Referee in Foreseeable Judgment-Call Situations*, 3 DePaul J. Sports L. & Contemp. Probs. 54, 65 (2005) ("It seems inherent in the role referees play, the monetary compensation provided, and the desire to prevent harm to athletes that referees would possess that 'special relationship' with the athletes and have some duty to protect or control the athletes they oversee."); Richard J. Hunter, Jr., *An "Insider's" Guide to the Legal Liability of Sports Contest Officials*, 15 Marq. Sports L. Rev. 369 (2005).

4. The National Association of Sports Officials has drafted a model statute restricting officials' liability, which sixteen states have adopted in one form or another. The model statute reads in part as follows:

> Sports officials who officiate athletic contests at any level of competition in this State shall not be liable to any person or entity in any civil action for injuries or damages claimed to have arisen by virtue of actions or inactions related in any manner to officiating duties within the confines of the athletic facility at which the athletic contest is played.

* * *

> Nothing in this law shall be deemed to grant the protection set forth to sports officials who cause injury or damage to a person or entity by actions or inactions which are intentional, willful, wanton, reckless, malicious or grossly negligent.

Is such a statute wise?

5. In *Carabba v. Anacortes School District No. 103*, 435 P.2d 936 (Wash. 1967), the court held that a school district could be held liable if an injury in a school-sponsored athletic contest was caused by the referee's failure to observe a "reasonable and prudent referee" standard. Does such a standard differ from the "abuse of his broad discretion" standard hypothesized in *Santopietro*?

6. Are sports officials the type of professionals who should be held to a "reasonable-and-prudent-member-of-the-profession" standard? Theoretically, at least, offi-

cials could be compensated at a wage high enough to allow them to purchase insurance and distribute the risk of poor officiating across the universe of sports officials the same way the medical profession distributes risk through malpractice insurance. Practically, however, are the parties who hire officials going to be willing to pay that additional wage?

7. Illinois has enacted the following statute, which insulates *volunteer* coaches and officials from negligence liability:

> [N]o person who, without compensation and as a volunteer, renders services as a manager, coach, instructor, umpire or referee * * * shall be liable to any person for any civil damages as a result of any acts or omissions in rendering such services or in conducting or sponsoring such sports program, unless the conduct of such person falls substantially below the standards generally practiced and accepted in like circumstances by similar persons rendering such services or conducting or sponsoring such sports programs, and unless it is shown that such person * * * kn[ew] or ha[d] reason to know that such act or omission created a substantial risk of actual harm to the person or property of another. It shall be insufficient to impose liability to establish only that the conduct of such person fell below ordinary standards of care.

745 Ill. Comp. Stat. 80/1.

8. If "professional" officials—i.e., those who are trained and paid for officiating—are made subject to a duty, while volunteers are not (*see* Note 7, above, and *Santopietro*'s footnote 17), the tort system will thereby inevitably discourage the use of professional officials. Will the result of such a regime be to decrease safety overall? If so, should the response be to impose a duty on all officials (professional and volunteer), or should it be to impose liability on none? If all officials bear a duty, will the tort system be creating an incentive for contests to go unofficiated?

9. Officials may be *owed* a duty of care by those in charge of athletic facilities if it is reasonable to anticipate a threat to the officials' safety. *See Toone v. Adams*, 137 S.E.2d 132 (N.C. 1964) (holding that any such duty, if it exists, was not breached when the facility provided two guards who were unable to prevent an assault on an umpire). *See generally* Carole J. Wallace, *The Men in Black and Blue: A Comment on Violence Against Sports Officials and State Legislative Reaction*, 6 Seton Hall J. Sports L. 341 (1996).

Patton v. United States of America Rugby Football, Union, Ltd. d/b/a USA Rugby

851 A.2d 566 (Md. 2004)

Opinion by Harrell, J.

On 17 June 2000, Robert Carson Patton, II, and his father, Donald Lee Patton, while at an amateur rugby tournament in Annapolis, were struck by lightning. Robert, a player in the tournament, was seriously injured, but survived. Donald, a spectator watching his son play, died. Robert and various other members of the Patton family filed suit in the Circuit Court for Anne Arundel County alleging negligence against the rugby tournament organizers, referee, and related organizations with regard to the episode.

* * *

Based on Appellants' amended complaint, we assume the truth of the following factual allegations:

Sometime during the early morning of 17 June 2000, Robert and Donald Patton arrived at playing fields adjacent to the Annapolis Middle School in Anne Arundel County, Maryland. Robert was to play rugby for the Norfolk Blues Rugby Club. Donald intended to support his son as a spectator. Robert and Donald, along with other participants and spectators, placed their equipment and belongings under a row of trees adjacent to the playing fields.

The rugby tournament was coordinated by Steven Quigg and was sanctioned by the United States of America Rugby Football Union, Ltd., d/b/a USA Rugby, and Mid-Atlantic Rugby Football Union, Inc. Rugby matches involving over two dozen teams began at approximately 9:00 a.m. and were planned to continue throughout the day. It was a warm, muggy day. The weather forecast for Annapolis was for possible thunderstorms. At some point prior to the start of the twenty minute match between the Norfolk Blues and the Washington Rugby Football Club ("the match"), a thunderstorm passed through the area surrounding the Annapolis Middle School. At the start of the match, rain commenced; lightning could be seen and thunder could be heard proximate to the lightning flashes. By this time, the National Weather Service had issued a thunderstorm "warning" for the Annapolis area.

Kevin Eager, a member of the Potomac Society of Rugby Football Referees, Inc., was the volunteer referee for the afternoon match in which Robert Patton was a participant. Under the direction of Eager, the match continued as the rain increased in intensity, the weather conditions deteriorated, and the lighting flashed directly overhead. Other matches at the tournament ended. Robert Patton continued to play the match through the rain and lightning and his father continued to observe as a spectator until the match was stopped just prior to its normal conclusion.

Upon the termination of the match, Robert and Donald fled the playing fields to the area under the trees where they left their possessions. As they began to make their exit from under the trees to seek the safety of their car, each was struck by lightning. Donald died. Robert Patton sustained personal injuries and was hospitalized, but recovered.

* * *

Appellants alleged that Appellees each had a duty to, but failed to, do one or more of the following acts:

"(a) Have and implement proper policies and procedures regarding the protection of players and spectators from adverse weather conditions and lightning;

"(b) Have and implement a policy regarding the safe evacuation of players and spectators from the fields of play at its matches when lightning is present;

"(c) Safeguard the health, safety, and welfare of the players and spectators at its matches;

"(d) Terminate the rugby match and tournament when lightning is present;

"(e) Monitor and detect dangerous conditions associated with its matches; and

"(f) Train, supervise, monitor and control actions of officials prior to ensure the safety of the participants and spectators from dangerous lightning strikes."

* * *

Appellants allege that a "special relationship" existed between Appellees * * * and Robert and Donald Patton sufficient to recognize the existence of a duty to protect the latter, the breach of which gave rise to an action for negligence. Appellants argue that:

A participant in a sporting event, by the very nature of the sport, trusts that his personal welfare will be protected by those controlling the event. Stated another way, it is reasonably foreseeable that both the player, and the player's father, will continue to participate in the match, as []long as the match is not stopped by the governing bodies in charge. It also is reasonably foreseeable that, when matches are played in thunderstorms, there is a substantial risk of injury from lightning. And finally, it is reasonably foreseeable that a father will not abandon his son, when he sees those who have assumed responsibility for his son's welfare placing his son in a perilous condition. * * *

Appellants essentially contend that the tournament organizers had a duty to protect Robert and Donald, and to extricate them, from the dangers of playing in and viewing, respectively, a sanctioned rugby match during a thunderstorm.

Appellees counter that "there is no 'special relationship' between Mr. Patton, Sr., Mr. Patton and the Appellees which would require the Appellees to protect and warn these individuals of the dangers associated with lightning." Appellees argue that they "had no ability to control the activities of players or spectators at any time," and "there is no evidence in the record that Mr. Patton, Sr. and Mr. Patton were dependent upon or relied upon the Appellees in any way, shape or form."

"[T]he creation of a 'special duty' by virtue of a 'special relationship' between the parties can be established by either (1) the inherent nature of the relationship between the parties; or (2) by one party undertaking to protect or assist the other party, and thus often inducing reliance upon the conduct of the acting party." We conclude that Appellants here did not establish by either of these methods a triable issue as to the existence of a "special relationship."

* * *

The element of dependence and ceding of self-control by the injured party that is needed [to trigger a "special relationship"] is absent in the present case.[5] There is no credible evidence that the two adults, Robert and Donald Patton, entrusted themselves to the control and protection of Appellees. * * *

* * * An adult amateur sporting event is a voluntary affair, and the participants are capable of leaving the playing field on their own volition if they feel their lives or health are in jeopardy. The changing weather conditions in the present case presumably were observable to all competent adults. Robert and Donald Patton could have sought shelter at any time they deemed it appropriate to do so.

* * *

Chief Judge Bell joins in the judgment only [without opinion].

Notes and Questions

1. Should the court have drawn a distinction between the duty owed to spectators and that owed to participants? How likely is it that a participant would withdraw from a game based on his own assessment that weather conditions make further participation unsafe?

---

5. There may be a degree of dependency and ceding of control that could trigger a "special relationship" in, for example, a Little League game where children playing in the game are reliant on the adults supervising them.

2. Would the case be decided differently if it arose out of a youth tournament? *Compare Patton* and *Maddox v. City of New York*, 487 N.E.2d 553 (N.Y. 1985) (holding that the plaintiff centerfielder for the New York Yankees assumed the risk of injury by playing baseball on a field he knew to be wet) with *Locilento v. John A. Coleman Catholic High School*, 523 N.Y.S.2d 198, 200 (App. Div. 1987) (refusing to apply *Maddox* to a case involving an amateur football game). As the court in *Maddox* explained, "a higher degree of awareness will be imputed to a professional than to one with less than professional experience in the particular sport." 487 N.E.2d at 556–57. Should the key question be the plaintiff's *experience* or his *status* as a professional or amateur?

3. If you agree with the court that adult participants and spectators bear responsibility for ensuring their own safety from hazardous weather, *shouldn't* parents, rather than coaches, league officials, and game officials bear that responsibility in youth games? What standard should be applied when the parents are absent? Can a coach reasonably refuse to play if the game official has not stopped the contest? If a coach does refuse to play because he perceives the field conditions as too dangerous, should a court be receptive to the team's appeal from the resulting forfeit? *Cf.* Chapter 3, *supra*.

4. *Patton* holds that the tournament officials owe no duty to protect the safety of players and spectators because there is no "special relationship." Alternatively, the court could have held that even if a special relationship existed, there is never a duty to warn someone of a weather condition he or she is capable of observing. *See Hames v. State*, 808 S.W.2d 41 (Tenn. 1991).

V. Injuries Caused by Defective Equipment

We have come a long way since the days of leather football helmets with no face guarding and the total absence of any head protection for players in Major League Baseball and professional hockey. (Hall of Fame goaltender Gump Worsley famously told reporters, "My face *is* my mask.") The heightened intensity of competition at all levels of sport, artificial surfaces, strength and weight programs, and other factors have led to an increase in the number and severity of sports-related injuries. Equipment manufacturers have responded by developing innovative, sophisticated forms of protection designed to insulate players from injury without compromising their performance. Notwithstanding the proper development and application of protective equipment, however, injuries still occur frequently, particularly in high-impact contact sports such as football and ice hockey. At times, the injury may be a product of equipment that is poorly designed, inappropriately marketed (*i.e.*, it fails adequately to warn potential users of its limits), or carelessly or insufficiently tested.

Everett v. Bucky Warren, Inc.
380 N.E.2d 653 (Mass. 1978)

QUIRICO, Justice. In this case the plaintiff seeks damages from the suppliers of a protective helmet he was wearing when, while playing in a hockey game, he was struck in the head by a puck and was seriously injured. The question before us is whether, on the various counts brought under both negligence and strict liability theories, the evidence was sufficient to support the verdicts for the plaintiff.

* * *

The controversies in this case revolve around the design of the protective helmet worn by the plaintiff when he was injured. It is described as a three-piece helmet because its protective components are three sections of high-impact plastic lined on the inside with shock foam. One piece covers the back of the head, extending from the nape up about six inches, and running horizontally between positions slightly behind each ear; the second piece, approximately two inches wide, rings the front of the head from the same positions, thus covering the forehead; and the third piece joins the tops of these two sections and covers the top of the head. This top piece is loosely connected to the other two sections by six strips of leather, each 1½ to 1¾ inches in width and 1½ to 2 inches in length. The side pieces are linked by a ¾ inch wide elastic strap, whose length is adjustable. The result of this three-piece design and loose method of linking the sections is that there are gaps within the helmet where no plastic piece covers. The gap between the top piece and the two side pieces ranges from ½ to ¾ of an inch. The gaps between the two side pieces vary with the size of the wearer's head and the tension with which the elastic straps are adjusted, and range from zero to ¾ of an inch. This three-piece design, characterized by the internal gaps, was somewhat unique, and there were available at the time of the plaintiff's injury and for some time prior thereto helmets that were designed as one-piece units and were therefore without such gaps.

When the injury occurred the plaintiff, who was approximately nineteen years old, was a post-graduate student and a member of the hockey team at the defendant New Preparatory School (New Prep) in Cambridge, Massachusetts. On January 10, 1970, the New Prep team went to Providence, Rhode Island, to play the Brown University freshman team. During the game the plaintiff, a defenseman, attempted to block the shot of a Brown player by throwing himself into a horizontal position on the ice, about ten to fifteen feet in front of the shooting player and perpendicular to the intended line of flight of the puck. The puck struck the plaintiff above and slightly back from his right ear, and penetrated into the gap of the helmet formed where the three helmet sections came together. As a result of this penetration the puck hit his head and caused a fracture of the skull. This serious injury subsequently required that a plate be inserted in the plaintiff's skull, and caused the plaintiff to have headaches that will continue indefinitely.

The helmet was being worn by the plaintiff on the night of his injury as a result of its being supplied to him through the following process. The helmet was manufactured by J.E. Pender (Pender), a proprietorship engaged in the manufacture of sporting goods and represented in this action by the defendant George Whittie, executor of the will of James E. Pender. In 1967 through 1969 Pender sold at least fourteen helmets of the type worn by the plaintiff to the defendant Bucky Warren, Inc. (Bucky Warren), a retailer in sporting goods, which in turn sold them to New Prep. The helmets had been specially ordered by Owen Hughes, the coach of the New Prep team, who was the person authorized by the school to make such purchases. They were painted in the colors of the school to match the team uniforms. Each player on the plaintiff's team was supplied with one of these helmets for practice and game use, although Hughes's testimony indicated that, had a player so wished, he could have worn a different helmet of his own choosing. Rather than purchasing his own helmet, the plaintiff chose to wear the one supplied to him by the school authorities.

The plaintiff brought this action claiming that, because of the gaps, the Pender helmet was defectively designed, and that therefore all three defendants, Pender, Bucky Warren, and New Prep, were liable to him in negligence for supplying him the helmet, and that the defendants Pender and Bucky Warren were also liable to him in tort on a strict liability theory. At trial, motions for directed verdicts were denied, and fourteen special questions were submitted to the jury. The jury found that all three defendants were negligent, that the helmet was not in a reasonably safe condition when sold by Pender and Bucky Warren, that the plaintiff's injury was caused by the condition of the helmet and the negligence of the defendants, and that the plaintiff himself neither assumed the risk of the injury nor was contributorily negligent. The plaintiff was awarded $85,000 in damages. After proper motions the judge, notwithstanding the jury verdicts, entered judgments in favor of all defendants on the negligence counts, holding that, as matter of law, the plaintiff assumed the risk of his injury. He entered judgment for the plaintiff for $85,000 on the strict liability counts, however, on the ground that assumption of the risk was not a defense to this cause of action. * * *

The issues raised here are whether there was sufficient evidence for the jury to find that: (a) the defendants Pender and New Prep were negligent, (b) the plaintiff was not negligent and did not assume the risk of his injury, and (c) the helmet was defective and unreasonably dangerous as sold by Pender and Bucky Warren.

* * *

1. Negligence. "A manufacturer is under a duty to use reasonable care to design a product that is reasonably safe for its intended use." W. Prosser, Torts §96, at 645 (4th ed. 1971). * * * The Pender helmet was designed by James E. Pender, who possessed no engineering background. It was intended to protect the vital areas of the head, the temples and cranium. It was designed in three pieces, however, not for safety reasons, but to facilitate adjustment. Pender indicated in his deposition—he was deceased at the time of trial—that the helmet was consciously designed so that there would be gaps between its sections when it was properly adjusted; the larger the head of the wearer, the larger would be the gaps. The jury could reasonably have concluded from the examination of the helmet that Pender knew, or should have known, that a puck could penetrate between the sections and cause serious injury to the wearer. Pender was aware that other manufacturers were producing helmets of a one-piece design, but he nevertheless failed to make any tests of his own helmet to determine its safety. We hold that this evidence was sufficient to support the answer of the jury that Pender was negligent in the design of the helmet.

We reach a similar conclusion with regard to the defendant New Prep. * * * As a supplier New Prep was required to exercise reasonable care not to provide a chattel which it knew or had reason to know was dangerous for its intended use. See RESTATEMENT (SECOND) OF TORTS §388 (1965). Hughes, as a person with substantial experience in the game of hockey, may be held to a higher standard of care and knowledge than would an average person. RESTATEMENT (SECOND) OF TORTS §289(b), Comment m (1965). * * * Since many of the teams that New Prep played prior to 1970 wore one-piece helmets, the jury could have found that Hughes knew, or should have known, of their availability. He conceded in his testimony that the one-piece helmets were safer than the Pender model since the gaps in the latter would allow for the penetration of a puck. There was sufficient evidence to permit the jury to decide whether, in these circumstances, the supplying of the helmet to the plaintiff was negligent conduct.

Having determined that the jury were warranted in finding negligence on the parts of the defendants, we turn now to a consideration of * * *assumption of the risk * * *. Unlike contributory negligence, assumption of the risk involves a subjective standard, keyed not to the knowledge or understanding of the hypothetical reasonable man, but to "what the particular plaintiff in fact sees, knows, understands and appreciates." RESTATEMENT (SECOND) OF TORTS §496D, Comment c (1965). * * * In order to rule that a plaintiff assumed the risk of his injury as matter of law, the facts must be so plain that reasonable men could draw only one inference. * * * The facts here are not so plain. The plaintiff testified that he did not know of any dangers that he was exposed to by wearing the helmet. He believed, he said, that it would protect his head from injury. The helmet had been supplied to him by a person with great knowledge and experience in hockey, a person whose judgment the plaintiff had reason to trust, and it was given to him for the purpose implied, if not expressed, of protecting him. On the other hand, the obviousness of the gaps in the helmet would support an inference that he was actually aware of the risks he ran. * * * But we do not think that these gaps were so large or so obvious as to require the conclusion, as matter of law, that the plaintiff possessed the awareness necessary to support an assumption of the risk defense. Rather it was the function of the jury to balance the obviousness of the helmet design against the plaintiff's testimony and the circumstances in which he received the helmet in order to arrive at a conclusion as to what the plaintiff knew at the time of the injury. * * *

* * *

2. Strict liability in tort. [T]he Supreme Court of Rhode Island [has] adopted the law of strict liability in tort as it is defined in the RESTATEMENT (SECOND) OF TORTS §402A (1965).[1] The plaintiff claims that the three-piece design of the Pender helmet, with the gaps in it, was defective and unreasonably dangerous as defined in the Restatement, and therefore that the manufacturer and retailer are liable to him. We hold that there was sufficient evidence to reach the jury on this theory. For a product to be in a defective condition it does not have to be the result of errors made during the manufacturing process; it is defective as well "when it is properly made according to an unreasonably dangerous design" and does not meet a consumer's reasonable expectation as to its safety. W. PROSSER, Torts §99, at 659 (4th ed. 1971). The focus is on the design itself, not on the manufacturer's conduct. Factors that should be weighed in determining whether a particular product is reasonably safe include "the gravity of the danger posed by the challenged design, the likelihood that such danger would occur, the mechanical feasibility of a safer alternative design, the * * * cost of an improved design, and the adverse consequences to the product and to the consumer that would result from an alternative design." In this case the gravity of the danger posed by the three-piece design was demonstrated by the injuries to the plaintiff. There was substantial evidence that tended to show that helmets of the one-piece design were safer than the Pender model, that these one-piece helmets were in manufacture prior to the plaintiff's injury, and that, while more expensive than the Pender helmets, they were not economically unfeasible. This evidence provided a sufficient basis for the jury's findings that the helmet was "unreasonably dangerous."

* * *

The judgments on the strict liability counts are affirmed. The judgments on the negligence counts are reversed with instructions that judgments be entered on the verdicts.

---

1. 402A provides:

(1) One who sells any product in a defective condition unreasonably dangerous to the user or consumer or to his property is subject to liability for physical harm thereby caused to the ultimate user or consumer, or to his property, if (a) the seller is engaged in the business of selling such a product, and (b) it is expected to and does reach the user or consumer without substantial change in the condition in which it is sold.

(2) The rule stated in Subsection (1) applies although (a) the seller has exercised all possible care in the preparation and sale of his product, and (b) the user or consumer has not bought the product from or entered into any contractual relation with the seller.

So ordered.

Notes and Questions

1. With respect to the negligence claim, the trial court, disregarding the jury's verdict, found that the plaintiff had assumed the risk of injury. What was the basis for this conclusion? Would the reviewing court's opinion, reversing the lower court, have changed if the plaintiff were a veteran professional hockey player? What if the plaintiff were a younger player, 11 or 12 years of age? Differentiating standards of duty and fault based upon age are not uncommon. For example, the Second Restatement of Torts, addressing contributory negligence, states that "the standard of conduct to which a child must conform for his own protection is that of a reasonable person of like age, intelligence, and experience under like circumstances." RESTATEMENT (SECOND) OF TORTS §464(2) (1965). *See, e.g., Gaspard v. Grain Dealers Mutual Ins. Co.*, 131 So. 2d 831 (La. Ct. App. 1961) (holding that a youth behaved as a reasonable person of his age would when he wiped his hands on his pants before swinging a baseball bat, which subsequently slipped, flew through the air, and injured another player).

2. The negligence claim against the manufacturer was predicated principally on the facts that: (1) the design of the helmet was defective and fell below the industry standard of care ("The helmet was consciously designed so that there would be gaps between its sections when it was properly adjusted. * * *"); and (2) the defendant failed to exercise any meaningful quality control ("[Pender] failed to make any tests of his own helmet to determine its safety.") Could a basis for the negligence claim also have been that the manufacturer had a duty to warn the users of the possible risks presented by the gaps in the helmet? Would the predicate for such a claim be obviated because the problems with the helmet were not latent, but, rather, obvious to the naked eye? *See Dudley Sports Co. v. Schmitt*, 279 N.E.2d 266, 275 (Ind. Ct. App. 1972); *see also* Karen A. Eager, *Products Liability: No Pain, No Gain! The Tenth Circuit Uses First Mini-Trampoline Lawsuit to Give Muscle to the Duty to Warn by Flexing the Duty to Test*, 35 WASHBURN L. J. 498 (1996).

3. In the original lawsuit, plaintiff had also claimed that defendant manufacturer had breached its "implied and express warranties of merchantability and fitness for use in the sale of the helmet." 376 Mass. at 281. These claims were "discontinued" prior to trial. Could plaintiffs have prevailed on these allegations? *See* U.C.C. §§2-314, 2-315.

4. Given the court's approach to the strict liability issue, and given the increasing speed and strength of today's athletes, is the manufacturer of sports equipment, particularly in sports like football and hockey, constantly vulnerable to suit? Will this fact escalate the costs of equipment due both to the diminution in the number of manufacturer/competitors and the prohibitive costs of insurance? *See* Shea Sullivan, *Football Helmet Products Liability: A Survey of Cases and a Call for Reform*, 3 SPORTS L. J. 233, 234 (1996).

Sanchez v. Hillerich & Bradsby Co.
104 Cal. App. 4th 703 (Cal Ct. App. 2002)

HASTINGS, J.

Appellant Andrew Sanchez, a pitcher, was seriously injured when struck by a line drive hit by an aluminum bat. He filed suit against the bat manufacturer and others alleging that the design and use of this particular bat significantly increased the inherent risk in the sport of baseball that a pitcher would be hit by a line drive. Defendants moved for summary judgment asserting primary assumption of the risk and that appellant would be unable to prove causation. The trial court granted summary judgment when it concluded that appellant would be unable to prove that his injuries resulted from the alleged increased risk the particular bat posed to pitchers. We reverse. Appellant presented sufficient evidence to establish that use of this particular bat significantly increased the inherent risk that a pitcher would be hit by a line drive and that the unique design properties of this bat were the cause of his injuries.

FACTUAL AND PROCEDURAL BACKGROUND

On April 2, 1999, appellant, pitching for California State University, Northridge (CSUN), was struck by a line drive off the bat of a player for the University of Southern California (USC), Dominic Correa. Appellant suffered serious head injuries from the incident. Correa was using an aluminum bat, the Air Attack 2, designed and manufactured by respondent Hillerich & Bradsby Co. (H&B).

USC was a member of the Pac-10, a collegiate athletic conference. The Pac-10 was a member of the National Collegiate Athletic Association (NCAA), a nonprofit organization of collegiate athletic conferences and other institutions. The NCAA establishes rules for equipment used in athletic events, including baseball bats. CSUN was a member of the NCAA, but not a member of the Pac-10.

The bat used by Correa was a newly designed hollow aluminum alloy bat with a pressurized air bladder which, according to its designer, substantially increases the speed at which the ball leaves the surface of the bat. Correa was supplied with the bat pursuant to an agreement between USC and H&B, which provided that USC would receive compensation for using H&B's Louisville Slugger equipment exclusively. At the time of the accident, the NCAA rules allowed the use of metal bats, and the bat was made in compliance with NCAA standards. However, prior to the start of the 1999 season, the NCAA notified athletic conferences under its umbrella, including the Pac-10, of the dangerous nature of the newer metal bats and of its decision to implement new rules to decrease the speed of the batted balls effective August 1, 1999. The Pac-10 implemented some of the proposed standards prior to the 1999 baseball season.

Prior to the commencement of the 1999 baseball season, appellant had signed a disclaimer form acknowledging that his participation on the team carried a risk of injury, specifically including brain damage, and consenting to assume the risk of such injury.

At the time of the injury, appellant and all of his team members were using metal bats, and appellant had used a metal bat in organized baseball games since he was six years old.

On March 17, 2000, appellant filed a lawsuit against H&B, USC, NCAA and Pac-10 asserting causes of action for products liability and negligence. Appellant later struck the product liability claim against USC and the Pac-10.

Each defendant moved separately for summary judgment. H&B's motion was based on the following grounds: (1) that appellant could not establish causation as a matter of law; (2) the action was barred by the doctrines of primary assumption of risk and express assumption of risk; and (3) that H&B was entitled to judgment because the bat was in compliance with rules established by the NCAA.

* * * Rhonda Hyatt, the head athletic trainer for CSUN, testified that when presenting the disclaimer form to baseball players, she normally would read to them the clause about assumption of risk word for word before they signed it. At deposition, appellant testified he was aware that pitchers were at risk for being hit by a line drive.

The motion by the NCAA also contended that the doctrine of primary assumption of risk barred appellant's claim against it and that appellant could not establish causation. In addition, it argued that it did not owe a duty to appellant because at the time of the accident the baseball community was in significant disagreement over the risk of aluminum bats. * * *

USC and the Pac-10 based their motion on primary assumption of risk, arguing that a pitcher being struck by a batted ball was a risk inherent in the sport of baseball.

In opposition to each of the motions, appellant argued that primary assumption of risk was not applicable because of an increased risk presented by the Air Attack 2 over that of other bats previously in use and that the increased risk was a substantial cause of appellant's injuries. In support, he submitted four declarations.

Jack Mackay, the designer of the Air Attack 2, declared that * * * the invention allowed a batter to hit a ball at speeds in excess of that which would have given a pitcher time to avoid being hit. As a result, he opined that the Air Attack 2 *substantially* increased the risk of a pitcher being hit by what he termed a "come backer." Mackay complained to his employers at the Louisville Slugger division of H&B about the increased risks of injuries, but the complaints were ignored and Marty Archer, president of the division, warned Mackay that he should not publicly discuss issues of safety.

William Thurston, a college baseball coach and editor of the NCAA Baseball Rules Committee from February 1985 to July 2000, had initiated an NCAA study tracking pitcher injuries from high-performance aluminum bats. He concluded that the Air Attack 2 *substantially* increased the risk of a pitcher being hit by a line drive over the risk associated with wood bats or earlier generations of nonwood bats. * * *

Appellant also submitted the declaration of James G. Kent, who had a Ph.D. in kinesiology. Based on his training and review of the evidence, he opined that the ball which struck appellant's head was traveling between 101 and 107.8 miles an hour, probably closer to the latter speed than the former. This would have left appellant a reaction time of .32 to .37 seconds to avoid the ball. This was below the minimum reaction time accepted by the NCAA and other organizations of .39 seconds. As a result, he concluded that appellant's head injury resulted from the increased danger posed by this particular bat.

The superior court granted the motions of H&B, USC and Pac-10 on the ground that appellant would not be able to prove causation. * * *

DISCUSSION

* * *

1. *Assumption of Risk*

* * *

When addressing the applicability of primary assumption of the risk, we analyze the nature of the activity and the role of each of the parties to that activity and decide as a matter of public policy whether the defendant should owe the plaintiff a duty of care. A defendant owes no duty of care to protect a plaintiff against risks inherent in a particular sport voluntarily played by the plaintiff. But the defendant owes a duty to participants not to increase the risk of harm over and above that inherent in the sport. The standards in the industry define the nature of the sport. If it is determined that the actions of a defendant did increase the risk of harm above that inherent in the sport, primary assumption of the risk is not available and the issue becomes one of secondary assumption of the risk.

A risk is inherent in a sport if its elimination (1) would chill vigorous participation in the sport; and (2) would alter the fundamental nature of the activity.

The essence of a baseball game is the contest between the defense, the pitcher and other players in the field, and the batter, for mastery over what happens to the pitched ball. The batter wants to hit the ball safely, usually away from the defense, so that the batter can advance on the bases. The defense wants to get the batter out, either by striking the batter out, or by causing the batter to hit the ball to a spot where one of the defensive players can make a play on it. Inherent in this mix is the risk that the pitcher, or any infielder, may have to catch, or avoid being hit with, a sharply batted ball. Appellant acknowledged he was aware of this risk. Thus, given the foundational facts of this case, a prima facie showing of assumption of the risk has been established. But appellant argued that use of the Air Attack 2 increased the risk above that inherent in the sport, and presented evidence on the issue. We now review that evidence.

At the time of the accident, the NCAA allowed the use of metal bats, and the bat in use was *apparently* in compliance with NCAA standards. It is undisputed that the Air Attack 2 was designed to cause the ball to come off the bat at a higher launch speed than with wooden bats and older metal bats. It is also undisputed that the inventor of the Air Attack 2 believed the Air Attack 2 *substantially* increased the risk of a pitcher being hit by what he termed a "come backer" and that he complained to his employers at H&B about these increased risks.

Additionally, the evidence submitted by appellant establishes that the Pac-10 and NCAA each believed that new generations of aluminum bats created a significant issue of safety. Before the incident at issue, the NCAA adopted new rules to regulate the exit speed of such bats, but postponed implementation of the rules until a date after this incident. On October 8, 1998, Thomas Hansen, commissioner of the Pac-10, sent a letter of protest to the NCAA about delayed implementation of the rules:

> I am writing on behalf of the Pacific-10 Conference Directors of Athletics to request that the NCAA reconsider its decision to postpone until August 1, 1999, a change in nonwood baseball bat specifications.

> We believe in light of the contents of your letter of August 28, 1998, that a change prior to the 1999 season is imperative. The comments of the NCAA Baseball Rules Committee and the NCAA Committee on Competitive Safeguards and Medical Aspects of Sports warn of the dangers of using the current bats. Since we consider the safety of competing student-athletes paramount, we believe an immediate change is in order since games are being played at this time. * * *

The NCAA not only believed that the newer aluminum bats created an increased risk of harm to players, it also believed that use of these bats changed the nature of the sport of college baseball. We quote from portions of a letter dated December 4, 1998, and sent by the NCAA Baseball Rules Committee to "Chief Executive Officers" "Directors of Athletics" "Head Baseball Coaches" and "Conference Commissioners":

> The NCAA adopted the new bat rule after a lengthy, careful and fair deliberative process. The baseball rules committee, composed of knowledgeable baseball coaches and administrators with many years of experience, has been concerned about runaway bat performance for many years. * * *
>
> * * * All interested manufacturers, experts, and other knowledgeable persons were invited to make presentations to the committee in open session. * * * *The committee was unanimously convinced that bat performance was indeed a safety risk to pitchers and infielders, that there has indeed been a change in the way the college game of baseball is played, and that the available evidence was more than sufficient to justify a change in the rule as soon as practically possible There is simply no question that aluminum bats substantially outperform traditional wood bats, that the risk of injury to pitchers and infielders is real, and that a performance limit on the aluminum bats was required to bring the game of baseball closer to its traditional form.* (Italics added.)

This case is similar to *Branco v. Kearny Moto Park, Inc., supra,* 37 Cal.App.4th 184. There, participants on bicycles raced around a motocross (BMX) course which contained "jumps" as part of the course. The plaintiff was injured when he crashed and struck the side wall of the landing area of what is described as "an expert caliber jump." (*Branco v. Kearny Moto Park, Inc., supra,* 37 Cal.App.4th at p. 187.) He filed suit and the defendants asserted primary assumption of the risk. The trial court granted summary judgment for defendants but the Court of Appeal reversed. "It is not unreasonable to expect a BMX course to refrain from utilizing jumps which by design create an extreme risk of injury. Certainly the jumps, and falls, are inherent to the sport, and under the doctrine of primary assumption of risk, there is no duty to eliminate the jumps entirely, and no duty to protect from injury arising from reasonably designed jumps. However, the sport does not inherently require jumps which are designed in such a way as to create an extreme risk of injury. Accordingly, premised on the duty not to utilize dangerously designed jumps, this case falls under the secondary assumption of risk category, and issues pertaining to [the plaintiff's] comparative fault are for the trier of fact to decide. [The plaintiff's] expert's opinions regarding the design of the jump create a triable issue of material fact whether the million dollar jump was designed in such a way as to create an extreme risk of injury." (*Branco v. Kearny Moto Park, Inc., supra,* 37 Cal.App.4th at p. 193, fns. omitted.)

Here, appellant's evidence raises a triable issue of material fact whether the design and use of the Air Attack 2 substantially increased the inherent risk appellant faced. The evidence also raises at least a triable issue whether defendants knew of and appreciated the nature of the increased risk. The letters from the Pac-10 and the NCAA clearly establish they were aware of the additional danger presented by the newer aluminum bats. The NCAA letter was addressed to all "Head Coaches" and from that we can infer that the USC head coach was placed on notice of the increased risk, since USC was under the NCAA's umbrella. Mackay's declaration states that he warned H&B of the increased risk.

If it is ultimately determined primary assumption of the risk does not apply here, the issue then becomes one of secondary assumption of the risk. Comparing the relative fault of plaintiff and defendants is a question of fact that must be resolved by a trier of fact and cannot be resolved by way of a summary judgment motion.

2. *Causation*

Respondents contended, and the trial court agreed, that because the speed of the ball leaving the bat was never established, no causation attributed to the increased risk of use of the Air Attack 2, if any, could be established. * * *

It is undisputed that Correa, using an Air Attack 2 manufactured by H&B, provided by USC, and approved by the NCAA, hit the ball that fractured appellant's skull. It is also undisputed that the Air Attack 2 was designed to and did increase the speed at which the baseball leaves the bat compared to other metal and wood bats. Thus, absent other factors (none are suggested) it follows that the ball must have reached appellant sooner than if Correa had used a bat other than the Air Attack 2. Dr. Kent opined that the ball that hit Correa was traveling at a speed of up to 107.8 miles per hour, giving appellant a reaction time of between .32 and .37 seconds, below the acceptable minimum time recognized by the NCAA.

* * *

We conclude the evidence presented by appellant is sufficient to create a triable issue of fact regarding causation.

* * *

Notes and Questions

1. Is this case good law after *Avila, supra* Part II?

2. Is it reasonable to place a duty on conferences, schools, coaches, or the players themselves to refrain from using equipment that has satisfied the NCAA's standards? How are those parties supposed to make a determination as to what equipment is safe? Are they likely to forego a piece of equipment that gives them an advantage, when the only risk of injury is to the *other* team?

3. If "[t]he standards in the industry define the nature of the sport," as the court says, shouldn't the fact that the bat satisfied applicable safety specifications be sufficient to defeat the plaintiff's claim? If not, what "standards" does the court mean?

3. Why would the NCAA delay implementation of the rule prohibiting the Air Attack 2 and bats like it? Should it matter if the ban was timed to take effect as the same time as a rule change helping batters (such as, for example, lowering the pitcher's mound) was to be implemented?

4. Do you think this case would be decided the same way if the NCAA itself had not concluded that the bat was unsafe? Does the holding of this case permit or require courts to assess for themselves the dangerousness of a piece of equipment?

5. Suppose an injured plaintiff put on evidence that the use of aluminum bats of any construction was unsafe. Assuming that the NCAA permits the use of some such bats, should the court be able to impose liability for injuries resulting from such legal equipment?

6. *Branco v. Kearney Moto Park, Inc.*, 37 Cal. App. 4th 184 (Cal. Ct. App. 1995), involved an allegation by an injured BMX rider that the track on which he was riding contained jumps that were too dangerous. The court held that although some jumps were inherent in BMX racing, "the sport does not inherently require jumps which are designed in such a way as to create an extreme risk of injury," and therefore primary assumption of the risk did not apply and summary judgment was inappropriate. Is that case distinguishable from *Sanchez*?

VI. Torts and the Written or Spoken Word: Defamation and the Sports Figure's Rights of Privacy and Publicity

Recall that the tort of defamation is subject to limitations imposed by the First Amendment. A "public figure" may recover for defamatory falsehoods only if the statements at issue were known by the defendant to be false or if they were made with "actual malice," that is, with reckless disregard for whether they were false or not. *See New York Times Co. v. Sullivan*, 376 U.S. 254 (1964). Private figures, by contrast, can recover damages under a lesser showing, though not as low as strict liability. *See Gertz v. Robert Welch, Inc.*, 418 U.S. 323 (1974). (A private-figure plaintiff must satisfy the "actual malice" standard to recover punitive damages, however. *Id.*) In the vast majority of cases, there is no question that sports personalities are public figures. The following case, however, presents an interesting exception: Can a person stop being a public figure after he leaves the limelight?

Time, Inc. v. Johnston
448 F.2d 378 (4th Cir. 1971)

RUSSELL, Circuit Judge. The defendant is the publisher of SPORTS ILLUSTRATED, a weekly periodical devoted to sports and athletics. Annually, it features its selection of "Sportsman of the Year". In 1968, it chose Bill Russell, a star on the professional basketball team of the Boston CELTICS, as its "Sportsman of the Year" and engaged George Plimpton, a well-known writer, especially in the field of sports, to write the feature article. In developing his article, Plimpton chose to quote from interviews he had had with persons acquainted with Russell and his exceptional talents as a basketball player. In quoting an interview with Arnold Auerbach, the coach of Russell with the CELTICS, Plimpton included in his article the following paragraph:

> "* * * That's a word you can use about him—he (Russell) 'destroyed' players. You take Neil Johnston—* * *, Russell destroyed him. He destroyed him psychologically as well, so that he practically ran him out of organized basketball. He blocked so many shots that Johnston began throwing his hook farther and farther from the basket. It was ludicrous, and the guys along the bench began to laugh, maybe in relief that they didn't have to worry about such a guy themselves."

The "Johnston" referred to in the quoted paragraph is the plaintiff. At the time of the incident referred to, he was an outstanding professional basketball player with the Philadelphia WARRIORS basketball team. He subsequently retired from professional basketball and is now the assistant basketball coach at Wake Forest University in Winston-Salem, North Carolina. Following the publication of the article, he sued the defendant, contending that he had been libeled in the quoted paragraph and had been "damaged (him) in his chosen profession, that of coaching basketball."

* * *

There can be no dispute that at the time of the events discussed in the challenged publication the plaintiff met the criteria of "a public figure". "Public figures", within the contemplation of the rule in *New York Times*, as enlarged by subsequent cases, are "those persons who, though not public officials, are 'involved in issues in which the public has a justified and important interest'" and "include artists, athletes, business people, dilettantes, anyone who is famous or infamous because of who he is or what he has done." Consonant with this definition, a college athletic director, a basketball coach, a professional boxer and a professional baseball player, among others, have all been held to be "public figures". The plaintiff, as he figures in the challenged publication, fits this definition of a "public figure". * * * He had offered his services to the public as a paid performer and had thereby invited comments on his performance as such. In a sense, he assumed the risk of publicity, good or bad, as the case might be, so far as it concerned his public performance. The publication in question related strictly to his public character. It made no reference to his private life, it involved no intrusion into his private affairs. It dealt entirely with his performance as a professional basketball player; it discussed him in connection with a public event in which the plaintiff as a compensated public figure had taken part voluntarily.

The plaintiff does not seriously question the defendant's premise that he was a "public figure" at the time of the event discussed in the publication; and the District Court apparently assumed in its decision that the plaintiff was such a "public figure". The plaintiff points out, though, that the event, to which the publication related, occurred twelve years before the publication and nine years after the plaintiff had retired as a professional basketball player. It is plaintiff's position that he had, at the time of publication, shed his character of "public figure" and that the New York Times standard was, therefore, inapplicable. This is the basic point of difference between the parties on this aspect of the case. The District Court accepted the plaintiff's view. In so doing, it erred.

The District Court relies for its conclusion primarily on a comment set forth in a note in Rosenblatt v. Baer (1966) 383 U.S. 75, 87, note 14: "To be sure, there may be cases where a person is so far removed from a former position of authority that comment on the manner in which he performed his responsibilities no longer has the interest necessary to justify the New York Times rule." This, however, is not such a case as was envisaged by Justice Brennan. The claim that plaintiff had retired as a player in 1958, nine years before the publication, is misleading. While plaintiff did retire as a player in 1958, he, by his own affidavit, "remained in organized professional basketball, until 1966." He thus identifies himself with professional basketball up to approximately two years of the publication in question. And, at the time of the publication itself, he was a college basketball coach, still involved as a public figure in basketball. Perhaps as a college basketball coach, he was not as prominently identified with the sport as in his playing days[, but] with his outstanding record, [he] had [not] become a forgotten figure among the many devotees of the game of basketball.

That even the plaintiff did not reckon his career as a professional basketball player forgotten is demonstrated by his claim in this case that a reflection on that career and on his eminence as a player damages him in his present occupation as a college basketball coach. By his claim for damages here, he is contending that his standing as a college basketball coach rests substantially on the public recollection and estimation of his former career as a professional basketball player; and it is for that reason he sues. It is because he is still engaged in basketball and because of the effect that any adverse comment on his record and achievements as a basketball star may have on his present position in basketball that he claims damage herein. It is manifestly inconsistent for him to contend that, when his basis for damage is thus grounded, his "public figure" career has become so obscure and remote that it is no longer a subject of legitimate public interest or comment.

The event to which the publication related remained a matter of public interest not simply because of its relation to plaintiff's own public career; it had an equal or greater interest as marking the spectacular debut of Russell in a career that was still phenomenal at the time of the publication. It was an event that had, in the language of one sports writer reporting it, a "tremendous" "psychological effect on the league". It was an event that was vivid in the memory of Auerbach at the time of the publication and likely in that of other followers of the sport. It is fair to assume that in the memory of basketball fans, the event described was neither remote nor forgotten; nor was it devoid of newsworthiness.

Moreover, mere passage of time will not necessarily insulate from the application of *New York Times Co. v. Sullivan*, publications relating to the past public conduct of a then "public figure". No rule of repose exists to inhibit speech relating to the public career of a public figure so long as newsworthiness and public interest attach to events in such public career. * * *

* * *

The plaintiff, by his cross-appeal, however, has raised the point that, even if defendant be entitled to a First Amendment privilege, the motion for summary judgment should have been denied because there was sufficient evidence in the record that the defendant had published the challenged item with actual knowledge of its falsity, or recklessly without regard to whether it was true or not and thereby lost its constitutional privilege. The District Court concluded to the contrary. * * * We agree that there is no basis in the record to support a finding of "knowing falsehood or reckless disregard" on the part of the defendant.

It is undisputed that Auerbach, whose statement is quoted in the allegedly offensive statement, was correctly quoted. So long as the press correctly quotes another's statement about a matter of legitimate public interest, does not truncate or distort it in any way, and properly identifies the source, recent decisions indicate that it may properly claim the protection of *New York Times*. * * * It is the plaintiff's contention, however, that the statement of Auerbach, though admittedly made by Auerbach and correctly quoted in the article, was known by the defendant to be false and defamatory and that, because of knowing falsity, the defendant is in no position to claim immunity under the doctrine of *New York Times*. To support such contention he points to two phrases as being knowingly false and defamatory. These phrases are "destroyed" and "psychologically destroyed", which he argues, taken in the context of the article and giving them their normal connotation, were libellous and were refuted by material in the defendant's own files. Manifestly, the challenged words were not used literally. No one reading the article would have assumed that Auerbach was stating that the plaintiff was actually and literally "destroyed", during the game being discussed. Auerbach was attempting to identify Russell's emergence as a star basketball player; he did that by recounting an event which, as he saw it, marked the beginning of Russell, the star, and incidentally, the eclipse of the plaintiff as star. In describing the event, he used phrases of some vividness, used them in a figurative, not literal, sense, used a form of hyperbole typical in sports parlance. *New York Times*, in its application, does not interdict legitimate or normal hyperbole. To deny to the press the right to use hyperbole, under the threat of removing the protecting mantle of *New York Times*, would condemn the press to an arid, desiccated recital of bare facts. * * * And the [interviews and reports of the game] available in the files of the defendant, so far from refuting this opinion that Russell had on the occasion in question "dominated" and outplayed the plaintiff, gave support to that conclusion and provided a rational basis for Auerbach's perhaps vivid characterization. * * * There was thus no basis for any conclusion that the defendant was in possession of any fact that would have justified on its part a "high degree of awareness of * * * probable falsity" of the statement made by Auerbach. * * * The District Court was accordingly clearly right in concluding that the record included "nothing * * * which would give substance" to a finding of "knowing falsity or reckless disregard" on the part of the defendant.

Affirmed in part, vacated in part, and remanded with directions that judgment be entered for the defendant.

Notes and Questions

1. Did the plaintiff place himself in a "Catch-22" situation by claiming that he was not a public figure (*i.e.*, no longer the basketball player that he was), but also claiming that, as a basketball coach, he was particularly victimized by statements disparaging his basketball talents?

2. Did the court, in its own way, chastise the plaintiff for being a little too oversensitive and litigious, particularly given the status of Bill Russell and his well-chronicled "domination" of most opposing players of his era? How relevant to the court's conclusion was the vernacular of the playground, where terms like "destroyed," "used," "buried," "schooled," and similar expressions, have become commonplace? Sports apparel manufacturers have even made substantial capital from incorporating this type of "in-your-face" jargon into their designs and advertisements.

3. Was plaintiff Johnston still a public figure at the time of the publication in question? The court correctly stated that he remained in basketball after his retirement, nine years prior to the publication giving rise to his lawsuit. Yet, he was hardly a household word at that time. Of greater pertinence, would those individuals following basketball accord him the notoriety associated with the typical "public figure"? A public figure is one "who has assumed the role of importance in the resolution of public affairs of general importance or concern to the people generally." PROSSER & KEETON §113, at 806; *see also Gertz v. Robert Welch, Inc.*, 418 U.S. 323, 352 (1974). In *Time, Inc. v. Firestone*, 424 U.S. 448, 453 (1976), the United States Supreme Court reiterated earlier pronouncements that "public figures" are persons who assume a position of unique prominence and place themselves at the "forefront of [a] particular public controversy in order to influence the resolution of the issues involved in it." Does Johnston come close to meeting this description? Clearly, his case was doomed from the moment that he was characterized as a public figure. *See* Mark Walton, *The Public Figure Doctrine: A Reexamination of* Gertz v. Robert Welch, Inc. *in Light of Lower Federal Court Public Figure Formulations*, 16 N. ILL. U. L. REV. 141, 147–50 (1995). There was little chance that he could establish actual malice, especially given the fact that one of the sources of the magazine's allegedly defamatory comments was Arnold "Red" Auerbach, resident NBA guru and icon.

4. In few areas is fame more fleeting than sports. Trivia buffs take great pleasure in recounting pedantic details of yesteryear's performers and performances. *See generally, e.g., Stump the Schwab* (ESPN Classic television program). Yet, by and large, many athletes labor in anonymity, even while they are playing, and quickly fade further into oblivion upon retirement. Thus, does it not seem appropriate to place some reasonable outside parameter on an athlete's tenure as public figure? For a thorough review of this

issue, see Elsa Ransom, *The Ex-Public Figure: A Libel Plaintiff Without a Cause*, 5 Seton Hall J. Sports L. 389 (1995).

One rationale for providing less protection to public officials and public officials than to private figures is that people in the public eye can command attention if they want to "set the record straight." Professor Ransom, commenting on judicial reluctance to embrace the notion of "public figure status abatement," argues that this rationale does not apply to people who have left the public eye long ago:

> The effect of this trend is that past conduct, no matter how prudent, lawful or remote in time, can forever impair one's ability to redress injury to one's reputation in a court of law. This rule can be particularly harsh for formerly well-known individuals who are defamed after they no longer have any realistic expectations of gaining access to the media for rebuttal.

Id. at 391. *See also Gertz*, 418 U.S. at 344. What do you think of Professor Ransom's argument? Are there other justifications for providing less protection to public figures? *See Cohen v. Marx*, 211 P.2d 320, 321 (Cal. Ct. App. 1949):

> [W]hen plaintiff sought publicity and the adulation of the public, he relinquished his right to privacy on matters pertaining to his professional activity, and he could not at his will and whim draw himself like a snail into his shell and hold others liable for commenting upon the acts which had taken place when he had voluntarily exposed himself to the public eye. As to such acts he had waived his right of privacy and he could not at some subsequent period rescind his waiver.

Cf. Cardtoons, L.C. v. Major League Baseball Players Association, 95 F.3d 959, 975 (10th Cir. 1996) (evaluating a right-of-publicity claim) ("[A] celebrity's fame may largely be the creation of the media or the audience."). Do you buy this "take-the-bitter-with-the-sweet" argument?

5. It will not surprise anyone who has listened to sports-talk radio that the First Amendment protects the expression of opinion (so long as that expression does not imply falsely the existence of facts). *See, e.g., Dancer v. Bergman*, 668 N.Y.S.2d 213 (N.Y. App. Div. 1998) (holding that an editorial charging that a jockey had "mailed in his second placing and refused to contest the issue from start to finish" was constitutionally protected).

6. Because damages in defamation actions are premised on the harm done to the plaintiff's reputation, there is the potential of a "defamation-proof" plaintiff, *i.e.*, someone whose reputation for a particular characteristic is so low that even a lie could not make that reputation appreciably worse. *See Guccione v. Hustler Magazine, Inc.*, 800 F.2d 298 (2d Cir. 1986) (holding that Penthouse publisher Bob Guccione's reputation for marital infidelity was so notorious as to make him judgment proof for a false statement on that topic). A plaintiff's reputation must be atrocious, however, for this "defense" to be a consideration. *Sprewell v. NYP Holdings, Inc.*, 772 N.Y.S.2d 188, 192 (N.Y. Sup. Ct. 2003), involved a defamation claim arising out of reports in the *New York Post* that basketball player Latrell Sprewell tried to punch a guest on Sprewell's yacht. The court rejected the defendant's argument that its reporting, even if false, could not damage Sprewell's reputation:

> [T]his court may take judicial notice of the widespread publication of articles concerning the 1997 incident involving Sprewell's alleged choking of his former coach, [P.J.] Carlesimo, during a practice. Considering the statements in

the Post articles in light of the reporting of this former incident, which is presumably known to the average sports reader, the court concludes that the prior publicity not only does not support, but cuts against, defendants' argument that a further imputation of violent conduct to plaintiff cannot increase the damage to Sprewell's reputation.

The court seems to be saying that it is one thing to choke a coach once, but quite another to engage habitually in sociopathic behavior. There is a limit to this logic, however. If a report falsely charged that Mike Tyson had once stolen a grade-school classmate's lunch money, would such a revelation damage Tyson's reputation?

Town & Country Properties, Inc. v. Riggins
457 S.E.2d 356 (Va. 1995)

COMPTON, Justice.

Code § 8.01-40(A) provides that if any person's name is used "for advertising purposes or for the purposes of trade," without first obtaining the individual's written consent, such person may sue and recover damages from the person, firm, or corporation so using the name "for any injuries sustained by reason of such use." The main issue in this appeal is whether the statute is unconstitutional as applied under the facts of this case to a corporation engaged in the sale of residential real estate.

The relevant facts are virtually undisputed. The plaintiff-appellee is John Riggins, formerly a prominent professional football player. * * * After playing five years with the Jets, Riggins was acquired by the Washington Redskins. He played for the Redskins for nine full seasons, completing his career as an active player in 1985. Because of his skill and accomplishments as a football player, Riggins was inducted into the Pro Football Hall of Fame in 1992. * * * As the result of his athletic exploits, Riggins became a celebrity nationwide and especially in the Washington, D.C. area.

The evidence showed that Riggins has been compensated over the years for use of his name in the endorsement of many products and has been paid for personal appearances at various functions. He always charges a fee for endorsements and always charges a personal appearance fee, except when his presence is connected with a charitable cause. His fees range from $5,000 to $90,000. He has been employed by Washington radio and television stations. Riggins currently works as a part-time commentator on an all-sports radio program in the metropolitan Washington area for which he is paid $40,000. The radio station advertises the fact that he works there.

Riggins testified these uses of his name presently are his "livelihood," saying, "I was very fortunate and had the talent to play at a level that was different from most of the people I played with. And I think I built a name which basically now to this day provides me with a living."

In 1991, the plaintiff and his wife, Mary Lou Riggins, were divorced. Pursuant to a property settlement agreement, the plaintiff conveyed his ownership interest in the marital home, located in Vienna, Virginia, to his former wife. Later that year, Ms. Riggins obtained a license as a real estate salesperson and became associated with defendant-appellant Town & Country Properties, Inc., in its Vienna branch office.

In 1992, she decided to sell the former marital home. To generate interest in the property, she arranged for a "brokers' open" to be held on the premises. Testimony described a "brokers' open" as "a solicitation of other brokers and sales associates to come view the house in the hope that they [will] know where the property is and they can find it comfortably and they will introduce it to their customers in the course of selling real estate."

In order to advertise the brokers' open, Ms. Riggins drafted, and arranged for the printing and distribution of, a flyer that is the focus of this controversy. The flyer is an eight-and-one-half by eleven-inch handbill printed with a photograph of the home's exterior near the center of the page. A partial reproduction of the flyer, not to scale, appears below.

BROKERS OPEN

June 16—11 AM to 1 PM

COME SEE...

John Riggins'

Former Home,

Photograph

$849,500

*Register to win an autographed football

Menu
Honey Baked Ham
Famous Rice Ring
Homemade Chocolate Cake and
Lemon Squares etc.

Directions: From 66, Rt. 123 North to a left on Hunter Mill Rd. Go 3.2 miles to a left onto Wickens. Take the first left onto Vickers Drive. Go to the Col-de-Sac and it's the second driveway.

10611 Vickers Dr.
Mary Lou Riggins
Home: 938-4199
Office: 938-5800

At the foot of the page on the left appears defendant's logo opposite Ms. Riggins' telephone numbers.

The printing company that prepared the flyer distributed 1,610 copies to real estate offices in Great Falls, McLean, Vienna, Oakton, and Tysons Corner. Approximately 78 persons attended the brokers' open. Following an "open house" on June 21 to show the home to the public, a contract of sale for $745,000 was executed on June 25. The purchasers did not see the flyer, but purchased the home as the result of a visit when it was open to the public. The defendant received a commission of $44,700 on the sale.

Plaintiff did not give his consent to the use of his name nor was he asked or contacted by either Ms. Riggins or any of defendant's principals requesting permission to use his name on the flyer. * * *

Plaintiff stated that when he first saw the flyer, he was "angry," "humiliated," and felt a loss of "integrity and dignity." Plaintiff said he felt "violated" and that his "livelihood" had been "threatened by this flyer." He stated, "I didn't even deserve a phone call. That's how little the people that did this thought of me, I guess." He said, "[T]his is not unlike somebody stole something from me. They clearly took my name and used it for their commercial purposes without any regard for me. I've had things stolen from me before and it is not a good feeling." He stated, "[I]f this is allowed, if this is okay, then basically the living or the life I am trying to live and the money I'm trying to earn is not going to be possible because my name belongs to everybody, it does not belong to me." He said that the flyer was "deceptive," because, at first glance, "I think John Riggins is going to be there. Then I see it's his former home and I'm somehow disappointed, and possibly angry at John Riggins for baiting me like that." * * *

In August 1992, plaintiff filed the present action against defendant seeking recovery of compensatory and punitive damages. In a three-count motion for judgment, plaintiff sought recovery for "statutory conversion" pursuant to Code § 8.01-40(A), trover and common-law conversion for misappropriation of his "name and reputation without his express written consent," and "breach of quasi-contract" based on defendant's alleged unjust enrichment at plaintiff's expense.

* * * On a special verdict form, the jury found in favor of the plaintiff on the conversion counts only, and fixed compensatory damages at $25,000 and punitive damages at $28,608.

* * *

First, defendant contends that the trial court's assessment of damages against it for an agent's disclosure of truthful, public information violates the free-speech provisions of the First Amendment to the United States Constitution and Article I, Section 12, of the Constitution of Virginia. * * *

Arguing that the utterance here is constitutionally protected "commercial speech," defendant says that the flyer did not suggest that the plaintiff endorsed defendant or the subject property, but "truthfully announced a luncheon to be held at a home for sale which was formerly owned by Mr. Riggins." Defendant contends, "A flyer stating that the Property is 'John Riggins' former home' when, in fact, the Property *is* John Riggins' former home, cannot be construed as misleading."

Noting that plaintiff's former ownership of the property was freely available to the general public from the Fairfax County land records and contending that "the identity of his ownership is an immutable characteristic" of the property, defendant argues that "Mr. Riggins has no privacy or property interest in it at all." Quoting *Cox Broadcasting Corp. v. Cohn,* 420 U.S. 469, 494–95 (1975), defendant says "interests in privacy fade when the information involved already appears on the public record."

* * * We do not agree with defendant's contentions.

Prior to 1890, no American court had granted relief expressly based upon invasion of the so-called "right of privacy." At the present time, however, the right is recognized in virtually all jurisdictions. W. Page Keeton Et Al., *Prosser and Keeton on The Law of Torts*

§ 117, at 849–51 (5th ed. 1984). Virginia is among a few states, including New York, that recognizes a right of privacy in a limited form by statute. * * *

Code § 8.01-40(A) provides that if a person's "name, portrait, or picture" is used for "advertising purposes or for the purposes of trade" without written consent, the person may maintain a suit in equity to prevent the use, and may sue and recover damages for any injuries resulting from such use. Code § 8.01-40(A) is substantially similar to §§ 50 and 51 of the New York Civil Rights Act. Therefore, as we interpret the statute in connection with the constitutional attack, we will look to New York courts for guidance.

Use for "advertising purposes" and use "for the purposes of trade" are separate and distinct statutory concepts. Claims based, as here, on the use of a name "for advertising purposes" have received a more liberal treatment by the courts than those based on use "for purposes of trade." The unauthorized use of a person's name as an integral part of advertising matter "has almost uniformly been held actionable." And, a name is used "for advertising purposes" when "it appears in a publication which, taken in its entirety, was distributed for use in, or as part of, an advertisement or solicitation for patronage of a particular product or service

Applying this test, we conclude that the defendant's flyer clearly is advertising material and a promotional publication. The placement on the document of defendant's logo and the agent's name and telephone numbers, as well as the wide distribution of the piece to a targeted audience leaves no doubt, as the testimony confirms, that the flyer was designed to enhance the probability of ultimate sale of the property.

We also conclude that plaintiff's name was used "for advertising purposes" in a manner forbidden by Code § 8.01-40(A). Ms. Riggins specifically directed the printer who set the type and distributed the flyer "to make the words John Riggins bigger than the other words" and to make them "stand out." Plaintiff's name, therefore, was an integral part of the flyer and cannot be deemed merely incidental to the flyer's clear commercial message.

Nevertheless, defendant seeks to avoid liability under the statute on the ground that the flyer is commercial speech protected from unwarranted governmental regulation by the First Amendment, as applied to the States through the Fourteenth Amendment. The defendant misapplies the Supreme Court's commercial speech cases to the situation presented here.

"The First Amendment's concern for commercial speech is based on the informational function of advertising." In the context of the Supreme Court's commercial-speech decisions, this real estate advertisement is not "informational."

* * *

Rather, the plaintiff's name was used strictly in a promotional sense to generate interest in the sale of real estate. The use was not relevant to dissemination of information to consumers about the physical condition, architectural features, or quality of the home. Simply, this is not the type of commercial speech accorded constitutional protection.

* * *

[Affirmed]

Notes and Questions

1. Why was the use of Riggins's name not "informational"? Are the facts here distinguishable from those in other First Amendment cases, which have protected the advertisement of the terms of sale of lawyers' services and prescription drugs?

2. The First Amendment permits states to restrict true, non-misleading commercial advertising of lawful conduct only when (1) the restriction is justified by a substantial government interest, (2) the restriction directly advances the substantial governmental interest, and (3) the restriction is no more extensive than necessary to further the governmental interest. *See Central Hudson Gas & Electric v. Public Service Comm'n,* 447 U.S. 557 (1980); EUGENE VOLOKH, THE FIRST AMENDMENT AND RELATED STATUTES: PROBLEMS, CASES AND POLICY ARGUMENTS 195 (2d ed. 2005). What is the governmental interest implicated here? Is it substantial? Does the statute directly advance the interest? Is the statute more restrictive than necessary?

3. Should the First Amendment *ever* permit the suppression of true, non-misleading commercial speech concerning lawful activity? *See 44 Liquormart, Inc. v. Rhode Island,* 517 U.S. 484 (1996).

4. Was there a risk here, as Riggins claimed, that his "livelihood" would be jeopardized if his name could be used in this way? Does/should it matter that, as the court reports, Riggins was earning other income from his radio show?

5. Is it fair that the current owners—the ones who bought the house from Ms. Riggins—cannot eventually advertise the house as having belonged to Mr. Riggins? Should they be able to recover the premium that they paid for the property? Do you think that Riggins would have sued if the advertisement were printed by anyone other than his ex-wife? Should the court treat the answer to that question as relevant?

The First Amendment question becomes more difficult when the celebrity's name is used not in an advertisement, but in the product itself:

John Doe, a/k/a Tony Twist v. TCI Cablevision, et al.

110 S.W.3d 363 (Mo. 2003), cert. denied 124 S. Ct. 1058 (2004)

STEPHEN N. LIMBAUGH, JR., Judge.

Appellant Anthony Twist, also known as Tony Twist, is a former professional hockey player in the National Hockey League. After learning of the existence of a comic book, titled *Spawn,* that contained a villainous character sharing his name, Twist brought misappropriation of name and defamation claims against respondents, the creators, publishers and marketers of *Spawn* and related promotional products. Respondents defended on First Amendment grounds. The circuit court dismissed the defamation count, but allowed the misappropriation of name count to go to trial, which resulted in a jury verdict in favor of Twist in the amount of $24,500,000. The circuit court, however, granted respondents' motion for judgment notwithstanding the verdict and, in the alternative, ordered a new trial in the event that its judgment notwithstanding the verdict was overturned on appeal. * * *

I.

Tony Twist began his NHL career in 1988 playing for the St. Louis Blues, later to be transferred to the Quebec Nordiques, only to return to St. Louis where he finished his career in 1999, due to injuries suffered in a motorcycle accident. During his hockey career, Twist became the League's preeminent "enforcer," a player whose chief responsibility was to protect goal scorers from physical assaults by opponents. In that role, Twist was notorious for his violent tactics on the ice. Describing Twist, a *Sports Illustrated* writer said: "It takes a special talent to stand on skates and beat someone senseless, and no one does it better than the St. Louis Blues left winger."

Despite his well-deserved reputation as a tough-guy "enforcer," or perhaps because of that reputation, Twist was immensely popular with the hometown fans. He endorsed products, appeared on radio and television, hosted the "Tony Twist" television talk show for two years, and became actively involved with several children's charities. It is undisputed that Twist engaged in these activities to foster a positive image of himself in the community and to prepare for a career after hockey as a sports commentator and product endorser.

Respondent Todd McFarlane, an avowed hockey fan and president of Todd McFarlane Productions, Inc. (TMP), created *Spawn* in 1992. TMP employs the writers, artists and creative staff responsible for production of the comic book. * * *

* * * In 1993, a fictional character named "Anthony 'Tony Twist' Twistelli" was added to the *Spawn* storyline. The fictional "Tony Twist" is a Mafia don whose list of evil deeds includes multiple murders, abduction of children and sex with prostitutes. The fictional and real Tony Twist bear no physical resemblance to each other and, aside from the common nickname, are similar only in that each can be characterized as having an "enforcer" or tough-guy persona.

* * * In the September 1994 issue, McFarlane admitted that some of the *Spawn* characters were named after professional hockey players, including the "Tony Twist" character: "Antonio Twistelli, a/k/a Tony Twist, is actually the name of a hockey player of the Quebec Nordiques." And, again, in the November 1994 issue, McFarlane stated that the name of the fictional character was based on Twist, a real hockey player, and further promised the readers that they "will continue to see current and past hockey players' names in my books."

In April 1996, *Wizard,* a trade magazine for the comic book industry, interviewed McFarlane. In the published article, "Spawning Ground: A Look at the Real Life People Spawn Characters Are Based Upon," McFarlane is quoted as saying that he uses the names of real-life people to create the identities of the characters. Brief biographies and drawings of the *Spawn* characters follow the McFarlane interview. The paragraph devoted to the "Tony Twist" character contained a drawing of the character accompanied by the following description:

> First Appearance: Spawn # 6
>
> Real-Life Persona: Tony Twist.
>
> Relation: NHL St. Louis Blues right winger.
>
> The Mafia don that has made life exceedingly rough for Al Simmons and his loved ones, in addition to putting out an ill-advised contract on the Violator, is named for former Quebec Nordiques hockey player Tony Twist, now a renowned enforcer (i.e. "Goon") for the St. Louis Blues of the National Hockey League.

Below the character description was a photo of a Tony Twist hockey trading card, in which Twist was pictured in his St. Louis Blues hockey jersey.

In 1997, Twist became aware of the existence of *Spawn* and of the comic book's use of his name for that of the villainous character. On one occasion, several young hockey fans approached Twist's mother with Spawn trading cards depicting the Mafia character "Tony Twist." Subsequently, at an autograph session Twist was asked to sign a copy of the *Wizard* article in which McFarlane was interviewed and Twist's hockey trading card was pictured.

In October 1997, Twist filed suit against McFarlane and various companies associated with the *Spawn* comic book (collectively "respondents"), seeking an injunction and damages for, *inter alia,* misappropriation of name and defamation, the latter claim being later dismissed. McFarlane and the other defendants filed motions for summary judgment asserting First Amendment protection from a prosecution of the misappropriation of name claim, but the motions were overruled.

At trial, McFarlane denied that * * * he or the other defendants had attained any benefit by using Twist's name. Twist, however, presented evidence that McFarlane and the other defendants had indeed benefited by using his name. For example, Twist introduced evidence suggesting that in marketing Spawn products, McFarlane directly targeted hockey fans — Twist's primary fan base — by producing and licensing Spawn logo hockey pucks, hockey jerseys and toy zambonis. On cross-examination, McFarlane admitted that on one occasion defendants sponsored "Spawn Night" at a minor league hockey game, where McFarlane personally appeared and distributed Spawn products, including products containing the "Tony Twist" character. Another "Spawn Night" was planned to take place at a subsequent NHL game, but the event never occurred. On the issue of damages, Twist, through purported expert testimony, offered a formula for determining the fair market value that McFarlane and the other defendants should have paid Twist to use his name. In addition, Twist introduced evidence that his association with the *Spawn* character resulted in a diminution in the commercial value of his name as an endorser of products. To that end, Sean Philips, a former executive of a sports nutrition company, testified that his company withdrew a $100,000 offer to Twist to serve as the company's product endorser after Philips learned that Twist's name was associated with the evil Mafia don in the *Spawn* comic book.

As noted, at the conclusion of the trial, the jury returned a verdict in favor of Twist and against the defendants jointly in the amount of $24,500,000.

II.

* * *

In this case, Twist seeks to recover the amount of the fair market value that respondents should have paid to use his name in connection with Spawn products and for damage done to the commercial value — in effect the endorsement value — of his name. Therefore, Twist's case, though brought as a misappropriation of name action, is more precisely labeled a right of publicity action — a point that both parties appear to concede in their briefs.

Despite the differences in the types of damages that may be recovered, the elements of the two torts are essentially the same. To establish the misappropriation tort, the plaintiff must prove that the defendant used the plaintiff's name without consent to obtain some advantage. In a right of publicity action, the plaintiff must prove the same elements as in a misappropriation suit, with the minor exception that the plaintiff must prove that the defendant used the name to obtain a *commercial* advantage. Restatement (Third) of Unfair Competition sec. 46; *see also* Restatement (Second) of Torts sec. 652C cmt. b (explaining that, in contrast, the misappropriation of name tort applies when plaintiff's name is used for commercial *or* non-commercial advantage). Given the similarity of elements of the two actions, Missouri cases analyzing the tort of misappropriation of name are pertinent to our recognition of a right of publicity claim.

* * *

To summarize, * * * the elements of a right of publicity action include: (1) That defendant used plaintiff's name as a symbol of his identity (2) without consent (3) and with the intent to obtain a commercial advantage.

In this case, the circuit court's entry of JNOV was based on a finding that Twist failed to make a submissible case on the commercial advantage element. In addition, and though the court implicitly held otherwise, respondents claim that the grant of JNOV also was justified because Twist failed to prove that his name was used as "symbol of his identity."

* * *

A.

Respondents' initial contention that Twist did not prove that his name was used as a "symbol of his identity" is spurious. To establish that a defendant used a plaintiff's name as a symbol of his identity, "the name used by the defendant must be understood by the audience as referring to the plaintiff." Restatement (Third) of Unfair Competition sec. 46 cmt. d. * * *

Here, all parties agree that the "Tony Twist" character is not "about" him, in that the character does not physically resemble Twist nor does the *Spawn* story line attempt to track Twist's real life. Instead, Twist maintains that the sharing of the same (and most unusual) name and the common persona of a tough-guy "enforcer" create an unmistakable correlation between Twist the hockey player and Twist the Mafia don that, when coupled with Twist's fame as a NHL star, conclusively establishes that respondents used his name and identity. This Court agrees. Indeed, respondent McFarlane appears to have conceded the point by informing his readers in separate issues of *Spawn* and in the *Wizard* article that the hockey player Tony Twist was the basis for the comic book character's name.

* * *

B.

* * *

[T]he commercial advantage element of the right of publicity focuses on the defendant's intent or purpose to obtain a commercial benefit from use of the plaintiff's identity. But in meeting the commercial advantage element, it is irrelevant whether defendant intended to injure the plaintiff or actually succeeded in obtaining a commercial advantage from using plaintiff's name. That said, it still was incumbent upon Twist to prove that respondents used his name intending to obtain a commercial advantage.

Twist contends, and this Court again agrees, that the evidence admitted at trial was sufficient to establish respondents' intent to gain a commercial advantage by using Twist's name to attract consumer attention to *Spawn* comic books and related products. * * * At a minimum, respondents' statements and actions reveal their intent to create the impression that Twist was somehow associated with the *Spawn* comic book, and this alone is sufficient to establish the commercial advantage element in a right of publicity action.

But this is not all. At trial, Twist introduced evidence that respondents marketed their products directly to hockey fans. For example, respondents produced and distributed Spawn hockey jerseys and pucks and sponsored a "Spawn Night" at a minor league hockey game where other Spawn products were distributed, including products featuring the character "Tony Twist." Additionally, Twist points to McFarlane's statement in the November 1994 issue of *Spawn*, in which he promised readers that "they will continue to see current and past hockey players' names in [his] books." This statement, Twist correctly contends, amounts to an inducement to *Spawn* readers, especially those who are also hockey fans, to continue to purchase the comic book in order to see the name Tony Twist and other hockey players. This is evidence from which the jury could infer that respondents used his name to obtain a commercial advantage.

* * *

III.

Having determined that Twist made a submissible case at trial, we next address whether the right of publicity claim is nevertheless prohibited by the First Amendment. * * *

Zacchini v. Scripps-Howard Broadcasting Co., 433 U.S. 562 (1977), is the first and only right of publicity case decided by the Supreme Court. The case involved the unauthorized broadcast of a videotape of the plaintiff's 15-second "human cannonball" act during a nightly news program. * * * In balancing the respective parties' interests, the Court held, "Wherever the line in particular situations is to be drawn between media reports that are protected and those that are not, we are quite sure that the First and Fourteenth Amendments do not immunize the media when they broadcast a performer's entire act without his consent." Because the *Zacchini* Court limited its holding to the particular facts of the case — the appropriation of plaintiff's "entire act" — it does not control the case at hand. Nonetheless, there are larger lessons that are certainly applicable.

First, the Court acknowledged * * * that the right of publicity is not always trumped by the right of free speech. Explaining the competing right of publicity interests, the Court observed that "[t]he rationale for protecting the right of publicity is the straightforward one of preventing unjust enrichment by the theft of goodwill. No social purpose is served by having the defendant get free some aspect of the plaintiff that would have market value and for which he would normally pay."

Second, the Court distinguished claims for right of publicity or name appropriateness from claims for defamation * * * and claims for "publicity that places plaintiff in a 'false light'" * * *. Because property interests are involved in the former categories but not the latter, the Court refused to apply the *New York Times v. Sullivan* "actual malice" standard that speech is privileged unless it was "knowingly false or was published with reckless disregard for the truth." As the Court later made clear * * *, *Zacchini* stands for the proposition that "the 'actual malice' standard does not apply to the tort of appropriation of a right of publicity. * * *"

Right to publicity cases, both before and after *Zacchini,* focus instead on the threshold legal question of whether the use of a person's name and identity is "expressive," in which case it is fully protected, or "commercial," in which case it is generally not protected. For instance, the use of a person's identity in news, entertainment, and creative works for the purpose of communicating information or expressive ideas about that person is protected "expressive" speech. On the other hand, the use of a person's identity for purely commercial purposes, like advertising goods or services or the use of a person's name or likeness on merchandise, is rarely protected.

Several approaches have been offered to distinguish between expressive speech and commercial speech. The Restatement, for example, employs a "relatedness" test that protects the use of another person's name or identity in a work that is "related to" that person. The catalogue of "related" uses includes "the use of a person's name or likeness in news reporting, whether in newspapers, magazines, or broadcast news * * * use in entertainment and other creative works, including both fiction and nonfiction * * * use as part of an article published in a fan magazine or in a feature story broadcast on an entertainment program * * * dissemination of an unauthorized print or broadcast biography, [and use] of another's identity in a novel, play, or motion picture. * * *" Restatement (Third) of Unfair Competition sec. 47 cmt. c at 549. The proviso to that list, however, is that "if the name or likeness is used solely to attract attention to a work that is *not related* to the identified person, the user may be subject to liability for a use of the other's identity in advertising. * * *" *Id.* (Emphasis added.)

California courts use a different approach, called the "transformative test," [which] "'* * * is essentially a balancing test between the First Amendment and the right of publicity based on whether the work in question adds significant creative elements so as to be transformed into something more than a mere celebrity likeness or imitation.'" * * *

The weakness of the Restatement's "relatedness" test and California's "transformative" test is that they give too little consideration to the fact that many uses of a person's name and identity have both expressive and commercial components. These tests operate to preclude a cause of action whenever the use of the name and identity is in any way expressive, regardless of its commercial exploitation. Under the relatedness test, use of a person's name and identity is actionable only when the use is solely commercial and is otherwise unrelated to that person. Under the transformative test, the transformation or fictionalized characterization of a person's celebrity status is not actionable even if its sole purpose is the commercial use of that person's name and identity. Though these tests purport to balance the prospective interests involved, there is no balancing at all — once the use is determined to be expressive, it is protected. At least one commentator, however, has advocated the use of a more balanced balancing test — a sort of predominant use test — that better addresses the cases where speech is both expressive and commercial:

> If a product is being sold that predominantly exploits the commercial value of an individual's identity, that product should be held to violate the right of publicity and not be protected by the First Amendment, even if there is some "expressive" content in it that might qualify as "speech" in other circumstances. If, on the other hand, the predominant purpose of the product is to make an expressive comment on or about a celebrity, the expressive values could be given greater weight.

Mark S. Lee, *Agents of Chaos: Judicial Confusion in Defining the Right of Publicity — Free Speech Interface,* 23 Loy. L.A. Ent. L. Rev. 471, 500 (2003).

The relative merit of these several tests can be seen when applied to the unusual circumstances of the case at hand. As discussed, Twist made a submissible case that respondents' use of his name and identity was for a commercial advantage. Nonetheless, there is still an expressive component in the use of his name and identity as a metaphorical reference to tough-guy "enforcers." And yet, respondents agree (perhaps to avoid a defamation claim) that the use was not a parody or other expressive comment or a fictionalized account of the real Twist. As such, the metaphorical reference to Twist, though a literary device, has very little literary value compared to its commercial value. On the record here, the use and identity of Twist's name has become predominantly a ploy to sell comic books and related products rather than an artistic or literary expression, and under these circumstances, free speech must give way to the right of publicity.

IV.

* * *

Because the verdict director allowed the jury to render a verdict for plaintiff without a finding that respondents *intended* to obtain a commercial advantage, and because the jury may well have determined that respondents obtained a commercial advantage even though they did not intend to do so, the verdict must be set aside.

* * *

For the foregoing reasons, the circuit court's judgment notwithstanding the verdict is reversed, the judgment granting a new trial is affirmed, * * * and the case is remanded.

All concur.

Notes and Questions

1. Keep in mind that the court in this case had to address two separate issues. First, it had to determine the scope of the state law right of publicity. Second, after determining that Twist had made out such a claim, the court had to determine whether the First Amendment's protection of the freedom of speech permitted a recovery under the state law claim. Recall that the same two-step formula is applicable in defamation cases, as courts must determine both whether there has been defamation and whether recovery for the defamation would be consistent with the First Amendment.

2. On remand, a new jury awarded Twist $15 million. Another motion for judgment notwithstanding the verdict was denied, and on appeal the decision was affirmed. If McFarlane petitions for certiorari from the Supreme Court, should the Court take the case? Recall from constitutional law that the United States Supreme Court is the authoritative interpreter of federal law, including the Constitution, but that the Court has no power to determine the meaning of state law. Accordingly, if certiorari is taken, it would be solely on the First Amendment question.

3. Do you think the court's "predominant use" test is manageable? If not, are you willing to accept the potentially conflicting applications of that test? Do you prefer the court's test, or the "relatedness" or "transformative" tests, as they are discussed in the opinion?

4. Suppose that instead of a comic book, *Spawn* were a novel. Does the result change? *Cf. Hicks v. Casablanca Records*, 464 F. Supp. 426 (S.D.N.Y. 1978).

5. What is the significance of McFarlane's use of Twist's name itself? Should there be a different result, on either the tort issue or the constitutional-law issue, if a character is readily identifiable as being based on a real person, but bears a different name? In this light, consider *Abdul-Jabbar v. General Motors Corp.*, 85 F.3d 407 (9th Cir. 1996) (discussing Kareem Abdul-Jabbar's claim that his right of publicity was infringed when General Motors used Abdul-Jabbar's former name, Lew Alcindor, in an advertisement):

> [The] "right of publicity is not limited to the appropriation of name or likeness." The key issue is appropriation of the plaintiff's identity. "It is not important how the defendant has appropriated the plaintiff's identity, but whether the defendant has done so * * * A rule which says that the right of publicity can be infringed only through the use of nine different methods of appropriating identity merely challenges the clever advertising strategist to come up with the tenth."

Id. at 414 (quoting *White v. Samsung Elec. Am., Inc.*, 971 F.2d 1395, 1398 (9th Cir. 1992)). *See also Newcombe v. Adolf Coors Co.*, 157 F.3d 686 (9th Cir. 1998) (involving the defendant's use of a drawing in which the plaintiff was identifiable); *Hirsch v. S.C. Johnson & Sons, Inc.*, 280 N.W.2d 129 (Wis. 1979) (involving the use of the football player Elroy Hirsch's nickname "Crazylegs" in promoting the defendant's shaving gel); *Motschenbacher v. R.J. Reynolds Tobacco Co.*, 498 F.2d 821 (9th Cir. 1974) (involving the defendant's depiction of distinctive markings on the plaintiff's race car); John McMillen & Rebecca Atkinson, *Artists and Athletes: Balancing the First Amendment and the Right of Publicity in Sport Celebrity Portraits*, 14 J. Legal Aspects of Sport 117 (2004); Brian M. Rowland, *Entertainment, Arts and Sports Law: An Athlete's Right of Publicity*, 76 Fla. Bar J. 45 (2002); Comment, *Stop the Presses! First Amendment Limitations of Professional Athletes' Publicity Rights*, 12 Marq. Sports L. Rev. 885 (2002).

6. *Twist* noted that *Spawn* was not a parody of, or commentary on, the real Tony Twist. If it were, it is quite likely that such expression would have been protected by the First Amendment. *Cardtoons, L.C. v. Major League Baseball Players Association*, 95 F.3d 959 (10th Cir. 1996) concerned a set of trading cards that depicted "players" such as "Treasury Bonds," "Ken Spiffy, Jr.," and "Egotisticky Henderson," whose real-life counterparts were readily identifiable. The cards made fun of the players by mocking their perceived greed and narcissism, among other characteristics. The MLBPA sued, claiming that the cards violated the players' right of publicity, and was rebuked by the court, which wryly noted "[t]he irony of MLBPA's counterclaim for profits from the cards." The court held that it was particularly appropriate to provide First Amendment protection to expressions of parody because celebrities will rarely license others to produce material that mocks them:

> Because celebrities are an important part of our public vocabulary, a parody of a celebrity does not merely lampoon the celebrity, but exposes the weakness of the idea or value that the celebrity symbolizes in society. Cardtoons' trading cards, for example, comment on the state of major league baseball by turning images of our sports heroes into modern-day personifications of avarice. In order to effectively criticize society, parodists need access to images that mean something to people, and thus celebrity parodies are a valuable communicative resource. Restricting the use of celebrity identities restricts the communication of ideas.

Id. at 972. Does this rationale protect derogatory expression more than praise? Should MLBPA be able to collect licensing fees from the publisher of a baseball card set on "the twenty-five greatest hitters in baseball" but not from the publisher of a set depicting "the twenty-five most overpaid crybabies in baseball"? One court suggested the difference is not whether the work criticizes or praises the plaintiff, but whether the work is advertising or not: "The difference between a 'parody' and a 'knock-off' is the difference between fun and profit." *White v. Samsung Electronics America, Inc.*, 971 F.2d 1395, 1401 (9th Cir. 1992). Does *Cardtoons* undermine that distinction or underline its wisdom?

7. Note that even though, generally speaking, use of celebrities' identities in advertisements violates their rights of publicity, media companies may promote themselves by reproducing prior, permissible uses of those identities, without gaining permission a second time. Thus, if a magazine legally writes a story about an athlete and features a photograph of him in connection with that story, it can advertise *itself* to potential subscribers by showing them the photo as an example of the material that appears in the magazine. *See Namath v. Sports Illustrated*, 371 N.Y.S.2d 10 (App. Div. 1975), *aff'd* 352 N.E.2d 584 (N.Y. 1976); *Montana v. San Jose Mercury News, Inc.*, 40 Cal. Rptr. 2d 639 (Cal. Ct. App. 1995); *Booth v. Curtis Publishing Co.*, 233 N.Y.S.2d 737 (App. Div.), *aff'd* 182 N.E.2d 812 (N.Y. 1962).

8. *Cardtoons* also involved a claim that the card set violated the players' intellectual property rights under the Lanham Act. The court held that there was no likelihood that the cards would be confused with traditional cards, and without a likelihood of confusion there could be no successful claim. Keep issues of the right of publicity in mind when you read Chapter 22's discussion of intellectual property.

Chapter 20

Torts and the Spectator

I. Balls and Pucks Leaving the Field of Play

The second pitch almost hit him in the head and he had to dive forward—across the dirt surrounding home plate and into the infield grass. Ball two. Everyone laughed at the explosion of dust created by Owen whacking his uniform; yet Owen made us all wait while he cleaned himself off.

My mother had her back to home plate; she had caught someone's eye—someone in the bleacher seats—and she was waving to whoever it was. She was past the third-base bag—on the third-base line, but still nearer third base than home plate—when Owen Meany started his swing. He appeared to start his swing before the ball left the pitcher's hand—it was a fast ball, such as they are in Little League play, but Owen's swing was well ahead of the ball, with which he made astonishing contact (a little in front of home plate, about chest-high). It was the hardest I'd ever seen him hit a ball, and the force of the contact was such a shock to Owen that he actually stayed on his feet—for once, he didn't fall down.

The crack of the bat was so unusually sharp and loud for a Little League game that the noise captured even my mother's wandering attention. She turned her head toward home plate—I guess, to see who had hit such a shot—and the ball struck her left temple, spinning her so quickly that one of her high heels broke and she fell forward, facing the stands, her knees splayed apart, her face hitting the ground first because her hands never moved from her sides (not even to break her fall), which later gave rise to the speculation that she was dead before she touched the earth.

JOHN IRVING, A PRAYER FOR OWEN MEANY 40 (1989).

Life imitates art as accidents similar to the one befalling the narrator's mother have been repeated myriad times in spectator sports ranging from baseball to golf. One example follows:

City of Coral Springs v. Rippe
743 So. 2d 61 (Fla. Ct. App. 1999)

GUNTHER, J.

* * *

[Plaintiffs Herbert and Helene Rippe] were attending a Little League game at Mullins Park, a multi-recreational facility owned and operated by the City. The chain link fence

1075

surrounding the baseball field is eight feet high behind home plate, while the remainder of the fence, including the area in front of the players' benches, is four feet high. Bleachers for spectator seating is provided behind the eight feet sections of the fence.

Helene was watching her son play in a Little League game from the bleachers. For a better view of the game, she moved in front of the players' bench, where the fence is only four feet high. Helene was struck with a foul ball, knocked unconscious, and suffered injuries. The Rippes sued and alleged negligence against the City. It is clear that throughout the trial the issue of the City's alleged negligence was related to the height of the fence. The jury concluded that Helene was 60% at fault and the City was 40% at fault. A final judgment of $130,000 was entered in favor of the Rippes.

* * *

[T]he City argues that there was no evidence of the City's knowledge of the alleged dangerous condition nor evidence of prior similar incidents presented, and without evidence of actual or constructive knowledge a duty to correct or warn does not arise. Further, the City contends that the Rippes failed to present any competent evidence which could have allowed the jury to conclude the City's knowledge of the condition was superior to Helene's.

In response, the Rippes contend that it is common knowledge that a batted ball could easily fly over a four foot fence. In addition, the Rippes argue that a previous tragedy is not a prerequisite to notice that a hazardous activity exists. Further, they maintain that the testimony indicated the City was fully aware of the possibility that a spectator standing behind the four foot fence could be hit with a batted baseball.

The Rippes rely upon the testimony of the park recreation manager to establish the City's knowledge of the dangerous condition, which would create a duty to warn or correct. The recreation manager testified that he did not have any knowledge of any prior similar incidents. In addition, the recreation manager testified,

> Q: Were you aware of the situations prior to this accident, you and members of the staff in the parks and recreation department, that parents had a tendency to view the game by looking over the four-foot fence?
>
> A: It's not what we had—it's not the intention of the field to have people standing by the four-foot fence. I'm not sure that anyone would have come up and said don't do that. I think the assumption is that we provide the bleachers behind a safe area, and if that somebody does stand by the four-foot fence, that they're watching the game and that they assume some risk of paying attention to the game that they're watching at what's going on.

This is the only evidence relied upon by the Rippes to establish the City's knowledge of the dangerous condition.

* * *

In the present case, the City's liability is based upon either: (1) its failure to warn the Rippes of a known dangerous condition; or (2) its failure to correct a known dangerous condition. The Rippes acknowledge that the danger of fly balls is common knowledge, and thereby essentially concede the City does not have a duty to warn of the condition. Notwithstanding the Rippes' concession that the condition was obvious, the City could be liable for failing to correct a known dangerous condition, provided the City should have anticipated spectator injury despite the obviousness of the danger. As explained in the Restatement (Second) of Torts, section 343A, comment f,

[T]here are situations in which the landowner can and should foresee that the dangerous condition will cause harm to an invitee despite its known or obvious danger. A reasonable probability to expect harm to an invitee from known and obvious dangers may arise under the following circumstances: If a landowner may expect that the invitee's attention might be distracted, so that he or she will not discover what is obvious, or will forget such discovery, or fail to protect himself or herself against it, and if the landowner may expect that the invitee will encounter the known or obvious danger, because, to a reasonable person, the advantages of such encounters would outweigh the apparent risk.

* * * Although there is no evidence of prior similar incidents in the present case, the jury could have inferred the City had knowledge that the height of the fence created a dangerous condition based upon the park recreation manager's testimony that the bleachers were provided in a safe area behind the eight foot fence. In addition, based upon this testimony, the jury could have concluded that the City should have and did expect that parents would choose to stand in front of the four foot fence rather than sit on the bleachers in a safer area. Further, it is reasonable to conclude that the City should have expected a Little League spectator's attention might become distracted, so that he or she would not discover, forget such a discovery, or fail to protect himself or herself from the obvious risk of being struck by a foul ball batted over a four foot fence. Moreover, it is foreseeable that parents may decide the advantage of positioning themselves behind the four foot fence for a better view of the game outweighs the apparent risk of being struck by a foul ball.

Therefore, the Rippes did present evidence upon which the jury could have inferred the City had knowledge of the dangerous condition. Further, it is reasonably foreseeable that a Little League spectator could be injured despite the obviousness of the danger. Thus, based upon the evidence presented, viewed in the light most favorable to the Rippes, the jury could have concluded the City negligently failed to correct a known dangerous condition.

* * *

Notes and Questions

1. The plaintiffs argued that the city had actual or constructive knowledge of the supposedly dangerous condition because "it is common knowledge that a batted ball could easily fly over a four foot fence." Why was it not an adequate *defense* for the City to point to the same common knowledge?

2. This opinion is unusually paternalistic in concluding that the city was bound to account for the likelihood that spectators would be distracted. Should the court instead have placed the risk of injury caused by the plaintiff's inattention on the plaintiff herself?

3. Is it good policy to encourage operators of athletic facilities to make every seat safe, or is it better to permit some spectators to have the advantage of an unobstructed view if they can protect themselves? Recall that the plaintiff moved from behind the backstop precisely to avoid the impediment that would have prevented her injury. In light of her choice, is her complaint about the city's negligence in failing to extend the higher fence tenable?

Because of the obvious relevance to the average fan, questions dealing with spectators struck by thrown baseballs, stray golf shots, post-collision stock cars and numerous other horror stories abound at cocktail parties as well as in courtrooms and classrooms.

No absolute rule of thumb emerges from the legions of cases dealing with this problem on every conceivable professional and amateur level. Yet, it is safe to say that, barring some intentional tort, most stadium owners, sports teams, and individuals will escape liability because of either primary or secondary assumption of risk. Recall that primary assumption of risk is equivalent to saying that the defendant owes no duty or has not breached a duty that does exist, while secondary assumption of risk is the plaintiff's conscious taking of an unreasonable risk. Thus, secondary assumption of the risk is more of a true defense in a tort action because it allows the defendant to avoid liability *after* its negligence has been proven. Of course, this defense has its limitations and, in appropriate circumstances, the alleged tortfeasor may find a court inhospitable to the argument that there was no duty to protect or that the spectator assumed the risk of injury. *See* MARTIN J. GREENBERG & JAMES T. GRAY, SPORTS LAW PRACTICE §11.08(1) (1998). Still, by and large, even when the jurisdiction in question has adopted a comparative fault approach, *see* Chapter 18, *supra*, the owners have emerged largely unscathed.

Friedman v. Houston Sports Ass'n
731 S.W.2d 572 (Tex. Ct. App. 1987)

DUNN, Justice.

* * *

The record reveals that 11-year-old Karen Friedman attended the Astros game on July 14, 1978. Karen was seated with her father and two family friends, Melvin Weiss and his daughter Penny. Karen and her father did not elect to sit in the screened area behind home plate that the appellee had provided for the protection of spectators. The record indicates that seats were available in this area. Instead, the appellants chose to sit several rows behind the first base dugout. In the bottom of the ninth inning, Karen and Penny left their seats, and walked down behind the first base dugout. Karen was hit near her right eye by a line-drive foul ball.

In the appellants' first, second, and third points of error, they argue that there was sufficient evidence to uphold the jury's verdict that the appellee was negligent in failing to warn of the danger of being struck by a baseball behind the first base dugout, and that this negligence was the proximate cause of Karen's injury. * * *

One of the grounds asserted by the appellee * * * is that there is no duty on the part of the owner of a baseball stadium to warn spectators of the open and obvious risk of injury from baseballs. This proposition is well settled as a matter of law in Texas. * * *

These cases do not eliminate the stadium owner's duty to exercise reasonable care under the circumstances to protect patrons against injury. However, they define that duty so that once the stadium owner has provided "adequately screened seats" for all those desiring them, the stadium owner has fulfilled its duty of care as a matter of law.

The appellants argue that these Texas cases no longer apply because of the present comparative negligence statute. The appellants misconstrue the purpose of comparative negligence. Comparative negligence does not create a duty; it simply allows partial recovery for a plaintiff who is no more than 50% at fault. The appellants in this case still have the burden to prove that the appellee owed them a duty to warn.

New York, a comparative negligence state, recently adopted the majority rule of limited liability for a baseball stadium owner. *Akins v. Glens Falls City School District*, 424 N.E.2d 531 (N.Y. 1981). * * * The court held that the owner was required to screen the most dangerous section of the field, the area behind home plate, and the number of protected seats so provided must be sufficient in number to accommodate the spectators who may reasonably be anticipated to desire protected seats on an ordinary occasion. Once this is done, the proprietor has fulfilled its duty of care imposed by law, and cannot be liable in negligence.

California has also abolished assumption of the risk and has adopted comparative negligence, while at the same time adhering to the traditional rule for baseball spectator injuries. *Rudnick v. Golden West Broadcasters*, 156 Cal. App. 3d 793 (1984). The California court stated that the stadium owner had only the limited duty to provide screened seats "for as many fans as may be reasonably expected to call for them on any ordinary occasion." If this is done, the stadium owner has "fulfilled its limited duty to spectators as a matter of law, and is entitled to summary judgment. * * * The chance to apprehend a misdirected baseball is as much a part of the game as the seventh inning stretch or peanuts and Cracker Jack."

Virtually all jurisdictions have adopted the limited duty of stadium owners to screen certain seats, and have held that where there is a screened area for the protection of spectators, and a fan elects to sit in an unscreened area, liability will be precluded even though injury arises.

* * *

We find that a stadium owner has no duty to warn spectators of the danger of foul balls. The stadium owner's duty is to provide "adequately screened seats" for all those desiring them.

* * *

COHEN, Justice, Concurring. American courts have refused, almost without exception, to allow sports spectators to recover for injuries caused by the open and obvious risks of the game. This rule is nowhere more clear than in baseball cases. The holdings are made as a matter of law on one or more of the following grounds: (1) the defendant had no duty to warn or protect the plaintiff from an open and obvious danger; (2) the plaintiff assumed the risk that was, or should have been, obvious to him; and (3) the plaintiff was guilty of contributory negligence by placing himself in a dangerous location.

* * *

Thus, adult plaintiffs must lose when their injuries result from the game's obvious hazards. As the majority states, this is also the rule in Texas. It may even be a good rule, when applied to adults. I am not convinced, however, that it is the rule, and certainly not a good rule, to apply this principle, as a matter of law, in a case involving an 11-year-old child as a plaintiff. Some 11-year-olds will know the dangers of baseball, and some will not. I cannot say, as a matter of law in every case and without exception, that those 11-year-olds who do not know of baseball's dangers lack the minimum level of "neighborhood knowledge" that society demands. In my opinion, a landowner who invites an unsupervised 11-year-old child to its premises should not be surprised if a court imposes liability upon finding that the child is less aware of some particular danger, and thus more in need of warning, than its parents or older siblings. Juries are well suited to make such distinctions, and we owe considerable deference to their verdicts when reviewing judgments n.o.v.

I nevertheless join the court's decision because I believe that any failure to warn this 11-year-old was excused, since she was accompanied by an adult responsible for her welfare. The law holds that there is no duty to warn adults. When a young minor enters a premises with a responsible adult, the landowner has a right to rely on the adult to protect the minor from dangers that are within the adult's "neighborhood knowledge." Thus, the neighborhood knowledge that the law requires of Robert Friedman [Karen's father] is imputed through him to Karen Friedman. In fact, Karen was generally warned about baseballs on the night of the accident by Melvin Weiss, and was told not to try to catch foul balls and to be careful when she approached the dugout.

The jury refused to find that Robert Friedman was negligent in failing to warn Karen about foul balls, in selecting seats behind the dugout, or in allowing Karen to leave her assigned seat. Yet Texas law holds, notwithstanding the jury's verdict, that Robert Friedman assumed this risk for Karen by allowing her to be at the place where she was injured. Although uncomfortable with this rule, as an intermediate appellate court justice, I am bound to follow it.

This does not mean that a duty to warn could never arise. An unsupervised 11-year-old invited into the stadium, despite his lack of "neighborhood knowledge," might be owed a warning, although his parents might be negligent for allowing him to attend without supervision.

With these reservations, I concur.

Notes and Questions

1. In this case, the court reinforced the view that a stadium owner's duty to exercise reasonable care does not include an obligation to warn spectators about the likelihood or danger of foul balls. Rather, it defined the duty as providing "adequately screened seats for all those desiring them." In an earlier portion of the majority opinion in which the court described the New York approach, the court seemed to embrace a description of the duty as one in which the stadium owner must "screen the most dangerous section of the field, the area behind home plate, and the number of protected seats so provided must be sufficient in number to accommodate the spectators *who may reasonably be anticipated to desire protected seats on an ordinary occasion.*" (Emphasis supplied.) Has this court held that an infinite number of screened seats must be made available upon demand? Is there a duty to provide 30,000 protected seats if the spectators make such a request on a given night? If not, a rule that permits stadium operators to screen only a small minority of seats effectively presents a fan who is unable to secure a protected seat with a Hobson's choice of going home or assuming the risk of injury. Should the law seek to avoid placing fans in such a position? *See Davidoff v. Metropolitan Baseball Club*, 463 N.E.2d 1219, 1222 (N.Y. 1984) (Cooke, C.J., dissenting). The Restatement's phrasing is that ballpark owners have a duty "to provide a reasonably sufficient number of screened seats to protect those who desire it against the risk of being hit by batted balls." Restatement (Second) of Torts § 493C. Practically, of course, virtually nobody asks for a shielded seat, and, as the *Rippe* case demonstrates, many spectators seek seats that are free of protective screens.

2. In the concurring opinion, Justice Cohen intimated that the result of this case might change if an uninitiated fan were victim of a foul ball. Should this factor affect the stadium owner's duty? In *Schentzel v. Philadelphia National League Club*, 96 A.2d 181 (Pa. Super. Ct. 1953), a woman was hit with a foul ball during what she claimed was the first baseball game she ever attended. Apparently her husband, who bought the tickets, asked for a seat under a protective screen, but the tickets he received were for seats 15–20 feet away from the screen. Modern notions of sexism aside, plaintiff argued

that ball clubs should take "'exceptional precautions' toward its women patrons, many of whom are ignorant of the hazards involved in the game." *Id.* at 184. The court rejected the argument, holding that she consented to the risk of injury, even without being aware of it. *See id.* at 185–86. Further, the court noted that though providing tickets for seats other than the ones requested might give rise to a breach of contract action, it had no relevance for negligence. *See id.* at 187.

3. The concurrence argues that stadium operators own no special duty to children who attend games, so long as the children attend games with responsible adults who will presumably warn and protect them. Should the same rule apply to adults who attend their first games in the company of more experienced companions? *Schentzel* did not reach the question, but noted that Mrs. Schentzel's husband "was thoroughly familiar" with the risk of foul balls (though apparently not as familiar with rules of grammar), as "established by his testimony on cross-examination. He stated, 'There is a million foul balls, maybe three or four or five in an inning, goes into the stand.'" *Id.* at 183.

4. Should stadium operators owe *any* duty of care to protect spectators from foul balls? Consider *Neinstein v. Los Angeles Dodgers, Inc.*, 229 Cal. Rptr. 612 (Cal. Ct. App. 1986) (dictum): "A person who fears injury always has the option of refraining from attending a baseball game or of sitting in a part of the park which is out of reach of balls traveling with sufficient velocity to cause harm." *Cf. Murphy v. Steeplechase Amusement Co.*, 166 N.E. 173, 174 (N.Y. 1929) (Cardozo, C.J.):

> The antics of the clown are not the paces of the cloistered cleric. The rough and boisterous joke, the horseplay of the crowd, evokes its own guffaws, but they are not the pleasures of tranquillity. The plaintiff was not seeking a retreat for meditation. Visitors were tumbling about the belt to the merriment of onlookers when he made his choice to join them. He took the chance of a like fate, with whatever damage to his body might ensue from such a fall. The timorous may stay at home.

5. Where the timorous have seated themselves behind a protective screen, the facility operators owe a duty to make reasonable efforts to ensure that the screen is effective. *See Berrum v. Powalisz*, 317 P.2d 1090 (Nev. 1957); *Edling v. Kansas City Baseball & Exhibition Co.*, 168 S.W. 908 (Mo. Ct. App. 1914).

6. Several states have enacted legislation providing that facility owners and operators are shielded from liability for injuries resulting from foul balls, but some statutes provide that immunity only when the facility warns of dangers, Colo. Rev. Stat. 13-21-120(5)(c), or "provide[s] protective seating that is reasonably sufficient to satisfy expected requests." Ariz. Rev. Stat. 12-554(A)(1).

7. Should courts draw a distinction between baseball and hockey? Some courts have argued that hockey's relative obscurity makes it less likely that patrons recognize the risks of attending a game, and for that reason impose a duty on arenas to protect fans. *See, e.g., Morris v. Cleveland Hockey Club*, 105 N.E.2d 419, 426 (Ohio 1952). Others treat the sports identically. *See Modec v. City of Eveleth*, 29 N.W.2d 453 (Minn. 1947); *Kaufman v. Madison Square Garden Corp.*, 284 N.Y.S. 808 (N.Y. App. Div. 1935). Professor Yasser suggests that there may be a move toward applying assumption-of-the-risk principles to both baseball and hockey, as hockey gains in popularity and the risks of the game become more well known. *See* Raymond L. Yasser, *Liability for Sports Injuries, in* Law of Professional and Amateur Sports § 15:26 (Gary A. Uberstine ed. 2002). Two state legislatures have immunized hockey facilities from liability for injuries to spectators from flying pucks. *See* 745 Ill. Comp. Stat. 52/10; Utah Code Ann. 78-27-62.

In part because "the direction and trajectory of the puck can be extremely unpredictable," one article suggests that the liability for injuries at hockey games should be expanded. *See* C. Peter Goplerud III & Nicolas P. Terry, *Allocation of Risk Between Hockey Fans and Facilities: Tort Liability After the Puck Drops*, 38 TULSA L. REV. 445 (2003). Do you find the argument persuasive? The question is hardly academic, as legislatures, courts, and commentators consider what responses are appropriate to incidents like the death of thirteen-year-old Brittanie Cecil, who was struck with a deflected puck which fractured her skull "and more critically caused her head to snap back violently, tearing her right vertebral artery." *Id.* at 446.

8. Should assumption of the risk apply to injuries caused when race cars, or parts of race cars, leave the track and strike spectators? *Compare Alden v. Norwood Arena*, 124 N.E.2d 505 (Mass. 1955), *and Arnold v. State*, 148 N.Y.S. 479 (App. Div. 1914), *with Blake v. Fried*, 95 A.2d 360 (Pa. Super. Ct. 1953).

Rinaldo v. McGovern
587 N.E.2d 264 (N.Y. 1991)

TITONE, Judge.

The issue in this appeal is whether a golfer who accidentally misses the fairway and instead sends the ball soaring off the golf course onto an adjacent roadway can be held liable in negligence for the resulting injury. Under the circumstances of this case, we hold that the defendant golfer incurred no tort liability for what amounted to nothing more than his poorly hit tee shot.

The present action arises out of an accident in which a golf ball driven by one of the two individual defendants soared off the golf course on which they were playing, traveled through (or over) a screen of trees and landed on an adjacent public road, where plaintiffs happened to be driving their automobile. The ball struck and shattered plaintiffs' windshield, with the result that plaintiff Roberta Rinaldo was injured. It is undisputed that both defendants, who were teeing off at the eleventh hole of the golf course, intended to drive their balls straight down the fairway and not in the direction of the trees. However, each defendant "sliced" his ball, causing it to veer off to the right. There is no evidence that either defendant was careless or guilty of anything other than making an inept tee shot.

Plaintiffs commenced the present action charging the individual defendants with negligence and failure to warn. On defendants' motion for summary judgment, the Supreme Court, Erie County, dismissed both causes of action, holding that defendants had no duty to warn plaintiffs of their impending tee shots and that defendants' conduct in mishitting their golf balls did not, without more, constitute actionable negligence. * * *

[W]hatever the extent of a golfer's duty to other players in the immediate vicinity on the golf course, a golfer ordinarily may not be held liable to individuals located entirely outside of the boundaries of the golf course who happen to be hit by a stray, mishit ball.

* * *

[T]he pertinent question here * * * is whether a warning, if given, would have been effective in preventing the accident. We conclude that, under the circumstances of this case, a warning would have been all but futile * * *. Even if defendant had shouted "fore," the traditional golfer's warning, it is unlikely that plaintiffs, who were driving in a vehicle on a nearby roadway, would have heard, much less had the opportunity to act upon, the shouted warning. Accordingly, * * * the possibility that a warning would have been effective here to prevent the accident was simply too "remote" to justify submission of the case to the jury.

Plaintiffs' cause of action based on the claimed negligence of the defendant golfer is similarly untenable. Although the object of the game of golf is to drive the ball as cleanly and directly as possible toward its ultimate intended goal (the hole), the possibility that the ball will fly off in another direction is a risk inherent in the game. [T]he presence of such a risk does not, by itself, import tort liability. The essence of tort liability is the failure to take reasonable steps, where possible, to minimize the chance of harm. Thus, to establish liability in tort, there must be *both* the existence of a recognizable risk *and* some basis for concluding that the harm flowing from the consummation of that risk was reasonably preventable.

Since "'even the best professional golfers cannot avoid an occasional "hook" or "slice,"'" it cannot be said that the risk of a mishit golf ball is a fully preventable occurrence. To the contrary, even with the utmost concentration and the "tedious preparation" that often accompanies a golfer's shot, there is no guarantee that the ball will be lofted onto the correct path. For that reason, we have held that the mere fact that a golf ball did not travel in the intended direction does not establish a viable negligence claim. To provide an actionable theory of liability, a person injured by a mishit golf ball must affirmatively show that the golfer failed to exercise due care by adducing proof, for example, that the golfer "aimed so inaccurately as to unreasonably increase the risk of harm."

No such proof was adduced here. In response to defendants' motion for summary judgment, plaintiffs submitted nothing more than the affidavit of a golf pro explaining that "slicing" is a common problem among inexperienced and experienced golfers alike and a deposition statement by defendant Vogel to the effect that his codefendant, McGovern, had such a problem. At most, this evidence, if ultimately proven to be true, would establish only what is obvious—that if one or both defendants teed off from the eleventh hole, there was a risk that one or both of their golf balls would travel off to the right in the direction of the road rather than the direction of the fairway. Plaintiffs' evidence did not, however, support the other element of the cause of action essential to plaintiffs' recovery, i.e., that defendant's actions with respect to this risk were negligent. Hence, plaintiffs' cause of action based on defendant's purported lack of due care was properly dismissed.

* * *

Ludwikoski v. Kurotsu

875 F. Supp. 727 (D. Kan. 1995)

LUNGSTRUM, District Judge.

* * *

On October 10, 1991, defendant and his associate were in Kansas City discussing business with two executives of Butler Manufacturing Company. * * * After lunch, the four men went to the Mission Hills Country Club to play golf. At that time, defendant was sixty-six years old and had been playing golf for nearly thirty years. He played golf dozens of times a year, had received professional training and, at one point, had a handicap of 22.

The golf game started at approximately 1:00 p.m. The weather was nice. Defendant did not consume any alcohol during the golf game. On each of the first seventeen holes, defendant's tee shot was straight down the fairway with no hook and only an occasional fade to the right. He had a smooth, consistent swing, knew how to hold the club, and understood the game and its rules of etiquette. * * *

The foursome arrived at the 18th tee at approximately 5:00 p.m. The 18th hole is basically a straight par 5 that parallels Belinder Road. A fence separates the golf course from the road, along with a row of trees. Defendant took the same amount of time and preparation before his tee shot as he did on the previous 17 holes. He did nothing different or unusual on the 18th tee. His intended line of flight for the ball was down the center of the fairway. He saw no one in his intended line of flight and neither he nor any other member of the foursome was aware that plaintiff was sitting in a car in a driveway across the street from the golf course. Neither defendant nor any other member of the foursome yelled any type of warning prior to the shot.

At approximately the same time the foursome arrived at the 18th tee, plaintiff was leaving an estate sale where she had been working all day. The estate sale was being held at a private home located on Belinder Road across the street from the golf course. The driveway of the house was approximately 100 yards north of the 18th tee. Plaintiff left the house and went to her car, which was parked on the street. She started her car and pulled into the driveway of the house where the estate sale was being held so she could turn around. As she did so, she saw a friend coming out of the front door of the house. As she was waiting to talk to her friend, the engine of her car running, defendant hit his tee shot.

Defendant's tee shot went straight for 25–30 yards and then hooked to the left. When defendant and his fellow golfers saw the ball begin to hook, they all yelled "FORE" as loudly as possible. The ball traveled over the perimeter fence, through a group of trees planted by the golf course to prevent errant shots from leaving the course, over Belinder Road, through another group of trees and into plaintiff's open car window, striking plaintiff in the eye and face. Defendant and his fellow golfers lost sight of the ball as it entered the first row of trees and did not see it again. Neither plaintiff nor the persons she was speaking with heard any type of warning prior to plaintiff being struck in the face by the ball.

Defendant and the other members of the foursome did not hear any response to their yells of "FORE," so the remaining three golfers hit their tee shots. As they proceeded up the fairway after the tee shots, they saw a man at or near the perimeter fence motioning to them to come over to the fence. They learned at that time that the ball had hit plaintiff, who was pointed out to them. That was the first time defendant or the other golfers had seen plaintiff or her car.

* * *

Plaintiff alleges that the defendant "caused a golf ball to be launched from the 18th tee in such a negligent and careless manner so as to leave the premises of the Mission Hills Country Club." She further alleges that as a result of defendant's negligence, she was struck in the face and eye with the ball, causing severe and permanent injuries. In essence, plaintiff proceeds on three separate negligence grounds, those being that: (1) defendant hit his tee shot in a negligent manner; (2) defendant failed to give a warning prior to hitting his tee shot; and (3) defendant gave an inadequate warning after hitting his tee shot.

In order to state a negligence claim under Kansas law, plaintiff must allege the existence of a duty, a breach of that duty, an injury, and a causal connection between the duty breached and the injury suffered. Whether a duty exists is a question of law.

It is generally established that the mere fact that a person is struck by a golf ball driven by a person playing the game of golf does not constitute proof of negligence on the part of the golfer who hit the ball, and that a golfer is only required to exercise reasonable care for the safety of persons reasonably within the range of danger of being struck by the ball.

The court finds that the plaintiff has put forward no evidence to support a finding by a reasonable jury that the defendant hit his tee shot in a negligent manner. The uncontroverted evidence is that plaintiff was an experienced golfer who plays dozens of times a year, that he has had professional training, and that he constantly practices. Further, the evidence is uncontroverted that plaintiff had consumed no alcohol prior to the time he hit his fateful tee shot, that he had a smooth consistent swing, that he knew how to properly hold the club, that his tee shots on the first seventeen holes were straight down the fairway with no hook and only an occasional fade to the right, that he took the same amount of time and preparation on the 18th tee as he did on the 17 previous tee shots, and that he did nothing different or unusual on the 18th tee.

Plaintiff comes forward with no evidence that controverts defendant's statement that he executed his shot on the 18th hole in the same manner as he did every other tee shot. Her only effort along those lines is a bald assertion that "[i]t is not unusual for a golfer to attempt to hit a longer shot on a par 5 hole by intentionally putting somewhat of a hook spin on the shot by rolling the wrists on the stroke. In this case, the fact that golfers often try such adjustments coupled with the fact that the ball did hook shows that defendant did indeed do something different on the 18th hole." The court finds this argument, even if it represents an accurate statement of golfing technique, is based on a generic reference as to what other golfers may do, merely invites speculation as to whether the defendant did so and does nothing to advance plaintiff's argument that defendant did not exercise due care in hitting his tee shot on the 18th hole.

The court also finds that under the factual circumstances of this case, defendant had no duty to give a warning prior to hitting his tee shot on the 18th hole. The general rule is that although a golfer about to hit a shot must, in the exercise of ordinary care, give an adequate and timely warning to those who are unaware of his or her intention to play and who may be endangered by the play, this duty does not extend to those persons who are not in the line of play if danger to them is not to be anticipated. * * *

In this case there is no question that plaintiff was not in the "foreseeable ambit of danger" when defendant struck his drive on the 18th tee. Plaintiff was sitting in a car in a driveway across the street from the golf course, which was past a perimeter fence and a group of trees planted by the golf course to prevent struck golf balls from leaving the course. The uncontroverted facts of this case show that, as a matter of law, plaintiff was outside the foreseeable ambit of danger as defined and applied by the courts and was not entitled to a warning prior to defendant's shot.

Plaintiff's final negligence claim is that defendant did not give a sufficient warning after he hit his tee shot on the 18th hole and realized that it might leave the course. Defendant has presented evidence that when he and his fellow golfers in his foursome saw the ball begin to hook and head over the trees towards Belinder Street, they all yelled "FORE" as loudly as possible. In attempting to controvert this evidence, plaintiff states that "[d]efendant and his fellow golfers did not yell a sufficient warning. Plaintiff and persons standing in the yard on Belinder did not hear any warning whatsoever." Plaintiff also presents her own affidavit statement and affidavits from the two persons who were in the yard with her stating that they "have had no problems with [their] hearing and can easily hear a shout from 100 yards away."

The court finds that plaintiff has not presented sufficient evidence to create a question of material fact as to the adequacy of defendant's warning following his recognition that his ball was heading off the course. The mere fact that plaintiff and the other persons standing in the yard did not hear the warning does not directly controvert defendants' evidence that both he and his fellow golfers yelled "FORE" as loudly as possible. Further, the affidavit statements of plaintiff and the two persons in the yard that they "had no problems with [their] hearing and can easily hear a shout from 100 yards away" is insufficient to create a fact question as to whether the warning was actually given. The general averments in the affidavit statements, which merely indicate that the persons can "hear a shout from 100 yards away," are not the same as an averment that they would have heard a warning shout had one been yelled by defendant. The affidavit statements fail to take into account that the shouts in question would be coming from across a street, behind two rows of trees, and would need to be audible over an idling car engine.

* * *

* * * Accordingly, the court finds that the affidavit statements are insufficient to rebut defendant's uncontroverted evidence that defendant yelled a warning after hitting his drive on the 18th tee.

* * *

[D]efendant's motion for summary judgment is granted.

Notes and Questions

1. Should the liability of a golfer depend in part on the defendant's ability consistently to hit the ball on the fairway? In other words, might an injury to a bystander be foreseeable if the golfer's control is notoriously poor? *Cf. Cook v. Johnston*, 688 P.2d 215 (Ariz. 1984) (taking into account the defendant's tendency to shank the ball).

2. Why does the doctrine of *res ipsa loquitur* ("the thing speaks for itself") not apply in these cases, such that negligence is presumed when the ball leaves the golf course?

3. According to these two cases, what is a golfer's duty to people outside the course who might be hit by a ball? What should it be?

4. Should golfers owe a duty to other golfers? Generally golf cases apply the same principles of primary assumption of the risk that we saw in the last chapter. *See, e.g., Yoneda v. Tom*, 133 P.3d 796 (Haw. 2006); *Schick v. Ferolito*, 767 A.2d 962 (N.J. 2001); *Monk v. Phillips*, 983 S.W.2d 323 (Tex. Ct. App. 1999). *But see Bartlett v. Chebuhar*, 479 N.W.2d 321 (Iowa 1992). Thus, mere negligence will not subject a defendant to liability, but reckless conduct—by, for example, hitting the ball without issuing a warning when someone is in the expected path of the ball—will.

5. Should golfers owe a different duty of care to homeowners whose land adjoins the course? The New York Court of Appeals has held that there is no duty to warn a homeowner before striking the ball because if warnings were given by each golfer, homeowners would soon ignore them. *See Nussbaum v. Lacopo*, 265 N.E.2d 762 (N.Y. 1970). The California Court of Appeals in one case, however, declined to apply assumption of the risk to a similar situation. *See Curran v. Green Hills Country Club*, 101 Cal. Rptr. 158 (Cal. Ct. App. 1972).

6. What should the liability of the golf course be, if its design results in balls being propelled into adjacent roadways and homes or if the design results in injuries to golfers

on adjacent holes? *Compare, e.g., Yoneda, supra,* and *Morgan v. FUJI Country USA, Inc.,* 40 Cal. Rptr. 2d 249 (Cal. Ct. App. 1995) (finding a question of fact as to the golf course's negligence), *with, e.g., Lincke v. Long Beach Country Club,* 702 N.E.2d 738 (Ind. Ct. App. 1998), and *Lemovitz v. Pine Ridge Realty Corp.,* 887 F. Supp. 16 (D. Me. 1995) (holding against liability). *See generally* David M. Holliday, Annotation, *Liability to One Struck by Golf Ball,* 53 A.L.R. 4th 282 (2004).

II. Liability for Unsafe Premises

Proprietors of sports arenas owe their invitees a duty of reasonable care to ensure that the facility is reasonably safe. Most sport-tort cases involving spectators concern risks peculiar to athletic contests, such as the risk of injury from balls and pucks that fly into the stands. But it is worth remembering that liability may attach for injuries that are not the direct result of action on the field of play. Consider the following cases:

Rockwell v. Hillcrest Country Club, Inc.
181 N.W.2d 290 (Mich. Ct. App. 1970)

J.H. GILLIS, Presiding Judge.

On July 27, 1963, a suspension bridge covering the Clinton river and located on the Hillcrest golf course, Mt. Clemens, Michigan, collapsed, dropping its occupants into the river below. Immediately before the bridge gave way, there were approximately 80 to 100 golf enthusiasts on the bridge, together with a golf cart. Among them were plaintiffs James and Ann Rockwell; they were spectators watching a tournament being played on the Hillcrest course. Ann Rockwell fell 25 feet, struck the water, and sustained serious injuries. This suit followed.

* * * Plaintiffs' complaint alleged negligence, including defendants' failure to warn tournament participants and spectators of the maximum capacity of the bridge. At trial, it was plaintiffs' theory that overloading caused the bridge to collapse and that defendants' negligence proximately caused plaintiffs' injuries. * * * A verdict was returned against [the Country Club] in the amount of $75,000 for Ann Rockwell and $2,500 for James Rockwell. Defendant Hillcrest Country Club's motion for judgment notwithstanding the verdict was denied and it appeals.

* * *

[T]the record clearly supports plaintiffs' pleaded contention that defendant Hillcrest County Club was under a duty to warn, by some reasonably appropriate means, tournament participants and spectators of the maximum capacity of the Clinton river bridge. The bridge itself was constructed in 1953. At that time, Woodrow Woody, defendant's president, was informed of the bridge's maximum capacity. He testified as follows:

Q. (By Mr. Fried, plaintiffs' counsel) Did you find out how many people could use the bridge:

A. I did.

Q. And what was that number?

A. Twenty-Five. As a safe factor. Not the capacity, but a safe factor.

Q. Mr. Woody, after you made that determination, after you found out that twenty-five people was the safe factor on that bridge, did you put a sign on the bridge?

A. Yes, sir.

Q. Did the sign say limited to twenty-five people?

A. It said capacity twenty-five persons.

Woody's testimony established that the defendant corporation had knowledge of a latent danger existing on premises occupied by the Hillcrest County Club. That more than 25 golf enthusiasts might—without notice of the safe capacity of the bridge—attempt to cross it during the tournament at the same time was a risk reasonably to be foreseen. Under these circumstances, the defendant corporation was obliged to warn its invitees, including plaintiffs, of the bridge's maximum capacity.

"[T]he obligation of reasonable care * * * extend[s] to everything that threatens the invitee with an unreasonable risk of harm. The occupier must not only use care not to injure the visitor by negligent acts, and to warn him of latent dangers of which the occupier knows, but he must also * * * take reasonable precautions to protect the invitee from dangers which are foreseeable from the arrangement or use. The obligation extends to the original construction of the premises, where it results in a dangerous condition." Prosser on Torts (3d ed.), §61 pp. 402–03.

Clearly preponderant proof also established that no forewarning was given to those crossing the bridge on the date of the tournament. Again we quote Woody's testimony:

Q. On July 27th, the date of this incident that's involved in this lawsuit, was there a sign on this bridge?

* * *

A. There was not a sign there. I looked at it and there was not a sign there, to my great disappointment.'

Q. * * * Did you on July 27, 1963, direct anybody to go down and control traffic on that bridge?

A. I did not.

* * *

[P]laintiffs' proofs show (1) that the bridge was constructed to hold 25 people safely; (2) when it collapsed there were 80 to 100 people on the bridge; (3) no sign was present warning those using the bridge of its safe capacity; (4) no marshals or other supervisory personnel were present to oversee proper use of the bridge; and (5) that the bridge collapsed, dropping its occupants into the river below. From these facts, we think it permissible to infer negligent causation. Reasonable men might draw a fair inference—as theorized by plaintiffs' counsel—that overload caused the bridge to collapse; and that, but for defendant's failure to forewarn those using the bridge of its safe capacity, the bridge would not have collapsed, injuring plaintiffs.

* * *

Neither are we of the view that the absence of expert testimony on plaintiffs' side of the case is fatal, as argued by defendant. * * * Whether, on the physical facts presented, the bridge collapsed because of overload is not a question beyond the understanding of ordinary lay minds. An elementary law of physics dictates that if more weight is placed on an object than it will hold, collapse will occur. We conclude that plaintiffs could sustain their burden of proof without production of expert testimony.

* * *

Rogers v. Professional Golfers Association of America
28 S.W.3d 869 (Ky. Ct. App. 2000)

BUCKINGHAM, Judge:

Linda A. Rogers * * * slipped and fell on a grassy hillside to the left of the seventeenth fairway at the Valhalla Golf Club during the playing of the 1996 PGA golf championship in Louisville, Kentucky, in August 1996. * * * We conclude the trial court properly granted summary judgment in favor of the PGA and Valhalla.

The PGA golf championship, one of the four major championships in the world of golf, was played at the Valhalla Golf Club in Louisville, Kentucky, over the four days of August 8–11, 1996. Thousands of spectators, including Rogers and her husband, who was a member of the golf club, attended the event to watch the golf action at the course.

A rainstorm hit the golf course on the first day of the tournament, and the course was still wet and muddy in places on the second day. When Rogers and her husband decided to leave the tournament at the conclusion of the first day, they proceeded from the area of the seventeenth green and eighteenth tee to the main entrance by way of the rough area along the left side of the seventeenth fairway. The rough in this area was grassy and hilly.

At the top of the rough area was a "tent village," which consisted of a gated area containing corporate booths or tents. In order to gain access into the tent village, a spectator was required to have a special ticket. If one could enter the tent village near the seventeenth green and proceed from one end to the other, then access to the main entrance could be had without walking over the grassy hillside. Although Rogers and her husband did not have special tickets to gain access to the tent village area, she requested and was granted permission to enter the area so as to walk from one side to the other to the main entrance in order to avoid the hillside because she had previously had knee surgery which continued to cause her concern.

On the second day of the tournament, Rogers and her husband again returned to watch the golf action, and later exited the main entrance to go to the merchandise tent to purchase various items of golf merchandise. They then decided to re-enter at the main entrance and proceed back toward the seventeenth green and eighteenth tee area. However, the guard or employee at the gate to the tent village would not let Rogers in the village area because she didn't have the proper ticket. Since she and her husband wanted to watch golf action in that area of the course, they proceeded across the grassy hillside toward the seventeenth green. While doing so, Rogers slipped and fell, injuring her leg.

* * *

As a tournament patron, Rogers was an invitee. Generally, the owner of premises to which the public is invited has a general duty to exercise ordinary care to keep the premises in a reasonably safe condition. However, "[r]easonable care on the part of the possessor of business premises does not ordinarily require precaution or even warning against dangers that are known to the visitor or so obvious to him that he may be expected to discover them."

Rogers testified that she had played golf approximately three times per year for ten years. As a result of this experience, she knew that golf courses have varying terrain, vegetation, and grass conditions. She also stated that she knew golf courses have hills, valleys, and undulating aspects of geography. In fact, she stated that she thought Valhalla was a little hillier than other courses.

Rogers also testified in her deposition that there was a significant rainfall on the day before she fell. She stated that the rainfall was so heavy that she had to wear different shoes to the second day of the tournament because her other pair was soaked from the rain. Nevertheless, despite having had a prior knee surgery which continued to cause her concern and despite seeing the hillside with its matted grass before traversing it, Rogers chose to proceed.

Rogers asserts that the grass was dry but the ground underneath was wet and slick and that the hazard was therefore not open and obvious. She argues that there was at least a factual issue in this regard. We disagree. Rogers could see the slopes on the hillside, could see the matted grass, and knew or should have known that the ground underneath could have been slick or wet due to the heavy rainfall on the prior day. Had she exercised ordinary prudence, she would have realized the danger from this hazard.

Rogers next contends that even if the hillside was an open and obvious hazard, the appellees were nevertheless not relieved of their duty to exercise ordinary care for her protection because they had reason to expect that she or other spectators would walk on the hillside despite the risk. In support of her argument, she cites *Wallingford v. Kroger Co.,* 761 S.W.2d 621 (Ky. Ct. App. 1988), wherein the court noted the following exception to the general rule governing natural and obvious outdoor hazards:

> There are, however, cases in which the possessor of land can and should anticipate that the dangerous condition will cause physical harm to the invitee notwithstanding its known or obvious danger. In such cases the possessor is not relieved of the duty of reasonable care which he owes to the invitee for his protection. * * *
>
> Such reason to expect harm to the visitor from known or obvious dangers may arise * * * where the possessor has reason to expect that the invitee will proceed to encounter the known or obvious danger because to a reasonable man in his position the advantages of doing so would outweigh the apparent risk.

Id. at 624–25, quoting the Restatement (Second) of Torts § 343(A) cmt. f (1965). In *Wallingford,* a delivery man slipped and fell on a delivery ramp that was slick with ice and snow after he had been denied entry into the store through a less hazardous entrance. We believe the facts of that case are distinguishable from those herein because in that case the delivery man had been allowed only one route into the store to make his delivery. In this case, however, Rogers was not forced to cross the hillside. There were other avenues to move around the golf course besides the one by the seventeenth fairway.

Rogers also argues that the hillside was not a natural outdoor hazard but was an "unnatural" one because the natural terrain had been altered from farmland to a stadium golf course. * * * We believe it is irrelevant as to whether the hillside may be considered a natural or unnatural condition. Even if the condition is man-made, the open and obvious rule would apply. * * * In short, we conclude the trial court properly held that the hillside was an open and obvious condition and that the appellees owed no duty to Rogers and other spectators who chose to proceed across it.

Finally, Rogers contends that the trial court erred in granting summary judgment to the appellees because it was premature due to her being denied complete and full discovery. * * * She asserts that further discovery was necessary to gather proof relative to the course design, the appellees' knowledge of any dangerous conditions, and the appellees' role in the construction, maintenance, and inspection of the course. Because we believe the hillside was an open and obvious condition as a matter of law, we conclude that further discovery was unnecessary.

The judgment of the Jefferson Circuit Court is affirmed.

Notes and Questions

1. The court concludes that the *Wallingford* case is inapplicable because Mrs. Rogers had an alternative route that she could have taken. (But she was turned-back when she attempted to take one such route.) Why is the availability of an alternative relevant? Is the court saying that given the alternative route, it was not foreseeable that Mrs. Rogers would have walked on the particular hillside that she chose? Were the alternative routes any safer than that one?

2. The Restatement (followed in *Wallingford*) holds that landowners can be liable for injuries caused by obvious dangers *if* the injury is foreseeable despite the obviousness. Restatement (Second) of Torts § 343A(1). Professor Dobbs notes that the Restatement position "has commanded almost complete acceptance where it has been expressly considered." Dan B. Dobbs, The Law of Torts § 235, at 604. Is *Rogers* faithful to the Restatement?

3. The court holds that there can be no liability because the condition of the hillside was open and obvious. Could the court have held that correcting the condition of wet grass on a golf course was not within the duty of reasonable care? Why did the court eschew that approach? The court in the following case found it appealing.

Daniels v. Atlanta National League Baseball Club, Inc.
524 S.E.2d 801 (Ga. Ct. App. 1999)

PHIPPS, Judge.

* * *

On July 8, 1994, [plaintiff Geraldine] Daniels attended an Atlanta Braves baseball game at Atlanta-Fulton County Stadium. She was an invitee of the Atlanta Braves. While exiting the stadium at the end of the game, Daniels slipped and fell on either a cup or liquid from the cup as she was walking down the stairs. Daniels contends the Atlanta Braves are liable for her injuries from the fall because they failed to exercise ordinary care in keeping the premises safe * * *.

At deposition, Daniels testified she did not know who dropped the cup on the stairs or how long it was there before she fell. She also testified that, at the time she fell, there were no employees of the Atlanta Braves or of the stadium in the immediate area.

* * *

To prove negligence in a slip and fall premises liability case, the plaintiff must show that (1) the defendant had actual or constructive knowledge of the foreign substance, and (2) the plaintiff lacked knowledge of the substance or for some reason attributable to the defendant was prevented from discovering it. Daniels does not claim the Atlanta

Braves had actual knowledge of the hazard which caused her fall. To establish constructive knowledge, Daniels must show that (1) an employee of the Atlanta Braves was in the immediate area of the hazard and could have easily seen the substance, or (2) the foreign substance remained long enough that ordinary diligence by the Atlanta Braves should have discovered it.

Because no employees of the Atlanta Braves or of the stadium were in the immediate area when Daniels fell, she must use the second method of proving constructive knowledge. Constructive knowledge may be inferred when there is evidence that the owner lacked a reasonable inspection procedure. * * *

Generally, on a motion for summary judgment, the owner must demonstrate its inspection procedures before the plaintiff must show how long the hazard has been present. But it would be unduly burdensome, if not impossible, for the Atlanta Braves to perform an inspection for trash on the stairs while tens of thousands of spectators are exiting the stadium.

While not an insurer of the invitee's safety, the owner/occupier is required to exercise ordinary care to protect the invitee from unreasonable risks of harm of which the owner/occupier has superior knowledge. The owner/occupier owes persons invited to enter the premises a duty of ordinary care to have the premises in a reasonably safe condition and not to expose the invitees to unreasonable risk or to lead them into a dangerous trap.

The cup on the steps was not an unexpected hazard at the end of the game. Just as a fan expects and assumes the risk of wild pitches, foul balls, and unintentionally thrown bats, a fan should reasonably expect and assume that trash will be dropped on the premises by the thousands of other fans exiting the stadium at the end of a game. The risk of a cup sitting on the aisle steps is not an "unreasonable risk of harm" for one exiting a baseball stadium at the end of a game.

Furthermore, requiring the Atlanta Braves to remove every article left by its fans, especially in the circumstances here when thousands of fans are in the aisles and on the steps, would effectively make the Atlanta Braves the insurer of the safety of all fans. And, accomplishment of this task would place too great a burden on the proprietor and the fans. Thousands of fans would be detained in their seats, long after the game was over, waiting for the aisles to be inspected.

Because we have found that inspection procedures under the specific circumstances presented here would be unduly burdensome, if not impossible, the burden now shifts to Daniels to come forward with some evidence of how long the cup and liquid were on the steps before her fall. Daniels admits that she cannot meet this burden. As a result, we affirm the trial court's grant of summary judgment in favor of the Atlanta Braves.

Cutrone v. Monarch Holding Corp.
749 N.Y.S.2d 280 (N.Y. App. Div. 2002)

[Per curiam]

* * *

The plaintiff, a spectator at a tournament roller hockey game, allegedly sustained injuries when he was assaulted by the defendant Christopher Ruggiero. The roller hockey rink was owned and operated by the defendants Monarch Holding Corp. and Rapid Fire Arena (hereinafter collectively Rapid Fire). Ruggiero, a player in the tournament, was sitting in the bleachers after he had been ejected from the game when suddenly and without provocation, he began yelling at the plaintiff. Ruggiero then jumped down from the bleachers, threw a garbage can in the plaintiff's direction, and immediately ran 15 to 20 feet to him. The plaintiff testified that Ruggiero then hit him in the back with a hockey stick, knocked out his tooth by punching him in the mouth, and struck his head and back several times with a metal folding chair. There was no evidence of any other interaction between the plaintiff and Ruggiero prior to the assault, nor was there any evidence of similar prior incidents at the arena. The plaintiff claims that Rapid Fire's failure to provide adequate security personnel and to take adequate steps to control and protect the spectators was negligent and the proximate cause of his injuries.

While landowners in general have a duty to act in a reasonable manner to prevent harm to those on their property, an owner's duty to control the conduct of persons on its premises arises only when it has "the opportunity to control such persons and [is] reasonably aware of the need for such control." Thus, the owner of a public establishment has no duty to protect patrons against unforeseeable and unexpected assaults, nor is it an insurer of its patrons' safety.

The movants demonstrated that the plaintiff was injured "as a result of a spontaneous and unexpected criminal act of a third party for which the defendant may not be held liable," and the plaintiff failed to raise a triable issue of fact in opposition. The circumstances of this case do not present a situation in which Rapid Fire's employees could reasonably have been expected to anticipate or prevent Ruggiero's assault of the plaintiff. Thus, the Supreme Court correctly granted Rapid Fire's motion for summary judgment dismissing the complaint insofar as asserted against them.

Notes and Questions

1. Under what circumstances should an arena owner be required to provide security to guard against assaults by players or fans? Should that duty extend to amateur events? Should the responsibility be placed on the home team, rather than the facility?

2. Suppose that a stadium balcony is perfectly safe for most patrons, but is perilous for the intoxicated fan who decides to lean over the railing to catch a foul ball, resulting in a fall and injuries. Should the law require the stadium to contain additional barriers for the benefit of the inebriated, even if doing so obstructs the vision of other spectators?

3. Intoxicated fans present dangers not only to themselves, but also to other fans and even persons outside of the stadium (to say nothing of the aggravation that they cause for people seeking to enjoy the game). As we are all aware, drunk driving causes thousands of injuries and deaths every year, despite efforts to promote designated drivers and awareness of alcohol's effects. In 2004, according to the National Highway Traffic and Safety Administration, 16,694 people died as a result of alcohol-related crashes. Of those deaths, 14,409 resulted from crashes when one driver had a blood alcohol content of 0.08% or more. *See Alcohol-Related Fatalities in 2004*, TRAFFIC SAFETY FACTS: CRASH STATS (NHTSA) Aug. 2005, at 1.

The liability of a sports facility and servers for injuries resulting from the drunk driving of their patrons is often subject to the limitations in each state's dram shop act. In *Verni v. Stevens*, 903 A.2d 475 (N.J. App. Div. 2006), for example, the court considered the liability of the New York Giants, Giants Stadium, and Aramark, the employer of the beer servers at the stadium, when an intoxicated fan drove home and caused an ac-

cident resulting in serious injuries. The fan consumed perhaps as many as eight six-
teen-ounce beers at the stadium through the start of the third quarter, and additionally
had three beers before the game and some drinks at two bars after leaving the stadium.
When the accident occurred, the fan's blood-alcohol content was 0.266%. One beer
seller appeared to violate stadium policy of not selling more than two beers to an individual at one time (a rule which was ignored by the server when the fan tipped the
server $10). Nevertheless, the only question relevant to the court was whether, in viola-
tion of New Jersey's dram shop act, a seller sold beer to the fan when he was "visibly intoxicated." Aramark's standard prohibited beer sales to persons who were "extremely
intoxicated."

As to the question whether the fan was visibly intoxicated when he bought his alcohol,
the court held that the plaintiffs could not introduce evidence of the history of Giants
Stadium's toleration for drunks and drunken behavior, resulting in a "culture of intoxication." To do so, said the court, would be to introduce character evidence to prove conformity with that character trait. N.J. R. Evid. 404(a); *see also* Fed. R. Evid. 404(a). Accordingly, the court remanded the case for a new trial without the prohibited evidence.

III. Spectators and Products Liability

Sports spectators are not only invitees at sports facilities, they are also consumers of
myriad products at sporting events, including such items as concessions, clothing, and
souvenirs. Where a defect in one of these products causes injury, the obviousness of the
defect may not insulate the seller or manufacturer from liability.

Bourne v. Marty Gilman, Inc.
452 F.3d 632 (7th Cir. 2006)

KANNE, *Circuit Judge.*

When Ball State student Andrew Bourne rushed onto a football field with a crowd
that tore down a goalpost, the post fell on his back and rendered him paraplegic. He
and his parents sued Gilman Gear, manufacturer of the post, in diversity under Indiana
law arguing that the post was defective and unreasonably dangerous because (1) it was
foreseeable that fans will tear down goalposts, (2) the average fan would not understand
the extent of the risk, and (3) there are alternative designs that would reduce that risk.
The district court granted summary judgment for Gilman Gear because the risk was
obvious. We affirm.

I. HISTORY

We have taken the facts of this sad but straightforward case from the parties' summary judgment papers, beginning with Bourne's testimony that, in October 2001 when
he was 21-years old, he attended his first-ever tailgating party outside the game. Near
the end of the fourth quarter, he joined a crowd to storm the field in celebration of an
imminent Ball State victory. Bourne himself did not rip down the post. He jumped and
tried to grab it, missed, and walked away. With his back to the post, he heard a snap,
and the post fell on his back, causing his injuries. Although he knew that the post
would collapse, he expected it to do so gradually.

As both parties agree, Ball State itself encouraged the crowd to pull down goalposts with a flashing sign on the scoreboard that read, "The goalpost looks lonely." Indeed, the school had earlier resolved that controlling the crowd might prove even more dangerous than letting it tear down the goalposts. (Ball State is not a party now because it settled for a paltry $300,000, a limit imposed by state tort reform in the 1970s.)

Neil Gilman, the president of Gilman Gear, testified that his company has known all along that fans sometimes tear down posts; he also described his company's posts. The posts, he explained, are about 40-feet tall and weigh 470 pounds. They are aluminum rather than steel because steel is heavier, harder to install, and tends to rust. And they are the so-called "slingshot" style with one vertical support holding up the structure. This slingshot style was introduced in 1969 so as to minimize the danger posed to players in the end zone by the old H-shaped goalposts with two vertical supports. Notably, Gilman Gear did not design the posts itself; instead, it bought the design in 1985. To facilitate "rolling" of the metal in its newly assumed manufacturing process, Gilman Gear switched to a different, less-brittle type of aluminum alloy than was used by the prior maker. When asked if his company had "considered engineering controls" to address hazards created by pulling down posts, Gilman said no.

To avert summary judgment, the Bournes submitted the affidavit of their expert, Vaughn Adams, a Ph.D. in Safety Engineering, who testified that reasonable manufacturers should foresee that goalposts will be torn down by fans. Adams compiled non-exhaustive numbers of football games in which students tore down posts: 16 in 2000, 10 in 2001, 17 in 2002, 12 in 2003, and 3 by October 2004. Adams also noted Gilman's testimony that he knew about some or all of those tear-downs (though not all were Gilman Gear posts). Additionally, Adams cited two newspaper articles reporting incidents of injury other than Bourne's, though he did not attempt to compile statistics.

In short, Adams's—and the Bournes'—theory is that, when fans try to pull them down, Gilman Gear's aluminum posts will at first bend but then suddenly "snap," abruptly falling on unwary fans whose lay knowledge of metallurgy lulls them into believing that goalposts fall gradually enough to permit a safe retreat. Adams, however, did not testify to any science on which he based his opinion. For example, he offered only speculation to support his premise that social and cultural pressure misleads the average fan into believing that goalposts collapse slowly enough that ripping them down is safe. Moreover, although he hinted that Gilman Gear's change in aluminum alloy in 1985 rendered the posts more dangerous, he cited no evidence comparing the posts before and after the change. Instead, his conclusions apparently rested on availability of alternative designs. The first of these alternative designs is the "double-offset gooseneck," which reinforces the single vertical support with another support right next to it. Second is a "hinged" goalpost, first introduced by the University of Iowa in the 1990s, which permits the athletic facility to lower the posts immediately after a game. (Gilman Gear itself began making and selling these posts after Bourne's injury; at least one other company makes them, too.) Third, there is the "fan-resistant" or "indestructible" goalpost made by Merchants Environmental Industries, Inc. This third kind is made out of steel, less likely to break than aluminum. But just as Adams did not conduct tests on any posts manufactured by Gilman Gear, he did not test any other company's posts or cite to any scientific data. Instead, he presented just a few marketing materials distributed by makers of these alternative designs. While posts like the one that injured Bourne cost $4,700 per pair, the hinged posts cost $6,500 and the "indestructible" posts between $23,000 and $32,000. The cost of the double-gooseneck rigs is not in the record. Adams assumed that a cost-benefit analysis shows the pricier alternatives to be preferable in light of their greater safety and lower rate of replacement. He also opined that Gilman Gear was negligent for failing to test its posts to determine when they would break.

In granting summary judgment for Gilman Gear, the district court held that Indiana law barred recovery for the Bournes because it was obvious to a reasonable person that a collapsing goalpost poses a risk of serious injury. The court reasoned that Andrew Bourne's subjective failure to appreciate the magnitude of the risk that a collapsing post might strike his back and take away the use of his legs did not alter the fact that the risk of injury was obvious as a matter of law and, consequently, that the post was not unreasonably dangerous. In so holding the district court acknowledged that in Indiana the so-called "open and obvious" rule is no longer an absolute bar to a claim under the Products Liability Act against a manufacturer, but the court reasoned that the principle remains relevant and, in this case, was decisive.

II. ANALYSIS

On appeal the Bournes maintain that the "open and obvious" rule cannot bar a claim for defective design under the Indiana Products Liability Act. Relying on *Mesman v. Crane Pro Servs.*, 409 F.3d 846, 849–52 (7th Cir. 2005), they insist that they can win despite the obviousness of the risk if they can nonetheless prove through the application of the classic formulation of negligence that Gilman Gear should have adopted a reasonable alternative design.

The relevant law is codified in the Indiana Products Liability Act. Ind. Code §§ 34-20-1-1 to 34-20-9-1. * * * A plaintiff bringing an action under the Act must establish that (1) he or she was harmed by a product; (2) the product was sold "in a defective condition unreasonably dangerous to any user or consumer"; (3) the plaintiff was a foreseeable user or consumer; (4) the defendant was in the business of selling the product; and (5) the product reached the consumer or user in the condition it was sold.

At the outset, we note that Indiana is a comparative-fault state and contributory negligence is not a complete bar unless the plaintiff bears more than 50% of the blame for his own injury. What is more, misuse is not a bar unless the misuse was "not reasonably expected by the seller." Likewise, the statute protects "any bystander injured by the product who would reasonably be expected to be in the vicinity of the product during its reasonably expected use." Mindful of these rules and Neil Gilman's testimony that this company actually foresaw the fans' vandalism, Gilman Gear does not argue that the claim should be barred on the basis of misuse or Bourne's fault. * * *

The only question presented by the parties is whether the goalpost was "in a defective condition unreasonably dangerous to any user or consumer." Actually, this is two questions because Indiana law requires the plaintiff to show that a product is both "in a defective condition" and that it is "unreasonably dangerous."

The district court started and finished its inquiry with the first prong, whether the post was "unreasonably dangerous." "Unreasonably dangerous" means "any situation in which the use of a product exposes the user or consumer to a risk of physical harm to an extent beyond that contemplated by the ordinary consumer who purchases the product with the ordinary knowledge about the product's characteristics common to the community of consumers." Applying that rule in this case, the district court decided that any reasonable person on the field should have known the general danger posed by a falling goalpost. Consequently, the court concluded, recovery was barred under precedent holding that a user's knowledge of a general risk precludes recovery even if he did not know the extent or specific degree of that risk. * * * Whether or not Andrew knew the post could suddenly "snap" and paralyze him, he should have known that it could fall and seriously injure him, and the district court considered that the end of the matter.

The Bournes' principal objection to this ruling is that the district court explained that their recovery was barred because the danger was "obvious" as a matter of law. They rely on our recent opinion in *Mesman* explaining that, after the Indiana legislature in 1995 expanded its code of products liability to cover all theories of liability including defective design, Indiana law no longer permits a manufacturer to avoid liability in a design defect case simply because a defect is "open and obvious." After all, a product may be designed with a feature that, although obvious, is nonetheless unreasonably prone to cause accidents. For example, a machine may have an exposed moving blade or other part such that the user, though he knows of it, may nonetheless slip and fall and cut off his hand. Since that injury is easily foreseeable and cheaply preventable by attaching a guard, the manufacturer ought not get off the hook. Indeed, that interpretation makes sense; the accident magnet is just as obvious to the designer as the user, and the rule should not work just one way.

* * *

Despite the use of some imprecise language here (the court should have said that the goalpost was not unreasonably dangerous as a matter of law, rather than declaring that the danger posed by the goalpost was obvious as a matter of law), the gist of the district court's ruling is sound. Indeed, the district court, like the *Mesman* court and the Indiana Supreme Court, expressly recognized that the "open and obvious" rule has been abrogated. The district court was correct, furthermore, that obviousness remains a relevant inquiry because, as noted above, the question of what is unreasonably dangerous depends upon the reasonable expectations of consumers and expected uses. In some cases, the obviousness of the risk will obviate the need for any further protective measures, or obviousness may prove that an injured user knew about a risk but nonetheless chose to incur it. Although obviousness typically factors in the equation for the jury (it is evidence but "not conclusive evidence"), there are some cases where the case is so one-sided that there is no possibility of the plaintiff's recovery. And the bottom line is that Indiana law does not permit someone to engage in an inherently dangerous activity and then blame the manufacturer.

Undeterred, the Bournes nevertheless maintain that, because the goalpost can be made safe * * *, a window remains open for them to show defective design because the goalpost exposed Andrew to a greater risk than he should have expected. * * * Even indulging that argument, the Bournes must lose because they cannot show a defect with the evidence that they have adduced.

A defective product is one sold in a condition "(1) not contemplated by reasonable persons among those considered expected users or consumers of the product; and (2) that will be unreasonably dangerous to the expected user or consumer when used in reasonably expectable ways of handling or consumption." Ind. Code § 34-20-4-1. That definition is decidedly unhelpful. But fortunately the statute more clearly explains that a plaintiff alleging a design defect cannot prevail without showing that the manufacturer was negligent. That requires applying the classic formulation of negligence: B < PL. *Mesman*, 409 F.3d at 849 (citing *United States v. Carroll Towing Co.*, 159 F.2d 169, 173 (2d Cir. 1947)). A caveat (hinted at above) is that there is no duty for a manufacturer to redesign a product that cannot be made safe * * *.

* * *

The Bournes' * * * expert's affidavit is their only evidence that the design is defective. But * * * Adams's testimony is comprised of mere conclusions. For the premise that fans are unaware of the risks, he offers only speculation that social pressure and publicity falsely assure them that pulling down posts is safe. (Perhaps seeing the weakness, the Bournes contend simply that people would not rip down posts if they knew the risks.) * * * Moreover, Adams does not provide a basis on which a finder of fact could evaluate the frequency of injuries caused by goalposts, or calculate the extent to which risk would actually be reduced by the alternative designs, or justify the cost of those alternatives relative to the benefits of aluminum posts. Although Gilman Gear points out such flaws, explaining that Adams's affidavit actually proves the infrequency of injury relative to the number of games, the Bournes retort simply that Adams's testimony was not meant to provide those statistics. As if unaware of their burden, they say neither statistics nor testing is required because the competitors actually sell safer (according to Adams) posts (although they are 38% to 700% more expensive). But that will not do: mere existence of a safer product is not sufficient to establish liability. Otherwise, the bare fact of a Volvo would render every KIA defective.

Finally, Adams does not even consider the possibility of unintended increases in risk to intended users, like the students or staff who would have to hurriedly lower the hinged post to police the crowd at the end of a game. But the costs of those incidental effects must be weighed in the balance. After all, Indiana neither requires manufacturers to be insurers nor to guard against all risks by altering the qualities sought by intended users.

III. CONCLUSION

Because the district court's conclusion that Indiana law does not require manufacturers to protect consumers and users from themselves is fundamentally correct, and because any jury's application of the B < PL formula based on this record would be mere speculation, we AFFIRM the judgment of the district court.

Notes and Questions

1. If you were responsible for replacing the fallen Ball State goal posts, would you replace them with the same model? If not, should that fact influence the outcome of this case?

2. The court's opinion indicates that the university itself settled the case against it. Was it negligent? How?

3. Suppose that instead of a fan being injured by a collapsed goal post at the conclusion of the game, this case involved a receiver who was injured by crashing into a goal post after running a "post pattern." What bearing should the obviousness of the risk have in determining whether the school or the manufacturer should be liable? What if the "H-style" post was used? If the base of the post were inadequately padded, who (if anyone) should be liable?

4. Decades ago, football positioned goalposts on the goal line. Predictably, such an arrangement led to several injuries and the NCAA responded in 1927 by moving the posts to the end line (at the back of the end zone). The NFL followed suit in 1974.

5. On July 21, 2006, a high-school football coach tried to move a steel goalpost and was killed when the post grazed a 7200-volt power line. *See* James Hart, *Girard, Kan., Coach Electrocuted*, Kansas City Star, July 22, 2006, at B2. If you represented the coach's executor in a suit against the school or the manufacturer of the goal posts, what would you have to prove?

Chapter 21

Criminal Law and Sporting Events

I. Introduction

Not only can sporting participants' conduct be deemed tortious, but it can also be deemed criminal. Like the situation involving the torts of assault and battery, however, consent may be a viable defense. *See* MODEL PENAL CODE §2.11(2)(b) (1962). Subsection (b) explicitly prescribes that consent to bodily harm or the conduct leading thereto is a defense if they "are reasonably foreseeable hazards of joint participation in a lawful athletic contest. * * *" If consent were not a viable defense to criminal actions, few "contact" sports would be as popular or profitable as they are now. Nevertheless, there must be limits to this consent: "You couldn't kill a person in a hockey game and not expect to be charged." RON FINN WITH DAVID BOYD, ON THE LINES: THE ADVENTURES OF A LINESMAN IN THE NHL 83 (1993). As one court explained, "Surely the authorities are not to turn a blind eye while the law of the jungle prevails." *Regina v. Henderson*, 4 W.W.R. 119, 127 (1976).

Several years ago, two National Hockey League players engaged in a fight on the ice (no surprises here). The players escalated the pugilism by leveling sticks at one another and striking damaging blows. One player, Boston Bruin Ted Green, suffered a fractured skull. Criminal charges were filed in Canada, but neither player was convicted. *Regina v. Green*, 16 D.L.R.3d 137 (Ontario Prov. Ct. 1970); *Regina v. Maki*, 14 D.L.R.3d 164 (1970). The court found that a professional hockey player recognizes the vigorous nature of a hockey game and, in a sense, consents to the possibility that he may be struck in a number of ways. At the same time, the court cautioned that such consent did not give players license to initiate, without provocation, assaults on opponents where serious injury could result. Professors Weistart and Lowell offer a precept:

> An athlete will not be subject to criminal liability for acts that are reasonably foreseeable aspects of the sport and which are not the result of intentional or reckless conduct having no reasonable relation to the sport.

WEISTART & LOWELL § 2.21, at 189. *See also* Chris J. Carlsen, *Violence in Professional Sports*, in LAW OF PROFESSIONAL AND AMATEUR SPORTS §§ 18:7–18:12, 18:20 (Gary A. Uberstine ed., 2002). Stated differently, the Weistart & Lowell formulation provides that criminal liability for actions taken in sporting competition will obtain only when either (1) the acts are not reasonably foreseeable, *or* (2) the acts are intentional or reckless *and* bear no reasonable relation to the sport. Thus, intentional conduct taken as part of the sport will not lead to liability, but criminal liability may result from intentional or reckless acts that are so extreme as to lack a reasonable relation to the sport, and consent to such actions will not be implied by the victim's mere participation.

If reckless play can lead to criminal liability, however, it raises the question whether criminal "recklessness" is any more blameworthy than the "recklessness" that is typically required before tort liability will be imposed. Unfortunately, the criminal cases do not resolve this question, merely using the "reckless" language without explicitly comparing the criminal standard to the tort one. Recalling the *Hackbart* case from Chapter 19, do you think that Hackbart's "reckless" action should have subjected him to the possibility of criminal prosecution?

Unfortunately, the Green-Maki incident has not been the last interaction between sports and criminal law. As you read the following cases, consider how you would draw the line between conduct that is rough enough to justify a penalty or suspension, and conduct that is so overly vigorous as to justify a criminal sentence. Note that your answer likely depends on the sport involved. Some assaults are regularly the subject of in-house discipline by sports leagues. In those instances, even if the conduct violates the rules of the sport, the action is contemplated by the rules and by participants, such that it is no great surprise when "assaults" occur. So although slashing and high-sticking violate the rules of hockey, courts would conclude that players consent to "normal" slashes. The tennis player, however, does not consent to similar slashes. Part of the difficulty in imposing liability—both civil and criminal—for actions taken in sporting events is that each sport has its own gray area of actions that are prohibited but within the expectations of participants.

Bear in mind, however, that the imposition of a suspension will not necessarily cause a court to stay its hand. In the extreme case where a player's conduct is so heinous that the league suspends the player for an extended time, the very severity of the suspension might indicate the appropriateness of the legal system's imposition of further penalties. Opinions differ on the question whether in-house discipline should, as a general matter, be sufficient to make the involvement of the legal system unnecessary. *Compare* Jennifer Marder, *Should the Criminal Courts Adjudicate On-Ice NHL Incidents*, 11 Sports L.J. 17 (2004), *with* Gregory Schiller, *Are Athletes Above the Law?: From a Two-Minute Minor to a Twenty-Year Sentence:* Regina v. Marty McSorley, 10 Sports L.J. 241 (2003).

Think also about practical factors that may influence the decision to prosecute and the shape this doctrine eventually will take. In the article referenced above, Schiller points to the difficulties in finding a pool of impartial jurors, and reports that "[i]n the only criminal trial of a professional athlete in the United States, *State v. Forbes*, the Judge was forced to declare a mistrial when the jury failed to agree, and it was believed that sports allegiances played a part." Schiller, *supra* at 252.

II. Crimes by Players: Assault on the Field or the Ice

Regina v. Cey

48 C.C.C. 3d 480 (Sask. Ct. App. 1989)[a]

Gerwing J.A.:

The Crown appeals the acquittal of the accused by a Provincial Court judge on a charge of assault causing bodily harm contrary to §245.1(1)(*b*) [now §267(1)(*b*)] of the Code.

---

a. Paragraphing has been altered for the convenience of the reader. [-Eds.]

The incident which gave rise to the charge occurred in the course of a hockey game. The hockey game was between two teams in the Wild Goose Hockey League, which is composed of amateur players of the average age of 24 to 28. The league was governed by the rules of the Canadian Amateur Hockey Association. The accused in the course of the game checked an opposing player. The incident was described by the referee, whose evidence was accepted by the trial judge, as follows:

> * * * Perry [the victim] was playing the puck, he had his [face] to the boards, approximately four feet away, three feet away from the boards. [Cey] came in from in front of the crease area, which is two feet past the goal line and held his stick out and checked him approximately, in the neck area. He did not make a jabbing motion, it was just he held his stick out and hit him.

* * *

At the time, the victim was facing the boards attempting to retrieve the puck. His face was pushed into the boards and he suffered injuries to his mouth and nose. He had to be carried from the ice and was found at the hospital to be suffering from a concussion and a whiplash. He was in hospital for approximately three days. The accused received from the referee a five minute penalty for cross-checking.

The complainant, although saying he had never been hit so severely before said, in examination-in-chief:

> Q. If I was to ask you—or tell you that it was a fair chance that in the course of a hockey game you were going to suffer these injuries that you did sustain November 27th, would you continue to play hockey?
>
> A. Yeah.

* * *

[T]he remarks of the trial judge make it clear he was not satisfied the accused had intended (a) to cause injury: "It was not a deliberate attempt to injure"; or (b) to apply any greater force to the victim than was customary in the game: "There was certainly no intention on the part of Cey to do anything else than what has really been the standard of play in hockey for a long time."

As for the consent of the victim, the trial judge appears to have taken the man's expressed willingness to continue to play the game, despite the injury, as having amounted to a consent to the bodily contact which had occurred:

> Would you, having suffered this kind of injuries you did, continue playing hockey? The answer was yes. That's your consent. He's accepted this basic standard of play.

Having made these findings the trial judge concluded by saying:

> Well, the one other area that I wanted to mention was the CAHA rules and the application of those. We have a check that was illegal under the provisions of CAHA rules, but it is acceptable, as a standard of play in what happens in the CAHA, say, if you check this way, this is what can happen to you. It will happen to you. It is a major and a game misconduct. This a long cry, a far cry from saying it bears penal consequences as an infraction of the Criminal Code of Canada. If you make a criminal out of a person who has committed an offence in a hockey game that says he shall get a five minute major and a game misconduct, if you make a criminal out of that person and, of course,

maybe you can if you can find that the offence committed was one which was intended deliberately to harm the other person. To cause him bodily harm, to, in the phrase used by the defence counsel, stop his career in hockey, cut it off. * * *

Assault for the purposes of §245.1(1)(b) was defined by then §244 [now §265], which reads in material part:

> 244. (1) A person commits an assault when
>
> (a) without the consent of another person, he applies force intentionally to that other person, directly or indirectly * * *

Consent to the application of force may be actual or implied * * *. Intentional bodily contact in the context of an organized sporting situation requires that implied consent be considered. Decisions in this jurisdiction * * * have contemplated that assaults in connection with hockey games may be such as to be beyond the scope of consent and hence an offence under the Code.

Many convictions for hockey violence * * * relate to incidents which occurred after play had been halted, but it is clear from other cases such as *Maki* * * * that the courts have considered assaults during the course of the game. Acquittals were entered in these cases but not expressly for that reason.

It is clear that in agreeing to play the game a hockey player consents to some forms of intentional bodily contact and to the risk of injury therefrom. Those forms sanctioned by the rules are the clearest example. Other forms, denounced by the rules but falling within the accepted standards by which the game is played, may also come within the scope of the consent.

> It is equally clear that there are some actions which can take place in the course of a sporting conflict that are so violent it would be perverse to find that anyone taking part in a sporting activity had impliedly consented to subject himself to them. * * *

In John Barnes' *Sports and the Law in Canada*, 2nd ed. (1987), it is stated:

> The primary issue in assault cases involving contact sports participants is whether the conduct falls within the ordinary implied consent of the game, or whether it exceeds this consent by reason of being deliberately and unnecessarily violent, the participant foresees, expects and agrees to the normal blows and collisions incidental to play but does not license the use of unlimited force against himself. * * *
>
> This case law recognizes that participants agree to the risk of blows provided they are unintentional, instinctive or reasonably incidental to the game: [quoting cases]

The cases to which the author refers illustrate the difficulty not only in determining the scope of the implied consent from case to case but in constructing a suitable framework by which that determination can be made.

Between, on the one hand, those forms of intentional bodily contact sanctioned by the rules and thus ordinarily included within the scope of the implied consent and, on the other, those forms which are beyond the rules and so violent as to be obviously excluded from consent, lie a host of others, many of which will present uncertainty. Since this is a matter of degree, the question becomes what, in general, is it that serves to distinguish those which exceed the ambit of the implied consent from those which do not.

Ordinarily consent, being a state of mind, is a wholly subjective matter to be determined accordingly, but when it comes to implied consent in the context of a team sport such as hockey, there cannot be as many different consents as there are players on the ice, and so the scope of the implied consent, having to be uniform, must be determined by reference to objective criteria. This is so with respect at least to those forms of conduct covered by the initial general consent. A fight between two players, where there may be additional, more specific consents, is perhaps another matter, but it is unnecessary to get into that.

As a general matter, conduct which is impliedly consented to can vary, for example, from setting to setting, league to league, age to age, and so on. In other words, one ought to have regard for the conditions under which the game at issue is played in determining the scope of the implied consent.

That case suggested, as well, that implied consent is limited both "qualitatively and quantitatively." By this we take it to mean that in determining whether, in any given case, the conduct complained of exceeds the scope of the prevailing implied consent, it is well to think in terms of (a) the nature of the act at issue and (b) the degree of force employed.

It is well, too, to think in terms of what most deeply underlies the issue, namely the risk of injury and the degrees thereof. Some forms of bodily contact carry with them such a high risk of injury and such a distinct probability of serious harm as to be beyond what, in fact, the players commonly consent to or what, in law, they are capable of consenting to. Such are the violent acts referred to earlier.

* * * Whether the accused *intentionally* applied force to the body of the victim must, of course, be determined in the context of that element of the offence, and if the body contact at issue should be found to have been unintentional, that of course will end the matter. On the other hand, should it be found to have been intentional, the trier of fact must then move on to determine whether the Crown has negatived consent. At that stage and for that purpose the accused's state of mind will form but one aspect of the whole of the circumstances to be looked to.

* * *

[T]he trial judge ought to have * * * determined as a matter of fact whether the action of cross-checking from behind across the back of the neck (assuming he found this to be the conduct intended by the accused), in such close proximity to the boards and with such force as was employed, was so violent and inherently dangerous as to have been excluded from the implied consent.

* * *

[T]he mere fact that a type of assault occurs with some frequency does not necessarily mean that it is not of such a severe nature that consent thereto is precluded. In a sport such as hockey, however, * * * [because] actions to which there is implied consent may in extraordinary circumstances cause harm[, liability should not be imposed whenever bodily injury is "caused."]

Thus, in summary, in my view the Provincial Court judge ought to have directed himself to the question of whether there was express or implied consent to this type of contact and whether the contact was of such a nature that in any event no true consent could be given. Accordingly, the acquittal is set aside and the matter is returned to the Provincial Court for a new trial.

Appeal allowed; new trial ordered.

Wakeling J.A. (dissenting):

* * *

But for the element of consent, the game of hockey involves a continuous series of assaults. Obviously, most of the body contact is consented to merely by the decision to participate in the sport. To determine at what point this consent disappears is not an easy task, but it must be identified in order to determine when a player moves from conduct calling for the imposition of a penalty into conduct which involves a criminal assault calling for a criminal conviction and sentence.

I conclude that a person who plays hockey expects the game to be played according to its rules, but recognizes that penalties are the appropriate sanction for disobedience. A player also expects that, in the heat of action, some contact will take place, which is dangerous and will therefore occasionally cause injury, even severe injury, but no injury is intended. This conduct will likewise call for a penalty, but not criminal charges, for it is such an integral part of the game that a player cannot expect to avoid it and therefore must be taken to have given his consent. There is a further classification of conduct which may or may not be brought about by the pace of the action, which is sometimes motivated by retaliation and, in any event, is intended to do bodily harm. I do not believe this level of conduct should be taken as consented to in any league or age group, and therefore should not be insulated from the assault provisions of the Code. It may even be that this is the point at which a player cannot legally give consent to such standard of violence. That there may be such a point has been suggested in the judgment of my colleague, but I find it unnecessary to determine that issue in this appeal, although I find the proposition essentially sound and attractive. It seems to me to be sufficient, at least for the purposes of this appeal, to conclude that playing hockey does not carry with it either specific or implied consent to violence that is employed with the intent to do injury. Otherwise, hockey leaves the category of sport and becomes a gladiatorial spectacle.

* * *

I wish only to add that it is not appropriate to conclude that everything done in the heat of action is necessarily consented to. I can perceive that in some circumstances violent action, even though taken in the heat of action, might be seen as such a marked departure from acceptable conduct that it must have been the result of a deliberate intent to injure, and that intention is the significant factor. I only mean to indicate that this intent to injure is more clearly identified where action has stopped and, conversely, is less likely to exist where it could be seen as an almost involuntary act motivated by the objective of enhancing the team's legitimate objective of winning the game.

Assuming then that one can conclude there is a general consent to violent physical contact, which takes place in the heat of action, I see no difficulty in concluding that while the trial judge may have provided some rather imprecise statements of the need to consider whether a consent had been given here, he did make some findings of fact which are adequate to support the application of what I perceive to be the appropriate standard. He found, for example, that this cross-check was done in the heat of action and without the intent to injure. That being so, it did not matter that he may have made the error of assuming that the willingness of the injured party to return to hockey was the equivalent of consent. When the trial judge said:

> So, I have to come to a conclusion that there was certainly no intention, on the part of Cey, to do anything else than what has really been the standard of play in hockey for a long time * * *

he must necessarily have decided that the accused did not intend to injure and his conduct was not beyond that which might reasonably be expected to occur in a physically violent sport. In my view, that forms an adequate basis for the conclusion that consent prevents the incident from being a criminal assault.

* * *

Notes and Questions

1. What should have been the effect of the victim's express willingness to endure the risk of the precise injury that he suffered?

2. In *Regina v. Jobidon*, 2 S.C.R. 714 (Can. 1991), the court held that one's consent to a bar fight was invalid, reasoning that there was no social utility in such a "sport" that should lead the courts to give it protection. The court opined, however, that "properly conducted games and sports" are "needed in the public interest" and therefore might be insulated from the rule against giving consent effect. Is the court referring to the public interest in spectator-entertainment, participant-recreation, both, or perhaps something else? What are the consequences of each potential answer? How is a court to assess the relative "social value" of sports? If a fistfight lacks social value, is boxing different? "Ultimate" fighting? Why or why not?

3. Why should sports be treated any differently from other activities with a risk of harm to participants? Should one be able to consent to a game of Russian Roulette? Sadomasochism? *See People v. Jovanovic*, 700 N.Y.S.2d 156 (N.Y. App. Div. 1999), *appeal dismissed* 735 N.E.2d 1284 (N.Y. 2000); Cheryl Hanna, *Sex Is Not a Sport: Consent and Violence in Criminal Law*, 42 B.C. L. Rev. 239 (2001).

4. Should there be a difference in the way courts approach these questions depending on whether the participants are amateurs or professionals? The next case arises from a notorious incident in the National Hockey League.

Regina v. McSorley

2000 BCPC 0116 (Provincial Court of British Columbia, 2000)[b]

[Kitchen, J.:]

This is my decision on the charge against Marty McSorley that he assaulted Donald Brashear with his hockey stick during a hockey game on February 21, 2000. * * * This is not the first time the issue [of the role of violence in hockey] has arisen, and it will not be the last, but it is a time when debate can focus on more than a theoretical problem. * * * If this is a trial of the game of hockey, the judge and jury are the Canadian public.

* * *

Mr. Hicks [counsel for the Crown, *i.e.*, the prosecutor], in his submission, explained why the act of McSorley in striking Brashear resulted in this charge being laid. It was as follows:

> "In our submission, that act is precisely why the law, the criminal law, has a place in the hockey rink. It is why the law refuses to sanction those acts as a matter of public policy. It is particularly significant when that act is carried out

---

b. Paragraph numbers have been deleted. In addition, some text has been re-arranged for clarity. [-Eds.]

in the National Hockey League at the highest level of the game in circumstances that are watched by millions of people for whom the game is important, many of whom play that game at a whole variety of levels. * * * It is way
beyond the scope of this game. * * * Mr. McSorley may have felt that there was
a need to deliver a message to his team that we don't quit, but you don't deliver
that message by putting another player's health and safety at risk, and that is
what happened in this case, we submit, and that is why it is a criminal act."

* * *

A related issue includes the question of whether the criminal law process should be
pre-empted where discipline procedures have been taken by the hockey authorities.
* * * There have been many cases before police discipline tribunals and medical licensing authorities where the public has been suspicious of the [internal-discipline] process,
fearing that those involved are getting special treatment or that the truth is being concealed. In my view, there should be a heavy onus on those purporting to pre-empt the
normal criminal process, particularly where it is a private organization such as a group
of hockey owners. Statutory bodies must act in the public interest; businessmen have
no such obligation.

* * *

The Rules of Hockey

* * *

[The NHL Official Rules] are only part of the picture. There is also an unwritten
code of conduct, agreed to by the players and officials, that is superimposed on the
written rules. This code of conduct deals mainly with situations where the written rules
are breached, and the code then comes into play.

* * *

There is a further complication. The referees and linesmen exercise considerable discretion in assessing penalties. This exercise of discretion is seen by them as setting guidelines
for the players so that the players will know what tolerance there will be for breaches of the
written rules. Presumably the players are then expected to govern themselves accordingly.
This requires the players to have a thorough knowledge of the written rules, a familiarity
with the unwritten code, and an understanding of the guidelines the referee is signaling to
the players during the game through his assessment and non-assessment of penalties.

* * *

The Game * * *

On February 21, 2000, the Vancouver Canucks and the Boston Bruins were both
struggling to make the playoffs. Vancouver jumped to an early lead. At 2:09 of the
first period,[c] following the first Canuck goal, McSorley and Brashear engaged in a
fight. At the midpoint of the same period, McSorley again attempted to fight with
Brashear, taking a penalty for doing so. Shortly afterward, Brashear himself was penalized for interfering with the Boston goalie. The second period was relatively un-

---

c. In hockey, the official time is the time that has *expired* in the period, even though the time
displayed on the scoreboard is the time *remaining* in the period. Thus, 2:09 of the first period means
that two minutes and nine seconds of game time have elapsed. The game clock would display 17:51,
indicating that seventeen minutes, fifty-one seconds remained in the first period. [-Eds.]

eventful, but Boston was more able to contend with the Vancouver scorers after the first period. At the midpoint of the third period, McSorley's teammate [Ken] Belanger was penalized for slashing Brashear. At the end of the period, with three seconds remaining on the clock, McSorley slashed at Brashear's head with his hockey stick, knocking him to the ice.

* * *

Looking at these earlier events in more detail, the first matter of significance to the Crown is the fight between Brashear and McSorley. This started with McSorley cross-checking Brashear from behind to get his attention. Both players promptly dropped their sticks and gloves and took a boxing stance, but the fight consisted mainly of clutching and grappling while blows were exchanged. This involved each player holding the jersey of the other in the area of the shoulders and upper arms, trying to get an arm free to deliver a blow without permitting the other to do the same. Brashear was much more successful at this than McSorley, delivering several heavy lefts to the side and top of McSorley's head, but with surprisingly little effect. * * * The fight ended with Brashear apparently delivering a heavy body blow and wrenching McSorley to the ice surface. McSorley did react to this; it is clear he was in considerable pain at this time. * * *

In any event, he promptly came to his feet after the linesmen intervened and skated off to the penalty box, showing no effects from the encounter. As McSorley, Vancouver Coach Marc Crawford, and Referee Bradley Watson said, the object of this fight was to raise the spirits of the Boston Bruins. The indifference shown by McSorley after experiencing such pain must have been inspiring to his teammates.

Brashear, for his part, skated past the Boston bench "dusting off" his hands, suggesting he had made short work of McSorley. This was obviously intended to upset the Boston players.

* * *

Ten minutes later, midway through the first period, the score was now 4-0 for Vancouver. McSorley approached Brashear from behind and cross-checked him to the ice. As Brashear was coming to his feet, helmet off, McSorley used his glove to swat Brashear about the head several times. Brashear failed to respond to this, and attempted to skate away. The referee gave McSorley three penalties for this—back to back two minute minors for cross-checking and roughing, and a ten minute [misconduct].

While the linesmen were separating McSorley and Brashear, a verbal exchange took place. This was described best by linesman Michael Cvik in his evidence:

> The two players came together and we go in to try to separate them and as we're trying to separate them, Donald is trying to break away because I don't think he wants to become involved at that point. Then we're trying to break them up and we can't because Marty has a hold of Donald's sweater and Marty says to Donald, "Come on, Don, You have to fight me again." And Don says, "No Marty, I'm not going to fight you. We're beating you four-nothing." * * *

During the power play on the McSorley four minute penalty,[d] Brashear was penalized for goalie interference. He had been positioning himself in front of the net to block

---

d. The standard penalty in hockey requires the offending player to be removed from the ice for a period of time (two minutes for "minor" penalties). During that time the penalized player's team plays with one fewer player than the number to which it would otherwise be entitled (usually resulting in a "power play," where the non-penalized team plays with five skaters and a goalkeeper, while

the view of the goalie and to deflect the puck. A Boston player had been pushing Brashear from behind and he suddenly removed himself to follow the puck into the corner. With the resistance removed, Brashear fell back onto the goalie. * * *

According to Referee Watson, from the Brashear penalty in the middle of the first period until the Belanger penalty in the middle of the third period, the game had settled down and play between the two teams had evened out. At 10:55 of the third period, Brashear was making a play to come from the corner to the front of the Boston net. Belanger slashed Brashear to prevent this and was given a penalty. During the stoppage in play, Brashear returned to the Vancouver bench, performing what the witnesses described as a Hulk Hogan pose for the benefit of the Boston bench. Once again this was an obvious attempt to antagonize the opposing players and it was effective. Boston complained to the referee but no action was taken; it was determined that the Boston players had been mocking him at the same time.

[The court recounted the play in the seconds preceding the slash, noting that as the game was ending, Brashear coasted through the neutral zone (centre ice), while McSorley took strides to catch up to him, ultimately reaching him at the Vancouver blue line with three seconds left in the game.]

As McSorley glides toward the point of impact, he is carrying his stick with both hands, left hand at the hilt and right hand about mid-shaft. He is seen to raise the stick briefly, then lower it. He draws his right hand toward the hilt, bringing the stick around on a horizontal plane in a baseball swing. As he brings the stick around, the shaft is turned so that the blade of the stick points up, with the stick impacting against the side of Brashear's head from the heel of the blade up the shaft for several inches. All of this happens very quickly; it is as fast as the swing of a bat or the swat of a fly.

* * * As [Brashear] is struck on the side of the head, his helmet is lifted out of position. Brashear's shoulder shrugs upward, an apparent reflex reaction to the blow of the stick. The shrug is his last purposeful movement. The blow is of significant force and Brashear is obviously stunned. He immediately loses balance and begins to fall back. In addition, his legs slew outward and he "does the splits," unable to support his weight.

McSorley then draws the stick back and slows to a stop, rotating his body so that he continues to directly face Brashear throughout as Brashear falls to the ice. McSorley then moves forward, bends over Brashear briefly, and continues past until he is taken by a linesman. He resists the linesman and is seen to shout across at other players before retreating with the linesman to the area of his own goal, facing an onslaught of Vancouver players.

* * *

As he collapsed to the ice, Brashear's neck muscles tensed, saving his head from full impact with the ice. His helmet was dislodged by the blow or the fall and did not protect him at this point. * * * As the medical evidence explained, he had a grand mal seizure before recovering consciousness. He suffered a grade three concussion and could not continue with physical activity for another month.

---

the "shorthanded" team plays with four skaters and a goalkeeper). Misconduct penalties, however, are different. Misconducts require that the offending player be removed from the ice for ten minutes, but the team suffers no penalty. Accordingly, McSorley's three penalties required that he sit in the penalty box for fourteen minutes, but the Bruins played below their usual on-ice strength for only four minutes. [-Eds.]

The Crown's Theory

Intention

* * * It is the position of the Crown that this body of evidence permits only two possibilities—that McSorley deliberately struck Brashear to the head without Brashear's consent, or that he recklessly struck him to the head, not necessarily aiming for the head directly. Recklessness in this case may be likened to wilful blindness—ignoring a known risk. On this secondary Crown theory the issue is whether McSorley aimed for the shoulder, choosing to ignore the danger of hitting the head.

If the blow to the head was intentional, it is common ground that it was an assault. Brashear himself said in evidence that he did not consent to being struck in that manner. The other witnesses agreed that stick blows to the head were not permitted in either the written rules, or the unwritten code. * * *

Recklessness

The other proposition of the Crown is much more difficult. McSorley's evidence, which I will examine in detail shortly, was to the effect that he intended to slash Brashear on the shoulder to get his attention so that they would fight. Brashear * * * agreed * * * that it was a deliberate blow to the head that he found objectionable. Implicit in this response was the likelihood that he would accept an accidental blow to the head, aimed elsewhere, as a risk of the game.

In addition there was a considerable body of evidence * * * in which witnesses agreed that slashes and cross-checks to various parts of the body, including the shoulders, were recognized as legitimate means of initiating fights. When they saw Brashear and McSorley on the ice together in the dying moments of the game, Crawford and Watson were both even expecting that McSorley might deliver a slash or cross-check to Brashear to start something. If the slash was intended for the shoulder, delivered with the intention of starting a fight, my conclusion would be that it was within the common practices and norms of the game.

* * * I must examine, then, the test to be applied in determining whether in law the risk was too great to be consented to by the players. * * * The question is, was the slash to the shoulder worth the risk, given all of the circumstances, including what had happened previously, and the time of the game?

* * *

Because Brashear was not interested in confrontation, only a very major slash might force him to respond, but this increased the danger of injury. The only benefit to be gained from all of this was that perhaps Boston might walk out of the building with a little more pride. The risk was not worth it. If McSorley was indeed aiming for the shoulder and missed, * * * the consent to accept such a risk must be vitiated or overridden.

This certainly does not conclude the matter. I have only concluded that a slash aimed at the shoulder was too dangerous for the players to consent to it. I have not concluded that McSorley was aware of this risk.

* * *

I therefore come to the final issue—what did Marty McSorley intend to do? I have said that if he intended to strike Brashear in the head, he is guilty of assault.

* * * In the last minute of play, it was clear that Boston would lose. McSorley said he was waiting for the final minute to run out when [coach] Jacques Laperriere ordered

him on to the ice with about twenty seconds left. There was no line change—he was the only player sent out. From his experience, and knowing his role on the team, this was a clear message to him to go out and finish things with Brashear. He said that he was not upset by the earlier fight, or the goalie interference, or the Brashear taunts to the Boston bench. His motivation for going after Brashear was twofold—to follow Laperrière's order, and to give Boston some pride to take into the next game. There was no anger.

* * *

Analysis

I will now consider some of McSorley's evidence in more detail, and begin with the issue of whether his hands were brought together to facilitate the slash. According to the game officials, this is a telling feature in determining a player's intent and whether a penalty should be assessed. * * *

Mr. McSorley's position is that he did not draw his hands together. My conclusion is that he did draw his hands together, and I have previously cited the footage on the videotape showing this. But I do not conclude the hand position has the significance it has to Mr. McSorley and the officials. Perhaps, if the hands were drawn together into the baseball position well prior to the swing, showing an intention to use the stick as a weapon and not for the purpose for which it was designed, the hand position would be significant. Where the hands are drawn together as part of the swing itself as was the case here, that may only be a matter of style, showing nothing of prior intention. Or it may be an attempt to extend the arc of a swing, such as when a batter is reaching for an outside pitch.

* * *

McSorley's view of the videotape is that as the blow is being struck, Brashear's shoulder dips, exposing Brashear's head to the force of the blow. My conclusion is that the shoulder did dip with Brashear's movement but it was a noticeable moment before the blow, and the shoulder appears to be rising at the moment of the blow. Even had it occurred as McSorley sees it, the movement of the shoulder is inconsequential and could not begin to account for the head being struck when aim has been taken for the top of the numbers on the arm, several inches lower.

Part of the evidence in this regard was the [] videotape from an ice level camera that McSorley believes shows the stick skirting the top of Brashear's shoulder before glancing up into the side of his head. This may well be the case. On my view, the line of the top of Brashear's jersey, overlaying his shoulder pads and his well-muscled shoulder, is very nearly in line with the side of his head in any event.

In conclusion, with regard to the shoulder, I must find that the movement of the shoulder was not a factor affecting the aim of McSorley.

* * *

McSorley said in evidence that the slash came when and as it did because he realized that Brashear was about to get away from him. He said, "I wasn't going to get to Donald, so I made a motion to stop Donald, to get him to stop and turn and fight." At another point he said, "The fact is he cut across and I wouldn't have been able to get to Donald. So I'm in a position to try and make Donald turn and fight me." I find this not to be accurate. As I have concluded, because Brashear had been gliding through the neutral zone, McSorley had more speed. Brashear's turn brought him across in front of McSorley, so that they were three feet or less apart. There was no indication that Brashear was going to begin skating. Brashear's turn had been a gradual one and any NHL player, particularly moving at a slightly higher speed as was McSorley, could have turned with him and closed the gap even more. It is simply not realistic to say that Brashear was about to get away.

McSorley recalled that he did not notice that the blow had struck Brashear in the head, nor did he see that he was injured until he moved over top of him. At the moment of impact, McSorley was squared off and facing Brashear directly. Their heads were the same level, about three feet apart. He could have almost reached out with his glove and touched Brashear's helmet. He maintained this view of Brashear by sliding to a stop, braking with his left skate and turning his body so that his orientation was always directly toward Brashear. Everything that had occurred had been right in front of him. There was no way he could have missed the impact of his stick, the dislodging of Brashear's helmet, and the fall to the ice as an obvious consequence of the blow. It cannot be that he was not aware of these things.

[McSorley] had an impulse to strike him in the head. His mindset, always tuned to aggression, permitted that. He slashed for the head. A child, swinging as at a Tee ball, would not miss. A housekeeper swinging a carpetbeater would not miss. An NHL player would never, ever miss. Brashear was struck as intended.

* * *

[T]here is another issue, not addressed by counsel, but one that I must consider. That is whether McSorley's hockey stick was a weapon at the time of the incident. A hockey stick is not designed as a weapon, but is often used as such to slash and cross-check other players. In other cases where persons are charged with simple possession of items not designed as weapons, the Crown must prove an intention to possess the items as weapons. The cases suggest there must be evidence that the possessor reflected on the nature of the item, and made the conscious choice to possess it for use as a weapon and not for its original purpose.

I find that that issue does not arise here. Every time a player uses a stick to apply force to another player, the stick is being used as a weapon and not to direct the puck as it was designed to do. Whether or not McSorley assaulted Brashear, he was using the stick as a weapon when he struck the blow.

Decision

Mr. McSorley, I must find you guilty as charged.

Notes and Questions

1. What potential injury-causing contact would pass the court's "worth the risk" test? Isn't every bit of physical contact, viewed in isolation, likely to appear to be an excessive risk? How can we say how much risk of injury is worth an incrementally better chance of winning a game?

2. People unfamiliar with hockey may be surprised to learn that there is a right way and a wrong way to be "tough" on the ice. Consider *Hockey Night in Canada* analyst, and former NHL coach, Don Cherry, commenting during *Hockey Night*'s "Coach's Corner" segment on Todd Bertuzzi's striking Steve Moore from behind: "You should never, ever do anything like this. * * * If you have a beef with somebody, and you want to do something, [you settle it] face-to-face. Face-to-face and you settle it that way. You do not sucker punch ever from behind." *See also* FINN, *supra*, at 42:

There is no place for violence or 'goon' tactics such as stick-swinging, but there is a place for fighting. * * * A collision in the corner that elevates into a fight is a way of letting off steam. Cheapshots, stick-swinging, or the other 'goon tricks' shouldn't be tolerated * * * but don't expect to remove anything as natural as the odd fight erupting out of the intensity of the struggle to win.

(Emphasis deleted).

3. What do you think was an appropriate response to Brashear's taunting of McSorley and his team? Was it cowardly of Brashear to decline to fight?

4. Do you read the court as saying that even conduct that is within the common practices and norms of the game cannot be consented to if the benefit is not worth the risk? Is such a rule wise? As with the cases on intentional torts, this question raises a point of the proper scope of judicial power: Should courts defer to the rules and cultures of each sport, or should they seek to reform the most dangerous aspects of sports through the imposition of liability?

5. Have we confused the culture or tradition of a sport with our concern for the economic viability of the enterprise? In other words, if the traditional way sports were played were unprofitable, would it yield to new approaches? As former NHL President Clarence Campbell stated, "[W]e are in the entertainment business and that can never be ignored. We must put on a spectacle that will attract people." Richard B. Horrow, Sports Violence: The Interaction Between Private Lawmaking and the Criminal Law 41 (1999).

One example of the adaptation of sports to economic pressures is the National Hockey League's response to a perceived desire on the part of the fans to see more scoring and wide-open skating. The league implemented several rule changes for the 2005–06 season and referees were directed to call many more penalties for infractions that would have gone unpenalized in years past, when the NHL's philosophy more closely resembled former Philadelphia Flyers' coach Fred Shero's quip that "[i]f it's pretty skating people want, let 'em go to the Ice Capades." Dave Schultz & Stan Fischler, The Hammer: Confessions of a Hockey Enforcer 189 (1981).

Likewise, rules and traditions that have remained constant may be in place precisely because of their economic value. We might see the persistence of fighting in hockey, for example, as reflecting a judgment by NHL owners that fans enjoy (and will pay to see) such violence, rather than a judgment about what conduct is "inherent" in a sport. To the extent that this cost-benefit analysis reflects the reasons sports are played as they are, how should it affect judicial decisions? *See generally* John C. Bridges, Making Violence Part of the Game: The Socio-Legal History of Violence in American Sport (1999).

6. What should Coach Laperriere's civil and criminal liability be for sending McSorley on the ice in the closing seconds of the game? Coaches have been known to place enforcers in games for the express or understood purpose of committing acts of violence. *See* Christian Ewell, *'Goons' Nothing New to Court*, Baltimore Sun, March 17, 2005, at 1E (discussing basketball's history of goon violence, which has culminated in Temple coach John Chaney's use of a substitute player to commit a hard foul, which resulted in breaking an opponent's arm).

7. In the United States, criminal law and tort law are traditionally regulated by the states, and the national government lacks the constitutional power to override state laws on those subjects, even if the effect of those laws is ultimately felt on the national economy. *See United States v. Morrison*, 529 U.S. 598, 615–19 (2000); *United States v. Lopez*,

514 U.S. 549, 564–65 (1995). *But see Gonzales v. Raich*, 545 U.S. 1 (2005) (permitting Congress to outlaw possession of marijuana because legalization by individual states would make it more difficult to suppress the interstate market for the drug). Obviously, different rules governing criminal and civil liability for participation in sports could cause huge problems for leagues that play games across the country or the continent (or the world). Would Congress have the power to impose criminal liability for acts of aggression in sports? In 1980 the House of Representatives considered a bill that would have imposed criminal liability for "excessive violence during professional sports events." The Sports Violence Act of 1980, H.R. 7903, 96th Cong. (2d Sess. 1980). Would Congress have the power to *forbid* state criminal prosecution for events in professional sports matches unless, for example, the defendant *intentionally* injured the victim?

8. Do you think that the popularity of sports violence portends defeat for any legislative effort to decrease it? If so, does the difficulty of passing legislation in this field reflect a failure of the political process and call for judicial action, or should it serve as a warning to the courts?

9. Are athletes more prone to violence "away from the job" than non-athletes? *See* Michael J. Cozzillio & Robert L. Hayman, Jr., Sports and Inequality 751–70 (2005); Carrie A. Moser, *Penalties, Fouls, and Errors: Professional Athletes and Violence Against Women*, 11 Sports L.J. 69 (2004); Note, *Out of Bounds: Professional Sports Leagues and Domestic Violence*, 109 Harv. L. Rev. 1048 (1996).

10. A related question is whether the criminal justice system should treat sports celebrities the same as other persons accused of crimes. Some argue that the athletes' role-model status should call for more serious punishment, while others point to the national publicity and career repercussions for athlete-offenders in arguing that shorter sentences for athletes are sufficient. *See generally* Michael M. O'Hear, *Blue-Collar Crimes/White-Collar Criminals: Sentencing Elite Athletes Who Commit Crimes*, 12 Marq. Sports L. Rev. 427 (2001). Does a sentence of "community service" serve an important public purpose even if it appears to be mollycoddling athletes and other celebrities?

11. What actions should leagues take to discipline college and professional athletes who commit off-the-field acts of violence? *See* Cozzillio & Hayman, *supra*, at 771–808; Deborah Reed, *Where's the Flag?: A Call for the NCAA to Promulgate an Eligibility Rule Revoking a Male Student-Athlete's Eligibility to Participate in Intercollegiate Athletics for Committing Violent Acts Against Women*, 21 Women's Rights L. Reporter 41 (1999); Anna L. Jefferson, *The NFL and Domestic Violence: The Commissioner's Power to Punish Domestic Abusers*, 7 Seton Hall J. Sports L. 353 (1997).

12. Should the criminal justice system schedule trials to accommodate athletes' schedules? *Cf. Clinton v. Jones*, 520 U.S. 681 (1997). Should athletes be able to serve sentences for minor crimes during the off-season?

III. Criminal Liability and the Sports Spectator

Just as players may be held accountable by the legal system for their actions in the playing arena if taken too far, spectators may similarly be held accountable for their actions during the events. But just as players have the freedom to engage in some conduct that would be criminal or tortious off the field, so too do spectators have the freedom to act in ways that would be inappropriate if done elsewhere, as the next case illustrates.

There have been very few prosecutions of unruly fans in the United States; one such prosecution produced the opinion reprinted below.

City of Cleveland v. Swiecicki

775 N.E.2d 899 (Ohio Ct. Apps. 2002)

JUDGE TERRENCE O'DONNELL:

Jeffrey Swiecicki appeals from a judgment of the Cleveland Municipal Court finding him guilty of disorderly conduct and resisting arrest in connection with his heckling of Russell Branyan, a Cleveland Indians baseball player, during a game at Jacobs Field. On appeal, Swiecicki claims the city failed to produce sufficient evidence to support his convictions. We agree, and therefore vacate the court's judgment and discharge him.

On September 25, 2001, Swiecicki and several friends attended the Indians game, sat in the left field bleachers at Jacobs Field, and heckled Indians' left fielder Russell Branyan throughout the game. During the seventh inning, Swiecicki yelled: "Russell Branyan, you suck. You have a big ass." This caught the attention of Jose Delgado, a Cleveland policeman who at the time worked as a security officer for the Cleveland Indians. Delgado motioned for Swiecicki to stop, but Swiecicki instead began to argue with Delgado. Delgado then approached Swiecicki's row and asked Swiecicki to come to him. When Swiecicki refused, Delgado went into the row and ordered Swiecicki to get up and go with him. When Swiecicki again refused, Delgado said "Well, we can do this the easy way or the hard way."

At that point, Swiecicki stood up and Delgado grabbed him in the "escort" position, that is, by one arm with both hands on the arm, and took him down the steps of the bleachers section. As they approached the tunnel to leave the bleachers section, Swiecicki began to argue again. Then as he jerked his arm out of Delgado's grip and pushed his arm away, Delgado said, "Now you are under arrest," turned him around, and placed him against the wall. Swiecicki's brother, Scott, then approached them. While Delgado motioned Scott to stop, Swiecicki broke from Delgado's grasp and turned around to face Delgado. As a result, Delgado, while telling Swiecicki to get down and to stop resisting, executed an "arm bar" by grabbing Swiecicki's arm, twisting it and locking it in a bond and finally brought him to the ground. He then handcuffed him and called on his radio for backup support; the officers who arrived to assist Delgado took Swiecicki to a holding room in the basement of Jacobs Field and later escorted him to jail.

Subsequently, Delgado signed two separate complaints charging Swiecicki with aggravated disorderly conduct * * * and resisting arrest * * *. Swiecicki entered pleas of not guilty and the court scheduled the matter for trial.

At the bench trial, Delgado testified that he observed Swiecicki carrying beers back to his seat several times during the game and saw him holding a beer in his hand when he yelled at Branyan. Wilfred Labrie, who worked as an usher, also testified for the city, stating that he heard some "foul and abusive" language.

Swiecicki testified in his own behalf, admitting that he heckled Branyan throughout the game. Five of his friends who attended the game testified that his comments during the game did not annoy them.

The court, after hearing the evidence, found Swiecicki not guilty of aggravated disorderly conduct but guilty of disorderly conduct and resisting arrest. The court sentenced him to a fine of $50 for disorderly conduct and a fine of $251 and one day in jail for resisting arrest.

* * *

Swiecicki maintains the evidence presented by the city does not support his convictions of disorderly conduct and resisting arrest.

* * *

Regarding the charge of disorderly conduct, the Codified Ordinances of the City of Cleveland provide, in pertinent part:

605.03 Disorderly Conduct; Intoxication

* * *

(b) No person, while voluntarily intoxicated shall do either of the following:

(1) In a public place or in the presence of two or more persons, engage in conduct likely to be offensive or to cause inconvenience, annoyance or alarm to persons of ordinary sensibilities, which conduct the offender, if he were not intoxicated, should know is likely to have such effect on others;

* * *

(e) Whoever violates this section is guilty of disorderly conduct, a minor misdemeanor. If the offender persists in disorderly conduct after reasonable warning or request to desist, disorderly conduct is a misdemeanor of the first degree.

At trial, the city assumed the burden to prove that Swiecicki was intoxicated, that he engaged in conduct likely to be offensive or cause inconvenience, annoyance, or alarm to persons of ordinary sensibilities, and that, if not intoxicated, he should know such conduct is likely to have that effect on others.

The only evidence the city produced to establish intoxication consisted of Delgado's testimony that he observed Swiecicki carrying beers several times back to his seat and holding a beer while yelling at Branyan. The city did not present Breathalyzer or blood alcohol evidence to establish intoxication, nor did it offer expert testimony. The evidence that Swiecicki carried or held beers, and even the inference that he had been drinking beer, is insufficient to establish intoxication.

Moreover, the city offered no evidence to establish that Swiecicki engaged in conduct likely to be offensive or to cause inconvenience, annoyance or alarm to persons of ordinary sensibilities. The charge here arose solely from Swiecicki's heckling of Branyan and yelling "Russell Branyan, you suck. You have a big ass."

Passionate baseball fans are emotionally involved in every play and customarily manifest their approval or disappointment with words or gestures. In Jacobs Field, the fans are in fact invited to yell and cheer via scoreboard prompting and even with the famous drum beat of John Adams. Appropriate conduct in this type of setting differs from what may be appropriate in a church, library, or orchestra hall. While persons of ordinary sensibilities might be offended, inconvenienced, annoyed, or alarmed by similar conduct in those other settings, the words uttered by Swiecicki to voice his displeasure at Branyan's lack of speed in a baseball game can hardly be perceived as offensive to ordinary sensibilities rising to the level of criminal disorderly conduct; some in attendance may even have shared his sentiments.

Likewise, the city failed to present evidence to establish that, if Swiecicki were not intoxicated, he should have known that his conduct was likely to offend, or cause inconvenience, annoyance, or alarm to persons of ordinary sensibilities.

Thus, the city's evidence is insufficient as a matter of law to support Swiecicki's conviction of disorderly conduct.

Regarding the charge of resisting arrest, section 615.08 of the Codified Ordinances of the City of Cleveland provides in relevant part:

> No person, recklessly or by force, shall resist or interfere with a lawful arrest of himself or another.

We recognize that in order to uphold a conviction for resisting arrest, it is not necessary for the prosecution to prove guilt of the underlying offense. However, the prosecution must prove that the defendant interfered with a lawful arrest. An arrest is "lawful" if the surrounding circumstances would give a reasonable police officer cause to believe that an offense has been or is being committed.

Swiecicki's heckling in these circumstances did not provide a reasonable police officer basis to believe that it constituted a criminal offense. Moreover, the transcript reveals that when asked on cross-examination what caused him to place Swiecicki under arrest, Delgado stated, "I was just going to escort him out until he jerked away from my hold and pushed my arm away. That's when I said he was under arrest." Thus, Officer Delgado, according to his own testimony, arrested Swiecicki because of his conduct committed while being escorted out of the stadium, not because of his belief that Swiecicki had committed the crime of disorderly conduct.

Applying the sufficiency standard, we therefore conclude the evidence here is insufficient to support a conviction of resisting arrest.

* * *

On the basis of the foregoing, the judgment of the court is vacated and Swiecicki is discharged.

* * *

Notes and Questions

1. After reading of Swiecicki's conduct, were you surprised to read that he had been observed carrying several beers to his seat? How should sports facilities control alcohol consumption by patrons to discourage unacceptable behavior? Should a facility be tortiously liable when alcohol served at a stadium contributes to fan-on-fan assault? *Cf.* Chapter 20, Part II.

2. What are the chances that Swiecicki would have been arrested and prosecuted if he had been heckling a *visiting* player?

3. The court concludes not only that there was insufficient evidence to support Swiecicki's disorderly-conduct conviction, but that the police officer lacked even probable cause to believe Swiecicki committed that offense. Do you agree?

4. What do you suppose would happen if someone upset with this holding stood outside the Cuyahoga County Courthouse and yelled at Judge O'Donnell that he "sucked" and had "a big ass"? *Cf. Bridges v. California*, 314 U.S. 252 (1941) (overturning a contempt conviction for a newspaper that published editorials about a pending sentencing proceeding); *Gentile v. State Bar*, 501 U.S. 1030 (1991) (stating that attorney speech can be punished only if it is substantially likely to prejudice a pending proceeding); *Standing Committee on Discipline v. Yagman*, 55 F.3d 1430 (9th Cir. 1995) (overturning the suspension of an attorney for calling a judge a buffoon); *In re Palmisano*, 70 F.3d 483 (7th Cir. 1995) (disagreeing with *Yagman*).

IV. Searches and Seizures at Sporting Events

In response to the September 11, 2001, terrorist attacks, security has been tightened in many public areas, and sports stadiums are not exceptions. The following case presents a constitutional challenge to the Tampa Bay Buccaneers' attempt to increase security by patting-down each fan as he or she enters the stadium.

The Fourth Amendment provides that the government may not conduct any "unreasonable" searches or seizures, and that any warrants must be supported by probable cause. Private parties are not restricted by the Fourth Amendment; like most other parts of the Constitution, that Amendment reaches only "state action," that is, government conduct. *See, e.g., Burdeau v. McDowell*, 256 U.S. 465 (1921); 1 JOSHUA DRESSLER & ALAN C. MICHAELS, *Understanding Criminal Procedure* § 4.04(D) (4th ed. 2006).

As a general matter, government officials may not conduct a search of an person (including a pat-down search) without individualized suspicion, that is, without suspecting the particular person searched has committed, is about to commit, or is in the process of committing a crime. Probable cause—that level of suspicion required for most searches and for all searches requiring warrants—is not necessary, however, if the suspect is only briefly detained and the search is limited to a pat-down of the outer clothing for discovery of weapons (not contraband). Instead, the government need satisfy only the lesser standard of "reasonable suspicion" for pat-down searches of persons believed to be armed and presently dangerous. *Terry v. Ohio*, 392 U.S. 1 (1968).

If weapons are discovered during the pat-down search, they may be seized. *Id.* Once the officer determines that the suspect is carrying no weapon, however, the officer may not search the suspect's pockets or perform any more intrusive search unless there is probable cause to believe that the suspect is carrying contraband. *See Minnesota v. Dickerson*, 508 U.S. 366 (1993).

Where the government has no individual suspicion, it ordinarily may not search or seize. There are exceptions to this general rule, where the Supreme Court has held that a search or seizure is "reasonable" even without any suspicion that the person searched is involved in a crime. Two common forms of legal, suspicionless searches and seizures are the sobriety checkpoint and the magnetometer search performed on persons entering certain government buildings (including, incidentally, the Supreme Court). *See Michigan Department of State Police v. Sitz*, 496 U.S. 444 (1990). To make such searches reasonable, the detention period must be brief, the intrusiveness must be minimal, and the primary purpose of the search must be the protection of the public—not law enforcement. *See Illinois v. Lidster*, 540 U.S. 419 (2004); *City of Indianapolis v. Edmond*, 531 U.S. 32 (2000). Are the searches in the following case "reasonable"?

Johnston v. Tampa Sports Authority
442 F. Supp. 2d 1257 (M.D. Fla. 2006)

[Whittemore, J.:]

* * *

The Tampa Bay Buccaneers, a NFL franchise, plays its home football games at [Raymond James] Stadium pursuant to the Buccaneers' Stadium Agreement with the

[Tampa Sports Authority ("TSA")]. * * * In August 2005, the NFL declared that all persons attending NFL games be physically searched before entering NFL stadiums. * * *

The TSA is a public entity created by the Florida legislature. Pursuant to that authority, the TSA operates the publicly-owned Stadium. During its September 13, 2005 board meeting, at the request of representatives of the NFL and Buccaneers, the TSA authorized pat-down searches of every person who enters the Stadium to attend Buccaneers games. Recognizing the constitutional implications of mass suspicionless searches, on advice of counsel, the TSA also voted to recommend that the Buccaneers refund ticket prices to any fan who objected to the pat-downs.

At the TSA's expense, private "screeners" were hired to physically pat down each patron as he or she enters the gate. Generally, the pat-down is performed above the patron's waist. If the security personnel observe suspicious bulges, the screener may pat the pockets and instruct the patron to empty them. The screener "conducts a visual inspection of the person by asking the person to extend his arms sideward and upward, parallel to the ground, with palms facing up, and then visually inspect[s] the person's wrists and arms for switches, wires, or push-button devices." The screener then conducts a "physical inspection by touching, patting, or lightly rubbing the person's torso, around his waist, along the belt line" and "touches, pats, or lightly rubs the person's back along the spine from the belt line to the collar line." Anyone found to be carrying contraband is detained while the police are summoned. Anyone who refuses to be patted down is denied entry into the Stadium.

Plaintiff has been a Buccaneers season ticket holder since the 2001–2002 season. To become a season ticket holder, he was required to pay a seat deposit in addition to the annual price of his tickets Plaintiff renewed his season tickets for the 2005–2006 season. At that time, he was not given notice that he would be subjected to a pat-down search before entering the Stadium. After the TSA adopted the pat-down policy, Plaintiff contacted the Buccaneers to complain. He was told that the Buccaneers would not refund his season ticket price. Even if Plaintiff were permitted to return his 2005–2006 tickets for a refund, he would lose the remainder of his seat deposit and would be relegated to the bottom of a long waiting list in the event he desired to purchase season tickets in the future. During the 2005–2006 season, Plaintiff attended several Buccaneers games. Prior to being patted down, he stated that he "do[es] not consent to the search."

* * *

* * * Defendants contend [that the policy does not violate the Constitution] because: (1) the TSA's role in implementing the pat-down policy does not constitute "state action"; (2) the pat-down searches are not unreasonable because the TSA demonstrated a "special need" and because the Plaintiff has no reasonable expectation of privacy at the NFL games; (3) Plaintiff impliedly consented to the pat-down search; and (4) the equities weigh in favor of public safety and against issuance of an injunction.

1. State Action

The Fourth Amendment to the United States Constitution and Article 1, Section 12 of the Florida Constitution guarantee the right to be free from "unreasonable searches and seizures. * * *" * * * A plaintiff must demonstrate that the alleged deprivation of constitutional rights was "caused by the exercise of some right or privilege created by the State or by a rule of conduct imposed by the State or by a person for whom the State is responsible."

Defendants contend the pat-downs were not performed by state actors because the TSA was not "acting in a governmental capacity" and was "not performing a governmental function" when it voted to implement the pat-down searches. According to Defendants, the TSA was acting as a "managing agent" pursuant to the Stadium Agreement it executed with the Buccaneers. Defendants maintain the TSA instituted the pat-downs because the Buccaneers requested that it do so, pointing out that the policy was "reasonably consistent' with rules for similar NFL stadiums" and therefore, the TSA was contractually obligated to implement the policy. Defendants' arguments are unpersuasive.

The TSA is a public agency created by the Florida legislature "for the purpose of planning, developing, and maintaining a comprehensive complex of sports and recreation facilities for the use and enjoyment of the citizens of Tampa and Hillsborough County, as a public purpose." The TSA cannot transform its actions as a public agency into that of a private actor simply because it has a contractual obligation to provide security for the Buccaneers games under the terms of the Stadium Agreement. When the TSA decided to implement the pat-down searches, it acted in its capacity as a public agency entrusted with the responsibility of maintaining the Stadium. Simply put, the TSA cannot contract away its public status. Likewise, it cannot contractually obligate itself to perform its responsibility to maintain the Stadium in an unconstitutional manner.

Similarly, that the pat-downs are conducted by a private security company does not insulate the searches from state action status. Contrary to the TSA's contention, the evidence demonstrates that the screeners who performed the searches were acting as instruments of the TSA for purposes of a state action analysis. The TSA voted to implement the pat-down policy, hired the security company to perform the pat-down searches, dictated the security company's duties, and paid the security company with taxpayer dollars. The alleged constitutional deprivation was caused by the exercise of a policy created and imposed by the TSA and implemented by people for whom the TSA was responsible. There is, therefore, a sufficiently close nexus between the TSA and the challenged conduct such that the conduct may be fairly treated as that of the TSA itself.

2. The Reasonableness of the Pat-Down Searches

"The Fourth Amendment requires government to respect the right of the people to be secure in their persons * * * against unreasonable searches and seizures. This restraint on government conduct generally bars officials from undertaking a search or seizure absent individualized suspicion." * * *

[A] search of an individual must be premised on "specific and articulable facts which, taken together with rational inferences from those facts, reasonably warrant that intrusion." [*Terry v. Ohio*, 392 U.S. at 21.] * * *

The "Special Needs" Exception

Recognizing that there are circumstances in which a compelling governmental interest will outweigh an individual's right to be free from suspicionless searches, the Supreme Court has carved out a narrow exception in instances where suspicionless searches are implemented "to further 'special needs' beyond the normal need for law enforcement." In order to justify the "special needs" exception, however, the risk to public safety must be "substantial and real." *Chandler* [*v. Miller*], 520 U.S. 305, 323 (1997). Accordingly, the "proffered special need * * * must be substantial—important enough to override the individual's acknowledged privacy interest, sufficiently vital to suppress the Fourth Amendment's normal requirement of individualized suspicion." There must also be a "concrete danger demanding departure from the Fourth Amendment's main rule," such that the hazard or threat is "real and not simply hypothetical." A "special need" cannot be demonstrated by the "gravity of the threat" alone or the "severe and intractable nature of the problem." In cases applying the "special needs" exception, some evidentiary justification for the suspicionless searches has been demonstrated.

* * *

Defendants contend the "special needs" exception justifies mass suspicionless pat-downs of NFL patrons because of the need to protect patrons against potential terrorist attacks. One cannot seriously dispute the magnitude of the threat of terrorism to this country or the Government's interest in eradicating it. In this regard, the TSA's "special need" to prevent terrorist attacks is "substantial," as that requirement is defined in *Chandler*. Likewise, any reasonable person appreciates the potential harm that would result from a terrorist attack at the Stadium. However, the gravity of the threat cannot alone justify the intrusiveness of a suspicionless search of Plaintiff's person. To warrant the intrusion on Plaintiff's fundamental right to be free from suspicionless pat-down searches, the specific threat that the TSA seeks to prevent, that of a terrorist attack on the Stadium, must be a "concrete danger," "real," and "not hypothetical." A generalized threat of a terrorist attack will not suffice. Although the record demonstrates a generalized threat of terrorism to large gatherings, the TSA has not met its burden of establishing a "substantial and real" risk of a terrorist attack at an NFL stadium.

During the preliminary injunction hearing, Roland Manteiga, a TSA board member, testified that prior to the TSA vote adopting the NFL's pat-down policy, there was no testimony or evidence of a particularized threat to NFL games or to the Stadium. The minutes of the September 13, 2005 board meeting confirm that although concerns of an attack were discussed, no evidence of a threat to NFL stadiums was presented. Moreover, in the aftermath of September 11, 2001, the TSA rejected pat-downs on two separate occasions, finding them unnecessary. * * * The minutes of the September 13, 2005 board meeting confirm that the TSA adopted the pat-down policy solely because of the NFL's mandate.

During the preliminary injunction hearing, the TSA presented testimony describing what the NFL relied on in mandating pat-downs at all NFL games. The information dealt primarily with threats to the transportation industry rather than sports or stadium events. Robert Hast, the NFL's Director of Event Security, testified that the NFL decided to implement the pat-down policy after the alert to the "transportation industry" was heightened.

While Hast testified that the NFL relied on information from "government agencies, the State Department, the FBI, the Secret Service, the New York Police Department, as well as the joint terrorist task force," he identified only two specific reports of terrorist threats. The first and most troubling report was a CBS news report from July 2002 that persons associated with terrorist groups had downloaded images from the internet of NFL stadiums in Indianapolis and St. Louis. However, according to the report, the FBI investigated that incident and determined that it presented no threat, "not even a perceived or implied threat." The FBI field director was quoted as saying there was no need to alter attendance policies at NFL games.

The second report relied on by the NFL was issued in April 2005 by the U.S. Department of State in its "Country Reports on Terrorism 2004." The Report included a summary of terrorist threats in Spain, which included an incident in March 2004 when a bomb was detonated on a commuter train and the arrest in November 2004 of individuals linked to a radical Islamic organization. The arrest reportedly disrupted "apparent plans" to bomb Spain's High court, Madrid's largest soccer stadium, office buildings and other public landmarks.

* * *

In summary, the evidence establishes that the NFL implemented a pat-down policy as a broad prophylactic measure in response to a general threat that terrorists might attack any venue where a large number of Americans gather. The TSA adopted that policy because it was "mandated" by the NFL and the Buccaneers and because the TSA believed it had a contractual obligation to do so. While the intentions underlying the pat-down policy are commendable, the evidence the TSA presented in support of a "special needs" exception is not sufficient to demonstrate the requisite "real" and "concrete danger" to public safety at the Stadium.

* * *

A finding of "special needs" based on evidence that supports only a general fear of terrorist attacks would essentially condone mass suspicionless searches of every person attending any large event, including, for example, virtually all professional sporting events, high school graduations, indoor and outdoor concerts, and parades. While a generalized threat of terrorism in this country and around the world is well documented, on this record, the TSA has not presented evidence that the threat of a terrorist attack on an NFL stadium is "concrete" or "real."[18]

Plaintiff's Privacy Interest

Putting aside that the TSA failed to demonstrate a "substantial and real" threat to NFL stadiums, the TSA has likewise not established that Plaintiff enjoys only a diminished expectation of privacy when attending an NFL game or that the TSA's interest in protecting patrons against terrorist attacks would be placed in jeopardy by a requirement of individualized suspicion. The Supreme Court has cautioned that only "[i]n limited circumstances, *where the privacy interests implicated by the search are minimal,* and where an important governmental interest furthered by the intrusion *would be placed in jeopardy by a requirement of individualized suspicion,* may a search be reasonable despite the absence of such suspicion." *Chandler* (emphasis added).

* * *

Defendants have presented no persuasive authority establishing that Plaintiff had a minimal expectation of privacy simply because he attends NFL games. To the contrary, the Eleventh Circuit has held that "[t]he text of the Fourth Amendment contains no exception for large gatherings of people." * * * Defendants' assertion that Plaintiff enjoyed a diminished or minimal expectation of privacy because he attended a Buccaneers game is * * * unpersuasive.

* * *

3. Implied Consent

Defendants contend the pat-down search is constitutional because Plaintiff consented to the search by repeatedly attending NFL games knowing in advance that he would either be subjected to a pat-down search or denied entry to the Stadium. In

---

18 As it has been applied, *Chandler*'s "substantial and real" standard does not require that the TSA establish that an attack on an NFL stadium is certain or imminent.

other words, Defendants contend that Plaintiff was not compelled to submit to the pat-down search, but rather consented to the search by choosing to attend the Buccaneers games.

This type of implied consent, where the government conditions receipt of a benefit (attending the Stadium event) on the waiver of a constitutional right (the right to be free from suspicionless searches), [is] invalid as an unconstitutional condition. Plaintiff's property interest in his season tickets and his right to attend the games and assemble with other Buccaneers fans constitute benefits or privileges that cannot be conditioned on relinquishment of his Fourth Amendment rights.

Regardless of the unconstitutional condition imposed on Plaintiff's admission to the Stadium, Plaintiff's conduct does not constitute implied consent because it was not voluntarily given, free from constraint. * * * "In order for consent to a search to be deemed voluntary, it must be the product of an essentially free and unconstrained choice." * * *

* * * Plaintiff was not notified of the pat-down policy prior to purchasing his 2005-06 season tickets. After the TSA adopted the pat-down policy, Plaintiff was informed that the Buccaneers would not refund the cost of his season tickets. Plaintiff was faced with the choice of either subjecting himself to the pat-down searches or losing the value of his tickets, parking pass, seat deposit and the opportunity to attend the Buccaneers games. Moreover, if he was refunded his ticket price and relinquished his tickets, he would have been placed at the bottom of a long waiting list if he desired to purchase season tickets in the future. It is undisputed that at each game he attended, Plaintiff clearly expressed his objection to submitting to the pat-down. Therefore, * * * this Court cannot conclude that Plaintiff's consent to the searches was voluntarily given, free of constraint.

Public policy does not and cannot justify mass suspicionless searches of those who choose to attend an NFL game at the Stadium. Utilizing mass suspicionless pat-downs simply goes too far. Moreover, enforcing the injunction leaves the TSA in the same posture it chose to maintain in the years before the pat-downs were implemented. The TSA will continue to utilize the same effective security measures to protect its patrons as it did before the NFL directed the use of pat-down searches. Those same procedures have been and continue to be used for non-Buccaneer events at the Stadium. While this Court recognizes a compelling public interest in preventing terrorism, the TSA has not justified the intrusion on Plaintiff's fundamental Fourth Amendment rights it seeks to impose.

* * *

* * * Accordingly, [t]he TSA is enjoined from conducting mass, suspicionless pat-down searches of every person attending Buccaneers games at Raymond James Stadium.

Notes and Questions

1. Drug testing of high-school and middle-school athletes is one type of suspicionless search that has been upheld. *See Vernonia School Dist. 47J v. Acton*, 515 U.S. 646, 650 (1995). That holding has been extended to permit suspicionless, random drug testing of students in any extra-curricular program, *Board of Education v. Earls*, 536 U.S. 822 (2002), but not to permit drug testing of all candidates for public office, *Chandler v. Miller*, 520 U.S. 305 (1997), or pregnant women suspected of abusing drugs, *Ferguson v. City of Charleston*, 532 U.S. 67 (2001). If the FBI conducted a program of random drug tests of NFL and MLB players, would such a program be constitutional?

2. How could the Buccaneers comply with *Johnston* and yet continue the pat-downs?

3. If you think the court was wrong to hold the pat-down program unconstitutional, do you feel differently about the screeners' authority to order fans to empty their pockets if the screeners observe "suspicious bulges"?

4. Was the court correct in concluding that Johnston's consent to the search was not "voluntary"? Is this case distinguishable from a municipal ordinance requiring pat-down searches of participants in a political protest? *See Bourgeois v. Peters*, 387 F.3d 1303 (11th Cir. 2004).

Chapter 22

Intellectual Property and Sports

I. Introduction

Professional sports is primarily a business of intangible assets. The producer of a tennis event does not need a manufacturing plant, heavy equipment, or a fleet of trucks to manufacture or distribute the product. The purchaser of a professional sports team receives player contracts, some uniforms and equipment, a stadium or arena lease, the name of the team with its associated marks, logos, mascot, history and traditions, and fan loyalty. As a member of a league, the team owner also receives the right to share in league revenue streams, reflected in contracts with television broadcast companies, sponsors, and manufacturers of licensed products. Similarly, the athlete who spends a career participating in nationally and internationally televised competitions may find that his or her name, public image, and photograph have tremendous marketing value coveted by commercial enterprises throughout the world. Therefore, there is a tremendous importance associated with the legal principles that define the intangible assets associated with sports and that prescribe the rights of event producers and athletes to limit the use by others of such intangible assets.

Historically, the business of professional sports involved the presentation of public exhibitions. In the early days of professional sports, the producers of events and the owners of teams engaged primarily in the enterprise of arranging athletic competitions and selling tickets, food, and beverages to the fans or spectators who were interested in watching the game or event. A sports team's sparse tangible assets were often limited to its uniforms and equipment. As sports developed in the early 20th century, unless the team owned a sports facility, the most important assets of an event producer or sports team were generally intangible assets—the contracts with the athletes and the lease with the stadium or the arena where the team played its games.

As time passed and sports became more established, the public interest in the team (and its league) or in the event (and its circuit of events) yielded the owner another intangible asset—goodwill. The fans' interest in the sport and loyalty to the team meant that future games or events would be well attended. The future revenue stream associated with that fan loyalty increased the value of the team or the event.

More recently, the greatest changes in the landscape of professional sports have been associated with the dramatically increasing importance of television. To a lesser, but still very important extent, the business has been altered by the increasing financial importance of sports sponsorship, the sale of licensed products, and the endorsement of products by professional athletes. The phenomenon of the fans' interest in the superstar as a central focus of team and league marketing has served to increase the significance of sports-related marketing of professional athletes.

From a legal standpoint, the result of these developments has been that the central actors in the sports business—leagues, teams, athletes, players associations, agents, event producers, and others—have a tremendous interest in protecting the intangible assets and property rights associated with their business operations. Television is such an important component of the sports business that an entire course could be devoted to sports broadcasting issues alone. The legal subjects that are associated with this general subject area are large in number and varied in content—copyright, trademark, rights of publicity and privacy, unfair competition, franchises and business opportunities, misappropriation, patents, and communications, to name just a few. A journey through all of those topics is far beyond the scope of this text, but, for the student or attorney seeking a full understanding of the business of sports, a short stroll through a few topics is essential.

This chapter initially focuses on the intangible asset that athletes create and own— the commercial value of their fame. The threshold questions center upon whether and to what degree limits should be placed on the commercial use by others of the name, image, picture, signature, caricature, biographical information, or likeness (which are often collectively referred to as the "identity") of a well-known athlete. The public's interest in athletes leads entrepreneurs to use athletes' identities in advertising and product development. Without legal protection, emanating from both statutes and the common law, athletes might find their identities used by others without permission on a regular basis. What are the parameters of an entrepreneur's use of an athlete's identity? *See, e.g., Palmer v. Schonhorn Enterprises, Inc.; Namath v. Sports Illustrated; Hirsch v. S.C. Johnson & Son, Inc.;* and *ETW Corporation v. Jireh Publishing, Inc.,* below.

The next stop considers the event producer's, team's or league's intangible assets— the commercial value of the public's interest in that event, team, or league. What limits are there on a business's sale of a product or service that capitalizes on consumers' interest in a sport, without permission from the professional league, teams, or events in that sport? *See, e.g., NFL Properties, Inc. v. New Jersey Giants, Inc.; NFL v. Governor of Delaware,* below.

Our stroll ends at the product created through the efforts of both the athletes and the owners of the events, teams, or leagues—the game or event itself and its transmission or recording. Who owns the broadcast? *See, e.g., Baltimore Orioles, Inc. v. Major League Baseball Players Ass'n.* Once the "owner" of the event or broadcast is determined, what rights does that "owner" have? What is the legal basis of the "owner's" rights? To what extent can the owner prohibit others from selling products that include information about the game or event, or the performance of the athletes during the event, or broadcasting or reporting about such game or event to others? *See, e.g., WCVB-TV v. Boston Athletic Ass'n; NBA v. Motorola, Inc.;* and *CBC Dist. and Marketing v. MLB Advanced Media, L.P.,* below.

As referenced above, there are countless additional issues that fall under the general rubric of intellectual property. Subtle and sophisticated patent law problems must be confronted by the manufacturers who produce the innovative race cars, tennis rackets, golf balls, and the myriad other equipment discussed in Chapter 13. Leagues, teams, television companies, the Federal Communications Commission, and Congress must address the issues presented by network, cable television, superstations, and pay-per-view broadcasts of sporting events. The importance of these communications issues can be gleaned from the multiple-year antitrust litigation between the NBA and the Chicago Bulls that is chronicled in Judge Easterbrook's opinions in the *Chicago Professional Sports Limited Partnership v. NBA* case in Chapter 12. This casebook reluctantly leaves those patent and communications law issues for other courses and other texts.

II. Athletes' Rights to Control and Restrict Commercial Use of Their Identities

Professional athletes typically are compensated by payment for their services—salaries and bonus provisions for team sport athletes, and prize money and appearance fees for athletes in individual sports. One other financial consequence of athletes' participation in public, televised sporting events is that fans and the public develop an awareness of, and interest in, many of the top athletes. The athlete's identity generally has commercial value.

There are many different ways that athletes' identities can be used to promote commercial endeavors. Athletes, like similar celebrities, can be identified as users of a particular product, and may recommend or "endorse" use of the product by others. Athletes endorse both "tools of the trade"—equipment associated with their sport (such as tennis players endorsing tennis shoes and rackets, golfers endorsing golf shoes, clubs or balls)—and unrelated products (*e.g.,* fast food restaurants, breakfast cereal, soft drinks, cameras, automobiles). Other products are not endorsed by anyone but include information about one or more athletes, such as books and magazines about sports in general, one particular sport or league, a particular team or an individual player.

In certain situations, the product itself may include pictures of athletes, with or without biographical or statistical information, such as posters, calendars, and trading cards. The players and statistics about their performances can also be incorporated into a wide variety of games, including board games, video games, computer games, and "fantasy" sports games, in which athletes' current performances benefit or cost the fictional teams. In addition, there are products that feature athletes' names, photographs, or likenesses—clothing, figurines, key chains, baseball bats, etc. Replica jerseys with the players' names and/or numbers are a huge industry. Products with an athlete's original signature are often in great demand. Athletes' identities are also associated with broadcast and video products—cartoons, highlight films, sports instructional videos, feature films, and humorous "blooper" films. Other ways in which the public's interest in athletes can be used commercially are limited only by entrepreneurs' imaginations.

Having identified possible commercial uses of athletes' identities, the question that remains is which uses require the athletes' permission. The answer is found in judicial decisions interpreting both the common law and statutory provisions. No one questions the value of athletes' and other celebrities' identities for commercial purposes—the issue is under what circumstances a player's identity constitutes "property," an asset that belongs to, and can only be used pursuant to a license from, that player. When does a product constitute free speech or news coverage about public figures and matters of public interest, as opposed to commercial misappropriation of an asset created through years of personal effort, culminating in recognition as a top professional athlete? What public policy considerations should influence the resolution of these issues?

Palmer v. Schonhorn Enterprises, Inc.

96 N.J. Super. 72; 232 A.2d 458 (1967)

HORN, J.S.C. Plaintiffs, well-known professional golfers and members of Professional Golfers' Association of America, seek an injunction and damages with respect to use of their names by defendant in conjunction with and as part of a game, the component parts of which are gathered in a paperboard box. The cover of the box has a large lithographic drawing of a golfer completing his swing and of a caddy holding a golf bag in the presence of spectators. The cover also bears the caption:

> "PRO-AM GOLF GAME. 18 Championship holes. Profiles and playing charts of 23 famous golfers. Yardage ruler. Ball markers. Tee. Flag. Score cards. Dice. AS CHALLENGING AND EXCITING AS GOLF ITSELF."

As part of the contents of the game, on each of 23 individual sheets of paper, entitled "Profile and Playing Chart," is the name of an internationally known professional golfer or a well-known personage accompanied by a short biography or profile. Each of the profiles contains admittedly accurate facts concerning their respective professional careers. Four of these 23 sheets contain the name and profiles of plaintiffs. It is these with which we are concerned.

Plaintiffs have never given their consent to the use of their names and profiles by defendant. As a matter of fact, each of them has requested that the information and his respective name be removed from said game. Defendant has refused to do so.

It is admitted for the purpose of these motions that the use of plaintiffs' names and biographies enhance the marketability of the game and public acceptance thereof. It is also admitted that plaintiffs derive substantial portion of their respective earnings from professional golf and the marketability of their names as professional golfers for endorsement purposes in commercial ventures. Plaintiffs contend that the use of their respective names reduces their ability to obtain satisfactory commercial affiliation by licensing agreements, and that such use is an invasion of their privacy and an unfair exploitation and commercialization of their names and reputations. In essence, the issue here is whether defendant, on the statement of facts detailed herein, has violated and continues to violate plaintiffs' rights of privacy. * * *

Recognition of the right of privacy is comparatively recent. It was unknown to the common law. *Reed v. Real Detective Publishing Co.*, 63 Ariz. 294, 162 P. 2d 133 (Sup. Ct. 1945). It was first discussed in an essay published in a law journal in 1860 but it never gained prominence until the article written by former U.S. Supreme Court Justice Brandeis, in collaboration with Frank Warren, was published in 4 Harv. L. Rev. 193 (1890). *Melvin v. Reid*, 112 Cal. App. 285, 297 P. 91 (D. Ct. App. 1931).

Defendant recognizes the existence of the right of privacy but insists that it has not violated plaintiffs' rights in this regard. It also asserts that plaintiffs have waived their rights of privacy because of their being well-known athletes who have deliberately invited publicity in furtherance of their careers.

Undoubtedly there are limits to the right of privacy. As observed in *Edison v. Edison Polyform & Mfg. Co.*, [73 N.J. Eq. 136 (Ch. 1907)], a man in public life may not claim the same immunity from publicity as a private citizen may. A public figure has been defined as a person who, by his accomplishments, fame or mode of living, or by adopting a profession or calling which gives the public a legitimate interest in his doings, his affairs and his character, has become a public personage. He is, in other words, a celebrity. Prosser on Torts, (3d ed. 1955), §112, p. 845.

Defendant says that since the information contained in the profiles is readily obtainable public data and available to all, it should not be denied the privilege of reproducing that which is set forth in newspapers, magazine articles and other periodicals. It further says that if there is no violation of the right of privacy to publish this same data and information in such forms of communication, it would seem to be incongruous to hold that it should be restrained from doing same.

Defendant relies on *Sidis v. F-R Pub. Corp.*, 34 F. Supp. 19 (S.D.N.Y. 1938) where it was held that publication of an article concerning the middle-age life of a former infant prodigy was not a violation of plaintiff's right of privacy. The decision was based on the fact that plaintiff's former fame made his life a subject of legitimate public interest and the account was truthful.

It also relies on *Gautier v. Pro-Football, Inc.*, 304 N.Y. 354, 107 N.E. 2d 485 (Ct. App. 1952). Here plaintiff, a well-known animal trainer, performed under contract before a large audience between halves of a professional football game. His contract provided that his act would not be televised without the written consent and approval of American Guild of Variety Artists. No consent was ever given. Recovery was denied on the basis that it was televised in connection with the main event, the football game, and no part of the television showing was connected with the commercial. It was held that

> "[T]he use of name or picture in a newspaper, magazine, or newsreel, in connection with an item of news or one that is newsworthy, is not a use for purposes of trade within the meaning of the [statute] * * *."

Both *Sidis* and *Gautier* were decided under a New York statute making it both a misdemeanor and a tort to make use of a name, portrait or picture of any persons for "advertising purposes or for the purposes of trade without the written consent." N.Y. Sess. Laws 1903, C. 132, §1-2, amended in 1921 as N.Y. Civil Rights Law, McKinney's Consol. Laws, c. 6, §50–51.

This statute has limited the extent of the right of privacy that exists in states which do not have such a statute. Prosser, op. cit. §112, p. 830.

As already adverted to, the law of privacy is of comparatively recent origin. The development as a result of social changes is defined by Professor Prosser as a "complex of four distinct kinds of invasions of four different interests tied together by the common name, but otherwise having almost nothing in common except that each represents an interference with the right of the plaintiff 'to be let alone.'" * * * He defined each of the four as follows: First, intrusion upon plaintiff's physical solitude or seclusion. Second, giving publicity of a highly objectionable kind with respect to private information about plaintiff, even though the information is true and no action would lie for defamation. Third, publicity which places plaintiff in a false light in the public eye. Fourth, appropriation, for defendant's benefit or advantage, of plaintiff's name or likeness.

The fourth one is the only one that touches the issues in this case. There is little doubt that a person is entitled to relief when his name has been used without his consent, either to advertise the defendant's product or to enhance the sale of an article. * * *

In the *Gautier* case the court stated, in addition to what has already been mentioned:

> "While one who is a public figure or is presently newsworthy may be the proper subject of news or informative presentation, the privilege does *not extend to commercialization of his personality through a form of treatment distinct from the dissemination of news or information.*"

In *Miller v. Madison Square Garden Corp.*, 176 Misc. 714, 28 N.Y.S. 2d 811 (S. Ct. 1941), it was held that an official program of a sporting event, published and sold at the place of the event by the promoter thereof, containing many photographs of contestants and prominent personalities of the sporting world, and numerous unrelated advertisements, was in a class different from a daily newspaper, and the publication of the picture and name of a person not connected with the sporting event was held to constitute a violation of the New York privacy statute. * * *

It is true that it has been held that the printing of a biography did not give rise to a cause of action, whether in book form * * * or in newspaper serial form * * *

It would therefore seem, from a review of the authorities, that although the publication of biographical data of a well-known figure does not per se constitute an invasion of privacy, the use of that same data for the purpose of capitalizing upon the name by using it in connection with a commercial project other than the dissemination of news or articles or biographies does.

The names of plaintiffs have become internationally famous, undoubtedly by reason of talent as well as hard work in perfecting it. This is probably true in the cases of most so-called celebrities, who have attained national or international recognition in a particular field of art, science, business or other extraordinary ability. They may not all desire to capitalize upon their names in the commercial field, beyond or apart from that in which they have reached their known excellence. However, because they presently do not should not be justification for others to do so because of the void. They may desire to do it later.

Perhaps the basic and underlying theory is that a person has the right to enjoy the fruits of his own industry free from unjustified interference. * * *

It is unfair that one should be permitted to commercialize or exploit or capitalize upon another's name, reputation or accomplishments merely because the owner's accomplishments have been highly publicized. The argument by defendant that it is not invading plaintiffs' rights of privacy because it does not advertise their names on the lid of the box, and because the purchaser does not know who the "23 famous golfers" are until he purchases and sees the contents, is not tenable. For the reasons already expressed, I find that plaintiffs' rights are violated notwithstanding. This is especially true in view of the admissions made for the purpose of these motions.

Judgment will be entered for plaintiffs and injunction will issue.

Notes and Questions

1. What was the nature of the plaintiffs' claim in the *Palmer* case? Was it a tort claim for invasion of the plaintiffs' right of privacy or was it a claim, grounded in quasi-contract theory, to prevent defendant's unjust enrichment? Or, has the court recognized an ownership interest in an asset—the marketable identity of each golfer—that has been misappropriated by the defendant?

2. Can an athlete sell, assign or license his or her identity on an exclusive basis to a third party, or does the athlete always retain the right to permit other use simply by releasing any claim for invasion of privacy? Can an exclusive licensee assert the athlete's right of privacy or "right of publicity" against an unlicensed third party? *See, e.g., Haelan Laboratories, Inc. v. Topps Chewing Gum, Inc.*, 202 F.2d 866, 867–69 (2d Cir. 1953). Is the issue a question of privacy, property, or publicity? *See Motschenbacher v. R.J. Reynolds Tobacco Co.*, 498 F.2d 821, 824–826 (9th Cir. 1974).

3. Would the recognition of a judicially enforceable "right of publicity" deter the development of worthwhile products that might otherwise promote the fan's interest in that sport? For example, after the *Palmer* decision, how would an entrepreneur secure licenses to use the names and statistical information of the world's top golfers in a game? In the major league team sports, the players generally yield group licensing rights to their players associations, which, in turn, enter into commercial licenses with the manufacturers of products that utilize the identities of a group of players. The players associations also police the unauthorized use of players' identities in group settings. *See, e.g., Uhleander v. Henricksen*, 316 F. Supp. 1277 (D. Minn. 1970).

4. Could Major League Baseball license a manufacturer of clothing to sell a jersey with the official team photograph of the 1969 New York Mets on the front of the jersey and various drawings and statistical facts on the front, back, and sleeves? Would the manufacturer need to secure a license from the photographer and each of the twenty-seven Mets players, their manager, and the coaches who appear in the photograph? *See Shamsky v. Garan, Inc.*, 167 Misc. 2d 149, 632 N.Y.S.2d 930 (Sup. Ct. N.Y. County 1995).

5. When an athlete or celebrity dies, should his or her "right of privacy" die as well? Or, has the athlete created an asset of continuing value that should be devisable to his or her heirs? *See Pirone v. MacMillan*, 894 F.2d 579, 585–586 (2d. Cir. 1990) (New York Civil Rights Law creating statutory protection for right of publicity was limited to living persons—publisher was free to use pictures of Babe Ruth and other dead baseball players in its baseball calendar). *See also Lugosi v. Universal Pictures*, 160 Cal. Rptr. 323, 603 P.2d 425 (1979), *Guglielmi v. Spelling-Goldberg Productions*, 25 Cal.3d 860, 603 P.2d 454, 160 Cal. Rptr. 352 (1979) (concerns fictionalized version of life of Rudolph Valentino). Should the right of publicity last as long as the duration of copyright protection under federal law—throughout the author's life plus fifty years?

5. In *Palmer*, the Court distinguished the dissemination of news or information from other commercial use of an athlete's likeness. Would the result in *Palmer* have been different if a newspaper ran in its pages a "fantasy golf" game in which participants selected a team of golfers, and the participants' success depended on the performances of the golfers that they had selected? Could a newspaper run a full-page color action photo of the star quarterback for the local football team, knowing that local readers would probably remove the page and use it as a poster? Does the answer depend on whether the quarterback is featured in posters that are being sold in local stores? If the newspaper ran a full-page photo of the quarterback as part of its coverage on the day after the team won the Super Bowl, could it later sell commemorative copies of that page of the paper? Consider those questions as you read the *Namath* case following immediately below.

Namath v. Sports Illustrated

363 N.Y.S.2d 276 (N.Y. Sup. Ct. 1975)

HAROLD BAER, JUSTICE: This is a motion to dismiss the complaint which seeks substantial damages under sections 50 and 51 of the Civil Rights Law. Plaintiff demands $ 250,000 in compensatory damages and $ 2,000,000 in punitive damages.

The defendant Time Incorporated publishes Sports Illustrated. In January, 1969, Sports Illustrated published photographs of the plaintiff. These photographs were admittedly newsworthy as plaintiff was the star quarterback of the "Jets" when they defeated the "Colts" in the Super Bowl. The gravamen of the plaintiff's complaint is that the magazine, in its advertising campaign during the latter half of 1972, used photographs in 10 advertisements to promote subscriptions. He demands damages for violation of his right of privacy and the wrongful use of his photograph without his written consent (Civil Rights Law, §§50, 51).

It is apparent from a reading of the complaint that plaintiff seeks damages, not for violation of his right of privacy but because he was deprived of substantial income from a "property" right. He earns substantial income for indorsement of many products. The contention is that this defendant should not be permitted to use his name or photograph without his written consent and without remuneration to him. Plaintiff states that in 1972 his commercial endorsements brought him income "in excess of several hundred thousand dollars." "His grievance is not the invasion of his 'privacy'—privacy is the one thing he did not want, or need, in his occupation." (Concurring opn., Desmond, J. in *Gautier v. Pro-Football*, 304 N. Y. 354, 361.) In that case it was pointed out that "claims based on use of a name or a picture for 'advertising purposes' * * * have received much more liberal treatment than those grounded on use 'for purposes of trade'." (*Gautier v. Pro-Football*, 278 App. Div. 431, 434.)

In connection with advertising, the courts of this State have held that incidental use of a name or likeness is not in contravention of the statute. * * * It is the *Booth* case [*Booth v. Curtis Pub. Co.*, 15 A.D.2d 343, aff'd, 11 N.Y.2d 907], on which defendant mainly relies. In that case, Holiday magazine had published a news article about a resort in the West Indies, accompanied by photographs of prominent guests. The plaintiff, Shirley Booth, the well-known actress, was photographed without objection, her picture appeared in the magazine and was republished six months later as part of an advertisement for Holiday. The Appellate Division held that there is no violation of the statute if the name and photograph are limited to establishing the news content and quality of the media:

> "Consequently, it suffices here that so long as the reproduction was used to illustrate the quality and content of the periodical in which it originally appeared, the statute was not violated, albeit the reproduction appeared in other media for purposes of advertising the periodical."

This was the extreme limit of "incidental use" and predicated upon the theory that the statute was not violated by a true and fair presentation in the news or from "incidental advertising" of the news medium in which she was properly and fairly presented.

There was a strong dissenting opinion by Justice Eager based on the case of *Flores v. Mosler Safe Co.* (7 N.Y.2d 276). However, as pointed out by Justice Breitel (now Chief Judge of the Court of Appeals), the *Flores* case involved the advertising for sale of defendant's products. It was a use for trade purposes and a classic example of collateral use. It was not a use incidental to the dissemination of news. The *Booth* decision emphasizes that the statute should be interpreted realistically, giving effect to the purpose as well as the language of the statute. * * *

This plaintiff raises the point that the defendant's advertisement was not an incidental use but became a collateral use with the passing of time, the make-up of the advertisements, the prominent use of plaintiff's name, the superimposed wording and the accompanying copy. He insists that these raise questions of fact that preclude summary judgment.

Photographs of Joe Namath appeared many times on the cover and in stories published by the defendant from July, 1965 through October, 1972. He admits that these were news-worthy and does not object to them. He does object to the use of his name and likeness in promotional material between September and December, 1972. In the defendant's promotional material, plaintiff's photograph was printed adjacent to a subscription application for Sports Illustrated. In most instances promotional material appeared alongside or below his picture. Magazines, popular with the male reader, included the words, "How to get Close to Joe Namath". In the publications read mostly by female subscribers, the inscription was, "The man you love loves Joe Namath". Plaintiff intimates that it may have been unobjectionable to him if they had substituted the word "football" where his name appeared. There is nothing degrading, derogatory or untruthful about the copy. The plaintiff does not doubt his popularity or newsworthiness or that the statement was fair comment. Admittedly, it was used to stimulate subscriptions but this is permissible. * * * :

> "It stands to reason that a publication can best prove its worth and illustrate its content by submission of complete copies of or extraction from past editions. Nor would it suffice to show stability of quality merely to utilize for that purpose a current issue. Moreover, the widespread usage over the years of reproducing extracts from the covers and internal pages of out-of-issue periodicals of personal matter relating to all sorts of news figures, of public or private statute, is ample recognition that the usage has not violated the sensibilities of the community or the purport of the statute * * *

> "To be sure, Holiday's subsequent republication of Miss Booth's picture was, in motivation, sheer advertising and solicitation. *This alone is not determinative of the question so long as the law accords an exempt status to incidental advertising of the news medium itself.*" (Emphasis supplied.)

[*Booth v. Curtis Pub. Co.*, 15 A.D. at 349]. * * *

It is understandable that plaintiff desires payment for the use of his name and likeness in advertisements for the sale of publications in which he has appeared as newsworthy just as he is paid for collateral indorsement of commercial products. This he cannot accomplish under the existing law of our State and Nation. Athletic prowess is much admired and well paid in this country. It is commendable that freedom of speech and the press under the First Amendment transcends the right to privacy. This is so particularly when a petitioner seeks remuneration for what is basically a property right—not a right to privacy.

The motion to dismiss the complaint is granted.

Notes and Questions

1. Was the decision in *Namath* limited to advertising that was used to "illustrate the quality and content of the periodical" or did it extend to any advertising that was designed to sell subscriptions to Sports Illustrated? Could Sports Illustrated sell a calendar that featured the covers from past issues? Could Namath have stopped the sale of T-shirts featuring a single Sports Illustrated magazine with Namath on the cover or several Sports Illustrated football-related covers, one of which included Namath's picture? Should it make a difference if Sports Illustrated produced and/or distributed the T-shirts, as opposed to merely licensing a T-shirt manufacturer in return for a royalty derived from the sales revenue generated?

2. The court in *Namath* relies on the *Gautier* case to distinguish advertising and trade. What is the difference between use of an athlete's identity for "advertising purposes" and its use "for purposes of trade"? Would a meaningful distinction depend upon whether the athlete's identity is sold, generating revenue directly, or is given away in the hope that the recipient will buy something later? Focusing on the questions in

Note 1, above, should *sales* of calendars or T-shirts constitute trade, while the inclusion in promotional material is advertising? If you accept that analysis, how would you treat T-shirts or calendars given to the first ten thousand fans who attend a professional sport team's "Sports Illustrated Day" or other sports team promotions (*e.g.,* "Bat Day")? What additional information about the promotion, if any, would facilitate your response?

3. The distinction between advertising and trade is often drawn in professional athletes' agreements with their leagues or the producers of events in which they participate. For example, tennis events are permitted by "agreements" specified in their rules to use the names of participating players to advertise the event. Similarly, the events generally may use footage from prior years as a promotional tool. Thus, the producers of Wimbledon can show past Wimbledon champions falling to their knees at the moment of victory in advertisements for their annual tournament, and can permit the licensed television company to use that footage to promote the upcoming broadcast ("Breakfast at Wimbledon on NBC"). However, they cannot authorize a television company to use Wimbledon footage of famous players to promote another product and cannot grant a product manufacturer the right to use footage of Roger Federer, Bjorn Borg, John McEnroe, or other Wimbledon competitors in the commercial. The product manufacturer generally must utilize Wimbledon footage without the identities of famous tennis players or must secure a license from the featured tennis players.

4. Rules of professional sports tours and circuits of events often contain language similar to the following:

> All players who enter any tournament that is part of the circuit agree to the following:

> I grant and assign to the circuit of events and the management of the tournaments and events that I enter or in which I participate, the right in perpetuity to make, use and show from time to time and at their discretion, motion pictures, still pictures, and live, taped or filmed television and other reproductions and other recordings in tangible form of me during said events, and to use my name, likeness, photograph, performance, voice, signature, and biographical data in any and all media, including, without limitation, for the purposes of advertising and promotion in connection with the circuit and the tournaments and events that are held as part of the circuit, without compensation to me, my heirs, devisees, executors, administrators or assigns.

> I agree to cooperate with the media and to participate upon request in reasonable promotional activities of the circuit and the tournaments and events that I enter or in which I participate, provided they are not in conflict with my playing or training schedule. I understand that such activities by me will not be represented as an endorsement by me of any product or company.

Is the player bound by such provisions contained in the circuit's rulebook in the absence of his or her expressed agreement to its terms? Should the general counsel for the circuit advise the circuit leadership to secure annually from every player an acknowledgement that there is consideration for the player's grant and assignment of rights, and that the player has read and understood the rules and agrees to be bound by them?

Hirsch v. S. C. Johnson & Son, Inc.
280 N.W.2d 129 (Wis. 1979)

HEFFERNAN, J.

Elroy Hirsch, the plaintiff, seeks damages for the unauthorized use of his nickname, "Crazylegs," on a shaving gel manufactured by the defendant, S. C. Johnson & Son, Inc. Johnson admitted in its answer that it knew that Hirsch is nicknamed "Crazylegs" and admitted that it marketed a product, a moisturizing shaving gel for women, under the name of "Crazylegs." It acknowledged that it had not received Hirsch's consent for the use of this nickname but also alleged that the name, "Crazylegs," was not exclusively used with reference to the plaintiff; and it denied any misappropriation or damage to the defendant. The case was tried for five days, and the motion to dismiss was brought at the close of the plaintiff's case.

Two legal issues surfaced as being controlling and were the subject matter of the motion to dismiss. The first is whether a cause of action for appropriation of a person's name for commercial use exists as a matter of Wisconsin common law. Johnson asserts that the cause of action for the appropriation of a person's name for trade purposes is part and parcel of the law of privacy and makes the further undisputed contention that the right of privacy has never been accepted in Wisconsin as a matter of common law and on numerous occasions has been rejected. The second issue is whether the plaintiff established a prima facie case of common law trademark or trade name infringement when he failed to allege or prove that his name had ever been used to identify a product or service.

We conclude that the plaintiff's pleadings and proof were sufficient to state a cause of action upon which relief can be granted under both theories. A cause of action for the appropriation of a person's name for trade purposes is different in nature from other privacy torts, and prior decisions of this court are not controlling. The appropriation cause of action protects not merely the right to be let alone but, rather, protects primarily the property rights in the publicity value of aspects of a person's identity.

In respect to the second issue, we base our conclusion upon the rationale that the trial court failed to consider the common law of trade name infringement (as distinguished from trademark infringement) and that, under trade name law, there need be no evidence of the prior marketing of a product or service under the plaintiff's nickname, "Crazylegs." It is sufficient to allege and prove the cause of action to show that "Crazylegs" designated the plaintiff's vocation or occupation as a sports figure and that the use of the name on a shaving gel for women created a likelihood of confusion as to sponsorship. We therefore reverse and remand the cause for a new trial. * * *

It is undisputed that Elroy Hirsch is a sports figure of national prominence. The testimony showed that Hirsch was an outstanding athlete at the Wausau (Wisconsin) High School, and thereafter he entered the University of Wisconsin in 1942. From the outset he proved to be a superstar of the era. In the fourth game of his first season of play at Wisconsin, he acquired the name, "Crazylegs." In that game, Hirsch ran 62 yards for a touchdown, wobbling down the sideline looking as though he might step out of bounds at any moment.

Hirsch's unique running style, which looked something like a whirling eggbeater, drew the attention of a sportswriter for the Chicago Daily News who tagged Hirsch with the nickname, "Crazylegs." It is undisputed that the name stuck, and Hirsch has been known as "Crazylegs" ever since. We take judicial notice of the fact that as recently as June 24, 1979, he was referred to as "Crazylegs" in the Madison newspaper, the "Wisconsin State Journal."

After the United States entered world War II, Hirsch left the University of Wisconsin and was assigned to Marine Corps Officer Training at the University of Michigan. He there participated in football, basketball, baseball, and track, and was the first person to earn four letters in one year at that school. His college and service athletic credits included 1942—All Big Ten, 1942—All American, Wisconsin, 1943—All American, Michigan, 1945—All Service El Toro Marines, and 1946—Most Valuable Player of the College All Star Game. He thereafter starred with the Chicago Rockets and the Los Angeles Rams, both professional teams. He also played professional basketball with the Racine, Wisconsin, Knights in 1948. He played football with the Los Angeles Rams from 1949 until 1957. During this period his professional achievements included 1951—All Pro NFL, 1952—Pro Ball Squad, 1953—All Pro NFL, and in 1970 he was named on the All Time All Pro Team for the first fifty years of football. He received numerous other athletic awards, and as recently as 1977 he received the Hickok Golden Link Award, one of the few recipients in history, on the basis of his outstanding traits of character, as well as for his athletic performance.

During his career as an athlete Hirsch did a number of advertisements, in all of which he was identified as "Crazylegs." After his active playing days, he was a general manager of the Rams football team and assistant to the president of the Rams organization. In 1969 he became athletic director of the University of Wisconsin.

In addition to there being evidence of numerous commercials which used the name, "Crazylegs," there was evidence introduced to show that a movie was made in the 1950s of his life called, "Crazylegs All American." This movie is still being shown on television. Hirsch stated that he had been protective of his name and what type product it was connected with. He stated that he refused to do cigarette advertising and that he declined to do any advertising for liquor and that he had a beer commercial withdrawn after he became the athletic director at the University of Wisconsin. In each case his nickname, "Crazylegs," was used to identify him.

There was evidence to show that the usual minimum compensation for the use of an athlete's name on an unrelated product was five percent of gross sales. Two expert witnesses testified, and it is undisputed that these witnesses were experts in the business of representing celebrities in the endorsement of products or in licensing the use of athletes' names for advertising purposes.

On the motion to dismiss, the defendants argued, and the court concluded, that a cause of action does not exist in Wisconsin for the unauthorized use of a person's name for the purposes of trade, even assuming, for the purpose of the motion, the factual finding that Johnson was using Hirsch's name without consent. The court also concluded, consistent with the defendants' argument, that an essential element of the cause of action for a common law trademark infringement was the prior use of the name, "Crazylegs," to identify goods or services and that Hirsch had not produced such proof.

We consider these causes of action separately.

The defendants conceded that "Crazylegs" is the plaintiff's nickname and that Johnson marketed a product under that name. It is clear from the record that the plaintiff presented sufficient credible evidence upon which a jury could find, as a matter of fact, that the name, "Crazylegs," identified Hirsch and that the use of that name had a commercial value to Johnson. The question dispositive of this appeal, although not of the case on retrial, is whether as a matter of law a cause of action exists for the unauthorized commercial use of the name, "Crazylegs." Subsequent to the operative facts in this case, the Wisconsin legislature in 1977 enacted sec. 895.50, Stats., under the general caption of the "Right of privacy." One of the definitions of "invasion of privacy" is included in the provisions of sec. 895.50(2) (b):

> "The use, for advertising purposes or for purposes of trade, of the name, portrait or picture of any living person, without having first obtained the written consent of the person. * * * *"

Under the law enacted by the legislature in 1977, Hirsch would now have a cause of action. This statute, however, was enacted after Johnson's "Crazylegs" product was taken off the market, and the question here presented is whether plaintiff had a cause of action under the common law. We conclude that he did.

The defendants' basic argument is that the right of privacy was never recognized by this court as a part of the common law. The defendants fortify this argument by pointing out that the statute enacted in 1977 denominates the unconsented use of a person's name for advertising purposes as an "invasion of *privacy*." (Emphasis supplied.) We conclude that the right of a person to be compensated for the use of his name for advertising purposes or purposes of trade is distinct from other privacy torts which protect primarily the mental interest in being let alone. The appropriation tort is different because it protects primarily the property interest in the publicity value of one's name. Because the previous decisions of this court declining to recognize a right of privacy have not dealt with the appropriation tort, they are not controlling. From almost the very outset of the recognition of the right of privacy, there has been an intermingling or confusion of the right of privacy and the right of control of the commercial aspects of one's identity.

* * *

The intermingling of the idea of the right of privacy and the right to control commercial exploitation of aspects of one's identity can be traced to one of the first cases to deal with the existence of a right of privacy. *Roberson v. Rochester Folding Box Co.*, 171 N.Y. 538, 64 N.E. 442 (1902). In *Roberson*, the New York Court of Appeals held that no right existed to protect a young woman from the unauthorized use of her portrait, captioned, "Flour of the Family," to promote the sale of flour. The decision provoked a storm of public disapproval, and the following year the New York legislature enacted a statute making it both a misdemeanor and a tort to use a name or a picture without consent for the purposes of trade. * * * During the next fifty years, the right of privacy was recognized by decision in most states and by statute in several others, so that by 1961, only three states, including Wisconsin, had not recognized the right. * * *

The defendants argue that this court's rejection of the right of privacy in other factual contexts constitutes a rejection of a cause of action for appropriation of the plaintiff's name for Johnson's commercial advantage. But Dean Prosser in his article has explained that the right of privacy as it has evolved is "not one tort but four," which are "distinct and only loosely related." Privacy, supra at 389, 422. He also states:

> "What has emerged from the decisions is no simple matter. It is not one tort, but a complex of four. The law of privacy comprises four distinct kinds of invasion of four different interests of the plaintiff, which are tied together by the common name, but otherwise have almost nothing in common. * * * *"

The four torts Prosser lists are:

> "1. Intrusion upon the plaintiff's seclusion or solitude, or into his private affairs.

"2. Public disclosure of embarrassing private facts about the plaintiff.

"3. Publicity which places the plaintiff in a false light in the public eye.

"4. Appropriation, for the defendant's advantage, of the plaintiff's name or likeness." (at 839)

The fourth tort—the tort of appropriation alleged by Hirsch in the present case—Prosser points out is "quite a different matter" * * * from the other three, because the interest is not so much a mental one as a proprietary one in the exclusive use of one's name and likeness. * * *

* * *

Because the right of publicity—the right to control the commercial exploitation of aspects of a person's identity—differs from other privacy rights, it is appropriate for this court to recognize a cause of action to protect this right, although other privacy rights were rejected in prior decisions of this court. Protection of the publicity value of one's name is supported by public-policy considerations, such the interest in controlling the effect on one's reputation of commercial uses of one's personality and the prevention of unjust enrichment of those who appropriate the publicity value of another's identity. * * * Moreover, where, as here, the record attempts to demonstrate that Hirsch over a period of years assiduously cultivated a reputation not only for skill as an athlete, but as an exemplary person whose identity was associated with sportsmanship and high qualities of character, and where the record demonstrates that much time and effort was devoted to that purpose, the rationale of *Mercury Record Productions, Inc. v. Economic Consultants, Inc.*, 64 Wis.2d 163, 218 N.W.2d 705 (1974), is appropriate. It is a form of commercial immorality to "reap where another has sown." * * *

The record is replete with evidence from which a jury could conclude that Elroy Hirsch's name indeed had commercial value. There was testimony that he had been paid for the use of the name in the past, and there was expert testimony by qualified persons who stated the reasonable compensation for the authorized use of his name or identity. That the tort is compensable is clear. * * *

The fact that the name, "Crazylegs," used by Johnson, was a nickname rather than Hirsch's actual name does not preclude a cause of action. All that is required is that the name clearly identify the wronged person. In the instant case, it is not disputed at this juncture of the case that the nickname identified the plaintiff Hirsch. It is argued that there were others who were known by the same name. This, however, does not vitiate the existence of a cause of action. It may, however, if sufficient proof were adduced, affect the quantum of damages should the jury impose liability or it might preclude liability altogether. Prosser points out "that a stage or other fictitious name can be so identified with the plaintiff that he is entitled to protection against its use." * * * He writes that it would be absurd to say that Samuel L. Clemens would have a cause of action if that name had been used in advertising, but he would not have one for the use of "Mark Twain." If a fictitious name is used in a context which tends to indicate that the name is that of the plaintiff, the factual case for identity is strengthened. * * *

The record shows that Johnson's first promotion of the product, "Crazylegs," was the sponsoring of a running event for women and the use of a television commercial similar to the "Crazylegs" cheer initiated at University of Wisconsin football games when Elroy Hirsch became athletic director. These facts may augment and further identify the sports context in which the name, "Crazylegs," has been particularly prominent. The question whether "Crazylegs" identifies Elroy Hirsch, however, is one of fact to be determined by the jury on remand, and full inquiry into that fact is not foreclosed by the defendants' concessions in the present procedural posture of the case.

Accordingly, we hold that a cause of action for appropriation of a person's name for trade purposes exists at common law in Wisconsin. The facts adduced in the plaintiff's case prima facie were sufficient for submission to the jury. The trial court erred when it concluded as a matter of law that Wisconsin cases which held that the right of privacy did not exist at common law in Wisconsin foreclosed the plaintiff from asserting a cause of action for the commercial misappropriation of his name and identity.

Additionally, Hirsch argued that the facts adduced established a prima facie case of common law trade name infringement. The trial court also ruled on this question as a matter of law. It concluded that the case did not involve trademarks or trade names because there was no evidence showing Elroy Hirsch's name or the name, "Crazylegs," had ever been connected with a service or a product. The position of the trial court and the position urged by the defendant on this appeal is that no cause of action for trade name infringement will lie unless it is alleged and proved that the alleged trade name, "Crazylegs," was used by the plaintiff to identify goods or services and distinguish them from others. We conclude that this is an erroneous view of the law.

The misuse of a trade name is a portion of the law of unfair competition. We stated in *J. I. Case Plow Works v. J. I. Case Threshing Machine Co.*, 162 Wis. 185, 155 N.W. 128 (1916), that the law of unfair competition is based on the maxim that, "One man may not reap where another has sown nor gather where another has strewn." * * * Common law trademark and trade name infringement is a branch of the law of unfair competition, and the principles used in each are substantially similar. *First Wisconsin National Bank of Milwaukee v. Wichman*, 85 Wis.2d 54, 60, 270 N.W.2d 168 (1978). "Passing off," or misrepresenting one's goods or services as those of another, and direct competition are no longer considered to be essential elements of a cause of action for unfair competition. * * * The modern approach to the law of unfair competition holds that:

> "[p]roperty rights of commercial value are to be and will be protected from any form of unfair invasion or infringement or from any form of commercial immorality. * * *" *Metropolitan Opera Ass'n, Inc. v. Wagner-Nichols Recorder Corp.*, 101 N.Y.S.2d 483, 492 (S. Ct. 1950); see, also, *Hogan v. A. S. Barnes & Co., Inc.*, 114 U.S.P.Q. 314, 316–19 (Pa. C.P., Philadelphia County, 1957).

As the discussion herein has demonstrated, the publicity value of a celebrity's name is built up by the investment of work, time, and money by the celebrity. The economic damage caused by unauthorized commercial use of a name may take many forms, including damage to reputation if the advertised product or service is shoddy and the dilution of the value of the name in authorized advertising. * * *

The court reached its conclusion that Hirsch proved no cause of action for common law trademark infringement because he proved only that the name, "Crazylegs," was used to identify himself and not to identify goods or services. In that conclusion the court was correct in stating that there was no proof that the name was used to identify goods or services.

The definition of "trademark" which was adopted by this court in *First Wisconsin, supra*, requires use in connection with goods and services. Such use, however, is not required where a name meets the definition of a trade name. The trial court failed to consider whether Hirsch's use of the name, "Crazylegs," met the definition of a trade name. Restatement 2d, Torts, sec. 716 (Tent. Draft No. 8, 1963), adopted as the common law of Wisconsin in *First Wisconsin, supra*, defined a trade name:

"A trade name is a designation which is used by a person to identify his business, vocation, or occupation, provided such use is not prohibited by legislative enactment or by an otherwise defined public policy."

Sec. 717 of the Restatement provided that one infringes a trademark or trade name if:

" * * * without a privilege to do so, he uses on or in connection with his goods, services or business a designation which so resembles the other's previously used mark or trade name as to be likely to

"(a) cause confusion, mistake or deception, or

"(b) cause prospective purchasers to believe that

"(i) the actor's goods or services are those of the other, or

"(ii) the actor's goods or services emanate from the same source as the other's goods or services, or

"(iii) the actor's goods or services are approved or sponsored by the other, or

"(iv) the actor's business is the business of, or is in some manner associated or connected with, the other, even though the actor does not use the designation with a purpose to deceive."

There was ample evidence for a jury to believe that "Crazylegs" designated Hirsch's vocation or occupation as a sports figure, first as a player and later in management and administration. There was also ample evidence to show the likelihood of confusion as to sponsorship of the product as the result of Johnson's use of the name, "Crazylegs."

Hirsch testified that there was actual confusion and that people told him that they assumed that he was sponsoring the product, and in fact he received orders for the product. For Hirsch to show that there was an infringement on the trade name, "Crazylegs," there was no necessity as a matter of law that the name had previously been identified with products and services. It was sufficient to show that the name was one used to identify Hirsch in this business or occupation and that the use of the name caused confusion or mistake in respect to the approval or sponsorship of the goods. The court erred in dismissing the cause of action for trade name infringement. * * *

We conclude that Elroy Hirsch made out a prima facie case under two separate theories: The appropriation of his name for purposes of trade, and infringement of a trade name under the common law. Nevertheless, substantial problems of proof stand in the way of the plaintiff's eventual success in this lawsuit. As a result of the motion of the defendants in the nature of a demurrer to the evidence, crucial facts which must be proved are conceded but only for the purpose of this appeal. Upon retrial under the appropriation theory, Hirsch must prove that the name, "Crazylegs," identifies him and that he has suffered damages based either on his loss or Johnson's unjust enrichment. Under the common law trade name-infringement theory, he must prove that "Crazylegs" designates his vocation or occupation and that there is a likelihood of confusion tending to make the public believe that he sponsored the Johnson product. These are questions which must be determined by the jury. Because the plaintiff's complaint was dismissed prior to a jury determination of the factual issues, the cause must be remanded for a new trial.

Judgment reversed and cause remanded for a new trial consistent with directions herein.

Notes and Questions

1. The *Hirsch* case held that the "right of publicity" extends beyond an athlete's photograph and name to nicknames, stage names, and other fictitious names. Is the determinative test whether consumers believe that the athlete has endorsed, or is associated with, the product? Or, is the test whether the business utilizing the name *intended* to capitalize on a positive association with the athlete? If the proper test is the former (consumers' belief), should a business that intended the latter (to reap what the athlete has sown) be estopped from defending on the basis that its effort to infringe an athlete's right of publicity was unsuccessful? On the other hand, if an effort to misappropriate a right of publicity is unsuccessful, either because the athlete is not as well known as had been thought or because the connection between the athlete and the product was not made sufficiently clear for consumers to perceive it, has the athlete suffered any injury that merits judicial intervention? If the alleged infringer's intent is not determinative, is it relevant? Why or why not? Can we reasonably infer the likely effect from the intent of the alleged infringer? *Compare Chicago Board of Trade v. United States*, 246 U.S. 231 (1918) (under antitrust laws, knowledge of anticompetitive intent may help a court assess the likelihood of anticompetitive effects).

2. Beyond photographs, names, nicknames and other fictitious names, what other types of identification can infringe upon an athlete's right of publicity? *See, e.g., Allen v. National Video, Inc.*, 610 F. Supp. 612, 622 (S.D.N.Y. 1985) ("any recognizable likeness"). Can a portrait of a nude black man on a stool in the corner of a boxing ring that is captioned "Mystery Man" infringe on World Heavyweight Boxing Champion Muhammad Ali's right of publicity if the portrait's facial characteristics resemble Ali's and a verse that accompanies the portrait refers to the man in the portrait as "the Greatest" (a common appellation for Ali)? *See Ali v. Playgirl, Inc.*, 447 F. Supp. 723, 725–27 (S.D.N.Y. 1978).

3. Can use of a well-known race car driver's distinctively decorated automobile in a cigarette commercial infringe upon the driver's right of publicity? *See Motschenbacher v. R.J. Reynolds Tobacco Co.*, 498 F.2d 821 (9th Cir. 1974).

ETW Corporation v. Jireh Publishing, Inc

332 F.3d 915 (6th Cir. 2003)

GRAHAM, District Judge. Plaintiff-Appellant ETW Corporation ("ETW") is the licensing agent of Eldrick "Tiger" Woods ("Woods"), one of the world's most famous professional golfers. Woods, chairman of the board of ETW, has assigned to it the exclusive right to exploit his name, image, likeness, and signature, and all other publicity rights. ETW owns a United States trademark registration for the mark "TIGER WOODS" (Registration No. 2,194,381) for use in connection with "art prints, calendars, mounted photographs, notebooks, pencils, pens, posters, trading cards, and unmounted photographs."

Defendant-Appellee Jireh Publishing, Inc. ("Jireh") of Tuscaloosa, Alabama, is the publisher of artwork created by Rick Rush ("Rush"). Rush, who refers to himself as "America's sports artist," has created paintings of famous figures in sports and famous sports events. * * *

In 1998, Rush created a painting entitled *The Masters of Augusta*, which commemorates Woods's victory at the Masters Tournament in Augusta, Georgia, in 1997. At that event, Woods became the youngest player ever to win the Masters Tournament, while setting a 72-hole record for the tournament and a record 12-stroke margin of victory. In the foreground of Rush's painting are three views of Woods in different poses. In the center, he is completing the swing of a golf club, and on each side he is crouching, lining up and/or observing the progress of a putt. To the left of Woods is his caddy, Mike "Fluff" Cowan, and to his right is his final round partner's caddy. Behind these figures is the Augusta National Clubhouse. In a blue background behind the clubhouse are likenesses of famous golfers of the past looking down on Woods. These include Arnold Palmer, Sam Snead, Ben Hogan, Walter Hagen, Bobby Jones, and Jack Nicklaus. Behind them is the Masters leader board.

The limited edition prints distributed by Jireh consist of an image of Rush's painting which includes Rush's signature at the bottom right hand corner. Beneath the image of the painting, in block letters, is its title, "The Masters Of Augusta." Beneath the title, in block letters of equal height, is the artist's name, "Rick Rush," and beneath the artist's name, in smaller upper and lower case letters, is the legend "Painting America Through Sports."

As sold by Jireh, the limited edition prints are enclosed in a white envelope, accompanied with literature which includes a large photograph of Rush, a description of his art, and a narrative description of the subject painting. * * * On the back of the envelope, under the flap, are the words "Masters of Augusta" in letters that are three-eighths of an inch high, and "Tiger Woods" in letters that are one-fourth of an inch high. Woods's name also appears in the narrative description of the painting where he is mentioned twice in twenty-eight lines of text. The text also includes references to the six other famous golfers depicted in the background of the painting as well as the two caddies. Jireh published and marketed two hundred and fifty 22½" × 30" serigraphs and five thousand 9" × 11" lithographs of *The Masters of Augusta* at an issuing price of $700 for the serigraphs and $100 for the lithographs.

ETW filed suit against Jireh on June 26, 1998, in the United States District Court for the Northern District of Ohio, alleging trademark infringement in violation of the Lanham Act ; dilution of the mark under the Lanham Act, ; unfair competition and false advertising under the Lanham Act; unfair competition and deceptive trade practices under [an Ohio statute]; unfair competition and trademark infringement under Ohio common law; and violation of Woods's right of publicity under Ohio common law. Jireh counterclaimed, seeking a declaratory judgment that Rush's art prints are protected by the First Amendment and do not violate the Lanham Act. Both parties moved for summary judgment. The district court granted Jireh's motion for summary judgment and dismissed the case. *See ETW Corp. v. Jireh Pub., Inc.,* 99 F.Supp.2d 829 (N.D.Ohio 2000)

II. Trademark Claims Based on the Unauthorized Use of the Registered Trademark "Tiger Woods"

* * *

ETW claims that Jireh infringed the registered mark "Tiger Woods" by including these words in marketing materials which accompanied the prints of Rush's painting. The words "Tiger Woods" do not appear on the face of the prints, nor are they included in the title of the painting. The words "Tiger Woods" do appear under the flap of the envelopes which contain the prints, and Woods is mentioned twice in the narrative which accompanies the prints.

The Lanham Act provides a defense to an infringement claim where the use of the mark "is a use, otherwise than as a mark, * * * which is descriptive of and used fairly and in good faith only to describe the goods * * * of such party [.]" 15 U.S.C. § 1115(b)(4); *see San Francisco Arts and Athletics, Inc. v. U.S. Olympic Comm.*, 483 U.S. 522 (1987) * * * In evaluating a defendant's fair use defense, a court must consider whether defendant has used the mark: (1) in its descriptive sense; and (2) in good faith. * * *

A celebrity's name may be used in the title of an artistic work so long as there is some artistic relevance * * * The use of Woods's name on the back of the envelope containing the print and in the narrative description of the print are purely descriptive and there is nothing to indicate that they were used other than in good faith. The prints, the envelopes which contain them, and the narrative materials which accompany them clearly identify Rush as the source of the print. Woods is mentioned only to describe the content of the print.

The district court properly granted summary judgment on ETW's claim for violation of its registered mark, "Tiger Woods," on the grounds that the claim was barred by the fair use defense as a matter of law.4

III. Trademark Claims Under 15 U.S.C. § 1125(a) Based on the Unauthorized Use of the Likeness of Tiger Woods

ETW has registered Woods's name as a trademark, but it has not registered any image or likeness of Woods. Nevertheless, ETW claims to have trademark rights in Woods's image and likeness. * * *

The Lanham Act defines a trademark as including "any word, name, symbol, or device, or any combination thereof" used by a person "to identify and distinguish his or her goods * * * from those manufactured or sold by others and to indicate the source of the goods, even if that source is unknown." 15 U.S.C. § 1127 * * * Not every word, name, symbol or device qualifies as a protectable mark; rather, it must be proven that it performs the job of identification, *i.e.*, to identify one source and to distinguish it from other sources. If it does not do this, then it is not protectable as a trademark.* * *

Here, ETW claims protection under the Lanham Act for any and all images of Tiger Woods. This is an untenable claim. ETW asks us, in effect, to constitute Woods himself as a walking, talking trademark. Images and likenesses of Woods are not protectable as a trademark because they do not perform the trademark function of designation. They do not distinguish and identify the source of goods. They cannot function as a trademark because there are undoubtedly thousands of images and likenesses of Woods taken by countless photographers, and drawn, sketched, or painted by numerous artists, which have been published in many forms of media, and sold and distributed throughout the world. No reasonable person could believe that merely because these photographs or paintings contain Woods's likeness or image, they all originated with Woods.

We hold that, as a general rule, a person's image or likeness cannot function as a trademark. Our conclusion is supported by the decisions of other courts which have addressed this issue. In *Pirone v. MacMillan, Inc.*, 894 F.2d 579 (2nd Cir.1990), the Second Circuit rejected a trademark claim asserted by the daughters of baseball legend Babe Ruth. The plaintiffs objected to the use of Ruth's likeness in three photographs which appeared in a calendar published by the defendant. The court rejected their claim, holding that "a photograph of a human being, unlike a portrait of a fanciful cartoon character, is not inherently 'distinctive' in the trademark sense of tending to indicate origin." *Id.* at 583. The court noted that Ruth "was one of the most photographed men of his generation, a larger than life hero to millions and an historical figure[.]" *Id.* The Second Circuit Court concluded that a consumer could not reasonably believe that Ruth sponsored the calendar:

[A]n ordinarily prudent purchaser would have no difficulty discerning that these photos are merely the subject matter of the calendar and do not in any way indicate sponsorship. No reasonable jury could find a likelihood of confusion.

Id. at 585. The court observed that "[u]nder some circumstances, a photograph of a person may be a valid trademark—if, for example, a particular photograph was consistently used on specific goods." *Id.* at 583. The court rejected plaintiffs' assertion of trademark rights in every photograph of Ruth.

In *Estate of Presley v. Russen,* 513 F.Supp. 1339, 1363–1364 (D.N.J.1981), the court rejected a claim by the estate of Elvis Presley that his image and likeness was a valid mark. The court did find, however, as suggested by the Second Circuit in *Pirone,* that one particular image of Presley had been consistently used in the advertising and sale of Elvis Presley entertainment services to identify those services and that the image could likely be found to function as a mark.

Here, ETW does not claim that a particular photograph of Woods has been consistently used on specific goods. Instead, ETW's claim is identical to that of the plaintiffs in *Pirone,* a sweeping claim to trademark rights in every photograph and image of Woods. Woods, like Ruth, is one of the most photographed sports figures of his generation, but this alone does not suffice to create a trademark claim.

The district court properly granted summary judgment on ETW's claim of trademark rights in all images and likenesses of Tiger Woods.[7]

IV. Lanham Act Unfair Competition and False Endorsement Claims, Ohio Right to Privacy Claims, and the First Amendment Defense

A. Introduction

ETW's claims under §43(a) of the Lanham Act, 15 U.S.C. §1125(a), include claims of unfair competition and false advertising in the nature of false endorsement. ETW has also asserted a claim for infringement of the right of publicity under Ohio law. The elements of a Lanham Act false endorsement claim are similar to the elements of a right of publicity claim under Ohio law. In fact, one legal scholar has said that a Lanham Act false endorsement claim is the federal equivalent of the right of publicity. *See* Bruce P. Keller, *The Right Of Publicity: Past, Present, and Future,* 1207 PLI Corp. Law and Prac. Handbook, 159, 170 (October 2000). Therefore, cases which address both these types of claims should be instructive in determining whether Jireh is entitled to summary judgment on those claims.

In addition, Jireh has raised the First Amendment as a defense to all of ETW's claims, arguing that Rush's use of Woods's image in his painting is protected expression. * * *

B. First Amendment Defense

The protection of the First Amendment is not limited to written or spoken words, but includes other mediums of expression, including music, pictures, films, photographs, paintings, drawings, engravings, prints, and sculptures. * * *

---

7. This includes ETW's claims of dilution under 15 U.S.C. §1125(c). Because Woods's likeness does not function as a trademark which is subject to protection under the Lanham Act, it follows that a dilution claim does not lie. * * *

Speech is protected even though it is carried in a form that is sold for profit * * * The fact that expressive materials are sold does not diminish the degree of protection to which they are entitled under the First Amendment. *City of Lakewood v. Plain Dealer Publ'g Co.*, 486 U.S. 750, 756 n. 5 (1988).

Even pure commercial speech is entitled to significant First Amendment protection. * * *

Rush's prints are not commercial speech. They do not propose a commercial transaction. Accordingly, they are entitled to the full protection of the First Amendment. Thus, we are called upon to decide whether Woods's intellectual property rights must yield to Rush's First Amendment rights.

C. Lanham Act False Endorsement Claim

The district court did not specifically discuss ETW's false endorsement claim in granting summary judgment to Jireh. The gist of the false endorsement claim is that the presence of Woods's image in Jireh's print implies that he has endorsed Jireh's product. * * *

False endorsement occurs when a celebrity's identity is connected with a product or service in such a way that consumers are likely to be misled about the celebrity's sponsorship or approval of the product or service* * *

In the ordinary false endorsement claim, the controlling issue is likelihood of confusion. This court has formulated an eight-factor test to determine the likelihood of confusion. *See Landham*, 227 F.3d at 626; *Wynn Oil Co. v. Thomas*, 839 F.2d 1183, 1186 (6th Cir.1988). However, for the reasons discussed below, we conclude that where the defendant has articulated a colorable claim that the use of a celebrity's identity is protected by the First Amendment, the likelihood of confusion test is not appropriate because it fails to adequately consider the interests protected by the First Amendment.

* * * [B]oth the Second Circuit and the Ninth Circuit have held that in Lanham Act false endorsement cases involving artistic expression, the likelihood of confusion test does not give sufficient weight to the public interest in free expression. Both courts rejected the "no alternative means" test. They held instead that the Lanham Act should be applied to artistic works only where the public interest in avoiding confusion outweighs the public interest in free expression. They agreed that the public interest in free expression should prevail if the use of the celebrity's image has artistic relevance, unless it is used in such a way that it explicitly misleads as to the source of the work. * * *

D. Right of Publicity Claim

ETW claims that Jireh's publication and marketing of prints of Rush's painting violates Woods's right of publicity. The right of publicity is an intellectual property right of recent origin which has been defined as the inherent right of every human being to control the commercial use of his or her identity * * * The right of publicity is a creature of state law[13] and its violation gives rise to a cause of action for the commercial tort of unfair competition. *Id.*

The right of publicity is, somewhat paradoxically, an outgrowth of the right of privacy. A cause of action for violation of the right was first recognized in *Haelan Labora-*

---

13 Approximately half of the states have adopted some form of the right of publicity either at common law or by statute.

tories, Inc. v. Topps Chewing Gum, Inc., 202 F.2d 866 (2nd Cir.1953), where the Second Circuit held that New York's common law protected a baseball player's right in the publicity value of his photograph, and in the process coined the phrase "right of publicity" as the name of this right.

The Ohio Supreme Court recognized the right of publicity in 1976 in *Zacchini v. Scripps-Howard Broadcasting Co.*, 47 Ohio St.2d 224, 351 N.E.2d 454 (1976). In *Zacchini*, which involved the videotaping and subsequent rebroadcast on a television news program of plaintiff's human cannonball act, the Ohio Supreme Court held that Zacchini's right of publicity was trumped by the First Amendment. On appeal, the Supreme Court of the United States reversed, holding that the First Amendment did not insulate defendant from liability for violating Zacchini's state law right of publicity where defendant published the plaintiff's entire act. *See Zacchini v. Scripps-Howard Broadcasting Co.*, 433 U.S. 562, 97 S.Ct. 2849 (1977). *Zacchini* is the only United States Supreme Court decision on the right of publicity.

There are few Ohio decisions defining the contours of the right of publicity in the aftermath of *Zacchini*. In *Vinci v. American Can Co.*, 9 Ohio St.3d 98, 459 N.E.2d 507 (1984), the Ohio Supreme Court merely reaffirmed its recognition of the right and devoted the remainder of its opinion to the issue of class action certification. Vinci was an Olympic gold medal weight lifter who brought a class action on behalf of himself and other Olympic athletes whose names and likenesses were used on a series of disposable drinking cups promoted by a partnership between the Minute Maid Corporation and the United States Olympic Committee. The Supreme Court of Ohio held that the action could be maintained as a class action. After remanding the case to the Cuyahoga County Court of Appeals, that court, with one judge dissenting, upheld the grant of summary judgment to the defendants, holding that "the mention of the athletes' names within the context of accurate, historical information was incidental to the promotion of the Dixie Cups by the partnership" and that the "reference to the athletes and their accomplishments was purely informational [.]" *Vinci v. American Can Co.*, 69 Ohio App.3d 727, 729, 591 N.E.2d 793, 794 (1990). * * *

When the Ohio Supreme Court recognized the right of publicity, it relied heavily on the RESTATEMENT (SECOND) OF TORTS, § 652.* * *

The RESTATEMENT originally treated the right of publicity as a branch of the right of privacy and included it in a chapter entitled "Invasion of Privacy." In 1995, the American Law Institute transferred its exposition of the right of publicity to the RESTATEMENT (THIRD) OF UNFAIR COMPETITION, Chapter 4, § 46, in a chapter entitled "Appropriation of Trade Values." The current version of the RESTATEMENT (THIRD) OF UNFAIR COMPETITION defines the right of publicity as follows:

> Appropriation of the Commercial Value of a Person's Identity: The Right of Publicity
>
> One who appropriates the commercial value of a person's identity by using without consent the person's name, likeness, or other indicia of identity for purposes of trade is subject to liability for the relief appropriate under the rules stated in §§ 48 and 49.

Id.

In § 46, Comment c, *Rationale for Protection*, the authors of the RESTATEMENT suggest that courts may justifiably be reluctant to adopt a broad construction of the right.

The rationales underlying recognition of a right of publicity are generally less compelling than those that justify rights in trademarks or trade secrets. The commercial value of a person's identity often results from success in endeavors such as entertainment or sports that offer their own substantial rewards. Any additional incentive attributable to the right of publicity may have only marginal significance. In other cases the commercial value acquired by a person's identity is largely fortuitous or otherwise unrelated to any investment made by the individual, thus diminishing the weight of the property and unjust enrichment rationales for protection. In addition, the public interest in avoiding false suggestions of endorsement or sponsorship can be pursued through the cause of action for deceptive marketing. Thus, courts may be properly reluctant to adopt a broad construction of the publicity right. See § 47.

In § 47, Comment c, the authors of the RESTATEMENT note, "The right of publicity as recognized by statute and common law is fundamentally constrained by the public and constitutional interest in freedom of expression." In the same comment, the authors state that "[t]he use of a person's identity primarily for the purpose of communicating information or expressing ideas is not generally actionable as a violation of the person's right of publicity." Various examples are given, including the use of the person's name or likeness in news reporting in newspapers and magazines.

The RESTATEMENT recognizes that this limitation on the right is not confined to news reporting but extends to use in "entertainment and other creative works, including both fiction and non-fiction." *Id.* The authors list examples of protected uses of a celebrity's identity, likeness or image, including unauthorized print or broadcast biographies and novels, plays or motion pictures. *Id.* According to the RESTATEMENT, such uses are not protected, however, if the name or likeness is used solely to attract attention to a work that is not related to the identified person, and the privilege may be lost if the work contains substantial falsifications. *Id.*

We believe the courts of Ohio would follow the principles of the RESTATEMENT in defining the limits of the right of publicity. * * *

In *Carson v. Here's Johnny Portable Toilets, Inc.,* 698 F.2d 831 (6th Cir.1983), a majority of this court, with Judge Kennedy dissenting, held that television comedian and talk show host Johnny Carson's right of publicity was invaded when defendant used the phrase with which Carson was commonly introduced on his television program. In *Carson,* we held that "a celebrity has a protected pecuniary interest in the commercial exploitation of his identity." *Id.* at 835.

In *Landham,* 227 F.3d at 625–26, this court held that Landham, a fringe actor who played supporting roles in several motion pictures, had failed to show a violation of his right of publicity when defendant marketed an action figure of a character he had played but which did not bear a personal resemblance to him. This court found that Landham had failed to show that his persona had significant value or that the toy invoked his persona as distinct from that of the fictional character he played.

There is an inherent tension between the right of publicity and the right of freedom of expression under the First Amendment. This tension becomes particularly acute when the person seeking to enforce the right is a famous actor, athlete, politician, or otherwise famous person whose exploits, activities, accomplishments, and personal life are subject to constant scrutiny and comment in the public media. * * *

In a series of recent cases, other circuits have been called upon to establish the boundaries between the right of publicity and the First Amendment. In *Rogers,* the Second Circuit affirmed the district court's grant of summary judgment on Rogers' right of publicity claim, noting that commentators have "advocated limits on the right of publicity to accommodate First Amendment concerns." That court also cited three cases in which state courts refused to extend the right of publicity to bar the use of a celebrity's name in the title and text of a fictional or semi-fictional book or movie.

In *White*, television celebrity Vanna White, brought suit against Samsung Electronics, alleging that its television advertisement which featured a female-shaped robot wearing a long gown, blonde wig, large jewelry, and turning letters in what appeared to be the "Wheel of Fortune" game show set, violated her California common law right of publicity and her rights under the Lanham Act. The Ninth Circuit, with Judge Alarcon dissenting in part, reversed the grant of summary judgment to defendant, holding that White had produced sufficient evidence that defendant's advertisement appropriated her identity in violation of her right of publicity, and that the issue of confusion about White's endorsement of defendant's product created a jury issue which precluded summary judgment on her Lanham Act claim. In so holding, the court rejected the defendant's parody defense which posited that the advertisement was a parody of White's television act and was protected speech.

A suggestion for rehearing *en banc* failed. Three judges dissented from the order rejecting the suggestion for a rehearing *en banc*. *See White v. Samsung Electronics America, Inc.*, 989 F.2d 1512 (9th Cir.1993). Judge Kozinski, writing the dissenting opinion, observed, "Something very dangerous is going on here. * * * Overprotecting intellectual property is as harmful as underprotecting it. Creativity is impossible without a rich public domain." 989 F.2d at 1513. Later, he commented:

> Intellectual property rights aren't free: They're imposed at the expense of future creators and of the public at large. * * * This is why intellectual property law is full of careful balances between what's set aside for the owner and what's left in the public domain for the rest of us[.]

Id. at 1516. In *Landham*, this court declined to follow the majority in *White* and, instead, cited Judge Kozinski's dissent with approval. *See* 227 F.3d at 626.

In *Cardtoons, L.C. v. Major League Baseball Players Assoc.*, 95 F.3d 959 (10th Cir.1996), the Tenth Circuit held that the plaintiff's First Amendment right to free expression outweighed the defendant's proprietary right of publicity. The plaintiff in *Cardtoons* contracted with a political cartoonist, a sports artist, and a sports author and journalist to design a set of trading cards which featured readily identifiable caricatures of major league baseball players with a humorous commentary about their careers on the back. The cards ridiculed the players using a variety of themes. The cards used similar names, recognizable caricatures, distinctive team colors and commentaries about individual players which left no doubt about their identity. The Tenth Circuit held that the defendant's use of the player's likenesses on its trading cards would violate their rights of publicity under an Oklahoma statute. Addressing the defendant's *First Amendment* claim, the court held:

> Cardtoons' parody trading cards receive full protection under the First Amendment. The cards provide social commentary on public figures, major league baseball players, who are involved in a significant commercial enterprise, major league baseball. While not core political speech * * * this type of commentary on an important social institution constitutes protected expression.

Cardtoons, 95 F.3d at 969. The Tenth Circuit rejected the reasoning of the panel majority in *White*, and expressed its agreement with the dissenting opinions of Judges Alarcon and Kozinski. * * * In striking the balance between the players' property rights and the defendant's First Amendment rights, the court in *Cardtoons* commented on the pervasive presence of celebrities in the media, sports and entertainment. The court noted that celebrities are an important part of our public vocabulary and have come to symbolize certain ideas and values:

> As one commentator explained, celebrities are "common points of reference for millions of individuals who may never interact with one another, but who share, by virtue of their participation in a mediated culture, a common experience and a collective memory." John B. Thompson, IDEOLOGY AND MODERN CULTURE: CRITICAL SOCIAL THEORY IN THE ERA OF MASS COMMUNICATION 163 (1990). Through their pervasive presence in the media, sports and entertainment celebrities come to symbolize certain ideas and values. * * * Celebrities, then, are an important element of the shared communicative resources of our cultural domain.

Cardtoons, 95 F.3d at 972.

The court observed that one of the justifications often given for the right of publicity is the furthering of economic goals such as stimulating athletic and artistic achievement by securing to celebrities the fruits of their labors and talents. The court then noted that major league baseball players' salaries currently average over one million dollars per year and commented:

> Such figures suggest that "even without the right of publicity the rate of return to stardom in the entertainment and sports fields is probably high enough to bring forth a more than 'adequate' supply of creative effort and achievement." * * * In addition, even in the absence of publicity rights, celebrities would still be able to reap financial reward from authorized appearances and endorsements. The extra income generated by licensing one's identity does not provide a necessary inducement to enter and achieve in the realm of sports and entertainment. Thus, while publicity rights may provide some incentive for creativity and achievement, the magnitude and importance of that incentive has been exaggerated.

Cardtoons, 95 F.3d at 974 (citation omitted). Noting that another justification for publicity rights is the prevention of unjust enrichment, the court observed that "Cardtoons added a significant creative component of its own to the celebrity identity and created an entirely new product." *Cardtoons*, 95 F.3d at 976. The Tenth Circuit affirmed the district court's ruling that the trading cards were expression protected by the First Amendment.

In *Hoffman v. Capital Cities/ABC, Inc.*, 255 F.3d 1180 (9th Cir.2001), the Ninth Circuit was again presented with a case involving the tension between the right of publicity and the First Amendment. The plaintiff, actor Dustin Hoffman, brought suit against a magazine and its publisher, seeking to recover on state law claims for the violation of his right of publicity, for unfair competition and for violation of the Lanham Act, based on allegations that the magazine used, without his permission, a still photograph from a motion picture to create a computer-generated image which falsely depicted him wearing fashion designer's women's clothes. * * *

In 1982, Hoffman starred in the movie *Tootsie*, playing a male actor who dresses as a woman to get a part on a television soap opera. In March, 1997, the defendant L.A. Magazine, Inc. ("LAM") published an issue of its magazine which contained an article entitled "Grand Illusions", which used computer technology to alter famous film stills to make it appear that the actors were wearing spring 1997 fashions. The article contained sixteen familiar scenes of famous actors from famous movies. In the photo of Hoffman, his head and the American flag appeared as they did in the original, but his body and the long sleeved, red dress were replaced by the body of a male model in the same pose, wearing a spaghetti-strapped, cream colored silk evening dress and high heeled sandals. The text on the page identified the still as from the movie *Tootsie* and read "Dustin Hoffman isn't a drag in a butter-colored silk gown by Richard Tyler and Ralph Lauren heels." * * *

The court concluded that LAM's publication of the altered *Tootsie* photograph was not commercial speech:

> Viewed in context, the article as a whole is a combination of fashion photography, humor, and visual and verbal editorial comment on classic films and famous actors. Any commercial aspects are "inextricably entwined" with expressive elements, and so they cannot be separated out "from the fully protected whole".

Hoffman, 255 F.3d at 1185. The court concluded that LAM was entitled to the full First Amendment protection accorded non-commercial speech which could be defeated only by proof of actual malice.

In *Comedy III Productions, Inc. v. Gary Saderup, Inc.,* 25 Cal.4th 387, 106 Cal.Rptr.2d 126, 21 P.3d 797 (2001), the California Supreme Court adopted a transformative use test in determining whether the artistic use of a celebrity's image is protected by the *First Amendment.* Saderup, an artist with over twenty-five years experience in making charcoal drawings of celebrities, created a drawing of the famous comedy team, The Three Stooges. The drawings were used to create lithographic and silk screen masters, which were then used to produce lithographic prints and silk screen images on T-shirts. Comedy III, the owner of all rights to the former comedy act, brought suit against Saderup under a California statute, which grants the right of publicity to successors in interest of deceased celebrities.

The California Supreme Court found that Saderup's portraits were entitled to First Amendment protection because they were "expressive works and not an advertisement or endorsement of a product." *Id.* at 396, 106 Cal.Rptr.2d 126, 21 P.3d at 802. In discussing the tension between the right of publicity and the First Amendment, the court observed:

> [B]ecause celebrities take on personal meanings to many individuals in the society, the creative appropriation of celebrity images can be an important avenue of individual expression. As one commentator has stated: "Entertainment and sports celebrities are the leading players in our Public Drama. We tell tales, both tall and cautionary, about them. We monitor their comings and goings, their missteps and heartbreaks. We copy their mannerisms, their styles, their modes of conversation and of consumption. Whether or not celebrities are 'the chief agents of moral change in the United States,' they certainly are widely used—far more than are our institutionally anchored elites—to symbolize individual aspirations, group identities and cultural values. Their images are thus important expressive and communicative resources: the peculiar, yet familiar idiom in which we conduct a fair portion of our cultural business and everyday conversation." (Madow, *Private Ownership of Public Image: Popular Culture and Publicity Rights* (1993)) 81 Cal. L.Rev. 125, 128.

Id. at 397, 21 P.3d at 803.

The court rejected the proposition that Saderup's lithographs and T-shirts lost their First Amendment protection because they were not original single works of art, but were instead part of a commercial enterprise designed to generate profit solely from the sale of multiple reproductions of likenesses of The Three Stooges:

> [T]his position has no basis in logic or authority. No one would claim that a published book, because it is one of many copies, receives less First Amendment protection than the original manuscript. * * * [A] reproduction of a celebrity image that, as explained above, contains significant creative elements is entitled to as much First Amendment protection as an original work of art.

Id. at 408, 21 P.3d at 810.

Borrowing part of the fair use defense from copyright law, the California court proposed the following test for distinguishing between protected and unprotected expression when the right of publicity conflicts with the First Amendment:

> When artistic expression takes the form of a literal depiction or imitation of a celebrity for commercial gain, directly trespassing on the right of publicity without adding significant expression beyond that trespass, the state law interest in protecting the fruits of artistic labor outweighs the expressive interests of the imitative artist.

> On the other hand, when a work contains significant transformative elements, it is not only especially worthy of First Amendment protection, but it is also less likely to interfere with the economic interest protected by the right of publicity. * * *

> Accordingly, First Amendment protection of such works outweighs whatever interest the state may have in enforcing the right of publicity.

Id. at 405, 21 P.3d at 808. Later in its opinion, the California court restated the test as follows:

> Another way of stating the inquiry is whether the celebrity likeness is one of the "raw materials" from which an original work is synthesized, or whether the depiction or imitation of the celebrity is the very sum and substance of the work in question.

Id. at 406, 21 P.3d at 809.

Finally, citing the art of Andy Warhol, the court noted that even literal reproductions of celebrity portraits may be protected by the *First Amendment.*

> Through distortion and the careful manipulation of context, Warhol was able to convey a message that went beyond the commercial exploitation of celebrity images and became a form of ironic social comment on the dehumanization of celebrity itself. * * * Although the distinction between protected and unprotected expression will sometimes be subtle, it is no more so than other distinctions triers of fact are called on to make in First Amendment jurisprudence.

Id. at 408-409, 21 P.3d at 811.

We conclude that in deciding whether the sale of Rush's prints violate Woods's right of publicity, we will look to the Ohio case law and the RESTATEMENT (THIRD) OF UNFAIR COMPETITION. In deciding where the line should be drawn between Woods's intellectual property rights and the First Amendment, we find ourselves in agreement with the dissenting judges in *White*, the Tenth Circuit's decision in *Cardtoons*, and the Ninth Circuit's decision in *Hoffman*, and we will follow them in determining whether Rush's work is protected by the First Amendment. Finally, we believe that the transformative elements test adopted by the Supreme Court of California in *Comedy III Productions*, will assist us in determining where the proper balance lies between the First Amendment and Woods's intellectual property rights. * * *

E. Application of the Law to the Evidence in this Case

The evidence in the record reveals that Rush's work consists of much more than a mere literal likeness of Woods. It is a panorama of Woods's victory at the 1997 Masters Tournament, with all of the trappings of that tournament in full view, including the Augusta clubhouse, the leader board, images of Woods's caddy, and his final round partner's caddy. These elements in themselves are sufficient to bring Rush's work within the protection of the *First Amendment*. The Masters Tournament is probably the world's most famous golf tournament and Woods's victory in the 1997 tournament was a historic event in the world of sports. A piece of art that portrays a historic sporting event communicates and celebrates the value our culture attaches to such events. It would be ironic indeed if the presence of the image of the victorious athlete would deny the work First Amendment protection. Furthermore, Rush's work includes not only images of Woods and the two caddies, but also carefully crafted likenesses of six past winners of the Masters Tournament: Arnold Palmer, Sam Snead, Ben Hogan, Walter Hagen, Bobby Jones, and Jack Nicklaus, a veritable pantheon of golf's greats. Rush's work conveys the message that Woods himself will someday join that revered group.

Turning first to ETW's Lanham Act false endorsement claim, we agree with the courts that hold that the Lanham Act should be applied to artistic works only where the public interest in avoiding confusion outweighs the public interest in free expression. The *Rogers* test is helpful in striking that balance in the instant case. We find that the presence of Woods's image in Rush's painting *The Masters Of Augusta* does have artistic relevance to the underlying work and that it does not explicitly mislead as to the source of the work.[18] We believe that the principles followed in *Cardtoons*, *Hoffman* and *Comedy III* are also relevant in determining whether the Lanham Act applies to Rush's work, and we find that it does not.

We find, like the court in *Rogers*, that plaintiff's survey evidence, even if its validity is assumed, indicates at most that some members of the public would draw the incorrect inference that Woods had some connection with Rush's print. The risk of misunderstanding, not engendered by any explicit indication on the face of the print, is so outweighed by the interest in artistic expression as to preclude application of the Act. We disagree with the dissent's suggestion that a jury must decide where the balance should be struck and where the boundaries should be drawn between the rights conferred by the Lanham Act and the protections of the First Amendment.

In regard to the Ohio law right of publicity claim, we conclude that Ohio would construe its right of publicity as suggested in the RESTATEMENT (THIRD) OF UNFAIR COMPETITION, Chapter 4 Section 47, Comment d., which articulates a rule analogous to the rule of fair use in copyright law. Under this rule, the substantiality and market effect

---

18. Unlike *Parks*, here there is no genuine issue of material fact about the artistic relevance of the image of Woods in Rush's print. *See Ruffin-Steinback v. dePasse*, 82 F.Supp.2d 723 (E.D.Mich.2000), aff'd, 267 F.3d 457 (6th Cir.2001) (likeness of members of Motown group "Temptations" used to promote televised mini-series and video cassette based on partly fictionalized story about group); *Seale v. Gramercy Pictures*, 949 F.Supp. 331 (E.D.Pa.1996) (use of plaintiff's name and likeness on cover of pictorial history book and home video clearly related to content of book and film).

of the use of the celebrity's image is analyzed in light of the informational and creative content of the defendant's use. Applying this rule, we conclude that Rush's work has substantial informational and creative content which outweighs any adverse effect on ETW's market and that Rush's work does not violate Woods's right of publicity.

We further find that Rush's work is expression which is entitled to the full protection of the First Amendment and not the more limited protection afforded to commercial speech. * * *

In balancing these interests against Woods's right of publicity, we note that Woods, like most sports and entertainment celebrities with commercially valuable identities, engages in an activity, professional golf, that in itself generates a significant amount of income which is unrelated to his right of publicity. Even in the absence of his right of publicity, he would still be able to reap substantial financial rewards from authorized appearances and endorsements. It is not at all clear that the appearance of Woods's likeness in artwork prints which display one of his major achievements will reduce the commercial value of his likeness.

While the right of publicity allows celebrities like Woods to enjoy the fruits of their labors, here Rush has added a significant creative component of his own to Woods's identity. Permitting Woods's right of publicity to trump Rush's right of freedom of expression would extinguish Rush's right to profit from his creative enterprise.

After balancing the societal and personal interests embodied in the First Amendment against Woods's property rights, we conclude that the effect of limiting Woods's right of publicity in this case is negligible and significantly outweighed by society's interest in freedom of artistic expression.

Finally, applying the transformative effects test adopted by the Supreme Court of California in *Comedy III,* we find that Rush's work does contain significant transformative elements which make it especially worthy of First Amendment protection and also less likely to interfere with the economic interest protected by Woods' right of publicity. Unlike the unadorned, nearly photographic reproduction of the faces of The Three Stooges in *Comedy III,* Rush's work does not capitalize solely on a literal depiction of Woods. Rather, Rush's work consists of a collage of images in addition to Woods's image which are combined to describe, in artistic form, a historic event in sports history and to convey a message about the significance of Woods's achievement in that event. Because Rush's work has substantial transformative elements, it is entitled to the full protection of the First Amendment. In this case, we find that Woods's right of publicity must yield to the First Amendment.

V. Conclusion

In accordance with the foregoing, the judgment of the District Court granting summary judgment to Jireh Publishing is affirmed.

CLAY, Circuit Judge, dissenting. Genuine issues of material fact remain for trial as to the claims brought by Plaintiff, ETW Corporation, under the Lanham Act, 15 U.S.C. § 1114 and § 1125, and Ohio common law for trademark infringement, unfair competition, and dilution; therefore, I would reverse the district court's judgment and remand the case for trial as to these claims. No genuine issue of material fact remains for trial that Defendant, Jireh Publishing, violated Plaintiff's right of publicity under Ohio common law; therefore, I would reverse the district court's judgment on Plaintiff's right of publicity claim and remand with instructions that the district court enter summary judgment in favor of Plaintiff. For these reasons, I respectfully dissent from the majority opinion. * * *

I. Trademark Claims Based on Defendant's Unauthorized Use of the Unregistered Mark— § 43(a) of the Lanham Act, 15 U.S.C. § 1125(a)

* * *

The majority's contention as set forth in footnote 5 of its opinion, that "Plaintiff's first amended complaint does not allege that Woods has used any specific image or likeness as a trademark," misses the point. That is, Plaintiff's complaint expressly takes issue with Defendant's unauthorized sale of Rush's print depicting Woods, and Plaintiff has proffered evidence to show that consumers are confused as to Woods being the sponsor or origin of the print, thereby establishing, particularly for purposes of summary judgment, that the image of Woods in Rush's print has been used as a trademark. * * *

The majority ignores this body of well established jurisprudence by holding that "as a general rule, a person's image or likeness cannot function as a trademark." Indeed, if a plaintiff alleging infringement in the unregistered mark of his image or likeness in the product of another brings forth evidence of consumer confusion, then the image or likeness of the plaintiff may very well be functioning "as a trademark" for purposes of § 1125(a). * * *

In support of its sweeping holding, the majority relies in part upon *Pirone v. MacMillan, Inc.,* 894 F.2d 579 (2d Cir.1990); however, a close reading of *Pirone* does not support the majority's position but instead follows the long line of cases establishing that a plaintiff may succeed on a claim under § 1125(a) for infringement of the unregistered mark of his likeness or image by bringing forth evidence of consumer confusion

* * *

Simply stated, contrary to the majority's contention, the jurisprudence clearly indicates that a person's image or likeness *can* function as a trademark as long as there is evidence demonstrating that the likeness or image was used as a trademark; which is to say, the image can function as a trademark as long as there is evidence of consumer confusion as to the source of the merchandise upon which the image appears. * * *

II. Lanham Act Unfair Competition & False Endorsement Claims— § 1125(a)

* * *

This dissent focuses on the majority's misapplication of the *Rogers* balancing test and resulting erroneous conclusion; however, this dissent should not be interpreted as endorsing the application of the *Rogers* test to the facts of this case. Rather, the point made by the dissent is that even under the *Rogers* standard, questions of fact remain precluding summary judgment. * * *

[I]n applying the *Rogers* balancing test to facts if this case, the majority fails to consider Plaintiff's survey evidence of consumer confusion and fails to do so under the scope of the Lanham Act relevant to the artistic work at issue. Instead, without any meaningful consideration whatsoever of Plaintiff's survey evidence, or for that matter any meaningful explanation of why Rush's print has artistic relevance for purposes of conducting a balancing of interests of any significance, the majority simply concludes that "the presence of Woods' image in Rush's painting *The Masters Of Augusta* does have artistic relevance to the underlying work and that it does not explicitly mislead as to the source of the work." Indeed, this is not the approach taken by the Second Circuit in *Rogers,* where the court specifically considered the survey evidence, and did so as to the specific form in which the false endorsement was made—a title to a motion picture, and found that although a factual dispute existed, it was not "genuine" for purposes of surviving summary judgment. *See Rogers*, 875 F.2d at 1001.

* * *

The majority's contention that this case is like *Rogers* because the survey evidence merely indicates that some members of the public would draw the incorrect inference that Woods had some connection with Rush's print fails to account for the differences in the type of survey evidence in this case as opposed to that in *Rogers*. In *Rogers* the survey evidence indicated that only about 14% of the consumers polled indicated that Ginger Rogers was "involved in any way with making the film[;]" however, in this case, 62% of the consumers polled indicated that they believed that Woods had an "affiliation" or "connection" with Rush's print, or "approved" or "sponsored" the print. *See* 875 F.2d at 1001 n. 8. And of particular significance, the *Rogers* court found that such survey evidence failed to create a *genuine* issue of fact for the jury. Here, on the other hand, considering the stark difference in actual consumer confusion between this case and *Rogers*, a genuine issue of fact has been demonstrated for purposes of allowing this matter to proceed. * * *

III. Trademark Claims Based on the Unauthorized Use of the Registered Mark— § 32 of the Lanham Act, 15 U.S.C. § 1114

Plaintiff brought suit against Defendant under § 32 for infringement of Plaintiff's registered mark, "TIGER WOODS." The mark appears on the back of the envelope containing Rush's print as well as in the narrative description of the print. * * *

As explained in the above sections, Plaintiff brought forth evidence of actual consumer confusion in this case sufficient to create a genuine issue of material fact for trial as to whether the prints upon which the registered mark appears or accompanies is an infringing use of the unregistered mark under § 43(a). Indeed, the fatal flaw in the majority's outcome as to Plaintiff's claims brought under § 43(a) is its failure to consider the evidence of actual consumer confusion proffered by Plaintiff, or any of the other factors looked to when determining consumer confusion. Thus, to conclude that Defendant's use of the registered mark is a fair use because the underlying work is not an infringing use is erroneous. * * *

The proper approach is to look at Defendant's use of the registered mark in the context of evidence of consumer confusion in order to determine whether the fair use doctrine can be applicable. *See Paccar Inc. v. TeleScan Techs., L.L.C.*, 319 F.3d 243, 255–56 (6th Cir.2003) (noting that "a finding of a likelihood of confusion forecloses a fair use defense") (citations omitted). Once again, the majority fails to engage in any meaningful inquiry into consumer confusion and instead simply concludes that because Defendant's print is an artistic expression, the use of the registered mark in association therewith constitutes a permissible fair use under the Act. This approach is in contravention to the application of the fair use doctrine and § 32 of the Act. *See id.* at 249, 255–56 * * *

IV. Dilution of the Mark under 15 U.S.C. § 1125

In Count II of its amended complaint, Plaintiff alleged dilution of the registered mark "TIGER WOODS" in violation of section 43(c) of the Act, 15 U.S.C. § 1125(c). The district court failed to engage in any independent analysis of Plaintiff's dilution claim, and instead simply found that the dilution claim fell prey to summary judgment for the same reasons that Plaintiff's trademark claims fell prey to summary judgment. *See ETW Corp. v. Jireh Publ'g, Inc.*, 99 F.Supp.2d 829, 834 (N.D.Ohio 2000). The majority likewise fails to engage in any independent analysis and simply concludes in footnote 7 of its opinion that "since Woods's likeness does not function as a trademark which is subject to protection under the Lanham Act, it follows that a dilution claim does not lie." Aside from its erroneous conclusion that Plaintiff has not brought forth evidence that Woods' image as portrayed in the print functions as a trademark, the majority's conclusion in this regard is perplexing and legally incorrect inasmuch as Plaintiff based its dilution claim on the registered trademark. * * *

The Lanham Act, as amended by the Federal Trademark Dilution Act of 1995, defines the term "dilution" as "the lessening of the capacity of a famous mark to identify and distinguish goods or services, *regardless of the presence or absence of*—(1) competition between the owner of the famous mark and other parties, or (2) *likelihood of confusion, mistake, or deception.*" 15 U.S.C. § 1127 (emphasis added). This Court has identified factors that a plaintiff must fulfill in order to succeed on a federal dilution claim," '(1) the senior mark must be famous; (2) it must be distinctive; (3) the junior use must be a commercial use in commerce; (4) it must begin after the senior mark has become famous; and (5) it must cause dilution of the distinctive quality of the senior mark.'" The Supreme Court recently made clear that in order to demonstrate dilution, the plaintiff must proffer objective evidence of actual dilution, "but that does not mean that the consequences of dilution, such as actual loss of sales or profits, must also be proved." Inasmuch as Plaintiff in the case at hand has brought forward evidence on each of these five elements of a federal dilution claim, the jury should be allowed to consider this claim as well.

V. Ohio Common Law Right of Publicity Claim

* * *

Although the right of publicity grew out of the right of privacy, the right of publicity has within it characteristics of other rights such that it has been described as a " '*sui generis* mixture of personal rights, property rights, and rights under unfair competition.'"

[S]ince *Haelan*, "[t]he right of a person, whether or not termed 'right of publicity,' to control the commercial value and exploitation of his or her name and likeness has received wide recognition by the courts." *Estate of Elvis Presley v. Russen*, 513 F.Supp. 1339, 1353 n. 6 (D.N.J.1981) (collecting cases). This Court has spoken on the right of publicity as follows:

> The right of publicity has developed to protect the commercial interest of celebrities in their identities. The theory of the right is that a celebrity's identity can be valuable in the promotion of products, and the celebrity has an interest that may be protected from the unauthorized commercial exploitation of that identity. In *Memphis Development Foundation v. Factors Etc., Inc.*, 616 F.2d 956 (6th Cir.1980), we stated: "The famous have an exclusive legal right during life to control and profit from the commercial use of their name and personality." *Id.* at 957.

Carson v. Here's Johnny Portable Toilets, Inc., 698 F.2d 831, 835 (6th Cir.1983) (analyzing right to publicity claim brought under Michigan common law).

* * *

Aside from the confusing development of the right of publicity, and aside from the many differences associated with the various state statutes in effect, the point of confusion most associated with the right of publicity law is its interplay with the First

Amendment. Each doctrine advances its own set of societal interests which often are in tension with one another. Those societal interests advanced by the right of publicity have been suggested to be that of "fostering creativity, safeguarding the individual's enjoyment of the fruits of her labors, preventing consumer deception, and preventing unjust enrichment." * * * * Two of the most frequently cited justifications for First Amendment free speech guarantees in this regard are the advancement of knowledge and search for the truth by fostering a free marketplace of ideas necessary to a democratic society, as well as the fulfillment of the human need for self-expression. *Id.* at 65–66. The tension between these interests is self-evident: while we want a free marketplace of ideas and expression, we wish to insure that any commercial value gained from that expression is not unjustly obtained through another's labors. *See Zacchini,* 433 U.S. at 576, 97 S.Ct. 2849 ("No social purpose is served by having the defendant [in a right of publicity case] get free some aspect of the plaintiff that would have market value and for which he would normally pay.").

B. Woods' Right of Publicity Claim in this Case

Zacchini v. Scripps-Howard Broadcasting Company is the sole case from the Supreme Court to directly address the right of publicity, and the case came to the Supreme Court by way of *certiorari* from the Ohio Supreme Court under Ohio common law. *See Zacchini,* 47 Ohio St.2d 224, 351 N.E.2d 454 (1976), *rev'd on other grounds,* 433 U.S. 562, 572, (1977) * * * The Court explained that the enforcement of the right of publicity claim was not at odds with the First Amendment inasmuch as "the rationale for [protecting the right of publicity] is the straightforward one of preventing unjust enrichment by the theft of good will. No social purpose is served by having the defendant get free some aspect of the plaintiff that would have market value and for which he would normally pay." *Id.* at 576.

Indeed, since *Zacchini,* "[t]he right of publicity has often been invoked in the context of commercial speech when the appropriation of a celebrity likeness creates a false and misleading impression that the celebrity is endorsing a product." * * * * "Because the First Amendment does not protect false and misleading commercial speech, and because even non-misleading commercial speech is generally subject to somewhat lesser First Amendment protection, the right of publicity often trumps the right of advertisers to make use of celebrity figures." In this case, to the extent that the district court was correct in characterizing Defendant's prints as expressive works and not as commercial products, even though Defendant was selling the prints for financial gain, the issue becomes what degree of First Amendment protection should be afforded to Defendant's expressive work.

[G]uidance is provided by the California Supreme Court because it has addressed the specific issue in a case nearly on all fours with that presented here; namely, *Comedy III Productions v. Gary Saderup, Inc.,* 25 Cal.4th 387, 106 Cal.Rptr.2d 126, 21 P.3d 797 (2001).

In *Comedy III,* the plaintiff, Comedy III Productions, which is the registered owner of all rights to the former comedy act known as The Three Stooges, filed suit against the defendants, Gary Saderup and Gary Saderup, Inc., seeking damages and injunctive relief for violation of, among other things, California's right of publicity statute in connection with the defendants' sale of T-shirts and lithographs bearing the image of the Three Stooges produced from a charcoal drawing done by Saderup. The defendants sold the T-shirts and lithographs without the plaintiff's consent, profiting $75,000 from the sale of these items. The trial court found for the plaintiff, and entered judgment in the amount of $75,000 as well as $150,000 in attorney's fees plus costs. *Id.* at 801. The court also issued a permanent injunction restraining Saderup from violating the statute by use of any likeness of The Three Stooges in lithographs, T-shirts, "or any other medium by which Saderup's artwork may be sold or marketed." *Id.* In addition, the trial court enjoined Saderap in several other respects regarding his marketing products in connection with The Three Stooges, but allowed Saderup's original charcoal drawing from which the reproductions were made to be exempt from the injunction. *Id.* at 801.

The defendants appealed, and the court of appeals modified the judgment by striking the injunction on the basis that the plaintiff had not shown a likelihood of continued violation of the statute, and that the wording of the statute was overbroad. *Id.* However, the court of appeals affirmed in all other respects, thereby rejecting the defendants' arguments that 1) his conduct did not violate the terms of the statute; and 2) in any event, his conduct was protected by the constitutional guaranty of freedom of speech under the First Amendment. *Id.* The defendants appealed to the California Supreme Court, which granted leave to address the two arguments raised by the defendants. *Id.* For purposes of the matter at hand, we focus on the Supreme Court of California's analysis of the First Amendment argument.

Relying on *Zacchini* and several cases from lower courts recognizing a celebrity's right of publicity, the court found that depictions of celebrities which amounted to little more than the appropriation of the celebrity's economic value, were not protected by the First Amendment.

* * *

Applying the transformative test to an artist's work at issue in *Comedy III,* the charcoal sketch made into lithographs and printed on T-shirts, the court found that the defendants' work was not protected inasmuch as the creative contribution was subordinated to the overall goal of creating a literal image of the Three Stooges to commercially exploit their fame. *Id.* at 811. In doing so, the court noted that when an "artist's skill and talent is manifestly subordinated to the overall goal of creating a conventional portrait of a celebrity so as to commercially exploit his or her fame, then the artist's right of free expression is outweighed by the right of publicity." *Id.*

Indeed, the rendition done by Rush is nearly identical to that in the poster distributed by Nike * * * Thus, although it is apparent that Rush is an adequately skilled artist, after viewing the prints in question it is also apparent that Rush's ability in this regard is "subordinated to the overall goal of creating literal, conventional depictions of [Tiger Woods] so as to exploit his * * * fame [such that Rush's] right of free expression is outweighed by [Woods'] right of publicity."

Accordingly, contrary to the majority's conclusion otherwise, it is clear that the prints gain their commercial value by exploiting the fame and celebrity status that Woods has worked to achieve. Under such facts, the right of publicity is not outweighed by the right of free expression. *See Comedy III,* 106 Cal.Rptr.2d 126, 21 P.3d at 811 (noting that the marketability and economic value of the defendant's work was derived primarily from the fame of the three celebrities that it depicted and was therefore not protected by the First Amendment).

I therefore respectfully dissent from the majority opinion affirming summary judgment to Defendant as to all of Plaintiff's claims.

Notes and Questions

1. Before the *ETW* case, it was generally understood in the sports industry that other than the *Namath v. Sports Illustrated* exception for newspapers and magazines, any

commercial use of the "identity" of an athlete—broadly defined to include his or her name, signature, picture, image, statistics or career information—without the athlete's consent was prohibited. Businesses interested in selling products (other than books, newspapers, or magazines) that featured any of those attributes of a player were advised that they needed to secure a license—from the player for the use of the player's "identity" and from the team or league if the athlete would be shown in his or her uniform. Manufacturers of a wide array of products—board games, video games, trading cards, posters, greeting cards, rotisserie-league and fantasy games, cups and mugs, dolls or action figures—would first secure a license from the appropriate players association (to which the players assigned their "group licensing rights"), agreeing to pay a specified percentage of the manufacturer's revenue to the players association. After the *ETW* case, the question was whether the decision only applied to works of art (in effect, limiting the decision to the particular facts presented in *ETW*), or whether it had much broader implications. What do you think?

2. Does *ETW* hold that use of a famous person's image, likeness, or picture can never violate the Lanham Act, even if consumers are misled to believe the famous person "sponsored" the use, unless it is a particular image, picture or a particular pose that has been "consistently used in the advertising and sale" of the famous person's products or services?

3. The Court in *ETW* says the defendant's prints are not commercial speech because they do not "propose a commercial transaction." What does that mean? Does it mean that only use of a photograph or likeness that advertises or endorses products or services are commercial speech? The defendant's prints were produced to be sold. Why isn't that a commercial transaction? If he had drawn the same picture or taken a photograph and used the picture or the photograph in an artistic poster, and printed 100,000 posters (without Tiger Woods' name appearing anywhere on the poster) for sale in sporting goods stores and mass merchandisers (e.g. Walmart, Target, Costco, Kmart), would the Court hold that was not commercial speech?

4. The Court states that "[T]he public interest in free expression should prevail if the use of the celebrity's image has artistic relevance, unless it is used in such a way that it explicitly misleads as to the source of the work." What is the definition of "artistic relevance"? Consider a collage with photos of ten famous African-American athletes from different sports, some living and some dead. What about a series of posters featuring Michael Jordan, Tiger Woods, Jackie Robinson, Rosa Parks, and Martin Luther King, Jr.? Based on the analysis in *ETW*, should there be First Amendment protection for a poster that consists of a photograph of Tiger Woods superimposed on top of a picture of the Earth, suggesting that Woods is a sports figure of worldwide importance (or just that given his recent successes, he must be feeling "on top of the World")? Could a fast food chain hire Rick Rush to draw twenty different famous athletes in an impressionist style, and put those drawings on its plastic cups along with information about each athlete's career (with or without using the athlete's name)?

5. The *ETW* Court cites approvingly excerpts from the California Supreme Court's decision in *Comedy III Productions, Inc. v. Gary Saderup, Inc.*, 21 P.3d 797 (2001), and interprets them to the effect that if a "work contains significant transformative elements" or whether the celebrity likeness is "one of the raw materials" that are "synthesized" to create the work, or perhaps even if, as is the case with the art of Andy Warhol, the artist is "able to convey a message" "[t]hrough distortion and the careful manipulation of context," the work should receive First Amendment protection from any right of publicity claim. Applying the concepts to the facts in *ETW*, the fact that the lithographs

also contained "images" of Augusta, Tiger Woods' caddy, and other famous golfers meant that Rush could sell the lithographs without having to pay any royalties to Woods. The Court says, "It would be ironic indeed if the presence of the victorious athlete would deny the work First Amendment protection." Do you find it ironic that adding Augusta and the likenesses of other athletes affords a Tiger Woods painting First Amendment protection? Does the Court really think the public is buying the lithograph because the course in the background is Augusta and a message is communicated that Tiger Woods will someday join a "revered group" of golfers, or do they perceive that they are buying a picture of Tiger Woods to hang on their wall? Is another possible interpretation of the lithograph that Tiger Woods is playing at Augusta, a golf course long criticized for its policies concerning women and minority groups, and his performance is being watched by the white golfers who preceded him? Does it matter?

6. When confronted with survey evidence that "62% of the consumers polled indicated that they believed that Woods had an 'affiliation' or 'connection' with Rush's print, or 'approved' or 'sponsored' the print," the *ETW* decision dismisses that evidence out-of-hand, on the basis that even though "some members of the public would draw the incorrect inference," that misunderstanding about Tiger Woods' involvement with the product "is so outweighed by the interest in artistic expression as to preclude application of the [Lanham] Act." The entire purpose of the Lanham Act is to prohibit activities that create "incorrect inferences" that mislead consumers. Do you agree with the dissent that the issue is a fact question for the jury or is the majority correct when it says the Court is responsible for "decid[ing] where the balance should be struck and where the boundaries should be drawn between the rights conferred by the Lanham Act and the protections of the First Amendment"?

7. In deciding whether Rick Rush is violating Tiger Woods' right of publicity, the Court considers that Tiger Woods is already earning millions of dollars from "authorized appearances and endorsements." The majority opinion also suggests that it believes Rush's lithographs put Tiger Woods in a positive light and will not reduce (and may even increase) the commercial value of his likeness. Does this mean that it is more permissible to sell unlicensed posters and pictures of very successful athletes and other individuals? Does a plaintiff in a right to publicity case have to prove that he or she would not have become a rock star or an athlete or an actor or actress if he or she had known that artists could sell pictures of them without consent? Suppose that as a result of the district court decision, a substantial number of manufacturers who had previously paid royalties to ETW based on sales of Tiger Woods video games, posters, coffee mugs, calendars, lunch boxes, backpacks, t-shirts, and other apparel, refuse to renew their licenses and start selling the same products with artistic renderings of Tiger Woods that contain "significant transformative elements." Would that be relevant as to whether Rush's products (and the other products) violate Tiger Woods' right of publicity?

8. The Court also states that "[p]ermitting Woods' right of publicity to trump Rush's right of freedom of expression would extinguish Rush's right to profit from his creative enterprise." If Rush's talent as an artist is substantial, he should be able to create lithographs of an unlimited number of subjects. All Tiger Woods is suggesting is that Rush should not be permitted to capitalize on and profit from the public's interest in Tiger Woods, by selling pictures of Tiger Woods. If Tiger Woods' likeness is an essential "raw material" in Rush's lithographs, why should Rush's creative enterprise be permitted to incorporate that raw material into its products and sell it, without having to pay anything to the person who created and is responsible for the raw material? Is that the unjust enrichment the right of publicity was designed to prevent? Would your view be dif-

ferent if Rush had approached ETW, seeking a license and had been turned down, or if he had approached ETW and been offered a license for $10 per lithograph, or had been offered a license that would require 20% of Rush's revenues to be paid to ETW? Do you believe it should affect your analysis if there were 5 other artists who had licenses from ETW and were paying royalties to ETW based on sales of their lithographs, but had told ETW that if Rush prevailed they would cease paying?

III. League, Team and Event Rights to Restrict Commercial Use of an Association with their Events

When a business seeks to capitalize on the public's interest in a professional athlete without seeking authorization from the athlete, courts had not experienced too much difficulty drawing lines differentiating permissible use (*e.g.*, the *Namath* case), from impermissible use (*e.g.*, the *Palmer* and *Hirsch* cases) until the *ETW* case came along. On the other hand, when a business seeks to capitalize on the public's interest in a sport, it is often difficult to determine whether the business should be required to seek authorization from the professional league or teams in that sport. Similarly, when teams with similar names seek to operate at the professional level in different leagues in the same sport or in different sports, ascertaining when consumer confusion is so great as to justify judicial intervention is no small task.

The legal analysis of these issues is not based on a single legal theory, but, rather, may implicate federal trademark law, federal copyright law, and a variety of common law theories—unfair competition, unjust enrichment, misappropriation, and other tort and contract theories, depending on the specific factual context in which the dispute arises. However, because federal trademark law plays a prominent role in the legal analysis, a short introduction to the basic concepts in this area is useful.

(A) An Introduction to the Basic Concept of Trademark Law

Modern trademark law traces its analytical underpinnings to efforts by craftsmen and members of guilds to identify who produced the goods that were sold in the marketplace. Unlike copyright law and patent law, which seek to afford the owner a property right or a legal monopoly over an invention or artistic work, trademark law is designed to provide information to consumers about the identity and origin of the goods and services that they purchase, from which the consumer can assess the likely quality. The modern trademark is now also a significant device for marketing and advertising.

The purposes of modern trademark law are to protect both businesses, which seeks to communicate with consumers, and the public at large, which pursues information about the goods and services that are offered for sale. Under the common law, the concept of a trademark has long been associated with causes of action for unfair competition and "passing off" asserted by the business that created the goodwill associated with the mark (*i.e.*, prohibiting competitors from passing off or "palming off" their wares as having been produced by another). By preventing others from utilizing his or her marks, a businessperson can protect the goodwill that has been created and the associated market demand for the products, by consistently offering goods and services of high quality. The trademark is afforded legal protection against infringement, both to protect the holder of the mark and his or her investment in the identification of the product, and to protect the public against the infringer's efforts to pass off different products as products made by the holder of the mark.

There are many different definitions of a trademark, but a definition suitable for our purposes is set out in the Lanham Act, the federal trademark statute:

> "The term 'trade-mark' includes any word, name, symbol, or device or any combination thereof adopted and used by a manufacturer or merchant to identify his goods and distinguish them from those manufactured or sold by others."

15 U.S.C. §1127. The Lanham Act also applies to services, but refers to them as "service marks." "A service mark is a symbol or combination of symbols used by a source of services to identify itself to the public and to create in the public consciousness an awareness of the uniqueness of the source and of its services." *M.B. Enterprises, Inc. v. WOKY, Inc.*, 633 F.2d 50, 53–54 (7th Cir. 1980). *See also* 15 U.S.C. §1127 ("The term 'service mark' means a mark used in the sale or advertising of services to identify the services of one person and distinguish them from the services of others.") The law generally considers service marks to be simply a particular kind of trademark, although for some purposes the differences are legally significant. In the context of professional sports, the same mark may be both a trademark and a service mark. For example, a team's marks and logos may identify for consumers both the services provided by the team to fans at the stadium or arena, and products that are officially licensed by the team for sale to the public at large.

Another Lanham Act term of significance is "trade name." A trade name is the name of the company or a corporate name used to identify the business itself. *See, e.g.*, 15 U.S.C. §1127. The Lanham Act distinguishes trade names and trademarks; it is the latter that are to be registered and protected. *See, e.g., Application of the Pennsylvania Fashion Factory, Inc.*, 588 F.2d 1343, 1345 (Ct. Cust. & Pat. App. 1978). Some trade names, such as the names of professional sports teams and leagues, are also used to identify the goods or services associated with that business; thus, they will be both trade names and trademarks or trade names and service marks, or all three. In the context of professional league sports, the names of professional sports leagues, the teams in those leagues, and league events (e.g. the Super Bowl, the World Series), as well as the logos, uniforms, and other identifying marks and symbols, are all subjects of potential trademark protection. Similarly, the names of circuits of events (*e.g.*, ATP Tour, PGA Tour) or individual events (*e.g.*, Wimbledon, the Masters golf tournament, the NCAA's March Madness, the Kentucky Derby, the various college bowl games, the New York City Marathon), and other marks and logos associated with those circuits and events, may be defended by their owners asserting claims against alleged infringers.

The theory underlying trademarks is that the merchant's use of the trademark serves the economic function of providing information to consumers. The trademark stamped or printed on goods or affixed to the packaging in which goods are sold, and the service mark included in the merchant's advertisements or displayed on the premises from which the merchant conducts business, all serve the function of providing the consumer with information about the source and quality of the goods or services.

Based on past experiences with the holder of the mark or in consuming goods or services that bore that mark, one can assess the quality of the products and the mark holder's overall responsiveness to the consumer's needs or desires. For example, the mark may indicate to the consumer that: (1) these goods are always of excellent quality;

(2) the business premises are always clean and well-maintained, with proper security for the consumer's well-being; (3) the mark holder stands by her product; (4) defective products will be replaced promptly or inadequate services remedied; and (5) the prices charged will be reasonable. Virtually every type of business, from airlines to fast food establishments, rely on their mark to communicate to the consumer information about the quality of their products or services and other aspects of their operations. Consumers are thereby provided with information with which they can make reasoned decisions about products or services that they might purchase.

Trademark law protects mark holders and their often substantial investments in advertising, promotional efforts, commitment to quality, and other means of establishing the identification of their products. At the same time, it protects the public against infringers' efforts to pass off their products as produced by the holder of the mark. The Lanham Act gives registrants of marks under the federal scheme a cause of action in federal court against persons who infringe on federally registered trademarks or service marks. 15 U.S.C. §114. The Trademark Counterfeiting Act of 1984 provides criminal penalties for anyone who "intentionally traffics or attempts to traffic in goods or services and knowingly uses a counterfeit mark on or in connection with such goods or services * * *" 18 U.S.C. §2320. In addition, state common law and statutory provisions protect trademark holders from infringing uses.

(B) Ambush Marketing and Free Riding

In the cases that follow this section, courts are called upon to adjudicate disputes concerning commercial ventures (including governmental entities) that are marketing a product or service that consumers typically associate with a sport or a particular professional league or team that competes in that sport. The owners of sports teams, leagues, and events are aware that their popularity, together with the media and fan attention and interest in their products and services have tremendous value.

For example, many consumers want to associate themselves with a particular sport, league, team, or sporting event. Fans and other consumers carry athletic bags that bear the marks and logos of sports organizations (e.g., U.S. Soccer, ATP Tour), wear team caps, use credit cards that bear team logos, and don shirts that identify particular sporting events (e.g., the 1997 U.S. Open Tennis Tournament). In these ways, the consumer may profess his or her loyalty to, and interest in, the sport, advertise to others that he or she is a fan of the home team and, perhaps, seek out and create a connection with others who share that loyalty or who root for the team's arch rival, or let the world know that he or she attended a prestigious event.

The various business participants in each professional sport, which may be referred to as the professional sport's "inner circle"—the leagues, circuits, owners, teams, event producers, players, players associations, television companies, sponsors, and equipment manufacturers—all seek to benefit from the commercial opportunities that result. In addition, businesses not within the "inner circle," and those with no legitimate association with the sport, may also attempt to capitalize on these business opportunities. The members of the inner circle will contend that they (or even a smaller subset of the inner circle) are the only businesses permitted to capitalize, and that all others need a license from those entities who control the sport. The inner circle will attack those entities who try to capitalize without a license as infringers, ambush marketers, or worse. The businesses that seek to capitalize without a license will contend that their conduct is protected as free speech, or simply is creative marketing and advertising that does not infringe upon anything that belongs to, or is legitimately controlled by, "inner circle" enterprises.

The outside businesses can use a wide variety of techniques. One approach is simply to utilize confusingly similar marks and logos; but that approach presents substantial litigation and liability risks. *See, e.g., NFL Properties, Inc., v. New Jersey Giants, Inc.* case, below. Another stratagem is to use images and themes that do not employ any official trademarks or logos. For example, companies that do not pay to become official sponsors of the Olympic Games may produce commercials, promotions, and other advertising that refer to the "Summer Games" or the "Winter Games." Similarly, the NCAA March Madness may be referred to as the men's collegiate basketball championships and the NCAA Final Four is the "men's college basketball finals." *See also NFL v. Governor of Delaware*, below.

When a business seeks to reach the fans who are attending a particular event or game, merely by purchasing vending space near the official venue or by flying over the venue with banners, it is possible to reach that audience and to capitalize on the efforts of the league, teams, or event producers who assembled that audience. In addition, as discussed earlier in this chapter, by employing one or more prominent athletes associated with a team or event, the outside business may create a public association between its products and the sports operation.

Another approach that has been employed is to use game or event tickets or officially licensed merchandise as the advertised prize for a sweepstakes or promotion. The prize may create the public assumption that the business running the sweepstakes is an official sponsor or is otherwise associated with the event, team, or league. On the other hand, even if consumers are aware that there is no official connection between the business and the event, league, or team, the business hopes that consumers' positive view of the professional sport and its inner circle may be transferred to the product associated with the sweepstakes.

When disputes about these business strategies are submitted to the courts, judges must assess which strategies are "fair" or permissible and which are "unfair," "improper," or unlawful. The inner circle sports businesses will attempt to convince the court that the conduct of the alleged infringer: (1) constitutes a theft or misappropriation of something created by the sports business that belongs to it; (2) deprives the sports business of such an important benefit that its deprivation will discourage other businesses from engaging in the effort to produce similar benefits in the future (similar to the idea that patent infringement will discourage invention and copyright infringement will discourage artistic and literary contributions); (3) rewards the infringer unjustly; and (4) advantages the infringer unfairly in his or her competition with the sports business, because the infringer can compete without having to incur the costs typically absorbed by the sports business.

One issue not likely to be addressed by the sports business suing an alleged infringer is the fact that even a clearly improper infringement may be a net benefit to the sport as a whole. For example, consider a computer software manufacturer's development and marketing of a very popular children's computer baseball game that educates users about the rules of baseball and statistical information about Major League Baseball players. The game may be the seed that yields a permanent crop of avid baseball fans which may be harvested by Major League Baseball and its teams for years to come. Those young fans in the future presumably will buy tickets to games, watch broadcasts of games, purchase licensed products, and teach their children to be the next generation of fans. Therefore, as the courts consider the legal and public policy questions associated with these disputes, there are difficult questions about where the appropriate lines should be drawn. What rights belong to the sports businesses? Which products, services, and advertisements are merely legitimate efforts to reach people who are interested in a sport and which are improper efforts to appropriate a right or asset that belongs to the professional league, team, or event?

You have already seen how this battle is waged between businesses and players, with the "right of publicity" and other legal theories as the rules of engagement. We now turn to consider the battle between outside commercial (or governmental) interests and the leagues, teams, and promoters that produce the games and events, and the rules of engagement that govern their combat.

National Football League Properties, Inc. v. New Jersey Giants, Inc.

637 F. Supp. 507 (D.N.J. 1986)

BARRY, District Judge. Plaintiff, the New York Football Giants, Inc., owns and operates the New York Giants, a major league professional football team which plays all of its home games in New Jersey yet eschews a New Jersey identification as resolutely as a vampire eschews the cross. Defendant, the New Jersey Giants, Inc., which is decidedly not a major league professional football team, was created and exists solely to illegally exploit the confusion engendered by the unwillingness of the team to correlate its name with the place it calls home. The other party to the case, plaintiff National Football League Properties, Inc. ("NFLP"), is the marketing arm of the twenty-eight present National Football League ("NFL") Member Clubs, and is licensed by those Clubs to use the NFL marks to promote the interests of the NFL and the Clubs while protecting those marks from infringement, dilution, misappropriation, and unfair competition.

Defendant, sensing an opportunity to exploit the anomaly of a team bearing the name of one state while playing in another, began to sell various items of sports-related apparel bearing the words "New Jersey GIANTS". Plaintiffs contend that defendant, as a result, has violated §32(1) of the Lanham Act, 15 U.S.C. §1114(1) and §43(a) of the Lanham Act, 15 U.S.C. §1125(a) (service mark infringement and unfair competition); the New Jersey Trademark Act, N.J.S.A. 56:3-13.11; common law trademark infringement and unfair competition; tortious misappropriation of good will; and tortious interference with business relationships. They seek, among other relief, a permanent injunction, various damage awards, and attorneys' fees, costs, and expenses.

This opinion, of necessity, will analyze the host of violations pressed by plaintiffs in light of the facts as found and the law as applicable. I note at the outset, however, that the testimony of the three principals of this three man defendant corporation, who are not themselves named as defendants, goes very far in and of itself towards proving the violations with which defendant is charged and the propriety of certain of the relief sought. These men testified that one of the purposes for starting the business and incorporating the name, as they had previously incorporated the name "New Jersey Cosmos", was to sell the corporate name to the Giants' football team; that the other purpose was to sell the merchandise to fans of the Giants' football team who would associate and "no doubt" did associate that merchandise with the team; that even though in its best year the company sold but $2263.85 of merchandise and operated out of a law office, a post office box, and the back seat of the car of one of the principals,

$30,000 worth of stock in the company has now been sold to three additional individuals; that two cease and desist letters were ignored with defendant, through its principals, continuing to do business and continuing to solicit business by means of radio spots which were intended to refer to the New York Giants' team and by means of advertisements in the "Giants News Weekly", a newsletter directed to Giants' fans and the subject of which was the team; and that these actions continued until such time as a temporary restraining order was entered with notice to but no appearance by any representative of defendant.

What came through from this testimony was an attempt to ride the New York Giants' coattails for one reason and one reason only—money. Defendant's attempt to foist upon the court a first amendment rationalization for its illegal actions and now to clothe those actions in justifications of "editorial content", "right to comment", and altruism are, in a word, incredible. Indeed, at no time from the inception of the New Jersey Giants, Inc., until the restraining order was entered was any hint given much less statement made in any ad placed in the print media or on radio or anywhere else that these individuals had any view about the team changing its name. Certainly, defendant's merchandise itself bearing the words "New Jersey GIANTS" over an outline of the State of New Jersey conveys no message whatsoever. And, I note, that separate and apart from the testimony of defendant's three principals, adduced on plaintiffs' case, defendant presented but one witness, an "expert" to whose opinion I accord no weight.

When all of the foregoing is considered together with the substantial additional evidence plaintiffs have presented, the conclusions I reach are inexorable. It is to that evidence and those conclusions that I now turn.

FINDINGS OF FACT

Each of the 28 Member Clubs of the NFL owns and operates a professional football team engaged in providing entertainment services by playing competitive professional football games in various cities throughout the United States. The NFL Constitution establishes the New York Football Giants' home territory as the area within a seventy-five mile radius of the City of New York and, thus, the Giants' fans are concentrated in the New York metropolitan area which includes portions of New York, New Jersey, and Connecticut.

In the New York Football Giants' sixty-year history, home games have been played at several locations in the New York metropolitan area: the Polo Grounds, Manhattan, New York (1925–1955); Yankee Stadium, Bronx, New York (1956–September, 1973); Yale Bowl, New Haven, Connecticut (1973–1974);[2] Shea Stadium, Queens, New York (1975); and Giants' Stadium, East Rutherford, New Jersey (1976–present). The New York Football Giants' decision to move to New Jersey was made in 1971 at which time an agreement was entered into with the New Jersey Sports and Exposition Authority under which the Giants agreed to play home games in East Rutherford, New Jersey, less than seven miles from midtown Manhattan, upon completion of the construction of Giants' Stadium. To maintain continuity of tradition, the Giants retained the name "New York Giants" when it began playing home games in New Jersey. This decision is embodied in the New York Football Giants' agreement with the New Jersey Sports and Exposition Authority.

---

2. The court notes that the Giants' foray into Connecticut was not necessarily by choice. During this period, the Giants were essentially homeless because Yankee Stadium was being renovated and suitable arrangements had not as yet been made at the other New York stadium.

To identify and distinguish their respective football teams and the entertainment services that they provide, the New York Football Giants and other NFL Member Clubs have adopted and have used in interstate commerce various names, logos, designs, color combinations, uniforms, and other identifying marks ("NFL marks"). The New York Football Giants' marks have been registered under federal law pursuant to the provisions of the United States Trademark Act of 1946, 15 U.S.C. §1051 et seq., ("the Lanham Act") and under the statutory laws of the states of New Jersey and New York. Among these registered marks are included the marks "Giants" and "New York Giants" which are service marks for entertainment services in the form of professional football games and exhibitions. The marks "Giants" and "New York Giants" have been continuously used by the Club since 1925, and throughout its

history the team has referred to itself and has been known by the media and fans as the "New York Giants" or the "Giants".

Because of the popularity of NFL football and the extensive media coverage it receives, the NFL marks, including those long standing marks of the Giants, are nationally recognized and have become well known in the metropolitan area in which each Member Club plays its home games. Moreover, the popularity of NFL football coupled with NFLP's promotional efforts which, as will become apparent, involved extensive advertising and culminated in an extraordinary volume of sales, have combined to create a public perception and consumer awareness that merchandise bearing the NFL marks is sponsored or authorized by the NFL and its Member Clubs. The NFL marks and, more particularly, "Giants" and "New York Giants," have achieved secondary meaning as identifiers of the NFL and its Member Clubs.

NFLP has established a licensing program in which it licenses selected companies to use the NFL marks on specific articles of merchandise and in approved promotional programs. NFLP has issued over one hundred national and local licenses for use of the NFL marks on a wide variety of merchandise including t-shirts, sweatshirts, caps, jackets, other wearing apparel, novelty items, sporting goods, toys and games and home furnishings, and apparel bearing the marks "Giants" and "New York Giants" has been manufactured and sold under NFLP license for many years. Moreover, the NFLP has established a quality control program in which it supervises and approves the conception, design, color combinations, production and distribution of all merchandise licensed to bear the marks of the Giants and other NFL Clubs.

Licensed articles of merchandise bearing NFL marks are sold by licensees throughout the United States in a wide range of distribution channels, such as mail order catalogs, major retail department store chains, and small retail sporting goods and athletic wear stores, including outlets in New York and New Jersey. NFLP's licensees have invested significant amounts of capital and have devoted substantial amounts of time to the production, marketing and promotion of merchandise bearing the NFL marks. For the four year fiscal period beginning April 1, 1980 and ending March 31, 1984, retail sales of NFLP licensed merchandise were in excess of four hundred million dollars ($400,000,000). NFLP derives income in the form of royalty payments from these retail sales. * * *

There is not nearly as much to say about the recent interloper that calls itself the New Jersey Giants, Inc. * * * Indeed, the New Jersey Giants, Inc. has engaged in no business other than the sale of unlicensed apparel bearing the mark "New Jersey GIANTS". Defendant's "New Jersey GIANTS" merchandise has been offered for sale and sold at retail outlets, including the Economy Store in Stanhope, New Jersey and Bowling Green Golf

Course Pro Shop. Additionally, defendant unsuccessfully attempted to sell its merchandise to the sports apparel buyer for Hermans' World of Sporting Goods' one hundred ten (110) stores, a major source of NFLP licensed merchandise, including that bearing the Giants' marks. Defendant also sold merchandise in the years 1981 to 1984 through direct mail order sales, with 25% of those customers ordering from eight states outside New Jersey.

By letter dated January 4, 1984, NFLP's attorneys requested that defendant cease and desist from the solicitation and sale of "New Jersey GIANTS" merchandise. No response was forthcoming. By letter dated February 13, 1984, NFLP's attorneys advised defendant that it would take legal action if defendant engaged in such conduct in the future. Again, no response was forthcoming. The NFLP presumed that defendant ceased its activities after the NFL football season ended, as consumer demand for merchandise bearing the NFL marks is highest during the NFL football season which begins in August with pre-season games and culminates with the NFL Championship Game known as the "Super Bowl" in late January.

But defendant neither ceased its activities nor changed its mark; rather, it escalated its business activities by placing ads on the radio commencing in the spring of 1984, placing large ads in the "Giants Newsweekly" in May and July 1984, and soliciting Hermans' World of Sporting Goods in the summer of 1984. Shortly before the NFL pre-season games began, NFLP learned that defendant was actively engaged in the advertising, offering for sale, distribution and sale of a line of sportswear bearing the inscription "New Jersey GIANTS" which included t-shirts, mesh shirts, sport shirts, sweatshirts, ¾-length sleeve football shirts, hooded sweatshirts, hats, golf hats, shorts, sweatpants, sweatsuits and windbreakers. The design of every item of defendant's "New Jersey GIANTS" merchandise displayed the word "GIANTS" more prominently than the descriptive geographic term "New Jersey" and used, on all but the earliest manufactured item, navy blue lettering, one of the Giants' team colors.

Defendant's "New Jersey GIANTS" merchandise competes directly with licensed NFL merchandise bearing the New York Football Giants' marks, because NFLP has licensed the same types of merchandise sold by defendant. Moreover, defendant's "New Jersey GIANTS" merchandise is likely to confuse consumers into believing that it is part of the wide array of licensed merchandise sponsored and approved by the New York Football Giants and available to the public through NFLP's licensing program.

But the Giants and NFLP have no control over defendant's business activities or over the nature and clearly inferior quality of the merchandise sold by defendant and, indeed, the quality of that merchandise does not satisfy the quality control standards imposed by NFLP on its licensees. The sale of inferior quality merchandise bearing the NFL marks, or colorable imitations thereof, will adversely affect NFLP's business including the poor impression of the NFL and its Member clubs that will be held by the consumer.

Because the demand for merchandise bearing the NFL marks is finite, any sales of unlicensed merchandise bearing those marks will cause direct economic harm to NFLP's licensees thus reducing the royalties payable by licensees to NFLP and reducing the size of the fund available for NFL Charities. Defendant's activities in the sale of its "New Jersey GIANTS" merchandise will interfere, as well, with NFLP's business and cause harm to its reputation and goodwill with licensees and retailers actively promoting the products of NFLP's licensees. If NFLP is unable to abide by its agreement to protect licensees from companies that use the NFL marks without authorization, licensees will lose confidence in the NFLP's licensing program and the value of a license will be impaired thus harming the business of NFLP.

Defendant's use of its trade name and the solicitation and sale of "New Jersey GIANTS" merchandise is also likely to confuse the public into believing that the New York Football Giants has changed the team's name to the New Jersey Giants or does not object to being referred to by that name. Neither is true, of course, and while one may wonder why the New York Giants resist a new name and may wish, perhaps, that it were otherwise, the fact remains that the Giants have the right to retain the long-standing goodwill and reputation they have developed in the name "New York Giants" and efforts in that regard will be undermined were defendant's conduct permitted to continue. * * *

CONCLUSIONS OF LAW

It is undisputed that "Giants" and "New York Giants" are valid service marks worthy of protection. Under the common law and the Lanham Act, owners of service marks and owners of trademarks are protected from other marks that are likely to cause confusion. However, assuming the New York Football Giants' marks are not distinctive marks, the Giants only have protection if their marks possessed secondary meaning at the time defendant commenced its use of them. * * *

Secondary meaning exists when the trademark is interpreted by the consuming public to be not only an identification of the product, but also a representation of the product's origin. * * * [It] is generally established through extensive advertising which creates in the mind of consumers an association between different products bearing the same mark. This association suggests that the products originate from a single source. * * * Once a trademark which could not otherwise have exclusive appropriation achieves secondary meaning, competitors can be prevented from using a similar mark. The purpose of this rule is to minimize confusion of the public as to the origin of the product and to avoid diversion of customers misled by a similar mark. * * *

A strong showing of secondary meaning in the marks "Giants" and "New York Giants" has been made.

In a case for service mark or trademark infringement and unfair competition, a plaintiff is entitled to a permanent injunction against a defendant by showing that that defendant's activities are likely to confuse consumers as to the source or sponsorship of the goods. * * * In order to be confused, a consumer need not believe that a plaintiff actually produced a defendant's merchandise and placed it on the market. Rather, a consumer's belief that a plaintiff sponsored or otherwise approved the use of the mark satisfies the confusion requirement. * * *

In a suit, as here, involving competing goods, the relevant factors to be considered in a determination as to whether a likelihood of confusion exists are:

(1) The degree of similarity between the owner's mark and the alleged infringing mark;

(2) The strength of the owner's mark;

(3) The price of the goods and other factors indicative of the care and attention expected of consumers when making a purchase;

(4) The length of time the defendant has used the mark without evidence of actual confusion;

(5) The intent of the defendant in adopting the mark;

(6) The evidence of actual confusion.

Scott Paper Co. v. Scott's Liquid Gold, Inc., [439 F. Supp. 1022,] 1036–37 [(D. Del. 1977), *rev'd on other grounds*, 589 F.2d 1225 (3d Cir. 1978)]. * * *

Defendant's mark "New Jersey GIANTS" is similar to the Giants' registered marks "New York Giants" and "Giants" and the dominant element of the mark — "Giants" — is identical, rendering those marks particularly confusing. * * * Confusion stems as well from defendant's misuse of the New York Giants' reputation and good will as embodied in the latter's similar marks. A defendant cannot escape the reach of the trademark laws by simply injecting a name in front of the allegedly infringed mark and claiming that this act differentiates or distinguishes the marks regardless of the similarity between or identity of the two marks without inclusion of the new name. * * *

The second *Scott* factor is similarly satisfied. Through extensive media coverage and commercial use, the NFL marks, including those of the Giants, are extremely strong, * * * and, accordingly, are entitled to a wide range of protection. * * *

With reference to the third *Scott* factor, the likelihood of confusion in this case is enhanced because both NFLP's licensed apparel bearing the Giants' marks and defendant's apparel, which is the same type of apparel, are low to moderately priced and purchasers will not exercise a high degree of care in determining whether the merchandise has been sponsored or approved by the NFL and the Giants. * * *

Defendant, which only began selling its merchandise in 1982 and had total sales of less than $5000.00 at the time its activities were halted by the restraining order, used the mark without evidence of actual confusion. In establishing the existence of a likelihood of confusion in actions such as this, however, there is no requirement that incidents of actual confusion be shown * * *, and such evidence is unnecessary where other factors so strongly suggest the likelihood of confusion. * * *

However, the consumer survey conducted by Dr. Jacoby and Guideline Research demonstrated substantial actual confusion and a substantial potential for further actual confusion. The results of the survey, which found that over 57% of respondents were actually and likely confused and that football fans were confused in even higher percentages (67%), is extremely strong evidence of likely confusion, * * * and far in excess of the evidence relied upon by courts for this purpose. * * *

Plaintiffs have established that the survey relied upon in this action was conducted in accordance with accepted principles of survey research. It is the type of study employed in the vast majority of market research and relied upon by experts in the field. * * *

Were this a case in which the defendant was acting in good faith, the court would point to the fact that defendant has adduced no survey evidence or testimony from any retailers or merchandisers, and has otherwise failed to provide any credible evidence to rebut plaintiffs' survey results (which corroborate plaintiffs' convincing evidential showing) that demonstrate both secondary meaning and a strong likelihood of confusion arising from defendant's activities. Here, little more need be pointed to than defendant's bad faith.[6]

---

6. The evidence of bad faith is so clear that the court will not even address defendant's offer to accompany prospective use of its infringing mark with a disclaimer.

Defendant's adoption of the mark New Jersey Giants with the hope or expectation that the Giants would acquire such mark from defendant at a profit to defendant and its principals manifests bad faith. Similarly, defendant Giants' bad faith in adopting the mark "New Jersey Giants" is evidenced by the admitted intention of its principals to have consumers associate its mark with the football Giants thereby breaching its duty to select a mark as far afield as possible from well known existing marks such as "New York Giants" and "Giants". * * * Moreover, defendant's continuation of its activities after receipt of plaintiffs' cease and desist letters constitutes bad faith and is deemed to be an actual and original intention to confuse consumers. * * *

Defendant's intentional, willful, and admitted adoption of a mark closely similar to the existing marks "Giants" and "New York Giants" manifested not only an intent to confuse but raised the presumption that there was a likelihood of confusion, thus shifting the burden of proof to defendant to establish that there was no likelihood of confusion arising out of the sale of its merchandise bearing the words "New Jersey GIANTS".[7] * * *

Defendant utterly failed to sustain its burden of proof at trial by failing to present any evidence to rebut the presumption that there was a likelihood of confusion and, for this reason alone, plaintiffs would be entitled to relief. When the appearance of defendant's merchandise and the conduct of defendant in advertising and marketing its merchandise are considered, the evidence that there is a likelihood of confusion is powerful. * * *

Defendant's use of the Giants' marks is likely to cause confusion or mistake or deceive purchasers of such merchandise as to the source, sponsorship or approval by the NFL and the Giants. It does not, however, constitute infringement of plaintiff Giants' service mark registrations in violation of §32 of the Lanham Act, 15 U.S.C. §1114(1).

* * * While service mark infringement is governed by the same principles as trademark infringement, there is a critical distinction—the distinction between goods and services. "While a trademark serves to identify and distinguish the source and quality of a tangible product, a service mark functions to identify and distinguish the source and quality of an intangible service." 1 McCarthy, Trademarks and Unfair Competition, §19.29 at 935 (2d ed. 1984 & 1985 Supp.) Here, the marks are used on a variety of goods and not used as to services. Moreover, the licensing and sale of this merchandise is beyond "entertainment services in the form of football games and exhibitions."

Plaintiffs would have me find that the sale of merchandise bearing the Giants' marks is designed to promote these entertainment services. The testimony, however, is that the professional football games, particularly if the team is successful, promotes the sale of the merchandise; indeed, the sale of the merchandise is a "direct offshoot" of the services the team provides on the field. Perhaps the game promotes the goods but there is nothing before me to suggest that the goods promote the game.

Defendant's use of the Giants' marks does constitute, however, the use of false designations of origin and false description or representation as to the source, sponsorship or approval of such merchandise by the NFL and the Giants in violation of Section 43(a) of the Lanham Act, §15 U.S.C. 1125(a). * * *

---

7. Similarly, courts have found a presumption of secondary meaning, unrebutted here, by a showing of deliberate and close imitation of or an attempt to capitalize on a senior user's mark. * * *

New Jersey has codified the common law authority of unfair competition at N.J.S.A. 56:4-1. As observed by the Third Circuit, "the federal law of unfair competition [as codified at §1125] is not significantly different, as it bears upon this case, from that of New Jersey." *SK & F Company v. Premo Pharmaceutical Lab., Inc.*, 625 F.2d 1055, 1065 (3d Cir. 1980). As it bears upon this case, having found liability under §43(a) of the Lanham Act, judgment will be entered for plaintiffs on the state law claim because defendant's use of the Giants' marks is likely to cause confusion or mistake or to deceive purchasers of such merchandise as to the source, sponsorship, or approval by the NFL and the Giants. Such conduct is also in violation of N.J.S.A. 56:3-13.11.

Defendant's conduct constitutes, as well, a tortious misappropriation of the goodwill and reputation of NFLP, the NFL and the Giants. * * *

Defendant's conduct further constitutes tortious interference with the business relationships of NFLP, the NFL and the Giants with NFLP's licensees, with retailers of licensed merchandise and with the ultimate consumers of licensed merchandise. * * *

The likelihood of confusion caused by defendant's conduct establishes that plaintiffs have been and will be irreparably harmed absent injunctive relief. Remedying the likelihood of confusion in the marketplace arising from defendant's conduct will protect the public interest. Plaintiffs are, therefore, entitled to a judgment and decree * * *

Notes and Questions

1. The New Jersey Giants were not a football team and were established primarily to profit from consumers' inability to distinguish between the New York Football Giants and the fictional New Jersey Giants. This fact made the court's task relatively easy. However, consider the case of the Baltimore Colts, who relocated to Indianapolis in 1984, as explained in Chapters 7 and 12. Could the NFL and the Indianapolis Colts prevent a football team in the Canadian Football League ("CFL"), with its principal place of business in Baltimore, from conducting business as the CFL Baltimore Colts? *See Indianapolis Colts, Inc. v. Metropolitan Baltimore Football Club Limited Partnership*, 34 F.3d 410 (7th Cir. 1994). Is the analysis of the Colts' effort to prevent a team from using their name in the city that they abandoned similar to the analysis of the Los Angeles Dodgers' efforts to prevent a restaurant in their old home town from operating under the name the Brooklyn Dodger Sports Bar and Restaurant? *See Major League Baseball v. Sed Non Olet Denarius*, 817 F. Supp. 1103 (S.D.N.Y. 1993).

2. The Colts are not the only relocating NFL team to be involved in trademark litigation with a team of the same name. When the Cleveland Browns were reincarnated as the Baltimore Ravens, they were sued by a wheelchair basketball team that had played in the same city, under the same name, for more than twenty years. *See* Complaint, *Baltimore Ravens Wheelchair Basketball Club, Inc. v. NFL Properties, Inc.*, Civ. No. 96-2208-WMN (July 17, 1996). The lawsuit was settled on undisclosed terms in October, 1996.

3. When the Washington Bullets of the NBA decided to change their team name to the "Washington Wizards," out of a concern that the term "Bullets" had a negative, pro-violence association, they ran into conflict with the Harlem Wizards, a comedic basketball team formed in the tradition of the better-known Harlem Globetrotters. Could the saturation of the market for licensed products by the NBA cause consumers to believe that the Harlem Wizards is an infringer in the spirit of the New Jersey Giants, seeking to appropriate fan interest in a major league professional sports team? *See Harlem Wizards Entertainment Basketball, Inc. v. NBA Properties, Inc.*, 952 F. Supp. 1084 (D.N.J. 1997).

4. Major League Baseball faced similar litigation when the Las Vegas Diamondbacks, a professional softball team, sued the Arizona Diamondbacks. *See* Complaint, *Las Vegas Diamondbacks v. Arizona Diamondbacks*, CV-S-95-344 (D. Neb. 1995). The plaintiffs were unable to prove a likelihood of consumer confusion, leading to a decision for the defendants.

5. Is the judicial concern about confusion and misidentification generally limited to teams in the same sport? Why should the Indianapolis Colts of the NFL have a claim against the CFL Baltimore Colts in another football league, while the San Francisco Giants of Major League Baseball have no apparent concerns about the New York Giants of the NFL? The NHL's Los Angeles Kings and the NBA's Sacramento Kings share the same state and the same nickname. There are also Panthers in Florida (NHL) and Carolina (NFL), Rangers in New York (NHL) and Texas (MLB), and for many years there were Oilers in Edmonton (NHL) and Houston (NFL). The New York Football Giants and MLB's Giants even shared the City of New York for many years, and the Cardinals played both baseball and football in St. Louis before Bill Bidwill relocated his NFL Cardinals to Arizona. Similarly, the Kansas City Wizards of Major League Soccer were evidently unconcerned about the new name for the NBA's team in Washington. In college sports, many NCAA schools share the same nickname, to such an extent that in the 1997 NCAA basketball tournament four teams were the Tigers, five teams were Cats (Bobcats, Bearcats and three Wildcats), and four teams were Golden (Golden Bears, Golden Hurricane, and two Golden Eagles). *See* Samuel Chi, College Basketball, *The San Francisco Examiner*, Mar. 10, 1997, at B-4. The NCAA final game matched the Arizona Wildcats and the Kentucky Wildcats. While those common nicknames may have been a chore for play-by-play announcers (and, perhaps, newspaper headline writers), they did not result in trademark litigation. How could a new professional sports team use those facts in defending a trademark lawsuit filed by an older, more established team from another city, but with the same team name?

6. As illustrated above, and as discussed in the reported decisions, knowledgeable sports fans are not likely to be confused in this area—they know that: (1) the Harlem Wizards are not the Washington Wizards; (2) the Baltimore CFL Colts (who were renamed the Stallions) played in a different professional football league (with slightly different rules on a longer field) than the Indianapolis Colts; and (3) the Clemson Tigers are not to be confused with the Princeton Tigers. Knowledgeable sports fans certainly would not go to the wrong game or purchase merchandise associated with the wrong team. Is the source of judicial concern a fear that a non-fan will erroneously purchase the wrong product? *But see* the discussion in *WCVB-TV v. Boston Athletic Ass'n*, below, regarding the exclusion of indifferent consumers when assessing the likelihood of confusion. In the case of the Indianapolis Colts, was the NFL more concerned about confusion concerning sponsorship or the unstated criticism of the 1984 Colts' middle-of-the-night relocation to Indiana that motivated the Baltimore fans' demand that the CFL name its Baltimore football team the Colts? Or, was NFL Properties trying to preserve its ability to sell or license others to sell old Baltimore Colts helmets, jerseys, and other memorabilia to consumers in Maryland? If the CFL Baltimore Colts could prove that one of the latter two concerns were the NFL's motivation in seeking to enjoin the use of the name "Colts," should that change the legal analysis?

7. If the issue is likelihood of confusion, could the CFL Baltimore Colts have solved the problem by advertising that the CFL team had absolutely no association with the National Football League? If the vast majority of the CFL Baltimore CFL Colts' licensed products will be sold in the State of Maryland, does it matter if consumers in Indiana or

California are likely to be confused? Consider those issues as you read about the NFL's lawsuit challenging the Delaware Lottery.

National Football League v. Governor of Delaware
435 F. Supp. 1372 (D. Del. 1977)

STAPLETON, District Judge: In August 1976, the Office of the Delaware State Lottery announced a plan to institute a lottery game based on games of the National Football League ("NFL"). Immediately thereafter, the NFL and its twenty-eight member clubs filed suit in this Court against the Governor and the Director of the State Lottery seeking preliminary and permanent injunctive relief barring such a lottery scheme. The State of Delaware intervened, and the complaint was amended to add a request that the Court create a constructive trust on behalf of the NFL clubs of all revenues derived from such a lottery. Finding no threat of immediate irreparable injury to the NFL, the Court denied the prayer for a temporary restraining order.

During the week of September 12, 1976, the football lottery games commenced. Upon defendants' motion, the Court dismissed plaintiffs' claims that the games violated the Equal Protection Clause of the Fourteenth Amendment and the Commerce Clause of the Constitution. With respect to twelve other counts, defendants' motion to dismiss or for summary judgment was denied. The lottery games continued through the season.

In late Fall, a six day trial on the merits was held. That was followed by extended briefing. The matter is now ripe for disposition. This Opinion constitutes the Court's findings of fact and conclusions of law on the questions presented.

FACTUAL BACKGROUND

The Delaware football lottery is known as "Scoreboard" and it involves three different games, "Football Bonus", "Touchdown" and "Touchdown II". All are weekly games based on regularly scheduled NFL games. In Football Bonus, the fourteen games scheduled for a given weekend are divided into two pools of seven games each. A player must mark the lottery ticket with his or her projections of the winners of the seven games in one or both of the two pools and place a bet of $1, $2, $3, $5 or $10. To win Football Bonus, the player must correctly select the winner of each of the games in a pool. If the player correctly selects the winners of all games in both pools, he or she wins an "All Game Bonus". The amounts of the prizes awarded are determined on a pari-mutuel basis, that is, as a function of the total amount of money bet by all players.

In Touchdown, the lottery card lists the fourteen games for a given week along with three ranges of possible point spreads. The player must select both the winning team and the winning margin in each of three, four or five games. The scale of possible bets is the same as in Bonus and prizes are likewise distributed on a pari-mutuel basis to those who make correct selections for each game on which they bet.

Touchdown II, the third Scoreboard game, was introduced in mid-season and replaced Touchdown for the remainder of the season. In Touchdown II, a "line" or predicted point spread on each of twelve games is published on the Wednesday prior to the games. The player considers the published point spread and selects a team to "beat the line", that is, to do better in the game than the stated point spread. To win, the player must choose correctly with respect to each of from four to twelve games. Depending upon the number of games bet on, there is a fixed payoff of from $10 to $1,200. There is also a consolation prize for those who beat the line on nine out [of] ten, ten out of eleven or eleven out of twelve games.

Scoreboard tickets are available from duly authorized agents of the Delaware State Lottery, usually merchants located throughout the State. The tickets list the teams by city names, e.g., Tampa or Cincinnati, rather than by nicknames such as Buccaneers or Bengals. Revenues are said to be distributed pursuant to a fixed apportionment schedule among the players of Scoreboard, the State, the sales agents and the Lottery Office for its administrative expenses.

THE PARTIES' CLAIMS

The core of plaintiffs' objections to Scoreboard is what they term a "forced association with gambling". They complain that the football lottery constitutes an unlawful interference with their property rights and they oppose its operation on a host of federal, state and common law grounds. Briefly stated, their complaint includes counts based on federal and state trademark laws, the common law doctrine of misappropriation, the federal anti-gambling laws, the Civil Rights Act of 1871 (42 U.S.C. §1983), the Delaware Constitution and the Delaware lottery statute.

The defendants deny that the state-run revenue raising scheme violates any federal, state or common law doctrine. Further, they have filed a counterclaim for treble damages under the Sherman and Clayton Acts for federal antitrust law violations charging, *inter alia*, that the plaintiffs have brought this litigation for purposes of harassment and that they have conspired to monopolize property which is in the public domain.

For the reasons which follow, I have determined that the plaintiffs are entitled to limited injunctive relief, in the nature of a disclaimer on all Scoreboard materials disseminated to the public. * * *

I. MISAPPROPRIATION

Plaintiffs have proven that they have invested time, effort, talent and vast sums of money in the organization, development and promotion of the National Football League. They have also convincingly demonstrated the success of that investment. The NFL is now a national institution which enjoys great popularity and a reputation for integrity. It generates substantial revenue from gate receipts, broadcasting rights, film rights, and the licensing of its trademarks.

There also can be no dispute that the NFL popularity and reputation played a major role in defendants' choice of NFL games as the subject matter of its lottery. Defendants concede that in making this election they expected to generate revenue which would not be generated from betting on a less popular pastime.

Based on these facts, plaintiffs assert that defendants are misappropriating the product of plaintiffs' efforts—or in the words of the Supreme Court, that the State of Delaware is "endeavoring to reap where it has not sown". *International News Service v. Associated Press*, 248 U.S. 215, 239 (1918) ("*INS*"). Thus, plaintiffs maintain the lottery must be halted and the ill-gotten gains disgorged. This Court has no doubt about the continuing vitality of the *INS* case and the doctrine of misappropriation which it spawned * * * I conclude, however, that plaintiffs' argument paints with too broad a brush.

The only tangible product of plaintiffs' labor which defendants utilize in the Delaware Lottery are the schedule of NFL games and the scores. These are obtained from public sources and are utilized only after plaintiffs have disseminated them at large and no longer have any expectation of generating revenue from further dissemination. This fact distinguishes the situation in *INS*.[3] In that case the Court recognized the right of INS to protection against misappropriation of the news it had collected for so long as that "product" still retained commercial value to AP. The court was careful to note that the injunction issued by the District Court limited the protection granted only until the time when "the commercial value as news to * * * [AP] and all of its * * * [customers had] passed away". 248 U.S. at 245. I do not believe the *INS* case or any other case suggests use of information that another has voluntarily made available to the public at large is an actionable "misappropriation".

Plaintiffs insist, however, that defendants are using more than the schedules and scores to generate revenue for the State. They define their "product" as being the total "end result" of their labors, including the public interest which has been generated.

It is undoubtedly true that defendants seek to profit from the popularity of NFL football. The question, however, is whether this constitutes wrongful misappropriation. I think not.

We live in an age of economic and social interdependence. The NFL undoubtedly would not be in the position it is today if college football and the fan interest that it generated had not preceded the NFL's organization. To that degree it has benefitted from the labor of others. The same, of course, can be said for the mass media networks which the labor of others have developed.

What the Delaware Lottery has done is to offer a service to that portion of plaintiffs' following who wish to bet on NFL games. It is true that Delaware is thus making profits it would not make but for the existence of the NFL, but I find this difficult to distinguish from the multitude of charter bus companies who generate profit from servicing those of plaintiffs' fans who want to go to the stadium or, indeed, the sidewalk popcorn salesman who services the crowd as it surges towards the gate.

While courts have recognized that one has a right to one's own harvest, this proposition has not been construed to preclude others from profiting from demands for collateral services generated by the success of one's business venture. General Motors' cars, for example, enjoy significant popularity and seat cover manufacturers profit from that popularity by making covers to fit General Motors' seats. The same relationship exists between hot dog producers and the bakers of hot dog rolls. But in neither instance, I believe, could it be successfully contended that an actionable misappropriation occurs.

The NFL plaintiffs, however, argue that this case is different because the evidence is said to show "misappropriation" of plaintiffs' "good will" and "reputation" as well as its "popularity". To a large extent, plaintiffs' references to "good will" and "reputation" are simply other ways of stating their complaint that defendants are profiting from a demand plaintiffs' games have generated. To the extent they relate to a claim that defendants' activities have damaged, as opposed to appropriated, plaintiff's good will and reputation, I believe one must look to other lines of authority to determine defendants' culpability. In response to plaintiffs' misappropriation argument, I hold only that de-

---

3. On this same ground, the case can be distinguished from *Zacchini v. Scripps-Howard Broadcasting Co.*, [433 U.S. 562 (1977)]. *Zacchini* upheld a performer's right of publicity in "an entire act that he ordinarily gets paid to perform". * * * The Delaware Scoreboard Lottery is not appropriating the very performances from which the NFL derives its earnings.

fendants' use of the NFL schedules, scores and public popularity in the Delaware Lottery does not constitute a misappropriation of plaintiffs' property.

In the event a differing analysis is determined to be appropriate in the course of appellate review, I should add that the plaintiffs have not demonstrated that the existence of gambling on its games, *per se*, has or will damage its good will or reputation for integrity. By this, I do not suggest that an *association* of the NFL with a gambling enterprise in the minds of the public would not have a deleterious effect on its business. Such an association presupposes public perception of NFL sponsorship or approval of a gambling enterprise or at least confusion on this score, and I treat this subject hereafter. I do find, however, that the existence of gambling on NFL games, unaccompanied by any confusion with respect to sponsorship, has not injured the NFL and there is no reason to believe it will do so in the future. The record shows that extensive gambling on NFL games has existed for many years and that this fact of common public knowledge has not injured plaintiffs or their reputation.

The most prevalent form of such gambling is the illegal form—office polls and head-to-head bets with bookies. Virtually every witness testified that he was familiar with illegal football pools and knew they were available in schools, factories and offices around the country. John J. Danahy, Director of Security for the NFL and a former member of the Federal Bureau of Investigation, estimated that millions of dollars a week are spent for illegal betting on football games and that such gambling provides a major source of income to organized crime.

In addition to the illegal gambling, the evidence shows that there is a substantial volume of legalized sports betting. In Nevada, sports betting, including betting on NFL games, has been legal since 1949. The parties have stipulated that sports betting in Nevada in the fourth quarter of the year, when the betting is primarily on football games, has reached the following levels:

1972	$ 873,318
1973	$ 826,767
1974	$ 3,873,217
1975	$ 26,170,328

These figures represent both "by event" or "head-to-head" betting and parlay card betting. In addition, pool card gambling on professional football has been legal in Montana since 1974. The NFL has not shown that any of this gambling, legal or illegal, has injured the reputation of professional football or the member teams of the NFL.

Some comment on the plaintiffs' survey evidence on this subject is in order. A market survey was conducted at the direction of the plaintiffs for use in this litigation. One of the questions asked of those surveyed was:

> Suppose there would be legalized betting on National Football League games which was run by a state agency in each of the various states. Do you think that the reputation of the National Football League would be better, stay the same or be worse than before legalized betting?

Those who responded that they thought the NFL's reputation would decline were asked in a follow-up question to explain why they thought so. Fifty percent of those responding in the "National" portion of the survey said that they believed the NFL's reputation would be hurt. Those who conducted the survey broke down the reasons given for that belief into four separate categories:

26% Will mean more crime

29% Opposed to betting
19% Throwing or fixing game
30% Takes sportsmanship out of the game

While these results do suggest that gambling on NFL games would adversely affect the NFL, there are several reasons why I cannot credit the data. Most importantly, there is the overwhelming evidence already reviewed that, in actual experience, widespread gambling, both illegal and state-authorized, has not hurt the NFL. That evidence is far more persuasive than survey results based on hypothetical questions.[7]

In addition, there are a number of problems with the form of question used in the survey. It asks the person responding, not whether he or she would think less of the NFL, but rather whether he or she thinks others would have less regard for the NFL. The response is by nature speculation and it is quite conceivable that many who would have no objection to state-run sports betting would assume that others would hold a different view. The question as asked did not elicit relevant information.

Moreover, the question assumed that every state would institute such a program. While it has been suggested that a few other states are considering football lotteries, I have no reason to believe that the Delaware scheme will be imitated by forty-nine other states. In any event, the issue before this Court is whether Delaware's Scoreboard games will injure the NFL's reputation. The question asked in the "national" survey addressed a far broader subject which the plaintiffs have not shown to be relevant.

Finally, the phrasing of the question did not emphasize a proposed system run independently of the NFL. As will be seen that may have influenced some responses.

II. TRADEMARK AND RELATED UNFAIR COMPETITION CLAIMS

The Delaware Lottery does not utilize the NFL name or any of plaintiffs' registered service marks for the purpose of identifying, as opposed to describing, the service which it offers. The name utilized for the football related betting games is "Scoreboard" and the individual games are identified as "Football Bonus", "Touchdown" and "Touchdown II". No NFL insignia or the like are utilized in the advertising. The cards on which the customers of the Delaware Lottery mark their betting choices, however, identify the next week's NFL football games by the names of the cities whose NFL teams are scheduled to compete against each other, *e.g.*, *Philadelphia v. Los Angeles, Washington v. Baltimore, etc.* It is stipulated that, in the context in which they appear, these geographic names are intended to refer to, and are understood to refer to, plaintiffs' football teams. It is in this manner that defendants have made it known that the Delaware Lottery offers the opportunity to bet on NFL football.

Undoubtedly when defendants print "*Philadelphia v. Los Angeles*", the public reads "*Philadelphia Eagles v. Los Angeles Rams*", and, in this sense, the words utilized by defendants have a secondary meaning. But I do not understand this fact alone to constitute infringement of plaintiffs' registered marks or unfair competition. Defendants may truthfully tell the public what service they perform, just as a specialist in the repair of Volkswagen cars may tell the public of his specialty by using the word "Volkswagen", and just as the manufacturer of a razor blade may advertise the brand names of the ra-

---

7. The survey itself bears out the conclusion that those with actual experience with state-run sports betting have far different views than those who are dealing with the question in the abstract. When Delawareans were asked whether the State's football lottery would injure the reputation of the NFL only 22% answered affirmatively. * * *

zors they will fit. The same rule prevails in the area of comparative advertising which utilizes the tradenames of competing products.

What one may not do, however, is to advertise one's services in a manner which creates an impression in the mind of the relevant segment of the public that a connection exists between the services offered and the holder of the registered mark when no such connection exists. Moreover, this legal prohibition imposes a duty to take affirmative steps to avoid a mistaken impression which is likely to arise from a truthful description of the service even though it does not literally suggest a connection.

This case presents a novel situation for application of these well established principles. After carefully reading all of the materials disseminated in connection with the Delaware Lottery, I cannot point to any specific statement, symbol, or word usage which tends to suggest NFL sponsorship or approval. At the same time, however, plaintiffs have convinced me that a substantial portion of the present and potential audience for NFL games believes that the Delaware Lottery is sponsored or approved by the NFL.

In what is denominated the "Delaware Special" portion of the market survey referred to above, 19% of the Delaware residents surveyed and 21% of those designated as "fans", either said that, as far as they knew, the legalized betting on professional football was arranged by the State with the authorization of the teams or said that it was conducted by the teams alone. Before answering, some of those questioned were shown a sample lottery ticket and others were not. The results did not vary significantly between the two groups. These figures establish that there is substantial confusion on the part of the public about the source or sponsorship of the lottery.

This Court perceives only one way to reconcile these survey results with the absence of any affirmative suggestion of sponsorship or approval in the Delaware Lottery advertising and materials. Apparently, in this day and age when professional sports teams franchise pennants, teeshirts, helmets, drinking glasses and a wide range of other products, a substantial number of people believe, if not told otherwise, that one cannot conduct an enterprise of this kind without NFL approval.

While defendants are guilty of no affirmative statements suggesting affiliation and may well not have foreseen that a substantial number of people would infer an association with the NFL, the fact remains that the ultimate result of their promotion of the Delaware Lottery is significant public confusion and the loss to the NFL of control of its public image. I conclude that this fact entitles plaintiffs to some relief.

The only monetary relief sought by plaintiffs—a judgment directing transfer of the proceeds of the Lottery to NFL Charities Incorporated—is inappropriate. These proceeds are not funds that the NFL would have harvested for itself in the absence of the Lottery. Nor is there any reason to believe that the retention by the State of any of these proceeds would result in unjust enrichment. I have previously held that Delaware has a right to profit from a demand for gambling created by NFL games. Relief is appropriate only because of the failure of the defendants to avoid an impression of sponsorship, and this record does not suggest that the proceeds of the Lottery were in any way augmented by any public perception of affiliation. Given the nature of the service provided, I strongly suspect that this limited perception had no effect on revenue.

To eliminate the confusion as to sponsorship, an injunction will be entered requiring the Lottery Director to include on Scoreboard tickets, advertising and any other materials prepared for public distribution a clear and conspicuous statement that Scoreboard is not associated with or authorized by the National Football League.

Officials of the Delaware Lottery volunteered early in this litigation to employ such a disclaimer. The NFL was dissatisfied with the proposal and, as a result, the Lottery Office took no steps to adopt it. Scoreboard tickets were inscribed with the statement, "The 'Scoreboard' Lottery is sponsored solely by the Delaware State Lottery". However, this appeared at the very bottom of the back of the tickets and was not included in defendants' advertising and other promotional materials.

The survey indicates that this approach to the problem was not sufficient to dispel the idea that the NFL was somehow associated with the Lottery. That survey does not suggest to the Court, however, that a prominent statement on all Scoreboard materials disclaiming any affiliation would be insufficient to protect plaintiffs' legitimate interests.

DEFENSES AND COUNTERCLAIMS

By way of affirmative defense, the defendants assert that the NFL is barred from obtaining any injunctive relief from this Court under the doctrines of acquiescence and unclean hands. I conclude that the defendants have established neither defense.

Acquiescence consists of conduct on the part of a trademark holder that amounts to "an assurance to the defendant, express or implied, that the plaintiff would not assert his trademark rights against the defendant". *McCarthy* §31:14. There was no acquiescence here. From the time the NFL learned that Delaware was considering a football lottery, it vigorously voiced its opposition and its belief that such a lottery was incompatible with the NFL's trademark rights.

The course of conduct of which the defendants complain is more consistent with an abandonment defense and it may be that that is the defense they intended to assert. *McCarthy* §31:14, explains the distinction:

> While plaintiff's failure to prosecute trademark uses by parties other than defendants may be evidence of plaintiff's acquiescence in defendant's use, such a failure is not acquiescence where the third party's usage is de minimus. Acquiescence should not be confused with abandonment of trademark rights. The defense of abandonment results in a loss of rights as against the world, while the defense of acquiescence merely results in a loss of rights as against one defendant. [Emphasis in original]

The defendant points to the NFL's failure to bring suit against other gambling related uses of NFL team names such as in the Nevada and Montana betting schemes, in tout sheets which publish predicted point spreads and in newspaper circulation contests.

It would appear that most of the examples the defendants cite are small scale and, in some cases, short lived uses of NFL registered marks. The NFL could reasonably have concluded that there was no risk that the public would be misled into believing that the NFL was involved in any way. And, as *McCarthy* notes, not every *de minimus* use must be pursued.

Football gambling in Nevada would appear to be the only large scale use of NFL names to which the defendants can point in support of their abandonment theory. Numerous representatives of the NFL testified that they considered the situation in Nevada unique and did not believe it posed the same kind of threat to their enterprise. Regardless of the validity of that judgment, an intent to abandon cannot be inferred from the mere failing to bring suit in Nevada. *See McCarthy* §17:5. This is particularly true when one considers the number of instances in which the NFL has brought suit or taken other measures to protect its trademark rights in non-gambling contexts.

Defendants' unclean hands defense is based on what it characterizes as NFL's trademark misuse in its licensing program. Relying on a blank licensing agreement form for proof of its allegations, the defendants complain that the NFL is guilty of using its trademark in violation of the antitrust laws. In particular, defendants claim that all licenses are exclusive, that they are available only in a package deal for the marks of all twenty-eight clubs, that minimum royalty payments are required to pay royalties at a single fixed rate. I need not consider whether these practices alone or together would constitute antitrust violations. The blank form defendants proffer is simply insufficient proof of how the NFL trademark licensing program operates.

In addition to relying on these alleged antitrust violations as the basis of an unclean hands defense, the defendants raise the antitrust claims affirmatively as a counterclaim for treble damages. The failure of proof is quite obviously just as fatal to the counterclaim. Moreover, defendants have not shown that they were injured by the allegedly anti-competitive practices.

CONCLUSION

For all of the reasons discussed in the foregoing Opinion, the Court will enter an Order (1) enjoining the defendants to include in publicly disseminated Scoreboard materials a clear and conspicuous statement that Scoreboard is not associated with or authorized by the National Football League. * * *

Notes and Questions

1. In light of the court's decision in *NFL v. Governor of Delaware*, could a shirt manufacturer market shirts that say "1997 Marathon: 26.2 Miles from from Boston to Hopkington, Massachusetts"? Would it change the analysis if the shirt (or the store that sold the shirt) had a prominent disclaimer: "This Shirt Is Not Affiliated with the Boston Marathon or the Boston Athletic Association"? *See Boston Athletic Ass'n v. Sullivan*, 867 F.2d 22 (1st Cir. 1989).

2. An official sponsor of the NCAA finds that its exclusive sponsorship is not renewed. In an effort to maintain its association with NCAA basketball in the minds of consumers, the sponsor advertises a college basketball promotion that features officially licensed NCAA merchandise. Should the sponsor's promotion be enjoined as a violation of trademark law and an improper misappropriation? *See Host Communications v. Kellogg Co.*, Civ. Action No. 94-26 (E.D. Ky. 1994) (preliminary injunction entered; court found that Kellogg created a false impression of affiliation and a likelihood of confusion as to whether the promotion was licensed by the NCAA or whether Kellogg was associated with the NCAA).

3. Following this 1977 decision by the United States District Court for the District of Delaware, it has generally been assumed by sports businesspersons and their counsel that there is no legal prohibition on the ability of a city or state (*e.g.*, Arizona for the Arizona Cardinals) to identify a professional sports team in advertisements and commercial products. Given the tight restrictions on use of players' names, likenesses, or biographical data, sports entrepreneurs have generally contracted for licenses from players in return for payment of royalties. Moreover, they have often sought to avoid paying leagues or teams by not mentioning the league or team or by using the city and state names for the teams and including a disclaimer similar to the one mandated by the court in *NFL v. Governor of Delaware*. These legal strictures have served to widen further the income dis-

parity between the most popular superstars and the other players in the league. If an advertisement features Michael Jordan, Patrick Ewing, Cal Ripken, Jr., Boomer Esiason, Joe Montana, or other athletes who are highly recognizable by consumers, there may be no need to show the athlete in his team's uniform or to mention the name of his team or the league and, in turn, no obligation to pay them royalties. The athletes whose names and faces are not as easily recognized may not have significant value to advertisers without identifying information—having the athlete wear the recognizable attire of his or her team or stating the name of the team in the advertisement. Use of the uniform or the name of the team or the league requires a license, thereby imposing additional costs on the advertiser and further reducing the amount likely to be offered to the athlete. Ironically, the more that leagues promote their players and raise their consumer profile, the more likely it is that advertisements and products utilizing the players' identities will not mention the leagues or their teams. However, leagues nevertheless seek to promote individual players because of a belief that fan interest in individual professional athletes translates to increased interest in teams, leagues, and sports. Does anyone doubt that the mid-1980s NIKE commercials and promotions featuring Michael Jordan and Spike Lee were among the most important promotions of the NBA, even though the Chicago Bulls and the NBA were never mentioned?

4. The specific problem at issue in *NFL v. Governor of Delaware*, state lotteries based on the outcome of professional sports events, was dormant for about ten years because Delaware terminated the games at issue for other reasons and other states were slow to follow Delaware's lead. Then, in the late 1980s, as lotteries became big business and major sources of revenue for state-funded operations, interest resurfaced. In 1989, Oregon conducted a lottery game based on the scores of NFL games, using only city names and including the prominent disclaimer discussed by the Delaware court. The NFL took no action, perhaps concerned about the collateral estoppel effect of *NFL v. Governor of Delaware*, and perhaps concerned that NFL protestations about the likely deleterious effects of an association with gambling would ring hollow given the history of gambling associated with the NFL, its owners, and its players. For a discussion of the latter topic, *see* Dan E. Moldea, *Interference: How Organized Crime Influences Professional Football* (1989).

Oregon followed its introduction of an NFL game with the announcement of a lottery game based on NBA scores, again using only city names and including a prominent disclaimer that the game was not sponsored by or associated with the NBA. In response, the NBA sued the lottery commission and others involved with the production of the game, asserting RICO claims and other claims under federal and state law. *See* Complaint, *National Basketball Ass'n v. Oregon State Lottery Comm'n*, C.A. No. 89-6470 MA (D. Or. 1989). The RICO claims and many of the NBA's other allegations did not survive a motion to dismiss, but the district court held that the NBA had met the threshold standard to state a claim under the Lanham Act and several state common law claims. *NBA v. Oregon State Lottery Comm'n*, C.A. No. 89-6470 MA (D. Or. 1990). The NBA-based lottery was not very successful and was discontinued by Oregon. As a result the case was settled without significant additional proceedings.

5. Fearing games in other states and concerned about the likely lack of judicial receptiveness to their challenges, the major professional sports leagues took the lottery issue to Congress while the NBA's case against the Oregon lottery was still pending. After several unsuccessful attempts to modify the Lanham Act to prohibit sports-based lotteries and other government authorized sports wagering, in 1992 Congress passed a criminal statute, the Professional and Amateur Sports Protection Act, which makes it unlawful, among other things, for

"a governmental entity to sponsor, operate, advertise, promote, license, or authorize by law or compact * * * a lottery, sweepstakes, or other betting, gambling, or wagering scheme based, directly or indirectly (through the use of geographic references or otherwise), on one or more competitive games in which amateur or professional athletes participate, or are intended to participate, or on one or more performances of such athletes in such games."

28 U.S.C. §§3701, *et seq.*, at §3702. The federal statute specifically exempts the Delaware and Oregon Lottery games, Nevada sports betting in casinos, and other gaming that was authorized by state statutes prior to the enactment of the federal statute. *Id.* at §3704. *See also* 1992 U.S.C.C.A.N., 102nd Cong., 2d Sess. at 3553–3567.

IV. Ownership of Broadcasts and the Right to Report on or Broadcast the Results of Games and Events

The cases discussed above chronicle many different conflicts between, on the one hand, the major professional sports leagues and teams or major professional events and, on the other hand, a variety of other sports teams and entities involved in marketing products and services related to professional sports. The same type of conflict occurs in another major sports arena—the audio, video, and "textual" broadcasting of professional sports events.

When a sports event is broadcast, advertisers know the demographics of the likely audience for that broadcast, and the owner of the broadcast can sell advertising time or another association with the broadcast to the businesses that want to pitch their products and services to the audience. In the early days of professional sports, events were "broadcast" over telephone wires and by telegraph. In 1921, baseball authorized the sale of the radio rights to the World Series for $3,000. See David M. Carter, Keeping Score: An Inside Look at Sports Marketing 11 (1996). More recently, television rights fees, including over the air networks, cable television, superstations, and pay-per-view have become of paramount importance. Television rights fees now constitute a majority of all of the revenue generated by the National Football League, its affiliates, and its thirty-two member clubs. Other methods, including pagers and the internet, may become important alternative broadcast media as technology advances. In a world of 500-channel television and broadcasts (including audio and video components) that may come over the air—by satellite, through cables, and by means of telephone lines and personal computers, the most sophisticated professional sports businesses are concerned about protecting their rights to control all potential means by which consumers can "view" their games and events.

In some cases, sports event producers sell all or a portion of the advertising time associated with a broadcast. With respect to the most successful sports events and the most successful professional sports leagues, television broadcast companies pay substantial rights fees to the event or the league in return for the right to sell the television broadcast advertising.

To some extent, the television company may offer advertisers an alternative opportunity to purchase an association with the professional sports league, game, or event. Rather than pay an event to be an official sponsor of that event (*e.g.*, the official soft drink) and to receive signage at the event, a business may choose to make a large purchase of advertising time and sponsor the broadcast of the event. If a viewer were to hear that "the NFL on NBC is brought to you by Pepsi," would the viewer know that

Coca-Cola is the official soft drink of the National Football League? Similarly, if there are Pizza Hut commercials on all of the local NFL broadcasts, will fans know that McDonald's, not Pizza Hut, is the official fast food restaurant of the NFL?

During the 1984 Winter Olympics in Lillehammer, Norway, the Wendy's hamburger chain bought substantial advertising time during CBS's broadcast and ran commercials with winter sports themes that included current and former Olympic athletes (*e.g.,* figure skater Kristi Yamaguchi). Subsequent consumer surveys in the United States suggested that a majority of people surveyed believed that Wendy's, not McDonald's, was an official Olympic sponsor.

The television company or radio station that pays a rights fee is pursuing exclusivity—it wants to be the only means by which the fan or consumer can "hear," "view" or experience the game or sports event without buying a ticket and attending the live event. With that exclusivity, the radio or television broadcaster will market to advertisers the opportunity to associate their products with the broadcast and to communicate with the listeners or viewers who tune in for the game or event. If the broadcast rights are not exclusive, the television company must share the audience with another broadcaster, thereby reducing the likely size of the audience, the value of the broadcast rights to that broadcaster, and the amount that the broadcaster is likely to pay the owner of the event or the team or league selling the rights.

The importance of television and other broadcast rights has rendered this area another fertile battleground for disputes about ownership, alleged ambush marketing, and claims of infringement, conversion, misappropriation, and unfair competition. Litigants have disputed the copyrightability of the broadcasts and the ownership of copyrights. *See, e.g., Baltimore Orioles v. Major League Baseball Players Ass'n,* below. Other cases have involved league and event efforts to enjoin a wide variety of unauthorized telephonic, audio, video, satellite, and microwave "broadcasts" about events and games in progress. *See, e.g., WCVB-TV v. Boston Athletic Ass'n, NBA v. Motorola,* below. The Second Circuit's landmark decision in the *Motorola* case was a major setback for leagues and event producers. Similarly, the lower court decision in the *CBC Distribution* case, below, may open the door for production, without a license, of many products that it was previously believed could not be produced over the objections of leagues, teams, or players. Questions about their proper interpretation and the likelihood that the *Motorola* and *CBC Distribution* cases will be followed by other courts will be a primary focus of litigants and sports lawyers for years to come.

As you read the following cases, consider their implications for the various participants in the business of sports—including leagues, teams, players, players associations, event producers, individual sport athletes, sponsors, and television companies. At the same time, think about the implications of these decisions as technology changes (for example, a pager, telephone, or personal computer may provide audio, video, graphic, and textual images). What objectives are the courts pursuing? Are they merely trying to interpret the relevant statutes and precedents, or are they crafting decisions that they believe will be the best for sports or best for society?

Baltimore Orioles, Inc. v. Major League Baseball Players Ass'n
805 F.2d 663 (7th Cir. 1986)

ESCHBACH, Senior Circuit Judge. The primary issue involved in this appeal is whether major league baseball clubs own exclusive rights to the televised performances of major league baseball players during major league baseball games. For the reasons stated below, we will affirm in part, vacate in part, and remand for further proceedings.

I

This appeal arises out of a long-standing dispute between the Major League Baseball Clubs ("Clubs") and the Major League Baseball Players Association ("Players") regarding the ownership of the broadcast rights to the Players' performances during major league baseball games. After decades of negotiation concerning the allocation of revenues from telecasts of the games, the Players in May of 1982 sent letters to the Clubs, and to television and cable companies with which the Clubs had contracted, asserting that the telecasts were being made without the Players' consent and that they misappropriated the Players' property rights in their performances. The mailing of these letters led the parties to move their dispute from the bargaining table to the courtroom.

On June 14, 1982, the Clubs filed an action * * * in which they sought a declaratory judgment that the Clubs possessed an exclusive right to broadcast the games and owned exclusive rights to the telecasts. Each count sought essentially the same relief, but was premised upon a different theory: Count I was based upon copyright law, in particular the "works made for hire" doctrine of 17 U.S.C. §201(b); Count II rested upon state master-servant law; Count III was predicated upon the collective bargaining agreement between the Clubs and the Players, including the Uniform Player's Contract; and Count IV was based upon the parties' customs and dealings.

On July 1, 1982, three major league players brought an action (entitled *Rogers v. Kuhn*, No. 82 C 6377) against the Clubs * * * The three players (whom we also refer to as the "Players") sought a declaration that the game telecasts misappropriated their property rights in their names, pictures, and performances, and also asked for damages and injunctive relief. The Rogers complaint asserted six claims for relief, based upon the Players' alleged property rights in their names, pictures, and performances, the doctrine of unjust enrichment, and sections 50 and 51 of the New York Civil Rights Statute, N.Y. Civ. Rights Law §§50–51. * * * [T]he parties stipulated to * * * consolidation of the two cases.

* * *

II

* * *

B. Copyright Claim

* * * The district court found that the Clubs, not the Players, owned a copyright in the telecasts as works made for hire and that the Clubs' copyright in the telecasts preempted the Players' rights of publicity in their performances. * * * Accordingly, it granted summary judgment and entered final judgment for the Clubs on this claim. The Players argue that the district court erred in holding that a baseball player's live performance, as embodied in a copyrighted telecast of the game, constitutes a work made for hire so as to extinguish the player's right of publicity in his performance.

1. Works Made for Hire Under 17 U.S.C. §201(b)

Our analysis begins by ascertaining whether the Clubs own a copyright in the telecasts of major league baseball games. In general, copyright in a work "vests initially in the author or authors of the work," 17 U.S.C. §201(a); however, "in the case of a work made for hire, the employer or other person for whom the work was prepared is considered the author * * * and, unless the parties have expressly agreed otherwise in a written instrument signed by them, owns all of the rights comprised in the copyright." 17 U.S.C. §201(b). A work made for hire is defined in pertinent part as "a work prepared by an employee within the scope of his or her employment." 17 U.S.C. §101. Thus, an employer owns a copyright in a work if (1) the work satisfies the generally applicable requirements for copyrightability set forth in 17 U.S.C. §102(a), (2) the work was prepared by an employee, (3) the work was prepared within the scope of the employee's employment, and (4) the parties have not expressly agreed otherwise in a signed, written instrument.

a. Copyrightability of the telecasts

The district court concluded that the telecasts were copyrightable works. We agree. Section 102 sets forth three conditions for copyrightability: first, a work must be fixed in tangible form; second, the work must be an original work of authorship; and third, it must come within the subject matter of copyright. *See* 17 U.S.C. §102(a). Although there may have been some question at one time as to whether simultaneously recorded live broadcasts were copyrightable, this is no longer the case. Section 101 expressly provides that "[a] work consisting of sounds, images, or both, that are being transmitted, is 'fixed' * * * if a fixation of the work is being made simultaneously with its transmission." Since the telecasts of the games are videotaped at the same time they are broadcast, the telecasts are fixed in tangible form. *See National Football League v. McBee & Bruno's, Inc.*, 792 F.2d 726, 731–32 (8th Cir. 1986); *see also* H.R. Rep. No. 1476, 94th Cong., 2d. Sess. 52 ("House Report"), reprinted in 1976 U.S. Code Cong. & Ad. News 5659, 5665.

Moreover, the telecasts are original works of authorship. The requirement of originality actually subsumes two separate conditions, *i.e.*, the work must possess an independent origin and a minimal amount of creativity.[6] * * * It is obvious that the telecasts are independent creations, rather than reproductions of earlier works.

As for the telecasts' creativity, courts long have recognized that photographing a person or filming an event involves creative labor. *See, e.g., Burrow-Giles Lithographic Co. v. Sarony*, 111 U.S. 53, 60 (1884). For example, one court held that the Zapruder film of the Kennedy assassination was copyrightable because it embodied many elements of creativity. Among other things, Zapruder selected the kind of camera (movies, not snapshots), the kind of film (color), the kind of lens (telephoto), the area in which the pictures were to be taken, the time they were to be taken, and (after testing several sites) the spot on which the camera would be operated. *Time Inc. v. Bernard Geis Associates*, 293 F. Supp. 130, 143 (S.D.N.Y. 1968). The many decisions that must be made during the broadcast of a baseball game concerning camera angles, types of shots, the use of instant replays and split screens, and shot selection similarly supply the creativity required for the copyrightability of the telecasts. *See* House Report at 52, reprinted in 1976 U.S. Code Cong. & Ad. News at 5665 ("When a football game is being covered by four television cameras, with a director guiding the activities of the four cameramen and choosing

---

6. It is important to distinguish among three separate concepts—originality, creativity, and novelty. A work is original if it is the independent creation of its author. A work is creative if it embodies some modest amount of intellectual labor. A work is novel if it differs from existing works in some relevant respect. For a work to be copyrightable, it must be original and creative, but need not be novel. (Thus, in contrast to patent law, a work that is independently produced by two separate authors may be copyrighted by both.) * * *

which of their electronic images are sent to the public and in which order, there is little doubt that what the cameramen and the director are doing constitutes 'authorship.'").

Furthermore, the telecasts are audiovisual works, which under §102[8] come within the subject matter of copyright. * * * The telecasts are, therefore, copyrightable works.

b. Employer-employee relationship

With regard to the relationship between the Clubs and the Players, the district court found, and the Players do not dispute, that the Players are employees of their respective Clubs. We add only that this finding is consistent with the broad construction given to the term "employee" by courts applying the "work made for hire" doctrine. * * *

c. Scope of employment

The district court further found that the scope of the Players' employment encompassed the performance of major league baseball before "live and remote audiences." * * * On appeal the Players argue that there exist genuine issues of material fact as to whether the performance of baseball for televised audiences is within the scope of the Players' employment. * * *

* * * Because of the Players' failure to point to any evidence to the contrary, we would not reverse the district court's finding that the performance of baseball before remote audiences is within the Players' scope of employment even if the Players had preserved their contention. * * *

d. Written agreements

Because the Players are employees and their performances before broadcast audiences are within the scope of their employment, the telecasts of major league baseball games, which consist of the Players' performances, are works made for hire within the meaning of §201(b). *See* Nimmer, §5.03[D] (the parties can change the statutory presumption concerning the ownership of a copyright in a work made for hire, but cannot vary the work's status as a work made for hire). Thus, in the absence of an agreement to the contrary, the Clubs are presumed to own all of the rights encompassed in the telecasts of the games. * * *

The Players further assert that the parties' traditional practice of devoting approximately one-third of the revenues derived from nationally televised broadcasts to the Players' pension fund establishes a genuine issue of material fact as to the ownership of the copyright in these telecasts. We disagree. The allocation of revenues from nationally televised broadcasts is determined by the parties' relative bargaining strength and abil-

---

8. Section 102(a) provides:

Copyright protection subsists * * * in original works of authorship fixed in any tangible medium of expression, now known or later developed, from which they can be perceived, reproduced, or otherwise communicated, either directly or with the aid of a machine or device. Works of authorship include the following categories:

(1) literary works;
(2) musical works, including any accompanying words;
(3) dramatic works, including any accompanying music;
(4) pantomimes and choreographic works;
(5) pictorial, graphic, and sculptural works;
(6) motion pictures and other audiovisual works; and
(7) sound recordings.

17 U.S.C. §102(a) (emphasis added).

ity. Depending on the Players' bargaining power, they can negotiate a greater or a lesser share of the national telecast revenues. Nevertheless, there is no relationship between the division of revenues from nationally televised broadcasts and the ownership of rights in those telecasts. For example, a motion picture star might negotiate to receive a certain number of "points" from a film's profits; however, that she shares in the film's profits does not mean that she owns some share of the copyright in the film. (Indeed, the producer most likely holds the copyright in the work.) Just as the ownership of points in a film's profits does not represent a proportionate ownership of the copyright in the film, the Players' receipt in the form of pension contributions of a certain fraction of the revenues from nationally televised broadcasts in no way suggests that they own any part of the copyright in the telecasts.

We thus conclude that there are no genuine issues of material fact as to the ownership of the copyright in the telecasts, and that the parties did not expressly agree to rebut the statutory presumption that the employer owns the copyright in a work made for hire. We, therefore, hold that the Clubs own the copyright in telecasts of major league baseball games.

2. Preemption under 17 U.S.C. §301(a)

Although the Clubs own the copyright to the telecasts of major league baseball games, the Players claim that broadcasts of these games made without their express consent violate their rights to publicity in their performances. For the reasons stated below, we hold that the Clubs' copyright in the telecasts of major league baseball games preempts the Players' rights of publicity in their game-time performances.

> Section 301(a) of Title 17 provides that all legal or equitable rights that are equivalent to any of the exclusive rights within the general scope of copyright as specified by section 106 in works of authorship that are fixed in a tangible medium of expression and come within the subject matter of copyright as specified by sections 102 and 103, whether created before or after that date and whether published or unpublished, are governed exclusively by this title. Thereafter, no person is entitled to any such right or equivalent right in any such work under the common law or statutes of any State.

17 U.S.C. §301(a). This provision sets forth two conditions that both must be satisfied for preemption of a right under state law; First, the work in which the right is asserted must be fixed in tangible form and come within the subject matter of copyright as specified in §102. Second, the right must be equivalent to any of the rights specified in §106. * * *

a. Section 102 test

The works in which the Players claim rights are the telecasts of major league baseball games. As established above, the telecasts are fixed in tangible form because they are recorded simultaneously with their transmission and are audiovisual works which come within the subject matter of copyright. The first condition for preemption is, therefore, satisfied.

The Players argue, however, that the works in which they claim rights are their performances, rather than the telecasts of the games in which they play, and that performances per se are not fixed in tangible form. They contend that, since the works in which they assert rights are not fixed in tangible form, their rights of publicity in their performances are not subject to preemption. We disagree. Under §101, "[a] work is 'fixed' in a tangible medium of expression when its embodiment in a copy* * *, by or under the authority of the author, is sufficiently permanent and stable to permit it to be perceived, reproduced, or otherwise communicated for a period of more than transitory duration." The Players' performances are embodied in a copy, viz, the videotape of the telecast, from which the performances can be perceived, reproduced, and otherwise communicated indefinitely. Hence, their performances are fixed in tangible form, and any property rights in the performances that are equivalent to any of the rights encompassed in a copyright are preempted.

It is, of course, true that unrecorded performances per se are not fixed in tangible form. * * * Because such works are not fixed in tangible form, rights in such works are not subject to preemption under §301(a). * * * Nonetheless, once a performance is reduced to tangible form, there is no distinction between the performance and the recording of the performance for the purpose of preemption under §301(a). Thus, if a baseball game were not broadcast or were telecast without being recorded, the Players' performances similarly would not be fixed in tangible form and their rights of publicity would not be subject to preemption. * * * By virtue of being videotaped, however, the Players' performances are fixed in tangible form, and any rights of publicity in their performances that are equivalent to the rights contained in the copyright of the telecast are preempted.

The Players also contend that to be a "work[] of authorship that * * * [is] fixed in a tangible medium of expression" within the scope of §301(a), a work must be copyrightable. They assert that the works in which they claim rights, namely their performances, are not copyrightable because they lack sufficient creativity. They consequently conclude that because the works in which they claim rights are not works within the meaning of §301(a), their rights of publicity are not subject to preemption. There is a short answer to this argument. Congress contemplated that "as long as a work fits within one of the general subject matter categories of section 102 and 103, * * * [section 301(a)] prevents the States from protecting it even if it fails to achieve Federal copyright because it is too minimal or lacking in originality to qualify." House Report at 131, reprinted in 1976 U.S. Code Cong. & Ad. News at 5747.[23] Hence, §301(a) preempts all equivalent state-law rights claimed in any work within the subject matter of copyright whether or not the work embodies any creativity. Regardless of the creativity of the Players' performances, the works in which they assert rights are copyrightable works which come within the scope of §301(a) because of the creative contributions of the individuals responsible for recording the Players' performances. Therefore, the Players' rights of publicity in their performances are preempted if they are equivalent to any of the bundle of rights encompassed in a copyright.

b. Section 106 test

A right under state law is "equivalent" to one of the rights within the general scope of copyright if it is violated by the exercise of any of the rights set forth in §106. * * * That section grants the owner of a copyright the exclusive rights to reproduce (whether in original or derivative form), distribute, perform, and display the copyrighted work. See 17 U.S.C. §106; see also Nimmer, §1.01[B][1]. Thus, a right is equivalent to one of the rights comprised by a copyright if it "is infringed by the mere act of reproduction, performance, distribution or display." Id. * * *

---

23. The reason that §301(a) preempts rights claimed in works that lack sufficient creativity to be copyrightable is to prevent the states from granting protection to works which Congress has concluded should be in the public domain.

In this case, the Players claim a right of publicity in their performances. As a number of courts have held, a right of publicity in a performance is violated by a televised broadcast of the performance. * * * Because the exercise of the Clubs' right to broadcast telecasts of the games infringes the Players' rights of publicity in their performances, the Players' rights of publicity are equivalent to at least one of the rights encompassed by copyright, viz., the right to perform an audiovisual work. Since the works in which the Players claim rights are fixed in tangible form and come within the subject matter of copyright, the Players' rights of publicity in their performances are preempted.

The Players argue that their rights of publicity in their performances are not equivalent to the rights contained in a copyright because rights of publicity and copyrights serve different interests. In their view, the purpose of federal copyright law is to secure a benefit to the public, but the purpose of state statutory or common law concerning rights of publicity is to protect individual pecuniary interests. We disagree.

The purpose of federal copyright protection is to benefit the public by encouraging works in which it is interested. To induce individuals to undertake the personal sacrifices necessary to create such works, federal copyright law extends to the authors of such works a limited monopoly to reap the rewards of their endeavors. * * * Contrary to the Players' contention, the interest underlying the recognition of the right of publicity also is the promotion of performances that appeal to the public. The reason that state law protects individual pecuniary interests is to provide an incentive to performers to invest the time and resources required to develop such performances. In *Zacchini v. Scripps-Howard Broadcasting Co.*, 433 U.S. 562 (1977), the principal case on which the Players rely for their assertion that different interests underlie copyright and the right to publicity, the Supreme Court recognized that the interest behind federal copyright protection is the advancement of the public welfare through the encouragement of individual effort by personal gain, *id.* at 576, and that a state's interest in affording a cause of action for violation of the right to publicity "is closely analogous to the goals of patent and copyright law." *Id.* at 573. * * * Because the right of publicity does not differ in kind from copyright, the Players' rights of publicity in their performances cannot escape preemption.

In this litigation, the Players have attempted to obtain ex post what they did not negotiate ex ante. That is to say, they seek a judicial declaration that they possess a right—the right to control the telecasts of major league baseball games—that they could not procure in bargaining with the Clubs. The Players' aim is to share in the increasingly lucrative revenues derived from the sale of television rights for over-the-air broadcasts by local stations and national networks and for distribution by subscription and pay cable services. Contrary to the Players' contention, the effect of this decision is not to grant the Clubs perpetual rights to the Players' performances. The Players remain free to attain their objective by bargaining with the Clubs for a contractual declaration that the Players own a joint or an exclusive interest in the copyright of the telecasts.

C. Master-Servant Claim

The Clubs sought a judgment "declaring (a) that the plaintiffs, as employers who create the product, Major League Baseball games, own all rights in and to Major League Baseball games, including the right to telecast them, and (b) that the Major League Baseball players, by virtue of their employment, have no rights in and to the product." * * * The district court found that the Clubs, as employers, retain all rights in their employees' work product. * * * It thus granted summary judgment and entered final judgment for the Clubs on this claim. On appeal, the Players argue that the district court erred in holding that their status as employees extinguished their rights of publicity in their performances.

In particular, the Players assert that they possess rights of publicity in their names, likenesses, and performances, * * * and that their rights of publicity prevent use of their persona without their express written consent. * * * They further argue that an employee's right of publicity bars an employer from using the employee's name, picture, or performance without the employee's consent, notwithstanding the master-servant relationship. * * * The Clubs respond by contending that, as employers, they possess all ownership interests in the work product that they hire the Players, as employees, to create, * * *, and that an employee's right of publicity does not prevent the employer from using the employee's performances when the performances are the very product that the employee was hired to create. * * *

The threshold issue that we must decide is what law governs the Clubs' master-servant claims. * * *

* * *

It would be understating matters to say that the conflicts question in this case is complex. The 26 Clubs are located in 14 states and in Canada. The Major League Baseball Players Association is an unincorporated association of individuals from most, if not all, the states and many foreign countries. The Players' contracts were negotiated and executed in various states and call for performance at stadiums across the country. The Players' rights of publicity might be violated wherever their performances are broadcast without their consent.

Because we cannot ascertain on the basis of the record before us the state or states whose law governs the Clubs' master-servant claim, we will vacate the district court's opinion and judgment with respect to Count II of the Baltimore Orioles complaint and remand this matter for further proceedings. On remand, the district court should determine the appropriate choice-of-law rule under Illinois conflicts law and should make the factual findings necessary to identify the state or states whose law controls. * * *

III

For the reasons stated above, the district court's judgment is AFFIRMED with respect to the Clubs' copyright claim and is VACATED with respect to the Clubs' master-servant claim and REMANDED for further proceedings consistent with this opinion and law.

Notes and Questions

1. The "films" divisions or affiliates of the professional sports leagues license the use of historical game footage for various purposes, including use in commercials for various products. For example, NFL Films has licensed Super Bowl footage of San Francisco 49ers' Joe Montana throwing a touchdown pass to wide receiver Dwight Clark. Does NFL Films' ownership of the copyright in the footage permit the inclusion of that footage in a commercial for a fast food restaurant, or would the restaurant need to receive permission from Montana and Clark? Does it matter if some consumers believe that Montana and Clark are endorsing the fast food restaurant? If the league owns the footage, what keeps it from using that footage for any purpose? For a criticism of some of the *Baltimore Orioles* case analysis, *see, e.g., Brown v.* Ames, 201 F.3d 654 (5th Cir. 2000). Melville B. Nimmer & David Nimmer, NIMMER ON COPYRIGHT §§ 101[B][1][c] and 209[F] 1999; David E. Shipley, "Three Strikes and they're Out at the Old Ball Game: Preemption of Performers' Rights of Publicity Under the Copyright Act of 1976," 20 ARIZ. ST. L.J. 369, 384–88 (1988), Shelly Ross Saxer, "Baltimore Orioles, Inc. v. Major

League Baseball Players Association" The Right of Publicity in Game Performances and Federal Copyright Preemption," 36 U.C.L.A. L. Rev. 861, 870 (1989). *See also, Leto v. RCA Corp.*, 355 F.Supp.2d 921 (N.D.Ill. 2004). *But see Ventura v. Titan Sports*, 65 F.3d 725 (8th Cir. 1995). Does the answer to this question depend on the proper construction of copyright law or the proper interpretation of the NFL's collective bargaining agreement with the NFLPA?

2. The *Baltimore Orioles* opinion focused on the copyright law of the United States. However, when the opinion turned to common law master-servant claims, the court noted that "the 26 Clubs are located in 14 states and in Canada." With the Montreal Expos and Toronto Blue Jays in the National and American Leagues, respectively, should the court have considered Canadian copyright law, at least with respect to broadcasts of games played in Canada? Compare the Morio case in Chapter 15, above, which restricted its holding concerning labor law violations by the North American Soccer League to the NASL teams in the United States. A related question has arisen in the context of certain Canadian laws that prohibit the use of permanent replacements for economic strikers. *See* Chapter 14, Section IX (A)(2).

3. What would have been the significance of a decision that Major League Baseball players shared ownership of the broadcast copyright or that the league could not authorize telecasts of games without the players' authorization? Would it have simply forced the players and clubs back to the bargaining table, to resolve that issue in an amendment to their collective bargaining agreement?

4. Are questions concerning players' rights to their performances mandatory subjects of collective bargaining under Section 8(d) of the National Labor Relations Act; 29 U.S.C. §158(a). *See* Chapter 14, Section VIII(B)(5). *See also NFL Players Ass'n*, Case No. 2-CB-12117, Advice Memorandum (April 29, 1988).

5. If the players association and the league negotiated an agreement that ceded a right to publicity arguably belonging to individual players, would such agreement be immune from antitrust scrutiny by virtue of the non-statutory labor exemption? *See generally* Chapter 9.

6. If the collective bargaining agreement contained language vesting the players with the broadcast rights to their performances, could an individual player surrender that benefit in exchange for certain club concessions. Would such individual, ad hoc, bargaining violate the exclusivity principle that establishes a certified or recognized union as exclusive collective bargaining representatives. *See* Chapter 14 Section, VIII (B)(5); Chapter 15, *Midland Broadcasting Co.*, 93 NLRB 455 (1951) and the *Notes and Questions* that follow.

7. What position did the players take concerning the copyrightability of their performances? Can a football player copyright a creative play that he authored or an end zone celebration dance that he devised? Can golfer Chi Chi Rodriguez copyright his pantomime celebration routine of wielding a golf club like a sword and then sheathing the club? Can MLB shortstop Ozzie Smith copyright his celebratory acrobatic flips after great plays? Consider the discussion in *Motorola*, below, regarding whether athletic events are copyrightable.

WCVB-TV v. Boston Athletic Ass'n
926 F.2d 42 (1st Cir. 1991)

BREYER, Chief Judge. The Boston Athletic Association ("BAA"), its licensing agent (ProServ), and Channel 4 (WBZ-TV) appeal the district court's refusal to enjoin Channel 5 (WCVB-TV) from televising the Boston Marathon. They point out 1) that the BAA has spent a great deal of money over the years promoting the annual Patriot's Day marathon event, 2) that it has registered the words "Boston Marathon" as a trade, or service mark, in connection with the event, 3) that it has licensed (for a fee) Channel 4 to broadcast the event on television, 4) that it has not licensed Channel 5 to broadcast the event or to use its mark, 5) that Channel 5 broadcast the event last year anyway, and intends to do so in 1991, simply by placing television cameras in the streets along the marathon route, and 6) that Channel 5 used the words "Boston Marathon" on the screen in large letters before, during, and after the event. They argue that Channel 5, by broadcasting the words "Boston Marathon" in connection with the event, violated federal trademark law. They asked the district court to issue a preliminary injunction, it refused to do so, and they have appealed that refusal.

In our view, the district court's refusal to grant the preliminary injunction was lawful. The dispositive legal issue concerns "customer confusion." A trademark, or service mark, is an "attention getting symbol" used basically, and primarily, to make clear to the customer the origin of the goods or the service. *See* 1 J. McCarthy, Trademarks and Unfair Competition §11.17 at 476 (2d ed. 1984). Trademark law prohibits the unauthorized use of such a mark, but only where doing so creates a "likelihood of confusion" about who produces the goods or provides the service in question. *See* 15 U.S.C. §1114(1); 15 U.S.C. §1125(a); *Boston Athletic Ass'n v. Sullivan*, 867 F.2d 22, 28–35 & n.11 (1st Cir. 1989). * * * Unless a plaintiff can convince a district court that it will likely show such a "likelihood of confusion" on the merits of its trademark claim (or can convince a court of appeals that the district court abused its discretion), it is not entitled to a preliminary injunction. * * * Yet, we cannot find in the record before us sufficient evidence of relevant customer confusion, arising out of Channel 5's use of the words "Boston Marathon," to require the district court to issue the preliminary injunction that the appellants seek.

Obviously, we do not have before us the common, garden variety type of "confusion" that might arise with typical trademark infringement. This is not a heartland trademark case, where, for example, plaintiff uses the words "Big Tom" to mark his apple juice, defendant (perhaps a big man called Tom) uses the same words (or perhaps similar words, e.g., "Large Tommy") on his own apple juice label, and plaintiff says customers will confuse defendant's apple juice with his own. * * * No one here says that Channel 5 is running its own marathon on Patriot's Day, which a viewer might confuse with the BAA's famous Boston Marathon.

Rather, BAA argues that the confusion here involved is somewhat special. It points to cases where a defendant uses a plaintiff's trademark in connection with a different type of good or service and a plaintiff claims that the public will wrongly, and confusedly, think that the defendant's product somehow has the plaintiff's official "O.K." or imprimatur. The Eleventh Circuit, for example, found trademark law violated when the defendant, without authorization, used the plaintiff's football team mark, a bulldog, not in connection with a different football team, but, rather, on his beer mugs. *See University of Georgia Athletic Ass'n v. Laite*, 756 F.2d 1535 (11th Cir. 1985). This circuit has found trademark law violated, when the defendant, without authorization, used this very appellant's foot race mark, "Boston Marathon," on his t-shirts, sold during the event, permitting the customer to wrongly or confusedly think that his t-shirts were somehow "official." *See Sullivan, supra.* BAA goes on to say that Channel 5's use of those words will lead viewers, wrongly, and confusedly, to believe that Channel 5 (like the t-shirt seller) has a BAA license or permission or authorization to use the words, i.e., that it broadcasts with the BAA's official imprimatur. It also notes that this court, in *Sullivan*, listed circumstances that create a "rebuttable presumption" of confusion. And, it quotes language from *Sullivan*, in which this court, citing *International News Service v. Associated Press*, 248 U.S. 215 (1918), said that the defendant's t-shirts were "clearly designed to take advantage of the Boston Marathon and to benefit from the good will associated with its promotion by plaintiffs," and that defendants obtained a "free ride" at the plaintiffs' expense; they "reap where [they have] not sown." *Sullivan*, 867 F.2d at 33. Appellants say that Channel 5 is doing the same here.

In our view, the cases BAA cites, and *Sullivan* in particular, do not govern the outcome of this case. Nor can we find a likelihood of any relevant confusion here. First, the *Sullivan* opinion, taken as a whole, makes clear that the court, in using the language appellants cite, referring to a "free ride," and taking "advantage" of another's good will, did not intend to depart from ordinary principles of federal trademark law that make a finding of a "likelihood of confusion" essential to a conclusion of "violation." As a general matter, the law sometimes protects investors from the "free riding" of others; and sometimes it does not. The law, for example, gives inventors a "property right" in certain inventions for a limited period of time; see 35 U.S.C. §§101 et seq.; it provides copyright protection for authors; see 17 U.S.C. §§101 et seq.; it offers certain protections to trade secrets. See generally 2 J. McCarthy §29.16. But, the man who clears a swamp, the developer of a neighborhood, the academic scientist, the school teacher, and millions of others, each day create "value" (over and above what they are paid) that the law permits others to receive without charge. Just how, when and where the law should protect investments in "intangible" benefits or goods is a matter that legislators typically debate, embodying the results in specific statutes, or that common law courts, carefully weighing relevant competing interests, gradually work out over time. The trademark statute does not give the appellants any "property right" in their mark except "the right to prevent confusion. * * *" And, nothing in *Sullivan* suggests the contrary.

Second, the "rebuttable presumption" of confusion that this court set forth in *Sullivan* does not apply here. We concede that the *Sullivan* court said that "there is a rebuttable presumption" of confusion "about the shirts' source or sponsorship" arising from the fact that the defendants used the words "Boston Marathon" on the shirts, which use made customers more likely to buy the shirts. The court wrote that when a manufacturer intentionally uses another's mark as a means of establishing a link in consumers' minds with the other's enterprise, and directly profits from that link, there is an unmistakable aura of deception. *Sullivan*, 867 F.2d at 35 (emphasis added). As we read these words, they mean that the *Sullivan* record indicated that the defendant wanted to give the impression that his t-shirt was an "official" t-shirt, a fact that, in the sports world, might give a shirt, in the eyes of sports fans, a special "cachet." It makes sense to presume confusion about a relevant matter (namely, official sponsorship) from such an intent, at least in the absence of contrary evidence.

Here, however, there is no persuasive evidence of any intent to use the words "Boston Marathon" to suggest official sponsorship of Channel 5's broadcasts. To the contrary, Channel 5 offered to "broadcast whatever disclaimers" the BAA might want—"every thirty seconds, every two minutes, every ten minutes"—to make certain no one thought the channel had any special broadcasting status. Nor is there any evidence that Channel 5 might somehow profit from viewers' wrongly thinking that the BAA had authorized its broadcasts. Indeed, one would ordinarily believe that television viewers (unlike sports fans who might want to buy an official t-shirt with the name of a favorite event, team or player) wish to see the event and do not particularly care about the relation of station to event-promoter. *See AMF, Inc. v. Sleekcraft Boats*, 599 F.2d 341, 353 (9th Cir. 1979) (when deciding whether there is confusion "the wholly indifferent [consumers] may be excluded") (cites omitted); 2 J. McCarthy §23.27 at 129 & n.20 (trademark law does not "protect those buyers who * * * [are] 'indifferent'" to the mark).

Third, and perhaps most importantly, the record provides us with an excellent reason for thinking that Channel 5's use of the words "Boston Marathon" would not confuse the typical Channel 5 viewer. That reason consists of the fact that those words do more than call attention to Channel 5's program; they also describe the event that Channel 5 will broadcast. Common sense suggests (consistent with the record here) that a viewer who sees those words flash upon the screen will believe simply that Channel 5 will show, or is showing, or has shown, the marathon, not that Channel 5 has some special approval from the BAA to do so. In technical trademark jargon, the use of words for descriptive purposes is called a "fair use," and the law usually permits it even if the words themselves also constitute a trademark. See 15 U.S.C. §1115 (b)(4)(statutory fair use defense); *Zatarains, Inc. v. Oak Grove Smokehouse, Inc.*, 698 F.2d 786, 796 (5th Cir. 1983) (fair use established if mark descriptive, not used in trademark sense, and used in good faith). If, for example, a t-shirt maker placed the words "Pure Cotton" (instead of the words "Boston Marathon") on his t-shirts merely to describe the material from which the shirts were made, not even a shirt maker who had a registered trademark called "Pure Cotton" could likely enjoin their sale. * * * As Justice Holmes pointed out many years ago, "when the mark is used in a way that does not deceive the public we see no such sanctity in the word as to prevent its being used to tell the truth." *Prestonettes Inc. v. Coty*, 264 U.S. 359, 368 (1924).

This is not a case where it is difficult to decide whether a defendant is using particular words primarily as a mark, i.e., as an "attention getting symbol," or primarily as a description. * * * Here there is little in the record before us to suggest the former (only the large size of the words on the screen); while there is much to show the latter (timing, meaning, context, intent, and surrounding circumstances). Consequently, the appellants have shown no real likelihood of relevant confusion.

We also note that the only federal court which has decided a case nearly identical to the one before us, a case in which a station planning to televise a public parade was sued by the parade's promoter who had granted "exclusive" rights to another station, reached a conclusion similar to the one we draw here. *See Production Contractors, Inc. v. WGN Continental Broadcasting Co.*, 622 F. Supp. 1500, 1504 (N.D. Ill. 1985). Reviewing the promoter's Lanham Act claim that the "unauthorized" broadcast would create a "false impression" of sponsorship, the court concluded that it fell "far short of establishing likelihood of confusion" among viewers that the defendant station was the "official" or "authorized" broadcaster of the parade. *See id.* at 1504–05. Similarly, we do not see how Channel 5's broadcast could likely confuse viewers that it bore the imprimatur of the BAA.

The BAA makes one further argument. It says that, because Channel 5, in earlier years, paid it for a license to use the mark for its broadcasts, Channel 5 is "estopped" from contesting the mark's "validity." The estoppel cases that BAA cites, however, all concern a challenge to the validity of a mark, a challenge absent here. * * * Regardless, we can find no case that would even prevent a challenge by a prior licensee, based upon post-license facts, after the license has expired. * * * We cannot think of any reason why such a licensee ought to be estopped; or why, a grant of a license should permanently immunize a trademark holder from legal attack. *Compare Lear, Inc. v. Adkins*, 395 U.S. 653 (1969) (estoppel doctrine does not apply to patent licensees) with *Beer Nuts, Inc. v.*

King Nut Co., 477 F.2d 326, 328–29 (6th Cir.), cert. denied, 414 U.S. 858 (1973) (estoppel doctrine does apply to trademark licensees).

Finally, we note that amici in support of appellants have raised various questions of state law. Appellants themselves, however, have not raised those questions; consequently, they are not properly before us. * * *

The district court's denial of the motion for preliminary injunction is Affirmed.

Notes and Questions

1. At the end of the opinion, Judge (now Justice) Breyer noted that questions of state law had not been raised by appellants and, therefore, were not considered. Is that the primary distinction between this case and *Zacchini v. Scripps-Howard Broadcasting Co.*, 433 U.S. 562 (1977)? In *Zacchini*, the television broadcasting company videotaped and broadcast the plaintiff's entire fifteen second "human cannonball" act after the plaintiff entertainer had requested that the television company not do so. The act was performed at a county fair in Ohio. The Supreme Court held that the federal Constitution did not prevent Ohio courts from ordering the defendant television company to compensate Zacchini for the misappropriation of his right of publicity. 433 U.S. at 575–79. The court expressed concern that "[t]the broadcast of a film of petitioner's entire act poses a substantial threat to the economic value of the performance," and upheld Zacchini's claim. *Id.* at 575. Does Channel 5's broadcast of the Boston Marathon pose a substantial threat to the economic value of the Boston Marathon? Why should Channel 4 pay a license fee when Channel 5 can broadcast without a license? Should there be a different outcome for misappropriation of an individual's performance and misappropriation of the performance of an event organized by an event producer? Is the reason for a different outcome: (1) the Boston Marathon failed to rely on state law misappropriation principles; (2) the Boston Marathon could be viewed from public locations without paying an admission fee, while the television company in Zacchini had to pay an admission fee to gain access to the county fair and Zacchini's performance; (3) The Boston Marathon had been broadcast, for years, by Channel 5, without objection from the event producer; or (4) the Boston marathon's owner, an association, only lost exclusive control over one revenue stream from one event, while Zacchini faced the possibility of forfeiting his livelihood and any reason to continue to perform his act?

2. The *Boston Athletic Ass'n* case was viewed by many commentators and sports business personnel as a decision that turned on Channel 5's historical broadcasting of the event and the need to run the 26.2 mile event on public streets. Prior to the First Circuit's decision, there had been a long, but not very recent, history of courts enjoining retransmission of radio broadcasts and other unauthorized play-by-play reporting of professional sports events while they were in progress, under common law theories of misappropriation, unfair competition, and unjust enrichment. *See, e.g., Pittsburgh Athletic Co. v. KQV Broadcasting Co.*, 24 F. Supp. 490 (W.D. Pa. 1938) (Pirates baseball games); *National Exhibition Co. v. Fass*, 133 N.Y.S.2d 379 (Sup. Ct.), *aff'd mem.*, 136 N.Y.S.2d 358 (App. Div. 1954), 143 N.Y.S.2d 767 (Sup. Ct. N.Y. County 1955) (New York Giants baseball games); *Twentieth Century Sporting Club, Inc. v. Transradio press Serv., Inc.*, 165 Misc. 71, 300 N.Y.S. 159 (1937) (boxing match); *Johnson-Kennedy Radio Corp. v. Chicago Bears Football Club, Inc.*, 97 F.2d 223 (7th Cir. 1938) (Chicago Bears football game). *But see Loeb v. Turner*, 257 S.W.2d 800 (Tex. Civ. App. 1953) (stock car auto race); *National Exhibition Co. v. Teleflash, Inc.*, 24 F. Supp. 488 (S.D.N.Y. 1936) (dissemination over telephone wires of play-by-play descriptions of baseball games).

The latter two opinions may have foreshadowed the decision in the *Boston Athletic Ass'n* case, as they both focused on the question of whether the play-by-play information was secured by the defendant from spectators who gained admission to an event by means of a ticket that expressly prohibited the broadcasting of the events witnessed.

In *Loeb v. Turner*, the court stated that South Mountain Speedway's admission ticket, which granted spectators a license to attend and watch the races but prohibited their taking pictures or relaying news of what they saw, was a valid enforceable contract. 257 S.W.2d at 802. However, the defendant radio station had merely listened to the authorized broadcast of the race and broadcast what it called a "recreated description," which the court described as a "production [that] was part factual and part imaginative." *Id.* at 801. The races took place in Phoenix, Arizona, and defendant's rebroadcasts were more than a thousand miles away, in Dallas, Texas. Therefore, the court found that there was no competition between the parties or any interference with the plaintiff's business, and affirmed the verdict for the defendants.

In *National Exhibition Co. v. Teleflash, Inc.*, the court denied the plaintiff's motion for an injunction and, in so doing, noted both that the admission ticket for the plaintiff's baseball games did not contain any limitation on a "ticket holder broadcasting, play-by-play, his own account of what is transpiring within his view" and that there was no evidence indicating that information originated from someone "within the plaintiff's enclosure where the game occurs." 24 F. Supp. at 488–89.

The best analysis and summary of the state of the law concerning these broadcasting issues prior to the *Boston Athletic Ass'n* and *Motorola* cases is found in Robert Alan Garrett and Philip R. Hochberg, *Sports Broadcasting*, in 2 *Law of Professional and Amateur Sports* (Gary A. Uberstine, ed., 1996).

3. As you read the following decision, which involves the NBA's efforts to prevent what the league considered free-riding on its substantial efforts to create a product of great fan interest, consider whether the Boston Athletic Association could prevent Channel 5 from broadcasting the Boston Marathon under a "'hot-news' INS-like claim"?

National Basketball Ass'n v. Motorola, Inc.

105 F.3d 841 (2d Cir. 1997)

WINTER, Circuit Judge. Motorola, Inc. and Sports Team Analysis and Tracking Systems ("STATS") appeal from a permanent injunction entered by Judge Preska. The injunction concerns a handheld pager sold by Motorola and marketed under the name "SportsTrax," which displays updated information of professional basketball games in progress. The injunction prohibits appellants, absent authorization from the National Basketball Association and NBA Properties, Inc. (collectively the "NBA"), from transmitting scores or other data about NBA games in progress via the pagers, STATS's site on America On-Line's computer dial-up service, or "any equivalent means."

The crux of the dispute concerns the extent to which a state law "hot-news" misappropriation claim based on *International News Service v. Associated Press*, 248 U.S. 215 (1918) ("INS"), survives preemption by the federal Copyright Act and whether the NBA's claim fits within the surviving INS-type claims. We hold that a narrow "hot-news" exception does survive preemption. However, we also hold that appellants' transmission of "real-time" NBA game scores and information tabulated from television and radio broadcasts of games in progress does not constitute a misappropriation of "hot news" that is the property of the NBA.

The NBA cross-appeals from the dismissal of its Lanham Act claim. We hold that any misstatements by Motorola in advertising its pager were not material and affirm.

I. BACKGROUND

The facts are largely undisputed. Motorola manufactures and markets the SportsTrax paging device while STATS supplies the game information that is transmitted to the pagers. The product became available to the public in January 1996, at a retail price of about $ 200. SportsTrax's pager has an inch-and-a-half by inch-and-a-half screen and operates in four basic modes: "current," "statistics," "final scores" and "demonstration." It is the "current" mode that gives rise to the present dispute. In that mode, SportsTrax displays the following information on NBA games in progress: (i) the teams playing; (ii) score changes; (iii) the team in possession of the ball; (iv) whether the team is in the free-throw bonus; (v) the quarter of the game; and (vi) time remaining in the quarter. The information is updated every two to three minutes, with more frequent updates near the end of the first half and the end of the game. There is a lag of approximately two or three minutes between events in the game itself and when the information appears on the pager screen.

SportsTrax's operation relies on a "data feed" supplied by STATS reporters who watch the games on television or listen to them on the radio. The reporters key into a personal computer changes in the score and other information such as successful and missed shots, fouls, and clock updates. The information is relayed by modem to STATS's host computer, which compiles, analyzes, and formats the data for retransmission. The information is then sent to a common carrier, which then sends it via satellite to various local FM radio networks that in turn emit the signal received by the individual SportsTrax pagers.

Although the NBA's complaint concerned only the SportsTrax device, the NBA offered evidence at trial concerning STATS's America On-Line ("AOL") site. Starting in January, 1996, users who accessed STATS's AOL site, typically via a modem attached to a home computer, were provided with slightly more comprehensive and detailed real-time game information than is displayed on a SportsTrax pager. On the AOL site, game scores are updated every 15 seconds to a minute, and the player and team statistics are updated each minute. The district court's original decision and judgment, *National Basketball Ass'n v. Sports Team Analysis and Tracking Sys. Inc.*, 931 F. Supp. 1124 (S.D.N.Y. 1996), did not address the AOL site, because "NBA's complaint and the evidence proffered at trial were devoted largely to SportsTrax." *National Basketball Ass'n v. Sports Team Analysis and Tracking Sys. Inc.*, 939 F. Supp. 1071, 1074 n.1 (S.D.N.Y. 1996). Upon motion by the NBA, however, the district court amended its decision and judgment and enjoined use of the real-time game information on STATS's AOL site. *Id.* at 1075 n.1. Because the record on appeal, the briefs of the parties, and oral argument primarily addressed the SportsTrax device, we similarly focus on that product. However, we regard the legal issues as identical with respect to both products, and our holding applies equally to SportsTrax and STATS's AOL site.

The NBA's complaint asserted six claims for relief: (i) state law unfair competition by misappropriation; (ii) false advertising under Section 43(a) of the Lanham Act, 15 U.S.C. §1125(a); (iii) false representation of origin under Section 43(a) of the Lanham Act; (iv) state and common law unfair competition by false advertising and false designation of origin; (v) federal copyright infringement; and (vi) unlawful interception of communications under the Communications Act of 1934, 47 U.S.C. §605. Motorola counterclaimed, alleging that the NBA unlawfully interfered with Motorola's contractual relations with four individual NBA teams that had agreed to sponsor and advertise SportsTrax.

The district court dismissed all of the NBA's claims except the first—misappropriation under New York law. The court also dismissed Motorola's counterclaim. Finding Motorola and STATS liable for misappropriation, Judge Preska entered the permanent injunction, reserved the calculation of damages for subsequent proceedings, and stayed execution of the injunction pending appeal. Motorola and STATS appeal from the injunction, while NBA cross-appeals from the district court's dismissal of its Lanham Act false-advertising claim. The issues before us, therefore, are the state law misappropriation and Lanham Act claims.

II. THE STATE LAW MISAPPROPRIATION CLAIM

A. *Summary of Ruling*

Because our disposition of the state law misappropriation claim rests in large part on preemption by the Copyright Act, our discussion necessarily goes beyond the elements of a misappropriation claim under New York law, and a summary of our ruling here will perhaps render that discussion—or at least the need for it—more understandable.

The issues before us are ones that have arisen in various forms over the course of this century as technology has steadily increased the speed and quantity of information transmission. Today, individuals at home, at work, or elsewhere, can use a computer, pager, or other device to obtain highly selective kinds of information virtually at will. *International News Service v. Associated Press*, 248 U.S. 215 (1918) ("INS") was one of the first cases to address the issues raised by these technological advances, although the technology involved in that case was primitive by contemporary standards. INS involved two wire services, the Associated Press ("AP") and International News Service ("INS"), that transmitted news stories by wire to member newspapers. *Id.* INS would lift factual stories from AP bulletins and send them by wire to INS papers. *Id.* at 231. INS would also take factual stories from east coast AP papers and wire them to INS papers on the west coast that had yet to publish because of time differentials. *Id.* at 238. The Supreme Court held that INS's conduct was a common-law misappropriation of AP's property. *Id.* at 242.

With the advance of technology, radio stations began "live" broadcasts of events such as baseball games and operas, and various entrepreneurs began to use the transmissions of others in one way or another for their own profit. In response, New York courts created a body of misappropriation law, loosely based on INS, that sought to apply ethical standards to the use by one party of another's transmissions of events.

Federal copyright law played little active role in this area until 1976. Before then, it appears to have been the general understanding—there being no caselaw of consequence—that live events such as baseball games were not copyrightable. Moreover, doubt existed even as to whether a recorded broadcast or videotape of such an event was copyrightable. In 1976, however, Congress passed legislation expressly affording copyright protection to simultaneously-recorded broadcasts of live performances such as sports events. *See* 17 U.S.C. §101. Such protection was not extended to the underlying events.

The 1976 amendments also contained provisions preempting state law claims that enforced rights "equivalent" to exclusive copyright protections when the work to which the state claim was being applied fell within the area of copyright protection. See 17

U.S.C. §301. Based on legislative history of the 1976 amendments, it is generally agreed that a "hot-news" INS-like claim survives preemption. H.R. No. 94-1476 at 132 (1976), reprinted in 1976 U.S.C.C.A.N. 5659, 5748. However, much of New York misappropriation law after INS goes well beyond "hot-news" claims and is preempted.

We hold that the surviving "hot-news" INS-like claim is limited to cases where: (i) a plaintiff generates or gathers information at a cost; (ii) the information is time-sensitive; (iii) a defendant's use of the information constitutes free-riding on the plaintiff's efforts; (iv) the defendant is in direct competition with a product or service offered by the plaintiffs; and (v) the ability of other parties to free-ride on the efforts of the plaintiff or others would so reduce the incentive to produce the product or service that its existence or quality would be substantially threatened. We conclude that SportsTrax does not meet that test.

B. *Copyrights in Events or Broadcasts of Events*

The NBA asserted copyright infringement claims with regard both to the underlying games and to their broadcasts. The district court dismissed these claims, and the NBA does not appeal from their dismissal. Nevertheless, discussion of the infringement claims is necessary to provide the framework for analyzing the viability of the NBA's state law misappropriation claim in light of the Copyright Act's preemptive effect.

1. *Infringement of a Copyright in the Underlying Games*

In our view, the underlying basketball games do not fall within the subject matter of federal copyright protection because they do not constitute "original works of authorship" under 17 U.S.C. §102(a). Section 102(a) lists eight categories of "works of authorship" covered by the act, including such categories as "literary works," "musical works," and "dramatic works." The list does not include athletic events, and, although the list is concededly non-exclusive, such events are neither similar nor analogous to any of the listed categories.

Sports events are not "authored" in any common sense of the word. There is, of course, at least at the professional level, considerable preparation for a game. However, the preparation is as much an expression of hope or faith as a determination of what will actually happen. Unlike movies, plays, television programs, or operas, athletic events are competitive and have no underlying script. Preparation may even cause mistakes to succeed, like the broken play in football that gains yardage because the opposition could not expect it. Athletic events may also result in wholly unanticipated occurrences, the most notable recent event being in a championship baseball game in which interference with a fly ball caused an umpire to signal erroneously a home run.

What "authorship" there is in a sports event, moreover, must be open to copying by competitors if fans are to be attracted. If the inventor of the T-formation in football had been able to copyright it, the sport might have come to an end instead of prospering. Even where athletic preparation most resembles authorship—figure skating, gymnastics, and, some would uncharitably say, professional wrestling—a performer who conceives and executes a particularly graceful and difficult—or, in the case of wrestling, seemingly painful—acrobatic feat cannot copyright it without impairing the underlying competition in the future. A claim of being the only athlete to perform a feat doesn't mean much if no one else is allowed to try.

For many of these reasons, *Nimmer on Copyright* concludes that the "far more reasonable" position is that athletic events are not copyrightable. 1 M. Nimmer & D. Nimmer, Nimmer on Copyright §2.09[F] at 2-170.1 (1996). Nimmer notes that, among other problems, the number of joint copyright owners would arguably include the league, the teams, the athletes, umpires, stadium workers and even fans, who all contribute to the "work."

Concededly, caselaw is scarce on the issue of whether organized events themselves are copyrightable, but what there is indicates that they are not. *See Production Contractors, Inc. v. WGN Continental Broadcasting Co.*, 622 F. Supp. 1500 (N.D. Ill. 1985) (Christmas parade is not a work of authorship entitled to copyright protection). In claiming a copyright in the underlying games, the NBA relied in part on a footnote in *Baltimore Orioles, Inc. v. Major League Baseball Players Assn.*, 805 F.2d 663, 669 n.7 (7th Cir. 1986), *cert. denied*, 480 U.S. 941 (1987), which stated that the "players' performances" contain the "modest creativity required for copyrightability." However, the court went on to state, "Moreover, even if the players' performances were not sufficiently creative, the players agree that the cameramen and director contribute creative labor to the telecasts." *Id.* This last sentence indicates that the court was considering the copyrightability of telecasts—not the underlying games, which obviously can be played without cameras.

We believe that the lack of caselaw is attributable to a general understanding that athletic events were, and are, uncopyrightable. Indeed, prior to 1976, there was even doubt that broadcasts describing or depicting such events, which have a far stronger case for copyrightability than the events themselves, were entitled to copyright protection. Indeed, as described in the next subsection of this opinion, Congress found it necessary to extend such protection to recorded broadcasts of live events. The fact that Congress did not extend such protection to the events themselves confirms our view that the district court correctly held that appellants were not infringing a copyright in the NBA games.

2. *Infringement of a Copyright in the Broadcasts of NBA Games*

As noted, recorded broadcasts of NBA games—as opposed to the games themselves—are now entitled to copyright protection. The Copyright Act was amended in 1976 specifically to insure that simultaneously-recorded transmissions of live performances and sporting events would meet the Act's requirement that the original work of authorship be "fixed in any tangible medium of expression." 17 U.S.C. §102(a). Accordingly, Section 101 of the Act, containing definitions, was amended to read:

A work consisting of sounds, images, or both, that are being transmitted, is "fixed" for purposes of this title if a fixation of the work is being made simultaneously with its transmission.

17 U.S.C. §101. Congress specifically had sporting events in mind:

The bill seeks to resolve, through the definition of "fixation" in section 101, the status of live broadcasts—sports, news coverage, live performances of music, etc.—that are reaching the public in unfixed form but that are simultaneously being recorded.

H.R. No. 94-1476 at 52, reprinted in 1976 U.S.C.C.A.N. at 5665. The House Report also makes clear that it is the broadcast, not the underlying game, that is the subject of copyright protection. In explaining how game broadcasts meet the Act's requirement that the subject matter be an "original work[] of authorship," 17 U.S.C. §102(a), the House Report stated:

When a football game is being covered by four television cameras, with a director guiding the activities of the four cameramen and choosing which of their electronic images are sent out to the public and in what order, there is little doubt that what the cameramen and the director are doing constitutes "authorship."

H.R. No. 94-1476 at 52, reprinted in 1976 U.S.C.C.A.N. at 5665.

Although the broadcasts are protected under copyright law, the district court correctly held that Motorola and STATS did not infringe NBA's copyright because they reproduced only facts from the broadcasts, not the expression or description of the game that constitutes the broadcast. The "fact/expression dichotomy" is a bedrock principle of copyright law that "limits severely the scope of protection in fact-based works." *Feist Publications, Inc. v. Rural Tel. Service Co.*, 499 U.S. 340, 350 (1991). "'No author may copyright facts or ideas. The copyright is limited to those aspects of the work—termed 'expression'—that display the stamp of the author's originality.'" *Id.* (quoting *Harper & Row, Inc. v. Nation Enter.*, 471 U.S. 539, 547–48 (1985)).

We agree with the district court that the "defendants provide purely factual information which any patron of an NBA game could acquire from the arena without any involvement from the director, cameramen, or others who contribute to the originality of a broadcast." 939 F. Supp. at 1094. Because the SportsTrax device and AOL site reproduce only factual information culled from the broadcasts and none of the copyrightable expression of the games, appellants did not infringe the copyright of the broadcasts.

C. *The State-Law Misappropriation Claim*

The district court's injunction was based on its conclusion that, under New York law, defendants had unlawfully misappropriated the NBA's property rights in its games. The district court reached this conclusion by holding: (i) that the NBA's misappropriation claim relating to the underlying games was not preempted by Section 301 of the Copyright Act; and (ii) that, under New York common law, defendants had engaged in unlawful misappropriation. *Id.* at 1094–1107. We disagree.

1. *Preemption Under the Copyright Act*

a) *Summary*

When Congress amended the Copyright Act in 1976, it provided for the preemption of state law claims that are interrelated with copyright claims in certain ways. Under 17 U.S.C. §301, a state law claim is preempted when: (i) the state law claim seeks to vindicate "legal or equitable rights that are equivalent" to one of the bundle of exclusive rights already protected by copyright law under 17 U.S.C. §106—styled the "general scope requirement"; and (ii) the particular work to which the state law claim is being applied falls within the type of works protected by the Copyright Act under Sections 102 and 103—styled the "subject matter requirement."

The district court concluded that the NBA's misappropriation claim was not preempted because, with respect to the underlying games, as opposed to the broadcasts, the subject matter requirement was not met. 939 F. Supp. at 1097. The court dubbed as "partial preemption" its separate analysis of misappropriation claims relating to the underlying games and misappropriation claims relating to broadcasts of those games. *Id.* at 1098, n.24. The district court then relied on a series of older New York misappropriation cases involving radio broadcasts that considerably broadened INS. We hold that where the challenged copying or misappropriation relates in part to the copyrighted broadcasts of the games, the subject matter requirement is met as to both the broad-

casts and the games. We therefore reject the partial preemption doctrine and its anomalous consequence that "it is possible for a plaintiff to assert claims both for infringement of its copyright in a broadcast and misappropriation of its rights in the underlying
event." *Id.* We do find that a properly-narrowed INS "hot-news" misappropriation claim
survives preemption because it fails the general scope requirement, but that the broader
theory of the radio broadcast cases relied upon by the district court were preempted
when Congress extended copyright protection to simultaneously-recorded broadcasts.

b) "Partial Preemption" and the Subject Matter Requirement

The subject matter requirement is met when the work of authorship being copied or
misappropriated "falls within the ambit of copyright protection." *Harper & Row, Inc. v.
Nation Enter.*, 723 F.2d 195, 200 (1983), rev'd on other grounds, 471 U.S. 539 (1985).
We believe that the subject matter requirement is met in the instant matter and that the
concept of "partial preemption" is not consistent with Section 301 of the Copyright Act.
Although game broadcasts are copyrightable while the underlying games are not, the
Copyright Act should not be read to distinguish between the two when analyzing the
preemption of a misappropriation claim based on copying or taking from the copyrightable work.

Copyrightable material often contains uncopyrightable elements within it, but Section 301 preemption bars state law misappropriation claims with respect to uncopyrightable as well as copyrightable elements. In *Harper & Row*, for example, we held that
state law claims based on the copying of excerpts from President Ford's memoirs were
preempted even with respect to information that was purely factual and not copyrightable. We stated:

> The [Copyright] Act clearly embraces "works of authorship," including "liter-
> ary works," as within its subject matter. The fact that portions of the Ford
> memoirs may consist of uncopyrightable material * * * does not take the work
> as a whole outside the subject matter protected by the Act. Were this not so,
> states would be free to expand the perimeters of copyright protection to their
> own liking, on the theory that preemption would be no bar to state protection
> of material not meeting federal statutory standards.

723 F.2d at 200 (citation omitted). * * *

Adoption of a partial preemption doctrine—preemption of claims based on misappropriation of broadcasts but no preemption of claims based on misappropriation of
underlying facts—would expand significantly the reach of state law claims and render
the preemption intended by Congress unworkable. It is often difficult or impossible to
separate the fixed copyrightable work from the underlying uncopyrightable events or
facts. Moreover, Congress, in extending copyright protection only to the broadcasts and
not to the underlying events, intended that the latter be in the public domain. Partial
preemption turns that intent on its head by allowing state law to vest exclusive rights in
material that Congress intended to be in the public domain and to make unlawful conduct that Congress intended to allow. This concern was recently expressed in *ProCD,
Inc. v. Zeidenberg*, 86 F.3d 1447 (7th Cir. 1996), a case in which the defendants reproduced non-copyrightable facts (telephone listings) from plaintiffs' copyrighted software.
In discussing preemption under Section 301(a), Judge Easterbrook held that the subject
matter requirement was met and noted:

> ProCD's software and data are "fixed in a tangible medium of expression",
> and the district judge held that they are "within the subject matter of copy-
> right". The latter conclusion is plainly right for the copyrighted application

program, and the judge thought that the data likewise are "within the subject matter of copyright" even if, after *Feist*, they are not sufficiently original to be copyrighted. 908 F. Supp. at 656–57. *Baltimore Orioles, Inc. v. Major League Baseball Players Ass'n*, 805 F.2d 663, 676 (7th Cir. 1986), supports that conclusion, with which commentators agree. * * * One function of §301(a) is to prevent states from giving special protection to works of authorship that Congress has decided should be in the public domain, which it can accomplish only if "subject matter of copyright" includes all works of a type covered by sections 102 and 103, even if federal law does not afford protection to them.

ProCD, 86 F.3d at 1453 (citation omitted). We agree with Judge Easterbrook and reject the separate analysis of the underlying games and broadcasts of those games for purposes of preemption.

c) *The General Scope Requirement*

Under the general scope requirement, Section 301 "preempts only those state law rights that 'may be abridged by an act which, in and of itself, would infringe one of the exclusive rights' provided by federal copyright law." *Computer Assoc. Int'l, Inc. v. Altai, Inc.*, 982 F.2d 693, 716 (2d Cir. 1992) (quoting *Harper & Row*, 723 F.2d at 200). However, certain forms of commercial misappropriation otherwise within the general scope requirement will survive preemption if an "extra-element" test is met. * * *

We turn, therefore, to the question of the extent to which a "hot-news" misappropriation claim based on *INS* involves extra elements and is not the equivalent of exclusive rights under a copyright. Courts are generally agreed that some form of such a claim survives preemption. *Financial Information, Inc. v. Moody's Investors Service, Inc.*, 808 F.2d 204, 208 (2d Cir. 1986), cert. denied, 484 U.S. 820 (1987) ("FII"). This conclusion is based in part on the legislative history of the 1976 amendments. * * * The crucial question, therefore, is the breadth of the "hot-news" claim that survives preemption.

In *INS*, the plaintiff AP and defendant INS were "wire services" that sold news items to client newspapers. AP brought suit to prevent INS from selling facts and information lifted from AP sources to INS-affiliated newspapers. One method by which INS was able to use AP's news was to lift facts from AP news bulletins. INS, 248 U.S. at 231. Another method was to sell facts taken from just-published east coast AP newspapers to west coast INS newspapers whose editions had yet to appear. *Id.* at 238. The Supreme Court held (prior to *Erie R. Co. v. Tompkins*, 304 U.S. 64 (1938)), that INS's use of AP's information was unlawful under federal common law. It characterized INS's conduct as

> amounting to an unauthorized interference with the normal operation of complainant's legitimate business precisely at the point where the profit is to be reaped, in order to divert a material portion of the profit from those who have earned it to those who have not; with special advantage to defendant in the competition because of the fact that it is not burdened with any part of the expense of gathering the news.

INS, 248 U.S. at 240.

The theory of the New York misappropriation cases relied upon by the district court is considerably broader than that of *INS*. For example, the district court quoted at length from *Metropolitan Opera Ass'n v. Wagner-Nichols Recorder Corp.*, 199 Misc. 786, 101 N.Y.S.2d 483 (N.Y. Sup. Ct. 1950), aff'd, 279 A.D. 632, 107 N.Y.S.2d 795 (1st Dep't 1951). *Metropolitan Opera* described New York misappropriation law as standing for the "broader principle that property rights of commercial value are to be and will be protected from any form of commercial immorality"; that misappropriation law developed "to deal with business malpractices offensive to the ethics of [ ] society"; and that the doctrine is "broad and flexible." 939 F. Supp. at 1098–1110 (quoting *Metropolitan Opera*, 101 N.Y.S.2d at 492, 488–89).

However, we believe that *Metropolitan Opera*'s broad misappropriation doctrine based on amorphous concepts such as "commercial immorality" or society's "ethics" is preempted. Such concepts are virtually synonymous for wrongful copying and are in no meaningful fashion distinguishable from infringement of a copyright. The broad misappropriation doctrine relied upon by the district court is, therefore, the equivalent of exclusive rights in copyright law.

Indeed, we said as much in *FII*. That decision involved the copying of financial information by a rival financial reporting service and specifically repudiated the broad misappropriation doctrine of *Metropolitan Opera*. * * *

In fact, *FII* only begrudgingly concedes that even narrow "hot news" INS-type claims survive preemption. *Id.* at 209.

Moreover, *Computer Associates Intern., Inc. v. Altai Inc.* indicated that the "extra element" test should not be applied so as to allow state claims to survive preemption easily. 982 F.2d at 717. "An action will not be saved from preemption by elements such as awareness or intent, which alter 'the action's scope but not its nature'. * * * Following this 'extra element' test, we have held that unfair competition and misappropriation claims grounded solely in the copying of a plaintiff's protected expression are preempted by section 301." *Id.* (citation omitted).

In light of cases such as *FII* and *Altai* that emphasize the narrowness of state misappropriation claims that survive preemption, most of the broadcast cases relied upon by the NBA are simply not good law. Those cases were decided at a time when simultaneously-recorded broadcasts were not protected under the Copyright Act and when the state law claims they fashioned were not subject to federal preemption. For example, *Metropolitan Opera*, 199 Misc. 786, 101 N.Y.S.2d 483, involved the unauthorized copying, marketing, and sale of opera radio broadcasts. As another example, in *Mutual Broadcasting System v. Muzak Corp.*, 177 Misc. 489, 30 N.Y.S.2d 419 (Sup. Ct. 1941), the defendant simultaneously retransmitted the plaintiff's baseball radio broadcasts onto telephone lines. As discussed above, the 1976 amendments to the Copyright Act were specifically designed to afford copyright protection to simultaneously-recorded broadcasts, and *Metropolitan Opera* and *Muzak* could today be brought as copyright infringement cases. Moreover, we believe that they would have to be brought as copyright cases because the amendments affording broadcasts copyright protection also preempted the state law misappropriation claims under which they were decided.

Our conclusion, therefore, is that only a narrow "hot-news" misappropriation claim survives preemption for actions concerning material within the realm of copyright. * * *

In our view, the elements central to an INS claim are: (i) the plaintiff generates or collects information at some cost or expense,. * * * ; (ii) the value of the information is highly time-sensitive,. * * * ; (iii) the defendant's use of the information constitutes free-riding on the plaintiff's costly efforts to generate or collect it,. * * * ; (iv) the defendant's use of the information is in direct competition with a product or service offered by the plaintiff,. * * * ; (v) the ability of other parties to free-ride on the efforts of the plaintiff would so reduce the incentive to produce the product or service that its existence or quality would be substantially threatened, * * * ("[INS's conduct] would render [AP's] publication profitless, or so little profitable as in effect to cut off the service by rendering the cost prohibitive in comparison with the return.")[8]

INS is not about ethics; it is about the protection of property rights in time-sensitive information so that the information will be made available to the public by profit-seeking entrepreneurs. If services like AP were not assured of property rights in the news they pay to collect, they would cease to collect it. The ability of their competitors to appropriate their product at only nominal cost and thereby to disseminate a competing product at a lower price would destroy the incentive to collect news in the first place. The newspaper-reading public would suffer because no one would have an incentive to collect "hot news."

We therefore find the extra elements—those in addition to the elements of copyright infringement—that allow a "hot-news" claim to survive preemption are: (i) the time-sensitive value of factual information, (ii) the free-riding by a defendant, and (iii) the threat to the very existence of the product or service provided by the plaintiff.

2. *The Legality of SportsTrax*

We conclude that Motorola and STATS have not engaged in unlawful misappropriation under the "hot-news" test set out above. To be sure, some of the elements of a "hot-news" *INS* claim are met. The information transmitted to SportsTrax is not precisely contemporaneous, but it is nevertheless time-sensitive. Also, the NBA does provide, or will shortly do so, information like that available through SportsTrax. It now offers a service called "Gamestats" that provides official play-by-play game sheets and half-time and final box scores within each arena. It also provides such information to the media in each arena. In the future, the NBA plans to enhance Gamestats so that it will be networked between the various arenas and will support a pager product analogous to SportsTrax. SportsTrax will of course directly compete with an enhanced Gamestats.

However, there are critical elements missing in the NBA's attempt to assert a "hot-news" *INS*-type claim. As framed by the NBA, their claim compresses and confuses three different informational products. The first product is generating the information by playing the games; the second product is transmitting live, full descriptions of those games; and the third product is collecting and retransmitting strictly factual information about the games. The first and second products are the NBA's primary business: producing basketball games for live attendance and licensing copyrighted broadcasts of those games. The collection and retransmission of strictly factual material about the games is a different product: e.g., box-scores in newspapers, summaries of statistics on television sports news, and real-time facts to be transmitted to pagers. In our view, the NBA has failed to show any competitive effect whatsoever from SportsTrax on the first and second products and a lack of any free-riding by SportsTrax on the third.

With regard to the NBA's primary products—producing basketball games with live attendance and licensing copyrighted broadcasts of those games—there is no evidence

---

8. Some authorities have labeled this element as requiring direct competition between the defendant and the plaintiff in a primary market. "In most of the small number of cases in which the misappropriation doctrine has been determinative, the defendant's appropriation, like that in *INS*, resulted in direct competition in the plaintiffs' primary market * * * Appeals to the misappropriation doctrine are almost always rejected when the appropriation does not intrude upon the plaintiff's primary market.", Restatement (Third) of Unfair Competition, §38 cmt. c, at 412–13; *see also National Football League v. Delaware*, 435 F. Supp. 1372 (D. Del. 1977). * * *

that anyone regards SportsTrax or the AOL site as a substitute for attending NBA games or watching them on television. In fact, Motorola markets SportsTrax as being designed "for those times when you cannot be at the arena, watch the game on TV, or listen to the radio * * *"

The NBA argues that the pager market is also relevant to a "hot-news" *INS*-type claim and that SportsTrax's future competition with Gamestats satisfies any missing element. We agree that there is a separate market for the real-time transmission of factual information to pagers or similar devices, such as STATS's AOL site. However, we disagree that SportsTrax is in any sense free-riding off Gamestats.

An indispensable element of an *INS* "hot-news" claim is free-riding by a defendant on a plaintiff's product, enabling the defendant to produce a directly competitive product for less money because it has lower costs. SportsTrax is not such a product. The use of pagers to transmit real-time information about NBA games requires: (i) the collecting of facts about the games; (ii) the transmission of these facts on a network; (iii) the assembling of them by the particular service; and (iv) the transmission of them to pagers or an on-line computer site. Appellants are in no way free-riding on Gamestats. Motorola and STATS expend their own resources to collect purely factual information generated in NBA games to transmit to SportsTrax pagers. They have their own network and assemble and transmit data themselves.

To be sure, if appellants in the future were to collect facts from an enhanced Gamestats pager to retransmit them to SportsTrax pagers, that would constitute free-riding and might well cause Gamestats to be unprofitable because it had to bear costs to collect facts that SportsTrax did not. If the appropriation of facts from one pager to another pager service were allowed, transmission of current information on NBA games to pagers or similar devices would be substantially deterred because any potential transmitter would know that the first entrant would quickly encounter a lower cost competitor free-riding on the originator's transmissions.[9]

However, that is not the case in the instant matter. SportsTrax and Gamestats are each bearing their own costs of collecting factual information on NBA games, and, if one produces a product that is cheaper or otherwise superior to the other, that producer will prevail in the marketplace. This is obviously not the situation against which *INS* was intended to prevent: the potential lack of any such product or service because of the anticipation of free-riding.

For the foregoing reasons, the NBA has not shown any damage to any of its products based on free-riding by Motorola and STATS, and the NBA's misappropriation claim based on New York law is preempted.

III. THE NBA'S CROSS-APPEAL

The NBA cross-appeals from the district court's dismissal of its false advertising claim under Section 43(a) of the Lanham Act, 15 U.S.C. §1125(a). This claim was based on a January 1996 Motorola press release stating that SportsTrax provides "updated game information direct from each arena" which "originates from the press table in each

---

9. It may well be that the NBA's product, when enhanced, will actually have a competitive edge because its Gamestats system will apparently be used for a number of in-stadium services as well as the pager market, resulting in a certain amount of cost-sharing. Gamestats might also have a temporal advantage in collecting and transmitting official statistics. Whether this is so does not affect our disposition of this matter, although it does demonstrate the gulf between this case and *INS*, where the free-riding created the danger of no wire service being viable.

arena" and on a statement appearing on the spine of the retail box and on the retail display stand that SportsTrax provides "game updates from the arena."

NBA argues that because STATS reporters collect their information from television and radio broadcasts, the information is not "direct from each arena" or even "from the arena." Motorola responds that the statement about information coming from the press table was an isolated remark occurring only in that press release. It also claims that the assertion that the game updates come "from the arena" is not literally false, presumably because the factual information does originate in the arena.

To establish a false advertising claim under Section 43(a), the plaintiff must demonstrate that the statement in the challenged advertisement is false. * * * However, in addition to proving falsity, the plaintiff must also show that the defendants "misrepresented an 'inherent quality or characteristic'" of the product. * * * This requirement is essentially one of materiality, a term explicitly used in other circuits. * * *

The district court found, "after viewing the complained-of statements in this action in their context," that "the statements as to the particular origin of game updates constitute nothing more than minutiae about SportsTrax." 939 F. Supp. at 1110. We agree with the district court that the statements in question are not material in the present factual context. The inaccuracy in the statements would not influence consumers at the present time, whose interest in obtaining updated game scores on pagers is served only by SportsTrax. Whether the data is taken from broadcasts instead of being observed first-hand is, therefore, simply irrelevant. However, we note that if the NBA were in the future to market a rival pager with a direct data-feed from the arenas—perhaps with quicker updates than SportsTrax and official statistics—then Motorola's statements regarding source might well be materially misleading. On the present facts, however, the complained-of statements are not material and do not misrepresent an inherent quality or characteristic of the product.

IV. CONCLUSION

We vacate the injunction entered by the district court and order that the NBA's claim for misappropriation be dismissed. We affirm the district court's dismissal of the NBA's claim for false advertising under Section 43(a) of the Lanham Act.

Notes and Questions

1. Prior to the NBA's lawsuit against Motorola, the National Football League had sued Stats, Inc. and SportsLine USA, Inc. *See* Complaint, *National Football League v. Stats, Inc.*, 95 Civ. 8547 (KMW) (S.D.N.Y. October 10, 1995). The NFL's lawsuit challenged Stats' creation of a text play-by-play description of NFL games, which had been transmitted to SportsLine and distributed over the internet. The NFL's case against SportsLine was settled prior to the Second Circuit's decision in the NBA's case against Motorola. Under the narrow "hot news" misappropriation test outlined in the *Motorola* decision, what information can an internet site provide about games while they are in progress? Can an internet site (such as SportsLine or the America On-Line site discussed in the court's opinion) provide play-by-play coverage of games that are broadcast on national television by simply watching those games and typing a factual description that does not utilize the commentary of the game announcers?

2. If the answer to the final question in Note 1 is "yes," can the internet provider depict the information graphically, by showing: a scoreboard with the same informa-

tion as the scoreboard at the game; generic cartoon runners (without identifying them by name) moving around the bases in baseball; or a replica of the ball moving down the field in football?

3. Does the *Motorola* decision, considered together with the right of publicity cases and the *Baltimore Orioles* decision, shed any light on the question of whether a pager or an internet site's factual description may include the names of the players and statistical information about their performances in the game? What use would you advise Motorola and Stats, Inc. that they can make of players' names and statistical information, in light of the right of publicity cases and the *Baltimore Orioles* decision considered earlier in this Chapter?

4. Can the play-by-play description of the game include the names of the teams or only the name of the city or state where they play their home games? If the play-by-play is over the internet, can the teams be identified by their logos? *Compare Motorola* with *NFL v. Governor of Delaware*, above.

5. Is the analysis of any of the above questions affected by whether the sports league has its own internet site that provides play-by-play coverage of games in progress?

6. Would it change the analysis if the internet site also included an audio component, which provided additional factual discussion of information about the teams and the players and analysis similar to, but not in any way derived from, the commentary provided by the play-by-play and "color" announcers on the league's television broadcasts? To what extent does the *Motorola* opinion prevent unfair competition claims or other common law claims, such as those considered in the cases cited in Note 2 following the *Boston Athletic Association* case?

7. Does the analysis change if the NFL can show that, as a result of the internet sites' ability to provide subscribers current, almost "real-time" information about all of the NFL games in progress (and those games that were played earlier in the day), certain fans are not watching NFL games that they would otherwise watch on television (thereby decreasing NFL television ratings) and canceling their subscriptions with the NFL to receive broadcasts (via pay-for-view cable or satellite television) of games not otherwise available for viewing in the local market? For example, gamblers who need to know scores and certain other statistics may prefer an internet datafeed to culling the data out of television broadcasts. How could the NFL or any other league ever prove that internet coverage, not including actually seeing the game in progress, "would so reduce the incentive to produce the product or service [the game or television broadcast?] that its existence or quality would be substantially threatened"—the fifth requirement identified by the Second Circuit for a "surviving 'hot-news' *INS*-like claim"? In the same way that the leagues went to Congress to stop state lotteries after they were disheartened by the courts' decisions in *NFL v. Governor of Delaware* and *NBA v. Oregon State Lottery Comm'n*, might you anticipate a congressional visit by professional sports leagues to seek legislative relief from the implications of the Second Circuit's holding?

8. As a public policy matter, should the outcome of the cases or the analysis of the issues be affected by whether the information being provided by means of a pager or an internet site is perceived (or marketed) as state-of-the-art news coverage or as an entertainment product that may become a substitute for attending the games, watching them on television, or listening to them on the radio? Should that policy decision be made by Congress or by the courts applying common law doctrines of the fifty states, to the extent that the common law is not preempted by federal copyright law?

C.B.C. Distribution and Marketing, Inc v.
Major League Baseball Advanced Media, L.P.
and Major League Baseball Players' Association
Case No. 4:05cv00252mlm (E.D. Mo. 2006)

MEDLER, UNITED STATES MAGISTRATE JUDGE. Before the court are the Motion for Summary Judgment filed by Intervenor/Counter Claimant Major League Baseball Players Association, the Motions for Summary Judgment filed by Plaintiff/Counter Defendant C.B.C. Distribution and Marketing, Inc. and the Motion for Summary Judgment filed by Defendant/Counter Claimant Major League Baseball Advanced Media, L.P. The parties have consented to the jurisdiction of the undersigned United States Magistrate Judge pursuant to 28 U.S.C. §636(c)(1).

I. BACKGROUND AND UNDISPUTED FACTS

The Players' Association is the bargaining representative for Major League baseball players and is comprised of almost all persons who are employed as Major League baseball players. Advanced Media was formed in 2000 by various owners of Major League Baseball teams to serve as the interactive media and internet arm of Major League Baseball. As part of its responsibilities Advanced Media is in charge of running Major League Baseball's internet site, MLB.com.

CBC, which uses the trade name CDM Fantasy Sports, is a Missouri corporation whose primary offices are located in St. Louis, Missouri. CBC markets, distributes and sells fantasy sports products, including fantasy baseball games accessible over the Internet. To date, the business of fantasy sports games is a multimillion dollar industry in the United States.

CBC offers its fantasy sports products via telephone, mail, e-mail, and the Internet through its website, www.CDMsports.com. CBC currently offers eleven fantasy baseball games, two mid-season fantasy baseball games, and one fantasy baseball playoff game. CBC provides lists of Major League baseball players for selection by participants in its games. Game participants pay fees to CBC to play its games and pay additional amounts to trade players. Prior to the start of the professional baseball season participants form their teams by "drafting" players from various Major League baseball teams. Participants or "owners" compete against other fantasy owners who have drafted their own teams. The success of one's fantasy team over the course of the baseball season is dependent on one's chosen players' actual performances on their respective actual teams.

In addition to fantasy sports games, CBC's website provides up-to-date information on each player to assist game participants in selecting players for and trading players on their fantasy teams. This information includes information which is typically found in box scores in newspapers such as players' batting averages, at bats, hits, runs, doubles, triples, home runs, etc * * * CBC also hires journalists to write stories relevant to fantasy owners, such as the latest injury reports, player profiles, and player reports.

CBC entered into license agreements with the Players' Association covering the period from July 1, 1995, through December 31, 2004. The 2002 License Agreement stated that it "represents the entire understanding between the parties and supercedes all previous representations." The court, therefore, need only address the terms of the 2002 License Agreement. The 2002 License Agreement stated that the Players' Association was acting on behalf of all the active baseball players of the National League and the American League who entered into a Commercial Authorization Agreement with the Players' Association; that the Players' Association in this capacity had the right to negotiate the Agreements and to grant rights in and to the logo, name, and symbol of the Players' Association, identified as the Trademarks, and "the names, nicknames, likenesses, signatures, pictures, playing records, and/or biographical data of each player," identified as the "Players' Rights"; and that CBC desired to use the "Rights and/or the Trademarks on or in association with the manufacture, offering for sale, sale, advertising, promotion, and distribution of certain products (the 'Licensed Products')."

The 2002 License Agreement included a no-challenge provision which provided that "during any License Period * * * [CBC] will not dispute or attack the title or any rights of Players' Association in and to the Rights and/or the Trademarks or the validity of the license granted." The 2002 License Agreement further stated that upon termination CBC would have no right "* * * to use in any way the Rights, the Trademarks, or any Promotional Material relating to the Licensed Products" and that upon expiration or termination of the License Agreement, CBC shall "refrain from further use of the Rights and/or the Trademarks or any further reference to them, either directly or indirectly. * * *"

Between 2001 and January 2004, Advanced Media offered fantasy baseball games on MLB.com without obtaining a license and without obtaining permission from the Players' Association.

In 2005, Advanced Media entered into an agreement (the "Advanced Media License Agreement") with the Players' Association whereby the Players' Association granted to Advanced Media a license to use "Rights and Trademarks for exploitation via all interactive media," with some exclusions.

On or around January 19, 2005, Advanced Media executive George Kliavkoff sent a request for proposals (the "RFP") to various fantasy game operators and providers including CBC. The RFP invited CBC to submit a proposal under which it would enter into a license agreement with Advanced Media and participate in Advanced Media's fantasy baseball licensing program for the 2005 season.

On February 4, 2005, Advanced Media offered CBC a license to promote Advanced Media's fantasy baseball games on CBC's website in exchange for a percentage share of all related revenue. In particular, Advanced Media stated that it was offering "a full suite of MLB fantasy games" and that CBC could use its "online presence and customer relationships, in conjunction with [Major League Baseball's] marks, to promote the MLB.com fantasy games to [CBC's] customers in exchange for a 10% revenue share from MLB.com on all related revenue." As such, Advanced Media was not offering CBC "a license to promote its own MLB fantasy game for the 2005 season."

On February 7, 2005, CBC filed the Complaint for declaratory judgment in the matter under consideration in which it alleges that it has a reasonable apprehension that it will be sued by Advanced Media if it continues to operate its fantasy baseball games. The Complaint further alleges that Advanced Media has maintained that it has exclusive ownership of statistics associated with players' names and that it can, therefore, preclude all fantasy sports league providers from using this statistical information to provide fantasy baseball games to the consuming public. CBC also seeks injunctive relief asking that Advanced Media and its affiliates be enjoined from interfering with CBC's business related to sports fantasy teams.

Advanced Media and the Players' Association, the latter of which intervened in this matter, assert counterclaims, including a contract violation based on the 2002 License Agreement between the Players' Association and CBC. Advanced Media and the Players'

Association further assert as a counterclaim that CBC violated the players' right of publicity based on CBC's exploiting the rights of players including their names, nicknames, likenesses, signatures, jersey numbers, pictures, playing records and biographical data (the "Player Rights") via all interactive media with respect to fantasy baseball games. Advanced Media and the Players' Association also seek injunctive relief and exemplary and punitive damages.

* * * On the record, in a teleconference of May 24, 2006, CBC clarified that when it speaks of statistics it is referring to players' names and performance records, also referenced as players' playing records or players' records; "player[s'] names plus their performance records are the only thing[s] at issue in this litigation." * * *

* * * [T]he only remaining issues before this court are whether the players have a right of publicity in their names and playing records as used in CBC's fantasy games; whether, if the players have such a right, CBC has, and is, violating the players' claimed right of publicity; whether, if the players have a right of publicity and if this right has been violated by CBC, such a violation is preempted by copyright law; whether, if the players have a right of publicity which has been violated by CBC, the First Amendment applies and, if so, whether it takes precedence over the players' claimed right of publicity; and whether CBC has breached the 2002 Licensing Agreement.

* * *

III. APPLICABLE LAW AND DISCUSSION
A. Right of Publicity:

* * *

The right of publicity is recognized by statute and/or common law in many states. Among those states recognizing the right of publicity is Missouri. [*Doe v. TCI Cablevision,*] 110 S.W.3d [363,]at 368.8 A fairly recent concept, according to the Sixth Circuit in *ETW Corporation v. Jireh Publishing, Inc.,* 332 F.3d 915, 929 (6th Cir. 2003), this right "was first recognized in *Haelan Laboratories, Inc. v. Topps Chewing Gum. Inc.,* 202 F.2d 866 (2nd Cir. 1953), where the Second Circuit held that New York's common law protected a baseball player's right in the publicity value of his photograph, and, in the process, coined the phrase 'right of publicity' as the name of this right." Subsequently, in *Zacchini,* 433 U.S. at 573, where a performer in a "human cannonball" act sought to recover damages from a television broadcast of his entire performance, the Supreme Court recognized that the right of publicity protects the proprietary interest of an individual to "reap the reward of his endeavors."(Mo. 2003) (en banc).[8]

* * *

The right of publicity is described in *Section 46 of the Restatement (Third) of Unfair Competition* (2005), Appropriation of the Commercial Value of a Person's Identity: The

---

8. In TCI a former professional hockey player known as Tony Twist brought suit regarding a comic book titled Spawn which included a character named "Anthony 'Tony Twist' Twistelli." *110 S.W.3d at 365–66.* The jury found in favor of the real Tony Twist and awarded him $ 24.5 million dollars. The trial court entered a judgment notwithstanding the verdict on the grounds that Twist had not made a submissible case. On appeal, the Missouri Supreme Court concluded that Twist had in fact made a submissible case. The court, however, remanded the matter based on an instructional error. Upon retrial, the jury awarded Twist $ 15 million dollars. The defendants filed an appeal asserting, among other things, that their use of Twist's name was protected speech under the *First Amendment.* The Missouri Court of Appeals, Eastern District affirmed the judgment of the trial court. *Doe v. McFarlane,* (Mo. Ct. App. June 20, 2006).

Right of Publicity. This Restatement provision states that "[o]ne who appropriates the commercial value of a person's identity by using without consent the person's name, likeness, or other indicia of identity for purposes of trade is subject to liability. * * *" Relying on the Restatement, the Missouri Supreme Court held in *TCI, 110 S.W.3d at 369*, that "the elements of a right of publicity action include: (1) That defendant used plaintiff's name as a symbol of his identity (2) without consent (3) and with the intent to obtain a commercial advantage." See also *Gionfriddo*, 94 Cal. App.4th at 409 ("The elements of [the tort of the right of publicity], at common law, are: '(1) the defendant's use of the plaintiff's identity; (2) the appropriation of plaintiff's name or likeness to defendant's advantage, commercially or otherwise; (3) lack of consent; and (4) resulting injury.'"). To prove a violation of one's right of publicity a plaintiff must establish that the defendant commercially exploited the plaintiff's identity without the plaintiff's consent to obtain a commercial advantage. *Carson v. Here's Johnny Portable Toilets, Inc.*, 698 F.2d 831, 835 (6th Cir. 1983). Thus, the court will proceed to determine whether the elements of the right of publicity are present in the matter under consideration.

1. Commercial Advantage Element of the Right of Publicity:

It is undisputed that CBC is using the players' names and playing records without the consent of the players * * * As such, the court must consider whether CBC's use of players' names in conjunction with their playing records in its fantasy baseball games utilizes the players' names as a symbol of their identities to obtain a commercial advantage and, if so, whether there is resulting injury.In TCI a former professional hockey player known as Tony Twist brought suit regarding a comic book titled Spawn which included a character named "Anthony 'Tony Twist' Twistelli." *110 S.W.3d at 365–66.* The jury found in favor of the real Tony Twist and awarded him $ 24.5 million dollars. The trial court entered a judgment notwithstanding the verdict on the grounds that Twist had not made a submissible case. On appeal, the Missouri Supreme Court concluded that Twist had in fact made a submissible case. The court, however, remanded the matter based on an instructional error. Upon retrial, the jury awarded Twist $ 15 million dollars. The defendants filed an appeal asserting, among other things, that their use of Twist's name was protected speech under the First Amendment. The Missouri Court of Appeals, Eastern District affirmed the judgment of the trial court. *Doe v. McFarlane*, 2006 Mo. App. LEXIS 876, 2006 WL 1677856 (Mo. Ct. App. June 20, 2006).

In regard to the commercial advantage element of the right of publicity, "it is *irrelevant* whether [a] defendant *intended to injure* the plaintiff." *TCI*, 110 S.W.3d at 371 (citing McCarthy, Rights of Publicity, § 3.28) (emphasis added). The *intent* must be *to obtain a commercial advantage*. Id. Evidence which shows that a defendant *intended to create an impression* that a *plaintiff is associated* with the defendant's product "alone is sufficient to establish the commercial advantage element in a right of publicity action." Additionally, using a plaintiff's name "to attract attention to [a] product" is evidence supporting a conclusion that a defendant sought to obtain a commercial advantage. For example, in *Henley v. Dillard Department Stores*, where it was uncontroverted that the defendant intended to use the plaintiff's name to make an advertisement "more interesting," the court found the requisite intent to use for commercial advantage. 46 F. Supp.2d 587, 592–93 (N.D. Tex. 1999) ("[The defendant] intended for [potential customers] to associate the expression 'Don's henley' with the Plaintiff Don Henley. Furthermore, * * * the ad's designer, admitted that she believed the expression Don's henley would catch the consumers' eye because of its similarity to the name 'Don Henley.'"). See also *Abdul-Jabbar v. Gen. Motors*, 85 F.3d 407, 415–16 (9th Cir. 1996) (quoting

Eastwood v. Superior Court for Los Angeles County, 149 Cal. App.3d 409, 198 Cal. Rptr. 342, 349 (1983) (finding a violation of the right of publicity where the defendant used "the plaintiff's birth name [to] attract[] television viewers' attention.").

Unlike cases where the commercial advantage element of the right of publicity has been found, there is nothing about CBC's fantasy games which suggests that any Major League baseball player is associated with CBC's games or that any player endorses or sponsors the games in any way. The use of names and playing records of Major League baseball players in CBC's games, moreover, is not intended to attract customers away from any other fantasy game provider because all fantasy game providers necessarily use names and playing records * * * As such, there is no triable issue of fact as to whether CBC uses Major League baseball players' names in its fantasy baseball games with the intent of obtaining a commercial advantage.

In regard to the commercial advantage element of the right to publicity and relying on *Palmer v. Schonhorn Enterprises, Inc.,* 96 N.J. Super. 72, 232 A.2d 458 (N.J. Super. 1967), the Players' Association and Advanced Media seek to draw analogy of the matter under consideration to use of a famous person's picture in a board game. As do the baseball players in the matter under consideration, the golfers in *Palmer* contended that "the use of their respective names reduce[d] their ability to obtain satisfactory commercial affiliation by licensing agreements." *Id. at 459.* Upon finding in favor of the golfers, however, the court in *Palmer relied upon the defendant's use of the golfers' pictures* and cited cases wherein recovery was permitted for an *invasion of privacy* where a picture of a famous person was used. *Id.* at 461

To the extent that *Palmer* involved the unauthorized use of professional golfers' names and playing records in the defendant's board games, the court acknowledges that Palmer has certain factual similarities to the matter under consideration, but with the critical exception that the defendant in *Palmer* used golfers' *pictures;* there is no allegation in the matter under consideration that CBC uses baseball players' pictures in conjunction with its fantasy baseball games; rather, the contention is that CBC uses players names in conjunction with their playing records * * * Unlike cases where there was an appropriation of a *likeness* to create the impression that a famous person endorsed a product, CBC's use of players' names in no way creates an impression that players endorse CBC's fantasy games. * * *

Most significantly *Palmer* was decided in 1967 and is inconsistent with more recent case authority including the Supreme Court's decision in *Zacchini.*[12] *Palmer* does not accurately reflect the concept of the right of publicity as articulated by the courts of various jurisdictions including the Supreme Court and, therefore, is not controlling in this matter.[13] In this regard, the court in *Palmer,* 232 A.2d. at 460, acknowledged that, at the

---

12. The Players' Association and Advanced Media also rely upon *Uhlaender v. Henricksen,* 316 F. Supp. 1277 (D. Minn. 1970), which case involved the defendant's use of baseball players' names, uniform numbers and statistical information in its board games. The baseball players in *Uhlaender,* as do baseball players in the matter under consideration, alleged that the defendant engaged in "'misappropriation and use for commercial profit of the names of professional major league baseball players without the payment of royalties.'" *Id.* 1279 (quoting the Complaint) * * * The court in *Uhlaender* found that the defendants engaged in the unauthorized appropriation of the players' "names and statistics for commercial use" and that, therefore, the baseball players were entitled to relief. *Id.* at 1283. Like *Palmer, Uhlaender* was decided early in the development of the recognition of the common law right of publicity and is inconsistent with more recent case authority including the Supreme Court's decision in *Zacchini.* As such, *Uhlaender* is not controlling.

13. The court in *Palmer* failed to consider the element of the right of publicity which requires that a defendant use a plaintiff's identity or persona. More recent authority reflects that use of a person's identity or persona is a critical element in establishing a right to recovery under a right of

time of the decision, recognition of the right of privacy itself was a relatively new concept.

The court finds, therefore, for the reasons fully set forth above that the undisputed facts establish that the commercial advantage element of the right of publicity is not met in the matter under consideration.

2. Identity Element of the Right of Publicity:

It remains to be determined in regard to the elements of the right of publicity whether CBC has, and is, using the players' names "as a symbol of their identity."

* * *

Indeed, not all uses of another's name are tortious; mere use of a name as a name is not tortious. *Id.* Rather, a name must be used as a *symbol of* the plaintiff's *identity* in a right of publicity action * * * CBC's mere use of Major League baseball players' names in conjunction with their playing records does not establish a violation of the players' right of publicity. CBC's use of the baseball players' names and playing records in the circumstances of this case, moreover, does not involve the character, personality, reputation, or physical appearance of the players; it simply involves historical facts about the baseball players such as their batting averages, home runs, doubles, triples, etc. CBC's use of players' names in conjunction with their playing records, therefore, does not involve the persona or identity of any player. Indeed, under the facts of this case there is no triable issue as to whether the persona or identity element of the right of publicity is present.

3. Policy Considerations Applicable to the Right of Publicity

* * * The *Restatement (Third) of Unfair Competition §46, Cmt. c* (2005), states that the justification for the right of publicity includes: (1) protection of "an individual's interest in personal dignity and autonomy"; (2) "secur[ing] for plaintiffs the commercial value of their fame"; (3) prevent[ing] the unjust enrichment of others seeking to appropriate" the commercial value of plaintiffs' fame for themselves; (4) preventing harmful or excessive commercial use that may dilute the value of [a person's] identity"; and (5) "afford[ing] protection against false suggestions or endorsement or sponsorship." "The right to publicity protects the ability of public personae to control the types of publicity that they receive. The right to publicity protects pecuniary, not emotional, interests." * * * This right protects a public figure's right to receive pecuniary gain for the commercial use of his or her likeness. *Haelan Labs.*, 202 F.2d at 868 ("[I]t is common knowledge that many prominent persons (especially actors and ball-players), far from having their feelings bruised through public exposure of their likenesses, would feel sorely deprived if they no longer received money for authorizing advertisements, popularizing their countenances, displayed in newspapers magazines, buses, trains and subways.").

* * *

All of the above the policy considerations are aimed at preventing harmful or excessive commercial use of one's celebrity in a manner which could dilute the value of a person's identity. However, CBC's use of Major League baseball players' names and playing records in fantasy baseball games does not go to the heart of the players' ability to earn a living as baseball players; the baseball players earn a living playing baseball and endors-

---

publicity theory. See e.g., *Cardtoons*, 95 F.3d at 968; *Carson*, 698 F.2d at 835; *Henley*, 46 F. Supp.2d at 597; *TCI*, 110 S.W.3d at 369, 372; *Gionfriddo*, 94 Cal. App.4th at 409.

ing products; they do not earn a living by the publication of their playing records.[20] Moreover, CBC's use of Major League baseball players' names and playing records does not give CBC something free for which it would otherwise be required to pay; players' records are readily available in the public domain. See id.

In fact, case law suggests that CBC's use of the names and playing records of Major League baseball players in the circumstances of this case actually enhances the marketability of the players. The plaintiffs in *Gionfriddo,* 94 Cal. App.4th at 413, who were baseball players themselves, argued that the baseball clubs used players' "information * * * to *increase interest in baseball,* with the belief that this would increase attendance at games." (emphasis added). Additionally, the court concluded in *Gionfriddo* that "the challenged uses [which] involve[d] statements of historical fact, descriptions of these facts or video depictions of them," would "likely" "enhance[]" the players' marketability. *Id.* at 415. As such, it cannot be said that CBC's use of the Major League baseball players' names and playing records in the circumstances of this case deprives the players of their proprietary interest in reaping the reward of their endeavors. * * *

In summary, the court finds that the undisputed facts establish that CBC does not use in its fantasy baseball games Major League baseball players' names separately or in conjunction with their playing records as a symbol of their identity; that CBC does not use players' names separately or in conjunction with their playing records with the intent to obtain a commercial advantage; that CBC's use of players' names separately or in conjunction with their playing records does not contravene the policy behind the right of publicity; and that, therefore, CBC has not and is not violating the players' claimed right of publicity. * * *

B. The First Amendment

* * *

Courts have found that First Amendment freedom of expression is applicable in cases where the subject matter at issue involved *factual data and historical facts.* For example, in *Gionfriddo,* 94 Cal. App.4th at 410, the court concluded that the "precise information conveyed * * * consist[ed] of factual data concerning [baseball] players [and] their performance statistics" and that, as such the *First Amendment* was applicable. The California court in *Gionfriddo* characterized the information conveyed by the defendant as "mere bits of baseball's history." Id. Significantly, the California court further held that the First Amendment protects "recitations of [baseball] players' accomplishments. 'The freedom of the press is constitutionally guaranteed, and the publication of daily news is an acceptable and necessary function in the life of the community.' (citations omitted). 'Certainly, the accomplishments * * * of those who have achieved a marked reputation or notoriety by appearing before the public such as * * * *professional athletes* * * * may legitimately be mentioned and discussed in print or on radio and television.'" Id. (citation omitted) (emphasis in original) * * *

Indeed, the manner in which CBC uses the names and playing records of Major League Baseball players in the context of its fantasy baseball games represents the accomplishments of Major League baseball players. The names and playing records of the

---

20. While not relying on these reports, the court notes that expert reports in the matter under consideration suggest that, in fact, fantasy sports games increase the commercial value of players' identities because the games encourage participants to attend live games, pay for television packages, or watch on television sporting events in which they otherwise would not be interested. See e.g., Saunders Expert Report PP 11–20; Thomas Decl. PP10.

baseball players as used by CBC are, in fact, "bits of baseball history" which educate the public about baseball. Most importantly, the statistical information about Major League baseball players, including their hits, runs, doubles, etc., which CBC disseminates, represents historical facts about baseball players. * * *

A defendant's *making a profit* does not preclude its receiving First Amendment protection. * * * The court finds, therefore, that CBC's deriving a profit from its use of the names and playing records of Major League baseball players in its fantasy baseball games does not preclude such use from having First Amendment protection. * * *

The First Amendment has been applied in the context of the right of publicity where the expression at issue *entertains* * * * Clearly, CBC's use of the names and playing records of Major League baseball players is meant to entertain game participants and persons using CBC's website. The court finds that this characterization, however, does not preclude CBC's use of players' names and playing records from receiving First Amendment protection.

Expression is not disqualified from First Amendment protection because it is *interactive.* Thus, "the breadth of the First Amendment" has been extended to "pictures, graphic design, concept art, sounds, music, stories, and narrative present in video games." The First Amendment is applicable to interactive expression because "literature is most successful when it 'draws the reader into the story, makes him identify with the characters, invites him to judge them and quarrel with them, to experience their joys and sufferings as the reader's own.'" As such, to the extent that CBC's use of the names and playing records of Major League baseball players in the circumstances of this case involves interaction among game participants and between game participants and CBC's website, such interaction does not preclude such use from being protected under the First Amendment.

The Players' Association suggests, to the extent expression is involved in the matter under consideration, that such expression is actually commercial speech and that it is, therefore, not protected under the First Amendment. * * *

"The Supreme Court has defined commercial speech as 'expression related solely to the economic interests of the speaker and its audience.'" Expression, however, is not commercial speech if it does not advertise another unrelated product, and speech is not transformed into commercial speech merely because the product at issue is sold for profit.

In the context of the matter under consideration, CBC communicates information about Major League baseball players; CBC does not use players' names and playing records for the purpose of advertising a product or services. As such, the court finds that CBC's use of the players' names and playing records is not commercial speech.

In summary and for the reasons fully set forth above, the court finds that the players' records which CBC provides are available to the public at large by watching games and are disseminated to the public in newspapers and by statistics providers; CBC uses players' names to convey information, the players' records, which information is already in the public domain. CBC's website encourages game participants to learn about players' playing records and can be said to provide an education in baseball. Further, CBC's games disseminate statistical information about baseball players; this statistical information is historical fact. Indeed, CBC's fantasy baseball games entertain participants based upon baseball history. *See id.* The fact that CBC derives a profit from its games does not preclude use of the players' names and playing records from being protected speech under the First Amendment. Likewise, to the extent that CBC's fantasy baseball games are interactive, use of players' names and playing records in the context of the games is not precluded from First Amendment protection. CBC's use of players' names and playing records in the context of this case is not commercial speech.

For these reasons the court finds that the First Amendment is applicable in the context of the right of publicity claim in the matter under consideration. The court further finds that CBC's use of the names and playing records of Major League baseball players in the context of the matter under consideration is speech which is protected under the First Amendment. * * *

Once it is determined that the First Amendment is applicable in the context of a claim of the right of publicity, courts balance "the right to be protected from unauthorized publicity * * * against the public interest in the dissemination of news and information consistent with the democratic processes under the constitutional guaranties of freedom of speech and of the press.'"

* * *

Upon considering whether the First Amendment takes precedence over a claimed right of publicity, courts "balance the magnitude" of restricting the expression at issue "against the asserted governmental interest in protecting" the right of publicity. As such this court must examine the importance of CBC's right to freedom of expression and the consequences of limiting that right. These consequences must be weighed against the effect of infringing on the Major League baseball players' claimed right of publicity. * * *

In order to apply a First Amendment balancing test this court must first identify the rights involved. Upon identifying the interests at stake in *Zacchini* the Supreme Court considered that a goal of the right of publicity is to "focus[] on the right of the individual to reap the reward of his endeavors" and that this goal has "little to do with protecting feelings or reputation." The Court further noted that, where a right to publicity is claimed, the individual's interest at issue is the right to receive the commercial benefit of the publication of allegedly damaging matter. Upon concluding that the First Amendment did not take precedence over the right of publicity in the circumstances of *Zacchini*, the Court distinguished cases where a person's name is used "for purposes of trade or the incidental use of a name or picture by the press" from those which *"go[] to the heart of [a person's] ability to earn a living"* and which involve *"the very activity by which the entertainer acquired his reputation in the first place."* Clearly baseball players make a living playing baseball and may capitalize on their fame by endorsing products. In the matter under consideration, however, CBC's use of the names and playing records of Major League baseball players does not interfere with the players' ability to reap financial reward from these endeavors. As stated above, CBC's use of Major League baseball players' names and playing records in the circumstances of this case, therefore, does not go to the heart of the players' ability to earn a living.

Additionally, economic incentive is also justification for the right of publicity, particularly "in the field[] of sports."[27] In regard to the economic incentive element at stake in the right of publicity, the court in *Cardtoons* made the following observation which is applicable in the circumstances of the matter under consideration:

---

27. Noting that there are noneconomic justifications for the right of publicity, the court in *Cardtoons, 95 F.3d at 975*, did state that, "[p]rofessional athletes may be more responsible for their celebrity status [than other celebrities], however, because athletic success is fairly straightforwardly the result of an athlete's natural talent and dedication. Thus, baseball players may deserve to profit from the commercial value of their identities more than movie stars."

[T]he additional *inducement for achievement* produced by publicity rights are often inconsequential because most celebrities with valuable commercial identities are already handsomely compensated. * * * [F]or example, * * * major league baseball players' salaries currently average over one million dollars per year, see Bill Brashler, *Booooooooooooooooo! Let's Hear It for Pampered, Preening, Overpaid Whiners: The Jocks,* Chi. Trib., July 28, 1996, (Magazine), at 12. Such figures suggest that "even without the right of publicity the rate of return to stardom in the entertainment and sports fields is probably high enough to bring forth a more than 'adequate' supply of creative effort and achievement." In addition, even in the absence of publicity rights, celebrities would still be able to reap financial reward from authorized appearances and endorsements. The extra income generated by licensing one's identity does not provide a necessary inducement to enter and achieve in the realm of sports and entertainment. Thus, while publicity rights may provide some incentive for creativity and achievement, the magnitude and importance of that incentive has been exaggerated.

Upon examining the interests involved in the right of publicity, right of publicity cases involving the value of one's performance, such as *Zacchini*, must be distinguished from right of publicity cases involving the economic value of one's identity. As the matter under consideration does not involve actual performances of the Major League baseball players but rather involves an allegation that CBC uses the players' identities, the incentive rationale is not compelling in the circumstances of the matter before this court.

Another economic justification for the right of publicity is that it "promotes the efficient allocation of resources." Id. "The efficiency argument is most persuasive in the context of advertising, where repeated use of a celebrity's likeness to sell products may eventually diminish its commercial value. The argument is *not as persuasive,* however, when applied to *nonadvertising uses.*" Significantly, the matter under consideration does not involve advertising.

Another "argument offered for rights of publicity is that they protect against consumer deception." * * * In the circumstances of the matter before this court, CBC's use of the names and playing records of Major League baseball players does not suggest that the baseball players are making representations in regard to the sale of any product. As such, there is no likelihood of confusion or deception in the context of the matter before this court.

It has been said that the right of publicity seeks to allow persons to enjoy the fruits of the goodwill which they have created. Indeed, professional athletes have responsibility for their celebrity status based on their athletic achievements; their fame, however, is nonetheless "largely [a] creation of the media or the audience." As such, balancing the scale in favor of the First Amendment in the circumstances of the matter before this court will not interfere with the ability of Major League baseball players to enjoy the fruits of their goodwill.

Another justification for the right of publicity includes the prevention of unjust enrichment. In the circumstances of the matter under consideration, as CBC merely uses players' names and playing records which are already in the public domain, there is no possibility of unjust enrichment.

In regard to the rights of the public which countervail the interests involved in the right of publicity, the public has an "interest in the dissemination of news and information consistent with the democratic processes under the constitutional guaranties of freedom of speech and of the press." * * * This court has found, in the circumstances of this case, that CBC's use of the names and playing records of Major League baseball players in its fantasy baseball games informs and entertains about the history of baseball. The public's interest in this suggests that the interests should be balanced in favor of the First Amendment rather than in favor of the right of publicity.

Also, it is significant in the matter before this court that if the players' right of publicity were to prevail over CBC's First Amendment right of freedom of expression, CBC's First Amendment right of freedom of expression would be totally extinguished; CBC would be unable to create and operate its fantasy games as the games cannot operate without the players' **names** *and* **playing records.** To the extent that Advanced Media and the Players' Association contend that they do not object to the use of players' playing records but rather only to their names, such use by CBC is not realistic; the records mean nothing without the names. For example, it would be meaningless and useless to its game participants for CBC to report that there were five home runs or ten singles in a baseball game without identifying the players who hit the home runs or singles. As such, CBC would be out of business if it were precluded from using in its fantasy games either players' names or their names in conjunction with their playing records. See e.g., *ETW Corp.*, 332 F.3d at 938 ("Permitting [Tiger] Woods's right of publicity to trump [the defendant's] right of freedom of expression would extinguish [the defendant's] right to profit from his creative enterprise).

In summation, the court finds that the First Amendment applies in the matter under consideration. Moreover, assuming, arguendo, that the players have a right of publicity in their names and playing records and that CBC has and is violating the players' right of publicity, the court finds, in the circumstances of this case, that the players' right of publicity must give way to CBC's First Amendment right to freedom of expression.

C. Federal Copyright Law:

* * * CBC and the Fantasy Sports Trade Association contend that, even if the players' have a right of publicity and this right was violated, federal copyright law preempts this right.

* * *

This court has found above that the names and playing records of Major League Baseball players in the context of CBC's fantasy games are factual information which is otherwise available in the public domain, including newspaper box scores * * * Clearly, the names and playing records of Major League Baseball players as used by CBC in its fantasy baseball games are akin to the names, towns and telephone numbers in a phone book, to census data, and to news of the day. Most significantly, players' names and playing records as used in CBC's fantasy games do not involve the *sine qua non* of copyright—originality. * * * This court finds, therefore, that, while the players' names and playing records in the context of CBC's fantasy games are arguably within the subject matter of copyright, the players' names and playing records as used by CBC in its fantasy games are not copyrightable. As such, the court further finds that copyright preemption does not apply in the matter under consideration.

D. The 2002 License Agreement:

The Players Association and Advanced Media contend that by operating its fantasy games without a license CBC is violating the 2002 Agreement pursuant to which CBC agreed not to use in any way the rights which were the subject of the 2002 Agreement beyond the term of the Agreement. * * *

First, to the extent the Players' Association and Advanced Media contend that CBC agreed not to use players' *identities* after the term of the 2002 Agreement, the court has found above that CBC has not and is not using players' identities in its fantasy games. * * *

In regard to a license of a patent, "licensees may avoid further royalty payments, regardless of the provisions of their contract, once a third party proves that the patent is invalid." *Lear,* 395 U.S. at 659, 667 (citation omitted). "Licensee estoppel" is not applicable where the "strong federal policy favoring the full and free use of ideas in the public domain" outweighs the public interest against the "competing demands of patent and contract law. * * *

* * *

Thus, Lear suggests that if the Players' Association, as a licensor, did not have the authority to license the players' names and playing records, the federal public policy of permitting and encouraging full and free competition of ideas takes precedence over the 2002 Agreement's prohibiting CBC's use of the names and playing records in the absence of a license.

In response to the argument that Lear is not applicable to the matter under consideration because it is a patent case, CBC argues, and this court agrees, that subsequent authority has extended Lear beyond the context of patent law. In *M & M Produce,* 335 F.3d at 131–32, the court considered the argument "that [a] no-challenge provision [in a license agreement] should not be enforced because it violate[d] the public policy embodied in the Lanham Act" and concluded that "'there can be no licensee estoppel involving a certification mark.'" Upon considering the applicability of Lear, the court in *M&M Produce,* 335 F.3d at 137, noted that "Lear itself recognized that federal policy embodied in the law of *intellectual property* can trump even explicit contractual provisions. * * * Lear makes clear that courts should weigh the federal policy embodied in the law of *intellectual property* against even explicit contractual provisions and render unenforceable those provisions that would undermine the public interest."

Upon concluding that Lear was applicable, the Second Circuit held in *M&M Produce,* that courts have "recognized that agreements related to *intellectual property* necessarily involve the public interest and have enforced such agreements only to the extent that enforcement does not result in a public injury." * * *

Advanced Media argues that Lear is not applicable in the matter before this court because it involves the right of publicity which is a creature of state and not federal law; as such, the strong federal interest as expressed in patent matters is not present. In *Zacchini,* 433 U.S. at 573, however, the Supreme Court held that in matters involving the right of publicity "the State's interest is closely analogous to the goals of patent and copyright law, focusing on the right of the individual to reap the reward of his endeavors and having little to do with protecting feelings or reputation." Thus, *Zacchini* establishes that Lear and its progeny are applicable to the matter under consideration where the players claim the right of publicity. As such, the public interests embodied in intellectual property law and those embodied in the right of publicity must be balanced to determine whether the challenged provisions of the 2002 Agreement should be enforced.

This court has concluded above that the First Amendment is applicable to CBC's claim that it is not required to have a license to use players' names and playing records in its fantasy games and that the First Amendment, in fact, prevails over the players' claimed right of publicity. Were the court to give effect to the no-challenge provision in the 2002 Agreement and to the provision prohibiting CBC from using the players' names and playing records without a license, information which is otherwise readily accessible would be removed from the public domain and CBC's First Amendment rights would be infringed. As such, balancing the interests in favor of CBC would facilitate enforcement of the First Amendment.

This court has also noted above that Major League baseball players make a living from playing baseball and from endorsements; that they are well compensated for these endeavors; but that CBC's use of players' names and records in its fantasy games does not go to the heart of the players' ability to earn a living. As such, balancing the interests in the matter under consideration in favor of CBC would have little impact on either the players' ability to earn a living or on their incentive for achievement.

The court, therefore, finds that in the circumstances of this case "the strong federal policy favoring the full and free use of ideas in the public domain" as manifested in the laws of intellectual property prevails over the challenged contractual provisions in the 2002 Agreement. As such, the court further finds that the no-challenge provision in the 2002 Agreement and the provision which prohibits CBC from using players' names and/or playing records without acquiring a license are unenforceable and void as a matter of public policy.

IV. CONCLUSION

For the reasons more fully set forth above, the court finds that the undisputed facts establish that the players do not have a right of publicity in their names and playing records as used in CBC's fantasy games and that CBC has not violated the players' claimed right of publicity. The court further finds, alternatively, that even if the players have a claimed right of publicity, the First Amendment takes precedence over such a right. The court further finds that the undisputed facts establish that the names and playing records of Major League baseball players as used in CBC's fantasy games are not copyrightable and, therefore, federal copyright law does not preempt the players' claimed right of publicity. Additionally, the court finds that the no-challenge provision of the 2002 Agreement between CBC and the Players' Association and the provision of this Agreement which prohibits CBC from using players' names and playing records after the expiration of the Agreement are unenforceable based on public policy considerations. The court finds, therefore, that declaratory judgment should issue in CBC's favor. As such, the court will order the Players' Association and Advanced Media to refrain from interfering with CBC's fantasy games in the manner proscribed by this court's decision.

Notes and Questions

1. In fantasy sports games, the names and performances of the athletes are the product. Whether it is "rotisserie league" or "fantasy" baseball or "fantasy" football, the entire game is simulated "buying" and "trading" of professional athletes, with the winners and losers determined solely by reference to the performance of the individual athletes on the field. The United States Magistrate Judge who decided the *CBC* case cited *Henley v. Dillard Department Stores* for the proposition that "using a plaintiff's name 'to attract attention to [a] product' is evidence supporting a conclusion that a defendant sought to

obtain a commercial advantage." Do you agree that a game that is based entirely on the names and performances of professional athletes, a game that consumers only purchase because they know it encompasses the performances of all (or virtually all) the players in a league, does not constitute using the "identity" of those players "with the intent of obtaining a commercial advantage"? Does the existence of trivia games (*e.g.,* Trivial Pursuit), which consist of trivia questions that often deal with the names, personalities, and facts and statistics about celebrities, public figures, and historical figures, support the Court's conclusion that the First Amendment permits CBC to produce its games without securing a license from all the players?

2. The Court distinguished *Palmer v. Schonhorn Enterprises, Inc.,* 96 N.J. Super. 72, 232 A.2d 458 (N.J. Super. 1967), on the basis that the golf board game in *Palmer* included use of the pictures of players in the game. Pictures obviously were not essential to the playing of the game at issue in *Palmer*—is there any indication in *Palmer* that the outcome would have been different if pictures of the players were not included?

3. The Magistrate Judge in *CBC* says *Palmer v. Schonhorn Enterprises, Inc.* and *Uhlaender v. Henricksen,* 316 F. Supp. 1277 (D. Minn. 1970), were "decided early in the development of the recognition of the common law right of publicity and [are] inconsistent with more recent case authority including the Supreme Court's decision in *Zacchini*." Do you agree? Does the *CBC* decision mean that manufacturers without any license can sell fantasy sports games, board games based on the historical performance of players, and video games in which the generic players (the players do not bear the image or likeness of the players whose name they bear) in the game are identified by the names of professional players (and perhaps perform better or worse depending on the statistics of the professional players whose names they bear)? Can the manufacturers combine the *CBC* decision with the decision in *National Football League v. Governor of Delaware* and identify the teams by their city names? For example, can the American League baseball team from New York (with players whose names and statistics correspond to the names and statistics of the players on the New York Yankees roster) play the National League baseball team from San Francisco in a board game or a video game, without any royalty owed to Major League Baseball, any Major League team, or any Major League Baseball player?

4. The *CBC* decision includes the statement that "CBC's use of the baseball players' names and playing records in the circumstances of this case, moreover, does not involve the character, personality, reputation, or physical appearance of the players." Did *Henley v. Dillard Department Stores* involve Don Henley's character, personality, reputation, or physical appearance? Did the use of the term "Crazylegs, " at issue in *Hirsch v. S.C. Johnson & Son, Inc.,* invoke Elroy Hirsch's character or persona, or just his nickname earned because he broke free for long runs as a football running back? For most professional athletes, what is their reputation beyond their ability to perform? Some athletes may have been on television enough that they are recognizable by the general public, but even many avid football and baseball fans would not be able to identify the photos of a substantial majority of the players whose statistics they know well. What do fans know of the character, personality, or reputation of a Major League Baseball pitcher beyond his reputation for winning games, having a low Earned Run Average, starting games or serving as a middle inning reliever or a "closer," or forcing opponents to hit into double plays? If a player is viewed as a "clutch" hitter or an outstanding fielder, it is primarily based on his statistical performance. Fans are interested in baseball players because they are "perennial .300 hitters" or they rarely commit errors in the field and are

therefore "Gold Glove" award winners. In many cases those statistics are their reputation, their persona, and their identity in the world of sports.

5. The Magistrate Judge observed that "CBC's use of Major League baseball players' names and playing records does not give CBC something free for which it would otherwise be required to pay; players' records are readily available in the public domain." Pictures of players are in the public domain, but that does not mean that a manufacturer can use those pictures in manufacturing and selling products. If a manufacturer prominently states that its video game is "unauthorized," can the manufacturer sell a Tony Hawk skateboarding video game or a Derek Jeter baseball game? Would the Court really say that the company manufacturing the Tony Hawk video game is not involved in commercial speech? How can the Court say a corporation selling a fantasy baseball game is not involved in commercial speech?

6. The *CBC* decision potentially puts at risk the ability of Major League Baseball players and their union, the Major League Baseball Players Association ("MLBPA"), to earn tens of millions of dollars each year from manufacturers of trading cards, video games, board games, and fantasy games. The *CBC* decision holds that current MLBPA licensees can simply stop paying royalties, based on the argument that the license agreements "undermine the public interest" and are therefore unenforceable. Those are the funds that make it possible for the players associations to operate, and to pay millions of dollars each year to the more than 750 Major League Baseball players and the more than 1,600 National Football League players. For young, non-superstar Major League Baseball players, their share of the MLBPA's licensing royalties from trading cards, video games, and fantasy games is not an insignificant portion of their income. Those are also the revenues that fund retirement accounts for current and former players and funded the NFL players' litigation against the NFL from 1987 to 1993 and the MLBPA strike funds that helped Major League Baseball players endure strikes and lockouts in their labor law struggles against Major League Baseball. Nevertheless, the Magistrate Judge concludes that "balancing the scale in favor of the First Amendment in the circumstances of the matter before this court will not interfere with the ability of Major League baseball players to enjoy the fruits of their goodwill" and ruling in favor of "CBC would have little impact on either the players' ability to earn a living or on their incentive for achievement." Should that be the test? If that is the test, should the outcome be the same if CBC were using pictures of the athletes as well, as long as no purchaser believed the use of pictures, names, and statistics was authorized? Would the answer be different if it concerned a fantasy soccer game about the performance of Major League Soccer players, who do not earn 7-figure salaries (many do not earn 6-figure salaries and some earn less than $25,000 per year) ? In the cases about "Crazylegs" Hirsch and Don Henley and Muhammad Ali (*Ali v. Playgirl, Inc.*, 447 F. Supp. 723 (S.D.N.Y. 1978)), was there ever any suggestion that in order to assert a right of publicity the plaintiff had to prove that he (or all football players, singers, or boxers) would not have worked as hard to achieve success if he did not have the right to prevent the defendant from using their name and/or likeness or the right to demand a royalty for such use? How could a plaintiff hope to prove that young athletes make decisions based on the amounts athletes receive from licensing revenue? Should the focus of cases concerning athletes' rights of publicity be on how much money the athletes make or on the extent to which the defendant is selling a product that is demanded by the public because the product is all about the name and identity of the athlete(s)?

7. How important to the Court is the fact that Major League Baseball did not offer CBC "a license to promote its own MLB fantasy game for the 2005 season," but rather

offered CBC the right to market Major League Baseball's fantasy game? Would the decision have been different if CBC simply decided it was no longer interested in paying a royalty for the right to license the players' names and statistics? The Court states that "it is significant in the matter before this court that if the players' right of publicity were to prevail over CBC's First Amendment right of freedom of expression, CBC's First Amendment right of freedom of expression would be totally extinguished; CBC would be unable to create and operate its fantasy games as the games cannot operate without the players' names and playing records." How does a decision not to license intellectual property to everyone give a potential licensee who is not offered a license a stronger First Amendment claim that leads to a decision that the intellectual property is not protected and is available without license to everyone?

8. In reading the *CBC* decision do you get the feeling that the Magistrate Judge, like Judge Padova in *Piazza*, is working too hard to make the law fit her conclusion, even to the point of mischaracterizing cases and characterizing the sale by a single competitor of competing fantasy sports games as a core First Amendment issue?

9. College football players are not permitted to license their names and likenesses because of NCAA rules. Therefore, they do not lose any money when a fantasy game is developed based on their names and statistics. If the businesses cannot proceed without a license they will lose their "First Amendment right" to produce such a game because a license is not available from anyone. Does that mean those college players do not have a right of publicity and cannot sue to enjoin commercial exploitation of their names and performances? Does it mean that anyone can produce NCAA fantasy sports games without securing a license from anyone?

10. The Court suggests that fantasy baseball games may generate interest in professional sports and thereby increase the profitability of those sports. The same may be true of gambling on sporting events; video games and trading cards; and photographs, posters and action figures of athletes that create a bond between the children who buy them and the athletes they depict. How is that relevant to whether the First Amendment permits a manufacturer to sell such products without the consent of the athletes who are a central component of all of those products?

11. Do the decisions in *National Basketball Ass'n v. Motorola, Inc.*, *ETW*, and *CBC* reflect a judicial hostility toward the control by professional sports leagues, players associations, and athletes of products associated with the leagues and highly-compensated professional athletes? As a matter of public policy, does the substantial public interest in sports and sports' importance in society support the view that businesses should be free to create products about athletes and the competitions in which they participate without having to compensate the athletes or their leagues? Should that decision be made by courts or by state or federal legislatures?

Chapter 23

The Player Agent and Sports

I. Introduction

Today sports agents, or representatives of individual professional athletes, occupy center stage in the theater of sports. They have climbed several rungs in the ladder of the sports industry's hierarchy since Charles Pyle first represented Harold "Red" Grange in his contract negotiations with the Chicago Bears. *See* Alec Powers, *The Need to Regulate Sports Agents,* 4 SETON HALL J. SPORTS L. 253, 255 (1994). For several years, club management chose to ignore those persons purporting to represent the athletes within the team's employ and, at times, retaliated against players who were so bold as to seek the services of outside counselors, lawyers, or agents. One humorous incident is illustrative: Supposedly, all-pro center Jim Ringo hired an agent to represent him in contract negotiations with his club, the Green Bay Packers. The revered Vince Lombardi, Packers' head coach and general manager, met briefly with the agent and quickly excused himself. When Lombardi returned, he advised the agent that Ringo had been traded, and that he should commence negotiations with the new team. *See* DAVID MARANISS, WHEN PRIDE STILL MATTERED 354 (1999); Michael A. Weiss, *The Regulation of Sports Agents: Fact or Fiction,* 1 SPORTS L.J. 329, 330 (Spring 1994). *See also* Jeffrey P. Crandall, *The Agent-Athlete Relationship in Professional and Amateur Sports: The Inherent Potential for Abuse and the Need for Regulation,* 30 BUFF. L. REV. 815, 815 n.2 (1981).

Several factors undoubtedly have contributed to the emergence of agents as dominant features of the sports landscape. Needless to say, free agency and salary arbitration have made salary negotiation the high stakes game that it has become. Other factors have contributed to the escalating salaries that have seriously upped the ante, including the evolution of players associations as viable and powerful trade unions, the periodic sprouting of rival leagues, and related developments. The derivative effect of the increases in the players' standard of living is a greater need for advice in the areas of estate planning, securities, tax, etc. *See* Powers, *supra,* at 256. The utility of an agent is by no means limited to player-club negotiations. The emergence of the athlete as folk hero, media darling, advertising plum, and industry spokesperson has expanded the range of commercial entanglement exponentially, and the agent's role has expanded in kind.

Finally, today's athletes are more sophisticated and more educated; they recognize the myriad problems that attend a seemingly uncomplicated contract negotiation, and they are savvy enough to acknowledge their own limitations in addressing these problems or following the lead of the top players in their sports. Ironically, the naïve athlete of the past, the individual most in need of outside counsel, typically was left to his own devices in dealing with his team. Doubtless, this phenomenon was largely a product of the player's failure to appreciate the value of third-party advisors or, in terms of job security, his fear of retribution for having the temerity to involve outsiders in the bargaining process.

A great deal of the literature treating the sports agent focuses upon three principal areas and levels of inquiry: (1) the prerequisites to become an agent and the duties and responsibilities that attend the representation of a professional athlete; (2) the pertinent regulations that govern an agent's eligibility and conduct; and (3) the abuses that have been perpetuated by unscrupulous, unqualified, or careless agents. In the following sections, we will discuss the standards (such as they are) for gaining recognition as an agent, as well as the various functions that an agent serves. We will delineate the agent's typical responsibilities, both from a general standpoint as well as from the perspective of specific sports and the idiosyncratic demands that they may exact. We will briefly address the attempts to regulate agents' conduct, including consideration of pertinent state legislation, regulations of the major sports' players associations (unions), NCAA rules, federal statutes, and professional codes of conduct. The overview of these efforts to monitor the activities of sports agents will yield evidence that, while they manifest a step in the right direction, they have yet to curb many of the recurring abuses. Lastly, we will consider examples of allegedly untoward agent conduct that has resulted in litigation at various levels, in both civil and criminal contexts. For excellent overviews of the law surrounding the sports agent enterprise, see Ted Curtis, *The Regulation of Sports Agents, in* Law of Professional and Amateur Sports §§ 1-1 *et seq.* (Gary A. Uberstine ed., 2005); Martin J. Greenberg & James T. Gray, Sports Law Practice Chapter 10, Appendix H (1998); Glenn M. Wong, Essentials of Sports Law Chapter 12 (3d ed. 2002).

II. Agents' Duties and Responsibilities

How does one become a sports agent? The cynical answer has been: "Open your mouth and declare yourself one." David Nightingale, *Are Agents a Pack of Parasites? Some Gouge, Lie and Cheat; Others Do Honest Competent Job*, The Sporting News, Feb. 6, 1987, at 11. *See also* Greenberg & Gray, *supra*, § 10.02, at 937. In truth, unless an agent is providing specific advice, such as a legal opinion, investment counseling, etc., there are few rules mandating minimum standards of expertise, experience, or competence. As discussed below, various governing regulations establish filing and registration requirements, but they are conspicuously devoid of any meaningful eligibility criteria.

The functions that an agent serves for his or her client run a wide gamut. Generally, the agent serves in various capacities as an athlete's representative, including lawyer, stock broker, tax consultant, estate planner, travelling secretary, public relations guru, etc. *See* Weiss at 329. *See also* Greenberg & Gray, *supra*, § 10.07, at 963–67; Robert P. Garbarino, *So You Want To Be a Sports Lawyer, or Is It a Player Agent, Player Representative, Sports Agent, Contract Advisor, Family Advisor or Contract Representative?*, 1 Vill. Sports & Ent. L. Forum 11 (1994). However, the function commonly associated with the sports agent and the duty that typically assumes the greatest importance is contract negotiations with the athlete's team. The agent's familiarity with all pertinent documentation (prior contracts, collective bargaining agreements, etc.), knowledge of all parties' financial conditions, awareness of contractual arrangements of other players and clubs, responsiveness to a player's immediate concerns, and sound business judgment are all crucial to successful dispatch of this function.

Judgment, in particular, can be critically important in assessing how hard to push contract negotiations. Agents and players must recognize that the players' interests are not always served by gaining increases in salary, if those additional funds are purchased at a cost of alienating one's teammates, coaches, fans, and others associated with the league. Nowhere was this lesson more vividly illustrated than in ex-Philadelphia Eagles receiver Terrell Owens's contract negotiations. Owens had completed one year of a seven-year, $49 million contract in 2005, when he hired notoriously aggressive agent Drew Rosenhaus and sought to renegotiate the contract. Owens threatened not to report to training camp and, though he did ultimately report to camp on time, his frequent conflicts with his head coach and his criticism of his own quarterback quickly foreshadowed Owens's departure from the Eagles. He was suspended from the club and released, later to be signed by the Dallas Cowboys. The episode destroyed Owens's reputation and made him — and Rosenhaus — the public faces of greed and self-centeredness in modern sports. In retrospect, at least, Rosenhaus's hard-line negotiating tactics seem to have backfired with Owens, though they often have been successful for other clients.

Another critical role that the agent assumes is that of conduit between the player and outside business opportunities — commercial endorsements. Athletes, for better or worse, have become role models, and their marketability knows few boundaries. The superstar may be presented with countless opportunities to act as spokesperson for, or otherwise to lend his name or image to, a particular product or service. The player's agent may be called upon to assess the prudence of such endorsement opportunities. This evaluation may entail numerous considerations, including the applicability of any contractual limitations or other legal restrictions upon such endorsement (e.g., conflicts with obligations to the team, prohibitions imposed by other endorsement deals, etc.), the impact upon the athlete's overall image, the quality of the product, and the effect upon future endorsement possibilities. An endorsement may yield immediate ego gratification and economic rewards but also may, in the long run, doom the athlete's chances for a wider range of endorsements over the life of his career. For example, an athlete who responds affirmatively to a request to pose in a notoriously risqué magazine may reap some short-term financial benefits, only to compromise a host of other opportunities to endorse more family-oriented products. Again, Terrell Owens provides a colorful example. In 2005, Owens appeared with *Desperate Housewives* actress Nicolette Sheridan in a skit introducing *Monday Night Football*. The skit had Sheridan approaching Owens in the locker room and, ahem, distracting him from his job. ABC later apologized for airing the clip, and the event further cemented Owens's reputation for egocentrism.

The agent's role in endorsement scenarios is multi-faceted. Not only must he or she appraise the utility and value of the particular endorsement, he or she must also negotiate the most favorable terms and payment options with due regard for the relevant tax consequences and other matters collateral to the contract at hand. If he or she does not possess the requisite experience or expertise to offer the proper advice in this regard, he or she should ensure that the athlete secures the appropriate counsel.

At times, the agent's job may include, or be limited to, a money-management function. This role may involve tasks as mundane as paying bills or filing tax returns and as sophisticated as offering advice on complex stock transactions or developing highly technical financial plans. *See generally* James W. Grossman, *Financial Planning for the Professional Athlete, in* LAW OF PROFESSIONAL AND AMATEUR SPORTS, *supra*, §§ 3-1 *et seq.* (2002). To the extent that the agent is immersed in investment advice or legal recommendations, he or she must comply with pertinent rules governing such pursuits. Failure to do so could visit harsh consequences upon the agent, including, but not limited to, the voiding of the agency agreement with the client and possible forfeiture of fees. *See, e.g.,* Investment Advisers Act of 1940, 15 U.S.C. §80b-1 *et seq.* (1940); AMERICAN BAR ASSOCIATION MODEL RULES OF PROFESSIONAL CONDUCT. *See also Zinn v. Parrish*, 644 F.2d 360 (7th Cir. 1981), *below.*

Of course, the responsibilities that an agent assumes will turn on the specific relationship with the athlete. The agent may provide only a narrow service due to limitations in expertise or interest, or he or she may be part of a large management group that offers a full panoply of comprehensive representation options. Further, the types of representation provided, the roles assumed, and the functions served will vary from player to player and from sport to sport. An agent should be aware that the needs of each client and the peculiarities of each sport will dictate different approaches and will require special levels of expertise.

For example, an agent representing a professional golfer or tennis player will undoubtedly perform services for those athletes that parallel the services provided to the athlete in traditional team sports. General advice regarding estate planning, accounting, investments, personal legal issues, post-athletic career vocational training, insurance, insulation from invasions of privacy and misuse of image, involvement in civic activities, and similar matters will likely apply "across the board," independent of the sports involved. However, other areas of counsel will require a specialized understanding of the athlete's particular sport and the potential opportunities and pitfalls that participation in each sport creates. The agent should be aware of the history, economics, and operational nuances of each sport, unique legal and commercial issues facing that sport, the competing players, and similar background data. By way of illustration, an agent representing a professional tennis player should be equipped to provide client advice in areas such as the circuit and non-circuit events that he or she should enter, the advisability of playing doubles and the most suitable doubles partners, the use and choice of practice partners, the location of practice courts (especially in areas in which the athlete is unfamiliar (*e.g.,* foreign sites)), interpretation of the rules and regulations governing play in the various circuits, selection of trainers and other medical advisors, travel arrangements (*e.g.,* hotel and airplane reservations, rental cars, etc.), and related services. Because there is no team affiliation, the tennis player is often left to fend for himself or herself in these areas, and the patient "hand-holding" of a conscientious agent can prove invaluable. Many of these same scenarios should apply in the context of a professional golfer or other "independent contractor" who does not enjoy the perks of team affiliation.

In addition to the foregoing distinctions between the needs of individual athletes and team players, there are critical differences involved in promoting the endorsement of the "tools of the trade." In individual sports, there are seemingly an infinite number of clothing and equipment manufacturers, and a potpourri of possible fashion options available to the participant. While team-sport athletes may endorse Nike or Reebok and other clothing/equipment manufacturers, they wear designated uniforms and ply their trade in accordance with the fashion dictates of the league. In individual sports, the products that the athlete endorses are part of each match's performance, and the athletes become veritable walking advertisements each time that they step on the court or course. Accordingly, the agent's dealings with the various manufacturers who provide the apparel and equipment assume added importance. Thorough research on tennis racquets, golf clubs, balls, shoes, etc., becomes an indispensable part of the agent's responsibilities in an individual-sport context.

Agents representing team-sports players have a major concern that does not afflict agents of athletes in individual sports—the predominance of collective bargaining representatives. As discussed in earlier chapters, the players in all major professional sports leagues are represented by unions. These unions (players' associations) are exclusive representatives for purposes of dealing with management about wages, hours, and working conditions. The line of demarcation between aggressively representing an individual player and encroaching upon the jurisdiction of the collective bargaining representative is not always clear. See Chapter 15, *Midland Broadcasting Co.*, 93 NLRB 455 (1951), and the *Notes and Questions* that follow; Wong, *supra*, § 12.5. Beyond this inherent tension, representation of the team-sports athlete has its own set of problems and demands. Intimate familiarity with the pertinent labor agreement and its restrictions is crucial. Unique provisions regarding salary arbitration, drug testing, special covenant limitations, and the like are overarching concerns in negotiating a player's standard contract. For example, the NBA-NBPA agreement contains a narrowly circumscribed list of provisions that may be included as special covenants in the standard NBA contract. Major League Baseball's special covenants are not nearly so limited, but do include prohibitions, such as limitations on the ability to negotiate incentive rewards for such individual accomplishments as home runs, RBIs, etc.

The concept of team affiliation also may suggest a somewhat different approach to community relations, local endorsements, participation in charitable causes, and other activities that take on heightened importance where one's home and place of business share a common locale. Likewise, cultivation of local business contacts may be a most prudent investment of time that could ensure the player's financial security long after his or her playing career has ended.

Again, the duties and responsibilities of a sports agent will vary from case to case. Suffice it to say that the agent should exercise care to avoid entering any area in which lack of experience or expertise compromises the client and visits charges of incompetence, or worse. In embarking upon a career as a sports agent, one should be mindful of specialized client needs, due both to the peculiar situation of the client as well as the idiosyncratic aspects of the sport in which he or she participates. The agent should also make every effort to become familiar with all governing rules and regulations, many of which are addressed immediately below.

III. Pertinent Regulations

Since the emergence of the sports agent as a significant and influential force in the sports industry, there have been repeated outcries for responsible legislation and regulation to govern the athlete-representation process. The criticism primarily has centered upon: "(1) income mismanagement; (2) excessive fees; (3) conflicts of interest; (4) incompetence; (5) overly aggressive client reimbursement practices * * *; (6) disruption of existing contractual relationships; and (7) misappropriation of funds entrusted to the agent by the athlete." Weiss, *supra*, at 331. In Part IV, below, we will address cases that deal specifically with such alleged abuses. *See also* Greenberg & Gray, *supra*, §§ 10.10, 10.12, 10.17; Curtis, *supra*, § 1:1; Kenneth L. Shropshire, Agents of Opportunity: Sports Agents and Corruption in Collegiate Sports (1990). It is commonly understood that these problems have arisen due to the increased athlete income and associated increases in agents' percentage-based fees, the rapid increase in the number of persons holding themselves out as agents, and the failure to develop governing rules that would establish minimum standards for eligibility and conduct. *See* Powers, *supra*, at 254.

As a result of the vociferous calls for regulation, several states, the major sports players associations, and the NCAA have attempted to promulgate meaningful rules to ordain appropriate guidelines for agent conduct, and to establish sanctions for failure to comply. The scope of these regulations varies from state to state and from sport to sport. Some measures that have been adopted in response to the concerns regarding agent incompetence and abuse follow below.

(A) The NCAA

Since 1984, the NCAA has attempted to monitor the activities of sports agents and, in some way, to govern their relationships with student-athletes who matriculate at its member institutions. The NCAA, however, has and had no authority to act as a self-appointed regulatory agency promulgating substantive rules with the force and effect of law. Agents, the target of the NCAA's attack, simply were beyond the association's jurisdiction. In an oft-quoted passage, agent Mike Trope crowed:

> The NCAA rules are not the laws of the United States. They're simply a bunch of hypocritical and unworkable rules set up by the NCAA. As an agent, I absolutely was not bound by them. NCAA rules are meaningless. The coaches themselves, the people who are supposed to be bound by them, don't abide by them either. Hell, nobody follows the NCAA rules.

GREENBERG & GRAY § 10.14(2)(d), at 1016. *See also* H.R. REP. No. 107-725 (2002):

> Unscrupulous agents, or their representatives, are willing to break the rules in order to sign promising student athletes to an agency contract. Agents are willing to do this because the fees that accompany the representation of a professional athlete are considerable, and the consequences that the agent will suffer in comparison to the athlete or school are limited or non-existent.

It became obvious at an early stage that the NCAA had no real power. In truth, the sanctioning arm of the NCAA only reaches as far as its own schools and, indirectly, the student-athletes of those institutions; it has no authority to seek legal reprisal against agents who engage in improper conduct or otherwise manifest indifference or incompetence. Accordingly, in an attempt to put some teeth into its regulatory function, the NCAA developed a registration system whereby agents would be required to enroll with the NCAA and commit to seeking and gaining athletic director approval before making contact with a student-athlete. *See* GREENBERG & GRAY § 10.14 (2)(d). Again, this registration regime was virtually impotent because the NCAA could do nothing other than remove a recalcitrant agent from the registration list. Accordingly, the NCAA rescinded its registration program in 1990. *Id.*

Nonetheless, the NCAA has persisted in playing some role in governing the relationship between agents and its student-athletes and, to that end, has promulgated a strict set of regulations circumscribing an agent's representation of student-athletes. As one commentator summarizes the restrictions, "a student-athlete risks losing his or her intercollegiate athletics eligibility by doing anything more than talking with an agent." Curtis, *supra*, at 1–11. And by "anything," Curtis means "anything." An athlete may not sign a contract with an agent, though a contract specifically limited to representation in one sport will not strip the athlete of eligibility in other sports. NCAA Div. I Bylaws §§ 12.1.2 (g), 12.3.1. A contract not specifically limited, however, will be applied to all sports and cost the athlete all of his eligibility. But not only are athletes prohibited from signing contracts; they are barred from accepting anything of value from an agent, even such incidentals as a meal at a restaurant, or transportation from school to the agent's office. *Id.* § 12.3.1.2. These regulations make it abundantly clear that incidental intrusion on these proscriptions will be grounds for the loss of the athletes' eligibility. For example, the prohibition on receiving benefits from an agent applies "even if the agent has indicated that he or she has no interest in representing the student-athlete in the marketing of his or her athletics ability or reputation *and does not represent individuals in the student-athlete's sport.*" *Id.* § 12.3.1.2 (b) (emphasis added). Student athletes may solicit advice from lawyers about professional contracts that have been offered them, but the lawyers may not take any part in the negotiation of the contracts lest they cause forfeiture of the athlete's eligibility. *Id.* § 12.3.2.

(B) State and Federal Legislation

The NCAA provides only one vehicle through which a university or athlete may seek to prevent an agent from engaging in unscrupulous activity vis-à-vis intercollegiate athletes. The tortious interference cause of action and other common law devices, together with claims predicated upon federal legislation such as the Federal Investment Advisers Act, 15 U.S.C. § 80b-1, and the Racketeer Influenced and Corrupt Organizations Act (RICO), 18 U.S.C. §§ 1961–1968, provide potential avenues of redress. In a case discussed below, federal prosecutors indicted two agents who had attempted to contract with student-athletes while they were still eligible to participate in intercollegiate athletics. In addition to claiming RICO violations as a result of threats of physical violence and threats to infringe upon the potential professional careers of student-athletes who refused to sign, federal prosecutors also claimed mail fraud, based upon the nature of the threats made by the agents and the attempts to induce student-athletes to falsify application forms and otherwise misrepresent their status to their member institutions. *See Walters v. Fullwood* and the discussion of *United States v. Walters* in the *Notes and Questions* that follow. *See also United States v. Piggie,* 303 F.3d 923 (8th Cir. 2002), *cert. denied* 538 U.S. 1049 (2003) (involving a fraudulent scheme to entice basketball players to play, and be paid for their participation, in an "amateur" league during the summer between high school and college).

Many states have attempted to respond to the crisis of sports-agent abuse by enacting legislation that, in varying degrees, governs the eligibility, qualifications, and standards of conduct for those persons seeking to represent athletes. Although the statutes cover a broad spectrum of regulatory reform, most laws include provisions dealing with registration and compliance requirements, basic qualifications, proscribed activities, enforcement mechanisms, and sanctions (both civil and criminal). Typically, these statutes establish a governing body, such as an administrative agency, to promulgate regulations and ensure compliance. *See* Powers at 268–70. Needless to say, these administrative schemes may present their own issues in terms of proper delegation of power and related constitutional questions. For example, what are the due process implications of refusing to certify an agent or disqualifying a certified agent? Whether an agent has a right to be heard in these circumstances may depend on whether the administrative agency seeks merely to deny an application or instead seeks to revoke privileges already granted. This application/revocation dichotomy has characterized much of the dialogue surrounding the privilege/entitlements due process debate. *See, e.g., Mathews v. Eldridge*, 424 U.S. 319 (1976); *Goldberg v. Kelly*, 397 U.S. 254 (1970); *Sumpter v. White Plains Hous. Auth.*, 278 N.E.2d 892 (N.Y. 1972). *Compare Greenholz v. Inmates*, 442 U.S. 1 (1979), *with Morrissey v. Brewer*, 408 U.S. 471 (1972).

A constant criticism of statutory responses to sports-agent abuse has centered upon the absence of meaningful enforcement power. Yet, recent legislation visits reprisals, both criminal and civil, upon recalcitrant agents. Generally, the criminal penalties can include fines, imprisonment, or both, and the transgressions may be identified as either felonies or misdemeanors. The civil penalties run a range of potential sanctions, including forfeiture of any right to reimbursement for payments made to athletes, refund of monies paid to agents, attorneys' fees, court costs, etc. *See* Uniform Athlete Agents Act § 16. Needless to say, if an agent's conduct amounts to a breach of contract or tortious act, common law causes of action will lie in which substantial damage awards may result. See Part IV, below. Thus, while incompetent or unscrupulous agents historically have escaped reprisals for their improper activity, several possible responses are now available, some of them carrying severe consequences.

The most significant effort to address abuses by agents has been the adoption of the Uniform Athlete Agency Act (UAAA). As of this writing, 34 states, plus the District of Columbia and the United States Virgin Islands, have adopted the Uniform Act. *See* <http://nccusl.org/Update/uniformact_factsheets/uniformacts-fs-aaa.asp>. "The [Act's] primary benefit lies not in any type of 'uniqueness,' but rather, in its nationwide uniformity." Diane Sudia & Rob Remis, *Athlete Agent Legislation in the New Millennium: State Statutes and the Uniform Athlete Agents Act*, 11 SETON HALL J. SPORTS L. 263 (2001). The Uniform Act requires agents to register, and a contract signed in violation of the Act "is void and no individual owes any money or other consideration under the contract." Robert N. Davis, *Exploring the Contours of Agent Regulation: The Uniform Athlete Agents Act*, 8 VILL. SPORTS & ENT. L.J. 1, 11 (2001). The registration process allows agents to take advantage of reciprocal registration between jurisdictions that have adopted the Uniform Act. *See* UAAA § 5(b).

Importantly, the Uniform Act not only requires agents to register, but also regulates the way in which they contract with student-athletes. Contracts must warn student-athletes that signing will jeopardize their eligibility. *Id.* § 10(c). Further, notice must be provided to the school's athletic director within 72 hours of the signing of the contract or before the next scheduled sporting event, whichever comes first. *Id.* § 11. If the student-athlete changes his mind after signing the contract, he has two weeks to cancel the contract, without penalty. *Id.* § 12.

In 2004, Congress passed the Sports Agent Responsibility and Trust Act, 15 U.S.C. § 7801 (SPARTA), which prohibits "deceptive acts or practices" by agents, and gives power to the Federal Trade Commission to enforce the prohibition. SPARTA largely duplicates the requirements of the Uniform Act, by imposing obligations on agents to register; to refrain from making deceptive claims in recruiting clients, post-dating contracts, or providing anything of value to student-athletes; and to notify the school's athletic director within 72 hours of signing a contract with a student-athlete. The federal law is not merely superfluous, however; its provisions are in addition to any others that state law imposes, and provides important protections in states that have not adopted the Uniform Act or any state-law version. Further, SPARTA closes a loophole in the Uniform Act and players' association regulations by imposing a registration requirement on agents who recruit students whose eligibility has expired but who have not yet been drafted. *See*

Sports Agent Responsibility and Trust Act: Hearing on H.R. 361 Before the Subcomm. on Commercial and Admin. Law of the H. Comm. on the Judiciary, 108th Cong. 4 (May 15, 2003) (statement of Rep. Osborne); R. Michael Rogers, *The Uniform Athlete Agent Act Fails To Fully Protect the College Athlete Who Exhausts His Eligibility Before Turning Professional*, 2 VA. SPORTS & ENT. L.J. 63 (2002). On the status of agent regulation after the UAAA and SPARTA, see generally Timothy Davis, *Regulating the Athlete-Agent Industry: Intended and Unintended Consequences*, 42 WILLIAMETTE L. REV. 781 (2006).

Finally, if the agent involved also happens to be a practicing attorney or member of the bar, then his or her actions will be governed by the American Bar Association Model Rules of Professional Conduct ("Model Rules") and pertinent state regulations monitoring attorneys' behavior. The Model Rules specifically prescribe standards of conduct for licensed attorneys in the areas of solicitation, advertising, fees, minimum competency, and conflicts of interest. *See* GREENBERG & GRAY § 10.18; Tamara L. Barner, Current Development, *Show Me the...Ethics?: The Implications of the Model Rules of Ethics on Attorneys in the Sports Industry*, 16 GEO. J. LEGAL ETHICS 519 (2003). Of course, difficult questions are presented by the sports agent/attorney who fulfills more than one need or serves in a dual capacity. Differentiating the practice of law from pure athlete representation is not easy. Indeed, to the extent that the two functions overlap, there is considerable likelihood that the Model Rules will govern the attorney's conduct. *See In re: Dwight*, 573 P.2d 481 (Ariz. 1978); GREENBERG & GRAY § 10.19; *see also In re: Horak*, 647 N.Y.S.2d 20 (App. Div. 1996). As the court in *Dwight* remarked:

> As long as a lawyer is engaged in the practice of law, he is bound by the ethical requirements of that profession, and he may not defend his actions by contending that he was engaged in some other kind of professional activity. For only in this way can full protection be afforded to the public, which is the court's role in the disciplinary process.

573 P.2d at 484.

Some have suggested that the additional regulation placed upon attorney-agents places them at a competitive disadvantage vis-à-vis non-attorney-agents, who need not abide by the Model Rules. *See, e.g.*, Mark Doman, *Attorneys as Athlete-Agents: Reconciling the ABA Rules of Professional Conduct with the Practice of Athlete Representation*, 5 TEX. REV. ENT. & SPORTS L. 37, 38 (2003). The additional regulations may mean that athletes would be well advised to hire attorney-agents. Because non-attorney agents have been able to make more grandiose claims about their services, however, many athletes have been lured into hiring them. *See, e.g.*, Gary P. Kohn, *Sports Agents Representing Professional Athletes: Being Certified Means Never Having to Say You're Qualified*, 6 ENT. & SPORTS L.J. 1 (1988); Stacey M. Nahrwold, *Are Professional Athletes Better Served by a Lawyer-Representative Than an Agent? Ask Grant Hill*, 9 SETON HALL J. SPORTS L. 431 (1999). It remains to be seen whether the Uniform Act or SPARTA will effectively counter this trend by requiring all agents to abide by norms that theretofore restricted the conduct of attorneys only. *See* Melissa Steedle Bogad, Note, *Maybe Jerry Maguire Should Have Stuck with Law School: How the Sports Agent Responsibility and Trust Act Implements Lawyer-Like Rules for Sports Agents*, 27 CARDOZO L. REV. 1889 (2006).

(C) Regulations of Agents by Players' Unions

As discussed throughout this text, the relationship between players' individual agents and players' collective bargaining representatives is somewhat unique. In private-sector labor relations, there are few analogues that replicate the unusual dynamic of athlete/employee being vigorously represented simultaneously at both a personal and collective level. Because a recognized or certified union is typically the exclusive representative regarding matters affecting wages, hours, and working conditions, this phenomenon seldom occurs in other industries. However, professional sports presents a special situation in which the only pragmatic approach is a modification of the exclusivity principle, and the union's ceding of certain bargaining prerogatives (*e.g.,* salary) to the individual (and his agent).

In earlier chapters, we touched upon the tension that can develop between agent and labor organization. At times, this tension is a product of the inherent responsibilities that attend the representation of an individual player who is also a member of a collective body. The "survival of the fittest" and the "one for all, all for one" concepts may not peacefully co-exist in this context. *See* Chapter 14, Part V; Chapter 15, *Midland Broadcasting Co.,* 93 NLRB 455 (1951) and the *Notes and Questions* that follow; *see also Notes and Questions* following *Detroit Lions, Inc. v. Argovitz, below.* Also, conflicts arise between agents. *See Smith v. IMG Worldwide, Inc.,* 437 F. Supp. 2d 297 (E.D.Pa. 2006).

Although agents and collective bargaining representatives both are presumably acting in the players' best interests, there are inevitably points at which these apparent allies are directly at odds with one another. Thus, it is not totally surprising that attempts would be made by one group to govern or exercise some oversight function over the other party. Such monitoring has assumed the form of players' association rules that regulate, to some degree, the agents who represent the unions' members. As discussed below, the exercise of this regulatory function has not always produced harmonious results.

No agent may negotiate team a contract on behalf of a player in any of the four major professional sports without registering with that sport's players' association. It was not always so. The National Football League Players Association ("NFLPA"), in 1983, was the first professional athletes' union to devise regulations to govern agents' representation of their player/members. These regulations are now embraced in the NFLPA Regulations Governing Contract Advisors ("NFLPA Regulations"). The NFLPA Regulations provide that "[n]o person (other than a player representing himself) shall be permitted to conduct individual contract negotiations on behalf of a player and/or assist in or advise with respect to such negotiations with NFL Clubs * * * unless he/she is * * * currently certified as a Contract Advisor pursuant to these regulations." The NFLPA Regulations address agent activity that includes: providing advice, counsel, information, or assistance to players with respect to negotiating standard player contracts with the player's team; giving recommendations to, and sharing information with, players as well as the NFLPA; handling funds paid to players as compensation for their services as NFL players; counseling players in the areas of tax, finance, and investments; and "any other activity * * * which directly bears upon the Contract Advisor's integrity, competence or ability to properly represent individual NFL players and the NFLPA in individual contract negotiations."

Application for membership as a contract advisor includes a questionnaire that requires the applicant to disclose (and to authorize a check of) background information regarding education, prior employers, bar membership (if the advisor is an attorney), professional licenses, conviction records, participation in any civil legal proceedings, references, and specific experience in the sports industry. The application must be accompanied by an application fee of $1650, which is in addition to an annual fee which is required upon certification, and the applicant will not be certified unless he or she has a four-year college or university degree as well as a master's or law degree (though exceptions from the master's- or law-degree requirement can be granted to applicants with sufficient negotiating experience), attends a two-day seminar given by the NFLPA, and passes an examination concerning "the Salary Cap, Player Benefits, NFLPA Regulations Governing Contract Advisors, and other issues relevant to player representation." NFL Players Association, Salary Cap and Agent Administration Department, *Agent Certification, at* <http://www.nflpa.org/RulesAndRegs/AgentCertification.aspx>.

Any contract advisor who seeks to represent an NFL player in individual contract negotiations must execute the NFLPA's standard representation agreement with the player, which delineates a description of the advisor's services to be rendered, compensation, dispute resolution mechanism, etc. Compensation is limited to a maximum of 3% of the player's salary. The Standard of Conduct section of the NFLPA Regulations lists examples of the standards that the contract advisor is expected to maintain and outlines specifically those types of activities that the NFLPA deems to be prohibited.

In the event that the contract advisor engages in improper activity, Section 6 of the NFLPA Regulations prescribes a detailed procedure for the registration of grievances, conduct of hearings, process of appeals, and imposition of sanctions. In addition, the NFLPA Regulations specifically describe the internal arbitration mechanism to be employed to resolve any disputes between contract advisors and players, as well as to appeal decisions adverse to the contract advisor with regard to the aforementioned complaint alleging improper conduct.

The NFL has begun regulating "financial advisors" as well as "contract advisors," in response to several instances of fraud and incompetence. Under the Player Financial Advisor Registration Program, begun in 2002, NFLPA-certified agents are prohibited from referring a player to any financial advisor who is not himself or herself certified. Certified financial advisors must provide their clients with quarterly statements detailing the status of their investments, and deceptive or fraudulent actions are prohibited. Specific warnings are required before a financial advisor and player can agree to place the player's money in any particularly risky investment. Further, the financial advisor must agree to allow a representative of the NFLPA, once authorized by the player, to audit the records concerning advice given to the player. *See* Curtis, *supra*, § 1-5; <http://www.nflpa.org/pdfs/FinancialAdvisors/NFLPA_code.pdf>.

The Major League Baseball Players Association likewise has developed its own set of standards governing the conduct of agents purporting to represent Major League Baseball players. The MLBPA Regulations closely parallel the NFLPA's Code of Conduct with regard to the application process, agent functions, standards of conduct, improper activities, filing of complaints, binding arbitration procedures, imposition of sanctions, etc. *See* MLBPA Regulations, Art. IV, §§ 3–6. One important distinction exists, however, regarding the fees that may be charged to the players. Article IV, § 4(F) of the MLBPA Regulations specifically precludes an agent from securing a fee for negotiating a salary unless the resultant net salary, after subtracting the agent's fee, exceeds the collective bargaining agreement's minimum for that year. Also significant is the fact that agents may not register with the MLBPA until a player designates the agent as his representative. *See* Curtis, *supra*, at § 1-5. Each of the other three sports permits an agent to register before a single player agrees to be represented by the agent. Another distinction, important to aspiring agents, is that the MLBPA—alone among the four associations—charges no registration fee for agents. *Id.*

The regulations promulgated by the National Basketball Players Association ("NBPA") track the NFLPA and MLBPA regulations in terms of applications, behavior, enforcement, etc. Applicants must pay an application fee of $100 and an annual fee of $1500. Any contracts that arise as a result of negotiations in which a player has been represented by a non-certified agent will be void. *See* NBPA Regulations, §§ 1, 2, & 4. The NBPA regulations also govern the fees that may be charged by the agent and, like the MLBPA regulations, circumscribe the amount of compensation that an NBPA-sanctioned agent may receive as a result of representing a player who is only awarded minimum compensation under the NBA-NBPA collective bargaining agreement. Unlike the MLBPA regulations, however, the agent negotiating such agreement shall receive a prescribed fee of $2,000 for the season in question. *See* NBPA Regulations, § 4(B)(1). Agents may collect a maximum fee of 4% for negotiating player contracts that exceed the league minimum. *Id.* § 4(B)(2).

Finally, the National Hockey League Players Association ("NHLPA") also has attempted to devise regulations to govern agents representing NHL players. The NHLPA regulations are patterned after the NFLPA, NBPA, and MLBPA regulations, and they close the loopholes mentioned previously. Applicants must pay a fee of $900 to begin the certification process.

Thus, the relevant collective bargaining representatives in the various professional sports have made some efforts to monitor the representation of their players. While the most significant limitation in this regard involves the failure to establish any meaningful minimum criteria or qualifications as barriers to entry, the development of some type of formal administrative device is a basis for some optimism. Further, it is likely that the omnipresent threat of litigation, the approbation or condemnation of strong unions, and the growing sophistication of the players will compel agents to approach their representation in a more responsible fashion.

Of course, players' associations must be mindful of governing the initial certification and monitoring agents in a fair and equitable fashion. Given the tension that is inherent in advancing the causes of athletes both as individuals and members of a collective, the potential for disputes between agents and unions is self-evident. The regulation of agents by the various players associations, particularly the disciplinary procedures employed and the sanctions imposed, have prompted challenges grounded in due process and antitrust. Thus far, the unions and their ability to govern the eligibility and activity of agents have emerged unscathed. However, a review of the agents' allegations reveals that they present issues warranting further attention and may serve as a caution to the players' associations that the power wielded is neither plenary nor untouchable. *See Collins v. NBPA*, 850 F. Supp. 1468, *aff'd per curiam*, 976 F. 2d 740 (10th Cir. 1992), discussed below and in Chapter 9, *supra*, and *Black v. NFLPA*, 87 F. Supp. 2d 1 (D.D.C. 2000), discussed in Chapter 16.

(D) Direct League Governance

In addition to regulation by players' associations effected in conjunction with the leagues as part of the collective bargaining relationship, the leagues themselves have flexed their muscles in terms of exercising direct control over certain agent activities and conduct. The following case illustrates that, in certain circumstances, professional sports leagues may impose their will upon player agents directly.

White v. National Football League
92 F. Supp. 2d 918 (D. Minn. 2000)

DOTY, District Judge. * * * This appeal arises out of a special master proceeding commenced by the National Football League Management Council ("NFLMC") in June

1999. The NFLMC alleges that the San Francisco 49ers and certain player agents entered into undisclosed agreements concerning player compensation, in violation of the NFL Collective Bargaining Agreement ("CBA") and the stipulation and settlement agreement in this case ("SSA"). In the underlying proceeding, the NFLMC has pursued discovery against player agents Leigh Steinberg, Jeffrey Moorad, and Gary Wichard. These agents have opposed discovery on the ground that they were not signatories to the CBA and SSA and are not subject to any penalty scheme provided in those agreements.

* * *

On February 18, 2000, after extensive briefing and oral argument on the status of player agents under the CBA and SSA, the special master issued a decision dismissing the player agents from the underlying proceeding. However, the special master also conditionally ruled that, if this court were to find that player agents were bound by the CBA and SSA, then player agents could be subject to penalties under Article XXIX, Section 3 of the CBA and Section XVI, Paragraph 3 of the SSA.

* * *

[T]he court must separately address the two fundamental issues raised by this dispute: (1) whether the contracting parties intended to bind player agents to the CBA and SSA and (2) whether, under the applicable legal rules, player agents have in fact been bound.

* * *

B. Did the Parties Intend to Bind Player Agents to the CBA and SSA?

* * *

The CBA and SSA contain a pair of provisions that, on their face, would appear to manifest the contracting parties' intent to bind player agents to the agreements. The first provision states:

> Binding Effect. This agreement *shall be binding upon* and shall inure to the benefit of the Parties hereto and their heirs, executors, administrators, *representatives, agents,* successors and assigns and any corporation into or with which any corporate party hereto may merge or consolidate.

CBA Art. LV, § 14; SSA § XXX, ¶ 2 (emphasis added). Notwithstanding the clarity of this provision, the special master concluded that it should be discounted on the ground that it is "mere boilerplate." * * * As the special master himself recognized, [however,] this provision is "utilized throughout the law to ensure continuity of obligation against those who stand in the shoes of a party." Further, "a court may not rewrite into a contract conditions the parties did not insert or, under the guise of construction, add or excise terms." Boilerplate or not, then, the court must take seriously the parties' broad declaration of "binding effect" in evaluating whether they intended to subject player agents to the CBA and SSA.[2]

---

2. While the special master did not address the issue, it is clear that player agents are among the "agents" and "representatives" contemplated in this provision. The CBA itself, and the standard NFL player contract, employ the term "agent" and "representative" to refer to player agents. Art VI, § 1; Art. XXIV, § 1; App. C, at ¶ 25. In addition, as the standard player contract makes explicit, the player agent acts as the "agent" of the individual member of the *White* class whom he represents. *See* CBA App. C, at ¶ 23 (referencing player's "rights as a member of the White class"); ¶ 25 (designating

Moreover, a second provision, addressing contract "certifications," makes it abundantly clear that the parties intended to bind player agents to the agreements. *See* CBA Art. XXIX; SSA § XVI. This provision sets forth the procedure by which the persons negotiating a player contract must certify the integrity of the contract under the CBA and SSA, and specifically instructs that "any player representative who negotiated the contract on behalf of the player" must execute the certification. CBA Art. XXIX, § 1(a); SSA § XVI, ¶ 1. It then provides:

> Any person who knowingly files a false certification required [above] shall be subject to a fine of up to $250,000, upon a finding of such violation by the Special Master. The amount of such fine as to a Club or non-player Club employee shall be determined by the Commissioner.

CBA Art XXIX, § 3; SSA § XVI, ¶ 1. As the special master stated, "the only sensible interpretation of [the penalty provision] is that it was intended to apply to any person who executes such a false certification with the intent the Player Contract involved will become effective." The special master thus found, and the court agrees, that the false certification provision empowers him to impose a fine on a player agent who executes a false certification.

Notwithstanding this finding, however, the special master concluded that his power to penalize player agents is negated by a separate provision in the CBA addressing the regulation of player agents:

> The NFLMC and the Clubs recognize that the NFLPA regulates the conduct of agents who represent players in individual contract negotiations with Clubs. The NFLMC and the Clubs agree that the Clubs are prohibited from engaging in the individual contract negotiations with any agent who is not listed by the NFLPA as being duly certified by the NFLPA in accordance with its role as exclusive bargaining agent for NFL players. * * * The NFLPA shall have sole and exclusive authority to determine the number of agents to be certified, and the grounds for withdrawing or denying certification of an agent. * * *

CBA Art. VI, § 1. The special master concluded that this provision vests in the NFLPA exclusive regulatory authority over player agents, thereby depriving him of jurisdiction to fine a player agent for submitting a false certification.

In reaching this conclusion, however, the special master made several interpretive errors. First, he read the word "exclusively" into the first sentence of this provision, thereby disregarding the principle that a court shall neither add nor remove terms in the service of construction. Second, he interpreted the agent regulation provision so as to create a direct conflict with the false certification provision, thereby disregarding the principle that a court shall make every reasonable effort to harmonize the terms of a contract. Third, he improperly downplayed the fact that, in a sentence appearing toward the end of the provision, the parties clearly demonstrate that they know how to assign "exclusive" authority to the NFLPA when they want to: "The NFLPA shall have *sole and exclusive* authority to determine the number of agents to be certified, and the grounds for withdrawing or denying certification of an agent." CBA Art. VI, § 1 (emphasis added).

---

player agent as "player's certified agent"). Finally, when player agents apply for certification to the NFLPA, they are expressly notified that they will be considered "[p]ersons serving * * * as the NFLPA's 'agent' pursuant to [the agent certification provision of] the CBA." NFLPA Regs. at 2.

[T]his provision appears to offer an example of very careful drafting, whereby the contracting parties achieve three important results: (1) they explicitly "recognize" that the NFLPA has direct regulatory authority over player agents; (2) they implicitly "recognize" that the NFLMC and the Clubs do not have direct regulatory authority over player agents; and (3) they leave open the possibility of some other regulatory arrangement by separate agreement of the parties, so long as the subject matter of that special arrangement does not involve determining "the number of agents to be certified, and the grounds for withdrawing or denying certification." In other words, this provision fully anticipates, and is wholly consistent with, the parties' decision in Article XXIX of the CBA to vest the special master with regulatory authority over player agents with respect to the issue of false certification.

In sum, after conducting a de novo interpretation of the relevant contractual provisions, the court concludes that the parties to the CBA and SSA clearly intended to bind player agents to those agreements.

C. Have the Player Agents Consented to Be Bound by the CBA and SSA?

This conclusion, however, does not end the court's analysis. As the special master aptly observed, "under basic common law contract doctrine, borne by simple justice, a [third party] cannot be bound to a contract without his or her consent in some form." * * *

Under common law contract doctrine, a third party may consent to the terms of a contract expressly through words or tacitly by conduct. *See* Restatement (Second) of Contracts § 19; ("The manifestation of assent may be made wholly or partly by written or spoken words or by other acts or failure to act."). Although silence does not ordinarily manifest assent, where the relationship between the parties is such that even a non-signatory would be expected to reply, silence can create a binding contract. *See* Restatement § 69 (silence will operate as acceptance: (1) "[w]here an offeree takes the benefit of offered services with the reasonable opportunity to reject them and reason to know that they were offered with expectation of compensation" and (2) "[w]here because of previous dealings * * *, it is reasonable that the offeree should notify the offeror if he does not intend to accept").

* * *

[T]he player agents have consented to be bound by the terms of the CBA and SSA. Several factors dictate this conclusion. First, player agents and the NFLPA are engaged in precisely the kind of special relationship that gives rise to principles of implied consent. Under federal labor law, the NFLPA has exclusive authority to negotiate with NFL clubs on behalf of NFL players. *See* National Labor Relations Act § 9(a) (codified at 29 U.S.C. § 159(a)). Player agents are permitted to negotiate player contracts in the NFL only because the NFLPA has delegated a portion of its exclusive representational authority to them. *See Collins v. NBA*, 850 F.Supp. 1468, 1475 (D.Colo.1991). In *H.A. Artists & Associates v. Actors' Equity Association,* the Supreme Court concluded that a closely analogous representational scheme—one involving theatrical agents who individually negotiated contracts for the members of an actors' union—demonstrated an "economic interrelationship" such that the agents must be defined as a "labor group" under federal labor law. 451 U.S. 704, 721–22 (1981). Because an almost identical "interrelationship" exists here, it is not legally tenable for player agents to claim that they are strangers to the core legal agreements entered into by the NFLPA and the players.

Second, player agents enjoy significant and ongoing economic benefits because of their relationship with the NFLPA and the players, benefits that flow directly from the

CBA and SSA. For example, Article VI of the CBA specifically bars NFL clubs from ne- gotiating with anyone other than an agent certified by the NFLPA, thereby granting cer- tified agents a powerful competitive advantage in the market for player-clients. And be- cause player agents are compensated under percentage-fee arrangements, the CBA and SSA directly benefit them by mandating guaranteed league-wide salaries and minimum club salaries. *See* CBA Art. XXIV; SSA § X. The legal consequence of this arrangement is clear: When third parties like the player agents silently reap the benefits of contractual agreements like the CBA and SSA, they cannot later disclaim the obligations these agreements impose on them. *See, e.g.,* Restatement § 69(1)(a).

Third, apart from manifesting consent through their conduct, certified player agents have expressly agreed to be bound by NFLPA agent regulations, which include specific provisions (1) requiring each certified player agent to become familiar with "applicable Collective Bargaining Agreements and other governing documents" and (2) prohibiting certified agents from "negotiating and/or agreeing to any provision in any agreement in- volving a player which directly or indirectly violates any stated policies or rules estab- lished by the NFLPA." NFLPA Regs. §§ 3.A(15); 3.B(10). There is no question that the CBA and SSA are among the "Collective Bargaining Agreements and other governing documents" and "policies or rules" referenced in these regulations. Thus, by expressly agreeing to represent players under these provisions of the NFLPA regulations, player agents have necessarily agreed to comply with the relevant terms of the CBA and SSA.

* * *

Finally, even if the NFLPA regulations did not expressly charge player agents with knowledge of the contents of CBA and SSA, no player agent can credibly argue that he is surprised by the penalty for false certification. The CBA and SSA govern the economics of professional football just as surely as the official NFL rulebook governs the game of professional football. To successfully negotiate with NFL clubs, player agents must be in- timately familiar with many aspects of the CBA and SSA, including their detailed rules about free agency, franchise player designation, guaranteed minimum salary, and salary cap operation. Further, to execute a valid player contract, agents must carefully follow the contract certification rules set out in Article XXIX of the CBA and Section XVI of the SSA. Indeed, the standard player contract, which must be used in each negotiation, and which the negotiating player agent himself must sign, directly quotes the contract certifi- cation provision. *See* CBA App. C ¶ 24. And it is precisely here, in the contract certifica- tion provision, that the player agent is warned that "[a]ny person who knowingly files a false certification * * * shall be subject to a fine of up to $250,000, upon a finding of such violation by the Special Master." CBA Art. XXIX, § 3; SSA § XVI, ¶ 3.

The agent's act of player contract certification thus places in bold relief the issue of consent presented by this dispute: It represents both the moment at which the player agent most clearly stands to reap the benefits of the CBA and SSA and the moment at which he is made most acutely aware of his obligations, and his potential liability, under those agreements. When the agent signs his name to the contract certification, fully informed of the rewards and obligations attaching to this act, he has manifested a consent to be bound by the CBA and SSA just as clearly as if he had signed the CBA and SSA themselves.

For all these reasons, the court concludes that the player agents are bound by the terms of the CBA and SSA. * * * Accordingly, the court must reverse the special master's decision insofar as it dismisses the player agents from the underlying proceeding.

* * *

IV. Agent Abuses and Related Litigation

Zinn v. Parrish

644 F.2d 360 (7th Cir. 1981)

BARTELS, Senior District Judge. [Agent and plaintiff Leo Zinn seeks] to recover agent fees due him under a personal management contract between him and the defendant Lemar Parrish. * * *

[Parrish defends, and the district court rendered a verdict for him,] on the grounds that the contract was void for Zinn's failure to register under the Investment Advisers Act of 1940, 15 U.S.C. §§ 80b-1 *et seq.* ("the 1940 Act"), and that Zinn had failed to perform his own obligations under the contract.

* * *

FACTS

* * * In the Spring of 1970, Parrish's coach at Lincoln University approached Zinn and informed him that Parrish had been picked by the Cincinnati Bengals in the annual National Football League draft of college seniors, and asked him if he would help Parrish in negotiating the contract. After Zinn contacted Parrish, the latter signed a one-year "Professional Management Contract" with Zinn in the Spring of 1970, pursuant to which Zinn helped Parrish negotiate the terms of his rookie contract with the Bengals, receiving as his commission 10% of Parrish's $ 16,500 salary. On April 10, 1971 Parrish signed the contract at issue in this case, which differed from the 1970 contract only insofar as it was automatically renewed from year to year unless one of the parties terminated it by 30 days' written notice to the other party. There were no other restrictions placed on the power of either party to terminate the contract.

Under the 1971 contract, Zinn obligated himself to use "reasonable efforts" to procure pro-football employment for Parrish, and, at Parrish's request, to "act" in furtherance of Parrish's interest by: a) negotiating job contracts; b) furnishing advice on business investments; c) securing professional tax advice at no added cost; and d) obtaining endorsement contracts. It was further provided that Zinn's services would include, "at my request efforts to secure for me gainful off-season employment," for which Zinn would receive no additional compensation, "unless such employment (was) in the line of endorsements, marketing and the like," in which case Zinn would receive a 10% commission on the gross amount. If Parrish failed to pay Zinn amounts due under the contract, Parrish authorized "the club or clubs that are obligated to pay me to pay to you instead all monies and other considerations due me from which you can deduct your 10% and any other monies due you * * *"

Over the course of Parrish's tenure with the Bengals, Zinn negotiated base salaries for him of $18,500 in 1971; $27,000 in 1972; $35,000 in 1973 (plus a $6,500 signing bonus); and a $250,000 series of contracts covering the four seasons commencing in 1974 (plus a $30,000 signing bonus). The 1974–77 contracts with the Bengals were signed at a time when efforts were being made by the newly-formed World Football League to persuade players in the NFL to "jump" to the WFL to play on one of its teams. By the end of 1973 season Parrish had become recognized as one of the more valuable players in the NFL. He was twice selected for the Pro Bowl game, and named by Sporting News as one of the best cornerbacks in the league. Towards the end of the 1973 season, the Bengals approached Parrish with an offer of better contract terms than he had earlier been receiving. By way of exploring alternatives in the WFL, Zinn entered into preliminary discussions with the Jacksonville Sharks in early 1974, but decided not to pursue the matter once he ascertained that the Sharks were in a shaky financial position. In retrospect, Zinn's and Parrish's decision to continue negotiating and finally sign with the Bengals was a sound one, for the Sharks and the rest of the WFL with them folded in 1975 due to a lack of funds.

Shortly after signing the 1974 series of contracts, Parrish informed Zinn by telephone that he "no longer needed his services." By letter dated October 16, 1975 Parrish reiterated this position, and added that he had no intention of paying Zinn a 10% commission on those contracts. In view of its disposition of the case, the district court made no specific fact finding as to the amounts Parrish earned during the 1974–77 seasons. Zinn claims that the total was at least $304,500 including bonus and performance clauses. The 1971 contract by its terms entitled Zinn to 10% of the total amount as each installment was paid, and Zinn claims that he has only received $4,300 of the amounts due him. Accordingly, this suit was filed to recover the balance * * *

In addition to negotiating the Bengals contracts, Zinn performed a number of other services at Parrish's request. In 1972 he assisted him in purchasing a residence as well as a four-unit apartment building to be used for rental income; he also helped to manage the apartment building. That same year Zinn negotiated an endorsement contract for Parrish with All-Pro Graphics, Inc., under which Parrish received a percentage from the sales of "Lemar Parrish" t-shirts, sweat-shirts, beach towels, key chains, etc. The record shows that Zinn made a number of unsuccessful efforts at obtaining similar endorsement income from stores with which Parrish did business in Ohio. He also tried, unsuccessfully, to obtain an appearance for Parrish on the Mike Douglas Show. Zinn arranged for Parrish's taxes to be prepared each year by H & R Block.

The evidence showed that, despite his efforts, Zinn was unable to obtain off-season employment for Parrish. In this connection, however, it was Zinn's advice to Parrish that he return to school during the off-season months in order to finish his college degree, against the time when he would no longer be able to play football. With respect to Zinn's obligation to provide Parrish with advice on "business investments," he complied first, by assisting in the purchase of the apartment building; and second, by forwarding to Parrish the stock purchase recommendations of certain other individuals, after screening the suggestions himself. There was no evidence that Zinn ever forwarded such recommendations to any of his other clients; he testified that he only did so for Parrish. In summing up Zinn's performance under the contract, Parrish testified as follows:

> Q: Did you ever ask Zinn to do anything for you, to your knowledge, that he didn't try to do?
>
> A: I shall say not, no.

DISCUSSION

I

We turn, first, to the district court's decision that Zinn's contract was void under the 1940 Act. The Act makes void any contract for investment advice made by an unregistered adviser. 15 U.S.C. §80b-15(b). The issue thus presented is whether Zinn was engaged by reason of the terms of his contract and all his activities thereunder in the business of advising others as to security transactions. If so, he was required to register as an investment adviser. 15 U.S.C. §80b-3(a). An investment adviser is defined under the Act as:

any person who, for compensation, engages in the business of advising others, either directly or through publications or writings, as to the value of securities or as to the advisability of investing in, purchasing, or selling securities, or who, for compensation and as a part of a regular business, issues or promulgates analyses or reports concerning securities.

15 U.S.C. §80b-2(a)(11).

The district court held that Zinn fell within the definitional requirements of the Act and was an investment adviser because: 1) the 1971 Management Contract stated that Zinn would provide advice on "business investments," and Zinn let others know by word of mouth that he was available as a personal manager, he was "holding himself out" to the public as an investment adviser; 2) Zinn "solicited the advice of others and transmitted to (Parrish) those investment recommendations, after screening by (Zinn)"; and 3) Zinn "accepted and invested funds sent to him" by Parrish for investment purposes. The court's conclusion, however, does not follow from its premises.

The 1940 Act was enacted as Title II of comprehensive regulations covering both investment companies and investment advisers. It was "the last in a series of Acts designed to eliminate certain abuses in the securities industry, abuses which were found to have contributed to the stock market crash of 1929 and the depression of the 1930s." *SEC v. Capital Gains Research Bureau, Inc.*, 375 U.S. 180, 186 (1963).

* * *

Among the factors the SEC looks to in determining whether someone "holds himself out" as an investment adviser are: "(t)he maintenance of a listing as an investment adviser in a telephone or business directory"; "the expression of willingness to existing clients or others to accept new clients"; or "the use of a letterhead indicating any activity as an investment adviser." The evidence showed that Zinn's listing in his office building directory was "Public Relations Consultant." His ad in the Chicago Yellow Pages was under the heading of "Public Relations." His letterhead did not contain the phrase "investment adviser" but only "Public Relations Consultant." The testimony showing that Zinn was, by word of mouth, available as a personal manager for both employment and business advice was not evidence that Zinn was available as an investment adviser.

The court failed to distinguish between ordinary business advice and advice on securities.[3] For example, Parrish purchased his own home and also an interest in an apartment building with the assistance of Zinn's advice, but this was not investment advice within the terms of the 1940 Act. Zinn was not engaged in a "common venture" with Parrish simply because he engaged in certain managerial tasks at Parrish's request with respect to the apartment building. Both Parrish and the district court relied too heavily on *First United Management Corp.*, (1973–74 Transfer Binder) Fed. Sec. L. Rep. (CCH) ¶ 79,742, which is in fact inapposite. There the SEC ruled that "the offer of * * * limited partnerships (in real estate) by First United to its (professional athlete) clients would constitute investment advice." Zinn made no offer to Parrish of a limited partnership interest in real estate, for in fact Parrish was the sole owner of the apartment building. Another factor which influenced the district court in reaching its conclusion that Zinn was an investment adviser was Parrish's testimony that he had sent Zinn about $1500

---

3. It is crucial to note that nothing in Zinn's contract obligated him to provide advice on securities investments * * * The Securities Acts were not designed to provide a remedy for every instance of a breach of common-law fiduciary duties. * * *

"to invest * * * in his company," in return for which he was to receive "something like 20 percent" on his investment. * * * [I]n our view [this arrangement] did not constitute advice to purchase a security in the form of an investment contract.

It is true that Zinn might have been compelled to register as an investment adviser, even if he limited his activities to screening the securities recommendations of others before passing them along to clients, if he made a business of such activities. But isolated transactions with a client as an incident to the main purpose of his management contract to negotiate football contracts do not constitute engaging in the business of advising others on investment securities. From the evidence, Parrish was the only one of his personal management clients to whom he transmitted securities recommendations from others.

Zinn was not a dealer or trader in securities and there was no evidence to indicate that he was financially interested in the securities recommendations he passed along. Therefore the conflict of interest at which the Act was aimed was not present here. In substance, his position was similar to that of a professional trustee whose advice to his clients on securities is "solely incidental to his duty as a professional trustee."

* * *

II

We consider next the district court's judgment that Zinn failed to perform the terms and conditions of his contract. Upon this issue, the district court made the following findings:

> The evidence was clear that (Zinn) did not, in fact, procure employment for (Parrish), did not obtain off-season employment for (Parrish), did not provide substantial investment advice, did not secure any more than the most superficial tax consultation and did not seek in any substantial respect endorsement contracts and other profitable marketing connections.

From these findings the court concluded that Zinn "was unable to and did not provide the services which he was obligated to provide by the contract under which he sues." We address the findings seriatim.

Employment Procurement

Zinn's obligation under the 1971 Management Contract to procure employment for Parrish as a pro football player was limited to the use of "reasonable efforts." At the time the contract was signed, Parrish was already under contract with the Cincinnati Bengals for the 1970–71 season, with a one-year option clause for the 1971–72 season exercisable by the Bengals. Parrish could not, without being in breach of his Bengals contract, enter into negotiations with other teams for the 1971–72 season. The NFL's own rules prevented one team from negotiating with another team's player who had not yet attained the status of a "free agent". At no time relevant to this litigation did Parrish become a free agent. Thus, unless he decided to contract for future services for the year following the term of the option clause with the Canadian or World Football League, Parrish's only sensible course of action throughout the time Zinn managed him was to negotiate with the Bengals.

Parrish had no objection to Zinn's performance under the professional management contract for the first three years up to 1973, during which time Zinn negotiated football contracts for Parrish. A drastic change, however, took place in 1974 when a four-season contract was negotiated with the Bengals for a total of $ 250,000 plus a substantial signing bonus. At that time, the new World Football League came into existence and its teams, as well as the teams of the Canadian Football League, were offering good terms to professional football players as an inducement to jump over to their leagues from the NFL. In order to persuade Parrish to remain with the team, the Bengals club itself first initiated the renegotiation of Parrish's contract with an offer of substantially increased compensation. This was not surprising.

Parrish claims, however, that Zinn should have obtained offers from the World Football League that would have placed him in a stronger negotiating position with the Bengals. This is a rather late claim. It was not mentioned in Parrish's letter of termination, and is entirely speculative. Given what Zinn accurately perceived as the unreliability of any offers he might have obtained from the WFL, his representation of Parrish during this period was more than reasonable. As the district court properly noted, prior to the signing of the 1974–77 series of football contracts the needs of the defendant, the services of the plaintiff, and the fees paid by the defendant for those services were all "relatively modest." We conclude that up to that point it is impossible to fault Zinn in the performance of his contract, nor can we find any basis for Parrish to complain of Zinn's efforts in 1974 with respect to procuring employment for him as a pro-football player.

Other Obligations

We focus next on the other obligations, all incidental to the main purpose of the contract. The first of these refers to "negotiating employment contracts with professional athletic organizations and others." Unless this is with respect to a professional football contract, it is difficult to understand to what "professional athletic organizations and others" refers. At all events, there is no claim that there was a failure to negotiate employment contracts with other athletic organizations. And the evidence clearly shows that Zinn performed substantial services in negotiating with the Bengals by letter, telephone, and in person when he and Parrish were flown at the Bengals' expense to Cincinnati for the final stage of negotiations on the 1974–77 series of contracts.

Zinn was further obligated to act in Parrish's professional interest by providing advice on tax and business matters, by "seek(ing) * * * endorsement contracts," and by making "efforts" to obtain for Parrish gainful off-season employment. Each of these obligations was subject to an implied promise to make "good faith" efforts to obtain what he sought. Under Illinois law, such efforts constitute full performance of the obligations. Until Parrish terminated the contract, the evidence was clear that Zinn made consistent, good faith efforts to obtain off-season employment and endorsement contracts. * * * Moreover, Zinn did give business advice to Parrish on his real estate purchases, and he did secure tax advice for him. Parrish fully accepted Zinn's performance for the years 1970, 1971, 1972, and 1973 by remitting the 10% due Zinn under the contract. Parrish was at all times free to discharge Zinn as his agent before a new season began. Instead, he waited until Zinn had negotiated a series of contracts worth a quarter of a million dollars for him before letting Zinn know over the phone that his services were no longer required. That call, coupled with Parrish's failure to make the 10% commission payments as they came due, was a breach of the 1971 contract. * * * Therefore Zinn has a right to recover a 10% commission on all amounts earned by Parrish under the 1974, 1975, 1976, and 1977 Bengals contracts.

* * *

Notes and Questions

1. Typical agreements between agents and the athletes they represent permit termination at will by either party, customarily after a brief notification period. Does this unilateral right to cancel rob the agreement of validity? If either party can cancel at will, is each promise illusory and thereby unsupported by the requisite consideration? *See* Chapter 4, Part IV(A). In numerous cases, courts have found that the existence of the notice provision or an implied notice provision derived from surrounding circumstances may be sufficient detriment to remove the illusoriness, thus eliminating the "consideration" problem. *See, e.g., Sylvan Crest Sand & Gravel Co. v. United States*, 150 F.2d 642 (2d Cir. 1945). *Compare Miami Coca-Cola Bottling Co. v. Orange Crush Co.*, 296 F. 693 (5th Cir. 1924).

2. Is there support in the Investment Advisers' Act for the court's indulgence of "isolated advice" about securities? The court stated that because Zinn was not a securities trader and, further, because there was no evidence to suggest any financial interest in securities advice, no conflict of interest existed. The court characterized the agent's recommendations as being somewhat beyond the evils that the statute sought to rectify. Do you agree that the statute was designed primarily to prevent the type of conflict of interest contemplated by the court? Or is it equally likely that the statute was devised to protect players and other advisees from imprudent or naive advice imparted by an individual not appropriately conversant or sophisticated in the securities business? Again, this point stresses the need to address problems stemming from agents' incompetence as well as deliberate and unlawful self-advancement.

3. In his counterclaim, Parrish alleged that Zinn had not performed his obligations under the contract, specifically in terms of his failure to secure offers from a rival football league that would have placed Parrish in a stronger negotiating position vis-à-vis the Cincinnati Bengals. The Second Circuit specifically overruled the district court's conclusion that Zinn had failed to perform his contractual obligations, holding that, in every respect, Zinn had exercised his best efforts and manifested good faith in attempting to secure outside endorsements, off-season employment, and other benefits for his client. Therefore, Parrish's repudiation of his contractual obligations in the face of Zinn's compliance with his responsibilities constituted a material breach justifying Zinn's lawsuit and his refusal to perform further.

The court excused Zinn from any obligations arising under his contract due to Parrish's material breach. The rationale was simply that the promises between Zinn and Parrish were constructively conditioned upon one another's substantial performance. The failure of either party to perform substantially constituted a material breach justifying both a suit to enforce the promise as well as a refusal to perform one's own duty. The constructive condition served as a duty trigger activating the other side's performance. Because Parrish failed to satisfy his obligations under the agreement, Zinn's duty did not arise, and he was excused from any further performance. At the same time, Zinn retained the right to sue Parrish for the material breach of his promise and to collect damages arising foreseeably from such breach.

Parrish learned a dear lesson—refusal to perform one's contractual duties under the assumption that the other side has materially breached or failed to substantially perform is frequently a risky and perilous proposition. If one party's breach is deemed to be trivial, and if the performance of the constructive condition constitutes substantial performance, then the other party's refusal to perform will, in and of itself, constitute a material breach, rendering that party subject both to a damage action and the first party's refusal to perform its obligations. Professor Farnsworth addressed this issue in the context of a breach taking the form of a delayed payment:

> Courts *** encourage the parties to keep the deal together by allowing the injured party to terminate the contract only after an appropriate length of time has passed. They restrain abuse of this power to terminate by denying the injured party the power to exercise it hastily. * * * Both in choosing to suspend and in electing to terminate, the injured party takes precipitous action at its own risk. * * * [T]hat party's decision "is fraught with peril, for should such termination, as viewed by a later court in the calm of contemplation, be unwarranted, the repudiator himself will have been guilty of material breach. * * * "
> (Citations omitted.)

E. Allan Farnsworth, Contracts § 8.15, at 633–34 (2d ed. 1990). *See also* Chapter 4, Part VI.

4. In assessing the validity of Parrish's claim, the court stated that each of Zinn's obligations was subject to "an implied promise to make 'good faith' efforts" to obtain for his client the various positions sought. The court found further that such efforts constituted "full performance" of any duties that Zinn assumed under the agreement. Although each of these requirements mandates good faith efforts, is the test purely subjective? What if Zinn had exercised good faith efforts to secure the employment, but a reasonable person in the position of the parties would find that there were additional matters that Zinn could have pursued to secure the requisite outside employment or endorsement for his client? Should the standard be one of an objective, reasonable person or one of subjective good faith?

Brown v. Woolf

554 F. Supp. 1206 (S.D. Ind. 1983)

STECKLER, District Judge. * * * The complaint * * * seeks compensatory and punitive damages and the imposition of a trust on a fee defendant allegedly received, all stemming from defendant's alleged constructive fraud and breach of fiduciary duty in the negotiation of a contract for the 1974–75 hockey season for plaintiff who was a professional hockey player. * * * During the negotiations in July 1974, the [Pittsburgh] Penguins offered plaintiff a two-year contract at $80,000.00 per year but plaintiff rejected the offer allegedly because defendant asserted that he could obtain a better, long-term, no-cut contract with a deferred compensation feature with the Indianapolis Racers, which at the time was a new team in a new league. On July 31, 1974, plaintiff signed a five-year contract with the Racers. Thereafter, it is alleged the Racers began having financial difficulties. Plaintiff avers that Woolf continued to represent plaintiff and negotiated two reductions in plaintiff's compensation including the loss of a retirement fund at the same time defendant was attempting to get his own fee payment from the Racers. Ultimately the Racers' assets were seized and the organizers defaulted on their obligations to plaintiff. He avers that he received only $185,000.00 of the total $800,000.00 compensation under the Racer contract but that defendant received his full $40,000.00 fee (5% of the contract) from the Racers.

Plaintiff alleges that defendant made numerous material misrepresentations upon which he relied both during the negotiation of the Racer contract and at the time of the subsequent modifications. Plaintiff further avers that defendant breached his fiduciary duty to plaintiff by failing to conduct any investigation into the financial stability of the

Racers, failing to investigate possible consequences of the deferred compensation package in the Racers' contract, failing to obtain guarantees or collateral, and by negotiating reductions in plaintiff's compensation from the Racers while insisting on receiving all of his own. Plaintiff theorizes that such conduct amounts to a prima facie case of constructive fraud for which he should receive compensatory and punitive damages and have a trust impressed on the $40,000.00 fee defendant received from the Racers.

Defendant's motion for partial summary judgment attacks plaintiff's claim for punitive damages, contending that plaintiff has no evidence to support such an award and should not be allowed to rest on the allegations of his complaint. Further, he claims that punitive damages are unavailable as a matter of law in a constructive fraud case because no proof of fraudulent intent is required. By his motion for summary judgment, defendant attacks several aspects of plaintiff 's claims against him. He argues (1) that plaintiff cannot recover on a breach of contract theory because Robert G. Woolf, the individual, was acting merely as the agent and employee of Robert Woolf Associates, Inc. (RWA), (2) that defendant's conduct could not amount to constructive fraud because (a) plaintiff alleges only negligent acts, (b) there is no evidence defendant deceived plaintiff or violated a position of trust, (c) there is no showing of harm to the public interest, and (d) there is no evidence that defendant obtained an unconscionable advantage at plaintiff's expense.

Turning first to the questions raised in the motion for partial summary judgment, the Court could find no Indiana case specifically discussing the availability of punitive damages in an action based upon the theory of constructive fraud. Cases from other jurisdictions reflect a division of authority. The Court concludes that Indiana courts would not adopt a per se rule prohibiting such damages in a constructive fraud action, but would rather consider the facts and circumstances of each case. If elements of recklessness, or oppressive conduct are demonstrated, punitive damages could be awarded. Indiana cases contain several formulizations of the tort of constructive fraud. Generally it is characterized as acts or a course of conduct from which an unconscionable advantage is or may be derived, or a breach of confidence coupled with an unjust enrichment which shocks the conscience, or a breach of duty, including mistake, duress or undue influence, which the law declares fraudulent because of a tendency to deceive, injure the public interest or violate the public or private confidence. Another formulization found in the cases involves the making of a false statement, by the dominant party in a confidential or fiduciary relationship or by one who holds himself out as an expert, upon which the plaintiff reasonably relies to his detriment. The defendant need not know the statement is false nor make the false statement with fraudulent intent.

The Court believes that both formulizations are rife with questions of fact, inter alia, the existence or nonexistence of a confidential or fiduciary relationship, and the question of reliance on false representations, as well as questions of credibility.

* * *

By reason of the foregoing, defendant's motions for partial summary judgment and for summary judgment are hereby DENIED.

IT IS SO ORDERED.

Notes and Questions

1. Constructive fraud has been described as both a tort and a contract concept. As a tort, it involves actions that give the perpetrator some type of unconscionable or unfair

advantage. In a contract context, constructive fraud is akin to duress, misrepresentation, or similar conduct that would render an agreement voidable at the behest of the victim party. Typically, a court will find constructive fraud, or imply the existence of a fraud, when "one party in a confidential or fiduciary relationship breaches his duty to another inducing justifiable reliance by the latter to his prejudice." *See Odorizzi v. Bloomfield School District*, 54 Cal. Rptr. 533, 539 (1964). Has the plaintiff in this case demonstrated the existence of such a course of conduct?

2. Assuming that a constructive fraud has been demonstrated, what measure of damages would be available? Again, the existence of fraud, duress, or similar untoward conduct will permit the victim to rescind the agreement and avoid all contractual obligations. However, the avoidance doctrines do not permit the party to sue on the contract as if it had been enforced, *i.e.*, recover full expectation damages putting him or her in the position that he or she would have been in had the contract been fulfilled. Further, even if defendant's activity amounted to a breach of contract, such breach would not result in an award of punitive damages. *See* RESTATEMENT (SECOND) OF CONTRACTS § 355. The purpose of relief in a contract action is compensatory—to put the non-breaching person in a position that he or she would have occupied had the contract been fully performed. Alternatively, the victim of the breach may receive reliance damages, which would return the victim to the status quo and provide recompense for any out-ofpocket expenditures in anticipation of the full performance of the agreement. Restitution damages, which also return the person to the status quo by preventing any unjust enrichment to the defendant and by requiring defendant to return any benefit received, may also be part of the damage calculus. However, punitive damages may be available in a tort action. *See id.* Therefore, alleging both tort and contract violations was a prudent course of action for the plaintiffs in this case because it expanded the range of relief potentially available to the plaintiff.

3. Defendant filed a motion for summary judgment in this case arguing that, assuming the existence of facts in a light most favorable to the plaintiff, defendant still demonstrated that he was entitled to dismissal as a matter of law. The court rejected the defendant's contentions that there were no unresolved factual claims, and that the matter was not appropriate for summary judgment. In particular, the court believed that numerous questions of fact were unresolved, including the truth of the defendant's representations, the reliance on such representations, and the confidential nature of the relationship between plaintiff and defendant. Do you agree that these matters, while factual, cannot be resolved through the deposition/summary judgment process? If defendant, by affidavit, had effectively rebutted plaintiff's factual allegations regarding the elements of the constructive fraud, and if plaintiff had failed to reply with his own affidavits establishing either a genuine issue of fact or sufficient facts to establish as a matter of law a breach of the contract or commission of the tortious act of constructive fraud, would summary judgment not have been appropriate in that situation?

4. What facts should the court attempt to adduce at trial in attempting to resolve the question whether or not defendant has, in fact,breached the contract or committed fraud?

Detroit Lions, Inc. v. Argovitz

580 F. Supp. 542 (E.D. Mich. 1984),
aff'd in relevant part, 767 F.2d 919 (6th Cir. 1985)

DeMASCIO, **District Judge.** The plot for this Saturday afternoon serial began when Billy Sims, having signed a contract with the Houston Gamblers on July 1, 1983, signed a second contract with the Detroit Lions on December 16, 1983. On December 18, 1983, the Detroit Lions, Inc. (Lions) and Billy R. Sims filed a complaint in the Oakland County Circuit Court seeking a judicial determination that the July 1, 1983, contract between Sims and the Houston Gamblers, Inc. (Gamblers) is invalid because the defendant Jerry Argovitz (Argovitz) breached his fiduciary duty when negotiating the Gamblers' contract and because the contract was otherwise tainted by fraud and misrepresentation. Defendants promptly removed the action to this court based on our diversity of citizenship jurisdiction.

For the reasons that follow, we have concluded that Argovitz's breach of his fiduciary duty during negotiations for the Gamblers' contract was so pronounced, so egregious, that to deny recision would be unconscionable.

Sometime in February or March 1983, Argovitz told Sims that he had applied for a Houston franchise in the newly formed United States Football League (USFL). In May 1983, Sims attended a press conference in Houston at which Argovitz announced that his application for a franchise had been approved. The evidence persuades us that Sims did not know the extent of Argovitz's interest in the Gamblers. He did not know the amount of Argovitz's original investment, or that Argovitz was obligated for 29 percent of a $1.5 million letter of credit, or that Argovitz was the president of the Gamblers' Corporation at an annual salary of $275,000 and 5 percent the yearly cash flow. The defendants could not justifiably expect Sims to comprehend the ramifications of Argovitz's interest in the Gamblers or the manner in which that interest would create an untenable conflict of interest, a conflict that would inevitably breach Argovitz's fiduciary duty to Sims. Argovitz knew, or should have known, that he could not act as Sims' agent under any circumstances when dealing with the Gamblers. Even the USFL Constitution itself prohibits a holder of any interest in a member club from acting "as the contracting agent or representative for any player."

Pending the approval of his application for a USFL franchise in Houston, Argovitz continued his negotiations with the Lions on behalf of Sims. On April 5, 1983, Argovitz offered Sims' services to the Lions for $6 million over a four-year period. The offer included a demand for a $1 million interest-free loan to be repaid over 10 years, and for skill and injury guarantees for three years. The Lions quickly responded with a counter offer on April 7, 1983, in the face amount of $1.5 million over a five-year period with additional incentives not relevant here. The negotiating process was working. The Lions were trying to determine what Argovitz really believed the market value for Sims really was. On May 3, 1983, with his Gamblers franchise assured, Argovitz significantly reduced his offer to the Lions. He now offered Sims to the Lions for $3 million over a four-year period, one-half of the amount of his April 5, 1983, offer. Argovitz's May 3rd offer included a demand for $50,000 to permit Sims to purchase an annuity. Argovitz also dropped his previous demand for skill guarantees. The May 10, 1983 offer submitted by the Lions brought the parties much closer.

On May 30, 1983, Argovitz asked for $3.5 million over a five-year period. This offer included an interest-free loan and injury protection insurance but made no demand for skill guarantees. The May 30 offer now requested $400,000 to allow Sims to purchase an annuity. On June 1, 1983, Argovitz and the Lions were only $500,000 apart. We find that the negotiations between the Lions and Argovitz were progressing normally, not laterally as Argovitz represented to Sims. The Lions were not "dragging their feet." Throughout the entire month of June 1983, Mr. Frederick Nash, the Lions' skilled negotiator and a fastidious lawyer, was involved in investigating the possibility of providing an attractive annuity for Sims and at the same time doing his best to avoid the granting of either skill or injury guarantees. The evidence establishes that on June 22, 1983, the Lions and Argovitz were very close to reaching an agreement on the value of Sims' services.

Apparently, in the midst of his negotiations with the Lions and with his Gamblers franchise in hand, Argovitz decided that he would seek an offer from the Gamblers. Mr. Bernard Lerner, one of Argovitz's partners in the Gamblers agreed to negotiate a contract with Sims. Since Lerner admitted that he had no knowledge whatsoever about football, we must infer that Argovitz at the very least told Lerner the amount of money required to sign Sims and further pressed upon Lerner the Gamblers' absolute need to obtain Sims' services. In the Gamblers' organization, only Argovitz knew the value of Sims' services and how critical it was for the Gamblers to obtain Sims. In Argovitz's words, Sims would make the Gamblers' franchise.

On June 29, 1983, at Lerner's behest, Sims and his wife went to Houston to negotiate with a team that was partially owned by his own agent. When Sims arrived in Houston, he believed that the Lions organization was not negotiating in good faith; that it was not really interested in his services. His ego was bruised and his emotional outlook toward the Lions was visible to [Argovitz's partner Gene] Burrough and Argovitz. Clearly, virtually all the information that Sims had up to that date came from Argovitz. Sims and the Gamblers did not discuss a future contract on the night of June 29th. The negotiations began on the morning of June 30, 1983, and ended that afternoon. At the morning meeting, Lerner offered Sims a $3.5 million five-year contract, which included three years of skill and injury guarantees. The offer included a $500,000 loan at an interest rate of 1 percent over prime. It was from this loan that Argovitz planned to receive the $100,000 balance of his fee for acting as an agent in negotiating a contract with his own team. Burrough testified that Sims would have accepted that offer on the spot because he was finally receiving the guarantee that he had been requesting from the Lions, guarantees that Argovitz dropped without too much quarrel. Argovitz and Burrough took Sims and his wife into another room to discuss the offer. Argovitz did tell Sims that he thought the Lions would match the Gamblers financial package and asked Sims whether he (Argovitz) should telephone the Lions. But, it is clear from the evidence that neither Sims nor Burrough believed that the Lions would match the offer. We find that Sims told Argovitz not to call the Lions for purely emotional reasons. As we have noted, Sims believed that the Lions' organization was not that interested in him and his pride was wounded. Burrough clearly admitted that he was aware of the emotional basis for Sims' decision not to have Argovitz phone the Lions, and we must conclude from the extremely close relationship between Argovitz and Sims that Argovitz knew it as well. When Sims went back to Lerner's office, he agreed to become a Gambler on the terms offered. At that moment, Argovitz irreparably breached his fiduciary duty. As agent for Sims he had the duty to telephone the Lions, receive its final offer, and present the terms of both offers to Sims. Then and only then could it be said that Sims made an intelligent and knowing decision to accept the Gamblers' offer.

During these negotiations at the Gamblers' office, Mr. Nash of the Lions telephoned Argovitz, but even though Argovitz was at his office, he declined to accept the telephone call. Argovitz tried to return Nash's call after Sims had accepted the Gamblers' offer, but it was after 5 p.m. and Nash had left for the July 4th weekend. When he declined to accept Mr. Nash's call, Argovitz's breach of his fiduciary duty became even more pronounced. Following Nash's example, Argovitz left for his weekend trip, leaving his principal to sign the contracts with the Gamblers the next day, July 1, 1983. The defendants * * * assert that neither Argovitz nor Burrough can be held responsible for following Sims' instruction not to contact the Lions on June 30, 1983. Although it is generally true that an agent is not liable for losses occurring as a result of following his principal's instructions, the rule of law is not applicable when the agent has placed himself in a position adverse to that of his principal.

During the evening of June 30, 1983, Burrough struggled with the fact that they had not presented the Gamblers' offer to the Lions. He knew, as does the court, that Argovitz now had the wedge that he needed to bring finality to the Lions' negotiations. Burrough was acutely aware of the fact that Sims' actions were emotionally motivated and realized that the responsibility for Sims' future rested with him. We view with some disdain the fact that Argovitz had, in effect, delegated his entire fiduciary responsibility on the eve of his principal's most important career decision. On July 1, 1983, it was Lerner who gave lip service to Argovitz's conspicuous conflict of interest. It was Lerner, not Argovitz, who advised Sims that Argovitz's position with the Gamblers presented a conflict of interest and that Sims could, if he wished, obtain an attorney or another agent. Argovitz, upon whom Sims had relied for the past four years, was not even there. Burrough, conscious of Sims' emotional responses, never advised Sims to wait until he had talked with the Lions before making a final decision. Argovitz's conflict of interest and self dealing put him in the position where he would not even use the wedge he now had to negotiate with the Lions, a wedge that is the dream of every agent. * * * [By way of example, the court noted that when the Gamblers made an offer to "untested rookie quarterback" Jim Kelly, Kelly's agent conveyed the terms of the offer to the NFL team that owned Kelly's rights, ultimately receiving a contract with the Gamblers that was only slightly less lucrative than the one the Gamblers made to Sims, who was "a former Heisman Trophy winner and a proven star in the NFL."] Argovitz did not follow the common practice described by both expert witnesses. He did not do this because he knew that the Lions would not leave Sims without a contract and he further knew that if he made that type of call Sims would be lost to the Gamblers, a team he owned.

On November 12, 1983, when Sims was in Houston for the Lions game with the Houston Oilers, Argovitz asked Sims to come to his home and sign certain papers. He represented to Sims that certain papers of his contract had been mistakenly overlooked and now needed to be signed. Included among those papers he asked Sims to sign was a waiver of any claim that Sims might have against Argovitz for his blatant breach of his fiduciary duty brought on by his glaring conflict of interest. Sims did not receive independent advice with regard to the wisdom of signing such a waiver. Despite having sold his agency business in September, Argovitz did not even tell Sims' new agent of his intention to have Sims sign a waiver. Nevertheless, Sims, an unsophisticated young man, signed the waiver. This is another example of the questionable conduct on the part of Argovitz who still had business management obligations to Sims. In spite of his fiduciary relationship he had Sims sign a waiver without advising him to obtain independent counseling.

* * * Moreover, Argovitz's failure to obtain personal guarantees for Sims without adequately warning Sims about the risks and uncertainties of a new league constituted a clear breach of his fiduciary duty.

* * * One cannot help but wonder whether Argovitz took his fiduciary duty seriously. For example, after investing approximately $76,000 of Sims' money, Argovitz, with or without the prior knowledge of his principal, received a finder's fee. Despite the fact that Sims paid Argovitz a 2 percent fee, Argovitz accepted $3800 from a person with whom he invested Sims' money. In March 1983, Argovitz had all of his veteran players, including Sims, sign a new agency contract with less favorable payment terms for the

players even though they already had an ongoing agency agreement with him. He did this after he sold his entire agency business to Career Sports. Finally, Argovitz was prepared to take the remainder of his 5 percent agency fee for negotiating Sims' contract with the Gamblers from monies the Gamblers loaned to Sims at an interest rate of 1 percent over prime. It mattered little to Argovitz that Sims would have to pay interest on the $100,000 that Argovitz was ready to accept. While these practices by Argovitz are troublesome, we do not find them decisive in examining Argovitz's conduct while negotiating the Gamblers' contract on June 30 and July 1, 1983. We find this circumstantial evidence useful only insofar as it has aided the court in understanding the manner in which these parties conducted business.

* * * We remain persuaded that on balance, Argovitz's breach of his fiduciary duty was so egregious that a court of equity cannot permit him to benefit by his own wrongful breach. We conclude that Argovitz's conduct in negotiating Sims' contract with the Gamblers rendered it invalid.

CONCLUSIONS OF LAW

* * *

In light of the express agency agreement, and the relationship between Sims and Argovitz, Argovitz clearly owed Sims the fiduciary duties of an agent at all times relevant to this lawsuit. * * *

* * * A fiduciary violates the prohibition against self-dealing not only by dealing with himself on his principal's behalf, but also by dealing on his principal's behalf with a third party in which he has an interest, such as a partnership in which he is a member.

* * * Where an agent has an interest adverse to that of his principal in a transaction in which he purports to act on behalf of his principal, the transaction is voidable by the principal unless the agent disclosed all material facts within the agent's knowledge that might affect the principal's judgment.

* * * The mere fact that the contract is fair to the principal does not deny the principal the right to rescind the contract when it was negotiated by an agent in violation of the prohibition against self-dealing * * *:

> The question, therefore, does not relate to the mala fides of the agent nor to whether or not a greater sum might have been procured for the property, nor even to whether or not the vendor received full value therefor. The self-interest of the agent is considered a vice which renders the transaction voidable at the election of the principal without looking into the matter further than to ascertain that the interest of the agent exists.

* * * Once it has been shown that an agent had an interest in a transaction involving his principal antagonistic to the principal's interest, fraud on the part of the agent is presumed. The burden of proof then rests upon the agent to show that his principal had full knowledge, not only of the fact that the agent was interested, but also of every material fact known to the agent which might affect the principal and that having such knowledge, the principal freely consented to the transaction.

* * * Argovitz clearly had a personal interest in signing Sims with the Gamblers that was adverse to Sims' interest—he had an ownership interest in the Gamblers and thus would profit if the Gamblers were profitable, and would incur substantial personal liabilities should the Gamblers not be financially successful. Since this showing has been made, fraud on Argovitz's part is presumed, and the Gamblers' contract must be rescinded unless Argovitz has shown by a preponderance of the evidence that he informed Sims of every material fact that might have influenced Sims' decision whether or not to sign the Gamblers' contract.

* * * We conclude that Argovitz has failed to show by a preponderance of the evidence either: 1) that he informed Sims of the following facts, or 2) that these facts would not have influenced Sims' decision whether to sign the Gamblers' contract:

a. The relative values of the Gamblers' contract and the Lions' offer that Argovitz knew could be obtained.

b. That there were significant financial differences between the USFL and the NFL not only in terms of the relative financial stability of the Leagues, but also in terms of the fringe benefits available to Sims.

c. Argovitz's 29 percent ownership in the Gamblers; Argovitz's $275,000 annual salary with the Gamblers; Argovitz's five percent interest in the cash flow of the Gamblers.

d. That both Argovitz and Burrough failed to even attempt to obtain for Sims valuable contract clauses which they had given to Kelly on behalf of the Gamblers.

e. That Sims had great leverage, and Argovitz was not encouraging a bidding war that could have advantageous results for Sims.

* * * At no time prior to December 1, 1983, was Sims aware of the material nondisclosures outlined above; accordingly, the defenses of ratification and waiver must be rejected.

* * * As a court sitting in equity, we conclude that recision is the appropriate remedy. We are dismayed by Argovitz's egregious conduct. The careless fashion in which Argovitz went about ascertaining the highest price for Sims' service convinces us of the wisdom of the maxim: no man can faithfully serve two masters whose interests are in conflict.

Judgment will be entered for the plaintiffs rescinding the Gamblers' contract with Sims.

IT IS SO ORDERED.

Notes and Questions

1. Problems surrounding conflicts of interest abound in the world of athlete representation. In this case, the controversy centered on the agent's blatant failure to observe minimum standards of propriety in the representation of his client. There is little doubt that the defendant agent placed himself in an untenable and indefensible position by representing a player who arguably would have an opportunity to play for a team in which Argovitz shared an interest. At times, the conflict of interest might not be so overt or may be more systemic (or institutional) in nature. For example, the relationship between an athlete and a collective bargaining representative, and the athlete and his or her individual agent, might not coincide quite as much as would be customarily expected. The collective bargaining representative has a duty to all members of the bargaining unit and, as such, may negotiate terms and conditions of employment that, while benefitting the unit as a whole, may disserve an individual. On more than one occasion, players have threatened litigation or even decertification of the union because they believed that they would have been better able to secure more advantageous terms

if they were free to negotiate on their own. As discussed in earlier chapters, the collective bargaining representative is the exclusive agent for all matters involving wages, hours and working conditions. Thus, any individual bargaining between a club and a player theoretically constitutes an unfair labor practice in violation of Section 8(a)(5) of the National Labor Relations Act as well as a likely breach of the collective bargaining agreement. However, recognizing that the skills and salary ranges of athletes are unique, collective bargaining agents have ceded certain "authority" to bargain on behalf of bargaining unit members and permitted the individual negotiation of matters above and beyond the minimum set by the collective agreement.

As discussed at numerous points earlier, Major League Baseball's collective bargaining agreement, among others, specifically provides that players may negotiate individually for salaries and special covenants that are beneficial to the player above and beyond the terms contained in the union contract. Notwithstanding the presence of these provisions permitting individual negotiations, countless subissues may still arise. For example, the players association may claim that a particular monetary increase provided a player in exchange for a minor concession detracting from the collective bargaining agreement is an attempt to "buy-out" the union contract on a piecemeal basis.

2. If a player participates in a sport that has a hard salary cap, there is some suggestion that a conflict of interest could exist whenever an agent represents two players on the same team. The rationale for this concern is that the representation of more than one player on a team creates a situation whereby any money secured by Player A derivatively is being taken from Player B and the remaining players in the team pool. Therefore, there is the potential that an agent will be less than vigorous in representing one player for fear that the gains secured will deplete the amount of available revenue to pay other team members that he represents. As one commentator has noted: "[T]he two athletes are each seeking the largest amount of possible compensation from a limited amount of resources. This is a win-lose, zero-sum situation in which one of the attorney's clients would win at the expense of the other athlete client." Jamie E. Brown, *The Battle the Fans Never See: Conflicts of Interest for Sports Lawyers*, 7 GEO. J. LEGAL ETHICS 813, 817 (1994). *See also* GREENBERG & GRAY, *supra*, § 10.17(1); Scott R. Rosner, *Conflicts of Interest and the Shifting Paradigm of Athlete Representation*, 11 UCLA ENT. L. REV. 193, 211–14 (2004). This type of potential conflict may also arise when an agent attempts to represent a player and a coach from the same club. Brown, *supra*, at 819–20; Rosner, *supra*, at 214–16. The regulations promulgated by the major professional sports unions explicitly address such situations and, in some instances, prohibit representation of players and any team managerial personnel. GREENBERG & GRAY, *supra*, §10.17(2).

3. If teams in a league refuse to negotiate with a player agent who is barred from certification by regulation of the players' union, are there antitrust ramifications? *See id.* § 10.16(5)(f). Is there a conspiracy among league members, or between the teams and the players association, that contravenes Section 1 of the Sherman Act? Assuming that these allegations raise colorable claims under Sherman 1, would either the statutory or non-statutory exemptions insulate the leagues, its members, and/or the union from antitrust liability? Several years ago, the United States Supreme Court addressed this question in the context of regulations governing agents for entertainers such as actors. These rules precluded agents who were not licensed by Actor's Equity (the stage actors' union) from representing their members. Agents contended that the regulations, which imposed various conditions upon agents' representation, violated the antitrust laws. The Court found that the labor exemption immunized the conduct from antitrust scrutiny.

See H.A. Artists & Assocs. v. Actors' Equity Ass'n, 451 U.S. 704, 712 (1981); Lionel S. Sobel, Professional Sports and the Law 727 (1977); Greenberg §10.16(5)(f)(ii). Claims by an agent that the NBPA's regulations limiting representation of its members to registered agents violated Sections 1 and 2 of the Sherman Act were likewise dismissed by virtue of the labor exemption. *See Collins v. NBPA*, 976 F.2d 740 (10th Cir. 1992); *see also* Greenberg & Gray §H-9 (Appendix), §§ 10.12 n.235, 10.16(5)(f)(ii). Would the statutory and non-statutory exemptions both be implicated in these situations given the unilateral promulgation of the regulations by the union in question as well as the league's agreement to honor such regulations? *See generally* Lori J. Lefferts, *The NFL Players Association's Agent Certification Plan: Is It Exempt from Antitrust Review?*, 26 Ariz. L. Rev. 699, 713–14 (1984) (concluding that neither the statutory nor non-statutory exemptions would insulate the NFLPA's regulations from potential antitrust reprisals). Would this commentator's conclusion or the Court's decisions in *Collins* and *Actors' Equity* be affected by the Supreme Court's recent proliferation of the exemption in *Brown v. Pro Football, Inc.*, 518 U.S. 231 (1996) (Chapter 9)? If this same activity involved the Major League Baseball Players Association, would the baseball exemption apply? *See* Chapter 8.

4. Because the players associations have taken an active role in the regulation of agent practices and conduct and because such involvement has indirectly become part of the collective bargaining process, the aforementioned state laws may encroach upon the jurisdiction of the National Labor Relations Board. Are issues such as governance of agents properly a matter for state involvement or are they pre-empted by federal law, at least insofar as unionized athletes or rank and file employees are concerned? *See San Diego Building Trades Council v. Garmon*, 359 U.S. 236 (1959); *Farmer v. Carpenters Local 25*, 430 U.S. 290 (1977); *Street, Elec. Ry. & Motor Coach Employees v. Lockridge*, 403 U.S. 274 (1971); *Martin v. Marine Engineers, National Maritime District 1*, 149 LRRM 2558 (E.D. La. 1994).

5. A classic illustration of the types of conflicts of interest that can arise occurred in connection with representation of athletes in the Major Indoor Soccer League. *See MISL and PROSPA and MISL Players Ass'n*, Decision and Direction of Election, November 15, 1983, Case No. 5-RC-11987, 5-RC-12001. There, two sports agents played critical roles in the establishment and maintenance of PROSPA, an association of soccer players organized as a collective bargaining representative. The Regional Director for Region 5 of the National Labor Relations Board found that PROSPA could be certified as collective bargaining representative, if it received the requisite number of votes from bargaining unit members, but that such certification would be suspended so long as any individual who represented individual soccer players held any "role, position or consultative capacity" within that organization insofar as its collective bargaining function was concerned. Some players associations explicitly prohibit their employees from representing individual players in negotiations with their clubs. Are these prohibitions appropriate? Is it fair to assume that a conflict of interest will automatically exist in these contexts, or are the unions attempting to eliminate the appearance of impropriety? Could it be argued that, given the inherent tension between a collective bargaining representative and an individual agent, the vast numbers of players involved, and the clear sacrifices that superstars must make in the name of some type of *esprit de corps*, some conflicts are to be expected and almost inevitable? *See generally* Greenberg & Gray, *supra*, §10.17(4).

6. The agent in *Argovitz* argued that he was not responsible for losses based on his principal's instructions. While it is true that an agent should generally not be accountable for losses directly resulting from adherence to orders from a person to whom he or she is directly responsible, should that rule of law apply when the agent occupies a posi-

tion plainly adverse to that of his principal? This situation is not unlike the old joke regarding children who kill their parents, only then to ask the court for mercy because they are now orphans.

7. The court in this case finds the existence of fraud or misrepresentation justifying rescission of the agreement. Generally, to establish fraud, the victim must prove a misrepresentation, including possibly a fraudulent non-disclosure, that was either material or deliberately deceitful and that induced the victim's justifiable and reasonable reliance. In this case, the court concluded that rescission was an appropriate remedy due to the defendant's egregious failure to represent his client properly. There is little question but that defendant's failure to disclose numerous aspects of his position constituted a perpetration of a fraud and a clear abuse of the fiduciary responsibilities that the agent owed to his principal. If the player had chosen to sue for damages rather than simply rescind the agreement and return to the status quo, what advice would you give him regarding the appropriate course of action? Could he have sued in both tort and contract? What would have been the advantages of either type of litigation in terms of the range of relief that would have been available?

8. In a typical contract avoidance situation, the victim's ability to disaffirm the agreement and return to the status quo could be compromised by evidence that the victim has ratified the agreement after the intrusive or disqualifying conduct or status has been removed (*e.g.,* duress, undue influence, etc.). Was ratification a viable argument in the *Argovitz* case? Clearly, any argument that the defendant could advance regarding ratification assumes the plaintiff's knowledge that the particular misrepresentation occurred. In this case, the court concluded that there was insufficient evidence to establish plaintiff's knowledge of numerous facts tending to perpetuate the misrepresentation and to accentuate the conflict of interest position in which the defendant had placed himself. Accordingly, the court summarily dismissed any contentions regarding the plaintiff's ratification of the agreement.

9. How relevant would it be if the deal negotiated by defendant were favorable to the plaintiff? Should a court assess whether or not a particular conflict of interest creates a "no-harm, no-foul" situation? Should the defendant be able to argue that, even in the absence of a conflict, no better deal could have been secured or that his "inside" position enabled him to do a better job for the plaintiff than he would have been able to do had no conflict existed? The court was unpersuaded by this argument, making it clear that the bad faith of the agent is not the critical factor to be considered in this context. Rather, "the self interest of the agent is considered a vice which renders the transaction voidable at the election of the principal without looking into the matter further. * * * " Do you agree?

10. A few players have chosen to "go it alone" in their dealings with club owners. In 1999, NBA superstar and budding actor, Ray Allen, negotiated his contract without the benefit of agent representation. He hired the late Johnnie Cochran at $500.00 an hour to serve in an oversight function to review the ultimate contract. By some estimates, Allen saved over one million dollars in agents fees and he landed a contract extension valued at over 70 million dollars.

Walters v. Fullwood

675 F. Supp. 155 (S.D.N.Y. 1987)

BRIEANT, Chief Judge. * * * Defendant Brent Fullwood * * * was an outstanding running back with the University of Auburn football team in Alabama. His success in

the highly competitive Southeastern Athletic Conference marked him as a top professional prospect. At an unspecified time during his senior year at Auburn, Fullwood
entered into an agreement with [World Sports and Entertainment ("W.S. & E."), a
corporation whose sole shareholders were plaintiff sports agents Norby Walters and
Lloyd Bloom]. * * * The agreement was dated January 2, 1987, the day after the last
game of Fullwood's college football career, and the first day he could sign such a
contract without forfeiting his amateur status under sec. 3-1-(c) of the N.C.A.A.
Constitution, quoted infra. The contract was arranged and signed for the corporation by plaintiff Bloom, and granted W.S. & E. the exclusive right to represent Fullwood as agent to negotiate with professional football teams after the spring draft of
the National Football League. Walters and Bloom were the corporate officers and
sole shareholders of W.S.&E. As a provisionally certified N.F.L. Players Association
contract advisor, Bloom was subject to the regulations of that body governing
agents, which require the arbitration of most disputes between players and contract
advisors.

On August 20, 1986, W.S. & E. paid $ 4,000 to Fullwood, who then executed a
promissory note in plaintiffs' favor for that amount. The note was secured by a pledge of:

> "a security interest in all of the players rights to receive payments under any ex-
> isting and or future contract or other agreement ("Player Contract") to which
> the Player may become a party relating to the Players services to or on behalf of
> any professional football team, if, as, and when such payments shall become
> due, including any insurance proceeds to which player may become entitled."

At various times throughout the 1986 season, plaintiffs sent to Fullwood or his family
further payments that totaled $ 4,038.

Reviewing substantially similar facts involving these same plaintiffs and a different
defendant in an unrelated case, Justice Altman of the New York State Supreme Court
concluded,

> "The underlying facts of the case reveal a pernicious practice of encouraging
> young college athletes to enter into deceptive agreements which are postdated
> so they can continue to play college football. The athletes thus act unethically
> and in violation of the rules of the National Collegiate Athletic Association[]
> and the National Football League[]."

Walters v. Harmon, 516 N.Y.S.2d 874 (N.Y. Sup.Ct. 1987). While neither plaintiffs nor
defendants have specifically admitted that the W.S. & E. agency agreement was post
dated, they have conspicuously avoided identifying the actual date it was signed. There
is a powerful inference that the agreement was actually signed before or during the college football season, perhaps contemporaneously with the August 20 promissory note,
and unethically postdated as in other cases involving these plaintiffs. No argument or
evidence has been presented to dispel this inference, and the Court believes the parties
deliberately postdated the contract January 2. Even if this likelihood is not accepted, it
is conceded by all parties and proven by documentary evidence that a security interest
was granted on Fullwood's future earnings from professional football, by the express
terms of the promissory note of August 20, 1986.

At some point prior to the N.F.L. spring 1987 draft, Fullwood repudiated his agreement with W.S.& E., and chose to be represented by defendant George Kickliter, an attorney in Auburn, Alabama. As anticipated, Fullwood was taken early in the N.F.L.
draft. The Green Bay Packers selected him as the fourth player in the first round; he
signed a contract with them, and currently is playing in his rookie season in the N.F.L.

In March, 1987, Walters and Bloom brought suit, * * * alleging (1) that Fullwood breached the W.S. & E. agency agreement, (2) that Fullwood owed them $ 8,038 as repayment for the funds he received during the autumn of 1986, which are now characterized as loans, (3) that Kickliter tortiously induced Fullwood's breach of the 1986 agreement, and (4) that Fullwood and Kickliter tortiously interfered with plaintiffs' contractual relations with other players by breaching or inducing the breach of the W.S.&E. agency agreement by Fullwood.[a]

* * *

Plaintiffs' claim for "interference with business relations"

* * *

In order to state a claim for tortious interference with existing contractual relations, a plaintiff must allege (1) the existence of a valid contract between plaintiff and another contracting party; (2) defendant's knowledge of that contract; (3) defendant's intentional procurement of a breach of that contract by the other party; and (4) damages * * * Plaintiffs have alleged neither Fullwood's knowledge of other contracts, nor his intentional procurement of any breach. Thus, no claim is stated.

If plaintiffs wish to have their complaint construed as alleging tortious interference with prospective economic advantage, they fare no better. Such a claim requires that "the defendant's sole motive was to inflict injury and that the defendant employed unlawful means to do so." * * * No New York case law has been advanced to or discovered by this Court establishing that the breach of a contract, standing alone, is sufficient to create liability for subsequent breaches by others of other contracts. Indeed such a proposition is frivolous on its face, and we decline to be the first to so hold. Absent rational allegations that Fullwood breached the W.S.&E. agency agreement through wrongful means, specifically to damage plaintiffs' business relations with others, no claim is stated upon which relief can be granted.

Treatment of defendants' motion to compel arbitration, and plaintiffs' surviving claims

* * *

* * * [The NCAA] constitution provides in relevant part that:

> "Any individual who contracts or who has ever contracted orally or in writing to be represented by an agent in the marketing of the individual's athletic ability or reputation in a sport no longer shall be eligible for intercollegiate athletics in that sport."

NCAA Constitution, sec. 3-1-(c). Section 3-1-(a) prohibits any player from accepting pay in any form for participation in his college sport, with an exception for a player seeking, directly without the assistance of a third party, a loan from an accredited commercial lending institution against future earnings potential solely in order to purchase insurance against disabling injury.

This Court concludes that the August 1986 loan security agreement and the W.S.&E. agency agreement between Fullwood and the plaintiffs violated Sections 3-1-(a) and 3-1-(c) of the N.C.A.A. Constitution, the observance of which is in the public interest of the citizens of New York State, and that the parties to those agreements knowingly betrayed an important, if perhaps naive, public trust. Viewing the parties as *in pari delicto*,

---

a. The court dismissed the claims against Kickliter for lack of personal jurisdiction. "[-Eds.]"

we decline to serve as "paymaster of the wages of crime, or referee between thieves" * * * We consider both defendant Fullwood's arbitration rights under the N.F.L.P.A. Agents' Regulations, and plaintiffs' rights on their contract and promissory note with Fullwood, unenforceable as contrary to the public policy of New York.

* * *

Absent these overriding policy concerns, the parties would be subject to the arbitration provisions set forth in section seven of the N.F.L.P.A. Agents' Regulations,[1] and plaintiffs' rights under the contract and promissory note with Fullwood also would be arbitrable. *See, Wood v. Nat'l Basketball Ass'n,* 602 F.Supp 525, 529 (S.D.N.Y. 1984), *aff'd,* 809 F.2d 954 (2d Cir. 1987). * * * However, under the "public policy" exception to the duty to enforce otherwise-valid agreements, we should and do leave the parties where we find them.

* * *

An agreement may be unenforceable in New York as contrary to public policy even in the absence of a direct violation of a criminal statute, if the sovereign has expressed a concern for the values underlying the policy implicated.

* * *

The New York State legislature has spoken on the public policies involved in this case, by expressing a concern for the integrity of sporting events in general, and a particular concern for the status of amateur athletics. *See, e.g.,* New York Tax Law § 1116(a)(4) (McKinney's supp. 1987) (granting tax exemption to any organization "organized and operating exclusively * * * to foster national or international amateur sports competition"); New York Penal Law §§ 180.35, 180.40 (McKinney's supp. 1987) (establishing criminal sanctions for sports bribery). Even were we not convinced of the legislative concern for the values underlying sec. 3-1-(c) of the N.C.A.A. Constitution, New York case law prevents judicial enforcement of contracts the performance of which would provoke conduct established as wrongful by independent commitments undertaken by either party. * * * Not all contracts inducing breaches of other agreements fall within this rule, but those requiring fraudulent conduct are unenforceable as contrary to the public policy of New York. * * * In the case before us, no party retains enforceable rights. To the extent plaintiffs seek to recover on the contract or promissory note signed by Fullwood, their wrongful conduct prevents recovery;[2] to the extent Fullwood seeks to compel arbitration, as provided for in the NFLPA Agents' Regulations, his own wrongs preclude resort to this Court.

* * *

Sections 3-1-(a) and 3-1-(c) of the N.C.A.A. Constitution were instituted to prevent college athletes from signing professional contracts while they are still playing for their schools. The provisions are rationally related to the commendable objective of

---

1. While defendants have sought to stay plaintiffs' action and compel arbitration of all claims under the Federal Arbitration Act ("F.A.A."), 9 U.S.C. §§ 3 & 4, both sides appear to have assumed that the arbitration agreement's effectiveness would be analyzed under [New York Law]. There is authority suggesting that a federal district court sitting on a diversity matter should apply the F.A.A. as federal substantive law. * * *

2. We note in passing that, as a provisionally certified N.F.L.P.A. agent, Bloom was bound by sec. 5(C)(1) of the N.F.L.P.A. Agents' Regulations, which forbids a contract advisor from "providing or offering to provide anything of significant value to a player in order to become the contract advisor for such player".

protecting the academic integrity of N.C.A.A. member institutions. A college student already receiving payments from his agent, or with a large professional contract signed and ready to take effect upon his graduation, might well be less inclined to observe his academic obligations than a student, athlete or not, with uncertainties about his future career. Indeed, he might not play at his college sport with the same vigor and devotion.

The agreement reached by the parties here, whether or not unusual, represented not only a betrayal of the high ideals that sustain amateur athletic competition as a part of our national educational commitment; it also constituted a calculated fraud on the entire spectator public. Every honest amateur player who took the field with or against Fullwood during the 1986 college football season was cheated by being thrown in with a player who had lost his amateur standing.

In August 1986, Brent Fullwood was one of that select group of college athletes virtually assured of a lucrative professional sports contract immediately upon graduation, absent serious injury during his senior year. The fruits of the system by which amateur players become highly paid professionals, whatever its flaws, were soon to be his. That is precisely why plaintiffs sought him out. Both sides of the transaction knew exactly what they were doing, and they knew it was fraudulent and wrong. This Court and the public need not suffer such wilful conduct to taint a college amateur sports program.

Conclusion

Plaintiffs' claims against defendant Kickliter are dismissed under Rule 12(b)(2), F.R.Civ.P., for lack of personal jurisdiction over that defendant. Plaintiffs' fourth claim is dismissed against defendant Fullwood under Rule 12(b)(6), F.R.Civ.P. for failure to state a claim on which relief can be granted. The first and second claims against Fullwood are dismissed with prejudice, and Fullwood's requests to stay this action and compel arbitration are denied, as the underlying agreements violate the public policy of New York, and the parties are *in pari delicto*. The Clerk shall enter final judgment.

SO ORDERED.

Notes and Questions

1. Plaintiffs in this case alleged that the agreement between defendants Fullwood and Kickliter was a product of Kickliter's tortious interference with the contractual relationship between plaintiffs and defendant Fullwood. The court dismissed plaintiffs' claim based on their unclean hands; their initial agency agreement with Fullwood violated the NCAA Constitution. The court therefore refused to enforce any arguable contract rights that plaintiffs may have had in their relationships with Fullwood. The court refused to act as a "referee between thieves" and enforce rights that allegedly arose under an illegal contract. Ironically, plaintiffs' action in securing the initial contractual arrangements with Fullwood may have constituted tortious interference itself. The relationship between Fullwood and his college is generally contractual in nature; therefore, any interference with such contractual relationship by entering into an agreement in violation of NCAA regulations, forfeiting the athlete's eligibility, and compromising the school's ability to participate in certain types of intercollegiate events, may be vulnerable to a claim of tortious interference. Generally, such interference is actionable if: (1) there is a contract or commercial relationship; (2) the alleged perpetrator of the tortious interfer-

ence is aware of this contract or commercial relationship; (3) there is *intentional* interference in such agreement or relationship; and (4) plaintiff suffers damages due to such
interference. *See* Richard P. Woods & Michael R. Mills, *Tortious Interference with an
Athletic Scholarship: A University's Remedy for the Unscrupulous Sports Agent*, 40 ALA. L.
REV. 141, 149 (1988). If, in fact, the relationship between a university and student-athlete is contractual, and the overwhelming consensus suggests that it is, then clearly the
deliberate attempts to enter into a relationship with a student athlete that compromises
the contractual relationship would seem to constitute a basis for a tortious interference
claim. *See Taylor v. Wake Forest University*, 191 S.E.2d 379 (N.C. Ct. App. 1972); *see also
Begley v. Corporation of Mercer Univ.*, 367 F. Supp. 908 (E.D. Tenn. 1973); *Gulf South
Conference v. Boyd*, 369 So. 2d 553, *cert. denied*, 192 S.E.2d (N.C. 1979).

In the Alabama Law Review article referenced above, Woods and Mills offer a creative response to the problem of unscrupulous agents tampering with college athletes.
Typically, such untoward dealings visit unpleasant consequences upon the university
and student-athlete, and no appropriate reprisal against the agent, because the NCAA
has authority to discipline only its own members. State legislation over the past several
years has attempted to address this problem and develop its own set of sanctions. However, the approach suggested by Woods and Mills would vest the school with a cause of
action to recover damages as a result of the agent's improper intrusion upon the contractual relationship between student-athlete and the educational institution. As the authors indicate, these damages may assume the form of lost revenues precipitated by the
declaration of the athlete's ineligibility for participation, loss of good will as an educational institution promoting amateur athletics, etc. They posit further that, even if
compensatory damages suffer as a result of uncertainty, there may be punitive damages
available given the "wanton disregard for the student-athlete's eligibility." *See* Woods
and Mills at 179.

2. In Chapter 6, we addressed the consequences of a party seeking injunctive relief
when it has engaged in its own inappropriate or illegal behavior. Courts will often deny
the availability of such an equitable remedy. In this instance, the court refused to indulge plaintiffs' claims and denied them any recompense. Was the agreement between
Fullwood and plaintiffs illegal? Was it simply inappropriate in terms of compliance
with NCAA rules? With regard to unclean hands, does the court have latitude to deny
relief any time that the party seeking relief has engaged in conduct that violates public
policy or, in some way, offends the sensibilities of the court? Should the standard be a
more exacting one in which the parties will not be deemed *in pari delicto* unless the
conduct is unlawful or illegal? *See further* Chapter 6 and compare *Weegham v. Killefer*,
215 F. 168 (W.D. Mich. 1914), with *Munchak Corp. v. Cunningham*, 457 F.2d 721 (4th
Cir. 1972).

3. If the court chose to retain jurisdiction over this matter rather than to "leave the
parties" where it found them, would this matter have been stayed pending resolution by
an arbitrator? If so, Section 5 of the National Football League Players Association Regulations, governing agents' representation of athletes, would generally require that the
matter be resolved through the arbitration process. An interesting question that is
spawned by such deferral is whether the New York arbitration law or the Federal Arbitration Act should be applied as the relevant substantive law polestar. Because the court
refused to order arbitration due to the parties' unclean hands, this issue was not resolved. Do you believe that this issue is one that should be decided under a federal substantive law analysis or under the laws of the state of New York? *See Walters & Bloom v.
Harmon*, 516 N.Y.S.2d 874 (Sup. Ct. 1987).

4. In 1991, Norby Walters, a plaintiff in the foregoing case, and another agent, Lloyd Bloom, were indicted by the United States government for mail fraud, prompted in part by secret representation agreements with college athletes who, subsequent thereto, continued to participate in college sports in violation of rules of the NCAA and various conferences. Because the student-athletes could only secure scholarships by dishonestly representing their status as eligible participants, presumably often through mail correspondence, and thereby fraudulently misdirecting scholarship funds, the mail fraud provisions of the United States Code were implicated. *See* 18 U.S.C. §1341. Further, these agents allegedly threatened players with serious bodily harm if they repudiated their contracts, thus giving rise to allegations of violations under RICO. Both agents were convicted and sentenced to prison terms. These convictions were overturned by the United States Court of Appeals for the Seventh Circuit based directly and indirectly upon the lower court's failure to issue appropriate jury instructions regarding defendant Walters' defense that he had operated on the advice of counsel. 913 F.2d 388 (7th Cir. 1990). After a remand, the Seventh Circuit once again overturned the district court's conviction of Walters, holding that the elements of mail fraud had not been established. *Walters v. United States,* 997 F.2d 1219 (7th Cir. 1993). *See also* Landis Cox, *Targeting Sports Agents with the Mail Fraud Statute: United States v. Norby Walters and Lloyd Bloom,* 41 DUKE L.J. 1157 (1992). In August of 1993, Bloom was found dead by gunshot in his Malibu, California home. The circumstances of his death remain sketchy; no weapon was found. Prior to his murder, Bloom had been resentenced to probation and community service.

5. In *People v. Sorkin,* 407 N.Y.S.2d 772 (App. Div. 1978), the court sentenced agent Richard Sorkin to a three-year prison term after he had pleaded guilty to grand larceny stemming from his misappropriation of players' money that he held as custodian. In addition to his poor investments, Sorkin had wagered extensively on professional sports using funds that clients had provided him for investment purposes. *See* Weiss at 331–32. This point illustrates that, while many problems surrounding agents' misuse of funds stem from their incompetence and naivete, there are also incidents in which the agents have engaged in blatant criminal activity. Unfortunately, in situations where agents have misappropriated funds, their own ineptitude and criminal conduct generally results in bankruptcy and an inability to compensate the players for monies that have been squandered. *Id. See also* Dunn at 1035.

6. The checkered history of former NHLPA Executive Director Alan Eagleson presents a striking illustration of the problems created by unscrupulous self-promoters. While serving as head of the hockey players' union, Eagleson allegedly engaged in numerous conflicts of interest ranging far beyond the appearance of impropriety created by his dual capacity as individual agent and union leader. Supposedly, he developed close relationships with NHL President John Ziegler, and various team owners, and these connections led to a series of collective bargaining agreements that may not have been in the best interests of the NHL players. *See generally* ROSS CONWAY, GAME MISCONDUCT (1995). The litany of Eagleson's alleged offenses eventually landed him in prison for racketeering, embezzlement, and fraud.

As discussed earlier, agents representing athletes in the four major professional sports leagues typically must comply with myriad requirements imposed by the players associations. Nevertheless, the following case illustrates that soliciting professional clients is generally a much simpler matter than soliciting athletes who are just completing their collegiate careers.

Speakers of Sport, Inc. v. ProServ, Inc.

178 F.3d 862 (7th Cir. 1999)

POSNER, Chief Judge. * * * Ivan Rodriguez, a highly successful catcher with the Texas Rangers baseball team, in 1991 signed the first of several one-year contracts making Speakers his agent. ProServ wanted to expand its representation of baseball players and to this end invited Rodriguez to its office in Washington and there promised that it would get him between $2 and $4 million in endorsements if he signed with ProServ—which he did, terminating his contract (which was terminable at will) with Speakers. This was in 1995. ProServ failed to obtain significant endorsement for Rodriguez and after just one year he switched to another agent who the following year landed him a five-year $42 million contract with the Rangers. Speakers brought this suit a few months later, charging that the promise of endorsements that ProServ had made to Rodriguez was fraudulent and had induced him to terminate his contract with Speakers. [The district court granted summary judgment to ProServ.]

* * *

Speakers could not sue Rodriguez for breach of contract, because he had not broken their contract, which was, as we said, terminable at will. Nor, therefore, could it accuse ProServ of inducing a breach of contract. * * * But Speakers did have a contract with Rodriguez, and inducing the termination of a contract, even when the termination is not a breach because the contract is terminable at will, can still be actionable under the tort law of Illinois, either as an interference with prospective economic advantage or as an interference with the contract at will itself. Nothing turns on the difference in characterization.

There is in general nothing wrong with one sports agent trying to take a client from another if this can be done without precipitating a breach of contract. That is the process known as competition, which though painful, fierce, frequently ruthless, sometimes Darwinian in its pitilessness, is the cornerstone of our highly successful economic system. Competition is not a tort, but on the contrary provides a defense (the "competitor's privilege") to the tort of improper interference. It does not privilege inducing a breach of contract—conduct usefully regarded as a separate tort from interfering with a business relationship without precipitating an actual breach of contract—but it does privilege inducing the lawful termination of a contract that is terminable at will. Sellers (including agents, who are sellers of services) do not "own" their customers, at least not without a contract * * * that is not terminable at will.

There would be few more effective inhibitors of the competitive process than making it a tort for an agent to promise the client of another agent to do better by him—which is pretty much what this case comes down to. It is true that Speakers argues only that the competitor may not make a promise that he knows he cannot fulfill, may not, that is, compete by fraud. Because the competitor's privilege does not include a right to get business from a competitor by means of fraud, it is hard to quarrel with this position in the abstract, but the practicalities are different. If the argument were accepted and the new agent made a promise that was not fulfilled, the old agent would have a shot at convincing a jury that the new agent had known from the start that he couldn't deliver on the promise. Once a case gets to the jury, all bets are off. The practical consequence of Speakers' approach, therefore, would be that a sports agent who lured away the client of another agent with a promise to do better by him would be running a grave legal risk.

* * *

Consider in this connection the characterization by Speakers' own chairman of Pro-Serv's promise to Rodriguez as "pure fantasy and gross exaggeration"—in other words, as puffing. Puffing in the usual sense signifies meaningless superlatives that no reasonable person would take seriously, and so it is not actionable as fraud. Rodriguez thus could not have sued ProServ (and has not attempted to) in respect of the promise of $2–$4 million in endorsements. If Rodriguez thus was not wronged, we do not understand on what theory Speakers can complain that ProServ competed with it unfairly.

The promise of endorsements was puffing not in the most common sense of a cascade of extravagant adjectives but in the equally valid sense of a sales pitch that is intended, and that a reasonable person in the position of the "promisee" would understand, to be aspirational rather than enforceable—an expression of hope rather than a commitment. It is not as if ProServ proposed to employ Rodriguez and pay him $2 million a year. That would be the kind of promise that could found an enforceable obligation. ProServ proposed merely to get him endorsements of at least that amount. They would of course be paid by the companies whose products Rodriguez endorsed, rather than by ProServ. ProServ could not force them to pay Rodriguez, and it is not contended that he understood ProServ to be warranting a minimum level of endorsements in the sense that if they were not forthcoming ProServ would be legally obligated to make up the difference to him.

It is possible to make a binding promise of something over which one has no control; such a promise is called a warranty. But it is not plausible that this is what ProServ was doing—that it was guaranteeing Rodriguez a minimum of $2 million a year in outside earnings if he signed with it. The only reasonable meaning to attach to ProServ's so-called promise is that ProServ would try to get as many endorsements as possible for Rodriguez and that it was optimistic that it could get him at least $2 million worth of them. So understood, the "promise" was not a promise at all.

* * *

We add that even if Speakers could establish liability * * * its suit would fail because it cannot possibly establish, as it seeks to do, a damages entitlement (the only relief it seeks) to the agent's fee on Rodriguez's $42 million contract. That contract was negotiated years after he left Speakers, and by another agent. Since Rodriguez had only a year-to-year contract with Speakers—terminable at will, moreover—and since obviously he was dissatisfied with Speakers at least to the extent of switching to ProServ and then when he became disillusioned with ProServ of *not* returning to Speakers' fold, the likelihood that Speakers would have retained him had ProServ not lured him away is too slight to ground an award of such damages. Such an award would be the best example yet of puffing in the pie-in-the-sky sense.

AFFIRMED.

Notes and Questions

1. Speakers argued that ProServ fraudulently induced Rodriguez to sever his relationship with Speakers. Judge Posner says that "in the abstract" the competitor's privilege does not encompass fraudulent promises. Nevertheless, the court holds that summary judgment was properly awarded to ProServ. Why?

2. Importantly, Rodriguez's initial contract with Speakers was terminable at will. Thus, there could be no claim that ProServ induced Rodriguez to breach the Speakers contract. How would you advise ProServ to solicit potential clients who are currently under contract with agents for set terms?

George Foreman Associates, Ltd. v. Foreman
389 F. Supp. 1308 (N.D. Ca. 1974)

[The question in this case is the validity of a contract, signed on December 1, 1972, between boxer George Foreman; his manager and trainer, Dick Sadler; and George Foreman Associates, Ltd. ("Associates"), a partnership. Foreman and Sadler argue that the contract is illegal under California regulations governing contracts between professional boxers and managers. Associates argues that it is not a "manager," and thus its rights under the contract do not depend on compliance with the regulations.]

PECKHAM, District Judge. * * * Under the 1972 Agreement, Foreman and Sadler are employed by Associates for participation in live boxing performances and for promotional activities in connection with those performances. Foreman and Sadler are given sole responsibility for the timing and location of all fights and for the negotiation of financial arrangements; Associates has no active part in any negotiations or promotional activities, except that it retains the right to approve or disapprove financial arrangements as long as such approval is not unreasonably withheld. Disputes as to the reasonableness of withholding of approval by Associates are to be referred to an arbitrator. Associates agrees to pay Foreman $10,000 per year for five years to cover training expenses, and an additional $25,000 per year for nine years, ending with the termination of the agreement on October 7, 1981. In exchange for these payments, Associates is given the right to receive 25 percent of Foreman's "promotional receipts," which include live gate and television receipts as well as virtually all receipts from endorsements and personal appearances. The payments from Associates to Foreman are to be "deemed satisfied" to the extent of any amounts received by Foreman as his share of his own promotional receipts; in effect, the payments from Associates to Foreman represent mere advances which are to be repaid to Associates out of Foreman's earnings.

* * *

Regulation of professional boxing in California falls within the province of the State Athletic Commission, established by Cal. Bus. & Prof. Code § 18620. The Commission is authorized to promulgate regulations in aid of the exercise of its statutory obligations. * * *

The Commission is granted sole authority and jurisdiction over the licensing of participants in boxing contests * * * as follows:

> The commission may license professional boxers * * * and * * * managers, trainers, and seconds of each.

> No such person shall participate in any boxing contest * * * or serve in the capacity of a * * * manager, trainer, or second, unless he has been licensed for that purpose by the commission.

> For the purpose of this section, the term "manager" means any person who does any of the following:

> (a) By contract, agreement, or other arrangement with any person undertakes or has undertaken to represent in any way the interest of any professional boxer in procuring or with respect to the arrangement or conduct of, any professional boxing contest in which such boxer is to participate as a contestant. * * *

> (b) Directs or controls the professional boxing activities of any professional boxer.

> (c) Receives or is entitled to receive more than 10 percent of the gross purse of any professional boxer for any services relating to such boxer's participation in a professional boxing contest. * * *

Failure to obtain a license, when one is required, is a misdemeanor.

In addition, the Commission has issued the following regulations * * *:

§256. Form of Contract. Contracts between boxers and managers * * * shall be executed on printed forms approved by the commission. The commission may approve a contract not on its printed form if entered into in another jurisdiction by non-residents of this state.

§257. Provisions of Contract. The original of all contracts entered into between managers and boxers must be placed on file with the commission at the time it is approved. * * * No manager or group of managers shall be allowed to participate in more than 33⅓ percent of the gross ring earnings of the boxer. * * *

§258. Execution of Contract. A contract is not valid between manager and boxer unless both parties appear at the same time before the commission or a commission representative and receives [sic] approval, unless otherwise directed by the commission. Except as hereinafter provided, no contract shall be approved between a manager and a boxer for a period exceeding three years.

* * *

Obviously the threshold determination which must be made is whether Associates falls within the applicable definition of "manager," since there is no other basis for bringing Associates within the jurisdiction of the California State Athletic Commission. As we have seen, the term "manager" is statutorily defined * * *; thus we need consider only whether Associates falls within any of the statutory categories.

Section 18674(b) [of the Cal. Bus. & Prof. Code] characterizes as a manager any person who "directs or controls the professional boxing activities of any professional boxer." As we have seen, paragraph 1(b) of the 1972 Agreement requires that all financial arrangements for Foreman's fights be approved by Associates, subject to the qualification that this approval not be unreasonably withheld. Even with this qualification of reasonableness, the approval power is a significant one; a partner in Associates has characterized this power as the right "to utilize its judicious and reasonable withholding of approval to obtain better and more favorable financial terms for such fight contracts," and in their legal arguments Associates recognize their approval power as a "substantive right to evaluate the offer on the merits, grant approval if warranted, or deny approval if such denial is reasonably called for under the particular circumstances." This approval is evidently not envisioned as a technical formality or a perfunctory matter; and the very real element of control which Associates derives from its approval right is in no way lessened by the prospect that the interests of Associates and Foreman will normally coincide, since there are situations in which, as counsel for Foreman has suggested, these interests may diverge, or in which the parties may differ in their perceptions of their short-term and long-term interests. The fact that disputes will be submitted to arbitration is likewise immaterial here, since the position of Associates may well be upheld by the arbitrator, and a control approved as "reasonable" is not thereby rendered any less of a restraint.

Another potential source of control over Foreman's boxing activities is found in paragraph 5 of the 1972 Agreement, which gives Associates a like power of approval or disapproval over Foreman's choice of a successor to Sadler, in the event that selection of a successor becomes necessary. Certainly the selection of a manager and trainer is one of a boxer's most important decisions.

Associates has volunteered, in its points and authorities, to waive the approval provisions of Paragraph 1(b); such a waiver is provided for in Paragraph 10 of the 1972 Agreement, which permits either party to waive the right to performance owed to it in the event that such performance is found to violate the laws of any jurisdiction. Such a waiver will not help Associates here, however, since we find below that the payment provisions of the Agreement are also sufficient to confer "manager" status upon Associates.

Section 18674(c) characterizes as a manager any person who is entitled to receive more than 10 percent of the gross purse of any professional boxer for services relating to such boxer's participation in a professional boxing contest. Associates quite rightly points out that one purpose of the 1972 Agreement was to eliminate Associates from the role of providing services in the negotiation and promotion of fights and various related rights; however, the Agreement does obligate Associates to advance money for training expenses and for travel expenses incident to training and boxing, and to guarantee Foreman $25,000 per year as compensation for his services as an employee of Associates. This court finds no reason why such payments should not, in keeping with the intent and purpose of the statute, be considered services relating to Foreman's boxing activities.

This interpretation derives considerable support and force from the history of state regulation of professional boxing in California and elsewhere. For many years, boxing was plagued by revelations of sordid abuses. Managers were accused of living off the earnings of impoverished fighters who received virtually nothing in return, having bartered away the right to their future earnings in exchange for the most meager present returns; close underworld connections often resulted in defrauding the public through the "fixing" of fights. These abuses ultimately prompted the extensive statutory and regulatory framework administered by the State Athletic Commission. * * * The statutes and regulations indicate a clear purpose to safeguard boxers against the temptation to mortgage their futures in exchange for relatively meager present consideration; in light of that purpose, it is appropriate and even necessary to interpret advance payments (such as those made to Foreman under the 1972 Agreement) as falling within the scope of the "services" which trigger the licensing requirement and other statutory protections.

In at least two respects therefore, this court finds that Associates falls within the statutory definition of "manager," and is hence subject to the jurisdiction of the State Athletic Commission. Once this determination is made, it is evident that the 1972 Agreement fails in numerous respects to comply with the applicable regulations governing boxer-manager contracts. The most significant violation was the failure of the parties to appear together before the Commission and secure its approval of the Agreement * * * ; in addition, the Agreement was not filed with the Commission, was not on a proper printed form or other approved form, and substantially exceeded the maximum term of three years.

These violations necessarily render the Agreement invalid and unenforceable, both by the express terms of the Commission's own regulations ("A contract is not valid between manager and boxer unless....") and by the recognized principle that a contract which violates the law cannot be enforced in an action founded upon the contract.

* * *

Associates argues that the Commission's jurisdiction, by statute, extends only to boxing matches in California, and that the Commission's rules are therefore inapplicable here since none of the bouts in question was sited in California. It is true that under § 18670, the Commission's jurisdiction is limited to bouts taking place in California; however, the regulations which the Commission has promulgated in aid of its exercise of that jurisdiction expressly cover all contracts between boxers and managers. There is no provision restricting the coverage of those rules to contracts relating to California boxing matches, and the court is certainly unable to say on this record that the Commission has exceeded its statutory mandate in purporting to regulate all boxer-manager contracts entered into in California.

Associates has further argued that summary judgment on this issue is inappropriate, since there is a factual dispute as to the purpose of the approval provision in the 1972 Agreement (Associates contends that the sole purpose of the approval clause is to assist them in acquiring information concerning Foreman's financial arrangements). As the earlier discussion of this provision indicated, the position of Associates on this issue has fluctuated; on some occasions, as noted, Associates has contended that the approval power is in fact a valuable substantive right going far beyond the mere acquisition of information. Thus, to the extent that there is a factual conflict on this issue, much of the conflict has been generated by Associates itself. Nevertheless, regardless of what evidence might be adduced as to the motive behind the clause, it is clearly within this court's province to find, as a matter of law, that the approval clause on its face vests sufficient power in Associates to trigger the application of the "directs or controls" provision of §18674(b).

* * *

On the basis of the preceding discussion, the court finds that there is no genuine dispute as to any material fact in this action, and that plaintiffs Foreman and Sadler are entitled to summary judgment as a matter of law.

* * *

[T]he 1972 Agreement must be deemed contrary to law and therefore unenforceable. Nevertheless, it is clear that this result threatens to work a substantial injustice upon Associates, which advanced substantial sums of money to Foreman and Sadler in reliance upon the 1971 and 1972 Agreements and which has received relatively little of its anticipated return. This fact is not a sufficient basis for enforcing the agreements themselves, since the private interests of the parties cannot overcome the interest of the state in the enforcement of its laws; however, where the public cannot be protected because portions of a transaction have already taken place, and where one party would be unjustly enriched at the expense of another, the courts have fashioned equitable remedies to mitigate the harshness of this result.

The present case seems a highly appropriate one for the application of this principle. Accordingly, as * * * Foreman and Sadler * * * will be ordered to reimburse Associates ... to the extent that such advances have not already been offset by payments to Associates.

* * *

Notes and Questions

1. The court gave the team "manager" a broad definition. Why?

2. How did the court circumvent the governing statute's limitation of jurisdiction to bouts occurring in California? Are the regulations that the Commission has promulgated regarding the scope of its jurisdiction valid? Could it be argued that those regulations constitute a usurpation of the state legislature's power to make laws?

3. The outcome of this case is extremely curious in terms of the remedy prescribed by the court. Although acknowledging that it could not enforce an illegal contract, a conclusion generally leaving parties where a court finds them, this court awarded com-

pensation characterized as equitable relief. Typically, equity is the last place that an "illegal" contractor will find solace. *See generally* FARNSWORTH, supra, § 5.9. Why did the court fashion such equitable remedy here? *See id.*

Table of Cases

Index